MW01201729

Pashto-English Dictionary
First Edition

Zeeya A. Pashtoon

Pashto-English Dictionary
First Edition

Zeeya A. Pashtoon

2009

DUNWOODY PRESS

Pashto-English Dictionary, First Edition

Copyright © 2009 McNeil Technologies, Inc.

All rights reserved.

No part of this work may be reproduced or transmitted in any form or by any means, electronic or mechanical, including photocopying and recording, or by any information storage and retrieval system, without the prior written permission of McNeil Technologies, Inc.

All inquiries should be directed to:

Dunwoody Press
6525 Belcrest Rd, Suite 460
Hyattsville, MD 20782
USA

ISBN: 978-1-931546-70-6
Library of Congress Catalog Card Number: 2009937483
Printed and bound in the United States of America

Table of Contents

Preface

This *Pashto-English Dictionary, First Edition* is intended for professional Pashto-to-English translators of modern Pashto written materials. It contains approximately 55,000 entries arranged alphabetically according to the Pashto alphabet.

The main sources for this dictionary are:

- *Afgansko-russkii slovar* (*Pashto-Russian Dictionary*, M. G. Aslanov, Martiros, N. A. Dvoriankov, Moscow, 1966, 994 pages)
- *Pashto-English Dictionary* (M.H. Rahimi, Academy of Science of Afghanistan, Kabul, 1979, 591 pages)
- *Pashto-Pashto Descriptive Dictionary* (Institute of Languages and Literature, Academy of Science of Afghanistan, Kabul, 2005, Vol. 1-4);
- *Daryab Dictionary* (Qalandar Momand, Peshawar, 1994, 1,325 pages)
- *Qamosona Pashto Dictionaries* (http://www.achakzai.de/j/)

The second edition of this dictionary is well underway. This new edition will be corpus-based and will include new headwords, new definitions, and new examples.

As always, the Publisher welcomes any comments, suggestions, corrections, and additions to the dictionary.

The Publisher
Dunwoody Press
Hyattsville, Maryland
November 2009

Acknowledgments

The publication of this *Pashto-English Dictionary, First Edition* has been made possible with the encouragement and support of many colleagues. In particular, I would like to express my deepest gratitude and sincere thanks to Thomas Creamer and Erin Gyomber for editorial support; to Aung Kyaw Oo for formatting the dictionary; to Patrick O'Sullivan, David Williams, Thomas Tucker, Alan Turnbull, Irina Knizhnik, and Melvin Deatherage for translation support; to Azizeh Babba and Mustafa Ajan Sayd for assistance in keyboarding the Pashto script; and especially to Naseer Honar Pashtoon for lending his expertise on both the Pashto language and Pashto lexicography.

Zeeya A. Pashtoon
McNeil Technologies, Inc.
Hyattsville, Maryland

Sample Entry

Headword

Homograph

Pronunciation

Sense number

Label

Definition

Subsense number

Alternate form

Gender

Cross Reference

اچول¹ achavә́l **1** *transitive* [*past:* وايي چاوه]. **1.** throw, fling, hurl, drop (from a height); throw out, cast پر مخکه اچول to throw on the ground بمونه اچول to drop bombs **1.2** to bring, knock down الوتکه پر ښکته راأچول to bring an aircraft down **1.3** throw on, throw over, put on بر ستن پر ځان اچول to cover with a blanket **1.4** to spread **1.5** to put, place, put together بار پر اوښ to lead a pack on a camel **1.6** to lay (eggs) **1.7** to strew, pour (in, into) مالګه اچول to sprinkle salt, salt **a** دانه اچول to strew seed, sprinkle grain **b** to sow **1.8** to pour, pour out یوه پترول اچول to refuel **1.9** to پیاله چای راواچوه pour me a cup of tea to give, feed (animals) **1.10** to fertilize, fertilize the soil **1.11** pass, give دوډی راواچوه pass me the bread **1.12** to register (mail) **1.13** to lower, let down, launch جهاز اوبو ته ور اچول launch a boat سر یي کښته واچاوه He hung his head. **1.14** to establish, set up (e.g., communications with someone) **1.15** to build **1.16** to bind, fasten (to) **1.17** to place, put, settle, lodge; assign a billet, quarter **1.18** to assign work, put to work **1.19** to send (to school) **1.20** to hand in (an application); institute (a suit) پر چا عرض اچول to bring a suit against someone **1.21** to entrust مسئولیت پر چا اچول to make someone responsible for something **1.22** to set aside, adjourn; drag out (an affair) سبا ! ته یي واچوه Put it off until tomorrow! **1.23** to draw up (e.g., a plan); sketch in, make a rough sketch or outline نقشه اچول to draw up a plan د چا پر ضد یوه نقشه اچول to plot something against someone **1.24** to make oneself out to be someone; pretend to be someone else; claim something as one's own property غوړونه یي کاڼه واچول He pretended to be deaf. **1.25** to start, set going; put into service, put into operation; utilize لښکر په جنګ کښي اچول to commit troops to battle **1.26** instill (in); install (in), establish د وطن محبت په زړو کښي اچول to inculcate love for the motherland **1.27** to make, produce, effect اور اچول to set on fire **a** سلام اچول to greet ځان اچول to throw oneself, rush **b** to make oneself out to be someone else, imitate someone else, pretend to be someone else ځان مړ اچول to pretend to be dead ځان پر ناجوړی اچول to feign illness, malinger **c** to expose oneself to something, subject oneself to something د چا سره انډیوالي اچول to be on friendly terms, establish friendship with someone **2** *m. plural* ☞ اچاوه¹ **1** *idiom* یو بل سره اچول quarrel

اچول² uchavә́l *transitive dialect* ☞ وچول

Pronounciation Guide

ا، آ، ا	ā	ā́	ښ	k̲h	
ب	b		ص	s	
پ	p		ض	z	
ت	t		ط	t	
ټ	ṭ		ظ	z	
ث	s		ع	'	
ج	dzh		غ	gh	
چ	ch		ف	f	
ځ	dz		ق	ḳ	q
څ	ts		ک	k	
ح	h		گ	g	
خ	kh		ل	l	
د	d		م	m	
ډ	ḍ		ن	n	
ذ	z		ڼ	ṇ	
ر	r		و	v/o/ó	ú/u/w
ړ	ṛ		ه	h	
ز	z		ی	aj	áj
ژ	zh		ې	e	é
ږ	g̣		ی	əj	ə́j
س	s		ي	i	í
ش	sh		ئ	əj	aj

Abbreviations and Labels

abbreviation

abusive

accounting

action noun

adjectival suffix

adjective

administration

adverb

adverbial prefix

adverbial suffix

adversative conjunction

affectionate

affirmative particle

Afridi

agriculture

anatomy

Arabic

archaeology

archaic

architecture

astronomy

attributive

auxiliary verb

auxiliary word

aviation

biology

botany

cards

causative

chemistry

chess

children's speech

collective

colloquial

combined with

combining form

comparative degree

compound

compound verb

conditional

conjunction

construction

contrastive conjunction

conventional formula

conversation

copulative

curse

demonstrative pronoun

demotic

denominative

derogatory

dialect

diminutive

diplomacy

directional pronoun

disjunctive conjunction

doublet

dual

dual number

Eastern

economics

electrical engineering

electronics

endearment

epistolary

ethnography

exclamation

expression

f.

feminine

feminine plural

feminine singular

figurative

finance

first person

first person past

first person plural

first person present

folk saying

folklore

future

future perfect

geography

geology

geometry

grammar

history

hunting

idiom

imperative

imperfect

imperfective

indeclinable

indefinite pronoun

independent perfective

indirect plural

indirect singular

intensifier

intensive particle

interjection

intransitive

invariable

ironic

jocular

law

library science

linguistics

literal

literally

literary

literature

m.

masculine

masculine plural

math

medicine

metallurgy

military

mining

music

mythology

negative particle

no plural form

noun of agent

noun suffix

number

numeral

oblique

oblique plural

oblique singular

obsolete

official

official abbreviation

onomatopoeia

optative

ordinal

parenthetic word

participle

particle

passive

past

past participle

past perfective

past stem

past tense stem

perfective

Persian

personal name

perspective aspect

philosophy

photography

physics

physiology

phytopathology

plural

poetic

polite

politics

possessive

postposition

postpositive

potential

predicate

predicative

prefix

prefixal verb

preposition

present

present participle

printing

productive verb

pronoun

proper name

proverb

railroad

regional

religion

saying

second person

second plural

second singular

secondary plural

separable part of present

separable part of verb

short plural

singular

sometimes plural

sometimes singular

sports

stem

suffix

superlative degree

swear word

tautological with

technology

textiles

theater

third person plural

third person singular

trade

transitive

used as the first element in compounds

used with

verb copula

veterinary

vice

vocative

vulgar

Waziri

Western

with numbers

word paired to

zoology

ا

ا ¹ alíf **1** the first letter of the Pashto alphabet **2** the number 1 in the abjad system **3** performs the following functions: **3.1** *the accented suffix of nouns derived from verbs*, e.g., خوځېدا motion گډېدا dance, dancing **3.2** *linking element in complex words.* e.g., مخامخ from house to house کور کور face to face **3.3** *indicates the vocative*, e.g., احمدا! oh, Ahmed! **3.4** *in verbs beginning with the phoneme "a" a separate part of the verb, in laconic sentences in the perfective aspect*, e.g., اچول، اخيستل etc. کتاب دي واخيست؟ هو، واٸي خيست Did you take the book? / Yes, I did.

ا ² u o *Eastern replaces the perfective aspect prefix*, e.g., ده اويل *instead of* ده وويل he said

آ ³ ā *vocative particle* oh, listen! آ هلکه، دلته راشه! Hey, boy, come here! آپلاره! Papa! Father! **2** *interjection* ah, aha

آ ⁴ ā *interjection, demonstrative pronoun colloquial* ☞ هغه ¹ يوه سري آبل ته وويل چه ... one told the other that …

ا ⁵ *official abbreviation* اخلاصمند

اً an án *Arabic adverbial prefix* e.g., ابداً eternally رسماً officially

آب ¹ āb *m.* āv *singular & plural* **1** water, moisture **2** brilliance, luster (of a precious stone) **3** honor, dignity, reputation آب تو بﻴدل، بﻴ آبه کول to disgrace, dishonor (someone) خپل آب ساتل to preserve one's honor هغه د آب سرى دٸ He is a respected man.

اب ² ab *m.* [*plural:* آبآ] *Arabic* father

ابا ¹ abā́ *m. Arabic* father ابا کول to regard as father; call (honorifically) father

ابا ² ibā́ *f. Arabic* refusal ابا کول ، ابا راوړل to refuse, decline, reject

ابا ³ ābā́ *m. Arabic plural of* اب ²

آبآت ☞ آباد

اباتوب abātób *m.* fatherhood

آباتي ābātí *f.* ☞ آبادي

آباد ābā́d **1** populated, settled, inhabited دغه ملک په پښتنو باندي آباد دٸ This district was settled by Afghans. **2** tilled, cultivated آبادي ځمکي cultivated lands **3** flourishing آباد دي وي زمونږ وطن! Long live our Native Land! **4** restored **5** well-nourished, fat (of animals)

آبادان ābādā́n **1** ☞ آباد **2** *m. plural* Abadan (city)

آباداني ābādā́ní *f.* **1** population, number of settlers **2** prosperity; well being **3** organization of public services and amenities; construction

آبادول ābādavә́l ابادول abādavә́l **1** [*past:* آباد يې کړ] *denominative, transitive* **.1** to populate, settle **1.2** to till, cultivate (the land); revitalize (e.g., the desert) **1.3** to restore **1.4** to provide with the amenities; construct تعمير آبادول to build a building **1.5** to promote development, promote prosperity خپل کور آبادول

figurative **a** to build one's house **b** to achieve prosperity; prosper **1.6** to create (e.g., favorable conditions) **2** *m. plural* آبادونه ☞

آبادونه ābādavә́na *f.* ابادونه abādavә́na *f.* **1** population **2** tilling, cultivation (land) **3** building, construction **4** prosperity; well being

آبادي ābādí *f.* ابادي abādí *f.* **1** populated place, domicile **2** ☞ آبادونه

آبادېدل ābādedә́l *denominative, intransitive* [*past:* آباد شو] **1** to be populated, be settled **2** to be tilled, be cultivated, have been tilled (of land) **3** to be built, be restored **4** to prosper, succeed

آبادېدنه ābādedә́na *f.* ابادېدنه abādedә́na *f.* **1** population **2** cultivation, tilling (land)

اباسيند abāsind *m.* Ind (river)

اباگنی abāganəj *f.* relatives, kinsmen (on the father's side), agnates (any paternal kinsmen)

آب انبار ābāmbár *m.* reservoir, pool

آبآ واجداد ābā-va-adzhdā́d *m.* ābā-u-adzhdā́d *Arabic plural* fathers and grandfathers, ancestors

اباً وجداً abán-va-dzháddán *Arabic* from generation to generation

آب ايستاده āb-i-istādā́ *f.* Ab-i-Istada (lake, near the city of Gazni)

ابائي abāí **1** ancestral **2** native ابائي هيواد native land

آباز ābbáz *m.* آب باز āvbáz **1** swimmer **2** sailor

آبازي ābbází *f.* آب بازي āvbází **1** swimming **2** aquatic sport

آبپاش ābpásh *f.* **1** pouring; watering آبپاش موټر watering machine **2** watering can

آبپاشي ābpāshí *f.* آب پاشي watering, irrigation

آبتاب ābtáb *m.* ☞ آب وتاب

آبتابه ābtābá *f.* ☞ آفتابه

ابتدا ibtidā́ *Arabic* **1** *f.* beginning, undertaking په لمړى ابتدا کښي in the very beginning له ابتدا نه from the very beginning په ابتدا *linguistics* ساکن cluster of consonants at the beginning of a word ابتدا کول to begin **2.1** firstly **2.2** for the first time

ابتدائي ibtidāí *Arabic adjective* **1.1** elementary; first-stage; first-echelon, primary ابتدائي مکتب elementary school ابتدائي تشکيل primary organization **2** rudimentary, primitive, weak (e.g., of a play) **3** *administration* junior ابتدائي مدير assistant department chief **4** *chemistry* elemental ابتدائي مواد raw material

ابتذال ibtizā́l *m. Arabic* **1** carelessness; negligence **2** meanness, baseness

ابتر abtár avtár *adjective* **1** destroyed; spoiled **2** useless; unnecessary; good-for-nothing

آبترازو abtarāzú *m. technology* level

ابترول abtaravә́l *denominative, transitive* [*past:* ابتر يې کړ] **1** to destroy, pull down **2** to spoil, make worse **3** to make useless, make unnecessary

ابتري abtarí *f.* **1** destruction, disintegration **2** spoiling, worsening, uselessness *idiom* پرﻴشاني او ابتري پيدا کول to cause confusion

ابتربدل abtaredól *denominative, intransitive* [*past:* ابتر شو] **1** to be destroyed, be pulled down **2** to be spoiled, be worsened **3** to be useless, be unnecessary

ابتكار ibtikár *m. Arabic* **1** initiative, undertaking ابتكار يي خپل كړ He/they displayed initiative. **2** invention

ابتكاري ibtikārí creative, full of initiative *idiom* ابتكاري انشا **a** impromptu **b** unique pronunciation

ابتل ubtál *m.* ابتله ubtála *f.* ☞ اويتل

ابته abatá *invariable* **1** unavailing, futile, unsuccessful **2** perished, destroyed ابته كول **a** render useless, futile **b** ruin, spoil

ابتهاج ibtihádzh *m. Arabic* **1** gaiety **2** pleasure **3** rejoicing, gladness

ابجد abdzhád *m. Arabic* abjad (i.e., the Arabic alphabet arranged according to the numberical values assigned to the letters, so-called from the first 4 letters ا, ب, ج, د i.e., 1, 2, 3, 4) د ابجد حساب alphabetic calculation, use of Arabic alphabet for numbers

ابجدي abdzhadí pertaining to the abjad (i.e., the Arabic alphabet arranged according to the numberical values assigned to the letters) ابجدي حروف the letters of the abjad

آبجو ābidzháu *m. plural* beer

ابجوشه abdzhúsha *f.* [*plural:* ابجوشي abdzhúshi] *often plural* "abjush" a variety of large, light-colored currant, the light "sabza" (a variety of currant having pale fruit- usually dried)

آبچكن ābchakán moire, having an undulating appearance or texture آبچكن بخمل velvet moire

ابحاث abhás *m. Arabic plural of* بحث ابحاث تاوده heated disputes, heated debates

ابحار abhár *m. Arabic plural from* بحر

آبخانه ābkhāná *f.* reservoir

ابخوره ābkhúra *f.* watering; a watering place

آبخوري ābkhurí *f.* āvkhurí mug (for water), flask, water bottle

ابد abád *m. Arabic plural* eternity ترابده constantly, eternally, forever, for good

ابداً abádan *Arabic* **1** constantly, eternally, forever, for good **2** quite, entirely ابداً خبر نه دئ He hasn't a clue. He doesn't know at all.

آبدات ābidát *m. Arabic plural from* آبد

آبدار ābdár āvdár **1.1** watery, humid, damp **1.2** juicy (of fruits) **1.3** sparkling, shining (of pure water, precious stones) **1.4** worthy, respected, glorious, honorable **1.5** tempered, hardened (steel) **2** *m.* **.1** butler **2.2** major-domo **2.3** person who affects irrigation

آبدارول ābdāravól *denominative, transitive* [*past:* آبداري يې كړ] glorify; esteem, honor, revere

آبداري ābdārí *f.* **1** glory, honor, dignity *f.* **2** hardening (steel)

آبداريدل ābdāredól *denominative, intransitive* [*past:* آبدار شو] to be glorified, be esteemed, be honored, be revered

ابداع ibdá' *f. Arabic* discovery, invention

ابدال abdál [1] avdál *m. Arabic* **1** saint; hermit, anchorite (solitary holy man) **2** *proper name* Abdal

ابدال ibdál [2] *m. Arabic* change, alteration

ابدالول ibdālavól *denominative, transitive* [*past:* ابدال يې كړ] change, alter

ابدالي abdālí *m.* avdālí *plural history* the Abdali (tribe, now called the Dur(r)ani)

آبدان ābdán *m.* āvdán tank, reservoir (for water)

آبده ābidá *f. Arabic m.* [*plural:* آبدات ābidát] sacred and holy thing

ابدي abadí *Arabic* **1** eternal, endless **2** life-long ابدي حبس life imprisonment

ابديت abadiját *m. Arabic plural* eternity

ابر abr *m.* cloud, storm cloud

ابرأ ibrá *f. Arabic* **1** liberation (e.g., from an obligation) **2** forgiveness (e.g., of a debt) ابرأ كول *compound verb* **a** to liberate (e.g., from a debt) **b** to forgive (e.g., a debt)

ابرار abrár *m. Arabic plural* [*singular:* بر] devout people, just men, saints

ابراز ibráz *m. Arabic* **1** discovery, revelation **2** demonstration ابراز كول *compound verb* **a** to discover, reveal **b** to demonstrate

ابرام ibrám *m. Arabic* urgent request ابرام كول to request urgently, demand

ابراهيم ibrāhím *m. Arabic proper name* Ibrahim, Abraham

ابراهيم خېل ibrāhimkhél *m.* birrimkhél *plural* **1** Ibrahimkheli (subdivision of a tribe) **a** of the Waziri-Utmanzaj **b** of the Gil'zaj-Sulimankhejlej **c** of the Zamusht **2** Ibrakhimkhejl (tribesman)

آبرساني ābrasāní *f.* آبرساني water supply د آبرسانى موټر water-tank truck

ابرك abrák *m. singular & plural* mica سپين ابرك Muscovite, white mica

آبرو ābráv [1] *m.* āvráv aqueduct د مستعملو اوبو آبرو irrigation ditch

آبرو ābrú [2] *m.* ābró *f. plural* honor, dignity, reputation آبرو وركول to do honor, respect آبرو پر مځكه تويول to shame, dishonor

ابرو abrú [3] *m.* [*plural:* ابران abruán] eyebrow

آبرومن ābrumán ābrumánd **1** honorable **2** deserving, respected, estimable

آبرومندانه ābrumandāná **1** deserving, estimable په آبرومندانه صورت in a deserving fashion or manner **2** in a worthy fashion or manner

ابره abrá [1] **1** right side (i.e., of clothing) **2** small shawl (worn at the waist) **3** sash, girdle **4** kashmir shawl **5** paper with a design (for wrapping or bookbinding)

ابره ibrá [2] *f.* harvest; picking (e.g., fruit)

ابرا ibrá [3] *f. Arabic* **1** needle **2** pointer

ابره ور ibravár pertaining to harvest or crops; fertile

ابري ¹ abrí cloudy

ابري ² abrí کاغذ ابري paper with design (for wrapping or bookbinding)

آبریز ābréz āvréz lavatory, latrine

ابرینم abrekhám m. plural ☞ ورېنم

ابرى ubṛə́j f. ☞ اوبړى

آبس ā-bás Well, that's it!; That's all!

اپس ډندى abasḍanḍáj ☞ اپس ډندى

آبشار ābshár m. waterfall

آبشناس ābshinás m. pilot (maritime)

ابطال ¹ ibtál m. Arabic 1 destruction 2 rejection medicine idiom د حس ابطال anaesthesia

ابطال ² abtál m. Arabic plural ابطال abtál m. from Arabic بطل

ابعاد ab'ád m. Arabic plural [singular: بعد] 1 distances 2 math dimensions, measurements

ابک abák m. affectionate Papa ابکه Oh Papa!

آبکند ābkánd m. ravine

آب کوثر āb-i-kavsár m. religion 1 water of the heavenly river Kavsar 2 nectar 3 proper name the Kavsar River (in NW Afghanistan)

آبګوټ ābgóṭ m. ☞ اگبوټ

آبګوشت ābgúsht m. āvgúsht bouillon

ابل abál 1 naked 2 barefoot ابلى پښې (to go, be) barefoot ابلى Eastern (to go, be) barefoot

ابلاغ iblā́gh m. Arabic notification, report, information

ابلاغول iblāgavál denominative [past: ابلاغ شو] to notify, report, inform

ابلاغېدل ibladadál denominative, intransitive [past: ابلاغ شو] to be communicated, be informed

ابلاغیه iblāgijná f. Arabic 1 (official) communication, communique حربي ابلاغیه situation report, SITREP (re military operations)

ابلتوب abltób m. nudity, nakedness

ابلق ablák ابلك ablák Arabic 1 motley, parti-colored 2 piebald 3 figurative two-faced, hypocritical ابلق سړى دئ He is a hypocrite.

ablán اوبلن ☞ ublán

ابلوخ ablúts 1 adult, of full legal age 2 youthful هلك ابلوخ teenager, lad, youth

ابلوخه ablústa 1 feminine singular of ابلوخ 2 f. girl

ابلوخېدل ablutsedál denominative, intransitive [past: ابلوخ شو] to attain adulthood, reach maturity

ابلول abálavál denominative, transitive ابل يې کړ [past: to 1 bare, expose 2 to take off someone's shoes

ابله ¹ abála f. plural of ابل

ابله ² abláh Arabic stupid, bad

ابلهانه ablahāná 1 stupid, foolish ابلهانه کلمي stupid words, foolish words 2 stupidly, foolishly

آبله کوبي ablakubí f. inoculation, vaccination

ابلهي ablahí f. Arabic foolishness, nonsense, folly

ابلېدل abáledál denominative, intransitive [past: ابل شو] 1 to be bared, be exposed 2 to have someone's shoes removed

ابلیس iblís m. Arabic devil, satan

آبمند ābmánd honorable, worthy, respected

ابن ibn m. [plural: ابنا abnā́] Arabic son (in proper names)

آبنا ābná f. آبناي ābnáj m. strait, sound د دردنیل آبنا Dardanelles

ابن سینا ibn-i-siná m. ibna-Sina, Avicenna (Arab physician and philospher, 980-1037)

آبنوس ābnús m. Arabic singular & plural black wood, ebony

آبنوسي ābnusí adjective of black wood, of ebony

ubána f. ☞ اوینه

ابو ¹ abú m. father (in proper names) ابوبکر Abubekr

ابو ² ubó Western oblique plural of اوبه

ابواب abvā́b m. Arabic plural of باب ¹

ابو الهول abulhául m. Arabic sphinx

ابوت ubuvvát m. Arabic 1 fatherhood 2 patriarchy

آبوتاب ābutāb m. آبوتاب 1 brilliance, splendor 2 dignity په آب وتاب ویل to speak importantly, speak with dignity, speak grandiloquently

ابو خاله ubudzála f. sponge

آب ودانه āb-u-dāná f. 1 subsistence, food 2 that which is necessary to exist

ابوس obús m. howitzer

ابوسي obusí adjective howitzer

آب وهوا āb-u-havá f. climate

ابویت abaviját 1 fatherhood 2 position or role of an ancestor or forefather

ابوین abavájn m. Arabic dual parents, father and mother

ابه ¹ abá ابه په دبه وهل to get by, live in poverty, live from hand to mouth

ابه ² abá m. abbot

ابهام ibhām m. Arabic 1 doubt 2 vagueness, uncertainty, confusion ابهام رفع کول to eliminate doubt, introduce clarity

آبي ¹ ābí ابي abí 1 moist, humid 2 pertaining to watering, irrigation 3 sky blue آبي سترګي sky-blue eyes 4 water آبي لاري water routes آبي قوه hydraulic power

ابى ² abáj f. [plural: ابى abə́j ابى ګاني abə́jgā́ni] 1 mama, mommy (affectionate form of address) 2 mom (form of address to an elderly woman) 3 (child's) nurse, nanny 4 servant, female worker

آبیا ābijá f. آبیا وهل to pace (i.e., special gait used in horsemanship)

ابیات abjā́t m. Arabic plural ☞ بیت ¹

آبیاري ābjārí f. watering, irrigation آبیاري کول to water, irrigate

آبیانه ābjāná f. collection or accumulation of water

ابیجان abidzhán m. Abidzhan (city)

ابیر abír m. singular & plural ambergris, fragrance, perfume

ابیض abjáz Arabic combining form white ابیضه بحیره White Sea

3

ابیضه بحیره abjáza buhajrá the White Sea

ابیه ور abjavár *dialect* fast, swift (horses, etc.)

ابیه وري abjavarí *f.* ☞ آبیا

اپ ap a به اپ او دوب برابرول to scrape together, accumulate, acquire with difficulty b to steal (something)

اپارتمان apārtmán *m.* 1 multiple dwelling house (of the European type) 2 apartment

آپت āpát *m.* ☞ آفت ؛ آپت و! That's bad!

ابته apatá ☞ ابته

اپرن aprán *m.* apron

اپره uprá 1 *adjective* foreign 2 *m. singular & plural* foreigner, foreigners

اپریت iprít *m. plural* yperite, mustard gas

اپریدي apridí *m. singular of* افریدي

اپریشن apréshán *m.* operation (surgical)

اپریل apríl *m.* April

آپرین āprín ☞ آفرین

اپس ډنډۍ apasḍanḍə́j to play "tip cat" (a game in which a pointed stick of wood is made to spring up from the ground by being struck on the tip with a stick, and is then batted as far as possible)

اپسوس apsós *m.* ☞ افسوس

اپۀل apə́l ابل اپلي پنبي *adverb* barefoot

اپلات aplā́t empty, nonsensical ویل اپلاتي to babble, talk nonsense, talk rot

اپلاتند aplātə́nd babbling, talking nonsense, talking rot اپلاتند سرۍ babbler, windbag

اپلاس iplā́s *m.* ☞ افلاس

اپلات aplát ☞ اپلات

اپلاتند aplatə́nd ☞ اپلاتند

اپلیت aplít *m.* babbler, windbag

اپن apín *m. plural* opium

اپنائن apinā́jn *m.* ☞ اپي ناین

آپندیسیت āpandisít *m. medicine* appendicitis

آپندیکس āpandíks *m. anatomy* appendix

اپوټه apuṭá 1 turned over, unscrewed 2 oppressed, despotized, enslaved

اپول apavə́l *transitive* ☞ هپول

اپه apá *f.* endeavor, striving

اپي apí [*plural:* اپیان apijján] 1 viper, adder 2 snake

اپیز apíz *m. colloquial* ☞ حافظ

اپیل apíl *m. regional law* 1 appeal اپیل کول to appeal 2 request for a new hearing

اپلۀل apelə́l *transitive* [*past:* و یې اپبلل] swallow, gulp down, ingurgitate

اپیم apím *m. plural* opium

اپیمچي apimchí *m.* اپیمي apimí *m.* opium smoker

اپین apín *m. plural* opium

اپي نین apinájn *m.* اپي ناین apinájn the Appenine peninsula د اپي ناین غرونه the Appenines

ات āt *Arabic plural suffix* 1 *usually used with Arabic nouns, and rarely for nouns borrowed from other languages*, e.g., احتیاجات necessities خواهشات wishes 2 *forms the second plural of Arabic nouns*, e.g., اخبارات newspapers

اتازونوي ēhtāzunaví atāzunaví pertaining to the United States of America; belonging to the USA; American

اتازوني ēhtāzuní atāzuní *m. & f.* the United States of America, the USA د اتازوني ولایتونه the United States of America, the USA

آتاشي ātāshé *m.* [*plural:* اتاشه گان ātāshegā́n] attaché نظامي آتاشي military attache

اتام atā́m *m.* 1 ☞ طعام 2 crumbs (of bread)

اتبار¹ itbár *m. regional* Sunday

اتبار² ittibár *m. colloquial* ☞ اعتبار

اتباري ittibārí *colloquial* ☞ اعتباري ؛ هغه دپر اتباري و I believed him.

اتباع¹ atbā́ 1 *masculine plural of* تبع 2 subjects, nationals خارجي اتباع foreign subjects, foreign nationals

اتباع² ittibā́ *f. Arabic* 1 obedience 2 following, shadowing someone 3 observation, maintenance (of principles)

اتجاه ittidzháh *f. Arabic* [*plural:* اتجاهات ittidzhāhā́t] 1 direction, course (of a ship, aircraft) 2 inclination, bent, aspiration 3 tendency

اتحاد ittihád *m. Arabic* 1 unity 2 union شوروي اتحاد Soviet Union د شوروي سوسیالیستي جماهیرو اتحاد Union of Soviet Socialist Republics, the USSR 3 union, bloc alliance تدافعي اتحاد defense alliance

اتحاد اسلام ittihād-i-islā́m *m.* Pan-Islamism

اتحاد نامه ittihādnāmá *f.* allied treaty

اتحادي ittihādí 1 union اتحادي جمهور union republic, federal republic 2 federal

اتحادیه ittihādijá *f. Arabic* 1 unified body, union د کارگرانو اتحادیه trade union د ټولي شوروي اتحادیي د تجارت اطاق All-Union Chamber of Commerce د شوروي لیکوالو اتحادیه Union of Soviet Writers د مللو اتحادیه *history* League of Nations 2 alliance, bloc نظامي اتحادیه military alliance

اتخاذ ittikhā́z *m. Arabic* 1 collection 2 reception, acceptance, taking اتخاذ کول *compound verb* a to collect b to receive, accept, take خپل تصمیمات یی اتخاذ کړي دي He decided.

اتر atár knowing, witting, informed په دي کار خبر او اتر نه یم I know nothing of this matter. I am not informed about it.

اتراغ utrā́gh *m.* اتراق utrā́ḳ *m.* stand, mooring, parking, halt, rest-stop اتراغ کېدل to be halted, be parked, be moored; have a rest-stop, arrange a halt

اترنگ atráng *m. singular & plural botany* henna, alkanna

اترول ataravə́l *denominative, transitive* [*past:* اتر یې کړ] to inform, notify

اتره atára *f.* trunk, body, torso

اتري atə́ri *doublet* خبري

اتربدل ataredə́l *denominative, intransitive* [*past:* اتر شو] to be informed, be notified

اتريش otrísh *m.* Austria

اتساع ittisā́' *f. Arabic* 1 broadening, expansion 2 extensiveness, magnitude, roominess, spaciousness

آتش ātásh *m.* ātísh 1 fire 2 gunfire د آتش خط آني آتش volley line of fire د آتش قوه firepower 3 *used as the first element in compounds,* e.g., آتش بازي fireworks

آتش افشان ātashfshā́n آتش انداز ātashandā́z 1 *adjective* flame-throwing 2 *m.* flame-thrower

آتش باري ātashbārí *f.* artillery fire

آتش بازي ātashbāzí *f.* fireworks

آتش پرست ātashparást *m.* fire worshipper

آتش پرستي ātashparastí *f.* fire worship

آتش خانه ātashkhāná *f.* 1 focus, pocket, center (e.g., infection) 2 shelf; lock, block, bolt (of a rifle, etc.); fuse, primer, detonator (armament)

آتش دار ātashdā́r 1 incendiary 2 pertaining to firearms آتش داره وسله weapon (firearm)

آتش فشان ātashfishā́n 1 pyrogenetic, volcanic آتش فشان غر volcano 2 *m.* flamethrower

آتش فشاني ātashfishāní *f.* volcanic eruption

آتشک ātashák *m.* 1 *agriculture* anthracnose (plant disease) د تاکو آتشک vineyard anthracnose 2 syphilis

آتش گير ātashgír *m.* tinder, wick

آتاشه atashé *m.* آتاشه ☞ ¹آتشي

²آتشي ātashí 1 *adjective* fire, pertaining to gunfire آتشي پرده curtain of fire 2 accumulated, amassed 3 bright 4 *figurative* given to anger, quick to anger *idiom* آتشي شيشه magnifying glass

اتصال ittisā́l *m. Arabic* 1 contiguity 2 joining, junction, tie, bond د اتصال کړۍ connecting link دچا سره اتصال ورکول to join, connect سره اتصال پيدا کول to join (something to something else), associate oneself with someone 3 continuity

اتصالي ittisālí *Arabic* joining, connecting

اتفاق ittifā́k *m. Arabic* 1 contiguity, coincidence 2 consent, agreement دچا سره اتفاق کول to come to an understanding, come to an agreement with someone ... چه لري اتفاق مسئلي دي د ټول all are in agreement with the fact that ... ... چه راغئ اتفاق دي په they have agreed that ... 3 unanimity د آراو اتفاق په consensus اتفاق سره a in concord, with mutual, common consent b unanimously 4 case, event, occurrence 5 good luck, success

اتفاقاً ittifā́kán *Arabic* 1 unanimously, by consensus 2 by chance, now and then

اتفاقي ittifākí *Arabic* accidental, fortuitous په اتفاقي صورت accidentally, by chance

اتکا ittikā́ *f. Arabic* 1 support 2 hope, reliance, expectation اتکا کول په، ...پر hope, reliance, expectation a to be

based (upon), be founded (upon) b to rely, depend, set hope upon (someone, something)

اتکائي ittikāí *military* supporting اتکائي ځای defended post, strong point

اتکړۍ atkar̪ə́j *f.* handcuffs, manacles

اتکو atkó *f.* اتکی atkə́j *f.* 1 mother (affectionate form of address) 2 grandmother (affectionate form of address)

اتل atál 1 courageous, brave, valorous 2 *m.* .1 distinguished person, talented person 2.2 epic hero 2.3 hero 2.4 champion

اتلاف itlā́f *m. Arabic* تلف ☞

اتلانتيک atlāntík *adjective* Atlantic

اتلتون ataltún *m.* اتلتون operational department (Soviet strategic, tactical term)

¹اتلس atlás *m.* 1 satin (cloth) 2 *proper name* Atlas

²اتلس atə́las *numeral* اته لس ☞

³اتلس atlás ☞ اطلس ¹

⁴اتلس átlas *m.* atlas (e.g., geographic reference)

اتلسم atə́lasə́m *ordinal* اته لسم ☞

اتلسه atlása *f. proper name* Atlasa

اتل لپرد atalégd *m. military* transfer, redeployment of troops

اتل وال atalvā́l *m. military* Chief of Operations Department

اتلواله atalvā́la *f.* talent, (personal) gift

اتم atə́m *ordinal* eighth

اتمام itmā́m *m. Arabic* completion, conclusion

اتمانځي utmāndzí *m. plural* ☞ اتمانزي 1 2 utmānzáj *m.* ☞ اتمانزي

اتمان خېل utmānkhél 1 *m. plural* the Utmankhejli 1a a tribe 1b a subdivsion of the Orakzai tribe 2 Utmankhejl (person)

¹اتمانزي utmānzí *m. plural* Utmanzi (a subdivision of (a.) the Waziri tribe; (b.) the Momandi tribe) 2 utmānzái *m. plural* the Utmanzai

اتمبار atambā́r *m.* ☞ اتمبار

اتموسفېر atmosfér *m.* atmosphere

آتن ātén *m.* Athens (city)

اتنا ēhtna *f.* Etna

اتنوگرافي ēhtnogrāfí *f.* ethnography

اننه utə́na *f. doublet* پوښتنه

اتنيم atə́ním *vice* اته نيم پر اتنيمي بجي at eight-thirty

اتن atán *m.* 1 the Atan (national dance) 2 dance اتن وهل، اتن اتن کول a to dance b to whirl in the air (of birds) اتن اچول

اتن وال atanvál *m.* one who dances the Atan; dancer

اتني ataṇí *adjective* dancing اتني ځوان dancer

¹اتو utú *m.* flatiron اتو کول flatiron اتو ماشين د *compound verb* to iron, press

²اتو ató *m. proper name* Ato

³اتو ató *oblique of* اته ²

اتوار itvār *m. regional* Sunday

¹اتوب atúb *m. dialect* a sweet odalda or pancake (cooked in butter)

اتوب ² atób *m. Eastern* sweet gruel; scrambled eggs

اتوریته otorité *f.* 1 power 2 authority

اتوکار otokár *m.* bus, intercity bus

اتوم atóm *m.* atom

اتومات atomát *m.* automatic device د اتومات مرکز automatic telephone station, automatic telephone switching installation

اتوماتیکي atomātikí automatic په اتوماتیکي ډول automatically اتوماتیکي کول to automate

اتومبیل atomobíl *m.* ☞ موټر

اتومي atomí اتومیک atomík *adjective* nuclear, atom اتومي انرژي atomic energy د اتومي ستېسن nuclear power station د اتومي وزن *physics* atomic weight

اتونی atonáj *m.* last person (e.g., in a queue), bringing up the rear

اته ¹ áta *f.* 1 cubit (measure of length) اته کول to measure a length 2 pace

اته ² atə *numeral* eight

اته ³ atá *f. regional* prison cell

اتهام ittihām *m. Arabic* accusation, suspicion

اتهامنامه ittihāmnāmá *f. Arabic* bill of indictment

اته انیزي atəanízaj *m.* half-rupee (eight annas in Indian money)

اته لس atálas *numeral* eighteen

اته لسم atálasəm *ordinal* eighteenth

اته ویشت atəvísht *numeral* twenty-eight

آتي ātí *Arabic* following, next, supervenient

اتیا atjá *numeral* eighty

اتیاً atíján *Arabic* afterwards, later on, subsequently, in the future

اتیات itjāt *m. colloquial* ☞ احتیاط

اتیتي atíte *f.* 1 patience 2 satisfaction اتیتي کول a to endure, stand, suffer b to content oneself with, be contented

آتیه ātijá *f. Arabic* future

اتاړی aṭaṛáj *f.* 1 country house, dacha 2 farmstead, villa (usually with two stories and a tower) 3 *Afridi* upper story

اټال aṭál 1 uneasy, worried 2 banned, not permitted, detained 3 unoccupied, unemployed 4 repulsed, repelled اټال کول ☞ اټالول اټال کېدل ☞ اټالبدل

اټالول aṭālavə́l *denominative, transitive* [*past:* اټال یې کړ] 1 to trouble, disturb, alarm 2 to detain, bother, obstruct 3 to prevent from working 4 to beat off, repel

اټالبدل aṭāledə́l [*past:* اټال شو] 1 to worry, be agitated, be alarmed 2 to be detained, be stoped 3 to be prevented from working 4 to be repulsed, be repelled

اټالبده aṭāledə́ *m. plural* 1 worry, agitation, alarm 2 delay, halt

اټاوا aṭāvá *f.* Ottawa (city)

اټراق uṭrák *m.* ☞ اتراغ

اټسکی atə́skaj *m.* sneezing اتسکی کول، اتسکی وهل to sneeze

اټک aṭák Atak (city) د اټک سیند the Ind River

اټکل aṭkál *m.* 1 supposition, guess, proposal غلط اټکل miscalculation, blunder د اټکل متار، اټکل وهل to suppose, guess a to divine, د اټکل په متار وهل وراجول to make a rough estimate

guess b to make a statement by guesswork 2 likening, comparison 3 judgement, opinion 4 check, test, trial

اټکلول aṭkalavə́l *denominative, transitive* [*past:* اټکل یې کړ] 1 to suppose, think, consider 2 to compare 3 to make a judgment concerning something; evaluate something تر حقیقت کم اټکلول، تر حقیقت لږ اټکلول to underestimate 4 to estimate 5 to check; test ځان اټکلول to check oneself

اټکلونه aṭkalavə́na *f.* 1 assumption, guess 2 comparison 3 evaluation 4 estimate 5 check, test

اټکلي atkalí 1 approximate, rough, near (as in guess, estimate) د اټکلي سنجش سره سم according to rough calculations 2 notional

اټکلبدل aṭkaladə́l *denominative, intransitive* [*past:* اټکل شو] 1 to be assumed, be considered 2 to be capable of comparison, be compared 3 to be evaluated 4 to be checked, be tested

اټکور aṭkór *m.* the application of a hot brick or other object to a sore spot

اټکورول aṭkoravə́l *denominative, transitive* [*past:* اټکورول یې کړ] to treat by applying a hot object to a sore spot

اټکوربدل aṭkoredə́l *denominative, intransitive* [*past:* اټکور شو] to be treated by the application of a hot object to a sore spot

اټکی ¹ aṭkáj *f.* hiccough اټکی کول to hiccough

اټکی ² uṭkáj *m.* pipe, flue

اټلس aṭlás *m.* atlas

اټلي ítəli *f.* ایطالیا

اټمبار aṭambár *m.* crowd, assemblage, gathering

اټمبارول aṭambaravə́l *denominative, transitive* [*past:* اټمبار یې کړ] 1 to assemble, unite 2 to arrange, put right

اټمبربدل aṭambraredə́l *denominative, intransitive* [*past:* اټمبار شو] 1 to be assembled, be united, be accumulated 2 to be arranged, be set right

اټودځي aṭodzáj *m.* bazaar, market

ات و سټ aṭ-u-sáṭ hither and thither, back and forth

اټوم aṭóm *m.* ☞ اتوم

اټوماتیکي aṭomātikí ☞ اتوماتیکي

اټومي aṭomí اټومیک aṭomík ☞ اتومي

اټومي وسله aṭūmí waslá *f.* dirty bomb

اټه ¹ aṭá *f.* ball, skein (of thread) اټه کول to wind, reel اټه کېدل to be wound, be reeled

اټه ² áṭa *f.* whim

اټه اوړه aṭa-oṛə́ *m. plural* finely-milled flour

اټي ¹ atə́j *f.* ☞ اته ¹

اټی ² atə́j *f.* ☞ هټی shop, store

اټي ³ ate *plural of* اته ¹

اټي ⁴ áti *plural of* اته ²

اټران aṭerān *m.* 1 spool, reel 2 pachisi, ateran (game with dice) *compound verb* اټران کول a to reel b to play pachisi

اټرل aṭerə́l [*past:* واټېره] 1 to suffer from indigestion, suffer from dyspepsia 2 to overeat, overfeed, be stuffed

اتهپرن aṭerán suffering from indigestion, suffering from dyspepsia

اتهپرنه aṭeróna *f.* indigestion, dyspepsia

اتنشن aṭenshán *regional military* Attention! (as a command) اتنشن کبدل *compound verb* to stand at attention

اتیوال aṭiwál *m.* shopkeeper

اثاث asās *m.* اثاث البيت asās-ul-bájt *m. Arabic* furniture; household furnishings; utensils

آثار āsắr *m. Arabic* **1** plural of اثر **2** ruins (antiquities), monuments تاريخي آثار ، عتيقه آثار historical monuments حفظ آثار hifs-i protection of ancient moments **3** works, writings, compositions

اثبات *m. Arabic* confirmation, proof په اثبات کښې يې سر و خوځاوه He nodded his head affirmatively. په اثبات رسول to confirm, prove دا هم د اثبات ته زه یې په اثبات رسولای شم I can prove it. رسېدلي ده چه ...It has been also proven that ... اثبات کبدل اثباتبدل *compound verb*

اثباتول isbātavál *denominative, transitive* [*past:* اثبات یې کړ] to confirm, prove

اثباتبدل isbātedál *denominative, intransitive* [*past:* اثبات شو] to be confirmed, be corroborated, be proven په لاس لیک اثباتبدل to be attested by signature

اثر asár *m.* [*plural:* اثرونه asarúna *Arabic plural:* آثار āsắr *plural:* اثرات asarát] **1** track دچا اثر مېندل to detect someone's tracks; find هیڅ اثر لاس ته رانغئ No tracks of any kind were detected. **2** sign, symbol **3** impression, influence, action, effect په ... اثر اچول ، په ... کښې اثر وربخښنل to influence, affect په ... کښې بد اثر وربخښنل ... to exert a bad influence upon... اثر لرل ، اثر کول ، اثر غورځول to influence... اثر غورځول to act, operate, exert influence on **4** leadership د ... اثر لاندي a under the influence ... **b** under the leadership ... **5** literary production, literary work *idiom* د ... له اثره ... as a result of ... په اثر کښي as a result, consequence of ...

اثره asrá *f.* اسره

اثري asarí bewitching, alluring

اثقال askāl *m. Arabic plural* **1** *from* ثقل **2** ballast

اثنا asnā *m. Arabic plural* **1** *from* ثني **2** interval, mean **3** interval of time, interval of space په اثنا کښي ... د in time ... in the course of ... په دغه اثنا کښي at that time, in the meantime

اثواب asvāb *m. Arabic plural of* ثوب

آثور āsúr *m. history* Assyria

آثوري āsurí **1** *adjective history* Assyrian **2** *m.* Assyrian (person)

اثیر asír *m. Arabic plural* ether

اثيوبي asjubí **1** *adjective* Ethiopian **2** *m.* Ethiopian (person)

اثيوبيه asjubijá *f.* Ethiopia

اجابت idzhābát *m. Arabic* **1** granting (satisfaction) of a request **2** favorable attitude **3** careful (attentive) hearing **a** اجابت کول to satisfy a request, respond to a request **b** to regard favorably **c** to give a careful (attentive) hearing

اجارت idzhārát *Arabic m.* اجاره idzhārá *f. Arabic* **1** lease, rental **2** lease, rental contract داجاري لیک ، داجاري حق a rent purchase (of land) **a** اجارت کول ، په اجارت اخیستل contract **3** lease, take on lease, rent **b** to assume ownership **c** to put (something) out to contract, contract (something) out **4** leased sector of land idiom د قرض او اجاري قانون *history* lend-lease law

اجاره اخیستونکی idzhārá akhistúnkaj *m.* leaseholder, lessee, tenant

اجاره دار idzhāradār *m. Arabic* **1** leaseholder, lessor, tenant **2** freeholder **3** contractor

اجاره داري idzhāradārí *f.* **1** lease, rent **2** possession based on lease

اجاره وال idzhāraväl *m.* اجاره دار

اجڑ udzáṛ dispersed, scattered, dissipated

اجاڑول udzāṛavál *denominative* to scatter, disperse, dissipate

اجاړېدل udzāṛedál *denominative* [*past:* اجاړ شو] to be scattered, be dispersed

اجاړېده udzāṛedá *m. plural* sparseness, dispersion

اجازت idzhāzát *m.* اجازه idzhazá *f. Arabic* **1** permission, authorization د چا په اجازت، د چا په اجازت سره with someone's permission بېله اجازي، بېله اجازي څخه without authorization د چا څخه اجازت اخیستل to receive someone's permission اجازت وړکول to request someone's permission اجازت غوښتل give permission, authorize اجازت کبدل *compound verb* to be authorized; be granted (rights, etc.) اجازه ده؟ May I? May one? Do I have your permission? اجازه ده it is allowed, One can, you may, **2** approval, sanction اجازت مېندل to have received approval, be sanctioned, be approved **3** right اجازت لرل to have the right

اجازه نامه idzhāzanāmá *f.* **1** license, authorization, certificate **2** pass, permit **3** admission (i.e., to premises); admittance

اجاغ udzhāgh *m.* hearth

آجال ādzhál *m. Arabic plural of* اجل

اجانیب adzhāníb *m. Arabic plural of* اجنبي

اجايي کبدل adzhājí to think only of food

اجب adzháb *colloquial* عجب

اجبار idzhbár *m. Arabic* compulsion; obligation اجبار کول to force, compel, oblige, constrain

اجباراً idzhbárán *Arabic* by force, compulsorily, by compulsion

اجباري idzhbārí *Arabic* compulsory, obligatory اجباري عسکري obligatory military service اجباري قوت لرل سیستم to be compelled (e.g., as a result of a court decision)

اجت adzhát *m. colloquial* حاجت

اجتماع idzhtimắ *f. Arabic* **1** *m.* [*plural:* اجتماعات idzhuma'ất] **1** meeting; gathering **2** *military* build-up, massing (of the enemy) **3** public, social life **4** [*plural:* اجتماعوي idzhtimắ'vi] society, collective

اجتماعاً idzhtima'ấn *Arabic* **1** in a social relationship **2** unanimously

اجتماعي idzhtimắ'í *Arabic* **1.1** public, social اجتماعي حيات public life اجتماعي نظام social system اجتماعي علوم social sciences

اجتماعي گرزول to socialize (the means of production) **1.2** *adjective* collective **2** *m.* [*plural:* اجتماعيون idzhtimā'ijún] sociologist

اجتماعيات idzhtimā'jā́t *m. Arabic plural* social problems, problems of public life, problems of social life; social life, public life

اجتناب idzhtināb *m. Arabic* **1** avoidance, evasion; removal **2** abstention ديوه شي څخه اجتناب كول to avoid, shun something, abstain from something

اجتهاد idzhtihā́d *m. Arabic* **1** diligence, endeavor, zeal **2** ☞ جهاد

اجداد adzhād *m. Arabic plural of* جد [1]

اجداد پرستي adzhdādparastí *f.* ancestor worship اجدادي *adzhdādí Arabic* ancestral, traditional

آجر [1] ā́dzhúr *m.* brick (baked in a kiln)

اجر [2] ádzhr *m.* ádzhar *Arabic* [*plural:* اجور udzhúr] **1** reward, recompense, compensation خپل زيار اجر ميندل to receive compensation for one's labor اجر وركول، صبر كوه، to compensate لري اجر لوى صبر *proverb* be patient, patience is liberally rewarded **2** pay, payment **3** repayment, retribution

اجرأ [1] idzhrā́ *f. Arabic* [*m. plural:* اجرآآت idzhrāā́t] fulfillment, implementation, accomplishment, realization د اجرأ قومانده *military* command of execution (i.e., as opposed to preparatory command) ديو شي اجرأ كول to carry (something) out اجرأ كول to accomplish تر اجرأ لاندي راوستل *compound verb* to fulfill, implement, accomplish, realize, carry out اجرأ كېدل *compound verb* to be fulfilled, be implemented, be accomplished, be carried out, be realized قانون په اجرأ اېښودل to put a law into effect

اجرا [2] udzharā́ *m. Arabic plural of* اجير

اجرام adzhrā́m *m. Arabic plural of* جرم، اسماني اجرام heavenly bodies

اجرايوي idzhrājaví اجرائي idzhrāí *Arabic* **1** executive اجرائيه قوه executive power اجرائيه كميته executive committee **2** administrative

اجرائيه idzhrāijá *f.* **1** executive power **2** administrator مدير administrative department, management directorate مدير اجرائيه mudír-i head of the management directorate

آجرپز ā́dzhurpáz *m.* bricklayer

آجرپزي ā́dzhurpazí *f.* firing, kilning bricks د آچرپزي داش kiln for firing bricks

اجرت udzhrát *m. Arabic* pay, recompense, wage اجرت لرل to receive pay د زيات اجرت ورکول to pay اجرت اخيستل to earn تقاضا لرل to demand an increase in wages or salary

اجرستان adzhristā́n *m.* Adzhristan (district)

اجره udzhrá *f. colloquial* ☞ حجره

آجري ā́dzhuń *adjective* brick

اجړه idzhṛá *m.* [*plural:* اجړه گان idzhṛagā́n] scoundrel, villain, rascal

اجزا adzhzā *m. Arabic plural* **1** *of* جز [2] **2** component parts, elements **3** matter **4** organs, members (or similar) د جملي اجزا *grammar* parts of a sentence اصلي اجزا **a** basic elements **b** principal parts (of a sentence)

اجسام adzhsā́m *m. Arabic plural* **1** *of* جسم **2** substances

اجسكي adzhóskaj *colloquial* pitiful, poor

اجغنه udzhghóna *f.* اجغونه udzhghóna *f.* goat's wool

اجل adzhāl *m. Arabic* [*plural:* آجال ādzhā́l] **1** end of life; hour of death; death زما خو نو اجل پوره شو *folklore* And now came my last hour, my end اجل نيولئ doomed; dying **2** limit; (fixed) term

اجلاپ adzhāp moral, pure (of a person)

اجلاس idzhlās *m. Arabic* session, sitting, conference كامل اجلاس plenum, plenary session اجلاس كول to confer, hold a conference

اجلاسي اجلاسيه idzhlāsí idzhlāsijá *singular & plural* اجلاسي غونډه plenary session, plenum اجلاسي دوره session

اجلئ adzháldzáj *m.* back of the head, occiput

اجل رسيده adzhál-rasidá doomed, dying

اجماع idzhmā' *f. Arabic* **1** *religion* unanimous decision or opinion of theologians **2** assembly, convocation **3** congregation, council

اجمال idzhmāl *m. Arabic* **1** short account, brief description, abstract, summary **2** short survey, compendium, resumé

اجمالاً idzhmālán *Arabic* briefly; concisely; in general, outline; as an abstract; summarily

اجمالي idzhmālí *Arabic* short, concise, recapitulative, summary

اجمل adzhmál *Arabic* **1** most beautiful; perfect **2** *m. proper name* Adzhmal, Ajmal

اجناب adzhnāb *m. Arabic plural of* جنب [1]

اجناس adzhnās *m. Arabic plural of* جنس ، صادراتي اجناس exports, export goods

اجنبي adzhnabí *Arabic* **1.1** strange, alien, foreign, outlandish اجنبي لغات foreign words **1.2** unfamiliar **2** *m.* [*plural:* اجنبيان adzhnabijā́n *Arabic* اجانب adzhāníb] **2.1** foreigner, alien **2.2** stranger

اجنبيت adzhnabijā́t *m. Arabic* condition of being alien or foreign; foreignness, alien

اجنټ adzhánṭ *m. regional* agent

اجنډا adzhenḍā́ *f.* اجنډه adzhenḍá *f.* agenda, order of the day د اجنډي جز گرځول to include in the agenda

اجنسي adzhensí *f.* **1** agency **2** organ (establishment, organization)

آجنه ādzhána *f.* woman who has completed a haj (i.e., pilgrimage to Mecca); pilgrim

اجوت adzhvát **1** united **2** side by side, next to; adjacent, contiguous

اجوت والى adzhvātvā́laj *m.* **1** joining, junction, connection, combination **2** bring next to, bring alongside; closeness of fit; contiguity

اجوتول adzhvatavә́l denominative [past: اجوت يې کړ past: اجوت يې کړ] to unite, join, connect, close

اجوتونه adzhvatavә́na f. joining, junction, addition, binding together

اجوته adzhváta ☞ اجوتول، اجوته کول adzhváta ☞ اجوته کبدل، adzhvatedә́l to unite

اجوتبدل adzhvatedә́l denominative [past: اجوت شو] unite; join, connect; close (up, in)

اجور udzhúr m. Arabic plural of اجر²

اجوره udzhurá f. Arabic pay; wages; compensation اجوره گټل to earn

اجوره کار udzhutakār hired, rented

اجوره کاري udzhurakārí f. Arabic work performed for pay; salary, earnings

اجوف adzhváf m. Arabic plural 1 of جوف 2 anatomy cavity 3 belly, interior 4 womb اجه údzha f. dialect leech

اجي adzhí m. colloquial hadji

اجيټن adzhiṭán m. اجيدان adzhidān m. colloquial adjutant

اجيداني adzhidāní f. duties of an adjutant

اجير adzhir m. Arabic [plural: اجيران adhirán Arabic plural: اجرا udzharā́] temporary worker

اجيري adzhirí hired, leased

وچ uch dialect ☞ اچ

آچار āchár pickles آچار اچول to pickle (literally and figuratively)

اچانک achānák regional suddenly; unexpectedly; all of a sudden اچانک سوال کول to make an unexpected request

اچاوه ¹ achāvә́ m. plural 1 throwing, flinging, hurling 2 knocking down 3 attacking, assaulting 4 filling in 5 pouring, pouring out 6 lowering; letting down, pulling down

اچاوه ² achāvә́ اچاوي achavój Western imperfect of اچول

اوچت uchát ☞ اوچت

اوچتوالی uchatvā́laj m. ☞

اوچتول uchatavә́l transitive ☞

اوچتبدل uchatedә́l intransitive ☞

اچرلي uchә́laj m. ☞ اچرلي

اچکزي ¹ achakzí m. plural ☞ اخکزي 1 2 achakzáj m. ☞ اخکزي 2

اچکل uchkúl m. six-month-old lamb

اچکۍ uchakój f. dialect small island, islet

اچمچ achmә́ch m. اچ موچ achmúch m. the game of tip cat (a game in which a pointed piece of wood called a cat is made to spring up from the ground by being struck on the tip with a stick and is then batted as far as possible)

اچو achú f. blackberry (the plant or the fruit)

اچول ¹ achavә́l 1 transitive [past: وايي چاوه] .1 throw, fling, hurl, drop (from a height); throw out, cast پر مځکه اچول to throw on the ground بمونه اچول to drop bombs 1.2 to bring, knock down الوتکه پر مځکه را اچول to bring an aircraft down 1.3 throw on, throw over, put on پر ستن پر ځان اچول to cover with a

blanket 1.4 to spread 1.5 to put, place, put together بار پر اوښ to lead a pack on a camel 1.6 to lay (eggs) 1.7 to strew, pour (in, into) a دانه اچول to مالګه اچول to sprinkle salt, salt strew seed, sprinkle grain b to sow 1.8 to pour, pour out یوه to pour me a cup of tea پټرول اچول پياله چای راواچوه to refuel 1.9 to give, feed (animals) 1.10 to fertilize, fertilize the soil 1.11 pass, give ډوډۍ راواچوه pass me the bread 1.12 to register (mail) 1.13 to lower, let down, launch جهاز اوبو ته ور اچول to launch a boat سر يې کښته واچاوه He hung his head. 1.14 to establish, set up (e.g., communications with someone) 1.15 to build 1.16 to bind, fasten (to) 1.17 to place, put, settle, lodge; assign a billet, quarter 1.18 to assign work, put to work 1.19 to send (to school) 1.20 to hand in (an application); institute (a suit) پر چا عرض اچول to bring a suit against someone 1.21 to entrust مسئوليت پر چا اچول to make someone responsible for something 1.22 to set aside, adjourn; drag out (an affair) سبا ! Put it off until tomorrow! 1.23 to draw up (e.g., a plan); sketch in, make a rough sketch or outline نقشه اچول to draw up a plan د چا پر ضد يوه نقشه اچول to plot something against someone 1.24 to make oneself out to be someone; pretend to be someone else; claim something as one's own property غوږونه يې کاڼه واچول He pretended to be deaf. 1.25 to start, set going; put into service, put into operation; utilize لنبکر په جنګ کښي اچول to commit troops to battle 1.26 instill (in); install (in), establish د وطن محبت په زړو کښي اچول to inculcate love for the motherland 1.27 to make, produce, effect اور اچول a to throw oneself, ځان اچول to greet سلام اچول to set on fire rush b to make oneself out to be someone else, imitate someone else, pretend to be someone else ځان مړ اچول to pretend to be dead ځان پر ناجوړي اچول to feign illness, malinger c to expose oneself to something, subject oneself to something د چا سره to be on friendly terms, establish friendship with انډيوالي اچول يو بل سره اچول someone 2 m. plural ☞ اچاوه 1 idiom quarrel

اچول ² uchavә́l transitive dialect ☞ وچول

اچولى uchvúlaj m. uchvólaj brow, forehead

اچوني achavunáj m. اچوني achavunáj f. miscarriage

اچونکى ¹ achavúnkaj present participle of اچول, نقب اچونکي توپ bomber بم اچونکي الوتکه، بم اچونکي طياره mortar

اچه achchá f. prop, support

اچهوت achhút regional 1 untouchable 2 m. member of the untouchable caste

اچبدل uchedә́l intransitive dialect ☞ وچبدل

اخذبتوب adzabatób m. flight, desertion

اخذبه adzába f. ☞ فرار

اخذباج adzábaj m. ☞ فراري

اخک atsák m. proper name Atsak

اخکزي atsakzáj m. plural ☞ اخکزي 1

اڅکزي 1 atsakzí *m.* اڅکزيان astaskiján *plural* the Achakzai (tribe) 2 atsakzáj *m.* the Achakzaj

اڅکيزه utskíza *f.* post, pole (of a tent)

اڅنل atsaṇól *transitive* [*past:* وايي څانه] 1 to level, make even, smooth over 2 to arrange, put right, adjust, regulate 3 *music* to tune 4 to baste, join loosely

اخه [1] atsá *f.* thighbone, femur

اخه [2] átsa *f.* 1 endeavor, aspiration 2 attempt, trial 3 rush 4 forward movement, advance اخه کول a to endeavor, strive b to try, attempt c to rush, throw oneself upon د دوی پر لور مي اخه وکړه I rushed him. d to conduct an advance

آحاد āhād *m. Arabic plural of* احد 2

احاديث ahādís *m. plural of* حديث

احاطه ihātá *f. Arabic* 1 encirclement, envelopment, action of surrounding 2 seige 3 enclosed place 4 fence, enclosure 5 understanding, comprehension احاطه کول *compound verb* a to encircle, envelop, surround b to beseige c to understand, comprehend 6 district, sphere

احاطه يي ihātaí *military* flanking, outflanking احاطه يي حرکت flanking movement

احاله ihālá *f. Arabic* transmission, handing over, presentation (of an award, etc.), delivery په محال احاله carrying to an absurdity

احتجاج ihtidzhádzh *m. Arabic* 1 protest 2 refusal

احتراز ihtiráz *m. Arabic* 1 care, caution, prudence, circumspectness, discretion د احتراز لاري راتلل to act with caution, act with discretion 2 avoidance, abstemiousness, temperance احتراز کول a beware of, be wary of, be careful b avoid, abstain from

احتراق ihtiráḳ *m. Arabic* burning, combustion; ignition د داخلي احتراق موتور internal combustion engine

احترام ihtirám *m. Arabic* 1 reprect, honor, esteem, deference, consideration, homage, respects (e.g., "last respects") په ډېر احترام قطعه د with great respect, with great esteem, د احترام گارد guard of honor د احترام شليک artillery salute د ځان د رتبي احترامات self-respect, self-esteem د رتبي احترام respect for rank چا احترام کول to pay respects, render homage to someone; treat someone with respect; esteem someone; take someone's opinion into consideration د چا احترام ته ورتلل to pay someone a courtesy visit 2 observance (of a law or custom), carrying out, accomplishment (of an obligation or duty) د بیطرفی احترام کول to observe neutrality

احتراماً ihtirāmán with deference, with respect احتراماً عرض کوم I have the honor to inform you ...

احتساب ihtisáb *m. Arabic* supervision of municipal authorities of the accuracy and correctness of weights and measures in the market

احتفال ihtifál *m. Arabic* 1 meeting, gathering 2 festival, fête, solemnity

احتکار ihtikár *m. Arabic* buying up or cornering the market on goods (for the purpose of speculation); profiteering; speculation احتکار کول to buy up goods; speculate

احتکاري ihtikārí *adjective* profiteering, speculative gouging

احتمال ihtimál *m. Arabic* 1 probability, possibility, supposition, likelihood دي احتمال نشته this is improbable; this is impossible په زیات احتمال سره in all probability 2 patience, endurance 3 chance, unexpectedness

احتمالاً ihtimālán *Arabic* probably, possibly

احتمالي ihtimālí *Arabic* probable; possible; supposed; conjectural; hypothetical, presumable; permissible *math* احتمالي نظریات theory of probability احتمالي ماضي *grammar* past conjectural (mood)

احتیاج ihtijádzh *m. Arabic* [*plural:* احتیاجونه ihtijādzhúna *Arabic plural:* احتیاجات ihtijādzhát] need, want, necessity ضروري احتیاج د وقت کښې pressing needs; basic requirements احتیاجات in case of necessity احتیاج لرل to need, require احتیاجات رفع کول to satisfy needs, satisfy requirements په زیات احتیاجات پوره کول احتیاج لوبدل a fall into extreme need

احتیاط ihtiját *m. Arabic* 1 care, caution, discretion, precaution په سره د ډېره احتیاطه very carefully زیات احتیاط سره not withstanding all the precautionary measures which were taken احتیاط کول to be careful 2 prudence 3 reserve, reserve supply د احتیاط بلوک *military* reserve platoon

احتیاطاً ihtijātán *Arabic* out of caution, as a precautionary measure, in any event

احتیاط کاره احتیاط کار ihtijātkára 1 careful, wary, provident 2 prudent

احتیاط کاري ihtijātkārí *f.* ☞ احتیاط 1, 2

احتیاطي ihtijātí *Arabic* 1.1 ☞ احتیاط کار and احتیاط کاره 1.2 spare, reserve احتیاطي بلوک *military* reserve احتیاطي عسکر *military* reserve platoon 2 *m. military* reservist

احجبه ahdzhibá *m. Arabic plural of* حجاب [1]

احد ahád *Arabic* 1 united, single, one 2 *m.* [*plural:* آحاد āhád] discrete (separate) person, individual, person

احداث ihdás *m. Arabic* [*plural:* احداثونه ihdāsúna *Arabic plural:* احداثات ihadāsát] 1 invention, innovation 2 finding, discovery (i.e., of resources) احداث کول a to invent b to find, discover (i.e., resources)

احدي ahadí *Arabic* single, separate, only

احدیت ahadiját *m. Arabic* 1 singleness, singularity (i.e., in math) 2 consent, assent 3 unity

احرار ahrár *m. plural* [*singular:* حر] 1 *history* freeborn, freemen 2 nobles 3 *politics* liberals

احراز ihráz *m. Arabic* 1 achievement (act of receiving), reception د احراز مقام the assumption of a post (e.g., of the president of a republic); entry into office 2 meaning, significance اول لمبر احراز کول to acquire paramount significance

احزاب ahzáb *m. Arabic plural of* حزب

احساس ihsās m. Arabic [plural: احساسونه ihsāsúna Arabic plural: احساسول ihsāsāt] feeling, sensation احساس کول موږ هيڅ د يخنی احساس نه کاوه، احساسول We compound verb ☞ did not feel the cold at all.

احساساتي ihsāsātí sensitive, emotional

احساسول ihsāsavól denominative, transitive [past: احساس يي کړ] سخته ډکه يي احساسه کړه He felt a strong shock. 2 to feel, sense to experience, feel

احساسېدل ihsāsadól denominative, intransitive [past: احساس شو] to be felt, be experienced

احسان ihsān m. Arabic 1 favor, grace, kindness, goodness له چا سره احسان کول to be gracious to someone, show kindness to someone د چا احسان منل to consider oneself obliged to someone زه د هغه هيڅ احسان نه منم I am not obliged to him for anything. وپر احسانونه مي ستا له لاسه لېدلي دئ You have done me much kindness. احسان پرما ډېر I am very much obliged to you. 2 gift, donation

احسان فراموشي ihsānfarāmushí f. thanklessness, ingratitude

احسان من ihsānmán مند ihsānmānd obliged, grateful, thankful to someone, have been shown much favor (by someone)

احسنت ahsánt Arabic excellent; bravo; well done

احصا ihsā f. Arabic 1 calculation; math calculus 2 enumeration, census, accounting احصا کول a to count, calculate b to enumerate

احصايوي ihsāijaví احصائي ihsāí statistical احصايوي معلومات statistical data

احصائيه ihsāijá f. Arabic [plural: احصائي ihsāijé m. plural: احصائيات ihsāijāt] 1 calculation, counting, tallying, census د نفوسو احصائيه a population census احصائيه اخيستل to calculate; conduct a census 2 statistics د احصائي رئيس Chief of the Statistical Directorate د احصائي مدير Chief of the Statistical Department د احصائي علم statistics (the science) 3 [plural: احصائيات ihsāiját] statistical information; data, numerical data

احصائيه نويس ihsāijanavís m. statistician

احضار ihzār m. Arabic 1 training (of personnel) د معلمينو احضارات training of teachers 2 summons (i.e., to court) 3 admission (i.e., of candidates) 4 draft, call up د خدمت دپاره احضار کول to draft or call up for military service 5 recall (i.e., of a diplomatic representative) احضار کول compound verb ☞ احضاريدل احضار کېدل، compound verb ☞

احضارنامه ihzārnāmá f. diplomacy letter of recall

احضارول ihzāravól denominative, transitive [past: احضار يي کړ] to train (personnel) 2 to summon (i.e., to court) 3 to admit (i.e., candidates) 4 to call up (into the army, etc.) 5 diplomacy to recall

احضاري ihzārí Arabic adjective training مکتب احضاريه maktáb-i history cadet corps

احضارېدل ihzāredól denominative, intransitive [past: احضار شو] to be trained (of personnel) 2 to be summoned (i.e., to court) 3 to be admitted (i.e., of candidates) 4 to be called up (into the army) 5 diplomacy to be recalled

احضاريه ihzārijá f. Arabic summons (to court), subpoena

احفاد ahfād m. 1 Arabic plural of حفيد 2 descendants

احقاق ihḳāḳ m. Arabic 1 the ascertainment of the truth, the establishment of the truth 2 recognition of the legal right, recognition of justice

احقر ahḳár Arabic comparative & superlative degree of حقير most contemptible, most paltry epistolary my most contemptible, worthless or paltry self

احکام ahkām m. 1 Arabic plural of حکم¹ 2 religion commandments

احکامات ahkāmāt m. second person plural of احکام

احلام ahlām m. Arabic plural of حلم

احمد ahmád m. proper name Ahmed احمد شاه Ahmed-Shah Durani, Ahmed-Shah Durrani

احمد زاي ahmadzāí m. plural ☞ احمد زي

احمد زي ahmadzí m. plural 1 the Akhmadzai (a sub-tribe of: a the Waziri Tribe; b the Sulayman Khel Tribe (in turn subordinated to the Gilzai); c the Ushtarani Tribe) 2 ahamadzáj m. Akhmadzai (person)

احمدي ahmadí Arabic pertaining to Mohammed (the founder of Islam); Mohammedan

احمديه ahmadijá f. Arabic the Akhmadija, the Ahmadiya (a Muslim sect)

احمر ahmár red صليب احمر بين المللي salíb-i International Red Cross Society

احمرار ihmirār m. Arabic reddening, redness

احمره بحيره ahmára buhajrá f. the Red Sea

احمق ahmáḳ Arabic 1 stupid, foolish 2 fool, dolt, ignoramus

احمقانه ahmaḳānā 1 stupid, foolhardy احمقانه کار و this was stupid 2 stupidly, in foolhardy manner

احمقتوب ahmaḳtób m. ☞ احمقي¹

احمق والی ahmaḳvālaj m. ☞ احمقي¹

احمقي¹ ahmaḳí f. stupidity, foodhardiness, a stupid trick

احمقي² ahmáḳi feminine plural of احمق

احواض ahvāz m. Arabic plural of حوض

احوال ahvāl m. singular & plural m. Arabic plural of حال [plural: احوالونه ahvālúna plural: احوالات ahvālát] 1 position, state (e.g., of health, affairs) د چا د حال او احوال ليکونکی biographer د احوال پښتنه کول، احوال پښتنه کول to make inquiries about health, ask about the state of affairs 2 circumstances (business, affairs, etc.) په تو لو احوالو کښي under any circumstances, in all cases بيا به تاسي ته احوال to notify someone و چا ته احوال ورکول راورم I'll let you know subsequently. I'll tell you afterwards what the story is. 3 conditions جوي احوال، هواييه احوال meteorological conditions

احوالات ahvālāt *m. second plural of* احوال zábt-i ضبط احوالات counterintelligence

احوالپرسي ahvālpursí *f.* احوال پنتل ahvālpukhtál *m. plural* احوال پونتنه ahvālpukhtána *f.* احوال پنتل ahvālpukhtál *m. plural* احوال پنتنه ahvālpukhtána *f.* 1 inquiry about the state of health, being informed about the state of health 2 exchange of courtesies, exchange of greetings پر احوال پنتلو وروسته having inquired about the condition of health, having exchanged courtesies, greetings

احوال ahvál *Arabic* slanting-eyed, squint-eyed

احيا ihjā *f. Arabic* 1 reanimation, resurrection, revival 2 restoration, rebirth احيا كول a to reanimate, resurrect b to restore, revive

احيان ahjān *m. plural of* حين

احياناً ahjānán *Arabic* 1 sometimes, at times 2 in the event that …, in case …, if …

آخ [1] ākh اخ akh *interjection* 1 used to express joy or satisfaction Good!; Excellent!; Bravo! 2 used to express regret اخ آخ آخ! كول to exclaim Ach!; exclaim Oh!; sigh

اخ [2] əx *interjection* gid-ap, ho! (or similar exclamation to urge on an ass)

اخاړه akhāṛa *f.* 1 poultice 2 plaster 3 application (as poultice or plaster)

اخبار [1] akhbār *m. Arabic of* خبر *singular & plural* [*plural:* اخبارونه akhbārúna *plural:* اخبارات akhbārāt] 1 newspaper 2 tidings, news

اخبار [2] ikhbār *m. Arabic* information, communication د اخبار قومانده *military* preparatory command

اخباروالا akhbārvālā *m.* 1 newspaper salesperson, newspaper carrier, newspaper deliverer 2 *colloquial* journalist

اخبارول ikhbāravál *denominative, transitive* [*past:* اخباري کړ] to notify, inform

اخباري [1] akhbāri 1 *adjective* newspaper, periodical (used in connection with information) اخباري نماينده گان press representatives 2 *documentary* اخباري فلم documentary film اخباري وقايع news items

اخباري [2] ikhbāri *Arabic adjective* that which serves to notify or inform; informational اخباري وجه *grammar* indicative mood

اخپل akhpál *dialect* ☞ خپل

اخپور [1] akhpór *colloquial* ☞ خپور

اخپور [2] əkhpór *m.* اخپوري khporí ikhporí soldier; rifleman (in extended line) د اخپور قسم ممتاز اخپور sniper extended line of riflemen

اختتام ikhtitām *m. Arabic* termination, finishing, completion, end په اختتام ميندل end, finish, come to an end, be over with, end in اختتام رسول to end, finish, complete, conclude, carry through, put a finish to

اختر akhtár *m.* akhtár 1 holiday, festival کوچنی اختر a the Feast of Ramadan b Ramadan (the 10th lunar month) لوی اختر a the

Feast of Kurbanbajram b Kurbanbajram (12th lunar month) دا اختر مو مبارک شه! Many happy returns of اختر کول to celebrate اختر پټ مبره نه دئ *proverb* When there's a holiday, everyone knows it. پردی اختر نيم اختر دئ Another's holiday is but half holiday. چه اختر تېر شو، نو نکريزي په ديوال وتپه *saying literal* When the holiday is over, throw away the henna. *figurative* Everything in its own time. *proverb* روژې چا نيولې، اختر چا وکړ Some fast, some feast; One man toils, another grows wealthy 2 good omen, good horoscope, good luck 3 *proper name* Akhtar

اختراع ikhtirā' *f. Arabic* [*plural:* اختراع گاني ikhtirā'ghāni *plural:* اختراعات *m.* [*plural:* ikhtirā'āt] *Arabic* invention, discovery اختراع کېدل اختراع کول to invent, discover *compound verb* to be invented, be discovered نوې اختراع راوېستل to invent, make a new discovery

اختراعي ikhtirā'í relating to invention or discoveries; inventive

اخترامباركي akhtārāmbarakí *f.* congratulations on a holiday

اختري [1] akhtarí 1 *adjective* holiday 2 sacrificial اختري کول to sacrifice

اختری [2] akhtərəj *f. proper name* Akhtari

اختصار ikhtisār *m. Arabic* 1 shortening, abbreviation, reduction د کسر اختصار reduction of a fraction 2 brevity, compression, conciseness په اختصار سره ويل د اختصار په ډول briefly, in short to set forth briefly, state briefly

اختصاراً ikhtisārán *Arabic* briefly, in short, in abbreviated form, in general outline

اختصاري ikhtisārí abbreviated اختصاري نښه abbreviated designation, conventional sign

اختصاص ikhtisās *m. Arabic* 1 participation, connection, anything to do with 2 peculiarity, characteristic quality 3 assignation, appropriation 4 specialization

اختصاصي ikhtisāsí 1 special, peculiar to 2 specialized

اختفا ikhtifá *f. Arabic* camouflage

اختلاط ikhtilāt *m. Arabic* 1 mixing, mixture, confusion, blending, merging 2 crossing 3 intercourse, contact د چا سره اختلاط کول to associate with someone 4 complication

اختلاف ikhtilāf *Arabic* [*plural:* اختلافونه ikhtilāfúna *Arabic plural:* اختلافات] 1 difference, disagreement, discord, divergence, discrepancy, contradiction, dissension مختصر اختلاف tiff, disagreement د چا سره اختلاف کول، د چا سره اختلاف را اخيستل to disagree with someone, quarrel with someone; differ with someone in viewpoint دوی اختلاف سره لري They disagree as to opinion. 2 break, breaking off, discrepancy, lack of correspondence 3 difference, distinction اختلاف لرل to differ from something 4 *math* difference

اختلافي ikhtilāfí disputable, contradictory اختلافي مواد disputed question, disagreements دا يوه اختلافي خبره ده، دا يوه اختلافي مسئله This is a moot point. ده

اختلال ikhtilāl *m. Arabic* 1 disorder, disorganization ويو کار ته اختلال وريبنبدل to be disordered, be disorganized 2 disturbances, disorders, sedition, agitation اختلال اچول to cause a disturbance, incite disorders

اختناق ikhtināḳ *m. Arabic* asthma

اخته akhtá *indeclinable* **1** subject to something; experiencing something هغه په غم اخته دئ He is mourning. **2** occupied, busy with something دى په کار اخته دئ He is occupied with work. اخته کول **a** to subject to something; plunge into something **b** to occupy, take up; involve in something **3** caught, captured, taken په دام اخته کول to net, catch in a net **4** having a musty or high smell (e.g., meat) اخته کېدل **a** to be subject to something, be subjected to something, experience something په قحط اخته کېدل to starve, famish, go hungry **b** to be occupied, be busy, be engaged in **c** to go bad, get high (meat) **5** *obsolete* castrated, emasculated

اخته والی akhtaválaj *m.* being busy, being employed

اختيار ikhtijār *m. Arabic* **1** will, choice, preference په خپل اختيار دئ He is free to act as he wishes. دا په خپل اختيار شوئ دئ This happened spontaneously. په خپل اختيار وي که نه voluntarily or not **2** authority, right, plenary power **a** of age **b** د خپل اختيار خاوند independent خپل اختيار فوق العاده اختيارات emergency powers تر خپل اختيار لاندي راوستل to decline power, right پربنسودل subordinate oneself ډېر اختيارات ورکول to grant broad powers **3** competence, jurisdiction, power زما په اختيار کښي نه دئ This is not within my competence (jurisdiction, power, etc.) اختيار لرل **a** to have, possess the wish or will **b** to rule, direct **c** to have the right, be empowered **d** to have plenary powers اختيار لری It's up to you. As you wish. زه اختيار نه لرم I don't want to. I cannot.

اختيار دار ikhtijārdār authorized, empowered, competent

اختيار داري ikhtiārdārí *f.* jurisdiction, competence

اختيار نامه ikhtijārnāmá *f.* power of attorney, written authorization

اختيارول ikhtijāraváləl *denominative, transitive* [*past:* اختيار يي کړ] **1** to choose, prefer استوګنه اختيارول to choose a residence, settle **2** to use, employ **3** to conduct (a policy) **4** to assume (a form), take on the air

اختياري ikhtijārí *Arabic* **1** voluntary **2** optional **3** arbitrary دا اختياري خبره نه ده There is no other choice.

اخ توخ akhṭúkh *m.* cough, intermittent coughing اخ توخ جوړول to cough, cough a little or intermittently; clear the throat

اخچه akhchá *f.* ☞ آقچه

اخچه يي akhchaí *adjective* Akhchai آخچه يي قالينی Akhchai carpets

اخذ akhz *m. Arabic* taking, reception, assumption, collection, receiving, receipt عسکري اخذ recruitment of an army, conscription into the army د اخذ عسکري مدير *ákhz-i* chief of the miltary conscription department د اخذ اطلاعات مدير *ákhz-i* chief of the information department اخذ کول *compound verb* **a** to take, assume, collect, receive **b** to call up (into military service) **c** to draw a conclusion, come to a conclusion دې نه دا مي نتيجه I came to this conclusion, that ... اخذ کړه چه ...

د اخذ الصوت اسباب akhz-as-sáut *m. Arabic* sound-locator, sound-ranger

آخذه akhzá *f.* radio receiver د آخذي ماشين radio receiver د لنډ موج shortwave receiver آخذه

آخر akhír akhər *Arabic* **1** last, final په آخرو ورغو کښي lately, in recent days تر آخره گريه جنګېدل to battle to the end, fight to the last drop of blood **2** *m.* [*plural:* آخرونه ākhirúna *plural:* akhərúna *Arabic plural:* اواخر avākhír] end آخر ته near the end, at the end, toward the end په دې آخره کښي at year's end, toward year's end آخر کول to end, complete آخر کېدل to be ended, be completed **3** finally, at last نو آخر Well, that's it!

اخراج ikhrādzh *m. Arabic* [*plural:* اخراجونه ikhrādzhúna *Arabic plural:* اخراجات ikhrādzhāt] **1** banishment, expulsion **2** exclusion, withdrawal, removal **3** extraction **4** expense, expenditures اخراجات کول to incur expenses, give rise to expenditures **5** export goods **6** evacuation

اخراجول ikhrādzhaváləl *denominative, transitive* [*past:* اخراج يي کړ] **1** exile, banish **2** exclude, withdraw; remove **3** extract

اخراجي ikhrādzhí *Arabic adjective* evacuation

آخرت ākhirát *m. Arabic* the next world, the life beyond ورځ Judgement Day آخرت ته بيول send into the next world لا تر اوسه آخرت نه دئ شوئ I still have to deal with you.

آخري ākhirí *Arabic* **1** last, final آخري حرف the last letter **2** definitive **3** conclusive آخري خبري the last word

اخرېدل akhiredəl *denominative* [*past:* اخر شو] to end, finish, come to an end, terminate, close

اخرين ākhirín آخريني ākhrináj last, final آخريني خبرونه ākhrináj the latest news

اخست ákhist *imperfect of* اخستل

اخستل akhistəl *transitive* ☞ اخيستل

اخسته akhistə *m. plural* ☞ اخيسته[1, 2]

اخ سخ akhsákh اخن akhən akhə́kh akhḳh *interjection* oh; ah

اخښت akhə́ḳht *m. plural* substance for putting up chinks or cracks in a wall

اخښل akhḳhə́l [*past:* وايي خښل] [*present:* اخړي] **1** to knead (dough) **2** *figurative* to inculcate, make habitual اخښل کېدل *passive* **a** to be kneaded (dough) **b** to be inherent, be innate

اخښنه akhḳhə́na *f.* yeast, leaven, leavening (of dough)

اخښونکی akhḳhúnkaj **1** *present participle of* اخښل **2** kneader (i.e., bakery worker whose duties consist of kneading dough)

اخښه akhḳhə́ *m. plural* ☞ اخښنه

اخښی ákhḳhaj *m.* [*plural:* اخښي ákhḳhi *plural:* اخښيان akhḳhiján] **1** brother-in-law (wife's brother), wife's sister's husband **2** sister's husband

اخطار ikhtár *m. Arabic* **1** warning, caution د اخطار کلمات words of warning اخطار کېدل to warn, caution اخطار ورکول to be warned **2** alarm, signal د اخطار زنګونه ووهل شول an alert was declared

اخفا ikhfā *f. Arabic* cover, concealment ستر او اخفا camouflage اخفا کول to camouflage

اخکل akhkól *transitive Eastern* ☞ اخنبل

اخگر akhgár *m.* 1 spark 2 hot coal 3 hot ashes

اخل akhól *transitive dialect* ☞ اخنبل

اخلاص ikhlās *m. Arabic* 1 sincerity د چا سره پوره اخلاص لرل to be sincere with someone 2 attachment, affection, devotion د زره له اخلاصه a sincerely, with all one's heart b with all one's strength, with all one's power په ډېر اخلاص سره a sincerely b devotedly, lovingly, tenderly c unanimously په اخلاص د چا خدمت کول to serve someone faithfully 3 diligence, industry

اخلاصمن ikhlāsmán اخلاصمند ikhlāsmánd 1 sincere 2 dedicated

اخلاف akhlā-f *m. Arabic plural of* خلف

اخلاق akhlāk *m. Arabic* 1 *plural of* خلق [2] 2 morals, moral system, ethics د اخلاقو قوانين high moral principles لوړ اخلاق ethical norms

اخلاقاً akhlākán *Arabic* morally, ethically

اخلاقي akhlākí *Arabic* 1 principled, moral, ethical ، اخلاقي تربيه moral upbringing د چا سره په اخلاقي توګه morally اخلاقي پالنه اخلاقي ملګرتيا کول to give someone moral support 2 *m. Arabic* [*plural:* اخلاقيون akhlākijún] moralist

اخلال ikhlāl *m. Arabic* 1 violation (e.g., of neutrality) 2 disarray, confusion, disorder

اخله واخیسته ákhla-vákhista *f.* skirmish, encounter, battle

اخلي ákhli *present tense of* اخیستل

اخلي پخلي akhláj-pakhláj *m.* cooking, preparation (of food), cookery د اخلي پخلي اسباب *akhlí-pakhlí* kitchen utensils

اخند akhúnd *m.* ☞ آخون

اخندزاده [*plural:* اخندزادگان akhundzādagán] descendant of an akhund (i.e., a Muslim ecclesiastic), akhundzadeh

اوخو ukhó ☞ اوخو

اخوا دبخوا akhvā-dekhvā *dialect* around, everywhere

اخوت ukhavvát *m. Arabic* 1 brotherhood, fraternity 2 *religion* community, commune

اخ وتوخ akh-u-ṭúkh *m.* cough, slight cough اخ وتوخ جوړول to cough; have a slight cough; clear one's throat

آخود akhúd *colloquial* Well, there you are!

اخ وډب akh-u-ḍáb *m.* skirmish; clash; battle

آخور ākhór *m.* manger, stall; stable

اخون akhún *m.* اخون akhún *m.* اخوند akhúnd *m.* [*plural:* آخوند] akhund (Muslim ecclesiastic, theological or religious teacher)

اخوندجي akhunddzhí *m.* akhund's (title and the form of address to him)

آخندزاده ākhundzādá *m.* ☞ اخندزاده

اخۍ ukhój *f.* witch

اخيار akhjár *m. Arabic plural* [*singular:* خير] virtuous people اخيار او اشرار good and bad people

اخير akhír recent, latest

اخيراً akhírán *Arabic* not long ago; recently, lately

آخري akhirí ☞ اخيري

اخير akhér *m.* 1 plaster 2 clay mixed with straw (used as plaster)

اخيرگر akhergár *m.* plasterer

اخيرل akheról *transitive* ☞ اخيرول

اخيرونه akheróna *f.* ☞ اخيرونه

اخيرول akheravól *denominative* [*past:* اخير يي کړ] to plaster, putty

اخيرونه akheravóna *f.* plastering, puttying, coating (i.e., with some substance like plaster or putty)

اخيريدل akheredól *denominative, intransitive* [*past:* اخير شو] to be plastered, be puttied

اخيستل akhistól *transitive* [*past:* وايي خيست *present:* اخلي] 1 to take دغه کتاب واخله take this book 2 to seize, conquer, capture, occupy, take possession of ښار اخيستل to capture a city, occupy a city 3 to buy, buy up, acquire, lay in a stock of ژمي ته دي څه اخيستي دي؟ What have you laid in for the winter? 4 to collect (e.g., taxes) 5 to accept, admit امتحان اخيستل to give an examination; examine 6 to receive امر اخيستل to receive an order, receive an instruction ځواب اخيستل to receive an answer ماموريت اخيستل to receive money روپۍ اخيستل to receive an assignment نښان اخيستل to receive a medal 7 to take (with oneself); drive (cattle) له ځان سره را اخيستل to take along or with oneself دا کتاب راواخله Take this book with you. 8 to catch, contract (a disease) مرض اخيستل to fall ill, become ill, be taken ill 9 to envelop (in flames) اور اخيستل to blaze up, catch on fire 10 to fall (into despair), be consumed, be seized (e.g., by panic) 11 to derive benefit (profit, advantage, etc.) د يو شي څخه فائده اخيستل to derive benefit from something, derive advantage from something د يو شي څخه خوند اخيستل to take pleasure in something 12 to borrow, adopt; give, present (an example) 13 to repulse, take away په زوره اخيستل to take by force له چا څخه وسله اخيستل to disarm someone 14 to shorten, take up (e.g., clothing) 15 to deprive له چا څخه تابع والي او رعيتي اخيستل to deprive of citizenship 16 to consider, regard ته يې همداسي واخله Consider it to be thus. 17 to observe, keep to; perform, execute (e.g., a ceremony) 18 to carry out, fulfill, satisfy (e.g., a whim, desire) عرض مي درواخله Satisfy my request. 19 to begin; venture; undertake د چا سره مخالفت اخيستل to begin a feud with someone. بوډۍ د خپل اولاد اوږدي قصې راواخيستې The old woman lauched into a long conversation about her children. 20 *approximates the sense and function of a compounding or auxiliary verb* پنه اخيستل to stride, قدم اخيستل ساه اخيستل to breathe اخيستل کېدل *passive* a to undertake b to be purchased, be obtained c to be collected, be levied d to be driven *idiom* سره اخيستل to be transmitted from one to another, be bequeathed له منځه څخه اخيستل to remove, eliminate; get rid of دنيکه نه واخله ترنمسي پوري from grandfather to grandson, د نيکه نه واخله تر نمسي پوري beginning with the grandfather and ending with the grandson

اخيستنه akhistóna *f.* ☞ اخيستنه [1]

اخیستوال akhistvāl *m.* tax collector

اخیستون akhistún *m.* ☞ اخیسته [1]

اخیستونکی akhistúkaj **1** *present participle of* اخیستل **2** infectious, contagious اخیستونکی مرض infectious disease, contagious disease **3** *m.* **.1** recipient, addressee **3.2** purchaser

اخیسته [1] akhistə́ *m. plural* **1** reception **2** taking (i.e., food, medicine), receipt د برخي د اخیستو دپاره for participation **3** taking, capture, seizing **4** purchase, acquisition دا څیز د اخیستو نه It is not worth buying this article. دئ **5** collection (e.g., of taxes) **6** *military* recruitment, bringing up to strength د لښکر recruitment into the army **7** adoption, borrowing اخیسته

اخیسته [2] akhistə́ *imperfect plural of* اخیستل

اخیسته اېنبوده akhistə́-iḵhhodə́ *m. plural* skirmish, clash

اخیستي [1] akhístaj *past participle of* اخیستل

اخیستئ [2] Western *imperfect of* اخیستل

ادا adā́ *f. Arabic* **1** implementation, execution, fulfillment **2** payment, pay, paying **3** utterance (of a sound, word) **4** expression (of some feeling or other) ادا کول *compound verb* **a** to implement, execute د وطن حق ادا کول to fulfill one's obligation to the Fatherland **b** to pay, make payment **c** to utter (a sound, word) **d** to set forth, formulate (a thought, sentence) **e** to express (e.g., gratitude) **f** to render (that which is due) **g** to perform, play (a role) ادا کېدل *compound verb* **a** to be fulfilled, be executed **b** to be paid **c** to be expressed (of gratitude) **d** to be performed (of a role)

آداب ādā́b *m. Arabic plural of* ادب

ادات adā́t *m.* [*plural:* ادوات advā́t] *Arabic* **1** means, instrument, device, tool, apparatus تحکیمیه ادات *military* entrenching tool **2** *grammar particle* د تاکید ادات intensifying particle **3** *grammar* preposition, postposition د عطف ادات conjunction د وضعیت ادات adverb of manner or mode **4** suffix

اداد idā́d *m. Arabic* requital, recompense, retribution

اداره idārá *f. Arabic* [*plural:* اداري idāré *Arabic plural:* ادارات idārā́t] **1** directing, directorate, management, administration, leadership د اور اداره *military* fire control کیفي اداره arbitrary rule اداره کول *compound verb* to direct, lead, manage خپل ځان اداره کول to manifest self-control **2** directorate, institution, office صحیح اداره کول apparatus (administrative) د اداري اعضا خفیه اداره counterintelligence د لوازماتو اداره quartermasters office د عسکري سیاسي اداره military-political directorate د عسکري صحي اداره military-medical directorate **3** bureau د اطلاعاتو اداره information bureau د معلوماتو ګیري اداره inquiry office **4** administration **5** editorial office **6** base (supply, etc.)

اداره چي idārachí *m.* **1** administrator, manager **2** leader, supervisor

اداره کوونکی idārá kavúnkaj **1** *m.* manager **2** *adjective* administrative

اداري idārí *Arabic* administrative; managerial; bureaucratic اداري هیئت administration, governing body, administrative apparatus;

اداري کاتب وېش clerk اداري board of directors adminstrative اداري عمومي مدیریت administrative directorate اداري لوازم division stationery

د فلم اداکار adākā́r *m.* artist, actor, performer (of a role) movie actor

د فلم اداکاره adākā́ra *f.* artist, actress, performer (of a role) movie actress

اداکاري adākārí *f.* performance (e.g., of a play), acting

ادامه idāmá *f. Arabic* prolongation; continuation ادامه ورکول to prolong, continue ادامه لرل to be prolonged, be continued

ادایات adājā́t *m. Arabic* ☞ اداکاري

ادایېنه adājə́na *f.* expression, statement, formulation

ادب adáb *m. Arabic* [*plural:* آداب ādā́b] **1** breeding, good breeding; politeness, civility, respect په ادب سره politely, respectfully د چا ادب کول to esteem someone, respect someone **2** literature تحریري ادب written language خلاقه ادب belles lettres **3** level of education شفاهي ادب folklore

ادبا udabā́ *m. Arabic plural of* ادیب

ادبار idbā́r *m. Arabic* misfortune, disaster

ادب ناک adabnāk ادب کوونکی adáb kavúnkaj well bred; polite; civil, respectable

ادبي adabí *Arabic* literary ادبي انجمن literary society

ادبیات adabijā́t *m. Arabic plural* literature بدیعي ادبیات belles lettres

ادبیانه adabijāná decent, proper, decorous (of conduct); civil (of an expression)

ادخال idkhā́l *m. Arabic* **1** introduction, establishment **2** inclusion

ادخالي idkhālí ادخالي لاري approaches

ادرار idrā́r *m. Arabic plural* urine ادرار کول to urinate

ادراک idrā́k *m. Arabic singular & plural* perception ادراک کول **a** to comprehend, understand **b** to perceive, feel **c** to guess

ادرس adrés *m.* address

ادرک adrák *m. plural* green ginger

ادرم adrám *m.* **1** influence, action, pressure (moral) پر چا ادرم کول to influence, put (moral) pressure upon پر چا ادرم کېدل to affect, have an effect on **2** shame

ادرول udravúl *transitive dialect* ☞ درول

ادریاتیک adriātík **1** *adjective* Adriatic ادریاتیک بحر the Adriatic Sea **2** *m.* the Adriatic seacoast

ادریدل undredə́l *intransitive* ☞ دریدل

ادعا iddi'ā́ *f. Arabic* claim, pretension, demand

ادعیات ad'ijā́t *m. Arabic plural of* ادعیه wish, desire خپل خالصانه ادعیات تقدیمول to send one's sincere best wishes

ادغام idghā́m *m. Arabic* **1** *linguistics* gemination **2** confluence, junction; tightening up, pulling together

ادکه adə́ka *f.* mommy, mama ادکي! Oh mamma!

ادکی adə́kəj *f.* **1** ☞ ادکه **2** mom (a form of address for one's mother or an elderly woman)

ادل بدل adál-badál **1.1** inconstant **1.2** disorderly, careless ادل بدل کول to mix up, confuse (e.g., words) **2** *m.* **.1** trade, commerce **2.2** oscillation

آدم [1] ādám *m.* ادم adám *m.* **1** *proper name* Adam آدم بابا Adam (the human progenitor) د بابا آدم د وختو old, antediluvian, of the time of Adam **2** man

ادم [2] adúm *m.* thigh

ادمان idmā́n *m.* physical training

ادم خان adamkhā́n *m.* **1** *proper name* Adamkhan **2** Adamkhan (designation of a number of settlements)

آدم خور ādamkhór *m.* cannibal

آدم خېل ādamkhél **1** *plural* the Adamkhejli (a sub-tribe of the Afridi) **2** *m.* Adamkhejl (person)

آدم زاد ādamzā́d *m.* man

آدم زاده ādamzāda *f.* woman

آدمي [1] ādamí *m.* ادماج ādamā́j *m.* man

آدمۍ [2] ādaмə́j *f.* woman

ادميرال admirā́l *m.* admiral

ادنا، ادنی adnā́ *Arabic indeclinable* **1** low (in position) **2** small, paltry, insignificant ادنی صدمه insignificant damage **3** low-quality, low standard

ادوات advā́t *m.* *Arabic plural from* ادات

ادوار advā́r *m.* *Arabic plural from* دور [1]

ادو بدو adú-badú *indeclinable* **1** *Eastern* swollen, bloated **2** *Western* beaten down ادو بدو کېدل to ache, hurt (of the body, from fatigue)

ادوری adúṛaj *m.* tanned buffalo hide

ادوزي adozí **1** *m.* *plural* the Adozai (a sub-tribe of Durrani) **2** *m.* adozā́j an Adozai (person)

ادوم adúm *m.* thigh

ادویه advijá *f.* *Arabic plural from* دوا [1] medicine, spice, medicinal herb

ادویه پاشي advijapā́shí *f.* *agriculture* sprinkling, spraying ادویه پاشي کېدل *compound verb* to sprinkle, spray ادویه پاشي کول *compound verb* to be sprinkled, be sprayed

ادویه فروش advijafurúsh *m.* pharmacist, apothecary

ادویه فروشي advijafurushí *f.* **1** commerce in pharmaceuticals **2** pharmacy

اده [1] udá ☞ هوده [1]

ادې [1] adé *m.* mommy, mummy (form of address to mother or older woman) د ادې زوی Mommy!; Mummy! ادي موري! mommy's boy ادي کول to regard as a mother, name or give the honorary title of mother

ادۍ [2] adə́j *f.* singular & plural ☞ اۍ [6]

ادیان adjā́n *m.* *Arabic plural from* دین [2]

ادیب adíb *m.* *Arabic* [*plural:* ادیبان adibā́n *Arabic plural:* ادبا udabā] man of letters, writer

ادیبانه adibāná *indeclinable* literary (of a literary work, style)

ادیبه adibá *f.* writer (woman)

ادیره adirá *f.* cemetery

ادیس آبابا adís-ābābā́ *f.* Addis Ababa (city)

ادېکولون adekolón *m.* *plural* eau-de-cologne

آدینه ādiná *f.* Friday

اواله aḓála *f.* shaft (of an underground irrigation channel)

اوانه aḓána *f.* ornamented cover or dust jacket of a book

اوانا aḓāṇá *f.* *regional* support په اوانه کېناستل to lean, rest upon

اواونه aḓāvṇa *f.* frame, framework

اور aḓár *m.* *regional* order اور ورکول to order, reserve (not a military order, but a commercial or customer order)

اوک aḓák *m.* leap-frog (the game)

اوني aḓanáj *m.* ☞ اوني

اوو aḓó ☞ هوو [1]

ادوری aḓúṛaj *m.* ادوری aḓuṛə́j *f.* ☞ اوري

اوکی aḓúkaj *m.* *dialect* bone

اوه aḓá *f.* **1** stop, (bus or tram) stand, station **2** base نظامي اوی military bases هوایي اوه airport **3** *military* post **4** blind (for bird-hunting)

اوی adáj *m.* fortifications around a city

اوی [2] áḓi *m.* *plural* ☞ هوي [1]

اوی [3] aḓí *plural from* اوی [1]

اوی [4] aḓé *plural from* اوه

اوی [5] aḓə́j *f.* singular & plural Ulmus foliacea (a kind of tree)

اوی [6] aḓə́j *f.* singular & plural fields or land surrounding a village

ادیپتر aḓipṭár *m.* اویتر aḓiṭár *m.* *technology* adapter

اوبل aḓél *m.* stone facing (for the shaft of an underground irrigation channel)

اذان azā́n *m.* *Arabic* **1** azan, call to prayer د اذان وخت prayer time اذان ویل to summon to prayer د خوار ملا پر اذان څوک نه تبروي *proverb* No one responds to the azan of a poor mullah. **2** crowing (of a cock) د چرگ پر اذان early, very early, with the roosters اذان کول to crow (of roosters)

اذربایجان azarbā́jdzhān *m.* Azerbaijan

اذربایجاني azarbā́jdzhāní **1** Azerbaijanian **2** *m.* **.1** Azerbaijanian (person) **2.2** Azerbaijani, the Azerbaijanian language

اذکار [1] izkā́r *m.* *Arabic* mention, reference اذکار کول to mention, refer to

اذکار [2] azikā́r *m.* *Arabic plural from* ذکر، اذکار کول to perform the ritual of zikr (i.e., remembering) or zeal (with reference to dervishes)

اذلت azallát *m.* *Arabic* baseness, meanness زه به څنگه دا اذلت پر ځان قبول کړم I cannot stoop to such baseness.

اذن izn *m.* *Arabic* authorization, permission اذن اخیستل to receive authorization د چا څخه اذن غوښتل to request authorization from someone چا ته اذن ورکول to authorize someone, permit someone

أذوغ azúgh *m.* آذوقه āzuķá *f. singular & plural* **1** provsions, rations, food آذوقي گدام supply base, provision depot **2** fodder (for cattle) د ژمي آذوقي برابرول to lay in fodder for winter

آذوقه رساني āzurķāsaní *f.* food supply

اذهان azhān *m. Arabic from* ذهن *plural* د تولني اذهان روښنانول to enlighten intellects

اذيت aziját *m. Arabic* torture, torment, oppression

اذيتول azijatavól *denominative, transitive* [*past:* اذيت يي کړ] **1** to torture, oppress **2** to annoy, bother, pester

آر ār *literal & figurative* basis, foundation په آر راوړل **a** to lay the foundation (of a building) *figurative* **b** to establish the main point of something **c** to evaluate as to merit *figurative* **d** to take someone into consideration *idiom* له آره in essence

آرا¹ āŕá *m. Arabic plural from* راي د آراو د ډېروالي په اثر، د آراو په اتفاق with a majority of votes د آراو په اتفاق unanimously اکثريت آرا-ji plebescite د آراو اختلاف disagreement

آرا² āŕá *used as the second element of a composite word* شهرآرا Shahrara (name of a section of Kabul)

ارابه¹ arābá *f.* ☞ ارابه

ارابه arābá *f.* volley

اراټ arāṭ *m.* ☞

اراخ arākh *m.* rākh **1** irrigation ditch **2** sluice; canal

ارادتاً irādātán *Arabic* intentionally, premeditatedly

اراده irādá *f. Arabic* **1** will د ارادي قوت strength of will په تينګه په پخه اراده with considerable decisiveness **2** intention, decision, wish (desire) اراده کول *official* **a** to command **b** to intend; desire; ...اراده مي کړې ده چه I have decided ..., I intend ... د قندهار اراده يې وکړه He decided to go to Kandahar. اراده لرل to intend, desire کومي خوا ته دي اراده ده؟ In which direction do you want to go? ر اتلل په اراده او تلل په اجازه *proverb* Come here freely, but leave only with permission. *idiom* د چا پر ضد بده اراده encroachment on someone, intrusion on someone

ارادي irādí **1** conscious په ارادي ډول consciously **2** volitional

ارارات arārát (Mount) Ararat

آراستگي ārāstagí *f.* **1** adornment **2** beauty

آراسته ārāstá *indeclinable* **1** adorned **2** well-dressed, smart, dressed-up آراسته کول **a** to adorn **b** to dress up

اراضي arāzí *m. Arabic plural* **1** *from* ارض **2** country, locality, district د جهت تعين په اراضي کښې orienting or getting familiar with respect to the area

اراکين arākín *m. plural from* ارکان persons holding high positions, leaders اراکين دولت arākín-i nobles, dignitaries

ارال arāl *m.* the Aral Sea

آرام¹ ārām **1** *m.* **.1** peace, rest په آرام سره peacefully, quietly آرام ورکول to allow to rest, soothe, make easier آرام ميندل to find peace, calm آرام نه لرل not to know peace په آرام کېدل to rest **1.2** comfort **2.1** peaceful, quiet **2.2** resting **2.3** peaceable آرام خلک peaceable people

آرامي¹ ārāmtjá *f.* ☞ آرامي¹

آرامچوکی ārāmchokój *f.* easy chair

آرامش ārāmísh *m.* calm

ارام طلب ārāmtaláb fond of comfort

آرامگاه ārāmgáh *m.* **1** stand, stopping place **2** burial-vault, mausoleum

آرامول ārāmavól *denominative, transitive* [*past:* آرام يې کړ] **1** to quiet **2** to eliminate (e.g., disorder)

آرامي¹ ārāmí *f.* **1** calm, peace آرامه آرامي utter calm **2** tranquillity **3** peace (i.e., absence of war) د جهان آرامي world wide peace

آرامي² ārāmí *m.* lazy person, lazybones

آرامي³ arāmí Armenian آرامي ژبه the Armenian language

آرامېدل ārāmedól *denominative, intransitive* [*past:* آرام شو] to soothe, quiet down زه مي پر آرام شو This soothed me. آرام شئ! *military* At ease! Order Arms!

آرايش ārājísh *m.* decoration, adornment; attire د آرايش خونه boudoir

ارايه irājá *f. Arabic* producing, presentation (of documents, etc.)

ارباب¹ arbáb *Arabic* **1** *masculine plural from* رب ارباب النوع gods (pagan) **2** *m.* [*plural:* اربابان arbābán] senior elder of a settlement or extended family; village elder

اربشه urbásha *f.* **1** barley corn **2** *dialect* life, existence

اربشي urbóshi *f. plural* barley

اربشين urbəshín *adjective* barley اربشينه ډوډی barley bread

اربشينه urbəshína *f.* **1** *singular of* اربشين **2** barley bread

اربکتيا arbaktjá *f.* the maintenance of order

اربکی arbakáj *m.* tribal constable (minor tribal official having police powers)

اربوز urbúz *m.* اربوزه urbuzá *f.* **1** muzzle **2** snout *idiom* اربوز! دئ ورک شه Be off with you! Don't bother me!

اربوشين urbushín ☞ اربشين

اربه¹ arabá *f.* **1** bullock cart, wagon, carriage **2** gun-carriage **3** د اربي سيم spoke **4** landing gear, داربي ډنده، wheel undercarriage (of an aircraft) *idiom* زما کار په تنگ دئ، که دي دا وار ته ؟اربه راوچلوله My affairs are going badly. Will you not help me? په دي ورځو کښي مي اربه بنده ده At present I am in straitened circumstances.

اربه² urbá *f.* tendon, ligament

اربه کښ arbakáķh draught (i.e., draught animal)

اربه لرونکی arabá larúkaj having a wheel; wheeled

آرت¹ ārt *m.* art

ارت² art arát **1** wide, spacious, extensive ارتي صحراوي extensive deserts ارته فاصله a great expanse د کميس غاړه ارته ده The shirt collar is large. **2** open ارت ځای an open space **3** open, free, exposed, pure (of air) په ارته هوا کښي in the open air 4 widely spread apart, bowed (of legs) پنښي يي ارتي دي He is bowlegged. *idiom* لر څه ارت ولاړو He stood off to the side.

آرتاو ārtāv *m.* ارتاو artāv *m.* 1 throw, toss 2 *Eastern* shot آرتاو *compound verb* ☞ ارتاو کېدل ارتاوول *compound verb* ☞ کول ارتاو ہدل

آرتاوز artāvúz *m.* ☞ ارتاویز

ارتاوول artāvəvə́l *denominative* [*past:* ارتاو یې کۍ] 1 to throw, fling, toss 2 *Eastern* to produce a shot, shoot

ارتاوی artavə́j *f. singular & plural* sun-dried currants

ارتاو ہدل artāvedə́l *denominative, intransitive* to be thrown, be flung

ارتاویز artāvíz 1 *m.* windbag ارتاویزي خبري 2 empty, insipid nonsense

ارتباط irtibắt *m. Arabic* connection, link, communication, intercourse, relationship د چا سره ارتباط لرل to have communication with someone پہ ... پوري ارتباط مېندل to establish communication with ... د خارجه ارتباطو مدیر chief of the foreign department

ارتباطچي irtibātchí *m. military* messenger, runner (liaison, orderly)

ارتباطچي گري irtibātchigarí *f. military* communications service

ارتباطي irtibātí *attributive* communication د بحر ارتباطي لاري maritime communications ارتباطي ادات *grammar* conjunction

ارتجاع irtidzhắ' *f. Arabic* 1 *politics* reaction 2 reactionary in character 3 regression, retrogradation 4 elasticity; resiliency 5 recoil (of a weapon)

ارتجاعي irtidzhā'í 1 reactionary 2 regressive 3 elastic; resilient ارتجاعي خاصه elasticity; resiliency

ارتجاعیت irtidzhā'ját *m.* 1 elasticity; resiliency 2 *literal & figurative* flexibility

ارتجالي irtidzhālí impromptu, written extemporaneously

ارتداد irtidād *m. Arabic* 1 desertion, treason, apostasy, deviation 2 renunciation 3 *religion* tergiversation, recreancy, backsliding ارتداد کول, ارتداد ته التجا کول a to apostatize from something, deviate from something b to reject, renounce (e.g., a faith)

ارتدادي irtidādí 1 disloyal ارتدادي سلوک disloyalty, treason 2 apostate

ارتزاق irtizắk *m. Arabic* nourishment, subsistence

ارتزاقي irtizāķí *Arabic attributive* food, produce ارتزاقي مواد food, produce

ارتزاقیات irtizākiját *m. Arabic plural* foodstuffs, produce

ارت زړه aratzṛə́ ارت زړی arətzə́raj 1 frank, honest, forthright (person) 2 generous, noble

ارتسام irtisām *m. Arabic* 1 representation, portrayal پہ زړه کښني نقش او ارتسام مېندل to stamp, impress itself upon; stick, be retained in memory 2 sign, mark

آرتست artíst *m.* ☞ ارتیست

آرتسته artístá *f.* ☞ ارتیسته

آرتستي artistí ☞ ارتیستي

ارتش irtísh *m.* the Irtysh (River)

ارتفاع irtifắ' *f. m. Arabic* [*plural:* ارتفاعات irtifā'ất] 1 altitude, height ټیټ ارتفاعات a low لوړ او هسک ارتفاعات a great height altitude د ارتفاع اقل حد *astronomy* perigee د ارتفاع اکثر حد *astronomy* apogee 2 thickness

ارتقا irtiķắ *f. Arabic* 1 rise (action); eminence, elevation 2 development, evolution د ژبي ارتقا development of language 3 growth, increase ارتقا کول to increase, rise, grow

ارتقايي irtiķāí evolutionary ارتقايي نظريه evolutionism, the theory of evolution د داروين ارتقايي فلسفه Darwinism

ارتکاز irtiķắz *m. Arabic* support, basis پر حقايقو تکيه او ارتکاز مېندل to rest upon facts

ارتنه artiná *f.* ☞ ارتينه

ارتوالی aratvắlaj *m.* ارت والی 1 width, spaciousness, extensiveness د مُلکي ارتوالی the extent of a territory 2 development (i.e., of a language); expansion (i.e., of trade) 3 tension 4 area (e.g., of a country) 5 diameter (e.g., of a wheel)

ارتوداکس artodắks 1 orthodox, canonical 2 Orthodox (i.e., pertaining to the Eastern Orthodox Church) ارتوداکس مذهب Orthodoxy (the Eastern Church)

ارتول ارتول [1] artavə́l arətavə́l *denominative, transitive* [*past:* ارت یې کۍ] 1 to widen, make extensive, make expansive 2 to spread widely, extend خپلي گوتي ارتول to extend the fingers 3 to disengage

ارتول [2] artavə́l *transitive* [*past:* ما وارتاوه] to throw, fling, toss

ارتون arətún *m.* width, spaciousness

ارتونه artavə́na *f.* 1 broadening, expansion 2 state of being widespread, state of being far-flung

ارتہدل arətedə́l *denominative, intransitive* 1 to widen, make spacious, make extensive 2 to be widely spread out, be widely extended 3 to be disengaged

ارتیست artíst *m.* 1 artist 2 painter

ارتیسته artísta *f.* actress, artist

ارتیستي artistí 1 artistic 2 artistically skillful, talented, pertaining to art generally

ارتینه artiná *f.* 1 woman 2 wife

آرټ [1] arṭ *m.* ☞ ارہټ

ارټ [2] aráṭ *m.* ☞ ارہټ

ارټ ساز araṭsāz *m.* master craftsman engaged in the construction of wells equipped with the noria (bucket-wheel)

آرټیست ārṭíṣṭ *m.* ☞ ارتیست

آرټیسته arṭísta *f.* ☞ ارتیسته

آرټیستي arṭisṭí ☞ ارتیستي

ارث irs *m. Arabic* inheritance مال پہ ارث پر پنبودل to leave a bequest of property

ارثي irsí *Arabic* hereditary; inherited

ارجاع irdzhắ' *f. Arabic* 1 return, recurrence 2 direction, address 3 institution (of an action, suit)

ارجل ardzhál **1** confused, muddled **2** *m.* the common people

ارجل و برجل ardzhál-u-bardzhál ارجل برجل ardzhál-bardzhál mixed, intermixed, disorderly, muddled

ارجمند ardshmánd **1** valuable, expensive **2** excellent

ارجنتاین ardshantājn Argentina

ارچه archá *f.* **1** archa (a kind of juniper bush) **2** kind of coniferous tree

ارچه کاري archakārí *f.* **1** plank panelling, planking; the wooden portion of a structure **2** cabinetwork, carpentry work

ارزبدل ardzedól *intransitive* ☞ ارزیدل

ارخالک arkhālók *m.* arkhaluk (an outer garment)

ارخنج arkhakh *m.* **1** ارخنج کنبل، ارخنج ایستل، ارخنج کول sobbing to sob, weep **2** asthma

آرداِبه ārdābá *f.* mash (food)

ارداوه ardāvá *f.* fodder (for cattle, barley or wheat)

اردل ardál *m.* **1** bodyguard **2** orderly, batman

اردلي ardalí *m. obsolete* orderly د اردلي سپاهیان household troops

اردن urdún *m.* اردنیه urdunijá *f. Arabic* Jordania

اردو urdú **1** *m.* **.1** army, forces افغان اردوي the Afghan Army صحرا اردو سیار اردو a land army بري اردو marines منظم اردو regular army د اردو عملیاتي اردو فعالي a field army د اردو ریاست Combined Arms Directorate (in the War Ministry) د احتیاط قوه the army reserve **1.2** *m. military* camp **1.3** *f.* Urdu (language) **2** *attributive* اردو ژبه the Urdu language اردو کتابونه books in Urdu

اردوبازار urdubāzār *m.* post exchange facilities

اردوگاه urdugāh *m. military* camp

اردووالا urduvālā *m.* Urdu speaker

اردویي urduí *attributive* army, forces

اردر ardár *m.* **1** order **2** instruction

اردي نېنس ardinéns *m. regional* edict

اري ¹ irŗáj *m.* ram (non-fat tailed breed)

اري ² irŗój *f.* sheep, ewe (non-fat tailed breed)

ارزاق arzāķ *m.* **1** *from* رزق **2** provisions, food stores, food supplies

ارزان arzán **1** cheap ارزان بې علته نه وي، گران بې حکمته Dear is dandy – cheap is shoddy. **2** cheaply

ارزان بیع arzānbája'ارزانباجه cheap

ارزانتوب arzāntób *m.* ارزانتیا arzāntjá *f.* cheapness

ارزان فروش arzānfurúsh selling cheaply

ارزان فروشي arzānfurushí *f. economics* dumping

ارزانوالی arzānvālaj *m.* cheapness, low prices

ارزانول arzānavól *denominative, transitive* [*past:* ارزان یې کړ] to reduce the price of

ارزانه arzāna *feminine singular from* ارزان

ارزاني arzāní *f.* cheapness

ارزانبدل arzānedól *denominative, intransitive* [*past:* ارزان شو] to fall in price, cheapen

ارزش arzísh *m.* ارزښت arzəkht *m.* **1** value د ډېر ارزښت وړ تحقیقات very valuable research لرل to be of equivalent worth, be of equal worth **2** *economics* cost استعمالي ارزش use value اضافي surplus value تبادلوي ارزش exchange value **3** significance ارزش ورکول to evaluate **4** evaluation

ارزگان uruzgán *m.* Uruzgan (city) د ارزگان اعلی حکومت، د ارزگان history ولایت Uruzgan Province

آرزو ārzó *f.* آرزو ārzú [*plural:* آرزوگاني ārzogāni *plural:* آرزووي] **1** wish, desire د کامیابي آرزو desire for success سره د ډېري آرزو despite a great desire **2** hope, expectation, expectancy آرزو لرل **a** to wish, desire آرزو مي درلوده چه... I wished that ... **b** to hope, expect **3** dream, daydream هغه ارزوگاني ناجرا پاتي شوي These dreams did not come true.

آرزومند ārzumánd desiring something, aspiring to something تلو ته ډېر آرزومن دئ He wants to go very much.

آرزومندي ārzumandí *f.* desire, wish, aspiration

ارزیدل arzedól *intransitive* [*past:* وارزید *present:* ارزي] to cost, be worth دا شي په دې قیمت نه ارزي This thing is not worth it. په دې پوهېدل هم ارزي That's worth knowing.

اربمي ¹ argamáj *m. Eastern* ☞ اربي

اربمي ² argamáj *f. Western* yawning, yawn اربمی کنبل to yawn

اربه urgə̄ *m. plural* ☞ اوربره

اربی argaj *m. Western* belching اربی ایستل، اربی بدول، اربی کول to belch

اربي بد argibád *m.* indigestion

ارسال irsál *m. Arabic singular & plural* shipping, sending هغه کتاب مي په ډاګ *compound verb* to send, ship, dispatch کول ارسال کړئ دئ I sent the book through the mail.

ارستوکراتیک aristokrātík aristocratic

ارستوکراسي aristokrāsí *f.* aristocracy د ارستوکراسي رژیم *history* aristocracy, the aristocratic form of government

ارسلان arslán *m.* arsalān *proper name* Arslan

ارسي urusí *f.* window with a frame capable of being raised and lowered

ارسېنک aseník *m. plural* arsenic

ارشاد irshád *m. Arabic* [*plural:* ارشادونه irshādúna *Arabic plural:* ارشادات irshādát] precept, lesson, instruction ارشادات کول و چا ته to give directions to someone; instruct someone

ارشو urshó *f.* [*plural:* ارشوگاني urshogāni *plural:* ارشووي urshóvi] common pasture; pasture; meadow

ارشیتکت arshitékt *m.* architect

ارشیف arshíf *m.* archive

ارض arz *m. Arabic* [*plural:* اراضي arāzí] earth, land

ارضي arzí *Arabic* **1** *attributive* land, earth; territorial **2** surface, land (as in land or ground forces)

ارغ arágh *m. plural* vodka

ارغشي arghasháj *m.* **1** clearing of the throat ارغشي کول to clear the throat **2** inhalation (when smoking)

ارغمان arghumán *m.* ☞ ارغوان

ارغنج arghándzh *m.* [*plural:* ارغنجونه arghandzhúna *plural:* ارغنجان arghandzhā́n] plum

ارغنجک arghandzhák *m.* kind of damson plum (the tree or its fruit)

ارغنجي arghandzháj *m.* cherry (the tree or its fruit)

ارغند arghánd *m.* [*plural:* ارغندونه arghandúna] *Western* [*plural:* ارغندان arghandā́n] paddle, bat (used in playing knucklebones) د ارغند لوبه the game of knucklebones

ارغنداب arghandā́b *m.* ارغنداو arghandā́v *m.* Argendab (river, district)

ارغنون arghańun *m. music* organ

ارغوان arghavā́n arghuvā́n ledum (marsh tea); pink acacia, *Cercis siliquastrum* زبر ارغوان *Sophora griffìthi*

ارغواني arghavā́ni purple, crimson

ارغوش arghúsh dark-complexioned

ارغوشول arghushavə́l *denominative, transitive* [*past:* ارغوش يې کړ] to make dark

ارغوشېدل arghushedə́l *denominative, intransitive* [*past:* ارغوش شو] to be made dark, tan

ارغومي [1] urghúmaj *m.* kid, young goat

ارغومي [2] urghúme *f. diminutive* goat

ارغون arghún *m. music* organ

ارغونچي arghuncháj *m.* rope, cord (braided from three strands) ارغونچي کول to twist a cord, plait a cord

ارغون arghún *m.* ☞ ارغند

ارغوي urghávaj *m.* palm (of the hand)

ارقام [1] arḳā́m *m. Arabic plural from* رقم

ارقام [2] irḳā́m *m. Arabic* spelling

ارک urə́k *dialect* ☞ ورک

اركاره [2] arkārá *f.* ☞ هرکاره

اركان arkā́n *m. Arabic plural* **1** *from* رکن **2** leaders, leadership, leadership apparatus ارکان دولت arkā́n-i higher official personages, dignitaries عسکري ارکان generals, general officers, higher command personnel **3** *military* staff, headquarters atkā́n-i harbijá-ji ارکان حربیه عمومیه، عمومي ارکان General Staff د عمومي ارکانو رئیس Chief of the General Staff

اركانحرب arkānikhárb *m.* ارکانحربیه arkāniharbijá *f.* staff

اركتیک arktík arctic

ورکزي urəkzí *m.* ☞ ورکزي

اركسترا arkestrā́ *f.* orchestra

اركسترائي arkestrāí *attributive* orchestra

اركیالودژست arkijālodzhíst *m.* archeologist

اركیالودژي arkijālodzhí *m.* archeology

ارگ arg *m.* fortress, citadel (primarily used of the Kabul Arg, the king's residents) د ارگ باغ the Arg Garden (in Kabul)

ارگان orgā́n *m.* organ (of political or government power)

ارگانه argāná *f.* food, nourishment

ارگانیزم orgānízm *m.* organism

ارگجه argadzhá mixed, heterogeneous

ارگه argā́ *m.* riding school, riding hall, riding arena

ارگمی argamáj *m. Eastern* ☞ اربمي [2] کول argamí he yawned

ارگنه arganá *f.* latticed door; door in form of grill

ارگون urgún *m.* Urgun (town, district) ارگون او کټواز Katawaz and Urgun

ارگی argáj ☞ اربی

ارم irám *m.* **1** Irem (legendary garden in Arabia) **2** *figurative* earthly paradise

ارمان armā́n *m.* **1** strong desire د چا ارمانونه پوره کول to carry out someone's desires د زړه ښخه يو ارمان لېري کول to fulfill a cherished desire **2** dream زما ارمان نه دئ ختلي I still dream about this all the time. په ارمان سره مړ شو He died without realizing his dreams **3** melancholy فتح خان ته بېکسي او يوازي توب *folklore* Fatekh-Khan grew melancholy in his ارمان ودرېدئ solitude. په دې شان په يې په زړه ارمان پاتي نه شي Thus he was inwardly at peace. **4** regret, repentance; grief ارمان لرل to regret something **a** ارمان کول to set one's heart at ease د زړه ارمان رژول to dream **b** to yearn **c** to regret; grieve; mourn over پر خپل تبر **a** to pity په چا پسي ارمان کول to regret the past شوي عمر ارمان کول someone **b** to miss someone! ارمان مه کوه، وکي ارمان به! Look out, you'll be sorry! ارمان I'm very, very sorry! ارمان ارمان دئ! I regret not having gone into town. ارمان دئ چه زه ښار ته تللئ واى *proverb* They are sorry when it is already too پس له زواله دئ late.

ارمانجن armāndzhén **1** desiring something; dreaming of something **2** grieving, yearning **3** regretting

ارماند armā́nd *m.* ☞ ارمان

ارماني armā́ni **1** desirable **2** ideal, perfect

ارمبه arambá *f.* ☞ رمبي

ارمچک aramchák *m. abusive* cur, mongrel

ارمړ urmə́ṛ **1** *m. plural* the Ormuri (also called Bakari or Bakisti; a nomadic people living in both Pakistan and Afghanistan south of Kabul) **2** *m.* Ormur (person)

ارمغان armaghā́n *m.* gift, souvenir; remembrance ارمغان پر پنبودل to keep in one's memory

ارمگی aramgáj *m.* shepherd's crook

ارمنستان armanistā́n *m.* ☞ ارمنیا

ارمني armaní **1** Armenian ارمني ژبه the Armenian language **2** *m.* Armenian (person)

ارمنیا arminijā́ *f.* arminijā́ Armenia

ارمولي urmúlaj *m.* armólaj diarrhea (in children)

آرموني ārmuní *f. music* harmony

ارمنیا [1] armunjā́ *f.* aluminum

آرمونیه [2] armunjā́ *f.* ☞

ارمونیک armuník *m.* accordion, concertina

ارمونیا armunijá *f.* harmonium لویه آرمونیه an organ

ارمبر urmég *m.* neck

ارمنیا armenjā́ *f.* ☞ ارمنیا

آرن ārán *m.* bugle (musical instrument)

آرند āránd *m.* ☞ آرن

ارنۍ urṇáj *m.* swaddling clothes

اروا arvā́ *f.* [*plural:* ارواګاني arvāgāni *plural:* ارواوي arvávi] **1** spirit **2** soul *idiom* اروا خُک کول، اروا خُک کېدل to think only of food سولول اروا **a** to be greedy (esp. for food) **b** to conduct oneself basely; toady, grovel, bootlick **c** to be stingy, be niggardly **d** to sniff at پر اروا اوبدل **a** to have a presentiment, have a foreboding **b** to think of, devise, invent; think up خدای دي نه کوي، څه دي پر اروا اوري؟ *literal* May God diminish the consequences! *figurative* What are you thinking of doing?

ارواح arvā́h *m. Arabic plural from* روح د ارواح په خوښی څه بخښنل to sacrifice something for a departed soul

ارواږۍ arvaṛáj *f. singular & plural* dandelion

ارواوبتوب arvāvəgtób *m.* ارواوبتیا arvāvəgtjā́ *f.* ارواوبوالی arvavəgválaj *m.* greed, avidity, insatiability

ارواوبږی arvāvə́gaj greedy, avid, insatiable

اروپا urupā́ *f.* Europe

اروپایي urupā́i **1** *indeclinable* European **2** European (person)

اروته arváta *f.* **1** woman **2** wife

اروړ ¹ aróṛ *m.* stutterer, stammerer

اروړ ² aróṛ *m.* **1** spite **2** envy

اروړه aroṛá **1** mixed, intermixed, muddled up اروړه کول to mix, intermix, muddle اروړه کېدل to be mixed, be intermixed, be muddled **2** *f.* ill-matched company, motley crew

اروړه توب aroṛatób *m.* blend, mixture

اروسي urusí *f.* ☞

اروګوی urugváj *m.* Urugvaj

ارومرو arumarú هرومرو

اروول arvavól *transitive* [*past:* وايي رواوه] **1** to oblige to listen **2** to read aloud

اروونې arvúne *f.* noise, sound تیزه اروونې sharp (loud, high-pitched) noise

اروي ¹ árvi *present tense of* اروېدل

اروې ² árve *present tense, second person of* اروېدل

اروېدل arvedól *transitive* [*past:* وايي روېدل *present:* اروي] *Western* to hear; listen; heed د اخبره په دواړو غوږو واروه Listen carefully to what I shall tell you. ... اروېدلي مي دي چه *arvedóli* I heard that ... اروېدلي به دي وي چه ... You probably heard that ... اروېدل کېدل *passive* to be heard نوم یې ښه اروبدل کیږي One hears good things about him. He enjoys a good reputation. He has a good name.

اروېدنه arvedóna *f.* hearing, audition

اروېدون arvedún *m.* تاسي د هغه په اروبدون کښي داسي ویل You said this about him; that he listened to what you said.

اروبدونکی arvedúnkaj **1** *present participle of* اروبدل **2** *m.* radio listener ګرانو اروبدونکو! Dear radio listeners!

اروېده arvedə́ *m. plural* **1** listening د دي خبري په اروبدو سره دپر په قهر شو Having heard of this, he became very angry. **2** rumors

آرویی árwajaj *m.* keyword

اره ¹ āra *f.* **1** saw (the tool) اره څکول to saw up, cut up **2** pruning saw *idiom* پر احمد اره و دو سره برابره ده Ahmed suffered a good deal of unpleasantness. Ahmed is in difficult straits.

اره ² āra *f.* foundation, groundwork

اره ³ urə́ *m. plural* ☞ اوره ¹

ارهټ arhaṭ well provided with a noria (i.e., water bucket wheel) *idiom* دي وران ارهټ نه سپی لیري شه *Eastern saying* Her tongue has been loosened. She is babbling all over the place.

ارهټي arhaṭí *attributive* well ارهټي مځکه land irrigated by means of a "noria" (i.e., water wheel)

ارهډ arháḍ *m.* ☞ ارهټ

ارهر arhár *m.* ارهرو arharú *singular & plural* dove pea, *Cajanus indicus*

اره کش arakásh *m.* sawyer, woodcutter

اره کشي arakashí sawing (of lumber)

اره ګل aragúl *m.* karakul (fur from the pelt of an Asian sheep)

ارهنډ arhánḍ *m. singular & plural* ارهنډه arhánḍa *f.* castor-oil plant د ارهنډي تېل وتبل castor oil

اري ¹ iráj *m.* ☞ اروري

اریان arjā́n اوس اریان یم چه څه به وکم حیران I am taken aback. I do not know what to do. اریان completely thunderstuck, dumbfounded, surprised

آریانا arjānā́ *f. history* Ariana (the western part of the Iranian plateau)

اریانتوب arjāntób *m.* اریانتیا arjāntjā́ *f.* ☞ حیرانتیا

اریانول arjānavól *transitive* ☞ حیرانول هغه یې په ځان پوري اریان کړه *folklore* He surprised everyone. ټوله یې په ځان پوري اریان کړه

اریاني ¹ arjāní *f.* ☞ حیراني

اریاني ² arjáni *f. plural* ☞ اریان

آریاني ³ ārjaní ☞ آریا یی

اریانېدل arjānedól *intransitive* ☞ حیرانېدل

آریایی ārjāi **1** *attributive* Aryan **2** *m.* Aryan (person)

ارېځ urjádz *f.* ارېځه urjádza *f.* [*plural:* ارېځي urjádzi] cloud, cloudiness ارېځ ده It is cloudy. It is overcast. هوا اریځ کیږي The weather is getting overcast.

اریړه ariṛá *f.* myrobalan (the tree or its fruit)

اریک شریک arik-sharík *m. regional* tribal feud, blood feud

آریائي árijan ☞ آریایي

ارئ ¹ irjáj *m.* dried rhubarb

ارئي ² irjáj *m.* ☞ اروي ¹

اړ اړ آر āṛ ār **1** *m.* **.1** obstacle; hinderance **1.2** error, delusion **1.3** cover, ambush اړ اخیستل to lie in ambush **1.4** hobbles; fetters, chains **1.5** colic **1.6** constipation **2** *predicative* **.1** connected, tied together **2.2** detained; apprehended **2.3** stuck; caught زما لاس اړ دئ **a** My arm is caught. My arm is entangled. **b** I am busy. I am engaged. **2.4** experiencing difficulties; being in need و هیڅ شي ته اړ نه وو ² اړول ☞ اړ کول He is in need of nothing. **2.5** compelled, forced اړ دئ چه ... He is compelled ... **2.6** muddled, confused; intricate, complex;

difficult to understand **2.7** very busy; absorbed, engrossed (e.g., in work) اړ وتل ☞ اړوتل **2.8** suffering from constipation اپړبدل ☞ اپړبدل idiom اړ او دوړ ☞ اړودوړ

اړا iṛā́ m. **1** driveler **2** ☞ اړام

اړام aṛā́m impudent, brazen

اړامنه aṛā́mna f. impudence, impertinence

اړاند aṛā́nd **1** detained **2** straitened, burdened **3** disordered, disturbed اړاند کول **a** to detain **b** to put restraint on; burden **c** to disturb اړاند کېدل **a** to be detained **b** to be straitened, be burdened **c** to be disturbed

اړايستل aṛistә́l transitive [past: اړ يې ايست] to compel, oblige

اړائي aṛājí f. bad harvest, crop failure

اړت [1] aṛā́t m. commission trade, trade on a brokerage commission

اړت [2] aṛә́t m. ☞ ارهټ

اړتاو aṛtā́v m. ☞ آرتاو

اړتوب aṛtób m. ☞ ارتیا

اړتون aṛtún m. prison

اړتي aṛatí m. broker; merchant; one who conducts business on the basis of brokerage commissions

اړتیا aṛtjā́ f. necessity, requirement, need و... ته اړتیا لرل to have a requirement for ... to have a need for ... د چا اړتياوي برابرول to satisfy someone's wants, د چا اړتياوي ليري کول satisfy someone's requirements د څوک د بل له اړتيا څخه ايستل to liberate, relieve someone of dependence

اړخ aṛkh **1** side پر اړخو په اړخ side by side د... on each side د... په اړخ ، د... د اړخ سره، د... و اړخ ته close by ..., at, near ... پر اړخ پربوتل to lie on one's side له خپله اړخه side by side with one پر اړخ بیدېدل to sleep on the right side پر اړخ لگول **a** to lean one's elbows (on); lean, rest (against) اوبنتل، اړخ بدلول **b** to go to sleep, rest **c** to suit, fit, be suitable, be proper اړخ لگېدل **a** to be up to, have within one's capacity **b** to calm, quiet, settle down from اړخ په اړخ اوري He moves from side to side. **2** edge (e.g., of a table); side کتاب د مېز و اړخ ته بل The book lies at the edge of the table. اړخ ته تېرېدل to cross over to the other side of the street **3** board (of a boat) **4** military flank **5** slope (of a mountain) **6** math edge, intersection **7** slant, aspect, point of view

اړخ لرونکی اړخدار ☞ اړخ دار aṛkhā́r

اړخک aṛkhák m. hunting battue (a method of hunting in which animals are driven into some place for the convenience of the shooters)

اړخ لرونکی aṛkh larúnkaj having edges, faceted, multifaceted اړخ لرونکی څيز، اړخ لرونکی جسم a cut pencil اړخ لرونکی پنسل polyhedron

اړخن aṛkhә́n **1** ☞ اړخيز **2** traversing a slope **3** going along something سړک د سيند په غاړه اړخن تللئ دئ The road goes along the riverbank. **4** bordering; edging

اړخي arkhaj m. **1** slope (of a mountain) **2** incline, declivity **3** anatomy true rib, upper rib

اړخيز arkhíz **1** side, lateral اړخيز څاينه side seats, seats at the sides of a hall or auditorium **2** extreme, outer, last, located on the edge **3** military flank, flanking اړخيزه حمله flank attack **4** angular, uneven **5** wide, flat idiom اړخيز گلوبيول physiology leucocyte, white blood cell ژوولپ او اړخيزه خبره کول to speak sharply

اردي urdí f. Eastern civil tunic, military formal coat

اړکی [1] arkáj m. aṛәkáj **1** staircase; stepladder **2** bar; bolt **3** part of a weaving machine

اړکی [2] arkә́j f. aṛәkә́j singular trap

اړکېده arkedә́ m. plural hinderance, delay بې اړکېدو without interference, without delay

اړگړه aṛgaṛá f. **1** stable **2** horse-breeding farm

اړلنگ aṛláng m. imagination, thought, idea

اړم [1] aṛám m. **1** crowbar; lever **2** bar, bolt اړم کول compound verb ☞ اړمبدل، اړمول compound verb ☞ **3** brake, hindrance **4** prop, support څان و يو شي ته اړم کول to rest, set (against)

اړم [2] úṛәm regional ☞ وړم

اړمن aṛimán m. "ariman" (an evil spirit, demon, devil)

اړمول aramavә́l denominative, transitive [past: اړم يې کړ] **1** to employ as a lever **2** to apply the tongue to the hard palate (in the pronunciation of retroflex consonants) **3** to rest against something; lean against something

اړمي aramáj m. ☞ اړم [1]

اړمبدل aṛamedә́l denominative, transitive [past: اړم شو] **1** to be employed in the capacity of a lever **2** figurative to set energetically to work دې چاري ته ښه اړم شوئ دئ He undertook this matter energetically.

اړناوی arnā́vaj m. **1** riches **2** solvency, richness

اړنگ aṛáng m. **1** doubt; vacillation **2** suspicion **3** blame اړنگ نيول **a** to doubt; vacillate **b** to suspect **c** to find deficiencies; blame

اړنگ-بړنگ aṛáng-baṛáng اړنگ دوړنگ aṛáng-duṛáng **1** doubting, uncertain, vacillating **2** confused, embarrassed

اړنگۍ aṛangә́j f. step, running board اړنگۍ اچول to backheel (i.e., to throw an opponent in wrestling by tripping him, throwing his heel over one's leg)

اړوالی aṛvā́laj m. ☞ اړتیا

اړوتړ aṛutáṛ m. **1** persuasion **2** measure

اړوتل aṛvatә́l intransitive [past: اړووت past: اړوزي] **1** to be occupied, be busy with something **2** to be obliged, be forced

اړودوړ aṛudúṛ m. **1** skirmish, melee; battle **2** argument, conflict, disagreement اړودوړ نبلول **a** to engage in battle **b** to create a conflict

اړوښتي aṛoḳhtaj m. economy

اړول ¹ aṛavól آړول aṛavól *transitive* [*past:* راوه وايي *present:* اړوي]
1 to move, stir 2 to shift, move elsewhere 3 to turn, turn over, leaf through د كتاب پاڼي اړول to leaf through a book 4 to transpose 5 to plow, dig, dig over again تمام پټي يي اړولي دئ He ploughed the entire field. He dug over the entire field. 6 to hold fast, bring to a stop, restrain 7 to take away, remove from the road 8 to put, put in, load 9 to load something from one place to another له غره نه اړول ، تر غره اړول to load (and transport) over the mountain 10 to throw repeatedly; throw across پنبه اړول a to cross the legs b to sit (e.g., on a horse) پنبه په پنبه اړول to cross the legs 11 to place in or convert to other circumstances or status اردو په شان اړول د روغي to convert the army to peacetime status 12 to translate (from one language to another) پښتو اړول to translate into Pashto 13 to drain (e.g., water) 14 to turn against (someone) 15 to attach a different meaning to something; turn things against someone 16 to inflict (damage, harm, loss), harm دښمن ته درانه تلفات اړول to inflict great loss on the enemy و چا ته مالي تاوان اړول to inflict material losses on someone بېړى ته زيان اړول to wreck a ship 17 to unload بار اړول to unload 18 to drop in, pay a call, stay somewhere بر چا اړول چه دا يوه مياشت كېږي to stay too long راباندي يي اړولي دي He has already been our guest for a month. دوى په كاروان سراى كښي واړول He stayed at the caravansarai. 19 to spend, pass (time) اړول را اړول a to turn over, overturn, topple b to change خان اړول to turn away from د چا د خبري څخه خان اړول not to listen to someone, to ignore

اړول ² aṛavól *denominative, transitive* [*past:* اړ يي كړ] 1 prevent, hinder 2 to detain, seize, catch 3 to place in a difficult situation 4 to force, compel, oblige, make

اړولئ aṛavólaj 1 *past participle of* اړول ¹ 2.1 muddled up 2.2 inappropriate, unseemly, obscene اړولي چاري aṛaváli a muddled matters b unseemly, indecent acts اړولي خبري aṛaváli a disconnected speech b grumbling, mumbling اړولئ بخت failure

اړوندج aṛvándzh *m.* 1 basis, foundation 2 leg (of a furniture piece) 3 supporting member

اړونه aṛavóna *f.* 1 turning over, capsizing, reversing 2 translation, transference 3 substitution, replacement 4 alteration

اړوونكى aṛavúnkaj 1 *present participle of* اړول ² 2 توري اړوونكى *grammar* preposition

اړوونى aṛawūńay *m.* adapter

اړوي ¹ áṛavi *present tense of* اړول ¹

اړوي ² áṛavi *present tense of* اړول ²

اړوي ³ áṛvi *vice of* اوړي ²

اړه ¹ āṛa *f.* furrow

اړه ² aṛá *f.* 1 relationship, connection, association; dependence 2 need, requirement; necessity و ، اړه لرل ... اړه لرلپه ... په سره

a to be connected with something, depend upon something هر كار په خپل وخت سره اړه لري Everything in its own time. اړه په ... b to belong to ته و ... b to need هوا ته اړه لرل to need fresh air 3 obstacle 4 iron stove lid, iron stove cover *idiom* اړه ايستل to relieve oneself, answer the call of nature

اړه ³ uṛá *m. plural dialect* ☞ اوره

اړه ⁴ áṛa *f. singular* ☞ اړ ²

اړكى ¹ aṛakáj *m.* ☞ اړكى

اړي ¹ aṛí *f.* ☞ اړكي 1, 3

اړي ² iṛáj *m.* ☞ اړري

اړي ³ aṛój *plural from* اړي ¹

اړېخي aṛídzáj *m.* guardroom, brig (place for short-term detention of arrestees)

اړېدل aṛedól *denominative, intransitive* [*past:* اړ شو] 1 to need, experience a need for; requirement 2 to be forced الوتكه ښكته كبدو ته اړه شوه The aircraft made a forced landing. 3 to be in great difficulties 4 to stay too long, linger on, stick

اړېدل uṛedól *denominative* [*past:* اړه شول] to be milled, be made into flour

اړكبده aṛedána *f.* اړبده aṛedá *m. plural* 1 ☞ اړكبده 2 need, requirement

اړېره aṛerá *f.* اوړى aṛeṛój *f.* the crosspiece of a noria (i.e., water wheel) to which the buckets are attached

اړېستل aṛjistól *transitive* ☞ اړېستل

اړېسه aṛisá boiled اړيسه غوښه boiled meat

اړيكتيايي سيسټم aṛiktjiāji sístəm *m.* communication system

اړېكنيو څار aṛíknajū tsár *m.* call waiting

اړېكى aṛekáj *m.* 1 need, requirement; necessity, requisite 2 relationship, connection تجارتي اړيكي تينگول aṛeki to strengthen trade links اړيكى لرل a to be in need, experience a need or requirement څه اړيكى راسره لري؟ What do you need from me? b to have a relationship, have a connection 3 obstacle, hinderance, difficulty اړيكي اچول a to establish a relationship connection b to hinder, put obstacles in the way, impede, hamper 4 *medicine* constipation 5 bolt, bar

اړېنه aṛína *f.* 1 need, requirement, necessity, requisite 2 dependence

آز āz *m. Arabic* 1 desire, passion 2 greediness, avidity

آزاد āzád azád 1.1 free, open, unrestricted په آزاده هوا كښي in the open air آزاد بحر the open sea a don't لاس يي آزاد پرېږده hinder him b let him go 1.2 independent; autonomous 2 *m.* 2.1 a free man 2.2 *proper name* Azad *idiom* آزاد وتل to pass completely through

آزادانه āzādāná 1.1 free, unrestricted آزادانه ژوندون لرل to live freely, lead an unrestricted life 1.2 independent 2.1 freely, unrestrictedly 2.2 independently

آزادخيال āzādkhijál freethinking

آزادخیالي āzādkhijālí *f.* freethinking; free thought

آزادګي azādagí *f.* ☞ آزادي[1]

آزادول āzādavál *denominative, transitive* [*past:* آزاد یې کړ] to free, liberate

آزاده āzāda **1** *indeclinable* ☞ آزاد[1] **2** *feminine singular from* آزاد

آزادي[1] āzādí *f.* **1** freedom د نطق او بیان آزادي freedom of speech د مطبوعاتو آزادي freedom of the press ، د تحریر او تقریر آزادي freedom of organization د عقیدي آزادي freedom تشکیلاتو آزادي of conscience د عملیاتو آزادي freedom of action د آزادي مجاهد the struggle for freedom د آزادي غوښتلو نهضت the liberation movement **2** independence

آزادی[2] āzādáj *m. proper name* Azadaj (diminutive of Azad)

آزادي خواه āzādikhā́h **1** freedom-loving **2** liberal

آزادي خواهي āzādikhā́hi *f.* **1** love of freedom **2** liberalism

آزادېدل āzādedál *denominative, intransitive* [*past:* آزاد شو] **1** to be liberated; be free **2** to receive freedom; be independent

آزادي دوست āzādidóst freedom-loving

آزادېده āzādedá *m. plural* liberation

آزادي غوښتونکی āzādí guk̲htúnkaj freedom-loving

آزار[1] āzā́r *m.* ازار azā́r *m.* **1** illness, disease **2** offense; injury وچاته په آزار کېدل to offend someone وچاته آزار رسول to take offense at someone **3** pursuit

ازار[2] izā́r *m.* breeches, loose trousers tucked inside boots

ازارول azāravál *denominative, transitive* [*past:* ازار یې کړ] **1** to offend; pain, injure **2** to pursue; pester, harass

ازاري azārí **1** *m.* sick person, patient **2** sick, ill, unhealthy

ازارېدل azaredál *denominative, intransitive* [*past:* ازار شو] to be offended; be grieved, be pained د چا څخه ازارېدل to be offended at someone

ازالت izālát *m.* ازاله izālá *f. Arabic* **1** elimination د غلطیو ازالت the elimination of errors **2** disappearance ازالت کول *compound verb* to remove, eliminate

ازان azā́n *m.* ☞ اذان

ازانګه azāngá *f.* زانګه zāngá **1** echo ازانګه اچول، ازانګه کول to ring, resound ازانګه کېدل to ring out, resound, reverberate (of an echo, sound)

ازبک uzbák *m.* Uzbek (person)

ازبکستان uzbakistā́n *m.* Uzbekistan

ازبکه uzbáka *f.* Uzbek (female)

ازبکي[1] uzbakí *attributive* ازبکي ژبه Uzbek, the Uzbek language

ازبکي[2] uzbáki *plural from* ازبکه

ازدحام izdihā́m *m. Arabic* assemblage, mob, crowd

ازدواج izdivā́dzh *m. Arabic* wedlock, marriage bond, marriage د چا سره ازدواج کول to enter into marriage with someone د ازدواج قانون matrimonial law

ازدیاد izdijā́d *f. Arabic* increase, augmentation ازدیاد کول to increase, augment

ازربایجان azarbajdzhā́n *m.* ☞ اذربیجان

آزردګي āzurdagí *f.* offense; injury, disorder, grief, displeasure

آزرده āzurdá *indeclinable* offended; injured, disordered, grieved له چا څخه آزرده کېدل to be offended at someone

آزرده خاطر āzurdakhā́tir ☞ آزرده دل āzurdadíl

ازرو azrú *m.* Azru (district, Pakti Province)

ازغکي azghakáj *m.* **1** prickle, thorn **2** *regional* mimosa, *Prosopis stephaniana*

ازغن azghán ☞ اغزن

ازغی azgháj *m.* **1** prickle, thorn هر چیري ګل وي، یو ازغی ور سره تل وي *proverb* There is no rose without thorns. **2** barbed wire دا زما په سترګو کښي ازغی دئ *idiom* It is like a sore on my eye.

ازګار uzghā́r ☞ وزګار

ازګارتوب uzgārtób *m.* ازګارتیا uzgārtjā́ *f.* ☞ وزګارتوب

ازګارول uzgāravál *denominative, transitive* ☞ وزګارول

ازګارېدل uzgāredál *denominative, intransitive* ☞ وزګارېدل

ازګری uzgəraj *m. Eastern* **1** large kid (i.e., young of goat) **2** *Western* goat

ازګي izgí *f.* spelling words out ازګي توري the alphabet

ازل azál *m. Arabic* eternity په تندي کښي مي نوشته دئ د ازل ټکي *folklore* Thus it was fated for me.

ازمار azmā́r **1** *m.* sly and cunning one; deceiver; cheat; intriguer **2** shrewd, crafty

ازمارتوب azmārtób *m.* shrewdness, craftiness, deceit, trickery, insidiousness

ازماینش āzmājísh *m.* ☞ ازماینت

آزماینشګاه āzmājishgā́h *f.* laboratory

ازماینت azmājə́k̲ht *m.* **1** verification, check, trial, test **2** experiment ازماینت کول، تر ازماینت لاندي نیول to experiment, carry out an experiment **3** roll call, muster

ازماینتي azmājə́k̲hti **1** *attributive* verifying, test; trial **2** experimental د ذروي ازماینتي چاودنو منع کول nuclear test ban

ازمایل azmājál *transitive* ☞ ازمینت ازمینه

ازماینه azmājə́na *f.* ☞ ازمینت

ازمودل azmudál *transitive* ☞ ازمویل

ازموده asmudá *indeclinable* experienced; worldly-wise ازموده کول to make experienced هغه ازموده سردار و He was an experienced military leader.

ازموده کار azmudakā́r tested, experienced; checked out

ازموینت azmojə́k̲ht *m.* azmujə́k̲ht ☞ ازماینت

ازموینتي azmojə́k̲hti ☞ ازماینتي پټي ازماینتي experimental field

ازمویل azmojál *transitive Western* [*past:* ویې ازمویه] **1** to verify; try, attempt **2** to experiment, test ځان ازمویل **a** to test, take stock of oneself **b** to be in training

ازموینځای azmujəndzā́j *m.* ازموینخای azmujə́ndzáj *m.* **1** experimental station **2** laboratory

ازموینه azmujə́na *f.* **1** verification, trial **2** experiment **3** temptation دا نړی د ازموینو نړی ده *proverb* Life is filled with trials.

ازمیونکی azumjúnkaj **1** *present participle of* ازمویل **2** tester, experimenter

ازمیر izmír *m.* Izmir (city)

ازمایښت azmajə́kht *m.* ☞ ازمیښت

ازماینتي azmajəkhtí ☞ ازمیښتی

ازمجل azmajə́l *transitive* ☞ ازمویل

ازمیښت azmejə́kht *m.* ☞ ازمویل

ازمیل azmejə́l *transitive* ☞ ازمویل

آزوت āzót *m. plural* nitrogen

آزوتي āzotí nitrogen, nitrogenous د آزوتي سري nitrogen fertilizers آزوتي سري فابریکه nitrogen-mineral (fertilizer) factory

ازور azór د ازور مجمع الجزایر the Azores Islands

ازوغ azúgh *m. singular & plural m.* ☞ ازوغه azughá *f.* اذوغي کوټه storeroom

آزوف āzóf *m.* د آزوف بحیره the Sea of Azov

ازوقه azuķá *f.* ☞ ازوغ

ازیل azejə́l *transitive* ☞ ازبیل

آژانس āzhāns *m.* **1** agency د خبر رسولو آژانس خبررسونکی آژانس telegraph agency د باختر آژانس the Bakhtar Agency د تاس آژانس TASS (Telegraph Agency of the Soviet Union) **2** bureau, office د سفر آژانس tourist bureau د معلوماتو information office د کار آژانس employment office

اژدر azhdár *m.* dragon

اژدهات azhdahā́t *m. singular & plural* bronze

اژغنجن uzhghəndzhə́n made of goat's wool

اژغونه uzhghúna *f.* ☞ اجغنه

اژبیل azhejə́l *transitive* [*past:* و یي اژبیه] to wind (threads)

ابرکه agbáka *f.* black martin (bird)

اورد ugd ☞ اوردو

اوردو ugdó *oblique plural of* اوردو د ... په اردو کښي along

اوردوالی ugdvā́laj *m.* ☞ اوردوالی

ابرمی agramáj *m.* ☞ اربمی

اوره ugá *f.* ☞ اوره

اګج agə́j *f. dialect* ☞ هګی

اګجل agəjə́l *transitive* [*past:* وايي ږیه] **1** to impel; incite, urge on **2** to twist (cord) **3** *carpentry* to saw into dovetail form

آس ās *m.* اس as *m.* [*plural:* اسونه asúna *plural:* آسان āsā́n] عرابه کش اس pack horse باري اس خسي اس gelding draught horse پر اس سپور mounted on a horse د اسونو طبیب *technology* horsepower د اس قوه veterinarian د اس څغلولو مسابقي میدان races د اس څغلولو مسابقه racetrack د اسونو ګله herd of horses اس څغلول a to ride a horse hard *figurative* b to make efforts; try c to think, reflect upon ته هم خپل اس وڅغلوه You also reflect upon it and think what to do. اس وهل a to ride horseback b to learn to ride horseback اسان یی نعلول They were shoeing horses چنګښو هم پنبی پورته کړي and even the frogs raised their little paws (i.e., everyone wanted to get into the act) اس دئ وي، په لاس دئ وي، اس لره په لاس لره *proverb* If you wish to control a horse you must know how to

handle it. اس خپله دانه پخپله زیاتوي *proverb* a good horse feeds itself اس یی په سوو ګټي، انسان یی په خولو ګټي *proverb* The hooves earn a horse's bread, but for man it is the tongue. اس که تکني دئ، میدان لنډ دئ *proverb* To a restive horse the public square is too small. زاړه اسونه تربي نه زده کوي *proverb* You can't teach an old horse to jump. (i.e., you can't teach an old dog new tricks)

آس² ās *m.* **1** millstone **2** milling of grain

آس³ ās *m.* **1** ashes (on a grate) **2** site of a fire; *figurative* home

آس⁴ ās *m.* myrtle

آس⁵ ās *m.* ermine

اسارت isārát *m. Arabic* **1** captivity **2** slavery; enslavement

اسارت آمیز isāratāméz **1** servile, slavish; اسارت آمیزه servitude اسارت آمیزه شرایط conditions of slavery **2** *attributive* slave

اساس asā́s *m. Arabic* [*plural:* اساسونه asāsúna *Arabic plural:* اساسات asāsā́t] **1** base, basis, foundation د ... پر اساس، د ... په on the basis of ... له اساسه څخه radically, fundamentally **2** principle

اساساً asāsán *Arabic* **1** in substance, in essence **2** fundamentally **3** in principle

اساسنامه asāsnāmá *f.* statute, regulation

اساسي asāsí *Arabic* **1** fundamental, basic اساسي اصول fundamental law, constitution اساسي قانون constitution **2** په اساسي ډول fundamentally, basically **3** in principle, in the main, in essence

اساطیر asātír *m. Arabic plural from* اسطوره

اسالیب asālíb *m. Arabic plural from* اسلوب

آسام āsā́m *m.* Assam

اسامبله asāmblá *f.* **1** assembly د متحده ملتو عمومي اسامبله General Assembly of the United Nations **2** meeting لویه اسامبله general meeting

اسامي asāmí *m. Arabic plural from* اسم

آسان¹ āsā́n اسان asā́n easy, uncomplicated, simple دا خو اسانه خبره This is quite easy to do. په اسانه ده easily

آسان² āsā́n *plural from* آس¹

اسانتر asāntár more easily

اسانتوب asāntób *m.* اسانتیا

اساني¹ sāntjā́ *f.* ☞ دا په خورا اسانتوب لاس ته راځي This is very easy to obtain.

اسانسور asānsór *m.* elevator; escalator

اسانګر asāngə́r *m.* accessibility, wizard

اسانول asānavə́l *denominative, transitive* [*past:* اسان یی کړ] to make easier اسانول سختي to lighten difficulties

اسانه asāna *feminine singular from* اسان¹ دا دپره اسانه ده چه It may very easily happen that ...

اساني¹ asāní *f.* **1** lightness, easiness په اساني سره easily **2** facilitation, assistance, furtherance په اساني پیښول to help و ... ته

someone, assist someone د درد اساني يې سوې ده؟ Has his pain subsided?

اساني asáni [2] *feminine plural from* آسان [1]

اسانیدل asānedál *denominative, intransitive* [*past:* اسان شو] to become easy, be made light (e.g., of work)

آسایش asajísh *m.* peace, rest آسایش کول to rest د چا آسایش خرابول to disrupt someone's rest

اسایلم asājlam *m.* asylum د اسایلم حق the right of asylum

اسباب asbấb *m. Arabic* **1** *plural of* سبب reasons; circumstances موجبه اسباب motivation; motives مجبره اسباب force majeure **2** [*plural:* اسبابونه asbābúna] equipment, weapons نقلیه اسباب means of transport, transport equipment د معیشت اسباب the means of existence **3** [*plural:* اسبابونه asbābúna] possessions; articles, utensils, baggage, equipment د خوب اسباب bedding اسباب او سامان equipment and situation

اسباب ساز asbābsáz *m.* plotter

اسباب سازي asbābsāzí *f.* intrigues

اسباپ asbáp *m. colloquial* ☞ اسباب

اسباق asbáķ *m. Arabic plural of* سبق

اسبانه asbānə́ *plural from* اسبون

اسبانه asbaná *feminine of* اسبون

څاسبون asbún *m.* [*plural:* اسبانه asbānə́] herder of horses

اسبونول asbunavál *denominative, transitive* [*past:* اسبون یې کړ] to make someone a horse herder, designate someone a horse herder

اسبونیدل asbunedál *denominative, intransitive* [*past:* اسبون شو] to become a horse herder, be designated a horse herder

اسبه asbə́ *m.* [*plural:* اسبانه asnānə́] اسبونول ☞ اسبه کول اسبون اسبونیدل ☞ اسبه کیدل،

اسپانیا ispānijá *f.* اسپانیه ispānijá *f.* Spain

اسپتال aspitál *m.* اسپتال aspitál *m.* hospital

اسپدواني aspandavāní *f.* horse races

اسپرانت aspirānt *m.* graduate student

اسپرانتور aspirāntúr *m.* course of graduate studies

اسپغول ispaghól *m.* plantain, *Plantago ispaghula*

آسپک āspák *m.* breastbone (bird)

اسپکي aspakáj *m.* hobby

اسپند ispánd *m. singular & plural perganum harmala*, wild rue

اسپندوس aspandós *m.* اسپندوسه aspəndósa *f.* polo اسپندوس کول to play polo

اسپندوکي aspəndúkaj *m.* pack (attached to the saddle)

اسپنه uspə́na *f.* ☞ اوسپنه

اسپه áspa *f.* [1] mare

اسپه aspá *f.* [2] **1** typhus **2** nettle rash **3** asthma

اسپي aspí [1] *indeclinable, attributive* horse, mounted اسپي ترصد mounted patrol

اسپي áspi [2] *plural from* اسپه [1]

اسپي aspé [3] *plural from* اسپه [2]

استا ustá *m.* **1** teacher استادبدل ☞ استا کېدل استا ☞ استادول **2** master, expert

استاتوب ustātób *m.* position or job of teacher, master, expert

استاځوالی astādzvalí *m.* استاځولي astādzvalí *f.* ☞ استازوالی

استازی astādzaj *m.* ☞ استازي

استاد ustád *m.* **1** teacher, instructor, tutor مشر استاد *regional* director of a school **2** master, expert د کار استاد master craftsman, brigade leader **3** professor

استادانه ustādāná **1** expert, craftsman **2** skillfully, in a masterful fashion

استادول ustādavál *denominative, transitive* [*past:* استاد یې کړ] to make into a teacher, make into master

استاده ustáda *feminine of* استاد

استادي ustādí [1] *f.* **1** *collective noun* teachers; teaching **2** craftsmanship; art

استادي ustádi [2] *m. from* استاده

استادیدل ustādedál *denominative, intransitive* [*past:* استاد شو] **1** to be a teacher **2** to be a master, be an expert

استاذ ustáz *m.* ☞ استاد تا پر کوم استاذ سبق ویلئ دئ؟ Under whom are you studying?

استاذه ustáza *feminine of* استاذ

استاذي ustāzí [1] *f.* ☞ استادي [1]

استاذي ustāzi [2] *plural from* استاذه

استازوالی astāzválaj *m. religion* the official mission of a religous body or the staff of such mission

استازي astāzaj *m.* **1** envoy, respresentative, delegate خپل استازي کول to send one's own man; send one's representative **2** spokesman (for feelings, hopes, etc.) **3** prophet

استاسیون istāsjún *m.* station د رادیو استاسیون radio station

استانبول istāmból *m.* Istanbul (city)

آستانه āstāná *f.* ☞ آستان

استاوالی ustāválaj *m.* ☞ استاتوب

استبداد istibdád *m. Arabic* despotism; autocracy

استبدادي istibdādí *Arabic indeclinable* despotic, autocratic

استتار istitár *m. Arabic* camouflage

استثمار istismár *m. Arabic* exploitation د انسانانو استثمار the exploitation of man استثمار کول *compound verb* ☞ استثمارول

استثمارچي istismārchí *m.* استثمارگر istismārgár *m.* exploiter

استثمارول istismāravál *denominative, transitive* [*past:* استثمار یې کړ] **1** to exploit **2** to use **3** to exploit (i.e., natural resources)

استثماریدل istimāredál *denominative, intransitive* [*past:* استثمار شو] **1** to be exploited **2** to be used; be exploited (e.g., of natural resources)

استثنا istisnấ *f. Arabic* [*plural:* استثناوي istisnấvi *plural:* استثناگاني istisnāgā́ni *m. Arabic plural:* استثناات istisnāā́t]

د ... په استثنا ببله استثنا without exception استثنا exception with the exception of ... استثنا کول to make an exception

استثنايي istisnāí *exceptional* په استثنايي مواردو کښي in exceptional circumstances په استثنايي ډول in the nature of an exception

استجابت istidzhābát *m.* استجابه istidzhābá *f. Arabic m.* [*plural:* استجابات istidzhābát] reaction, response

استحاله istihālá *f. Arabic* change, transformation, transition (from one state to another); metamorphosis کيفي استحالي qualitative changes

استحصال istihsāl *m. Arabic* 1 getting, receiving 2 production استحصال کول *compound verb* to produce 3 [*plural:* استحصالات istihāsālāt] manufactured article production

استحصالول istihsālavól *denominative, transitive* استحصالول istihsālavól to produce, manufacture, make

استحصالېدل istihsāledól *denominative, intransitive* استحصالېدل istihsāledól to be produced, be manufactured, be made

استحضار istihzār *m. Arabic* summons, invitation

استحقاق istihķāķ *m. Arabic* [*plural:* استحقاقونه istihķāķúna *Arabic plural:* استحقاقات istihķāķā́t] 1 virtue, merit 2 ability; competence; right 3 allowance, allocation, ration ورځنی استحقاق daily ration مقوي استحقاق augmented ration

استحقاقي istihķākí استحقاقيه istihķākijá 1 due, due to 2 *attributive* ration, pertaining to a ration or allocation

استحکام istihkā́m *m. Arabic* [*plural:* استحکامونه istihkāmúna *Arabic plural:* استحکامات istihkāmā́t] 1 strengthening, consolidation 2 *military* reinforcement, fortification چوبي او زميني استحکامات سپک استحکامات bunker fortifications of a field (temporary) nature 3 combat engineering د استحکام کنډک combat engineer battalion

استحکامچي istihkāmchí *m.* combat engineer

استحکامچي ګري istihkāmchigarí *f.* combat engineering

استحکامي istihkāmí 1 reinforced, fortified استحکامي حرب static warfare 2 *attributive* combat engineer, engineer استحکامي قطعه combat-engineer unit

استحمام istihmā́m *m. Arabic* bathing د استحمام جامه bathing suit

استخاره istikhārá *f. Arabic* fortunetelling (by means of books, by strung beads concerning the outcome of matters planned or in the future)

استخبار istikhbár *m. Arabic* [*plural:* استخبارونه istikhbārúna *Arabic plural:* استخبارات istikhbārā́t] notification, finding out, reconnoitering; information د استخباراتو ځانګه information department

استخبارات istikhbārā́t *m. Arabic plural* 1 *from* استخبار 2 intelligence data, intelligence 3 intelligence (agent)

استخدام istikhdā́m *m. Arabic* 1 hiring for work, acceptance for a job د ملي استخدام اداره hiring directorate 2 employment, use استخدام کېدل *compound verb* ☞ استخدامول استخدام کول *compound verb* ☞ استخدامېدل

استخدامول istikhdāmavól *denominative, transitive* [*past:* استخدام يي کړ] 1 to accept, take on for work, sign (someone) on for a job کاريګران استخدامول to hire workers 2 to employ, use

استخدامي istikhdāmí hired

استخدامېدل istikhdāmedól *denominative, intransitive* [*past:* استخدام شو] 1 to be accepted for a job, be signed on for a job 2 to be used, be employed

استخراج istikhrādzh *m. Arabic* 1 development, extraction (e.g., of natural resources) 2 extraction استخراج کول *compound verb* ☞ استخراجول استخراج کېدل *compound verb* ☞ استخراجېدل

استخراجول istikhrādzhavól *denominative, transitive* [*past:* استخراج يي کړ] 1 to extract (esp. natural resources) 2 to obtain, extract, mine 3 *figurative* to reprimand

استخراجي istikhrādzhí pertaining to the extraction of mining (esp. natural resources) د حفريات استخراجي the mining of ore

استخراجېدل istikhrādzhedól *denominative, intransitive* [*past:* استخراج شو] 1 to be extacted, be mined (esp. natural resources) 2 to be extracted, be mined

استخلاص istikhlā́s *m. Arabic* deliverance, liberation

استخوان ustukhā́n *m. ostokhán* 1 bone 2 stone (of a fruit) ☞ هډ

استخوان بندي ustukhānbandí *f. ostokhānbandí* 1 skeleton, frame, framework 2 structural framework

استخوان کاري ustukhānkārí *f. ostokhānkārí* structural work, skeletal work

استدراج istidrádzh *m. Arabic* gradualness د استدراج په توګه gradually

استدراک istidrák *m. Arabic* understanding; the ascertainment of meaning; cognition

استدعا istid'á *f. Arabic* [*plural:* استدعاوي istid'ávi *plural:* استدعاګاني istid'āgā́ni] 1 request, entreaty 2 inquiry 3 complaint د استدعا اداره bureau of complaints

استدعانامه istid'ānāmá *f.* application, petition

استدلال istidlā́l *m. Arabic* 1 conclusion, inference 2 production of proofs; reasoning; arguments; reason, justification منطقي استدلال to advance arguments 3 په ... پوري استدلال کول arguments in proof of ...

آستر āstár *m.* استر astár *m.* 1 lining (of clothing); the wrong side 2 socle (of a wall)

استر astár *m.* mule

استراحت istirāhát *m. Arabic* rest; peace د استراحت کور rest home استراحت کول to rest

استراخان astrākhā́n *m.* Astrakhan (city)

استراليا astralijá *f.* ☞ استراليا د استراليا اتحاد the Australian Union

استراليائي astralijaí 1 *attributive* Australian 2 *m.* Australian (person)

استريل usturdál *m.* back part, hind part, back; rear

استرحام istirhā́m *m. Arabic* request, entreaty (for mercy, quarter) د چا څخه استرحام کول to request mercy of someone

استرداد istirdád *m.* 1 request for return, request for claiming 2 taking away 3 restoration

استرضا istirzā́ *f. Arabic* 1 request for agreement 2 agreement 3 satisfaction

استرکاري astarkārí *f.* cementing of masonry; plastering

استرکش astarkásh *m.* asuarkásh *military* driver

استرونوم astronóm *m.* astronomer

استرونومي astronomí *f.* astronomy

استره usturá *f.* razor

استری [1] ustráj *Western* 1 last, latest استري خبرونه *ustrí* the latest news په دې استري وخت کښي the little finger استري ګوته *ustrí* recently 2 at last استرى یې کالي واغوستل He has got dressed at last.

استرى [2] usturé *plural from* استره

استري [3] ustrí *f. regional* flatiron استري کړئ سوټ a suit which has been pressed استري کول *compound verb* to press, iron

آستریا āstrijā́ *f.* استریا astrijā́ *f.* Austria

آستریایي āstrijaí استریایي astrijaí 1 *attributive* Austrian 2 Austrian (person)

استرلیا استرالیا astrelijā́ *f.* ☞ استرالیا

استرلیایي استرالیائي astreljāí ☞ استرالیائي

استسقا istisḳā́ *f. Arabic medicine* dropsy

استشهاد istishhā́d *m. Arabic* summoning as a witness په . . . استشهاد کول a to summon as a witness b to attest to

استصواب istisvā́b *m. Arabic* 1 approval 2 consultation; solicitation of opinion

استضادي istizādí antagonistic

استضاع istizā' *f. Arabic* inquiry

استطاعت istitā'at *m. Arabic* 1 force, strength 2 resources; means; assets 3 ability

استطلاع istitlā' *f. Arabic* 1 investigation, research 2 explanation, information *idiom* د استطلاع مینه inquisitiveness

استعاره isti'ārá *f. Arabic* [*plural:* استعاري isti'āré] *m. Arabic* [*plural:* استعارات isti'ārát] extended meaning, metaphor; picturesque expression, figurative expression; allegory استعارات راوړل to adduce metaphors

استعاري isti'ārí figurative, metaphorical, allegorical

استعانت isti'ānát *m. Arabic* request for help; appeal for help

استعباد isti'bā́d *m. Arabic* enslavement

استعجاب isti'dzhā́b *m. Arabic* astonishment, amazement په استعجاب کتل to regard with astonishment, be astonished, be surprised, be amazed

استعداد isti'dā́d *m. Arabic* 1 ability, gift, talent استعداد لرل to be able, have ability 2 predisposition, bent

استعفا isti'fā́ *f.* استعفی *Arabic* retirement, going into retirement استعفا کول to retire استعفا ورکول to resign, put in for retirement استعفا قبلول to accept resignation, accept retirement

استعلام isti'lā́m *m.* استعلامیه isti'lāmijá *f. Arabic* 1 inquiry 2 inquest

استعمار isti'mā́r *m. Arabic* 1 settlement 2 colonization استعمار کول *compound verb* to colonize 3 colonialism

استعمارپرست isti'mārparást *m.* استعمارجو isti'mārdzhú *m.* استعمارچي isti'marchí *m.* استعمارګر isti'margár *m.* 1 colonizer 2 imperialist

استعماري isti'mārí colonial, colonializing

استعمال isti'mā́l *m. Arabic* use, utilization, application په . . . کښي استعمال پیدا کول to find an application for . . .

استعمالول isti'mālavᵊl *denominative, transitive* [*past:* یې] to use, utilize, apply بد استعمالول misuse

استعمالي isti'mālí *Arabic* 1 having been in use, used, secondhand 2 practical

استعمالیدل isti'māledᵊl *denominative, intransitive* [*past:* شو] to be in use, be used, be employed, be applied

استغاثه istighāsá *f. Arabic* 1 request, entreaty, petition د چا څخه استغاثه کول to ask someone (for cooperation, assistance) عرض او استغاثه کول to intercede, solicit, petition 2 suit, complaint

استغراق istighrā́ḳ *m. Arabic* 1 absorption 2 concentration 3 rapture

استغفار istighfā́r *m. Arabic* appeal for forgiveness; repentance استغفار الله Lord have mercy!

استغنی ، استغنا istighnā́ *f. Arabic* absence of need; material independence; (being) provided for, sufficiency د یو شي څخه استغنا کول to manage without something د یو شي څخه استغنا کبدل not to need something

استفاده istifādá *f. Arabic* use; utilization یو شی په خپل کار او استفاده کښي راوستل، یو شی په خپل کار او تر استفادي لاندي راوستل to use, utilize something د یو شي تر استفادي لاندي راتلل to be used, be utilized د یو شي څخه بده استفاده کول to use something

استفاده جو istifādadzhú *m.* exploiter

استفاده جوي istifādadzhuí *f.* exploitation

استفاده وي istifādaví *economics* استفاده وي ارزش use value

استفسار istifsā́r *m. Arabic* inquiry د چا څخه استفسار کول to inquire of someone

استفهام istifhā́m *m. Arabic* question د استفهام علامت question mark

استفهامي استفهامیه istifhāmijá *Arabic* interrogative استفهامي ضمائر interrogative pronoun

استقامت istikāmát *m. Arabic* 1 steadfastness, persistence 2 straightforwardness, frankness, plaindealing 3 decency 4 direction, side د شمال پر استقامت in a northern direction

استقبال istiḳbā́l *m. Arabic* 1 meeting, reception د جشن په استقبال on the occasion of the forthcoming holiday د چا استقبال کول to receive, meet someone د هغه استقبال وشو a meeting was arranged for him استقبال کول *compound verb* a to receive, meet b to comment on something 2 future 3 *grammar* future tense

استقبال کوونکی istiḳbā́l kavúnkaj 1 *present participle of* استقبال کول *m.* 2 istikbā́l kavúnki *m. plural* those attending the meeting

استقرا istiḳrā́ *f. Arabic* 1 conclusion, inference; induction استقرا کول to make an inference, draw a conclusion

استقرار istiḳrā́r *m. Arabic* 1 strengthening, stabilization 2 settling; transition to a settled way of life 3 confirmation, ratification

استقراض istiḳrā́z *m. Arabic* 1 granting of a loan, granting of credit, crediting 2 receiving credit د چا څخه استقراض کول to borrow, receive a loan from someone, be given credit

استقصا istiḳsā́ *f. Arabic* 1 attainment of the limit, end 2 intensified study

استقلال istiḳlā́l *m. Arabic* 1 independence د استقلال جشن Independence Day, Independence Holiday 2 steadfastness; resoluteness

استقلالي istiḳlālí 1 independent 2 steadfast; resolute

استکار ustakā́r *m.* 1 village craftsman, rural craftsman 2 master craftsman

استکشاف istikshā́f *m. Arabic* 1 *military* reconnaissance, intelligence, scouting 2 research

استکشافي istikshāfí *Arabic attributive military* reconnaissance, intelligence, scouting 2 research استکشافي هیئت expedition

استگاه istgā́h *m.* stand, stop, station هوایي استگاه airport

ایستل istál *transitive Western* ☞ ایستل

استلزام istilzā́m *m. Arabic* 1 demand 2 acknowledgement of necessity استلزام کول a to demand b to acknowledge necessity

استماع istimā́' *f. Arabic* audition; hearing (i.e., witnesses) استماع کول *compound verb* to listen, hear

استمداد istimdā́d *m. Arabic* request for help, request for assistance

استمرار istimrā́r *m. Arabic* 1 duration 2 persistence, steadfastness 3 past tense of the imperfective aspect, the imperfect

استمراري istimrārí *Arabic* 1 *attributive* prolonged, durative 2 *grammar* pertaining to the imperfect استمراري ماضي past tense of the imperfective aspect, the imperfect

استناد istinā́d *m. Arabic* 1 reference to something د کابل د خبر په استناد referring to the communication from Kabul 2 support د استناد نقطه *military* a strong point 3 *military* reinforcement, support

استنباط istinbā́t *m.* ☞ استنتاج It د دې څخه استنباط کیږي چه ... follows from this that ...

استنبول istamból *m.* Istanbul (city)

استنتاج istintā́dzh *m. Arabic* logical inference, logical conclusion; deduction استنتاج کول to draw an inference, draw a conclusion; deduce, conclude داسي استنتاج کیدی شي چه ... *Eastern* One may infer that ...

استنطاق istintā́ḳ *m. Arabic law* interrogation, investigation د چوک تر استنطاق لاندي نیول to interrogate someone

استنکار istinkā́r *m. Arabic* 1 disapprobation 2 aversion

استوا istivā́ *f. Arabic* 1 balancing, equilibration 2 parallelism *idiom* د استوا خط the equator

استوار ustuvā́r 1 *literal* strong, hard, firm 2 steady, firm, steadfast

استواري ustuvārí *f.* 1 *literal* hardness, firmness 2 steadiness, firmness, steadfastness

استوانه ustuvāná cylinder

استواني ¹ ustuvāní cylindrical استواني میل shaft

استواني ² ustuvāné *plural of* استوانه

استوایي istivāí equatorial; tropical استوایي افریقا Equatorial Africa استوایي اقلیم equatorial climate

استوزی astózaj *m.* ☞ استازی

استوژه astózha *f. Eastern* استوربنه astogə́na *f.* استوره astóga ☞ استوگنه

استوگن astogə́n living, residing, staying somewhere استوگن کېدل to settle, reside, stay somewhere په هوټل کېني استوگن کېدل to stay at a hotel

استوگندزای astogəndzáj *m.* 1 residence, abode 2 hostel, dormitory

استوگنه astógna *f.* astogə́na *f.* استوگه astóga *f.* استوگیه astógja *f. dialect* 1 residence, stay, sojourn د مبلمنو د استوگني ځای a guest room b residence استوگنه کول، استوگنه لرل to live, stay, sojourn استوگنه نیول to settle somewhere, reside somewhere, stay somewhere 2 life, existence 3 residence, abode

استوگجای astogjáj *m. dialect* resident

استول astavál [*past:* وایي ستاوه] to send, dispatch, direct احوال استول to dispatch information, send news, communicate سلام استول to send a greeting شیان استول to dispatch goods

استوني estoní 1 Estonian استوني ژبه the Estonian language 2 *m.* Estonian (person)

استونیا estonijā́ Estonia

استوني پته astone patá *f.* mailing address

استوني لړ astáwūne laṛ, astone láṛ *m.* mailing list

استوني ننکه astone náḳhka *f.* shipping label

استوونکی astavúnkaj 1 *present participle of* استول 2 *m.* sender

استهزا istihzā́ *f. Arabic* mockery

استهزا آمیزه istihzāāméz آمیزه istihzāāméza *attributive* mocking

استهلاک istihlā́k *m.* 1 liquidation (e.g., of a debt) 2 consumption 3 amortization استهلاک کول *compound verb* a to liquidate (e.g., a debt) b to consume c to amortize استهلاک کېدل a to be liquidated (e.g., a debt) b to be consumed c to be amortized

استهلاکي istihlākí *attributive* consumers' استهلاکي تعاون consumers' cooperative

استتیک estetík 1 *m.* aesthetics 2 aesthetic, artistic

استتیکي estetikí *attributive* aesthetic

استبدل astedál *intransitive* [*past:* واستېد] 1 to live, reside 2 to be, abide, stay, make a stop

استبدونکی astedúnkaj **1** *present participle of* استبدل **2** inhabitant, resident

استیذان istizắn *m. Arabic* authorization استیذان اخیستل to receive authorization

استیصال istisál *m. Arabic* **1** destruction, annihilation **2** demolition

استیلا istilá *f. Arabic* **1** conquest; capture استیلا کول *compound verb* to conquer, capture, seize استیلا کیدل to be conquered, be captured, be seized **2** supremacy **3** epidemic

استیلائي istilāí *attributive* epidemic

آستین āstín *m.* sleeve

استیناف istináf *m. Arabic law* appeal; reclaim د استیناف محکمه appeals court, appelate court

استرالیا astrāljá *f.* ☞ استرالیا استرالیا

استحکام *abbreviation from* اسح

اسحاق ishāḵ *m. Arabic proper name* Isaac, Yitzak

اسحاقزی ishāḵzí *m. plural* **1** the Iskhakzai (tribe) **2** *m.* ishāḵzáj Ikshakzai (tribesman)

اسحق ishāḵ *m.* ☞ اسحاق

اسد asád *m. Arabic* **1** lion **2** *astronomy* Leo (constellation) **3** Asad (the fifth month of the solar year; July-August)

اسدالله asadullá *m. Arabic proper name* Asadullah

اسر usr *m. Arabic* **1** captivity **2** *medicine* retention of urine

اسرا usará *m. Arabic plural from* اسیر

اسرار asrár Arabic plural from سر حربي اسرار military secret **2** اسرار israr *m. Arabic* keeping of a secret اسرار کول to keep a secret

اسراف isráf *m. Arabic* wastefulness, prodigality

اسرافیل asrāfíl *m. Arabic religion* **1** Asraphel (one of the four archangels) **2** seraph (angel of the highest rank)

اسرائیل isrāíl *m.* **1** Israel بني اسرائیل Israelis, Jews **2** Israeli (person)

اسرائیلی isrāílí **1** *attributive* Israeli **2** *m.* Israeli (person)

اسره asrá *f.* hope; dream اسره کول to hope; dream

اسرهت asrəhát *m. vice* استراحت

اسری asarí *indeclinable* enchanting; charming; attractive

آس زغل aszghál *m.* horseman

آس زغلونه aszghalabəna *f.* horse races

اسستنت asistánt *m.* assistant, aide

اسطوره asturá *f. m.* [*plural:* اساطیر] fable; myth

اسعار as'ár *m. Arabic plural* **1** *from* سعر **2** currency خارجه اسعار foreign currency **3** *finance* draft (payable abroad in foreign currency)

اسعاری as'ārí *attributive* currency اسعاری سیستم monetary system اسعاری معاملات currency operations

اسغل asghál *m.* horse thief

اسف asáf *m. Arabic* regret

اسفالت asfált *m. plural* asphalt

اسفالت کاری asfāltkāri *f.* paving with asphalt

اسفل اسافلین asfal-us-sāfilín *m. Arabic religion* nether world, nether regions

اسفناک واقعات asafnák regrettable, unfortunate, sad lamentable occurrences

اسقاط iskát *m. Arabic* miscarriage; premature birth; abortion اسقاط کول to miscarry; give birth prematurely; effect an abortion

اسقاط iskát *m. Arabic religion* **1** interment, burial **2** alms given at burial services

اسقف uskúf *m.* bishop لوی اسقف archbishop

اسک isk *m.* ☞ هسک

اسک ask *dialect* ☞ هسک

اسکات iskát *m. Arabic* **1** calming **2** pacification; calm

اسکادر eskádr *m. military* squadron, naval squadron

اسکادریل eskādríl *m. military* squadron, air squadron

اسکان iskán *m. Arabic* transition to a settled life; settling

اسکایي iskāí *history* **1** Sakian, Shakian (referring to an era beginning in 78 A.D. with the rule of Kanishka, one of the rulers of the Kushani governments called in India shaki) **2** *m. plural* the Shaki

اسکلیت iskelét *m.* skeleton

اسکلیت بندي iskeletbandí *f.* frame, framework د ودانی اسکلیت بندي framework of a building

اسکندر iskandár *m. proper name* Alexander, Iskander

اسکندریه iskandarijá Alexandria

اسکبرل askerál *transitive* [*past:* و یې اسکېره] to make sorry, make unhappy

اسکبرلی askerálaj pitiable, unhappy, wounded by fate

اسکبرنه askeróna *f.* misfortune, ill-fortune, disaster

اسکیمو eskimó *m.* Eskimo (person)

اسل ásəl just right, exactly right, well-fitting (e.g., of clothing) دا خولی زما پر سر اسله ده This (embroidered) skullcap is just for me. دا موزه اسله ده These shoes fit perfectly.

اسلاف aslāf *m. Arabic* سلف *plural* **1** *from* سلف **2** ancestors

اسلام islám *m. Arabic* **1** Islam, the Mohammedan religion, the Muslim world **2** religious orthodoxy, religiousness

اسلام آباد islāmābád *m.* Islamabad (city)

اسلام قلعه islāmka'lá *f.* Islamkala (border point)

اسلامي islāmi *Arabic* **1** Islamic, Mohammedan **2** orthodox اسلامي علوم theology (Muslim)

اسلامیت islāmiját *m.* Islam, Mohammedanism

اسلاو islắv *m.* Slav (person) د اسلاو ژبي the Slavic languages

اسلاوي islāví *m.* **1** Slavic **2** *m.* Slav (person)

اسلحه aslihá *f. Arabic* **1** *plural of* سلاح **2** weapon; armament پټه اسلحه personal weapon انفرادي اسلحه concealed weapon جارحه اسلحه automatic weapon اوتوماتیکي اسلحه bladed weapons ناریه اسلحه firearm (cold steel) د اسلحي په زور by force of arms

اسلحه جوړونکی aslihá dzhoṛavúnkaj **1** *attributive* manufacturing arms, arms اسلحه جوړونکي کارخانه arms factory; munition factory **2** gunsmith

اسلحه خانه aslihakhāná *f.* arsenal

اسلحه دار aslihadár *m. military* chief of supply (in the field)

اسلحه سازي aslihasāzí *f.* arms production, armaments

أسلم aslám *m. Arabic proper name* Aslam

اسلوب aslúb *m.* [*plural:* اساليب asālíb] *Arabic* **1** method, way د اسلوب تربيي methodology **2** style د كتاب اسلوب the style of a book

اسلول aslavә́l asә́lavә́l *denominative, transitive* [*past:* اسل يي كړ] to adjust to, fit to, adapt to *idiom* پر پښتنو وراسلول كوئي to teach someone a lesson, punish

اسلېټ islét *m.* **1** (school) slate **2** *plural* slate (roofing)

اسلېدل asledә́l asә́ledә́l *denominative, intransitive* [*past:* اسل شو] to be suitable, to suit, be just right

اسلېده asledә́ *m.* asә́ledә́ *plural* fitness, conformity

اسم ism *m. Arabic* [*plural:* اسمونه ismúna *Arabic plural:* اسما asmá *plural:* اسامي asāmí] **1** name, appellation **2** *grammar* د اشارې اسم، اسم اشاره *ísm-i* demonstrative pronoun د تصغير اسم، اسم تصغير *ísm-i* a diminutive د تفصيل اسم، اسم تفصيل *ísm-i* the comparative degree جمع اسم *ísm-i* collective noun, plural number جنس اسم، خاص اسم *ísm-i* tribal name, noun ذات اسم *ísm-i* proper name زمان اسم *ísm-i* adverb, temperal circumstances صفت اسم *ísm-i* adjective صوت اسم *ísm-i* onomatopoeic word عام اسم، اسم عام *ísm-i* common noun فاعل اسم *ísm-i* numeral عدد اسم *ísm-i* noun of action, agency مجموع اسم *ísm-i* collective noun, مذكر اسم، اسم مذكر *ísm-i* masculine noun مشتق اسم، مشتق اسم *ísm-i* productive noun the indeterminate mood, infinitive, masdar (type of verb معنی اسم *ísm-i* abstract noun مفعول اسم *ísm-i* passive participle, the object of an action مكان اسم *ísm-i* adverb, circumstances of place منسوب اسم، منسوب *ísm-i* relational adjective موصوف اسم، موصوف *ísm-i* definitive (i.e., adjective limiting the significance of noun) موصول اسم، موصول *ísm-i* relative pronoun مونث اسم، اسم مونث *ísm-i* feminine noun نکره اسم *ísm-i* common noun **3** invocation, incantation, exorcism پر چا باندي اسم ويل to pronounce an incantation over someone شب اسم *ísm-i military* password

اسما asmā́ *m. Arabic plural from* اسم

اسمار asmár *m.* Asmar (district, Nangrahar Province)

اسماعيل ismā'il *m. Arabic proper name* Ismail, Izmail

اسماعيل خيل ismā'ilkhél **1** *m. plural* Ismailkheili (a subdivision of the Chagarzi tribe) **2** *m.* Ismailkheil (tribesman)

اسماعيلزي ismā'ilzí **1** *m. plural* the Ismailzai (a subdivision of the Usmanzai Tribe and of the Orakzai Tribe) **2** ismā'ilzáj *m.* Ismailzai (tribesman)

اسماعيلي ismāílí *Arabic* **1** Ismailitic **2** *m.* Ismailian (person)

اسماعيليه ismā'ilijá *f. Arabic* Ismailism; the teachings of the Ismailians

آسمان āsmán *m.* اسمان asmán *m.* sky, heavens په بره آسمان كښي high in the sky آسمان وك ستوريو له a sky studded with stars; a

starry sky نن آسمان شين دئ The weather is clear today. پرون آسمان صاف و آسمان ته كتل، د آسمان Yesterday was a clear day. ستورو ته كتل a to look at the sky, look at the stars *figurative* b آسمان ته ختل *literal* to put on airs, take pride in, be puffed up to become elevated, rise up high *figurative* to become "stuck-up" آسمان مځکه ګڼل *literal* to think that the sky is the earth *figurative* to fail to understand something سر دي آسمان ته رسېږي او عقل دي تر پنبو لاندي كېږي *proverb literal* Though he grows to the sky, a fool is a fool *figurative* A fool's a fool for that! چه آسمان ته غونډي ولي، نو پخپله پري لګي *proverb* He who throws clods at the sky will himself be injured by them. چه آسمان ته توكي، نو پخپل مخ يي راپر بوځي *proverb* He who spits at the sky will soil himself thereby. د آسمان كټ *astronomy* Ursa Major (the constellation) د آسمان كټ دئ *saying* Nothing can be done without it's presence. چا ته د آسمان ستوري ښودل to punish someone cruelly په آسمان كښي ستوري شمېرل، د آسمان ستوري شمېرل a If you try to count the stars in the sky, you'll be agape. b to undertake an impossible task د اسمانه ښنوروا راكښته كول to be extremely tall, be lanky آسمان راچپه كېدل to have trouble afoot; have a dangerous situation arise آسمان پر چپه كېدل to fall into misfortune; be in danger آسمان نړېدل a to be beset by great misfortune b to have trouble fall like snow on one's head

اسمان ښک asmantsák very high

اسمان ښكالی asmāntskālaj *m.* skyscraper

اسمان ښكالكی asmāntskáləkaj *m.* bat, flying mouse

آسمان خراش āsmānkharásh high-altitude آسمان خراش عمارت high building; skyscraper

اسمان خوله asmānkhulá antiaircraft اسمان خوله توپ antiaircraft gun

اسمان ښكلوونکی asmān shkә́lavúnkaj very high

اسمان لار asmānlár *f.* اسمان لاره asmānlára *astronomy* the Milky Way

اسماني [1] asmāní **1** celestial; heavenly اسماني كاڼي meteorite **2** azure, light blue, sky blue **3** religious, spiritual, sacred **4** *figurative* foolish, absurd اسماني خبري كول a to speak nonsense b to boast; fabricate; invent; lie c to joke, jest *idiom* اسماني كول to go far away; be missing, to اسماني كېدل to leave جانانه، ولاړي، اسماني شوې *folklore* Dear one, thou hast gone away; thou art missing.

اسماني [2] asmānә́j **1** *feminine singular and plural from* اسماني [1] *f. plural* foolish nonsense اسماني كول، اسماني ويل to talk foolish nonsense

آسماني رنگ asmāniráng azure, sky blue اسماني رنگي سترگي sky-blue eyes

اسمايي غر asmāí Mount Asmai (in Kabul)

اسماعيل isma'íl ☞ اسمعيل

اسمي ismaí *Arabic indeclinable grammar* nominal, substantive

اسناد [1] isnád *m. Arabic* **1** reference to someone **2** substantiation **3** *grammar* subtatic relationship

اسناد² asnād *m. Arabic plural from* سند د اسناد پور loan-bonds کنبل شوي نومه اسناد bonds payable to bearer literary بي نومه اسناد monuments

اسنسیون asunsjón *m.* Asuncion (city)

اسو asú *m. regional* Asu (the sixth month of the Hindu calendar; September - October)

آس والا āsvālā *m.* horseman

آسوان asuān *m.* Aswan د آسوان بند the Aswan Dam

اسود asvád *Arabic* black

آسودگي āsudagí *f.* ☞ آسوده گي

آسوده āsudá *indeclinable* 1 quiet, peaceful 2 satisfactory, happy 3 content; satisfied

آسوده حال āsudahā́l 1 successful, prosperous 2 content

آسوده حالي āsudahāli *f.* contentment; satisfaction

آسوده گي āsudagí *f.* 1 rest, peace, calm 2 prosperity, well-being 3 material success 4 comfort

اسوري usurí *f.* د اسوري دریاب the Ussuri River

اسوگلاس isoglā́s *m. linguistics* isogloss

اسوېلجن asveldzhán grieving over, mourning over

اسوېلکی asvelkáj *m.* ☞ اسوپلي

اسوېلن asvelán mourning over, grieving over

اسوپلی asveláj *m.* 1 yawn 2 deep breath, sigh سوړ اسوپلی a heavy sigh; deep breath سوړ اسوپلی کول to sigh heavily; breath deeply 3 shivering (from cold) اسوپلی کول a breath; sigh b shiver (from cold)

اسهال ishā́l *m. Arabic* diarrhea

اسهام ashā́m *m. Arabic plural from* سهم¹ د اسهامو خاوندان shareholder, stockholder

اسهامي ashāmí *Arabic attributive* joint stock; share اسهامي شرکت joint-stock company

اسي¹ así *Eastern* áse ☞ هسي

اسي² así 1.1 stingy, niggardly, avaricious اسي کېدل to be stingy, to stint 1.2 unfortunate, luckless 2 *m.* .1 miser 2.2 luckless wretch

اسی³ asáj *m.* 1 hoarfrost 2 *dialect* fog, mist

اسی⁴ asə́j *feminine singular from* اسي²

آسیا¹ āsjá *f.* asijā́ 1 ☞ ژرنده¹ 2 used in geographic designations چهار آسیا Charasiya (settlement)

آسیا² asijā́ *f.* Asia جنوب شرقي آسیا Southeast Asia وسطي آسیا Central Asia کوچنی آسیا، وړه آسیا Asia Minor (peninsula)

آسیاب āsijā́b *m.* mill

آسیابي āsijābí *f. history* collection (of tax-in-kind) from mills

آسیانه āsijaná *f.* whetstone

آسیاوان āsjāvā́n *m.* āsijāvā́n miller

آسیائي āsijāí *attributive* Asiatic

آسیب āséb *m.* misfortune, trouble, disaster

اسي توب asitób *m.* stinginess, avarice

اسید asíd *m.* acid پروسیک اسید prussic acid

اسیر asír *m. Arabic [plural:* اسیران asirā́n *Arabic plural:* اسرا usarā́] اسیر کول، اسیر نیول prisoners of war د جگړي اسیران to take captive اسیر کېدل to surrender

اسیري asirí *f.* captivity

اسیستانت asistā́nt *m.* assistant

اسسر asasár *m. regional* member of a jury

اسیموت asimút *m.* azimuth

اسېمه asemá *f.* hunting mare

آش¹ āsh *m.* 1 dumpling 2 food; meal, soup 3 kasha هغه آش ، هغه کاسه *saying* Same old soup warmed over. 4 tannin extract پوست ته آش ورکول *compound verb* to tan آش کول to tan leather

اش² ash *m. children's speech* ass, donkey

اشا ashā́ *f.* 1 misfortune, trouble, disaster 2 danger

اشارات ishārā́t *m. Arabic plural from* اشاره

اشارت ishārát *m. Arabic* ☞ اشاره

اشارتاً ishārátán *Arabic* by means of a hint

اشارتي ishāratí *attributive* signal اشارتي کارتوس signal cartridge

اشاره ishārá *f. Arabic [plural:* اشاري ishāré *Arabic plural:* اشارات ishārā́t] 1 sign, symbol, mark دبپلتون اشاره ددا dash د punctuation marks عجامیه اشارات exclamation point اشاره 2 signal, sign د در بدو اشاره یې the Morse alphabet مورس اشارات وکړه He made a sign indicating that one should halt. 3 *grammar* demonstrative pronoun د اشاري ضمیر demonstrative pronoun 4 *military* signal, bugle call حربي اشاره military signal (prearranged short order) د هجوم اشاره the signal for attack وخه ته صبح اشاره reveille 5 sign, token, mark 6 indication په چا پوري اشارات کول to point to something 7 hint اشاره کول to drop a hint to someone

اشاره چي isharāchí *m.* signalman

اشاره یي ishāraí 1 *attributive* signal 2 *grammar* demonstrative

اشارتوب ashartób *m.* اشارتیا ashartjā́ *f.* اشاروالی ashāṛvā́laj *m.* 1 bitter taste 2 *figurative* cruelty د . . . . سره اشارتوب کول to act cruelly, treat someone cruelly

اشاړي¹ ashāṛáj *m.* dried fruit with a bitter pit

اشاړي² ashāṛí *f.* bitter taste

اشاعت isha'át *m. Arabic [plural:* اشاعات ishā'ā́t *f. singular:* اشاعه ishā'á *plural:* اشاعي ishā'é *m. Arabic plural:* اشاعات ishā'át] 1 publication; edition د اشاعاتو اداره *regional* publishing house 2 dissemination (e.g., of learning, points of view)

اشباح ashbā́h *m. plural Arabic from* شبح

اشباع ishbā' *f. Arabic* 1 satiation 2 saturation 3 satisfaction (i.e., of requirements)

آشپاز āshpáz *m.* اشپز ashpáz *m.* cook

آشپزخانه āshpazkhāná *f.* kitchen

آشپزي āshpazí *f.* cookery, cuisine

اشپیر ashpír *m.* 1 conversation *f.* 2 noise, din, hubub

اشتباه ishtibā́h *f. Arabic* 1 doubt; suspicion; skeptical attitude

د اشتباه په there is no doubt that ... په دې كښې هيڅ اشتباه نشته چه ... to have doubts about someone, regard someone سترگو ورته كتل with suspicion 2 mistake, blunder اشتباه كول a to doubt b to err, blunder اشتباه مي نه ده كړي 2 I have not erred.

اشتباهي ishtibāhí 1 suspicious; dubious 2 erroneous

اشتراط ishtirā́t m. *Arabic* provisional state; agreement

اشتراك ishtirā́k m. *Arabic* 1 participation 2 subscription (to a newspaper, etc.) اشتراك كول a to take part, participate b to subscribe (to a newspaper) د مجلي اشتراك to subscribe to a newspaper 3 *military* cooperation, teamwork

اشتراكات ishtirākā́t m. *Arabic plural* 1 *from* اشتراك 2 general outlines, the big picture سره اشتراك لرل to have in common

اشتراك كوونكى ishtirāk kavúnkaj m. 1 participant 2 subscriber

اشتراكي [1] ishtirākí *Arabic obsolete* 1.1 socialist 1.2 collective, common, general 2 m. Socialist

اشتراكي [2] ishtirākí f. اشتراكيت ishtirākiját m. *obsolete* socialism; communism د لومړى اشتراكى دوره the epoch of primitive communism

اشترانی ashtarāní m. *plural* 1 the Ashtarani (tribe) 2 ashtarānáj m. Ashtaranaj (tribesman)

اشتعال ishti'ál m. *Arabic* 1 ignition 2 provocation (deliberate instigation of an incident)

اشتغ ashtágh m. dried apricot (without the pit)

اشتغال ishtighā́l m. *Arabic* occupation, taking, capture, seizure اشتغال كول *compound verb* a to seize, capture, occupy b to hold, fill (e.g., a post, position)

اشتقاق ishtiḳā́ḳ m. *Arabic* derivation (of words) د الفاظو اشتقاق word derivation اشتقاقات derivative words

اشتوكه ashtóka f. peace, conciliation

اشتها ishtihā́ f. *Arabic* 1 desire 2 appetite د چا اشتها راوستل to arouse an appetite in someone اشتها مي بنده ده I've lost my appetite.

اشتهار ishtihā́r m. *Arabic* 1 proclamation, announcement; publication اشتهار كول to proclaim, announce; publish; make a public announcement of 2 proclamation, declaration 3 poster

اشتهاري ishtihārí *Arabic regional law* مجرم اشتهاري criminal seeking to avoid punishment

آشتي āshtí f. conciliation

اشتياق ishtijā́ḳ m. *Arabic* 1 strong desire, yearning اشتياق كول to desire passionately 2 passionate desire

آشتي جو āshtidzhú m. ☞ آشتي طلب

آشتي جويي āshtidzhuí f. ☞ آشتي طلبي

آشتي طلب āshtitalā́b m. conciliator

آشتي طلبي āshtitalabí f. spirit of conciliation

اشتام ishṭā́m m. *regional* paper bearing an official seal

اشخار ashkā́r m. potash *idiom* نبستي په اشخار ډبرول to split hairs, quibble

اشخاص ashkhā́s m. *Arabic plural from* شخص

اشخوركه ashkhoráka f. child's bib

اشر [1] ashár m. help, assistance ☞ حشر

اشر [2] ashár *Arabic* 1 unpleasant, disagreeable 2 indecent, unseemly

اشرار ashrā́r m. *Arabic plural from* شرير

اشراف ashrā́f m. *Arabic plural* [*plural:* اشرافان ashrāfā́n] aristocrats, aristocracy, elite, nobility

اشربه ashribá m. *Arabic plural from* شراب

اشرپي ashrapí f. *Western* اشرپۍ ashrapə́j f. *Eastern* 1 gold, gold coin piece 2 *proper name* Ashrafi

اشرف ashráf *Arabic* 1 most noble, most radiant 2 m. .1 prince 2.2 *proper name* Ashraf

اشرفي [1] ashrafí f. ☞ اشرپي

اشرفۍ [2] ashrafə́j f. 1 Ashrafi 2 *botany* marigold

اشري asharí 1 immoral, dissolute; wicked 2 obstinate; wrong-headed

اشعار [1] ash'ár m. *Arabic plural from* سعر [1]

اشعار [2] ish'ár m. *Arabic* information, notification

اشعه ash'á m. *Arabic plural from* شعاع

اشغال ishghā́l m. *Arabic* 1 occupancy 2 entry into (a position) د ماموريت اشغال occupying a position 3 seizure, capture, occupation

اشغالول [1] ishghalabə́l *denominative, transitive* [*past:* اشغال يي كړ] 1 to be the occupant (e.g., of a job) 2 to seize, capture, occupy

اشغالي ishghalí *attributive* occupation

اشغالبدل [1] ishghāladə́l *denominative, intransitive* [*past:* اشغال شو] 1 to be filled, be occupied (i.e., a job) 2 to be captured, be occupied

آشفتگي āshuftagí f. 1 confusion, concern, alarm, worry; disorder 2 calamity, misfortune

آشفته āshuftá *indeclinable* worried; downcast

آشفته حال āshuftahā́l 1 worried; downcast 2 impoverished

اشقار ashḳār m. potash, caustic soda

آشك [1] āshák m. meatballs made of meat and flour

اشک [2] ashk m. *poetic* tears

اشكال [1] ishkā́l m. *Arabic* difficulty, trouble; impediment بې له څه without special difficulties اشكالات پېښول to hamper, create difficulty; impede خپل اشكال حل كول to eliminate an obstacle; get out of a difficult situation

اشكال [2] ashkā́l m. *Arabic plural from* شكل

اشكشم ishkashím m. Ishkashim (settlement, district)

اشكمش ishkamísh m. Ishkamish (settlement, district)

اشكي ashkí *interjection* well done, bravo

آشنا āshnā́ اشنا اشنا āshnā́ 1 m. .1 close friend, chum, buddy له چا سره آشنا څخه په سختي كېدل to make friends with someone كښې لاس مه اخله Do not forget a friend in misfortune. 1.2 acquaintance 1.3 beloved one 2.1 acquainted with something 2.2 knowledgeable about something د آشنا حقيقت سره آشنا شو He got to know the truth.

آشنا āshnā́j m. ☞ اشناى

اشنايه ashnāja 1 *f.* .1 female friend 1.2 female acquaintance 1.3 beloved (female) 2 *feminine singular of* اشنا 2 اشنايه پيغله young woman acquaintance

آشنائي āshnāī اشنائي *f.* ashnāī .1 friendship; acquaintance نژدي د چا سره آشنائي کول، د close friendship; close acquaintance آشنائي چا سره آشنائي لرل to befriend, carry on a friendship, be close to someone زما ورسره ډيره آشنائي ده I am on very close terms with him. ده دغه سره آشنائي ښه نه ده It is not worth being his friend.

اشنغر ashnaghár *m.* Ashnagar, Khashtnagar (district near Peshawar)

اوشنل ushnə́l *transitive* ☞ اوشنل

اشوا ashvá disgraced اشوا کول to disgrace اشوا کېدل to be disgraced

آشوب āshúb *m.* 1 noise 2 confusion, anxiety, alarm, worry 3 calamity, misfortune

آشوب کن āshubkún *m.* alarmist; person given to panic

اشوره ashurá *f.* ☞ عاشوره

آشول āshól *m.* noise, hubub, cry آشول کول to make a noise, make a hubub, make a din, cry out

اشه [1] ásha *interjection* get going (cry used by one who is driving an ass)

آشه [2] āshá *f. proper name* Aisha آشه ښه ده که گله؟ مه يوه ويني، مه بله *saying* They make a good pair!

اشهاد [1] ishhád *m. Arabic law* 1 summoning as a witness 2 establishment of a fact with the assistance of witnesses

اشهاد [2] ashhád *m. Arabic plural from* شاهد

اشجا ashjá *m. Arabic plural from* اشيا [1] معدني شي minerals

اشيا eshjá *f.* Asia

آشيانه āshjāná *f.* 1 nest 2 cell 3 dot, point 4 hangar د طيارو آشيانه hangar

اڼ akh *m.* 1 consideration; scrutiny 2 patience

اڼکه ukhka *f.* tear اڼکي تويول to shed tears

اڼکي [1] ukhki *plural from* اڼکه

اڼکۍ [2] ukhkə́j *f.* praying mantis (insect)

اينبودل ikhodə́l *transitive* ☞ اينبودل

اصابت isābát *m. Arabic* 1 hit (on a target) په هدف اصابت کول to hit the target 2 accuracy (e.g., of a comparison); preciseness (of an expression) 3 perspicacity

اصالت asālát *m. Arabic* 1 nobility, decency 2 firmness of character 3 personal responsiblity 4 personal representation 5 substance, essence

اصالتاً asālátán *Arabic* 1 from oneself personally, personally 2 fully 3 as a matter of fact, in point of fact

اصالت وجودي asālatvudzhudí *f. philosophy* existentialism

اصحاب ashā́b *m. Arabic plural from* صاحب [*plural:* اصحابان ashābān] associates of Mohammed

اصدار isdár *m. Arabic* export د وريو اصدار the export of wool

اصرار isrár *m. Arabic* insistence, persistence, persistent demand; determination, pertinacity د ډېر او مکرر اصرار په واسطه thanks to

to په پرلو شي باندي اصرار کول repeated and determined demands insist upon something

اصراف [1] asrā́f *m. Arabic plural from* صرف

اصراف [2] isráf *m. Arabic* extravagance

اصطبل istábl stable, horse-barn

اصطکاک istikák *m. Arabic* friction اصطکاک کول to rub against

اصطکاکي istikākí *physics* static اصطکاکي برق static electricity

اصطلاح istilā́ *f. & m.* istilāh *Arabic* 1 phrase, expression, locution, idiom په بله اصطلاح in other words 2 term تخنيکي اصطلاحات technical terms

اصطلاحاً istilāhán *Arabic* 1 idiomatically 2 technically 3 as it is officially designated, as they say, as one says

اصطلاحي istilāhí *Arabic* 1 phraseological 2 idiomatic اصطلاحي خبره an idiom 3 special, technical (esp. of a term)

اصغر asghár *Arabic* junior; lesser, little

اصغري asgharí minimal

آصف āsáf *m. Arabic* 1 *proper name* Asaph 2 *figurative* wise counselor

اصفهان isfahán *m.* Isfahan (city)

اصل asl *Arabic* 1 *m.* [*plural:* اصلونه aslúna *Arabic plural:* اصول usúl] .1 basis, base, root د مصدر اصل the stem of a verb 1.2 article (of a law); statute 1.3 fact; substance; principle په اصل in essence, in substance; in actuality; factuality 1.4 کښي origin; race; family (extended) په اصل a by origin; by family b originally 1.5 original 1.6 *economics* fixed capital 1.7 classifier used in counting trees, saplings سل اصله نهالگي saplings 2 *attributive* .1 real, veritable اصل حقيقت ويل to speak the solemn truth اصله خبره داده چه... the main point is that ... 2.2 proper اصل تول proper weight په اصل ميان کښي in the very center 2.3 suitable dimensions, proper dimensions 2.4 *economics* fixed (of capital) *idiom* توره په اصل غوڅول کوي *proverb* A good saber cuts according to its blade.

اصلاً áslán *Arabic* 1 in fact; all intents and purposes; in essence 2 by origin, descent, family

اصلاح islā islāh *f. & m. Arabic m.* [*plural:* اصلاحات islahát] 1 correction; emendation; amendment 2 improvement د حيواني نسل اصلاح improvement of a breed of cattle 3 reform د تشکيل اصلاح reorganization اصلاح کول *compound verb* a to correct; amend b to improve; mend, repair c to carry out a reform d to carry out land-reclaimation work اصلاح کېدل *compound verb* a to be correctd b to be improved; be mended c to be reformed

اصلاح طلب islāhtaláb *m. Arabic* reformer

اصلاح طلبانه islāhtalabānā 1 reform; reformative; reformatory 2 in a reform manner, in a reformative manner

اصلاحي islāhí reform, reformative, reformatory

اصل بست aslbást *m. military* personnel د اصل بست جز وتام personnel unit

اسلول aslavə́l *transitive* ☞ اصلول

اصله [1] ásla *feminine singular of* اصل [2]

34

اصله ásla ☞ اصل ²

اصلي aslí *Arabic* 1 real, veritable, true 2 natural; innate اصلي ورېښم natural silk 3 practicable; effective 4 inborn 5 native اصلي ژبه native language 6 basic, fundamental 7 chief, main اصلي قوتونه *military* main forces 8 literal; authentic نقل اصلي يې څه شو؟ Where is the original? 9 اصلي own (one's) اصلي اوبه territorial waters 10 original په اصلي صورت in the original form

اصلي بڼه aslí báṇa *f.* لومړنۍبڼه lūmṛanájbáṇa prototype

اصلیت asliját *m. Arabic* nature, property, essence, being

اصلي حافظه aslí hāfizá *f.* virtual memmory

اسلبدل asledál *intransitive* ☞ اسلبدل

اصناف asnáf *m. Arabic plural from* صنف

اصوات asvát *m. Arabic plural from* صوت اصوات د تحسين shouts of approval د افسوس اصوات exclamations of regret د نفرین اصوات curses

اصول usúl *m. Arabic plural from* اصل [*plural:* اصولات usulúna *Arabic plural:* اصولونه usulát] 1 principles, bases اساسي اصول basic laws; constitution کلیه اصول basic propositions 2 system; method په دې اصول سره different ways, methods دول دول اصولونه according to such a principle د برلیس اصول the Berlitz Method په پخواني اصول سره after the index cardfile system کارت اصول old way, after the former fashion 3 order, system بندیگری د the slave-owning system اصول

اصولاً usúlán *Arabic* 1 basically, for the most part 2 according to statute; according to law; according to the legal code

اصولات usulát *m. second plural of* اصول

اصولنامه usulnamá *f.* 1 statute; legislation 2 regulations داخلي اصولنامه regulations

اصولي usulí *Arabic* 1 basic, of principle, pertaining to principle 2 systematic, methodical 3 based on a constitution, based on legislation; constitutional, legal اصولي رخصتي leave of absence stipulated by law 4 correct, legal

اصیل asíl *Arabic* 1.1 noble, of high birth 1.2 thoroughbred; purebred اصیل حیوانات purebred cattle 1.3 real, genuine, natural 1.4 fundamental 1.5 firm 2 *m. proper name* Asil

اصیلتوب asiltób *m.* noble origin, noble birth

اصیل زاده asilzādá noble, highborn, of noble origin

اضافت izāfát *m. Arabic* 1 addition, augmentation 2 *grammar* the expression of the genitive relationship by the use of the construct or izafet form of two nouns د اضافت علامت the izafet sign

اضافگي izāfagí *f.* ☞ اضافه گي

اضافه izāfá *Arabic* 1.1 addition, augmentation, accretion د هغه besides that په هغه اضافه over and above that اضافه څخه اضافه to increase pay تنخواه اضافه کول to add, increase کول 1.2 development 2 *attributive* 1. exceeding 2.2 *economics* surplus اضافه تولید surplus product

اضافه توب isāfatób *m.* اضافه والی izāfaválaj *m.* اضافه گي izāfagí *m.* 1 addition, augmentation 2 development د کرهني اضافه توب the development of agriculture اضافه توب کول to increase, grow

اضافي izāfí *Arabic* 1 additional, supplemental اضافي ارزش *economics* surplus value اضافي تولید *economics* surplus product 2 *grammar* pertaining to "izafet" د اسم اضافي حالت the "izafet" state, construct state اضافي مرکب genitive case

اضحلال izhilál *m. Arabic* dissolution, liquidation د شرکت اضحلال liquidation of a state stock company

اضحی az-hā *f. Arabic* sacrifice عید اضحی íd-i the Feast of Sacrificial Offering اضحی کول to offer a sacrifice, make a sacrificial offering

اضحیه iz-hijá *f. Arabic* sacrificial offering اضحیه کول to offer a sacrifice, make a sacrificial offering

اضداد azdád *m. Arabic plural from* ضد ¹

اضداد izdád *m. Arabic* 1 opposition 2 *philosophy* antithesis اضدادو مبارزه conflict of opposites 3 contradiction داخلي اضداد internal contradiction

اضرار azrár *m. Arabic plural from* ضرر ¹

اضرار izrár *m. Arabic* harmful influence ²

اضطراب iztiráb *m. Arabic* 1 agitation; concern, alarm پېنبنول to agitate; cause concern, cause alarm 2 oscillation برقي اضطرابات electrical oscillation; oscillations of an electrical current

اضطرابي iztirābí *Arabic* concerned, anxious اضطرابي حالت اعلان شو a the alarm was sounded b a state of emergency was declared

اضطرار iztirár *m. Arabic* 1 extreme necessity 2 hopeless situation, desperate situation; desperation, despair

اضطراري iztirārí 1 unusual, extreme, extraordinary اضطراري غونډه extraordinary session 2 په اضطراري حالاتو کښې in extreme cases forced

اضلاع azlá *m. Arabic plural from* ضلع

اضیاف azjáf *m. Arabic plural from* ضیف

اطاعت itā'át *m. Arabic* 1 obedience, submission, subservience د پتو سترگو اطاعت بلا قید او شرط unquestioning obedience blind obedience د چا اطاعت کول to obey, submit to someone 2 respect, esteem 3 *military* subordination

اطاق uták *m.* 1 room د تجربو او تجزیو اطاق experimental laboratory 2 chamber د تجارت اطاق Chamber of Commerce

اطام atám *m.* food, meal اول اطام بیا کلام *proverb* Eat first – talk later. ☞ طعام

اطبا atibbá *m.* اطبه atibbá *Arabic plural from* طبیب

اطراح ittirá *f. & m.* ittirāh *Arabic* 1 *physiology* excretion 2 waste matter, offal, garbage

اطراحي ittirāhí اطراحي مواد، اطراحیه مواد *physiology* excretion

اطراد itrád *m. Arabic* banishment اطراد کول to banish

اطراف atráf *m. Arabic plural from* طرف

اطرافي atrāfí **1** outlying, peripheral اطرافي سیمي outskirts; periphery **2** *m.* [*plural:* اطرافیان atrāfiján] circle of associates, cronies; colleagues, close associates

اطراق utrāk̲ *m.* ☞ اتراغ

اطریش otrísh *m. obsolete* Austria

اطفا itfā́ *m. Arabic* extinguishing of a fire

اطفال atfā́l *m. Arabic plural from* طفل

اطفائي itfāí *Arabic attributive* fire اطفائیه عمله firemen; fire company اطفائي موټر fire engine

اطلاع ittilā́ *f. Arabic m.* [*plural:* اطلاعات ittilā'ā́t] **1** information د اطلاعاتو وزارت Ministry of Information د اطلاعاتو شعبه Information Bureau اطلاع لاس ته راورل to obtain information **2** communiqué, news وروستنی اطلاع ... د رنګون the latest news د رنګون ... اطلاع ده چه There is a dispatch from Rangoon to the effect that ... **3** knowledge, state of being conversant with اطلاع یې کمه وه He was very poorly informed. **4** notification, notice اطلاع کول *compound verb* to communicate, notify, inform اطلاع ورکول to notify, inform

اطلاعاً ittilā́'an *Arabic* as a matter of information درته وکئ می عرض اطلاعاً I have the honor to inform you.

اطلاعاتي ittilā'ātí *attributive* information اطلاعاتي آژانس Information Agency

اطلاع دهي itlā'dihí *f.* informing, making cognizant

اطلاعیه ittilā'ijá **1** notification, information **2** communiqué

اطلاق itlā́k̲ **1** reference (to something) **2** giving a name; designation **3** granting of a divorce (to a woman) اطلاق کول *compound verb* ☞ اطلاقول

اطلاقول itlākavál *denominative, transitive* [*past:* اطلاق یې کړ] **1** to relate to something, refer to something **2** to name, designate **3** to grant a divorce (to a woman)

اطلس [1] atlás *m.* د اطلس اوقیانوس the Atlantic Ocean *manshúr-i history* د اطلس منشور the Atlantic Charter اطلس غرونه the Atlas Mountain

اطلس [2] atlás *m. Arabic* satin

اطلسي atlasí *Arabic* **1** satin, made of satin **2** *m.* black eunuch

اطمینان itminā́n *m. Arabic* **1** confidence, reliability د اطمینان ور favorable, satisfactory **2** verification; confirmation اطمینان کول **a** to believe in something, be certain of something **b** to verify, confirm دیو شي څخه و چا ته اطمینان ورکول to assure someone of something **3** receipt (i.e., of a letter) د اطمینان جواب ورکول peace, calming, tranquility د زړه اطمینان spiritual peace

اطمینان بخش itminānbákhsh اطمینان ببنونکی itminān bak̲húnkaj

اطمیناني itminā́ní **1** satisfactory; favorable **2** calming **3** reliable; reassuring

اطوار atvā́r *m. Arabic plural from* طور [1]

اظلال azlā́l *m. Arabic plural from* ظل

اظهار izhā́r *m. Arabic* **1** statement, utterance, speech اظهار نظر *iz-hār-i* expression of one's opinion, views, point of view **2** evidence, testimony زباني اظهار oral testimony, deposition اظهارول *compound verb* ☞ کول

اظهارنامه izhārnāmá *f.* **1** statement **2** notification

اظهارول izhāravál *denominative, transitive* [*past:* اظهار یې کړ] **1** to state; say; express (opinion, etc.) **2** to testify, give evidence

اظهاریدل izhāredál *denominative, intransitive* [*past:* اظهار شو] to be stated, be said, be expressed

اظهر uzhúr *m. Arabic plural from* ظهر [2]

اعاجیب a'ādzhíb *m. Arabic plural from* اعجوبه

اعاده i'ādá *f. Arabic* **1** return; restitution **2** restoration **3** renewal; resumption **4** repayment (e.g., of a debt) اعاده کول *compound verb* **a** to return **b** to restore **c** to renew **d** to repay, discharge (e.g., a debt)

اعاشه i'āshá *f. Arabic* **1** provisions; victuals حیواني اعاشه forage, provender د اعاشي ضابط food supply chief **2** nourishment, subsistance

اعانتاً j'ānatán *Arabic* in the form of a donation

اعانه i'āná *f. Arabic* **1** donation د اعاني او مرستي مجلس charity evening affair **2** payment, dues د حزب اعانه party dues

اعتبار i'tibā́r *m. Arabic* **1** faith, confidence پرچا اعتبار کول، پرچا اعتبار دي نشته to trust, have confidence in someone اعتبار دي لرل One cannot depend on you. سپک سړی دئ، اعتبار یې نشته He is a frivolous man, and does not enjoy people's confidence. خلقو ور It was believed that he was very rich. باندي د ډېر د ولت اعتبار کاوه **2** *economics* credit تجارتي اعتبار بانکي اعتبار bank credit commercial credit **3** importance, weight; authority; reputation **4** *law* effect, implementation, force (of a law) د اعتبار ور effective, operative د اعتبار موده period of validity (of a treaty) **5** authorization; authority **6** basis, grounds پـه دي اعتبار چـه... on the grounds that ... پـه اعتبار د ... . in view of the fact that ... **7** certificate of immunity, safe-conduct; guarantee

اعتبارلیک i'tibārlík *m.* اعتبارنامه i'tibārnāmá *f.* **1** mandate, warrant, certificate **2** *diplomacy* credentials **3** *finance* letter-of-credit

اعتبارول i'tibāravál *denominative, transitive* [*past:* اعتبار یې کړ] to give credit

اعتباري i'tibārí **1** enjoying confidence, reliable **2** *attributive* credit اعتباري معاملات credit operations **3** conditional, tentative; nominal

اعتدال i'tidā́l *m. Arabic* **1** justice **2** moderation (e.g., in viewpoints) **3** steadiness, even-tempered *idiom* د شپو او روځو اعتدال equinox

اعتدال پسند i'tidālpasánd **1** just, fair **2** moderate (e.g., of viewpoints) **3** counterbalanced, countervailing

اعتدال پسندي i'tidālpasandí *f.* **1** justice **2** moderation (e.g., in viewpoints) **3** steadiness, even-temperedness

اعتدالي i'tidālí **1** ☞ اعتدال پسند **2** *m.* [*plural:* اعتدالیون i'tidālijún] اعتدالي *Arabic* moderate, person of moderate views

اعتذار i'tizā́r *m. Arabic* apology, excuse

اعتراض i'tirā́z *m. Arabic* [plural: اعتراضونه i'tirāzúna *Arabic plural:* اعتراضات i'tirāzā́t] **1** objection, reclaim **2** protest **3** remonstrance دا اعتراض خو دي ټهيک دئ *dialect* Your remonstrance is a just one. اعتراض کول **a** to object **b** to protest **c** to remonstrate **4** attack, hostile action **5** *finance* protest of a bill

اعتراضنامه i'tirāznāmá *f.* written protest

اعتراض والا i'tirāzvālā́ **1** *m.* critic **2** *attributive* objecting

اعتراف i'tirā́f *m. Arabic* **1** acknowledgement **2** confession په يو شي کښي اعتراف کول، پر يو شي اعتراف کول **a** to confess to something **b** to confess one's sins, unburden oneself

اعتصاب i'tisā́b *m. Arabic* [plural: اعتصابونه i'tisābúna *Arabic plural:* اعتصابات i'tisābā́t] strike, work stoppage عمومي اعتصاب general strike معکوس اعتصاب lockout اعتصاب کول to strike, carry out a work stoppage

اعتصاب شکن i'tisābshikán *f.* strikebreaker, scab

اعتصاب کوونکی i'tisāb kavúnkaj striker

اعتصابي i'tisābí **1.1** *attributive* strike **1.2** *attributive* walkout **1.3** pertaining to a work stoppage **2** *m.* striking worker, striker

اعتصام i'tisā́m *m. Arabic* **1** steadfastness **2** self-preservation

اعتقاد i'tiḱā́d *m. Arabic* faith, confidence اعتقاد لرل to believe in, trust زه پر تا اعتقاد نه لرم، زه پر تا باندي اعتقاد نه لرم I don't trust you. I don't believe you.

اعتلا i'tilā́ *f. Arabic* development

اعتماد i'timā́d *m. Arabic* **1** trust, confidence اعتماد متقابل *i'timā́d-i* mutual trust پرچا بشپړ اعتماد لرل to have full confidence in someone د اعتماد وړ deserving of confidence, reliable **2** reliance, confidence, certitude دوی پر خپل ځان او نفس اعتماد او باور نه لري They are not self-confident. **3** expectation, hope, reliance پرچا اعتماد کول **a** to express confidence in someone **b** to have strong expectations, have confidence (in, of, for someone)

اعتماد بالنفس i'timādbinnáfs *m.* اعتماد بنفس i'timādbanafás self-confidence, self-reliance

اعتمادنامه i'timādnāmá *f. diplomacy* credentials اعتمادنامه وړاندي کول to present credentials

اعتمادي i'timādí reliable, trustworthy, dependable

اعتنا i'tinā́ *f. Arabic* attention, concern, anxiety د اعتنا په نظر کتل to be considerate of someone و چا ته اعتنا کول to pay attention to someone; be concerned about someone دوی دي خبري ته ډېره اعتنا لري They are paying a great deal of attention to this.

اعتیاد i'tijā́d *m. Arabic* [plural: اعتیادات i'tijādā́t] habit, wont

اعجاب¹ a'dzhā́b *m. Arabic plural from* عجب

اعجاب² i'dzhā́b *m. Arabic* **1** astonishment **2** pleasure **3** complacency, self-satisfaction

اعجاز i'dzhā́z *m. Arabic* miracle, wonder

اعجازي i'dzhāzí wonderful, miraculous

اعجامیه i'dzhāmijá *Arabic* علامات اعجامیه punctuation marks

اعجوبه a'dzhubá *f. Arabic* miracle, wonder, phenomenon

اعدا a'dā́ *m. Arabic plural from* عدو

اعداد¹ a'dā́d *m. Arabic plural from* عدد

اعداد² i'dā́d *m.* preparation

اعدادي i'dādí **1** preparatory **2** middle, secondary (of a school)

اعدادیه i'dadija *Arabic* **1** *feminine singular from* اعدادي **2** *f.* middle, secondary school, gymnasium (i.e., high school) د اعدادیي مکتب secondary school

اعدام i'dā́m *m. Arabic* execution, capital punishment په اعدام سره to condemn to death پرچا د اعدام حکم کول sentenced to death محکوم death, sentence someone to death اعدام کول *compound verb* ☞ اعدامېدل *compound verb* ☞ اعدام کېدل، اعدامول

اعدامول i'dāmavə́l *denominative, transitive* [past: اعدام يي کړ] to sentence to death, condemn to death

اعدامېدل i'dāmavə́l *denominative, intransitive* [past: اعدام شو] to be sentenced to death, be condemned to death

اعراب a'rā́b *m. Arabic plural from* عرب

اعرابیان a'rābijā́n *m. second plural from* اعراب

اعراض a'rā́z *m. Arabic plural of* عرض³

اعراف i'rā́f *m. Arabic religion* purgatory *idiom* دا ځای د اعراف ځخه هم بد دئ This is a veritable Hell.

اعزا a'izzā́ *m. Arabic plural from* عزیز

اعزاز i'zā́z *m. Arabic* honor; esteem; respect د چا په اعزاز in honor of someone

اعزازي i'zāzí *Arabic attributive* honor اعزازي پهره honor guard, guard of honor; ceremonial guard

اعزام i'zā́m *m. Arabic* sending, dispatching

اعزامي i'zāmí *Arabic* expeditionary اعزامي اردو expeditionary forces اعزامي هیئت delegation, mission

اعشار a'shā́r *m. Arabic plural from* عشر

اعشاري a'shārí *Arabic math* decimal اعشاري کسور decimal fraction

اعشاریه a'shārijá *Arabic math* اعشاریه عدد number with a decimal fraction

اعصاب a'sā́b *m. Arabic plural from* عصب

اعصر a'súr *m. Arabic plural from* عصر

اعضا a'zā́ *m. Arabic plural from* عضو

اعطا i'tā́ *f. Arabic* gift, presentation of gifts; granting, bestowing

اعظم azā́m **1.1** big, high **1.2** great, most important, greatest امام اعظم *imā́m-i* the great Imam, Imam Knanifa (the founder of the Knanifite Sect) **1.3** maximum, most high **2** *m. proper name* Azam

اعظمی u'zmā *f. singular from* اعظم په اعظمي توګه استفاده کول to make maximum use of

اعلی¹ a'lā́ ☞ اعلی

اعلا² i'lā́ *f. Arabic* height, loftiness

اعلا ترین a'lāterín the best

اعلام i'lâm *m. Arabic* **1** notification, information; announcement د هوایي خطر اعلام air-raid alarm **2** news, communication اعلام کول *compound verb* ☞ اعلامول

اعلام a'lâm *m. Arabic plural from* علم

اعلامول i'lāmavə́l *denominative, transitive* [*past:* اعلام يي کړ] **1** to notify, inform, announce **2** to express (e.g., sympathy) **3** to declare

اعلامېدل i'lāmadə́l *denominative, intransitive* [*past:* اعلام شو] to be announced

اعلاميه i'lāmijá *f. Arabic* communiqué; declaration

اعلان i'lân *m. Arabic* [*plural:* اعلانونه i'lānúna *Arabic plural:* اعلانات i'lānât] **1** announcement بې له اعلانه without announcement; without warning **2** advertisement تجارتي اعلانات commercial advertisement روښانه شوئ اعلان illuminated sign اعلان کېدل، اعلانول *compound verb* ☞ اعلانول اعلانېدل *compound verb* ☞

اعلانول i'lānavə́l *denominative, transitive* [*past:* اعلان يي کړ] to announce

اعلانېدل i'lanedə́l *denominative, intransitive* [*past:* اعلان شو] to be announced

اعلم a'lâm *Arabic* most knowing, most informed والله اعلم *religion* Since God knows best, Allah will direct the matter.

اعلی a'lấ *Arabic* **1.1** highest نظامي اعلی حاکم highest governor اعلی حاکم military governor اعلی حکومت district **1.2** of the highest quality; excellent اعلی پوستین a short fur jacket of the highest quality ډېر اعلی It could not be better. **2** excellent (grade, evaluation) *idiom* په اعلی درجه کوښښس کول to make every effort

اعلاترین a'lātarín ☞ اعلی ترین

اعلیحضرت a'lāhazrát *m. Arabic* His Highness! اعلیحضرتا! Your Highness! (as a form of address)

اعم a'ấm *Arabic* universal, general

اعما i'mấ *f. Arabic* blinding, dazzling; blindness, dazzled state

اعمار a'mấr *m. Arabic plural* ☞ عمر

اعمار i'mấr *m. Arabic* creation

اعماق a'mấḳ *m. Arabic plural from* عمق اعماق کشفول to explore the depths

اعمال a'mấl *m. Arabic plural from* عمل

اعمالات a'mālất *m. second plural from* اعمال

اعمالاتخانه a'mālātkhāná *f.* workshop

اعمق a'máḳ *Arabic* deeper, deepest

د المر عالي نبنان *official abbreviation and* المر عالي نبنان ا، ع، نبنان Chevalier of the Order of the Sun, Second Degree

اعور a'vár *Arabic* **1** *m. anatomy* blind gut, cecum اعوره کلمه blind gut, cecum **2** one-eyed, blind in one eye

اعیان a'jấn *m. Arabic plural* **1** *from* عین **2** distinguished, noble people, the nobility د اعیانو مجلس Senate, Upper House, House of Lords

آغا aghấ اغا aghā [*plural:* آغایان āghāján *plural:* اغاګان aghāgán *Arabic plural:* آغایون āghājún] **1** mister, Agha **2** prince **3** master *idiom* لوی آغا older brother

آغاتوب āghātób *m.* supremacy, mastery, rule, sway

اغاجان aghādzhán *m. proper name* Agadzhan

آغاز āgház *m.* beginning آغاز کول *compound verb* to begin, undertake, start up مقاله يي آغاز کړه He began the speech.

اغاز agház *m. technology* wedge

آغایون āghājún *Arabic plural from* اغا

اغتذا ightizâ *f. Arabic* nourishment

اغتذائي ightizâí **1** relating to nourishment **2** digestive اغتذائي تشویش digestive disorder

اغتشاش ightishâsh *m. Arabic* mutiny, revolt اغتشاشات وشوه disturbances occurred, disorders occurred

اغتصاب ightisâb *m. Arabic* **1** seizure, taking away **2** expropriation

اغذیه aghzijá *f. Arabic* food, meal د حیوانانو اغذیه fodder, forage

اغر aghár *m.* drawing a bowstring, stretching a bowstring اغر کول to draw a bowstring, stretch a bowstring

اغر aghə́r self-satisfied, complacent

اغراض aghấz *m. Arabic plural from* غرض

اغراق ighrâḳ *m. Arabic* exaggeration

اغ روغ، اغروغ aghrúgh *m. singular & plural* fraud, swindling, trickery

اغز ughúz *m.* [*plural:* اغزان ughuzán] walnut (thin-shelled)

اغزکی aghzakáj *m.* kind of mimosa, *Prosopis stephaniana*

اغزن aghzə́n prickly, spiny اغزن مزی barbed wire *idiom* اغزنه لاره thorny path

اغزنول aghzənavə́l *denominative, transitive* [*past:* اغزن يي کړ] to make prickly, cause to be spiny

اغزنېدل aghzənedə́l *denominative, intransitive* [*past:* اغزن شو] to be prickly, be spiny; prick, sting

اغزی aghzáj *m.* **1** prickle, thorn د اغزو تار *Eastern* barbed wire هر ګله سره اغزی وي *proverb* No rose is without thorns. **2** splinter **3** *figurative* bitter taste, pain; bitterness د بېلتون اغزی the bitterness of separation **4** *dialect Fagonia cretica* (a kind of plant) **5** *dialect Sonchus arvensis* (a kind of thistle) په حلوا کښې مي اغزی وموند *proverb literal* I found a thorn in the halva. *figurative* A fly in the ointment. د ژوند د لاري د اغزیو څخه ځان نه غورول Do not be afraid of difficulties in the course of your life.

اغزیانه aghzijāṇa *f.* thorn-bush thickets

اغږ aghg *present stem of* اغږل *and* اغنبل

اغږل aghgə́l *transitive* [*past:* و يې اغږل *present:* اغږي] to knead; mix (dough)

اغږنه aghgə́na *f.* اغږه aghgə́ *m. plural* kneading, mixing (dough)

اغږونکی aghgúnkaj **1** *present participle of* اغږل **2** *m.* dough mixer, dough kneader (special worker in a bakery)

اغستل aghistə́l *transitive dialect* ☞ اخیستل

اغستل aghustə́l *transitive* ☞ اغوستل

اغوسته aghustə́ *m. plural* ☞ اغوستنه

اغرل aghḳhə́l *transitive* ☞ اغربل

اغفال ighfā́l *m. Arabic* fraud, deception اغفال کول *compound verb* ☞ اغفالول ، اغفال کېدل *compound verb*

اغفالول ighfalavə́l *denominative, transitive* [*past:* اغفال یې کړ] to cheat, swindle; lead into error, delude

اغفالېدل ighfāledə́l *denominative, intransitive* [*past:* اغفال شو] to be swindled, be cheated

اغل¹ āghíl *m.* āghál āghúl enclosure, corral (for cattle)

اغل² āghə́l 1 mixed, kneaded (of dough) 2 blended, intermingled

اغلاط aghlā́t *m. Arabic plural* ☞ غلط

اغلب aghlā́b *Arabic* 1 having preference, having advantage 2 *m.* majority, greater part 3.1 for the most part 3.2 in all probability اغلب دئ چه هغه به تللئ وي In all probability he went there.

اغلباً aghlábán *Arabic* for the most part; ordinarily

اغلی aghə́laj 1 beautiful, elegant, refined 2 pleasing, pleasant, nice 3 excellent 4 fitting, proper

اغماز ighmā́z *m. Arabic* indulgence, spoiling; condescension اغماز کول a to show indulgence towards b to be a hypocrite, act contrary to conscience

اغوا ighvā́ *Arabic* 1 instigation, incitment, provocation 2 seduction 3 calumny, libel اغوا کول a to instigate b to provoke c to seduce d to slander, calumniate, libel

اغواگري ighvāgarí *f.* 1 disturbance 2 instigation, provocation 3 breach of discipline

آغود āghúd *m. plural* 1 malt 2 rotting flour, spoiled flour

آغودول aghudavə́l *denominative, transitive* [*past:* آغود یې کړ] to prepare malt, make malt 2 to malt (go through the process of making a malt)

آغودېدل aghudedə́l *denominative* [*past:* آغود شو] to be swindled

اغوړ aghúr *m.* vengeance اغوړ ایستل to take vengeance

اغوز aghúz *m. plural* ☞ اوربره

اغوستل aghustə́l aghostə́l *transitive* [*past:* وایي غوست] [*present:* اغوندي] 1 to put on (clothing) خپل کالي اغوستل to dress oneself, get dressed 2 to pull over oneself (i.e., a blanket) 3 to wrap up in something هغه مي په یوه شړی کبنی واغوست I wrapped him in an overcoat. 4 to clothe in some sort of uniform

اغوستن aghustán *m.* attire, clothing د اغوستن شیان clothing

اغوستنه aghustə́na *f.* اغوسته aghustə́ *m. plural* the act of putting on clothing, dressing د اغوستني کالي clothing

آغوش āghósh *m.* 1 embrace, به آغوش کبنی نیول to embrace, clasp in the arms 2 an armful 3 *figurative* bosom, lap

اغوند aghúnd *present stem of* اغوستل

اغوندول aghundavə́l *necessitive verb, transitive* [*past:* وایي غونداوه] to compel to put on, dress

اغه aghá *regional colloquial* ☞ هغه¹,²

اغیار aghjā́r *m. Arabic plural* 1 *from* غیر 2 [*plural:* اغیاران aghjārā́n] stranger; outsider; foreigner د اغیار څخه خالي *literal* without outsiders, in the absence of outsiders

اغېر aghér *m.* 1 dyspepsia, indigestion 2 illness accompanied by nausea

اغېرل agherə́l *dialect* 1 [*past:* واغېره] *intransitive* to suffer from indigestion, suffer from dyspepsia 2 [*past:* و یې اغېره] *transitive* to cause nausea

اغېرلئ agherə́laj 1 *past participle of* اغېرل 2 *m.* person suffering from dyspepsia, person suffering from indigestion

اغېری agéraj suffering from dyspepsia, suffering from indigestion

اغېرېدل agheredə́l *intransitive* [*past:* اغېر شو] to vomit, throw up هغه اغېر شوئ دئ He is nauseous. He is vomiting.

اغېزه ناک aghezanā́k ☞ اغېزناک aghezdzhə́n

آغېزه āghezá *f.* اغېزه aghezá *f.* 1 influence, action د دوا آغېزه the action of a medicine په یوه شي کښي آغېزه کول to have an influence on something پر چا آغېزه کول to act upon someone, influence someone 2 result; effect 3 conclusion د دې خبری څخه دي څه آغېزه وکښه؟ What conclusion did you draw from this?

اغېزه کوونکی aghezá kavúnkaj اغېزه ناک aghezanā́k effective, operative

اغیل āghíl ☞ اغل¹

اف¹ uf *interjection* 1 ugh! اف، څومره ناولي کوټه ده! Ugh! What a filthy room! 2 oh, ah اف، څه بده ورځ ده! Oh! What a calamity! اف، نن څنگه گرمي ده! Whew! How hot it is today! اف کول to exclaim oh!, exclaim ah!

اف² *abbreviation of* افغاني

افات āfā́t *m. Arabic plural* 1 *from* آفت 2 *agriculture* pest د نباتاتو افات agricultural pests د کرهني د آفاتو دفع the struggle with agricultural pests insects and other pests harmful to crops

افادوي ifādaví expressive; eloquent د ژبي افادوي قدرت expressiveness of language; eloquence, facility of language

افاده ifādá *f. Arabic* 1 expression د بیان او افادې ډول a manner of expressing a thought, a formulation, a statement (esp. written) د یو لفظ معنی افاده کول *compound verb* to communicate, express افاده کېدل *compound verb* to express the meaning of a word *compound verb* to be communicated, be expressed 2 usefulness, benefit, utility د چا سره افاده لرل to be of use to someone 3 *law* testimony, evidence

افادیت ifādiját *m.* efficaciousness, utility, benefit

افاضه ifāzá *f. Arabic* exact description, circumstantial description; pithiness

افاغنه afāginá *m. Arabic plural from* افغان

اف اف¹ ut-úf ☞ اف

آفاق āfā́ḳ *m. Arabic plural from* افق

افاقه ifāḳá *f. Arabic* recovery, restoration (to health)

آفاقي āfāḳí objective

آفت āfā́t 1 *m.* [*plural:* آفتونه āfatúna *plural:* آفات āfā́t] *Arabic* misfortune, distress, disaster په آفت اخته کېدل to suffer آفت ورته

تر بیکاری لوی پیښن شوئ misfortune has befallen them *proverb* آفت نشته There is no greater misfortune than idleness. **1.2** damage or loss from agricultural pests **2** *attributive* په دغه آفت at the time of this heavy rain

آفتاب āftā́b *m.* the sun

آفتابه āftābá *f.* pitcher (for washing the hands, etc.)

آفتابه لگن aftābalagán *m.* pitcher and basin (for washing)

آفتابي āftābí **1** sunny **2** yellow **3** faded

افتاده uftādá *indeclinable* **1** cheerless, downfallen **2** unfortunate; abased

افتتاح iftitā́ iftitáh *f. & m. Arabic m.* [*plural:* افتتاحات iftitāhā́t] beginning, ceremonial opening افتتاح کول *compound verb* to begin, open (e.g., a meeting) افتتاح کېدل *compound verb* to have begun, be opened (e.g., of a meeting)

افتتاحي iftitāhí *Arabic* relating to an opening; introductory افتتاحیه وینا introductory speech

افتخار iftikhā́r *m. Arabic* [*plural:* افتخارونه iftikhārúna *Arabic plural:* افتخارات iftikhārā́t] **1** glory; honor په افتخار سره gloriously لرل **a** to be famed for **b** to have the honor افتخار کول **a** I have the honor to … **2** pride افتخار لرم چه … **a** to be proud of, take pride in **b** to have the honor افتخار کوم چه … **a** I pride myself in the fact that … **b** I have the honor to … **3** *proper name* Iftikhar

افتخاري iftikhārí *Arabic* honorable افتخاري ریاست the honorable presidium

افترا iftirā́ *f. Arabic* slander, lie; calumny, obloquy

افتراض iftirā́z *m. Arabic* assumption, hypothesis *idiom* د افتراض کلمات moral words and turns of phrasing, moralizing and turns of expression

افتراق iftirā́ḳ *m. Arabic* **1** parting, separation **2** disconnection; juncture **3** dissidence, split

افخم afkhám *Arabic* excellent, magnificent, outstanding

افراد afrā́d *m. Arabic plural* **1** *from* فرد **2** *military* personnel, complement عسکري افراد privates, soldiers; enlisted personnel موظفه افراد enlisted reserve بحري افراد seaman, sailors احتیاطي افراد enlisted personnel on active duty د مخابرې افراد signal corpsmen نوي افراد recruits, rookies

افراز ifrā́z *m. Arabic* **1** section, compartment, apportionment **2** *physiology* secretion

افراط iffrā́t *m. Arabic* **1** excess **2** extreme; excessiveness افراط کول **a** to give oneself up to excesses **b** to go to extremes, run to excesses

افراطي ifrātí *Arabic* **1** extreme; ultra- **2** *m.* [*plural:* افراطیان ifrātiján *Arabic plural:* افراطیون ifrātijún] extreme elements, extremists; ultras افراطي افروز afróz compound expression illuminating (or similar) جهان افروز illuminating the world (of the sun)

افروزه afruzá *f. proper name* Afruza

آفریده āfridá *indeclinable* created

آفریده گار āfridagā́r *m.* creator, maker

1 افریدي afridí *m.* apridí *plural* Afridi (tribe) **2** afridáj *m.* apridáj *m.* Afridi (tribesman)

افریقه afriḳá *f.* ☞ افریقا

افریقائي afriḳāí **1** African **2** *m.* African (person)

افریقا afriḳá *f.* Africa د افریقي براعظم the African mainland, African continent د جنوبي افریقي جمهوریت the South African Republic د مرکزي افریقي جمهوریت the Central African Republic جنوب غربي افریقه Southwest Africa

آفرین āfrín āprín **1** praise, approval د آفرین وړ بلل to consider praiseworthy چا ته آفرین ویل to praise someone, approve of someone! آفرین ستاپه همت شه! You've done excellent work! **2** *interjection* good, wonderful, bravo

آفرینش āfrinísh *m.* creation, making

افزار afzā́r *m.* implement, tool, instrument د جراحی افزار surgical instruments

افزارداني afzārdāní *f.* box, case, bag for tools or instruments

افزایش afzājísh *m.* addition; increase

افزوده afzudá *indeclinable* increased, enlarged

افسار afsā́r *m.* halter

افسانوي afsānaví *attributive* fairy tale; legendary; mythical

افسانه afsāná *f.* **1** fable; tale, fairy tale د افساني په ډول like a fairy tale **2** invention, fiction د افسانو افسانه ده This is sheer invention. This is pure fiction. **3** *regional* novel, romance

افسانه نگار afsānanigā́r *m. regional* novelist

افسر ¹ afsár *m.* crown, diadem

افسر ² afsár afsā́r *m. regional* **1** officer بحري افسر ، جهازي افسر naval officer کمان افسر commander; general officer commanding نظامي افسران officers **2** civil servant, public employee افسر مال afsár-i tax official

افسرده afsurdá *indeclinable* **1** freezing; congealing **2** fading, withering **3** *figurative* sad, cheerless, depressed **4** *figurative* disheartened, dispirited

افسرده دل afsurdadil ☞ افسرده 3, 4

افسري afsari *attributive regional* officer, pertaining to officer rank or office

افسوس afsós apsós **1** *m.* د افسوس اصوات expressions of regret افسوس ښکاره کول، افسوس څرگندول to express regret پر چا افسوس کول **a** feel sorry for, pity someone **b** to regret زه افسوس کوم چه … I regret that … **2** *interjection* woe, alas

افسوسناک afsosnā́k worthy, deserving of regret; sad افسوسناک اوضاع a sad situation

افسون afsún *m.* witchcraft, sorcery; spell, incantation افسون کول to bewitch, charm, put under a spell

افسون گر afsungár *m.* sorcerer, magician, enchanter, wizard

افسون گره afsungára *feminine of* افسون گر

آفسېټ āfseṭ *m.* offset (printing)

افشا ifshā́ *f. Arabic* disclosure, publicity افشا کول *compound verb* to disclose (a secret); give publicity to something

افشار afshā́r *m. singular & plural* Afshar (Turkic tribe)

افشان afshā́n *compound* disseminating, spreading غازافشان chemical mortar

افضل afzál *Arabic* 1.1 most virtuous 1.2 best, excellent *m.* 2 *m. proper name* Afzal'

افضلیت afzaliját *m. Arabic* excellence

افطار iftā́r *m. Arabic* the first meal taken after a (religious) fast افطار کول to eat after having fasted

افعال afʿál *m. Arabic plural from* فعل

افغان afghā́n avghā́n 1 *m.* [*plural:* افغانان afghanā́n *Arabic plural:* افاغنه afāghiná] Afghan (person) 2 *attributive* Afghan افغان اولس the Afghan people

افغان پېژندونکی afghā́n pezhandúnkaj *m.* Afghanist (academic specialist)

افغانستان afghā́nistān *m.* Afghanistan

افغاني afghā́ni 1 *attributive* Afghan معاصر افغاني ادب modern Afghan literature افغاني مطبوعات the Afghan press 2.1 *f.* Afghani, the Afghan language, Pashto 2.2 [*plural:* افغانۍ afghanə́j] Afghani (monetary unit) نیمه افغانۍ one-half Afghani

افغانېدل afghānedә́l *denominative, intransitive* [*past:* افغان شو] to become Afghan, become an Afgan; be Afghanized

افق ufúḳ *m. Arabic* [*plural:* افقونه ufkúna *Arabic plural:* آفاق afā́k] 1 horizon مرئي افق the visible horizon د توپچي افق *military* artillery fire area 2 *figurative* mental outlook, mental horizon

افقي ufukí horizontal خط افقي horizontal line افقي تمرکز *economics* horizontal concentration *idiom* افقي حرکت کول to move forward, advance

افکار afkā́r *m. Arabic plural from* فکر د افکارو بدلول exchange of opinions عمومي افکار، عام افکار the general opinion د افکارو حالت frame of mind

افگار afgā́r avgā́r 1 injured, hurt 2 mutilated; covered with wounds

افلاس iflā́s *m. Arabic* 1 poverty, want 2 insolvency, bankruptcy د چا په خصوص د افلاس حکم صادرول to declare someone bankrupt

افلاک aflā́k *m. Arabic plural from* فلک

افلاتې aflā́te *f. plural regional* ☞ اپلات

افلیج iflídzh *m. Arabic* paralysis افلج وهل to paralyze افلج وهلئ سری a paralytic

افندي afandí *m.* effendi, mister

افواج afvā́dzh *m. Arabic plural from* فوج

افواه afvā́ afvā́h *f. & m. Arabic* [*plural:* افواګاني afvāgā́ni *Arabic plural:* افواهات afvāhā́t] rumor بې اساسه افواګاني خپرول to spread groundless rumors

افواهي afvāhí pertaining to rumors دا افواهي خبره ده There is a rumor that …

افول ufúl *m. Arabic* setting (of the sun); decline, going down کول to set (of the sun)

افوه úfuh *interjection* ugh

افهام ifhā́m *m. Arabic* exclamation; interpretation ژبه د افهام او تفهیم یوه وسیله ده Language is a means of communication.

افبر afér *m.* ☞ شارژدافبر

آفیسر āfisár *m. regional* ☞ افسر[2]

افیمچي afimchí *m.* opium smoker

افیون afjún *m. plural* 1 opium 2 *figurative* narcotic, dope

آق[1] āḳ 1 white 2 *used in geological designations* آق تپه Aktepa

ا، ق[2] *abbreviation from* د اس قوه horsepower

آقا āḳā́ *m.* ☞ آغا

اقالیم aḳālím *m. Arabic plural from* اقلیم

اقامت iḳāmát *m. Arabic* 1 stay, sojourn, residence اقامت لرل to live, stay, settle 2 *religion* precise observance (of some rite) اقامت کول a to live, stay, settle b to stand and sit (during prayer) c to pray diligently اقامت ویل to pray diligently

اقامتگا، اقامتگاه، اقامتگا، اقامت گا iḳāmatgā́ iḳāmatgā́h 1 *f. & m.* place of residence; residence 2 *military* army reception center

اقامه iḳāmá *f. Arabic* 1 settling, placing, accomodation 2 presentation, presenting, institution (of a suit) دعویٔ اقامه کول to initiate legal action, institute a suit

آقایون āḳājún *m. Arabic plural from* آقا

آقایي āḳāí *f.* supremacy, rule, sway

اقبال iḳbā́l *m. Arabic* 1 prosperity; well-being; material success 2 good luck; luck 3 *Eastern law* consent; acknowledgment د جرم اقبال کول، د اقبال دعویٔ دخلول to admit one's guilt; plead guilty 4 *proper name* Ikbal

اقبالمن iḳbālmán iḳbālmánd 1 prosperous, flourishing 2 happy

اق پق aḳ-páḳ ☞ هک پک

اقتباس iḳtibā́s *m. Arabic* 1 adoption, borrowing 2 extract, quotation *idiom* د اقتباس علامت quotation marks

اقتباسول iḳtibāsavә́l *denominative, transitive* [*past:* اقتباس یې کړ] to adopt, borrow

اقتدا iḳtidā *f. Arabic* imitation; following someone's example اقتدا کول to imitate, follow someone's example

اقتدار iḳtidā́r *m. Arabic* 1 strength, power, might 2 authority د چا اقتدارات لرول exercising authority د اقتدار خڼتن to limit someone's authority, reduce someone's rights 3 superiority پریو شي اقتدار میندل a to triumph over something b to surmount something 4 mastery

اقتراح iḳtirā́ iḳtirāh *f. & m. Arabic f.* [*plural:* اقتراګاني iktirāgā́ni *plural:* اقتراحگاني iktirāhgā́ni *m. Arabic plural:* اقتراحات iktirāhā́t] 1 improvisation 2 initiative, creativeness 3 suggestion (e.g., to play, have a good time) 4 casting of lots (in foretelling, etc.)

اقتصاد iḳtisā́d *m. Arabic* economics; the economy ملي اقتصاد the national economy د ملي اقتصاد وزارت Ministry of the National

اقتصاد علم Economy د اقتصاد مجله political economy Iktisad (the periodical)

اقتصاداً iķtisādán economic, in an economic sense

اقتصاد پوهاند iķtisādpohǻnd *m.* اقتصاددان iķtisāddǻn economist

اقتصادي iķtisādí **1.1** economic, pertaining to the economy د هیواد اقتصادي قوه the economic power of the country economic policy نوی اقتصادي سیاست *history* the New Economic Policy اقتصادي ساختمان the economic structure **1.2** economical, profitable, economically advantageous **2** *m.* [*plural:* اقتصادیان iktisādijǻn *Arabic plural:* اقتصادیون iktisādijún] economist

اقتصادیات iķtisādiját *m. Arabic plural* economics; economic problems د ملي اقتصادیاتو شورا the Council for the National Economy

اقتصادي پوه iķtisādipóh *m.* economist

اقتضا iķtizǻ *f. Arabic* [*plural:* اقتضاگانی iķtizāgǻni *m. Arabic plural:* اقتضاءات iķtizāǻt] *Arabic* **1** need, necessity, want **2** requirement, demand

اقتفا iķtifǻ *f. Arabic* movement, folowing, taking after د چا په اقتفا following, taking after someone

آقچه āķchá *f.* Akcha (city, district)

اقدار aķdǻr *m. Arabic plural from* قدر

اقدام [1] iķdǻm *m. Arabic* [*plural:* اقدامونه iķdāmúna *Arabic plural:* اقدامات iķdāmǻt] **1** measure, arrangement باید هر راز اقدامات وشي it is necessary to take all measures **2** speech, oral presentation **3** *military* operation اقدامات کول to conduct operations **4** endeavor, effort

اقدام [2] aķdǻm *m. Arabic plural from* قدم [1]

اقداماتي iķdāmātí executive (of authority, organs)

اقدس akdās *Arabic* most sacred, holy

اقرار iķrǻr *m. Arabic* **1** acknowledgement, admission, confession صحیح شرعي اقرار *law* a confession in accordance with the observance of Shariat (i.e., the Moslem code of religious and civil law based on the Koran) اقرار یې کړئ دئ او ځان یې ملامت He admitted that he was guilty. **2** attestation, affirmation اقرار کوم چه... I attest that ..., I affirm that ...

اقرارنامه iķrārnāmā *f. Arabic law* contract (written), agreement; obligation

اقرارول iķrāravól *denominative, transitive* [*past:* اقرار یې کړ] **1** to admit, confess, acknowledge **2** to attest, affirm

اقراریدل iķrāredól *denominative, intransitive* [*past:* اقرار شو] **1** to have admitted, have confessed, have acknowledged **2** to have attested, have affirmed; be attested, be affirmed

اقرب aķráb ☞ اکرب

اقربا aķribǻ *m. Arabic plural* [*singular:* قریب] relatives, relations; kinfolk

آقرباط āķrabǻt *m.* Akrabat (city, northern Afghanistan)

اقساط aķsát *m. Arabic plural from* قسط

اقسام aķsám *m. Arabic plural from* قسم [1]

اقصی، اقصا aķsǻ *Arabic* distant, far شرق اقصی *sharḳ-i* the Far East

آقطي āķtí āķtá *f. Arabic botany* elder

آقگل āķgúl *m.* akgul (a kind of karakul, i.e., Asian sheep or its wool, fur or pelt)

اقل aķál *Arabic* least; minimal, smallest حد اقل minimum

اقلاً aķállán *Arabic* at least, although, at a minimum, not less than

اقلام aķlǻm *m. Arabic plural from* قلم د صادراتو اقلام، صادراتي اقلام items of export عمده اقلام principal export items

اقلیت aķalliját *m. Arabic* minority ملي اقلیتونه national minorities

اقلیم iķlím *m. Arabic* [*plural:* اقالیم aķālím] **1** climate بری اقلیم continental climate سخت اقلیم severe climate **2** region, district; country, land area; territory **3** *geography* belt, zone

اقلیم شناسي iķlimshināsí *f.* climatology

اقلیمي iķlimí climatic

اقمار aķmǻr *m. Arabic plural from* قمر **1** fellow travelers **2** satellites

اقوات aķvát *m. Arabic plural from* قوت [2]

اقوال aķvál *m. Arabic plural from* قول [1]

اقوام aķvám *m. Arabic plural from* قوم د متحده اقوامو موسسه the United Nations Organization

اکا akǻ *m.* **1** uncle (father's brother) **2** elderly man; adult man

اکابیر akābír *m. Arabic plural* [*singular:* کبیر] **1** grown-ups **2** adults د اکابرو تعلیم the eradication of illiteracy

اکاخیل akākhél **1** *m. plural* Akakhejli (a subdivision of the Afridi tribe of Tirakh) **2** *m.* Akakhejl (person)

اکادمي akādemí *f.* academy د ساینس اکادمي the Academy of Sciences

اکادمیک akāḍémik *m.* اکاډمیک akāḍémik *m.* اکاډمیکي akāḍemīkí *m.* academician

اکاډمي akāḍemí *f.* ☞ اکاډمي

اکاړ akāṛ **1** cruel, fierce, severe **2** hostile, inimical

اکاړی akāṛaj [1] ☞ اکاړ

اکاړي akāṛí [2] *f.* cruelty, ferociousness, severity; oppression اکاړي کول **a** to demonstrate cruelty **b** to oppress

اکاړیتوب akaṛitób *m.* cruelty, ferociousness, severity

اکب ukúb *m.* grandeur, greatness

اکبار ikbǻr *m.* a kind of buckthorn

اکبر akbār *Arabic* **1** greatest, most high **2** *m. proper name* Akbar

اکبری akbarój *f. regional* kind of candy, kind of sweetmeat

اکپک akpák ☞ اک پک

اکتساب iktisǻb *m. Arabic* **1** acquisition; gain; money-grubbing **2** preparation, training

اکتسابي iktisābí **1** acquired; earned, gained **2** preparatory, preliminary اکتسابي درس academic training *idiom* اکتسابي تابعیت naturalization

اکتشاف iktishǻf *m. Arabic* [*plural:* اکتشافونه iktishāfúna *Arabic plural:* اکتشافات iktishāfǻt] **1** discovery, invention **2** research

3 intelligence, scouting, reconnaissance **4** development, progress

اكتشافي iktishāfī *Arabic* **1** *attributive* research **2** *attributive* intelligence; reconnaissance اكتشافي الوتكه reconnaissance aircraft

اكتفا iktifā́ *f. Arabic* contentment, satisfaction په يو شي اكتفا كول to be contented, be satisfied with something د يو شي دپاره اكتفا كول to be enough for something

اكتوبر aktóbr *m.* October

اكتيف aktíf active, aggressive

اكټ akṭ *m.* **1** theatrical presentation, act **2** acting, stage acting

اكټينګ ákṭing *m.* performance, acting (on the stage) اكتينګ كول to act, perform (on stage)

اكثر aksár *Arabic* **1** the many; the majority, the greater part په اكثرو هيوادونو كښي in the majority of countries **2** principally, for the most part, mostly, in the majority of cases, mainly; in general; often, usually اكثر داسي وي it usually happens thus **3** higher, highest اكثر حد the maximum

اكثراً aksárán ☞ اكثر 2

اكثره aksára **1** *feminine of* اكثر **2** principally, for the most part, mostly, in the majority of cases, mainly

اكثريت aksariját *m. Arabic* majority بسيط اكثريت a simple majority مطلق اكثريت an absolute majority د آراو اكثريت majority of votes اكثريت لرل to have a majority

اكر akár *m.* giddiness, dizziness

اكرا ákrā́ *f.* Akkra (city)

اكرام ikrắm *m. Arabic* respect, esteem په ښه اكرام with great respect, very respectfully د چا اكرام كول to treat someone with respect

اكره ikráh *m. Arabic* aversion, repugnance, disgust, loathing

اكرب akrāb **1** poor اكرب سړى a poor man, poor person **2** *m.* poor peasant

اكرب توب akrabtób *m.* poverty, want

اكربكر akarbakár *m. plural regional* **1** expression, look **2** character, spirit (of a time, epoch)

اكربه akrába *feminine singular from* اكرب

اكرم akrám *Arabic* **1** most generous, most bountiful, most gracious **2** *m. proper name* Akram

اكرم المخلوقات akram-ul-makhluḳắt *m. Arabic* crown of creation, mankind

اكرمه akráma *f. dialect* fourth finger

اكرى akarój *f. plural* ruins

آكړ ¹ ākóṛ *m.* oh dear uncle (as a form of address)

اكړ ² akáṛ **1** childless; fruitless, barren **2** despairing

آكسايد āksắjd *m.* oxide

اكسرېز iksréz *m.* eksréz *plural* **1** x-rays **2** x-ray room

آكسيجن āksidzhán *m.* oxygen

اكسير aksír *m. Arabic* **1** elixir **2** alchemy اكسير اعظم aksír-i a panacea

آكسيژن aksizhán *m.* oxygen

اكسلبټر akseleṭár *m.* pedal, accelerator په اكسپلبټر پنبه اينبودل to depress the pedal with the foot

اكل akl *m. Arabic* food, nourishment د اكل څيزونه foodstuffs

اكليل aklíl *m. Arabic* coronet

اكمال ikmā́l *m. Arabic* **1** completion, end **2** execution (e.g., of a commercial order) **3** *military* replenishment د جبخاني اكمال replenishment of ammunition **4** supply اكمال كول compound اكمالبدل *compound verb* ☞ اكمال كبدل، اكمالول *verb*

اكمالاتي ikmālātí **1** *military* pertaining to resupply **2** *attributive* supply, of supply

اكمال كوونكى ikmā́l kavúnkaj **1** *attributive* supply, of supply **2** *m.* member of supply services

اكمالول ikmālavól *denominative, transitive* [*past:* اكمال يي كړ] **1** to complete, finish, end **2** to fill an order **3** *military* to replenish, resupply **4** to supply

اكمالي ikmālí ☞ اكمالاتي

اكمالبدل ikmāledól *denominative, intransitive* [*past:* اكمال شو] **1** to be completed, be finished **2** to be filled (of an order) **3** *military* to be replenished, be resupplied **4** to be supplied

اكمل akmál *Arabic* **1** completed **2** maximal; highest possible

اكملاتور akumulātór *m.* storage battery

اكناف aknā́f *m. Arabic plural from* كنف *idiom* د كور اكناف personal plot, land allocation (of a collective farmer)

اكنون aknún *literary* at once, now

اكوادور ekvā́dor *m.* Ecuador

اكوان akuvā́n *m. plural children's speech* little children, children

اكو بكو áku-báku *m.* **1** kind of bird **2** kind of children's game **3** *dialect* person with protruding eyes

اكوردېون akordeón accordion

اكوړ akóṛ *m.* [*plural:* اكوړان akoṛā́n] walnut

اكوړخېل akoṛkhél **1** *m. plural* Akorkhejli (subdivision of the Khammok tribe) **2** *m.* Akorkhejl (tribesman)

اكوړه akoṛá *f.* Akora (capital city of the Khammok tribe)

اكوړى akoṛáj *m.* Morocco

اكوزي akozí *m. plural* **1** Akozai (a subdivision of the Yusufai tribe) **2** akozáj Akozai (tribesman)

اكوك akúk *m. plural* **1** unripe fruit اكوك كول، اكوك نيول to set (as of fruit) **2** the juice of unripe fruit; a seasoning made from unripe fruit

اكونومي ekonomí *f.* economics

اكونومست ekonomíst *m.* economist

اكونوميك ekonomík *m.* economics

اكي ikí *f. obsolete* iki, pice (i.e., 1/30 of a rupee)

اكيډيمي akaḍemí *f. regional* academy

اګاهو agavú ☞ اګاوو

آګاه āgāh **1** experienced, learned, informed آګاه كول to inform, notify آګاه كېدل to be informed, know **2** conscious

آګاهمن āgāhmán ☞ آګاه

اگاهو agāhú *regional* **1** sharp-sighted; farsighted **2.1** beforehand, in advance, in good time **2.2** earlier د دي نه لږ اگاهو somewhat earlier نه کاله اگاهو nine years ago

آگاهي āgāhí *f.* information, notification

آگبوت agbút *m.* agbót *regional* steamboat

اگدر agdár strong, robust

اگر agár [1] *m.* **1** base person, low person; toady, sycophant **2** slave

اگر agár [2] *conjunction* if, though اگر چه، اگر که although

اگر agár [3] *m. regional* **1** kind of perfume **2** aloe

اگربگر agár-bagár *m. regional* bustle, turmoil

اگرمای agramáj *m.* ☞ اړدمی

اگره ugrá [1] *f.* ☞ اوگره

اگره agára [2] *feminine of* اگر

اگرېمان agremán *m. diplomacy* agrément (i.e., the granting of diplomatic recognition to a diplomatic representative by the state to which he is to be accredited) د چا اگرېمان ورکول to accord agrément to someone

اگست ágəst *m.* agást August

اگل agál *m.* ditch, drainage ditch

اگن agán *m. mirafra cantillans* (a kind of lark)

اگواړی agvāṛəj *f.* reins

اگوچي agúchi اگوچي کول *a* to be exhausted (with), break down from *b* to strive to attain (something)

آگه āgáh ☞ آگاه ما آگه که له مطلبه Let me know what the story is. Let me know what is happening.

اگی agə́j *f. singular & plural dialect* egg, eggs تلبدلي اگی omelet *idiom* د اگی بچی an innocent baby پہ اگی کښنی چونہبدل *literal* to sing while in the egg *figurative* to be very adroit, be dexterous ☞ هگی

اگېل agejə́l اگېيل agəjúl *transitive* [*past:* ده و اگېبه] **1** to irritate, annoy **2** to incite, instigate **3** to abrade, rub sore **4** to sew up (i.e., a sack)

آل āl [1] *m. Arabic singular & plural* children, posterity د آدم آل the human race آل مال، آل او آل posterity آل او اولاد، آل مال household and property

ال al [2] cord connecting the yoke with the main beam of a plow

آل āl [3] scarlet, red

ال al [4] *interjection* hey, look, look here

ال al [5] *Arabic* the definite article in the Arabic language; before the "sun" letters ت، ث، د، ذ، ر، ز، س، ش، ص، ض، ط، ظ، ل، ن *it is assimilated by these sounds, and is read accordingly with them; i.e., the phoneme /l/ of the article preceding a "sun" consonant is not only assimilated but has the effect of doubling the consonant phoneme in question;* الرحمن *ar-rahman* التاريخ *at-tarikh; etc. It is pronounced in Pashto in borrowed compound words as "ul," "ur," "ut," etc. e.g.,* عبد الرحمن *abdurraham*

الا alā [1] *f.* run; running; rush وچا ته الا کول to run up to someone, rush up to someone

الا illā [2] *Arabic* **1** excluding, besides, aside from **2** however

الاالا alā-alā heave-ho, all-together (or similar expression used as a cry in unison when doing heavy work)

الابلا alā-balā **1** all, altogether **2** quite, completely *idiom* کول to worry, to be disturbed, be alarmed

الاپ alā́p *m. regional* solo part, melody پہ ... الاپ کول to lead the singing, strike up a tune, begin to play

آلات ālát *m. Arabic plural* ☞ آلت

الاج alā́dzh *m.* الاجگر alā́dzhgár *m.* **1** skutcher, operator of a combing machine in a cotton mill **2** hand combing flax, beating cotton

الاجه alā́dzha *feminine of* الاج

الاجي alā́dzhí [1] *f.* wooden gin or spike revolving barrel (for separating the cotton from the seeds of the cotton plant) کول to skutch, gin cotton, free the cotton from the seeds

الاجي alā-dzhi [2] *plural of* الاجه

الاچه alāchá *f.* ☞ الچه

الاچي ilāchí *f.* cardamom (the plant or the spice)

الارغه alārghá *m.* falcon (bird)

الاستي alā́sti *indeclinable* disappearing; unseen

الاسکا alāskā *f.* Alaska

الاشه alāshá *f.* jaw, maxilla

الاغبهدي alāghbahdí *f.* manufacture of silver and gold, lace, braid, etc.

الاکولنگ alākuláng *m.* swings

الال alā́l ☞ حلال

آلام ālā́m [1] *m. Arabic plural from* الم

الام alā́m [2] ☞ کلام

الاو alā́v *m.* flame; bonfire

الاورتي alāvrə́ti *f. plural* **1** ill-considered action الاورتي پيبنبه کول *a* to act rashly **2** nonsense **3** improvisation الاورتي ويل *b* to talk nonsense *c* to improvise; make something up

آلايش ālájísh *m.* **1** profanation **2** soiling, defilement, spoiling

الب elb *m.* د الب درياب the Elbe River

البا elbā́ *f.* the Island of Elba

البانيا albānijá *f.* البانيه albānijá *f.* Albania

البانيائي albānijājí Albanian البانيائي ژبه the Albanian language

البته albátta *Arabic* of course, undoubtedly; to be sure; without fail

البرز elbúrz *m.* البروس elbrús *m.* Mount Elbrus

البسه albisá *m. Arabic plural* [*plural:* البسي albisé] dress (in the general sense), clothing

البشاکه albushā́ka *f.* token, sign, indication

البم albúm *m.* ☞ البوم

البند ilbánd *m.* summer pasture, mountain pasture

البنگ albúng mute

البوم albúm *m.* album

البومين albumín *m. chemistry* albumen البومن، البومين

الپ ālp *m.* the Alps د الپ غرونه the Alps

الپي الا alpi-alá *indeclinable* ruined; bereft of resources الپي الا کبدل کول to ruin الپي الا کبدل to be ruined

آلت ālát *m. Arabic* [*plural:* آلتونه ālatū́na *Arabic plural:* آلات ālā́t] instrument, tool, device, apparatus, contrivance حفريه آلات *military* entrenching tool د موسيقي آلات *d* musical instruments ماشين آلتو توليد machine tools د آلاتو توليد machine-tool manufacture; toolmaking; instrument manufacture

التائي altā́j *m.* 1 Altai د التائي غرونه the Altai Mountains 2 paws of a fox pelt

التباس iltibā́s *m. Arabic* confusion, vagueness التباس کول to confuse, muddle up التباس مخه نيول to avoid confusion, avoid vagueness

التجا iltidzhā́ *f. Arabic* running for shelter; seeking asylum التجا کول to run to shelter; seek asylum و چا ته التجا کول to turn to someone for assistance

التزام iltizā́m *m. Arabic* debt; obligation

التزامي iltizāmí *Arabic* under obligation; obliged *idiom* التزامي حال *grammar* present tense of the perfective aspect

التفات iltifā́t *m. Arabic* 1 esteem; honor; courtesy 2 attention د و چا ته التفات کول a to attract someone's attention جلبول to show respect, honor for someone b to pay attention to someone

التماس iltimā́s *m. Arabic* earnest request; entreaty; supplication و چاته التماس کول, له چا څخه التماس کول to entreat, supplicate someone التماس لرل to earnestly request, address a request التماس کوونکی iltimā́s kavúnkaj *m.* applicant, petitioner; one addressing a request

التهاب iltihā́b *m. Arabic medicine* inflammation

التهابي iltihābí inflammatory التهابي پړسوب inflammation

التيماتوم ultimātúm *m.* ultimatum التيماتوم ورکول to present an ultimatum

التيمتر altimétr *m.* التي متر altimeter

الجزائر aldzhazā́ir *m. Arabic plural* الجزاير aldzhazājír *m.* Algeria (state, city) د الجزاير د خلکو دموکراتيک جمهوريت People's Democratic Algerian Republic

الجزايري aldzhāzajirí 1 Algerian 2 Algerian (person)

الجزيره aldzhazirá *f.* Algeria (state, city)

الجه uldzhá *f.* trophy, captured equipment, military loot, booty الجه کول *compound verb* to acquire as trophies, obtain as captured equipment

الجيان aldzhiā́n *m. plural* water plants

الجيريا aldzhirijá *f.* Algeria (state, city)

الچکان alchakā́n *m. plural* handcuffs, manacles

الچه alachá *f.* alacha (spotted or striped cloth)

ايلچي ilchí ☞ ايلچي

الحاد¹ ilhā́d *m. Arabic* heresy, atheism

الحاد² alhā́d *m. Arabic plural from* لحد

الحاصل alhāsíl *Arabic* in a word, in one word, in short چه الحاصل in short

الحاق ilhā́ḵ *m. Arabic* 1 joining, annexation 2 appendix, supplement 3 contiguity, junction

الحاقول ilhāḵavól *denominative, transitive* [*past:* الحاق يي کړ] 1 to join, annex 2 to apply; supplement; adjoin

الحاقېدل ilhāḵedól *denominative, intransitive* [*past:* الحاق شو] 1 to be joined, be annexed 2 to be applied, be supplemented

الحاقيه ilhāḵjá *f.* 1 appendix, supplement 2 extension, wing (of a building)

الحان alhā́n *m. Arabic plural from* لحن

الحمدالله alhamdulillá́h *Arabic* thanks to God, glory to God, praise to Allah

الخ ilákh *Arabic* and so on, and so forth, etc.

الدر alḍár *m. Eastern* penholder (for letter-writing)

الرياض arrijā́z *m. Arabic* ☞ رياض

الزام ilzā́m *m. Arabic* 1 charge, accusation; conviction په چا باندي الزام *Eastern law* to accuse someone, charge 2 reproof, blame, censure 3 shame, disgrace

اولس¹ uláˊs *m.* ☞ اولس

الستي alásti unexpectedly, against all expectations الستي پېښېدل to happen unexpectedly

الستيکي elastikí flexible; elastic

الستيکيت elastikiját *m.* flexibility; elasticity

السلام عليکم as-salám 'aléjkum *Arabic* Peace unto you, Peace be with you; Hello, Goodbye

السلوادور elsalvādór *m.* El Salvador

السنه alsiná *m. Arabic plural from* لسان

السي¹ alsí *m. plural Eastern* flaxseed د السو تېل flaxseed oil

السي² uləsí ☞ اولسي

الش alísh ☞ اليش

الشول alishavól *transitive* ☞ اليشول

الشېدل alishedól *intransitive* ☞ اليشېدل

الغا¹ ilghá́ *f. Arabic* cancellation, annulment; abolishment الغا کول *compound verb* to cancel, annul; abolish

الغا² alghá̋ بلغا کول to make a noise, create a hubub

الغاسه¹ alghāsá́ *f.* piece of bread taken in order to allay one's hunger

الغاسه² alghāsá́ upset, saddened الغاسه کېدل to feel upset over

الغاوتلغاو alghá́v-talghá́v *m. regional* ☞ الغوتلغو

الغتان alghatā́n restless, active (of a child)

الغرض algharáz *Arabic* in a word, in short, in brief

الغوتلغو alghú-talghú 1 noise, din 2 confusion

الغه alghá́ *f.* ring, hoop *idiom* الغه کول to dupe, deceive someone ☞ حلقه

الف alíf *m.* ☞ ا¹ aliff (the name of the first letter of the Afghan-Arabic alphabet) *idiom* الف هېڅ نه لري I am as poor as a church mouse. د الف په شان دربدل to stand at attention

الفاظ alfā́z *m. Arabic plural from* لفظ

الفبا alifbā́ *f.* alphabet; ABC book د الفبا په ترتیب according to the alphabet, in alphabetic order

الفبائي alifbají alphabetic, pertaining to the alphabet

الف بې alifbé *f.* د الف بې له مخي according to the alphabet, in alphabetic order

الفت ulfát *m. Arabic* closeness, intimacy; affection; friendship د چا سره الفت کول to enter into a friendship with someone الفت میندل to strike up a friendship with someone

آلفته āluftá *indeclinable* 1 upset, annoyed 2 unhappy آلفته کول a to upset b to make unhappy آلفته کېدل a to be upset, be annoyed b to be unhappy

الف بي alifbé *f.* alphabet; ABCs; ABC book د مورس الف وبي the Morse code, Morse alphabet

القا ilkā́ *f. Arabic* persuasion; suggestion; incitement القا او تائید کول to suggest insistently; persuade

القاب alkā́b *m. Arabic plural from* لقب رسمي القاب official titles

القاح ilkā́h *m. biology* impregnation, fertilization د تخم القاح impregnation, fertilization مصنوعي القاح artificial insemination

القصه alkissá *Arabic* 1 in a word, in short, in brief 2 finally

الک alə́k *m.* ☞ هلک

الکترون elektrón *m.* [*plural:* الکترونه elekrronúna *plural:* الکترونات elektronā́t] electron

الکتروني elektroní electronic الکتروني نظریه، الکتروني ثوري electronic theory د حساب الکتروني ماشین electronic computer

الکترونیک elektroník *m.* electronics

الکترون elektrón *m.* ☞ الکترون

الکتروني elektroní ☞ الکتروني

الکوزائي alkozājí *m. plural* ☞ الکوزي

الکوزي 1 alkozí *m. plural* Alkozai (one of the Durrani tribes) 2 alkozáj *m.* Alkozai (tribesman)

الکول alkól *m. Arabic plural* alcohol

الکویت alkuvájt *m.* Kuwait

الکه 1 ulká *f. obsolete* 1 province 2 proprietorship

الکه 2 alə́ka *vocative from* الک

الکی ژبه alkə́j zhə́ba *f.* الکی ژبۍ alkə́j zhəbə́j *f. anatomy* uvula *idiom* و احمد ته مي الکی ژبه ولوېده چه دغه کتاب دي راکه I used all my persuasion to get Ahmed to give me his book.

الگه alága *f.* barren (e.g., of a cow)

الله alláh *Arabic* 1 *m.* God, Allah الله! Oh my God! 2 *interjection* I swear *proverb* الله پاک او دربار يي هم پاک He is destitute. He is poor as a church-mouse.

الله اکبر allahuakbár *Arabic* 1 Allah is great! 2 used as a battle cry by troops going in to attack 3 Thanks be to God; Glory to God; Praise be to God

الله خیر allah-khájr *Arabic* God forbid!

الله داد allahdā́d *m. proper name* Allahdad

الله یار allahjā́r *m. proper name* Alajar, Alayar

الم 1 alā́m *m. Arabic* [*plural:* الامونه alamúna *Arabic plural:* آلام ālā́m] 1 grief; sorrow 2 torment, torture *idiom* الم سور اخیستل a to suffer from gluttony, be insatiable b to be impatient

الم 2 alám *m.* ☞ هلم

الماآتا almā-atā́ *f.* Alma Ata (city)

الماری almārə́j *f.* cupboard, cabinet with shelves د کتابو الماری bookcase دېوالي الماری wall cupboard د الماری کلپ ده the cupboard is open

الماس almā́s *m. singular & plural* 1 diamond 2 small scissors, clippers

آلمان ālmā́n *m.* Germany

آلماني 1 ālmānaví ☞ آلماني

آلماني ālmāní ālmānáj 1 German آلماني ژبه ālmāni German language 2 *m.* German (person)

الماوور alamāvár ☞ المناک

الميپا المپیا olimpjā́ *f.* لوبي المپیا the Olympic Games, the Olympiad

المپیک alimpík olimpík 1 olympic 2 *m.* the Olympic Society (of Afghanistan)

المپیکي alimpiki olimpikí olympic

المر almár *m.* ☞ لمر د المر عالي نښان the Order of the Sun, Second Degree د المر اعلی نښان the Order of the Sun, First Degree

المره almará *f.* Almara (district, Khost)

المغرب almaghrib *m.* almaghréb 1 Morocco 2 countries of the Magreb (i.e., those in northwest African Arabic-speaking lands)

المغربي almaghribí almaghrebí 1 Moroccan 2 *m.* Moroccan (person)

الم غلم alam-ghalám 1.1 good-for-nothing, dissolute 1.2 reckless 2 *m.* .1 intriguer, plotter; cheat, swindler 2.2 nonsense, fiddlesticks 2.3 inarticulateness 2.4 *dialect* swindle, fraud, trickery

المناک alamnā́k 1 agonizing, painful 2 sad, melancholy; sorrowful

المنیوم almunijúm *m. plural* المونیم almunijə́m *m. plural* aluminum

المه ulmá *f.* ویره المه fine weather, clear weather

المیه alamijá ☞ په الميه طرز المناک sadly, dolorously

النگار alingár *m.* the Allingar River

النگه alangá *f.* wall

آلو 1 ālú *m.* [*plural:* آلوگان ālugā́n] plum

آلو 2 āló *interjection* hello

الو 3 alú *m. regional* potato

الو 4 aló ☞ للو

الو 5 aló *m. proper name* Alo

الو 6 ulú *m.* kindling wood (i.e., dead brush, fallen branches)

الو 7 uló̀v *m.* ☞ اولو 2

الواح alvā́h *m. Arabic plural* ☞ لوح

الوار alvā́r *m. plural* wood; lumber; timber (logs)

الوان alvā́n *Arabic* **1** *m. plural of* لون **2** *m.* cotton print, brightly-colored cloth (used for shawls, dresses)

آلوبالو ālubālú *m. singular & plural* cherries

آلوبخارا ālubukhārā́ *f.* Bukharian plum; prunes

الوت¹ alvút *m.* flight کول الوت to fly away, take off

الوت² alvút *imperative of* الوتل

الوتک alvuták alvaták **1** flying **2** being fledged, becoming fledged (of nestlings)

الوتکه alvutáka *f.* aircraft, airplane ببری ورونکي الوتکي aircraft carrier بم غورزونکي ويشتونکي توپ الوتکي antiaircraft gun حربي الوتکه bomber د military aircraft, بم اچوونکي الوتکه airdrome الوتکو میدان ground-attack aircraft ښکاري بريد الوتکه fighter aircraft جتي الوتکه jet aircraft, دجټ الوتکه

الوتل alvutál alvatál *Eastern* **1** الوزي *present tense* والوت *past* وابه لوزي *future perfective intransitive* **1.1** to fly **1.2** to take off; be launched (in air) **1.3** to be blown up **1.4** *electrical engineering* to burn out **1.5** to fly away; be detached, be broken off **1.6** to blow; rise (of the wind) نن سور باد راالوزي A cold wind is blowing today. سيلی والوته A blizzard is blowing up. **1.7** to evaporate, lose fragrance, go flat (of a concentrate solution, perfume); disappear, volatilize, disappear into thin air **1.8** to fade, lose color (of paint, dye) **1.9** to turn yellow; grow pale (a face) بنه یي الوتي ده دغه ده مخه ښخه رنگ والوت He grew pale. **2** *m. plural* **2.1** flight, flying **2.2** explosion *idiom* نفس يي والوت He died. **a** رنگ يي والوت He lost his head. **b** He grew pale. اوبه یي عقل دي والوت! You have gone out of your mind. الوتلي دي He has sunk down (morally).

الوتنه alvutə́na *f.* **1** flight; flying **2** explosion **3** take-off

الوتونکی alvutúnkaj **1** *present participle of* الوتل **2** *attributive* flying, pertaining to flight بم الوتونکی cruise missile

الوته alvutə́ *m. plural* ☞ الوتنه

آلوچه āludzhá *f.* آلوچه aluchá *f.* alycha (a kind of damson)

الوڅ alvúdz *present stem of* الوتل

الوځول alvudzavál *transitive* ☞ الوزول

الوڅه alutsá *f.* الوڅه alótsa alycha (a kind of damson) *idiom* سترگي الوڅه کول to screw up one's eyes

آلود ālúd *combining form* stained, soiled, covered with blood خون آلود gory, bloodstained

الوداعي alvidā́í *attributive* parting, valedictory الوداعي سلام farewell, leave-taking الوداعي سلام ته تلل to pay a farewell visit; go/say goodbye

آلوده āludá *indeclinable* stained, bloodstained

الوزول alvuzavál **1** *transitive* وا بي لوزي *future prefective* وائي *present tense* **1.1** to make to fly, arise, rise up; toss up, throw up کوتره الوزول to release pigeons **1.2** to pilot (an aircraft) **1.3** to blow up پل په هوا الوزول د to blow up a bridge توپ په مخ کښی الوزول، په توپ کښی الوزول to shoot one who has been lashed to the muzzle of a cannon (a form of capital punish in former times) **1.4** to fan (flames) **1.5** to winnow (grain)

1.6 to blow off, carry away (by wind) **1.7** to evaporate **1.8** to separate, detach, chip off; chop off; break off **1.9** *electrical engineering* to burn through, burn out فيوز الوزول to burn out a fuse **1.10** to break, break up د سر ماغزه الوزول to smash one's skull **1.11** to kill, get someone out of the way **1.12** to spend frivolously; squander, waste, throw to the winds **2** *m. plural* **2.1** piloting (e.g., an aircraft) **2.2** explosion

الوزوونکی alvuzavúnkaj **1** *present participle of* الوزول **2** *m.* pilot, flier

الوزي alvúzi *present tense of* الوتل

اولس ulús *m.* ☞ اولس

اولسي ulusí ☞ اولسي

الول alvál **1** sinuous, tortuous **2** collapsing, tumbling down پربوتل to collapse, tumble (in ruins) **3** disorderly

الومنيوم aluminijúm *m. plural* aluminum

الون بلون alun-balún *m.* concern, alarm توله شپه مي په الون بلون تېره کړه I spent the whole night in a state of alarm.

الونجا alunjā́ in hiding; disappeared from sight، تر سترگي الونيا کول، ستر سترگي الونيا کېدل to be hidden from sight, disappear, vanish

الوول aluvál ☞ الول

الوييل alvojál *transitive* [*past:* وايي لوويه] **1** to burn **2** to fry, grill **3** to torture, torment

الوهيت uluhiját *m. Arabic* **1** deity **2** divinity

الوی¹ alávaj álvaj **1** fried, grilled **2** tortured, tormented

الوژ² alvə́j *f.* roasting of an ear of corn

الوېزان alvezā́n upset, pained, grieved

الوېښ alvéǩh *m. plural* light wind, breeze

آله ālá *f. Arabic* **1** device; tool, apparatus; contrivance; machine tool د ساز آله musical instrument د مساحي آله rangefinder د نشر آله radio transmitter د چا د لاس آله **2** *figurative* a tool د آلي کرېدل to be a tool in someone's hands **3** *grammar* agent اسم noun of agent

اله iláh *m. Arabic* God

الها ilahā́ *Arabic interjection* oh God

الهام ilhā́m *m. Arabic* [*plural:* الهامونه ilhāmúna *Arabic plural:* الهامات ilhāmā́t] **1** suggestion; inducement الهام کول *compound verb* to suggest to someone **2** inspiration الهام اخيستل to inspire **3** stimulus, incentive

اله بله alá-balá *f.* cry, howl

اله ټيک alatsík *m.* thawed patch

اله ستي alásti *f. plural* rashly spoken word

اله گوله ála-gúla *f.* اله گله alá-gulá *f.* **1** riot, revolt, sedition; disturbances **2** noise اله گوله کول **a** to rebel, revolt; instigate disturbances **b** to make a noise, be noisy

الهنگ alháng *m. regional* **1** sorrowful weeping **2** torments, agonies, sad experiences

اله ورتي alavráti *f. plural* ☞ اله ستي

اله وی alávaj *interjection* **1** ow, it hurts **2** ouch

آلهه ālihá *m. Arabic plural* divinity

الهي ilahí *Arabic* **1** divine; celestial, heavenly **2** *interjection* oh God

الهيات ilahiját *m. Arabic plural* theology

آلي [1] ālí *attributive* toolmaking; used for making tools

الى [2] aláj *interjection* **1** oh, oh really, my God دا دي څه وکړه الى! Oh! Oh! What have you done!

الياس iljás *m. Arabic proper name* Ilyas

الياف aljáf *m. Arabic plural from* ليف

اليافي aljáfí *Arabic* fibrous اليافي جسم a fibrous substance

اليت پليت alit-palít *regional* **1** turned head over heels **2** *m.* disorders; disturbances

الي ځلي áli-dzáli *f. plural* request for forgiveness, request for absolution

الپسکا aleská *f.* Alaska

اليش alísh substituted, replaced

الیشنگ alisháng *m.* the Alishang River

الیشول alishavól *denominative, transitive* [*past:* الیش یې کړ] **1** to change, exchange, replace کالي الیشول to change (one's clothes) **2** to change, alter پوست الیشول to shed hair (of animals) *passive* الیشېدل کېدل

الیشېدل alishedól *denominative, intransitive* [*past:* الیش شو] to be changed, be exchanged, be replaced سره الیشېدل to alternate, take turns اوبه په توبن الیشېږي The water is turning to steam. **2** الیشېدونکی

الیشېدونکی alishedúnkaj **1** *present participle of* الیشېدل changeable, unstable, inconstant

الیشېده alishedó *m. plural* **1** substitution; change د عنوان الیشېده a change of address **2** change, alteration, transformation

الیف alíf *m. plural* drying oil

اِلېکشن ilekshán *m. regional* elections; electoral campaign

الیوشان aliushán د الیوشن جزيري the Aleutian Islands

الیه ilájh *Arabic combining form* مشار الیه mentioned in passing, referred to

الویل alejól *transitive* الویل

آم [1] ām *m.* ام am *m.* امه

ام [2] um اوم

ام [3] um *f.* umm *Arabic* mother

ام [4] um هم

اما ammā *Arabic conjunction* however, but هم اما however

اماج amádzh *m.* اماچ amách *m.* omelet with greens

آمادگي āmādagí *f.* **1** readiness, preparation **2** procurement د ازوغ آمادگي procurement of fodder

آماده āmādá *indeclinable* **1** ready; prepared ... موږ ته آماده يو چه We are ready. **2** laid in, prepared **a** آماده کول to prepare, make ready **b** to lay in, store, ready آماده کېدل **a** to be ready, be prepared **b** to be laid in, be stored, be readied **3** susceptible (to illnesses)

امارت imārát *m. Arabic* **1** emirate, principality **2** power, authority

امارگه umārgá *f.* boil (on children)

امازون amāzón *m.* the Amazon River

اماکن amākín *m. Arabic plural from* مكن

آمال āmāl *m. Arabic plural from* امل [3]

ام البلاد umm-al-bilád *f. Arabic history* the Mother of Cities (i.e., Balkh)

آماله [1] amālá *f. Arabic* enema

اماله [2] imālā *f. Arabic linguistics* softening of a vowel sound

امام imám *m. Arabic* **1** imam; chief priest; spiritual leader **2** religious minister (leader of prayer) **3** *figurative* leader, teacher

امامت imāmát *m. Arabic* the rank of imam

امان amán *m. Arabic* **1** security; calm په امان کېدل د يو شي څخه to be protected from something **2** mercy; pardon, amnesty امان بخښنل to spare, show mercy to امان غوښتنل to ask for mercy; ته امان ورکول throw oneself at the mercy of the conqueror چا to spare, show mercy to, forgive someone, give amnesty to someone *idiom* په امان! د خداى Goodbye!

امانت amānát *m. Arabic* **1** honesty, conscientiousness, decency امانت ساتل to be honest **2** goods or money put into escrow or loaned for temporary use **3** custody **4** guardianship, trusteeship **5** power of attorney **6** *finance* deposit, account امانت اېښودل to make a deposit, deposit, deposit money into an account وجوه هغه چه خلق يي په بانکو کښي امانت ږدي the total assets deposited by a population in banks **7** security; calm

امانت دار amānatdár *Arabic* **1** honest, conscientious, decent; worthy of confidence **2** *m.* trustee, custodian, guardian

امانت داري amānatdārí *f.* honesty, conscientiousness, decency په پوره امانت داری completely honestly

امانت کار amānatkár *Arabic* امانت دار

امانت کاري amanatkārí *f.* devotion; honesty

امانت گر amānatgár امانت دار

امانت گري amānatgarí *f.* امانت داري

امانتي amānatí **1** deposited to an account **2** place in trust, given into custody زما روپۍ د هغه سره امانتي دي He has charge of my money. **3** under guardianship

امان جن amāndzhán sorrowful, sad

اماني [1] amāní **1** relating to the rule of King Amanully-Khan **2** *f. history* amani (a coin minted in the time of Amanully-Khan)

اماني [2] amāní *Arabic* sound, worthy of confidence (of money, goods, property) اماني کول to entrust, deposit, make a deposit **a** روپۍ اماني کول to keep money (in a safe place) **b** روپۍ اماني اېښودل to put money aside

اماني [3] amāní *Eastern* quite; all; entirely, in full

امب amb *m.* the Amb River

امبا umbá *f.* bleating of sheep

امبار ambár *m.* **1** sewage; manure **2** fertilizer د امبار جوړولو کارخانه agricultural fertilizer factory; chemical fertilizer plant مځکي ته امبار اچول، مځکي ته امبار ورکول to fertilize the soil امبار خورل to be fertilized **3** storehouse, barn **4** heap, pile (of manure) **5** haystack, hayrick **6** trash, rubbish

امبارخانه ambārkhāná *f.* **1** storeroom **2** warehouse **3** *regional* barn; grain-storage facility

امبارکښ ambārkákh *m.* one who collects dung, manure, etc. for use as fertilizer

امبالوج ambālój *f.* seat with canopy (on the back of an elephant), howdah

امبریالوجي embriālodzhí *f.* embryology

امبر چمبر ambár-chambár *regional* **1** wound around, twined around, wrapped (i.e., with a blanket) **2** interlaced گوتي امبر چمبر کول to interlace the fingers

امبور ambúr *m.* ☞ انبور

امبولانس ambuláns *m.* ambulance

امبوه ambóh ☞ انبوه

امبه ambá *f.* mango (tree or its fruit)

امپراتریس impirātrís *f.* empress

امپراتور impirātúr *m.* emperor

امپراتوري impirāturí امپراطوریت impirāturiját *m.* empire

امپریالزم impirjālízm *m.* imperialism

امپریالیست impirjālíst *m.* imperialist

امپریالیستي impirjālístí *indeclinable* imperialistic

امپول ampúl *m.* ampule

امت ummát *m. Arabic* religious community, flock

امتثال imtisāl *m. Arabic* following, obedience to someone د فرمان امتثال in execution of the order په امتثال

امتحان imtihān *Arabic* **1** test, check-up د چا امتحان کول to test someone **2** examination تقریري امتحان oral examination زباني امتحان to take an examination امتحان اخیستل to pass an examination امتحان ورکول He failed the examination. امتحان یې نامنظور شو

امتحانول imtihānavól *denominative, transitive* **1** [*past:* امتحان یې کړ] to check up on, test **2** to examine

امتحاني imtihāní *Arabic* **1** *attributive* test, check-up **2** examination

امتداد imtidād *m. Arabic* **1** extent, stretch, duration د سرک په امتداد کښي for the duration of the journey, along the route **2** prolongation, extension امتداد ورکول to prolong, extend

امتدادي imtidādí *Arabic* continued, extended, prolonged

امتزاج imtizā-dzh *m. Arabic* **1** blend; blending **2** *chemistry* combination

امتناع imtinā' *f. Arabic* refusal, rejection; abstention from something دیو شي څخه امتناع کول to reject, abstain from something

امتناعي imtinā'í preventative, deterrent امتناعي تدابیر preventative measures امتناعي طب *medicine* prophylaxis

امتنان imtinān *m. Arabic* thankfulness, gratitude د چا څخه امتنان کول to thank someone, express gratitude to someone

امته amtá *f.* **1** reliance, hope, expectation **2** wish, desire امته کول **a** to hope, entertain hope, have expectations **b** to wish

امته دار amtadār **1** hoping for something **2** achieving, attaining something

امتیاز imtijāz *m. Arabic* [*plural:* امتیازونه imtijāzúna *Arabic plural:* امتیازات imtijāzắt] **1** difference, distinction; peculiarity د قومیت امتیاز ورکول national traits to distinguish, differentiate امتیاز لرل **a** to be distinguished, be differentiated **b** to occupy the first places لوږ _ میندل to be distinguished for, be notable for امتیاز پري گران وي It is hard to tell them apart. **2** advantage; privilege **3** *economics* concession امتیازات ورکول to grant concessions

امتیازنامه imtijāznāmá *f. Arabic economics* concessive agreement

امتیازي imtijāzí *Arabic* **1** distinctive, different from; special امتیازي معاش special rate; special pay rate **2** advantaged; privileged; preferred **3** *economics* concessional امتیازي سیمه settlement, concession (e.g., the International Settlement in Shanghai in pre-1949 China)

امثال amsál *m. Arabic plural from* مثل [1, 2]

امحا imhắ *f. Arabic* destruction, annihilation دښمن امحا کول destruction of the enemy

امحاکار imhākắr destroying, annihilating امحاکار اور annihilating fire

آمد āmád *m.* **1** arrival **2** income, receipts **3** assets; resources **4** *combining form* capable of use کار آمد useful, necessary; fit, suitable

امداد imdād *m. Arabic* assistance, support مقدماتي امداد first aid مالي امداد pecuniary aid

امدادي imdādí *Arabic military* auxiliary امدادي لښکر reinforcement

آمدن āmadán *m. plural* **1** arrival **2** income; receipts آمدن او مصرف income and expenditures

آمدني āmadaní *f.* income

آمدورفت āmad-u-ráft *m.* **1** arrival and departure; traffic; regular roundtrip traffic between two points **2** intercourse, connection, communication آمدورفت کول **a** to ply (a route) **b** to visit, frequent

آمر [1] āmír *m. Arabic* [*plural:* آمران āmirắn *Arabic plural:* آمرین āmirín] **1** chief د شعبې آمر department chief **2** staff officer **3** leader; manager **4** sovereign **5** person who gives commissions or instructions to others

امر [2] amr *m. Arabic* [*plural:* امرونه amrúna *Arabic plural:* اوامر avāmír] **1** order, instruction عملیاتي امر operational order تر امر لاندي subordinate د چا تر امر لاندي under someone's orders; subordinate to someone پر چا امر کول، و چاته امر ورکول to order someone, command someone امر صادرول to issue an order و چاته امر فرمایل to command someone **2** *grammar* imperative mood

امر [3] ámr *m.* ámər *Arabic* [*plural:* امور umúr] matter, affair, the state of affairs, the circumstances دا طبیعي امر دئ چه ... It is understood that ... It is natural that ...

امرا umrắ umarắ *m. Arabic plural from* امیر

امراض amrắz *m. Arabic plural from* مرض

امیران amirắn *m. plural* **1** *from* امر **2** senior officer complement

امرير amrbár *m. Arabic* messenger, orderly, runner منصبدار امرير liaison officer

امريري amrbarí *f. Arabic* the job of orderly, messenger or runner

امرت amrút *m.* guava (the fruit)

امرسه amrasá *f.* "amrasa" (a kind of a sweet dish made of flour, boiled butter and syrup)

امروت amrút *m.* امرود amrúd *m.* 1 ☞ امرت 2 pear (the fruit)

امروزه amrozá *regional* on the very same day

آمره āmíra *f.* head, chief (female)

امري amrí *Arabic* وجه امري *grammar* imperative mood

آمريت āmiriját *m. Arabic* 1 authority, supremacy د چا تر آمريت لاندي راتلل to be under someone's authority 2 leadership; management آمريت كول a to lead, be chief b to command, have someone at one's disposition 3 job, post, position

امريكا amriká *f.* America د امريكا متحده اضلاع، د امريكا متحده ولايتونه، د امريكا متحده رياستونه the United States of America شمالي امريكا North America جنوبي امريكا South America مركزي امريكا Central America

امريكائي amrikāí امريكني armikaní *regional* 1 American 2 *m.* American (person)

امريكه amriká *f.* ☞ امريكا

امړی umŕáj ☞ لمړی [1]

امزری əmzaráj *m. Eastern* tiger په خپل كور كښي سپي هم امزری وي *proverb* In one's own home the dog is a tiger. د امزري په غار *proverb literal* in the tiger's lair lie كښي د امزري بچي پراته وي tiger cubs *figurative* Like father, like son. اوده امزری ولي *saying* Do not awaken a sleeping tiger. وينبوي؟

امزولی amzólaj *m.* ☞ همزولی [1]

امسا amsá *f.* stick, walking stick, staff

امسته amastá *f.* 1 arrangement, adaptation 2 *agriculture* scion, graft

امضا imzá *f. Arabic* signature د امضاٴ ځای the place for a signature امضاٴ كول *compound verb* to sign امضاٴ كېدل to be signed

امغانه əmghānā *f. dialect* groin

امغلن umghalán 1 unripe 2 embryonic, incipient, rudimentary

امكان imkán *m. Arabic* possibly; feasibility د امكان پر قدر، د امكان په صورت كښي to the extent possible امكان تر اندازي پوري if possible د امكان لرل impracticable د امكان د دائرې څخه بهر to have the possibility ... امكان لري چه... It is possible that ... د ورتگ امكان to turn out to be possible; come true امكان پيداكول دا كار د امكان نه لري دئ It is... يې هم نه و will be difficult to bring this matter to fruition. He could not even come.

امكان بخش imkānbákhsh possible; practicable

امكاني imkāní *Arabic* امكاني وجه، امكاني صيغه *grammar* the potential form

امل amál *m.* 1 aim, goal, object, end, purpose د ساتني له امله for defense purposes دغه مطلب ته د رسېدلو له امله For the sake of attaining this goal. 2 reason, basis د ... له امله for the reason

له همدې امله ده چه that ..., in view of the fact that ..., because ... هم له دې امله چه ... ... for this very reason, that ...

امل amál *m.* drug addiction [2]

امل amál *m. Arabic* [*plural:* املونه amalúna *Arabic plural:* آمال āmā́l] hope, expectation [3]

املا imlā́ *f. Arabic* 1 dictation املا ليكل to transcribe diction املا ويل to dictate 2 spelling, orthography معياري املا standardized spelling املا دي غلطه ده You write with errors.

املاك amlā́k *m. Arabic plural from* ملاك 2 chief of د املاكو مدير the directorate of state property

املائي imlājí orthographic

املوك amlúk *m.* املوكه amúka *f. plural* a kind of persimmon *idiom* د املوكو په تول راغئ *saying* He suffered along with his pals.

امله amlá *f.* ☞ امله كول حمله to attack someone او چاته امله كول

آمله āmlá *f.* a kind of myrtle

املي amalí *m.* 1 smoker 2 drug addict 3 drunkard [1]

املى imlə́j *f. botany* tamarind [2]

املجل amlejə́l *transitive* [*past:* واملېبه ده] to hide, conceal

امن amn *m. Arabic* 1 security, tranquillity, peace امن كول a to secure (e.g., tranquillity, peace) b to make secure جهاني امن په to مسئله په امن فيصله كول to threaten the peace خطر كښي اچول settle a question by peaceful means په امن و امان كښي ژوندون كول to live peacefully, live in tranquillity بيا امن امان شه *Eastern* Complete tranquillity was reestablished. 2 order [1]

امن amə́n thoughtful, serious [2]

امن imə́n calming, consoling [3]

امنا amaná *f.* consent, assent امنا كول to agree, assent

امن پسند amnipasánd peace loving امن پسند خلك peace loving people

امنته amantá *f.* snow mixed with rain, sleet

امن كوت amankóṭ *m.* 1 asylum, refuge, place of refuge 2 stronghold

امنول amənavə́l *denominative, transitive* [*past:* امن يې كړ] to calm, soothe

امنه اماني amína-amāní *f.* peace, tranquillity

امنيت aminiját *m. Arabic* 1 security, tranquillity د امنيت شورا، امنيت مجلس Security Council 2 *military* protection, security

امنيتي aminijatí pertaining to security

امنېدل aminedə́l *denominative, intransitive* [*past:* امن شو] to be calmed

امنيه amnijá *f. Arabic* 1 security امنيه مجلس، امنيه شورا Security Council 2 security police

آمو āmú *m.* د آمو درياب، د آمو سيند the Amu Darya River

امواج amvā́dzh *m. Arabic plural from* موج د برق امواج electrical currents

اموال amvā́l *m. Arabic plural from* مال

اموخت amókht *m.* 1 habit د يو شي سره اموخت نيول to grow accustomed to something 2 practice, custom, wont

اموخته amokhtá amukhtá *indeclinable* **1** knowing something; being accustomed to something زه په سګرېټو اموخته نه يم I do not have the smoking habit. **2** tamed; tame اموخته کول **a** to train په زيار اموخته کول to train for work **b** to tame, domesticate اموخته کېدل **a** to be trained; make oneself familiar with **b** to be tamed بلا په بسم الله نه منع کېږي *proverb* It is hard to break bad habits. اموخته باز *idiom folklore* the serene falcon

اموختگي amokhtagí *f.* **1** state of being tame, state of being domesticated **2** knowledge of locality

امور umúr *m. Arabic plural from* امر جاري امور current matters خيريه امور philanthropy, charity

امور² amúr *m.* the Amur River

امورات umurā́t *m. second plural from* امور¹

آموز āmúz āmóz *combining form* سبق آموز instructive نو آموز novice نو آموزه افراد recruits

امومت umumát *m. Arabic* **1** maternity **2** matriarchy

امونيا amonijā́ *f. chemistry* ammonia, ammonium hydrate

امونيک amonják *chemistry* ammoniac

امه¹ áma *f.* mango (the tree or its fruit)

امه² umә́ *from* اومه²

امه³ umá ☞ اومه³

امهال imhā́l *m. Arabic* postponement; delay, procrastination

امي¹ amí *m.* ignoramus

امي² ammí *Arabic* ummí *Eastern* **1** illiterate, uneducated **2** *m. & f.* ignoramus

امياني¹ amjāní *f.* handbag, purse, wallet, money belt

امياني² amjāní *f. plural from* امي² ²

آمېب āméb *m.* āmíb amoeba

آمېبك āmebík آمېبك پېچ amebic dysentery

امبد uméd *m.* umíd *m.* **1** hope, expectation مخالف د دي امبد څخه despite expectations زما د دي کار څخه امبد ختلئ و I lost hope for this. د ژوند څخه يي امبد ختلئ و He gave himself up completely to despair. امبد کول to nourish a hope, hope ... امبد کېږي چه to give rise to hope, instill hope امبد ورکول to nourish hope, hope that ... امبد لرل There is no hope that this matter will succeed. ... قوي امبد مي دئ چه I hope very much that ... د هغه د جوړېد و هيڅ امبد نشته There is no hope for his recovery. زه در ته په امبد کېني وم **a** I rely on you. **b** I expect you. بي امبده شيطان دئ *proverb* While there is life there is hope. **2** *proper name* Umed

امبدافزا umedafzā́ امبد بخښونکی uméd bakhkhúnkaj giving rise to hope, reassuring

امبدوار umedvā́r **1.1** hoping for something ... زه امبدوارم چه I hope that ... **1.2** optimistic mood **2** *m.* candidate, competitor

امبدوارول umedvāravól *denominative, intransitive* [*past:* امبد يي کړ] to give rise to, instill hope

امبدواره umedvā́ra *f.* pregnant

امبدواري¹ umedvārí *f.* **1** hope, expectation **2** pregnancy

امبدواري² umedvāri *plural from* امبدواره

امىده amidá *m. & f.* namesake

امير amír *m. Arabic* [*plural:* اميران amirā́n *Arabic plural:* امرا umarā́] **1** ruler; emir; prince; nobleman اميران و وزيران noblemen **2** military leader **3** *proper name* Amir

اميرال amirā́l *m.* اميرالبحر amir-ul-báhr *m. Arabic* admiral

اميرانه admirāná *Arabic* princely

اميرزاده amirzādá **1** *m.* son of an emir; prince; young son of a prince **2** *f.* daughter of an emir; princess; young daughter of a prince

اميري amirí **1** pertaining to an emir, princely **2** *f.* **.1** emir's, prince's court **2.2** emirate, principality آمبز اميري āméz *combining form* being mixed up; mixed, blended رنگ آمبز painted, colored

امبزان amezā́n *m.* the Amazon River

آمبزش āmezísh *m.* blending, mixture

امبل amél *m.* **1** necklace **2** wreath; garland **3** *proper name* Amel لاسونه امبل کول *idiom* to throw one's arms around someone's neck

آمين¹ āmín *Arabic* **1** amen; so be it **2** *m.* amen آمينونه ويل to say amen آمين آمين تا سره! *idiom Eastern* I wish you the same!

امين² amín *Arabic* **1** correct, reliable, conscientious دپه امين سړی دئ He is a very reliable person. **2** *m.* **.1** confidential agent, proxy **2.2** guardian **2.3** arbitrator **2.4** *proper name* Amin, Emin امين الدين Aminuddin امين الله Aminulla

امين توب amintób *m.* guardianship; trusteeship

امينکي amínki amen, so be it

امين والی aminvā́laj *m.* reliability, faithfulness, conscientiousness

آن¹ ān *m. Arabic* instant, moment هرآن all the time; every minute په يوه آن، په يوه آن کښي in an instant, at once, instantly, immediately in a twinkling آن تمامول *idiom* to try with all one's might آن مي پر تمام کئ چه راسه، نه راغئ *Western* I tried to persuade him in every way, but he did not come. د هغه اوس آن *Western* He is at death's door. آن منل to submit to, be reconciled with اوستري ته يي آن ومانه In the final analysis they submitted to their fate. In the end they were reconciled to their lot.

آن² on **1** exactly; precisely **2** right up to پوري ان تر... even up to ..., right up to

آن³ ān *plural suffix usually for animate nouns* باز بازان hawk *plural* hawks

انا anā́ *f.* [*plural:* اناگانی anāgā́ni *plural:* اناوي anā́vi] grandmother انا کېدل **a** to be a grandmother **b** to mature early; become mature early, become grown up (of a girl) **c** to grow wise, be wise انا مړه شوه، تبه يي وشلېده *idiom* This matter is already a thing of the past.

آناً ā́nán *Arabic* instantly, at once, right away

اناب anā́b *m. plural botany* any member of low shrubs of the Buckthorn family

اناتوم anātóm *m.* anatomist

اناتومي anátomí 1 f. anatomy حيواني اناتومي animal anatomy نباتي اناتومي plant anatomy 2 anatomical

اناتیتی anatə́j f. blindman's-bluff (the children's game)

اناثي inásí Arabic feminine, woman's ليسه اناثیه، اناثي ليسه lisá-ji women's secondary school

انادول anādól m. Anatolia

انار anár m. singular & plural pomegranate د انار دانه pomegranate (the fruit) د انار شربت pomegranate juice د انار اوبه pomegranate syrup د انار پوستکي ☞ انار پوست

انارپوست anārpóst m. pomegranate rind

اناردره anārdará f. Anardara (district)

آنارشي ānārshí f. anarchy

آنارشیزم ānārchizm m. anarchism

آنارشیست ānārshíst m. anarchist

آنارکي anārkí f. ☞ آنارشي

اناركیزم anārkízm m. 1 anarchism 2 anarchy

انارواٌلا anārvālá m. seller of pomegranates

اناطول anātól ☞ انادول

انافلس anáfeles m. anopheles mosquito, malarial mosquito

انانس anáns m. regional announcement, notice

انانگه anāngá f. cheek

انانیت ananiját m. Arabic 1 egotism 2 arrogance

اناواٌت anāvā́t m. dialect 1 damage, loss 2 ☞ اناوت

اناواٌلی anāvā́laj m. position of a grandmother (in a family)

اناوٌت anāvát m. scrap business, scrap

انائي unā́i m. د انائي دره the Unai Pass

انائي anā́ji m. fool, blockhead

انبار ambár m. ☞ امبار

انبارخانه ambārkhāná f. ☞ امبارخانه

انباروٌل ambāravə́l denominative [past: انبار یې کړ] 1 to put (down, together, in, on) 2 to put or lay (in, on) لاندي باندي انباروٌل to pile one on another 3 to drift (e.g., of snow)

انباریدٌل ambāredə́l intransitive [past: انبارشو] 1 to be put, be placed, be piled (on one another) 2 to be drifted

انبالٌی ambālə́j f. ☞ امبالي

انبساط inbisát m. Arabic 1 gaiety, joy, delight 2 broadening, expansion

انبور ambúr m. tongs, pincers

انبوه amboh 1 numerous 2 m. crowd, gathering (of people)

انبوهي ambohí f. abundance, plenty

اٌنبه ambá f. mango

انبیا anbijá m. Arabic plural from نبي

انبیق ambík m. انبیک ambík m. still, distillation apparatus

انتاج intā́dzh m. Arabic 1 production; creation 2 produce; product 3 work (of art, literature, etc.)

انتارکتک antārktík m. Antarctica د انتارکتک قاره the continent of Antarctica

انتان intán m. festering, suppuration, abscessing انتان لرل to fester, suppurate

انتان antán m. history the Entente

انتباٌ intibá f. intibáh Arabic 1 cheerfulness, courage 2 awakening د انتباه دوره the Renaissance 3 vigilance, circumspection

انتباهنامه intibāhnāmá f. appeal, leaflet, broadside

انتجاع intidzhá' f. Arabic foraging

انتحار intihár m. Arabic suicide

انتحال intihál m. Arabic plagiarism

انتخاب intikháb m. Arabic 1 election, selection, choice بیا نوی انتخاب انتخابول compound verb ☞ انتخاب کول reelection 2 biology selection طبیعي انتخابدل compound verb ☞ انتخابدل، کېدل natural selection

انتخابات intikhābā́t m. Arabic plural from انتخاب elections پټ انتخابات secret ballot د انتخاباتو اصولنامه election statute عمومي انتخابات electoral district د انتخاباتو دائره electoral law د انتخاباتو حق انتخابات direct elections مستقیم انتخابات general elections نوی انتخابات reelection

انتخاباتي دوره intikhābātí electoral, pertaining to elections the term of a convocation or session (e.g., of a parliament)

انتخاب کوونکی intikháb kavúnkaj m. elector, voter

انتخابول intikhābavə́l denominative [past: انتخاب یې کړ] to elect

انتخابوونکی intikhabāvúnkaj 1 present participle from انتخابول 2 elector; voter

انتخابي intikhābí 1 electoral; voting 2 sports elimination

انتخابېدٌل intikhābedə́l denominative [past: انتخاب شو] to be elected په ریاست نوی انتخابېدٌل to be elected مجدداً انتخابېدٌل He was elected chairman. انتخاب شو

انتخابېدونکی intikhābedúnkaj 1 present participle from انتخابېدٌل 2 person elected, candidate elected

انتداب intidā́b m. Arabic mandate

انتدابي intidābí Arabic mandate, pertaining to mandate

انتراسیت antrāsít m. plural anthracite

انترس interés interest

انترکس antráks m. medicine malignant anthrax

انترنېشنلزم interneshanalízm m. internationalism

انتروپولودژي antropolodzhí f. anthropology

انتروشی antróshaj m. sneezing

انتساب intisáb m. Arabic 1 relationship, connection; belonging 2 origin, provenance 3 preface, foreword

انتشار intishár m. Arabic [plural: انتشارونه intishārúna Arabic plural: انتشارات intishārát] Arabic 1 dissemination (e.g., of rumors) 2 publication, promulgation د راډیو انتشار installation of radio receivers on a broad basis a انتشار میندل to be disseminated (of rumors) b to be published, be promulgated 3 dispersion 4 finance issuance

انتصاب intisáb m. Arabic establishing, fixing, setting, designating

انتصابي intisābí having been fixing; set, designated

انتصار intisár m. Arabic victory

انتظار intizā́r m. Arabic 1 waiting, awaiting د انتظار خونه، د انتظار having waited for a while ترلرِ انتظار وروسته انتظارخانه ☞ کوټه to wait, await انتظار ايستل، انتظار کښل، انتظار کول، په انتظار اوسېدل For whom is he waiting? هغه د چا انتظار کوي؟ They expect that … انتظار کږي چه ... وکئ I waited all day ستاسي انتظار لرم I am waiting for you. 2 hope, expectation

انتظارخانه intizā́rkhānā f. 1 reception room 2 waiting room

انتظام intizā́m m. Arabic 1 order ښه انتظام organization, orderliness 2 administration, management 3 arrangement, organization 4 measure انتظام کول a to administer something, manage something b to adjust, put something to rights د چايو a to set up tea-drinking, arrange tea-drinking b to انتظام کول prepare tea و يو شي ته انتظام ورکول to arrange something, organize something, adjust something انتظام پيدا کول to be arranged, be organized, be adjusted 5 regularity 6 installation; equipment idiom د وجود انتظام carriage, bearing

انتفاع intifā́' f. Arabic utilization, use

انتقاد intiķā́d m. Arabic criticism ادبي انتقاد literary criticism تر انتقاد لاندي راتلل to be انتقاد کول، انتقاد نيول subjected to criticism, be criticized

انتقال intiķā́l m. Arabic 1 transport, transportation 2 passage, transition 3 demise, passing, death انتقال کول a compound verb b to die 4 infection د مرض انتقال infection 5 انتقالول ☞ transference (e.g., of energy at a distance)

انتقالول intiķālavál denominative [past: انتقال يې کړ] 1 transfer; transport 2 assignation (e.g., of property rights)

انتقالي intiķālí 1 portable, transportable 2 transitional (e.g., of period) 3 progressive (of a movement)

انتقام intiķā́m m. Arabic 1 vengeance, retribution د چا څخه انتقام to avenge someone 2 repression اخيستل

انتورپ antvérp m. Antwerp (city)

انتومولوژي entomolozhí f. entomology

انتها intihā́ Arabic 1 f. end, edge; terminal point 2 attributive extreme, last, maximum تر انتها درجي پوري to the utmost degree, to the extreme degree

انتهاپسند intihāpasánd m. extremist

انتهائي intihāí 1 final, extreme, last, maximum انتهائي چابکوالی the ultimate speed, maximum velocity انتهائي حدود limit 2 senior, older

انتبي entebbé f. Entebbe (city)

انتي تېز antitéz antithesis انتيتيبز antitéz antithesis

انتي سائكلون antisā́jklon m. anticyclone

انتي سېرم antiserúm m. anti-diphtherial serum

انتيک antík antique, ancient انتيک او زاره شيان antiquities

انتيکه antiká f. rarity, rare thing, rare object

انتيل antíl د انتيل جزيري the Antilles (Islands)

انتن antén m. antenna چوکاتي انتن loop antenna د استقامت انتن directional antenna

انترانيټ intrāneṭ m. انترانېټ intrāneṭ intranet

انترنېشنلزم interneshanalízm internationalism

انتوشى anṭóshaj m. انتوشاج anṭóshaj m. sneezing; sneeze

انجام andzhā́m m. 1 end, conclusion, outcome په انجام رسول، انجام to be انجام مېندل ورکول to end, conclude, complete; execute ended, be concluded, be completed How will انجام به يې څه وي؟ انجام کېدل، انجامول ☞ compound verb this come out? انجامېدل ☞ compound verb 2 end, tip 3 extremity

انجامول andzhāmavál denominative [past: انجام يې کړ] to end, finish, complete, execute وظيفه انجامول to carry out his duties

انجامېدل andzhāmedál denominative [past: انجام شو] to be ended, finished, be completed; be executed, be carried out

انجذاب indzhizā́b Arabic 1 attraction, gravity د انجذاب قوه an attractive force 2 enthusiasm, bent, attraction

انجروت andzharút m. plural gum of milk vetch

انجړ andzhář 1 m. tangled skein 2.1 tangled, confused; in a tangle 2.2 complex د انجړي کلاوي سربنودل literal to tangle the skein

انجكشن indzhéksjon m. انجکشان indzhekshán m. injection, infusion; vaccination, inoculation انجکسيون کول to give an injection; an infusion, an inoculation

انجکه indzháka f. moan (of a person who is ill)

انجماد indzhimā́d m. Arabic 1 thickening, congealing, freezing د انجماد درجه freezing-point 2 hardening, thickening, callosity انجماد مېندل a to congeal, freeze b to harden 3 figurative state of being phlegmatic; apathy

انجمن [1] andzhumán m. 1 society, organization; meeting د کشافان The Afghan Boy Scout Organization 2 commission; committee د تحقيق انجمن preparatory committee; committee for legislative proposals 3 literary society

انجمن [2] andzhumán m. Andzhuman (valley, district in Badakhshan) د انجمن غاښى Andzhuman Pass

انجن indzhín m. [plural: انجنونه indzhinúna plural: انجنان indzhinā́n] 1 motor; engine د تېلو انجن internal combustion engine 2 locomotive د ريل انجن railroad engine

انجن خانه indzhinkhāná f. 1 railroad depot 2 machine room, engine room

انجنير indzhinír m. engineer د معدن انجنير mining engineer

انجنيري indzhinirí 1 attributive engineering 2 technology; subject matter of engineering

انجوري andzhorí f. kind of vegetable

انجه índzha f. ☞ هنجه

انجير andzhír m. medicine scrofula

انجيل [1] indzhíl m. gospel

انجيل [2] indzhíl m. Indzhil, Injil (district)

انچ inch m. inch

انچارج inchā́rdzh m. regional manager; administrator, head, chief

انچي inchí f. distance equal to an inch

انځر indzár m. singular & plural fig انځرو ونه fig, fig tree

انځکی andzəkáj f. moan (of a sick person)

انځور andzór *m.* **1** drawing, design انځور کول، انځور کښل to draw; cover with drawings **2** style

انځور کښلو وزله andzór kķhalū wázla *f.* imaging device

انځور کښنه andzorķshóna *f.* drawing

انځورگر andzorgár *m.* artist; graphic artist

انځورول andzoravúl *denominative* [past: انځور یې کړ] *Eastern* to draw; cover with drawings

انځوریز andzoríz drawn; covered with drawings, covered with designs; pictorial انځوریز لیک hieroglyphic letter, hieroglyphic document

انځوریز جال andzūríz dzhál *m. computer science* video network

انځیر indzír *m.* ☞ انځر

انځۍ intsə́j *f.* woolen thread د وړیو انځۍ woolen thread

انحراف inhiráf *m. Arabic* **1** deviation, digression انحراف کول to diverge, digress **2** *politics* deviation **3** *technology* deviation; derivation

انحرافي inhiráfí **1** *m.* deviationist **2** evasive, deviational

انحصار inhisár *m. Arabic* **1** monopoly د خارجي تجارت انحصار foreign trade monopoly **2** siege **3** quota for a certain person; reserving (credits, etc.) for an individual

انحصارات inhisárát *m. plural* **1** *from* انحصار **2** administration of state monopolies

انحصارول inhisáravúl *denominative* [past: انحصار یې کړ] **1** to monopolize **2** to reserve something for someone

انحصاري inhisárí monopolistic په انحصاري ډول monopolistically, on a monopolistic basis

انحصاریدل inhisáredə́l **1** *denominative* [past: انحصار شو] **.1** to be monopolized; be the object of a monopoly **1.2** to be reserved for someone **2** *m. plural* **.1** monopoly د مبوي انحصاریدل a monopoly in fruits **2.2** reserving

انحطاط inhitát *m. Arabic* **1** lowering, fall **2** decline, depression **3** disintegration; breakdown, ruin

انحلال inhilál *m. Arabic* **1** liquidation, annulment **2** dismissal (e.g., of parliament) **3** *economics* decline, depression **4** decline of forces, weakening **5** disintegration, decomposition

اند ¹ and *m.* **1** thought, reflection **2** worry, alarm; anxiety, cares

اند ² and *m.* 500-year time period

انداخت andákht *m.* shooting; firing مستور انداخت firing from concealment د انداخت میدان artillery salute د مراسمو انداخت firing range

انداختي andākhtí *attributive military* fire-; firing-

انداز andáz *combining form* **1** throwing, casting لنگر انداز casting anchor مین انداز mortar **2** *m.* **.1** style of expression, manner of expression **2.2** *regional* pose

اندازه andāzá *f.* **1** measure; dimensions په ډېره اندازه، په لویه اندازه to a considerable extent; on a large scale تر کمه اندازه to what extent? to what degree? په دې اندازه، په دې اندازه سره to such an extent یوه اندازه some quantity د حاجت په اندازه سره to the extent

په ممکنه اندازه excessively great تر اندازي زیات necessary تر کمه اندازه دا ښه والی ! excessive له اندازي وتلئ extent possible په ممکنه What good is this! تر یوي اندازي to a certain extent اندازه کول، اندازه لگول، اندازه اخیستل to the extent possible اندازه واتن *compound verb* **a** to measure something له خپلي اندازي څخه پښنه وړ measure a distance **b** to weigh, evalute اندي ایینول to undertake a task which is beyond one's strength or capabilities په خپله اندازه کوښښ کول to try to the extent of one's capabilities له اندازي نه زیات بارول to overload, load down excessively اندازه کېدل *compound verb* **a** to be measured, to come to **b** to be weighed, be evaluated **2** د ارزاقو اندازه norm ration scale **3** total (e.g., of a debt) **4** inner sole

اندازه گیری andāzagirí *f.* measuring, measurement د اندازه گیری آلات measuring instruments

اندازي andāzí *combining form* throwing دست اندازي encroachment on someone's rights

اندام andám *m.* **1** body; frame, figure **2** اندامونه extremity extremities, arms and legs

اندامان andāmán *m.* د اندامان بحیره the Andaman Sea

اندامور andāmavár tall, big

اندخوی andkhój *m.* Andkhoj (city, district)

انداراب andaráb *m.* **1** Andarab (district in Badakhshan) **2** Andarab (embankment in Kabul)

اندراج indirádzh *m. Arabic* **1** item, entry (e.g., in a periodical) **2** an entry on a list

اندرپایه andarpājá *f.* staircase

اندرکه andarká *f.* اندرکۍ andərkə́j *f.* short coat, short jacket

اندرمیعاد andár-i-mi'ád *regional* timely, on time

اندړ ¹ andə́ṛ **1** *m. plural* the Andary (Gilzaj tribe) **2** *m.* Andar tribesman **3** *m. plural* the Andar District

اندړ ² andə́ṛ *m.* yellow-colored songbird

اندکی indikáj *m. dialect* ☞ انکی

اندورا andorá *f.* Andorra د اندورا ښار Andorra (city)

اندوس índús *m.* the Indus River

اندوکارد endokárd *m. anatomy* endocardium

اندومان andomán *m.* ☞ اندامان

اندونیزیا indonezijá *f.* Indonesia

اندونیزیائي indonezijájí **1** Indonesian **2** Indonesian (person)

آنده ¹ ánda *f.* انده ánda *f.* thought, consideration

انده ² ində́ *m.* ☞ اینده

انده ³ índa *f.* full gulp انده کول to gulp; gulp down (liquid)

اندر andér *m.* **1** pitch darkness **2** misfortune

اندرۍ anderə́j *f.* crowd

اندیس ándís *m. plural* د اندیس غرونه the Andes

اندیشه andeshá *f.* ☞ اندېښنه

اندېښمن andeķhmón troubled, perturbed

اندېښنه andeķhná *f.* **1** concern; anxiety; thought اندېښنه کول to be concerned about someone, be anxious about someone اندېښنی be extremely worried, be alarmed, وهل، په اندېښنو کښي لوېدل to be extremely worried, be alarmed, be very concerned څه اندېښننه لرل to experience worry, to be worried, to have apprehensions 2 foresight

انديکاتور indikātór *m.* ☞

انډره anḏə́ra *f. anatomy* large intestine

انډو anḏú *m.* unripe boll of the cotton plant

انډوخر anḏokhar *m.* 1 ☞ لتپير 2 *figurative* crowd, assemblage

انډول¹ anḏól *m.* metal mortar

انډول² anḏvál *m.* 1 steadiness, equilibrium, balance 2 equal د چا انډول کول a to balance; equalize (in weight) b to compare په انډول کېږي لوبدل سره to measure oneself against someone 3 equivalent; equal amount

انډولي anḏolí 1.1 stable, brought into equilibrium 1.2 swinging, rocking to and fro 1.3 equivalent, of equal worth 2 *f.* equivalence; equal in meaning

انډونيزيا inḏoneshjā́ *f.* ☞ اندونېښيا

انډی¹ anḏáj *m.* 1 bale, load اندی کول to load up, load with 2 side

انډی² anḏəj *f.* soup

انډېری anḏeráj *m.* mat

انډیز anḏiz *m. plural* ☞ انډیس

انديکاټر indikā́ṭar *m.* log of incoming and outgoing papers; record log د انديکاټر کتاب a logbook for incoming and outgoing documents

انډی کونډی anḏáj-kunḏáj *f.* entertainment; treating of guest to refreshments

انډيوال anḏivál *m.* anḏevál 1 companion, friend; comrade 2 table companion 3 traveling companion; fellow traveler 4 accomplice

انډيواله anḏivála anḏevála *feminine of* انډيوال

انډيوالي andivālí *f.* andevālí 1 companionship; friendship, comradeship د چا سره انډيوالي اچول to take up with someone; enter into a friendship with someone 2 sharing food with; dining together with (noun indicating a habitual or frequent condition) 3 *figurative* common dish

انرجي inardzhí *f.* انرژي enerzhí *f.* energy

انزجار inzidzhā́r *m. Arabic* aversion, disgust په انزجار with aversion

انزکی anzəkáj *m.* bright child

انزوا inzivā́ *f. Arabic* 1 solitude, seclusion, retirement 2 isolation د انزوا سياست isolationism

انزواپسند inzivāpasánd *m. politics* isolationist

انزواپسندي inzivāpasandí *f.* 1 *politics* isolationism 2 isolation

انزور anzór *m.* ☞ انگور

انجکسيون inzheksjón *m.* ☞ انژکسيون

انس uns *m. Arabic* 1 attachment, affection; sympathy; friendship 2 sociability

انساب ansā́b *m. Arabic plural* 1 *from* نسب 2 familial relations 3 pedigree, genealogy

انساج ansā́dzh *m. Arabic plural* 1 *from* نسج 2 *anatomy* tissues

انسان insā́n *m. Arabic* man انسان primitive man انسان تر لومړنی انسان *proverb* Man is harder than stone, yet more tender than a blossom. انسان سخت, تر گل نازک دئ کاڼي

انساناني insānā́ni *plural from* انسانه

انسان پرست insānparást *m.* ☞ انسان دوست

انسان پرستي insānparastí *f.* ☞ انسان دوستي

د انسان پېژندنی عالم insānpezhandə́na *f.* anthropology انسان پېژندنه anthropologist

انسان دوست insāndóst *m.* humanist

انسان دوستي insāndostí *f.* humanism, philanthropy, love of mankind

انسان شناسي insānshinā́sí *f.* knowledge of people; life experience

انسانه insā́na *feminine of* انسان

انساني insāní 1 human (race, shape, form, likeness) 2 living, human انساني تلفات له لاسه ورکول manpower to sustain manpower *idiom* انساني علوم the humanities

انسانيت insāniját *m. Arabic* 1 humaneness, humanity 2 mankind

انسپکټر inspeḳtár *m. regional* 1 inspector 2 chief پوليس انسپکټر officer-in-charge of a police station

انستيتو instú *m. & f.* انستيتوت institút *m.* انستيتوت insṭiṭuṭ *m.* institute

انسجام insidzhā́m *m. Arabic* 1 order, state of order 2 smoothness

انسداد insidā́d *m. Arabic* 1 obstruction; blockage 2 *medicine* embolism, thrombosis 3 *figurative* restraint

انسيکلوپيديا ansiklopedijā́ *f.* encyclopedia

انسلېټر insuleṭár *m. technology* insulator

انسولېټاډ insuleṭā́ḍ *technology* insulating انسولېټاډ سيم insulating wire

انسياق insijā́ḳ *m. Arabic* obedience

انشأ inshā́ *f. Arabic* 1 compilation, spelling; composition 2 structure, construction 3 correspondence 4 style د انشأ کتاب handbook of style انشأ کول *compound verb* a to draw up, write; compose b to structure, construct

انشعاب inshi'ā́b *m. Arabic* 1 branching off; ramification 2 branch

انصاب ansā́b *m. Arabic plural from* نصب

انصاري ansārí *m. singular & plural* the Ansari (an ethnic group of sheiks among the Afghans and Pushtuns among whom are found descendants of the original associates of Mohammed in Medina)

انصاف insāf *m. Arabic* justice انصاف کول a to be just to someone b *figurative* to give that which is due ... چه دا دئ د انصاف حق justly speaking ..., justice requires that ... دا تهمت له انصافه بهر This accusation is unjust. تاسي انصاف وکئ دئ Judge for yourself. انصاف په تا نسته You are unjust. نو ما انصاف وکئ چه ... I have justly judged that ...

انصافاً insāfán *Arabic* justly, in justice, in conscience

انصاف پسند insāfpasánd انصاف خوښونکی insāf khaḵhavúnkaj

انصاف دار insāfdār انصاف نواز insāfnavāz just

انصاف نوازي insāfnāvazí *f.* justice

انضباط inzibā́t *m. Arabic* order, discipline

انضباطي inzibātí disciplinary انضباطي جزا ، انضباطي تنبيه، disciplinary punishment

انطباع intibā́' *f. Arabic* imprint, impression

انطباعات intibā'ā́t *m. Arabic plural* 1 *from* انطباع 2 publication, printed work 3 publishing house د انطباعاتو عمومي مديريت publishing department, publications department

انطباعي intibā'í polygraphic

انطباق intibā́ḵ *m. Arabic* 1 reference, allusion 2 adaptation, adjustment انطباق ميندل ، انطباق لرل to adapt, adjust

انعام in'ā́m *m. Arabic* 1 favor, grace 2 reward, recompense نقدي انعام monetary reward, recompense انعام ورکول to give recompense, reward

انعامي in'āmí انعامي مزكه land which has been deeded over or settled upon someone

انعدام in'idā́m *m. Arabic* disappearance; absence; nonexistence مخ پر انعدام a disappearing b on the wane (of the moon)

انعقاد in'iḵā́d *m. Arabic* convocation; opening د كنفرانس انعقاد opening of a conference انعقاد ميندل to take place (e.g., a conference)

انعكاس in'ikā́s *m. Arabic* 1 reflection; reflex انعكاس كول to reflect 2 response *literal* a to be reflected انعكاسات پيدا كول b to receive responses

انفاذ infā́z *m. Arabic* realization, bringing into existence, execution, fulfillment of something

انفجار infidzhā́r *m. Arabic* explosion; burst (i.e., of a shell) انفجار كول to explode; burst

انفجاري infidzhārí exploding; bursting; demolition

انفراداً infirā́dán *Arabic* individually; personally

انفرادي infirādí *Arabic* 1 individual, personal انفرادي وجود individuality 2 *regional* separate; one-man; solitary انفرادي حبس solitary confinement

انفراديت infirādijā́t *m. Arabic* individuality

انفس anfús *m. Arabic* subject

انفسي anfusí *Arabic* subjective

انفصال infisā́l *m. Arabic* 1 separation 2 solution of a problem انفصال ورکول to solve a problem

انفعال infi'ā́l *m.* 1 shame; embarrassment, confusion 2 grief, vexation عصبي انفعالات depression, depressed state 3 عاطفي انفعالات emotional experiences 4 reaction, response خفيف انفعال weak reaction

انفعالي infi'ālí 1 depressed, despondent انفعالي جذبه ، تاثر انفعالي depression, despondency 2 vexatious, painful; unpleasant, irritating

انفكاك infikā́k *m. Arabic* tearing, rending

انفلاسيون enflāsijón *m. economic* inflation

انفلاق infilā́ḵ *m. Arabic* ☞ انفجار *idiom* د حوصله انفلاق كوي Patience is exhausted.

انفلاقي infitaḵí *Arabic* explosive انفلاقيه مواد explosive substances انفلاقي فيوز demolition bomb انفلاقي بم time-delay fuse انفلاقي تخنيك pyrotechnics

انقباض inḵibā́z *m. Arabic* 1 curtailment; decrease in scope, pressure, compression or volume; crumpling, puckering 2 *medicine* constipation 3 *physiology* systole 4 *figurative* depression, despondency

انقره anḵará *f.* Ankara (city)

انقسام inḵisā́m *m. Arabic* 1 division انقسام ميندل to divide; fractionate; dismember 2 *biology* division (of a cell); fission

انقضا inḵizā́ *f. Arabic* end, expiration (of a term, deadline)

انقطاع inḵitā́' *f. Arabic* 1 interruption; discontinuance په لږ غوڅوالی ورکول to interrupt, discontinue 2 break, disruption او انقطاع سره with minimal disruption

انقلاب inḵilā́b *m. Arabic* 1 revolution اجتماعي انقلاب social revolution صناعتي انقلاب the Industrial Revolution فلاحتي انقلاب the Agrarian Revolution 2 overthrow, coup 3 wrongness, falseness, variability *idiom* شمسي انقلاب *astronomy* solstice

انقلابي inḵilābí *Arabic* 1 revolutionary انقلابي شاعر revolutionary poet 2 *m.* [*plural:* انقلابيان inḵilābijā́n *Arabic plural:* انقلابيون inḵilābijún] revolutionary

انقياد inḵijā́d *m. Arabic* obedience, submissiveness د چا سره انقياد كول to be subordinate; be obedient, be submissive to someone

انكار inkā́r *m. Arabic* negation, nonrecognition; repudiation د يو هغه شي څخه انكار كول to deny, not recognize, repudiate someone *Eastern* ده تګ نه دی څخه He refused to leave. دا انكار نه لرم I cannot deny this.

انكاري inkārí refusing, declining انكاري كېدل to refuse, decline

انكسار inkisā́r *m. Arabic* 1 breakage; fracture 2 *physics* refraction 3 *figurative* regret; repentance

انكشاف inkishā́f *m. Arabic* 1 development; growth; upsurge; progress اقتصادي او مدني انكشاف economic and cultural development انكشاف كول *compound verb* to develop انكشاف ميندل to be developed, grow; progress 2 discovery; research

انكشافي inkishāfí 1 انكشافي پلان plan of development 2 *attributive* research

انكه ¹ anə́ka *f. children's speech* granny, grandmother

ان كه ² ánki 1 even 2 inasmuch as

انكى inkáj *m.* 1 weeping of a bride (at the time of the plaiting of the braids) 2 weeping

انګ ang *m.* 1 spirit of contradiction 2 sense, meaning

انګا ingā́ *m.* weeping of a newborn

انګار angā́r 1 *m.* hot coals; hot ashes انګار كول to cause coals to heat up; cause coals to flame up سور انګار كېدل to flame of (of coals) 2 burning; sparking; sparkling *idiom* په سره انګار كېدل a to worry b to sit on coals; be troubled

انگارا angārā́ *f.* the Angara River

انگبرل angāról *transitive dialect* ☞

انگاره angārá *f.* stubble

انگارى [1] angāráj *m.* poor man who gathers wheat, etc. which has fallen in the field after the harvest; gleaner

انگاري [2] angāré *plural from* انگاره

انگارى [3] angāráj *f.* disease of camels

انگارى [4] angāráj *feminine of* انگاري [1]

انگازه angāzá *f.* 1 rumor, common talk مگر دا انگازه عملي نه شوه However, this rumor has not been confirmed. انگازه، انگازه گډول، ... ده چه to spread a rumor, disseminate a rumor اچول There are rumors to the effect that ... 2 echo انگازي کول to ring out, resound (e.g., a song)

انگاف angāf *m.* chink, slit (in stonework, masonry)

انگافکاري angāfkārí *f.* patching chinks in stonework with lime mortar

انگبين angabín *m. plural* honey

انگچه angachá *f.* intention

انگر [1] angár *m.* ☞

انگر [2] angár *m.* ☞ هنگر

انگرکى angarkáj *m.* fire, campfire or bonfire which has been lit by children

انگر منگر angár-mangár angór-mangór کول انگر منگر to make excuses for; shirk, elude

انگروزه angruzá *f.* ☞ انگازه [1]

انگرى anguráj *f.* ☞ اندركه

انگرېز angréz angríz 1 *m.* Englishman 2 English

انگرېزي angrezí angrizí 1 English انگرېزي سركار *regional* the English government 2 *f.* the English language انگرېزي يي زده ده He knows the English language. انگرېزي راته نه څي I do not know the English language.

انگړ angáŕ *m.* 1 fence 2 yard, court

انگشت angúsht *m.* finger

انگشتانه angushtāná *f.* 1 ring; seal-ring 2 thimble

انگشت زني angushtzaní *f.* interference, meddling

انگشت نما angushtnumá well-known

انگل angál *m.* 1 confused affair; involved quarrel; slanderous affair 2 noise; confusion

انگلس inglís *m. regional history* pension

انگلس خور inglishkhór *m. regional history* 1 person receiving a pension 2 one receiving a miserable pittance

انگلستان inglistán *m.* England

انگلوساکسون anglosāksón 1 *attributive* Anglo-Saxon 2 *m.* Anglo-Saxon انگلوساکسون خلک the Anglo-Saxons

انگليز anglíz *m.* انگليس inglís anlís *m.* 1 Englishman 2 England

انگليسي inglisí 1 English انگليسي كانال the English Channel 2 *f.* the English language

انگن əngón *m.* ☞ انگر انگن

انگور [1] angúr *m. plural* grapes د انگورو باغ د انگورو تاک vineyard انگور چغال خوري بښه *proverb* The jackal eats the best grapes. grapevine

انگور [2] angór *m.* agreement, adjustment, putting into order

انگور [3] əngór *f.* [*plural:* انگبندي əngénde] *Eastern* daughter-in-law

انگورتوره angurtóra *f.* black solanum

انگوري angurí 1 *attributive* grape انگوري باغ vineyard 2 *m.* vineyard tax

انگورى angóṛaj *m.* small pomegranate, miniature pomegranate

انگوزه anguzá *f.* ☞ انگازه

انگولا [1] angolá *f.* 1 howl, howling (of a dog, jackal) انگولا کول to howl, begin to howl (of a dog, jackal) 2 moaning, weeping

انگولا [2] angólá *f.* Angola

انگولل angolól [*past:* انگولو و يي] to howl, begin to howl (of a dog, jackal)

اينگه ingá *f.* ☞ انگه

انگهار əngahár *m. Eastern* groans

انگى [1] angáj *m.* cheek

انگى [2] angáj *m. Eastern* sneezing; sneeze

انگى [3] ingə́j leapfrog

انگى [4] ingə́j *f.* echo

انگيا angijā́ *f.* ☞ بنيان

انگټى angeṭáj *f.* brazier; hearth

انگبرل angeról *transitive* [*past:* انگبره و يي] 1 think, suppose, assume 2 to imagine, fancy 3 to weigh, consider, reason through, assess 4 to calculate (e.g., losses)

انگبرنه angeróna *f.* 1 assumption 2 imagination, imagining, notion 3 assessment, consideration 4 calculation (e.g., of losses)

انگبز angéz *combining form* exciting, evoking هيجان انگبز worrying, alarming

انگبندي əngénde *plural Eastern from* انگور [3]

انند anánd joy; delight; enjoyment

اننگ [1] anáng *m.* 1 pomegranate 2 cheek

اننگ [2] anáng *m.* anə́ng distance between the little finger and the thumb; span

اننگورى anánguṛaj *m.* pomegranate

اننگى anangáj *m.* cheek

انناس anannā́s *m.* pineapple

انوار anvā́r *m. Arabic plural from* نور [1]

انواع anvā́' *m. Arabic plural f. plural* 1 *from* نوع 2 *biology* species د انواعو په داخل کښي interspecific د انواعو ترمنځ intraspecific

انود anód *m. physics* anode

انور anvár *Arabic* 1.1 brightest, most brilliant 1.2 most radiant, most shining 2 *proper name* Anwar, Enver

انول anavól [*past:* وايي ناوه] to compel someone, quiet down, pacify

انونیم anoním *m.* anonymous work; anonymous letter; anonymous writer

انویس invájs *m.* invoice

آنه [1] āná *f.* saddlebow, pommel

آنه [2] āná *f.* anna (Indian coin) د آنې تکس stamp having a 1 anna value

آنه [3] āná *adjectival and adverbial suffix; indeclinable* a مردانه courageous, brave b bravely, courageously

انهاک inhák *m. Arabic* exhaustion, depletion, attrition

آنه بهانه āná-bahāná *f.* trick, guile, evasion آنې بهانې کول a to trick; elude b to make excuses

انهدام inhidám *m. Arabic* destruction, annihilation

انه ناس ananás *m.* ☞ اننناس

آنې [1] āní *Arabic* 1 sudden, surprise آنې اور a surprise fire b volley 2 momentary, instant

آنې [2] āné *plural from* آنه [1, 2]

انی [3] anə́j *f.* grandmother, grandma, granny

انې [4] áni *f.* āne *suffix plural Eastern* بگیانې girls بگیانې carriages

انیاب anjáb *m. Arabic plural from* ناب [1]

انې بانې ané-bāné *f. plural regional* tricks, evasions

انیز aníz *combining form regional* consisting of so many annas اته انیز 8 anna coin

انیس anís *m. Arabic* 1 friend 2 comrade in arms

انیلین anilín *m. chemistry* aniline

انغنج aṇagándzh *m.* ball game

انل aṇə́l *transitive* [*past:* و یې انل] to pound; grind into powder; crush; smash to pieces; grind up

انول aṇavól *transitive* [*past:* و یې انول] 1 to gather, gather in (a harvest) 2 to pick (flowers, berries) 3 to choose, select

او [1] au av *conjunction* 1 *copulative* and آدم او درخانی Adam and Durkhani هلک نژدې شو ودرېد The boy came up and stood there. 2 *adversative conjunction* but احمد مکتب ته ولاړ او محمود کورته Ahmed went to school, but Makhmud stayed home. او که but if او یا or else

او [2] o 1 hey, oh او موري!، او احمده! Mamma!, Mommy! Hey Ahmed! 2 *particle regional* yes

او [3] av 1 go on (or similar cry by which one drives a cow) 2 *m. children's speech* cow

او [4] ou *m.* howl (of a wolf, jackal) او کول to howl, begin to howl

او [5] u *Eastern indicator of the perfective aspect instead of* و

اواخر avākhír *m. Arabic plural from* آخر 2 په دې اواخرو کښې for the last time

آوار [1] āvā́r āvar ☞ اوار هوار

آوار [2] āvā́r *m. regional* ore; stolen goods

آوارگي āvāragí *f.* 1 wandering, vagabondage, travelling 2 dissipation

آوارول āvāravól *transitive* ☞ هوارول

آواره [1] āvā́ra 1.1 homeless, wandering 1.2 dissolute 2 *m.* wanderer, vagrant

اواره [2] avā́ra *f.* plain

آواره گرد āvāragárd *m.* wanderer, vagrant

آواربدل āvāredə́l *intransitive* ☞ هواربدل

آواز āvā́z *m.* 1 voice, sound د آواز نه گړندی supersonic, په لوړ آواز، loudly آواز ټیټول to lower the voice په لوړ آواز سره to raise the voice, to intensify the sound; make louder چا ته آواز to call someone ... چا ته آواز کول to cry out to someone ورته آواز وکړه! Call him. آواز وکړ چه ... He whispered to me that آواز لرل to answer someone پر چا آواز کول، پر چا باندي آواز کول to resound په ډېرو چیغو می آواز کښېنستلئ دئ I became hoarse from shouting. د احمد آواز ډډ شوئ دئ Ahmed has matured; his voice has deepened. ښه آواز د غوږو دوا ده *proverb* A pleasant voice is a pleasure. 2 rumor, talk, talking *idiom* په هغه د مرگ آواز وشو He was sentenced to death.

آوازخوان āvāzkhā́n *m.* singer

آوازدار āvā́z larúnkaj 1 ringing; sounding; آواز لرونکی sound آوازدار فلم sound film 2 *linguistics* vowel آوازدار صوت vowel sound

آوازه āvāzá *f.* ☞ انگازه

اواسط avāsít *m. Arabic plural from* وسط

اوامر avāmír *m. plural from* امر [2]

اوان avā́n *m. Arabic plural* period, time

آوانس āvā́ns *m.* advance; payment on account

آوانسي āvānsí *attributive* advance آوانسي حواله an advance

اوان avā́ṇ *m. plural* the Avans (people of northwest India)

اوایل avāíl *m. Arabic plural* 1 *from* اول 2 the first days of the month; the first days of the week په راتلونکي هفتې په اوائلو کښې At the beginning of next week.

اوب [1] ub *m.* whim, caprice

اوب [2] ob *m.* Ob River

اوباز avbā́z *m.* ☞ آباز

اوبازي avbāzí *f.* ☞ آبازي

اوباش avbā́sh 1 riffraff, rabble 2 tramp; vagrant

اوباشي avbāshí *f.* libertinism, debauchery

اوبال aubál ubál *m. Arabic* delinquency; sin, fault اوبال گټل to perpetrate a misdemeanor; to transgress, commit an offense اوبال ور په غاړه شو He committed an offense.

اوبال گر ubālgár aubālgár *m.* sinner

اوبتل ubtál *m.* obtál [*plural:* اوبتلان ubtalā́n] اوبتله ubtala *f.* submarine

اوبجن ubdzhə́n ☞ اوبلن

اوبچي obchí *m.* warrior

اودل [1] د ☞ obə́l *transitive* [*present:* اوبي یې *past:* اوبیده یې] 1 loom 2 to knit (e.g., a scarf) اوبدلو ماشین

اوبدنه obdə́na *f.* 1 weaving 2 knitting

اوبدوب ubḍúb *m.* ☞ اوبتل

اوبرژ ubrə́j *f.* green algae

اوبزه ubə́za *f.* moth (clothes)

اوبژن obzhə́n ☞ اوبجن

اویسپی ubəspáj *m.* otter

اوبخت obə́khht *m.* juniper

اوبلن oblə́n ublə́n 1 watery; liquid 2 juicy, fresh

اوبلن توب obləntób *m.* 1 wateriness 2 juiciness; freshness

اوبلوبنی oblókhaj *m.* tank (water)

اوبنی ubənáj 1 watery; water 2 blue

اوبڼه ubə́na *f. anatomy* placenta, afterbirth

ابوغاله ubodzắla *f. botany* river sponge, freshwater sponge

اوبوخته ubúkhta *f.* juniper

اوبوس obús *m.* howitzer

اوبوسه ubúsa *f.* 1 swampy place, bog; marsh; moist ground, swampy ground 2 irrigated land

اوبول obavə́l 1 *denominative* [*past:* اوبه یې کړ] to irrigate; flush مځکي په کاریزو اوبول to irrigate the land with the help of kiarizes (i.e., underground irrigation canals) اوبول کېدل *passive* to be irrigated 2 *m. plural* irrigation, flushing

اوبومور ubumór *f.* insect of the cricket family

اوبونه obavə́na *f.* irrigation; flushing

اوبه¹ obə́ *f.* ubə́ *plural* 1 water ایشیدلي اوبه boiling water تپتي warm water تومي اوبه saltwater ترخي اوبه ground water اوبه freshwater خوبي اوبه turbid water تودي اوبه hot water خوري اوبه chemistry heavy water رنبي اوبه، پاکي اوبه، صافي اوبه pure water, clear water رواني اوبه running water سړي اوبه cold water, very cold water د boiling water یخي اوبه، سوي اوبه well water د چینلو اوبه drinking اوبه دڼا اوبه rainwater باران اوبه water د حیات اوبه آب حیات د واورو اوبه melt water اوبه په غاړه on the shore of a stream or river د اوبو ډېروالی flood, abundance of water اوبه راوستل to conduct water, irrigation ditch یو تر بله د څا څخه اوبه to sprinkle water on one another, lap اوبه شیندل to draw water from a well اوبو ته وراچول، په اوبوکنبي ګډول to launch into the water (e.g., a boat) په سرو اوبو ګډېدل to scald oneself اوبه راوړه! Bring water! اوبه په چپو راغلي The water was rising. ډېرې علاقي تر اوبو لاندي شوي دي Many districts suffered from floods. 2 liquid په خوله کنبي اوبه راشي saliva د خولې اوبه the saliva flows 3 juice (of meat, fruits) د مېوو اوبه 4 fruit juice temper (of metal) 5 *veterinary* (bone) spavin 6 *figurative* honor, dignity اوبه خرول a to stir up the water b to evade, avoid something c to drag the business out اوبه درول to disgrace someone اوبه یې په سترګو کنبي ودرېدي He disgraced himself. اوبه مي ورخ تبري شوي I am ashamed. This تر اوبه د چا سره غلبلول matter cannot be put to rights. اوبه to be careful with someone *f.* اوبه کول *compound verb* a to irrigate, flush b to melt, melt down c to dissolve d to sell, market اوبه کېدل *compound verb* a to be irrigated, be flushed b to be melted, be melted down c to thaw d to be turned into water (of steam) e to grow thin غوښي دي اوبه شوي دي You have grown very thin. اوبه ورکول a to give water, give to اوبه کېدل to be ashamed

drink b to supply with water c to irrigate, flush d to temper (metal) تر اوبو د مخه څاولي کښل *literal* to take off one's shoes without going into the water *figurative* to be in a hurry, act rashly په د سترګو اوبه یې وتلي He lost all shame and conscience. زړه مي سړې اوبه تویې شوۍ .I was stupified اوبو اخیستئ و خاشې ته *proverb* A drowning man will grasp even at a straw. د مراٻو اوبو بهرپره اوبه د سره پای له *proverb* Still waters run deep. خړي دئ *proverb literal* Water grows turbid from its source. *figurative* A fish rots from its head. اوبه توري *regional* ocean تورو اوبو ته تلل to be sentenced to exile for life

اوبه² obé *f.* obá Obe (city, district)

اوبه تله obətalá *f.* water level; level

اوبه خور ubəkhór 1 subject to irrigation, requiring irrigation 2 *m.* 1. drinking bowl, fountain 2.2 *figurative* sources 2.3 *regional* irrigation; flushing اوبه خور کول to irrigate; flush 2.4 *regional* watering place

اوبه رنګی obərángaj light blue اوبه رنګی الماس corundum; blue carbuncle

اوبه لګول obə́lagavə́l *m. plural* irrigation; flushing

اوبه واری obəváraj *m.* اوبه وری obəváráj *m. regional* street cleaner (with water)

اوبي¹ óbi *f.* the Ob (river)

اوبي² obí *present tense from* اوبدل

اوبدل obedə́l *denominative* [*past:* اوبه شو] 1 to be irrigated; be flushed 2 to absorb, take in 3 to drink, quench thirst (of animals)

آوپاش āvpāsh *m.* worker engaged in watering (streets, flowers, etc.)

آوپاشي āvpāshí *f.* flushing, watering د آوپاشی ماشین street-watering truck آوپاشي کول to flush, water

اوپره uprá ☞ اپره

اوپړي پوپړي upə́ṛi-pupə́ṛi *f. plural* conversation about widely divergent matters

اوپېرا operá *f.* opera

اوتاد avtād *m. Arabic plural* [*singular:* وتد] important people, big wheels

اوتار avtār *m. Arabic plural from* وتر³

اوتر avtár 1 frightened 2 alarmed; downcast; distressed اوتر کول اوتربدل ☞ اوترول اوتر کبدل ☞

اوتراق otrắ́k *m.* halt, stopping place

اوتراوتر avtár-avtár scared, frightened اوتر اوتره وضع frightened appearance اوتراوتر کتل to look upon with fright

اوترائي utrājí *f. regional* descent (from a mountain)

اوترتوب avtartób *m.* اوتروالی avtarválaj *m.* 1 perturbation, panic 2 pain, distress

اوترول avtaravə́l *transitive* [*past:* اوتر یې کړ] 1 to frighten 2 to alarm; distress, grieve

اوترتوب ☞ avtarí *f.* اوتري

اوتربدل avtaredэl *transitive* [*past:* اوتر شو] 1 to be frightened 2 to be alarmed; be perturbed

اوتو utú *m.* flatiron اوتو برقي electric iron اوتو کول to press, iron

اوتو [2] úvato óvato *past perfective Eastern from* وتل

اوتوبوس avtobús *m.* bus

اوتوجن *technology* autogenous اوتوجن سيم جوش autogenous welding

اوتوماتيک otomātík اوتوماتيکي otomātíkí automatic

اوتوموبيل avtomobíl *m.* automobile د اوتوموبيل صنائع the automobile industry

اوتوموبيل سازي avtomobilsāzí *f.* automobile manufacture د اوتوموبيل سازی فابريکه automobile plant

اوته avtá اوته اوته هبره سي! May you know no rest!

اوتي پوپري úte-búte *f. plural Eastern* 1 ☞ اوپري پوپري 2 delirium د ليوني اوتي بوتي the disconnected speech of an insane person, the delirium of a madman

اوتاوا otāvэ́ *f.* Ottawa (city)

اوتکروپ aútkrop *m. geology* exposure of a stratum or deposit at the surface

اوتوپيا uṭopjā́ *f.* Utopia

اوتوپيائي uṭopjājí Utopian

اوج audzh *m. Arabic* 1 zenith; apogee 2 *military* leader of the vanguard د اوج ترصد point of the vanguard; lead patrol of the vanguard 3 *aviation* ceiling

اوجار udzhā́ṛ ☞ ويجار *idiom* اوجار شه Damn you!

اوجارول udzhaṛavэ́l *transitive* ☞ ويجارول

اوجاري udzhā́ṛí *f.* destruction, devastation

اوجري udzhráj *m. regional* organ meats, entrails

آبجوشي avdzhúshi *f. plural* ☞ آبجوشي

اوجه [1] údzha *f. regional* leech

اوجه [2] údzha *f.* ☞ وژه

اوجي udzhэ́j *f. children's speech* insect (small)

اوچ uch *Eastern* ☞ وچ

اوچت uchát 1 high اوچت نيول to stand, jump up اوچت پاڅبدل rise; lift 2 loud (of the voice) 3 steep (of a road) 4 *regional* afore-cited *idiom* سايه اوچته اخيستل to puff (quietly)

اوچت توب uchattób *m.* uchattjā́ *f.* uchatvэ́laj *m.* 1 height 2 rise, increase 3 loudness (of a noise) 4 steepness (of a road)

اوچتول uchatavэ́l *denominative, intransitive* 1 [*past:* اوچت يي کړ] 1 lift; raise 2 to raise, heighten 3 to make loud, intensify (e.g., a sound) 4 to emphasize; accent something 5 *regional* to clear away plates and dishes 6 to cause, occasion (harm, injury, etc.)

اوچت توب uchatjā́ *f.* ☞ اوچتيا

اوچتبدل uchatedэ́l *denominative, intransitive* 1 [*past:* اوچت شو] 1 to rise, rise above, heave up 2 to ascend 3 to be loud, be intensified (e.g., a sound) 4 to rise up, get up د روانبدو دپاره اوچت شوم I got up to leave. 5 to rise, ascend (of celestial objects) 6 *regional* to come into existence, appear, be born

اوچتبده uchatdэ́ *m. plural* 1 raising (e.g., the flag) 2 rise, increase 3 intensification (e.g., of a noise) 4 rising, ascension 5 ascent د نمر اوچتبده sunrise 6 origin, emergence, appearance, conception

اوچ کسکر uchkaskár *regional* completely dry

اوچکی [1] uchakэ́j *f.* islet

اوچکی [2] uchakáj emaciated; lean

اوچولي uchúlaj *m. Eastern* forehead, brow

اوچوني [1] uchúnaj *m.* six-month-old lamb

اوچوني [2] uchúne *f.* young ewe (which has not yet lambed)

اوچه [1] uchá *f.* ☞ اچه

اوچه [2] úcha *f. singular dialect from* اوچ

اوچي پوچي úche-púche *f. plural Eastern* nonsense, drivel

اوڅار avtsár apparent, evident; well-known

اوڅارول avtsāravэ́l *denominative, intransitive* [*past:* اوڅاريي کړ] to reveal, explain; make manifest, make evident

اوڅاربدل avtsāredэ́l *denominative, intransitive* [*past:* اوڅار شو] to come to light, turn out, be manifest, be apparent

اوڅکک avtsэkák *m. botany* fumitory, fumaria (annual herb whose dried leaves are used in the preparation of tonics and alteratives)

اوخ ukh *interjection* oy, oh

اوخوتسک okhótsk *m.* د اوخوتسک بحيره the Sea of Okhotsk

اوبنه [2] úkha *f. Eastern* ☞ اوبنه

اوبنی [1] ávkhaj *m. dialect* ☞ اوبنی

اوخی [2] ukhэ́j *f. children's speech* boogeyman, bugbear

اوخي [3] úkhe *plural from* اوخه

آوخبزي āvkhezí high-water, flooding

اود [1] od *m.* plaiting (of mats, etc.)

اود [2] aud *m.* reservoir, pond

اودال avdэ́l *m.* saint; religious anchorite or hermit

اودالي avdālí *m. plural* ☞ ابدالي

اودان avdэ́n *m.* ☞ آبدان

اودخبل udkhél 1 *m. plural* the Udkhejli (a sub-tribe of the Gilzai) 2 *m.* Udkhejl (tribesman) 3 Udkhejl' (name of various settlements)

اودر odér *m.* the Oder (river)

اودرول udravúl *transitive Eastern* ☞ درول

اودربدل udredэ́l *intransitive Eastern* ☞ دربدل

آودس āvdás *m.* اودس avdás *m.* ablution, washing (body) آودس ماتول تازه کول to effect ablution, wash the body *idiom* to urinate, answer the call of nature

اودس مات avdasmā́t *m. transitive* اودس مات ته تلل to go to take care of nature's call

اودس ماتی avdasmātэ́j *f.* evacuation (of the bowels), defecation

اودل [1] odэ́l udэ́l 1 *transitive* [*present:* او يي *present:* اودي *past:* [او يي اود .1 to weave 1.2 to twist, twine 1.3 to plait (braids) اودل کبدل *passive* a to be woven b to be twisted, be twined 2 *m. plural* ☞ اودنه

اودل ² avdál *m. proper name* Avdal

اودنه odəna *f.* **1** weaving **2** twisting, twining **3** plaiting (braids)

اودونکی ¹ odúnkaj *m.* weaver

اودونکۍ ² odúnke *f.* weaver (female)

اوده ¹ udá *f.* **1** conspiracy, charm, exorcism **2** witchcraft

اوده ² udə́ *Eastern* ☞ ابیده غرق اوده one who has fallen into a deep sleep

اوده ³ udá *f. singular from* اوده ²

اودي ¹ udé *plural from* اود ¹

اودي ² udí *present tense from* اودل ¹

اودېسه odesá *f.* Odessa (city)

اودل odə́l *transitive* [*past:* وی اوده] to arrange, put right, adjust

اودنی ovdə́naj *m.* small chador, small veil (for women, children)

اور or *m.* ur **1** fire; conflagration د اور غر ☞ د اور گاډی volcano ناگاه اور لنبه شو اورگاډی the fire suddenly blazed up **2** gunfire, fire, firing د اور خط line of fire اور شدید ویو a hurricane of fire شي ته اور اچول **a** to set something on fire اور اخیستل to catch fire, ignite **b** *figurative* to hurry, hasten **c** *figurative* to anger suddenly, flare up اور بلول **a** to set afire, start a fire **b** to open a strong fire پر دښمن اور بلول to open up a strong fire on the enemy **c** *figurative* to drive out of one's wits اور کول to open fire, fire اور گډول **a** to set fire to **b** to spread discord **c** to evoke discontent **d** to spoil اور وژل، اور مړ کول، اور گل کول **a** to light a fire اور لگول ☞ اور لتول **b** to cause a fire, set a fire د جنگ اور لگول to fan the fire of war, unleash war **c** *figurative* to enrapture په کور باندي اور ولگېد house caught fire خو ځایه اورونه ولگېدل Fires broke out in several places. چه اور ولگېږي هغه وخت اوبه نه وي *proverb* Whenever fire breaks out there's no water to be found. اور په خوله ورل **a** to hurry, hasten **b** *figurative* to be stingy, be greedy اور له خپله سره وژل to arrange one's affairs by oneself (without outside help) پر اور کول **a** to roast on a spit **b** *figurative* to torture, torment **c** *figurative* to worry پر اور کېدل **a** to be roasted on a spit **b** to be tortured, be tormented **c** not to sit quietly, squirm پر اور نیول **a** to subject to fire **b** *figurative* to torment, torture په اور کېدل **a** to burn down اور کنبي اچول **a** to set on fire اور پوري کول to throw into the fire **b** *figurative* to torture, torment روپی و اور ته to squander money, throw money to the wind اور ته نیول **a** to hold to the fire **b** *figurative* to oppress اور ته خپل و پردي یو *proverb* It's all one to the fire, whether it's yours or another's اور او اوبه یو ځای نه شي دي *literal* Fire is incompatible with water. *figurative* These are incompatible things.

آور āvár *combining form* bringing, possessing خنده آور ludicrous, laughable

اوراخیسته orakhistə́ *m. plural* **1** fire, conflagration; burning; ignition **2** *figurative* hurry, haste

اوراد avrād *m. Arabic plural from* ورد

اوراره orārə́ *m.* ☞ وراره ¹

اوراق avrā́ḳ *m. Arabic* **1** *from* ورق **2** archive; office; registry د اوراقو مدیر chief of the archives (office)

اورال urā́l *m.* the Urals د اورال دریا the Ural River د اورال غرونه the Urals, the Ural Mountains

اورانیوم urānijúm *m. chemistry* uranium

اوراورکی ororə́kaj *m.* glowworm, firefly

اوربخړی orbatsə́raj *m.* **1** spark **2** hot-tempered person

اوربشه orbə́sha *f.* ☞ اربشه

اوربشي orbə́shi *f. plural* barley د اوربشو اوبه beer

اوربشین orbəshín *attributive* barely اوربشینه ډوډۍ barley bread

اوربل ¹ orbál Fire! (as a command)

اوربل ² orbál *m.* **1** lock, curl; bang, forelock **2** *personal name* Orbal

اوربلک orbalák *m.* **1** fire lighter **2** furnace man **3** steel (formerly used in lighting a fire) **4** syphilis

اوربلوونکی orbalavúnkaj *incendiary* اوربلوونکی بم incendiary bomb

اوربندي orbandí *f.* cessation of fire, end of firing

اوربوز orbúz *m.* muzzle, snout, (ugly) face *idiom* چا ته اوربوز نیول to hang around someone خله بوت اوربوز نیسي؟ What are you in a huff about? دي ورک شه اوربوز! Be off! Get away!

اوربوشه orbúsha *f. Eastern* ☞ اربشه د اوربوشي په میاشت اربشه In a month will be the barley harvest.

اوربه orbá *f.* heating chamber for a bath

اوربېړی orbeṛ́j *f.* steamboat

اورپالی orpə́laj *m.* fire worshipper

اورپښت orpə́kht *m.* [*plural:* اورپښتونه orpəkhtúna *plural:* اورپښتان orpəkhtā́n] nocturnal moth

اورتون ortún *m.* temple of fire worshippers

اورته ¹ avráta *f.* **1** woman **2** wife

اورته ² aórtá *f. anatomy* aorta

اورتک orṭák *m.* flint (of a flintlock rifle)

اوردو urdú *m. & f.* ☞ اردو

اوربره urgə́ *m. plural* **1** colostrum, beestings **2** milk of a cow which has just calved with spice added

اورس urús *m. obsolete* ☞ روس

اورسي ¹ urusí *obsolete* ☞ روسي

اورسي ² ursí *f.* window with frame which can be raised

اورشو urshó *f.* ☞ ارشو

اورشیند غر orshínd ghar *m.* volcano

اورښت orə́kht *m.* اورښته orə́khta *f.* fall of showers, rain سخت اورښت و A heavy rain fell.

اورښتی ² orəkhtə́j *f.* ☞ باراني

اورغالی orghā́laj *m.* **1** fireplace, hearth **2** heating box, chamber **3** blast furnace

اور غورځوونکی or ghurdzavúnkaj غر اور غورځوونکی غر volcano

اورغوی urə́vaj *m.* palm (of the hand)

اورغی urə́j *f.* soot

اورکزي ¹ orə́kzi *m. plural* the Orakzai (tribe) **2** orəkzáj *m.* Orakzai (tribesman)

اوركوټ avarkóṭ *m. regional* overcoat, greatcoat

اوركى orakáj *m.* glowworm, firefly

اورگاډه اورگاډی orgā́ḍa *f.* اورگاډی orgā́ḍaj *m.* اورگاړی orgā́raj *m.* **1** train; rolling stock برقي اورگاډی electric train, electric railway **2** د اورگاډي سړک *orgā́di* railroad د اورگاډي لار لار اورگاډي تېسن *orgā́di* railroad station

اورگان orgā́n *m.* نشراتي اورگان press organ قضائي اورگان judicial organ

اورگډی orgā́ḍaj *m.* troublemaker

اور لرونکی orlarúnkaj fire (i.e., firearms) اور لرونکې وسله firearm

اورلړلی orlaŕólaj troubled (e.g., times)

اورلړونی orlaŕúnaj *m.* poker *idiom* اورلړونی سړی troublemaker, instigator, ringleader

اورلگوونکی orlagavúnkaj incendiary اورلگوونکی بم incendiary bomb

اورلگیت orlagít *m.* urlagít *singular & plural* matches د اورلګیتو کارخانه match factory یوه دانه اورلګیتو دبلی box of matches اورلګیت a match

اورلگیتوالا orlagitvālā́ *m. singular & plural* seller of matches

اورلګید orlagíd *m.* ☞ اورلګیت

اورلګېدنه orlagedóna *f.* **1** fire, conflagration **2** flash, outbreak

اورلوبی orlóbi *f. plural* fireworks

اورمړ ormóṛ [1] *m.* person in whose home there is a deceased member

اورمړ omóṛ [2] *m.* the Ormur, the Baraki (nationality)

اورمږک ormagák *m.* salamander

اورمل urmál *m. Eastern* fig tree

اورمېږ ormeg *m.* neck

اورنگ اوتان orang-utā́n *m.* orangutan

اورنوسی ornúsaj *m.* coal tongs

اورنی oranáj *attributive* fire د اورنی غر خوله volcano اورنی غر volcano crater

اورنی oraṇáj *m.* swaddling clothes نر ځوی په اورني نه پېژبري *oraṇi proverb* A brave son is discerned while still in swaddling clothes

اوروالا orvālā́ *m.* furnace man; stoker

اوروپا urupā́ *f.* ☞ اروپا

اوروركی orəŕókaj *m.* glowworm, firefly

اور وژونکی or vazhúnkaj *attributive* fire اور وژونکې عمله firefighting company اور وژونکی موټر fire engine

اورول oravól [1] *transitive* [*past:* و یې اوراوه] **1** to throw, throw down **2** to strew **3** to cause (rain) دا اوریځ ډبلی اوروي This storm cloud will bring rain.

اورول avravól [2] *transitive* [*past:* وایې راوه] **1** to announce something, proclaim something; state something, express something; read out something. دلته دا خبره اورول غواړم I want to say here that … **2** to compel to listen **3** to issue (an order) *idiom* یوه یې راته وویله، سل مي ورته واورولی *proverb* He spoke but a word to me, I spoke a hundred to him; I am not in his debt.

اوره ovró [1] *m. singluar & plural* **1** cloudlet لمر په اورو کښی پټ شي The sun is hidden behind the clouds **2** cataract

اوره a'vra [2] *imperative, imperfect from* اوربدل [2]

اوري óri urí *present tense of* اوربدل [1]

اوري a'vri *present tense of* اوربدل [2]

اورى aoráj [3] *m.* ☞ اهورى

اورى oráj [4] *m. Eastern* lamb

اورى orə́j [5] *f.* **1** gum (mouth) **2** *anatomy* root bed of the nail *idiom* نوک اورى نه سره جلا کېږي We (you, they) are inseparably linked with one another.

اورئ a'vrəj [6] *Eastern second person plural of* اوربدل [2]

اوریا orjā́ *f.* rain

اوریاخېل urijakhél **1** *m. plural* the Uriyakhejli (a subdivision of the Gilzai) **2** *m.* Uriyakhejl (tribesman)

اوریامېچ orjāméch *m.* rain gauge

اوري پوري óri-póri اوري پوري وتل to pass through

اوریځ orjádz *f.* uréz [*plural:* اوریځي urjádzi] cloud; storm cloud توره اوریځ threatening storm-cloud خړه اوریځ grey cloud د دوړو اوریځ cloud of dust نن ډېره اوریځ ده It's very cloudy today. نن ورځ اوریځ ده Today it's overcast.

اوربدل oredól [1] *intransitive* [*present:* اوري *present:* اوربږي *past:* واوربده] **1** to pour (of rain), come down (of rain, snow) باران اوري It's raining. چه اوربږي باران، مزي کوي خوران When it rains the poor peasants rejoice (in hopes of of a good harvest) **2** to strike (of lightning)

اوربدل avredól [2] آوربدل avredól *Eastern transitive* [*present:* اوري *past:* ده واوربدل] **1** to hear **2** to listen وایي وربدل *past:* to resound (e.g., of sound) ☞ اروبدل *passive* کېدل

اوربده oredó [1] *m. plural* falling of showers د شبنم اوربده formation of dew

اوربده avredó [2] *m. plural* ☞ لیدو او اوربدو کښی ډېر فرق وي اروبده *Eastern* It's one thing to hear, another to see.

اوریز oríz [1] *firey, pertaining to fire

اوریز awríz [2] *m.* اوریزه awriza غریزه ghagíz audio

اوریز uréz [3] *f. dialect* ☞ اوریځ

اورېږي orégi *present of* اوربدل [1]

اورینوکو orinokó *f.* د اورینوکو دریاب the Orinoco River

اورېی orjə́j *f. dialect* gum (of the mouth)

اوړ avṛ *present stem of* اوښتل

اوړاندي uṛańde *Eastern* ☞ وړاندې

اوړدو uṛdú *m. Eastern* ☞ اردو

اوړدی uṛdí *f. regional* uniform; tunic

اوړل uṛól *transitive dialect* ☞ وړل

اوړم ávṛəm [1] *Eastern* ☞ اوښتل

اوړم óṛəm [2] *Eastern* ☞ وړم اوړم کال last year

اوړمبی uṛumbáj *dialect* ☞ وړنبی

اوړنی oraṇáj [1] *m.* small veil (worn by Moslem women)

اوړنی orəṇáj [2] *attributive* summery, summer

اوروبۍ uṛobáj *m.* **1** mash (watery or semiliquid food) **2** syrup (in jam)

اوروکی uṛúkaj *dialect* ☞ وروکی [1]

اوروول oṛavól *denominative, intransitive* [*past:* اوره یې کړل] **1** to grind, mill **2** to pulverize, break in pieces; grind to powder

اوړه [1] oṛá *m.* اوړ uṛá *plural* **1** flour د اوړو گل ، پاسته اوړه coarse-grained flour, coarse flour د اوړو کولو ماشین flour-milling machine; milling equipment اوړه ببخي سرکه سوه The dough has turned sour. اوړه په کور کښې نه لري، تنور یې پر بام جوړ کړئ دئ *proverb* They don't even have flour in the house, but still they're installing a stove. **2** powder اوړه کول *compound verb* ☞ اوړول اوړه او اوبه کول **a** to pound, abrade, grind **b** to boil until soft اوړه او اوبه کېدل [1] *compound verb* ☞ اوبدل **a** to be crushed, be pounded, be transformed into powder **b** to be boiled soft **c** to have learned by rote سبق مي داسي اوړه او اوبه شو I learned the lesson by heart. میده میده اوړه کول **a** to grind, mill finely **b** to hem and haw *idiom* اوړه په اوړه ، منت یې څه؟ *saying* We're even. What is there to thank me for?

اوره [2] ávṛa *f.* instrument, device, tool

اوړه والا oṛávālā *m.* flour merchant, flour dealer اوړه خرڅونکی oṛə́khartsavúnkaj *m.*

اوړی [1] óṛaj *m.* **1** summer د اوړي ځای óṛi summer place, vacation place **2** summer harvest

اوړي [2] ávṛi *present tense of* اوبنتل

اوړي [3] ávṛi *plural from* اوړه [2]

اوړدل [1] oṛedól *intransitive* [*past:* اوړه شول] **1** to be ground, be milled **2** to be pulverized, be broken into pieces, be ground into powder

اوړدل [2] avṛedól *intransitive* ☞ اوبنتل شپه واوړېده It is past midnight.

اوړدونکی [2] avṛedúnkaj **1** *present participle of* اوړدل [2] **2** changeable

اوز [1] uz *m.* goat

اوز [2] oz **1** *m.* negligible quantity, insignificant sum **2** several, some

اوزار avzár *m. Eastern* weapon, arm تږ اوزار pɣ blunt weapon افزار ☞ sharp weapon

اوزان avzán *Arabic plural from* وزن

اوزبک uzbák *m.* ☞ ازبک

اوزبکي [1] uzbakí ☞ ازبکي

اوزگار uzgár *dialect* ☞ وزگار

اوزگوری uzgóṛaj *m.* ☞ ازگری uzgúṛaj *m.*

اوزون ozón *m. chemistry* ozone

اوزه uzá *f.* she-goat ☞ وزه

اوزی [1] ózaj *m.* forearm

اوزی [2] úzi *Eastern* ☞ وزي

اوزغوني uzhúni *f. plural* goat's wool

اوژی ozhój *f.* oilcake

اوږد ugd **1** lengthy, long لار نه ده اوږده The road is not all that long. **2** protracted, prolonged اوږد سفر کول to accomplish a protracted journey

اوږدبریتی ugdbritaj mustachioed, mustached

اوږدغوری ugdvágaj **1** lop-carcd, having lop-ears **2** *m. abusive* dolt, lop-eared fool, ass

اوږدوالی ugdvấli د غربي ساحل په اوږدوالي کښې *m.* **1** length along the western shore **2** prolongation, extension (e.g., of a treaty); dragging out (e.g., of talks) *idiom* و چا ته د عمر اوږدوالی غوښتل To wish someone a long life.

اوږدول ugdavól *denominative, intransitive* [*past:* اوږد یې کړ] **1** to lengthen **2** to extend; prolong (as in to extend a treaty); drag out (talks) **3** to lead, conduct, lay **4** to extend, stretch out, pull out لاس اوږدول، لاس را اوږدول، لاس در اوږدول، لاس ور اوږدول **a** to stretch out the hand **b** to encroach upon زمونږ و خواته یې لاس اوږد They encroached upon our country. دومره پښې اوږدوه چه څومره کړ Cut one's coat according to the cloth. *idiom* بیره دي برستن وي to grow a beard اوږدول

اوږده [1] ugdá *f. singular from* اوږد

اوږده [2] ugdó *m. plural from* اوږد

اوږده [3] ugdó *m. plural* length د سرحد په اوږدو کښي along the border

اوږده مېرجانه ugdá megjấna *f.* cayenne pepper

اوږدېدل ugdedól *denominative, intransitive* [*past:* اوږد شو] **1** to be lengthened **2** to be continued, be prolonged; be extended (e.g., a treaty); be dragged out (of a talk, etc.) **3** to be conducted, be laid, be applied **4** to be stretched, be pulled out **5** to reach or occupy some space

اوږدری ugráj *m.* entrails, offal

اوږم ogm *m. obsolete* moon

اوږمی ogmáj *f.* ugmáj moon; moonlight

اوږه [1] ogá *f. Eastern* ugá shoulder اوږه په اوږه، اوږه پر اوږه shoulder to shoulder; side by side منگی پر اوږه with a pitcher on the shoulder توپک پر اوږه تکیه to shrug the shoulders اوږه ښورول to shoulder a rifle زما پر اوږه تکیه ووهه Lean on me. اوږبی یې to د چا اوږه سپکول He is broad-shouldered. *idiom* سره ارتي دي A په ښه زوی سره د پلار اوږه سپکه وي help, be a help to somebody good son is help to a father اوږه کښنل **a** to get rid of something **b** to shun, reject, avoid something اوږه کښنېکښنل to strive, bend the back و کارته اوږه څني خالي کول to rid oneself of something و دي کارته می اوږه لگول، و کار ته اوږه ورکول to undertake the work و چا اوږه ورکول This matter is beyond my powers. اوږه نه لگېږي to help someone, lend assistance to someone; support someone پر اوږه اخیستل to strive tenaciously و کارته اوږه نیول to take something upon oneself, undertake something د چا پر اوږه ولاړېدل، د چا پر اوږه دربدل to help, give assistance, support someone **a** پر اوږه گرزول to bear on one's shoulders **b** *figurative* to make much of د چا سره اوږه په اوږه کېدل to help one another,

---

د چا د اوړو بار کېدل support one another to live at someone's expense; be a burden to someone.

اوره ²úga *f.* garlic ☞ هوره

اوړه پک ogapák *military* Shoulder Arms! (as a command)

اوږه ور ogavár broad-shouldered

اوږی ¹ogáj *m.* oka (a unit of weight equal to about 14 kgs.)

اوږی ²ógaj *Eastern* ☞ وږی ²

اوږی ³ogə́j *f.* ugə́j necklace (of silver and gold coins)

اوس os us **1** at once, now, at the present time اوس اوس **a** just now, now; not long ago **b** recently, lately اوس دستي now, just now اوس به نو ځو just now اوس به نو ځو They just now left., تر اوسه up to now, until this time, so far تر اوس لا ښه better تر اوسه پوری than before سر له اوسه ښښنت اوس just now **a** just now **b** hence forward, in the future د دا اوس right now, at the present time د کار د اوس نه شروع still لا تر اوسه، اوسه ځخه لا just now لا تر اوسه، اوسه ځخه لا کره Get on with the matter immediately. **2** *attributive* at the present time

اوسا osə́ ☞ هوسا

اوسار avsár *m.* bridle assembly (of a harness)

اوسارول avsāravə́l *denominative, intransitive* [*past:* اوسار یی کړ] **1** to bridle **2** to subjugate; subordinate

اوساکا osākā́ *f.* Osaka (city)

اوسان avsā́n *m.* **1** feeling **2** presence of mind, self-control, bravery *idiom* تللی اوسان reckless

اوسپنتوری ospəntógaj *m.* file

اوسپنتوکی uspəntúkaj *m.* roofing iron

اوسپنخړی ospənkhə́ṛaj *m.* slag; cinder

اوسپنکښ uspənkáx̌ *m.* magnet

اوسپنمزی uspənmə́zaj *m.* iron wire

اوسپنه óspəna *f.* uspə́na iron اومه اوسپنه د اوسپني تختي iron ore خوړه sheet iron ترخه اوسپنه *obsolete* pig-iron (low quality) اوسپنه چه توده نه شي، هومره به اوږده نه شي high-quality iron *proverb* strike while the iron is hot د اوسپني لار dا railroad د اوسپني نیني چیچل دي *saying* It's a very difficult matter.

اوسپنیز ospəníz *adjective* iron

اوستا avastā́ *f.* avesta

اوستری ustráj *Western* **1** last; terminal; final, conclusive خبرونه د خط په اوستری کښی یی ustrí the latest news **2** *m.* end لیکلي و چه ... at the end of the letter he wrote that ... *idiom* اوستری خور the 6th month of the lunar year

اوستریا avstrijā́ *f.* ☞ آستریا

اوستریائي avstrijāí ☞ آستریائي

اوستکار ustakā́r *m.* ☞ استاد

اوستکاری ustakārí *f.* ☞ استادی

اوسط avsát *Arabic* **1** middle, average اوسط راز, اوسط رقم average (middling) size په اوسط ډول, په اوسط صورت on the average **2** intermediate

اوسطلبي avsattalabí *f.* moderation

اوسلو osló *f.* Oslo (city)

اوسمهالول osmahālawə́l *compound verb* update, to update

اوسنی osə́n ☞ اوسنی

اوسنگو usangú quick, fast; high-speed

اوسنی osanáj present, contemporary, existing

اوسول osavə́l *transitive* [*past:* و یی اوساوه] to settle someone, lodge someone

اوسه ¹ósa ☞ اوس

اوسه ²ósa *imperative perfective and imperfective of* اوسېدل خوش اوسه! همېش بیدار اوسه! Be forever vigilant! Rejoice!

اوسی ¹osáj *m.* male gazelle, *Gasella subgutterosa*

اوسی ²ósi *present tense of* اوسېدل

اوسی ³óse *second person singular present tense of* اوسېدل ! جوړ Be healthy! روغ اوسی! Be healthy! ژوندی اوسی! Live long! تل کامیابه اوسی! I wish you success! په خیر اوسی!

اوسی ⁴osə́j *f.* female gazelle, *Gasella subgutterosa*

اوسئ ⁵ósəj *second person plural present tense of* اوسېدل هر کله اوسئ! I wish you long life! خبر May reknown come to you!

اوسبچی osecháj *m.* knucklebone (piece in a game, the bone of an antelope)

اوسېدل osed *intransitive* [*present:* اوسی *past:* واوسېده *present:* اوسېږي] to live, reside; abide; settle, take up one's residence; be, be located دی د ټول عمر په کابل کښی اوسېدلئ دئ He has lived in Kabul all of his life. *idiom* دئ باید د ... ښخه با خبره اوسی He should know that ... *proverb* چه اوسی، په خوی به د هغوسی You learn from your companions.

اوسېدنه osedə́na *f.* اوسېده osedə́ *m. plural* life; residence, domicile; sojourn د اوسېدو ځای place of residence; residence

اوسېدونکی osedúnkaj **1** *present participle from* اوسېدل **2** *m.* resident

اوسېلجن avseldzhə́n **1** sighing **2** *m.* a whiner

اوسېلل avselə́l *transitive* [*past:* ده واوسېلل] **1** to sigh **2** to grieve, be distressed **3** to whine, complain in a tiresome way

اوسېلنه avselə́na *f.* **1** deep breathing, sigh **2** grieving **3** whining

اوسېلی avseláj *m.* ☞ اسوېلی

اوش osh whoa (or similar command to halt an ass)

اوشا ushā́ command to urge on a camel

اوشنل ushnə́l *transitive* [*past:* و یی اوشنه] to unwind; untwist; dismiss; untwine

اوشی úshi *Eastern* ☞ وشي

اوشین avshín *m.* order

اوښ ¹ux̌ *m.* camel د اوبښانو five camels پنځه اوبښه ، پنځه اوبښان غاړی چا نیولي دي؟ *saying literal* Who dares seize a camel by the neck? *figurative* Do not enter into combat with the strong. اوبښ د باره ولوېدئ، د غرغره ونه لوېدئ *Western proverb literal* The camel cries out in complaint before the load is on his back. He is old but his former habits remain. اوبښ په غلبیل نه درنیږي *saying* A sieve will not burden a camel. اوبښ ته یی ویل بازی وکه! ده *saying literal* Tell a camel: "Play a bit!" He'll جړنګان خراب کړه

tear up a melon field. *figurative* Tell a fool to pray to God and he'll bang up his forehead. اوش تره، بیاخني ځه *saying literal* Tie up a camel, and get out of the way. *figurative* Be careful. اوښ تر پله لاندي نه شي پټېدای *proverb literal* You can't hide a camel under a bridge. *figurative* Murder will out. که اوښان کوې، نو ورونه دنگه کنبرده *saying* If you keep camels, build tall gates. گوره چه اوښ په کوم اړخ څملي *saying literal* Observe what side the camel kicks on. *figurative* Keep a sharp eye out and you'll survive. اوښ تې ویل دا غاړه دي ولي کړه ده؟ ده ویل کوم څای مي سم دئ؟ اوښ تې ویل دا غاړه دي ولي کړه ده؟ ده ویل کوم څای مي بیا سم دئ؟ *saying* They asked the camel, "Why do you have a crooked neck?" He answered, "And what do I have that is straight? د اوښ په شا سپو وخورم *saying literal* I sat upon a camel, but the dogs bit me. *figurative* I brought disgrace upon myself.

اوښ ² uḳh *interjection* oh, ah

اوښاره uḳhā́ra *f. zoology* praying mantis

اوښبونه ¹ ushbānə́ *plural from* اوښبون

اوښبانه ² uḳhbānə́ *plural from* اوښبنه

اوښبنه uḳhbaná *feminine of* اوښبون

اوښبني ¹ uḳhbaní *f.* camel herder (as an occupation)

اوښبنې ² uḳhbané *plural from* اوښبنه

اوښبون uḳhbun *m.* اوښبنه uḳhba *m.* [*plural:* اوښبانه uḳhnanə́] camel driver, camel herder

اوښبه توب uḳhbətób *m.* اوښبه والی ushbəvā́laj *m.* camel driver (as an occupation)

اوښت ávuḳht *past stem of* اوښتل

اوښتل avuḳhtə́l [*present:* اوړي *past:* واوښت *past:* واوړېده] *Eastern* اوښتل 1 to overturn; turn; wallow (in mud) 2 to cross (a mountain); climb over (a fence); cross, get across something 3 to change, switch; change into something; shift (to another situation) هوا د خپل حال څخه اوښتل the weather has shifted اوښتي to change one's situation, undergo change موسمونه واوښته را واوښته The seasons of the year have come and gone. شپې او ورځي اوښتي days and nights have passed; time has gone by د ده بنه پر بله اوښتي ده His appearance has altered. 4 to abandon something; reject something; diverge from something, deviate from something له بد خویه _ to reeducate oneself; break bad habits 5 to be inflicted درانه تاوانونه او تلفات ورواښتل They have inflicted heavy losses (losses) 6 to exceed 7 to turn (of a road) 8 to bump into, run into (someone) 9 to be translated په پښتو اوښتل to be translated into the Pashto language 10 to flood (water) په پسرلي اوبه له دې In spring this place is flooded with water. خایه واوښتي 11 to be dislocated 12 to be circulated (capital) چه غواړي نو پرې واوړي *saying* Here is that which you have striven for.

اوښتنه avuḳhtə́na *f.* اوښته avuḳhtə́ *m. plural* 1 turning, turn, shift 2 wallowing (in the mud) 3 crossing (a mountain); climbing over (a fence); passing over (anything) 4 shifting; changing into something; a transfer over to another situation 5

د زماني په اوښتو سره *idiom* refusal, repudiation of something with the passage of time

اوښتونکی avuḳhtúnkaj 1 *present participle of* اوښتل 2 changeable

اوښته رااوښته avuḳhtə́-rāavuḳhtə́ *m. plural* 1 change 2 wrongness, falseness

اوښ غوئي uḳhghvajáj *m.* [*plural:* اوښ غوائي] giraffe

اوښکه uḳhka *f.* tear اوښکي تویوونکی غاز tear gas او ښنکي کول to lachrymate (of the eyes) هغه اوښنکو کښي موسکي شوه *Eastern* She smiled through her tears. سترگو ته او ښنکي راغلي Tears welled up in the eyes.

اوښکبجن uḳhkedzhə́n tearful, lachrymose

اوښکینی uḳhkináj *m.* rancorous person

اوښلن uḳhlə́n teary; lachrymal; full of tears (eyes)

اوښ مرغه uḳhmərghə́ *m.* 1 yellow griffon (vulture) 2 ostrich

اوښمرغی uḳhmərghaj *m.* اوښملغی ushmə́lgháj *m. botany* haloxylon (small tree or bush native to Central Asian desert country)

اوښ والا uḳhvālā́ *m.* nomad who owns a camel

اوښه ¹ úḳha *f.* female camel

اوښه ² óḳha *f. Eastern* tear اوښي ويني ګډي وډي تويول to weep bloody tears

اوښی ¹ ávḳhaj *m.* [*plural:* اوښي ávḳhi *plural:* اوښیان ávshijā́n] 1 wife's brother, brother-in-law 2 sister's husband

اوښي ² oḳhí *m. plural* mane (of a horse)

اوښي ³ uḳhi *plural of* اوښه ¹

اوښي ⁴ óshẹ *plural of* اوښه ²

اوښیمه uḳhemá *f.* female camel in heat

اوښینی oḳhené اوښینی سترگي eyes filled with tears

اوصاف avsáf *m. Arabic plural of* وصف

اوضاع avzā' 1 *m. plural of* وضع 2 *f.* position, situation; status داخلي اوضاع the internal situation سیاسي اوضاع the political situation اوضاع ډېره خرابه معلومېږي the situation is catastrophic اجتماعي اوضاع social relationships

اوطاق otā́q *m.* room; premises; chamber د پهري اوطاق guardroom

اوطراق otrā́q *m.* bivouac, halt

اوعیه av'ijá *m. Arabic* 1 *plural of* وعا 2 *anatomy* vessel د وینو اوعیه blood vessels

اوغز ughz *m.* [*plural:* اوغزان ughzan] *dialect* walnut

اوغم ughə́m *m.* pride; honor اوغم کول to honor, do honor, render homage

اوقات ¹ avḳā́t *m. Arabic* 1 *plural of* وقت 2 times, moments, circumstances عادي اوقات the usual circumstances

اوقات ² avḳā́t *m. Arabic* 1 *plural of* قوت 2 produce, victuals, food

اوقاف avḳā́f *m. Arabic* 1 *plural of* وقف 2 waqf, wakf (ecclesiastical property; an Islamic endowment of property to be held in trust and used for a charitable or religious purpose) د اوقافو مدیریت the management or direction of one or more waqfs

اوقیانوس okjānús *m.* ocean اوقیانوس کبیر *okjānús-i* the Pacific Ocean

اوقیانوسیه okjānosijá *f.* Oceania (island)

اوقیه ukijá *f. Arabic* ounce

اوک uk **1** protruding **2** on end, erect, upright اوک کېدل to be placed on end, be made to stand erect

اوکا oká *f.* the Oka (river)

اوکراین، اوکرائن ukráin ukrājín *m.* the Ukraine

اوکرائني، اوکرایني ukrāiní **1** Ukrainian اوکرائني ژبه the Ukrainian language **2** Ukrainian (person)

اوکلی ukaləj *f.* wooden mortar

اوک¹ úka *feminine singular of* اوک 1

اوکه² auká *conjunction* ☞ که 3

اوکه³ úka *dialect* ☞ وکه

اوکیناوا جزیره okināvá *f.* د اوکیناوا جزیره Okinawa (island)

اوګار avgár **1** *m.* sufferer **2** suffering; experiencing, going through مور او پلارخورا ور سره اوګار دي Her parents have gone through a lot on her account.

اوګد ugd *Eastern* ☞ اوږد

اوګرائي ugrājí *f. Eastern* **1** receipt of the cost of goods in installment payments **2** payment, dues; share

اوګره ugrá *f.* ográ *f.* groats; thin gruel اوګره کول to cook groats *idiom* اوګره د احمد په تلوار نه سپړې *saying* One must wait خخه تو سوه، ویل یې نصیب مي نه وه *proverb* to blame one's failures on fate

اوګرائي ugrājí *f.* ☞ اوکرائي

اوګړه ugṛá *f.* ☞ اوګره

اوګنده ugándā *f.* ugáṇḍa *f.* Uganda

اوګوټ avgóṭ *m. regional* steamship بحري اوګوټ seagoing steamship ☞ اګبوت

اوګه¹ ogá *Eastern* ☞ اوږه

اوګه² úga *f. Eastern* ☞ هوږه

اوګی¹ ogáj *m.* ☞ اوږی 1

اوګی² ugəj *f.* kind of tree

اوګی³ ogəj *f.* Ogaj (city, northwest Pakistan)

اول avvál *Arabic* **1.1** first د لمبر اول **a** first number; first place **b** paramount **c** excellent (appraisal) په اول رئیس chairman ژمي He went to Kandahar at the beginning of the کنبی قندهار ته ولاړ winter. **1.2** beginning; elementary **1.3** former **2** *m.* [*plural:* اوائل avail] beginning د پسرلي په اوائلو کنبی at the beginning of spring له اوله قسمت مي خراب و I had no luck from the beginning. که چیري یې له اوله داسي کړي وای نو . . . If he had done it that way at once, then . . . **3.1** first, in the beginning, first off اول هغه *Eastern* He treated me well from the very ماسره ښه سلوک کاوه beginning. **3.2** in the first place **3.3** formerly, earlier **3.4** already څراغ خو ئي اول مړ کړئ و He has already put the candle already out. **3.5** before, earlier, until د روانېدو نه اول before leaving, before departure

اولاً avválán *Arabic* first of all; to begin with; before all else

اولاد avlád *m. Arabic plural from* ولد [*plural:* اولادونه avlādúna] progeny; children, descendants, offspring اولادونه، اولاد راورل، راورل to produce progeny

اولاده avlādá *f.* **1** progeny **2** descent

اولان اودې ulān-udé *f.* Ulan-Ude (city)

اولانباتور ulān-bátór *m.* Ulan-Bator (city)

اولجه¹ uldzhá *f.* ☞ الجه

اولجه² uldzhá intricate, complex اولجه کول to tangle, embroil; complicate اولجه کېدل to be tangled, be embroiled; become complicated

اولس uləs *m.* ☞ ولس

اولسواله uləsvála *f.* ☞ ولسواله

اولسي uləsí ☞ ولسي

اولل oləl *transitive dialect* ☞ ولل

اولمپیک olimpík ☞ المپیک

اولنی avlanáj avalanáj **1.1** previous, former, late **1.2** initial, elementary, early **1.3** first, primary **1.4** ancient **2** *m.* avlaní *plural* ancestors

اولو¹ avlú *m.* oló *f. singular & plural* syrup

اولو² uləv *m.* horse (of a courier)

اولو³ ulú *Arabic* possessing, having

اولوالامر ululāmr *m. Arabic plural* commanders; chiefs; the leadership

اولوالعزمي ulula'zmí *Arabic* resolution, resoluteness

اولوس ulús *m.* ☞ ولس

اولوسي ulusí ☞ ولسي

اولوی¹ avlávaj **1** fried, roasted, grilled **2** *figurative* worn out with suffering

اولوی² ulaví courier's; pertaining to a courier

اوله¹ ol *m.* [*plural:* اولان olan] flock of nursing ewes all with lambs of the same age and development

اوله² avvála *feminine singular of* اول

اولیا avlijá *m. Arabic plural* **1** *from* ولي² **2** holy men **3** parents and guardians of children **4** leader, manager, person in authority

اولیانوسک uljánovsk *m.* Ulyanovsk (city)

اولیت avvaliját *m. Arabic* superiority; priority, advantage د اولیت to have a prior right or advantage مقام نیول حق لرل to occupy first place

اولیګارشي oligārshí *f.* oligarchy

اولین avvalín the first, the very first

اوم¹ um om اومه uma *f.* umə́ *m. plural* اومي umé *f. plural* **1** raw, not fully cooked اوم غوندي a bit raw **2** unripe, green **3** unfinished, partly processed اومه خښته raw brick, adobe اومه مواد شیان، raw material **4** undressed (of hide, pelt) اوم پوست undressed hide اومه څرمن raw leather **5** not well-adjusted; downcast **6** immature, inexperienced *idiom* تر اومه مځکه لاندي زیار کښل to work underground (of miners)

اووم² uvə́m ovə́m ☞ اووم

اومان umā́n *botany* ephedra (a genus of jointed, nearly leafless desert shrubs)

اومتوکپاڼه ūmtūkpā́ṇa *f. computer science* datasheet

اومتوکپاڼی لید ūmtūkpāṇe *computer science* líd datasheet view

ارمته umatá *f.* snow mixed with rain, sleet

اومړی umə́raj woven of raw silk اومړی کول to make raw-silk thread

اومسوی umsə́vaj burnt (of food) اوم سوی کول to let food burn اوم سوی to burn سوی کېدل

اومغړی umghə́raj اومړی ☞

اومغلن umghalán semi-raw, not completely cooked

اموالی umvā́laj *m.* 1 state of being half or partly cooked 2 unripeness, greeness 3 state of being unprocessed 4 state of not being in proper adjustment 5 immaturity, inexperience

اومه umə́ *m.* اومان ☞ [1]

اومه umə́ *m. plural* اوم ☞ [1]

اومه umá *f. singular from* اوم [1]

اومه ovə́ma *f. numeral singular from* اوم [2]

اومه خوله umá-khulá immature, inexperienced (of a person)

امېد uméd *m.* امبد ☞

امېدوار umedvā́r امبدوار ☞

امېدواره umedvā́ra *f.*

امېدواري umedvārí *f.* [1]

امېدواري umedvāri *plural of* امبدواره [2]

اونتاریو ontārijó *f.* د اونتاریو غدیر Lake Ontario

اونس auns *m.* ounce

اونگ aváng *m.* mortar

اونه úna *f. dialect* ونه ☞

اونی unáj *m.* onáj idle talker, windbag [1]

اونی uvanə́j *f.* ovanə́j week [2]

اونی úne *plural of* اونه [3]

اونېگا onegā́ *f.* د اونېگا غدیر Lake Onega

اونس auṇs *m.* اونس ☞

اونی uṇáj *m.* diaper

اوورکوټ ovarkóṭ *m. regional* overcoat, greatcoat

اوبنتل avuḳhtə́l *intransitive* اوبنتل ☞

اودل ovə́l *transitive dialect* اودل ☞

اووم ovvúm uvvə́m *ordinal* seventh

اوونی uvanə́j *f.* week

اووه ovvə́ uvə́ *numeral* اوه ☞ [2] اووه ستوری *astronomy* asterism consisting of seven stars *history* اووه کشوره the Seven Nations of the East (China, Turkestan, Hindustan, Turania, Iran, East-Rome, and Syria-Sham)

اووي ovví اوي ☞ [1]

اوه ová *f.* 1 cut place, chipped place 2 blister; pimple [1]

اوه uvə́ ová *numeral* seven اوه دېرش thirty-seven اوه نیم seven and a half [2]

اوه oh *interjection* oh [3]

اوهام avhā́m *m. Arabic plural from* وهم

اوهامي avhāmí 1 vacillating, doubting 2 doubtful

اوه ډزی ovə́dázaj *m.* seven-shot rifle

اوه کلن ovəkalán seven-year اوه کلن پلان Seven-Year Plan

اوه نی uvanə́j *f.* wcck اوه کی

اوه ورځنی ovəvradzánaj weekly

اوي oví *singular & plural* 1 comb, fleshy crest (of a bird) 2 mane (of a horse) [1]

آوي aví اوي aví irrigational; pertaining to flushing or watering آبي ☞ [2] [1]

اوی uj *m.* promise, word (of honor) [3]

اویا avjā́ *numeral* seventy [1]

اویا au jā́ او ☞ [2] [1]

آبیانه āvijā́ná *f.*

اوبجه avédzha *f.* country, locality, territory

اوبر avéṛ *m. medicine* inhalation

آوېز āvéz *combining form* دست آوېز document

اوبزان avezā́n اوبزاند avezā́nd hanging

اوبزاندول avezāndavə́l *denominative, transitive* [*past:* اوبزاند یې کړ] to hang, suspend

اوبزاندبدل avezāndedə́l *denominative, intransitive* [*past:* اوبزاند شو] to hang, be suspended

اوبنبته uvkhtá *f.* juniper

اوینه ujnə́ *m.* ojnə́ *singular & plural* termite (insect)

اودل úji *present tense of* اودل او یی [1]

آه āh 1 *m.* sigh آه کنبل ساړه آهونه heavy sighs, آهونه ایستل sigh b to gasp 2 *interjection* ah

اها ahā́ *particle* 1 oh but … aha 2 *interjection* my اها څه ښه خوند کوي My, but this is tasty!

آهار āhā́r *m.* 1 starch کالیو ته آهار ورکول to starch linen 2 *textiles* to size

اهار āhā́r *m.* 1 intense heat, heat 2 *regional* hottest month of the year

آهاک āhā́k *m.* آهک ☞

اهالي ahālí *m. Arabic plural from* اهل [1]

اهتمام ihtimā́m *m. Arabic* 1 zeal, diligence 2 concern, attention اهتمام کول a to try b to take care of, concern oneself about اهتمام ورکول to give attention to 3 editing

اهدا ihdā́ *f. Arabic* 1 dedication (of a book) 2 gift, presentation

اهداد ihdād *m. Arabic* punishment اهداد ورکول to punish, chastise

اهداف ahdāf *m. Arabic plural from* هدف

اهدانامه ihdānāmá *f. law* settlement, deed

اهرام ahrā́m *m. Arabic plural from* هرم

اهر ahár *m.* اهار ☞

آهستگي āhistagí *f.* 1 slugishness 2 mildness

آهسته āhistá 1 slow; quiet آهسته کول to delay, detain, stop 2 slowly, quietly

آهستگي āhistagí *f.* آهسته گي ☞

آهک āhák *m. plural* lime

آهکي āhakí *attributive* lime

د اهل ahl *Arabic* **1** *m.* [*plural:* اهالي ahālí] people, population
نورو دينو اهل heterodox people **2.1** *predicative, attributive*
worthy **2.2** able **2.3** knowing something; trained to do
something **2.4** fit, suitable

اهل ايمان ahl-i-imán *m. plural* a believer

اهل حديث ahl-i-hadís *m. plural* Waqqabites, Mujtadhids (Muslim
sectarian religious teachers)

اهل سنت ahl-i-sunnát *m. plural* Sunnites

اهل قلم ahl-i-halám *m. plural* writers

اهل کار ahl-i-kár *m. plural* office workers, employees, workers

اهل کسبه ahl-i-kasabá *m. plural* craftsman

اهل وعيال ahl-u-'ajál *m. plural* goods and chattel, the entire
household

اهلي ahlí *Arabic* domestic, domesticated, tame

اهليت ahliját *m. Arabic* **1** professional qualification, speciality **2**
ability

اهليت نامه ahlijatnāmá *f.* driver's license

اهم ahám *Arabic* more important, most important تر ټولو لمړی او
اهمه وظيفه the foremost and most important task

اهمال ihmál *m. Arabic* negligence, carelessness

د اهميت وړ ahammiját *m. Arabic* significance; importance
significant, important خورا ډېر اهميت لرل to have great
significance اهميت له اهميت څخه لوېدل to lose its significance
ډېر اهميت ورکول to take on significance, be important ميندل to
give great significance خورا اهميت ورکول to give great
significance to هيڅ اهميت نه ورکول not to attribute the slightest
significance to

آهن āhín *m. āhán singular & plural* iron

آهن باب āhinbáb *m. plural* iron; article made of iron

آهن چادر āhán-i-chādár *m.* sheet iron, roofing iron

آهن ربا āhinrubá *f.* magnet

آهن کوب āhinkób *m.* hammer

آهنگ āháng *m.* **1** melody, musical theme, tune **2** sounding,
sound په نه آهنگ کول to sound **3** tone, intonation *idiom*
آهنگ آهنگ willy-nilly

آهنگ دار āhangdár melodic, tuneful

د سل تکي āhingár *m.* آهن گر āhingár smith, blacksmith
زرگر، يو د آهنگر، سل تکي د زرگر، يو د آهنگر برابر دئ *proverb* One
hundred blows of the jeweler's hammer are equal to one of the
blacksmith's.

آهنگري āhingarí *f.* blacksmith's work د آهنگري دکان smithy, forge

آهنه āhiná *f.* mirror

دی په خان آهني ضبط لري āhiní *adjective* iron *idiom* He has
excellent self-control.

آهو āhu *m.* **1** antelope **2** wild goat **3** *poetic* gazelle ☞ هوسی

آهواز āhváz *m.* Ahvaz (city)

آهوچشم āhucháshm having the eyes of a gazelle

اهورامزده ahurāmazdá *m.* Ormuzd (Zoroastrian diety)

آهوري āhoráj *m.* **1** mustard د آهوري تپل āhori mustard oil **2**
colza, cole-seed

اهور ahúr *m.* century; epoch

آهين āhín *m.* ☞ آهن

آهنگر āhingár *m.* ☞ آهنگر

آهينه āhiná *f.* mirror

ای [1] aj eh *interjection* hey, oh زويه! ای Sonny! My Son!
احمده! Hey, Ahmed!

ای [2] aj *demonstrative pronoun dialect* this, these

آيا ājá *particle* really, indeed آيا دا خبره رښتياده؟ Is this really true?
آيا څه به راته وايي؟ Really! What is this that they are telling me?
آيا څه به وي؟ Will something really happen?

آيات āját *m. Arabic plural from* آيت

اياز ajáz *m. proper name* Ajaz

ايالت ijālát *m. Arabic* district; province; state

ايالتي ijalatí *adjective* district

ايام ajám *m. Arabic plural from* يوم [2]

اېبره کيلي aebrá kilí *f.* product key

ای بک ajbák *m. singular & plural*

ابونيت ebonít *m. plural* ebonite, ebony

ايت aját *m. Arabic* [*plural:* آيات ājāt] Koranic verse

ايتالوي itālaví **1** *adjective* Italian **2** *m.* Italian (person)

ايتاليا itālijá *f.* Italy

ايتام ajtám *m. Arabic plural from* يتيم

اېترنېټ ajitarneṭ *m.* ethernet

ائتکال i'tikál *m. Arabic geology* washing, erosion

ايتلاف itiláf *m.* ائتلاف i'tilaf *m. Arabic* coalition, bloc

ائتلافي i'tilāfí *adjective* coalition, coalitional

د يو جلا آيتم په حيث په اجنده کښې نيول ājtám *m.* point, item
introduce a specific point into the agendā

اېتو etó *possessive pronoun second singular Afridi familiar* **1**
your **2** thy (all gender and number forms)

اېتوسو etóso *possessive pronoun plural Afridi polite* your

ايتالوي iṭālaví ☞ ايتالوي

ايتاليه íṭáli *f.* ايتاليجا iṭālijá *f.* Italy

اېتم [1] étəm *m.* atom

آيتم [2] ājtám *m.* ☞ آيتم

ايثار isár *m. Arabic* **1** donation **2** generosity

د ايجاب idzhâb *m. Arabic* [*plural:* ايجابونه idzhâbuna *Arabic
plural:* ايجابات idzhâbat] **1** need, necessity **2** requirement
د وخت د ايجابو سره سم depending on the requirements of the
moment **3** *trade* commission, order

ايجابول idzhabāvəl *denominative, intransitive* [*past:* ايجاب يې کړ]
1 to call for, stipulate **2** to demand, require (e.g., expenditures)

ايجابي idzhābí *Arabic* required, necessary

ايجاد idzhâd *m. Arabic* **1** creation, foundation; organization **2**
invention **3** act of forming, act of organizing ايجاد کول
compound verb **a** to create, found, organize **b** to invent **c** to

form, design ایجاد کېدل ایجاد مېندل compound verb **a** to be created, be founded, be organized **b** to be invented **c** to be formed, be designed

ایجادکاري idzhādkarí *f.* creativity, creative work

ایجړا idzhṛā́ *m.* ایجړاگی idzhṛāgáj *m.* ایجړی idzhṛáj *m.* **1** cunuch **2** pederast

ېجنت édzhānṭ *m.* **1** پولتیکل ایجنت political agent **2** representative

ایجنتي edzhanṭí *f.* ایجنسي édzhensí *f.* agency

اېجنی edzháne *doublet word* to پېژنې

اېجین edzhíjən Aegean د اېجین بحیره the Aegean Sea

ایخودل ikhodál *transitive dialect* ☞ اینبودل

ایخول ikhavál *transitive* [*past:* وی ایخاوه] to compel a camel to lie down

ایداد idā́d *m.* ☞ اهداد

ایدیال idjā́l *m.* ideal

ایدیالي idjālí *adjective* ideal

اېډمیرال eḍmirā́l *m.* admiral

آیدیا ajḍijā́ *f.* idea

اېډي کانگ eḍikáng *m. regional* aide-de-camp

ایذا izā́ *f. Arabic* **1** damage, loss **2** anxiety, trouble ایذا رسول **a** to inflict damage; harm **b** to trouble, disturb

ایر ajr *m.* ☞ اترلېند

ایر[2] ir obtained; received

ایر[3] er ☞ هېر[1]

ایراد irā́d *m. Arabic* **1** pronunciation, articulation (e.g., of speech); proclamation (statement, declaration, etc.) **2** mention **3** production of proofs **4** objection; cavil کوم ایراد پر نشي نیول کېدای It's impossible to find fault with him.

ایرادول irādavál [*past:* ایراد یې کړ] to pronounce, articulate (e.g., speech); proclaim (a statement, etc.) یو نطق یې ایراد کړ He made a speech.

ایران irā́n *m.* Iran

ایراني irāní irānáj **1** Iranian **2** *m.* Iranian (person)

ایراوادي irāvādí *f.* the Irawaddy River

ایرب iráb curved, crooked ایربه لیکه curved line

اېرړی erṛáj *m.* ☞ اړړی[1]

ایرکوتسک irkútsk *m.* Irkustsk (city)

آیرلېند ājrlénd *m.* اترلېند Ireland

ایرم irám *m.* coral

ایرن irán ash grey

ایروپز iropáz **1** base **2** cowardly

آېرودینامیک āerodināmík *m.* aerodynamics

آېرودینامیکي āerodināmikí aerodynamic

آېروستات āerostā́t *m.* balloon

ایره irá *f.* ایري iré *usually plural* ash, ashes ایري کول reduce to ashes, incinerate ایري کېدل **a** to be burnt up, to smoulder, be reduced to ashes **b** *figurative* to burn with shame ایري ورکول **a** to strew with ashes **b** to deprive of something, *figurative* to

avoid someone **c** *idiom* ډېري ایري په سر اچول to sprinkle the head with ashes; grieve deeply له خاورو څخه ولاړبدل، پر ایرو کښېنستل to make an error in calculation, miscalculate سره ایري کول to embroil someone with someone else ایري په خوله کېدل to fail to be awarded something, be passed over مخ نه یې ایري وچېهېدې He grew pale.

ایری[1] iráj *f.* idle talk ایری وهل to prate, talk nonsense

ایري[2] iré *plural of* ایره

ایریان irijā́n *m.* Irian

اېریال érijál *m.* antenna

اېرېوان erevā́n *m.* Erevan (city)

اېړ iṛ *m. obsolete* fleet

ایراب iṛā́b *m.* kind of bitter shrub

ایز íz ایزه íza *adjectival suffix place after vowels:* څلور فقره ایز consisting of four points

ایزتی izatə́j *f. proper name* Izati

ایزوتوپ izotóp *m.* isotope

ایزومېر izomér *chemistry* isomer

اېگ eg *m.* ☞ ابر هیر

ایرد igd *present stem of* اینبودل

اېگدي ígdi *present tense of* اینبودل

ایسار isā́r ☞ حصار

ایسارتیا isārtjā́ *f.* delay; stop

ایساړول isāravál *denominative, transitive* [*past:* ایساړي یې کړ] **1** to delay, stop **2** to besiege, blockade **3** *figurative* to place in a difficult position **4** to limit, restrict, put restraint upon

ایساړبدل isaredál *denominative, intransitive* [*past:* ایساړ شو] **1** to be delayed, be detained, be stopped **2** to wait دلي ایسار شه wait here **3** to be beseiged, be blockaded **4** *figurative* to find oneself in a difficult situation **5** to be limited, be constrained

ایست ist *imperfective of* ایستل

ایستاده istādá ☞ آب ایستاده

ایستگا istgā́ *m. & f.* ایستگاه istgā́h *m.* [*plural:* استگاهونه istgāhúna *f. plural:* استگاوي istgā́vi] stand, stop دبهریو ایستگا harbor

ایستل istál *Western* **1** *transitive* [*present:* باسي *past:* وی ایست] **1.1** to throw out, discard; chuck out توره له **1.2** extract, take out تبکي څخه ایستل to unsheathe a saber **1.3** to take off (a shoe, article of clothing) پنی ایستل to take off someone's shoes کالي ایستل to undress **1.4** to rake out (e.g., ashes) **1.5** to extract, obtain سکاره ایستل to mine coal, extract coal **1.6** to exclude; dismiss له ... څخه چا نوم ایستل to leave someone's name off ..., to exclude someone from ... **1.7** to turn out, issue (production, money, etc.) اخبار ایستل to issue paper money نوټونه ایستل to publish a newspaper **1.8** to start, put into operation **1.9** to let out (air from a tire, balloon) **1.10** to expell, evict; turn out; dismiss څوک په تاخت له کوره ایستل to put out of the house **1.11** to invent; think up, devise **1.12** to unharness آس له بگي څخه وباسه! Unharness the horse! **1.13** to show, extend something (for inspection) **1.14** to tear out, pull out **1.15** to extract (e.g., a tooth) **1.16** *chemistry & physiology* to isolate, secrete **1.17** to remove, get rid of, liquidate له من‌حه ایستل to remove, get rid of, liquidate **1.18** to withdraw (e.g., troops from a country); evacuate **1.19** to send out, put in front (i.e., a detachment) **1.20** to build (a road); dig (a canal) **1.21** to transfer (to another place) **1.22** to export **1.23** to drain (water) **1.24** to express (i.e., gratitude) **1.25** to emit (a sound) **1.26** to come upon, get on (the trail of) **2** *m. plural* ☞ د ورېښمو ایستل ایستنه silkworm breeding, sericulture

ایستنه istə́na *f.* **1** throwing away, rejection, chucking out **2** extracting, taking out **3** taking off (shoes, clothing) **4** raking out (i.e., ashes) **5** extracting, obtaining, mining د سکرو ایستنه mining of coal **6** exclusion; elimination, leaving out **7** output, issuing (production, money, etc.) **8** starting, putting into operation **9** dispatch; eviction **10** banishment **11** invention; thinking up, conceiving **12** tearing out, extraction **13** removal, extraction (of a tooth) **14** *chemistry & physiology* isolation, secretion **15** elimination, removal, liquidation **16** withdrawal (i.e., of troops) **17** forward emplacement (of a detachment) **18** building, laying (a road); digging (a canal) **19** export **20** draining, drainage (of water) *idiom* د لغتو ایستنه word production

ایستونی estoní **1** Estonian ایستونی ژبه Estonian language **2** Estonian (person)

ایستونیا estonijā́ *f.* ☞ استونیا

ایسته istə́ ¹ *m. plural* ☞ ایستنه

ایسته ísta ² at the side (of something) را ایسته over here, on this side ایسته کول **a** to remove; eliminate **b** to draw back (i.e., curtain); clear (dishes away, etc.) **c** to get rid of, eliminate (a defect) **d** to satisfy (requirements, etc.) ایسته بدل to move off, go away, withdraw خلق سره ایسته شول the people stepped aside د ځایه ایسته شه! Be off! Get away! ایسته شه! Get away from here! Get out of here! *idiom* په ایسته له دې From here on, in future ... له ۲۳ کالو را په ایسته It's been twenty-three years already ...

آیس لبند ājslend *m.* Iceland

آیس لبندي ājslendí **1** Icelandic آیس لبندي ژبه the Icelandic language **2** Icelander (person)

ایسند isə́nd fitting, suitable, proper

ایساول esavə́l *transitive* [*past:* و یې ایساوه] adorn, beautify

ایسی íse ¹ ☞ ایسته ²

ایسی íse ² *present of* ایسبدل

ایسبدل isedə́l *intransitive* [*past:* وایسبده] to seem to be, appear to be, present itself as ضرور ایسی to be, seem to be, appear to be necessary بد ایسبدل to please; present a pleasing appearance بنه ایسبدل not to please; be unpleasant

ایشله ishála *f.* dance performed by females

ایشلی eshə́le *f.* pancake

ایشنا ishnā́ eshnā́ *f.* **1** boiling **2** fermentation **3** *figurative* excitation; agitation; fit, paroxysm

ایشند ishə́nd **1** boiling **2** *figurative* aroused, excited, agitated

ایشول ishavə́l *transitive* [*past:* و یې ایشول] **1** to boil **2** to bring to fermentation **3** *figurative* to arouse, excite, agitate

ایشولی ishavə́li boiled ایشولي شیدې ishavə́li boiled milk ایشولئ هگی soft-boiled egg

ایشی ishí *present of* ایشبدل

ابشیا eshjā́ *f.* ☞ آسیا ²

ایشبدل eshedə́l *intransitive* [*present:* ایشپري *past:* وایشبده present:* ایشی] **1** to boil; boil up **2** to ferment; be in a state of fermentation **3** *figurative* to be aroused, be excited, be agitated; be irritated, be annoyed پرله ایشبدل to flare up **4** to seethe

ایشبدلی اوبه ishedə́laj **1** *past participle of* ایشبدل **2** boiled ایشبدلئ ishedə́li boiled water, boiling water (for tea)

ایشبدنه ishedə́na *f.* **1** boiling **2** fermentation **3** *figurative* arousal, excitation; irritation

ایشیک آغاسي ishikāghāsí *m. history* master of ceremonies

ابنبل eḳhə́l iḳhə́l *transitive dialect* ☞ اینبودل

ایبنو iḳhov *imperfective of* ایبنوول

ایبنود iḳhod *imperfective of* ایبنوول

ایبنودل iḳhodə́l *transitive Eastern* eshodə́l [*present:* ږدي *Western* چو *past:* کښني یې ږنود ایردي] **1** to put, place; stand, install; locate و مرغانو ته دام ایبنودل Place the chair there. کئ هلته کښبنږده place a net on birds یوی خوا ته ایبنودل to put aside, move aside, move out of the way **2** to put in هنداره ایبنودل to install a windowpane **3** to plant (i.e., trees) **4** to put aside (for a reserve) **5** to create, develop **6** to lay or place upon someone (i.e., responsibility) **7** to invest (capital) **8** to pay in (money) **9** to lay, build (i.e., a road)

ایبنودنه iḳhodə́na *f.* **1** establishment, putting, placing, arrangement; location **2** planting (i.e., trees) **3** setting aside (for a reserve) **4** investment (capital) **5** laying, building (i.e., a road)

ایبنوده iḳhodə́ ¹ iḳhodá *imperfective of* ایبنودل

ایبنوده iḳhodə́ ² *m. plural* ☞ ایبنودنه

ایبنول iḳhavə́l ishovə́l *transitive dialect* ☞ ایبنودل

ایبنوونه ishoّvə́na *f.* ☞ ایبنودنه

ایبنئ iḳhaj *past participle of* ایبنودل

ایصال isā́l *m.* **1** joining, conjunction; contiguity **2** assistance (i.e., in attaining a goal) **3** progress (in some matter)

ایضاً ájzán *Arabic* also, as well

ایضاح izā́ izā́h *f. Arabic m.* [*plural:* ایضاحات izahā́t] explanation, elucidation, illustration ایضاح کول to explain, elucidate, illustrate

ایطالوی itālaví **1** Italian **2** *m.* Italian (person)

ایطالیا itālijā́ *f.* Italy

ایغ egh ¹ *pronoun Afridi* ☞ هغه ¹

ایغ egh ² protruding, sticking out

ایغ سترگی estárgaj **1** jolly **2** smart, quick, spritely

ایغ نبغ eghnégh **1** stiff with cold **2** stiff **3** *figurative* artificial, unnatural

اېغو eghó *pronoun Afridi* ☞ هغو

اېغوی eghúj *pronoun Afridi* ☞ هغوی

اېغه égha *feminine of* ایغ[2]

اېفا ifā́ *f. Arabic* **1** execution (i.e., of an obligation); fulfillment (i.e., of a promise) **2** payment, clearing (i.e., of a debt)

اېفاد ifā́d *m. Arabic* sending, delegation

اېقاظ iḳā́z *m. Arabic* awakening

اېکتر ektár *m. regional* actor

اېکتریس éktrís *f. regional* actress

اېکر ekr *m.* acre

اېکسرې eksré *f.* اېکس رېز eksréz *m. plural* x-ray, x-rays د اېکسرې ماشین x-ray apparatus د اېکسرې موسسه x-ray room

اېکوادور ekvādór *m.* Equador

اېکي[1] ikí *f.* copper coin, copper, penny توري ایکی a trifle

اېکي[2] ekí only, sole

اېکېډېمي ekéḍemi *f. regional* academy

اېل[1] el *m.* tribe, clan

اېل[2] el il **1** quiet; tame; domesticated (of animals) **2** submissive, obedient ☞ اېلول، اېل کول ☞ اېل کېدل، اېلبېدل

آېل[3] ājl *m. plural* **1** oil **2** petroleum

اېلاپ elā́p *m.* snake plant (a medicinal plant)

اېلاق ilā́ḳ *m.* ☞ اېلبند

اېلاقي ilā́ḳi relating to summer pasture ایلاقي خونه a summer house

اېلاني elāní *f.* submissiveness

اېلبند ilbánd *m.* summer pasture, mountain medow

اېلجاري ildzhārí iladzhārí ☞ ایله جاري

اېلچي ilchí *m. obsolete* **1** ambassador **2** herald, messenger

آېلسویچ ājlsvích *m. technology* oil switch

اېلغار ilghā́r *m.* ☞ ایلغر ilghár *m.* attack, raid

اېل والی elvā́laj *m.* submissiveness

اېلول elavól *denominative* [*past:* اېل یې کړ] **1** to pacify; tame **2** to conquer; subjugate, subordinate to

ایله ilá **1.1** free, discharged, released ایله کول *a* to free; discharge, release *b* to exude (i.e., gas) *c* to evacuate ایله کېدل *a* to be freed, be discharged, be released *b* to be leaked out (i.e., gas) *c* to be evacuated **1.2** itinerant, wandering **2.1** hardly, barely زه ایله ایله رنا شوم زه ایله باج شوم I had a narrow escape. It is just beginning to dawn. **2.2** just, only ایله اوس only now ... ایله اوس خبر شوم چه I just now noticed that … مونږ به ایله دوډی شروع کړي وه چه ... We had only just sat down to eat when … **2.3** in all, in toto

ایله جاري iladzhārí **1.1** voluntary; pertaining to military volunteers **1.2** partisan **2.1** *m.* volunteer; militia volunteer **2.2** a partisan

ایله گردي ilagardí *f.* vagabondage, vagrancy

ایلې[1] íle íli here, over here, this way

ایلی[2] iláj *f.* ☞ هیلی[1]

ایلی[3] ilí *f.* liquid mud

اېلهېدل eledál *denominative, intransitive* [*past:* ایهل شو] **1** to be tamed **2** to be conquered, be subjugated, be subordinated

اېلهېدنه eledána *f.* اېلبېدنه eledána *m. plural* **1** taming, domesticating **2** conquering, conquest, subjugation, subordination

اېلکترونیک elektroník *m.* electronics

اېلکترونیکي elektronikí electronic

اېما imā́ *f. Arabic* sign, hint; nod

ایماق ajmā́ḳ **1** *m.* people, tribe **2** *m. plural* the Ajmaks (a nationality) **3** *m.* Ajmak (tribesman)

ایماقي ajmā́ḳí *adjective* Ajmak ایماقي پسه Ajmak sheep

ایمان imā́n *m. Arabic* **1** faith, belief; persuasion ثابت ایمان deep conviction ایمان راوړل، په ایمان راوړل to believe in something **2** conscience; conscientiousness, honesty, decency په ایمان ویل to confess honestly

ایماندار imāndā́r **1** correct, true, devoted; reliable ایمانداره ښنځه devoted wife ایماندار شي! May they have faith in thee! (a wish) **2** conscientious, honest, decent **3** convinced **4** devout, pious

ایمانداري imāndārí *f.* **1** faithfulness, devotion; reliability **2** sincerity; conscientiousness, honesty, probity د ایمانداري کار کول *a* to be faithful, be devoted *b* to be honest; be decent; be sincere

ایماني imāní pertaining to religion, religious

اېمبولېنس embuléns *m. regional* ambulance; emergency medical vehicle

اېمن emán quiet, peaceful; peace loving

اېمن والی emánvā́laj *m.* calm; peaceableness

اېمنه emána **1** *feminine singular of* اېمن **2** *f. proper name* Emina

اېمو emó *possessive pronoun Afridi* my ☞ زما

ایمه ajmá *f. history* estate, fief

ایمه دار ajmadā́r *m. history* owner of a fief, feudal landlord

اېنټي یونیټ فرنټ énți-junịt frant *m. regional history* movement opposing the creation of a single united province of West Pakistan

اېنچ inch *m.* inch *idiom* د خپل وطن هر اېنچ خاوره Every inch of one's native land.

اېنځر indzár *m.* ☞ انځر

اېنداره indā́ra *f.* **1** mirror **2** glass ☞ هنداره

اېندتوب indətób *m.* اېندوالی indəvā́laj *m.* reservation of an animal for productive or breeding purposes

آېنده[1] ājandá **1** future; approaching, coming **2** *f.* future د آېنده ته a future time; in the future په آېنده دپاره in future نژدی آېنده کښي in the near future آېنده ته وخندول to put off to the future

اېنده[2] ində *m.* [*plural:* ایندان indā́n] *agriculture* sire, stud (ram, bull, etc.) اېنده کول to reserve for breeding اېنده کېدل to be reserved for breeding

اینده ³ índa *f.* drink, gulp به يوه اينده چنبل to drink off at one draught, يوه اينده کول drink a lot *idiom* ځان يوه اينده وهل to dress up, dress smartly اينده کول

اینده ⁴ indá *f.* colza, cole, rape

اینکه ajnáka *f. usually plural* اينکي ajnáki glasses, spectacles اينکه پر سترگو ايښودل a to wear glasses b to put glasses on

اینگه ingá engá *f.* inga (the female companion of a new bride chosen from among her relatives, and who lives in the house of her husband for some time after the wedding)

اینه inā *f. anatomy* liver

يوازي evázaj ايوازى iváżaj *dialect* ☞ ايواحى

ايوان ¹ ajván *m. colloquial* 1 ☞ حيوان 2 child

ايوان ² ajván *m.* hall, gallery

ايوان عام ajván-i-'ám *m. regional* the House of Commons

ايوب ajúb *m. Arabic proper name* 1 Ayub 2 *proper name* Job

ايوب زي 1 ajubzí *m. plural* the Ayubzi (tribe) 2 ajubzáj *m.* Ayubzai (tribesman)

آیه ājá *f. Arabic* ☞ آيت

اى هي ēhé *interjection* hey, look here, ahoy

آئین āín *m.* 1 rite, ceremony; custom, procedure 2 law; legal code; statute; regulations د آئين څخه بهر unlawful

آئینه āiná *f.* mirror برقي آئينه signal mirror آئينې ته کتل to look in the mirror

آئینه خانه āinakhāná *f.* room, chamber; small room usually in the upper part of a dwelling

آئینه ساز ainasáz *m.* mirror stand, mirror holder

ب

ب ¹ be 1 the second letter of the Pashto alphabet 2 the number 2 in the abjad system

ب ² *official abbreviation* بسالت مند

ب ³ ☞ به ¹

ب ⁴ bi *Arabic preposition or prefix used with Arabic words* بالخاصه especially, particularly بالذات personally, in person

ب، ا *abbreviation* د باختر آژانس the agency Bakhtar باختر آژانس the news agency Bakhtar

با ¹ bā *children's speech* bah-bah (imitating sheep)

با ² bā ☞ بيا

با ³ bā *Farsi preposition or prefix indicating the presence of some quality or attribute* باادبه well brought up باهميت important; significant

بادبه bāadaba well brought up

بانصافه bāinsáfa honorable, honest; just

باهميت bāahamiját bāahammiját important, significant

باب ¹ bāb *m. Arabic [plural:* بابونه bābúna *Arabic plural:* ابواب abváb] 1 door 2 number used when counting buildings, schools, etc. 3 chapter, section (of a book) 4 question, problem, matter دي باب کښي relative to this; about this; for this reason

باب ² bāb 1 *predicate* suitable; widespread; brought into use; accepted 2 *m.* spreading, dissemination 3 *combining form* plurality, collectivity خشک باب dried fruit خوراکه باب groceries

بابا ¹ bābá *m.* 1 *vocative* father! بابا جانه! Father! 2 *vocative* Grandfather! 3 grandfather 4 [*plural:* باباگان bābāgán] ancestors *idiom* د بابا غر Kokhibaba Range

بابا ² bābá *children's speech* بابا يي که! Beat him!

باباجي bābādzhí *m.* grandfather

بابازي bābāzí *m. plural* Babazi (a subdivision of the Momands)

باب المندب bāb-al-mandáb *m.* د باب المندب آبنا Bab-el'-Mandeb Strait

بابائي bābāhí *f.* 1 fatherhood 2 *figurative ironic* good deed; patronage څه بابائي را باندي کوي چه ماته يي را کوې؟ Have you decided to be my benefactor with this?

بابت bābát *m. Arabic* question, problem د دي له بابته relative to this, concerning this; in connection with this د چا په بابت کښي relative to, in relation to someone

بابر bābúr *m.* 1 lion 2 *proper name* Babur, Baber بابر پادشاه Sultan Babur د بابر باغ the Garden of Babur (in Kabul)

بابر ¹ bābur *m.* ☞ بابر ²

بابر ² bābŗ 1 *m. plural* Babyr (tribe) 2 Babyr (person) 3 *proper noun* Babyr

بابک bābək *m.* بابکو bābkó *m.* bābəkó *m. vocative* father, papa (as a term of endearment)

بابل bābúl *m. Arabic history* Babylon

بابو ¹ bābó *m. vocative* father, papa

بابو ² bābú *m.* 1 clerk; office worker, employee (from local inhabitants, in India) د بابوگان دفتر office workers 2 gentlemen; chiefs

بابو ³ bābó *f.* older sister

بابوزي 1 bābuzí *m. plural* Babuzai (tribe) 2 bābuzáj Babuzaj (person)

بابول bābavól *denominative, transitive* [*past:* باب يې کړ] to spread, disseminate; bring into use

بابولاله bābulála *f.* wedding lament (a lamentation of the bride at the wedding rite) *idiom* بابولالي ويل to speak nonsense

بابونه ¹ bābúna *m. plural of* باب ¹

بابونه ² bābavəna *f.* spreading, dissemination; bringing into use

بابي ¹ bābí 1 *m. plural* Babi (tribe) 2 bābáj *m.* Babi (person)

بابی ² bābáj *f.* 1 bride (brother's wife) 2 mother, auntie (familiar form of address to an elderly woman)

بابیدل bābedól *denominative, intransitive* [*past:* باب شو] to be spread around, be disseminated; be used; be accepted, be usual

بابیدنه bābedəna *f.* بابیده babedə *m. plural* dissemination, spreading

بابیری bāberáj *m.* 1 recurrence, relapse (of a sickness) پر بابیری تبي He's sick again with a fever. 2 price increase د انگورو بابیری وکئ He raised the price of grapes. 3 addition to bride money, increase in the amount of bride amount (after bargaining) يي پر وکئ

بابېز bābéz **1** unimportant, mediocre **2** vain, futile تول کوښښونه يې بابېز شول all of his efforts were futiles **3** bad, base (of a person) **4** bad, nasty (of a word)

بابېزوالی bābezvālaj *m.* low quality; mediocrity

بابېزوکی bābezúkaj **1** bad (diminutive form) **2** thin, puny

بابېزول bābezvál *denominative, predicate* [*past:* بابېز يې کړ] to spoil something; break off some matter

باتجربه bātadzhribá experienced; having experience, practice

باتدبیره bātadbíra bright, sharp, quick (on the uptake)

باتکلیفه bātaklífa difficult, heavy, burdensome; full of grief, deprivation باتکلیفه کال a bad year, difficult year

باتور¹ bātúr bātór **1.1** mighty **1.2** heroic; brave; courageous **2** *m.* **.1** hero; brave man **2.2** *proper name* Batur

باتور² bātúr *m.* bātór pupil (of the eye)

باتوره bāturá *f.* thorn-apple

باتوري bāturí *f.* bātorí *f.* heroism; courage, bravery, daring باتوري کول to show heroism; be courageous

باتی¹ bātáj *m.* large saucepan

باتی² bātój *f. singular & plural* **1** wick, fuse **2** *medicine* probe

باتبری¹ bāteráj *m.* quail

باتبری² bāteráj *f.* female quail

باتینگر bātingár *m.* **1** tomato **2** *dialect* asafetida (a gum resin)

بات bāṭ *m.* whetstone, hone بات کول *compound verb* to sharpen (on a whetstone)

باتاره bāṭára *f.* large hail

باتک bāṭúr baṭók boastful

باتلی bāṭláj *m. diminutive* pail د اوبو باتلی a pail of water

باتو bāṭú *m.* braggart; haughty person, boastful person

باتول bāṭavól *m.* **1** *denominative* [*past:* بات يې کړ] to sharpen (on a whetstone) **2** [*past:* وي يې باتاوه] *figurative* to incite, arouse

باته bāṭa *f. usually plural* باتي bāṭi boasting, bragging, باتي کول، باتي وهل، باتي ویستل to boast, brag

باتهرست bāṭhárst *m.* Baterst (a locality)

باتبدل bāṭedól *intransitive* ☞ باته and باتي کول to brag, boast

باتیگن bāṭigán *m.* baṭegán *m.* [*plural:* باتيگن bāṭigán *plural:* باتینگن bāṭegán باتیگن bāṭingán *m. plural:* باتینگن bāṭingán] tomato

باثروته bāsarváta wealthy, well-to-do

باثمره bāsamára fruitful; sucessful

باج bādzh *m. history* tribute, tax باج ورکول to pay tribute, pay tax

باجدار bādzhdár *m.* ☞ باجگیر

باجره bādzhrá *f.* kind of sorghum, *Holcus spicatus*

باجر bādzháṛ *m.* downpour

باج گذار bādzhguzár *m. history* one paying tribute or tax

باجگیر bādzhgír *m. history* collector of tribute

باجنجاله bādzhandzhála strained, tense; intensive باجنجاله کال intensive year

باجور bādzhaváṛ *m.* Badzhaur

باجوری bādzhaváṛaj *m.* inhabitant of Badzhaur, Badzhaurian

باجه¹ bādzhá *f.* **1** brass band **2** *music* رغول باجه to play (of an orchestra) *idiom* د خولي باجه harmonica دگوتو باجه harmonium

باجه² bādzhá *m.* brother-in-law (wife's sister's husband)

باچا bāchá *m.* [*plural:* باچهان bāchahán] **1** king **2** title of a sayyid or descendent of followers of the prophet

باچاجي bāchādzhí *m. vocative* master, sayyid

باچر bāchár *m.* ☞ باجر

باچهه bācháha *f.* [*plural:* باچهانی bāchahāni] **1** queen **2** queen bee

باچهی bāchahí *f.* kingdom

باحسه bāhíssa sympathethic; responsive

باخبره bākhabár bākhabára informed, knowledgeable باخبره informed circles له یو شي څخه باخبر کېدل to be informed, be knowledgeable in something; to recognize, find out something

باختر bākhtár *m. history* **1** Baktriya **2** د باختر آژانس نشراتي موسسه the Bakhtar (news) agency

باختری bākhtarí *history* **1** of or from Baktriya **2** person from Baktriya *idiom* باختري ژبي Iranian languages

باخکه bākhkhó *imperfect from* بخښل

باخملی bākhmalój *f.* ☞ بخملی

باخو bākhú *f.* fairy-tale witch

باد¹ bād *m.* **1** wind د سهل باد پاسنی باد wind from the mountains د نور خاته باد north wind د قطب باد west wind د قبلي باد south wind د لوري باد east wind سور باد را والوت the wind is blowing a cold باد وهلئ wind blew **a** beaten by the wind **b** having caught cold **c** *figurative* gone insane **2** air (in a balloon, ball, etc.) باد ورکول to inflate, pump up (a balloon, ball, etc.) **3** wind (intestinal), flatus **4** rheumatism (in the joints); arthritis باد فرنگ *bád-i* **a** erysipelas **b** St. Anthony's fire **c** syphilis **5** *figurative* breathing, blowing (of the wind) **6** *figurative* boastfulness, bragging باد کول *compound verb* ☞ بادول *idiom* باد بند و oppressive hot weather remained **a** to brag, boast **b** په توره باد وهل to make a show of bravery **c** to pursue a useless task باد پیمانه کول to beat the air, mill the wind دا د باد پیمانه ده this is a vain undertaking باد الوزول to babble foolishness, speak nonsense باد سپکول to insult, humiliate, shame; to degrade

باد² bād *colloquial* ☞ بعد خو عمر باد after a while

بادار bādár *m.* master (in relation to a servant), sir (landed gentry)

باداره bādára *f.* [*plural:* بادارانی bādāráni] mistress (in return to a servant), ma'am

بادري bādārí *f.* dominion په چا باندي باداري کول to hold sway over someone

بادام bādám *m.* **1** almond tree سنگي بادام، کلک بادام almond with hard shell کاغذي بادام almond with soft shell **2** kind of embroidery **3** woman's adornment worn over the temples (in a form resembling an almond)

بادامچه bādāmchá *f.* **1** wild almond **2** ☞ بادام 2, 3

بادامه bādāmá *f.* snowstorm

بادامي bādāmí 1 almond-like (of the eyes); oval 2 cream-colored; brown; beige

بادبان bādbán m. 1 sail 2 lampshade

بادباندار bādbāndár بادباني bādbāní adjective sailing بادبانداره کښتی sailboat

بادبرک bādbarák m. botany baby's breath

بادبیزی bādbezáj m. 1 ventilator 2 fan

بادپخ bādpákh m. ☞ بادرو¹

بادپنسی bādpəkháj m. fast runner

بادپکه bādpaká f. ☞ بادبیزی

بادپوژن bādpuzhón haughty, arrogant

بادپیزي bādpezí f. nonsense, foolishness, absurdity بادپیزی کول to do something stupid; behave thoughtlessly, act carelessly

بادپیما bādpajmā́ swift as the wind بادپیما بېړی a fast ship

بادجړی bāddzhaŕój f. 1 downpour 2 snowdrift

بادخور bādkhór m. بادخورک bādkhorák m. kestrel, windhover (a kind of falcon)

بادخوره badkhoŕá f. 1 tuberculosis of the skin, lupus vulgaris 2 tumor 3 final stage of syphilis

بادر¹ bādə́r m. period of time corresponding approximately to February

بادر² bādúr ☞ بهادر

بادرانه bādurāná ☞ بهادرانه

بادرب bādráb m. snowdrift

بادرنگ bādráng m. بادرنگ bādráng [plural: بادرنگان bādrangā́n plural: bādrəngā́n] cucumber

بادرو¹ bādráv m. 1 opening in the wall (for ventilation) 2 small hinged pane for ventilation

بادرو² bādró m. regional second month of monsoons (August-September)

بادري bādurí f. ☞ بهادري

بادشاه bādshā́h m. 1 king, padishah 2 sayyid, lord, sir 3 queen bee 4 proper noun Badshah

بادشاهانه bādshāhāná 1 regal, royal 2 in a regal manner

بادشاه زادۍ bādshāhzādə́j f. princess

بادشاهي bādshāhí 1 regal, royal 2 f. kingdom, realm بادشاهي لرل to hold sway

بادغېز bādghéz m. airhole, vent (in a stove)

بادغیسات bādghisā́t m. plural Badghisat (a region)

بادغیسي bādghisí adjective of or from Badghisat بادغیسي وړی Badghisat wool

بادفرنگ bā-d-i-farang m. 1 erysipelas 2 St. Anthony's fire 3 syphilis

بادقته bādiḳḳáta attentive

بادکښ bādkákh m. 1 flue 2 ventilator

بادکوبه bādkobá f. snowstorm

بادکوبه bādkujá f. snowdrift

بادگوله bādgolá f. medicine colic

بادماغه bādimāgha sensible, clever, quick-witted; thoughtful

بادمنگ bādmáng adjective fast

بادنجان bādindzhā́n m. eggplant

بادوامه bādavā́m بادوامه badāvā́ma firm, solid; lengthy, lasting سکاره اور لري بادوامه coal burns a long time

بادوان bādvā́n m. ☞ بادبان

بادور bādúr ☞ بهادر

بادورانه bādurāná ☞ بهادرانه

بادوري bādurí f. ☞ بهادري

بادوری bādvəraj 1 knocked down by the wind 2 m. fallen grain, fallen fruit

بادوکی bādúkaj m. 1 breeze 2 figurative stupid person 3 figurative spineless person; someone lacking character

بادول bādavól denominative, transitive [past: باد يې کړ] 1 to winnow (grain) 2 to pour, spread (earth, etc.) 3 figurative to squander, toss to the wind

بادونه bādavóna f. winnowing (grain)

باده bādá f. wine

بادهوا bādhavá f. snake (made of paper)

بادي bādí 1.1 filled with air or gas; aerial 1.2 wind (powered) بادي ژرنده windmill 1.3 pneumatic 1.4 figurative flighty, empty-headed 1.5 figurative haughty (of a person) 2 m. .1 someone suffering from rheumatism 2.2 agriculture winnower (of grain) 2.3 swift camel بادي کول to winnow (grain) a بادي کېدل to be winnowed (of grain) b to suffer rheumatism

بادیان bādjā́n m. star anise

بادیښ bādíkh m. flue (in a stove)

بادهوا بادي گن bādigán m. ☞

باډاسکه bāḍáska f. wave وهل باډاسکي to be agitated, be covered with waves; to seethe, boil up

باډاسکي bāḍáski f. plural hide-and-seek (children's game)

باډر bāḍár 1 m. regional borderline (of tribes); border, boundary 2 relating to a tribal boundary

باډاسکي bāḍáski f. plural ☞

باډگول bāḍgól m. 1 reins 2 string; rope, cord

باډنگ bāḍńg m. 1 cucumber 2 figurative blockhead, stupid person

باډو bāḍú m. 1 blockhead, stupid person 2 coward

باډول bāḍól m. teapot

باډي bāḍí f. باډۍ bāḍə́j f. body (of a car); hull (of a ship)

بار¹ bār 1 m. .1 load, burden; pack بار تړل a to fasten a load, secure a pack figurative b to succeed in something, obtain something بار نه سي تړلای He'll hardly succeed in this. بار وړل a to transport a load, carry a load b m. plural transfer a load, transport of a load د بارونو گاډی a cart 1.2 figurative load; oppression د چا تر بار لاندي تلل to load heavily دروند بار بارول to be subservient, to subordinate oneself to someone 1.3 fruit بار کول، بار نیول to bear fruit بار راوړل to set (development of fruit after pollination) 2 predicate .1 loaded, laden 2.2 figurative overwhelmed (with worries) *idiom* بار ځني ترل to receive benefit from someone

بار ² bār *m.* one time, once باربار often

بار ³ bār *m.* 1 field; plain 2 *combining form* هندوبار Hindustan

باران bārā́n *m.* rain رنگی باران ، نری باران a fine and intermittent rain مصنوعي باران a heavy rain, a downpour گڼ باران ، موږ باران *agriculture* irrigation by sprinkling ميده باران a light rain, a shower ننۍ د باران ورځ ده today is a rainy day باران اورئ it's raining باران ودربدئ *Western* it has stopped raining

باراني ² bārānkóṭ *m.* ☞ باراني

باران ګی bārāngáj *m.* rain shower

باراني ¹ bārāní *adjective* rainy; monsoon باراني هوا rainy weather

باراني ² bārānə́j *f.* umbrella; raincoat, mackintosh

باراني ³ bārānə́j *f.* dry-farming land (i.e., without artificial irrigation)

باربردار bārbardár *adjective* freight, cargo; cartage

باربرداري bārbardārí *f.* 1 transport, transfer of freight, cargo collective 2 animal-drawn transport; draft animals

باربند bārbánd *m.* enclosure, pen (for cattle)

باربندي bārbandí *f.* 1 loading, loading up 2 packing **a** باربندي کول to load **b** to pack

باربلیز bārbelíz stray, ownerless (of cattle)

باربلیزه bārbelíza 1 *f. singular from* باربلیز 2 unmarried, single (woman)

بارتنگ bārtáng *m. botany* plantain

بارتري bārṭarí *f. trade* clearing (of accounts)

بارجامه bārdzhāmá *f.* 1 duck (a kind of sailcloth) 2 double bag or sack

بارچالاني bārchālāní *f.* shipping of cargo; dispatching

بارخاک bātsā́k *m.* gusset (in a shirt)

بارخو bārkhú *m.* cheek

باردار bārdár 1 of a load 2 fruit bearing 3 covered with fruit

بارداره bārdára 1 *feminine singular of* باردار 2 *f.* pregnant

بارده bāridá *Arabic plural* بارده مناطق the Arctic

باریز bāríz *Arabic* 1 apparent, obvious 2 successful (of a person)

بارسلونا bārselonā́ *f.* Barcelona (city)

بارک ¹ bārák *m. proper name* Barák (eponym of the Barakzái tribe)

بارک ² bārák *m.* barracks; wooden barrack, hut

بارک لله bārakallá *Arabic interjection* bravo! well done!

بارکزي bārakzí 1 *m. plural* Barakzái (tribe) *m.* 2 Barakzáj (tribesman)

بارکش bārkásh *m.* scoop, bucket (of a lifting wheel)

بارکښ bārkáx *adjective* 1.1 pack; cartage; draught 1.2 humble, meek 2.1 rope for tying on a pack 2.2 beast of burden

بارکښي bārkáxí *f.* carrying; transport of cargo **a** بارکښي کول to work at carrying; transport cargo **b** to transfer, drag loads

باراکه bārāka *f.* baráka (a kind of wool fabric)

بارګاه bārgā́h *m.* palace, mansion; royal tent

بارنامه bārnāmá *f.* invoice, waybill نقلیه بارنامه bill of lading

بارنتس bārénts د بارنتس بحیره Barents Sea

باروبونه bārubuná *f.* travel gear; pack; baggage

باروت bārút *m. plural* gunpowder *idiom* بی باروتو تکان کول *literal* to try to shoot with no gunpowder *figurative* to undertake a useless venture; to act for no purpose

باروتخانه bāruthkhāná *f.* powder store

بارود bārúd *m. plural* ☞ باروت

بارودسازي bārudsāzí *f.* manufacture of powder

بار وړونکی bār vṛúnkaj *adjective* of a load; pack بار وړونکی جهاز cargo ship بار وړونکی ډوده pack animal

باروزي bārozí 1 *m. plural* Barozái (tribe) 2 bārozáj *m.* Barozáj (tribesman)

بارول ¹ bāravél *denominative, transitive* [*past:* باریی کړ] 1 to load, pack 2 to ship, send

بارول ² bāravél *transitive* [*past:* و یی باراوه] to stir up (against); to instigate

بارومتر bārométr *m.* barometer

بارونه bāravéna *f.* 1 loading, packing 2 shipping, sending

باره ¹ bārá *f.* په دی باره کښنی in this respect دیو شي په باره کښنی about, concerning something په همدغه باره کښنی relative to the same thing

باره ² bā́ra *f.* 1 fortification; rampart 2 large dam 3 barrier, obstruction, obstacle

باره ³ bārá *particle* 1 and behold 2 even **a** باره راغئ And behold he has come **b** Even he has come

باره سنگها bārasinghā́ *m. regional* deer

باري ¹ bārí *m. Arabic* God; divine being, deity

باري ² bāráj *m.* crowbar

باري ³ bārí 1 draught (of cattle) 2 fruitful, fruitbearing (of a tree)

باري ⁴ bāri bāre *modifies force of imperative* 1 come on let's!; one time, once چه باري ما پربرده just let me 2 in a word, briefly, that is to say

باریاب bārjáb deserving of a reception or an audience

باریابیدل bārjābedól *denominative, intransitive* [*past:* باریاب شو] to be deserving of a reception or an audience

باریدل bāredól *denominative, intransitive* [*past:* بار شو] 1 to be loaded up 2 to be packed, be wrapped 3 *figurative* to be burdensome, be a burden for someone 4 to migrate

باریدنه bāredóna *f.* باربده bāredə́ *m. plural* 1 loading; packing 2 wrapping up; packaging 3 migration

باریک bārík 1 thin; narrow 2 tender; soft 3 *figurative* delicate, sensitive (of a question) 4 *figurative* penetrating **a** باریک کول to refine; make thinner, narrow **b** to soften, make tender *idiom* و یوی خبری ته باریک کېدل to go carefully into something; investigate something

باریک بین bārikbín penetrating, shrewd, perspicacious; understanding something to a fine degree

باریکي bārikí *f.* 1 fineness; narrowness 2 tenderness; softness 3 *figurative* sensitivity, delicacy 4 *figurative* acuteness, shrewdness باریکي کول to be penetrating, show acuity

بار bāṛ *m.* volley, salvo; firing بار کول to fire a volley بار چلول to carry on firing

بارخو bāṛkhú *m.* بارخه bāṛkhə́ *m.* ☞ بارخو

بارک bāṛə́k *m. botany* saxaul (haloxylon)

بارواک bāṛvák careless, negligent

باره ¹ bārá *f.* rent; freight charge; payment (for passage, accommodations, etc.) باره اخیستل، باره خورل to collect rent, freightage, payment for something باره ورکول to pay in rent, freightage; to make payment په باره اخیستل *compound verb* to rent, hire, charter په باره ورکول to rent out

باره ² bā́ra *f.* 1 temporary fence 2 enclosure (for cattle)

باره ³ bārá *f.* the Bara (river) د باري وریجي bara rice (a high-quality rice)

باری ¹ bāṛáj *m.* 1 pay, reward for work; remuneration 2 bribe 3 food used for a cow or goat when milking

باری ² bāṛí *m.* servant, worker باري نیول to hire a servant or worker

باری ³ bāṛə́j *f.* 1 fence 2 front garden 3 garden plot 4 cultivated earth 5 *military* parapet 6 society

باری مار bāṛemár *m.* hired worker

باز ¹ bāz *m.* [*plural:* بازان bāzā́n *plural:* بازونه bāzúna] 1 kind of hawk (usually the female, *Accipiter gentilis*) 2 hunting bird 3 *proper name* Baz *idiom* د زینبي باز پر ربدي گل نه کښیني Zejnáb doesn't want to marry Redáj Gúl. پر مونږ یې باز نه کښیني he doesn't love us خیالي بازونه یې په ښکار پربنبي ور daydreams

باز ² bāz *m. dialect* bamboo

بازار bāzā́r *m.* 1 bazaar, marketplace بازار ته تلل to go to the marketplace اوس د کشمشو بازار گرم (تود) دئ there's now a great demand for raisins اوس د وړیو بازار سوړ دئ the demand now for wool is bad 2 *figurative* area, sphere, arena

بازاري bāzārí 1 of the bazaar, market *m.* 2.1 tradesman at a marketplace 2.2 town-dweller 2.3 commonplace person

بازخواست bāzkhā́st *m.* making accountable; punishment

بازدار bāzdā́r *m. hunting* falconer

بازرسي bāzrasí *f.* ☞ وارسي

بازل bāzə́l *transitive* [*past:* و یې بازه] 1 to lose (e.g., money) 2 to squander, waste 3 *theater* to play (a role) 4 to give (a bribe)

بازنه bāzna *f.* 1 loss (e.g., of money) 2 wastefulness, extravagance

بازو bāzú *m.* 1 hand, arm 2 side (e.g., of a bed) 3 hinge (of a door) 4 *military* flank 5 small lever

بازوبند bāzubánd *m.* bracelet (worn on the forearm)

بازي bāzí *f.* 1 game بازي playground د بازیو میدان toys د بازي اسباب to play with someone 2 deception و چاته بازي کول to play بازي ورکول to deceive

بازیچه bāzichá *f.* toy

بازیگر bāzigár *m.* بازینگر bāzingár *m.* 1 player 2 conjurer 3 rogue; swindler *regional idiom* بازیگر کمتر tumbler pigeon

باس ¹ bās *m.* latrine

باس ² bās *present verb stem from* ایستل

باسار bāsár madman

باستاني bāstāní ancient

باسفورس bāsfoṛús *m.* the Bosphorus د باسفورس آبنای the Bosphorus (strait)

باسمچي bāsmachí *m.* 1 basmach (member of anti-Soviet movement in Central Asia) 2 *adjective* basmach

باسمه bāsmá *f.* tightly-woven textile (used for curtains)

باسنه bāsə́na *f.* 1 conclusion 2 extracting; an extract

باسواد bāsavā́d باسواده bāsavā́da literate باسواد کول to teach reading and writing

باسوادي bāsavādí *f.* literacy

باسه bāsá *f.* ☞ بایکر

باسي bāsí 1 not fresh, rotten 2 stale (of bread)

باسیلي bāsilí bacillary

باشرفه bāsharáfa 1 honest; noble 2 honored

باشقر bāshkír *m.* Bashkir

باشقري bāshkirí *adjective* Bashkir باشقري ژبه the Bashkir language

باشکوه bāshukúh باشکوهه bāshukúha magnificent, luxurious

باښ bāx *m.* steed with a white star on its forehead and white stockings

باښنه گی bāxhagə́j *f.* ☞ باښنه گی

باښنه bākhá *f.* kind of hawk (female)

باښنه گی bākhagə́j *f.* hawk moth, sphingid

باښین bākhín *m.* kind of hawk (male)

باصحته bāsihháta well, healthy

باصره bāsirá *f. Arabic* sight د باصري حس sight

باضبطه bāzábta disciplined

باطري bātrí *f.* باطري bātarí ☞ بتري

باطل bātil *Arabic* 1 invalid, null, revoked 2 futile, vain, useless باطلبدل ☞ باطل کېدل، باطلول ☞ باطل کول

باطلاق bātlā́ḳ *m.* swamp; bog

باطلنامه bātilnāmá *f.* letter about rescinding a warrant, notification refusing an assignment

باطلوالی bātilválaj *m.* futility, vainness, needlessness

باطلول bātilavə́l *denominative, transitive* [*past:* باطل یې کړ] 1 to annul, revoke, declare invalid 2 to make futile, vain, useless

باطلېدل bātiledə́l *denominative, intransitive* [*past:* باطل شو] 1 to be invalid, be revoked, lose force 2 to be useless, needless

باطن bātín *m. Arabic* 1 interior, inside 2 *figurative* innermost thoughts *idiom* باطن روند nearby, limited

باطني bātiní *Arabic* 1 internal 2 *figurative* hidden; innermost

باطومي bātúmi *m.* Batúmi (city)

باعث bā'ís *m. Arabic* [*plural:* باعثونه bā'isúna *Arabic plural:* بواعث bavā'ís] reason, cause د یوشي په باعث because of something; due to something

باعثتیا ba'istjá *f.* cause, (underlying) condition

باعد bā'id *Arabic* distant

باعظمته bā'azamáta majestic; magnificent; grand

باعمله bā'amálá energetic, active (of a person)

باغ bāgh *m.* **1** garden باغ عمومي municipal garden باغ بالا *bāgh-i* Bagibala (palace in Kabul) **2** kitchen garden, vegetable garden **3** Bagh (center of Tirach, region of the Aphridian tribes)

باغ باغ bāghbā́raj باغبهرج bāghbāgh quite satisfied; beaming زړه يې باغ باغ ورى کېږي to give great joy, make very happy زړه ضرور باغ باغ ورى کېږي he's beaming from joy; he's very contented the spirit rejoices unwittingly

باغبان bāghbán *m.* ☞ باغوان

باغچه bāghchá *f.* **1** flower bed; flower garden **2** vegetable garden

باغدار bāghdár *m.* **1** gardener **2** owner of a garden **3** market gardener

باغداري bāghdārí *f.* gardening, horticulture باغداري کول to practice gardening

باغلي bāghlí *m.* bāghulí *m. plural* beans of the field

باغ والا bāghvālā́ *m.* gardener, horticulturist

باغوان bāghvā́n *m.* **1** gardener **2** market gardener

باغواني bāghvāní *f.* **1** gardening, horticulture **2** market gardening باغواني کول **a** to practice gardening **b** to practice market gardening

باغوت bāghút *m.* **1** *medicine* mumps **2** *anatomy* parotid gland

باغولي bāghulí *m. plural* ☞ باغلي

باغي¹ bāghí **1** garden, horticultural **2** market-gardening

باغي² bāghí *m. Arabic* insurgent, striker; rebel کېدل _ to go on strike, raise a rebellion; to rebel

باغى³ bāgháj *m.* reserve, preserve

باغيانه baghijāná *f.* rebellious; unruly باغيانه حرکت rebellion

باغيچه bāghichá *f.* ☞ باغچه

باغيرته bāghajráta *Arabic* valiant, worthy of glory

بافت bāft *m.* **1** weaving **2** knitting **3** braiding the hair **4** kind of woman's hairdo

باقاعده bāḳā'idá repaired, restored; regular

باقاعدگي bāḳā'idagí *f.* **1** state of good repair; regularity **2** agreement; harmony په باقاعده گى سره **a** in good repair; regularly **b** harmoniously; in an orderly way

باقي bāḳí *Arabic* **1** remaining **2** *m.* **.1** arrears **2.2** *math* difference

باقيات bāḳijā́t *m. Arabic plural* **1** arrears **2** survivals, relics

باقي مانده bāḳimāndá **1** remaining **2** *m.* remainder

باک bāk *m.* **1** fear, fright; anxiety; unrest باک کول to be afraid, take fright; ده باک په و نه کړ he's not afraid of this **2** concern *idiom* هيڅ باک نشته! no problem, it's all right!

باکتري bākterí *f. & m.* باکتريا bākterijā́ *f.* bacteria اوږده باکتريان bacilli

باکتريولوژي bākterjolozhí **1** *f.* bacteriology **2** bacteriological

باکتريا bākterijā́ *f.* ☞ باکتري

باکسنگ bāksíng *m.* ☞ بکسنگ

باکفايت bākifājā́t talented, gifted; capable, skillful

باکفايته bākifājā́ta efficient, capable, qualified

باکماله bākamā́la skilled; learned, erudite

باکو¹ bākó *m.* **1** elder brother **2** *proper name* Bako

باکو² bākú *m.* Baku (city)

باکه سارى bākasāraj *m.* short-horned ram

باکى bākáj *f.* vomiting; vomit

باکيفه bākájfa pleasant باکيفه ژوند a life full of pleasures

باگاژ bāgā́zh *m.* baggage

باگډور bāgḍór *m.* reins

باگره bāgára *f.* باگو bāgó *f.* باگولى bāgoláj باگوه bāgáva *f.* witch; hag

باگه bāga *f.* bragging, boasting باگه کول to brag, boast

بالا bālā́ **1.1** above, from above; high up **1.2** higher **1.3** over, above, more than **2** upper, located in the upper part of something

بالاباد bālābā́d *m.* southwest wind

بالاپوښ bālāpóḳh *m.* topcoat, overcoat

بالاجمال bilidzhmā́l *Arabic* in short, concisely, in general outline

بالاحصار bālāhisā́r *m.* Balahisar (fortress in Kabul)

بالاخانه bālākhāná *f.* **1** upper story of a house; superstructure **2** balcony

بالاخره bilākhirá *Arabic* finally, at last

بالامرغاب bālāmurghā́b *m.* Bala-Morghab, Bala-Murghab (town)

بال بال bālbā́l ☞ باغ بارى

بال بچدار bālbachdár *adjective regional* family, having a family بال بچ دار سرى يم I have a family.

بالبداهه bilbadāhá *Arabic* suddenly

بالبديهه bilbadihá *Arabic* ex promptu, without preparation

بالت bālét *m.* ballet

بالتيک bāltík د بالتيک بحيره Baltic Sea

بالتيکي bāltikí *adjective* Baltic

بالتى bāltájáj *f.* [*plural:* بالتى گانى bāltəjgā́ni] **1** bucket **2** (galvanic) element وچه بالتى dry element

بالتيک bālṭík ☞ بالتيک

بالتيکي bālṭikí ☞ بالتيکي

بالخاصه bilkhāssá *Arabic* especially, in particular

بالخش bālkhásh *m.* د بالخش غدير Lake Balkhash

بالخصوص bilkhusús *Arabic* especially, in particular

بالذات bizzā́t *Arabic* by its nature, in essence

بالستيک bālistík bāllistík **1** ballistic بالستيک ليري ويشتونکى تغوندى intercontinental ballistic missile **2** *m.* ballistics

بالشويزم bālshevísm *m.* Bolshevism

بالشويک bālshevík **1** *m.* Bolshevik **2** *adjective* Bolshevik

بالیخت bālíkht *m.* [*plural:* بالښتان bālikhtān *plural:* بالښتونه bālikhtúna] pillow

بالیختک bālikhták *m.* بالښتوگټى bālikhtgoṭáj *m.* **1** small pillow, cushion **2** padding, packing, separator (of wood or similiar material)

بالضرور bizzarúr *Arabic* certainly; without fail

بالطبع bittáb' *Arabic* in point of fact, in essence

بالعکس bil'áks *Arabic* on the contrary د دې بالعکس despite this

بالعموم bil'umúm *Arabic* generally, in general

بالغ bālígh *Arabic* 1 grown-up; mature; of age 2 *m.* grown man د بالغانو تعليم كورس campaign against illiteracy courses to end illiteracy

بالفرض bilfárz *Arabic* let's suppose; supposedly

بالفعل bilfé'l *Arabic* in fact, actually

بالقان bālḵā́n *m.* [*plural:* بالقانات bālḵānā́t] Balkans د بالقان جزيزه نما the Balkan peninsula

بالكل bilkúl bilkúll *Arabic* altogether, absolutely, completely

بالكچي bālkachí *m.* بالكي bālkí *m.* follower of a fakir (learning from him and serving his needs)

بالمثل bilmísl *Arabic* analogous; identical, the same

بالمقابل bilmukābil *Arabic* in reply; in exchange; in turn

بالنتيجه binnatidzhá *Arabic* as a result

بالنگ bāláng *m.* [*plural:* بالنگان bālangā́n] large wild orange tree

بالن bālán *m.* [*plural:* بالڼ bāláṇ] 1 fuel 2 dung-brick fuel 3 kind of roast (meat)

بالو bālú *m. regional* beast of prey

بالون bālón bālún *m.* 1 balloon 2 rubber ball 3 balloon, aerostat

بالوني bāloní spherical

باله bāláʹ *imperfect from* باله كېدل، بلل to be called

بالۍ bālə́j *f.* earrings

باليستيك bālistík ☞ بالستيك

باليگی bāligáj *m.* foundling

بالين bālín *m.* ☞ بالنت

باليوس bālijús *m.* Balijus (ancient name of the Kandahar Province)

بام bām *m.* 1 roof 2 top (of a carriage) 3 flooring, planking

باماكو bāmākó *f.* Bamako (city)

بامبر bāmbár *m.* ☞ بامبن

بامبره bāmbára *f.* flame

بامبن bāmbán *m.* Brahmin

بامبڼه bāmbáṇa *f.* ☞ بامبره

بامبو bāmbú *m.* buzzing (of insects) [1]

بامبو bāmbú *m.* bamboo [2]

بامبوره bāmburá *f.* top (the toy)

بامبېر bāmbér *m.* noise, uproar, commotion بامبېر كول to make noise, make a racket

بامره bāmára *f.* edge; border, hem, edging

بامل bāmə́l *transitive* [*past:* و يې بامه] to strike up a friendship, maintain friendship, befriend

بامڼه bāmáṇa *f.* thick smoke

بامونکی bāmúnkaj 1 *present participle from* بامل 2.1 *m.* tutor, educator 2.2 friend

بامه bāmá *f.* end of winter [1]

بامه bāmə́ *imperfect from* بامل [2]

بامه bắma *singular oblique from* بام [3]

باميان bāmijā́n *m. sometimes plural* Bamian (city) د باميان معبر، باميان ولايت Bamian Province د بامياؤ معبر Bamian Pass

باميه bāmjá *f.* okra, *Hibiscus esculentus*

بان bān *m. regional* missile, rocket [1]

بان bān *m.* Bonn (city) [2]

بان bắn *m. suffix* doer of an action باغبان gardener [3]

بانټ bānṭ *m.* part, a part (of a car and so forth)

بانجاني bāndzhāní violet, lavender

بانجن bāndzhán *m.* [*plural:* بانجن bāndzhə́ṇ] eggplant تور بانجن eggplant سره بانجن، سوركي بانجن tomato رومي بانجن tomatoes د بانجنو اوبه tomato juice

بانجو bāndzhú *m.* newly-born puppy

باندو bāndó *f.* military band

باندونگ bāndúng *m.* Bandung (city in West Java, Indonesia)

باندي bāndi bānde *Eastern* 1 *combined with the preposition* پر (*Eastern* په) *or without it* .1 on (on the surface of something) زما كتاب پرميز باندي دئ my book is on the table باندي كول to stand or put onto something, load onto something باندي كېدل to be placed, put or loaded onto something 1.2 with, with the help of په چا باندي with the help of someone په يو شي باندي with the aid of something 2.1 *adverb* on him, her, it; on them; onto him, her, it 2.2 to him, her, it; to them احمد باندي پرغ كرل Ahmed shouted to him. 2.3 around him, her, it, them ټوله باندي راتول دي everyone gathered around him

باندي والی bānditób *m.* ☞ باندي والی

بانديني bāndinájj 1 upper 2 someone else's, another's 3 external, foreign

باندي والی bāndiválaj *m.* 1 height 2 *figurative* superiority

بانډار bānḍár *m.* ☞ بندار

بانډه bānḍá *f.* 1 pen for cattle (summer pasturing); fence behind which cattle are driven 2 small village 3 camp of nomads, cattle herders 4 settlements 5 body, torso 6 *used in geographical place names* گوجروبانډه Gudzharobanda (an inhabited locality) [1]

بانډه bānḍə́ *m. proper name* Banda [2]

بانډه bānḍá destroyed, annihilated; killed, fallen [3]

بانډه وال bānḍawál *m.* بانډه چي bānḍachí *m.* 1 one who is living at a mountain pasture 2 villager, peasant, farmer

بانډبسی bānḍesáj *m.* بانډپچی bānḍecháj *m.* 1 nomad herdsman, shepherd; one who lives on the steppe 2 summer resident in the country

بانډپسي bānḍesí *f.* summer camp, area where nomads make camp in the summer

بانر bānə́r *m.* leaf of the date-palm tree

بانس bāns *m.* bamboo

بانشاطه bānishā́ta *adjective* cheerful, buoyant, hale and hearty (of a person)

بانك bānk *m.* bank تجارتي بانك bank of commerce, commercial bank زراعتي بانك agricultural bank ملي بانك، دكرهني بانك national bank د افغانستان بانك Afghan Bank, Bank of Afghanistan دولتي بانك state bank, government bank

بانكدار bānkdár *m.* banker, bank owner

بانكداري bānkdārí *f.* banking business

بانكر bānkár *m.* ☞ بانكدار

بانس bānks *m.* ☞ بانس

بانكسي bānksí *adjective* bamboo

بانك لرونكى bānk larúnkaj *m.* ☞ بانكدار

بانكنوت bānknót *m.* bank note

بانكنوت bānknóṭ *m.* bank note

بانكه ¹ bānká *f.* ankle bracelet ☞ بانكه

بانكه ² bānká *m.* ☞ بانكي ¹ bānkí *m.* بانكيا

بانكي ¹ bānkí *m.* ☞ بانكيا

بانكي ² bānkí *adjective* bank, banking

بانكيا bānkjā́ *m.* 1 dandy, fop 2 conceited person

بانگ bāng *m.* 1 crow, crowing (of a rooster) 2 muezzin's call to prayer بانگ ويل ،بانگ كول *compound verb* a to crow (of a rooster) b to call to prayer (of a muezzin)

بانگورى ¹ bāngóṛaj *m.* tongs (blacksmith's)

بانگپرى ² bānguṛáj *m.* cockerel, young rooster ☞ بانگپرى

بانگي ¹ bāngí *m.* 1 بانگي چرگ crowing rooster 2 muezzin

بانگي ² bāngí *m.* yoke (for carrying buckets, etc.)

بانگي ³ bā́ngí *m.* Bangui (capital of the Central African Republic)

بانگپرى bāngeṛáj *m.* cockerel, young rooster

بانو ¹ bānó *m.* 1 kind of insect 2 kind of apricot

بانو ² bānó *f.* 1 lady 2 Bannu (city in northern Pakistan)

بانه bāná *f.* pretext, excuse بانه ورته غوښتل to look for an opportunity to harm somebody

باني bāní *m. Arabic* founder, initiator

بانين bānín *m.* falcon

بان bāṇ *m.* rope made of palm leaves

بانس bāṇs *m.* 1 bamboo 2 bamboo rod, pole

بانكه bāṇká *f.* ankle bracelet

بانو bāṇu *m.* [*plural:* بانوگان bāṇugán] eyelash بانو اينبودل پر بانو a to close the eyes b *figurative* to die c to blink پرچا بانو درنول *idiom* to have evil designs towards someone دچا بانو درنبدل a to be insidious b to be sad دچا بانو مراوي كول to insult

بانوكه bāṇoká *adjective* tipsy, drunk

بانه bāṇá *m. plural* eyelashes

بانپچغ bāṇechógh *m.* swing, seesaw

باو bāw *m.* syphilis

باوجدانه bāwidzhdā́na *adjective* honest, conscientious, decent, respectable

باوجود bāwodzhód in spite of, despite, not withstanding, against د دغه باوجود in spite of this

باور bāwár *m.* faith, confidence په چا باور په ځان self-confidence دچا په to trust somebody, to rely on somebody باوركول، په چا باورلرل to believe someone's words خوله باوركول ...باور لرم چي I am sure that...

باورچي bāwarchí *m.* 1 cook 2 messenger

باورچي خانه bāwarchikhāná *f. regional* kitchen

باور كارت bāwar kārṭ *m.* credit card

باوري bāwarí *adjective* reliable, trustworthy; earnest په باوري ډول earnestly

باوپرى ¹ bāwṛə́j *f.* plateau

باوپرى ² bāwṛə́j *f.* large well

باوسير bāwsír *m. singular & plural* piles, hemorrhoids

باولل bāwlə́l *transitive* [*past:* ويي باوله] to train for hunting (a bird or a dog)

باولنه bāwlə́na *f.* training to hunt, training for hunting (a bird or a dog)

باوله ¹ bāwəlá *adjective* dull, stupid; ignorant

باوله ² bāwlə́ *imperfective of* باولل

باولى ¹ bāwláj *m.* bait (used in training hunting birds or dogs) باولل ☞ وركول

باولى ² bāwláj *adjective* 1 feigning bravery, pretending to be brave 2 pretending to be business-like, efficient

باولى ³ bāwlí *m.* place where a bird or dog is training for hunting

باولى ⁴ bāwlə́j *f* 1 path or stairs leading to a well or kahriz 2 reservoir near a well, chute for water

باوو bāwú *m.* ☞ باهو

باوي bāwí *m.* syphilitic

باهر bāhár ☞ بهر بيگا له ځما ډوډۍ باهر ده in the evening I don't eat at home

باهمي bāhamí *adjective* collective, joint; common باهمي بقا life together

باهنر bahonár *adjective* skillful, able

باهو bāhú *m.* bracelet (for arms or legs)

باى bāj 1 *m.* .1 loss (in sports, gambling, etc.) 1.2 loss, waste 2 *first separable syllable of the verb* بايلل پام كوه چي ځان باى نلي! look out, don't get lost!

بايت bājṭ *m. computer science* byte

بايد bā́jád *adverb* should, must, ought to, is necessary بايدڅه وكو؟ What ought one to do?, What should be done?; *sometimes combines with the hortative particle* دئ بايددئ چي سره ووينو it is necessary that we meet

بايده bā́jdá, bā́jidá 1 should, must, ought to, is necessary دى چي بايده We ought not to موږ بايده نه دئ چي ولاړ سو go ولاړ سي He ought to go 2 *f.* due, appropriate دود او بايده كول observe wedding rites

بايسكل bā́jskə́l, bā́jsicál *m.* bicycle

بايسكل سوار bā́jskalsawár, bā́jsklsawár *m.* bicyclist

بايسكوپ bā́jskóp *m. regional* motion picture projector

بايع bāí ' *m. Arabic* seller, vendor

بايقال bājḳál *m.* Baykal

بايكاټ bājḳáṭ *m.* boycott بايكاټ كول *compound verb* to boycott

بايكر bājkáṛ *m. Salvadora persica* (a kind of tree)

بايلات bājlát *m.* 1 loss; defeat په جنگ كښي بايلات كول suffer defeat in war, in battle 2 loss, waste

بايلل bājlə́l 1 *transitive* [*past:* و يي بايلود] .1 to lose, to be defeated 1.2 lose something; forfeit something 2 *m. plural* .1 loss; defeat

2.2 loss, waste of something بايله ځان idiom get lost! ځان مه بايله Don't get lost!

بايلنه bājlə́na f. **1** loss; defeat **2** loss, waste of something

بايلودل bājlodә́l transitive dialect ☞ بايلل

بايلودى bājlódaj past participle of بايلودل خپل قيمتي وخت يي بايلودى They lost valuable time بايلودى زړه idiom a heart in love

بايلول bājlawә́l transitive dialect ☞ بايلل

بايولوجي bajólodzhí f. biology

بايولوجيكي biolodzhikí adjective biological

بايي 1 bājí m. regional old chap, old fellow

بايي 2 bājí interjection well بايي ته هرڅه چه وايې وايه Well, you can say what you want.

ببر 1 babár m. lion

ببر 2 babә́r **1** tousled, shaggy, disheveled **2** hairy **3** dense, thick (of wood) **4** figurative angry, cross, irate

ببرستنى babәrstónaj m. type of English rifle

ببرسرى babәrsáraj adjective tousled, shaggy, disheveled

ببرغوړى babә́rghwágaj m. English 11-round rifle

ببرک 1 babrák m. proper noun Babrák

ببرک 2 bәbrák m. castor (textile)

ببرول babәrawә́l, babarawә́l denominative, transitive [past: ببر يې کړ] **1** to tousle, ruffle, rumple **2** figurative to anger, to enrage

ببرى 1 babráj m. [plural: ببريان babriján and ببري babrí] shaggy hunting dog

ببرى 2 babә́raj, babráj m. basil

ببريدل babәredә́l, babaredә́l denominative, intransitive [past: ببر سو] **1** become tousled, become shaggy, disheveled **2** figurative, colloquial to snap at, bristle

ببغى babә́gháj, babagháj poor; unfortunate

بيليوگرافي bibliogrāfí f. bibliography

ببو 1 babáw m. elf, goblin (fantastic being that frightens children)

ببو 2 babó f. disease of horses

ببو 3 babó f. mother (form of addressing a mother or an old woman)

ببوتتى bәbotátaj m. ببوتى bәbotátaj f. hoopoe

ببوځى bәbódzaj m. damper (in a flue)

ببوزى bәbózaj, bәbuzaj m. **1** fan برقي ببوزى electric fan compound verb to fan **2** sail **3** kingfisher, halcyon

ببوکى babúkaj m. hoopoe

ببى 1 babáj m. snipe (bird)

ببى 2 babáj f. **1** older sister **2** sis (form of addressing an older sister) **3** wise and beautiful woman

ببزنه babézna f. shivers, shivering, chill, fever

بپاري bipārí, bapārí m. ☞ بيپاري

بت 1 but m. idol, statue

بت 2 bat m. stone masonry (the walls of a well, kahriz, etc.)

بتاره batára, bәtára f. club, cudgel

بتاليون batāljón m. battalion

بت پرست butparást m. idolater, idol-worshiper

بتخاک butkhā́k m. Butkhak (inhabited place near Kabul)

بتخانه butkhāná f. idol

بتر batár worst; very bad

بت شكن butshikán m. **1** history religion iconoclast **2** person who combats prejudice, outdated ideas, beliefs

بتک baták m. بتكه batáka f. flask; water bottle, canteen

بتكه 1 batáka f. flask; water bottle, canteen

بتكه 2 batáka f. goose

بتكى 1 batakáj m. flask, water bottle

بتكى 2 butkój f. gold coin; gold piece

بتله batála f. young chicken, pullet

بتون bitón m. plural concrete بتون كول compound verb to cover with concrete, lay concrete

بته 1 báta f. goose

بته 2 butá f. type of embroidery

بتي 1 bátí, batí f. glue, starch; size, sizing

بتي 2 batí f. fallow land, fallow

بتي 3 batí, bәtí f. reproach, rebuke بتي كول compound verb to reproach, rebuke

بتى 4 batój f. **1** candle **2** wick

بټ baṭ m. **1** oven for baking brick, kiln **2** griddle for frying kernels of corn or peas **3** hot, burning desert **4** figurative success, good luck

بټرى baṭří, baṭarí f. [plural: بټرى baṭrój or baṭarój and بټري گاني baṭrigā́ní or baṭarigā́ní] battery د ذخيري بټري storage battery

بټ سترگى baṭstórgaj goggle-eyed, lobster-eyed

بټ سوره baṭsóra f. coarse-ground flour

بټ سورى baṭsúraj m. straw remaining after threshing; straw left on the threshing floor

بټک baṭák ☞ بټ سترگى

بټل baṭál m. motar (for grinding hashish or naswar) بټل كول compound verb to grind in a mortar (hashish or nasvar)

بټله baṭála f. ☞ بټله

بټن baṭә́n f. regional button; push-button, call-button

بټوه baṭwá f. regional bag, handbag (lady's, etc.)

بټه 1 baṭá f. **1** fish and rice **2** dialect unseasoned boiled rice porridge

بټه 2 báṭa f. thumb بټه گوته thumb

بټي 1 baṭí f. barley juice, extracted liquid from barley

بټى 2 baṭój f. stove, kitchen range برقي بټى electric stove اټومي بټى atomic reactor بټى كول compound verb to fry, to grill

بټي 3 báṭe f. barley porridge

بټي بيابان báṭebjābán hot, sweltering desert

بټجارى baṭjāráj m. بټي والا baṭiwālá m. **1** vendor of sweets and roasted kernels **2** baker

بج 1 budzh m. [plural: بجان budzhán] seed (e.g., of a melon, watermelon)

بج 2 badzh m. sound during milking

بج [3] badzh *m.* log (a segment of the trunk of a tree when stripped of branches)

بجرا budzhŗá lazy

بجرانگي budzhŗángi *f. plural* rags

بجز badzhúz *Arabic* with the exception of, excepting, excluding, except

بجل budzhúl *f.* [*plural:* بجلي budzhúli ☞] د چا بجل شکېدل بجلکه *idiom* to have success, be lucky in something د ریدي گل اوس بجل .شکه سوېده، هره خوا یې راسته ده Just now Reday Gul is having luck in everything بجل یې مړه ده He was unlucky.

بجل باز budzhulbáz *m.* player of the knucklebones game

بجلکه budzhláka, budzhuláka *f.* 1 ankle, anklebone 2 knucklebone; بجلکه کول *compound verb* to play knucklebones

بجلي [1] bidzhlí *f.* 1 electricity د بجلي صنعت electric industry 2 lantern, flashlight; lamp 3 spark

بجلي [2] budzhuli *plural of* بجل

بجه badzhá *f.* [*plural:* بجي badzhe] اوس څو بجي دي؟ hour What time is it? پر اته بجي، په اته بجي، پر اتو eight o'clock بجو، په اتو بجو at eight o'clock نیمه یوه نیمه بجه an hour and a half بجه half an hour

بجی badzháj *f. children's speech* breast, chest

بچ bach *m.* 1.1 border, edging; edge, rim 1.2 rescue, rescuing; defense, protection 2 *predicative* defended, protected بچ کول *compound verb* ☞ بچېدل بچ کېدل *compound verb*

بچاو bachāw, bacháw *m.* بچاوتیا *f.* 1 protection, protect بچاوکول *compound verb* ☞ بچاوبدل بچاوکېدل *compound verb* 2 بچاوبدل *regional* to save

بچاوکېدنه bachāwkedóna *f.* defense, protection

بچاون bichāwón, bachāwan *m.* بچاونه *f.* large floor covering, canvas

بچاوول bachāwawól *denominative, transitive* ☞ بچول

بچاوېدل bachāwedól *denominative, transitive* ☞ بچېدل

بچت bachát *m.* supply, reserve, savings بچت کول *compound verb* to be created (of reserves, supplies) بچت کېدل *compound verb* to accumulate (of savings)

بچرتوب bachartób *m.* girlhood

بچره bachará *f.* girl

بچری [1] buchárəj *m.* young donkey, foal of an ass

بچری [2] bacháraj *m.* 1 tassel on the tail (of an ox) 2 ☞ بچکري

بچک [1] bachák *m.* 1 assistant, helper (e.g., of a irrigation system controller, miller) 2 apprentice

بچک [2] bachák *m.* tobacco wastage

بچکری bachákraj *m.* tip of a knout

بچکک bachakák *m.* [*plural:* بچکي bacháki *m.*] ☞ بچک [2]

بچگانه bachagāná children's, child's

بچندر bachandár *m.* stepson

بچو bachó *m. & f. slang* my child (address)

بچوري [1] bachúri *m. plural* stockings

بچوری [2] bachúraj *m.* 1 young of animals; young birds 2 mask

بچوکی bachúkaj *m.* 1 string, lace 2 toe (of shoes) 3 ribbon (for the hair)

بچول bachawól *denominative, transitive* [*past:* بچ یې کړ] to save, rescue; defend, guard

بچونگړی bachúngáŗaj *m.* 1 baby, child 2 the young of animals; young birds

بچوی bacháwaj *m.* 1 ☞ بچکری 2 ribbon (for the hair)

بچه [1] bachá *m.* lad, fellow

بچه [2] bácha *onomatopoeia* cry used in driving goats

بچه گرد bachagárd *m.* critical age (of a boy)

بچه گوته bachagúta, bachagwáta *f.* fourth finger, ring finger

بچه مرد bachamárd 1 *m.* young man; young stalwart, brave man, man of courage 2 *adjective* brave, courageous

بچه مرده bachamárda 1 *m.* young man; young stalwart, brave man, man of courage 2 *adjective* brave, courageous

بچی [1] bacháj *m.* [*plural:* بچي bachí *and* بچیان bachiján] 1 child, baby 2 sonny, lad (form of address) 3 young of animals and birds

بچی [2] bəcháj, bacháj *f.* base, foot of a wall

بچی [3] bacháj *f.* darling, dear one (addressing one's child)

بچی بچی bachíbachí, bəchíbəchí *onomatopoeia* cry used in driving goats

بچېدل bachedól *denominative, intransitive* [*past:* بچ سو] to escape, rid oneself of, shake off; to be protected

بچېدنه bachedóna *f. plural* بچېده bachedə́ *m.* rescuing, saving, deliverance

بخه budzá *f.* termite, white ant

بخخگی butskhagə́j *f.* handbag

بخخه butskhá *f.* ☞ بخخه

بخرکی batsə́rkaj *m.* small spark

بخری batsə́raj *m.* 1 spark 2 *figurative* little, few 3 *figurative particle* grain (of gold, etc.) 4 spray

بحث bahs *m. Arabic* [*plural:* بحثونه bahsúna *and Arabic* ابحاث abhás] 1 argument; debate, discussion وروسته تر دېر بحث څخه after long debate د بحث په مینځ a very heated argument بنه گرم بحث intervene in an argument 2 consideration (of an کښې وردنگل issue, of a question) د یوشي بحث کول ، د یوشي څخه بحث کول to discuss something; consider a matter

بحر bahr *m. Arabic* [*plural:* بحرونه bahrúna *and Arabic* ابحار abhár] 1 sea شمالي منجمدبحر ocean اوقیانوسي بحر، بحري محیط the Arctic Ocean، د هندبحر هندی بحر، the Indian Ocean 2 meter (in poetry); rhythm; metrics

بحرالکاهل bahr-ul-kāhíl *m. Arabic* the Pacific Ocean

بحران buhrán *m. Arabic* crisis اقتصادي بحران economic crisis; سیاسي بحران political crisis

بحراني buhrāni *Arabic* critical, crucial; dangerous, perilous (of a situation)

بحرپیمایي bahrpajmājí *f.* navigation

بحروبر báhr-u-bár, bahr-u-bár on land and sea

بحري bahrí *Arabic* marine, sea; naval بحري قوه navy بحري جريانات sea currents; بحري سفر (sea) voyage

بحرين bahrájn *m.* Bahrain, Bahrain Islands

بحريه bahrijá *f. Arabic* fleet جنگي بحريه merchant fleet تجارتي بحريه navy حربي بحريه،

بحيره bahirá *f. Arabic* sea توره بحيره the Black Sea

بخار bukhấr *m. Arabic* [plural: بخارونه bukhāruna and *Arabic* بخارات bukhārất] 1 steam; vapor د سکرو بخار (charcoal) fumes, carbon monoxide بخار کېدل *compound verb* to evaporate بخار ورکول *compound verb* to be evaporated to steam, stew 2 rash

بخارا bukhārấ *f.* Bukhara

بخارالود bukhārālúd بخاراره bukhārdấra saturated with steam; water vapor بخارالوده هوا saturated air

بخارست bukhārést *m.* Bucharest

بخاري [1] bukhārí *adjective* steam بخاري بېړۍ، بخاري کښتۍ steamship

بخاري [2] bukhārój *f.* oven; stove; hotplate; fireplace عادي بخاري iron stove د برېښنا بخاري، برقي بخاري electric hotplate د تنور د ګبس بخاري gas stove

بخت [1] bakht *m.* luck, good fortune د ښه بخته fortunately د ... پرېبخت سپرېدل چه و he was unsuccessful be a minion of fortune بخت شا ورته سوه، بخت یې بیده سو Good fortune turned away from him. بخت یې تور سو He was unlucky; بخت یې خلاص سو He was lucky, بخت یې ویښ سو بخت یې بیدار شو He's started having good luck.; بخت په لغته وهل to be the cause of one's own destruction or ruin

بخت [2] bukht, bukhót busy, occupied (with doing something) په کار We're occupied with the matter په کار باندي بخت یو سره بخت يو We're busy with the case

بخت توب bukhttób *m.* بخت تیا bukhttjấ *f. and* بختوالی bukhtwấlaj *m.* (state of) being busy; occupation

بختور bakhtawór, bakhtawấr 1 happy, fortunate, lucky بختوره زمانه happy time زه دي بختور یم I am happy. 2 joyous, festive په دې بختوره ورځ کښي on this joyous, festive day

بختول bukhtawól *denominative, transitive* [past: بخت یې کړ] to be busy, be occupied with affairs, with work; to enlist (someone) in participating in something

بختونه bukhtawóna *f.* enlisting, involving (someone) in something

بخته [1] bấkhta *oblique singular of* بخت [1]

بخته [2] *feminine singular of* بخت [2]

بختيا bukhtjấ *f.* صنعتي بختيا لرل بخت توب to be engaged in industry, work in industry

بختيار bakhtjấr, bakhtijấr 1 fortunate; satisfactory 2 *m.* .1 *plural* Bakhtiars (tribe) 2.2 *proper noun* Bakhtiar

بختياري bakhtajārí, bakhtaijārí *f.* prosperity, success

بختېدل bukhtedól *denominative, intransitive* [past: بخت سو] to be busy with something, work at something; be enlisted in participating in something

بختېده bukhtedó *m. plural* working in something په تجارت بختېده work in commerce

بخچه bukhchá *f.* بخچه bukhtsá *f.* بخڅګی bukhtsagój *f.* 1 bundle (with belongings); bundle; packet 2 bag, pouch (with sewing articles)

بخره [1] bákhra *f.* ☞ برخه

بخره [2] bakhóra *f. dialect* ☞ خبره

بخره ور bakhrawár happy, fortunate

بخش bakhsh *m.* part, portion, share

بخشش bakhshish *m.* بخښ bakhkh *m.* 1 gift, present 2 award بخشش کول *compound verb* a to give b to award 3 tip, gratuity 5 forgiveness, pardon بخشش ورکول *compound verb* a to give a tip b forgive *idiom* صاحب بخشش *idiom sāhib-i-bakhshish* kind, merciful; all-forgiving

بخښاوو bakhkhāwú 1 generous 2 kind, merciful; all-forgiving

بخښخ bakhkhókh *m.* بخښنت bakhkhókht *dialect* ☞ بخشش

بخښل bakhkhól *transitive* [past: ويي باخښنه] 1 to give, present 2 to show mercy, grant pardon; forgive 3 to release from payment (of taxes) 4 to exert influence

بخښندوی bakhkhəndúj, bakhkhəndój 1 generous 2 *m.* benefactor

بخښنه bakhkhóna *f.* 1 giving, donating 2 forgiveness بخښنه غوښتل *compound verb* to beg forgiveness, pardon بخښنه کول *compound verb* a to give a present b to forgive بخښنه وکئ! Pardon me! 3 gift, present دطبیعت بخښنه gift of nature

بخل [1] bukhól *m. Arabic* stinginess, greed, avarice بخل کول *compound verb* to be greed

بخل [2] bakhól *transitive* ☞ بخښل

بخله bakhula *f.* ☞ بخوله

بخمل bakhmál *m.* [plural: بخملونه bakhmaluna and بخملان bakhmalấn] velvet

بخمله bakhmála *f. proper noun* Bakhmala

بخملي [1] bakhmalí *adjective* velvet

بخملي [2] bakhmalój *f.* بخملي bakhmalí *m.* red bug

بخن bakhón, bakhun *suffix* -ish (or similar used with the names of colors) سوربخن reddish

بخن بخن bakhánbakhán, bakhunbakhun parti-colored, variegated; of different colors

بخنه bakhóna *f.* ☞ بخښنه

بخنی bakhónaj *m* dyer

بخور [1] bukhur *m. Arabic* incense

بخور [2] bəkhwór *m. hunting* feeding bird بخورکېدل *compound verb* to feed (of a bird)

بخور و نمير bukhur-u-namír *m.* starvation ration د بخور و نمير په حال to live on short rations, be half-starved; کښي شپي او ورځي تېرول drag out a miserable existence

بخوری bakhuraj *m.* 1 ☞ بو [1] 2 stuffed calf (placed next to a cow that has lost its calf)

بخول bakhwál *m. anatomy* diaphragm زړه تر بخول وتل *idiom* to desire something passionately

بخوله bəkhwóla *f.* trouble, misfortune په بخوله اخيستئ (one who has) gotten into trouble, (one who has) come to grief

بخى bakhə́j *f.* type of sewing, kind of stitch بخى وهل، بخى پركول *idiom* to decorate; praise, laud

بخيل bakhíl *Arabic* **1** *m.* miser, skinflint, stingy greedy person **2** stingy, miserly

بخيلي bakhilí *f.* stinginess, miserliness بخيلي او حسدكول to be stingy, miserly, greedy

بخيه bakhiá *f.* ☞ بخى

بد bad **1** bad, wicked بده خبره داده چي ... ، بده داده چي ... the trouble is that ... بده به نه وي كه لومړى تيلفون راكړي It wouldn't be bad if you call first **.1** evil; بدبدكتل look with malice **2** *m. plural* **.1** evil; trouble, unpleasantness بد وررپښي شول He has had a misfortune. د هغه درسره بد Don't wish anyone evil. **2.2** bad things چا بد مه غواره You acted badly. تا بد كړي دي He has treated you badly. بد وكړل *compound verb* to swear; to scold و چا ته بد ويل to speak ill of someone, give a bad report about someone خپل بد په خپله وايم mea culpa **2.3** fine بد وركول to establish the size of a fine بد تاكل to pay a fine *idiom* to be hateful to د چا بد راتلل، د چا څخه بد راتلل someone ته پرې بد مه كړه Please don't take offense at this هغه بالكل He was not at all offended. فكرى يي بد دئ He is upset. خه بد ونه منل to be angry زه له دي خولۍ نه بد ورم I don't like this hat.

بداخلاقه badakhlā́qa **1** immoral **2** ill-bred, unmannerly بداخلاقه سړى boor

بداخلاقي badakhlā́qí *f.* **1** immorality **2** lack of breeding

بداروا badārwá stingy, greedy

بداروايي badārwā́jí *f.* stinginess, greed, cupidity

بداستعمال badisti'mā́l *m.* [*plural:* بداستعمالات badisti'mālā́t] abuse, misuse; د صلاحيت بداستعمال abuse of power

بداصل badáșl of low birth, of low origin

بداعت bedā'át *m. Arabic* innovation, novelty

بدامني badāmní *f.* breakdown, disorganization, anarchy

بداهت badā́hat *m. Arabic* obviousness په بداهت سره پوهېدل to see clearly, understand well

بدائت bedā́jat *m. Arabic* undertaking; measure

بدبخته badbákhta **1** unfortunate, ill-fated **2** unfit **3** stupid

بدبختي badbakhtí *f.* trouble, misfortune; haplessness; له بدبختي نه unfortunately

بدبوړى badbóṛaj gloomy, morose; troubled, distressed

بدبويه badbója smelly, stinking, fetid

بدبويي badbují *f.* stench, stink

بدبين badbín **1** *m.* **.1** pessimist **1.2** distrustful, untrusting person **2.1** pessimistic **2.2** mistrustful

بدبيني badbiní *f.* **1** pessimism **2** distrust, lack of confidence in

بدپوره badpóraj unpunctual, tardy, late (of a debtor, for example); unreliable (of a person)

بدپوزى badpózaj gloomy; dissatisfied, discontented

بدتر badtár ☞ بتر

بدترين badtarín worst, very worst

بدتفاهم badtfāhúm *m.* misunderstanding

بدتيا badtíá *f.* **1** malice, harm, trouble **2** depravity

بدجوله baddzhawlá *indeclinable* plain, homely; ugly, hideous

بدچاروكى badchā́rukaj *m.* villain, scoundrel

بدچلاوه badchalāwá بدچلند badchalánd dissipated, dissolute, good-for-nothing

بدحاله badhā́la in poor condition

بدحالي badhā́lí *f.* poor condition

بدخرڅه badkhártsa *m.* بدخرڅى badkhártsaj spendthrift, prodigal, squanderer

بدخشان badakhshā́n *m.* Badakhshan د بدخشان ولايت Badakhshan Province

بدخصلته badkhasláta having bad character, immoral

بدخواه badkhwā́h, badkhā́h **1** *m.* enemy, foe **2** unfriendly, hostile

بدخولى badkhúlaj swearing, using foul language

بدخونده badkhwánda **1** unpalatable **2** unpleasant

بدخوندي badkhwándí *f.* **1** unpleasant taste **2** unpleasantness

بدخويه badkhója **1** immoral; wicked **2** disobedient, unruly, undisciplined

بدخوئي badkhojí *f.* **1** immorality; malice **2** disobedience, lack of discipline

بدديانتي baddijānatí *f.* dishonesty

بدډوله baddáwla *indeclinable* **1** homely; ugly, hideous بدډوله كول *compound verb* to disfigure **2** bad, nasty

بدذات badzā́t *m.* scoundrel; mean, underhanded low person

بدذاتي badzātí *f.* baseness, meanness

بدر badár, badr *m.* **1** ☞ بدر **2** cotton tree

بدر bádər *m. Arabic* full moon

بدرالدين badruddrín *m. Arabic proper noun* Badruddin

بدرد badrád *m. plural* invective, abusive language; foul language چاته بدرد ويل to scold someone

بدررفت badarráft *m.* outflow, runoff, drainage

بدرقاني badraqāní *f.* ☞ بدرگاني

بدرقه badraqá *f.* ☞ بدرگه

بدركند badarkánd *m.* cotton tree resin

بدرگاني badragāní *f.* payment for escorting, fee for convoying

بدرگه badragá *f.* **1** guard, convoy, escort, accompanying د بدرگي convoy vessel د پښتنو بدرگه ورسره وه He was escorted by a convoy of Pashtoons **2** funeral feast

بدرنگ badráng unattractive, plain; ugly, hideous په بدرنگ كېدل *idiom* to disgrace oneself

بدرنگول badrangawə́l *denominative, transitive* [*past tense* بدرنگ يي کړ] **1** to shame somebody **2** to deceive, let somebody down **3** to portray somebody in a bad light

بدرنگه badránga ☞ بدرنگ

بدرنگي badrangí *f.* ugliness, hideousness

بدرو badráw *m.* water escape

بدره badrá *f. Arabic* **1** sack of money **2** 10,000 Dirham (monetary unit of Morocco)

بدري ¹ badrí *f.* **1** stumbling بدري خوړل *compound verb* to slip, stumble **2** *Western* harm, damage بدري ميندل *compound verb* to suffer loss; ruin oneself **3** anxiety, uneasiness, worry

بدرى ² badrə́j *f. proper noun* Badri

بدړ badáṛ *m.* Euphrates poplar

بدزبانه badzabắna بدژبۍ badzhabə́baj cursing, swearing, using abusive language

بدرغه badgágha بدرغۍ badgághe spoiled, ruined (of a woman who has had a miscarriage or who has had a still-born baby)

بدسترگى badstə́rgaj shameless, brazen, insolent

بدستور badastúr in order, OK; as before, as usual

بدسلوک badsulúk unsociable, treating somebody poorly, slighting someone

بدسلوکي badsulukí *f.* slighting, treating someone badly

بدشاگوم badshāgúm unfortunate, unhappy, ill-stared, hapless

بدصورت badsurát unattractive, plain; ugly, hideous

بدعا badu'ā́ *f.* curse, damn بدعاكول *compound verb* to curse په بدعا يادول to curse at someone

بدعت bid'át *m. Arabic* **1** innovation **2** *religion* heresy

بدغږ badgháǵ **1** harsh-sounding **2** *m.* sharp sound

بدغوني badghúnaj coarse, crude, impolite, discourteous

بدفال badfā́l ominous, sinister

بدفالي badfā́lí *f.* misfortune, bad luck بدفالي نيولئ unfortunate, unhappy

بدفعله badfé'la ☞ بدكار

بدبخته badbákhta ☞ بدقسمته badqismát

بدبختي badbakhtí *f.* ☞ بدقسمتي badqismatí

بدكار badkā́r **1.1** sinful **1.2** wicked بدكاره سړى villain, scoundrel, fiend, monster **1.3** disobedient **2** *m.* villain, scoundrel, fiend, monster

بدكاري badkārí *f.* **1** sin **2** evil deed, crime **3** disobedience, state of being out of control

بدكردار badkirdā́r ☞ بدكار

بدكرداري badkirdā́rí *f.* ☞ بدكاري

بدگذرانه badguzrā́na ☞ بدسلوكه

بدگذراني badguzrā́ní *f.* **1** ☞ بدسلوكي **2** strained relations, discord, lack of harmony

بدگمانه badgumā́na **1** suspicious, distrustful **2** dubious, suspect, shady

بدگماني badgumā́ní *f.* **1** suspiciousness, mistrust, distrust **2** doubt

بدگوى badgúj, badgój *m.* one who abuses, slanderer

بدگويي badgují, badgojí *f.* malignant gossip, scandal, reviling; slander

بدل ¹ badál *m. Arabic* **1** substitute, substitution ده دى په بدل instead of دچا شي په بدل رايول to substitute something for something سره خيالات بدل رابدل كول exchange views with someone **2** revenge دچا څخه بدل اخيستل to take revenge on someone **3** compensation, indemnity **4** equivalent

بدل ² badál **1** of poor quality **2** of low birth

بدلاري ¹ badlārí *f.* waywardness, dissipation بدلاري كول *compound verb* to lead a dissipated life

بدلارى ² badlā́raj good-for-nothing, wayward, dissipated

بدلامى badlā́maj ☞ بدكار

بدل زن badəlzán *m.* singer

بدلمنه badlamə́na بدلمني immoral, lewd, debauched (woman)

بدل مېچ badəlméch, badalméch *m.* rhyme

بدلول badlawə́l, badalawə́l **1** *denominative, transitive* [*past:* بدل يي] جامه بدلول *compound verb* to be surmounted, be overcome **1.2** بدلول ... په to turn into something **2** *m. plural* ☞ بدلون

بدلون badlún *m.* بدلونه badlawə́na *f.* **1** replacement, substitution, exchange په بدلون كښي دیوشي in exchange for something **2** compensation, indemnity **3** change; transformation په حال كښي څه بدلون راغئ the situation has changed somewhat

بدله ¹ badə́la *f.* song بدلي ويل *compound verb* to sing a song په بدله لويول to lull someone دخوب بدلي ويل to sing the praises of someone, laud someone

بدله ² badlá *f.* **1** revenge دچا څخه بدله اخيستل to take revenge on someone **2** replacement, substitution, exchange دى په بدله كښي instead of that **3** *regional* compensation, indemnity

بدلي ¹ badə́lí *m.* singer

بدلي ² badə́li *plural of* بدله ¹

بدلي ³ badlé *plural of* بدله ²

بدلېدل badledə́l *denominative, intransitive* [*past:* بدل سو] **1** په بدلېدلو to be changed, to be substituted, to be exchanged **2** ... په سره to turn / change into something

بدلېده badledə́ *m. plural* **1** substitution, exchange **2** change into something; accompanying by something

بدماري ¹ badmārí *f.* simulation, sham, pretense

بدمارى ² badmā́raj *m.* malingerer

بدماش badmā́sh *m.* ☞ بدمعاش

بدمخي ¹ badmə́khí *f.* ugliness, hideousness

بدمخى ² badmə́khaj **1** unattractive, plain; ugly, hideous **2** shameless

بدمرغه badmə́rhga unfortunate, unhappy بدمرغه سړى failure (a person)

بدمرغي badmə́rghí *f.* bad omen, ill omen

بدمستي badmastí *f.* drinking bout, binge بدمستي كول drink heavily

بدمعاش badma'ā́sh *m.* **1** scoundrel, blackguard; bandit, thug, gangster **2** dissipated person

بدمعاشي badma'ā́shí *f.* **1** banditry **2** dissipation

بدمعرفي badma'rifí *f.* portraying in a bad light, discrediting دچا بدمعرفي كول to discredit someone

بدمعمله گي badma'milagí *f.* unscrupulousness, lack of integrity, lack of conscientiousness

بدن badán *m.* body, trunk

بدنام badnā́m 1 to have a bad reputation, be in bad repute; disgraced, be dishonored 2 shameful, disgraceful

بدناموسي badnā́musí, badnā́mosí *f.* shame, disgrace, dishonor; bad reputation

بدنامول badnā́mawә́l *denominative, transitive* [*past:* بدنام يې کړ] dishonor, disgrace, discredit

بدنامي badnā́mí *f.* bad reputation; shame, dishonor خونه بدنامي ده! What a shame!

بدناميدل badnā́medә́l *denominative, intransitive* [*past:* بدنام سو] be disgraced, be dishonored, be discredited; disgrace oneself

بدنصيبه badnasíba *indeclinable* unfortunate

بدنمايه badnumája بدنماى badnumā́j unattractive; ugly, hideous

بدنه badaná *f.* fuselage (of an aircraft)

بدني ¹ badaní physical, bodily, corporal بدني تربيت physical culture بدني ورزش physical exercises, calisthenics

بدني ² badnә́j, badanә́j *f.* small basin for washing, water container with a spout (usually made of copper or aluminum)

بدنيته badnijáta 1 unfortunate, unlucky 2 ominous, sinister 3 ill-intentioned, malicious; unfriendly, hostile, ill-disposed

بدنيتي badnijatí *f.* malice, malicious intent, ill-will, hostility

بدو badú cross, angry, bad-tempered

بدوالى badwā́laj *m.* poor quality; negative side

بدودي badodí *f.* harm; damage

بدورد badwә́rd hostile, inimical

بدورده badwә́rda *indeclinable* unfortunate, unhappy

بدورگه badwә́rga cross, angry, bad-tempered

بدورگېدل badwәrgedә́l *intransitive* [*past:* بدورگ شو] to get angry

بدورى badúraj *m.* ☞ بدووى

بدور badwә́ŗ dangerous (of a person)

بدورول badwәŗawә́l *denominative, transitive* [*past:* بدور يې کړ] to consider (to be) harmful, consider (to be) dangerous

بدورېدل badwәŗedә́l *denominative, intransitive* [*past:* بدور شو] to be harmful, be dangerous

بدورمه badwágma *indeclinable* fetid, stinking, bad-smelling

بدوک badúk *m.* بدوکى badúkaj *m.* scoundrel, villain; worthless person, a bad lot

بدول badawә́l *denominative, transitive* [*past:* بد يې کړ] make bad, worsen, spoil

بدون bidún *Persian preposition combines with the postposition* له without, except له بدون

بدوي badawí *m. Arabic* bedouin, nomad

بدويت badawiját *m. Arabic* nomadic way of life

بده ¹ báda 1 *feminine singular of* بد 1 2 *f.* .1 harm; trouble, misfortune; د ښې او بدي توپيرکول distinguish good and evil; په چاته په بده ککړېدل to regard someone maliciously; په بده کتل to get into trouble 2.2 bad; په بدو اوښتل a to worsen, get worse (e.g., of the condition of a wound) b to engage in nefarious business, take the path of wrong; go bad, become corrupted (of a person) بده وراړول a

to cause harm b shame, discredit هغه بدي اخيستئ دئ a he has become pitiable b he got lost c he lost consciousness

بده ² budá *f. textiles* weft, woof

بده ³ budh *m.* Buddha بده مذهب Buddhism

بده ويرانه báda-u-birā́na *f.* ☞ بده ويرانه

بده ورځ bádawradz *f.* rainy day; trouble; need; difficult position په بده . Misfortune befell Walo-jaan. ولوجان بدي ورځي اخيستئ دئ وچاته بدي ورځي fall into poverty ورځ اخته کېدل ، په بده ورځ ککړېدل کول to pester someone with requests, importune someone

بده ويرانه báda-wirā́na *f.* disturbance, discord, sedition بده ويرانه پېنبول a to create a disturbance b to make much mischief بده ويرانه پېنبېدل a to be raised (of a disturbance) b to happen, occur (of a misfortune)

بدي ¹ bádí *f.* 1 evil, harm, misfortune 2 deadly hostility, enmity 3 *Eastern* hatred, enmity د هغه ورور زما بدي شي ، د هغه د ورور زما بدي شي I hate his brother. بدي کول *compound verb* to sin

بدي ² bádi *Eastern* bade 1 *feminine plural of* بد 1 2 *oblique case singular of* بده ¹ 2

بدى ³ badә́j wicked, malicious; worthless, good-for-nothing (of a person)

بدى ⁴ badә́j *f.* bank of a canal subject to erosion

بدى ⁵ badә́j *plural of* بدي ¹

بديا badjā́ *f.* 1 evil, harm, misfortune 2 depravity, perversity

بديا badjā́ *f.* ☞ بېديا

بديدار badidā́r *m.* بدي دار deadly enemy, person who is in a state of deadly enmity or who has committed an act of bloody vengeance (murder, wounding, etc.)

بديداري badidā́rí *f.* بدي داري the custom of blood revenge

بدېدل badedә́l *denominative, intransitive* [*past:* بدشو] 1 to grow worse, spoil 2 to become unsuitable; be ruined 3 to perish

بديع badí' *Arabic* remarkable, wonderful, wondrous

بديعه badi'á *f. Arabic* [*plural:* بدائع badā́i'] *m. Arabic* wonderful thing, amazing thing

بديعي badi'í *Arabic* rhetorical

بديهي badihí *Arabic* clear, obvious بديهي ده it is clear, it is obvious

بﮉ ¹ baḍ equal, identical

بﮉ ² buḍ one-armed, having one arm

بﮉ ³ bәḍ clear په بﮉه ويل to speak clearly; speak bluntly

بﮉا buḍā́ 1 old; aged, advanced in years 2 *m.* old man, elder دسړي نه بﮉا جوړول to make someone (look) older

بﮉاگري baḍāgarí *f.* ☞ بﮉايتوب

بﮉال baḍā́l *m.* wine

بﮉاى baḍā́j 1 *m.* rich man 2 rich, wealthy

بﮉايتوب baḍājtób *m.* wealth, substance

بﮉاﮋنه baḍājә́na *f.* enrichment, gain

بﮉاﮋول baḍājavә́l *denominative, transitive* [*past:* بﮉاى يې کړ] to enrich, make rich

بﮉاﮋي baḍājí *f.* ☞ بﮉايتوب بﮉائي *idiom* په يو شي بﮉائي کول to be proud of something

بڊبول baḍból truthful; righteous

بڊبول توب baḍboltób *m.* بڊبولتیا baḍboltjá *f.* بڊبولوالی baḍbolválaj *m.* truth; veracity; truthfulness, uprightness

بڊگال baḍagál *m.* fluff on the flower cluster of the cat-tail (used in construction)

بڊگي bəḍəgí *f.* vagrancy

بڊو baḍú *m.* bribetaker

بڊوﮈی baḍúḍaj *m. anatomy* kidney

بڊوکی baḍúkaj *m.* kidney (of a sheep, goat)

بڊوگی buḍogáj *m.* old boy, old chap

بڊولی baḍólaj *m.* clay pitcher

بﮈه báḍa *f.* 1 belt or cord worn with wide pants 2 target, goal 3 waning moon 4 bribe *idiom* بﮈي راغنﮢل to roll up one's sleeves, get down to work بﮈي په چا پسې پورته کول to pursue someone persistently 5 بﮈي وهل to take up something, take up some business

بﮈها buḍhá ☞ بﮈا

بﮈی buḍáj *m.* old man

بﮈی buḍáj *f.* old woman

بﮈی baḍáj *m.* person with no arms, armless person

بﮈي báḍi *f. plural* bribe بﮈي اخیسﺗل، بﮈي خورل to take a bribe بﮈي ورکول to give a bribe

بﮈي خور baḍikhór bribe-taker

بﮈي مار baḍimār *m.* bribe-giver

بذر bazr *m. Arabic singular & plural* grain for sowing, seed

بزگر bazgár *m.* ☞ بزگر

بزگره bazgára *f.* ☞ بزگره

بزگري bazgarí *f.* ☞ بزگري

بذله bazlá *f. Arabic* joke; witticism

بذله گو bazlagú *m.* بذله گوی bazlagúj wit; joker, comedian

بذله گوی bazlaguí *f.* wit, wittiness

بر bar *f.* barr *Arabic* dry land (as opposed to the sea)

بر bar *m.* breast, chest

بر bar *m.* width (of fabric, etc.)

بر bar 1.1 upper بریﺒﻨﺗون Afghan living in the mountain region (in Afghanistan) 1.2 having conquered, having come out on top بر a کﯧﺪل to ascend, go up b to conquer, win out 2 *m.* top د بره a from above b from the mountains, from the north, from Afghanistan (with reference to Afghans)

بر bər *m. astronomy* eclipse د نمر بر eclipse of the sun *idiom* a مﺪمان b سﻠﭘﻮﺍﻟﮑﺮ sleepwalker

بر bər *m.* 1 branch with small leaves (e.g., of a tamarisk) 2 leafy top of root vegetables (e.g., of carrots)

برابر brābár barābár 1.1 equal, identical نزدې په برابر شمبر almost equally, in equal parts 1.2 suitable, appropriate, fit, useful 1.3 favorable 1.4 proper, fitting 1.5 parallel 1.6 uniform برابر uniform heat په برابره توگه، په برابر ﮈول تودوالی uniformly 2.1 equally, indentically یو برابر in equal amounts; on a par (with), on an equal footing 2.2 in accordance (with something) په نمونه سره

په ... سره برابر، according to model 2.3 parallel, along ... برابر سره برابر parallel to something, alongside something 2.4 uniformly 2.5 directly برابر کورته ﺡﯤ go directly home *idiom* دوه برابره پر وخت in time twice as much

برابرتیا brābartjá *f.* برابربنت brābarbént *m.* barābarókht برابروالی brābarválaj *m.* barābarválaj 1 correspondence 2 uniformity 3 equality, sameness 4 agreement; coordination 5 regulation, adjustment

برابرول brābaravól barābaravól *denominative, transitive* [*past:* برابر کﺮ] 1 to balance; equalize, make even 2 to bring into agreement 3 to arrange 4 to fit, adapt 5 to supply; stock د خوړلو مواد برابرول to lay in provisions 6 to prepare; create 7 to arrange, organize 8 to fold, pack کالي سره برابرول to fold clothing 9 to tune (e.g., a radio) *idiom* ویو کار ته ﺡان برابرول to be engaged in business

برابرونه brābaravóna *f.* barābaravóna ☞ برابري 3-9

برابري brābarí *f.* barābarí 1 equality 2 parallel direction هغه غرونه چه د ساحل په برابري پراته دي mountains which stretch along the shore 3 fitting, adjustment 4 correspondence, agreement 5 supply; stock 6 preparation; creation 7 arrangement 8 folding, packing 9 tuning (a radio)

برابرﯧﺪل brābaredól barābaredól *denominative, intransitive* [*past:* برابر شو] 1 to balance; equalize, become even 2 to be sufficient, be enough د حیواناتو د پوﻟﻮ دپاره واﺑﻨﻪ نه برابرﯦﺮي there is not enough grass for pasturing the cattle 3 to come into correspondence, come to an agreement 4 to be arranged, be adjusted 5 to be fitted, be accommodated 6 to be supplied, be stocked 7 to be prepared, be created 8 to be arranged, be organized 9 to be folded, be packed 10 to be tuned (e.g., a radio receiver)

برأت barā'át *m.* barất *m. Arabic* 1 remmittance (money) د معاش برأت check or order for receipt of pay or maintenance *finance* 2 bill of exchange, transferable bill د برأت صدور payment of a note; issuance of a note برأت صادروونکی، برأت ورکوونکی issuer of a promissory note د برأت قبول acceptance of a bill of exchange

برات barất *m. Arabic* fourteenth day of the eighth month of the lunar year when funeral banquets are customarily celebrated

براﺟﻪ brádza *f.* tick (on a camel or great-horned cattle)

براده burādá *f.* sawdust, filings د اوسپني برادي iron filings

بروﮈکاست brádkāst *m.* ☞ بروﮈکاست

برار bərār *m.* growth, development

برازاویل brāzāvíl *m.* Brazzaville (city)

برازندگي barāzandagí *f.* honor, merit

برازیل brāzíl *m.* Brazil

برازیلیا brāzilijá *f.* Brasilia (city)

براعظم barria'zám *m.* continent

براعظمي barria'zamí continental

براق burāk *m.* embankment; rampart

برالا barālā 1 evident, open 2 manifestly, openly; (to speak) frankly

برالبوالی brālbválaj *m.* pregnancy; gestation; being in foal, etc.

برالبه brālba pregnant; gestating; in foal, etc.

برالبیدل brālbedə́l *denominative, intransitive* [*past:* برالبه شوه] to be fruitful; be pregnant; become pregnant; be with young, in foal, etc.

برامد barāmád discovered, revealed, disclosed برامد کېدل to be discovered; turn up somewhere

برآمده barāmadá *f. regional* veranda

بران burrān cutting; sharp

برانچ brānch *m.* branch, section

برانډه bərānda *f.* cry, scream برانډه کول to cry out, howl

برانش brānsh *m.* gills; branchiae

برانشي brānshaj *m.* gill, branchia

برانگیزانده barāngizāndá provocative (of actions)

براوډه brāvḍa *f.* bragging, boasting براوډي وهل a to boast, brag b to lay claim to something c to pretend to be someone

براورد barāvúrd *m.* 1 estimate 2 valuation

براونه barāvə́na *f.* victory

براهماپوترا brāhmā-putrā *f.* the Brahmaputra (river)

براهوی brāhúj *m.* Brahui (nationality of a people living mainly in western Pakistan)

براهین barāhín *m. Arabic plural from* برهان

برائت barā'át *m. Arabic* 1 *law* acquittal 2 release (e.g., from obligations) 3 purity, innocence

برای راست barāji-rāst *regional* truly; in actuality, in fact

برایه barājə́ برائي barājí yesterday evening برایه ماښام last night برایه شپه late last night

برباد barbād 1.1 ruined 1.2 annihilated; destroyed; crushed 1.3 wasted, spent 2 down with! let perish!

بربادول barbādavə́l *denominative, transitive* [*past:* برباد يې کړ] 1 to ruin 2 to annihilate, crush, destroy 3 to waste, throw to the wind

بربادي barbādí *f.* 1 ruin 2 annihilation, destruction 3 squandering 4 nonsense, foolishness

بربادېدل barbādedə́l *denominative, intransitive* [*past:* برباد شو] 1 to perish, be lost 2 to be annihilated, be crushed, be destroyed 3 to be squandered

بریت bərbə́t [1] *m.* haughtiness; pride

بریت barbát [2] *m.* guitar

بربره burburá *f.* bubble (on the surface of water)

بربری bərbəráj [1] *m.* propeller (of a ship or airplane)

بربری burburáj [2] *m.* 1 kindling 2 leaves (e.g., of the tamarisk)

بربری barbarí [3] 1 barbarian 2 *m.* a barbarian

بربری barbarí [4] *m. plural* ☞ هزاره 1

برباس barbás *m.* بریست barbást *m.* 1 property; belongings, things 2 success

بربک burbə́k *m.* thorn apple, hawthorn

بربکی burbəkáj *m.* ☞ بوبکی

بربنډ barbə́nḍ 1 naked, bare 2 bare, without vegetation (of mountains) 3 *obsolete* easily armed, easily equipped, easily instigated

برېنډتوب barbəndtób *m.* برېنډتیا barbəndtjá *f.* برېنډوالی barbəndvālaj 1 nakedness, bareness 2 absence of vegetation (on mountains)

برېنډول barbəndavə́l *denominative, transitive* [*past:* برېنډ شو] to bare, uncover, strip, lay bare

برېنډېدل barbəndedə́l *denominative, intransitive* [*past:* برېنډ شو] 1 to be uncovered, be laid bare, be stripped 2 to be denuded (of vegetation on mountains)

بربوزک barbuzák *m.* mountaineer's bow

برپا barpā́ 1 raised, erected, constructed 2 established; founded, based برپا کول a to raise, erect, construct b to establish, found, base 3 برپا کېدل a to be raised, be erected, be constructed b to be established, be founded, be based

برپي barpí foolishly brave

برتانوي britānaví British

برتانیه britānijá *f.* England لویه برتانیه Great Britain

برتري bartarí *f.* superiority ظاهره برتري لرل to be clearly superior

برته bartá *f.* boiled eggplant without butter

برته bírta *f.* ☞ ببرته

برتي bartí *f.* 1 ☞ بهرتي 2 *technology* soldering

برج burdzh [1] *m. Arabic* brədzh [*plural:* برجونه burdzhúna *plural:* برجان burdzhán *Arabic plural:* بروج burúdzh] 1 tower; fort; stronghold; blockhouse 2 sign of the zodiac 3 month of the solar year گرڅېدونکی برج aviation (gun-) turret

برج bardzh [2] *m.* 1 thin bark of a tree (used for paper); birch-bark 2 birch tree

برجاو bardzhā́v 1 full, filled 2 thickly populated

برجتو bardzhətú *m.* trouble-maker

برجد bardzhád established, fixed, set up

برجستگي bardzhastagí *f.* 1 protuberance, bulge, projection 2 superiority تر نورو برجستگي لرل to surpass others

برجسته bardzhastá 1 outstanding د برجسته خلک eminent people برجسته خدمتونو په نسبت for outstanding service 2 precisely, distinctly a برجسته ویل to speak distinctly b to emphasize (in speech)

برجک bardzhák *regional* برجک bardzhák full, filled برجق کول to fill د کمره د خلقو نه برجقه شوي ده the room was filled with people برجق کېدل to be full, be filled; fill up

برجگی burdzhagáj *m.* turret

برجو bardzhú *f.* 1 whetstone, touchstone برجو کانی whetstone, touchstone 2 cheek 3 kidney stones

برخ brədz *f.* [*plural:* برخي brə́dzi] peritoneum

برچول brachavə́l *denominative, transitive* [*past:* برچ یې کړ] to anger; annoy, irritate

برچه barchá *f.* flat bayonet د برچو جنگ bayonet battle برچه پک *military* Fix bayonets! (as a command)

برخبر bartsér 1 evident, clear 2 raised (to the surface) برخبر کول ☞ برخبرېدل ☞ برخبر کېدل، برخبرول

برخبرول bartseravə́l *denominative, transitive* [*past:* برخبر یې کړ] 1 to exhibit, show, display 2 to raise (to the surface)

برخېره bartséra *feminine singular from* برخېر

برخېرېدۇل bartseredۇl *denominative, intransitive* [*past:* برخېر شو] **1** to be exhibited, be shown, be displayed **2** to be raised, rise up (to the surface)

برحال barhál existing, current (of a government, etc.)

برخاست barkhāst *m. regional* **1** closing (e.g., of a session) **2** firing, removal (from a job)

برخلاف barkhilāf opposed (to someone, something) د ، دي برخلاف دي په برخلاف despite that; counter to that (in defiance of that)

برخليک barkhlík *m.* fate, lot

برخو barkhú *m.* ☞ بارخو

برخاست barkhāst *m.* ☞ برخاست

برخوردار barkhurdár **1.1** fortunate, happy, prosperous برخوردار کېدل to be happy, fortunate **1.2** making use of something **2** *m. polite* son ستاسي د برخوردار نوم څۀ دئ؟ What is your son's name?

برخونه barkhúna *f.* ☞ بالاخانه

برخه bárkha *f.* brákha *f.* **1** part; portion د پنځې برخه share; portion, lot له درو څخه دوې برخي shareholder; partner د برخي خاوند two thirds برخه برخه in part, partially, by parts د يوشي يوه برخه جوړول to be a part of something دوې برخي کېدل to be divided in half, into two parts پر دوو برابرو برخو باندي ويشل to divide into two equal parts, split in half له يو شي څخه برخه اخيستل، له يو شي څخه برخه ميندل **a** to own a part; to be a shareholder **b** to promote, assist, be conducive to something د يو شي څخه لويه برخه لرل to play a large role be worthy of something پوره برخه لرل to utilize something in full measure يو شي په برخه ورکول to provide someone with something د چا په برخه کېدل to pass on to someone (inheritance); for someone to get what's coming to him **2** portion of land, allotment of land **3** *military* flight (3-4 aircraft) sub-unit *idiom* برخه لټول to seek happiness

برخه خور barkhakhór *m.* **1** co-owner **2** landowner **3** member of a commune

برخه لرونکی bárkha larúnkaj *m.* **1** participant **2** shareholder

برخه من barkhamۇn having a portion

بردار bardár **1** a width of … **2** wide, broad; of double width (of fabric)

برداشت bardásht *m.* **1** patience **2** firmness, steadfastness **3** advance (in pay) برداشت کول **a** to endure, bear **b** to take an advance on your pay **4** introduction, forward (e.g., in a book)

برداشتول bardáshtavۇl *denominative, transitive* [*past:* برداشت يې کړ] to endure, be patient

بردگي bardagí *f.* slavery د بردگي دوره epoch of slavery

بردوباى burdubáj *m.* victory and defeat

برده bardá [*plural:* برده گان bardagán] **1** *m.* slave **2** *f.* female slave; female captive

برره barára *f. botany Periploca aphylla* (a kind of bush)

برزاله barzála *f.* eyelid

برزخ barzákh *m.* **1** isthmus, neck (of land) **2** receptivity; susceptibility

برزو bۇrzú *m.* padded pants, quilted trousers

برس burs *m.* ☞ برش

برسات barsát *m.* **1** rainy season **2** monsoon نیکبنی برسات monsoon from India

برساتي barsātí *f.* raincoat

برست brest *m.* Brest (city)

برسراقتدار barsar-i-iḳtidár *regional* being in power, being in office

برشول bursavۇl *transitive* ☞ برشول

برشېر barsér *obsolete* ☞ برخېر

برسېر barsér *m.* interface

برسېرنی barserۇn barserۇnáj superficial, external

برسېره barséra over, above, more than something; apart from, besides something برسره پر دي، برسره پر هغه moreover, in addition

برخېرول brakhۇrávۇl ☞ کول

برش brash *m.* barásh [*plural:* برشان brashán *plural:* barashán] brush دمسواک برش toothbrush برش کول *compound verb* ☞ برشول

برش burísh *m.* cutting (out)

برشته birishtá roasted, fried, grilled برشته کول to roast, fry, grill

برشول brashavۇl *denominative, transitive* [*past:* برش يې کړ] to clean with a brush

برطانوي britānaví British

برطانیه britānijá *f.* England لویه برطانیه Great Britain

برطرف bartaráf dismissed (from a job), fired برطرف کول ☞ برطرفېدل برطرف کېدل، ☞

برطرفول bartarafavۇl *denominative, transitive* [*past:* برطرف يې کړ] to dismiss (from a job), fire

برطرفي bartarafí *f.* dismissal (from a job), firing

برطرفېدل bartarafedۇl *denominative, intransitive* [*past:* برطرف شو] to be dismissed (from a job), be fired

برعکس bar'áks on the contrary

برعلیه bar'alijá contradictory

برغ bragh *m.* **1** fold **2** layer

برغت burghút *m.* steppe cat (caracal)

برغته burghúta *f.* steppe cat (the female) (caracal)

برغتی barghuṭáj *m.* ☞ برغوتی

برغزووي barghazúvi *f. plural* nonsense, foolishness

برغښکی barghۇ́khaj *m.* upper jaw

برغنډ barghánḍ *m.* **1** notch (on a log, etc.) **2** wound (stab wound) **3** piece (of meat)

برغو barghú *m.* **1** borer, drill, auger **2** bayonet

برغوت burghút *m.* ☞ برغت

برغوته burchúta *f.* ☞ برغته

برغوتی barghuṭáj *m. medicine* mumps

برغوږی barghvágaj *m.* earring

برغولی barghۇláj *m.* lid, cover (of a kettle, etc.)

برغونی barghúnaj ☞ غبرگونی

برف پاک barfpāk *m.* snowplow

برفدان barfdā́n *m.* reservoir for snow

برفک barfák *m.* Barfak (village, town)

برف کوچ barfkúch *m.* snow avalanche

برفي barfī́ *f.* cream and sugar frozen in small bars (a kind of confection)

برق bark *m. Arabic* 1 lightning 2 electricity د برق څراغ electric light, د برق فابريکه electric power station

برقرار barkarār 1 established, founded ☞ برقرار کول 2 برقراريدل ☞ کېدل، firm, hard

برقرارول barkarāravál *denominative, transitive* [*past:* برقرار يې کړ] 1 to establish, found 2 to make fast, firm

برقراري barkarārí *f.* 1 founding, establishment 2 firmness, hardness

برقراريدل barkarāredál *denominative, intransitive* [*past:* برقرار شو] to be founded, be established

برقعه burk'á *f.* veil, yashmak (worn by Moslem women)

برق والا barkvālā́ *m.* electrician

برقه burká *f.* ☞ برقعه

برقي barkí 1 electric برقي څراغ electric light, برقي پايه stoplight برقي تداوي electrotherapy برقي کول to electrify 2 *m.* electrician

برکات barakát *m. Arabic* [*plural:* برکتونه barakatúna *Arabic plural:* برکات barakát] 1 blessing, benediction 2 influence د چا له برکته thanks to someone, because of someone 3 well-being, prosperity د زمري له کوره برکت تللئ دئ، د زمري له کوره برکت ټول شوئ دئ Prosperity has left Zmaraj's house 4 *proper noun* Barakat

برکتي barakatí fruitful, fertile

برکنړ barkunáṛ *m.* Barkunar (region)

برکه baráka *f.* kind of fabric from camel fur

برکۍ barakə́j *f.* large bag (for hauling straw)

برکي برک barakí-barák *m.* Baraki-Barak (city)

برکي راجان barakí-rādzhán *m.* Baraki Rajan (town or village)

برگ brag [1] 1 variegated, motley, many-colored; skewbald 2 *m.* leper *idiom* برگ برگ کتل to look at angrily

برگ barg *m.* [2] 1 leaf برگ غوږپړي leaves are falling برگ رژېږي leaves are are coming out 2 slice برگ برگ کول to cut into thin slices (e.g., meat) 3 fighting equipment

برگت burgút *m. proper name* Burgut

برگد brigíd *m.* birgíd *obsolete* brigadier general

برگرندۍ bargrandə́j *m.* ☞ برگرندی

برگزيده barguzidá chosen, selected, elected; picked

برگ سترگی bragstə́rgaj having a cataract on the eye

برگشت bargásht *m.* 1 return 2 turn, turning د برگشت نقطه turning point

برگوته bargúta *f.* little finger, little toe

برگه bargá *f.* [1] 1 beam, girder 2 raft

برگه brága [1] 1 *feminine singular from* برگ 1 2 *feminine for* برگ [1] 2

برگۍ bragáj *m.* [1] leper

برگ يالی bragjāláj motley, variegated; spotted

برلاسی barlā́saj strong, powerful, authoritative

برلک barlák *m.* scarecrow

برله barláh on behalf (of someone)

برلين barlín *m.* Berlin (city)

برم bram *m.* power له برمه لوېدل، له برمه پرېوتل to wear oneself out, grow weak (of a person)

برما barmā́ *f.* Burma د برما اتحاديه Union of Burma

برمانو barmāṇú *m.* savage, barbarian

برمته bramatá *f.* baramatá (unauthorized) driving away of cattle, etc. برمته کول *compound verb* to drive away cattle; to seize property

برمل barmál *m.* Bar Mil (region in Paktia province)

برملا barmalā́ ☞ برالا

برمند barmə́nḍ ☞ برېنډ

برمندتيا barmənḍtjā́ *f.* ☞ برېنډتوب

برمندول barmənḍavál *denominative, transitive* ☞ برېنډول

برمندېدل barmənḍedál *denominative, intransitive* ☞ برېنډېدل

برمنگهم birminghám *m.* Birmingham (city)

برمه barmá *f.* auger, gimlet د سکرو د برمي ماشين auger (for drilling wells) د برمي برج derrick برمه کول a to drill b to cut through (air, of an airplane propeller, etc.)

برمه کار barmakār *m.* driller; drill operator

برمه کاري barmakārí *f.* drilling برمه کاري کول *compound verb* to drill

برمه ئي barmají used for or related to drilling, boring

برميالی bramjāláj strong, great; mighty

برن bern *m.* barn *m.* Bern (city)

برناحقه barnāháḳa برناحقي barnāháḳe in vain, for nothing

برنج biríndzh *m.* brass

برند brand 1 cheerful 2 coquettish, playful 3 attentive 4 having come out against someone 5 *dialect* opened wide (of the eyes) چا ته برند کېدل a to come out against someone; attack someone *dialect* b to be wide-eyed

برندول brəndavál *denominative, transitive* [*past:* برند يې کړ] to furrow one's brows; frown

برندېدل brəndedál *denominative, intransitive* [*past:* برند شو] 1 to frown 2 to become angry

برنډه baranḍá *f.* 1 veranda 2 deck

برنی baranáj [1] 1 *adjective* yesterday برنی شپه last night, yesterday evening 2 stale (of bread)

برنی baranáj [2] upper (living or located in the mountains) برنی کلی mountain village

برنی ولتا baranə́j voltā́ *f.* ☞ بره ولتا

بروټی barotaj *m.* [1] bundle of brushwood

بروټی barvə́taj *m.* [2] ☞ دسترخان

بروج burúdzh *masculine plural Arabic from* برج [1]

بروډکاست broḍkā́st *m.* radio broadcast; broadcasting د بروډکاست په ذريعه by radio, on the radio بروډکاست کول *compound verb* to broadcast over radio بروډکاست کېدل *compound verb* to be broadcast by radio

بروره baróṛa *f.* Ornithodorus (a kind of tick, carrier of typhus or tick fever)

بروز burúz *m. Arabic* manifestation, disclosure, revelation; appearance بروز کول to become manifest, be revealed; appear

بروق burók *m.* ☞ براق

بروکسل bruksél *m.* Brussels (city)

برونشیت bronshít *m.* bronchitis

بروڼي barvúṇaj *m.* 1 part of a bucket chain or noria 2 spot (of a wheel)

بروی barváj 1 sticky 2 *figurative* boring, tiresome بروی کول **a** to stick on, glue on **b** *figurative* to bore بروی کېدل **a** to stick (to), adhere **b** *figurative* to be fed up, be bored

بره bára *feminine singular of* بر 4

برهان burhán *m. Arabic* [*plural:* برهانونه burhānúna *Arabic plural:* براهين barāhín] convincing proof, argument براهين راايستل to introduce convincing proof or arguments

بره خونه bára khúna *f.* ☞ بالا خانه

برهگوندی baragáṛa *f.* ☞ برهگوندی

برهم barhám 1 mixed, mixed up 2 spoiled برهم کېدل، ☞ برهمېدل برهمول

برهمن brahmán *m.* Brahmin

برهمول barhamavól *denominative, transitive* [*past:* برهم یې کړ] 1 to mix, mix up, confuse 2 to spoil 3 to ruin, destroy

برهمېدل barhamedól *denominative, intransitive* [*past:* برهم شو] 1 to be mixed, be mixed up, be confused 2 to be spoiled, spoil 3 to be ruined

بره ولتا bára voltá *f.* Upper Volta د بري ولتا جمهوریت Republic of Upper Volta

بری baráj 1 *m.* victory; success بری کول، بری گټل، بری میندل، بری ورل **a** to win a victory over someone, conquer, overcome someone **b** to overcome, master something

بري barrí 2 *Arabic* 1 land (as opposed to marine, air) بري لښکر ground army 2 continental بري اقليم continental climate

بري barí 3 *Arabic* 1 innocent (of), not guilty 2 freed (from obligations, etc.)

بريا barjá *f.* ☞ بريا

بري الذمه barij-uz-zimá *Arabic* 1 exonerated, found innocent 2 freed (from payment of a debt, from carrying out something) بري الذمه کېدل **a** to be justified **b** to be liberated, be freed (from payment of a debt, from doing something)

برياله barjála *f.* air hole, vent, safety value; smoke vent

بریالی barjaláj 1.1 triumphant, victorious 1.2 succeeding in something; having achieved success بریالی کېدل **a** to triumph, win, conquer **b** to succeed, attain success په امتحان کښې بریالی کېدل to pass an examination 2 *m.* .1 victor; champion د گرندیتوب بریالی champion in racing 2.2 *proper name* Barjalaj

برياليتوب barjālitób *m.* success, victory دوی ته تر دې لا زيات برياليتوب غواړو We wish them even greater success.

برت bret *m.* moustache خپل برت په خمڅه اړول **a** twirl your moustache **b** *figurative* to make a show of bravery برتونه څوړول **a** to be cowardly **b** to stint, grudge *idiom* تاوول ده خپل برتونه **a** he rejoiced (in) **b** he gave himself airs

برتانيه britānijá *f.* ☞ برتانيا

برېخ brekh *m. Eastern* ☞ برېښ 2

برید brid *m.* 1 attack, assault 2 beginning, starting point, access برید کول **a** to attack **b** to approach something, begin something

برید buríd *m.* 1 separation 2 absence 3 border

برید جنرال briddzhenrāl *m.* major-general

برید جنرالي briddzhenrālí *f.* rank of major-general

برېدل baredól bəredól *intransitive* [*past:* و برېده] to grow (of living creatures, organisms)

برېدليک bridlík *m.* foreward

بريدمن bridmán *m.* lieutenant لمړی بريدمن 1st lieutenant دوهم بريدمن 2nd lieutenant دريم بريدمن 3rd lieutenant

بريدمني bridmaní *f.* rank of lieutenant

برېز brez *f.* bug

برېزر brezár *m.* morning, dawn

برېزري barezaráj *m.* breakfast

برېزن brezón *m.* برېزن bregón *m.* bleat, bleating برېزن کول to bleat

برېښ brekh *m.* 1 inflammation of the lungs, pneumonia تبه برېښ inflammation of the lungs, pneumonia 2 sharp pain in the side برېښ کول **a** to be ill with inflammation of the lungs, be ill with pneumonia **b** to have a pain in the side

برېښ brekh *m.* glitter, shine, gleaming د توري برېښ **a** the glitter of a sable *figurative* **b** flourishing arms برېښ کول **a** to shine, glitter, gleam *figurative* **b** to flourish arms, threaten war

برېښناليک brékhlik *m.* ایمبل اجیمل brekhnálik e-mail

برېښناليک پته brékhlik páta *f.* e-mail address

برېښند brekhónd ☞ برېښنن

برېښنا brekhnā *f.* [*plural:* برېښناگاني brekhnāgáni *plural:* برېښناوي brekhnāví] 1 shine, glitter, gleam 2 lightning 3 electricity; electric light د برېښنا فابريکه electric power station د برېښنا ميټر electric meter 4 *proper name* Brekhna

برېښناچي brekhnāchí *m.* electrician

برېښناوال brekhnāvál electric

برېښند brekhónd gleaming, shining, resplendent, dazzling

برېښول brekhavól *transitive* [*past:* و یې برېښناوه] 1 to cause to shine, cause to glisten ايندره برېښنول to admit rays of sunlight 2 to dazzle with brilliance *figurative idiom* غاښونه برېښنول to set the teeth on edge توره برېښنول to flourish arms, threaten war

برېښېدل brekhedól *intransitive* [*past:* وبرېښنبده] 1 to shine, glisten 2 to seem to be, be represented as something 3 to be visible غاښونه مي برېښني، مي برېښنبري I set my teeth on edge.

برېښيزي سوداگري کارت brekhizé sawdāgarój kārṭ *m.* Electronic Business Card

برېک brek *m.* brake برېک کول to brake, apply the brakes

بریک آب barikáb *m.* Barikab (town, village, region)

بریکت brikét *m.* بریکت briként *m.* بریکت brikét *m.* briquette

بریگیډیر brigeḍír *m. colloquial* brigadier general

بري لیک barilík *m.* certificate; diploma

بریمن barajmán ☞ بریمن کیدل، بریالی to conquer, achieve success

بړ baṛ *m.* banyan (tree)

بړاس bṛās *m.* 1 vapor, steam د اوبو بړاس water vapor, steam 2 evaporation د سکرو په بړاس اخته کیدل fumes د سکرو بړاس to be poisoned by charcoal fumes بړاس کبدل *compound verb* to evaporate

بړانډه baṛānḍa *f.* flame with smoke

بړبړ baṛbaṛ 1 loudly; authoritatively, angrily بړبړ بغبدل، بړبړ ویل to speak loudly, angrily, with authority 2 *Eastern* often, constantly بړبړ راشه، بړبړ راشئ Come more often! Glad to see you!

بړبړی bṛbṛáj 1.1 loudly conversing 1.2 angered (of a camel) 2 *m.* roar, noise (of water)

بړباس baṛbás *m.* magnificence, grandeur

بړبنکی buṛbukhkáj *f.* whirlwind; sandstorm, tornado

بړبنگ buṛbáng 1 *m.* .1 horsetail, *Equisetum* 1.2 ruler, ferule (used for punishment in school) 2 *figurative* shallow, stupid

بړبوزه baṛbóza *f.* violent trembling

بړبوزی baṛbuzáj *m.* insulting talk بړبوزی اچول to say insulting things بړبوزی کول to insult, humiliate; offend with words; mock, scoff at

بړبوکیزه barbūkiza *f.* pop-up (e.g., ads, menus)

بړبوکی bṛbukáj *f.* ☞ بوړبوکی

بړچ bṛch *m.* 1 wraith 2 sneezing بړچ وهل، پرچا بړچ وهل a to become angry at someone b to sneeze

بړچول bṛchavál *transitive* [*past:* و یي بړچاوه] to cause to sneeze

بړچیدل bṛchedál *intransitive* [*past:* و بړچیده] to become angry

بړستن bṛastón *f.* [*plural:* بړستني bṛastóni] 1 blanket 2 *figurative* cover د واورو بړستن snow cover

بړق bṛaq بړق وهل، تولو بړق خندل to laugh loudly, guffaw Everyone laughed.

بړگړندی baṛgaṛandáj *m.* بړگندی bargandáj *m.* exchange of greetings بړگړندی کول to exchange greetings, say hello

بړنگ baṛáng *word paired to* ارنگ

بړو baṛú *m.* weaver's beam

بړوا baṛvā *m.* 1 profligate, libertine 2 procurer, pander, pimp

بړواتوب baṛvātób *m.* بړوائي baṛvājí *f.* 1 profligacy 2 pandering 3 baseness بړواتوب کول a to be profligate b to pander c to commit some base act

بروت bṛut *m. botany* Cyperus

بروس bṛus bṛos 1 morose, gloomy; angry, sullen 2 irritated, annoyed 3 out of sorts بروس بروس very angrily, sternly

بروستوب bṛustób *m.* بروستیا bṛustjá *f.* بروسوالی bṛusválaj *m.* 1 sternness, sullenness 2 vexation, annoyance 3 discomposure

بروس مروس bṛus-mṛus very angry, sullen

بروسول bṛusavól *denominative, transitive* [*past:* بروس یې کړ] 1 to anger 2 to annoy, vex 3 to upset, disconcert

بروسېدل bṛusedól *denominative, intransitive* [*past:* بروس شو] 1 to become angry 2 to be vexed, be annoyed 3 to be out of sorts, be disconcerted

بروی baṛvój *feminine for* بروا

بروی توب baṛvəjtób *m.* 1 looseness (of a woman) 2 procuring (said of a woman)

بوړه buṛá *f.* ☞ بوړه [1]

بړه گړه baṛagaṛá *f.* greeting; inquiring after someone's health د چا سره بړه گړه کول to greet someone, say hello to someone

بړی buṛáj [1] *m. Eastern* rifle, gun; ten-shot rifle

بړی buṛój [2] *f.* rectal prolapse بړی راوتل a to slip out of place (the rectum) b *figurative* to (over) strain oneself; tire; be played out *figurative* c to grow decrepit d *figurative* to become poor

بړیا barǰá *f.* payment بړیا کول *compound verb* to pay, make payment بړیا کبدل *compound verb* to be paid

بړیاینه barǰājóna *f.* payment

بریڅ baréts 1 *m. plural* Baretsy (tribe) 2 *m.* Barets (tribe member)

بریڅي bṛetsí [1] *m. plural* ☞ بریڅ 1

بریڅی bṛetsáj [2] *m.* ☞ بریڅ 2

بریدل buṛdól *intransitive* [*past:* وبړیده] to bellow, snort (of an angry camel)

برینچغ baṛincágh *m.* 1 gyroscope; top (the toy) 2 swings 3 merry-go-round

بز bəz *m.* buz *m.* [*plural:* بزونه bəzúna *plural:* بزونه bzúna buzúna] goat

بزاز bazzáz *m. Arabic* trader in cotton textiles

بزازي bazzāzí *f.* cotton textile trade دبزازي دکان cotton textile shop

بزاقي bazāǩí *Arabic* بزاقي غدي salivary glands

بزبز bəzbáz *m.* ☞ بزهار

بزدل buzdíl fainthearted, cowardly

بزدلي buzdilí *f.* faintheartedness, cowardice

بزرگ buzúrg bzərd 1 large, big; great; grandiose, mighty 2 *m.* saint *idiom* بزرگه میاشت Rajab (seventh month of the lunar year, Muslim calendar)

بزرگوار buzurgvár 1 respected 2 great

بزرگواري buzurgvārí *f.* بزرگي buzurgí *f.* greatness; mightiness

بزغلی buzghaláj *m.* sprout, shoot

بزغندج buzghúndzh *m.* gall on the pistachio (tree)

بزغندجر bəzghandzhór feeble, sickly; frail, puny; thin, emaciated بزغندجر ځان یې دئ he is frail; he's thin

بزک buzák *m.* karavajka (a kind of bird, ibis family, *Plegadis falcinellus*)

بزکشي buzkashí *f.* buzkashi (*literally:* goat wrestling, a national sport in which horsemen compete to carry the headless body of a goat to the goal)

بزکی buzkáj *m.* ☞ بزهار

بزگر bazgár bazgə́r *m.* [*plural:* بزگر bazgə́r *plural:* بزگران bazgarãn *plural:* بزگران bazgərãn] 1 peasant, farmer 2 sharecropper

بزگره bazgára *f.* peasant girl, peasant woman

بزگري bazgarí *f.* 1 farming 2 sharecropping

بزل buzə́l *transitive* verb [*past:* وي بزه] 1 to quilt 2 to mend, patch, sew on a patch

بزله bazlá *f.* ☞ بذله

بزم bazm *m.* feast, banquet

بزمي bazmí lyric (of poetry) بزمي شاعر lyric poet

بیزو bizó *f.* ☞ زو

بزول bəzávəl *transitive* [*past:* و يي بزاوه] to play (on the violin, etc.)

بزه¹ bza *f.* she-goat *idiom* د چا څخه بزه جوړول to shame someone, disgrace someone ☞ وزه²

بزه² buzá *f.* patch (on garments)

بزه³ búza *f.* moth

بزه⁴ bazá *f.* fault, guilt; sin بزه کول to sin

بزه⁵ bza ☞ بژه

بزهار buzəhár *m.* buzzing (of insects)

بزه گار bazagár *m.* culprit, sinner

بزه گاره bazagára *f.* culprit, sinner (of a female)

بزی¹ bizáj *m.* knucklebone (of cattle)

بزي² bze *plural of* بزه¹ ⁵

بزي³ buzé *plural of* بزه²

بزي⁴ buzé *plural of* بزه³

بزي⁵ bazé *plural of* بزه⁴

بزیری bazéraj *m.* flag, banner

بژرکوالی bzhərkvãlaj *m.* ☞ بژرکوالی

بژرکی bzhə́rkaj ☞ بژرکی

بژه buzhá 1 *indeclinable* 1. torn, torn off 1.2 cut off 1.3 slaughtered 2 *f.* slaughter, massacre 2.2 sacrificial offering بژه کول a to tear, tear off b to cut, chop off c to slaughter d to make a sacrificial offering بژه کېدل a to be torn off b to be cut off c to be slaughtered d to be brought as a sacrifice

بږ buǵ *m.* ☞ بږهار

بربرانک bugbugãnák *m.* top (the toy)

بردنگی bugdəngáj *m.* mountain finch, brambling

بږرکوالی bgərkvãlaj *m.* 1 energy, decisiveness 2 fury

بږرکی bgə́rkaj 1 energetic, decisive 2 infuriated

بږلکه bgálga *f.* shout, scream بږلکه کول، بږلکه وهل to shout, cry out

بږناول bugnavə́l *transitive* [*past:* و يي بږناوه] 1 to frighten; cause to tremble 2 to depress, cause extreme distress; disturb, upset, worry

بږنېدل bugnedə́l *intransitive* [*past:* وبږنېده] 1 to be frightened; be startled 2 to be depressed, be extremely distressed; be worried

بږول bugavə́l *transitive* [*past:* و يي بږاوه] to fling, throw, chuck

بږوه bəǵóva *f.* Afghan fox, vixen, *Vulpes nana*

بږه buǵá ☞ بژه بره

بږهار bugahár *m.* 1 ☞ بزهار 2 drone (e.g., of an airplane) 3 babbling (of a brook)

بږج bagaj *m.* spasm; convulsion بږی اخیستل، بږی نیول بږی bági a to be seized with convulsions or spasms b to get a cramp پنښه مي بږی I've got a cramp in my leg. وینیوله c *figurative* to be frightened d *figurative* to be nervous e *figurative* to be beside oneself *figurative* to burn with impatience

بږدل bugedə́l *intransitive* [*past:* وبږیده] 1 to buzz (like insects) 2 to drone (e.g., like an airplane) 3 to babble (a brook)

بږدونکی bugedúnkaj *m.* (electrical) buzzer

بس¹ bas 1 *indeclinable* sufficient بس کول to end, finish; cease بس دئ!، بس دي! Enough! That'll do! بسېدل ☞ کېدل 2 enough Okay! 3 *conjunction* only ... چه دئ مطلب يو لا بس خو ځما I have only one wish 4 *particle* and only, that's all! بس چه دئ!، و بس! that's the whole story for you; there you are, that's the whole story!

بس² bus *m.* plural ☞ بوس¹

بسا basã *often* بسا اوقات

بساړه busáṛa *f.* ☞ بوساړه

بساط bisãt *m.* *Arabic* 1 bedding; thick broadcloth 2 furnishings, furniture 3 chessboard

بساک basák *m.* *botany* anther (the part of the stamen that contains the pollen)

بسالت basãlát *m.* *Arabic* bravery, courage, daring

بسالت مند basãlatmánd brave (in the title of a lieutenant)

بسباسه bəsbãsá *f.* *botany* mace

بسپن bəspə́n *m.* بسپنه bəspə́na *f.* 1 donation, offering بسپن ټولول to collect donations 2 material aid to a suffering kinsman 3 help (of a material sort) 4 grant, subsidy بسپن ورکول a to make an offering b to render material assistance to a suffering kinsman c to help (materially) d to give a grant

بسپه baspá *f.* crumb

بست¹ bast *m.* personnel; staff دائمي بست permanent personnel

بست² bast *m.* refuge, sanctuary

بست³ bust *m.* Bust (city)

بستان bustãn *m.* 1 ☞ بوستان 2 *proper noun* Bustan

بستر bistár *m.* بستره bistará *f.* 1 bed, couch 2 bed (of a river)

بستره ایز bistaraíz بستره یز bistarajíz rated for a certain number of beds (of a hospital, etc.)

بستري bistarí pertaining to a bed; bedridden (of a patient); recumbent

بسته¹ bastá *f.* 1 bunch, bundle; sheaf; pack 2 bolt, catch 3 leather briefcase (for books, writing materials)

بسته² bãsta enough, that will do

بسته کار bastakár *m.* assembler, installer (of equipment)

بسته کارخانه bastakãrkhãná *f.* assembly shop (in a factory)

بسته کاري bastakãrí *f.* assembly, installation

بستیا bastjã *f.* sufficiency بستیا کول to be sufficient; to satisfy

بسره basrá *f.* hawk used for hunting

بسکټ biskíṭ *masculine plural* بسکوت

بسکټبال baskiṭbãl *m.* basketball

بسکر baskár *m.* avenger

بسکره baskóra *f.* voluntary help (e.g., during wheat harvest, road building)

بسکوت biskót بسکيت biskít *m. plural* **1** cookies **2** spongecake, biscuits

بس کيده baskedó *m. plural* completion, end, conclusion; cessation

بسم الله bismillá *Arabic* **1** in God's name بسم الله الرحمن الرحيم in the name of God (who is) the most gracious and the most merciful (words with which Muslims begin some activity) **2** *f.* beginning بسم الله کول to begin something, undertake something

بسمک basmák *m.* murrain, cattle plague

بسمل bismill *Arabic* **1** slaughtered (of cattle) **2** brought as sacrifice بسمل کول a to slaughter (cattle) b to bring as a sacrifice بسمل کیدل a to be slaughtered; to be brought as sacrifice

بسندول basnḍól *m.* trickery; deception بسندول کول to trick, deceive

بسنه basóna *f.* ☞ بسوالی

بسواسه bisvāsá *f.* bisvasa (a unit of area equal to 1/20 of a bisva or 488 square meters)

بس والا basválā *m.* bus driver

بسوالی basválaj *m.* sufficiency, satisfactoriness

بسوه bisvá *f.* bisva (unit of area equal to 1/20 of a jerib or 975 square meters)

بسيا basjá **1** sufficient **2** *regional* processed, cultivated, tilled **3** *regional* populated, settled بسيا کول a to satisfy b *regional* to cultivate, work, till c *regional* to populate, settle بسيا کيدل a to be sufficient b *regional* to be cultivated, be tilled c to be populated

بسيار bisjár a lot; very

بسيارخور bisjārkhór voracious, gluttonous

بسياوالی basjāválaj *m.* satisfaction with something د يو شي بسياوالی کول to be satisfied with something

بسيدل basedól *denominative, intransitive* [*past:* بس شو] **1** to be enough, to suffice **2** to end, be ending, be completed; to cease

بسره baserá *f.* **1** twilight (when birds return to their nests) **2** nest; perch, roost بسره کول to sit on a perch **3** stay of a bird at its perch **4** night's lodging (usually of bird hunters)

بسيط basít *Arabic* **1** wide, broad **2** simple, uncomplicated, elementary

بسيطيدل basitedól *denominative, intransitive* [*past:* بسيط شو] **1** to be wide, be broad **2** to be simple, be elementary; become simpler

بش bash *m.* main beam, girder

بشاش bashshásh *Arabic* cheerful; animated, lively

بشاشت bashshāshát *m. Arabic* cheerfulness; gaiety, merriment; animation, gusto په بشاشت سره cheerfully; in a lively or animated manner

بشال bushál *m.* honeysuckle

بشپړ bəshpóṛ **1** full, complete, exhaustive **2** finished, completed, fulfilled **3** utmost, every possible **4** perfect, absolute; superior **5** of full value **6** adult, mature, grown up **7** satisfied (e.g., of requirements)

بشپړتوب bəshpəṛtób *m.* بشپړتيا bəshpəṛtjá *f.* **1** fullness, sufficiency **2** completeness, finish **3** perfection; superiority **4** full value **5** maturity **6** satisfactory (e.g., of requirements)

بشپړک bəshpəṛák clever, bright, quick-witted بشپړکي خبري کول to talk like an adult (of a child)

بشپړوالی bəshpəṛválaj *m.* ☞ بشپړتوب

بشپړول bəshpəṛavól *denominative, transitive* [*past:* بشپړ يې کړ] **1** to make full, make exhaustive; to exhaust **2** to finish, complete; fulfill **3** to satisfy (e.g., requirements) **4** to develop

بشپړونه bəshpəṛavóna *f.* ☞ بشپړتوب

بشپړيدل bəshpəṛedól *denominative, intransitive* [*past:* بشپړ شو] **1** to be full, be exhaustive **2** to be completed, be fulfilled **3** to be satisfied (of requirements) **4** to be developed

بشپړيدنه bəshpəṛedóna *f. m.* بشپړيده bəshpəṛedó *plural* **1** completion, end **2** development

بشر bashár [1] *m. Arabic* person نوع بشر náu'-i humanity, humankind, the human race

بشر bashár [2] *m.* body

بشريالونکی bashár pālúnkaj humane, philanthropic

بشرپيژندنه basharpezhandóna *f.* ☞ بشرناسي

بشردوست bashardóst *m.* humanist

بشردوستي bashardostí *f.* humaneness, philanthropy د بشردوستي فلسفه humanism

بشرناسي basharshināsí *f.* **1** anthropology **2** ethnography

بشرويه bushrujá *f.* bushruya (a kind of handcrafted fabric)

بشره bashrá *f. Eastern* **1** face, physiognomy; exterior; (outward) appearance **2** *biology* thin skin, epidermis

بشري basharí *Arabic* **1** human بشري ټولنه human society **2** humanitarian *idiom* بشري قوا work force

بشريت bashariját *m. Arabic* humanity, mankind

بشقاب bushḳáb *m.* dish

بشكال bəshakál *m. regional* **1** rainy season **2** monsoon

بشكالي bəshakālí *f. regional* harvest year, good year (for a crop)

بشكه bóshka *f. botany* **1** lepidium (a genus of herbs) **2** Erophila

بشل búshál *m.* bushel

بشاندنج bashándzh *m.* reputation, fame, honor

بشير bashír suffering night blindness

بخباوو bakhāvú ☞ بخناوو

بخنتنه bukhtóna *f.* **1** quagmire, bog, swamp **2** being stuck (in a quagmire, swamp)

بوبنتول bukhtavól *transitive* ☞ بنتول

بوبنتيدل bukhtedól *intransitive* ☞ بنتيدل

بشكال bakhakál *m.* ☞ بنبكال

بشكالي bakhakālí *f.* ☞ بنبكالي

بنبكوله bakhkóla *f.* unpleasantness; misfortune, disaster

بنبگلوي bəkhgólaví *f.* **1** security **2** quiet, calm

بخنبل bakhól *transitive* ☞ بخنبل

بښنه baḵẖə́na *f.* forgiveness, pardon دتلو نه یې ببنښنه وغوښنته He said he was sorry, but he must leave د ببنني دعا کول *religion* to pray for the repose of the departed

بصارت basārát *m. Arabic* sharp-sightedness; perspicacity

بصایر basāír *m. Arabic plural from* بصیره

بصره basrá *f. Arabic* Basra (city, Iraq)

بصیر basír *Arabic* **1** seeing **2** penetrating, perspicacious **3** clever; knowledgeable

بصیرت basirát *m. Arabic* **1** vision, sight **2** perspicacity د بصیرت حق ادا کول to show one's perspicacity **3** knowledge, (possession of) information

بصیرمن basirmán observant

بصیره basirá *f. Arabic* ☞ بصیرت

بطري batrí *f.* بطریه batrijá *f.* battery

بطلان butlán *m. Arabic* **1** vanity **2** worthlessness, uselessness **3** annulment, invalidity

بطن batn *m. Arabic* **1** *anatomy* ventricle د زړه بطن heart ventricle **2** belly, paunch

بطني batní *Arabic anatomy* abdominal, visceral بطني کخوړه swim bladder

بطه báta *f.* duck

بطي batí *Arabic* slow بطي کېدل to slow down په بطي صورت slowly (of movement)

بطیطه batitá *f.* larva, grub; maggot

بعث ba's *m. Arabic* **1** incitement **2** reason, cause **3** *religion* resurrection

بعث و نشر ba'sunáshr *m. religion* resurrection

بعد ba'd bād *Arabic* after, afterward د دي بعد in future, henceforward شپږ شپږ میاشتي بعد after every six months

بعض ba'z *Arabic* certain, some بعض وخت sometimes; from time to time

بعضاً bá'zán sometimes, at times, from time to time

بعضي bá'zi bá'ze ☞ بعض certain months بعضي میاشتي

بعید ba'íd *Arabic* far, removed, distant شرق بعید sharḵ-i the Far East *grammar* بعیده ماضي pluperfect, past perfect tense

بعینه ba'ajna *regional* exactly, precisely

بغ¹ bəgh *m.* heron

بغ² bugh *m.* roar, howl; cry, shout

بغارگ bghārg ☞ غبرگ

بغاره bughā́ra *f.* cry; outcry بغاري کول to cry out, shout; to howl, wail هغه په بغارو سو he cried out, he started wailing

بغاوت baghāvát *m. Arabic* insurrection, strike, revolt, mutiny

بغبغو baghbaghú sandpiper

بغبغي bughbugháj *m.* **1** honking (of an automobile) **2** horn, bugle; trumpet, pipe

بغداد baghdād *m.* Baghdad (city)

بغدادی baghdādáj baghdādí *adjective* (of) Baghdad *idiom* بغدادی کوتره turtledove

بغدر baghdár *m.* **1** [*plural:* بغدر baghdə́r] hammer [*plural:* بغدرونه] **2** [*plural:* bughdarúna] dumbbell (for exercise)

بغرگ bgharg *dialect* ☞ غبرگ

بغرگول bghargavə́l *transitive* ☞ غبرگول

بغرگولی bghargoláj twin, one who is a twin

بغرگه bghárga *f.* **1** valley between two mountains **2** woman who has borne twins بغرگېدل bghargedə́l *intransitive* ☞ غبرگېدل

بغرنج bughrándzh complicated, mixed up

بغره¹ bughrá *f.* veil, yashmak; shawl بغره پر سرکول to wear a veil, put on a veil

بغره² baghə́ra *f.* burrow (of a rabbit)

بغری¹ bagharáj *m. swearword* procurer, pander, pimp

بغری² baghrə́j *f.* **1** mortar **2** mortar for husking rice

بغض bughz *m. Arabic* enmity, hatred; malice د دښمنانو بغض hatred of enemies

بغضیت bughziját *m.* bitterness, animosity په چا کښي بغضیت پیدا کول to embitter someone, arouse someone's animosity

بغل baghál *m.* **1** armpit **2** side, edge د سړک په بغل on the side (of a road, etc.) **3** edge (of material); curb **4** embrace *idiom* د چا څخه a to avoid someone بغل خالي کول b not to support someone

بغلان baghlán *m.* Baghlan (city) د بغلان ولایت Baghlan Province

بغل کشي baghalkashhí *f.* بغل گیري baghalgirí *f.* embrace د چا سره بغل کشي کول to embrace (someone) to hug one another

بغمه bughmá *f.* envy

بغنه baghaná *f.* lambskin

بغول bughavə́l *transitive* [*past:* و یې بغاوه] to force someone to cry out

بغهار bughahā́r *m.* shouts, cries, wails

بغی¹ bughə́j *f.* horn

بغی² baghí *Arabic* rebellious

بغېدل bughedə́l *intransitive* [*past:* وبغده] to shout; begin shouting, cry out

بغیر baghájr *preposition* besides; except; without بغیر څمونږ نه except us بغیر له ښځو په کور کښي څوک نه وو ، بغیر د ښځو په کور کښي Besides women, there was no one in the house څوک نه وو

بغیر bagháṛ suspicious

بق buḵ بق کول to open (e.g., the eyes)

بقا baḵā́ *f. Arabic* **1** duration, length **2** eternity, immortality بقا لرل a to last, continue b to be eternal, be immortal **3** existence

بقال bakkā́l *m. Arabic* grocer; greengrocer

بقایا baḵājā́ *m. Arabic plural* **1** *from* بقیه ، بقایا د خوړو scraps, leftovers, remnants **2** survivals

بقبق baḵbā́ḵ *m.* ☞ بک¹

بقچه buḵchá *f.* ☞ بخچه

بقه baḵá *f.* ☞ بکا

بقیه baḵijá *f.* [*plural:* بقیي baḵijé *Arabic m. plural:* بقایا baḵājā́] *Arabic* **1** remainder **2** debt, arrears

بک ¹ bak *m.* chatter, gossip; nonsense بک بک کول to speak nonsense

بوک ² buk ☞ بوک

بکا bakā́ *f.* frog

بکاری bakā́raj *m.* courier

بکاول bakāvál *m.* *regional* cook

بکاین bakājā́n *m.* بکاینه bakājā́ṇa *f.* Indian ash-tree, Indian lilac, *melia azedarach*

بک بکی bakbakáj *m.* chatterbox, gossip

بکتر baktár *m.* armor; armor-plating

بکتری bakterí *f. & m.* بکتریا bakterijā́ *f.* ☞ باکتري

بکتریولوژي bakterjolozhí *f.* ☞ با کتریولوژي

بکتریا bakterijā́ *f.* ☞ باکتریا

بکره bakóra *f.* بکری bakrój *f.* flint

بکس ¹ baks *m.* handbag, purse; drawer; box د لاس بکس briefcase خریطه بکس (change) purse, wallet *military* map case د روپو بکس

بکس ² bakás *obsolete* 1 insignificant 2 a few, not many

بکسکی bakáskaj a few, not many, a little

بکسنگ báksing *m.* boxing

بکلوریا bakaloreā́ *f.* baccalaureate, bachelor's degree

بکوا bakvā́ *f.* بکواه bakvā́ *f.* 1 dry, parched earth 2 *regional* Bakva

بکوره bakóra *f.* kurkut (dried balls of strained sour milk)

بوکول ¹ bukavál *denominative, transitive* ☞ بوکول

بوکول ² bukavál *denominative, transitive* [past: بک یې کړ] to make hunchbacked; arch, hunch; make prominent, make protuberant, make hunched up

بکاینه bukjā́ṇa *f.* ☞ بکاین

بوکېدل ¹ bukedál *denominative, intransitive* ☞ بوکېدل

بوکېدل ² bukedál *denominative, intransitive* [past: بک شو] to be hunchbacked; be arched, be hunched; be protuberant, be prominent

بگار bəgā́r bread, crumbled into ajran (a drink made from sour milk)

بگاښ bugā́kh *m.* mediation بگاښ کول to be (a) mediator; settle a conflict; reconcile

بگت ¹ bugát *m.* means, way په دې بگت in such a way, in this way

بگت ² bəgát stupid; shallow (of a person)

بگتو bəgatú singer of folk songs (in particular the بگتي bagati)

بگته bugúta *f.* business, matter

بگتي bagatí *f.* bugtí folk song (performed by two singers)

بگر bagár *m.* custom, habit

بگرام bagrā́m *m.* Bagram (city)

بگرامی bagrā́mí *m. plural* Bagrami (town near Kabul)

بگړی bagrój *f.* turban بگړی ترل a to put on a turban b to wear a turban *idiom* بگړی دي د سره لوېدل to disgrace oneself مه لوبږه! I wish you success!

بگرگل bagrəjgúl *m.* camomile

بگل bigl *m.* *regional* *music* horn, bugle

بگلولی ¹ bagalolə́j *f.* ☞ بو

بگلی buglā́j *m.* baglā́j heron

بگڼ bugə́ṇ *m.* gadfly

بگڼول bugṇavál *transitive* ☞ بڕنول

بگڼه bəgā́ṇa *f.* blackberries; bramble, blackberry bush

بگڼېدل bungṇḍál ☞ بڕنېدل

بگوری ¹ boguрí *f.* attack of dog (with howling and snarling)

بگوری ² baguрí tousled, dishevelled (of the hair)

بگوڕا bagoрā́ *f.* curds, cottage cheese

بگوڕه ² bəgoрá *f.* ☞ بکوره

بگوڕی bəgoрáj *m.* buffalo calf

بگوه bagóva *f.* ☞ بروه

بگی bagə́j *f.* carriage, buggy, two-wheeled cart

بگی خانه bagəjkhāná *f.* building or place where carriages are kept

بگل bəgél *m.* 1 quail that has been defeated in battle 2 deserter

بگینه baginə́ *m. plural* ☞ گبینه

بگی والا bagəjvālā́ *m.* بگی وان bagəjvān *m.* 1 coachman 2 drayman

بل ¹ bal burning, on fire

بل ² bə́l 1 other, different بل راز a other, different b in another way یو په بل پسې one بله پلا another time بل څوک someone else یو تر بله گی after another یو تر بله by one another, at one another's یو تر بله مین دي they are living together ژوندون کوي they are in love with each other یو تر بله سره گران دي di they love each other; they are dear to one another د یو بل احترام او عزت mutual respect یو د بله سره ترون mutually, with each other یو د بله سره غونډ شوه mutual agreement یو له یو د بل سره خُخه they have gathered together بله، یو له بله لیری کېدل *Eastern* from one another to depart, go away from each other یو و بل ته to each other 2 next, following (day, year, etc.) بله روغ a (on) the next day b the future بل سبا day after tomorrow بله هفته next week بل کال ته next year بل کال د بل په شکنه غوړونه مه سوحه 3 another's *saying literal* don't burn your ears in someone else's soup *figurative* don't interfere in someone else's business *idiom* یوه خبره بله ده ... it must be added that ... او بل داچه ...، بله دا چه .... and here's something else ... , moreover

بل ³ bal *Arabic conjunction and particle* ☞ بلکه

بلا ¹ balā́ *f. Arabic* 1 misfortune, disaster په بلا اخته کېدل to encounter misfortune بلا دي واخلم! let all your misfortunes fall on me!; I'm ready to do anything for you! (an expression of obedience, agreement) په بلا ککېدل a to suffer misfortune b to grow poor, become impoverished 2 witch, hag بلا گاني ملاگاني یوي بلا و بلي ته ویل اوخ! the Evil one نر بلا devil; wood-goblin *saying* one hag said to another: Aaghh! (both are pretty) 3 (conversational) piece, item, gimmick دا بله څه بلا ده؟ What sort of a thing is that? What is it? *idiom* سنک بلا اخیستئ دئ Sanak is very greedy! بلا دي رنده سه! I wish you success! د هغه بلا رنده سوه، که نه He was lucky; he might have drowned! غرق سوئ و! په یو کار کبنی to be outstanding in something بلا کول په دې کار کبنی دي بلا وکړه! You have shown (us) wonders!

بلا ² balā́ *word paired with* سلا

بلا ³ bilā *Arabic preposition, prefix* without بلا استثنى without exception بلا توقف without delay

بلا احتراز bilāihtiráz *Arabic* carelessly, incautiously, imprudently

بلا استثنى bilāistisnā *Arabic* without exception, making no exception

بلابتر balābatár *m.* 1 odds and ends, all kinds of things 2 rubbish, trash, junk

بلاتن balātón *m.* Balaton (lake)

بلاتوقف bilātavaḳúf *Arabic* urgently

بلاربوالى blārbválaj *m.* ☞ برالبوالى

بلاربول blābaválaj *denominative, transitive* [*past:* بلاربه يې کره] to fertilize; impregnate; to cover

بلاربه blārba ☞ برالبه

بلابېدل blābedál *denominative, intransitive* ☞ برالبېدل

بلاره bulāra *f. hunting* decoy (bird)

بلاشرط bilāshaṛt *Arabic* unconditional بلاشرط تسليم unconditional surrender

بلاغ balāgh *m. Arabic* communication; notification

بلاغت balāghát *m. Arabic* eloquence

بلاغند balāghúnḍ *m.* [*plural:* بلاغندان balāghunḍān] *botany* Bengal quince, marmelo

بلاک blāk *m.* 1 *politics* bloc يو بلاک جوړول to create a bloc 2 group (of settlements)

بلاکم وکاست bilākamukāst without a pass

بلاناغه bilānāghá *Arabic* بلاناغي bilānāghé regularly, without change; without fail

بلانده bálānda *f.* girl who has come of age

بلانګوری blāngúṛaj *m.* dormouse

بلانه bilāṇa *f.* moan, groan

بلاواسطه bilāvāsitá *Arabic* direct, straight

بلاوهلئ balávahólaj 1 remaining idle, loafing 2 *m.* loafer, idler, sponger

بلبل ¹ bulbúl *m.* 1 nightingale بلبل هزار داستان nightingale 2 "bulbul" (name given a number of birds with bright plumage or which sing beautifully)

بل بل ² balbál shining, gleaming, lustrous

بل بل ³ bálbál 1 varied, diverse 2 different, all kinds

بلبله ¹ bulbúla *f.* female nightingale

بلبله ² balbalá *f.* د وزيرو بلبله dance of the Wazirs

بلبلج balbaláj *m.* torch, flare

بلجيک bildzhik *m.* Belgium

بلجيکي bildzhikí bildzhukáj 1 Belgian 2 *m.* Belgian (person)

بلجيم bildzhijúm *m.* ☞ بلجيک

بل چيري bál chíri in another place

بلدځايګه báldzājgá another's; strange, alien

بلخ balkh *m.* Balkh (city and region) د بلخ ولايت Balkh province بلخ درياب Balkh river

بلخاب balkháb *m.* Balkhab region

بلخاش balkhásh *m.* Lake Balkhash

بل خوا bálkhvā *Eastern* 1 in the other direction 2 on the other side

بلخه bálkhá *f. textiles* warp

بلد balád *m. Arabic* 1 *m.* .1 guide; conductor; escort 1.2 country, nation 1.3 city 2.1 being knowledgeable about something; knowing something; being acquainted with someone or something دی خلقو سره ډېر بلد دئ he knows these people very well 2.2 accustomed; mastered; having adapted to …

بلدوزر buldozér *m.* bulldozer

بلدول baladavál *denominative, transitive* [*past:* بلد يې کړ] 1 to acquaint with, familiarize 2 to train, school (in)

بلده ¹ baladá *f. Arabic* small town, locality

بلده ² baláda *f. feminine singular from* بلد ²

بلدي ¹ baladí *Arabic* municipal, (of the) city; communal

بلدى ² baladáj *m.* Baladaj (village near Qandahar) د بلدي د ګوروان په وسه baladí … *saying* the same thing happened to him as to the shepherd from Baladi (this shepherd was known for his greed, which always turned out to his disadvantage)

بلديت baladiját *m. Arabic* knowledge of something; familiarity with someone, with something په دي کار کښي بلديت لري he is familiar with this work

بلدېدل baladedál *denominative, intransitive* [*past:* بلد شو] 1 to be informed, be knowledgeable; be acquainted with someone or something; become acquainted 2 to get used to; familiarize (oneself); adapt (oneself)

بلديه baladijá *f. Arabic* municipal authority; municipality; city council بلديه رياست municipal authority, municipality, city council رئيس بلديه raísi-i head of the municipal authority; mayor of the city; chairman of the city council

بلديه وي baladijaví municipal, (of the) city; communal

بلډنګ bilḍíng *m.* tall building

بل رازوالى bálrāzválaj *m.* distinction, difference

بلرغو blarghú *m.* not in agreement

بل سبا bálsabā *m.* day after tomorrow

بل شانته bálshānta in another way, a different way, otherwise

بلشويزم bolshevízm *m.* ☞ بالشويزم

بلشويک bolshevík *m.* ☞ بالشويک

بلغا bulaghā *Arabic* eloquent; expressive

بلغار bulghār بلغار باد gentle breeze, zephyr (in the spring)

بلغارستان bulghāristān *m.* ☞ بلغاريا

بلغاري bulghārí 1 Bulgarian بلغاري ژبه the Bulgarian language 2 *m.* Bulgar, Bulgarian (person)

بلغاريا bulghārijā *f.* بلغاريه bulghārijá *f.* Bulgaria

بلغاکه bulghāka *f.* 1 noise; shouting; wailing 2 mourning بلغاکي کول a to make noise; to shout; wail b to mourn (over)

بلغم balghám *m. Arabic* phlegm; mucus (e.g., from the nose)

بلق balḳ *m.* ☞ برق

بلقيس bilḳís *f. proper noun* Bilkis, Belkis

بلوک ¹ blək ☞ بلوک

بلک ² balk *m. dialect* glistening, shining بلک وهل to glisten, sparkle

بلكمشر bləkmə́shr *m.* ☞ بلوكمشر

بلكه bálki **1** *adversative conjunction* but, but also نه فقط دري بلكه not three but four pupils came **2** *emphatic particle* (and) even خلور شاگردان راغلل

بلكه² balə́ka *f. dialect* campfire

بلگ balg *m.* leaf (of a tree, etc.)

بلگراد belgrǻd *m.* Belgrade (city)

بل گئیخ bə́l gaídz *m.* day after tomorrow in the morning (morning after next)

بلل balə́l *transitive* [*present:* بولي *past:* وبي باله] **1** to name, enumerate **2** to call; invite; convoke د شپي را بلل، در بلل، ور بلل **2** I was invited to dinner دوی دپاره یې ویلم **3** to consider, suppose, think پریو شي نه بلل to consider it better, prefer something **4** to announce **5** to sing loudly, sing cheerfully لندی بلل to sing (folk) songs

بللگی bə́lalgə́j *f.* **1** woman who gives birth each year **2** cattle which give increase each year

بلمگی bə́lmágaj بلمنگه bə́lmánga tasteless, flavorless

بلندخه blándza *f.* saxaul (Haloxylon, a small tree or shrub of Central Asia)

بلند bilánd bulánd **1.1** high, tall; exalted **1.2** loud, resounding **1.3** *figurative* successful, unusual **2** *m. proper noun* Biland, Buland

بلندپایه bilandpājá excellent, outstanding

بلندپرواز bilandparvā́z flying high, soaring

بلندپروازي bilandparvāzí **1** high-altitude flight **2** (upward) flight, take-off *idiom* د بلندپروازی آسمان *literal & figurative* the empyrean, the highest reaches of heaven

بلندره blándra *f. Afridi* **1** invitation **2** blándra *f.* reception; entertaining (as by a host)

بلندهمت bilandhimmát **1** valiant **2** noble; magnanimous

بلندهمتي bilandhimmatí *f.* **1** valor **2** nobility; magnanimity

بلندي¹ bilandí *f.* height, altitude

بلندی² bilandáj *m. proper noun* Bilandaj

بلنگ blang **1** fresh, young, green **2** bright (of colors) **3** beautiful, attractive

بلن لیک baləlík *m.* (written) invitation

بلنه balə́na *f.* **1** naming, enumeration **2** invitation; summons; call **3** announcement; pronouncement **4** reception مابنامي بلنه evening reception

بلو¹ baló *m. proper noun* Balo نه مرو ملک شو بلو *proverb literal* When there were no brave men, even Balo became a leader *figurative* When there are no fish, even a crab is a fish

بلو² biláv *m.* ☞ بیلاو

بلوا balvā́ *f.* disorder; disturbance; sedition, revolt بلوا کول to create disturbances; instigate rebellion

بلوجستان baludzhistán *m.* Baluchistan (province, Iran)

بلوجي baludzhi **1** *adjective* Baluchi **2.1** *m.* Baluchi (person) **2.2** *f.* Baluchi (language)

بلوچ balóch *m.* ☞ بلوخ¹

بلوجستان baluchistā́n *m.* ☞ بلوجستان

بلوجي baluchí ☞ بلوچي

بلوخ¹ balúts *m.* **1** Baluchi (person) **2** *proper noun* Baluts

بلوخ² blots *m.* ☞ بلوس

بلوخه¹ balútsa *f.* **1** Baluchi (female) **2** *proper noun* Balutsa

بلوخه² blótsa *f.* ☞ بلوس

بلوخي balutsí ☞ بلوجي

بلودل blodál *transitive* ☞ بلوسل

بلوده blávda *f.* stumbling; getting stuck خورل بلوده to stumble

بلور bulúr *m. Arabic* **1** crystal **2** cut glass, crystal

بلوري bulurí بلورین bulurín *Arabic* **1** (of) crystal, crystalline **2** (of) crystal, cut glass

بلوس blos *m.* blaus **1** collision; touching, contact **2** insulting; causing distress

بلوسل blosál blausál [*past:* وبي بلوسه] **1** to touch, brush against **2** to rub, rub down, massage **3** to cause revulsion; alienate (someone); irritate **4** to bite (of a dog)

بلوسوالی blosválaj *m.* blausválaj hostility, enmity; repulsion, antipathy بلوس والی کول to nourish a hatred, nourish an antipathy

بلوسول blosavál blausavál *transitive* [*past:* وبي بلوساوه] to evoke enmity; to alienate (someone); to irritate

بلوسه blósa *f.* **1** ☞ بلوس **2** ☞ بلوسوالی

بلوسبدل blosedál blausedál *intransitive* [*past:* وبلوسیده] **1** to collide, run into; brush against; touch **2** to be distressed, be out of sorts **3** to hate; nourish hostility, nourish antipathy **4** to interfere, meddle **5** to encroach upon (someone, something), infringe **6** to offend, insult (someone)

بلوسبدنه blosedə́na *f.* **1** collision; brushing (against), grazing **2** distress, disorder, confusion **3** hatred; revulsion, enmity, hostility

بلوط balút *m. Arabic* **1** oak (lithocorpus) **2** acorn

بلوغ bulúgh *m. Arabic* maturity, manhood; ripeness; majority (coming of age) د بلوغ تر وخته before coming of age

بلوک blúk *m.* bulúk *military* platoon د استحکام بلوک sapper platoon

بلوکات bulukā́t *m. plural* suburbs د کابل بلوکات suburbs of Kabul

بلوکاد blokā́d *m.* blockade, encirclement اقتصادي بلوکاد economic blocade په بلوکاد گیر کول to blockade, encircle, surround

بلوکمشر blukmə́shr *m.* bulukmə́shr *military* lieutenant

بلوکي blukí bulukí *adjective military* (of a) platoon بلوکي قطار platoon column

بلول balavál *denominative, transitive* [*past:* بل یې کړ] to set on fire

بلون balún *m.* ☞ بلنه

بلونگری bilóngraj *m.* kind of polecat, *Vormela peregusna*

بله¹ balá *f. regional* bayonet; pike, lance

بله² bála *feminine singular of* بل¹

بله³ bəla *feminine singular of* بل²

بلهوس bulhavás بل هوس *Arabic* capricious, whimsical, fickle; greedy, stingy, miserly

بلۍ ¹ baləj *f.* **1** cornice; eaves **2** pole (for pushing a boat) **3** bolt, bar **4** roof

بلې ² balé *Arabic particle* yes, certainly

بلیارد biljärd *m.* billiards; billiard table

بلېچون blechún *m. history* sling (weapon)

بلېدل baledə́l *denominative, intransitive* [*past:* بل شو] to burn; catch fire

بلېږدل bleghdə́l *intransitive* **1** to be wrapped in swaddling clothes **2** to become entangled, become confused

بلېږدول bleghadavə́l *transitive* بلېږدول bleghadavə́l **1** to swaddle, wrap in swaddling clothes **2** to entangle, confuse

بلېط bilét *m.* ticket

بلیغ balígh *Arabic* eloquent; expressive

بلیغي balighí considerable, large, big

بم ¹ bum *m.* ☞ بوم ²

بم ² bam *m.* [*plural:* بمونه bamúna *plural:* بمان bamə́n] bomb خرابونکی بم atomic bomb د هیدروجن بم hydrogen bomb اتومي بم bمونه اچول، incendiary bomb سوونکی بم high explosive bomb اورول، بمونه غورځول to drop bombs, bomb; bombard

بم ³ bam *m.* low tone; bass (voice)

بم اچوونکي الوتکه، بم بم اچوونکی bam achavúnkaj *adjective* bombing اچوونکي طیاره bombardier

بم انداز bamandáz *m.* **1** *obsolete* bomb-thrower **2** depth-charge gun بمب bomb *m.* ☞ بم ²

بمبار bambár *m.* بمبارد bambárd *m.* bombardment بمبار کول *compound verb* ☞ بمباربدل *compound verb* ☞ بمباربدل، بمباردول to undergo bombardment تر بمبار لاندي نیول to subject to bombardment

بمباردماني bambārdəmāní *adjective* bombardment

بمباردول bambārdavə́l *denominative, transitive* [*past:* بمبارد یې کړ] to bomb, bombard

بمباري bambārí *f.* bombardment پر ... بمباري کول to bomb, bombard تر بمباری لاندي راتلل to subject to bombing تر بمباري لاندي نیول to undergo bombing

بم اچوونکی bambārí kavúnkaj ☞ بمباري کوونکی

بمبره bambóra *f.* hornet

بمبل bambál *m. plural* **1** *botany* ear without seed, seedless ear **2** inflorescence of corn **3** panicle of a reed **4** thick beard

بمبولۍ bamboláj *m.* wicker corn-bin

بمبه bambá *f.* pump

بمبئي bambai *f.* Bombay (city)

بمپر bampár *m.* **1** bumper, buffer **2** shock absorber

بملۍ bamləj *f.* balmy (a small drum held under the arm)

بمه ¹ bumá *f.* pike, lance

بمه ² báma *f. dialect* ☞ لم ²

بن ¹ bin *m. Arabic* son

بن ² bən *f.* one of the wives (in relation to another under polygamy)

بن ³ bon *m.* bonn Bonn (city)

بنا ¹ binā́ *f. Arabic* **1** building, structure **2** basis بنا پر دې ، بنا په دې on this basis, د ... بنا کول ، بنا پر څه on the basis of something دتلو بنا یې ... **a** to plan, contemplate, undertake; decide; بنا کېده **a** to be وکړه he decided to go **b** to undertake something built **b** پر بنا، په بنا to be based on something **3** *philosophy* superstructure

بنا ² banná *m. Arabic* mason; builder

بنات banát *m.* (heavy, coarse) cloth

بنات النعش banāt-un-ná'sh *m. Arabic plural astronomy* the Big and Little Bear (i.e., Ursa Major and Ursa Minor)

بناتي banātí of (coarse) cloth

بنارس banārás *m.* **1** Varanasi (India) **2** *proper name* Banaras **3** striped silk

بنایات bināját *m. Arabic* building

بناعلیه binā'alájhi *Arabic* in view of what has been said, in view of the foregoing

بنبل bambál *m. plural dialect* **1** awn, beard (of corn, grain) **2** sheaf (of wheat); tuft (of grass)

بنت bint *f.* [*plural:* بنتي bínti] *Arabic plural* daughter

بنتک binták *m.* flick (of the fingers); insult, slight, blow

بنج ¹ bandzh *m.* **1** horse chestnut **2** henbane

بنج ² bandzh *m.* banádzh trade

بنجارگي bandzhāragí *f.* fancy goods, haberdasher's trade د بنجارگی سامان haberdashery, fancy goods

بنجاره ¹ bandzhārá *f.* haberdashery; fancy goods

بنجاره ² bandzhārá *m. regional* tradesman in grocery items

بنجخ bandzhákh *m.* thick branches

بنجي ¹ bundzháj *m.* **1** person with a small nose **2** person with a collapsed nose (due to syphilis)

بنجی ² bandzhə́j *f. botany* cassia

بنچ bench *m.* ☞ بنچ

بنچک bunchák *m.* basis, essence

بنڅي ¹ bundzáj *m.* son of one wife (under polygamy), stepson

بنڅۍ ² bundzə́j *f.* daughter of one wife (under polygamy), stepdaughter

بند band **1** *m.* **.1** bonds, ties, nets **1.2** incarceration **1.3** captivity, bondage له بنده آزادول، د بنده آزادول، له بنده خلاصول، د بنده خلاصول to free from imprisonment, free from captivity **1.4** dam, weir **1.5** *anatomy* joint د بندو خور rheumatic fever **1.6** node (on the stem of a plant) **1.7** bandage, binding **1.8** spell, incantation **1.9** measure; size **1.10** *geography* mountain range, ridge بند ترل **a** to build a dam, dam **b** to take measures **c** to decide, make a decision خپل بند یې سره وتړه چه ... **d** they have decided that ... **d** to prepare (something) **2** *predicate* **.1** blocked (of a roadway); closed, cut off (of movement); closed (e.g., of a border) **2.2** cut short, stopped; held back, restrained **2.3** forbidden (of a custom, etc.) **2.4** arrested, imprisoned **2.5** captured **2.6** stuck (in a swamp, mudhole) **3** *attributive* stuffy, close, sultry, stifling بنده خونه، بنده کوټه a stuffy room

بندار bandā́r *m.* punishment

بنداژ bandā́zh *m.* 1 tire, band (of metal) 2 bandage 3 dressing; binding د بنداژ پاکټ *military* individual field dressing, first-aid packet بنداژ کول to apply a dressing, dress (a wound)

بندبست bandubā́st *m.* ☞ بندوبست

بندبند bandbánd by part, in parts

بندپسور bandpsor *m.* bandwidth

بنداج bandídzh *m.* ☞ بنداژ

بندخ bandúkh *m.* ☞ بندق

بندي خانه bandkhā́nā *f.* ☞ بندي خانه

بندر bandár *m.* 1 port, harbor 2 approach, access (road), pass (in the mountains) 3 parking place; halting place; moorage 4 center (e.g., for trade)

بندر عباس bandara'bā́s *m.* Bender-Abbas (Iran, city)

بندرگاه bandargā́h *m.* port; harbor

بندري bandarí 1.1 *adjective* port 1.2 obtained through the Persian Gulf (of goods) 2 *f.* kind of imported chintz

بنداژ bandā́zh *m.* ☞ د بندژ محل، د بندژ ځای بنداژ dressing station

بندش bandísh *m.* 1 obstacle 2 blockade (e.g., economic)

بندښت bandə́kht *m.* 1 stagnation, standstill 2 dead-end (e.g., in negotiations)

بندق bakdúk̦ *m. history* musket

بندکی bandakáj *m. botany* mare's tail, *Equisetum*

بندگان bandagā́n *masculine plural from* بنده

بندگي bandagí *f.* slavery

بندوالی bandvā́laj *m.* 1 interment, arrest 2 captivity 3 jamming کلپ بندوالی پیدا کوي the lock is beginning to jam

بندوس bandubā́s *m. colloquial* بندوبست bandubā́st *m.* bandobā́st 1 measure 2 organization, arrangement بندوس کول a to take measures; put through a measure b to arrange, organize

بندوخ bandúkh *m.* ☞ بندق

بندول[1] bandavə́l *denominative, transitive* [*past:* بند یې کړ] 1 to barricade (the roadway); cut off (motion, movement); close (e.g., a border) 2 to cut short, suspend, halt; restrain, hold back مواجب بندول to hold back payment د وراندي تلو مخه بندول to halt an attack 3 to forbid (a custom, etc.) 4 to arrest, incarcerate, imprison 5 to capture 6 to drag in, suck in (of a swamp, mudhole) 7 to imprint, impress *idiom* په الفاظو بندول to expound, set forth; describe

بندول[2] bandavə́l *denominative, transitive* to log off

بنده bandá *m.* [*plural:* بندگان *plural:* بنده گان bandagā́n] 1 slave, slave-laborer; bondsman 2 *religion* God's slave; simple person, otherworldly person

بندگي bandagí *f.* ☞ بنده گي

بندي bandí[1] 1.1 arrested, imprisoned 1.2 taken captive 2 *m.* 1. person under arrest; prisoner بندي کول to arrest, imprison, lock up 2.2 captive بندي نیول to take prisoner, capture

بندي bandə́j[2] *f.* 1 (female) person under arrest, prisoner 2 (female) captive 3 neckerchief 4 *regional* bracelet

بندیاتي bandijā́tí *f.* imprisonment دبندیاتي موده بښنل to pardon

بندیانول bandijānavə́l *denominative, transitive* [*past:* بندیان یې کړ] to arrest, imprison

بندي توب banditób *m.* arrest, imprisonment

بندي خانه bandikhānā́ *f.* prison

بندیدل bandedə́l *denominative, intransitive* [*past:* بند شو] 1 to close, be closed خوله یې بنده شوه he became silent 2 to be blocked (of a roadway); be closed off (of movement) 3 to be cut short, be stopped, be restrained 4 to be prohibited (of a custom, etc.) 5 to be arrested, be imprisoned, be thrown in prison 6 to be captured 7 to fall into, get caught in (e.g., a net, a snare) 8 to get stuck (in a swamp, in a quagmire) 9 to shut oneself up; close up

بندیز bandíz *m.* 1 obstacle, hindrance; limitation اقتصادي بندیزونه economic limitations بندیز ایسته کول to remove the obstacles, limitations 2 struggle, campaign (e.g., against rumors) 3 *dialect medicine* constipation

بندیگري bandigarí *f.* slavery, enslavement

بندیوان bandivā́n *m.* 1 prisoner, person under arrest 2 captive

بنډار banḍār[1] *m.* feast, banquet بنډار کول to arrange a feast, feast

بنډار banḍār[2] *m.* chat

بنډارخونه banḍārkhūna *f.* chatroom

بنډاري banḍārí *m.* carouser; convivial fellow

بنډل banḍál *m.* 1 bundle, bunch, pack 2 skein (of thread) 3 bale, package

بنډه bánḍa *f.* part, portion, share

بن زی bənzáj[1] *m.* ☞ بنڅي[1]

بن زی bənzə́j[2] *f.* ☞ بنڅي[2]

بنزین benzín *m. plural* gasoline

بنست bənzə́ţ *m.* 1 foundation 2 *figurative* basis, foundation 3 *philosophy* base, basis

بنغازي benghā́zí *m.* Benghazi (city, Libya)

بنفش bináfsh ☞ بنفشي

بنفشه binafshá *f.* violet

بنفشي binafshí *adjective* violet (color)

بنک bank *m.* ☞ بانک

بنکاک bankā́k *m.* Bangkok (city, Thailand)

بنگ bang[1] *m.* 1 Indian hemp 2 hashish

بنگ bəng[2] *m.* bung 1 buzzing (of insects) 2 jingling; strumming 3 whispering

بنگ bang[3] *combined with* رنگ

بنگال bangā́l *m.* د بنگال بحیره، د بنگال خلیج Bay of Bengal Bengal

بنگتی bangatə́j *f.* 1 desert brambling (a kind of finch) 2 kind of children's game

بنگړه bangṛá *f.* dance (among the Hataki, a tribe in the Kandahar region)

بنگړی bangṛáj *m.* bracelet

بنگړی بنگړی bangṛáj-bangṛáj collapsed, in ruins; destroyed

بنگريوال، بنگري وال bangṛiwál *m.* 1 trader in bracelets 2 magician 3 traveling showman with a trained monkey

بنگښ bangáx̌ 1 *m. plural* the Bangashes (tribe) 2 *m.* Bangash (tribesman)

بنگښات bangax̌át *m. plural history* area of the Bangash

بنگښه bangáx̌a 1 *feminine for* بنگښ 2 *proper noun* Bangasha

بنگله bangalā *f.* 1 bungalow, villa; little house 2 palace

بنگينه bangína *f.* ☞ بنگی³

بنگوری bangóraj *m.* ☞ بگبل 1

بنگورک bangoṛák *m.* fortuneteller, soothsayer

بنگول bəngavál bungavál *transitive* [*past:* و يي بنگاوه] 1 to cause to buzz, cause to hum 2 to cause to jingle

بونگه bungá¹ *f.* ☞ بنگه

بنگه bánga² *f.* ☞ بنگ¹

بنگي bangí¹ *m.* 1 drug addict 2 *figurative* person drunk with love; someone in love

بنگي bangi² *m.* sweeper, yardman

بنگی bungáj³ *m.* harp

بنگی bungáj⁴ *m.* 1 buzzing (of insects) 2 jingling, strumming *idiom* بنگی پر لرل to be shy

بنگی bangáj⁵ *m.* roan horse

بنگي bangí⁶ *m.* Bangi (city)

بنگېدل bungedál *intransitive* [*past:* وبنگېده] 1 to buzz (of insects) 2 to jingle

بنو banú¹ *f.* Banow, Banu, (town, region)

بنو banó² *m. Arabic* ☞ بني¹

بنو báno³ *oblique plural from* بن²

بنوچی banucháj *m.* بنوڅی banutsáj *m.* Banuchi (inhabitant of Banow)

بنوښ binavx̌ *m.* [*plural:* بنوښان binavx̌án] ash tree

بنون banú *m.* banún ☞ بنو¹

بني baní¹ *m. Arabic singular & plural* son; sons; descendents د بشر ټول بني نوع آدم، بني آدم the whole human race بني اسرايل Jews

بنی banə́j² *f.* bellows (of a blacksmith) *idiom* په بني باد كبنبوتل to become poor, impoverished *idiom* زړې بني ته رنگ وركول *saying* to perform some worthless task; to dress up an old woman

بنياد bunjád *m. Arabic* foundation, basis بنياد كېدل *compound verb* ☞ بنيادبدل *idiom* بنياد كېنبل to eradicate; destroy right down to the foundation د هغه د كورنۍ بنياد وخوت his whole family perished

بنيادم baniādám *m. Arabic singular & plural* people, mankind

بنيادم توب baniādamtób *m.* human qualities

بنيادي bunjādí basic; fundamental

بنيادبدل bunjādedál *denominative, intransitive* [*past:* بنياد شو] to be created, be founded

بنيان banján *m.* 1 knitwear, knitted item 2 jersey 3 t-shirt, (sailor's) striped vest

بنيان بافي banjānbāfí *f.* knitwear production

بنېر bunér *m.* Buner (region)

بنېروال bunerwál *m.* inhabitant of the Buner region

بنيه binjá *f. Arabic* 1 build, frame, (bodily) constitution 2 bunjá a structure b position, situation

بن baṇ¹ *m.* garden, orchard

بن baṇ² *m.* ☞ بنگ²

بن buṇ³ *m.* rope (made of rush, etc.)

بنرېژ bəṇrézh *m.* بنرېژون bəṇrezhún *m.* moult, moulting (of birds)

بن سات baṇsát *m.* gardener

بن سترگی buṇstórgaj weak-sighted, having poor eyesight

بنکه baṇáka¹ *f.* feather بنكي سره شكول a to fight (e.g., of fighting cocks) b *figurative* to quarrel

بنكه baṇká² *f.* ☞ بنكی²

بنكی buṇkáj¹ *m.* ☞ بنگ²

بنكی baṇkə́j² *f.* (small) garden

بن وال baṇvál *m.* gardener

بنگول buṇavál *transitive* ☞ بنگول

بنه baṇá¹ *f.* 1 face; aspect, appearance بنه الوتل a to grow pale, change countenance بنه يي والوته he grew pale; he changed countenance b to fade, turn yellow, wither c *figurative* to show cowardice, take fright 2 aspect, image, form بنه گرزبدل a to change, change countenance بنه يي بالكل اوبنتي ده he has changed greatly; he's completely unrecognizable b *figurative* to be lost, be confused بنه بدلول a to change, to be transformed b to change (one's clothes) د . . . په بنه كېدل to take on the appearance or the form of something 3 nature (of a person) *idiom* بنه خاوري كېدل a to die b to grow weak, weaken (of a person) *idiom* بنه دي مه سه خاوري! I wish you a long life!

بنه báṇa² *f.* 1 feather (of a bird) بنه غورځول to moult (of birds) 2 fin (of a fish)

بنهار buṇəhár *m.* 1 buzzing (of insects) 2 whispering 3 muttering

بنه الوتئ baṇá alvútaj 1 grown pale; having a changed countenance 2 faded, turned yellow; withered 3 *figurative* having shown cowardice, having been frightened

بنه بنه baṇabaṇá various, diverse; all kinds of بنه بنه كول to vary, diversify بنه بنه كېدل to be varied, be diversified

بنی bəṇáj¹ *m.* weeping willow

بنی baṇáj² *m.* gardener

بنيا banjá half-opened, slightly opened بنيا كول to open slightly بنيا كېدل to be opened slightly

بنيار baṇjár *m.* dyer

بنيالی baṇjāláj beautiful; bright; well-dressed, elegant

بنېنچغ baṇechágh *m.* ☞ بهرين چغ

بنېدل buṇedál *intransitive* [*past:* وبنېده] 1 to buzz (of insects) 2 to whisper 3 to mutter

بنېژ baṇézh *m.* ☞ بنرېژ

بنيه banjá *m.* [*plural:* بنيه گان *plural:* بنيهگان banjagán] shopkeeper, petty tradesman

بو bav¹ *m.* 1 scarecrow 2 boogeyman (an imaginary being used to frighten children)

بو ² bau bo *interjection* goo-goo! (interjection used to make a baby smile)

بو ³ bu *m.* ☞ بوی ¹

بو ⁴ bu *m.* 1 thorn, prickle 2 syphilis

بو ⁵ bo *separable part of the verb* بوتلل

بوا boā *m.* boa (constrictor)

بواری buvāraj *m.* 1 young animal weaned from its mother 2 skin, hide, pelt

بواسیر bavāsír *m. Arabic plural* hemorrhoids

بواعث bavā'ís *m. Arabic plural from* باعث

بوالهوس bulhavás *Arabic* 1.1 capricious 1.2 lightheaded 1.3 sensual 2 *m.* .1 capricious person 2.2 lightheaded, flighty person 2.3 sensual nature

بوالهوس ناكي bulhavasnākí *f.* بولهوسي bulhavasí *f.* 1 capriciousness 2 flightiness 3 sensuality

بوب bob pure, unadulterated بویه پښتو pure Pashto

بوبول bobavə́l *denominative, transitive* [*past:* بوب یې کړ] to clean, free from impurities

بویه ¹ bobá *f.* money in the money-box (saved at home and put to no use)

بویه ² bóba *feminine singular of* بوب

بوبی bobə́j *f.* sister (addressing an older sister or an elderly woman)

بوبیدل bobedə́l *denominative, intransitive* [*past:* بوب شو] to be cleaned, be freed from impurities

بوت ¹ but *m.* young man

بوت ² but *m.* ☞ بوت ²

بوب ³ bot *past of* بپول ¹

بوتاړ butā́ṛ *m.* snout, muzzle; mug

بوتکی ¹ butkáj 1 *m.* lad, youth 2 having grown a bit بوتکی کېدل to grow up (a bit)

بوتکی ² butkə́j 1 *f.* girl 2 *feminine singular from* بوتکی

بوتکی ³ butkéj *f.* ☞ بتکی ²

بوتل butál *m.* [*plural:* بوتلونه butalúna *plural:* بوتلان butalā́n] *Western* bottle

بوتلل botlə́l *transitive* [*past:* بوت یې , *imperative perfective* بوزه] *perfective of* بپول ¹

بوتلئ botə́laj *past participle from* بوتلل

بوته ¹ botá *f.* ☞ برمته

بوته ² búta *f.* girl

بوته ³ botə́ *past from* بپول ¹

بوته ⁴ bóta *feminine past of* بپول ¹

بوتی botáj *m.* young camel

بوتئ bótəj *Western past of* بپول ¹

بوت ¹ buṭ morose, sullen زړه یې بوټ وتلئ دئ He is morose.

بوت ² buṭ *m.* [*plural:* بوټونه buṭúna *plural:* بوټان buṭā́n] *Western* shoe, footwear یوه جوړه بوټ a pair of shoes د بوټانو گنډلو فابریکه a shoe factory دبوټو گنډلو فابریکه a shoe factory

بوټبا buṭbá *m.* person who collects brushwood for fuel

بوټ پالش buṭpā́lish *m. regional* boot polish

بوټ دوز buṭdúz *m.* shoemaker, cobbler

بوټ رنگوونکی buṭ rangavúnkaj *m.* bootblack (a person who shines boots or shoes)

بوټ سوري buṭsurí *m. plural* chaff

بوټکه buṭə́ka *f.* girl

بوټکی buṭkáj *m.* ☞ بوتکی ¹

بوټني bótaní *baġ* بوټني botanical gardens

بوټ وربوزي buṭvərbuzí *f.* dissatisfaction د چاسره بوټ وربوزي کول to express your dissatisfaction to someone

بوټی ¹ bútaj *m.* 1 bush 2 plant (general designation) بېکاره بوټی د botany بوټو پوهنه د بوټی weeds دارو بوټی búṭi medicinal plants بوټی کنښل a botanist بوټو پوه a to uproot; root out b *figurative* to extirpate, eliminate 3 brushwood 4 [*plural:* بوټي búṭi] thickets 5 pattern, design (embroidered or drawn) *idiom* بوټی دي وخپړه! Go away! Get lost! *idiom* د احمد خوارکي بوټی وخوت Poor Ahmed is altogether ruined.

بوټی ² buṭáj *m.* 1 crop-eared animal 2 miscarriage

بوټی ³ boṭáj *m.* fillet (steak)

بوټی پوهاند buṭipohā́nd *m.* botanist

بوټید buṭíd wearing European footwear

بوج bodzh *m.* 1 burden, weight 2 volume, dimension

بوجود bavudzhúd despite, in spite of

بوجه ¹ budzhá *f.* 1 stopper, plug 2 gag

بوجه ² bodzh *m. regional* burden, weight

بوجی budzhéj *f.* bag, purse

بوچ buch *m.* 1 animal with a clipped ear or ears; animal with a mutilated muzzle 2 person with a flattened or sliced nose

بوچخړی buchkhə́ṛaj *m.* scarecrow (in a garden)

بوچر buchə́r *m.* kind of small melon

بوچری ¹ buchə́raj *m.* sluice gate (of an irrigation ditch)

بوچری ² buchṛáj *m.* young snake

بوچک buchák *m.* kind of melon

بوچنی ¹ buchúnaj *m.* miller's helper

بوچنی ² buchuní *f.* portion of ground flour (a remuneration for the miller's helper)

بوچی bucháj *m.* ☞ بوټی ² 1

بوغ budz بوغ buts 1 angry, enraged 2 insulted 3 sticking out (usually refers to the ears) 4 having pricked up one's ears بوغ کېدل a to be angry, be infuriated b to be offended c to stick out, protrude بوغ بوغ کېدل a to bristle; get into a fight b to be shy, be timid; feel uncomfortable (of a woman who has caught sight of outsiders)

بوغل bodzə́l *m.* stone wall, stone fence

بوغ buts ☞ بوغ

بوخکی butsakáj *m.* 1 ☞ پوخکی 2 pommel (of a saddle)

بوخول butsavə́l *denominative, transitive* [*past:* بوغ یې کړ] 1 to anger, infuriate 2 to insult 3 suspiciously to prick up one's ears

بوخبدل butsedə́l *denominative, intransitive* [*past:* بوغ شو] 1 to become angry; be enraged 2 to be offended 3 to protrude (said usually of ears) د ده غوږونه بوخ شول He listened carefully. He pricked up his ears.

بوخت [2] bukht bukhə́t ☞ بخت

بوختول bukhtavə́l transitive ☞ بختول

بوخته bukhtá f. to marinate, soak for shish kebob (meat)

بوختېدل bukhtedə́l intransitive ☞ بختېدل

بوخښی bukhtsə́j f. ☞ بخښه

بود [1] bud m. 1 being, existence, life 2 exaction, (money) recovered 3 proceeds (from selling something) بود کول compound verb ☞ بودول

بود [2] bud m. storehouse for hay (plastered with clay)

بود [3] bud m. 1 quick-wittedness 2 bright, clever person بود سړی clever person, sensible person په بودي يي پوهېدل to know the point of something

بودا budā m. ☞ بوډا 1.2

بوداپست budāpést m. Budapest (city)

بودائي budājí ☞ بوډائي

بودتون budtún m. (heathen) temple

بودجوي buddzhaví budget-related, budgetary; relating to a financial estimate

بودجه buddzhá f. budget; (financial) estimate

بودلنه bodlə́na f. stupid; dullness

بودله bodlá bodlaj stupid, dense, dull-witted

بودول budavə́l denominative, transitive [past: بود يې کړ] 1 to receive; exact 2 to gain, make (when selling something) idiom خپل حق بودول to achieve your rights

بوده [1] budá f. woof (of a fabric)

بوده [2] bodá m. singular & plural [plural: بوده گان bodagān plural: بودگان bodagán] cattle (beast or beasts of burden)

بوده [3] budá f. amount received, proceeds; amount exacted

بوده رو bodaráv m. cart track; caravan trail

بودېدل budedə́l denominative, intransitive [past: بود شو] 1 to be received, be exacted 2 to be gained (at the sale of something)

بوډا buḍā 1.1 m. old man 1.2 m. Buddha 2 attributive adjective old بوډا سړی old man بوډا کېدل to grow old

بوډاگی [1] buḍāgáj m. (little) old man

بوډاگی [2] buḍāgə́j f. old woman

بوډائي buḍājí Buddhist, (of) Buddha

بوډوگی [1] buḍogáj m. ☞ بوډاگی

بوډوگی [2] buḍogə́j f. ☞ بوډاگی

بوډی [1] buḍáj m. 1 (venerable) old man, elder; spiritual advisor 2 bad omen

بوډی [2] buḍə́j f. 1 old woman, old lady 2 f. attributive adjective old بوډی تال، د بوډی بنځه old woman idiom بوډی تال rainbow idiom astronomy د بوډی کټ، بوډی کټ the Great Bear (Ursa major) idiom بوډی نيول to grow numb (e.g., of a foot)

بوډی [3] boḍə́j f. ☞ بادهوا

بوډی [4] boḍáj f. skull, cranium

بور [1] bor brown

بور [2] bavr m. 1 leopard 2 proper name Bavr

بور [3] bor m. fruit ☞ بار [1] 3

بور [4] bur m. ☞ بر [6]

بور [5] bor m. caliber

بور [6] bor m. waist, loins idiom بور دي مات سه! Out of my sight! بور يي مات دئ he's very tired

بورا [1] bavrā́ 1 m. moth 2 f. butterfly

بورا [2] burā́ f. cellar; basement

بوراني borāní بوراني borānə́j f. dish made from eggplant with meat and sour milk

بوربوکی borbukə́j f. burbukə́j f. ☞ بوربکی

بورجل bordzhál m. [plural: بورجلونه bordzhalúna f. plural: بورجلي bordzháli] 1 dwelling; habitation 2 trench 3 ambush

بورچنډه burchanḍá f. woman whose baby died in infancy

بورخنگ burkháng m. tub, trough (for mixing dough); kneading trough; unleavened dough

بورد bord m. بورډ borḍ m. 1 sign, signboard 2 commission, council

بورډوالا borḍvālā m. member of a commission, council member

بورژوا burzhuā́ 1 m. bourgeois 2 adjective bourgeois

بورژوازي burzhuāzí 1 f. bourgeoisie 2 adjective bourgeois

بورس burs m. exchange په بورس کښې معاملات exchange operations

بورغو burghú m. pipe (for smoking)

بورقه burḳá f. ☞ برقعه

بورکس boráks m. chemistry borax

بورنه borná f. بورنه borṇá f. flour (for breading fried foods)

بوروندي burundí m. Burundi (country, Africa)

بوره [1] burá f. sawdust, filings د لرگيو بوره sawdust

بوره [2] burá f. granulated sugar

بوره [3] buṛá f. woman who has lost her son! بوره وراره سې! May your son die and your brother too!

بوره [4] bóra feminine singular of بور [1]

بوری [1] bavráj m. 1 anatomy gall, bile 2 bitter taste, bitterness

بوری [2] buráj ☞ بوری [3]

بوری [3] búri بوري بلا fright (object inspiring fear); witch, hag

بوری [4] buri f. بوری boráj f. bag, sack د بوري سند jute

بوری [5] bavrə́j f. corn, callus

بوریا burijā́ f. mat, matting

بوریک borík boric, boracic بوریک ايسيد boric acid

بوڼ [1] boṛ m. roast (meat)

بوڼ [2] boṛ په عقل بوڼ unintelligent

بوڼبک buṛbák slow-witted, muddle-headed

بوڼبکی boṛbukə́j f. buṛbukə́j sandstorm, whirlwind

بوڼه [1] bávṛa f. búṛa plateau, tableland

بوڼه [2] boṛá 1 unfinished, uncompleted 2 out of order بوڼه کېدل a to be unfinished b to be out of order, not working properly

بوڼی [1] buṛə́j f. ☞ بوری [3]

بوڼی [2] buṛáj m. projection, protuberance, prong

بوری [3] buṛáj **1** with a cut off or mutilated nose, lip, ear, etc.; with a dull or stupid face **2** with a chipped edge (of dishware) **3** broken, smashed

بوری [4] boṛáj *m.* plug, stopper; plugging, stopping up

بوړی [5] boṛə́j *f.* bunch of lucerne

بوړی [6] bóṛi nonsense بوړي خبري کول to speak nonsense

بوړی [7] boṛáj *m.* pattern on felt

بوړی بوړی bóṛi-bóṛi بوړي بوړي ورته پرپوتل **a** to stretch out, sprawl **b** *figurative* to achieve something; strive toward something, dream of something هغه و د دي کارته بوړي بوړي پروت دئ He dreams about this work.

بوز buz *m.* **1** buzzing (of insects) **2** crack, crackle, crackling (sound)

بوزبو buzbú *m.* owlet

بوزبوزکه buzbuzə́ka *f.* بوزبوزی buzbuzáj *m.* **1** ☞ بوز **2** grumbling, muttering

بوزغلی buzghə́láj *m.* sprout, shoot

بوزه bozá *f.* **1** bouza (fermented beverage); koumiss (fermented mare's milk) **2** soured food

بوزه [2] bozá *f.* glossy ibis, *Plegadis falcinellus*

بوزه [3] bozá one who does not observe fasting

بوزه [4] bóza *perfective imperative of* بپول [1]

بوزی بنده buzibandá **1.1** guileless, openhearted **1.2** silent, taciturn **2** *m.* **.1** guileless, openhearted person; simpleton **2.2** taciturn person

بوزیدل buzedə́l *intransitive* **1** to buzz (of insects) **2** to sour, be suitable (of dough)

بوزینه boziná *f.* morocco (leather)

بوژومبوره buzhumburá *f.* Bujumbura (capital of Burundi)

بوږ [1] boẓ **1** indistinct, hoarse, husky (of the voice) **2** sore (of the throat)

بوږ [2] boẓ collected, located together بوږ درومل to go together

بوږغاړی bogghā́ṛaj **1** with a muffled, hoarse voice **2** with a sore throat

بوږنول bugnavə́l *transitive* ☞ برنول

بوږنیدل bugnedə́l *intransitive* ☞ برنیدل

بوږه bogá *f.* **1** secluded place **2** neighborhood **3** ☞ بوښه

بوس [1] bus *m. plural, less often singular* **1** finely cut straw, chopped straw **2** chaff, bran, siftings, peels د اورو بوس bran *idiom* بوس ورکول to deceive with flattery توبوسو لاندي اوبه بپول to trick

بوس [2] bus ☞ بوغ

بوسات busā́t *m.* influence, effect بوسات کول to influence; have an effect, have an influence on

بوساړه [1] busāṛá *f.* **1** stack of hay or straw which has been plastered with clay **2** hollow object **3** *figurative* lazybones *idiom* هسي بوساړه کبدل to strut, to be puffed up, be important

بوساړه [2] busāṛá *f.* blow, stroke

بوساري busāṛí *f.* propaganda بوساري کول to conduct propaganda, propagandize

بوستان bostā́n *m.* flower bed; array

بوس خوسی buskhusáj *m.* stuffed calfskin

بوسر busə́r *m.* smoldering ashes

بوسکارل buskārə́l *transitive* [*past:* و یې بوسکاره] to urge on, drive (a hoarse, mule, etc.)

بوس ماسو busmāsú *m.* toady, lickspittle

بوسول busavə́l *transitive* ☞ بوخول

بوسه busá inflated, swollen

بوښت boẓ̌t stuck (in mud), bogged down (in a swamp, in a mudhole)

بوښت توب boẓ̌ttób *m.* ☞ بوښنت والی

بوښتنه boẓ̌tə́na *f.* getting stuck (in mud), getting bogged down (in a swamp or mudhole)

بوښت والی boẓ̌tvā́laj *m.* **1** flabbiness, limpness; inertia, sluggishness **2** ☞ بوښتنه

بوښتول boẓ̌tavə́l *denominative, transitive* [*past:* بوښنت یې کړ] **1** to drag in, suck in (of a swamp, mire) **2** to plunge (into), dig (into) (of claws, etc.)

بوښته bóẓ̌ta *f.* **1** mire, bog, swamp **2** *figurative* stagnation, standstill; swamp

بوښتیدل boẓ̌tedə́l *denominative, intransitive* to get stuck (in the mud), get bogged down (in a swamp, quagmire)

بوښند buẓ̌ə́nd sad, depressed, dispirited

بوښنه bávẓ̌a *f.* barren desert *idiom* پر بوښنو گرزیدل to be a hermit, be a recluse پر بوښنو مخ نیول **a** to go crazy **b** to be a hermit, be a recluse

بوغ [1] bugh *m.* bowl, saucer (made of wood)

بوغ [2] bogh **1** rough (of a voice) **2** unpleasant; ugly

بوغ توب boghtób *m.* بوغ تیا boghtjā́ *f.* **1** roughness, coarseness **2** ugliness

بوغده boghdá *f.* ☞ پیشقوضه

بوغلی bughláj *m.* bright kerchief (such kerchiefs are given by the bride's family to guests at the wedding)

بوغمه boghmá *f.* edema, swelling (in the throat)

بوغو bughú *m. music* trombone

بوغ توب boghvā́laj *m.* ☞ بوغ توب

بوغول boghavə́l *denominative, transitive* [*past:* بوغ یې کړ] to make coarse, make rough (of the voice)

بوغه boghá *f.* intoxication from smoking hashish or strong tobacco

بوغیدل boghedə́l *denominative, intransitive* [*past:* بوغ شو] to grow coarse (of the voice)

بوق buḳ *m. Arabic* pipe; horn

بوقلمون buḳalamún *m. Arabic* **1** chameleon **2** Himalayan pheasant

بوقه boḳá *f. regional* ☞ بوکه

بوک [1] bok *m.* **1** hump (of a camel, zebu) **2** rise, raising; eminence **3** protuberance, prominence, bulge

بوک ² buk 1 fallen into ruins 2 overturned, toppled بوک اړول to topple, overturn بوک اوښتل to be toppled, overturned

بوک ¹ bokán m. ☞ بوک

بوک بوک bukbúk بوک بوک کېدل a to dissemble, play the hypocrite b to pose, act

بوکر bokár conic, conical

بوکه ¹ bokrá f. ☞ بوکه

بوکه ² bukrá f. ☞ برقعه

بوکړی bukə́raj weaned (of a baby)

بوکسنگ bóksing m. boxing بوکسنگ کول to engage in boxing

بوکول bukavə́l denominative, intransitive [past: بوک يې کړ] to knock down, bring down; to overturn, topple

بوکه boká f. bucket (of leather or wood)

بوکېدل bukedə́l denominative, intransitive [past: بوک شو] to be knocked down; be overturned, be toppled; overturn, topple

بوگ bog rotted within; hollow, empty

بوگړی bogə́raj m. 1 land given to the clergy for their use free of charge 2 parcel of land allotted to farm workers as payment 3 land use whereby sharecropper and owner split produce fifty-fifty

بوگړا ¹ bugṛá 1 slaughtered (of cattle) 2 slaughtered (by a predator or plunderer) 3 figurative victim بوگړا کول a to slaughter (cattle) b to tear apart (said of a predator) c figurative to torment, torture بوگړا کېدل a to be torn to pieces, be slaughtered (of cattle) b to be torn to pieces (by a predator) c figurative to be victimized, suffer harm

بوگړا ² bugṛá f. chickpea

بوگنول bogənavə́l transitive Eastern ☞ برنول

بوگوتا bogotá Bogata (city)

بوگه bugá f. watermelon

بول ¹ bol m. 1 word, promise 2 speech 3 rumor, talk; fame, repute

بول ² baul m. Arabic plural ☞ بولي ²

بول ³ bol present tense verb stem from بلل

بولان bolán m. the Bolan Pass (West Pakistan)

بولاني bolāni f. small pie with vegetables

بولټ bolṭ m. 1 bolt 2 latch د دروازي بولټ کول to latch the door idiom چا د ژبې بولټونه خلاصول to loosen someone's tongue

بولدوزر buldózér m. bulldozer

بولشویزم bolshevízm m. بالشویزم

بولشویک bolshevik m. بالشویک

بولغه bulghá f. ☞ بېلگه

بولقه bulká f. ☞ برقعه

بولک ¹ bolə́k ☞ بلوک

بولک ² bolák consignment of goods

بولل bolə́l transitive ☞ بلل

بوله ¹ bóla f. female relatives of bride treating groom's relatives to boiled rice

بوله ² bóla imperative, imperfective from بلل

بوله ³ bolá word paired with سوله

بولۍ ¹ bolə́j f. command; instruction, ordinance

بولي ² báuli m. plural urine لوی بولي بولي کول to urinate

بولي ³ bóli present tense of بلل

بولۍ تڼۍ bolə́j taṇə́j f. command button

bolivijá f. Bolivia بولیویا

بوم ¹ bum m. native

بوم ² bum m. owl; tawny owl (Bubo bubo)

بوم ³ bum 1 m. nation; land; region 2 familiar (with the territory, the road, etc.)

بوم ⁴ bom slack, lazy (of willpower)

بومي bumí local, indigenous

بومیا bumjá m. 1 guide, escort 2 imam, leader of prayer 3 basis بومیا کول to substantiate, base

بومیاگلوي bumjāgalví f. 1 the title of imam 2 leadership

بومیه bumjá f. ☞ بدرگه

بون bon m. bonn m. Bonn (city)

بونجی bundzháj m. ☞ بنجی ¹

بوند bund m. a drop

بوند buṇḍ 1 short 2 clipped, trimmed

بونډه bónḍa: بونډه گوته index finger

بونډی buṇḍáj 1 m. 1.1 truncheon, baton 1.2 cattle with docked tails 2 quite short

بونسټ bonsáṭ m. ☞ بنسټ

بونگه bongá f. bungá f. ransom (from imprisonment, etc.) په بونگه to pay ransom (for a captive, etc.) خلاصول

بونگی bongáj with nose cut off

بونگېدل bungedə́l intransitive [past: و بونگېد] to growl, curse; mutter

بونه ¹ buná f. ☞ باروبونه

بونه ² buná f. 1 anus 2 seat, buttocks

بونه ³ buná f. hunting lying low (as by a grouse or quail at the appearance of a bird of prey)

بونه ⁴ buná f. slaughter, massacre

بونه ⁵ buná filled, with a full stomach

بونیا bonjá acquainted, familiar

بونیاک bunjā́k ☞ بوي ناک

بونېدل bonedə́l intransitive ☞ بنېدل

بون ¹ boṇ m. medicine atrophic rhinitis, ozena

بون ² buṇ m. ☞ بڼ ³

بون ³ buṇ m. boṇ m. ☞ بنگ ² بوڼ چاته وهل to whisper to someone بوڼ نه وهل not to utter a word; not to make a sound

بون بسیر buṇbasír weak-sighted

بونول buṇavə́l boṇavə́l transitive ☞ بنگول

بونه buná f. ☞ بوڼه

بونهار buṇəhā́r m. ☞ بزهار، بوڼه هار

بونی ¹ buṇáj m. cartilage (of the nose)

بونی ² buṇáj nasal

بونېدل buṇedə́l boṇedə́l intransitive ☞ بنېدل

بوو bavú m. ☞ بو ¹

بوواري buvāráj m. ☞ بوواری

بهار buhā́r *m.* ☞ بهار ¹

بوهاری buhāráj *m.* **1** small child who has been weaned **2** young animal just weaned

بوی buj ¹ *m.* smell بد بوی bad smell, odor نبه بوی pleasant smell; aroma بوی راتلل ،... د بوی تلل ،... د **a** to smell, give off an odor **b** *figurative* to indicate ("smack of") the approach of something نبه بویونه خپرول **to be fragrant بوی کښل a** to sniff, smell (at) **b** *figurative* to be greedy, envious بوی کول to go bad, go rotten د چا بوی ولاړېدل **a** to gain a bad name; be scandalized **b** to be caught in adultery

بوي bávi ² *blending of the particle* به *and the linking verb* وي

بویا bujā́ *f. botany* licorice

بویاره bujārá *f.* **1** insignificant or hardly noticeable trace **2** model, specimen

بوی کښ bujkáx̌ greedy, envious

بوین bujə́n smelly, foul-smelling

بوي ناک،بویناک bujnā́k **1** giving off an odor **2** smelly, foul-smelling **3** *regional* fragrant

بوینسرآیرس buénos-ā́jres *m.* Buenos Aires (city)

بویول bujavál *denominative, transitive* [*past:* بوي یې کړ] to sniff, smell (at); sniff around

بویه bója ¹ ought, should, must اوس بویه چه ښارته ولاړ سي He should now go to town.

بویه bojá ² *f.* grass and straw used for fertilizer, green fertilizer

بوی يي bují *f.* ☞ بوی ¹

بویېدل bujedál *intransitive* [*past:* وبویېده] **1** to smell, give off an odor **2** to go bad, become rotten

به bə ba ¹ *particle* **1** *forms future tense* زه به لیکم I shall write زه به ولاړشم ولیکم I shall write (something) زه به ولاړه شم I'll go I'm going **2** *expresses repetition of an action when used with forms of the past tense* هغه به راغئ he would call on, he would come هغه به راغلئ و کار کاوه he worked (usually) **3** *expresses modalities* هغه به راغلئ که تاویلي وای، it's a pity he hasn't come راغلئ و If you had said (it), he would have come

به beh ² *f.* better

بها bahā́ ¹ *f.* price, cost

بها bahā́ ² *f.* brightness; sparkling

بهادپ bahādáp expensive; valuable

بهادر bahādúr **1** brave, valiant **2** *m.* .**1** brave man, hero **2.2** Bogatyr (fabled hero)

بهادرانه bahādurāná **1** brave, valiant **2** bravely, valiantly

بهادري bahādurí *f.* bravery, valor, heroism په وطن په مدافعه کښي يې he displayed valor while defending his native land په بهادري وکړه بهادری سره bravely, valiantly; heroically

بهار bahā́r *m.* spring

بهاند bəhānd **1** running, flowing **2** liquid بهاند مواد liquids

بهانه bahāná *f.* pretext, cause; excuse; evasion, trick, subterfuge بهانه کول ، بهانه نیول to seek a pretext, seek an excuse

بهانجا bahānjá valuable, expensive

بهان bihā́n *m.* [*plural:* بهانان bihaṇā́n *plural:* بهانونه bihāṇúna] foal, colt

بهان گی bihāṇgáj *m.* small colt, foal

بهانه bihā́ṇa *f.* filly (foal)

بهبود behbúd **1.1** healthy, well **1.2** regulated, organized, arranged **1.3** flourishing, thriving **2** *m.* ☞ بهبودي ¹

بهبودي behbudí ¹ *f.* **1** health **2** arrangement, organization **3** well-being; prosperity

بهبودي behbudí ² *f.* large knife, dagger

به بی bəbə́j *f. proper noun* Babi

بهتان buhtā́n *Arabic* lie, slander بهتان ویل to lie, slander

بهتر behtár بهتره behtára better تر دي بهتر څه شي دئ؟ What could be better? دا بهتره ده چه ... ، بهتره ده چه ... (it will be) better, if ... بهتره بلل ، بهتره ګنل **a** to prefer **b** to consider a blessing

بهتري behtarí *f.* **1** improvement **2** advantage; preference **3** well-being; prosperity

بهترین behtarín the best; of superior quality; outstanding *idiom* د دي لغت په بهترینه معنی in the best sense of the word

بهر bahár **1.1** from without, externally, on the outside د ... نه څو له ... بهر at a distance of several miles from ... میله بهر beyond the limits of something د له ښاره بهر outside the city دروازي نه بهر behind the door **b** at, beside, near **1.2** abroad بهر **a** from without, externally, on the outside **b** from abroad بهرول بهر ☞ بهر ایستل، بهر کول تلل to go out (from somewhere) کېدل، **a** to be led out; be expelled, be driven out, be exiled **b** to go out, leave (from some place) **c** to be extracted, pulled out **d** to be released, be freed بهر لپرل **a** to send **b** to send abroad بهر ته وتل، **a** to go out (from somewhere) **b** to come forward, project; appear (publicly) **2.1** external, outer بهر ور outside door **2.2** foreign **2.3** going beyond the framework (of something)

بهراس bharā́s *m.* ☞ براس

بهر په بهر bahár-pə-bahár **1** from the outside; on the outside, from without **2** far from something; beyond the limits of something

بهرتي bharatí *f.* recruitment بهرتي کول *compound verb* to recruit بهرتي کېدل *compound verb* to be recruited, be enlisted, be won over

بهرني baharanáj **1** outer, exterior بهرني دروازه outer gates **2** done, produced outside the home **3** another's; alien, foreign

بهرول baharavál *denominative, transitive* [*past:* بهر یي کړ] **1** to lead out; drive out, banish, expel **2** to extract, take out **3** to release, free **4** to thrust out, display on the outside

بهره bahrá ¹ *f.* **1** share, portion **2** wealth **3** use; advantage; profit

بهره bahrá ² *m. regional* waiter

بهره برداري bahrabadārí *f.* use, utilization; exploitation; operation

بهره من bahramán بهره مند bahramánd fortunate, happy; flourishing, thriving بهره من کېدل to be happy; fourish

بهره مندي bahramandí *f.* happiness, good fortune; prosperity; well-being

بهره ور bahravár بهره یاب bahrajáb 1 flourishing 2 deriving profit or benefit from; gaining 3 having been awarded something; having received something

بهزاد behzád *m. proper noun* Behzad

بیهسود bihsúd *m.* bejsúd Bikhsud, Bejsud (region in the Dajizangi district and in Nangarhar)

بهشت bihísht *m.* paradise

بهشتي bihishtí 1 heavenly 2 *m. jocular* water-carrier

بهنت bihiḵht *m.* ☞ بهشت

بهنتي bihiḵhtí ☞ بهشتي

بهگن bhagán *m.* gadfly

بهلول bahlól *m. proper noun* Bahlol

بهم bahám together, with one another

بهنه bahná [1] *f.* top (the toy)

بهنه bahóna [2] *f.* lock of hair left with children as a vow or promise

بهوت bhut *m. regional* evil spirit, demon

بهوتان bhután *m.* بهوتان bhután *m.* Bhutan (region in Indian)

بهوتي bhuṭí 1 *adjective* (of) Bhutan 2 native of Bhutan

بهوج bhudzh *m.* Himalayan birch tree, *Betula utilis*

بهوج پتر bhudzhpatár *m.* 1 birch bark 2 papyrus

بهوس bhus *m. plural* ☞ بوس [1]

بهول bahavál *transitive* [*past:* و یي بهول] 1 to turn on, run (water) 2 to spill (blood) 3 to send regularly (e.g., food, provisions)

بهي bihí [1] *f.* improvement; development بهي کول to improve, develop

بهي bihí [2] *m.* quince, quince tree

بهي bəhój [3] *f.* 1 steps down a well 2 well with steps

بهانيه bahjáṇa ☞ بهانيه

بهبدا bahedá *f.* ☞ بهبدنه

بهبدل bahedál baedál *intransitive* [*past:* وبهبده] 1 to flow, run; flow out 2 to flow, be shed (of blood)

بهبدنه bahedóna *f.* baedóna 1 current, course (of water) 2 shedding, spilling (of blood)

بهیر bahír *m.* 1 transport and equipment of an army 2 large accumulation; great many, horde, multitude 3 line, stream (of people); caravan 4 chain (of events) 5 race; dynasty 6 process, development

بهیرگر bahírgár *m.* processor

بهیمیت bahimiját *m.* cruelty, savagery

بی bəj [1] *children's speech* 1 *f. & m.* sore بی کول to hurt, make painful بی کبدل to be hurt 2 watch out, be careful

بي be [2] *f.* name of the letter ب

بي be [3] *combination of the particle* به *and the pronoun* يي ته بي و ويني؟ Will you see him (her, them)?

بي be bi [4] *preposition usually in combination with* د . . . څخه *or* له ما . . . څخه without; except, with the exception of بي ما without me بي له ديله without interruption, unceasingly, continously بي له توقفه

immediately, quickly, without delay بي له يوخوکسانو with the exception of several people

بي be bi [5] *prefix* without, not بيباکي recklessness, foolhardiness بي ځايه inappropriate, useless, empty

بیا bjá bijá [1] 1 again, anew بيا به کله سره وو وينو؟ When shall we meet again? د بيا دپاره again بيا بيا again and again, repeatedly 2 after that, then بيا مکتب ته ځم then I go to school 3 back بيا ورکول to return *idiom* بيا هم still, nevertheless, however بيا نو all the same; (and) what is more په تبره بيا په زیاته بیا especially; all the more بیا نور بیا to be continued چه تا چه، بیا چي especially, particularly وويل، هغه بیا وشوه It happened just as you said.

بیا bjá [2] *prefix* re- (or similar indicating renewal or repetition of an action) بیاموندل a to find again b to acquire, gain c to return d to restore بیا تنظيمول to reorganize

بیا انتخاب bjáintikháb *m.* reelection

بي آب beáb 1 shameless 2 disgraced, dishonored, shamed بي آب کول to disgrace, dishonor, shame

بیابان biābán *m.* bejābán desert, wasteland

بیاباني biābání uninhabited, deserted, desert

بي آبرو beābrú disgraced, dishonored, shamed

بي آبرويي beābruí *f.* ☞ بي آبي

بي ابري beibré barren, sterile

بي آبول beābavál *denominative, intransitive* [*past:* بي آبه یي کړ] to disgrace, dishonor

بي آبه beába ☞ بي آب

بي آبي *f.* disgrace, dishonor

بیا بیا بیا bjá bjá bjá hunter's cry used to summon falcon

بي آبدل beābedól *denominative, intransitive* [*past:* بي آبه شو] to be disgraced, be dishonored

بیاپیلون bjápájlūn *m.* reboot

بیا تعمیر bjáta' mír *m.* restoration (of something destroyed)

بي اتفاقه beittifáka unfriendly; disunited, separated, alienated کول _ to separate, alienate

بي اتفاقي beittifákí *f.* 1 disagreement, divergence; disharmony 2 contradiction

بیاتي bjátí *f.* [*plural:* بیاتي bjatój *plural:* بیاتیګاني bjátigáni] scissors *compound verb* بیاتي کول to cut with scissors; cut (out) کالي بیاتي کول to cut a dress out کول

بي اثره beasára 1 without leaving a trace; futile, unsuccessful; ineffective; fruitless (e.g., of one's efforts) 2 ineffectual, vain, useless

بي اثري beasarí *f.* futility; ineffectiveness; fruitlessness (e.g., of one's efforts)

بي اجرا beidzhrá unfulfilled

بي اجله beadzhála sudden, unexpected

بي احتياطه beihtiáta 1 careless 2 carelessly

بي احتياطي beihtiátí *f.* carelessness

بي اختياره beikhtijára 1 involuntary 2 involuntarily

بي ادب beadáb **1** ill-bred **2** disrespectful

بي ادبي beadí *f.* **1** poor breeding **2** disrespect

بيارته bjárta ☞ بهرته

بيارغي خځلنۍ bjáraghe khadzálnǝj *f.* recycle bin

بي آرزو beārzó unreliable

بي عزته beárza ☞ بي ارزه

بي ارزي bearzí *f.* disrespect, lack of respect

بي اساسه beasása without any basis, unjustified, groundless, unsound

بياسته bjásta *f.* cable; cord, rope

بي اسرې beasré **1** pitch-dark **2** hopeless **3** deprived of one's share; unfortunate

بي اصوله beusúla disorderly, without system (of life)

بياض bajáz **1** *m.* *Arabic* **.1** whiteness **1.2** notebook **2** white

بي اعتباره bei'tibára **1** not to be trusted, untrustworthy; discredited بي اعتباره کول to deprive of trust; discredit **2** ineffective; invalid

بي اعتمادي bei'timádí *f.* distrust

بي اعتنا bei'tiná inattentive, careless, negligent

بي اعتنائي bei'tinái *f.* inattention, carelessness, negligence

بي اقتداري beiḳtidárí *f.* **1** incompetence **2** lack of skill, clumsiness

بي الايشه beālājísha disinterested; unselfish

بي التفات beiltifát inattentive; impolite

بي التفاتي beiltifátí *f.* inattention; discourtesy

بيالوجي bajālodzhí *f.* biology

بيالوجي پوه bajālodzhipóh *m.* biologist

بيالوژيکي جنگ bjālozhikí dzhang *m.* biological warfare

بياله bjālá *f.* *dialect* ☞ واله

بي امان beamán merciless, relentless

بي اماني beamání *f.* mercilessness, relentlessness په بي اماني سره mercilessly

بياموندل bjāmundǝl *transitive* [*present:* بيامومي *past:* بيا يي موند] بياميندل bjāmindǝl [*present:* بيامومي *past:* بيا يي ميند] **1** to find ورپسي ډېر وگرځېدم، لاکن بيا مي نه موند again I looked for him a long time, but again I didn't find him **2** to return **3** to acquire, obtain **4** to restore (e.g., independence)

بيان bajǝ́n *m.* *Arabic* [*plural:* بيانونه bijānúna *Arabic plural:* بيانات bajānát] **1** explanation, exposition; description په بيان راورل to explain, expound **2** utterance, pronouncement; appearance; statement, declaration د بيان حق لرل to have a right to speak **3** story, narrative بيان کول *compound verb* ☞ بيانول

بي انتظام beintizám undisciplined, disorganized; disorderly; disordered, unsettled

بي انتظامي beintizámí *f.* lack of dicipline; disorganization; disorder, confusion, upset, derangement

بي انتها beintihá endless, limitless

بي انتهائي beintihái *f.* endlessness, infinity

بي اندازه beandáze extreme, extraordinary, excessive بي اندازې روپۍ to throw one's money about, squander خرڅول

بي انصاف beinsáf **1** unscrupulous **2** unjust, unfair

بي انصافي beinsāfí *f.* **1** unscrupulousness **2** injustice په هغه باندي ډبره بي انصافي شوی ده They treated him very unfairly.

بي انکشاف beinkisháf undeveloped; underdeveloped

بيان نامه bajānnāmá *f.* announcement, declaration

بيانول bajānavǝ́l *denominative, transitive* [*past:* بيان يي کړ] **1** to explain; to expound, tell, describe ما د هغه نوره قصه بيان کړه I told what else was the matter with him/it. **2** *f.* to express; announce

بيانه bajāná *f.* ☞ بيعانه

بيانېدل bajānedǝ́l *denominative, intransitive* [*past:* بيان شو] to be clarified, be explained; be set forth, be told; be described

بيان bijāṇ *m.* ☞ بهان

بي آواز beāvāz *linguistics* consonant بي آواز صوت consonant sound

بي اوبه beóba waterless, arid بي اوبه مځکي waterless lands, arid lands

بياودانول bjāvadānavǝ́l **1** *denominative, transitive* [*past:* بياودان يي کړ] to restore (something destroyed) **2** *m.* *plural* restoration (of something destroyed)

بي اولاده beavlāda childless

بي اولادي beavlādí *f.* childlessness

بي اهميته beahammijáta insignificant; unimportant دا بي اهميته شی دئ That is of no importance.

بي ايمانه beimān ☞ بي ايمان

بي ايمانتوب beimāntób *m.* **1** treachery; dishonesty; baseness **2** cowardliness بي ايمانتوب کول **a** to behave treacherously **b** to be cowardly

بي ايمانه beimāna **1** untrue, treacherous; dishonest; base, mean **2** cowardly دی ډېر بي ايمانه سړی دئ **a** he's a dishonorable person; he's a scoundrel **b** he's a coward

بي ايماني beimāní *f.* ☞ بي ايمانتوب

بيائي bijān *present tense of* بيول [1]

بيباخېل bibākhél *m.* *plural* Biba-khel' (a clan of the Djadran tribe)

بي بار bebār barren, fruitless

بي باکه bebāka **1.1** careless, carefree **1.2** incautious **1.3** unsuitable; unscrupulous, dishonest **2.1** carelessly, without a care **2.2** incautiously

بي باکي bebākí *f.* **1** carelessness, lightheartedness **2** lack of caution **3** unseemly behavior **4** reckless bravery, foolhardiness

بي بال وير bebāl-u-par helpless

بي بال وېري bebāl-u-parí *f.* helplessness

بي باوره bebāvára uncertain

بي بخت bebákht unfortunate, unhappy

بي بختي bebakhtí *f.* bad luck

ببودي bebudǝj *f.* ☞ بهبودی [2]

بي برخي bebárkhi deprived (of something); disinherited; unfortunate, hapless

بي بار bebára ☞ بي بر

بيبکه bibǝ́ka *f.* *diminutive of* بي بي [1] 3, 4

بي بها bebahā priceless

بي برخي bebahrá ☞ بي بره

بي بي ¹ bibí *f.* بیبي [*plural:* بي بیاني bibijāni] **1** lady **2** princess **3** elder sister **4** grandmother, grandma *idiom* بي بي اوښه praying mantis ☞ بخملی ¹

بي بي ² bebé *f. children's speech* **1** book **2** lesson **3** paper

بیپاري bepārí *m.* client (purchaser)

بیپاما bepāma ☞ بي فکر

بي پاجابه bepājāba بي پایاوه bepājāva bottomless (of the sea) *idiom* څوک بي پایابه کول to destroy, liquidate someone

بي پایه bepāja **1** limitless, endless **2** of unknown origin, without clan or tribe **3** uncertain, unreliable, inconstant

بي پتول bepataból *denominative, transitive* [*past:* بې پته یې کړ] to disgrace, defame, discredit

بي پته bepáta **1** dishonest; untrue, treacherous, insidious **2** unworthy of respect بي پته کیدل ☞ بي پتبدل

بي پتي bepatí *f.* **1** disloyalty, treachery, craftiness **2** shameful business

بي پتبدل bepatedól *intransitive* [*past:* بې پته شو] to be disgraced, be dishonored

بي پرته bepárta **1** shameless **2** talkative

بیپرتي bepartí *f.* **1** shamelessness **2** talkativeness بیپرتي ¹

بیپرتي ² bepártaj gluttonous, voracious

بي پر دگي bepardagí *f.* **1** failure (of woman) to wear a veil **2** open face, uncovered face **3** disgrace, dishonor

بي پرده bepardá disgraced, shamed بي پرده کول **a** to disgrace **b** to ruin بي پرده کیدل **a** to be disgraced, be shamed بي پرده مه سي! Don't shame yourself, Preserve your honor! **b** to fall into poverty, be ruined

بي پر دگي bepardagí *f.* ☞ بي پر دگي

بي پردي bepardé **1** without a veil, uncovered (of the face) بي پردي کول to uncover the face **2** close (of relationship) بي پردي یار close friend

بي پروا beparvā **1** careless, unconcerned **2** hasty, rash, unconsidered **3** inattentive; discourteous

بي پروایي beparvāí *f.* **1** carelessness, lack of concern **2** hastiness, rashness **3** inattention; discourtesy

بیپل bipál *m.* ☞ بلاغند

بي پولي bepulí *f.* lack of money, impecuniousness

بیت ¹ bajt *m. Arabic* [*plural:* بیتونه bajtúna *Arabic plural:* ابیات abját] *Arabic* **1** couplet (verse of two lines) **2** song

بیت ² bet *m.* reed, rush

بیت ³ bajt *m. Arabic* house, heart, family

بیت ⁴ bet *m. dialect* espionage

بیتاب، بیتاب betāb **1** weak, grown weak **2** impatient **3** aroused, disturbed, upset

بیتابه betāba uneasy, restless, agitated

بي تابي betābi *f.* **1** powerlessness, weakness **2** impatience **3** uneasiness, agitation

بي تار betār wireless

بیتار ² bajtār *m.* ☞ بیطار

بي تاریخه betāríkha undated

بیت الخلا bajtulkhalā *f. Arabic* bathroom, toilet

بیت المال bajt-ul-māl *m. Arabic* **1** treasury **2** escheat

بیت المقدس bajt-ul-muḳaddas *m.* Jerusalem (city) د بیت المقدس ښار Jerusalem (city)

بیت بافي betbāfí *f.* manufacture of wicker furniture

بي تجربگي betadzribagí *f.* inexperience, innocence

بي تجربه betadzhribá inexperienced, innocent

بي ترتیب betartíb بي ترتیبه betartíba disorderly, untidy; irregular

بي ترتیبي betartibí *f.* disorder; irregularity

بي ترس betárs ☞ ناترس

بیتري betrí *f.* ☞ بیتري

بي تعلیمي beta'alimí *f.* illiteracy; lack of education

بي تکلفه betakallúfa **1** simple, plain **2** unconstrained, natural

بي تکلفي betakallufí *f.* **1** simplicity, plainness **2** naturalness, freedom from constraint

بي تکلیفه betaklífa simple, plain ساده بي تکلیفه ډوډۍ a simple treat

بي تمیز betamíz reckless, rash, hasty

بي تمیزي betamizí *f.* recklessness, hastiness, rashness بي تمیزي کول to behave recklessly, behave hastily

بي توجه betavadzhdzhúh **1** inattentive **2** discourteous

بي توجهي betavadzhdzhuhí *f.* **1** inattention **2** discourtesty

بي توقع betavaḳḳó' unreliable

بیتومن bitúman *m. plural* shale, slate

بیتون betón *m. plural* concrete

بیتي betí *m. dialect* spy, scout

بیت ¹ beṭ *m.* **1** reinforcement, help, assistance بیت ورکول to help, send reinforcements **2** good tempering (of steel)

بیت ² beṭ *m.* steppe

بیتري beṭrí *f.* battery

بیتک beták *m.* **1** male half (of a home) **2** *Eastern* living room

بیتني ¹ bejṭaní *m. plural* Betani (tribe) **2** Betanaj (member of Betani tribe)

بیته bíṭa *f.* foot (of a mountain)

بي ثبات besabāt unstable, inconstant, changeable

بي ثباتي besabātí *f.* instability, inconstancy, changeableness

بي ثمره besamára fruitless, vain, futile

بي ثمري besamarí *f.* fruitlessness, futility, vainness

بي جان bedzhān inanimate; dead; lifeless

بیجک bidzhák *m.* way bill, invoice; bill

بیجلي bidzháli *f. plural* a game of babki, knucklebones بیجلي کول to play babki, knucklebones

بجوري bedzhoṛé incomparable; superlative, remarkable

بیچ bech *m.* bich *m.* possibility

بیچارگي bechāragí *f.* **1** poverty, need, destitution **2** helplessness په ډېره بیچارگی with great difficulty, just barely *idiom*

بیچاره ¹ bechárá **1.1** poor, destitute **1.2** helpless; powerless **2** *m.* [*plural:* بیچاره گان bechāragán] **.1** poor man **2.2** poor devil

بي چاره ² bechāra out of work, nothing to do

بې چارگي bechāragí f. ☞ بې چاره گي

بيچانه bichāṇa f. Eastern بيچاوڼه bichāuṇa f. bed بيچانه غورول to make (up) a bed

بې چورته bechúrta thoughtlessly, rashly

بې چورتي bechurtí f. thoughtlessness, rashness

بې چيني bechejní f. regional agitation; uneasiness, alarm

بېځانه bedzāna insensible; lifeless

بېځايه bedzāja 1.1 unsuitable, useless, empty په بېځايه کارو to be idle, loaf, do nothing 1.2 knocked out, forced out بېځايه کول to knock out, force out 1.3 له ځايه بېځايه کول to move, shift, displace 2 in vain, for nothing; out of place, not to the point بېځايه گډېدل to interfere inappropriately (into someone else's affairs, in a conversation) بېځايه خبري مه کوه! ، بېځايه مه وېږره! Don't chatter to no purpose! ... بېځايه به نه وي It's not out of place to mention that ...

بې ځنډه bedzánḍa urgently, quickly, without delay

بې خښتنتنه betsaḵẖtána ownerless

بې کس betsók ☞ بې کوک

بې کسي betsoktjá f. ☞ بې کوکتيا

بې کسه betsóka ☞ بې کوکه

بېڅه bétsa f. kind of grass used as fodder; fodder grass

بې څه betsә́ useless

بېحاصله behāsíla fruitless, futile, (in) vain, idle

بې حاله behāla 1.1 feeling ill; weakened 1.2 faint 2 insensible, fainted

بې حالي behālí f. 1 ill feeling; weakness 2 faint

بې حده behádda 1 limitless, unlimited; huge بې حده ډېر an enormous quantity, a whole lot 2 boundlessly, infinitely

بې حرکته behapakáta motionless, unmoving, immovable

بې حرکتي behapakatí f. 1 immobility 2 passivity

بې حرمت behurmát 1 not respected 2 shamed, disgraced

بې حرمتي behurmatí f. dishonor, disgrace

بې حسابه behisāba countless, huge

بې حسه behíssa grow numb; insensible, unfeeling

بې حوصله behavsilá 1 impatient 2 unbearable 3 sluggish (of a person) 4 downhearted, depressed

بې حوصله گي behavsilagí f. 1 impatience 2 intolerability 3 sluggishness 4 depression, downheartedness

بې حيا، بېحيا behajā immodest, shameless, bold; cynical

بې حياتوب behajā́tób m. بې حيائي behajāí f. immodesty; shamelessness, boldness, cynicism

بې خاونده bekhāvә́nda ownerless

بې خبره bekhabár بې خبره bekhabára unknowledgable, uninformed, ignorant د خطر څخه بې خبر وو They didn't know of the danger. خوک بې خبر له... څخه ځان بې خبر کول نيول to ignore something idiom to take someone unawares

بې خبري bekhabarí f. 1 ignorance بېخبري بيانول to claim ignorance 2 rudeness, bad manners

بېخجن bekhdzhә́n well-founded, sound, serious

بېخدار bekhdār بېخداره نباتات root plants

بې خرتى bekhraṭáj m. unconsidered behavior, rashness بې خرتى کول to behave recklessly

بې خرڅه bekhártsa moneyless, impecunious بې خرڅه کېدل to be ruined, be left without money or means

بې خطره bekhatár بې خطره bekhatára safe, secure

بې خطري bekhatarí f. safety, security

بېخ کني bekhkaní f. ruin, destruction, extermination

بېخدار bekh larúnkaj ☞ بېخدار

بېخ نيوى bekhnívaj m. literal establishing bases; laying a foundation

بېخواب bekhāb sleepless

بېخوابي bekhābí f. insomnia, sleeplessness

بې خوبه bekhóba ☞ بېخواب

بې خوبي bekhóbaj ☞ بېخواب

بېخوابي bekhobí f. ☞ بېخوابي

بېخوده bekhúda 1 having lost consciousness, fainted 2 drunken 3 having lost self control بېخوده کول a to cause to faint b to make drunk, intoxicate c to drive to distraction بېخوده کېدل a to lose consciousness, fall into a faint b to get drunk c to lose one's self control

بېخودي behudí f. 1 loss of consciousness, unconsciousness 2 intoxication

بې خوښي bekhvákhaj unwillingly, without wanting to

بې خوښي bekhvakhí f. unwillingness, reluctance

بې خولي bekhulé 1 meek, uncomplaining, submissive 2 stumbling (in speech); confused, distracted بې خولي کېدل a to be meek, be uncomplaining b to stumble (in speech); to be confused, be distracted

بې خونده bekhvánda 1 unpalatable; tasteless 2 poor; (having been) ruined 3 disordered, out of order بې خونده کېدل a to grow poor; to ruin oneself, to be ruined b to become disordered 4 absurd, senseless, foolish بې خونده خبري کول to talk nonsense, talk foolishness

بې خوندي bekhvandí f. lack of taste, bad taste

بې خوېش bekhésh without kith or kin; homeless, stateless

بېخي bekhí bikhí 1 altogether; absolutely; very دا بېخي دروغ دي That's an out-and-out lie 2 (with negation) not at all, not in the least

بې خيري bekhajrí f. uselessness

وله bed m. willow tree ☞ بېد

بېدار bedār 1 vigilant, unsleeping 2 watchful, indefatigable 3 conscious; deliberate; aware

بېدارول bedāravál denominative, transitive [past: بېداري کړ] 1 to awaken, wake (someone) up 2 to urge caution, watchfulness 3 to foster awareness

بېداري bedārí f. 1 vigilance; keeping awake; awakening; (military) reveille د بېداري اشاره blowing of reveille 2 reality دا خوب لېدل وو او نه بېداري وه That was in a dream, and not in reality. 3

awakening, appearance (of a feeling) **4** vigilance **5** awareness
بیداری اچول **a** to show watchfulness **b** to show awareness

بیداریدل bedāredэl *denominative, intransitive* [*past:* بیدار شو] **1** to wake up, awaken, arise **2** to awaken, appear (of a feeling) **3** to be vigilant **4** to be aware **5** to beware (of), be careful (of)

بی داغ bedāgh unsullied, clean

بیدانه bedāná seedless (of raisins, berries, etc.)

بی درده bedárda hard, callous, pitiless

بی دردي bedardí *f.* callousness, ruthlessness

بی درکه bedárka not covered by income, exceeding income (of an expense)

بی درنگه bediránga quickly, without delay

بی دل bedíl **1** grieved, distressed, sad, depressed **2** *poetic* passionately in love

بی دماغه bedimāgha bedamāgha hot-tempered, irritable

بی دماغي bedimāghí *f.* bedamāghí *f.* shortness of temper, irascibility, irritability

بیدمشک bedmúshk *m.* Egyptian willow tree

بی دمه bedáma **1** lifeless **2** disobedient

بیدو bedú **1** the same **2** exactly, to the letter

بی دوا bedavā incurable

بی دودي bedodí *f.* inobservance of a custom

بیدول bidavэl *denominative, transitive* [*past:* بیده یې کړ] to put to sleep, lull

بی دولت bedavlát **1.1** not wealthy, poor, propertyless **1.2** unfortunate, unsuccessful **2** *m.* **.1** poor man **2.2** failure, unlucky person

بی دولتي bedavlatí *f.* **1** unluckiness **2** poorness, poverty

بیدونه bidavэna *f.* putting to sleep, lulling

بیده ¹ bidэ بیده bidá *f. m.* [*plural:* بیده bidэ *f. plural:* بیدې bidé] **1** sleeping **2** *figurative* dozing; latent, unused

بیده ² bedá *f.* dried green forage in bunches; hay

بیده ³ bidá *feminine singular of* بیده ¹

بیدیا bedjā *f.* plain; steppe

بیدیاني bedjānáj **1** *adjective* of the plain, steppe **2** unpolished, uncouth

بیدیدل bidedэl *denominative, intransitive* [*past:* بیده شو] **1** to sleep; to fall asleep **2** *figurative* to remain in ignorance

بیدیدنه bidedэna *f. m.* [*plural:* بیدیده bidedэ] dream; sleep د بیدیدنه سامان bedclothes

بی دین bedín **1** unbeliever **2** *m.* godless person, atheist

بیدیني bediní *f.* godlessness, atheism

بی ډپه beḍába absurd, senseless

بی ډوله beḍávla **1** shapeless, formless **2** ugly **3** ill-bred

بیډون beḍavэn uncouth, unpolished

بی ډوي beḍaví *f.* fearlessness

بی ډهی beḍáj *f.* knucklebone (of an animal, used in games)

بی ذوقه bezávka **1** tasteless, bad tasting **2** insipid, vapid, flat; unsalted

بیر ¹ ber *m. botany* jujube, *Zizyphus*

بیر ² bir *m. plural* beer یو بوتل بیر a bottle of beer

بیرا berā *m.* ☞ بیره ³

بیران berān **1** having lost consciousness, unconscious **2** frozen in one's tracks, gone dumb, stunned

بیرانول ¹ berānavэl *denominative, transitive* [*past:* بیران یې کړ] to render unconscious, cause to faint

بیرانول ² berānavэl *transitive* ☞ ورانول

بیرانه berāna *feminine singular of* بیران

بیراني ¹ berāní *f.* **1** loss of consciousness **2** stupor, stupefaction

بیراني ² berāni *feminine plural of* بیران

بیرانیدل ¹ berānedэl *denominative, intransitive* [*past:* بیران شو] to lose consciousness, faint

بیرانیدل ² berānedэl *denominative, intransitive* ☞ ورانیدل

بی راه berāh **1** good-for-nothing, dissipated; undisciplined **2** mistaken, in error **3** unprincipled, unscrupulous

بی راهي berāchí *f.* **1** uselessness, dissoluteness; lack of discipline **2** error, delusion **3** unscrupulousness

بیرته bérta bírta **1.1** back په بیرته back بیرته اخیستل to take back, take away بیرته پاته کېدل، بیرته پاتي کېدل، بیرته پاتېدل to lag behind (in movement, in study, in development, etc.) بیرته تلل to return بیرته کول to look back **a** to force back **b** to remove; to send away **c** to dismiss **d** to clear away, clean up دا کتاب له مېزه بیرته کئ clear this book off the table **e** to remove (e.g., difficulties) **f** to open (the door; a shop, courses, etc.) **g** to take off (clothing) بیرته کئ! As you were! (military command) بیرته کېدل **a** to retreat, back off; to go away **b** to resign, relinquish a post بیرته گرځېدل، بیرته گرځېدل **a** to move backwards, go from **b** to return **c** *figurative* to back out of (one's word or promise) بیرته ورکول to give back, return **1.2** at some distance, a little way off **1.3** again, anew **2** away, off دلاري بیرته شه Off the road!; Stand Aside!; Away! **3** *predicate* **.1** forced back **3.2** removed, sent away **3.3** cleared away **3.4** open (of a door or window; of a shop, courses, etc.) **3.5** removed (of clothing) **3.6** behind (in movement, in studies, in development, etc.)

بیرته ³ bértapāte ☞ بیرته پاتي

بیرته پاتي توب bertapātetэб *m.* backwardness

بیرته راتگ bertarātág *m.* return

بی رحمانه berahmāná **1** cruel, ruthless **2** cruelly, ruthlessly

بی رحمه beráhma stern, cruel, ruthless بی رحمه زمانه bleak time, bleak times

بی رحمي berahmí *f.* sterness, cruelty, ruthlessness په خورا بی رحمي، بیرحمي very sternly, cruelly, ruthlessly، په زیاته بیرحمي سره

بیرخانه birkhāná *f.* alehouse, pub

بیرړا berṛā *m.* lark

بیرستر beristár *m. regional* lawyer

بی رضا berizā willy-nilly, against one's will; reluctantly

بیرغ bajrágh *m.* banner, flag; signal flag بیرغ درول to hoist a flag بیرغ جگول، بیرغ رپول، بیرغ اوچتول to raise the flag

بيرغ والا bajraghvālā́ m. standard bearer

بيرغ bajrák m. ☞

بیرگال bergál m. water skin from ox hide

بیرل berál m. barrel, cask

بیرلو berló f. attack

بیرلووال berlovā́l m. aggressor

بیرندوکی berəndúkaj cowardly, fearful

بیرنگ ¹ beríng د بیرنگ آبنای بحیره Bering Straits buhajrá-ji Bering Sea

بیرنگ ² beríng m. bearing

بیرنگ ³ bajráng beráng relating to additional payment

بیرنگه beránga colorless

بیرن beráṇ m. wild clover

بی روی berú ☞ بیرو

بیروت bejrút m. bajrút m. Beirut (city)

بی روحه berúha بی روح berúh 1 lifeless, unanimated, inanimate 2 apathetic, listless 3 heartless; soulless

بی روزگاره berozgāra without income, without pay; needy

بی روزگاری berozgārí f. absence of income, absence of pay; want, need

بیراول beravə́l transitive [past: و یی بیراوه] to frighten, scare idiom د خپله لاسه بیراول to be afraid of flying into a rage

بیرون birún berún outside, from without; on the outside د بیرون طرف from without بیرون ته ووځه! regional Get out! idiom له چاپ خخه نه بیرون کبدل to go out of print بیرون غورزول to weed

بیرون نویس birunnavís berunnavís written out (of a word, phrase, etc.), copied out بیرون نویس کول to write out, make an excerpt

بیرونی beruní external, exterior

بی روی berúj shameless; bold, coarse; uncouth

بیره ¹ béra f. fear, fright بیره کول to be afraid, to take fright

بیره ² béra f. ☞ بیر ¹

بیره ³ berá m. [plural: بیرگان bergán plural: بیره گان beragán] regional 1 servant; lackey 2 waiter

بی ریا berjā́ sincere, straightforward

بی ریائی berjāí f. sincerity

بیربدل beredə́l intransitive [past: وبیربده] to fear, take fright; be afraid of

بیریل beril m. plural beryl (mineral)

بیریلیوم beríljúm m. plural beryllium

بیر beṛ m. crowd (of people)

بیرا beṛá 1 stupid; ignorant 2 m. stupid person, dumbbell; simpleton

بیرکی beṛəkáj f. boat

بیره ¹ bíṛa f. 1 hurry, rush; urgency په بیره سره quickly, hurriedly; urgently په ډیره بیره very quickly, most urgently د کار بیره trouble, efforts په یو شی کښی بیره جوړول to hurry with something 2 striving بیره کول to strive for, seek to gain (something)

بیره ² beṛá f. raft

بیری ¹ beṛə́j f. vessel, ship; barge; boat د بیری د پاسه on board تبل وړونکي بیری ferry (boat) د تناو بیری freighter بارووړونکي بیری tanker عسکر الوتکي وړونکي بیری، aircraft carrier طیاره وړونکي بیری landing boat مسافر وړونکي بیری passenger ship د پیاده کوونکي بیری spaceship فضائي بیری minesweeper idiom نقب تولوونکي بیری He was unlucky. He had bad luck. هغه بیری و اوښته

بیری ² beṛə́j m. ☞ بابیری

بیری ³ beṛə́j f. regional shackles, chains; hobble

بیری چلوونکی beṛə́j chlavúnkaj m. captain of a ship

بیریوال beṛəjvā́l m. بیری وال beṛəjvā́lā́ m. boatman, ferryman

بیزار bezār dissatisfied; upset, angered

بیزارول bezāravə́l denominative, transitive [past: بیزار یې کړ] to repel, call forth enmity, disgust

بیزاری bezārí f. dissatisfaction, irritation

بیزاریدل bezāredə́l denominative, intransitive [past: بیزار شو] figurative to experience, feel repulsion, hostility; to turn away from someone هغه ټول څخنی بیزاره سول They all turned from him.

بی زاوي bezāví f. need, want

بی زبانه bezabāna bezubāna speechless, dumb

بی زره bezṛə́ 1 downcast, gloomy 2 weak-spirited, cowardly 3 timid

بی زره توب bezṛətób m. بی زره والی bezṛəvā́laj m. 1 despondency, depression 2 faintheartedness, cowardliness 3 timidity

بیزل bezél transitive [past: و یې بیزه] to darn; mend; sew inconspicuously

بی زمین bezamín بی زمینه کلیوال bezamíng landless a بی زمین landless peasant b the landless peasantry

بیزو bizó 1 f. [plural: بیزوگانی bizogā́ni] monkey 2 m. [plural: بیزوگان bízogán] male monkey idiom د بیزو پرهار څنی جوړول a to exaggerate some matter b to drag out some business

بی زوره bezóra weak, powerless

بیزه bezá f. dailect ☞ وزه ²

بی ژبی ¹ bezhə́baj 1 dumb, speechless 2 untrustworthy, treacherous

بی ژبي ² bezhə́bi f. breaking a promise, treachery

بیگدن begdə́n m. weathercock; fickle person, changeable person

بی غه begágha linguistics consonant

بی ږوږه begvága 1 noiselessly, without noise 2 without a murmur بی ږوږه منل to agree without a murmur

بی سا besā inanimate بی سا شیان inanimate objects بی سا نمونه grammar inanimate nouns

بی سابقی besābiḱá unusual, unheard of, without precedent

بی ساری besāraj unusual, unprecedented; without equal په بی ساری اندازه besāri of unusual proportions

بی سا besāh ☞ بی ساه

بی سترگو bestə́rgo eyeless, blind

بی ستره besátra 1 uncovered; bare, naked 2 dishonored, disgraced

بی ستری besatrí f. 1 baring, uncovering, denudation 2 figurative dishonor, disgrace

بېستۍ bestə́j *f.* besatə́j *f.* kind of fabric, coarse calico

بې سدتیا besədtjā́ *f.* loss of consciousness; faint

بېسدول besədavə́l *denominative, transitive* [*past:* بېسده يې کړ] to cause to faint, render unconscious

بې سده besə́da 1.1 having lost consciousness, fainted, insensible 1.2 stupid 1.3 *figurative* inebriated بې سده کول a to cause to lose consciousness, cause to faint b to drive insane c *figurative* to make drunk بې سده کېدل a to lose consciousness, faint b to become foolish c *figurative* to get drunk 2 unusually, unbelievably بې سده ښنه سړی دئ He is an exceptionally fine person.

بې سدي besədí *f.* fainting fit, unconsciousness, loss of consciousness

بې سرايت besirājā́t disinfected بې سرايت کول to disinfect

بې سروسامان besar-u-sāmā́n 1 disinherited, deprived of a livelihood, needy 2 stupid

بې سروساماني besar-u-sāmā́ní *f.* 1 need, a difficult material situation 2 stupidity, foolishness

بې سره besára neglected; stray, homeless; leaderless بي سره او بي سره a tramp b بي سره او بي ښکره سری neglected; stray ښکره disorderly, chaotic, poorly organized

بې سره والی besaravā́laj *m.* neglect

بې سري besarí *f.* 1 ☞ بې سره والی 2 disorder

بېسواده besavā́da illiterate

بېسوادي besavā́dí *f.* illiteracy

بې سود besúd bearing no interest بې سود روپۍ non-interest-bearing loan

بې شانه besijāl ☞ بې سيال

بې سپکه beséka weak, powerless; feeble

بې سيم besím wireless بېسيم تېلگراف radio-telegraph

بې شانه beshāna unusually, extraordinarily, exceptionally

بې شبهه beshúbha undoubted, indubitable; definite

بې شرمه beshárma shameless; obscene, indecent; immodest بي خان بي شرمه کول to become insolent

بې شرمي besharmí *f.* shamelessness; obscenity; immodesty

بې شک beshák بېشک beshákk بې شکه besháka بېشکه beshákka 1 undoubted, irrefutable, indisputable 2 undoubtedly, indisputably, absolutely, certainly بې شک! بې شکه بې شکه! Certainly!

بې شماره beshumā́ra innumerable, countless

بې شمځی beshamdzə́j invertebrate

بې شمبره beshméra ☞ بې شماره

بې بنځي beḳhə́dzi unmarried, single, bachelor

بې بنې beḳhé useless, futile; needless, good-for-nothing

بې صبر besábr بې صبره besábra impatient

بې صبري besabrí *f.* impatience

بې ضرر bezarár harmless, inoffensive

بې ضرري bezararí *f.* harmlessness, inoffensiveness

بيطار bajtār *m. Arabic* veterinarian

بيطاري bajtārí *f.* veterinary medicine

بې طاقته betāḳáta 1 grown weak, collapsed; weak 2 impatient

بې طالعه betālí'a unfortunate, unhappy

بې طبقاتو betabaḳāto classless بي طبقاتو جامعه classless society

بېطرف betaráf neutral

بې طرفانه betarafānā́ neutral, neutralist بي طرفانه سياست policy of neutrality

بې طرفدار betaraftdār impartial, unbiased

بېطرفه betaráfa ☞ بېطرف

بېطرفي betarafí *f.* neutrality د بېطرفي ماتول to violate neutrality بېطرفي مراعات کول to observe neutrality

بې طمعه betám'a disinterested; unselfish

بې طمعي betam'aí *f.* disinterestedness, unselfishness

بيع báj' *f.* báj'a *f. Arabic* ☞ بيعه¹ د بيع قطعي قباله deed of purchase بيع وفا báj'-i document concerning sale

بيعانه baj'ānā *f.* deposit, advance

بيعت baj'át *m. Arabic history* recognition of authority (of a feudal lord); vow to serve faithfully; oath of a vassal (to his suzerain) د چا سره بيعت کول to acknowledge someone's authority, pledge loyalty (to a suzerain)

بېعدالتي be'adālatí *f.* injustice, unfairness

بې عزته be'izzát ☞ بې عزته

بې عزتول be'izzatavə́l *denominative, transitive* [*past:* بې عزته يې کړ] to dishonor, disgrace

بې عزته be'izzáta dishonored, disgraced بې عزته کول to dishonor, disgrace

بې عزتي be'izzatí *f.* dishonor, disgrace

بېعقل be'áḳl stupid; foolhardy, reckless *saying,* بېعقل وړاندي ځي، A stupid person goes وروسته نه ګوري، عاقل وړاندي ځي، وروسته ګوري ahead and doesn't look back; a clever person goes ahead, but looks back

بېعقل توب be'aḳltób *m.* stupidity; foolhardiness, recklessness

بېعقله be'áḳla ☞ بېعقل

بېعقلي be'aḳlí *f.* ☞ بېعقل توب

بې علاقې be'alāḳé unconcerned, neutral, indifferent

بې علمه be'ílma ignorant; uneducated

بې علمي be'ilmí *f.* ignorance; lack of education

بيع نامه baj'nāmá *f.* deed of purchase

بيعه báj'a *f.* ☞ بيعه¹ a expensive, dear b at a high price, dearly د چا سره بيعه کول to sell to someone

بې عيب be'ájb بې عيبه be'ájba perfect, irreproachable

بې غاښو beghāḳho toothless

بې غرض begharáz 1 disinterested, unselfish; uninterested 2 carefree, unconcerned; careless

بې غرضانه begharazānā́ 1 unselfish (of behavior) 2 unselfishly

بې غرضه begharáza ☞ بې غرض

بې غرضي begharazí *f.* 1 unselfishness, disinterestedness; lack of interest 2 unconcern, lightheartedness; carelessness

بې غږه baghága 1 noiseless; quiet 2 noiselessly; quietly

بغمه **begháma 1** carefree, unconcerned; peaceful په بغمه زړه in a carefree manner; peacefully بغمه اوسه! Don't worry! **2** secluded; sheltered; cozy

بغمي **beghamí** *f.* lightheartedness, lack of concern; peacefulness د پره بغمي spiritual tranquility په د پره بغمي very lightheartedly, in a most unconcerned manner

بې غوره **baghávra 1** rashly, without thinking **2** negligently, carelessly

بې غوري **beghavrí** *f.* **1** rashness **2** negligence, carelessness د بې غوری او غفلت په سترګه کتل to have a careless attitude toward something

بغيرته **beghajráta 1** shameless; disgraceful, dishonorable **2** timid; fainthearted, cowardly **3** mean, base

بغيرتي، بې غيرتي **beghajratí** *f.* **1** shame, dishonor **2** timidity; faintheartedness, cowardice **3** meanness, baseness

بې فائدې **befáidé 1** useless دا بې فائدی کار دئ That's no help. **2** of no use, in vain

بې فقاري **befaḳārí** invertebrate بې فقاریه حیوانات invertebrate animals

بې فکر **befíkr 1** carefree, unconcerned; frivolous **2** inattentive, careless, negligent

بې فکري **befíkrí** *f.* **1** lightheartedness, lack of concern; frivolity **2** inattention, negligence بې فکري کول to exhibit inattentiveness, carelessness; to neglect, disregard **3** thoughtless, inability to think things out **4** rashness

بې فهمه **befáhma** slow-witted, dull, dense

بې قاعدګي **beḳā'idagí** *f.* irregularity, incorrectness; anomaly

بې قائده **beḳā'idá** incorrect, irregular; anomalous

بې قاعدیوالی **beḳā'idaválaj** *m.* ☞ بقاعدګي

بې قائدي **beḳā'idé** ☞ بې قائده

بې قدره **beḳádra 1** unworthy, contemptible **2** useless, good-for-nothing

بې قدري **beḳadrí** *f.* **1** unworthiness, contemptibility **2** uselessness

بې قراره **beḳarāra 1** uneasy, anxious کول _ to worry **2** inconstant, unstable, changeable

بې قراري **beḳarārí** *f.* **1** uneasiness, anxiety **2** inconstancy, instability, changeableness

بې قصور **beḳusúr** innocent (of), not guilty

بې قيد، بې قيده **beḳájd beḳájda** undisciplined; unbridled, ungovernable

بې قيدي **beḳajdí** *f.* lack of discipline, dissoluteness; unruliness

بیک¹ **bjak** *m.* **1** harpoon **2** oar

بک² **bek** *m.* younger brother of a khan; bek

بېکار بېکاره **bekār bekāra 1.1** idle بېکار ناست دئ He sits idle. **1.2** apathetically **2** unemployed بېکار خلق، بېکاره سړي *saṛí* the unemployed **3** *m.* unemployed person

بېکاري **bekārí** *f.* **1** unemployment **2** idleness

بیکال **bajkāl** *m.* د بیکال غدیر Lake Bajkal

بې کچ **bekách** unmeasurable, unlimited, infinite

بې کډي **bekáḍi 1** non-nomadic, non-migrating **2** *adjective* unmarried, single, bachelor

بې کسه، بېکسه bekás، بېکس **bekása 1** without a breadwinner (of a family) **2** without close friends or relatives; lone, solitary **3** defenseless, unprotected

بې کسي، بېکسي **bekasí** *f.* **1** lack of a bread-winner (in a family) **2** loneliness, being alone **3** defenselessness

بې کماله **bekamāla** uneducated; undeveloped; ill-bred

بېکن **bekán** *m.* beacon

بې کوره **bekóra 1** homeless **2** single, unmarried, bachelor, without family

بېگ **beg** *m.* ☞ بیګ

بېګا **begā 1** last night, yesterday evening بېګا شپه last night; yesterday evening د بېګا نه this evening, tonight بل بېګا since evening night before last **2** *m.* yesterday evening, last night

بېګار **begār** *m.* **1** forced labor, hard labor; labor obligation په بېګار نيول to recruit to a labor obligation **2** corvée

بېگاري **bagārí 1** mobilized for compulsory labor **2** *m.* worker recruited by force or one fulfilling a labor obligation

بېګانګي **begánagí** *f.* estrangement; separation, alienation

بېګانه **begāná 1** alien, unfamiliar; strange, foreign بېګانه خلق unfamiliar people, strangers د چا څخه ځان بېګانه نيول to shun someone **2** foreign, from another country

بيګاني **begánaj** *adjective* (of) yesterday بيګاني شپه last night

بېګاه **begāh** ☞ بېګا

بېگتوت **begtút** *m.* Begtut (village near Kabul)

بې ګټي **begáṭi 1.1** useless, vain **1.2** unsuccessful, having no result **2.1** uselessly, vainly **2.2** unsuccessfully, futilely

بېګذراني **beguzarāni** *f.* need

بېگر **begór** *m.* monal (Himalayan pheasant, *Lophophorus*)

بې ګرزه **begárza 1** without dust **2** dust-free, clean بې ګرزه هوا air free of dust, pure air

بېگړا **begṛā** languid; lazy

بيگل **bigál** *m.* bugle, horn, trumpet

بېګم **begám** *f.* Miss (in addressing foreign females)

بېګناه، بیګنا **begunāh** innocent

بېګناهي **begunāhí** *f.* innocence خپله بېګناهي ثبتول to prove one's innocence

بېگانی **beganáj** ☞ بيګاني

بېگی **begój** *f. cards* the queen

بېل¹ **bel** particular; separate; another په بېل ډول particularly; separately دا بېله خبره ده that's another matter, that's a special question

بېل² **bel** *m.* shovel; spade د استحکام بېل sapper shovel

بېل³ **bel** *m.* ☞ بلاغند

بېل بېل **belābel** ☞ بېلابېل

بی لاري belāri 1 without roads; impassable 2 *figurative* erring, mistaken بی لاري گرزیدل a to wander, roam b *figurative* to err, to be mistaken 3 *figurative* unprincipled 4 *figurative* lawlessness

بی لاري belārí f. 1 absence of roads 2 *figurative* error, delusion 3 *figurative* unscrupulousness 4 *figurative* lawlessness

بیلان bilān m. بیلانس bilānas m. *finance* balance (sheet) کالنی بیلان yearly balance بیلان ترتیبول to compile a balance

بیلاو belāv m. touchstone; whetstone

بیل بیل bel-bél 1 various, different په بیل بیل ځای a in different places b in special cases په بیله بیله ډول in different ways بنه ځرگندیدل to appear in various forms 2.1 in detail; point by point 2.2 especially; individually, separately بیل بیل ته for each one individually د بیل بیل نه each has individually

بیلتانه beltāná *oblique singular of* بیلتون

بیلتون beltún m. بیلتیا beltjá f. 1 separation, parting بیلتون ننامار پر لاري پروت دئ Separation, the serpent, lay in his path (from a song) بیلتانه وسوم، غم ایري کړم *folklore* Separation has consumed me; grief has turned me to ashes. 2 distinction 3 alienation, separation 4 *regional* divorce (from one's wife)

بیلچه belchá f. small shovel

بی لحاظ belihāz crude, coarse, impolite

بیلدار beldār m. 1 unskilled laborer (who uses a shovel) 2 sapper, combat engineer

بیلډنگ bílḍíng m. tall building

بیلزوم beluzúm superfluous, excessive, leftover

بی لزومه beluzúma excessively, unnecessarily, superfluously

بی لږ و ډیر be lǝg-u-ḍér 1 irreproachable 2 fully, completely, altogether

بی لفظي belafzí f. ☞ بی لوظي

بیلک belák m. 1 gifts sent by a bridegroom to his bride's home 2 rival, competitor

بیلگه belgá f. 1 (piece of) evidence; trace, track, sign بیلگه موندل to find evidence; to hit upon a trail 2 sign, mark, indication

بیلل belǝl *transitive* ☞ بایلل

بیلماز belmāz 1 (someone) not completing his prayers 2 menstruating

بیلمانځتیا belmāndztjá f. ☞ بیلمانځي

بیلمانځه belmāndzǝ ☞ بیلماز

بیلمانځي belmāndzí f. 1 noncompletion of prayer 2 menstrual period

بیلنه belǝna f. 1 ☞ بیلوالی سره کول to be separated, be divided, be disunited 2 separation, parting 3 distance, space, interval

بیلنه bilána belána f. rolling pin (for rolling out dough)

بیلنه bajlǝna f. loss

بیلنی belǝnaj m. *botany* mint

بیلواله belvála f. بیلوالی belválaj m. 1 separation, division, disconnection د کارو بیلواله distribution or assignment of obligations 2 difference, distinction 3 weaning 4 parting, separation

بیلوروس belorús White Russian, Byelorussian

بیلوروسي belorusí *adjective* 1 White Russian, Byelorussian ژبه the White Russian language, Byelorussian 2 White Russian, Byelorussian

بیلوروسیه belorusijá f. Byelorussia

بی لوظي belavzí f. breaking one's word or promise بی لوظي کول not to keep one's word, to break a promise

بیلول belavǝl *denominative, transitive* [*past:* بیل یي کړ] 1 to separate, divide, disconnect 2 to distinguish, differentiate 3 to wean 4 to part, separate

بیلونه belavǝna f. 1 ☞ بیلوالی 2 weaning

بیله belá f. 1 trough, gutter (for draining of water) 2 branch (of a river) 3 small island; sandbar, shallows

بیله béla *preposition* ☞ بی

بیله belá f. whistle

بیله béla *feminine singular of* بیل

بیلیدل beledǝl *denominative, intransitive* [*past:* بیل شو] 1 to be separated, be divided, be disconnected 2 to be distinguished, be differentiated 3 to be weaned 4 to be diverted (of a canal) 5 to part, separate (from someone)

بیم bim m. 1 fear, fright, scare, apprehension 2 ☞ بیمه

بیم bim m. 1 root of the cattail 2 ☞ مورلی

بیمار bimār 1 sick; feeling indisposed 2 dejected *idiom* بیماري a languid eyes b sleepy eyes *idiom* په زره بیمار یم I'm sick سترگي at heart.

بیمارپرستي bimārparastí f. care for a sick person کول to look after a sick person

بیمارخانه bimārkhāná f. hospital

بیمارول bimāravǝl *denominative, transitive* [*past:* بیماري یي کړ] to cause (someone's) illness, make sick; provoke (someone's) indisposition

بیماري bimārí f. sickness; indisposition

بیماریدل bimāredǝl *denominative, intransitive* [*past:* بیمار شو] to get sick, be sick

بی مالگي bemālgi *indeclinable* fresh, unsalted

بی ماله bemāla indigent, poor

بی مایگي bemājgí f. poverty, indigence

بی مبالاتي bemubálāti f. carelessness, lack of concern; improvidence, lack of thrift

بی متري bemátri weak, powerless

بی مثاله bemisāla بیمثاله، بی مثال، بیمثال unexampled, unparalleled, incomparable

بی مجاله bemadzhāla powerless, weak, helpless

بی محاله bemahálla 1 inappropriate, irrelevant 2 inappropriately, inopportunely

بی مختوب bemǝkhtób m. 1 shamelessness, impudence 2 inattentiveness, rudeness 3 indifference

بی مخه bemǝkha 1 shameless, impudent 2 inattentive, impolite 3 indifferent

بی مختوب ☞ .bemakhí *f* بی مخي [1]

بی مخه ☞ bemə́khaj [2]

بی مرمي bemarmí blank (catridge), dummy

بی مروت bemuruvát 1 inhuman, cruel, heartless 2 uncultured 3 mean, base

بی مروتي bemuruvatí *f.* 1 inhumanity, cruelty 2 boorishness, uncivilized ways 3 baseness, meanness

بی مراني bemərāni inhuman, cruel

بی مزگي bemazagí *f.* 1 absence of flavor (in a food), tastelessness 2 colorless, inexpressiveness 3 coolness, discord (between friends)

بی مزه bemazá 1 tasteless, bad-tasting 2 colorless, inexpensive 3 unpleasant 4 grown wearisome; become boring

بی مزي bemázi بی مزي تېلگراف بسيم besím وايرليس wājarlis wireless radio telegraph

بی مزیه خبری اتری bemazija khabəreatə́re *plural* wireless communication

بیمصرفه bemasráfa unsuitable, unnecessary

بی معنی bema'nā bema'ní 1 senseless, absurd; stupid 2 vain, foolish, futile

بی مغزه bemághza 1 stupid 2 insubstantial; emasculated

بی ملاحظي bemulāhazé 1 hasty, precipitate, unconsidered 2 impartial, unbiased

بی مناسبه bemunāsíba 1 inappropriate, irrevelant بی مناسبه به نه وي ... it won't be out of place ... 2 unsuitable (of food)

بی منع bemán'a 1 free, clear, unimpeded 2 freely, without hindrance

بی موجب bemudzhíb 1 causeless; pointless 2 without cause, without reason

بیمورد bemauríd inappropriate; unsuitable بیمورده به نه وي It won't be inappropriate (to announce, to say, etc.)

بی موقع bemauḱe' 1 inappropriate, unsuitable 2 inopportune, untimely 3 excessive (of expenditures)

بیمي bimá *f.* insurance د بیمي موسسه insurance company د ترانزیت بیمه accident insurance د پینبو بیمه اجرت insurance payment زراعتي بیمه life insurance د حیات بیمه freight insurance د سوگبدلو بیمه insurance against natural disasters in agriculture د غلا بیمه fire insurance د صحي بیمه theft insurance د صحي بیمه health insurance بیمه کول property insurance *compound verb* to insure بیمه کېدل *compound verb* to be insured, take out insurance

بی مهر bemíhr unfriendly, hostile

بی مهري bemihrí *f.* unfriendliness, hostility

بیمه کوونکی bimá kavúnkaj *m.* insurer

بیمه کېدونکی bimá kedúnkaj *m.* insured

بی میلي bemajlí *f.* unwillingness, disinclination

بی مینی bemíni unfriendly, reserved; unobliging, discourteous

بی مینی توب beminitób *m.* unfriendliness, reserve; discourtesy

بین bín *m.* whistle, pipe, flute [1]

بین الملل bajn *Arabic preposition, prefix* between, among international بین الناس among people [2]

بدبین bín *used as the second part of a compound verb* pessimist خوشبین optimist [3]

بینا bināsighted (not blind), seeing; sharp-sighted

بی ناغي benāghé strictly, rigorously, necessarily

بین الدولي bajn-ul-dául *Arabic* بین الدول بین الاقوامي bajn-ul-aḵvāmí بین الملل bajn-ul-milál *Arabic* بین الملل bajn-ul-milalí international; world (wide) بین الاقوامي جنگ world war د بین الاقوامي قانون international law بین الاقوامي حقوق، بین الاقوامي حق، بین الاقوامي کاریگرو بین الملل موسسه the 'Internationale'

بین النهرین bajn-an-nahrájn *m.* bajn-un-nahrájn *m. Arabic* Mesopotamia, Mesopotamian lowlands (between the Tigris and the Euphrates Rivers)

بی نام benām inglorious, infamous

بی ناموس benāmús dishonorable, disgraceful

بی ناموسي benāmusí *f.* dishonor, disgrace

بینائي bināí *f.* 1 vision 2 sharp-sightedness

بین باجه binbādzhá *f.* bagpipes

بینت bent *m.* 1 reed, rush 2 stick; cane په بینت وهل to strike, beat with a stick بینتو نه خورل to be beaten with a stick

بی نتیجي benatidzhé futile, unsuccessful, vain, purposeless بی نتیجي پاتبدل to prove to be unsuccessful, futile

بینچ bench *m.* bench

بیندي bendí *f.* colored mark between the eyebrows (worn by Hindus)

بیندۍ bində́j *f. regional* okra, *Hibiscus esculentus*

بی نزاکتي benazākatí *f.* tactlessness, indelicacy

بینش binsh *m.* bench *technology* main girder

بی نصیبه benasíba 1 done out of, disinherited; deprived of 2 unworthy of 3 unsuccessful حریص بی نصیبه وي the greedy person is unsuccessful *idiom* له ژونده بی نصیبه کېدل to perish

بی نصیبي benasibí *f.* 1 haplessness; deprivation (of one's share) 2 lack of success

بی نظم benázm unregulated, unorganized; disorderly

بی نظمي benazmí *f.* lack of regulation, disorderliness; disorder *idiom* د خوب بی نظمي restless sleep

بی نظیره benazíra without equal, unusual, unheard of, unprecedented

بینگ bing *m.* root of the erianthus (plume grass)

بینگرۍ bingrə́j *f. botany* loofah

بی مالگي ☞ benamák بی نمک

بی ننگه benánga 1 shameless, impudent 2 base, mean, low 3 cowardly

بی ننگي benangí *f.* 1 shame, dishonor 2 disgraceful behavior, lowdown behavior 3 baseness, meanness 4 cowardliness, faintheartedness

بینوا benavā bínavá poor; very needy, unfortunate

بی نوایي benavāí *f.* poverty, indigence

بی نومه benúma nameless, unknown

بینه bajiná *f. Arabic* irrefutable proof

بې نهايته benihájáta boundless, infinite

بيني biní *used in names of populated areas* بيني حصار Bini Hissar

بې نيازه benijáza **1** well-to-do, well-off; not needing (anyone or anything); independent بې نيازه كول to make indepedent, provide for د ... څخه بې نيازه كېدل to become independent **2** well-to-do

بې نيازي benijází *f.* **1** independence (from someone, something) **2** independent nature **3** well-being

بيني حصار binihisār *m.* Bini Hissar (suburb of Kabul)

بې واده bevādə́ *adjective* unmarried, single, bachelor

بې واره bevāra suddenly, unexpectedly

بې واسطې bevāsité direct, straight

بې واک، بېواکه، بېواک bevāk بې واكه ، بېواكه bevāka **1.1** weak; helpless, powerless **1.2** involuntary **1.3** indecisive **2.1** weakly; helplessly, without power **2.2** involuntarily **2.3** indecisively

بې واكي ، بېواكي bevākí *f.* **1** weakness; helplessness, powerlessness **2** indecisiveness, indecision

بيواى bivā́j *potential form of verb* بېول [1]

بې وټه bevā́ṭa pure, unadulterated

بې وجدانه bevidzhdā́na unscrupulous, dishonest

بې وخته bevákhta inopportunely; at a bad time

بيورو كراتيكي bjurokrātiki bureaucratic

بيورو كراسي bjurokrāsí *f.* bureaucracy

بهوره [1] bevrá *f.* **1** oppression **2** injustice

بهوره [2] bévra **1.1** obvious, evident **1.2** candid, frank (of a conversation) **2.1** obviously, evidently **2.2** candidly, frankly

بهوره bevā́ra unsuitable, inappropriate

بهوزله bevázla ☞ بې وزلي

بې وزلي [1] bevázli **1** poor, indigent, destitute يوه بهوزله ښڅه beggar woman **2** helpless

بې وزلي [2] bevazlí *f.* bevazalí *f.* بهوزلي توب bevazlitób *m.* بهوزلي والى bevazlivā́laj *m.* **1** poverty, need, indigence **2** helplessness

بې وزني bevazní *f.* weightlessness د بې وزنى حالت condition of weightlessness

بې وس bevás بهوسه bevása powerless بې وس كول to force, compel بې وسلې كول bevaslé unarmed بې وسلې كېدل to disarm (intransitive) to disarm

بې وسلې كولl bevaslé kavə́l *m. plural* disarmament

بيو شيمي bioshimí *f.* biochemistry

بيوطنه bevatána banished, exiled; without a homeland, homeless, stateless له وطنه بيوطنه كول to banish, exile

بيوطني bevataní *f.* banishment, exile

بيوفا bevafā not keeping one's word, not fulfilling one's promises; untrue, untrustworthy; traitorous

بې وفائي bevafāí *f.* بهوفائي betrayal of one's word, breaking a promise, infidelity, untrustworthiness, treachery, betrayal بې وفائي كول to betray one's word, to break a promise, act treacherously; to betray

بيوفزيك biofizík *m.* biophysics

بې وقته bevákta inopportunely, not in time (late); at an ill-advised time

بهوقوف، بې وقوف bevukúf **1** stupid, slow-witted, senseless **2** uniformed, ignorant, lacking culture, uneducated

بې وقوفي bevukufí *f.* **1** dullness, stupidity, senselessness **2** ignorance

بيوگراف biográf *m.* biographer

بيوگرافي biográfi *f.* biography خپله بيوگرافي autobiography

بهول [2] bajavə́l *transitive* ☞ بهول

بهولوژيست bajolodzhíst *m.* ☞ بهولوژي پوه

بهولوژي bajólodzhi *f.* ☞ بهولوژي

بهولوژي پوه bajolodzhipóh *m.* بهولوژي دان bajolodzhidán *m.* ☞ بيولوژي پوه

بيولوژي biolozhí **1** *f.* biology **2** biological

بيولوژي پوه biolozhipóh *m.* بيولوژي دان biolozhidán *m.* biologist

بيولوژيكي biolozhikí biological

بهوله bevála artless, unsophisticated; sincere

بيوه [1] bivə́ *imperfect of* بهول [1]

بيوه [2] bivə́ *m. plural* **1** taking away, carrying off, stealing **2** building, breaking (e.g., a road)

بهوه [3] bevá *f.* widow

بهوبري bevéri brave, fearless

بيه [1] bája *f.* **1** price, cost په ارزانه بيه at a low price په ډېره لوړه بيه at a very high price په مناسبه بيه سره at a matching price بيه نه درلودل to set a price بيه كول to ask a price, price **a** to depreciate, be devalued **b** to be priceless; be without equal له بئي *figurative* **a** to beat down the price **b** to spoil (something) په اچول بيه وركول to sell **2** sale and purchase; business, transaction تجارتي بيه ماتول closing a deal د بئي انعقاد بيه تړل to close a deal بيه *trade* to cancel a deal **3** subsciption price, payment

بيه [2] bijá *f.* growth

بهاند behánd *m.* ☞ بهان

بهو behú **1** wild **2** frightened بهو كول **a** to make wild **b** to frighten بهو كېدل **a** to be wild; run wild **b** to be frightened بيو كېدل **a** to be tactless, be rude **b** to do something incompetently

بهودگي behudagí *f.* uselessness, superfluousness, superfluity; senselessness, absurdity

بهوده behudá useless, unnecessary, superfluous; senseless, absurd

بهوده گوی behudagoj *m.* chatterer, windbag, idle talker

بهوده گوئي behudagoí *f.* foolishness, idle chatter, nonsense, idle talk

بهوش behósh بهوشه behósha without feeling, unconscious, in a faint بهوش شه *dialect* He has lost consciousness.

بهوشي behoshí *f.* loss of consciousness, fainting spell بهوشي ته نژدي close to fainting

بهوښ behókh بهوښنه behókha ☞ بهوش

بهوښي behokhí *f.* ☞ بهوښي ، بې هوښني

بهووالج behuvā́laj *m.* **1** wildness, savagery **2** fright

بې هيبه behajbáta brave, fearless, intrepid

بی هېڅه behétsa to no purpose, without cause, for nothing; not for anything

بی هيلي behíli disillusioned بی هيلي کول to disillusion بی هيلي کېدل to be disillusioned

بهېدل bajedə́l *intransitive* ☞ بهېدل

بهير bajír *m.* ☞ بهير

پ

پ [1] pe the third letter of the Pashto alphabet

پ [2] pə *combining form of the preposition* په، پکښې in him, in her, in them, پکار a *necessary, indispensable* b *utilized*

پا [1] pā *m.* foot, leg ☞ پای

پا [2] pā 1 *a separable prefix in the verbs* پاڅېدل *and* پاڅول in short phrases پانه څو He did not arise

پابند pābánd 1 *m.* chains; fetters 2.1 connected, linked, bound; fettered 2.2 linked with something, depending on something; limited, constrained by something 2.3 taking something into account; observing something د وخت پابند punctual هغه د وخت ډېر پابند دئ He is very precise. He is very puntual. د قانون پابند observing the law *pābánd* يو شي ته پابند کېدل، په يو شي پابند کېدل to take something into consideration; observe something

پابندي pābandí *f.* 1 linking, fettering; chaining 2 link or connection with something; depending upon something; limitation, constraint upon something 3 consideration, investigation, observation (of something) پابند کول a to make dependent upon something; b to consider something; investigate something; observe something

پاپ pāp *m.* پاپا pāpā *m.* Pope (supreme head of the Catholic Church) د روم پاپ The Pope of Rome

پاپ پاپ پاپ pāp-pāp-pāp *interjection* the call of a hen or a sound of endearment made when chucking someone under the chin

پاپړ pāpə́r *m.* thin cookie made from groundpea flour and cooked in hot oil *proverb* د سلو پاپړو يو ډانګ بس دئ *literal* A single stick of firewood is sufficient to bake a hundred pea-flour cookies *figurative* He works best who knows his trade. Work goes with a swing under the master's hand.

پاپکه pāpə́ka *f. botany Scorzonera* (black salsify)

پاپلي pāpə́li *f. plural* first uncertain steps of a child پاپلي کول to walk unsteadily (of a child)

پاپوا pāpuā́ *f.* Papua

پاپوتکر pāpoţkúr decent, honest

پاپوش pāpúsh *m. regional* پاپوښه pāpósha *f.* shoe

پاپوکه pāpúka *f.* caraway root

پاپی pāpój *f. children's speech* foot, paw

پاتا pātā́ *f.* 1 prayer for the dead, rite for the dead پاتا لوستل to read the first chapter of the Koran at the rites for the dead پاتا ورکول to conduct the service for the dead 2 prayer for the dead, ceremonial meal on occasion of death پاتا اخيستل، پاتا کول a to conduct rites for the dead b to arrange a funeral meal پر پاتا کښېنستل to

attend rites for the dead b to pray for the deceased; attend memorial services for the dead

پاتاخوان pātākhān *m.* person who reads the first chapter of the Koran at service for the dead

پاتالوژي pātālozhí *f.* ☞ پاتولوژي

پاتالوژيکي pātālozhikí ☞ پاتولوژيکي

پاتان pātán stairway, staircase

پاتاو pātā́v *m. Western* large irrigation ditch

پاتخه pātə́kha *f.* step; rung; tread (of a stair)

پاترون pātrón *m.* boss, supervisor

پاتره pātrá *f.* scab

پاتکول pātakavə́l *transitive* ☞ پاتول

پاتنده pātə́nda 1 remaining 2 durable, stable 3 constant

پاتو [1] pā́to *f.* dialect ☞ پاته [1]

پاتو [2] pātó *f.* پاتو pātú *m.* 1 patú *m.* red caterpillar بيبي پاتو red caterpillar 2 name of a bird 3 pātó *f. proper name* Pato

پاتوڅنه pātotsə́na *f. usually plural* پاتوڅني pātotsə́ni maidenhair fern, *Adiantum capillus veneris*

پاتول pātavə́l *denominative, transitive* [*past:* پاته يې کړ] to stop; detain

پاتولوژي pātolozhí *f.* pathology

پاتولوژيکي pātolozhikí pathological

پاته [1] pā́ta 1 *adjective singular & plural* remaining, rest of پنځه اويا افغاني پاته دي Seventy-five Afghans are left. پاته لري to be continued 2 lagging behind; being behind زما ساعت پاته دئ My watch is slow. پاته کول، پاته کول to disturb someone, prevent someone from working پاته کېدل ☞ پاتېدل

پاته [2] pātá *f.* ☞ پاتا

پاته مری pātamə́raj *m.* inheritance; property, that which is left as a legacy

پاته وری [1] patavə́raj *m.* heir, inheritor

پاته وړی [2] pátavaṛe *f.* heiress

پاتې [1] pā́te *Eastern* ☞ پاته پاتې راتلل to lag, be behind

پاتې [2] pātáj *m.* bozbash (dish made from peas, evoking extreme thirst) *saying* وخوره پاتي ، کښېنه پر لښتي If you eat bozbash, you'll stay drinking at the brook awhile.

پاتېدل pātedə́l *denominative, intransitive* [*past:* پاته شو *past:* إپاتې شو] *Eastern* 1 to stay, remain په کور کښې پاتېدل to remain at home 2 to be abandoned, be forgotten کتاب را نه په مېز پاتې شو I left a book on the table. 3 to miss (also in combination with بېرته and وروسته in various meanings) ساعت مي د ريل نه بېرته پاتېدل to miss a train My watch is slow. *idiom* د . . . څخه پاتېدل Not to have the possibility of doing something. د تګ څخه پاتېدل to stop, get stuck

پاتېدونی pātedúnaj lasting, protracted

پاتېده pātedə́ *m. plural* ☞ پاتې کېده

پاتېشون pāteshún *m.* پاتېشونکی pāteshúnkaj *m.* leftovers (food)

پاتې کېده pātekedə́ *m. plural* 1 delay 2 a lag

پاتېکېدل pātekedə́l *intransitive* ☞ پاتېکېدل

پاته مری pātemə́raj *m.* ☞ پاتی مری

پات pāṭ *m.* section of field 50 meters long and 60 meters wide

پات ² pāṭ *m. theater* part, role

پاتخ pāṭə́kh *m.* shoebrush

پاتک pāṭák *m. regional* ☞ پهاتک

پاتکی ¹ pāṭkáj *m.* 1 small place (town); nook 2 small piece 3 scrap, fragment 4 verse, poem 5 witchcraft, sorcery 6 fortunetelling

پاتکی ² pāṭkáj *m.* tread of a stairway

پاتی pāṭaj *m.* پاتی pāṭí *f.* 1 leather loop (of a sling, slingshot) 2 ring on the bow-shaped tool of a wool-beater

پاجامه pādzhāmá *f.* 1 wide trousers 2 pajamas

پاچا pāchá *m.* [*plural:* پاچهان pāchāhán *plural:* پاچایان pāchāján] 1 king, shah 2 queenbee *idiom* په اندبننو ځان پاچا کول to be addicted to impractical dreams, build castles in the air

پاچاخزک pāchakhə́zák *m.* 1 breed of short-legged roosters 2 kind of fireworks

پاچاگل pāchāgúl *m. botany* Malcolmia

پاچاوزیرک pāchāvazirák *m.* kind of game

پاچائي pāchājí *f.* ☞ پادشاهي

پاچه pāchá *f.* 1 sheep's feet (food) 2 ☞ پایخه

پاچهي pāchahí 1 *f. colloquial* ☞ پاچهي کول پادشاهي to rule over, govern 2 kingly, royal *idiom* پاچهي لار highway, main roadway

پاڅول pātsavə́l *transitive* [*past:* پا یي څاوه] 1 to raise, awaken پا یي نه خولو He did not awaken him 2 to turn against someone or something 3 to incite or induce to do something 4 to evoke or elicit (feelings of some kind)

پاڅیدل pātsedə́l *intransitive* [*present:* پاڅي، پاڅيري *future:* پابه څي، پانڅبد پا نه خبد، He did past: پاڅبد] هغه به پاڅي 1 to get up, rise چه ودربدي نه شوي، نو پاڅبدي ولي؟ not get up *Eastern proverb literal* If you can't stand up why bother to arise. *figurative* One should not undertake this work 2 to wake up 3 to come out against someone or something دوی د روښان مخي ته را پاڅبدل He came out against Roshan. مقابلي ته پاڅبدل to oppose, resist 4 to spring up, arise, appear to engender (of some feeling) *idiom* طبيبان تري پاڅبده *Eastern* The doctors refused to treat him.

پاڅبده pātsedə́ *m. plural* 1 rising, lifting; awakening 2 coming out, speaking against someone or something

پاخسه pākhsá *f.* ☞ پخسه

پاخه pākhə́ *masculine plural of* پوخه

پاداش pādásh *m.* 1 compensation 2 reward; recompense 3 retribution 4 revenge

پادري pādrí *m.* 1 priest, minister ستر پادري bishop 2 [*plural:* پادریان pādrijān] the clergy

پادزهر pādzáhr *m. plural* bezoar from Persian pad-zar (protecting against poison, an antidote for snakebite)

پادشاه pādisháh *m.* [*plural:* پادشاهان pādisāhán *plural:* پادشایان pādishāján] 1 king; padishah 2 the title of a Sayd 3 *proper name* Padishah

پادشاهي ¹ pādshāhí *f.* 1 kingly, royal د افغانستان پادشاهي حکومت the Royal Government of Afghanistan; پادشاهي دولت kingdom 2 *f.* .1 kingdom 2.2 royal power; throne

پادو pādāv *m.* messenger; boy who runs errands

پادواني pādavāní *f.* job of messenger

پادوکالی pādo-kālé Pas de Calais (the Straits of Dover)

پاده pádá *f.* herd of cattle د مېښو پاده a herd of buffalo پردی پاده پوول to work as a herdsman

پاده وان pādavā́n *m.* herdsman

پاده pā́da *f.* 1 ribbon 2 bandage 3 tailoring basting; act of basting 4 sinew (in the neck)

پار ¹ pār *m.* attention (paid) to someone *idiom* د خدای په پار، for goodness's sake, for God's sake د خدای پار دئ!

پار ² pār *m.* 1 incitement, instigation 2 will, power, authority ورکول a to incite b to give someone free rein c to dismiss someone

پار ³ pār *doublet* وار

پارا ² pārā́ *f.* ☞ پاره

پارازیت pārāzít *m.* parasite

پارازیتي pārāzití parasitical

پارازیتولوژي pārāzitolozhí *f.* parasitology

پراشوت pārāshuṭ *m.* ☞ پراشوتي

پراشوتي pārāshutí ☞ پراف

پاراف pārāf *m. diplomacy* قرارداد پاراف کول to initial a treaty

پاراگوای pārāgváj *m.* Paraguay

پاراگویي pārāgvají 1 Paraguayan 2 *m.* Paraguayan (person)

پارامریبو pārāmaribó *f.* Paramaribo (city)

پارتي ¹ pārtí *adjective history* Parthian

پارتي ² pārtí *history* ☞ پارتي 1

پارتیا pārtijá *f. history* Parthia

پارتیزان pārtizā́n *m.* partisan

پارتیزاني pārtizāní *adjective* partisan پارتیزاني نهضت the partisan movement

پارت pārṭ *m. theater* part, role پارت لوبول، پارت تمثیلول to play a part

پارتي pārtí *f.* 1 *politics* party 2 *regional* evening affair, party

پارچاو ¹ pārcháv *m.* drain, drainpipe

پارچاو ² pārchav́ 1 empty دکان پارچاو پروت و the shop was empty 2 inactive, inoperative, non-working, out of action, operation

پارچاوول pārchāvavə́l *denominative, transitive* [*past:* پارچاو یي کړ] to stop, hold up, detain

پارچاوېدل pārchāvedə́l *denominative, intransitive* [*past:* پارچاو شو] to be stopped, be held up 2 to be inactive, do nothing, be out of operation (e.g., of a machine)

پارچل pārchál *m.* crushed fruit, bruised fruit, rotten fruit

پارچنگ pārcháng *m.* 1 wooden staircase 2 stair tread

پارچنگی pārchangáj *m.* short flight of stairs

پارچه pārchá *f.* [*m. plural:* پارچي pārché] [*plural:* پارچه جات pārchadzhāt] piece; fragment; part پارچه کول *compound verb* a to divide into parts **b** to split (the atom) پارچه کېدل *compound verb* **a** to be divided into parts **b** to be split (of the atom) **2** cloth **3** splinter, fragment د گولي پارچه shell fragment, piece of shrapnel **4** bucket (of a noria or waterwheel)

پارچه باب pārchabā́b *m.* cloth, woven fabrics, textiles

پارچه بافي pārchabā́fī **1** *f.* weaving **2** weaving, weaver's

¹ پارس pārs *m. history* Persia

² پارس pārás *m.* philosopher's stone د پارس تېره philosopher's stone

پارسا pārsā́ **1** abstinent, temperate **2** chaste **3** pious, devout

پارساتی pārsā́taj attentive

پارسائي pārsā́ī *f.* **1** abstinence, temperance **2** chastity **3** piety, devotion

پارسل pārsál *m.* [*plural:* پارسلونه pārsalúna *Arabic plural:* پارسلات pārsalā́t] sending

پارسنگ pārsáng *m.* **1** makeweight (something thrown onto a scale to bring the weight to a desired value) **2** counterweight, counterpoise

پارسڼه pārsáṇa *f.* Parsee woman

¹ پارسي pārsí **1** *f.* Farsi; the Persian language; the Tajik language; پارسي ژبه Farsi; the Persian language; the Tajik language **2** *m.* Parsee (person)

² پارسی pārsə́j *f.* ☞ پارسڼه

پارسي خوان pārsikhā́n *m.* پارسي وان pārsivā́n *m.* Farsi speaker, Persian speaker, Tajik speaker

پارک pārk *m.* **1** park د کولتور پارک cultural park **2** pool (i.e., place where fleets of various motor vehicles are kept or stored) د موترانو پارک automotive pool, motor pool

پارکال pārkā́l *m.* **1** grandeur, greatness, glory **2** power, strength, force پر پارکال سپرېدل to achieve power, come to power د پارکاله لوېدل to become weak, become decrepit

پارگین pārgín *m.* cesspool

پارلمان pārləmā́n *m.* Parliament

پارلماني pārləmā́nī parliamentary پارلماني هيئت parliamentary delegation

پارلبمنټ pārlemā́nṭ *m. Eastern* ☞ پارلمان

¹ پارو pārú *m.* **1** rake **2** oar, paddle پارو وهل to row, rake (with rakes, paddles)

² پارو pārú *m.* manure, fertilizer

پاروسازي pārusāzí *f.* production of fertilizer

پاروکی pārukə́j *f.* comb

پارول paravál *transitive* [*past:* و يي پاراوه] **1** to incite; provoke **2** to tease (an animal) **3** *figurative* to arouse, excite (feelings of one kind or another); to stimulate, agitate **4** *figurative* to inspire; fill with enthusiasm; encourage

¹ پاره pārá *f.* piece; part

² پاره pārá *f. chemistry* mercury

پاره چنار pārachinā́r *m.* ☞ پاره چنار

پاريس pārís *m.* Paris (city)

پاريسي pārisí pārisáj **1** Parisian **2** *m.* Parisian (person)

¹ پار pāṛ *m.* scaffolding; scaffold

² پار pāṛ ☞ پارو

پاربندنج pāṛbāndzh *m.* chestnut; chestnut tree

² پارس pāṛás *m.* ☞ پارس

¹ پارسي pāṛsí *f.* پارسو pāṛsó *f.* ☞ پارسي

پارسي خوان pāṛsovā́n *m.* پرسوب pāṛsób *m.* ☞ پرسوب

پارسي بان pāṛsibā́n *m.* پارسي وان pāṛsivā́n *m.* ☞ پارسي خوان

پاركی paṛkə́j *f.* verse, poem; song (short)

پارو pāṛú *m.* **1** charm; witchcraft, sorcery **2** snake charmer; fakir, conjuror; sorcerer; magician; shaman, medicine man

² پارو pāṛugár *m.* ☞ پارو

پاروگري pāṛugarí *f.* charm; magic, sorcery; primitive medicine (herbs, ritual, etc.)

¹ پاره pāṛá *f.* **1** baker's paddle, baker's shovel (for handling hot baked goods) **2** board or paddle for moving wash around in a laundry tub **3** part of a corn-husker

² پاره pāṛá *f.* **1** *agriculture* blemish, flaw **2** *figurative* unfinished work

پاره چنار pāṛachinā́r *m.* Parachinar (settlement in Pakistan near the Afgban border)

پازه وال pāzvā́l *m.* ☞ پازه وال

پازه pāza *f.* **1** affair, matter; activity; work په پازه اچول to set in motion; use, employ **2** counsel, advice, admonition **3** boldness, courage **4** quickness, promptness, efficiency **5** attention to someone پازه کول **a** to act **b** to give advice, give admonition **c** to demonstrate courage **d** to show promptness, demonstrate efficiency پازه لرل to produce an effect, influence

پازه pāza *f.* dim, weak light

پازه وال pázaval *m.* worker, colleague, employee, functionary

پازیکه pāzikā́ ☞ پاکیزه

پاژوله pāzholá *f.* stocking of goat's wool

پاگ pāg *m.* swelling, tumor

پاگول pāgavə́l *transitive* ☞ پرسول

¹ پارو pāgá *f.* ☞ پارو

پاگېدل pāgedə́l *intransitive* ☞ پرسېدل

¹ پاس pās **1** up, upward; above, overhead; higher د .... د پاسه above something; from above something; over, beyond something تر حد له پاسه excessively, beyond measure **2.1** upper **2.2** above-mentioned, above-indicated; aforesaid

² پاس pās *m.* **1** ointment (for treating mange in animals) **2** application of ointment (to animals suffering from mange)

³ پاس pās *m.* **1** guarding, protection **2** nursing, tending, looking after; care, concern; attention **3** esteem, respect

⁴ پاس pās *m.* **1** passing a course (of instruction) پاس کېدل *compound verb* to take an examination; to finish school **2** acceptance, adoption, confirmation (e.g., of a law) **3** *sports* pass پاس کول to pass, execute a pass **a** پاس ورکول to pass a course (of

instruction) مكتب پاس كول to finish school **b** to accept, adopt, confirm (e.g., a law) **c** *sports* to pass, execute a pass

پاس ⁵ pās *present stem of* پاسېدل

پاسبان pāsbān *m.* sentinental, guard

پاسپوټ pāspóṭ *m. Eastern* پاسپورت pāspórt *m.* passport د پاسپوټ passport officer پاسپوټ ویزه کول to stamp a visa on a passport

پاسپورتي pāsportí *adjective* passport

پاسپورټ pāspórṭ *m.* ☞ پاسپوټ

پاسپورتي pāsportí ☞ پاسپورتي

پاست pāst *m.* gratitude

پاستل pāstél *m. art* pastel, pastel drawing

پاسته ¹ pāstə 1 *masculine plural of* پوست ² 2 *oblique singular of* پوست ² په پاسته بغ ويل to speak affectionately, softly

پاسته ² pāsta *feminine doublet* ناسته

پاستی pāstaj *m.* 1 chapati (a sweet flat cake) 2 dewlap (of an animal)

پاسخ pāsúkh *m.* answer پاسخ ورکول to answer

پاسداري pāsdārí *f.* 1 guarding, protection, defense 2 care; charge; concern پاسداري كول **a** to guard **b** to care for; have charge over; to concern oneself about

پاسره pāsrá *f.* 1 economy, savings پاسره کول to effect economies, save 2 reason, cause

پاسرگر pāsragár پاسره وال pāsravāl thrifty, economical

پاسۀ pāsə́l *transitive [past:* وی پاسه] 1 to tend to someone, care for somebody; concern oneself about someone; pay attention to someone 2 to treat an (animal) for mange

پاسلۀ pāslə́l *transitive* ☞ پاسل ¹ ځان پاسلل **a** to take care of oneself, look after oneself **b** to dress up, dress in a showy or ostentatious fashion

پاسلنه pāslə́na *f.* پاسلودنه pāslodə́na *f.* 1 gratitude 2 reproach

پاسلول pāslavól *transitive [past:* وی پاسلاوه] 1 to turn something over for custody or trust; to have confidence in, trust someone 2 باسلپيل ☞

پاسلون pāslún *m.* 1 watchman, guard 2 پاسلونه ☞ 1

پاسلونه pāslavə́na *f.* 1 care; concern; charge (as to have charge or responsibility for children); attention 2 reproach

پاسلوینه pāslojə́na *f.* reproach

پاسلیۀ pāslejə́l *transitive [past:* وی پاسلپيه] to remind of a service rendered; to reproach

پاسنگ pāsáng *m.* ☞ پارسنگ

پاسنه pāsə́na *f.* 1 پاسلونه ☞ 1 2 fattening up (of cattle)

پاسنی pāsənáj 1 upper 2 *attributive* mountain, living "up there" (from the point of view of Peshawar i.e., living in Kabul, Gazni, Kandahar, etc. and for residents of Kandahar, i.e., living in Kabul, Gazni, etc.) پاسنی پښتون ⁴ بر ☞ 3 aforementioned, above-indicated; above-mentioned; پاسنی باد wind from the mountains (chinook, foehn)

پاسو pāsú 1.1 humble, meek 1.2 low, base 2 *m.* scoundrel, villian

پاسوال pāsvál *m.* ruler, padishah

پاسوال زی pāsvalzáj *m.* prince, ruler's son

پاسوالی pāsválaj *m.* 1 predilection, inclination 2 guard 3 care, charge, tending, taking care of

پاسوان pāsván *m.* 1 watchman, guard 2 herdsman

پاسوالي pāsvā́ní *f.* ☞ پاسوالي

پاس ورونکی pās vṛúnkaj *m.* elevator; hoist

پاسوگلوي pāsugalví *f.* 1 modesty, humility 2 lowness, baseness

پاسول ¹ pāsavə́l *transitive* ☞ پاڅول

پاسول ² pāsavə́l ☞ پاسل

پاسېدل pāsedə́l *intransitive* ☞ پاڅېدل

پاسیف pāsíf passive (of measures)

پاسیفیک pāsifík *m.* the Pacific Ocean

پاش pāsh ☞ فاش

پاشان pāshān sparse, scattered, diffused پاشان كول ☞ پاشل پاشان كېدل to dissipate (one's energies), disperse, scatter; be scattered, be dispersed

پاشتقی pāshtáke *f. plural* stairs, staircase

پاشتک pāshták *m.* ceiling beam, rafter

پاشتوک pāshtúk *m.* crossbeam, ceiling plank

پاشۀ pāshól *transitive [past:* وی پاشه] 1 to pour (water on) 2 to spurt, splash 3 to strew; scatter; spill 4 to sow تخم پاشل to sow seed, disperse seed 5 to disperse, drive away باد اورېځي سره وپاشلي the wind dispersed the clouds پاشل كېدل *passive* **a** to be poured **b** to be watered **c** to be splashed **d** to be strewn, be scattered **e** to be sown, disintegrate, be destroyed, be torn down

پاشلي pashálaj 1 *participle from* پاشل 2 uncoordinated, odd پاشلئ pashə́li uncoordinated notes, uncorrelated notes یادداشتونه

پاشي pāshí *f. second element in compound* آبپاشي watering, flushing

پاغنده pāghundá *f.* 1 mass, bunch (of cleaned cotton or wadding) 2 flakes (of snow) 3 puffs (of smoke) پاغونده

پافشاري pāfishārí *f.* insistence, persistence پافشاري کول to insist on something; persist in something

پاک pāk 1 clean, neat 2 holy, sacred; پاکه زمکه sacred land 3 innocent

پاکټ pākáṭ *m.* 1 (official) package, envelope 2 بنداژ ☞

پاکټونه pākaṭū́na *m. plural* packets

پاکدامن pākdāmán ☞ پاکزری

پاکړه pākṛá *f.* packsaddle

پاکزری pākzə́raj 1 pure; chaste, innocent 2 modest

پاک ساک pāk sák pure and immaculate, absolutely pure

پاکستان pākistán *m.* Pakistan

پاکستاني pākistāní پاکستانای pākistānáj 1 Pakistanian 2 Pakistanian (person)

پاکنفسي pāknafasí *f.* 1 purity, chastity, innocent 2 sincerity, candor 3 decency, honesty

پاکنویس pāknavís پاکنویسه pāknavísa clean, fair, written in a clean or fair copy پاکنویس کول to write a fair copy, write a clean copy

پاکنویس کېدل to be written out in a clean copy, be written out in a fair copy

پاکنویسول pāknavisavә́l *denominative, transitive* [*past:* پاکنویس یې کړ] to write out in a clean copy, write out in a fair copy

پاکنویسي pāknavisí *f.* execution (writing) of a clean copy, execution of a fair copy

پاکوالی pākvā́laj *m.* **1** ☞ پاکي¹ **2** tidiness (premises)

پاکول pākavә́l *denominative, transitive* [*past:* پاک یې کړ] **1** to clean, clear; wipe, wipe dry غاښونه پاکول to brush the teeth بوټونه پاکول clean shoes کوټه پاکول to tidy the premises **2** to wash; wash clean; wash thoroughly **3** to pay off (a debt); settle an account حساب پاکول to pay up, settle, settle an account

پاکه¹ paká *f.* wide cotton cloth

پاکه² pā́ka *feminine singular of* پاک

پاکه³ pākә́ *imperfect of* پکل²

پاکي¹ pākí *f.* cleanliness, neatness, tidiness

پاکي² pākí *f.* razor

پاکېدل pākedә́l *denominative, intransitive* [*past:* پاک شو] **1** to be cleaned; be cleaned up; be wiped up; be wiped clean **2** to be washed; be washed thoroughly; be washed clean **3** to be paid up (debts); be settled (accounts)

پاکېده pākedә́ *m. plural* **1** cleaning up; cleaning; wiping clean, wiping dry **2** washing; washing clean, washing thoroughly **3** payment (debt); settlement (account)

پاکېزګي pākizagí *f.* **1** cleanliness, tidiness **2** chastity

پاکیزه pākizá **1** clean, pure; tidy, neat **2** chaste

پاکیزه خصلت pākizá-khaslát chaste

پاګل pāgál *m. regional* **1** abnormal person; psychopath **2** extravagant person; spendthrift

پاګل خانه pāgalkhāná *f. regional* psychiatric hospital, clinic

پال¹ pāl *m.* **1** abstention پال کول to abstain; be wary of **2** *agriculture* blemish, flaw; lapse, balk in plowing **3** beginning, commencement **4** ☞ تپش

پال² pāl ☞ فال

پال³ pāl *m.* hollow

پال⁴ pāl *m.* plowshare

پالان pālā́n *m.* پالانه pālā́na *f.* packsaddle

پالش pálish *m. plural* **1** polish; action of polishing پالش کول *compound verb* to polish پالش کېدل *compound verb* to be polished **2** polishing agent, varnish

پالک¹ pālák *m. plural* spinach

پالک² pālák *m.* foster child, ward

پالکانه pālkāná *f.* smoke vent, window in roof, skylight

پالکوری pālkóraj *m.* storeroom (for agricultural implements)

پالکۍ pālkә́j *f.* elephant saddle, howdah

پالل pālә́l *transitive* [*past:* و یې پاله] **1** to protect, care for, guard **2** to bring up, raise کوچنیان پالل to bring up children, rear children **3** to cultivate, develop someone or something د کار محبت پالل to instill or inculcate a love for work **4** to cherish, foster **5** to caress

6 to look after, tend مېلمه پالل to show hospitality **7** to feed, nourish, suckle (a child) **8** to observe (e.g., a law)

پاللئ pālә́laj *past participle of* پالل لور پاللې adopted daughter

پالندوی pāləndúj *m.* ☞ ساتندوی

پالنګ pālā́ng *m.* large wooden bed (with painted legs)

پالنګر pāləngór *m.* خدماتي کمپیوټر khidamā́ti kampjúṭər سرور sarwár server

پالنګپوښ pālangpóg̣h *m.* bedspread, counterpane

پالنه pālә́na *f.* **1** development; education **2** instruction; training نظامي عمومي پالنه universal military training **3** care د چا پالنه کول to care for; be concerned about someone **4** bestowing of gifts upon a new bride at the time of the first visit to her home by her parents

پالوال pālvā́l **1** abstemious, moderate **2** devoted, loyal

پالوان pālvā́n *m.* ☞ پهلوان

پالوده pāludá *f.* sweet jelly dish; jam

پاله¹ pāla *f.* plowshare

پاله² pālá *f.* wedge (wooden)

پاله پدری pālá-padrí without fail; willy-nilly

پالی pāláj *m.* **1** *agriculture* lapse, balk (in plowing) **2** diet **3** kind of children's game

پالېز pāléz *m.* melon field; kitchen garden

پالېز کاري pālezkārí *f.* melon farming, truck gardening

پالېزوان pālezvā́n *m.* melon grower, truck gardener

پالیسي¹ pālisí *f.* policy, politics

پالیسي² pālisi *f.* insurance policy

پام pām *m.* attention په پام سره attentively, with attention زما پام نه و I didn't pay attention. I didn't notice. پام غلطول to divert the attention پام غلطېدل to be distracted (of attention) پام کول to pay attention to something; look after something پام کوئ Pay attention! Look out! پام کوه چه و نه لوېږې Watch out! Don't fall! پام لرل to be riveted, drawn (of the attention) و... ته پام کېدل to be concerned about something له پامه وتل to be left without attention, be forgotten, be unnoticed

پامال pāmál ☞ پایمال

پامالول pāmālavә́l *denominative* ☞ پایمالول

پامان pāmā́n *vice* د خدای پامان! So long! Au revoir! په امان

پامته دار pāmtadā́r **1** expecting something; counting on something **2** *regional* reproaching, rebuking

پامته داري pāmtadārí *f.* expectation of something; reproach for something

پام لرنه pāmlarә́na *f.* care for something; concern about something, attention to something; seeing to something د افرادو د د کرهنې پاملرنه care of public health صحت پاملرنه looking after the sowing (of crops) پاملرنه کول to tend to something; be concerned about something; pay attention to something; see to something

پام لرونکی pām larúnkaj attentive, concerned

پامول pamavә́l *transitive* ☞ فهمول

پاملرونکي ☞ پامیالی pāmjālā́j

پامېدل pāmedә́l *intransitive* ☞ فهمېدل

پامیر pamír *m.* 1 the Pamir د پامیر غرونه the Pamir 2 [*plural:* پامیرات pāmirā́t] the Parmirs

پاناما pānāmā́ *f.* پانامه pānāmá *f.* Panama (country and city) د پاناما کانال، د پانامي کانال the Panama Canal

پاندان pāndā́n *m.* box for betel (Asiatic plant whose leaf is chewed with betel nut as a narcotic)

پاندري pāndrә́j *f.* silk and gold threads, braided into the hair (braids) of a bride

پانډه pā́nḍa *f.* firewood basket

پانسمان pānsmā́n *m.* bandage, dressing *attributive* د پانسمان کوټه bandage پانسمان کول to bandage, dress

پانسي pānsí *f.* ☞ پهانسي

پانسیون pānsijón *m.* boarding school

پانکراس pānkriā́s *m.* *anatomy* pancreas

پانګ pā́ng *m.* ☞ پان 1

پانګوال pāngvā́l *m.* capitalist

پانګه pā́nga *f.* 1 capital صنعتي پانګه خصوصي پانګه private capital مالي پانګه industrial capital د بانک پانګه bank capital financial capital دایمي پانګه constant capital اصلي پانګه basic capital جاري پانګه د پانګي تمرکز working capital د لګښت پانګه variable capital concentration of capital پانګه اچول، پانګه اېښودل to invest capital پانګه لرل to have capital, possess capital 2 *figurative* property; value; wealth; resources طبیعي پانګي natural resources, wealth *idiom* د صبر پانګه په کار ده One should be patient.

پانګه لرونکی pānga larúnkaj *m.* capitalist

پانګه ور pāngavár *m.* capitalist

پانګه وري pāngavarí *f.* capitalism

پانوس pānús *m.* ☞ فانوس

پانه pānā́ *f.* 1 wedge (wooden) 2 stocks, rack (for torture, punishment) a پانه ورکول to drive a wedge, split, cleave b to lock up in stocks

پانیات panjā́t *m.* lesson; conclusion, moral د . . . څخه پانیات کول to extract a lesson from; draw a conclusion from پانیات کېدل to serve as a lesson

پانیاتي pānjā́ti 1 instructive 2 learning a lesson from something 3 exemplary, model; serving as an example for others (of a person)

پان pāṇ [1] *m.* precipice; steep bank; abyss پورته گورم پرانگ دئ، کښته گورم پان دئ *proverb literal* Above I see a leopard, below I see an abyss. *figurative* Caught between a rock and a hard place. د پان په a سر ولار standing at the edge of an abyss b at the edge of the grave *figurative* nari‌ نري پان ته دربدل a to stand at the edge of an abyss b to be extremely quick-tempered, not to control oneself; to be unstable

پان [2] pāṇ *m.* starch

پانرېژ paṇrézh *m.* 1 fall 2 autumn

پانکۍ paṇakә́j *f.* (small) leaf

پانو [1] paṇú *m.* salad lettuce

پانه [2] pāṇo *oblique plural of* پانه

پان [3] pāṇó *oblique plural of* پان [1]

پانوځی pāṇodzā́j *m.* 1 bookstore 2 book trade

پانه pāṇa *f.* 1 leaf, leaflet (of a plant) د چایو پانه tea leaf, leaflet د گل پانه a petal وني پاڼي کوي The trees are starting to be covered with leaves. The trees are growing green. د توت د پاڼي په شان رپېدبدل to tremble like an autumn leaf 2 sheet (of paper) 3 page پاڼي کتل to turn over the pages; look at every page 4 note, document, paper 5 leaflet; newspaper 6 ☞ پلوان 7 card (playing) ستا پاڼه زوروره شوه You have won. 8 [*plural:* پاڼي pāṇi] a leaves, foilage b archive د تاریخ پاڼي Archives (the institution) د پاڼو مدیریت the Annals of History c playing cards

پاڼي pāṇe *f.* 1 fate, good fortune پاڼي یې وگرزېده His luck has betrayed him. 2 leaflet 3 sterile flower

پانژ paṇә́j *f.* knocking out a nut with a nut (a game)

پانیرژون paṇirəzhún *m.* fall (the season)

پاڼي رژونکی pāṇi razhavúnkaj fall, autumnal (of trees)

پاڼیز pāṇíz 1 foliate; composed of thin layers or flakes 2 consisting of so-many pages or sheets اته پاڼیزه ورځپاڼه an 8-page newspaper

پاو [1] pāu *m.* pāo *m.* *regional* 1 fourth, fourth part of something د پاو باندي څلور بجي a quarter past four پاو کم اوه بجي a quarter to seven 2 ¼ "sir" ☞ سیر

پاو [2] pāu *m.* pound دوه پاوه pāva two pounds

پاو [3] pāo *vice* ☞ پای پنج پاو

پاوتل pāutál *m.* sediment, deposit

پاورهاوس pāverhāus *m.* *regional* electric power station, powerhouse

پاورقي pāvaraḳí *f.* 1 footnote, note 2 feature article (in a newspaper)

پاولی pauláj *m.* coin in a necklace

پاویلیون pāviljón *m.* pavilion

پاها pāhá *f.* cotton batting (which is placed under a bandage when a dressing is being made)

پای pāj *regional* pāe *m.* 1 leg پای مرد a pāj-i human leg b *figurative* flight, escape 2 end, termination د پای حکم final decision (of a Supreme Court) د کال په پای کښي at the end of the year تر پایه finally, in conclusion, at last په پای کښي until the end پای یې څه؟ In the final years of his life د خپل ژوند د پای په څوکلو What will this end with? یو کار پای ته رسول to finish, complete, bring a matter to its conclusion; execute a piece of work پای ته رسبدل to be finished, be completed, be brought to a conclusion 3 consequences (of an illness) *idiom* پای کول *compound verb* to plumb, measure the depth (e.g., of a river)

پایاب pājā́b [1] *m.* 1 ford; shoal 1.2 *proper name* Payab 2 shallow, not deep, suitable for fording

پایان pājā́n *m.* end, conclusion

پایاو pājā́v *m.* ☞ پایاب

پایاوي pājā́ví cheerful, joyous, buoyant

پایبند pājbánd *m.* ☞ پابند

پایپ pājp *m.* pipe پایپ څکل to smoke a pipe

پای پای pāj-pāj *children's speech* quietly, softly, gently پای پای تلل to walk softly پای پای کول to direct gently, conduct gently, carry gently

پای تاوی، پای پیچی pājpéchi *f. plural* پای تاوی، pājtavé *f.* leg wrappings, puttees

پایتخت، پای تخت pājtákht *m.* capital (city)

پای ته pájta *vice* پای

پایخور pājtsór *m.* 1 end, completion, termination 2 person bringing up the rear 3 remains or remainder, left-overs (food)

پایڅه pājtsá *f.* 1 trouser leg 2 hems of the legs of wide Middle-Eastern trousers; trouser cuffs 3 wide Middle-Eastern trousers *idiom* د پایڅې په رگ پسې تلل، دپایڅې رگ پالل to be on friendly terms with wife's relatives

پایدار pājdár steady, stable; strong, firm

پایداري pājdārí *f.* steadiness, stability; strength, firmness

پایدان pājdán *m.* running board, footboard (of a vehicle, carriage, etc.)

پایدو pājdáv *m.* بادو

پایزار pājzár *m.* shoe

پای زیب pājzéb *m.* ankle bracelet

پاینت pajəkht *m.* durability, immutability, stability پاینت لرل to be durable, be immutable, be stable پاینت کول to last, endure چېی چپایی ډېر پاینت ونه کئ silence did not last long; the silence did not long endure

پایکوب، پایکو pājkó *f.* پایکوب pājkób *m.* rice huller; grain huller; treadle-operated rice huller, crusher, huller for rice and other grains مېخانیکی پایکو motor-driven rice huller د شولې په پایکو میده کول to hull rice

پایکوټ pājkóṭ *m.* rice cleaner, man engaged in the cleaning of rice

پایکیله pājkilá *f.* boundary, limit (of a plot of land)

پایگاو pājgáv *m.* paygav (a measure of land equal to half kul'ba, amount of land that can be plowed in one season by an ox-team)

پایگاه pājgá *f.* پایگاه pājgáh *f.* 1 foot (of a mountain) 2 *military* bridgehead; springboard for attack

پایل [1] pājə́l *m.* corn bread

پایل [2] pājl *m. electronics* battery اتومی پایل atomic reactor

پایلات pājlát *m.* disturbance; mutiny پایلات کول to create a disturbance; incite to mutiny

پایلاتی pājlātí mutinous پایلاتي کېدل to rebel, revolt

پایلامه pājlāmá *f.* 1 sign, symbol, token 2 banner

پایلوټ pājlóṭ *m.* پیلوټ

پایله pájla *f.* bracelet with bells (for the ankle, leg)

پایمال pājmál 1 crushed 2 destroyed 3 trampled

پایمالول pājmālavə́l *denominative, transitive* [*past:* پایمال یې کړ] 1 to crush 2 to destroy 3 to crudely suppress, infringe upon, violate د چا حقوق پایمالول to violate or infringe on someone's rights 4 to suppress (feelings)

پایمالي pājmālí *f.* 1 destruction 2 crude violation; infringement 3 suppression (of feelings)

پایمالېدل pājmāledə́l *denominative, intransitive* [*past:* پایمال شو] 1 to be suppressed 2 to be destroyed 3 to be violated, be infringed upon 4 to be suppressed (of feelings) *idiom* غلیمان مو پایمال سه! May your enemies disappear!

پائنڅه pāintsá *f.* پایخه

پای نخ pājnákh *m.* fruit-bearing branch of a grapevine

پاینده pājandá 1 durable; constant; enduring 2 *proper name* Payanda, Painda

پایندی pājəndáj پاینده [1]

پاینک pājnák *m.* rim or edge of the scabbard of a saber

پائنو pānáv inundated پائنوه زمکه low place, depression, flooded land, marshy land

پایڼه pājə́na *f.* strength; duration; constancy

پایڼی pājənáj last, final, conclusive

پایو pājáv *m.* float, floating structure

پایول pājavól *transitive* [*past:* و یې پا یاوه] 1 to prolong life; sustain life in someone 2 to settle 3 to conclude, complete 4 to measure the depth (i.e., of a river)

پایه pājá *f.* 1 foundation, groundwork, basis 2 column; mast 3 supporting member; pier (bridge) 4 step 5 wheel; wheels 6 piece, item (a counting word for machines, equipment) دوې پایې ماشینونه two pieces of machinery (i.e., two machines) 7 dignity; grade, rank 8 *figurative* level (of development)

پائي [1] pājí *f.* 1 rein; reins; bridle 2 hobbles

پائي [2] pājí *present of* پایېدل

پائي [3] pāí *f. regional* pice (small Indian coin, worth a quarter anna)

پایېدل، پائېدل pājedə́l pāedə́l 1 [*present:* پائي *intransitive past:* و پایده] 1.1 to last 1.2 to be strong, be firm 1.3 to live, exist 2 *m. plural* life, existence

پایېدنه pājedə́na *f.* پاینت

پائېکو pājkó *m.* پایکو

پاب [1] pəbāb *vice* په باب باب

پبي [1] pabí 1 *m. plural* Pabi (settlement between Peshawar and Naushera) 2 *m. plural* Pabi (tribe) 3 pabáj *m.* Pabi (tribesman)

پبی [2] pabə́j 1 *f.* پبي [1] 2 *feminine of* پبی 3

پپ pap *m.* small scoop (of a shopkeeper)

پپاخه papákha papə́kha *f.* "papkha" (a tall hat, usually of sheepskin)

پپړ papə́ṛ *adjective* big (of ears)

پپړ غوبر papə́ṛ ghvag *m.* burdock

پپنا pupənā destroyed, annihilated پپنا کول to destroy, annihilate پپنا کېدل to be destroyed, be annihilated

پپوس [1] pəpús *m.* lungs

پپوس [2] pəpús *m.* 1 coward 2 dawdler

پپۍ [1] papə́j *f.* kiss

پپۍ [2] papə́j *f. diminutive children's speech* foot

پت [1] pat *m.* honor, dignity; respect *idiom* د مېره په پت کېنېنستل، د to remain a widow مېره پر پت کېنېنستل

پت ² pat *m. plural* **1** fine goat's wool **2** undercoat (the fine wool growing beneath the outer wool of goat's, sheep) **3** nap, pile (textiles)

پت ³ pit flat; flattened, flattened out ☞ پيت

پت ⁴ pit *m.* core, pith, heart, pulp (e.g., of elder wood)

پت ⁵ pət *doublet* تت

پتا pətā *vice* پتا څه سوي دئ؟ په تا What happened to you?

پتاړی pətāŕáj *f.* board upon which the body of a deceased person is washed په پتاري کول **a** to wash the body of the decease **b** *figurative* to teach a lesson, punish severely

پتار pətāŕ *m.* large basket with a narrow opening

پتاسه patāsá *f. Eastern* **1** piece (of sugar) **2** kind of candy or sweetmeat مدام د پتاسو باران نه کېږي *proverb literal* Sweets do not fall from the sky forever *figurative* Good things do not last forever.

پتاقي patāqí *f.* cap, percussion cap

پتانه patānə́ *oblique singular of* پتون

پتاو pitāv **1** sunny **2** *m.* sunny side

پتاوی pitāvaj *m.* **1** sunny side (of a mountain) **2** warm and sunny winter day پتاوي ته کښېنستل، پتاوي کول *pitāvi* to sit in the sun, bask in the sun

پتخول patkhavə́l *transitive* [*past:* و يې پتخاوه] to cause to perspire freely

پتخه patə́kha *f.* revolver

پترک patrák small-eared (used for a particular breed of sheep)

پترکی patrakáj *m.* **1** scab **2** ☞ پتری ¹ **3** shaving, chip

پترول petról *m. plural* ☞ پترول

پترول کښي petrolkashí *f.* extraction of oil, output of oil

پتره patrá *f.* ☞ پتری ¹

پتری ¹ patrāj *m.* **1** crampon (iron, brass) پتری کول to fasten together with crampons; rivet, clinch **2** adornment, decoration

پتری patŕəj *f.* double hepatic duct (of sheep)

پتري والا patrivālá *m.* **1** trader in hardware, iron-monger **2** kind of German-made rifle

پتر patár *m.* ☞ پتن ²

پتک ¹ paták *m.* flask, water bottle ☞ بتک

پتک ² paták *m.* paper (card on which thread is wound)

پتک ³ paták bald

پتکی ¹ patkáj *m.* wool, hairy coat, hairy covering

پتکی ² patakáj *m. diminutive form of* پتک ¹

پتکی ³ pitkáj *m.* **1** bird **2** squab, shorty (of a person)

پتلون patlún *m.* [*plural:* پتلونونه patlunúna *plural:* پتلنونه patlanúna] trousers, breeches پتلون اغوستل **a** to wear trousers **b** to be clothed in trousers

پتلون پوش patlunpósh dressed in European style

پتلبز patléz *m.* پتلبس patlés *m.* **1** *agriculture* graft پتلبز کول to graft **2** organization, arrangement

پتلبسول patlesavə́l *denominative, transitive* [*past:* پتلبس مي کړ] *agriculture* to graft, make a graft

پتليک patlík *m.* diploma

پتنسی pitnásaj *m.* ☞ پتنوس

پتنگ patáng *m.* **1** nocturnal moth; moth, butterfly; clothes moth **2** پتنگ په a kite **3** moth (used as a synonym for one who is in love) شمعي عاشق دئ ځکه ځان پري سبزي *folk saying* The moth falls in love with the candle and is burned up in its flame. **4** *proper name* Patang

پتنوس patnús *m.* [*plural:* پتنوسان patnusā́n *plural:* پتنوسونه patnusúna] salver, tray

پتنوم patnúm *m.* ☞ لقب

پتنونه patanúna *masculine plural of* پتون

پتنه pitná *f.* **1** riot, mutiny; disturbance **2** enmity; struggle; vengeance زره پتنه family feud

پتن ¹ patán *m.* **1** wheel (of a spinning wheel) **2** ☞ پتنگ

پتن ² patán *m.* **1** ferrying, crossing by ferry (river) **2** landing, dock, wharf د پتن ډبوه lighthouse beacon

پتوا patvā *f.* ☞ فتوا

پتور patúr *m.* brassiere, bodice

پتون patún *m.* [*plural:* پتنونه patanúna] thigh, haunch

پتونی patunáj *m. botany* petunia

پتونی patúṇaj lagging behind all, last

پته ¹ patá *f.* branch, offshoot (of a tribe)

پته ² patá *f.* **1** sign; trace پته لگول، پته ايستل to get on the track of; track; shadow **2** páta address

پته ³ pə́ta *f.* silt, mud, ooze

پته ⁴ páta *f.* playing card پتي کول to play cards

پته پته patá paṭá *f. computer science* address bar

پتي ¹ páti **1** estimable, honorable; respectable **2** honest; decent

پتي ² paté *f. feminine plural of* پته ^{1, 2}

پتي ³ páti *plural of* پته ⁴ and پته ²

پتي ⁴ patáj *m.* ☞ پاتی ²

پتي ⁵ patə́j *f.* division of property

پتي ⁶ patə́j *f.* alphabet

پتي ⁷ pitáj *m. regional* ☞ پتکی ³

پتير patír ☞ فطير

پتيره ¹ patíra **1** *feminine singular of* پتير **2** *f.* unleavened bread دوډی unleavened bread

پتيره ² pətéra especially

پتيبل patəjə́l *transitive* ☞ پتيبل

پتيله patilá *f.* ☞ پليته ¹

پتيبل patejə́l *transitive* [*past:* و يې پتيبه] **1** to divide; divide up **2** to decide, make a decision

پت ¹ paṭ *m.* **1** step, rung **2** panel, element (of a door) **3** layer (of cloth) **4** pan (of a scale)

پت ² paṭ *m.* **1** bark of a tree; bark stripped from a tree پت اړول to remove bark from a tree, debark **2** tanning extract from bark

پت ³ paṭ *m.* delirium; fever پت نيولئ دئ He is delirious. He is in a state of delirium. He has a fever.

پټ ⁴ paṭ puṭ **1** hidden, concealed پټ ځای refuge; secluded place **2** secret, clandestine, covert پټ په پته a پټ قرارداد secret agreement دا څه پته خبره نه ده secretly, clandestinely; surreptitiously This is not a secret. ... پته دي نه وي چه The fact ought not to be concealed that ... له ځان سره پټ ساتل to conceal, keep secret نو خبره یې پته واچوله to disregard, pay no heed to He pretended that nothing had happened. **3** latent, hidden, inner, secret **4** closed, private پټ مجلس closed session **5** clothed, covered (of parts of the body) **6** *regional* stricken by misfortune *idiom* څوک د تعلیم نه پټ ساتل Not to allow to learn, to keep in ignorance.

پټ ⁵ paṭ *doublet* غټ

پټ ⁶ paṭ *doublet* لټ

پټاپټ paṭāpaṭ *m.* blindman's bluff (the game)

پټاټې paṭāṭé *f. plural* potato

پټاخه paṭākhá *f.* **1** *military* percussion cap **2** *regional* fly-swatter

پتاخبدار توپک paṭākhedár muzzleloading rifle

پټار paṭār piebald, skewbald; spotted, stripped; having white socks (of a horse)

پټاره paṭāra *f.* **1** ribbon, strap **2** stripe (leather, bark) **3** stripe (on uniform trousers)

پتاس pəṭās *m. chemistry* potash

پتاسه pəṭāsá *f.* waste material from sugar cane

پتاخه paṭakha *f. Eastern* ☞ پتاخه

پتانستان paṭānistán *m. obsolete* ☞ پښتونستان

پټ پټ paṭ paṭ secretly, clandestinely; furtively, surreptitiously

پټ پټاڼی paṭpaṭānaj *m. regional* پټ پتانی pəṭpəṭānaj *m.* blindman's bluff (the game) پټ پتانړی کول to play blindman's bluff

پټ پنهم pəṭpinhám **1** completely hidden, concealed **2** top secret

پټ پوهاند pəṭpohānd *m.* magician, wizard

پټ تیا pəṭṭjā *f.* ☞ پټ والی

پتوخ pəṭúkh pəṭókh rude, cruel, harsh

پتوخ والی pəṭukhvālaj *m.* rudeness, cruelty, harshness

پتوخول pəṭukhavá [*past:* پتوخ یې کړ] to cause to become rude or cruel; cause to become harsh

پټ خولی pəṭkhúlaj taciturn, not talkative; reticent

پتوخبدل pəṭukhedál *denominative, intransitive* [*past:* پتوخ شو] to grow coarse, grow rude, grow cruel; grow harsh

پترول peṭról piṭról **1** *m. plural* gasoline د پترولو تانک gasoline pump **2** oil

پترولی peṭrolí piṭrolí *adjective* **1** gasoline **2** oil

پتری paṭṛój *f.* track (of a railroad)

پتکاری paṭkārí *m. plural* aluminum

پتکه ¹ paṭáka *f.* young hen, pullet

پتکه ² paṭəká *f.* **1** threat **2** reprimand, scolding پتکه کول a to threaten b to reprimand, scold

پتکه ³ paṭáka *f.* cottage cheese

پتکه ⁴ paṭká *f.* **1** belt, sash **2** kind of noose, snare, lariat

پتکی paṭkáj *m.* small turban *idiom* د مشرتوب پتکی the position of leader or head پتکی د چا په پښو غورزول to throw oneself at someone's feet; to beseech someone for assistance

پتکی ² puṭakáj tiny, small; insignificant

پتکی ³ pəṭəki ☞ تڼکی ¹

پتگنی puṭganój *f.* ambush پتگنی کول to set up an ambush

پټ لمسه pəṭlamésa *f. computer science* blind carbon copy (bcc, e.g., of email)

پټلی paṭlój *f. singular & plural* rail, rails; railroad tracks

پتم paṭám *m.* sluice gate of a yaryk (i.e., irrigation channel)

پتن paṭán *m.* dock, landing

پتنگ paṭáng *m.* ☞ پتنگ

پتنوس paṭnús *m.* ☞ پتنوس

پټ نوم paṭnúm *m.* تبرنویی password

پتنه puṭóna *f.* **1** ☞ پتونه **2** secret

پتو ¹ paṭú *m.* [*plural:* پتوان paṭuán *plural:* پتوگان paṭugán] patu (woolen shawl or rug) پتو اودل to weave a patu

پتو ² paṭó *oblique plural of* پتی ¹

پتو ³ páṭo *oblique plural of* پټ ⁴

پتوار paṭvár *m.* پتواري patvārí *m. regional* **1** rural accountant, village accountant; rural clerk, village clerk **2** land surveyor

پتوالی pəṭvālaj *m.* **1** ☞ پتونه، پټ والی **2** secret

پتوخ paṭúkh ☞ پتخ

پتوسکی pəṭúkaj *m.* leather trunk (for transporting load on pack animals)

پتوکی ¹ pəṭúkaj *m.* ☞ پوتکی

پتول paṭavál puṭavál *denominative, transitive* [*past:* پټ یې کړ] **1** to hide, conceal, take away, remove **2** to cover, cover up **3** to conceal (from), keep secret حقیقت پتول to conceal the truth, hide the real state of affairs **4** to classify (documents, etc. as secret) **5** *Eastern* to steal ځان پتول a to hide, conceal oneself b to cover oneself up, muffle oneself up (in something) خپل ځان ټول پټ کړه to cover or wrap oneself up properly c to conceal or not tell one's real name, be incognito ځان له سترګو څخه پتول to lie in hiding, lie low سترګی پتول a to shut one's eyes (to) b to disregard, ignore; fail to notice زه غوارم چه لاړشم اوله تا نه هم سترګي پتی کړم I want to go away and never see you again.

پتون paṭún *m.* cover, concealment; sanctuary, refuge (for wild game, wild fowl, etc.) دپتون خورا بنه ځای دئ This is a very secluded place.

پتونه pəṭavóna *f.* **1** hiding, clearing, taking away **2** covering, screening **3** concealment

پتونی ¹ puṭúne *f.* ambush

پتونی ² paṭónaj *m.* woolen shawl, woolen rug

پتوه paṭvá *f.* **1** galloon, braid, lace **2** cord **3** purse

پتوه گر paṭvagór *m.* patvagár *m.* maker of gold lace, braid, etc.

پته ¹ páṭa **1** *f.* secret د چا په پته behind someone's back **2** *feminine plural of* پټ ⁴

پته ² paṭá f. 1 board 2 panel

پته ³ puṭá f. 1 strip (of bark, cloth) 2 metal fastening or clamp

پته ⁴ paṭá f. 1 complaint 2 deed, document

پته خوله paṭakhulá taciturn, uncommunicative; reclusive پته خوله کول a to compell to be silent b to neutralize (the enemy's fire) پته خوله ناست دئ He sits there in silence.

پتهان paṭhán m. regional Pathan, Pushtun

پتهانستان paṭhānistán m. obsolete ☞ پښتونستان

پته دار paṭadár striped

پته دانه páṭa dāná f. regional shashlik made from ram's kidneys and heart

پته کوډ paṭākóḍ m. barcode

پتی ¹ paṭáj m. area which has been sown, field under crops کوچنی پتی a small field; a bed prepared for a crop

پتی ² paṭə́j f. 1 bandage په پتی لګول a to apply a bandage, dress پښه باندی پتی لګول to bandage the leg b to calm, soothe 2 suspenders د جرابو پتی suspenders 3 garters د پتلانه پتی garters 4 strip (of cloth); ribbon, tape 5 board 6 strap, belt

پتی ³ paṭáj f. 1 model, example (for correspondence or practice) 2 ABC book, primer

پتی ⁴ paṭé plural of پته ²

پتی ⁵ paṭí 1 f. plural secret 2 feminine plural of پت ⁴

پتی ⁶ paṭí masculine plural of پتی ¹

پتیاد paṭjád m. cache

پتی پالا paṭí-pālá 1 secret, concealed 2 disordered, distressed

پتیخ paṭíkh ☞ پتخ

پتی دار paṭedár having a stripe of contrasting color on the neck (of animals)

پتیدل paṭedál puṭedál denominative [past: پت شو] 1 to be hidden, be concealed 2 to be covered; cover, wrap oneself په واورو پتیبدل to be covered with snow 3 to hide, lie hidden, set (of heavenly bodies)

پتیدنه paṭedána f. 1 m. [plural: پتیده paṭedə́] hiding; concealment د پتیدو ځای نشته to have nowhere to hide, have no place of concealment

پتیره paṭéra f. 1 main beam of a building 2 boards (collectively) 3 log, beam

پتی لن paṭelán m. textiles weaver's beam پتی لن، پتی لن

پتیمو paṭemú m. damnation

پج padzh m. ☞ پچنه

پچنه padzhána f. 1 scratch 2 cut

پچواب padzhaváb vice ☞ جواب په جواب

پچه padzhá f. 1 oven (for firing bricks or pottery, for the manufacture of glass) 2 furnace, forge 3 blast furnace

پچه وال padzhavál m. bricklayer

پچ ¹ puch unfit, unsuitable, bad

پچ ² pach m. flower pattern on glass, iron, etc.

پچاری pəchāṛáj f. 1 hobbles, chains 2 outer cord of a woven cot or bed

پچ خولی puchkhúlaj foulmouthed

پچرک pachṛák m. eyehole in a belt

پچکولمه puchkulmá f. large intestine (of animals)

پچکي puchəkí m. having set its fruit (cucumbers)

پچموزی pəchmozé f. mockery, ridicule

پچن pəchən 1 weak, puny 2 ugly, not good-looking

پچنه pachána f. 1 lancet 2 cut, scratch

پچواری pichvāṛáj f. ☞ پچواري

پچوری pəchúraj m. regional ☞ دوپته

پچونی pachúnaj regional tiny, minute

پچوی pachávaj m. tail-tuft (of a cow)

پچه ¹ pácha f. púcha f. 1 dung, droppings (of sheep, goats, etc.) په پچه اچول to defecate (of sheep, goats, etc.) 2 pertaining to lot پچه پرختل by lot Western a to draw lots, win b to become the owner of something, pick up or acquire something پچه کول to cast lots پچه سره اچول to draw lots پچه ورل to effect the casting of lots پچی اچول to have a drawing, a lottery idiom پر پچه ختل a to perform a stupid action, get involved in a dumb operation b to act in a conceited manner, put on airs

پچه ² pácha f. ripples (on water) پچه کول to cover with ripples, trouble (water)

پچه ³ pácha f. kiss

پچه ⁴ pachá f. branches (used in covering a roof)

پچي ¹ pacháj f. woven basket (of reed)

پچي ² pucháj f. ☞ پچکي

پچي ³ páchi feminine plural of پچه ^{1, 2}

پچیز pachíz m. پچیس pachís m. pachisi, parcheesi (ancient boardgame resembling backgammon, played on a cruciform board)

پځای pədzáj 1 on the spot, at the location 2 executed, carried out پځایول ☞ پځای کول

پځایول pədzājavál denominative, transitive [past: پځای یی کړ] to fulfill (e.g., an obligation)

پخول padzavál transitive ☞ پزول ¹

پخ pəts 1 dull, blunt پخه چاره dull knife ☞ پخ کول 2 پخول dull, stupid, slow-witted 3 crude, rough 4 steep, preciptous

پخسانی pətsānaj 1.1 insignificant, small; tiny, scanty 1.2 rare, fortuitous 2 m. small piece, fragment of something; crumb, pinch

پخستوب pətstób m. پختیا pətsjā f. blunting, dulling (of a knife, etc.)

پخسنگ pətsáng vice ☞ خنگ په خنگ

پخسنی patsónaj پخانی

پخسوالی pətsválaj m. ☞ پختوب

پخول pətsavál denominative, transitive [past: پخ یی کړ] 1 to dull, blunt, obtund 2 figurative to confuse idiom د دښمن سره یی پخی کړي دي They dealt with the enemy.

پخسونه pətsavóna f. dulling, blunting (of a knife, etc.)

پخه ¹ pátsa f. stitch

پخه ² pátsa feminine singular of پخ

پخه ³ pətsə́ vice ☞ خه په خه

پخی patsə́j f. ☞ پیخکی

پخښدل pətsedə́l [past: پخ شو] 1 to be dulled, be blunted, be obtunded 2 *figurative* to grow dull, sink into torpor

پخښر pətsér *vice* په خبر 1 like, resembling 2 similar

پخ¹ pəkh *m.* tetter, mange; scab

پخ² pəkh *m.* 1 sniffing (of a cat) 2 exclamation or cry by which a child is frightened

پخ³ pakh *m.* 1 trap, snare 2 fetters, manacles

پخ⁴ pəkh *m.* loud guffaw; burst of laughter

پخاټی pikhāṭi *f. plural* پخاری pikhāṛaj *m.* wool clotted with dung (at or near the tail of a sheep)

پخپله pəkhpə́la pəkhpúla 1 (my, thy, his, her, etc.) -self; personally زه به پخپله ورسم I will go to him myself. 2 willingly; voluntarily, of one's own free will 3 by oneself, spontaneously

پخت pukht *m. Eastern* ☞ پښت²

پختگي pukhtagí *f.* 1 ripening 2 *figurative* maturity; wisdom; experience

پختورګی pukhtavórgaj *m. Eastern* ☞ پښتورگی

پخته¹ pukhtá 1 ☞ پوخ² 2 basic, fundamental (of a structure, construction) 3 training (of a falcon, a hawk)

پخته² pakhtá *f.* cotton

پخته کار pakhtakār *m.* cotton grower

پخته کاري¹ pakhtakārí *f.* cotton growing, cultivation of cotton

پخته کاري² pukhtakārí *f.* paving, tarring

پخساک pakhsā́k *m.* 1 grief; sorry; melancholy; chagrin 2 envy

پخساول pakhsavál *transitive* [past: و يي پخساوه] 1 to grieve; upset 2 to anger, enrage 3 to invoke envy, cause envy

پخسوی¹ pakhsə́vaj *Western* boiled, cooked

پخسوي² pākhsaví *present tense of* پخسول

پخسه pakhsá *f.* layer of a pisé (beaten clay) wall د پخسي دېوال pisé wall پخسه وهل to lay, put in place, make a pisé wall

پخسېدل pakhsedə́l *intransitive* [past: و پخسېده] 1 to grieve (for); be sad; be melancholy; be distressed 2 to strive for something; try to get something 3 to envy, covet هغه راته پخسېږي He envies me. د ده دولت ته پخسېده He covets his (i.e., another's) wealth.

پخسېدنه pakhsedə́na *f.* 1 grief, sadness, melancholy 2 striving after something 3 envy

پخسيه pakhsijá *adjective* liquid, fluid

پخشاك pakhshāk *m.* ☞ پخساك

پخشو pakhshó quiet

پخشوی pakhshə́vaj ☞ پخسوی¹

پخكړئ pakhkáṛaj *compound past participle of* پخول ښه دوډۍ يې پخكړي وه He cooked a good meal.

پخل pəkhə́l *m.* preparation of irrigated land which is under a rice crop

پخلا pukhlá reconciled پخلا کول a to reconcile b to come to an agreement, settle (a question, etc.) پخلا کېدل to be reconciled هغوی په ډېره خواری سره پخلا شوي دي They reconciled them with great difficulty.

پخلاتوب pukhlātób *m.* [plural: پخلاکېده pukhlākedə́] *m.* پخلاوالی pukhlāvə́laj *m.* reconciliation

پخلاوی pakhlāvaj *m.* cook

پخلان pakhlán *m.* cookery, culinary work

پخلنځ pakhlándz *m.* kitchen

پخلنگ pakhláng *m.* cooking, preparation of food

پخلوځی pakhlózáj *m.* kitchen

پخلی¹ pakhláj *m.* 1 cooking, preparation of food د پخلي اسباب، د پخلي کال cooking equipment د پخلي ځای pakhlí kitchen 2 cookery 3 baking (bricks) 4 maturity; wisdom

پخلي² pə́khli *f. plural* ☞ چخره

پخلي³ pukhə́le *f.* ☞ پوخلی

پخلېدځی pakhlédzáj *m.* ☞ پخلوځی

پخن¹ pəkhə́n 1 downy, having a nap 2 rug or shawl with nap or pile

پخن² pakhán *m.* mineral

پخوندی pəkhəndáj *m.* ☞ پخوندی

پخوا pəkhvá 1 before پخوا له دې څخه before this, before this time پخوا تر هر څه first of all, له هر شي څخه پخوا before this پخوا تر دې first and foremost د دوی تر راتلو پخوا before their arrival 2 earlier, before; in former times, in the past پخوا پخوا a long time ago 3.1 previous, former په پخوا زمانو کښي in former, previous times د پخوا ځني since former times, dating from former times په پخوا راهيسي in comparison with what used to be, in comparison with the previous circumstance نسبت و پخوا ته more than تر پخوا زيات as before, as د پخوا په ډول، لکه د پخوا په خبر before previously 3.2 ancient د پخوا پخوا نه *Eastern* له ډېره پخوا راهيسي from ancient times 4 ☞ خوا ☞ په خوا

پخواترپخوا pəkhvātərpəkhvá beforehand, in good time

پخوالی pəkhvə́laj *m.* ☞ پخلی¹

پخواني pəkhvắnaj 1.1 old, ancient; very old پخواني شيان pakhvā́ni antiquities له پخوانيو زمانو څخه of old, from ancient times 1.2 previous, preceding, foregoing, early 1.3 former, ex- 2.1 person living in ancient times 2.2 پخواني pakhvā́ni *plural* ancestors

پخواني توب pəkhvā́najtób *m.* antiquity

پخوړ pəkhóṛ *m.* juice, extract

پخوړول pəkhoṛavál *m.* [past: پخوړ يې کړ] *denominative, transitive* to squeeze out, press out

پخول pakhavə́l *denominative, transitive* [past: پوخ يې کړ] 1 to cook, prepare (food) 2 to cause to become ripe; facilitate ripening 3 to bake, fire (brick) 4 to pave, tar 5 *figurative* to cause to be, make experienced, make mature; make wiser through experience *idiom* سترگه پخول to acquire a good eye

پخولا pəkholā *regional* ☞ پخلا

پخوله¹ pəkhóla *f.* whooping cough

پخوله² pəkhulá *vice* ☞ خوله ا خوله

پخولی pəkhvaláj *m.* پخون pakhún *m.* ☞ پخلی¹

پخوندی pəkhvandáj *m.* 1 joint (of an animal's leg) 2 knot 3 buttonhole

پخوونکی pakhavúnkaj **1** *present participle of* ووډی پخوونکی baker **2** *m.* cook; baker

پخوونی pakhavúnaj *m.* cook; baker

پخه[1] pə́kha *f.* **1** wool undercoat (wool-bearing animals) **2** down, pile

پخه[2] pakhá *feminine singular of* پوخ

پخی[1] pəkháj **1** mangy; suffering from mange (or similar skin disease); scabby **2** person suffering from the itch or other skin disease characterized by scabs **3** lousy fellow

پخی[2] pə́khi *f. plural* dandruff, scruff

پخیدل pakhedə́l *denominative, intransitive* [*past:* پوخ شو] **1** to be cooked, be prepared (of food) **2** to be fired, be baked (of brick) **3** to be prepared, be mixed (of cement) **4** to be paved, be tarred **5** to ripen, mature **6** *figurative* to become experienced, become wise **7** to come into one's own (of seasons of the year); come on, begin, fall (e.g., of night) چه شپه پخه شوه، کلي ته ورسیدل They arrived in the settlement when night had far advanced. **8** *figurative* to be tormented, suffer

پخیده pakhedə́ *m. plural* ☞ پخلی[1]

پخیر pəkhájr *vice* پہ خیر، پخیر اوسې! All the best!

پخل pəkhél *m.* **1** employment or use of a sudorific **2** sweating, profuse sweating پخل کول to induce sweating, evoke perspiration

پخلوالی pəkheválaj *m.* sweating, profuse perspiration

پداسی pədāsi *vice* ☞ پہ داسي

پدری pidarí padarí paternal پدري حصه پدري زمکه hereditary land patrimony (inheritance)

پدغه pədágha *vice* ☞ پہ دغه[1]

پدل padl *m.* padə́l *m.* **1** influence پدل کول to influence something **2** fear, terror پدل وراتول *idiom* a پدل ماتول to break from being too shy, wean from being too shy b to make more adroit

پدننه pədənə́na پدننه کښې pədənə́nakkhi inside, within ☞ دننه

پدود pədód like, as, how

پدول padúl *m.* **1** gossip, scandalmonger **2** deceiver, cheat

پدوله padúla *f.* **1** gossip, scandalmonger (women) **2** deceiver, cheat (woman)

پدولي padulí *f.* **1** fraud, deception **2** (unauthorized) disclosure of a secret

پدوی pədúj *vice* ☞ پہ دوی[2]

پدی pədé *vice* ☞ پہ دی[2]

پدید padíd clear, evident, manifest

پدنگ pádíng *m.* pudding

پدول pədául *vice* ☞ پہ ډول[1]

پده padá *f.* **1** species of willow (lit. the old willow) **2** species of popular (lit. the variegated-leafed poplar)

پذیرائي pazirāí *f.* meeting; reception پذیرائي کول to meet

پر[1] par *m.* **1** sail of a windmill **2** blade or flat board of a water wheel **3** wing **4** fin (of a fish) *idiom* پر وهل a to knock one's ankle together while walking b to stretch, stretch out c to procede (from) پر څنې وهل to be afraid of someone, fear someone

پر[2] pər pur *Western* **1** *preposition usually in compound with the suffix* باندي; *feminine nouns in* ə (a, a) *may not be subject to inflexion;* **1.1** on (to designate location on the surface of an object, the direction of an action, and also places and expanses) پر پر چوکی، پر چوکی باندي on the chair پر میز، پر میز باندي on the table **1.2** in (to indicate the location where some action is taking place) پر دکان کښینستل *literal* to sit in a shop *figurative* to trade **1.3** to (to indicate direction toward) د برما لار پر چین the road from Burma to China **1.4** at, during, in etc. (in designating time) پر نیمه شپه at midnight د طوفان پر وخت during or in the midst of the storm پر دېرشم کال in his/her 30th year of life **1.5** in, into (to convey the general sense of distribution) پر درو تقسیمول divide 3 into … **1.6** by (to indicate the route or means of travel) د بحر پر لاري by sea پر لاري تئ He went by road (i.e., land travel) **1.7** on (to indicate the direction of an action upon a specific object) پر سر وهل to beat on the head **1.8** over, above (to indicate the location of someone, something higher than something else, above it) زمونږ پر over, above us الوتکه پر ښارگرزیده سر باندي the aircraft circled over the city **1.9** after (to indicate the sequence of events or objects) پوښتنه پر پوښتنه question after question **1.10** for (to indicate the reason, cause, or goal) پر ناموس for the sake of honor پر ښار جنگونه the battle for the city پر یوه مڅکه دعوه competition for land پر څه باندي؟ For what reason? **1.11** at, with (to indicate a person associated with an action) پر ملا سبق ویل to study with a mullah پر خیاط کالي گنډل to work at a tailor's (shop) **1.12** *used to designate dates* د جون پر۱۵ June 15th **2.1** on him, on her, on it, on them هغه چوکی واخله او پر کښینه Take this chair and sit on it. **2.2** concerning him, about her, concerning it, about them څه پر ولیکئ write something about him **2.3** for him, for her, for it, for them یوه داسي روځ به پر راشي چه … the day will come for him (her, them) when … **2.4** according to him, according to her, according to it **2.5** for him, for her, for them

پر[3] pər sound imitative of the flight (take-off) of birds (whirrr) پر وهل to take wing, fly up, take off

پر pur *combining form* full, filled پرآشوب filled with alarm, uneasy

پرا prā *separable initial prefix of the verb* پرانیتل، پرانستل، *in laconic phrases* پرا می نه نسته *Eastern* I didn't open it

پراته prātə́ *masculine plural of* پروت

پراتیک prātík *m.* practice

پراټه parāṭá *f.* layered pastry

پراچه parāchá *m.* [*plural:* پراچه گان parāchagán پراچه گان *plural:*] **1** cotton textiles trader; peddler **2** ☞ پراچي[1]

پراچي parāchí **1** *m. singular & plural* Parachi (a nationality) **2** *f.* Parachi (language)

پراخ prākh pirákh **1** wide, extensive, spacious **2** open (i.e., a brow)

پراخ پزی prākhpázaj having a flattened nose

پراختیا prākhtjā *f.* **1** ☞ پراخوالی **2** *military* deployment, dispersal

پراخوالی prākhválaj *m.* **1** extensiveness, spaciousness **2** territory, area **3** broadening, increase **4** development پراخوالی ميندل to widen; increase; develop (i.e., trade)

پراخول prākhavól *denominative, transitive* [*past:* پراخ يي کړ] **1** to widen, increase **2** to develop (i.e., trade) *idiom* سينه پراخول a to expand the chest **b** to accomplish a feat; perform a feat of valor

پراخه prákha pirākha *feminine singular of* پراخ

پراخه باند prākhábánd *m.* broadband

پراخي prākhí *f.* pirākhí ☞ پراخوالی *idiom* د سينې پراخي quiet, tranquility

پراخېدل prākhedól *denominative, intransitive* [*past:* پراخ شو] **1** to be widened; be increased **2** to be developed (i.e., trade)

پرار pirār [1] *m.* ☞ فرار

پرار pərār [2] *m.* ☞ پرهار [1]

پراړول pirāravól *denominative, transitive* ☞ فرارول

پراړه pirāra *f.* ☞ فرار

پراړېدل pirāredól *denominative, intransitive* ☞ فراربدل

پراز pərāz *vice* ☞ په راز ☞ راز [1]

پرازيتولوژي parāzitolozhí *f.* parasitology

پرازيتي parāzití parasitic

پراژېکتور prāzhektór searchlight

پراسراره purasrāra mysterious, full of mystery, enigmatic

پرآشوب purāshúb uneasy, anxious; tense پرآشوب وخت uneasy time, time of anxiety

پراشوت parāshút *m.* parachute د پراشوت فن parachute jumping (as sport)

پراشوتي parāshutí **1** *adjective* parachute پراشوتي عسکر parachute units **2.1** *m.* parachutist **2.2** *f.* parachute jumping

پراگ prāg *m.* Prague (city)

پراگندگي parāgandagí *f.* diffusion, sparseness

پراگنده parāgandá diffused, dispersed پراگنده کول to diffuse, disperse

پراگوی parāgváj *m.* ☞ پاراگوی

پرامن purámi purámna calm, equable

پرانتل prānətól *transitive* ☞ پرانيتل

پرانتنه prānətóna *f.* پرانست prānóst *m.* opening (the act) پرانتنه کول to open

پراچه parāchá پراچه

پرانستل pranəstól *transitive* ☞ پرانيتل

پرانستئ prānístaj **1** open په پرانستو سترگو with open eyes **2** wide, spacious

پرانستي سرچينه prāniste sarchiná *f. computer science* open source

پرانسي prānsé *f. colloquial* the French language

پراني parāní *second element in compounds* سرنگ پراني exploding, blasting

پرانيت prānít *past of* پرانيتل پرانيت کېدل to be opened

پرانيتل prānitól *transitive* [*present:* پرانيڅي *past:* پرانئ نيت] **1** to open **2** to open (i.e., to found or establish, e.g., a school or other establishment) **3** to untie, loosen (i.e., a knot) **4** to unfold, unroll **5** untwist, unreel **6** *figurative* to explain پرانيتل کېدل *passive* **a** to be opened **b** to be opened (i.e., to found or establish, e.g., a school or enterprise) **c** to be untied (e.g., a knot) ډوډۍ پرانيتل to make a living

پرانيځ prānidz *present stem of* پرانيتل

پرانيستل pranistól *transitive* ☞ پرانيتل

پراوېز parāvéz *m. regional* eaves (of a roof)

پراها prāhā *f.* Prague (city)

پرائمري prājmari *regional* primary (of a school)

پوراينه purājóna *f.* ☞ پوراينه

پرباندي púrbāndi *a compound of the preposition* پر *and the suffix or postposition* باندي ☞ پر [2]

پرپانو parpaṇú *m. botany* colocynth

پرپر pərpər quickly, animatedly پرپر راتويبدل to flow, stream, roll (i.e., of tears); to flow in a stream or current

پرپرکی pərpərakáj *m.* screw, propellor (i.e., of an aircraft)

پرپی purpáj caught, captured

پرت prat pərt [1] **1** shallow, empty, useless **2** inappropriate, out of place **3** distant, remote **4** maimed, disfigured **5** flabby, flaccid, weak

پرت pərt [2] connected, linked, attached

پرتاب partáb *m.* range (of an arrow, bullet, etc.)

پرتاگه partāgə̣ *oblique singular of* پرتوگ

پرتاو partáv *m.* throwing, flinging, hurling پرتاو کول *compound verb* to throw, fling, hurl پرتاو کېدل *compound verb* to fall, fall down, collapse

پرتگال partugál *m.* Portugal

پرتگالي partugālí partūgaláj **1** Portuguese **2** *m.* Portuguese (person)

پرتل partál *m.* **1** equipment, outfit **2** gear of a horseman or nomad (which is carried on a horse, camel, etc.)

پرتله partalá *f.* **1** equilibrium, equipoise, balance **2** weighing **3** *figurative* evaluation پرتله کول a to balance **b** to weigh **c** *figurative* to consider, think over; evaluate پرتله کېدل a to be balanced, be evened up **b** to be weighed **c** *figurative* to be considered, be evaluated

پرتم partám *m.* horror; terror; fear له پرتمه from terror, from fear پر پرتم کېدبي in horror

پرتوگ partúg *m.* wide, Middle-Eastern trousers *idiom* پرتوگ ايستل، پرتوگ کبدل to take off one's belt; to grow insolent

پرتوگابش pártugáx̣ pártugāsh belt, girdle (used to hold up wide Middle-Eastern trousers) *idiom* پرتوگابن په شلبدل to overtax one's strength, overtax oneself

پرتوگ پوښ partugóx̣ partugókh wearing wide Middle-Eastern pants, dressed in oriental fashion

پرته práta [1] **1.1** *feminine singular of* پرت [1] **1.2** foolish, stupid, nonsensical, confused پرته ويل، پرته گەبدل to talk nonsense **2** *f.* quarrel, discord ورسره يي پرته ده He is at odds with him/them.

پرته práta [2] *preposition Eastern* without; except, apart from, over and above پرته لدي aside from this, apart from this

پرته ³ pratá *feminine singular of* پروت

پرته ورته práta-varta confused, chaotic

پرتي práti *f. plural* 1 of پرت ¹ 2 nonsense, gibberish پرتي ویل to talk nonsense, speak rubbish

پرچ ¹ prəch *m. regional* plate; dish; saucer

پرچ ² prəch *m.* 1 sneezing 2 snorting (of an animals)

پرچاو parcháv پارچاو ²

پرچتۍ parchatáj *m.* 1 straw awning or eave on a beaten-clay (pise) wall (protection from weather) 2 hut with a straw or wooden roof 3 coating of clay mixed with straw

پرچل ¹ parchál unsuitable, bad; below quality standard

پرچل ² prəchól *transitive* [past: و یې پرچل] to sneeze

پرچم parchám *m.* 1 lock, curl, ringlet; forelock 2 banner, flag 3 *botany* stamen

پرچول prəchavól *causative* [past: و یې پرچاوه] to cause sneezing, evoke sneezing

پرچون parchún *m.* groceries

پرچه parchá *f.* 1 issue (of a magazine, newspaper) 2 excerpt, clipping (from a magazine, newspaper)

پرچی prəcháj *m.* sneezing

پرچدل prəchedól [past: و پرچېده] to sneeze

پرځای pərdzáj purdzāj 1 fitting, proper 2 appropriate 3 executed, carried out 4 living somewhere پرځای کول a to execute, carry out b to settle پرځای کېدل a to be executed, be carried out b to be settled

پرځندانه pərdzandānó (of a pregnant woman) near her time, in the last month of pregnancy

پرځول pərdzavól *transitive* ☞ پرزول

پرځبدل pərdzedól *intransitive* ☞ پرزبدل

پرځنگبدل pərtsxangedól *denominative, intransitive* [past: پرځنگ شو] to stand aside, make way

پرحرارت purharatát passionate, ardent (of feelings)

پرخ ¹ parkh *m.* injustice پرخ کول to act unjustly

پرخ ² pərkh *m.* severe cold, hard frost

پرخلاف pərkhiláf against, contrary to ☞ خلاف

پرخم ¹ pərkhám *m.* brush or tuft of the tail (animal)

پرخم ² parkhám *m.* 1 ☞ پرچم 2 fan 3 fly swatter

پرخوا purkhvá supporting someone, something; siding with someone ☞ خوا

پرخوالی purkhvávălaj *m.* help, assistance, support

پرخول parkhavól *transitive* [past: و یې پرخول] to squirt water, spurt water (with the mouth); to sprinkle; to moisten, wet

پرخه pərkha *f.* 1 dew پرخه پربوته dew has fallen 2 light shower

پرخیز parkhíz unjust

پرخیل pərkhíl *m.* ☞ پښخبل

پرداخت parkdákht *m.* 1 expense 2 payment 3 use of something د قوت پرداخت application, employment (of force)

پراختي pardākhtí *adjective* payment

پردار pardár 1 winged 2 having blades, fans, paddles, etc.

پرداز pardáz *m.* execution; fulfillment; finishing (work of final nature in craft, etc.)

پردازي pardāzí *f. second element of compounds* انشا پردازي composing; writing letters

پردل purdíl 1 bold, brave 2 *m. proper name* Purdil

پردو ¹ prادó *oblique plural of* پردی

پردو ² pardó *oblique plural of* پرده ¹

پرده ¹ pardá *f.* 1 curtain; bed curtain; jalousie, blinds 2 screen د نری پرده لوگي پرده smoke screen 3 covering, casing, membrane د زړه پرده *anatomy* pleura د ډنگ پرده membrane *anatomy* pericardium 4 layer د خاوره پرده یوه stratum of earth 5 screen د سینما پرده cinema screen 6 *figurative* cover (of night, etc.) 7 پرده پورته کول to reveal a secret، پرده خیرل اخیستل to raise a curtain, expose تا نه څه پرده ده I have nothing to hide from you. په پرده یې راته وویل He told me in secret. 8 seclusion, solitary life; seclude life (of women) 9 secluded life 10 part, action, activity, act (of a play) 11 picture 12 frame (of film) 13 *figurative* camouflage پرده کول، پرده پر، پرده پراچول *compound verb* پرده غوړول to hide, cover up پرده کېدل *compound verb* to be hidden, be covered up

پرده ² pərdó ☞ ده ²

پرده بندي parabandí *f.* seclusion, secluded life (of a female)

پرده پوښ pardapóẋ 1 keeping a secret; concealing 2 *m.* custodian of a secret, keeper of a secret

پرده پوښي pardapoẋí *f.* paradapoẋhi *f.* keeping a secret; concealment

پرده دار pardadár secret, confidential

پرده داره pardadára *f.* female leading a secluded way of life (for cultural and traditional reasons)

پرده داري pardadārí *f.* 1 trust, confidence 2 concealment, dissimulation

پردی pradáj prədaj 1.1 foreign, strange, alien, another's پردی ژبه foreign body پردی دهقاني کول to plow and sow for another; work as a farm laborer پردی کټ تر نیمو شپو دئ *proverb* One can use another's bed … till midnight 1.2 foreign پردی ژبه foreign tongue pradí په پردي ملک کښې foreign goods پردي شیان to alienate پردی کول abroad پردی کېدل to become alienated 2 *m.* 1 foreigner; alien; stranger له پردو لاسه خلاصول to deliver from the foreign yoke د پردو تسلط foreign domination 2.2 great-great-grandson

پردی توب prədajtób *m.* alienation; estrangement

پردېس pardés *m.* 1 wanderer 2 traveller 3 visitor

پردېسنه pardesóna *f.* pardesí *f.* 1 wandering; journeying; journey 2 vagrancy

پردېسي توب pardesitób *m.* the wandering life

پردېسبدل pardesedól *denominative, intransitive* [past: پردېس شو] to 1 wander; roam; travel 2 to be a tramp; be on the road

پرړ priṛ ☞ پربړ

پرړوالی priṛválaj *m.* ☞ پربړوالی

پرزحمت purzahmát hard, difficult; troublesome پرزحمته ازموینه a difficult experience

پرزو ¹ pirzó ☞ پپرزو

پرزه ² purzó *oblique plural of* پرزه

پرزول pərzavə́l *transitive* [*past:* و يي پرزاوه] 1 to throw down on the ground; to overcome (in wrestling) زه يي ويپرزولم He threw me. He wrestled me down. 2 *m. plural* wrestling پرزول كول *sports* to wrestle

پرزوه pirzavá *f. feminine singular of* پرزو ¹

پرزه purzá *f.* [*plural:* پرزې purzé *plural:* پرزه جات purzadzhə́t] *Arabic* part; component د موټر پرزې parts for a car

پرزه فروشي purzafurushí *f.* sale of components, parts, etc. (e.g., of machines, cars)

پرزېدل pərzedə́l *intransitive* [*past:* وپرزېده] to fall, topple

پرس pres *m.* pressing, compressing د پرس دستگاه a press (machine) پرس كول *compound verb* to press پرس كېدل *compound verb* to be pressed

پرسان pursán 1 asking, inquiring about 2 *m.* inquiry, request, questioning

پرسپېکتيف perspektíf *m.* perspective (in architecture, drawing, painting)

پرست parást 1 worshiping something; bowing, making obeisance to something 2 paying court to someone taking care of, troubling onself about someone 3 *the second elemental of compounds* آتش پرست fire-worshiper

پرستار parastár *m.* 1 person who is taking care of or showing concern about another 2 hospital attendant, hospital orderly

پرستاره parastára *f.* nurse; female hospital attendant; child's nurse

پرستاري parastāri 1 care of the sick 2 hospital work د پرستاري مكتب training courses for hospital attendants

پرستش parastísh *m.* worship, veneration; cult د چا پرستش كول to bow down before someone, venerate someone; honor someone د يوشي پرستش كول to worship something

پرستي parastí *combining form* worship of something بت پرستي idolatry

پرستيژ prestízh *m.* prestige, authority خپل پرستيژ تسليمول to lose prestige, lose face, lose authority خپل پرستيژ ته صدمه رسول to undermine one's authority, cause the loss of or damage to one's authority or prestige

پرسد pursə́d 1 state of being conscious, aware 2 intelligent

پرسوزه pursóza full of emotion, heartfelt

پرسونال personál *m.* پرسونل personál *m.* personél *m.* staff, personnel پرسونال فني experts, technical and engineering workers

پرش parísh *m.* 1 beating, throb, palpitation د زړه پرش heartbeat پرش كول to beat, throb, palpitate 2 flight, flying

پرشا pərshá *adverb* back, backwards پرشا بول a to drive off b to lead back, take back پرشا تلل to step back, retreat پرشا ځغلول to beat back (the enemy)

پرشتيا pərishtjá *vice* ☞ رشتيا په رشتيا

پرشكال parshakál *m.* rainy season, monsoon season

پرشور ¹ purshór 1 animated, lively (e.g., a city) 2 energetic (of an action)

پرشور ² parshór *m.* Parshor (the ancient name of the city of Peshawar)

پرېښته piriḵtá *f.* piriḵtá *f.* 1 angel 2 *proper name* Pirishta, Firishta

پرېنه pə́rḵha *f.* pə́rḵha *f.* mushroom, *Russula foetens idiom* پرېنه كېدل to harden, become hard *idiom* وچه پرېنه كېدل to stint, grudge, skimp *idiom* كومه پرېنه په تا ولگېده؟ What has gotten into you? What has happened to you?

پرضد pərzíd pərzídd *Western* against, opposed to someone or something ☞ ضد

پرغرور purghurúr ambitious; arrogant

پرغز parghə́z *m.* 1 arrow with an iron tip (for children's games) 2 fainting fit, swoon پرغز كېدل *compound verb* to lose consciousness, lose one's senses, fall in a swoon 3 rage, fury پرغز نيول a to lose consciousness, be deprived of one's senses, fall in a swoon b to get into a rage, fly into a fury

پرغزتيا parghaztjá *f.* irritability, edginess

پرغزي pargazí 1 nervous, irritable, edgy 2 convulsive, spasmodic

پرقيمت purḵimát valuable پرقيمت ارشادات valuable instructions

پركال ¹ parkár ☞ پركال

پركار ² purkár 1 full, filled, crowded; stuffed (with) 2 well-made, well put-together

پركاري purkārí *f.* 1 stuffing (of a stuffed animal) 2 *technology* filling in with rubble

پركال ¹ parkā́l *m.* compasses, dividers

پركال ² parkā́l *regional* weak, sickly, puny

پركالتيا parkāltjá *f.* پركالوالى parkālvā́laj *m.* weakening, debilitation

پركالول parkālavə́l *denominative, transitive* [*past:* پركال يې كړ] to weaken, debilitate

پركالېدل parkaledə́l *denominative, intransitive* [*past:* پركال شو] to grow weak, become sickly

پركټى ¹ pərkaṭáj *m.* stepson

پركټى ² pərkaṭə́j *f.* stepdaughter

پركبن purkaḵ purkaḵ pulling the bowstring to its limit

پركن parkán پركنډ parkā́nḍ *m.* landmark

پركي ¹ parəkí *f.* bread baked on a stone

پركى ² purkáj *m.* taking wing (birds)

پركار pargā́r *m.* ☞ پركال ¹

پرگټى ¹ pərgaṭáj *m.* ☞ پركټى ¹

پرگټى ² pərgaṭə́j *f.* ☞ پركټى ²

پرگنه parganá *f.* Pargana (general term for district or state in India)

پرگويي purguí *f.* gossip, idle talk زياته پرگويي مي وكړه I began to chatter idly.

پرگه pargá *f.* tribe, nationality

پرگى pərgáj pirgáj *m.* acorn

پرل ² pərə́l *transitive* ☞ پېرل

پرله pórla *Western* **1** placed alongside, located alongside; adjoining **2.1** around, round بيبو سر مي پرله ګرزي my head is going around پرله وخرخبده طبيعت يي پرله Bibo has begun to whirl about from joy. **2.2** continuously, all the time **2.3** entirely, completely طبيعت يي پرله واوښت His character has completely changed.

پرله باندي pórlabāndí **1** folded **2** placed one upon the other

پرله پسي pərlapacé *Western* **1.1** successive, consecutive **1.2** continuous, uninterrupted, unbroken **2.1** successively, consecutively **2.2** continuously, uninterruptedly, unbrokenly *idiom* پرله پسي لمبر latest issue, current issue (of a newspaper)

پرله پسبوالی pərlapasevālaj *m. Western* **1** sequence, succession **2** continuity

پرله پوري pórlapuri **1** connected; attached (to) **2** sequential **3** fit (for), suitable **4** well-built; beautiful زينبه پرله پوري وه Zejnab was good-looking.

پرله پوري والی pórlapurivālaj *m. Western* **1** joining; contiguity **2** sequence **3** fitness, suitability **4** beauty, comeliness

پرله وهلئ pórla vahálaj *Western* portly, fat

پرليکه pórlika په کرښه pókarkha *computer science* online

پرم prəm ☞ پرن

پرمان parmắn *m.* ☞ فرمان

پرمايل parmā́jəl *transitive* ☞ فرمايل

پرمخ pərmə́kh purmə́kh *Western* **1** before someone, in front of someone, ahead of someone **2.1** forward, ahead پرمخ بيول to successfully develop, execute something *dialect* **a** پرمخ درومبدل to go ahead, move forward, advance **b** to develop, make progress **2.2** completely, entirely, fully پرمخ منع کول to forbid absolutely, ban categorically پرمخ ځه، پرشا ګوره! *saying* Go and have a look around! **b** پرمخ درومبدل **a** پرمخ تلل to disappear, be missing, get lost زما کتاب پرمخ ولاړ My book is missing.

پرمختگ pərməkhtág *m.* purməkhág **1** movement forward, attack پرمختگ وکې! *military* Forward! (as a command) **2** development, progress

پرمختلئ، پرمخ تللئ pərmə́kh tlálaj developed, advanced (e.g., of a country)

پرمختله pərmə́khtlə́ *m. plural* پرمختوب pərməkhtób *m.* پرمختيا pərməkhtjā́ *f.* پرمخ تگ پرمخ يون pərməkhjún *m.* ☞ pərmə́khjún

پرمنگان permangā́n *m.* potassium permanganate

پرمهره parmuhrá *f. hunting* divination (used by those hunting wildfowl) پرمهره اچول، پرمهره غورځول to cast spells, predict through paranormal means or charms

پرمهره parmerá *f.* mushroom

پرنا pərnā́ *f.* **1** drowsiness; lassitude پرنا ول to nod (in sleepiness); cause sleepiness

پرنا paraná *f.* **2** د پرنا درياب the Parana River

پرناله parnālá *f.* gutter, drainpipe

پرناوری parnāvə́raj **1** sleepy, drowsy پرناوړي سترګي parnāvórí sleepy eyes **2** sluggish, flaccid **3** pensive

پرناوه parnāvá *f.* ☞ پرناله

پرنج prandzh *m.* sneezing

پرنجل prəndzhál *transitive* [*past:* وي يي پرنجل] to sneeze

پرنجول prəndzhavál *causative* [*past:* وي يي پرنجاوه] to cause sneezing

پرنجونکی prəndzhavúnkaj sternutatory پرنجونکی غاز sternutatory (sneezing) gas

پرنجی prəndzháj *m.* sneezing

پرنجبدل prəndzhedál *intransitive* [*past:* وپرنجبده] to sneeze

پرنجبدنه prəhdzhedóna *f.* sneezing

پرنځل prəndzál *transitive* ☞ پرنجل

پرنځی prəndzáj *m.* ☞ پرنجی

پرنځبدل prəndzedál *intransitive* ☞ پرنجبدل

پرنده parandá *m.* [*plural:* پرندگان *plural:* پرنده گان parandagā́n] bird

پرنړ prəṇ *regional* ☞ پرن

پرنس prins *m.* prince

پرنسپل príncipál *m. regional* principal (chief officer, dean of a college)

پرنسيپ prinsíp *m.* principle د پرنسيپ له مخي out of principle

پرنفوس purnufús populous

پرنگی pərangáj *m.* **1** Englishman **2** European

پرن prəṇ **1** turning sour; curdling **2** coagulating, clotting (of blood)

پرني prəṇi *f.* sweet thin gruel, kissel (a kind of blanc mange)

پرو parú paró *m.* **1** hot wind, simoom

پرو paró *oblique plural of* پر **2**

پرو paró *oblique plural of* پره **3**

پرو purú useless, empty, void **4**

پروا parvá *f.* **1** attention; concern د چا پروا کول، د چا په څه پروا کول to pay attention to someone or something هغه پروا يي په دي ونه کړه He paid no attention to this. **2** agitation, anxiety دا پروا نه It doesn't matter! پروا مه کوه! Don't worry! لري!

پرواز parvā́z *m.* **1** flight, flying د پرواز آله flying machine, aircraft **2** *figurative* (upward) flight, ascent

پروان parvā́n *m.* Parvan, Parwan (a city, former name of Jebel-us-Siraja) د پروان ولايت Parvan Province, Parwan Province

پروانگي parvā́nagí *f.* commission, errand; instruction, directions

پروانه parvā́ná *f.* **1** nocturnal butterfly, nocturnal moth (usually in poetry) **2** propellor, screw (e.g., aircraft)

پروانه parvā́ná *f. history* **2** **1** instruction, directions; writ; patent **2** pass, safe-conduct document; passport

پرواه parvá *f. obsolete* ☞ پروا

پروپاگاند propā́gánd *m.* پروپاگاند propā́gánd *m.* propaganda پروپاگاند چلول، پروپاگاند کول to conduct propaganda; propagandize

پروپاگندچي propā́gandchí *m.* propagandist, propaganda specialist

پروپاگندي propā́gandí propagandistic

پروپاگنډ propā́gánḍ *m.* ☞ پروپاگاند

پروپاگنډچي propā́gánḍchí *m.* ☞ پروپاگندچي

پروپاگنډي propā́gánḍí ☞ پروپاگندي

پروپاگنډه propā́génḍa *f. regional* propaganda

پروپيلر propéller *m.* propellor, screw (e.g., of an aircraft)

پروت prot *m.* پرته pratá *f.* **1** *m.* [*plural:* پراته pratá *f. plural:* پرتي praté]. **1.** lying دئ baandi prot کتاب پر مهز باندي پروت دئ The book is lying on the table. زه دري ورځي ناجوړه پروت وم I was sick in bed for three days. **1.2** living, being somewhere اتمان خپل د تیراه په خواوشا کښي پراته وه The Utmankhejli live in the Tirakh district. **1.3** standing (of furniture) **1.4** consisting of something; inherent in, characteristic of something or someone **2** *m. military* prone position د پروت وضعیت the prone position پروت! Prone position! (command)

پروتست protést *m.* protest وچاته پروتست وړاندي کول to make a protest to someone; protest to someone

پروتستان protestán *m.* Protestant

پروتست protést *m.* ☞ پروتست

پروتوپلاسم protoplásm *m.* protoplasm

پروتوکول protokól *m.* **1** minutes, record of proceedings, report **2** agreement, understanding **3** protocol unit; ceremonial usage, protocol

پروته próta *f.* act of lying down, being in a prone position په پروته *adverb* lying down, in lying or prone position د پروتي اتن kind of Afghan round dance

پروتون protón *m.* proton

پروتي peróte¹ *f.* ☞ پپروتي

پروتئ prótaj² ☞ پروت

پروت parváṭ *m.* **1** strong man; husky fellow **2** hero

پروټتوب parvaṭtób *m.* پروټ والی parvaṭválaj *m.* strength, might

پرودشکتور prodshektór *m.* پروجکتور prodzhiktór *m.* searchlight

پرور parvár *m. second element of compounds* روح پرور for the soul, spiritual

پروردگار parvardigár *m.* God, the All-High

پرورش parvaríkh *m.* پرورښ parvaríkh *m.* parvaríkhh **1** nourishment, feeding, fattening up **2** breeding, cultivation, raising د حیواناتو پرورش animal breeding د پنبي پرورش cotton farming وربښمو د چنجیانو پرورش silkworm breeding, sericulture **3** tending, care, charge, fostering پرورش اخیستل **a** to breed, multiply; be cultivated **b** to be cherished, be fostered **4** training (e.g., of specialists)

پرورل parvarál *transitive* [*past:* و یې پرواره] **1** to feed, nourish **2** to breed; cultivate **3** to rear, educate, foster

پروړ proṛ *m.* [*plural:* پروړونه proṛuna *plural:* پرړونه praṛúna] *Western* straw اوبه تر پروړ لاندي بوول *saying literal* to conduct water under straw *figurative* to be very shrewd

پروړوالا proṛválá *m. singular & plural* person trading in straw; fodder merchant

پروړه próṛa *f.* coarse rice straw

پروژه prozhá *f.* project, scheme, design

پروژکتور prozhektór *m.* searchlight

پروسۀ paroság **1** *m.* last year **2** in the year past, during last year

پروسني parosəgán پروسکلني paroskalanáj پروسبني parosəganáj *Eastern* last year's پروسبن کال **a** last year **b** in the year just past

پروسه parósa *Eastern* پروسه کال **a** last year **b** (sometime during) last year

پروسیک prusík حامض پروسیک prussic acid, hydrocyanic acid

پروشیا prushijá *f.* Prussia

پروخول proḵhavál proḵhavál *transitive* [*past:* و یې پروخباوه] to twist, twirl, revolve, rotate

پروغرام proghrám *m.* ☞ پروگرام

پروف pruf *m. printing* galley proof

پروفیسر profésór *m.* professor

پروفیسري profesorí *f.* **1** teaching in an institution of higher learning **2** professorship; the rank of professor

پروفیسور profesór *m.* ☞ پروفیسر

پروفیل profíl *m.* profile, side view

پروکساید peroksájd *m.* peroxide, hydrogen peroxide

پروگرام prográm *m.* **1** program; plan; rough draft **2** order, routine **3** intention, purpose

پرول paravál *transitive* [*past:* و یې پراوه] **1** ☞ پارول پخول **2** to make run, drive, urge on **3** to steal

پرولدودی proldódaj *m.* **1** mediation, the action of performing as a commercial broker or middleman; commission (commercial) **2** *adjective* commission

پرولل prolál *transitive* [*present:* پرولي *past:* و یې پروله] to sell, market

پرولنه prolána *f.* sale, marketing

پرولوگ prológ *m.* prologue

پرولتار proletár *m.* proletarian

پرولتاري proletári proletarian

پرولبتر proletár *m.* ☞ پرولتار

پرولبتریت proletariját *m.* proletariat

پرون parún yesterday پرون شپه **a** last night **b** yesterday night پرون سهار، د پرون ورځ **a** the day just past **b** yesterday یسترده morning نن پرون lately; in our time بل پرون the day before yesterday تر پرونه پوري until yesterday

پروني parunáj **1** *adjective* yesterday, yesterday's پرونی شپه the night before last **2** preceding, past; former

پرولل provúl *transitive Eastern* ☞ پرولل

پرولنه provúna *f. Eastern* ☞ پرولنه

پروبخی parvédzaj *m.* sieve پروبخی خپل سل سوري نه ویني او د کوزي دوه سوري ویني *saying literal* The sieve does not see its hundred holes, but sees the two openings of a water pitcher. *figurative* To see a mote in the eye of another, and not to see a beam in one's eye

پرویز parvíz *m. proper name* Parviz

پروبخی parvédzaj *m.* ☞ پروبخی

پروین parvín **1** *m. plural astronomy* the Pleiades (star cluster) **2** *proper name* Parvin

پره pará¹ *f.* **1** blade, paddle (of a water wheel, etc.) **2** edge, rim **3** row, line; column; rank په پره تلل to walk in columns, march, walk or move in extended rank order په پره دربدل to be placed standing in a row **4** grouping, group; company پره جنبه clique-formation, cliquishness پره تړل، پره کول **a** to place in a row **b** to group **c** to create a grouping په ... پسې ځان پره کول to join, adjoin someone or something پره پره **a** in groups **b** in rows **c** on end, upended پره کول to place in a row; spread out in a chain **5** peak (of a mountain)

پره ² pará *f.* search; raid, roundup په ... پسې پره کول، پره کول to seek for, make a search; organize a raid

پرهار ¹ purhár parhár *m.* **1** wound گزک شوئ پرهار ulcer **2** blow, injury دپر پرهارونه خورل **a** to be wounded **b** to be beaten severely

پرهار ² purəhár *m.* noise made by the flapping of a bird's wings at take-off

پرهارباد purhārbád *m.* monetary recompense for a wound

پرهارپانه purhārpāṇa *f.* plantain; plantain leaf

پرهارژن purhārdzhón پرهارزه purhārzə́ پرهارژلج purhārzhə́laj پرهارجن purharzhón wounded; injured پرهارجن کول to wound; injure پرهارجن کبدل to be wounded; be injured

پرهاری ¹ purhāráj *m.* surgeon

پرهاری ² purhārí ☞ پرهارجن

پره بندي parabandí *f.* **1** grouping **2** squabbles; spats

پره دار ¹ paradár furnished with blades, equipped with paddles

پره دار ² paradár *m.* supporter, participant, member of a group

پرهر parhár *m.* ☞ پرهار ¹

پرهارپانه purharpāṇa *f.* ☞ پرهارپانه

پرهسر pərhosə́g *m.* ☞ پروسبر

پرهسرنی pərhosəganáj ☞ پروسبرنی

پره ول paravúl *transitive Eastern* ☞ پارول

پره هی parəháj *m.* auger (for drilling stone)

پرهیز parhéz *m.* **1** abstinence, moderation; restraint **2** diet **3** fast (from foods forbidden to be consumed during a fast) پرهیز کول **a** to abstain from something **b** to observe a diet **c** to observe a fast پرهیز ماتول **a** to violate a diet **b** to break a fast

پرهیزدانه parhezāná *f.* diet

پرهیزکار parhezkār **1** abstinent, moderate **2** devout, pious

پرهیزکاری parhezkārí *f.* **1** abstinence **2** observation of a diet **3** observation or keeping of a fast

پړی ¹ pre **1** cut off; cut; chopped off **2** clipped, trimmed **3** broken off, torn off

پړی ² pre *Eastern a combination of the preposition* پر *and the pronoun* ئي، یې **1** on him, onto her, on them; on top of something **2** concerning, about him, her, them; in relation to him, her, them **3** for him, for her, for them **4** with his, her, their help; thanks to him, her, them; this; because of this زړه یې پړی وسو He pitied him (her, them).

پړی ³ parə́j *f.* shovel (for digging irrigation canals)

پړی ⁴ parí *f.* fairy, peri (mythical being in Persian folklore having female form, but formed of fire and descended from the fallen angels)

پړی ⁵ pre *a separable verbal prefix, accented in the perfective aspect* پربنودل to leave پربوتل to fall

---

پریادي parjādí *m.* ☞ فریادي

پرجال parjāl *m.* **1** enclosed place where nomads live **2** curtain; blind

پریان parijān *m.* ☞ پریان

پریبستل preistə́l *transitive* ☞ پریبستل

پری اینبکه preiḵhə́ka preiḵhə́ka divorced woman, divorcee

پرېباس prébās *present stem of* پریبستل

پربدل prebdə́l *transitive* ☞ پربل

پربل prebə́l *transitive* [*present:* پربی یې *past:* و یې پربه] beat, strike

پرتوریا pretorijā́ *f.* Pretoria (city)

پرپت ¹ pareṭ *m. Eastern* **1** د پربت ځای parade assembly area (for a military operation) پربت کول to organize a parade **2** roll-call

پرپت ² paréṭ *m.* **1** kind of haircut **2** pleat (in clothing)

پرچ prech *m.* saucer

پربدل ¹ predə́l *transitive Eastern* ☞ پربنودل

پربدل ² paradə́l *intransitive* [*past:* وپرید] to run, retreat, chicken out

پربده préda *Eastern vice* پربده

پربړ ¹ paréḍ *m.* ☞ پربت

پریړ priṛ preṛ thick, fat پریړ کول to consolidate, thicken پریړ کبدل to condense, thicken, become thicker

پریړتوب priṛtób *m.* پریړتیا priṛtjā پریړوالی priṛvālaj *m.* fatness, thickness, compactness

پریړول priṛavə́l *denominative, transitive* [*past:* پریړ یې کړ] to consolidate, thicken

پریړبدل priṛedə́l *denominative, intransitive* [*past:* پریړ شو] to condense, thicken, become thicker

پرهبز pəréz paréz *m.* ☞ پرهیز

پرهبزانه parezānā *f.* diet

پرهبد pregd *present stem of* پربنودل

پرهبدل pregdə́l *transitive* ☞ پربنودل

پربړه pregá starving, suffering from hunger, having or suffering from crop failure

پریسه prisá *f.* idle woman; woman who loafs

پرپش parésh پریشان pareshān preshán **1** upset, distressed **2** agitated, alarmed; worried **3** absent-minded, incoherent پرپش کول ☞ پرپش کبدل، پرپشانول **a** to be upset over, grieve **b** to be worried, be agitated **c** to become absent-minded, become incoherent د کور له خوا پرپش کبدل to worry about home **4** sorrowful (of thoughts, meditation) **5** tossed about, disordered (of hair)

پرپشان حال pareshānhál **1** disturbed, grieved; alarmed **2** embarrassed, confused

پرپشانول preshānavə́l *denominative, transitive* [*past:* پرپشان یې کړ] **1** to upset, grieve **2** to disturb, agitate **3** to scatter, spread

پرپشانه preshāna **1** ☞ پرپشان **2** *feminine singular of* پرپشان

پرپشاني preshāní pareshāní *f.* **1** disorder, grief **2** melancholy; sorry **3** worry, agitation **4** distraction, innattention **5** unpleasantness

پرپختته pərikhtá perikhtá *f.* angel

پرپخاکه preḵhə́ka preḵhə́ka *f.* ☞ پری اینبکه پرپبنبکه

پرپخل preḵhə́l preḵhə́l *transitive Eastern* ☞ پربنودل

پرېبنودل preẖhodál preshodə́l *transitive* [*present:* پرېپرېدي *past:* پرې [پرېنود] **1** to leave, abandon **2** to let pass; let go; admit, allow **3** to release (e.g., on bail) **4** to curtail, call a halt to جگړه پرېبنودل to break off the battle, curtail military operations **5** to allow, authorize پرېپرده چه ولاړشي Allow me to leave. Let پرې مي پرده چه خُم him go. Let them go. **6** to desert, leave (a wife); give a divorce (to a wife) **7** to give up (a place) *idiom* لوی سړي خو لا پرېپرده Not to mention grown-up people.

پرېبنودنه preẖhodə́na preẖhodə́na *f.* [*plural:* پرېبنوده preẖhodə́ preẖhodə́] *m.* **1** leaving, abandonment **2** stopping, cessation **3** permission, leave, authorization **4** desertion (of a wife), divorce

پرېخوَل preẖhvál *transitive* پرېبنودل preẖhovál *transitive* ☞ پرېبنودل

پرېبنودنه preẖhovə́na preẖhovə́na *f.* ☞

پرېخه preẖhə́ preẖhə́ *imperfective dialect* ☞ پرېبنودل

پرې فابريکي prefābriké prefabricated (of houses)

پرېفکس prefíks *m.* prefix

پرېکارد perikárd *m. anatomy* pericardium, pericardial sac

پرېکتون prektún *m.* military tribunal, court

پرېکرون prekrún *m.* **1** solution, answer (to, of a problem) **2** understanding, arrangement **3** break (i.e., in diplomatic relations)

پرېکړه prékṛa *f.* **1** ☞ پرېکړون پرېکړه د خولي a verbal understanding **2** handsome or good-looking face; beautiful exterior, appearance

پرېکوَل prekavál **1** *transitive* [*past:* پرې يې کړ]. **1.1** to cut; cut off; sever **1.2** to clip (the nails) **1.3** to interrupt (e.g., a speech) **1.4** to cut down, fell **1.5** to break off (e.g., diplomatic relations) **1.6** to pay, pay off (a debt) **1.7** to solve, answer (e.g., a question, a problem) **2** *m. plural* ☞ پرېکون *passive* ☞ پرېکوَل کېدل

پرېکون prekún *m.* **1** answer, solution (e.g., to a question, a problem) **2** betrothal, engagement د واده پرېکون betrothal, engagement **3** agreement concerning the wedding expenses

پرېکونه prekavə́na *f.* **1** cutting; severing; cutting off **2** clipping (nails) **3** cutting down, felling **4** breaking off (e.g., diplomatic relations) **5** paying off, paying up (a debt) **6** answer, solution (e.g., to a question, problem)

پرېکوونی prekavúnaj *m.* cutting tool; chisel

پرېکېدل prekedál *intransitive* [*past:* پرې شو] **1** to be cut, cut off **2** to be cut off, be severed **3** to be clipped (nails) **4** to be cut down **5** to be broken off (of diplomatic relations) **6** to be paid up, be paid off (of a debt) **7** to be answered, be solved (of a question, problem)

پرېگډ pregd *Eastern* ☞ پرېبرد

پرېمان premān *m.* ☞ پرېبان

پرېمان premān ☞ پرېبان

پرېمیشتل premishtál *intransitive* ☞ پرېمیشتل

پرېمیندزل premindzál *transitive* ☞ پرې منڅل

پرېمیشتل premishtál *intransitive* [*past:* پرېمیشت شو] to be settled; live; dwell

پرېمیندزل premindzál *transitive* [*past:* پرې يې مینڅه] **1** to wash; مخ يې پرې مینڅه he washed himself **2** to launder ☞ مینڅل

پرین prin *m.* **1** *anatomy* diaphragm **2** kind of children's game

پرینب parájnḅ *m.* arrangement, organization, setting something in motion

پرینی parajnáj *m.* organizer, arranger of something

پریني priṇí *f.* ☞ پرني

پرېبو prév parév *m. dialect* ☞ پیرو

پرېبواته prevātə́ *m. plural* **1** fall د پرېبوتو سره سم having fallen; at the fall, drop (of) **2** the going down (of), setting (of the sun) لمر په پرېبوتو و The sun has set.

پرېبوار parivár fairy-like

پرېبوان preván *m. anatomy* placenta

پرېبوان preván abundant, abounding in

پرېبواني prevāní *f.* abundance, plenty, profusion

پرېبوتل prevatál *intransitive* [*present:* پرېبوزي *past:* [پرېبووت] **1** to fall, drop **2** to lie down (to sleep) **3** to flow into (of a river) **4** to set, go down (of the sun) **5** to be perpetrated (of a raid) زمونږ په کلي باندي داره پرېبوتله A raid was carried out on our village. **6** to be owing from someone, impose upon someone (of a tax, fine) **7** to fall upon, go for, fling oneself at پرېبوتو باندي موټر هغه *Eastern* He jumped into the car. **8** to be lacking, not to have (appetite) **9** to set up camp, arrange a rest stop **10** to descend, ride down (from a mountainous locale to one lower down; e.g., from Kabul to Peshawar)

پرېبواتنه prevatə́na *f.* ☞

پرېبوته preváta *f.* ☞ پېبروتی

پرېبوتئ prevátaj **1** *past participle of* پرېبوتل **2** backward قام پرېبوتئ a backward nation

پرېبنودل prevdál *transitive* ☞ پرېبنودل

پرېبوَل prevlál **1** [*past:* پرې يې وله] *transitive* **1.1** to wash; wash thoroughly **1.2** to launder **1.3** to clean, brush (the teeth) پرېبوَل کېدل *passive* **a** to be washed out, be washed, be thoroughly washed **b** to be laundered **c** to be cleaned, be brushed (teeth) **2** *m. plural* ☞ پرېبوللو مبز پرېبوله د مخ د washbasin

پرېبوَن prevlə́n *m.* پرېبولنه prevlə́na *f.* پرېبوله prevlə́ *m. plural* **1** washing (out); bathing **2** laundering **3** brushing, cleaning (teeth)

پرېبوینڅل previndzál *transitive* ☞ پرېبوینڅل

پرېباسته prejāstə́ *m. plural* **1** throwing down, dropping, throwing off **2** flinging, throwing, throwing away **3** shooting, firing **4** overturning **5** lying down to sleep **6** divorce (of a wife by husband)

پرېباستل prejəstál *transitive* [*present:* پرېباسي *past:* [پرې يې يست] **1** to throw down, drop, throw off **2** to fling, hurl, throw; throw away **3** to shoot, fire **4** to compel to lie down, put lying (an animal) **5** to topple, overturn **6** to abandon, desert (a wife); divorce, grant a divorce (to a woman)

پرېباستل prejəẖtál prejəẖtál *transitive dialect* ☞ پرېباستل

پر pəṛ پړ pṛa *f.* پړه pṛə *plural* پړي pṛe *plural* **1** guilty, culpable پړېدل ☞ پړ کېدل ، پړول ☞ پړکول **2** overcome, conquered

پړ pəṛ *m.* **1** layer **2** story, floor

پر ³ paṛ *m.* bridge

پر ⁴ puṛ *m.* wedging, fastening with a wedge

پر ⁵ pəṛ *intensive particle* پرخم completely turbid; dark-brown پر غور very greasy

پراته paṛātá *f.* pastry or flour product similar in size and composition to a tortilla but made with wheat flour

پراخ prākh ☞ پراخ

پراق pṛāk *m. regional* 1 tap 2 knock

پراکی pṛākáj *m.* quick-tempered man, hot-headed man

پرانگ pṛāng *m.* snow leopard, *Uncia uncia*; leopard *idiom* د هغه پرانگ دئ خبرو He likes to chatter. He is a gossip.

پرانگ پيش pṛāngpísh *m.* wild cat

پرانگه ¹ pṛānga [*plural:* پرانگي pṛāngi *plural:* پرانگاني pṛāngā́ni] *feminine of* پرانگ

پرانگه ² paṛánga *f.* thin stripe (e.g., in cloth)

پرانه ورانه pṛána-vṛána *f.* 1 game of chance 2 bet

پراو paṛā́v *m.* 1 rest stop, discount 2 stop (e.g., for a bus route) پراو by stages, by phases

پرپوس paṛpús *m.* 1 pluck (i.e., the heart, liver and lungs of a slaughtered animal, especially as used for food) 2 *figurative* scoundrel

پرتوب paṛtób *m.* 1 guilt 2 defeat, loss

پرتوغاښ paṛtughā́ḳh *m.* partughásh *m.* ☞ پرتوگاښ

پرتوگ paṛtug *m.* ☞ پرتوگ

پرته pṛáta *f.* net, snare

پرتيا pəṛtjā́ *f.* ☞ پرتوب

پرخوب paṛtsób *m. dialect* ☞ پرسوب

پرده paṛdá *f.* ☞ پرده *regional* دپردي خبري secrets, mysteries په پرده in secret, secretly کشي

پرده پوش paṛdapóḳh paṛdapósh ☞ پرده پوښ

پرسمن pṛasmə́n 1 rotten, spoiled 2 blown up, swollen up

پرسنده pəṛsə́nda 1 swollen, inflated 2 sulking, angry ناست و He sat sulking.

پرسوب paṛsób *m.* swelling پرسوب کول to swell پرسوب نه کمېږي The swelling is not going down.

پرسول pəṛsavə́l *transitive* [*past:* و يې پرساوه] to inflate, fill up (with air, with gas), blow, fan بڼي پرسول to blow air through a bellows 2 to cause a swelling, swelling; cause the development of a swelling or tumor 3 to rise, arise (waves) 4 *figurative* to anger someone 5 *figurative* to incite against someone *idiom* ځان پرسول to become conceited, become swellheaded

پرساونه pəṛsavə́na *f.* inflation, filling up (with air, gas); blowing

پرسېدل pəṛsedə́l *intransitive* [*past:* وپرسېده] 1 to swell, swell up; become inflated; become distended 2 to be inflated, be filled (with air, gas); become inflated; get distended 3 to puff up 4 to rise (of dough) 5 to surge, make swells (of waves) 6 *figurative* get huffy, grow angry

پرسېدنه pəṛsedə́na *f.* 1 swelling, swelling up; tumescence 2 filling up (with air, gas); blowing (i.e., bellows, fan) 3 distention

پرغښه pəṛghə́sha *f.* knot in a sash (for holding pants up)

پرق ¹ paṛák *m.* strop (for sharpening a straight razor)

پرق ² pṛak *m.* 1 crack, crash, crackle (as a noise) 2 smack, slap, blow 3 cuff, box, clout

پرق ³ pəṛák *m. regional* sparkling, glittering پرق وهل to sparkle, glitter دتندر پرق وه lightning flashed *idiom* په مزغو کښي مي پرق شه I suddenly remembered. It suddenly occurred to me.

پرق پرق pṛakpṛúk *m.* rustling (of silk cloth, etc.)

پرقول paṛakavə́l *transitive* ☞ پرکول

پرقېدل paṛakedə́l *intransitive* ☞ پرکېدل ²

پرک ¹ pṛak *m.* ☞ پرق ²

پرک ² paṛk *m.* 1 group of people (10-20 persons) 2 *military* half of a platoon (an eighth of a company) 3 crowd 4 flock, pack 5 flock of sheep (numbering 5 to 20)

پرک ³ pəṛák *m.* 1 oscillation; agitation; trembling پرک خوړل to shake to and fro; be agitated; tremble 2 sparkling, twinkling 3 summer lightning 4 seething, bubbling

پرک ⁴ pṛək *m.* string of pearls

پرکا pṛakā́ *m.* ☞ پرکهار ²

پرکمشر paṛkmə́shr *m. military* noncommissioned officer; sergeant; company quartermaster sergeant

پرکول pṛəkavə́l *transitive* [*past:* و يې پرکاوه] 1 to disturb, shake; sway 2 to pull, tug 3 to set to trembling 4 to be in the grip of a fever *idiom* لاسونه پرکول to applaud, clap

پرکه paṛká *f.* puṛáka *f.* ☞ پرته

پرکهار ¹ pṛakahā́r pəṛakahā́r *m.* summer lightning

پرکهار ² pṛakahār *m.* 1 crack, crash, crackle 2 shuffling, smacking (or similiar sound)

پرکی ¹ paṛkáj *m.* 1 shinbone, tibia; bone into which avian metatarsals insert 2 ankle پرکي مي واوښت I've dislocated my foot.

پرکی ² pə́ṛkaj *m.* cord

پرکی ³ paṛkə́j *f.* trap, snare (for birds)

پرکی تر paṛkajtár *m.* puttees

پرکېدل ¹ paṛkedə́l *intransitive* [*past:* وپرکېده] 1 to shake to and fro; be agitated; tremble 2 to vibrate 3 to seethe, bubble up 4 to fear, be afraid of

پرکېدل ² pṛakedə́l *intransitive* [*past:* وپرکېده] to sparkle, twinkle, shine, beam

پرم pṛam *m.* ☞ پرن

پرمبی paṛambə́j *f.* bubble (in water)

پرمخ pəṛmə́kh پرمخي pəṛmə́khi 1 lying face up, lying prostrate on one's back پرمخ پرپوتل، پرمخ را پربوتل to fall flat on one's back; to sprawl on one's back 2 turned over (on the back), toppled over پرمخ کول to turn, topple over پرمخ کېدل a to fall sprawled on one's back b to be turned or toppled over on one's back

پرنگ ¹ pṛəng *m.* ☞ پرينگ ¹

پرنگ ² pṛang *m.* 1 mischief, prank, trick 2 a leper

پرنگ ³ pṛəng *m.* hypocrite, two-faced person

پرنگی pṛangáj *m.* leper, person ill with leprosy

136

پرنه pṛə́na *f.* 1 compulsion, coercion 2 censure, blame

پرنه ورنه pṛə́na-vṛə́na *f.* ☞ پرانه ورانه

پروالی pəṛválaj *m.* ☞ پرتوب

پروپی paṛúpaj *m.* ☞ چارک

پروستي pṛósti *f. plural* cooked grains of the maize or corn plant

پروکی pṛúkaj *m.* 1 cord 2 ribbon, tape; thin braid

پروکی ² paṛúkaj *m.* small bridge; ship's bridge

پروکی ³ paṛúkaj small herd of sheep

پرول paṛavə́l *denominative* [past: پری یې کړ] 1 to find guilty; convict 2 to defeat, conquer, overcome

پرومبه pṛumbā *f.* پرومبی pṛumbé *usually plural* serum

پروند paṛvánd strong, robust

پرونه paṛavə́na *f.* 1 finding of guilty; conviction 2 infliction of a defeat, gaining of a victory

پرونی paṛúnáj *m.* shawl, veil, large chador پرونی په سر کول to be covered with a chador; wear a chador

پروهنه pəṛvahə́na *f.* surveying of lands

پروهونکی pəṛ vahúnkaj *m.* surveyor

پره ¹ pṛa paṛa *f. dialect* 1 censure, condemnation, (legal) conviction پره اړول a to censure, convict, accuse b to inflict defeat, conquer, overcome 2 fine 3 compulsion, coercion 4 injustice چاته د پري گوته نیول a to consider someone guilty b to consider someone unjust

پره ² púṛa *f.* lining

پره ³ pṛa *f. feminine singular of* پی ¹

پره ⁴ pṛə *m. masculine plural of* پی ¹

پره تکي pṛatáki *f. plural* fluttering (of a bird) پره تکي وهل to flutter (of a bird)

پره څمکني paṛatsamkaní *m. plural* 1 Parachamkani (tribe) 2 *m.* Parachamkanaj (tribesman)

پره لیک pṛalík *m.* obligation

پره ول paṛavúl *transitive regional* ☞ پرول

پرهه paṛhá *f. dialect* shoe, slipper

پری ¹ pə́ṛaj *m.* rope, cord, string دشگو پړی غبنتل *saying literal* to braid rope from sand *figurative* to mill about, beat the air د چا پړی په غاړه کښي اچول to subordinate someone, enslave someone

پری ² puṛə́j *f.* horse-drawn scoop (for leveling a field, scraping earth from it, or spreading something evenly over it), horse-drawn device for cleaning irrigation channels

پری ³ pəṛə́j *f.* 1 construction materials (stone, etc.) prepared for the building of a house 2 planks or poles which compose a roof

پریخ pṛikh flat-nosed; flattened

پریخ پزی pṛikhpázaj snub-nosed; having a flat nose

پریدل pəṛedə́l *denominative, intransitive* [past: پړشو] 1 to be guilty, be to blame; commit an offense 2 to suffer defeat 3 to be unjust 4 to lose (in sport)

پریس pṛis 1 fat, stout; corpulent 2 ugly (of a face)

پریس والی pṛisválaj *m.* stoutness; corpulence

پریم pṛim *m.* 1 clot (of blood) 2 ball, lump

پرن pṛin *doublet* خوپرین

پرینگ ¹ pṛing *m.* 1 sobbing پرینگ وهل to sob پرینگ او پرینگ moaning, whining پرینگ او پرونگ weeping (of children) 2 exclamations of "Oh" and "Ah"

پرینگ ² pṛing *doublet* کپرینگ

پرینگهار pṛingəhār *m.* continuous crying (of children)

پری والا pəṛajvālā *m.* rope merchant

پربلون prevláng *m.* ☞ پربلون

پز پربکړی که شرم paz prekə́raj 1 having the nose cut off درلودای ، دچې نوم بی نه اخیست *proverb* If he-who-was-deprived-of-his-nose experienced shame, he would not recall the knife. 2 shameless

پزره ² pəzṛə́ *vice* ☞ په زره ☞ زره ²

پزغمی pazghamáj *m.* nose ring

پزکی pazakə́j *f.* small nose

پزول ¹ pazavə́l *transitive* [past: و یې پزاوه] to smell, sniff, sniff around; snuff

پزول ² pəzavə́l *transitive dialect* [past: و یې پزاوه] to wound

پزونی pzúnaj *m.* lancet

پزوهل pazvahə́l *transitive* [past: پز ئې واهه] 1 to squeeze out; press out 2 to press; mash 3 to bleed, cause the flow of blood

پزه paźa *f. Western* 1 nose پته پزه، پلنه پزه، چته پزه flat nose, snub nose پزه تکوهل، پزه سونکل to blow the nose; to clear the nasal passages by blowing پزه کنبل ، پزي نبنن وهل to become sharp, become pointed (of the nose, from thinness, etc.) پزه وینول to cause a nosebleed a پزه پربکول to cut off the nose b *figurative* to disgrace, shame 2 muzzle, snout *idiom* تر پزي مور full up to the neck (food) *idiom* a تر پزي ډکېدل to eat to satiety, stuff oneself b to grow angry, become wrathful *idiom* تر پزي رسېدل to be in very difficult straits, be reduced to extremities پزه تروه کول، پزه کړول to get angry, pout a پزه نه درلودل to be without a nose b not to have a conscience, be shameless, be brazen c to be ashamed of پزه په هوا to have one's nose in the air, be proud پزه مچ نه پربنیودل to be arrogant, be haughty, be proud په پزه خط کبل a to be inferior, submit to someone b to apologize to someone

پزی ¹ pázi *plural of* پزه

پزی ² pazáj *m.* flair, feeling (for)

پزي ³ pazí *f.* portliness, corpulence

پزیدل ¹ pəzedə́l [past: و پزیده] to be wounded; receive a wound; get wounded

پزیدل ² pəzedə́l *intransitive* [past: و پزیده] to boil, begin to boil

پزین puzín *adjective* made of matting, bast matting, matting

پژهرکی pəzhárkaj 1 energetic, enterprising 2 ready to attack 3 angry

پژمردگي pazhmurdagí *f.* 1 fading, drooping 2 *figurative* depression, grief

پژمرده pazhmurdá 1 faded, drooping, withered 2 *figurative* depressed; sad

پژواک pazhvák *m.* echo

پژی pə́zhaj *m.* ☞ پړی

پیر ¹پوډ ☞ .m pug

پیړی póɣaj *m.* body, trunk, torso

پس ¹ pas **1.1** after, later, after that, afterwards درې میاشتي پس three months later, after three months شو ورځي پس several days later, after several days **1.2** subsequently **2** *preposition, postposition* پس له غرمي ،پس له هغه څخه ۱. after that, after after noon, in the afternoon د دې پس، د دې پسه after me پس له ما in the future **2.2** beyond something, beyond the limits of something پس د غزني څخه beyond Gazni

پس ² pis *m.* arrogance, haughtiness; pride

پس ³ pus *m.* pəs whisper *idiom* پس اچول to release gas; blow a fizzer

پس ⁴ pəs *dialect* ☞ پیخ

پسات pəsāt *m.* **1** evil **2** mutiny, revolt; riots; disturbance **3** schism, split پسات کول **a** to cause harm, harm somebody **b** to stir up mutiny, revolt; cause a disturbance **c** to introduce a schism

پساتي pəsātí *m.* rebel; rioter

پساره psārə́ *singular oblique of* پسور

پسان ¹ psān *m.* grindstone, whetstone

پسان ² psān *Western plural of* پسه ¹

پس انداز pasāndāz *m.* economy, savings پس انداز کول *compound verb* to save, economize, put aside as a reserve پس انداز کېدل *compound verb* to be saved, be put aside as a reserve د خلقو پس انداز شوي پيسې national economies د پس انداز صندوق، د پس انداز بانک savings bank

پساڼی pisā́ɳaj *m.* ☞ پخاڼی

پساو pəsā́v *m.* **1** leftovers from soup **2** brushwood, driftwood swept to the banks by a river current

پس پا paspā́ withdrawing, departing پس پا کېدل to withdraw, depart

پس پرده paspardá secret, hidden; suppressed; undercover

پس پس ¹ páspas more rarely; rarely

پس پس ² puspús: پس پس خبري whispering back and forth to one another پس پس کول to whisper, whisper in someone's ear په خپلو کنبي یې پس پس وکړل they were whispering to one another

پس پسی puspusáj *m.* pəspəsáj *m.* پس پسی کول whispering, whispering back and forth

پست ¹ post *m.* ☞ پوسته ¹

پست ² past **1** low پسته لار low mountains پست غرونه road running on a slope **2** *figurative* low, base

پست ³ pust *doublet* سست

پستال postā́l پستال کارټ postcard

پستاندار pistāndā́r پستاندار حيوانات mammals

پستری pastrí *f.* pastries

پستکی ¹ pastakáj **1.1** soft, yielding **1.2** mild, tender **2** *m.* lobe of the ear, earlobe

پستکی ² pustə́kaj *m.* ☞ پوستکی

پستکی ³ pastakə́j *f.* **1** sweet child, my dear (form of address to a little girl) **2** *proper name* Pastakaj

پستنه pəstə́na پستنه تلل، پسته جاروتل **a** to return, come back **b** to step back, recede, depart پستنه کول to return, give back, turn back پستنه کېدل to return, step back

پستو ¹ pastú *m.* back room, storeroom; pantry

پستو ² pastó *oblique plural of* پوست ²

پستوالی pəstvā́laj *m.* **1** softness, tenderness **2** *figurative* gentleness, meekness

پستوره pasturə́ *m. plural* finely-ground flour, the finest wheaten flour

پستوکی pəstúkaj *m.* ear lobe

پستول pastavól *denominative, transitive* [*past:* پوست یې کړ] **1** to soften **2** to knead **3** to grind, pulverize **4** to loosen, hoe, dig all over again (earth) **5** to boil soft **6** *figurative* to render gentle, tender, tractable

پستونی pastavúnaj *m.* Indian lime-tree, *Grewia oppositifolia*

پستوور pastavór *m.* ☞ پسته وور

پسته ¹ pistá *f.* pistachio (tree)

پسته ² pastá **1** *feminine singular of* پوست ² پسته ډوډۍ soft bread پسته خاوره soft clay **2** *f.* liquid, fluid

پسته ³ pásta after, later; after that, then, afterwards ☞ پس ¹

پسته ⁴ postá *f.* ☞ پوسته ¹

پسته ⁵ pásta *feminine singular of* پست ²

پسته ⁶ pəsta *interjection* Giddyap! Get going!

پسته وور pastavór *m.* light rain

پستي ¹ pastí meanness, baseness ځان پستي ته ورکول to stoop to the performance of base acts, act basely, do a mean, or base thing

پستي ² postí postal پستي خط post-office line پستي پارسل package sent by parcel post

پستي ³ pasté **1** *feminine plural of* پوست ² پستي وړی soft wool **2** *f.* posterior part of the tongue

پستي ⁴ posté *plural of* پوسته ¹

پستېدل pastedól *denominative, intransitive* [*past:* پوست شو] **1** to soften, grow soft **2** to be kneaded **3** to be ground, be pulverized **4** to be loosened, be hoed **5** to be boiled soft **6** to be gentle, be tender, be tractable

پستيز pastíz soft, tender

پست posṭ *m.* پسته posṭa *f.* ☞ پوسته ¹

پستي posṭi ☞ پستي ²

پسخاک paskhǎk *m.* ☞ پخساک

پسخانه paskhāna *f.* ☞ پستو ¹

پسخند pəskhánd *m.* mockery; gibe پسخند وهل to mock (at); to jeer (at)

پسخندي pəskhandí **1** *m.* scoffer **2** *f.* scoffer (female)

پس خورده paskhurdá *f.* leftovers; remains of a meal

پسخه paskhá *f.* ☞ پخسه

پسخېدل paskhedól *intransitive* ☞ پخسېدل

پسرلنی psarlanáj spring, vernal

پسرلی psarláj *m.* spring, springtime پسرلي in spring په پسرلي کنبي د ژمي ترګل spring has come, spring has arrived پسرلی شو

اور ښه دئ psarlí *proverb* A fire in winter is better than the flowers in spring. *proverb literal* په يوه گل نه پسرلی كېږي One flower does not make a spring *figurative* One swallow does not make a summer. **2** *proper name* Psarlaj

پسرو pasráv **1** *m.* follower **1.2** [*plural:* پسروان pasraván] followers; suite, retinue **2** dependent; successive, sequential

پسرور psəravór wide, broad, expansive, spacious

پسرول pəsaravúl *denominative, transitive* [*past:* پسر يې كړ *dialect* to don, put on (headgear) قراقلي پسرول to put on a caracul cap, wear a caracul cap تاج پسرول to crown (a king)

پس صبا passabā the day after tomorrow

پسکاوڼ puskāvə́ṇ *m.* **1** one who emits gases **2** coward, faint-hearted, pusillanimous fellow

پسکاوڼه pskavə́ṇa *f.* hawthorn

پسکی [1] pəskáj *m.* whisper

پسکی [2] pəskə́j puskə́j *f.* gases (intestinal) پسکی اچول to emit gases *idiom* د كارغه پسکی crow

پسل pasl *m.* time of the year, season

پسله pásla ☞ پس [1]

پسماندگي pasmāndagí *f.* backwardness

پسمانده pasmāndá **1** *f.* leftovers, remains of a meal **2.1** remaining; surviving **2.2** backward

پسماني pasmāní *f.* **1** incompleteness **2** lag

پسمن pismə́n arrogant, haughty, proud

پسمنظر pasmanzár *m.* background

پسند pasánd **1** selection, choice, approval **2** *combining form* **a** approved, pleasing دل پسند pleasant, nice **b** approving, acknowledging امن پسند peaceful, pacific

پسندول pasandavól *denominative, transitive* [*past:* پسند يې كړ] **1** to approve **2** to prefer, select

پسندېدل pasandedól *denominative, intransitive* [*past:* پسند شو] **1** to be approved; to please **2** to be preferred, be selected

پسندیده pasandidá **1** approved **2** preferred, selected **3** pleasant; pleasing

پسنی pśsnaj *m.* ☞ پسونی

پسنبدل pəsnedól *intransitive* [*past:* و پسنبده] to whisper, speak in a whisper

پسوا pasvā́ behind the back of, in someone's absence

پسور psor *m.* width, breadth په پساره in depth

پسورور psoravór ☞ پسرور

پسوریز pəsoríz landscape

پسول [1] psol *m.* **1** necklace of coins; necklace **2** adornment, decoration

پسول [2] pə́savul *transitive dialect* ☞ پښول

پسولل psolól *transitive obsolete* ☞ پسولول

پسولنه psolə́na *f.* decoration (the action)

پسولول psolavól *transitive* [*past:* و يې پسولاوه] to adorn, attire someone

پسولبدل psoledól *intransitive* [*past:* و پسولبده] to be dressed up, be well-attired, dress oneself up, deck oneself out

پسونه psúna *plural of* پسه [1]

پسونی pasúnaj *m.* **1** ambush په پسوني كېني كېنبنستل pasúni to lie in ambush چاته پسوني جوړول to set up an ambush for somebody د پسوني له ځايه پورته نيول to hide oneself in ambush, conceal oneself له پسوني pasúni to come out of ambush **2** man lying in ambush

پسه [1] psə *m.* [*plural:* پسونه psúna] *Western* [*plural:* پسان psə́n] **1** ram, sheep د پسو روزنه sheep breeding، د پسو مالداري wild mountain sheep (ram) تركي پسه ram of the Gissar breed هزاره گي پسه ram of the Khazar breed غلجائي پسه ram of the Gilzaj breed **2** *dialect* small horned domestic animals in general (sheep and goats collectively) **3** *figurative* blockhead, dimwit

پسه [2] pusá *f.* bread made from the seeds of the mastic tree

پسه [3] pása after د دي پسه به زيار كاړو in the future we will try

پسه روزونکی psə rozúnkaj *m.* shepherd, one who raises or breeds sheep

پسهار pusəhār *m.* پسهاری pusəhā́raj *m.* ☞ پس پسی

پسي [1] pisí arrogant, haughty; proud

پسي [2] pəsé pasé pse *dialect* pasí **1** *postposition, either in conjunction with the preposition* په *or without it, and sometimes with* د **.1** after, immediately after يو په بل پسي one after the other يو د بل پسي one after the other **1.2** for (to designate a purpose or goal) په ډاكټر پسي تلل to go for a doctor ما پسي دفتر ته راشه to go on business Come pick me up at the office **1.3** for (to designate a person from whom it is necessary to obtain something) په ما پسي وليكئ Write this down for me. **2** for him, for me, for them پسي ورسه go after them, go for them **3** after, afterwards اوڼ څان ، پسي جهان *proverb literal* One's shirt is rather close to one's body. *figurative* Charity begins at home. Self comes first. **4** *in connection with verbs* پسي اخيستل ، پسي را اخيستل **a** to follow someone; pursue some one; chase someone بيبو پسي راواخله Follow after Bibo! **b** to track down, keep a watch on someone په چا پسي کبدل، په چا پسي لگبدل **a** to go after, follow someone **b** to pursue someone په چا پسي تلل، پربوتل **a** Ahmed follows Mahmud **b** احمد په محمود پسي ځي Ahmed imitates Mahmud; په يو كار پسي کبدل **a** to undertake some work or other **b** to plan, conceive something دوی په دي پسي شول They planned that they would do thus ... چه ... په چا پسي کتل to follow someone پسي گرځبدل to look for, search for پسي لټول to obtain something **5** *verb intensifier* پسي ډبرول to increase all the more, develop; increase, augment

پسي [3] pə́se *f.* **1** entertainment and refreshment (on the occasion of the birth of a daughter) **2** recompense (to a shepherd in connection with the lambing time with sheep, and the seasonal bringing forth of kids by goats)

پسبدل [1] pusedól *intransitive* [*past:* وپسبده] to whisper, converse in whipers

پسبدل [2] pəsedól *denominative, intransitive dialect* ☞ پښبدل

پسبره pəséra besides, moreover پسبره كول besides پسبره پردې **a** to put aside, defer as less important **b** to place on top, put on the surface **c** to display something پسبره كېدل **a** to turn out to be superfluous **b** to be placed on top, be located on the surface **c** to appear

پسي شا paseshá behind the back

پسيكولوژي psikolozhí *f.* psychology

پسين pasín **1** subsequent **2** late; last

پسينه pasiná [1] *f. grammar* affix, suffix

پسينه pasiná [2] *f.* late sowing, late crop

پسيه pasjá [3] *f.* ☞ پسي [2]

پشا pəshá *vice* زما پشا په شا in back of me; behind me

پشان pəshấn پشاني peshấni like دپخوا پشان as before, as formerly

پش پش pish-pish *interjection* Pussy! pussy! (to call a cat)

پش پش پش pash-pash-pash used to call a camel

پشت pusht [1] *m.* **1** back **2** ☞ پنت [1] **3** pool, reservoir (for irrigation system) **4** support, prop

پشت pəsht [2] *m.* laying (of eggs)

پشت pusht [3] *Eastern* ☞ پيشت

پشت pəsht [4] *interjection* Shoo! (to a cat)

پشتاره pushtārá *f.* **1** basket (of flowers) **2** armful; burden

پشترود pushtrúd *m.* Pushtrud (district)

پشتک pishták *m. regional* **1** short and tubby person; dwarf **2** resourceful person

پشتگير، پشت گير pushtgír *m.* assistant

پشتگيره ، پشت گيره pushtgíra *f.* assistant (female)

پشتول pishtvál *m.* ☞ پيشتول

پشته pushtá [1] *f.* **1** foothills **2** hillock **3** ridge (of mountains) **4** low ridge

پشته pōshta [2] *interjection* ☞ پشي [4]

پشتي pushtí [1] *f.* **1** support, prop, assistance پشتي كول to support, help **2** dust cover, folder **3** prop, support

پشتي pishtáj [2] **1** undersized, stunted **2** *m.* terrier (breed of dog)

پشتيبان pushtibán *m.* **1** patron, protector, defender **2** assistant

پشتيباني pushtibāní *f.* **1** patronage, protection **2** help; assistance

پشبرلي psharláj *m.* ☞ پشبرلى [1]

پشكاب pishkáb *m.* plate

پشك pishák *m.* **1** *medicine* ringworm **2** carrion crow (bird)

پشكاب pishkáb *m.* ☞ پشقاب

پشكال pashakál *m. Eastern* the period of time from July to November; the rainy season

پشكالي pəshkālí *m. plural* hay, dry grass

پشكنډى pishkandáj *m.* kitten

پشكى pəshkáj *m.* ☞ پنكى [1]

پشلا pəshálá behind the back, in the absence of پشلا ويل to talk behind the back of, gossip

پشم pashm [1] *m. singular & plural* wool

پشم pashám [2] *m.* light rain

پشمک pashmák *m.* kind of halvah

پشمكه pashmáka *f.* ☞ زمى

پشمي pashmáj [1] *m.* two-year-old camel

پشمي pashmí [2] woolen پشمين pashmín woolen پشمي توكران woolen fabrics

پشمينه pashminá **1** ☞ پشمي [2] **2** *f.* **2.1** (heavy, coarse) cloth; woolen cloth **2.2** fine sheep's wool

پشمينه بافي pashminabāfí *f.* wool weaving د پشمينه بافي فابريكه woolen mill, cloth factory, textile mill

پشنگ pisháng *m.* lead horse (in a caravan)

پشنگوري pishəngúraj *m.* kitten

پشو pishó *f.* cat *saying literal* پي او د پشو پاسواني to send a cat to watch the milk *figurative* to send a fox to watch the chickens; send a goat to watch the cabbages ☞ پيشو

پشوپړى pishopṛáj *f.* game played with a ball

پشوخټ pishokhút *m.* galls (abnormal growth on plants)

پشورمه pishórma *f.* marmot

پشوگى pishogáj *m.* kitten

پشول pəshavál *transitive* ☞ پنبول [1]

پشولمى pisholəmáj *f. botany* hedge-mustard, Sisymbrium

پيشونگړى pishóngṛaj *m.* ☞ پيشونگړى

پشه pashá [1] *f. usually in compounds* **1** gnat, mosquito **2** *cards* spades د پشي ماتكه queen of spades

پشه písha pósha [2] ☞ پشي [4]

پشه بند pashabánd *m.* mosquito netting

پشهار pəshahár *m.* ☞ پنبهار

پشه خانه pashakhāná *f.* elm (tree)

پشه خورک pashakhurák *m.* flycatcher (bird of the finch family)

پشه يي pashaí **1** *m. plural* Pashai (nationality) **2** *m.* Pashai (member of the nationality group) **3** the Pashai language

پشي pishí [1] *f.* [*plural:* پشياني pishijấni] kitten, cat *idiom* د پشى لنگون څنى جوړول to exaggerate, drag out or complicate a matter د پشيانو سترگي ترل to be extremely stingy, be niggardly *idiom* پشي پشي كېدل **a** to fawn upon, truckle to **b** to pretend to be wretched or unhappy

پشي pisháj [2] *m.* [*plural:* پشيان pishiján] cat

پشي pəsháj [3] *f.* handfuls of unripe wheat, (small) bundles of unripe wheat

پشي póshe [4] *interjection* scat پشي كول to drive a cat away; to say "Scat!" پشي شه Scat!

پشي pəsháj [5] *m.* ram or goat with short ears

پشېدل pəshedál *intransitive* ☞ پنبېدل

پشبرل psherál *m.* ☞ پشبرلى [1]

پشبرله pshérla *f.* ☞ پشبرلى [2]

پشبرلي psherláj [1] *m.* [*plural:* پشبرليان psherliján *plural:* پشبرلي psherlí] young ram in the second year

پشبرلى psherláj [2] *f.* [*plural:* پشبرلياني psherlijấni] young ewe in the second year

پشيشا pəsheshá *dialect vice* پسي شا

پشه ئي pashaí ☞ پشه ئي

پنښ pə́kh *m.* **1** *Western* blacksmith د پنښ کور چه وسو ، هومري بنه شو *saying literal* Once burned down, the smith's house is rebuilt better. *figurative* Good can come out of evil. **2** smith's bellows

پنښ pukh *m.* hissing (i.e., of a snake); rustling (of leaves); the noise of the wind

پنښارتوال pkhārtavál *m.* fiancé

پنښارته pkhā́rta *f.* ☞ پنښه ارته

پنښانگه pkhā́nga *f.* **1** angle, corner **2** angular part (of a water skin, etc.)

پنښ بنی، پنښبنی pə́khanáj smith's bellows

پنت pe̱kht *m.* **1** family, clan, tribe پنت يې ونړيد Their family has died out. **2** generation, posterity پنت په پنت from generation to generation په اوه پنته کښي unto the seventh generation

پنت pukht *m.* ☞ تلخان

پنښتانه pakhtanə́ *m.* oblique singular of پنښتون

پنښتل pukhtə́l *transitive* ☞ پوښتل

پنښتنخا pukhtunkhā́ *f.* پنښتنخوا pukhtunkhvā́ pakhtunkhvā́ *f.* Pushtunkhva (the ancient name for the country of the Afghans); Afghanistan and Pashtunistan

پنښتنواله pə̱khtənvā́la *f.* پنښتنوالی pə̱khtənvā́laj pukhtunvā́laj *m.* the Customs and Conventions of the Afgans; the Code of Honor of the Pashtoons

پنښتنه pukhtə́na *f.* ☞ پوښتنه

پنښتنه pakhtə́na pukhtaná **1** *f.* [*plural:* پنښتني pakhtané] Afghan woman, Pashtoon woman **2** *f. adjective* Afghan پنښتنه ښځه Afghan woman, Pashtoon woman

پنښتني pakhtané *plural of* پنښتنه

پنښتني pakhtaní Afghan, Pashtoon

پنښتو pə̱khtó pakhtó pukhtó *Eastern* **1** *f.* **.1** the Pashto language, the Afghan language پنښتو ويل **a** to speak Pashto **b** to teach Pushtu **1.2** ☞ پنښتنواله **1.3** honor, dignity; decency; modesty **2** *adjective* Afghan پنښتو ژبه the Pashto language, the Afghan language پنښتو تولنه "Pushtu Tolana", the Pashto Academy (in Kabul) پنښتو اکاډمي the Pashto Academy (in Peshawar) **a** پنښتو کول to observe or abide by the Code of Honor of the Afghans **b** *compound verb* to translate into Pashto پنښتو کېدل *compound verb* to be translated into Pashto

پنښتوپالنه pakhtopā́lə́na *f.* interest in the Pashto language

پنښتوپوهاند pakhtopohā́nd *m.* پنښتودان pakhtodā́n Afghanist; specialist in the Pashto language

پنښتورگه pukhtavə́rga *f.* پنښتورگی pukhtavə́rgaj *m. anatomy* kidney

پنښتوژبی pakhtozhə́baj *adjective* Pashto speaker

پنښتون pakhtún pə̱khtún *Eastern* pukhtún **1** *m.* **.1** [*plural:* پنښتانه pakhtā́nə́] Afghan, Pashtoon د پنښتانه ملت، د پنښتانه قوم the Afghan **1.2** ☞ لر **2** ☞ لر پنښتون **1.2** لر پنښتون **1** بر **4** بر پنښتون people Pashtoon, Pakhtun **2** *adjective* Afghan, Pashtoon پنښتون قام the Afghan people پنښتانه زلمیان Afghan Youth پنښتانه جرگه Pukhtun Dzhirga (the Organization of Pushtuns living in India)

پنښتنخوا pakhtunkhvā́ *f.* ☞ پنښتنخا

پنښتونستان pakhtunishtā́n *m.* Pushtunistan

پنښتونستانی pakhtunistā́náj pakhtunistā́ní **1** *adjective* Pushtustanian **2** *m.* native of Pushtustan, Pushtun

پنښتونکوټ pakhtunkóṭ *m.* Pashtunkot (district, admininistration center)

پنښتونگلوي pakhtungalví *f.* پنښتونوالی pakhtunvā́laj *m.* پنښتنواله pə̱khtunvalí *f.* ☞ پنښتنواله

پنښته pukhtá *f.* **1** hillock **2** low ridge

پنښتی pukhtáj *f.* rib; ribs *idiom* زره مي پر پنښتی شو I felt relieved, I felt as though a weight had been lifted from me

پنښتی pukhtáj *f.* dust cover, folder

پوښتبدل pukhtedə́l *transitive* ☞ پوښتبدل

پنښکی pukhkáj *m.* ☞ پنښ

پنښکي pə̱khi *dialect* ☞ پکنښي

پنښندی pkhandaj *m.* **1** bracelet (worn on the legs by children up to the age of seven) **2** leg irons

پنښنگه pkhə́nga *f.* wooden pitchforks with two tines

پنښوخوا pkhókhba *f.* south

پنښوکي pkhúki *f. plural* boot leg, stocking leg

پنښول pukhavə́l *transitive* [*past:* وي يې پنښاوه] **1** to cause hissing, cause sputtering, cause sizzling **2** to inflate (blacksmith's bellows) **3** *figurative* to anger

پنښوندی pə̱khvandáj *m.* leg irons

پنښویه pkhója *f. grammar*; spelling, orthography

پنښه pkha *f.* **1** foot پنښه په رکاب **a** foot in the stirrup **b** ready for the road دوي پنښي یي درلودي، دوي unsteady, unstable په یوه پنښه دربدلئ یي نوري پورکوي *folk saying literal* He had two legs and used two more *figurative* May God give him (extra) legs **2** leg (e.g., of a chair) **3** branch (of a tribe), clan; generation **4** *technology* hammer (in a crusher) پنښه اچول to kick **a** پنښه اخیستل to begin to walk, walk (of a child) **b** پنښه ارتول to walk, stride quickly پنښه خلاصول، to authorize the fiancé to visit the bride-to-be (*literally:* to take the hobbles off) **a** پنښه ایندول to step in, enter **b** to go forward, stride پنښه پر یو شي تېرول to look through the fingers at something **a** پنښه تولول to move the feet away **b** to refuse something پنښه نیول **a** not to go somewhere **b** *figurative* to look for grounds, seek a pretext **c** to halt; linger; loiter **d** *figurative* to waver, show indecision پنښه ترکنده واریستل to try to arrange a match, propose a young man as a husband پنښه وهل to stamp with the hoof (of a horse) په ... پنښي ایندول **a** to ride roughshod over someone's rights **b** to trample, press down **c** to enter, step in پنښي پسي لغول to be run off one's legs looking for something پنښي تناکي کول **a** to develop a callous on the foot **b** *figurative* to be in a great hurry **c** to seek, make an intensive search, run off one's legs looking for something پنښي تکول **a** to stamp the feet **b** *figurative* to hurry پنښي تینگول to resist پنښي **a** پنښي خرل، پنښي خرندي کول تینگي لگول to be very careful **b** to refuse پنښي مښکي ته نه رسېدل *Eastern* to be beside oneself with joy; be walking on پنښي په زمکه نه لگېدل

پنبي سپكول، پنبي غخول air to prepare to flee, prepare to depart پنبي غزول a to stretch, extend the legs *figurative* b to loaf, idle پنبي كنبل a to move the legs aside b *figurative* to avoid, shun پنبي لندي لندي كبدل someone a to be tottering on one's legs (from exhaustion), to strain one's strength to the breaking point b to resolve not to go پنبي نه پر چا ورتلل to have no desire to go to see پنبي پنبي را اخيستل، پنبي پنبي ور someone پر پنبو درول، په پنبو to go on foot پر پنبو تلل to grow bolder اخيستل درول a to stand on the feet (e.g., a child) b *figurative* to put someone back on his feet; help someone c to set someone against another to incite against someone پر پنبو دربدل، په پنبو دربدل a to stand upright b *figurative* to be independent په پنبو كښي رغنتل to fall down at someone's feet, entreat بوټ په پنبو كول to wear boots; put on shoes په پنبو كښي ور لوبدل، په پنبو كښي در لوبدل to throw oneself at someone's feet; bow the head to someone's, beseech someone تر پنبو لاندي كول a to throw beneath the feet b to cross, traverse (e.g., a desert) c to trample on someone's right d to ignore (advice, etc) تر پنبو لاندي كبدل a to be thrown beneath the feet b to be trampled (of someone's rights) پر پنبه خر ختل south side, south *idiom* د پنبي خوا *idiom* to have been through a lot in life *idiom* پر يوه پنبه ورته دربدل to be devoted to someone a د چا د پنبو خاوري كبل پنبه پر پنبه اړول to sit idly by to treat someone meanly b to slander, calumniate *idiom* د چا د پنبو خاوري كبدل to subordinate oneself to someone *idiom* د پنبو پر سر ناست و He was د پنبو پر سر ژوند كول to lead nomadic life *idiom* squirming. He couldn't sit still د پنبو څخه لوبدل to be tottering on one's feet (from fatigue, etc.) د پنبو له تربه لوبدل a to strain one's strength to the breaking point, get tired b to grow decrepit, become weak

پنبهار pəkhahár *m.* پنبهاری pəkhahárraj *m.* 1 noise, roar (of the wind) 2 heavy nasal breathing 3 hissing (e.g., a snake)

پنبه ارتون pəkha-artún *m.* پنبه ارته pəkha-árta *f.* پنبه ارتي pəkha-aratí *f.* 1 visit by a fiancé to the family of the bride-to-be (after the betrothal) 2 fete or celebration in the home of the bride-to-be (after the betrothal)

پنبه سوری pəkhasúraj *m.* chicken tied to the leg of the horse of the bride-to-be (it is slaughtered at the entrance of the house of the fiancé)

پنبه نيولئ pəkha-nivólaj 1 lingering 2 hesitatingly پنبه نيولئ راننه وت He entered hesitatingly.

پنبه وندی pəkhavəndáj *m.* hobbles; leg irons, fetters

پنبي[1] pḳhəj *f. botany* rhubarb سپينه پنبي *literal* (white rhubarb) edible rhubarb سره پنبي *literal* (red rhubarb) medicinal rhubarb

پنبي[2] pḳhe *plural of* پنبه

په پنبو پنبي ابلي رواني وي pḳhe-áble *Eastern* 1 barefoot پنبي ابلي They (women) went barefoot 2 *adjective* barefooted

پنبهدل pəkhedól *intransitive [past:* وپنبهده] 1 to hiss (e.g., of a snake) 2 *figurative* to be angry, be in a bad temper چا ته پنبهدل to be angry with someone

پنبهدنه pḳhedóna *f.* hissing (e.g., snake)

پنبي لوخ pḳhelúts *adjective* barefooted, barefoot

پنبهمان pḳhemán regretting; repenting ☞ پنبهمان كبدل پنبهانبدل

پنبهمانتوب pḳhemántób *m.* پنبهمانتيا pḳhemántjá *f.* repentance, regret

پنبهمانول pḳhemānavól *denominative, transitive [past:* پنبهمان يې كړ] to compel to repent or to regret (something)

پنبهمانه pḳhemána *f.* 1 ☞ پنبهمان 2 *feminine singular of* پنبهمان

پنبهماني pḳhemāní *f.* repentance, regret په شوي كار پسي پنبهماني مه كوه do not regret the past

پنبهمانبدل pḳhemānedól *denominative [past:* وپنبهمان شو] to repent (of) be sorry, regret

پنين pikhín *m.* Pishin (city)

پنبي يبل pḳhéjabl barefoot, barefooted

پطرول pitról petról *m. plural* ☞ پترول

پطرولي pitrolí petrolí ☞ پطرولي منابع پطرولي oil deposits

پطريك patrijárk *m.* پطريك patriják *m.* patriarch

پطلانه patlānə *oblique singular of* پطلون

پطلون patlún *m.* trousers (European type)

پعوض pə'iváz *vice* ☞ عوض په عوض د دي چه ... instead of (introducing adverbial clause)

پغمان paghmán *m.* Pagman (city and district of Kabul province) د پغمان غر the Pagman Mountain Range

پغنه paghná *f.* hoeing soil, loosening soil پغنه كول *compound verb* to hoe پغنه كبدل *compound verb* to be hoed

پفك pufák *m.* air rifle

پقير pakír *m. Eastern vice* فقير

پك[1] pək 1.1 bald, hairless 1.2 mangy 2 bald man; hairless man دوه پك، هغه هم سره ورك *folk saying* Two bald men and still they don't get along.

پك[2] puk *m. regional* 1 opportune time; propitious moment پك خطا كبدل not to use, to allow a propitious occasion to slip by 2 turn (as in "it's your turn") 3 fate, lot, portion, destiny 4 *pak* time

پك[3] vesló *m.* oar, scull, paddle

پك[4] pak *m.* dandruff, scuff

پك[5] pak ☞ هك پك

پكار pəkár necessary, needful, requisite څه شي دي پكار دئ؟ What do you require? هيڅ مي پكار نه دئ I don't need anything. پكار وو چه زه تللئ واى I would have to go.

پكارول pəkāravól *denominative, transitive [past:* پكار يې كړ] to use, employ, utilize

پكاربدل pəkāredól *denominative, intransitive [past:* پكار شو] 1 to be used, be employed, be utilized 2 to be necessary

پكت pakt *m.* pact دفاعي پكت defense pact

پكتيا paktijā́ *f. history* Paktia د پكتيا ولايت the Province of Paktia

پكتينگ pikatíng *m.* picketing پكتينگ كول to picket

پكر[1] pákar *m.* 1 begging, beggary 2 alms پكر كول to beg; ask for alms پكر وركول to give alms

پكر[2] pákər ☞ فكر

پکر [3] pəkár clash; quarrel

پکرول pəkaravál *transitive verb* [*past:* وېيې پکراوه] **1** to scratch **2** to disturb (i.e., wasps) **3** *figurative* to anger, irritate

پکرېدل pəkaredál *intransitive* [*past:* وپکرېده] **1** to be scratched **2** to be disturbed (e.g., of wasps) **3** *figurative* to be angered, be irritated

پکر [1] pəkár **1** poor **2** *m.* pauper

پکر [2] pəkər *m.* wood, timber (pine)

پکړه pəkaṛa *feminine singular of* پکړ [1]

پکست pəkásta پکسته on purpose, intentionally, deliberately پکست کول to do something on purpose or intentionally

پکسمت paksimāt *m.* rusk

پېکښي pékkhi پکښي pəkkhe *Eastern* **1** in him, her, it, them يو مکتوب يې وراستولئ او پکښني ويلي يې دي چه ... He wrote him a letter in which it was written that … **2** among them

پکل [1] pakál *m.* **1** light screening (of reed, rush, matting) **2** wattle fencing

پکل [2] pəkál *transitive* [*past:* وېيې پاکه] to take up with the tongue from the palm of the hand (i.e., medicine)

پېکو pekó ☞ پکه

پکوالی pəkválaj *m.* baldness

پکوڼ pəkóṛ *m.* winter cap

پکوړا pəkavṛā *f.* ground haricot or French beans cooked with onion and red pepper

پکول pəkól *m.* ☞ پکوړ

پکوم pəkúm *vice* ☞ په کوم کوم

پکوڼی pəkuṇə́j *f.* divorced woman who has remarried

پکه [1] paká pakká *f.* **1** fan پکه وهل to fan **2** damper, stove door

پکه [2] paká *f.* **1** small handful of something **2** fine powder (medicine) پکه وهل to take up on the tongue from the palm of the hand (i.e., food medical powder)

پکه [3] pə́ka *feminine singular of* پک [1]

پکه [4] peká *f.* bran, siftings (e.g., of maize)

پکه باښه pə́ka bāṣ́ha *f.* carrion crow

پکه تيږه pə́ka tíga *f.* ☞ پله تيږه

پکه يې pakaí pakkaí پکه شکل pakashákl pakkashákl fan-shaped (of an antenna)

پکی [1] pakáj *m.* **1** fan **2** ventilator fan د بجلی پکی electric fan

پکی [2] pəkáj pukáj *diminutive* somewhat bald, a bit thin on top

پکی [3] pə́ki ☞ پکښني

پکی [4] pekí *present tense of* پکل [2]

پکی [5] paké *plural of* پکه [1,2]

پکی [6] peké *plural of* پکه [4]

پکبدل pəkedál *denominative, intransitive* [*past:* پک شو] to grow bald; have one's hair grow thin or fall out

پگر pagaṛ *m.* ☞ پگڼ

پگړه pagóṛa *f.* **1** collective work; assistance; پگړه کول to work collectively, work together, work jointly **2** *obsolete* to exterminate a hostile tribe to the last man

پگړی pagṛój *f.* large turban *idiom* د خاني پگړی ورترل to elect or choose as khan

پگړیوالا pagṛəjvālā *m.* man wearing a turban

پگڼ pagán *m.* pagún *regional* Pagan (the eleventh month of the Indian calendar, February-March)

پگڼه pagóṇa *f.* ☞ پگړه

پل [1] pal *m.* **1** sole (of foot) پل اخيستل، پل پېژندل to identify footprints **a** پل اېينودل، پل پر پله اېينودل **2** footprint **a** to step in, enter پل په پله اېينودل **b** to follow in the steps or tracks (of) **b** *figurative* to imitate پل ورکول to cover up tracks; to hide, cover پل لگول to follow the tracks, shadow د چا پل to be on the track of (e.g., a thief) وركول to lose someone's trail پل پر پل *literal* to take a step forward يو پل نور هم وراندي تلل پل په توره *idiom* to pursue پل پسي اخيستل، پل پل اېينودل، اېينودل to nourish a fierce hatred وهل

پل [2] pal *m.* millstone

پل [3] pul *m.* [*plural:* پلونه pulúna *plural:* پلان pulán] *Western* bridge د پله محصول plə bridge toll پل ترل to throw a bridge (across a river) اوښ تر پله لاندي نه سي پټېدای *proverb literal* You can't hide a camel under a bridge *figurative* "Murder will out" *idiom* ځان پل کول to display endurance, demonstrate patience; stand one's ground

پل [4] pil *m.* ☞ پيل [2]

پل [5] pól *m.* pil **1** moment, instant **2** minute

پل [6] pól **1** liberated from something **2** forgiven **3** justified, vindicated پل کول ☞ پلول [1]

پل [7] pól castrated, neutered پل کول ☞ پلول [3]

پل [8] pal **1** *doublet* دل **2** *doublet* دل

پلا plā *f.* **1** time, occasion يوه پلا خو پلا once, one time several times, repeatedly په يوه پلا *colloquial* at once, at one go اوله پلا، the first time, at first د لمړی پلا دپاره for the first time, د لمړی پلا تر درو پلا زيات more than three times خلورمي پلا دپاره for the fourth time په دي پلا another time بله پلا this time **2** end, terminal, terminus, one-way trip *idiom* په پلا کول، په پلا پسي تلل to travel on business

پلاتين plātín *m. plural* platinum

پلاټ plāṭ *m.* idea, topic

پلار [1] plar *m.* [*plural:* پلارونه plarúna *Eastern plural:* پلارونه plārúna *plural:* پلاران plārán] father پلار په پلار from generation to generation پلار نيکه ancestors **2** founder *idiom* ستاسو موټر د موټرانو پلار دئ! *Eastern* You have the best of automobiles!

پلار [2] pólār *vice* ☞ په لار لار

پلارتوب plārtób *m.* پلارتيا plārtjā́ *f.* fatherhood

پلارخېل plārkhél *m.* father's tribe د ناوي پلارخېل the tribe of the bride-to-be on her father's side; the bride's patrilineal tribe

پلارگلوي plārgalví *f.* fatherhood د پلار گلوی د پلار گلوی ويناوي کول، نصيحتونه ورکول to make a paternal admonition

پلارمړی plārmə́raj **1** deprived of a father, having lost a father, orphaned **2** *m.* orphan

پلاروالی plārvålaj *m.* پلارولي plārvalí *f.* ☞ پلارتوب

پۀلاره pۀlāra *vice* ☞ لار ، په لاره

پلاز plāz *m.* throne

پلازمېنی plāzménaj *m.* capital

پلاس ¹ pۀlås *vice* ☞ لاس ، په لاس

پلاس ² plās *m.* pliers

پلاستر plāstár *m.* 1 plaster (construction material) 2 *medicine* plaster

پلاستک plāstík *m.* پلاستیک plastic

پلاستیکي plāstikí *adjective* plastic

پلاسمه plāsmá *f. biology* plasma

پلاسنتا plāsentá *f. anatomy* placenta

پلال pۀlål *m.* پلاله plåla *f.* straw (usually rice)

پلان ¹ plān *m.* plan د پلان سره سم ، سم له پلانه سره according to plan, in accordance with the plan پلان انکشافي داقتصادي plan for developing the national economy د پلان پنځه کلن Five Year Plan د پلان وزارت Ministry of Planning پلان په اساس *attributive* planning, plans پلان تطبیقول to carry out a plan, execute a plan پلان جوړول to draw up a plan, plan

پلان ² pulån *Western plural of* پل ³

پلان ³ plān *pronoun* ☞ فلان

پلانده plånda *f. sports* wrestling

پلانکی plānkáj *pronoun* ☞ فلان

پلان گذاري plānguzārí *f.* پلاننگ plāníng *m.* planning

پلانول plānavól *denominative, transitive* [*past:* پلان یې کړ] to plan, draw up plans

پلانه ¹ plåna *oblique of* پلان ¹

پلانه ² plåna *feminine singular of* پلان ⁴

پلانی plānáj *pronoun* ☞ فلان

پلانبر plānēr *m.* glider

پلانه ¹ plåṇa *f.* 1 water conveyed in a water-skin from afar 2 large water-skin full of water

پلانه ² pۀlåṇa *f.* 1 threshing floor 2 packsaddle

پلاو pulåv *m.* 1 pilaf 2 groats *idiom* خیالي پلاو پخول to build castles in the air; fantasize

پلپ palp *m.* antenna, palpus

پل پتي palpۀtí *f.* eradicating tracks; concealment پل پتي کول to eradicate tracks, eliminate footprints; to hide, cover up

پلپوټ palpóṭ 1 hidden, secret 2 hushed-up (of an affair, mater) پلپوټ کول to eradicate tracks; hide; cover up

پل پیسه pulpajsá *f.* bridge toll

پلت plat *m.* 1 plot, small piece of ground 2 sketch 3 project, idea

پلتری pۀlatráj *f.* squatting on one's haunches, sitting cross-legged پلتری وهل to squat on one's hunches

پل تگ paltág *m.* following someone; pursuing someone

پلتند plåtənd tossing restlessly (of a sick person) برائي بی تبه وه ، کړی ... شپه پلتند و Yesterday he came down with a fever, and he tossed restlessly all night.

پلته paltá *f.* palitá 1 fuse, wick 2 cord

پلتری pۀlatۀj *f.* ☞ پلتری

پلت plaṭ *m.* ☞ پلت

پلتل pۀlatۀl [*past:* و یې پلاته] 1 to look for, search for, seek out, trace عیبونه پلتل to ferret out deficiencies 2 to search 3 to investigate

پلتمن plaṭmۀn ☞ پلتند

پلتن pۀlṭۀn *f. regional military* 1 infantry regiment 2 infantry

پلتند plaṭənd 1 ☞ پلتند 2 inquisitive, curious

پلتنه ¹ pۀlaṭۀna *f.* 1 inquests, inquiries 2 search 3 investigation علمي پلتني scientific investigations پلتني کول a to look for, search for b to find something c to do research تپلتني لاندي نیول to carry out an investigation; to subject to an investigation 4 *military* د پلتني محلي جنگونه reconnaissance encounters of local importance 5 examination; check

پلتنه ² palṭána *f.* ☞ پلتن

پلتنی pۀlṭənáj *m. Eastern colloquial* soldier

پلتون ¹ pۀlaṭún *m.* inquiry

پلتون ² plaṭún *m. regional military* platoon

پلتونکی pۀlaṭúnkaj 1 *present participle of* پلتل 2 *m.* investigator

پلچک pulchák *m.* little bridge

پلغ pləts long and thick (of goat's wool, etc.)

پلغی plۀtse *f. plural* long, thick wool (e.g., goat's)

پلغور plۀtsevár having long wool

پل خمري ، پلخمري pul-i-khumrí Pul-i-Khumri (city)

پلرگنی plۀrganáj *f.* relatives, relations (on the father's side)

پلرنی plaranáj paternal پلرنی تاتوبی fatherland

پلس pils *m.* scales (fish)

پل ساز pulsåz 1 *adjective* bridge-builder 2 *m.* bridge construction

پل سازي pulsāzí *f.* construction of bridges, bridge construction

پلستري plۀstۀrí *f.* stocking

پلشته pۀláshta *f.* prostitute

پلغټ palghát pۀlaghát 1 fast walk, quick pace په پلغټ تلل to walk quickly 2 *dialect* quickly, at once اس مي پلغټ پرېنود، لاکن لاندي I quickly urged the horse on (after him), but did not مي نه کړ overtake him.

پلغټي palghaṭí *f.* swiftness, quickness

پل غټ palghalát 1 good-for-nothing, useless 2 hypocritical 3 base

پلک ¹ pۀlk *m.* blacksmith's hammer, sledgehammer

پلک ² pilk *m.* 1 eyelid 2 instant, moment

پلک ³ plak *tautological with* کلک

پلکش palkásh *m.* scraper, scoop, shovel

پلکه ¹ pۀlka *f.* 1 nail 2 button, knob 3 *botany* fruit stalk *idiom* د پلکو کول to beat up, pound, beat د پلکو کېدل to be beaten up, pounded on

پلکه ² pۀlká *f.* hilt (of a saber)

پلکی palakáj *f.* iron pintle locking the plowshare to the plowbeam

پلگ plag *m. electronics* plug

پلگواښه palgvåkha *f.* ☞ پل گواښه

پلمه palmá *f.* pretext, occasion, excuse, subterfuge, ruse پلمې تراشل، پلمه جوړول، پلمه کول to seek refuge in excuses, resort to ruses; use cunning, use guile *idiom* پلمه ویل to slander, discredit

پلن [1] plən plan 1 broad, wide, expansive په پلنو in depth 2 obtuse (angle) *idiom* ځان پلن اچول to play the simpleton

پلن [2] palə́n *obsolete* pedestrian, related to walking, on foot

پلنپاڼی plənpáṇaj *m.* cabbage

پلن پزی plənpázaj flat-nosed, snub-nosed

پلن والی pləntób *m.* پلن تیا pləntjá *f.* ☞ پلن والی

پلندر plandár *m.* [*plural:* پلندرونه plandarúna] stepfather

پلندۍ plandə́j *f.* 1 marsh, swamp 2 *figurative* betrayal, cheating, swindling

پلنډه plánḍa *f.* 1 load, burden 2 kit; knapsack

پلنډي planḍí *m.* porter; stevedore

پلن سری plənsáraj *m.* 1 wooden spade 2 blockhead, fool

پلنغوړی [1] plənghvagaj *m.* elephants

پلنغوړې [2] plənghváge *f.* cow, female elephant

پلنگ paláng *m.* bed

پلنگ پوښ palangpóḳh *m.* bedspread, coverlet

پلن والی plənválaj *m.* 1 width; breadth; expanse 2 square, plaza

پلنول plənavə́l *denominative, transitive* [*past:* پلن یې کړ] 1 to widen; make extensive, extend 2 to throw down and pound someone

پلنېدل plənadə́l *denominative, intransitive* [*past:* پلن شو] to be widened; be extended

پلو [1] paláv *m.* paláu pə́láv 1 side, direction, flank سویل پلو south side سویل پلو ته to the south, on the south ښی پلو right side ښی پلو ته on the right, to the right کین پلو، کینه left side کس پلو، گس پلو ته on the left, to the left نه هغه پلو . . . . د across, on the other side دغه کتاب د look here (this way) دي پلو ته وگوره، دي پلو ته وگوره یو پلو ته Put this book alongside of that one! هغه کتاب په پلو کېږده! له . . . . د پلوه *literal & figurative* to stand aside کېدل **a** from the point of view of . . . **b** *the subject of the action in the passive voice is expressed with the assistance of this location* د حکومت له پلوه ترتیبات نیولي شوي دي Measures were taken by the government 2 *figurative* relationship له اقتصادي پلوه in an economic relationship 3 width, panel (i.e., of a tent, pavilion); side, lateral wall 4 border, edge د چمن پلو the edge of a forest glade پلو په مخ اچول to cover the face with the edge of something; cover up with the edge of something *idiom* پلو غوټه کول to ask someone for help, assistance پلو نیول **a** to support someone, be on someone's side **b** to ask for forgiveness د چا په پلو کېدل، د چا پر پلو کېدل **a** to be on someone's side پلانی زما پلو ته دئ so and so is on my side, so and so supports me **a** د پلو روی ورول to ask for help (a woman) **b** to ask forgiveness (a woman)

پلو [2] pə́lo *oblique plural of* پلی [1]

پلو [3] puló *oblique plural of* پل [3]

پلو [4] plo *oblique plural of* پله [1]

پلواری palvá̱raj *m.* پلواری palvá̱raj *m.* tea rose

پلواښه palvá̱ḳha *f.* pulvá̱ḳha 1 loop, frog (for a button) 2 hobbles 3 lasso, lariat

پلوالی pə́lvă̄laj *m.* forgiveness

پلوان pulvá̄n *m.* bridge builder

پلوخه plótsa *f.* palótsa *botany* Indian acacia, *Acacia modesta*

پلور plor *m.* 1 price 2 selling, sale; buying and selling (i.e., trading); transaction

پلورتون plortún *m.* market

پلورتولی plorṭólaj *m.* company

پلوردزی plórdzáj *m.* shop; place where something is sold د کتابونو پلورځی bookstore

پلورل plorə́l 1 [*past:* وی یې پلوره] *transitive* to sell پرچا باندي پلورل، په to sell to someone *passive* چا باندي پلورل کېدل to be sold 2 *m. plural* selling; sale د پلورلو مامور sales agent د پلورلو او پېرودلو مدیر manager of a (the) commercial section

پلورنه ploró̱na *f.* selling, sale

پلورونکی plorúnkaj 1 *present participle of* پلورل 2 *m.* vendor

پلوری ploráj merchant; trader

پلورینه ploríː̄na *f.* selling, sale

پلوره plóṛa *f.* anteroom, hall, lobby

پلوس plós *m botany* purging cassia, *Cassia fistula*

پلوسه plósa *f.* ☞ پلوخه

پلوشه palvashá *f.* 1 ray د لمر پلوشې sunbeam, ray of the sun پلوشی to sparkle (diamond) 2 tongues (of flame) *idiom* د علم پلوشی luminary of science

پلواښه pulvá̱ḳha palvəḳhá ☞ پلواینه

پلوغوټه pə́lavghúṭa *f.* palavghúṭa 1 money given by the head of a household to relatives (on the occasion of a family celebration) 2 money given by a financé to his bride (at the first meeting)

پلول [1] pə́lavə́l pə́lavə́l pulavúl *denominative Eastern* [*past:* پل یې کړ] 1 to release, liberate 2 to forgive حق پلول to forgive someone for sins or an offense (upon setting out on a journey); bless someone for the road 3 to justify

پلول [2] palavə́l *denominative, transitive* [*past:* اپل یې کړ] to pace off, measure by pacing (i.e., land)

پلول [3] pə́lavə́l *denominative, transitive* [*past:* ایل یې کړ] to castrate, neuter پلولئ پسه gelding پلولئ اس castrated ram, castrated buck

پلوند palvánḍ 1.1 fat, portly, stout 1.2 stupid; dimwitted, obtuse 2 *m.* .1 fat person 2.2 blockhead

پلوندتوب palvanḍtób *m.* پلوندتیا palvanḍtjá *f.* پلوندي palvanḍí *f.* 1 stoutness, obesity 2 stupidity 3 ☞ پهلواني

پلونه [1] pə́lavə́na *f.* 1 liberation 2 forgiveness 3 justification

پلونه [2] palavə́na *f.* pacing off, measuring by paces (i.e., land)

پلونه [3] palúna *plural of* پل [1]

پلونه [4] pulúna *plural* پل [3]

پلوه palá̄va *oblique of* پلو [1]

پلوی [1] pə́laví palaví 1.1 being alongside, neighboring, adjoining 1.2 having contiguous plots of land 2 *m.* partisan, supporter پلوی

کول to be a supporter (of a person, idea, etc.), support someone or something

پلوی ² palaváj *m.* the outside or further ox (of a team engaged in grinding grain on a circular threshing floor)

پلوی ³ palavэ́j *f.* 1 fully-grown girl 2 palavэjā́ni women, the women's half of the house

پلوي ⁴ palaví *m.* kind of mulberry

پلویغ pólavídz *m.* neighbor

پله ¹ plá *f.* pólá 1 tendon; sinew, ligament 2 nerve خپلي پلي په خپله قبضه کښي راوستل to hold oneself in check; to display self-control 3 muscle 4 vegetable fiber *idiom* پلي وهل to nourish a fierce hostility or hatred; to hate

پله ² pulá *f.* [*plural:* پلي pulé] cooked corn kernels

پله ³ palá *f.* pallá pólá pan (of scales) پله خوربدل to outbalance, weigh (all or a quantity) 2 panel (of a door), half a double door 3 convenient occasion; auspicious moment 4 advantage پله پر پیدا کول to overcome, overpower

پله ⁴ palá *f. dialect* edge; flank, side *idiom* پله نیول، پر پله دربدل to support, help

پله ⁵ púla plэ *oblique singular of* پل ³

پله ⁶ píla *f.* cow, female elephant

پله ⁷ pála *f. feminine singular of* پل ⁷

پله ⁸ plэ *oblique singular of* پل ¹,³

پله ایلی pólailэ́j *f.* coot (the bird)

پله پسی pólapasé *☞* پرله پسی

پله پسی توب pólapasetób *m.* پله پسی والی pólapasevā́laj *m.* sequence; continuity; uninterruptedness

پله پوري póla-púri póla-póre *Eastern* 1.1 adjoining, situated alongside 1.2 closed, shut (e.g., doors) پله پوري کول a to join, connect b to close, shut 1.2 پله پوري کبدل a to be joined, to abut (upon) b to be closed, be shut 2 nearby, with one another, near, right up against د ښار سره پله پوري close by the city

پله تیره platíga *f.* asbestos

پلی ¹ pólaj 1 *m.* [*plural:* پلي póli] .1 pedestrian د پلیو لار sidewalk پلی کول a to set down b to dismount پلی کبدل a to alight; come off of b to dismount 1.2 infantryman 1.3 [*plural:* پلي pэ́li] infantry د پلیو تعلیمگاه Infantry Officers Training School 1.4 *chess* pawn 2 on foot *idiom* د عقله پلی stupid, dimwitted, one who has lost possession of his faculties

پلی ² pэ́lэj *f.* 1 pod د موټو پلی pod of *Phaseolus aconitifolius* (a kind of bean) 2 clove (of garlic) 3 bundle of cut willow withes

پلی ³ palэ́j *f.* spoke (of a wheel)

پلی ⁴ pluэ́j *f. ☞* پله ²

پلی ⁵ pulэ́j *f.* blister, bump

پلی ⁶ plé pэ́lé *plural of* پله ¹

پلی ⁷ pulé *plural of* پله ²

پلی ⁸ palé pallé *plural of* پله ³

پلی ⁹ palé *plural of* پله ⁴

پلیت ¹ palít 1 muddy, soiled 2 defiled 3 disgusting, nasty, base

پلیت ² plet *m. ☞* پلیت

پلیتکه palitáka *f.* 1 fuse, wick 2 flame, (small) light

پلیتول palitavэ́l [*past:* پلیت یی کړ] 1 to soil, muddy 2 to defile

پلیتونی pэ́litúnaj *f.* bobbin, spool

پلیته ¹ palítá *f.* 1 fuse, primer (of a weapon) 2 corn ear with husk which has just formed

پلیته palíta *feminine singular of* پلیت ¹

پلیتي palití *f.* 1 mud 2 manure 3 *figurative* vileness, baseness, loathsomeness

پلیتبدل palitedэ́l *denominative* [*past:* پلیت شو] 1 to be soiled, be muddied 2 to be defiled

پلیت plet 1 *photography* plate 2 *regional* dish, plate

پلیتفارم pleṭfā́rm *m.* پلیتفارم railroad platform

پلیتن pэ́leṭэn *m.* پلی تن weaver's beam

پلید palíd *☞* پلیت ¹

پلیدي palidí *f. ☞* پلیتي

پلیس pulís *m. ☞* پولیس

پلبکو pólekó *m.* water-powered rice huller

پلیگون poligón firingrange

پلبل pólél *m. plural ☞* فلبل

پلبور plevr *m. anatomy* pleura

پم pam *m.* 1 scab; itch; mange 2 dandruff 3 bran, siftings 4 crumbs

پمبچو pumbachó *f.* پمبچه pumbachá *f. ☞* پمبچو

پمبه ¹ pumbá *f. ☞* پنبه

پمبه ² pambá *f.* crumbs

پمبه چیني pambachiní *f.* پنبه چیني pambachiní *☞*

پمبی pambáj *m.* 1 cattle shed; stable 2 *☞* پمبه ²

پمبچو، پمبی چو pumbechú *m.* pumbechó *f.* 1 stalk of cotton plant, Asiatic cotton plant, *Gossypium asiaticum* 2 dry cotton boll

پمپ pamp *m.* pump

پندانه pumdā́na *f. ☞*

پمن pamэ́n scabby; mangy, suffering from the mange

پمن کور pamэnkóṛ *m. regional* 1 scab; itch 2 leprosy

پمن کوري pamэnkoṛí *m. regional* 1 mangy, scabby 2 leprous

پمنول pamэnavэ́l *denominative, transitive* [*past:* پمن یی کړ] to infect with scab, infect with mange

پمنه pamэ́na *f. regional* scab; itch

پمنبدل pamэnedэ́l *denominative, intransitive* [*past:* پمن شو] to be infected with scab (rash); be covered with mange

پمبچو pamechú pumechú *☞* پمبچو

پن pun *m. dialect ☞* پم

پنا panā́ *f.* 1 refuge, asylum, shelter, safe haven, cover 2 protection, guardianship, patronage پنا غوښتل a to request asylum; seek asylum b to request protection, patronage پنا کول *compound verb* a to give shelter, grant asylum, hide b to defend, act as patron ځان پنا کول a to seek asylum; lie in hiding, be hidden b to be protected پنا کبدل to conceal oneself, hide oneself, disappear لۀ غرۀ نه پنا شو The sun was hidden behind the mountain د لمر

سترگو نه پنا کېدل to be out of sight (hidden from the eyes) له سترگو پنا کېدل a to be concealed, be hidden, be out of sight b to come running for protection or patronage c to avoid (something) *idiom* پنا په خدای to come running for protection or patronage پنا پخدای غوارم! له دی نه! God protect us from this! God forbid!

پنا ² panā پنا کول to remove, eliminate, take away

پنا ³ pənā *f.* 1 pouring; sprinkling پنا کول to pour, sprinkle 2 drizzling rain پنا کېدل a to flow b to drizzle

پناځای panādzáj *m.* پناگاه panāgáh *f.* ☞ گاه

پنامخ pənāmúkh behind someone's back, in someone's absence

پنامه pənāmá *vice* ☞ په نامه نوم

پنا ¹ panáh *f.* ☞ پنا

پناهځای panāhdzáj *m.* ☞ پناه گاه ¹

پناه گاه panāhgā *f.* panāhgáh 1 shelter, asylum د غازو پناه گاه gas-proof shelter 2 *military* د بمو پناه گاه dugout بمب پناه گاه bomb shelter 3 پناه گاه ترل to fence in 4 *figurative* asylum, shelter وروستی last refuge, shelter پناه گاه نیول to find shelter

پناهگزین panāhguzín *m.* پناه گیر panāhgír *m.* refugee

پناه ورکونکی panáh varkavúnkaj *m.* patron

پناه ورونکی panáh vrúnkaj 1 appealing for help 2 *m.* refugee

پناهي panāhi *f.* 1 shelter, asylum 2 protection, patronage پناهي نیول a to seek asylum b to seek protection, seek patronage

پندانه pumbādāná *f.* ☞ پنبه دانه

پنبه pumbá pambá *f.* cotton د پنبي اومه raw cotton *attributive* د پنبي cotton پنبي بوتی، د پنبه بوتي cotton plant د پنبي پلورل turning over of cotton, delivery of cotton د پنبي تیارول cotton procurement د پنبي کرنه، د پنبه و کرنه planting of cotton د پنبي کرهنه cotton grower د پنبي کرونکی cotton production د پنبي د پاکولو کارخانه sowing cotton, planting cotton د پنبي کښت cotton mill د پنبي د تیارولو *attributive* cotton procurement د پنبي د کرهني *attributive* cotton-planting *attributive* cotton growing

پنبه بافي pumbabāfí *f.* cotton weaving د پنبه بافی فابریکه cotton-weaving mill

پنبه چیني pumbachiní *f.* cotton picking, cotton harvesting

پنبه کاري pumbakārí *f.* cotton growing, cotton production

پنبئي pumbaí cotton, of cotton پنبئي توتی، پنبئي منسوجات، پنبئي یي، پنبئي توکران cotton fabric

پنجاب pandzháb *m.* Punjab

پنجابي pandzhābí pandzhābáj 1 *adjective* Punjabi 2 *m.* Punjabi (person)

پنجالۍ pandzhālə́j *f.* small window

پنج پاو pandzhpáo *m.* پنج پای pandzhpáj *m.* Pandzhpao (one of the two principal branches of the Durrani)

پنج پولی pandzhpulí *f.* panjpuli (Afghan 5 pul coin)

پنج تار pandzhtár *m.* panjtar (five-stringed musical instrument)

پنجده pandzhdéh *m. & f.* Panjdeh (a district)

پنجره pandzhará *f.* pandzhərá پنجری pandzharə́j *f.* 1 (window) lattice, grille 2 (latticed) window 3 cage (for birds); open-air cage; voliere

پنجشنبه pandzhshambá *f.* Thursday

پنجشېر pandzhshér *m.* Pianjshir (district)

پنجشېري pandzhsherí pandzhsheráj 1 Pianjshirian 2 Pianjshirian (person)

پنج صومه pandzhsumá *f.* 1 five-sum (i.e., monetary unit) 2 *history* gold 5 sum coin

پنج غشی pandzhghisháj *m.* پنج غنبی pandshghakháj *m.* 1 rake 2 wooden pitchfork

پنجک pandzhák *m. history* tax amounting to one-fifth share of a harvest پنجک اخیستل پنجک ټولول to levy or collect a tax amounting to one-fifth part of a harvest

پنجکوره pandzhkorá *f.* Pandzhkora (district, Peshawar)

پنجکی pandzhakáj *m.* 1 crossbar of sling (weapon), sling grip 2 door handle, door knob

پنجه ¹ pandzhá *f.* 1 hand (from the wrist to finger-tips), hand and five outstretched fingers 2 foot, sole 3 paw 4 claw, talon په پنجو نیول to seize with the paws or claws 5 fork (eating utensil) *idiom* د یوې موضوع سره پنجه to measure one's strength چا سره پنجي ورکول په دوه ی باندي پنجه راکښ to deal with a subject, treat a theme نرمول کول to cut slashes into bread dough (to bake it more thoroughly)

پنجه ² pandzhá *f.* the Pyandzh River آب پنجه *āb-i* the Pyandzh River

پنجه بابا pandzhabābá *f.* crab

پنجه چنار pandzhachinár *m.* plane tree

پنجهزاری pandzhhazārí *f. history* post or function of chief of a detachment of fifty men د پنجهزاری منصب ☞

پنجه گی pandzhagí *f. military* cartridge clip

پنچر panchár puncture (tire)

پنغ pundz *m. obsolete* creation, origin

پنځټکیز pindztakíz five-shot (of a rifle)

پنځخند pindztsə́nḍ pentagonal

پنځروپیه گیز pindzrupagíz *m.* five-rupee bank note

پنځسویز pindzsavíz *m.* 500-afghan, rupee, etc. bank note; five-hundred denomination bill

پنځکابلیزه pindzkāblíza *f. obsolete* a five-Kabul-rupee coin

پنځه کلن pindzokalán ☞ پنځکلن

پنجکوړه pandzkorá *f.* ☞ پنځکوړه

پنځگوټی pindzgvóṭaj pentagonal

پنځه گون pindzəgún pindzəgúnaj ☞ پنځگونی

پنځلس pindzə́las *number* fifteen

پنځلسم pindzə́lasə́m *ordinal* fifteenth د پنځلسمي شپه ☞ برات ²

پنځلسورځنی pindzə́lasvradzanáj every two weeks, semi-weekly; پنځلس ورځنی معاش fortnightly pay

پنځم pindzə́m *ordinal* fifth *idiom* د جاسوسانو پنځمه نمره فرقه fifth column

پنځوس pindzós *number* fifty

پنځوس پولی pindzospuláj *m.* pindzospulí *f.* fifty-pul coin, half afghani

پنځوس مشر pindzosmə́shr *m. history* commander of a fifty-man detachment

پنځول pəndzavə́l *transitive* [*past:* و یی پنځاوه] 1 to create 2 to fill up (e.g., a bag) 3 to cause to be successful 4 to increase, multiply

پنځون pəndzún *m.* 1 nature, creation 2 origin, provenance

پنځونه pəndzavə́na *f.* creation (the act)

پنځه pindzə́ 1 *number* five پنځه ورځی a five days b *figurative* human life (shortness, etc.) 2 group of five, fivesome کار چه د پنځو شي، هغه خراب شي *proverb literal* If the matter is delegated to five, then it will go wrong. *figurative* Too many cooks spoil the broth.

پنځه ² pə́ndza *f.* ☞ پنځونه

پنځه بنا pindzə baná *m. plural religion* the five principles of Islam (Kalima: Recital of the Creed; Namaz: Performance of Divine Worship (prayer) five times daily; Fasting: Fasting in the month of Ramadan; Zakat: alms (legal and determined); there are also voluntary alms (sadaqat); Hadj: Pilgrimage to Mecca)

پنځه پوره pindzəpóra five-story پنځه پوره عمارت five-story building

پنځه څنديز pindzətsəndíz *m.* 1 pentagon 2 pentagonal

پنځه څوکیز pindzətsukíz five-pointed پنځه څوکیز ستوری five-pointed star

پنځه ډزی pindzəḍázaj five-shot (of a rifle)

پنځه غبنی pindzəghakháj *m.* six-year-old camel (i.e., one entering the 6th year, being fully 5-years old)

پنځه کسیز pindzəkasíz five-man (consisting of five men)

پنځه کلن pindzəkalán پنځه کلنی pindzəkalanáj five-year پنځه کلن پلان five-year plan

پنځه ګون pindzəgún پنځه ګونی pindzəgúnaj 1 quintuple, consisting of five parts پنځه ګون اصول panchashila (the five principles of peaceful coexistence) 2 five-fold

پنځلس pindzə́las *number* ☞ پنځلس

پنځه ویشت pindzəvísht *number* twenty-five

پنځه یکه pindzəjaká one-fifth

پنځی ³ pəndzə́j *f.* sack (for smoking materials)

پنځبدل pəndzedə́l *intransitive* [*past:* وپنځبده] 1 to be created 2 to be filled (with) 3 to have success

پنځیز pindzíz consisting of five parts, quintuple

پنځه pantsá *f.* ☞ دای

پند ¹ pand *m.* 1 advice, instructions, moral admonition پند ورکول to give advice د یوه شي څخه پند اخیستل to derive a lesson for oneself from something 2 wisdom 3 rule of conduct 4 *dialect* ruse, deception, guile پند ورته اینبودل، پند ورسره کول to deceive

پند ² pand *m.* 1 distance 2 removal; departure; leaving; exit 3 journey پند کول to go away; to leave; to depart; to exit

پند ³ pənd *m.* enmity

پندار pindár *m.* 1 imagination; opinion 2 conceit په ډبر پندار ویل to speak haughtily

پندانه pundāná *f.* cottonseed

پندتیا pandtjá *f.* 1 wisdom 2 opinion; cleverness

پندنامه pandnāmá *f.* 1 book of advice; instructions, precepts 2 testament

پند ورکوونکی pand varkavúnkaj *m.* preceptor

پندوک pundúk *m.* bud; blossom

پندول pandúl *m.* pendulum

پنده ¹ púnda *f.* 1 ☞ پونده ² 2 decorative mountings on a saber scabbard

پنده ² pónda *f.* ☞ بری ¹

پندی ¹ pəndə́j *f. botany* Erophila verna

پندی ² pundə́j *f.* 1 ☞ پونده ² 2 steel or iron tip of a spear or javelin

پندیر pandír *m. plural* ☞ پنیر

پندیرک pandirák *m.* ☞ پنډهرک

پنډ ¹ panḍ *m.* 1 pack, bale 2 load, pack (animal), burden (head) پو پنډ واښه bundle of hay 3 *figurative* burden, incubus

پنډ ² panḍ *m.* large dam, weir پنډ اچول to build a dam

پنډ ³ pənḍ *m.* punḍ [*plural:* پنډان pəndā́n punḍā́n] 1 detachment; group 2 tumor, swelling; lump 3 *anatomy* vagina

پنډ ⁴ pənḍ *m.* punḍ 1 steel (for striking fire from flint) پنډ اوبکری steel 2 firing pin, hammer (of a flintlock rifle)

پنډ ⁵ pənḍ 1.1 fat; fatty; stout پنډ سری fat person پنډه ستن thick needle 1.2 rude; sharp 1.3 rounded up; assembled 1.4 *Waziri* mustered, assembled (people) 2 fat person *idiom* کور دی ودان، ووی دی پنډه! May your house be a full goblet! Live in wealth!

پنډار pənḍā́r *m.* crowd

پنډاره pənḍāra *f.* payment; collection (for musicians)

پنډاو چرګ pənḍā́v chərg *m.* fighting cock, gamecock

پنډاور panḍavə́r covered with down (of a fledgling)

پندبکری punḍbakrə́j *f.* steel (for striking fire from flint)

پنډت panḍít *m.* pundit (title of an educated Hindu)

پنډتوب pənḍtób *m.* ☞ پنډوالی

پنډتون pənḍtún *m.* ☞ پند غالی ¹,²

پنډته panḍə́ta *f.* mockery, ridicule, gibe

پنډتیا pənḍtjā́ *f.* ☞ پنډوالی

پنډغالی ¹ pənḍghā́laj *m.* cattle shed; pen (cattle) sheep pen, sheepfold

پنډغالی ² pənḍghā́laj *m.* place where guests are received and entertained

پنډغلی pənḍghaláj *m.* piece of leather attached to the heel for walking

پنډک punḍák *m.* blossom

پنډکی ¹ punḍkə́j *f.* bandage; piece of cloth applied with adhesive to a wound پر زخمو پنډکی اینبودل to bandage a wound

پنډکی ² panḍakə́j *m.* ☞ پنډوکی

پنډګر pənḍgár *m.* craftsman engaged in making steels (for striking fire from flint)

پنډل panḍə́l *m.* 1 boundary strip; berm of road 2 ☞ سنګر

پنډو ¹ pənḍó *f.* assemblege, mob, crowd (people)

پنډو [2] **pánḏo** *oblique plural of* پنډه [1]

پنډو [3] **pənḏó** *oblique plural of* پنډ [1-4]

پنډوالی دپر پنډوالی **pənḏvālaj** *m.* **1** obesity **2** stoutness, embonpoint corpulence

پنډور **pənḏavár** having thick calves, fat-legged

پنډوس **pənḏós** *m.* پنډوسان **pəndosắn** *plural:* پنډوسونه **pənḏosúna**] ball د واوري په پنډس کول to play ball **2** ball, clod پنډوسونه یو بل سره ویشتل to play with snowballs, have a snowball fight **3 pənḏús** [*plural:* پنډوسان **pənḏusán**] fat man

پنډوسکه **pənḏoska** *f.* پنډوسکی **pənḏóskaj** *m.* پنډوسه **pənḏósa** *f.* ball, small ball پنډوسکه کول to play ball

پنډوکمار **panḏukmár** *m.* **1** porter **2** petty thief

پنډوکی **panḏúkaj** *m.* پنډوکی **panḏúke** *f.* **1** small load, burden; knapsack; bundle **2** sheaf (e.g., of letters)

پنډول **[1** پنډ یی کړ **pənḏavál punḏavál** *denominative, transitive* [*past:* to make fat, fatten **2** to make look fat, overfill **3** to drive cattle (into a herd); bring together (people for a feast, for conversation) **4** to round up (cattle into a herd); bring together (people for a feast, for conversation)

پنډولگر **pənḏolgár** *m.* گر cotton harvester

پنډولی [1] **panḏoláj** *m.* share of cotton given by the owner of the field to a hired worker for harvesting the cotton

پنډولی [2] **panḏolí** *f.* picking, harvesting cotton or fruit for pay پنډولي کول to pick or harvest cotton or fruit for pay

پنډولی [3] **pənḏoláj** *f.* sheet, bedding (onto which fruit is dumped from the tree)

پنډون **pənḏún** *m.* **1** ☞ پنډغالی [1,2] **2** round-up, drive (of cattle)

پنډه [1] **pánḏa** *f.* **1** burden; bundle, sheaf **2** alms, charity

پنډه [2] **pəńḏa** *feminine singular of* پنډ [5]

پنډه [3] **pə́nḏa** *f.* **1** heated iron **2** piece of clay taken up by a spade

پنډه [4] **pánḏa** *f.* party of guests served in turn

پنډی [1] **panḏáj** *m.* [*plural:* پنډیان **panḏiján**] porter; stevedore

پنډی [2] **punḏój** *f.* **1** *anatomy* shin; calf (leg) **2** *technology* funnel, cone **3** wooden trunk, chest, box

پنډي [3] **pinḏí** *f.* *regional colloquial* Rawalpindi (city)

پنډي [4] **pánḏi** *feminine plural of* پنډ [5] پنډي وریجي plump-kerneled rice, mealy rice

پنډی [5] **pənḏáj** *f.* iron tip, point

پنډیدل **[1** پنډ شو **pənḏedál** *denominative, intransitive* [*past:* to become thicker, condense, thicken **2** to grow fat, put on weight, grow stout **3** to swell up; become swollen **4** to be rounded up (in a herd, flock); stick together (in flocks) **5** *dialect* to assemble (of people); throng

پنډیرک **panḏirák** *m.* mallow, hollyhock, marsh mallow

پنډیری **panḏeráj** *m.* wicker corncrib

پنډیور **pənḏevár** long-legged

پنر **panár** *m.* ☞ فنر

پنس [1] **puns** *numeral* five hundred

پنس [2] **pens** *m.* penny (coin)

پنساري **pansārí** *m.* **pansāráj** dealer in paints, oils, and related sundries

پنسری **pənsóraj** *m.* ☞ راشبیل

پنسری **pansaráj** *m.* *dialect* ☞ سپنسي

پنسل **pinsál** *m.* **pansil pensíl** [*plural:* پنسلونه **pinsalúna pansilúna pensilúna** *Western plural:* پنسلان **pinsalán pansilán pensilán**] pencil د پنسل قلم pencil

پنسل پاک **pinsalpák pensilpák** *m.* eraser (pencil)

پنسلین **penisilín** *m.* *plural* penicillin

پنسن **pinsán** *m.* *Eastern* ☞ پنسل

پنشن **pinshán** *m.* *regional* pension

پنشني **pinshaní** *m.* *regional* pensioner

پنگ [1] **pəng** *m.* hum, buzz, drone

پنگ [2] **pang** *tautological with* رنگ

پنگ پانگ **pingpáng** *m.* ping-pong, table tennis

پنگلی **punglój** *f.* **pungóláj** native wind instrument similiar to the Persian zurna

پنگول **pəngavál** *transitive* ☞ بنگول

پنگه [1] **pánga** *f.* ☞ پانگه

پنگه [2] **pungá** *f.* bud پنگه وهل to bud

پنگه [3] **pánga** *f.* deep-bedded river (flowing through a plain or a forest)

پنگه وال **pangavál** *m.* capitalist

پنگی [1] **pungój** *f.* **1** reed (for native wind instrument similiar to the Persian zurna) **2** smooth depression, hollow

پنگی [2] **pungój** *f.* peddler's wares

پنگی [3] **pungój** *f.* door hinge

پنگی [4] **pungój** *f.* budlet, small bud

پنگی [5] **pəngáj** *m.* ☞ منجله

پنگی فروش **pungəjfurúsh** *m.* peddler, travelling, itinerant merchant

پنل **pinál** *transitive* ☞ پینل

پنهم **pinhám** **1** concealed; hidden **2** secret, secure, mysterious

پني [1] **pináj panáj** *m.* *botany* **1** *Western* agnus castus, Kochia **2 panáj** *Eastern* beard-grass, Andropogon muriaticum **3** *dialect* vetiver, Cuscus-Vetiveria zezanoides

پني [2] **1** *m.* **paní** *plural* Pani (tribe) **2 panáj** *m.* Pani (tribesman)

پنیر **panír** *m.* *plural* cheese

پنیرک **panirák** *m.* ☞ پنډیرک

پنیرمایه **panirmājá** *f.* clabber, curds (for cheese)

پنیری **panerí** **1** garden **2** *attributive* flowers

پنیک **paník** *m.* panic

پڼ **pəṇ** full, filled

پڼاکي **puṇáki** *f.* *plural* bounds, leaps (of an animal) پڼاکي وهل to leap, bound (of an animal)

پڼاو **paṇáv** *m.* competition, contest

پڼسی **paṇsáj** *m.* *dialect* ☞ سپنسي

پڼل **puṇál** *m.* soft inner seed portion of the pit of a fruit

پڼوډزی **paṇódzáj** *m.* پڼوخی **panodzaj** *m.* entrance hall, lobby

پنول [1] pəṇavə́l *transitive* [*past:* پنه يې کړ] to pour (on, upon); water, irrigate

پنول [2] puṇavə́l *transitive* [*past:* وې يې پناوه] to skin, pare, peel; clean (seeds)

پنه [1] paṇá *f.* slippers (Middle-Eastern type)

پنه [2] páṇa *f.* **1** pouring; irrigation, watering پنه کول *compound verb* to pour (on); irrigate, water پنه کېدل to be poured; be irrigated **2** initial irrigation (of a field)

پنه [3] pəṇə́ páṇa gathered around, forming a group around somebody; surrounding somebody پر چا پنه کېدل to be assembled or grouped around somebody; surround somebody

پنی [1] paṇí *m.* paṇáj ☞ پني [2]

پني [2] paṇé *plural of* پنه [1]

پنی گنډونکی paṇé ganḍúnkaj *m.* slipper maker, shoemaker

پو [1] pu *m.* no plural form **1** blowing, breathing پو کول ☞ پو پوکول **2** *linguistics* aspiration *idiom* پو او چو ☞ پوکېدل، کېدل، incantation

پو [2] pu light, lightweight

پو [3] pu *m.* raids, investigations, searches

پو [4] pu *children's speech* **1** *m.* fire **2** hot پو کېدل *compound verb* to burn up

پو [5] po *f.* the Po (river)

پو [6] po *dialect* ☞ پوه [1]

پواره puvārá *f.* fountain

پوار pəvā́r **1** dirty, unclean, foul پوار کېدل to be dirty, be unclean **2** *m.* guttersnipe

پواره pəvā́ra *feminine singular of* پوار

پوپ تنی puptanáj *m.* hoopoe (bird)

پوپک [1] pupák *m.* [*plural:* پوپکونه pupakúna *plural:* پوپکان pupakā́n] *Western* air rifle

پوپک [2] popák *m.* pompon

پوپکه pupáka *f.* popáka **1** bump; swelling **2** pompon

پوپل popál *m.* **1** Popal (branch of the Dur(r)ani tribe) **2** Popal (tribesman) **3** *proper name* Popal

پوپلزائي [1] popalzā́i *m. plural* پوپلزي popalzí *m. plural* Popalzai (branch of the Dur(r)ani tribe) **2** پوپلزی popalzáj Popalzaj (tribesman)

پوپلین poplín *m.* poplin (cloth)

پوپنا pupəṇā́ annihilated, destroyed پوپنا کول to annihilate, destroy پوپنا کېدل **a** to be annihilated, be destroyed **b** to die out, be extinct

پوپی pupáj *m.* **1** bat **2** ☞ تاتکه

پوت [1] pot *m.* thin felt (used for oriental robes)

پوت [2] put *m.* son

پوتاس potā́s *m. plural* پوتاسیم potasijum *m. plural* potassium پوتاس پرمنگنبت potassium permanganate

پوتکژ potakə́j *f.* necklace

پوتل pavtál *m.* garbage, waste

پوتلی potláj *f.* large doll; puppet, marionette

بوته púta *f.* ox hide (without the head, and legs)

پوتی potə́j *f.* **1** face, image **2** stitched book **3** notebook; blank notepad

پوت [1] pot *m.* **1** hide **2** skin, rind پوت ارول **a** to skin, flay **b** to peel, debark, decorticate

پوت [2] poṭ *m.* **1** misfortune, grief **2** disagreement, discord; dissention

پوت [3] poṭ social gathering, party

پوت [4] puṭ ☞ پت [4]

پوت [5] puṭ *tautological with* لوت

پوتاس potā́s *m. plural* ☞ پوتاس

پوتسکی puṭə́skaj *m.* ☞ پوتس [2,3]

پوتکی [1] poṭə́kaj *m.* **1** skin پوتکی کنبل خام پوتکی pelt **2** hide skin, flay **3** skin, peel, rind, pellicle پوتکي کول ...د potóki **a** to clean; remove, strip off (hide, etc.) **b** *figurative* to thrash, beat up someone *idiom* پوتکی اچول to worry about, torment oneself د انسان کلک پوتکی دئ *saying* the man is hardy

پوتکی [2] poṭəkáj small hill, hillock

پوتکیوالا poṭəkajvālā́ *m. singular & plural* tanner

پوتگنی puṭganə́j *f.* **1** shelter; asylum; secluded place **2** ambush

پوتول puṭavə́l *transitive dialect* ☞ پتول

پوتونی puṭúne *f.* ambush

پوتی [1] poṭáj *m.* [*plural:* پوتی poṭi *plural:* پوتیان poṭijā́n] hill, small mountain

پوتی [2] púṭaj *m.* pṓṭaj **1** small piece **2** fragment of some substance **3** crumb (e.g., bread) پوتی کول، پوتی پوتی کول *compound verb* to cut up carelessly; crumble پوتی کېدل، پوتی پوتی کېدل to be crumbled; be divided into bits **4** pigmy, dwarf

پوتی [3] puṭáj *m. Eastern* small box

پوجي pudzhí *f.* **1** weeding; thinning out **2** pruning (of branches) پوجي کول **a** to weed; thin out **b** to prune (branches)

پوچ puch **1** stupid, senseless, absurd; frivolous پوچ ویل to talk nonsense, talk drivel پوچ او رد ویل No nonsense! پوچ مه وایه! to use foul language **2** bad, evil (of a disposition) **3** spent (cartridge case)

پوچات puchā́t *m. plural* empty words, mere words, absurdity

پوچخولتوب puchkhultób *m.* پوچ خولتیا puchkhultjā́ *f.* foul language

پوچخولی puchkhúlaj swearing, using foul language

پوچک puchák *m.* empty cartridge casing, spent cartridge casing

پوچ کاږ puchkā́g *m.* cartridge-case ejector

پوچکه puchā́ka *f.* freshly-set melon-fruit

پوچ گو puchgó *m.* windbag

پوچ گویي puchgoí *f.* idle talk پوچ گویي کول to talk nonsense; engage in idle talk

پوچ ورد puchurád *m.* **1** nonsense, rubbish **2** verbal abuse پوچ ورد ویل to use foul language

پوچول puchavə́l *denominative* [*past:* پوچ یې کړ] **1** to dupe, make a fool of **2** to fire (cartridges) **3** to bring to naught (e.g., someone's action)

پوچه [1] púcha *feminine singular of* پوچ

150

پوچه ² púcha *f. Western* ☞ پچه

پوچی puchәj *f.* unripe melon

پوغ paudz *m.* ☞ فوغ

پوغۍ pavdzí *f.* ☞ فوغۍ

پوتسکه putská *f.* potsáka corn which has reached a state of milky ripeness

پوتسکی ¹ potsәkáj *m.* ear lobe

پوتسکی ² potsakәj *f.* mushroom

پوتسه ¹ pótsa *f.* cottage cheese; cheese of curdled milk پوتسه کېدل to curdle

پوتسه ² potsá *f.* garbage, waste

پوتسی ¹ potsәj *f.* ear lobe

پوتسی ² potsәj *f.* skein of wool (for yarn-making)

پوتسی ³ potsáj *m.* cotton ball

پوخ pokh پخه pakhá *f.* [*plural:* پاخه pākhә *f. plural:* پخې pakhé] 1 ripe, mature 2 ready, prepared (for the table), cooked 3 experienced, able, skillful *proverb* د پاخه استاد دېگ ورو ورو پخبري *literal* With a good cook, the meal is prepared slowly. *figurative* Haste makes waste. 4 wordly, having a view tempered by life 5 well-considered, well-thought-out (e.g., an answer) 6 elderly; old; of a ripe or mature age 7 reliable, tested (e.g., method) 8 not liable to fade (cloth); fast (dye) 9 پوخ سرک paved paved road, paved highway 10 learned by heart, learned 11 active (e.g., of trading) پاخه مواد finished articles پخه خښته fire-baked bricks پوخ دښمن a sworn enemy; fierce foe دوستي firm friendship پوخ کاغذ *regional* stamped paper; تعمیر capital construction پخه مقاله پوخ لیکل well-written article (official) form اساسي او پوخ گام اخیستل، اساسي او پوخ قدم اخیستل to take a decisive step, take decisive measures seriously wounded

پوختوب pokhtób *m.* پوختیا پوختوب، پوخ توب pokhtjá *f.* 1 ripeness, maturity 2 experience, skillfulness 3 fastness (of dyestuffs)

پوخړی pukhřәj *tautological with* سوخړی

پخلا pukhlá ☞ پخلا

پوخلی pukhәle *f. plural* ☞ پخوله ¹

پوخلی توخلی pukhәle-tukhәle *f. Eastern* whooping-cough

پوخنا pokhná well-developed, mature, smart (of a child)

پوخوالی pokhválaj *m.* ☞ پوختوب، پوخوالی، پوخ والی

پوخول pokhvúl *transitive dialect* ☞ پخول

پوخه pókha *f.* leather strip

پوخېدل pokhedәl *intransitive* ☞ پخېدل

پودر pudár *m. singular & plural* 1 powder د غاښونو پودر tooth powder 2 any substance consisting of ground or pulverized particles

پودرپاشي pudarpāshí *f.* pulverization, sprinkling

پوده ¹ pudá *f. textiles* woof, weft

پوده ² pudá putrid, rotten; worm-holed پوده کول to let rot پوده کېدل to become rotten; putrify

پوده والی pudaválaj *m.* 1 rotting 2 rottenness; putrification

پودر puḍár *m. singular & plural* ☞ پودر

پوډري puḍarí powdered, pulverent

پوډینگ puḍíng pudding

پور ¹ por *m.* 1 debt; credit; loan د اوږدې مودې پور extended credit; long-term loan د پور سند commercial bond, debenture پور او اجاره *history* د نقد پور cash, monetary loan; credit په پور د پور په صورت as a Lend-Lease on loan, as a loan, on credit loan, in the form of a loan پر چا باندي دي پور دئ؟ Who is in debt to you? د چا پور راباندي دئ؟ لس روپۍ پور راباندي دئ. I owe ten rupees. To whom are we in debt? پور اخیستل to take out a loan, incur a debt, obtain credit خپل پور اخیستل to recover a debt پور ادا کول، پور پور غوښتل to pay off a debt to ask about the granting of a loan خپل پور غوښتل to demand payment of a debt پور ورکول *compound verb* to be in debt to recover a debt پور کول lend, make a loan, offer credit په پور کېدي ډوب و He is up to his په پور سره پلورل، مالونه په پور سره پلورل neck in debt. to sell on credit پور پرغاره، پور پرغاره، مبره په پور اخیستل to buy on credit مرداره *saying* debt on the back and the sheep is dying (descriptive of the hopelessness of a situation) پور د مېنې لور دئ *saying* Debts spoil relationships. 2 blood-feud debt د مړي د پور بدله vengeance for one killed پور اخیستل، انتقام او پور اخیستل to take revenge for a murder پوره، ورک دي کړه دوه کوره! *saying* Ah blood feud, thou has ruined two houses! پور پری کول *idiom* to die

پور ² pore *Eastern* ☞ پوری ¹ 2, 3

پور ³ púr *used in geographic names* سلطان پور Sultanpur (settlement near Dzhalalabad)

پوراینه purājәna *f.* پورائي purāí *f.* 1 execution, implementation 2 creation of reserves (i.e., of provisions) پوراینه نیول، پوراینه کول to create reserves (i.e., of provisions)

پورتاتیف portātíf portable; transportable

پورت اف سپین port-af-spén *m.* Port-of-Spain (city)

پورترت portrét *m.* portrait

پورتگال portugál *m.* Portugal

پورتگالي portugālí portugāláj 1 *m.* Portuguese (person) 2 *adjective* Portuguese

پورتنی portanáj 1 upper, higher, topmost 2 above-mentioned, above-cited, foregoing *idiom* په پورتني جهان کښي portaní *literal* In the Upper Heaven *figurative* in the Other World, in Heaven

پورتوپرنس portopréns *m.* Port-au-Prince (city)

پورتونوو pórtonovo *f.* Porto-Novo (city)

پورته pórta 1.1 above, overhead د پورته څخه from above د پورته نه نیولي تر ښکته from top to bottom 1.2 upwards, to the top په پورته upwards, upwards from ... 1.3 above (of a quoted text, etc.) 2.1 upper 2.2 higher 2.3 above-mentioned, above-cited, foregoing په دي پورته بیان کښي شک نشته The foregoing does not evoke doubts. پورته تلل a to rise up, climb up b to grow, increase, rise (prices) را پورته کول a to hoist up b to increase (e.g., prices) در پورته کول a to take, attract, draw to oneself d to close (e.g., a book) ور پورته کېدل a to ascend, climb up b to rise up, tower, raise, elevate c to grow, increase, rise (e.g., prices) d to arise, spring up, appear ... داسي مسئله پورته شوه a question such as this arose ... پورته دي وي زمونږ بيرغ! Raise the banner higher! *idiom* پورته کښته ورته کېدل to toady

پورته تگ portatág *m.* 1 ascent 2 climbing heights (e.g., aircraft)

پورته کېده portakedə́ *m. plural* پورته والی portaválaj *m.* 1 height, altitude 2 rising, ascent 3 rise (e.g., prices) 4 superiority

پورچ porch *m. regional* porch; portico

پوردار pordár *m.* creditor

پورژنی porzhənáj 1 exiled 2 *m.* .1 exile 2.2 wanderer (i.e., religious pilgrim)

پورغو porghú *m.* porghó joint working of land by two or more families

پورکونکی por kavúnkaj *m.* debtor

پور لرونکی por larúnkaj *m.* lender, creditor

پورنوم pórnūm *m.* alias

پوروال porvál *m.* پور والا porvālā́ *m. singular & plural* creditor

پور ورکوونکی por varkavúnkaj *m.* lender, creditor پور ورکوونکی مملکت lender state, creditor government

پوروړی poravə́raj 1.1 in debt to somebody; obtaining funds on credit from somebody 1.2 obliged to somebody 2 *m.* .1 debtor 2.2 avenger; one engaged in a blood fued

پورول poravə́l *denominative, transitive* [*past:* پوريې کړ] to borrow; assume a debt, take on a loan; obtain on credit

پوره purá 1 full, whole, entire 2 executed, effected; implemented 3 finished, completed 4 satisfactory, exhaustive (of an answer) د زما هري خبري جواب يې پوره راکئ He delivered an exhaustive response to my questions. 5 sufficient (e.g., of a supply of air) په پوره ډول in full; completely پوره کول a to execute, effect, implement b to finish, complete c to satisfy; exhaust احتياجات پوره کول to satisfy requirements d to cover, defray (i.e., expenses) e to supplement f. to compensate (e.g., losses) پوره کېدل a to be executed, be effected, be implemented b to be finished, be completed c to be satisfied, be exhausted d to be covered, be defrayed (e.g., expenses) e to be supplemented f. to be compensated, be made good (e.g., losses)

پوره کېده purakedə́ *m. plural* 1 execution, putting into effect, implementation 2 finishing, completion د پنځلسو ورځو تر پوره کېدو in two week's time, in two weeks 3 satisfaction (e.g., of requirements) 4 covering, defrayment (e.g., expenses) 5 supplement 6 compensation (e.g., for losses)

پوره والی puraválaj *m.* 1 fullness, state of being full 2 execution, putting into effect, implementation 3 finishing, completion 4 satisfactoriness (e.g., answer to a question)

پوري póri púri póre *Eastern* 1.1 abutting, bordering something 1.2 closed, covered 1.3 affixed to something, presented along with something 1.4 connected with, depending upon something 1.5 located on the other shore, on the other side دبحر پوري خوا beyond the sea پوري غاړه a the other (river) bank, the opposite

bank b the other side, the opposite side له سرک نه پوري غاړه لوي را پوري پټي وو There are large fields on the other side of the road. پوري غاړه this bank of the river c beyond the Amu-Darya (from the Afghan's point of view) پوري کلي يې کښني يي کور دئ He lives in a settlement beyond the river. پوري غاړي the transriparians, inhabitants of Central Asia (from the Afghan point of view) 2 *postposition* .1 in combination with په (*Eastern* د), without it (indicates that an action is directed at someone or something to) ما آس په ونه پوري وتاړه I tied the horse to the tree. 2.2 *in combination with* په 2.2a by (indicates the person or object which one is touching) په لاس پوري مي واخيست I took him by the hand. 2.2b about (indicates the subject or theme of a conversation) کرهنه پوري خبره وشوه، په کرهنه پوري خبره وشوه We were talking about farming. 2.2c at (indicates the direction of an action with reference to someone) چا پوري خندل، په چا پوري خندل to laugh at someone, mock someone 2.3 *in combination with* تر (*Eastern* د) *or without it* 2.3a to, up to (indicates the limit or boundary of something in space) تر ښاره پوري دري up to the knees زنګانه پوري، تر زنګانه پوري It is three kilometers to the city کيلومتره دئ 2.3b until, before (indicates a time limit) تراوسه پوري until the present time تر پنځو بجو پوري prior to five o'clock 3 through (used in combination with the particle را "ra" which is used as a verb prefix having a directional sense) را پوري کېدل to pass through 4 to him, to us, to them ټول به پوري حيران يو This will be a surprise to us all.

پوري [2] póre *contraction of the postposition* پوري *and the preposition* یې

پوري [3] pori *separable verbal prefix* (accented or stressed in perfective verbs) 1 trans- پوري ايستل to procede across (some obstacle, space, barrier) 2 *indicates direction of action beyond a given point or continuation of an action to excess* 3 action of attaching, direction of action from above downward پوري کول a to close b to enclose c to sew on

پوري ووري pori-óri ☞ پوري اوري

پوري يې pori-istə́l *transitive* [*present:* پوري باسي *past:* پوري ايستل to procede across something

پوري راووري póri-rāpori پوري راپوري there and back, back and forth

پورژنی porezhənáj ☞ پورژنی

پوري يې کړ pori-kavə́l *transitive* [*past:* پوري کول] 1 to close; close down ور پوري که! Close the door! 2 to affix 3 to place against; move up to 4 to sew onto په خت پوري لستوني پوري کول to sew a sleeve onto a shirt 5 to glue, affix, stick onto 6 to attribute (a writing) to someone 7 to crumble (make crumbs) په مستو ډوډی پوري که! Crumble the bread into sour milk! 8 to lubricate, anoint (with grease, ointment) رانجه په سترګو پوري کول to color the eyes with kohl *idiom* اور پوري کول to set fire to

پوري کونی pórikunaj *m. Western* پوري کوونی porekavúnaj *m. Eastern* food, victuals

پوري کبدل pori-kedál *intransitive* [*past:* پوري شو] **1** to be closed, be closed down ور پوري شو the door was closed **2** to be affixed, be placed against **3** to be moved up to **4** to be sewn on to **5** to be attributed to someone (a piece of writing); to cast (aspersions) په نورو پوري کبدل، ور پوري کبدل to be communicated (of a disease)

پوري کبدونکی porikedúnkaj **1** *adjective* adhesive **2** infectious کبدونکی ناروغي epidemic, epizotic

پوري واته porivātá *m.* پوربواته porevātá *plural* ford, crossing (river, etc.)

پوري وتل porivatál پوربوتل porevatál **1** [*present:* پوري وزي *past:* پوري وت] *intransitive* to cross, traverse (rivers, etc.) په لانبو پوري وتل to swim across, float, sail across، په چپو پوري وتل، په گدار پوري وتل *m. plural* ford, crossing (river, etc.)

پوري واته porivatóna *f.* ☞ پوري وتنه

پوري ووري póri-vóri **1** through; right through تر یوشي پوري ووري پوري ووري وتل، پوري ووري ختل to pierce something اخیستل to pass through **2** alongside زمونږ کلي سره پوري ووري دئ Our villages are side by side **3** on all sides

پوري وهل pori-vahál *transitive* [*past:* پوري یي واهه] **1** to push, nudge مامه پوري وهه! Don't push کراچی پوري وهل to shove underwater me! **2** to bring up to something

پوري ایستل pore-vestál *transitive Eastern* ☞

پور por **1** *m.* **1** large mat, mat **2** sugar-cane waste

پور puṛ *m.* poṛ **1** layer, stratum پوړ پر پور **a** in layers **b** gradually پوړ پر پوړ توبدل، پوړ پر پوړ پربکبدل **a** to become stratified **b** to disintegrate; collapse **c** to unravel (cloth) **2** story, floor یو پوړ one-story دوه پوره کوټی two-story house **3** deck د جهاز پور ship's deck **4** *figurative* stage (e.g., of development)

پوړ poṛ **1** *m.* juvenile **2.1** almost ripe (fruit) **2.2** undercooked (food)

پوړ puṛ *m.* hobbles

پوړ poṛ *tautological with* سوړ

پوړ poṛ *tautological with* زوړ

پوړا puṛā calm, confident

پوراینه puṛājóna *f.* **1** confidence, tranquility; calm پوراینه ورکه! Calm him! **2** reassurance

پوړجگول pūṛdzhagawál *compound verb* to upgrade

پوړنده puṛónda *f.* **1** hot ashes **2** friable, loose, powdery soil. پوړنده خاوره friable soil

پوړنده توب puṛandatób *m.* پوړنده تیا puṛandtjā *f.* puṛandótjā پوړنده والی puṛandóválaj *m.* friability (of soil)

پوړنی poṛúnaj *m.* poṛúnaj **1** feminine covering; chador **2** cover (e.g., of night)

پوړوندوالی puṛuntób *m.* پوړوند تیا puṛundtjā *f.* پوړونده توب puṛundválaj *m.* ☞

پوړنی poṛúnaj *m.* ☞

پوره poṛá calm, tranquil په پوره زړه tranquilly زړه پوره کول to calm, pacify لره pacify زړه یي پوره شو He became calm.

پوړه puṛá *f.* grain shovel

پوړه póṛa *feminine of* پوړ

پوړه púṛa *oblique singular of and with number of* پوړ

پوره زړه poṛazrá calm, peaceful, confident, satisfied

پوره زړه توب poṛazṛatób *m.* پوره زړه والی poṛazṛaválaj *m.* calmness, confidence; satisfaction

پوړها poṛhá ☞ پوړه

پوړی puṛáj *f.* pauṛáj **1** *Western* step, rung **2** *Eastern* stairs پوړونه کوز شم I came downstairs. **3** stool **4** *figurative* level, stage پوړی په پوړی gradually

پوړی puṛáj *f.* **1** ☞ پلکش medicine **2** powder

پوريز puríz poṛíz *combining form* دری پوريز three-storied خو پوريز multi-stage rocket, multi-stage missile تغوندی

پزپربکرئ pozprekóraj ☞ پزپربکرئ

پوزه póza *f. Eastern* **1** nose, prow (of a ship, rocket) پته پوزه، چیته پوزه سونول snub nose to clean out the nose, blow the nose **2** cape, promontory *idiom* پوزه په دیوال پاکوي He's very poor; He's poor as a church mouse; *idiom* پوزه یي پربکرې شوه He has digraced himself. He has brought shame upon himself. *idiom* په پوزه مچ نه This bored تر پوزي راغلی یم He is very hot-tempered. *idiom* پربردي me. I'm fed up to the eyes with this. *idiom* **a** He تر پوزي یي راوستم exasperated me. **b** He made my life unbearable. *idiom* ځما دپوزي He stuck to me like a leech. *idiom* د پوزي سر یي غوند دئ He is growing. He's not a child any more. *idiom* د پوزي په لیکه ځه! Walk erect! چه د پوزي یي نیسې، نو ساه یي خبړي He's in a critical state. He's so frail.

پوزی puzáj *m.* small mat (for sleeping); mat

پوزې póze *feminine plural of* پوزه

پوزیترون pozitrón *m. physics* positron

پوزیشن pozishán *m. regional* **1** position **2** posture, state

پوژي puzhí *f.* ☞ پوجي

پوړ pug *m. Western* **1** puff, breath **2** splashing, spraying پوړ وهل to spurt (from the mouth) **3** noise (made by a smith's bellows) **4** steam

پوړ pug *m.* dregs; remains; waste

پوړل pugál pogál *transitive* [*past:* و یي پوړل] to spray, sprinkle (from the mouth); spray (from a sprayer)

پوړلی pugalaj *m.* pump; sprayer

پوړول pugavál *transitive* ☞ پوړل

پوس pos *colloquial* **1** ☞ پوست **2** fat, plump (of cattle)

پوپسک pupusák *m.* forest bettle (plant parasite)

پوست post *m.* **1** hide پوست ورکول to shed hair, moult (of animals) **2** bark, rind **3** pelt **4** skin, peel (of fruit) **5** head, pod (of poppy) پوست کنبل، پوست کول **a** to flay, skin **b** to peel (fruit, vegetables) **c** to peel, skin (bark, rind) **d** to beat up, thrash *idiom* پوست خیري پر to consider something impossible or unrealizable *idiom* په پوست ور ننوتل *idiom* په پوست ننوتل to be penniless پوست سکه وهل to insinuate, worn oneself into someone's confidence *idiom* تر پوست خنجبدل to reproach, reject a kind act *idiom* پوست خنجول

oppress, torment about a favor which has been done to or by someone *idiom* له پوسه وتل to put on weight, grow heavy

پوست ² post پسته pasta' *f. m.* [*plural:* پاسته past *f. plural:* پستې pasté] soft; tender

پوست باب postbāb *m.* furs, pelts

پوستر postár *m.* ☞ پوستر

پوست غاړی ¹ postghāṛaj obedient, quiet, submissive

پوست غاړي ² postghaṛí *f.* obedience, humility, submissiveness

پوستک posták *m.* piece of leather

پوستکالي postkālí *m. plural* software

پوستکی postákaj *m.* قره قلی پوستکی **1** pelt **2** lamb-fleece pelt caracul lamb-fleece pelt **3** peel, skin (of fruit) **4** bark, rind **5** shell (egg) **6** *Eastern* lobe (ear)

پوست والی postvālaj *m.* softness, tenderness

پوستول ¹ postavál *denominative, transitive* [*past:* پوست یې کړ] **1** to skin, flay **2** to peel (fruit, vegetables) **3** to strip off (bark)

پوستول ² postavál *transitive* ☞ پستول

پوسته ¹ postá *f.* **1** mail, postal service هوايي پوسته airmail د پوستي بکس post-office box د پوستي تکس postage پذريعه stamp **2** post; outpost د پوستي قراول outpost, battle outpost هوايي مخابري پوسته aviation communications outpost **3** *military* combat team **4** د قوماندي پوسته command post

پوسته ² pósta *oblique singular of* پوست ¹

پوست باشي postabāshí *m.* chief of a border outpost detachment

پوسته خانه postakhāná *f.* postal service; postal administrative office; post office

پوسته رسان postarasān *m.* postman, mail carrier

پوستي ¹ postí postal

پوستي ² postí *m.* drug addict, opium smoker

پوستي ³ postí *m.* **1** mollycoddle **2** loafer; lazybones, idler

پوستبدل ¹ postedál *denominative, intransitive* [*past:* پوست شو] **1** to be skinned; be flayed **2** to be peeled (of fruits, vegetables) **3** to be stripped off (of bark)

پوستبدل ² postedál *intransitive* ☞ پستبدل

پوستین postín *m.* [*plural:* پوستینونه postinúna *plural:* پوستینان postinān] *Western* (sheep's) skin, fleece coat گلدار پوستین embroidered sheepskin coat *idiom* د بل په پوستین کښې لوبدل، د بل په پوستین کښې ننوتل to say spiteful things about

پوستینچه postinchá *f.* pustincha, sleeveless fur jacket

پوستینچي postinchí *m.* پوستین دوز postindúz ☞ پوستین گندونکی پوستین دوزي postinduzí furriery, the fur business

پوستین گندونکی postín gaṇḍúnkaj *m.* furrier (fur craftsman), fur dresser

پوستر postár *m.* poster; advertisement رنگه پوستر colored poster

پوسکی puskáj *m.* ☞ پسکی ¹

پوسل posál *transitive* [*past:* و یې پوسه] **1** to tend (e.g., a sick animal) **2** to calm, comfort **3** to raise, nurse, foster

پوسل توب posáltób *m.* پوسل تیا posáltjā *f.* ornamentation, decoration

پوسلول poslól *transitive* ☞ پسلول

پوسل توب posálvālaj *m.* ☞ پوسل والی

پوسنه posóna *f.* pusóna nursing, tending (e.g., a sick animal)

پوسه ¹ pusó *dialect* ☞ پسه

پوسه ² posá *f.* garbage

پوسه ³ púsa *f.* dish made from the fruit of the khinjak tree, *Pistacia khinjak*

پوش posh Take care! Look out!

پوشاک poshāk *m.* clothing, attire

پوشیده poshidá **1** secret, clandestine, unknown دا لا تر اوسه پر مورږ پوشیده او پته ده This has not been known to us up to now. **2** in secret, surreptitiously

پوښ poḳh *m.* poḳh **1** covering; sheathing; puttees; cover د بالښت pillowcase د ماشیندار پوښ machine-gun barrel-jacket د توری پوښ sheath **2** armor پولادي پوښ steel armor-plate **3** tablecloth پر مېز پوښ واچوه to set the table; spread the tablecloth **4** clothing, clothes, dress; attire **5** costume and finery (of a bride) **6** binding (of a book) **7** *figurative* shielding, hiding, concealing

پوښاک poḳhak *m.* clothing, attire

پوښتل puḳhtál *transitive* [*past:* و یې پوښتنه] **1** to ask (about), question یو سوال پوښتل to put a question to **2** to ask (for), request, require د هغو څخه ځواب پوښتي An answer from them is required.

پوښتنپانه puḳhtánpāna *f.* questionnaire

پوښتنه puḳhtána *f.* **1** question د پوښتنه کول to ask, put a question to د یوي پوښتني چا پوښتنه کول to ask about, inquire about someone د ځان نه پوښتنه کول to answer a question د ځواب ویل to work out a problem, try to find the answer to a question د چا پوښتني له راتلل to visit, call on someone; go and inquire about someone د مریض په پوښتنه سری مکی ته رسېږي پوښتنه کول to visit a sick person *proverb* If he keeps inquiring a man will find his way to Mecca (e.g., one should not fear to ask questions)

پوښتنه اتنه puḳhtána-utána *f.* questions, questioning پوښتنه اتنه کول to question

پوښته ¹ puḳhtá *f.* **1** low mountain **2** hillock

پوښته ² puḳhtó *imperfective aspect of* پوښتل

پوښتی puḳhtój *f.* rib غتي پوښتي upper ribs کچي پوښتي lower ribs

پوښتبدل puḳhtedál *transitive* ☞ پوښتل

پوښاښ poḳháḳh *m.* **1** clothing, attire **2** sheathing, covering **3** roof, roofing

پوښل poḳhál *transitive* ☞ پوښنول

پوښنه poḳhóna *f.* ☞ پوښنس

پوښنول poḳhavál *transitive* [*past:* و یې پوښناوه] **1** to dress ځان پوښنول to dress oneself, put clothing on (oneself) **2** to cover, lay a cover on, cover up **3** to bind (book) **4** to put, put away (i.e., a sabre into a sheath) **5** *construction* to put sheathing on, install cladding *passive* **a** to be covered, be laid (a cover), be covered up **b** to be bound (a book) **c** *construction* to be sheathed; have exterior cladding installed (e.g., a house, a ship)

پوښی póḳhaj *f.* folder

پوښیده pǒkhedá ☞ پوڅنبده

پوصوله pusulá *f.* compass; surveying compass

پوکانه pukáṇa *f.* ☞ پوقانه

پوک puk *m.* ☞ پو¹

پوک puk² *m.* ☞ سوک¹

پوکانه pukāṇa *f.* 1 bubble (e.g., in water) 2 (urinary) bladder د لانبو swim bladder (in fish) 3 inflated (leather) bag *idiom* د یوي پوکانه to burst like a soap bubble پوکاني غوندي چول

پوکاڼی pukaṇój² *f.* ☞ پوکڼی

پوکل pukól *transitive* ☞ پوکي *proverb* په شیدو سوئ مستي پوکي Once burned, twice shy. د چا په زړه تازه روح پوکل ، د چا په زړه to inspire, encourage (someone) کڼبي نوی روح پوکل

پوکلور poklór *m.* folklore

پوکڼی pukaṇój¹ *m.* *music* 1 pukanay (native wind instrument similiar to the Persian zurna) 2 clarinet

پوکڼی pukaṇój² *f.* 1 urinary bladder 2 bubble (e.g., in water)

پوکول pukavól [*past:* وی یې پو کاوه] *transitive past:* 1 to blow on something, cool something 2 to blow up, inflate ژي پوکول to inflate a wineskin 3 to fan, kindle (fire) اور پوکول to fan a fire 4 to blow out, extinguish ډېوه پوکه to blow out or extinguish the lamp 5 to play (a wind instrument) پوکڼی پوکول to play reed pipe 6 to blow away (e.g., dust) 7 *figurative* to inspire (e.g., a life) نوی روح یې را پو کم He put a bit of heart in us.

پوکونه pukavóna *f.* 1 inflation (e.g., of a ball) 2 fanning, kindling (e.g., a bonfire) 3 blowing out (e.g., a fire)

پوک وهونکی puk vahúnkaj *music* wind instrument پوک وهونکي آله wind instrument

پوکی pukáj *m.* 1 ☞ پو¹ شپپلی ته پوکی ورکول to play the reed pipe 2 *music* trumpet 3 blowtorch

پوکېدل pukedól *intransitive* [*past:* و پوکېده] 1 to be inflated, be blown up 2 to be fanned, be kindled (e.g., a bonfire) 3 to be blown out, be extinguished, put out 4 to be blown away (e.g., dust)

پوکیوال pukajvál ☞ پوک وهونکی

پوگ pog¹ hollow, empty

پوگ pug² *m.* ☞ پوړ¹

پوگ pog³ *m.* ☞ پوړ²

پوگار pugár *m.* [*plural:* پوگر pugór] 1 bellows 2 blowtorch 3 bellows operator

پوگه pugá *f.* ☞ پوړ¹

پول pul¹ *m.* 1 money د پول نرخ تر نظم لاندي راوړل to regulate the currency rate ډېر پولونه خرڅول to spend a good deal of money 2 pul (Afghan coin, worth 1/100th of an afghan) ژړ پول a brass pul

پول pul² *m.* ☞ پل³

پول pul³ *m.* cataract

پول pol⁴ *m.* Pole (person)

پولاد polád *m.* pulád 1 *plural* steel 2 *proper name* Polad, Pulat

پولادسازي polādsāzí *f.* steel-smelting business د پولادسازی فابریکه a steel mill

پولادي polādináj *adjective* steel

پولاو puláv *m.* ☞ پلاو *Eastern* د چرگ پولاو chicken pilaf

پول پوښ pulpóx̌ *m.* small bridge

پولتیکي politikí political پولتیکي او اجتماعي مسائل political and social problems

پولت بیورو politbjuró Politbureau

پولتیس paulṭís *m.* *medicine* poultice, embrocation

پولتیکل poliṭíkal *regional* political

پولدار puldár rich, monied (of a person)

پولس polís *m.* *singular & plural* ☞ پولیس

پولک pulák *m.* double-wedge (for attaching the iron plowshare to the frame of the plow)

پولهند póland *m.* ☞ پولنند

پولندي polandí polandáj 1 Polish 2 *m.* Pole (person)

پولونیا polonijā́ *f.* ☞ پولنند

پوله púla¹ *f.* 1 edge, boundary (of a field) 2 earthen wall; embankment 3 boundary strip 4 border, frontier; state frontier پوله وهل to violate the frontier 5 barrier, obstacle

پوله pulá² *f.* 1 cooked grain 2 lump, bump

پوله púla³ *oblique with numerals from* پول¹ 50 pul پنځوس پوله

پوله púla⁴ *oblique of* پول²

پوله polá⁵ *f.* cataract

پولی puláj polój¹ *f.* 1 armful, pile (thornbush, brushwood) 2 bound sheaf (e.g., of lucerne, clover)

پولی pulój² *f.* 1 bump 2 ulcer, sore د زړه د پاسه مې پولی ولاړي دینه *folk saying* My heart is covered with wounds. 3 corn, callus

پولی pulój³ *f.* sparkles

پولي pulí⁴ monetary پولي سیاست monetary policy

پولي تخنیک politekhník *m.* polytechnic school د پولي تخنیک انستیتوت polytechnic institute د پولي تخنیک موسسه

پولیتک poliṭík *m.* *regional* politics, policy

پولیتکي poliṭikí *regional* political, policy

پولیس polís *m.* *singular & plural* 1 *attributive* police د پولیس سپاهي police خفیه پولیس secret police پولیس کفتان *regional colloquial* police chief 2 police officer, policeman

پولیسوالا polisvālá *m.* *singular & plural colloquial* police officer

پولیسي polisí 1 *adjective* police پولیسي سپی bloodhound 2 *adjective* detective

پولیکلینیک polikliník *m.* polyclinic

پولیگون poligón *m.* firing range

پولهند pólénd *m.* ☞ پولهند pólénd *m.* Poland

پولندي polendí polendáj ☞ پولنند

پولینزیا polinezijā *f.* د پولینزیا جزیري the Polynesian Islands

پولیو polijó poliomyelitis د پولیو ضد واکسین anti-poliomyelitis vaccine پولیو مرض

پومبه pumbá *f.* ☞ پنبه

پون pun *m.* ☞ پم

پوندانه pundāná *f.* د پوندانۍ کیسه پندانه a in the nature of play or a game b empty talk, idle talk

پوندغلی pundghǝláj *m.* heel (of a shoe)

پوندګلوی pavandgalví *f.* پوندګلي pavandgalí *f.* nomadic economy; cattle raising

پونده [1] pavandá povandá *m. singular & plural* 1 povindah, nomadic cattle herder; nomadic trader 2 steppe dweller

پونده [2] púnda *f.* 1 heel پونده کول، پونده وهل *compound verb* to spur, put spur to آس یې پونده ورکول He put spur to his horse. a پونده ورکول to spur (on) b to move on with a job, get on with a matter; determine to do something پونده ورته کول a to use the heel (spur) b to get to work, get on with it 2 *technology* socket; coupling element 3 stern (ship)

پونده توب pavandatób *m.* ☞ پوندګلوی

پوند [1] punḍ *m.* ☞ خپه [1]

پوند [2] paunḍ *m.* 1 pound sterling 2 pound (measure of weight)

پوندکه punḍǝka *f.* greens, vegetable

پوندکی [1] punḍkǝj *f.* ☞ پنډکی [1]

پوندی [2] punḍǝj *f.* ☞ پونده [2]

پونړی punṛǝj *f.* ☞ پونی [2]

پونس puns پون سو púnsu *numeral colloquial* five hundred

پونګ pung *m.* bank (the financial institution)

پونګپاڼی pungpāṇaj *m.* bank note

پونګه [1] pungá *f.* ☞ پنګه [2]

پونګه [2] púnga *f.* ☞ پانګه [1]

پونګلی [1] pungalǝj *m.* 1 reed pipe 2 reed, oboe, hautboy

پونګلی [2] pungalǝj *m.* پونګی pungǝj *f.* 1 table-top (of a mountain) 2 merchandise (of an itinerant peddler)

پونه puná *f.* 1 light rain; rain showers 2 spraying (from the mouth) پونه کول to spray (saliva from the mouth)

پون [1] paunḍ *m. Eastern* ☞ پوند [2]

پون [2] punḍ *m.* kind of match used in former times

پوناکه puṇāka *f.* پونکه puṇǝka *f.* ☞ پناکی

پونی ponǝnaj *m.* ☞ پوړنی

پونول punavǝl *transitive* [*past:* و یې پوناوه] 1 to hollow out 2 to gnaw out, eat away

پونه puṇa *f.* leap, amble

پونی [1] púnaj *m.* ☞ سپونی

پونی [2] puṇǝj *f.* skein, hank (of woolen yarn) په سر کنبی یې لا پونی نه Out of a ser of wool, he did not twist even one *literal* وه ریشلی skein. *figurative* He did not do 1/100th of the task he was to do.

پونیدل puṇedǝl *intransitive* [*past:* وپونېده] 1 to be hollowed out 2 to be hollow; be eaten out 3 to leap, bound; amble

پونیول puṇjavǝl *transitive* [*past:* و یې پونیاوه] 1 to gnaw (e.g., of a mouse) 2 to crack, crack (with the teeth); shell (nuts, seeds, etc.)

پووړه pǝvóra *f.* lazy woman

پوول povǝl povúl puvúl *transitive Eastern* [*present:* پیائي *past:* و یې پووه] to graze *idiom* پر خپل سر پوول to act independently, not seeking advice

پوون pavún *m. dialect* English pound

پوونده povandá *m.* ☞ پونده [1]

پوونه povǝna *f.* pasturage, pasture

پووه [1] povǝ́ povǝ́ ☞ پووی povaj *Western imperfective aspect of* پوول

پووی [2] povǝ́ *interjection* Aha!

پوه [1] poh 1.1 intelligent, quick (on uptake), clever; sensible 1.2 wise 1.3 expert, able پوه استکار skilled craftsman 1.4 erudite, knowledgeable پوه کسان experts سری باید پوه وي چه ... one should know that ... 2 *m.* 1 sage; scholar 2.2 expert

پوه [2] poh *m. regional* tenth month of the Hindu calendar (December - January)

پوه [3] puvá *f.* moist, arable land

پوه [4] puh *m.* ☞ پو [1]

پوها pohā *interjection* Aha! Well, well!

پوهان pohā́n *plural of* پوه [2]

پوهاند pohā́nd *Western* 1 *m.* 1 scholar اجتماعي پوهاند sociologist پښتو پوهاند، د پښتو پوهاند Pashto specialist 1.2 expert; expert in his field 1.3 professor emeritus 2.1 erudite, knowledgeable 2.2 prudent, reasonable

پوهاوه póhāvǝ *imperfective aspect of* پوهول

پوهپنا puhpanā ☞ پوپنا

پوهر [1] puhǝ́r *m.* large mat

پوهر [2] puhǝ́r پوهړی poharaj 1 stupid, imbecilic 2 crude, uncultivated, uncouth 3 dirty, slovenly 4 clumsy, ungainly

پوهښت pohǝ́kht *m.* knowledge, state of being informed

پوهلنډی pohlanḍáj dull-witted, unskilfull

پوهنتون pohǝntún *m.* university; academy (educational establishment); institute د کابل پوهنتون Kabul University

پوهنځی pohǝndzǝ́j *m.* 1 institute (educational establishment) د پوهنځی پیغله female university student 2 university department د موسیقی پوهنځی conservatory

پوهند pohǝnd intelligent, erudite

پوهندوی pohǝndój *m.* 1 scholar 2 (academic) specialist; expert

پوهنمل pohǝnmál *m.* senior lecturer, docent

پوهنوال pohǝnvál *m.* professor

پوهنه pohǝna *f.* 1 knowledge, cognition پوهنه رڼا ده knowledge is light پوهنه لرل to have learning 2 learning; science طبیعي پوهني natural history د پوهنو ټولنه Academy of Sciences 3 education د پوهني وزارت Ministry of Education 4 instruction; training حربي پوهنه او روزنه military training

پوهنیار pohǝnjár *m.* teacher (in an institution of higher learning); assistant (junior member of a teaching or research staff)

پوهنیال pohǝnjál *m.* expert, specialist, authority

پوهو pohó *interjection* oho, aha

پوهوالی pohvǝ́laj *m.* 1 comprehension, cleverness; intelligibility 2 wisdom 3 ability, skillfullness

پوهوتلی pohvatǝ́laj understandable, accessible to understanding

پوهول pohavǝl 1 [*past:* و یې پوهاوه] *transitive* 1 to explain, elucidate, explicate; make understand ځان پوهول to make out, understand 1.2 to teach (students) 1.3 to inform, let know, acquaint **1.4** to let know beforehand, warn **1.5** to give a few tips, advise **2** *m. plural* ☞ پوهونه

پوهاول‎-راپوهاول pohavə́l-rapohavə́l *m. plural* mutual understanding; relationship سره پوهول را پوهول mutual understanding; relationship

پوهاونه pohavɔna *f.* **1** explanation, elucidation **2** teaching (students) **3** information, intelligence, data **4** warning, admonition **5** exhortation, homily

پوهوهو pohohó *interjection* ah-ha-ha

پوهه póha¹ *f.* **1** reason, intellect **2** comprehension **3** realization, understanding پـه پوهه، په پوهه سره **a** consciously **b** reasonably **4** knowledge; learning عادتي پوهه practical accomplishments, learning

پوهه póha² *feminine singular of* پوه¹

پوهيالی pohjālə́j **1.1** clever, bright **1.2** circumspect **2** *m.* teacher (in a higher institution of learning)

پوهېدل pohedə́l poehdə́l **1** [*past:* پوه شو *intransitive past:* وپوهېد past: وپوهېده]. **1** to understand, comprehend, grasp ته زما په خبره Did you understand me? پوه شوی؟ **1.2** to know, understand په هغه ښه پوهېږي to understand foreign languages ... خارجي ژبو پوهېدل It is well known to him that ... څه پوهېږي؟ How do you know that? ... هغه Everybody knows that ... هر څوک ورباندي پوهېږي چه He doesn't know anything. He doesn't understand anything. په هيڅ نه پوهېږي **1.3** to find out; notice هپڅوک ورباندي پوه نه شو No one found out about this. Nobody noticed this. **1.4** to know how to ته Do you know how to write? په ليک پوهېږي؟ **1.5** to find out about, inquire into هيڅ په حال پوه نه شو He didn't find anything out about it. He didn't inquire into it. **1.6** to notice, feel something په ښخني We did not feel the cold. هيڅ نه پوهېدو **1.7** to resolve, sort out, analyze (some problem) سبا به سره پوه شو We'll figure it out tomorrow. Tomorrow we'll come up with the explanation. **1.8** *ironic* to settle up with, get even with someone! ستاسره به پوه شم! I'll get even with you! I'll show you! **2** *m. plural* ☞ پوهېده

پوهېدل راپوهېدل pohedə́l-rapohedə́l *m. plural* mutual understanding; intercourse

پوهېدنه pohedə́na *f.* cognition, learning, study دشفاهي ادبیاتو پوهېدنه the study of folklore

پوهېده pohedə́ *m. plural* familiarization, informing

پوی poj¹ *dialect* ☞ پوه¹

پوی poj² *m.* ☞ پو

پوينگ pujə́ng *m.* vine (grape) beginning to bear fruit

پویول pojavə́l *transitive* ☞ پوهول¹

پویه pója¹ *f. dialect* ☞ پوهه¹

پویه pujá² *f.* clothes moth

پویه pojá³ *f.* trot, amble

په pə¹ *dialect* pa **1** *preposition in several cases the noun governed by it is not inflected.* **.1** *in combination with the postposition* کي, *or without it:* **a** in (used to designate place, direction, or location) په کوټه کښي، په کوټي کښي in the house په کور کښي in the room دسمال په جیب کښي اینبودل to put a handkerchief in the pocket

په هغه خوا on the other side **b** on (used to designate the place or surface on which something is located) په اوږه کښي on the shoulder د دوی کور زمونږ په کوڅه کښي دئ They live on our street. په بازار کښي خرڅول to sell in the bazaar په دغه جلسه کښي in this meeting **c** at; at the time of something in; during (indicates time or term) د دمارچ په میاشت کښي last year په تېر کال کښي in March په امتحان کښي on Friday جمعې په روځ at the examination; at the time of the examination په شا تللو کښي پسرلي *psarlí* in spring at the time of the retreat, during the retreat په هره مرحله کښي **at** each stage **d** into (indicates the general meaning of distribution) په دوو برخو وېشل to divide into two parts **e** for, in the course of, in (indicates duration of time) په دغه دری روځي کښي for these three days په یوه روځ for a day, in one day په څلورو ساعتو کښي، په څلور for four hours, in the course of four hours **f** from ... to ... (indicates transfer from one to another analogous object, forming a bound form) کور په کور from house to house, in each house لاس په لاس from hand to hand **g** from ... to ... (indicates a constant repetition in time, making a bound form) کال په کال from year to year, annually میاشت په میاشت from month to month, monthly **h** along (indicates the object or surface over which someone or something is moving or proceeding) په لار کښي نه سو تلای He could not go along the road **i** among, with (indicates location or stay among or with someone, a group) په پښتنو کښي among the Pashtoons, with the Pashtoons په مونږ کښي among us, with us **j** *used to indicate multiplication and short numerical correspondences* یو یه دوه 2x2=4 دوه په دوو کښي څلور by 2 times, twice as much **k** *indicates percent* په سل کښي دېرش (by) thirty percent, (by) 30% **1.2** *Eastern in conjunction with the postposition* باندي *and without it:* **a** on; at (indicates the place or surface where someone or something is located, or where some action is taking place, and also indicates the person or object to which the action is directed) هغه په بام وخوت He went up on the roof. کتاب په مېز باندي کېږده Put the book on the table. دوی په مېز They are eating at the table. په څان باندي دوی خوري to control oneself په څان باندي حاکمیت لري **b** at (indicates the time or term of something) په لس بجي at 10 o'clock **c** for so much; for such and such amount (indicates compensation, reward, or price received for something) په پیسو باندي خرڅول to sell for money په لس روپي خرڅول to sell for ten rupees **d** *indicates the person or object by means of which an action is accomplished* لاس په صابون باندي مینځل to wash the hands with soap په خیاط باندي کالي گنډل to have clothing made by a tailor بادام په غاښ مه ماتوه Don't crack the almond with your teeth. ما په منشي باندي چټی ولیکله The letter writer wrote a letter for me. I had a scribe write a letter for me. **e** *indicates the person or object to which something else relates or pertains* دا چاره په ما ده I'm responsible for this. I'll take this upon myself. **f** *indicates the limit of an action, the attainment of a goal* تلل تلل، په بره بازدره ورغلل They kept going and going and they got to Bara-Bazdary. **1.3** *in conjunction with the postposition* سره *or without it:* **a** with (indicates the means or method by which an action is accomplished) په قلم باندي ليکل to write with a pen په قلم سره ليکل to write with a pen په دغه روپو غنم رانيسه Buy wheat with this money. **b** at; at the time of (indicates the time, or beginning of an action or process) د نوي کال په شروع کېدو سره with the advent of the New Year; at the beginning of the New Year په رسيدو سره at the arrival (of); ... having arrived ... **c** with; in (indicates the condition or character of the action accomplished) په لويه علاقمندۍ with great interest په وار او آرام سره ژوند کول to live peacefully نوبت سره in turn, in its turn په لويي پيماني سره in great quantity (scope) په زور with force په کلکه firmly, with firmness **d** in the presence of; when there is a ... (indicates the presence of something) په سپوږمۍ شپه رونه وي It is light at night when there is a moon. **e** according to (in accordance with something, on the basis of something) په مقرري on the basis of the election په انتخاب according to nomination, appointment **f** hundreds, thousands (indicates a large quantity, in general round numbers) په لکو موټران hundreds of thousands of automobiles په زرګونو پښتانه، په زرونو thousands of Pashtoons په زرهاو پښتانه، په زرها پښتانه **1.4** *in conjunction with the postposition* پسې **a** for, after (indicates the goal or purpose of an action) زه په ميوه پسې بازار ته ځم I am going to the market for fruit. هلکه، په چا پسې راغلئ يې؟ Boy! for whom have you come? په اصلاح پسې کېدل to send for someone په چا پسې کول to strive for improvement **b** following, behind (indicates following after someone) احمد په ما پسې ځي Ahmed is coming behind me. Ahmed is following me. **1.5** *in conjunction with the postposition* پوري **a** to (indicates an object which is attached or fastened to something) آس په ونه پوري وتړه tie the horse to a tree **b** *indicates belonging, dependence; relationship to someone or something* په هيڅ حزب پوري ارتباط نه لرل not to belong to any party; to be non-party په محيط پوري اړه لرل to depend on the environment **a** *indicates location close to or near something* په خوله پوري at the entrance (to a cave, etc.) **b** to the mouth (to bring nearer) **c** with (indicates consumption, eating together with something else) په دغو انگورو پوري ډوډۍ وخوره Eat some bread with these grapes. **2** *adverb* **.1** for it, for them هنداره هم په رانيسه Also get some glass for this (i.e., for this money). **2.2** with the help of this or these; by means of this or these **2.3** because of this; about this په دبر خوشحاله يم I am very glad about this. I rejoice because of this.

په[2] *pa f.* **1** plaster **2** splints

پهاټک phāṭák *m. regional* **1** entrance **2** gate

پامانی pəamāní *f.* خدای په امانی، د خدای په امانی farewell, parting

پهانسي phānsí *f.* gallows پهانسي کول *compound verb* to hang پهانسي کېدل *compound verb* to be hung

پباندې pəbānde *adverb Eastern* **1** on it (any gender); on them; on this **2** by means of this; it

په پسې pə pasé *adverb* **1** after him, her; after them په پسې کول to send someone after په چا پسې کېدل **a** to follow after someone;

accompany someone **b** to strive after something **2** afterwards, after something او په پسې رخصت شو And he left afterwards.

په پوري pə́ pori pə́ puri *adverb* to something; in the presence of something

پښتنی phataní *regional* Afghan, Pathan ☞ پښتني[2]

پاشتوک pachá *f.* ☞ په چه

په ځای pə dzáj **1.1** settling, populating **1.2** setting, reducing (of a fracture, dislocation) **1.3** executed, completed, brought to a finish په ځای کول **a** to settle **b** to reduce, set (of a fractured, dislocated joint) **c** to execute, complete, bring to a finish په ځای کېدل **a** to be settled **b** to be set, be reduced (of a joint) **c** to be executed, be completed, be brought to a finish **2** opportunely, apropos, at the proper time ستا ويل په ځای وو You spoke to the point.

په ځای کونه pədzājkavə́na *f.* **1** settling, colonization **2** reduction, setting (of an injury to a joint) **3** execution, completion, bringing to a finish

په څټ تلونکی pətsəṭ tlúnkaj very backward, reactionary, retrograde

په څنگ pətsáng **1** secluded, solitary په څنگ ځای a secluded place **2.1** alongside, near, close by په څنگ کېناست *Eastern* He sat alongside. **2.2** along

په څنگ pətsangavə́l *denominative, transitive* [*past:* په څنگ يې کړ] **1** to push aside, remove, move to one side **2** to set apart **3** to set aside, grant a postponement

په څنگ pətsangedə́l *denominative, intransitive* [*past:* په څنگ شو] **1** to stand aside, withdraw to the sidelines **2** to be set apart **3** to be postponed, be set aside

په څو pə tsó how much, for how much دسګريتو قطي په څو ده؟ How much does a pack of cigarettes cost? دا ختکي په څو خرخوئ؟ How much are you selling these melons for? دا په څو کېږي؟ How much does this cost?

په څه ډول والی pətsəḍaulvә́laj *m.* **1** quantity **2** circumstances (of a matter)

په حال pə hāl conscious, comprehending

پخپله pəkhpə́la ☞ په خپله

په دې کي pə dé ki pə dé ke *Eastern* **1** now then; at this time **2** among, including **3** in the meantime, meanwhile

پهر[1] pahár *m. Eastern* **1** watch (e.g., sentinel, guard) **2** time, occasion

پهر[2] puhár indecent

پهر[3] pəhár *vice* په هر پهر ځای کېږي everywhere

په رنگول pərangavə́l *denominative, transitive* [*past:* په رنگ يې کړ] to paint, color

په رنگېدل pərangedə́l *denominative, intransitive* [*past:* په رنگ شو] to be painted, be colored

پهرول pahravúl *transitive Eastern* ☞ پارول

پهره pahrá *f. regional* pehrá ☞ پیره[1]

پهره دار pahradā́r *m.* ☞ پیره دار

پهره دار خانه pahradārkhāná *f.* ☞ پیره دار خانه

پهر pahár *m.* slanderer

پیړی pehŕój *f. regional* ☞ پیړی ¹

په زړه پوري pə zŕə puri **1** pleasant (e.g., a smell) **2** interesting, entertaining; attractive **3** sincere, cordial

په زړه کول pəzŗəkavál *m. plural* په زړه کونه pəzŗəkavóna *f.* memorization, learning by heart

په زړه کوونی pəzŗəkavúnaj *m.* instruction, aide-mémoire, note

په زیاته pə zjáta **1** especially; particularly **2** moreover **3** also

پستنه pə stəná ☞ پستنه

لکه ورته *m.* pə səmon analog

په شا لیکنه pəshālikóna *f.* endorsement (of a promissary note)

په شاني pəshān پیشاني pəshāní like, similiar (to)

په شنو کونه pəshnokavóna *f.* maintaining cattle on green fodder or pasturage

په ښه په ښه pə x̌ə pə x̌ə for good, favor, benefaction دچا په ښه ورتلل to be useful to someone, go to someone for a favor

[په غاښ یې ک pəghax̌havál *denominative, transitive* [*past:* په غاښ یې کړ] to seize something with the teeth, bite

[په قار یې ک pəḳāravál *denominative, transitive* [*past:* په قار یې کړ] to anger, enrage

[په قار شو pəḳāredál *denominative, intransitive* [*past:* په قار شو] to be angry, be enraged

پکار pəḳār ☞ په کار

پکارول ¹ pəḳāravál *denominative, transitive* ☞ په کارول

پکارول ² pəḳāravál *denominative, transitive* ☞ په قارول

پکاربدل ¹ pəḳāredál *denominative, intransitive* ☞ په کاربدل

پکاربدل ² pəḳāredál *denominative, intransitive* ☞ په قاربدل

پکنبي páki *Eastern* pəke ☞ پکنبي

پکو pəkó ☞ په کو

په ګرده pəgárda **1** in entirety, fully **2** collectively, together, jointly

[په لاس یې ک pálāsavál *denominative, transitive* [*past:* په لاس یې کړ] to deliver, entrust

پهلو pahlú *m.* side (of a question), aspect رقم رقم پهلوګان لرل to have various aspects

پهلواړی pahlvāŗaj *m. regional botany* white dog-rose

پهلوان pahlaván *m.* **1** *sports* wrestler; athlete **2** champion **3** hero; folk-hero

پهلواني pahlavāní *f.* **1** *sports* wrestling **2** heroism

پام pahm *m. Eastern* ☞ پام

په متي pəmáṭi *interjection* aha, oho

پر مخ pəmə́kh ☞ پر مخ

پر مخ تګ pəməkhtág *m.* ☞ پر مخ تګ

په مخ تللئ pəmə́kh tlólaj advanced, developed (i.e., of a country)

په مخه pəmə́kha toward په مخه راتلل to meet halfway هغه زما په مخه راغئ I went to meet him.

په مخه ویل pəmə́khax̌á *f.* pəmə́khax̌á leave-taking, farewell ننه ویل to say goodbye

پامول pahmavál *transitive Eastern* ☞ پامول

پهن دار pahandár wide, expansive, broad

په ها pəhā́ *interjection* aha, oho په ها خو مره لیري دئ! Oh, how far away he is!

په هاها pəhāhā́ *interjection* ☞ په هوهو

هوا پهوا pəhavā́ *vice* ☞ په هوا

پورته phórta ☞ پورته

په ورو ورو pəvróvro little by little, slowly

پوهول pəhavál *transitive* ☞ پوهول

په هو هو pəhohó *interjection* oh-ho-ho

پهه pahá́ *f.* **1** coating (substance) **2** bandage, binding **3** ointment

په یاد pəjád memorized, mastered, studied

[په یاد یې ک pəjādavál *denominative* [*past:* په یاد یې کړ] **1** to remember, recall **2** to memorize, learn by heart

[په یاد شو pəjādedál *denominative* [*past:* په یاد شو] **1** to be remembered; be recalled, come to mind **2** to be memorized, be learned by heart

پوهیدل pəhedál *intransitive* ☞ پوهیدل

[وي یې پهلاوه pəhelavál *transitive* [*past:* وي یې پهلاوه] **1** to spread, spread out **2** to unroll **3** to scatter, strew **4** to disseminate; expand

[وپهلبده pəheledál *intransitive* [*past:* وپهلبده] **1** to be spread, be spread out **2** to be unrolled **3** to be scattered, be strewn **4** to be disseminated; be expanded

پی ¹ paj *m.* [*plural:* پیونه pajuna]. **.1** tendon, sinew **1.2** foundation, base **1.3** print, track (feet) **1.4** ford, crossing **1.5** place between two rivers **1.6** cutting; chopping **1.7** layer of earth dug up by shovel پی وهل to shovel, dig پی کول *compound verb* **a** to cut a tendon **b** to chop, chop down **c** to leave tracks, footprints **d** to cross (a river, ford) **e** to measure, plumb the depth (e.g., of a river) **1.8** possession, ownership دچا پر پی کول to transfer into someone's possession دچا پر پی کبدل to belong to someone, to be in someone's possession **2** behind, immediately after *idiom* پی ورل to understand, apprehend the sense, get the hint; find out the meaning

پی ² pəj *f. plural m. plural Eastern* **1** milk **2** milky juice (plant), latex **3** *dialect* ☞ هسته *idiom* دوی د یو بل سره پی او شکره دي They are very friendly. They always keep together.

پی ³ pe pe, name of the letter پ

پی ⁴ pe *Eastern* ☞ پری ²

پیاده ² *military abbreviation of*

پیاخه ¹ pjáatsa *f.* rice or wheat bread, rice or wheat flat-cake

پیاخه ² pəjátsa *f.* **1** part (hair) **2** bell-bottoms (trousers)

پیاخله ¹ pjákhla *f.* **1** silk cuff **2** piping (on collar, sleeve)

پیاخله ² pjákhla *f.* **1** preparation of vegetable extract **2** sweating (of a sick person) پیاخله کول to make sweat, cause to sweat (a patient)

په یاد pəjád ☞ په یاد

پیادګي pijādagí *f.* the work of a courier or deliveryman پیادګي کول to work as a courier, be a delivery man

په یادول pəjādavál *denominative, transitive* ☞ په یادول

پیاده pijādá **1** *adjective* **.1** pedestrian **1.2** *adjective military* infantry عسکر پیاده infantry قطعه پیاده infantry unit **2** *m.* **.1** pedestrian **2.2** courier, deliveryman **2.3** infantryman **2.4** *chess* pawn **3** on foot

پياده پا pijādapā́ پياده پای pijādapā́j on foot

پياده رو pijādaráv *m.* sidewalk

پياده روي pijādaraví *f.* going on foot, walking

په يادبدل pəjādedál *denominative, intransitive* ☞

پيارژندي pjārzhəndí *f.* watering land at night

پيارگنده pjārgónda *f.* ☞ چارند

پيارمه pjārma *f.* **1** crupper (harness part) **2** rope (specifically that which laces the netting of a bed to the frame) **3** drive belt (of a spinning wheel) **4** *figurative* property obtained by dishonest means

پيارمه خور pjārmakhór *m.* extortionist

پيارمه ور pjārmarvár having a large fatty tail (sheep) پيارمه ور پسه ram with large fatty tail

پياز pijāz *m. usually plural* onions, onion نيش پياز، نوش پياز spring onions پياز دﻩ وي ، په نازدي وي *proverb literal* Even if it's only onions, let them be (given) with kindness. *figurative* It's not the gift, it's the thought that counts.

پيازکی pjāzəkáj *m.* wild onions

پيازه pjāza **1** *f.* miscarriage, abortion **2.1** missing, disappeared; perished **2.2** damaged, spoiled پيازه کول **a** to abort; have a miscarriage **b** to abort, destroy, damage, spoil پيازه کېدل **a** to be aborted **b** to be missing, disappear; perish **c** to be damaged, be spoiled

پيازي pjāzí reddish

پياسه pjása *f.* channel (of a river, stream)

پياغله pjā́ghla *f.* **1** ☞ پياخله **2** scarf, muffler

پياغله pjā́ghla *f.* ☞ پياخله

پياگي pjā́gi *f.* knee tendons

پياخله pjā́lkha *f. dialect* embroidery, needlework

پياله pijāla *f.* **1** piala (footed teacup), cup د چايو پياله cup of tea دشرابو پيالي ډکول to fill cups with wine **2** basin, bowl **3** pan (of a flintlock rifle)

پيالۍ pijālə́j *f.* small teacup

پيالي pijālé *plural of* پياله

پيام pajām *m.* ☞ پيغام

پيانده pjā́nda **1** lock (hair) **2** beautiful

پيانگ يانگ piāng-jā́ng *m.* Pyongyang (city)

پيانو pjānó *f.* piano پيانو وهل to play the piano

پيانو وهونکی pjāno vahúnkaj *m.* pianist

پياورکی pjāvərkaj *m. botany* spurge, *Euphorbia*

پياور pjāvər ☞ پياوری

پياورتوپ pjāvərtób *m.* پياورتيا pjāvərtjā́ *f.* پياوروالی pjāvərválaj *m.* **1** courtesy, good breeding **2** mind, quick-wittedness **3** development, strengthening

پياوری pjāvə́raj **1** courteous, well-bred **2** quick-witted, understanding, able **3** outstanding **4** vigorous **5** able, excellent (i.e., a marksman) **6** strong, powerful, robust په اقتصادي لحاظ

strong, developed (economically) پياوری کول to develop, strengthen پياوری کېدل to be developed, be strengthened **7** talented; skillful, expert

پياورتوب پياوری توب pjāvərajtób *m.* ☞

پياي píjāj *present stem of* پوول

پيپ pip *m.* **1** can (i.e., for gasoline) **2** barrel

پيپ pajp *m.* **1** pipe (smoking) **2** pipe

پيپري piprí *f.* lean meat

پيپلاج piplájm. kind of elongated pepper

پيپني pepnáj *f.* dress, gown

پيت pit **1** flat **2** shallow (e.g., of a dish) **3** flat-bottomed (of a boat) چيت ☞

پيتاوه pajtāvá *f.* puttees

پيتاوی pitāvaj *m.* ☞ پتاوی

پيت پوزی pitpózaj پيت پوزي pitpúzaj having a flat nose; snub-nosed

پی تړی petáraj *m.* warehouseman; superintendant of a depot or warehouse

پيتال pitál *m.* tin plate

پيتنسی pitnásaj *m.* ☞ پتنوس

پيتول pitavə́l *denominative, transitive* [*past:* پيت يې کړ] **1** to flatten, flatten down **2** to press down په ځمکه پوري ځان پيتول to press oneself to the earth, flatten oneself to the ground

پيته pəjíta *f. usually plural* پيتي pəjíti deposit, film (on the teeth)

پيته píta *feminine singular of* پيت

پيته pitá *f.* tape measure; tape (for measuring)

پيتي pití *f.* پيتی pajtí *Eastern* پيتی petáj *m. Western* ☞ پاتی

پيتي pitáj flat-nosed, snub-nosed پيتی توپک *dialect* Snyder rifle

پيتي píti *plural of* پيته

پيتي pité *plural of* پيته

پيتېدبل pitedál *denominative, intransitive* [*past:* پيت شو] **1** to be flattened **2** to be pressed down

پيټ piṭ *m. plural* peat

پيټ peṭ **1** *m.* **.1** damnation پټ دي شي ورباندي! May he be damned! پټ پر ويل to curse **1.2** shame, disgrace **2** *interjection* phooey **3** quite, on the whole

پيټ peṭ *m.* ☞ پټی

پيټار peṭār *m.* **1** woven basket with a top **2** woven cage, woven container (for snakes kept by fakirs)

پيټک peṭák *m.* **1** gift from relatives of the bride-to-be given to the young man (on the occasion of the unveiling of the fiancé's face) **2** gift to a child from relatives (soon after its birth) **3** woman's decoration worn at the temples

پيټل peṭə́l *transitive* [*past:* ويي پيټه] to curse

پيټلئ peṭə́laj damned

پيټن peṭán *m.* **1** aversion **2** indignation; displeasure

پيټو peṭú *m.* cursing someone

پيټو peṭó *plural oblique of* پټی

پيټوار peṭvár *m.* ☞ پټار

پېټی peṭáj *m.* **1** load; pack; bale **2** *figurative* burden; weight د اوږدو پېټی burden, weight د مشکلاتو پېټی excessive burden, burden too great to bear پېټی پر لبهّ اخیست کبری *proverb literal* They are picking up the burden. *figurative* There is no other way out. تا د چا پېټی نه دئ پورته کړئ You gave assistancc to no one. *idiom*

پېټی [2] peṭáj *f.* **1** sword belt **2** belt, girdle **3** bale, pack

پېجاو pedzháv pure, unalloyed پېجاو کول to purify پېجاو کبدل to be purified

پېجمخ والی pedzhmǝkhválaj *m.* beauty

پېمخی pedzhmókhaj ☞ پیمخی

پېچ [1] pech *m.* **1** bend, twist; turn **2** crookedness **3** screw; wood screw **4** dysentery آمبي پېچ amoebic dysentery **5** *regional* cramps پېچ کول a to wind, coil; turn b to screw in; twist in c to pin down with a hold (wrestling) d *figurative* to betray e *figurative* to complicate, muddle up پېچ ورکول to revolve, twist, turn round and round

پېچ [2] pech *m.* Pech (river, district in Nuristan) د پېچ دره the Pech Valley

پېچ تاب pechtāb *m.* **1** difficulty **2** emotional agitation, anxiety **3** screwdriver

پېچ تو pechtáv *m.* screwdriver

پېچ درپېچ pechdarpéch winding, tortuous

پېچش pechísh *m.* **1** dysentery **2** colic

پېچک pechák *m.* **1** skein, hank (of thread, yarn) **2** spool; bobbin

پېچ کاري، پېچکاري pechkārí *f.* **1** injection, shot, hypodermic injection پېچکاري کول to give a shot, give an injection, administer a hypodermic injection **2** syringe, hypodermic syringe

پېچل pechól *transitive* [*past:* وی پیچه] **1** to revolve, turn **2** to wind round; wind پېچل سر to turn away, turn to one side پېچل کبدل *passive* ☞ پیچبدل

پېچلی pechólaj **1** twisted **2** turned; wound; wound around **3** complex; complicated; involved; unclear (e.g., of a problem) پیچلی a to wind round b to be twisted; be wound; be wound around c to be complicated; be involved; be unclear

پېچموزي pechmózi *f. plural* پېچمی pechmój *f.* mockery پېچموزي وهل to laugh, laugh at someone

پېچواړی pechvāṛáj *f.* hobbles, fetters

پېچوتاب pechutāb *m.* ☞ پېچ وتاب 1, 2

پېچوخم pechukhám winding, twisting

پېچورا pechorā *f.* د پېچورا دریاب the Pechora River

پېچومه pechúma *f.* rise, ascent, upgrade slope (e.g., in the mountains)

پېچومی pechúmaj **1.1** winding, twisting **1.2** roundabout پېچومی لار a roundabout road **2** *m.* .1 rise, slope; uphill grade **2.2** turn, bend (in a road) **2.3** *figurative* turning point, crisis

پېچه [1] pechá *f.* little pigtail (braided lower than the ear)

پېچه [2] péchá *imperative of* پېچل

پېچه [3] pechó *imperfective of* پېچل

پېچی [1] píche *dialect* closed, shut خوله پېچی کړه! Shut up! Be quiet!

پېچی [2] pechí *present tense of* پېچل

پېچی [3] peché *plural of* پېچه [1]

پېچیدګي pechidagí *f.* **1** complication **2** intricacy **3** complexity

پېچېدل pechedól *intransitive* [*past:* وپېچیده] **1** to move around, revolve **2** to be wound around; be wound up **3** to coil

پېچیده pechidá ☞ پیچلی

پېچیدګي pechidagí *f.* ☞ پېچیده ګی

پېخ pets *m.* **1** patience, endurance **2** *dialect* evil

پېخانی petsáṇaj ☞ پخانی

پېخکی pítska *f.* پېخکی pitskój *f.* **1** hem (of a shirt) **2** cuff (e.g., of trouser leg) **3** tip, corner (of a shawl, chador, etc.) **4** *figurative* side, aspect (of a question, etc.)

پېخل petsól *transitive* [*past:* وی پېخه] to bear, endure (e.g., grief)

پېخنه petsóna *f.* patience, endurance, long-suffering

پېخول petsóvál *m.* **1** side panel of a tent **2** screen; partition

پېخونی petsúnaj *m.* ☞ پسونی

پېخه [1] petsá *f.* **1** portion, part **2** lot **3** ☞ پېخه کول to bear, suffer, endure

پېخه [2] pítsa *f.* ☞ پېخکه

پېخه [3] pétsa *f.* annoyance, pestering, bothering په پېخه کبدل to annoy, bore, pester

پېخه [4] pétsa *imperative imperfective of* پېخل

پېخه [5] petsó *imperfective aspect of* پېخل

پېخ pekh *m.* spur (of a rooster)

پېخاره pikháṛa *f.* dung, droppings (of sheep, goat)

پېخاله pikhála *f.* droppings (of a bird)

پېخر pekhór *m.* large quantity; profusion په پېخر کبدل to become abundant

پی خرڅوونکی pǝj khartsavúnkaj *m.* milkman, one who sells milk

پېخبدل pekhedól *intransitive* ☞ پېنبدل

پیدا pejdā **1** created; produced **2** born **3** appearing; forming; arising **4** discovered, found **5** obtained; acquired **6** evoked, endangered (e.g., difficulties) پیدا کول a to create; produce b to discover, find c to acquire, obtain, get d to evoke, engender, give rise to (i.e., difficulties) پیدا کبدل a to be created; appear, arise د دوی په مینځ کښی مخالفت پیدا شو Disagreements arose between them. b to be discovered, be found c to be obtained, be gotten, be extracted d to appear, show itself e to turn out, prove to be, arise f to be born په خطا پیدا شوئ illegitimate, born out of wedlock ته په کم ښار کښی پیدا شوئ يي؟ In what city were you born? g to be found, be met داسي خلق لږ پیدا کبری It is rare to encounter such people. h to breed (cattle) i to be produced, be manufactured

پیداکوونکی pajdā kavúnkaj *m.* **1** creator, maker **2** producer

پیداکېده pajdākedó *m. plural* **1** creation; appearance, origin **2** discovery **3** acquisition, obtaining **4** descent **5** birth

پیداګوژي pedāgozhí *f.* pedagogy موسسه پیداګوژي muassasá-ji پیداګوژی pedagogic institute

پیداوار pajdāvār *m. plural* **1** production, output; product; goods د سکرو معدني پیداوار mineral riches **2** mining, extraction د سکرو coal mining

پیداوڼنت pajdāvúnkht *m.* pajdāvukht **1** provenance, descent; origin; birth په پیداوڼنت کښي by descent **2** living creature; creature

پیدایش pajdājísh *m.* ☞ پیدایښي

پیدایښي pajdājishí inborn, innate, congenital

پیدایښ pajdajọ́kh *m.* pajdajọ́kht پیدایننت *m.* pajdajọ́kht **1** creation; appearance, beginning **2** birth **3** output; product **4** production

پی درپی pajdarpáj **1** sequential; uninterrupted **2** successively; uninterruptedly

پیر[1] pir *m.* **1** old man, elder **2** pir (Muslim spiritual guide)

پیر[2] per *m.* **1** turning; turn دستي سپرو په بېرته پیر وکړ The horsemen immediately turned back. **2** bend, twist پیر خوړل **a** to revolve; turn; turn around **b** to coil **3** *figurative* falseness

پیر[3] pir *m.* Monday

پیراهن perāhán *m.* **1** shirt, blouse **2** dress (female's)

پیرایه piraja *f.* **1** adornment, appointments; attire **2** embellishment **3** *figurative* appearance

پیرزو perdzó *Eastern* ☞ پیرزو

پیرزوینه perdzojọ́na *f.* ☞ پیرزوینه

پیرزی pérdzáj *m.* post, place of assignment

پیرړ perář[2] ☞ پیر[1]

پیرړتوب perəřtób *m.* پیرړوالی perəřválaj *m.* corpulence; stoutness

پیرزاده pirzādá *m.* offspring of a pir (i.e., spiritual guide)

پیرزو perzó **1** proper, fitting, worthy پیرزو کول to award, favor, consider worthy of something پیرزو کېدل to be worthy, deserve something دا انعام زما په تا پیرزو دئ I consider you worthy of this reward. یه، نو دغه خواري مي پر تا نه پیرزو کېږي No, I do not want you to suffer so. **2** desired, wished پیرزو لرل **a** to consider worthy, deserving of something **b** to desire someone (to have) something **3** pleasant, pleasing *idiom* بده یي نه ده درباندي پیرزو He doesn't wish you evil. ستاسي په نور تکلیف نه یم پیرزو I don't want to disturb you any longer. مګر زماني پیرزو نکړه However, time ordained otherwise. بار اچول نه پیرزو کوم I don't wish to burden anybody.

پیرزوناک perzonāk *m.* پیرزوونکی perzovúnkaj *m.* well-wisher

پیرزووالی perzoválaj *m.* پیرزوینه perzovúna *f.* پیرزوینه *perzojọ́na f.* **1** awarding **2** wish, desire هر ډول پیرزووالی بنه پیرزووالی good wishes پر چا پیرزووالی لرل، لرل to wish (someone) all the best **3** favor, inclination, consideration to someone; courtesy په پیرزووالي considerately, courteously چاته د پیرزویني ست کول *perzojọ́ni* to show consideration to someone **4** advantage, preference **5** indulgence, favor, goodwill, kindness پیرزووالی غوښتل to ask a favor, ask for indulgence

پیرزویونی perzojúnaj **1** kind; well-wishing **2** gracious **3** kind, considerate

پیرس pérís *m. regional* Paris (city)

پیرکی[1] perakáj *m.* pirakáj small pie (with vegetable filling) د تناره پیرکی small pie baked in a tonur (i.e., earthen oven) د تبی پیرکی small pie cooked in a skillet

پیرکی[2] pirkáj *m. diminutive of* پیر[1]

پیرګر pergọ́r imitating

پیرګی[1] pirgáj *m.* acorn ☞ پرګی

پیرګی[2] piragáj *m.* wooden shovel (for shoveling snow)

پیرګی[3] pirgáj *m. diminutive of* پیر[1]

پیرل[1] pirọ́l *transitive* ☞ پیرودل

پیرل[2] perọ́l *transitive* [*past:* وئ یی پیره] to braid, plait (e.g., a net, a mat)

پیرمحمد pir muhammád *m. proper name* Pir Muhammed

پیمخی permọ́khaj ☞ پیمخی

پیرنګ peráng *m.* **1** the Christian world **2** Europe

پیرنګی perangáj *m.* **1** Englishman پیرنګیان افسران English officers **2** European (person) **3** Christian (person)

پیرینی piriné د پیرني غرونه Pyrenees, the Pyrenees Mountains

پیرنه[1] perọ́na *f.* plainting, braiding (e.g., nets, mats)

پیرنه[2] perọ́na *f.* ☞ پیرودنه

پیرو[1] pajráv *m.* **1** follower, adherent **2** member of a sect

پیرو[2] piró *m. affectionate* پیرمحمد

پیرو[3] perú *m.* Peru

پیروان[1] perván *m. anatomy* placenta

پیروان[2] pajraván *plural of* پیرو[1]

پیروتی pervátaj *m.* pervátaj perváte *f.* **1** bindweed (plant) **2** lianas (general term for climbing plant in tropical climates)

پیرود peród *m.* buying; procurement

پیرودل perodọ́l pirodọ́l *transitive* [*present:* پیري *past:* وئ یی پیرود] to buy, procure, stock up

پیرودنه perodọ́na *f.* purchasing; procuring; stocking up

پیرودونکی perodúnkaj **1** *present participle of* پیرودل **2** *m.* purchaser

پیرودی peródaj bought (up); procured

پیروژه perozá *f.* ☞ پیروژه

پیروزی[1] peruzí *f.* victory

پیروزی[2] perozáj *m.* strainer, filter (of cloth, muslin)

پیروژه perozhá *f.* turquoise

پیرونکی perúnkaj **1** *present participle of* پیرل[2] **2** *m.* weaver (of nets, mats)

پیرونه pervọ́na پیروني pervọ́ne *f.* **1** *singular & plural astronomy* the Pleiades **2** *f. proper name* Pervyna *idiom* اوس پیرونه لګېدلي ده Autumn came on.

پیروی perọ́vaj perávaj *m.* cream د اومو شیدو پیروی sour cream پر sour cream **a** to grow dark before one's eyes **b** to get into a rage پر سترګو پیروی اوبدنتل idiom سترګو پیروی راتلل **c** to be angry with someone *idiom* سترګو یي پیروی نیولئ دئ **a** he became blind **b** he became intensely hungry

پیروی pajraví *f.* **1** emulating someone; escorting, accompanying someone د چا په پیروي سره in company with someone **2** imitating someone **3** observing, maintaining something (as a law or custom, tradition) **4** *law* conducting a trial د مقدمي پيروي a trial

پیره perá *f.* pajrá **1** guard (body of men); protection, security وراندي پیره advance guardpost پیره درول to set up a guard, institute security په هغو باندي سخته پیره ولگېده to guard, protect پیره کول They were under increased security. **2** *Eastern* time, occasion دوه پیری ولاړ او راغئ He came and went two times. **3** case *idiom* په پیره تلل to travel on business

پیره دار peradár *m.* pajradár sentry, guard

پیره دارخانه peradárkhāná *f.* sentry box

پیره داري peradárí *f.* guarding, carrying out security measure, performing the duties of an armed-guard detachment د پیره داری وظیفه guard duty, guard service

پیرکی perakáj *m.* ☞ پیره کی [1]

پیره والا peravālá *m.* ☞ پیره دار

پیری peráj [1] *m.* evil spirit, jinn, demon *idiom* پر سترگو پیری راتلل **a** to grow dark before one's eyes **b** to go into a rage **c** to be angry with someone *perí* ته پیری وهلئ یی؟ Are you losing your mind? Has the evil one bewitched you?

پیری perí [2] pirí **1** *present of* پیرودل، پیرل **2** *m.* purchase, buying پیری پلور buying and selling, trading پیری کول to buy, procure

پیری pirí [3] *f.* **1** old age; declining years **2** the position of a pir (i.e., spiritual advisor), or a murshid (i.e., spiritual counsellor)

پیری peráj [4] *f.* fairy

پیرې peré [5] *f.* *plural* imitating, mimicking

پیریان perján perijān *plural of* پیری [1] *idiom* پیریان اوبه mirage

پیریانه perjāná *f.* wicked fairy, witch

پیریاني perjaní perjānáj **1** devilish; demoniac **2** possessed, dominated by an evil spirit

پیریني periní *f.* ☞ پرنی

پیرینېز pirinéz *m.* *plural* the Pyrenees

پیړ peṛ [1] *m.* **.1** mortar (wooden) **1.2** press (for obtaining must from berries) **1.3** squeezing (juice from berries) **2.1** stout; corpulent; fat **2.2** large, big پیړه منه a large apple **2.3** coarse, thick (e.g., of cloth)

پیړ peṛ [2] *tautological with* زبر

پیړتوب peṛtób *m.* ☞ پیړوالی

پیړزه peṛza *f.* pile of earth

پیړمار peṛmár *m.* worker engaged in the cooking of must

پیړمخ peṛmákh turned over, overturned پیړمخ کول to invert, overturn

پیړمن peṛmán *m.* lazy fat man, lazy fatso

پیړو peṛú peṛó *m.* pay of a herdsman or shepherd [1]

پیړو peṛó *oblique of* پیړی [1] [2]

پیړو peṛó *oblique plural of* پیړ [1] [3]

پیړوالی peṛvālaj *m.* **1** stoutness; corpulence **2** coarseness (e.g., of cloth)

پیړوده peṛóda coarse, harsh

پیړه péṛa *f.* **1** lump, ball (of dough) **2** sweet dish made of cream and sugar [1]

پیړه péṛa *feminine singular of* پیړ [1] [2]

پیړی peráj [1] *f.* **1** century, age له پیړی په پیړی from century to century, from one century to another په پیړو پیړو for centuries, in the course of centuries پیړی رژول to last for centuries **2** generation (30 years)

پیړی peráj [2] *f.* stool; bench

پیز pez *m.* repairing; darning, mending

پیزار pajzár *m.* slippers; payzars (a kind of Afghan footgear with turned-up toes)

پیزاره pajzārá *f.* pedestal

پیزل pezál *transitive* [*past:* وی یې پیزه] to repair; darn, mend

پیزو pezó *f.* peso (monetary unit)

پیزو pezú *present tense first person singular of* پیزل

پیزوان pezvān *m.* **1** nose ring (female adornment) **2** single (swingle)- tree (for harnessing horse to a plow) **3** ring or wooden plug threaded through a camel's nostril to control the animal **4** muzzle (for a calf)

پیزواني pezvānáj *m.* pezvāní **1** bullock or ox with muzzle **2** *figurative* docile person, meek person **3** ☞ جغ لنډی

پیزه péza [1] *f.* **1** ledge (on a mountain) **2** pinnacle (mountain), peak **3** *dialect* nose **4** crown **5** point, spike پیزه جوړول to sharpen

پیزه pezá [2] *f.* *medicine* incontinence of urine

پیزې péze [1] pézi *plural of* پیزه [1]

پیزي pezí [2] pezáj faded, withered پیزي کېدل to fade, wither

پیزي pezáj [3] *f.* reading haltingly پیزی توري ABC's, alphabet پیزی کول **a** to read haltingly **b** to write or pronounce haltingly

پیزتوب pezitób *m.* **1** flabbiness **2** fading, withering

پیزېدل pezedál *intransitive* [*past:* و پیزېده] to droop, fade, dry up

پیزي والی pezivālaj *m.* ☞ پیزتوب

پېژاند pezhānd **1** familiar **2** *m.* connoisseur; expert

پېژندگلوي pezhāndgalví *f.* ☞ پېژند گلوي

پېژندل pezhāndál *transitive* ☞ پېژندل

پېژانده pezhāndá *m.* *plural* pezhāndá *f.* **1** cognition, understanding of something **2** familiarity with someone or something

پېژن pézhan *present stem of* پېژندل

پېژنتون pezhantún *m.* *military* directorate of personnel

پېژند pezhánd *m.* *military* personnel, cadre

پېژند گلوي pezhandgalví *f.* پېژند گلي pezhandgalí *f.* **1** familiarization or acquaintance with something; cognition or knowledge of something پېژند گلوي می ورسره نشته I am not acquainted with him. **2** recommendation د پېژند گلوی علایق friendly relations **3** registration; inventory-taking

پېژندل pezhandál **1** [*present:* وی یې پېژاند *past:* پېژني] *transitive* **.1** to know someone, be acquainted with someone ته ما پېژنی؟ Do you know me? چا ته ور پېژندل، چا ته پېژندل to acquaint someone with someone or something; to present to someone اجازه راکوئ چه یو خپل دوست ستاسي حضور ته درپېژنم Permit me to introduce my friend to you. **1.2** to recognize someone په دي مینخ کښني دوی یو بل سره ښه پېژني They knew one another well by this time. **1.3** to understand, get to know, grasp **1.4** to know something **1.5** to recognize someone or something په رسميت پېژندل to recognize officially (e.g., a government) سره پېژندل to distinguish something د چا په حضور کښې پېژندل to be presented to someone څخه پېژندل کېدل to distinguish one from another **2** *m. plural* ☞ پېژندنه

پېژندنه pezhandə́na *f.* **1** acquaintanceship د چا، د چا سره پېژندنه کول to become acquainted with someone **2** appelation, designation **3** description, depiction **4** knowledge; study سره پېژندنه self-knowledge ځان پېژندنه د اقليم پېژندنه climatology

پېژندوال pezhandvál *m. military* chief of the personnel directorate

پېژندون pezhandún *m.* ☞ پېژندنه

پېژندوی pezhəndúj pezhəndój **1.1** knowing, informed **1.2** familiar پېژندوی کسان acquaintances **2** *m.* acquaintance

پېغل peghə́l *transitive Western* [*past:* و يې پيغه] **1** to make a cut or notch **2** to cut; chop, chop off, cut off **3** *medicine* to amputate

پيس [1] pes *m.* **1** *m.* leprosy **2** leprous

پيس [2] pis *m.* vanity; arrogance په پيس کول، په پيس کېدل to be vain; be arrogant

پيساڼی pisāṇaj *m.* ☞ پخانی

پيسټ peṣṭ *m.* paste د غاښو پيسټ toothpaste

پيسړ pesə́ṛ ugly; unattractive پيسړ ګڼل a to consider ugly, think unattractive b to despise

پيښکه péska *f.* ☞ پيښکه

پيښکۍ piskə́j *f.* ☞ پيښکۍ

پيسلی pisláj *m.* section of land over which water passes at the time of irrigation

پيسمن pismə́n vain; arrogant

پيسه pajsá pesá *f. Eastern* **1** small coin, pice **2** *usually plural* پيسې pajsé pesé *Eastern* pesé **3** money د پيسي خاوند rich man, monied person پيسه اخيستل a to take money b to take bribes

پيسه دار pajsadár monied, well-to-do

پيسه دوستي pajsadostí *f.* avarice, greed

پيسي [1] pesí *m.* leper

پيسی [2] pisáj *m.* fop, dandy

پيسي pajsé pesé *Eastern plural of* پيسه

پيسي والا pesevālá *m. Eastern* rich man, monied individual

پيش [1] pesh **1.1** in front, ahead; before **1.2** forward **1.3** earlier, formerly, first تر ټوله پيش first of all پيش کول a to bring forward; advance; present b to adduce, offer (an example, a quotation) **2** *m. linguistics* pesh, zamm (the supralinear symbol ' for the short vowels /u/ or /o/)

پيش [2] pish *m. dialect* cat

پيشاره pishára *f.* **1** mockery په چا پيشاري کول to laugh at someone **2** attack **3** smirk, grin

پيشاک pishák *m.* scab; mange

پيش آمد peshāmád *m.* **1** event, occurence **2** approach, behavior پيش آمد يې زشت و They were rude. They conducted themselves rudely. د چا سره پيش آمد کول to conduct yourself in relation to someone else, behave toward someone

پيشان peshán **1** forward, front **2** advanced

پيشانه peshāná *f.* **1** sitting room **2** *dialect* pantry, storeroom

پيشاني peshāní *f.* ☞ تندی [1]

پيش اهنگ peshaháng *m.* **1** pioneer, member of the pioneer organization **2** vanguard, advance party

پيش بند peshbánd *m.* **1** martingale (harness component) **2** apron

پيش بندي peshbandí *f.* **1** prudence, foresight **2** care, caution پيش بندي کول a to be prudent, be foresighted b to be careful, be cautious

پيشبين peshbín **1** prudent, foresighted **2** careful, cautious

پيشبيني peshbiní *f.* prevision, foresightedness; prudence پيشبيني کول *compound verb* to foresee, envisage پيشبيني کېدل *compound verb* a to be foresighted, to have envisaged b to have anticipated

پيشپړانگ pishpṛáng *m.* panther

پيش پيش پيش pish-pish-pish *interjection* here kitty-kitty-kitty

پيشت [1] pisht *tautological with* خيښت

پيشت [2] pisht *interjection* Scat!

پيشتر peshtár **1** former, previous **2** earlier, before

پيشتری pishtáraj *m.* kind of sweet green vegetable

پيشتول pishtvál *m.* **1** lintel (of a door) **2** ceiling **3** main ceiling beam

پيش خانه peshkhāná *f.* ☞ تهروري

پيش خبري peshkhabarí *f.* ☞ پيشگويي

پيشخور peshkhór extravagant, living on credit, living beyond one's means

پيشخوري peshkhorí *f.* **1** life on credit, extravagance **2** grain on loan against a future harvest (as collateral)

پيش خيمه peshkhajmá *f.* **1** tent sent ahead of a military unit on the march **2** herald, harbinger

پيشدار peshdár *m. military* vanguard; advance party

پيشدست peshdást **1** outstripping the others, running ahead **2** swift, quick, adroit

پيشدستي peshdastí *f.* **1** outstripping, running ahead **2** swiftness, quickness, adroitness

پيشران، پيش ران peshrán *m.* breechblock (of a rifle)

پيشرس peshrás early, ripening early, early-ripening

پيشرفت peshráft *m.* **1** moving forward, progress **2** success, advancement **3** *military* offensive, attack پيشرفت کول a to move forward b to produce successes c to attack

پيشرفت غوښتونکی peshráft ghuḳhtúnkaj progressive

پيشرو peshráv **1** *m.* **.1** advancement, moving forward پيشرو وهل to go forward **1.2** doubt, fear **1.3** preface **1.4** person who is advancing **1.5** predecessor **2.1** front, anterior **2.2** preceding

پيشروي peshraví *f.* advancement, moving forward پيشروي کول to move forward, advance

پيش فکري peshfikrí *f.* foresight پيش فکري کول to be foresighted

پيش قوضه peshḳábza *f.* ☞ پيش قبضه

پیشقدم peshkadám **1** advanced, vanguard, moving forward پیشقدمه *figurative* forward, advanced detachment, vanguard **2** *m.* herald, precursor, forerunner تولگی

پیشقدمي peshkadamí *f.* **1** advance, advancement, moving ahead **2** offensive **3** initiative

پیش قراول peshḳarāvúl *m. military* **1** vanguard, advance units **2** patrol

پیش قوضه peshḳávza *f.* peshkavza (a kind of large double-edged knife) (په پیش قوضه وهل to stab with a peshkavza

پیشک peshák *m. medicine* leprosy, Hanson's disease

پیشکار peshḳár *m.* **1** manager (e.g., of property) **2** overseer

پیشکاري peshḳārí *f.* **1** direction, management **2** the work of an overseer

پیشکه pisháka *f.* pussy, pussycat

پیشکي peshakí *f.* پیشگي ☞ ¹

پیشکی peshḳáj *m.* leper, Hanson's disease sufferer ²

پیشگویي peshgoí *f.* peshguí prediction, forecast, prognosis هیڅ د هوا د حالاتو پیشگویي نه شم کولای I can say nothing in advance. پیشگویي کول **a** to predict, forecast **b** to make a prognosis, make a forecast (e.g., of the weather) پیشگویي کول *compound verb* to predict, forecast

پیشگي peshgí *f.* peshagí advance, advance money, deposit

پیشل peshál *transitive* [past: پیشه یي و] to cool (stirring with a spoon)

پیشلره peshlára *f.* پیشلری pishláraj *m.* پیشتری ☞

پیش لمی peshlamáj *m. Western* پیش منی ☞

پیشمنډی peshmanḍáj *f.* mockery

پیشمنی ، پیش منی peshmanáj *m.* meal completed before daybreak (during Ramadan)

پیشنهاد peshnihád *m.* [plural: پیشنهادونه peshnihādúna plural: پیشنهادات peshnihādāt] *Arabic* proposition, suggestion پیشنهاد کول **a** to introduce a proposal, propose **b** to submit proof د محکمي و حضورته پیشنهاد کول to submit evidence to a court

پیشني peshaní *fashionable* پیشني جامي fashionable clothing

پیشو pishó *f.* cat پیشو یي د غوښو څوکیداره کړه *proverb* to set a cat to guard meat, set a goat to watch the cabbages

پیشوا peshvá *m.* **1** leader, chief **2** *history* peshwa (title of the leader of the Mahrattas in India)

پیشوبازي pishobāzí *f.* toadying, bootlicking پیشوبازي کول to toady, be a bootlicker

پیشوپړی pishopṛáj *f.* tug-of-war (the game)

پیشور peshavár *m.* artisan; workman

پیشورز peshvórz *m.* overskirt (worn by a dancer)

پیشوگی pishogáj *f.* **1** kitty, pussycat **2** hairy caterpillar

پیشول peshavál *denominative* [past: پیش یي کړ] **1** deliver; bring to someone **2** close, lock, bolt (e.g., a door) **3** to fasten to, join, unite **4** to bring forward, set (e.g., conditions) دا شرطونه یي ورته پیش کړه He placed the following conditions before them. **5** to present (with)

پیشومپړی pishompráj *f.* game with a ball

پیشونگوری pishóngraj *m.* pishongóraj *m.* kitten

پیشاونه peshavóna *f.* **1** presentation; delivery **2** closing, locking (e.g., a door) **3** attaching, joining (to) **4** bringing forward (e.g., conditions) **5** proposal, overture

پیشوای peshváj *f.* ladle, scoop

پیشه peshá *f.* **1** trade, craft; profession **2** practice; habit ¹

پیشه peshá *f. regional* **1** testimony, evidence پیشه درجول to take down testimony **2** appearance (in court) ²

پیشه ور peshavár *m.* پیشور ☞

پیشي pishí *f.* cat پیشي پیشي کېدل **a** to try to ingratiate oneself with, make up to, fawn upon **b** to make up to ¹

پیشی pisháj *m.* cat ²

پیشي peshí *f.* **1** precedent **2** conduct, conducting (of a trial) د مقدمي د پیشی په وقت at the time of the (courtroom) trial ³

پیشی pisháj *f.* **1** small nose ring (female decoration) **2** hairy caterpillar **3** purse ⁴

پیشي péshi *f. plural children's speech* pee-pee, urine پیشي کول to pee-pee, urinate ⁵

پیشبدل peshadál *intransitive* [past: پیش شو] **1** to be delivered; present oneself to someone **2** to be closed, be locked, be bolted (e.g., of a door) **3** to be attached, be joined **4** to be closed up (of a wound) **5** to join, converge **6** to be put forth, be proposed (conditions)

پیشین peshín *m.* **1** the afternoon **2** namaz (Muslim prayer offered after noon)

پیپن peḳh *m.* peḳh پیش ☞ ¹ 2 ¹

پیپن peḳh peḳh **1** going on, occurring را پیپنی چاري happening to me, happening to us; experienced by me, experienced by us څه مصیبت پیپن دئ؟ What kind of misfortune befell? **2** *predicative* front, anterior to, first, moved up front ²

پیپن peḳh peḳh *tautological with* هبن ³

پیپناو peḳhāv peḳhāv *m.* **1** humorous prank, trick; eccentricity; to be engaged in pranks, perform practical jokes عجیبه پیپناوونه کول **2** mockery, ridicule پیپناو کول to ridicule **3** occurrence, event

پیپناور peḳhāvár peḳhāvár *m.* پیپنور ☞ ¹

پیپناوو peḳhāvú peḳhāvú *m.* **1** imitator **2** scoffer

پیپنکاخ peḳhkáḳh peḳhkáḳh *m.* پیپنکبنی peḳhkaḳhí peḳhkaḳhí *f.* gift; present پیپنکبنی ورکول to give a gift

پیپنو peḳhú peḳhú *m.* پیپناوو ☞

پیپنور peḳhavár *m.* peḳhavár Peshawar (city) د پیپنور حوزه Peshawar District ¹

پیپنور peḳhavár *m.* carpet maker, weaver of palases (a kind of napless carpet) ²

پیپنوری peḳhavráj peḳhavráj **1** *attributive* Peshawar **2** *m.* resident of Peshawar ¹

پیپنوری peḳhavráj *feminine singular of* پیپنوری ¹ ²

پیپنول peḳhavál *denominative, transitive* [past: پیپن یي کړ] **1** to cause, provoke خرابي پیپنول to destroy زیان پیپنول to inflict harm, cause damage پښنول تکليف چاته و to trouble, disturb someone 2 to render assistance; create (conditions) پښنول اساني to facilitate something

پښنه [1] péḵha péḵha *f.* 1 occurrence; happening; incident اختلافي پښنه conflict څه پښنه ده؟ What happened? What's the matter? دردمنه پرون يوه پښنه وشوه Yesterday the following incident occurred د پښنې د خداى پښنې دي Everything is from God. a sad event نه تښتته نه وه You can't do anything about it. There's nowhere to go. 2 occurrence, appearance د خطري پښنې په وخت کښي In the event of the occurrence of danger پښنه کول a to begin b to appear by chance, arise by chance

پښنه [2] peḵhá peḵhá *f.* 1 mimicking; mocking دا د پښني کسب پربرده Stop teasing. د خولي پښني کول to imitate someone; mock someone 2 imitation د چا پښني کول to mimic someone

پښنه [3] peḵhá *f. regional* ☞ پيشه [2]

پښنه مار peḵhamár peḵhamár 1 imitating 2 *m.* mimic, imitator

پښنی [1] peḵháj *m.* ☞ پښنه مار

پښنی [2] péḵhi *plural of* پښنه [1]

پښنی [3] peḵhé *plural of* پښنه [2]

پښنېدل peḵhedəl 1 *intransitive* [*past:* پښېن شو] 1.1 to happen, occur; go on; arise ... چه پښنېبري داسي لږ پر It rarely happens that ... نه پوهېږم څه راپښېن شوي دي I don't know what happened to me. تا ته تعجب در نتيجه ځني پښنېبري This will lead to sad consequences. ... پښنېبري It is a surprise to you that ... 1.2 to be found, find oneself, happen to be; run into دلته څنګه پر ده پښېن شو He met him. پښېن شوئ يئ؟ How did you happen to get here? 1.3 to come into sight; appear 1.4 to be caused; cause, inflict (e.g., losses) ورپښېن شو نقصان Considerable injury was done him. Considerable injury was done them. 2 *m. plural* occurrence, appearance

پښنېدونکی peḵhedúnkaj 1 *present participle of* پښنېدل 2 possible, probable

پښنېده peḵhedə *m. plural* occurrence, appearance

پښني گر peḵhegár *m.* clown, buffoon

پيغام pajghám peghám *m.* message; utterance د چا په نامه يو پيغام to address someone with a formal message صادرول

پيغامبر pajghāmbár *m.* ☞ پيغمبر

پيغلتوب peghəltób *m.* 1 virginity, chastity 2 girlhood, girlhood years په پيغلتوب کښي in girlhood years

پيغلتون peghəltún *m.* girlhood, girlhood years

پيغلوکی peghlúke *f. dialect* little girl

پيغله péghla *f.* unmarried girl, unmarried woman, spinster په کور ناسته پيغله old maid

پيغم pajghám *m.* ☞ پيغام

پيغمبر pajghambár *m.* prophet پيغمبر گل، پيغمبربوتی arnebia (a kind of decorative plant)

پيغور peghór *m.* reproach; judgement; censure, rebuke, reproof سره to reproach; censure; pass judgement; rebuke, reprove ورکول يو شي پيغور گڼل to be ashamed of something پيغرونه ورکول to blame one another دا موږ ته لوى پيغور دئ This is a great reproach to us.

پيغورول peghoravál *denominative* [*past:* پيغوري کړ] 1 reproach; reprove; judge; 2 reprimand, censure; rebuke

پيغورېدل peghoradál *denominative, intransitive* [*past:* پيغور شو] to be judged; be reproved

پکه [1] pajk *m.* fan اور ته پيک وهل to fan a fire ☞ پکه

پيک [2] pik *m.* funnel for pouring oil

پيک [3] pik *m.* peak (of a peak cap, military service cap)

پيکپ pikáp *m.* pickup (vehicle)

پيکتوب pikatób *m.* ☞ پيکه توب

پيکټ pikáṭ *m.* picket; outpost

پيکر pajkár *m.* 1 figure; body 2 *figurative* personality traits; character

پيکړه pajkəṛá *f.* 1 chains, shackles 2 *hunting* nooses, snares (for trapping birds) 3 *figurative* knotty problem; scandalous, maliciously litigious affair

پيکل pajkál *m.* 1 chain 2 clothesline 3 roller of spiny or thorny material (used in threshing)

پيکو pajkó *m.* 1 ☞ پايکو 2 tool or device for cutting noodles

پيکن pekín *m.* پيکنگ peking *m.* Peking (city)

پيکوی pekávaj *m.* ribbon (for the hair)

پيکه pekə́ piká 1 disordered; confused پيکه کول a to disorder; embarrass, confuse b to spoil c *figurative* to poison (e.g., a life) پيکه کېدل to be disordered; be embarrassed, be confused 2 pale (color) 3 tasteless, unpalatable 4 unpleasant

پيکه توب pekətób pikatób *m.* پيکه والی pikaválaj *m.* 1 confusion; bashfulness; shyness 3 paleness 4 bad taste, tastelessness

پيکی [1] pekáj *m.* bangs (cut straight across) پيکي پرېکول a to cut of the bangs b to announce to a young unmarried woman that she is to be engaged (married)

پيکي [2] piké *f.* dive (of an aircraft) الوتکه د پيکي څخه را ايستل to pull an aircraft out of a dive

پيکيالی pekjāláj wearing bangs

پيل [1] pajl *m.* beginning, initiative په څه باندي پيل کول، و څه ته پيل کول to begin something; set about something; undertake something په دخپل ژوند پيل کار پيل کول، پيل ورته اينوندل to start a job, begin a task دولسم کال پيل کوي He is in his twelfth year.

پيل [2] pil *m.* elephant پيل چه مري ، يو زنګون اوبه يې په نس کښي وي *folk saying* Even after death an elephant has a barrel of water in his belly. پيل چه ژوندي وي ، يو لک او چه مړسي دوه لکه قيمت لري *folk saying* A live elephant is worth a hundred thousand rupees, and when he dies is worth twice as much. *idiom* د پيل غوږ *Eastern* twigs (a pastry) د پيل په غوږ کښي بيدېدل to doze, look stupid, look dumb; yawn

پيل [3] pejál *transitive* ☞ پيپل

پيلات pajlāt *m.* 1 disturbance; disorders, riots 2 fraud, swindling, cheating

پيلاتي pajlātí *m.* troublemaker

پيلاتيتوب pajlātitób *m.* 1 stirring up trouble, sedition 2 cheating; cheating at games

پیلار pelár *m.* curtain; blind پیلار اچول to pull the blinds, close the curtains

پیلامه pajlāmá *f.* **1** basis, foundation, base **2** sign, token **3** disposition, temper

پیلبو peləbó pelabó *f.* lightning پیلبو کېدل to flash (as lightning)

پیلپا pilpá *f.* **1** elephantiasis sufferer **2** *medicine* elephantiasis

پیلپیلکه pilpiláka *f.* praying mantis (insect)

پیلخانه pilkhāná *f.* stable or stall for elephants چه پیل ساتي ، پیلخانه به جوړوي *proverb* He who would keep an elephant must pay for a stable.

پیلار pilár *m.* pillar, column د سرحد پیلار frontier marker

پیلستی pelástaj growing up, growing stronger پیلستی کېدل to grow up, grow stronger

پیلغوړه pilghvága *f.* twigs (pastry)

پیل مرغ pilmúrgh *m.* turkey, Tom turkey

پیلنه pelána *f.* farewell, leave-taking پیلنه کول to say good-bye, take leave

پیلوا pelvá *f.* ☞ پیلبو

پیلوان pilván *m.* elephant keeper, mahout

پیلوت pilót *m.* pilot, flyer اتوماتیکي پیلوت automatic pilot

پیلوته pilóta *f.* [*plural:* پیلوتاني piloṭáni] female pilot, woman flyer ښځه پیلوته female aviator

پیلوتي piloṭí *f.* the profession of flying, piloting د پیلوتۍ ښوونځی، flight school د پیلوتۍ شاگردان flying school students, flight cadets

پیلوځی pelvódzaj *m.* پیلوزی pelvózaj *m.* brush, kindling; kindling wood

پیلوړ pajlór *m.* پیل ومټ pelumáṭ *m.* **1** effort, diligence **2** care, concern

پیلون pajlūn *m.* boot, launch

پیلون چلیز pajlūn chalíz *m.* *computer science* boot drive

پیلونه ¹ pelavóna *f.* ☞ بایکړ

پیلونه ² pajlavóna *f.* undertaking, initiative

پیله ¹ pelá *f.* cocoon (of a silkworm) د پیلې تربیه silkworm breeding, sericulture پیله جار ایستل دپیلې چنجی silkworm to spin a cocoon (of the worm)

پیله ² píla *f.* cow, female elephant

پیله کشي pelakashí *f.* silkworm breeding, sericulture

پیله ور pelavár *m.* silkworm breeder

پیله وري pelavarí *f.* ☞ پیله کشي

پیلی ¹ pajlé *f.* *plural* leg bracelets, ankle bracelets

پیلی ² pelé *plural of* پیله ¹

پیلیار peljár *m.* ☞ پیلار

پیمال pajmál *m.* occupation, trade

پیمال وال pajmālvál *m.* artisan, handicraftsman

پیمان pajmán *m.* **1** promise; assurance; consent **2** obligation پیمان کول to make a commitment پیمان تړل to promise; assure عهد او to be obliged *idiom* د اطلس پیمان the Atlantic Charter پیمان کول

پیمانه pajmāná *f.* **1** measure; dimensions; scale په یوه معینه پیمانه in a certain quantity په لویي پیمانې سره in large proportions په جهاني پیمانه on a terrestrial scale پیمانه کول *compound verb* to measure **2** cup, goblet

پیمایش pajmājísh *m.* **1** measure, standard **2** bound, limit

پیمایشي pajmājishí *f.* metrology

پی مختوب pəjməkhtób *m.* پی مخ والی pəjməkhválaj *m.* beauty, attractiveness; good looks

پی مخی pəjmókhaj **1** beautiful, attractive; good-looking **2** beardless

پیمل peməl *transitive* [*past:* و یې پیمه] to measure

پیمی ¹ pemáj *m.* ☞ پیمایش

پیمی ² pemí *present tense of* پیمل

پین ¹ pin *m.* powder (medicine)

پین ² pin *m.* pin

پینټ pajnṭ *m.* *regional* **1** point **2** *sports* point (in counting scores)

پنځه pindzó ☞ پنځه غنبی ☞ پنځه غاښبی ☞ پنځه

پېنده pénda *f.* **1** common dish or bowl **2** dinner party, party at table, table-mates

پېنډۍ penḍáj *f.* stone base, buttress of a column

پنسل pensíl *m.* pencil

پینغ pajnógh *m.* appendicitis

پینگ pujáng *m.* **1** vine **2** support for a vine

پینگ پونگ pingpóng *m.* ping-pong

پینگن pingón impatient; unable to endure

پینگو pengó *f.* **1** child's swing **2** cradle

پینل pinól *transitive* [*past:* و یې پینه] to lick up from the palm of the hand, take up from the palm of the hand with the tongue (e.g., medicine)

پینه ¹ piná *f.* **1** trough (for dough); wooden basin **2** patch (e.g., for a shoe) پینه وروړل، پینه کول to patch **3** brace, support (for a wall)

پینه ² pína *f.* dish

پینه دوز pinadúz *m.* itinerant cobbler; cobbler

پیني piní *f.* world, universe

پینغ pinégh *m.* *medicine* **1** constipation **2** colic **3** volculus (a twisting of the intestine upon itself that causes obstruction)

پېڼه peṇá *f.* **1** turn **2** time

پېوار pevár *m.* the Pevar Pass, the Pewar Pass د پېوار دره the Pevar Valley, the Pewar Valley

پی واز pəjváz *m.* temporary cooperative operation for the collection of milk for making butter and cheese for the winter

پیوچ pevúch *m.* pine tree

پېودل pevdól *transitive* ☞ پیپل

پېودنه pevdóna *f.* **1** composition; composing **2** arranging, setting going; regulating **3** stringing, threading together; planting, seating in place

پېودون pevdún *m.* order

پېوده pevdó *m.* *plural* ☞ پېودنه

پیوره pəjvә́ra pəjvúra milch, milk (of a cow) دا دپره پیوده غوا ده This cow gives much milk.

پیوست pajvást pevást *Eastern* 1 affiliated, adjoining, contiguous د هغه کور ځما له کور سره پیوست دئ His house is right next to mine. 2 *m.* .1 conjunction; contiguity; junction 2.2 friendship; closeness 2.3 *dialect* gap; crack; break

پیوستگي pajvastagí *f.* conjunction; contiguity; connection پیوستگي کول to join, conjoin; connect; affix

پیوستون pajvastún pevastún *m. Eastern* 1 joining; contiguity 2 friendship, closeness 3 merging, unification

پیوسته pajvastá 1.1 joined; affiliated 1.2 close 2 always, constantly; continuously

پیوسته ابرو pajvastá-abrú having eyebrows which are joined

پیوستبدل pajvastedә́l *denominative, intransitive* [*past:* پیوسته شو] 1 to join; adjoin له چاسره پیوستبدل to join someone, be on someone's side 2 to become close friends, start a friendship

پیوکی pevúkaj *m.* ☞ پیکوی

پیول pajvә́l *transitive* [*past:* پی یې کړ] 1 to chop down (a tree) 2 to plumb, measure the depth (e.g., of a river)

پیوند pajvánd *m.* 1 joining; coupling 2 repairing, mending, patching 3 *agriculture* grafting 4 rapprochement, friendship پیوندول idiom دوینو پیوند blood relationship ☞ پیوند کول

پیوندول pajvandavә́l *denominative, transitive* [*past:* پیوند یې کړ] 1 to join, adjoin 2 to mend, patch 3 *agriculture* to graft

پیوندي pajvandí 1 patched 2 *agriculture* grafted

پیوندبدل pajvandedә́l *denominative, intransitive* [*past:* پیوند شو] 1 to join; interlock 2 to be patched 3 to be grafted

پیونر pionér *m.* pioneer (member of the Pioneer Organization)

پیه [1] pája *f.* bandage, dressing (for the eyes)

پیه [2] pajá *f.* moth, clothes moth

پیبدل pajedә́l *denominative, intransitive* [*past:* پی شو] 1 to be cut down (of a tree) 2 to be plumbed, be measured (e.g., the depth of a river)

پیر pajér ☞ پهر

پیکی pejә́kaj *m.* ☞ پیکوی

پیل pejә́l *transitive* [*past:* وبې پیبه] 1 to put together, make up; gather, assemble 2 to arrange, organize, regulate, adjust 3 to plant, seat, string مرغلري پیبل پی یل to string pearls on a string ستن پیبل to thread a needle

پیبلئ pejә́laj 1 made up; gathered 2 arranged, regulated 3 planted, seated, strung; pulled through, threaded

پیوده pejánd *m.* ☞ پیبینه پی ینه pejә́na *f.* پی یند

پیوی pejә́vaj *m.* ☞ پیکوی

ت

ت te 1 the fourth letter of the Pashto alphabet 2 the number 400 in the abjad system

تا [1] tā *oblique form of the pronoun* ته 1 *used as an object with transitive verbs in the present and future tenses, and also in the imperative mood* راغلم چه تا ووینم I came to see you. 2 *used as a subject with transitive verbs in the ergative* "you", "by you" تا وواهه you killed him تا وخندل you laughed تا وویل you said 3 *used with prepositions, postpositions and adverbs* تا باندي، په تا باندي on you تا تاپوري، په تا پسي a beyond you b about you *Eastern* to تا کبني په تا کبني، وتا ته، تا له، تا له *Eastern* to you تا څني، تا څخه، له تا څخه، تا نه، له تا نه by you; from you تا کي، په تا کي in you تا دپاره *Eastern* for you تا سره *Eastern* with you تا غوندي *Eastern* like you, similar to you تا لاندي *Eastern* beneath you, under you

تا [2] tā *f.* 1 layer; sheet دوه تا یوه تا single دوې تا *Eastern* دوه تا double 2 fold, crease 3 bend, twist

تا [3] tā *f.* 1 sound 2 noise; roar, rumble

تا [4] tā تا کول to set down, land (e.g., a plane); land, disembark (troops, etc.) تا کبدل to alight (e.g., of a bird); land (e.g., in a plane); disembark

تا [5] tā 1 up to something 2 *conjunction* in order to

تاب tāb *m.* power, might دیو شي تاب نه لرل not to have the strength to do something زه یې د جنگ تاب نه لرم I don't have the strength to fight with him. I don't have the strength to fight with them.

تاب [2] tāb *m.* 1 ☞ تاو [2] 2 brightness, radiance, sparkling; light

تاب [2] tāb *m.* bend, twist

تابان tābā́n shining, radiating, sparkling

تابخانه tābakhāná *f.* ☞ تاوخانه

تابدار tābdā́r winding, twisting

تابدار [2] tābdā́r ☞ تابان

تابدان tābdā́n *m.* 1 window (glassed-in, e.g., in a roof); small window 2 small hinged pane for ventilation

تابستان tābistā́n *m. poetic* summer

تابع tābe' tābí' *Arabic* 1.1 subordinate; dependent 1.2 submissive, obedient د چا تابع کبدل to be subordinate, submit to 1.3 agreeable, in agreement with something; corresponding to something 2.1 *m.* [*plural:* تابعین] tābe'in *m. plural:* تبعه taba'á] supporter, adherent; follower 2.2 [*plural:* اتباع atbā' *plural:* تبعه taba'á *plural:* توابع tavābí'] subject, national

تابعدار tābe'dā́r [*plural:* توابع] 1 subordinate; dependent 2 submissive, obedient 3 devoted هغه مي تابعدار دئ He obeys me without question. He is devoted to me.

تابع داري tāb'dārí *f.* 1 subordination; dependence 2 submissiveness 3 devotion تابع داري کول a to submit (to), obey b to show one's devotion

تابع گلوي ‏ tāb'galví f. تابع والى ‏ tābe'válaj m. تابعيت ‏ tábe'ját m. Arabic allegiance; citizenship

تابعين ‏ tābe'ín m. Arabic plural from تابع

تابلو ‏ tābló f. 1 picture; poster 2 view, panorama 3 table, plate 4 list

تابلیت ‏ tāblét m. tablct, pill

تابوت ‏ tābút m. Arabic coffin

تابوتگر ‏ tābutgár m. coffin-maker, undertaker

تابه ‏ ¹ tābə́ imperfect of تبل ¹

تابه ‏ ² tābə́ oblique of the suffix توب تر مشرتابه لاندي ‏ under direction

تابه خانه ‏ tābakhāná f. ‏ تاوخانه

تابيا ‏ tābjā́ ready, made, done

تابين ‏ ¹ tābín m. ‏ تابعداري

تابين ‏ ² tābín m. arrangement, adjustment تابين کول ‏ to arrange, adjust تابين کبدل ‏ to be arranged, be adjusted

تابيه ‏ tābijá f. تعبیه

تاپ ‏ tāp m. top (of a carriage)

تا ‏ ³ ¹ tā́ pase ‏ تا پسي

تاپه ‏ ¹ tāpá f. ‏ تپه

تاپه ‏ ² tāpə́ imperfect of تپل

تاتار ‏ tātā́r m. Tatar

تاتاره ‏ tātā́ra f. Tatar (female)

تاتاري ‏ tātārí adjective 1 Tatar تاتاري ژبه ‏ the Tatar language 2 the Tatar language

تاترین ‏ tātərín m. hell, the underworld, the nether regions

تاتمل ‏ tātmə́l m. تاتمول ‏ tātmúl m. strong desire, dream a تاتمل نيول ‏ to experience a strong desire; dream b to feel sympathy, sympathize

تا ‏ ³ ¹ tā́ ta ‏ تا ته

تاتي ‏ tātí f. decrepit old woman

تاثر ‏ ta'assúr m. Arabic [plural: تاثرات ta'assurát] 1 impressionability 2 impression 3 grief, sorrow 4 regret, chagrin

تاثير ‏ tāsír m. Arabic [plural: تاثیرونه tāsirúna Arabic plural: تاثیرات tāsirát] 1 impression, effect; influence, action پر... باندي تاثير کول ‏ to influence, affect someone; make an impression on someone په... کښي تاثير کول ‏ پر چا باندې تاثير کول ‏ to impress someone په... تاثیر لرل، په... تر تاثير لاندي ‏ to have an influence نيول، تر تاثير لاندي راوستل ‏ to influence, affect 2 physics induction

تاج ‏ tādzh m. 1 botany crown 2 comb, crest (of a bird) تاج خروس ‏ tā́dzh-i cock's comb b Amaranthus, amaranth 3 bookshelf

تاج بخش ‏ tādzhbákhsh m. emperor, suzerian

تاجپوشي ‏ tādzhposhí f. coronation, accession to the throne

تاجدار ‏ tādzhdár 1 crowned, enthroned m. 2 king, monarch

تاجر ‏ tādzhír 1 m. Arabic [plural: تاجران tādzhirán Arabic plural: تجار tudzhdzhár] merchant tradesman کوچنی تاجر ‏ petty tradesman 2 attributive merchant, trade تجاره طبقه ‏ merchants (as a group)

تاجک ‏ tādzhík m. Tajik

تاجیکستان ‏ tādzhikistán m. Tajikistan

تاجکه ‏ tādzhíka f. Tajik (female)

تاجکي ‏ tādzhikí adjective 1 Tajik تاجکي ژبه ‏ the Tajik language 2 f. the Tajik language

تاجیک ‏ tādzhik m. ‏ تاجک

تاجیکستان ‏ tādzhikistán m. ‏ تاجکستان

تاجکه ‏ tādzhíka f. ‏ تاجکه

تاجیکي ‏ tādzhikí ‏ تاجکي

تاجيل ‏ tādzhíl m. Arabic 1 postponement, delay 2 law suspended sentence

تا ‏ ³ ¹ tā́ dzəni تاخه ‏ tā tskha ‏ تا خُني

تاخ ‏ tākh m. ‏ تاخچه

تاخت ‏ tākht m. 1 gallop په تاخت خُغلول ‏ at a gallop to urge on, whip up to a gallop په تاخت خُغلبدل ‏ to go at a gallop 2 attack تاخت کول ‏ a to gallop, race b to attack, carry out a raid on someone

تاخت و تاراج ‏ tākht-u-tārā́dzh m. wholesale pillage تاخت و تاراج کول ‏ compound verb to plunder, pillage, ravage

تاخچه ‏ tākhchá f. shelf; niche (used as a bookshelf) idiom په کار ‏ تاخچه کښي اينبودل ‏ to shelve, put off some matter

تاخوم ‏ tākhúm m. ‏ تاغه

تاخون ‏ tākhún m. 1 alarm, uneasiness 2 heartache

تاخیر ‏ tākhír m. Arabic slowdown, delay, procrastination; postponement تاخير کول ‏ to put off, delay; linger with something, stall

تاداو ‏ tādā́v m. تاداى ‏ tādā́j m. foundation (of a building), تاداو اينبودل، a تاداو کينل، د تاداو تیره اینبودل ‏ to lay a foundation (for a building) b to found, create (a school, a direction in something)

تادي ‏ ¹ tādí f. 1 hurry, haste 2 quickness, swiftness, promptness تادي کول ‏ a to hurry, rush b to be prompt

تادیه ‏ ² ta'addí f. Arabic ‏ تادس

تادیب ‏ tādíb m. Arabic 1 punishment, means of exerting pressure 2 correction, rehabilitation تادیب کول ‏ a to punish b to correct, rehabilitate

تادیه ‏ tādijá f. m. Arabic [plural: تادیات tādiját] payment (of taxes, dues); payment (of a check) تادیه کول ‏ د تادیاتو قابلیت ‏ solvency compound verb to pay (taxes, dues) تادیه ‏ to pay (a check) تادیه کبدل ‏ compound verb to be paid (of taxes, dues); be paid (of a check)

تار ‏ ¹ tār m. 1 thread 2 string 3 anatomy chord, ligament دآواز ‏ تارونه ‏ vocal chords 4 warp (of a fabric) 5 yarn, thread 6 wire; conductor 7 colloquial telegram د تار خبر ‏ telegram تار اخیستل ‏ to receive a telegram a تار وروهل ‏ to send a telegram تار لبرل ‏ to issue a telegram, send a telegram b to call, phone idiom تار ورسره اچول، ‏ ورسره درلودل ‏ a to be friendly with b to have a love affair with

تار ‏ ² tār m. plural تارکول

تاراج ‏ tārā́dzh m. theft, pillage; plundering; robbery, piracy تاراج کول ‏ compound verb to rob; plunder; destroy

تاران ‏ tārán m. botany knotweed

تاربرقي ‏ tārbarkí f. Eastern colloquial telegraph

تارپتار ‏ tārpətár تار په تار ‏

تارپتارول ‏ tārpətāravə́l denominative, transitive ‏ تار په تار تارول

تار په تاربدل ☞ *denominative, intransitive* تارپتاردل tārpətāredál

تار په تار tārpətā́r 1 separately, apart 2.1 scattered, thrown about 2.2 dispersed, strewn about 2.3 wind blown (of hair); fluffed up (of feathers) 2.4 tossed, sprawled (of a sleeper, sick person) تار په تار کبدل، تاربه تارول ☞ تار کول

[تار په تار یې کړ :past] *denominative, transitive* 1 to scatter, throw about 2 to disperse 3 to dishevel (hair); fluff up (feathers)

[تار په تار شو :past] *denominative, intransitive* تارپتاردل tārpətāredál 1 to be scattered, be thrown about 2 to be dispersed 3 to go away, disperse, break up (e.g., from a meeting) 4 to be disheveled (of hair); be fluffed up (of feathers) 5 to toss about (of a sleeper or a sick person)

تارپیدو tārpedó *f. military* torpedo

تار په تار ☞ تارتار tārtā́r

تارخه tārkhə́ *m. Eastern plural of* تریخ

تارک tārík *Arabic* 1 leaving, abandoning 2 *m.* deserter

تارک الدنیا tārik-ud-dunjā 1 having turned away from this world 2 *m.* hermit, anchorite, recluse

تارکبن tārkákh *m.* spider

تارکول tārkól *m. plural* تار کولو سرک tarred road

تارکۍ tārkə́j *f.* small spider

تارگر tārgár *m. regional* telegraph

تارلومه tārlúma *f.* snares, traps

تار tārú [1] *m.* francolin (a kind of patridge) تور تارو francolin *idiom* تارو یو مرغه دئ چه چا ونیو د هغه دئ *saying* the one who is bold is the one who has eaten

تارو [2] tārú *m. Eastern* collar beam (part of a harness)

تار په تار ☞ تاروتار tārutā́r

تاروگی [1] tārugáj *m.* hawkmoth, sphinx

تاروگی [2] tārugə́j *feminine of* تارو [1]

[او یې تاراوه :past] *transitive* تاراول tārawál 1 to put in (e.g., to thread a needle) 2 تار په تارول

تارونار tārunā́r thin, frail تارونار کبدل a to be thin, be gaunt b *figurative* to wither, be consumed (from grief, bitterness)

تاروه tārvə́ *Eastern masculine plural of* ریو

تاری tāri *attributive* cotton تاري توکران cotton fabrics

تاریخ tārîkh *m. Arabic* [plural: تاریخونه tārikhúna *Arabic plural:* تواریخ tavārîkh] 1 date تاریخ په شلم د on the twentieth (day) په مقرر تاریخ on the appointed day 2 chronology تاریخ میلادي Christian chronology دهجرت تاریخ Muslim chronology 3 history د افغانستان تاریخ history of Afghanistan تاریخ پوهان historians

تاریخ پوه tārikhpóh *m.* historian

تاریخچه tārikhchá *f.* concise history

تاریخ دان، تاریخدان tārikhdā́n *m.* historian, history expert

تاریخ لیکونکی tārîkh likúnkaj ☞ تاریخ نگار tārikhnigā́r *m.* 1 historian 2 chronicler, annalist

تاریخ نگاري tārikhnigarî *f.* history

تاریخ لیکونکی ☞ تاریخ نویس tārikhnavîs *m.*

تاریخ وار tārikhvā́r on certain days

تاریخي tārikhí *Arabic* historical

تاریزي آلي tāríz *stringed instruments*

تاریک tārik 1 dark, somber 2 *m. history* Tarik (name given to Bajazid Ansari, founder of the Roshani sect, by his enemies)

تاریکه tārîka 1 *feminine singular of* تاریک [1] 2 *f.* darkness, gloom

تاریکي tārikí 1 *f.* darkness, gloom 2 *m. history* the Tariki (name for followers of the Roshani sect)

تاری ☞ تارین tārín

تاړ tāṛ *m.* 1 gang, band of robbers په کلي تاړ پربوت Bandits fell upon the village. 2 robbery تاړ کول to rob 3 boulder; large rock

تارا tāṛā́ تارا کول to plunder, rob

تاراک [1] tāṛā́k *m.* misfortune

تاراک [2] tāṛák *m.* ☞ تارا

تاړه [1] tāṛá ☞ تارا

تاړه [2] tāṛá unfortunate

تاړه [3] tāṛə́ *imperfect of* تړل

تاړي tāṛí *f. plural* hand-clapping, applause د تاړیو په پړکار کښې thunderous applause تاړي کول، تاړي وهل to clap, applaud

تاز tāz *m.* cicada

تازه tāzá *exclamation* really and truly

تازر tāzár *m.* bath towel

تازک tāzík *m.* ☞ تاجک

تازگي tāzagí *f.* 1 freshness 2 newness; novelty

تازه tāzá *indeclinable* 1 fresh تازه ډوډۍ fresh bread 2 new, fresh نن دا کتاب اوس تازه چاپ شوئ؟ څه تازه خبر دئ؟ What news is there today? This book is hot off the press. 3 glowing (of health) تازه په fresh and flowering 4 succulent, unwithered تازه کول a to freshen, renew b to change, replace c to wash up (hands and face before prayer) d to promote good health تازه کبدل a to be refreshed, be renewed b to be changed c to perform ablution (before prayer) d to be health, be in the pink e to liven up, cheer up په تازه ورحوکبني in recent days تازه اوسي Be well! Good luck! (God) bless you! تازه روح ورکول to inspire, rouse, hearten تازه مبلمه newborn

تازه دم tāzadám fresh, new تازه دم لښکرونه fresh troops, new units

تازه دماغ tāzadimā́gh *Eastern* satisfied احمد تازه دماغ شه Ahmed remained satisfied.

تازه والی ☞ تازه گي tāzavā́laj *m.* تازگي tāzagí *f.*

تازي tāzí *m.* borzoi (dog) تازي سپی male borzoi

تازیانه tāzijāná *f.* lash, whip تازیانه وهل to lash, whip

تازه ☞ تاگه tāgá *dialect*

تاس [1] tās *m.* copper bowl; basin

تاس [2] tās *m.* Tass (Russian news agency)

تاسپاني tāspáni *f. plural* card game

تاسف tāssúf *m. Arabic* regret تاسف کول، تاسف خورل to regret, deplore په باب تاسف ښکاره کول د. . . to express regrets in connection with something

تاسلج tāsláj *m.* basin, wash basin

تاسو tā́su tāso *Eastern* تاسي tāsi *Eastern* tāse *proper name second person plural* **1.1** you (used as subject of an action in all tenses and also in the imperative) تاسو چرته ځئ؟ Where are you going? **1.2** you (as object of an action in an ergative construction) تاسو چا ووهلاست Who beat you? **2** *oblique* **.1** you (as a direct object with transitive verb in the present or future tense) مونږ به کله تاسو وینو؟ When will we see you? **2.2** you (as subject of an action in an ergative construction) تاسو څه کول؟ What were you doing? **2.3** *with preposition, postpositions and adverbs* تاسو **a** behind تاسو باندي، په تاسو پسي، په تاسو باندي on you, at you **b** about you تاسو پوري to you, و تاسو ته، تاسو ته to you، له تاسو دپاره by you, from you تاسو نه، له تاسو څخه، له تاسو څخه *Eastern* for you تاسو سره *Eastern* with you تاسو غوندي *Eastern* like you, similar to you تاسو لاندي *Eastern* beneath you, under you **3** you (used as a polite form in place of ته) تاسو کله راغلي يئ؟ *Eastern* When did you arrive?

تأسيس tāsís *m. Arabic* [*plural:* تأسيسونه tāsisúna *Arabic plural:* تأسيسات tāsisā́t] **1** foundation, institution, creation, organization تأسيس کول، تأسيسول *compound* تأسيس *compound verb* ☞ **2** organization; institution **3** gathering, meeting

تأسيسات tāsisā́t *m. Arabic plural* **1** *from* تأسيس **2** institutions; facilities نظامي تأسيسات military sites

تأسيسول tāsisavə́l *denominative, transitive* [*past:* تأسيس يي کړ] **1** to found, create, organize **2** to build, erect

تأسيسيدل tāsisedə́l **.1** [*past:* تأسيس شو] *denominative, intransitive* **1.1** founded, be created, be organized **1.2** to be built, be erected لوی بندونه تأسيس شوي دي Several large dams have been built. **2** *m. plural* foundation, creation

تاش tāsh *regional* card game

تاش پتاش tāshpətā́sh scattered, sparse, thrown about

تاشقرغان tāshḳurghā́n *m.* Tashkurghan (city, also called Kholm)

تاشکند tāshkānd *m.* Tashkent (city)

تاشله tāshə́la wide and shallow (of dishes)

تابنه tāḳhá *f.* lisle thread

تاغار tāghár *m.* **1** clay trough, clay tub **2** kneading trough **3** bowl for fruit **4** lime pit

تاغارک tāghārák *m.* person with dropsy

تاغگه tā́ghga *f.* ☞ تاغه

تا غوندي tā́ ghunde *Eastern* ☞ تا 1 **3**

تاغه tā́gha *f.* hackberry, hackberry tree

تافته tāftá *f.* taffeta (material)

تاق tāḳ unpaired, odd

تاقچه tāḳchá *f.* ☞ تاخچه

تاقي tāḳí banded (of a bird)

تاک 1 ták *m.* steep incline, precipice *idiom* تاک له تاکه کول to deprive of shelter تاک له تاکه کېدل to be homeless; be without shelter

تاک 2 tāk *m.* [*plural:* تاکونه tākúna *Western plural:* تاکان tākā́n] grapevine

تاک 3 tāk **1** odd (-numbered) **2** solitary **3** odd (not paired)

تاکاو tākā́v *m.* cellar, basement

تاکتيک tāktík *m.* tactics

تاکداري tākdārí *f.* wine growing, viticulture

تاکره tākará **1** at your house, at your home **2** to your house, to your home

تاکستان tākistā́n *m.* vineyard

تاکيد ta'kíd *m.* tākíd *Arabic* affirmation; confirmation; emphasis تاکيد کول to affirm, confirm; emphasize

تاکيداً ta'kídán *Arabic* categorically, persistently

تاکيدي ta'kidí *Arabic* final, categorical, peremptory تاکيدي حکم peremptory decision

تال 1 tāl *m.* **1** copper basin **2** salt pit

تال 2 tāl hand-clapping (in time to music) تال کول to clap hands

تالا tālā́ **1** *f.* robbery **2** robbed, pillage, destroyed تالا کول *compound verb* to subject to robbery تالا کېدل *compound verb* to be robbed

تالاب tālā́b *m.* **1** pool, reservoir **2** pond

تالاترغا tālā-tārghā́ *f.* plunder, pillage

تالاتوب tālātób *m.* تالاتيا tālātjá *f.* robbery; plunder, pillage

تالار tālār *m.* large hall

تالا کوونکی tālā́ kavúnkaj *m.* robber

تالاگر tālāgár *m.* robber

تالان tālā́n *m.* robbery; burglary تالان جوړول to rob

تالاني tālāní amassed by robbery

تالاو tālā́v *m.* ☞ تالاب

تالاوالا tālāvālā́ *f.* تالاوالی tālāvālə́j *m.* تالاينه tālájə́na *f.* ☞ تالاتوب

تا لره tā́ lara *Eastern* ☞ تا 1 **3**

تاليکان tāliḳā́n *m. colloquial* تاليخان tālikhā́n *m. plural* Talikan (city)

تالگر tālgár *m.* composer

تالم tāllúm *m. Arabic* suffering, torment; grief

تالن tāllin *m.* Tallin (city)

تالنده tālə́nda *f.* thunder د تالندي ټکهار peals of thunder

تالو tālú *m.* palate تالو لوبدل to have a sore palate *idiom* د سفرکولو تالو ورته لوبدلئ دئ He very much wanted to complete the journey.

تاله 1 tālá *f.* **1** small stream, brook **2** narrow and shallow gully

تاله 2 tālá *f.* meadow grass

تا له 3 tā́ la *Eastern* ☞ تا 1 **3**

تاله 4 tālá *f.* ☞ تالا 1

تاله 5 *f.* Tala (populated place)

تاله 6 tālə́ *oblique singular of* تول 1

تاله و برفک tālá-u-barfák *m.* Tala barfaq (Bazar-e Taleh, region)

تالی 1 tālə́j *f. Eastern* round dish (of copper, etc.)

تالی 2 tālé ☞ طالع

تالی 3 tālé *plural of* تاله 1

تاليف tālíf *m. Arabic* [*plural:* تاليفونه tālifúna *Arabic plural:* تاليفات tálifā́t] **1** composition writing; compilation (of a textbook, etc.) **2** work (of literature), composition تاليف کول *compound verb* ☞ تاليفبدل ، تاليف کېدل *compound verb* ☞ تاليفول

تاليفول tālifavә́l *denominative, transitive* [*past:* تاليف يې کړ] to compose, write; compile (a textbook, etc.)

تاليفيدل tālifedә́l *denominative, intransitive* [*past:* تاليف شو] to be written, be composed; be compiled (of a textbook, etc.)

تاليم tālím *m.* ☞ تعليم

تالي من tālemә́n happy, fortunate

تام tām tāmm *Arabic* full; complete تام استقلال full independence

تاماس tāmā́s *m. proper name* Tohmas

تامبه [1] tāmbá *f.* copper سره تامبه red copper

امبه [2] *f.* tent

تامبر tāmber *m.* 1 large smooth rock 2 cliff

تامبړی tāmberә́j *f.* oar

تامل tāmmúl *m. Arabic* thought; consideration تامل کول a to think; think over, consider, weigh b to ponder, hesitate, linger

تامين tāmín ta'mín *m. Arabic* securing, providing (with); guarantee

تامينول tāminavә́l *denominative, transitive* [*past:* تامين يې کړ] to secure, provide (with); to guarantee

تامينيدل tāminedә́l *denominative, intransitive* [*past:* تامين شو] to be secured, be provided (with); be guaranteed

تان [1] tān *m.* piece, item (manufacture)

تان [2] tān *m.* 1 melody, harmony 2 creation, arrangement 3 *regional* disposition, temperature

تامبه tāmbá *f.* ☞ تامبه [1]

تاند tānd 1.1 fresh, young 1.2 green, turning green, sprouted (of grain) 1.3 fresh, cool ورمه تانده fresh breeze 2 *m.* growth (of plants)

تاندتيا tāndtjā́ *f.* freshness, greenness (of plants)

تاندلبان تاندلبند tāndləbā́n tāndləbánd died young, died prematurely تاندلبان کيدل to die young, die prematurely

تاندوبه tāndóba حُمکه تاندوبه river-irrigated land

تاندول tāndavә́l *denominative, transitive* [*past:* تاند يې کړ] to freshen, refresh (*literally and figuratively*)

تاندوله tāndóla *f. botany* goosefoot, orach

تانده tā́nda *f.* 1.1 green shoot 1.2 cow which has calved (for the first time) 2 *feminine singular of* تاند 1

تانسته tānistá *f.* 1 warp (of a fabric) 2 spider's web *idiom* تانسته جاروتل to take to going somewhere (e.g., going for a walk)

تانک tānk *m.* 1 tank 2 cistern 3 د تيلو تانک gasoline pump

تانکدار tānkdā́r *adjective* tank

تانک ماتوونکی tānk mātavúnkaj *military* anti-tank توپ تانک ماتوونکی anti-tank gun

تانکټ tānkét *m. military* light tank, tankette

تانگ tāng *m.* saddle-girth, belly-band

تانگانيا tānganikā́ *f.* Tanganyika

تانيث tānís *m. Arabic* 1 *grammar* feminine gender 2 *biology* female sex

تانه tāņá *f.* 1 outpost, security detachment (border, police) 2 *regional* police station *idiom* په چا باندي تانه کيدل *regional* to stay too long as someone's guest, wear out one's welcome

تانه دار tāņadā́r *m. regional* chief (of a border outpost or a police security detachment)

تاني دار tāņedā́r *m. regional* district police chief

تاو [1] tāv 1 *m.* .1 bend, twist; distortion تاو خورل a to bend, twist b to be dislocated 1.2 twisting, winding تاو اخيستل to rotate, spin, whirl تاو کول، تاوول *compound verb* ☞ *compound verb* a د تاو ورکول to walk around, circle څخه تاو کنبل دليري *compound verb* ☞ تاوبدل، a to bend, twist (something) b to wind, wrap c to spin, rotate, whirl (something) 2.1 *predicate* bent; distorted 2.2 rotated, twisted

تاو [2] tāv *m.* 1 heat, temperature زيد ډير تاو لري Zejid has a high temperature. هوا ډېره توده ده، له حُمکي تاو جگيږي It's very hot, the earth is blazing hot. 2 sunstroke تاو پرهوتئ affected by sunstroke 3 ardor, passion د تاوه ډک خيالات fervid imagination 4 anger 5 power, might *idiom* په تاو، په تاو سره quickly, soon تاو خورل to fade, wither away

تاوان tāvā́n 1 *m.* .1 harm, injury; loss مالي تاوان material damage چاته تاوان ورارول، و چا ته تاوان ورسول to inflict a loss on someone; cause someone harm تاوان کبدل to suffer injury, incur losses 1.2 compensation, indemnity د جنگ تاوان reparations تاوان اخيستل to receive compensation تاوان ورکول to indemnify, compensate 1.3 burdening تاوانول *compound verb* ☞ تاوان کول 2 *predicate* burdened (with something) *idiom* د حان تاوان risk

تاواني tāvāndzhә́n ☞ تاوان جن

تاوان رسوونکی tāvā́n rasavúnkaj harmful; injurious; unprofitable

تاوانول tāvānavә́l *denominative, transitive* [*past:* تاوان يې کړ] 1 to cause harm, inflict injury or loss 2 to burden 3 to spend, use up

تاوانه tāvā́na 1 *oblique singular of* تاوان 2 *feminine singular of* تاوان [2]

تاواني tāvāní 1 unprofitable 2 maimed, mutilated

تاوانيدل tāvānedә́l *denominative, intransitive* [*past:* تاوان شو] to be unprofitable

تاوتاو tāvtā́v crooked; twisting, winding

تاوته tāvtá *f.* ☞ تافته

تاوخانه tāvkhāná *f.* heating device placed under the floor

تاوده tāvdә́ *m. plural from* تاوده راتلل تود a to get excited, become impassioned b to take up some matter heatedly

تاوده ساره tāvdә́ sāṛә́ *m. plural* تاودی tāvdáj *m.* onion soup

تاور tāvár *m.* ☞ تاور

تاوراتاو tāvrātā́v crooked; winding تاوراتاو حرکت کول a to twist, wind; تاوراتاو کبدل to tack (a boat) *idiom* په درو کبني دا to twist, wind غبر تاوراتاو شو That shout echoed through the canyons.

تاووز tāvúz *m. proper noun* Tavuz

تاوس tāús *m.* peacock

تاوول tāvavә́l *Eastern* tāovúl *denominative, transitive* [*past:* تاويې کړ] 1 to bend, twist; distort 2 to wind, wrap (around) 3 to twirl, turn, whirl 4 to roll (up), coil to roll down 5 to wrap (up) 6 to entwine 7 to wind (up) in quantity

تاوون tāvún *m.* تاوونی tāvunáj *m.* plague; widespread death

تاوه ‫¹‬ tāvá *f.* **1** small barrier (to keep moisture in a field) **2** small parcel of land

تاوه ‫²‬ tāvá ☞ تبی

تاوی ‫¹‬ tāváj *m.* **1** screwdriver **2** screw

تاوپ ‫²‬ tāvé ☞ تابع

تاوپ ‫³‬ tāvé *colloquial for* تا ويل

تاويتک tāviták *m.* golden amulet, talisman

تاوېدل tāvedə́l *denominative, intransitive* [*past:* تاو شو] **1** to bend, twist; be distorted **2** to turn to the side (of a car, a road) **3** to be wounded, be wrapped **4** to rotate, wind, circle around **5** to be rolled (up) **6** to be wrapped up **7** to be entwined, twine oneself round **8** to be wound up (in quantity) **9** to hover (e.g., of smoke) **10** to turn toward someone

تاوېده tāvedə́ *m. plural action noun from* تاوېدل

تاويز tāvíz *m.* تعويذ

تاويل ‫¹‬ tāvíl *m.* ta'víl *Arabic plural* [*plural:* تاويلونه tāvilúna *plural:* تاويلات tāvilát] explanation, interpretation, commentary تاويل کول false rumors to explain, interpret, clarify کاربه تاويلات، بد تاويلات دا خبره دوه تاويله لري That can be taken two ways.

تاويل ‫²‬ tāvíl *m.* ☞ تحويل

تاويلدار tāvildár *m.* ☞ تحويلدار

تاويلول tāvilavə́l *intransitive* ☞ تحويلول

تاه ‫²‬ tāh *f.* ☞ تا

تاهر tāhár **1** *m. plural* Takha (Tahar) tribe **2** *m.* Takhar (person)

تائب tāíb *Arabic* repenting, penitent, repentant

تايگا tājgá *f.* taiga

تايوان tājván *m.* Taiwan

تايه tājá *f.* ☞ تهيه

تائد tāíd *m.* تاييد tājíd *m. Arabic* **1** confirmation, corroboration **2** strengthening; support د هغه په تائيد with his support تائيد کول *compound verb* ☞ تائيدول، تائيدول کېدل *compound verb* **3** thesis

تائيدول tāidavə́l *denominative, transitive* [*past:* تائيد يې کړ] **1** to confirm, corroborate **2** to support, lend support

تائيدي tāidí **1** confirming, corroborating **2** providing support, supporting

تائيدېدل tajdedə́l *denominative, intransitive* [*past:* تائيد شو] **1** to be confirmed, be corroborated **2** to be supported

تائيلبند tāiléṇḍ *m.* ☞ تائيلبند

تب tab *m.* **1** antidote **2** poultices **3** grinding; massage **4** liquid ointment

تبا təbấ *colloquial for* ته به وايی

تبادلوي tabādulaví *economics* exchange تبادلوي ارزش exchange value

تبادله tabādulá *f. Arabic* exchange د تبادلې په ډول on the basis of exchange د افکارو تبادله an exchange of opinions د کتابو تبادله exchange of books جنس په جنس تبادله barter تجارتي تبادله trade د چا سره تبادله کول *compound verb* to exchange for something تبادله کول to trade with someone

تبار tabār *m.* family, clan, trade

تبارز tabārúz *m. Arabic* **1** clearing up; clearness, clarity **2** appearance, origin, beginning

تباشير tabāshír *m.* chalk

تباه tabāh perished, destroyed تباه کول to destroy تباه کېدل to be perished; be destroyed

تباه حال tabāhhál annihilated; destroyed

تباه کونکی tabāhkún ☞ تباه کونکی tabāh kavúnkaj destructive, ruinous; pernicious

تباهي tabāhí *f.* destruction; ruin; death

تباين tabājún *m. Arabic* **1** antagonism; contradiction **2** opposition; antithesis

تبت tibát *m.* **1** Tibet; the Tibetan region **2** angora wool

تبتي tibatí **1** Tibetan **2.1** *m.* Tibetan, inhabitant of Tibet **2.2** *f.* the Tibetan language

تبجن tabdzhán someone sick with fever

تبحر tabahhúr *Arabic* in-depth knowledge of something علمي تبحر erudition

تبخ tabáx *m.* ☞ تبق

تبخک tabakhə́k *m.* black-throated thrush

تبخی ‫¹‬ tabəkháj *m.* tabakháj **1** iron sheet (for baking bread) **2** *anatomy* pelvis

تبخی ‫²‬ tabakhə́j *f.* raven

تبخير tabkhír *m. Arabic* **1** steaming, evaporating **2** smoking, fumigating

تبدل tabaddúl *m. Arabic* [*plural:* تبدلونه tabaddulúna *Arabic plural:* تبدلات tabaddulát] change, alteration

تبديل tabdíl *m. Arabic* **1** change, substitution **2** change, transformation په يو شي تبديل ميندل to turn into something **3** move, transfer (in one's job)

تبديلاً tabdílán *Arabic* on the basis of a transfer (in one's job)

تبديلول tabdilavə́l *denominative, transitive* [*past:* تبديل يې کړ] **1** to change, substitute, replace **2** to change, transform, alter **3** to move, transfer

تبديلي tabdilí *f.* **1** change, substitution, replacement **2** change, transformation **3** move, transfer (in one's work)

تبديلېدل tabdiledə́l *denominative, intransitive* [*past:* تبديل شو] **1** to be changed, be replaced **2** to be changed, be transformed **3** to be moved, be transferred (in one's work)

تبذير tabzír *m. Arabic* squandering, wastefulness په تبذير سره بندول to squander, spend senselessly

تبر ‫¹‬ təbə́r *m.* tabár [*plural:* تبرونه təbərúna *plural:* tabarúna *Western plural:* تبران teberán *plural:* tabarán] axe *idiom* ترتبر لاستي درنول to incur expenses out of proportion with one's income

تبر ‫²‬ təbə́r pocket (in the top of a dress)

تبرا tabarrā́ *f. Arabic* forgiveness, pardon

تبرزين tabarzín *m. history* halberd; pole-axe

تبرع tabarró' *f. Arabic m.* [*plural:* تبرعات tabarro'ất] gift; giving د تبرع په توګه in the form of a gift

تبرغان tabarghán *m.* marmot

تبرک[1] tabarrúk *m. Arabic religion* asking a blessing

تبرک[2] təbərák *m.* 1 ☞ اچار 2 pillar of the water-lifting wheel

تبرگای təbərgáj *m.* small axe, hatchet

تبری[1] turbáj *m.* notch on an arrow

تبری[2] tabarrā *f. Arabic* ☞ تبرا

تبریز tabríz *m.* Tabriz (city)

تبریک tabrík *m. Arabic* [*plural:* تبریکونه tabrikúna *Arabic plural:* تبریکات tabrikát] greeting, congratulation و چا ته د جشن په مناسبت تبریک ویل to greet someone with a holiday wish و چا ته د نوي کال تبریک ویل to wish (someone) a "Happy New Year" تا ته تبریک وایم I congratulate you. تبریک استول، تبریک لیرل to send greetings

تبریکي tabrikí *Arabic* of or related to a greeting تبریکي پیغام message of greeting, message of congratulation تبریکیه عریضه address (written greeting)

تبسم tabassúm *m. Arabic* smile تبسم کول to smile

تبصره tabsirá *f. Arabic* note, comment; explanation, commentary پر یو شي تبصره کول، د یو شي له خصوصه تبصره کول to make a note explaining something; clarify, comment on something لکه چه د خارجي مطبوعاتو تبصره کړي ده judging by commentaries in the foreign press تبصره نه کول to refrain from comment

تبع tabá' *m. Arabic* [*plural:* اتباع atbā'] follower; supporter, adherent دی د ده تبع دئ He is his supporter. تبع تابعین *religion* friends of the followers of Mohammed

تبعه taba'á *m. Arabic plural from* تابع[2]

تبعید tab'íd *m. Arabic* exile تبعید کول *compound verb* to exile تبعید کېدل *compound verb* to be exiled

تبعیدگاه tab'idgáh *m.* place of exile

تبعیض tab'íz *m. Arabic* discrimination نژادي تبعیض racial discrimination

تبق tabák *m.* ☞ تبک tabak *m. veterinary* foot-and-mouth disease

تبکی tubakáj *f.* ☞ تبکی

تبل[1] tabál *transitive* [*past:* و یې تابه] 1 to make poultices 2 to massage (with ointment)

تبل[2] tabál *m.* 1 embarrassment, confusion; shame تبل خورل to be embarrassed; be ashamed 2 fear, apprehension تبل کول to fear, be afraid of

تبلول tabálavál *transitive* [*past:* و یې تبلاوه] to embarrass; to shame

تبلی tabláj *f.* tambourine

تبلېدل tabáledál *intransitive* [*past:* و تبلېده] to be embarrassed; be ashamed

تبلیغ tablígh *m. Arabic* [*plural:* تبلیغونه tablighúna *Arabic plural:* تبلیغات tablighát] 1 propaganda 2 announcement, report; notification تبلیغ کول a to propagandize b to announce, report something; notify about something تبلیغ کول *compound verb* ☞ تبلیغېدل، تبلیغول *compound verb* ☞ تبلیغ کېدل،

تبلیغاتي tablighātí ☞ تبلیغي

تبلیغچي tablighchí *m.* propagandist

تبلیغول tablighavál *denominative, transitive* [*past:* تبلیغ یې کړ] to announce something, report something; to notify about something

تبلیغي tablighí propagandistic تبلیغي کوشش کول to propagandize, conduct a propaganda campaign

تبلیغېدل tablighedál *denominative, intransitive* [*past:* تبلیغ شو] to be announced, be reported

تبنه tabána *f.* 1 application of poultices 2 massage (with ointment)

تبنی[1] tabánaj *m.* flat fragment of rock

تبنی[2] tubnáj *f.* board (for dough)

تبور tabúr *m.* brassiere

تبون tabún *m.* compensation for being wounded or crippled (provided according to the adat, traditional law of an Islamic area)

تبه tába *f.* fever زه تبي نیولئ یم، په ما تبي راغلي ده I have a fever. I'm sick with a fever. سه یکه برائي مي تبه وه Yesterday I was feverish. پخه تبه، ژړي تبه، زبری تبه intermittent fever وارېره تبه، درېمه تبه د ژري تبي میاشي malaria-carrying د پخي تبي میاشي mosquito, anopheles سره تبه، سره لري تبه shivering, chills شپږره تبه، typhus تبي حرکات *idiom* وچکی تبه، اوچکی تبه، لو تبه، لویه تبه feverish movements

تبه بربنډ təbabrékh *m.* inflammation of the lungs

تبی[1] təbáj tubáj *m.* 1 pouring hot oil (over food) 2 preparation of a sauce تبی کول a to pour hot oil (over food) b to prepare a sauce 3 ☞ تبی[2]

تبی[2] tabáj *f.* clay frying pan د تبی ډوډی، تبی ډوډی bread baked on a clay frying pan *idiom* تبی توده! *children's speech* It's hot! (said when an object being sought is nearby)

تپ[1] tap *m.* crowd, assemblage, mob

تپ[2] təp *m. Western* 1 birthmark تور تپ birthmark 2 wart

تپ[3] tap perished; destroyed تپ کبدل ☞ تپبدل، تپ کول ☞ تپول[1]

تپ[4] tap *exclamation* Go get him! (cry to dogs on a hunt when closing in on a wild animal)

تپ[5] tap *combining form with adjectives which indicate color* تپ تور absolutely black, pitch black تپه تیاره outer darkness, pitch darkness

تپ[6] tap ☞ تاپ

تپا təpá *f.* agitation, excitement; uneasiness, disturbance

تپاس tapás *m.* 1 searches, inquiries 2 trying تپاس کول a to seek, search for b to try

تپاق tapák *m.* ☞ تپاک[3]

تپاک tapák *m.* 1 zeal, fervor, diligence 2 mad, passionate love 3 greed, avidity تپاک یې نه ماتبري His greed know no limits. 4 agitation, excitement; unrest, disturbance تپاک وهل، تپاک اخیستل to be filled with zeal; try very hard b to love madly, love passionately c to be greedy d to be agitated, upset تپاک لرل a to love someone b to respect someone *idiom* په خورا تپاک ځغستل race, run swiftly چا ته ډېر په تپاک لاس ورکول to shake someone's hand firmly

تپال tapál *m.* clay (for plastering walls)

تپاند[1] tapánd *m.* trowel (mason's, plasterer's tool)

تپاند tapā́nd **1** blazing **2** excited, upset

تپانده tapā́nda *f.* ☞ تپاند[1]

تپانده tapā́nda *feminine singular of* تپاند[2]

تپ تپ taptáp *exclamation* Go get him! (hunter's cry to his dog at the lair of a wild animal)

تپتپنۍ təptəpanáj *m.* popgun (children's toy)

تپرکی tapórkaj *m.* scab, scabs

تپړا taprā́ *f.* taparā́ burnisher (potter's tool)

تپک tapák *m.* **1** beating of a drum, drumbeat **2** blow to the back of the head

تپل tapól *transitive* [*past:* و يې تاپه] **1** to mold, form (from clay, etc.) **2** to coat (with) besmear **3** to glue (on), glue together **4** to accumulate, amass; collect, gather **5** to thrust (something on someone) against his will پر چا يوه معاهده تپل to force an agreement on someone

تپند təpánd greedy

تپندی tapəndáj *m.* ☞ تپاند[1]

تپنه tapóna *f. action noun from* تپل

تپڼا tapṇā́ *f.* tapanā ☞ تپړا

تپو tpo *exclamation* whoa (or similar to stop horses)

تپور tapór *m.* **1** brassiere **2** embroidered sleeveless blouse (worn by young women)

تپوس təpós *m.* tapús *Eastern* tapaús *Eastern* question له چا نه تپوس کول to ask someone د چا تپوس کول to ask after, inquire about someone

تپول təpavól[1] *transitive* [*past:* و يې تپاوه] to upset, disturb

تپول tapavól[2] *denominative, transitive* [*past:* تپ يې کړ] to destroy, ruin, annihilate

تپول tapavól[3] *denominative, transitive* [*past:* تپ يې کړ] to urge on, drive (a dog into the lair of a wild animal)

تپه təpá[1] *f.* **1** mountain, hill, mound; high place **2** family, part of a tribe **3** region, province **4** *used for designation of populated places* قره تپه Karatapa

تپه tápa[2] *feminine singular of* تپ[3, 5]

تپه زار tapazā́r *m.* mountainous, hilly locality

تپی tapáj[1] *m.* ☞ تپ[2]

تپی tapáj[2] *f.* pressed dung (used as fuel)

تپي tapí[3] *present tense of* تپل

تپېدل tapedól[1] *denominative, intransitive* [*past:* تپ شو] **1** to perish, die **2** to be destroyed

تپېدل tapedól[2] *intransitive* [*past:* وتپېده] to beat, flutter (of the heart)

تت tət[1] **1** thick, compact; dense (of crops) د تته اورېځ thick clouds غنم تت فصلونه dense sowing of wheat **2** with strong roots; stocky

تت tət[2] **1** faint, weak تته رڼا faint light **2** muffled (of a sound); inaudible, poorly heard **3** dark (of a color) **4** pale (of the lips) **5** *figurative* faint (of a hope) *idiom* تت ژوند a cheerless life, a drab existence

تت tət[3] تت اوبت وتل **1** to lose one's head; become confused or embarrassed **1** to freeze, be rooted to the ground

تتبع tatabbó' *f. Arabic m.* [*plural:* تتبعات tatabbo'ắt] research; inquiry; study (of some problem) تتبعات کول to engage in research; to research, investigate, study (some problem)

تتر tatár *m. proper noun* Tatar

تتری tatráj *m.* tataráj porphyry (rock)

تتری tətṛáj tətaṛáj tutṛáj tətaṛáj mumbling, speaking incomprehensibly

تتمه tatimmá *f. Arabic* supplement; enclosure, appendix

تت والی، tətvā́laj[1] *m.* **1** thickness; denseness (of sowing) **2** stockiness; rootiness

تت والی، tətvā́laj[2] *m.* **1** faintness, weakness (of light) **2** incomprehensibility, unclearness (of a sound)

تتول tətavól[1] *denominative, transitive* [*past:* تت يې کړ] to make compact, compact, thicken, make dense

تتول tətavól[2] *denominative, transitive* [*past:* تت يې کړ] **1** to make faint, weak (of light); to lower, dim (a light) **2** to muffle, lower, turn down (a sound; e.g., in a receiver)

تتوه tatáva *f.* turtledove

تته tắta[1] *feminine singular of* تت[1, 2]

تته tətá[2] ☞ توری[1]

تتي téti[1] *feminine plural of* تت[1, 2]

تتی tatáj[2] *f.* **1** dewlap (of a camel) **2** front, belly (of reptiles) *idiom* څوک تر تتی لاندي کول to grieve تتی په مڅکه پوري منښلول maliciously to avenge someone

تتی tatáj[3] *f.* wooden measure for grain

تتېدل tətedól[1] *denominative, intransitive* [*past:* تت شو] **1** to be compact, be thick, be dense; thicken **2** to be stocky; be strong-rooted

تتېدل tətedól[2] *denominative, intransitive* [*past:* تت شو] **1** to be faint, be weak; grow dim د سترگو رڼا مي تته شوه My eyesight has dimmed. **2** to be muffled, be incomprehensible (of a sound) **3** *figurative* to be erased (from the memory)

تثبيت tasbít *m. Arabic* **1** confirmation **2** establishment تثبيت کول *compound verb* ☞ تثبيتول تثبيتېدل *compound verb* ☞ تثبيت کېدل

تثبيتول tasbitavól *denominative, transitive* [*past:* تثبيت يې کړ] **1** to confirm **2** to establish **3** to make firm, make steady

تثبيتېدل tasbitedól *denominative, intransitive* [*past:* تثبيت شو] **1** to be confirmed دا خبره تثبيت شوه This report has been confirmed. **2** to be established

تجار tudzhdzhā́r *m. Arabic masculine plural of* تاجر

تجاران tudzhdzhārā́n *m. second plural of* تاجر

تجارب tadzhāríb *m. Arabic plural of* تجربه

تجارت tidzhārát *m. Arabic* trade, commerce خارجي تجارت foreign trade د خارجي تجارت وزارت، د خارجه، داخلي تجارت internal trade تجارت وزارت ministry of foreign trade تجارت کول to trade

تجارت پيشه tidzhāratpewá trader, person occupied in trade

تجارتخای tidzhāpatdzāj *m.* store

تجارتخانه tidzhāratkhāná *f.* trading company, trading house

تجارتي tidzhāratí *Arabic adjective* trade, commercial تجارتي معاهده trade agreement, commercial contract تجارتي معامله trade operation, business deal

تجانس tadzhānús *m. Arabic* uniformity, homogeneity

تجاوز tadzhāvúz *m. Arabic* [*plural:* تجاوزونه tadzhāvuzúna *Arabic plural:* تجاوزات tadzhāvuzắt] 1 encroachment, infringement 2 border violation, intrusion, aggression 3 excess, exceeding (e.g., exceeding one's authority) له اختیاراتو څخه تجاوز exceeding one's commission د نورو پر تجاوز کول *a* to encroach (upon) infringe د حقوقو تجاوز کول to encroach upon another's rights *b* to violate borders; invade, commit aggression *c* to exceed *d* to commit a misdemeanor

تجاوزات tadzhāvuzắt *m. Arabic plural* 1 *from* تجاوز 2 misdemeanors; violations

تجاوزکارانه tadzhāvuzkārāná ☞ تجاوزي

تجاوزکوونکی tadzhavúz kavúnkaj *m.* aggressor

تجاوزي tadzhāvuzí 1 encroaching (upon something) 2 violating borders; aggressive 3 exceeding (e.g., authority)

تجاویز tadzhāvíz *m. Arabic plural from* تجویز

تجاهل tadzhāhúl *m. Arabic bookish* تجاهل کول to feign ignorance, pretend not to know

تجدد tadzhaddúd *m. Arabic* 1 renewal, renovation 2 novelty, newness

تجددپسندي tadzhaddudpasandí *f.* love for everything new

تجدید tadzhdíd *m. Arabic* 1 renewal, resumption (e.g., of negotiations) 2 rebirth, revival

تجدیدنظر tadzhid-i-nasár *m.* revision, review (e.g., of a court decision)

تجدیدول tadzhdidavól *denominative, transitive* [*past:* تجدید یې کړ] 1 to resume (e.g., negotiations) 2 to revive

تجدیدېدل tadzhdidedól *denominative, intransitive* [*past:* تجدید شو] 1 to be resumed (e.g., negotiations) 2 to be revived, to revive

تجربوي tadzhribaví ☞ تجربي

تجربه tadzhribá *f. Arabic* [*plural:* تجربي tadzhribé *Arabic m. plural:* تجارب tadzhāríb] 1 experiment, test تجربه کول *a* to perform an experiment, experiment *b compound verb* to check, test verify تجربه کېدل *compound verb* to be checked, be tested 2 experience, skill دا په تجربه رسېدلې ده چه ... It has been shown in practice that ... د ډېرو شیانو تجربه لرل to have great experience د تجربي څخه وتل *a* to pass through a test *b* to gain experience, acquire skill

تجربه کار tadzhribakắr experienced تجربه کار سړی experienced person

تجربه کاري tadzhribakārí *f.* experience

تجربه گا tadzhribagắ *f.* تجربه گاه tadzhribagáh *m.* experimental station, testing station

تجربي tadzhribí experimental په تجربي توگه، په تجربي ډول as an experiment

تجرید tadzhríd *m. Arabic* 1 isolation; seclusion 2 abstraction; abstracting

تجریدول tadzhridavól *denominative, transitive* [*past:* تجرید یې کړ] 1 to isolate, separate 2 to abstract

تجریدي tadzhridí 1 isolated; secluded 2 abstracted

تجریدېدل tadzhridedól *denominative, intransitive* [*past:* تجرید شو] 1 to be isolated, be separated 2 to be abstracted

تجزیه tadzhzijá *f. Arabic* 1 analysis; breakdown (into component parts) کیمیاوي تجزیه chemical analysis 2 division (into parts) تجزیه کول *compound verb a* to analyze to break down (into component parts) tadzhzijá *f.* b to divide (into parts) تجزیه کېدل *compound verb a* to be subjected to analysis; be broken down (into component parts) *b* to be divided (into parts) *c* to fall apart, disintegrate

تجزیه ئی tadzhzijádzáj *m.* تجزیه خانه tadzhzijakhāná *f.* laboratory

تجسس tadzhassús *m. Arabic* 1 investigation; search; prospecting 2 *military* conducting reconnaissance 3 tracking, shadowing 4 secret service, spying, espionage تجسس کول *a* to investigate; look for, search for; prospect for *b military* to conduct reconnaissance *c* to track, follow, spy upon

تجسم tadzhassúm *m. Arabic* embodiment, personification تجسم پیداکول to be embodied, be personified

تجلي tadzhallí *f. Arabic* 1 shine, brightness; radiance; sparkling 2 *figurative* glory

تجمع tadzhammó' *f. Arabic* accumulation, gathering, collection; concentration تجمع کول to amass, gather; concentrate; accumulate

تجمل tadzhammúl *m. Arabic* luxury, elegance

تجن tadzhán *m.* Tedzhen River (in Russia; in Afghanistan and Iran called the Harirud River)

تجویز tadzhvíz *m. Arabic* [*plural:* تجویزونه tadzhvizúna *Arabic plural:* تجاویز tadzhāvíz] 1 proposal تجویز وړاندي کول to introduce a proposal 2 decision, decree; resolution زیر تجویز *zír-i regional law* one awaiting a decision تجویز کول to decide, decree

تجهیز tadzhhíz *m. Arabic* [*plural:* تجهیزونه tadzhhizúna *Arabic plural:* تجهیزات tadzhhizắt] equipment; arms; ammunition د تجهیزاتو کارخانه munition factory تجهیز کول *compound verb* to equip, arm

تچ ¹ tich *m.* sheath (of a sword, dagger)

تچ ² təch *dialect* ☞ تش

تحت taht *Arabic* 1 *m.* bottom, lower part of something 2 *preposition* lower (than something); under (something) تحت صفر táht-i below zero (of temperature) 3 *forms part of Arabic words* تحت البحري *a* underwater *b* submarine

تحت الارضي taht-ul-arzí *Arabic* underground تحت الارضي مواد depths (of the earth)

تحت البحري taht-ul-bahrí *Arabic* 1 underwater 2 *f.* submarine

تحت الحمایگي taht-ul-himājagí *f.* protectorate

تحت الحمایه taht-ul-himājá mandated, under protection, under wardship

تحتانی tahtāní *Arabic* lower

تحدید tahdíd *m. Arabic* 1 limitation (e.g., in one's rights) 2 establishment, determination (of something) 3 demarcation (of borders)

تحدیدول tahdidavól *denominative, transitive* [*past:* تحدید یې کړ] 1 to limit (e.g., in rights) 2 to establish, determine something 3 to demarcate (borders)

تحدیدیدل tahdidedól *denominative, intransitive* [*past:* تحدید شو] 1 to be limited (e.g., in rights) 2 to be established, be determined 3 to be demarcated

تحریر tahrír *m. Arabic* [*plural:* تحریرونه tahrirúna *Arabic plural:* تحریرات tahrirā́t] 1 writing, written account تحریر کول to write down, jot down تحریر کېدل to be written (down) 2 language, style (of a writer)

تحریراً tahrírán *Arabic* in writing, in written form

تحریرات tahrirā́t *m. plural Arabic* 1 *from* تحریر 2 official papers; correspondence; paperwork (in business) د تحریراتو دائره office تحریراتو مدیر office chief, boss

تحریری tahrirí written په تحریری ډول in written form, in writing

تحریص tahrís *m. Arabic* inducement; incentive; instigation, incitement د کلمات تحریص *idiom grammar* hortatory particles

تحریف tahríf *m. Arabic* distortion

تحریک tahrík *m. Arabic* [*plural:* تحریکونه tahrikúna *Arabic plural:* تحریکات tahrikā́t] 1 putting into motion 2 movement (political, religious, etc.) 3 urging; incitement چا ته تحریک ورکول to urge someone, force someone; incite someone 4 stimulus

تحریکول tahrikavól *denominative, transitive* [*past:* تحریک یې کړ] to urge, motivate; incite د ... مرګ ته تحریکول to incite to murder

تحریم tahrím *m. Arabic* prohibition

تحسر tahassúr *m. Arabic* grief, affliction

تحسین tahsín *m. Arabic* approval; praise تحسین کول to approve; praise چاته آفرین او تحسین ویل to praise someone

تحسین‌نامه tahsinnāmá *f.* certificate of merit

تحشید tahshíd *m. Arabic military* assembly (of troops)

تحصیل tahsíl *m. Arabic* 1 receipt, acquisition د اطلاعاتو تحصیل receipt of information 2 collection, levying (of a tax, etc.) 3 study, learning; education د تحصیل سامان educational supplies; textbooks تحصیل کول to receive an education 4 *regional* section, region (tax collection)

تحصیلدار tahsildā́r *m.* 1 *regional* head of a region 2 tax collector

تحصیلداري tahsildārí *f.* 1 position as a tax collector 2 collection of taxes

تحصیلول tahsilavól *denominative, transitive* [*past:* تحصیل یې کړ] to levy (a tax); receive, recover (a debt)

تحصیلي tahsilí *adjective* educational, school; training تحصیلي کال school year

تحصیلیدل tahsiledól *denominative, intransitive* [*past:* تحصیل شو] to be collected (of a tax); be recovered (of a debt)

تحفظ tahaffúz *m. Arabic* 1 maintaining (a discipline) 2 keeping (a secret) 3 defense, safeguard 4 caution; precaution

تحفه tuhfá *Arabic* 1 *f.* gift, present چا ته تحفه ورکول *a* to give someone a present or tribute *b* to treat someone 2.1 rare, uncommon 2.2 beautiful, excellent

تحقق tahaḳúḳ *m. Arabic* confirmation of something, certification of something

تحقیر tahḳír *m. Arabic* contempt; scorn; degradation; humiliation تحقیر کول *compound verb* ☞ تحقیرول

تحقیرول tahḳiravól *denominative, transitive* [*past:* تحقیر یې کړ] to despise; scorn; humiliate; insult

تحقیق tahḳíḳ *Arabic* 1 *m.* [*plural:* تحقیقونه tahḳiḳúna *Arabic plural:* تحقیقات tahḳiḳā́t] .1 investigation, legal inquiry; inquest 1.2 check, verification 1.3 study, research تحقیق کول *a* to investigate, conduct an inquiry *b* to check out, verify *c* to study, perform research 2 *attributive* true, correct; verified 3 .1 truly, correctly 3.2 really

تحقیقاتي tahḳiḳā́tí تحقیقي tahḳiḳí 1 investigative 2 of or relating to an inquiry 3 verified, checked

تحکیم tahím *m.* [*plural:* تحکیمونه tahkimúha *plural:* tahkimúha *Arabic plural:* تحکیمات tahkimā́t] strengthening, reinforcing, making firm

تحلیل tahlíl *m. Arabic* [*plural:* تحلیلونه tahlilúna *Arabic plural:* تحلیلات tahlilā́t] 1 analysis; parsing د وینو تحلیل analysis of blood د جملې تحلیل parsing of a sentence 2 *chemistry* solution تحلیل کول *compound verb* ☞ تحلیلول، تحلیل کېدل *compound verb*

تحلیلول tahlilavól *denominative, transitive* [*past:* تحلیل یې کړ] 1 to make analysis (e.g., of blood) 2 to analyze, investigate, look into; to parse 3 to dissolve (something)

تحلیلیدل tahliledól *denominative, intransitive* [*past:* تحلیل شو] 1 to have completed an analysis (e.g., of blood) 2 to be analyzed; be parsed 3 to be dissolved

تحمل tahammúl *m. Arabic* 1 patience, endurance تحمل کول *compound verb* to be patient; endure په مشکلاتو تحمل کول to endure difficulties د تحمل نه کار اخیستل to show endurance 2 submissive, obedience, humility

تحمیل tahmíl *m.* 1 burdening 2 imposition (e.g., of an agreement)

تحمیلول tahmilavól *denominative, transitive* [*past:* تحمیل یې کړ] 1 to burden, load, make difficult 2 to impose جبراً تحمیلول to impose by force 3 to lay on

تحمیلي tahmilí imposed (e.g., of an agreement) تحمیلي معاهده an agreement imposed by force

تحول tahavvúl *m. Arabic* [*plural:* تحولونه tahavvulúna *Arabic plural:* تحولات tahavvulā́t] 1 change, transformation, evolution یو شي ته تحول ورکول to change something, transform something 2 turning point, transition په یو شي سره تحول میندل to turn into something; be replaced by something

تحولول tahavvulavól *denominative, transitive* [*past:* تحول یې کړ] 1 to change, transform 2 to re-work, process (e.g., raw materials)

تحویل tahvíl *m.* tāvíl *Arabic* 1 transfer for safekeeping, handing over for safekeeping 2 what has been hand over for safekeeping; pawning, mortgaging 3 change, transfer (to another system of measurement, etc.)

تحویلخانه tahvilkhāná *f.* storage, storage room; warehouse

تحویلدار tahvildár *m.* 1 keeper, custodian 2 manager of a warehouse or storage facility جنسي تحویلدار manager of a storage warehouse or depot 3 *military* quartermaster 4 cashier; paymaster نقدي تحویلدار cashier

تحویلول tahvilavól *denominative, transitive* [*past:* تحویل یې کړ] 1 to transfer, submit for storage 2 to change, transform 3 to change, transfer (to another system of measurement, etc.)

تحویلیدل tahvoledól *denominative, intransitive* [*past:* تحویل شو] 1 to be transferred for storage be given over for storage 2 to be changed, be transformed 3 to be changed, be transfered (to another system of measurement, etc.)

تحیات tahiját *m.* *Arabic* [*plural:* تحیات tahiját] greeting پر چا تحیات ویل to greet someone

تخار tohkár *m.* takhár ☞ تخارستان د تخار ولایت Takhar Province

تخارستان tokháristán *m.* Takharistan (region in northeastern Afghanistan in former times)

تخالف takhālúf *m.* *Arabic* 1 difference, distinction 2 contradiction

تخت takht *m.* throne په تخت کښېنستل to ascend to the throne یا تخت یا تخته *saying* either the throne or the slab

تخت روان tákht-i-raván *m.* sedan chair

تختک takhták *m.* small board

تخت گاه takhtgáh *m.* ☞ پایتخت

تخت نشین takhtnishín *m.* king

تخت نشیني takhtnishiní *f.* accession to the throne; succesion to the throne

تخته takhtá 1 *f.* 1.1 blackboard پر تخته لیکل to write on the board 1.2 sheet (of paper) 1.3 slab (e.g., of a marble) 1.4 *technology* shield 1.5 piece (used in counting rugs, hides, sheets, etc.) 2.1 densely woven (of a fabric) 2.2 densely packed تخته کول *compound verb* 2.2 a to level, flatten b to weave densely c to cram in, stuff

تخته بندي takhtabandí *f.* veneering with boards; lining, facing

تخته پاک takhtapák *m.* rag (for wiping the school blackboard)

تخته پوښ takhtapókh *m.* 1 wooden flooring, planking 2 platform

تخته سنگ takhtasáng *m.* 1 flagstone (shale) 2 stone stab

تخته نرد takhtanárd *m.* game of cards

تخته یي کمپیوتر tákhtají kampjūṭór *m.* *computer science* table PC, desktop

تختی takhtój *f.* 1 small board 2 small tabular listing; small plate with inscription

تخځ takhódz *f.* ☞ تخز

تخرگ tkharg *m.* arm-pit د هغه ښه تخرگونه لانده سوه He was greatly shamed. He was embarrased. تخرگ ته کول to take without permission; take with oneself

تخرگی tkhərgáj *m.* gusset (in shirt)

تخریب takhríb *m.* *Arabic* 1 destruction د تخریب بم high-explosive bomb د تخریب تجزئي *biology* products of decomposition 2 sabotage, wrecking 3 spoilage, breakage

تخریبي takhribí *adjective* of a wrecker, of a saboteur تخریبي فعالیت wrecking activity, sabotage

تخز təkhóz *f.* ☞ ترښخ

تخصص takhassús *m.* *Arabic* 1 specialization 2 specialty لرل a to have a specialization b to be a specialist, have a specialty

تخصصي takhassusí special; specialized

تخصیص takhsís *m.* *Arabic* [*plural:* تخصیصونه takhsisúna *Arabic plural:* تخصیصات takhsisát] 1 purpose, earmarking, setting apart (for something); assignment (under something) 2 assignation, appropriation, allocation تخصیص کول *compound verb* تخصیص میندل *compound verb* تخصیص کېدل، تخصیصول ورکول ☞ تخصیصېدل

تخصیصول takhsisavól *denominative, transitive* [*past:* تخصیص یې کړ] 1 to intend, earmark, set aside (for something); to assign (under something) 2 to appropriate, allocate

تخصیصیدل takhsisedól *denominative, intransitive* [*past:* تخصیص شو] 1 to be intended, be earmarked, be set apart (for something); to be assigned (under something) 2 to be appropriated, be allocated

تخصیصیه takhsisijá *f.* *Arabic* appropriation, allocation د معارف تخصیصیه appropriation for education

تخطي takhattí *f.* *Arabic* 1 aggression 2 encroachment, infringement 3 error, mistake تخطي کول a to commit aggression b to encroach (upon something) c to err, be mistaken

تخطیط takhtít *m.* *Arabic* 1 outline 2 sketch, draft

تخطي کوونکی takhattí kavúnkaj *m.* aggressor

تخفیف takhfíf *m.* *Arabic* 1 relief, softening, weakening 2 discount; lowering (of a price) 3 curtailment (e.g., of arms) تخفیف کول، تخفیف ورکول a to relieve, soften, weaken b to make a discount; to lower (a price) c to curtail (e.g., arms)

تخلص takhallús *m.* *Arabic* 1 takhallus (a literary pseudonym) 2 nickname

تخلف takhallúf *m.* *Arabic* violation, non-observance, non-fulfillment

تخلیق takhlíḳ *m.* *Arabic* 1 creation, making تخلیق میندل to be created 2 upbringing, education تخلیق کول *compound verb* ☞ تخلیقول

تخلیقول takhliḳavól *denominative, transitive* [*past:* تخلیق یې کړ] 1 to make, create 2 to bring up, educate

تخلیقي takhliḳí creative

تخلیه takhlijá *f.* *Arabic* 1 evacuation 2 unloading تخلیه کول *compound verb* a to evacuate b to unload 3 isolation, solitude 4 deviation; evasion

تخم [1] tukhm *m.* **1** seed (of fruit) **2** seed, grain تخم شیندل، تخم اچول **a** to sow **b** *figurative* to sow the seeds of dissension **3** breed (of cattle) *idiom* تخم کنبل، تخم ورکول، تخم ختل to die out to destroy, exterminate تخم دي شین سه! May your family grow and prosper!

تخم [2] tákham *m.* **1** spit **2** steam (e.g., from a pot)

تخمپاکي tukhmpākí *f.* cleaning of grain د تخم پاکی ماشین grain cleaner, grader, screening machine

تخمخ t, تخ مخ takhmókh **1** *interjection* pah, phooey **2.1** shamed, embarrased **2.2** scattered; disconnected, incoherent

تخمدان tukhmdán *m. botany* ovary

تخمریز tukhmréz sown تخم ریزه مځکه sown land

تخم ریزي tukhmrezí *f.* **1** sowing, crops **2** spawning تخم ریزي کول **a** to sow **b** to spawn

تخم شندونکې آله، تخم شندونکی tukhm shindúnkaj سوونکی ماشین sowing machine, seed drill

تخمگذاري tukhmguzārí *f.* laying of eggs

تخم وال tukhmvál flowering (type) تخم وال زرغونیز flowering plant

تخمه [1] tukhmá *f.* **1** origin **2** breed **3** seed-bud نر تخمه sperm وهل to shoot up (of crops)

تخمه [2] tukhmá *f. Arabic medicine* indigestion, dyspepsia

تخمي tukhmí **1** seminal, seed تخمي کېدل to go to seed **2** uninoculated; ungrafted **3** productive (of a hen)

تخمیر takhmír *m. Arabic* fermentation; *figurative* ferment

تخمیز tukhmíz ☞ تخم وال

تخمین takhmín *m. Arabic* **1** supposition, guess **2** estimate, approximation (of something), calculation; draft, preliminary outline تخمین کېدل، تخمینول *compound verb* ☞ تخمینېدل *compound verb* ☞

تخمیناً takhmínán *Arabic* approximately, about

تخمینول takhminavól *denominative, transitive* [*past:* تخمین یې کړ] **1** to suppose **2** to estimate, make an approximation, calculate

تخمیني takhminí **1** imaginary تخمیني ټکی imaginary point **2** conjectural; hypothetical; approximate د تخمیني سنجش له مخي according to an approximate count, approximately په تخمیني ډول supposedly; approximately

تخمینېدل tahkminedól *denominative, intransitive* [*past:* تخمین شو] **1** to be proposed, be intended **2** to be determined approximately, be calculated

تخنث takhannús *m. Arabic* delicacy; softness; effeminacy

تخنول tokhmavól *transitive* [*past:* و یې تخناوه] to tickle *idiom* اعصاب تخنول to stimulate nerves

تخنېدل tokhnedól *intransitive* [*past:* و تخنېده] to feel a tickling sensation

تخنیک tekhník *m.* technique, technology, engineering

تخنیکدان tekhnikdán *m.* technician, technically qualified person

تخنیکي tekhnikí technology تخنیکي آلات، تخنیکي وسائل technical machinery, technical equipment تخنیکي پوهان technicians, technologists, engineers

تخنگ tokháng *m.* strong desire, strong wish; attraction

تخنول tokhavól *transitive* ☞ تخنول

تخوني tokhunáj voracious, gluttonous

تخه [1] tokhá *f.* curds, cottage cheese تخي تخي شیدي curdled milk

تخه [2] tokhá *f.* تخی tokháj *m.* tickling

تخېدل tokhedól ☞ تخنېدل *intransitive idiom* سترگي مي تخېږي، ورته کتلای نه سم I'm ashamed to look at him.

تخیل takhajjúl *m. Arabic* **1** imagination, fantasy د تخیل قوت power of imagination **2** supposition, assumption **3** idea

تخیلي takhajjulí **1** imaginary; assumed **2** fantastic **3** romantic; dreamy

تدابیر tadābír *m. Arabic plural* **1** *from* تدبیر **2** plans

تدارک tadārúk *m. Arabic* [*plural:* تدارکونه tadārukúna *Arabic plural:* تدارکات tadārukất] **1** preparation; stock-piling **2** supply تدارک کول **a** to prepare; stock up **b** to supply, fit out

تدارکات tadārukất *m. Arabic plural* **1** *from* تدارک **2** half-finished products, billets, blanks **3** *military* rations, pay and allowances

تداعي tadā'í *f. Arabic psychology* association

تدافع tadāfú' *f.* defense

تدافعي tadāfú'í *Arabic* defense; defensive تدافعي توان defensibility, defensive capability

تداوي tadāví *f. Arabic medicine* treatment; therapy په... تداوي کول *compound verb* to treat (with something)

تدبر tadabbúr *m. Arabic* judgment, good sense, reasonableness; foresight, prudence

تدبیر tadbír *m. Arabic* [*plural:* تدبیرونه tadbirúna *Arabic plural:* تدبیرات tadbirất *plural:* تدابیر tadābír] **1** measure احتیاطي تدبیر cautionary measures, precautions **2** means **3** inventiveness, resourcefulness له خپل تدبیر څخه کار اخیستل to show resourcefulness **4** good sense تدبیر کول **a** to take measures **b** to carry out some measure **c** to show resourcefulness **d** to be sensible

تدخین tadkhín *m. Arabic* smoking

تدرج tadarrúdzh *m. Arabic* gradual movement; gradual transfer

تدریج tadrízh *m. Arabic* **1** gradualness په تدریج، په تدریج سره gradually, by degrees **2** gradation

تدریجاً tadrídzhán *Arabic* gradually

تدریجي tadridzhí gradual په تدریجي ډول gradually

تدریس tadrís *m. Arabic* [*plural:* تدریسونه tadrisúna *plural:* تدریسات tadrisất] teaching, study (of something) د تدریساتو ریاست Directorate of Institutions of Learning (in the Ministry of Education of Afghanistan) تدریس کول *compound verb* ☞ تدریسول تدریسېدل *compound verb* ☞

تدریسول tadrisavól *denominative, transitive* [*past:* تدریس یې کړ] to teach, give lessons

تدریسي tadrisí *Arabic adjective* learning; teaching تدریسي کتابونه textbooks, educational aids تدریسي مدیر director of studies

تدریسېدل tadrisedól *denominative, intransitive* [*past:* تدریس شو] to be studied, be taught (in schools, etc.)

تدفین tadfín *m. Arabic* burial, funeral

تدقیق tadḳíḳ *m. Arabic* [*plural:* تدقیقونه tadḳiḳúna *Arabic plural:* تدقیقات tadḳiḳắt] **1** careful study, meticulous research **2** check, verification تر تدقیق لاندي نیول، تر تدقیق لاندي کول **a** to study in detail; search thoroughly **b** to verify

تدویر tadvír *m. Arabic* **1** starting, start up د فابریکې تدویر starting a factory **2** work, functioning

تدوین tadvín *m. Arabic* **1** composition, compilation (e.g., of a collection of stories, of a textbook) **2** codification د قوانینو او تدوین مدیریت legislative department (in ministries of Afghanistan) **3** entry, writing in تدوین کول *compound verb* ☞ تدوینول

تدوینول tadvinavә́l *denominative, transitive* [*past:* تدوین یې کړ] **1** to compose, compile (e.g., a collection of stories or articles, a textbook) **2** to codify, classify, systematize

تذبذب tazabzúb *m. Arabic* indecision, uncertainty, vacillation د یوه شي تذبذب لرل uncertainty about something او تردید vacillate, be indecisive تذبذب نه لرل to carry out something unwaveringly

تذخیر tazkhír *m. Arabic* accumulation د اوبو تذخیر accumulation of water reserves

تذکار tazkár *m. Arabic* reminder; remembrance; reference (to) د چا تذکار کول to make mention of someone; recall someone

تذکر tazakkúr *m. Arabic* **1** reference (to); reminder (about); information, notification **2** discussion تذکر ورکول **a** to remind; inform, notify **b** to discuss

تذکره tazkirá tazkará *f. Arabic* **1** passport د تابعیت تذکره passport; personal identification; residence permit **2** certificate **3** note; reminder د رخصت تذکره dismissal notice **4** short biographies (of famous people, poets, etc.) تذکرة الشعرا biographies of poets with examples of their poetry; anthology

تذکیر tazkír *m.* **1** *grammar* attributing masculine gender to a word **2** *grammar* masculine gender **3** *biology* male sex

تذلیل tazlíl *m. Arabic* humiliation, degradation, abasement

تذمیم tazmím *m. Arabic* obligation تذمیم کول to undertake an obligation, pledge oneself, undertake

تر ¹ tәr **1** *preposition in Western dialect words of feminine gender ending in "o" may not be inflected* **1.1** *independently or in combination with* پوري **1.1a** to, up to (indicating a distance) تر کابله پوري I'm going (as far as) to the city. ښار ته ځم **1.1b** to, up to, till (indicating an interval of time) له سهاره تر ماښامه from morning till evening تر کمه پوري؟ Until what time? تر نن روځي پوري up to this day تر مرګه until death **1.1c** How long? to, up to (indicating a quantitative limit) تر شلو پوري وشمېره count up to twenty **1.1d** across (e.g., going across something) تر ولې to jump across a stream تر رود پوري وتل، تر وله غورځېدل cross a river **1.1e** through; past (e.g., through or past something) تر ښار تېرېدل to go through town; go past a town; pass by a town **1.2** *in combination with* لاندي **1.2a** under (e.g., lower than something, from the lower part of something) تر مېز لاندي under the table لاس تر سر under the earth; subterranean تر ميخکي لاندي، مېخکه لاندي

تر موټر لاندي کېدل put your arm under your head لاندي کښېږده to be struck by a car تر واورو لاندي کېدل to be covered by snow **1.2b** *in expressions with the verb* نیول، تر ترکتني لاندي نیول to examine, take under observation تر روزني لاندي نیول to educate, bring up; cultivate, foster **1.3** out of, from (indicates direction of an action from somewhere, from within something) زلمی تر کور راووت Zalmaj went out of the house. تر سترګو مي څاڅکي تویېږي Tears poured from my eyes. **1.4** with someone, with something (with the postposition تر پلار سره، سره with my father یو تر بله سره ګډول to mix with one another **1.5** above, more than, over (indicates exceeding some number or quantity) تر یو کیلومتر تجاوز کوي more than one kilometer; it exceeds one kilometer تر لس زره متره تجاوز نه no more than ten thousand meters تر دوه کاله ډېر کېږي چه ... کوي more than two years have passed since ... **1.6** than (indicates comparative and superlative degrees) احمد تر تا مشر دئ Ahmad is older than you. زه نن تر تا وروسته راغلم Today I came later than you. **2** *adverb* **.1** from him, from her; from them منګر په سبق کښي تري ګل But in their studies Gulbashara overtook him. بشره تر تېره وه **2.2** without him, without her; without them; without it ضرورت نشته، تر It's not necessary, we'll get along without it. تر به شو *idiom* تر هغه to the point that; as much as, to such a تر دي پوري چه، پوري چه degree تر هر کار دمخه، تر هر څه د مخه first of all

تر ² tre *Eastern* ☞ ترې ⁵

تر ³ tar damp, wet

تر tár *suffix showing comperative degree in borrowed words* بدتر worse

ترا ¹ tәrá ☞ طرح

ترا ² trā *f.* ☞ تراه

ترا ³ tará *suffix indicating comperative and superlative degrees* ښه ترا better, best لوی ترا greatest

تراب taráb *used with* خراب

ترابیع tarābí' *m. Arabic plural of* ربیع

تراپي tr̃api *present tense of* ترپل

تراټ ¹ tәráṭ *m. Eastern* trot (gait); fast pace په یوه تراټ آس at a run آس په تراټ وهل to ride at a trot په تراټ پرېنبودل، آس په تراټ خوشي کول to drive a horse تراټ کول to run swiftly

تراټ ² trãṭ *m.* **1** ☞ ترټ ¹ **2** spur

تراټه tr̃áta *f.* **1** zig-zag embroidery (on silk) **2** edging, piping **3** ☞ تراډه

تراټی tr̃áṭaj brittle, fragile

تراژدي tradzhedí *f.* ☞ تراجېدي

تراحیم tarāhím *m. Arabic plural of* ترحیم

تراخ trākh *onomatopoeia* bang, boom

تراخه trákhә *dialect masculine plural of* تریخ

تراډه tr̃áḍa **1** stripe, streak تراډه ایستل to cut off a strip **2** ribbon, tape

ترار trār **1** upset; disturbed **2** perplexed; in confusion; in a panic

تراره trārá *f.* **1** agitation, anxiety **2** perplexity; confusion; panic په چا تراره کول to confuse someone, upset someone

تراړ trāṛ *m.* three-year-old camel

تراړه trāṛa **1** *f.* **.1** pebbles, shingles **1.2** rocky place **1.3** foot (of a mountain) **2** *attributive* **.1** pebbly **2.2** stony, rocky

تراوزو tarāzí *m.* scales; spring-balance د تراوزو پله cup on a set of scales د تراوزو پله خوربدل to outweigh (on scales) *idiom* غوږونه یې ترازوګان دي He has huge ears. He is lop-eared.

ترازووان tarāzuván *m.* weigher

ترازه tarāzá [1] *f.* **1** chunk, bit, piece د ختکي ترازي جوړول to cut a melon into pieces ترازه ترازه کول to cut in slices **2** shred, scrap; string (e.g., of fabric) ترازه کول to tear into shreds, tear into strips ترازه کبدل to be torn, be shredded

ترازه trāza [2] *f.* large dam (for irrigation)

تراژدي، تراژیدي trāzhedí **1** *f.* tragedy **2** *attributive* tragic

تراژیک trāzhík tragic

تراش tarāsh *m.* **1** cutting **2** forming, shaping **3** chopping knife, chopper **4** form, shape, aspect **5** shaving

تراشل trāshǝl tarāshǝl *transitive* [*past:* وی تراشه] **1** to cut **2** to wipe off, scrape off **3** to shave **4** to trim **5** to confine, limit **6** to sculpt **7** to scrape (parquet) *idiom* له خانه تراشل to compose, think up خان ملنگ تراشل to pretend to be a fakir

تراشه tarāshá *f.* **1** shaving, filing **2** piece, bit of something

تراشی tarāsháj *m.* scraper

تراشبدل tarāshedǝl *denominative, intransitive* [*past:* تراش شو] **1** to be cut, be trimmed, be cut off **2** to cut one's hair, have a hair-cut **3** to be polished **4** to be carved (of stone) تراش شوئ هیکل sculpture, statue

تراغ tarāgh *m.* **1** fold, wrinkle **2** bend, twist **3** circle, ring

ترافیک trāfík *m.* traffic (on the street, etc.) د ترافیک کنترول regulation of street traffic د ترافیک مدیریت Department of Traffic Regulation (in Afghanistan)

ترافیکي trāfīkí road, highway; transportation-related ترافیکي نښني او علامي road signs

تراک trāk *m.* **1** crack, split **2** cracking noise **3** cut, groove, notch (e.g., on the barrel of a gun)

تراکتور trāktór *m.* [*plural:* تراکتورونه trāktorúna *plural:* تراکتوران trāktorán] **1** tractor **2** truck tractor

تراکم tarākúm *m. Arabic* **1** accumulation, concentration **2** pile, heap

ترام trām *m.* ☞ تراموی

ترامبیه trāmbjá *f.* stairway

تراموی trāmvája *m.* streetcar, tram

ترامه trāmá *f.* **1** sheet metal for roofing **2** lampshade

ترانځه trándza *f.* stickiness, adhesiveness

ترانزیت trānzít *m.* transit

ترانزیتي trānzití *adjective* transit

ترانسپورت trānspórt *m.* transportation, transport, conveyance د اشخاصو ترانسپورت passenger conveyances, passenger conveying

ترانه tarāná *f.* **1** song **2** hymn ملي ترانه state hymn ترانه ویل **a** to sing **b** to sing a hymn

تران trāṇ *m.* beginning

ترانه trāṇa *f.* anger; malice ترانه کول to fly into a rage; be angry

تراورس trāvárs *m.* sleeper (railway car)

تراوسه tǝr ósa تراوسه پوري tǝr ósa póri until now

تراوه tǝrāvá *f.* woven bag, woven sack (for transporting dirt)

تراوی tǝrāvé *f.* تراویح tarāvíh *f. Arabic plural* additional prayer or service (performed during Ramadan)

تراه taráh *m.* ☞ تره [2]

ترائي turāí *f.* loofah, luffa

ترب tǝrb turb [*plural:* تربان tǝrbán *plural:* turbán] **1** radish **2** horseradish

تربارى tarbáraj *m.* clothes rack; cloak-room

تربت turbát [1] *m. Arabic* **1** grave; tomb, burial vault; mausoleum **2** *used in geographical names* تربت حیدری turbát-i Turbat-i Haidari (town)

تربت tarbát [2] **a** تربت کول **1.1** compressed, squeezed **1.2** stuffed to press, squeeze **b** to stuff, pack in تربت کبدل **a** to be pressed **b** to be stuffed, be packed in **2** *m.* **.1** stuffiness, closeness **2.2** maladjusted person, disturbed person

تربچه trubchá *f.* radish

تربد turbúd *m.* turbád turbíd *botany* jalap (root, a laxative or purgative)

تربرونه tǝrburúna *plural of* تربور

تربره tǝrbǝrá *oblique singular of* تربور

تربگني trabganí *f.* **1** relationship through grandparent (as cousins) **2** enmity, rivalry (usually between close relatives) تربگني کول to show hostility, show rivalry **3** relationship, similarity

تربوڅه turbutsá *f.* radish leaves, radish tops

تربوخته tarbúkhta *f.* something which smells bad, something which gives off a foul odor تربوخته هوا bad smell, foul odor

تربوختی tǝrbúkhti *f. plural* stale air, stuffiness

تربور tǝrbúr *m.* [*plural:* تربرونه tǝrburúna *Western plural:* تربوران tǝrburán] cousin (on the father's side) تربور د لستوني مار دئ *saying* A cousin is a snake in one's bosom.

تربگني tǝrburgalví *f.* تربوری tǝrburí *f.* ☞ تربور گلوی

تربوزک tǝrbuzák *m.* ☞ تمبوزک

تربوزه tarbúza *f.* kind of silk embroidery

تربیت tarbiját *m. Arabic* **1** upbringing; teaching د کوچنیانو تربیت the upbringing of children, teaching of children **2** breeding (of animals) د حیواناتو تربیت animal husbandry تربیت کبدل *compound verb* **a** to be raised, brought up, taught **b** to be bred (of animals) *idiom* جسمي تربیت، د بدن تربیت physical education

تربیتي tarbijatí **1** ☞ تربیوي **2** preparatory

تربیع tarbí' *m. Arabic* [*plural:* ترابیع tarābí'] **1** phase (of the moon) **2** square **3** squaring, quadrature

تریبون tribjún *m.* tribune; platform, chair (at a university); department (of a university)

تربیوي tarbijaví educational; pedagogic

تربیا tarbijá *f. Arabic* ☞ تربیه تربیت عقلي development of mental ability تربیه او تعلیم educational work د تربیي پوهان teachers, pedagogues

تربیه خانه tarbijákhāná *f.* farm

ترپ [1] trap 1 *onomatopoeia* .1 clop, clop-clop 1.2 bang, crack, boom 2. 1 jump; leap, bound د ترپ وهل to jump; leap, bound خپل ځایه ترپ لګول to leap up from one's place 2.2 flight, escape ترپ یا خرپ یا ترپ کول to flee, run *saying* Either a blow from the saber or flight ترپ او تروپ tread, tramp, clatter (of hooves) *idiom* له تربه لوېدل to weaken, lose one's strength, wear oneself out

ترپ tərp *m.* turp ☞ ترب

ترپا trəpā́ *f.* 1 tramp, clatter (e.g., of camel's hooves) 2 convulsive twitch, shaking, quivering (of a wounded animal or bird) 3 slaughter (of an animal, bird)

ترپال tarpā́l *m.* ترپالین tarpālín *m.* canvas top (of a vehicle), awning

ترپان tərpā́ṇ *m. botany* plantain

ترپوچه tərpuchá *f.* turpuchá ☞ تربوڅه

ترپري ترپري traparój-traparój *children's speech* clippety-clop ترپري کول to stamp one's feet

ترپړ [1] trapáṛ *m.* [*plural:* ترپړ trapóṛ] 1 rags, old clothes; rubbish 2 garbage, waste 3 defective goods, rejects

ترپړ [2] trəpóṛ *m.* loafer, idler, lazy-bones

ترپکه trəpáka *f.* [*plural:* ترپکي trəpáki] 1 stamping, treading ترپکي وهل، کول a to stamp, tap one's foot b *figurative* to insist, persist ته لا تراوسه ترپکي وهې؟ Do you continue to insist on your own way? په ترپکو راتلل to come hopping 2 fluttering, quivering

ترپل [1] trəpól *transitive* trā́pi [*present:* تراپي *past:* ویې تربه] 1 to oil, grease, lubricate 2 to lay in, lay on, pack; stack in a pile

ترپل [2] trəpól *transitive* [*present:* تراپي *past:* ترپل ویې traplól *transitive past:* ویې ترپلو، ویې ترپلود، ویې ترپلل] 1 to jump; to gallop 2 to run swiftly 3 to run off, disappear زه له توري نه ترپلم *literal* I don't run from the saber. *figurative* I'm not afraid of battle.

ترپلنه traplóna *f.* 1 jumping; galloping 2 fast running 3 running away, ducking out

ترپلو trapló *past tense stem of* ترپلل

ترپلود traplód *past tense stem of* ترپلل

ترپله [1] trápla *imperfective imperative of* ترپلل

ترپله [2] trápla *f. military* movement at a run across some area, rush, bound

ترپندی trapandáj *m.* ترپونکی trapúnkaj *m.* 1 rock thrown into shallow water (for going across) 2 [*plural:* ترپندي trapandí *plural:* ترپونکی trapúnki] river crossing of stones or rocks

ترپول [1] trapavól *transitive* [*past:* ویې ترپاوه] 1 to cause to jump, cause to gallop 2 to cause to run swiftly 3 to put to fight 4 to pull (by the tail feathers, of a bird)

ترپول [2] trəpavól *transitive* [*past:* ویې ترپاوه] 1 to oil carelessly, lubricate carelessly 2 to beat, strike, thrash, drub

ترپه trapá *f.* 1 jump; gallop 2 dance, dancing

ترپهار trapəhár *m.* 1 stamping, trampling 2 beating (e.g., of wings), clapping

ترپی trapáj *m.* 1 gait, step, walk 2 sound (of steps); tramp (of feet)

ترپیدل trapedól *intransitive* [*past:* و ترپیده *past:* و ترپید] 1 to beat, tremble, pound, shake 2 to jump; hop, skip 3 to stamp, tramp; tap one's foot 4 to tremble, shake, quake (e.g., from fright) 5 to twitch convulsively, shake, flutter (of a wounded or dying animal or bird) 6 *figurative* to bustle about, run around, fuss

ترپیدو tarpedó *f.* ☞ تارپیدو

ترت [1] trat *m.* whip; *history* knout

ترت [2] turt 1 instantly, momentarily, in a flash 2 quickly, hurriedly

ترتاب tartā́b *m.* 1 regret; sorrow, sadness ترتاب کول to regret; grieve, be sad *saying* په تبر پسې ترتاب نسته You can't get back what's been lost.

ترتر tartár ترتر سپی male borzoi (dog)

ترتری tartaráj *m.* 1 stammerer, stutterer 2 stammering, stuttering 3 kind of bird

ترتلو tərtólo *m.* ترتله tərtóla eternally, forever

ترتیب tartíb *m. Arabic* [*plural:* ترتیبونه tartibúna *Arabic plural:* ترتیبات tartibā́t] 1 order, routine; arrangement په دې ترتیب a in that order b in such a way د روحني کارونو ترتیب په order of the day د کلو په ترتیب سره by years; in chronological order په ترتیب in order regulated, put in (good) order 2 disposition, arrangement; distribution 3 measure

ترتیبات tartibā́t *m. Arabic plural* 1 *from* ترتیب 2 measures ترتیبات نیول to take measures

ترتیب وار tartibvár in order, by turn

ترتیبول tartibavól *denominative, transitive* [*past:* ترتیب یې کړ] 1 to arrange, put into order 2 to organize, regulate 3 to compile (e.g., lists); write (a report) 4 to dispose, arrange, set out 5 to deploy 6 to form (units)

ترتیبي tartibí *ordinal*

ترتیبیدل tartibedól *denominative, intransitive* [*past:* ترتیب شو] 1 to be put into order, fall into order 2 to be arranged, be organized; be regulated 3 to be compiled (e.g., a list); be written (of a report) 4 to be disposed; be deployed 5 to be formed (of units) ترتیب سئ! Fall in!

ترتیزک taratezák *m. singular & plural* watercress, *Lepidium sativum*

ترټ trat *m.* ☞ ترت [1]

ترټاپ tartā́p *m.* ☞ ترتاب

ترټل tra̱tól *transitive* [*past:* ویې تراټه] 1 to swear, curse; scold, reprimand, tell off 2 to banish, drive off

ترټنه tra̱tóna *f.* 1 scolding, reprimand 2 banishment, exile

ترټه tra̱tá *f.* woven corn-bin (shaped like a barrel)

ترجمان tardzhumán *m. Arabic* 1 translator, dragoman 2 one who expressed others' wishes, opinions, feelings, etc. 3 representative, envoy, messenger

ترجماني tardzhumāní *f. Arabic* **1** work of a translator, work of a dragoman **2** expression of someone's wishes, opinions, feelings, etc.

ترجمه tardzhumá *Arabic* translation (from one language into another) لفظي ترجمه word-for-word translation ترجمه کول *compound verb* to translate په پښتو ترجمه کول، په پښتو باندي ترجمه کول to translate into Pashto ترجمه کړی کتاب translated book

ترجيح tardzhíh *f.* tardzhí *Arabic* preference د ترجيح حق right of preferential acquisition ته ترجيح ورکول، پر... باندي ترجيح کول prefer someone, prefer something په ... ترجيح لرل to surpass someone, surpass something; be preferred to someone, be preferred to something

ترجيحاً tardzhíhán *Arabic* preferably

ترجيع tardzhí *f. Arabic* **1** return **2** repeating, repetition

ترجيع بند tardzhi'bánd *m.* ballad (with a refrain of two rhymed half-verses)

ترچ trach **1** *m.* sneezing **2** *interjection* ah-choo

ترچل trachól *intransitive* [*past:* و يي ترچل] to sneeze

ترچه trácha *f.* ترچهار trachahā́r *m.* sneezing

ترځ [1] tradz *m.* ترخ trats *m.* interval of time په دې ترځ کښي along with this, at the same time as this; by the way, incidentally د خپلي وينا په ترځ کښي in one's own speech د ژوندون په ترځ کښي in the course of life

ترخ [2] trats *m. Eastern* **1** edge; side په ترخ **a** obliquely, slantwise **b** sideways **2** edging, border, hem **3** crude word, sharp word *idiom* چا ته په ترخ کتل to look askance at someone, look suspiciously at someone په ترخ کښي ويل to speak secretly

ترخکون tratskún attractive

ترخو tər tsó ترخوپوري tər tsó pori ترخو چه tər tsó chi until

ترحم tarahhúm *m. Arabic* pity, sympathy ترحم کول to be sorry (for), feel pity, have sympathy د چا پر حال ترحم کول to be sorry for someone; take pity on someone

ترحيم tarhím *m. Arabic* [*plural:* تراحيم tarāhím] prayer for the repose of the soul (of the dead) د ترحيم مجلس funeral gathering

ترخ [1] trakh *m.* ☞ تخرگ

ترخ [2] trakh *m.* ☞ ورخ

ترخان [1] tarkhā́n *m. history* person freed from payment of tribute or taxes

ترخان [2] tarkhā́n *m.* ☞ ترخون

ترخځ tərkhádz *f.* wedge, gusset (in a shirt)

ترخول tərkhavól *denominative, transitive* [*past:* تريخ يي کړ] to make bitter; over-pepper

ترخون tarkhún *m. botany* tarragon

ترخه [1] tárkha *f. botany* wormwood

ترخه [2] tərkhó **1** *masculine plural of* تريخ **2** *m. plural* pepper تور ترخه black pepper سره ترخه red pepper

ترخه [3] tərkhá *feminine singular of* تريخ

ترخه [4] tárkha *f.* crack, split; slit, crevice ترخي چاودل to crack, split

تريخ توري tórkha toraj *f.* ☞ ترخه توری

ترخي [1] tórkhé **1** *feminine plural of* تريخ **2** *f. plural figurative* bitterness, a bitter feeling په ژوندون کښي يې ډېري ترخي او خوږي ليدلي دي In life he saw much grief and joy.

ترخي [2] tórkháj *f.* chamomile

ترخي [3] tarkhí *f.* frosts, cold spells

ترخېدل tórkhedól *denominative, intransitive* [*past:* تريخ شو] to become bitter, have a bitter taste, turn rancid; be over-peppered

ترخيص tarkhís *m. Arabic* **1** dismissal, disbandment **2** *military* transfer to the reserve

تردد taraddúd *m. Arabic* **1** indecision, vacillation, doubt without hesitating **2** running regular trips تردد کول **a** to be indecisive, hesitate **b** to run (between), make regular trips

ترديد tardíd *m. Arabic* **1** declining, refusal; denial, refutation څای نشته incontestably, undeniably **2** indecision, hesitation, doubt څه ترديد نشته undoubtedly

ترديدول tardidavól *denominative, transitive* [*past:* ترديد يې کړ] to decline, reject, turn down; deny, refute

ترديدي tardidí declining, rejecting; denying, refuting

ترديدېدل tardidedól *denominative, intransitive* [*past:* ترديد شو] to be refused, be denied; be refuted

ترديف tardíf *m. Arabic* **1** movement, proceeding **2** to string, thread

تر ډېره tər ḍéra ☞ تر ډېر، ډېر

تروري [1] traṛí *m. plural* small clouds

تروري [2] tráṛe *f. plural Eastern combining form with* مندي

ترز tarz *m.* ☞ طرز

ترزبان tarzubā́n talkative

ترزنى tərzónaj *m.* cattle which have just been purchased and brought home

ترورږمى taragmój *f. Western* ☞ تروږمى

ترس [1] tars *m.* **1** fear, fright **2** sympathy, pity I څما ترس پري راغئ felt sorry for him.

ترس [2] tórs *m.* **1** ☞ ترخ [2] **2** inclined, sloping

ترسا tarsā́ *m.* non-Moslem; pagan; Christian

ترسان tarsā́n timid, skittish

ترسب tarassúb *m. Arabic* settlement (of alluvia) د ترسب دوره *geology* alluvium

ترست trast *m.* trust (industrial or business)

ترستيشيپ trastishíp *m.* **1** guardianship, trusteeship **2** patronage, sponsorship

تر سره tər sára تر سره کول، تر سره کېدل، سر ☞

ترسرى [1] tarsəráj *m.* bridle; headband

ترسري [2] tórsári *m.* tarsóri *plural* freckles ترسري کېدل، ترسري لوېدل to be covered with freckles

ترسري مخى tórsári-mókhaj freckled

ترسکون traskún somewhat salty

ترسکنول traskunavól *denominative, transitive* [*past:* ترسکون يې کړ] to make salty, salt slightly

ترسکون traskún ☞ ترسکن

ترسند tərsə́nd keeping away, avoiding something; indifferent, apathetic, unconcerned

ترسندوالی tərsəndvā́laj m. avoidance (of something); indifference, apathy

ترسندول tərsəndavə́l denominative, transitive [past: ترسند یې کړ] to remove, free

ترسندېدل tərsəndedə́l denominative, intransitive [past: ترسند شو] to keep away (from something); be indifferent, be unconcerned

ترسیب tarsíb m. Arabic geology sediment (of a rock layer), sedimentation

ترسیبي tarsibí geology sedimentary

ترسیري társijari geology tertiary, ternary

ترسیم tarsím m. Arabic image, representation, description; exposition, account

ترسیمول tarsimavə́l denominative, transitive [past: ترسیم یې کړ] 1 to represent, describe; expound 2 math to describe دائره ترسیمول to describe a circle

ترش tursh 1 sour (to the taste) 2 figurative unsatisfied, dissatisfied; irritable 3 figurative gloomy, morose

ترشا tərshā́ 1 postpositive behind, after; in a back of ورو ورو یې ترشا He followed slowly after him. 2.1 behind ترشا پاتېدل to lag behind ځان د نورو ترشا کول to lag behind others 2.2 back ترشا اچول to put off, postpone ترشا گرز! About face! (as command) ترشا کېدل to retreat, fall back ترشا کول to repel, fight off (e.g., an attack) مقابل طرف ترشا وهل to throw back (an opponent) ☞ شا

ترشاپاتې tərshāpā́te backward (of a country)

ترشاتگ tərshātág m. [plural: ترشاکېده tərshākedə́] m. withdrawal, retreat, departure

ترشح tarashashóh f. Arabic m. [plural: ترشحات tarashshohāt] 1 physiology secretion 2 leakage (of rumors) ترشح کول a to ooze out, exude b to leak (of rumors)

ترش روی turshrúj ترش رو turshrú dissatisfied, having a sour expression; sullen, gloomy

ترش رویي turshruí f. dissatisfied expression, dour expression; sullenness, moroseness

ترش مزه turshmazá sour (to the taste)

ترشوالی، ترش والی turshvā́laj m. sour taste

ترشي turshí f. 1 salted food(s) 2 chemistry acid

ترخنځ tərkhə́dz f. ترخنز tərkhə́za f. ترخنزه tərkhə́za 1 adze 2 wedge, gusset (in a shirt)

ترېنکه trékhka f. path, small road

ترصد tarassúd m. Arabic [plural: ترصدونه tarassudúna Arabic plural: ترصدات tarassudā́t] 1 observation هوایي ترصد aerial observation 2 waiting; temporizing 3 shadowing

ترصدگاه tarassudgā́h m. observation point

ترغا targhā́ combining form with تالا

ترغاره tərghā́ra 1 serving as a debt, serving as an obligation; laid upon someone, entrusted to someone (literally: around the neck) و چا ته ترغاره کول، را ترغاره کول، ور ترغاره کول to assign

someone (responsibility); obligate someone; thrust upon someone, foist upon someone چا ته ترغاره کېدل، را ترغاره کېدل، در ترغاره کېدل، ور ترغاره کېدل to be assigned to someone (responsibility); to be obligated

ترغاک targhā́k m. 1 storm 2 waste (plot of) land, waste ground

ترغلوني tərghalúnaj m. medicine mastitis

ترغوني tərəghúne [1] f. darkness, dusk 2 attributive چه ترغوني ماښام سو when it got dark, when twilight fell

ترغونی tərəghúnaj [2] ancient, old; antique

ترغه tərghá 1 sparse, scattered, thrown about 2 diffused, dispersed, driven away ترغه کول a to scatter, throw about b to disperse, drive away ترغه کېدل a to be scattered b to be driven off, be dispersed

ترغیب targhíb m. Arabic encouragement, incentive و چاته ترغیب کول، و چاته ترغیب ورکول to encourage someone, inspire someone

ترغه ☞ ترغۍ ترغوٰی targhə́j - targhə́j

ترفع taraffó' f. Arabic haughtiness; arrogance

ترفیع tarfí' f. Arabic [plural: ترفیعگاني tarfi'gāni m. Arabic plural: ترفیعات tarfi'ā́t] promotion (at work) د ترفیع فرمان edict on promotion (in one's position, profession) د رتبې ترفیع promotion in rank ترفیع کول to receive a promotion (at work)

ترفیعاً tarfi'án Arabic by way of a promotion (at work)

ترقي tarakkí f. Arabic [plural: ترقی tarakkə́j m. Arabic plural: ترقیات tarakkijā́t] 1 forward movement 2 progress, development; success attainment ترقي غوښتل to strive for progress د یو کار ته ترقي ورکول to further the progress, further the development of something, develop something 3 growth, increase (of taxes, etc.) ترقي کول، ترقي مېندل a to progress, develop; be successful b to grow, increase (of taxes, etc.)

ترقیخواه tarakiparvár ترقي پرور tarakikhāh progressive; striving for progress

ترقېدل tarkedə́l intransitive [past: و ترقېده] dialect to double up (from pain)

ترقیم tarkím m. Arabic numeration, numbering

ترقي یافته tarakijāftá progressive, advanced; developed

ترک trak m. germination, sprouting; growth [1] ترک وهل to germinate, sprout, grow

ترک trak [2] m. 1 knock, thump; blow 2 tread, tramp ترک کول a to knock; to strike b to tramp, tread

ترک trak [3] m. reservoir (of a churn or press)

ترک trak [4] m. decorative edging of a rug (made of woolen threads)

ترک turk [5] m. 1 Turki (member of ethnic group with Turkic a language) 2 Turk 3 history soldier 4 poetic handsome youth

ترک tark [6] m. Arabic 1 leaving, abandoning 2 refusal of something ترک کول a to leave, abandon b to refuse something

ترک tark [7] m. 1 crack, split; cleft, fissure 2 crack, crackling (sound) 3 hoof disease (in horses, mules, etc.)

ترکا trəkā́ f. ☞ ترکهار

ترکاري tarkārí f. verdure; vegetable, vegetables

ترکاري والا tarkāriwālā *m.* greengrocer

ترکاڼ tarkā́ṇ *m.* carpenter ترکاڼ کېدل to be a carpenter; do carpentry work

ترکاڼک tarkāṇák *m.* woodpecker

ترکاڼي [1] tarkāṇī́ *f.* carpentry; carpentry work

ترکاڼي [2] 1 tarkāṇī́ *m. plural* Tarkini (also called Tarkanis, Tarkalani, Tarkalanis, name of a tribe) 2 tarkāṇáj *m.* Tarkini (tribesman)

تراکتور traktór *m.* ☞ تراکتور

ترکزي 1 tarakzī́ *m. plural* the Tarakzi (a subdivision of the Mohmands) 2 tarakzáj *m.* Tarakzi (tribesman)

ترکستان turkistā́n *m. history* Turkestan

ترکښ tarkáx *m. history* quiver

ترکلاڼي 1 tarkalāṇī́ *m. plural* Tarkalani (tribe) 2 tarkalānáj *m.* Tarkalani (tribesman)

تر کله tər kə́la ترکله پوري tər kə́la pori until what time, until when, how long

ترکمان turkmā́n *m.* [*plural:* ترکمانان turkmānā́n *Arabic plural:* تراکمه tarākimá] Turkmen

ترکمانه turkmā́na *f.* Turkmen (female)

ترکماني turkmānī́ 1 Turkmen ترکماني ژبه Turkmen (language) 2 *f.* Turkmen (language)

ترکمن turkmán *m.* ☞ ترکمان

ترکمنستان turkmanistā́n *m.* Turkmenistan

ترکمنه turkmána *f.* ☞ ترکمانه

ترکمني turkmaní ☞ ترکماني

تر کمه tər kə́ma تر کمه پوري tər kə́ma pori until what time, till when, how long

ترکڼ tərkə́ṇ *m.* tradesman (one who has come to a village from the city)

ترکوپره tərkopára 1 often, frequently 2 a lot, much

ترکودی trakódaj *m.* plant

ترکول [1] trakavə́l *transitive* [*past:* و يې ترکاوه] 1 to strike, hit, knock 2 to whip, lash

ترکول trakavə́l *denominative, transitive* [*past:* ترک يې کړ] to abandon, leave (behind)

تر کومه tər kúma تر کومه پوري tər kúma pori ☞ ترکمه

ترکوڼی tarkúṇaj *Eastern* diseased (of a plant)

ترکه [1] tariká *f.* tarká *Arabic* inheritance, inherited property

ترکه [2] turka *f.* 1 Turkish female 2 *f. poetic* beloved, sweetheart, girlfriend

ترکه [3] tarká *f.* twig, shoot (of a tree)

ترکهار trəkəhā́r *m.* ترکهاری trəkəhā́raj *m.* 1 tramping, clatter (of hoof beats) 2 crack, cracking (sound)

ترکي [1] turki 1.1 Turkic 1.2 Turkish ترکهار ژبه Turkish (language) 1.3 gizzar (breed of sheep) 2 *f.* the Turkish language ترکهار ويل to speak Turkish

ترکی [2] tərəkáj dark-complexioned

ترکی [3] trakə́j *f.* soured milk

ترکی [4] tarakə́j *f.* cluster of rocks (apart from a mountain ridge)

ترکي [5] 1 tərə́ki *m. plural* Taraki (tribe) 2 tərə́kaj *m.* Taraki (tribesman)

ترکی [6] trakə́j *f.* (young) goldfinch

ترکيب tarkíb *m. Arabic* 1 compilation 2 *chemistry* compound, composition 3 *linguistics* sentence, phrase, combination of words 4 *philosophy* synthesis

ترکيب بند tarkibbánd *m. literature* verse form with a refrain at the end of each stanza consisting of two rhymed half-verses

ترکيبي tarkibí *Arabic* 1 composite, complex, complicated 2 synthetic

ترکېدل trakedə́l *intransitive* [*past:* و ترکبده] 1 to strike (against), knock oneself (against), bump (against) 2 to grow, sprout

ترکي ورکي tárki-várki scattered, thrown about, dispersed

ترکيه turkijá *f.* Turkey

ترگ targ *m.* perforation of the bladder (in cattle)

ترگمۍ tərgmə́j *f. Eastern* ☞ تپه تياره او توره ترگمۍ وه تروږمۍ It was pitch dark.

ترلاس لاندي tərlā́slāndi subordinated, subordinate, subject to

ترلاس لاندي والی tərlāslāndiwálaj *m.* subordination

تر لاندي tər lā́ndi 1 *adverb* underneath ترلاندي کول to put under something, shove under لاس ترلاندي که slip your hand under ترلاندي کبدل to crawl under something, stand under 2 under something

ترلغوني tarləghúnaj *m. veterinary* foot-and-mouth disease

ترله [1] tərlá *f.* tərlə́ [*plural:* ترلي tərlé *plural:* ترلي ګاني tərlegā́ni] cousin (female), daughter of an uncle on the father's side ترله کول *children's speech* to consider as a cousin; to call cousin

ترله [2] tárla *Western* with one another; from one another ترله تبرول to make peace with each other; to reconcile که هرڅو توره شپه سي، مور او خور ترله بنکاره سي *proverb* However dark the night, you can still tell the mother from the daughter. ترله تبريدل to be reconciled *idiom* a ترله وتل to become angry ولي ترله ووتې؟ Why did you get angry? b to overdo it, try too hard (e.g., when treating someone)

ترم [1] turúm *m.* trumpet, horn; bugle

ترم [2] turúm *m.* [*plural:* ترمونه turumúna *plural:* ترمان turumā́n] 1 stallion 2 stud-horse, male (of species)

ترم [3] tərám *m.* ☞ تمبل

ترموز tarmāzə́ *oblique of* ترموز

ترمائي tərmājí *m.* grapes of the last harvest

ترمباز trambā́z *m.* ox closest to the center of the threshing floor (during the threshing of grain)

ترمتی turumtáj *m.* hawk or falcon used for hunting

ترمچي turumchí *m.* trumpeter, horn-player, bugler پر ترمچي يو پو دئ *proverb* The trumpeter's business is only to blow.

تر مخ tər məkh ترمخه tər mə́kha 1 *postpositive* in front of something, by something د کور ترمخ in front of the house, by the house 2 earlier, already ☞ مخ

ترمله trámla *f.* rice water, water in which rice was washed

ترمنځ tər mándz ترمنځه tər mándza ☞ ترمینځ

ترمنه trámna *f.* **1** moist arable soil **2** swamp; swampy hollow, pool (in a bog)

ترموز tarmúz *m.* thermos, thermos flask

ترمه tráma *f.* **1** sediment **2** clay; dirt **3** ☞ ترمنه **4** crack, cracking

ترمي tarmí *exclamation* cry shouted by shepherds when driving sheep

ترميانځ tər mjándz ☞ ترمینځ

ترمي ترمي tarmí-tarmí *Eastern* **1** scattered, dispersed **2** fragmented, broken up, disrupted ترمي ترمي کول *a* to scatter *b* to break up ترمي ترمي کېدل *a* to be scattered *b* to be broken up

ترميذي tarmizí tərmizí *history* of Termez (city)

ترميره tarmirá *f.* watercress, *Nasturtium officinale*

ترمیم `tarmím *m. Arabic* [*plural* ترميمونه tarmimúna *Arabic plural:* ترميمات tarmimā́t] **1** repair د موټرو د ترميم کارخانه auto repair shops **2** recuperation; strengthening, fortification (of the organism); correction (in a law, etc.) ترميم کول *compound verb* ☞ ترميمبدل، ترميمول *compound verb* ☞

ترميم کاري tarmimkārí *f.* repair works

ترميمول tarmimavә́l *denominative, transitive* [*past:* ترميم يې کړ] **1** to repair, fix **2** to revive (health); fortify (the organism) **3** to introduce a correction, introduce an amendment (into a law, etc.)

ترميمبدل tarmimedә́l *denominative, intransitive* [*past:* ترميم شو] **1** to be repaired, be fixed **2** to be revived (of health); be fortified (of the organism) **3** to be corrected, be modified, be amended (of a law, etc.)

ترمینځه trándza **1** *feminine singular of* ترنځ **2** *f.* darkness, gloom (during an eclipse)

ترنځى trandzáj *m.* emaciated person

ترمینځ tər mjándz ترمینځه tər mjándza *postpositive* **1** between **2** across یوه ورځ ترمینځ in a day ☞ یوه ورځ ترمینځ بله ورځ

ترمینل tarminal د ترمینل وډانی airport terminal

ترناو tarnā́v *m.* **1** chute, gutter (for drainage of water) **2** aqueduct **3** channel, groove, trough **4** *technology* water cooling tower **5** pass between mountains

ترنج tarándzh *m. singular & plural* camel's thorn

ترنج turúndzh *m. botany* citron, *citrus medica*

ترنج turándzh **1** wrinkled, creased; folded **2** tough, coarse

ترنجبين tarandzhubín *m. singular & plural* manna, sugary juice on the camel's thorn

ترنجوکى trandzhukáj *f.* skein of silk, skein of yarn

ترنجه trandzhá *f.* sharp stone (used by shepherds instead of a knife when slaughtering sheep)

ترنجوکى trandzháj *f.* ☞ ترنجوکى

ترنځ trandz **1** thin, gaunt **2** stunted, poor (of crops)

ترنځکى trandzəkáj skinny, thin

ترنځول trandzavә́l *denominative, transitive* [*past:* ترنځ يې کړ] to torture, exhaust, dry up

ترنځى trandzáj *f.* stream of water

ترنځېدل trandzedә́l *denominative, intransitive* [*past:* ترنځ شو] to grow thin, wither away

ترهند tə́rənd ☞ ترهند

ترنداره trandā́ra *f.* aunt (on the father's side)

ترهندتوب tərəndtób *m.* ترندتيا tərəndtjā́ *f.* ☞ ترهندتوب

ترندي trándi *plural of* ترور

ترندۍ trandáj *f.* **1** attack, assault **2** influx of guests **3** cry, shout

ترنز tranz ☞ ترنځ

ترنزکه tranzə́ka *f.* snapping the fingers

ترنزکى tranzəkáj ☞ ترنځکى

ترنزول tranzavә́l *transitive* ☞ ترنځول

ترنزى tranzáj *m.* ☞ ترنځى

ترنزى tranzә́j *f.* ☞ ترنځى

ترنزېدل tranzedә́l *intransitive* ☞ ترنځېدل

ترنک tarnák *m.* **1** rage, anger, wrath **2** *figurative* the appetite of a wolf

ترنک tarnák *m.* Tarnak (River)

ترنکوخه trankútsa *f.* ☞ ترنکوخه

ترنکى tərnəkí angry, raging

ترنگ trəng *m.* **1** strumming, playing (on the rabab) **2** knock, knocking; crack, cracking (noise)

ترنگ trang *m.* **1** *diminutive* (little) hour **2** striking (a gong); striking (of a clock)

ترنگ trang with a hanging (drooping) spike (of grains ready for harvest) ترنگ کېدل to ripen

ترنگ trang *m.* area for games

ترنگا trəngā́ *f.*

ترمچي turungchí *m.* ☞

ترنگر trangə́r *m.* string bag for carrying hay or straw

ترينگلى tringə́laj *m.* ☞

ترنگن trangə́n *m.* ☞

ترنگو trəngú *m.* سارنگ

ترنگوخه trangútsa *f.* sling (as a weapon)

ترنگول trəngavә́l *transitive* [*past:* يې ترنگاوه و] **1** to play (on the rabab) **2** to knock; produce a crackling sound

ترنگه trangá *f.* smooth and level board

ترنگهار trəngahā́r *m.* ترنگى trəngáj *m.* **1** strumming, sounding, the sound (of a rabab) **2** tapping; crackling

ترنگېدل trangedә́l *intransitive* [*past:* و ترنگېده] to jingle, sound (of a rabab)

ترنه tréna *dialect* ☞ تری

ترنیکه tərnikə́ *m.* great-great-grandfather

ترنى tarṇáj *m. regional* customs (duty)

ترو tro **1** hence, therefore **2** then, thereupon

تروالى turvā́laj *m.* sourness, acidity; acid

تروبى trobáj *m.* vinegar

تروپ trup *combining form with* ترپ

تروتازگي tarutāzagí *f.* **1** freshness, newness **2** *figurative* liveliness, gaiety

تروتازه tarutāzá **1** very fresh **2** *figurative* lively, cheerful تروتازه کېدل **a** to freshen **b** to come to life, revive, become cheerful شادي تروتازه شو Shadi revived, Shadi grew cheerful

تروټ troṭ *m.* loss, injury تروټ خورل to incur a loss و چا ته تروټ رسېدل to be detrimental for someone

تروټمن troṭmə́n detrimental, unprofitable

تروټه troṭá **1** *f.* loss, injury دا شی را باندي تروټه دئ I incur a loss on this تروټه کول to incur a loss **2** *attributive* unprofitable تروټه مال unprofitable commodity تروټه کېدل *compound verb* to prove unprofitable

ترڅو tróchi *dialect* ☞ ترڅه

ترور tror **1** *f.* [*plural:* ترندي trándi *plural:* ترېندي trénde *plural:* تروراني trorāni] **1** aunt (on father's side) ترور کول *children's speech* ☞ ترورول **1** ترور کېدل *children's speech* to be considered an aunt, be called an aunt تر ترور نیمه مور به ده *beh proverb* there is no friend like your mother **2** aunt, auntie (direct address)

ترور tərúr **2** **1** confused; distracted, dismayed, perplexed **2** out-of-sorts, upset, disordered

ترور terrór **3** *m.* terror

ترورتوب tərurtób *m.* تروروالي ترورتیا tərurtjā́ *f.* ☞

ترورزوی trordzúj **1** *m.* Eastern ☞ ترورزی

ترورځی trordzə́j **2** *f.* Eastern ☞ ترورزی

ترورزی trorzáj **1** *m.* cousin (son of an aunt on father's side)

ترورزی trorzə́j **2** *f.* cousin (daugther of an aunt on father's side)

ترورکۍ troráke *f.* auntie

ترورمېره trormerə́ *m.* uncle (husband of aunt on father's side)

ترورواله tərurvā́laj *m.* **1** confusion; dismay, perplexity **2** upset, discomposure

ترورول troravə́l **1** *denominative, transitive* [*past:* ترور یې کړه] *children's speech* to consider as one's aunt; to call aunt

ترورول təruravə́l **2** *denominative, transitive* [*past:* ترور یې کړ] **1** to confuse **2** to upset, distress

تروری troráj **1** *m.* fox; vixen

تروری trorə́j **2** *f.* تروري trorí *f.* [*plural:* تروري troráj *plural:* trorə́j ترورياني trorəjā́ni] auntie

ترورېدل təruredə́l *denominative, intransitive* [*past:* ترور شو] **1** to become confused, become flustered; get lost **2** to become upset, become distressed

تروړه troṛá **1** *f.* storm (when the whole sky is covered with dark rain clouds)

تروړه tróṛa **2** *f.* golden thread (for women's shoes, slippers)

تروړی taroṛə́j *f.* fox

تروږمی trogmáj *f.* tərogmáj dark and moonless night; darkness د تروږمی زور *idiom* the power of darkness

تروسکه təróska and here ...

تروش trush *word paired with* تنگ

تروشي turúshi *dialect* تروشي اوبه salty water

تروښنول troḵhavə́l *transitive* [*past:* وي یې تروښناوه] **1** to spend economically, spend frugally; be stingy **2** to steal, appropriate another's possession

تروښېدل troḵhedə́l *intransitive* [*past:* وتروښنبده] **1** to be spent economically, be spent frugally **2** to be appropriated

تروکه tərvə́ka *f.* تروکی turvə́kaj *m.* tərvə́kaj *m.* *botany* sorrel جوگا تروکه kind of sorrel with tubers

تروگی trogáj *m.* *botany* spurge, euphorbia

ترهول təravə́l *transitive* ☞ ترهول

تروم tərúm **1** *m.* ☞ ترم

تروم tərúm **2** *m.* ☞ ترم

ترومی trúmaj *m.* sip of water

ترونگزی turungzí **1** *m.* *plural* Turungzi (tribe) **2** turungzáj *m.* Turungzi (tribesman)

ترونه trúna *plural of* تره ☞

تروه tərvə́ turvə́ **1** *masculine plural of* تریو **2** *m.* *plural* **1.** something sour to the taste, sour (-tasting) stuff **2.2** ferment; leaven په اوږو کبني تروه اچول to leaven dough

تروه tərvá turvá **2** **1** *feminine singular of* تریو **2** *f.* vinegar

تروی tarváj *m.* **1** *botany* spurge, euphorbia **2** jalap (root)

تروې tarvé *f.* turvé **1** *feminine plural of* تریو **2** *f.* *plural* ☞ شلومبې

تروپت tarvét *m.* astrology

تروپتی tarvetáj **1** *m.* astrologist

تروپتی tarvetə́j **2** *f.* fortune-teller

ترویج tarvídzh *m.* *Arabic* **1** spreading, dissemination; inculcation, indoctrination; implanting **2** development د صناعت ترویج development of industry ترویج ورکول ☞ ترویجول

ترویجول tarvidzhavə́l *denominative, transitive* [*past:* ترویج یې کړ] **1** to spread, disseminate, make available; inculcate, introduce, implant **2** to develop د صناعت ترویجول to develop industry

ترویدل tərvedə́l *denominative, intransitive* [*past:* تریو شو] **1** to be salty **2** to be sour; turn sour; turn (sour)

تروير tarvír *m.* **1** deception, fraud **2** depression, sadness

تره trə **1** *m.* [*plural:* ترونه trúna] uncle (on father's side) تره کول *children's speech* to consider as an uncle; be called uncle

تره tra **2** *f.* **1** repulsion **2** fear د یو شي څخه تره کول **a** to have an aversion for something **b** to fear, be afraid of something *idiom* خوب یې په لیمو کبني تره شویدئ He can't sleep

تره tərá **3** *f.* mill-race

تره tará **4** *f.* musk melon

تره tərá **5** *f.* body (of a person, animal)

تره tára **6** *suffix* ☞ ترا

ترها tarhā́ *f.* trahá **1** fright, fear **2** fearfulness, timorousness ترها کول to be afraid, take fright

ترهاو tirhā́v *m.* *Eastern* one-third, a third

تره پر trapə́ṛ *f.* rag; waste

ترتېزک taratezák *m.* ☞ تره تېزک

ترہ خبل tarakhél 1 *m.* *plural* Tarakheli (tribe) 2 *m.* Tarakheli (tribesman)

ترهرہ tarhará *f.* ☞ ترهہ

ترهرہ tarhára *f.* dangerous moment

ترهغو tər haghó ترهغو پوري tər haghó pori ترهغو څو tər haghó tso ترهغہ tər haghá ترهغي پوري tər haghé pore ☞ ترخو

ترہ کي taráki *m.* *plural* Taraki (a subdivision of the Gilzaj)

ترهگري ضد tárhagárəj zíd counter terrorism

ترهند tərhónd 1 fearful, timorous 2 restive (of animals, esp. horses)

ترهند توب tərhəndtób *m.* ترهندتیا tərhəndtjá *f.* ترهندوالی tərhəndválaj *m.* 1 timidity, timorousness; fearfulness 2 restiveness (of an animal)

ترور tərhúr ☞ ترور [2]

ترهورتیا tərhurtjá *f.* ترهوري tərhurí *f.* 1 uneasiness, unrest; commotion, confusion 2 fright, alarm

ترهول tərhavəl trahavəl *transitive* [*past:* و يي ترهاوه] to frighten; scare away

ترهہ tráha *f.* 1 fear, fright 2 fearfulness, timorousness 3 uneasiness, anxiety, alarm د . . . څخه ترهہ کول، د . . . نه ترهہ کول *a* to be afraid *b* to be uneasy, be alarmed

ترهېدل tərhedəl trahedəl *intransitive* [*past:* وترهېده] 1 to be afraid, take fright 2 to be uneasy, be alarmed

ترهېده tərhedə́ *m.* trahedə *plural* 1 fear, fright 2 uneasiness, anxiety, alarm

تري tarí [1] *m.* *plural* *Eastern* granulated sugar

تري tarí [2] *f.* 1 water (as contrasted to the dry land) 2 waterway 3 moisture

تری traj [3] *m.* ☞ تره [4]

تری traj [4] *m.* water from the mountains for irrigation

تري tre [5] *Eastern* 1 *adverb* from him, from her, from them خپل He هغہ تري رخصت شو کتاب تري واخله Take your book from him. went away from them. 2 out of it, out of them 3 across it, across them; through it, through them

تری tarə́j [6] *f.* stilling pit of a mill

تری tráj [7] *f.* tarə́j 1 gorge, ravine 2 road along a precipice 3 stream between mountains

تری tarə́j [8] په تري ویل secretly, on the sly په تري ویل to speak in secret

تریاک tarják *m.* *plural* 1 opium preparation (used against snakebite) 2 opium

تریاکي tarjáki *m.* opium smoker

تریپولي tripolí *f.* Tripoli (city)

تریت tərít *m.* soaked oil-cakes (feed for cattle)

تری تم taráj-tam disappeared, vanished, lost تری تم کېدل، تری تم ورک کول taráj-tam کېدل to vanish, disappear, be lost تری تم سې! Get lost! The devil take you!

تریخ trikh ترخہ tərkhá *m.* [*plural:* ترخہ tərkhə́ *f.* *plural:* ترخي tərkhé] 1 bitter (to the taste) 2 salty, brackish (of water) تریخ درياب، ترخي اوبہ *a* sea water *b* the sea 3 *figurative* strict,

stern 4 *figurative* heavy, difficult, bitter د ده اوقات هم ترخه وي Life is hard for him. 5 *figurative* bitter, unpleasant (of words) 6 hot-headed, temperamental ترخي خبري کول to speak the bitter truth *a* د تریخ غورپ تېرول *idiom* difficulties of the time په هغه دا خبره ډېره ترخه ولگېده to suffer a little; to master something That distressed us terribly.

تریخ بخن trikhbəkhə́n 1 somewhat bitter 2 somewhat salty

تریخ تیا trikhtób *m.* ☞ ترخه تیا توب

تریخ توری trikh torə́j *f.* kind of vine

تریخ تیا trikhtjá *f.* ترخوالی trikhválaj *m.* 1 bitter taste, bitterness 2 brackishness, saltiness (of water) 3 *figurative* strictness, sterness 4 *figurative* bitterness (of words) 5 *figurative* distress, grief 6 *figurative* tiff, disagreement

تریخول trikhavə́l *denominative, transitive* [*past:* تریخ یې کړ] 1 to make bitter 2 *figurative* to spoil (a mood); poison (one's pleasure, one's life) *idiom* خان ورته ډېر تریخول to try still harder

تریخي tríkhaj *m.* 1 bile, gall 2 malice تریخي لرل to feel malice toward someone, be inclined against someone 2 *idiom* د دښمن پر اینه تریخي درلودل to inspire terror in an enemy to be decent, be honorable

تریخېدل trikhedə́l *denominative, intransitive* [*past:* تریخ شو] 1 to become bitter; have a bitter taste 2 *figurative* to be spoiled (of a mood); be poisoned (one's pleasure, one's life)

ترهېدل təredə́l *intransitive* ☞ ترهېدل

تریرہ triṛa *f.* 1 scorching of earth from intense heat 2 ☞ ترري [1]

تریرہ tréṛa [2] *f.* *history* transport and equipment of an army

تریز triz *m.* *botany* chicory

تریگہ triga *f.* flat cake fried in oil

تریل tarél *f.* *regional* tray

ترلاندي tre lánde *Eastern* ☞ تري لاندي

تریلر trelár *m.* trailer

تریلي trelə́j *m.* pool, reservoir

ترین tarín 1 *m.* *plural* Tarini (tribe) سپین ترین، تور ترین branches of the Tarini 2 *m.* Tarin (tribesman)

ترین tren [2] *m.* train برقي ترین electric train

تریناک tarəjnák wild, unbridled

ترندارہ trendára *f.* ☞

ترینگر tringár *m.* *music* triangle (the instrument)

ترینگلی tringə́laj [1] *m.* 1 moody person, morose person 2 dissatisfied person تریو ترینگلي مه راته درپرېه Don't stand in front of me with a sour look on your face.

ترینگلی tringlə́j [2] *f.* finger snap to the forehead

ترېنہ tréna *dialect* ☞ تري [5] نور صبر ترېنه ونه شو He couldn't stand it. His patience wore thin.

تریو triv تروه tərvá *f.* turvá *f.* *m.* [*plural:* تروه tərvə́ *plural:* turvə́ *Eastern plural:* تاروه tārvə́ *f.* *plural:* تروي tərvé *plural:* turvé] 1 *a* تروي اوبہ sour (to the taste) 2 salty, brackish (of water, soup) و چاته تندی تریو نیول، و چا ته تریو وچولی کول salt water *b* sea water 2 to look at someone with a dissatisfied expression

تری والی tarəjvắlaj *m.* secrecy

تریو بخوند trivbəkhə́n trivbakhvánd **1** somewhat sour; acidic **2** somewhat salty, brackish (of water)

تریوتندی triv tandáj *m.* **1** dissatisfied expression, sour expression **2** gloomy expression, sullen expression په تریوتندي *triv tandí* sullenly **a** with a dissatisfied expression, with a sour expression **b** sullenly تریوتندی نیول **a** to be dissatisfied **b** to be sullen

تریوتوب trivtób *m.* تریوتیا trivtjá *f.* ☞ تریووالی

تریوخوری trivkhvə́gaj *m.* sweet-and-sour drink, syrup (made from water, honey, vinegar and lemon)

تریوخوندی trivkhvándaj ☞ تریوبخن

تریوری trevŗáj *m.* cucumber

تریوکی trivkáj *m.* marinade; pickles

تریومخی trivmə́khaj sullen, morose; dissatisfied

تریوناک trivnắk **1** slightly sour **2** slightly salty

تریونگولی trivngólaj *m.* trivngúlaj ☞ اچار

تریووالی trivvắlaj *m.* **1** sourness, acidity; acid دغه لیمو بی شانه تریووالی This lemon is unbelievably sour. **2** *chemistry* acidity لری

تریوزمه trivvázma ☞ تریوبخن

تریوول trivavə́l *denominative, transitive* [*past:* تریو یی کړ] **1** to make sour; **2** pickle, ferment *idiom* تندی تریوول to take on a dissatisfied expression; to become angry; gaze angrily

تریوبدل trivedə́l *denominative, intransitive* [*past:* تریو شو] to become sour; sour, turn sour *figurative* to become apathetic

تریه təŗjá cry used when driving sheep

تړ ¹ taŗ *m.* **1** conclusion (of a treaty, of an alliance) **2** agreement, treaty, alliance **3** condition **4** knot (in thread, rope, etc.) **5** dam **6** refuge, sanctuary **7** ☞ ملاتړ

تړ ² taŗ *m.* large rock

تړازه taŗāzá *f.* ☞ ترازه ¹

تړاک ² tṛāk ☞ تراک ¹

تړاقی tṛākə́j *f. Eastern* band or bandage on the thigh تړاقی کول to tie the thighs with a band or bandage

تړاک ¹ taŗák *m.* **1** row, column; string (e.g., of horses), series **2** side

تړاک ² tṛāk *onomatopoeia* bang (sound of firearms)

تړاگی taŗāgə́j *f.* ☞ تراقی

تړانگه tŗānga *f.* **1** strip (of fabric, leather, etc.) **2** piece, small piece; slice **3** patch of land **4** ☞ تناکه

تړانگه تړانگه tŗānga-tŗānga تړانگي تړانگي tŗāngi-tŗāngi **1** torn into strips or pieces (fabric, leather, etc.) **2** cut into pieces or slices تړانگه تړانگه کول **a** to tear into strips or pieces **b** to cut into pieces; slice, cut up تړانگه تړانگه کېدل **a** to be torn into strips or pieces **b** to be cut into pieces; be sliced, cut up

تړاو təŗáv *m.* **1** string for measuring land **2** relationship, connection

تړبوخه taŗbókha *f.* تړبوخی taŗbukháj *m.* stuffiness, stale air; heat نن تړبوخه ده Today it's stifling.

تړپ tŗap **1** *onomatopoeia* bang, boom **2** *m.* **.1** muffled blow, muffled knocking **2.2** haste; impatience

تړپول tŗapavə́l *transitive* [*past:* یی تړپاوه و] **1** to wave, cause to flutter **2** to strike **3** to force to jump, force to gallop **4** to throw upward **5** *figurative* to disturb

تړپهار tŗapəhár *m.* **1** hoof beats (of an animal) **2** knocking, noise

تړپبدل tŗapedə́l *intransitive* [*past:* وتړپیده] **1** to sway, flutter, flap **2** to strike (against), hit **3** to jump, gallop **4** to be thrown, be tossed **5** *figurative* to be anxious, show impatience

تړژی taŗuráj ☞ تړژی

تړتک taŗták *m.* impatience

تړژی taŗzhə́baj stammering, stuttering

تړس tŗas *onomatopoeia* crack

تړک ¹ tŗak *m.* ☞ تک ² 2

تړق ² taŗák *m. regional* heat, heat of day

تړک ¹ tŗak **1** *onomatopoeia* bang **2** *m.* **.1** knock; crack **2.2** clap, bang **a** banging, slapping, clapping **b** cracking (sound); crackling تړک او تړوک **a** to knock **b** to clap **3** blow تړک وهل to strike **4** clicking (with the tongue) ورکول

تړک ² taŗák *m.* ☞ تلکه

تړک ¹ 2 تړوک تړک tṛak̃ *f.* tṛakár *m.* tṛaktŗúk *m.* ☞ تړکا

تکه ¹ tŗáka *f.* **1** lightning **2** ☞ تړکه

تړکه ² tuŗká *f.* heated oil

تړکهار tṛakəhár *m.* ☞ تړکار

تړل taŗə́l *transitive* [*past:* یی تاړه و] **1** to connect, tie, bind **2** to fasten, secure; reinforce آس په ونه پوري وتړه Tie the horse to the tree. **3** to harness آس په گاډۍ پوري تړل to harness a horse to a cart **4** to combine, unite; knock over, knock down دستکونه تړل to knock down boards **5** to put on (a veil) **6** to fill in, close up (a hole, etc.) **7** to build (a bridge, a dam) **8** to close, shut **9** to obstruct (a roadway); to close off (movement, traffic) **10** to close down (a plant, institution, etc.) **11** to conclude (a treaty, contract, agreement) شرط تړل to make a bet شرط یی را سره وتاړه او با یی لود He made a bet with me and lost. **12** to fix, set, appoint (a time, etc.) **13** to call, convene مجلس تړل to call a session **14** to ascribe د بل بنه کار په ځان پوري تړل to ascribe another's services to oneself ځان وربوري to dedicate to someone د چا د نوم سره تړل **15** to dedicate تړل کېدل to join someone, associate (oneself) with someone *passive* **a** to be harnessed **b** to be closed, be shut **c** to be concluded

تړلئ taŗə́laj **1** *past particle from* تړل **2.1** closed دروازه تړلې وه the door was closed **2.2** dependent, depending (on someone, something) زما تگ د هغه د راتگه پوري تړلئ دئ My departure depends upons his arrival. **3** obligated, obliged **4** of one piece, integral, solid

تړلیک taŗlík *m.* agreement, contract

تړم ¹ taŗm təŗə́m **1** warm ترمه هوا warm weather **2** hot, burning (of tears)

تړم ² taŗə́m *first person present of* تړل

تړمبه tŗumbá *f.* ☞ ناتار ²

تړمتوب taŗmtób *m.* تړمتیا taŗmtjá *f.* تړموالی taŗmválaj *m.* tepidness

ترمول taṛmavә́l *denominative, transitive* [*past:* ترم يي کړ] to heat up; to make warm, warm

ترمبدل taṛmedә́l *denominative, intransitive* [*past:* ترم شو] 1 to warm up, be heated 2 to be warm

ترنګ [1] taṛáng *m.* unassailable cliff

ترنګ [2] tṛáng ☞ ترنګ [1]

ترنګا tṛangá *f.* ترنګهار tṛangahә́r *m.* ☞

ترڼه taṛә́na *f.* 1 binding, linking 2 reinforcement 3 harnessing 4 joint, connection, compound 5 filling in, covering up (a hole, etc.) 6 closing (of some institution) 7 conclusion (of a contract or agreement) 8 convocation (of something) *idiom* د چا سره د زړه ترڼه لرل to nourish affection toward someone

تروبای taṛubáj *m.* pump

تروپ tṛup *onomatopoetic* bang, smack

تروک tṛuk *word paired with* ترک [1] 2

ترومبي tṛumbé *f. plural* warm buttermilk

ترون [1] taṛún *m.* 1 conclusion, ratification (of a treat, contract, agreement) د قرارداد تحريري ترون written formulation of a contract 2 contract, agreement ترون کول to conclude a contract or agreement; reach an agreement 3 convening (of a legislature, etc.) 4 connection, interconnection; relationship د چا سره د عمر ترون کول to connect your life with someone 5 measure (action to be taken) 6 knot (thread, string) 7 string 8 dedication (book)

ترون [2] taṛūn *m. computer science* باندره protocol

ترونی taṛúnaj *m.* 1 band; bandage 2 strips of bast

تره [1] tára *f.* path; way, road پر خپله تره حُه! Go home! Get out of here! Go away! *idiom* په تره کښي ګرزېدل a to walk about looking important b to make a show of bravery

تره [2] tára *f.* 1 promise; obligation تره کول to make conditional (upon); cause, bring about 2 intention

تره [3] tára *f.* 1 rock, cliff 2 rocky place 3 watershed 4 steep hillock

تره [4] taṛá *imperfective imperative of* تړل

تړی [1] taṛáj *m.* stammerer, slutterer

تړي [2] taṛí *present tense of* تړل

تړئ [3] taṛә́j *present tense, second person plural of* تړل

تریسکي tṛíski *f. plural* experiences (esp. those endured, suffered through); difficulties

تریسمار tṛismә́r *m.* intense heat, sultriness

تریکه tṛíka *f.* 1 uneasiness, anxiety 2 pain

تزار tzār *m.* czar, tsar

تزاري tzārí *adjective* czar, tsar

تزايد tazājúd *m. Arabic* 1 growth, increase, increment, augmentation 2 development تزايد مېندل a to grow, increase, multiply b to develop, be developed

تزريق tazríḳ *m. Arabic medicine* injection; infusion تزريق کول *compound verb* to make an injection; make an infusion

تزکيه tazkijá *f. Arabic* purification, cleansing, cleaning; تزکيه کول to clean, cleanse, purify

تزلزل tazalzúl *m. Arabic* oscillation, wavering (*literally and figuratively*); instability په اراده کښي تزلزل راوستل to shake the will

توزن tuzә́n ☞ تزن

تزنبدل tuznedә́l *intransitive* [*past:* وتزنېده] to be upset, be distressed, grieve

تزوج tazavvúdzh *m. Arabic* marriage تزوج او جوړه کېدل to enter into matrimony, get married

تزويج tazvídzh *m. Arabic* marriage, matrimony; giving (someone) in marriage

تزوير tazvír *m. Arabic* 1 deceit, forgery 2 dissembling, pretense, hypocrisy, falseness

تزويري tazvirí feigned, hypocritical, false, insincere *literal* تزويري کالي اغوستل to be camouflaged, be disguised

تزی tә́zaj *m.* 1 centerpost of a tent 2 inflorescence of corn

تزئيد tazjíd *m.* [*plural:* تزئيدونه tazjidúna *Arabic plural:* تزئيدات tazjidә́t] addition, supplement; increase, multiplication تزئيد کول to add, supplement; increase; multiply

تزئين tazjín *m. Arabic* ornament, decoration تزئين کول *compound verb* to decorate تزئين کېدل *compound verb* to be decorated; adorn oneself

تزئيني tazjiní *Arabic* decorative تزئيني بوټي decorative plants *idiom* تزئيني لوازم decorations

تګل tagál *m. dialect* outfitting, equipment, supplies

تګم tágəm *m.* smell, foul odor

تګمجن tagəmdzhán smelly, foul-smelling

تږی tә́gaj 1 tormented by thirst زه تږی يم I'm thirsty. تږی او وږی و He wanted both to eat and to drink. تږی کول to cause thirst 2 a تږی کېدل thirsting (for something) striving (toward something) to thirst, be thirsty, be tormented by thirst b to thirst for, desire (something), strive (toward something) علم ته دپر تږی دئ He very much wants to learn. *idiom* تر اويو تږی پوري ايستل، تر ولې تږی پوري ايستل to deceive, dupe, swindle; twist around one's finger

تږی والی tә́gajvә́laj *m.* thirst

تس [1] təs 1 ☞ تش [1] 2 thrown, tossed, strewn تس کول to throw, toss تس کېدل to be thrown, be tossed

تس [2] təs *m. exclamation* cry used for getting a camel to rise up

تسامح tasāmúh *m. Arabic* condescension, indulgence, leniency; softness

تسانيد tasānúd *m. Arabic* solidarity

تساوي tasāví *f. Arabic* equality, equal amount (e.g., an equal number of votes)

تسبک tasbák sticking out, sticking up

تسبه tasbá *f.* ☞ تسپه

تسبيح tasbíh *f.* tasbíh [*plural:* تسابيح tasābíh] *Arabic* 1 *religion* praise of God 2 rosary, prayer beads, tasbih

تسپه taspá *f.* rosary bead; prayer beads تسپي ويل، تسپي اړول to recite a prayer going through a rosary (prayer beads)

تسخير taskhír *m. Arabic* conquest; subjugation; mastery د فضا تسخير conquest of space تسخير کول *compound verb* to conquer; subdue; master تسخير کېدل *compound verb* to be conquered; be subjugated

تسخين taskhín *m.* **1** warming, heating **2** heating مرکزي تسخين central heating تسخين کول **a** to warm, heat (up) **b** to heat

تسر tusár *m.* tussah silk

تسريع tasrí *f. Arabic* acceleration, speeding up

تسطيح tastí *f.* tastíh *Arabic* smoothing out, leveling

تسعير tas'ír *m. Arabic* **1** *economics* conversion د قرض تسعير، دپور conversion of a loan **2** evaluation **3** *finance* course, rate of exchange

تسکره taskará *f.* sedan (chair); litter; stretcher

تسکره چي taskarachí *m.* hospital attendant, medical orderly

تسکوره təskóra *f.* **1** curved shovel, crooked shovel تسکوره وهل to dig **2** *dialect* wedge axe, wood cleaver

تسکين taskín *m. Arabic* **1** calming, reassuring تسکين کول *compound verb* تسکين ورکول to calm, reassure تسکين کېدل *compound verb* to become calm, calm down په اذهانو کښي تسکين to act reassuringly **2** *linguistics* marking a "sokun"

تسلسل tasalsúl *m. Arabic* **1** sequence; consecutiveness د واقعاتو تسلسل a chain of events د خبرو تسلسل پرېکول to interrupt someone's speech د خبرو تسلسل خراب شو The conversation was deteriorating. د خبري تسلسل ساتل to continue speaking **2** series **3** numbering of pages, pagination

تسلط tasallút *m. Arabic* **1** dominion, sway **2** force (e.g., of a law) قانون تر تسلط لاندي تغيير natural change

تسلي tasallí *f.* تسليت tasliját *m. Arabic* consolation, reassurance د خو د زړه تسلي مي و چا تسلي کول to console, calm, reassure someone نه شوه But that did not reassure me.

تسلي بخش tasallibákhsh **1** consoling, reassuring **2** satisfactory

تسليح taslíh *m. Arabic* arms; arming تسليح کول to arm, equip with weapons

تسليحاتي taslihātí relating to arms, armament

تسليخ taslíkh *m. Arabic* slaughter (of cattle) تسليخ کول *compound verb* to slaughter (cattle)

تسليم taslím *m. Arabic* **1** surrender, capitulation بله شرطه تسليم unconditional surrender **2** submissiveness, obedience **3** handing over, passing **4** delivery (of some goods) **5** [*plural:* تسليمات taslimāt] greeting **6** recognition, acknowledgment

تسليمول taslimavól *denominative, transitive* [*past:* تسليم يي کړ] **1** to hand (over), transmit, pass (along) ځان تسليم که! Give up! **2** to deliver, turn over (an item)

تسليمي taslimí *f.* **1** handing over, passing (along) **2** receiving, reception د مکتوب د تسليمي دستخط receipt for delivery of a letter

تسليمېدل taslimedól *denominative, intransitive* [*past:* تسليم شو] **1** to surrender, capitulate **2** to be transmitted, be handed over **3** to be supplied, be delivered (of goods)

تسليمېده taslimedó *m. plural* **1** surrender, capitulation **2** handing over, passing along **3** reception, receipt (of goods)

تسمه tasmá *f.* **1** leather strip **2** belt

تسمه غور tasmaghvár *m.* wax for boots

تسميه tasmijá *f. Arabic* name, designation تسميه کول *compound verb* to name, call

تس نس tasnás tas-u-nás to eat (food) تس نس کول تس نس ونس

تسويد tasvíd *m. Arabic* sketch; draft (of an executive decision, etc.) تسويدول تسويد کول *compound verb* ☞

تسويدول tasvidavól *denominative, transitive* [*past:* تسويد يي کړ] to make a sketch; compile the draft (of an executive decision, etc.)

تسويه tasvijá *f. Arabic* **1** leveling; smoothing out; tamping down, flattening **2** regulating, arranging; resolution (of a question) **3** repayment (of a debt) تسويه کول *compound verb* **a** to level, equalize; smooth over; tamp down, flatten **b** to regulate, arrange; resolve (a question) **c** to pay back (a debt)

تسهيل tashíl *m. Arabic* **1** facilitation, advantage **2** [*plural:* تسهيلات tashilāt] advantageous, favorable conditions تسهيلات پېښبنول a to facilitate, grant advantages **b** to create favorable conditions

تش¹ təsh **1.1** empty; hollow تش منگی empty jug or pitcher لاسه، دښمن مي ته يي *saying* an idle hand – you're my enemy **1.2** د تش ټوپک نه دوه کسه ډارېږي *proverb* an unloaded weapon is twice feared (both by the owner and by his enemy) **1.3** blank (of a cartridge) **1.4** deprived (of something), free (from something) د شخصي اغراضو څخه تش ملگری an unselfish friend **1.5** empty, pointless تشي خبري empty words, pointless words په تشي خبري کول to speak empty or pointless words; jabber nonsense تشو خبرو سري تېرايستل to deceive with empty promises **2** only; just, hardly **3** *military* Unload! (a command) *idiom* تشه ورځ Saturday تش په نامه **a** false, self-styled so-called; fictitious; nominal

تش² tash *m.* ☞ تشت

تشاکل tashākúl *m. Arabic* similarity, resemblance

تشبانی təshbā́ṇaj *m.* unarmed person

تشبث tashabbús *m. Arabic* [*plural:* تشبثونه tashabbusúna *Arabic plural:* تشبثات tashabbusāt] **1** initiative, beginning **2** trying, endeavor, zeal, diligence **3** attempt **4** address (to someone) تشبث کول **a** to begin **b** to try, show zeal **c** to make an attempt **d** to adress (someone)

تشبيه tashbíh *m. Arabic* [*plural:* تشبيهونه tashbihúna *Arabic plural:* تشبيهات tashbihāt] **1** comparison تشبيه کول to compare; to liken تشبيه لرل to be similar **2** allegory; metaphor

تشپانی təshpā́ṇaj *m.* ☞ تشبانی

تشت tasht *m.* basin; wash-tub (for laundering)

تشتپاک tashtpák *m.* toady, lickspittle

تشتت tashattút *m. Arabic* **1** complication; mix-up څوک په تشتت اخته کول to mix up someone, confuse someone **2** complication, confusion (of an exposition) **3** absentmindedness

تشتور təshtor **1** absolutely empty **2** devastated, laid waste تش تور درول to devastate, ruin, lay waste **3** with empty hand, empty-handed تش تور بېرته راتلل to come back with nothing, come back empty-handed

تشتیا təshtjấ *f.* emptiness; void

تشتینه tashtiná *f.* meat on the jawbone of a sheep or other animal

تشجیع tashdzhí' *f. & m. Arabic* incentive; encouragement و چاته تشجیع ورکول to encourage someone, cheer up someone

تشخانه tashkhāná *f.* primer, igniter, detonator

تشخص tashakhkhús *m. Arabic* **1** importance **2** distinction, peculiarity, characteristic **3** determination, establishment

تشخیص tashkhís *m. Arabic* **1** recognition; identification **2** establishment, determination **3** diagnosis د امراضو تشخیص diagnostics

تشخیصول tashkhisavól *denominative, transitive* [*past:* تشخیص یې کړ] **1** to recognize; identify; get to know **2** to determine, establish **3** to make a diagnosis

تشخیصي tashkhisí **1** diagnostic **2** distinctive تشخیصیه خصوصات distinctive features

تشخیصېدل tashkhisedól *denominative, intransitive* [*past:* تشخیص شو] to be established, be determined

تشدد tashaddúd *m. Arabic* **1** strengthening; aggravation د مرض تشدد شو the illness was aggravated **2** cruel treatment; force نه کار اخیستل to resort to force

تشدید tashdíd *m. Arabic* **1** strengthening; aggravation **2** *grammar* doubling a consonant by using the tashdid

تشریح tashrí *f.* tashríh *m. Arabic* [*plural:* تشریحات tashrihất] **1** description; explanation, commentary تشریحات کول to give an explanation, provide clarification; describe in detail **2** analysis **3** dissection; post-mortem **4** anatomy د تشریح علم anatomy *idiom* د تشریحاتو علامت conventional sign, symbol

تشریحول tashrihavól *denominative, transitive* [*past:* تشریح یې کړ] **1** to describe; explain, clarify, comment upon **2** to analyze, figure out **3** to dissect

تشریحي tashrihí **1** anatomical **2** analytical تشریحي ژپوهنه analytical linguistics **3** explanatory

تشریحېدل tashrihedól *denominative, intransitive* [*past:* تشریح شو] **1** to be described; to be explained; be commented upon **2** to undergo analysis **3** to be dissected

تشریع tashrí' *f. Arabic* legislation; issuance of laws

تشریعي tashri'í *Arabic* legislative تشریعي سلطه legislative authority

تشریف tashríf *m. Arabic* **1** to do an honor **2** *polite* visit; arrival تشریف راوړل، خپل تشریف راوړل to pay a visit, deign to come لرل to deign to attend, be present; honor by one's presence **3** *polite* departure, leavetaking تشریف وړل to deign to leave, depart

تشریفات tashrifất *m. Arabic plural* **1** *from* تشریف **2** ceremonial, ceremony; formalities **3** protocol section د تشریفاتو عمومي مدیریت، د تشریفاتو عمومي ریاست protocol department

تشکارل tushkāról *transitive* ☞ شکارل

تشکر tashakkúr *m. Arabic* gratitude, expression of gratitude د ډېر تشکر سره with deep gratitude د چا څخه د یو شي تشکر کول to thank

someone for something; express one's gratitude تشکر د چا په مقابل کښې څرګندول to express one's gratitude to someone

تشکرنامه tashakkurnāmá *f.* letter of gratitude

تشکل tashakkúl *m. Arabic* ☞ تشکیل

تشکیل tashkíl *m. Arabic* organization, foundation, creation, formation, arrangement د تشکیلاتو مدیر chief of the administrative department د مځکي تشکیلات land-tenure regulations اداري administrative division د . . . څخه تشکیل مېندل to be formed, consist of something یو شي ته تشکیل ورکول to compile, make, constitute something

تشکیلول tashkilavól *denominative, transitive* [*past:* تشکیل یې کړ] to organize, found, create; form کابینه تشکیلول to form a cabinet

تشکیلېدل tashkiledól **1** [*past:* تشکیل شو] **1.1** to be organized, be founded, be created, be formed; form نوی تشکیلېدل to be created, be organized anew, be reorganized **1.2** to consist of something, be made up of something **2** *m. plural* ☞ تشکیل

تش لاسی təshlấsaj **1** poor, indigent, penniless **2** with empty hands, empty-handed, with nothing

تش مغزه təshmághza hollow

تشمیل tashmíl *m. Arabic* enclosing, enveloping, taking in; scope, range

تشناب tashnấb *m.* تشناو tashnấv *m.* washroom; wash basin

تشنج tashannúdzh *m. Arabic* spasm; convulsion

تشنگ tasháng *m. medicine* dropsy

تش والی، تشوالی təshvấlaj *m.* **1** emptiness, void **2** *anatomy* cavity

تشوش tashavvúsh *m. Arabic* **1** confusion; commotion **2** disorder, upset وظیفوي تشوشات *medicine* functional disorders عصبي تشوش nervous disorder, nervous shock

تشول təshavól *denominative, transitive* [*past:* تش یې کړ] **1** to empty (out), free **2** to unload **3** to discharge (a firearm) **4** to pump out (e.g., air) **5** to deprive of something, leave without something *idiom* زړه تشول **a** to become angry **b** to lay bare one's heart

تشونه teshavóna *f. action noun from* تشول

تشویش tashvísh *m. Arabic* unrest, agitation, alarm دا د تشویش سبب نه دئ، دا د تشویش خبره نه ده That causes no alarm.

تشویق tashvíḳ *m. Arabic* encouragement, incentive; assistance, help چا ته تشویق ورکول to encourage, urge (on); render assistance to someone

تشویقول tashviḳavól *denominative, transitive* [*past:* تشویق یې کړ] to encourage, urge on

تشه təsha *f.* **1** air, atmosphere **2** *physics* vacuum, void

تشهیر tashhír *m. Arabic* **1** publication, promulgation, proclamation **2** *history* form of punishment where the criminal was put on display at a pillory or astride a donkey تشهیر کول **a** to publish, promulgate, proclaim **b** *history* to put into a pillory or seat on a donkey (as a punishment for crime) تشهیر موندل to be put into a pillory or seated on a donkey

تشی təshaj *m.* **1** side; iliac region **2** groin **3** empty place, free place **4** *physics* vacuum, void

تشبدل¹ təshedə́l *denominative, intransitive* [*past:* تش شو] **1** to be emptied, be freed, become empty گاډی له خلګو تش شو *regional* The train emptied out. **2** to be unloaded (of cargo) **3** to be unloaded (of firearms) **4** to be pumped out (e.g., of air) **5** to be deprived of something, be left without something خوله له غاښو څخه تشه شوه all his teeth fell out **6** to be worthless, be useless

تشبدنه təshedə́na *f. action noun from* تشبدل

تنبت təkht *present tense stem of* تنبتبدل

تنبتن təkhtán *m.* ☞ څنبتن

تنبتند təkhtə́nd unsociable, introverted, withdrawn تنبتند سری unsociable person, introverted person; lone wolf, loner

تنبتول¹ təkhtavə́l *transitive* [*past:* وی تنبتاوه] **1** to drive off, steal (cattle) آس تنبتول to steal a horse **2** *Eastern* to steal, abduct, hijack **3** to put to flight **4** to abduct, kidnap, carry off (a girl, another man's wife) **5** to be engaged in smuggling, be engaged in the movement of contraband

تنبتونه təkhtavə́na *f. action noun from* تنبتول د تنبتوني مال contraband (goods)

تنبتي təkhtí *present tense of* تنبتبدل

تنبتبدل təkhtedə́l *intransitive* [*present:* تنبتي *past:* وتنبتبده] **1** to run; to run away, make off تنبتبدل د ځان له وبری to save oneself by flight تنبته چه تنبته run for all you're worth **2** to desert **3** to shirk (work, studies); to avoid *idiom* اور ته به کنبښنو چه ساره رانه و تنبتي Let's sit by the fire to warm ourselves. شونډي یې سپیني تنبتبدلي وي His lips grew pale.

تنبتبدلئ təkhtedə́laj **1** *past participle from* تنبتبدل **2** *m.* deserter

تنبتبده təkhtedə́ *m. plural action noun from* تنبتبدل

تنبل təkhə́l *intransitive* ☞ تنبتبدل

تنبول təkhavə́l *transitive* ☞ تنبتول

تصاحب tasāhúb *m. Arabic* possession, ownership; mastery, seizure; taking possession (of property, etc.) تصاحب کول *compound verb* to take possession of, master; acquire as your own property

تصادف tasādúf *m. Arabic* **1** meeting **2** incident, chance (happening), coincidence تصادف کول *compound verb* **a** to meet **b** to find, discover by chance تصادف کبدل *compound verb* **2 a** to meet with **b** to be found by chance **c** to coincide

تصادفاً tasādúfán *Arabic* by chance, unexpectedly, accidentally

تصادفي tasādufí *Arabic* chance, unexpected, accidental, unintentional په يو تصادفي رقم سره by chance, unexpectedly, accidentally *idiom* تصادفي محاربه encounter battle

تصادم tasādúm *m.* [*plural:* تصادمونه tasādumúna *Arabic plural:* تصادمات tasādumā́t] **1** د تصادم واقعه collision, accident **2** skirmish, encounter هوايي تصادم aerial encounter تصادم کول **a** to collide, run against, run into **b** to take place (of an encounter, skirmish)

تصاعد tasā́ed *m. Arabic math* progression هندسي تصاعد geometric progression

تصانيف tasāníf *m. Arabic plural from* تصنيف

تصاويب tasāvíb *m. Arabic plural from* تصويب

تصحيح tashí *f.* tashíh *Arabic* correction; correcting تصحيح کول *compound verb* to correct, put right; make corrections, read proofs, correct proofs تصحيح کبدل *compound verb* to improve, reform; be corrected *idiom* سرک تصحيح کول to level a road, straighten a road

تصدير tasdír *m. Arabic* export

تصديق tasdík *m. Arabic* **1** confirmation; affirmation **2** ratification **3** attestation, certificate تصديق کول *compound verb* **a** to confirm; affirm; to certify **b** to ratify تصديق کبدل *compound verb* **a** to be confirmed; be affirmed; be certified **b** to be ratified

تصديقاً tasdíkán *Arabic* تصديقاً لاس لیک کول to witness, certify (a document)

تصديق نامه tasdiḳnāmá *f.* **1** testimonial or certificate given upon completion of studies at an institute or school تعلیمي تصدیق نامه certificate **2** ratification document **3** witness, testimonial; document; certificate د بيمي تصدیق نامه insurance policy

تصرف tasarrúf *m. Arabic* [*plural:* تصرفونه tasarrufúna *Arabic plural:* تصرفات tasarrufā́t] **1** ownership, possession; use of something د چا په تصرف کښي under someone's authority; at someone's disposal **2** seizure په تصرف راوستل، په تصرف راوړل to seize something, possess something; get hold of something تصرف کول *compound verb* ☞ په خپل تصرف کول to seize, take possession of د چاپه تصرف کبدل **a** to turn out to be under someone's authority **b** to be seized by someone

تصرفول tasarrufavə́l *transitive* [*past:* تصرف یې کړ] **1** to possess, own; use something **2** to seize, take possession of

تصريح tasrí *f.* tasríh *Arabic* explanation; clear, precise instruction; clarification, amplification تصریح کبدل *compound verb* to be explained, be cleared up; be clarified, be made precise (of a deadline, etc.)

تصريف tasríf *m. Arabic grammar* **1** inflection **2** declension **3** conjugation

تصريفي tasrifí *Arabic grammar* morphological; relating to inflection تصريفي بل رازوالی morphological distinctions

تصغير tasghír *m. Arabic* diminution, lessening, decrement اسم تصغير ísm-i *grammar* diminutive

تصفيه tasfijá *f. Arabic* **1** clarification **2** solution, resolution (of a problem, question) **3** liquidation, removal (e.g., of disagreement) دتصفيي مامورين abolition commission **4** cleaning, cleansing; purification; filtration; refining د تبلو تصفيه petroleum distillation **5** payment (e.g., of a share) **6** *politics* purge تصفيه کول *compound verb* **a** to clarify **b** to resolve (a question, problem) **c** to liquidate; remove (e.g., disagreement) **d** to pay (e.g., a share) **e** to clean, filter, refine **f** to concentrate (ore) **g** *politics* to carry out a purge تصفيه کبدل *compound verb* **a** to be clarified **b** to be resolved (a question, problem) **c** to be liquidated, be removed (e.g., disagreement) **d** to be paid (e.g., a share) **e** to be cleaned, be filtered, be refined **f** to be enriched, be concentrated (e.g., of ore) **g** *politics* to pass through a purge

تصفیه خانه tasfijakhāná *f.* petroleum refining plant

تصمیم tasmím *m. Arabic* [*plural:* تصمیمونه tasmimúna *Arabic plural:* تصمیمات tasmimã́t] decision تصمیم نیول، تصمیم کول to make a decision

تصمیم نامه tasmimnāmá *f.* resolution; decree

تصنع tasannó' *f. Arabic* pretense; affectation, artificiality

تصنعي tasanno'í feigned; affected, artificial تصنعي احساس insincere feelings

تصنیف tasníf *m. Arabic* [*plural:* تصنیفونه tasnifúna *Arabic plural:* تصانیف tasāníf *plural:* تصنیفات tasnifã́t] 1 compliation, composition, writing (of books) 2 composition, work 3 distribution 4 *biology* classification

تصور tasavvúr *m. Arabic* [*plural:* تصورونه tasavurúna *Arabic plural:* تصورات tasavvurã́t] 1 imagination; representation; supposition 2 idea تصور کول *compound verb* ☞ تصورول *compound verb* ☞ تصوربدل

تصورول tassavvuravól *denominative, transitive* [*past:* تصور یې کړ] to imagine; suppose, presuppose

تصوري tasavvurí *Arabic* 1 imagined, imaginary 2 *philosophy* subjective

تصوریت tasavvurijã́t *m. regional* imagination د تصوریت فلسفه idealism

تصوربدل tasavvuredól *denominative, intransitive* [*past:* تصور شو] to be proposed, be intended; be represented داسي تصوربري چه ... it is proposed that ...

تصوف tasavvúf *m. Arabic religion* 1 Sufism 2 mysticism

تصویب tasvíb *m. Arabic* [*plural:* تصویبونه tasvibúna *Arabic plural:* تصویبات tasvibã́t *plural:* تصاویب tasāvíb] 1 approval, acceptance, sanction 2 decree, resolution تصویب کول *compound verb* a to approve, accept, sanction b to decree, make a resolution تصویب کبدل *compound verb* a to be approved, be accepted, be sanctioned b to be decreed

تصویبنامه tasvibnāmá *f.* decision (regarding confirmation of a government proposal); decision (of legislative body)

تصویر tasvír *m. Arabic* 1 description, representation 2 picture, portrait تصویر کول *compound verb* ☞ مناظر تصویرول to paint landscapes

تصویروالا tasvirvālá *m.* artist; portrait painter

تصویرول tasviravól *denominative, transitive* [*past:* تصویر یې کړ] 1 to describe, represent 2 to draw

تضاد tazã́d *m. Arabic* 1 opposition; contrast 2 contradiction, antagonism 3 *literary* antithesis, contrast 4 *philosophy* antithesis

تضامن tazāmún *m. Arabic* 1 reciprocity 2 collective responsibility; collective guarantee; solidarity

تضامني والى tazāmunivã́laj *m.* ☞ تضامن 2

تضرع tazarró' *f. Arabic* 1 entreating; humble supplication 2 humility, meekness

تضمین tazmín *m. Arabic* 1 guaranteeing; guarantee دیوشي تضمین کول to guarantee something 2 use of a quote from the work of one poet to another when writing verse

تضمینول tazminavól *denominative, transitive* [*past:* تضمین یې کړ] to guarantee; vouch for; ensure

تضمینبدل tazminedól *denominative, intransitive* [*past:* تتضمین شو] to be guaranteed; be assured

تضیق tazjík *m. Arabic* 1 squeezing; pressing (upon) 2 *physics* pressure 3 oppression 4 limitation

تطابق tatābúk *m. Arabic* correspondence, similarity, likeness; coincidence دمحیط سره تطابق حاصلول to adapt to one's environment

تطبیق tatbík *m. Arabic* [*plural:* تطبیقونه tatbiķúna *Arabic plural:* تطبیقات tatbiķã́t] 1 observation of something 2 application, use 3 realization, fulfillment د تطبیق وړ a applicable b realizable, fulfillable 4 practice 5 adaptation 6 collation, comparison

تطبیقات tatbiķã́t *m. Arabic plural* 1 *from* تطبیق 2 applied studies; practical training 3 *military* exercise

تطبیقول tatbiķavól *denominative, transitive* [*past:* تطبیق یې کړ] 1 to observe something 2 to apply, use 3 to realize, fulfill 4 to practice 5 to adapt ځان تطبیقول to adapt oneself 6 to coordinate, bring into correspondence

تطبیقي tatbikí *Arabic* 1 applied; practical 2 comparative

تطبیقبدل *denominative, intransitive* [*past:* تطبیق شو] 1 to be applied, be used 2 to be realized, be carried out, be fulfilled په علمي میدان کښني تطبیقبدل to be realized; be applied in actuality 3 to be practiced; practice, have practice (in) 4 to be observed 5 to coordinate, be brought into correspondence 6 to be collated, be compared

تطرف tatarrúf *m. Arabic* 1 excess 2 extreme

تطمیع tatmí' *f. Arabic* inducement, prompting; encouragement, incentive

تطور tatavvúr *m. Arabic* [*plural:* تطورونه tatavvurúna *Arabic plural:* تطورات tatavvurã́t] 1 change, transformation, conversion تطور او تغیر ورکول to change, undergo a change تطور میندل change, alter (something) 2 improvement, change (for the better)

تطویل tatvíl *m. Arabic* 1 lengthening, elongation 2 tightening ببفایدي تطویل delay, procrastination

تظاهر tazāhúr *Arabic* [*plural:* تظاهرونه tazāhurúna *Arabic plural:* تظاهرات tazāhurã́t] 1 manifestation, disclosure تظاهر کول to be revealed, be disclosed 2 showing, demonstration د تظاهر دپاره for show, ostentatious په خپله پوهه باندي تظاهر کول to be puffed up about one's knowledge

تعادل ta'ādúl *m. Arabic* 1 equilibrium خپل تعادل ساتل to preserve an equilibrium 2 balance, proportion; conformity 3 balance (sheet) تجارتي تعادل balance of trade 4 *figurative* moderation, restraint

تعارض ta'ārúz *m. Arabic* contradiction; counteraction, opposition دیوشي سره تعارض لرل to contradict, act counter to something

تعارف ta'ārúf *m. Arabic* 1 treat, regalement دچا تعارف کول to treat someone, regale someone 2 exchange of courtesies 3 custom 4 acquaintance تعارف غایبانه دهغه acquaintance by correspondence سره دي تعارف شته که نه؟ د چا په Are you acquainted with him? تعارف ویل to acquaint with someone to present someone, acquaint, introduce someone

تعاطي ta'ātí *f. Arabic* exchange د افکارو تعاطي exchange of opinions د معاونت تعاطي mutual assistance

تعاقب ta'āķúb *m. Arabic* 1 following one another 2 succession, sequence 3 replacement, alternation, interchange

تعالي¹ ta'ālí *f. Arabic* 1 eminence, elevation, raising 2 high praise, extolment

تعالى² ta'ālā *Arabic religion* Most High (epithet for God)

تعامل ta'āmúl *m. Arabic* 1 interaction 2 *chemistry* reaction کیمیاوي تعامل chemical reaction 3 reaction تعامل کول to react 4 ملي حقوقیه او جزائیه تعاملات customary law, adat law custom

تعاون ta'āvún *m. Arabic* 1 mutual assistance 2 interconnection, interdependence 3 cooperation

تعاوني ta'āvuní *Arabic* cooperative تعاوني کول to cooperate

تعبد ta'abbúd *m. Arabic* 1 slavery, imprisonment 2 *religion* asceticism

تعبیر ta'bír *m. Arabic* [*plural:* تعبیرونه ta'burúna *Arabic plural:* تعبیرات ta'birắt] 1 expression, turn of speech غلط تعبیر incorrect expression 2 explanation, interpretation 3 description, representation د تعبیر قوت expressiveness تعبیرکول *compound verb* ☞ تعبیربدل *compound verb* ☞ تعبیرول، تعبیرکېدل 4 term

تعبیرول ta'biravól *denominative, transitive* [*past:* تعبیر یې کړ] 1 to explain, interpret 2 to describe, represent 3 to formulate

تعبیري ta'birí *phraseological* دژبي تعبیري پانگه phraseology

تعبیرېدل ta'abiredól *denominative, intransitive* [*past:* تتعبیر شو] 1 to be explained 2 to be described, be represented په یوه نامه تعبیربدل to be named, be designated, be called

تعبیوي ta'bijaví *Arabic military* tactical تعبیوي مانوره tactical maneuvers

تعبیه ta'bijá *f. Arabic military* tactics

تعبیه دان ta'bijadắn *military* tactician تعبیه دان قوماندان

تعجب ta'adzhdzhúb *m. Arabic* astonishment, amazement تعجب کول to be astonished, be amazed دي خبري ته تعجب دئ چه... Here's what's amazing … په تعجب کښي کېدل to be astonished, be amazed تعجب ورل to amaze, astonish

تعجب آوار ta'adzhdzhbāvár تعجب ناک ta'adzhdzhubnắk amazing, astonishing

تعجیز ta'dzhíz *m. Arabic* causing unrest تعجیزات او تعرضات *military* harrassment

تعداد ta'dắd *m. Arabic* number, quantity د طبع تعداد circulation of a publication

تعدي ta'addí *f. Arabic* 1 encroachment, infringement 2 violence; oppression تعدي کول *a* to infringe, encroach (upon) *b* to commit an act of violence; oppress

تعدیل ta'díl *Arabic* [*plural:* تعدیلونه ta'dilúna *Arabic plural:* تعدیلات ta'dilất] 1 correction; improvement 2 straightening, straightening

out (a line, road, etc.) 3 regulation; adjustment تعدیل کول *compound verb* ☞ تعدیلول

تعدیل نامه ta'dilnāmá *f.* amendment (to a law, etc.)

تعدیلول ta'dilavól *denominative, transitive* [*past:* تعدیل یې کړ] 1 to correct; improve 2 to straighten (a line, a road, etc.) 3 to regulate; adjust

تعذیب ta'azíb *m. Arabic* 1 torture, suffering 2 punishment

تعذیبول ta'azibavól *denominative, transitive* [*past:* تعذیب یې کړ] to torture

تعذیبېدل ta'azibedól *denominative, intransitive* [*past:* تعذیب شو] to be tortured, suffer

تعرض ta'arrúz *m.* [*plural:* تعرضونه ta'arruzúna *plural Arabic plural:* تعرضات ta'arruzất] attack; offensive پر چا باندي تعرض کول to attack someone, move against someone تعرض شروع کول to go on the attack, cross over to the offensive

تعرضي ta'arruzí *Arabic* 1 *adjective* offensive, attack تعرضي محاربه offensive battle 2 aggressive (of a pact, etc.)

تعرفه *f. Arabic* 1 tariff 2 time-table, schedule 3 list

تعریف ta'ríf *m. Arabic* [*plural:* تعریفونه ta'rifúna *Arabic plural:* تعریفات ta'rifất] 1 description; definition; characteristics 2 eulogy; praise; honorable mention دیو شي تعریف کول to praise someone تعریف کېدل، تعریفول *compound verb* ☞ تعریف کول *compound verb* ☞ تعریفېدل

تعریف نامه ta'rifnāmá *f. military* instructions, manual

تعریفول ta'rifavól *denominative, transitive* [*past:* تعریف یې کړ] 1 to describe; determine; characterize 2 to praise, eulogize

تعریفېدل ta'rifedól *denominative, intransitive* [*past:* تعریف شو] 1 to be desecribed; to be defined; to be characterized 2 to be praised

تعز ta'íz *m.* ta'ízz Taizz (city, south Yemen)

تعزیت ta'ziját *m. Arabic* 1 sympathy, condolence د تعزیت خط letter with an expression of sympathy 2 mourning

تعزیت نامه ta'zijatnāmá *f.* letter with an expression of sympathy

تعزیر ta'zír *m. Arabic* 1 punishment (not provided by the sharia, but determined by the judge) 2 punishment (of a criminal)

تعزیرول ta'ziravól *denominative, transitive* [*past:* تعزیر یې کړ] 1 to impose a punishment (not provided in the sharia, but determined by the judge himself) 2 to punish (a criminal)

تعزیري ta'zirí not provided for by the sharia but determined by the judge himself (of a punishment) تعزیري مجازات punishment (determined by the judge himself)

تعزیرېدل ta'ziredól *denominative, intransitive* [*past:* تعزیر شو] 1 to undergo punishment (not provided by the sharia, but determined by the judge) 2 to be punished (of a criminal)

تعزیه ta'zijá *f. Arabic* 1 ☞ تعزیت 2 tazia (a Shiite mystery play)

تعصب ta'assúb *m. Arabic* 1 fanaticism 2 impatience 3 passion (for something) 4 prejudice, bias

تعطیل ta'tíl *Arabic* 1 *m.* 1.1 time of rest د تعطیل روغ non-working day, holiday 1.2 cessation, suspension (of work, etc.); break دري کاله تعطیل د ملازمت *official* removal from a job for three years (as a punishment) **1.3** closing (of an enterprise) تعطیل کول *compound verb* ☞ تعطیلول **2** *predicate adjective* **.1** stopped, suspended (of work, etc.) **2.2** closed (of an enterprise) تول رسمي دوایر تعطیل وو no institutions were working, all institutions were closed

تعطیلول ta'tilavәl *denominative, transitive* [past: یې کۍ تعطیل] **1** to cease, suspend (work, etc.); have a break, have a recess **2** to close (an enterprise)

تعظیم ta'zím *m. Arabic* greetings; rendering homage, doing honors د هغه یې ښه تعظیم وکئ *military* saluting They greeted د تعظیم رسم him respectfully. They paid him great honors.

عفن ta'affún *m. Arabic* decay, rot, putrefaction

تعقل ta'aќúl *m. Arabic* **1** reason **2** understanding, awareness

تعقلي ta'aќulí reasonable, judicious, intelligent

تعقیب ta'ќíb *m. Arabic* **1** following after someone یو د بل په تعقیب one after another د چا تعقیب کول to follow after someone, not to lag behind someone, not to lose touch **2** pursuit, chase **3** realization, fulfillment (of hopes, aspirations) *idiom* د چا د سرنوشت to share someone's fate په لیک سره تعقیب کول *official* to تعقیب کول confirm in writing

تعقیبات ta'ќibất *m. Arabic plural* **1** *from* تعقیب **2** prosecution, being taken to court قانونیه تعقیبات answering before the law تر جزائي تعقیباتو لاندي راوستل instituting criminal proceedings (against)

تعقیبول ta'ќibavәl *denominative, transitive* [past: یې کۍ تعقیب] **1** to carry out, fulfill (a policy, a course, etc.) **2** to pursue someone, follow (after) someone **3** to keep track of something د دنیا واقعات to keep track of world events تعقیبول

تعقیبیدل ta'ќibedәl *denominative, intransitive* [past: شو تعقیب] **1** to be carried out, be put into effect (of a policy, course, etc.) **2** to be pursued **3** to be realized (of hopes, aspirations)

تعقید ta'ќíd *m. Arabic* **1** entanglement, complexity, vagueness, obscurity **2** tying of a knot

تعقیم ta'ќím *m. Arabic* sterilization

تعلق ta'allúќ *m. Arabic* [plural: تعلقونه ta'alluќúna *Arabic plural:* تعلقات ta'alluќất] **1** relation, connection سیاسي تعلقات diplomatic relations په یو شي تعلق لرل، په یو شي پوري تعلق لرل to bear a relationship to something دچا سره تعلق لرل to support relations with someone **2** acquaintance **3** *history* taluk, taluka (administrative region in India)

تعلقات ta'alluќất *m. Arabic plural* **1** *from* تعلق **2** questions relating to a matter

تعلم ta'allúm *m. Arabic philosophy* cognition

تعلیق ta'líќ *m. Arabic* **1** hanging, suspending, fastening **2** postponement **3** talik (a style of writing)

تعلیقه ta'liќá *f. Arabic* **1** appendix (to a book, etc.) **2** note (in the margins), marginalia

تعلیقي ta'liќí **1** postponed, delayed **2** conditional (of a verdict or sentence in court) **3** overhanging, impending

تعلیل ta'líl *m. Arabic* **1** clarification of a reason په تعلیل پسي درومل to explain a reason **2** reference

تعلیلي ta'lilí causal تعلیلي استدلال reason, justification

تعلیم ta'lím *m. Arabic* **1** teaching; learning تعلیم اخیستل to study, learn تعلیم کول to teach **2** *military* drill training

تعلیمات ta'limất *m. Arabic plural* **1** *from* تعلیم **2** preparation; training, schooling اساسي تعلیمات general preparation لوړ تعلیمات higher education

تعلیماتنامه ta'limātnāmá *f.* instructions; manual; regulation

تعلیماتي ta'limātí ☞ تعلیمي

تعلیمخانه ta'limkhāná *f.* educational facility; study room, auditorium; riding school

تعلیمگاه ta'limgắ *f.* ta'limgáh *regional* institution of learning, educational institution

تعلیمنامه ta'limnāmá *f. military* regulations د محاربي تعلیمنامه field manual

تعلیمي ta'limí *Arabic* **1** educational تعلیمي کال school year تعلیمي سابقه، تعلیمي حالت training received; education received تعلیمي جبه خانه *military* drill cartridges, rounds educational aids تعلیمي سامانونه **2** instructive, didactic

تعلیمیافته ta'limjāftá **1** learned; educated تعلیم یافته د فرانسي تعلیم یافته educated in France **2** *military* senior soldier

تعمق ta'ammúќ *m. Arabic* immersion (e.g., in thought); thoughtfulness په غور او تعمق سره thoughtfully

تعمیر ta'mír *m. Arabic* [plural: تعمیرونه ta'mirúna *Arabic plural:* تعمیرات ta'mirất] **1** construction **2** building **3** *figurative* creation, construction د نوي ژوند تعمیرات building a new life

تعمیراتي ta'mirātí تعمیري ta'mirí *adjective* building, construction تعمیراتي کارگران the construction industry تعمیراتي صنایع construction workers, builders **2** *figurative* creative, constructive

تعمیل ta'míl *m. Arabic* carrying out, fulfillment, realization تعمیل تعمیل کۍدل، تعمیلول *compound verb* ☞ کول *compound verb* ☞ تعمیلۍدل

تعمیلول ta'milavәl *denominative, transitive* [past: یې کۍ تعمیل] to carry out, fulfill, realize

تعمیلۍدل ta'miledәl *denominative, intransitive* [past: شو تعمیل] to be enacted, be fulfilled, be realized

تعمیم ta'mím *m. Arabic* dissemination, popularization; inculcation تعمیم پیداکول to be disseminated, be popularized; take root تعمیم کول *compound verb* to disseminate, popularize; inculcate تعمیم کۍدل *compound verb* to be disseminated; take root

تعویذ ta'víz *m. Arabic* amulet, talisman

تعویض ta'víz *m. Arabic* **1** substitution, replacement **2** recompense, compensation

تعویضول ta'vizavәl *denominative, transitive* [past: یې کۍ تعویض] **1** to subsitute, replace **2** to make up for, compensate

تعویضۍدل ta'vizedәl *denominative, intransitive* [past: شو تعویض] **1** to be changed, be replaced **2** to be compensated

تعویق ta'víќ *m. Arabic* postponement, delay, procrastination

تعهد ta'ahhúd *m. Arabic* **1** obligation **2** contract, agreement (for work, supply of something) تعهد کول a to obligate oneself, pledge

b to reach agreement (on work, supplies of something) **c** *compound verb* to make conditional (upon), cause, bring about تعهد كېدل *compound verb* to be conditioned (by)

تعهداً ta'ahhúdán *Arabic* on an oath تعهداقبول to promise on an oath

تعهد نامه ta'ahhudnāmá *f.* written pledge, obligation in writing

تعیین *m. Arabic* definition, determination; establishment, fixing; appointment د ځمكي پر سر تعیین setting a price قیمت تعیین position finding

تعیینول ta'ajjunavál *denominative, transitive* ☞ تعیینول

تعیین ta'jín *m. Arabic* determination; establishment; fixing, setting تعیین كول *compound verb* ☞ تعیینول to orient oneself to the terrain د ځمكي پرمخ ځای تعیین كول *compound verb* ☞ تعیینبدل

تعیینات ta'jinā́t *m. Arabic plural* **1** *from* تعیین **2** *military* one day's ration

تعیینول *denominative, transitive* [*past:* تعیین يې کړ] to determine; to establish; to fix, set

تعیینبدل *denominative, intransitive* [*past:* تعیین شو] to be defined, be established; be fixed, be set

تغ [1] təgh *m.* helmet

تغ [2] təgh *m.* **1** whistle (of a bullet) **2** crackling (of meat being fried)

تغ [3] tugh *m.* ☞ توغ [1]

تغاده taghādá *f.* ☞ تقاضا

تغار taghā́r *m.* ☞ تاغار

تغارك təghārák *m. medicine* dropsy

تغاري təghārí *m.* person suffering from dropsy

تغدري təghdarí *f. zoology Chlamydotis undulata* (large crane of the steppe)

تغذیه taghzijá *f. Arabic* nourishment; feeding دتغذيې فعل خرابول to cause indigestion

تغزل taghazzúl *m. Arabic* lyric poetry; lyrics

تغزلي taghazzulí lyrical (of poetry)

تغلقي tughluḳí *history* relating to the Tughluq Dynasty (of India)

تغمه taghmá *f.* blow from a whip, blow from a stick

تغند təghənd ☞ سركنده

تغندی təghándaj *m.* basin, bowl

تغنول təghnavál *transitive* [*past:* و يې تغناوه] to roast; burn, scorch

تغني taghanni *f. Arabic* singing

تغول [1] təghavál *transitive* [*past:* و يې تغناوه] to roast badly

تغول [2] tughavál *transitive* ☞ توغول

تغندی tughundáj *m.* ☞ توغندی

تغیر [1] taghajjúr **1** *m. Arabic* **.1** change; alteration كمي تغیرات *philosophy* qualitative changes كيفي تغیرات *philosophy* quantative changes د تغیر پكنبي راوستل to introduce changes تغیر مېندل، تغیر كول، تغیر خورل، تغیر موندل to change, be transformed وضعیت مهم تغیر ندئ موندلئ the situation has not materially changed تغیر وركول to change, alter **1.2** dismissal (from a position) **1.3** difference, distinction **2** *predicate* **.1** changed, altered **2.2** replaced

تغیر [2] taghír *m. colloquial* change, alteration

تغیرول taghiravól *denominative, transitive* [*past:* تغیر يې کړ] **1** to change, alter **2** to replace

تغیري taghirí *f.* تغیربده tagiredə́ *m. plural* **1** change, alteration **2** replacement, substitution

تغیربدل taghiredól *denominative, intransitive* [*past:* تغیر شو] **1** to change, be changed *m.* **2** to be replaced

تغیر taghjír *m. Arabic* ☞ تغیر

تف [1] taf *m.* steam

تف [2] tuf *m.* **1** spitting **2** spit, spittle

تفاریق tafārík *m. Arabic plural from* تفریقه

تفاسیر tafāsír *m. Arabic plural from* تفسیر

تفاله tufalá *f.* oilcakes; concentrates (for cattle)

تفاوت tafāvút *m. Arabic* difference, distinction لرل تفاوت to differ, stand out

تفتیش taftísh *m. Arabic* **1** audit; inspection د تفتیش هیئت audit commission **2** customs inspection; checking (of passports at a border)

تفحص tafahhús *m. Arabic* **1** interrogation, interview; search **2** test, trial

تفحصاتي tafahhusā́ti *adjective* test, trial

تفرع tafarrú' *f. Arabic* **1** branching, forking **2** branch (of industry, etc.)

تفرعات tafarru'ā́t *m. Arabic plural* **1** *from* تفرع **2** particulars; details

تفرقه tafriḳá *f. Arabic* **1** division, separation **2** disagreement; split, schism تفرقه غوښتونكى schismatic; separatist; sectarian تفرقه اچول to create dissent

تفریح tafrí tafríh *Arabic* [*plural:* تفریحگاني tafrigā́ni *plural:* tafrihgā́ni] *m. Arabic* [*plural:* تفریحات tarfihā́t] **1** distraction, amusement, gaiety **2** leave, vacation د تفریح رخصت *official* leave for rest **3** rest, vacation د تفریح وخت school interval, break *idiom* د تفریح باغ culture and rest park

تفریح گاه tafrihgā́h *m.* resort

تفریحي tafrihí amusing, entertaining په ډېر تفریحي سبك ليكل to write in an entertaining way

تفریخ tafríkh *m. Arabic medicine* incubation د تفریخ دوره incubation period

تفریط tafrít *m. Arabic* carelessness, negligence د تفریط له لاسه from carelessness, from negligence

تفریق tafrík *m. Arabic* **1** distinction, difference **2** discrimination **3** *math* subtraction

تفریقول tafriḳavól *denominative, transitive* [*past:* تفریق يې کړ] **1** to distinguish, tell the differnce (between) **2** to discriminate, practice discrimination **3** *math* to subtract

تفریقه tafriḳá *f. Arabic f.* [*plural:* تفریقې tafriḳé *m. Arabic plural:* تفاریق tafārík] interval, distance (between)

تفسیر tafsír *m. Arabic* [*plural:* تفسیرونه tafsirúna *Arabic plural:* تفاسیر tafāsír *plural:* تفسیرات tafsirā́t] **1** explanation, commentary

دخپل موقف تفسیر کول to set forth one's own position **2** *religion* commentary on the Koran **3** *description* (of something)

تفسیرول tafsiravә́l *denominative, transitive* [*past:* تفسیر یې کړ] to explain, elucidate, provide commentary

تفسیرېدل tafsiredә́l *denominative, intransitive* [*past:* تفسیر شو] to be explained; explain oneself; to be provided with commentary

تفصیل tafsíl *m. Arabic* [*plural:* تفصیلونه tafsilúna *Arabic plural:* تفصیلات tafsilā́t] **1** detailed account د ويناو تفصيلات detailed account of the speeches, detailed account of presentations تفصيل کول to expound in detail, give a detailed account **2** detail په تفصيل سره in detail, exhaustively

تفصيلاً tafsílán تفصيلوار tafsilvā́r *Arabic* in detail, thoroughly

تفصيلي tafsilí *Arabic* detailed, thorough په تفصيلي ډول in detail; thoroughly

تفضيل tafzíl *m. Arabic* **1** superiority **2** preference **3** *grammar* superlative (degree)

تفکر tafakkúr *m. Arabic* **1** reflection, meditation; deliberation **2** thoughtfulness, pensiveness **3** worry, concern **4** thought, thinking تفکر کول **a** to reflect upon, think over **b** to fall into deep thought **c** to worry about **d** to think

تفکير tafkír *m. Arabic* deliberation, consideration; reflection, meditation

تفکيک tafkík *m. Arabic* **1** division, separation, fragmentation **2** *physics* splitting, fission د اتومي هستۍ تفکيک splitting the atom, nuclear fission

تفنگ tufáng *m.* rifle ☞ توپک

تفنگچه tufangchá *f.* revolver, pistol

تفنگ ساز tufangsā́z *m.* gunsmith

تفنگ سازي tufangsāzí *f.* manufacture of hand guns, manufacture of rifles

تفنن tafannún *m. Arabic* **1** erudition, learning **2** study of the sciences د تفنن دپاره with cognitive purposes **3** art, skill, ability

تفوق tafavvúḳ *m. Arabic* **1** superiority تر چا تفوق لرل، پر چا تفوق لرل to excel, stand above (someone), stand out (among others) پر چا تفوق حاصلول to gain ascendancy over someone **2** supremacy فضائي تفوق *military* air supremacy

تفويض tafvíz *m. Arabic* handing over, delivery, transmission کول *compound verb* to hand over, transmit, deliver

تفهم tafahhúm *m. Arabic* understanding, comprehension, grasp

تفهيم tafhím *Arabic* **1** *official* information, notification **2** explanation, elucidation; annotation

تقابل taḳābúl *m. Arabic* **1** meeting, reception تقابل **2** taḳābúl *m. astronomy* opposition **3** conflict (of views, interests)

تقادم taḳādúm *m. Arabic* antiquity, olden times

تقارب taḳārúb *m. Arabic* **1** rapprochement **2** *poetry* kind of a meter in verse

تقارير taḳārír *m. Arabic plural from* تقرير

تقاضا taḳāzā́ *f. Arabic* [*plural:* تقاضاگاني taḳāzāgā́ni *m. Arabic plural:* تقاضي taḳāzí] requirement; demand to require; to present a demand, submit a demand تقاضا کول to need something

تقاعد taḳā'úd *m. Arabic* retirement with pension

تقاليد taḳālíd *m. Arabic plural* **1** *from* تقليد **2** tradition; custom

تقبيح taḳbíh *f. Arabic* condemnation, censure, criticism

تقبيحول taḳbihavә́l *denominative, transitive* [*past:* تقبيح يې کړ] to condemn, censure; discredit, defame; criticize

تقدس taḳaddús *m. Arabic* **1** holiness; piety **2** respect, reverence

تقدم taḳaddún *Arabic* **1** movement ahead, movement forward; an offensive **2** *figurative* progress تقدم کول **a** to move forward; to advance **b** *figurative* to develop

تقدير taḳdír [1] *m. Arabic* evaluation دیو شي لوړ تقدير کول to put a high value on something

تقدير [2] taḳdír *m. Arabic* **1** proposition, hypothesis **2** condition په دې تقدير چه ... on the condition that ... **3** fate, predestination

تقديراً taḳdírán *Arabic* in fact, actually

تقديرنامه taḳdirnāmá *f.* certificate of progress and good conduct (in school)

تقديرول taḳdiravә́l *denominative, transitive* [*past:* تقدير يې کړ] to value, appreciate; render (someone) his due

تقديري taḳdirí تقديري قوت fate, lot, predestination

تقديس taḳdís *m. Arabic* sanctification, consecration; deification, worshipping

تقديم taḳdím *m. Arabic* **1** presentation, presenting; delivery, handing (over) **2** present, tribute تقديم کول *compound verb* ☞ تقديمول

تقديمول taḳdimavә́l *denominative, transitive* [*past:* تقديم يې کړ] **1** to present, give; hand over, deliver **2** to present with و چاته *idiom* تبريکات تقديمول to send one's respects to someone سلامونه تقديمول to send greetings

تقر taḳór *m.* astrakhan (fur)

تقرب taḳarrúb *m. Arabic* approach, drawing near, closing in تقرب کول to draw near, draw together *idiom* یوې دعوي ته تقرب کول to lay claim to something, have pretensions to something

تقرر taḳarrúr *m. Arabic* **1** appointment د تقرر عزت ميندل *official* to be awarded an appointment تقرر ميندل to be appointed **2** function, responsibility, appointment

تقريب taḳríb *m. Arabic* **1** drawing near, approach **2** coming (e.g., of a holiday) *idiom* په دې تقريب on this account, in connection with this

تقريباً taḳríbán *Arabic* approximately, about تقريباً لس کاله پخوا about 10 years ago

تقريبي taḳribí *Arabic* approximate

تقرير taḳrír *m. Arabic* [*plural:* تقريرونه taḳirúna *Arabic plural:* تقارير taḳārír] **1** confession, declaration **2** announcement, pronouncement; speech, word; public appearance, speech افتتاحي introductory word د تقرير آزادي freedom of speech تقرير کول **a** to confess, declare **b** to speak out; to come forward with a speech, make an announcement; appear د تقریر دپاره بلل to give someone your word

تقریر کوونکی takrír kavúnkaj *m.* orator

تقریظ takríz *m. Arabic* 1 review 2 criticism تقریظ او تنقید rubric, heading, section of criticism (in a newspaper or magazine) 3 praise

تقسیم taksím *m. Arabic* [*plural:* تقسیمونه taksimúna *Arabic plural:* تقسیمات taksimất] 1 *military* .1 division; partition, section; distribution, allocation 1.2 *math* division لاندي تقسیمونه حل کړئ solve the following problems using division 2 *military* deployment garrisoning; disposition 3 classification, classification scientific *idiom* تقسیم اوقات taksím-i order of the day ملکیه تقسیمات administrative division

تقسیمول taksimavól *denominative, transitive* [*past:* تقسیم یې کړ] 1.1 to divide; partition, separate; distribute, allocate 1.2 *math* to divide 2 *military* to deploy *idiom* تقسیم یې کړه او حکومت پري کوه! Divide and conquer!

تقسیمېدل taksimedól *denominative, intransitive* [*past:* تقسیم شو] 1 to be divided; be separated; be distributed 2 *math* to be divided

تقسیمېده taksimedó *m. plural* division; separation, parting; distribution, allocation *math plural* division

تقصیر taksír *m.* [*plural:* تقصیرونه taksirúna *Arabic plural:* تقصیرات taksirất] 1 omission, negligence 2 fault, blame, transgression, sin دخپل تقصیر په اثر through one's own fault تقصیر کول to commit a sin, be guilty of an offense

تقصیردار taksirdár having committed an offense, (having been) guilty of wrongdoing

تقطیع taktí' *f. Arabic* 1 format (of a book) 2 scansion (of verses) تقطیع کول to scan (verses)

تقلب takallúb *m. Arabic* deceit, deception, cheating (at games), swindling

تقلبي takallubí false, fake

تقلید taklíd *m. Arabic* 1 imitation; copying تقلید کول، تقلید د ... د ... کول to imitate; copy 2 following (a spiritual leader)

تقلیدي taklidí 1 imitative 2 false, counterfeit, unnatural

تقلیل taklíl *m. Arabic* 1 diminution, lessening, decrease تقلیل مېندل to lessen, decrease, get smaller 2 insufficiency, lack, deficit

تقنینی takniní *Arabic* legislative

تقنینیه takninija *f. Arabic* legislative body

تقوی takvấ *f. Arabic* piety اهل تقوی áhl-i God-fearing people

تقویت takviját *m. Arabic* ☞ تقویه

تقویم takvím *m. Arabic* 1 evaluation, valuation 2 device; regulating, putting into (good) order 3 *astronomy* calendar 4 almanac

تقویه takvijá *f. Arabic* 1 strengthening; reinforcing, making firm; development (e.g., of trade) دجسم تقویه fortifying one's health تقویه کول *compound verb* to strengthen; fortify, reinforce, make firm; develop (trade) *compound verb* تقویه کېدل، تقویه مېندل to

become strong; be fortified; become firmer, be consolidated; develop (e.g., of trade)

تقي taki *Arabic* pious, devout

تقاجد takajúd *m.* 1 trying, diligence, industry; effort, endeavor 2 worry, concern

تقیه takijá *f. Arabic* piety, devoutness

تک ¹ tak *m.* run, running, race تک کول to run; bustle, fuss

تک ² tak *m.* locust

تک ³ tǝk *combining form with colors for intensification* تک تور jet black, black as tar تک سپین very white, white as snow تک سور blood red, scarlet

تک ⁴ tak *m.* supposition

تکاپو takāpú *m.* 1 bustle, fuss, bother 2 search تکاپو کول a to run around, fuss, bother b to run around, ransack in search of something

تکاثر takāsúr *m. Arabic* abundance

تکاثف takāsúf *m. Arabic* thickening; concentration

تکاسل takāsúl *m. Arabic* 1 laziness 2 carelessness, negligence

تکافو takāfú *m. Arabic* 1 equivalence, identity 2 authenticity, trustworthiness 3 payment, covering (of expenditures)

تکالیف takālíf *m. Arabic plural* 1 *from* تکلیف 2 responsibilities, obligations (e.g., of an employer)

تکامل takāmúl *m. Arabic* 1 improvement; development, progress تکامل مېندل to improve; develop 2 finish, completeness تدریجي تکامل evolution

تکاملي takāmulí evolutionary تکاملي سیر، تکاملي عمليه process of improvement, process of development; evolution; progress

تکان takấn *m.* 1 push, shove دتگ په وخت کښي تکان خورل to rock or sway while walking 2 shaking تکان ورکول to shake; rock, stir up

تکاهل takāhúl *m. Arabic* carelessness, negligence تکاهل کول to display carelessness, display negligence

تکبر takabbúr *m. Arabic* conceit, haughtiness, arrogance

تکبیر takbír *m. Arabic religion* pronunciation of the formula الله اکبر! God is great!

تکت tikát *m.* ☞ ټکټ

تکت پولي tikatpulí *f.* ☞ ټکټ پولي

تکتک takták *m.* knocking, tapping تک تک کول to knock, tap د ور ترشا تک تک کول to knock at the door

تک تنها tak-tanhấ absolutely alone; all by oneself

تکثر takassúr *m. Arabic* 1 *biology* reproduction 2 increase, growth; development تکثر کول a *biology* to reproduce, multiply b to increase, grow; develop

تکثیر taksír *m. Arabic* multiplication; increase in quantity; augmentation in number, augmentation in personnel strength

تکثیف taksíf *Arabic* thickening, condensing

تکذیب takzíb *Arabic* refutation; being caught in a lie, exposure (as a liar, etc.) تکذیب کېدل، تکذیبول *compound verb* ☞ تکذیبېدل *compound verb* ☞

تکذیبول takzibavә́l *denominative, transitive* [*past:* تکذیب یې کړ] **1** to refute **2** to catch in a lie, expose

تکذیبیدل takzibedә́l *denominative, intransitive* [*past:* تکذیب شو] **1** to be refuted **2** to be caught lying, be exposed (as a liar, etc.)

تکرار takrā́r *m. Arabic* **1** repetition د درسو تکرار repetition of lessons **2** renewal *compound verb* ☞ تکرار تکرارول میندل **a** to repeat, be repeated; learn by rote **b** to be renewed, resume **3** *Eastern* argument; altercation سبب د تکرار څه وه؟ What caused the argument?

تکرارول takrāravә́l *denominative, transitive* [*past:* تکرار یې کړ] **1** to repeat; learn by rote, memorize **2** to renew **3** *Eastern* to argue

تکراري takrārí tikrārí **1.1** repeated; recurring **1.2** *Eastern* peevish, shrewish **2** *m. Eastern* squabbler, wrangler; debater

تکراریدل takrāredә́l *denominative, intransitive* [*past:* تکرارشو] **1** to repeat, be repeated دا واقعه بیا تکرارشوه This incident has occured again. **2** to be renewed, resume

تکر خور takr xor *m. technology* shock-absorber

تکري tukrí *f.* **1** basket **2** chute, gutter, trough

تکریم takrím *m. Arabic* **1** esteem, respect **2** [*plural:* تکریمات takrimā́t] honors

تکړښت takŕә́xht *m.* sport

تکړه ¹ tukŕá *f.* pebble

تکړه ² takŕá *indeclinable* **1** healthy, strong تکړه اوسه! Be well! To your health! **2** hale and hearty; full of strength and energy, energetic تکړه کول **a** to make healthy, make strong; fortify **b** to invigorate, fill with energy ځان تکړه کول to encourage oneself, spur oneself on تکړه کیدل **a** to be healthy, be strong; fortify **b** to be vigorous, be energetic **3** healthy, not infected by disease (of crops)

تکړه توب takŕatób *m.* تکړه تیا takŕatjā *f.* تکړه والی takŕavā́laj *m.* **1** health; strength, power **2** heartiness; cheerfulness; vigorousness

تکړی takŕә́j *f.* patch (for garments)

تکفین takfín *m. Arabic* wrapping in a shroud (the deceased)

تکل takál *m.* **1** intention; aspiration **2** attempt; trying د ... تکل کول **a** to intend; to strive (for) **b** to try, attempt **3** exercise *idiom* د اوده کېدو په تکل شوم I was going to sleep.

تکلاسی، تک لاسی tak-lā́saj **1** energetic; active **2** quick, agile; adroit; cunning

تکلف takallúf *m. Arabic* **1** ceremoniousness; constraint; artificiality **2** ceremony; etiquette; formality **3** efforts, work(s) تکلف کول to try, make an effort

تکلم takallúm *m. Arabic* conversation, speech تکلم کول to carry on a conversation, talk, chat

تکلیف taklíf *m. Arabic* [*plural:* تکلیفونه taklifúna *Arabic plural:* تکالیف takālíf] **1** difficulty; uneasiness, constraint; labor, efforts تاسوته زما په وجه ډېر بې له تکلیفه without difficulty, without fuss تکلیف کول I caused you a great deal of worry. to worry, fuss تکلیف ورکول to feel uneasy, worry تکلیف لرل to make difficult; cause worry **2** ceremony; etiquette **3** obligation, debt

اخلاقي تکلیف moral duty *idiom* ساده ، بې تکلیفه ډودی simple food, modest refreshment

تکم tukә́m *m.* race; breed, species

تکمه tukmá *f.* **1** button **2** *medicine* hemorrhoid **3** knob (e.g., of a doorbell)

تکمیل میندل takmíl *m. Arabic* **1** completion; fulfillment **2** perfection **a** to be completed, be finished; be fulfilled **b** to be improved, be perfected; improve

تکمیلول takmilavә́l *denominative, transitive* [*past:* تکمیل یې کړ] **1** to complete, finish; fulfill **2** to improve, perfect

تکمیلیدل takmiledә́l *denominative, intransitive* [*past:* تکمیل شو] **1** to be completed, be finished; be fulfilled **2** to be improved, be perfected

تکمیلیده takmiledә́ *m. plural* **1** completion, ending **2** improving, perfecting

تکنالوجست teknālodzhíst *m.* technologist, engineer

تکنالوژي teknālodzhí *f.* ☞ تکنالوجي

تکنالوژي teknālozhí *f.* technology

تکنالوژیکي teknālozhikí technological تکنالوژیکي عملیات technological process

تکنیک tekník *m.* technique; engineering; equipment

تکاپو tak-u-pú *m.* ☞ تک و پو

تکوین takvín *m. Arabic* **1** creation **2** forming, organizing **3** conception; origin

تکه ¹ tiká *f.* piece

تکه ² tiká *f.* ☞ تیکه

تکه ³ tәká ungelded (of a ram, billy goat)

تکه تپارکه tәka-tapárka *f.* hurry, haste, rush

تکه دار tikadár *m.* ☞ تېکه دار

تکی tәkә́j **1** paired, forming a pair **2** غوږونه تکی کول to prick up one's ears, be on the alert

تکیه takjá *f.* ☞ تکیا

تکیف takajjúf *m. Arabic* accommodation, device, fitting

تکیناباد takinābád *m.* Takinabad (city, ancient name for the city Kandahar)

تکیوان takivā́n *m.* prop (for fruit trees)

تکیه takjá *f. Arabic* **1** leaning (against) **2** support, rest, prop *compound verb* **a** to put, place توپک پر اوږه تکیه کول to put rifle on your shoulder **b** to lean, rest (against) ودیوال ته تکیه کول to lean against the wall **c** *figurative* to hope, count on پر ځان تکیه کول to rely on oneself په نورو باندي تکیه کول to rely on others **d** *military* to based (on) **3** pillow; head of the bed **4** dwelling of a fakir (i.e., dervish) *idiom* دغې اطلاع په تکیه on the basis of this report هغه دلي تکیه وهلي ده He has made himself at home here. په تکیه کښي دم وهل to pause for breath, take a breath

تکیه کلام takjakalā́m *m. Arabic* saying, catch phrase; popular expression

تکیه گاه takjagā́h *m. military* **1** base هوایي تکیه گاه airbase **2** bridgehead; beachhead **3** fortified post, strong point

تكييف takjíf *m. Arabic* 1 forming; organizing 2 adapting, adjusting 3 regulating

تگ tag *m.* 1 movement په تگ كښي on the move; in motion مخكښني تگ movement ahead, forward movement د تگ ډول gait (of horses) 2 conduct, behavior 3 relationship, connection 4 action, act, deed تگ كول a to walk, go, move b to behave c to maintain relations, maintain communications د خپلوي په توگه تگ كول to maintain friendly relations d to act, take action 5 gait, walk, step 6 dispatch; departure تگ اجازه غوښتل to request permission to leave لاري د تگ نه idiom ☞ تگ راتگ او تگ راتگ the truck broke down وه

تگا tigá *f.* patience تگا لرل to endure, bear *idiom* تگا وهل to be out of breath; puff, pant

تگاب tagáb *m.* ☞

تگاو tagáv *m.* 1 Tagab, Tagao (city, region) 2 *used in geographical names* شرين تگاو، شيرين تگاب Shirin Tagab (river)

تگ راتگ tagrátág *m.* 1 coming and going; arrival and departure 2 movement (back and forth, to and fro); communication د موټرو تگ راتگ travel here and there (of automobiles); automobile traffic, automotive transportation 3 exchange of visits; acquaintance, familiarity; contact تگ راتگ كول a to come and go b to go back and forth (of transport) c to associate (with)

تگړی tagə́raj *m.* 1 scrap, piece (of material) تگړی ايستل to tear off a piece تگړی تگړی كول to tear into pieces 2 ☞ تنبی¹ *idiom* تگړی اړول to exploit unscrupulously, oppress

تكسي گلپا tekusigalpá́ *f.* Tegucigalpa (capital, Honduras)

تگلی tagə́laj *m.* trampled area, tamped (down) area

تگ ليار tagljár *m.* regulation

تگ وپو tag-u-pú *m.* تگ ودو tag-u-dáv *m.* ☞ په تگ وپو كښني to rush about; fuss, bustle about

تگی tagə́j¹ *f.* board, bulletin board

تگی tə́gaj² *Eastern* ☞ تړی

تگير tagír *m.* dam (for disturbing water during irrigation)

تل tal¹ *m.* 1 bottom; bed (of a river) د بحر په تل كښني on the bottom of the sea تل كبدل to drown 2 level area, smooth area 3 basis, foundation (of something) 4 depths دزمكي په تل كښني in the lower regions of the earth 5 cavity, hollow 6 precipitation; sediment *idiom* د زړه په تل كښني in the depths of one's soul, deep in one's heart

تل tal² *m.* tall *Arabic* 1 hill, rise, raised place *m.* 2 Tal (city)

تل tə́l³ 1.1 always, constantly هغه تل سبق وائي He is constantly occupied. دروغ تل نه چلپږي *saying* You won't go far on a lie. 1.2 forever, eternally تل ته تله، تل تتله، تل تا تله *obsolete* تل تر تله forever, eternally تل دي وي سوله! Let there be lasting peace! 2 *m.* eternity د تل نوم گټل to be reowned through the ages

تل til⁴ *m.* ☞ تېل

تل ابيب talabíb *m.* Tel Aviv (city)

تلاتوب tə́látób uneasiness, agitation, anxiety

تلاړه tlári̇́ga *f.* shred, piece (of fabric, etc.)

تلاست tlāst *Western imperfect, second person plural of* تل¹

تلاش tə́lā́sh *m.* ☞ تلاښ

تلاشي talāāshí *f. Arabic Eastern* ☞ تلاښي

a تلاښ tə́lā́kh *m.* 1 trouble, fuss, worry 2 *Eastern* search تلاښ كول to fuss, bustle, trouble about b to search, enquire (into)

تلاښي tə́lā́khí *f.* search تلاښي اخيستل to search (the premises, etc.)

تلاطم talātúm *m. Arabic* 1 splash, splashing (of waves) 2 agitation, anxiety, worry

تلافي talāfí *m. Arabic* 1 compensation; replacement 2 catching up, repairing (an omission)

تلاكی talākə́j *f.* divorced wife ☞ طلاق

تلانگه talánga *f. literal & figurative* echo

تلاو talā́u *m.* man-made pool; reservoir; basin

تلاوت talāvát *m. Arabic* reading (usually of the Koran)

تلاوه tə́lāvá *f.* oppression

تلاوی tə́lávaj *m.* sugar molasses storage tank

تلای tlāj *conditional and potential form of* تل¹

تلب taláb¹ ☞ طلب

تلب taláb² *combining form with* تور

تلبر talbár *m.* 1 large chute, large gutter 2 *figurative* surface (of the sea, ocean)

تلبري talbarí *m.* glutton, gormandizer

تلبيس talbís *m. Arabic* deception, deceit, swindling, cheating

تلپاتی tə́lpā́taj eternal, everlasting

تلپچه talpəchá *f.* overhang of a roof, eaves

تلتک tə́ltakák *m.* [*plural:* تلتكونه tə́ltakúna *Western plural:* تلتكان tə́ltakā́n] 1 blanket 2 *Eastern* bed *idiom* د واورو تلتک a covering of snow, a blanket of snow

تلخ talkh bitter

تلخان talkhā́n *m.* ground mulberrys and walnuts (baked and sliced into squares)

تلخه tə́lkha *exclamation* go away, scat (used when chasing away dogs)

تلخي talkhí *f.* 1 bitter taste, bitter substance; bitterness 2 *figurative* grief, sorrow

تلذذ talazzúz *m. Arabic* 1 amusement, pleasure, enjoyment 2 savoriness, relish

تېلسكوپ tiliskóp *m.* teleskóp ☞

تل شين tə́l shín evergreen

تلطيف taltíf *m. Arabic* goodness, kindness; favor, charity; attention

تلغاک talghák *m.* 1 noise, din 2 thunder storm

تلف taláf *Arabic* 1 *m.* [*plural:* تلفونه talafúna *Arabic plural:* تلفات talafát *plural:* اتلاف atlā́f] .1 destruction, death 1.2 loss; casualty تلفات وراړول، تلفات وررسول to sustain losses تلفات وركول to inflict losses تلفات وريبنبدل، تلفات وررسبدل to suffer losses, sustain losses 1.3 annihilation, destruction تلف كول *compound verb* ☞ تلفول 2 *predicate* .1 perished; killed 2.2 annihilated, wiped out 2.3 spent, exhausted (of assests, means) 2.4 lost (e.g., of time)

تلفظ talaffúz *m. Arabic* pronunciation, accent تلفظ كول *compound verb* to pronounce, articulate

تلفول talafavәl *denominative, transitive [past:* تلف يي كړ] **1** to destroy; kill ځان تلفول ، ځانونه تلفول to destroy oneself **2** to annihilate **3** to squander, waster (means) **4** to lose (e.g., time)

تلفېدل talafedә́l *denominative, intransitive [past:* تلف شو] **1** to be killed **2** to perish, be lost تخمونه ټول تلف شول all the seeds perished **3** to be annihilated **4** to be squandered (of means) **5** to be lost (e.g., of time)

تلفېده talafedә́ *m. plural* **1** death, destruction, ruin **2** annihilation **3** loss (e.g., of time)

تلفیق talfík *m. Arabic grammar* combination; composition; word order د جملو تلفیق word order in a sentence

تلقي talaḳḳí *f. Arabic* meeting; reception, receipt (of some report, news, etc.) تلقي كول *compound verb* to meet; receive (some report, news, etc.) *idiom* طرز تلقي position with respect to, relationship towards

تلقيح talḳí *f.* talḳíh *Arabic* **1** inoculation **2** impregnation

تلقین talḳin *m. Arabic* **1** exhortation, admonition, inspiration د بري تلقین كول *compound verb* to edify, exhort, inspire *compound verb* to inspire fear **2** *religion* sermon, homily

تلكه taláka *f.* mousetrap; trap; snares

تلگراف tiligrǻf *m.* telegrǻf **1** telegraph په تلگراف سره by telegraph په تلگراف كښي احوال وركول to communicate by telegraph **2** telegram

تلگرافچي tiligrǻfchí *m.* telegrǻfchí telegraphist

تلگرافخانه tiligrǻfkhāná *f.* telegrǻfkhāná telegraph office

تلگرافي tiligrāfí telegrāfí **1** *adjective* telegraph, telegraphic راديو radiotelegraph **2** *m.* telegraphist, telegrapher

تلگرام tililgrǻm *m.* telegrǻm telegram چاته تلگرام وركول، چاته تلگرام استول to telegraph, send someone a telegram

تلل [1] tlәl **1** *intransitive* ځي *present tense* تئ *imperfect* تله *imperfect tense* ولاړ به شي *past tense* ولاړ به شي *future tense* ځه *imperfective imperative* ولاړ شه *perfective imperative*. **1.1** to go دوی ښار ته ځي They are going to town. **1.2** to go, run (of a mechanism) ساعت مي وراندي ځي My watch is fast. **1.3** to leave, depart, go away, set out; fly away (of birds, a plane) ته لا نه يي ؟ Haven't you left yet? تلل راتلل to come and go **1.4** to lead, go (of a road) دا لار چيري تللي ده؟ دا لار چيرته تللي ده؟ Where does this road lead? **1.5** to flow (of a river) **1.6** to flow out (of sap, etc.) **1.7** to pierce, penetrate (of a thorn, sliver) **1.8** to pass (of time) عمر تللئ دئ youth has passed ځلمي توب ولاړ years (have) passed **1.9** to disappear **1.10** to be spent, be exhausted (of money, materials) **1.11** *used with adverbs and adjectives:* بېرته تلل to return وراندي تلل to advance, move on **2** *m. plural* **1.** walking, going **2.2** leaving; departure, flight (of birds, a plane) **2.3** passage (of time) **2.4** loss, expenditure (of money, materials) **2.5** fading away, disappearance *idiom* رنگ يي تللئ و He turned pale. له دنیا ځخه ولاړ He died. He has departed this world.

تلل [2] talә́l *transitive [present:* تلي *past:* وي تاله و يي] **1** to weigh; *figurative* to consider ځان تلل to be weighed **2** to determine the weight of something by tossing it up; to estimate the weight of something **3** *figurative* to test someone, put someone to the test ما وتاله ، په دوستي كښي كلك دئ I have tested him, he is true to his friends **4** to compare **5** *figurative* to weigh, consider

تللو tlә́o *Eastern* ☞ تلو

تلئ [1] tlә́laj *past participle of* تلل [1]

تلئ [2] talә́laj *[past:* تلل] *past participle of* تلل [2]

تلم [1] tәm *first person past of* تلل [1]

تلم [2] talә́m *first person past of* تلل [2]

تلمتى tulumtáj *m.* ☞ ترمتى

تلمدام tә́lmudǻm eternally, forever تل مدام، تلمدام

تلمید tilmíz *m.* talmíz *Arabic* pupil

تلمیذي tilmizí talmizí *Arabic adjective* school, pupil's

تلنځي tlә́ndzáj *m.* appointed place, meeting place

تلنگه talә́nga *f.* ☞ تلنگي [1]

تلنگي [1] talә́ngi *f. usually plural* sole (of foot, boot) *idiom* تلنگي شلېدل to run your feet off looking for something

تلنگي [2] tilingí **1** *m. regional* Indian soldier ☞ گوره **2** *m. plural* Telugu (Dravidian people of India)

تلنلار tlә́nlǻr *f.* **1** line of movement; course; track **2** *figurative* direction

تلنه [1] tlә́na *f.* ☞ تلل [2]

تلنه [2] talә́na *f. action noun from* تلل [2]

تلو [1] tlo *Eastern imperfect of* تلل [1]

تلو [2] tlu *feminine plural of* تلل [1]

تلو [3] tlo *oblique plural of* تله [4]

تلوار talvǻr *m.* hurry, haste په تلوار، په تلوار سره hastily, hurriedly چيري داسي په تلوار ځي؟ زما تلوار دئ I'm in a hurry. Where are you going in such a hurry? پر ښو تلوار ، پر بدو تلوار كول to hurry, rush تامل *proverb* in the good hurry, in the bad be slow

تلوارگندى tavārgándaj precipitate, rash, hasty; hurried

تلواري tavārí fast, swift, quick; skillful, dexterous

تلوال talwǻl *computer science* default

تلوترک talotarák *m.* agitation, uneasiness تلو ترک كول to disturb, agitate

تلوث talavvác *m. Arabic* pollution, contamination (of water, food products)

تلوسه tavasá *f.* **1** uneasiness, deep agitation تلوسه كول to disturb, agitate, upset **2** strong desire ستا لیدو ته مي ډېره تلوسه وه I would very much like to see you. تلوسه لرل **a** to be impatient, be upset; worry **b** to have a strong desire **c** to await

تلول [1] tә́lavә́l *transitive [past:* وي تلاوه و يي] **1** to roast, fry (in butter, oil) **2** to toss, throw, fling **3** to release from one's hands, drop

تلول [2] taval *m.* **1** swiftness; haste **2** agitation, uneasiness تلول كول **a** to hurry **b** to worry, to be upset

تلول [3] talvál abundant, plentiful

تلول ⁴ talvál roasted, broiled; fried, grilled

تلول ⁵ tálavәl denominative, transitive [past: تل يې کړ] to immortalize, perpetuate

تلول ⁶ talavәl denominative, transitive [past: تل يې کړ] 1 to immerse (in liquid) 2 to drown

تلوله talvála f. worry, anxiety, agitation

تلولئ ¹ past participle of تلول

تلولئ ² tәlvaláj 1 dismayed, perplexed; stunned 2 m. lively person, active person idiom زړه مي په دي سودا کښني تلولئ و I was quite upset, I was nervous.

تلون ¹ tlun m. ☞ تلل ² 1

تلون ² talún m. weighing, weighing out

تلون ³ talavvún m. Arabic inconstancy, fickleness ستا طبيعت تلون کښني دئ، ستا طبيعت په تلون کښني دئ Eastern You are fickle.

تلونکی ¹ tlúnkaj 1 present participle of تلل ¹ 2 m. passerby, traveler

تلونکی ² talúnkaj present participle of تلل ²

تلونه talavәna f. roast, roasting

تلونی ¹ tlúnaj ☞ تلونکی ¹

تلونی ² talúnaj ☞ تلونکی ²

تلويث talvís m. Arabic 1 contamination, pollution (of water) 2 spoiling; damage 3 soiling, dirtying, staining

تلويزيون televizjón m. tilivizjón ☞ تپلويزيون

تله ¹ tәlá f. 1 scales دتلی ستن pointer on scales 2 standard, criterion داوپو تله level (geodesy) 3 میزان ☞ 5, 6

تله ² tála f. sole (of the foot) idiom a تله پر تبرول، تله پر کشول to gloss over, conceal (defects) b to settle (an argument, quarrel) c to practice witchcraft, practice sorcery

تله ³ tlә imperfect plural of تلل ¹

تله ⁴ tlә m. plural ☞ تلل ¹ 2 تله او راتله ☞ تله راتله

تله ⁵ tla imperfect feminine of تلل ¹

تله راتله tlә-rātlә m. plural movement, running (back and forth between points) پلي تله راتله walking, going

تلی ¹ taĺj m. 1 sole د بوټو تلی sole 2 foot 3 palm تلی وهل to lick (off) one's palms (e.g., powder) 4 bottom (e.g., of a river) 5 peritoneum 6 agriculture threshing floor

تلی ² tiláj f. 1 shank (of an arrow) 2 straw 3 stalk (of a reed, etc.)

تلی ³ tali present tense of تلل ²

تلئ ⁴ tlәj 1 Western imperfect of تلل ¹ 2 Eastern imperfect second person plural of تلل ²

تلی ⁵ tle 1 imperfect second person singular of تلل ¹ 2 imperfect feminine plural of تلل ¹

تلی ⁶ tәlé plural of تله ¹

تلی ⁷ táli plural of تله ²

تلئ ⁸ tәlaj past participle of تلل ¹

تلی پت talipáṭ m. pan (of a scale)

تلبدل ¹ tәledәl intransitive [past: وتلبده] 1 to be roasting, be frying 2 figurative to be in torment

تلبدل ² taledәl denominative, intransitive [past: تل شو] 1 to settle; form a sediment 2 to slide, slip 3 to be thrown about, be dispersed, be scattered

تليز tәlíz constant, perpetual

تليسک talisák m. seed (of a grape)

تلين talín m. taalín تلينه tlína f. 1 anniversary تلين پر ځای کول to celebrate an anniversary 2 funeral banquet held a year after someone's death

تلبوار tlevár talevár m. ☞ تلوار

تلبوارګندی tlevārgándaj adjective hurrying, making haste

تم ¹ tam 1 m. constancy 2 predicate adjective lingering; residing, spending time, being someplace

تم ² tam word paired with تور

تم ³ tәm colloquial contraction of the pronoun ته and the conjunction هم

تماتر tamáṭar m. regional tomato

تماثل tamāsúl m. Arabic likeness, resemblance, similarity تماثل سره لرل to be similar, resemble; look like

تماثلي tamāsulí similar, like

تماثيل timāsíl m. Arabic plural from تمثال

تماچه tamāchá f. tumāchá Arabic Eastern pistol شپږ ډزي تماچه، شپږ میله تماچه six-shooter

تمادي tamādí f. Arabic time period, interval of time

تمارض tamārúz m. Arabic feigning an illness

تماس ¹ tamás m. Arabic 1 contiguity 2 contact, connection د چا سره تماس پيدا کول، د چا سره تماس لرل، د چا سره په تماس کښني کبدل to establish or maintain communication or contact with someone يو په بله سره تماس کول to establish contact with one another د هغو سره تماس راغلئ دئ contact has been established with them 2 grammar agglutination

تماس ² tamás m. proper noun Tohmas

تماشه tamāshá f. Arabic ☞ تماشا

تماشابین tamāshābín m. تماشاچي tamāshāchí m. ☞ تماشه بین

تماشاخانه tamāshākhāná f. تماشاگاه tamāshāgáh m. ☞ تماشه خانه

تماشگیر tamāshgír m. Eastern ☞ تماشه بین

تماشه ¹ tamāshá f. tәmāshá spectacle, entertainment a تماشه کول to watch a spectacle b to admire 2 tmāshá tumāshá attributive adjective strange, odd تماشه سری دئ He's a strange one. تماشه خبري strange talk, unaccustomed speech

تماشابین tamāshabín m. تماشاچي tamāshachí m. 1 spectator, observer 2 idler, scatterbrain

تماشه خانه tamāshakhāná f. place of spectacles, spectacle (theater, circus, etc.)

تماشه کوونکی tamāshá kavúnkaj m. spectator, observer

تماشه گاه tamāshagáh m. ☞ تماشه خانه

تمغه tәmághá f. 1 fur cap with ear flaps 2 cowl (worn by hunters of fowl)

تماکو tamākú m. plural tobacco

تمام tamā́m *Arabic* **1.1** all, the whole, the entire تمامه روځ all day, the whole day **1.2** finished, completed **2** *m.* end, completion, finish تمام کېدل، تماول *compound verb* ☞ تمام کول *compound verb* ☞ تمامېدل *idiom* زه يې تمام يم I shall take care of this matter. That's something I can handle.

تماماً tamāmán *Arabic* altogether, in full; for once and all, finally, completely, definitely

تمام تمت tamā́m-tamát completed, finished تمام تمت کېدل to end, finish, be completed

تمام توب tamāmtób *m.* تمام تيا tamāmtjā́ *f.* finish, completeness

تمام شد tamāmshúd *economics* تمام شد قيمت، تمام شد نرخ cost

تمامۍخت tamāmóxht *m.* تماموالى tamāmválaj *m.* **1** completion, end, ending **2** finish, completeness

تماول tamāmavól *denominative, transitive* [*past:* تمام يې کړ] **1** to end, finish, complete **2** to complete one's schooling

تمامى tamā́maj ☞ تمام 1

تمامي tamā́mi [2] *f.* end, completion, finish

تماميت tamāmiját *m. Arabic* wholeness, integrity د خاوري تماميت، اراضي تماميت territorial integrity

تمامېدل tamāmedól *denominative, intransitive* [*past:* تمام شو] **1** to end, conclude, come to an end تمام شو the end (e.g., of a book) **2** to expire, elapse (of a time period); become invalid (of a contract, etc.) **3** to run out, be sold out (e.g., copies of a book) **4** to turn out, turn out to be په زيان تمامېدل to prove (to be) useful په مفاد تمامېدل to prove harmful; cause harm **a** to prove harmful; cause harm **b** to prove unprofitable; bring a loss **5** to cost, come to مصارف يې خورا گران تمامېږي That costs a great deal.

تمامېده tamāmedó *m. plural* ☞ تماموالى

تمانچه tamānchá *f.* تمانچه tumānchá **1** ☞ تماچه **2** clamp, vice (used by a potter)

تمايل tamāgúl *m. Arabic* inclination; predilection (for); aspiration; tendency

تمب tamb *m.* camp, nomad encampment

تمباکو tambākú *m. plural* tobacco

تمبړى tambóraj *m.* board for rolling out dough

تمبکه tambóka *f.* beehive

تمبگۍ tambagój *f.* shutter (of a door, window)

تمبل tumbúl *m.* **1** tambourine **2** drum

تمبل باز tumbulbā́z *m.* drummer

تمبو tambú *m.* **1** tent **2** wattle fencing, wooden fencing (at the entrance to a house, tent) **3** snares

تمبور tambúr *m.* ☞ تنبور

تمبوزک tambuzák *m.* **1** snout (of an animal) **2** muzzle **3** bridge (of the nose)

تمبوزى tambúzaj *m.* bridge (of the nose)

تمبوگى tambugáj *m.* **1** small tent **2** spider web

تمبه tambá *f.* **1.1** bolt, catch, bar, lock **1.2** shutter (of a door, window) **1.3** crowd, gathering, throng; group, bunch (of people) تمبي تمبي in groups, in bunches **1.4** pillar, building support **2**

predicate adjective **.1** pressed against **2.2** put against, leaned against

تمبېدل tambedól *intransitive* [*past:* وتمبېده] to fall away, fall off, slip

تمبېزه tambéza *f.* ☞ تمبوزک

تمبوزى tambúzaj *m.* bridge (of the nose)

تمت *Eastern word paired with* تمام

تمتراق tamtarā́k *m.* greatness, grandeur, magnificence; pomp

تمترى tamtaráj ☞ تري تم

تمتع tamattó' *f. Arabic* **1** trial, touch; taste, experience **2** use تمتع کول *compound verb* **a** to try; feel, touch; to taste, experience **b** to use, make use of

تمثال timsā́l *m. Arabic plural* [*plural:* تمثالونه timsālúna *Arabic plural:* تماثيل timāsíl] image; portrait

تمثيل tamsíl *m. Arabic* **1** comparison; likening تمثيل جوړول to make a comparison **2** allegory; fable تمثيل ويل **a** to make a comparison **b** to speak in allegory **3** play, representation تمثيل کول *compound verb* ☞ تمثيلېدل، تمثيل کېدل **4** *compound verb* ☞ representation

تمثيلول tamsilavól *denominative, transitive* [*past:* تمثيل يې کړ] **1** to compare; liken **2** to represent, be an example, personify **3** to play, represent

تمثيلېدل tamsiledól *denominative, intransitive* [*past:* تمثيل شو] **1** to compare; be likened to **2** to be personified **3** to be represented

تمجيد tamdzhíd *m. Arabic* **1** praise, eulogy تمجيد کول to praise, laud, eulogize يوشي ته تمجيد ويل to praise something **2** prayer (made an hour and a half before sunrise or sunset)

تمچو tamchú *m.* bolt, catch, bar, lock

تمځای tamdzā́j *m.* parking, stop (for buses, etc.) تم ځای، تمځای

تمځری tamdzóraj *m.* Indian partridge, *Francolinus*

تمدن tamaddún *m. Arabic* civilization

تمديد tamdíd *m. Arabic* time extension, prolongation (of an agreement, etc.)

تمديدول tamdidavól *denominative, transitive* [*past:* تمديد يې کړ] to extend the time period, prolong (an agreement, etc.)

تمديدېدل tamdidedól *denominative, intransitive* [*past:* تمديد شو] to be extended, be prolonged (of an agreement, etc.)

تمرد tamarrúd *m. Arabic* **1** stubbornness **2** disobedience, insubordination

تمرکز tamarkúz *Arabic* concentration د پانگي تمرکز concentration of capital د توليداتو تمرکز concentration of production و... ته تمرکز و پانگي ته تمرکز ورکول to concentrate capital ورکول to concentrate تمرکز نيول *compound verb* to be concentrated, to concentrate (intransitive) تمرکز لرل، تمرکز ميندل to be concentrated تمرکز کېدل to be concentrated, to concentrate (intransitive)

تمرهندي tamr-i-hindí *m.* tamár-i-hindí tamarind

تمرين tamrín *m. Arabic* **1** exercise **2** repetition

تمرينات tamrinā́t *m. Arabic plural* **1** *from* تمرين **2** training

تمزق tamazzúk *m. Arabic* **1** tearing; break, gap, rupture, severance

تمساح timsā́h *Arabic* African crocodile

تمسخر tamaskhúr *m. Arabic* **1** ridicule, gibe; irony **2** smile, grin په تمسخر *a* sarcastically, with irony **b** with a smile, with a grin

تمسخرآمېز tamaskhurāméz sarcastic; ironic

تمسق tumúsk *m.* kind of apricot with a reddish color

تمسک tamassúk *m. Arabic* promissory note, receipt for a debt

تمکین tamkín *m. Arabic* **1** solidity; steadiness; worthiness **2** restraint, unflappability, coolness په هيڅ حالت کښې خپل تمکين د لاسه *a* نه ورکول ډېر تمکين لرل to be always unflappable, keep one's cool to be very solid, be very steady **b** to possess great self-control, have great coolheadedness

تملق tamallúk *m. Arabic* ☞ تملک 1

تملک 1 tamalúk *m.* flattery, servility; toadying, bootlicking په تملک خوشحالېدل to love flattery

تملک 2 tamallúk *m. Arabic* ownership, possession

تملیک tamlík *m. Arabic law* **1** coming into possession **2** granting ownership

تمن tumán *m.* **1** tribe (among the Baluchis) **2** crowd, throng **3** detachment په تمن تمن in detachments **4** twenty (in counting money)

تمندار tumandár *m.* leader of a tribe (among the Baluchis)

تمنا tamanná *f. Arabic* **1** request **2** wish, desire تمنا کول *a* to request **b** to wish تمنا لرل *a* to have a request **b** to have a wish; to have a propensity toward something *idiom* د تمنا ماضي *grammar* optative subjunctive mood

تمنچه tamanchá *f. regional* ☞ تماچه

تمني tamanní *f. Arabic* wish desire چا ته ډېر ښه تمنيات څرګندول to wish someone the best of everything

تموج tamavvúdzh *m. Arabic* [*plural:* تموجونه tamavvudzhúna *plural:* تموجات tamavvudzhā́t] agitation, vacillation; vibratory movement *idiom* برقي تموجات electric waves

تموز tammúz *m.* tamóz *Arabic* **1** summer heat **2** July

تموس tamús *m.* **1** itch; *figurative* urge **2** summer heat

تمول 1 tamavál *denominative, transitive* [*past:* تم يې کړ] **1** to restrain, hold back دا سړی لږ تم کړه چه څما څه چاره ده ورسره Hold this fellow a little while, I have some business with him. **2** to support someone to help someone

تمول 2 tamavvúl *m. Arabic* **1** wealth; well-being **2** enriching, enrichment

تمه táma *f.* ☞ طمع *idiom* د ژوند تمه يې زبښته کمه وه His life was hanging by a thread.

تمهید tamhíd *m. Arabic* **1** introduction; foreword **2** arrangement, settlement **3** spreading (out)

تمېدل tamedál *denominative, intransitive* [*past:* تم شو] **1** to be held up, stand (idle) تر ډېره پوري ورته تم شوم، رانه غئ I waited for him a long time, but he didn't come. **2** to bear, endure; stand one's ground

تمیز tamíz *m. Arabic* تمییز tamjíz *m. Arabic* **1** preference و...ته تميز ورکول to show one's preference **2** distinction تميز کول to distinguish, single out **3** *law* cassation د تميز رئيس head of the

appeals department (in the Afghan Ministry of Justice) *idiom* تميز لرل to be reasonable, be sensible

تن 1 tan [*plural:* تنونه tanúna *with numbers plural:* تنه tána] **1** body مونږ دري تنه يو to dress **2** person لباس په تن کول There are three of us. لاس په لاس او تن په تن idiom څلور تنه ښځي four women *idiom* و چاته تن ورکول، و چاته تن جنګېدل to engage in hand-to-hand combat ايسېدول *a* to be attentive to someone **b** to reckon with someone; يو کار ته تن نه ورکول agree with someone **c** to yield to someone fail to resolve something په تن کښې وينه وچېدل *a* to be exhausted, be worn out **b** to lose one's head, be taken aback

تن 2 tan *m.* ton ☞ تن 1

تنا taná *f.* thunder

تناره tanā́ra *oblique of* تنور

تنازع tanāzó' *f. Arabic* **1** argument, dispute **2** battle, struggle د البقا struggle for existence

تن آسائي tanāsāí *f.* delicacy, softness

تناسب tanāsúb *m. Arabic* proportion; symmetry; correlation په همغه تناسب in accordance with this په تناسب سره proportionately; symmetrically ښه تناسب proportionality

تناسبي tanāsubí proportionate, symmetrical

تناسخ tanāsúkh *m. Arabic religion* metempsychosis, passing of the soul at death into another body

تناسخي tanāsukhí believing in metempsychosis

تناسق tanāsúk *m. Arabic* ☞ تناسب

تناسل tanāsúl *m. Arabic* reproduction, propagation

تناسلي tanāsulí *Arabic* sexual تناسلي آلات، تناسلي جهاز sexual organs

تناظر tanāzúr *m. Arabic* symmetry

تنافر tanāfúr *Arabic* mutual repugnance

تناقص tanāḳús *m. Arabic* **1** lessening, cutting short, abbreviation **2** insufficiency, lack

تناقض tanāḳúz *m. Arabic* **1** contrast; opposition **2** contradiction

تناو tanāv *m.* **1** string; rope د تناو بېړی ferry (-boat) **2** tanáb tanab (a measurement of ground which varies in different regions: between one-fourth and one-half acre) **3** vine (of a melon, squash) تناوونه غزول to put forth vines **4** *figurative* fetters, bonds *idiom* د مخکي تناوونه لنډېږي distance no longer has any meaning, there no longer are great distances ☞ طناب

تناوب tanāvúb *m. Arabic* **1** attention, interchange, rotation **2** *agriculture* crop rotation

تناوى tənāvájm *m.* rope for fastening tent sections to stakes

تنبل 1 tambúl *m.* ☞ تمبل

تنبل 2 tambál lazy

تنبلي tambalí *f.* laziness

تنبو tambú *m.* ☞ تمبو

تنبور tambúr *m.* **1** tambur (stringed instrument like a mandoline); tambourine **2** *dialect* drum

تنبورچي tamburchí *m.* **1** tambur player; tambourine player **2** *dialect* drummer

تنبه ‏tambá *f.* ☞ تمبه

تنبه ‏tanabbóh *f. Arabic m.* [*plural:* تنبهات tanabbohất] **1** forewarning, forestalling **2** inducement, incentive

تمبزه ‏tambezá *f.* ☞ تمبزک

تمبزى ‏tambezáj *m.* ☞ تمبزى

تنبيه ‏tanbí *f.* tanbíh *Arabic* **1** teaching, homily, sermon **2** warning, caution; reminder تنبيه کول، تنبيه ورکول **a** to teach, preach **b** to warn, caution, forewarn; remind

تن پرور ‏tanparvár **1** soft, effeminate, delicate **2** lazy; not mobile, slow-moving *idiom* تن پرور سړى glutton, gourmand

تن پرورى ‏tanparварí *f.* **1** softness, delicacy; effeminacy **2** laziness, idleness **3** gluttony

تن په تنا ‏tanpətaná *f. obsolete* self-preservation, self-defense

تنتړى ‏tántaráj *adjective* stammering, stuttering

تنتنا ‏tántaná *f.* **1** cries; shouts **2** glory **3** news; novelty **4** echo **5** grandeur, luxury, pomp

تن توش ‏tantósh *m.* grocery bag

تنته ‏tantá *f. textiles* warp تنته کغلول to stretch the warp

تنځړى ‏tandzáraj *m.* ☞ تمځرى

تنخاه ‏tankhá *f.* تنخواه tankháh pay (from work), salary

تند ‏tund **1** fast, quick **2** caustic, acrid (e.g., of food, a smell) **3** coarse, sharp په تنده لهجه coarsely, sharply تند الفاظ coarse words, sharp words **4** irascible, unrestrained, hot-tempered **5** irritable, short-tempered تند خوى **a** irascibility, lack of self-control **b** irritability **6** strong, heavy (of the wind, rain) تند کول ☞ تندول تند تند کول *idiom* تندبدل ☞ کبدل، to show ostentatious zeal or ardor

تند ‏tand ☞ تاند

تنداره ‏tindára *f.* aunt, wife of an uncle (on the father's side)

تندخوى ‏tundkhój **1** irascible, unrestrained, hot-tempered **2** irritable

تندر ‏tandár *m.* lightning

تندرا ‏tundrá *f.* tundra

تن درست ‏tandurúst healthy, strong, robust

تندرستوالى ‏tandurustválaj *m.* تن درستي tandurustí *f.* health, strength

تندره ‏tándra *f.* **1** eclipse سپوږمي تندري ونيوه an eclipse of the moon took place **2** *figurative* misfortune, calamity تندري وهلئ دئ a disaster befell him **3** ☞ تندر

تندره ‏tundurá *f.* ☞ تندوره

تندرى ‏tandáraj *m.* new bark (of a pine tree, etc.)

تندزبان ‏tundzabán **1** eloquent, expressive **2** caustic, coarse

تيندک ‏tinadák *m.* ☞ تيندک

تندک ‏tundak nervous, irritable

تندل ‏tandál *transitive* ☞ تنډل

تندمزاج ‏tundmizádzh hot-tempered, irascible

تندوالى ‏tundválaj ☞ تندي

تندوبه ‏tundóba *f.* تندوبى tundóbaj *m.* fountain

تندور ‏tandúr *m.* ☞ تنور

تندور ‏tindór *f.* ☞ تنداره

تندوره ‏tundurá *f.* **1** cascade, waterfall **2** steep slope

تندورى ‏tindóraj cartilage (of the nose)

تندول ‏tundavál *denominative, transitive* [*past:* تند يي کړ] **1** to make fast; speed up, hasten **2** to make sharp, make caustic **3** to behave rudely **4** to make irascible, make hot-tempered

تندولى ‏tandólaj *m. botany* portulaca

تندونى ‏tandúŋaj *m.* ☞ چندونى

تندوى ‏tandváj *m.* tandəváj **1** *anatomy* diaphragm **2** cartilage (of the nose)

تنده ‏tənda *f.* **1** thirst تندي وهلئ يم I'm overcome by thirst. په ما تنده لګېږي I'm thirsty. **2** lack of water, lack of moisture **3** *figurative* desire, wish تنده ماتول **a** to quench one's thirst **b** *figurative* to satisfy a desire *idiom* د فايدي اخيستلو تنده thirst for gain د شهرت تنده longing for glory

تنده ‏tandá *f. botany* camel's thorn

تنده ‏túnda *feminine singular of* تند

تنده غرى ‏təndaghóraj *m. Eastern* person sick with dropsy

تندى ‏tandáj *m.* **1** forehead, brow ده تندى پراخ دئ He has a broad forehead. **2** slope (of a mountain) **3** upper jamb of a door **4** part of a wall under a cornice **5** level (of water in a river, stream) **6** heading, title *idiom* په ورين تندى *tandí* with a content expression; joyfully په تريو تندى *tandí* with a dissatisfied, sour expression; morosely تريو تندى سړى a morose person تندى تريول to make a dissatisfied expression; frown; be angry تندى چا ته مه تريووه to be affable and affectionate with everyone دا يې په تندى کښې ليکلي دي، that was pre-ordained for him, that was دا يې په تندى کښې نوشته دي fated for him تندى غوټه کول to contemplate evil تندى تريو نيول he تندى يي وغوړيد to be satisfied, be content سره تلل، تندى وغوړيدل flourished; he grew cheerful تندى داغل to grieve, regret

تندي ‏tundí *f.* **1** swiftness, speed په تندى سره quickly, hurriedly چا تندي کول to hurry someone په تلو کښي تندي جوړول to quicken the pace په تلو کښي يي تندي شروع کړه He began to hurry. **2** sharpness; causticity, sarcasm **3** crudeness, harshness **4** irascibility, touchiness

تندى ‏tandáj **1.1** young تندى ورى unweaned lamb تندى هلک baby, infant **1.2** immature; unripe **2** *m.* **.1** young (of animals) **2.2** young tree **2.3** sprout, shoot

تندى ‏təndáj round

تندياره ‏tandjára *f.* ☞ تنداره

تندېدل ‏tundedál *denominative, intransitive* [*past:* تند شو] **1** to be fast, be swift; hasten, speed up **2** to be sharp, be caustic **3** to be coarse, be harsh **4** to get excited, become impassioned **5** to grow stronger (e.g., the wind, rain)

تنډل ‏tandál *transitive* [*past:* ويي تانده] **1** to make; form; prepare **2** to arrange **3** to fix, correct; repair

تنډو ‏tandú *colloquial* big-bellied, pot-bellied, large-waisted, chubby

تنرونه ‏tanarúna *plural of* تنور

تنزانيا ‏tanzānijá *f.* Tanzania

تنزرى ‏tanzáraj *m.* ☞ تمځرى

تنزل tanazzúl *Arabic* lowering, reduction, fall (of prices) تنزل کول to go down, fall (of prices)

تنزیل tanzíl *m. Arabic* 1 lowering, letting down 2 reduction (in prices); discount 3 *finance* discounting (of bills, etc.) 4 reception (of guests)

تنزیلول tanzilavól *denominative, transitive* [*past:* تنزیل یې کړ] 1 to lower, reduce (prices) 2 *finance* to discount (bills, etc.)

تنزیلېدل tanziledól *denominative, intransitive* [*past:* تنزیل شو] 1 to go down, to fall (of prices) 2 *finance* to be discounted (of bills, etc.)

تنسته tanistá *f.* 1 fabric, material 2 spider's web 3 *textiles* warp 4 frame (of a rug weaving loom)

تنشا tanshá *f.* splendor, glory

تنشن tanshán *m.* tenshán *physics* tension

تنظیم tanzím *m. Arabic* 1 organization, arrangement; regulation, putting in order د تنظیماتو مدیریت organizational department 2 compilation (of a document, etc.) 3 composition (of verses) 4 *military* correction (of firing), adjustment تنظیم کول *compound verb* ☞ تنظیمېدل ، تنظیم کېدل 5 *physics, chemistry* structure

تنظیمول tanzimavól *denominative, transitive* [*past:* تنظیم یې کړ] 1 to organize, arrange; regulate, set in order; adjust د مناسبات تنظیمول to regulate relations 2 to compile (a document, etc.) 3 to compose (verse) 4 *military* to adjust (firing)

تنظیمېدل tanzimedól *denominative, intransitive* [*past:* تنظیم شو] 1 to be organized, be arranged; to be regulated, be put in order; go well, come right 2 to be compiled (of a document, etc.) 3 to be composed (of verse) 4 *military* to be adjusted (of fire)

تنظیمیه tanzimjá *f. Arabic* تنظیمیه ریاست organizational committee (for enacting reforms and the reorganization of the provincial bureaucracy) د تنظیمي رئیس raís-i تنظیمیه chairman of the organization committee

تنفس tanaffús *m. Arabic* breathing د تنفس جهاز ، د تنفس آله respiratory organs د تنفس لوله trachea, windpipe تنفس کول *compound verb* to inhale, breathe in صافه هوا تنفس کول to inhale fresh air, breathe fresh air

تنفیذ tanfīz *m. Arabic* setting in motion, carrying out; confirmation (of a verdict) *idiom* بشري تنفیذ People's Court

تنفیذي tanfizí *Arabic adjective* executive تنفیذي سلطه executive authority

تنقید tanķíd *m. Arabic* criticism پرچا تنقید کول، پرچا باندي تنقید کول، پرچا تنقید نیول، پرچا باندي تنقید نیول to criticize, subject someone to criticism پرما تنقید مه نیسه! Don't condemn me!

تنقیدي tanķidí critical تنقیدي لیکونکی critic

تنقیص tanķís *m. Arabic* reduction, abbreviation

تنقیط tanķít *m. Arabic grammar* punctuation د تنقیط اصول rules of punctuation

تنکج tankáj 1.1 tender; fine, delicate تنکی لښته small twig 1.2 fresh 1.3 early تنکی لمر morning sun, sun at sunrise تنکی غرمه

time before noon, morning 2 *m.* .1 baby, infant 2.2 suckling; whelp

تنکجوالی tankajválaj *m.* تنکی والی tankajtjá *f.* تنکی تیا tankajtób *m.* تنکی توب 1 tenderness; fineness, delicacy 2 freshness

تنگ tung *m.* [*plural:* تنگان tungán] *plural* jug, pitcher

تنگ tang 1 narrow; cramped, crowded; tight, 2 insufficient, scanty, limited 3 constrained, straitened, difficult تنگ ژوند تېرول to be in straitened circumstances, live in need په تنگ کېدل، په تنگ راتلل a to wind up in a difficult situation b to be in torment, suffer د خوب له لاسه په تنگ راغلئ و He was excruciatingly sleepy. c to become confused; become upset د یو شي څخه په تنگ کېدل to be in torment, suffer from something ډېر په تنگ شو it become very difficult for him څوک تنگ نیول to oppress someone

تنگاچه tungāchá *f.* 1 bench 2 platform; scaffold

تنگ تروش tangtrúsh very tight, narrow

تنگ توب tangtób *m.* تنگتیا tangtjá *f.* 1 narrowness, tightness 2 insufficiency, lack, scantiness 3 difficulty, straits 4 need, poverty

تنگ چشم tangcháshm 1 miserly; greedy 2 envious

تنگ چشم والی tangchashmválaj *m.* تنگ چشمي tangchashmí *f.* 1 miserliness; greed 2 envious

تنگ حال tanghál poor, needy

تنگ حالي tanghālí *f.* need; straited circumstances

تنگ حوصله tanghavsilá talkative, unable to keep a secret

تنگخولی tangkhúlaj *m.* jug or pitcher with a narrow neck

تنگ دست tangdást 1 poor, needy 2 miserly, stingy

تنگ دستي tangdastí *f.* 1 need, indigence 2 miserliness, stinginess

تنگ دل tangdíl miserly, stingy

تنگ دلي tangdilí *f.* miserliness, stinginess

تنگستن tangstán *chemistry* tungsten

تنگسه tangsá *f.* تنگسیا tangsjá *f.* 1 poverty, want 2 difficult situation; straits د تنگسۍ په وخت کښي at a difficult time

تنگ غارو tang-i-ghārú *m.* Tangigaru (a ravine near Kabul)

تنتنگلاسی tanglāsaj poor, needy

تنگنا tangná *f.* ravine, gorge

تنگ نظري tangnazarí *f.* shortsightedness; narrowness (of views)

تنگوالی tangválaj *m.* ☞ تنگ توب

تنگول tangavól *denominative, transitive* [*past:* تنگ یې کړ] 1 to make narrow, narrow; make (too) tight; to pinch 2 to disturb; burden; constrain, hamper 3 to presecute; oppress

تنگه tangá *f.* 1 tree trunk 2 bodice (of a dress)

تنگه tangá *f.* ☞ تنگه

تنگه tánga *feminine singular of* تنگ

تنگي tangí *f.* tangí *f.* 1 narrowness; tightness 2 narrow part of something 3 insufficiency, lack, scantiness, limitation 4 difficult situation; straits 5 need, poverty په زیاتي تنگي سره اخته کېدل to fall into want, be very needy

تنگی tangáj *m.* 1 ravine, gorge; narrow valley; pass 2 pouch for dried cheese 3 *used in geographical names:* نری تنگی Naraj-Tangaj Ravine

تنگې [3] tangé *plural of* تنگه [1, 2]

تنگېدل tangedə́l *denominative, intransitive* [*past:* تنگ شو] **1** to grow narrow; become crowded **2** to be tight, be constrained; be in a tight or difficult situation **3** to be in torment, suffer **4** to be bored, experience boredom

تنگ غارو tangighārú *m.* ☞ تنگ غارو

تنگي وال tangivál made in local Afghan workshops (small arms, etc.)

تنميه tanmijá *f. Arabic* growth, development

تنور tanúr *m. Arabic* [*plural:* تنورونه tanurúna *plural:* تنرونه tanarúna] tanur (i.e., an oven built in the ground) د تناره ډوډۍ bread or flat cakes baked in a tanur *idiom* **a** د آسمان په تناره کښني beneath a sultry sky **b** in the heat په چا دنیا تنور کول to oppress someone, create intolerable conditions for someone

تنورپاک tanurpák *m.* shovel for digging ash out of an underground oven (i.e., a tanur)

تنوع tanavvó' *f. Arabic* **1** variety, diversity; heterogeneity **2** *biology* formation of species; differentiation by species

تنول [1] tənavə́l *transitive* [*past:* و یې تناوه] **1** to rumble, roar (with laughter, etc.) **2** *figurative* to resound (of glory, etc.)

تنول [2] tənavə́l *transitive* [*past:* و یې تناوه] to draw out into thread

تنومن tanumán تنومند tanumánd fat, obese; full

تنویر tanvír *m. Arabic* **1** illumination, lighting د تنویر گېس gas for lighting **2** enlightenment, instruction عمومي تنویر general education, schooling

تنویرول tanviravə́l *denominative, transitive* [*past:* تنویر یې کړ] **1** to illuminate **2** to enlighten

تنویري tanvirí **1** *adjective* lighting, illuminating تنویري مصارف expenses for lighting **2** educational

تنه taná *f.* **1** body, frame, torso **2** trunk (of a tree) **3** fuselage (of an airplane) **4** hull (of a ship)

تنها tanhā́ **1** solitary, lone **2** only

تنهائي tanhāí *f.* loneness; loneliness; isolation

تنی [1] tné tané *Eastern* ☞ تری

تنی [2] tané *plural of* تنه

تنی [3] tanə́j stammer(ing), stutter(ing)

تنبدل [1] tanedə́l *intransitive* [*past:* وتنبده] to peal, rumble (of thunder)

تنبدل [2] tanedə́l *intransitive* [*past:* وتنبده] **1** to be drawn out into a thread **2** *figurative* to become nice, become dear, become lovable

تنی نا tənajnā́ *f.* ☞ طنطنه

تن [1] tə́n *m.* song; verse, poetry

تن [2] taṇ *m.* تنا taṇā́ *f.* **1** thunder **2** roaring (of a tiger, lion, etc.) تنا کول to roar (of a tiger, lion, etc.)

تناکه taṇā́ka *f.* blister, bump; corn, callus تناکي کول to develop calluses تناکي کېدل to be covered with blisters; be covered with corns *idiom* دلاس په تناکو گټل to live by one's own labor تناکه چاودل **a** to calm, quiet, soothe; bring to reason; bridle, curb **b** to despair (of)

تنتنا taṇṭəṇā́ *f.* ☞ تنتنا

تنکار tənəkár *m. chemistry* borax, sodium borate

تنول tənavə́l *transitive* [*past:* و یې تناوه] **1** to beat up; slaughter **2** to slaughter, butcher (cattle)

تنهار təṇəhár *m.* **1** thunder **2** roaring (of a tiger, lion, etc.)

تنی [1] taṇáj *m.* bellyband (of a harness)

تنی [2] taṇə́j *f.* **1** lace (shoelace, drawstring of a dress); bands, ribbons **2** belts, straps (of a pack-saddle, etc.) **3** button **4** button (e.g., on a doorbell) تنی ته فشار ورکول، تنی کښني منډل to press a button **a** د بوټ تنی وتړه! Tie your shoelaces! **b** to tie (bands, ribbons) **c** to button (up) تنی را شلول، تنی تنی شلول **a** تنی در شلول، تنی ور شلول to tear off (ribbons, bands, a button) **b** *figurative* to shame, disgrace **c** *figurative* to labor, strain, (over) tax oneself په کار کښني می تنی وشلولې I overtaxed myself at work. **d** *figurative* to entreat, request **e** *figurative* to cry, wail, moan **f.** *figurative* to toil, endeavor; puff, pant

تو [1] tu *m.* **1.1** spittle; spitting تو کول to spit **1.2** steam, vapor **1.3** scornful relationship **2** *interjection* phooey, pah تو دي په تا وي! Confound you! Be damned!

تو [2] to *oblique plural of* تی [1]

تو [3] tav *m.* ☞ توت [1]

تو [4] to ☞ تو تو تو

تو [5] to *Western* ☞ توی [2]

توابع tavābí' *m.* **1** *plural from* تابع [2] 2 **2** possessions

تواتو təvātáv *m.* **1** gaining money underhandedly **2** pocketing money تواتو کول **a** acquire money dishonestly **b** to pocket money

تواچي tavāchí *m.* helper of the village elder

توارث tavārús *m. Arabic* heredity

تواره təvārá *f.* wicket or wooden fence at the entrance to a house or tent

تواریخ tavāríkh *Arabic masculine plural of* تاریخ

توازن taʐún *m. Arabic* equilibrium, stability, steadiness د قواو توازن balance of power توازن ورکول ذ هني توازن rest, calmness **a** to destroy the equilibrium **b** *figurative* to lose one's temper

تواضع tavāzó' *f. Arabic* **1** humility, meekness په تواضع humbly, meekly **2** attention to someone **3** refreshments په...، تواضع کول to treat someone to something

توافق tavāfúk *m. Arabic* unanimity; agreement توافق سره کول **a** to reach agreement **b** to accommodate oneself ورسره توافق لرل to be in agreement ورسره توافق مېندل to accomodate oneself

توالت tuālét *m.* توالېت **1** toilette **2** toilet

توان tvắn tuván tavān *m.* **1** power, might, mightiness تر خپله توانه according to one's strength **2** armed forces, troops هوايي توان پوري *regional* air force عسکري توان armed forces *idiom* له توانه ورته وتل to be consumed by desire; to be unable to refrain from something

توانا tvānā́ tuvānā́ tavānā́ **1** mighty, powerful, energetic **2** all-powerful

توانائي tvānāí tuvānāí tavānāí *f.* might, power, mightiness

توانول [1] tvānavə́l tuvānavə́l tavānavə́l *transitive* [*past:* و یې تواناوه] to make strong, make powerful; fortify **2** to enforce; support;

to encourage **3** to nourish, fortify (with food) هلک په شیدو توانول to nourish a child with milk

تواني tvāní *f.* tuvāní tavāní might, power, strength

توانیدل tvānedól tuvānedól tavānedól *intransitive* [*past:* وتوانېده] **1** to be able, be capable, have strength (to) **2** to fortify oneself (by eating, drinking something)

توب tób *suffix forming abstract masculine nouns* سپین توب whiteness سری توب humanity

توبرکلوز tuberkulóz *m.* tuberculosis

توبره tobrá *f.* tubrá purse; bag, sack

توبری tubráj *m.* **1** point (of an arrow) **2** quill (of a feather)

توبري túbri *f. plural* cross-shaped embroidery

توبگار tobagā́r *m.* ☞ توبه گار

توبه tobá taubá *Arabic* **1** *f.* **.1** repentance; plea for forgiveness توبه می دي وي! I repent! May I be forgiven! I won't do it again! توبه کښل، توبه وېستل to repent, be sorry, ask forgiveness **1.2** *used with* اوس اې توبه شوې ده، هې or اې they have now repented of that **2** *exclamation* **.1** ستا له خیره می I'm sorry!, I won't do it again! توبه، سپی رانه لری کړه! *proverb* I don't need your alms, just call off the dog! **2.2** I can't express ..., I can't find words ... *idiom* توبه دونه خوشحاله سوم چه توبه! Ugh! I was so overjoyed that I can't even express it.

توبه tobá *f.* Toba (mountain, village in Baluchistan)

توبه گار tobagā́r *m.* penitent person, repentant person

توبیخ tavbíkh *m. Arabic* scolding; rebuke; censure, reprimand

توبیخي tavbikhí reproving; disapproving ماضي توبیخي *grammar* form of the perfect expressing a shade of blame or censure

توبین tobín *m.* infringement of the law, offense

توپ top *m. military* piece of ordnance, gun, cannon جگ خوله توپ، د طیارو هوایي توپ، طیاره وېشتونکی توپ، دافع توپ antiaircraft gun ویشتل توپ long-range gun **a** to fire from a cannon **b** *figurative* to shoot off one's mouth, boast توپ ایله کول، to fire from a cannon توپ خلاصول

توپ top *m.* **1** piece, item; piece (of textile) **2** ball, small ball

توپان tupā́n *m.* **1** storm, hurricane **2** *figurative* great achievements, remarkable matters **3** *figurative* misfortune, disaster; unpleasantness *idiom* توپان سری energetic person ☞ طوفان

توپان tupā́n *m.* colored trim (on a dress)

توپانچه tupānchá *f.* ☞ توپنچه

توپانه tupāná by the piece (of textiles) توپانه پلورل، توپانه ورکول to sell textiles by the piece

توپانۍ topānə́j *f.* nonsense, foolishness

توپبازي topbāzí *f.* game of ball توپ بازي کول to play ball

توپچي topchí *m. military* gunner, artilleryman

توپخانه topkhānā́ *f.* **1** artillery د توپخانې فعالیت artillery fire **2** battery (artillery)

توپړ topə́r *m.* blow, jolt

توپړک tupṛák *m.* sheepskin coat, hareskin coat

توپسازي topsāzí *f.* production of guns

توپک topák *m. plural Eastern* [*plural:* توپک topə́k *plural:* توپکونه topakúna *Western plural:* توپکان topakā́n] rifle; gun; handgun شکاري وېشتل توپک sportsman's rifle هغه توپک ویشتل to fire from a rifle توپکه، مه دي خوله سه، مه دي کونه! شه توپک ولي He shoots well. *saying* Rifle, you should get lost for good!

توپک گری topakgáraj *m.* gunsmith

توپک لېچ topakléch *m.* butt of a rifle, butt-stock of a rifle

توپک والا topakvālā́ *m. military* gunner (in a plane, tank)

توپ لرونکی top larúnkaj (person) having a gun or guns بېړی gunboat

توپنچه topanchá *f. Western* توپنگچه topangchá *f.* pistol, revolver

توپڼي topə́ṇi *m.* ☞ توتنکی

توپوغرافي topoghrāfí *f.* توپوگرافي topogrāfí **1** *f.* topography **2** topographic

توپه tópa *f. Eastern* gun, cannon

توپیر tavpér *m.* taupír difference, distinction هیڅ توپیر پکښې نشته they are not at all distinguishable from one another توپیر کول to differ (from), stand out

توت tut *m.* [*plural:* توت tut *Western plural:* توتان tutā́n] mulberry tree, mulberry (fruit) برنجي توت mulberry tree د توت ونه mulberry tree بی دانه توت kind of mulberry tree تور توت mulberry without seeds سیمیا توت، کشمشي توت، مرواري توت black mulberry kind of mulberry دوه توته اهمیت نه ورکوي *literally* He's not worth two mulberries. *figuratively* He's not worth two cents.

توت tavt fried in oil, roasted in oil

توتا totā́ *m.* [*plural:* توتایان totājā́n] parrot

توتا totā́ *f. regional* vitriol

توت خوره tutkhvərá *f.* finch (the bird)

توتر tavattúr *m.* **1** tension **2** exhaustion

توتریت tavatturiját *m. Arabic medicine* emaciation; asthenia (loss of bodily strength) عصبي توتریت neurasthenia

توتړی tutṛáj *m.* stammerer, stutterer

توتنبه totónbha *f.* flat and soft stone

توتکرکی totakarkáj *m.* توتکری totakaráj *m.* **1** male swallow **2** kind of fringe (girls' hair style)

توتکه tutóka *f.* **1** larynx **2** conduit for millstones **3** reed pipe

توتکه tutóka *f.* fascine, faggot, bundle of sticks

توتکی totakáj *m.* ☞ توتکرکی

توتکۍ totakə́j *f.* [*plural:* توتکی totakə́j *plural:* توتکیاني totakəjā́ni] barn swallow

توتلی totólaj *m.* rag, cloth, pad (for removing a kettle from the fire)

توتنی totónaj *m.* small shovel of a salt worker

توتنکی totónkaj *m.* توتنی totónaj *m.* **1** shaving, filing **2** gold filings

توتو tutú **1** *interjection* cry used when calling chickens **2** *m. children's speech* hen, bird

توتوتو tototó cry used when calling a dog

توته tutá *f.* **1** bobbin, spool **2** ☞ توله

توتي totí *m.* [*plural:* توتیان totijā́n] parrot

توتی ² tútaj ground, ground off, rounded off

توتیا totijā́ f. chemistry zinc oxide

توجه tavadzhdzhó f. tavadzhdzhá Arabic attention په لوړه توجه with great attention د توجه وړ worthy of attention دیو شي و خواته توجه کول to turn your attention to something و یو شي ته پوره توجه لرل to devote proper attention to something په دی کښي ستاسو توجه ضروري ده You should pay attention to this question. توجه ځان ته راگرځول to attract attention to oneself

توجیه tavdzhí tavdzhíh Arabic 1 military laying (gunnery), aiming (small arms) 2 settling (e.g., an argument) 3 regulating (accounts, etc.) توجیه کول compound verb a to aim (guns) b to settle (e.g., an argument) c to regulate (accounts, etc.)

توحید tavhíd m. Arabic 1 unity, unification 2 standardization

توخانه tavkhāná f. ☞ تاوخانه

توخته tokhtá f. calmness, restraint

توخری tokhə́raj m. توخه tokhá f. butter-milk, whey

توخي ¹ tokhí m. plural the Tokhi tribe 2 tokháj m. Tokhi (tribesman)

توخیر tavkhír m. combing; scratching

توده تود tod tavdá f. [plural: تاوده tāvdə́ m. plural: تودي tavdé] f. 1 hot توده لمبه a burning تود باد، تود ورښ a hot wind, sultry wind نن هوا توده ده It's hot out today. 2 warm توده اوبه hot water wind (of clothing) 3 figurative warm, affable, cordial په ډېر تاوده زړه چاته مبارکي ورکول to greet someone warmly 4 figurative hot; fiery; animated; agitated د دوی تر منځ خبري خورا تودي دي They are arguing heatedly. توده وینا animated conversation 5 figurative lively, boisterous (e.g., of trade) 6 figurative tense, heated, bitter (of a battle, struggle) تود راتلل، تود پر راتلل a heatedly to take something up b to become excited idiom تود تود کېدل a to take to someone, visit often, inform someone b to work earnestly

تودښ tavdə́kh m. تودښت tavdə́kht m. 1 heat, sultriness 2 heating (up) 3 figurative warm greeting په ډېر تودښ د چا پذیرائي کول to greet someone very warmly

تودڼی tavdə́ne f. oven, furnace

تودوالی todvā́laj m. 1 heat, sultriness 2 heating; heating up د تودوالي آلی heating apparatus 3 figurative warmth, affability, cordiality 4 figurative zeal; passion; liveliness; anxiety 5 figurative liveliness, activity (e.g., of trade) 6 figurative tension, bitterness (of a battle, struggle)

تودوبن tavdobə́n m. تودوبی tavdobáj m. bathhouse

تودوخه tavdókha f. تودوخي tavdúkha f. تودوخې tavdókhe f. tavdúkhe 1 heat, sultriness; stuffiness نن تودوخه ده It's hot today. 2 heating (up)

تودوکی tavdúkaj 1 moderately hot 2 close, stuffy, stifling

تودول tavdavə́l denominative, transitive; past [past: تود یی کړ] 1 to heat (up), warm اوبه تودول to heat water 2 to fire up (e.g., an oven) ما بخاری توده کړه I fired up the oven. 3 to heat, provide heat 4 figurative to make warm, make cordial (e.g., a meeting, reception) 5 figurative to stimulate, arouse; upset; animate;

ځان تودول inflame a to warm up, be heated up b to become zealous, liven up ځوک پر تودول to encourage, incite someone to something 6 figurative to enliven, activate (e.g., trade) 7 to make tense, make bitter (a battle, struggle)

توده ¹ tudá f. 1 heap, pile 2 embankment (of railroad, road) 3 hill; burial mound 4 mountain-mass 5 mass (of people), crowd 6 mound of sand (used as archery target) 7 the Tude party (in Iran)

توده ² tavdá f. onion soup

توده ³ tavdá feminine singular of تود

تودېدل denominative, intransitive [past: تود شو] 1 to be warmed, be heated, warm up بخاری توده کړه چه تود شم Heat the oven so that I can warm up. 2 to be heated (of a house, room) 3 figurative to be warm, be cordial (e.g., of a reception, meeting) 4 figurative to be zealous, be aroused, be agitated; grow lively; become inflamed پر تودېدل to become active; undertake some matter ardently 5 figurative to liven up, grow active (e.g., of trade) 6 figurative to flare up, intensify, become more bitter (of a battle, struggle)

تودي سړي tavde-saṛé f. plural trials, difficulties ډېري تودي سړي لېدل to experience a great deal in one's lifetime

تودیع tavdí' f. Arabic 1 deposit; depositing تودیع کول compound verb to deposit 2 farewell, parting

تودیع کوونکی tavdí' kavúnkj m. depositor

تود toḍ m. loss

تور ¹ tor m. net, netting د تور په وسیله کب نیول to catch a fish with a net تور غورول، تور اچول a to cast out a net تور ورته اچول b figurative to arrange intrigues, set a trap for someone

تور ² tor m. 1 fear, fright 2 stubbornness, obstinacy تور خورل a to fear, be frightened b to be stubborn, be obstinate, be disagreeable

تور ³ tor 1.1 black; dark توره تخته blackboard توره شپه dark night رنگ یي ډېر تور He is very dark-complexioned. 1.2 dark-complexioned; sunburnt, brown; tanned دئ 1.3 covered (with clothing, of parts of the body, in common law) 1.4 figurative guilty 1.5 figurative disgraced, shamed 2.1 m. [plural: تورونه torúna] something black, black object [plural: تورونه torúna] pupil د سترگو تور pupil of the eye 2.2 زما د سترگو تورا! You, my beloved! 2.3 [plural: توران torán] dark-complexioned person, very dark skinned person 2.4 [plural: تورونه torúna] figurative slander په ناحقه to slander د چا تور پوري کول، په چا تور پوري تړل، په چا تور پوري ویل د څه شي په تور یی He is slandering me unjustly. تور را پوري موربي توره لوخړه On what charge did they arrest him? idiom نیولئ دئ؟ thick smoke توره خاوره تور بازار black market توره ورځ a black day black earth ☞ تور او سپین توري لښکري obsolete numerous troops د چا تور پر تندي کېدل، و چا ته تور پر تندي کېدل to be not overfond of, not to like someone تور خورل to grow dark in one's eyes په تور اوربل کبني سپین لګېدل، په تور کبني سپین لګېدل to begin to turn gray; age پر توره سپین کول to oppress someone

تورا torá f. obsolete slander, calumny

توران ¹ turā́n m. history Turan

توران toरán *m.* black Kandahar grape

توران toरán *plural of* تور 2, 3

تورانه toरána *f.* ☞ توره انا

تورانه toरána *f. proper name* Torana

توراني toरānáj *m.* 1 peevish person 2 scandalmonger; tale-bearer

توراڼۍ toरāṇə́j *f.* ☞ توره انا

توربخت torbákht unhappy, unfortunate

توربختوالی torbakhtválaj *m.* توربختي torbakhtí *f.* misfortune

توربختي torbákhtaj ☞ توربخت

توربخن torbəkhə́n توربخون torbəkhún blackish, somewhat black

توربخی torbə́khəj *f.* seam, stitch

توربرښ turbrékh *m.* 1 saber rattling 2 bragging توربرښ کول a to rattle sabers, threaten war b to brag

توربورگلوي turburgalví *f.* ☞ تربگنی

توربین turbín *m.* turbine

تورپوستکی torpóstəkaj تورپوستی torpóstaj 1 black, colored 2 *m.* Black (person)

تورپیکۍ torpekə́j *f. proper noun* Torpeki

تورپیل torpíl *m. military* torpedo په توربیل ویشتل to torpedo

تورت turt *m.* direct person, candid person

تورتاریک tor-tारík absolutely black, pitch-black, blacker than black توري تاریکي اوریځي black storm clouds

تورتاوده tortāvdə́ *m. plural* onion soup

تورتپ tortáp *m.* ☞ تورتم

تورتپی tortə́paj having a black birth mark

تورتلب tor-taláb 1 absolutely black, pitch-black, blacker than black 2 burned to the ground تورتلب کېدل to burn to the ground کباب پر دوست مي زړه تورتلب شو the shish-kebab has burned *idiom* With all my heart I pitied my friend. With all my heart I became sorry for my friend.

تورتم tortám 1 darkness, elemental darkness ډيوه مره شوه، يو په يو تورتم شو The candle burned out, immediately darkness ensued. 2 completely black, blackest black; very dark تورتم ځنگل thick forest

تورتیپ tortíp *m.* ☞ تیپ

تورتیبلی tortejə́laj very dark-complexioned تورتیبلی کېدل to be very dark-complexioned; get a deep suntan

تورجان tor-dzhā́n *m. proper noun* Torjan

تورخم torkhám *m.* Towr Kham (border point near Pakistan)

تورخیل torkhél *m.* [*plural:* تورخیلونه torkhelúna] *plural* male slave

تورخیله torkhéla *f.* female slave

تور دریاب tor darjā́b *m. obsolete* the Black Sea

توردلی tordaláj *m.* 1 small black bird related to the stonechat 2 *proper noun* Tordalaj

توررڼ toraṛə́j *f.* black wheat-ear (bird, member of chat family)

توررزڼ torzə́ṛaj pernicious; noxious

توريزم turízm *m.* tourism

تورزن turzə́n 1 *m.* fine swordsman; brave person 2 brave, noble, courageous

تورزن توب turzəntób *m.* courage, nobility, bravery

توربیری torgíraj with a black beard

تورسپین tor-spín *m.* 1 secret, something mysterious, suspicious دي کېږي څه تورسپین شته په Something's not right here. 2 literacy (ability to read and write) له تورسپین نه خبر نه دئ He can't read at all. د مور له برکته په تورسپین خبرشوم Thanks to my mother, I learned to read.

تورسترگی torstə́rgaj black-eyed, dark-eyed

تورسرکه torsaróka *f.* scarecrow

تورسرې torsáre *f.* widow

تورسکاڼ torskā́ṇ dark-bay (horse's color)

تورشان torshán blackish, somewhat black

تورغر torghár Towr Ghar (mountain range)

تورغړی torghə́ṛaj *m.* forearm

تورغنډۍ torghunḍə́j *f.* Towraghondi, Tor Ghundai (a border settlement)

تورغوړ torghváṛ *m.* oil for lamps; rape-oil, colza-oil

تورغوړگی torghvágaj 1.1 uneducated; stupid 1.2 disobedient 2 *m.* 2.1 uneducated person; stupid person 2.2 disobedient person 2.3 caracal, steppe lynx, *Felis caracal*

تورک torák *m. proper noun* Torak

تورک təvərák *m.* dismantling, unscrewing (of a gun)

تورک turk *m.* Turk

تورکڼي torkáṇi *m.* 1 soot, lamp-black 2 blight (disease of cereal grains)

تورکه torə́ka *f.* black starling (the bird)

تورکي torkí *m.* ☞ تورکڼي

تورکی torəkáj 1 black 2 *m.* 2.1 lure (for catching starlings) 2.2 *proper noun* Torykaj 2.3 wheat infected with blight

تورکی torəkáj *m.* syllable په تورکي یې ووایه! Read by syllables!

تورگاړ torgā́ṛ *m.* اشخار

تورگل torgúl *m. proper noun* Torgul

تورگمی torgamáj *m.* ت *obsolete* ☞ توربخون

تورلال torlā́l *m.* variety of grape

تورلشي torlə́shi *m. plural* variety of wheat with a black awn

تورلمی torlə́maj *m.* 1 marten 2 *dialect* badger

تورم turám *m.* horn ☞ ترم

تورمخکه torməkháka *f.* custom where children carry an animal skin stuffed with rags around the village and collect alms for the poor

تورمخی tormə́khaj guilty; to blame, at fault

تورن turə́n *m.* turán *military* captain; staff captain جگ تورن captain تورن جنرال lieutenant-general

تورن toरə́n *m. obsolete* ☞ تور 2, 3

تورنج turúndzh *m.* ☞ ترنج

تورنگړی tornagə́raj ☞ توربخون

تورني turaní *f.* rank of captain, title of a captain

توروالی torvā́laj *m.* 1 blackness 2 darkness of one's complexion

توروانجه torvā́ndzha *f.* nutmeg flower, *Nigella sativa*

تورويور tor-u-bór *m. colloquial* essence of the matter, heart of the matter په تورويور چوک پوهول to explain the heart of the matter to someone

تور و سپين tór-u-spín black and white (printer, TV)

تورول[1] toravə́l *denominative, transitive [past:* توري کړ] **1** to blacken; make dark, darken **2** *figurative* to discredit, blacken, smear; shame, disgrace **3** د کتاب مخونه تورول، کاغذ تورول to write; cover with writing **4** to dye, darken (the eyebrows) *idiom* عملنامه تورول to be guilty (of) ملک تورول to desolate a country, ravage a nation

تورول[2] toravə́l *transitive [past:* و یې توراوه] **1** to frighten away, scare off **2** *figurative* to repulse (by one's looks, by one's actions)

توره[1] túra *f.* **1** saber; sword جنگ د تورو سره د توري بند sword-belt توره ایستل، توره کښل hand-to-hand combat to draw (your) sword څوک چه توره به باسي، په توره به مرشي who lives by the sword, dies by the sword **a** توره برېښنبول to draw one's sword **b** to rattle one's saber, threaten war توري ته لاس کول to fence توري چلول to take up the sword په تورو کبدل to be cut down, be chopped up د تورو باران له تورو تپرول to cut up with swords پرې جورول to cut down, chop up; slaughter توره لښته کول to surrender, lay down arms ډال اچول to rattle with a sword **2** *figurative* valor, courage, bravery د هغه توري سری دئ He's a brave man. توره درلودل to be strong and brave; be valiant, be brave توره کول **a** to show valor, demonstrate courage, exhibit bravery **b** to excel in something توره وهل **a** to cut with a sword توري نور ځوانان وهي، منصب سدو خوري *proverb literally* The young men cut with their sabers, but Sado receives higher rank. He lets someone else do the dirty work. **b** *figurative* to show valor, demonstrate courage, exhibit bravery *idiom* د دلائلو توري کَلبدي په باد توره وهل **a** a heated argument was taking place to boast, brag **b** to make a show of bravery **c** to grind water in a mortar; be engaged in a useless business

توره[2] torá *f.* **1** detachment of warriors from the tribes توره لرل to have armed forces, have soldiers **2** nomads' camp **3** small village

توره[3] torá *f.* **1** concern; sadness **2** enmity, hostility **3** bile, gall

توره[4] tóra *f.* **1** *obsolete* coin with a value equal to 2 "paise"; penny **2** wedding expenses (payment for musicians, etc.)

توره[5] tóra *f.* **1** hill, mound **2** *agriculture* fallow, land lying fallow **3** rain-cloud, storm-cloud

توره[6] tóra *feminine singular of* تور[3] **1**

توره انا tóra aná *f.* black drongo, *Dicrurus*

توره بحیره tóra buhajrá *f.* the Black Sea

توره بډه tóra baḍá *f.* pitch darkness, outer darkness

توره بلا tóra balá *f.* **1** witch, hag **2** misfortune, calamity

توره پانه tóra páṇa *f.* violet

توره تبه tóra tə́ba *f.* **1** brucellosis **2** *dialect* typhus, spotted fever

توره تتی tóra tatə́j *f.* blackbird

توره تياره tóra tjårá **1** *f.* full darkness **2** *attributive* توره تیاره اوريځ dark cloud

توره تېښته tóra teḵhta *f.* strong repulsion, strong adversion

توره ټوخله tóra ṭukhə́la *f.* ☞ توره غاره

توره دربله tóra dərbilá *f.* ☞ توره دربه tóra dərbá *f.* ☞ تورتم

توره شمه tóra shə́ma *f.* black tent (of nomads)

توره غاره tóra ghárá *f.* whooping cough

توره غندی tóra ghunḍə́j *f.* Towraghondi (border village)

توره لښته tóra lə́khta *f.* *botany* round-leaved cotoneaster

توري[1] **1** turí *m.* torí *plural* Turi (tribe) **2** turáj *m.* toráj Turi (tribesman)

توري[2] tóraj *m.* **1** letter په تورو ویل to read letter by letter; read haltingly توري په توري لوستل tóri pə tóri ... to read carefully **2** word سپين توري پرکول to confirm one's own opinion

توري[3] tavə́ri *m. plural* **1** home furnishings; household goods توري اخیستل to lead a nomadic life, migrate **2** mats

توري[4] tóraj *m.* spleen

توري[5] toráj *m.* توری toráj *f. botany* loofah

توري[6] torí restive; balky; shy دا آس توري دئ This horse is restive.

توري[7] túri *plural of* توره[1]

توري[8] tóri *f. plural* **1** *from* تور[3] **1 2** *from* توره[4, 5]

توري[9] toráj **1.1** black **1.2** dark-complexioned **2** *m.* dark-complexioned person

توری[10] toráj *f.* horn (trumpet)

توری[11] túre go away (or similar cry used to chase away a dog)

توری[12] toré *plural of* توری[2, 3]

توريالتيا turjāltjá *f.* valor, courage, bravery

توريالی turjāláj **1** valourous, brave, courageous **2** *m. proper noun* Turjalaj

توريالی توب turjālitób *m.* ☞ توريالتيا

توریانی torjāṇə́j *f.* martin, swift (the bird)

توري اوبه tóri obə́ *f. plural* **1** dark sea water **2** sea; ocean **3** *regional* exile, penal servitude **4** glaucoma

توري ايکی tori ikə́j *f. plural* change, small change (coins)

توریت[1] torét tavrít *m. Arabic religion* Torah, Pentateuh

تورېت[2] tavrét *m.* astrology

توري تپی túri-tápi *Eastern* túre-tápe توري تپي کول to beg, entreat, request

تورېتون tavretún *m.* study of astrology, work in astrology

تورېتی tavrétaj *m.* astrology

تورید tavríd *m. Arabic* import

تورېدل[1] toredə́l *denominative, intransitive [past:* تور شو] **1.1** to blacken, grow dark, darken **1.2** *figurative* to be accused, be blamed **1.3** *figurative* to be disgraced, be shamed **2** *m. plural* **.1** darkening, dimness **2.2** eclipse د سپوږمی تورېدل lunar eclipse **2.3** *figurative* shame, disgrace

تورېدل[2] toredə́l *intransitive [past:* وتورېده] **1** to be frightened **2** to run away, flee (after being frightened) کرک را ځخه وتورید The quail took fright and flew away. **3** to be stubborn دا آس ډېر تورېږي This horse is very restive.

تاوريدول tavridavə́l *denominative, transitive* [*past:* تاوريد يې کړ] to import

تاوربل turél *m. military* turret; ring mount

توريم torijúm *m. plural chemistry* thorium

توريجمار turəjmā́r *m.* horn-player, trumpeter

تورشک turshák *m.* reproach; blame, censure

توری ¹ toṛə́j *f.* 1 aunt (on mother's side) توری کول to consider as an aunt; call auntie 2 aunt, auntie (as a familiar form of address)

توری ² tuṛáj 1 stammering توري خبري کول tuṛi to stammer, slutter 2 *m.* stammerer, stutterer

توری زی toṛəjzáj *m.* cousin (son of mother's sister)

توری زی toṛəzə́j *f.* cousin (daughter mother's sister)

توزن tuzán 1 base, ignoble 2 cowardly 3 *figurative* vain, futile, unavailing توزنه هیله a vain hope, futile hope

توزیع tavzí' *f. Arabic* 1 spreading, dissemination 2 delivery, distribution, allocation (of income, etc.) توزیع کول *compound verb* a to spread, disseminate b to deliver, distribute; allocate توزیع کېدل *compound verb* a to be spread b to be allocated

توژنه tózhna *f.* meadow, (forest) glade

توربل togə́l *transitive* [*past:* یې توربه] 1 to plane, shave; cut, hew 2 to grind, round off, machine 3 to scrape 4 *figurative* to sharpen, whet; polish, perfect

توربلي togə́le *f.* shaving, filing

توربند togónd *m.* lathe operator, turner

توربندی togəndáj *m.* plane (tool for planing wood)

توربنه togə́na *f. action noun from* توربل

توربونی togúnaj *m.* scraper

توربی ¹ togə́j *f.* ☞ توربندي

توربی ² togí *present tense of* توربل

توس ¹ tus *m.* sniffing of a track by a dog

توس ² tavs *m.* 1 powerful thirst 2 heat, sultriness, hot spell

توس ³ tos *m.* slice of white-bread toast

توسط tavassút *m. Arabic* mediation, assistance, aid د چا په توسط with someone's help

توسعه tavsi'á *f. Arabic* 1 spread, dissemination; broadening و يوشي ته توسعه ورکول to be spread, be disseminated; broaden, ميندل to develop, broaden, expand something 2 extent, stretch 3 expansion توسعه غوښتل to strive for expansion

توسل tavassúl *m. Arabic* fastening, uniting; connecting, linking

توسن ¹ tosán reason, cause

توسن ² tosán *m.* spirited steed

توسن ³ tusə́n *m.* 1 bloodhound 2 greedy person

توسند ¹ tavsánd burning from the heat (hot weather)

توسند ² tusánd 1.1 greedy 1.2 voluptuous 2 *m.* bloodhound

توسندک tusandə́k *m.* 1 bloodhound 2 greedy person; grasping person, money-grubber

توسول tavsavə́l *transitive* [*past:* یې توساوه] to evoke a strong desire

توسه tósa *f.* means; facilities; rememdy

توسبدل tavsedə́l *intransitive* [*past:* و توسېده] 1 to become impassioned, become excited; become irritated, become annoyed 2 to strive for, wish for passionately 3 to fade (crops, due to lack of precipitation) 4 to dry up (of milk in the breast)

توشدان toshdán *m. regional military* cartridge pouch

توشک toshák *m.* 1 mattress 2 reversible rug

توشل tavshál 1 shallow (of a dish, saucer) 2 flat-bottomed (of a boat)

توشول toshavə́l *transitive* [*past:* و يې توشاوه] to set a dog onto

توشه toshá *f.* provisions for the road

توش خانه toshakhāná *f.* storeroom, pantry

توشی tavsháj *m.* 1 wooden bowl, wooden dish 2 fruit carried away by the groom as he departs from the bride

توښ ¹ tavx̌ *m.* steam; vapor د ابو توښ water vapor; steam; steaming

توښ ² tox̌ paying attention, attentive

توښ ³ tūx̌ *m. computer science* source, resource

توښه tox̌á *f.* ☞ توشه

توښی tavx̌áj *f.* stove, oven

توصل tavassúl *m. Arabic* setting up of communication(s), establishment of contact توصل کول to set up communication(s)

توصیف tavsíf *m. Arabic* definition, characterization; description توصیف کول to define, characterize; describe

توصیه tavsijá *f. Arabic* 1 recommendation, advice 2 will, testament توصیه کول a to recommand, advise b to leave (to), bequeath

توصیه نامه tavsijanāmá *f.* letter of recommendation

توضو tavazzú *Arabic religion* ablution before prayer

توضیح tavzí *m. & f.* tavzíh *Arabic m.* [*plural:* توضیحات tavzihāt] 1 explanation, clarification 2 observation, note توضیح کول *compound verb* to explain, clarify توضیح کېدل *compound verb* to become clear, be explained توضیحات ورکول to provide explanations

توطیه tautijá *f. Arabic* intrigue; machinations

توغ ¹ tugh *m.* togh 1 banner 2 hackberry tree, *Celtis*

توغ ² togh *m.* entertainment arranged by an intermediary to reconcile hostile parties

توغل tughál *m.* توغم toghám *m.* 1 sweat-cloth, saddle-cloth 2 long drawn-out rain

توغمه tughmá *f.* anger, wrath توغمه کول to put into a rage, anger په توغمه کېدل to fly into a rage, become angry

توغمه ناک tughmanā́k enraged; angry

توغندی tughandáj *m.* rocket, missile فضائي توغندی space rocket نقلیه توغندی rocket carrier

توغول ¹ tughavə́l *transitive; past tense* [*past:* و يې توغاوه] 1.1 to drag along the ground 1.2 to throw away, toss 1.3 to put (into orbit, e.g., a spaceship) مدارته توغول to put into orbit 2 *m. plural*

1. dragging along the ground **2.2** throwing away, tossing (away) **2.3** putting into (orbit) د توغولو راکټ rocket carrier

توغول ² tughavәl *transitive dialect* [*past:* و يې توغاوه] to steal, rob

توغونه tughavә́na *f.* ☞ توغول ¹ 2

توغه ¹ tógha *f.* expiation of guilt

توغه ² toghá *f.* fig, fig tree

توغېدل ¹ tughedә́l *intransitive* [*past:* و توغېده] **1** to be dragged along the ground **2** to be thrown, be tossed (away) **3** to be put (into orbit, e.g., of a space ship)

توغېدل ² *intransitive* [*past:* و توغېده] **1** to be stolen **2** to leave surreptitiously; slip away

توفیق tavfíķ *m. Arabic* [*plural:* توفیقونه tavfiķúna *Arabic plural:* توفیقات tavfiķā́t] **1** favor; mercy; charity **2** success; realization of one's desires **3** settlement, arrangement, agreement **4** *proper noun* Tevfik

توقع tavaķķú' *f. Arabic m.* [*plural:* توقعات tavaķķ'ā́t] expectation, hope د توقع پر خلاف despite one's expectation دټولوتوقوعاتو په خلاف in spite of all expectations توقع لرل، توقع کول to hope (for)

توقف tavaķķúf *m. Arabic* stop, delay بله توقف ځخه، بله توقفه quickly, without delay توقف کول to linger, tarry

توقف گاه tavaķķufgā́h *m.* stopping-place; stop, parking space

توقیف tavķíf *f. Arabic* **1** arrest **2** hold-up, delay (of baggage, goods, etc.) **3** stopping, delaying توقیف کول *compound verb* ☞ توقیفېدل *compound verb* ☞ *military idiom* د توقیف کېدل، توقیفول توقیف اور defensive fire

توقیفول tavķifavә́l *denominative, transitive* [*past:* توقیف یې کړ] **1** to arrest **2** to delay (baggage, goods, etc.) **3** to stop, hold up

توقیفېدل tavķifedә́l *denominative, intransitive* [*past:* توقیف شو] **1** to be arrested **2** to be delayed (of baggage, goods, etc.) **3** to be stopped; stop

توک ¹ tuk *m.* spit, spittle توک کول to spit *idiom* توک سهل to endure, bear, suffer, stand

توک ² tok *m.* ☞ تکم

توکانئ tukāṇә́j *f.* **1** spittoon **2** kind of children's game

توکبنسټ tókbәnsәṭ *m. computer science* database

توکپټه tókpaṭá *f. computer science* toolbar

توکرکی tokә́rkaj *m.* tavkә́rkaj **1** broken piece of pottery **2** fragment توکرکي توکرکي الوتل to crack; fall to pieces

توکری tokә́raj *m.* tavkә́raj fragment توکری کول to break off a fragment

توکری tokaṛáj *m.* scraper

توکل ¹ tavakkúl *m. Arabic* **1** hope په چا توکل کول to hope (for), count on (someone) **2** *proper noun* Tavakkul

توکل ² tukә́l *transitive* [*past:* و يې توکل] to spit, spit out لارې توکل to spit *idiom* پر ځان توکل، ځان ته توکل، پر بېره توکل to commit a blunder, play the fool خپلي لارې توکل او بېرته اخیستل، خپلي ناري توکل to reproach for some good that's been done خپلي او بېرته اخیستل

ناري چه سري توکي، بیائي نه اخلي *Eastern proverb* one should not be reproached for a good deed

توکلي ¹ tavakkulí chance, accidental; done at random chosen at random

توکلی ² tukә́laj *past participle of* توکل ²

توکم ¹ tukә́m *m.* ☞ تکم

توکم ² tukә́m *first person present of* توکل

توکنی ¹ tukaṇí *f.* swearing, verbal abuse, bad language

توکم ² tukaṇә́j *f.* ☞ تکم

توکل 2 ☞ ¹ [توبي کړل] tukavә́l *denominative, transitive* [*past:* figurative to speak inopportunely

توکه túka *f.* advantage, profit, use

توکه tokā́ *f.* corn-cob

توکه ³ tuká *imperfective imperative of* توکل ²

توکی ¹ tokáj *m.* **1** kind, type **2** thing

توکی ² tóki *f. plural computer science* elements

توکی ³ tukí *present tense of* توکل

توکي توکي tóki-tóki **1** curled in ringlets (of hair) **2** different, various, varied

توکېدل tukedә́l *denominative, intransitive* [*past:* توک شوه] to be spit out

توکیو tókjó *f.* Tokyo

توگ tog *m.* ☞ توگه

توگو ¹ togó *f.* Togo

توگو ² tógo *oblique plural of* توگه

توگولېند togolénd *m.* ☞ توگو ¹

توگه tóga *f.* **1** method, way; type, kind پر دې توگه، په دې توگه in such a way, thus ؟ څه توگه سري دئ؟ What sort of a person is he? په سمه توگه regularly, evenly, directly ښه توگه good, fine په بله توگه in a different way, variously د مثال په توگه for example, as an example **2** part; component دا دوا درې توګي ده this medicine consists of three components

توگی togáj *m.* **1** group, row, line (of people) **2** part; component

تول ¹ tol *m.* weight اتومي تول atomic weight په توله by weight, according to weight تول لرل to weigh *idiom* تول ترازو *astronomy* the Scales, Libra هره خبره په تول تلل to weigh, consider, think over each word

تول ² tul *m.* **1** grain (almost ripe) **2** field; melon patch **3** fixed property د تول خاوند rich man, person of property

تول ³ tul *m.* **1** ☞ تولان **2** rolling down (from a hill)

تول ⁴ tval **1** equal (in weight) تول کول to balance **2** *m.* balance, equilibrium خپل تول ساتل to preserve a balance

تولان tulā́n *m. literally* the walk of a partridge *figurative* graceful walk

تولاجی tulājí mattress

تولد tavallúd *m. Arabic* birth تولد کېدل *compound verb* to be born

تولک tulák *m.* molt, molting (of birds)

تولکه tuláka *f.* whistle, pipe

تولگر tolgár *m.* weigher

تولند tuländ *adjective* rolling down

تولنده tulánda *f.* widgeon (a kind of duck)

تولوالی tvalvắlaj *m.* equilibrium, balance

تولول¹ tolavәl *denominative, transitive* [*past:* تول يې کړ] to weigh

تولول² tvalavәl *transitive* [*past:* تول يې کړ] to balance

تولول³ tulavәl *transitive* [*past:* و يې تولاوه] to roll (something)

تولونه¹ tolavóna *f. action noun from* تولول¹

تولونه² tvalavóna *f. action noun from* تولول²

تولونه³ tulavóna *f. action noun from* تولول³

توله¹ tulá *f.* 1 siren, horn, whistle 2 pipe, fife 3 *anatomy* auditory passage 4 tube, pipe د تولي په شان tubular

توله² tolá *f.* tola (an Indian measure of weight equal to the weight of a silver rupee, 180 grains)

توله³ tvála *feminine singular of* تول⁴ 1

تولی¹ tuláj *m.* inflorescence, plume of a reed or rush

تولی² tulé *plural of* توله¹

تولی³ tolé *plural of* توله²

تولی⁴ tuláj *f.* 1 fife, reed pipe 2 flue 3 spent cartridge *idiom* د تولی تنفس windpipe

تولی⁵ toláj *f.* 1 scales (for weighing silk) 2 root of paddy rice

تولی⁶ tavlój *f.* cup, piala (i.e., Asian handleless cup)

تولیا tavlijắ *f.* towel

تولید tavlíd *m. Arabic* 1 production, manufacture د برق تولید production of electric energy 2 birth

تولیدات tavlidất *m. Arabic plural* 1 *from* تولید 2 product; production اجتماعي توليدات social product 3 birthrate

تولیداتي tavlidấtí ☞ توليدي مو سبي industrial enterprises توليداتي قواوي productive forces

تولیدل¹ tvaledәl *denominative, intransitive* [*past:* تول شو] to balance, be balanced

تولیدل² tuledәl *intransitive* [*past:* وتولېده] to roll (somewhere)

تولیدول tavlidavәl *denominative, transitive* [*past:* تولید يې کړ] to produce, manufacture

تولیدوونکی tavlidavúnkaj 1 *present participle of* تولیدول 2 *m.* 1. producer; sire 2.2 د برق تولیدوونکی *technology* generator

تولیدي tavlidí 1 production; productive تولیدي وسایل means of production توليدي روابط industrial relations 2 *figurative* fruitful

تولیدبدل tavliledәl *denominative, intransitive* [*past:* تولید شو] 1 to be produced, be manufactured 2 to arise, spring up, be created

تولیا tavlijắ *f.* towel

تومار¹ tumắr *m.* ☞ طومار

تومار² tumắr *m.* 1 itch; urge 2 scab, rash

توماشه tumāshá *f.* ☞ تماشه

تومان tumắn *m.* 1 twenty rupees شپیر تومانه افغانی one hundred twenty afghanis 2 toman, tuman (Persian, Iranian monetary unit) 3 *history* ten thousand 4 *history* region, province

تومانچه tumānchá *f.* pistol, revolver

توماندار tumāndár *m.* leader of a tribe (among the Baluchis)

تومبار tumbắr *m.* instigation تومبار کول to instigate, incite

تومبسکی tumbóskaj *m.* ☞ ؤومبسکه

تومت tomát *m.* ☞ تهمت

تومن¹ tumán *m.* ☞ تومان

تومن² tumán *m.* warm milk

تومن³ tumán *m.* grain for sowing

تومنه tvámna *f.* tómna 1 ferment, leaven د پنیر تومنه، د پوخي تومنه ferment for cheese تومنه کول to ferment, leaven 2 *figurative* essence, substance 3 ☞ تومن³

تومنه گیاه tomnagijắ tomnagijäh *f. botany* ascomycetes (a class of fungi)

تومنی tumóṇaj warm, lukewarm

تومه tómá *f.* 1 ☞ تومنه 2 falcon feed 3 fatty piece of meat

تون¹ tun *m. obsolete* 1 homeland, motherland 2 dwelling, abode بی خایه تونه without kith or kin, stateless; homeless

تون² tvan *m.* hut, shack, hovel

تون³ tun *m.* toona, *Cedrela toona*

تون tún *suffix of masculine nouns* 1 *indicates abstract notions and condition* کنډتون widowhood 2 dwelling-place, receptacle مېږتون ant-hill چرتون sheath, scabbard وروکتون kindergarten

توناژ tonắzh *m.* tonnage

تونبیا tonbiẩ *m. singular & plural* 1 thread of combed (refined) cotton 2 combing of cotton (before spinning) تونبیا کول to comb cotton (before spinning)

تونده túnda *f.* 1 food, dish 2 enmity, hostility

تونس¹ tauns *m.* wrath, anger, rage

تونس² tunís *m.* Tunisia د تونس ښار the city of Tunis

تونگ¹ taváng *m.* 1 basket with a cover (for clothing); cardboard box (for ribbons, etc.) 2 pan, tray (of a baker)

تونگ² tung *m.* tuváng 1 storehouse, depository 2 clay pitcher

تونگ³ tung sparse, scattered, strewn about

تونگه túnga *f.* maiden

تونگی¹ tongáj *m.* tavangáj basket, purse, small case

تونگي² túngi *plural of* تونگه

تونل tunél *m.* tunnel

تونه tvána *f.* ☞ تومنه

تونه toṇá *f.* exterior, outside

تونی toṇój *f.* 1 suitcase 2 cupboard, enclosed shelf

توول tovәl *transitive* ☞ تویول

توه¹ tóva *f.* dregs of milk

توه² tóva *f.* small bank, small earthen wall (for holding back water in a field)

توه³ tavá *f.* mulberry tree

توه⁴ tavá *f.* taste (for something); desire, inclination

توهړ toháṛ *m.* upas-tree, *Antiaris toxicaria*

توهم tavahhúm *m. Arabic* 1 imagination 2 supposition; suspicion 3 superstition

توهین tauhín *m. Arabic* insult

توی¹ tóvaj *m.* herd of goats

توی ² toj 1.1 poured (out); spilled 1.2 strewn, scattered 1.3 knocked down (of fruit from trees) 1.4 dropped (e.g., of a bomb) 1.5 cast (of type-face) 2 m. .1 stream 2.2 channel, bed (along which runs a stream) idiom توی تلل to be lost, perish for nothing

توی ³ toj m. ☞ بنادي ¹

تویالکه tojálka f. kettle, boiler

توی توی toj-tój interjection oh-oh

تویند tojánd pouring (forth), spilling (out), flowing (out)

تویل tojavə́l denominative, transitive [past: توی یې کړه] 1 to pour; spill 2 to stew, scatter 3 to knock down (fruit from trees); shake down (leaves) 4 to drop (e.g., bombs) 5 to cast (type-face) idiom د وطن په لیار وینی تویل to spill one's blood for the fatherland

تویونه tojavə́na f. 1 pouring out; spilling 2 strewing, scattering 3 dropping (e.g., of bombs) 4 casting (type-face)

تویېدل tojedə́l denominative, intransitive [past: توی شوه] 1 to be poured, pour, spill, overflow 2 to fall, flow (into, of a river) 3 to scatter, be scattered, be strewn 4 to be knocked down (of fruit); to fall (of leaves) 5 to be dropped (e.g., of bombs) 6 to be cast (of type-face) 7 to fall out (of teeth) 8 to wear out (of clothing, shoes)

تویېدنه tojedə́na f. action noun تویېده tojedə́ m. action noun plural from تویېدل د وینو تویېده bloodletting, bloodshed

ته ¹ tah f. 1 fold, bend 2 bottom, underside idiom ته و بلا feet up ته و بلا کول to dig up, to dig across (a garden, etc.)

ته ² tə Eastern imperfect of تلل ¹

ته ³ tə proper name second person singular you (direct form) a as subject of an action with intransitive verbs in all tenses and with transitive verbs in present and future tenses, and also in the imperative mood: ته به ولاړ شي؟ What are you saying? ته څه وایي؟ Will you leave? ته به زمونږ معلم یې؟ You, probably, are our teacher? ته څه You go! b as object of the action in an ergative construction: ته څا کښینولي؟ Who woke you up?

ته ⁴ ta postposition in connection with the preposition و; or without it; a indicates the addressee of an action: تا ته وایم I am speaking to you. ما احمد ته خط ولېږه I sent Ahmed the letter. b indicates the place to which an action is directed: پغمان ته ځي They are going to Paghman. دا کاغذ پوستي ته یوسه Take this letter to the post office. زه کارته ځم I am going to work. کوڅي ته راوتل to go out onto the street کورته ځو We are going home. c indicates the location of something: د پامیر سهیل ته south of the Pamirs افغانستان شمالي خوا ته تاجکستان پروت دئ Tajikistan is located north of Afghanistan. d indicates the person or object toward which an action is directed: دوی خولې ته he came to his father پلار ته راغئ ورل to lift bread to your mouth e indicates the object for which some action is undertaken هري غلي او نبات ته مځکه په راز راز ډول یوې کوي for each grain and plant the ground is plowed differently f indicates the goal or purpose of an action: دلته اوبو ته راغلم I came here for water. ستا پوښتنې ته راغلئ یم I came to inform you. g indicates the place near which something is happening: موږ مېز ته

تولھ مېز ته ناست وو we sit at the table کښینبنو everyone sat at the table h indicates the time of an action or a certain period of time: صبا ته (on) the next day; (on) the next morning; next morning i indicates appearance, likeness with someone or something: هغه دی کټ مټ و آصف ته سوئ مور ته تللئ دئ He takes after his mother. دئ He's the image of Asaf.

تهاجم tahādzhúm m. Arabic [plural: تهاجمونه tahādzumúna Arabic plural: تهاجمات tahādzhumát] attack; invasion; intrusion تهاجم کول to attack; invade; intrude

تهاتر tahātúr m. Arabic clearing (of accounts); clearing account, paper transfer

تهان thān m. 1 ☞ تان 2 cattle-shed, cow-house, pig-sty

تهانه tahāná f. ☞ تهانه

تهانه دار tahānadár m. ☞ تهانه دار

تهانه tahāná f. 1 gate; barrier; outpost 2 border post, police post

تهانه دار tahāṇadár m. chief of an outpost, head of a border station

تهجي tahadzhdzhí f. Arabic reading by syllables, reading haltingly تهجي کول to read haltingly, spell out

ته خانه tahkhāná f. cellar, basement

تهداب tahdā́b m. تهداو tahdā́v تهدای tahdā́j m. 1 foundation (of a building) د تهداب مراسم the ceremony of laying the cornerstone (of a building) 2 figurative basis, foundation تهداب اچول، تهداب وهل a to lay the foundation (of a building); lay a foundation, establish a basis

تهدید tahdíd m. Arabic [plural: تهدیدونه tahdidúna Arabic plural: تهدیدات tahdidát] 1 threat; scare سره له تهدیداتو despite threats تر تهدید لاندي نیول to threaten 2 danger

تهدیدآمېز tahdidāméz تهدیدامېزه tahdidāméza threatening

تهدیدول tahdidavə́l denominative, transitive [past: تهدید یې کړ] to threaten

تهذیب tahzíb m. Arabic 1 culture, civilization 2 improvement in manners; moral upbringing

تهذیبي tahzibí Arabic cultural, cultured تهذیبي روابط cultural ties تهذیبي ژوند a cultured life, refined life; cultural life

تهران tehrā́n m. Tehran (city)

تهلکه tahliká f. tahluká 1 destruction, ruin; death 2 agony, death pangs

تهلکه دار tahlikadár destructive, perditious; dangerous

تهمت tuhmát m. tomát tohmát Arabic 1 accusation, blame 2 slander تهمت اچول، تهمت ترل، تهمت ویل a to accuse (of something) تهمت وهل b to slander (someone) to blacken, censure, critize 3 suspicion

تهمتي tuhmatí tomatí tohmatí 1.1 suspicious 1.2 defamed, discredited; slandered 2 m. slanderer

تهن tahə́n deep (e.g., a gully, river)

تهنه təhə́na f. 1 hollow area, low-lying area; swampy region 2 slope; inclination, descent

تهي tihí 1 empty 2 *figurative* vain, idle *idiom* ديو شي څخه پهلو تهي کول a to refrain from something b to move away, keep aloof from something

تهي دماغ tihidimágh 1 stupid 2 vacuous, shallow (of a person)

تهيدل təhedál *intransitive* [*past:* وتهيده] to tremble, shiver

تهيه tahjá *f.* tahijá *Arabic* 1 procurement, purchase (of provisions) 2 finding (of means) 3 preparation, training (of personnel) تهيه کول *compound verb* a to purchase, procure (provisions) b to obtain acquire (means) c to prepare, teach (personnel) معلمان تهيه کول to prepare teachers تهيه کېدل *compound verb* a to be purchased b to be obtained (means) c to be trained; train, prepare oneself (personnel)

تي ¹ taj *m.* [*plural:* تي ti *plural:* تيونه tajúna] nipple (of the breast); breast تي د تي غوټول d te ṭhukhe pərbukol to suckle له تي څخه پرېکول to wean تي يي کوډ شو she has lost her milk *idiom* د چا سره تي رودل to fraternize with someone

تي ² te *f.* te, name of the letter ت

تي ³ te *contraction* a the pronouns ته and يي تي ويني؟ Do you see him? b the postposition ته and the pronoun دا کتاب واخله، عمر تي يوسه Take this book, carry it to Omar.

تي ⁴ te *Eastern* ☞ تري ⁵

تئ ⁵ təj *Western dialect imperfect of* تلل ¹

تيا tjá *suffix of feminine nouns, indicates abstract concepts or an abstract condition* آسانتيا a facilitation; relief b lightness; easiness c privilege; advantage

تياتر tjātr *m.* theater

تيار tajár 1 ready, prepared ډوډۍ تياره ده Dinner is ready. 2 finished, completed 3 agreeable, ready (for something) مونږ دي ... ته تيار يو چه We are ready to go in order to ... ; We agree that ... 4 stout, full; obese, corpulent *idiom* خو تيار ليونى دئ He has gone completely mad. دا تيار مرګ دئ That's sure death.

تيارخور tijārkhór *m.* 1 parasite, sponger, idler 2 person provided with full support (lodging, food and sometimes clothing) 3 *regional* servants (of a khan, etc.)

تيارول tajāravál *denominative, transitive* [*past:* تيار يي کړ] 1 to prepare (food) 2 to train, prepare someone, prepare something ځان تيارول to be prepared, be trained 3 to stock up, procure 4 to force, encourage د زوى مينې هر څه ته تيار کړ Love for his son forced him to go to all lengths. 5 to feed (cattle)

تيارونه tajāravóna *f.* 1 preparation, training 2 procurement

تياره tiārə tjárá tiārá 1 *f.* darkness تپه تياره، توره تياره full darkness تياره وه tiārá تکه توره تياره وه it became pitch black, it was pitch black څه توره سترګو يي تياره راغله Everything grew dark before her eyes. تياره وه، څه انا وروسته پاته وه. څه توره تياره وه، څه انى وروسته پاته وه *proverb literally* in part it was dark, in part grandma herself was late *figurative* there were a lot of different reasons 2 *attributive adjective* dark; immersed in darkness تياره ماښام dark evening تر تياره ماښامه until late at night تياره کول a to darken, make dark,

make obscure b to darken, cloud تياره کېدل to grow dark, become dark, darken *idiom* د زړه تياره depression, dejection, despondency

تياراج tajāráj *m.* tajārí *f.* 1 preparation د امتحان تيارى preparation for an examination د جشن تيارى preparations for a holiday تيارى نيول، وخه ته د تيارى کول د څه د پاره تيارى کول، د څه د پاره تيارى نيول to prepare, ready (oneself) train د امتحان په تيارى سره اخته و He prepared for his examinations. 2 preparedness 3 procurement (e.g., of produce) 4 provision, fitting out (with); acquisition (of) (something needed for a household)

تياريدل tajāredál *denominative, intransitive* [*past:* تيار شو] 1 to prepare (oneself), get ready, train تيارسئ! *Western* At ease! (command) 2 to be manufactured, be processed 3 to put on weight, grow stout

تياربده tajāredá *m. plural* 1 preparation 2 manufacture, processing

تويالکه tjálka təjálka *f.* ☞ تويالکه

تيانشان tjánshán *m.* Tien Shan (mountains)

تبون tebún *m. religion* ablution with sand تبون وهل to perform ablution with sand

تيپ ¹ tip *m.* 1 row تيپ تړل to form rows, line up in ranks 2 detachment; squadron

تيپ ² tip *m.* 1 type (model) د موټر نوى تيپ a new model car 2 *literature* type

تيپچه tipchá *f. hunting* bird-call (for quail)

تيت tit 1 scattered, dispersed 2 widespread, instilled تيت په ترک ☞ تيت پترک 3 *military* line (formation), extended order (formation)

تيتان titán *m.* titanium

تيتانوس tetānús *m.* tetanus

تيت پترک tit-patrák تيت پرک تيت پترک tit-parák 1 dispersed, driven off 2 routed, defeated تيت پترک کول a to disperse, drive off b to rout, defeat

تيتری titrój *f.* marinated mushrooms

تيتوالى titválaj *m.* 1 scattering, dispersing; disseminating 2 spreading, instilling 3 absent-minded, inattention

تيت پترک tit-u-parák ☞ تيت وپرک

تيتول titavól *denominative, transitive* [*past:* تيت يي کړ] 1 to scatter, disseminate 2 to spread, instill 3 to determine, regulate (the flow of gas, steam, etc.)

تي تي ¹ ti-tí *interjection* cry used when calling chickens

تيتى ² titój *f. children's speech* baby chick

تيتيدل titedól *denominative, intransitive* [*past:* تيت شو] 1 to be scattered, be disseminated 2 to be spread (around), be instilled; spread, take root 3 to be determined, be regulated (of a supply of gas, steam, etc.)

تيتي کاکا titikāká *f.* Titicaca (lake on the border of Peru and Bolovia)

تبځل tedzál *transitive* [*past:* و يي تبخه] to force to run, to drive, chase

تبخل tetsól *transitive* [*past:* و يي تبخه] 1 to pierce, run through 2 to drill, bore through 3 to stab, spear (someone) 4 to stuff, fill 5 to devour

تبخنه tetsə́na *f.* 1 piercing, running through 2 drilling 3 stabbing (of someone) 4 stuffing, filling

تبخی tetsə́j¹ *f.* auger; drill

تبخي tetsí² *present tense of* تبخل

تخنیک tekhník *m.* ☞ تخنیک

تخنیکدان tekhnikdā́n ☞ تخنیکدان

تخنیکي tekhnikí ☞ تخنیکي

تبخوری tajkhóraj *m.* nursing baby

تیر tir¹ *m.* [*plural:* تیران tirā́n] 1 arrow; shaft 2 log; beam, girder 3 mast 4 firing, shooting; a shot

تبر ter² 1.1 past; last تبر کال last year تبر ځل، تبر وار last time تبره شپه late evening; late in the evening تبره هفته last night, yesterday evening تبره زمانه last week تبره زمانه old times, times long past دا خو د تبري زماني خبره ده These are matters of days long past. 1.2 passed, spent (of time) 1.3 devoted, loyal, true 1.4 near, close تبر ته ور پلاره! Dear father! زړه ته را تبر close; dear 1.5 sacrificing تر خپل سر و مال تبر sacrificing everything پر وطن تبر یی خپل ځان دئ He is sacrificing himself in the name of the Motherland. 1.6 renouncing (something), denying oneself (something) 2 *m. regional* deception تبر ورکول to deceive *idiom* په تبر پسي ترتاب نسته notwithstanding; moreover تبر تر دي ، تبر له دي *proverb* you cannot turn back the past تبر پر تبر گڼل to finish with the past, bury the past تبر تر تبره exceptional, unusual; huge تبر، تبر پر تبر، تبره په تبره let bygones be bygones

تیر tir³ *m.* bare mountain-top

تیرا tirā́ *f.* ☞ تیرا

تبران terā́n¹ 1 permitted; accepted, usual; popular, current 2 current

تیران tirā́n² *plural of* تیر¹

تیرانا tirānā́ *f.* Tirana (capital, Albania)

تیرانداز tirāndā́z *m.* shot from a bow

تیراندازي tirāndāzí *f.* shooting from a bow

تیراوال tirāvā́l *m. invariable plural* inhabitant of the Tirah region (western Pakistan)

تیراه tirā́h *m.* Tirah (region in western Pakistan)

تبرایستل teristə́l *transitive* [*present:* تبر یی باسي *past:* تبر یی ایست *past:* تبر یی یوست] to deceive, fool; delude, mislead

تبرایستنه teristə́na *f.* error, delusion د ځواني تبرایستني the sins of youth

تبرایسته teristə́ *m. plural* deception, swindling, cheating

تیرائي tirā́i 1 of Tirah, from Tirah تیرائي عالم population of Tirah, inhabitants of Tirah 2 *m.* inhabitant of Tirah

تبربلی terbalə́j *f.* end of a beam which juts out from a porch or wall

تبربوزی terbúzaj *m.* kind of stitch *idiom* سره تبربوزی کول to do somehow or other, do any old way

تیرپرتاب tirpartā́b *m.* 1 distance an arrow flies 2 ☞ تیرکش

تیرجمیر tiradzhmír *m.* Tirajmir (mountain)

تیرپرتاب tirrā́s ☞ تیرپرتاب

تبرسری tersarā́j *m.* bridle

تبرسو térsu *numeral obsolete* three hundred

تبرسولی tersulā́j *m.* leftovers, scraps (of fodder)

تبرغمل terghamál *m.* تبرغمی terghamáj *m.* oppression; violence, force

تیرک tirák *m.* axle (of a millstone)

تیرکش tirkásh *m.* تیرکښ tirkā́kh *m. architecture* embrasure; *military* loophole, embrasure

تبرگه térga *f.* 1 partition 2 rope with which the crupper is attached to the saddle blanket

تبرمتی termətáj *m.* pony

تبرنه terə́na *f.* 1 passing, going past 2 forgiveness, pardon 3 oppression

تیارو tjaró *regional oblique plural of* تیاره

تبرواته tervātə́ *m. plural* 1 deception 2 error; oversight; mistake

تبر و بیر ter-u-bér 1.1 more or less suitable; approximate 1.2 changing, alternating تبر و بیر وتل to change, alternate 2 sooner or later

تبروت پته terwat paṭá *f. computer science* error bar

تبروتل tervatə́l *intransitive* [*present:* تبروزي *past:* تبروت] 1 to be deceived; err, be mistaken 2 to examine, look over; over look

تبروتنه tervatə́na¹ *f. action noun from* تبروتل طباعتي تبروتني misprints, errata

تبروتنه tervatə́na² *f. computer science* bug (i.e., error)

تبرور terór *m.* terror

تبروری tervaráj *m.* very light load sent well in advance during a move (by nomads)

تبرول teravə́l¹ *denominative, transitive* [*past:* تبر یی کړ] 1 to spend (time) د رخصتی روځي په غرونو کښي تبرول to spend one's leave in the mountains دري روځي یی هلته تبري کړي He spent three days there. مال د سیند to have fun, amuse oneself 2 to lead across ساعت تبرول ځخه تبرول to lead cattle across the river 3 to suffer, endure, bear زحمت پر ځان تبرول to endure difficulties, suffer deprivation 4 to introduce (facts, data); to quote مثالونه تبرول to give examples متل تبرول to quote a proverb افسانی تبرول to tell tales 5 to swallow گولی یی تبره کړه He swallowed the pill. 6 to strain, filter 7 to pass off as something یو شي پر خپل نامه تبرول to pass something off as one's own *idiom* له نظره تبرول to scrutinize; look over قصه یی تبره کړه He told how the matter stood.

تبرول teravə́l² *denominative, transitive* ☞ تبره¹ *and* تبره کول

تبرون terún *m.* ☞ تبری

تبرونی terúnaj near, close, native, own; dear ترما هغه ور تبرونی دئ He is dearer to them than I am. تبرونی خپلوان terúni close relatives

تی روی tajrə́vaj *m.* 1 nursing baby 2 suckling

تبرویسته tervestə́na *f.* ☞ تبرایسته

تبره terə́¹ تبرہ تبرا terá *f. m.* [*plural:* تبره teró *f. plural:* تبری teré] 1 sharp, biting تبره چوړکی terá sharp knife تبره توره terá sharp saber 2 penetrating; fixed, intent تبره کتنه terá intent look 3 sharp, caustic هغه یی تبره ژبه لري، ژبه یی تبره ده terá He has a sharp tongue. **4** harsh, coarse تېره *terá* a harsh word **5** bold, decisive **6** clever, quick تېره سړی *a* bold person, decisive person *b* clever person توره تېره كول *a* to sharpen *terá* to sharpen a saber *b* to make penetrating; make intent *c* to make sharp, make caustic *d* to make harsh, make crude *e* to make bold, make decisive *f.* to make clever, make quick تېره كېدل *a* to be sharp, be biting; become sharp, become pointed چوړكې ښه تېره سوې ده *terá a* the knife has been sharpened well *b* to be penetrating *c* to gaze intently *d* to be sharp, be caustic *e* to be harsh, be coarse *f.* to be clever, be quick

تېره² *téra* **1** *feminine singular of* تېر² په تېره كښې in the past, formerly **2** *oblique singular of* تېر² له تېره كاله since last year *idiom* په تېره، بيا په تېره، په تېره بيا particularly, in particular; especially (since) بيا په تېره د هغه ورځي راهيسي ... particularly from the day when ...

تېره³ *tirá* **1** dark (in color) **2** gloomy, dismal, somber

تېره توب *terətób m.* **1** sharpness (e.g., of a knife) **2** intentness (e.g., of a gaze) **3** sarcasm **4** harshness, coarseness **5** boldness, decisiveness **6** cleverness, quickness

تېره كاوه *terəkāvə́ m. plural* sharpening

تېره والی *terəvā́laj m.* ☞ تېره توب

تېر هېر *ter-hér* long-past, forgotten

تېرى *teráj m.* **1** exceeding, excess **2** violation **3** outstripping; forestalling **4** violence; oppression **5** encroachment, infringement (e.g., upon someone's rights) **6** aggression تېرى كول *a* to go beyond what is permissible, do something uncalled for سختي خبري دي ورته وكړي، ډېر تېرى دي وكړ You spoke with him harshly and went too far. *b* to exceed, surpass *c* to violate *d* to outstrip, overtake تر چا په سبق كښي تېرى كول to overtake someone in studies *e* to commit violence; oppress *f* to infringe, encroach (e.g., upon someone's rights) په چا تجاوز او تېرى كول to infringe upon someone's rights; make an attempt on someone's life *g* to commit aggression *idiom* تر خوله تېرى كول، تر خولۍ تېرى كول *a* to be impertinent (to) *b* to say too much زما په حق كښي ډېر تېرى وسو I suffered greatly. I endured much.

تېرېدل *teredə́l* **1** *denominative, intransitive [past:* تېر شو].* **1.1** to pass (of time) په كوكه تېر شو a year passed **1.2** to go past, cross يو كال تېر شو تېر شه! to go along the street, pass down the street تېرېدل Pass! تر سرحد را تېرېږئ پر كينه خوا to cross the border go along the left side, keep to the left تر ما تېر شو او زه يي و نه ليدم He passed by and didn't notice me. تېرېدل او راتېرېدل to move back and forth, scurry about; travel about, move around **1.3** to flow (of a river) ارغنداب د قندهار څخه تېرېږي The Arghandab flows through Kandahar. **1.4** to occur, take place **1.5** to cross something تر له خپل سر او مال څخه to cross a river **1.6** to sacrifice تېرېدل to sacrifice life and property, sacrifice everything له ځانه تېرېدل to sacrifice oneself **1.7** to decline, turn down (something); renounce تر خپلو مطالباتو تېرېدل to renounce one's own demonds خپلي پادشاهۍ تېر شو He has renounced the throne. **1.8** to exceed,

تر اندازي تېرېدل to be excessive, exceed **1.9** to forgive تر گناه ورتېرېسو He forgave him his fault. **1.10** to be acknowledged; be famed, be renowned **1.11** to ignore, forget about (something) ته له ننگه او ناموسه تېر شوئ يې You have forgotten about honor. هيڅوك تر رښتيا ويل نه تېرېده Everyone was telling the truth. **1.12** to be swallowed **1.13** to be in foal, be in yean **2** *m. plural* ☞ تر جهان تېر سو، تر دنيا تېر سو *idiom* He has died, he's departed this world.

تېرېدنه *teredóna f.* ☞ له ځان څخه تېرېدنه selflessness

تېرېدونكى *teredúnkaj* **1** *present participle of* تېرېدل **2** passing, changeable, transitory, liable to decay **3** *m.* passerby

تېرېدونى² *teredúnaj* ☞ تېرېدونكى

تېرېده *teredə́ m. plural* **1** passing, proceeding, movement په كانال د شپږو مياشتو تېرېدو، د شپږو كښي تېرېده movement along a canal مياشتو په تېرېدو باندي in the course of six months **2** outstripping; forestalling **3** infringement, encroachment **4** refusal (of something) ترځان تېرېده self-sacrifice

تېرى كوونكى *teraj kavúnkaj m.* **1** transgressor **2** user of force; violator **3** aggressor

تېريوال *terajvál m.* aggressor

تېرې وېرې *tére-vére* تېرى وېرى جامي rags

تېس¹ *tez m.* ☞ تېز

تېز² *tez* **1** sharp, pointed; cutting **2** caustic, burning hot **3** fast, swift **4** quick-moving **5** harsh, coarse; persistent **6** bright (of color, light) تېزه رڼا bright light **7** sharp (of thinking, hearing, seeing) ده تېز ذكاوت درلود He had a sharp mind. He was smart. په تېزي سترگي لري He's sharp. He hears well. اوربدو كښي تېز دئ He has keen eyesight. **8** penetrating, sharp **9** deep (of feelings)

تېز³ *tiz m. vulgar* تېز اچول، تېز وهل، تېز ويشتل farting to fart

تېزاب *tezáb m.* **1** nitric acid **2** mordant; pickle, dip

تيزارتى *tizártaj* تېزاوﻦ *tizāvə́n* ☞ تيزن

تېزپر *tezpár* **1** swift in flight **2** *m.* pratincole (a swallow-like shore bird of the genus *Glareola*)

تېزتگى *teztágaj* swift, rapid (of a current)

تېزرفتار *tezraftár* passenger (conveyance) تېزرفتار موټر passenger car, automobile

تېزرگ *tizrág m.* **1** ankle-bone **2** *military* tumbler (part of the lock of a machine-gun)

تېس *tezís m.* **1** thesis **2** dissertation تېزس ليكل to write a dissertation

تېزفكر *tezfíkr* quick (to understand), bright, clever

تېزفهم *tezfáhm* intelligent, bright, keen-witted

تېزفهمي *tezfahmí f.* intelligence; brightness, quickness (of wit)

تېزقلم *tezkalám m. ironic* hack writer

تېزل *tezə́l transitive* ☞ تېخل

تيزن *tizə́n* **1** *vulgar* one who fouls the air **2** *m.* coward

تېزندى *tezandáj m.* تېزندۍ *tezandə́j f.* **1** noose (for hanging) **2** lasso

تبزوالی tezválaj *m.* **1** sharpness (e.g., of a knife) **2** causticity, hotness **3** swiftness, impetuousness په خورا تبزوالي *tezváli* very quickly **4** harshness, coarseness **5** energy, drive, push **6** brightness (of light, color) **7** keenness (of mind, hearing, sight) **8** sharpness, ability to penetrate **9** strength, intensity

تبزول tezavə́l *denominative, transitive* [*past:* تبز يي کړ] **1** to sharpen **2** to make caustic **3** to quicken (steps); speed up; drive faster (e.g., a car) **4** to make harsh, make coarse **5** to sharpen, intensify; strain (thought, hearing, sight) **6** to refresh one's memory, repeat لوستونه تبزول to report one's lessons **7** to make sharp, make penetrating **8** to increase, add on (light, fire)

تبزه téza **1** *feminine singular of* تبز [2] **2** *f.* rapid reading

تبزي tezí *f.* ☞ تبزوالی

تبزیدل tezedə́l *denominative, intransitive* [*past:* تبز شو] **1** to be sharp, be pointed **2** to be caustic, be burning hot **3** to quicken the pace, speed up **4** to hurry **5** to grow stronger (of the wind) **6** to increase, grow brighter (of light); flare up (of flame) **7** to be sharp, be keen (of thought, hearing, sight)

تبږکه tigáka *f.* sharp wooden strip or chip (used as a knife)

تیږه tíga *f.* **1** stone; cobble-stone; boulder د ژرندي تیږه mill-stone د لاري a stone house د تیږو کور coal د تیرو سکاره granite د برنجي تیږه stone in the road **b** *figurative* obstacle, hindrance قیمتي تیږه precious stone تیږه اړول **a** to turn over a stone **b** *figurative* to take an important step **c** *figurative* to rejoice, be glad تیږه ایښودل to lay a stone (marking the ending of military action and a peace agreement, a practice in former times) په خبره ایښودل to put a stop to some business تیږه غورځول **a** to throw a stone; toss a stone (as a sport) **b** *figurative* to get something out of your head, forget about it تیږه ماتول to break up a stone (indicating a resumption of hostilities) د تیږي نه غوړ ویستل *Eastern* to squeeze butter from stone, do the impossible په یوه تیږه دوه مرغۍ ویشتل *Eastern proverb* to kill two birds with one stone **2** rock رسوبي تیږي *sedimentary* rock **3** *medicine* stones د مثاني تیږه stones in the urinary tract په اینه کبني یې تیږه ده He has stones in his liver.

تبس tes *m.* **1** dissertation د داکټری تبس doctoral dissertation **2** thesis

تبسه tesá *f.* economy, thrift

تبش tesh *m.* plowshare

تبش خولی teshkhválaj *m.* cone-shaped hood, cowl

تبشه teshá *f.* adze *idiom* و ځان ته تبشه وهل to work for oneself

تبنتول teḵtavúl *transitive dialect* ☞ تبنتول

تبنته téḵta *f.* flight, escape مخ په تبنته کېدل run, flee ځان په تبنتي ته ناﺥاره کول to put to flight له پېښي نه تبنته نشته *proverb literally* cannot be passed by *figurative* whatever will be, will be

تبنتیدزای teḵtidzáj *m.* refuge, harbor

تبنتیدل teḵtedə́l *intransitive dialect* ☞

تیغ tegh *m.* **1** scimitar; sword; blade **2** edge (of a knife, etc.) **3** sprout, shoot تیغ وهل **a** to cut with a saber **b** to sprout, put out sprouts

تیغنه téghna *f.* **1** iron frying pan (for baking flat cakes) **2** sword, saber **3** shoot, sprout تیغنه وهل to sprout, put out sprouts

تیغون tujghún [1] *m.* **1** white hawk, white falcon (or similar bird of prey with white coloration) **2** albino (animals)

تیغون teghun tighún [2] **1.1** golden-winged **1.2** shining **2** *m.* blade of Damascus, patterned steel; sword (of Damascus steel)

تیغه teghá *f.* **1** edge (of a knife, etc.) **2** blade

تیفو tifó *f.* تیفوئد tifoíd *m.* typhoid (fever)

تیقین tajjakín *m. Arabic* affirmation د تیقین کلمات *grammar* affirmative words, particles

تیک tjak [1] **1** sticking up, sticking out **2** tall, strapping **3** extended, stretched تیکول ☞ تیک کول [1]

تبک tek [2] تبک کریچ! *military* Return sabers! (as a command)

تیک والی tjakválaj *m.* **1** tallness, height **2** quality of being stretched or drawn out

تیکول tjakavə́l [1] *denominative, transitive* [*past:* تیک یې کړ] **1** to stand on end **2** to stretch out, draw out, extend

تبکول tekavə́l [2] *transitive* [*past:* و یې تبکاوه] to put into its sheath (a saber)

تیکه tiká *f.* ☞ تبک [1, 2]

تیکه tjáka *feminine singular of* تیک [1]

تبکه téka *f.* تبکی tékaj *m.* **1** sheath, scabbard **2** *biology* shell, membrane

تیکیدل tjakedə́l *denominative, intransitive* [*past:* تیک شو] **1** to stick out **2** to grow (of people, animals) **3** to stretch, extend

تبکیر tekír *m.* **1** searching for lice **2** pursuit, chase په تبکیر کول، to purse someone **3** attention تبکیر کبني کېدل

تیگا tigá *f.* ☞ تیگه [2]

تیگریس tigrís *m.* Tigris (River)

تبگسی گلپه tegusigálpa *f.* Tegucigalpa (capital, Honduras)

تیگه tíga *f. Eastern* ☞ تیږه [1]

تیگه tigá *f.* shortness of breath تیگه وهل to be short-winded *idiom* تیگه نه لرل to be impatient; be nervous

تبل tel *m. usually plural* **1** oil د ترکودیو تبل، د نباتاتو تبل، نباتي تبل vegetable oil د شرشمو تبل rapeseed oil د پنداني تبل cottonseed oil د زغرو تبل linseed oil د کنځلو تبل sesame seed oil **2** petroleum (oil) **a** د تبلو ایستل crude oil خاورو تبل buttermaking, dairy work **b** extraction of crude oil د تبلو وړلو کبني oil-carrying ship د تبلو صافولو کارخانه oil-processing plant **3** fuel; gasoline; kerosene د تبلو ټانک gasoline pump د موټر تبل بندول to turn off a motor

تبلپکه telpáka *f.* cap

تبل دار teldár **1** oil-bearing **2** oily; relating to butter or crude oil

تبل داني teldāní *f.* oil can, lubricator

تي لرونکی ti larúnki تي لرونکي حیوانات *mammals*

تبلسکوپ teliskóp *m.* telescope

تبلفون telifún *m.* telifón 1 telephone په تبلفون کښي by telephone بي ستا تبلفون radiotelephone 2 conversation over the phone سيم تبلفون دئ You're wanted on the phone. تبلفون کول to talk by phone; تبلفون ور وکه telephone call him by phone

تبلفونخانه telifunnkhānā *f.* telifonkhána telephone central office, telephone exchange

تبلفوني telifuní telifoní 1 *adjective* telephone رابطه تبلفوني telephone communication تبلفوني راديو radiotelephone تبلفوني خبر ورکول مخابره telephoned message, phonogram to telephone 2 *m.* telephone operator

تبل کشي telkashí *f.* butter-making; oil manufacture

تبلگراف teligrắf *m.* 1 telegraph 2 ☞ تبلگرام

تبلگرافي teligrāfí 1 *adjective* telegraph, telegraphic 2 *m.* telegraphist, telegraph operator

تبلگرام teligrắm *m.* telegram

تبلو teló *f.* 1 binding the teats of the ewe or she-goat (so that the lambs or kids will not take milk) 2 bandage or dressing on the breasts of a nursing mother (so the baby will not feed there)

تبل وړونکی موټر tel vủúnkaj tank truck; (gasoline) fueling truck تبل وړونکي بېړي tanker

تبلويزيون televizjón *m.* tilivizjón 1 television 2 television set تبلويزيون درول to turn the TV on تبلويزيون لگول to turn the TV off

تيله tilá *f.* cord of golden thread, golden lace; golden braid

تيله داره tiladắra تيله دارخولۍ gold-embroidered skull cap (as worn in Central Asia)

تيلی [1] tiláj *m. Eastern* 1 match تيلی لگول، تيلی وهل to light a match 2 box of matches 3 ☞ تربلی

تبلي [2] telí 1 *m. Eastern* dealer in dry or salted foods (and also chemicals) 2.1 *adjective* kerosene تبلي څراغ kerosene lamp 2.2 *adjective* oil

تبلی [3] telə́j *f.* small bag, pouch (for money); purse

تبلی [4] telə́j *f.* oil-can, lubricator

تبلی [5] tiláj *f. Western* ☞ تيلی [1]

تيلی [6] tiláj *f.* 1 large flat-slice (e.g., of a melon) 2 match 3 splinter, chip (of wood)

تبلفون telefón tilifún *m.* ☞ تبلفون

تبلفون خانه telefonkhānā *f.* tilifunkhānā ☞ تبلفون خانه

تبلفوني telefoní tilifuní ☞ تبلفوني

تيم tə́jam *colloquial contraction of the pronouns* ته, يې *and the conjunction* هم تيم وغواړه! You also ask!

تيمار timắr *m.* تيمارداري timārdārí *f.* 1 caring for a sick person 2 tending a horse (covering it with a horse-cloth, etc.) تيمار کول a to care for a sick person b to tend a horse

تيمبوزک timbuzák *m.* ☞ تينبوزک

تيمچه timchá *f.* handbag, rug (given by villagers to a bride)

تيمم tajamúm *m. Arabic religion* ablution with sand تيمم وهل to perform the ritual of ablution with sand

تيمني tajmaní *m. plural* Taimani (a tribal group)

تيمور timúr *m. proper noun* Timur

تينبوزک timbuzák *m.* tembuzák 1 bridge (of the nose) 2 snout, muzzle; *figurative* mug 3 bridle

تينبوزی timbúzaj *m.* tembúzaj snout, muzzle; *figurative* mug

تين تبرک tinterák *m.* dragon-fly

تينداره tindắra *f.* aunt (father's brother's wife)

تيندک tindák *m.* 1 jump, skip, hop 2 stumbling تيندک خورل to stumble تيندک په تيندک a to jump, leap b to stumble تيندک وهل زغاستل to run bending to the ground from time to time; make a rush 3 *colloquial* snag, obstacle; failure

تيندکه tindáka *f.* 1 stream 2 fountain تيندکه وهل to gush out (in a stream), well up

تيندلک tində́lák stumbling, halting

تيندوبی tindóbaj *m.* ☞ تيندکه

تيندوړی tindóṛaj *m.* تيندوړی tindóṛaj *m.* nose cartilage, nose septum

تيندوڼی tindóṇaj *m. anatomy* helix (folded rim of cartilage around the outer ear)

تيندوی tində́vaj *m.* cartilage

تبنس tenís *m.* tennis

تينکی tenkáj *m.* ☞ تيندوری

تبنگ teng *m.* 1 coffin; grave 2 burial

تينگړی [1] tingṛáj *m.* dish, plate

تينگړی [2] tingṛáj *m.* blow (flick of the fingers) to the forehead

تبنول tenavál *m.* Tanaol (khanate of Amb)

تيوب tjub *m.* 1 tire inner tube 2 tube (of toothpaste, etc.)

تيور tajvár having nipples

تبوري teorí *f.* [*plural:* تبوريگاني teorigā́ni] theory

تبوزه tévza *f.* cave

تيرا دبل فوېگو tjerrā́ del-fuégo *f.* Tierra del Fuego (archipelago, southermost tip of South America)

تبيل tejə́l *transitive* [*past:* ويي تبيه] to fry, simmer (in oil)

تبيلي tejə́li *f. plural* fried liver; fried giblets

تبينکی tejə́nkaj *m.* ☞ تيندوری

تبيني [1] tejə́naj *m.* quantity of peas, etc., cooked at one time in a frying-pan

تبيني [2] tejə́ni *f. plural* ☞ تبيلي

تبيني والا tejə́nivālā́ *m.* seller of liver, vendor of giblets

تئيي tajjí *f.* wet nurse

ت

ت ṭe the fifth letter of the Pashto alphabet

ټاب ṭāb *m.* regret, repentance

ټابلت ṭắblet *m.* tablet, pill

ټاپ [1] ṭāp *m.* 1 ☞ چاپ 2 ☞ تاپ

ټاپ [2] ṭāp *m. regional* 1 top, top part (of a carriage) 2 lid, cover

ټاپ تيپ ṭāptíp *m.* ټاپ تيپ tāptíp 1 sluggishness; inertia 2 shuffling (slippers, etc.) 3 man of declining years; old man, elder

ټاپل ṭāpə́l *transitive* [*past:* ويي تاپه] 1 to mark, note, mark off 2 to stamp, brand 3 to emasculate, castrate

ټاپۍلج **1** *past participle of* ټاپل **2** marked, branded

ټاپندزای *m.* ☞ چاپخانه

ټاپنه *f.* **1** stamping, branding **2** emasculation, castration, gelding

ټاپو *m.* [*plural:* ټاپوګان ṭāpugắn *plural:* ټاپوان ṭāpuắn] **1** island **2** bank, sandbank

ټاپوره *f.* washboard, scubbing board (for laundry)

ټاپوړۍ *f.* crutches

ټاپول ṭāpavál *transitive* ☞ چاپول

ټاپوزمه ṭāpuvázma *f.* peninsula

ټاپه ṭāpá *f.* **1** seal, stamp ټاپه لګول to seal **2** mark, brand **3** trace design (for embroidery)

ټاپه رس ṭāparás *m.* sunflower

ټاپی [1] ṭā́paj *m.* **1** time, period په خپل ټاپي ṭápi in one's time **2** *medicine* crisis **3** friendship, connection with someone

ټاپی [2] ṭāpaj *m.* seal engraver, engraver of seals

ټاپۍ [3] ṭāpə́j *f.* **1** ☞ ټاپه **1, 2** **2** mark or seal on a pile of threshed grain (placed in order to guard against misappropriation)

ټاپي ټاپي ṭápi-ṭápi packed, chock-full, full to overflowing

ټاپېدل ṭāpedə́l *intransitive* ☞ چاپېدل

ټاټ [1] ṭāṭ *m.* **1.1** boasting, bragging **1.2** foppery, dandyism تات کول **a** to brag, boast **b** to be a fop, play the dandy په تات کېدل، تات وهل

ټاټ [2] ṭāṭ *m.* **1** canvas; sacking **2** oilcloth

ټاټکه ṭāṭə́ka *f.* ☞ پاپکه

ټاټولی ṭātválaj *m.* **1** incline, declivity **2** curvature

ټاټوب ṭāṭob *m.* **1** rest, peace ټاټوب نیول to rest **2** life, existence ټاټوب کول **a** to rest **b** to quiet **c** to live, exist

ټاټوبه ṭāṭóba *f.* ټاټوبی ṭāṭóbaj *m.* **1** home, residence د یتیمانو ټاټوبه orphan asylum; children's home **2** base (e.g., aviation) **3** bed (of a river)

ټاټوکه ṭāṭúka *f.* ☞ پاپکه

ټاټول ṭāṭavál *denominative* [*past:* ټات یې کړ] **1** to coddle, care for **2** incline, bend **3** to bow, bend, curve

ټاټه ṭāṭá suitable, proper, appropriate

ټاټي ṭāṭí *m.* fop, dandy

ټاټۍ [2] ṭaṭə́j **1** *f.* **1.1** lullaby, cradle song **1.2** cradle, crib ټاټۍ خورل to rock, be rocked; be lulled ټاټۍ کول to sleep in a cradle ټاټۍ وهل to rock, rock back and forth; to lull **2** *interjection* hush-a-bye, lullaby

ټاټۍ [3] ṭaṭə́j *f.* ☞ پټتی

ټاټېدل ṭaṭedə́l *denominative* [*past:* تات شو] **1** to be inclined, be bent **2** to be bowed, be curved

ټاخ ṭākh *m.* ☞ تاخت

ټاری ṭáraj *m.* **1** tower (of a fort) **2** branch (of a fir tree)

ټاس [1] ṭās *m.* **1.1** crack, crackling **1.2** clap, bang **1.3** shot **2** *interjection* snap, bang, bam

ټاس [2] ṭās *m.* large turban

ټاغ ṭagh ټاغی tahgáj **1** goggle-eyed **2** ox-eyed

ټاق [3] ṭāḳ ☞ تک

ټاقر ṭāḳár ☞ تاقر ټاکر

ټاک [1] ṭāk *m.* Bengali quince, *Aegle marmelos*

ټاک [2] ṭāk *m.* ☞ تک [3]

ټاک [3] ṭāk sour

ټاک [4] ṭāk marked, branded (of cattle)

ټاک ټوک ṭākṭúk *m.* utensils, household goods and chattel; decor, furniture ټاک ټوک برابرول to obtain utensils

ټاکر ṭākə́r **1** old, decrepit **2** *m.* old man, elder

ټاکس ṭāks *m.* *regional* tax; assessment

ټاکل ṭākə́l *transitive* [*past:* ویې ټاکه] **1** to establish, fix; determine **a** to fix a time ساعت ټاکل، ګړۍ ټاکل **b** to set a watch, clock **2** to appoint (e.g., to a post); choose **3** to select, pick (people) **4** to assign to do something, designate for some duty or other **5** to stamp, brand, mark ټاکل کېدل **a** to be established, be fixed; to be determined **b** to be destined for something

ټاکلی ṭākə́laj *past participle of* ټاکل په ټاکلي وخت کښي at the appointed time د یوه ټاکلي پروګرام په اساس according to a predetermined (worked out in advance) program; according to plan

ټاکنده ṭākənda ټاکنده غرمه diurnal solar maximum; hottest part of the day; extreme heat

ټاکنه ṭākə́na *f.* **1** establishment, determination **2** assignment (to a post, duty)

ټاکو [1] ṭākú *m.* **1** thief **2** robber

ټاکو [2] ṭākú *m.* **1** foot-and-mouth disease **2** cattle plague, cattle murrain; epizootic **3** *figurative* misfortune, disaster

ټاکو [3] ṭākú **1** importunate, tiresome, troublesomely insistant (of a person) **2** intriguer, schemer

ټاک ټوک ṭak-u-ṭúk *m.* ☞ ټاک و ټوک

ټاکور ṭākór *m.* ☞ تکور [1]

ټاکه ṭākə́ *imperfective of* ټاکل

ټاکۍ [1] ṭākə́j *f.* **1** patch (on footgear, of leather or rubber) **2** cork **3** ripened boil, furuncle **4** overfed person **5** overfed, surfeited cattle یوه _ دربدل **a** to swell, swell up **b** to overeat **6** reservoir, water storage basin

ټاکي [2] ṭākí *present tense of* ټاکل

ټاکۍ [3] ṭākə́j *present, second person plural of* ټاکل

ټاکي [4] ṭāki *f.* *plural* bangs, cracks (noises)

ټال [1] ṭāl *m.* swings (children's toy) د اندبیننو په ټال زنگېدل to swing, rock ټال خورل **a** to swing on swings **b** to flutter in the wind (curls) *idiom* په آسمان کښي د بوډۍ ټال راختلئ دئ a rainbow appeared د فکر په ټال کښي کېنبوتل to become pensive, become thoughtful د اندبیننو په ټال زنگېدل to vacillate, be indecisive

ټال [2] ṭāl *m.* delay; postponement ☞ ټالېدل ټال خورل ټالول [1] ټال اچول to delay, check (i.e., the advance of troops) بې له ټاله ټال ورکول to notify, inform without delay اطلاع ورکول

ټال [3] ṭāl *m.* **1** knot (in a tree) **2** commercial scales

ټال [4] ṭāl *m.* **1** cobweb ټال اچول to spin a web **2** lariat, lasso

ټال [5] ṭāl *tautological with* تول

تالاوٙ ṭālāvә́ *imperfective of* تالول [1, 2]

تالمتال ṭālmaṭál *m.* guile, trick تال متال كول to dodge, evade, shirk

تالمتالول [تالمتال يې كړ] ṭālmatālavә́l *denominative, transitive [past:* 1 to deceive someone, mislead somebody 2 to use guile, trick, try to get out of

تالمتالوونكى ṭālmatālavunkaj 1 *present participle of* تالمتالول 2 *m.* 2.1 deceiver 2.2 sly, cunning person; dodger, shirker

تالمتالېدٙل [تالمتال شو] ṭālmaṭāledә́l *denominative, intransitive [past:* to be deceived; swallow the bait, be a sucker

تالمتول ṭālmaṭól *m.* 1 verbosity 2 تالمتال ☞

تالول [و يې تالاوه :past] ṭālavә́l [1] *transitive* to swing, swing back and forth

تالول [و يې تالاوه :past] ṭālavә́l [2] *transitive* 1 to delay, hold back ولي مي دومره تالوي؟ Why are you delaying me so? 2 to delay, drag out, put aside; extend, prolong اجرا تالول to delay, put off the execution of something

تاله ṭālá *f.* wholesale sales

تالېدٙل [وتالبده :past وتالبد :past] ṭāledә́l [1] *intransitive* to rock, rock back and forth

تالېدٙل [وتالبده :past وتالبد :past] ṭāledә́l [2] *intransitive* 1 to delay; linger; slow down 2 to stand idle (e.g., of the transport) 3 to be put aside; be dragged out; be prolonged, last

تالبده ṭāledә́ *m. plural* 1 to delay, halt دوه ساعته تالبده a two-hour delay 2 postponement

تامباري ṭāmbári *f. plural* cries, wails; howl, loud weeping تامباري وېستٙل to cry, wail, howl; bawl, weep loudly

تامبوسى ṭāmbúsaj *m.* sleet

تامته ṭāmṭá *f.* stalk (corn)

تانټاري ṭānṭáre *f. plural Eastern* تامباري ☞

تانټس ṭānṭás dull-witted, of limited intelligence; stupid

تانتوبى ṭānṭobә́j *f.* throng (of people), crowd تانتوبى كول to throng, crowd

تانټه ṭānṭá *f.* تامته ☞ تانټې ورسره چیچل to compete, contend, vie (with someone)

تانك ṭānk *m.* 1 tank 2 reservoir; cistern; vat د اوبو تانك cistern, water-tank

تانكدار ṭānkdár *adjective military* tank; armored تانكداره قوه armored (tank) troops

تانك ماتوونكى ṭānk mātavúnkaj *military* antitank توپ تانك ماتوونكى antitank gun

تانكى [1] ṭānkә́j *f. military* tank; small tank د الوتكي تانكى له تېلو ډکول to fuel up an airplane

تانكي [2] ṭānkí *military* tank تانكي ټولګى tank unit

تانګ [1] ṭāng *m.* rumor, talk

تانګ [2] ṭāng *m.* 1 lambing time 2 *figurative* appropriate time, right moment *m.* 3 definite time, definite term

تانګ [3] ṭāng *m.* column, post serving as a buoy

تانګ [4] ṭāng *m.* تانګو ☞

تانګاري ṭāngāri *f. plural* تامته ☞

تانګتوره ṭāngturá *f. botany* thorn apple, *Datura stramonium*

تانګر ṭāngár *m.* residue of corn (maize) straw (e.g., on the threshing floor)

تانګو ṭāngú *m.* wild pear (tree)

تانګه [1] ṭánga *f.* domestic pear (tree)

تانګه [2] ṭānga *f.* tanga, two-wheeled carriage

تانګه وال ṭāngavāl *m.* تانګه والا ṭāngavālá *m.* cabbie, tanga-driver, tanga-wallah

تانګى [1] ṭāngáj *m.* table mountain; flat-topped hill

تانګى [2] ṭāngә́j *f.* تانګو ☞

تانګي وال ṭāngevāl *m.* تانګي والا ṭāngevālá *m. regional* تانګه وال ☞

تانه ṭāná *f.* تهانه ☞

تاور ṭāvár *m.* turret, watchtower

تاه ṭāh *m.* 1 pronounciation, accent 2 speech, converse, conversation

تايپ ṭājp *m.* 1 printing; typewriting د تايپ ماشين typewriter تايپ كول *compound verb* to print (on a typewriter) تايپ كېدٙل *compound verb* to be typed up 2 type, typeface

تايپيست ṭājpíst *m.* typist (male)

تايپيسته ṭājpísta *f.* typist (female)

تاير ṭājr *m.* tire (automobile)

تايل ṭājl *m.* د تايل تيږه tile

تايم ṭājm *m.* تيم [4] ☞

تائي ṭaí *f.* necktie تائي تړل to tie a tie, knot a necktie

تائيلند ṭailend *m.* Thailand

تبر ṭabar *m.* تبٙر ṭabә́r 1 family (often wife) 2 clan, tribe 3 people د پښتون تبر the Afghan people 4 dynasty, (dynastic) clan

تبردار ṭabardár *m.* family man

تبٙر ṭabә́r *m.* تبر ☞

تبكى ṭubakáj *m.* تٙبكاج tәbakáj 1 dimple, hollow 2 hole (used in a game)

تبكي تبكي ṭubakí-ṭubakí uneven, having pits or potholes, bumpy

تبلى [1] ṭubalә́j *f.* تٙبلاج tәbalә́j ☞

تبلى [2] ṭablә́j *f.* children's game played with marbles

تپ [1] ṭap 1 *m.* 1.1 clap; clapping, clattering تپ له دواړو لاسه خېژي *saying* Clapping takes two hands 1.2 knock; stamping, tramping 1.3 blow, smack 1.4 slap (in the face) تپ كول *compound verb* 2 *interjection* Smack! Slap! Bang! تپ وهل ☞ تپول

تپ [2] ṭap *m.* 1 wound, wounding; maiming, mutilation تپ يې ډېر ژور دئ His wound is very deep. تپ ګنډٙل to suture a wound دا تپ د څه شي دئ؟ By what means was this wound inflicted? تپ خورٙل to receive a wound 2 indemnity for mutilation, wergeld 3 mark, brand, scar 4 spot, blemish

تپ [3] ṭap 1 *tautological compounding element for adjectives and participles* quite, completely, extremely (indicates an extreme degree of the quality) تپ تيت a very low b very flattened, pressed down تپ خراب completely spoiled دا ښڅه تپ ړنده ده This woman is totally blind. زه تپ ستړى يم I am utterly at the end of my forces. تپ لوند wet clear through, wet to the skin تپ نژدې right up next to تپ وبريدلئ scared to death **2** *predicative* quite, entirely دى تپه نه تري Don't let him dam up the irrigation ditch completely. چلاو مي تپ ودرېدئ **a** to come to a halt My affairs have تپ درېدل come to a standstill. **b** *figurative* to stop short (speech), not to know what to say next

تپ ⁴ ṭap thin, gaunt

تپا تپ و تپ ṭapã́ *f.* ☞

تپال ṭəpãl *m.* **1** [*plural:* تپالان ṭəpãlãn] *history* herald, harbinger **2** [*plural:* تپالان ṭəpãlãn] postman, mailcarrier **3** [*plural:* تپالونه ṭəpãlúna] message, communication تپال ورل **a** to convey news; communicate, deliver a message **b** to gossip, spread gossip

تپالوک تپالي ṭəpãlí **1** communicating something **2** gossiping

تپ پت ṭap-pə́t petty; trivial په تپپتو خبرو سرخوړول tipí ptí xbəri trifles to rack your brain, knock your brains out over trivialities

تپ تپ ṭapṭáp *m.* **1** knock, rap (caused by two objects hitting together) **2** *figurative* threat تپ تپ کول **a** to knock, rap **b** *figurative* to threaten, intimidate

تپټپاڼی ṭapṭapãṇãj hide-and-go-seek (the children's game)

تپټپني ṭapṭapanãj *m.* motorcycle

تپټور ṭapṭór sequential

تپرا ¹ ṭaparã́ *m.* **1** wanderer **2** person uprooted from his home **3** rolling stone, rootless wanderer

تپرا ² ṭaparã́ *f.* shivering, chill; shudder

تپرا ³ ṭaparã́ *f.* assumption of responsibility, assumption of guilt

تپرا ⁴ ṭaparã́ **1** circumspect, cautious **2** broken-spirited, scared

تپرېدل ṭaparedə́l *intransitive* [*past:* وتپرېده] **1** to walk blindly; grope one's way **2** to reel (e.g., from weakness) **3** to tremble, shiver **4** to be agitated, be distressed, be grieved, be shattered **5** to be circumspect, be careful

تپر tapár *m.* **1** sailcloth; canvas, sacking **2** cloth woven from artificial fiber **3** straw rope or braid for tying sheaves

تپرا ṭaparã́ *f.* **1** potter's burnishing tool **2** trowel; smoother

تپس تپوخ ṭapə́s *m.* ☞

تپساری تپسوری ṭapsóraj **1** dependent on someone; needing someone; something **2** cowed, downtrodden (of a person)

تپک تپرا ṭapák *m.* ☞

تپکی ṭəpəkãj sick, powerless, weak

تپگی ¹ ṭapgãj *m.* slight wound

تپگی ² ṭapgãj *m.* **1** burrow, hole **2** ditch

تپل تاپل ṭapə́l *transitive* ☞

تپلن ṭaplən **1** spotted, stained **2** pitted, pockmarked

تپلي ¹ ṭə́laj *m.* **1** spot **2** stamp, mark, brand; sign **3** freckle

تپلي ² ṭapə́laj **1** tired; sluggish, weak **2** *m.* castrated cattle

تپن ¹ تپلن ṭapə́n ☞

تپن ² ṭipán *m.* light breakfast, light lunch

تپنا تپرا ṭəpənã́ *f.* ☞

تپنه ṭapə́na *f.* idle wandering, idling

تپڼ ṭapə́ṇ *m.* **1** bag **2** تپر ³ ☞

تپو ṭapú *m.* tower, turret, watchtower

تپوتپ ṭapuṭáp *m.* **1** clap, clatter (noise) **2** (act of) clapping, slapping (e.g., on the shoulder)

تپوخ ṭapúts *m.* **1** kite (the bird) **2** sluggard **3** flabby person, sluggish person, dawdler

تپوس تپوخ ṭapús *m.* ☞

تپوک ṭapúk *m.* fur coat

تپوک ṭapúk *m.* slap (in the face)

تپول ṭapavə́l *denominative, transitive* [*past:* تپ يې کړ] **1** to close, slam to, close with a bang (e.g., a book) **2** to turn off, switch off (e.g., radio) **3** to stamp the foot, tamp **4** to knock **5** to hit, strike پرچا شا _ to clap, slap on the back (condescendingly) **a** to cast aspersions on someone **b** to throw all of the work and responsibilities of the household on someone

تپه ¹ ṭapá *f.* **1** لندی ☞ **2** note **3** card (playing) **4** working of miracles

تپه ² ṭápa *f. singular of* تپ ³, ⁴

تپه ³ ṭápa *f.* skylight, window (in the ceiling of a lower floor room)

تپه تغره ṭápa-ṭaghára *f.* destitution, extreme poverty پر چا تپه تغره پر هغه دنيا کېدل to leave someone without the means of subsistence تپه تغره شوه He fell into destitution.

تپهار تپ تپ ṭapahã́r *m.* ☞

تپط ¹ ṭəpáj *m.* **1** birthmark **2** black mark, black star (on an animal's forehead) **3** gout

تپی ² ṭapí **1.1** wounded تپي کول to wound someone تپي کېدل to be wounded **1.2** pitted, pockmarked **2** *m.* wounded man

تپی ³ ṭapáj *f.* pressed dung (used as fuel)

تپی ṭapé *plural of* تپه ¹

تپی ṭápí *plural of* تپه ²,³

تپین تپلن ṭapín ☞

تت تت ¹ ṭət *m.* ☞

تتار تر ṭətã́r *m.* ☞

تتپت تت پت ṭətpə́ṭ *m.* ☞

تت ¹ ṭət *m.* **1** boasting, bragging **2** conceit, arrogance

تت ² ṭəṭ *m. Eastern* copper

تت ³ تيت ṭiṭ ☞

تتار ṭəṭã́r *m.* coppersmith

تتاری ¹ ṭəṭã́raj *m.* sandpiper

تتاري ṭəṭã́ri *f. plural* noise, cry

تتاون ṭəṭãvə́n *m.* [*plural:* تتاون ṭəṭãvən] **1** braggart, boastful person, bragger **2** arrogant person

تتپت تت پت ṭəṭpə́ṭ *m.* idle talk, verbiage

تتخه تتر ṭaṭə́kha *f.* ṭaṭár *m.* ṭaṭər *m.* **1** breast **2** paunch, belly (e.g., of a fish) **3** crown (of the head) *idiom* د مرجاني تتخه باندي اور لگېده *Eastern* Mardzhana burned within.

تتری ¹ ṭaṭráj *m.* تتری brassiere

تتری ² ṭaṭráj *f.* sleeveless jacket, vest

تتری ³ ṭaṭráj **1.1** boastful **1.2** garrulous **2** *m.* **.1** braggart, boaster **2.2** loquatious person, gabby person, babbler

ټتنگ țațáng *m.* 1 desert سور ټتنگ burning desert 2 Tatang (region in Nangrakhar)

ټتنگه țațangá *f.* shrike (the bird)

ټتو țatú *m.* 1 pony 2 bridge (of a violin)

ټتوغى țațúghaj *m.* ټتوى țațóvaj *m.* kite (the bird)

ټټه țóța *f.* 1 bragging, boasting 2 chatter, idle talk

ټتى ¹ țațáj *m.* 1 braggart, boaster 2 loquatious person, idle-talker 3 dandy, fop 4 coward

ټتى ² țațáj *f.* [*plural:* ټتیانی țațájāni] 1 small caravansarai, guest house 2 enclosure made of matting 3 toilet, latrine

ټتي țáți *plural of* ټته

ټچ ¹ țach *m.* 1 clap, bang 2 blow 3 faint shot (sound)

ټچ ² țach *m.* strength, force د ټچ وتل to grow faint, weaken

ټچ ³ țach 1 insignificant, of little importance 2 cheap

ټخ ¹ țakh *tautological with* ټوخ

ټخ ² țukh *m.* ☞ ټوخ

ټخ ټخ țǝkhțǝkh loud, booming د خندا ټخ ټخ loud laughter; guffaw

ټخ و ټوخ țakhțúkh *m.* ☞ ټوخ و ټخ

ټخله țukhóla *f.* ☞ ټوخله

ټخلى țukhalój *f.* 1 cap with earflaps 2 nightcap with earflaps

ټخمخ țakhmákh scattered; dispersed

ټخ و ټوخ țakhuțúkh *m.* slight cough تخ و ټوخ یی دئ He/she has a slight cough.

ټخول țukhavól *transitive* ☞ توخول

ټخى țúkha *f.* ټخاى țukháj *m.* ☞ توخى

ټخبدل țukhedól *intransitive* ☞ توخبدل

ټخبدنه țukhedóna *f.* cough; slight cough

ټر țǝr *m.* ټرا țǝrá *f.* ☞ ترهار

ټراک țrák *m.* țǝrák garden warbler (the bird)

ټرام țrām *m.* streetcar (trolley)

ټرام چلوونکى țrām chalavúnkaj *m.* streetcar (trolley) conductor

ټران țrān *m.* uproar, rumble

ټرت țǝrt *m.* ☞ ترهار

ټرتپرت țǝrtpórt *m.* ☞ nonsense, rubbish, absurdity ټرتپرت اچول to talk nonsense, spread drivel abroad

ټرتهار țǝrthár *m.* ☞ ترهار

ټرتر țǝrtór *m.* 1 chatter 2 fuss; uproar, rumble

ټرم țarm *m. regional* semester

ټرول țǝravól *transitive* [*past:* و یی ټراوه] to have a laxative effect, cause a bowel movement

ټروونه țǝravóna *f.* diarrhea, loose stools

ټرهار țǝrǝhár *m.* 1 nonsense, rubbish, absurdity ترهار وهل to talk nonsense, spread drivel 2 *vulgar* fart

ټرى țre *f. regional* tray

ټربدل țǝredól *intransitive* [*past:* وټریده] 1 to talk nonsense, spread rubbish; talk drivel 2 to suffer from an upset stomach, have indigestion

ټز țaz *m.* ☞ تس ²

ټس ¹ țǝs *m.* 1 dull noise 2 hissing

ټس ² țas 1 *m.* .1 crash; crackle تس ختل to crash; crackle 1.2 blow په شاه تس وهل to strike تس ورکول to receive a blow تس خورل to hit someone on the back 2 *interjection* knock; bang

تسا țasá *f.* ☞ تسهار

تس توس țastús *m.* 1 exchange of fire, clash 2 skirmish; collision 3 confusion; uproar, rumpus 4 crackling تس توس کول a to have an exchange of fire, skirmish b to fight, struggle c to make an uproar, make a racket d to crash, crackle

تسک țǝsák *m.* ☞ تسکى ¹

تسکى ¹ țǝskáj *m.* 1 coward 2 scoundrel, villian

تسکي ² țǝskí *f.* țiskí 1 laziness 2 slowness

تسکى ³ țǝskáj *m.* 1 hissing, snorting 2 sobbing

تسکبدل țǝskedól *intransitive* [*past:* وتسکبدل] 1 to hiss, snort 2 to sob

تسلک țǝslák *m.* ☞ تسک

تس مس țǝsmós flabby, apathetic, sluggish

تسهار țasahár *m.* crack, crackling

تسبدل țǝsedól *intransitive* ☞ وزبدل

تغ țǝgh *m.* 1 squawk (e.g., of a trapped bird) 2 bellow; crying, scream (of a child) تغ کول a to squawk b to bellow, roar, weep

تغ țágh *m.* jay (the bird)

تغ țagh *m.* eyelid

تغ پغ țǝghpǝgh *m.* ☞ تغ پغ ¹

تغ تغى țaghțagháj *m.* ☞ تغ تغى ²

تغر țaghár *m.* 1 palas (napless carpet), coarse carpet تغر اودل to weave a palas (napless carpet) 2 saddle cloth 3 rag *idiom* د تحقیقاتو تغر غورول to carry out extensive investigations

تغره țaghára *f.* ☞ ټپه تغره

تغکى țighakaj *m.* 1 epizootic disease (of chickens) 2 head cold

تغن țaghan 1 *m.* [*plural:* تغن țaghǝn] .1 person of weak character 1.2 coward 2.1 coughing, suffering from a cough 2.2 noisy

تغول țǝghavól *transitive* [*past:* و یی تغاوه] 1 to make whine, cause to whimper 2 to torture 3 to make weep 4 to gnash the teeth 5 to express unwillingness

تغهار țǝghǝhár *m. plural* 1 wheeze, wheezing sound 2 cough

تغي ¹ țághi تغي سترگي with wide eyes, eyes popping out په تغو سترگو to open the eyes wide (from surprise); goggle, gawk کتل

تغى ² țǝgaj *m.* epizootic disease (of birds)

تغبدل țǝghedól *intransitive* [*past:* وتغبده] 1 to squawk (of trapped birds, etc.) 2 to weep, behave capriciously (of a child)

ټک țak *m. regional* ☞ ټک ³ لاسونه سره ټق تق وهل to clap, strike the hands together

تقار țaķár *m.* tread, tramp

تقالي țaķālí sharp-witted, clever, astute تقالي سرى clever man

تقر țaķáŕ *m. regional* ☞ ټکر ¹

تقول țaķavól *transitive* [*past:* و یی تقاوه] 1 to censure; criticize (from a hostile point of view), run down 2 to swear at, tell off 3 to punish

تقونه țaķavóna *f.* abuse; censure

تقهار ṭakahár *m.* knocking, crackling; continued sharp sound as of something breaking, rapping, etc.

تک [1] ṭak *m.* 1 border, frontier, boundary 2 border region; border territory, border zone 3 inherited land

تک [2] ṭak *m.* 1 stitch; basting, tacking تک کبل to sew with large stitches; tack 2 hole (in the earth for setting in a plant)

تک [3] ṭak *m.* [*plural:* تکونه ṭakúna *Western plural:* تکان ṭakā́n] 1 knock, tap (in driving nails etc.) تک وهل to knock, strike, hit 2 noise of a shot 3 firing, shot تکان کول to fire, effect firing بې توپک تک دا to fire blanks b to act to no purpose باروتو تکان کول a this rifle misfires 4 تک له تکه کبدل to die suddenly, die unexpectedly *figurative* censure; reproach; criticism *idiom* تک له to attain immediate success, succeed تکه اوبنتل، تک او مایه کبدل from the very beginning

تک [4] ṭak *m.* 1 ☞ تاکو [2] 2 large boil, abscess (e.g., on the throat)

تک [5] ṭuk *m.* ☞ توک [1]

تک [6] ṭak *m.* wooden sun-clock (for determining times for irrigation, etc.)

تک [7] ṭak *m.* enigma, mystery, riddle

تکا [1] ṭaká *f.* ☞ تکهار

تکا [2] ṭuká growing تکا کول to grow (of grass, etc.)

تکارکی ṭakā́rkaj *m.* 1 bald spot, bare place (e.g., in a meadow) 2 barren ground

تکاله ṭəkā́la *f. tautological with* توقه

تکان ṭəkā́n *m.* 1 stumbling (e.g., a horse) 2 ☞ تکان

تکان ṭakā́n *plural of* تک [3]

تکانگر ṭakāngár *m.* thresher (e.g., of corn, maize)

تکانه [1] ṭakāná *f.* 1 size, dimensions 2 border, limit تر یوی معلومداری تکانې پوري to a certain extent; in a certain measure 3 region, area

تکانه [2] ṭikāná *f. regional* 1 habitation, home, dwelling place, residence تکانه کول to live, reside تکانه کبدل to settle, settle oneself تکانه لگول a to settle, settle (elsewhere) b to determine, decide c to arrange, organize تکانه لگبدل a to settle, take up residence b to be determined, be decided 2 border, limit

تکاو ṭikā́v *m. regional* abode, location تکاو کول *compound verb* to settle, settle (elsewhere); quarter, billet تکاو کبدل *compound verb* ☞ تکاوبدل

تکاوه [1] ṭəkāvə́ *imperfective third person singular of* تکول

تکاوه [2] ṭəkāvə́ *m. plural* ☞ تکونه [1]

تکاوبدل ṭikāvedə́l *denominative, intransitive* [*past:* تکاو شو] to settle, take up residence

تکټ ṭikáṭ *m.* [*plural:* تکټونه ṭikaṭúna *Western plural:* تکټان ṭikaṭā́n] 1 ticket د گاډی تکټ railway ticket د مېلمستیا تکټ invitation card د تکټ کمره ticket window, ticket office 2 note 3 stamp (postage)

تکټپولي ṭikaṭpulí *f. economics* 1 dividend 2 rate (e.g., currency exchange)

تکتک [1] ṭakták *m.* ☞ تکتکه

تکتک [2] ṭakták تک تک 1.1 knock, tap 1.2 tramp, tread 1.3 tick, ticking (of a clock) 2 *interjection* .1 knock-knock 2.2 tick, ticktock

تکتکانه ṭakṭakā́na *f.* 1 woodpecker 2 cam (in a mill-apparatus)

تکتکانی ṭakṭakā́naj *m.* 1 children's game 2 ☞ تکتکانه

تک تک تک ṭak-ṭak-ṭák *interjection* drip-drip-drip

تکتکه ṭakṭáka *f.* stitch

تکتکی [1] ṭaktə́kaj *m.* cam (as part of the apparatus of a flour-mill)

تکتکی [2] ṭakṭakə́j *f.* 1 ☞ تکتکی [1] 2 wryneck (bird)

تکتکی [3] ṭaktáki *plural of* تکتکه

تکټ گهر ṭikaṭghár *m. regional* ticket office

تکتوک ṭaktúk *m.* exchange of fire

تکر [1] ṭakár *m.* 1 collision; blow 2 stumbling تکر خورل a to collide with something, strike against something; to fall upon something b to stumble against something له نقب سره تکر خورل to fall upon a mine تکر وهل، تکر کول to push, push off 3 detriment, loss عقل په تکر حاصلېږي ورکول *proverb* one experienced man is worth more than two greenhorns

تکر [2] ṭukár *m.* [*plural:* تکرونه tukərúna *Western plural:* تکران tukərā́n] 1 piece, part 2 cloth, fabric تکر نخي cotton cloth, cotton fabric تکر تکر کول to tear, cut in pieces تکر کبدل to be torn apart, be cut up into pieces

تکرگیر ṭakargír *m. technology* shock absorber

تکره ṭukrá *f.* ☞ تکر [2]

تکری [1] ṭikráj *m.* 1 shawl; kerchief for wear on the head 2 chador

تکری [2] ṭukráj *f.* tray, basket

تکرې ṭukré *plural of* تکره

تکر ṭukṛ *m.* ☞ تکر [2]

تکړه ṭukṛá *f.* ☞ تکر [2]

تکس ṭikás *m.* ☞ تکټ

تکسره ṭaksára *f.* house sparrow, *Passer domesticus*

تکسری ṭaksáraj تک سری، 1 suffering from an epidemic disease 2 scabby, worthless, rotten 3 shameless, impudent 4 stubborn, persistent *idiom* تک سری شی! May you drop dead! May you rot!

تکسي ṭaksí *m. & f.* [*plural:* تکسیان ṭaksijā́n *f. plural:* تکسیاني ṭaksijāni] تکسي موټر taxi taxi

تکسي والا ṭaksivālá *m.* chauffeur, taxi driver

تکک ṭikák full to overflowing, full to the brim

تککه ṭakáka *f.* 1 crossbar, projecting piece on a spade providing thrust for the foot; crossbeam 2 pedal

تکلاس ṭaklā́s تکلاستی ṭaklā́staj 1 adroit, smart, quick 2 businesslike, efficient 3 well-aimed, accurate (of a shot) 4 bold, brave

تک لاستی والی ṭaklāstajvā́laj *m.* تکلاستجتوب taklāstajtób *m.* 1 adroitness 2 efficiency 3 accuracy 4 boldness, bravery

تیکله ṭikála *f.* ☞ تیکله

تکمخی ṭikmə́khaj تک مخی، pockmarked, pitted

تکن ṭəkə́n speckled, spotted

تاکنده ṭákənda ☞ تاکنده

ټکنه [1] ṭəkána *f.* **1** seal, stamp **2** mark, brand

ټکنه [2] ṭəkə́na *f. singular of* تکن

ټکنی [1] ṭakanáj **1** obstinate; retarding; balky آس تکنی balky horse **2** fearful **3** vacillating تکنی کول to cause to be timorous, cause to be indecisive تکنی کبدل a to be obstinate, be restive, be jib; bc balky آس که تکنی دئ، میدان لنډ دئ *saying* although the horse be restive, there's not far to go to overcome the reluctant lender **b** to be indecisive, to act indecisively

ټکنی [2] ṭakanə́j ☞ تاکنده په دې تکنی غرمه څله ځي؟ Where are you going in such heat?

ټکانه ṭakáṇa **1** ☞ تاکنده **2** *adjective* midday **3** meridional

ټکوپو ṭakupú died unexpectedly, passed suddenly

ټک و توک ṭakuṭúk *m.* **1** exchange of fire **2** knock, persistant tapping

ټکوچ ṭəkóch *m.* stitching, basting, tacking

ټکور [1] ṭakór *m.* poultices, fomentations تکور کول *compound verb* تکورول ☞

ټکور [2] ṭakór *m.* **1** song; melody تکور کول to sing **2** beating (of a drum)

ټکور [3] ṭakúr *m.* ☞ توته

ټکورټکورول ṭukurṭukravə́l *denominative, transitive* [*past:* تکورټکور یی کړ] to tear apart, tear into pieces

ټکورول ṭakoravə́l *denominative* [*past:* تکور یې کړ] to make poultices

ټکوری ṭəkoráj *m.* ☞ کتوری

ټکوربدل ṭakoredə́l *denominative* [*past:* تکور شو] to be applied (of a poultice)

ټکول ṭəkavə́l *transitive* [*past:* و یې تکاوه] **1** to pound, crush, grind; کورکمن تکول to grind turmeric **2** to thresh, beat out grain from the husk درمن تکول to thresh grain **3** to forge, hammer (e.g., iron) **4** to scutch, swingle (wool, cotton) **5** to beat, clean (e.g., carpet, clothing) **6** to beat, thrash someone **7** to knock ور تکول to knock on the door ور وتکول شو someone is knocking at the door **8** to stamp **9** to click ژبه تکول to make a clicking sound with the tongue **10** to beat (a drum) **11** to chop (meat) *idiom* سر تکول to live in poverty, endure extreme want

ټکولئ ṭəkavə́laj **1** *past participle of* تکول **2.1** pounded, crushed **2.2** ground **2.3** forged, hammered **2.4** beaten clean (e.g., carpet, clothes) **2.5** minced, chopped تکولي غوښه meatballs, chopped meat (a food dish)

ټکونه ṭakavə́na *f.* **1** pounding, crushing **2** threshing, beating out grain from the husk **3** forging, hammering **4** scutching (wool, cotton) **5** beating clean (e.g., carpet, clothes)

ټکونه ṭakúna *plural of* تک [1-7]

ټکوهل ṭakvahə́l *transitive* [*past:* تک یې وهل، تک وهل *past:* تک یې] **1** to beat, beat clean; beat (carpet) **2** to shake, swing ونه تک to shake a tree **3** to affix, hammer in موږي تک وهل to impale, drive a spear in **4** to clap the hands لاسونه یې سره تک وهل They clapped their hands. سره تک وهل to bang up, batter (of kitchenware)

ټکوهنه ṭakvahə́na *f.* **1** beating; banging up, battering **2** shaking up **3** affixing with nails, driving in **4** clapping the hands

ټکه [1] ṭáka *f.* **1** meteorite **2** lightning **3** *figurative* misfortune, disaster تکه پرلوبدل a misfortune is occurring څه تکه درولوبده؟ What has happened to you? تکي وواهه *taki* **a** Lightning struck him. **b** *figurative* Misfortune befell him. *idiom* تکي رژول to perform miracles تکه ښکاره کول to express surprise, be surprised, be amazed

ټکه [2] ṭaká *m.* [*plural:* تکه گان ṭakagán] **1** ibex, mountain goat **2** male goat (leader of flocks)

ټکه [3] ṭuka *f.* shaft (of the *karez* irrigation system)

ټکهار ṭəkahár *m.* **1** exchange of fire **2** knock, persistent rapping **3** rattle, crackle **4** tramp **5** *figurative* hard freeze, frost **6** *figurative* intense heat, sultriness

ټکه پوست ṭakapóst *m.* leather from the hide of a mountain goat

ټکه چال takachál **1** *m.* sleepy person **2** drowsy, sleep کبدل _ to doze, slumber

ټکه مستي ṭáka mastí *f.* ☞ مستي

ټکی [1] ṭəkaj *m.* **1** period, point په تکوشوئ ځای dotted line **2** *linguistics* diacritical mark **3** speck, spot; mark **4** letter **5** mouthful, drink (of water) **6** point, place **7** question, issue په تکي زه په باندي هم نه پوهبږي *ṭ́ki* He has no understanding of this issue. دې تکی پوه شوئ یم I understand this. *idiom* په تکي *ṭ́ki* then and there, at once تکي په تکي exactly, precisely د زره تکی dream

ټکی [2] ṭikáj *m.* leather circular piece at the end of a spindle or spinning device (e.g., a distaff)

ټکی [3] ṭikáj *m.* ☞ تیک [3]

ټکی [4] ṭəkə́j *f.* **1** flat cake **2** disk (solar, lunar) **3** target (archery) **4** distych, couplet, landay **5** loop (of a sling) **6** red spot (in nettle rash) *idiom* هر یو پر خپله تکی اور اړوي، د چا په چا غرض نسته *proverb* charity begins at home

ټکی [5] ṭəkə́j *f.* guffaw تکی تکی خندل to guffaw

ټکي [6] ṭ́ki *plural of* تکی [1]

ټکي [7] ṭáki *plural of* تکه [1]

ټکې [8] ṭuké *plural of* تکه [3]

ټکیالی ṭəkjāláj **1** spotted, speckled **2** *linguistics* having a diacritical mark (of a letter)

ټکي تکي ṭúki-ṭuki ṭ́ki-ṭəki **1.1** rent, torn into rags **1.2** spattering, drizzling (of rain) **1.3** ☞ تکیالی **2** exactly, precisely

ټکیدل ṭakedə́l *intransitive* [*past:* و تکبده] **1** to be beaten, be hammered **2** to resound, be heard (of a knock) دروازه وتکبده There was a knock at the door. Someone knocked at the door. **3** to be beaten clean, be beaten out (of clothes etc.) **4** ☞ تورکبدل **5** to walk slowly, shuffle, drag along, trudge slowly along **6** to be forged

ټکی لرونکی ṭəkaj larúnkaj ☞ تکیالی

ټکي مکي ṭ́ki-məki *colloquial* تکي مکي بنودل to study reading and writing

تگ [1] tag *m.* **1** petty thief, swindler, cheat; fraud **2** robber

تگ [2] tag *m.* ☞ تک [3]

تگۇل ṭagǘl transitive [past: تاگه وي] 1 to cheat, swindle; defraud, dupe 2 to rob

تگمار ṭagmā́r m. ☞ تگ 1 1

تگۇنه ṭagǘna f. ☞ تگي

تگي ṭagí f. cheating, swindling; fraud, sharp practice تگي کول to cheat, defraud ځان پر تگي اچول to pretend

تگۇي-تورۇي ṭagǘj-ṭorǘj ده تگي توري کول to cheat, swindle; defraud, dupe

تل 1 ṭal m. 1 log raft تل ترل to fasten or bind logs together in a raft 2 batch (of goods) 3 traveling companion, fellow traveler د چا سره تل کيدل to be united, be in an association with some other person ځان تل کول to unite with, join someone 4 tribe

تل 2 ṭal m. 1 quarter (of a town, village) 2 crops; area under crops; patch, strip 3 thicket 4 meadow د گلونو تل meadow in bloom 5 the fourth part of a settlement's land idiom تل ترکول to inflict defeat on someone

تل 3 ṭal m. Tal (city)

تل 4 ṭal 1 thick, dense تل فصلونه abundant crops 2 figurative plentiful, rich تل کول a to make thick, thicken; make dense, solidify b to make plentiful تل کيدل a to be thick, thicken; be dense, become dense b figurative to be plentiful, be rich

تلتوب ṭaltób m. concomitancy, accompaniment

تلفون ṭilifún m. ☞ تيلفون

تلیگراف ṭiligrā́f m. 1 telegraph 2 telegram

تلیگرام ṭiligrā́m m. telegram

تلگی ṭalgáj m. 1 diminutive of تل 2 2 small farm 3 small cultivated field

تل والی talvǻlaj m. 1 thickness; density 2 figurative abundance, plenty

تم 1 ṭam m. 1 barking; growling, snarling تم وهل to bark; growl, snarl 2 smacking the lips

تم 2 ṭam 1 thick; dense 2 figurative abundant, plentiful

تم 3 ṭim m. barrel

تم 4 ṭim tin

تماغه ṭəmāghá f. officer's service cap

تمباري tambā́ri f. plural weeping; wailing تمباري وهل to weep; cry out

تمبکه ṭambə́ka f. candlestick

تمبل 1 ṭambúl 1 fat, stout, chubby 2 lazy, sluggish idiom تمبل ملخ grasshopper

تمبل 2 ṭumbǘl transitive ☞ تومبل

تمبوس ṭambús ☞ تنبوس

تمبه tambá f. 1 assemblage, throng 2 medicine constipation تمبه کيدل compound verb a to assemble, gather (of people) خلق سره تمبه شوي دي people gathered in a crowd b to suffer from constipation 3 bolt, bar; lock idiom زره مي داسي تمبه دئ چه ... My heart is sinking because …

تمتم ṭamṭám m. Eastern 1 light carriage, cart 2 motorcycle

تمتی ṭamṭáj m. 1 short-handled shovel 2 brief topic

تمتبری ṭamṭeráj m. shorty, person of short stature

تمتل 1 ṭamṭél m. 1 snipe (the bird) 2 sandpiper

تمتل 2 ṭamṭél m. assemblage of people, crowd

تم تیلا ṭamṭilā́ m. ☞ تمتبل 1

تیمک ṭimák m. ☞ تیمک 1

تمول ṭamavə́l transitive [past: تماوه وي] to make bark, make growl, make snarl

تمبدل ṭamedə́l intransitive [past: تمبده و] to bark; to snarl, growl

تن ṭan m. ton لس زره تنه 10,000 tons

تنبکه tambə́ka f. 1 wasps' nest; beehive 2 oven for extraction of tar

تنبل ṭumbə́l transitive ☞ تومبل

تنبوس ṭambús تنبل tambel 1 swelling, swelling up 2 fat, stout, chubby

تنته 1 ṭanṭá f. stalk (of corn, maize)

تنته 2 ṭanṭá f. uproar; confusion, agitation

تند ṭanḍ 1.1 stout, portly; corpulent سرى _ a fat man 1.2 swollen; swollen up 2 m. 1. steer; buffalo calf 2.2 ☞ تندوب

تندتوب ṭanḍtób m. obesity, stoutness; corpulence

تندتوت ṭanḍtút m. kind of large white Kandahar mulberry

تندغرکی ṭanḍghərə́kaj تندکی ṭanḍakáj diminutive somewhat obese; a little paunchy; a bit chubby

تندو ṭanḍú 1 m. fat man; pudgy fellow 2 fat; pudgy

تندوالی ṭanḍvǻlaj m. ☞ تندوب

تندور ṭanḍór m. 1 roasting of pine kernels on red-hot sand 2 piling up of things, accumulation of things

تندول ṭanḍavə́l denominative, transitive [past: تندو يې کړ] 1 to put on weight 2 to inflate, blow up; pump up idiom تنده يې کړه She became pregnant (out of wedlock)

تندوبک ṭanḍvék m. span

تنده 1 ṭánḍa f. 1 assembly; meeting تنده کول to organize an assembly تنده کيدل to meet, assemble 2 crowd, assemblege دا څه تنده ده؟ What is this assembly? 3 award; prize

تنده 2 ṭə́nḍa f. brow idiom په غوړيدلي تنده affably

تنده 3 ṭánḍa 1 singular of تنډ 2 pregnant تنده ښځه pregnant (out of wedlock) 3 with calf; in foal تنده کيدل تندېدل idiom تنده خره kind of game تنده غالبوزه bumblebee

تندېدل ṭanḍedə́l denominative, intransitive [past: تند شو] 1 to put on weight, grow stout 2 to swell up, swell m. 3 to become pregnant (out of wedlock)

تنگ 1 ṭang m. ṭəng 1 knock 2 sound (of metal vessels, etc.) 3 jingling تنگ کيدل a to clink b to jingle 4 music sounds, notes

تنگ 2 ṭung m. Eastern posterity

تنگ 3 ṭing ☞ تینگ

تنگا ṭangā́ f. تنگار ṭangā́r m. ☞ تنگهار

تنگ تکور ṭang-ṭəkór m. 1 music sounds, notes (of music) 2 party, carousal

تنگتونگ ṭangṭúng m. 1 tapping (of a hammer) 2 jingling; strumming (e.g., on a violin) 3 noise (made by a knife and fork); clanging (of pots)

تنگسال ṭangsál *m.* mint (where money is struck)

تنگول ṭangavál *transitive* [*past:* او یی تنگاوه] 1 to clink, tap with something 2 to strum with something 3 to strum or pick at something 4 to play (on stringed and percussion instruments)

تنگه ṭangá *f.* 1 *obsolete* tenga (coin equal to ⅓ Afghan) 2 money; riches, substance

تنگهار ṭangahár *m.* 1 knock; persistent tapping 2 sound (of rifle, pots and pans, etc.) 3 jingling 4 noise (of music)

تنگیدل ṭangedál *intransitive* [*past:* او تنگیده] 1 to clink 2 to squeak 3 to jingle 4 to sound (of musical instruments)

تنن ṭanán 1 cowardly 2 lying, mendacious

توبخی ṭubəkháj *m.* high sand dune

توبکی ṭubəkáj *m.* 1 hole 2 pit, abyss

توباج ṭubáj *m.* sand dune overgrown with grasses

توپ ¹ ṭop *m.* 1 jumping; jump; leap قدمدار توپ triple jump لوړ توپ high jump دنیزی توپ broad jump, pole vault توپ اچول، a to jump; to leap له خوشحالی نه توپونه وهل، توپ کول، توپ وهل jump for joy b to jump, do competition jumps لوړ توپ وهل to do the high jump c to recoil, jump away, jump aside په توپ کېدل to begin to jump په توپو تلل to run hopping and skipping, hop and skip *proverb* توپ وهه چه له پښو ونه لوبرې Don't bite off more than you can chew. Pride cometh before a fall. 2 beating د زره توپونه the beating of a heart, heartbeat

توپ ² ṭop *m.* 1 heap; pile 2 stack, rick, straw stack 3 built-up pile, arranged stack د لرگو توپ woodpile 4 *trade* premium, bonus (added to goods purchased) 5 stupa (a hemispherical or cylindrical tower serving as a Buddhist shrine) 6 cap with earflaps

توپ ³ ṭup *tautological with* تپ ¹

توپ تپانی ṭopṭəpānáj *m.* competitive jumping (high jump)

توپخن ṭupkhán *m.* pile, heap (i.e., of earth)

توپک ṭopák *m.* ☞ توپک چقمقي توپک flintlock باتیدار توپک musket توپک سینی سره نیول to come to present arms د چرو توپک shotgun رخدار توپک rifle توپک musket *regional military*

توپکچی ṭopakchí *m. regional* 1 rifleman 2 sniper

توپک گری ṭopakgə́raj gunsmith

توپک والا ṭopakvālā́ *m.* rifleman; man armed with a rifle

توپکی ṭopakáj *f.* clumsily covered arch or vault of an irrigation system

توپل ṭopál *m.* 1 crown, coronet 2 headgear; cap 3 peak (e.g., of a mountain)

توپن ṭopán *m.* world, universe

توپنای ṭopnáj *m.* traveler, wayfarer

توپنی ¹ ṭopanə́j *f.* pile (of earth, etc.)

توپنی ² ṭopənáj *m.* 1 man-of-the-world; well-traveled person 2 children's game

توپوگرافي ṭopogrāfí *f.* topography

توپه ṭópa *f. dialect* miracle, performance of a miracle

توپی ¹ ṭopə́j *f.* 1 cap, helmet قراقلي توپی fez ترکی توپی caracul cap; high conical lambskin hat 2 crown (of a hat); upper part of a cap

3 bowl (of a tobacco pipe) 4 ridge, hill 5 small hill, mound (on a grave) 6 hooded cloak (of a bird hunter) 7 ☞ د پتاقي *idiom* توپی گل وبنبنتانو توپی camomile wig

توپی ² ṭopí *m.* 1 *obsolete* groom 2 jumper

توپییدار ṭopidár *regional* توپیدار توپک muzzleloader (rifle)

توتار ṭotár *m.* knife (butcher's)

توتکه ṭoṭká *f.* 1 spell, incantation توتکه کول to charm away (an illness) 2 amulet 3 gift made by the bridegroom's family to the relatives of the bride

توتکه چی ṭoṭkachí *m.* توتکه مار ṭoṭkamár *m.* sorcerer, witch doctor, quack; exorcist

توتکی ṭoṭəkáj *f.* 1 kneecap, patella 2 wooden bowl 3 femur

توته ṭoṭá *f.* 1 piece, small piece; part توته کول *compound verb* to tear, tear to pieces a توتی توتی کول to cut up carelessly, tear into small pieces b to break up, pulverize توتی توتی کېدل a to be torn up, be torn up into small pieces b to be broken up, be pulverized 2 sector, plot یوه توته ځمکه plot of land 3 note; chit 4 patch توته نخی توته to apply a patch, patch 5 fabric, cloth اینسودل، توته گندل cotton fabric, cotton cloth *idiom* یوه توته جنگ وشه a cruel battle had arisen *idiom* زړونه توتی کول to trouble, grieve

توتی ¹ ṭuṭáj *m.* thigh

توتی ² ṭuṭə́j *f.* [*plural:* توتی ṭuṭáj *plural:* توتی گانی ṭuṭəjgáni] 1 wooden goblet; bowl 2 tankard

توتی ³ ṭutí *f.* 1 boasting, bragging 2 slander

توتی ⁴ ṭavṭáj *m.* box

توتل ṭoṭál *m.* ☞ تمتپل ¹

توخ ṭukh 1 *m.* cough توخ وهل اخ او توخ جوړول to cough to have a slight cough 2 clearing of the throat

توخل ṭukhál *transitive* [*past:* او یی توخل] to cough

توخله ṭukhála *f.* توخلی ṭukhə́laj *m.* whooping cough توخله یې پ ده He has whooping cough.

توخلی ² ṭukhaláj *f.* quilted, hat, padded cap

توخول ṭukhavál *transitive* [*past:* او یی توخاوه] 1 to cause to cough 2 to have a tickle in the throat

توخه ṭúkha *f.* ☞ توخ

توخهار ṭukhəhár *m.* intermittent coughing, slight coughing

توخی ṭukháj *m.* cough وچ توخی a dry cough توخی یې دئ He has a cough توخی نیولی یم *tukhi* … I have a cough.

توخیدل ṭukhedál *intransitive* [*past:* وتوخیده] to cough پر توخبرم I have a bad cough.

توری ¹ ṭuráj *m.* small ear of corn

توری ² ṭoráj *m.* ☞ چلمچی

توری ³ ṭoráj *tautological with* تگی

توس ¹ ṭos *m.* piece of toasted white bread

توس ² ṭus *tautological with* تس

توسان ṭusán *m.* large hailstones (in spring)

توغ ṭugh 1 bent, curved, distorted 2 stooped, kyphotic, hunchbacked

ټوغ ټوغ ṭughtugh 1 extremely curved, distorted 2 markedly hunchbacked 3 hunched up ټوغ ټوغ کېدل a to sit with hunched back; hunch oneself up b to huddle oneself up c to sneak silently past

ټوغک 1 ṭughak m. ټوغکی ṭughakáj m. plague, epizootic (of birds, poultry)

ټوغکی 2 ṭughəkáj diminutive of ټوغ

ټوغول ṭughavəl denominative, transitive [past: ټوغ يې کړ] 1 to bend, curve, twist 2 to arch, hunch

ټوغېدل ṭughedəl denominative, intransitive [past: ټوغ شو] 1 to be bent, be curved, be distorted, be twisted 2 to stoop, become bent

ټوقا toḳā́ m. blacksmith

ټوکړ tuḳáṛ m. ☞ ټاکړ

ټوقمار toḳmár m. fool; jester, joker, clown

ټوقه ṭóḳa f. joke; anecdote; ټوقي او ټکالي fun and games ټوقه کول to joke, jest دا ولي په چا پوري ټوقه کول to ridicule somebody idiom درباندي داسي ټوقه وشوه؟ Why has this happened to you?

ټوقه تکاله tóḳa-təkā́la f. 1 joke, pleasantry 2 humor

ټوقي 1 toḳí m. ☞ ټوقمار

ټوقي 2 tóḳi ṭóḳe Eastern plural of ټوقه

ټوک 1 tuk m. [plural: ټوکونه ṭukúna plural: ټوکان ṭukā́n] Western 1 piece, part ټوک ټوک کول to cut into parts 2 charity, alms ټوک غونډول، ټوک ټولول to beg, live by begging, live on charity 3 volume لومړی ټوک Volume One idiom و چاته ټوک ورکول to rebuff someone (in a dispute)

ټوک 2 tok thick (of cloth)

ټوک 3 ṭuk tautological with تک

ټوکا 1 ṭukā́ m. growth, germination (of seeds)

ټوکا 2 ṭukā́ m. ☞ ټوقا

ټوکار ṭukár m. 1 aversion; hostility ټوکار خوړل to grow cold towards, lose interest; feel an aversion to something اوس مي ددي کار څخه ټوکار وخوړ This matter bored me. This had become repugnant. 2 knife, butcher's knife

ټوکخوار ṭukkhár m. lickspittle, toady

ټوکر 1 ṭukər m. ☞ ټوکر 2

ټوکر 2 ṭukár m. cage (for birds)

ټوکر 3 toḳər old person, one who has lived a long life

ټوکره 1 ṭukrá f. ☞ ټوکری 1

ټوکره 2 toḳrá f. large basket

ټوکری 1 ṭukráj m. 1 piece, small piece of something ټوکری کېدل to fall to pieces, disintegrate 2 length (of cloth) 3 blanket, coverlet

ټوکری 2 toḳráj f. 1 basket 2 peddler's tray

ټوکړې 3 ṭukré plural of ټوکره 1

ټوکړې 4 tokré plural of ټوکره 2

ټوکرېل ṭukrejəl transitive [past: وي ټوکرېه] to cut (carelessly) up into pieces; cut into pieces, cut into bits

ټوکر 3 tokəṛ ☞ ټوکر

ټوکړه ṭukṛá f. ټوکړژ ṭukṛəj f. ☞ تکر

ټوکل ṭukəl transitive [past: وي ټوکه] 1 to pound; crush, grind, husk (corn, etc.) 2 to cut into chops (meat) 3 to hew, cleave asunder (with a stone, sledgehammer) 4 to hem (cloth) 5 to hit, strike, beat someone

ټوکلی 1 ṭukláj m. sewing (by hand)

ټوکلئ 2 ṭukəlaj 1 past participle of ټوکل 2 chopped off ټوکلي غونډه a chop (cut of meat)

ټوقمار toḳmár m. ☞

ټوکول ṭukavəl transitive [past: وي ټوکاوه] 1 to grow, cultivate 2 figurative to evoke, bring forth (e.g., sympathy)

ټوکه 1 ṭóka f. ☞

ټوکه 2 ṭuká f. dry cow

ټوکه 3 tuka f. well shaft (of a kariz, or irrigation system)

ټوکی 1 toḳí m. ☞

ټوکی 2 túkaj m. 1 part, piece دوه ټوکي کېدل to break in half 2 length (piece of cloth) 3 cloth, cotton textiles ورپنبمین ټوکي túki … silk fabrics

ټوکی 3 ṭukáj m. ☞

ټوکي 4 tóki plural of ټوکه 1

ټوکې 5 ṭuké plural of ټوکی 2

ټوکي 6 túki plural of ټوکه 3

ټوکي 7 ṭukí m. cotton fabrics dealer

ټوکیا ṭukjā́ f. large knife, large butcher's knife; kitchen knife

ټوکي تکالي tóki-təkāli f. plural jokes, pleasantries; humor

ټوکېدل ṭukedəl intransitive [past: وټوکېده] 1 to grow, germinate, put out shoots, sprouts 2 to swell, swell up 3 to ripen (of ears of corn, etc.)

ټوکېدنه ṭukedəna f. 1 germination 2 swelling, swelling up 3 ripening (of ears of corn, etc.)

ټوکیو tokjó f. Tokyo

ټول 1 ṭaul m. ṭval towel (Turkish, terrycloth)

ټول 2 ṭol m. obsolete ☞ ټولی 1

ټول 3 ṭol pronoun 1 all ټوله دنیا the entire city ټوله ښار the entire world ټول خپلوخپلو کورونو ته ولاړل All are working. له ټولونه Everyone left for home. تر ټولو ښه better than everyone زیات more than everyone 2 predicative those who have gathered خلق ټول وه The people have assembled.

ټول 4 ṭul m. tulle (cloth)

ټول ټال ṭol-ṭā́l as soon as, all-in-all

ټولتون ṭoltún m. meeting place; collection point

ټول زرمی ṭolzérmaj m. state treasury

ټولگر ṭolgár m. [plural: ټولگر ṭolgər plural: ټولګران ṭolgərā́n] beggar, pauper, mendicant

ټولګی ṭolgáj m. ټولګی ṭolgəj f. 1 class (in school); year (in a university) 2 group, small detachment; formation مخنی ټولګی forward flock 3 small flock 4 association, society, organization

ټولګیوال ṭolgəjvál m. classmate, schoolmate

ټوللیک ṭollík m. 1 office 2 ledger

ټولمشر ṭolmə́shr *m.* ṭolmə́shər **1** commander (commanding general officer) لوی ټولمشر Commander-in-Chief **2** emir, ruler

ټولمشري ṭolməshrí *f.* **1** command group **2** control element, leadership **3** governing, government

ټولنپوهه ṭolənpóha *f.* social science

ټولنه ṭoló́na *f.* **1** meeting; conference; council فوق العاده ټولنه extraordinary session ټولنه کول to meet; arrange a meeting په زما کور کښي زمونږ ټولنه وشوه We met at my place. **2** society; organization د دوستی ټولنه پښتو ټولنه the Pashto Academy Friendship Society **3** population **4** *biology* society **5** commission د پلټني ټولنه control commission **6** [plural: ټولني ṭoló́ni] circles, spheres سياسي ټولني political circles *idiom* د ټولني روغ ورځ the Diplomatic Corps دیپلوماتیکه ټولني Friday

ټولو ṭólo *f. oblique plural of* ټول³

ټولواک ṭolvā́k *m.* ټولواکمن ṭolvā́kmán *m.* monarch, ruler, king

ټولواکي ṭolvā́ki *f.* monarchy, kingdom

ټولول ṭolavə́l *denominative* [past: ټول یي کړ] **1** to gather گلونه ټولول to gather flowers معلومات ټولول to collect information کلکسیون شیان ټولول، ټولول to assemble a collection **2** to take in, bring in (harvest) **3** to convene, convoke **4** to join, unite **5** to pile up, accumulate, amass (wealth) **6** to lift up, retract (hand, leg, landing gear, etc.) خپل دي ټولي کړه! Pull your legs in! *idiom* to decrease, contract, shrink دیو شي څخه ځان ټولول to decline (something)

ټوله ṭóla¹ **1** *feminine singular & masculine plural of* ټول³ **2** in all, sum, total ټوله پنځه کسه راغلي وو In all, five men came.

ټوله ṭolá² *f.* begging, mendicancy

ټوله تاله ṭóla-ṭā́la *feminine singular of* تال ټول

ټولی ṭoláj¹ *m.* **1** group, detachment **2** company

ټولی ṭoló́j² *f.* **1** group **2** detachment (100 to 200 men) **3** company; batallion (i.e., artillery) د سپرو ټولی squadron

ټولېدل ṭoledə́l *denominative, intransitive* [past: ټول شو] **1** to be assembled; be mustered; be convoked ټول شئ! Fall in! **2** to be gotten in, be gathered (harvest) **3** to be acquired, be amassed **4** to be retracted (e.g., aircraft landing gear) **5** سره ټولېدل to be compressed (lungs); be contracted (muscles)

ټولیمشر ṭoləjmə́shr *m.* ṭoləjmə́shər captain (army)

ټولیمشري ṭoləjmə́shrí *f.* captaincy, rank of captain

ټوم ṭum *m. Eastern* **1** instigation, incitement دا چاره یي د احمد په ټوم وکړه He did this at Ahmed's instigation. **2** advice, counsel

ټومب ṭumb *m.* **1** prick, jab **2** ټوم

ټومبل ṭumbə́l *transitive* [past: ویي ټومبه] **1** to nail, affix (with a pin, tack) **2** to plunge in, stick into **3** to dig into, pick (e.g., the teeth) **4** to extract (a splinter, etc.) **5** to beat an opponent (e.g., of a cock in a cockfight)

ټومبونی ṭumbúnaj *m.* غاښن ټومبونی toothpick

ټومبېدل ṭumbedə́l *intransitive* [past: وټومبېده] **1** to be nailed, be tacked, be pinned **2** to be plunged into, be stuck into

ټونډینه ṭunḍína *f.* ear, cob (of corn)

تونس ṭunís *m.* Tunis

ټونگ ṭung *m.* ṭong **1** irritation, arousal, excitement ټونگ ورکول to irritate; excite **b** to instigate, incite **2** advice, counsel ټونگ سره to negotiate about something; decide jointly **3** lancet; scapel

ټونگاره ṭungā́ra *f.* **1** pinch **2** peck **3** irritation; excitement **4** incitement, instigation, provocation ټونگاره اچول ☞ ټونگربیل

ټونگره ṭungrá *f.* ☞ ټونگه¹

ټونگربیل ṭungrejə́l ṭongrejə́l *transitive* [past: وی یي ټونگربیه] **1** to pinch **2** to peck (of a bird) **3** to irritate, rouse, arouse **4** to instigate a quarrel, incite a quarrel, provoke to a quarrel **5** to play dirty tricks in an underhanded manner **6** to curse, abuse, revile, insult

ټونگل ṭungə́l *transitive* [past: وی یي ټونگه] to get someone's attention (by beckoning with the finger, or a slight wink)

ټونگوره ṭungóra *f.* ☞ اینگه

ټونگول ṭungavə́l *transitive* ☞ ټونگربیل

ټونگه ټونگه túnga ṭonga¹ *f. Eastern* beak ټونگه وهل to peck ټونگه کول to peck to death

ټونگه tónga² *f.* **1** joint, phalange (of the finger) **2** back of the leg

ټیک ṭhik *regional* ☞ تیک⁴

ټهیکټاک ṭhikṭhā́k *regional* زه ټهیکټاک یم I am not hurt. I'm OK. هر څه ټهیکټاک دي All is in order.

ټهیکه ṭhíka **1** *feminine singular of* ټهیک **2** *f. regional* rightness زه په ټهیکه یم I am right.

ټی te *f.* name of the letter ټ

ټی بی tebé *f. regional* tuberculosis ده د ټی بی ده He is ill with tuberculosis.

ټیپچه ṭipchá *f.* ☞

ټیپر ṭepə́r *m.* [plural: ټیپرونه ṭepərúna plural: ټیپر ṭepə́r] *Eastern* turnip, rutabaga

ټیپرکی ṭepə́rkaj *f.* short person

ټیپی ṭepə́j *f.* stomach, craw (of a bird)

ټیټ ṭiṭ **1** low, low-lying; undersized, stunted ټیټه ځمکه plain, depression **2** bent, stooping ټیټ ټیټ راتلل to steal up on, sneak up on; creep, slink **3** crooked, bent **4** lower, located below **5** lowest in tone (of sound) **6** *figurative* base, mean, low (of a person) په ټیټ خواهشات to scorn, despise **7** vile, debased ټیټو سترگو کتل lower appetites, base cravings

ټیټاری ṭiṭā́raj *m.* lapwing, pewit

ټیټاکی ṭiṭā́kaj *m.* land holdings, property

ټیټال ṭiṭā́l *m.* **1** meanness, baseness; degradition (moral) **2** cunning, fraud ټیتال خوړل to be deceived, be cheated **2** ټیټال کول **a** to act basely, act viley **b** to cheat, swindle, deceive

ټیټپاس ṭiṭpā́s *m.* flattery, adulation, servility; cringing

ټیټ پیټ ṭiṭ-píṭ **1** quite low **2** bent down

ټیټتوب ṭiṭtób *m.* shortness, smallness of stature

ټیاتر ṭíatr *m. regional* theatre

ټیټسترگی ṭiṭstə́rgaj ashamed, with downcast eyes

تیت شانته țitshấnta rather low, rather short; small of stature, small of height تیت شانته غرونه low mountains

تیتکه țitká *f. medicine* nettle rash, contact dermititis of vegetative origin

تیتکی țitakáj 1 short, short of stature 2 *m.* short person

تیتکي țitáki *f. plural* 1 jerking 2 twitching, kicking تیتکي وهل a to jerk the legs, twitch the legs b to kick, kick one another

تیتکۍ țitakə́j *f.* kneecap

تیتکي țiṭke *plural of* تیتکه

تیت مزاجه țitmizádzha *m.* low, mean, base

تیتوالی țitvấlaj *m.* 1 short stature, shortness 2 bend, curvature 3 fall, lowering, reduction د قیمت تیتوالی reduction of prices 4 submissiveness, humility 5 degradation (moral)

تیتول țitavə́l *denominative, transitive* [*past:* تیت یې کړ] to incline, bend, bow 2 to curve, distort 3 to lower, hang (e.g., the head) 4 to bring down, reduce 5 *figurative* to be little (e.g., the role, the significance)

تیته țíta 1 *feminine singular of* تیت 2 *f.* .1 low place, low country, lowland; depression, hollow لاندي په تیته کښي سیند بهېږي The river is flowing below in the lowland. 2.2 baseness, lowness 2.3 unpleasantness تیته وچاته ویل to say unpleasant things to somebody

تیته پیته țíta-píta 1 *f.* worship, adoration تیته پیته کول to bow down, bend low 2 *feminine singular of* تیت پیت

تیتی țiṭáj hunchbacked, kyphotic

تیتي țíti *Eastern* țíte 1 *feminine plural of* تیت 2 *plural of* تیته

تیتۍ țiṭə́j 1 *f. singular of* تیتی 2 *f.* clay bowl

تي تي تي țe-țe-țé cry to call a buffalo

تیتیدل țiṭedə́l *denominative, intransitive* [*past:* تیت شو] 1 to stoop, bend, bend down چاته را تیتیدبل to bow د احترام په دود تیتیدبل to bow down before someone 2 to go down, set (of the sun) 3 to fall; sink, descend

تیر țajr *m.* ☞ تایر

تېرج țeráj *m.* Teraj (city)

تیز țiz *m.* ☞ تیز

تیس پیس țispís sluggish, lazy

تېسن țesə́n *m.* 1 station د اورگاډی تېسن railroad station تېسن په تېسن trip after trip 2 center (e.g., tourist center)

تېغ țegh *m.* belch تېغ کبنل، تېغ ایستل to belch, burp

تیغ țigh *m.* small ball, marble

تیغ تمبه țighțambá 1 suffering from indigestion 2 *figurative* disordered, grieved, sad

تیغ سترگی țighstə́rgaj google-eyed, popeyed, exopthalmic

تیغکه țighákа *f.* shrike

تیغکی țighákaj *m.* تیغی țigháj *m.* ☞ تغکی

تپک țek *m.* 1 stop د تپک کول stop, tram stop to stop, halt, take a break د تپک ځای مو نشته There is nowhere for us to stay. لږ تپک وکه Wait a bit! 2 peace, rest 3 break, intermission *idiom* د پلار و نیکه تپک ancestral homestead

تپک țek *m.* 1 temple خولی پر یوه تپک اینبی wearing the cap askew, wearing the skullcap askew 2 ornament worn on the temple 3 kind of embroidery

تیک țik *m.* 1 decoration or ornament worn on the forehead 2 gold ornament worn in the nostril

تیک țik 1.1 true, correct; extract دا خبر بالکل تیک دئ This communication is perfectly correct. 1.2 fitting, appropriate 2.1 precisely, exactly تیک په پنځه نیمو بجو مو حرکت وکاوه We left at precisely five-thirty. 2.2 fully, completely

تیکاله țikālá *f.* lark (the bird)

تپکانو țekānú *m.* true state of affairs

تپکانه țekaná *f.* 1 lease 2 order, job (at work) 3 lodging, dwelling, abode

تپکاو țekấv *m.* 1 stop, rest stop; halt, (bus, tram, etc.) stop; shelter د چا په کور کښي تپکاو کبدل to stay at someone's house 2 existence; residence 3 peace په تپکاو نه پرچاکېدل a to be uneasy, be alarmed; not to find a place for oneself b not to have the means of subsistence *idiom* رو رو مي خیالات په تپکاو شول I gradually collected myself.

تپکاول țekāvə́l *denominative, transitive* [*past:* تپکاو یې کړ] 1 to settle 2 to call a halt, arrange a stop 3 to arrange to stay overnight with someone 4 *figurative* to calm

تپکاوبدل țekāvedə́l *denominative, intransitive* [*past:* تپکاو شو] 1 to settle 2 to stay overnight, arrange to stay the night 3 to calm down, compose oneself

تپکتاکه țektấka *f.* rug with a nap

تیک خولی توپ țijakkhulaj țikkhúlaj antiaircraft gun

تپکدار țekadấr *m.* ☞ تپکه دار

تیکرج țikráj *m.* [*plural:* تیکري țikrí] *Western* [*plural:* تیکریان țikrijấn] shawl, chador

تکس țikás *m.* ☞ تاکس

تپکس țeks *m. regional* ☞ تاکس

تپکسي țeksí *m. & f.* ☞ تکسي

تیکله țikála *f.* 1 bread; flat cake غلمینه تیکله د جوارو wheat bread تیکله د ردنو millet cake corn bread 2 phonograph record

تیکلی țikaláj *m.* 1 circle; disk (of the sun, solar) 2 phonograph record

تیکلۍ țikalə́j *f.* flat cake; small loaf

تي کوزي țikózi *m.* quilted cover for a teapot

تپکاول țekavə́l *transitive* ☞ تپکاول

تپکه țeká *f.* agreement to deliver something; contract په تپکه اخیستل to conclude an agreement to deliver something; undertake a contract for something

تیکه țiká *f.* 1 tika (red mark on the forehead of Hindu women, formerly with religious significance) تیکه وهل، تیکه اینبودل to place a tika on the forehead 2 tag, label *idiom* تیکې اوربدل to be a heathen, be a pagan

تیکه țíka *feminine singular of* تیک

تپکه دار țekadấr *m.* supplier, contractor

تیکی ṭikə́j *f. diminutive of* تیک [3] *idiom* تیکی اچول to put verses from another song into a ghazal (i.e., Arabic verse form)

تیکې [2] ṭeké *plural of* تیکه [1]

تیکې [3] ṭiké *plural of* تیکه [2]

تیکېدل ṭikedə́l *intransitive* [*past:* تیک شو] to settle, take up residence

تیگه ṭigá *f.* gaunt or emaciated cow, cow in poor condition

تېگی ṭegáj *m.* kind of elongated yellow melon

تپل ṭel *m.* push, shove; nudge; pushing through ☞ تپل وهل

تپلټال [1] ṭelṭál *m.* jumping; game, pastime; diversion, recreation تپل ټال کول to jump; amuse oneself, have a good time

تپلټال [2] ṭilṭál *m.* 1 delay, hold-up; procrastination 2 din, uproar

تپلفون ṭelefún *m.* ☞ تیلفون

تپلگراف ṭeligráf *m.* ☞ تیلگراف

تپلگرافي ṭeligráfi ☞ تیلگرافي

تپلگرام ṭeligrám *m.* ☞ تیلگرام

تپل ماتپل ṭelmáṭel *m.* 1 crush, crowding; mass of people د ژوندانه تپل ماتپل کول to push, shove; push or shove one another 2 vanity تپل ماتپل worldly vanity

تپلمار ṭelmár *m.* 1 shoving, pushing (e.g., a wheelbarrow) 2 ☞ تپله مار

تپلوهل ṭelvahə́l *transitive* [*past:* تپل یې واهه] 1 to push, shove; push, shove one another 2 to give up, reject, push aside *idiom* ما آواز په ښکته تپل واهه I lowered my voice.

تپله ṭelá *f.* 1 trees and bush (carried down by a river) 2 mash 3 stone dam 4 flotsam (any object carried down by the current of a river, etc.)

تپله مار ṭelamár *m.* parasite, sponger, freeloader

تپلیا ṭeljá *m.* 1 mower, one who mows 2 *dialect* groom

تپلی پرنتر ṭeleprinṭár *m.* teletype

تیم [1] ṭim *m. sports* team

تیم [2] ṭim *m.* tin

تیم [3] ṭim *m.* [*plural:* تیمونه ṭimúna *Western plural:* تیمان ṭimán] 1 (metal) barrel 2 can, tin can

تیم [4] tajm *m. regional sports* half, period

تیمک [1] ṭimák *m.* main member of a hipped roof, strut, support

تیمک [2] ṭimák *m.* 1 small barrel, small keg 2 small metal container, can

تینخی ṭenkháj *m.* 1 boaster 2 poseur

تینس ténis *m.* tennis د تینس ډگر tennis court

تینک ṭenk *m.* ☞ تانک

تینگ ṭing 1.1 firm, stiff, rigid تینگ تکر 1.2 thick, strong, tough thick fabric تینگ پړی strong rope 1.3 forceful, intense تینگه آرزو an intense desire 1.4 viscous (e.g., a syrup) 1.5 reliable, worthy of trust 1.6 persistent, persevering تینگ تینگ کېدل a to be stubborn, be unyielding b to stint, grudge 1.7 firm, decisive 1.8 stable, constant (of a rate of monetary exchange) 2 firmly, strongly; energetically تینگ دربدل to affix firmly تینگ ترل to oppose, resist; stand up firmly for one's own *idiom* پر دنیا تینگ stringy, misery, tightfisted; greedy, grasping

تینگار ṭingár *m.* 1 steadfastness; firmness په مړانه او تینگار in a manly and steadfast manner د تینگار خاوند a steadfast person, manly person 2 persistence, decisiveness په خورا تینگار، په ډېر very persistently په یوه کار کښې تینگار کول to display persistence in some matter په تینگار ویل to emphasize, point out 3 resistance, counteraction 4 toughness, strength

تینگاو ṭingáv *m.* order; organization, arrangement

تینگتوب ṭingtób *m.* تینگتیا ṭingtjá *f.* ☞ تینگار

تینگر ṭingə́r *m.* ☞ ترنگر

تینگری ṭingrəj *f.* blow to the brow, slap on the brow تینگری وهل to strike the brow, slap the brow

تینگل ṭingə́l *m.* shoenail, cobbler's nail

تینگوالی ṭingválaj *m.* ☞ تینگار

تینگول ṭingavə́l *denominative, transitive* [*past:* تینگ یې کړ] 1 to make firm, make stiff, make rigid 2 to strengthen; fasten, secure; fasten together 3 concentrate 4 to hearten, put heart into د سړی خطر په مخ کښې تینگول to hearten into people in the face of threatening danger ځان تینگول، خپل ځان تینگول a to get stronger, become stronger b to counteract ځان د بېری و مخي ته تینگول not to yield to fear 5 to strengthen, enhance, develop (friendly relations, etc.)

تینگون ṭingún *m.* ☞ تینگار

تینگه ṭínga 1 *feminine singular of* تینگ 2 *f.* 1 persistence, decisiveness نو می دا په تینگه په زره کښې وه I became decisive. I firmly decided. په تینگه انکار کول to reject decisively ... په تینگه سره We require ... We insist that ... 2.2 craw, stomach (in birds)

تینگی ṭingí *m.* ☞ تینگل

تینگېدل ṭingedə́l *denominative, intransitive* [*past:* تینگ شو] 1 to harden, become hard, set 2 to become strengthened; be fastened tight, be consolidated; be fastened together 3 to be concentrated 4 to intensify 5 to be thickened, be condensed 6 to insist, persist (in) 7 to be enhanced, be strengthened, be developed (of friendly relations etc.) 8 to resist, hold out, endure

تیوب ṭjub *m.* د موتر تیوپ ṭjup *m.* 1 inner tube inner tube (automotive) 2 tube

ث

ث se 1 the sixth letter of the Pashto alphabet 2 the number 500 in the abjad system

ثابت sābít *Arabic* 1 established, proven; inconvertible, irrefutable, clear دا ثابته خبره ده چه ... ، دا یوه ثابته خبره ده چه ... It has been established that ... 2 sure, firm, steadfast 3 steady, stable 4 fixed *idiom* ثابت بالون captive balloon

ثابت قدم sābítḳadám *Arabic* 1 sure, firm, steadfast 2 loyal, devoted; constant ثابت قدمه ښنځه a faithful wife, devoted wife 3 consecutive

233

ثابت قدمي sābítķadamí *f.* 1 stability, firmness, unshakability 2 faithfulness, devotion, constancy 3 sequence

ثابتول sābíṭavól *denominative, transitive* [*past:* ثابت يې کړ] 1 to make sure, make firm, make steadfast; consolidate, strenghten 2 to make steady, stabilize 3 to establish, prove, confirm 4 to make immoveable

ثابته sābitá *Arabic* 1 *feminine singular of* ثابت 2 *f. Arabic m.* [*plural:* ثوابت savābít] *astronomy* fixed star

ثابتېدل sābitedól *denominative, intransitive* [*past:* ثابت شو] 1 to be sure, be firm, be steadfast; become firmer, be strengthened 2 to be stable, become stabilized 3 to be established, be proven; be confirmed; be incontrovertible, be indisputable 4 to turn out to be مهلک ثابتېدل to result in destruction, prove fatal ناکام ثابتېدل to turn out to be unsuccessful, fail 5 to result in, follow from, to be the consequence of something دا دې څخه ثابتېږي چه ... It follows from this that …

ثالث sālís *Arabic* 1 *numeral* third ثالث بلوک مشر *obsolete* junior lieutenant 2 *m.* arbitrator, arbiter, umpire

ثالثاً sālísán *Arabic* thirdly, in the third place

ثالثي sālisí *f. Arabic* arbitration, arbitrational tribunal

ثانوي sānaví *Arabic* 1 secondary ثانوي تعليمات secondary education 2 second 3 secondary, minor, subordinate ثانوي اهميت لرل to have a secondary meaning

ثاني sāní *Arabic numeral* second ثاني غندمشر lieutenant colonel *idiom* خپل ثاني نه لرل to be unrivalled, have no competitor

ثانياً sāníján *Arabic* secondly, in the second place

ثانيه [1] sānijá *f. Arabic* second (unit of time)

ثانيه [2] sānijá *numeral feminine of* ثاني

ثانيه گرد sānijagárd *m.* second hand (clock, watch)

ثبات sabát *m.* subát *Arabic* 1 firmness; constancy ثبات ښکارول to show firmness; constancy خپل مقصد باندي ثبات persistency in the attainment of a goal, purposefulness 2 soundness, stability, firmness

ثبت sabt *Arabic* 1 *m.* .1 firmness; constancy 1.2 entry on a list, record, registration 1.3 recording (on film, etc.) 2 *predicative* 1. entered on a list, recorded, registered 2.2 recorded (on film, etc.)

ثبتول sabtavól *denominative, transitive* [*past:* ثبت يې کړ] 1 to enter on a list, record, register 2 to record (on film, etc.)

ثبتېدل sabtedól *denominative, intransitive* [*past:* ثبت شو] 1 to be entered on a list, be recorded, be registered 2 to be recorded (on microfilm, etc.)

ثبوت subút *m. Arabic* 1 confirmation, proof; establishment of fact; verification ثبوت ته رسول، ثبوت کول to confirm, prove, establish a fact; verify په ثبوت رسېدل، ثبوت ته رسېدل to be confirmed, be proven, be established 2 steadiness, firmness, steadfastness 3 constancy, stability 4 *law* basis of a claim

ثروت sarvát *m. Arabic* 1 riches, wealth 2 property

ثروتمند sarvatmánd rich, wealthy, well-to-do, propertied, well-off

ثروتمندي sarvatmandí *f.* riches, wealth

ثروتي sarvatí ثروتي منابع natural resources

ثريا surajá *f. Arabic astronomy* the Pleiades

ثعلب مصري sa'labmisrí *m. Arabic singular & plural botany* salep

ثقافت saķafát *m. Arabic* culture قديم ثقافت ancient culture

ثقافتي saķāfatí ثقافي cultured ثقافتي علايق، ثقافتي روابط cultural ties

ثقالت saķālát *m. Arabic* gravity, weight; weightiness

ثقت siķát *m. Arabic* ☞ ثقه

ثقل siķl *m. Arabic* [*plural:* اثقال asķál] 1 gravity, mass, weight 2 load

ثقه siķá *Arabic* 1 *f.* trust, confidence 2 deserving of trust, reliable, loyal, trustworthy ثقه معلومات reliable information

ثقيل saķíl *Arabic* 1 heavy 2 difficult (e.g., of languages) 3 lazy; phlegmatic 4 difficult to digest, indigestible 5 hard, burdensome *idiom* ثقيل ماشيندار medium machine gun, MMG

ثلاث salás *Arabic numeral literary* three

ثلث suls *m. Arabic* third part, third د آراو دوه ثلثه two-thirds of the votes

ثمر samár *m. Arabic* 1 fruit 2 produce, foodstuffs 3 benefit, advantage 4 progeny 5 results, issue

ثمردار samardár *m.* 1 bearing fruit, fruitful 2 productive 3 producing progeny, prolific

ثمرقند samarķánd *m.* Samarkand (city)

ثمره samará *f. Arabic* [*plural:* ثمري samaré *m. Arabic plural:* ثمرات samarát] 1 fruit 2 results, issue د بې پروايي ثمري the results of carelessness 3 progeny, offspring 4 *proper name* Samara

ثمين samín *Arabic* 1 valuable, expensive; precious 2 *m. proper name* Samin

ثمينه saminá 1 *feminine singular of* ثمين 2 *f. proper name* Samina

ثنا sanā *f. Arabic* praise, eulogy; panegyric ثنا ويل to praise, eulogize; extole

ثناخوان sanākhán *m.* panegyrist

ثناخواني sanākhāní *f.* praise, eulogy; glorification ثناخواني کول to praise, eulogize; glorify

ثنايا sanājá *m. Arabic plural* front teeth, incisors

ثنويت sanaviját *m. Arabic philosophy* dualism

ثنى sinā *f.* [*plural:* اثنا asná] *Arabic* 1 bend; turn 2 fold

ثواب savāb *m. Arabic* 1 recompense, reward, award (for a good deed) ثواب گټل، ثواب لرل a to be awarded b to deserve an award 2 good deed ثواب کول to perform a good deed, do good

ثوابت savābít *m. Arabic plural of* ثابته

ثوابي savābí *m.* person rewarded for a good deed

ثوب saub *m. Arabic* [*plural:* اثواب asváb *plural:* ثياب sijáb] 1 wearing apparel, apparel, clothing 2 *classifier used in counting articles of clothing*

ثوباړى sobāṛaj *m. regional* ☞ څوباړى

ثور saur *m. Arabic* 1 bull, bullock, ox 2 *astrology* Taurus (the constellation) 3 Saur (the second month of the solar year; 21 April-21 May)

ثې se *f.* the name of the letter ث

ثياب sijáb *m. Arabic plural of* ثوب

ثيبه sijibá *f. Arabic* newly wed, woman who has just married

ج

ج ¹ dzhim *m.* 1 the seventh letter of the Pashto alphabet 2 the number 2 in the abjad system

ج ² 1 جواب *abbreviation* 2 جل جلاله *abbreviation* 3 جلالتمآب *abbreviation* 4 جلد ¹ *abbreviation*

جابر dzhābír *Arabic* 1 oppressive; coercive; despotic جابر حكومت despotism, tyranny; violence 2 despot, tyrant; oppressor; aggressor

جابرانه dzhābiráná 1 forcible, compulsory جابرانه نظام despotism, tyranny; force 2 forcibly, by force, compulsorily

جابه dzhābá *f.* 1 skin oil container with a spout 2 ☞ جعبه

جابى ¹ dzhabáj *f.* 1 short skirt; tutu 2 man's pleated shirt

جابى ² dzhabáj *f.* leg bracelets

جاپ dzhāp *m.* muttering of prayers

جاپان dzhāpån *m.* Japan بحيره جاپان، د جاپان بحيره the Sea of Japan د جاپان جزيرى the islands of Japan

جاپانی dzhāpāni dzhāpānáj .1 Japanese 1.2 *m.* Japanese (person) 2 *f.* dzhāpāni Japanese, the Japanese language

جاپرى dzhāpari *f.* sheepskin coat

جات dzhāt *plural suffix ending for nouns ending in a vowel* عراده جات carriages مېوه جات fruits

جاجه dzhādzh *m.* 1 supposition, surmise; idea 2 anxiety, concern جاج وهل a to suppose, surmise b to worry about something *idiom* جاج پكښې اچول to call something into question, doubt something

جاجه dzhākhá *f.* pile of brush, stack of kindling wood

جادو dzhādú *m. singular & plural* magic, witchcraft; sorcery جادو كول to enchant

جادوگر dzhādugár *m.* 1 sorcerer, magician, wizard 2 conjurer, magician

جادوگره dzhādugára *f.* witch, sorceress

جادوگرى ¹ dzhādugari *f.* witchcraft, sorcery

جادوگرى ² dzhādugári *plural of* جادوگره

جاده dzhāddá *f. Arabic* road عمومي جاده highway, surfaced road

جاونگ dzhāḍáng old, decrepit, senile

جاوى dzhāḍáj *f.* 1 old and skinny cow-camel 2 *abusive* old crone

جاذب dzhāzíb *Arabic* 1.1 attractive, attracting 1.2 absorbing, taking in, imbibing 2 *m.* blotting paper

جاذبه ¹ dzhāzibá *f. Arabic* attraction د جاذبې قوه *physics* attractive force, gravity

جاذبه ² dzhāzíba *feminine singular of* جاذب

جاذبيت dzhāzibiját *m.* attractiveness

جار ¹ dzhār *m.* victim, sacrifice, obligation جار كېدل *compound verb* جار ¹ جاربدل ☞ *idiom* جار قربان چاته ويل to dote upon someone

جار ² dzhar *m.* declaration, proclamation جار وهل to announce, proclaim په جار مخالفت كول to speak out openly against someone

جار ³ dzhār *m.* 1 pen (for cattle) 2 temporary fence (constructed on a threshing floor of reeds, etc.) 3 enclosed area for trapping quail 4 reed corral, rush corral 5 manure pile, dunghill

جاريستل dzhāristál *transitive* [*present:* جارباسي *past:* ويي جاريوست *past:* ويي جاريست] 1 to turn back 2 to wind, roll up, twist 3 to weave, weave together 4 to vomit; feel nauseous

جارجيا dzhārzhijá *f.* Georgia

جارچي dzhārchí *m.* 1 town crier 2 herald

جارچي باشي dzhārchibāshí chief crier, herald

جارح dzhāríh *Arabic* sharp, keen-edged (of a tool)

جارحانه dzhārihāná 1 decisive, crucial (of a military offensive, etc.) 2 جارحانه عمليات active operation جارحانه حمله crucial offensive aggressive

جارحيت dzhārihiját *m.* decisiveness

جارغلى dzhārghóláj *m.* hearth; trivet

جاركبده dzhārkedé *m. plural* self-sacrifice

جاركنى dzhārkənáj *f.* 1 place near the hearth where fuel is stored 2 wood shed

جارو dzhārú *m. f. regional* broom جارو كول *compound verb* a to sweep, sweep up كوټه جارو كول to sweep the room د برق د جارو كولو ماشين vacuum cleaner برقي جارو b *figurative* to lick off, lick up *idiom* د چا كور ور جارو كول to rob someone

جارواته dzhārvātó *m. plural* 1 rotation 2 turning; shunting aside 3 return د جاروتو په وخت كښې upon returning 4 getting stuck; falling (e.g., into a net) 5 interweaving, weaving together 6 swaddling, winding, twisting together

جاروتل dzharvatál *intransitive* [*past:* جارووت *present:* جاروزي *past:* و جارووت] 1 to revolve, rotate 2 to turn, shunt, turn aside 3 to return 4 to get stuck, fall (e.g., into a net) مرغه په دام كښې جارووت The bird fell into the net. 5 to interlace, intertwine د ونو سرونه يو تر بله سره جارواته The treetops were intertwined. 6 to swaddle, twist, wrap around 7 to be woven, be woven together 8 to fall off, fall away, separate

جارواتنه dzhārvatóna *f.* ☞ جارواته

جاروكبن dzhārukákh sweeper; trash man

جاروگى dzhārugáj *f.* broom, sweeper; whisk broom

جارول ¹ dzhāravál *denominative, transitive* [*past:* جار يې كړ] to sacrifice ځان جارول to sacrifice oneself

جارول ² dzhāravál *denominative, transitive* [*past:* جار يې كړ] 1 *textiles* to warp 2 to clean (with a brush)

جاروونى dzhāravúnaj 1 *m.* .1 shawl, dress (woman's) 1.2 *textiles* warping frame 2 *adjective* weaving

جاروپستل dzhārvestál *transitive Eastern* ☞ جارايستل 1

جارى ¹ dzhāraj *m.* dzhāri sacrifice, obligation

جارى ² dzhāri *Arabic* 1 moving, moving from one place to another 2 current, present جاري كال the current year 3 occuring, being conducted سخت جنگونه جاري وو a bitter battle occured 4 being in circulation, current (of money) **5** effective (of a law, etc.) جاري كول **a** to move, move from one point to another **b** to put into circulation (of money) **c** to put into effect (a law etc.) جاري كېدل **a** to be moved, be moved from one point to another **b** to go on, result from **c** to be in circulation (e.g., money) **d** to go into effect (a law, etc.) **e** to flow, stream خپل سفر جاري ساتل to continue one's journey *idiom* حساب جاري *accounting* current account

جارياسته dzharjāstə́ *m. plural* **1** return **2** reeling, winding, coiling **3** twisting, twining, torsion **4** vomiting

جاربدل[1] dzhāredə́l *denominative, intransitive* [*past:* جار شو] to be sacrificed *saying* جار دي شم I am ready to do all for you. I am your slave. جار دي شم، ولي را سره خوابدى يي؟ My dear fellow, why are you offended at me? د وطن تر سر جاربدل to give one's life to one's country

جاربدل[2] dzhāredə́l *denominative* ☞ جاروتل

جارايستل dzhārjəstə́l *transitive* ☞ جارايستل

جاريستنه dzhārjəstə́na *f.* ☞ جارياسته

جاړ[1] dzhāṛ *m.* purging (the stomach), taking a laxative جاړ كول to purge (the stomach), take a laxative

جاړ[2] dzhāṛ *m.* **1** thickets, bushes; undergrowth **2** uncultivated land

جاړه[1] dzhā́ṛa *dialect imperfective imperative of* جړل

جاړه[2] dzhāṛə́ *imperfective of* جړل

جاړه[3] dzhā́ṛa *f.* thorny bush, shrub

جازباند dzhāzbānd *m.* جازبند dzhāzbánḍ *m.* jazz

جازم dzhāzím *Arabic* preemptory, categorical

جاسوس dzhāsús *m. Arabic* spy, (military) scout; one engaged in investigative work

جاسوسي dzhāsusí **1** *f.* espionage, agent-intelligence, intelligence collection جاسوسي كول to spy, engage in espionage, do intelligence collection

جاغر dzhāghúr *m.* جاغور **1** magazine, magazine case of a firearm **2** breech assembly of a firearm **3** goiter (in humans)

جاغوردار dahārghurdár *adjective* magazine (of a firearm)

جاغوري dzhaghurí *f. & m. plural* Dzhaguri (district)

جاغه dzhāghá *f.* collar (of a shirt)

جاكارتا dzhākārtá *f.* Jakarta (city)

جاكت dzhākát *m.* جاكټ dzhākáṭ *m.* **1** jacket **2** kind of caracul

جاكړ dzhākáṛ *m.* storm

جاكى dzhākáj **1** curdled, coagulated (of milk, blood, etc.) **2** thickened, congealed

جاگنى dzhāgənáj *m.* stag, bull (of certain horned animals), leader of a herd

جاگير dzhagír *m. history* jagir (fiefdom, land granted to a feudal noble in return for military and other services)

جاگيردار dzhāgirdár *m.* **1** *history* feudal lord, overlord of a jagir **2** landowner

جاگيرداري dzhāgirdārí *f.* **1** *history* feudalism, the jagir system **2** ownership of manorial land

جال[1] dzhāl *m.* custom, rule جالول *compound verb* ☞ جالول

جال[2] dzhāl *m.* **1** net; seine جال اچول to toss a net, cast a net **a** to put a net in place جال غوړول **b** *figurative* to set a snare; use cunning **2** netting د والي بال جال *idiom* **د** volleyball net اوبنكو جال floods of tears

جال[3] dzhāl *m.* ☞ جعل

جال[4] dzhāl *m.* شبكه shabaká *computer science* network

جال چليز dzhāl chalíz *m. computer science* network drive

جالدار dzhāldár netted, reticular

جالار dzhālár *m. regional* edging, hem

جالگى[1] dzhālagáj *m. religion* Goliath

جالگى[2] dzhālagə́j *f.* **1** grillwork (in a window) **2** netting inserts of a chador (for the eyes)

جاله وان dzhālaván *m.* ☞ جاله وان

جالوغ dzhālúgh *m.* horse cloth, horse blanket

جالول dzhālavə́l *denominative, transitive* [*past:* جال يې كړ] to bring into use, make a custom of, make a habit of, make a rule (to act in some way)

جاله[1] dzhā́la *f.* **1** nest جاله كول to make a nest, weave a nest **2** hangar **3** beehive **4** spider web

جاله[2] dzhālá *f.* **1** raft (of timbers, logs) د بارونو جاله barge **2** sheet on which mulberries are shaken from the bush **3** lace جاله جوړول to weave lace, plait lace, crochet lace

جاله[3] dzhālá *f. regional* calamity, misfortune

جاله وان dzhālaván *m.* **1** rower, oarsman; boatman **2** ferryman **3** raftsman **4** Dzhalavan (district, Baluchistan)

جالي dzhālí *f.* جالى dzhālə́j *f.* **1** netting **2** gauze, cheesecloth **3** metal screening **4** kind of (embroidery) stitch **5** spider web **6** *botany* duckweed

جاليدار dzhālidár reticular; having a network

جالېدل dzhāledə́l *denominative, intransitive* [*past:* جال شو] to be observed as a custom or rule

جام[1] dzhām *m.* **1** cup; goblet **2** vessel **3** mirror جمشېد dzhām-i the enchanted mirror of Emperor Jamshed (which showed him whatsoever he desired)

جام[2] dzhām *m.* jam

جامباز dzhāmbáz *m.* **1** pack camel, transport camel **2** camel which has not yet been loaded

جامبره dzhāmbə́ra *f.* jujube

جامبره dzhāmbṛá *f.* thickets, brake; bushes

جامد dzhāmíd *Arabic* **1** frozen **2** hard, stiff **3** inorganic جامدي مادي، جامد مواد inorganic substances

جامدني dzhāmdāní dzhāmadāní **1** *f.* kind of muslin with flowers woven into it **2** having a flowered ornamentation, flowered

جامع dzhāmí *Arabic* **1.1** full, comprehensive **1.2** consisting, composed of **1.3** rich in content, substantial مختصره او جامعه وينا **a** brief but substantive and meaningful speech **1.4** principal, central (used of mosques) **2** *f.* [*plural:* جامع گاني dzhāmi'gāni *Arabic plural:* جوامع dzhavāmí] principal mosque, main mosque د جامع مسجد main mosque

جامعه ¹ dzhāmi'á *f. Arabic* [*plural:* جامعي dzhāmi'e *Arabic f. plural:* جوامع dzhavāmí] 1 society; group, body 2 league, community, commonwealth

جامعه ² dzhāmi'á *Arabic feminine plural of* جامع

جامعه ملل dzhāmi'á-ji-milál *f. history* League of Nations

جامكى dzhāmakáj *m.* shorts, short pants

جامن dzhāmán *m.* جامنو dzhāmanú *m. botany Eugenia jambolana*

جامه ¹ dzhāmá *f.* 1 clothing, dress جامي بدلول، جامه اليشول *a* to change clothes *b figurative* to change, alter, transform جامه تولول to straighten (e.g., the hem of a dress) جامه ماتول to wrinkle a dress, crumple a dress جامي غورځول *a* to remove clothing, throw off clothing, get undressed *b figurative* to lose one's mind جامي كتل *a* to take off clothing *b figurative* to die, depart this world 2 fitting out, equipping (with uniform) 3 color of hide (of cattle) *idiom* د عمل جامه وراغوستل to change, alter, transform to effectuate, put some affair in motion وبره يې د يقين جامه واغوسته His apprehensions were confirmed.

جامه ² dzhāma *f.* ☞ زامه

جامه كښ dzhāmakákh *m.* bath attendant

جامه ور dzhāmavár cut out into a dress (of material)

جان dzhān *m.* 1 life 2 soul 3 beloved one, loved one 4 *affectionate* dear, my soul ښادي جان!، ښادي جانه! Dear Shadi! Shadi My Soul! پلار جان!، پلار جانه! Dear Father!

جانان dzhānān *m.* loved one, beloved one

جانب dzhaníb *Arabic* 1 *m.* [*plural:* جوانب dzhavāníb] [*plural:* جانبين dzhānibájn] side; direction دواړه جانبه both sides مقابل جانب the opposing side د جانبينو په خوښی سره with the consent of both sides اطراف او جوانب the environs 2 in the direction (of)

جانباز ¹ dzhāmbáz *m.* ☞ جامباز

جانباز ² dzhānbáz *m.* جانبازي dzhānbāzí *f.* effort, endeavor; labor, difficulty جانباز كول، جانباز وهل to try, endeavor, take trouble (to)

جانبداري dzhānibdārí *f.* partiality, bias

جانبي dzhānibí *adjective* lateral, side

جانجو dzhāndzhó ☞ جانجي ²

جانجي ¹ dzhāndzhí *m.* participant in the bridegroom's procession at a wedding

جانجي ² dzhāndzháj 1 sluggish; weak 2 lazy

جانجيتوب ¹ dzhāndzhitób *m.* 1 sluggish; weakness 2 laziness

جانجيتوب ² dzhāndzhitób *m.* participation in a wedding procession

جانجبدل dzhāndzhedál *denominative, intransitive* [*past:* جانجي شو] 1 to grow weak; grow sluggish 2 to grow lazy

جانخاني dzhānkhānáj *f.* large bag made of coarse material

جاندار dzhāndār lively, animated

جاندم dzhāndóm *m.* dzhāndúm ☞ جهنم

جانشين dzhānishín *m.* successor; deputy

جانفشان dzhānfishán selfless, dedicated, self-sacrificing جان فشان

جانفشاني dzhānfishāní *f.* 1 selflessness, dedication, self-sacrifice 2 zeal; enthusiasm جانفشاني كول *a* to display dedication, demonstrate self-sacrifice *b* to display zeal, work with enthusiasm

جانكټ dzhānkáṭ *m. colloquial* ☞ جاكټ

جان كندن dzhānkandán *m.* death agony

جان نثار dzhānnisár selfless; ready to sacrifice oneself

جان نثاري dzhānnisārí *f.* selflessness; readiness for self-sacrifice; self-sacrifice

جانور dzhānvár *m.* جانور dzhānvár *m.* 1 animal; wild beast 2 bird (usually one which has been trapped)

جانوله dzhánvala *f.* ☞ ژاوله

جانه ¹ dzhāna *vocative of* جان ښادي جانه! Dear Shadi!

جانه ² dzhāna *f.* darling, dearest, dear بيبو جانه!، بيبو جاني! Dear Bibo! darling! Dear Bibo!

جاني ¹ dzhāni *Eastern* dzhāne *vocative of* جانه بيبو جاني! Bibo darling! Dear Bibo! خور جاني! Dear little sister!

جاني ² dzhānáj *f. proper name* Dzhani

جاني ³ dzhāní *Arabic* 1 sinful; criminal 2 *m.* criminal

جاني خېل dzhānikhél 1 *m. plural* the Dzhanikhejli (a branch of the Mangal Tribe) 2 Dzhanikhejli (tribesman)

جاوا dzhavā́ *f.* Java (island)

جاوجي dzhāvdzhój *f.* 1 edging; selvage 2 hem

جاويدان dzhāvidán ☞ جاوداني

جاويداني dzhavidāní *f.* ☞ جاويداني

جاوله dzhā́vla *f.* ☞ ژاوله

جاويد dzhāvíd جاويدان dzhāvidán eternal, deathless

جاويداني dzhāvidāní *f.* eternity, immorality

جاه dzhāh *m.* high position, office; high rank, rank; title of office

جاه طلبانه dzhāhtalabāná ambitious

جاه طلبي dzhāhtalabí *f.* ambition

جاهل dzhahíl *Arabic* 1 ignorant; stupid 2 *m.* ignoramus, fool

جاهلي dzhāhilí *f.* جاهليت dzhāhiliját *m. Arabic* ignorance; stupidity

جاه وجلال dzhāh-u-dzhalā́l *m.* grandeur, glory

جاى dzhāj *m.* ☞ ضرور جاى، ځاى toilet, latrine

جاى بند dzhājbánd restive (of a horse)

جايداد dzhājdád *m.* 1 real estate 2 property, estate د كليسا جايداد ecclesiastical property

جائز dzhāíz *Arabic* 1 lawful, legal; right, correct 2 permissable, allowed; admissible جائز كول *a* to award, grant; adjudge *b* to permit, allow

جائزه ¹ dzhāizá *f.* 1 reward; recompense; prize د سولي بين المللي International Peace Prize 2 winnings (in a lottery, etc.) 3 *regional* inspection جائزه اخيستل to review, inspect

جائزه ² dzhāizá *feminine singular of* جائز

جايزه ورونكى dzhāizá vrúnkaj *m.* laureate, prize winner

جاي ضرور dzhāj-i-zarúr *m.* toilet, latrine

جايگير dzhājgír *m.* property, estate

جايگيردار dzhājgirdār *m.* landowner

جايگيرداري dzhājgirdārí *f.* ☞ جاگيرداري

جبار dzhabbár *Arabic* 1 potent, powerful 2.1 *m.* giant, colossus 2.2 tyrant, despot

جباړه dzhabāṛá *f.* sleet جباړه ده، جباړه وريږي It is sleeting. Sleet is falling.

جبال dzhabāl *m. Arabic plural of* جبل

جبان dzhabā́n *Arabic* 1 cowardly بې زړه او جبان سړی a coward 2 *m.* coward

جب جوب dzhabdzhúb ☞ جبه جوبه

جبر dzhábr *m.* dzhábar *Arabic* 1 force; violence, compulsion په جبر سره، له جبر نه by force, forcibly, violently 2 injustice

جبراً dzhábrán *Arabic* forcibly, by force

جبران dzhubrā́n *m. Arabic* compensation, damages د خساري جبران **a** compensation for losses **b** forfeiture (of assets for breach of contract) د يوشي جبران کول to compensate, reimburse

جبرانتيا dzhubrāntjā́ *f.* compensation, indemnification په جبرانتيا in the form of compensation, in the form of an indemnity

جبرانول dzhubrānavál *denominative, transitive [past:* جبران يې کړ] 1 to compensate, indemnify 2 to cover (a deficit) 3 to eliminate (deficiencies)

جبرلوټ dzhabərlóṭ *m.* kind of rifle

جبروت dzhabarút *m. Arabic* omnipotence

جبری [1] dzhabráj *m.* garter (for sock, stocking)

جبري [2] dzhabrí *Arabic* 1 forcible, compulsory, obligatory 2 inevitable, unavoidable

جبری [3] dzhabrój *f.* sock, stocking

جبل [1] dzhabál *m. [plural:* جبال dzhabāl] *Arabic* mountain د جبل توپ mountain gun, mountain cannon

جبل [2] dzhəbál *m.* crowbar

جبل السراج dzhabalussurā́dzh *m.* Dzhabalussuradzh

جبل الطارق dzhabal-at-tārík *m. Arabic* Gibraltar د جبل الطارق آبنا، جبل الطارق آبناى the Straits of Gibraltar

جبلت dzhibillát *m. Arabic* natural quality, innate quality, innate characteristic; character, nature

جبلي [1] dzhabalí *Arabic* mountainous

جبلي [2] dzhibillí *Arabic* natural, innate, inborn

جبن dzhubn *m. Arabic* cowardice, pusillanimity

جبه [1] dzhabá *f.* dzhəbá 1 swamp 2 marshy field

جبه [2] dzhubbá *f. Arabic* jubba (masculine outer dress with wide sleeves)

جبه [3] dzhabéh *m. Arabic history* armor; shirt of mail

جبه [4] dzhə́ba *f.* oil tank (on a press)

جبه [5] dzhə́ba *f. dialect* ☞ ژبه

جبه جوبه dzhabá-dzhubá *Eastern* soaked, steeped (in blood)

جبه خانه dzhəbakhāná *f.* 1 arsenal 2 ammunition

جبه زار dzhabazā́r *m.* swampy locality, bog, swamp

جبهه dzhabhá *m. Arabic [plural:* جبهې dzhabhe *plural:* جبهات dzhabāt] front د جبهې ترشا united front يوه متحده جبهه in the rear جبهې ته لېرل to send to the front

جبی [1] dzhəbój *f.* 1 ☞ ژبی 2 stripe (on cloth, etc.)

جبی [2] dzhabé dzhəbé *plural of* جبه [1]

جبی [3] dzhubbé *plural of* جبه [2]

جبي [4] dzhə́bi *plural of* جبه [4]

جبي [5] dzhə́bi *plural of* جبه [5]

جبيره dzhabirá *f. Arabic* 1 *medicine* bandage; splint 2 ☞ جبران

جبين dgabín *m. Arabic poetic [plural:* جبينان dzhabinān] brow, forehead

چپالی dzhəpamārgó چپامرگو dzhəpamārgó *f.* wholesale deaths, high mortality

چپر dzhəpár *m.* worn-out or broken agricultural implements; trash, junk

جت [1] dzhat *m.* shape; appearance

جت [2] dzhat Jat (a group of nomadic tradesmen in western Afghanistan)

جت [3] dzhet ☞ جټ [3]

جت بولي dzhatbolí *f.* impertinence جت بولي کول to be impertinent, be cheeky

جته dzhatá *f.* group, detachment

جتئ dzhatəjí baseborn, of lowly birth

جټ [1] dzheṭ *m.* ☞ جټ [3]

جټ [2] dzhaṭ *m.* Jat (socio-ethnic group)

جټپول dzhaṭpól *m.* 1 cunning 2 magic

جټکه dzhiṭká *f.* ☞ جيټکه

جثه dzhussá *f. Arabic* body, torso

جج [1] dzhadzh *m.* double chin

جج [2] dzhadzh *m. regional* judge

جچکی dzhdzhakáj *m.* ☞ چجه

ججلداخ dzhidzhildā́kh *m.* cicada

ججوره dzhadzhurá *f.* ججوری dzhadzhúraj *m.* 1 crop (of birds), maw 2 dewlap (in animals) 3 ☞ جج [1]

ججوی dzhadzhój *m. botany* anemone

ججه dzhadzhá *f. history* tax (imposed on non-Moslems)

ججی [1] dzhidzháj *m.* pheasant

ججی [2] dzhudzhój *f.* ☞ چوچی [2]

جخ dzhakh *m.* dzhukh 1 ☞ جک [1] 2 bubble (on the surface of water)

جخت dzhukht 1.1 situated alongside; located very close to; abutting, adjoining 1.2 paired, forming a pair 1.3 flat, even, smooth, level 1.4 *regional* exact, correct 2.1 close to; alongside, very closely جخت ولاړ وه They were standing alongside. 2.2 regularly, evenly, smoothly 2.3 *regional* precisely, correctly 2.4 at once *idiom* د .... سره along with ...

جختوالی dzhukhtvā́laj *m.* (the acts of, or states of) adjoining, abutting; being located alongside (of)

جختول dzhukhtavál *denominative, transitive [past:* جخت يې کړ] to put alongside, place alongside, place very close 2 to press (to), clasp (to) سينې پوري جختول to clasp to the breast 3 to select a pair 4 to mate (of animals)

جختي dzhukhtí *f.* ☞ جفتي

جختېدل dzhukhtedál *denominative, intransitive [past:* جخت شو] 1 to be alongside, be very close to; to abut; to adjoin 2 to press oneself (to, against) **3** to approach one another; to be a pair **4** to be mated (of animals)

جد dzhad *m.* dzhadd [*plural:* اجداد adzhdád] *Arabic* **1** grandfather **2** forefather

جد dzhid *m.* dzhidd *Arabic* endeavor, effort; diligence

جدا dzhudá *adjective* **.1** section; separate, solitary; isolated **1.2** separated; severed, parted **1.3** alienated **1.4** special دا جدا خبره ده This is a special (peculiar) problem. **1.5** separate (i.e., a seperate peace) جدا کول *a* to separate, disjoin; isolate *b* to sever, part جدا کبدل *a* to be separated, be disjoined; be isolated *b* to be separated, be severed, be parted **2.1** separately, apart; in isolation **2.2** specially, peculiarly

جداً dzhíddán *Arabic* assiduously, zealously, diligently, vigorously

جدا جدا dzhudá-dzhudá ☞ جدا 2

جدار dzhidár *m. Arabic* wall, divider, partition *idiom* د تتر جدار chest, thorax, rib cage

جدا کبده dzhudákedə *m. plural* **1** section, sectioning, disconnection, isolating **2** parting, leave-taking

جداگانه dzhudagáná **1** special, extraordinary (of a representative) **2** specially

جدال dahidál *m. Arabic* quarrel, argument; squabble, row

جداول dzhadávíl *Arabic masculine plural of* جدول

جدائي dzhudáí *f.* parting يو له بله يي جدائي نه درلوده They did not part. They did not take leave of one another.

جدر dzhadár *m. Arabic* root, basis

جدل dzhadál *m. Arabic* dispute, argument

جدوار dzhadvár *m.* zedoary root (rhizome of *Curcuta zedoaria*)

جدوجهد dzhidd-u-dzháhd *m.* efforts, endeavors

جدول dzhadvál *m. Arabic* **1** table **2** list **3** manuscript copy, enumeration **4** ruled sheet, sheet of graph paper **5** column of a table, column of a page **6** schedule (of tasks, duties, etc.) **7** *grammar* paradigm

جدول کشي dzhadvalkashí *f.* drawing, sketch د جدول کشي اسباب *drawing instruments*, case of drawing instruments

جدولي dzhadvalí ruled, ruled off into squares

جده dzhiddá *f.* Jidda

جدي dzhadí *m. Arabic* **1** *astronomy* Capricorn (the constellation) **2** Jadi (the 10th month of the solar year; 22 December - 20 January)

جدي dzhiddí *Arabic* **1** assiduous, fervid; active, energetic, vigorous **2** serious (of a question, etc.) **3** bold, quick

جدي dzhaddí *Arabic* pertaining to forefathers, ancestral

جديانه dzhiddijáná decisive (of measures, etc.)

جديت dzhiddiját *m. Arabic* **1** zeal, fervor; activity, energy په جديت سره diligently; actively; energetically **2** criticality, critical in nature (of a problem); seriousness (of a question, etc.) **3** boldness

جديد dzhadíd *Arabic* new; contemporary

جديداً dzhadídán newly

جديدالاسلام dzhadid-ul-islám *Arabic* newly converted to Islam (of the Nuristani)

جديدالتاسيس dzhadid-ut-tāsís *Arabic* newly founded, newly established

جديدالزرع dzhadid-uz-zár' *Arabic* newly acquired (of lands)

جديدي Jadidí (name given to the Kafiri-Nuristani after their conversion to Islam)

جذاب dzhazzáb *Arabic* **1** absorbing, fascinating جذابه قصه absorbing story **2** attractive

جذابي dzhazzābí *f.* جذابيت dzhazzābiját *m.* **1** fascination **2** attractiveness

جذام dzhuzám *m. medicine* leprosy

جذب dzhazb *m. Arabic* **1** attraction, allurement **2** leaning, bent **3** absorption, soaking up **4** *physics* gravity, attraction جذب کول *compound verb* ☞ جذب کبدل، جذبول *compound verb* ☞ جذبول

جذبات dzhazbát *Arabic* **1** *masculine plural of* جذبه **2** spirit انقلابي revolutionary

جذباتي dzhazbātí emotional

جذبول dzhazbavól **1** *denominative* [*past:* جذب يي کړ] **.1** to attract, fascinate **1.2** to draw, pull (up) **1.3** to absorb, soak up **1.4** *physics* to attract (magnetically) **2** *m. plural* **.1** attraction, fascination **2.2** adducing **2.3** absorbing, soaking up **2.4** *physics* attraction د مګکي جذبول gravitation

جذبه dzhazbá *f.* [*plural:* جذبي dzhazbé *Arabic m. plural:* جذبات dzhazbát] **1** strong feeling **2** enthusiasm; animation; ecstasy **3** agitation, emotion

جذبدل dzhazbedól *denominative, intransitive* [*past:* جذب شو] **1** to be attracted, be fascinated **2** to be absorbed, be soaked up **3** *physics* to be attracted (magnetism)

جذر dzhazr *m. Arabic* **1** *math* root جذر تربيعي quadratic root جذر حاصلول to extract a root **2** descent, extraction

جر dzhar *m.* ford

جر dzhar *m.* **1** small irrigation ditch; ditch, gutter جر ايستل to construct an irrigation ditch or conduit **2** cleft, fissure

جر dzhar dzharr *m. Arabic* **1** drawing (as wire); carrying away **2** *grammar* oblique case د جر حرف preposition, postposition

جر dzhar **1** confused, muddled up **2** obstinate **3** jaded, feeling down, defeated, beaten down

جراپه dzhurápa *f.* sock, stocking

جرات dzhurát *m.* **1** boldness, daring, courage جرات ميندل to grow bold, grow brave **2** resolution, determination *a* په جرات سره to display boldness, display daring, display courage *b* to behave decisively, act resolutely *c* to dare, take the liberty of د وتلو جرات مي نه شو کولئ *Eastern* I did not dare to leave.

جراثيم dzharāsím *m. Arabic plural* microorganisms

جراح dzharráh *m. Arabic* surgeon

جراحت dzharāhát *m. Arabic* wound; ulcer; sore

جراحي dzharrāhí *f. Arabic* **1** surgery د جراحي آلات surgical instruments د جراحي د عملياتو مبز operating د جراحي چاقو lancet د

table 2 [*plural:* جراحی dzharrahə́j *plural:* جراحيگاني dzharrahigani] surgical operation

جرار dzharrā́r *Arabic* 1 warlike, bellicose; brave 2 battle-worthy, fit for combat

جراسک dzhərāsák *m.* cricket

جرائد dzharāíd *m. Arabic* 1 *plural from* جريده 2 the press

جرايل dzharājə́l *m.* ☞ جزايل

جرائم dzharāím *Arabic masculine plural of* جريمه

a جرائم پيشه سرى dzharāimpeshá criminal, felonious جرائم پيشه criminal

جرب dzharáb *m. Arabic* scab, rash, mange

جربى dzharpáj garrulous

جرثقيل dzharr-i-saķíl *m.* crane, derrick

جرجير dzhirdzhír *m. Arabic botany* watercress

جرح dzharh *f.* جرحه dzhárha *f. Arabic* wound

جرړه ¹ dzhə́rra *f.* 1 rootlet, root (of a plant) 2 cotton

جرړه ² dzhírra *f.* ☞ چرړه

جرزايل dzharzājə́l *m.* ☞ جزايل

جرس dzharás *m. Arabic* bell, hand bell

جرعه dzhur'á *f. Arabic* mouthful, drink

جرقه dzharķá *f.* spark د برق جرقه electrical spark

جركني dzharkaní *f.* action of digging a ditch (in order to drain a swamp)

جرگه ماو dzhərgāvú *m.* ☞ جرگه مار

جرگټو dzhirgáṭu *m.* جرگوال dzhərgavāl *m.* member of a jirga (council)

جرگه dzhə́rga *f.* dzhirgá dzhargá 1 jirga, council of elders, council of tribe or clan members; gathering, assembly لويه جرگه، لو جرگه The Loya Jirga (convenes to decide the most important questions) 2 meeting, conference, gathering; convention د ليكوالو جرگه Conference of Writers جرگه كول to meet, confer; conduct a meeting, hold a conference د چا سره جرگي كول to conduct a meeting with someone جرگه كېدل *compound verb* a to take place (of a jirga, an assembly) b to meet, assemble (at a jirga, assembly) c to meet, confer 3 commission 4 the adat (traditional Islamic law code) 5 matchmakers (go-betweens between parents of prospective couples) په چا جرگه كول to send matchmakers, send marriage brokers *idiom* رسمي جرگي official circles

جرگه گى dzhərgagə́j *f.* 1 commission, committee 2 colloquium; seminar

جرگه مار dzhərgamár *m.* an expert in adat (traditional Islamic law)

جرگه وال dzhərgavāl *m.* جرگه والا dzhərgavālā́ *m.* 1 member of a jirga 2 marriage broker, go-between in arranging a marriage

جرم ¹ dzhurm *m. Arabic* fault, misdemeanor; crime د جرم مرتكب criminal

جرم ² dzhirm *m.* dzhirmúna *Arabic* [*plural:* جرمونه dizhirúna *Arabic plural:* اجرام adzhrā́m] *physics* body, mass آسماني اجرام heavenly bodies

جرم ³ dzhurm *m.* Dzhurm (city)

جرمن dzharmə́n *m.* 1 Germany 2 German

جرمني dzharmə́ní 1.1 *m.* Germany 1.2 German (person) 2 *adjective* German

جرموړه dzharmoṛá *f.* ☞ جرموړه

ژرندگري dzhrandagáraj ☞ ژرندگري

ژرنده ¹ dzhrə́nda ☞ ژرنده

جندره ² dzhahránda *f.* ☞ جندره

جرندى dzharandáj *m.* 1 shaft regulating the speed of revolution of the millstones in a mill 2 sliding latch (of a door)

شرنگ dzhrang *m.* ☞ شرنگ

ژورنالست dzhurnalíst *m.* ☞ ژورنالست

جرنېل dzharnél *m. colloquial* general جرنېل ملكي general (chief of tribal militia) ☞ جنرال

جرنېلي dzharnelí 1 *adjective* pertaining to the rank of general; general's 2 *f.* rank of general *idiom* جرنېلي سړک highway, main road

جره ¹ dzhará *m.* bachelor, unmarried man

جره ² dzhurrá *m.* [*plural:* جره گان dzhurragā́n *plural:* جره يان dzhurrajā́n] hawk (male)

جره ³ dzhará *f.* ☞ جره ¹

جره توب dzharatób *m.* جره والى dzharavā́laj *m.* single life, unmarried condition

جري ¹ dzharrí *Arabic grammar* inflected, variable حالت جري oblique form

جري ² dzharé *plural of* جره ³

جريان dzharajā́n *m.* dzhirjā́n *Arabic* [*plural:* جريانونه dzharajānúna *Arabic plural:* جريانات dzharājanā́t] 1 movement, circulation; flow د هوا جريان circulation of air 2 flow, course (of time, events, etc.) 3 progress (of a matter, etc.) جريان لرل to be conducted, be carried on 4 trend (political, social) 5 *electronics* current متناوب جريان alternating current مستقيم جريان direct current پوزيتيف جريان positive electrical current منفي جريان negative electrical current *idiom* جريان شكم dzharajā́n-i- *idiom* dysentery

جريانات dzharajānā́t *m. Arabic* 1 *plural of* جريان 2 events سياسي جريانات political events 3 processes اجتماعي جريانات social processes 4 process (of development, growth)

جريب dzharíb *m. Arabic* jerib (an area measurement equivalent to 1952 sq. meters) جريب كول *compound verb* ☞ جريبول

جريب كش dzharibkásh *m.* surveyor

جريبول dzharibavál *denominative, transitive* [*past:* جريب كړ] 1 to measure in jeribs 2 to carry out surveying work

جريده dzharidá *f. m. Arabic* [*plural:* جريدي dzharidé] *m. Arabic* [*plural:* جرائد dzharāíd] newspaper (not a daily); magazine; periodical

جريده ليكونكى dzharidá likúnkaj *m.* journalist

جريز dzhəríz *m.* sweet gruel, porridge

جريمانه dzharimaná *f.* جريمانه كول to fine

جريمه dzharimá *f. Arabic* [*plural:* جريمي dzharimé *m. Arabic plural:* جرائم dzharāím] fine

جړ ¹ dzhaṛ *m.* **1** root (of a tree) **2** poison جړ ورکول to administer poison, poison *idiom* جړکول to be rooted in something

جړ ² dzhaṛ **1** tangled, entangled (of threads, etc.) **2** complex, complicated (of a problem) جړکول **a** to tangle, tangle up (threads, etc.) **b** to complicate (a problem) جړکېدل **a** to be tangled, be tangled up (thread) **b** to become complicated, get complicated (a problem, question) **c** to rush about, rush from one side to another

جړ ³ dzhuṛ *m.* **1** seething, boiling, bubbling up **2** rumbling (in the stomach) جرجر کول to rumble **3** babbling, murmur (of a brook) جړکول **a** to boil, seethe, bubble up **b** to babble, murmur

جړا dzhaṛá *f.* ☞ ژړا

جړمبو dzharambó sluggish, slack; weakened, enervated

جړنگو dzhaṛángú *m.* **1** purging cassia, *Cassia fistula* (a medicinal plant) **2** Egyptian willow

جړاو dzhaṛắv decorated with precious stones ☞ جړاو کول جړاوول

جړاوول dzhaṛavavál *denominative, transitive* [*past:* جړاو یې کړ] **1** to decorate with precious stones **2** to place in a setting (diamond)

جړاوه dzhaṛावá *f.* kind of decoration or ornament of precious stones

جړاوېدل dzhaṛavedál *denominative, transitive* [*past:* جړاو شو] to be decorated with precious stones

جړپړ dzhaṛpáṛ *m. medicine* laxative

جړجر dzhaṛdzhóṛ empty, useless

جړجړی dzhuṛdzhuṛáj *m.* waterfall, cascade, cataract

جړق dzhaṛk *m.* جرک dzhaṛk *m. regional* jolt, shove, shock, tremor ځما زړه یو جړق او خور My heart skipped a beat. My heart went pitapat.

جړکانی dzhaṛkắnaj *m.* dzhuṛkắnaj increase, supplement

جړکژروک dzhaṛkzhṛúk *m.* shaking, jolting, bumps

جړل dzhaṛál *transitive* ☞ ژړل

جړمړی dzhaṛmóṛáj *f.* antidote (for poison)

جړموړه dzhaṛmoṛá *f.* **1** *medicine* nettlerash جرموړه کول to suffer from nettlerash **2** lump (from the bite of an insect)

جړند dzhuṛónd *m.* ☞ جلغ

جړنگاوو dzṛəngāvú *m.* rattle

جړنگهار dzhṛəngahắr *m.* جړنگی dzhṛangáj *m.* sound of small bells, sound of chimes

جوروبی dzhuṛobáj *m.* dzhəṛobáj ☞ جوروبی

جړول dzhaṛavál *transitive* ☞ ژړول

جړه ¹ dzhaṛá *f.* rose

جړه ² dzhaṛá *f.* root (of a tree) *idiom* جړي وېستل *regional* to root out, to eradicate, eliminate

جړي ¹ dzhaṛí *f.* **1** bark (of a dog) **2** cry, noise, din, uproar جړي وهل **a** to go for while barking (dog) **b** to howl, cry out

جړي ² dzhaṛój *f.* foul weather, bad weather, rains, downpours په تېره میاشت کښې ډېري جړي وې Last month there were many heavy showers.

جړی ³ dzhaṛój *f.* root of a plant used as an antidote for snakebite

جړي باجړي dzhaṛí-bādzhaṛí *f. plural* mud, slush

جړېدل dzhaṛeḍál *intransitive* ☞ ژړل

جړېدنه dzhaṛeḍóna *f.* dialect ☞ ژړا

جز ¹ dzhəz *m.* **1** hissing **2** bite (of snake, scorpion, wasp) جز کول to hiss **b** *compound verb* to bite, sting جز کېدل **a** to hiss **b** to be bitten, be stung

جز ² dzhuz *m. Arabic* [*plural:* جزونه dzhuzúna *Arabic plural:* اجزا adzhzắ] **1** part, particle; portion, component of something else د یو شي جز گرزیدل to be a component of something else **2** edition (of a literary work); part (of a book) **3** printed page

جزا ¹ dzhazắ *f.* [*plural:* جزاگاني dzhazagắni *Arabic plural:* جزاوي dahazắvi] **1** punishment, retribution د یو شي جزا گرزیدل to be punished, suffer punishment; pay (for) جزا ورکول to punish, inflict punishment upon په جزا محکومول to sentence, impose sentence upon په جزا محکومېدل to be sentenced, have sentence imposed **2** outcome, conclusion **3** *grammar* main clause (in conditional sentence)

جزا ² dzhəzắ *f.* ☞ جزهار

جزاک الله dzhazák-alláh *Arabic* **1** May Allah reward him! **2** bravo; well-done; excellent

جزائر dzhazáir *m. Arabic plural* **1** *of* جزیره ☞ الجزائر **2**

جزایري dzhāzirí **1** Algerian **2** *m.* Algerian (person)

جزایل dzhazájəl *m.* long-barreled musket

جزایلچي dzhazájəlchí *m.* musketeer, soldier armed with a musket

جزائي dzhazári *Arabic* **1** punitive **2** criminal جزائي تدابير اداري disciplinary measures

جزبازي dzhuzbāzí *f.* hopscotch

جزبیز dzhizbíz *f.* game of knucklebones ☞ بجل

جزبندي dzhuzbandí *f.* stitching جزبندي کول to stitch (e.g., commercial stitching of pages in books, pamphlets)

جزدان dzhuzdán *m.* **1** notebook **2** folder (for paper)

جزر dzhazr *m. Arabic* ebb tide

جزغاله dzhizghālá heating up, roasting

جزکی dzhəzkáj *m.* ☞ جز ¹

جزم dzhazm *m. Arabic* **1** truncation, cutting off د جزم علامه sukun (the name of the supralinear symbol, which indicates that no vowel sound follows) **2** amputation **3** decision *idiom* د جزم قوي روح decisiveness

جزو dzhuzv *m. Arabic* ☞ جز ²

جزوتام dzhuzutám *m. Arabic military* unit; formation (at any level) حربي جزوتام combat unit

جزوکاري dzhuzvkārí *f.* detail work, fine details

جزوکل dzhuz-u-kúl fully, in full

جزول dzhəzavál *transitive* [*past:* و یې جزاوه] **1** to cause hissing, cause sputtering **2** to sting, bite **3** to fry, roast, grill

جزوي dzhuzví *Arabic* insignificant جزوي تاوان slight damage, insignificant loss

جزهار dzhəzahār *m.* جزهاری dzhəzaháraj *m.* hissing, sputtering (e.g., of roasting meat)

جزېدل dzhəzedál *intransitive* [*past:* وجزیده] to hiss, sputter (e.g., of roasting meat)

جزیره dzhazirá *f. Arabic* [*plural:* جزیري dzhaziré *Arabic plural:* جزائر dzhazáir] island

جزیره غوني dzhaziraghúne *f.* جزیره نما dzhaziranumá peninsula

جزیه dzhizjá *f. Arabic* poll tax; tax; land tax

جزئي dzhuzí *Arabic* 1 petty, insignificant 2 personal, separate, private

جزئیات dzhuzijāt *m. Arabic plural* details, particulars; minutiae نور جزئیات other details

جرږ dzhǝg *m.* blow or stroke with a knife (in butchering cattle)

جرږکی dzhǝgkáj *m.* sound of flowing or streaming blood

جرږگی dzhǝggáj *m.* hedgehog

جرغمه dzhǝ́gma *f.* eyelid

جرږهار dzhǝgǝhár *m.* ☞ جرږکی

جس dzhas *m. plural* ☞ جست

جسارت dzhasārát *m. Arabic* bravery, courage, valiance; audacity

جسامت dzhasāmát *m. Arabic* size, sizes; scope; magnitude

جست dzhast *m. plural* zinc

جست dzhǝst جست دربدل to stand rooted to the ground جست غورَهُبدل to make a strong leap; rush headlong

جستجو dzhustudzhó *f.* searches جستجو کول to search

جست وخبز dzhust-u-khéz *m. philosophy* great advance, great leap forward

جسته dzhisǝtá *f.* kind of woman's slipper

جستي dzhastí zinc; zinc-plated جستي اوسپنه galvanized-iron sheeting

جستي dzhisǝté *plural of* جسته

جسد dzhasád *m. Arabic* 1 body, corpus د مري جسد cadaver 2 hull, frame, fuselage

جسر dzhisr *m. Arabic* pontoon, pontoon bridge

جسم dzhism *m. Arabic* [*plural:* اجسام adzhsám] 1 body مایع جسم *physics* liquid body ابخدار جسم *math* polyhedron 2 deposit معدني جسم *geology* continous deposit

جسماني dzhismāní *Arabic* corporeal; physical جسماني سپورت physical training; gymnastics

جسماً dzhísmán *Arabic* corporeally; physically جسماً او روحاً physically and morally

جسمي dzhismí *Arabic* 1 corporeal, physical جسمي ضعف physical weakness 2 material; substantive

جسور dzhasúr *Arabic* brave, bold, valorous جسور سرى brave lad, valorous fellow

جسورانه dzhasurāná boldly, bravely, valorously

جسیم dzhasím *Arabic* cumbersome, massive

جشکی dzhǝshkáj *m.* hedgehog

جشن dzhashn *m.* holiday, festival جشن کول to celebrate جشنونه نیول to arrange festivities د ۲۵ کال جشن په هَای رسول to celebrate a 25th anniversary

جشی dzhíshaj *m.* agrimony, burdock

جعبه dzha'bá *f. Arabic* 1 drawer (e.g., of a table) 2 bellows (of a smithy) 3 box *idiom* د آواز جعبه *anatomy* larynx

جعبه يي ساز dzha'baí expanding, expandable *idiom* جعبه يي accordion

ج،ع،ج *official abbreviation* the title of the prime minister جناب عاليقدر جلالتمآب

جعفر dzha'fár *m. proper name* Jafar

جعفري dzha'farí *m. botany* marigolds

جعفري dzha'farí *f.* grating, grill

جعل dzha'l *Arabic* 1 *m.* counterfeit, falsification 2 *predicative* fake, counterfeit, falsified جعل کول *compound verb* to counterfeit, falsify

جعلسازي dzha'lsāzí *adjective* pretense; shame; dissembling

جعل کاري dzha'lkārí *f.* forgery, falsification

جعلي dzha'lí 1 ☞ جعل 2 imaginary; unreal; deceptive

جغ dzǝgh dzhugh *m.* 1 yoke جغ د کولبي yoke of a plow 2 *figurative* yoke, oppression

جغ dzhǝgh *m.* hissing, sputtering (e.g., of roasting meat)

جغا dzhǝhá *f.* ☞ جرهار

جغات dzhǝghát *m.* effort, labor

جغانغه dzhǝghanēghá *f. botany* amaranthus, cock's comb

جغاول dzhǝghāvól *m.* 1 necklace 2 collar (e.g., for a dog)

جغبوز dzhǝghbúz *m.* blacksmith

جغتو dzhghatú *m.* Jaghatu (district)

جغدي dzhughdí 1 roasted 2 burned up

جغرافي dzhughrāfí geographic

جغرافیا dzhughrāfijá *f.* geography د جغرافیا عالم geographer

جغرافیایي dzhughrāfijāí geographic

جغرافیه dzhughrāfijá *f.* ☞ جغرافیا

جغرافیه دان dzhughrāfijadán *m.* geographer

جغرى dzhugharój *f.* formation of sores (on the toes from dirt, pollution)

جغ لندی dzhughlandáj *m. agriculture* one of a pair of wooden members on each side of a yoke through which the animal's head is inserted

جغله dzhaghalá *f.* gravel, crushed stone, riprap جغله اچول to surface a road with gravel

جغن پری dzhǝghǝnpóraj *m.* rope fastening the yoke to the pole of a cart

جغندر dzhughandár *m. singular & plural* ☞ چغندر

جغنډ dzhǝghánḍ *m.* ☞ ژغنډ

جغنډه dzhǝghǝnḍó *m.* ☞ ژغنډه

جغوندی dzhǝghunḍáj *m.* ☞ جغ لندی

جغه dzhǝghá *f.* ☞ جیغه

جغهار dzhǝgahár *m.* ☞ جرهار

جغی dzhigháj *m.* 1 woven wicker litter (for transporting corpses) 2 wicker basket

جغبدل dzhughedól *intransitive* [*past:* وجغبده] 1 to pester, be importunate 2 را جغبدل، در جغبدل، ور جغبدل to display persistence

جغبدلی dzhughedólaj 1 *past participle of* جغبدل 2.1 importunate 2.2 persistent

جفا ¹ dzhafá *f. Arabic* **1** oppression, suppression **2** cruelty **3** offense, injury جفاکول **a** to oppress, suppress **b** to act cruelly toward someone **c** to injure, offend جفاورل **a** to endure oppression **b** to bear, put up with injury, insult

جفاکار dzhafākár **1** cruel **2** *m.* .**1** oppressor **2.2** offender

جفاکاري dzhafākārí *f.* **1** oppression; violence **2** cruelty **3** insult, injury

جفت ¹ dzhuft **1** *m.* pair خلور جفته بوټ four pairs of boots **2** paired; even جفت عداد even numbers

جفت ² dzhuft ☞ جخت

جفتکه dzhuftáka *f.* kicking with both feet جفتکه وهل to kick with both feet

جفتي dzhuftí *f. agriculture* mating, breeding, coupling جفتي کول to mate, couple

جق جق dzhakdzhák *m.* **1** cackling, clucking **2** chatter **a** جق جق کول to cackle, cluck **b** to chatter, speak without a break

جک ¹ dzhak *m.* small waterbug جک وهل **a** to talk nonsense **b** to be occupied with trivia or nonsense; do stupid things جک! مه وهه Don't act stupidly!

جک ² dzhak *m.* churn; oil press

جکت dzhakát *m.* ☞ جاکت

جکړ ¹ dzhakář *m.* storm, thunderstorm

جکړ ² dzhakář sluggish; lazy

جکړ ³ dzhikář *m.* destruction, ruin

جکه جکه dzháka-dzháka *f.* protracted quarrel; altercation

جگ ¹ dzhag *m.* jug, pitcher

جگ ² dzhəg dzhig **1** high, towering, elevated جگ کور tall house جگه سیمه height **2** tall, strapping **3** upright, vertical **4** high (of voice, noise) په جگ غږ ويل to cry out **5** high (of price) جگول ☞ high-priced جگ کول

جگار dzhəgár *m.* heat of battle

جگتوب dzhəgtób *m.* جگتیا dzhigtób *f.* جگتیا dzhəgtjá *f.* dzhigtjá ☞ جگوالی

جگتورن dzhəgturán *m.* captain

جگ جگ dzhig dzhíg sound by which a bull is urged on to fight جگ کول to urge a bull to fight

جگجگی ¹ dzhəgdzhigí *m.* جگجگی dzhəgdzhigə́j *f.* butting (as of horned animals)

جگجگی ² dzhəgdzhəgə́j *f.* coaxing, prevailing upon

جگ جور dzhəg-dzhór completely healthy; in the pink

جگ خوله dzhəgkhulá جگ خوله توپ antiaircraft cannon

جگر dzhigár *m. combining form* liver

جگرخوار dzhigarkhár جگرخور dzhigarkhór جگرخون dzhigarkhún suffering

جگرخوني dzhifarkhuní *f.* **1** suffering ډېري جگرخوني پر راغلي دي He has suffered a lot. **2** grief

جگري dzhigarí **1** crimson **2** hepatic

جگر ¹ dzhəgár *m.* hut or temporary cabin (for hunters, etc.) made of straw and brush

جگړاوو dzhagrāvú pugnacious جگړاوو سړی دئ He is a quarrelsome fellow.

جگرن dzhagrə́n *m.* **1** *military* major **2** warrior, soldier **3** *plural obsolete* troops

جگرني ¹ dzhagrənáj **1** fighting **2** military جگرني قوتونه troops, forces

جگرني ² dzhagrəni *f. military* the rank of major; the title of major دجگرني رتبه the rank of major

جگروال ¹ dzhagravál ☞ جگرني

جگرول dzhagravúl *transitive dialect* ☞ جنگول

جگړه dzhagrá *f.* dzhəgára **1** war دنړی جگړه، عمومي جگړه world war ذروي جگړه imperialist war امپریالیستي جگړه civil war داخلي جگړه thermonuclear war, nuclear war سره جگړه cold war د جگړې طاقت combat effectiveness **2** battle, clash, engagement, skirmish; conflict **3** struggle طبقاتي جگړه class struggle, class warfare سیاسي جگړه political struggle د ژوندون جگړه struggle for existence د ضدینو جگړه، د اضدادو جگړه *philosophy* struggle of antitheses, struggle of oppsing viewpoints **4** fight **5** quarrel; argument په جگړه کېدل **a** to come into conflict **b** to quarrel جگړه کول **a** to go to war, conduct warfare **b** to engage in battle, join a battle **c** to carry on a struggle, struggle **d** to fight **e** to quarrel, argue

جگړه مار dzhagramár **1** *m.* .**1** warlike, bellicose man, warrior **1.2** troublemaker **1.3** warmonger **2** *attributive* .**1** combat; warring جگړه مار عسکر active army, army in the field **2.2** bellicose **2.3** peevish

جگړه ناک dzhagranák disputed جگړه ناک مورد a moot point, case in dispute

جگړیال dzhagarjál جگړیالی dzhagarjāláj **1** bellicose **2** combat, combative; warring

جگړیځ dzhagərídz جگړئی dzhagrə́i combat, operational جگړیځ ډگر the field of battle

جگړیدل dzhagredə́l *intransitive dialect* ☞ جنگیدل

جگکتوری dzhəgkatóraj *m.* glass

جگن dzhagán sedge

جگناتی dzhəgnātə́j *f.* kind of unbleached muslin

جگواله dzhəgvála *f.* جگوالی dzhəgválaj **1** altitude; height د مثلث جگواله the altitude of a triangle **2** stature

جگول dzhəgavə́l *denominative, transitive* [*past:* جگ یی کړ] **1** to raise, raise slightly لاس جگول to raise the hand بیرق جگول to raise the flag **2** to compel to stand up, make rise **3** to rise into the air (e.g., a plane) **4** to thrust (a point) into نښتر جگول to sting (of a wasp, etc.) **5** to stir up, foment (mutiny, rebellion) **6** to develop, move forward **7** to raise (prices) **8** to mount (a horse, etc.) *idiom* فصل جگول to gather in the harvest

جگه ¹ dzhə́ga *f.* altitude, height; summit; eminence; raised place, highland جگه او تیټه mountains and valleys

جگه ² dzhigá *f.* married woman

جگه ³ dzhə́ga *feminine singular of* جگ ²

جگی ¹ dzhigə́j *f.* entreaty جگی، جگی کول، جگی کول *a* to entreat *b* to obtain the favorable notice of someone, get on the good side of someone

جگی ² dzhəgáj rather high

جگي جگي dzhəgí-dzhəgí welcome (as a greeting)

جگېدل dzhəgedə́l *denominative* [*past:* جگ شو] 1 to tower up, rise, rise up, go up 2 to get up, mount, ascend په بام جگېدل to get up on the roof په غره جگېدل to ascend the mountain 3 to climb (aircraft), make an ascent د تعظیم دپاره جگېدل to arise in order to greet, pay respect to someone گئیز په څو بجو جگېږې؟ When do you get up in the morning? 4 to rise (get louder, of noise) 5 *figurative* to ascend the heights, succeed 6 to rebel, rise up against someone څوی پلار ته نه جگېږي A son does not rebel against his father.

جگېده dzhəgedə́ *m. plural noun of agent from* جگېدل

جل ¹ dzhal *m.* 1 hot wind; simoon جل وهل *a* to be destroyed or be ruined by a simoon *b* to have sunstroke

جل ² dzhal *m. dialect* moat (around a castle)

جل ³ dzhal *m.* skylark (the bird)

جل ⁴ dzhul *m.* 1 hiding; concealment 2 limitation, constraint

جل ⁵ dzhə́l *f.* [*plural:* جلي dzhə́li] girl

جل ⁶ dzhal *m.* 1 hedge 2 gateway 3 thorn bushes used as a windbreak around a house

جل ⁷ dzhálla *Arabic* ☞ جل جلاله

جلا ¹ dzhalá *f.* dzhilá *Arabic* exile, separation

جلا ² dzhalá *f. Arabic* polishing; imparting luster; burnishing جلا ورکول to polish, burnish

جلا ³ dzhə́lá 1.1 separate; disconnected; withdrawn; severed 1.2 weaned (from the breast) 1.3 drained (of a canal, irrigation channel) هغه فکر نه راځخه جلا كول *a* to separate; divide; part کېږي This thought will not leave. *b* to be weaned (from the breast) *c* to be drained (canal, irrigation ditch) 2 separately, apart, aloof جلا اوسېدل to live separately, live apart, live alone

جلاب ¹ dzhulá́b *m. Arabic* laxative جلاب کول to take a laxative جلاب ورکول to administer a laxative

جلاب ² dzhallá́b *m. Arabic* 1 secondhand dealer, speculator 2 herdsman, cattle dealer

جلات dzhə́lát 1 *m.* .1 brave person 1.2 *proper name* Jalat 1.3 ☞ جلاد 2 *attributive* cruel, inhuman

جلاتوب dzhə́látób *m.* 1 separation 2 solitude

جلاجل dzhuládzhíl *m.* bells (hung from the neck of a camel, etc.)

جلاد dzhallá́d *m. Arabic* executioner

جلادي dzhala2dí *f.* 1 occupation of executioner 2 cruelty, heartlessness

جلار dzhalá́r *m.* irrigation wheel (worked on a stream bank)

جلال dzhalá́l *m. Arabic* greatness, glory

جلال آباد dzhalálábád *m.* Jelalabad (city)

جلال الدین dzhalāluddín *m. Arabic proper name* Jelal-ed-din

جلالتمآب dzhalālatmaáb *m. Arabic* (his) Excellency (in addressing by title)

جلال کوټ dzhalālkóṭ *m.* ☞ جلال آباد

جلاله dzhə́lala *f.* spring

جلاوالی dzhalāvā́laj *m.* 1 separation, division 2 parting 3 estrangement

جلاوطن dzhalāvatán dzhilāvatán *Arabic* 1 *m.* .1 banishment 1.2 emigre 1.3 exile 1.4 emigration 2 pertaining to emigration جلاوطن کول to expel, exile جلاوطن کېدل to leave one's native land, emigrate

جلاوطنه dzhalāvatā́na dzhilāvatā́na emigre, one who has emigrated

جلاوطني dzhalāvataní *f.* dzhilāvataní 1 emigration 2 banishment

جلایش dzhilājísh *m.* ☞ جلا ²

جلب ¹ dzhalb *m. Arabic* 1 attraction (of attention) 2 involvement (in something) 3 *military* call-up د افرادو جلب summons to military service 4 *physics* attraction

جلب ² dzhalá́b *m.* dzhilá́b د چا جلب کول، دچا سره جلب کول جلو to escort someone

جلباب dzhalbá́b *m. Arabic* 1 veil 2 bed curtain of netting (protection against flies)

جلب النظار dzhalb-un-nazár *m. Arabic* attraction of attention جلب النظار کول to attract attention

جلبل ¹ dzhalbá́l 1 *m.* .1 experience, suffering جلبل کول *compound verb* to torment, inflict suffering upon جلبل کېدل *compound verb* to suffer, experience suffering 1.2 brightness 2.1 *predicative regional* burned down 2.2 burned 2.3 *figurative* infuriated, hot-tempered

جلبل ² dzhalbál adorned; dressed up جلبل کول to adorn; dress up جلبل کېدل to be adorned; be dressed up

جلبلي dzhalbə́lí sparkling, radiant, glittering

جلبنگ dzhalbáng *m.* جلبنگي dzhabangí *f.* 1 stinging nettle 2 *dialect* reed

جلبول dzhalbavə́l *denominative, transitive* [*past:* جلب يې کړ] 1 to attract (attention) 2 to involve in something, attract to something 3 to call up (to military service)

جلبي ¹ dzhalbí *m. military* draftee

جلبي ² dzhalabə́j *f.* ☞ ځلوبی

جلبېدل dzhalbedə́l *denominative, intransitive* [*past:* جلب شو] 1 to be attracted (of attention) 2 to be involved in something, be attracted to something 3 to be called up, be drafted (for military service)

جلت dzhalt 1 agile, quick; fast (of a horse) 2 rapid, hurried

جلته dzhə́lata *f.* 1 corncrib made of wicker material 2 woven basket *idiom* ځان په جلته ورسره اچول to adjoin, join oneself to someone

جلتي dzhaltí *f.* جلتیا dzhaljá́ *f.* 1 agility; speed (of horse) 2 rapidity, haste په پوره جلتي سره *a* swiftly; rapidly *b* quickly, hurriedly, in a hurry جلتي کول to hurry, hasten

جل جلاله dzhalladzhalála *religion* greatest

جلد ¹ dzhild *m. Arabic* 1 binding (of a book) 2 volume 3 issue, copy (of a book, magazine) د چاپ شمېر ۱۰۰۰ جلده an edition of 1,000 copies 4 *anatomy* skin 5 *classifier for counting pelts or skins*

جلد ² dzhald *Arabic* ☞ جلت

جلدک dzhaldák Jaldak (place name)

جلدگر dzhildgár *m.* bookbinder

جلدي ¹ *Arabic* **1** epidermal, skin جلدي ناروغۍ، جلدي رنځونه skin disease **2** leather جلدي صنائع the leather industry

جلدي ² dzhaldí *f.* ☞ جلتي

جلريز dzhalríz *m.* Jalriz (district)

جلسه dzhalsá *f. Arabic* [*plural:* جلسي dzhalsé *Arabic plural:* جلسات dzhalsā́t] **1** conference; meeting, (mass) meeting جلسه کول to confer; conduct a meeting, a (mass) meeting **2** session

جلغ dzhilágh *m.* tendril (of a climbing plant)

جلغوزه dzhalghuzá *f. botany Pinus gerardiana* (a pine tree with edible nuts) **2** nut tree

جلغه ¹ dzhalghá *f.* hide, pelt; sheepskin

جلغه ² dzhilghá *f.* bad comrade, bad fellow-traveler

جلف dzhilf *Arabic* featherbrained, frivolous

جلک dzhalák *m. technology* bobbin

جلکوټي dzhálkóṭe *f.* ☞ جلکی

جلکه dzhálká *f.* push, shove, jolt, bump

جلکی dzhilkáj *f.* girl, little girl

جلگه dzhálgá *f.* **1** plain; steppe **2** small meadow; pasture; grassplot

جلگه يي ورۍ dzhálgaí a variety of wool

جلناني dzhanānáj *f. regional* kitchen

جلندر dzhalandár *m.* Jalandar (city, Punjab)

جلندرۍ ¹ dzhalandəráj *m.* mill wheel

جلندرۍ ² dzhálandaráj *f.* **1** top (the children's toy) **2** oilcloth

جلو dzhiláv *m. Arabic* **1** bridle, rein, reins د آس جلو نيول to lead a horse by the reins **2** retinue; escort د چا په جلو کښي تلل to escort somebody, accompany someone *idiom* د خولۍ جلو ښستول to speak without thinking

جل و بل dzhal-u-bál ☞ جلبل

جلودار dzhilavadár *m.* **1** escorting, accompanying someone **2** led, on a lead (of pack animals); groom's

جلوس dzhulús *m. Arabic* **1** accession to the throne; rein د جلوس لسم کال the 10th year of the reign **2** *regional* procession, parade

جلوگيري dzhilavgirí *f.* interruption, halt; forestalling, forbidding د پيشرفت جلوگيري کول to halt an assault, break off an attack

جلوه dzhalvá *f. Arabic* **1** brightness, radiance **2** the nuptial adornment of a bride

جلوه گاه dzhalvagáh *m.* nuptial throne

جلوه گر dzhalvagár **1** bright, radiant, sparkling **2** flirting, conquettish

جلوه گري dzhalvagarí *f.* **1** brightness, radiance, glitter **2** conquettishness

جلوي dzhilaví located up front, in front

جلي ¹ dzhalí *Arabic* **1** manifest, clear, obvious **2** well-defined, large (of writing, etc.) دا اطلاع په لويو او جلي حروفو خپره شوې ده This communication was printed in large letters.

جلی ² dzhaláj *f.* **1** cry, roar; noise, uproar **2** barking (of a dog) جلی کول **a** to cry out, roar; make an uproar, cause a din, create a racket جلی وهل، **b** to bark (of dogs)

جلي ³ dzhilé *f.* jelly

جلی ⁴ dzhiláj *f.* girl, little girl, young girl

جليا dzhaljā́ جليا بليا dzhaljā́-baljā́- *regional* **1** flaming, burning **2** burned up, burned **3** *figurative* infuriated **4** *figurative* burning (with hatred) جليا کول **a** to catch fire, begin to burn **b** to burn **c** to be infuriated **d** to burn (with some emotion, e.g., shame)

جليل dzhalíl *Arabic* **1** great, glorious **2** esteemed (in official correspondence)

جلی مار ¹ dzhalajmár *m.* shouter

جلی مار ² dzhálajmár *m.* ladies' man; lady-killer

جم ¹ dzham *m.* dzhamm *Arabic* **1** concentration of people, crowd **2** clan, tribe **3** ☞ جمله **4** mob attack **5** lead small-shot (rifle)

جم ² dzham *m.* storm, hurricane with rain; thunderstorm

جم ³ dzhəm turf ☞ چم ³

جم ⁴ dzham ☞ جمشيد

جم ⁵ dzham *abbreviation* جمرود

جمات dzhumā́t *m.* mosque

جماتي dzhumātí **1** at prayer in a mosque **2** *m.* devotee or attendant of a mosque

جماد dzhamā́d *m. Arabic* [*plural:* جمادونه dzhamādúna *Arabic plural:* جمادات dzhamādā́t] mineral; mineral deposit; inorganic substance

جماداني dzhamādāní *f.* ☞

جمادي dzhamādí *Arabic* inorganic; solid (of a body)

جمادي الاخره dzhumādā' lāukhrá *f. Arabic* ☞ جمادي الثاني

جمادي الاول dzhumādā' lāvvál *m.* جمادي الولي dzhumādā'lulā́ *f. Arabic* Jumadalula (fifth month of the lunar year)

جماد-اس-ساني dzhumād-as-sāní *f.* dzhumādi-as-sāní *Arabic* Jumadasani (sixth month of the lunar year)

جماع dzhimā́ *f. Arabic* copulation

جماعت dzhamā́'at *m.* dzhumā'át *Arabic* **1** crowd **2** meeting **3** mosque **4** class (in school) **5** *regional* organization (association)

جمال dzhamā́l *m. Arabic* beauty, gracefulness

جمال الدين dzhamāl-ud-dín *m. Arabic proper name* Jamal-ud-din

جمال فروشي dzhamālfurushí *f.* coquetry

جمال گوته dzhamālkoṭá *f.* جمال کوته dzhamālgoṭá *f.* Croton seeds, castor oil tree seeds, (*Croton tiglium*, a laxative)

جمالي dzhamālí **1** esthetic **2** beautiful, gracious

جمامه dzhamāmá *f.* indau (oil-producing plant)

جماهير dzhamāhír *m. Arabic plural of* جمهور

جمباز dzhambā́z *m.* ☞ جامباز

جمبر dzhambạ̌r *m.* rags; dilapidated, worn-out clothing

جمبک dzhambák ☞ جنبق

جمبوري dzhamborí *f.* boy-scout rally

جمبوبښ dzhəmbúkẖ crowd

جمبه dzhambá *f.* ☞ جنبه

جمجکړه dzhamdzhakṛá *f.* storm

جمجمه dzhamdzhamá *f. Arabic* skull, cranium

جمدار dzhamdắr *history* pin

جمدر [1] dzhamdór *m.* sword

جمدر [2] dzhamdár *m.* wild oats

جمرود dzhamrúd *m.* Jamrud (river, fortified place near Peshawar)

جمشېد dzhamshéd *m. proper name* Jamshid, Jamshed

جمع dzhám' *f.* dzhám'a *Arabic* 1 collection, concentration; conjuction *military* جمع سئ! Fall in! (as a command) 2 *grammar* plural number 3 *math* addition اجزا جمعي addition د جمعي عمل items 4 total, sum جمع کول *compound verb* a to collect; concentrate; join together *math* b to add جمع کېدل *compound verb* a to be collected; be concentrated; be joined together b to shrink (of cloth) c *math* to be added

جمعاً dzhám'an *Arabic* 1 in unison, together 2 in the aggregate; in toto, in sum

جمع آوري dzham'āvarí *f.* collection; gathering; procurement

جمع خرچ dzhama'khárch *m.* credit and debit account

جمع دار dzhama'dắr *m.* جمعدار 1 *military obsolete* officer rank 2 *regional* overseer, guard (prison) 3 *regional military* junior lieutenant

جمعگي dzhuma'gí *f. obsolete* 1 scholarship money, stipend paid to pupils on Fridays 2 gift from pupils to a teacher offered on Fridays

جمع نظام dzham'nizắm *m. military* close order

جمعه [1] dzhum'á *Arabic* 1 *f. Arabic* Friday په جمعه weekly 2 *m. proper name* Juma

جمعه [2] dzhám'a *f.* ☞ جمع

جمعي dzhám'i *plural of* جمع

جمعیت dzham'ijất *m. Arabic* 1 meeting; society, association جمعیت العلما Council of Ulemas (Muslim theologians, scholars, Islamic law specialists) 2 population 3 *grammar* plurality 4 riches 5 quiet, tranquility

جمعیت خاطر dzham'ijatkhātír *m.* quiet, tranquillity

جم گل dzhamgúl *m.* kind of caracul

جمګنى dzhəmgənáj *adjective* winter

جمګي dzhumagí 1 weekly 2 Friday

جملتاً dzhumlátán *Arabic* in toto, in sum, total

جمله dzhumlá *f. Arabic* 1 aggregate, sum, total, in total دهغو له from their number, including د دې جملي، دهغو د جملي څخه from this quantity 2 [*plural:* جملي dzhumlé] *m. Arabic* [*plural:* جملات dzhumlất] phrase, sentence 3 words

جمله بندي dzhumlabandí *f.* 1 combination of words in a sentence 2 phraseology

جملي dzhəmólí *m. plural* twins

جمنازیم dzhimnắzijúm *m.* جمنازیوم 1 gymnasium 2 stadium

جمناستیک dzhimnāstík *m.* gymnastics

جمنېزیم dzhimnézijúm *m.* ☞ جمنازیوم

جمو dzhamú *m.* Jammu (province)

جم و جوش dzham-u-dzhósh *m.* 1 confluence, accumulation 2 abundance, profusion (e.g., of flowers)

جمود dzhumúd *m. Arabic* 1 freezing; thickening; hardening 2 hardness, rigidity 3 *figurative* stagnation د تجارت جمود stagnation in trade; economic stagnation

جمه [1] dzhumá *f.* ☞ جمعه [1]

جمه [2] dzháma *f.* ☞ جمع [1]

جمهور dhumhúr *m. Arabic* 1 [*plural:* جماهیر dzhamahír] republic د شوروي سوسیالیستي جماهیرواتحاد the Union of Soviet Socialist Republics د جمهور ریس President of the Republic 2 concentration (of people)

جمهوري dzhumhurí *Arabic* republican

جمهوریت dzhumhurijất *m. Arabic* republic; the republican system

جمهوریت dzhumhurijất *m.* جمهوري خوا guḳhutúnkaj *m.* dzhumhurikhắn *m.* republican

جمهوریه dzhumhurijá *Arabic* جمهوریه ریس president of a republic

جمی dzhómaj *m. dialect* ☞ ژمی

جمیا dzhamjá *f.* ☞ جمامه

جمیکا dzhamájkā *f.* Jamaica (island)

جمیله dzhamilá *f. proper name* Jamila

جن [1] dzhən *f. dialect* girl, little girl

جن [2] dzhin *m.* dzhinn *Arabic* evil spirit, devil, demon; jinn

جن dzhón *adjectival suffix* غمجن sad, sorrowful

جناب dzhanắb *m. Arabic* 1 His Excellency (title of high rank) 2 Master, Mister, Honorable Sir جناب عالي Master, Mister, Sir معلم صاحب Honored Teacher (form of respectful address to a teacher)

جناح dzhanáh *m. Arabic* 1 wing; side 2 *military* flank

جناحي dzhanāhí *Arabic* 1 side, lateral 2 *military* flank, flanking جناحي حرکت flanking fire جناحي اور wide enveloping movement around the flank

جنازه dzhināzá *f.* dzhanáža 1 obsequies, burial services 2 corpse, deceased د چا جنازه شخول، د چا جنازه وړل to bury somebody, inter someone

جناور dzhanāvár *m.* 1 wild animal 2 bird (usually a game bird)

جنایت dzhinājất *m. Arabic* crime جنایت کول to commit a crime

جنایت کار dzhinājatkắr one who has committed a crime جنایت کار انسان، سړی a criminal

جنایت کارانه dzhinajatkārāná criminal; felonious

جنائي dzhináí *Arabic* criminal; felonious جنائي حادثه criminal indictment جنائي انسان criminal; felon; perpetrator of a crime

جنب dzhanb *m. Arabic* [*plural:* جنوب dzhunúb *plural:* اجناب adzhnāb] flank, side

جنوب dzhunúb *Arabic religion* defiled, impure

جنباز dzhambắz *m.* جنبازه dzhambāzá *f.* 1 uneven gait 2 wave (e.g., on a river) جنباز وهل a to ride bumpily, drive bouncing up b to wave, covered with waves

جنبان dzhumbắn 1 quivering, vibrating 2 shaking, oscillating

جنبش dzhumbísh *m.* 1 choppiness, oscillation; rocking, jolting 2 development, progress

جنبق dzhambák جنبك dzhambák dense, crowded *idiom* جنبق ستوري *astronomy* the Pleaides

جنبه dzhambá *f.* جنبه dzhumbá *Arabic* 1 crowd 2 group, grouping; clique پره جنبه cliquishness; discords 3 aspect, perspective 4 tendency 5 *grammar* aspect د فعل جنبه the aspect of a verb 6 support جنبه کېدل *compound verb* to be a follower, be a partisan of someone; associate oneself with someone 7 suite, retinue

جنبه دار dzhambadár 1 partial, biased 2 *m.* partisan, supporter

جنبه داري dzhambadārí *f.* partiality, bias

جنبه مار dzhambamár *m.* member of a group

جنت dzhanát *m.* dzhannát *Arabic* heaven, paradise جنت الفردوس heavenly gardens, paradisiacal gardens

جنتري dzhantarí *f.* calendar زره جنتري old style (in chronology)

جنتي dzhannatí 1 inhabitant of paradise 2.1 heavenly 2.2 marvelous, wonderful يوه ښکلي جنتي شپه a marvelous night

جنج dzhandzh *m.* nuptial procession

جنجلرى dzhandzháṛaj fading, withering

جنجال dzhandzhál *m.* 1 agitation, anxiety, trouble جنجال اخيستل to worry (about), take trouble (to) 2 complication, difficulty سياسي جنجالونه political complications 3 quarrel; scandal جنجال کول a to worry, disturb, alarm b to create complications, cause difficulties c to quarrel with, start a row 4 unpleasantness 5 load, burden 6 unpleasant personality

جنجالي dzhandzhālí 1.1 anxious, troubled; embarassing 1.2 disputed مسايل جنجالي vexed question, moot question 1.3 unpleasant 1.4 onerous 2.1 *f.* complication, difficulty 2.2 *f.* unpleasantness 2.3 troublemaker, mischief-maker

جنجړ dzhandzháṛ *m.* جنجړک dzhandzhaṛák *m. botany* hedge mustard, *Sisymbrium*

جنجړى [1] dzhandzhaṛáj duty, responsibility; obligation

جنجړى [2] dzhandzhaṛáj *f. botany* bindweed, *Convolvulus*

جنجن [1] dzhandzhán *m. botany* pigeon pea, *Cajanus indicus*

جنجن [2] dzhandzháṇ *m.* cartridge case

جنجن [3] dzhandzháṇ *m.* 1 red chintz 2 inflamed wound

جنجى [1] dzhandzháj *m.* [*plural:* جنجي dzhandzhí *plural:* جنجيان dzhandzhiján] participant in the bridegroom's procession

جنجى [2] dzhandzháj *f.* participant in the bridegroom's procession

جنحه dzhunhá *f. Arabic* fault, breach of conduct, manners

جند [1] dzhund *m.* basis, essence

جند [2] dzhund *m.* piece (of pastry, etc.)

جندر dzhandór *m.* ☞ جند [1]

جندره [1] dzhandóra *f.* rake

جندره [2] dzhandrá *f.* padlock جندره کول to padlock

جندره [3] dzhándra *f.* جندرى dzhandráj *f.* 1 wire-drawing machine (of jewelers, etc.) 2 screw-cutting device 3 form for straightening shell cases

جندکه dzhhindóka *f.* small coin

جند dzhaṇḍ 1 standing, vertical 2 firm, stable

جندا dzhaṇḍá greedy, grasping

جنده dzhaṇḍá *f.* جندى dzhunḍój *f.* 1 flag; banner 2 *Eastern* signal flag جنده وهل to communicate by flag signals

جنراتور dzhenerātór *m. technology* generator

جنرال dzhanrál *m.* جنرال dzhenerál 1 *military* general بريد جنرال major-general تورن جنرال lieutenant-general ډگر جنرال colonel-general ستر جنرال general of the Army 2 general-, general's جنرال قونسل consul-general

جنرالي dzhanrālí 1 pertaining to a general 2 rank of general

جنرېټر dzheneréṭer *m.* ☞ جنراتور

جنس dzhins *m. Arabic* [*plural:* جنسونه dzhinsúna *Arabic plural:* اجناس adzhnás] 1 sort, kind; variety 2 species, breed (of animals) 3 thing; commodity د جنس په جنس بدلولو a separately *economics* trade on the principle of net-balance د اجناس تبادله *economics* trade on the commodity circulation 4 *biology* sex 5 make (e.g., of automobile)

جنساً dzhínasán *Arabic* in nature, by nature

جنسي dzhinsí *Arabic* 1 goods, commodity, pertaining to things, articles, material جنسي تحويلدار warehouse manager 2 sexual

جنسيت dzhinsiját *m. Arabic* 1 grade; quality 2 homogeneity, uniformity 3 *biology* sex

جنغوڅه dzhanodzá *f.* جنغوزه dzhanozá *f.* جنغوزى dzhanozáj *m.* 1 ☞ جلغوزه 2 percussion cap

جنکوالى dzhinkawálaj *m. dialect* virginity

جنکۍ dzhinakój *f.* [*plural:* جنکى dzhinakój *plural:* جنکياني dzhinakəjáni] girl, little girl, young girl

جنگ [1] dzhang *m.* 1 fight, battle, engagement سينه په سينه جنگ hand-to-hand combat د جنگ ميدان single combat کره په ککره جنگ the field of combat, field of battle په چاورل to attack someone 2 war حقه war of liberation د آزادي جنگ world war عمومي جنگ just war ذروي جنگ unjust war, aggressive war تجاوزي جنگ cold war سوړ جنگ nuclear war, thermonuclear war و چاته په جنگ ور ولاړېدل to go to war, attack someone 3 struggle 4 quarrel; brawl; fistfight جنگ اچول a to stir up war b to start a quarrel, start a row په جنگ سره اچول set to fighting (cocks, quail) جنگ کول a to conduct a battle, battle b to war, carry on a war c to struggle, conduct a struggle جنگ کول d to quarrel; row; fight جنگ نښتول a to join battle b to start a war

جنگ [2] dzhung *m.* 1 collection of something 2 chrestomathy, collected writings

جنگ [3] dzhung camel calf

جنگ اچونکى dzhang achavúnkaj *m.* 1 instigator of war 2 brawler, troublemaker

جنگ ازموده dzhangazmudá experienced in battle, battle-hardened

جنگ اندازي dzhangandāzí *f.* starting of a war جنگ اندازي کول to incite to war, start a war

جنگيالى dzhangāvár ☞ جنگ آور

جنگ آوري dzhangāvarí *f.* war; conduct of military operations

جنگ بوټی dzhangbútaj *m.* ivy

جنگجو dzhangdzhú جنگجوی dzhangdzhúj 1.1 bellicose 1.2 rowdy; pugnacious 2 *m.* .1 warmonger, one who incites war 2.2 rowdy, brawler, troublemaker

جنگ جویي dzhangdzhuí *f.* 1 bellicosity 2 pugnacity

جنگ ځای dzhangdzáj *m.* field of battle, field of combat; location of military operations, arena of military operations

جنگ دیده dzhangdidá experienced in battles, experienced in military matters

جنگره¹ dzhangərá battle-worthy; combatative جنگره لښکر a battle-worthy army

جنگره² dzhangrá *f.* pitchfork

جنگ ریز dzhangréz *m.* 1 field of battle, field of combat 2 withdrawl while fighting battles

جنگړه¹ dzhangəṛá ☞ جنگره¹

جنگړه² dzhangṛá *m.* thicket, bushes

جنگړه³ dzhungaṛá *f.* ☞ جونگړه

جنگل dzhangál *m.* ☞ ځنگل woods; bushes

جنگل باغ dzhangalbāgh *m.* grove; park; stands of trees

جنگلباني dzhangalbāní *f.* forestry

جنگلک dzhangalák *m.* Jangalyak (district of Kabul)

جنگله¹ dzhangə́lá *f.* 1 grille window 2 parapet; railing on a roof; border rail

جنگله² dzhanglə́ *oblique singular of* جنگل

جنگلي dzhangalí *adjective* 1 pertaining to tree, forest, or lumber 2 wild

جنگنی dzhangənáj *m.* goat kid born in winter

جنگ و جدل dzhang-u-dzhadál 1 struggle 2 conflict; collision

جنگوری dzhangúraj *m.* skirmish, fight, encounter

جنگول dzhangavə́l *transitive* [*past:* و یې جنگاوه] 1 to cause to go to war; compel to engage in warfare 2 to cause to collide, incite two parties to fight, set dogs on یو دبل په مقابل کښې سره جنگول a to incite to war, compel to fight against one another b to collide with one another; quarrel with one another

جنگه¹ dzhangá *f.* plow handle

جنگه² dzhangá *f.* excessive profits; excess profits

جنگه³ dzhúnga *feminine of* جنگ³

جنگي¹ dzhangí 1 *m.* warrior, soldier 2.1 warlike; military جنگي کارنامي military warrior جنگي طیاره military aircraft جنگي ځوان warrior feats جنگي مهمات ammunition 2.2 bellicose جنگي روح warlike spirit; bellicosity 2.3 *military* operational, line, front-line جنگي افراد line personnel 2.4 *literature* epic

جنگی² dzhungáj *m.* camel calf

جنگی³ dzhungáj well-cut, well-formed (of clothing, etc.)

جنگی⁴ dzhungáj *m.* long woolen stockings

جنگی⁵ dzhungáj *m.* (short) jacket

جنگی⁶ dzhungə́j *f.* thicket, grove, coppice; planting (of mulberry bushes)

جنگیالی dzhangjālə́j 1 bellicose *m.* 2 warrior, soldier

جنگيالي توب dzhangjālitób *m.* bellicosity

جنگېدل dzhangedə́l *intransitive* [*past:* وجنگېده] 1 to war; wage war تر پایه پوری جنگېدل to wage war to a (victorious) conclusion 2 to struggle د آزادی دپاره جنگېدل to struggle for freedom 3 to engage in conflict a د چا سره جنگېدل، د چا په مقابل کښي جنگېدل to war with another party b to engage in conflict with someone 4 to quarrel په خپل منځ کښي جنگېدل to engage in dissention with someone; cause feuds 5 to allude to, touch upon

جنگېده dzhangedə́ *m. plural* 1 conduct of war 2 struggle for something 3 fight 4 quarreling

جن نیولئ dzhin nivə́laj possessed, obsessed

جنیوا dzhiníva *f.* Geneva (city)

جنوب¹ dzhanúb *m. Arabic* south د ښار په جنوب کښي south of the city جنوب شرقي dzhanub-i southeast جنوب شرق southeasterly جنوب غربي dzhanub-i southwest جنوب غرب dzhanub-i southwesterly

جنوب² dzhumub *m. Arabic plural of* جنب¹

جنوب ختیز dzhanubkhatíz southeasterly

جنوب لوېدیز dzhanublvedíz southwesterly

جنوبي dzhanubí southern

جنوبي ختیز dzhanubikhatíz ☞ جنوب ختیز

جنوبي لوېدیز dzhanubilvedíz ☞ جنوب لوېدیز

جنوتاړی dzhənutā́raj *m.* tender youth, delicate youth

جنوټی dzhənote *f.* little girl

جنوري dzhanvarí *f.* January

جنون dzhunún *m. Arabic* madness, insanity

جنوني dzhununi mad, insane

جنی¹ dzhnə́j *f.* dzhinə́j *Eastern* ☞ جلی⁴

جني² dzhinni *Arabic* 1 obsessed; possessed 2 obstinate, stubborn

جنین dzhanin *m. Arabic biology* fetus, embryo

جن جن dzhəndzhə́n *m.* kind of cartridge

جنجنک dzhandzhuṇák *m.* person given to subterfuges or excuses; person who is evading something

جنه جنه dzhəna-dzhəna *f.* subterfuge, excuse; evasion; equivocal بېله په جنه جنه څخه without subterfuges, without excuses جنه جنه کول evasively to use evasions, try to get out of

جو¹ dzhav *m. Arabic* air, atmosphere

جو² dzhav *m. singular & plural botany* oats ☞ اوربشي

جواب dzhaváb *m. Arabic* 1 answer قطعي جواب a definite answer مترددانه جواب an indefinite answer, evasive answer; a refusal, declination جواب کول to quarrel, altercation, wrangling جواب سوال answer جواب میندل to receive an answer 2 dismissal, discharge 3 refusal جواب ورکول a to give an answer b to fire, release c to dismiss څه سوال ، هغسي جواب *proverb literally* As the question is, so is the answer. *figurative* Do unto others as you would have them do unto you.

جواب ده، جوابده dzhavābdéh responsible, carrying responsibility, responsible for something

جوابدهي dzhavābdehí *f.* responsibility

جوابنامه dzhavābnamá *f.* written answer

جوابي dzhavābí *Arabic* given in answer, answering مقابل او جوابي اقدامات countermeasures

جوار¹ dzvār *m.* dzavār *plural* maize, corn نري جوار sorghum غټ جوار maize, corn

جوار² dzhivār *m. Arabic* vicinity; proximity د هغه په قرب او جوار near to him; in proximity to him

جوار پاکي dzhavārpākí *f.* shelling maize, shelling corn

جواركره dzhuvārkára *f.* section of land sown with maize or corn; field with corn, maize crop

جواريگر dzhavārgár *m.* ☞ جواركره

جواركره dzhvārgára *f.* ☞

جواري¹ dzhvārí *m.* dzhuvārí *plural, sometimes singular* maize, corn

جواري² dzhvārí *f.* card game; gambling game

جواري³ dzhvāráj *m.* corn bread

جواريگر dzhavārigár *m.* card player; gambler

جوارينه dzhvārína *f.* ☞ جواري³

جواز¹ dzhavāz *m. Arabic* 1 authorization, pass جواز لرل to be permitted 2 licence 3 certificate, document 4 diploma (certification of completion of an institution of learning) 5 permission

جواز² dzhavāz *m.* press (for extracting juice, oil, etc.)

جوازليك dzhavāzlík *m.* جوازنامه dzhavāznamá 1 licence 2 certificate, document

جوال dzhvāl *m.* dzhuvāl bag, sack *idiom* ځان په جوال كښي ورسره اچول to support someone (in an affair or an undertaking) د چا سره په جوال كښي لوبدل to have dealings with a fool

جوالي dzhvālí *m.* dzhuvālí porter; stevedore

جوالي توب dzhvālitób *m.* dzhuvālitób work of a porter or stevedore

جوامع dzhavāmí' *m. Arabic plural of* جامع² and جامعه¹

جوان dzhavān ☞ ځوان

جوانب dzhavāníb *m. Arabic plural of* جانب

جوان بخت dzhavānbákht ☞ ځوان بخت

جوان توب dzhavāntób *m.* ☞ ځوان توب

جوان مرد dzhavānmárd *m.* ☞ ځوان مرد

جوانوان dzhavānvān *m. botany* Amni copticum, Trachyspermum copticum (a kind of herb)

جوانه¹ dzhivaná *m.* dzhiuvaná calf, bull calf in the third year

جوانه² dzhavāná *f.* sprout جوانه وهل to sprout

جواني dzhavāní *f.* ☞ ځواني

جواني دانه dzhavānidāná *f.* pimple

جواهر dzhavāhír *m. Arabic* 1 *plural of* جوهر 2 [*plural:* جواهرونه dzhavāhirúna *Arabic plural:* جواهرات dzhavāhirāt] precious stone; jewel

جواهر خانه dzhavāhirkhāná *f.* storage place for valuables or jewels; precious stones

جواهري dzhavāhirí *m.* jeweler

جوباته dzhubātá *f.* sheet, towel (for wiping, drying)

جوبړ dzhobə́ŗ *m.* dewlap

جوبل dzhóbə́l *dialect* ☞ ژوبل

جوبلول dzhoblabə́l *transitive* ☞ ژوبلول

جوبله dzhóbla *f. dialect* ☞ ژوبله

جوبلبدل dzhoblbə́d *intransitive* ☞ ژوبلبدل

جوبه dzhobá *f.* market

جوپ dzhup ☞ چپ

جوپه dzhopa *f.* 1 caravan جوپي لار، جوپه كول caravan road جوپه كول to be in the caravan transport business; in groups 2 group, pile 3 turn (as in "your turn") 4 batch (of goods) جوپه جوپه pile

جوپه انگړ dzhopaanghə́ŗ *m.* caravansari

جوپه مشر dzhopamə́shər *m.* caravan leader

جوپه وال dzhopavál *m.* member of a caravan

جوت¹ dzhavát clear, evident; elucidated; established

جوت² dzhavt 1 adjoining 2 په جوت كښي سره ناست sitting alongside forming a pair; even

جوتك dzhavták 1 adjoining 2 close

جوتكي dzhavtaki *f. plural* 1 constellation of two stars 2 jumps, leaps 3 jerking the feet

جوتول¹ dzhavtavə́l *transitive* [*past:* وېى جوتاوه] to harness, harness up, hitch up

جوتول² dzhavtavə́l *denominative* [*past:* جوت يې كړ] to make clear, apparent; explain; establish (through explication)

جوتونه dzhavatavə́na *f.* explanation; establishment (i.e., of a fact)

جوتي¹ dzhotí dzhavtáj *adjective* 1 draught, draft, work 2 domestic جوتي حيوانان a draft, work animal b domestic animals 3 *regional* commonplace, everyday

جوتى² dzhutáj *f.* slipper; shoe (woman's)

جوتبدل dzhavatedə́l *denominative, intransitive* [*past:* جوت شو] to become clear, become evident; be explained; be established

جوت¹ dzhuṭ 1 sad 2 vain, idle, futile 3 spurned, rejected

جوت² dzhuṭ *m.* buffalo calf

جوت³ dzhuṭ *m. plural* jute

جوتول dzhutavə́l *denominative, transitive* [*past:* جوت يې كړ] 1 to grieve, upset 2 to reject, spurn 3 to spend vainly, spend uselessly

جوته¹ dzhoṭá *m.* ☞ جوت²

جوته² dzhuṭá *f.* garbage; leavings, leftovers

جوته³ dzhuṭá false, counterfeit

جوتى dzhuṭáj *f.* 1 swinging جوتى وركول to rock, swing 2 nodding, drowsing جوتى خورل a to rock b to nod, drowse

جوجوره dzhudzhúra *f.* جوجورى dzhudzhúraj *m.* 1 dewlap 2 double chin 3 craw, crop (of a bird) 4 *military* magazine (of a rifle, revolver)

جوجه ماجوجه dzhúdzha-mādzhúdzha *f.* God and Magog

جوجيدسو dzhodzhisú *m. sports* jiujitsu

جخت dzhukht ☞ جخت

جختول dzhukhtavə́l *denominative, transitive* ☞ جختول

جختوالى dzhukhtválaj *m.* ☞ جختوالى

جود dzhud *m. Arabic* generosity

جودر dzhavdár *m. denominative, transitive* **1** ☞ جمدر **2** wild rye, *Secale cereale Afghanicum*

جور [1] dzhavr *m. Arabic* violence جور کول to coerce, torture, torment

جور [2] dzhavór ☞ ژور

جور [3] dzhor *m.* quality of being well-cooked (of rice)

جورتیا dzhavartjá *f.* ☞ ژورتیا

جورج ټون dzhordzhṭáun *m.* Georgetown (city)

جورس dzhavrás *m.* Javras (kind of apple)

جورکه dzhoráka *f.* ☞ چورکی

جورمله dzhormóla fat (of cattle)

جورنالست dzhurnālíst *m.* ☞ ژورنالست

جورواالی dzhavarválaj *m.* ☞ ژوروالی

جوری [1] dzhuráj *m.* جوری dzhuráj *f.* tankard, quart (measure used in the sale of sour milk)

جوری [2] dzhuráj edging

جوري [3] dzhaváre *f. plural dialect* ☞ جور [2]

جوریدل dzhuredól *intransitive* [*past:* وجوریده] to penetrate (into the organism, of poison, etc.)

جوړ [1] dzhoṛ **1.1** adjusted, organized; being in order **1.2** healthy, whole, unharmed جوړ یې؟ Are you well? روغ جوړ quite hale and hearty ورسره د جوړ او روغ پوښتنه کول to inquire of someone about the health of his relatives **1.3** sufficient په لښتي کښي جوړي اوبه There is enough water in the aryk **1.4** convened (of a conference) **1.5** ready; prepared; made ready **2.1** indeed, quite **2.2** precisely, just جوړ نن just today, on this very day **2.3** at once, immediately **2.4** accordingly **2.5** just right (of dress)

جوړ [2] dzhuṛ *m.* ☞ جړ [3]

جوړاب dzhoṛáb **1.1** *m.* handsomeness; beauty; elegance **1.2** *m.* appearance, form **2** beautiful (of clothing)

جوړابدل dzhoṛābedól *denominative, intransitive* [*past:* جوړاب شو] **1** to grow prettier **2** to take shape, form

جوړانگه dzhuṛánga *f.* **1** strip of old cloth **2** icicle

جوړاوه dzhoṛavó *imperfective of* جوړول

جوړتازه dzhoṛtāzá *f.* جوړتازي دپاره والاړیدل to arise in order to greet جوړتازه کول *Eastern* to exchange greetings

جوړتوب dzhoṛtób *m.* جوړتیا dzhoṛtjá *f.* **1** health **2** well-being **3** state of being well-adjusted, regulated **4** readiness; preparation, training

جوړجوړی dzhuṛdzhuṛáj *f.* small waterfall, cascade

جوړښت dzhoṛókht *m.* **1** construction, structure, building under construction د جوړښت مواد construction materials **2** creation, formation **3** production, manufacturing, making **4** agreement, harmony زمونږ او د دوی جوړښت نکېږي We do not get along with them. **5** compact, agreement د چا سره جوړښت کول to enter into a compact, come to an agreement with someone **6** system (of government organization) **7** composition, make-up د هوا کیمیاوي

جوړښت the chemical composition of air *idiom* بدني جوړښت build, frame

جوړکانی dzhoṛkắṇaj *m.* stone (monument) erected as a token of peace

جوړلیک dzhoṛlík *m.* **1** reconciliation, peaceful settlement **2** peace treaty

جوړنگ dzhuṛáng *m.* ☞ جلغ

جوړواالی dzhoṛválaj *m.* **1** health **2** agreement, harmony **3** state of being in adjustment, well-regulated state

جوړوب dzhuṛúb *m.* splash (water)

جوړویی dzuṛobáj *m.* waterfall

جوړول dzhoravól [*past:* جوړ یې کړ] **1.1** to build, construct; weave (nest) **1.2** to produce, manufacture, make **1.3** to put in order, regulate, adjust **1.4** to create, form; shape **1.5** to rehabilitate **1.6** to sew لباس جوړول to sew a dress **1.7** to cut hair **1.8** to heal, cure **1.9** to lay out (a park, garden, etc.) **1.10** to settle (a quarrel) **1.11** to draw up, form up (in a rank) **1.12** to arrange, convoke, call, convene (a meeting, conference, etc.) **1.13** to draw up, draft (e.g., a plan, document) **1.14** to compose (a story, song, etc.) **1.15** to set up, start (a hubub, noisy row, etc.) **1.16** to dress up; to array (in) **1.17** to be a part of something **1.18** to get, obtain (e.g., passport) **2** *m. plural* ☞ جوړښت

جوړولو [1] dzhoṛaválo *oblique plural of* جوړول

جوړولو dzhoṛaválo *Eastern imperfective of* جوړول *vice* جوراوه

جوړونه dzhoṛavóna *f.* ☞ جوړښت

جوړه [1] dzhóṛa *f.* harmony, peace زما د هغه سره جوړه نه ده I will not get along with him. له هغو He sided with him. هغه يې ورسره جوړه کړ سره جوړه لري They came to an agreement with them.

جوړه [2] dzhóṛa *feminine singular of* جوړ

جوړه [3] dzhoṛá *f.* **1** pair خلور جوړي بوټ four pairs of shoes **2** match; rival د رباب په وهلو کښي يې جوړه نه درلوده There was none equal to him in playing the rubab. **3** clothing sent by the bridegroom to the bride جوړه ورکول to send clothing to the bride **4** song with two singers alternating

جوړی [1] dzoṛáj *f.* gown of cotton cloth (cut in a form-fitting manner)

جوړی [2] dzhuṛáj *f.* **1** small waterfall, cascade **2** singing (of children)

جوړي [3] dzhóṛe really, indeed; just, on the point of

جوړیدل dzhoredól *denominative, intransitive* [*past:* جوړ شو] **1** to build for someone, be built; be woven, be made (of a nest) **2** to be produced, be manufactured, be made **3** to be put in order, be adjusted; be created, be formed; be shaped **4** to be created, be formed; be shaped; arise **5** to be rehabilitated **6** to be sewed **7** to be shorn, have the hair cut **8** to get better, recover په ښان جوړیدل to get better, recover **9** to heal (of a wound) **10** to be laid out (garden, park, etc.) **11** to be settled (quarrel) **12** to be drawn up, be formed up (in a line) **13** to be arranged, be convened, be called, be conducted (a meeting, conference) **14** to be drawn up, be drafted (plan, document) **15** to be composed (story, song, etc.)

16 to be started up (noisy row) **17** to be dressed up, be arrayed in **18** to consist of something **19** to get along with someone **20** [*past:* وجوړیده] to be decided; set about an affair or piece of business

جوړیده dzhoṛedá *m. plural* **1** construction, structure **2** production, manufacture, making **3** putting into order; adjusting **4** creation, forming; shaping; origin **5** rehabilitation **6** sewing; needlework **7** haircut **8** recovery, return to health **9** healing (of a wound) **10** laying out (garden, park, etc.) **11** settling (a quarrel) **12** forming up, drawing up (in a line) **13** arrangement, convening, conducting (a meeting, conference, etc.) **14** drafting, drawing up (plan document, etc.) **15** composition (story, song, etc.) **16** construction, design (e.g., aircraft)

جوز dzhavz *m. Arabic plural* nut; nuts جوز هندي betel nut

جوزا dzhavzá *f. Arabic* **1** *astronomy* Gemini **2** Javza (the third month of the solar year; May-June)

جوزبویه dzhavzbujá *f.* ☞ جوزه

جوزجان dzhozdzhán *m. history* Jozjan (district) د جوزجان ولایت Jozjan Province

جوزه dzhavzá *f.* nutmeg

جوس dzhavás *m.* **1** field, square **2** courtyard (of a house)

جوسر dzhavsár closely adjoining; located alongside

جوسرول dzhavsaravól *denominative, transitive* [*past:* جوسر یې کړ] to place up against; place alongside

جوسریدل dzhavsaredól *denominative, intransitive* [*past:* جوسر شو] to adjoin closely; take up a position alongside

جوسه¹ dzhusá *f.* face

جوسه² dzhavsa *f.* wall cupboard

جوش dzhosh *m.* **1** disturbance; excitement **2** ardor, fervor, elan, enthusiasm په جوش سره بدلي ویل to sing with fervor **3** boiling جوش وهل، په جوش راتلل **a** to begin to boil **b** to boil **4** passion **5** welding جوش ورکول to weld **6** to grow together, knit up جوش خورل **a** to begin to boil **b** to boil **c** to grow together, knit

جوشانده dzhoshāndá *f.* medicinal extract, decoction

جوش وخروش dzhoshkharósh *m.* ☞ جوش وخروش

جوشناک dzhoshnāk exciting, rousing (of a speech, of words)

جوش و خروش dzhosh-u-kharósh *m.* ardor, fervor, elan, enthusiasm

جوشول dzhoshavól *denominative, transitive* [*past:* جوش یې کړ] **1** to boil **2** to pour boiling water over, scald

جوښت dzhuḳht dzhuḳhht ☞ جخت

جوغ¹ dzhugh *m.* ☞ جغ

جوغاړکی dzhuāṛkaj *m.* **1** dimple **2** bottom (of a dish, pot)

جوغدي¹ dzhudí subject to, dependent on

جوغدي² dzhudí roasted جوغدي کول to roast جوغدي کېدل to be roasted

جوغړی dzhuǝráj *m.* hole; crack; opening

جوغړی dzhuṛáj *m.* pit

جوغوندر dzhuundár *m.* beet

جوغه dzhughá *f.* ☞ جیغه

جغبدل dzhughedál *intransitive* ☞ جغبدل

جوف dzhauf *m. Arabic anatomy* cavity

جوک¹ dzhuk *m.* weight

جوک² dzhuk *m.* **1** place where a camel lays to rest **2** melting down (boiling down sugar)

جوک³ dzhavák *m.* linnet

جوکل dzhukól dzhakól *transitive* [*past:* جوکه یې و] to weigh

جوکمار dzhukmár *m.* fire man, fire tender (in the boiling down of sugar)

جوکوب dzhaukób coarsely ground, crushed (of corn) جوکوب کول to grind coarsely, crush

جوکه dzhúka *f.* leech *idiom* په کاڼي جوکه نه لګېده It was of no avail. It was useless.

جوکبدل dzhukedál *intransitive* [*past:* وجوکېده] to be weighed

جوگ dzhog *m. figurative* vegetation eaten by camels (*literally:* camel bush)

جوگي dzhogí **1** *m.* **.1** anchorite; hermit; beggar, dervish **1.2** breed of pigeons **2** *predicative* yellow جوگي رنگ yellow color

جولا dzholá *m.* [*plural:* جولاگان dzholāgā́n *plural:* جولایان dzholāján] **1** cloth, fabric **2** spider د جولا څاله spider web

جولاگاډی dzholāgā́ḍaj *m.* velocipede

جولاگري dzholāgarí *f.* weaving, textile industry

جولاگک dzhulāgák *m.* spider mite (an insect pest of cotton and other plants)

جولاگی dzholāgáj *m.* spider

جولان dzhavlán *m.* dzhavalán *Arabic* **1** rotation, circulation **2** wandering, roving

جولان گاه dzhavlāngā́h *m.* riding school

جولاه dzholáh *m.* ☞ جولا

جولائي¹ dzholā́i *f.* ☞ جولاگري

جولائي² dzhulā́j *m.* dzhulā́ji July

جوله¹ dzholá *f.* ☞ جل¹

جوله² dzhavlá *f.* form, shape د ښان د ښنځي په جوله کول to dress up as a woman

جوله³ dzholá *f.* ☞ جوانوان

جولی dzholáj *f.* **1** hem (of a dress) **2** bosom چا ته جولی غوړول to beseech someone on one's knees

جوم dzhum *m.* [*plural:* جومونه dzhumúna *Western plural:* جومان dzhumán] piece of turf picked up with a shovel

جومبر dzhumbár *m.* **1** cattle with a very large dewlap **2** man dressed in baggy clothes

جومولونگما dzhomolungmā́ *f.* Jomolungma (formerly Everest)

جومه dzhumá *f.* ☞ جمعه¹

جون dzhun *m.* June

جوند dzhvand *m. dialect* ☞ ژوند

جوندون dzhvandún *m. dialect* ☞ ژوندون

جوندی dzhvandáj *dialect* ☞ ژوندی

جونډی dzhunḍáj *m.* pompom

جونکی dzhunakáj *f. dialect* ☞ جنکی

جونگ ¹ dzhong *m.* ☞ جونگی ¹

جونگ ² dzhong *m.* notebook

جونگرا dzhongṛā́ lazy; indolent

جونگره dzhongərá *f.* جونگری dzhongṛə́j *f.* **1** shack د وينو جونگره (temporary) cabin **2** hut; lodge

جونگری dzhongṛə́j *f.* frame by which the weaver's beam is fastened to the loom

جونگڼه dzhongəṇá *f.* ☞ جونگره

جونگوڼا dzhunguṇá *m.* uncultivated person

جونگی ¹ dzhongáj *m.* baby camel, camel calf

جونگی ² dzhongáj *m.* increase, raise (above what is fitting or appropriate)

جونه *dialect plural of* جن ¹

جونی dzhunə́j *f. dialect* ☞ نجلی ²

جوور dzhuvə́r *m.* pool, reservoir; pond

جوول dzhovúl *Eastern* ☞ ژوول

جووه dzhová *f.* shaft or channel for irrigation

جوهر dzhavhár *m. Arabic* [*plural:* جواهر dzhavahir *plural:* جوهرات dzhavharā́t *plural:* جوهرونه dzhavharúna] **1** precious stone; jewel, valuable **2** flash (e.g., of a blade) **3** extract; essence **4** *chemistry* alkaloid; acid; compound د گوگرو جوهر sulphate **5** *figurative* substance, essential quality **6** *figurative* valor **7** *figurative* merit, virtue

جوهردار dzhavhardā́r **1** shining, flashing **2** *figurative* efficient, businesslike; experienced

جوهره dzhavharí **1.1** essential **1.2** painted, colored **1.3** aniline (of dyes) **2** *m.* jeweler

جوهره dzhuhaṛá *f.* fold; crease, wrinkle

جوی ¹ dzhuj *m.* irrigation shaft; small irrigation ditch or channel جوی کول to build a system of irrigation shafts or irrigation ditches

جوی ² dzhavví *Arabic* atmospheric, meterologic جوي اوضاع meteorologic conditions

جویر dzhojír *m.* جویر dzhəvér *m.* **1** puddle (after a rain) **2** gutter

جویک dzhuják *m.* small irrigation shaft or channel

جویل dzhojə́l *transitive* ☞ ژویل

جویه dzhojá *f.* ☞ جویک

جویی dzhoí *f.* hem (of a dress)

جه ¹ dzhah *m.* unity; harmony, accord

جه ² dzhah **1** obstinate, disobedient **2** resolved to resist to the end جه کول to insist (on) جه کبدل to show stubborn resistance

جهاد dzhihā́d *m. Arabic religion* **1** jihad, holy war against infidels and invaders **2** vigorous struggle; merciless conflict

جهاربوتی dzhhāṛbútaj *m. botany* variety of rue

جهاز ¹ dzhahā́z *m. Arabic* **1** ship, boat جنگي جهاز combat vessel هوايي جهاز space ship *Eastern* کوزميکي جهاز aircraft **2** *biology* vessel **3** *physiology* تنفس جهاز د respiratory system د وينې دگرځېدو جهاز *physiology* circulatory organs **4** device, apparatus اخذي جهاز د radio receiver

جهاز ² dzhihā́z جهازجل dzhihā́z *m. Arabic* **1** dowry (of a bride) **2** decor, furniture

جهازرانی dzhahārā́ní *f.* navigation, shipping د جهازرانی شرکت shipping company

جهازسازي dzhahāzsazí *f.* shipbuilding د جهازسازی کارخاني shipyard, dockyard

جهازوان dzhahāzvā́n *m.* **1** sailor, seaman **2** navigator; helmsman, pilot

جهازي dzhahāzí *m. regional* sailor

جهالت dzhahālát *m. Arabic* savagery, barbarism; ignorance

جهان dzhahā́n *m.* dzhihā́n **1** world, universe **2** people *idiom* په سترگو نه لېدل to give oneself airs

جهان افروز dzhahānafróz *figurative* that which illuminates the world (of the sun) (*literally:* illuminating the world)

جهان بینی dzhahānbiní *f.* **1** (world) outlook **2** knowledge of the world

جهان حیرانوونکی dzhahā́n hajrānavúnkaj striking, staggering, surprising the world

جهان دیده dzhahāndidá having seen much, worldly; experienced, worldly-wise

جهان سوز dzhahānsóz committing the entire world to flames (epithet of a conqueror)

جهان گرد dzhahāngárd **1** having travelled over the world **2** *m.* traveller; tourist

جهان گیر dzhahāngír **1** having conquered the world (epithet of an emperor) **2** *m. proper name* Jehangir

جهان وطني dzhahānvataní **1** *f.* cosmopolitanism **2** cosmopolitan

جهاني dzhahāní *adjective* world جهاني اقتصاد the world economy جهاني آرامي او سوله the world in its entirety

جهت dzhihát *m. Arabic* **1** side, direction **2** reason, basis د دې د دې له جهته، له دې جهته for this reason, therefore د دې له جهته for this reason د همدغه جهته precisely because of this, for this very reason

جه جه dzhahdzháh call used in driving cattle

جهد dzhahd *m. Arabic* striving, effort جهد او کوښښ کول to try, endeavor, make efforts

جهر ¹ dzhahr *m. Arabic* ☞ جار ² په جهر سره loudly, publicly, for all to know

جهر ² dzhihr *m.* jikhr (a dance performed by men)

جهگره dzhagṛá *f. regional* ☞ جگره

جهل dzhahl *m. Arabic* **1** ignorance, lack of knowledge **2** recklessness, foolhardiness جهل کول a to be ignorant b to display recklessness

جهم جکم dzhhmdzhakaṛ *m.* thunderstorm

جهنده dzhhandá *f.* dzhhandá *f. regional* banner

جهنم dzhhannám *m. Arabic religion* hell, firey Gehenna د جهنم کنده the Nether Regions

جهنمي dzhahannamí *Arabic* infernal, hellish

جهود dzhahúd *m.* ☞ یهود

جهول dzhahúl *Arabic* extremely ignorant, backward

جهوله dzhahulá *f.* ☞ جوله[1]

جهیز dzhahéz *m.* dowry (of a bride)

جهیل dzhil *m.* lake جهیل سرقول Lake Sarykul' د ارال جهیل the Aral Sea کسپین جهیل the Caspian Sea

جی[1] dzhaj *m.* ☞ ژی[1]

جی[2] dzhəj *f.* ☞ ژی[2]

جي dzhi *regional* lord, master (as a form of address)

جي dzhí *suffix* ☞ چي

جیالوجستي dzhiālodzhistí 1 geological 2 *m.* geologist

جیالوجي dzhiālodzhí جیالوژي dzhiālozhí 1 *f.* geology 2 geologic

جب dzheb *m. Arabic* 1 pocket په جب کښي باد handbag لاسي جب to be penniless 2 gift of food sent to a fiancé by the bride's relatives

جیباته dzhibātá *f.* جیبټه dzhibaṭá *f.* 1 coverlet 2 sheet, towel (for drying off)

جبي dzhebí *adjective* pocket

جیتی dzhitáj *m.* round, flat pebble

جټ[1] dzheṭ *m.* dzhiṭ *botany* restharrow

جټ[2] dzheṭ *m.* Jet (third month of the Hindu calendar, May-June)

جټ[3] dzheṭ *m.* place near the hearth (used for storing pressed-dung fuel)

جټ[4] dzheṭ jet جټ الوتکه jet aircraft

جیټکه dzhiṭká push, shove, bump, jolt جیټکه خورل to receive a push, shove, bump or jolt جیټکي ورکول to push, shove, etc.

جیجری dzhidzhráj *f.* iron or brass milk pail

جیجي[1] dzhidzhe *f. plural children's speech* breast

جیجی[2] dzhidzhaj *m.* Himalayan pheasant

جیحون dzhejhún *m. Arabic* د جیحون سیند *histroy* the Amu-Darya River دریای جیحون dariā-ji Amu-Darya River

جید dzhajád *Arabic* prominent, eminent (of an eclesiastic), saintly, venerable

جیره dzhirá *f.* ration, allowance; standard ration

جیره بندی dzhirabandí *f.* allotment, rationing (of food, etc.); allocation by ration card د جیره بندی اصول ration card system

جبرمه dzhégma *f.* ☞ زبرمه

جبسل dzhesál *transitive* [past: و یې جبسه] to oppress; offend

جیغه dzhighá *f.* 1 plume (on a hat, headdress) 2 crest (of a bird)

جیکت dzhekát *m.* ☞ جاکټ

جهل[1] dzhel *m. colloquial* ☞ جهل

جهل[2] dzhel *m.* prison جهل خورل to be in prison

جهل[3] dzhel *m.* 1 column of prisoners 2 bucket on a noria (or water wheel)

جهلخانه dzhelkhāná *f. Eastern* ☞ جهل[2]

جیلغ dzhilógh *m.* 1 crupper (harness) 2 saddlecloth 3 cluster (of nuts) 4 row

جیم[1] dzhim *m. Arabic* name of the letter ج

جیم[2] dzhim *m.* ticking (cloth)

جیم[3] dzhim *m. hunting* pitfall trap for wolves

جین dzhin *m. technology* 1 gin 2 ginning (of cotton)

جیناکی dzhinākój little girl

جنجر[1] dzhindzhár *m. botany* 1 ☞ جنجن 2 nutmeg flower, Nigella

جینجرک dzhindzhoṛák gift of food sent on the first day of the wedding from the home of the relatives of the bride

جینجو dzhindzhó weak, feeble

چینگ dzhing ☞ چینگ

جینگا dzhingā́ 1 unthinking 2 dumb; taciturn

جینگ دار dzhingdā́raj open-mouthed; with bared teeth

جینگر dzhingóṛ 1 cowardly 2 weak, puny (of a child) 3 flabby

جینگول dzhingavál *denominative, transitive* ☞ چنگول

جینگیدل dzhingedál *intransitive* ☞ چنگیدل

جینوا[1] dzhinivā́ *f.* Geneva (city)

جنوا[2] dzhénuā *f.* Genoa (city)

جینی dzhinój *f.* young woman, girl

جیو dzhiv *children's speech* Yes, yes! Of course! I'll do everything for you!

جیورجیا dzhijordzhjā́ Georgia

چ

چ che the eighth letter of the Pashto alphabet (also called چیم chim)

چا chā *oblique form of the preposition* څوک 1 who (used as the subject of the action in and the ergative construction) چا وواهه؟ Who beat him? دا واله چا راوستي ده Who built this irrigation system? 2 who, whom (used with prepositions, postpositions and adverbs) توپک دي پر چا خرخ کړئ دئ؟ *Western* To whom did you sell the rifle? خپل کالي په چا گنډي؟ Who made that dress for you? په چا کښي؟ For someone? دا د چا کور دئ؟ In whom? Whose house is this? له چا سره ځي؟ د چا سره ځي؟ With whom are you going? *Eastern* له چا څخه، د چا څخه، د چا نه (at) someone's چا ته، و چا ته، چاله to whom (place)

چاباره chābára *f.* efficient woman; good housekeeper

چابړی chābṛój *f.* pan of weighing scales

چابک chābúk chābák 1 quick, swift; lively; agile, prompt 2 rapid, fast چابک ځي He is going very fast.

چابک تگی chābaktágaj چابک تگی موټر light vehicle

چابکتوب chābaktób *m.* چابکتیا chabəktja *f.* ☞ چابکي[1]

چابک دست chābukdást ☞ چابک

چابک دستی chābukdastí *f.* ☞ چابکي[1]

چابکول chābəkavál *denominative* [past: چابک یې کړ] to hasten, act more quickly گامونه چابکول to hasten one's steps

چابکي[1] chābəkí chābukí *f.* 1 quickness, swiftness; liveliness, agility; promptness 2 speed, velocity په چابکی سره quickly; promptly چابکي کول a to be prompt, be adroit b to hasten, hurry

چابکی[2] chābukój *f.* cockroach

چابکیدل chābəkedál *denominative, intransitive* [past: چابک شو] to be hurried, be hastened

چاپ[1] chāp 1 *m.* .1 printing, print د چاپ صنعت the printing industry ☞ چاپ کول to bring out, له چاپه وتل، له چاپ نه وتل چاپول

253

publish **1.2** composition (typographic) **1.3** lithographic stone **1.4** impression, imprint **1.5** edition چاپ اول first edition **1.6** to print a pattern (on cloth, paper) **1.7** brand (factory) **2.1** printed **2.2** published, issued

چاپ ² chāp *m. military* caliber

چاپ ³ chāp *m.* ☞ مغازه

چاپت chāpót *m.* **1** booklet or list of written instructions **2** cutting **3** incision

چاپخانه chāpkhāná *f.* printshop, publishing house

چاپراخ chāprákh **1** open, wide-open **2** spacious, wide

چاپکه chāpóka *f.* dried-dung fuel cakes

چاپگر chāpgár *m.* printer

چاپلاخه chāpólákha *f.* ☞ چلاخه

چاپلوس chāplús *m.* toady, flatterer; lickspittle

چاپلوسي chāplusí *f.* bootlicking, flattery

چاپ والا chāpvālā *m.* **1** printer **2** stamp-press operator

چاپول chāpavól *denominative, transitive* [*past:* چاپ یې کړ] to print بیا چاپول to reprint

چاپونه chāpāvóna *f.* printing, print

چاپه chāpá *f. archaeology* **1** composition (typographic), چاپه کول چاپه وهل to print **2** lithographic stone **3** pattern (on cloth, paper) **4** large sheaf **5** ☞ چامپه ²

چاپه خانه chāpakhāná *f.* ☞ چاپخانه

چاپي chāpí **1** *f.* **1** massage **2.1** massaged چاپي کول to give a massage; massage چاپي کېدل to be massaged **2.2** printed; published

چاپېدل chāpedól *denominative, intransitive* [*past:* چاپ شو] to be printed

چاپېر chāpér **1.1** round, around د باغ چاپېر around the garden **1.2** in full, quite, in entirety **2** environment, surroundings **3** ambient (air, environment) *idiom* د... په چاپېر کښې concerning, about, with regard to چاپېر سیند ocean

چاپېرول chāperavól *denominative, transitive* [*past:* چاپېر یې کړ] **1** to surround, besiege **2** to wind up, reel up **3** to embrace, clasp to oneself

چاپېره chāpéra ☞ چاپېر د مېز نه چاپېره کېناستل to sit down at table

چاپېریال chāperjál *m.* environment, surroundings, circumstances

چاپېرېدل chāperedól *denominative, intransitive* [*past:* چاپېر شو] **1** to be surrounded; be besieged **2** to be wound up, be rolled up, be reeled in **3** to envelop, surround چاپېرېدل په شان را کمربند د to envelop something

چاپېره chāpéra *f.* buffet, slap in the face

چاټ chāṭ *m. anatomy* perineum

چاټۍ chāṭój *f.* **1** large clay pitcher **2** partition in a tanur oven **3** clay storage vessel for grain

چاجوشه chādzhúsha *f.* ☞ چایجوش

چاچي ¹ chāchí *regional* chāchój *f.* **1** aunt (wife of father's brother) **2** Auntie (address to wife of father's brother)

چاچي ² chāchój *f. children's speech* paw, hand (i.e., palm) چاچي وهل clap hands, pat-a-cake

چاخول ¹ chākhavól *transitive dialect* [*past:* چاخاوه یې و] to hurry

چاخول ² chākhól swift pace, headlong running

چاخبدل chākhedól *intransitive dialect* [*past:* چاخبده و] to hurry, hasten

چاد chād *m.* Chad

چادار chādár *m.* **1** coverlet **2** sheet **3** chador

چادرنشینه chādarnishína بنګه a female hermit, anchorite; woman following the rule of the solitary life b woman wearing the chador

چادري chādarí *f.* chador

چادي chādí **1.1** simple; open-hearted; trustful **1.2** stupid, unintelligent **2** *m.* [*plural:* چادیان chādiján] simpleton; dope, fool

چادي توب، چادیتوب chāditób *m.* **1** simplicity; open-heartedness; credulity **2** stupidity; imbecility

چادي چکمار chādí-chakamár **1** very stupid **2** *m.* idiot, fool

چار chār *m. dialect f.* [*plural:* چاري chāri *Eastern plural:* چاره chāre] ☞ چاره ¹ څنه چار؟ How are things? Is everything alright? چار دي ښه شه! I wish you success!

چارابرو chārabrú *m.* youth

چاراندام chārandám *m. plural religion* ablution, lavabo

چارآئینه chārāiná *f. history* hauberk, shirt of mail; armor

چارباغ chārbágh *m.* **1** garden, park (with intersecting alleys) **2** Charbag (setttlement)

چاربیته chārbájta *f.* **1** poetic strophe consisting of four verses **2** *colloquial* quatrain **3** ballad

چاربجتي chārbajtí *m.* singer

چارپا chārpá *m.* ☞ چارپای

چارپاره chārpārá *f.* **1** crushed rice, ground rice **2** explosive, bullet

چارپای chārpáj *m.* [*plural:* چاریایان chārpāján] **1** quadruped, animal **2** domestic animal, beast

چارپائي chārpāi *f.* wooden bed

چارپېر chārpér ☞ چاپېر

چارتار chārtár *m.* چارتاره chārtāra *f.* chartar (stringed musical instrument)

چارتراش chārtarásh *m.* boards, lumber, planks

چارج chārdzh *m. electrical engineering* **1** charge مثبت چارج positive charge منفي چارج negative charge **2** charging

چارجول chārdzhavól *denominative, transitive electrical engineering* [*past:* چارج یې کړ] to charge

چارجبدل chārdzhedól [*past:* چارج شو] *electrical engineering* to be charged

چارچاپېر، چارچاپېره chārchāpér chārchāpéra ☞ چاپېر

چارچشم chārcháshm *m.* **1** expectation **2** appointment

چارچلند chārchalánd *m.* **1** move, course (of business, etc.) **2** lifestyle

چارچوب chārchób *m.* frame (of a door, window)

چارچوبۍ chārchobә́j f. 1 latrine, lavatory 2 bathing shed, dressing booth 3 ☞ چارچوب

چاردزۍ chárdzáj m. ☞ کارخانه

چارخانه chārkhāná f. 1 checkered cloth 2 chess-board

چارخول chārkhól m. چارخولی chārkhvaláj m. ☞ چرخول

چارخولک chārkhvә́lák m. cock's comb

چاردانگ chārdāng m. four points of the compass چاردانگ عالم chārdāng-i the entire world

چاردانګي chārdāngí m. male falcon

چارده chārdéh ☞ چهارده

چاربوالي chārdevālí f. 1 fence 2 rampart, wall (around a city)

چاراهي chārrāhí f. 1 crossroads 2 square

چارزانو chārzānú m. sitting with crossed legs چارزانو کښېنستل to sit with crossed legs

چارسال chārsál m. horse in its fourth year

چارسو chārsú m. 1 crossroads 2 plaza, square 3 Charsu (a bazaar in Kandahar)

چارشانه chārshāna 1 robust, strong 2 colloquial friendly

چارشنبه chārshambá f. Wednesday د چارشنبې ورځ چارشمبه، چارشنبه Wednesday

چارښاخه chārx̌ákha four-tined pitchfork

چارک chārák m. charak (a quarter of a sir, measure of weight equivalent to 1766.4 gm.)

چارکنج chārkúndzh m. charkunj (a kind of pastry)

چارکی chārә́káj m. one charak weight

چارگر chārgár m. ☞ کارگر

چارگل chārgúl m. [plural: چارګلان chārgulān] silver ornament in the form of a flower (worn in the left nostril)

چارگلی chārguláj m. camomile

چارگنده chārgә́nda f. ☞ چارنده

چارمغز chārmághz m. [plural: چارمغزان charmaghzan] walnut

چارناچار chārnāchár چارناچاره chārnāchára 1 willy-nilly, against one's will منلوته چارناچار تيار شوم I was forced to agree against my will. 2 without fail

چارند chárәnd m. چارنده chárәnda f. gutter (around a hipped roof)

چارندوکی chārәndúkaj active; hard-working, assiduous

چارنی chárónaj m. artisan

چارو chārú m. diligent man, hard worker

چاروغه chārógha f. usually plural چاروغي chāróghi charyki (a kind of shoe)

چاره chára f. 1 work چاره کول to work 2 affair د خارجه چارو وزير Minister of Foreign Affairs

چاره chārá 1 means, way out هيڅ چاره يې نه کېږي It's impossible to do anything with him. څه چاره؟ How to correct the matter? How to set things right? ... مگر څه چاره but what can one do ... 2 medicine, medication

چاره ساز chārasáz f. 1 assistant 2 healer

چاره سازي chārasāzí f. 1 aid, assistance, succor 2 healing, cure

چاره گر chāragár m. ☞ چاره ساز

چاره سازي chāragarí f. ☞ چاره گري

چاري chārí f. regional چارۍ chārә́j f. 1 wooden tool for making terraces used in irrigation 2 shoulder blade

چاريار chārjár plural religion four caliphs (successors of Mohammed)

چاريک chārják m. 1 fourth part, a fourth 2 ☞ چارک

چاري کار، چاربکار chārekár m. 1 sharecropper (one who works for a quarter of the crop harvested) 2 farm laborer

چاربکار chārikár m. plural Charikar (city)

چاري کاري، چاربکاري chārekari f. sharecropping

چارا chārá 1 m. .1 stammerer 1.2 ignoramus 2.1 stammering; speaking thickly 2.2 stupid 2.3 poorly educated, ignorant

چاراتوب chārātób m. چاراوالی chārāvә́laj m. 1 stammering; confused articulation 2 stupidity 3 ignorance

چاره chārá chaṛe f. [plural: چڼي chaṛó] 1 knife 2 short sword 3 razor د سر چاره razor 4 large knife, butcher's knife idiom چاره ورته کنبل to nourish enmity for someone, hate someone idiom تر چاره لاندي ساه اچول a to be close to death b to be tormented, suffer idiom چاره ورته تېره کول terá to contemplate someone's murder idiom چاره کول to oppress someone idiom چاره پرغاړه وراينبول to betray someone, cheat someone (in buying and selling) idiom خپله چاره په اويو کنبي لبدل to foresee, have a premonition of disaster idiom په پڅه چاره د وجود غوښي بېلول to torture, torment

چاره گر chārәgár m. cutler

چارۍ chārә́j f. ☞ چاري

چاشني chāshní f. 1 test, tasting (of food) چاشني کول to taste food 2 relish, condiment

چاغ chāgh 1 healthy 2 fleshy, obese, fat 3 lively, adroit

چاغتوب chāghtób m. چاغتیا chaghtjá f. چاغښت chaghә́x̌ht m. چاغوالی chāghvә́laj m. stoutness, embonpoint

چاغول chāghavә́l denominative, transitive [past: چاغ یې کړ 1 to grow healthy; put on weight 2 to become plump, become stout 3 to fatten up

چاغونه chāghavә́na f. 1 stoutness 2 fattening up

چاغبدل chāghedә́l denominative, intransitive [past: چاغ شو 1 to put on weight 2 to grow stout, get fat

چاغ chāk ☞ چاغ

چاقو chāḳú m. pen-knife

چاقوساز chāḳusáz m. cutler, knife maker

چاقوسازي chāḳuzāzí f. manufacturer of knives

چاک chāk m. 1 crack, split; hole (in a wall, etc.) 2 cut, slit; knick چاک کول a to crack b to cut, slit, make an incision چاک کېدل a to be cracked b to be cut, be cut open

چاکر chākár m. servant, attendant

چاکري chākarí f. 1 service, serving 2 dependence

چاکلېت chāklét m. چاکلېت chāklét m. plural chocolate

چاکو chāḳú m. ☞ چاقو

چاکي chākí 1 cracked, having a crack 2 torn 3 slit; cut, incised

چاگله chāgә́la f. leather water-bag, canteen

چال ¹ chāl *m.* **1** movement, moving **2** action, operation, work **3** trick; ruse; fraud چالونه intrigues, tricks چال کول to use cunning **4** habit, conduct **5** *chess* move چال سنجول to think over a move **6** yarn (of 40 threads) **7** vomiting

چال ² chāl *m.* **1** pit, abyss **2** *anatomy* cavity

چال ³ chāl *m.* Chal (district in Badakhshan)

چالاک chālák چالاکه chālā́ka ☞ چابک 1

چالاکي chālākí *f.* ☞ چابکي ¹ 1

چالان chālán *m.* **1** starting up, putting into operation; winding up, cranking up **2.1** acting, operating **2.2** running, showing (a film) **2.3** brisk (of trade)

چالانول chālānavól *denominative, transitive* [*past:* چالان یې کړ] **1** to bring a case to court **2** to start up, put into operation; crank up, start (a motor, etc.) **3** *regional* to institute criminal proceedings **4** to send, dispatch

چالانیدل chālānedól *denominative, intransitive* [*past:* چالان شو] **1** to be taken to court (of a case) **2** to operate, be started, be cranked up (of a motor, etc.) **3** to be sent, be dispatched

چالباز chālbā́z *m.* swindler, rouge, cheat, cunning person

چالتار chāltár *m.* chaltar (kind of Muslim head-covering or turban)

چال چلند chālchaláhd *m.* **1** conduct **2** ☞ چارچلند

چالچودي chālchodí *f.* fraud; swindle; cunning

چالان chālán *m. economics* invoice

چاله ¹ chála *f.* mare

چا له ² chá la *Eastern* ☞ چا ² 2

چالي chālí *f.* ☞ چال ¹ 5

چامبېل chāmbél *m.* چامبېلي chāmbelí *m.* white jasmine, *Jasminum grandiflorum*

چامپ chāmp *m.* chop (meat)

چامپه ¹ chāmpá *f.* wave, waves (in water) چامپې وهل to be agitated, splash (of water)

چامپه ² chāmpá *f.* champa (measure of length equivalent to the width of the palm of the hand)

چامته chāmtá *f.* ☞ چمته

چان chān *m.* church (ecclesiastical) bell

چامپه chāmpá *f.* ☞ چامپه ¹

چانته chāntá *f.* ☞ چمته

چاندماری chāndmārój *f.* **1** firing (rifle, etc.) **2** execution by shooting چاندماری کول **a** to shoot **b** to execute by shooting **c** shooting, riflery

چاندني chāndaní *f. Eastern* **1** case for a rug **2** coverlet (for a bed)

چاندي chāndí purified (of adulterants) چاندي کول to purfiy (of adulterants, contaminants) د معدن چاندي اخیستل to enrich ore, concentrate ore

چانډه cháṇḍa *f.* **1** piece, slice (e.g., of melon) **2** share (of profits)

چانس chāns *m.* **1** chance **2** luck, fortuity

چانطه chāntá *f.* ☞ چمطه

چانغ چوغ chānghchúgh *m.* scream, squeal; cries چانغ چوغ جوړول to set up a howl, scream

چانک chānák *m.* ☞ چاینک

چاند ماری chānmārój *f.* ☞ چان ماری

چان chāṇ **1** *m.* **.1** sieve, strainer **1.2** screening (through a sieve) **1.3** strainer چان کول *compound verb* ☞ چڼل **2.1** strained (through a sieve) **2.2** separated, filtered **2.3** purified **2.4** selected, chosen

چاڼول chāṇavól *denominative, transitive* ☞ چڼل

چاڼه chāṇá *f.* rafter

چاڼي ¹ chāṇí *m.* dung-beetle

چاڼی ² chāṇój *f.* **1** sieve **2** strainer

چاڼیدل chāṇedól *denominative, intransitive* ☞ چنڼیدل

چاوجی chāvdzhój *f.* edge, hem (of clothing)

چاود chāvd *m.* slit; crack د زړه په چاود with great tension, with great stress

چاودل chāvdól *intransitive* [*present:* چوي *past:* وچاود] **1** to burst, crack open; crack, split مځکه وچاوده the earth split, the earth cracked **2** to explode بم وچاود a bomb exploded **3** *literally* to grieve, be upset; *figurative* to eat one's heart out له غمه وچاودم I ate my heart out with grief.

چاودنه chāvdóna *f.* explosion

چاودول chāvdavól *transitive* ☞ چول ³

چاودونکئ chāvdúnkaj **1** *present participle of* چاودل **2** explosive, exploding چاودونکي مواد *chāvdúnki* explosive substance

چاوده chāvda *f.* cut (on the skin of the hand, leg); ulceration, ulcer

چاودیدل chāvdedól *intransitive* ☞ چاودل

چاودینک chāvdinák bold; impertinent, insolent

چاول chāvól *m.* [*plural:* چاولونه chāvólúna *Western plural:* چاولان chāvólā́n] plumb-bob, level

چاوله chávla *f.* sluice-gate (of an irrigation shaft, well)

چاوڼی chāvṇój *f.* permanent military garrison town

چاوه chāvá *f.* tea with molasses and ginger (medicine for cold)

چاه chāh [*plural:* چاهان chāhā́n] well

چاه آب chāhā́b *m.* Chahab (settlement in Badakhshan)

چاه کن chāhkán *m.* well-digger

چای chāj *m.* چای chāe *f. plural* tea تور چای، توری چای black tea چای مو وچښنبه tea-room د چای هوټل green tea شین چای، شنی چای We were drinking tea. د غره چای St. John's Wort

چایجوش chājdzhósh *m.* tea-kettle برقي چایجوش electric tea-kettle

چایخانه chājkhāná *f.* tea khana; tea-room

چای خوري chājkhurí *f.* tea drinking د چای خوری ظروف tea service, tea things (dishes)

چایدان chājdā́n *m.* tea caddy

چایصاف chājsā́f *m.* چایصاف کن chājsā́fkún *m.* tea strainer

چایل chājól *m.* spotted covering of lace (for the face), chador

چاینک chājnák *m.* چاینکه chājnáka *f.* tea-kettle

چائي chāji *f.* چایه chāje *plural* ☞ چای

چبقپاک chubukpā́k *m.* ground chalk (for cleaning pots, etc.)

چپ ¹ chup *m.* ☞ چف

چپ ² chəp chup keeping silent چپه خوله a taciturn b silently چپ
Be quiet! Shut up! کَه! خان چپ نيول to be silent; keep still

چپ ³ chap 1 left (of the hand, side) 2 contradicting something,
hindering something له قانون څخه چپ خوځېدل to break the law
قدم اينبودل to resist; interfere with, hinder someone 3 deprivcd of
something 4 in error; incorrect; mendacious له حقيقت څخه چپ فکر
پيدا کول to lead astray, disorient 5 unsuccessful; mistaken; bad 6
dissolute

چپاته chəpáṭa f. kind of slipper

چپاو chapáv m. 1 raid; invasion چپاو کول a to raid b to rob 2
offensive چپاو اچول a to hasten, hurry (in some matter or other) b
to attack چپاو اخيستل to display impatience, be in a hurry about
something په يوه چپاو تلل to be in an excessive hurry a چپاو پر ورل
to make a surprise attack b to appear suddenly

چپاول chapávul m. history cavalry patrol

چپاوول chapāvavál denominative [past: چپاو يې کړ] to raid, pillage

چپاوي ¹ chapaví 1 predatory 2 quick, hurried 3 attacking
فوځونه attacking troops

چپاوي ² chapāví row (as in rowboat), propelled by oars

چپاوېدل chapāvedál denominative, intransitive [past: چپاو شو] to be
plundered

چپه چپائي chupājí f. ☞ چپه چپائي

چتوب ¹ chəptób m. چتيا chəptjá f. taciturnity, silence

چتوب ² chaptób m. opposition, contradictoriness

چپت ¹ chapáṭ m. ☞ چيرغټ

چپت ² chəpáṭ m. idle-talker, windbag, talker

چپته ¹ chəpáṭa f. wooden pole for reinforcing adobe walls

چپته ² chapáṭa f. healthy girl, strong girl

چپته ³ chəpáṭa f. frivolous woman, gossip

چپ چاپ chəpchāp chupchāp 1 taciturn 2 quietly

چپ چاپیر chapchāpér چپ چاپیره chupchāpéra ☞ چاپیر

چپ چور chapchúr 1.1 smashed, broken 1.2 shattered 2 m. robbery

چپر chapár m. 1 messenger, courier 2 runner

چپراس chaprás m. loop, noose

چپراسي chaprāsí m. 1 courier, deliveryman, messenger د هوتل
a hotel servant (boots) b waiter c runner (messenger)

چپرغټ chaparghát m. healthy boy, healthy man; brawny fellow

چپرکټ chaparkáṭ m. bed, cot

چپرګی chapárgaj m. twig; shoot, sucker (of a tree)

چپره chaprá f. leather-dresser, currier's knife

چپری chapráj m. small reservoir

چپراخه chapəṛákha m. ☞ چپراخه

چپراسي chapṛāsí m. ☞ چپراسي

چپرتاخ chapaṛṭákh f. چپرتاخ chaparbákh m. چپردخ chəpaṛdákh m.
kind of game

چپروس chaprús m. ☞ چاپلوس

چپروسي chaprusí f. ☞ چاپلوسي

چپری chapṛí f. lean meat

چپری چپرو chapṛí-chapṛó f. lazy woman

چپښ chapákh flat-footed

چپک chapák squint-eyed, cross-eyed; slant eyed; one-eyed چپکي
سترګي squinting eyes, slanted eyes سترګي چپکي کول to cast a
sidelong glance, look sidelong at

چپکو chapəkú m. left-hander

چپکه chəpáka f. dried dung (used for fuel)

چپلاخه chapalákha f. slap, cuff چپلاخه وهل to slap in the face په يوه
proverb the faces of 100 men smart چپلاخه د سلو کسو مخ خوږېږي
from one slap in the face

چپلاسي chaplāsí m. ☞ چپلاسي

چپلکه chapláka f. worn-out slipper

چپلی chaplə́j f. ☞ څپلی

چپنده chapə́nda f. wooden bowl, flat dish

چپنک chapanák m. child's coat

چپنه chəpána f. jacket, caftan

چپوالی ¹ chapválaj m. opposition

چپوالی ² chəpválaj m. silence

چپوښ chapúkh ☞ چپښ

چپ غروپ chəp-və-ghrúp taciturn د چا چپ غروپ يو کول to compel
someone to be silent چپ غروپ يو کېدل to fall silent

چپول ¹ chəpavál denominative, transitive [past: چپه يې کړ] to kiss

چپول ² chəpavál chupavál denominative, transitive [past: چپ يې کړ]
to compel to be silent; muffle; turn off (i.e., a radio)

چپول ³ chapavál denominative, transitive [past: چپه يې کړه] 1 to turn
over, invert, upset 2 to change, alter لاره چپول to alter course;
diverge from the route 3 to avert something, keep something bad
from happening

چپول ⁴ chapavál transitive [past: وي يې چپاوه] to suck

چپول ⁵ chəpól 1 squint-eyed, squinting; one-eyed 2 deformed

چپونی chapúnaj m. end-piece of soap

چپه ¹ chapá f. 1 oar 2 wave 3 gust (of wind) 4 attack (i.e., of
malaria) چپه وهل a to rake b to be agitated, splash (water) c to
heave, wave (of a grain field) d to blow in gusts (wind) e to
attack suddenly; pelt with stones (in hunting birds) 5 medicine
crisis

چپه ² chápa 1 f. opposition په چپه کښي on the other hand, on the
contrary په چپه کښي کېدل to resist 2 feminine singular of چپ ³

چپه ³ chápa f. kiss چپه اخيستل to kiss one another چپه ورکول to kiss

چپه ⁴ chapá overturned, upset چپه کول a to turn over, invert, upset
b to change, alter c to shoot down (e.g., a plane) d to derail
(e.g., a train) e to spill, spill out چپه کېدل a to be turned over, be
inverted, be upset b to fail پر چپه لار پنبه اخيستل، چپه لار نيول، پر چپه
لار تلل to be diverted from the path; be driven off course

چپه ⁵ chápa 1 feminine singular of چپ ² 2 f. silence يو بل ته په چپه
کتل to regard one another in silence

چپه چپائي chəpa-chəpājí f. چپه چپيا chápa-chupjá f. complete silence,
muteness; silence دې چپي چپائي ډېر پايښت نه کئ This silence did not
last very long.

چپه کبن chapakákh m. oarsman

چپه یی chapaí oared, row (of a boat)

چپی chapáj squint-eyed, squinty; slant-eyed; one-eyed

چپیدل chapedól *denominative, intransitive* [*past:* چپ شو] to be silent; fall silent چپ شه! Be still!

چپیدل [past: چپه شو] ² chapedól **1** *denominative, intransitive* to be turned over, be inverted, be upset **2** to be changed, be altered **3** to be averted **4** to be saved, escape

چپیره chapéra *f.* ☞ چپلاخه

چت ¹ chat *m.* **1** roof **2** ceiling **3** awning **4** story (of a building) **5** deck

چت ² chit ☞ چیت ²

چت پت chit-pit ☞ چیت پیت

چت دپوه chatdevá *f.* chandelier; candelabrum

چتر ¹ chatr chatór *m.* camel in its fourth year

چتر ² chatór **1** *m.* **.1** blemish (from a scab, wound); scar **1.2** bald spot, bare place چتر کبدل to grow bald سر یو چتر درول to shave one's head **1.3** curl, lock of bangs (of a woman) **2** clean, purified

چتر ³ chátr chátr *m.* **1** umbrella, parasol **2** awning, overhang (of a roof) *idiom* چتر نجات parachute

چترال chitrál chatrál *m.* Chitral

چترالي chitrālí chitrāláj **1** Chitralian **2** *m.* resident of Chitral

چترکی chatrakáj **1** short of stature, short **2** *m.* shrimp, shorty

چتری chatráj *f.* **1** umbrella, parasol **2** even, smooth land **3** scar

چترئي chatrəjí bald, having bald patches

چترر chatór *m.* factory mark

چتکی ¹ chətkáj chətakáj *m.* warbler (bird)

چتکی ² chótkaj چتکی چتکی a little bit, a bit

چتله chatlá ground up, pulverized

چتنی chatnáj *f.* ☞ چتنی

چیتول chitavól *denominative, transitive* ☞ چیتول

چته ¹ chatá *f.* **1** beehive **2** wasps' nest

چته ² chatá **1** *f.* **.1** storey **1.2** roof **2** دوه چته کور two-storied house *idiom* تر چته وتل a to overdo it, go too far b to تر چته اوښتل *idiom* lose one's temper

چتی ¹ chótaj *m.* **1** ☞ چتکی ¹ **2** titmouse

چتی ² chútaj *m.* peg, hinge (of a door)

چیتبدل ¹ chitedól *denominative, intransitive dialect* ☞ چیتبدل

چتیز chatíz اوه چتیزه مانی seven-storied building

چت ¹ chat **1.1** unmarried (man), single **1.2** hare-brained, frivolous, dissolute **1.3** corrupt **1.4** perished, ruined, annihilated چت دي وي زمور دښمنان! May our enemies perish! **1.5** unclean, dirty **1.6** shaven; beardless, with beard shaven **1.7** tipsy, intoxicated **1.8** *Western* smart, keen, bright **2** *m.* **.1** unmarried man, single man, bachelor **2.2** idler, playboy; profligate man; scapegrace **3** fully, quite

چت ² chat *m.* **1** bowl (for a dog) **2** slop-pail **3** dirty dish, dirty vessel

چتاکی chatākój *f.* **1** quarter of a khurd ☞ خورد **2** quarter of a pound **3** trifle, small thing, bagatelle

چتاوت chatāvát *m.* unexpected strike, sudden strike (e.g., at an enemy)

چت پت chatpát **1** defeated, destroyed **2** finished, completed چت پت کول a to destroy, spoil b to smash, destroy c to end, finish چت کبدل a to be defeated, be destroyed b to be ended, be finished

چتک ¹ chuták *m. dialect* ☞ ختک

چتک ² chaták **1** quick, swift; spry, agile, smart **2** quickly, swiftly, smartly چتک ولاړ شه! Run (and fetch something)! Go quickly (to get something)!

چتک تسمه chataktasmá *f.* belt, cincture

چتکتوب chataktób *m.* چتکتیا chataktjā *f.* چتکوالی chatakvā́laj *m.* ☞ چتکی ¹

چتکول chatakavól *denominative, transitive* [*past:* چتک یې کر] **1** to hasten, speed up **2** to hurry, make haste

چتکه chitká *f.* **1** red calico, chintz **2** spot

چتکه دار chitkadár spotted, dotted (of cloth)

چتکی ¹ chataki *f.* speed, swiftness; spryness, agility, smartness په چتکی، په چتکی سره quickly, swiftly, smartly

چتکی ² chótkáj *m.* swearing, cursing, rough language

چتکی ³ chutkój *f.* pinch چتکی کول to pinch

چتکبدل chatakedól *denominative, intransitive* [*past:* چتک شو] **1** to be sped up, be hastened **2** to be hurried along, be made to get a move on

چتل chatál dirty; soiled; clogged with dirt چتلی اوبه polluted water

چتل والی chataltjā́ *f.* چتل تیا، چتلتیا chataltób *m.* چتلتوب، چتل توب chatalvā́laj *m.* uncleanness, dirt, condition of being clogged or clotted with dirt

چتلول chatalavól *denominative, transitive* [*past:* چتل یې کر] to dirty, soil; clog with dirt

چتلبدل chataledól *denominative, intransitive* [*past:* چتل شو] to be dirtied, be soiled; be clogged with dirt

چتنی chatní *f.* [*plural:* چتنیاني chatnijā́ni] chutney

چتو ¹ chatú *m.* wooden mortar

چتو ² cható چتوکول، چتو او لرو کول a to squander, spend, waste b to spoil, mar, ruin something

چتو ³ cható *f.* empty-headed person, frivolous person

چتول ¹ chatavól *denominative, transitive* [*past:* چت یې کر] **1** to ruin, spoil **2** *dialect* to end, complete

چتول ² chatavól *denominative, transitive* [*past:* چت یې کر] to devour, eat up

چتو و لرو cható-u-laró ☞ چتو ²

چته chatá *f.* usury

چته cháta *feminine singular of* چت ¹

چتی ¹ chatí **1.1** stupid, absurd; frivolous, useless **1.2** harmful, inflicting damage on a matter or situation **2.1** *f.* dissipation چتی کول to lead a dissipated life **2.2** stupidity, absurdity چتی ویل to talk nonsense, speak rubbish

چتی ² chatój *f.* **1** ☞ چیتی **2** chador

چتی ³ chutí *f.* ☞ چوتی ²

چتي ⁴ cháṭi *feminine plural of* چت ¹ 1

چتيات chaṭijã́t *m.* چتيات ويل to speak nonsense, talk rot

چتي برو chaṭibaró *f.* stuff and nonsense, rubbish

چتېدل chaṭedál *denominative, intransitive* [*past:* چت شو] **1** to perish; deteriorate **2** *dialect* to be ended, be finished (to dic)

چج chadzh *m.* sieve; tray (for sorting grain); screen چج کول to sort or grade grain or corn on a special tray

چجک chadzhák *m.* trigger (on a firearm)

چجکی ¹ chadzhkáj *m.* ☞ چجه

چجکی ² chadzhkə́j *f.* rib, ribs

چجه chadzhá *f.* **1** weir (for catching fish) **2** ribs **3** leafy tops (of carrots) **4** fencing; wattle fencing **5** eaves **6** *medicine* splints

چچ chach *m.* ☞ چج

چچاړی chəchã́ṛaj *m.* island, islet

چچخه chichə́kha *f.* generation; progeny; clan چچخه يې وخته His clan has died out.

چچرن chachṛə́n **1** watery **2** ☞ چخرک

چچروبن chachṛobə́n **1** swollen, waterlogged (of food which has been allowed to stand overnight) **2** ☞ چخرک

چچل chichə́l *transitive* ☞ چیچل

چچنه chəchã́na *f.* ☞ چرچنه

چچو chachó *f.* breast (female); nipple

چچوگی chachogə́j *feminine diminutive of* چچو

چچه ¹ chachá *f.* Chach (district in northwestern Pakistan)

چچه ² chácha cry used in driving goats

چچی ¹ cháche *f. children's speech* hand, patty

چچی ² chíchaj ☞ غابنى چيچي

چخ ¹ chəkh **1** stuck into چخ کول ☞ چخول **2** *m.* hitching post (in a stable)

چخ ² chikh *interjection* Get away! (cry used to drive a dog off)

چخا chkhā *children's speech* doggie, dog

چخپیت chəkhpít **1** crushed down; baggy **2** *figurative* trampled, downtrodden

چخپیتول chəkhpitavə́l *denominative, transitive* [*past:* چخپیت یې کړ] **1** to trample, trod down **2** *figurative* to trample (down); oppress

چخپیتېدل chəkhpitedə́l *denominative, intransitive* [*past:* چخپیت شو] **1** to be pressed down, be crushed down **2** *figurative* to be trampled upon, be downtrodden

چختاړ chəkhtáṛ crushed down; pressed down

چختاړول chəkhtāṛavə́l *denominative, transitive* [*past:* چختاړ یې کړ] to press, crush, trample

چختاړېدل chəkhtāṛedə́l *denominative, intransitive* [*past:* چختاړ شو] to be trampled, be trodden down

چختان chəkhtã́ṇ ☞ چختاړ

چخچای chəkhchã́j *m.* sharp stake (for weeding)

چخړ chəkhã́ṛ *m.* mud, slush

چخړبا chakhṛabá *f.* **1** mud, slush ببخي چخړبه ده solid mud, very muddy **2** waste, extravagance چخړبه کول **a** to muddy, make muddy **b** to dilute; dissolve; blend **c** to squander, waste (money)

چخړبه کبدل to be turned into mud, be turned into slush; be thinned out, get slushy

چخرک chəkhṛák چخړن chəkhṛə́n having suppurating eyes

چخروبن chəkhṛobə́n watery

چخروبنول chəkhṛobənavə́l *denominative, transitive* [*past:* چخروبن یې کړ] to cause to become watery

چخروبنېدل chəkhṛobənedə́l *denominative, intransitive* [*past:* چخروبن شو] to become watery

چخړه chə́khṛa *f.* mucus and pus (from inflamed eyes) چخړه یې لیدلې وه He has seen a lot in his lifetime.

چخکی chakə́kaj *m.* intestinal worm

چخل chikhə́l *transitive* ☞ چخول

چخله chikhála *f.* dragonfly

چخن chikhə́n **1.1** suppurating (of eyes) **1.2** dirty **1.3** tarnished (of a mirror, glass) **2** *m.* person with suppurating eyes *idiom* چخني خبري biting words, sharp words

چخول chikhavə́l *transitive* [*past:* و یې چخاوه] **1** to prick; stick into; plunge, thrust into **2** to drive away (e.g., wasps) **3** to drive into, implant

چخونیا chikhunjã́ **1** inflamed (e.g., eyes) **2** rotting, decaying (of food) **3** unfit, bad چخونیا کول **a** to inflame, cause inflammation **b** to spoil, rot (produce) چخونیا کبدل **a** to be inflamed **b** to be rotted (of food)

چخړه ¹ chíkha *f.* ☞ چخړه ¹

چخه ² chíkha *interjection* ☞ چخ ²

چخه ³ chə́kha ☞ څخه ¹

چخه ⁴ chákha ☞ چغه ¹

چخی ¹ chíkhi *f. plural* ☞ چخړه

چخی ² chíkhe ☞ چخ ²

چخی ³ chíkhe *colloquial* somewhat, a bit, a little

چدام chadã́m *m. archaeology* the eighth part of a tola ☞ توله

چدئ chídəj *vice* چه دئ ☞ چه

چدل chəẓ́ál *m.* clay dish filled with food

چدوسکی chəẓ́úskaj *m.* چدوکی chəẓ́úkaj *m.* rind (of a melon, etc.)

چر ¹ chur *m.* [*plural:* چران churā́n] basin, reservoir (e.g., in the shaft of an irrigation system) چرکول to construct (such a) reservoir چرکبدل to be washed away, be eroded

چر ² char **1** *m.* ☞ چړ ¹ **2** custom

چر ³ chər *m.* **1** chirping, twittering **2** noise (made by ripping cloth) **3** chatter (of children) **4** rubbish, stuff and nonsense; poppycock

چر ⁴ char ☞ چلر ¹

چر ⁵ chur ☞ چور ⁵

چر ⁶ cháre *Eastern* ☞ چبری

چراتی charātə́j *f. archaeology* pebbles used instead of lead shot

چرار chərã́r *m.* ☞ چر ³

چراسپه charã́spa *f.* **1** rope (of goat hair, for tethering horses) **2** straps (for carrying rifles) **3** leather straps **4** means of fastening a pack on a camel

چراغ chirágh *m.* [*plural:* چراغان chiraghán] **1** ☞ خراغ **2** [*plural:* چراغان] **a** candles; lamps **b** illumination چراغان کول **a** to light, illuminate **b** to provide illumination

چراغک chiraghák *m.* **1** small lamp; lampion **2** glow-worm, firefly

چراگاه charágǎ charagáh *f.* pasture

چراوی charǎvaj *m.* imitator, emulator; man who imitates or copies another person

چرب charb ☞ خورب

چربانگ charbǎng *m.* ☞ چرگ بانگ

چرب دست charbdást agile; energetic

چرب زبان charbzabán charbzubán smooth-talking, flattering

چربل charbál *m.* reins (braided of cord)

چربوری charburáj *m.* filet (meat)

چربه charbá *f.* oiled paper; tracing paper

چربی charbí *f.* lard; grease

چرت churt *m.* **1** reflection; thought; contemplation چرت وهل **a** to think, reflect **b** to doze چرت پکښني وهل to think about something چرت مه ورانوه! Don't get upset!

چرت chart *m.* **1** stream (of water) **2** sound (of spitting)

چرتکی chartəkáj *m.* funnel

چرتکی churtakáj inconstant, unstable

چرت وری churt vəraj reflective; pensive

چرته chartá *f.* ☞ چرده

چرته chárta *Eastern* ☞ چیری

چرتي churtí ☞ چورتي

چرټ chiráṭ *m.* (Indian) cigar د چرټو ډبلی box of cigars

چرچر charchár *m.* ☞ چرچر کول **a** to chirp, twitter **b** to engage in idle talk, talk stuff and nonsense

چرچرانکی charchərǎnkaj *m.* cicada

چرچرک charchərák *m.* چرچری charchəráj *m.* idle talker, windbag

چرچن charchán *m.* [*plural:* چرچن charchán] common sparrow

چرچنه charchóna **1** *feminine of* چرچن *f.* **2** hen sparrow

چرچور charchúr cut up into small pieces

چرچورکی charchurakáj *f.* چرچوری charchuráj *f.* cricket

چرچه charchá *f.* ☞ چرچه

چرخ charkh *m.* ☞ خرخ 1, 2

چرخل charkhál *m.* چرخول charkhvál *m.* **1** cock's comb **2** end of a chalma (turban) worn by Muslim men

چرخوله chirkhvála *f.* *botany* amaranthus, coxcomb

چرخولی charkhvaláj *m.* **1** ☞ چرخل **2** handle (of a lid of a kettle)

چرخه charkhá *f.* distaff

چرده chardá *f.* **1** color of the face **2** complexion **3** color, shade (of an animal's fur)

چرروت charurút *m.* twitter, chirping

چرره chírṛa *f.* rag

چرس chars *m.* *plural* hashish

چرسي charsí *m.* hashish smoker; drug addict

چرغ chargh *m.* gerfalcon, *Falco cherrug*

چرغزه charghóza *f.* coot (the bird)

چرغغ charghág *m.* ☞ چرگ بانگ

چرک chirk *m.* mud, dirt

چرک chrək *m.* stiches, sharp pain (in the side)

چرک chrək *m.* ☞ چرکه

چرکی charkáj *m.* **1** talk, chatter, gossip **2** squawking (of a starling, a mynah bird)

چرکېدل chrəkedál *denominative, intransitive* [*past:* چرک شو] **1** to have a stitch or shooting pain (e.g., in the side) **2** to experience a shooting pain

چرکین chirkín **1** dirty **2** filthy, defiled چرکین کول **a** to soil, dirty, besmirch **b** to defile

چرگ chərg *m.* rooster د چرگ غوښني chicken meat د چرگانو روزنه the poultry industry, poultry breeding *idiom* دوی ورته حلال کړي They were devoted to him. They were absolutely subordinate to him.

چرگ chrag **1.1** piebald; spotted; parti-colored **1.2** striped **1.3** clever, shrewd **2** *m.* star, white blaze (on the brow of an animal)

چرگبانگ chərgbáng *m.* **1** crowing of a cock و چرگ بانگ the first cocks began to crow (it was early) **2** dawn, daybreak, early morning

چرگبانگي chərgbāngí *f.* ☞ پیشلمی

چرگ برگ chrag-brág **1** piebald; spotted; parti-colored **2** striped *idiom* چرگي برگي سترگي wide-open eyes

چرگ خالی chərgkhǎlaj *m.* hen-house, chicken-coop

چرگغ chərggágh *m.* ☞ چرگ بانگ

چرگ سابه chərgsābó *m.* *plural* spinach

چرگغغ chərgghág *m.* ☞ چرگ بانگ

چرگک chərgák *m.* hoopoe

چرگ ناری chərgnāré *f.* *plural* ☞ چرگ بانگ

چرگ ناری chərgnāráj *m.* serving guests chicken (meat)

چرگوتی chərgótaj *m.* cockerel

چرگوری chərgúraj *m.* chick د چرگورو وښتلو ماشین incubator

چرگه chórga *f.* [*plural:* چرگي chórgi *plural:* چرگاني chərgāni] hen *proverb* چرگي له د ستني داغ هم بس دئ Everything seems threatening to a small man.

چرگی chərgáj having a star, with a white blaze on the brow (of an animal)

چرگی chərgój *f.* hearth

چرگی chərgáj *m.* long-tailed cat

چرگی برگی chragáj-bragáj ☞ چرگی

چرگین chərgín hen's, chicken's, gallinaceous

چرلاو churláv chərláv *m.* **1** factory **2** machine, motor

چرلائي churlājí *f.* amaranth, *Amaranthus polygamous*

چرلټ churláṭ quite, completely

چرلکی churlúkaj *m.* heel, counter (of a shoe)

چرلندی churlandáj *m.* ☞ چرلندي

چرلند churlánḍ charlánd *m.* no-account, good-for-nothing, base fellow

چرلندی churlandáj *m.* rattle (child's toy)

چورلول churlavә́l *transitive* ☞ چورلول

چرلی churlә́j *f.* **1** churli (children's game played with nuts) **2** top

چورلېدل churledә́l *intransitive* ☞ ماشيندار

چرلی غرب chәrlajghráb *m. dialect* ☞ ماشيندار

چرم charm *m.* leather ☞ څرمن

چرم باب charmbáb *m. plural* leather goods

چرمباز chrambáz charambáz *m.* outside ox in the row (when using animals in threshing)

چرمينکی charmәkhkә́j *f.* چرمنبی charmәkhә́j *f.* lizard

چرمک charmák *m.* leather ring in which an axle is place

چرمګر charmgár *m.* leather worker, currier

چرمګري charmgarí *f.* **1** leather business, leather production **2** job or work of a currier

چرموچرک chәrmuchrák **1** baby; boy-child **2** little

چرمور charmór ☞ چختار

چرمورول charmoravә́l *transitive* ☞ چختارول

چرمه chәrmá *f.* braided cord

چرمين charmín چرمي charmí **1** leather, leathern **2** leather-dressing

چرمينه charmená charminá *f.* harness traces, straps

چرند chәrónd **1** garrulous **2** windbag, idle talker

چورندک churәndák *m.* ☞ چورندک

چرنک charanák *m.* [*plural:* چرنک charanә́k] چرنگ chrang *m.* spurge, euphorbia

چرنوزیوم chernozjóm *m.* chernozem, black earth

چروده chróda *f.* pit, hollow, depression

چروک chrok *m.* **1** short period of time **2** customary time period during which irrigation water is released in a field (usually three hours)

چره ¹ chará *f.* **1** shot (for a firearm) د چرو توپک shotgun **2** shrapnel fragment (from a shell) د چرو بم high explosive shell

چره ² chará *f.* **1** irrigation ditch (in a melon, cotton field) **2** drainage ditch

چرهار chәrahár *m.* chirping, twittering, squawking چرهار کول to chirp, twitter, squawk (birds)

چري ¹ cháre *Eastern* ☞ چیري

چری ² chәrә́j *f.* variety of plum

چری ³ charә́j *f.* pot with a lipped edge

چری دار charedár چری دار توپک shotgun

چرېدل chәredә́l *intransitive* [*past:* وچرېده] **1** to chirp, twitter, squawk (birds) **2** to cry out **3** to moan

چرېکار ¹ charekár *m.* ☞ چاري کار ¹

چرېکار ² charekár *m.* imperial (beard)

چرئیز charaíz چرئیز توپک shotgun

چر ¹ char *m.* **1** shoal, hank, sandbar **2** *Eastern* ford (of a river) په چر پوري وتل to ford by wading **3** heavy rain, downpour **4** crackling (of roasting meat)

چر ² char *m.* collection of produce among the populace (for a mullah or for guests)

چر ³ chur *m.* **1** hinge (of a door) **2** crack, split

چر ⁴ char *m.* shaft (of a lance, spear) *idiom* چر په چا ایستل، چر په چا گدول to slay (by spearing), pierce repeatedly (with a lance, spear)

چراح chәráh *m.* **1** slashing wound, penetrating wound **2** ulceration (on the heel)

چرانگو chәrāngú *m.* tendril (of a vegetative stalk)

چراو charáv *m.* slaughter, butchery, carnage چراو گدول to slay, slaughter

چراوه chәrāvá *f.* water leaking or percolating from an irrigation well, etc.

چرپ chrap *m.* چرپا chrapá *f.* **1** smacking or chomping of the mouth and lips **2** splashing (of water) چرپ او چروپ **a** loud chomping **b** forceful splashing

چرپن chrapә́n *m.* **1** idle-talker, windbag **2** garrulous

چرپول chrapavә́l *transitive* [*past:* وي چرپاوه] **1** to smack (lips); to chomp خوله چرپول to smack; chomp **2** to splash, splash out (water)

چرپهار chrәphár *m.* چرپی chrapáj *m.* ☞ چرپ

چرپېدل chrapedә́l *intransitive* [*past:* وچرپیده] **1** to smack; chomp **2** to squelch; tramp (i.e., through mud) **3** to be splashed, be splashed out (water) **4** to impoverish, make destitute

چرتون chartún *m.* sheath, scabbard

چرچکه charcháka *f.* harrow

چرچوبن charchobә́n watery, aqueous

چرچوبي charchobә́j *f.* ☞ چارچوبي

چرچه charchá *f.* out-door party, merrymaking, feasting چرچي وهل ، چرچي کول to have an out-door party, feast, make merry

چرچی charchaí چرچئ ي charchají *m.* playboy

چرغه chargha *f.* sharp stone (used in slaughtering cattle)

چرق charák *m.* splash of pouring water

چرقاو charḳáv *m.* sprinkling; watering, irrigating چرقاو کول to sprinkle, spray, water

چرک chrak *m.* **1** fountain **2** splash **3** crackling **4** latch (door)

چرکانی charḳā́ṇaj *m.* grindstone

چرکاو charḳáv *m.* ☞ چکراو

چرکه chrә́ka *f.* stitch, shooting pain

چرکی charәkә́j *f.* چرکی charḳáj *m.* small knife, pocket-knife

چرنگ chrang ☞ شرنگ

چرو charú **1** base **2** *m.* **.1** base person; scoundrel, ne'er-do-well **2.2** cadger

چروبن charobә́n watery, aqueous

چروبی ¹ charobáj *m.* waterfall

چروبی ² charobáj *m.* salt-dryer, merchant dealing in salted and pickled foods

چروبی ³ charubáj *m.* dyer

چروتوب charutób *m.* baseness, meanness

چروس charús *m.* ☞ چرو 2

چروکی charokә́j *f.* ☞ چرکی

چرونگ chrung *m.* چرونگا chrungā́ *f.* چرونگهار chrungәhár *m.* peeping, cheeping (of nestlings)

چرونگی chṛungáj *m.* pouring, streaming (of water)

چرونگېدل chṛungedál *intransitive* [*past:* و چرونگېده] to emit cheeping, peep (of nestlings)

چروی chaṛávaj *m.* dyer

چړه chóṛa *f.* 1 piece, slice (e.g., of watermelon, melon) 2 pin, hinge (door)

چړهار chuṛahár *m.* 1 sputtering (of roasting meat) 2 chirping (of birds) 3 babbling (of running water)

چړي ¹ chaṛí *m.* 1 cadger, beggar 2 man collecting offerings or gifts (e.g., for a mullah)

چړي ² chaṛé *plural of* چاړه

چړیا chaṛjá engaged, occupied, busy

چړیاگر chiṛjāgár *m. regional* zoo, zoological garden

چړیتوب chaṛitób *m.* service; servitude

چړیس chaṛəsón dirty, slovenly

چسپ chasp *m.* 1 adhesiveness, stickiness; viscosity 2 ☞ چسپان

چسپان chaspán 1 adhesive, gummy, sticky, gluey 2 tight-fitting, close-fitting (of garments) چسپان پتلون close-fitting pants

چسپانده chaspánda quick, swift; lively; spry, bright

چسپناک chaspnák ☞ چسپان

چسپول chaspavál *transitive* [*past:* و یې چسپاوه] to cling, adhere; to stick, stick on; stick together

چسپېدل chaspedál *intransitive* [*past:* و چسپېده] to adhere, adhere to; stick to, stick together

چست chust quick, swift, lively; versatile

چستي ¹ chustí *f.* swiftness, agility, promptness

چستي ² chustáj *m.* ☞ چوستی

چشته chíshta *abbreviation* څه شي ته why, for what reason

چشتي ¹ chishtí *m.* Chishti (an order of dervishes)

چشتی ² chəshtáj *f.* ☞ چوستی

چشکله cháshkəla ☞ څنبکله

چشل chshəl *transitive* ☞ چنبل

چشم chashm *m.* [*plural:* چشمان chashmán] 1 eye 2 look, glance *idiom* چشمان به راه in expectation, expectantly

چشم بندي chashmbandí *f.* 1 (hypnotic) suggestion 2 eyewash (deliberate faking of the true situation)

چشم دید chashmdíd چشم دید گواهي کول to testify

چشمک chashmák *m.* winking چشمک وهل to wink

چشمکه chashmáka *f.* [more often *plural:* چشمکي chashmáki] glasses, spectacles

چشمه chashmá *f.* 1 spring, source, small stream of potable water 2 *Eastern* ☞ چشمکه

چشمي chashmé *f. plural* glasses چشمي په سترگو لگول to put on glasses

چشی ¹ chisháj *m.* burrs of burdock or xanthium (sticking to a sheeps wool)

چشی ² chishaj *contraction of* څه شي؟ What?

چنباک chnbák *m.* drink, beverage

چنتن chəkhtán *m.* ☞ څنتن

چرتون chakhtún *m.* ☞ چرتون

چنجه chakhchá *f.* splinter, chip (of wood)

چنکوری chəkhkúraj *m.* 1 spout (e.g., of a teapot) 2 tap, faucet, cock

چنبل chkhól chəkhól *transitive* [*past:* و یې چنبل] 1 to drink چای to drink چنبل to drink tea څنوروا چنبل to drink soup 2 to absorb, take up, soak up

چنن chkhən *m.* چننگ chkhang *m.* drink, beverage د چنبن اوبه drinking water چنن کول to drink

چننوکی chəkhnúkaj *m.* small water-skin, leather canteen

چنبوبی chkhubáj *m.* drink, beverage

چنبول chəkhavál *transitive* [*past:* و یې چنناوه] to give to drink

چغ ¹ chəgh *m.* 1 screen of reeds, rushes 2 snare

چغ ² chəgh chigh *m.* 1 cry 2 squeak

چغ ³ chagh ☞ چاغ

چغا chəghá *f.* چغار chughár *m.* 1 chirping, singing (of birds) 2 jingling

چغار chəghár *m.* ☞ چغهار

چغاره chighára *f.* 1 cry, wail 2 chirping, singing (of birds)

چغانغه chəghágha *f.* ☞ چغانغه

چغال chaghál *m.* jackal *proverb* چغال انگور خوري ښه the jackel eats the best grapes

چغالي chaghālí 1 low-grade (of apricots) 2 deserted, desolate, abandoned (of a place, a square) چغالي کول a to bare, strip b to abandon 3 latticed; made of fencing چغالي ور wicket-gate

چغانغه chaghángha *f.* mint

چغاول chəghāvál *m.* ☞ جغاول

چغبغ chəghbəgh *m.* din, uproar

چغبوز chəghbúz *m.* blacksmith

چغتا chaghatá *m. history* the Chagataj (the tribe to which Tamurlane belonged)

چغتار chaghtár *m.* ☞ چلتار

چغته chaghtá chaghatá *f.* snipe (the bird)

چغتی chaghatáj *m. history* member of the Chagataj tribe

چغټ chaghóṭ dirty

چغ چغ chighchígh *m.* 1 cackling 2 noise, din 3 chatter

چغچی chaghchój *f.* ☞ چغزی ²

چغر chaghár 1 having a cataract چغره سترگه a cataract on the eye 2 cross-eyed

چغرسترگی chagharstórgaj with a cataract on the eye

چغرو chaghrú *m.* eagle-owl

چغربه chaghṛəbá *f.* 1 noise, din, racket 2 altercation, row

چغرکه chəghṛáka *f.* bread from lightly fermented dough

چغزي ¹ chaghzí fragile, brittle

چغزی ² chaghzój *f.* walnut kernel (a variety of soft walnut)

چوغ سترگی chəghstórgaj ☞ چغ سترگی

چوغک chughók *m.* ☞ چغک

چوغکه chughóka *f.* ☞ چغکه

چغکی chəghkáj *m.* noise, din, uproar

چغل ‎¹‎ chughúl *m.* ☞ چغلگوی

چغل ‎²‎ chighíl *m.* sieve, strainer, sifter

چغلبازي chəghálbāzí *f.* visit by the bridgegroom to the home of the bride prior to the wedding

چغلبه chəghlabá *f.* noise, din; howling, screams

چغلگوی chughulgúj *m.* چغلمار chughulmār *m.* scandalmonger; slanderer; schemer *proverb* د چغلگوی مخ همیشه توروی A scandalmonger's face is ever dark.

چغلماري chughulmārí *f.* ☞ چغلي

چغل والا chighilvālá *m.* worker who sorts or sifts corn kernels

چغلول ‎¹‎ chughálavál *denominative, transitive* [*past:* چغل یې کړ] to engage in scandalmongering or intrigue; spread scandal, calumniate

چغلول ‎²‎ chighilavál *transitive* [*past:* چغل یې کړ] to sift, screen

چغله ‎¹‎ chughúla *f.* bettle

چغله ‎²‎ chaghlá linear dimensions, length and breadth (of an object)

چغلي chughulí *f.* scandal; slander; intrigue چغلي کول ☞ چغلول ‎¹‎

چغلي خور chughlikhór *m.* ☞ چغلمار

چغلیدل chughuledál *denominative, intransitive* [*past:* چغل شو] to be slandered

چغمټ chəghmáṭ fat; fattened up

چغمټه chaghmə́ṭa *f.* unleavened bread

چغمغي chaghmaghí ☞ چقمقي

چغندر chughundár *m.* beet قندي چغندر sugar beet

چغنۍ chaghanáj *m.* 1 hand gin for separating the cotton boll from the seeds 2 stork

چغنۍ وال chaghanajvál *m.* scutcher, carder of cotton

چغ وغ chəghupə́gh *m.* noise, din, uproar

چغول chəghavál *transitive* [*past:* وي چغاوه] 1 to make shout, cry out 2 to cause to chirp, cheep or twitter 3 to cause to squeal 4 to cause a quarrel

چغه ‎¹‎ chə́gha *f.* 1 shout, outcry چغي عمومي general approval په ورته مي ډېري چغي ووهلي I was shouting, crying out چغو چغو shouting at him for a long time. 2 alarm (upon the attack on a village, etc.) 3 Chiga (detachment used to repel robbers) په داري پسي په چغه تلل to pursue a gang

چغه ‎²‎ chughá *f.* ☞ چوغه

چغه ‎³‎ chígha *interjection* Get away! (cry used to chase dogs away)

چغهار chəghəhár *m.* 1 creak (of wheels, doors, etc.) 2 shout, outcry

چغه سراج chaghasarā́j *m.* Chagasaraj (settlement)

چغی chugháj *m.* person having his eyes screwed up

چغبدل chəghedál *intransitive* [*past:* وچغبده] 1 to shout, cry out 2 to chirp, cheep, twitter, burst into song (of birds) 3 to squeal 4 to quarrel, raise a din

چغي مير chəghimír *m.* chief of a Chigi ☞ چغه ‎¹‎ 3

چف chuf *m.* 1 puff (wind) 2 charm, spell چف کول a to blow b to extinguish c to heal with a charm or by spells

چفته chaftá chiftá *f.* lathe, slat (wooden)

چفول chufavál *denominative, transitive* [*past:* چف یې کړ] 1 to blow 2 to extinguish 3 to heal with a charm, with spells

چغر chakár *m.* ☞ چکر

چقر chikár *m.* ☞ چکر

چقره chikára *f.* ☞ چکړه

چقماق chakmák *m.* چقمق chakmák *m.* flint

چقمقي chakmakí چقمقي توپک flinklock rifle

چقندر chukundár *m.* ☞ چغندر

چاقو chakú *m.* ☞ چاقو

چقوري chukurí *f.* pit; pot-hole

چقه chuká *f.* cackling چقه وهل to cackle

چک ‎¹‎ chak *m.* 1 honeycombs 2 wasps' nest 3 timber or masonry frame of a well 4 disk 5 short jacket made of goat's wool

چک ‎²‎ chak *m.* 1 group چک په چکه in groups 2 ☞ چکه ‎¹‎

چک ‎³‎ chak *m.* Chak (settlement)

چک ‎⁴‎ chik *m.* ropes or traces used to yoke bullocks or camels to a chigir or noria (Persian type irrigation wheel)

چک ‎⁵‎ chek chik *m.* [*plural:* چکونه chekúna chikúna *Western* چکان chekán chikán] check د بانک چک bank check د چکونو کتاب check book

چک ‎⁶‎ chek *m.* Czech

چک ‎⁷‎ chek *m.* checkered cloth

چک ‎⁸‎ chik *colloquial* No!

چک chák *adjectival suffix* rather, somewhat, -ish سپین چک whitish

چکاک chəkák *m.* drink, beverage خوراک او چکاک food and drink

چک چاپېر chakchāpér ☞ چپ چاپېر

چکچک chikchík cry used in driving a donkey

چکچکي chakchákí *f.* چک چکي کول *plural* applause چک چکي کول to applaud, clap

چکر ‎¹‎ chakár *m.* 1 circle; round, beat; circuit 2 stroll یو چکر لګول to stroll, take a walk په چکر وتل a to complete a ride around b to go out for a stroll چکر وهل a to circle b to walk, have taken a stroll

چکر ‎²‎ chikár *m.* چکري chikári cry used to drive a goat

چکړ chikáṛ *m.* [*plural:* چکړونه chikaṛúna *f. plural:* چکړي chikáṛe] *Eastern* 1 liquid mud; slush 2 bog, marsh

چکړاو chakṛáv *m.* 1 liquid mud; slush 2 downpour, heavy rain 3 sprinkling

چکړه chakṛá *f.* bullock-cart; two-wheeled cart (with a team of harnessed bullocks)

چکړي ‎¹‎ chikáṛi *f. plural* cackling

چکړي ‎²‎ chakṛí *f.* ☞ چکړه

چکړي ‎³‎ chakṛé *plural of* چکړه

چکړی ‎⁴‎ chakṛə́j *f.* short jacket made of goat's wool

چکس chakás *m.* ☞ چگس

چکش chakúsh *m.* hammer

چکخو chakkhú *m.* cassia (medicinal plant)

چکله ‎¹‎ chaklá *f.* 1 drop, droplet 2 sip

چکله ‎²‎ chaklá *f.* district, province

چکله ³ chaklá *f.* unleavened bread

چکلی chaklój *f.* 1 whirlpool 2 toothed cogwheel of a nori (Persian water-wheel) 3 top (the children's toy)

چکلټ chaklét *m. plural* chocolate

چکمار chakmā́r ☞ چادي

چکمک chakmák *m.* ☞ چقمق

چکمن chakmán *m.* چکمنه chakmána *f.* cloth jacket

چکمه chakmá *f.* 1 shoe 2 short jacket

چکن chəkán chikán *m.* 1 chakan (patterns made on cloth by means of colored beeswax) 2 kind of embroidery

چکن دوز chəkandóz *m.* master-craftsman working in the art of chakan (decoration of fabric with colored beeswax) ☞ چکن

چکن دوزي chəkandozi *f.* decoration of fabric by the chakan method ☞ چکن

چکو ¹ chakú *m.* left-handed person

چکو ² chəkó *m. children's speech* hand

چکو ³ chakú *m.* ☞ چاقو

چکوتره chukutrá *f.* grapefruit

چکوچکو chko-chkó cry used for calling calves

چکور chəkúr quick, prompt, smart

چکوړی chaķoŕáj *m.* [*plural:* چکوړیان chaķoŕijā́n] new-born calf

چکوسلواکي chekoslovākí *f.* چکوسلواکیا chekoslovākijā́ *f.* Czechoslovakia

چکه ¹ chaká *f. Western* hand *idiom* چکه کشول to slap in the face

چکه ² chaká *f.* 1 coagulated and expressed milk-curds, cottage cheese مستی چکه کول to squeeze or express sour milk, cottage cheese 2 unleavened bread

چکه ³ chaká چکه اغزن experienced (professional) thief چکه غل extremely thorny, densely covered with spines or thorns (of a bush)

چکه دانه chakadāná *f.* fruit or berry of a plant of the honeysuckle family

چکي ¹ chekí Czechoslovakian

چکي ² chā́ki *f. plural children's speech* palm (of the hand)

چکي ³ chə́ke cry used to drive a goat

چکي ⁴ chaké *plural of* چکه ¹, ²

چکي ⁵ chakój *f.* 1 small piece, scrap, morsel (e.g., of soap, fat) 2 pastry, small loaf 3 pig (iron), ingot د سربو چکی lead ingot 4 fat tail (sheep) 5 core (fruit) 6 cell (prison)

چکي ⁶ chəkój *f.* [*plural:* چکیاني chəkəjāni] girl (child)

چکي ⁷ chakój *f. dialect* islet

چکي ⁸ chakí *f. hunting* lure, bait

چکي چکي chikí-chikí cry used to call a goat

چکیده chakidá 1 clotted, coagulated (sour milk) 2 *f.* expressed curds, cottage cheese

چگټ chagáṭ *m.* cotton seed

چگس chagás *m.* perch, roost (for a raptor such as a falcon or hawk trained for the hunt)

چگه chəga *f.* [*plural:* چگاني chəgāni] *children's speech* eye

چل chal *m.* 1 artifice, deception; subterfuge, trick 2 way, method 3 rotation, circulation چل کول a to deceive b to put into motion 4 trap (for foxes) 5 turn 6 existence چل کېدل a to be put in motion, be activated b to exist 7 conduct, behavior *idiom* ټوک په چل نیول a to knock someone off balance with a shove; to deceive or take someone in *idiom* څه چل دئ؟ What's going on? What does all this mean? *idiom* په ده څه چل شوئ دئ؟ What is the matter with him?

چلان chəlā́n *m.* چلاند chəlā́nd 1.1 turning, dealing with 1.2 started, put into motion 1.3 operational, working 1.4 flowing (of a liquid) 1.5 marketable (of goods) 2 *m.* .1 invoice 2.2 rotation, circulation 2.3 winding up, getting moving, starting 2.4 action on a matter (in court, etc.)

چلاو ¹ chalā́v *m.* 1 means of existence; sustenance چلاو می بند شو I lacked the wherewithal for existence. 2 life, existence 3 dealing with someone دی سړي سره می چلاو نه کېږي I cannot get along with that man.

چلاو ² chilā́v *m.* ☞ چلو

چلاوصاف chilāvsā́f *m.* colander

چلباز chalbā́z *m.* cunning person, fraud, cheat, swindler چل باز،

چلبازي chalbāzí *f.* guile, cheating; fraud, swindle چل بازي،

چلتار chaltā́r *m.* dervish's headband (of goat's wool)

چلچراغ chilchirā́gh *m.* chandelier

چلچل chalchál *m.* چلچله chalchalā́ *f.* 1 vanity, haste, confusion 2 disputes, disagreements (on the route)

چلخی ¹ chalkhój *f.* top (the children's toy)

چلر ² chulúr *m.* sly individual; fraud, cheat, swindler

چلر ² chulár *m.* incompetent, awkward or stupid person

چلښت chaláķht *m.* ☞ چلنت 1

چلښت لیکه chaláķhtlíka *f.* course, direction

چلغوزی chalghúzaj *m.* ☞ جنغوزی

چلغه chalghá *f.* ☞ چغله ²

چلقت chalkát *m. history* 1 quilted greatcoat (soldier's) 2 coat of mail

چلک chilák *m.* jerrycan (for kerosene, gasoline)

چلکه chaláka *f.* agitation, ripple (on water)

چلگری chalgóraj *m.* weaver of carpets

چلم chiləm *m.* [*plural:* چلمونه chiləmúna *Western plural:* چلمان chiləmā́n] chilim, narghile, water-pipe چلم څکول to smoke a waterpipe

چلمچي chiləmchí *m.* [*plural:* چلمچیان chiləmchijā́n] large brass or tin basin used as a wash-basin

چلمکښ chiləmkáķh *m.* water-pipe smoker

چل مل chalmál *m.* cheating, fraud هیڅ چل مل نشته There is no fraud.

چلمي chiləmí 1 چلمي تمباکو tobacco for a water-pipe 2 *m.* ☞ چلم کښ

چلن chalán *m.* 1 habit; style 2 conduct; behavior 3 ☞ چلند *idiom* چلنه غوټه a nautical knot

چلند chalánd **1** *m.* **.1** currency, (process of) circulation (money) turnover, (monetary) circulation د پيسي چلند اچول *economics* to put money into circulation دا روپۍ چلند نه لري This currency has gone out of circulation. **1.2** work, operation, functioning **1.3** force, effect (of a law, etc.) **1.4** movement, traffic (transportation) **1.5** conduct, behavior **1.6** *trade* good market **1.7** threshing **1.8** gusting (of wind) **2.1** operating, working well (e.g., a motor) **2.2** spry, animated **2.3** current; in circulation

چلندول chalandavól *denominative, transitive* [*past:* چلند يي کړ] **1** ☞ چلول **2** to put into force (e.g., a law)

چلندي chalandí current; in circulation

چلندېدل chalandedól *denominative, intransitive* [*past:* چلند شو] **1** ☞ چلول **2** to be put into force (e.g., a law)

چلني chalaní marketable (e.g., goods)

چلو chaláv chiláv *m.* rice kasha, groats

چلوته chaloṭá *f.* **1** cunning; ruse; fraud; swindle **2** manner, conduct

چل ول، چلول [1] chalvál *m.* **1** cunning, ruse **2** tricks, intrigues, machinations

چلول [2] chalavól *transitive* [*past:* و يي چلاوه] **1** to put into circulation (e.g., money) **2** to move; put into motion, start (e.g., a car) **3** to drive (e.g., an automobile) **4** to carry on, carry out (trade, gunfire, etc.) **5** to direct, manage **6** to use for draught or packing transport اوښان چلول to be in the business of goods transport by camel **7** to introduce (a custom) *idiom* خپله ورځ چلول to live out (life)

چلولي chalvalí *m.* ☞ چلباز

چلون chálún *m.* currency, circulation (of money), liquid movement

چلوونکی chalavúnkaj *present participle of* چلول **2** supervisory apparatus, management

چله [1] chalá *f.* flood, inundation چله راغله The water overflowed the banks.

چله [2] chalá *f.* silver earring (worn by men)

چله [3] chilá chillá *f.* **1** forty-day fast **2** period of winter cold spells

چله [4] chála *f.* treatment of another person, behavior (with relation to another)

چلي [1] chalí *m.* ☞ چلباز

چلي [2] cháli *plural of* چله [4]

چلي [3] chilí *m.* Chile

چلي [4] chaláj چلي مخ pinched face

چلي [5] chale *plural of* چله [1, 2]

چلي [6] chilé chillé *plural of* چله [3]

چلي [7] chaláj *f.* ear (of corn, grain, etc.)

چلي [8] chaláj *f.* colored thread (used to embroider a pattern on the toe of a slipper)

چلیپا chalipá *f.* cross (Christian)

چلېدل chaledól *intransitive* [*past:* وچلېده] **1** to act, operate, work, function **2** to move, shift, displace, to be in motion **3** to go, ply (back and forth) د کابل او قندهار په منځ کښي سرويسونه چلېږي Buses run between Kabul and Kandahar. **4** to blow (of the wind) **5** to be open to traffic (of a road) **6** to move, be in circulation (money)

7 to carry on, conduct (trade, gunfire, etc.) **8** *figurative* to prosper **9** to swim, float په دي سيند کښي کښتۍ چلېدلای شي This river is navigable **10** to live, exist هغه يواځي په خپله تنخواه چلېږي He lives on his salary alone. *idiom* سره چلېدل to be compatable, fit, suit

چلېدنه chaledóna *f.* چلېده chaledó *m. plural* **1** movement, traffic **2** circulation **3** sale

چلي کار، چلبکار [1] چاري کار chalekár *m.* ☞

چليگر chóligár *m.* cheat, fraud, swindler

چم [1] cham *m.* **1** gait **2** trick, ruse چمونه يي زده دي He's a clever boy. **3** aspect, look د مسافر په چم Having the appearance of a traveler. **4** method, way

چم [2] cham *m.* **1** part, branch (of a tribe); clan **2** quarter, district چم چم quarter after quarter; district after district

چم [3] chóm *m.* **1** clod of clay (picked up in a spade) **2** turf, sod

چماچار chamáchár *m.* cricket

چمباز chambáz *m.* ☞ چلباز

چمبازي chambází *f.* ☞ چلبازي

چمبر chambár *m.* ☞ چنبر

چمبر خيال chambarkhjál *m.* melon

چمبر [1] chambár *m.* patterned calico

چمبر [2] chambár *tautological with* امبر

چمبړي chambaráj *m.* inflated leather bag used in fording a river

چمبه chambá *f.* **1** paw; claws (of a bird) **2** tambourine **3** circle, rim *idiom* تر چمبه صافېدل to overpower, overcome something تر چمبه لاندي کېدل to subdue, subjugate someone تر چمبه لاندي کول to be subjugated, be subordinated احمد مي اوس تر چمبه لاندي دئ Ahmed is now in my hands. Ahmed is now in my power.

چمبه کښنه chambakákha *f.* kind of bread

چمبي chambáj *m.* ☞ چمبه 3

چمبېل چمبېلي chambél chambelí *m.* ☞ چنبېلي

چمتاره chamtára *f.* violin

چمتو chamtú **1** ready, prepared تيار او چمتو يو we are ready, we are fully prepared **2** adapted, fit **3** produced, manufactured چمتو کول **a** to prepare, manufacture **b** to adapt, fit, adjust **c** to produce, make چمتو کېدل **a** to get ready, prepare for **b** to adapt oneself to, to be adapted

چمتوکېده chamtukedó *m. plural* چمتووالی chamtuválaj *m.* **1** readiness, consent چمتوکېده څرگندول to express readiness (to do something) **2** preparedness **3** adjustment, accomodation

چمته chamtá *f.* **1** powder flask **2** pouch **3** kitbag د شا چمته knapsack, haversack

چمټي chamṭáj *m.* capital (of a column)

چمجي chəmdzháj *m.* ☞ چنجي

چمچک chamchák *m.* چمچک chamchák *m.* cymbals

چمچوړي [1] chamchúráj *m.* **1** dipper, scoop **2** ladle

چمچوړي [2] chamchuráj *m.* **1** dipper, scoop **2** ladle

چمچه chamchá *f.* ☞ څمڅی

چمچه مار chamchamár *m.* cobra

چمچی chamchə́j *f.* ☞ څمچی

چمړدی chamaṛdáj *m.* rice-husker

چمغړک chamghaṛák *m. dialect* ☞ چنغړک

چمکار chamkár sparkling, shining

چمکلی chamkaléj *f.* female's forehead decoration made of coins

چمکني chamkaní *m.* ☞ څمکني

چمګاوند ، چم ګاوند chamgávənd *m.* 1 neighborhood (in regard to a quarter, street) د چم ګاوند سری neighbor 2 neighbor

چمګر chamgár shrewd, cunning, wily

چم ګواند chamgavánḍ *m. regional* 1 neighbor (with respect to quarter, street) 2 neighbor (with respect to quarter, street) 3 quarter, street 4 environment, ambience

چمله chamlá *f.* Chamla (province)

چمن [1] chamán *m.* 1 meadow, grass-plot 2 flower-bed

چمن [2] chamán *m.* Chaman (city)

چمن زار chamanzā́r *m.* meadow

چمني [1] chamaní 1 turning green 2 flowering

چمني [2] chimnə́j *f. regional* lamp-chimney

چم و خم chamukhám *m.* graceful walk, smooth gait

چموسه chamúsa *f.* 1 rawhide shoe 2 snowshoes

چموکی chamúkaj *m.* sly person, cunning person, cheat

چمه chəmá *f.* strumpet

چمیار chamjár *m.* 1 currier, leather worker 2 shoemaker

چنار chinár *m.* [*plural:* چناران chinārā́n] 1 poplar نیله چنار silver poplar 2 plane tree

چنارو chināró *f. proper name* Chinaro

چنانچه chunánche *conjunction* as چنانچه د لندن څخه وايي ... As reports from London say …

چناو chanáv *m.* initial flow of water in an irrigation shaft or channel system

چنبر chambár *m.* 1 *anatomy* clavicle 2 fence, wall (around a house, castle, etc.) 3 circle, disk 4 rim, thin rim

چنبلی chambelí *m.* ☞ چامببل

چنج chundzh *m.* aversion چنج څني کول to harbor an aversion to something; abhor something

چنجړی chandzhə́raj *m. dialect* ☞ تمځری

چنجن chindzhə́n 1 worm-eaten; spoiled 2 *figurative* unpleasant

چنجنتوب chindzhəntób *m.* چنجنتیا chindzhəntjā́ *f.* چنجنوالی chindzhənválaj *m.* 1 worminess, corruption, rottenness 2 caries, decay (of the teeth)

چنجنول chindzhənavə́l *denominative, transitive* [*past:* چنجن یې کړ] 1 to cause to become wormy 2 to deteriorate through decay (teeth)

چنجنېدل chindzhənedə́l *denominative, intransitive* [*past:* چنجن شو] 1 to become wormy, be wormy 2 to rot, decay (teeth)

چنجوغی chindzhúghaj *m.* khingjak, mulberry (fruit)

چنجول chundzhavə́l *transitive* [*past:* و یې چنجاوه] 1 to feel sick 2 to cause nausea

چنجوی chandzhúj *m.* three-tined fork (used by nomads to cut grain)

چنجی chindzháj *m.* [*plural:* چنجیان chindzhijā́n] 1 worm د مځکي earthworm چنجی ، د ختو سور چنجی 2 small insect; insect

چنجېدل chunzhedə́l *intransitive* [*past:* و چنجېده] 1 to experience nausea 2 to feel nauseous

چن چنی chanchaṇ́j *f.* rattle mounted on a stick

چند [1] chand 1 how much 2 bit 3 *combining form* دو چند twofold; twice, double دری چند thrice, triple څلور چنده quadruple *idiom* هر چند چه although

چند [2] chand *m. proper name* Chand

چندان chandā́n چنداني chandáni so, so much, such دا چندان اسان کار نه This دا جواب چندان صحیح نه دئ This is not such a simple matter. و answer is not all that simple.

چنداول chandāvúl chandāvól *m.* ☞ چنداول

چیندخ chindákh *m.* ☞ چیندخ

چندرو chandrú *m.* dew

چندری chindrə́j *f.* 1 hopscotch 2 jumping on one leg

چندر chandáṛ *m. plural* sandalwood tree د چندرو ونه sandalwood

چندل chandə́l jumping on one leg, hopping on one foot

چندنی chandnə́j *f.* 1 white cloth (laid down on a carpet) 2 *music* time, measure

چندن chandán *m. plural* ☞ چندر

چندن هار chandaṇhár *m.* sandalwood beads

چندول chandavól *m.* ☞ چنداول

چندونی chandóṇaj *m. anatomy* auricle

چنده [1] chindá choice, select چنده کول to choose, select

چنده [2] chandá *f.* 1 collection of varied resources (e.g., among relatives) 2 donation

چندی chandáj *m. history* poet

چندین chandín 1 so much 2 much

چندال chandál *m.* 1 man of lowly origins 2 sweeper, trash collector 3 childless man 4 unfortunate man, hapless man

چنداول chanḍāvól *m. history* rearguard

چندولی chanḍaválaj *m. history* leader of the Kazalbashi or professional military rearguard in British times

چنډت chanḍə́ṭ poor, indigent

چنډخه chinḍákha *f.* frog

چنډن chanḍán *m. plural* ☞ چندر

چنډه chánḍa *f.* share, portion

چنډي chunḍí *f.* pinch (e.g., of salt)

چنغاله [1] changhālə́ *plural of* چنغول

چنغاله [2] changhāla *f.* ☞ چنغله

چنغړک changhaṛák *m.* Adam's apple, larynx

چنغله changhalá *f.* fiancee, betrothed

چنغول changhól *m.* [*plural:* چنغاله changhālə́] fiancé, betrothed

چنگ [1] chang *m.* 1 chang (a kind of cymbals) 2 harp

چنگ [2] chang *m.* 1 paw, pad 2 hand (extended, spread), palm with all five fingers extended

چنگ [3] chung *m.* cupped hand, handful

چنگ [4] chang *m.* hook (for drawing a bucket up from a well, etc.)

چینگ ching ☞ چینگ 5

چنگانس chungā́kh m. 1 crab, crayfish 2 ☞ سرطان 3, 4

چنگال changāl m. ☞ چنگ 2

چنگ چینگ chungching m. groanings, moanings چنگ چینگ کول to groan, moan

چنگړ changáṛ m. good-for-nothing, scoundrel

چنگبس chungákh m. toad

چنگبنه chungákha f. frog د ونو چنگبنه frog, tree-frog

چنگک changák m. 1 hook (used for pulling a flatcake out of a tanur oven) 2 fish-hook د چنگک مزي fishing-rod د چنگک لکړه small wood, copse

چنگکي changakí hooked, unciform (of a beak, etc.)

چنگل changúl f. [plural: چنگلي changúli] talons

چنگل changúl m. changul (measure of land equal to fifteen dzharibs or a quarter kul'ba)

چنگن chəngán m. miser

چنگو changú m. lapwing (bird)

چنگوټی changotáj m. puppy

چنگوری changúraj m. piece, fragment (e.g., of rock)

چینگول chingavál denominative, transitive ☞ چینگول

چنگي chungí f. local duty, municipal tax

چنگی changáj cross-eyed, squinteyed

چینگبدل chingedál denominative, intransitive ☞ چینگبدل

چن ماری chanmāráj f. ☞ چاند ماری

چنه chóna f. 1 province, district, regional subdivision 2 quarter (of a city, town) 3 external wall (of a house) 4 partition, thin wall 5 edge of a roof 6 figurative patronage, protection

چنه chaná f. dispute over price or a commercial transaction چنه وهل to bargain

چنه chaná f. jaw

چنی chanáj m. basin, bowl

چنی chanáj f. frost, light frosts چنی وهلی nipped by frost

چنی chənáj roan (color of a horse)

چن chuṇ m. ☞ چون

چن chaṇ m. 1 sifting (through a sieve) 2 straining, filtration 3 choice, selection 4 gathering, collecting, picking (berries, etc.) 5 weeding چن کول compound verb ☞ چنل

چن chaṇ m. brush (for thatching roofs)

چناخه chaṇākha f. disease of the joints, arthritis

چناسک chənāsák 1 moldy, covered with mold 2 stinking, fetid

چناسکه chənāka f. چناسه chənāsa f. mold, mildew چناسي کول to grow moldy, be covered with mold

چنچن chaṇchán m. چنچن [plural: چنچن chaṇchán] sparrow

چنچنک chaṇchanák m. little sparrow

چنچنکه chaṇchanáka f. چنچنه chaṇchóna f. 1 hen sparrow 2 general sparrow 3 small bird

چنکاو chaṇkāv m. چنکاو chaṇkāv m. ☞ چکراو

چنل chuṇál chəṇál transitive [past: چنل و یي چنه] chaṇavál denominative, transitive [past: چن یي کړ] 1 to strain, filter 2 to

sift (through a sieve) 3 to choose, select 4 to gather, pick (berries, etc.) 5 to weed, weed out

چنونکی chəṇúkaj m. fine sieve

چنه chaná f. chick-pea, Cicer arietinum

چنی chaṇáj m. sandal lace, sandal thong

چنیا chuṇjá violet

چنیاتوب chuṇjātób m. violet (the color)

چناسه chaṇjása f. ☞ چناسه

چنبدل chuṇedál chəṇedál intransitive [past: و چنبده past: چن سو] 1 to sift (through a sieve) 2 to be strained, be filtered out 3 to be filtered through 4 to be chosen, be selected 5 to be gathered, be picked (berries, etc.) 6 to be perceptible, be seen (through the trees, etc.) 7 to be weeded (out)

چو chav m. 1 crack, slit 2 cleft, fissure 3 shallow ditch, trench

چو chu m. ☞ چف

چو cho chu Giddap! (cry used to encourage a horse to continue)

چوار chvār hanging, pendent

چوارول chvāravál denominative, transitive [past: چوار یي کړ] to hang, hang up, suspend

چواره chəvára f. 1 dried fig 2 infant's pacifier made from dried fig

چواربدل chvāredál denominative, intransitive [past: چوار شو] to be hung up, be suspended

چواړی chuvāṛí m. 1 sweeper 2 dark-complexioned person

چوب chob m. 1 tree 2 stick, staff 3 mace

چوتره chobtará f. stage, platform

چوبرن chobṛán ignorant

چوبک chobák m. drumstick

چوبی chobí wooden

چوپ chup 1 ☞ چپ 2 ☞ ساکن

چوپاړ chopā́ṛ m. چوپال chopál m. 1 platform 2 awning 3 hut

چوپان chopán m. shepherd

چوپتیا chuptjá f. silence, quiet

چوپته chopáṭa f. beam (for reinforcing a wall); brace

چوپر chupór piebald; dappled

چوپر chopáṛ m. 1 work, service چوپر وهل to work, serve 2 waiting upon, serving د چا چوپر کول to wait upon, serve someone 3 serving, service د وطن چوپر serving the country

چوپرن chupṛán 1 having inflamed eyes 2 weak-eyed, having poor eyesight

چوپړی chopráj m. 1 servant, attendant 2 waiter idiom اوتوماتیکي چوپړی، میخانیکي چوپړی a robot

چوپړی chopráj f. 1 attendant 2 waitress

چوپل chopál chupál transitive [past: و یي چوپه] to suck, suck in, imbibe

چوپنی chopanáj m. bubble (e.g., of soap)

چوپول chupavál transitive ☞ چپول 2

چوپه chúpa feminine singular of چوپ

چوپه چپیا chúpa-chupjá f. چپه چپیا

چوپبدل chupedál intransitive ☞ چپبدل

چاپير ☞ chavpér چپپر

چوتانگی chotāngə́ *m. plural* چوتانگی chotāngə́j *f.* metal ring around a pack saddle (camel's)

چونتره ☞ .chotará *m* چوتره

چوتی chotáj *m.* 1 femoral ligament 2 swimming trunks 3 rope used for tying a pack to a camel

چوټ [1] chuṭ *m.* chintz, printed cotton

چوټ [2] chuṭ *m.* 1 ☞ چرټ [1] 2 sufficient

چوټانداز choṭāndáz *m.* guess, conjecture

چوټول choṭavə́l *denominative, transitive* [*past:* چوټ يې کړ] 1 to drag, drag along 2 to steal

چوټه [1] choṭá *f.* matter; concern *idiom* یک چوټه کارکول to work continually

چوټه [2] chəváṭa *f.* sandal *idiom* د چوټي تر بنده رسول to win a law suit

چوټي [1] choṭí uncombed, disheveled

چوټي [2] choṭí *f. Eastern* 1 leave, holidays چوټي اخیستل to take a holiday, vacation 2 release, dismissal (from a job) چوټي ورکول to dismiss, fire someone

چوټېدل choṭedə́l *denominative, intransitive* [*past:* چوټ شو] 1 to be dragged, drag 2 to be stolen 3 *figurative* to cope with something 4 to attain victory

چوجکی chudzhakə́j *f.* ☞ چچکی [2]

چوجی chudzhə́j *f.* ☞ چوچی [2]

چوچ choch *m.* custom, tradition

چوچاړی chuchā́ṛaj *m. regional* island

چوچو chuchú *m. children's speech* birdie, bird

چوچی [1] chucháj *m.* nestling

چوچی [2] chuchə́j *f.* pheasant

چوچی [3] chucháj *regional* weak-eyed, having poor eyesight

چوخ [1] chokh 1 crooked, bent 2 curved; stooping, round-shouldered

چوخ [2] chukh acute (e.g., of an angle)

چوخت chukht ☞ جوخت

چوخته chókhta *f.* cave

چوخرن chukhṛón ☞ چخرن

چوخره chukhṛá *f.* ☞ چخره

چوخکه chukháka *f.* ☞ چخله

چوخل chukhál *m.* skis, snowshoes

چوخله chukhála *f.* ☞ چخله

چوخلی [1] chukhalə́j *f.* tall hat

چوخلی [2] chukhláj *m.* sharp stake, sharp spike (for taking the kernels from ears off corn)

چوخمخی chukhmə́khaj pitted, pocked, nicked

چوخنی chúkhni *f. plural* pus, gum (in the eyes)

چوخول [1] cvhokhavə́l *denominative, transitive* [*past:* چوخ یې کړ] 1 to incline, bend 2 to distort

چوخول [2] chukhavə́l *transitive* ☞ چخول

چوخوله chukhvúla *f.* چوخونی chukhúnaj *m.* ☞ چخله

چوغه [1] chokhá *f.* ☞ چوغه

چوخه [2] chókha *f.* 1 curvature; distortion 2 crookedness; round shoulders

چوخی chukháj 1 pitted, pocked 2 hump-backed; stooped; round-shouldered

چوخېدل [1] chokhedə́l *denominative, intransitive* [*past:* چوخ شو] 1 to be inclined, be bent 2 to be distorted

چوخېدل [2] chukhedə́l *intransitive* [*past:* و چوخېده] to pierce, penetrate, be stuck into

چودل chavdə́l *intransitive* ☞ چاودل

چودن chudán *m. plural* pig-iron د چودنوحاصلات smelting of pig-iron

چودني chudaní *attributive* cast iron چودني دېگ boiler

چودهري chaudhrí *m.* 1 shift-foreman 2 senior man (in various groups)

چودی chavdáj *m.* sweat-cloth, saddle-cloth

چور [1] chur 1.1 powder 1.2 sawdust 1.3 small fragment 2 *predicative* .1 indented 2.2 *figurative* tormented, tortured چور کول to suffer, be tormented

چور [2] chur *m.* robbery, raid, foray چور کول to rob چور کېدل to be robbed

چور [3] chur *m.* [*plural:* چوران churán] 1 rut 2 ravine 3 gully

چور [4] chur *m.* sharp stone (for slaughtering cattle)

چور [5] chur *Eastern* 1 all, fully, as a whole 2 completely, quite; absolutely, conclusively چور را څخه هېر شوه I completely forgot about that.

چوربل churdál *m.* [*plural:* چوربلونه churbalúna *plural:* چوربل churbə́l] hair-rope

چورت [1] churt *m.* ☞ چرت چورتونه د ځان سره وهل to become pensive

چورتي churtí pensive

چورت churə́t *m.* ☞ چرت

چورچورک churchurák *m.* mole-cricket (insect)

چورچورکی churchurakáj *m.* چورچوری churchurə́j *f.* cricket

چورکی chorkə́j *f.* teal (the bird)

چورلاو churlā́v *m.* machine; motor

چورلټ churláṭ ☞ چور [5]

چورلټه churláṭa *f.* revolution; circling, turning

چورلک churlák *m.* 1 revolution; circling, turning چورلکونه خوړل to circle, soar (of birds etc.) 2 turns, revolutions (of machines, wheels)

چورلکه churláka *f.* چورلکی churlákaj *m.* 1 wooden top 2 spout (e.g., of a teapot) 3 toe (of a shoe)

چورلندی churlandáj *m.* ☞ چورلکه [1]

چورلول churlavə́l *transitive* [*past:* و یې چورلاوه] to circle, turn, revolve

چورله چورله churlá chorə́la *f.* inlet aperture of an irrigation well or canal system; cofferdam

چورلېڅج churlédzaj *m.* axle, shaft (of a machine, wheels)

چورلېدل churledə́l *intransitive* [*present:* چورلي *present:* چورلبري *past:* وچورلېده] 1 to turn, rotate, revolve, spin around نن مي ډېر سر

چورلي My head is spinning around a lot today. **2** to circle (of an aircraft) **3** to revolve (machine, wheels); operate (of mechanisms)

چورمچور chormachór churmachúr **1** cut up into pieces, cut up carelessly **2** *m.* man who is hopelessly in love

چورن churə́n chorə́n *m.* **1** ☞ چورله **2** drainage ditch

چورندک churəndák *m.* warbler (the bird)

چورنگ chavráng *m.* **1** fencing **2** cutting off the four feet of an animal with one blow of a sword

چوره¹ churá *m.* hernia

چوره² chúra *f.* dark and gloomy ravine

چوره³ chúra *feminine singular of* چور¹ 2

چوری¹ churáj *m.* **1** servant **2** dancer

چوری² churáj *f.* **1** housemaid, domestic servant **2** dancer

چوری³ chavráj *f.* swatter (flies)

چوري⁴ churí *f. regional* shortbread, small and rich loaf

چوړ¹ chuṛ *m.* **1** pin, hinge (door) **2** splitting with a wedge

چوړ² chavṛ destroyed; annihilated; ruined کور دي چوړ شه! May your house be destroyed! (curse)

چوړا churā́ *m.* bracelet

چوراغ churágh *m.* **1** crevice (in a rock, cliff wall) **2** cleft **3** channel (river) **4** ravine

چورچورک churchurák *m.* child

چورک churák *m.* lock, bolt; bar

چوړکی choṛkə́j *f. dialect* ☞ چوروکی

چوړو churú *m.* black-billed thrush

چوروکی choṛukáj *m. dialect* small knife

چوړول¹ churavə́l *transitive* [*past:* و يې چوړولي] to release (water onto the fields)

چوړول² chavravə́l *denominative, intransitive* [*past:* چوړ يې کړ] to destroy, annihilate; ruin

چوړهار churṓhár *m.* gurgling or rippling of water (i.e., the sound)

چوړی choṛáj *m.* sweeper

چوړيدل¹ chavṛedə́l *denominative, intransitive* [*past:* چوړ شو] **1** to be destroyed, be annihilated; go into a decline **2** to be ruined

چوړيدل² chuṛedə́l *intransitive* [*past:* و چوړيدي] to flow (of water)

چوړيل churajə́l *transitive* [*past:* و يې چوړيدي] to caulk

چوز chuz *m.* young falcon, young hawk (as yet untrained)

چوزه chúza **1** *feminine of* چوز **2** beautiful woman, beauty

چوزی chúzaj tender, soft

چوس chus *m.* **1** insignificant thing **2** *anatomy* third stomach (of ruminants) **3** peritoneum **4** entrails

چوسار chavsár *m.* file

چوستی chústaj *m.* ☞ چوس

چوسه chosá *f.* lassitude; laziness

چوشک choshák *m.* **1** pacifier (infant's) **2** sucker (plant, animal organ)

چوښتی chúkhtaj *m.* abomasum, rennet bag (a division of the stomach of ruminants)

چوښکه chúkhka *f.* spout of a teakettle, etc.

چوغ chugh having the eyes screwed up سترگي چوغي نيول to screw the eyes up

چوغالی choghāláj *m.* **1** stopping place for camels **2** cesspool

چوغبوغ chughbúgh noise, disorder

چوغری chughəráj green; blossoming, burgeoning (of buds)

چوغک chughák *m.* arid plain mimosa, jinjak (a medicinal plant)

چوغکه chughə́ka *f.* **1** sparrow **2** small bird

چوغل¹ chughál *m.* skis

چوغل² chughə́l *m.* **1** gossip; scandal-monger; intriguer **2** sieve, strainer; sifter

چوغلي chughlí *f.* piece of scandal; tale-bearing چوغلي کول to carry gossip; inform on, tell tales about

چوغ و بوغ chugh-u-búgh *m.* ☞ چغ بغ جوړ شه و بوغ *Eastern* to raise a ruckus

چوغه choghá *f.* chughá kaftan (long Eastern-style outer robe)

چوغی chugháj **1** becoming stooped; stooping **2** hunchback

چوغبدل chughedə́l *intransitive* ☞ چغبدل

چوک¹ chavk *m.* **1** market square د چوک بازار Chawk, the bazaar in Kabul **2** crossroads **3** small paved area in front of an entrance door or shop **4** small raised porch or platform around a mosque

چوک² chuk *m.* **1** reduction **2** alleviation (e.g., of one's fate) **3** suppression (of anger, etc.) **4** loss, damage **5** blunder چوک ايستل **a** to reduce **b** to soothe, quite; mitigate **c** to suppress anger, etc. **d** regret, sorrow

چوک³ chok kneeling (of a camel)

چوک⁴ chuk cross-eyed, one-eyed

چوک⁵ chavk *m.* chauk something well or bravely done; something done conscientiously

چوک⁶ chuvák *m.* staff for measuring the water-level in an irrigation-well

چوک⁷ chok *dialect vice* څوک

چوکاټ chokā́ṭ *m.* **1** frame, framework **2** landing-gear, chassis **3** door-post, door-jamb **4** *military* personnel, cadre **5** diagram **6** structure (system) **7** boundaries, limits

چوکاټي chokā́ṭi *adjective* frame چوکاټي انتن loop (frame) antenna

چوک چوکه chukchúka *f.* gossip, hearsay; rumors چوک چوکه کېدول to spread a rumor چوک چوکه ده چه ... There is a rumor that …

چوکر chokár *m.* ☞ چوکړ¹

چوکړ¹ chokár servant

چوکړ² chokáṛ blind

چوکسترگی chukstə́rgaj cross-eyed, one eyed

چوکل chokə́l *transitive* ☞ جوکل

چوکول¹ chokəvə́l *denominative, transitive* [*past:* چوک يې کړ] to make a camel kneel *idiom* د چا و کور ته اوښ چوکول **a** to inflict damage on someone's house **b** to do something unpleasant to someone

چوکول² chavkavə́l *denominative, transitive* [*past:* چوک يې کړ] to behave well, behave as one should, do conscienciously

269

چوکول ³ chukavә́l *transitive regional* [*past:* و یې چوکاوه] to plant (e.g., a tree)

چوکه ¹ chuká *f.* 1 pike, lance 2 sharp pain, stabbing pain 3 dipping into something 4 small quantity, few چوکه کول a to split b to dip in, stick into, pierce c to plant (trees etc.) چوکه کېدل a to be split b to be pierced, be penetrated c to be planted (of trees, etc.)

چوکه ² chuká *f.* ☞ تیکه ²

چوکۍ ¹ chavkә́j *f.* chokә́j *plural* 1 chair, seat د زده کړې چوکۍ school desk پر چوکۍ کښېنول to sit on a chair 2 guard post, guard unit 3 visit to a holy place, pilgrimage چوکۍ اخیستل to make a pilgrimage, visit holy places

چوکۍ ² chukә́j a little bit

چوکیدار chavkidā́r *m.* څوکیدار، چوکي دار

چوکېدل chokedә́l *denominative, intransitive* [*past:* چوک شو] 1 to be kneeling (of a camel) 2 to be bent (under a heavy load) *idiom* گوره چه اوښ په کوم ارخ چوکېږي *saying* If we live long enough, we will see the outcome.

چوکېدل ² chavkedә́l *denominative, intransitive* [*past:* چوک شو] to be well done, be conscientiously done

چوکي ساز chokәjsā́z *m.* joiner

چوگان chavgā́n *m.* polo mallet

چوگان بازي chavgānbāzí *f.* polo (mounted)

چول ¹ chol *m.* steppe, arid grasslands

چول ² chul *m.* ☞ چون ¹

چول ³ chavә́l *transitive* [*past:* و یې چاوه] 1.1 to split, cleave 1.2 to detonate, blast 2 [*past:* وچاوه] *intransitive* .1 to burst, crack; split apart 2.2 to be blown up, be blasted 2.3 to be exploded, be detonated 2.4 to suffer, be tormented

چول ⁴ chavә́l *separable part of verb* اچول

چولاوه cholāvá dying of thirst

چولک ¹ cholák *m.* wet snow, snow mixed with rain

چولک ² cholák *m.* uncircumcised penis of a child

چولول chulavә́l *denominative, transitive* [*past:* چوله یې کړه خوله] چولول to gape, yawn, open the mouth wide

چوله ¹ cholá *f.* crevice, crack

چوله ² chóla gaping, with open mouth چوله خوله کول ☞ چولول

چولی ¹ chavә́laj *past participle of* چول ³

چولی ² cholә́j 1 shirt (with tucks at the waist) 2 torn or broken snare

چولۍ ³ cholә́j *f.* ☞ چولک ²

چوم chom *m.* ☞ چم ³

چومبۍ chombә́j *m.* pestle (mortar)

چومړدی chumәrdáj *m.* main beam of a rice-husker

چومل chumә́l *transitive* [*past:* و یې چومه] to kiss

چومی chumáj *m.* childhood disease

چون chun *conjunction* 1 insofar as 2 as

چومبیل chumbél *m.* large bowl of a fakir

چونتره chontará *f.* chauntará 1 awning 2 platform; rise, elevation

چونتی ¹ chonṭáj one-armed, armless

چونتي ² chunṭí *f.* large braid of hair

چوندی chundáj *m.* hopping on one leg

چونډۍ chunḍә́j *f.* ☞ چنډۍ

چونکه chúnke *conjunction* insofar as, for

چونکی chunkáj 1.1 shameless, impudent 1.2 obscene, indecent 2 *m.* ☞ سارنگ

چونگ ¹ chung *m.* 1 handful 2 share, part of something 3 fragment

چونگ ² chung *m.* [*plural:* چونگان chungā́n] 1 peep (of nestling) 2 immature thought; poorly-thought out advice 3 slander

چونگاښ chungā́ķh *m.* ☞ چنګاښ

چونگښه chungә́ķha *m.* ☞ چنګښه *idiom* چونگښي تلل to be occupied with a meaningless or insignificant matter

چونگ کنگ chungkíng *m.* Chongqing (Chungking, Chinese city)

چونگن chungә́n whining, pitiable, pathetic

چونگوښه chungúķha *f.* ☞ چنګښه

چونگول chungavә́l *transitive* [*past:* و یې چونگاوه] to make a child cry چونگي چونگي کول ☞ چونگی ¹ to crush, grind up چونگي چونگي ورکول to do or produce a bit at a time

چونگی ¹ chungáj *m.* ☞ چنګي 2 payment in kind (to a smith, barber, etc. for services) چونگي اخیستل a to collect a local tax چونگي ټولول b to take payment in kind

چونگی ³ chungáj *m.* chirping (of nestling)

چونگی ⁴ chungáj one-armed; armless

چونگېدل chungedә́l *intransitive* [*past:* و چونګېده] 1 to weep; sob 2 to rumble (of the stomach)

چون و چرا chun-u-cherā́ *f.* 1 quarreling; altercation 2 (nagging, pestering) queries

چونه ¹ chóna *f.* old woman

چونه ² chuná *f.* lime لنده چونه quicklime اوبه نه رسېدلي چونه slaked lime د چونې اوبه limewater, calcium hydroxide suspension چونه کول to whitewash ډبره limestone

چونه گچ chunagách *m. plural* 1 alabaster 2 *attributive* clad in stone or brick; whitewashed

چونه یي chunají *adjective* limestone

چونی ¹ chunáj *m.* 1 dwarf 2 tiny, small

چونی ² chunә́j *f.* ruby

چونی ³ chavnә́j *f.* ☞ چونی ²

چون ¹ chuṇ *m.* 1 fold, pleat; layer, sheet دا ټوکر چوڼ نه خوري This cloth will not wrinkle. 2 pin, pivot (of a door); hinge (of a door) چوڼ وهل a to utter, whisper b to chirp, emit chirping

چون ² chuṇ *m.* 1 whisper 2 chirping (of nestling)

چونا chuṇā́ *f.* ☞ چوڼار

چون چون ¹ chuṇchúṇ *m.* chirp, chirping د چون چون بڼ chirp

چون چون ² chuṇchúṇ ☞ چونلئ

چونچونه chuṇchúṇa *f.* ☞ چنچنه

چونکی chuṇkáj *m.* 1 twittering 2 babbling (of water) 3 crackling, sputtering (in roasting)

چونل chunál *transitive* [*past:* وي چونه] **1** to sift **2** to strain, filter **3** to select, choose **4** to gather (e.g., in making a dress) *idiom* پزه چونل to wrinkle up the nose

چونلئ chunálaj plicated, folded

چونول chunavál *transitive* [*past:* وي چوناوه] **1** to make a bird sing or squawk **2** to release water with a gurgling sound

چونول chunavál *transitive* ☞ چونل

چونهار chunahár *m.* chirping, twittering (of birds) د چنچنو چونهار خبري One can hear the twittering of sparrows.

چونی ¹ chunáj madrasa student

چونی ² chavnáj *f.* chonáj caserne چونی عسکري military post

چونیا ¹ chunjá *m.* **1** song-bird **2** nightingale

چونیا ² chunjá violet

چونیدل ¹ chunedál *intransitive* [*past:* و چونیده] **1** to sing, chirp (of birds) **2** to gurgle (of water)

چونیدل ² chunedál *intransitive* [*past:* و چونیده] **1** to be sifted; be strained, be filtered **2** to be gathered into folds or pleats, be wrinkled (of clothing)

چوو chavú *m.* wind accompanied by wet snow

چوه ¹ chavá *f.* large woven basket

چوه ² chavá *f.* **1** grassy glade, hollow **2** small irrigation well (in a melon field)

چوهاری chuháraj dirty, base, vile

چوهره chuhrá *f.* pleat, tuck, gather

چوهری chuhráj *m.* **1** trash-picker **2** man belonging to the scavenger, trash-picker, trash-collector **3** outcast, untouchable

چوهن chuhan *m.* cast-iron, pig-iron

چه ¹ cha *f.* chah *m.* **1** shade **2** cover, shelter; protection

چه ² chi chə che *conjunction* **1** that (introduces a subordinate clause) هغه وويل چه ... He said that ... **2** who, which (introduces a determinant subordinate clause) هغه هلک چه نوم يي احمد دئ ... The boy who is called Ahmed ... هغه کور چه موږ پکښني اوسو The house in which we live **3** when (introduces temporal subordinate clauses) ته چه احمدته ورغلي ﭤه يي درته وويل When you came to Ahmed what did he say to you? ما چه يو طرف بل طرف وکاﺗه يوه ونه مي ولېدله When I looked I saw a tree. **4** since, for, because (introduces a subordinate clause of causality) چه خوا بېربرېم ... since I am very much afraid **5** in order that, so as to (introduces a subordinate clause of purpose) راغلم چه تا ووينم I came in order to see you. **6** if, whenever (introduces a conditional subordinate clause) چه ﺗه ﺧﻲ، نو زه ﺧﻨﮕه پاﺗه سم؟ If you depart, how can I remain? *idiom* چه و، يو سوداگر و *folklore* once upon a time there was a merchant

چه chá *diminutive suffix* باغچه small garden

چهار chahár *numeral* **1** four **2** used as the first or second element of compounds چهار آسیاب Charasiya (district)

چهاربرجک chahārburdzhák *m.* Chaharburjak (settlement)

چهارتراش chahārtarásh *m.* boards, planks

چهارده chahardéh *f.* چهاردهي chahārdehí *f.* Chardekhi (district and plain near Kabul)

چهارراهي chahārrahí *f.* crossroads

چهارشنبه chahārshambá *f.* Wednesday

چهارکونجه chahārkuńdzha quadrangular

چهارنعل chahārná'l chārná'l *m.* gallop (gait)

چهارکار ¹ chahárkár *m.* ☞ چاري کار

چهاریکار ² chārikár *m.* Charikar (city)

چاونی chhāuńoj *f.* ☞ چاونی

چایل chahājál *m.* ☞ چایل

چهت chhat *m.* ☞ چت *regional* د چهت پکی punkah, ceiling fan

چهل قدمي chihilkadamí *f.* short stroll چهل قدمي کول to stroll, go for a walk

چلی chahlój *f.* ☞ چلی ⁸

چای ¹ chaj *m.* چی chəj *f.* ☞ چای

چه ² chi ☞ چه ²

چی ³ che *f.* the name for the letter چ

چی ⁴ che *combination of the conjunction* چه *and the preposition* يي همدغه کار دئ چی کوم I am busy with this very matter.

چی chí *suffix of agent* تماشاچي spectator, نندارچي observer باورچي cook

چی ایشي chəjíshe *f. dialect* teapot, teakettle

چیت ¹ chit *m.* ☞ چیت

چیت ² chit **1** crushed; crumpled; flattened **2** flat, plane

چیتا chitá *f.* Chita

چیت پیت chit-pít crushed; flattened out

چیتر chitár *m. Eastern* Chitar (the 12th month of the Hindu calendar; March-April)

چیتره chitrá *f. regional* rags

چیتول chitavál *denominative, transitive* [*past:* چیت یی کړ] to crush; flatten out لړم چیتول to crush a scorpion

چیتیدل chitedál *denominative, intransitive* [*past:* چیت شو] to be crushed, be crumpled up, be flattened down

چیت chit *m.* chintz, printed cotton

چیتی chitój *f. Eastern* **1** note; letter **2** invoice

چیچړ chichár chichór [*plural:* چیچړ chichór] **1** *m.* **.1** fold **1.2** wrinkle **1.3** red-tape merchant, petty functionary **2.1** wrinkled **2.2** knotty, gnarled (of a stick)

چیچړول chicharavál *denominative, transitive* [*past:* چیچړ یی کړ] **1** to fold, make folds **2** to wrinkle

چیچړه chichrá *f.* **1** soft little clod or lump of something **2** crumpled object **3** lean meat

چیچړی chichrój *f.* very small louse

چیچړیدل chicharedál *denominative, intransitive* [*past:* چیچړ شو] **1** to form folds or pleats **2** to wrinkle up

چیچک chichák *m.* **1** chicken-pox **2** infection of fruit trees by scale-insects

چیچکه chicháka *f.* pullet

چیچل chichál *transitive* [*past:* ويي چیچه] **1** bite, masticate, gnaw شوندي په غاښو چیچل to bite one's lips (in anger) خپلي شوندي چیچل to chew one's lips **2** to sting, stick (with a sting, point) **3** to nibble (e.g., sunflower seeds) **4** to chew, chew thoroughly **5** to gnaw around (a bone) **6** to curse, berate **7** to grind, chatter (the teeth) *idiom* چاته غاښونه چیچل to have it in for someone

چیچونکی سپی chichúnkaj vicious dog

چیچی chicháj *m.* [*plural:* چیچیان chichiján] **1** fledgling, chick **2** young (of animals, e.g., cub, calf) چیچیان راوړل a to hatch out chicks b to give birth to young د ماهي چیچی fry, fingerlings (fish)

چیخا chikhá *f. children's speech* bow-wow (dog)

چیختاړ chikhtáṛ چختاړ

چیخل chikhál *transitive* چخول

چیخله chíkhla *f.* stick, staff

چیخن chikhán **1** dirty **2** suppurating

چیخن توب chikhəntób *m.* چیخن والی chikhənválaj *m.* dirt, mud

چیخوړی chikhúṛaj *m.* rags

چیخي chíkhi *f. plural* چخړه

چی دمی chəjdamáj *f.* teapot, teakettle

چیرته chérta *Eastern* چیري

چیرره chírṛa *f.* rag

چیرا chirá *f.* turban with narrow twisted folds

چیري chéri *Western* chíri chére **1** where (to)? چیري ځې؟ Where are you going? هغه چیري تللئ دئ؟ Where is he going? **2** where (at)? چیري به دي ووینم؟ Where will I see you? **3** (to) somewhere, anywhere **4** (at) somewhere; anywhere, somewhere or other **5** once; someday چیري چیري a here and there b sometimes چیري I sometimes see Ahmed. چیري احمد وینم *idiom* که چیري if, in the event that **5** *idiom* که چیري ضرورت پیښ شي If the necessity arises

چیر chiṛ *m.* **1** sticky substance **2** gum; mucilage; pitch, resinous secretion

چیر cheṛ *m.* **1** exertions **2** obstinacy **3** altercation; dispute

چیرچاړ cheṛchāṛ *m. Eastern* [*plural:* چیرچاړي cheṛchāṛe] **1** joke **2** gaiety د چاسره چیرچاړ کول a چیرچاړ کول to joke with someone b to enjoy oneself

چیرچاړي cheṛchāṛe *f. plural regional* enjoyment, delight, pleasure چیرچاړي کول to take pleasure in

چیرل cheṛál *transitive* [*past:* وي چیره] **1** to oppress; disturb **2** خیرل

چیز chiz *m.* ځیز

چیستان chistán *m.* riddle, mystery

چیستکی chistákaj **1** soft **2** juicy

چیشن cheshán hirsute; shaggy, touseled

چیشنول cheshənavál *denominative, transitive* [*past:* چیشن یې کړ] to disarrage, tousled

چیشنیدل cheshənedál *denominative, intransitive* [*past:* چیشن شو] to get disarranged, get tousle

چینبل chikhál *transitive* چنبل

چیخن chikhán drinking; drink

چیغار chighár cry of a bird

چیغه chígha *f.* چیغي پورته کول to cry out, yell په چیغه ویل چغه to cry out, make a loud declaration

چیکړ chikáṛ *m.* چکړ

چیلم chilám *m.* چلم

چیلی cheláj chiláj *Eastern* kid

چیم chim *m.* name of the letter چ

چین chin *m.* **1** picking, gathering, harvesting (cotton, vegetables) **2** selection, choice

چین chin *m.* China د چین د خلکو جمهوریت the People's Republic of China د شرقي چین بحیره the South China Sea د جنوبي چین بحیره the East China Sea

چینجن chindzhán *m.* چنجن

چینجی chindzháj *m.* چنجی

چینچاړی chinchāṛaj *m.* cricket

چیندخ chindákh *m.* crab

چیندخ خور chindakhkhór *m.* heron

چیندخه chindákha *f.* چندخه

چینگ ching open, gaping (of a mouth, beak)

چینگ خولی chingkhúlaj with wide-open mouth, with gaping maw (animal)

چینگ داری chingdaráj *m.* scoffer, mocker

چینگول chingavál *denominative, transitive* [*past:* چینگ یې کړ] to open, gape (mouth, beak)

چینگهار chingəhár *m.* whining and crying (of a child)

چینگیدل chingedál *denominative, intransitive* to be open, be gaping (of a mouth, beak)

چینه chiná *f.* spring, source د سیند چینه the sources of a river د نفتو چینی oil deposits

چینی chiní *m. Eastern* sugar

چینی chiní chináj **1.1** *adjective* Chinese **1.2** china چینی سامانونه chinaware, china service د چینی جوړولو فابریکه ceramics factory, pottery **2** *m.* Chinese (person)

چینی chináj **3** piebald (of a horse)

چینی chiní *f. combining form* construction, laying, installing سنگ چینی stone facing

چینی باب chinibáb *m. plural* **1** articles of porcelain and pottery; porcelain or pottery table service **2** silicates

چینی خرڅونکی chiní khartsavúnkaj *m.* چینی فروش

چینی دان chinidán *m. Eastern* sugar-bowl

چینی فروش chinifurúsh *m.* dealer in tableware (porcelain, china, pottery, etc.)

چینی هند chinihínd *m.* Indo-China (peninsula)

چیڼی chiṇáj *f.* chisel

چی chəjé چي

ځ

ځ dze the ninth letter of the Pashto alphabet

ځا dzā ☞ ځای

ځابۀ dzābә́ *imperfect of* ځبل

ځاپۀ dzāpә́ *imperfect of* ځپل

ځاځي dzādzí *m. plural* 1 the Dzadzi, Jaji (a tribe) 2 dzādzáj *m. & f.* [*plural:* ځاځيان dzadzaijā́n] Dzadzi, Jaji

ځاځي ميدان dzādzi-majdā́n *m.* Dzadzi-Majdan (a district in Khost)

ځاڅل dzātsә́l *intransitive* [*past:* وځاڅه] to get angry, grow enraged

ځار dzār *m.* sacrifice, oblation ☞ جار

ځاردزار dzārdzā́r *m.* clamor, outcry

ځار و دزار dzār-u-dzahā́r *m.* 1 I am prepared to do everything for you (conventional formula) 2 blessing, farewell ځار و جار کول to bless, address in parting

ځارول dzāravә́l *denominative, transitive* [*past:* ځاري کړ] to offer a sacrifice, sacrifice *idiom* a تر سر ځارول to wave, wave over the head (as a hat, flag) b to lift up and throw an opponent to the ground (as in wrestling) ☞ جارول[1]

ځاربدل dzāredә́l *denominative, intransitive* [*past:* ځار شو] to be offered in sacrifice ☞ جاربدل[1]

ځاږل dzāgҙ́l *transitive* [*past:* ویې ځاږه] *history* to scratch

ځاکۍ dzākә́j *f.* armful of wheat

ځاګلۍ dzāglә́j *f.* 1 cage (for animals) 2 (snug, little) home *idiom* د تتر ځالګۍ *anatomy* rib cage

ځاله dzāla *f. Eastern* nest *idiom* په یوه ملک د بدی ځاله this world ☞ جاله[1] کښي ځاله کول to settle, settle down somewhere

ځالۍ dzālә́j *f.* 1 nest; (snug, little) home ځالۍ جوړول to build a nest 2 hangar

ځام dzām *abbreviation vice* ته ځام نه وي تللئ؟ so څه وایم څه وام So, you didn't go?

ځامن dzāmә́n *plural of* ځوی

ځامه dzāmә́ *imperfect of* ځمل

ځان dzān *m.* 1.1 body ځان مي لرمی سو A nettle-rash has broken out on my body. زه په ځان نه وم ښه I felt bad. I was sick. 1.2 soul, spirit 1.3 life 1.4 private parts (of the human body) 2 *m.* 1 *reflexive pronoun* oneself ځانه self-respect د ځان عزت one's own, one's particular د ځانه ځخه دفاع کول to protect oneself, defend someone د ځانه ځخه پوښتنه کول to ask oneself a question د خپل ځان for one's own self *Eastern* د ځان سره، د خپل ځان سره، ځان سره، ځانه سره، له ځانه سره a with oneself (when speaking of a single individual) b to oneself (e.g., to think) with themselves (many people) د ځان غوندي like oneself ځان ته my self, yourself, himself (etc.) په ځان نه پوهبدم ځانته I was, as it were, without consciousness a چوک په ځان کول to bring someone to, bring back to consciousness b to make someone think better of, make someone see reason ځان پوري یې وخندل He laughed at himself. د دی او خپل ځان یوازي په یوازي ژوند to brag, boast ځان باتي او لافي او وهل

د خپله ځانه کوي He lives by himself. He lives completely alone. ځانه ، خپله ځانه! ندئ راضي He is dissatisfied with himself. چه په ځان Each person thinks of himself first. Charity begins at home. کښني ويني ، په جهان کښني يې ويني *proverb* to judge others by oneself 2.2 *employed in connection with transitive verbs by a reflexive verb* a ځان اچول to hurl oneself on, fall upon b to give oneself out as another person (to pretend to be someone else), imitate someone else, emulate another person c to subject or expose oneself to something ځان تودول to warm oneself ځان خرابول to ruin oneself *idiom* د چا خبري پر ځان تېرول، د چا خبري پر ځان وړل to put up with someone; calmly obey someone و چاته یو شی په ځان ورکول to transfer something of value to someone; yield or bestow something upon someone دا قلم واخله ،ستا ئي په ځان Take this pen, it is yours

ځان پالنه dzānpālә́na *f.* egotism, self-love

ځان پالونکی dzānpālúnkaj ځان پالی dzānpālaj egotistical, selfish

ځان پرستي dzānparastí *f.* ☞ ځان پالنه

ځان په ځان dzānpәdzā́n separate; isolated

ځانته dzā́nta 1.1 to oneself, for oneself, for or to ones very self; by one's own self 1.2 toward oneself 2.1 separate, by own self, alone 2.2 particularly, specially; concerning ځانته به د در سره خبري a I will speak a bit with you alone. b I will have a little talk with you in particular. ځانته کول to seclude, separate, isolate ځانته کبدل to be secluded, be separated, be isolated 3.1 reserved, unsociable هغه ځانته سری دئ He is a reserved. He is an unsociable man. 3.2 special دا ځانته اهميت لري This has a special significance. 3.3 *diplomacy* extraterritorial

ځان ځارونی dzān dzāravúnaj self-sacrificing; selfless

ځان ځانته dzāndzā́nta 1 personally 2 separately, specially

ځانځاني dzāndzāní *f.* 1 egotism, self-love 2 disconnectedness دځان ځانو ډزي single rounds (of gunfire) 3 seclusion 4 limitedness

ځانځولۍ dzāndzolә́j *f.* playful rocking a child back and forth by the hands and feet ځان ځولۍ کول to amuse a child by swinging it back and forth by hands and feet

ځان ځومری dzāndzomә́raj weak, puny

ځان خورگي dzānkhurgí *f.* dzānkhvurgí dzānkhurgí dzānkhuragí 1 exhaustion 2 depression 3 irritation a ځان خورگي کول to be exhausted b to experience depression c to be irritated

ځان خوښي[1] dzānkhvakhí *f.* self-sacrifice

ځان خوښی[2] dzānkhvákhaj self-satisfied, complacent

ځاندار dzāndā́r 1 lively, animated 2 *m.* lively topic; living creature ځاندار

ځانداري dzāndari *f.* 1 life 2 animation

ځاندره dzāndә́ra *f.* form; shape

ځان ستاينه dzānstājә́na *f.* self-praise

ځان ښکارونه dzānҙ̌kāravә́na *f.* pretense, hypocrisy

ځان ښودنه dzānҙ̌odә́na *f.* display of one's personal qualities; posing

ځان غلاکول dzānghlakavә́l *m. plural* self-aggrandizement, self-deceit

ځان غوښتل dzānghuķhtól *m.* ځان غوښتنه dzānghuķhtəna *f. plural* egotism, self-love

ځان غولوونکی dzān ghulavúnkaj deceiving oneself

ځانکدن dzānkadán *m.* ☞ ځان کندن

ځان کښل dzānkķhəl *m. plural* seclusion

ځان کندن، ځانکندن dzānkandán *m.* death-throes, mortal agony

ځنگل dzāng *present stem of* ځنگل

ځانګرتیا dzāngərtjã *f.* 1 specialization 2 peculiarity

ځانګړی dzāngə́raj 1 special, particular 2 distinctive 3 independent

ځانګو dzāngó *f. Eastern* [*plural:* ځانګووي dzāngóve] cradle ☞ زانګو

ځانله dzā́nla ☞ ځانله ژوند کول to live by oneself

ځانلګړی dzānlagə́raj

ځانله والی dzānlavā́laj *m.* solitude, seclusion

ځانمنتوب dzānməntób *m.* ځانمني dzanmə́ni *f.* self-satisfaction

ځان منونی dzānmanúnaj ځا نمنی dzānmənáj self-satisfied

ځانور dzānavə́r *m.* living being, living creature

ځان وزګاری dzānvəzgã́raj without work, unoccupied

ځانه dzā́na 1 My Soul! My Dear! My Darling! (as a form of address) 2 *oblique of* ځان

ځانه dzānə́ *imperfect of* ځنل

ځان ځاني، ځانه ځاني dzānadzā́ni *f.* ☞

ځان هېروونکی dzān heravúnkaj self-sacrificing; selfless ځان هېروونکی مزاج self-sacrifice; selfessness

ځاني dzāni 1 corporeal, physical 2 human, personnel (of casualties) ځاني تلفات losses, casualties (from personnel strength) 3 subjective

ځانه dzā́na *f. dialect* ☞ زانه

ځاڼی dzā́naj *m.* crane (the bird)

ځاو dzāv March!, On the double!

ځای dzāj *Eastern* dzāe *m.* 1 place, site خالي ځای، تش ځای unoccupied place, empty seat ځای ځای here and there ځای کوم ځای ناست، ځای خالي کول to yield a place, give up a seat و؟ *Eastern* Where did he sit? 2 locale, location; inhabited location, built-up area د غزني په واغز ځای کښې زیږېدلئ دئ He was born in Baguz, near Gazni. میمنه یو تجارتي ځای دئ Mejmene is a trade center. د هغه ځای from those places, of that place تاسي به کم Where are you د کم ځای یې؟ Where are you going? ځای ته ولاړسئ؟ from? د هغه ځایه څخه Where do you come from? د کم ځایه راځي؟ د دې ځایه، له دې ځایه، د دې ځایه، له from there له هغه ځایه څخه everywhere, an all sides, دی ځایه ته from here هر ځای، هر ځای wherever a ځای پر ځای on the spot b everywhere there and now, on the spot, at once b here and there په ځينو ځايو in places, here and there 3 premises; house, residence; کښې building ستا ځای چیري دئ؟ the master of the house د ځای خاوند Where is your house? ځای ته راغلو We arrived at our own place. 4 bed په ځای نموتل to make a bed ځای ته اچول to go to bed 5 *military* position 6 portion, share څلور ځایه کول to divide into four parts 7 echelon; establishment; work-place a لوړ ځای high place b high

echelon 8 case, instance دا افعال په ډېرو ځایونوکي استعمالېږي These verbs are employed in many situations. 9 basis, grounds for something د افسوس ځای دئ appropriate condolences 10 job, position ځای وهل to receive a job, get a position ځای پربنول to go into retirement a ځای پر ځای کول to put in place b to calm c to a ځای لرل ځایېدل kill on the spot *compound verb* ☞ be, be located b to be appropriate c to take place, happen ځای نیول a to occupy a place; lodge b to take place, eventuate c to replace someone زمونږ زیار او زحمت به ځای نیولئ وي Our efforts will not be in vain. d چا ځای وهل a to compare with, match with someone; catch up with someone b to jump as far as another پر دتولو غوښتني یې پر ځای a to effect, bring about ځای کول، په ځای کول پر ځای کېدل، په ځای ځایول b He fulfilled the petition of all. په ځای ځایېدل a to be effectuated, be brought about b ☞ کېدل په ځای راوړل، په ځای راوستل to come to oneself (after a faint) راتلل ځای ته رسېدل، تر ځایه to bring something to a conclusion, execute احمد ځای ته ورسېده a to reach, achieve, attain something رسېدل Ahmed reached home. b to attain a goal c *figurative* to get a good job, obtain a good position d *figurative* to make one's way in the world e to reach a specific age د بنځي ځای ته رسېدل to reach maturity (of a girl) a تر ځایه رسول a to bring, deliver to a place b *figurative* to help to get on in the world *idiom* د .... په ځای کښي Send your brother ورور دي په خپل ځای کښبني راواستوه instead of instead of yourself. په خپل ځای، په خپل ځای کښبني appropriate, apt, as it should be په بد ځای کښبني inappropriate, out of place, inept د خندا surprisingly د تعجب ځای دئ at one sitting, at a stretch ځای a to سره یو ځای کول funnily يو ځای دئ together, jointly convoke, convene b to unite, unify سره یو ځای کبدل a to assemble, gather ډېر خلک سره يو ځای سوي دي Many people were assembled b to be unified, be united يو ځای واقع کبدل to coincide, happen at the same time تر هغه ځايه چه امکان و insofar as it was possible

ځی dzāj ☞ ^{2} ځای

ځای بند dzājbánd fattened up in a stall (of cattle)

ځایداد dzājdã́d *m.* ☞ جایداد

ځای غلی dzājghə́ləj *f.* woman in childbirth

ځایګی ^{1} dzājgáj *m. diminutive* small town ځای ځايګی *colloquial* residence

ځايګي ^{2} dzājəgí right here, on the spot ځایګي ويشتل to slay on the spot

ځای ناستی ^{1} dzājnā́staj *m.* 1 substitute; deputy 2 successor

ځای ناستي ^{2} dzājnāstí *f.* acting tenure of office; office of deputy

ځای وال dzājvā́l settled (in contrast to nomadic)

ځای ول dzājavə́l *denominative, transitive* [*past:* ځای یې کړ] 1 to embody; to lodge, accommodate; to put in, install, establish 2 to hold, include, incorporate 3 to enter (e.g., on a list) 4 to fix, reinforce (in memory)

ځائي dzājí 1 settled; local ځائي خلک، ځائي وګړي natives, local population 2 stable, invariable 3 firm, solid 4 appropriate, suitable *idiom* ځائي کبدل to appear, arise

ځايېدل dzājedə́l *denominative, intransitive* [*past:* ځای شو] **1** to be embodied; be lodged; be established; be disposed **2** to be incorporated, be contained, be included in **3** to be entered, be recorded (e.g., on a list) **4** to be fixed, be reinforced (in memory) ته زمونږ په مينځ كښي نه ځايېږي You are out of place among us.

ځب dzab[1] hirsute, hairy

ځب dzab[2] *interjection* bang

ځبځب dzabdzáb small, reduced in size

ځبږيری dzabghíraj having a broad or thick beard

ځبل dzabə́l *transitive* [*past:* و یی ځابه] **1** to crush, pulverize **2** to chop (meat) **3** to wink **4** to beat, thrash **5** *figurative* to oppress **6** *figurative* to degrade **7** to affect, strike (of a disease) **8** to destroy, defeat

ځبله dzábla[1] with one another, among ourselves, themselves, yourselves; mutually ځبله باندي **a** placed together; placed in a pile **b** pleated; in pleats

ځبله dzabə́la[2] *f. imperfect of* ځبل

ځبلج dzablaj **1** *past participle of* ځبل **2** unhappy مصيبت ځبلی suffering *idiom* دار ځبلي خلگ frightened people, panic-stricken people

ځبن dzabán dzabə́n **1.1** crude, rough **1.2** rude; uncouth **1.3** ignorant **2** dzabán *m.* idiot, imbecile; ignoramus

ځبول dzəbavúl *transitive* [*past:* و یی ځباوه] to blink (the eyes)

ځبېدل dzabedə́l *denominative, intransitive* [*past:* ځب شو] **1** to be thick, grow thick **2** to be plentiful, be abundant

ځبېنل dzbeḵə́l *transitive* ☞ زبېنل

ځبېنند dzbeḵónd **1** suctorial; sucking out, sucking dry **2** soaking up into itself; absorbing كاغذ ځبېنند blotting paper

ځپل dzapə́l *transitive* ☞ ځبل انفلوينزا بدبد ځپلئ یم ځبل I have a bad case of influenza.

ځدځا dzədzā́ *f.* sizzling (of roasting meat)

ځدزبوكج dzadzbókaj *m.* ځدزغولی dzadzgúlaj *m.* cracklings, cracknels

ځدزرل dzədzerə́l *transitive* ☞ ځیځبدل

ځخه dzə́kha *dialect* ☞ څخه[1]

ځدران dzadrắṇ **1** *m. plural* Dzadrani, Jadrani (tribe) **2** *m.* Dzadran, Jadran (tribesman)

ځرځ dzərdz *m.* ☞ زرع

ځرځ ستر‌گج dzerdzstórgaj ☞ زرع

ځری dzáraj[1] *m.* **1** spy, espionage operative, secret police agent **2** back-sight (gun); sight ځری لگول، ځری اخيستل to aim, take aim **3** *Eastern* guide, conductor

ځری dzarə́j[2] *f.* food ☞ زری

ځريځه dzarídza *f.* safflower, *Carthmus tinctorious*

ځراوه dzaṛavə́ *imperfect of* ځرول

ځرند dzəránd ☞ زرند

ځرندول dzəṛandavə́l *transitive* ☞ زوږندول

ځروبج dzəṛobáj *m.* waterfall, cataract

ځرول dzaṛavə́l *transitive* [*past:* و یی ځراوه] **1** to hang, hang up, suspend **2** to lower, let down **3** to hang, lower (the head)

ځړه dzə́ṛa *f.* attack of a dog

ځړېدل dzaṛedə́l *intransitive* [*past:* و ځړيد] **1** to hang, be hung **2** to be lowered, be let down **3** to hang over اوريځ پر كلي راځړيده A storm cloud hung over the village. **4** to be hung down (of the head) **5** to droop (of flowers) **6** *figurative* to cling (e.g., to the past)

ځز dzez *m.* ☞ ځزكی dzəzkáj *m.* ځړهار dzəzəhár *m.* sizzling، ځزلرل ځزوهل to sizzle

ځز dzəg[1] *m.* **1** dam of loose earth (allowing water to percolate through) **2** sandy bank of an irrigation channel (allowing water to percolate through) **3** drifts of sand and gravel

ځز dzəg[2] *m.* whistle of a bullet

ځږه dzəga[1] *f.* **1** stomach pains **2** birth pangs

ځږه dzəga[2] *f.* hillock

ځښت dzəḵht **1** severe; sharp **2** very, too much, exceedingly (used as an intensifying word) دا ځښته توده كوټه ده It ځښت ښه very good is very hot in this room ډېر ځښت very much

ځښكله dzəḵhkóla when, at the time when

ځغ dzegh *m. dialect* ☞ جغ[1,2]

ځغاست dzghāst[1] *m.* **1** run **2** raid

ځغاست dzghāst[2] *imperfect of* ځغاستل

ځغاستا dzghāstā́ *f.*

ځغاستل dzghāstə́l *intransitive* ☞ ځغاست

ځغاسته dzghāstə́ *m. plural* run, running, race

ځغاله dzəghālá *f.* small lump of dough

ځغامه dzghāmə́ *imperfect of* ځغمل

ځغستا dzghastā́ *f.* run په ځغستا on the run, at a run په ځغستا پيل كول to break into a run

ځغستل dzghastə́l *intransitive* [*present:* ځغلي *past:* وځغاست] to run

ځغل dzghə́l[1] *present stem of* ځغستل

ځغل dzghə́l[2] *f. present stem of* ځغبدل

ځغلا dzghalá *f.* run; races; horseraces د ځغلا ميدان **a** racetrack **b** *figurative* arena

ځغلاوه dzghalāvə́ *imperfect of* ځغول

ځغلند dzghalónd **1** running; racing **2** at a run; at a gallop

ځغلندی dzghólandáj pitiable; poor

ځغلول dzghalavə́l *transitive* **1** to make run; urge on; drive **2** to put to flight; drive away **3** to drive off (horses, etc.) **4** to flush (game); drive out (of a lair, den) **5** to lay in (a water conduit, etc.) **6** to extend (a pipeline) **7** *literally* to put out (e.g., roots)

ځغله dzghála *imperfective imperative singular of* ځغستل

ځغلي dzghalí[1] *present of* ځغبدل، ځغستل

ځغلی dzghaláj[2] *imperfective imperative plural of* ځغستل

ځغلېدل dzghaledə́l *intransitive* [*present:* ځغلي *past:* وځغلیده] **1** to run **2** to rush, race; proceed quickly (of automotive vehicles, ships) **3** to flee, be put to flight **4** to be laid down (of water conduits, pipe, etc.) **5** to extend (of a pipeline)

څغلېدۀ dzgaledӭ *m. plural* **1** run **2** flight, escape **3** swift motion (of automotive vehicles, ships) **4** laying (of waterline) **5** extent, laying down (of pipeline)

څغم dzgham *m.* absorption ☞ زغم

څغمدژن dzghamdzhэn **1** reserved; restrained **2** patient

څغمل dzghamӭl *transitive [past:* ويي څغامه] **1** to suffer, endure, put up with **2** to absorb رڼا څغمل to absorb light اوبه څغمل to absorb water

څغول dzэgavӭl *transitive [past:* وي څغاوه] to cause sizzling

څغوندڅغول dzghundzavӭl *transitive [past:* وي څغوندڅاوه] **1** to cause to twist or wind **2** to turn, invert, turn over

څغوندڅیدل dzghundzedӭl *intransitive [past:* و څغونڅۀبدل] **1** to be twisted **2** to be turned, be inverted

څغېدل dzэghedӭl *intransitive [past:* وڅغۀبده] to sizzle

څک ¹ dzak *m.* ☞ څگ ¹

څکلول ² dzuklavӭl *transitive [past:* وي څکلاوه] to torture, torment

څکلیدل dzukledӭl *intransitive [past:* وڅکلۀبده] to be tortured, be tormented

څکدن dzakadán *m.* ☞ څان کندن

څکه dzӭka *conjunction* therefore, for this reason هغه در څخه خوابدی دئ څکه نه درځي He has a grudge against you, therefore he will not come. څکه چه because نو څکه therefore, and so, that's why

څگ ¹ dzag *m.* foam څگ کول د صابون soapsuds to whip up foam or suds څگ کېدل to froth, foam څگونه الوتل to foam up, arise (of foam, suds)

څگ ² dzag *m.* oil press; container for pressing oil

څگال dzgāl *m.* bread crumbled into soup

څگخور dzagkhór *m.* water-bird; seagull

څگر dzigár *m.* **1** *anatomy* liver څگر چینجی hepatic bile duct **2** breast **3** *figurative* bravery, valor; manhood *idiom* خون څگر مه خوره! Don't overstrain yourself! Don't try too hard!

څگرگوش dzigargósh **1** dear, beloved **2** near, related

څگرور dzigarvár brave, valorous; manly

څگروی dzgarváj *m. dialect* ☞ څگروی

څگري dzigarí **1** hepatic **2** dark-red

څگلانه dzaglӑna *f.* skin-bag for sour milk

څگلن dzaglэn foamy

څگروی dzgerváj *m.* moan څگروی کول to moan

څل ¹ dzal *m. [plural:* څلونه dzalúna *Eastern f. plural:* څلي dzále] time دوه څل the second time په لمړي څل for the first time دویم څل twice دپر څل in the first instance, in the first place دلمړي څل دپاره often, many times, repeatedly یوڅل، دوه څله، یودوه څلي *Eastern* دیوه څله، یونیم څله two times پوڅل نیم several times څوڅله abruptly, all at once یو څل بیا once again, once more د دوهم څل دپاره for the second time

څل ² dzӭl *m. [plural:* څلان dzэlān] horse cloth; saddlecloth *m.* ironic *idiom* پر چا څل اینبول to subordinate oneself to someone

څلا dzэlӑ *f.* ☞ جلا

څلادار dzэlādár shining (of hair, fleece)

څلاند dzэlӑnd dzalӑnd **1** shining, sparkling, radiant **2** *figurative* clear, evident **3** *figurative* outstanding, distinguished, brilliant هغه د ادب یو څلان ستوری دئ He is an outstanding writer. څلان کول **a** to make to shine, make to sparkle **b** *figurative* to make clear, make evident **c** to single out from others څلان کېدل **a** to shine, sparkle, be radiant **b** *figurative* to be clear, be evident **c** to be outstanding, be singled out from others, be conspicuous

څلبل dzalbál ☞ څلان

څلبلاند dzalbalānd **1** agitated **2** deranged; distressed

څلبلاندیدل [څلبلاند] dzalbalāndedӭl *denominative, intransitive [past:* to be agitated **2** to be deranged, be distressed

څلبلی dzalbӑláj ☞ څلاند

څلځی dzáldzaj *m. anatomy* mammillated extension of the temporal bone

څلنب dzalӭkht *m.* glitter, radiance, sparkle

څلک dzalk *m. Eastern* **1** flash, sudden combustion **2** glitter, radiance **3** reflection, gleam

څلکان dzalkӑn gleaming, radiating, sparkling

څلکیدل dzalkedӭl *intransitive dialect* ☞ څلبدل

څلل dzalál *m. dialect* ☞ ضرر

څلما dzalmӑ *f.* ☞ زلما

څلموتی dzalmótaj *m.* ☞ زلموتی

څلمی ¹ dzalmáj *m.* ☞ زلمی ¹

څلمی ² dzalmáj *f.* ☞ زلمی ²

څلمیتوب dzalmitób *m.* ☞ زلمیتوب، څلمي توب

څلمیگوتی dzalmigótaj *m.* little fellow

څلمینه dzalmína *f.* ☞ زلمیتوب

څلند ¹ dzalánd ☞ څلان

څلند ² dzalánd ☞ ظالم 2

څلند ستوری dzalánd stóraj *m. astronomy* Sirius (the star)

څلندوکی dzalandúkaj gleaming, sparkling, radiating

څل و بل dzalubál bright, sparkling

څلوبی ¹ dzalobáj *m.* mirage

څلوبی ² dzalobáj *f.* jalibi (sweet made of flour, sugar, and oil)

څلوکه dzalúka *f.* cardiac blood-vessels

څلول dzalavӭl *[past:* وي څلاوه] *transitive* to make to gleam or sparkle, be radiant; give a luster to

څلون dzalún *m.* **1** double skin-canteen **2** bag

څله ¹ dzíla *f.* **1.1** derangement, distress **1.2** worry, alarm **2** deranged, distressed

څله ² dzála *oblique singular used with numeral from* څل ¹

څلی ¹ dzále *f. plural Eastern* ☞ څل ¹

څلي ² dzáli *f. plural* ☞ الي څلي

څلیدل dzaledӭl *intransitive* **1.1** *[past:* وڅلۀبده] to gleam, sparkle, be radiant; twinkle په اسمان کښي ستوري څلېږي The stars are twinkling in the sky. وړاندي د موټر برق و څلېده The headlights of cars gleamed ahead. **1.2** *m. plural figurative* to be radiant, glow (e.g., from joy) **2** *m. plural* **.1** gleam, sparkling; radiance; twinkle **2.2** heat lightning د ستورو څلېدل heat lightning

خَلِدَنه dzaledə́na *f.* خَلِدَنه dzaledə́ *m. plural* gleam, sparkling, radiance; twinkling د ستورو خَلِدَنه the twinkling of stars

خَم ¹ dzəm *first person present of* تلل 1

خَما dzmā dzəmā *pronoun Eastern* ☞ زما

خُمب dzumb *m. dialect* twinkling, winking, blinking

خَمل dzamə́l *transitive* ☞

خَمبیدل dzambedə́l *intransitive* [*past:* وخَمبیده] to drag oneself along, trudge

خَمری dzmaráj *m. Eastern* ☞ زمری

خُمکَنی dzməkənáj *adjective Eastern* 1 land, ground 2 *figurative* of the earth, mundane, practicable *idiom* خُمکَني توت wild strawberries, domestic strawberries خُمکَني چینجي earthworms

خُمکَوال dzməkaвál *m. Eastern* peasant farmer

خُمکه dzmə́ka *f. Eastern* 1 earth, land خُمکه جگه height, elevation 2 floor (of a room) 3 the world ☞ مَخکه

خَمل dzamə́l *transitive* [*past:* و یې خَامه] to blink, screw up the eyes; to squint (from sunlight)

خُمنَر dzməng *dialect* ☞ زمونَر

خُمنه ¹ dzmə́na *f.* promise خُمنه کول to promise

خُمنه ² dzamə́na *f.* blinking

خُمور dzmug خُمونَر dzmúng خُمونِره dzmúnga *pronoun* ☞ زمونَر

خُني dzíne ☞

خَنازه dzənazá *f.* ☞ جنازه

خَناور dznaвár *m.* [*plural:* خَناوران dznaвarə́n خَناور dznaвə́r *dialect plural:* dzənaвə́r] wild beast, animal د خَناورو باغ zoo, zoological park

خَناورتوب dznaвartób *m.* feral disposition; brutality; savagery

خَمبَل dzambə́l *transitive* ☞ خَمل

خَمبَول dzambawə́l *transitive* [*past:* و یې خَنباوه] 1 to make to wink, make to squint 2 to shake, quiver 3 to move, budge

خَمبیدل dzambedə́l *intransitive* [*past:* وخَمبیده] 1 to blink 2 to oscillate, shake to and fro 3 to stir, budge

خَنج dzandz *m.* alum

خَنخَری dzandzərə́j *f.* carpet pattern

خَنخَلبَر dzzndzlér *m.* tassels used to decorate a tent or marquee

خَنخَول dzəndzawə́l *transitive* [*past:* و یې خَنخاوه] 1 to drop دارو خَنخَول to drop medicine (into eyes, nose, etc.) 2 to distill, alembicate

خَنخه dzə́ndza *f.* centipede

خَنخَی dzandzə́j *f.* small chain (for jewelry)

خَنخَبیدل dzandzedə́l *intransitive* ☞ خَنخَبیدل

خَنخَیر dzandzír *m.* 1 chain 2 shackles 3 bonds, ties *idiom* د استعمار خَنخَیرونه شلول to break the chains of colonialism

خَنخَیرکه dzandziráka *f.* kind of embroidery pattern in the form of a small chain

خَنخَیر لرونکی تراکتور dzandzír larúnkaj caterpillar tractor

خَنخَوال dzankhvál *m. anatomy* pericardium

خَنډ dzanḍ *m. anatomy* 1 delay; holdup; lateness په خَنډ slowly, gradually خَنډ کول to linger, tarry زر وي یا په خَنډ وي sooner or later خَنډ خورل to linger 2 a stop

خَنډمَن dzanḍmə́n 1 slow; long-drawn out; protracted 2 tardy

خَنډَن dzandən خَنډَنی dzandanaj old, ancient *idiom* خَنډَن غوري rancid oil

خَنډَنی dzanḍənáj 1 tardy دی په خَواب کښې لر خَنډَنی شو He is late with an answer. 2 slow, gradual *idiom* خَنډَنی کوکو petunia

خَنډوالی dzandvə́laj *m.* ☞ خَنډیده

خَنډول dzanḍawə́l *transitive* [*past:* و یې خَنډاوه] to detain; drag out; tput aside خَنډول کیدل *passive* to be detained; be dragged out, be put aside, be postponed

خَنډی dzanḍój *f.* ☞ خَونډی

خَنډیدل dzanḍedə́l *intransitive* [*past:* وخَنډیده] 1 to be detained; be late, be overdue; inger, tarry زر راخَه چه ونه خَنډیږي! Go more quickly! Don't delay! 2 to be dragged out; be put aside, be postponed 3 to stand for a time, sit there (of food)

خَنډیده dzanḍedə́ *m. plural* 1 delay, holdup; lateness 2 protraction; deferment

خَانکندن dzankadán *m.* خَنکندن dzankandán *m.* ☞

خَنگ ¹ dzang *m. dialect* ☞ زنگ

خَنگَر dzangár unconscious, senseless خَنگَر کیدل to lose consciousness

خَنگَل ¹ dzangál *m.* [*plural:* خَنگَلونه dzangalúna *plural:* خَنگَلات dzangalā́t] *Arabic* 1 forest; grove گني خَنگَل thick forest تور خَنگَل dense forest په خَنگله کښي in the forest د خَنگل محافظ forester خَنگل ساتونکی 2 thickets 3 wasteland, waste ground *idiom* خَنگل ویستل to weed, eliminate weeds

خَنگَل ² dzangə́l *transitive* ☞ زنگل ¹

خَنگَلباغ dzangalbágh *m.* grove; park; tree plantings

خَنگَلباني dzangalbāní *f.* timber industry

خَنگَله dzanglə́ *oblique singular of* خَنگَل ¹

خَنگَلي dzangalí 1 *adjective* 1.1 forest, timber 1.2 wild, savage 2 *m.* savage *idiom* خَنگَلي وبینته disheveled, disarranged

خَنگوری dzangúraj *m.* bunch of grapes, cluster of grapes

خَنگَول dzangavúl *transitive Eastern* ☞ زنگول

خَنگَبیدل dzangedə́l *intransitive Eastern* ☞ زنگبیدل ¹

خَنگَبیده dzangedə́ *masculine plural of* خَنگَبیدل

خَنَل dzanə́l *transitive* [*past:* و یې خَانه] to anneal, harden (a javelin tip, etc.)

خَنه dziná *f.* ☞ زینه

خَني dzə́ni dzíni *Eastern* dzíne 1 *dialect postposition* out of, from, at (in the presence of or in possession of) د بنار خَني out of the city, from the city تا خَني کتاب شته؟ Do you have the book? 2 *adverb* in their, in his, in her (possession); from him, from her, from them زما کتاب خَني واخله Take my book away from him. خَني ولاړسه Depart from him 3 *pronoun* ☞ خَیني ¹

خَنکَی dzəṇkáj *m.* 1 *dialect* ☞ زنکی ¹

خَنَی dzánaj *m. Eastern* 1 ☞ زنی ¹ 2 schoolboy

خَو ¹ zo پروسږکال خَوکړیٔ دئ to be born خَوکول He was born last year.

خَو ² dzu *first person plural present of* تلل 1

خَواب dzaváb *m.* ☞ خَواب

خواب لوښی dzavāblútsaj quick-witted, resouceful

خوابي dzavābí *m.* one who has rejected, rejectee

خواک dzvāk *m.* life, existence د پلار خواک ښه دئ (My) father is living well

خواله dzvála *f.* ☞ خومنه

خوان dzvān dzəván 1 *m.* .1 young man, youth 1.2 fine young fellow 1.3 real man; noble man, generous man 1.4 *Eastern* warrior, soldier 2.1 young, youthful خوان آس young horse خوانه ونه young tree, sapling خوان خوان ښودل to try to look young 2.2 under age *idiom* خوان ختل to turn out to be a fine fellow لوی خوان *religion* Lojdzvan, the Pir Baba (the title of the founder of the Sufi Order of the Qadiriya", Abdul Quadir Beidel Gilyani)

خوان بخت dzvānbákht 1 happy, lucky 2 gifted, talented

خوان توب dzvāntób *m.* youth; youthfulness

خوانکه dzvānáka *f.* pimple

خوانکی dzvānəkáj 1 *m.* young lad 2 young, youthful

خوانکی dzvānakáj *f.* freckle

خوانگه dzvánga *f.* pinch خوانگه کول to pinch one another

خوان مرد dzvānmárd *m.* 1 fine young fellow 2 valorous man; daredevil 3 noble man, generous man, magnanimous man

خوانمردي dzvānmardí *f.* 1 valor, courage 2 nobility, generosity, magnanimity د چا سره خوانمردي کول to display nobility with regard to another

خوانمرگ dzvānmárg *adjective* person who had died young; having died in youth

خوانمرگي dzvānmargí *f.* death in youth

خوانمرد dzvānmárd *m.* ☞ خوانمرد

خوانمردي dzvānmardí *f.* ☞ خوانمردي

خوانول dzvānavәl *denominative, transitive* [*past:* خوان یې کړ] to make look young; rejuvenate

خوانه dzvāna 1 *feminine singular of* خوان 2 *f.* [*plural:* خواناني dzvānāni] young girl, unmarried woman

خواني dzvāní *f.* 1 youth; youthfulness خپله خواني کول to enjoy youth 2 valor, courage 3 nobility, generosity, magnanimity ښه خواني generosity; hospitality 4 beauty

خواني مرگ dzvānimárg *attributive* having died in youth خواني مرگ سي! *curse* May you drop dead!

خوانېدل dzvānedәl *denominative, intransitive* [*past:* خوان شو] 1 to grow young again, seem to grow a bit younger 2 to be nubile, start to develop (of children) 3 to develop

خوانېدنه dzvānedәna *f.* خوانېده dzvānedә *m. plural* youth, state of being young

خواوله dzvávla *f.* ☞ خومنه

خواونه dzvávna *f.* soup

ژویل dzóbәl *dialect* ☞ ژویل

ژوبلول dzoblavәl *transitive* ☞ ژبلول

ژوبلېدل dzobledәl *intransitive* ☞ ژبلېدل

خوځات dzavdzát *m. dialect* 1 descent, origin 2 clan, family ☞ زوزات

جوجه ما جوجه dzúdzaj-mazúdzaj *m. dialect* ☞ خوجی ما خوجی

خور dzaur *m.* 1 oppression 2 grief, distress ☞ جور

خور dzur intelligent, clever, bright

خورابي dzurābi *f. plural dialect* stockings

خورتوب dzurtób *m.* خورتیا dzurtjā *f.* خوروالی dzurvālaj *m.* 1 intelligence, cleverness, brightness 2 keen hearing 3 keen eyesight

خوراورل dzravravәl *transitive* [*past:* و یې خوراوه] 1 to torture, torment 2 to distress 3 to irritate

خوره dzúra *f.* cooking of food

خوربدل dzavredәl *intransitive* 1 to suffer, be a prey, be tormented 2 to be distressed 3 to be irritated

خوربدل dzuredәl *intransitive* [*past:* وخوربده] to be re-cooked, be warmed up (food)

خوربده dzravredә *m. plural* 1 suffering, torment 2 distress 3 irritation

خوربده dzavredә *imperfect of* خوربدل

خور dzvaṛ low; gently sloping خور لور uneven, broken (of terrain)

خورند dzvaṛәnd 1 hanging, suspended خورند پل suspension bridge 2 flying, fluttering

خورندول dzvaṛandavәl *denominative, transitive* [*past:* خورند یې کړ] 1 to hang, suspend 2 to flap, stream

خورندونه dzvaṛandavәna *f.* 1 hanging, suspension 2 flapping, fluttering, streaming

خورندېدل dzvaṛandedәl *denominative, intransitive* [*past:* خورند شو] 1 to hang, be suspended 2 to flap, flutter, stream

خوروالی dzvaṛvālaj *m.* 1 descent, slope 2 brokenness (of terrain)

خوروبای dzvaṛobáj *m.* waterfall

خورول dzvaṛavәl *denominative, transitive* [*past:* خور یې کړ] to lower; bring down; reduce, demote

خوره dzvára *f.* lowering لوړه او خوره a raising and lowering ډبري extremely broken terrain b *figurative* reversal of fortune, vicissitudes of fate لوړي او خوري مځکي

خوره dzvára *feminine singular of* خور

خورای dzvaṛáj *m.* ☞ خوړی

خورېدل dzvaṛedәl *intransitive* [*past:* خور شو] 1 to descend, come down 2 to dismount

خوز dzoz *m. Eastern* ☞ زوز

خوزخانه dzozkhāná *f. Eastern* temporary cabin made of brushwood

خوزه dzóza *f. Eastern* ☞ زوز

خوږ dzvag *m.* noise

خوش dzokh *m.* boiling hot water خوش لوښی boiler; kettle اوبو ته خوش ورکول to boil water

خوشا dzokhā́ *f.* زوښنا

خوشول dzokhavәl *transitive* [*past:* و یې خوښولې] to boil hot water

خوغاله dzughālá *f.* ☞ زغاله

خوکره dzókṛa *f.* birth

خول dzul *m.* 1 snowstorm; hard frost 2 prolonged rain; bad weather

خولنه dzavlāná *f.* ☞ خولنه

خُولی dzoláj *f.* ☞ جولی

خُوم dzum *m. Eastern* ☞ زوم ¹

خُومنه dzvámna *f.* soup

خُونډی dzunḍáj *m.* pompom; tassel

خُوی dzoj *m.* dzvaj [*plural:* خامن dzāmə́n] *Eastern* son

خُویک dzojə́k *m. Eastern* little son, sonny

خُوی والی dzojgalví *f.* ☞ خُوی گلوي

خُوی مری dzojmə́raj *m.* man who has lost a son

خُوی والی dzojvā́laj *m.* ولي خُوی dzojvalí *m.* obligations and the rights of a son

خه dzə *personal pronoun Eastern* I ☞ زه

خه ² dza *imperfective imperative of* تلل ¹ 1

خي dze *f.* name of the letter ع

خي ² dze *second person present of* تلل ¹ 1

خي ³ dzi *present tense of* تلل ¹ 1

خئ ⁴ dzəj 1 *imperfective imperative of* تلل ¹ 1 2 *second person plural present tense of* تلل ¹ 1

خی ¹ dzáj *m. Eastern* ☞ زی

خی dzaj dzáj *m. suffix* place اټوخی bazaar

خب dzeb *m.* ☞ جب

خيدزه رل dzidzerə́l *transitive* [*past:* وي يي خيځبره] 1 to chop, crumble, crush 2 to beat, thrash someone 3 *figurative* to bawl out, tell off

خير dzir 1 *m.* .1 fixed, intent stare, scrutiny په، خير کتل، په خير کول to stare intently, scrutinize 1.2 to investigate something 1.3 attention خير اچول ته شي پوره يوه ويه to pay a lot of attention to something ... چه شي خير دي ډپر One should pay special attention in that ... ته په خير کېدل ...و a to look intently at, scrutinize b to pay close attention to someone or something c to pay attention to someone or something خير سئ! Attention! 2 *attributive* .1 intent, attentive خيري سترگي intent stare 2.2 investigating, looking into something... ته خير کېدل a to scrutinize, look closely at b to investigate, look into something

خير ² dzir *m.* 1 peep 2 ☞ زير ³

خير ³ dzir *m.* kind of soft leather from Iran

خيرتوب dzirtób *m.* خيرتيا dzirtjā́ *f.* 1 ☞ خُورتوب 2 attention

خيرک dzirák *dialect* ☞ زيرک

خبرمه dzérma *f.* ☞ زبرمه

خيره dzirá *f.* 1 share, portion 2 ☞ جيره

خيگ dzig ☞ زير ²

خيگتوب dzigtób *m.* خيرتيا dzigtjā́ *f.* 1 hardness, firmness 2 rudeness, crudeness 3 severity, cruelty

خبرمه dzégma *f.* eyelid

خبرنده dzégənda *f.* ☞ زبرنده

خبرنه dzegə́na *f. Eastern* birth د خبرني نبته birthday

خيرتوب dzigvā́laj *m.* ☞ خيرتوب

خبرول ¹ dzegavúl *transitive Eastern* ☞ زبرول ¹

خبرول ² dzigavə́l *denominative, transitive* ☞ زبرول ²

خيره ¹ dzigá *feminine singular of* خير

خيره ² dzigə́ *masculine plural & oblique singular of* خير

خبريدل ¹ dzegedə́l *Eastern intransitive of* زبريدل ¹

خبريدل ² dzigedə́l *denominative, intransitive* ☞ زبريدل ²

خبريده dzegedə *m. plural Eastern* ☞ خبرنه

جبسل dzesə́l *transitive* ☞ جبسل

خير dzig *Eastern* ☞ خير

خيگر dzigár *m.* ☞ خگر هغه ډپر په خيگر تنگ دئ a He is very nervous. b He is burning with impatience.

خيگرور dzigarvár ☞ خگرور

خبگول dzegavə́l *transitive Eastern* ☞ زبرول ¹

خيگه ¹ dzigá *Eastern* ☞ خيره ¹

خيگه ² dzigə *Eastern* ☞ خيره ²

خبگېدل dzegedə́l *intransitive Eastern* ☞ زبريدل

خبل ¹ dzel *m.* 1 ☞ جهل 2 stubbornness; obstinacy; unyieldingness

خبل ² dzel *m.* 1 coupled buckets of a noria (well) 2 column (of prisoners, etc.)

خبلي ¹ dzelí *m.* 1 boor 2 blockhead

خبلی ² dzeláj *f.* 1 branch, shoot, scion (of a grapevine) 2 breed (of animals, etc.) *idiom* غم يې د عمر خبلی وچي کړی Grief consumed him

خين dzin *m.* [*plural:* خينان dzinā́n] saddle

خينو ¹ dzinó *oblique plural of* خينه ¹

خينو ² dzíno dzínu *oblique plural of* خيني ¹

خينو ³ dzíno *oblique plural of* خين

خينه ¹ dzina *f.* ☞ زينه

خينه ² dzína *folklore present tense of* تلل ¹ خي ³ *vice*

خيني ¹ dzini *indefinite pronoun usually plural* 1 some خيني وخت sometimes, at times ...په خينو خينو خايو کښي in some places ...خيني...خيني some ..., others ... 2 dzíne *Eastern postposition* ☞ خني

خيني ² dziné *plural of* خينه ¹

خ

خ tse the tenth letter of the Pashto alphabet. In some dialects it is pronounced as "s" and can be accordingly changed by the letter س and frequently خ changes to چ

خا tsā *m.* [*plural:* خهان tsahán *plural:* خاهان tsāhán *f. plural:* خاگاني tsāgáni *plural:* خاوي tsấvi] 1 well د خا اوبه well water 2 bore hole ژور خا deep well د تبلو خا oil well 3 mine د سکرو خا coal mine 4 *figurative* abyss, chasm *idiom literally* و چا ته خا کندل to undermine *figuratively* to cut the ground out from under someone *proverb* چه ته چا ته خا کيني، پخپله به پکښي ولوبري Don't dig a pit to trap another, you may fall into it yourself د خان دپاره خا کينل *proverb* to fall into one's own trap

خابون tsābún *m.* soap ☞ صابون

خاپاڼی tsāpā́ṇaj to almost fall

خاپېر tsāpér ☞ چاپېر

خاپېره ¹ tsāpéṛa *f.* ☞ خيره

خاته ¹ tsātə́ *m. plural* licking

خاته ² tsātə́ *imperfect* ☞ ختل

ښاڅکوټی tsātskóṭaj *m.* small drop, droplet د اوبو ښاڅکوټی droplet of water

ښاڅکی tsātskaj *m.* drop یو ښاڅکی اوبه drop of water ښاڅکی ښاڅکی drop by drop له ښاڅکی باران اوري It drizzles. It's drizzling. ښاڅکی سیند جوړیږي *proverb* From a drop (of water) a river forms.

ښاڅوکی ☞ ښاڅکوټی tsātsúkaj *m.*

ښاڅي tsātsi *present of* څڅېدل

ښادر tsādár *m.* 1 sheet, bed sheet 2 clock, mackintosh, raincoat; cape, mantle د اوبي ښادر cloak 3 shroud, mantle 4 mask د ریاکاری ښادر خپل ښادر سره mask of hypocrisy, pretense, sham *idiom* ښادر پنبې غزول پکار دي *proverb* to cut one's coat according to the cloth ☞ چادر

ښادری tsadarí *f.* chador

ښار ¹ tsar *m.* 1 observation, scrutiny, close supervision تر ښار او کتني لاندي نیول to bring under close scrutiny چا لرل ښار لرل to put someone under scrutiny 2 intelligence gathering, reconnaissance د ښار الوتکه reconnaissance aircraft 3 shadowing ښار کول a to observe, watch, put under surveillance b to find out, reconnoiter, collect information, gather intelligence, observe, put under surveillance c to shadow, have someone shadowed d to wait for, lie in wait for *idiom* لیري ښار کول to look far ahead

ښار ² tsar *m. history* tsar, czar, emperor

ښارا tsārā́ *f.* pit (for storage of grain and other agricultural products) ښارا کول *compound verb* to bury in a pit ښارا کېدل *compound verb* to be buried in a pit

ښارانی tsārānáj *adjective* steppe, wilderness; wild (of animals, birds)

ښاربنکه tsārókhka *f.* ☞ ښاربنکه

ښار کوونکی tsār kavúnkaj *adjective* sharp-sighted, vigilant, attentive, careful, intent

ښارل tsāról *transitive* [*past:* و یې ښاره] 1 to observe, put a watch or observation into effect 2 to collect information, gather intelligence, carry out reconnaissance, reconnoiter 3 to shadow, follow, pursue 4 to note, notice 5 to ascertain (e.g., the reason) 6 to be on the watch for, be in wait for, lie in wait for 7 to try to find, investigate, find a way, find the means

ښارنتون tsārəntún *m. military* 1 veterinary practice 2 veterinary administration

ښارند tsaránd recording, registering, monitoring (of a device)

ښارندوی tsārəndúj tsārəndój 1 *m.* .1 boy scout د افغانستان د ښارندوی تولنه Afghan Boy Scouts 1.2 *history* Pioneer 2 ☞ ښارند

ښارنه tsaróna *f.* 1 surveillance, observation; supervision, scrutiny 2 intelligence collection, reconnoitering 3 shadowing ښارنه کول a to observe; put under surveillance b to collect intelligence c to shadow, pursue

ښارو tsārú *m.* ☞ ښاری ¹

ښاروال tsārvā́l *m.* guard, sentry, sentinel, patrol, watch

ښاروالی tsārvālí *f. military* sentry, guard

ښارونکی tsārūnkaj *m.* 1 observer 2 guard, sentry, sentinel

ښاروی tsā́rváj *m.* [*plural:* ښاروی tsā́rvé *plural:* ښارویان tsārvijā́n] cattle, livestock ستا څو ښاروي دي؟ How many head of cattle do you have? د ښارویو سري، د ښارویو څري draught animals د کار ښاروي manure (as fertilizer)

ښاروي پالنه tsārvipālə́na *f.* livestock breeding, cattle breeding, animal husbandry

ښاره ¹ tsārá *f.* ☞ چاره ¹

ښاره ² tsārá *f.* pit into which juice flows when sugar cane is squeezed in a press

ښاره ³ tsārə́ *imperfect of* ښارل

ښاره ⁴ tsā́ra ☞ ښاره څونه

ښاره ساز tsārasā́z *m.* ☞ چاره ساز

ښاره سازي tsarasāzí *f.* ☞ چاره سازي

ښاری ¹ tsā́raj *m.* [*plural:* ښاري tsā́ri *plural:* ښاریان tsā́rijan] 1 patrol, round 2 scout 3 detective, plainclothes policeman

ښاري ² tsārí tsar's, czar's, royal

ښاري ³ tsāri *present tense of* ښارل

ښارو tsārú *m.* ښاره tsā́ra *f. anatomy* peritoneum

ښاړی ¹ tsā́ṛaj *m. medicine* disease of the hair (in which the hair is cut off) ښاړی کول to be cut, be cut off (of the hair)

ښاړی ² tsā́ṛaj *m. zoology* Bengali bustard د غره ښاړی mountain bustard

ښاغ tsāgh *m.* blood-money (custom of the payment of a sum of money to guarantee withholding of vengeance for the death of a clan member in a vendetta)

ښاشی tsā́shaj *m.* ☞ ښاښی

ښاښ tsā́ķh *computer science m.* axis

ښاښت ¹ tsā́ķht *m.* time from sunrise to noon; morning; breakfast time د لوږي ښاښت تکنده کپنپنستل *idiom* پوخ ښاښت غرمه ☞ to be hard up, starve, go hungry

ښاښت ² tsāķht *m.* charm written on paper (given to a sick child who swallows it with water)

ښاښتی ¹ tsaķhtáj *m.* breakfast; lunch

ښاښتی ² tsaķhtí *adjective* morning

ښاښنکه tsā́ķhka *f.* pink starling

ښاښه tsā́ķha *f.* spun yarn

ښاښی tsā́ķhaj *m.* axle (of a wheel); spindle (of a spinning wheel)

ښاک tsāk *m.* 1 ☞ چاک 2 *medicine* migraine

ښاکه tsāka *f.* ښاکی tsākaj *f.* 1 summit (of a mountain), peak 2 corner of a chador

ښاگی tsāgáj *m.* small well

ښالاک tsālák ☞ چابک

ښاله tsā́la *f.* watchman's shelter (in a melon field)

ښامره tsāmra *dialect* ☞ څومره

ښاندو tsāndú *m.* ☞ ساندو

ښانده tsāndə́ *m. plural* 1 shaking out; shaking up 2 knocking down, shaking down (fruits from a tree) 3 flapping (of wings) 4 brandishing (sabers)

خانده ² tsāndə́ *imperfect tense of* خندل ¹

خانګ tsāng *m.* **1** bones (of the wing of a bird) **2** wing خانګونه وهل a to flap wings **b** to strive for freedom, seek freedom **3** *dialect* ☞ خانګه ¹

خانګ غوخ tsāngghvə́ts **1** with clipped wings **2** *figurative* helpless; unfortunate

خانګوړی tsāngúṛaj *m.* twig, sprig, shoot

خانګه ¹ tsā́nga *f.* **1** branch, bough (of a tree) **2** branching off (of something), offshoot **3** branch (of industry) **4** branch (office), affiliated branch; department (of an establishment) **5** pike, spear, lance **6** district, region

خانګه ² tsā́nga *f.* stab of pain; ache; dull pain خانګي کول to feel a stab of pain; ache; hurt; be painful

خانګي وانګي tsā́ngi-vā́ngi **1.1** in off-shoots **1.2** in pieces **2.1** flabby, flaccid; lazy **2.2** decrepit; weak; feeble

خانګيز tsāngíz *adjective* **1** local, regional **2** partial **3** *library science* specialized, subject

خاڼی tsāṇáj *m.* gleaner, after the grain harvest

خاو tsāv *m.* ☞ خار ¹

خاوار tsāvā́r *m.* **1** false hair **2** decorating the hair, styling of hair (of young women)

خاوتی tsāvtáj *m.* **1** migraine **2** *regional* intermittent fever

خاه tsāh *m.* [*plural:* خهان tshā́n *f. plural:* خاه ګاني tsāhgā́ni] ☞ خا د خا artesian well *idiom* د زني خاه dimple on the chin ارتبزين خاه

څبله ¹ tsə́bla ☞

خبوتی tsabótaj *m.* short chador

خپ tsap *m.* winnowing tray, tray for winnowing and sorting grain خپ وهل to winnow grain with a winnowing tray

خپ ² tsap *m.* **1** slapping (the leg of a camel) خپ او خوپ sound of a camel's tread **2** tread, footfall, tramp

خپ ³ tsap *m.* kiss

خپا tsapā́ *f.* ☞ خپهار

خپاخه tsapātsá *f.* small mound of earth along the outer walls of a peasant's house for insulation against the cold and used as a bench in good weather

خپاری ¹ tsapā́ṛaj *m.* **1** lump, snowball; cold of earth or clay **2** handful (of water, when drinking from a stream, etc.)

خپاری ² tsapā́ṛaj *m.* tread, footfall

خپان tsapā́n **1** *m.* waterspout; typhoon; strong gale **2** *adjective* stormy (of the sea, etc.)

خپاند tsapā́nd *adjective* stormy (of the sea, etc.)

خپان tsəpā́ṇ *m.* row, column

خپانی tsapaṇaj *adjective* unbalanced, unsettled; disorganized, confused; embarrassed, perplexed

خپتی tsapatáj *m.* خپتژ tsəpatə́j *f.* unleavened flat bread

خپتسپانه tsaptsapā́na خپخپانی tsaptsapā́naj خپخپاڼی tsaptsapā́ṇaj **1** disordered, disturbed, unsettled; pained, grieved **2** unfortunate, ill-fated, ill-starred, luckless خپخپانه کول a to disturb, throw into confusion, unsettle; pain, grieve **b** to make unhappy, leave

destitute خپخپانه کبدل a to be thrown into disorder, be disrupted, make unhappy **b** to be unlucky, be unfortunate, be indigent, be destitute

خپخپی ¹ tsaptsəpáj *m.* ☞ خپ ¹

خپر tsapə́r *m.* **1** *agriculture* drag harrow, threshing rake **2** flat summit, crown (of a mountain); flat cake, crumpet

خپر tsápar *m.* **1** cornice (of a roof) **2** hut

خپرغوږی tsaparghvághaj lop-eared

خپرکی tsapə́rkaj *m.* **1** twig, sprig, shoot **2** heap, pile (e.g., of stones) **3** shavings, cuttings, chip **4** chapter (of a book) **5** scale, flake, scute; plate, lamella, squama; husk **6** scale (of a fish)

خپره tsapə́ra *f.* prop, support

خپری tsapə́raj *m.* **1** small piece, bit; scrap **2** pile (e.g., of stones) **3** flat summit (of a mountain) *idiom* د واورو خپری tsapə́ri flakes of snow

خپر tsapə́ṛ *f.* خپراخه tsaparā́kha *f.* خپره tsapə́ṛa *f.* leg (of a camel, elephant); paw (e.g., of a tiger) خپری وهل a strike with the claws (of an animal) **b** *figurative* to approach, be near, be imminent (e.g., of darkness); envelop, creep over

خپری ¹ tsaparə́j *f.* **1** crossbar (on the handle of a spade, shovel) **2** *sports* hockey stick

خپری ² tsaprəj *f.* ☞ خپلی

خپنه tsapə́kha *f.* bedroom slippers, slippers (for indoor wear); worn-down shoes, old shoes

خپک tsapák ☞ خپق 1, 2

خپک tsapák *m.* **1** hunk of bread **2** tsapak (a unit of measurement equal to the width of four fingers pressed firmly together) **3** snow flakes; snow-flake **4** small section of land

خپکه tsapə́ka *f.* ☞ رفيده

خپکی tsapakáj *m.* game of chance خپکی وهل to play a game of chance

خپلاخه tsapə́lā́kha *f.* ☞ چلاخه

خپلاک tsaplā́k *adjective* **1** thick, dense **2** trampled (by feet) خپلاک کول to trample (with feet) خپلاک کبدل to be trampled (with feet)

خپلاک والی tsaplākvā́laj *m.* **1** thickness, density **2** state of being trampled, state of being overwhelmed

خپلک tsaplák *m.* **1** tough, stiff (of leather, etc.) **2** *m.* **.1** band, strip (of old leather, etc.) **2.2** old shoe

خپلور tsapə́lvár long-legged

خپلی tsaplə́j *f.* **1** sandals woven from grasses, leather, etc. **2** prize for marksmanship or equestrian skills

خپلی ګند tsaplə́jgánd *m.* reimbursement, fee (e.g., for delivery and driving of cattle, for a doctor's visit)

خپن غوږی tsapənghvághaj *m.* earlobe

خپنی tsapanə́j *f.* plow handle, plow shaft (used to direct the plow)

خپوتکی tsapútkaj *m.* خپوتی tsapútaj *m.* **1** small face veil (usually worn with the chador); veil **2** small turban

خپول ¹ tsapól *m.* **1** luxuriant hair, flowing hair **2** thick hair

خپول tsapavә́l transitive [past: و يي خپاوه] **1** to winnow grain with a winnowing tray خپ ☞ **2** to agitate, shake **3** to put into disorder, disarrange

خپولتسۀنی tsapoltsә́ṇaj **1** with hair in disarray **2** ☞ خپولی خپی

خپولږيری tsapolgíraj with disheveled beard, with tangled beard

خپولی tsapólaj **1** disheveled, tangled, matted خپولی کول to dishevel, tousle خپولی کېدل to be disheveled, be mussed up **2** m. person with disheveled hair

خپونۀکی tsapuṇә́kaj m. خپونی tsapóṇaj m. **1** kerchief (worn as headgear) **2** small veil covering the upper half of the face (with slit or lace allowing vision) **3** strainer, filter

خپه tsapá f. **1** wave د بې سيم خپی، د راډيو خپی radio waves د بحر خپی sea waves نوراني خپی light waves برقي خپی electrical waves وهل to be covered with waves, be agitated (of a river, etc.); get smashed, smash (of the shore by waves) **2** oar **3** gust (of wind) **4** attack of a raptor on its prey **5** medicine bout, attack (e.g., of fever); intensification, sudden worsening (of an illness) **6** fit, attack, seizure; faint, syncope خپه وهل **a** to be covered with waves, be hit, be splashed (of a shore by waves) **b** to row (with oars) **c** to blow (of a gust of wind) **d** to swoop down on prey **e** to become acute (of an illness) **f** to have an attack (of an illness) **g** to faint, swoon

خپه tsapá ☞ چپه⁴

خپهار tsapәhár m. **1** ☞ خپ² **1 2** lapping (of waves) **3** sound of winnowing grain

خپیاکه tsapjáka f. **1** beehive, honeycomb **2** kind of fuel made of pressed and dried manure in the shape of a brick **3** flat, having a flat form; flat object

خپيدل tsapedә́l intransitive [past: وخپیده] **1** to be covered with waves, be choppy, be rough (of a river, etc.); knock against, hit against, batter; lap, wash, splash against (of waves on a shore) **2** to steam, emit steam; hover, soar **3** to be sorted (of grain at winnowing when impurities and chaff are removed by air currents)

خپيره tsapéṛa f. box on the ear, slap in the face خپیره وهل، خپیره ورکول to give someone a box on the ear, give somebody a slap in the face په يوه خپیره ډېر مخونه خوږيږي proverb from a single slap in the face many cheeks are stinging پر مخ يوه خپیره ګڼل to consider a slap in the face, insulting

خپيره tsapeṛá f. plateau, tableland, high ground; height, elevation

خت tsәṭ m. [plural: ختونه tsәṭúna plural: ختان tsәṭán] **1** back of the head, occiput خت ګرول **a** to comb the back of the head **b** figurative to be puzzled, be perplexed; be confused; be embarrassed; be lost, get lost, disappear چوک په خت کښې وهل to give someone a slap **2** summit (of a mountain) **3** reverse of something, back of something; rear side, back; rear چوک په خت بهول to turn someone back, cause to go in the opposite direction په خت تلل to go back; depart په خت درومل **a** to go out, step back, retreat **b** to disappear په خت کول to turn over, turn upside down; turn inside out خت ګرزول **a** to turn away, turn aside **b** figurative to be

dissatisfied, be discontented, be displeased **c** figurative to dissent, disagree idiom پر خت بارول to make somebody responsible for something پر خت باربدل to be taken under somebody's wing خت ته اچول to forget, put something out of one's mind په ختوی يې حلال کړم He cut me with a knife (i.e., wounded me with words or actions)

ختال tsaṭál m. plural resin, gum; tar, pitch; asphalt

ختک tsuṭә́k m. tstә́k hammer

ختکوری tsәṭkóraj adjective ruined, destroyed; homeless

ختکه tsә́ṭka f. calico, cotton print material

ختکی tsuṭә́káj m. hammer, mallet

ختل tsaṭә́l transitive [past: و يي خاته] **1** to lick, lick all over **2** to lap, lap up idiom د چا سر ختل to starve (out of stinginess, miserliness)

ختلی tsaṭә́laj m. flatterer, toady, brown-noser, suck-up

ختمخ tsәṭmә́kh m. lining (i.e., of a garment), backing, padding

ختمخی tsәṭmә́khaj adjective plain, homely, uncomely

خت مری tsәṭ marә́j f. anatomy cervical vertebra

ختمېری tsәṭmerә́j f. anatomy occipital fossula

ختوت، خت وت tsaṭvát **1** m. apoplexy, stroke, sudden death **2** adverb suddenly **3.1** loving at first sight **3.2** untimely dying; suddenly dying; dying young په چا خت وت کېدل **a** to fall in love with someone at first sight خت وت کېدل **b** to die untimely, die an untimely death; die young خت وت شئ! Drop dead!

ختول tsaṭavә́l causative verb [past: و يي ختاوه] **1** to cause to lick, cause someone to lick something clean **2** to compel to lap (up something)

ختونی tsaṭúnaj **1** m. blotting paper **2.1** sucking out, drying **2.2** licking off, licking away

خته tsáṭa f. full bag, filled sack; full saddlebag, full pack (of a pack animal)

خته tsáṭa f. **1** base (of a tree trunk) **2** geometry side, bound, foot of a perpendicular **3** figurative stout woman, fat lady **4** figurative thickset man, robust fellow

ختی tsaṭә́j f. back edge, blunt edge (of a saber, etc.)

ختی tsaṭә́j f. bouquet of flowers

خچه tsә́cha cry to drive goats

خچه tsә́chi vice خه چه

خځله tsidzlá f. ☞ سجده

خځ tsats m. field thistle, common thistle

خځا tstsá f. ☞ خځبده

خځبکی tsatsbekáj m. **1** ☞ کځوک **2** medicine angina

خځبکی tsatsbékaj خځپکی tsatspékaj bright, smart; quick, prompt, adroit

خځند tsatsә́nd خځنده tsatsә́nda flowing, running, having a leak

خځوب tsatsób m. dropping, dripping, trickling; seepage, leakage

خځوبکی tsatsóbkaj m. drop of rain

خځوبی tsatsóbaj m. **1** dripping, trickling; دا کوټه خځوبی کوي This room leaks. **2** cornice (of a roof)

282

خُشوبی ² tsatsobáj *m.* **1** spring, source, wellhead from which waters flows drop by drop **2** dropping, dripping (water); soaking through, leakage, trickle, drip

خُشوری tsatsórí *m. plural* leftovers (food)

خُشول tsetsavál *transitive [past:* وی خُشاوه] to drip, pour out drop by drop خُشول کیدل drop, drip, trickle; pour drop by drop; soak through, permeate, impregnate *idiom* تر پوست خُشول to reproach concerning a good deed that has been performed

خُشون tsatsún *m.* ☞ خُشوب

خُشی tsatsáj *f.* groove, gutter, through, channel; drain pipe, catchment pipe

خُشیدل tsatsedál *intransitive [present:* خُشی *past:* وخُشیده] to drip, be poured drop by drop; soak through, permeate, infiltrate

خُشیده tsatsedá *m. plural* dropping, dripping, trickling, soaking through, permeation, leakage

خُخ tsakh *m.* death rattle of slaughtered cattle

خُخاک tskhāk *m.* miscarriage; stillborn baby

خُخخُخکي tsakhtskhák i *m. plural* fine drops (of rain)

خُخړه ¹ tskháṛa *f.* anger, ire, wrath

خُخړه ² tskháṛa *f. regional* robbery, pillage, plundering

خُخکو tsakhkú *m.* ☞ چکنو

خُخکي tskhák i *f.* mutton

خُخل tskhál *transitive* ☞ خُخول 1, 2, 4, 5

خُخو tsákho a little, some, somewhat, slightly, rather خُخو خُخو a little, a little at a time; not much خُخو را خُخه کښېنه sit down for a little while with me

خُخول tskhavál *transitive [past:* وی خُخاوه] **1** to stuff, pack, fill with; shove in, push in, put into, shove into, slip into, squeeze into, cram in **2** to press in **3** to drag (e.g., the hem of one's robe), pull, haul **4** to break, split, crack (e.g., nuts); stick, plunge, pierce **5** to peck, pick (e.g., one's nose)

خُخه ¹ tskha tsákha *postposition in combination with the prepositions* د *or* له **1** from, whence, out of (indicates the direction of an action from somewhere or from which something comes) له ښارو خُخه from the city له غرو خُخه from the mountains **2** from, out of, of (indicates the source of a receipt of something or the origin or provenance of something) له رفیق خُخه پوښتنه وکه ask your friend د ورور خُخه دي کتاب واخله Take the book from your brother. **3** at, with, by, of (indicates the state of belonging) ستا زما کتاب ستا خُخه دئ؟ Do you have a watch? خُخه ساعت ستا ته؟ Do you have my book? **4** by, near, close to, besides, around د دیوال خُخه near the wall, close to the wall, by the wall **5** *in the Eastern dialect the preposition is often omitted*: ښار خُخه near the city, around the city

خُخه ² tskhá *colloquial abbreviation* خُه خبرېم How would I know? خُخه چه احمد راغلئ دئ که نه I don't know whether Ahmed arrived or not.

خُخه ³ tskha *past tense of* خُخل

خُخه ⁴ tsákha ☞ خُخو

خُخېدل ¹ tskhedál *intransitive* ☞ خُخکېدل

خُخېدل ² tskhedál *intransitive [past:* وخُخیده] **1** to be stuffed into, be squeezed into, be crammed into **2** to be pressed in, be pressed into **3** to be compressed **4** to be stuck, be thrust, be stabbed into (e.g., a pin, knife)

خُخېده tskhedá *m. plural* **1** sticking into, squeezing into **2** pressing in, pressing into **3** compressing

خر ¹ tser *m.* **1.1** peep, chirp, squeak **1.2** sound of a cloth or frabic tearing **1.3** driving on snow, sliding on snow **2** *figurative* frightened, scared, startled یو خر کېدل to be afraid of, fear, dread *idiom* خر وهل to jump, leap

خر ² tsar *m.* ☞ خُر

خرا tsará *f.* ☞ خُرا

خراغ tsrāgh *m.* tsirāgh ☞ چراغ د برق خُراغ electric bulb لاسي خُراغ small flashlight

خراغدان tsrághdán *m.* candlestick

خراگاه tsarāgáh *m. dialect* pasture

خراو tsaráv *m.* ☞ خُراو

خرب tsarb tsurb ☞ خُورب

خربښت tsarbákht *m.* plenitude, completeness; fatness, obesity; corpulence, stoutness

خربول tsarbavál *denominative, transitive [past:* خرب یې کړ *past:* خُورب یې کړ] to fatten

خربه tsarbá *feminine singular of* خرب *and* خُورب

خربېدل tsarbedál *denominative, intransitive [past:* خرب شو *past:* خُورب شو] to put on weight, gain weight, grow fat, put on flesh

خرپ tsrap *m.* flapping (its) wings خرپ وهل to flap wings

خرول tsaravál *transitive [past:* وی خُرپاوه] to flap wings ☞ سرپول

خرپېدل tsrapedál *intransitive [past:* وخُرپیده] to quiver (of wings) ☞ سرپېدل

خردځای tsardzáj *m.* ☞ خُرا

خرخ ¹ tsarkh **1** *m.* **.1** wheel **1.2** propeller (i.e., of an aircraft) **1.3** grinding wheel, grindstone **1.4** rotation, revolution; turning په خرخ اچول **a** to start (e.g., an engine) **b** to begin, initiate (an operation, an action) **1.5** approach (from the side, in passing) **1.6** puncture, puncture wound **1.7** *figurative* luck, good fortune **1.8** sky, heaven **2** pierced, penetrated; stabbed خرخ کول to prick, sting, stab, run through, transfix خرخ کېدل to be stabbed, be pierced *idiom* د صنعتي خُرخونه گرندي کول to hasten the development of industry د اوبو خرخ turbine

خرخ ² tsarkh *m.* ☞ چرغ

خرخ ³ tsarkh *m.* Tsarkh (settlement, Logar Province)

خرخکه tsarkháka *f. regional* ☞ ساړکه

خرخلرگی tsarkhlargáj *m.* tsarkhalgáj *m.* ☞ خُرخوکی

ترخند tarkhónd **1** *m.* **.1** scratch, abrasion ترخند لگېدل to be scratched, get a scratch **1.2** catching on, brushing against **2** revolving, rotating

خرخندوکی tsarkhandúkaj *m.* ☞ چورلندوی

خرخنی tsarkhanáj *m.* خرخوبی tsarkhobaj *m.* whirlpool, eddy, vortex

څرخوکی tsarkhukáj *m. textiles* spool, bobbin; reel, reeling frame, swift, coiler

څرخول tsarkhavól *transitive* [*past:* وي څرخاوه] 1 to rotate, turn 2 to start, trigger, actuate 3 سره څرخول، را څرخول to surround, enclose, encircle 4 to turn, swing (the line of a front)

څرخه tsarkhá *f.* 1 wheel 2 spinning wheel څرخه کول، څرخه ورپښل to spin on a spinning wheel *idiom* د اوبو څرخه turbine

څرخه tsárkha *feminine singular of* څرخ 1 2

څرخی tsarkháj *m.* 1 spool, bobbin, reel 2 spinning wheel څرخی پوری کول a to start a spinning wheel, begin spinning b to start a quarrel څرخی شلول a to stop a spinning wheel, quit spinning b *figurative* to cease a quarrel څرخی ورپښل a to spin on a spinning wheel b *figurative* to drag out a quarrel

څرخی tsarkháj 2 *m.* ☞ چرغ

څرخي tsarkhí 3 wheeled, equipped with wheels *idiom* څرخي توپه *Eastern* Maxim machine gun

څرخي tsarkhí 4 *present tense of* څرخیدل

څرخي tsárkhi 5 *feminine plural of* څرخ 1 2

څرخیدل tsarkhedól *intransitive* [*present:* څرخي *present:* وڅرخبږي] [*past:* وڅرخیده] 1 to revolve, rotate, turn, turn around, whirl, spin, go round مځکه پر لمر راڅرخي The earth rotates around the sun. 2 to start up, be started (i.e., of a motor) 3 to be surrounded 4 to be turned (to the left, right, etc., of a front tine) 5 to concern something, apply to something, relate to something

څرخند tsarkhónd *m.* ☞ څرخبند

څرخنه tsókha *f.* 1 massage 2 trace, track, sign, footprint

څرک tsrək 1 *m.* 1 search; reconnaissance, reconnoitering; finding out چا څرک اخیستل to make inquiries about, find out about someone د . . . څرک اخیستل to come upon a track, find a trace څرک کول، څرک ایستل مي پسي اخیستئ دئ I came upon his footprints. a to find out surreptitiously, reconnoiter د احمد د ځای څرک يي وایست He found out where Ahmed lives. b to look for, search, find, track; find tracks, find traces of something; track, shadow ما د خپل کتاب څرک وایست I searched out and found my book. 2 criminal investigation department 3 advanced guard د څرک ټولګی advanced guard units

څرک tsrək 2 *m.* rising لمر څرک وهي the sun is rising

څرکه tsrəká *f.* 1 radiance; aureole, aureola; luster, brilliance, brilliancy 2 dropping, dripping, trickle

څرکبه tsrəkbá *m.* [*plural:* څرکبانه tsəkbánə] 1 detective, plainclothes policeman 2 scout 3 *dialect* watchman, guard

څرکول tsrəkavól *transitive* [*past:* وي څرکاوه] to make sparkle, make glitter; make brilliant, make lustrous; polish; give a gloss, give a luster to

څرکیدل tsrəkedól *intransitive* [*past:* وڅرکیده] to sparkle, glitter; shine, beam

څرگند tsagánd tsəgánd evident, obvious, clear, distinct, apparent, manifest; definite څرګند جواب نه ویل to not give a definite answer

دا څرګنده ده چه . . . ، دا څرګنده خبره ده چه . . . It is clear that … It is obvious that …

څرګندوالی tsargandvālaj *m.* څرګندنه tsargandəna *f.* څرګندتوب tsargandtób *m.* obviousness, lucidity, clarity; certainty, definiteness

څرګندلمبسه tsargandlamesá *f. computer science* carbon copy

څرګندول tsargandavól *denominative, intransitive* [*past:* څرګند يي کړ] 1 to make evident, make clear, make obvious; bring to light, make know; elucidate, clear up, explain 2 to express, manifest, reveal, give evidence of 3 to set forth (reasons, a position, etc.)

څرګندونه tsargandavóna *f.* 1 revelation, exposé; elucidation, clarification, clearing up 2 expression, term, manifestation, display 3 account, statement, presentation (of a reason, position, etc.) 4 advertisement, announcement (e.g., in a newspaper)

څرګندیدل tsargandedól *denominative, intransitive* [*past:* څرګند شو] 1 to become clear, become obvious, become evident; be made manifest; be explained; be exhibited, be displayed څرګنده شوه چه . . . It was explained that … 2 to be expressed, be displayed 3 to be set forth (e.g., reasons, a position)

څرګه tsárga *f.* brown owl, *Athene poctua*

څرل tsaról *intransitive* ☞ څریدل 1

څرمنکی tsarmə́khkáj *f.* ☞ شرمبنکی

څرمن tsarmán *f.* [*plural:* څرمني tsarmóni] pelt; skin (animal, human) د پخو څرمنو سامان skin پخه څرمن hide, pelt (uncured) خامه څرمن leather goods د څرمني د پخېدو کارخانه leather factory *idiom literally* I'll sell your skin! *figurative* څرمن به دي وباسم I'll skin you alive! څرمن يي د ښو ه ه کړه He gave him a thrashing. د سپي په څرمن کښي يي په مخ اچولي ده He lost shame and conscience. مي يوه کوډی نشته I am penniless. I don't have a cent to my name.

څرمنوالا tsarənvālá *m.* tanner, leather dresser, worker in the tanning industry

څرمنی tsarmənáj 1 *adjective* leather

څرمني tsarmóni 2 *feminine plural of* څرمن

څرمه tsórma 1 *f.* edge, brim له څرمي نه، له څرمي a from the beginning and to the end b quite, entirely, totally له څرمي وژل to annihilate, exterminate 2 *adjective* near, close, located alongside of 3 *adverb* near, close to, not far, not distant ور څرمه کول a to push up to something, move up to someone b to draw, attract ور څرمه کیدل a to move closer, draw nearer to something, move up to someone b to come into contact with, run across, meet up with

څرمي tsarmí *adjective* leather څرمي بالا پوښ leather overcoat

څرنده tsarónda passing (a ball)

څرنگوالی tsarangvālaj *m.* ☞ څرنگه والی

څرنگه tsáranga ☞ a څرنگه چه خنگه b so far as, as far as څرنگه چه . . . هغسي to the extent that …, then …

څرنگوالی tsarangavālaj *m.* 1 shape, form 2 way, mode, aspect

څروتکه tsarvátka *f.* ☞ سکروټه

څرول tsaravә́l *transitive* [*past:* و یي څراوه] to pasture (sheep), shepherd; graze cattle, pasture cattle, tend grazing cattle

څېرونکی tsiruńkaj ☞ څرونکی

څروی tsarváj *m.* **1** scarecrow **2** target, shooting mark **3** limit, bound

څروي ² tsaraví *present of* څرول

څرا ¹ tsará *f.* ☞ څارا

څره ² tsira *f.* tsә́ra saw څره لور kind of scythe

څره ³ tsә́ra *f.* fertilization, manuring د مال څره manure (as fertilizer) ځمکي ته څري ورکول to fertilize the soil, manure the soil

څره ⁴ tsra *interjection* all is in order, everything is OK, everything is going well

څری ¹ tsaráj *m.* **1** load carried balanced on the head **2** netting in which straw is transported

څری ² tsә́raj *m.* څرو tsә́rә́j *f.* yellow rose

څری ³ tsә́raj *m.* **1** running (e.g., of ink) **2** spreading, spread (of a disease); infection, contagion

څری ⁴ tsә́raj *f.* predator thrush, robber thrush

څری ⁵ tsaráj *f.* wooden abutment (support for main beam)

څري ⁶ tsaré *plural of* څره ¹

څري ⁷ tsiri tsә́ri *plural of* څره ²

څري ⁸ tsә́ri *plural of* څره ³

څرېدل ¹ tsaredә́l *intransitive* [*past:* وڅرېده] **1** to graze, pasture; browse **2** to feed (of poultry)

څرېدل ² tsәredә́l *intransitive* [*past:* و څرېده] to defecate, evacuate the bowels

څریکه tsríka *f.* tsiríka ☞ څریکه

څر tsaṛ *m. Western* pasturage څړ ته بیول to graze, pasture څړ کول to drive (cattle) out to pasture

څړا tsaṛá́ *f.* څړاو tsaṛáv *m.* څرځای tsaṛdzáj *m.* pasturage, common pasture

څرک tsṛak **1** *m.* dripping, falling in drops څرک او څروک constant dripping **2** *interjection* sound of dripping water

څرکه tsṛ́ka *f.* **1** agitation, nervousness, concern, uneasiness, alarm **2** emotional pain, distress **3** noise, hubbub, disorder

څرکهار tsṛakәhár *m.* ☞ څرک ¹

څرل tsaṛәl *intransitive* ☞ څرېدل ¹

څرمنی tsaṛmә́naj *m.* څرمونی tsaṛmúnaj *m.* spring (the season)

څرنۍ tsaṛnә́j *f.* ☞ څری

څراول tsaravә́l *transitive* ☞ څرول

څره tsará **1.1** secluded, solitary; lonely, retired **1.2** single, unmarried **1.3** traveling without luggage, traveling unburdened **2** *m.* [*plural:* څره گان tsaṛagán] pedestrian

څره پانه tsará pā́ṇa *f.* lettuce

څره توب tsaṛatób *m.* **1** solitude, seclusion **2** loneliness **3** unmarried life, single life

څره خشمه tsaṛákhәshma *f.* saw (the tool)

څره گي tsaṛagí *f.* ☞ څره توب

څره لار tsaṛalár *f.* [*plural:* څره لاري tsaṛalári] **1** path **2** sidewalk

سره لوه tsaṛalә́re *f. regional*

څره نازه tsaṛanáza *f.* ☞ څره خشمه

څره وات tsaṛaváṭ *m.* ☞ څره لار

څره وری tsaṛavә́raj *m.* traveler with little or no luggage, traveler able to travel along a footpath

څری ¹ tsaṛáj *m.* servant

څری ² tsaṛә́j *f.* **1** crown (of the head) **2** forelock, bangs (of hair) **3** summit (of a mountain) **4** hoop-like frame of a large tent

څرېدل tsaṛedә́l *intransitive* ☞ څرېدل

څرېدونکي tsaṛedúnkaj **1** *present participle of* څرېدل **2** حیوانات ruminant (animal)

څریک tsiṛík *m.* څریکه tsṛíka *f.* **1** sharp pain, acute pain; colic pains **a** څریکي وهل، څریکي کول to be ill with, be down with, ache پنښي مي My feet hurt. **b** to throb **2** *medicine* shock, stroke **3** splashes (e.g., of mud, raindrops) *idiom* بده څریک inferior breed, base lineage

څره وری tsaṛáj-vә́raj *m.* ☞ څرو وری

څری tsaṛә́ghaj *m. dialect* ☞ سری

څسي tsә́si ☞ څشي

څنکله tsәshkә́la ☞ څنکله

څشي tsә́shi *children's speech* what, what's this

څناک tskhā́k *m.* drinking; drink, beverage

څنختن tsә́khtán *m.* **1** master, boss, owner, proprietor; possessor, holder **2** husband; man څنتن کول to marry (of a woman) *idiom* د قوي ارادي څنتن کمال څنتن کېدل to reach perfection person with a strong will, resolute person

څنتن والی tsә́khtantób *m.* څنتن تیا tsә́khtantjā́ *f.* څنتن توب position or obligation of a boss, owner, etc. tsәkhanbálaj *m.*

څنتنه tsә́khtána *f.* mistress, proprietress; owner, holder

څنتول tsә́khtavә́l *transitive dialect* ☞ تینتول

څنته tsә́khta *f.* cooking, meal preparation

څنتبدل tsәkhtedә́l *intransitive dialect* ☞ تینتبدل

څنخوری tsә́khtsóraj *m.* ☞ تسکوره

څنکله tsә́kkә́la **1** how, in what way **2** so far as, so long as, since

څنکو tsakhkú *m.* ☞ چکینو

څنکوری tsakhkuṛaj *m.* skin; pelt (of an animal)

څنل tskhә́l *transitive dialect* ☞ چنل

څنندی tskhandáj *m.* smooth sloping rock (which children roll)

څنبول tskhavә́l *transitive* [*past:* و یي څنباوه] to drag along, pull, draw ☞ څخول

څنی tsә́khaj *m.* calf

څنبدل tskhedә́l *intransitive* [*past:* وڅنبده] **1** to crawl, creep along **2** to drag oneself, crawl along; be dragged; stretch oneself; to drag on, last a long time ☞ څکېدل

څنبده tskhedә́ *m. plural* **1** creeping, crawling په څنبدو تلل to move by crawling, propel oneself forward by crawling; creep up to, creep under **2** dragging, pulling, hauling; drawing wire

څک ¹ tsak *m.* tsәk *medicine* sharp pain, acute pain; lumbago

څک ² tsak *m.* ☞ څرک

څک ³ tsak **1** upright **2** straight, straightforward څک ودرېد He stood (there) as if rooted (in the ground). **3** *adjective* alert څک کول **a** to stand erect **b** to straighten **c** to prick up the ears, be alert خپل غوږونه څک کړه آس The horse pricked up his ears. څک کېدل **a** to stick out, stand out, jet out **b** to straighten one's back, draw oneself up **c** to prick up one's ears سړی څک شو لکه چه څه یې واورېده The man pricked up his ears as though he had heard something.

څکا tskā *f.* څکاک tskāk *m.* ☞ څناک ·

د آسمان څکالکی ، آسمان څکالکی tskálkaj *m.* bat (the animal) bat

څکالی tsakálaj *m.* **1** [*plural:* څکاليان tsakāliján] bat (the animal) **2** [*plural:* څکالي tsakáli] piece of old leather or fur **3** [*plural:* tsakáli] the crust of flat-bread adhering to the sides of a tanur (i.e., traditional Afghan oven)

څکپاڼی tsakpāṇáj *m.* turnip tops

څکشو tsakshú *m.* څکنبو tsakkhú *m.* ☞ چکنبو

څکل ¹ tsakúl *m. history* special land holdings granted to special individual peasants early in the nineteenth century

څکل ² tsəkál *m.* **1** short distance, sgement of a road **2** section of land

څکل ³ tskəl *transitive* [*past:* وۍ څکل] **1** to drink, take (water, medicine) **2** to smoke چلم څکل to smoke a hookah

څکل ⁴ tsakál tsekál *transitive* [*past:* وۍ څکه] to try, taste, take a sip of

څکل پکل tsakal-pakál *m.* beginning of the snow thaw (at the end of winter)

څکالکی tsəkálkaj *m.* ☞ څکالکی

څکندن tskindán *m.* **1** trial, test, taste, tasting څکندن وهل to test, try, taste **2** taste; aroma, fragrance

څک والی tsakválaj *m.* straightness

څکوړی tskoṛáj *m.* ☞ چکوړی

څکول ¹ tsakvál *m.* ☞ څکل ¹

څکول ² tskavál *causative* [*past:* وۍ څکاوه] **1** to give to drink, water (cattle), make to drink **2** to smoke

څکول ³ tskavál *transitive* [*past:* وۍ څکاوه] **1** to drag, lug, take things somewhere, carry; pull خپل ځان پر مځکه باندي څکول، خپل نس پر مځکه باندي څکول to crawl, creep; move from one place to another by crawling **2** to unsheathe, bare (a saber, etc.) **3** to attract څکول سره to fight, clash ☞ څخول

څکول ⁴ tsakavál *denominative, transitive* ☞ څک کول ، څک

څکولي ¹ tsakóli *m. plural dialect* ☞ څکالي ³

څکوۍ ² tskavólaj *past participle of* څکول ^{1,2}

څکونداره tskundãra *f.* pinch, nip, tweak

څکوندل tskundál tskondál *transitive* [*past:* وۍ څکونده] to pinch, nip, tweak

څکونډی tskunḍáj *f.* ☞ سکونډی

څکونه ¹ tskavóna *f. physics* **1** wire-drawing **2** bent (for), inclination (for), attraction (to) attraction, gravitation, gravity

څکونه ² tsakúna *plural of* څک ¹

څکه ¹ tsáka *f.* **1** test, trial, testing, assaying څکه کول to try, test, sample; *metallurgy* to assay **2** to take a sip (of) د پرونه رائیسي مي I haven't had a bite to eat since yesterday. د دوۍ څکه نده کړی

څکه ² tskə *m. plural* **1** drinking; drink, beverage **2** drink of (something)

څکه ³ tsáka *f.* cliff, precipice; abyss, chasm

څکه ⁴ tsáka ☞ څکه

څکه ⁵ tsáka *feminine singular of* څک ³

څکی ¹ tsukáj *m.* bag, pouch (carried over the shoulder), knapsack, shoulder-pack

څکی ² tskaj *m.* **1** basket for commodities (hanging from a ceiling) **2** clothes-line, rope (for drying laundry)

څکی ³ tskaj *m.* kernel (nut of almond, etc.)

څکی ⁴ tsəke cry used to drive goats, calves

څکی ⁵ tsáki *plural of* څکه ³

څکی ⁶ tski *present tense of* څکل

څکېدل ¹ tskedəl *intransitive* [*past:* وڅکېده] پر نس څکېدل **1** to crawl **a** to crawl on the belly; do the leopard-crawl *figurative* **b** to crawl before, cringe (before); lick the boots (of) **2** to drag, trail **3** to pull closer

څکېدل ² tskedál *denominative, intransitive* ☞ څک ، څک کېدل ³

څکېړل tsəkeṛál *transitive* [*past:* وۍ څکېړه] to catch in a net or trap

څکېندن tsəkindán *m.* ☞ څکندن

څگک tsəgak *m.* spinning wheel, distaff (manual)

څگل tsagál *m. history* otrub, holdings (land granted by a landowner to certain peasants for use in addition to their normal acreage)

څگی ¹ tsəgaj *m. dialect* ☞ سبی

څگي ² tsəge ☞ څکی ⁴

څلاخل tsalātsál lost, fallen, perished, killed

څلرم tsalarám *ordinal Western* fourth

څلگه tsálga *f.* jet, spurt, stream, (of water)

څلندر tsilindár *m.* cylinder

څلور tsalór *numeral* four څلور زره four thousand څلور سوه four hundred څلور خوندی the four sisters (the name of four months of the lunar year; i.e., لمړی خور، دویمه خور، دریمه خور، څلرمه خور ☞) څلور خواوي خور cardinal points of compass, four directions (North, South, East, West) *idiom* په څلورو دئ He is a fool.

څلوراربه tsalorarabá four-wheeled څلوراربه گاډی carriage; barouche

څلورارخی tsalorárxaj quadrilateral, four-sided; tetrahedral

څلوربرغه tsalorbrágha *adjective* folded up in fours; stacked in fours څلوربرغه کول to stack, pile, pile up in fours (letter, note, memo, report, etc.)

څلوربول tsalorból **1** walking on all fours **2** ☞

څلوربولی tsalorbólaj *adjective* four-legged, quadruped څلوربولی څلوربولي tsalorbóli four-legged animals, quadruped animals په حيوانات *tsalorbóli* on all fours

خلور پېنيز خلورپينيځی tsalorpkhídzaj خلورپيني tsalórpkhaj خلور بولی ☞ tsalorpkhíz

خلورخُنډی tsalortsónḍaj *m.* tetragon, quadrangle, square

خلورخانيز tsalorkhāniz *adjective* squared, checkered, graph (paper, cloth)

خلورستايه tsalorsitājá *m. plural* Sunni Muslims

خلورغاښې tsalorghā́khe female camel in her sixth year

خلورغښهای tsalorghəkháj bull or ox in the sixth year

خلورګوټی tsalorǵvóṭaj *adjective* quadrangular, square

خلورلاره tsalorlára *f.* [*plural:* خلور لاري tsalorlári] *usually plural* crossroad, crossing

خلرم tslorə́m tsalorə́m *Eastern* ☞ خلرم

خلورماشينه tsalormāshína four-motored, four-engine الوتکه خلورماشينه four-engine aircraft

خلورورېزی tsalorvrézaj *m.* youth whose mustache is just sprouting

خلوريغ tsalorídz quadrangular

خلوريڅه tsalorídza *f.* خلوريزه tsaloríza rubayat, quatrain (poetry, prosody)

خلوېنت tsalvékht *numeral* forty

خلوېنت کلن tsalvekht kalan *adjective* (of) forty years, forty year

خلوېنتم tsalvekhtə́m *ordinal* fortieth

خلوېنتمه tsalvekhtə́ma *f.* forty days after a death (day on which a religious memorial service is held)

خلوېنتي tsalvekhtí [1] *m.* elected member of a clan or tribe chosen to maintain order or propriety during a trip or overnight stay

خلوېنتي tsalvekhtí [2] 1 *f.* .1 forty days after birth 1.2 fortieth day after death 1.3 *colloquial* the sum of 40 afghanis, 40 rupees, etc. 2 forty (referring to afghanis, rupees, etc.)

خلوېنت يکه tsalvekhtjaká *f.* 1/40th part (in a tax payment)

خله tsilá [1] *f.* 1 forty coldest days of the year 2 forty hottest days of the year 3 forty day fast and religious rite (among dervishes)

خله tsalá [2] *f.* 1 wish, inclination, desire 2 dream, day-dream

خله tsə́lá [3] *f.* confidence (in), certitude (in)

خله tsə́la [4] *interrogative* what for, why, for what purpose

خله مست tsilamást bearing or enduring the cold well

خله وال tsilavál *m. religion* experiencing a forty day trial, going through a forty day initiation or passage (similar to a Christian monastic novitiate for those seeking to be Muslim clerics or clergy)

خلی tsə́laj [1] *m.* 1 column; pillar 2 pyramid; obelisk; stone cairn erected over a grave; monument, memorial 3 stone cairn or pile used as a target for archery practice 4 end-mark, boundary mark; road milestone سرحدي خلی frontier marker 5 tower or hut constructed as a watch or guard structure for crops 6 finger, ring 7 article (of a law); codex د پښتو خلی the Afghan or Pashto code of honor; traditional Pashto or Afghan law 8 custom, usage

خلی tsə́ləj [2] *botany* catkin, amentum

خلی خولی tsə́laj-tsúlaj *m.* 1 ascent and descent 2 provisions (for the road)

خلبرويشت tsalervisht *numeral* twenty-four

خلبرويشتم tsalervishtə́m *ordinal* twenty-fourth

خلبن tslekh *m.* خلبنت tslekht *m.* 1 glue 2 sticky substance

خلبن ناک، خلبنناک tslekhnā́k sticky, gluey, adhesive

څم tsam 1 *dialect* ☞ سم [1]

سمځ tsməts *f.* ☞ څمځ

مڅرک tsamtsaŕkej *m.* ☞ څمڅربکی

څمڅکی tsamtsəkáj *m.* tadpole

څمڅلکی tsamtsəlkáj *m.* dragonfly

څمڅه tsamə́tsa [1] *f.* ☞ څمڅی

څمڅه tsamə́tsa [2] *f.* stockade or shelter dug below the surface (for sheep)

څمڅه منګور tsamtsamangór *m.* cobra (snake)

څمڅی tsamtsə́j *f.* 1 spoon 2 ladle, soup ladle *idiom* د هري کټوي څمڅی a person who sticks his nose in everywhere; interfering in everything

څمغبلی tsamghélaj *m.* 1 smallish old tent 2 scarecrow

څمغبلی څمغبلی tsamghéli-tsamghéli *adjective* dry, dried up, parched (of soil) څمغبلي کبدل to dry up, grow parched

څمکني tsamkaní 1 *m. plural* Tsamkani (a tribe) 2 tsamkanáj Tsamkani (tribesman)

څملاستل tsamlāstál *intransitive Eastern* [*present:* څملي *past:* څملاست] to lie down for a bit, have a nap زه اوس څملم خوب راځي I'll lie down, I want to sleep.

څملاسته tsamlāstá *m. plural* lying down in bed د څملاستو ځای نه و There was no place to lie down and sleep.

څملول tsamlavál *transitive* [*past:* وي يي څملاوه] 1 to lie down in bed, lie down and go to sleep 2 to throw down; to roll on the ground (in a fight)

څملبدل tsamledál *intransitive* ☞ څملاستل

څمنګی tsəmangáj *m.* 1 processed pelt, skin, leather 2 piece of leather in which bread is packed prior to baking it

څموخی tsamutsáj *adjective* bald, bald-headed

څمول tsamól 1 melancholy, sad 2 injured, wounded

څمولول tsamolavál *denominative, transitive* [*past:* څمول يې کړ] 1 to pain, grieve 2 to injure, wound

څمولبدل tsamoledál *denominative, intransitive* [*past:* څمول شو] 1 to be pained, be grieved 2 to be injured, be wounded

څميار tsamjáŕ *m.* shoemaker ☞ چميار

څمياري tsamjārí *f.* shoemaker's trade

څنار tsinář *m.* [*plural:* څناران tsinārā́n] poplar (the tree) ☞ چنار

څنډ tsanḍ [1] *m.* shaking, jolting; shaking up oscillatory, vibratory motions په څنډ وهل to shake, oscillate, vibrate

څنډ tsənḍ [2] *m. obsolete* horizon

څنډل tsənḍól tsanḍól [1] [*past:* وي يي څانده] 1 to shake, shake out; shake up غاليچه تغر څنډل to beat dust out of a (reversible) rug ځان څنډل to rouse oneself (of a bird), shake its wings 2 to beat (fruit from a tree) 3 to flap (its wings) 4 to brandish (a saber, etc.) 5 to sweap aside, reject (criticism)

خنډل [2] tsandál *m.* bare ground on a mountain top

خنډول tsəndavúl [*past:* وي خنډاوه] to oscillate, vibrate, sway, swing, rock, shake

خنډوهل tsandvahól *transitive* [*past:* يي خنډ واهه] to knock out (a wedge); break open or down (a door), smash (a window), drive out, dislodge (an enemy); beat out (dust); shake out, fall (by shaking)

خنډه tsə́nḍa *f.* 1 edge کتاب د میز پر خنډه دئ The book is lying on the edge of the table. د ... په خنډه along the edge of something 2 skirt flap, lower edge of clothing 3 shore, bank, coast 4 side (of a road), curb 5 *military* boundary, border, flank, wing 6 *math* edge, side 7 section, sphere, realm 8 territory, country 9 outskirts

خنډیدل tsəndedól *intransitive* [*past:* وخنډیده] to oscillate, vibrate, vacillate, sway, swing; vibrate; shake

خنگ tsang *m.* 1 side, near, next to, by, beside, around, about د خنگه a next to, near, around د ... تر خنگه، د ... ، د ... په خنگ کښي next to, near, around something زما په خنگ کښي کښېنه *Eastern* sit next to me b along خنگ په خنگ، خنگ پر خنگ along the road د سړک په خنگ close to په خنگ تلل to walk alongside 2 side (of a ship) 3 slope (of a mountain) 4 side (e.g., left, right, wrong, right) او دواړو خنگ لگول، خنگ اینډول، خنگ اچول from both sides to rest on or lean on one's elbows, lean on, lean against د چا څخه خنگ کول a to turn away from someone b *figurative* to avoid, shun someone c to fear, be apprehensive of someone پر خنگ کول to remove, put to one side, put out of the way د یوشي له خنگه تېرېدل go around something *idiom* د غوږو له خنگه تېرول to disregard, give no ear (to)

خنگه tsángra *dialect* ☞ خرنگه

خنگری tsangrój *f.* armful (of hay, straw, etc.)

خنگزن tsangzán 1 slanting, oblique, crooked, curved, away 2 overturned خنگزن کېدل a to heel, list, careen b to turn over, overturn *idiom* خنگزنه سپوږمۍ moon on the wane

خنگل tsangól *f.* tsəngál خنگله tsangóla *f.* tsəngóla [*plural:* خنگلي tsangóli tsəngóli] elbow خنگل پر ... لگول to lean with one's elbows (on something)

خنگلی tsangólaj *m.* خنگلی tsanglój *f.* first or last pole of a tent

خنگوﺍﺧﮊی tsangváḳhaj *m.* ☞ خنگپرېدی [2]

خنگپرېدی tsangvéghdaj *m.* 1 carrying sling, carrying strap, rifle sling 2 cushion, pillow (for sitting)

خنگه [1] tsangá tsəngá 1 scattered, spread (about), flung (about), sown, disseminated, disbursed 2 sparse (of sowing, seeding, planting, forest, trees)

خنگه [2] tsə́nga *interrogative pronoun* 1 what, what kind of هغه خنگه خنگه به نه وي که ... سړی دئ؟ What sort of person is he? 2.1 how ... خنگه چه مي درته ویلي وو، هم هغسي کار وکه Would it be good if ... You should do as I told you. 2.2 what for, why خوانه ، خنگه راغلي Young man, why did you come here? 2.3 how 3 why is this

لکه *idiom* دا بیا خنگه Why is this so? Why did this happen? خنگه چه just as ... , exactly as ... , exactly!

خنگه [3] tsánga ☞ خنگ

خنگواﻟﻰ tsəngaválaj *m.* 1 quality 2 state, status, condition; state of affairs

خنگی [1] tsangáj *m.* tether with a ring (in the nose, for cattle)

خنگی [2] tsangój *f.* stone arch of a kahriz (or near horizontal underground water-collecting gallery)

خنگیز tsangíz side, lateral

خنل tsanól *transitive* [*past:* وي څانه] to shake, shake out, cause to fall by shaking, shake up

خنور tsanúr *m.* May (the month)

خنی [3] tsnəj *f.* ☞ نخی

خنکه tsə́nḍka *f.* tsuṇ́ka 1 lock, curl, ringlet 2 cork, plug, spigot 3 filiform (threadlike) stigmata of maize or corn

خنکی tsuṇakój *f.* 1 peys (the long uncut side-looks or side-burns of orthodox Jews worn traditionally in accordance with biblical and talmudic rules) 2 topknot, tuft of hair

خنه tsə́ṇa *f.* [*plural:* خنی tsə́ṇi] 1 locks, curls, ringlets 2 filiform (hairlike) stigmata on the racemes of maize or corn 3 *proper name* Tsuna

خنی کوکو tsəṇəjkokó *m.* ☞ سمبل

خو [1] tsav *m.* ☞ خوی [1]

خو [2] tso 1 *pronoun* .1 *interrogative* how much, how many خو زامن خوکسه راغلي وو؟ How many sons do you have? خو کسه راغلي؟ How many people came? خو د څوکلو یمي؟ What time is it? له خو مودي How old are you? 1.2 *indefinite pronoun* some, several له څه مودي نه، خو عمر دمخه *Eastern* for some time راهیسته sometimes ago 2 *indefinite numeral* several, some quantity, often, more than once خو واره مي ورته وویل several times خوخو واره spoke to him several times. *idiom* خوخو په خوقسمه ، په خوخو differently, in different ways خو خو چته many-storied, multistory a ترخو، ترخو پوري as long, as long as, til what time, for how long b in order to, in order that زه داسي وایم تر خو وپوهېږئ [1] speak thus so that you would understand. تر خو چه، تر خو پوري چه a until, as long as b د خو پوري چه in order that خو تر خو؟ What time exactly? How long?

خوار tsvár *m.* patience, endurance, staunchness; inflexibility

خوارلس tsvárlas *numeral regional* fourteen

خوارخیز tsoáṛxíz 1 complicated (of a question) 2 many sided, having multiple aspects

خوب tsvab *m.* 1 passion, passionate love, strong desire 2 aspiration (for), striving (for); yearning خوب لرل a to thirst (after), crave, strongly desire; to aspire (to), strive (for), aspire (to) b to long (for)

خوباری tsobáṛaj *m.* flat paddle-like instrument for beating laundry and stirring in the washing process

خوپ [1] tsup ☞ خوپ

خوپره tsoprá *f.* yarn which has become entangled

 څوټ tsoṭ *m.* **1** sally, sorteé, attack, raid **2** damages, injury څوټ کول a to organize a sally, sorteé, attack or onslaught; accomplish a raid b to inflict injury, do harm

څوټک tsuṭák *m.* hammer

څوټی سراب tsuṭajsərâb esteemed individual

څوچنده tsochánda several times قوت څوچنده زیاتول to become more powerful, build up strength

څوځی tsudzáj *m.* gonorrhea

څوخ tsuts *m.* **1** dolphin **2** greedy, avid, covetous person

څوخلن tsutslə́n greedy, covetous, avid

څوخينک tsutsinák *m.* **1** cricket **2** name of a bird

څورب tsorb tsvarb څربه tsarbá *f.* څوربه tsvárba *m.* [plural: څاربه tsârbə́ *f.* plural: څربي tsarbé plural: څوربي tsvárbi] heavy, plump, fat, obese

څوربتوب tsorbtób tsvarbtób *m.* څوربتیا tsorbtjấ tsvarbtjấ *m.* څوربوالی tsorbválaj tsvarbválaj *m.* stoutness, corpulence, plumpness, fatness; obesity

څوربول tsorbavə́l *denominative, intransitive* ☞ څربول

څورکه tsúrka *f.* side

څورگه tsurgá *f.* **1** steppe **2** side **3** foreign country, distant land

څورلس tsvárlas *numeral* fourteen

څورلسم tsvarlasə́m *ordinal* fourteenth *idiom* د څورلسمي سپوږمی half moon (i.e., moon of the 14th day)

څورله tsorlá *f.* wild pig, wild boar

څورلی ¹ tsurláj *m.* borer, drill, perforator; gimlet

څورلي ² tsvarlí *m. regional* rider, horseman

څورلی ³ tsvarlə́j *f. regional* riding (horses)

څورلېځی tsúrledzáj *m.* axis; axel

څورنگ ¹ tsavráng **1** trampled, stamped on, crushed **2** slaughtered, massacred; blood-stained, bloody

څورنگ ² tsoráng molley, variegated, many colored, parti colored, of different colors

څورنگ ³ tsuráng *m. regional* ☞ سرنگ ¹ 2

څورنگتوب ¹ tsavrangtób *m.* ☞ څورنگ والی ¹

څورنگتوب ² tsorangtób *m.* ☞ څورنگ والی ²

څورنگتیا ¹ tsavrangtjấ *f.* ☞ څورنگ والی ¹

څورنگتیا ² tsorangtjấ *f.* ☞ څورنگ والی ²

څورنگ والی ¹ tsavrangválaj *m.* state of being blood-stained, blood-stained condition

څورنگ والی ² tsorangválaj *m.* **1** diversity of colors **2** *figurative* of mixed character, motley character, motley nature

څورنگول ¹ tsavrangvə́l *denominative, intransitive* [*past:* څورنگ یې کړ] **1** to stamp vigorously, tramp, tramp down, tramp under foot **2** to beat, thrash په وینو څورنگول to beat until bloody

څورنگول ² tsorangavə́l *denominative, intransitive* [*past:* څورنگ یې کړ] to make variegated, make multi-colored, cover with paint (of varied colors)

څورنگېدل ¹ tsavrangedə́l *denominative, intransitive* [*past:* څورنگ شو] **1** to be trampled (down) **2** to be beaten, be thrashed

څورنگېدل ² tsorangedə́l *intransitive* [*past:* څورنگ شو] to be motley, be vari-colored, be partly-colored; become brightly colored

څوری ¹ tsuráj *m.* sharp stone used as knife

څوری ² tsváraj tsóvraj *m.* څوری tsvárəj *f.* **1** provisions, victuals, provender (for the road) **2** reserve of foodstuffs or rations څوری و چا ته څوری ورکول to gather, collect provender en route اخیستل get ready, pick someone up en route ما نو اوس څوری و شا ته اچولئ دئ I had already picked up provisions en route.

څور tsaváṛ *m.* **1** staff or rod tied or fastened between a bull's legs to prevent him from getting separated from the herd **2** horse-cloth **3** membranous flesh (around the navel of a domestic animal, cattle)

څوړ ² tsuṛ *m.* ☞ څاړه

څوړ ³ tsuṛ **1** let down, lowered, hauled down **2** bent, curved, crooked **3** bent, curved back (of cattle) **4** disfigured, mutilated **5** emaciated, underfed (of a child) **6** stale (of food) *idiom* څوړي سترگي with shame, disgrace, infamy, shamed, disgraced څوړ غوړونه ولاړ He emerged shamed. He emerged embarrassed

څوړغوړ tsuṛghvaǵ ashamed, embarrassed

څوړمنی tsoṛmə́naj *m.* spring (the season)

څووړنگ tsovṛáng *m.* portion (at the time when a butchered animal carcass is being cut up)

څوړنگه tsoṛánga *f. agriculture* seedling, sapling, young plant

څوړوالی tsuṛválaj *m.* **1** omission, lapse **2** curvature, flexion, bend, crookedness **3** disfigurement, deformity, malformation **4** emaciated state, emaciation (of an infant, small child) **5** stale state, spoiled condition (of food)

څوړول tsuṛavə́l *denominative, transitive* [*past:* څوړ یې کړ] **1** to lower, reduce, sink, decline **2** to bend, fold, twist, distort **3** to disfigure, deform, mutilate, maim **4** to starve, exhaust (a child)

څوړی ¹ tsuṛaj *m.* tsoṛaj bull with horns bent back

څوړی ² tsoṛə́j cow with horns bent or curved back

څوړېدل tsuṛedə́l *denominative, intransitive* [*past:* څوړ شو] **1** to get down, go down, descend; go down, be reduced; sink; hang down; settle; lie down; go down **2** to be bent; to twist, sag; bend, bow, stoop; become bent; become crooked **3** to be disfigured, be mutilated, be maimed **4** to be underfed, be emaciated (of a small child, infant)

څوړین tsoṛín *m.* piece of leather or old wineskin spread on a (flat) stone when washing laundry by means of a valka or wooden paddle bat

څوز tsvaz *m.* essence; product of distillation

څوزی ¹ tsúzaj *m.* bedding made of matting; litter for domestic animals

څوزی ² tsúzaj *m.* chicken, chick, pullet

څوس tsus *m.* څوس وهل a to roam, rove, scour about (of a dog in search of food) b *figurative* to obtain wealth, pursue a career (in search of monetary success, reknown, etc.)

خوسن tsusán roaming, roving, scouring, sniffing around (of a dog in search of food)

خوسېدل tsusedól *intransitive* [*past:* وخوسېده] to roam, rove, scour, sniff around (of a dog in search of food)

خوښتى tsvaxhtáj *m. textiles* **1** shuttle (in carpet weaving) **2** corner (of the mouth) **3** spout (of a jug)

خوښکورى tsukhkóraj *m.* خوښکه tsúkhka *f.* [*plural:* خوښکي tsúkhki] spout (of a tea pot, etc.)

خوښى [1] tsukháj *m.* spout (of a tea pot, etc.)

خوښى [2] tsukháj *f.* spout (of a tea pot, etc.)

خوک [1] tsuk *m. dialect* ☞ سوک

خوک [2] tsok **1** *pronoun* **.1** *interrogative and relative, direct sense form* (oblique چا) *pronoun* **1.1a** who (used as the subject of an action in intransitive verbs in all tenses, and in transitive verbs in the present and future tenses) ددى خوک راغئ؟ Who has arrived? په کور خاوند خوک دئ؟ ترپايه Who is the master of this house? دى وائي چه ... خوک So nobody really knew this ... پورى و نه پوهېدل Some people say ... **1.1b** whom (used as the object of an action in intransitive verbs in the present and future tenses and in the grammatical construction) خوک ويني؟ Whom do you see? خوک وواهه؟ Whom did he beat? **1.2** *indefinite pronoun* anyone, anybody; someone, somebody په کورکښى خوک سته؟ Is anybody home? **2** *attributive* some, a kind of, a certain خوک مېلمه a certain guest *dialect* خوک نه خوک، خوک نه خوک سړى somebody or other, someone, somebody **3** *m.* **.1** man, person هغه خوک چه this person that, the one who درى تنه بل خوک three others اى هغه خوکه چه ... oh, that person who ... ; oh, the one who ... (in address) **3.2** important person, big-wig

خوک بازي tsukbāzí *f. regional* boxing

خوکرى tsukráj *m.* ☞ چکرى

خوکرېدل tsukrejól *transitive* [*past:* و يى خوکربيل] to cut (meat), prepare (sausage meat)

خوکړ tsukáṛ *m.* **1** man with a thick beard **2** *literature* Kyosa (a personage occuring in folk literature)

خوکربيل tsukól *transitive* ☞

خوکلن tsokallón زينبه خوکلنه ده؟ How old are you? ته خوکلن يې؟ How old is Zeynab?

خوکني tsavkaní *m. plural* **1** ☞ خمکني **2** Chamkani (Pakistani town near the Afghan border)

خوکه tsúka *f.* **1** top, apex; crown (of a tree, of the human head) **2** sharp peak (of a mountain), pinnacle **3** sharp tip; point, spike (of a knife, spearhead, etc.) خوکه کول to become shapened, become pointed **4** advance, forward patrol (mounted or foot) *idiom* د پښو په خوکو دربدل to stand on tiptoe

خوکه ور tskavór pointed

خوکى [1] tsukáj **1** wicker rack (for transporting plates, dishes, crockery) **2** bag, pouch

خوکى [2] tsokáj *m.* tsavkáj ☞ خوکيدار

خوکى [3] tsaukáj tsokáj **1** guard, watch, patrol د جهازونو تر خوکى لاندى guarded by ships, convoyed by ships خوکى درول to set up a sentry post, establish a sentry post, post a guard خوکى کول to guard, protect, watch **2** deputy's credentials **3** *regional* customs post **4** stool بازوداره خوکى arm-chair, easy chair **5** position, stand د دولت خوکى نيول to occupy a position **6** post, job, position government job, post تشه خوکى vacancy

خوکى [4] tsokáj *f.* **1** small round loaf of bread **2** vow to make a pilgrimage خوکى اخيستل to make a vow to complete a pilgrimage

خوکى جوړوونکى tsokáj dzhoṛavúnkaj *m.* joiner, cabinet-maker

خوکيدار tsokidár *m.* tsavkidár watchman, guard, sentry, sentinel

خوکيداري tsokidārí *f.* **1** guarding, protection, patrolling د ساحل خوکيداري coast-guard, patrolling the coast **2** *Eastern* tax on a home

خوگل tsavgál *m.* bran

خوگير tsavgír *m.* hunter lying in wait for game

خول tsvál **1.1** blown to pieces خول خول in shreds, rags, ragged **1.2** moth-eater **2** *m.* little piece, scrap; rag, shred

خولگى tsolgój *f.* chisel, gouge

خولند tsvolánd greedy, stingy, niggardly

خوله tsolá *f.* shirt made of coarse and thick lining cloth or material

خولى [1] tsvaláj *m.* خولى tsolój ☞ خورلى

خومره tsómra tsúmra **1.1** how much (by quality, amount, weight) په کلى دى گونى کښى خومره غنم دي؟ How much wheat in this bag? خومره وخت دي هورى تېر کئ؟ How far to the village? How much time did you spend there? **1.2** as far as, so far as, how خومره به ما ته معلومه ده چه In so far as I know How good it would be! خومره ښه هوا لگېږي How pleasant(ly) the breeze is blowing **2** خومره ... ، هغومره ... the ..., the ... (e.g., the more the merrier; the hotter, the better) او بيا خومره شمال ته دا غر ځي ، هغومره يې خوکى لوړېږي The farther these mountains extend to the north, the higher their peaks are.

خومره والى tsomraválaj *m.* quantity, amount, number

خومبره tsómbra tsúmbra ☞ خونبره

خونتى tsontáj armless (missing one arm)

خونخى tsontsój ☞ څمخى

خوند tsəvánd disquieted, uncalm, troubled

خوندي tsóndi *dialect* ☞ خومره

خونډه tsúnḍa *f.* fringe; border, edging ☞ خنډه

خونگرى tsungóraj *m.* small loaf of unleavened bread (given to children while warm in the presence of the children's illness چومى)

خونه tsóna tsúna ☞ خومره

خونه څاره tsóna-tsára **1** and so that's it **2.1** *f.* avoiding, evading **2.2** squabble, hassle **a** خونه څاره کول to avoid, evade **b** quarrel, wrangle, squabble (with)

خونه والى tsonaválaj *m.* quantity, amount, number

خوني [1] tsóni tsúne *dialect* ☞ خومره

خوني [2] tsunáj *m.* waste products of cane sugar manufacture

خوني [3] tsunój *f.* figured cotton cloth (for clothing, etc.)

خُوني موني tsúni-múni *regional* **1** brilliant, glittering **2** polished, burnished

خُونکه tsuṇə́ka *f.* ☞ خُنه

خُونول tsuṇavə́l *transitive* ☞ سونول

خُونه tsúṇa *f.* ☞ خُنه

خُوني ور، خُونبور tsuṇevə́r **1.1** with a forelock **1.2** with ringlets, with curls **2** *m.* brother-in-law

خُول tsvavə́l [¹] *transitive* [*past:* و يې خُواوه] to cause pain

خُول tsavavə́l [²] *transitive* [*past:* و يې خُواوه] to design, devise or project something

خُووم tsovə́m tsovúm *pronoun interrogative* what, how, which (according to the account) نن د مياشتي خُوومه ده؟ What date is today?

خُوه tsva [¹] *f.* hoof (of horse)

خُوه tsóva [²] *f.* ☞ خُويه

خُوهټ tsoháṭ lazing around, loafing

خُوهره tsuhrá *f. medicine* hernia, rupture

خُووم tsohə́m *pronoun* ☞ خُووم

خُومره tsóhamrə *dialect* ☞ خُومره

خُوى tsávaj [¹] *m.* **1** ambush په خُوى کښېنستل، خُوى کول to organize an ambush, lie in ambush **2** refuge, asylum, shelter

خُوى tsoj [²] *m. regional* hare

خُويه tsójə *f. regional* doe-hare

خُوبدل tsvedə́l *intransitive* [*past:* وخُوبده] to be ill with, be down with, have sharp pains (of fingers and toes when they are frost-bitten)

خُووم tsojə́m *Eastern* ☞ خُووم

څاه tsah [¹] *m.* ☞ څاه

څه tsə [²] *dialect* tsi **1** *pronoun* **.1** *interrogitive* what (being the subject in intransitive verb, or the object of the action in ergative constructions, it is regarded usually as a plural) پر مېز باندې څه پراته What is lying on the table? څه وايې؟ What are you saying? دي؟ *di* What else? څه وکم؟ What can I do? دا څه دئ؟ *di* What is this? تا څه کول؟ What did you do? دا څه اوربدلي دي؟ *di* What did you hear? دا نجلۍ ستا څه ده؟ How is this girl related to you? نوم دي څه دئ؟ What is your name? د څه دپاره؟ What for? Why? څله ☞ څه ته، څه له [⁴] څه کول to do something with someone, for someone or to someone په تا مې څه کړي دي؟ What did I do to you? **1.2** *interrogitive pronoun* what, how, what kind of, how څه حال دي دئ؟ How are you? What is ستا تره څه نوم What is this? دا څه شي دئ؟ What? څه شي دئ؟ What? needed? اوه، دا څه بې بختي ده! Oh, what a درلود؟ What is your uncle's name? misfortune! **1.3** *indefinite pronoun* something, anything څه ووايه say something خواره څه something nice يو نوي څه something new بل څه *proverb* better something تر نه څه بيا څه ښه دئ than nothing **2.1** several, some, a few, any (amount) څو ورځي هر څه ☞ هرڅه بل راڅه چه دا د لوى عمارت ته څه نژدې سو several days ago مخکېني Let's walk a bit closer to this large building. څه قدر، څه قدري a little bit, some, partly **2.2** to a certain extent, to a certain degree **3** *particle* really (in emotional speech it is placed at the end of a phrase) روند يې څه؟ Are you really blind? *idiom* پـه تا يې څه؟ What business is it of yours? What has this got to do with you? څه وخت چه when, at that time, since پـه ډېر څه for a large sum of money a خُه لږ شاني …څه، ...څه little, just a bit, …څه…څه partly … , (and) partly … ; not only …، but also … څه راغلي دي او څه راغلي نه دي some arrived, but some did not ته څه وايي او زه څه وايم you say one thing and I (say) another څه شل يا څه شل نيمي *proverb* it's twenty or twenty and a half (e.g., a small difference is of little import) څه کېدل a to happen, come to pass **b** to get to, disappear to, become of زما کتاب … څه شوکه Where did my book disappear to? … څه شو که that is تا څه څه ولېدل؟ What exactly because … څه څه that is, just exactly did you see?

څهان tsahã́n [¹] *plural of* څاه

څهان tsahã́n [²] *plural of* څه

څه خو tsə́xo [⁴] ☞ څخه

څه ډول tsə́ḍaul how, in what way

څه رنگه tsəránga ☞ څرنگه

څهره tsirá tserá [¹] ☞ څهره

څه شان tsə́shān how په څه شان؟ how, in what manner, in what way

څه شي tsə shaj what ☞ شى [¹]

څه طور tsə́taur how; in what way, in what manner

څه ناڅه tsənātsə́ څه نه څه tsənatsə́ somewhat; in some measure, to some degree; almost, approximately

څه وڅه tsə-u-tsə́ *indefinite pronoun* **1** something **2** *m. plural euphemism* shameful parts, indecent parts; the naughty parts (the genitals, etc.)

څې tsi [¹] *vice* دئ څه شي *colloquial* what's this څه راکه! ، ته what is this, give it to me (show it to me)

څې tse [²] *f.* name of the letter څ

څې tse [³] *acquisition of prepositional characteristics* څه *and* يې څې؟ ‌کوي *proverb* څې کوي چه نې کوي؟ Why is this yours? Why take it upon yourself, if you don't need it? (e.g., a person who refuses just for appearnce's sake, but then goes ahead and takes it upon himself)

څېته tsetá *f.* dull side or edge of a saber

څيخل tsixə́l *transitive* ☞ سيخل

څېر tser *m.* likeness, resemblance په دې څېر so, thus, like this, this way, in that way ستا په څېر like you دا چا په نظر کښې د سړي په څېر نه ورځي They do not consider him to be the man. One does not consider him to be the man.

څيراوه tsirāvə́ [¹] *m. plural* **1** rupture, tearing, laceration **2** disruption; cleaving, cutting; cleavage, separation, division **3** operation, operating; opening (of a wound, an abscess, a boil)

څيراوه tsirāvə́ [²] *imperfect of* څيرول

څيرخولى tsirxvə́láj *m.* eggplant

څيرسترگى tsirstə́rgaj [¹] impudent, impertinent, insolent

څيرسترگي tsirstərgí [²] *f.* impudence, impertinence, insolence, cheek څيرسترگي ويل to speak insolently

څيرګۍ tsirgə́j *f.* strip, narrow sector of a field

څيرل tsirál *transitive verb* [*past:* وى يې څيره] 1 to tear, rend 2 to cleave, split, break 3 to kill (of a beast of prey) 4 to operate, open a wound, open a boil

څيرلى ¹ tserláj *m.* kid (young goat)

څيرلئ ² tsirə́ləj 1 *past participle of* څيرل 2 impudent, impertinent, insolent; disrespectful څيرلي خبري کول *a* to speak plainly, speak in plain terms *b* to speak impertinently (of children) *idiom* څيرلئ کار کول to undertake a difficult affair

څيرلى tserláj *feminine of* څيرلى ¹

څيرمه tsérma 1 *f.* .1 corner (e.g., of a kerchief) 1.2 edge, side 2 aside! څيرمه کتاب کيږده! Put the book aside! 3 *predicative* .1 directed at, directed toward 3.2 aspiring to څيرمه کول *a* to put aside *b* to throw, fling *c* to send, direct څيرمه کيدل *a* to stand aside, step aside, move away from, keep away from *b* to be sent, be dispatched; make for, make one's way toward *c* to aim at, aspire to, strive for

څيروالى tsirválaj *m.* state of being broken or torn; state of being torn to pieces

څيرول tsiravál *transitive* ☞ څيرل

څيرونکى tsirúnkaj 1 *present partcicple of* څيرل 2 predatory, raptoral څيرونکي حيوانان tsirúnki wild beasts, predators, څيرونکي ساکښان predatory animals

څيره ¹ tserá *f.* 1 appearance, exterior, looks, look, aspect; face په څيره پيژندل to recognize by his/her face 2 look, view, form, shape 3 drawing, picture, painting, portrayal, image 4 portrait; snapshot, photograph 5 wreath or garland of flowers worn by a groom on his wedding day 6 *figurative* mask 7 *figurative* character, characteristic property

څيره ² tsíra *f.* rise (sunrise)

څيره ³ tséra *f.* scarecrow (in a field)

څيره ⁴ tsíra *f.* 1 cut, section 2 strip, band (of paper, cloth); rag, shred, scrap څيره جورول to cut into strips; tear into strips

څيره کښ tserakákh *m.* 1 portraitist 2 artist

څيره کښي tserakakhí *f.* 1 representation 2 portrait (painting)

څيره گر tseragár *m.* ☞ څيره کښ

څيري ¹ tsíri tsíre *Eastern* 1 torn, lacerated, torn asunder څيري کالي راغئ He arrived all in rugs. 2 cut 3 cracked (i.e., skin); split; cut (up) 4 cut out; split څيري کول *a* to tear, tear asunder; tear up *b* to slit, section, lay open *c* to cleave, split *d* to cut out څيري کيدل ☞ څيريدل

څيري ² tsiráj *m.* piece (of food, cloth, etc.)

څيري ³ tserə́j *f.* directions (explanation), instructions

څيري ⁴ tsirí *present tense of* څيرل

څيرجر tserjár *m.* ☞ څيره گر

څيري پيري tsíri-píri څيري څيري *dialect* all torn into shreds; in rags; ragged

څيريدل tsiredál *intransitive* [*past:* وخيريده *past:* څيري شو] 1 to break, burst, tear, explode 2 to be torn, be tattered; be spit, be cut, be slit 3 to crack, burst, disintegrate; be broken up; be hammered flat; be cloven, be split ځمکه وخيريده the earth cracked, the earth fissured 4 to be split open 5 to be operated upon; be opened (of a wound, a boil, etc.)

څپرل tserə́l 1 *transitive* [*past:* وى يې څپره] .1 to consider, examine, discuss something 1.2 to investigate, explore, examine 1.3 to find out about (a deposit of one, etc.), reconnoiter, collect data (intelligence, etc.) 2 *m. plural* ☞ څپرنه

څپرنپال tserənpál *m.* president of the Afghan Academy

څپرندوى tserəndój *m.* member (active) of the Afghan Academy

څپرنمل tserənmál *m.* senior scientific worker

څپرنوال tserənvál *m.* corresponding member of the Afghan Academy

څپرنه tserə́na *f.* 1 investigation, discussion of something 2 investigation د لغاتو څپرنه investigation of vocabulary items, study of lexical items; lexicography د ... په شاوخوا کښي څپرنه کول، په ... *a* to investigate, discuss something *b* to explore, investigate 3 *law* inquest, investigation ابتدائي څپرنه preliminary inquest, preliminary investigation 4 to find out about, investigate (a layer of ore) تر څپرني لاندي نيول *a* to investigate something *b* to investigate, research *c* to investigate, inquiring into *d* to explore (source of something)

څپرنيار tserənjár *m.* junior scientific worker

څپرونکى tserúnkaj 1 *present participle of* څپرل 2 *m.* assistant or teacher in a higher institution of learning, teacher, instructor

څيره tsíra *f.* 1 row, line, rank, file 2 band, crowd 3 flock; herd (of horses), shoal (of fish), flock (of birds) 4 *hunting* round-up د څيري خلق *obsolete a* advance guard *b* *hunting* beaters

څپرى ¹ tserə́j *f.* 1 evergreen oak, *Quercus baloot* غوره څپري large-leafed oak سپيرکى څپري small-leafed oak 2 crown, top

څيري ² tsíri *plural* ☞ څيره

څپرى ³ tseri *present tense of* څپرل

څيز tsiz *m. Eastern* thing, object دا څه څيز دئ؟ What is that?

څيزمه tsézma *f.* څپرمه tséghma *f. dialect* eyelid

څپنتن tsekhtán *m. dialect* ☞ تنبتن

څپنتول tsekhtavál *transitive dialect* ☞ تنبتول

څپنته tsékhta *f.* ☞ تنبته

څپنتبدل tsekhtedə́l *intransitive dialect* ☞ تنبتبدل

څپنل tsekhə́l *transitive dialect* ☞ چنبل

څيکل tsikál *transitive* [*past:* وى يې څيکه] to hack, chop up (viscera, etc.)

څيکه tsíka *f.* top or peak of turban

څپلمه tsélma *f.* 1 edge, side د کلي په څپلمه دده مي کور دئ *Eastern* My house is on the edge of the village. 2 trench, emplacement, foxhole; position *idiom* له څپلمي نه quite, very; د څپلمي *idiom* راتلل to come unexpectedly, appear unexpectedly; pop in without notice ☞ څيرمه

څيله tsíla *f.* ☞ څيره

څيلى ¹ tsiló́j *f.* سيلى ²

څيلى ² tselə́j *f.* rope, cord

چیندخ tsindzáḳ *m. dialect* ☞ څینځبن

څینځبنه tsindzə́kha *m. dialect* frog

چنگبن tsingə́kh *m. dialect* ☞ څینگبن

څینگبنه tsingə́kha *f. dialect* ☞ چنگبنه

څنور tsinavár *m.* ☞ خنور

څینی tsinə́j *f. dialect* ☞ نښی³

ح

ح¹ he hā-ji-huttí **1** the eleventh letter of the Pashto alphabet **2** the number 8 in the abjad system

ح² *official abbreviation for* **1** من حمیت **2** حربي

حاتم hātím *m. Arabic personal name* Hatim (especially as the name for an Arab of the tribe, as the personification of generosity)

حاجب hadzhíb *m. Arabic* [*plural:* حاجیان hādzhibān *Arabic plural:* حجاب hudzhdzháb *plural:* حجبه hadzhabá] porter, doorman; watchman

حاجت hādzhát *m. Arabic* [*plural:* حاجتونه hādzhatúna *Arabic plural:* حاجات hādzhát] necessity, requirement حاجت نشته There is no need. It isn't necessary. حاجت کېدل to need, have need of someone or something که ستا حاجت شي If you have need of it *idiom* حاجت کول، د حاجت دپاره وتل to answer the call of nature

حاجتمند hādzhatmán **1** needy; poor **2** *m.* pauper; poor peasant

حاجتمندي hādzhatmandí *f.* need; destitution; poverty

حاجز hādzhíz *Arabic* **1.1** impending **1.2** separating, isolating **2** *m.* impediment, obstacle

حاجي hādzhí *m. Arabic* haji (a Moslem who has made a pilgrimage to Mecca)

حاد hād *Arabic* acute (i.e., angle)

حادث hādís *Arabic* new, fresh

حادثه hadisa *f.* [*plural:* حادثي hādisé *Arabic m. plural:* حادثات hādisāt *Arabic plural:* حوادث havādís] **1** event; incident; occurrence; happening داسي حادثه پېښنه شوه Such an event occurred. **2** accident حوادث شوم wreck, crash; accident **3** a phenomenon (of nature)

حاذق hāzíḳ *Arabic* skillful, experienced; intelligent; wise

حار hār *Arabic* hot مناطق حاره *manātíḳ-i* hot, tropical countries; the tropics

حارص hārís *Arabic* **1** greedy, grasping, stingy **2** strongly desiring, thirsting for something; striving for something

حازي hāzí *m. plural* حازي خېل hāzikhél *m. plural* the Hazi, the Hazikhejli (a branch of the Yusufzai tribe)

حاسد hāsíd *Arabic* **1** envious **2** *m.* envious person

حاسه hāssá *f. Arabic* [*plural:* حواس havás] feeling د کتلو حاسه viewpoint د بویولو حاسه sense of smell, olfactory sense

حاشیه hāshijá *f. Arabic* [*plural:* حاشیي hashije *Arabic m. plural:* حواشي havāshí] **1** edge; edging; selvage **2** note in the margin of a book or manuscript, marginalia

حاشیه نویسي hāshijanavisí *f.* marginalia, commentary (on the margins of a publication, etc.) حاشیه نویسي کول to comment (in a publication, etc.)

حاصل hāsíl *Arabic* **1.1** receiving, obtaining **1.2** achieving, getting **2** *m.* [*plural:* حاصلات hāsilát *plural:* حواصل havāsíl] **1** harvest **2.2** revenue, income **2.3** product; production **2.4** *figurative* result, total; consequence; outcome, conclusion حاصل کول **a** to yield a harvest, bear (of land) دا مځکه ډېر حاصل کوي This land yields a big crop. **b** to bring in revenue **c** to yield a result **3** *predicative* **.1** received, obtained **3.2** achieved **3.3** determined (by right, law) حاصل جمع *math* sum حاصل او معنی د meaning حاصل دا چه، حاصل دا دئ چه the meaning of life ژوندون معنی او حاصل د کلام، د خبري حاصل *obsolete* in a word; succinctly stated

حاصلخېز hāsilkhéz fruitful; high-yield حاصل خېزه مځکه fruitful, productive land

حاصلخېزي hāsilkhezí *f.* fruitfulness; high-productivity

حاصلول hāsilavə́l **1** to [حاصل يي کړ *denominative, transitive* [*past:* get; to obtain معرفت یو شی ځان ته حاصلول to obtain something خپل مطلب حاصلول to acquire knowledge حاصلول to attain one's goal **2** to attain, achieve **3** to turn out, put out, produce **2** *m.* حاصلول *present participle of*

حاصلونکی hāsilavúnkaj **1** *present participle of* حاصلول **2** *m. economics* producer

حاصلي hāsilí fruitful; high-yield

حاصلېدل hāsiledál **1** to [حاصل شو *denominative, intransitive* [*past:* be gotten; be obtained **2** to be attained, be achieved (e.g., of success) **3** to be procured, be acquired **4** to be produced, be turned out **5** to flow out of, be the consequence of something نتیجه حاصلېدل to produce a result

حاضر hāzír *Arabic* **1.1** present, appearing; on hand, available تول دغه دئ حاضر دئ! Here he is! **1.2** present (of حاضر کسان at present time, situation) دی په هيڅ وخت کي و دی ته present **1.3** ready for something حاضرول حاضر نه دئ He will never agree with this. حاضر کول ☞ *amr-i* امر حاضر **2** *m.* the present (time) حاضرېدل ☞ حاضر کېدل، *grammar* imperative mood

حاضراً hāzírán *Arabic* at the present time, at the present moment

حاضرباش hāzirbásh *m.* **1** bodyguard **2** servant, attendant د حاضرباش کار کول to attend

حاضرجواب hāzirszhaváb resourceful; witty

حاضرجوابي hāzirdzhavābí *f.* resourcefulness; wittiness

حاضروالی hāzirválaj *m.* **1** presence; availability **2** readiness **3** agreement, consent

حاضرول hāzíravə́l **1** [حاضر يي کړ *denominative, transitive* [*past:* to bring, convey **1.2** to prepare for something **1.3** to summon, assemble عمومي مجمع حاضرول to call a general meeting **1.4** to compel; force, make to do something **2** *m. plural* **.1** delivery **2.2** preparation for something **2.3** summons **2.4** compulsion

حاضري hāzirí *f.* **1** appearance, showing up for work; presence **2** *military* roll-call, muster حاضري کول to call the roll, take attendance **3** time sheet (for logging workers in and out) د حاضري

293

کتاب time-keepers log کول امضا حاضري ،حاضري ليکل to sign in (workers) 4 *military* call-up (to active duty) 5 *regional* lunch راورل حاضري to have lunch

حاضرېدل hāziredә́l *denominative, intransitive* [*past:* حاضر شو] 1 to appear, arrive, show up; participate 2 to be ready for something 3 to agree دي ته نه حاضرېدل They did not agree on this.

حاضرين hāzirín *m. Arabic plural* those present, those participating

حافظ hāfiz *m. Arabic* 1 custodian, guardian 2 person who has committed the Koran to memory 3 Hafiz (a classical poet of the 16th century)

حافظ الله hāfizullá *m. Arabic proper name* Hafizulla

حافظه hāfizá *f. Arabic* memory

حاکم hākím *Arabic* 1 *m.* .1 hakim; head; chief of a province or district; governor لوی حاکم governor اعلی حاکم chief of a province 1.2 *Eastern* judge 2 *attributive* .1 governing; ruling 2.2 dominating 2.3 command حاکم ځای *military* command post

حاکمانه hākimāná 1 imperious, commanding; overbearing 2 authoritative حاکمانه مشري authority, power

حاکم نشين hākimnishín administrative; regional حاکم نشين ځای administrative center

حاکمه hākíma *f.* 1 empress, sovereign 2 mistress

حاکمي hākimí *f.* government of a province, region or district

حاکمیت hākimiját *m. Arabic* 1 supremacy; authority د شوروي حاکمیت په وخت کښی during the years of Soviet power, in the Soviet period 2 jurisdiction 3 competence 4 sovereignty 5 ownership, possession 6 action, influence a پر لرل حاکمیت to master, possess b to act (upon), influence *idiom* پر چا حاکمیت ښنکاره کول to love to command or have at one's disposition

حاکي hākí *Arabic* speaking; relating; stating ... دا خبر حاکي دئ چه This communication states that ...

حال hāl *m. Arabic* [*plural:* حالونه hālúna *Arabic plural:* احوال ahvál] 1 position, situation; circumstance حال ويل to relate or tell about the circumstances of a matter حال يې و نه وايه They did not say what it was about. a خپل حال ويل to tell about oneself; to talk about one's situation b to lay out, expound proofs c to reveal one's secret, be frank وچا ته د ىوه شي حال ورکول to inform someone about something چاته حال استول to let someone know about something د چا حال اخيستل to inquire about someone سره حال معلومول to find out about one another 2 (current) reality 3 health, condition of health ستاسي حال څه دئ؟ How do you feel? How is your health? How are you? 4 *grammar* the present tense *idiom* او حال دا دئ چه meanwhile; in reality; whereas; at the same time په هر حال سره while, because په داسي حال کښي چه in any case په هیڅ حال کښي not in any case

حالات hālā́t *Arabic masculine plural of* حالت

حالانکه hālā́nki *vice* او حال دا whereas, while

حالت hālát *m. Arabic* [*plural:* حالتونه hālatúna *Arabic plural:* حالات hālā́t] 1 position, situation; circumstance هوايي حالت meteorological conditions طبيعي حالت the normal state, natural

زما حالت بالکل اوښتئ دئ I have completely reformed. 2 *grammar* case

حالتي hālatí *adjective grammar* case, pertaining to case, case-related

حالي hālí *Arabic* 1 knowing, informed 2 contemporary

حامل hāmíl *Arabic* 1 conveying; transporting, carrying 2 *m.* .1 ferryman 2.2 bearer of this, bearer 2.3 holder (of a bond)

حامله hāmilá *Arabic* 1 *feminine singular of* حامل پیسکه pregnant (woman) 2 *f.* .1 pregnant woman 2.2 transmitter (of ideas, etc.)

حامله گي hāmilagí *f.* pregnancy

حامي hāmí *m. Arabic* protector, defender, patron; savior

حاوي hāví *Arabic* containing, holding

حائز hāíz *Arabic* possessing, owning

حائل hāíl *Arabic* 1 hindering, impeding 2 *m.* [*plural:* حائلونه hāilúna *Arabic plural:* حوائل hāvāíl] .1 obstacle, impediment, hindrance 2.2 barrier, hurdle د رودو حائل حائلېدل watershed

حائلېده hāiledә́l *denominative, intransitive* [*past:* حائل شو] to be or serve as an obstacle or barrier

حب hab habb *m. Arabic* [*plural:* حبوب hubúb] 1 corn 2 fruit

حب hub hubb *m. Arabic* love; affection د دنیا حب نه یم اخیستئ *folklore* Worldly matters do not hold me prisoner.

حباب hubā́b *m. Arabic* bubble صابون حباب soap bubble

حب الذات hubb-uz-zā́t *m. Arabic* self-love, egotism

حب الغیر hubb-ul-ghájr *m. Arabic* altruism

حب النفس hubb-un-náfs *m. Arabic* حب الذات

حب الوطن hubb-ul-vatán *m. Arabic* patriotism

حبطه hubatá حبته

حبس habs *m. Arabic* arrest, imprisonment عمري حبس، دائمي حبس life imprisonment حبس کول *compound verb* حبس کېدل، حبسول حبسېدل *compound verb*

حبسول habsavә́l *denominative, transitive* [*past:* حبس یې کړ] to arrest, imprison

حبس هوا habs-i-havā stuffy, stifling (of air)

حبسېدل habsedә́l *denominative, intransitive* [*past:* حبس شو] to be arrested, be imprisoned

حبشستان habashistā́n *m.* حبشه habashá *f.* Ethiopia; Abyssinia

حبشي habsháj habshí habashí 1 Ethiopian; Abyssinian 2 Black; African

حبطه habatá *Arabic* useless, good-for-nothing

حبوب hubúb *Arabic masculine plural of* حب

حبوبات hububā́t *m. second person plural of* حبوب 1 grain, grains 2 cornbread, food, cereals 3 leguminous plants

حبیب habíb *Arabic* 1 favorite, beloved 2 *m. proper name* Habib

حبیب الله hubibullá *m. Arabic proper name* Habibulla

حبیبیه habibijá *f.* Habibiya (a lycee in Kabul thus named for the Emir Habibulla)

ح پ *abbreviation* حربي پوهنځی military college

حتم hatm *m. Arabic* 1 obligation; commitment 2 solution (of a problem) د يوه امر قطع او حتم definitive solution to a problem

حتماً hátmán *Arabic* without fail, certainly, absolutely

حتمي hatmí *Arabic* obligatory, indispensable, absolute حتمي تعليم obligatory training دا زموږ دپاره لازمي او حتمي ده We are obliged to do this ... دا حتمي ده چه It is necessary to ...

حتمي الوقوع hatmi-ul-vuķú *Arabic* unavoidable, inevitable

حتميت hatmiját *m. Arabic* binding force; indispensability, unavoidability

حتى hattá *Arabic* 1 *conjunction* even; so, that 2 *preposition* until; right unto; till; while 3 *combining form* حتى الامكان insofar as possible

حتيات hatiját *m.* ☞ احتياط

حتى hatt-āl-imkán حتى المقدور hatt-āl-māķdúr *Arabic* حتى الوسع hatt-āl-vús *Arabic* insofar as possible; as much as possible; to the best of one's ability

حج hadzh *m.* hadzhdzh *Arabic* hadj, pilgrimage to Mecca

حجاب¹ hidzháb *m.* [*plural:* حجابونه hidzhābúna *Arabic plural:* حجب hudzhúb *Arabic plural:* احجبة ahdzhibá] 1 shawl, veil 2 membrane; partition حاجز حجاب hidzháb-i *anatomy* diaphragm 3 modesty; bashfulness *idiom* په حجاب د شپي under cover of night

حجاب² hudzhzháb *Arabic plural of* حاجب

حجار hadzhdzhár *m. Arabic* lapidary; stonemason

حجاري hadzhdzhārí *f.* lapidary work

حجاز hidzház *m. Arabic* Hejaz

حجام hadzhdzhám *m. Arabic* barber who uses cupping-glasses or bloodletting

حجامت hadzhāmát *m. Arabic* 1 use of cupping-glasses; bloodletting 2 shave; haircut حجامت جوړول to get a haircut حجامت کول to give a haircut

حجانى hadzhāŋə́j *f.* ☞ اجانى

حجب¹ hadzhb *m. Arabic* concealing, covering up

حجب² hudzhúb *Arabic masculine plural of* حجاب¹

حجت hudzhdzhát *m. Arabic* 1 proof, argument, logical proof کول to prove, present arguments, give logical proof 2 *economics* document, promissory note; I.O.U

حجتي hudzhdzhatí 1 *m.* .1 expert debater 1.2 faultfinder 2 peevish; troublesome

حجر hadzhár *m. Arabic* [*plural:* احجار ahdzhár] stone, rock

حجراتي hudzhrātí *biology* cellular

حجره hudzhrá *f. Arabic* [*plural:* حجرې hudzhré *Arabic m. plural:* حجرات hudzharát] 1 *Eastern* guestroom (in rural villages) حجره to have a guestroom 2 lodging ته بيګاه د چا په حجره کښې وي؟ At whose place did you stay yesterday? په مسجد کښې يې حجره ده ونيوله He practically lives at the mosque. 3 cell (of a honeycomb) 4 *biology* cell

حجم hadzhm *m.* hudzhm *Arabic* 1 volume, capacity, cubic content د بېړۍ حجم the displacement of a ship خپل د حجم له مخي in volume

حجم لويول to increase in volume 2 format (of a book) 3 size, bulk, scale د کارو حجم volume of operations 4 output (of an enterprise)

حد had hadd *m. Arabic* [*plural:* حدونه hadúna *Arabic plural:* حدود hudúd] 1 limit, boundary د ښار په حدودو کښې within the city limits يو حد تلل to go a considerable distance پر خپل حد within limits, within the norm, within boundaries په حدودو د 8 بجو around 8 hours تر څخه حده پوري، تر يوه حده as possible د توان تر حده پوري تر داسي حده پوري چه to a certain extent, to a certain degree څه حده، تر تر ډېره حده پوري ... to such a degree that ... ; to the extent that ... تر ممکنه حده پوري in a significant degree or measure ډېره حده، a تر حده زيات، تر حده پورته، تر حد تېر insofar as this is possible د اکثر حد د پاره درې کاله infinitely, boundlessly; excessively, too much b infinite, boundless حد ترل a maximum of three years حد تېرېدل to limit تر حد تېرى کول to go beyond the permissible limits, depart from the framework or bounds of something a ☞ تر حد تېرى کول تر حد تېرېدل b to encroach on something د وکالت د حدود څخه تېرى to exceed authority 2 *religion* punishment for crime (established by shariat, the canonical law of Islam) *idiom* حد بلوغ hád-i; hádd-i majority; maturity حد کول *regional* a to exaggerate, overplay b to overstate

حدبخشي hadbakhshí *f.* demarcation, delimitation

حدت hiddát *m. Arabic* sharpness, zeal; fury

حدس hads *m. Arabic* offer, proposal, surmise دا حدس درست و This surmise has turned out to be true. ده ښه حدس وهلئ دئ He guessed right.

حدوث hudús *m. Arabic* novelty

حدود hudúd *Arabic masculine plural of* حد

حديث hadís *m. Arabic* [*plural:* حديثونه hadisúna *plural:* احاديث ahādís] *religion* hadis (tradition about Mohammed)

حديقه hadiká *f. Arabic poetic* garden

حذا hazá *f. Arabic military* dressing حذا نيسئ! *military* Dress! (as a command)

حذر hazár *m. Arabic* fear, dread; caution حذر کول to be fearful; be wary of حذر کېدل to be fearful; be wary

حذف hazf *m. Arabic* 1 dropping (e.g., a letter, a prefix) 2 *abbreviation* حذفول compound verb ☞

حذفول hazfavə́l *denominative, transitive* [*past:* حذف يې کړ] 1 to drop (e.g., a letter, a prefix) 2 to abbreviate

حر hur hurr 1 free, independent 2 *m.* [*plural:* احرار ahrár] liberal

حرارت harārát *m. Arabic* 1 heat, hot weather 2 temperature حرارت درجې تر صفر پورته دئ 8 The temperature (of the air) is 8 degrees above zero.

حراست hirāsát *m. Arabic* guarding; tending; caring for حراست کول to guard; to tend; to take care of; to watch over

حرام harám *Arabic* 1 unauthorized 2 impermissible, forbidden (by shariat, i.e., Islamic canon law); repudiated حرامه نفقه inedible, unclean, forbidden food *idiom* حرام خوړل a to take a bribe b to appropriate another's property c to be a scoundrel

حرام خوار harāmkhār حرام خور harāmkhór **1.1** living on unearned income **1.2** living at another's expense **2.1** *m.* parasite, sponger **2.2** cheat, swindler **2.3** rascal

حرام خوري harāmkhorí *f.* **1** parasitism; sponging **2** cheating, swindling

حرامزادگي harāmzadagí *f.* **1** meanness **2** cheating; swindling حرامزادگي کول **a** to commit a base action **b** to cheat, swindle

حرامزاده harāmzādá **1** indeclinable base **2** *m.* [*plural:* حرام حرامزاده، حرام زاده harāmzādagán] .**1** cheat **2.2** good-for-nothing; زادگان، زادگان scoundrel

حرامغز harāmághz *m.* spinal chord

حرامول harāmavól *denominative, transitive* [*past:* حرام یې کړ] **1** to forbid **2** to spoil, render useless; make inedible, defile

حرامونی harāmúnaj **1** useless, base, mean **2** *m.* good-for-nothing, scoundrel

حرامي harāmí *m.* **1** good-for-nothing, scoundrel **2** bandit

حرامېدل harāmedál *denominative, intransitive* [*past:* حرام شو] **1** to be impermissible, be forbidden **2** to go bad, put out of commission; be defiled

حرب harb *m. Arabic* war وزیر حرب *vazír-i* Defense Minister

حربي harbí **1** military حربي ښوونځی، حربي پوهنځی military school حربي خدمت military service حربي فابریکه armaments plant, munitions factory **2** *adjective* combat, operational

حربیه harbijá *Arabic* ☞ حربي چیف directorate of حربیه ریاست chief directorate of artillery and technical supply (of the Ministry of Defense)

حرج hárdzh *m.* háradzh constraint, difficulty; critical situation د حرجه څخه وتل to surmount a difficulty

حرص hirs *m. Arabic* **1** greed, avidity, cupidity **2** passionate desire حرص کول to desire passionately, lust after

حرف¹ harf *m. Arabic* [*plural:* حرفونه harfúna *plural:* حروف hurúf] **1** letter (of the alphabet) په حروفو لیکل to write out in full **2** *grammar* participle نفي حرف negation **3** *grammar* preposition

حرف² hiráf *Arabic masculine plural of* حرفه

حرفت hirfát *m. Arabic* [*plural:* حرفات hirfắt *f. Arabic* حرفه hirfa *plural:* حرفي hirfé *m. Arabic plural:* حرف hiráf] **1** trade, craft اهل حرفت áhl-i artisans **2** occupation; field of work

حرفه یي hirfaí *adjective* handicraft, trade حرفه یي ښوونځی trade school

حرفي harfí *Arabic* **1** in letters **2** literal **3** *grammar* prepositional (i.e., phrase)

حرکات harakất *masculine plural* **1** *of* حرکت **2** *military* operations د حرکاتو عمومي مدیر chief of the operations department (in the General Staff)

حرکاتي harakātí **1** *military* operational **2** mobile, transportable

حرکت harakát *m. Arabic* [*plural:* حرکتونه harakatúna *Arabic plural:* حرکات harakất] **1** movement, travel د حرکت آله motor په حرکت کښې دي لښکري په حرکات the troops are on the march ته حرکت ورکول، و... راوستل to move, put into motion **2** departure, leaving کول ...د څخه حرکت to proceed (from), depart; go out, set

out **3** ☞ نهضت **4** action, conduct, behavior **5** *linguistics* diacritical mark indicating a short vowel

حرکتي harakatí **1** lively (of games) **2** *physiology* motor

حرم harám *m. Arabic* **1** harem **2** sacred place, shrine الحرم place of worship in Mecca

حرمت hurmát *m. Arabic* esteem, respect

حرمخانه haramkhāná *f.* حرم سرای haramsarāj *m.* harem

حرمین haramájn *m. Arabic plural religion* Mecca and Medina

حروف hurúf *m. Arabic plural* **1** *of* حرف **2** type

حروفچین hurufchín *m.* compositor

حروفچیني hurufchiní *f.* **1** typographic composition, typesetting **2** work of typesetting

حروفي hurufi *typographic* حروفي دستگاه printing press

حریان harján ☞ حیران

حریان دریان harján-darján extremely surprised; startled, stunned

حریت hurriját *m. Arabic* freedom

حریت خواه hurrijatkháh ☞ آزادي خواه

حریر harír *m. Arabic* silk, silk cloth

حریص harís *Arabic* avaricious, mean حریص کېدل to become avaricious, become mean; be greedy, be mean

حریف haríf *m. Arabic* [*plural:* حریفان harifán *Arabic plural:* حرفا hurafắ] **1** rival, competitor, opponent **2** *regional* client **3** *regional* partner

حریق haríḱ *m. Arabic* fire

حزب hizb *m. Arabic* [*plural:* حزبونه hizbúna *Arabic plural:* احزاب ahzáb] party, political کمونستي حزب Communist Party

حزبي hizbí *Arabic attributive* party

حزم hazm *m. Arabic* prudence, caution, circumspection په حزم او احتیاط سره رفتار کول to act cautiously, behave circumspectly

حس his *m.* hiss *Arabic* sensation, feeling حس کول *compound verb* حسېدل *compound verb* ☞ حس کېدل، حسول

حساب hisáb *Arabic* **1** *m.* [*plural:* حسابونه hisābúna *Arabic plural:* حسابات hisābắt] .**1** counting; calculation, computation; count; enumeration حساب کتاب accounting جاري حساب current account د حساب آله، د حساب ماشین calculator, calculating machine د حساب میتر meter (device) حساب پاکول to settle accounts (with) د چا سره حساب لرل to settle an account with someone حساب ورکول to have an account with someone حساب ورکول to submit a financial report; render an account په خپل حساب او خیال غلط تلل to make an accounting error دا په هیڅ نه وي حساب This isn't worth anything. **1.2** arithmetic **1.3** grouping, category **1.4** account, payment, retribution د حساب ساعت را نژدې دئ The hour of retribution is approaching. **2** *predicative* being reckoned, being counted, taking into account

حسابدهي hisābdihí *f.* book-keeping; accountancy حسابدهي ورکول to render an account (of resources, sums of money)

حساب گیر hisābgír *m.* meter (in various senses); tally-clerk

حسابول hisābavә́l *denominative, transitive* [*past:* حساب يې کړ] **1** to compute, calculate, count up, reckon up **2** to be enumerated, be reckoned, be counted (in a statistic, list, etc.)

حسابي hisābí *Arabic* **1** accounts, accounting حسابي مامورين accounting clerks **2** arithmetical **3** financial, fiscal حسابي دوره fiscal period حسابي کال fiscal year **4** economical, thrifty

حسابدل hisābedә́l *denominative, intransitive* [*past:* حساب شو] **1** to be settled, be calculated, be tallied up **2** to be considered, pass for دا قاليني د ښو قالينو په جمله کښي حسابږي These rugs are considered to be good. **3** to amount to **4** to be enumerated, be listed somewhere

حساس hassā́s *Arabic* **1** sensitive; sympathetic, responsive; impressionable; receptive **2** punctilious, meticulous **3** sensitive (of an instrument, etc.) **4** vulnerable

حساسول hassāsavә́l *denominative, transitive* [*past:* حساس يې کړ] **1** to render sensitive, render receptive **2** *radio* to tune

حساسيت hassāsijā́t *m. Arabic* **1** sensitivity; sharpness, responsiveness; impressionability; receptiveness **2** punctiliousness, fussiness **3** sensitivity (of an instrument, etc.)

حسام hasā́m *m. Arabic* sword

حسام الدين hasāmuddín *Arabic proper name* Hasamuddin

حسان hisā́n *Arabic masculine plural of* حسن [1]

حسب hasb *Arabic* **1** *m.* counting, quantity; size; measure **2** according to, in accordance with, as حسب الوعده in accordance with the promise, as promised حسب الامر in accordance with your order, according to your instructions حسب المعمول as usual, as customary

حسد hasád *m. Arabic* envy د حسد وړ enviable (of fate etc.) حسد کول، حسد لرل to envy

حسد ناک hasadnā́k envious

حسرت hasrát *m. Arabic* grief, sorrow, melancholy حسرت خوړل **a** to grieve, suffer; long for **b** to dream, think

حسن husn [1] *m.* [*plural:* حسنات husnā́t *plural:* حسان hisnā́n] **1** beauty, charm; elegance, grace **2** *combining form* حسن خلق good behavior حسن مثال an example

حسن hasán [2] *Arabic* **1** beautiful **2** *m. proper name* Hasan *idiom* د حسن حسين مياشت، د حسن و حسين مياشت the month of Muharram (the name of the first month of the lunar year)

حسنات husnā́t *Arabic* **1** *masculine plural of* حسن [1] **2** good, the good

حسن انتخاب husnintikhā́b *m. Arabic* happy choice

حسن انتظام husnintizā́m *m. Arabic* **1** proper adjustment, good organizational order **2** state of good discipline

حسن بيان husnbajā́n *m. Arabic* eloquence

حسن تفاهم husntafāhúm *m. Arabic* mutual understanding

حسن تکئيف husntakjíf *m. Arabic* fitness, suitability

حسن تلقي husntalaķí *m. Arabic* ☞ حسن ظن

حسن خط husnkhát *m. Arabic* **1** calligraphy **2** beautiful handwriting

حسن خلق husnkhúlķ *m. Arabic* good behavior

حسن سلوک husnsulúk *m. Arabic* ☞ حسن گذاره

حسن سيرت husnsirát *m. Arabic* good conduct

حسن ظن husnzán *m.* husnzánn حسن قبول husnķabúl *m. Arabic* favor, favorable relation

حسن گذاره husnguzārá *f.* good treatment; courtesy

حسن مثال husnmisā́l *m. Arabic* example

حسن محافظه husnmuhāfizá *f. Arabic* good care

2 حسن معامله husnmu'āmalá *f. Arabic* **1** ☞ حسن گذاره conscientiousness

حسن نظر husnnazár *m. Arabic* ☞ حسن ظن

حسن نيت husnniját *m. Arabic* good intention

حسن همجواري husnhamdzhuvārí *f.* good-neighborliness

حسود hasúd *Arabic* **1** envious **2** *m.* envious person

حسول hisavә́l *denominative, transitive* [*past:* حس يې کړ] to feel, sense

حسي hissí *Arabic* **1** substantial; tangible; capable of being felt **2** sentimental **3** sensitive **4** emotional

حسيات hissiját *m. Arabic plural* feeling, sensation; mood حربيه حسيات warlike spirit

حسبدل hisedә́l *denominative, intransitive* [*past:* حس شو] to be felt, sensed

حسين husájn *Arabic* **1** beautiful **2** *proper name* Husain

حسيني husajní red, pink (in names of flowers, birds) حسيني انگور ladies fingers (a variety of grape) حسيني قاز flamingo (the bird)

حشر hashr *m. Arabic* **1** assembly, assemblage, crowd, concourse (of people) **2** *religion* resurrection from the dead د حشر روځ Day of Judgement, Day of the Final Judgement

حشره hasharā́ *f. Arabic* [*plural:* حشري hasharé] *Arabic m.* [*plural:* حشرات hasharā́t] **1** insect, bug ضرر رسوونکي حشرات harmful insects **2** reptile

حشره خورونکي hasharā́ khvarúnkaj insectivorous

حشمت hashmát *m. Arabic* **1** splendor, magnificence; grandeur **2** a numerous retinue

حشمت مآب hashmatmā́b *Arabic* (His) Excellency (form of address of presidents of republics)

ح، بن *abbreviation* حربي ښوونځی military academy

حصار hisā́r *Arabic* **1** *m.* **.1** stronghold, fort, fortification **1.2** fence, wall بالا حصار Bala Hisar (fortress in Kabul) **1.3** encirclement, siege, blockade **1.4** roadblock **1.5** *figurative* difficulty, obstacle **2** *predicative* **.1** at bay (of an animal) **2.2** besieged, blockaded **2.3** *figurative* placed in a difficult position **2.4** limited, restricted

حصارول hisāravә́l [*past:* حصاري يې کړ] **1** to surround, besiege, blockade **2** to arrange a battle (for game); hunt (game) **3** to drive to the wall, into a corner **4** to detain, stop

حصاربدل hisāredә́l *denominative, intransitive* **1** to be encircled, be besieged, be blockaded **2** to be hunted down, be brought to bay (of game) **3** *figurative* to be driven into a corner **4** to be detained, be stopped

حصر hasr *m. Arabic* **1** limitation, hindrance **2** blockade حصر كول **a** to restrict, hinder **b** to blockade

حصص hisás *Arabic plural masculine plural of* حصه

حصول husúl *m. Arabic* **1** acquisition; receipt حصول كول *compound verb* **2** حصولبدل، حصولول *compound verb* ☞ production

حصولول husulavə́l [*past:* حصول يې كړ] **1** to obtain, receive **2** to take, seize

حصولبدل husuledə́l *denominative, intransitive* **1** to be obtained, be received **2** to be taken, be seized

حصه hissá *f. Arabic* lot, part, portion; share, allocation حصه كول to divide, divide into parts, distribute

حصه دار hissadár *m.* participant; co-owner, partner; shareholder

حصير hasír *m. Arabic* mat

حضار huzzár *Arabic masculine plural* **1** *of* حاضر **2** those present, the audience, the public

حضارت hazārát *m. Arabic* **1** settled (way of) life; location in (a certain) place **2** civilization, material culture **3** living, habitation, life

حضر hazár *m. Arabic* **1** settled way of life; life in one's own home **2** peacetime د حضر په وخت كښې in peacetime

حضرت hazrát *m. Arabic* **1** majesty, highness (form of address for monarchs and high-ranking persons); hazrét (title of ecclesiastical persons) حضرت عيسى Jesus Christ **2** presence

حضرت امام صاحب hazratimāmsáib *m.* Hazrat-Imam-Saib (city)

حضري hazarí *Arabic* **1** leading a settled life; urban **2** pertaining to peacetime *idiom* حضري فرقه *military* regular division

حضور huzúr *m. Arabic* **1** presence د چا په حضور كښې، د چا په حضور in someone's presence په خپل حضور سره personally, face-to-face حضور لرل to grant an audience حضور كښې منل to attend, honor with one's presence **2** *Eastern* Your Grace (form of address to a high-ranking personage) **3** *epistolary* You, Your Grace (in writing to high-ranking personages, instead of ستاسي په حضور (تاسي) I am reporting to Your Honor. *idiom* حضور! Yes Sir! عرض كېږي Sir!

حضوراً huzúran *Arabic* personally, in the actual presence of

حضوري huzurí چمن حضوري chamán-i Parade-ground (in Kabul)

حظ haz *m.* hazz *Arabic* [*plural:* حظونه hazúna *plural:* hazzúna *Arabic plural:* ظ huzúz] **1** pleasure; enjoyment; bliss, happiness خونه حظ! What a pleasure! حظ ځني اخيستل to enjoy, savor, receive pleasure **2** pleasant taste **3** scent

حفاري haffārí *Arabic* **1** dug up, dug out, excavated حفاري فعاليت excavations **2** *military* entrenching

حفاظت hifāzát *m. Arabic* guard, defense, protection د .... حفاظت كول to guard, defend, protect د ځان حفاظت كول to be guarded, be protected, be defended

حفاظتي hifāzatí protective, defensive, guard

حفر hafr *m. Arabic* digging, excavation, dug-up area

حفريات hafriját *m. Arabic plural* **1** excavations حفريات كول to excavate **2** work of sappers or military engineers د حفرياتو كنډك sapper battalion, engineer battalion

حفظ hifz *m. Arabic* **1** guard, defense, protection; custody, storage **2** memory **3** memorization, rote-learning حفظ كول *compound verb* **a** to guard, defend, protect **b** to memorize, learn by heart حفظ كېدل *compound verb* **a** to be guarded, be protected **b** to be memorized, learned by heart

حفظ الصحه hifz-us-sihá *f. Arabic* **1** hygiene; sanitation **2** public health

حفظ ما تقدم hifzmātaḳḳadúm *m. Arabic medicine* prophylactic

حفظيه hifzijá *f. Arabic* guard, guardianship; custody, storage

حفيد hafíd *m. Arabic* [*plural:* احفاد ahfād] grandson

حفيظ الله hafizullá *m. Arabic proper name* Hafizulla

حق haḳ haḳḳ *Arabic* **1** *m.* [*plural:* حقونه haḳúna *m. Arabic plural:* حقوق haḳúḳ] **.1** right, law د خپل سرنوشت د ټاكلو حق the right to self-determination د كار حق the right to work د حقوقو پوهنځی، فاكولته the Faculty of Law د بيان حق لرل to have the right to (free) speech د رای حق لرل to have the right to vote په ما دي حق to trample on someone's rights حقوق تر پښو لاندي كول دئ چه You make this request of me rightly. **1.2** belonging to by law حق ادا كول to give that which is determined, give that which belongs rightly by law **1.3** pay, emolument (for labor) **1.4** truth, rightness, justice دا ټول حق او حق ستا په جانب دئ You are right. حقيقت دئ This is the veritable truth. له حقه نه تېرېدل not to deviate from the truth **1.5** God حق تعالى God, the All-High **2** *attributive* **.1** belonging by right **2.2** veritable, real, genuine **2.3** correct, true دا كار حق او صحيح دئ This is true. This is correct. **2.4** just *idiom* حق نمك hák-i faithfulness, devotion **a** د چا په حق كښې in respect to, with reference to, relating to someone **b** for someone's sake د خدای حق punishment for a crime against the will of God, punishment for a crime against religion د چا ته د استاذ حق وركول to recognize or acknowledge someone as master or as teacher *idiom* **a** د چا حق پر ځای كول to give someone his due, reward someone according to his just deserts **b** to threaten someone **c** to punish someone, teach someone a lesson د چا حق ☞ څوك په خپل حق رسول پر ځای كول

حق [2] huḳ حق وهل to vomit, feel sick; belch

حقاً haḳḳán *Arabic* **1** in truth, actually, indeed **2** justly

حقارت haḳārát *m. Arabic* **1** disdain, scorn **2** humiliation چا ته په ډېر حقارت كتل **a** to scorn someone **b** to humiliate someone

حق حيران haḳariján ☞ حق حيران

حق الاجاره haḳḳ-ul-idzhārá *f. Arabic* rent

حق الانحصار haḳḳ-ul-inhisár *m. Arabic* monopoly, monopolistic law

حق الزحمه haḳḳ-uz-zahmát *m.* حق الزحمه haḳḳ-uz-zahmá *f. Arabic* honorarium; compensation for labor; wages

حق الله hakk-ul-láh *m. Arabic* **1** religious laws **2** crime against religion **3** punishment for a crime against religion

حق العبد haḵḵ-ul-á'bd *m. Arabic law* **1** civil laws **2** crime against the civil laws **3** punishment for crimes against the civil laws

حقانه haḵḵāná just, correct, right

حقاني haḵḵānī *Arabic* **1** just; impartial **2** divine

حقانيت haḵḵāniját *m. Arabic* **1** justice; impartiality **2** the rightness (of a judgment, etc.)

حقائق haḵāíḵ *m. Arabic* **1** *plural of* حقيقت **2** facts, reality حقائق پټول to conceal the facts, conceal the reality حقائق مينده كول to establish the facts

حقبين ، حق بين haḵḵbín just

حقبيني haḵḵbiní *f.* justice

حق پرست haḵḵparást حق پسند haḵḵpasánd just, fair

حق تلفي haḵḵtalafí *f.* flouting of rights; the infringement of rights حق تلفي كول to flout rights, trample upon rights

حق حيران haḵḵhajrán astonished, astounded, extremely surprised

حقدار ، حق دار haḵdár **1.1** having a right to something **1.2** lawful دوى هم د دې حق حق دار دي They have a legal right to this. ځان حق حق دار بلل to consider oneself in the right **2** owner, master

حقدوست haḵḵdóst *m.* owlet, *Athene noctua*

حق شناس haḵḵshinás **1** just **2** grateful, thankful

حق شناسي haḵḵshināsí *f.* **1** justice **2** thanks, grateful recognition

حق گوی haḵḵgój [1] speaking the truth, truthful

حق گويي haḵḵgoí [2] *f.* veracity

حقله haḵlá *f. regional* ☞ حقله د هغه كال په حقله in comparison with that year

حقمن haḵḵmán ☞ حقدار

حق ناحق haḵḵnāháḵ haḵḵnāháḵḵ willy-nilly

حقوق huḵúḵ *m. Arabic plural of* حق [1] **1**

حقوق شناس huḵuḵshinás ☞ حق شناس

حقوق شناسي huḵuḵshināsí *f.* ☞ حق شناسي

حقوقي huḵuḵí *Arabic* juridical حقوقي مشاور legal advisor

حقه haḵá haḵḵá [1] **1** legal, just; inalienable حقوق حقه legal rights حقه غوښتنه lawful demand **2** doubtless

حقه háḵḵa [2] *feminine singular of* حق [1] **2**

حقير haḵír *Arabic* **1** base, contemptible, paltry, pathetic **2** humble, obedience څوک د چا په نظر كښي حقير گرزول to lower someone in someone's eyes **3** modest, simple, rather poor

حقيرانه haḵirāná shameful, degrading

حقيري haḵirí *f.* **1** baseness, contemptibility, insignificance **2** humility, obedience **3** modesty; simplicity, poverty

حقيقت haḵiḵát *m. Arabic* [*plural:* حقيقتونه haḵiḵatúna *Arabic plural:* حقائق haḵaik] **1** truth, verity نسبي حقيقت *philosophy* relative truth مطلق حقيقت absolute truth حقيقت ويل to speak the truth هغه د حقيقت غل دئ He is hiding the truth. **2** essence, being, substance حقيقت دا دئ چه ... the fact is that ... مگر حقيقت بل و But the fact is otherwise. **3** actuality, reality, fact; real thing د حقيقت لرل realism, a realistic approach حقيقت خوښولو حس realism, a realistic approach حقيقت ميندل، حقيقت مونده كول to correspond to reality to effect, realize

---

د حقيقت په سترگو كتل to see in its true light له حقيقت څخه غاړه غړول to be ignorant of the fact

حقيقتاً haḵiḵátán *Arabic* actually, indeed

حقيقتبين haḵiḵatbín *m.* realist

حقيقةً haḵiḵátán *Arabic* ☞ حقيقتاً

حقيقي haḵiḵí **1.1** actual, factual, real **1.2** genuine, natural حقيقي تول natural wool حقيقي وزن the actual weight **2** *m. Arabic* [*plural:* حقيقيون haḵiḵijún] realist

حقيقي توب haḵiḵitób *m.* actuality, reality

حكاك hakkák *m. Arabic* carver; engraver

حكاكي hakkākí *f.* carving; engraving

حكام hukkám *m. Arabic plural of* حاكم

حكايت hikāját *m. Arabic* [*plural:* حكايتونه hikijātúna *m. Arabic plural:* حكايات hikājāt *f. Arabic* حكايه hikājá *plural:* حكايي hikājé *m. Arabic plural:* حكايات hikājāt] hikayat, story, tale, fable د يو شي څخه حكايت كول to relate a tale, tell a story about something و چاته حكايت كول to tell someone a story

هك پك hakpák ☞ حقله

حكله haklá *f.* ☞ حقله

حكم húkm húkəm [1] *m. Arabic* [*plural:* حكمونه hukmúna hukəmúna *Arabic plural:* احكام ahkám] **1** order, command, instruction; injunction حكم وركول to issue an order, issue an instruction **2** sentence, decision (of a court) د شرعي حكم a decision based on Shariat حكم ماتول to alter the decision (court) حكم كول to **a** to order, command; enjoin **b** to sentence, judge **c** په ... باندي حكم كول to give judgment concerning something **3** property, quality حكم لرل **a** to be equivalent, be equal to **b** to operate (a law) **4** basis د تجربي په حكم on the basis of experience **5** *proper name* Hukm *idiom* څه حكم دئ؟ As it will please you! چه څنگه ستاسو حكم وي! What is your command? What would you like? حكم نشته! No entry!; Forbidden! Not authorized!

حكم hakám [2] *m. Arabic sports* umpire, referee

حكم hikám [3] *m. Arabic* wise saying, aphorism

حكماً húkmán *Arabic* no doubt, of course

حكمت hikmát *m. Arabic* **1** wisdom; reason **2** ability **3** *proper name* Hikmat

حكمتي hikmatí **1.1** shrewd, adit **1.2** wise (of a saying, proverb) **2** *m.* shrewd person

حكم جان hukəm-dzhán *m. proper name* Hukumjan

حكمدار hukmdár *m.* sovereign, ruler, monarch

حكمران hukmrán *m.* chief, administrator

حكمراني hukmrāní *f.* authority, administration

حكم فرما hukmfarmá **1** ruling, ordering **2** effective (of a law)

حكم فرمائي hukmfarmājí *f.* **1** supremacy **2** effectiveness (of a law) حكم فرمائي كول **a** to rule **b** to be effective, be operative (of a law)

حكمنامه hukmnāmá *f. regional* order (written)

حكم منونكى hukm manúnkaj obedient, submissive

حکمي hukmí *Arabic* **1** not tolerating an objection, categorical **2** effective, effectual (of a medicine) *idiom* حکمي اتفاق unity of opinion

حکمیت hakamiját *m. Arabic* arbitration; mediation حکمیت تجارتي trade negotiations

حکومت hukumát *m. Arabic* **1** government د افغانستان حکومت *history* the Afghan government, the government of Afghanistan د افغانستان پادشاهي حکومت the Royal Afghan Government **2** region; province; district لوی حکومت district; province, state اعلی حکومت province **3** central authority, government د شوروي حکومت په کلونو during the years of Soviet power حکومت کول **a** to direct, govern **b** to rule **4** regime, social structure قومي حکومت societal structure **5** government *idiom* نظامي حکومت، لښکري حکومت، د د نظامي حکومت اعلان کول martial law *idiom* عسکري حکومت حال to declare martial law

حکومتي hukumatí **1.1** governmental **1.2** state **2** *f.* **.1** administrative region, province or district **2.2** region; province; district لویه حکومتي province

حکیم hakim *m. Arabic* **1** wise man; thinker, philosopher **2** *Eastern* tabib (i.e., native medical practitioner); physician **3** *proper name* Hakim

حکیمانه hakimaná **1.1** wise, reasonable **1.2** philosophical حکیمانه آثار philosophical writings **2** wisely; reasonably

حکیمي hakimí *f.* practice of traditional medicine

حل hal hall *m. Arabic* **1** solution, resolution (of a question, problem, etc.) د حل لاره میندل to find a way of solving a problem **2** solution, dissolution **3** analysis; investigation حل کول *compound verb* ☞ حلول ¹ حلبدل *compound verb* ☞ حل کبدل

حلاج haládzh *m. Arabic* carder, scutcher of cotton

حلاجي halādzhí *f.* separation of the cotton fiber from the seeds; carding, scutching or ginning of cotton حلاجي کول to separate the cotton fiber from the seed; to scutch, card or gin cotton

حلال halál *Arabic* **1** authorized **2** permitted, authorized (by Shariat or Islamic law) حلاله نفقه pure food (as contrasted to حرام)

حلالول halālavól *denominative, transitive* [*past:* حلال یې کړ] **1** to authorize, permit (according to Shariat or Islamic law) **2** to cut up, butcher (cattle, fowl duly observing the rules of Moslem tradition in the slaughter of animals) *idiom* ورته حلال کړي چرګان وو They were his devoted friends.

حلالبدل halāledól *denominative, intransitive* [*past:* حلال شو] **1** to be permitted, be authorized (according to Shariat, or Islamic law) **2** to be butchered (of cattle, fowl with due observance of the Moslem tradition in the slaughter of animals) **3** to be deprived of life, to perish

حلاوت halāvát *m. Arabic* sweetness, joy; enjoyment, pleasure

حلبه hulbá *f. Arabic* fenugreek

حلبي halabí *f.* tin-plate

حلبي halabí dzhoṛavúnkaj *m.* حلبي ساز halabisāz *m.* tin-smith حلبي جوړوونکی

حل طلب halltaláb debatable, requiring resolution

حلف haláf *m.* hilf *Arabic* oath, vow

حلق halḳ *m. Arabic* larynx; throat; gullet *idiom* د ظریف خان حلق تریخ دئ Zarif Khan suffered, Zarif Khan perished

حلقه halḳá *f.* **1** ring; hoop **2** circle, radius د الوتنو حلقه average radius of operation **3** circle (of people) د رقص حلقه dance circle *idiom* د سترګو لاندي حلقي *Eastern* circles around the eyes په . . . . د د هغه کتاب په حلقه about, concerning حلقه about this book

حلقه بگوش halḳabarósh *m.* servant, slave حلقه به گوش غلام servant, slave

حلم hilm *m. Arabic* softness (of character) حلم کول to demonstrate a soft manner, behave in a weak way

حلوا halvā *f. Arabic* halvah; sweets هره ورځ اختر نه وي چه څوک حلوا وخوري *saying literal* Every day is not a holiday on which halvah is eaten. *figurative* All good things must come to an end.

حلوایي halvāí [*plural:* حلواییان halvāijān] confectioner

حلول hallavól ¹ *denominative, transitive* [*plural:* حل یې کړ halvāijā́n] **1** to solve, resolve (a question, problem, etc.) **2** to dissolve **3** to break down, decompose **4** to analyze **5** to digest, assimilate (food)

حلول hulúl ² *m. Arabic* **1** lowering, hauling down **2** embodiment (of an ideal, etc.)

حلبدل halledól *denominative, intransitive* [*past:* حل شو] **1** to be solved, be resolved (of a question, problem, etc.) دا مسئله اوس حل شوي ده This problem has already been solved. **2** to be dissolved **3** to be (analytically) investigated **4** to be analyzed **5** to be digested, be assimilated (of food)

حلیم halím *Arabic* **1** gently, quiet; courteous civil **2** *m. proper name* Halim

حلیمه halimá *f. Arabic proper name* Halima

حلیه huljá *f. Arabic* **1** exterior, appearance **2** adornment; apparel, attire

حما hummā́ *f. Arabic* heat, fever, high temperature لکه داره حما typhus, spotted fever راجعه حما relapsing typhus

حماست hamāsát *m.* hamāsá *f. Arabic* valor in battle, courage

حماسي hamāsí *Arabic literary* **1** epic حماسي قصي epos **2** heroic

حماقت himāḳát *m. Arabic* stupidity; dull-wittedness; slow-wittedness

حمال hammā́l *m. Arabic* stevedore, porter

حمام hammā́m *m. Arabic* (public) bath حمام کول to bathe in a public bath

حمامک hammāmák *m.* natatorium, swimming-pool

حمامي hamāmí *m.* bath-attendant

حمایت himāját *m. Arabic* **1** defense, protection, custody د ځان self-defense د مبندو او اطفالو حمایت the protection of motherhood and infancy حمایت کبدل *compound verb* to be protected, be in protective custody **2** support; patronage; protective influence **3** *military* cover **4** *politics* trusteeship حمایت کول *compound verb* **a** to protect, have in care **b** to give support to; have under one's patronage; protect by means of one's influence **c** *military* to cover **d** *politics* to establish a trusteeship over

حمايتي اصول حمايوي himājaví patronal; guardian حمايتي economics protectionism د گمرک حمايتي محصولات protective tariffs

حمايه himājá *f. Arabic* ☞ حمايت

حمايتي وي himājaví ☞ حمايه وي

حمد hamd *m. Arabic religion* eulogy; thanksgiving

حمل¹ halm *m. Arabic* 1 conveyance; transporting; transportation; dispatch 2 pregnancy; conception *idiom* يو شى په بې عقلى حمل کول to ascribe or attribute something to thoughtlessness

حمل² hamál *m. Arabic* 1 lamb, young ram 2 *astronomy* Aries, the Ram (the constellation) 3 Hamal (the first month of the solar year; March-April)

حمل ونقل haml-u-háķl *m.* 1 transport 2 conveyance; transporting د حمل ونقل موټر transport, troop-ship حمل ونقل بېړى transportation vehicle (for transport of goods and personnel) د حمل ونقل موټرونه transportation vehicles

حمله hamlá *f. Arabic* [*plural:* حملې hamlé *plural:* حملات hamalất] 1 attack, offensive, offense, assault متقابله حمله counterattack پر چا حمله راوړل to assault someone, attack someone هوايي حمله aerial attack د چا څخه حمله کول **a** to repulse, take away from someone **b** to steal from someone حمله شروع کول **d** to go over to the attack توپو تر حملې لاندي راتلل to undergo artillery fire حمله کول **a** to carry out an attack, mount an offensive, attack **b** to affect (of an illness) حملې اچول **a** to attack **b** to throw oneself, fling oneself over something تر حملې لاندي کول to subject to an attack 2 *figurative* blow of fate, shock

حمله آور hamlaāvár attacking, assaulting, advancing

حمله يي hamlaí shock, assault, striking a decisive blow حمله يي اردو shock army

حميت hamiját *m. Arabic* 1 feeling of honor; a feeling of personal dignity 2 high-minded ardor, zeal 3 patriotism

حميت مند hamijatmánd *official* the title (form of address) of a colonel

حميد hamíd *Arabic* 1 praiseworthy, worthy of praise 2 *proper name* Hamid

حميد الله hamidullá *m. Arabic proper name* Hamidullah

حميده hamidá *Arabic* 1 *feminine singular and plural of* حميد 2 *f. proper name* Hamida

حنا hinā hinná *f. Arabic* henna

حنابند hinābánd hinnābánd *m.* cloth wet with a henna solution (used to color hair, hands)

حنائي hināí hinnāi color of henna, reddish-brown

حنجره handzhará *f. Arabic* larynx, throat کښتنى حنجره the windpipe وربنېنمينه حنجره pleasant voice

حنجره يي handzharají *linguistics* pharyngeal

حنظل hanzál *m. Arabic* colocynth, bitter apple, citrellus colocynthus

حنفي hanafí *Arabic* pertaining to the Hanif sect or Hanafi

حنيف haníf *m. Arabic* Orthodox (fundamentalist) Moslem

حوا havắ *f. proper name* Eve

حوادث havādís *Arabic masculine plural of* حادثه

حواس havắs *m.* haváss *Arabic masculine plural of* حاسه

حواشي havāshí *Arabic* 1 *masculine plural of* حاشيه 2 suite, retinue

حواصل havāsíl *Arabic masculine plural of* حاصل 2

حوالات havālất *Arabic masculine plural* 1 *of* حواله 2 *regional* jail, lockup

حوالجات havāladzhất *Arabic masculine plural of* حواله 3

حوالدار havāldár *m.* 1 *regional* sergeant 2 non-commissioned officer (in the infantry)

حوالداري havāldārí *f.* 1 *regional* position of sergeant 2 position of NCO (in the infantry)

حواله havālá *f. Arabic* [*plural:* حوالي havālé *Arabic m. plural:* حوالات havālất] 1 handling, delivery (e.g., of a package, baggage) 2 transfer of property or of the rights to property 3 *Arabic* [*plural:* حوالي havālé *plural:* حواله جات havāladzhất *plural:* حوالجات havāladzhất] *trade* transfer of payment; money order; grant (of funds); bill of exchange حواله اخيستل **a** to take an assignment **b** to receive money 4 reference to a source 5 *regional* arrest, imprisonment حواله کول *compound verb* **a** to deliver (e.g., a package, baggage) **b** to transfer (property, etc.) **c** to assign (a room in a hotel, etc.) **d** to transfer (money and payment) **e** *regional* to arrest, imprison **f** *figurative* to deal a blow يو ښه سوک يې ور حواله کړ He dealt him a heavy blow with his fist. حواله کېدل *compound verb* **a** to be delivered (e.g., of baggage, package) **b** to be transferred (of money, payment) **c** to be arrested, be imprisoned حواله ورکول **a** to give an assignment **b** to refer to … *idiom* د هغه حواله لا سره شوه He laughed all the more.

حواله اخيستونکى havālá akhistúnkaj 1 *present participle of* حواله اخيستل 2 *m. trade* 1. executor of an assignment 2.2 recipient of money

حواله دار havāladár *m.* ☞ حوالدار

حواله نامه havālanāmá *f.* promissory note

حواله ورکوونکى havālá varkavúnkaj *present participle of* حواله ورکول حواله ورکوونکى شخص guarantor, principal (person empowered by another to act for him)

حوائج havāídzh *Arabic masculine plural of* حاجت

حوت hut *m. Arabic* 1 kind of large fish 2 *astronomy* Pisces (the constellation) 3 Hut (the 12th month of the solar year; February-March)

حوره húra *f.* حوري hurí *f. Arabic* houri د جنت حوره houri (heavenly maiden)

حوزه havzá *f. Arabic* 1 district, region 2 territory square, plaza

حوصله havsilá havsalá *f. Arabic* 1 endurance, patience, self-possession; firmness لويه حوصله لرل Be patient! حوصله لويه کړئ! to have patience; be very patient, be self-possessed; be very firm د چا حوصله تنگول I'm losing patience. حوصله مي پسته شوي ده to discourage **2** stomach, craw (of a bird)

حوصله دار havsiladár patient, self-possessed; firm

حوض háuz *m. Arabic* [*plural:* احواض ahvā́z] reservoir, water-storage basin; pond

حوضچه hauzchá *f.* small water-storage basin, reservoir

حوضه hauzá *f.* **1** *geography* basin د دونبس حوضه the Don Basin **2** ☞ حوزه

حولي havlí *f.* حوېلي havelí *f. Arabic* residence, house, building; country estate

حى ¹ haj hajj *Arabic* living, live

حې ² he *f.* the name of the letter ح

حيا hajā́ *f. Arabic* shame, shyness, timidity, bashfulness حيا کول to be bashful

حيات hajā́t *m. Arabic* life, existence د حيات طرز way of life او ممات مسئله question of life and death

حياتي hajātí *Arabic* **1** vital; full of life حياتي مهمي مسئلي vitally important problems **2** live, alive حياتي کيميا biochemistry

حياتيت hajātijāt *m. Arabic* vitality, viability, tenacity of life

حياسوز hajāsóz repulsive; obscene حياسوز کنزل *Eastern* foul language

حيث hajs *m. Arabic* **1** relation له اقتصادي حيثه in economic relationships **2** له هره حيثه in all respects په حيث in the capacity (of), in the role (of) له دي حيثه چه ... د يو شي in view of that ... حيث لرل to take something into consideration

حيثيت hajsijāt *m. Arabic* **1** prestige, reputation, dignity د حيثيت ساتنه to preserve one's prestige **2** په حيثيت in the capacity of, in the role of د ديپلومات په حيثيت in the capacity of a leader د مشر په حيثيت in the role of a diplomat حيثيت لرل to carry out someone's role

حيدر hajdár *m. Arabic* **1** lion **2** *personal name* Haidar, Hayder

حيدرآباد hajdarābā́d *m.* Haidarabad (city and a former principality in India, the name of several population centers)

حيران hajrā́n *Arabic* amazed, surprised, stunned حيران پاته شو He was surprised ... زه دي خبري ته حيران يم چه I am surprised at that ...

حيرانتيا hajrāntjā́ *f.* surprise, amazement و چا ته په حيرانتيا کتل to look at someone with surprise

حيرانول hajrānavól *denominative, transitive* [*past:* حيران يې کړ] to surprise, stun, astonish

حيراني hajrāní *f.* **1** ☞ حيرانتيا **2** surprise, unexpectedness خوشحاله حيراني pleasant surprise

حيرانېدل hajrānedól *m. denominative, intransitive* [*past:* حيران شو] to be amazed, be surprised, be astounded, be stunned

حيرانېده hajrānedá *m. plural* amazement, surprise

حيرت hajrát *m. Arabic* ☞ حيرانتيا د حيرت وړ worthy of surprise, surprising حيرت راوړل to surprise, amaze

حيض hajz *m. Arabic medicine* monthlies, menstruation

حيضه hajzá *f.* woman at the time of her menstruation

دپر حيف دئ چه ... حيف hajf *Arabic* **1** حيف دئ! It's a pity! It grieves me very much that ... It's a great pity that ... **2** useless, good-for-nothing

حيله ¹ hilá *f. Arabic* shrewdness, trickery حيله کول to employ trickery

حيله ² hilá only just, only حيله اوس only now, just now

حيله باز hilabā́z *m.* ☞ حيله ساز

حيله بازي hilabāzí *f.* ☞ حيله سازي

حيله حواله hila-havālá *f. regional* trickery, wiles; cheating, intrigue

حيله ساز hilasā́z *m.* shrewd person; cheat

حيله سازي hilasāzí *f.* shrewdness; cheating

حيله گر hilagár *m.* ☞ حيله ساز

حيله گري hilagarí *m.* ☞ حيله سازي

حيله ناک hilanā́k shrewd; crafty

حين hin *m. Arabic* [*plural:* احيان ahjā́n] time, season, period

حيوان hajvā́n *m. Arabic* [*plural:* حيوانان hajvānā́n *Arabic plural:* حيوانات hajvānā́t] animal, livestock; cattle د في راس حيوان حاصل productivity of cattle د حيواناتو تربيه animal husbandry

حيوانداري hajvānparvārí *f.* ☞ حيوان پرواري

حيوان توب hajvantób *m.* brutishness, baseness

حيوانداري hajvāndārí *f.* animal husbandry; cattle-raising

حيوان شناس hajvānshinā́s *m.* zoologist

حيوان شناسي hajvānshināsí *f.* zoology

حيوان لرونکی hajvān larúnkaj *adjective* cart, pack

حيواني hajvāní *Arabic adjective* animal حيواني پوست hide of an animal حيواني آفات forage **a** حيواني اعاشه damage (to agriculture) caused by insects, birds and rodents **b** illnesses of farm animals حيواني توليدات production resulting from animal husbandry

حيوانيت hajvānijāt *m. Arabic* ☞ حيوان توب

حيوي hajaví *Arabic* **1** vital; physiological **2** vitally important

خ

خ khe **1** the twelfth letter of the Pashto alphabet **2** the number 600 in the abjad system

خاب khāb *m.* ☞ خوب

خاپ khāp *m.* ☞ خپ

خاپوړي khāpótsi *f. plural* ☞ خاپوخي

خاپوړت khāpoṛát *m.* reptile, serpent

خاپوړن khāpoṛón creeping, crawling خاپوړن حيوانات serpents, snakes

خاپوړي khāpóṛi *f. plural* creeping, crawling; crawling over خاپوړي کول، خاپوړي وهل to crawl, creep; crawl over

خاتر khātór *m.* ☞ خاطر

خاتم khātím *m. Arabic* **1** seal; sealring **2** mosaic, inlay

خاتمه khātimá *f. Arabic* **1** end, termination, completion, conclusion خاتمه مېندل to be ended, be terminated, be completed, be closed, be adjourned (of a meeting) و ... ته خاتمه ورکول to end, terminate, complete; close, adjourn (i.e., a meeting) **2** *grammar* ending

خاته khātә́ *m. plural* **1** lifting, rising, ascent **2** climbing up, clambering up **3** rise, rising, د لمر خاته sunrise **4** mounting, entrainment, embussment (on some form of transport)

خاته khātә́ *imperfect of* ختل

خاته khā́ta *f.* book

خاتيغ khātíz خاتيز khatíz ☞ ختيغ

خاټول khāṭól *m.* **1** tulip **2** *proper name* Khatol

خاچونی khāchúṇaj *m. dialect* nightingale

خاخی khākhә́j *f. Eastern* ☞ بناخی

خادم khādím *m. Arabic* [*plural:* خادمان khādimā́n *plural:* خدام khuddā́m *plural:* خدم khadám] servant, attendant آلي خادم robot

خادمه khādimá *f. Arabic* maid, (female) servant; domestic

خادمه khādəma *f.* خادمۍ khādəmә́j *f.* mountain hadama (a kind of lizard with a bristly back); vampire, vampire bat

خاده khādá *f.* **1** pole, stake (2.5 cm. thick) **2** pole or wooden tablet at the head of a grave; grave marker **3** [*plural:* خادي khādé] fence

خار khār *m.* thorn, spine خار وهل **a** to spear, stick **b** *figurative* to prevent; thwart; harm, injure

خار khār *m. Eastern* ☞ بنار

خارانۍ khārānáj *m.* south wind

خارپوټه khārpótsa *f.* ☞ خارپوټي

خارج khāridzh *Arabic* **1.1** external, surface له خارج نه from without **1.2** foreign, external, alien, pertaining to other countries than one's own **2** *m.* foreign parts د خارجه څخه from abroad په خارج کښي abroad, overseas

خارجول khāridzhavә́l *denominative, transitive* [*past:* خارج یي کړ] **1** to exile, depart **2** to exclude, discharge, fire **3** to evacuate **4** *mining* to mine, extract معدن خارجول to mine ore **5** to extract (e.g., natural) gas

خارجه khāridzhá *Arabic feminine plural of* خارج *combining form* د خارجه وزير Minister of Foreign Affairs د خارجه امورو وزير, د خارجه چارو وزارت Ministry of Foreign Affairs

خارجي khāridzhí *Arabic* **1.1** external, exterior خارجي صورت external appearance **1.2** strange, outside, alien خارجي شيان foreign admixtures (in wool etc.) **1.3** foreign, external, overseas, pertaining to that which is beyond the borders of a country خارجي سياست external policy خارجي تجارت foreign trade خارجي مالونه import خارجي پولونه foreign currency **2.1** *m.* خارجي پيسي foreigner **2.2** *history* Harijit (a member of a Moslem sect which did not recognize Ali as the successor of Mohammed)

خارجېدل khāridzhedә́l *denominative, intransitive* [*past:* خارج شو] **1** to be exiled, be deported **2** to be dropped, be dismissed, be fired **3** to be evacuated **4** *mining* to be mined, be extracted **5** to be processed, be extracted (e.g., gas)

خارجېده khāridzhedә́ *m. plural* **1** exile, deportation **2** exclusion, dropping, dismissal, discharge **3** evacuation **4** mining, extraction د کانو خارجېده mining of ore **5** processing, extraction (e.g., gas)

خار خوټۍ khārkhuṭә́j *f.* ☞ خار خوړی

خارخور khārkhór *m.* puncture vine, *tribulus terristris*

خارخورۍ khārkhvuṛә́j *f.* **1** babbling, murmuring **2** gurgling, seething خارخورۍ وهل **a** to babble, murmur **b** to gurgle **3** *dialect* river, stream **4** gulf, abyss, whirlpool **5** broken terrain, rough terrain

خاردار khārdā́r thorny, spiny

خارش khārísh *m.* **1** mange **2** itch خارش کول to scratch, scratch deeply

خارښت khārә́kht *m.* **1** mange خارښت اخيستل to be inflected with mange **2** itch خارښت کول to itch, feel itchy

خارښتول khārəkhtavә́l *denominative, transitive* [*past:* خارښت یي کړ] to itch, scratch

خارښتي khārəkhtí **1** itchy; mangy, afflicted with mange خارښتي بزه mangy she-goat **2** lustful man **3** scoundrel

خارښتبدل khārəkhtedә́l *denominative, intransitive* [*past:* خارښت شو] to get itchy, itch

خارق العاده khārik-ul-'ādá *Arabic* exceptional, unusual خارق العاده پيبنه unusual event, extraordinary incident

خارک khārák *m.* meat-grinder frame

خارکوف khārkóf *m.* Kharkov (city)

خارگيري khārgirí *f.* thorn-hedge enclosure or fence

خارو khāró *f.* ☞ بنارو

خارو khārú *m.* **1** spur (of a rooster) **2** comb (of a rooster)

خارو khā́ro *oblique plural of* خار

خارونۍ khāronә́j *f. Eastern* ☞ بنارونۍ

خاره khārá *f.* virgin land, undeveloped land خاره دښته bare steppe جنگ په خاره ښه دئ نه په شودياره *proverb* It is better to conduct a war on the steppe than on cultivated land.

خاري khārí *Eastern* ☞ بناري

خارپوټي khārpótsi *f. plural* **1** crawling on all-fours خارپوټي کول to crawl on all-fours **2** crawling along په خارپوټو تلل **a** to crawl, crawl on all-fours **b** to crawl along, move by means of crawling

خازه khāzá **1** fading, withering خازه کېدل to fade, wither **2.1** *f.* blade of glass **2.2** trifle, bit, bagatelle

خازه khāzá *f.* ☞ خاده

خاښخاښ khāgkhā́g *m.* ☞ خاشخاش

خاسه khāsá *f.* muslin

خاسه khāsá ☞ خاصه خاسه ډوډۍ special high-quality bread

خاشاک khāshák *m.* kindling; bruswood

خاشخاش khāshkhā́sh *m.* poppy-seed د خاش خاش غوټه، خاش خاش head, pod or capsule of poppy

خاشنه khāshnә́ خاشنه khāshnә́ *m. plural regional* ☞ خرشين

خاشه khāshá *f.* **1** pinch **2** crumb **3** piece (e.g., meat) **4** particle of something **5** litter, trash د جارو خاشي، خاوري او خاشي litter, trash **6** a speck (in the eye) *idiom* په خاشه نه اينبول to idle خاشي ماتول to impede, hinder something

خاشه khāshá *f.* skin ailment of children

خاشه پنا khāshapṇā́ avaricious, stingy, niggardly

خاشه کیڼ khāshakáẖ *m.* native practitioner who will heal the illness

خاص khās khāss *Arabic* **1** special, particular, private, individual خاص اثر special influence په هر خاص حال کښي in each particular instance په ځينو خاصو وختو کښي in special cases په خاص خاصه خوا private rooms ډول، په خاصه توګه especially, particularly (in a bath-house) **2** only, solely خاص بيا especially, in particular *idiom* خاص و عام *proper name* خاص نوم to know the common people, the elite and the lowly

خاصاً khāssátán *Arabic* especially

خاصره khāsirá *f. Arabic* side لگن خاصره lagán-i *anatomy* pelvis

خاصكر khāskár *regional* especially

خاص كنړ khās kunáṛ *m.* Khas-kunar (district on the middle reaches of the Kunar River)

خاصم khāsím *Arabic* hostile, inimical

خاصمانه khāsimāná hostile, inimical خاصمانه حرکت hostile act

خاصه khāssá *Arabic* **1.1** special, particular; private, individual **1.2** superlative, excellent; choice **1.3** privileged **2** *f.* [plural: خاصي khāssé *m. Arabic plural:* خواص khavvás] properly, native quality; peculiarity; distinguishing characteristics فطري خاصي natural quality, innate quality *idiom* خاصه سپاهيان *regional history* life-guards خاصه ململ muslin, guaze

خاصه دار khāssadár *m. regional* mercenary soldier from various Afghan tribes (who guarded roads, mountain passes, serving under the British and furnishing his own rifle)

خاصه وردار khāssavardár *m.* feudal bodyguard

خاصيت khāsiját *m. Arabic* [plural: خصائص khasāís] **1** peculiarity; innate quality, quality **2** merit, virtue **3** advantage, benefit

خاضع khāzí *Arabic* obedient, docile

خاطر khātír *m. Arabic* **1** thought, meditation **2** memory له خاطره ايستل to forget something په خاطر کښي ساتل to keep in memory, remember **3** soul, spirit خاطر يي ناارام و He was worried. خاطر جمع د هغه خاطر ښه جمع شو to be calm; be unworried, not to be upset کول He calmed down. **4** disposition, favor; attention (paid) to someone *idiom* په خاطر... د For God's sake! د خدای خاطر وکړه someone *idiom* ... له خاطره for the sake of, because of د چا د خاطره تربدل to grieve someone, distress someone

خاطرات khātirāt *Arabic masculine plural of* خاطره [1]

خاطرآزرده khātirāzurdá upset, sad

خاطرپريشان khātirpreshán worried, distressed; upset

خاطر جمع khātirdzhám *Arabic* calm; confident; composed اوسه! Be calm!, Don't worry!

خاطر جمعي khātirdzham'í *f.* calmness; confidence; composure; spiritually peaceful د چا ته خاطر جمعي ورکول to calm someone down

خاطر خواه khātirkhā́h **1** desired; to one's liking; pleasant **2** satisfactory

خاطر خواهي khātirkhā́hí *f.* **1** desireability; pleasantness **2** satisfaction

خاطردار khātirdár ☞ خاطرخواه

خاطرداري khātirdārí *f.* ☞ خاطرخواهي

خاطرمانده khātirmāndá ☞ خاطر پريشان

خاطرنشان khātirnishán **1** imprinted in memory, remembered **2** favorite

خاطره khātirá [1] *f. Arabic* [plural: خاطري khātiré *m. plural:* خاطرات khātirāt] **1** recollection, reminiscence زاړه خاطرات recollections, reminiscences of the past **2** impression **3** thought, meditation

خاطره khātíra [2] *oblique singular of* خاطر

خاغلی khāghálaj *Eastern* ☞ ښاغلی

خاک khāk *m.* **1** land, ground **2** earth, dust *idiom* خاک په سر submissive, gentle

خاکپا khākpá *f.* **1** earth; ground under one's feet **2** nothing; nothingness

خاکرېز khākréz *m.* Khakrez (settlement near Kandahar)

خاکسار khāksár **1** obedient, mild, gentle **2.1** *m. proper name* Khaksar **2.2** *history* member of the Moslem Youth Organization Khaksar (in India)

خاکساري khāksārí *f.* obedience, gentleness

خاکسترداني khākistardāní *f.* **1** ash-tray **2** ash-pit, ash-bin (of a furnace, stove)

خاکستررک khākistarák *m.* mildew (a disease of grapevines)

خاکنوري khākkhorí *f.* labor; work for hire خاکنوري کول to work for wages

خاکلی khākálaj ugly, unattractive

خاکنا khāknā́ *f.* خاکنای khāknáj *m. geography* isthmus

خاکه khāká *f.* **1** coal dust **2** dust **3** broken rice (unfit for use) **4** sketch, rough drawing

خاکي khākí [1] **1** grey-green, khaki; brownish-grey **2** dusty **3** ☞ *idiom* خاکي برالبدل خاکسار **a** to be with calf; in yean (ewe); in foal **b** to give birth out of wedlock

خاکی khākáj [2] *m.* **1** ditch **2** pit, hole (used in a game)

خاکيان khākiján *m. plural* one of the dervish brotherhoods

خاګاه khāgáh د خاورو خاګاه کول **a** to destroy; annihilate **b** to ravage خاورو خاګاه کېدل **a** to die, perish; be annihilated **b** to be ravaged

خاګلی khāgálaj *Eastern* ☞ ښاغلی

خاګينه khāginá *f.* scrambled egg, omelet

خال khāl [1] *m.* **1** birthmark, naevus **2** beauty spot (on the cheek) **3** speck, spot **4** gold ornament worn on the brow *idiom* د چيچک خال وهل to vaccinate (against smallpox)

خال khāl [2] *m. agriculture* scraper

خالپوڅي khālpótsi *f.* خالپوري khālpóri *f. plural* ☞

خال خال khāl-khál **1** spotted, specked **2** rarely; here and there; in places

خالد khālíd *Arabic* **1** eternal, immoral **2** *m. proper name* Khalid

خالدار khāldár **1** birthmarked, having a naevus **2** spotted, specked

خالص khālís *Arabic* **1** pure, genuine, real, natural زر خالص pure, red gold خالص مس pure copper خالصي شيدي whole milk **2** sincere, pure-hearted

خالصانه khālisāná ☞ خالص [2]

خالصه khālisá *f.* *Arabic* **1** state property **2** fallow land, virgin, uncultivated land دا کار د خالصی دل نه و *proverb* *literally* This isn't kasha from Khalisa. (Khalisa is a settlement near Peshawar) *figurative* This is not an easy matter.

خالق khālíķ *m.* *Arabic* **1** Creator, Maker (an epithet of God) **2** *proper name* Khalik, Khaliq

خالکوبي khālkobí *f.* vaccination (against smallpox)

خاله khālá *f.* aunt, auntie (maternal)

خالي khālī *Arabic* **1.1** idle, idling; free, unemployed خالي کول to idle; free, liberate څای خالي کول *a* to vacate a place *b* to honor, greet someone by rising خالي کېدل to be idle; become free; become empty **1.2** pure خالي اوبه pure water **1.3** deprived of something **1.4** unpopulated **1.5** خالي ورځ Saturday **2** only, just خالي دومره ... It is only that ... **3** *m.* *regional* Saturday *idiom* خالي خبره ده چه *a* خالي لاس تلل with empty hands *b* unarmed, weaponless to go away empty-handed, get nothing for one's pains *b* to earn nothing ميدان خالي کول to flee the field of battle, abandon the battlefield

خالي توب khālitób *m.* ☞ خالي والی

خاليگاه khāligá *f.* خاليگا khāligáh **1** lacuna, gap, blank **2** break **3** interruption (e.g., in elecrical service) **4** *anatomy* cavity

خالي والی khālivә́laj *m.* **1** emptiness **2** unemployment

خام khām **1** raw, unripe, immature خام مواد raw materials **2** unstable, not fast (of dyestuff, color) **3** *figurative* inexperienced, unskilled **4** of un-kiln baked brick, adobe **5** idle; good-for-nothing دا خام فکر دئ مګر This is an idle dream.

خامتا khāmtә́ *f.* coarse calico *idiom* زره سپينه خامتا کېدل to fast; be greedy for food

خامتايي khāmtāí cotton خامتايي توته cotton cloth

خامخا khāmakhá willy-nilly, whether one wishes it or not

خامزوری khāmazúraj *m.* kind of medicinal plant

خامسوز khāmsóz خام سوز uncooked, raw

خامک khāmák *m.* **1** ☞ خامک دوزی **2** shoots of a vine, suckers of a vine خامک وهل to prune the suckers from a vine

خام کار khāmkә́r awkward, unskilled; inexperienced

خام کاري khāmkārí *f.* awkardness, lack of skill, inexperienced

خامکدوزي khāmakdozí *f.* sewing done with untwisted threads

خام لېتی khāmletә́j *f.* **1** thin gruel **2** poultices خام لېتی ايښودل to apply poultices

خاموش khāmósh taciturn, silent; quiet, still خاموش طبيعت taciturnity خاموش! خاموش! *regional* Shut up! Be still!

خاموشانه khāmoshāná **1** taciturn, silent; dumb **2** taciturnly, silently

خاموشي khāmoshí *f.* silence, stillness, quiet هري خواته خاموشي وه Silence reigned everywhere. خاموشي لوی کمال دئ *proverb* Silence is golden.

خامول khāmavә́l *denominative, transitive* [*past:* خام يي کړ] to breach (trust, confidence)

خامه khāmá *f.* **1** pen, reed pen **2** *botany* pistil

خامه khāmá earthen, dirt خامه سړک dirt road

خامه کاري khāmarkārí *f.* road-bed (dug out in the preparitory work for road-building)

خامي khāmí *f.* **1** unripeness, immaturity **2** inexperience, unskillfulness **3** lack of completion, insufficiency

خان کول ، خان khān *m.* **1** khan (leader of a tribe or tribal family) که خان یې په یاران یې، که یاران *compound verb* to become khan کېدل نه وي، خاوري د بيابان یې *proverb* If thou art khan, it is thanks to your henchmen; Without thy henchmen thou would'st be the dust of the desert. چه پخپله څان ته خان وائي، خان نه دئ *proverb* Because thou callest thyself khan, thou will not be khan. د ، دا چه ورانه ده *proverb* Everything bad comes from the khan. خانه ده **2** landowner, feudal chief; prince **3** khan (honorific title joined with the proper name) احمد خان Ahmed-Khan

خان آباد khānābád *m.* Khanabad (city)

خانتما khāntamá **1.1** proud; arrogant, haughty, pretentious **1.2** exceedingly greedy, avaritious **2** *m.* **.1** dreamer, visionary **2.2** conceited person

خانجی khāndzháj *m.* lust; sensuality

خانچه khānchá *f.* ☞ خوانچه

خان خاني khānkhāní *f.* feudal segmentation, territorial fragmentation

خاندان khānadán *m.* **1** family, family group; home, hearth **2** dynasty, tribe

خانداني khānadāní **1** family, familial **2** dynastic, tribal

خاندور khāndór *m.* خاندوره khāndóra *f.* blazing campfire, flame

خانده khānda *imperative of* خندل

خاندي khāndi *present tense of* خندل

خانزاده khānzādá *m.* son of a khan

خانشين khānashín *m.* Khanashin (district)

خانصاحب khānsāhíb *m.* Lord Khan; Khan-Sahib (title in India)

خانقه khānaķá *f.* خانكا khānķá *Arabic* **1** monastery **2** cell (ecclesiastical); cloister (of a Sufi, an aesthetic religious monk)

خانگره khángra *f.* dandruff, scruff

خان گل khāngúl *m.* *proper name* Khangul

خانم khānə́m *f.* خانوم khānúm Madam, Mrs.

خانمان khānumán *m.* environment of a home

خان ملا khānmullá *m.* chief mullah

خانمه khanə́ma *f.* **1** Madame **2** *polite* spouse, wife

خانواده khānavādá *f.* family; tribe

خانول khanavә́l *denominative, transitive* [*past:* خان یې کړ] to designate a khan; choose a khan

خان و مان khān-u-mә́n *m.* ☞ خانمان

خانه khāná *f.* **1** residence, house; room **2** compartment (of a cupboard, table) **3** matchbox **4** column; (table, page) **5** *combining form* بالاخانه balakhaná superstructure, attic garret *idiom* خانه آباد! I wish you success!

خانه khә́na *vocative and oblique singular of* خان

خانه آبادي khānaābadí *f.* well-being; easy circumstances, prosperity

خانه بدوش khānabadósh nomadic خانه بدوش قبايل nomadic tribes

خانه پری khānapurí entered (onto a list)

خانه خانه khāna-khāná consisting of compartments (cupboard, table, desk, etc.)

خانه خراب khānakharáb 1 ruined, destroyed 2 unfit, shallow (of a person) 3 خانه خراب! The Devil take you!

خانه خرابي khānakharābí f. ruin, destruction

خانه دار khanadár m. head of a house, head of a family

خانه داري khānadārí f. household management

خانه زاد khānazád born of a slave-woman

خانه سامان khānasāmán m. man in charge of property (in a home); logistical manager (in an enterprise); superintendent (of a building)

خانه نشين khānanishín sitting at home; retired, not working

خانه واده khānavādá f. ☞ خانواده

خاني 1 khāní f. 1 history د خيوي خاني Khivi Khanate 2 reign of a khan 3 position of khan 4 title of khan 5 authority, sovereignty

خاني 2 khānáj m. khanaj (measure of weight equal to 8 "kabul siras" or 56 kg.)

خانيڅی khānídzaj خاني خاني khāne-khāné compartment (a desk, cupboard) څلور خانيڅي الماري cupboard with four compartments

خانېدل khānedól denominative, intransitive [past: خان شو] to become khan, be khan

خانيز khāníz ☞ خانيڅی 1

خاڼی khā́ṇaj m. gopher

خاواک khāvák m. Khavak (a pass) د خاواک کوتل the road which passes through the Khavak

خاوال khāvál m. 1 pit, hollow 2 pen, fold (for sheep, on the steppe or the mountains)

خاور khāvár m. east; the east

خاور گاړی khāvargā́ṛaj m. quarry (where clay for pottery production is obtained)

خاوره khā́vra f. 1 soil, land مړه خاوره infertile land د متّه خاوره clay خاوري تبل petroleum 2 country, land, province 3 territory 4 usually plural خاوري khā́vrí dirt; dust خاوره الوزول پر to raise dust سر خاوري بادول a to sprinkle dust on the head (in grief, distress) b to regret خولۍ ته خاوري اچول a to endure, keep silence b to be satisfied with little د کوڅي خاوري چاڼول not to leave a stone upon request د پنبو خاوري خوړل a to die b to be in extreme want خاوري کول a to harm someone b to calumniate someone compound verb a to turn to dust b to destroy خپل ژوند خاوري کول to ruin one's life ځان خاوري کول to try hard, strive with all one's might خاوري کېدل compound verb to die, perish يي پر سر شوی د چا د پنبو خاوري کېدل Things didn't go his way. He is unlucky. to subordinate oneself to someone, be under somebody's thumb خاوري په خوله پوري مښل to pretend to be poor, feign poverty څوک پر خاورو نه درلودل to be without a penny, be without means پر خاورو لوېدل to do someone much harm; trip someone up اچول to suffer; fall into a distressed state د چا رزق په خاورو لړل a to inflict damage upon someone b to play a dirty trick on someone خاورو ته تلل to die, become dust خاورو ته سپارل to commit to the earth, bury د خاورو څخه پورته کول a to extricate someone from need or poverty;

render assistance (to a poor man, to one in dire need) b to caress, comfort someone د خاورو څخه ولاړېدل a to rise up from the ground b figurative to stand on one's feet, begin to live well د خاورو څخه ولاړېدل او پر ايرو کښېنستل literally to arise from the dust and fall in the ashes figurative to miscalculate

خاوري 1 khā́vri plural of خاوره

خاوري 2 khā́vre intensifier Eastern هغه به په دې خاوري پوه شي څه! Can he really understand this!

خاوری 3 khāvráj m. 1 forest; thickets 2 green clay (used in dying cloth)

خاوري پېژندل khā́vri pezhandól m. plural soil science

خاورين khāvrin 1 earthen; clay خاورين تبل kerosene خاورين لوبني clay vessel 2 (mixed) with sand, clay (of grain) 3 turbid (of water) 4 figurative mild, meek idiom خاورين چينجي earthenworms, rainworms

خاوند khāvónd m. 1 master, owner, possessor د کور خاوند master of the house 2 malik (i.e., tribal leader) 3 proprietor; he who owns something; he who has some quality or other افغانستان د بري اقليم خاوند دئ Afghanistan is characterized by a continental climate. د د شادى خاوند a man قلم خاوندان writers د پيسو خاوند a rich man د ژبي خاوند who is coping (successfully) with fate the possessor of د رتبو او مقامونو خاوندان a tongue (descriptive of an eloquent man) high ranks د څومره عمر خاوند دئ؟ How old is he? 4 man who is the head of a family 5 God خاوند بلل to appeal to God

خاويار khāvjár m. caviar, roe (of fish)

خايدک khājdák m. ☞ خيدک

خائېدل khāedól intransitive Eastern ☞ ښائېدل

خائسته khāistá Eastern ☞ ښايسته

خائن khāín Arabic 1 perfidious 2 m. traitor, betrayer

خائنانه khāinānā treacherous

خايه khājá f. testicle

خباثت khabāsát m. Arabic 1 dishonesty; venality 2 corruptness

خباروسک khabárovsk m. Khabarovsk (city)

خبث khubs m. Arabic malice; insidiousness, perfidy

خبر khabár Arabic 1 m. .1 piece of news, news, report, information تازه خبر fresh piece of news, fresh news, news وروستني خبرونه the latest news د هرات خبر دئ They communicate the news from Herat. خبر اخيستل to receive news, find out; be informed خبرونه راتللl to be in receipt of (of communications, information) خبر رسول to communicate, report راورل to communicate, notify; inform, transmit information د خبر رسولو آژانس news service, telegraph agency 1.2 notice, notification خبر ورکول و چاته to notify, give notification to someone 2 attributive knowledgable, well-informed خبر يم I know ... هر څوک په دي باندي خبر دئ چه ... خبره نه Everybody knows that ... هر څوک په دي ورباندي خبر دئ چه ... I don't know (says a woman) له خبرو مجالسو څخه from informed circles

خبرال دوتنه khabrál dūtána f. computer science log file

خبرتوکي khabártóki computer science f. plural data

خبرتیا khabartjá f. 1 knowledge, possession of information سرسري او ناقصي خبرتیاوي superficial knowledge دی هیڅ زما د تلو څخه خبرتیا نه لري He knows nothing about my trip. 2 notification, information

خبرتیاوو پته khabártjiāū patá computer science f. information bar

خبرڅانى khabartsā́naj m. scandalmonger

خبردار khabardár Arabic 1.1 careful, attentive خبردار کول to warn someone خبردار اوسه!، خبردار! Be careful! 1.2 knowledgable, well-informed 2 Look out! Stand aside!

خبرداري khabardārí f. 1 carefulness 2 knowledge, possession of information

خبر ډله khabár ḍála f. د خبرونو ډله də khabarūnū́ḍála computer science newsgroup

خبررسان khabarrasā́n m. correspondent

خبررساني khabarrāsaní f. information د خبررسانۍ آژانس news agency, telegraph agency

خبرشنوي khabarshinaví gossip

خبرغل khabarghál m. scandal-monger

خبرغلا khabarghlā́ f. piece of scandal

خبرغوړی khabarghvágaj submissive, meek

خبرگیر khabargír m. informer, spy

خبرلوڅ khabarlóts khabarlúts ☞ خبرلوڅى [1]

خبرلوڅى [1] khabarlótsaj khabarlútsaj 1 loquatious, talkative 2 eloquent

خبرلوڅي [2] khabarlutsí f. khabarlotsí 1 loquaciousness, talkativeness 2 eloquence 3 noise 4 expressiveness (e.g., eyes)

خبرلوس khabarlós ☞ خبرلوڅ

خبرلوسي khabarlosí f. ☞ خبرلوڅي [2]

خبرمزی khabarmázaj m. telephone

خبرول khabravál khabaravál denominative, transitive [past: خبر یې کړ] 1 to communicate, inform, notify, make known (to); give information (to) د چا خان خبرول to be acquinted with something له حاله خبرول to inquire about someone 2 to invite (to a wedding, as a guest, etc.)

خبرونه khabaravána f. 1 communication, notice, notification, provision of data 2 invitation (to a wedding, as a guest, etc.)

خبره khabára f. 1 word خبره کول to speak, utter a word یوه خبره کوم Here is what I want to say. د چا په خبره لوبدل to interrupt someone د خلي نه مي خبره هم نه اوښه اوږده شوه I was rambling (speech) سوه وتى Eastern And I couldn't say a word 2 [plural: خبري khabári] words; conversation, talk په خبرو خبرو preface لمري خبري موبر لندي خبري during the conversation, at the time of the talk زموږ خبري کول a to speak I دا خبري کول ضروري بولم چه ... consider it necessary to say ... b to have a talk, converse تر خبري Not one word د ده د جرأت خبري له خولو نه دي لوبدلي تبردل to forget of his valor crossed his lips. 3 matter, question, problem; something مگر دومره خبره ده چه ... The thing is that ... لویه خبره داده چه ... The big problem is that ..., the main thing is that

دا خبره د ... This is the essence of the matter. اساسي خبره دا ده ... زه درته یوه خبره کوم It is necessary to say that ... غواړم وړ ده چه to tell you something. څه کم زیات د اتیا کالو خبره ده It was eighty years ago. په خبره سرخلاصبدل to comprehend, understand مونږ باید په دي خبره ځان پوه کړو This is what we must understand. idiom خبره تیرول to submit to دا څه خبره ده؟ What does this mean? د چا سره خبره جگول to pick a quarrel with someone خبري بي کول، لکي یي You did not agree with me. خبره دي نه منله کړې کول literally to talk well, but to fall flat at the end

خبري khabári plural of خبره

خبري اتري khabári-atári f. plural 1 negotiations اقتصادي خبري اتري negotiations on economic questions 2 conversation, talk خبري اتري سره کول to converse, have a talk 3 discussion, debate, disputation د خبرواترو په نتیجه کښې a as a result of negotiations b as a result of conversations or talks c as a result of discussion or debate خبري اتري کول a to conduct negotiations b to have a conversation, talk c to discuss, debate, analyze, review

خبرجال khabarjál 1 loquacious, talkative 2 m. .1 spokesman for some group's views 2.2 representative (e.g., of an enterprise of some sort) 2.3 radio-announcer 2.4 correspondent idiom خبريال غړی correspondent-member (of an academy, society)

خبريالي [1] khabarjālí f. 1 news agency 2 representation

خبريالى [2] khabarjāláj 1 garrulous, gabby 2 m. scandal-monger

خبردل khabredál khabaredál denominative, intransitive [past: خبر شو] 1 to find out, be in the know, be well-informed, be informed ټول ورباندي خبربري Everyone knows about that. 2 to be invited (to a wedding, as a guest, etc.) 3 to notice, remark تر څو هغه ځان نه خبردو چه ... He did not suceed in collecting himself.

خبرده khabredá m. plural knowledge, state of well-informed

خبري مبري khabári-mabári f. plural ☞ خبري اتري [1]

خبریه khabarijá Arabic خبریه جمله grammar narrative sentence

خبط khabt m. Arabic 1 thoughtlessness, inability to think things through; stupidity 2 false step, blunder

خبیث khabís Arabic 1.1 disgusting, nasty; vile 1.2 malignant 2 m. Evil Spirit, Evil One

خبیر khabír Arabic well-informed, knowledgeable خبیر مجلسونه informed circles

خپ khap 1 m. .1 cicatrice, scar 1.2 typographic error 1.3 blemish, spot 2.1 hidden, secret خپ خپ secretly, on the sly 2.2 unclear, indistinct idiom خپ وهل to swipe, steal

خپاره khpará masculine plural & oblique singular of خپور

خپت khupát dialect ☞ بخت [2]

خپرتیا khpartjá f. ☞ خپورتیا

خپرنه khparána f. ☞ خپرونه

خپرول khparavál 1 denominative, intransitive [past: خپور یې کړ] to spread; disperse; dispel 1.2 to open wide; unfold 1.3 to spread, disperse, circulate (rumors, publications, etc.) 1.4 to transmit, communicate, announce 1.5 to publish, make public, issue, print

1.6 to settle (in a new place) **1.7** to extend, spread out **2** *m.* plural ☞ خپرونه

خپرونه khparavə́na *f.* **1** dispersion; dispersal **2** opening; unfolding **3** distribution, spreading, circulating (of rumors, publications, etc.) **4** transmission, communication, announcement **5** publication, publishing, issue, printing, press **6** settling, settlement **7** extending

خپره khpará *feminine singular of* خپور

خپرېدل khparedə́l *denominative, intransitive* [past: خپور شو] **1** to disperse, go away خلک خپاره سول The people dispersed. **2** to be opened, be unfolded **3** to be spread, be circulated, be distributed (of rumors, publications, diseases, etc.) **4** to be transmitted, be communicated, be announced **5** to be published, be issued, be printed **6** to be settled **7** to be spread out, be extended (e.g., of clouds)

خپرېدونکی khparedúnkaj *present participle of* خپرېدل ناروغتيا infectious disease

خپرېده khparedə́ *m.* plural ☞ خپورتيا

خپر khapə́r *f.* khəpə́r **1** paw **2** foot, sole of foot **3** hand (with fingers spread) *idiom* د چا سره خپړي لګول **a** to fight with someone **b** to quarrel with someone خپړي سره ورکول to contend with, measure one's strenght

خپر khapə́r *m.* whirlwind, tornado

خپړه khapə́ṛa *f.* khə́pə́ṛa ☞ خپر

خپسکه khəpə́ska *f.* خپسه khapə́sa *f.* ravings; nightmare خپسي نيول to torment (of a nightmare)

خپاک khapák *m.* stonesmith, masonry smithy

خپاکه khapə́ka *f.* ☞ خپکه

خپکی khapakáj *m.* hypocrite, two-faced person

خپکی khapakə́j *f. Eastern* nightmare خپکی نيول to torment (of a nightmare)

خپګان khapagán *m.* **1** sadness, depression, melancholy **2** discomposure, grief په ژوند کښي ډېري خوشحالي او ډېر خپګانونه وي There are many joys and sorrows in life. خپګان کول **a** to grieve, be depressed, be melancholy **b** to be discomposed, be grieved **3** discord, quarrel ☞ خفقان

خپګي khapagí *f.* discomposure, grief

خپل khpə́l **1** *possessive pronoun* one's own خپل کور يي دئ He has his own house. په خپل to the end of one's life د خپل عمر تر اخره پوري له خپله انده، په خپل among themselves, etc. مينځ کښني، په خپله کښني involuntarily, unwittingly **2** *m.* [plural: خپلوان سره، د خپل ځان دپاره khpə́lvān] relative نژدي خپل close relative لیري خپل distant relative **3** native, blood, by birth ستا خپل ورور څه نومېږي؟ What is your blood brother's name?

خپل چاري khpə́lčắṛaj *m.* خپل چاروکی khpə́lčắrúkaj *m.* khpə́lčáraj *m.* **1** egoist; mercenary person **2** obstinate person; wilful person

خپل سر khpə́lsār obstinate, self-willed; wilful

خپل سرتوب khpə́lsartób *m.* obstinacy, wilfulness; capriciousness

خپل سری khpə́lsáraj **1** foolish (of a person) **2** independent

د خپلګلوی khpə́lgalaví *f.* **1** relationship **2** friendship مناسبات friendly relations

خپلواک khpə́lvák independent, self-governing; autonomous; free

خپلواکي khpə́lvākí *f.* independence, condition of being self-governing; autonomy; freedom د خپلواکي اختر Independence Day holiday کورنی خپلواکي autonomy

خپلواکی khpə́lvắkaj ☞ خپلواک

خپلوالی khpə́lvắlaj *m.* ☞ خپلګلوي

خپلوان khpə́lvān **1** plural ☞ خپل **2** *attributive* related خپلوانه ښځه (female) relative

خپلول khpə́lavə́l *denominative, transitive* [past: خپل يي کړ] **1** to take possession of, seize; conquer **2** to get, receive; obtain استقلال خپلول to receive independence **3** to acquire (e.g., new lands) **4** to assimilate, memorize **5** to bring together, link; have at one's disposal **6** to pardon

خپلولي khpə́lvalí *f.* خپلوي khpə́lví *f.* **1** relationship **2** friendship خپلولي کول **a** to become related to **b** to be friends with; become friends with د خپلوی بنا اېښودل to start a friendship **3** friendliness

خپله khpə́la *feminine singular of* خپل

خپله khpə́la *Eastern* ☞ پخپله

خپلېدل khpə́ledə́l *denominative, intransitive* [past: خپل شو] **1** to become a relative of **2** to be brought together, be friends

خپم khpam **1** killed, smashed **2** *m.* scab, mange

خپنځ khpandz streching out on the ground

خپنځل khpandzə́l *transitive* [past: و يي خپانځه] to lay out; throw down on the ground

خپند khpand ☞ خپنځ

خپند khpand *m.* large ball or skein of cleaned wool or cotton

خپندل khpandə́l *transitive* ☞ خپنځل

خپ و چوپ khpuchúp quietly, secretly

خپوثي khapótsi *f.* plural ☞ خاپوړي

خپور khpor **1** *f.* خپره khpará خپاره khpārə́ *m.* plural خپري khparé *f.* plural **1.1** dispersed; scattered **1.2** uncovered; unfolded **1.3** spread, circulated (of rumor, publications, etc.) **1.4** transmitted, communicated, announced **1.5** published, issued; printed **1.6** settled **1.7** extended, streched out **2** soldier, warrier (in an extended line of riflemen)

خپورتيا khportjá *f.* خپوروالی khporvắlaj *m.* **1** dispersion; dispersal **2** opening; unfolding **3** spreading, circulation (of rumors, publications, etc.) **4** transmission, communication, announcement **5** publishing, issuing (of a publication) **6** settling (in a new place)

خپورول khporavə́l *denominative, transitive* ☞ خپرول

خپورېدل khporedə́l *denominative, intransitive* ☞ خپرېدل

خاپوړي khapóṛi *f.* plural ☞ خاپوړي

خپه khpə *m.* plural tinder, touchwood ☞ خو

خپه khapá ☞ خفه

خپه khpa *f. Eastern* ☞ پنبه

خپه khə́pa *feminine singular of* خپ

خپی khapáj scarred, having a cicatrice

خپی khapáj f. 1 rope (of cotton, wool, hemp) 2 lead, rein, halter

خت khət m. shirt

ختا khatá f. ☞ خطا

ختامي khitāmí Arabic concluding ختاميه وينا a concluding word

ختای khatáj m. history China

ختايي khatāi f. ☞ خطايي

ختر khatár m. ☞ خطر

خترناک khatarnák ☞ خطرناک

ختل khatál intransitive [present: خيژي past: وخوت] 1 to arrise, rise; climb up, clamber up غره ته ختل to climb a mountain, ascend a mountain پر ځينو باندي ختل to climb the stairs 2 to rise (of celestial bodies) لمر را وخوت the sun rose 3 to break out, swell up (of a pimple); appear, develop (of an abscess, a boil) 4 to attack; seize 5 to weigh approximately دا غنم به څونه وخيژي؟ How much do you think this wheat will come to? 6 to turn out to be د هغه څخه هزره He proved to be a shallow person. idiom د کار څخه يي سری وخوت He concluded the work. په امتحان کښي ښه وخوت گوټي وختي passed the examination.

ختم khatm m. Arabic 1 m. .1 end, termination, conclusion, completion 1.2 ☞ ختمه 2 predicative concluded, completed

ختمول khatmavál denominative, transitive [past: ختم يي کړ] to end, conclude; finish, complete; terminate (e.g., a meeting)

ختمه khatmá f. Arabic reading from the Koran (on the seventh, or fortieth day after death)

ختمبدل khatmedál denominative [past: ختم شو] 1 to be ended, be concluded, be completed; be terminated (e.g., a meeting) 2 grammar to terminate (in)

ختمبده khatmedá m. plural termination, conclusion, completion; closing (e.g., of a meeting)

ختن khután m. Khotan (city, district)

ختنه khatóna f. ☞ خاته

ختنه khatná f. ختنه سوري khatnasurí f. Arabic religion circumcision, the ritual of circumcision ختنه کول compound verb to perform the rite of circumcision

ختو kható dialect imperfect of ختل

ختو kható oblique plural of خاته

خته khóta f. 1 rag 2 ☞ خت

ختي kháti f. plural ☞ جوړه 3

ختی khətáj f. undershirt

ختيز khatídz ختيز khatíz 1 eastern 2 m. east; the East ليري ختيځ the Far East منځنى ختيځ the Middle East نژدي ختيز the Near East

خټ khə́t m. 1 hill; knoll 2 bank (of clouds)

خټ khut m. ☞ خوت

ختبه khatbá m. ☞ ختگر

ختبل khatbél m. sediment; dregs

خټخټ khutkhút m. ☞ خوت په خټ خټ خندل to laugh loudly, guffaw

ختک khaták 1 m. plural the Khattaki (tribe) 2 m. Khattak (tribesman)

ختک khaták m. [plural: ختک khatók plural: ختکان khatakán] stink-bug, darkling-beetle

ختک khaták m. ختکان khatakán unripe melon (used as an ingredient in marinades)

ختکنی khutkanáj m. boiler

ختکنی khutkanáj f. regional pot; small pot, jar

ختکول khutkavál transitive regional ☞ خوتول

ختکی khatakáj m. melon دوه ختکي په لاس نيول khatakí proverb literal to take two melons in one hand figurative to bite off more than one can chew

ختکی khətkáj m. small knoll; hillock

ختکبدل khutkedál intransitive regional ☞ خوتکبدل

ختکي والا khatakivālá m. melon seller

ختگر khatgár m. bricklayer; mason

ختگري khatgarí f. bricklaying, masonwork

ختمار khatmár m. ☞ ختگر

ختماله khatmālá f. ختموبی khatmúkhaj m. trowel (for plaster, mortar)

ختنکه khutnáka f. saucepan

ختوبی khatóbaj m. turbid water

ختولن khatolán muddy, dirty

خټه kháta 1 f. ختي kháti usually plural .1 mud لار ختي ده the road is very muddy په ختو لړلئ soiled, muddied 1.2 also khúta clay پخه خته clay used for mortar or plaster چيني خته kaolin د تناره refractory clay ختی کول to plaster; to make a pise wall 1.3 figurative ferment, leaven; colloquial spirit 1.4 figurative origin, descent هغه خته بارکزی دئ His descent is from the Barakzai (tribe). 2.1 thick, viscous; sticky 2.2 turbid; dull په ختو غورزول to shame, discredit په ختو کښي مبنتل to stick, get stuck in

خټه khúta f. ☞ خوته

ختی khətáj m. corn-stubble

ختي kháti plural of خته 1

ختين khatín pise, adobe

خج khadzh m. foam

خج khadzh m. grammar accent

خجالت khadzhālát m. Arabic shame; inhibitation, embarrasment; shyness خجالت کښل to be shamed; be inhibited, be embarrassed

خجسته khudzhastá khudzhistá happy, blessed

خجل khadzhíl Arabic 1 shamed 2 bashful; inhibited, shy

خجو khadzhó m. proper name Hadjo

خج والا khadzhvālá ☞ خجي

خجونکی khadzhúnkaj 1 skittish, fast (of a horse) 2 rebounding (of a ball) 3 with a waddling gait

خجي khadzhí grammar stressed

خچپچ khachpách fine, crumbled, in crumbs

خچپچول khachpachavál denominative, transitive [past: خچپچ يي کړ] to crumble

خچپچبدل khachpachedál denominative, intransitive [past: خچپچ شو] to crumble, break into small pieces

خچخچونی khachkhəchúnaj *m.* 1 tumbling 2 reversing, reversal 3 ricocheting تلل په خچخچونی a turn summersalts b to turn over c to ricochet

خچر khachór *m.* mule

خچړه khachóra *f.* 1 pus, suppuration (in the eyes) 2 wax (in the ears)

خچل khəchól *transitive* [past: خاچه وئ] to fling, shove

خچن khəchón 1.1 slimy 1.2 muddy, dirty 2 *m.* guttersnipe, slut

خچوکی khəchúkaj *m.* morsel, small piece (of meat)

خچه khácha *f.* 1 bouncing (of a ball) 2 falling short, shortfall (bullet, etc.) خچه کېدل a to bounce (a ball etc.) b to fall short (a bullet etc.)

خچی مچی گوته khácha gúta *f.* خچه گوته khácháj gúta *f.* khácháj-macháj gúta *f.* little finger

خڅله khadzóla *f.* 1 trash, rubbish; garbage 2 [*plural:* خڅلي khadzóli] waste, waste products

خڅوکی khadzúkaj *m.* 1 crack, crevice (in a floor) 2 small quantity of something

خڅله khatslá *f.* hangnail

خڅوڅکی khatsútskaj *m.* 1 morsel 2 crumbs 3 chaff

خڅوزه khatsúza *f.* خڅوزی khatsúzaj *m.* 1 mini-morsel 2 bit

خڅوسکي khatsúski *m. plural* sawdust

خخول khakhavúl *denominative, transitive Eastern* ☞ بنخول

خخبدل khakhedól *denominative, intransitive Eastern* ☞ بنخبدل

خدا khudá *m.* ☞ خدای

خداداد khudādā́d God-given

خدای زده khudāzdá ☞ خدای زده

خدام khuddā́m *Arabic masculine plural of* خادم

خدانخواسته khudānakhāsta *regional* May God spare us! God forbid!

خداوند khudāvánd *m.* ☞ خدای

خدای khdā́j khudā́j *m.* God خدای کول that to appeal to God خدای بللل if God grants, with God's help خدای دي نه خبر! God knows! خدای اوبنه idiom May God forbid! کړي! *zoology* praying mantis خدای میاشت Radjab (month) د خدای شرمول to disgrace oneself

خدای بنبلئ khudā́jbaḳhólaj 1 *m.* the deceased 2 deceased, passed away

خدای پاماني khudā́jpāmāni *f.* خدای په اماني khudā́j-pə-āmāni *f.* farewell, parting د چا سره خدای پاماني کول to say farewell, part with someone

خدای خه khdā́jkhá khudā́jkhá *vice* خدای خبر ☞

خدایرحم khudā́jráhm *m. proper name* Khudajrahm

خدای زده khdā́jzdá khudā́jzdá disgraced, unworthy

خدای رو khdā́jgú khudā́jgú khudā́jgó khudā́jgó Oh God!; Oh! Oh!

خدای شته khdā́j shta khudā́j shta I swear to God!; As God is my witness!

خدای ناخواسته khudā́j nākhāstá May God forbid!

خدای نظر khudā́jnazár *m. proper name* Khudajnazar

خدایه khudā́ja O God!; Oh Lord!

خدایي khudā́i 1 divine 2 *f.* divinity *idiom* خدمتگار *regional history* Red Shirt

خدرزي 1 kidərzí *m. plural* the Khidarzai (one of the Yusufzai tribes) 2 kidarzáj *m.* Khidarzai (tribesman)

خدشه knadshá *f. Arabic* fear, alarm

خدعه khad'á *f. Arabic* deception, shrewdness, strategm حربي خدعه military strategm *idiom* نظر ته خدعه ورکول optical illusion

خدم khadám *m. Arabic plural* ☞ خادم

خدمت khidmát *m. Arabic* [*plural:* خدمتونه khidmatúna *Arabic plural:* خدمات khidamā́t] 1 service خدمت دولتي خدمت ، ملکي خدمت government service عسکري خدمت military service 2 attendance upon; helpfulness; services و چاته خدمت کول، د چا خدمت کول a to serve someone; be of service, be helpful to someone b *figurative* to beat up, thrash someone 3 service, good deed, favor ستاسي زما I am at your service (I am there to serve you) خدمت ته حاضر یم یو خدمت به نه وکي؟ Will you not do me a favor? 4 merit (or services deserving merit) برجسته خدمتونه outstanding services 5 care (for the sick) خدمت کول a to serve b to provide services; service c to be helpful, do favors d to care for (the sick) 6 formula of respectful address or mention ... ما د هغوی په خدمت دا په خدمت کي I courteously said to His Honor that ... عرض کړئ و چه یی ولاړ سو He respectfully stood up before them.

خدمتگار khidmatgā́r *m.* servant, attendant د خدای خدمتگار *regional history* a Red-shirt

خدمتگاره khidmatgā́ra *f.* serving-girl; attendant (female)

خدمتگاري khidmatgā́ri *f.* 1 service 2 services (e.g., municipal); good-turn, kindness, help

خدمتگذاري khidmatguzārí *f.* services

خدمتي khidmatí 1 assiduous; attentive 2 assisting, serving

خدنگ khadáng *m.* 1 silver poplar 2 arrow of silver poplar 3 ☞

خندق khadokhél 1 *m. plural* the Hadokhejli (tribe) 2 *m.* Hadokhejl (tribesman)

خدیجه khadidzhá *f. Arabic proper name* Hadija (particularly the name of Mohammed's wife)

خيل khaḍál *m.* sheep-dog; wolfhound

خيل بيل khaḍal-baḍál quite healthy

خر khar *m.* [*plural:* خره khrə] ass, donkey پر خره سپور، په خره سپور stride a donkey په خپل خره سپور دئ او نه د خره سپرلی riding a donkey خني را کبنته کبري *literal* He sits upon his donkey, and will not descend. *figurative* His is stubborn. He is headstrong. په خره سپرول to sit upon a donkey د خره پر لکی سپربدل a to be despairing *literal* to set upon a donkey's tail *figurative* to be importunate د دوو خرو دانه نه وبشل *literal* to be unable to divide corn between two donkeys *figurative* to be a fool خپل خر تر ختو پوری ایستل *figurative* to take care of oneself *literal* to draw one's own donkey out of the mud b to shame, put to shame *idiom* په خبره کبني خر کډول، په خبره کبني خر گوډول to rudely interrupt someone

خر² khər *m.* 1 snore 2 whine خر وهل a to snore b to whine

خراب kharā́b *Arabic* **1** bad خرابه هوا bad weather **2** destroyed **3** spoiled

خرابات kharābā́t *Arabic masculine plural of* خرابه¹

خراباتي kharābātí *m.* debauche

خراب تراب kharā́b-tarā́b **1** spoiled **2** utterly destroyed كول **a** to spoil **b** to destroy utterly خرابي ترابي جامي old clothes, worn-out clothing

خرابتيا kharābtjā́ *f.* ☞ خرابي¹

خرابوالى kharābvā́laj *m.* ☞ خرابي¹

خرابول kharābavə́l *denominative, transitive* [*past:* خراب يې كړ] **1** to spoil; make worse **2** to destroy **3** to break *idiom* پيسې خرابول to squander (money) *idiom* دماغ خرابول to fatigue (the brain)

خرابه¹ kharābá *f. Arabic* [*plural:* خرابې kharābé *Arabic m. plural:* خرابات kharābā́t] **1** ruins, remains **2** desert

خرابه² kharā́ba *feminine plural of* خراب

خرابي¹ kharābí *f.* **1** deterioration د هوا خرابي **a** worsening of the weather **b** bad weather **2** spoiling **3** worthlessness **4** destruction **5** accident **6** ruination **7** unpleasantness, misfortune دا پيدا شوې خرابي ده چه ... the trouble is that …

خرابي² kharā́bi *feminine plural of* خراب

خرابېدل kharābedə́l *denominative, intransitive* [*past:* خراب شو] **1** to become worse; be spoiled **2** to be destroyed **3** to be broken **4** to have an accident **5** *figurative* to be insulted, be hurt, be injured

خرابېده kharābedə́ *m. plural* ☞ خرابي¹

خراپ kharā́p khə́rāp ☞ خراب

خراپول kharāpavə́l *denominative, transitive* ☞ خرابول

خراپېدل kharāpedə́l *denominative, intransitive* ☞ خرابېدل

خراج khirā́dzh *m. Arabic history* tax, duty, tribute

خراجي khirādzhí *f. history* taxable land

خراد kharrā́d kharā́d *m. regional* lathe

خرادي¹ kharrādí kharādí *f.* **1** machining **2** metal turning work, lathe work خرادي كول *compound verb* **a** to machine **b** *figurative* to sharpen, hone (e.g., style) خرادي كېدل *compound verb* **a** to be machined **b** to be sharpened, be honed (e.g., of style)

خرادي² kharrādí *m. regional* ☞ خراط

خراړه khrā́ṛa *f.* black-breasted sand-grouse

خراسان khurāsā́n *m.* Khorasan

خراساني khurasānáj **1** Khorasanish **2** *m.* native of Khorasan

خراش kharā́sh *m.* **1** scratch, abrasion **2** laceration, ragged wound

خراشكي khrā́shkaj khərāshkaj *m.* phlegm ويني لرونكي خراشكي bloody phlegm

خراشول kharāshavə́l *denominative, intransitive* [*past:* خراش يې كړ] **1** to scratch **2** to lacerate, tear

خراط kharrā́t *m. Arabic* lathe-operator

خراطي kharrātí *f.* lathe operation د خراطي دستگاه lathe

خرافات khurāfā́t *m. Arabic plural* fable

خرام khirā́m *m. regional* branch, bough

خربانه kharbā́nə *plural of* خربه and خربون

خربشو kharbəshú kharbishó خربشوى kharbəshúj kharbishój *m.* **1** wild boar, wild hog **2** *abusive* swine

خربشويه kharbəshója *f.* swine

خربنه kharbaná *f.* donkey-driver (female)

خربون kharbún *m.* [*plural:* خربانه kharbā́nə *m.* خربه kharbá [*plural:* خربانه kharbā́nə donkey-driver, ass-drover

خرپ khrap *m.* خرپا khrapā *f.* **1** crack, crash خرپ او خروپ crackle, crackling **2** crunch

خرپانډى kharpā́nḍaj *m.* dormouse (rodent)

خرپت kharpát *m.* powdered medicine خريت كول to lick powdered medicine from the hand

خرپل khrapə́l *transitive* ☞ خرپول

خارپوڅى kharpótsa *f.* خرپوسه kharpósa *f.* ☞ خرپوڅه

خرپول khrapavə́l *transitive* [*past:* و يې خرپاوه] **1** to beat, beat up, thrash someone **2** to eat (e.g., carrots) with a crunching noise, crunch

خرپهار khrapəhā́r *m.* خرپى khrapáj *m.* **1** crack, crackle **2** crunch **3** tread, tramp

خرپېدل khrəpedə́l *intransitive* [*past:* خرپ شو] **1** to be beat up **2** to crack, crackle **3** to crunch

خرتوب khartób *m.* stupidity, ignorance

خرت khrát khərát fat, weighty, stout, portly; fatty

خرتول khraṭavə́l *denominative, transitive* [*past:* خرت يې كړ] to make fat, fatten up

خرته¹ kharā́ta *f.* large turban of a mullah

خرته² khraṭá *m.* [*plural:* خرتان khraṭā́n] rascal, swindler

خرتى khərtáj *m.* foam

خرتيت khartít *veterinary* glanders

خرتېدل khraṭedə́l *denominative, intransitive* [*past:* خرت شو] to grow fat, get heavy, become stout

خرجدال khardzhadā́l *m.* **1** Antichrist **2** villain

خرجگجگلى khardzhəgdzhəgalə́j *m.* kind of children's game

خرجيگه khardzhíga *f.* bag (used for carrying a load on an ass) خرجگه، خرجيگه

خرچ khrach *m.* **1** crack, crackle **2** crunch **3** gnashing, grinding; squeak

خرچول khrəchavə́l *transitive* [*past:* و يې خرچاوه] **1** to crack, crackle **2** to crunch **3** to gnash, grind; squeak

خرچهار khrəchahā́r *m.* خرچى khracháj *m.* **1** crackle, crackling **2** crunch **3** gnashing, gritting; squeak

خرچېدل khrəchedə́l *intransitive* [*past:* وخرچېد] **1** to crack, crackle **2** to crunch **3** to gnash, grind, squeak

خرڅ¹ kharts **1** *m.* **.1** expense, expenditure, spending, outlay, expenses د لاري خرڅ travel expenses په خرڅ رسېدل to be consumed, be used up **1.2** sale, selling دا آس د خرڅ دئ؟ Is this horse for sale? **1.3** tribute; tax, duty **2** *predicative* **.1** spent, expended **2.2** sold

خرڅ² khrats *m.* ☞ خرچ

خرڅاوو khartsāvú *m.* spendthrift, wastrel; embezzler

خرڅښت khartsákht *m.* expenditures, expenses, outlays دونه خرڅښت دئ؟ کار په څه What are these expenses for?

خرڅ گیر khartsgír *m.* customs duty collector

خرڅلا khartslá *f. dialect* خرڅلان khartslán *m. dialect* خرڅلاو khartsláv *m.* خرڅلون khartslún *m.* sale, disposal by sale, selling

خرڅوړی khartsóraj *m.* 1 rags, tatters 2 dust cloth 3 *regional* short person

خرڅول khartsavól *denominative, transitive* [*past:* خرڅ یې کړ] 1 to sell, vend پر چا خرڅول to sell to someone پر خارجه مملکتو خرڅول to sell abroad 2 to expend, spend

خرڅون khartsún *m.* sale, selling, vending د خرڅون بازار seller's market د خرڅانه دپاره for sale

خرڅونکی khartsavúnkaj 1 *present participle of* خرڅول 2 *m.* merchant شیدي خرڅونکی milkman, one who sells milk

خرڅه khártsa *feminine singular of* خرڅ 1 2

خرڅي khartsí 1 extravagant 2 *m.* spendthrift, wastrel

خرڅېدل khartsedól *denominative, transitive* [*past:* خرڅ شو] 1 to be sold 2 to be spent, be expended

خرڅېده khartsedó *m. plural* 1 sale, selling د خرڅېدو بازار seller's market 2 expenditure, spending, expense, expenses

خرخاري kharkhārí *f.* 1 jumps, leaps 2 stupidity, ignorance

خرخچ kharkhóch *m. no plural form* staircase

خرخشه kharkhəshá *f.* خرخښه kharkhəkhá *f.* 1 noise, disturbance 2 quarrel 3 doubt, vacillation خرخشه کول a to make a noise, cause a disturbance b to quarrel c to doubt, vacillate 4 riff-raff

خرخوړی kharkhóraj *m.* gulf, abyss

خرخول kharkhvól *m.* shears (for clipping sheep)

خردځال khardadzhál *m.* خرجدال

خردماغ khardamágh khardimágh 1 stupid 2 stubborn

خرډک kharḍók *m.* خرډیک kharḍík *m.* scopalamine, *scopolia praealta* (a medicine plant)

خرړار khrərá̄r *m.* خرړاری khrəráraj *m. regional* snore

خرړول khrəravúl *transitive* [*past:* خرړول یې] *dialect* to snore

خرړېدل khrəredól *intransitive* [*past:* خرړیده] *dialect* to snore

خرزیری kharzeráj *m. medicine* jaundice

خرس khirs *m.* bear

خرسک khursák *m.* خروسک

خرسک kharsák *m.* jumping for joy خرسک کول to jump for joy

خرسند khrasónd 1 breaking, splitting 2 *figurative* brainless

خرسوار kharsavár *m.* person riding on a donkey

خرسور kharsór *m.* dunce, blockhead, fool

خرش khrəsh *m.* heavy nasal breathing

خرشبون kharshabún *m. history* Kharshanun (one of the ancestors of the Afghan tribes, the Yusufzai, the Momands, the Khalils, etc.)

خرشکه khróshka *f.* pimple

خرشن kharshín *m.* خرشین

خرشونډی kharshúnḍaj *m.* person with a hairlip

خرشونډی kharshunḍáj *m.* muzzle of a bull

خرښبدل khrəshedól *intransitive* [*past:* وخرښبده] to breath heavily through the nose

خرشین kharshín *m. usually plural* [*plural:* خرشینه kharshinə́] dung (of a horse of donkey), manure

خرطوم khartúm *m.* 1 خرتم 2 hose

خرطوم khartúm *m.* Khartoum (city)

خرغوړی kharghvágaj *m. botany* marshmallow

خرفه khurfá *f. botany* portulaca

خرقه khirḳá *f. Arabic* rags; hairshirt (of an aesthetic, a dervish)

خرقه پوش khirḳapósh *m.* dervish

خرک kharák *m.* خارک *idiom* to play dirty tricks on someone

خرک kharák *m. zoology* wood-louse

خرکار kharkā́r *m.* carter, drover who transports goods by donkey-caravan; drover of asses

خرکاري kharkārí *f.* cargo transport (animal), transport on donkey-back خرکاري کول to be engaged in the transport of goods by donkey-caravan

خرکاو kharkā́v *m.* خرکاو ماتول to water wheat immediately after sowing په خرکاو کي کېدل to be unwatered after sowing (of wheat) خرکاو ماتبدل to be watered immediately after sowing (of wheat)

خرکی khurkáj *m.* 1 snore 2 wheeze 3 purring (of a cat) کول a to snore b to wheeze c to purr

خرکی kharakój *f.* blacksmith

خرکېدل kharkedól *intransitive* [*past:* وخرکېده] 1 to grow luxuriantly 2 to become full, become rounded

خرگټ khargáṭ *m.* خاره

خرگی khargáj *m.* 1 small pin 2 part of a flintlock rifle 3 bridge (stringed musical instrument)

خرل kharól *transitive* [*past:* ویې خاره] to tear to pieces; tear and scatter, tear up and strew around *idiom* پنښي خرل to be insistant upon, persist in

خرلنځه kharlándza *f.* kind of oak tree

خرلوډگلی kharloḍəgóláj *m.* crowd of people, noisy assembly خرلوډگلی جوړول to create an uproar, make a disturbance کبدل to instigate or bring about a noisy assembly

خرم khurrám 1.1 pleasant, enjoyable 1.2 joyful, merry, content 2 *proper name* Khurram

خرما khurmā́ *f.* date هم خرما او هم ثواب date-palm خرما ونه to perform a charitable act and earn merit (both dates, and an action which pleases God)

خرمائي khurmāí light-brown chestnut

خرمدل khurramdíl *m. proper name* Khurramdil

خرمستي kharmastí *f.* 1 games; pranks, practical jokes 2 drunken party, carousal 3 debauch خرمستي کول a to play; play tricks b to get drunk, carouse c to engage in debauchery

خرمندی kharmandáj rotund; miniature; tiny

خرمهره kharmuhrá *f.* cowry (a shell used in India for money)

خرنار kharnā́r *m. botany* mullein

خرنج khrandzh *m.* disturbance, strife

خرنده khránda *f.* scratch

خرندي khərándi *f.* خرندي کول *a* to tear up; tear up and scatter to tear up and strew about *b figurative* to be insistent, be stubborn

خرندل khrandól *transitive* [*past:* وي خرانده] **1** to make a hole; bore; drill **2** to torture, torment

خرنل kharnál *m.* mountain rush, Arundo

خروار kharvár *m.* **1** harvar (a measure of weight equal to a 8 Kabul sera, or 565.280 kg) **2** load which can be carried by an ass

خروار kharvár *m.* Kharvar (settlement, Gazni District)

خروپ khrup *tautological compound with* خپ

خروتي **1** kharotí *m. plural* Kharoti (one of the Gilzai tribes) **2** kharoṭáj *m.* Kharotai (tribesman)

خروتی kharoṭáj *m.* measure for corn

خروج khurúdzh *m. Arabic* **1** departure, exit **2** expulsion **3** *biology* excretion

خرورگ kharvárg *m.* ☞ خرورگ

خرورا khrorā́ *f.* خرورک khrorák *m.* kharorák kind of wild edible grass

خروری khəróraj **1** vicious (of an animal) **2** predatory, wild

خروسک khurosák *m. medicine* croup

خروش kharósh *m.* خروښ khroṣh *m.* **1** noise **2** unruly actions, riotous conduct **3** disturbance

خروکی kharúkaj *m.* **1** scab (on a wound); incrustation **2** scar, suture

خرول khravól *transitive* [*past:* وي خراوه] to cut, clip, shave (the hair, beard, etc.) ☞ خریل

خرول khəravól *transitive* [*past:* وي خراوه] to cause to squeak

خرول khrul *m.* wooden stopper for a jug

خرومږ kharomág *m.* stupid and ill-tempered man

خرومه khromá *f.* food, sustenance

خره kharā́ *f.* **.1** pile, heap (of ground corn) **1.2** stack (of wood) **2** *predicative* placed in a pile, heap or stack

خره khrə *plural and oblique singular of* خر

خره khra *f.* she-ass

خرهاړ khərəhā́ṛ *m.* **1** squeak **2** snore

خرهپکه khórapkha هغه ورته خره پنبه شو he insisted; he persisted

خری khəráj *m.* **1** blister, lump **2** corn, callus

خری khóraj **1** *m.* hangnail **2.1** stubborn, obstinate **2.2** *dialect* living, animate

خریجات khariját *m. Arabic* ☞ خرتوب

خرید kharíd **1** *m.* purchase, buying, obtaining **2** bought, obtained خرید کول to buy, obtain, procure

خریدار kharidā́r *m.* **1** purchaser **2** *poetry* admirer of a beautiful woman

خریداري kharidārí *f.* purchase, buying, obtaining د خریداریو مدیر chief of supply, chief of procurement department

خریدل kharedól *intransitive* [*past:* وخریده] **1** to snore **2** snore په خریدلو یې شروع وکړه He began to snore.

خرید و فروش kharid-u-furúsh *m.* buying and selling

خریری khəreráj *m.* **1** drink made of curds and whey (i.e., sour milk similar to Caucasian airan but diluted with fresh milk) **2** *botany* mushroom خریری کول *compound verb a* to spoil (some matter) **b** to beat, break خریری کیدل *a* to be spoiled (some matter) **b** *compound verb* to be beaten, be broken خریری خیدک کیدل to protrude (of eyes)

خریز khríz *m.* khiríz **1** stubble (of cotton, alfalfa) **2** spur (of a rooster) **3** spit, skewer **4** crow-bar (tool)

خریطه kharitá *f. Arabic* map خریطه جغرافیائي geographic map

خریف kharíf *m. Arabic* **1** autumn **2** kharif (autumnal sowing)

خریل khrəjól khrajól khrijól *transitive* [*past:* وي خرایه] to cut, shave, clip (hair, beard) خریل کیدل *passive* to be cut, be clipped, be shaved

خریمه kharemáf she-ass in heat خریمه کیدل to be in heat (a she-ass)

خریل khrejól *transitive* ☞ خریل

خر **1** khaṛ **1** grey **2** brown; khaki color **3** dark خړه اوریځ a dark cloud خړ گهیځ early morning dusk **4** turbid خړي اوبه turbid water خړي سترگي turbid eyes **5** overcast خړه هوا overcast weather **6** unbleached (cloth) **7** *figurative* ashamed, embarrassed **8** *figurative* vague, uncertain, confused (times)

خړ **2** khuṛ *m.* noise made in vomiting, expectorating or spitting خړ وهل *a* to vomit, throw up *b* to expectorate, spit

خړاس khṛās flat

خرانکه khəṛānáka *f.* pipit (the bird)

خرانگه khəṛā́nga *f.* bough, twig

خراو khəṛáv ☞ خروب

خراوه khṛāvá *f.* fighting of dogs

خربخن khəṛbakhən grayish

خرپ khṛap *m.* **1** crash; crunch خرپ کول *a* to crack, crash *b* to crunch **2** tramp, tread

خرپر khəṛ-pə́ṛ **1** completely gray **2** dust-covered; soiled, dirty **3** cloudy, confused; tense خړ پړ کیدل *a* to become dirty, get soiled *b figurative* to get complicated; become tense

خرپرتیا khəṛpəṛtjá *f.* **1** dirt, mud **2** *figurative* tension (relations, position)

کرپوڅه kaṛpótsa *f.* ☞ خارپوشي خرپوڅه

خرپ و خروپ khṛap-u-khṛúp *m.* cracking, cracking, rustling

خرپول khṛapavól *transitive* [*past:* وي خرپاوه] **1** to cause a crackle **2** to thrash, beat up

خرپهار khṛapəhā́ṛ *m.* **1** crackle, rustle; knock **2** crunch **3** clicking of teeth

خرپی khṛapáj *m.* tread, tramp

خرپیدل khṛapedól *intransitive* [*past:* وخرپیده] to strike against and fall

خرتم khaṛtám *m.* trunk, proboscis *idiom* خرتم اچول to brag, boast about

خرتي khṛáti *f. plural* nonsense, idle talk خرتي کول to talk nonsense, engage in idle talk

خرت khṛaṭ *m. plural regional* mucous, nose-drippings, snots

خرجن khərdzhən 1 brown 2 dark 3 turbid, dirty

خرز khrəz *m.* خرس khrəs *m.* 1 dry cough 2 crunch 3 crash, crack 4 noise of a shot 5 clap, bang خرز وهل a to cough dryly b to crunch c to crack d to resound (of a shot) e to bang

خرسا khrəsã́ *f.* ☞ خرسهار

خرسترگی khərstə́rgaj 1 grey-eyed 2 embarrassed, ashamed

خرس و خروس khrəs-u-khrús *m.* 1 ring, ringing, rattle (saber) 2 crunch 3 cracking, crashing

خرساول khrəsavə́l *transitive* [*past:* و يي خرساوه] 1 to bring forth, cause a dry cough 2 to make a cracking or crashing noise

خرسهار khrəsahár *m.* خرسی khrəsáj *m.* 1 dry cough 2 crunch 3 crash, crack

خرسیدل khrəsedə́l *intransitive* [*past:* و خرسید] 1 to cough dryly 2 to crunch 3 to crack, crack 4 to clap, bang, slap 5 to strike against

خرکی ¹ khuṛkáj *m.* ☞ خرکی ²

خرکی ² khəṛkáj turbid; dust-covered

خرگاوه khərgāvá *f.* silt

خرل khəṛə́l *transitive* [*past:* و يي خرل] to defecate

خرلمی khəṛlə́maj *m.* squirrel

خرمور khəṛmór *m.* ☞ خراره

خرن khəṛə́n gluttonous, voracious

خرنج khrandzh *m.* dissention, disturbance خرنج اچول to cause dissention

خرند khṛand *m.* 1 stump 2 stubble (of wheat, rice)

خرنه khəṛə́na *f.* defecation

خروالی khəṛvã́laj *m.* 1 turbidity; sediment 2 *figurative* disorder, grief

خروب khəṛób 1 richly watered, copiously irrigated 2 watered (of a horse)

خروب گری khəṛobgáraj *m.* plaster, mortar

خروبول khəṛobavə́l *denominative transitive verb* [*past:* خروب يي کړ] 1 to water; fill up with water, irrigate 2 to plaster with a clay mortar, stucco *idiom* سترگي خروبول a to charm (with beauty, etc.) b to admire (the sight, appearance) د بنیایت ننداره خروبول to enjoy beauty

خروبی ¹ khəṛobáj *m.* mortar, stucco of clay (for covering, stuccooing a wall) خروبی کول to prepare clay stucco, mortar

خروبی ² khəṛóbi *feminine plural of* خروب

خروبیدل khəṛobedə́l *denominative, intransitive* [*past:* خروب شو] 1 to be watered; be filled up with water; be irrigated 2 to be plastered with clay mortar, be stucoed

خروپړ khəṛ-u-pə́ṛ ☞ خرپر

خروپی khəṛopáj *m.* thick yogurt-like dish heated up

خرورگ khəṛvárg *m.* ram older than four years

خرورگه khəṛvárga *f.* ewe older than four years

خروز khaṛúz *m.* 1 noise of a shot 2 a clap, bang

خروس ¹ khaṛús 1 cowardly 2 *m.* coward

خروس ² khṛus *m. tautological compound word with* خرس

خروسکه khṛúska *f.* 1 thick smoke 2 repulsive smell; stink

خړول khəṛavə́l *denominative, transitive* [*past:* خړي يي کړ] 1 to dye grey, color grey 2 to trouble, disturb اوبه خړول او کب نیول to catch fish in trouble waters 3 *figurative* to shame, embarrass, confuse

خړه ¹ khə́ṛa *f.* 1 stream-borne silt 2 sediment په شنه خړه early in the morning, at dawn د ماښام په خړه تیاره کښني at twilight, in the evening خړه دنیا the transitory world

خړه ² khə́ṛa *feminine singular of* خړ

خړی ¹ kharáj 1 gluttonous, voracious 2 garrulous

خړی ² khəṛáj *f.* ☞ خرانکه

خړي ³ khə́ṛi *plural of* خړه ¹

خړی پړی khəṛáj-pəṛáj *f.* 1 simplification, oversimplification 2 humiliation

خړیت khṛit snub-nosed, pug-nosed

خړیدل khəṛedə́l *denominative, intransitive* [*past:* خړ شو] 1 to dye grey, color grey 2 to trouble, roil, grow dim 3 to be covered with dust, get dirty 4 *figurative* to grow ashamed, be embarrassed 5 to grow worse, worsen (circumstances)

خریس ¹ khris 1 person in the pink of health; very large person; giant 2.1 huge, healthy (a person) 2.2 enormous

خریس ² khris *tautological with* تور

خرین khuṛín ☞ خورین

خز ¹ khaz khazz *m.* 1 fur 2 *regional* sable (both the animal and the fur) 3 pole-cat, ferret

خز ² khaz khazz *m. Arabic* kind of rough silk

خزان khazã́n *m.* 1 autumn 2 *predicative* .1 fading, losing freshness, wan 2.2 *figurative* withering, growing old حالت يي مراوي او خزان وي he is growing old; he is withering away

خزانه khazānã́ *f.* khizāná *Arabic* 1 treasury 2 depository, storehouse 3 *military* chamber (breech of a weapon)

خزانه چي khazānachí *m.* ☞ خزانه دار

خزانه خانه khazānakhānã́ *f.* Treasury, Exchequer

خزانه دار khazānadár *m.* 1 treasurer 2 ☞ خزانه يي

خزانی khazānaí having a chamber, having a breech (of a firearm) خزانه يي

خزانی khazānaí autumnal

خزانیدل khazānedə́l *denominative, intransitive* [*past:* خزان شو] 1 to fade, grow wan 2 *figurative* to grow old, age

خزدوکه khazdóka *f.* 1 dung-beetle 2 *dialect* beetle of the Tenebrionidae family 3 small insect

خزری khazə́raj 1 *m.* bread crumbs 2 tiny

خزله khazə́la *f. dialect* ☞ خځله

خزنده khazandá 1 *m. & f.* [*plural:* خزندي khazandé *m. plural:* زیانداره خزنده گان khazandagã́n] .1 reptile, snake 1.2 insect harmful insect 1.3 *f. plural* snakes, reptiles 2 creeping, crawling خزنده حیوانات serpents, snakes, reptiles

خزه ¹ khazá *f.* 1 ambush (for hunting) 2 basin, bowl

خزه ² khə́za *f. dialect* ☞ بنځه

خژ khəzh *m.* خژا khəzhā́ *f.* خژ او پر خبرکي wheeze (in the chest) خژ کول to wheeze (in the chest)

خژهار khəzhahár *m.* ☞ خبرکی

خبر khug ☞ خوبر ²

خبرکی khəg *m.* ☞

3 خز ¹ ☞ khag *m.* خبر ³

خبرکی کول khəgkáj *m.* wheeze (in the chest) to wheeze (in the chest)

خوربرول khugavúl *transitive dialect* ☞ ²

خبرهار khəgahár *m.* ☞ خبرکی

خبربدل khugedól *intransitive dialect* ☞ ²

خس ¹ khas *m. plural* brushwood *idiom,* دا د یوه خس قدر اهمیت نه لري، دا د یوه خس قدری اهمیت نه لري This has no value whatsoever.

خس ² khas *m. plural* 1 meat 2 *anatomy* placenta

خسا khsā́ khusā́ stinking, evil-smell خسا هوا foul air خسا کول to cause to be stinking, cause to be evil-smelling خسا کبدل to stink, be stinking, be foul-smelling

خسارات khasārā́t *Arabic masculine plural of* خساره *and* خسارت

خسارت khasarát *m. Arabic* ☞ خساره

خساره khasārá *f. Arabic* [*plural:* خساري khasāré *Arabic plural:* خسارات khasārā́t] detriment, losses, loss, damage, waste خساره پوره کول to recoup a loss خساره مبندل to suffer damage, incur loss خساره غوښتل دعوٰی کول to bring action to recover damages خساره پیښه شوي ده damage was caused دٻر خسارات او تلفات ورورسبده They suffered great losses.

خساوجه khusā́vdzha *f.* خساوزه khusā́vza *f. dialect* iris bulb

خسبانه khasbānə́ *masculine plural of* خسبه *and* خسبون

خسبون khasbún *m.* خسبه khasbá *m.* [*plural:* خسبانه khabānə́] gatherer of brushwood

خس پوبن khaspóḵẖ *m.* 1 *military* wolf's hole (tank trap, covered and camouflaged) 2 snare, trap

خست khissát *m. Arabic* 1 miserliness, niggardliness 2 baseness, meanness

خستگي khastagí *f.* weariness, exhaustion بې له خستگی tireless, impervious: to exhaustion

خسته ¹ khistá *f.* stone (of a fruit)

خسته ² khastá tired, exhausted خسته او ستړی سوئ tired, exhausted

خسته کن khastakún exhausting

خس خس khaskhás petty, very small, in small bits خس خس کول to crumble

خسر khusə́r *m.* khusúr 1 father-in-law (wife's father) 2 father-in-law (husband's father)

خسران khusrā́n *m. Arabic* damage, harm; injury خسران راورل to inflict damage, harm; harm

خسرگنی khusarganə́j *f.* relatives on either the husband's or wife's father's side

خسۍ khasə́raj *m.* 1 straw 2 twig, branch 3 trash 4 worthless thing *idiom* خسۍ اچول to cast lots

خساک khasák *m.* bedbug, *Cimex lectularius*

خسکي khasakí low quality (of fruit) خسکي توت white mulberry

خسمان khasmā́n *m.* guarantor

خسمانه khasmā́na *f.* 1 care, concern; charge; service د چا خسمانه او to serve, be of service to someone 2 guard, protection خسمانه کول *compound verb* a to care for, concern over something; watch over; serve b to guard, protect خسمانه کبدل to take something upon oneself

خسمانه گر khasmānagár *m.* خسمانه وال khasmānaval 1 person caring for or concerning himself about another person 2 one who guards or protects another, protector 3 guarantor

خسماني khasmānáj *m.* guarantor

خسڼی khasə́ṇaj khəsā́ṇaj ☞ خسری

خسوزه khasúza *f.* ☞ خڅوزه

خسی ¹ khsáj khusáj *m.* calf

خسی ² khasí *m.* 1 castrated animal; gelding, beast who has been altered, ox 2 gelded, castrated خسی کول to geld, castrate خسی کبدل to be gelded, be castrated

خسی ³ khsə́j khusə́j *f.* heifer

خسیس khasís *Arabic* 1 greedy, miserly 2 base, mean 3 repulsive, unpleasant

خسیل khasíl *m.* grain mowed prior to ripening and used for fodder

خشاک khashā́k *m.* brushwood; wood; firewood

خیشت khisht khusht ☞ خبشت

خشتول khishtavúl *Eastern* khushtavúl *transitive* ☞ خبشتول

خشته khashtá *dialect* ☞ بنایسته

خشتبدل khishtedól *intransitive* ☞ خبشتبدل

خشک khushk dry, withered, dessicated

خشکاوه khushkāvá *f.* dry valley

خشک دماغ khushkdamā́gh crazy, mad, insane

خشک دماغي khushkdamāghí *f.* insanity, madness

خشک سالي khushksālí *f.* drought, dry year

خشک دماغ khushkmā́ghz ☞

خشک دماغي khushkmaghzí *f.* ☞

خشکه ¹ khushká *f.* dry land (as opposed to the sea)

خشکه ² khushká *f.* boiled rice, steamed rice, cooked rice

خشکي khushkí *f.* 1 dryness 2 drought

خشم khashim *m.* khishm wrath, anger, rage خشم ورغلئ he became angry, he became enraged

خشمبدل khashmedól *intransitive* [*past:* وخشمبده] to become enraged

خشنگ khasháng malicious

خشنود khushnúd content, satisfied, contented

خشنودي khushundí *f.* contentment, satisfaction, gratification

خشڼه khushaṇə́ *m. plural* dung (of horse, ass)

خشوع khushú' *f. Arabic* ☞ خضوع

خشونت khushunát *m. Arabic* harshness, rudeness په دٻر خشونت ویل to be rude to; cut short, snub

خوشی khúshaj ☞ خوشی ²

خشیت khashját *m. Arabic* fear, terror

خشیل khashíl *m.* small quantities of brushwood washed up by wave-action on shore

خبن khaḵẖ ☞ بنخ

خنتک khəkhták *m.* gore, gusset in a dress or trousers *idiom* خنتک ټيرل to commit a dishonorable deed

خنت کاري khəkhtkārí *f.* bricklaying

خنتگ khəkhtág *m.* خنتگی khəkhtagáj *m.* ☞ خنتک

خنته khə́khta *f.* 1 brick د ډبرو خنته، خنبه ډبره rough-finished stone د سمنټو خنته cinder-block 2 *figurative* element, component, composite part په خنته بيانول to lay out or expound point by point *idiom* د يوي نيمي خنتي شی neither one thing or another; something inferior

خنم khəkhm *m.* ☞ خشم

خنمبدل khəkhmedə́l ☞ خشمبدل

خنبول khəkhavə́l *transitive* ☞ بنخول *idiom* په چا خوله خنبول to seize someone (of a dog)

خنبي khakhí *m. plural* the Khashi (a branch of the Afghans encompassing all of the Yusufzai tribes)

خنبدل khakhedə́l *intransitive* ☞ بنخبدل

خنبدنه khakhedə́na *f. dialect* ☞ بنخبدنه

خنبينه khukhína *f.* ☞ خوبنينه

خصائص khasāís *Arabic masculine plural of* خاصيت

خصايل khasāíl *Arabic masculine plural of* خصيله

خصلت khaslát *m. Arabic* personality, nature, character (of a person)

خصم khasm *m. Arabic* [*plural:* اخصام akhsám] enemy, foe

خصمانه khasmāná 1 hostile, unfriendly 2 hostility, in an unfriendly manner

خصوص khusús *m. Arabic* 1 peculiarity 2 relationship, respect په دی خصوص کښی in this respect, with regard to this, about this له هره خصوصه in all respects

خصوصاً khusúsán *Arabic* 1 especially, in particular 2 privately, personally, individually

خصوصي khususí *Arabic* 1 particular; private په خصوصي لحاظ in particular خصوصي پانگه ، خصوصي سرمايه private capital 2 special; confidial; secret 3 personal خصوصي سکرتر private secretary

خصوصيات khusuijā́t *Arabic masculine plural of* خصوصيت

خصوصيت khususijāt *m. Arabic* [*plural:* خصوصيتونه khususijatúna *Arabic plural:* خصوصيات khususijā́t] 1 detail, particular 2 peculiarity; characteristic; specific; property کيمياوي خصوصيات chemical property 3 proximity, close relationship, intimacy د چا سره خصوصيت لرل to have close relations, be intimate with someone

خصي khasí *m.* ☞ خسي²

خصيله khasilá *f. Arabic* [*plural:* خصيلي khasilé *Arabic m. plural:* خصايل khasāíl] manner, style اخلاقي خصائل moral quality

خضر khizr *m. regional* 1 friend of the Prophet Moses 2 Prophet Elijah

خضوع khuzú *f. Arabic* humility; submission, obedience و يو شي ته خضوع کول to resign oneself to something, submit to something

خط khat *m.* khatt *Arabic* [*plural:* خطونه khatúna *Arabic plural:* خطوط khutút] 1 letter, correspondence د چا سره خط او کتابت to carry on a correspondence with someone 2 line, mark مستقيم خط a straight line منحني خط a curved line منکسر خط a broken (dotted) line د خپور خط استوا *khátt-i* the equator خط دفاعي *military* forward edge of battle area military line of defense خط کښل ، خط وهل a to write, inscribe b to make a line, draw 3 rail, rails; line (of a railroad) 4 fuzz (on the face)

خطا khatā́ *f. Arabic* mistake, blunder دا لويه خطا ده This is a serious mistake. دا دوی گناه او خطا نه ده بلکه انسان له proverb Man is prone to error. خطا نه خالي ندئ خطا ايستل to swindle, deceive خطا کول a to knock over, lead into error b to let down slowly (a staff), strike (with a staff on the head) c to toss, throw خطا کبدل to repeat a mistake بيا بيا خطا کول *compound verb* a to miss b to go astray c to fall (stumble) پښه يي خطا سوه a His feet went out from under him (from a tree branch etc.) b He stumbled خطا کبدل را *compound verb* a to collapse, fall; to roll away b to deviate (from a theme) خطا وتل a to be deceived b to err, make a blunder په خطا کښي لوبدل to make a mistake, miscount بی له خطا خبري کول to speak without hesitation

خطاب khitā́b *m. Arabic* 1 title خطاب ورکول to give a title 2 address, appeal, turn to or address someone with a speech or an appeal

خطابه khitābá *f. Arabic* speech, sermon د خطابې کرسی، د خطابې منبر tribune, podium (for an orator)

خطاط khattā́t *m.* calligrapher

خطاطي khattātí *f. Arabic* calligraphy

خطاکار khatākā́r *m.* sinner

خطاکاري katākārí *f.* mistake, error, blunder

خط السير khatt-as-sájr *m. Arabic* 1 current د برق خط السير electric current 2 way, flow 3 course, direction 4 line

خطا وتل khatāvatə́l *m.* خطا وتنه khatāvatə́na *f. plural* 1 mistake, blunder 2 deception د سترگو خطا وتل optical illusion

خط آهن khátt-i-āhan *m.* railroad

خطا يستلئ khatājəstə́laj deceived

خطايي khatāí 1 *f.* mistake, blunder 2 inaccurate, untrue خطايي ډز a shot that missed, a miss b a shot into the air

خطبه khutbá *f. Arabic religion* hutba (holiday sermon containing a reference to the reigning noble)

خط پش khátt-i-pesh *m. military* forward line

خطر khatár *m. Arabic* [*plural:* خطرونه khatarúna *Arabic m. plural:* اخطار akhtár] 1 danger; threat; risk وطن په خطر کښي دئ the Fatherland is in danger دپر لوی خطر danger to life د ځان خطرات خطر او ولاړ شوئ دئ a danger arose, a threat arose و چاته خطر وړاندي کول to be in danger په خطر کښي لوبدل to create great danger د خطر سره مخامخ کبدل to create a threat to someone to meet face-to-face with danger 2 alarm هوايي خطر air-raid alarm د هوايي خطر زنگ وهل air-raid warning announcement د هوايي خطر اعلام to announce an air-raid warning

خطرات khatarā́t *Arabic masculine plural of* خطره

خطرناک khatarnā́k dangerous, risky خطرناکه لاره uneasy road, dangerous road

خطرناكوالى khatarnākvális m. خطرناكيت khatarnākijāt m. danger دا څومره خطرناكوالى نه لري This is not so dangerous.

خطره khatrá f. Arabic [plural: خطرى khatré Arabic m. plural: خطرات khatarāt] 1 danger; threat تر خطري لاندى نيول to place under threat, threaten 2 alarm, warning 3 risk

خط فاصل khatt-i-fāsíl m. border, frontier

خط كښ khatkásh m. خط كښ khatkákh m. ruler, straightedge

خط لرونكى kat laruńkaj lined خط لرونكى كاغذ lined paper, ruled paper

خط مشي khátt-i-mashí f. Arabic [plural: خطوط مشي khutú-i-mashí] 1 itinerary, line (of travel) 2 politics course (of action) د سياست خط مشي، سياسي خط مشي political course

خط مط khatmát m. letter, correspondence خط مط استول to send letters, dispatch letters

خطمي khatmí f. Arabic botany marshmallow, Althaea

خط لرونكى khatvālá ☞ خط لرونكى

خطوط khutút 1 f. Arabic plural of خط 2 routes, itineraries

خطيب khatíb m. Arabic 1 preacher 2 orator

خطير khatír Arabic 1 serious, great (of responsibility, etc.) 2 esteemed, honored

خفا khifá f. Arabic secret د خفا د پردې شا ته hidden (of difficulties, etc.)

خفاش khuffásh m. Arabic bat

خفت khiffát m. Arabic 1 lightness, lightness in weight 2 insignificance (e.g., of a problem) 3 light-mindedness 4 humiliation, insult

خفقان khafakán m. Arabic 1 despair 2 depression د خفقان افكار despondent thoughts 3 palpitation

خفك khafák m. marten

خفگان khafagán m. ☞ خفقان

خفگي khafagí f. grief, derangement, disorder

خفه khafá Arabic 1.1 upset, grieved زړه مي خفه دئ I am upset, I am distressed 1.2 angry, dissatisfied 1.3 suffocated, smothered 1.4 figurative dispirited خفه كول a to upset, grieve b to anger, annoy c to suffocate, lie heavy on d figurative to oppress, stifle خفه كيدل a to fall into confusion; grieve b to be angry (with), be annoyed (with) له ما نه مه خفه كيږه Don't be angry at me! c to choke 2 f. asthma, asphyxiation

خفه كوونكى khafá kavúnkaj 1 present participle of خفه كول 2 asphyxiating خفه كوونكى غازونه asphyxiating gases

خفي khafí Arabic hidden, secret

خفيف khafíf Arabic 1 light (of industry) 2 military manual, hand, light 3 insignificant; unimportant 4 linguistics palatalized (of phonemes)

خكل khukál transitive dialect ☞ ښكل

خكل khkul transitive dialect ☞ ښكل ښكل كول

خگ khug Eastern ☞ خوړ

خگلن khugálən m. خوگلن

خل khal m. 1 faith, assurance 2 trust, confidence

خلا khalá f. Arabic 1 anatomy cavity د خولي خلا oral cavity 2 emptiness 3 alienation د دوى تر مينځه يوه خلا پيدا كيږي There was a noticeable alienation between them.

خلعت khalát m. ☞ خلعت

خلاص khlās ☞ خلاص

خلاصتون khlāstún m. ☞ خلاصيده

خلاصول khlāsavál denominative, transitive ☞ خلاصول

خلاصيدل khlāsedál denominative, intransitive ☞ خلاصيدل

خلاص khlās khalās Arabic 1 free, liberated, saved, delivered 2 unoccupied, not busy (with work, matters) 3 دكان خلاص دئ open the shop is open 4 unsealed (letter, package) 5 deprived of something 6 completed, finished idiom خلاصه هوا open, fresh air

خلاصتاً khulāsátán Arabic brieflly, succinctly خلاصتاً ذكر كول to mention briefly

خلاصوالى khlāsvális m. 1 freedom 2 idleness, unemployment 3 opening, unsealing (letter, package) 4 completion, finishing

خلاصول khlāsavál denominative, transitive [past: خلاص يي كړ] 1 to free, set free, set at liberty; save, deliver 2 to open (a door, a shop) 3 to dismiss (from a job) 4 to open, unseal (a letter, a package) 5 to unload (a gun) 6 to finish, complete 7 to settle, eliminate (a conflict, etc.) 8 to untie (e.g., a knot) 9 to untangle (threads) idiom د خلكو غوږونه خلاصول to educate the people idiom لار خلاصول to open up a road (e.g., in the mountains)

خلاصون khlāsún m. 1 deliverance, salvation, liberation 2 settling (dispute)

خلاصه khlása 1 feminine singular of خلاص 2 unmarried woman (daughter, sister)

خلاصه khulāsá f. Arabic the heart of a matter, crux of a matter; deduction, conclusion خلاصه دا چه ، خلاصه خبره دا چه succinctly speaking خلاصه كول compound verb to summarize, speak succinctly

خلاصى khlāsáj m. khalasi f. 1 salvation, deliverance خلاصى ميندل to save oneself, escape 2 running dry, failing; decreasing 3 khlāsáj m. dialect break in relations

خلاصيدل khlāsedál khaladél intransitive [past: خلاص شو] 1 to become free, escape, get out 2 to be open 3 to get fired (from a job); to get out of (i.e., responsibility) 4 to come to an end, end, finish, come to completion سمستر خلاص شو the semester is ended 5 to be opened, be unsealed (letter, package) 6 to be unloaded (a gun) 7 to deliver, give birth, calve, kitten, foal 8 to run out, to be expended

خلاصيدون khlādedán m. خلاصيدنه khlādedána f. dialect خلاصيدون khlāsedún m. ☞ خلاصيده

خلاصيده khlāsedá m. plural 1 liberation, deliverance, salvation 2 opening 3 dismissal (from work) 4 termination, completion 5 opening, unsealing (letter, package) 6 unloading (a gun) 7 delivering (birth), birth, giving birth, calving, kittening

خلاف khilā́f Arabic 1 m. 1.1 breaking, infraction د وعدې خلاف كول to break a promise 1.2 opposition 1.3 contradiction

د يو شي په خلاف ، د يو شي ۱۷ رايي پر خلاف د ۲۰ رايو ۱۷ votes to 20 پر خلاف contrary to something **2** contradicting, contradictory خلاف له عقله، له حقيقت نه خلاف contradictory, not corresponding to reality

خلافت khilāfát *m. Arabic* **1** *history* caliphate (government) **2** office of caliph **3** successor د خلافت چوخه اغوستل to be someone's successor

خلاف رفتاري khilāfraftārí *m.* misdemeanor

خلاف قانون khilāf-i-kānún *regional* illegal, illicit

خلاف ورزي khilāfvarzí *f.* **1** infraction of a law or custom **2** crime, misdemeanor

خلاق khallā́ķ *m. Arabic* creator, maker

خلاقه khallāķá creative خلاقه ليكوال writer, creative worker

خلاقيت khallāķiját *m. Arabic* creative work ادبي خلاقيت literary creativity

خلال khilál *m. Arabic* **1** defect, flaw; imperfection **2** disorder

خلاملا khalāmalā **1** sincere (of friendship) **2** frank, open په خلاملا ويل to speak frankly, talk in plain terms

خلائق khalāík *Arabic masculine plural of* خليقه

خلبوري khulbúraj *m.* ☞ خولبوري

خلپل khalpál *m.* brush, brushwood

خلپه khulpá *f.* ☞ خرفه

خلتم khaltúm *m.* ☞ خرتم

خلته khaltá *f.* bag د بيدبدلو خلته sleeping bag

خلجي khildzhí *m. plural history* Hilji (a people living in Afghanistan in the Middle Ages)

خلخنډه khalkhaṇḍá deformed

خلش khalísh *m.* **1** suspicion **2** obstacle

خلش khalísh *m.* stitch

خلص khullás *Arabic* **1** pure, unadulterated **2** short په خلص ډول in resume form

خلط khalt *Arabic* **1** *m.* **.1** mixture, admixture **1.2** blend **2** *predicative* blended خلط کېدل to mix (with) *intransitive* to mix

خلع khal' *f. Arabic* **1** removal **2** abolition

خلع khul' *f. law* **1** divorce at the instigation of the woman **2** cutting a son off from his inheritance

خلعت khil'át *m. Arabic* ceremonial robe

خلع سلاح khal'-i-silāh *f.* disarmament خلع سلاح کول *compound verb* to disarm خلع سلاح کېدل *compound verb* to disarm

خلعه khál'a *f.* ☞ خلع

خلف khalāf *m. Arabic* [*plural:* اخلاف akhlā́f] **1** successor **2** son

خلفا khulafā́ *Arabic masculine plural of* خليفه

خلفي khalafí **1** rear, back **2** subsequent

خلق khalķ *m. Arabic singular & plural* **1** nation, people, the people **2** *plural* people; inhabitant لوى خلق important people **3** creation, making خلق کول *compound verb* to make, create خلق کېدل *compound verb* to be made, be created

خلق khulķ *m. Arabic* [*plural:* اخلاق akhlā́ķ] **1** disposition, temperament; character **2** breeding *idiom* خلق يې تنگ شو he got angry; he became disturbed

خلقت khilķát *m. Arabic* **1** creation, making **2** world, society; people **3** temperament; nature (of a person)

خلقتاً khilķátán *Arabic* by nature

خلق تريخي khulķtrikhí *f.* anger, discomposure خلق تريخي ور پيښنه شوه he was angry; he got upset

خلقه khalķá *f. obsolete* nation, people

خلقه khálķa *oblique singular and vocative of* خلق

خلقي khilķí *Arabic* natural, innate; inherent, characteristic (of)

خلقي khalķí popular, of the people

خلک khalk *m.* ☞ خلق

خلکه khilká *f.* **1** ☞ خرقه اوږدده خلکه (Eastern-type) robe **2** apron

خلگ khalág *m.* khalg *m.* ☞ خلق

خولگی khulgə́j *f.* ☞ خولگی

خلل khalál *m. Arabic* **1** loss, damage, harm **2** hindrance, interference خلل کول، خلل رسول **a** to inflict damage, harm **b** to hamper, interfere with *idiom* ستا دماغ کښې خلل راغلئ دئ *Eastern idiom* You have gone out of your mind.

خلم khulm *m. history* hul'm ☞ تاشقرغان

خلنج khalándzh *m.* [*plural:* خلنجان khalandzhā́n] mulberry (white or red, with pits)

خلنځه khalə́ndza *f.* oak

خلوت khalvát *m. Arabic* **1** solitude, loneliness **2** closed meeting, private property

خلوت khlot empty, hollow

خلوت خانه khalvatkhāná *f.* **1** room (in the men's half of the house) **2** cell (ecclesiastical)

خلوت نشين khalvatnishín **1** retiring, withdrawing **2** *m.* hermit

خلوتي khalvatí **1** *m.* **.1** confidant **1.2** hermit **2.1** confidential, secret **2.2** secluded

خلود khulúd *m. Arabic* eternity, immortality

خلوص khulús *m. Arabic* sincerity, candor

خلوندونی khalvandúnaj *m.* cord for fastening up a bag; lace

خلوېته khálvéta empty, hollow

خله khulá *f.* khulá ☞ خوله

خلی khólaj *m.* **1** sprout **2** blade of grass **3** straw **4** litter, garbage, trash *idiom* خلی يې سپين شوه His beard has gotten a bit grey د غل *proverb* په بيره خلی وي Murder will out; the guilty mind eventually betrays itself

خلیته khalitá *f.* ☞ خلته

خليج khalidzh *m. Arabic* bay د بنگال خليج the Bay of Bengal خليج فارس khalídzh-i the Persian Gulf

خليفه khalifá *m. Arabic* [*plural:* خليفگان khalifagā́n *Arabic plural:* خلفا khulafā́ *plural:* خلائف khalāíf] **1** *history* Caliph **2** successor **3** polite form of address (e.g., to a tailor and other craftsmen)

خليق khalíķ *Arabic* **1** kind, gracious **2** *m. proper name* Khalik

خليقه khaliķá f. Arabic m. [plural: خلائق khalāíķ] 1 nature, disposition, character 2 creature

خليل khalíl m. Arabic 1 religion true friend (an epithet of Abraham) 2 proper name Khalil 3 m. plural Khalili (tribe) 4 Khalil (tribesman)

خليلي¹ khalilí m. plural Khalili (tribe)

خليلي² khalilí khalili (a variety of early-ripening grape, dark red in color)

خم¹ khum m. khum (a large clay jar for the storage of water, wine, oil, etc.)

خم² kham bending, bowing; curving

خمار¹ khumár m. Arabic 1 drunkenness; hangover 2 intoxication (from love) 3 languor (in the eyes)

خمار² khimár m. ☞ قمار

خماره khumára f. proper name Khumara

خماري khumārí 1 intoxication 2 languorous, languid (of eyes) خماري سترگي languorous eyes

خما زوری khəmāzúraj m. Withania coagulans (a plant yielding a ferment for cheese)

خمبه khambá f. large woven basket (for storing corn, grain); corn-bin, granary

خمبیره khambirá f. dialect ☞ خمیره

خمپار khumpár m. Eastern mortar (weapon)

خمپاره khumpārá f. khampārá siege gun

خمتا khamtā́ f. ☞ خامتا

خمت khamát 1 chubby and pink (of a baby) 2 stocky

خمچه khamə́cha little finger, pinky خمچه پښتۍ لور lower rib خمچه گوته

خمچي khamə́che f. plural Eastern bread made of broken rice or millet

خمری khumrə́j f. mug for drinking (clay, metal)

خمس khums m. Arabic fifth part, fifth

خمسور¹ khamsór m. fall of leaves, the beginning of autumn

خمسور² khamsór 1 spontaneous, unceremonious 2 sociable

خمسورتيا khamsortjā́ f. 1 spontaneity, informality 2 friendship, sociability

خمسوز khamsóz ☞ خامسوز

خمسه khamsá f. Arabic 1 pentad (five poems unified into a single entity, e.g., by Nizami, and Navoi) 2 five senses (sight, hearing, smell, touch, and taste)

خمن khamə́n bent, crooked

خمندک khamandə́k m. zoology tick

خم و چم kham-u-chám m. shrewdness, tricks

خمود khumúd m. Arabic 1 extinguishing, extinction 2 medicine loss of the power of speech

خمول khamavə́l denominative, transitive [past: خم يې کړ] 1 to bend, bow 2 to distort

خمیځ khamídz ☞ خمن

خمېدل khamedə́l denominative, intransitive [past: خم شو] to bend; bow; be deformed, be distorted

خمیر khamír Arabic 1 fermented (of dough) خمیره دوډی sourdough bread 2 m. .1 dough 2.2 pasta 2.3 figurative nature

خمیره khamirá 1 feminine singular of خمیر 2 f. .1 leaven 2.1 ورگډول to leaven (dough) 2.2 dough اوره خمیره شي the dough is rising د خمیري مزری Eastern literal a lion made of dough a weak and puny man

خمېز khaméz slightly bent; inclined

خمېزول khamezavə́l denominative, intransitive [past: خمېز يې کړ] to bend slightly; incline

خمېزېدل khamezadə́l denominative, intransitive [past: خمېز شو] to bend slightly; incline

خنازیر khanāzír m. Arabic plural 1 from خنزیر 2 medicine scrofula

خناق khunáķ m. Arabic diphtheria

خنثی khunsā́ f. Arabic neutralization, paralysis

خنجاره¹ khundzhā́ṛa f. rags

خنجاره² khundzhā́ṛa f. 1 millet 2 oil-cake

خنجر khandzhár m. dagger

خنجرخطی khandzharkhatáj m. ornament in the form of a dagger

خنجري khandzharí striped (of silk cloth)

خنجک khəndzhák m. khindzhak (a kind of pistachio tree) ☞ شنی²

خنجکی khandzhakáj m. plug, spigot; bung

خند khand m. court for playing knucklebones خند خند the game of knucklebones

خندا khandā́ f. laughter خندا کول a laughable b senseless د خندا وړ to laugh په خندا تشي په خندا دئ he laughs to fall down laughing

خندان khandā́n 1 m. laughter; smile د خندان قصه anecdote, joke 2 poetry laughing, smiling

خنداناک khandānā́k laughable

خندرکی khandə́rkáj m. ☞ خندکی

خندق khandáķ m. Arabic 1 ditch; moat 2 trench

خندک khandák m. corral, paddock behind which cattle are driven

خندکی khandəkáj m. mastiff, pointer (breed of dog)

خندل khandə́l transitive [present: خاندي past: و يې خندل] to laugh, jeer at, deride ده پر وخندل Don't laugh at him. ورپوري مه خانده He laughed for a long time. دوی سره خاندي They are laughing.

خندني khandə́ni 1 mocking, sarcastic 2 funny خندني شی له ځان نه جوړول to become a laughing stock 3 pleasant, lifegiving

خندول khandavə́l transitive [past: و يې خنداوه] to make laugh

خنده آور khandaāvár laughable, funny

خندي khandí ☞ خوندي⁴

خندېدل khandedə́l intransitive [past: وخندېده] to laugh; guffaw; giggle

خندیل khundijə́l transitive [past: و يې خندیه] to preserve, safeguard, guard

خنډ khaṇḍ m. dialect [plural: خنډونه khaṇḍúna] dialect [plural: خنډان khandā́n] 1 stump, stubble 2 spur (on a rooster) 3 figurative hindrance, obstacle, impediment اغزي او خنډونه نبغ شول

319

Every kind of obstacle arose. ‫پيدا‬ ‫خنډونه‬ ‫لوی‬ ‫کښي‬ ‫لاره‬ ‫په‬ ‫شي‬ ‫يو‬ ‫د‬
‫کول‬ ‫خنډونه‬ ‫لوی‬ ‫کښي‬ ‫لاره‬ ‫په‬ ‫شي‬ ‫يو‬ ‫د‬ to create serious
obstacles in someone's path ‫کول‬ ‫ليري‬ ‫خنډونه‬ to eliminate obstacles
‫کول‬ ‫پيدا‬ ‫کښي‬ ‫لاره‬ ‫په‬ ‫خار‬ ‫او‬ ‫خند‬ to encounter obstacles

‫خنډکی‬ khanḍəkáj ☞ ‫خنډی‬

‫خنډل‬ khanḍál m. male of the keklik, keklik

‫خنډمنډ‬ khənḍmə́nḍ m. shrimp, short person

‫خنډن‬ [1] khanḍə́n m. wormseed root, *Curcuma zerumbet*

‫خنډن‬ [2] khanḍə́n knotty, gnarled (of wood)

‫خنډی‬ khənḍáj short, short in stature

‫خنزير‬ khinzír m. *Arabic* [*plural:* ‫خنزيران‬ khinziṛā́n *Arabic plural:* ‫خنازير‬ khanāzír] pig, boar

‫خنک‬ khunúk cold, cool

‫خنکي‬ khunukí f. cold, coolness

‫خنگ‬ [1] khing embarrassed; ashamed

‫خنگ‬ [2] khing m. sage

‫خنگتيا‬ khingtjā́ f. embarrassment; shame

‫خنگره‬ khóngra m. 1 dandruff 2 plaque (on the teeth) 3 scale, deposit

‫خنگری‬ khangráj m. *textiles* reed (of a loom)

‫خنگول‬ khingavə́l *denominative, transitive* [*past:* ‫خنگ‬ ‫يي‬ ‫کړ‬] to embarrass, shame

‫خنگيدل‬ khingedə́l *denominative, intransitive* [*past:* ‫خنگ‬ ‫شو‬] to be embarrassed, be ashamed

‫خنه‬ khṇa f. ☞ ‫ننه‬

‫خو‬ [1] khu m. *plural* 1 tinder 2 kind of sugar cane

‫خو‬ [2] kho khu m. *plural* 1 you see, you know, (emphasis) ‫ته‬ ‫تاسي‬
‫خو‬ ‫ويلي‬ ‫مي‬ ‫خو‬ ‫هغه‬ you know, I told you, I (emphasis) told you
‫دئ‬ ‫تللئ‬ ‫دي‬ ‫کار‬ ‫په‬ ‫کول‬ ‫خو‬ ‫څه‬ you see, he left; he (emphasis) left
you know, one must do something 2 however, but ‫خو‬ ‫وايي‬ ‫ښه‬ ‫ته‬
‫شته‬ ‫هم‬ ‫خبره‬ ‫بله‬ ‫يوه‬ you speak well, but the fact is…, you are
right, but the fact is… ‫خو‬ … ، ‫هم‬ ‫څه‬ ‫که‬ although…, but… 3
of course, that is so ‫ده‬ ‫داسي‬ ‫خو‬ of course, that is so ‫دا‬ ‫هم‬ ‫بيا‬ that's all
very well and good, but (emphasis)… 4 f. but, hindrance ‫غټه‬ ‫يو‬
‫شته‬ ‫خو‬ that's a big "but".

‫خو‬ [3] kho khu *Eastern vice* ‫بنو‬ [2]

‫خوا‬ khvā f. 1 side, direction ‫خوا‬ ‫پښنو‬ ‫د‬ south ‫خوا‬ ‫دا‬ here, hither ‫هغه‬
‫خوا‬ there, thither a ‫خوا‬ ‫دي‬ ‫پر‬ along this side; on this side b in that
direction, here ‫خوا‬ ‫ښي‬ ‫پر‬ a along the right side, on the right side
b to the right side, to the right ‫خوا‬ ‫ښی‬ ‫زما‬ to my right ‫خوا‬ ‫کينه‬ ‫پر‬ a
along the left side, on the left side b to the left side, to the left ‫په‬
‫خوا‬ ‫کيني‬ ‫چا‬ ‫د‬ near ‫پخوا‬ ‫ته‬ ‫خوا‬ ‫کيني‬ ‫زما‬ to my left ‫خوا‬ ‫پر‬ ، ‫خوا‬ ☞
someone, next to someone ‫خوا‬ ‫بلي‬ ‫له‬ from the other side ‫يوي‬ ‫له‬
‫خوا‬ from one side ‫شو‬ ‫روهي‬ ‫را‬ ‫خوا‬ ‫پر‬ ‫کور‬ ‫د‬ he started home ‫خوا‬
‫دي‬ ‫روهي‬ ‫را‬ ‫خوا‬ ‫په‬ ‫زما‬ ، ‫دي‬ ‫روهي‬ ‫را‬ ‫خوا‬ ‫هغه‬ they are coming to me
‫خوا‬ ‫هغه‬ ‫خوا‬ ‫دي‬ ، ‫خوا‬ ‫هغه‬ ‫خوا‬ ‫دي‬ *Eastern* here and there, hither and thither, in
all directions; back and forth, there and back ‫تگ‬ ‫راتگ‬ ‫ته‬ ‫خوا‬ ‫هغه‬ ‫خوا‬ ‫د‬
to go back and forth, there and back ‫د‬ ، ‫خوا‬ ‫له‬ … ‫د‬ ‫راتگ‬ ‫او‬ ‫کول‬
‫څخه‬ ‫خوا‬ ‫له‬ a from the direction… b *with the help of this turn of a*

phrase, the subject of the action of a passive voice is expressed ‫د‬
‫دي‬ ‫شوي‬ ‫نيول‬ ‫ترتيبات‬ ‫خوا‬ ‫له‬ ‫وزارت‬ measures were taken by the
ministry ‫خوا‬ ‫دوه‬ ‫خواته‬ ‫و‬ ‫ماښام‬ ‫د‬ bilateral ‫هري‬ ‫له‬ towards evening
‫څخه‬ ‫خوا‬ ‫يوې‬ a from all sides b all-around, comprehensively ‫خوا‬
‫کيدل‬ ‫ته‬ to step aside, avoid 2 direction (of the wind, etc.) ‫د‬ ‫نن‬
‫الوزي‬ ‫باد‬ ‫خوا‬ ‫له‬ ‫شمال‬ a northern wind is blowing today 3 country,
region, province ‫پښتونخوا‬ an old name for the country of the
Afghans ‫خوا‬ ‫مشرقي‬ the Eastern province ‫خوا‬ ‫جنوبي‬ the Southern
province 4 relation, connection ‫کښي‬ ‫خواو‬ ‫ټولو‬ ‫په‬ in all respects 5
mood, desire ‫کيږي‬ ‫مي‬ ‫ته‬ ‫خوا‬ I want (to eat, to drink, etc.) ‫پته‬ ‫خوا‬
‫سوه‬ ، ‫پوته‬ ‫خوا‬ ، ‫کول‬ ‫کار‬ ‫خوا‬ ‫ماته‬ ‫په‬ not to feel appetite disappeared
like working, without desire 6 soul, heart ‫شوه‬ ‫بده‬ ‫ورخَوه‬ ‫خوا‬ ‫زما‬ I
took offense at him ‫کيدل‬ ‫خوا‬ ‫په‬ ‫خوا‬ a to live in
perfect harmony b to become close ‫بدول‬ ‫خوا‬ a to offend b to
distress, upset ‫بدبدل‬ ‫خوا‬ to be offended, be distressed, be upset ‫خوا‬
‫توربدل‬ to arouse, arouse disgust, instill hostility, dislike ‫ورتوربدل‬ ‫خوا‬
to feel, have a feeling of disgust; feel hostility; no longer love, fall
out of love ‫ټولول‬ ‫خوا‬ to calm down !‫کړئ‬ ‫راټوله‬ ‫مو‬ ‫خوا‬ calm down!
‫اړول‬ ‫را‬ ‫خوا‬ ‫بله‬ ‫پر‬ to turn everything upside down ‫اړول‬ ‫را‬ ‫خوا‬ ‫سپينه‬ ‫پر‬
a to beat until loss of consciousness b to learn inside information
‫سپيدل‬ ‫خوا‬ ‫څخه‬ … ‫د‬ a a to calm down b to take revenge ‫سړبدل‬ ‫خوا‬
to grow cold, fall out of love b *figuratives* to be satiated, gorged
‫کبدل‬ ‫شنه‬ ‫خوا‬ to offend, distress, upset ‫کول‬ ‫شنه‬ ‫خوا‬ to be offended,
be distressed, be upset ‫کول‬ ‫خوا‬ ‫هغه‬ ‫او‬ ‫خوا‬ ‫دي‬ ‫ځان‬ *Eastern* to avoid
an answer, decline (by making excuses) ‫کبدل‬ ‫خوا‬ ‫پر‬ ‫چا‬ ‫د‬ to take
someone's side, be for someone ‫گرزول‬ ‫خوا‬ to feel nauseous ‫خوا‬
‫گرزبدل‬ a to throw up, vomit b to feel, to feel, have a feeling of
disgust ‫ورگرزبدل‬ ‫خوا‬ ‫پر‬ a to visit, to drop by b to come back to
one's mind, come to mind ‫هوارول‬ ‫خوا‬ ‫پر‬ ‫د‬ ‫خبري‬ to win over to
someone's side; persuade, convince somebody ‫يخول‬ ‫په‬ ‫خوا‬ ☞ ‫خوا‬
‫کړه‬ ‫يخه‬ ‫خوا‬ ‫دښمن‬ ‫په‬ ‫احمد‬ ‫سړول‬ Ahmed took revenge on the enemy
‫يخه‬ ‫په‬ ‫مي‬ ‫خوا‬ a to achieve a goal b to take revenge ‫يخبدل‬ ‫په‬ ‫خوا‬ a
‫شوه‬ ‫خوا‬ ‫له‬ ‫روحي‬ ‫د‬ ، ‫خوا‬ ‫د‬ ‫روحي‬ ‫د‬ I took revenge on the enemy ‫د‬ in the
daytime ‫خوا‬ ‫له‬ ‫شپي‬ ‫د‬ at night ‫خوا‬ ‫هره‬ everywhere, all places, all
‫وغبرزده‬ ‫ورسره‬ ‫کي‬ ‫خوا‬ ‫په‬ ‫زما‬ to intercede with him on my behalf ‫سوو‬ ‫د‬
‫خوا‬ ‫دي‬ ‫په‬ ‫را‬ ‫کالو‬ … it's already been hundreds of years that…

‫خوابدوالی‬ khvābavә́laj m. ☞ ‫خوابدی‬ [2]

‫خوابدی‬ [1] khvābádaj 1 offended ‫کبدل‬ ‫خوابدی‬ ‫څخه‬ ‫چا‬ ‫د‬ to be offended
with someone 2 distressed, upset ‫کول‬ ‫خوابدی‬ a to offend b to
distress, upset ‫کبدل‬ ‫خوابدی‬ ‫څه‬ ‫پر‬ to be upset with someone

‫خوابدی‬ [2] khvābadí f. 1 offense 2 distress, upsetting 3 indigestion

‫خواپوتگي‬ khvāpuṭagí f. 1 dejection ‫احساسول‬ ‫خواپوتگي‬ to be dejected
2 distress, upsetting

‫خواپوته‬ khvāpúṭa 1 distressed 2 offended 3 distress, upsetting
‫کبدل‬ ‫خواپوته‬ to repel, spoil one's appetite

‫خواپوتگي‬ khvāpuṭagí f. ☞ ‫خواپوتگي‬

‫خواپخوا‬ khvāpəkhvá side by side

خواتورن خواتوری khvātóraj 1 distressed, sad خواتورن کول to distress, sadden خواتورن کېدل to be distressed, be saddened 2 disgusting, unpleasant

خواټولوالی khvāṭolválaj *m.* calm

خواټولی khvāṭólaj calm خواټولی کول to calm down خواټولی کېدل to be calmed down

خواجه khādzhá *m.* [*plural:* خواجگان khādzhagán] 1 khojja (a rich merchant or landowner) 2 eunuch

خواخپوروالی khvākhporválaj *m.* distress, upsetting

خواخوږتوب khvākhugtób *m.* khvākhvugtób ☞ خواخوږی [superscript 2]

خواخوږی [superscript 1] khvakhúgaj khvakhvúgaj sympathetic, compassionate; responsive

خواخوږي [superscript 2] khvākhugí *f.* khvākhvugí 1 sympathy, compassion; responsiveness د چا سره خواخوږي کول to sympathize with someone 2 good deed; help

خوار khvār 1.1 poor; pitiful خوار سړی *a ... saṛáj* poor peasant **b** ... *saṛi* poor peasants, the poor خوار او غريب ژوند a miserable existence 1.2 *Eastern* thin, emaciated 2 *m.* .1 a poor man 2.2 [*plural:* khvārán] poor, poor people 2.3 poor devils

خوارځواکی [superscript 1] khvārdzvákaj weak, powerless

خوارځواکي [superscript 2] khvārdzvākí *f.* weakness, powerlessness

خوارزم khavārízm *m.* Khorezm

خوارژواکی khvārzhvákaj poor

خوارکوټی khvārkóṭaj *m.* poor devils

خوارکی khvārəkáj 1 *m.* poor fellow, poor devil 2.1 rather poor 2.2 modest, simple

خوارنجوکی khvārəndzhúkaj pitiable, wretched

خوارنجی khvārəndzháj gaunt, thin, emaciated

خواروالی khvārválaj *m.* leanness

خوارول khvāravól *denominative, transitive* [*past:* خوار یې کړ] 1 to make unhappy, make miserable 2 to offend, humiliate 3 to annoy, bother, torment 4 to weaken, make weak خپل ځان خوارول to get tired, become tired 5 to blow up (e.g., a bridge, pier) 6 to discredit, bring into disrepute (e.g., a law, custom)

خواره [superscript 1] khvārə́ *m. singular & plural Eastern oblique of* خور [superscript 3] خواره ☞ خپرېدل خواره کېدل خپرول ☞ کول

خواره [superscript 2] khvā́ra *feminine singular of* خوار [superscript 1]

خواره واره khvārə́-vārə 1 spread about; scattered in various directions خواره واره کول to spread around, scatter, throw around in various directions 2 uncoordinated, uncoupled *a* خواره واره کېدل to spread, scatter, be thrown about in different directions **b** to be uncoordinated, be uncoupled

خواري [superscript 1] khvārí *f.* 1 heavy labor; physical work خواري کول to toil, tire out by one's labor 2 *dialect* work ښه خواري یې پیدا کړې ده He found good work. 3 poverty, destitution; lack of means; extreme need, want *idiom* دا مسافري سخته خواري وه This journey was very exhausting.

خواري [superscript 2] khvāri *feminine plural of* خوار [superscript 1]

خوارېدل khvāredə́l *denominative, intransitive* [*past:* خوار شو] 1 to live in poverty; be destitute 2 to be wretched, be unhappy 3 to be offended, be humiliated 4 to grow weak, become thin 5 to worry

خواریکښ khvārikáx 1 doing physical labor 2 working, laboring, toiling خواري کښ لره، خواري کښ خلق workers 3 hardy, capable of endurance

خواره [superscript 1] khvārə́ *m. plural* 1 food, comestibles; nourishment نباتي خواره vegetable food خواره سکه food and drink 2 eating, eating up

خواره [superscript 2] khvārə́ *imperfect plural of* خورل

خواږه khvāgə́ 1 *masculine plural and oblique singular of* خوږ [superscript 2] 2 *m. plural* .1 sweet, candy 2.2 *figurative* pleasant thing

خواست khvast *m.* khast 1 wish وستری خواست last wish (of a dying man) 2 request 3 entreaty, supplication 4 begging

خواستغی khvāstə́ghaj exhausted خواستغی کېدل to die of exhaustion

خواستگاري khāstgārí *f.* khvāstgārí match-making

خواستگر khāstgaṛ *m.* beggar

خواستگري khāstgarí *f.* begging

خواشینی، khvāshínaj 1 offended 2 grieved, distressed خواشینی کول *a* to offend **b** to grieve, distress

خواشیني [superscript 2] khvashiní *f.* 1 offense د خواشیني ور کار regrettable occurrence 2 grief, distress 3 dissatisfaction

خواښې khvā́x̌he *f.* [*plural:* خواښپاني khvāx̌hejáni] خواښه khvā́x̌ha *f.* 1 wife's mother 2 husband's mother

خواښپتوب khvāx̌hetób *m.* state of being a mother-in-law

خواښیخېل khvāx̌hikhél *m. plural* relatives of a mother-in-law on either the husband's or wife's side

خواص khavā́s 1 *Arabic masculine plural of* خاصه 2 the nobility; the bosses; upper classes

خواگرځن khvāgərdzə́n repulsive; nauseating

خواگرځوونکی khvā gərdzavúnkaj emetic

خواگرځی khvāgərdzáj *m.* khvāgərdzí *f.* nausea; vomiting

خواگرزن khvāgərzə́n ☞ خواگرځن

خواگرزی khvagərzáj *m.* khvāgərzí *f.* ☞ خواگرځی

خوالو khvālú *m.* confidant, trusted person

خواله khvāla *f.* 1 secret of the heart; innermost thoughts 2 frank conversation, talk خواله کول to confide a secret (to); be candid with د زړه خواله یې را سره وکړه He opened his heart to me. He imparted his secret to me. څوک مې نشته چه خواله ورسره کم I don't have anyone to share with. I don't have anyone to open my heart to. *a* خواله ویل to betray a secret, let a secret out **b** to confess د ورورگلوی خواله کول to be close friends

خواله ساتی khvālasátaj 1 knowing how to keep a secret 2 *m.* confidant, trusted person

خوا مخواه khāmakhā́h ☞ خواه مخواه

خان [superscript 1] khān 1 literate 2 singing

خان [superscript 2] khān *m.* خانچه khānchá *f.* tray

خانمخواه khānakhā́h ☞ خواه مخواه

خواندن khāndán *m.* singing

خواننده [1] khānandá to teach reading and writing خواننده کول to eliminate illiteracy ناخوانه خلق خواننده کول to learn to read and write, become literate خواننده کېدل to become literate

خواننده [2] khānandá مرغان خواننده songsters (of birds)

خواوخاطر khvá-u-khātír *m.* memory خواوخاطر ته راوستل to remember

خوا وشا khvā-o-shā *Eastern* ☞ شاوخوا په خوا وشا کبني around, about

خواه [1] khāh 1 *combining form* wishing, desiring خیرخواه well-wisher 2 *conjunction* though, let خواه ... خواه both ... and ...; خواه په ښار کي، خواه په کلي کي both in the city and in the country

خوا [2] khvā *f.* archaeology ☞ خوا

خواهش khāhísh *m.* [*plural:* خواهشونه khāhishúna *Arabic plural:* خواهشات khāhishā́t] wish, desire; request د چا له خواهشه سره سم in accordance with someone's wish or request

خواهشمند khāhishmánd 1 wishing, having the wish, having the desire خواهش من دئ چه دلته راځي He wants to come here. 2 *m.* interested party

خواه مخواه khāmakhā́ willy-nilly; inevitable; without fail زه خواه مخواه *Eastern* Whether I wanted to or not, I had to go to the city. ښار ته ولاړم

خوایخی khvājákhaj *m.* vengeance, revenge

خوب [1] khob *m.* 1 sleep له خوبه uneasy sleep مظطرب او پریشانه خوب sleepy eyes د خوب خونه bedroom د خوب اسباب bed ډکي سترګي cloths خوب راوړل to put to sleep, lull; inspire sleep, plunge into sleep خوب نه راځي I can't sleep. خوب یې زنګوي He is dozing. خوب یې وړي vri he is dozing; he wants to sleep خوب کول to sleep خوب لیدل to dream په درانه خوب بیده وه She was in a profound sleep. خوبونه پربرده! Wake up! Awake! د خوب د قاصدانو لاس ته ځان سپارل to be deep in sleep تږی په خوب کښي د اوبو ډونډونه ویني *proverb* "The thirsty man dreams of a lake د ویبني خوب day dream 2 dream

خوب [2] khub *poetry* good

خوبا khubā́ *f.* dear, beloved

خوبان khubā́n *f. plural* beauties

خوبانۍ khubānə́j *f.* sweet dried apricot

خوبائي khubāi *f.* 1 beauty 2 advantage, superiority

خوبجن khobdzhán sleepy, somnolent; drowsy

خوبځای khóbdzáj *m.* lodging for the night

خوبروی khubrúj 1 handsome 2 *m.* handsome man, Adonis

خوبرویه khubrúja 1 beautiful 2 *f.* a beauty

خوب صورت khubsurát beautiful

خوب و خیال khob-u-khjál *m.* dreams, daydreams

خوبولی khobavə́laj *Eastern* sleeping خوبولی غوندي وم I had a nap. I dozed off.

خوبي khubí *f.* 1 beauty 2 advantage, superiority 3 something pleasant 4 good *idiom* په خوبۍ سره excellently, in superior fashion

خوبیالی khobjālaj *dialect* sleeping; sleepy

خوپ khup *m.* 1 sultriness 2 fog

خوت khot *imperfect of* ختل

خوټ khuṭ *m.* boiling, the action of boiling

خوټباد khoṭbā́d *m.* hernia

خوټ خوټی khoṭkhuṭə́j *f.* bowling (the game)

خوټکښ khuṭkā́kh *m.* toad

خوټکی khuṭkáj *m.* ☞ خوټ

خوټکېدل khuṭkedál *intransitive* [*past:* و خوټکېدل] *regional* to boil; boil up

خوټول khuṭavál *transitive* [*past:* و یې خوټاوه] 1 to bring to a boil, boil; cook by boiling هګی خوټول to boil eggs 2 to pour boiling water upon 3 *figurative* to anger

خوټه khóṭa khóṭa *f. anatomy* male child's sexual organ

خوټ هار khuṭhār *m.* action of boiling or boiling over

خوټی khoṭáj small

خوټېدل khuṭedál *intransitive* [*past:* وخوټېدل] 1 to boil, cook by boiling 2 to anger; get angry ماغزه یې وخوټیده He got angry. He flew into a rage. د غضب اور و خوټیده Anger shook him. Anger seized him.

خوجک khodzhák د خوجک کوتل the Khodjak Pass (south of Kandahar)

خواجه [2] khodzhá *m.* ☞ خواجه

خوچی khócha ☞ غوچي

خوځند khvadzónd starting, moving; oscillating

خوځندکه khvadzəndə́ka *m.* insect; small insect; mite

خوځندی khvadzəndáj ☞ خوځند

خوځول khvadzavál *transitive* [*past:* و یې خوځاوه] 1 to move, shift عسکر را خوځول to move troops 2 to shake, oscillate, sway, flap, flutter هوا د کړکیو پردي وخوځولي The wind shook the window curtains. 3 to cause to shake, shake 4 to send, dispatch 5 to put in motion, turn on (i.e., motor) 6 to agitate زړونه خوځول to cause cardiac disturbance a ځان خوځول to move, stir, budge b to collect, assemble; be concerned with collections خوځول کېدل *passive* to be put in motion; be started up (e.g., a motor)

خوځوونکی khvadzavúnkaj 1 *present participle of* خوځول 2 *m.* figurative motivating force; source

خوځېدل khvadzedál *intransitive* [*present:* خوځي، خوځېږي *past:* وخوځیده] 1 to move, budge په خپل ځای کښي سره خوځېږي He is fidgeting in his seat. 2 to shake, oscillate, sway, flap, flutter 3 to proceed, set out, depart 4 to operate, work (e.g., a motor) 5 to worry 6 to develop (e.g., of a culture) 7 *grammar* to have a diacritical mark, have a vowel sign

خوځېدنه khvadzedə́na *f.* خوځېده khvadzedá *m. plural* 1 motion, movement لاس او پښي مي د خوځېدو نه دي I can't move; I can budge neither hand or foot. 2 oscillation, swaying, fluttering 3 setting out, departure, exit 4 operation (of a motor) 5 worry 6 development (e.g., of a culture)

خوخ khuts *m.* خوخکی khutskáj *m.* ☞ خوټ

خوخول khutsavál *transitive* ☞ خوټول [1]

خوخه khutsá *f.* crack

خوتپدل khutsedál *intransitive* [*past:* 1 و خوتپده [2 to bubble up; boil

خود khud 1 *combining form* self خود ارادیت self-determination خود پرستي self-love, egotism 2 *pronoun* self, oneself په خوده کبدل to come to oneself, regain consciousness 3 therefore 4 *particle* but نو خود … or so … therefore

خود اختیار khudikhtijār 1 independent 2 *regional* of age

خوداختیاري khudikhtijārí *f.* 1 independence 2 *regional* majority (i.e., being of age)

خودآرا khudārā 1 well-dressed, smart 2 arrogant

خودارادیت khudirādiját *m.* self-determination د خوداراديت حق right of self-determination

خوداعتمادي khudi'timadí *f. regional* self-assurance

خودبخود، خودبه خود khudbakhúd unintentionally, of itself

خودبین khudbín self-assured, self-reliant; vainglorious; haughty

خودبيني khubiní *f.* self-assurance, self-reliance; vaingloriousness; haughtiness

خودپرست khudparást *m.* egotist, egoist خودپرست کول to display egotism

خود پرستي khudparastí *f.* egotism, self-love

خودبسند khudpasánd ☞ خودبین

خودپسندي khudpasandí *f.* ☞ خودبيني

خود بخود khudpəkhúda ☞ خود په خوده

خود خواه khudkhāh egotistical, egotistic خود خواه سړی egotist, egoist

خوددارانه khuddārāná 1 careful, cautious 2 reserved, restrained خوددارانه هرکلی کول to greet someone in a restrained manner

خودداري khuddārí *f.* abstinence; evasion, digression ديو شي څخه خودداري کول to abstain from, evade something, avoid something

خودرای khudrāj 1 obstinate; willful; headstrong 2 self-confident, having a high opinion of oneself

خودرائي khudrāí *f.* 1 obstinance; self-will 2 self-assurance, self-importance

خودرنگ khudráng 1 natural, having its natural color (of hair, etc.) 2 fast, stable (of dyestuff) *idiom* خودرنگ قلم fountain pen

خودرو khudrú خودروی khudrúj wild (of plants)

خودروبي khudruí *f.* growth under natural condition

خودساخته khudsākhtá forced, affected په خودساخته رسوخ with forced composure

خودستای khudsitáj ☞ خودبین

خودستائي khudsitaí *f.* ☞ خودبيني

خودسر khudsár wilful; stubborn

خودسرانه khudsarāná wilfully

خودسر khudsára ☞ خودسر

خودسري khudsarí *f.* 1 arbitrariness

خودښکه khudkhka خودڅکه khudəkhka really and truly; in very truth

خودغرض khudgharáz 1 self-interested, mercenary-minded 2 interested (in)

خودغرضي khudgharazí *f.* 1 cupidity, profit 2 interest (in) دوی د خودغرضي نه کار اخلي They are biassed.

خودکار khudkár self-acting; automatic

خودکام khudkām undisciplined; wilful; headstrong

خودکامي khudkāmí *f.* indiscipline, lack of discipline; willfulness; self-will

خودکرده khudkardá home-made

خودمختار khudmukhtár independent; self-governing, autonomous

خودنما khudnumā vain

خودنمائي khudnumāí *f.* vanity

خودي khudí *f.* 1 pride; vanity 2 individuality, peculiarity

خور[1] khor *f.* [*plural:* خوندي khvándi *Eastern plural:* خوېنده khvénde] sister د تي خور foster sister *idiom* ربيع ☞ لمري خور ☞ خلرمه خور جمادي الاولي ☞ دريمه خور ربيع الثاني ☞ دويمه خور جمادي الثاني

خور[2] khvar *m.* 1 crust, peel, rind; skin (fruit) خور اړول to peel; take the skin off 2 scab خور اوښتل to come off (scab) خور خور covered with scabs خور ورکول to tan a skin 3 scales, scale (fish, etc.) *idiom* خور اچول to moult, shed (of animals)

خور[3] khor ☞ خپور

خور[4] khur *present stem of* خوړل

خور[5] khór *combining form* eating something up, making use of something, eating or corroding something مورچه خور eaten by rust میراث خور heir بډه خور bribe-taker

خورا khvarā khvárā very, highly; exceedingly خورا لږ very little دوبي په دغو ځايو کي خورا ډېر تود دئ The summer in these provinces is very hot. دغه خورا ښه کتاب دئ This is a very good book. خورا شمالي نقطه The northernmost point.

خوراره khurārá *f.* leprosy

خوراک khvarák khorák *m.* 1 food, nourishment, victuals د خوراک شیان foodstuffs, food products طبي خوراک dietetic food لوی خوراک *Eastern* staple food (i.e., rice) 2 eating; drinking; ingesting food دچايو خوراک tea drinking

خوراکه khorāká *f.* food, victuals, fodder د خوراکي مواد food products, foodstuffs, comestibles

خوراکه باب khorākabáb *m.* 1 eating, food consumption 2 food products

خوراکي[1] khorākí khvarākí *adjective* 1 nourishing; edible; food خوراکي مواد، خوراکي شیان food products, comestibles, victuals خوراکي مواد صنایع food industry 2 fodder 3 provision, food

خوراکي[2] khorāké *plural of* خوراکه

خورجین khurdzhín *m.* saddlebag

خورجینه khurdzhína *f.* padded hat, quilted cap

خورځه khurdzá khurdzá *f.* [*plural:* خورځي khurdzé *plural:* خورځیاني khurdzijāni] niece (sister's daughter)

خورخل khorkhál *m.* ☞ خورخول khorkhvál *m.* ☞

خورد khurd 1 little, small; paltry, insignificant 2 *m.* khurd (a measure of weight equivalent to a fourth of a pound or 110 grams)

خورده بین khurdabín petty; captious; pedantic

خورده بيني khurdabiní *f.* pettiness; captiousness; pedantry

خورده فروش khurdafarósh *m.* retail merchant

خورده فروشي khurdafaroshí *f.* retail trade خورده فروشي کول to conduct retail trade

خوراک khvərák *m.* خوراک

خوړکه khoṛóka *f.* little sister, sis

خوړکي ¹ khorakí ☞ خوراکي شیان food products, foodstuffs

خوړکۍ ² khorakə́j *f.* little sister, sis

خورلنده khorlánda *f.* خورلنه khorláṇa 1 tribes-woman 2 fellow-tribes woman (so the members of the clan call a young woman who marries into another clan or tribe)

خورمه ¹ khurmá khormá *f.* fuzz (on the chin, face)

خورمه ² khúrma *f.* 1 cloudburst, downpour 2 pimples (on the face)

خورنده khurandá *m.* 1 (big) eater 2 glutton

خوړنه khvarə́na *f.* Eastern ☞ خپرونه

خوړول ¹ khuravə́l khoravə́l *causative form of* خوړل [*past:* ويي] 1 to feed 2 to entertain, treat رابانديي يي ډېر ښه خوراک [خوراوه] خوړولئ دئ He entertained me well.

خپړول ² khvaravə́l *denominative, transitive* ☞ خپړول

خورون khvarún *m.* Eastern 1 development د ادب خورون development of literature 2 intensification د تیاري د خورون په وچه because of the twilight

خوروور khor-vór Eastern خوړه وره khvará-vará *f. m.* [*plural:* خوواره واره khvārə́-vārə́ *f. plural:* خوړي وړي khvaré-varé] 1 spread about; scattered 2 dispersed

خوړه ¹ khurá *f.* 1 rust 2 gangrene; ulcer 3 corrosive substance (e.g., acid)

خوړه ² khvará *feminine singular of* خور ³

خوړهار khurəhár *m.* snore, snoring

خوړه یی khorajaj *m.* ☞ خوړئ

خوړی ¹ khavráj *m.* 1 pit from which clay is removed or taken; quarry 2 origin, provenance

خوړي ² khorí *f.* the relations or relationship of sisters

خوړي ³ khori *vocative of* خور ¹

خوړی ⁴ khavrə́j *f.* lum *idiom* خوړي پرایشول to give heat

خوړي khorí *combining form* خوشخوړي conoisseurship

خوړیدل ¹ khvaredə́l *intransitive Eastern* ☞ خپړیدل

خوړیدل ² khuredə́l *intransitive dialect* [*past:* وخوړبده] 1 to treat oneself (to); regale oneself (with) 2 to eat, feed

خوړیده khvaredə́ *m. plural Eastern* disintegration, breakdown; decomposition

خاورین khavrin khurin ☞ خاورین

خوړینگه khkoringá *f.* 1 betrothed sister 2 female friend, girl friend (of women)

خوړینگۍ khoringə́j *f.* 1 friendship among women 2 *diminutive of* woman-friend

خوړیی khvəraják khoraja *m.* [*plural:* خوړیونه khvərajúna *plural:* خوړیان khorajā́n] nephew (son of one's sister)

خوړ ¹ khvaṛ *m.* 1 ravine, gully; hollow 2 brook

خوړ ² khuṛ *m.* ☞ خۍ ²

خوړ khoṛ *imperfect of* خوړل

خوړسکه khuṛóska *f.* ☞ خوړسکه

خوړل khvaṛə́l 1 *transitive* [*present:* خوري ويي *past:* خوړ ويي] 1 .1 to eat, take (something, some food); eat a little په چا خوړل to eat; dine ډوډۍ خوړل to entertain, treat someone 1.2 to drink چای خوړل to drink tea شراب خوړل to drink wine 1.3 to take (medicine) 1.4 to bite; to sting 1.5 to pierce, transfix (with an arrow) 1.6 to appropriate (the property of another) 1.7 to take money, accept money (as a bribe) 1.8 to suffer (defeat, etc.) شکست خوړل to suffer defeat 1.9 to take, swear (an oath) قسم خوړل to take an oath, swear 1.10 to hit against, hurt oneself 1.11 *regional* to test, subject to a test 1.12 to receive (a shock, a flow) 2 *m. plural* .1 food, nourishment, edibles دخوړلو شیان، دخوړلو مواد nutriment, food products 2.2 taking (of medicine) 2.3 biting 2.4 appropriation (of the property of another) *idiom* غوته خوړل to dive

خوړنځی khvarə́ndzaj *m.* dining room, refectory

خوړنگ khvəráng *m.* food, nourishment

خوړو khvaṛó *oblique plural of* خواړه ¹

خوړوځای khvaṛodzā́j *m.* ☞ خوړنځی

خوړونکی khvaṛúnkaj خوړونکی سپی vicious dog

خوړوني khvaṛúni *m. plural* foodstuffs

خوړه ¹ khvára *f.* 1 sandy bottom (of a river, ravine) 2 dry stream, arroyo 3 alluvium, drift

خوړه ² khvaṛá *f.* 1 offering, gift (to a mullah, etc.) 2 refreshments sent to the bride by the fiancé 3 refreshments served in connection with a betrothal لو خوړه wedding feast 4 pension 5 *dialect* food for servants

خوړهار khuṛnár *m.* ☞ خۍ ²

خوړه مشر khvaṛamə́shr *m.* one of the masters-of-ceremony at a wedding feast

خوړه وال khvaṛavə́l *m.* participant at a wedding feast

خوړین khvṛin khuṛín 1 boiled soft; overcooked خوړینه اوګره kasha boiled soft خوړینه غوښه overcooked meat 2 overripe; soft, mushy (of fruits, vegetables) 3 soft, friable

خوړین پرین khuṛín-prin 1 boiled very soft 2 overripe

خوړینتوب khvṛintób khuṛintób *m.* خوړین والی khvṛinvā́laj khuṛinvā́laj *m.* 1 state of being boiled soft; state of being overcooked 2 overripeness 3 softness, friability

خوړینول khvṛinavə́l khuṛinavə́l *denominative, transitive* [*past:* ايي کړ] 1 to boil soft; overcook 2 to soften, make friable

خوړینیدل khvṛinedə́l khuṛinedə́l *denominative, intransitive* [*past:* خوړین شو] 1 to boil soft; overcook 2 to over ripen; soften, get mushy (of fruits, vegetables) 3 to become soft, become friable; make soft مځکه خوړینه شوي ده The soil became soft.

خوځول khvazavə́l *transitive Eastern* ☞ خوځول

خوځیدل khvazedə́l *intransitive Eastern* ☞ خوځیدل

خوږ ¹ khug khvə́g 1 *m.* pain, ache د سر خوږ headache سره له خوږو despite the pain 2 *predicative & attributive* painful (of a part of the body) ښی لاس مي خوږ دئ My right hand hurts. خوږ ښای

painful place; an injury *idiom* دزره خوږ with great effort, with strain, with stress

خوږ [2] khog خوږ khvagá *f. m.* [*plural:* خوږ khvāgə́ *f. plural:* خواږه khvagə́] 1 sweet 2 tasty 3 pleasant خوږه غاره melodious voice, pleasant voice 4 intimate (of friends) دا خوږ نقل دئ This is an interesting story. خوږي خوري Dear sister!

خوږتوب khogtób *m.* خوږتیا khogtjá *f.* ☞ خوږوالی

خوږلوری khogalóraj sweet-sour; rather sour

خوږم khugə́m *m.* jasmine

خوږمن khugmə́n khvəgmə́n خوږمند khugmánd 1 suffering, grieving 2 empathetic; sympathetic هغه ډبل په غم خوږمن دئ He is responsive to the misfortunes of others. خوږمن کول ☞ خوږمنول خوږمنیدل ☞ خوږمن کیدل

خوږمنول khugmənavə́l *denominative, transitive* [*past:* خوږمن یې کړ] to make suffer, torture

خوږمنیدل khugmənedə́l *denominative, intransitive* [*past:* خوږمن شو] to suffer; grieve (for)

خوږوالی khogválaj *m.* 1 sweetness, sweet taste 2 euphoniousness 3 intimacy (of friends)

خوږوبی knvagobáj *m.* 1 sherbet 2 syrup

خوږوکه khvagúka *f.* 1 relish, condiment 2 hors d'oeuvre

خوږول [1] khvagavə́l khogavə́l *denominative, transitive* [*past:* خوږ یې کړ] 1 to make sweet, sweeten 2 to delight someone, give someone pleasure or enjoyment

خوږول [2] khugavə́l *denominative, transitive* [*past:* خوږ یې کړ] to wound; injure; cripple

خوږه khvagá 1 *feminine singular of* خوږ [2] 2 *f.* candy, sweet, sweet dish

خوږکی khvagakáj sweetish

خوږلوری khvagalóraj ☞ خوږ لوری

خوږه والا khvagavālá *m.* sweets seller

خوږه وله khvagā-vóla *f. botany* liquorice

خوږي khvagé *feminine plural of* خوږ [2]

خوږیدل [1] khvagedə́l khogedə́l *denominative, intransitive* [*past:* خوږ شو] 1 to be sweet; be sweetened 2 to receive, get pleasure, get enjoyment 3 to be near, be dear (to); become close friends (with)

خوږیدل [2] khvugedə́l khvəgedə́l *denominative, intransitive* [*past:* خوږ شو] to injure oneself; hurt oneself; become crippled

خوږیده [1] khvagedə́ *m. plural* 1 sweetness 2 sweetening

خوږیده [2] khugedə́ *m. plural* pain, ache د سر خوږیده headache

خوسا khusá ☞ خسا

خوساوند khusaḍánḍ *m.* septic field, septic tank, sewage disposal pit

خوساوژه khusávzha *f.* kind of ferule (group of herbs related to parsley)

خوست khost *m.* Khost (district in Pakhti province and an area in northeast Afghanistan)

خوستوال khostvál *m.* inhabitant of Khost, Khostian

خوستی khostáj 1 Khostic, relating to Khost خوستي چاره dagger from Khost 2 *m.* ☞ خوستوال

خوسکی khuskáj *m.* خوسی [1] khusáj *m.* calf

خوسی [2] khusáj *m.* game in which the player stands on one leg and attempts to overthrow one another

خوش khush 1.1 good, pleasant 1.2 joyous, merry خوش او خرم joyous, merry 2 *combining form* good, pleasant خوشحال content, joyful

خوشاتر khushātaṛ *m.* flatterer; toady

خوش اخلاق khushakhlā́ḳ virtuous, moral

خوش اخلاقي khushakhlā́ḳí *f.* virtue; morality

خوشحال khushāl ☞ خوشحال

خوشحالول khushālavə́l *denominative, transitive* ☞ خوشحالول

خوشحالي khushālí *f.* ☞ خوشحالیدل

خوشحالیدل khushāledə́l *denominative, intransitive* ☞ خوشحالیدل

خوش آمد khushāmád *m.* 1 flattery; toadying خوش آمد کول to flatter, toady (to) 2 to compliment

خوش آمدگر khushamādgár *m.* [*plural:* خوش آمدگر khushamadgə́r] flatterer; toady

خوش آمندي khushāmandí *f. plural* flattery; toadying دچا خوش امندي کول to flatter someone; toady to someone

خوش اندام khushāndā́m shapely, well-formed

خوش آواز khushāvā́z possessing a good voice, having a pleasant voice; mellifluous, melodious; tuneful

خوش آوازي khushāvāzí *f.* possession of a good voice; mellifluence, melodiousness; tunefulness

خوش آیند، خوش آیند khushājánd 1 favorable 2 pleasant خوشایند خاطرات pleasant memories

خوشوی khushāí خوشائي khushājə́ khushāī *plural of* خوشایه

خوشبخت khushbákht happy, successful موږ خوشبخته یو چه ... We are happy that …

خوشبختانه khushbakhtāná fortunately

خوشبختي khushbakhtí *f.* happiness, luck, good fortune

خوشبو khushbú خوشبوی khushbúj خوشبویه khushbúja aromatic, sweet-smelling, perfumed

خوشبویي khushbuí *f.* scent, fragrance, pleasant odor

خوش بیان khushbajā́n eloquent

خوشبین khushbín *m.* optimist

خوشبیني khushbiní *f.* optimism

خوش پوشاک khushposhā́k well-dressed

خیشت khusht *dialect* ☞

خوش ترکیب khushtarkíb 1 good looking, pleasing to the sight 2 well-formed

خوشحال khushhā́l 1.1 content; joyous, merry; happy خوشحال یم چه I am glad to see you here. تاسي دلته وینم 1.2 lively, animated 2 *m. proper name* Khushhal'

خوشحالتیا khushhāltjá *f.* ☞ خوشحالي

خوشحالول khushhālavə́l *denominative, transitive* [*past:* خوشحال یې کړ] to cheer, gladden خپل زړه خوشحالول to take comfort (in), rejoice (in)

خوشحالي khushhālí *f.* **1** gladness; merriment; pleasure ... د خوشحالي دي چه ... I am delighted that ... It is gratifying that ... **2** liveliness

خوشحالبدل khushhāledól *denominative, intransitive* [*past:* خوشحال شو] to rejoice in, enjoy oneself زره مي خوشحالبري My spirit rejoices.

خوشخبرک khushkhabarák *m.* magpie (the bird)

خوشخبري khushkhabarí *f.* glad news

خوشختي khushkhátaj khushkháttaj *m.* خوشخط khushkhát khushkhátt *m.* calligrapher

خوش خلق khushkhúlk easy to get along with; of good character

خوشخوان khushkhā́n tuneful, harmonious, melodious

خوشخوني khushkhāní *f.* **1** tunefulness; harmoniousness, melodiousness **2** pleasant singing (of birds)

خوشخور khushkhór **1** loving to eat well **2** *m.* gourmand

خوشخوري khushkhorí *f.* gourmandise

خوشخوي khushkhój ☞ خوش خلق

خوش دل khushdíl خوشدل merry, joyful, full of joie de vivre

خوشدوخت khushdúkht well-tailored

خوشرنگ khushráng beautiful; beautiful in color, of a beautiful coloration (cloth); beautifully feathered (bird)

خوش سلوک khushsulúk civil, affable, well-mannered

خوش سلوكي khushsulukí *f.* civility, affability, courtesy

خوش صحبته khushsuhbáta sociable

خوش طبع khushtáb' merry, full of joie-de-vivre

خوش طبعي khushtab'i merriment, joie-de-vivre دچا سره شوخي او خوش طبعي كول to joke with someone

خوش قسمته khushḳismatá happy

خوش قسمتي khushḳismatí *f.* happiness, success

خوشكي khushakáj *m.* loafer, idler

خوشگذران khushguzarán **1** living for one's own pleasure **2** *m.* bon-vivant, playboy

خوش گذراني khushguzarāní *f.* **1** life for one's own pleasure **2** merriment, entertainment د خوش گذراني سندري merry songs

خوش گو khushgó خوش گوی khushgój eloquent

خوش لباس khushlibā́s well-dressed, smart

خوش مزه khushmazá **1** tasty, tasteful **2** interesting, attractive

خوشنما khushnamā́ khushnumā́ **1** beautiful; pleasant, pleasing **2** nicely put-together

خوشنويس khushnavís *m.* calligrapher

خوشنويسي khushnavisí *f.* calligraphy

خوشوقت khushváḳt خوش وقت joyful; happy

خوشوی khushój *m.* [*plural:* خوشائي khushāí *plural:* خوشايه khushājə́] maure; dung

خوشه khosá *f.* **1** ear, spike (e.g., of wheat) **2** cluster, bunch

خوشه چين khoshachín *m.* person who gathers ears or spikes of grain (after the harvest); gleaner

خوشهوا khushhavā **1** having good air; sweet-smelling **2** having a good and healthful climate

خوشي khushi *f.* ☞ خوښي

خوشي khúshi khúshe *indeclinable* **1.1** deserted, unpopulated خوشي كور deserted, empty house **1.2** fired, discharged (of a shot) **1.3** master less, without supervision (of cattle) خوشي كول **a** to discharge, fire (a shot) **b** to let go, release **c** to cede, yield (to) **d** to liberate (territory) خوشي كبدل to be let go, be released, be discharged **1.4** useless, in vain; futile خوشي ناسته idleness خوشي خبره idle chatter; empty talk; nonsense خوشي ويل to ramble on, talk nonsense, talk rubbish **1.5** crazy, deranged **2** in vain, without effect, to no avail وخت خوشي تبرول to waste one's time هغه كوښښونه مو خوشي توی ولاړل Our efforts were useless. *idiom* خپل نظر خوشي كول to fix one's gaze, regard, stare fixedly

خوشي khushí *f.* Khushi (district, Logar Province)

خوښي په خوشي khúshe-pə-khushe easily, without the slightest difficulty

خوښ khvaḳh **1** pleasant, nice, good **2** pleasing; preferred; desired زما منې خوښي دي I like زما دغه كتاب خوښ دئ I like that book. apples. **3** content, satisfied, glad زما (له ما) سره خوښ يې؟ Are you satisfied with me?

خوښناوه khvaḳhnāvə́ *imperfect of* خوښنول

خوښت khuḳht *dialect* ☞ خیښت

خوښتیا khvaḳhtjā́ *f.* **1** gladness, joy, delight **2** pleasure, satisfaction

خوښ من khvaḳhmə́n wanting something, desirous of something

خوښن khvaḳhə́n content, satisfied

خوښنوالی khvaḳhvā́laj *m.* ☞ خوښتیا

خوښنول khvaḳhavə́l *denominative, transitive* [*past:* خوښ يې کړ] **1** to دا خبره يي خوښنوم I don't like this room. زه دا كوټه نه خوښنوم approve کړه He has agreed to this. **2** to prefer, choose **3** to love, like something

خوښنوونکی khvaḳhavúnkaj **1** *present participle of* خوښنول **2** *m.* supported, adherent, advocate

خوښه khváḳha *f.* **1** desire; wish په خوښه willingly, voluntarily له زه به ستا خپلي خوښي سره سم in accordance with one's own desire خوښه وکړم I will carry out your wish. خوښه دي چه چای وڅنو؟ Do you wish to drink tea with me? هغه د خپلي خوښي دئ He is free to do as he wishes. **2** will په خپله خوښه موخپله ده As you please! خوښه خپل سرنوشت ټاكل to define one's own position, decide one's own fate

خوښه khváḳha *feminine singular of* خوښ

خو ښه kho ḳhə all right, good, very well, O.K.

خوښي khvaḳhí *f.* joy, gladness, pleasure ... دا د خوښي ځای دئ چه I am delighted to note that ... د چا د خوښي زبری كول to transmit glad tidings to someone خوښي كول to rejoice, make merry خوښي څرگندول to express joy, خوښي ور خرابول to spoil someone's pleasure په ډېره خوښي دي ته حاضر شول He agreed to this very willingly.

خوښي khuḳháj *m.* expenses for the wedding paid for by the groom's family; foodstuffs for the wedding feast delivered by the groom's family to the bride's home

خوښېدل khvakhedә́l *denominative, intransitive* [*past:* خوښ شو] **1** to like زما دغه فلم مي خوښېدو I liked that film. ستا راتگ مي خوښ دي I like to walk. I like walks. **2** to be content; to rejoice دپر به در څخه خوښ سم *idiom* Your arrival delighted me. I shall be very grateful to you.

خوښينه khuḵhína khoḵhína *f.* sister-in-law

خوف khauf khof *m. Arabic* fear, terror

خوفناک khaufnák khofnák dangerous; frightful, terrible

خوگ [1] khug *m.* boar, wild boar; pig

خوگ [2] khug *m. Eastern* ☞ خوړ [1]

خوگ [3] khog *Eastern* ☞ خوړ [2]

خوگلن khuglә́n *m.* smouldering flame or fire

خوگياڼي [1] khugjáṇi *m. plural* Khugiani (tribe) **2** khugjāṇáj *m.* Khugiani (tribesman)

خول [1] khol *m.* **1** helmet د سر خول helmet **2** sheath, case, holster (of a firearm) **3** casing (cartridge)

خول [2] khol *m.* light autumn frosts

خولبوړی khulbúraj *m.* stopper; plug

خولبول khulból broken up; minced; ground خولبول کول to break, break up; grind; mince خولبول کېدل to be broken up, be minced, be ground

خولپوټی khulpúṭaj **1** keeping silent **2** *m.* **.1** damper, oven door **2.2** lid د چاينک خولپوټی teapot lid

خولگی khulgә́j *f. diminutive* **1** mouth **2** kiss (on the mouth) سپينه خولگی خولگی دي راکه! Kiss me!

خولم khvә́lә́m stained, soiled

خولن khvalә́n sweaty

خولواښی khvalvā́ḵhaj *m.* string, twine; cord

خولوندی khulvandáj *m.* ☞ خولبوړی

خوله [1] khulá khvlә́ khulә́ *Eastern* kholá *f.* **1** mouth; lips; jaws, maw (animal) د خوله پيڅي کړه oral cavity خوله مي وتلی ده Shut your mouth! My lips have become chapped. **2** opening, mouth (of a mine, a ravine, etc.) **3** crater (of a volcano) **4** rims (of table vessels, dishes) د ډک په خوله brimful **5** neck (of a vessel) **6** muzzle (of a gun); barrel **7** point, edge (of a knife, etc.) دچری خوله پخه ده the knife has become dull **8** cuff; (coat, jacket) cuff دلستوني خوله cuff; (coat, jacket) cuff **9** *poetry* mouth, lips دا خبره د ټولو په خولو کښی لوېدلې ده from mouth to mouth Everyone is talking about this. This is on everyone's lips. نو بيا In such a case I will speak. د خان د خولي خبر شوم I heard خوله زما ده it from the khan. I heard it from the lips of the khan. خپله خوله هم *saying literal* قلا ده هم بلا One's mouth is both a stronghold and a misfortune. *figurative* My tongue is my own worst enemy. **10** said, expressed by someone د ورور په خوله يې هيڅکله باور ونه کړ He never believed what his brother said. د بل چا د خولي څخه from the words of strangers **11** kiss خوله اخيستل to kiss خوله ورکول to kiss (i.e., exchange kisses) خوله اچول *a* to attack someone with invective or curses *b* to be given to biting (e.g., of a horse) خوله اړول *a* to talk to no purpose *b* to be cheeky *c* to

خوله بويول، خوله پلټل، خوله کتل to query, make inquiries about, try to find out وازه خوله پاتېدل *a* to be startled, be rooted to the ground *b* to repent of خوله پر يو شي پتول to reject something, give something up خوله يې پته سوه He died. خوله اوبه پرېردي، خوله *curse* May you drop dead! خوله دي پته سه! to My (his etc.) mouth is watering. اوبه کېږي خوله پرېکول to speak, utter a word د چا سره په خوله به خوله کېدل، خوله په ورسره وهل to quarrel, have strong words with someone خوله په خوله نه ړدي *Eastern* He is a crybaby. He is constantly howling (of a child) خوله ترل *a* to compel silence, shut someone up *b* to give a bribe, buy (person) خوله چوله کول to smack the lips خوله چپول to begin to speak, start to utter a word خوله چينگول *Eastern* to ask for mercy خوله اسمان ته ختل to be surprised, be astounded خوله يې و اسمان ته وخته He was astounded. He was thunderstruck خوله خلاصول *a* to open, open wide the mouth *b* to begin to speak, start to speak چه خوله خلاصه سي، قندهار ته به ځو خوله خلاصېدل When we break the fast (i.e., when Ramadan comes), we will go to Kandahar. دوی ته هم د مرگ خوله خلاصه شوی ده Death also threatens them. خوله خوڅول to speak خوله يې و نه خوڅوله He didn't say a word. خوله خوري، سترگي شرمبېري *Eastern saying literal* The eyes are ashamed as the mouth eats. دچا خوله خوړول to give sweets, treat to dessert خوله کول *compound verb a* to tell off *b* to force to admit one's guilt خوله يې وخوندېده *a* he liked this *b* He dared. He became bolder. خوله يې نه درېږي *a* He (she, etc.) speaks ceaselessly. *b* He (she, etc.) speaks inappropriately. خوله نه ورته He و ختکي ته يې خوله نه درېږي can't wait; he wants to eat. درېږي He wouldn't say no to a melon. ټول يوه خوله دي All were of one mind. د تاريخ پوهان په دغه مسئله يوه خوله نه دي Historians do not have a single view of this problem. بي خولي، بي زبانه دئ *Eastern* He is not talkative. خوله يې سره to chatter without a let up خوله ستړي کول *Eastern* He decided to speak. خوله سنبالول *Eastern* to hold back خوله دي سنبال کړه Don't rattle on so! *a* to خوله په غلطه بنورول lie, prevaricate *b* to talk more than necessary خوله سمه بنورول *a* to speak the truth *b* to speak appropriately or aptly خوله يې بده نه ده *Eastern* He uses foul language. He swears. خوله يې طوی طوی شوه *Eastern* He was dumbfounded. خوله غوړي کول *a* to blurt out a secret, blab *b* to content oneself (with), to be satisfied خوله کړول، خوله کړه کړه کول to beg of, try to get someone to do something خوله گرزول ☞ خوله *a* to talk, speak, converse with someone خوله لگول *b* to be silent to spread, flair up (of an epidemic) اړول خوله مسکول *a* to use foul language *b* to take an oath خوله نيول *a* to fall silent, ډکه خوله to smile broadly to smile be silent *b* to abstain (from eating); be on a diet خوله اسمان ته نيول to live in poverty, starve خوله وازول *a* to speak indecently *b* to swear, curse خوله وازه نيول to get lost, get confused *a* خوله دي وچه سه! خوله وچېدل That thou mayest die! *b Eastern* to be thunderstruck خوله وراړول ، خوله وراچول to request something ورگزول *a* to try to get something *b* to make a request, intercede for someone خوله ورهکول، خوله ورخوړول to beg, cadge خوله ورانول

to give a bribe, suborn دچا خوله ورماتول to rudely interrupt, interrupt someone خوله په مومو وهل to fall silent, become silent خوله ویته نیول، خوله ویره نیول a to smirk stupidly; show the teeth b to be reproached c to bite the tongue خولې مي وینښتان وکړل I spoke about this many times. It bores me to have to speak about this. خوله پر لاس لګول a to try with all one's might b to be greedy پر خوله نه راوړل to keep a secret, hold one's tongue په خوله لاس اینودل to fail to mention, omit mention of something Eastern په خلاصه خوله بلل to shut up, compel to be silent په ډکه خوله پوښتنه کول to call someone loudly to ask loudly, ask at the top of one's voice په خوله سره to regret, deplore something په خوله کي تویول to compose, invent or make up something for the purpose of self-justification په خوله مي نه جوړېږي Eastern I can't make up my mind. په خوله کي سره جوړول چه تا خوله to decide to say something سره جوړوله ، زه بیا وپوهېدم You have not spoken, as I already guessed. په خوله کښي اور وړي Eastern He is very able. He is very imaginative. په خوله کښي ژړي اوبه درېدل a to disgrace oneself b to grow poor, fall into need, become destitute; to starve په خوله کي د سره توکل to reach an understanding, see eye to eye with someone د هغه په خوله کول to obey someone, follow someone's advice چا په خوله کنبي مه ئه، په خوله یي مه کېږه Don't believe him. په خوله کي لومه ده Eastern I am in his power. I depend upon him. لویدل a to remember someone's words b to speak lucidly c to interfere in another's quarrel په خوله مي نه دئ He does not obey me. په خوله کښي یي زه ورکړم Eastern He dumps his guilt on me. ښوک په خوله خوله په معلومات ورکول to transmit orally, communicate ښوک په کي وهل to interrupt someone, interrupt someone's speech تر خولې تیربدلل to receive ښه خوله یادول to speak well of someone more than is due تر خولې تپري کول to speak more than necessary, not to know how to hold one's tongue تر خولې ډک دئ crowded, chock-a-block تر خولې ژړي اوبه بهېدل a to grow weak b to become destitute, fall into need خولې ته قلف اچول، خولې ته کلپ اچول to be silent, fall silent دچا خولې ته کتل to await instructions from someone دخولي الم کلام ورسره نه کوم Eastern I don't agree with them at all. دخولي پلاو پخول He is a poor orator. دخولي Eastern to fantasize, dream; build castles in the air دخولي جلوستبدل to blurt out; say too much جلوستول to escape one's lips (a word) دچا د خولي ښخه خبري کښل to ask someone a question دا د خولي خبري نه دي Eastern This is no joke. This is not a joking matter. دخولي خندا affected smile, affected laugh خندا ورسره لرل to be friendly with someone on the surface; be insincere د خولي سر واښی یي نشته He wags his tongue. He's a talker. دخولي خوند یی بد شو He is immoderate in his demands. دخولي نه کارغان مه الوزه Take care, don't let the cat out the bag! له خولې وتل to escape the lips (of a word) دخولي نه ناسولتي باسي He is rude. دا کلمه له خولو لوېدلي وه This word has already been forgotten. وړه خوله Eastern Hold your tongue! خولي نه څه مه باسه! غټه خبره saying He's cheeky. He doesn't restrain himself. خولي، ډېري خبري proverb The words of man are like the ocean

waves. د خولي خوند، د ګېډي ویر Eastern proverb Your eyes are bigger than your stomach. خوارې خولي، ښرې خبري proverb literal poor mouths, rich words figurative He's a braggart. په خوله خوږ، په زړه کوږ proverb literal He speaks sweet words, but his heart is crooked. figurative the mailed fist in a velvet glove په خوله مسلمان، په زړه کافر proverb A Moslem in speech, but a kafir (i.e., unbeliever, infidel) at heart. چه خوله سپینه لرم، یاران مي ډېر، چه خوله سپینه لرم، نو یاران مي ډېر proverb The rich man has many hangers-on; the beauty has many suitors.

خوله [2] khvalá khvə́lá f. usually plural خولي khvalé sweat, perspiration مریض په خولو خولي تویول ، خولي کول to sweat, perspire خوله ورکول The patient was covered in perspiration کښي ډوب دئ to make to sweat freely په خوله کي باد وهل to thrust (alternately) into heat and cold وچلي نه یي خولي رواني وي He works by the sweat of his brow.

خوله [3] khvála f. ☞ خولي [1]

خوله ور khulavár khvə́lavár eloquent; sharp-tongued

خولي [1] khvalə́j f. 1 hat; skullcap; cap; headgear زرینه خولي gold-embroidered skullcap 2 technology cowl, cowling

خولي [2] khulé plural of خوله [1]

خولي [3] khvalé plural of خوله [2]

خولېدل khuledə́l intransitive [past: وخولېد] to press down, squeeze; press down

خولي والا khvalə́jvālā́ m. 1 hatter, hat-maker 2 man wearing a skullcap

خوم khum m. ☞ خم idiom خوم خراب شو false rumor set in motion

خومار khumár m. ☞ غبار idiom خومار نه په خوړل ، قمار not to care less, to be bothered in no way (by some matter)

خوماري [1] khumārí m. plural peach, peaches

خوماري [2] khumārí f. ☞ خماري

خومري khumráj f. 1 clay jar, clay jug 2 pail

خومبنی khúmkhaj m. dusty, hot day

خون [1] khun m. 1 blood 2 murder, bloodshed خون کول to spill blood, commit murder idiom خون جګر خوړل khún-i to overtax oneself in working

خون [2] khuván ☞ ښوون

خوناب khunáb m. poetry bloody tears

خوناړینه khunārína f. ferocity; bloodthirstiness

خوناق khonā́k m. angina

خون آلوده khunāludá bloodstained, bloody

خون بها khunbahā́ f. wergeld, payment (to a clan, family, etc.) in compensation for a death

خونجاړه [2] khundzhā́ṛa f. ☞ خنجاړه

خونخوار khundkhár 1 bloodthirsty 2 cruel, savage

خونخواري khunkhārí f. 1 bloodthirstiness 2 cruelty, ferocity, savagery

خوند khvand m. taste خوند ښه خوند good taste, pleasant taste تسي، pleasant خوند کول a to taste, try b to be to the taste, please ستاسي کتاب ډېر خوند It's so pleasant when … څه ښه خوند کوي که …

راکئ I liked your book very much. دا فلم خوند نه راکوي That film has no appeal. دا انگور ډير ښه خوند لري a to taste good These grapes are very tasty. b to be interesting, excellent ديو شي په خوند خورل to enjoy, revel in something ښخه خوند اخيستل to eat with pleasure *idiom* د خوند ځای a pleasant placc

خوندار، خون دار khundár 1 full-blooded 2 *m.* .1 man engaged in obtaining vengeance for the murder of a relative, avenger of a family murder 2.2 avenger

خوندور khvandór خوندناک khvandnák خوندنی khvandənáj خوندن khvandavār 1 tasty, tasteful, pleasant 2 interesting خوندن بحث interesting discussion

خوندول khvandavól *transitive* [*past:* و يې خونداوه] to delight

خوندي khvándi *plural of* خور[1]

خوندي[2] 1 khundí *m. plural* Khundi (tribe) 2 khundáj *m.* Khundaj (tribesman)

خوندي[3] khvandí defended; guarded; protected خوندي کول a to keep (i.e., a secret) b to watch over, guard (a flock, herd, crops) c to safeguard (health, honor) خوندي کېدل a to be safeguarded (e.g., a secret) b to be kept safe, watched over (flock, herd, crops) c to be safeguarded (health)

خوندي[4] khwandí ساتل sātól *computer science* save

خونديتوب khvanditób *m.* safety; preservation

خوندېدل khvandedól *intransitive* [*past:* خوله يې وخوندېده وخوندېدله] a He liked this. b He dared. He became more bold.

خوندي والی khvandiválaj *m.* ☞ خونديتوب

خون ریز khudréz *m.* cut-throat; murderer

خونريزي khunrezí *f.* bloodshed; slaughter خونريزي کول to spill blood, slay, murder

خونړی khunaráj 1.1 sanguinary, bloody 1.2 heavy (of losses) 1.3 bloodthirsty 1.4 bad, rotten; dangerous; threatening 2 *m.* murderer

خون سرد، خونسرد khunsárd 1 cold-blooded, calm 2 indifferent, unconcerned

خون سرده حيوان، خونسرده khunsárda cold-blooded animals

خون سردي، خونسردي khunsardí *f.* 1 calm د خونسردی نه وتل to lose self-control 2 indifference, unconcernedness

خونکار khunkár *m.* murderer

خونگرم khungárm ardent, hotheaded (of a person)

خونه khúna *f.* 1 house خونه دي ودانه May your house prosper! 2 room بدروم بدروم bedroom د انتظار خونه vestibule; reception room, waiting room 3 drawer (of a desk, cabinet) 4 *figurative* building, system

خونه[2] khavnó *m. plural* khavóna *f.* olive tree

خوني[1] khunáj *m.* 1 strewing or sprinkling the newlyweds (with flowers, etc. at the wedding) 2 gift (to the betrothed couple or to newlyweds)

خوني[2] khuní 1.1 bloody, bloodstained 1.2 sanguinary (of a battle, etc.) 2 *m.* murder

خوني[2] khunín ☞ خوني[1]

خوی[1] khvaj *m.* 1 wooden spade 2 wedding

خوی[2] khoj *m.* personality, character خصلت خوی personality, character

خوید khvid *m.* green forage, fodder

خبښ kheḵh *m.* ☞ خبښ

خوجاول[1] khojavól [*past:* و يې خوجاوه] *transitive* to cause inflammation, give rise to suppuration

خوجاول[2] khvajavól *transitive Eastern* ☞ بنوجول

خوجېدل[1] khojedól *intransitive* [*past:* وخوجېده] to suppurate, become inflamed

خوجېدل[2] khvaedól *intransitive Eastern* ☞ بنوجېدل

خي[1] khe *f.* the name for the letter خ

خي[2] khe getting down and remaining on the knees (of a camel) خي کېدل to get down and stay on the knees (of a camel); kneel to be kneeling (of a camel)

خي[3] khəj *children's speech* No, no! Nasty!, Don't touch!, Don't eat!

خيابان khiābán *m.* 1 avenue, pathway (in a garden) 2 flower-bed

خيار[1] khiár *m.* cucumber

خيار[2] khijár *m. Arabic* right to vote; choice; judgment

خياست khjāsát *m.* ☞ خاصيت

خياط khaját *m. Arabic* tailor د خياط دکان tailor's shop

خياط خانه khajātkhāná *f. Arabic* tailor's shop, tailor's workshop

خياطه khajā́ta *f.* seamstress, dressmaker

خياطي khajātí *f.* tailoring, tailor's work خياطي کول to do tailoring, work as a tailor

خيال khjā́l khajā́l *m. Arabic* [*plural:* خيالونه khjālúna *plural:* khajālúna *Arabic plural:* خيالات khajālā́t] 1 thought, meditation, idea, concept دا خيال کوم I think, I suppose ... زه ما خيال کاوه چه think that ... په خپل اوږده خيال کښي ډوب و He was deeply pensive. ډېرو کسانو ته دا خيال را پيدا شو چه ... Such an idea arose in the minds of many people. دهغې سره په لور خيال و She thought of her daughters. خيال پکښي وهل to think of something 2 opinion (زما په عام خيال دا دئ چه ... in my opinion The general opinion is as follows ... د دوی خيال اختلاف disagreement ... خپل a They think that ... b Their opinion is as follows ... زما هم دا خيال دئ خيال څرگندول to express an opinion I am of that opinion too. د چا سره خيالات بدلول to exchange opinions 3 imagination, notion, concept خيال وهل to suppose, imagine ... ده ته دا خيال راغئ چه It appeared to him, It seemed to him that ... 4 dream revery; fantasy د شمايلي په خيال کښي ورک و He dreamed of Shamayle. 5 supposition; intention خيال مي دئ چه قندهار ته ولاړسم I intend to go to Kandahar. خيال لرل to mean to, decide to do something چه خيال دي بدل نه شي! Don't think it over! 6 attention د خيال ساتل a to memorize b to be attentive 7 mood 8 whim, fancy 9 reflection 10 anxiety 11 *khajāl* pride, creation of self-esteem 12 *khajāl* ghost; apparition 13 *khajāl* decoration

خيال پرست khajālparást *m.* dreamer, visionary

خیال پرستي khajālparastí *f.* fantasizing

خیالمن khjālmə́n 1 willful 2 coquettish 3 imaginary; fantastical

خیالو khjāló Oh my beloved! Oh my dream!, My dear!

خیالوتکی khjalótkaj flirtatious

خیالور khjālavə́r 1 dressing in the latest style; fashionably up-to-date 2 dressed up

خیالي khajālí *Arabic* 1 imaginary, fictive 2 fantastic خیالي دنیا the world of dreams of fancies خیالي پلاو (پلاوونه) پخول to build castles in the air, fantasize 3 proud, haughty; romantic

خیالی khjālə́j *m. proper name* Khialaj

خیالی khjālə́j *f.* 1 dear, beloved 2 *proper name* Khiali

خیام khajjā́m *m. Arabic* 1 tentmaker 2 Omar Khayyam

خیانت khijānát khajānát *m. Arabic* 1 treason, perfidy, betrayal د چا سره خیانت کول to behave perfidiously with someone; betray someone 2 misappropriation د چا په امانت زوجیت خیانت a to misappropriate property held in trust b to abuse another's trust

خیبر khajbár *m.* 1 د خیبر دره، خیبر کوتل the Khyber Pass د خیبر غرونه the Khyber Mountains 2 *history* Khyber (settlement in Arabia)

خیبري khajbarí 1 *adjective* Khyber 2 *m.* inhabitant of the Khyber Gorge

خیت khit turbid

خیته khíta *f.* line mark سمه خیته straight line ماته خیته dotted line

خیتو kheṭú 1.1 big-bellied, pot-bellied 1.2 gluttonous 2 *m.* person having a paunch

خیتور kheṭavə́r ☞ خیتو 1

خیته khéṭa *f.* 1 belly, paunch, tummy په مره خیته خوراک خوړل to eat one's fill 2 hold (of a ship) *idiom* د خبري پر خیته ختل to interrupt, break in on someone's words a تر خیتي لاندي کول to put forcibly down b to put down, subordinate تر خیتي لاندي کېدل a to be put down forcibly b to be suppressed, be subordinated

خیتور kheṭavə́r ☞ خیتو 1

خیج khedzh *Eastern present stem of* ختل

خیږول khedzhavúl *transitive Eastern* ☞ خیژول

خیچن khichə́n ☞ خڅن

خید khid *m. Eastern* ☞ خوید

خیدک khajdák *m.* 1 yogurt; curdled soured milk 2 cheese in molds

خیر khajr *Eastern* kher *Arabic* 1 *m.* [*plural:* اخیار akhjā́r] 1.1 good, blessing, good deed, boon خیر او شر good and evil 1.2 well-being خیر دي وي! well, prosperously! په خیر سره I wish you prosperity! I wish you success! خیر دئ! خیر یوسې! I wish you prosperity. I wish you all the best. چا ته خیر یوسي کول to wish someone prosperity, wish someone all the best خیر به شي all will be well, all will end up all right خیر سفر غوښتل *khájr-i* to wish someone a happy trip 1.3 alms, charity خیر غوښتل to ask for alms, ask for charity 1.4 *used in proper names* خیر محمد Khajr-Muhammed 2 *particle* خیر دئ! So be it!, O.k.!, Let it be! O.k.! All right! 3 *combining form* well *idiom* په خیر راغلې! Welcome!,

Glad you're here! د خبره چېرې ځې؟ Where are you going now? *idiom* که نه وي خیر! If it doesn't work out it's no great pity!

خیر khir 1 furious 2 obstinate

خیرات khajrā́t *m. Arabic* 1 matters pleasing to God! 2 good deeds, philanthropy; charity (usually distributed at funerals) خیرات کول to do good deeds, perform philanthropy; distribute alms (usually at funerals) 3 tip, gratuity

خیرات خوار khajrātkhā́r *m.* خیراتخور khajratkhór *m.* person receiving voluntary contributions (e.g., a clergyman)

خیراتول khajratāvə́l *denominative, transitive* [*past:* خیرات یې کړ] to sacrifice (a sheep, bull, etc.); distribute alms (usually at funerals)

خیراتي khajrātí 1 designated for distribution in the form of charity 2 *regional* charitable, philanthropic خیراتي هسپتال hospital for the poor (supported by donations)

خیراتېدل khajrātedə́l *denominative, intransitive* [*past:* خیرات شو] 1 to be sacrificed (of sheep, a bull, etc.) 2 distributed in the form of alms (usually at funerals)

خیراخلونی khirakhlúnaj easily soiled

خبرازه kherāzá ☞ شبرازه

خیرالدین khajruddín *m. Arabic proper name* Khajruddin

خیرالله khajrullā́ *m. Arabic proper name* Khajrulla

خیراندېشي khajrāndeshí *f.* good intentions; benevolence; benevolent attitude; friendship

خبرڅوتوب kherdzətób *m.* shame; embarrassment; bashfulness

خبرڅه kherdzə́ bashful; ashamed خبرڅه کول to embarrass; shame خبرڅه کېدل to be embarrassed; be ashamed

خیر خواه khajrkhā́h 1.1 benevolent, kindly 1.2 kindhearted 2 *m.* philanthropist; well-wisher

خیر خواهي khajrkhāhí *f.* 1 benevolent attitudes 2 kindly feelings

خیرک khajrák *m. diminutive of* خیر 1.4

خیر محمد khajrmuhammád *m. personal name* Khajr-Muhammed

خیرن khirə́n 1 dirty, soiled; slovenly 2 *figurative* base

خیرنول khirənavə́l *denominative, transitive* [*past:* خیرن یې کړ] to soil, make dirty

خیرنېدل khirənedə́l *denominative* to be soiled, become dirty

خیرو khajró *diminutive affectionate of* خیر

خیرو khajró *f.* ☞ خیري

خیره khíra *f.* 1 dirt, mud د شپیلۍ خیره دغوږ ear-wax 2 slag, dross *idiom* د زره نه خیري لیري کول to make amends for an injury which has been inflicted

خبره kherá *f. Eastern* ☞ نبرا

خیره khájra *oblique singular of* خیر

خیره khirá dim, bull; blinded

خیری khiráj *m. Eastern* ☞ خیره

خیری khajrí *m.* mallow گل خیري *gúl-i* mallow

خیری khajrí *Arabic* charitable, philanthropic

خیري khájri *vice* خیر وي *regional* که خیري if all goes successfully

خبری kheré *plural of* خبره

خيرت khajriját *m. Arabic* **1** good, good deed; well doing **2** well-being خير خيرت **a** good, the good, blessing **b** well-being

خيريه khajrija *m. Arabic* charitable خيريه موسسات charitable institution

خېز khez *m* jumping, leaping خېز کول **a** to lcap up; jump up, bob up and down **b** to fall upon, go for خېز وهل ، خبزونه وهل to leap, jump *idiom* په يوه خېز in a flash *idiom* سيند په خېزونو روان دئ The river bore its water along headlong.

خبزان khezán jumping up, leaping up and down, hopping

خبزش khezísh *m.* upward flight, ascent د خېزش لیک runway

خېژ khezh *present stem of* ختل

خبژول khezhavól *transitive [past:* و یې خبژاوه] **1** to raise, raise slightly خبژول څوک په سولۍ to hang someone **2** to help to climb up (e.g., in a tree) **3** to raise (prices)

خبر khig *m. [plural:* خبرونه khigúna *plural:* خبران khigán] scab نيول خبرونه to be covered with scabs *idiom* دزره خبرونه mortal insults

خبرن khigán covered with scabs

خبرون khegún *m. Himalayan cedar*

خبشاوه kheshává *f.* weeding

خيشت khishtá *f. m. [plural:* خيشته khishtó *f. plural:* خيشتي khishté] wet, moist, raw

خيشت پيشت khisht-pisht wet through; soaking wet

خيشتول khishtavól *denominative, transitive [past:* خيشت يې کړ] to wet; dampen; soak

خيشته khishtó [1] *masculine plural of* خيشت

خيشته khishtá [2] **1** *feminine singular of* خيشت **2** *f.* snails

خيشتبدل khishtedól *denominative, intransitive [past:* خيشت شو] to become wet, become soaked; get wet

خبشکي kheshkí **1** *m. plural* Kheshki (tribe) **2** kheshkáj *m.* Kheshkaj (tribesman)

خبشوم kheshúm *m.* nasal cartilage

خبشومي kheshummí *linguistics* nasal

خبښ khekh *m.* relative, relation

خبښواله khekhvála *f.* ☞ خبيني [1]

خبښه khékha *f.* [1] female relative, female relation

خبښه khikhá *f.* [2] ☞ نبښينه

خبښني khekhí *f.* [1] relationship, relationship by marriage د چا سره to be a relative خبښني لرل

خبښني khékhi *plural of* خبښنه [1]

خبک khik *m.* خبگ khig *m.* large inflated skin (used for fording streams)

خبگ khig *m.* [2] *Eastern* ☞ خبر

خبگ khig *m.* [3] ☞ خوبد

خبگړي khigráj *m.* skin bag, skin bottle

خبل khel *m.* [1] **1** Khel (tribal subdivision), clan; extended family; *used as a compounding element in tribal names* سليمان خيل the Sulejmankhejli tribe **2** *used in geographic names* ماشوخيل Mashukhel (settlement in southern Afghanistan) **3** *history* cavalry squadron

خبل khəjól [2] *transitive Eastern* ☞ بنودل

خبلخانه khelkhaná *f.* **1** clan; tribe **2** dynasty

خبله khelá *f.* **1** nonsense **2** empty, void, worthless

خبله خند khelakhánd empty, void, worthless

خبله خندي khelakhandí *f.* nonsense, rubbish, idle talk

خيم khim **1** frozen **2** thick

خبمه khemá khajmá *f.* tent, marquee, pavilion خبمه درول to pitch a tent خبمه وهل *figurative* to jump (behind, onto), run up

خبنتۍ khəntój *f.* **1** small fry **2** act of climbing a tree (by the method of clasping the arms around the trunk and pressing the chest thereto)

خينجاړي khindzháří spoiled, bad

خنگ khing ☞ خنگ [1]

خينگتيا khingtjá *f.*

خينگول khingavól *denominative, transitive* ☞ خنگول

خينگبدل khingedól *denominative, intransitive* ☞ خنگبدل

خينو khíno *vice* بنه نو *dialect* all right, very well (qualified concession)

خيه khja *vice* بنه يي *dialect* good, very well

د

د dāl [1] the thirteenth letter of the Pashto alphabet; the number 4 in the abjad system

د də, da [2] *dialect* di *prepositon* **1** of (or similar possessive used for expressing belonging, relationship to someone or something) د پلار father's house کور د دوست ورور friend's brother د گلو بوی aroma of flowers **2** measure (or similar used in the meaning of a measure or portion of same substance) د چایو پياله **a** a cup of tea **b** tea cup **3** from, at (or similar usually in combination with the postposition نه، څخه *Eastern* expressing origin د کوره from the house د بازار from the market د خياط څخه from the tailor's ☞ څخه **4** for, for the sake of (or similar used in combination with the postposition دپاره) د کار دپاره for the work **5** *Eastern* than (or similar used in combination with the postposition نه when comparing) بازگل د ټولو نه مشر دئ Bazgul is older than everyone **6** *Eastern* under (used in combination with لاندي، لاندې below something, from beneath something) د مېز لاندي under the table **7** with, together with, jointly with (or similar used with سره for expressing commonality) د ورور سره with brother, together with brother **8** *used in combination with nouns expresses qualitative and relative adjectives* د ژمي wintry د خوند tasty د غره mountainous, wild **9** *forms compound prepositions and adverbs* د **a** دپاره for; for the sake of, because of **b** outside, outwardly د باندي، باندي on the outside **b** on, etc. د تاريخ کتاب history book بيا *Eastern* Then he started talking about going to the movies. يي د سينما د تلو وويل He knocked him to the ground. د مځکي يي وويشت

د di [3] *pronoun* ☞ دي [3]

د di [4] *particle* ☞ دي [4]

دا dā *pronoun oblique of* دي **1** *demonstrative* **a** this, these دا کور this house دا ښځه this woman دا کتابونه these books په دي کور in this house **b** *with words of feminine gender occasionally not inflected* په دا کوټه کښي in this room **c** *substantive* this, that دا څه شي دئ؟ what is that? **d** *in complex sentences may replace the subject in the second clause* د دوبي هوا توده ده او د ژمي دا سره ده In summer the weather is warm, but in winter it is cold **2** *personal pronoun, third person singular, feminine* she, it دا چيري ځي؟ Where is she going? دا څه کوي؟ What is she doing? مگر دا ده چه ... however, the point is that... دا هم ده چه ... besides (that), in addition (to that), furthermore بله دا چه and what's more; besides (that) که دا نه وي to be brief, in short لنډه يي دا otherwise, in the contrary case دا کېږي چه it may happen, it's possible او يا دا ده چه or else; or, otherwise دا دئ ، دا ده There it is! دا دئ راغلم Well, I have come. دا دئ چه Here's why. *Eastern* نو دا دئ چه **a** therefore **b** exactly

داب dāb *m. Arabic* **1** wooden axle (a simple mechanism with a wheel for lifting water from a reservoir for irrigating small fields) **2** custom; established ways **3** situation; condition

داباشي dābāshí *m.* foreman

دابه ¹ dābá *f. Arabic* quadruped; wild animal; livestock

دابه ² dābə́ *imperfect of* دبل

داتکی dātkáj *m. regional botany* Grislea Tomentosa

داتوره dāturá *f. botany* thorn apple

داج ¹ dādzh *m.* bride's dowry

داج ² dádzh *m.* darkness, gloom, obscurity

داخل dākhíl *Arabic* **1** entering, in-coming **2** internal ☞ داخله ² **3** participating, taking part in something **4** entered, included (e.g., on a list) داخل دفترکول *regional* file papers **5** accepted, enrolled (in school, etc.) **6** contained in something; being a part of something

داخلول dākhilawə́l *denominative, transitive* [*past:* داخل يي کړ] **1** to bring in(to), introduce (e.g., forces, troops) **2** to enter, include, insert (e.g., on a list) **3** to accept, enroll (in school, etc.)

داخله ¹ dākhilá *f. Arabic regional* entrance ده بنده ده داخله the entrance (is) closed داخلي کارډ pass, permit

داخله ² dākhilá *f. and plural, Arabic from* داخل وزارت داخله ministry of internal affairs, interior ministry د داخله چارو وزير minister of internal affairs

داخلي ¹ dākhilí **1** internal داخلي تجارت domestic trade ، داخلي جگړه boarding school **2** په مدرسه کښي داخلي شق داخلي جنگ civil war *m.* native of a country

داخلي ² dākhilé *plural of* داخله ¹

داخلېدل dākhiledə́l, dākhledə́l *denominative, intransitive* [*past:* داخل سو] **1** to enter, go in, drive in **2** to lead دا لاره کابل ته داخلېږي This road leads to Kabul **3** to be included, be entered, be enrolled (e.g., on a list) **4** to be accepted, be enrolled (in a school, etc.) **5** to get deeper into, penetrate deep into a territory **6** to be contained, be

part of something داخلېدل ورکارته يو کار to be busy with some work; get down to work

داد ¹ dād *m.* **1** scream, shout for help د چا په داد رسېدل to help someone **2** complaint; demand for justice; request for fairness داد ورکول give someone his due

داد ² dād *m.* gift, present; kindness, favor داد کول *compound verb* to give, present

داد ³ dā́d *m. suffix used in proper names* سخي داد Sakhidad

دادا ¹ dādā́ *m.* **1** father دادا کېدل *compound verb* to become a father **2** *dialect* older brother

دادا ² dādā́ *f. diminutive* sis, sister

داداتوب dādātób *m.* fatherhood, paternity

داداجي dādādzhí *m. regional, slang* **1** father, daddy **2** my good fellow (in addressing an old friend familiarly)

دادخواه dādkhā́h **1** *m.* plaintiff **2** demanding justice

دادخواهي dādkhāhí *f.* **1** request for help **2** demand for justice, demand for fairness دادخواهي کول *compound verb* to demand justice, appeal for fairness

دادرس dādrás *m.* rescuer, savior; intercessor

دادرسي dādrasí *f.* **1** justice **2** support, intercession

دادک dādák, dādə́k *m. slang* dad, daddy

دادگر dādgár *m.* ☞ دادرس

دادوبېداد dād-u-bedā́d *m.* دادوفرياد dād-u-farjā́d *m.* shouts for help دادوبېدادکول *compound verb* to call for help

دار ¹ dār *m.* **1** picket, stake **2** pillar, column **3** gallows, gibbet په دار کول , دار ځړول to hang someone on a gibbet

دار ² dār *m. Arabic* **1** house, dwelling, abode **2 a** chamber, house دارالعموم house of commons **b** house, residential building دارالايتام orphanage

دار ³ dā́r *suffix* possessing something, having something وسله دار armed دوامدار lasting (of peace)

دارالاقامه dār-ul-iqāmá *f. Arabic* hostel

دارالامان dār-ul-āmā́n *m. Arabic* **1** place of peace, tranquility **2** Darulaman (district of Kabul)

دارالانشا dār-ul-inshā́ *f. Arabic* secretariat (e.g., of the UN)

دارالايتام dār-ul-ajtā́m *m.* orphanage

دارالتحرير dār-ul-tahrír *m.* office, chancellery شاهي دارالتحرير *history* the king's personal chancellery

دارالحرب dār-ul-hárb *m. Arabic* **1** front, theater of military operations **2** *religion* land of unbelievers, land of infidels

دارالحکومه گي dār-ul-hukumagí *f.* governor's administration, governor's office, provincial government, provincial administration

دارالخلافه dār-ul-khilāfá *f. Arabic* **1** *regional* capital (city) **2** *history* Teheran

دارالرياست dār-ul-rijāsát *m. Arabic* capital, principal city of a principality

دارالسلطنه dār-ul-saltaná *f. Arabic* capital city

دارالسلام dār-ul-salā́m *m. Arabic* **1** place of peace, place of tranquility **2** Dar-es-Salaam

دارالشوری dār-ul-shurá *f. Arabic history* council (consultative body)

دارالعلوم dār-ul-'ulum *m. Arabic* academy دارالعلوم عربیه *dār-ul-'ulum-i-'arábiya* عربي دارالعلوم Sacred Academy (in Kabul)

دارالعموم dār-ul-'umum *m. Arabic* house of commons

دارالعوام dār-ul-'awám *m. Arabic* parliament (in Canada)

دارالفنون dār-ul-funún *m. Arabic* 1 university 2 Darulfunun ☞ دارالامان²

دارالمعلمین dār-ul-mu'allimín *m. Arabic* teacher training institute

دارایی dārājí *f.* دارائي 1 property 2 financial assets

دارباز dārbáz *m.* acrobat

دارچینی dārchiní *m.* cinnamon

دارکش dārkásh *m.* hangman, executioner

دارکوب dārkób *m.* woodpecker

دارنگه dáranga 1 *demonstrative pronoun* that, those په دارنگه ځایو Do not walk in those places کېنبي مه ګرځه 2 thus, in that way

دارو dārú *m. plural* 1 medicine; potion; drug داروکول *compound verb* to treat medically داروکېدل *compound verb* to be treated 2 *Eastern* gunpowder دارومردک *ammunition* داروگولی ammunition

دارودرمان dārudrmān *m.* دارودرمل dārudarmál *medicine* treatment

داروغه dārughá *m.* [*plural:* داروغگان dāroghán] *history* 1 head or chief of a district 2 head of a prison, prison warden 3 *regional* police inspector

داروگر dārugár *m.* 1 doctor 2 person who manufactures gunpowder

داره dára *f. usually plural* داري وهل ، داري کول dári 1 spray *compound verb* to splash, spatter, sprinkle; spurt ويني داري وهي Blood is spurting. اوښکو داري وکړې Tears began to flood. 2 *Eastern* current (of a river); stream

داري dārí *suffix of abstract nouns of feminine gender* وفاداري fidelity, devotion

داریال dārjál *m.* tambourine داریال وهل *compound verb* to play the tambourine

داریال وهونکی dārjál wahúnkaj *m.* playing (on) the tambourine

دارین dārájn *m. dual number Arabic from* دار² religion both worlds, this world and the one beyond the grave

دارک dáŗak ☞ دارو¹

دارل dáŗəl *transitive* [*past:* وېی داړه] 1 to bite; tear; gnaw دغه مېږه A wolf killed this sheep. شرمین داړلي ده 2 *figurative* to lecture, rebuke; give a telling off, give a scolding

دارو¹ dāŗú *f.* داړی dáŗəj toothy, having large teeth

دارو² dāŗó *oblique plural of* داړه¹

داړونکی 1 *present participle of* داړل 2 predatory, preying (of wild animals)

داړه¹ dāŗá *f.* 1 foray, raid; attack داړه اچول *compound verb* داړه کول *compound verb* داړه غورځول *compound verb* to attack, assault, fall upon (of a gang) 2 armed gang

داړه² dāŗá *f.* canine tooth; fang (of an animal)

داړه³ dāŗá *imperfective of* داړل

داړه مار dāŗamár *m.* bandit, robber

داړه ماري dāŗamārí *f.* banditry, robbery

داړي¹ dáŗi *plural of* داړه²

داړي² dárí *present tense of* داړل

داړی³ dāŗə́j *feminine singular of* دارو¹

داړې⁴ dāŗé *plural of* داړه¹

داړه مار dāŗemár *m.* ☞ داره مار

داړي ماري dāŗemārí *f.* ☞ داره ماري

داستان dāstán *m.* tale, story; short story, fairy tale; legend

داستان ويونکی dāstán wajúnkaj *m.* narrator; storyteller

داسکاله dāskālá *f.* cultivation, hoeing, breaking up, loosening (of soil)

داسي dási داسې dáse *Eastern* 1 *demonstrative pronoun* such ګاهي يې داسي I like this kind of book very much. لکه داسي He has never seen anything like it. such 2 thus, so, this way داسي نه ده That isn't so. داسي نه ده؟ Isn't that so? داسي مه کوه! That is not permitted! ډېر داسي سوي دي چه It often happened in such a way that... داسي نه چه This does not mean that... لکه داسي چه thus, for example او داسي نور and so forth and so on, etc, etc.

داش dāsh *m.* 1 oven (for firing bricks and clay pots), kiln 2 oven (e.g., for baking bread) برقي داش او نغری electric stove عمومي مديريت Directorate or Administration for the Production of Construction Materials

داشت dāsht *m.* strength, stability, durability داشت لرل to be strong, have stability

داښ dāx *m.* داښت dāxt ☞ داش

داښی dāxí baked in an oven (of bread)

داعي dā'í *m. Arabic* 1 instigator 2 plaintiff

داغ¹ dāgh *m.* 1 *literal & figurative* spot, stain, blot; slur داغ لګول ، داغ ورکول *compound verb* a to soil something b *figurative* to shame someone; stain 2 brand داغ اېښنودل *compound verb* to brand (as with a branding iron) 3 to prick with a hot needle (a form of medical treatment) 4 ☞ روغنداغ

داغ² dāgh *suffix used in geographic names (mountain)* قره داغ Karadag (the mountain)

داغدار dāghdár 1 soiled, dirtied, stained 2 *figurative* shamed, disgraced, sullied, stained

داغسر dāghsár *m.* tree sparrow, hedge sparrow, *Passer montanus*

داغل dāghál *transitive* [*past:* وېی داغه] 1 to burn; sear; scorch; cauterize 2 to brand 3 *figurative* to shame, disgrace له غمه داغلی *idiom* broken-hearted

داغمه dāghmá 1 worn out, unserviceable 2 *f.* scrap, salvage

داغمه خانه dāghmákhāná *f.* scrap depot, salvage dump

داغول dāghawál *denominative, transitive* ☞ داغل

داغه dágha *demonstrative pronoun* ☞ دغه¹

داغي dāghí spotted, stained

داغېدل dāghedál *denominative, intransitive* [*past:* داغ سو] 1 to be burned, be scorched, be cauterized 2 to be spotted, have spots 3 to be branded, have a brand 4 to cicatrize 5 *figurative* to be shamed, be disgraced

دافع dāfi' *Arabic* **1.1** repulsing, beating back (e.g., an attack, an onslaught) (د تانكو دافع توپ د الوتکي دافع توپ antitank gun antiaircraft gun **1.2** defending **1.3** prompting, motivating, inducing دافعه قوه، دافع قوت motive, inducement, incentive; impulse **2** *m.* [*plural:* دوافع dawāfi'] incentive, impulse, stimulus

دافع طياره dāfi'-i-tajārá دافع هوا dāfi'-i-hawā zenith, overhead; (more often antiaircraft) دافع طياره توپ antiaircraft gun

داقدر dā́qadár, dā́kadár so much, so many ☞ دومره

داکار dākā́r *m.* Dakar

داکتر dāktár *m.* **1** physician, doctor **2** doctor (the academic degree)

داکتره dāktára *f.* woman doctor, female physician

داکتری dāktārí **1** *f.* **.1** work of a doctor; medical work **1.2** graduate study for the doctor's degree د داکتری تیز doctoral dissertation **2** medical; doctor's

داکه dākā́ *f.* muslin; gauze, cheesecloth

دال dāl *m. Arabic* name of the letter د

دال dāl *m. plural* pulse (a variety of peas)

دالان dālā́n *m.* **1** lounge, hall; vestibule **2** covered passageway; corridor **3** veranda

دالته dā́láta, dā́lta *adverb* there (near you, at your place)

دالچيني dālchiní *m. plural* ☞ دارچيني

دام dām *m.* net; snare; trap دام اچول، دام ايندودل *compound verb literal & figurative* to cast a net; set a trap

دام dām *contraction of the pronoun* دا *and the conjunction* هم دا هم دا This is also harmful. دا تاوان لري

دامادخېلي dāmādkhelí *m. plural* fiancé's relatives, relatives of the groom

دامان dāmā́n *m.* **1** skirt, hem of a skirt **2** foot (of a hill, mountain) **3** valley **4** summer pasture **5** Daman (the territories near the Suleiman mountains inhabited by Afghans) خبره د دامان هوسی شوه *proverb* These words were futile.

داماني dāmānáγ *m.* resident of the Daman

دامدار dāmdā́r *m.* trapper, bird snare, fowler; hunter

دامن dāmán *m.* ☞ دامان

دامنه dāmaná *f.* **1** foot (of a mountain); region, district

دامنه داره dāmanadā́ra دامنه لرونکی dāmaná larúnkaj, دامبار dāmjā́r **1** vast, broad, wide, extended **2** long, prolonged, protracted, drawn out

دان dān **1** fog, haze **2** dust cloud **3** dim, dark

دان dán *suffix* knowing something پښتودان knowing Pashto

دان dán *suffix* vessel چایدان tea caddy

دانا dānā́ **1.1** wise **1.2** learned **2** *m.* [*plural:* دانا dānā́ and دانايان dānājā́n] sage, wise man

داناجي dānājí *f.* دانائي knowledge; wisdom

د انترنېټ پالنوال də intárneṭ pālánwā́l *m. computer science* Internet service provider

د انترنېټ جرګېځ də intárneṭ dzhárgídz *m. computer science* Internet forum

دانسته dānistá **1** known; well-known, noted **2** *f.* knowledge

دانش dānísh *m.* knowledge; science

دانشگاه dānishgā́h *f.* school

دانشمند dānishmánd **1.1** learned; knowledgeable; erudite **1.2** wise **2** *m.* **.1** learned man, erudite man **2.2** wise man, sage

دانشمندي dānishmandí *f.* learning, erudition; wisdom

دانگ dāng *m.* jump; leap, bound دانگ وهل *compound verb* to jump; leap, bound

دانگ dāng *m.* **1** one-sixth of something; **2** coin with the value of one-sixth if a drachma or dinar **3** side, part or neighborhood of a city **4** side

دانگ dāng *present tense stem of* دنگل، دانگل

دانگل dāngə́l *transitive* ☞ دنگل

دانگوری dāngúṛaj *m.* cucumber

دانگول dāngawə́l *transitive* ☞ دنگول

دانگی dāngáj *m.* stove (for frying kernels of maize)

دانگی dāngáj *m.* **1** run, running **2** flight, escape

دانگي دانگي dā́ngi-dā́ngi torn into pieces دانگي دانگي کول *compound verb* to tear, rip into pieces

دانگېدل dāngedə́l *intransitive* ☞ دنگېدل

دانه dāná *f.* **1** grain; kernel واښه او دانه forage دانه ټولول *compound verb* to bring in the harvest **2** granule, grain د واوري دانه snowflake **3** dot, speck, spot; pea **4** boil, abscess; pimple **a** د کال دانه blackhead; pimple **b** ulcer (from an oriental sore) **5** piece, copy شپېته دانې مڼي sixty apples یوه دانه هندوانه one watermelon

دانه dāná *f.* gate valve, water gate ☞ دهانه

دانه خوره dānakhóra, dānakhurá *f.* feeding trough, feed box, feeder

دانه دار dānadā́r **1** grainy, granular, granulated; having kernels **2** spotted, mottled; with spots

دانه دانه dānádāná **1.1** by the kernel **1.2** by the piece **2** scattered, dispersed

داني dāní *suffix* vessel صابون داني، صابون داني soap dish

دانيوب dānjúb *m.* Danube

داو dāw *m.* stake (in a game)

داوتي dāwutí *f.* ☞ داودي

داود dāud *m. Arabic* دائد *proper noun* Daud, David

داودزي dāúdzí **1** *m. plural* Daudzi (a tribe) **2** *m.* dāúdzáy Daudzai

داودي dāwudí *f.* chrysanthemum

داوس dāus *m.* **1** scoundrel, blackguard **2** coward

داوطلب dāwtaláb *m. Arabic* **1** volunteer **2** pretender, claimant, aspirant **3** plaintiff **4** person who wishes to participate in an auction, bidder **5** instigator (of war), warmonger

داوطلبي dāwtalabí *f.* auction

داون dāwán *m.* veil; shawl (woman's)

داوه dāwá *f. usually plural* داوه وهل، داوې dāwé *compound verb* to argue ☞ دعوه

داوي dāwí, dāwáj **1** *m. plural* Dawi (a tribe) **2** *m.* Dawai

داسي dā́hase *pronoun* ☞ داسي

داهمره dāhúmra *adverb* so many, so much, this many ☞ دومره

داهومي dāhomé *f.* Dagomeya

داهي dāhí *Arabic* **1** talented, capable **2** skilful, able

دای dāj *m.* course of masonry (in a wall) دای د اینبودل *compound verb* to lay the foundation stone (of a building)

دایر dājir, dājár دائر *Arabic* **1** moving, set in motion; revolving **2** working, operating, turned on (e.g., of a machine) **3** established, founded **4** instituted, brought (of a suit, a legal action) دایرکول *compound verb* ☞ دایربدل *compound verb* دایرول

دائرت المعارف dājiratuma'āríf, dāirat-al-ma'āríf *m.* دایرة المعارف *Arabic* ☞

[دایر یی کړ] dājirawól دائرول **1** *denominative, transitive* [past: to move, set in motion, turn **2** to put into operation, turn on (e.g., a machine) **3** to establish, found **4** to institute, bring (a suit, a legal action)

دایروي dājrawí دائروي circular, round دایروي حالت circle, round dance

دایره dājirá *f. Arabic* **1** circle دایره قوسي semicircle دایري *d dialect* face **2** circle, دایره ساعت circumference, circle محيط cycle **3** radius of action; range of action, flight range **4** *m. plural, Arabic* دوایر dawāyir institution دوایر مملکتي government institution idiom geography د طول دایره degree of latitude دایره geography د عرض دایره degree of longitude په چا دایره تنگول to nonplus somebody, put somebody in a bind

دایرة المعارف dāirat-al-ma'āríf *m. Arabic* encyclopedia پښتو دایرة المعارف The Pashto Encyclopedia

دائرة المعارفي dājratuma'ārifí, dāirat-al-ma'ārifí دایرة المعارفي معلومات encyclopedic knowledge encyclopedic

دایره وي dājrawí دائره وي حالت circular; cyclic(al) دایره وي (cyclic) recurrence

[دایر سو] dājiredól دائربدل **1** *denominative, intransitive* [past: to move, be put into operation, be turned on (e.g., of a machine) **2** to be established, founded, instituted **3** to be instituted, be brought (of a suit or legal action)

دایزانگي dājzāngí *f.* Dajzangi (district and province)

دایک dājók *m.* [plural: دایکان dājókán] spangle, sequin

دایکندي dājkundí *f.* Daikundi (province, Central Afghanistan)

دایم dājóm, dāím *Arabic* constant, eternal; stable, lasting; long, prolonged, protracted دایم دي وي افغانستان! *saying* Long live Afghanistan!

دائماً dājímán *Arabic* constantly, always, forever

دایمي dājimí, dāimí دائمي *Arabic* **1** constant, permanent, eternal دایمي نماینده permanent representative **2** stable, lasting; long, prolonged, protracted **3** دایمي حبس life دایمي life sentence

دایمیت dājimiját دائمیت *m. Arabic* constancy; eternity

داین dāín *m. Arabic law* creditor; lender

دایي dājí دائي dāí *f.* nurse, wet nurse دایي مور nurse, wet nurse

دباب dabáb *m.* bragging, boasting

دبابو dabābú boastful

دباغ dabágh *m. Arabic* tanner, currier

دباغت dabāghát *m.* ☞ دباغي

دباغ خانه dabāghkhāná *f.* tannery

دباغي dabāghí *f.* dressing, currying, tanning; leather business دباغي کول *compound verb* to tan, dress leather

دباندنی dəbāndináj **1** ☞ دباندینی **2** *m.* foreigner

دباندي dəbāndi, dəbānde **1.1** outside (of); on the outside of; beyond له مرکزه دباندي a not in the center b outside of Kabul تر بنوونخي دباندي دباندي They were situated تر بنار دباندي یي واړول outside of school outside the city. دباندي ایستل *compound verb* a to extract b to دباندي راوتل select, pick out, single out **1.2** outside, on the street *compound verb* to go out (onto the street, etc.) **1.3** abroad دباندي مړ سو He died while abroad **2** *predicate* external; going beyond, going outside something **3** *attributive* ☞ د دباندي بنکته دباندینی *idiom* down د هیواد په دباندي او دننه کښي outside and inside the country له دباندي څخه from abroad

دباندینی dəbāndináj, dibāndináj **1** external, foreign د دباندینی وزارت، ministry of foreign affairs **2** exterior, outside **3** strange, alien, other's; (from) outside

دباندي [2] dəbānde *Eastern* ☞ دباندي

دباو dabáw *m. Eastern* **1** pressure **2** influence په دباو سره peremptorily **3** pomp, splendor

دبت dibít, debét *m. accounting* debit

دبدبه dabdabá *f. Arabic* **1** pomp, splendor په ډېره دبدبه with great ceremony **2** *regional* fear, terror

دبړ dabáŗ fat, stout, plump

دبز dabáz heavy, coarse (of cloth)

دبستان dabistán *m.* school

دبکه dabká *f.* intimidation, threat

دبل dāból *transitive* [past: دابه وي] drive in, hammer in, sink (into the ground)

دبلن dablín *m.* Dublin

دبله dabóla *f.* bin

دبلاج dabláj *m.* [plural: دبلي dablí and *Western* دبلیان dabliján] box; jar, pot (tin) can د چایو دبلی tea caddy

دبه dabá *f.* **1** vessel for oil **2** leather wineskin

دبي [1] dabí ripening in straw or leaves (of fruit)

دبی [2] dabáj *m.* **1** cudgel, club **2** washing beetle (for doing laundry)

دبیز dabíz ☞ دبز

دپ [1] dəp **1** *m. dialect* sweltering heat, stuffiness دپ سو It became stuffy **2.1** close, stuffy, stifling **2.2** to become deaf **2.3** cloudy, overcast, gloomy دپ کېدل *compound verb* a to be close, be stuffy b to become deaf غوږونه یې دپ سول He went deaf c to be cloudy, be overcast

دپ [2] dap *paired word with* هپ

دپاره dəpāra, dapāra, dipāra لپاره *postposition less often preposition, alone or in combination with the preposition* د **1** for the sake of; because of; for دپیسو د کار دپاره for the work ستا دپاره for you دپاره for the sake of money د څه دپاره؟ What for? **2** for (used when denoting a time period) د څو ورځو دپاره for several days همیشه دپاره forever **3** for something, against something (of a medication,

د سل د مرض دپاره دوا medication for (remedy for something) tuberculosis نو د همدي دپاره This is why.

دپاري dəpáre *contraction of the postposition* دپاره *and the pronoun* يي

دپاسه dəpā́sa, dapā́sa, dipā́sa *postposition in combination with the preposition* د *or Eastern without it* 1 above, over, on top of something دکور دپاسه above the house 2 besides, in addition to, over, in excess of دنومورو کتابونو دپاسه in addition to the books mentioned ...چه کبري کاله شل دپاسه څه It's been over twenty years already since...

دپتيا dəptjā́, daptjā́ *f.* ☞ دپه

دپاره دوپړي dəpáre-dupáře *f. plural* د خولې دپړي دوپړي foolish thing, nonsense

دبکه dapká *f.* ☞

دپلوم diplóm *m.* diploma

ديپلومات diplomā́t *m.* ☞ ديپلومات

ديپلوماتي diplomātí ☞ ديپلوماتي

ديپلوماسي diplomāsí ☞ ديپلوماسي

دپلومه diplómá *f.* ☞ دپلوم

دپه dəpa 1 *f.* stuffiness, stuffy air, foul air 2 *feminine singular from* دپ 2 دپه هوا stuffiness, stuffy air, foul air

د تېروتني خبرال də terwatəní khabrā́l *m. computer science* error log

دجاج dudzhā́dzh *m.* domestic fowl, poultry

دجال dadzhā́l *m. Arabic* 1 antichrist 2 swindler

دجله dadzhlá, didzhlá *f. Arabic* the Tigris River د دجلي سيند the Tigris

دچ dach ☞ ځ

د چا də chā́ *pronoun* whose ☞ څوک

دوچار duchár ☞ دوچار

دځان dədzā́n one's, one's own, his own, her own ☞ ځان

دځانول dədzānawə́l *denominative, transitive* [*past:* دځان يې کړ] take something; acquire something

دخالت dəkhālát, dikhālát *m. Arabic* 1 interference; intervention دخالت کول *compound verb* to interfere 2 relationship, relation, connection

دخانيات dukhānijiā́t, dukhānijiā́t *m. plural Arabic* tobacco products د دخانياتو استعمال smoking

دخل dákhl *m. Arabic* 1 income, profit 2 relationship, relation, connection دخل کول *compound verb* to interfere دخل لرل *compound verb* a to have a relationship or connection with something; take part or to participate in something; play a part or to have a role in something b to have access to something

دخمه dakhmá *f.* 1 corner, nook دخمه نيول، په دخمه کښېنستل *compound verb* to hide or conceal oneself 2 tomb, sepulcher; grave 3 ambush

دخول dukhúl *m. Arabic* entry; invasion, encroachment

دخيل dakhíl *Arabic* 1.1 borrowed (of a word) 1.2 close, intimate (of a friend) 2 *m.* agent, proxy, accredited representative

دد dad *m.* wild animal, beast

د دوتنه نوم شاتاړی də dawtəná nūm shātā́ṛay *m. computer science* file name extension

د دوتنه ځانگړني لنتيال də dawtəná dzāngáṛne jakhtjā́l *m. computer science* file allocation table (FAT)

د دوی də dúj, də dój *pronoun* their, theirs ☞ دوی 2 3

د ده da də́ *pronoun* his ☞ ده 2 3

د دې də dé *pronoun* her, hers ☞ دې 2 3 د دې کبله، د دې له کبله for this reason

د دې نه da déna *Eastern instead of* د دې څخه from this

در dar *m.* 1 door 2 *figurative* access

در dur, durr *m. Arabic* pearl

در dər, dar 1 *pronoun, second person singular & plural* 1.1 to you, for you (combinations with postpositions and adverbs are to be found in their alphabetical order) 1.2 to you, with you (denotes the one to whom the action is addressed, functioning as an adverbial indirect object, placed before the predicate) دا کتاب مې در وباخښنه I gave you this book. څه در کبري؟ What's the matter with you? څه در وسوه؟ What happened to you? 1.3 *with certain verbs of motion indicates the direction of the action* درورسېدم I came to see you. يه، زه به نسم در No, I won't be coming. 2 *verbal prefix* زه تاسي ته خپله کتابچه درکوم ،درتلل ،درکول and others I am giving you my notebook.

دري dri *numeral* ☞ در

درازه drā́za *f.* 1 *anatomy* fontanel 2 earthquake

دراست dirāsát *m. Arabic* studies; study

درافتنگ drā́ftíng *m.* drawing, drafting د درافتنگ سامان drawing implements

درافشاني durāfshā́ní, durrāfshā́ní *f.* eloquence

دراک darā́k, darrā́k *Arabic* shrewd, keen-witted, ingenious, intelligent د راکه قوه shrewdness

دراماتورژي drāmāturzhí *f.* ☞ درامه نويسي

درآمد darāmád *m.* profit; income; receipts

درامه drāmá *f.* play, drama منظومه درامه play in verse

درامه نويس drāmanawís *m.* playwright, dramatist

درامه نويسي drāmanawisí *f.* dramaturgy

درانده drāndə́ *dialect masculine plural of* دروند

درانه drā́nə 1 *m. plural of* دروند 2 *m. plural* heavy load, weight

دراني durānaj *m. plural* 1 Durani (tribe) 2 Durani 3 *m. proper noun* Duranai, Duranay

دراني durānə́j *f.* 1 Durani woman 2 *proper noun* Durani

دراوه darāwə́ *imperative of* درول

درايي darājí *f.* درائي darāí striped taffeta

درب drab *m. plural* 1 species of meadow grass, *Poa cynosuroides* 2 meadow, grassland

درب drab 1 *interjection* boom, bang 2 *m.* 2.1 noise, sound, crash, din; knocking, rattling; rumble, hum درب وهل *compound verb* to make a noise, rumble; knock, rattle 2.2 lie, falsehood درواغ او درب He lied blatantly. يې ډېر وويل

درب drab *m.* scab, mange

دربا drabā *f.* ☞ دربهار

دربار darbār² *m.* **1** court, palace (of the monarch) د دربار وزير court minister احمق د دربار جستر court jester **2** audience, reception درباركول *compound verb* to arrange an audience or reception

درباري darbārí **1** *m.* courtier **2** court

دربان darbān *m.* gatekeeper, doorkeeper

درباندي dárbāndi, dárbānde *pronoun* **1** for you **2** with you داخه چار ؟درباندي وشو *Eastern* What happened to you? **3** with your help, with your assistance **4** to you, for you درباندي گران و He was dear to you.

دربچه darbachá *f.* **1** window **2** small cupboard

دربدر darbadár homeless; poor; destitute, impoverished; ruined دربدركول *compound verb* **a** to ruin **b** to squander (money)

دربدرباني drabdrabānaj *m.* hide-and-seek (children's game) درب درباني كول *compound verb* to play hide-and-seek

درب دروب drabdrúb *m.,* درب دروپ drabdrúp *m.* scuffle, fight, brawl

دربدري darbadarí *f.* homelessness; poverty, destitution

دربر darbə́r ☞ دبر

درب drabə́l¹ *transitive* [*past:* وبي درابه] to compress, squeeze, ram, tamp

درب drabə́l² *intransitive* [*past:* ودرابه] to fall with a crash; collapse, cave in

دربل durbál, dərbál³ *m.* hobble, fetters

دربلول durbalawə́l, dərbalawə́l *denominative, transitive* [*past:* دربل يې كړ] to hobble

دربله dárbla, drablá¹ *f.* **1** pressed manure **2** clump of mud

دربله darbilá, durbilá² *paired word with* توره completely dark

دربلج durbəláj *m.* fetters

دربلي dərbəláj¹ *f.* **1** tripod **2** type of swing

دربلي darbaláj² *f. regional* joy, rejoicing, jubilation

دربلبدل durbaledə́l, dərbaledə́l *denominative, intransitive* [*past:* دربل شو] to be hobbled, be fettered

دربند darbánd **1** *m.* **.1** gorge, narrow mountain pass **1.2** bolt, bar **2** taken prisoner, captured; imprisoned

درب و دروب drab-u-drúb, drab-wə-drúb *m.* **1** thunder, crash, roar, din, noise **2** *figurative* festival, celebration په ډېر درب و دروب with ceremony

دربول drəbawə́l, drabawə́l *transitive* [*past:* وبي درباوه] **1** to stamp (one's foot) **2** to beat (a drum) **3** to shake, shake up **4** to beat, hit, strike, thrash (somebody)

دربه drə́ba, drába *f.* darkness, the dark, gloom

دربهار drəbahár *m.* **1** noise, din **2** beating (of a drum) **3** stamping دربهاركول *compound verb* **a** to make noise, thunder, rattle, clank **b** to beat (a drum) **c** to stamp *idiom* د زړه دربهار the beating of the heart

دربهتوب drəbatób *m.* ☞ دربه

دربدر، دربدره darbadár ☞ در په در

دربي drabaj *m.* ☞ دربهار

دربدل drabedə́l *intransitive* [*past:* و دربهده] **1** to thunder, crash, rumble, rattle, clank **2** to rumble from footsteps, hoof beats, etc.

دربهدونكي drabedúnkaj *music* دربهدونكي آلي drabedúnki ālé percussion instruments

دربله darbelá *f.* ☞ دربله¹

دريسي dárpase *adverb* after you دريسي به درځو We will go after you.

دربدر، دربدره darpadár ☞ در په در

درتگ dartág *m.* arrival at your place or house

درتلل dartlə́l *intransitive* [*present:* درځي *imperfect:* درتئ *past:* درغئ] to go to your house or place زه سبا درځم Tomorrow I am planning to come to your house. زه به درسم I will come to your place ژر راسه! Come here quickly! درغلم! I'm coming!

درته dárta *adverb* **1** to you, for you **2** to you, to your place or house **3** next to you, beside you

درج dardzh *Arabic* **1** *m.* inclusion, insertion, entry, entering, recording **2** *predicate* included, inserted, entered, recorded

درجات daradzhā́t *m. plural Arabic from* درجه

درجول dardzhawə́l *denominative, transitive* [*past:* درج يې کړ] include, insert, enter, record

درجه dardzhá, daradzhá *f. Arabic* [*plural:* درجي daradzhé *and m. plural Arabic* درجات daradzhā́t] **1** degree د يوي درجي پوري to a certain degree د مقايسي درجي in varying degree په متفاوتو درجاتو *grammar* degree of comparison **2** category, type, sort, class لومړى a first category, first class **b** first-class **3** rank, title **4** sort درجه ورکول *compound verb* to sort **5** degree (measure of temperature) د حرارت درجه، د تودوخي درجه، د تودوالي درجه temperature د تودوخي درجه تر ۴۰ پوري رسېږي The temperature reaches 40 degrees. په آخري درجي پوري، په extremely اخره درجه absolutely په درجو much

درجه بندي daradzhabandí *f.* **1** classification **2** sorting, grading, classifying درجه بندي کول *compound verb* **a** to classify **b** to sort

درجبدل dardzhedə́l *denominative, intransitive* [*past:* درج شو] to be included, be entered (e.g., on a list)

درچل drəchə́l *intransitive* [*past:* ودرچبده] to sneeze

درچول drəchawə́l *transitive* [*past:* وبي درچاوه] to cause to sneeze, make someone sneeze

درز dardz *m.* ☞ درز¹

دردزني dárdzəni ☞ درخه

درځه dárdza *imperfective imperative of* درتلل درځه چه ځو! Let's go!

درځي dárdzi *present tense of* درتلل

درتسخه dártsəkha you have..., do you have...; from you خو روپي زما قلم درخه دئ؟ Do you have my pen? درخخه دي؟ How much money do you have?

دريچه durə́tsa *f.* ☞ دريچه

درخاني durkhānə́j *f. proper noun* Durkhani (the name of the heroine of the legend "Adam-khan and Durkhanay")

درخته drákhta *f. Western* tree مبوه داره درخته fruit tree

درخو durkhó *f. diminutive, slang of* درخاني Durkho

درخواست darkhwā́st, darkhā́st *m.* درخواستي darkhwā́stí *f.* **1** request; petition, application **2** inquiry **3** desire, wish درخواستي کول *compound verb* **a** to request; make an application, petition **b** to make an inquiry **c** to desire, wish

درد dard *m.* **1** pain; suffering درد کول *compound verb* to hurt (e.g., of the arm, etc.) **2** anxiety په آینده سرنوشت مو زړه درد کوي We are worried about the future **3** offense, injury گل مکی ته درد ورغئ Gulmaki took offence **4** *plural* labor, childbirth د درد خبري *idiom* sad news په درد خوړل، په درد لګیدل *idiom* **a** to be useful, be of use **b** to be appropriate, be suitable

دردآلود dardālū́d agonizing, painful

دردانیل dardāníl *m.* the Dardanelles

دردر dardór *m.* sound of rain

دردمن دردمند dardmánd **1** painful, hurting (e.g., of an arm, etc.) **2** angry, cross (of a person) **3** sympathetic

دردناک dardnā́k **1** painful, sore (e.g., of an arm, etc.) **2** sad, melancholy, sorrowful

دردول dardawól *transitive* [*past:* ویې درداوه] **1** to anger, make angry **2** to distress, upset **3** to offend, hurt someone's feelings

دردبدل dardedól *intrinsive* [*past:* ودردېده] **1** to get angry, become angry **2** to be distressed, be upset, be sad زړه یې دردبدلئ دئ He is upset **3** to be offended, take offense

درز [1] darz *m.* **1** crack, fissure **2** *military* breakthrough, penetration درز اچول *compound verb,* درز جوړول *compound verb* **a** to form a crack, make a fissure **b** *military* to break through, penetrate د دښمن په استحکاماتو کښي درز جوړول to penetrate the enemy's defense **3** seam, hem درز ګنډل *compound verb* **a** to stitch, sew **b** *figurative* to settle, arrange, patch up a misunderstanding د چا په مینځ کښي درز اچول *idiom* to introduce dissension in the ranks of someone, cause a quarrel between, put someone against someone

درز [2] draz, drəz **1** *interjection* boom, bang **2** *m.* crash, din, thunder درز او دروز ☞ درز دروز

درز [3] dəráz *m.* **1** platform **2** embankment (low mound of earth along the sides of a peasant house)

درزا drazā́ *f.* ☞ درزهار

درزدروز drazdrúz *m.* **1** roar, thunder, rumble, rumbling **2** crackling, rattle

درزن darzán, dərzán *m.* dozen یو درزن جرابي a dozen socks

درزنده drazónda, darazónda *f.* **1** *anatomy* fontanel **2** flat top (of a mountain)

درزنی drəzanáj *m.* plain, flat terrain

درزول drazawól *transitive* [*past:* ویې درزاوه] **1** to hit, beat hard (a drum) **2** to stomp (with the feet) **3** to beat, bang (e.g., on a door)

درزهار drazahár *m.* درزی *m.* **1** footfall, tread, tramp **2** rumble, roar, thunder **3** crackling, rattle **4** *figurative* torture, torment, agony

درزی drazáj ☞ درزهار

درزی darzí *m.* tailor

درزبدل drazedól *intransitive* [*past:* ودرزېده] **1** to crack, crackle, creak **2** *figurative* to torment oneself, worry, eat one's heart out

درس dars *m. Arabic* [*plural:* درسونه darsuna *and Arabic* دروس durus] lesson د درس سامان school supplies د درس کتاب textbook د درس شرح کول *compound verb* to study to explain a lesson د ... درس ورکول *compound verb* to study درس لوستل *compound verb* to teach, instruct, give lessons

درسال darsā́l *m.* ☞ درشل

درست [1] drəst, drast *pronoun* all, everyone, everything درست عالم پوهېږي everyone knows

درست [2] drust, durust **1.1** correct, right, true دا درسته ده چي That's true **1.2** careful, industrious, punctual, conscientious درست کول *compound verb* ☞ درستول [2] **2.1** correctly, right **2.2** carefully, industriously, conscientiously

درستول [1] drəstawól *denominative, transitive* [*past:* درست یې کړ] to complete, conclude, bring to an end; fulfill, execute, carry out

درستول [2] drustawól *denominative, transitive* [*past:* درست یې کړ] **1** to correct, put right **2** to organize, arrange

درستون darstun (one who is) appealing to you, (one who is) turning to you (with a request, etc.)

درسته [1] dərastá, darastá *f.* weapons, arms, armament درسته اغوستل *compound verb* to arm oneself

درسته [2] drusta *feminine singular of* درست [2]

درسته والا dərastawā́lā *m.* gunsmith, armorer, small-arms technician

درستي [1] drustí, durustí *f.* **1** quality of being business-like, efficient, sensible and serious **2** honesty, integrity په درستی سره honestly

درستی [2] drəstáj, drastáj *m.* objective witness

درستبدل drəstedól *denominative, intransitive* [*past:* درست سو] to be concluded, be consummated, be ended or brought to an end

درسګاه darsgā́h *m.* school; educational institution

درسو [1] dársu *Western present tense perfective aspect first person plural of* درتلل

درسو [2] dársó *oblique plural of* درس

درسي [1] darsi educational, academic; school درسي ګرامر school grammar (textbook) درسي ملا teacher, instructor (in a madrasa) درسي پروګرام curriculum درسي کوټه classroom; auditorium

درسي [2] dársi *Western present tense perfective aspect second person singular of* درتلل

د رسي کیلي də rasi kilí *f. computer science* access key

درشاهي dərshājigā́n] درشايي، درشائي :*plural*] dərshāhí *m.* threshold, (of a door)

درشل dərshól, darshál *f.* [*plural:* درشلي dərshóli] **1** threshold (of a door or figuratively) **2** jamb (of a door) د هېچا په درشل سر نه ټیټوي *idiom* He doesn't bow his head to anyone.

درشونډی darshunḍáj *m.* snout, muzzle

درښودل [1] darkhodól *transitive* [*present:* دربنیي :*past* در ویې ښود] to show you **2** to teach you ☞ ښودل

درغل [1] darghál **1.1** counterfeit, fake, forged, false **1.2** treacherous **2** *m.* **.1** scoundrel, villain **2.2** embezzler (of public funds)

درغل [2] darghál surrounded

درغل [3] darághl *verb stem past tense of* درتلل

338

درغلندي darghalandí *f.* درغلنه darghalanəna *f.* ☞ درغلي

درغلول darghalawə́l *transitive* [*past:* درغلاوه ويي] **1** to worry, harass, bother **2** to hamper, hinder, impede someone **3** to entice, lure

درغلئ [1] dáraghləj *dialect in place of* درغئ

درغلي [2] darghalí *f.* **1** deception, fraud; slyness, cunning, guile **2** treacherousness, betrayal, perfidy

درغلی [3] darghaláj *m.* **1** deceiver; swindler, cheat, rogue **2** cunning person, sly person

درغلی [4] daraghə́laj *past participle of* درتلل

درغن draghə́n *f.* [*plural:* درغني draghə́ni] flagstone (stone on which people grind pepper, etc.)

درغنی draghə́naj *m.* crowd, crush

درغن draghə́ṇ *m.* ☞ درغن

درغوږ darghwág *m.* درغوگ darghwág *Eastern* **1** brand, mark **2** nicked ear, notched ear (of livestock) **3** sacrificial animal

درغول darghól *m.* **1** wash-out, erosion (river bank through which water pours during high water or heavy rain) **2** break (water) د بند اوبو درغول وکئ Water burst the dam. **3** narrow valley

درغئ dáraghə́j *Western past tense of* درتلل

درک [1] dark, dárak *m. Arabic* **1** sign, indication, symptom **2** comprehension, understanding درک کول *compound verb* to understand زما اوسني حال نه سي درک کولای You cannot understand my current situation. **3** source of revenue, income له دې شي درکه as a result of له همدغه درکه څخه a for this (very) reason b from this very source; it is precisely from here

درک [2] darák *m.* water gate (of an irrigation ditch or ark)

درک [3] drak *m.* floor

درکره darkará in your house, at your house or place

درکڼ [1] drakə́ṛ *f.* **1** outer rim of a wheel **2** rim of a sieve

درکڼ [2] darkáṛ **1** prominent, protruding **2** consecutive, successive

درکڼ [3] drə́kə́ṛ *m.* log (of wood)

درکڼئ darkə́ṛaj *past participle of* درکول

درکښي dárkҳe in you

درکول darkawə́l *transitive* [*past:* در يي کړ] to give (to) you, issue to you

درکېدل darkedə́l *intransitive* [*past:* درکړل سو] *regional* to be given or issued to you

درگ [1] drag *m.* ☞ درگهار

درگ [2] drag *m.* forest, woods; grove

درگا dragá́ *f.* ☞ درگهار

درگاه dargā́h *m.* **1** palace **2** doorway

درگ دروگ dragudrúg *m.* loud footsteps

درگذر darguzár *m.* forgiveness, pardon

درگرده dargárda *adv.* **1** completely, entirely **2** constantly **3** repeatedly

درگوټي dargóṭe *f.* thicket, brush; grove

درگ و دروگ drag-u-drúg *m.* ☞ درگ دروگ

درگورکول dargór درگور dargór *compound verb* to abandon, give up, cease doing something; forget something

درگه [1] də́rga *f.* **1** thicket of bushes, cane or rushes; heart of the forest **2** reed, cane, rush

درگه [2] dargáh *m.* ☞ درگاه

درگه [3] drə́ga *f.* flight, escape; rout

درگهار dragahár *m.* درگی drəgáj *m.* **1** sound of footsteps **2** beating (of the heart), heartbeat

درگهي dargəhí *m.* **1** cupboard (for dishes); buffet **2** pantry, larder, storeroom

درگوټي درگی dargə́j *f.* ☞ درگوټي

درله dárlara ☞ درته

درلود dárlod *past tense of* لرل

درلودلئ darlodə́laj *dialect past participle of* لرل

درلودنه darlodə́na *f.* **1** property, fortune **2** estate, holdings, possessions

درلول darlowə́l *transitive* ☞ لرل

درلوئ darlowə́laj *dialect past participle of* لرل

درلوونکی darlowúnkaj *dialect* **1** *present participle of* درلول **2** *m.* **2.1** owner, possessor (of a car, carriage, etc.) **2.2** bearer (e.g., of a letter, complaint), complainant

درله də́rla *adverb* ☞ درته

درم dram *m.* **1** drumbeat, roll of a drum **2** thundering noise (of cannon), gun (i.e., cannon) fire

درمان darmā́n *m.* medicine, medication, remedy

درماندگي darmāndagí *f.* **1** indigence, poverty, impecuniosity **2** fatigue, weariness

درمانده darmāndá **1** needy, indigent **2** weary, fatigued

درمب dramb *m.* درمبا drambā́ *f. onomatopoeia* drumbeat درمب او درومب *idiom* drum-roll

درمبول drambawə́l *transitive* [*past:* ويي درمباوه] to beat the drum

درمبهار drambahár *m.* drumbeat

درمسال daramsā́l *m.* Hindu temple

درمغول daramaghól, darməghól confused, mixed up, tangled

درمکښ drəmkā́ҳ, dramkā́ҳ *m.* awl (of harness maker, sadler)

درمل [1] darmál *m.* **1** medicine, medication **2** medical treatment, doctoring درمل کول *compound verb* to treat, doctor

درمل [2] durmál *m.* **1** unripe fruit, green fruit **2** young fellow

درملتون darmaltun *m.* pharmacy, drug store

درمل جوړوونکی darmal dzhoṛawúnkaj *m.* pharmacist, druggist

درملگر darmalgár *m.* doctor

درمل واکي darmalwākí *f.* pharmacy business

درملي [1] darmalí *f.* medical treatment, doctoring

درملی [2] darmaláj *m.* doctor

درملیار darmaljár *m.* ☞ درملگر

درمن darmə́n *m.* **1** wheat being threshed درمن بادول *compound verb* to winnow grain درمن کېدل *compound verb* to be threshed درمن کوټل، میده کول *compound verb* to thresh grain or wheat **2** shock (of hair)

درمن ځای darməndzáj *m.* threshing floor

درمند darmónd **1** *m.* ☞ درمن **2** *attributive* level, smooth, (of the earth)

درمندځای darmənddzáj *m.* ☞ درمن ځای

درمنده darməndá *f.* skein, hank (of wool)

درمندی darməndáj [superscript 1] *m.* grain left on the threshing floor after threshing

درمندې darməndé [superscript 2] *plural of* درمنده

درمنه darmaná *f.* wormwood, santolina, *Artemisia cina*

درمول ډل durmolḍál *m.* thicket of rushes, cane

درمه durmá *f.* **1** rushes, cane **2** shepherd's pipe (musical instrument) **3** barrel (of a shotgun)

درناوی drənáwaj *m.* **1** weight **2** respect په درناوی respectfully (close of a letter) دیو شي درناوی ورکول to show respect, to value something, hold something dear **3** celebration or feast in honor of **4** seriousness, earnestness, solidity **5** *literal & figurative* preponderance

درنجی drandzháj *m. regional* ritual (e.g., kalyad)

درند drund ☞ دروند

درنتیا drandtjá *f.* ☞ درندښت drandókht *m. dialect* **1** weight **2** *figurative* burden

درندوالی drandwálaj *m. transitive* ☞ درنول drandawól ☞ درنول

درنده darandá [superscript 1] **1** predatory, savage درنده حیوانات beasts of prey **2** *m.* [*plural* درنده گان *and* درندگان darandagán] predatory animal, beast of prey

درنده drandá [superscript 2] *dialect feminine singular of* دروند

درنده d55ráda [superscript 3] *f.* rain cloud, storm cloud

درندی dr66dáj *m.* liver disease (of sheep)

درنېدل drandedól *intransitive* ☞ درنېدل

درنښت dranókht *m.* ☞ درناوی

درنگ dráng, diráng [superscript 1] *m.* delay, procrastination; hold back درنگ کول *compound verb* to delay, hold back, wait لږ درنگ وکړه! Wait for a minute!

درنگ drang [superscript 2] *m.* **1** peal, ringing **2** knocking ☞ درنگ او درونگ درنگ درونگ

درنگ drang [superscript 3] *m.* mine (for salt); deposit (of minerals)

درنگا drangá *f.* ☞ درنگهار

درنگ درونگ drangdrúng *m.* **1** jingling, clinking, clanking **2** knocking, rapping

درنگول drangawól *transitive* [*past:* ویې درنگاوه] to ring, elicit a ringing sound

درنگه drangá *f.* carrion, dead animal

درنگهار drangahár *m.* درنگی drangáy *m.* ring, ringing, peal, tinkling

درنگېدل drangedól *intransitive* [*past:* ودرنگېده] to ring, sound (of a musical instrument)

درندوالی dr66nwála *f.* ☞

درنول dranawól *denominative, transitive* [*past:* دروند یې کړ] **1** to make heavier, increase the weight of **2** *figurative* burden (with) **3** to make reliable, serious

درنه draná [superscript 1] *feminine singular of* دروند ☞ درخخه

درنه draná [superscript 2] *Eastern* ☞ درخخه

درنې drané *feminine plural of* دروند

درنېدل dranedól *denominative, intransitive* [*past:* دروند شو] **1** to become heavier, increase in weight سترگي په باڼو نه درنېږي *proverb* a burden of one's own choice is not felt (*literally:* the eyelashes do not burden the eyes) **2** to outweigh, overbalance **3** *figurative* to be burdened **4** to be solid, be reliable, be serious; be staid, be sedate

درو dro [superscript 1] *f.* [*plural:* درووې drówe] *Eastern* ☞ دروه

درو dro [superscript 2] *oblique of* درې [superscript 3]

درواخله dárwākhla *phrase* take it, take with you

درواز darwáz *m.* Darvaz (region in Badakhshan)

دروازگی darwāzagój *f.* door

دروازه وان darwāzawān *m.* ☞ دروازه وان

دروازه darwāzá *f.* door دروازه بېرته کول لویه دروازه gate; wicket *compound verb* to open the door or gate دروازه پیشول ، دروازه پوري *compound verb* to close the door or gate دروازه تړل ، دروازه کول *compound verb* to knock at the door or gate د بند دروازه تکول sluice, lock

دروازه وان darwāzawān *m.* **1** door-keeper, doorman **2** goalkeeper

دروازي darwāzí, darwāzáj [superscript 1] Davraz

دروازي darwāzé [superscript 2] *plural of* دروازه

درواغ dərwágh *m. Western usually plural* lie, deception درواغ کول *compound verb* to deny, disclaim, to refute, disprove درواغ ویل *compound verb* to lie, deceive د درواغو منزل لنډدئ *proverb* a lie has short legs ☞ دروغ

درواغجن dərwāghdzhón **1** lying, untruthful, mendacious; false, fake, sham; deceptive **2** *m.* liar, deceiver, cheat, imposter

درواغجني dərwāghdzhóní *f.* falsity, mendacity

دروان darwán *m.* دروانچي darwānchí *m.* doorman, doorkeeper

دروب drub دروپ drup *paired word with* درب

د روځي də rwádzi during the day, in the day-time, by day

درود durúd, dərúd *m.* **1** praise **2** blessing(s), benediction درود ویل *compound verb* **a** to praise, laud, extol **b** to bless

درودگر drudgár *m.* miller

درور dror *f. dialect* ☞ ندرور

درورل darwról *transitive* [*present:* درېږي ووړ *past:* درورپي] bring to you, take to you ☞ وړل

دروړن dərwaṛón *m.* دروړنگ darwaṛng *m.* summer cypress (used for making brooms)

دروړونکی darwṛúnkaj **1** *present participle of* درورل **2** *m.* bearer (of a letter, etc.) د دي لیک درورل the bearer of this letter

دروز druz *m.* thunder, roar, din دروز شو، دېوال ولوېد A crash was heard, the wall crumbled.

دروزگر druzgár *m.* carpenter

دروزه drúza *f.* **1** straw د دروزو ټوپۍ *regional* straw hat **2** *regional* stubble, stubble field

دروږ darwág *m.* brand

دروږي darwagí **1** branded, having a brand **2** *figurative* attached, devoted, loyal **3** *figurative* convinced of something **4** being made a sacrifice

دروس durús *m. Arabic plural of* درس

دروستل darwəstəl *transitive* [*present:* درولي, *past:* در یې وست] to lead, take to you ☞ راوستل

دروغ darógh, dərógh **1** *usually plural* lie, untruth, deceit بیخي دروغ barefaced lie, outright lie صاف دروغ *patent lie* په دروغو ځان ناجوړه او *to malinger* د دروغو خبري false words, lying words د رنځور اچول په دروغو گواهي false evidence, false testimony, perjury **a** falsely, deceitfully **b** in vain, for nothing دروغ ویل *compound verb* to lie, to deceive **2** *attributive and predicative* false, lying, deceiving, deceitful هغه زما خبره دروغ وگڼله lie یوه دروغ خبره He thought that I was lying.

دروغجن dəroghdzhə́n دروغژن dəroghzhə́n ☞ درواغجن

دروغگوی dəroghgój *m.* liar, deceiver

دروغگویي dəroghgojí *f.* lie, deceit; falsity, mendacity

دروغه daroghá *m.* chief, head د بندي خاني دروغه warden (of a prison)

دروگ drug *paired word with* درگ

درول darawə́l *transitive* [*past:* و یې دراوه] **1** to stop, halt, detain, delay موټر دلته ودروه Stop the car here آس ودروه! Stop the horse! سړی لږ ودروه Detain that man for a bit **2** to put, place, set **3** to rouse someone, get someone up, make someone get up **4** to appoint, put into a particular job **5** to bring in, introduce, put in place **6** to advance, field (an army, troops) **7** to stop, discontinue, break off

درولي dárwali [1] *present tense of* دروستل

درولی darawə́laj [2] *past participle of* درول

دروم drum [1] *m.* **1** roar (of a tiger) **2** din, roar, firing (of weapons)

دروم drum [2] march (as a command)

دروم drum [3] *present stem from* درومل *and* درومبدل

درومل drumə́l *intransitive* [*past:* ودرومبده] **1** to set off, start out, go, leave **2** to follow someone or something ☞ په ... پسې

درومئ drumə́j *imperfective imperative plural of* درومل

درومبدل drumedə́l *intransitive* [*past:* ودرومبده] **1** to set off, start out, go, leave, depart **2** په چا پسې درومبدل to pursue, chase someone

درون darún inside

درونته daruntá *f.* Darunta (populated place near Jalalabad)

دروند drund *f.* [درنه], *dialect* درنده, *m. plural* درانده, درانه *dialect, f. plural* درني *dialect* [درندې] **1** heavy دروند بار heavy load **2** heavy, difficult, burdensome; onerous **3** deep, hard, fast (of sleep) **4** deep (of shade and shadow) په درانه سیوري in deep shade **5** weighty, convincing دروند دلیل convincing argument **6** dear; respected, esteemed زمونږ ډېر دروند مېلمه our esteemed guest **7** influential **8** expressing respect, esteem په درانه, په درنه سترگه کتل، دروند کېښودل to treat with respect نظر کتل, دروند ولاړېدل

compound verb to treat respectfully **9** staid, sedate, serious, reliable ځان دروند او موقر ساتل to bear oneself in a dignified manner **10** dear, expensive, valuable **11** important, significant **12** high (of taxes and duties) پنځه زره تنه دروند جهاز a ship with a displacement of five thousand tons په غوږو دروند hard of hearing, a little deaf درنه دعوت formal reception درنه ډوډۍ great entertainment, food and drink دروند بغ thud, deep sound

دروند باری drundbáraj *m. military* supply train

درونتیا drundtjá *f.* درندوالی drundwálay *m.* **1** weight, heaviness **2** difficulty, onerousness **3** weight, convincingness, persuasiveness **4** respect, esteem **5** influentialness, quality of being influential **6** seriousness, reliability sedateness **7** value **8** importance, significance **9** weight, onerousness (of taxes, etc.)

دروندمزاج drundmizádzh serious, thoughtful

درندول drundawə́l *transitive* ☞ درنول

درندهډی drundháḍaj noble, high-born, blue-blood

درندېدل drundedə́l *intransitive* ☞ درنېدل

درونگ drung *paired word with* درنگ

درونه daruná *f.* core, pith, heart

درونی druṇáj, dərwaṇáj *m.* thicket of reeds or cane

دروول drowúl *transitive dialect* ☞ دروهل

دروه dro, droh [1] *f.* [*plural:* دروهوي drówe, dróhwe] *dialect m.* [*plural:* دروهونه drohúna] **1** deceit, deception, cunning, subterfuge دروه خورل *compound verb* to be deceived دروه ورکول *compound verb* to deceive, dupe, trick **2** hatred, malice

دروه dərə́wa [2] right now, immediately, in a flash

دروهل drohə́l *transitive* [*past:* و یې دروهه] **1** to deceive, dupe **2** to be hypocritical, dissemble

دروهلی drohə́laj **1** *past participle of* دروهل **2** treacherous

دروهنه drohə́na *f.* **1** deception, trickery, cheating **2** hypocrisy

دروهول drohawə́l *transitive* ☞ دروهل

دروهونکی drohúnhaj **1** *present participle from* دروهل *m.* **2.1** deceiver, fraud, trickster **2.2** hypocrite

دروهه dróoha [1] *f.* ☞ دروهنه

دروهه drohá [2] *imperfective imperative from* دروهل

دروهي dróhi [1] *plural of* دروهه [1]

دروهي drohí [2] *present tense of* دروهل

دروهبدل drohedə́l *intransitive* [*past:* ودروهبده] to be deceived, be tricked

دروی dórwaj, dárwaj *m.* ☞ درمه

دروېزه darwezá **1** *f.* beggary, destitution **2** *f.* alms دروېزه ټولول *compound verb* to collect alms **3** *m. history* Darveza (the opponent of Bayazid Ansari)

دروېش darwésh *m.* dervish

دروېشانه darweshāná *attributive* dervish

درويشت dərwísht *numeral* twenty-three

دروېش خېل darweshkhél **1** *m. plural* Darveshkheyli (a branch of the Vaziri tribe) **2** *m.* Darveshkhejl

دروبشي darweshí *f.* dervishism

دروبشۍ darweshə́j *f.* bow for training, training bow

دروی والا dərwajwālā́ *m.* seller of reeds and cane, reed and cane vendor

درویه dərúja on the basis of something; in accordance with something, according to something

دره dará, darrá *f.* [*plural:* دري daré, darré *and m. Arabic plural* دره جات darajā́t, darrajā́t] **1** valley **2** gorge, ravine, mountain pass

دره durá, dirrá *f. Arabic* lash, whip, knout

دره جات daradzhā́t, darradzhā́t *m. Arabic plural of* دره

درهد کې darhádke it doesn't matter, it's okay, don't cry (said to a child when he falls)

دره صوف daráji-suf *m.* Darajisuf (valley in northern Afghanistan)

درهم dirhám *m.* **1** dirham (Iraqi coin) **2** *history* drachma

درهم برهم darhám-barhám درهم وبرهم darhám-u-barhám mixed up, confused درهم برهم کبدل *compound verb* to confuse درهم برهم کول *compound verb* to be (or to get) confused, be tangled, be mixed up

دره وال darawā́l ☞ دري وال

درهيسته dárhista to you, to your side

دري darí *f.* Dari (language)

دري darə́j *f.* cotton rug

دري daré, darré *plural of* دره

دري dre three (in combination with tens دري dri numeral) دري زره three دري زره سل او دري one-hundred three دبرش thirty-three thousand دري واره all three سره دري واړه three (together), the three (of us, of them, etc.)

دریاب darjā́ *f.* ☞

دریال darjā́ *f.* ☞

دریاب darjā́b *m.* **1** river دریاب تور Kabul River دریاب کابل سمندر دریاب Black Sea دریاب د لوی ocean دریاب بالتیک Baltic Sea *figurative* stream, flow (e.g., of goods) دریاب کښې خیال په د *idiom* in (day)dreams

دریابي darjābí *attributive* **1** river, fluvial **2** sea, maritime دریابي حمل ونقل sea transport دریابي مرغان sea birds

دري اتیا driattā́ *numeral* eighty-three

دریاچه darjāchá *f.* lake

دري ارخیز dreaṛkhíz three-sided

دریافت darjā́ft *m.* understanding دریافت کول *compound verb* to understand

دریال darjā́l *m.* tambourine

دریان darjā́n *paired word with* حریان

دریاوال darjāwā́l *m.* tambourine player

دریاواله darjāwā́la *f.* tambourine player (female)

دري اویا driawjā́ *numeral* seventy-three

دریای آمو darjājiāmú *m.* Amu Dar'ya

دري بنده drebánda *numeral* consisting of three parts, tripartite

دري پنخوس drippindzós fifty-three

دري پنځکی drepetsə́kaj triangular

دریچه darichá *f.* **1** window; door **2** hatch (e.g., of a ship) **3** *figurative* loop-hole

دریځ dərídz *m.* **1** platform, rostrum **2** *figurative* position, point of view

دري څلوبښت dritsalwékht *numeral* forty-three

دري څنډی dretsə́nḍaj **1** triangular **2** *m.* triangle

دریڅه daritsá *f.* ☞ دریچه

دري خپل darikhél دریخپل *m. plural* Darikhejli (a branch of the Dzadran tribe) **2** *m.* Darikhejl

دریدځای dareddzáj دربدځی dareddzáy *m.* **1** platform, rostrum **2** stage **3** stand, parking place; stop; station

دریدل daredə́l **1** *intransitive* [*past:* ودرید، ودرېده] **1.1** to stop; stand ساعت ودرید The clock stopped. موټر ودرید The car stopped. **1.2** to stand up, rise **1.3** to cease, end, stop; pause باران ودریدئ *Western* The rain stopped. **1.4** to stand too long, become stale, be no longer fresh (of water) **1.5** to keep, fulfill (one's word, one's promise) **1.6** چاته دربدل *compound verb* to wait for someone **1.7** to be based (on), be founded (on), rest (on) **1.8** withstand, stand up against د چا مخي ته دربدل *compound verb* to stand up to someone **1.9** to stand up for, come out for (or to speak in favor of) someone or something; defend someone or something **1.10** to become or fall silent, stop talking خوله یې نه دربري He talks incessantly **1.11** to be appointed, be named (to a position, post); to be elected, be chosen **1.12** to be enrolled (in a military unit) **2** *m. plural* ☞ دربده

دریدلي اوبه daredə́ləj **1** *past participle from* دربدل **2** standing دریدلي اوبه standing water

دریدنه daredə́na *f.* دربده daredə́ m. plural **1** stop, parking space, parking lot د بهري د پیری pier, dock, wharf **2** rising, standing up **3** ceasing; stopping, cessation; checking, pausing **4** fulfilling (one's word, a promise) **5** چا ته دربدنه waiting for, awaiting someone **6** establishing, founding **7** defending someone or something **8** ceasing to talk, falling silent **9** appointing or appointment (to a position, job); election **10** enrolling, enlisting (in a military unit)

دري دبرش dridérsh *numeral* thirty-three

دربر dreg *imperfective imperative, short form from* دربدل halt (as a command)

دربر daré g *present tense stem of* دربدل

دري شپیته drishpetə́ *numeral* sixty-three

درېشي dreshí *f.* suit عسکري درېشي military uniform د درېشی خاوند man in a suit

دري شبرلی dresherláy دري شبرلی dresherláy four-year-old ram

درېشيوالا dreshiwālā́ *m.* man in a suit

دري ښاخه drekhā́khəy *f.* دري ښاخی dreṛkhā́khə fork

دربنکی dreṛkhkáj *m.* chamber, rein (in a bridle)

دريغ drégh, darégh *m.* regret; sigh of regret دریغ خوړل *compound verb* to regret د یوچا څخه دریغ کول *compound verb* to refuse

د یوشي څخه دریغ کول someone *compound verb* to renounce something, waive, decline

دریغول dreghawә́l *denominative, transitive* [*past:* دریغ یې کړ] to refuse جان مه دریغوه! Don't refuse!

دریغه drégha *interjection* alas, what a pity

دری کسیز drekasíz consisting of three persons (of a committee, delegation, etc.)

دری گون dregún, دریگونی dregúnay threefold, triple; trilateral, tripartite دري گون اتحاد *history* The Triple Alliance د انگلستان دریگونی قواوي the armed forces of England (land, naval and air)

دریم drəjә́m, drejә́m 1 *ordinal* third دریمه ورځ every other day دوره *geology* Tertiary period 2 *m.* ☞ دریمگړی

دریمان drimán *m.* ☞ دریمگړی

دریم توب drəjəmtób *m.* mediation, arbitration دریم توب کول *compound verb* to mediate

دری مخی dremә́khaj three-sided, trilateral, tripartite

دریمگړی drəjəmgә́raj *m.* mediator, arbitrator, arbiter

دری منزله dremanzalá three-stage

دریمه drəjә́ma 1 *feminine singular of* دریم 2 *f.* 1 the third day of a wedding 2.2 the third day after a death

دری میاشتنی dremjāshtanáj published once a quarter (of a magazine)

دریناژ drenázh *m.* drainage

درینگ dring 1 *m.* 1 hard soil, firm ground, hardpan 1.2 forest; pine forest 2 hard, compact, dense د درینگه ویشتل *compound verb* a to discourage, dishearten, puzzle, perplex b to lead someone into failure; spoil or frustrate someone's plans

درینگل dringawә́l *transitive* [*past:* و یې درینگه] to pull (on), draw taut (e.g., a rope)

درینگول dringawә́l *denominative, transitive* [*past:* درینگ یې کړ] to pull (on), draw taut (e.g., a rope)

درینگه drínga *f.* درینگی dringáy *m.* ☞ درینگ 1

درینگبدل dringedә́l *denominative, intransitive* [*past:* درینگ شو] to be pulled (on), drawn taut (e.g., of a rope)

دری نوی driniwí *numeral* ninety-three

درېو dréwo *oblique plural of* دری 1

درېواړه drewā́ṛa *numeral* (all) three

دري وال darewā́l *regional* of local manufacture, made locally (of a gun)

درېور drajwár *m.* driver, chauffeur

درې ورگ drewárg *m.* درې ورگی drewárgay *m.* three-year-old camel

دریا darjá *f.* ☞ دریال

دریا باز darjabā́z *m.* ☞ دریاوال

دری یم drejə́m *numeral* ☞ دریم

در daṛ *m.* 1 large scales, weighing machine 2 packaging weight, weight of packaging در نیول ، دروهل *compound verb* counting or not counting the weight of packaging

درد daṛd *m. Eastern* ☞ درد

در در daṛ-dáṛ [*f.* دره دره dáṛa-dáṛa] 1 broken 2 smashed, shattered, split 3 torn to pieces, ripped to shreds 4 divided into parts 5 cut (up) در در کول *compound verb* a to break, break up b to hit, stab, break, split c break into pieces d divide into parts e to cut, chop در در کېدل *compound verb* a to be broken, break b to break, get broken c to be torn into pieces, be ripped to shreds d to be divided into parts e to be cut, be chopped

دردنگ dəṛdáng *m.* jumping, leaping (for joy) دردنگ وهل *compound verb* to jump (for joy) په یو دردنگ at once, in a flash, in an instant, in no time

دردول daṛdawә́l *transitive* ☞ دردول

دردېدل daṛdedә́l *intransitive* ☞ دردبدل

درکه daṛaká *f.* 1 threat by firearm 2 threat, intimidation په چا درکه کول، په چا درکي کول a to threaten someone with a firearm b to threaten, intimidate someone

درواجی darwājí *m.* 1 weigher 2 *regional* grain merchant

دره dára *f.* 1 board د شطرنج دره chess-board د خوني غوړېدلي دري wood flooring 2 leaf of a folding door 3 single-panel door 4 strip of something 5 height (of a person) 6 crack, split, cleft 7 lobule, section, slice 8 makeweight دره وهل *compound verb* to make up the weight 9 springboard

دره دره dára-dára *feminine singular of* در در

دره دوره dára-dúra *f.* noise, din, racket دره دوره جوړول *compound verb* to make noise, make a hubbub

درج daṛáj *m.* 1 drop 2 measure (for liquids)

درۍ daṛә́j *f.* 1 foil 2 spangles, decorations made of foil د بوډۍ په سر نوي درۍ اېنبودل *proverb* to do something foolish (*literally:* to decorate the head of an old woman with new spangles)

درۍ daṛә́j *f.* seer (a measure of weight) یو درۍ غنم one seer of wheat

دری دری dáṛi-dáṛi *feminine plural of* در

دساتیر dasātír *m. Arabic plural of* دستور

دسایس dasājís *m. Arabic plural of* دسیسه

دسپلاسه daspəlā́sa *dialect* immediately, at once, instantly, right now

دسپلین disiplín *m.* discipline دسپلین کول *compound verb* to discipline دسپلین ساتل *compound verb* to observe discipline, maintain discipline

دست dast *m.* 1 arm 2 elbow (a measure of length)

دست dast *m.* feces, excrement, stool

دستا dəstā́ *dialect* ☞ ستا

دستار dastā́r *m.* turban

دست انداز dastāndā́z *m.* one who encroaches on someone's rights; oppressor; tyrant; enslaver

دست اندازي dastāndāzí *f.* encroachment (on someone's rights); violence, coercion; robbery, pillage, plundering

دستاني dastāné *plural f. Eastern* gloves دستاني په لاس کول *compound verb* a to put on gloves b to wear gloves

دست آویز dastāwéz *m.* document; obligation

دست بازي dastbāzí *f.* misuse, abuse (e.g., of one's official position)

دست بردار dastbardár one who has refused something, one who has renounced something

دست بسته dastbastá respectfully

دست پاک dastpåk *m.* table napkin, serviette

دست پناه dastpanáh *m.* 1 hilt of a saber 2 master, expert craftsman

دست تنگ dasttáng needy, poor

دست تنگي dasttangí *f.* need, poverty

دستخط dastkhát *m.* 1 receipt 2 signature دستخط كول *compound verb* to sign, sign one's name

دستر خوان dastarkhån *m.* table with food; covered table پر دسترخوان راتولېدل *compound verb* to be about setting the table دسترخوان هوارول *compound verb* to sit down to eat كښېنستل *compound verb* to spread tablecloth; prepare refreshments

دسترس dastrás 1 accessible, reachable, attainable, achievable 2 *m.* accessibility, attainability, achievability په دسترس كښې اېنبودل *compound verb* to make accessible, attainable

دسترنج dastrándzh *m.* labor, work (physical)

دست شوی dastshój *m.* ☞ دشوی

دست فروش dastfarósh *m.* peddler, hawker

دست فروشي dastfaroshí *f.* peddling, hawking

دستک ¹ dasták *m.* record, register

دستک ² dasták *m.* rafter, truss

دستكښ dastkáḵẖ دست كله *f.* glove

دستكول dastkól *m.* handbag, reticule

دستكى ¹ dastakáj *m.* 1 rafter, truss 2 cross beam, cross piece

دستكى ² dastakój *f.* bread of a special baking

دستگا،دستگاه dastgå, dastgåh *f.* [*plural:* دستگاوي dastgåwi *and rarely m. plural* دستگاهونه dastgåhúna] 1 machine tool, machine; apparatus; installation, plant برق دستگاه electric motor 2 equipment, machinery 3 factory, plant; (work)shop 4 *regional military* battery 5 apparatus, machinery (e.g., government, state)

دستگير dastgír *m.* 1 patron, protector 2 handle, grip, lever 3 *proper noun* Dastgir

دستگيري dastgirí *f.* patronage, protection

دست لاپ dastlåp *m.* دست لاف dastlåf *m.* initiative (in trade)

دستمال dastmål *m.* ☞ دسمال

دستمايه dastmājá *f.* plow handle

دستمبول dastamból *m.* fragrant and small-fruited melon

دستور dastúr *m.* [*plural:* دستورونه dasturúna, *Arabic* دستورات dasturát *and* دساتير dasatír] 1 rule, custom د دنيا دود او دستور خو دا دئ That is the custom in the world. 2 direction, instructions, order, directive; manual, handbook, guide 3 accepted established payment (for a doctor, a barber, etc.) 4 *regional* ceremony 5 [*plural:* دستوران] vizier, advisor, counselor په هر دستور چه وي by any means يو دستور بندول *compound verb* to abolish, liquidate

دستورالعمل dastur-ul-'amál *m. Arabic* 1 instructions, directions 2 procedure

دستوري dasturí *f. trade* 1 brokerage, commission 2 discount

دسته dastá *f.* 1 group, detachment, party 2 *history* druzhina, prince's bodyguard 3 sheaf; bundle; bunch 4 bouquet 5 handle, grip, lever 6 skein, hank 7 quire of paper دساز دسته ، د موسيقى dastá orchestra

دسته بندي dastabandí *f.* grouping; cliquishness

دسته دار dastadår 1 having a grip, with a handle 2 *m. history* druzhina leader, leader of the prince's bodyguard

دستي dastí 1.1 manual (of labor) 1.2 handicraft, hand-made, cottage industry 2 right now, immediately اسلم ته ووايه چه دستي دي راشي Tell Aslam to come immediately.

دستيار dastjår *m.* assistant

دستي پدستي dastipədastí right now, immediately

دسخط daskhát *m.* ☞ دستخط

د سره də sára quite, entirely, totally, completely د سره كول *compound verb* to bring to an end, finish, complete

دسكله daskalá *f.* glove

دسكونت diskónt *m. trade* discount, discount of a bill

دسلاپ daslåp *m.* ☞ دست لاپ

دسمال dasmål *m.* 1 kerchief د پزي دسمال ، د جېب دسمال handkerchief دسمال وركول *compound verb* to present the guests with kerchiefs (during the betrothal ceremony, of the fianceé) دسمال وړل *compound verb* to become engaged (*literally:* to wear the kerchief) د دسمال مجلس a party on the occasion of a betrothal 2 towel

دسماله dasmālá *f.* plaster, dressing

دسمبر disámbr *m.* December

دسيسه dasisá *f. Arabic* [*plural:* دسيسي dasisé *and m. plural Arabic* دسايس dasāyís] 1 intrigue, machinations 2 plot, conspiracy; evil intent

د شپې də shpé at night

دشت dasht *m.* ☞ دښت

دشلمه dishlamá *f.* candy (with tea)

دشمن dushmán *m.* ☞ دښمن

دشمني dushmaní *f.* ☞ دښمني

دشوی dəshúj *m.* basin (for washing up)

دښت daḵẖt *m.* دښته *f.* steppe; semi desert

دښتي daḵẖtí wild دښتي څاروي wild animals دښتي چرگ pheasant

دښمن duḵẖmán *m.* [*plural:* دښمنان duḵẖmanån *and* دښمن duḵẖmán] enemy, foe, opponent

دښمنانه duḵẖmānāná 1 hostile 2 hostilely, with hostility

دښمنداره duḵẖməndārá, دښمن دار، دښمندار duḵẖməndår having a deadly enemy

دښمنول duḵẖmənawál *denominative, transitive* [*past:* دښمن يې كړ] to make an enemy

دښمني duḵẖmƏní *f.* hostility, hatred; enmity; spite, malice سخته دښمني ferocious hatred د چا سره دښمني لرل to quarrel with someone, be at loggerheads with someone

دښمنېدل duḵẖmənedál *denominative, intransitive* [*past:* دښمن شو] to be an enemy

دښن dukhén *m.* ☞ دښمن

دښنه dukhné *plural of* دښن

دښمني dukhní *f.* ☞ دښمني

دعا du'ā *f. Arabic* [*plural:* دعاگاني du'āgāni *and* دعاوي du'āwi] 1 prayer یوه دعا راته وکه! Pray for me! 2 blessing

دعاگوئ du'ágódzh 1 praying for someone 2 blessing someone

دعوا da'wā *f.* ☞ دعوه

دعوت da'wát *m. Arabic* 1 invitation دعوت کول *compound verb* to invite 2 reception دعوت کېدل *compound verb* a to be invited موږ د احمد کور ته دعوت شوي وو We were invited to Ahmed's. b to take place, be held (of a reception) یو دعوت شوئ و a reception was held دعوت ورکول *compound verb* to invite a د چاته د ډوډۍ دعوت ورکول to invite someone for dinner b to arrange a reception, put on a reception c *figurative* to draw in, to attract

دعوتنامه da'watnāmá *f.* 1 invitation card 2 message

دعوه da'wá *f. Arabic* 1 suit, (legal) action; claim, complaint, grievance تجارتي دعوٰي trade conflicts, trade claims زه له دعوٰي نه I am rejecting legal action. دعوه شوئ مال disputed property د دعوو وکیل agent; lawyer 2 assertion; declaration دعوه کول *compound verb* a to claim, to file a claim b to assert, affirm; declare زه دا دعوه نشم کولای چه ... I cannot assert that ...

دعویدار da'wadār *m.* دعوه گیر da'wagír *m.* ☞ دعویدار

دعوي¹ da'wí *m. Arabic law* respondent, defendant

دعوٰی² da'wā *f. Arabic* ☞ دعوه اقبال دعوٰی iqbāl-i ... taking an action or suit under review دا دعوٰی چه ... the assertion that... دعوٰی کول *compound verb* a to claim, lodge a claim, file suit; demand preference د شفعي د حق دعوٰی کول، په چا دعوٰی to assert; declare b کول، په چا دعوٰی لرل to accuse, charge, indict, prosecute someone

دعوي³ da'wé *plural of* دعوه

دعویدار da'wādār *m.* 1 plaintiff 2 claimant 3 supporter

دغ digh ☞ دق

دغا daghā *m.* deception, fraud په دغا حاصلول *compound verb* to obtain fraudulently

دغدځی daghdzáj paralyzed (of the extremities)

دغدغه¹ daghdaghá *f. Arabic* 1 noise, hubbub, racket 2 alarm, agitation

دغدغه² daghdaghá *f.* throne

دغدغی¹ daghdagháj *m.* 1 rain and sun(shine) 2 ray (of sunlight)

دغدغی² daghdagháj *m.* deceiver, cheat, swindler; rogue

دغدوغ daghdúgh *m.* deception, fraud; cunning, slyness; trick, dodge, subterfuge

دغسي dághasi, dághase 1 *demonstrative pronoun* that kind of, that sort of 2 like this, like that, in such a way, thus, and so ☞ داسي

دغلته daghálta 1 here 2 right here; right then

دغو¹ dágho *oblique plural of* دغه¹

دغو² dighó *oblique plural of* دغه² د هیواد دغو کره تللئ وم I went to visit Hewad's relatives.

دغومره daghúmra دغونه daghúna, daghóna 1 that's the kind of 2 so much, so many دغومره چه ... as much as

دغوی dighój, daghój *plural of* دغه²

دغه¹ dágha [*oblique m.* دغه dəghə, *f.* دغي daghé] *demonstrative pronoun* this, these په دغي سیمه کښي ، په دغي سیمي کښي in this region په دغي موده کښي in this period دغه دئ! a There he is! b دغه ده! There! دغه ده! There she is! دغه دي There they are! دغه گری immediately دغه هغه ، هغه دغه one thing and another

دغه² daghá *personal pronoun, third person singular* [*oblique m.* دغه dəghə, *f.* دغي daghé] 1 he, she, it (used as the subject of the action with intransitive verbs in all tenses and with transitive verbs in the present and future tenses) 2 him, her (used as the object of the actiion in ergative constructions) دغه واخله take her

دغه³ dəghə *oblique of* دغه¹

دغه⁴ dəghə 1 *oblique case of* دغه² 2 *colloquial* hey

دغه رنگي dágharange دغسي سي ، دغسي dághasi, dághase *regional, pronoun* ☞ داسي¹

دغي daghé *oblique feminine of* دغه¹,²

دف daf *m.* tambourine

دفاتیر dafātír *m. Arabic plural of* دفتر³

دفاع difā' *f. Arabic* defense, protection د دفاع defensive د ملي دفاع ministry of defense د یوشي څخه دفاع کول to defend something د خپلي آزادی څخه دفاع کول to defend one's liberty د ځانه دفاع کول to defend oneself

دفاعي difā'í defensive, defense دفاعي خط personal defense دفاعي توان defensive power د دښمن په دفاعي استحکاماتو کښي سوری کول to break through enemy defenses

دفتانگ diftáng *linguistics* diphthong

دفتر daftár *m.* [*plural:* دفترونه daftarúna *and Arabic* دفاتیر ، دفاتر dafātír] 1 book ورځنی کل دفتر ledger تجارتي دفترونه trade books دفتر journal, log 2 register, listing 3 office, bureau 4 hereditary land خپل دفتر ancestral land

دفتربردار daftarbardár *m.* ☞ دفتردار

دفترخانه daftarkhāná *f.* 1 office, chancellery, bureau 2 office space, office premises, office room

دفتردار daftardár *m.* 1 clerk; office worker 2 accountant; bookkeeper

دفترداري daftardārí *f.* 1 clerical work, office work, business correspondence 2 accounting, bookkeeping

دفتري daftarí 1.1 office, bureaucratic پښتو ژبه دفتري کول to introduce Pashto into office work 1.2 official, office په دفتري وخت کښي during office hours 2 *m.* owner of hereditary land; land owner

دفع daf' *f.* 1 repelling, repulse (of a strike, attack) 2 withdrawal; removal; expulsion, banishment, exile 3 *law* defense 4 push, impulse, impetus, incitement دفع کول *compound verb* a to beat back, repel, repulse (a strike, attack) b to withdraw; remove; expel, banish, exile c *law* to defend d to push, incite to something دفع کېدل *compound verb* a to be beaten back, be repulsed (of a strike, attack) **b** to be withdrawn; be removed; be expelled, be banished, be exiled

دفعتاً daf'tán *Arabic* at once; suddenly, all of a sudden ☞ دفعةً

دفعدار daf'adár *m. regional* sergeant, junior noncommissioned officer (in the cavalry)

دفعه‎¹ dáf'a *f.* ☞ دفع

دفعه‎² daf'á *f. Arabic* time

دفعه دار daf'adár *m. regional* ☞ دفعدار

دفن dafn *m. Arabic* burial, interment دفن كول *compound verb* to bury, inter

دق diq *Arabic* **1** bored, weary دق كېدل *compound verb* to be bored دق رنځ سو He became bored. **2** *m.* **.1** wasting fever consumption, pulmonary tuberculosis **2.2** boredom, depression

دقايق daqájaq *m. Arabic plural of* دقیقه

دقت diqát *m. Arabic* **1** attention, care په دقت ، په دقت سره attentively په خاص دقت او غور سره with special attention دیوي مسئلې په شا وخوا كښې ډېر غوراو دقت كول to discuss a problem in detail غور او دقت او غور لازم دئ great attention is required باید دقت وسي چه ... دقت لاندي نيول to discuss something in detail care should be taken so that… **2** accuracy

دقه diqá only دقه یو only (of a child)

دقه مال diqamál *m.* **1** boredom, tedium, melancholy **2** loneliness

دقیق daqíq *Arabic* **1** attentive, careful **2** diligent, industrious, assiduous پر دقیق نظام كاركول to work very diligently **3** perspicacious, astute د اروبدو دقیق حس keen ear **4** small, tiny (in size) دقیق حیوانات واړه او microorganisms **5** fine, delicate **6** accurate, true

دقیقاً daqíqán *Arabic* attentively, carefully

دقیقانه daqiqaná **1** accurate, precise **2** accurately, precisely, exactly

دقیق والی daqiqwáľaj *m.* **1** attentiveness, carefulness **2** diligence, industriousness, assiduousness **3** perspicacity **4** delicacy **5** accuracy, trueness, fidelity

دقیقه daqiqá *f. Arabic* [*plural:* دقیقې daqiqé *and m. plural Arabic* دقایق daqāyaq] **1** minute, moment هره دقیقه لس every minute دقیقې كم اته بجي دي، اتو بجو ته لس دقیقي پاته دي، اته بجي دي په لس دقیقي كم Ten minutes before eight. **2** detail

دقیقه رس daqiqarás inquisitive, curious, searching, keen

دقیقه گرد daqiqagárd *m.* minute hand

دقیقه ئیز daqiqajíz minute دری دقیقه ئیز three-minute

دقیقې daqiqé *plural of* دقیقه

دك‎¹ dak *m.* cause; occasion, basis, grounds

دك‎² dik *m.* ☞ دق دك زغملو *compound verb* **a** to endure pain, bear pain **b** to strain oneself working, overdo it at work

دك‎³ duk *m.* ☞ دوك‎²

دكان dukán *m. Arabic* [*plural:* دكانونه *and rarely Arabic* دكاكين] shop, store **2** workshop

دكانچه dukānchá *f.* **1** counter **2** bench **3** platform, floor, deck **4** plank bed

دكاندار dukāndár *m.* merchant, dealer, trader

دكانداري dukāndārí *f.* trade, business of a shopkeeper

دكان والا dukānwālá *m.* shopkeeper

دكتاتور diktātór *m.* dictator

دكتاتوري diktātorí *f.* دكتاتوريت diktātoriyát *m.* dictatorship د كاريگرو دكتاتوري dictatorship of the proletariat

دكترين doktrín *m.* doctrine

دكتور doktór *m.* ☞ داكتر

دكتورا doktorā́ *f.* **1** doctorate, doctor's degree **2** period and process of preparing the doctoral dissertation

دكتوره doktóra *f.* ☞ داكتره

دكتوري doktorí ☞ داكتري

د كمه də kə́ma from where? د كمه راځي؟ Where are you coming from?

دكن dakán *m.* Dekan, the Dekan plateau

دكني dakaní **1** *attributive* Dekan **2** *m.* Dekan (native or resident of the Dekan)

دكوراسيون dekorāsjón *m. theater* scenery, set

دكن dakhán *m.* ☞ دكن

دكني dakhní, dakhaní ☞ دكني

دكۍ dəkə́j *f.* **1** milk pail **2** large pitcher, jug

د كېږنكلي تيكلي يواز- لوستي ياد də kéẋhkali ṭiklí jawāz lwə́staj jā́d *m. computer science* compact disc read-only memory (CD-ROM)

دكيكه dakiká *f.* ☞ دقیقه

دكيكه گر dakikagár *m.* ☞ دقیقه گرد

دگ dag *m.* ☞ دگی

دگل‎¹ dagə́l *m.* rebuke, reproach

دگل‎² dagál *m.* mast

دگلي‎¹ dagəlí *f.* ☞ دگل‎¹

دگلي‎² dagalí mast, masted يو دگلي جهاز single-masted vessel

دگلى‎³ dagə́laj grateful, thankful, obliged to someone

دگى dəgáj *m.* **1** butcher block **2** feldspar **3** gold tube, silver tube (a decoration on a woman's breast)

دل‎¹ dil **1** *m.* heart; soul **2** *used as the first or second part of compound words* دلارام beloved دلاور brave خوش دل cheerful

دل‎² dal *m.* **1** grouts **2** bean porridge, bean gruel

دل‎³ dal *m.* loss دل تلل *compound verb* to go to the dogs, go to rack and ruin, be wasted, come to nothing

دلا جانه dilādzhā́na *f. proper noun* Dila-dzhana

دلار dalár *m.* dollar

دلارام dilārám *m.* **1** beloved, sweetheart, lover **2** Dilaram (inhabited place near Kandahar)

دلارامه dilārā́ma *f.* beloved, sweetheart, lover, mistress

دلازار dilāzár *m* **1** offender, one who give offense **2** tormentor, torturer **3** beloved

دلازاري dilāzārí *f.* **1** offense; grief, chagrin, distress **2** torment, torture; anxiety, uneasiness, distress **3** cruelty

دلازاك dilāzák **1** *plural m.* Dilazaki (a tribe) **2** *m.* Dilazak

دل آزرده dilāzurdá upset, distresse

دلاسا dilāsá *f.* [دلاساینه dilāsáyə́na دلاسه‎¹ dilāsá] *f.* comfort, consolation; kindness په دلاسه دلاسه very affectionately دلاسا كول

د ورکول دلاسا، *compound verb* to calm, console; reassure; soothe دلاساینی دپاره ویل to say something in consolation; console, calm دلاسه لاس ☞ لاس [لاس and د] from] da lása دلاسه کول *compound verb* to seize, take possession of, master دلاسه وتل *compound verb* to be lost, disappear

دلاک dalák *m. Arabic* barber دلاک دکان barber shop

دلاکخانه dalākkhāná *f.* barber shop

دلاکي dalākí *f.* haircut and shave دلاکی اسباب shaving articles

دلال dallāl *m. Arabic* 1 broker, middleman د مالو دلال commission agent, factor د بورس دلال stock broker 2 procurer, pimp

دلالت dalālát *m. Arabic* evidence, proof; reason, argument دا دلالت کوي پر دی چه ... This proves that…

دلالي ¹ dallālí broker('s), brokerage (attributive) دلالي معاملات brokerage operations

دلالي ² dallālí *f.* 1 brokering, brokerage دلالي کول *compound verb* to engage in the business of brokering, be in the brokerage business 2 commission business د دلالی اجرت compensation or fee paid to the middleman or broker upon consumation of a business deal

دلاندي ,ترلاندِ dəlāndɪ dəlā́nde *Eastern* ☞ ترلاندي

دلاور dilāwár 1 brave, daring, bold 2 *m. proper noun* Dilawar

دلاوري dilāwarí *f.* bravery, daring, boldness دلاوري کول *compound verb* to be notable for bravery, daring; be a bold spirit, be a daredevil

دلایل dalājal *m. Arabic plural* دلایل

دلبار dalbár *m. Eastern* ☞ دربار

دلباري dalbārí *m.* ☞ درباري

دلبر dilbár *m.* 1 beloved, sweetheart 2 *proper noun* Dilbar

دلبره dilbára *f.* 1 beloved, sweetheart, darling 2 *proper noun* Dilbara

دلبري dilbarí *f.* charm, fascination دلبري کول *compound verb* to charm, fascinate

دل بستگي dilbastagí *f.* attachment, affection; love; enthusiasm, passion (for something)

دل بسته dilbastá fallen in love; become attached to; been carried away

دلبند dilbánd *m.* pluck (the heart, liver and lungs of an animal when used for food)

دل پسند dilpasánd pleasant, attractive دلپذیر dilpazír

دل پل dalpál very rumpled; badly trampled; very baggy

دلتا deltā́ *f. geography* delta

دلتنگ diltáng depressed, despondent, sad, melancholy

دلتنگي diltangí *f.* depression, despondency; sadness, melancholy

دلته dálta 1 here دلته راشه! come here! دلته او هلته here and there دلته و چه to walk there and back 2 at that time, then دلته او هلته تلل it's at that time دلته ده چه that's why

د لټون ماشین də laṭūn māshín *m. computer science* search engine

دل جوی dildzhój 1 comforting, consoling; caressing 2 captivating, charming

دل جوئي dildzhojí *f.* 1 consolation, comfort; kindness 2 charm دل جویي کول *compound verb* a to comfort, console; soothe b to captivate, charm, fascinate

دلچسپ dilchásp 1 pleasant, attractive; captivating, fascinating 2 interesting

دلچسپي dilchaspí *f.* 1 attractiveness 2 interest, personal interest په یوه with great interest فردي دلچسپي vested interest پوره دلچسپی د یو شي to be interested in something موضوع کښي دلچسپي اخیستل په دېره دلچسپي لرل to be extremely interested in something

دلخراش dilkharā́sh sad; heart-rendering, heart-breaking

دل خسته dilkhastá aggrieved, distressed, depressed, dejected

دل خواه dilkhā́h loved, long wished for, desired

دل خواهي dilkhāhí *f.* 1 good will 2 favorable attitude

دلداده dildādá enthusiastic, easily carried away

دلدار dildár beloved, young man, lad, boy

دلداره dildára *f.* دل داره 1 beauty, very good-looking female 2 beloved, sweetheart, darling

دلداري dildārí *f.* دل داري comforting, calming, quieting

دلدل daldál *m.* bog, swamp, marsh دلدل لاره *astronomy* the Milky Way

دلدل زار daldalzā́r *m.* swampy terrain

دلده daldá *f.* groats

دل ربا dilrubā́ 1 captivating, fascinating, charming 2 *f.* beloved, sweetheart, darling, dear one

دل ربائي dilrubājí *f.* fascination, charm, beauty

دل سرده dilsárda دل سرد dilsárd 1 indifferent, unconcerned, inattentive; callous, hard-hearted 2 cool, composed; cold-blooded

دل سردي dilsardí *f.* indifference, lack of concern, inattention; coolness, equanimity, composure

دل سوز dilsóz 1 compassionate, soft-hearted; sympathetic; responsive 2 touching, moving

دل سوزه dilsóza beloved, sweetheart

دل سوزي dilsozí *f.* pity, compassion; sympathy; responsiveness

دلفریب dilfaréb دلکش dilkásh captivating, charming, attractive, engaging

دلکشا dilkushshā́ gladdening the heart, inspiring delight د دلکشا مانی Dilkusha (palace in Kabul)

دلگیر dilgír sad, doleful, woebegone, melancholy

دلگیري dilggirí despondency, dejection, grief, sadness, sorrow, melancholy

دل dalə́ *m.* exhaustion, over-fatigue; fatigue, weariness

دلن dalə́n *m.* bog, swamp, marsh

دلو dalw *m. Arabic* 1 pail, bucket 2 *astronomy* Aquarius (the constellation) 3 Dalwa (the eleventh month of the solar year; January-February)

دلول dalawə́l *denominative, transitive* [*past:* دل يې کړ] to husk, pearl; mill, grind (into groats)

دلوه dálwa *f.* ☞ دلو

دله dəla *dialect instead of* درته

دله خپک dalakhapák *m.* دله گک beech martin, stone martin, *Mustela foina*

دلی [1] daláj *f.* **1** stack; rick **2** pile (e.g., of rocks) **3** pile, stack (of firewood) دلی کول *compound verb* **a** to stack (up) **b** put into a pile (e.g., stones) **c** to stack (up) (firewood) **d** to demolish, raze (a house) دلی کېدل *compound verb* **a** to be piled, be stacked (up) **b** to be piled, be heaped up (of rocks) **c** to be piled, be stacked up (e.g., of firewood) **d** to fall to the ground, tumble down

دلی [2] dalé, dlé ☞ دلته دلی دوری here and there

دلېته daléta ☞ دلی

دلېدل daledál *denominative, intransitive* [past: دل شو] to be ground into groats

دلېر dilér brave, bold, daring

دلوري dilerí *f.* ☞ دلېري

دلېري dəlíri from afar, from far away, from a distance

دلېگه dlegá *f.* waste land

دلیل dalíl *m. Arabic* [plural: دلیلونه and Arabic plural: دلایل، دلائل] reason, argument, proof; evidence همدا دلیل دئ چه It's for this reason دا دلیل راورل This remains to be proved *compound verb* to produce proofs or reasons; argue, prove, demonstrate

دلیلي dalilí convincing, persuasive; conclusive, evidential; well-founded, sound

دم [1] dam *m.* **1** breathing, respiration; inhalation and expiration, inhaling and exhaling دم اخیستل *compound verb* to sigh **2** sigh, deep breath دم نیول *compound verb* **a** to inhale **b** to breathe, sigh, heave a sigh دم وهل *compound verb* **a** to breathe **b** to talk, converse دم تری وخوت They sat with bated breath. دم ختلي ناست وو For a moment he couldn't breathe. **3** instant, moment دم تر دمه perpetual یو دم right now **4** fraud, deceit, trickery دم ورکول *compound verb* **a** to expire (to breathe one's last) **b** to deceive, trick **5** steam د دېگ دم steam from a boiler **6** bellows (blacksmith's) **7** special form of exorcism when people blow on the sick one دم اچول ، دم کول ، دمول *compound verb* **a** to blow; fan تر آخري دمه دفاع کول ، تر at each step دمول په هر دم او هر قدم **b** ☞ قدم تر آخره دمه دفاع کول to defend oneself to the last breath

دم [2] dam *m.* blade, edge (of a knife, etc.)

دما [1] dəmá *dialect pronoun* ☞ زما

دما [2] damá *f.* ☞ دمهار

دماغ dimágh *m. Arabic* **1** brain لوی دماغ cerebellum کوچنی دماغ cerebrum brain, cerebrum ستا دماغ خراب شو You've gone out of your mind. د دماغ لوست دماغ ته سپارل to remember what's been read **2** mood د دنیا دماغ والی good mood, cheerfulness د دماغ دنیا the world of dreams **3** nose **4** *regional* arrogance, haughtiness د ده دماغ خاوند و He was well.

دماغجن [3] dəmāghdzhən ☞ دماغي

دماغچه dimāghchá *f* ☞ کنډی [1,2]

دماغخانه dimāghkhāná *f.* **1** cranium **2** brain

دماغه dimāghá *f. geography* cape

دماغي dimāghí **1** brain **2** mental, intellectual دماغي کارکوونکی mental worker دماغي مشغولا intellectual work **3** *regional* arrogant, haughty

دنبال dumbál *m.* ☞ دمبال

دمباله [1] dumbālá *f.* ☞ دمدار [1]

دمباله [2] dumbālá *f.* carpet or embroidered khurdzhin (for keeping valuables)

دمبخود dambakhúd **1** taciturn, reticent, silent **2** with bated breath, (while) holding one's breath

دمبوره damburá *f.* domra (Russian stringed folk instrument) دمبوره وهل *compound verb* to play the domra

دمبول dambawál *transitive* ☞ دمول

دمبله dambelá *f.* ☞ دمباله [1]

دمپخته dampúkhta *m.* دم پخت chicken pilaf

دم پدم dampədám constantly, continuously; every instant

دمپینگ dampíng *m.* dumping د دمپنگ نرخونه cut prices, throw-away prices (prices below the costs of production)

دم پدستي dampədastí دم په دم ☞ دم پدم

دمچي dumchí *f.* strap tied around the rump of a donkey or horse

دمخنی dəməkhanáj **1** front **2** former, proceeding, ex- **3** early

دمخه [1] dəmákha **1.1** in front, from the front هغه دمخه ولاړ و He was standing in front. **1.2** forward, ahead هغه دمخه شو He went on ahead **1.3** earlier, before, formerly; until, by; already دمخه مي ورته ویل I spoke to him previously څرنگه چه دمخه ذکر سوه As has already been noted earlier لا دمخه beforehand تردې دمخه before this تر هر څه دمخه ، تر هر شي دمخه before everyone ترهرچا دمخه first and foremost زما دمخه ، زما څخه دمخه ، ترما دمخه before me هغه زما څخه دمخه دئ He passed me (by). **1.4** long ago, a long time ago **1.5** ago څلور قرنه دمخه ، څلور پیړی دمخه four centuries ago **2** د یو شي دمخه according to something, in accordance with something **3** ☞ دمخنی

دمخه [2] dəmákha *f.* seeing off, leave-taking, saying one's good-byes دمخه دي بنه! Good-bye!

دمخه توب dəməkhatób *m.* دمخه والی the act of preceding, coming before

دمخی [1] dəmákhe earlier, before ☞ دمخه [1]

دمخی [2] dəmákhe *contraction of* دمخه [1] *and the pronoun* يې

دمدار [1] dumdúr *m.* rear guard

دمدار [2] damdár elastic

دم درحال damdarhál دم در حاله in a flash, in an instant, at once

دمدره damdará *f.* heddle (in a loom)

دم دستي damdastí now, at this moment

دم دلاسا damdilāsá [1] *f.* **1** دم دلاسه comfort, consolation; kindness, affection دم دلاسا ورکول *compound verb* to calm, comfort; soothe, caress **2** *predicate* calmed, comforted; soothed, caressed

دمدمه [1] damdamá *f.* **1** pride **2** arrogance, hautiness

دمدمه [2] damdamá *f.* bastion; battery

دمرده damardá *f.* wooden lever

دومري ، دومره dúmra ☞ دمري ، دمره

دمري damṛə́j *f. regional* damr (a small coin equal to ⅛ of a paisa, a paisa is 1/100 of a rupee)

دم ساز damsā́z **1** concordant, harmonious **2** *m.* close friend; confidant

دم سازي damsāzí *f.* **1** concord, harmony **2** close friendship; intimacy

دمشق dimáshq *m.* Damascus

دمک¹ damák *m.* hand-powered iron roller (for leveling and smoothing roads)

دمک² damák *m.* moment, instant, flash

دمکی damakə́j *f.* comma

دم گر ، دمگر damgár *m.* دم گري *m.* sorcerer, conjurer, exorcist

دمل¹ damə́l *transitive* [*past:* دمل يي و] **1** to bewitch a sick person by blowing on him **2** to blow (of the wind) **3** to break, begin (of the dawn)

دملی² damlə́j *f.* ☞ دمري

دمو dəmú *m.* confluence of two rivers

دموکراتيکي demokrātikí democratic

دموکراسي demokrāsí *f.* democracy

دمول damawə́l *denominative, transitive* [*past:* دم يي کړ] **1** to make, brew (tea) **2** to stew, braise (meat, vegetables) **3** to bewitch a sick person by blowing on him

دمه¹ dáma **1** *f.* rest; peace, tranquility; respite دمه جوړول، دمه کول، دمه نيول *compound verb* to rest, take a break, take a breather د شپې دمه مو په هوټل کي وکړه We rested overnight at the hotel دمه ورکول *compound verb* to allow to rest, give a break; be resting **2** resting, taking a break, taking a respite, at rest **3** *predicate* rested

دمه² damá *f.* **1** snowstorm, blizzard **2** fog

دمه³ də́ma *f.* indigestion, dyspepsia

دمهار dəmahár *m.* roar, rumble (of cannon) د توپو دمهار خوت There was the roar of cannon.

دمه ځای damadzáj *m.* place of rest, resting place

دمه گير damagír دمه لوی resting, reposing

دمبدل¹ damedə́l *denominative, intransitive* [*past:* دم شو] **1** to be made, be brewed (of tea) **2** to stew, braise (of meat, vegetables)

دمبدل² damedə́l *denominative, intransitive* [*past:* دم شو] to become silent, grow quiet, stop talking; fade away, subside

دن dan *m.* pitcher, jug, ewer

دنامه dənāmə́ existing in word only, nominal, fictitious

دناو danáw *m.* last irrigation of wheat before it ripens

دنبال dumbā́l *m.* rear, the rear part of something; rear echelon د چا په دنبال in pursuit of someone

دنباله dumbalá peduncle, stalk, stem; escape

دند¹ dund **1** dim, dark **2** *m.* **.1** fog, haze **2.2** dust cloud

دند² dund *m.* roar, rumble (of artillery)

دندانا dandāná *f.* **1** tooth, cog دندانه دندانه toothed, geared; notched, crenulated **2** small waterfall; bar, shallow, shoal; rapids

---

دندانه دار dandānadā́r دندائي dandānayí **1** toothed; notched **2** irregular, uneven (of a shoreline)

دند کنډ dandkánḍ *m. regional* ivory

دندن شکن dandanshikán *m.* Dandanshikan (the gorge and the pass)

دندوکار¹ dandukā́r *m.* ☞ دند¹²

دندوکار² dandukā́r *m.* ☞ دند²

دنده¹ dánda *f.* **1** obligation, duty خپله دنده اجراکول ، خپله دنده ترسره رسول to carry out one's duty **2** well-being, happy life

دنده² danndá *f.* **1** mallet (for a game, e.g., croquet) **2** spoke (of a wheel)

دنسطر ، دنستر dnestr *m.* Dnestr River

دکانچه dunkāchá *f.* ☞ دکانچه

دنگ¹ dəng *m.* **1** jump, leap **2** rice mill **3** swing (with a board)

دنگ² dəng tall, strapping يو لوړ دنگ سړی tall person دنگه مانۍ tall building

دنگ³ dang drunk, intoxicated

دنگ دنگ dəngdáng *m.* trembling دنگ دنگ کېدل *compound verb* to shiver, shudder (from the cold)

دنگ غاړي dəngghā́ṛaj having a long neck, long-necked

دنگل dangə́l **1** *transitive verb* [*present:* دانگي *past:* وي دنگل] to jump (up), leap (up), skip, hop د لوړو پولو څخه رادانگي to jump off a cliff **1.2** وردنگل، پردنگل *compound verb* to attack, assault, fall upon someone **2** *m. plural* **.1** jump **2.2** swoop, pounce

دنگله dangəlá *f.* quarrel, discord, strife

دنگو dangú *m.* boiled beans, boiled pulses (kidney beans, peas); bean kasha

دنگوالا dangwālā *m.* rice mill worker

دنگول dangawə́l *transitive* [*past:* وي دنگاوه] **1** make (someone) jump, jump up **2** to throw, toss up, put

دنگېدل dangedə́l *intransitive* [*past:* ودنگېده] **1** to jump, leap; skip, hop **2** to be thrown, be tossed, be put

دنمارک danmárk *m.* Denmark

دننني danənanáj internal, inner دننني ديوال interior wall دننني کارونه internal affairs

دننه danə́na **1.1** inside دننه څه شي دئ؟ What's inside there? **1.2** into, in, inside دننه راتلل *compound verb* to go in, walk in, enter دننه کول *compound verb* **a** to put in, push in(to); insert **b** to introduce, bring in (to somewhere) دننه کېدل *compound verb* **a** to go or walk in(to), enter **b** to be put into, be pushed into; be inserted **2** *attributive* internal, inner په دننه فرانسه کښي in France د درې ورځو دننه in the course of three days

دننې danə́ne *dialect* ☞ دننه

د نوي ټکنالوژۍ دوتنه سيستم də nawi ṭiknālozhə́y dawtaná sistə́m *m. computer science* NTFS (New Technology File System)

دنه¹ dána *f.* spring of a kahriz

دنه² daná *f.* necklace

دني¹ daní **1** Danish **2** *m.* Dane

دني² daní *Arabic* mean, vile, low

دنیا dunjā́ f. Arabic **1** the world, the universe پر دنیا in the world له دنیا تربدل حيواني دنیا human-kind بشري دنیا the animal world compound verb to leave this world, die ، تر دنیا تېر سو له دنیا ولاړ He (has) left this world. زړه دنیا the Old World نوي دنیا the New World **2** wealth دنیا مومبدل ، په دنیا گتل compound verb to get rich **3** worldly matters (as distinct from spiritual) د دنیا کارونه worldly matters دنیا د ارهت منگوتی دئ proverb good fortune and bad luck are close neighbors

دنياپرست dunjāparást **1** wealth-loving **2** indulging in worldly pleasures; hungry to get everything from life

دنياپرستي dunjāparastí f. **1** love of wealth **2** a passion for worldly pleasures; the desire to get everything from life

دنيادار dunjādā́r m. rich man

دنياداري dunjādārí f. wealth

دنياگۍ dunjāgə́j f. **1** world **2** sorry world

دنياوال dunjāwā́l m. inhabitant of the world

دنياوي dunjāwí ☞ دنيوي

دنيايي ، دنيائي dunjājí **1** world **2** ☞ دنيوي

دنپر dnepr m. Dnepr

دنيوي dunjawí Arabic world, worldly; secular, temporal

دن دن dəṇdə́n m. sound of the rabab

دنيا daṇjā́ m. botany coriander

دو [1] daw m. run, running !په دو! ، په دو دو دو را running about دو کول compound verb squander (money); waste (money)

دو [2] daw m. **1** auction دو پر وهل compound verb Western to participate in an auction **2** raising the stakes (in a game) دو وهل compound verb to raise the stakes (in a game)

دو [3] du m. ☞ دوک [1]

دو [4] du in combinations with tens instead of دوه دوبرش thirty-two

دو [5] du, do a second time, for the second time دوباره (over) again دوزبانه two-faced

دوا [1] dawā́ f. Arabic [plural: ادويه and Arabic دواگاني] medicine, medication دوا خوړل compound verb to take medicine دوا کول compound verb to treat, cure دوا کېدل compound verb to be cured

دوا [2] duā́, dwā f. **1** prayer ☞ دعا **2** gold amulet

دوآب Duā́b, doā́b m. **1** the area between two rivers, interfluvial region **2** Duab, Doab (the names of a number of inhabited places)

دوابه duābá f. **1** ☞ دوآب **2** Doaba (region in the Peshawar District)

دواپاشي dawāpāshí f. spraying (of crops) دوا پاشي کول compound verb to spray (crops)

دواپړ dawāpáṛ praying

دوات dawā́t m. Arabic ink-well, ink-pot, inkstand

دواتيا duatjā́ numeral eighty-two

دوا جوړوونکى dawā dzhoṛawúnkaj m. pharmacist

دواخانه dawākhāná f. pharmacy, drug store

دوادنم duādénúm m. anatomy duodenum

دواره dəwā́ra at once; suddenly; all of a sudden دواره نيول compound verb to catch unawares, take by surprise

دواړه dwā́ṛo oblique of دواړه

دواړه dwā́ṛa pronoun both (in the Western dialect, the feminine the form دواړي خواوي ، دواړي خواري dwā́ṛi is also used) both له دواړو خواوو from both sides دواړه يو دي That is one and the same thing.

دواساز dawāsā́z m. pharmacist

دواسازي dawāsāzí f. preparation of medications, the pharmacist's specialty/business

دوافروش dawāfarósh m. pharmacist, druggist

دوافع dawāfi' m. Arabic plural of دافع [2]

دوام dawā́m m. Arabic continuation; duration ، دوام لرل ، دوام کول دوام ميندل compound verb to continue, be in progress, last دوام ورکول compound verb to continue, go on with, proceed

دوامدار dawāmdā́r دوام لرونکى long, protracted, prolonged; enduring, lasting (of peace)

دوامداري dawāmdārí f. دواموالى length, duration; lasting (of peace)

دواوه duāwá f. ☞ دوابه

دواويا duawjā́ numeral seventy-two

دواوين dawāwín m. Arabic plural of ديوان [2]

دواير ، دوائر dawājír m. Arabic plural of دائره [4]

دوايي dawājí f. دوائي dawāí **1** medicine **2** (medical) treatment

دوب dub m. **1** scorching heat **2** pot, boiler

دوباجه dubādzhá ☞ دوچند، دوچنده

دوباره dubārá **1** again, anew, once more **2** and now

دوباره dubā́ra hybrid (of domestic fowl)

دوباره وداني dubārá-wadāní f. restoration or reconstruction (of a city, etc.)

دوباړج dubā́ṛaj m. battledore, beetle (for washing laundry)

دوباله dubālá f. biplane (طياره is meant)

دوبدجن dubdzhón stinking, fetid; rotting, putrescent

دوبدو dubadú face-to-face

دوبگنۍ dobganáj ☞ دوبنى

دوبگوړى dubgúṛaj m. **1** dacha, country cottage, cabin, summer place **2** summer pasture (in the mountains)

دوبلن dúblin m. Dublin

دوبندي dubandí f. junction, confluence (of rivers)

دوبنى dobənáj summer, relating to summer

دوبنه dobána f. ☞ دوبى

دوبل duból m. ☞ دوه بول

دوبي [1] dobí m. washerman, man or boy who does the laundry

دوبي [2] dóbaj m. summer په دوبي in (the) summer د دوبي خونه dacha

دوبى [3] dobə́j f. laundress

دوبي خانه dobikhāná f. laundry

دوبل dubél m. **1** place where two rivers join, confluence **2** islet, small island

دوپ dup *m.* scorching heat, extremely hot, sultry weather دوپ شو The hot weather has arrived.

دوپای dupā́j two-legged, two-footed

دوپتی duptə́j *f.* cardboard binding, paperback

دوپت dupát double, two-fold, dual, binary

دوپته dupaṭá *f.* 1 shawl, yashmak (for young women) 2 cloak with a border

دوپړ dupáṛ *m.* 1 calamity, disaster; misfortune, trouble 2 feeling or condition of being upset; distress, affliction, disorder

دوپړه dupṛá *f.* tambourine

دوپړي dupuṛí *f.* 1 *medicine* bulimia 2 disorder, feeling upset; distress

دوپنځوس dupindzós *numeral* fifty-two

دوپه dopá *f.* ☞ دوکه [superscript 1]

دوتار dutā́r *m.* ☞ دمبوره

دوتاني dutā́ṇi 1 *m. plural* Dutani (a tribe) 2 *m.* Dutanay

دوتر dawtár *m.* heriditary land ☞ دفتر [superscript 4]

دوتري dawtarí *m.* ☞ دفتري [superscript 2]

دوتنه dawtəná *f* cover (of a book), file

دوتنه سیستم dawtəná sistə́m *m.* دوتنه سیستم dawtəná sestə́m *computer science* file system

دوتنیار dawtanjā́r *m.* bookbinder

دوجانبه dudzhānibá two-sided, bilateral, joint دوجانبه ارتباط two-way communication

دوچار duchā́r meeting, encountering someone په یو شي دوچار کېدل to encounter, meet someone; bump into something; undergo something; get into a particular situation; encounter a particular circumstance

دوچنده duchánda دوچندان duchandā́n دوچند duchánd twice, twice as much دوچنده کول *compound verb* to double, redouble دوچنده کېدل *compound verb* to be doubled

دوڅلوېښت dutsalwéxht *numeral* forty-two

دوختنی dəwakhtanáj former, past

دوخته dəwákhta early

دود dod [superscript 1] *m.* 1 custom, habit, usage; rite دود اېښودل *compound verb* establish the habit دود پالل ، دود اجرا کول *compound verb* to observe the custom 2 dowry (bride's) 3 treating, entertaining 4 ceremony د ... په دود kind of

دود dud [superscript 2] *m.* 1 smoke دود کول دودول [superscript 1] *see* 2 sacrifice, victim د زړه دود deep sigh

دودآلوده dudāludá smoked

دودبایده dodbā́jda *m. plural* wedding customs

دودپالنه dodpālə́na *f.* observing customs

دودجن duddzhə́n 1 smoky 2 smoked

دوددان duddā́n *m. regional* milk jug, pitcher for milk

دودکادود dudkādúd *m.* fire ناڅاپه دودکادود جوړ شو Suddenly a fire broke out.

دودکښ dudkáx *m.* chimney, (smoke)stack, flue

دودو dawdáw running, at a run, at the double په دودو راتلل *compound verb* to run up to, come running up to

دودوزن doduzə́n expected by custom (of the dowry, etc.)

دودول dudawə́l [superscript 1] *denominative, transitive* [*past:* دود یې کړ] *regional* to smoke (a cigarette); smoke, cure (i.e., meat)

دودول dodawə́l [superscript 2] *denominative, transitive* [*past:* دود یې کړ] to introduce a custom; instill, implant

دودول dodawə́l [superscript 3] *transitive* [*past:* ویې دوداوه] to rebuke, give a dressing down, scold, criticize, abuse verbally

دوده dudá *f.* 1 hearth for cooking food 2 soot

دودي dudí [superscript 1] smoke دودي پرده *military* smoke screen

دودي dodí [superscript 2] usual; customary, relating to a custom; established by custom

دودیالی dodjāláj cultured, refined, well-bred, well brought up

دودېدل dudedə́l [superscript 1] *denominative, intransitive* [*past:* دود سو] 1 to be smoked (of a cigarette) 2 to be smoked, be cured

دودېدل dodedə́l [superscript 2] *denominative, intransitive* [*past:* دود سو] to become custom; be introduced; be established

دودېرش dudérsh *numeral* thirty-two

دودیه dudjá *f.* ☞ دود [superscript 2]

دور daur [superscript 1] *m. Arabic* [*plural:* دورونه daurúna *and Arabic* ادوار adwā́r] 1 period; time 2 going around د دنیا د دور سیاحت circumnavigation of the world 3 rotation, revolution دور ورکول *compound verb* to rotate, revolve

دور dur [superscript 2] 1 distant, remote 2 far, a long way, far off دور کول *compound verb* to remove, take away دور کېدل *compound verb* to be removed, be taken away 3 *used as the first part of word compounds* دوربین a far-sighted b far-seeing, foreseeing, prudent لیري ☞

دور dur [superscript 3] *m.* ☞ دوړ [superscript 1]

دورا dəwrā́ ☞ دورایه

دوران daurā́n, dawrā́n *m. Arabic* 1 time, period; epoch استعماري دوران the epoch of colonialism 2 rotation; turn-over, circulation د وینو دوران *economics* circulation of capital سرمایي دوران the د وینو د دوران جهاز ، د دوران جهاز circulation of the blood circulatory system 3 flight (e.g., around the world)

دوراندېش durandésh foreseeing, prudent, far-sighted, prescient

دوراندېشي durandeshí *f.* foresight, prescience دوراندېشي کول *compound verb* to be far-sighted, be prescient

دوراني dawrāní 1 rotating, rotational, rotary 2 *military* turning (movement), envelopment

دوراهي durāhí *f.* fork in the road

دورایه dəwrā́ja from a distance, from afar, from far away

دوربه durbá *f.* bad weather, rainy weather

دوربین durbín 1.1 far-sighted 1.2 farseeing, prescient 2 *m.* spyglass; binoculars نجومي دوربین field glasses صحرائي دوربین telescope

دوربیني durbiní *f.* 1 far-sightedness 2 foresight, prescience

دورسنجي dursandzhí *f.* ☞ دورفکري

درشل durshál *m.* ☞ درشل

دورفکري durfikrí *f.* foresight, prescience

دورگه سری duragá دورگ durág hybrid; half-breed, first hybrid half-breed

درمه durmá *f.* ☞ درمه

دورنگي durangí *f.* 1 duplicity 2 double-dealing 3 inconstancy

دورنما durnumá *f.* view, panorama; vista

دورنویسي durnawisí *f.* د دورنویسی آله teletype

دوروسته dəwrústo دوروسته dəwrústa from behind, behind

دوره dawrá, daurá *f. Arabic* 1 epoch; period د کمونیزم دوره the epoch of communism 2 stage, level 3 turn-over, circulation, rotation دوره کول *compound verb* to circle (of an airplane, etc.) 4 term or duration of a convocation (of a legislative body) اجلاسیه دوره session 5 going around, making the rounds; making an inspection tour, journey, tour په دوره وتل to go on an inspection tour له دوری نه بېرته راتلل to return from a trip 6 reign

دوري ¹ durí *f.* distance, range

دوري ² duri here

دوري ³ dawré, dauré *plural of* دوره

دوري ⁴ duré there, on that side of ځان دوری کول *compound verb* to dodge, evade

دوریدل dauredól *denominative, intransitive* [*past:* دور شو] to turn, turn to

دوربده dauredó *m. plural* turning د وینی دوربده circulation (of the blood)

دور ¹ dur *m.* weaver; carpet weaver

دور ² daur *m. plural* 1 Dauri (the tribe) 2 *m.* Daur

دور ³ dur deceptive, false, untruthful, deceitful

دوراندي dəwŕánde *Eastern* 1 in front, in front of 2 forward

دوردورکه durduráka *f.* sand storm

دورن durón false, deceitful, lying, mendacious

دورول durawól *transitive* [*past:* ویي دوراوه] 1 to sprinkle, dust 2 to raise dust ترخه زهر دورول *proverb* to be the bane of someone's existence

دوره ¹ dúra *f.* 1 sand storm; dust storm 2 dust هوا صافه وه، هیخ دوري نه وي The air was clear, there was no dust at all. 3 powder (tooth powder, etc.) دوره کول *compound verb* a to reduce to ashes b to smoke دوري ویشتل *compound verb* to throw dust in (someone's) eyes دوري په ایستل a to ruin someone b to be completing a deal څوک په دوره ایستل a to turn out, kick out, evict b to fire, sack (from a job)

دوره ² doŕá *f.* 1 gibe, sneer, taunt; jest 2 exaggeration, hyperbole

دوره پاکي duṛapākí *f.* برقي دوره پاکي vacuum cleaner

دوره مار doṛamár *m.* scoffer, mocker; joker, jester

دوري ¹ dúṛi *plural of* دوره

دوړۍ ² dawŕój *f.* dinar (coin)

دوریت duṛít *m.* wandering, roaming دوریت کول *compound verb* to wander, roam

دوریدل duṛedól *intransitive* [*past:* ودوریده] to spill, scatter, run out, pour

دوزانو کښېنستل duzānú *compound verb* to kneel, get on one's knees; sit having gone down on both knees

دوزبان duzabán two-faced, hypocritical

دوزباني duzabāní *f.* duplicity, hypocracy; double-dealing دوزباني کول *compound verb* to be hypocritical, dissemble; be a double-dealer

دوزخ dozákh *m.* ☞ دوزخ

داودزي dauzí *m. plural instead of* داودزي

دوږخ dogákh *m.* hell, nether world

دوږخي dogakhí hellish, infernal

دوساله dusālá two-year-old horse

دوسپنه duspaná *f.* chains, irons, fetters

دوست dost 1 *m.* .1 friend ځوک دوست په زړه پوري دوست dear friend دوی سره دوستان سوه لرل to love someone They have become دوستان دیښمن ښه دئ ترببعقل دوست هوښنیار friends. *proverb* a smart enemy is better than a stupid friend 1.2 *proper noun* Dost 1.3 liking something, supporter of, adherent of something علم دوست loving science 2 *attributive* friendly, amicable د دوست افغانستان خاوره the territory of friendly Afghanistan

دوستانه dostāná 1 friendly, amicable دوستانه خبري friendly talk دوستانه روابط friendly relations 2 in a friendly way, amicably 3 *f. regional* friendship پخه دوستانه strong friendship

دوستاني dostā́ni *plural of* دوسته

دوستدار dostdár *m. epistolary* I; your humble servant

دوست محمد dost-muhammád *m. proper noun* Dost Muhamad

دوسته ¹ dósta *f.* [*plural:* دوستاني] (female) friend دوسته پیغله dear friend (female)

دوسته ² dósta *oblique singular of* دوست

دوستي dostí, dustí *f.* 1 friendship سره دوستي کول to be friends with دچاسره د دوستي تار نښلول، دچاسره د دوستي ترون کول make friends with someone 2 relationship by marriage دوستي کول *compound verb* to become related (to)

دوستی dostáj *m. diminutive of* دوست محمد

دوسخانه duskhāná *f.* corn bin, crib, silo

دوسي dausí *f.* 1 meanness 2 cowardice 3 shame

دوسیه dosjá *f.* dossier, file; folder

دوش dawísh *m.* running, race; harness races

دوشاخه dushākhá *f.* 1 bipod (machine gun, etc.) 2 *technology* fork برقي دوشاخه electrical plug

دوشاله dushālá *f.* large shawl یوه کشمیری دوشاله cashmere shawl

دوشپته dushpetó *numeral* sixty-two

دوشس dushés *f.* duchess

دوشنبه dushambá *f.*, دوشنبي dushambé 1 Monday 2 Dushanbe

دوشي doshí *m.* Doshi

دوشبرلی dusherláj *m.* two-year-old ram

دوبنا dokhá *f.* compote, stewed fruit

دوبناخه dokhákha *f.* bipod (machine gun, etc.)

دوښخې duk̲h̲akhé *f. plural* person's lower extremities (from the thigh to the foot)

دوطرفه dutarafá **1** on both sides; double-sided; two-way **2** there and back, round-trip (of a ticket)

دوغښ dughák̲h̲ *m.* ☞ دربخ

دوغونه dughóna *dialect* ☞ دغونه

دوفصله زمکه dufáslá زمکه land yielding two harvests a year

دوک ¹ duk *m.* **1** consumption, tuberculosis دوک ورولوېدئ He came down with consumption. **2** anger, spite, malice; hostility, enmity **3** irritation, dislike **4** envy دوک سره لرل **a** to nurse mutual enmity **b** to envy each other

دوک ² duk *m.* spoke

دوک ³ dwak *m.* two-year-old colt

دوکال dukál *m.* drought-stricken year

دوکان dukán *m.* ☞ دکان

دوکترين doktrín *m.* doctrine

دوکتور dokt̲ór *m.* ☞ دکتور

دوکړه dukṛá *f.* **1** drum; kettle-drum دوکړه وهل *compound verb* to beat the drum **2** step, tread; rung

دوکمه dukmá *f.* **1** button **2** knob, push button

دو يې کړ dukawál *denominative, transitive* [*past:* دو يې کړ] to make a (concerted) effort, apply oneself

دو کول djkawál *denominative, transitive* [*past:* دوک يې کړ] to torment; oppress

دوکه doká *f. Eastern* deception, fraud دوکه خوړل *compound verb* to be deceived, be tricked دوکه کول *compound verb* **a** to decieve, trick someone **b** to cheat, defraud someone دوکه چاته ورکول *compound verb* to deceive, trick someone

دوکه duka **1** *imperative of* وکول ¹ **2** Come on!, Come on! (shouts of approval while working)

دوکه مار dokamár *m. Eastern* swindler, cheat

دوکه ماري dokamārí *f. Eastern* swindle, fraud, trickery

دوکی ¹ dukáj *m.* small spindle

دوکي ² doké *plural of* دوکه ¹

دوکېدل dukedál *denominative, intransitive* [*past:* دوک شو] **1** to be sick with consumption **2** to torment oneself over, suffer torments **3** to become irritated, get annoyed

دوگ dug *m.* **1** smoke **2** pain **3** rage, fury دوگ کول *compound verb* to make someone angry دوگ کېدل *compound verb* to be angry

دوگانه dugáná *f.* seedling (of a grapevine)

دوگړ dugáṛ *m.* small quantity, little, few دوگړ اوړه a small handful of flour

دوگړه dogṛá *f.* small drum (held under the arm while being played)

دوگزه dugazá *f.* large net for catching hawks; snare

دوگغرن dugghaṛén **1** smoky, sooty **2** dirty, muddy

دوگی dugáj *m.* smoke ☞ لوگی

دوگېدل dugedál *intransitive* [*past:* ودوگېده] to speak slowly, speak in measured tones, speak leaving pauses in one's speech

دول duwál *m. Arabic plural of* دولت

دولاغي dulāg̲h̲í *f.* women's sharovary

دولت dawlát *m. Arabic* [*plural:* دولتونه dawlatúna *and Arabic* دول duwál] **1** (the) State حائل دولت *history* republic جمهوري دولت buffer state مشترکه دولت *regional* (British) Commonwealth وزير د دولت مامورین minister without portfolio government employees **2** power, authority **3** wealth **4** *proper noun* Daulat

دولت آباد dawlatābā́d *m.* Daulatabad (city in northern Afghanistan)

دولت آبادی dawlatābādáj Daulatabad دولت آبادی قاليني Daulatabad carpets

دولت زي dawlatzí **1** *m. plural* Davlyatzi (the tribe) **2** *m.* Daulatzay

دولتمند dawlatmánd rich, wealthy

دولتمندي dawlatmandí *f.* wealth

دولت والی dawlatwā́laj *m.* State system, State organization, statehood

دولتي ¹ dawlatí **1** state, national دولتي تشکیلات state system دولتي مال government employees **2** government government property

دولتي ² dulatój *f* kicking دولتي وهل *compound verb* to kick

دوولس dwólas *numeral* ☞ دولس

دوولسم dwolasóm *numeral* ☞ دولسم

دولکوټ dulkóṭ *m.* row of meat stalls

دولوزه dulā́wza insincere دولوزه سوي ، دولوظه You broke your word.

دولي dawlí *Arabic* ☞ دولتي

دومره dumra, dómra دومري dumre, dómre so much, so many, so, to the extent, to the degree خُومره ... دومره as much... as... لېکن دومره خبره ده چه...، خو خبره دومره ده چه...، مگر دومره قدرته ده مگر دومره ده چه ...، However, the fact of the matter is that... دونه ☞ ...مگر دومره ويلی شم چه *Eastern* I can only say that...

دومنده dwamandá *f.* area between two rivers

دومه ¹ domá *f.* low fire (for boiling milk, etc.)

دومه ² dúma *f.* ☞ دا دومي هم و نه چسپیدي لومه *idiom* Even this ruse didn't succeed.

دومینیکا dominikā́ د دومینیکا جمهوریت Dominican Republic

دوند dund ☞ دند

دونکاچه dunkāchá *f. regional* ☞ دکانچه

دونی dunaṇój *f.* ☞ دوهی

دونوي duniwí *numeral* ninety-two

دونه dúna, dóna دومري dúni, dóni so much, so many, so, to the extent, to the degree د دي چیت قیمت دونه گران نه دئ This chintz is not that expensive. دونه بوره دي بس ده؟ Will this much granulated sugar be enough? فقط دونه وسو Here's what happened.

دوني duní *f.* meanness, baseness

دونی dunṇój *f.* **1** vessel for milk, milk jug **2** milk pail (earthenware)

دوو dwo *oblique case of* دوه

دووس dawús *m.* scoundrel, villain, rascal

دووسي dawusí meanness, baseness دووسي کول *compound verb* to do a mean act

دوولس dwólas *numeral* twelve

دوولسم dwolasóm *numeral* twelfth

دوولسمه dwolasə́ma *f.* twelfth day of the third month in lunar calendar, birthday of Muhammad د دوولسمي ورځ the birthday of Muhammad

دوه dwa **1** *numeral (f. Western* دوی dwe, *Eastern* دوو dwó ، دوه و، دواو dwáwo) two دوه دوه خلور دي two times two is four ، په دوه دوه خبرو باندي *Eastern* on two questions **2** two (used as the first part of word formations) دوه گونی double; two-fold *proverb* د دوو ییسو اهمیت هم نه ورکول خلور several have not the faintest respect for

دوه ارخیز dwaaṛkhíz double, two-way; bilateral, two-party

دوهان duhā́n *m.* camp fire, bonfire

دوه انیز dwa-aníz *m.* two anna coin

دوه برغه dwabrágha double, two-fold

دوه بول dwabúl *m.* man, biped

دوه بی dwabáj *m.* ☞ دوه بی

دوه پتی dwapəṭáj double, two-fold

دوه پتیز dwapaṭíz **1** folding (of a door) **2** *zoology* bivalve

دوه پسوری dwapsóraj ☞ دوه پتی

دوه پنبیزه dwapkhíza دوه پنبیزه dwapkhíz two-legged, two-footed, bipedal

دوه پوړه dwapuṛá two-story

دوه پهار dwa pahā́r *m.* post meridiam time, p.m. time

دوه تاریز dwatāríz two-stringed

دوه جانبه dwadzhāníba bilateral, mutual

دوه چته dwachatá two-story

دوه چنده dwachánda ☞ دوچند

دوه خایه dwadzā́ja دوه خایه کول *compound verb* to divide into two parts

دوه خلی dwakhə́le *f.* fork, pitchfork

دوه دونه dwadóna ☞ دوچند

دوه زره dwa zə́ra *numeral* two-thousand

دوزړی dwazṛə́ray دوه زړی *dwazóray* vacillating; uncertain په دوه زړه dwazórai و/ دوه زړه کېدل to vacillate, be uncertain, be in a state of uncertainty

دوه ژبی یز dwazhəbajíz دوه ژبی *dwazhə́bat* **1** bilingual **2** insincere; two-faced

دوه ژبی dwazhəbí *f.* دوه ژبی کول *compound verb* **a** to express oneself unclearly **b** to confuse (a question)

دوه ژواکي dwazhwā́ki *m. plural* amphibians

دوه سوه dwa sáwa *numeral* two hundred

دوه سوه وم dwasawawə́m *ordinal* two-hundredth

دوه ښاخه dwakhākhá *f.* **1** fork (in the road) **2** corner

دوغبرگه dwaghbárga double, two-fold

دوه غنبی dwaghə́khaj *m.* four-year-old bull or ox

دوه کسیز dwakasíz **1** consisting of two persons **2** for two persons; double (bed)

دوه گرای dwagrā́j Step out!, Wide step! (as a command)

دوه گرایه dwagrā́ja **1** twice **2** double, twice (as much)

دوه گوری dwagóraj cross-eyed; one-eyed, blind in one eye

دوه گون dwagún **1** both, two **2** double, two-fold **3** two-Afghan coin (or note)

دوه گونی dwagúnaj **1** double, two-fold **2** double-faced, two-faced

دوه لاري dwalārí *f.* دوه لاریخه dwalārídza cross-roads; parting of the ways

دوه لاسی dwalā́saj having two hands دوه لاسي سلام کول to make namaste

دوه لکه dwa láka *numeral* two-hundred thousand

دوهم dwahə́m *numeral* second دوهم غنډمشر *obsolete* lieutenant colonel دوهم فرقه مشر *obsolete* major general

دوه مخی dwamə́khaj **1.1** two-sided, bilateral **1.2** two-faced **2** *m.* double-dealer

دوهمه خور dwahə́ma khor *f.* ☞ خور[1]

دوه نلیز dwanalíz دوه نلیز توپک double-barrelled (shot)gun

دوه نیمه dwaníma divided into two parts, divided in half دوه نیمه کول *compound verb* to divide into two parts, divide in half, halve

دوه واریخ dwawārídz repeated

دوه والی dwawā́laj *m.* **1** duality **2** double quantity

دوه ورگی dwawárgaj *m.* two-year-old camel

دوه وزروالا dwawazarwālā́ دوه وزر والا حشرات *zoology* Diptera (flies, mosquitoes, etc.)

دوه ویشت dwawísht *numeral* twenty-two

دوه ویشتم dwawishtə́m *ordinal* twenty-second

دوهه duhá *f.* monk's cell (among the Shiites)

دوه همره dwahúmra double, twice (as much)

دوهی duhə́j **1** hearth **2** smoking room, opium den (of dervishes)

دوه یز dwajíz twin; double

دوی diwí[1] *contraction of the particle* دی *and the copula* وي

دوی doj[2] ☞ دود[1]

دوی duj[3] *personal pronoun, third person plural* **1.1** they (as the subject of the action in all tenses) دوی څوک دي؟ Who are they? دوی چیري ځي؟ Where are they going? **1.2** them (as the object of the action with transitive verbs in ergative constructions) دوی یی راوستل He bought them. **2** *oblique* **.1** them (as the object of the action with transitive verbs in the present and future tenses) ته دوی وینی؟ Do you see them? **2.2** they (as the subject of the action with transitive verbs in ergative constructions) دوی څه وویل؟ What did they say? دوی یو اس واخیست They bought a horse. **2.3** them (used with prepositions, postpositions and adverbs) پر دوی on them **2.4** their (in combination with the preposition د as a possessive pronoun) د دوی کور their house ذهین دوی راغلل Zaheen and his relatives' friends came.

دوی dwe[4] *Western numeral feminine of* دوه

دویال dūjā́l *computer science* binary

دویاله دوتنه dūjā́la dawtə́na *f. computer science* binary file

دویچه dujchá *f.* **1** gutter or channel for irrigation (in melon fields and gardens) **2** trough at a well (into which water for live stock is poured)

دویز dawíz *m.* **1** scoundrel **2** coward

دويستي dəwísti *f. plural* bride's girlfriends (who accompany her singing wedding songs)

دويل duál *m.* دويل duel

دويم dwajə́m *ordinal* second

دويي dují *f.* **1** discord, dissension, split راوستل دويي کښني ... په to introduce discord **2** duplicity

ده ¹ deh **1** *m.* village **2** *used in geographic names* ده سبز Dehisabz (an administrative region of Kabul Province)

ده ² də *oblique of* دی ¹ *pronoun* **1** him, it (in combination with prepositions and postpositions) و ده to him ده ته په ده کښني in it ته وواېه له ده سره tell him with him **2** he (as the subject of the action with transitive verbs in ergative constructions) ده وویل he said وکړه ده پوښتنه he asked **3** his (in combination with the preposition د as a possessive pronoun) کتاب ده ده his book د لاس خوږېږي his arm hurts

ده ³ da *copula, third person singular present tense, f.* **1** is چوکی دا this is a chair تخته ده this is a board **2** is (often used in sentences where the word خبره is understood) چه ده صحيح دا ... it is true that... چه ده معلومه ... it is known that... باندي مېز پر کتابچه ده the notebook is on the table

دها dahā́ *f. Arabic* **1** talent, giftedness **2** skill, know-how

دهاتي dehātí country, rural, rustic

دهانه dahānā́ *f.* **1** mouth (of a river) **2** bit; curb, curb-bit

ده باشي dahbāshí *m.* foreman

دهتوره dahturá *f. botany* datura, thorn-apple, *Datura; common d.* jimsonweed, *Datura stranmonium*

دهر dahr *m. Arabic* **1** epoch, time **2** custom **3** success **4** danger **5** atheism, godlessness

دهراؤد dahrāúd *m.* دهراؤد Daraud (inhabited place in Kandahar Province)

دهرم شاستر dharmshāstár *m.* Hindu laws, the laws of Brahminism

ده سبز dehisábz *m.* ده سوز Dekhisabz (administrative region in Kabul Province)

دهسي dáhasi *pronoun* ☞ داسي

دهشت dahshát *m. Arabic* panic دهشت کښني په in a panic

ده صومه dahsumá *f.* ten rubles, ten-ruble note

دهقان dehqā́n *m.* **1** peasant, plowman, farmer, dekhkanin

دهقاني dehqāní **1** peasant **2** *f.* **.1** the occupation of farming **2.2** the metayaage system کول دهقاني *compound verb* **a** to engage in agriculture **b** to be a metayer

دهله dahlá́ *f.* ☞ دهله

دهلول dahlawə́l *transitive [past:* دهلاوه یې و] to scare, frighten; intimidate

دهله dahlá *f.* Dahla (inhabited place near Kandahar)

دهلي dehlí, dehláj *m.* Delhi دهلي نوی New Delhi

دهلبدل dahledə́l *intransitive [past:* ودهلېد] to be frightened; fear; shake, tremble, shudder from fear

دهلېز dahléz *m.* **1** passage(way); lobby, ante-room, hall(way) **2** *anatomy* auricle, atrium

ده مزنگ dehimazáng *m.* Dehmazang (a neighborhood in Kabul)

دهند dhund *m. regional* fog

ده نشين dehnishín settled (as contrasted to nomadic)

دهنه dahaná *f.* ☞ دهانه

دهور dəhór *m.* weaver

دهوکه dhoká *f. regional* deception, fraud ☞ دوکه ²

دها dahá *f.* first ten days of the month of Moharram

دئ ¹ dəj دی day, də *Eastern copula third person singular, present tense, Western* **1** is دا مېز دئ this is a table **2** is, is located کتاب پر مېز باندي دئ the book is on the table

دي ² *non-emphatic pronoun second person singular (it cannot begin a sentence)* **1** you (familiar form, as the subject of the action with transitive verbs in ergative constructions) وخوړه؟ دي ودوډۍ Have you had dinner? **2** you (familiar form, as the object of the action with transitive verbs in the present and future tenses) دي به کله وينم؟ When will I see you? **3** your (as possessive pronoun) ورور Did راوستي دي پلار ته Where did your brother go? دي چيري ولاړ؟ your father bring you?

دي ³ دی دی *modal-hortative particle (it cannot begin a sentence)* let وواېي دوی دي دلته راځي. Let him say. Let them go there.

دي ⁴ di *copula third person plural present tense* **1** are کتابونه چا د دا Whose notebooks کتابچي دي؟ دا د چا Whose books are these? دي؟ are these? **2** are, are located باندي دي مېز پر کتابونه The books are on the table.

دی ⁵ daj *third person singular (oblique* ده) *pronoun* **1** he, it (as the subject of the action with intransitive verbs in all tenses and with transitive verbs in the present and future tenses) دی چيري ځي؟ Where is he going? دی څه کوي؟ What is he doing? **2** him, it (as the object of the action with transitive verbs in ergative constructions) دی یي وليد They saw him.

دي ⁶ de *oblique of* دا *pronoun* **1** her, it (in combinations with prepositions and postpositions) په دي کښني **a** in this **b** at this time **c** in it, in her چه دپاره دي د **a** in order to **b** because of, on account of (the fact that) **2** she, it (as the subject of the action with transitive verbs in ergative constructions) دي وویل she said **3** her (in combination with the preposition د as a possessive pronoun) دي مور her mother

دي ⁷ de *Western contraction of the particle* دی *and the pronoun* يي خندول باندي ځان پر ديار تول *proverb* to become a laughing-stock

ديار djār *m.* country, province

ديار djār *m.* Himalayan cedar, deodar, *Cedrus deodara*

ديرلس djā́rlas *numeral* ☞ ديرلس

ديالكتيک djālektík *m.* dialectics پوه ديالكتيک dialectician

ديالكتيكي djālektikí dialectical ماتريالزم ديالكتيكي dialectical materialism

ديانت dijānát **1** honesty; decency **2** piety, religiosity

ديانتدار dijānatdā́r honest, decent

ديانت داري dijānatdārí f. honesty, decency

دبب deb m. evil spirit, demon

دبت débet m. economics debit

دبچك dibchík m. staff, pikestaff

دبوسه débtsa f. دبسه débsa f. ☞

دپارتمان depā́rtmán m. 1 section, bureau 2 department

ديپلوم diplóm m. diploma ديپلوم انجنير graduate engineer

ديپلومات diplomā́t m. diplomat

ديپلوماتي diplomā́tí 1 diplomatic 2 m. diplomat

ديپلوماتيك diplomā́tík diplomatic كور ديپلوماتيك diplomatic corps

ديپلوماسي diplomā́sí 1 diplomatic ديپلوماسي پاسپورت diplomatic passport 2 f. diplomacy

دپو depó f. 1 warehouse, storehouse 2 depot دپو كول compound verb to put together, accumulate, amass دپو كېدل compound verb to be put together, be accumulated

دپوزيت depozít m. 1 finance deposit 2 mining deposit

دېخوا dékhwā here

ديد did m. 1 vision ديدكول compound verb to see ده يې تيز دئ He is sharp-eyed. 2 rendezvous, meeting

ديدان didā́n m. rendezvous, meeting سرى يې په ديدان نه مړېږي One can't see enough of her.

ديدبان didbā́n m. 1 sight; rear sight (of a shotgun) 2 tower 3 observer; scout

ديدني didaní f. 1 what (I) saw, what (I) experienced 2 privations, hardships, disasters, ordeals

ديدوان didwā́n m. regional ديدبان ☞

دير dir m. Dir د دير رياست the principality of Dir

دبر dir, der 1 late, tardy 2 long ago, a long time ago, for a long time

ديرپا derpā́ firm, durable, stable, steady

دبرش dersh numeral thirty

دبرشم dershóm ordinal thirtieth

ديرك dirák m. 1 mast 2 pole (of a tent), tent pole

ديركتيف direktíf m. directive

ديرلس djárlas numeral thirteen

ديرلسم djarlasóm ordinal thirteenth

دبره derá f. 1 dwelling, shelter; residence د دبري خاوند head of the house خپلي دبري ته راغلو We came home. 2 stopping place camp, temporary quarters دبره كول ، دبره كبدل ، دبره لگول ، دبره نيول compound verb a to settle, take up residence b to pitch, set up (camp), encamp 3 hut 4 used in geographical names دبره اسماعيل خان Dera Ismail Khan, دبره غازي خان Dera Ghazi Khan (both cities in north-west Pakistan)

ديره dajrá f. tambourine

دبره جات deradzhā́t m. plural Deradzhat districts in Dera Ghazi Khan and Dera Ismail Khan (Pakistan)

ديزانتري dizāntarí ☞ پيچ

ديزل dízél m. diesel (engine)

ديزل آيل dizelā́jl m. fuel

دبزنفكسيون dezinfeksjón m. disinfection دبزنفكسيون كول compound verb to disinfect

دبس des m. country (usually in India)

دبسي desí 1 Indian (of merchandise, etc.) 2 local

دبسيمتر decimétr m. decimeter

ديغ digh m. dialect ☞ دق²

دبكه deká f. push, impulse, impetus

دبگ deg m. 1 boiler د بخار دبگ steam boiler 2 pot, pan, saucepan

دبگان degā́n m. Degan (the name of Tajiks in the south of Afghanistan)

دبگاني degā́ní Tajik دبگاني ژبه the Tajik language, Farsi

دبگچه degchá f. دبگچی degcháy m. ☞ دبگلی

دبگدان degdā́n m. hearth; trivet

ديگر digár other, different

دبگلای deglā́j m. دبگوری degúray m. pot; pan

دبگی degáj m. ☞ دبگلی

دبگي degí cleaned (for cooking grain) دبگي كول compound verb to clean (grain for cooking)

ديله dajlá f. cards ten-spot

ديلي dilé dialect here

ديم¹ dájam contraction of the pronoun دى¹ and the conjunction هم

ديم² díjam contraction of the particle دي¹ and the conjunction هم

دبموكرات demokrā́t 1 democratic دبموكرات شاعر poet-democrat 2 m. democrat

دبموكراتيك demokrā́tík democratic، دبموكراتيك سنترالزم، دبموكراتيك مركزيت democratic centralism

دبموكراتيكي demokrā́tikí democratic

دبموكراسي demokrāsí 1 f. democracy دبموكراسي كول compound verb a to democratize b democratization 2 democratic پردبموكراسي اساس on democratic principles

دبميسبزون demisezón light-weight (coat, worn in spring or fall)

دين¹ dajn m. Arabic [plural: دينونه daynúna and Arabic ديون duyún] debt (monetary)

دين² din m. Arabic [plural: دينونه dinúna and Arabic اديان adyā́n] 1 religion 2 used in proper names محمددين Muhammaddin

دين³ dajn m. beginning

دينار dinā́r m. Arabic 1 dinar (Indian coin equal to 0.1 paisa) 2 history gold coin, gold piece 3 dinar (the monetary unit in Iraq)

ديناميت dināmít m. dynamite

ديندار dindāra 1 believing, religious 2 virtuous

دبنشين denishín ☞ ده نشين

دينگ ding jutting out, sticking out, protruding, projecting دينگ دربدل compound verb to jut out, protrude, stick out دينگ دينگ كبدل compound verb to swell, rise

ديني dinawí Arabic religious, spiritual ديني علوم theology

دينه dína literary used in place of دي³ ☞ نه⁶

دبنه déna Eastern used in place of دي نه ، پخوا له دبنه before this دبنه وروسته after this

ديني dinī *Arabic* **1** religious ديني پوه religious holidays ديني روحي theologian **2** foster, adoptive ديني زوی foster child

دينيات dinijāt *m. plural Arabic* theology; religion class (in school) (*literally:* God's Law)

دېو dew *m.* **1** devil, evil spirit ☞ دېب **2** giant **3** demon

دېوال dewāl *m.* دېوار dewā́r *m.* **1** wall **2** *anatomy* wall دېوال ته سر proverb to be obstinate, persist, refuse stubbornly دېوالونه تمبه کول proverb The walls have ears. هغه راسره دېوال په هم غوږونه لري proverb اوسي He lives next door to me.

دېوالي dewālī wall دېوالي جريده wall newspaper دېوالي ساعت wall clock

ديواليا diwāljā́ *m. regional* bankrupt

دېوان[1] dewā́n, diwā́n *m.* divan, collection of a poet's poems (arranged in alphabetic order of rhythm and by genre)

دېوان[2] dewā́n, diwā́n *m.* [*plural:* دېوانونه dewānúna, diwānúna *and Arabic* دواوين dawāwín] court; tribunal دېوان حرب dewā́n-i-harb, diwā́n-i-harb military tribunal

دېوان[3] dewā́n *m. proper noun* Devan

دېوانخانه dewānkhāná, diwānkhāná *f.* court, courthouse, courtroom

دېوانگي dewānagī *f.* madness, insanity, the state of being possessed

دېوانه dewāná **1** mad, insane **2** foolish **3** *literary* madly in love

دېواني dewānī, diwānī **1** judicial **2** *law* civil دېواني حاکم judge for civil cases دېواني قانون the civil code

دېوبند dewbánd *m.* Dewband (inhabited place in India where the Muslim sacred academy د دېوبند دارالعلوم is located)

دېوده dewda *f.* salute, welcoming volley (of a detachment of tribal warriors) دېوده کول *compound verb* to greet or salute with a volley (of a detachment of tribal warriors)

دېوسه dewsá *m.* [*plural:* دېوسه گان] **1** corner (in a tent, where people usually eat and where the dishes are kept) **2** rack, counter (for dishes) **3** low mound of earth along the walls of a peasant's house

دين dujún *m. Arabic plural of* دين[1]

دیوه مخه تلل də jawə́ mə́kha completely, entirely; together دیوه مخه ورل to carry everything away دیوه مخه ورل everyone is to go away

ديويزيون diwizjón division

ډ

ډ the fourteenth letter of the Pashto alphabet; retroflex (cerebral) d

ډاپ ḍāp *m. printing* reprint (e.g., of an article)

ډاډ ḍāḍ *m.* **1** calming, quieting, soothing, comfort, consolation ډاډ کېدل، ډاډ مېندل *compound verb* to be quieted, be consoled ډاډ ځان self-calming زړه یې ډاډ شو *Eastern* His heart was quieted. **2** confirmation, assurance د لېک د رسېدو څخه ډاډ راکئ confirm receipt of the letter ډاډ ورکول *compound verb* **a** to calm, console **a** to console **b** to confirm; assure **3** certitude, زړه ډاډ ورکول confidence, sureness په ډاډ سره with confidence د اوستري برې

په تا نو زه ډاډ ډاډ گندول express confidence in the ultimate victory نه کوم I have lost faith in you.

د ډاډگېرنې ور ḍāḍgerə́na *f.* comforting, consolation reassuring ډاډگېرنه ورکول *compound verb* to calm, quiet, reassure, console

ډاډونه ḍāḍówarkawə́na ډاډ ورکونه .ḍāḍóna *f* **1** reassurance, comforting, consolation **2** confirmation, assurance

ویې *and* ډاډ یې کړ *and* ډاډول ḍāḍawə́l *denominative, transitive* [*past:* ډاډاوه] **1** to console, comfort, soothe **2** to confirm; assure

ډاډه[1] ḍā́ḍa *f.* **1** ear of corn of milky-wax ripeness ډاډه اچول *compound verb* to form ears of milky-wax ripeness (of corn, maize) **2** unripe ear of maize or ears of grain roasted on a fire ډاډه کول *compound verb* to roast unripe ears of maize or ears of grain

ډاډه[2] ḍāḍá **1** calmed, soothed; calm, assured ډاډه کول، ڈاډه گرزول *compound verb* to calm, soothe ډاډه کېدل *compound verb* to calm down, regain one's composure; be convinced of, be certain of something زړه یې ډاډه شو He calmed down. ډاډه اوسه! Be calm! **2** quiet, peaceful (of life)

ډاډینه ḍāḍína *f.* confidence, certitude, assurance

ډاډېدل ḍāḍejə́l *transitive* ☞ ډاډول

ډار ḍār *m.* **1** fear, dread, terror; apprehension هیڅ ډار دار نه راسره ونه وي I won't be the least bit afraid. ډارکول، ډار په زړه کېنبي لرل *compound verb* to be frightened, feel frightened, be afraid (of), to dread; fear **2** threat

ډارځپلی ḍārdzapə́laj frightened, terrified, scared

ډارن ḍārə́n **1** timid, timorous, cowardly **2** *m.* coward

ډارول ḍārawə́l *transitive* [*past:* و یې ډاراوه] to threaten; frighten, intimidate

ډارونزم ḍārwinízm *m.* Darwinism

ډاره ḍára *f.* **1** hut, cabin **2** awning (above a door, etc.)

ډارېدل ḍāedə́l *intransitive* [*past:* ډار شو *and* ډارېده] to be afraid, fear, be apprehensive له تیاري نه ډارېدل to be afraid of the dark

ډاک ḍāk *m. regional* the post, the mail په ډاک لېږل، په ډاک کي استول to send by mail

ډاکټر ḍākṭár *m.* doctor, physician د سترگو ډاکتر ophtalmologist

ډاکټري ḍākṭarī *f.* **1** the occupation of a doctor; medical work د ډاکټري آلات medical instruments **2** medical

ډاکخانه ḍākkhāná *f.* post office

ډاکه مار ḍākú *m.* ☞ ډاکو[1]

ډاکوالا ḍākwālá́ *m.* ☞ ډاکي[1]

ډاکوتوب ḍākutób *m.* ☞ ډاکه[1] ḍāká *f.* **1** the act of carrying out a raid **2** postal delivery (the occupation)

ډاکه[1] ḍāká *m.* ډاکوتوب *regional* raid ډاکه اچول، ډاکه غورځول *compound verb* to carry out a raid

ډاکه[2] ḍāká *f.* ☞ ډاگه[2]

ډاکمار ḍākamár *m.* robber, bandit

ډاکي[1] ḍākí *m.* **1** postman, letter-carrier **2** courier

ډاکي[2] ḍāké *plural of* ډاکه[1,2]

ډاکي مار ḍākemár *m. regional* ☞ ډاکه مار

ډاگ ¹ ḍāg *m.* ☞ ډاك

ډاگ ² ḍāg **1** *m.* **.1** dale, plain, flatland (as contrasted to forest or mountains) لوړ ډاگ plateau **1.2** steppe **1.3** barn floor, threshing floor **2** level and bald, flat and barren (of land, terrain) دنمن ډاگ له ډاگه وهل *compound verb* to destroy the enemy او ډبر کول to remove, push aside پرسپین ډاگ غابن وتل to overpay, pay dearly for something; miscalculate, make a mistake in counting پر سپین ډاگ غابن ایستل **a** to deceive, fool **b** to get somone to cut the price of something, let something go cheap

ډاگول ḍāgawól *denominative, transitive* [*past:* ډاگ يې کړ] to destroy; devestate, lay waste to, ravage

ډاگه ¹ ḍāgá *f.* **1** post, pole, column **2** beam, joist **3** shaft; flagstaff, flagpole په ډاگه ويل to speak frankly, speak without beating about the bush

ډاگه ² ḍāgá *f.* muslin (fabric)

ډاگه ³ ḍā́ga *f.* ☞ ډاگ ²

ډاگي ¹ ḍāgí *m.* ☞ ډاكي ¹

ډاگي ² ḍāgí steppe

ډاگى ³ ḍāgáj *m.* **1** lecher, rake **2** squanderer, spendthrift **3** person with a large protruding forehead

ډاگۍ ⁴ ḍāgə́j *f.* low mound of earth along the walls of a peasant's house

ډاگېدل ḍāgedól *denominative, intransitive* [*past:* ډاگ شو] to be destroyed, be devastated, be ravaged

ډال ¹ *m.* the name of the letter ډ

ډال ² ḍāl *m.* **1** shield **2** *technology* washer, gasket, spacer; rest, stop د ډال په لاس *politics* buffer state غليم ته ډال نيول، د ډال رياست، د ډال مملكت توره ډال اچول to advance against the enemy with arms in hand دربدل to surrender, capitulate ډال نيول *compound verb* to parry, to deflect a blow سيني مو ډال کړي دي we are prepared to repulse

ډال باز *m.* ropewalker ☞ داربار

ډالر *m.* dollar

ډال غاړى ḍālghā́ṛaj *m.* warrier with shield; warrier in full regalia

ډالفين ḍālfín *m.* dolphin

ډال و ډيل ḍāl-u-ḍíl *m.* dressing stylishly, dress smartly په ډال وډيل کي کېدل to dress in the latest fashion

ډالۍ ḍālə́j *f.* **1** watchtower **2** basket (of flowers) **3** present, gift; souvenir ډالۍ کول *compound verb* to present with something, make a present of something **4** cradle

ډامبورى ḍāmbúraj *m.* granary, storehouse; warehouse

ډانډ ḍānḍ *m.* shaft; stalk, stem

ډانډس ḍānḍə́s *m.* ډانډس ḍānḍə́s bow (of a cotton comber, carder)

ډانډس والا ḍānḍəswālā́ *m.* ډانډسى ḍānḍəsay cotton comber, cotton carder

ډانډسى ḍānḍəsaj *m.* ډانډس والا ḍānḍəswālā́ cotton comber, cotton carder

ډانډسي ḍānḍəsí *f.* work of a cotton comber

ډانډوغ ḍānḍúgh **1** lagging, falling behind **2** to bring up the rear (of a column, of a procession)

ډانډوكى ḍānḍwukáj *f.* swimming

ډانډول ḍānḍól *m.* stick with torches at the ends (which is twirled rapidly)

ډانډولى ¹ ḍānḍólaj *m.* person who is grabbed by the hands and feet and swung about (in a game)

ډانډولۍ ² ḍānḍoláj *f.* game in which someone is grabbed by the hands and feet and swung about

ډانډى ¹ ḍā́nḍaj *m.* cluster or bunch of grapes

ډانډى ² ḍānḍáj *m.* short stick, baton

ډانډى ³ ḍānḍáj *m.* **1** flame **2** ☞ ډنډى ¹ **3** beam, girder, joist, rafter **4** balance beam (of scales)

ډانس ḍāns *m.* dance ډانس يې ښه زده دئ She is a good dancer.

ډانشل ḍānshál *m.* dancing

ډانگ ḍāng *m.* **1** club, cudgel **2** mace **3** shaft, staff اوبه په ډانگ وهل *proverb* to beat the air

ډانگلكۍ ḍānglakə́j *f.* **1** flycatcher of paradise (a bird) **2** *regional* drongo (a bird)

ډانگو ḍāngú *m.* lanky fellow, spindleshanks, spindlelegs, gangling fellow

ډانگورى ḍānguráj *m.* ډانگورۍ ḍāngurə́y *f.* crutch; cane, walking-stick

ډانگه ḍānga *f.* **1** leg (from the thigh to the foot) **2** pole (telegraph, etc.) **3** mast

ډانگى ḍāngáj *m.* **1** step **2** club, cudgel

ډانگى ³ ḍāngáj *f.* *botany* twinflower

ډاونى ḍāwónaj *m.* shawl, veil, yashmak

ډای اکسیډ ḍājaksíḍ *m.* *chemistry* dioxide کاربن ډای اکسیډ carbon dioxide

ډب ¹ ḍab **1** *m.* **.1** pit, hole **1.2** puddle **1.3** whirlpool, eddy **2.1** standing, stagnant (of water) ډبي اوبه stagnant water اوبه ډبي کول *compound verb* to dam, impound **2.2** having stayed, having delayed ډب دربدل *compound verb* to linger, stay too long, stop

ډب ² ḍab *m.* **1** *interjection* boom, bang **2** *m.* **.1** knock, rumble, din, roar ډب ختل *compound verb* **a** to knock **b** to fall with a great noise, fall with a crash **c** to be heard (of a sound) **d** *figurative* to lose stature, lose respect **2.2** blow ډب ورکول *compound verb* to strike, hit **2.3** loss ډب خورل *compound verb* to suffer a loss, incur a loss ډب وروستل *compound verb* to cause damage or loss **2.4** greatness, grandeur

ډب ³ ḍab *m.* **1** force, strength, power, might **2** form; shape **3** conduct, behavior

ډبا ḍabā́ *m.* ☞ ډبهار

ډبالى ḍabāláj *m.* earthen corncrib

ډباوى ḍabā́waj *m.* stamp, die (for stamping or minting coins, etc.)

ډبتبر ḍabtér *m.* favus, mange, scabies

ډبډبنای، ḍabḍabnáj 1.1 indecisive; vascillating, wavering 1.2 ډبډبنی کېدل *compound verb* a to be in a state of indecision, waver, vascillate b to be alarmed, be disturbed, be worried 2 *m.* 1. indecision 2.2 alarm, agitation, anxiety, worry

ډبډنگ ḍubḍáng *m.* lout, bumpkin

ډبډوب [1] ḍabḍúb *m.* clash of arms, skirmish

ډبډوب [2] ḍabḍúb 1 unconscious, lifeless, numb 2 having lost one's head

ډبډی ḍabḍáj sick

ډبر ḍəbár destroyed, annihilated; ruined

ډبرتیا ḍəbartjã *f.* ☞ ډبروالی

ډبرکی ḍabarkə́j *f.* pebble

ډبروالی ḍabarwã́laj *m.* destruction, annihilation; ruin

ډبرول ḍabarawə́l *denominative, transitive* [*past:* ډبر يې کړ] to destroy, annihilate; ruin

ډبره [1] ḍabára *f.* 1 stone, rock د ډبرو کور stone house، ښنکلي ډبري cornerstone د بنست لومړی ډبره precious stones 2 rock قیمتي ډبري idiom ډبره پر ، ډبره اویو ته اچول ، ډبره اویو ته غورځول اینبول idiom to keep a secret; raise someone's hopes by promising a high price (in trade) ډبره غورځول او سر تر لاندي نیول idiom a to be pugnacious b to start a quarrel ډبري ته سرنیول idiom to be stubborn, persist in د ډبري دوره *archeology* Stone Age

ډبره [2] ḍabrá *f.* black-bellied ryabok

ډبري [1] ḍibrí *f.* nut, female screw

ډبری [2] ḍabrə́j *f.* snare for birds

ډبربدل ḍabaredə́l *denominative, intransitive* [*past:* ډبر شو] to perish, die

ډبرین ḍabarín stone, stony; rocky

ډبرینه ḍabarína *f.* rocky terrain

ډبل [1] ḍabl, ḍabál 1 double ډبله تنخواه double pay ډبل تار telegram with paid reply ډبله دروازه folding door 2 large ډبله قالینه large carpet ډبله ډوډۍ European bread (in the shape of a loaf, long loaf, etc.)

ډبل [2] ḍábl, ḍábəl *m. regional military* double-time march, rapid march ډبل کول ، ور ډبل کول *compound verb* to urge someone on; hurry someone په ډبل وتل *compound verb* to hurry, rush ډبل کېدل to come out quickly, come running out

ډبلکوټ ḍablkóṭ *m.* coat; overcoat

ډبلل ḍablə́l *intransitive* [*past:* و ډبله] to part from someone, say goodbye to someone

ډبلین ḍablín *m.* Dublin

ډبلو ḍəbəlú *m.* ډبلی [1] ḍabaláy 1 battledore, paddle (for doing the laundry) 2 rolling pin 3 bread made from flour of various grains ډبلی [4] ☞

ډبلی [1] ḍabláj *m.* ☞ ډبلی

ډبلی [2] ḍabalə́j *f.* wooden mallet, wooden beetle (for breaking up clumps of earth)

ډبلي مار ḍablimár *m.* conjurer; juggler

ډبلي ماري ḍablimārí *f.* 1 comjuring tricks 2 juggling

ډبن ḍabə́n dug up, in holes, in pits and bumps

ډبو [1] ḍəbú stout, fat, obese, corpulent

ډبو [2] ḍabó *oblique of* ډبه

ډب واخ ḍabuãkh *m.* ☞ اخ و ډب

ډب وډوب ḍabuḍúb, ḍabwəḍúb *m.* 1 assault and battery; fight, brawl 2 noise, uproar, hubbub ډب وډوب اچول *compound verb* a to fight, brawl, start a fight b to make noise, raise a din, create a hubbub

ډبوس ḍəbús puffy

ډبول ḍabawə́l *transitive* [*past:* و يې ډباوه] 1 to beat, strike; knock, bang on ډبول دروازه پننه *compound verb* to knock on a door *compound verb* to stamp one's foot 2 to beat, beat up, beat unmercifully

ډبه [1] ḍabá *f.* 1 place of assembly 2 raised platform, scaffold; low mound of earth along the walls of a peasant's house 3 platform, rostrum 4 *railroad* car ډبه درجه اوله first-class car 5 crossroads, crossing 6 center (of a market)

ډبهار ḍabəhár *m.* knocking, rapping; din, thunder, roar; crackling, rattle

ډبي [1] ḍabí *feminine plural of* ډب 2

ډبی [2] ḍabáj *m.* 1 club, cudgel 2 battledore, paddle (for washing the laundry) 3 box

ډبی [3] ḍubə́j *f.* bottle gourd, crookneck squash for snuff

ډبی [4] ḍubə́j *f.* trembling, tremor; quivering, twitching ډبی وهل *compound verb* to tremble, quiver زړه يې ډبی ووهلئ His heart was fluttering.

ډبی [5] ḍabə́j *f.* net, snare

ډبی [6] ḍabə́j *f. regional* sleeping compartment (on a train)

ډبجالی ḍabjãláj well-bred; courteous, civil

ډبېدل ḍabedə́l *intransitive* [*past:* و ډبده] to be beaten up, be given a thrashing

ډپ [1] ḍap *m.* puddle, pool

ډپ ḍap *m.* 1 loss چاته ډپ ورسول to cause a loss 2 conceit په ډپ کي کېدل to get a swelled head

ډپ [2] ḍəp *m.* 1 hill; mound, knoll, hillock 2 hill near a village where people take walks 3 pile of earth ډپ ډپ کول *compound verb* to be covered with bubbles (of dough)

ډپتي [3] ḍiptí *m.* assistant ډپتي کمېشنر *regional* district chief

ډپلوم ḍiplóm *m.* ☞ دیپلوم

ډپه ḍápa *f.* 1 platform, scaffold 2 low mound of earth along the walls of a peasant's house

ډت ḍət *m.* 1 noise of ginning of cotton 2 smack, slap

ډتن ḍətə́n 1.1 cowardly 1.2 mean, vile, low, underhanded 2 *m.* 1. coward 2.2 scoundrel, villain, rascal

ډتي [1] ḍaə́ti *f. plural* 1 digging up the soil (by a hen) 2 rubbish, nonsense

ډتی [2] ḍətáj ☞ ډتن

ډچ ḍach *m.* Dutchman, Hollander

ډچکه ḍə́chka *f.* **1** amble ډچکي وهل *compound verb* to amble په ډچکو اچول to trot one's horse **2** sumptuousness, splendor, magnificence **3** fame, glory, respect **4** trembling, tremor

ډچول ḍəchawə́l *transitive* [*past:* ډچاوه یي و] to make a horse go at a pace, pace a horse

ډچه ḍə́cha *f.* ☞ ډچکه

ډډ [1] ḍaḍ **1** *m.* **.1** hollow **1.2** low, dull sound; hoarse voice; bass, basso **2** *attributive* **.1** hollow; empty **2.2** low, dull (of a sound); rough, hoarse (of a voice) آواز یي لږ ډډ سو He became hoarse. **3** swollen

ډډ [2] ḍaḍ *m.* ☞ ډډو [2]

ډډبد ḍaḍ-báḍ **1** *m.* man who has died young **2** swollen

ډډبېکی ḍaḍbekə́j *f.* *anatomy* mastoid bone

ډډتوب ḍaḍtób *m.* ډډتیا *f.* hollow; empty space; cavity, void

ډډزنی ḍaḍzə́naj *m.* *anatomy* temple

ډډګی ḍaḍə́gj *f.* ☞ راشپبل

ډډم ḍaḍə́m *m.* weed

ډډنکی ḍaḍə́nkaj *m.* *anatomy* lower jaw, mandible

ډډنه ḍaḍə́na *f.* search

ډډو [1] ḍəḍú *m.* **1** narghile, hookah **2** fat man

ډډو [2] ḍaḍú *m.* quinsy, tonsillitis

ډډو [3] ḍaḍó *oblique plural of* ډډی

ډډوالی ḍaḍwā́laj *m.* ☞ ډډتوب

ډډوزه [1] ḍaḍúza *f.* **1** acrid smoke, fumes **2** dense smoke **3** haze, fog

ډډوزه [2] ḍaḍúza *f.* *regional* ☞ دروزه

ډډوښی ḍaḍwəkháj *m.* earring

ډډول ḍaḍawə́l *denominative, transitive* [*past:* ډډ یي کړ] **1** to inflate; blow, fan **2** to empty, make hollow, hollow out **3** *figurative* to lead someone astray

ډډون ḍaḍún *m.* search, investigation ډډون کول *compound verb* to search for

ډډه [1] ḍáḍa *f.* **1** direction د کلي څنلمه northerly direction شمال ډډه the outskirts of the village **2** side په ډډه ډډه side by side ، ډډه اچول *compound verb* **a** to lean on, lean sideways **b** to take something on oneself ډډه اړول *compound verb* to turn away, turn aside ... ډډه څخه a to step aside, yield the right-of-way, let someone go ahead **b** *figurative* to avoid, shun; evade, shirk **c** to refrain, abstain (e.g., from voting) د چا څخه ډډه کېدل ، د چا څخه ډډه گرزبدل to avoid someone ډډه لگېدل *compound verb* **a** to lean on, lean sideways **b** to calm down, compose oneself **c** to cope with (an assignment, etc.) **d** to be inclined toward something گرجبدو ته دي ډډي نه لگي؟ Wouldn't you like to go for a walk? ډډه ورکول *compound verb* **a** to lean on, lean sideways **b** to undertake to do something with enthusiasm بهر لور ته ډډه وهل to lean out (of the window) a to set په ډډه کول to lie down on one's side په ډډه پربوتل aside **b** to remove, resolve (e.g., differences) د ... نه څان ډډي ته a to avoid something **b** to hide oneself, cover oneself (e.g., کول from the rain) ... ته ډډه ورورل to reach, amount to (of monetary sums) زما ډډه بغمه وي I am not worried.

ډډ [2] ḍaḍá *f.* clod, clump (of soil); cup (of a hookah)

ډډ بده ḍáḍa-baḍa *f.* woman who has died young

ډډ یي ḍaḍají **1** dull, dim-witted, obtuse **2** flabby; lazy, indolent

ډډی [1] ḍaḍáj *m.* **1** dummy calf (which is placed next to a cow that has recently lost its calf) **2** pillow

ډډی [2] ḍaḍə́j *f.* powder flask

ډډی بدی ḍaḍáj-baḍáj swollen, bloated (from illness)

ډډیدل ḍaḍedə́l *denominative, intransitive* [*past:* ډډ شو] **1** to swell (up); distend, become distended; be puffed up, be swollen **2** to become rough, become hoarse (of the voice) **3** to become hollow, form a hollow

ډډیي ḍaḍají ☞ ډډ یي

ډرام ḍrām *m.* ☞ درامه

ډراماتیست ḍrāmātmíst *m.* ☞ درامه لیکونکی

ډراماتیک ḍrāmātmík *drāmawí* dramatic

درامه ḍrāmá *f.* drama; play تراجبدي درامه tragedy کومبدي درامه comedy د درامي لیکل dramaturgy

درامه لیکونکی ḍrāmá likúnkaj *m.* playwright, dramatist

ډران ḍarán *m.* **1** lowing, mooing; bellow(ing) ډران وهل *compound verb* to moo; bellow **2** shout, cry, scream, shriek

ډرایور ḍrājwár *m.* driver, chauffeur د لاری ډرایور a truck driver

ډرایوري ḍrājwarí *f.* driving (an automobile, etc.) د درایوری کار کول to be a driver, be a chauffeur

ډربل ḍərpál *m.* **1** toady, sycophant, bootlicker **2** parasite; scoundrel, blackguard; lout, boor

ډربلي ḍərpalí *f.* **1** sycophancy, toadyism, flattery, fawning ډربلي کول *compound verb* to grovel **2** caddishness, loutishness

ډربلی ḍarpaláj *m.* kind of vegetable

ډرسک ḍərsák *m.* assemblage, crowd

ډرودژاني ḍərodzhā́ni *f.* ☞ ډری

ډرهار ḍərəhā́r *m.* nonsense, rubbish ډرهار! Nonsense!

ډری ḍarə́j *f.* gibe, sneer, taunt ډری وهل *compound verb* to make fun of, mock, make a fool of, insult

ډرایور ḍrajwár *m.* ☞ ډرایور

ډرایوري ḍrajwarí *f.* ☞ ډرایوري

ډز [1] ḍaz, ḍəz *m.* [*plural:* ډزونه ḍazúna, ḍəzúna *and f. plural Eastern dialect* ډزي ḍáze, ḍéze] shot ډز کول *compound verb* to shoot (at), fire (at) له توپک نه ډز کول to shoot a gun ډزی کول *compound verb* to shoot, fire ډز وهل *compound verb* to take a shot (at), fire a shot (at)

ډز [2] ḍəz **1** stupid, dumb (of a person) **2** *m.* **.1** a stupid person, dummy **2.2** windbag, babbler

ډزدز ḍazdáz *m.* ډز ډوز ḍazdúz *m.* exchange of shots, firing, skirmish

ډزوال ḍazwál *m.* rifleman

ډزوغرپ ḍazughŗáp **1** *m.* skirmish, clash **2** in a flash, in the twinkling of an eye

ډزول ḍazawə́l *transitive* [*past:* ډزاوه یي و] **1** to beat, thrash (with a stick) **2** to shoot, fire

ډزهار ḍəzəhā́r *m.* shots, shooting, firing, fire

ډزي [1] ḍázaj *used as the second part of word formations* لس ډزي ټوپک a ten-round rifle

ډزې [2] ḍáze, ḍəze *f. plural of* ډز [1]

ډزېدل ḍazedə́l *intransitive* [*past:* وډزېده] to be thrashed, be beaten up badly

ډسک ḍesk *m.* table; (school) desk

ډسکې ḍə́ski *f. plural* lie; lying ډسکې وهل *compound verb* to (tell a) lie

ډسمبر ḍisámbr *m.* December

ډسمس ḍismís *regionalism* discharged, demobilized, demobbed ډسمس کېدل *compound verb* to be discharged, be demobbed

ډغ ḍəgh *m.* **1** *medicine* Basedow's disease, exophthalmic goiter **2** kind of bird **3** *regional* person with bulging eyes, goggle-eyed person

ډغډغۍ ḍəghḍəghə́j *f.* children's game

ډغره ḍaghə́ra *f.* **1** pushing **2** butting **3** collision ډغره خوړل *compound verb* to collide, bash against ډغره وهل *compound verb* **a** to push **b** to butt **c** to collide د رنګارنګ پېښو سره ډغرې وهل to encounter various events **4** surf, breakers

ډغرې [1] ḍəghə́ri *f. plural* twaddle, idle talk

ډغرۍ [2] ḍagharə́j *f.* butting ډغرۍ وهل to butt

ډقره ḍaqə́ra *f.* ☞ ډغره

ډک [1] ḍuk *m.* ☞ ډغ [2]

ډک [2] ḍək *m.* oak leaf

ډک [3] ḍak **1** full, filled; overfilled د اوبو ډکه کوزه ، د اوبو څخه ډکه کوزه ، په اوبو ډکه کوزه pitcher full of water سالون له خلکو څخه ډک و the room was full د اوبو ډک خوړ deep creek فضا د شور نه ډکه وه The air was full of noise. زړه مې ستا په مينه ډک دئ My heart is full of love for you. **2** abounding in something **3** charged, loaded دا ټوپک ډک دئ This gun is loaded. **4** sated, satiated **5** *figurative* pregnant دغه سياست له ډېرو خطرو نه ډک دئ This policy is fraught with danger.

ډک [4] ḍak *m.* **1** collision ډک خوړل *compound verb* to collide with **2** mercenary motive; self-interest ډک لرل *compound verb* to have a selfish motive

ډکار ḍakā́r *m.* belch(ing), eructation ډکار کښل ، ډکارونه ايستل *compound verb* to belch

ډکال ḍukā́l *m.* **1** drought **2** death by starvation **3** sudden death

ډکتوب ḍaktób *m.* ډکتيا ḍaktyā́ *f.* ☞ ډکوالی

ډکتور ḍakṭór *m.* ☞ ډاکټر

ډکتوري ḍakṭorí *f.* ☞ ډاکټري

ډکره ḍukrá *f.* tambourine

ډکشنري ḍíkshinarí *f.* dictionary ډکشنري ليکل *compound verb* to compile a dictionary

ډکوالی ḍakwā́laj *m.* **1** fullness **2** filling (up)

ډکول ḍakawə́l *denominative, transitive* [*past:* ډک يې کړ] **1** to fill (up), pack; stuff بکس په کتابونو ډکول to pack a suitcase with books پياله په چايو ډکول to pour a full cup of tea د قهوې نه پياله ډکول *Eastern* to pour coffee into a cup ډوغل ډکول *compound verb* to fill in a hole کارتوس ډکول *compound verb* to load a cartridge غاښ ډکول *compound verb* to fill a tooth **2** to charge, load ټوپک ډکول *compound verb* to load a gun **3** to stuff, cram کوچنوټي له خوږو ډکول to stuff a child with sweets **4** to incite, instigate و جنګ ته ډکول to instigate a quarrel د يو شي ځای ډکول to replace something

ډکه [1] ḍaká *f.* **1** blow, stroke; collision; push, shove د وګړو ډکې او تمبې crowd **2** confinement (in a prison), incarceration **3** mirage **4** the shadow of a fairy or ghost (said to bring on trouble) ډکه وهل *compound verb* **a** to push **b** to cast a shadow **5** state of frenzy, state of being possessed ډکه خوړل *compound verb* **a** to receive a blow **b** to be frenzied **6** *regional* rout, destruction (of the enemy)

ډکه [2] ḍaká *f.* Dacca

ډکه [3] ḍáka *f.* **1** *singular of* ډک [3] **2** pregnant (of animals)

ډکه [4] ḍaká *f.* **1** caravan stopping place **2** embankment, quay **3** occurrence, happening, event, incident

ډکه [5] ḍaká *f.* obligation

ډکه خوله ḍáka khulá with wide-open mouth, with mouth agape

ډکه ناک ḍakanā́k raging, frenzied, possessed, obsessed

ډکې [1] ḍáki *f. plural of* ډک [3] زما سترګې هم ډکې ډکې کېدې I wanted to sleep.

ډکی [2] ḍə́kaj *m.* **1** stalk, stem; shoot, sprout **2** small bush, shrub **3** fluff, down (on the beard) په ږيره کښې يې تور ډکی کم وو There were few black hairs in his beard.

ډکۍ [3] ḍakə́j *f.* rise سخته ډکۍ a sharp rise

ډکېدل ḍakedə́l *denominative, intransitive* [*past:* ډک سو] **1** to be filled, be packed, be stuffed سترګې په اوښکو ډکې سوې tears welled up in the eyes **2** to be charged, be loaded **3** to be crammed, be stuffed **4** to be pregnant (of animals) **5** to be induced, be incited

ډګ ḍəg *m.* **1** log **2** hearth, bonfire **3** ☞ ډوبله

ډګډګلی ḍagḍəgaláj *m.* collapse (in the economy, etc.)

ډګډګی ḍəgḍəgáj *m.* ☞ ټکټکۍ

ډګ ډګی ḍəgḍagáj *f.* rocky, uneven terrain

ډګر ḍəgə́r *m.* **1** steppe; field د جګړې ډګر field of battle **2** area, square **3** ground, area, site, (e.g., take-off and landing ground) د الوتکو ډګر airfield ، هوايي ډګر الوتکه پر ډګر راکښته سوه The plane landed. د ستېشن ډګر platform **4** arena; field ډګر ته راوتل **a** to appear in the arena, become well known **b** to be divulged (of a secret) **5** sphere of action, use, application ډګر ته راايستل to put into practice په وچ ډګر پرېښودل *proverb* to leave with nothing

ډګر جنرال ḍəgərdzhanrā́l *m.* general of the army

ډګر جنرالي ḍəgərdzhanrā́lí *f.* rank of general of the army

ډګرمن ḍəgərmán *m.* lieutenant colonel

ډګرمني ḍəgərmaní *f.* rank of lieutenant colonel

ډګروال ḍəgərwā́l *m.* colonel

ډګروالي ḍəgərwā́lí *f.* rank of colonel

ډګره ḍagə́ra *f.* waste land, vacant land

ډګري ḍigrí *f.* **1** decree, decision of a court **2** (advanced) academic degree

ډګلند ḍuglánḍ *m.* trot (horse's gait of 200 meters per minute) په ډګلند تلل *compound verb* to go at a trot, trot په ډګلند وهل to trot a horse,

ډګله ḍəglá *f.* riding breeches, narrow trousers

ډګه ḍə́ga *f.* sex organ, penis

ډګى ḍagáj *m.* skinny calf (male)

ډل [1] ḍal *m.* shovel for mounding up beds and for digging irrigation ditches

ډل [2] ḍal *m.* rendered fat, melted fat د غوړي رنده rendered fat

ډل [3] ḍal *m.* 1 grove 2 group, detachment

ډلګى [1] ḍalgáj *m. diminutive of* ډل [3] 2

ډلګى [2] ḍalgáj *f.* military squad, section

ډلګى مشر ḍalgəjmə́shər *m.* military squad leader, section leader

ډلوګى ḍalogə́j *f.* old vixen, sly old woman

ډله ḍála *f.* 1 group; union, society د زده کوونکو يوه ډله a group of pupils 2 society, company; collective په دوی ډله کښي in their collictive په خپله ډله کښي in one's circle 3 crowd ډله ډله a by groups b in crowds 4 row, group د آسيا ډېر هېوادونه ، چه افغانستان هم په دي ډله کښي دئ ... Many countries of Asia, including Afghanistan ... 5 *biology* class 6 herd; flock; school د ماهيانو ډله a *biology* class of fish b school of fish 7 system (e.g., river system) د لوګر د سيند په ډله کښي in the Logar river system 8 type, category 9 *politics* class د کاريګرانو ډله the working class 10 *politics* party ملي ډله the nationalist party 11 grove کتونکى ډله editorial board ساکنه ډله *linguistics* consonant cluster

ډله يېز ḍalajíz ☞ ډله ييز

ډله وال ḍalawál *m.* fellow-worker, colleague

ډله ييز ḍalajíz pertaining to the collective; collective, group; social ډله ييزي چاري affairs of the collective

ډلى ḍaláj *f.* 1 trash bin; garbage pail 2 manure bag 3 bag for gathering figs 4 snow drift 5 pile (of hay, grass)

ډم [1] ḍəm, ḍum *m.* 1 barber ډمان خونه وو ولي نېستى ډمان کړو *saying* Hunger is no joking matter (*literally:* we weren't barbers, necessity forced us) 2 musician; singer (among the tribes)

ډم [2] ḍam 1 *m.* .1 pond; lake 1.2 spot, stain ډم لګول *compound verb* to soil ډم لګېدل *compound verb* to be soiled 2 *attributive* ډمي اوبه stagnant water ډم ورول *compound verb* to suffer failure

ډم [3] ḍam *m.* beat(ing) (of a drum), drumbeat

ډمامه [1] ḍamāmá *f.* drum; kettledrum ډمامه وهل to beat the drum

ډمامه [2] ḍamāma *f.* hole, pit; cavity, depression; pot-hole

ډمامي ḍəmámi اوبه ډمامي stagnant water

ډمان ḍəmā́n *plural of* ډم [1]

ډمبره [1] ḍambə́ra *f.* bumblebee

ډمبره [2] ḍambára *f.* ☞ ډنبره [2]

ډمبک ḍumbák *m.* drum

ډمبکى ḍumbakáj *m.* small drum

ډمبه ḍambá *f.* trowel

ډمبهار ḍambəhā́r *m.* beat(ing) (of a drum); sounds (of a tambourine)

ډمپينگ ، ډمپينگ ḍámpíng *m. economics* dumping

ډمتوره ḍamturá *f. botony* datura

ډم ډوم ḍamḍúm *m.* drumbeat

ډمگى [1] ḍamgáj *m.* pond

ډمگى ، ډم گى [2] ḍəmgáj *m. diminutive of* ډم [1]

ډموکراسي ḍemokrāsí *f.* ☞ دموکراسي

ډمول ḍamawə́l *denominative, transitive* [*past:* ډم يې کړي] to hold back the water; turn into a swamp, swamp

ډمه ḍə́ma, ḍúma *f.* [*plural:* ډمي ḍə́mi and ډماني ḍəmā́ni] 1 (female) singer 2 hairdresser (who dresses a bride)

ډمي [1] ḍə́mi *feminine plural of* ډمه

ډمي [2] ḍámi اوبه ډمي swamp ☞ ډم [2]

ډمي [3] ḍəmé *f.* children's game

ډمېدل ḍamedə́l *denominative, intransitive* [*past:* ډمي شوي] 1 to stagnate, stand too long (of water) 2 to turn into a swamp, become a swamp

ډمېره ḍaméra *f.* bumblebee ☞ ډنبره [1]

ډنبره ḍambára *f.* sumac (kind of tree) د ډمبرو لرګي جوړول *idiom* to thrash someone, beat someone up

ډنډ ḍanḍ 1 *m.* .1 lake 1.2 puddle 1.3 fertile valley 1.4 shimmering surface (of a mirror, etc.) 2 *attributive* په ډنډو اوبو in stagnant water ډنډ کېدل *compound verb* to stagnate, stand too long (of water) کوڅي ډنډ شوي ډمبدل The streets were covered with puddles. ☞ د سمندر شين ډنډ The blue expanse of the ocean. د لمبدو ډنډ the blue sea د اوبو شين ډنډ swimming pool خبره په ډنډ گډه شوه *idiom* things came to a standstill

ډنډا ḍanḍā́ *f.* ☞ ډنډوره

ډنډاپ ḍanḍā́p *m.* ☞ ډانډپ

ډنډاره [1] ḍanḍārá *f.* 1 stalk; stem, trunk 2 twig, sprig, shoot

ډنډاره [2] ḍanḍārá *f.* bumblebee

ډنډاس ḍanḍā́s *m.* ☞ ډانډپ

ډنډاکى ḍanḍākaj *m. anatomy* pelvic bone

ډنډالى ḍanḍālaj *m.* town-crier, herald

ډنډاو ḍanḍā́w *m.* ☞ ډنډ [1]

ډنډر ḍanḍə́r *m.* 1 ☞ ډنډاره [1] 2 ring of an earring (put into the nose) 3 scape 4 stalk with ear attached

ډنډغر ḍanḍəghə́r *m.* straw residue (after feeding livestock)

ډنډکى ḍanḍəkáj *m.* kichri-kurut (a porridge dish)

ډنډگلى ḍanḍgúlaj *m.* lotus

ډنډوب ḍanḍób insensible, unfeeling, numb

ډنډورچي ḍanḍorchí *m.* town-crier, herald

ډنډوره ḍanḍorá *f.* 1 proclaiming, announcing (by drumbeat) ډنډوره گرزول ، وهل *compound verb* to make public 2 good repute, fame

ډنډورچى ḍanḍorchí *m.* ☞ ډنډوره چي

ډنډورى ḍanḍóraj *m.* ☞ ډانډى [1]

ډنډوکاري ḍanḍukā́ri *f. plural* yelling, shouting ډنډوکاري وهل *compound verb* to yell, shout

ډنډوکى ḍanḍúkaj *m.* 1 pond; pool 2 puddle

ډنډول ḍanḍawə́l *denominative, transitive* ☞ ډمول

ډنډه [1] ḍanḍá *f.* 1 club, stick (for ball games) 2 (balance) beam (of a scale) 3 handle (of a toothbrush) 4 trunk; stalk

ډنډه ² ḍánḍa *f.* 1 section of a field in the form of a long strip (on which rice is grown) 2 windrow (for water retention) ډنډی اچول *compound verb* to make windrows (for water retention)

ډنډا کېلک ḍanḍá kelák *m.* 1 *sports* polo 2 ☞ ډی ²

ډنډی ḍanḍə́j *f.* 1 (balance) beam (of a scale) ډنډی وهل *compound verb* to give short weight, cheat in weighing 2 ear lobe

ډنډېدل ḍanḍedə́l *denominative, intransitive* ☞ ډمبدل

ډنډیي ḍanḍəjí *f.* outrunner, trace-horse

ډنگ ¹ ḍəng *m.* 1 ring or sound of metal 2 sounds (of music)

ډنگ ² ḍang surprised, astonished, startled, staggered

ډنگا ḍangá *m.* ☞ ډنگهار

ډنگالۍ ḍangālə́j *f.* kind of damson plum

ډنگ ډونگ ḍəngḍúng *m.* ☞ ډنگ ودونگ ښه په ډنگ ډونگ واده کول to celebrate a wedding solemnly

ډنگر ¹ ḍangár, ḍəngə́r *m. Peshawar* 1 *singular and plural* cattle, neat cattle 2 [*plural:* ḍəngə́r] bull; ox

ډنگر ² ḍangár, ḍəngə́r thin, skinny, gaunt, emaciated

ډنگرک ḍəngərák *diminutive* skinny little

ډنگرکه ḍəngəráka 1 *feminine singular of* ډنگرک 2 *f.* pileate mushroom

ډنگروالی ḍangərwā́laj *m.* thinness, leanness

ډنگرک ¹ ḍəngərə́j ☞ ډنگری

ډنگلی ² ḍingarə́j *f.* ☞ ډنگلی

ډنگلی ḍingalə́j *f.* sweep, shadoof (of a well)

ډنگ ودونگ ḍang-wə-ḍúng *m.* sounds (of music and singing) بی ډنگ ودونگ واده a poor wedding (one without music and singing)

ډنگول ḍangawə́l *transitive* [*past:* و یي ډنگاوه] 1 to beat the drum 2 to announce, notify (by beating the drum) 3 to play (the rebab, etc.) پر خپل سر ډنگول to act on one's own responsibility, at one's own risk

ډنگهار ḍəngəhār *m.* beat(ing) (of a drum); sounds (of a tambourine)

ډنگېدل ḍangedə́l *intransitive* [*past:* وډنگېده] to sound, ring out, resound (of music)

ډنگیدوال ḍangiḍwā́l wide open (of a door, a gate)

ډنمارک ḍanmārk *m.* Denmark

ډنمارکي ḍanmārkí 1 Danish ډنمارکي ژبه Danish (language) 2 Dane

ډوب ḍub 1 immersed (in a liquid); submerged, sunken 2 *figurative* to be lost in thought, be plunged into thought, be absorbed in thought ډوب تللی to be upset about, be discouraged خپه ډوب تللی to be surprised (at someone, something) ډوب ورته تلل یي؟ What are you upset about? اندېښنو کښی ډوب کښناست *Eastern* He was lost in melancholy thoughts.

ډوبلن ḍublə́n with an uneven gait (of a horse)

ډوبله ḍúbla *f.* uneven gait

ډوب ماکو ḍubmākú *m.* torpedo, mine

ډوبول ḍubawə́l *denominative, transitive* [*past:* ډوب یي کړ] to immerse (in a liquid); sink (e.g., a ship) خپل غم په شرابو ډوبول to drown one's sorrows in wine

ډوبۍ ḍubáj *m.* snuffbox (for chewing tobacco)

ډوبېدل ḍubedə́l *denominative, intransitive* [*past:* ډوب شو] 1 to be immersed (in a liquid); sink 2 to disappear (of water in the sand) 3 to set (of the sun) 4 *figurative* to meditate, be immersed in thought 5 to lose consciousness په ننداره ډوبېدل to be carried away by the spectacle

ډوبېدونکی ḍubedúnkaj *present participle of* ډوبېدل نور ډوبېدونکی دی *Eastern* The sun is setting.

ډوپکنۍ ḍupkanə́j *f.* hillock, heap, mound

ډوپۍ ¹ ḍupə́j *f.* underground reservoir

ډوپۍ ² ḍupə́j *f.* lameness, limping ډوپۍ وهل *compound verb* to limp, be lame

ډوډ ḍuḍ *m.* lotus blossom

ډوډا ḍuḍá *f.* 1 thistle 2 boll or pod of the poppy

ډوډوزه ḍoḍóza *f.* ☞ ډوزه ¹

ډوډه ḍoḍá *f.* 1 ☞ ډوډا 2 corn bread

ډوډی ¹ ḍuḍáj *m.* 1 *anatomy* ilium 2 children's game

ډوډی ² ḍúḍaj *m.* spy

ډوډۍ ³ ḍoḍə́j *f.* ډوډی ḍoḍé 1 bread; flat bread توره ډوډۍ black bread د تنور ډوډۍ bread baked in a tandoori سپینه ډوډۍ white bread د تناره ډوډۍ white bread baked in an oven د تبی ډوډۍ fry-pan bread د ډابی ډوډۍ bread baked in a pan د سیلو ډوډۍ formed bread ډبله ډوډۍ European-style bread په ډوډۍ باندي یوه ډوډۍ رانیسه buy one flat bread 2 meal, dinner د غرمي ډوډۍ lunch د مانبام ډوډۍ ، د شپی ډوډۍ supper, dinner د ډوډۍ خورلو خونه، د ډوډۍ خونه، د ډوډۍ خورلو کوټه، د ډوډۍ کوټه ، د د ډوډۍ سامان table setting د ډوډۍ کمره dining room ډوډۍ خورل *compound verb* to eat, dine د غرمي ډوډۍ کول to dine, have lunch هغه زموږ سره to sit down at the table, start a meal ډوډۍ ته کښېنستل به ډوډۍ کښي شریک و He dined with us. 3 entertaining, treating ډوډۍ کول ، د چا ډوډۍ کول ، ډوډۍ ورکول *compound verb* to treat ډوډۍ ته تلل to go for dinner ډوډۍ ته غوښتل to invite for dinner د تدریس له لاري ډوډۍ پیداکول to live by lessons

ډوډۍ پخوونکی ḍoḍə́j pakhawúnkaj *m.* 1 cook 2 baker

ډوډۍ غرپ ḍoḍəjghṛáp 1 voracious, gluttonous 2 *m.* glutton

ډوډۍ کغالی ḍoḍəjkughā́laj *m.* tandoori (oven for baking bread)

ډوډۍ مار ḍoḍəjmár *m.* hospitable person

ډوډۍ والا ḍoḍəjwālā́ *m.* baker

ډور ḍor *m.* 1 bottom-land deciduous forest, flood-plain forest 2 hollow; cavity; empty space, void

ډوره ¹ ḍorá torn, ripped ډوره کول *compound verb* to tear, rip

ډوره ² ḍorá *f.* ☞ ډوری 1

ډورۍ ¹ ḍuráj *m.* scarecrow

ډورۍ ² ḍoráj *f.* 1 grave 2 Dori (river to the south of Kandahar)

ډوریا ḍorjā́ *f.* thin striped fabric (used for the veil)

ډوزک ḍuzák *m.* 1 chatterbox, windbag 2 *abusive* person suffering from flatulence

ډوزک ¹ ḍuzə́n *m.* ☞ ډوزن

ډوزه ḍúza *f.* 1 rubbish, nonsense ډوزه خبره nonsense 2 exaggeration ډوزي وهل *compound verb* a to talk nonsense b to exaggerate

دوزي ۱ ḍúzi *f.* **1** *plural of* دوزه **2** desperate lies

دوزی ۲ ḍuzáj **1** shallow (of a person) **2** lying, mendacious

دوغ ḍugh *m.* cough

دوغل ۱ ḍughál *m.* hole, pit; depression; hollow, cavity **2** crater **3** precipice, abyss, gulf **4** cough

دوغل ۲ ḍughə́l *transitive* ☞ توخل

دوغن ḍughán *m.* [*plural:* دوغن] coughing person; patient who suffers from a persistent cough

دوغول ḍughawə́l *transitive* ☞ توخول

دوغېدل ḍughedə́l *intransitive* ☞ توخېدل

دوک ḍuk *m.* small branch, twig مرغه پر دوک وچېږي *proverb* there is a terrible cold spell (*literally:* a bird grows stiff on the branch, a bird freezes on the branch)

دوکال ḍukál *m.* ☞ وکال

دوکړه ḍukṛá *f.* tambourine

دوکه ۱ ḍuká *f.* **1** *textiles* strand of five threads **2** cluster or bunch of dates

دوکه ۲ ḍoká *f.* cunning, slyness; ruse, trick, subterfuge

دوکه ۳ ḍoká *f.* slut

دوکه مار ḍokamár *m.* deceiver, trickster, swindler, cheat

دوکی ḍúkaj *m.* **1** brushwood **2** fluff, down پر مخ يې دوکی شنه کېږي His beard has begun to grow.

دوګره ۱ ḍográ **1.1** poor (of a person) **1.2** not deserving trust, untrustworthy **2** *m.* **.1** poor man **2.2** fellow-traveler, traveling companion

دوګره ۲ ḍográ *m.* Dorga (a people of India)

دوګره مست ḍogramást *m. collective noun* the poor

دوګل ḍugə́l *m.* being upset, being distressed; dispondency, dejection, grief, sorrow

دوګول ḍugawə́l *transitive* [*past:* وﯥ دوګاوه] to reproach; censure, reprimand

دوګي ḍogí *m.* person who tidies up the village and does errands for the villagers

دول ۱ ḍaul, dawl *m.* **1** kind, type; way, means د ... پر دول ، د ... په دول in the capacity of something د اختصار پر دول ، په اجمالي دول ، په موقتي دول temporarily په لنډ دول in brief؟ په څه دول؟ پر څه دول؟ In what way? په دې دول ، په همدې دول ، پر دغه ، پر دغه دول of such a type په آزادانه دول freely په ډېر ښه دول very good په دول In such a way په اتوماتيکي دول automatically په واضح دول clearly خالص دول in pure form دا دول نده that's not so په لانديني دول in the following way پر هر دول چه وي in another way په بل دول completely په پوره دول however that may be په يوه دول by no means په هيڅ دولو anyhow دول دول of a different sort په رخصتي دول on leave **2** sort, grade, quality اول دول اوره grade-A flour **3** kind, nature, character د صادراتو دول په بېلو بېلو کلونو کښي the kind of exports in various years **4** brand, make (e.g., of a car); system, type نوي دول الوتکه aircraft of a new design نوي دول دولت a new type of government **5** style **6** smartness of dress, dandyism **7** *grammar* aspect (of verbs)

دول ۲ ḍol *m.* **1** drum دول وهل د چغي دول alarm *compound verb* to beat the drum **2** hopper, feed bin, funnel (of a mill) **3** pail **4** toothed wheel of a water-lifting wheel (which the working ox is closest to) نخل د چا په دول *saying* to dance to somebody's tune

دول ۳ ḍul *m.* slow gait, slow walk

دولاډنګه ḍolāḍánga *f.* **1** chilren's game (a song sung door-to-door in early spring) **2** *abusive* blockhead, dunderhead **3** slacker, idler, loafer

دولبره ḍolbərá *f.* ☞ دول ۲

دول ټکور ḍolṭəkór *m.* ☞ دول ټيل

دولچه ḍolchá *f.* **1** small washtub (for washing up and for laundry) **2** small bucket (at a well)

دولچي ḍolchí *m.* drummer

دولډال ḍolḍál *m.* ☞ دول ټيل

دول ډبلی ḍol-ḍabaláj *m.* household utensils; goods and chattels

دولډيل ḍoldíl *m.* **1** dress, attire, finery **2** dressing in the latest fashion, foppery, dandyism دول ډيل جوړول *compound verb* to play the dandy دول ډيل کول *compound verb* to dress up

دولک ḍolák *m.* ☞ دولکی **1** small drum دولک وهل ، دولک ټکول to drum **2** box

دولکي ḍoləkí *m.* drummer

دولول ḍulawə́l *transitive* [*past:* وﯥ دولاوه] to drive, urge on slowly

دوله ۱ ḍolá *f.* **1** hole, pit; depression **2** ravine **3** rut, groove **4** *dialect* dense forest, pine forest څوک په يوه دوله کښي اچول *idiom* to play a mean trick on someone

دوله ۲ ḍáula *oblique singular and short form plural of* دول ۱

دولي ۱ ḍaulí **1** *m.* dandy, man of fashion, fop **2** beautiful; smart, well-dressed; adorned دولي ښار beautiful city دولي کول *compound verb* to dress up

دولی ۲ ḍawaláj *m.* wealth, property

دولی ۳ ḍoláj, ḍuláj *f.* palanquin (in which a bride is customarily carried) د پېريانو دولی *idiom regional* sandstorm

دولېدل ḍuledə́l *intransitive* [*past:* و دولېده] to go slowly, walk slowly

دولی مار ḍoləjmár *m.* palanquin bearer

دومارل ḍumārə́l *transitive* [*past:* وﯥ دوماره] **1** to incite, instigate something **2** سترګي دومارول to lower one's eyes

دومبسکه ḍumbə́ska *f.* knob, protuberance

دومبک ḍumbák *m.* **1** tambourine **2** chat (a bird of the thrush family)

دومبکه ḍumbə́ka *f.* female chat (a bird of the thrush family)

دمبکی ḍəmbəkáj *m.* small drum; tambourine, gong

دومبوری ḍumboráj *m.* pile (of manure). dung hill, manure heap

دومبکی ḍumkáj *m.* ☞ دومبکی

دون ḍon *m.* the Don (river)

دنډ ۱ ḍonḍ *m.* ☞ دنډوره

دنډ ۲ ḍunḍ killed, dead, lost

دونډاکی ḍunḍákaj *m.* pelvic bone

ﮈﻮﻧﮓ¹ ḋong *m.* **1** stealing (of livestock), cattle-rustling **2** seizure (e.g., of property) **3** robbery, raid ﮈﻮﻧﮓ ﻮﻫﻞ *compound verb* **a** to steal, rustle (cattle) **b** to seize (e.g., property) **c** to carry out a raid

ﮈﻮﻧﮓ² ḋong *m.* **1** arrogance, haughtiness **2** mockery, sneer, gibe

ﮈﻮﻧﮓ ﮈﻮﻧﮓ ḋungḋúng *m.* **1** refusing, making excuses **2** grumbling ﮈﻮﻧﮓ ﮈﻮﻧﮓ ﻛﻮﻝ *compound verb* **a** to refuse, make excuses **b** to grumble

ﮈﻮﻧﮕﺮﯼ ḋungráj *f.* **1** oar; paddle **2** ladle

ﮈﻮﻧﮕﻠﻪ ḋunglá *f.* sweep, shadoof (at a well)

ﮈﻮﻧﮕﻦ ḋungán grumbling, peevish, querulous

ﮈﻮﻧﮕﻪ¹ ḋónga *f.* waist

ﮈﻮﻧﮕﻪ² ḋónga *f.* mockery, sneer, gibe

ﮈﻮﻧﮕﻬﺎﺭ ḋungəhár *m.* buzzing (of flies, etc.)

ﮈﻮﻧﮕﯽ¹ ḋongí *m.* mocker, scoffer

ﮈﻮﻧﮕﯽ² ḋongí carrying out an assault or raid

ﮈﻮﻧﮕﯧﺪﻝ ḋungedál *intransitive* [*past:* ﮈﻮﻧﮕﯧﺪ ﻮ] **1** to grumble, express one's displeasure **2** to sob

ﮈﻮﻭﻝ ḋəwúl *m.* small sheatfish

ﮈﻮﻫﺮ ḋuhár **1** aged, advanced in years, superannuated **2** weakened, enfeebled

ﮈﻮﯼ ḋoj *m.* anxiety, uneasiness

ﮈﻮﻳﮋﻥ ḋiwízhán *m.* *regional* division

ﮈﻫﺎﻛﻪ ḋəháka *f.* ten

ﮈﻬﻞ ﮈﺍﻭﻝ ḋhelḋául *m.* *regional* ☞ ﮈﯦﻞ

ﮈﯼ¹ ḋaj *m.* *textiles* weaver's beam support

ﮈﯼ² ḋəj *f.* **1** tip-cat (a children's game) ﮈﯼ ﻛﻮﻝ *compound verb* to play tip-cat **2** fringe

ﮈﯧﺒﺎﻙ ḋibák *m.* **1** precipice; slope, hill-side **2** ☞ ﮈﯧﻮ

ﮈﯧﺒﻮ ḋibó *f.* Oenanthe opstholeuca (an Old World thrush)

ﮈﯧﺒﯽ ḋibáj *f.* milk pail

ﮈﭙﺎ ḋepá *m.* servant, part of the retinue of, in the service of

ﮈﻳﭙﻠﻮﻣﺎﺕ ḋiplomát *m.* diplomat

ﮈﻳﭙﻠﻮﻣﺎﺗﯽ ḋiplomātí **1** diplomatic **2** *m.* diplomat

ﮈﻳﭙﻠﻮﻣﺎﺗﻴﻚ ḋiplomātík diplomatic

ﮈﻳﭙﻠﻮﻣﺎﺳﯽ ḋiplomāsí **1** *f.* diplomacy **2** diplomatic

ﮈﻳﭻ ḋich *m.* **1** splendor, magnificence **2** being overdressed, overdressing

ﮈﻳﭽﻪ ḋícha *f* **1** jerking; jumping **2** waves

ﮈﻳﮈﺍﻧﻪ ḋiḋāná *m.* sweeper

ﮈﻳﮈﻡ ḋiḋám *m.* ☞ ﮈﯦﺪﻡ

ﮈﻳﺪﻩ¹ ḋída *f.* volley

ﮈﻳﺪﻩ² ḋída *f.* **1** cork, stopper, plug **2** bushing **3** shaft in the center of the lower millstone (on which the upper millstone rotates) **4** journal (of an axle, shaft)

ﮈﻳﺪﻩ ḋeḋá **1** satiated, sated **2** patient **3** calm, quiet, tranquil

ﮈﭘﺮ ḋer **1.1** numerous; large ﭘﻪ ﮈﭘﺮﻩ ﺧﻮﺑﯽ، ﭘﻪ ﮈﭘﺮﯼ ﺧﻮﺑﯽ ﺳﺮﻩ with the utmost pleasure ﮈﭘﺮ ﺧﻪ much ﮈﭘﺮ ﻣﻮﺩﻩ ﻛﯧﺒﺮﯼ ﭼﻪ ﻧﻪ ﺩﯼ ﺭﺍﻏﻠﯥ He has not come for a long time. ﮈﭘﺮ ﻣﻮﺩﻩ ﻛﯧﺒﺮﯼ ﭼﻪ ... It's a long time ago ﮈﭘﺮﻩ ﻣﻮﺩﻩ ﭘﺲ much later ﻟﻪ ﮈﭘﺸﻪ ﮈﭘﺮﻩ ﺗﺒﺮﻩ ﻭﻩ It was late night. ﻧﻮ now

ﺗﺮ ﮈﭘﺮﻩ ﭘﻮﺭﯼ، ﺩ ﮈﭘﺮﯼ ﻣﻮﺩﯼ ﺧﺨﻪ for a long time now ﮈﭘﺮﯼ ﻣﻮﺩﯼ ﺧﺨﻪ ﻧﺎﺳﺖ ﻭﻭ They sat for a long time. ﮈﭘﺮ ﻏﻮﻧﺘﻞ to ask a high price ﭼﻪ ﮈﭘﺮ ﻭﺍﻳﯽ، ﻟﺮ ﺧﯧﮋﯼ *proverb* He who talks a lot does little. ﮈﭘﺮﯼ ﺧﻮﻟﯽ, ﮈﭘﺮﯼ ﺧﺒﺮﯼ، *proverb* many mouths, many words (there are as many minds as there are heads) **1.2** frequent; abundant; large ﮈﭘﺮ ﻛﯧﺒﺪﻝ *compound verb* to give a large harvest ﮈﭘﺮ *compound verb* **a** to be frequent; be abundant (e.g., of rains) ﭘﻪ ﭘﺴﺮﻟﯽ ﻛﯽ ﺑﺎﺭﺍﻥ ﮈﭘﺮ ﻛﯧﺒﺮﯼ In spring there is abundant rainfall **b** to have an abundant crop, be abundant (of the harvest) ﺳﺮﻛﺎﻝ ﻏﻨﻢ ﮈﭘﺮ ﺳﻮﯼ ﺩﯼ This year the wheat crop was good **2** *adverb.* **1** very, much ﮈﭘﺮ ﺧُﻠﻪ، ﮈﭘﺮ ﻛﻠﻪ very little ﮈﭘﺮ ﻟﺒﺮ at maximum ﮈﭘﺮ ﺗﺮ ﮈﭘﺮ very much ﮈﭘﺮ ﺧُﻠﻪ very often ﮈﭘﺮ ﻭﺭﻭ ﻭﺭﻭ very slowly **2.2** often ﺗﻪ ﺩﻟﺘﻪ ﮈﭘﺮ ﺭﺍﻏﻠﯥ ﻳﯥ You used to come here often.

ﮈﭘﺮﺍﻥ ḋerán *m.* ﮈﭘﺮﺍﻧﯽ *f.* manure pit; dump ﺩ ﮈﭘﺮﺍﻥ ﭘﻴﺪﺍ! Such trash!

ﮈﭘﺮﭘﻮﺭﻩ ḋerpurá multistory

ﮈﭘﺮﺗﻮﺏ ḋertób *m.* ﮈﭘﺮﺗﻴﺎ ḋertyā́, ﮈﭘﺮﺑﻨﺖ ḋeráxht *m.* ﮈﭘﺮﻭﺍﻟﯽ ḋerwálay *m.* **1** increase, growth; augmentation ﺩ ﺧﻠﻘﻮ ﮈﭘﺮﺗﻮﺏ the increase in population ﺩ ﺗﻮﻟﻴﺪﺍﺗﻮ ﮈﭘﺮﺗﻮﺏ growth of production، ﮈﭘﺮﺗﻮﺏ ﻛﻮﻝ to increase ﻣﺦ ﭘﻪ ﮈﭘﺮﺗﻮﺏ ﺑﯧﻮﻝ to increase (crop yields, etc.) **2** strengthening **3** development **4** abundance, plenty **5** majority ﺩ ﺁﺭﺍﺅ ﭘﻪ ﮈﭘﺮﺗﻮﺏ a majority of votes **6** multiplicity, numerical strength

ﮈﭘﺮﻭﻝ ḋerawál *denominative, transitive* [*past:* ﮈﭘﺮ ﻳﯥ ﻛﺮ] **1** to increase, augment; multiply ﭘﻨﮕﯽ ﮈﭘﺮﻭﻝ increase capital **2** to strengthen **3** to develop ﻛﺮﻫﻨﻪ ﮈﭘﺮﻭﻝ to develop agriculture **4** to further increase (wealth, etc.)

ﮈﭘﺮﻭﻧﻪ ḋerawóna *f.* **1** auction **2** increase, augmentation **3** development, growth

ﮈﭘﺮﻩ¹ ḋerá *f.* ☞ ﮈﭘﺮﻩ¹

ﮈﭘﺮﻩ² ḋéra *feminine and oblique singular of* ﮈﭘﺮ¹ ﺗﺮ ﮈﭘﺮﻩ ﭘﻮﺭﯼ long time

ﮈﭘﺮﻩ ﺟﺎﺕ ḋeradzhát *m. plural* ☞ ﮈﺑﺮﻩ ﺟﺎﺕ

ﮈﭘﺮﯼ¹ ḋeráj *m.* ☞ ﮈﭘﺮﺗﻮﺏ

ﮈﭘﺮﯼ² ḋeráj *f.* **1** pile; heap ﮈﭘﺮﯼ ﻛﻮﻝ *compound verb* to dump, put into a pile **2** hill; hillock **3** manure pile, dung heap

ﮈﭘﺮﯦﺪﻝ ḋeredál *denominative, intransitive* [*past:* ﮈﭘﺮ ﺳﻮ] **1** to increase, grow; be augmented **2** to intensify **3** to develop **4** *biology* to multiply, reproduce

ﮈﭘﺮﯦﺪﻩ ḋeredá *m. plural* **1** increase, growth; augmentation ﺩ ﺍﺟﻮﺭﯼ ﮈﭘﺮﯦﺪﻩ increase in wages **2** strengthening **3** development **4** *biology* reproduction

ﮈﻳﺰﺍﻳﻦ ḋizā́jn *m.* drawing, figure; sketch, draft

ﮈﻳﺰﻝ ḋizál *m.* diesel

ﮈﻳﺰﻝ ﺁﻳﻞ ḋizalā́jl *m.* diesel, heavy fuel oil

ﮈﻳﺲ ḋis very full, satiated ﮈﻳﺲ ﻛﻮﻝ *compound verb* to satiate ﮈﻳﺲ ﻛﯧﺪﻝ *compound verb* to be satiated

ﮈﻳﺴﯥ ḋesé *f.* corn-cob

ﮈﻳﻜﺘﻪ ḋiktá *f.* dictation

ډیگ ďig having an uneven gait (of a horse)

ډيگ ډيگو ډigdigó *f.* uneven gait په ډيګ ډيګو تلل to go at an uneven gait

ډيګلَن ďiglәn ☞ ډويلن

ډيګله ďiglá ☞ ډويله

ډيل [1] ďil *m.* delay; being late; procrastination بې له ډيلي immediately ډيل کول *compound verb* to be delayed; be late ډيل لګول *compound verb* to delay; postpone, drag out

ډيل [2] ďil *m. dialect* ☞ ډول [1]

ډيل ډيل ďilďaul *m.* ☞ ډول ډول

ډيلو ďeláw *m.* ☞ ډيل [1]

ډيل وډال ďiluďál *m.* dressing in the height of fashion, dandyism, fopishness ډيل وډال جوړول *compound verb* to dress up

ډيلول ďilawә́l *denominative, transitive* [*past:* ډيل يې کړ] to delay; postpone, drag out

ډيله ďíla *f.* cypress-grass, *Cyperus* (a medicinal plant)

ډيلی ďeláj *m.* ☞ دهلي

ډيليدل ďiledә́l *denominative, intransitive* [*past:* ډيل شو] to be delayed; be late (for)

ډيمبه ďimbá *f.* oarlock

دېموکرات ďemokrāt ☞ دېموکرات

ډينډاپ ďinďáp *m.* cotton comber, cotton carder

ډينگ [1] ďing 1 *m.* stork 2 tall; leggy, lanky

ډينگ [2] ďing *m.* lullaby ډينگ ويل to sing a lullaby

ډينگ [3] ďing *m. Western* windbag, braggart

ډينگار ďingár *m.* boasting, bragging, vainglory

ډينگاز ďingāz feeble, frail, weak

ډينگ ډينگو ďingďingó *f.* ډينگي دينگ ďingďingáy *m.* 1 ☞ ډيگ ډيګو ډينگ ډينگو کول to sing a lullaby 2 lullaby

ډينگری ďingráj *f.* 1 mushroom 2 sweep, shadoof (at a well) 3 oar, paddle

ډينگلی ďinglә́j *f.* sweep, shadoof (at a well)

ډينی ďenáj *m.* ☞ وی [1]

ډيوالي ďewālí *m.* bankrupt

ډيوټ ďewáṭ *m.* candlestick; pedestal (for a lampion, etc.)

ډيوټي djuṭí *f. regional* 1 duty, watch 2 manning one's post 3 service obligation خپله ډيوټي کول a to do one's job; be on duty b to fulfill one's service obligation, carry out one's duty

ډيوډ ďewáḏ *m.* 1 aromatic candle (lit for a wedding) 2 candlestick, earthenware stand (for a lamp) 3 long earring

ډيوډی ďiwḏáj *f.* 1 porch; hall, corridor 2 iron decorations on a parapet

ډيولا ďiwlá *m,* small sheatfish, catfish

ډيوه ďewá *f.* 1 lamp, lantern; oil lamp, lampion د خاورو د تېلو ډيوه kerosene lamp 2 *figurative* luminary بله ډيوه a burning lamp b *figurative* luminary (of the mind, etc.)

ډيوه خولی ďewakhwólaj pouting, with puffed-out cheeks (of a baby who is getting ready to start crying) ډيوه خولی کېدل to get ready to cry

---

ډييه ďijá *f.* street platform (where villagers gather and sit)

ذ

ذ zāl 1 the fifteenth letter of the Pashto alphabet 2 the number 700 in the abjad system

ذات zāt *Arabic* 1 *m.* [*plural:* ذوات zavāt] .1 human being, person همايوني ذات دا لاندي ذوات the persons mentioned below His Royal Highness 1.2 individual د ذات احترام self respect 1.3 essence, substance په خپل ذات کښي the heart of the matter in essence, essentially 1.4 caste هغه له ذاته پراچه دئ He is of the Paracha caste. 2 *attributive* خو ښځه ذات وه څه يې کولی شو؟ Well she was just a woman; what could she do?

ذاتاً zātán *Arabic* 1 in substance; in essence, by virtue of one's nature 2 personally speaking; by one's self; notwithstanding

ذات البين zātulbájn *m. Arabic plural* interrelationships

ذات البيني zātulbajní mutual روابط ذات البيني interrelationships اختلافونه ذات البيني differences, disagreements

ذاتي zātí *Arabic* 1 inherent, innate, natural 2 *adjective* pertaining to personnel, personnel 3 personal اغراض ذاتي mercenary aims, venal motives

ذاتيه zātijá *f. Arabic* 1 personality, person ذاتيه څانگه department of personnel, personnel department 2 *philosophy* subjectivism

ذاکر zākír *Arabic* remembering, recalling

ذاکره zākirá *f. Arabic* memory

ذال zāl *m. Arabic* the name of the letter ذ

ذائق zāíḳ *Arabic* tasting, trying, trying the flavor (of)

ذائقه zāiḳá *f. Arabic* taste

ذبح zabh *f. Arabic* ☞ ذبحه

ذبحگاه zabhgāh *m.* slaughterhouse, abattoir

ذبحه zábha *f.* 1 slaughter (of cattle) 2 sacrifice (of animals), immolation ذبحه کول a to slaughter (cattle) b to sacrifice (animal)

ذبذبه zabzabá *f. Arabic* [*plural:* ذبذبي zabzabé *m. Arabic plural:* ذبذبات zabzabā́t] oscillation

ذبه zába *f.* ☞ ذبحه

ذبيح zabíh *f. Arabic* sacrifice, sacrificial animal ذبيح الله the sacrifice to God, Allah's victim (an epithet of Ismael, the son of Abraham)

ذخائر zakhāír *Arabic masculine plural of* ذخيره

ذخيره zakhirá *Arabic* 1 *f.* [*plural:* ذخيري zakhiré *m. Arabic plural:* ذخائر zakhāír] .1 reserve, stock د لغاتو ذخيره vocabulary ذخيره کول *compound verb* to reserve اوبه ذخيره کول to save, lay in a stock of water ذخيره کېدل *compound verb* to be reserved, be put aside in reserve 1.2 storage depot د تېلو ذخيره oil storage depot 1.3 [*plural:* ذخيري zakhiré] deposit معدني ذخيري ore deposits د تبلو petroleum reserves 2 د سکرو ذخيرې coal deposits ذخيرې *attributive* spare, reserve

ذرات zarrā́t *m. Arabic plural* ☞ ذره

ذرائع zarāī' *m. Arabic plural* ☞ ذريعه

ذروي zarraví atom; nuclear; atomic ذروي جنگ atomic war بم ذروي atomic bomb وسله ذروي nuclear weapon

ذره zarrá *f. Arabic* [*plural:* ذري zarré *m. plural:* ذرات zarrā́t] **1** atom **2** minute particle; grain; speck of dust ذرات راديواكتيف radioactive particles ذري ذري كول *compound verb* to tear into very small pieces ذره كېدل *compound verb* to be torn into very small pieces **3** *biology* blood corpuscle سرې ذري hemocytes, red blood corpuscles

ذره بين zarrabín *m.* **1** magnifying glass لاسي ذره بين **2** microscope

ذري zarrí atomic; nuclear ذري قواوي atomic energy

ذريعه zari'á *f. Arabic m.* [*plural:* ذرائع zarāī'] means; method په ... د by means of something

د دي په ذريعه، د دي په ذريعه باندي by means of, د ډاک په ذريعه by mail in this way د حمل او نقل ذرائع transport equipment; vehicles

ذريه zurriá *f. Arabic* posterity; family; generation

ذكا zuká *f. Arabic* quick-wittedness, comprehension; perspicacity

ذكاوت zakāvát *m. Arabic* cleverness, quick-wittedness تېز ذكاوت quickness on the uptake

ذكر zíkr *m.* zíkər *Arabic* **1** mention, mentioning دلته دا خبره هم ... It must be mentioned here that ذكر ور ده چه ذكر كول *compound verb* to mention ذكر كېدل *compound verb* to be mentioned پاس ذكر شوي ذوات the abovementioned persons ... It دا هم بايد ذكر شي چه ... is also necessary to mention څرنګه چه دمخه ذكر سوه، څرنګه چه ذكر يي دمخه تېر شو As has been mentioned earlier **2** *religion* reading of the Koran **3** repetition of the Divine Epithets; dervish rites

ذكريا zakarijā́ *m. Arabic proper name* Zachariah

ذكي zakí *Arabic* **1** quick-on-the-uptake; quick, quick-witted **2** *m. proper name* Zaki

ذلت zillát *m. Arabic* baseness, meanness

ذليل zalíl *Arabic* **1** contemptible, base, mean **2** degraded, humiliated ذليل كېدل ☞ ذليل كول، ذليلول

ذليل توب zaliltób *m.* ذليل تيا zaliltjā́ *f.* ذليل والى zalilvā́laj *m.* ☞ ذلت

ذليلول zalilavə́l *denominative, transitive* [*past:* ذليل يي كړ] **1** to cause to become base or mean **2** to humiliate

ذليلېدل zaliledə́l *denominative, intransitive* [*past:* ذليل شو] **1** to be base, be mean **2** to be degraded, be humiliated

ذم zam zamm *m. Arabic* censure; reproof; abuse ذم كول to censure, reprove; abuse

ذمت zimmát *m. Arabic* ذمه zimmá *f. Arabic* responsibility نور كار زما ذمه، نور كار زما ذمه ده The rest is my responsibility. ذمت وهل ذمت، كول to undertake

ذمه بردار zimmabardā́r accountable, responsible, bearing the responsibility for something, taking upon oneself ذمه بردار كېدل to answer (for), assume the responsibility for something; to take upon oneself

ذمه ګي zimmagí requiring the payment of a debt ذمه ګي دين subject to payment (of a debt)

ذمه وار كس ذمه بردار ☞ ذمه وار zimmavā́r responsible person

ذمه واري zimmavārí *f.* responsibility

ذمي zimmí *m. Arabic* devoted Moslem

ذو zu *Arabic combining form* possessing, having, possessor legal ذواليد legal competent person

ذوات zavā́t *Arabic masculine plural of* ذات

ذوالجلال zuldzhalā́l *religion* All-High (an epithet of God)

ذوالفقار zulfiḱar *m.* **1** *proper name* Zulfiqar **2** ☞ ذوالفقار

ذوالقرنين zulḱarnájn *m. Arabic* Twin-Horned (an epithet of Alexander of Macedon)

ذواليد zuldáj *m. Arabic legal* competent person

ذواليدي zuljadí *f.* original (as contrasted to a copy)

ذوب zaub *m. Arabic* fusing, melting

ذوجنسين zudzhinsájn *m. Arabic plural botany* bisexual flowers

ذوحياتين zuhajjātájn *m. Arabic* amphibian

ذوق zauḱ *m. Arabic* **1** wish, desire **2** enjoyment, pleasure **3** taste د ذوق خاوندان experts, connoisseurs په ذوق برابر appealing to one's taste; confirming to one's taste ذوق اخيستل to taste ذوقونه او فكرونه راز راز وي *proverb* There is no agreement on tastes.

ذوقمن zauḱmán *m.* lover, enthusiast of something

ذوالفقار zulfaḱar *m. Arabic* **1** *religion* Cleaver of Vertebrae (an epithet of the sword of Ali) **2** *proper name* Zulfakar, Zulfaqar

ذهن zihi *m. Arabic* mind, intellect; comprehension كه په ذهن مي هر څومره زور كړ، راته ياد نه شول No matter how much I strained my memory I couldn't recall. نومونه يي د ذهن نه ووتل Their names have flown from my memory. په ذهن سره ضربول to increase in intellect ذهن حاضر نه و My head is working poorly.

ذهن نشين zihinashín imprinted upon the memory; understandable, mastered ذهن نشين كول to memorize, master

ذهني zihní *Arabic* mental, intellectual ذهني آزادي freedom of thought ذهني جمود sluggishness, intellectual limitation

ذهنيات zihnijā́t *m. Arabic plural* psychology, frame of mind

ذهنيت zihniját *m. Arabic* **1** manner of thought, cast of mind; frame of mind **2** intellect **3** psychology, psyche غلامانه ذهنيت slave psychology **4** ideology

ذهير zahír ☞ زهير

ذهين zahín *Arabic* **1** intelligent, reasonable, sensible **2** perspicacious, incisive

ذي zi ☞ ذو

ذي الحجه zilhidzhdzhá *f. Arabic* Zilhija (the name of the 12th month of the lunar year when pilgrimages are usually made)

ذي القعده zilḱa'dá *f. Arabic* Zilqada (the name of the 11th month of the lunar year)

ذي دخل zidákhl *Arabic* included in, consisting of something, enclosed

ذي حجه zihidzhdzhá *f.* ☞ ذي الحجه

ذي حق zihákḱ *Arabic* **1** having, possessing a right, competent **2** meriting something

ذي روح، ذيروح، ذي روح zirúh *Arabic* **1** animate انیمته animate noun **2** *m.* living being

ذي صلاحيت zisalahiját *Arabic* competent

ذي علاقه، ذيعلاقه zi'aláḵá *Arabic* (materially) interested

ذي القعده zi̱ḵa'dá *f.*

ذيل¹ zajl zel *Arabic* **1** *m.* **.1** bottom **1.2** addition **2** the following

ذيل² zajl *m.* kind, type; variety هر ذيل مېوي every variety of fruit زيل¹ ☞

ذيلاً zájlán *Arabic* **1.1** below **1.2** herewith **2** the following

ذبلدار zeldā́r *m. regional* chief of a province

ذينفع zináf *Arabic* interested (materially)

ر

ر re rā **1** the sixteenth letter of the Pashto alphabet **2** the number 300 in the abjad system

را¹ rā **1** *personally directive pronoun, first person singular & plural* **1.1a** to us, to me دا هم را معلومه ده چه This is also unknown to us **1.1b** towards us, to us, to me **1.1c** about us, me را خبر يي چه زه ګوروان وم You do know that I used to be a shephard. You do know about me that I used to be a herdsman. **1.1d** on us, on me را په قهر شه *dialect* He got angry at us. **1.2** to us, to me, for us, for me (designates the target of an action functioning as the indirect object of a verb, standing before the predicate or direct object) تيلفون راوكه Call us, me (on the phone) up! چاى را واچوه! Pour us, me some tea! **1.3** to me, to us; with me, with us; here; over to the people (with several verbs of motion, indicates the direction of action) ستا خط راسبدلئ دئ Your letter came to me. Your letter came to us. الوتکي را الوزول to shoot down an aircraft لمر راوخوت the sun rose د تګ روغ را نژدې ده The departure day is near. **1.4** (to) home, to one's own place پر يوولس بجي را رخصت سوو We set out for home at eleven o'clock. **2** *used as a productive verb prefix:* راتلل، راکول، رانيول، راوړل، راوستل

را² rā *vice* راکه قلم را! Give me a pen!

را³ rā *f.* the name for the letter، ر ثقيله را the name for the letter ړ

رااخيستل rāakhistə́l [*present:* را يي واخيست *past:* را يي اخلي] **1** to take, take along with one **2** to scoop up, borrow something **3** to proceed along a road اخيستل ☞ **.1** را يي ويست *past:* را يي راباسي rāistə́l **1** *transitive [present:* را يي ويست *past:* bring out (from somewhere, to somewhere) میدان ته رايستل to bring out on to the field **1.2** to raise chicks **1.3** to extract, take out **1.4** to mine, extract (ores); get **1.5** to think up, devise **2** *m. plural* ☞ ايستل رايسته ☞

رايسته¹ rāistə́ *m. plural* ☞ رايسته

رايسته² rā́ista ☞ راهيسي

راباندي rābāndi rābānde **1** on us, on me **2** because of us, me **3** to us, for us; to me, for me ته راباندي ګران يې You are dear to me راباندي ناوخته شو *idiom* I am late.

رابر rābár *m. plural* rubber د رابر ونه **a** rubber tree **b** ficus

رابرسازي rābaṛsāzí *f.* rubber industry

رابړي rābǝṛí *adjective* rubber

رابط rābít *Arabic* joining, unifying

رابطه rābitá *f. Arabic [plural:* رابطي rābité *m. plural:* روابط ravābít] *Arabic* link; relation, connection د چا سره رابطه اچول، د چا په ... سره رابطه پيدا کول to establish a connection with someone پوري رابطه لرل to have a connection with someone or something رابطه قطع کول to break off رابطه سره لرل to be in mutual touch روابط شلول to disrupt relations communication

رابلل rabalə́l **1** *transitive [present:* رابولي *past:* را يي باله] to summon; invite; convoke **2** *m. plural* invitation; convocation بلل ☞

رابيا¹ rābjā́ *f.* large waterskin

رابيا² rābijā́ *f. proper name* Rabiya

رابېل rābél *m. plural* رابېلي rābelí *m. plural* jasmine-yellow

راپاتې rāpā́te remaining; left over

راپدېخوا rapǝdekhvā́ ☞ را په دې خوا، راپدي خوا

راپرمخ rapermə́kh راپرمخ کېدل to attack us or me; move, move in this direction

راپرپيستل rāprejəstə́l *transitive [present:* راپرپباسي *past:* را پري ايستل را يي پري يست] **1** to knock to the ground, overthrow **2** to descend (e.g., from a mountain)

راپسي rə́pase after us, me oneself هغه راپسي روان و He walked after us or me راپسي سئ! Follow me! (as a command)

راپوټ rāpóṭ *m.* ☞ راپورت

راپور rāpór *m.* report دا راپور ندئ تصديق سوئ This report has not been confirmed.

راپورت rāpórt *m.* **1** report; account; communication راپورت کول to report; give account, a report **2** (formal written) report; announcement

راپورتاژ rāportā́zh *m.* reporting

راپورتر rā́portér *m.* **1** reader of a report, speaker **2** reader of a report, seminar leader **3** reporter

راپورته rāpórta **1** down to us, down to me **2** down (to) here راپورته کول to bring up, raise راپورته کېدل **a** to move up, ascend **b** to overflow (a river)

راپوري rə́pori **1** in our, my presence; with us; with me **2** to us, to me **3** on, at us, me هغه به راپوري وخاندي He will laugh at us, me **4** ☞ پوري¹ **3** *idiom* راپوري غاړه This bank of the river.

راپدېخوا rāpǝdekhvā́ since such a time, since such times، راپه دبخوا د لږي مودي را په دې خواه recently

رات rāt *m.* clientele (of a barber)

راتب rātíb *m. Arabic* food, rations

راتګ rātág *m.* **1** arrival **2** coming, approach د مودي راتګ The approach of the deadline

راتلای rātlā́j *conditional form of* راتلل

راتلل rātlə́l *intransitive [present:* راځي *imperfective* راتئ *Western* راته *Eastern past:* راغئ *imperfective imperative* راځه *perfective*

راشه [*imperative*] 1 to arrive; come running up to (animals), come flying (birds) راغله كورته I arrived home کله به راشي؟ When will you come to our (to my) house? په تلوار راتلل to come tearing along *Eastern* که هغه راته، نو را دي شي If he decides to come, let him come 2 to approach (of a time) پسرلی راغئ او تیر شو Spring has come and gone 3 to eventuate, happen زما په ژوند کښې هیڅ تغیر No changes of any kind have occurred in my life 4 to undergo, experience something 5 to fall under (the influence) د احمد تر تاثیر لاندي راغلئ دئ He fell under Ahmed's influence 6 to occur, be used (of words, expressions) 7 to come through, arrive (documents) *idiom* هغه په مخه راغئ، په لاس راتلل I ran into him د چا په لاس ته راتلل a to be received لاس ته راتلل to fall into someone's hands b to obtain, secure; be derived چای راغلي They brought tea کوهی د اوبو په ډکیدلو پر حرکت راتلل to put into motion ماته انگریزي ژبه نه راغئ *Eastern* The well slowly filled with water. راځي English is hard for me.

راتلنه rātlə́na *f.* ☞ راتلل [1]

راتلو rā́tlo *Eastern imperfect of* راتلل

راتلونکی rātlúnkaj 1 *present participle of* راتلل 2 future, coming; approaching; following په نژدې راتلونکي زمانه کښې In the near future راتلونکي هفته next week, the following week

راتله rātlə́ *m. plural* 1 advent, coming, arrival هغه په راتلو کښې دئ He is just coming. 2 approach, coming د ماښام د راتلو سره with the approach of evening 3 receipt (of documents) [1]

راتله rātlə́ *imperfect plural of* راتلل [2]

راتله rā́tla *imperfect feminine plural of* راتلل [3]

راتلئ rātləj ☞ راتئ

راتویدل rātojedə́l *intransitive* [*past:* راتوی شوه] to flow; drip ☞ توییدل

راته rā́ta 1 to us, to me; (up) to us, me; for us, me راته ووایه tell us, tell me راته ویل به یې He was speaking to us or me [1]

راته rātə́ راتئ rā́təj *Western for* راتلل [2]

راټول rā́ṭol gathering, assembling

راټولیدل rāṭoledə́l *denominative, intransitive* [*past:* راټول شو] to gather, assemble; meet ☞ ټولیدل

راټولیده rāṭoledə́ *m. plural* assemblage د راټولیدو ځای meeting place

راته rā́ṭəj *imperfect of* رتل

راج rādzh *m.* 1 authority; government 2 the State [1]

راج rādzh *m. regional* builder; mason [2]

راجا rādzhá *m.* 1 prince; grandee; Rajah (princely title) 2 emperor

راجپوت rādzhpút *m.* Rajput (Indian nationality)

راجپوتانه rādzhputāná *f.* Rajputana (province, India)

راجستان rādzhastán *m.* Rajastan (province, India)

راجستراسیون rādzhistrāsión *m.* registration

راجستری rādzhistarí 1 registered راجستري کول to register 2 registered (i.e., mail) راجستري لیک استول to send by registered mail

راجع rādzhé' *Arabic* pertaining to someone or something; relating to someone or something دغه کار د ده خونبی او ارادي ته راجع دئ It depends on his wishes and desires و چا ته راجع کول to direct or send

... ته راجع کیدل to relate to someone, pertain to something

راجعه rādzhi'á *medicine* حما راجعه recurring typhus

راجگان rādzhagán *masculine plural of* راجه

راجه rādzhá *m.* ☞ راجا

راچاپیر rāchāpér surrounding هغه محیط چه پر راچاپیر وي His surrounding environment

راځ rādz *m.* راز

راځنی rā́dzəni ☞ راځخه

راځه rā́dza *imperfective imperative of* راتلل 1 come here 2 let's چه یو کتاب رانیسو Let's buy a book

راځي rā́dzi *present of* راتلل [1]

راځئ rā́dzəj *second person present plural of* راتلل [2]

راتسار rātsár overturned, reversed

راځخه rā́tskha 1 at, with us, me 2 from us, me راځخه ولاړ He left us or me

راتسکول rātskavə́l *transitive* [*past:* را و یې څکاوه] 1 to pull up 2 to stuck in, absorb ☞ څکول

راتسکیدل rātskedə́l *intransitive* [*past:* را و څکیده] 1 to drag up 2 to soak into, be absorbed ☞ څکیدل

راحت rāhát *Arabic* 1 *m.* 1 tranquillity د راحت خوب tranquil sleep راحت کول to rest 1.2 *proper name* Rahat 2 At Ease! (as a command) *idiom* راحت کئ! *military* Order Arms! (as a command)

راحت بخښونکی rāhatbákhḵh rahat bakhḵhúnkaj comfortable, snug (of furnishings, etc.)

راحت طلب rāhattaláb *m. Arabic* sybarite

راخ rākh *m.* 1 person 2 party

راخاته rākhātə́ *m. plural* rising (of the sun) د نمر د راختو په وخت کښې at sunrise

راختل rākhatə́l 1 *intransitive* [*past:* راوخوت] to rise (of the sun) 2 *m. plural* rising (of the sun)

راخاتو rākható *oblique plural of* راخاته

راخکل rākhkə́l *transitive* ☞ راکښل

رادار rādár *m.* radar installation; radar equipment

رادو rādáv رادو که! Run to us; To me!

راده rā́da *f.* colored edging (cloth) [1]

راده rādá *m. dialect* swift horse; ambler (i.e., horse) [2]

راده rādə́ *oblique plural of* رود [3]

رادیپلو rādepaláv *Eastern* ☞ راپه دي خوا

رادیکال rādikál 1 radical 2 *m.* a radical

رادیو rādijó *f.* [*plural:* رادیووي rādijóvi] رادیوگاني rādijogắni *plural:* radio; radio-receiver د کابل رادیو، د کابل رادیو Radio Kabul په رادیو د رادیو خپرونی by radio, via radio د رادیو وسیله، د رادیو په ذریعه radio broadcast د رادیو نشریات radio transmission د رادیو مبصر radio announcer, radio commentator د رادیو آخذي ماشین radio receiver د رادیو اوریدونکی radio listener, په رادیو کښی اوریدل radio-auditor په رادیو کښی اوریدل to listen to the په رادیو لگول to announce on the radio په رادیو کښي اعلان کول radio

راديو گل کول، راديو چوپول، راديو تپول to turn the radio on راديو مړه کول to turn the radio off

راديواکتيفي rādijoaktíf radioactive راديواکتيف مواد radioactive substances راديواکتيف کول to render radioactive راديواکتيف کېدل to be radioactive

راديواکتيفيت rādioaktifiját m. radioactivity

راديوتلفوني rādijotelefoní radiotelephonic راديوتلفوني مخابره radiotelephone communication

راديوتلگرافي rādiotelegrāfí radiotelegraphic

راديويي rādijoí pertaining to radio راديويي پروگرام radio program راديويي خپرونه radio transmission

راديو rādijó f. ☞ راديو مړه کول Western to turn the radio off

راديواېلېکترونيک rādijoelektroník m. radio electronics

راديويي rādijoí ☞ راديويي

راډيټر rādijeṭár m. 1 radiator 2 electric stove, electric cooker

رارسېدل rārasedól 1 intransitive ☞ رسېدل 2 m. plural ☞ رارسېده

رارسېده rārasedə́ m. plural arrival; coming; advent

راهروی rāravój m. ☞ راهروی

راړه rāṛá f. bread made from the flour of various cereals

راز [1] rāz m. 1 type; kind; variety هر راز of every kind د راز of a different kind; various, all possible په راز فکرونه various thoughts هغه راز of such a kind خه راز خواهش لري؟ What is his desire? 2 way, fashion; method په دغه راز thus, in this way هر راز چه وي by whatever means possible, in any way at all مخصوص راز by a special method بل راز کېدل to be transformed, turn into, become

راز [2] rāz m. secret راز ساتل to keep a secret راز ويل to reveal a secret

رازبېري rāzberí f. raspberry

رازدار rāzdār 1 reliable; knowing how to keep a secret 2 m. confidant

رازدارانه rāzdārāná mysterious (of a tone), trustworthy

رازداري rāzdārí f. keeping of a secret

رازغلول rāzghavəl transitive [past: راو يي زغلاوه] to fetch, bring on the run ☞ غلول

رازق rāzíḳ Arabic 1 feeding, giving food, nourishing 2 m. .1 All-high, God 2.2 proper name Raziq

رازوباز rāzubāz m. Western personality, character

راز-و-نياز rāz-u-nijáz m. 1 frank talk رازونياز د چا سره کول to be frank with someone 2 conversation between lovers

راژوندی rāzhvandáj becoming animated, livening up, taking heart, reviving

راس rās m. ra's [plural: راسان rāsān plural: رؤوس ruús] Arabic 1 head; management, supervisory body د ....په راس کښې at the head of something, someone 2 geography cape 3 head (in counting cattle) سل راس مال hundred head of cattle

راساً rásān Arabic directly, immediately

راس-امېد rās-i-uméd m. Cape of Good Hope

راس بابا rās bābā m. Cape Baba

راسبري rāsbarí f. raspberry

راست rāst 1.1 direct, regular, even 1.2 true, correct 1.3 just 1.4 right راسته لاس، راست لاس right hand 2.1 definitely 2.2 truly, correctly

راستانه rāstānə́ masculine plural of راستون

راستباز rāstbāz upright, conscientious

راستبازي rāstbāzí f. uprightness, conscientiousness

راستکار rāstkár 1 upright, honest; conscientious 2 just, unprejudiced

راست گو rāstgój direct, straightforward, sincere, frank

راست گويي rāstgoí f. directness, veracity, sincerity, frankness

راستمن rāstmán ☞ راستکار

راستونول rāstanavə́l denominative, transitive ☞ راستونول

راستنه rāstaná feminine singular of راستون

راستني rástané feminine plural of راستون

راستونېدل rāstanedə́l intransitive ☞ راستونېده

راستونېده rāstanedə́ m. plural return

راستون rāstún راستنه rāstaná f. m. [plural: راستانه rastānə́] f. [plural: راستني rāstané] returning to us or me here, to one's own (place)

راستونول rāstanavə́l denominative, transitive [past: راستون يې کړ] 1 to return to us or me here 2 to return to us or me here

راستونېدل rāstunedə́l denominative, intransitive [past: راستون شو] to return (from a journey, etc.)

راسته [1] rāstá f. line, series (e.g., of products) د بزازانو راسته manufactured line, line of manufactured goods

راسته [2] rásta feminine singular of راست

راستي rāstí f. 1 directness, straightforwardness, veracity, honesty راستي کول to behave honestly 2 truth, sincerity په راستي کښې in actuality, actually

راسخ rāsíkh Arabic firm, unwavering په راسخ ډول firmly, unwaveringly راسخ لرل to make a firm decision

راسره rāsara with us, with me دوی راسره تلل They went with us or me

راسن rāsən m. 1 produce, food-products 2 food-ration

راسه [2] rása Western ☞ راشه

راسي [1] ráse Eastern ☞ راهيسي

راسي [2] ráse Western perspective aspect second person of راتلل

راسيونل rasionál rational, efficient راسيونل گرځول a to rationalize, improve b rationalization, improvement

راش rāsh 1 m. grain on the threshing floor 2 usually predicative په غرو کښې واوره راش ده A thick layer of snow lies on the mountains.

راشبېل rāshbél m. wooden spade

راشتلی rāshtáläj m. corn scattered in the field or on the threshing floor (by custom belongs to the hired hand or sharecropper)

راشن rāshán m. regional food-ration

راشه [1] rāshá rāshə́ f. [plural: رشي rāshé] 1 ☞ رشه [4] 2 produce, food-products

راشه [2] rásha perfective imperative of راتلل

راشه درشه to د چا سره راشه درشه کول rāsha-dársha *f.* contact, relations associate with someone د هر چا سره ښه راشه درشه کوه Be pleasant to everyone

راشی rāsháj *m.* avalanche

راښکل rāẖkól *transitive* ☞ راښنکل

راښکو rāẖkó *f. & m.* draw-bench, wire-drawing machine

راښکودل rāẖkodól *transitive* [*present:* را کاږي *past:* را يي ښکوده] *dialect* to draw, drag, pull *idiom* په سختی يي سا راښنکوده He breathed heavily.

راښنکول rāẖhkól *m.* basket

راښنکون rāẖhkún *m.* 1 attraction, involvement 2 enthusiasm (for), passion (for)

راښکۀ ¹ rāẖhkə́ *past of* راښنکل

راكښنه ² rāẖhkə́ *m. plural* ☞ راكښنه

راښنودل rāẖhodól *intransitive* ☞ ښنودل

راضي rāzí *Arabic* satisfied, content; agreeable (to) زه ځني راضي يم I'm satisfied with them. د چا څخه راضي satisfied with someone راضي کول څوک to convince someone, make someone agree راضي کېدل to be satisfied, be content; agree to په کمه درجه نه راضي کېږي He doesn't want to concede.

راضي نامه rāzināmá *f.* peaceful settlement, amicable agreement; compromise settlement

راغ rāgh *m.* 1 meadow 2 hillock, knoll

راغ rāgh *past stem of* راتلل

راغيب rāghíb *Arabic* desiring, striving for something; avid for something د علم راغب striving for knowledge

راغځى rā́ghdzáj *m.* راغزه rāghdzə́ *m.* ☞ راغه

راغلو ¹ rā́ghlo *dialect* 1 ☞ راغئ 2 rāghlu *past plural of* راتلل

راغلو ² rāghə́lo *oblique plural of* راغلئ ¹

راغلئ ¹ rāghə́ləj *past participle of* راتلل

راغئ ² rāghləj ☞ راغلئ

راغوښتل rāghukhtól [*present:* را و يي غوښت *past:* را و يي غواړي] 1 to order, reserve; subscribe 2 to summon; invite ☞ غوښتل

راغونډ rāghvónḍ rāghúnd gathered; assembled ټول راته راغونډ دي Everyone gathered around me

راغونډول rāghvənḍavól rāghundavól *transitive* [*past:* راغونډ يي کړ] to gather ☞ غونډول

راغونډېدل rāghvənḍedól rāghundedól *intransitive* [*past:* راغونډ شو] to assemble, gather ډېر خلق راغونډ شوي دي Many people had assembled ☞ غونډېدل

راغه rāghə *m.* [*plural:* راغه گان rāghəgán *plural:* رغونه raghúna *plural:* راغونه rāghúna] 1 dale; meadow 2 plain (stoney, sandy) په غرو او رغو کښي in the mountains and the plains

راغئ rā́ghəj *past perfective of* راتلل

رافضي rāfizí *m. Arabic* heretic, apostate

رافضي توب rāfizitób *m.* apostasy

رافع rāfé' *Arabic* ascending, rising

راک ¹ rāk *m.* ☞ راگ

راكت rākét *m.* rocket, missile راكت باليستكي ballistic missile راكت ويشتونکی راکت، ليري ويشتونکی راکت intercontinental missile راكت شغول، راكت توغول missile-equipped vessel د راكت توغولو ميدان missile-base لرونکي الوتکه launch a missile

راكتي rāketi *adjective* missile راكتي عسکر missile troops

راكټ rā́kíṭ *m.* rā́ket ☞ راكت

راكټي raketí ☞ راكتي

راكد rākíd *Arabic* 1 stagnant 2 immobile

راكوړ rā́kər̄ *past of* راكول

راكوړه rā́kṛa 1 *perfective imperative of* راكول 2 *past feminine of* راكول

راكوړه وركوړه rā́kṛa-vārkṛa *f.* 1 exchange 2 receiving and disbursement

راكوړئ rākə́r̄əj 1 *past participle of* راكول 2 given, given out

راكس ¹ rākás *m.* demon, devil

راكس ² rāks *m.* oxen (used in grinding grain)

راكش rākásh 1 pulled; dragged 2 thrown on to; thrown out راكش کول a to draw; attract b to throw on, throw out راكش کېدل a to be drawn, be attracted b to be thrown on, be thrown out

راكښن rā́kẖh ☞ راكښني

راكښنته rākẖhə́ta 1 lower down, subordinate, inferior, lower-ranking (of an organization) 2 below; (down to) here راكښنته کول a to lower b to help down راكښنته کېدل a to descend b to alight, disembark له ربل نه راكښنته کېدل a to alight from a train b to flow down c to make a landing

راكښنته کول rākẖhə́takavól *m. plural* descent, lowering, reduction ځمكي ته راكښنته کول landing

راكښنته کېده rākẖhə́takedə́ *m. plural* descent; landing ځمكي ته راكښنته کېده landing

راكښل rākẖhól *transitive* [*present:* را و يي کښين *past:* را کاږي] 1 to take out, extract 2 to procure 3 to draw, pull something in 4 to drag به زوره يي پښي د ځان پسي راكښنلي He barely shuffled along 5 to gather, assemble (e.g., troops) 6 to draw, illustrate 7 to draw, delineate, illustrate ☞ کښل

راكښنه rākẖhə́na *f.* 1 dragging up 2 attracting 3 attractiveness

راكښوبی rākẖhóbaj *m.* pump

راكښۀ ¹ rākẖhə́ *past of* راكښل

راكښنه ² rākẖhə́ *m. plural* 1 taking out; removal 2 mining, extraction 3 pulling out something 4 dragging 5 assembling, gathering (e.g., troops)

راكښي rā́kẖhe 1 among us 2 in us, in me

راكوزوَل rākuzavól *denominative, transitive* ☞ كوزول

راكوزېدل rākuzedól *denominative, intransitive* ☞ كوزېدل

راكول ¹ rākavól *transitive* 1 prefixal verb [*past:* را يي کړ] 1.1 to give را يي کړ to us, give to me 1.2 to sell to us, to me 2 [*past:* را و يي کړ] to do something for someone تليفون راوکه Telephone me.

راكول ² rākúl *m.* rake

راكه rā́ka *perfective imperative of* راكول

راكي ¹ rā́ki *perfective present of* راكول

راکې ² răke *perfective present second person of* راکول

راکې ³ răke ☞ راکېنۍ

راکېد۪ل rākedә́l 1 *Eastern intransitive & passive prefixal verb* [*present:* را کېږي *past:* راشو *past:* سزا به] to give itself, be given to us خۀ را وشوه؟ ☞ کېدل [*past:* را وشوه] I will be punished 2 What has happened to me?

راگ ¹ rāg *m.* trousers, breeches

راگ ² rāg *m.* melody; song راگ ویل to sing

راگرځول rāgәrdzavә́l *transitive* ☞ راگرزول

راگرځېد۪ل rāgәrdzedә́l *intransitive* ☞ راگرزېدل

راگرځېدۀ rāgәrdzedә́ *m. plural* return; way back د راگرځېدو پۀ وخت while returning, while on the way back کې بنۍ

راگرزول rāgәrdzavә́l *transitive* [*past:* راوي گرزاوه] 1 to turn 2 to restrain; impede; deter from something ☞ گرزول

راگرزېد۪ل rāgәrzedә́l *intransitive* [*past:* راو گرزېده] to return ☞ گرزېدل

راگیر rāgír envelopped, enclosed; grasped; surrounded

راگیرول rāgiravә́l *transitive* [*past:* راگیر یې کړ] 1 to capture, occupy 2 to fill, fill up

رالاندي کول rālā́ndi kavә́l *transitive* ☞ لاندي کول

راله rā́la *Eastern* رالره rā́lara ☞ راته ¹

رالېږونکی rālegúnkaj *m.* sender (of a letter)

رالېبنل rālékhә́l *computer science* download, to download

رام ¹ rām obedient, docile

رام ² rām *m. proper name* Ram

رامبېل rāmbél *m. plural* yellow jasmine

رامت rāmát *m. colloquial* ☞ رحمت

رامبنت rāmә́sht *m.* music

رامکان rāmkā́n *m.* double-weight plaid shawl

راموسی rāmusáj *m.* musk-deer

ران rắn *suffix of actor* طیاره ران pilot, flyer

رانت rānt *m.* rent

رانجن rāndzhә́n dark-grey; the color of antimony

رانجۀ rāndzhә́ *m.* antimony د رانجو معادن deposits of antimony

رانځړه rāndzŕә *m. plural* ☞ رنځړه

رانده rāndá banished; cast-out, rejected رانده کېدل to be banished

راندمان rāndemā́n *m.* 1 manufacturing; production 2 productivity

رانسکورول rānaskoravә́l *transitive* ☞ نسکرول

راننواته rānәnavātә́ *m. plural* entrance د راننووتو دروازه gate; entrance

راننوت۪ل rānәnavatә́l *intransitive* ☞ ننوتل

رانه rắna *Eastern* ☞ راڅخه

رانیو۪ل rānivә́l 1 *transitive* [*past:* راو یې نیو] 1. to catch, seize, take 1.2 *prefixal verb* [*past:* را یې نیو] to buy, purchase, obtain 2 *m. plural* د رانیولو قیمت purchase price

رانیونه rānivә́na *f.* ☞ رانیوه

رانیونکی rānivúnkaj 1 *present participle of* رانیول 2 *m.* purchaser

رانیوۀ rānivә́ *m. plural* buying, purchasing, procuring

رانۀ rāṇә́ *masculine plural of* رون ¹

رانۍ rāṇә́j *f.* 1 ranee (title of nobility) 2 *derogatory* princess, ladyship

رانیزي ¹ rāṇizí *plural* the Ranizai (tribe) 2 ranizáj *m.* Ranizai (tribesman)

راواتۀ rāvātә́ *m. plural* 1 origin, appearance 2 going, setting out د راوتو ځای the sources of a river

راوت۪ل rāvatә́l *intransitive* [*present:* راوزي *past:* راووت *past:* راوووت] 1 to go out, come out, move out کتاب لۀ طبعي څخه راووت The book has already been published. 2 to begin, commence, flow out (of a river) 3 to resound, be heard (of a shout, etc.) 4 to show oneself, put oneself forth 5 to turn out to be 6 to appear, arise

راودېخواته rāvәdekhvā́ta ☞ راپه دې خوا

راوروسته rāvrústa late; subsequent; last, latest پۀ راوروسته کېبنۍ، recently راوروسته وخت کېبنۍ

راوړ ¹ rắvuṛ *past of* راوړل

راوړ ² rắvṛ *present stem of* راوړل

راوړ۪ل rāvṛә́l *transitive* [*present:* راوړي *past:* را یې وړ *past:* را یې وووړ] 1 to bring, deliver, convey 2 to obtain, extract 3 to bring in, mention مثل راوړل to present an example 4 to give birth to بنځي یې زوی راوړ His wife gave birth to a son. 5 to effect, accomplish پر چا هجوم راوړل to attack someone a to receive b to seize c to obtain لاس ته راوړل

راوړۀ ¹ rāvṛә́ *m. plural* delivery, bringing, transport

راوړه ² rắvṛa *past feminine of* راوړل

راوړه ³ rắvṛa *imperfective imperative of* راوړل

راوړئ ¹ rāvә́ṛәj *past participle of* راوړل

راوړي ² rắvṛi *present of* راوړل

راوست rắvust *past of* راوستل

راوستای rāvәstā́j *conditional form of* راوستل

راوست۪ل rāvustә́l rāvә́stә́l 1 *transitive* [*present:* راولي *past:* رٲ rắvali *past:* را یې ووست rājevust] .1 to bring, deliver someone یې ووست 1.2 to obtain, extract لاس ته راوستل to obtain, get, achieve something 1.3 to force 1.4 to bring water to, irrigate 1.5 to bring about (e.g., revolution) 1.6 to advance arguments راوستل کېدل *passive voice* a to be brought, delivered b to be obtained, extracted c to be conducted, led through 2 *m. plural* ☞ راوستنه *idiom* میدان ته سړی راوستل to push forward fighters

راوستنه rắvustә́na *f.* ☞ راوسته ¹ rāvustә́ *m. plural* 1 bringing, delivering something 2 obtaining, extracting 3 forcing 4 bringing water to; irrigating 5 bringing about (e.g., revolution) 6 bringing or advancing arguments

راوسته ² rắvusta *feminine past tense of* راوستل

راول rắval *present stem of* راوستل

راووست ¹ rắvust *past tense of* راوستل

راووست ² rāvúst *imperfect of* راوستل

راوه rāvá *f.* ointment

راوي rāví *m. Arabic* narrator, teller (of a story)

راوئ rāvә́j *Western past tense of* راوړل

راوېست۪ل rāvestә́l *transitive* ☞ وېستل

راوبستون rāvestún *m.* **1** innovation, novelty نوی راوبستون innovation, novelty **2** invention

راه rāh *m. combining form* road, way راهبر conductor, guide

راهبر rāhbár *m.* **1** conductor, guide **2** leader

راهبري rāhbarí *f.* **1** duties and obligations of a conductor or a guide **2** leadership راهبري کول **a** to be a conductor or a guide, do the work of a conductor or a guide **b** leader

راهدار ¹ rāhdár *m.* collector of road or transit duties, tax collector

راهدار ² rāhdár striped (e.g., cloth)

راهداري rāhdārí *f.* **1** road duty, transit duty, tax, toll **2** pass **3** safe-conduct pass **4** passport

راهرو rāhráv *m.* passage; corridor; vestibule

راهروی rāhraváj *m.* traveller

راهزن rāhzán *m.* robber, bandit

راهزني rāhzaní *f.* robbery, banditry

راهسازي rāhsāzí *f.* roadbuilding

راهسته rāhista راهسي rāhisi ☞

راهسکبدونکی rāhaskedúnkaj **1** rising **2** growing up راهسکبدونکی نسل rising generation

راهگذر rāhguzár *m.* راهروی ☞

راهنما rāhnumá *m.* راهنمای rāhnumáj **1** conductor, guide **2** guidebook **3** leader

راهنمائي rāhnumāí *f.* leadership د چا تر راهنمائي لاندي under someone's leadership راهنمائي کول *compound verb* **a** to lead something or somewhere **b** to lead someone

راهوار rāhvár *m.* ambler (i.e., horse)

راهي rāhí رهي ☞

راهيټ rāhíṭ *m. regional* old age

راهسته rāhista over here, to us, over to where I am

د راهيسي rāhisi since, since such-and-such a time, since the time of د هغه راهيسي، د هغه وخته راهيسي چه since, since the time when د اسد د مياشتي راهيسي since last year پروسبرکاله راهيسي since the month of Asad? د څو مياشتو راهيسي Since when? د کله راهيسي؟ It has been several months already; several months ago

رای rāj *m. Arabic* [*plural:* آرا آرآ ārā] **1** opinion د رای، رای څرگندول to express an opinion, speak out د چا نه بد رای کول to form a poor opinion of someone **2** vote (in elections) د رای حق، د مشوري رای right to vote د تجویز رای deciding vote د ورکولو حق consultative vote, opinion د آراو اتفاق unanimously د آراو د by a majority of votes ... آرای عمومیه ārā-ji plebescite د چا دپاره رای ورکول to vote, cast one's vote for someone په عمومي، برابر، مستقیم او مخفي رای voting رای اخیستل general and direct elections by secret ballot *idiom* د چا په رای چلبدل to follow someone's bidding ☞ رایه

رایات rāját *m.* رعیت ☞

رایتول rājatavál *denominative, transitive* [*past:* رایت یې کړ] to subordinate, subjugate

رائج rāídzh *Arabic* **1** in circulation (i.e., money) **2** disseminated, sought after, popular **3** generally accepted

رائجول rāidzhavál *denominative, transitive* [*past:* رائج یې کړ] **1** to introduce, put into circulation (i.e., money) **2** to disseminate, put into general use

رائجبدل raidzhedál *denominative, intransitive* [*past:* رائج شو] **1** to be put into circulation, be in circulation (i.e., money) **2** to spread **3** to be generally accepted

رایدهي rājdihí *f.* rājdehí voting

راهروی rājraváj *m.* رای روی ☞

رایسته ¹ rājistá *m. plural* **1** deduction, conclusion **2** breeding, raising (of chicks) **3** *math* extraction (of a root) **4** mining, extraction (of mineral deposit) **5** thinking up, invention

رایسته ² rájista رایسی rájisi راهیسي ☞

رایگان rājgán **1** free, gratuitous **2** for nothing, gratis

رای گیري rājgirí *f.* voting; referendum عامه رای گیري referendum پټه secret ballot پنکاره رای گیري open balloting

راین rājn *m.* Rhine River

رای ورکونکی rāj varkavúnkaj *m.* voter, participant in elections

رایست rájúst *imperfect of* رایستل

رایه rāja *f.* رای ☞ ¹ د رایو په اکثریت، په ډېرو رایو by a majority of the votes د ۳۷ رایو by 50 votes to 37 د ۵۰ رایو په مقابل کښي په ۳۷ رایو طرفداره رایه، مثبته رایه unanimously د رایو په اتفاق tie votes برابري رایه vote for رایه ورکول to vote ممتنعه رایه ورکول to abstain from voting په ډېرو رایو غوره to elect by secret ballot د پټو رایو له لاري انتخابېدل کول to elect by a majority vote

رای ورکونکی rája varkavúnkaj ☞ رایه ورکونکی

رائي ¹ ráji *plural of* رایه

رایې ² ráje *compound of the pronouns* را *and* یې

رائي ³ rāji *present tense of* ریل ²

رایې ⁴ ráe *f. oblique* رای ☞

رب ¹ rab rabb [*plural:* ارباب arbáb *plural:* ربان rabán rabbán] **1** sir, master **2** Lord, God

رب ² rub *m. Arabic* syrup; juice د بهي رب quince juice

ربا ribā *f. Arabic* usury, extortion

رباب rabāb rəbāb *m. Arabic* rabab, rebab (a stringed instrument played by plucking or strumming) سم رباب the lute رباب وهل to play the rabab

ربابي rabābí *m.* rabab player

رباخور ribākhór *m.* usurer, extortioner

رباط rabāt ribát *m. Arabic* **1** rabat caravansarai, inn **2** *used in geographic names* آق رباط Akrabat **3** Rabat (city)

رباعي rubā'í *f. Arabic* [*plural:* رباعیگاني rubā'igáni رباعیاني rubā'iáni *Arabic m. plural:* رباعیات rubā'iját] rubai, quatrain

رب النوع rab-an-náu *m. Arabic* God, divinity (of primitive people)

ربانی rabbāní *Arabic* divine

ربح ribh *f. Arabic* profit

ربړ ¹ rabáṛ *m.* **1** disquiet, alarm بی له ربړ نه without trouble د بېلتون ربړ ورکول to trouble, alarm **2** غم او ربړ bitterness of parting **3** suffering, tortures; deprivation **3** oppression **4** difficulties, troubles

رابر rabár [2] *m. plural* ☞ رابر

ربراو rabráv *m. dialect* ☞ ربره

ربراول rabṛavól *transitive* [*past:* ربراوه يي و] **1** to disturb, alarm **2** to torture, torment **3** to oppress **4** to cause trouble **5** to place in a difficult position

ربړه rabṛá *f.* ☞ ربر [1]

ربړي rábṛi *plural of* ربره [1]

رابري rabaṛí rabəṛí ☞ رابري [2]

ربریالی rabərjālój hardworking, industrious

ربړې جبړې rabṛe-dzhabáṛe *f.* rabə́ṛe-dzhabə́ṛe *plural Eastern* **1** difficulties; complications **2** quarreling

ربریدل rabṛedól *intransitive* [*past:* وربریده] **1** to worry, be anxious, be alarmed **2** to feel unhappy د چا له لاسه ربریدل to be oppressed (by someone)

ربریز rabṛíz **1** worried, alarmed **2** troublesome; peevish

ربګوکی rabagúkaj poor, pitiable, weak

ربط rabt *m. Arabic* link; relation, connection ربط کلمه *grammar* copulative verb

ربع rub' *f. Arabic* 4th part, ¼ th of something یو متر او ربع 1¼ meters دري ربع ¾

ربغر rabəghóṛ *m.* poor family

ربغړی rabəghə́ṛaj **1** poor **2** naked

ربل rából [1] **1** accepted, agreed upon **2** deserving; worthy of something

ربل raból [2] *transitive* ☞ ربل

ربل rabl [3] *m.* ☞ پېرزوینه

ربلول rablavól *denominative, transitive* [*past:* ربل يي کړ] **1** to accept, be approved **2** to consider worthy, think deserving of something

ربلونکی rablúnkaj ewel-ess, motherless (of a lamb)

ربلیدل rabledól rabóledól *denominative, intransitive* [*past:* ربل شو] **1** to be accepted, be approved **2** to deserve, be worthy of something

رب نمانځونی rabnmāndzúnaj God fearing

ربنیدل rabnedól *intransitive* ☞ ربنیدل

ربنوکی rabaṇúkaj *m.* **1** sturdy child **2** bright, smart child

ربڼه rabaṇá *f.* ربڼی rabaṇə́j *f.* **1** shaft of light; gleam **2** morning wind which sweeps away the clouds

ربنیدل rabṇedól *intransitive* [*past:* وربنید] to be afraid, fear; be frightened

ربیع rabí' *f. Arabic* spring; spring harvest *idiom* ربیع الاخر، ربیع الثانی assāní name of the fourth month of the lunar year ربیع الاول name of the third month of the lunar year

ربینه rabiṇá *f.* membrane

رپ rap [1] *m.* moment; flash د سترګو په رپ، د سترګي په رپ instantaneously, in the wink of an eye

رپ rap [2] *m.* niche; shelf; baggage shelf ☞ رف

رپ rap [3] *m.* slap, clap (on the back, shoulder) اوږدي ته رپ ورکول to slap on the shoulder

رپا rapá *f.* **1** blinking, flashing **2** vibration

رپت rapát *m.* communication, report

رپک rapák *m.* shelf, bracket (for tableware)

رپکندی rapkandáj *m.* water-clock

رپند rapónd **1** trembling, blinking **2** fluttering

رپندی rapandáj *m. Eastern* ☞ رپی [1]

رپورت rapóṭ *m.* ☞ راپورت

رپوتچي rapoṭchí *m.* رپوتي rapoṭí *m.* **1** spy; informer **2** snitch; tattle-tale

ریپورت ripóṭ *m. regional* report د راتلو ریپورت کول *military* to report on events

رپاول rapavól *transitive* [*past:* رپاوه يي و] **1** to blink (the eyes) **2** to oscillate, sway, flap باد بیرغونه رپوي The wind causes the banners to flutter. *idiom* په سترګه رپولو کښ instantaneously, in a flash, in the wink of an eye

رپاونه rapavóna *f.* **1** blinking **2** oscillating, swaying

رپهار rapahár *m.* noise, uproar

رپی rapáj [1] *m.* **1** shivering وربانده رپی راغئ He was thrown into a fit of shivers. He began to shiver. **2** banner, flag

رپی rupə́j [2] *f.* ☞ روپی

رپي rapí [3] *present of* رپیدل

رپیدل rapedól *intransitive* [*past:* وربپیده] **1** to quiver; shiver د ډبري ستومانۍ نه مي پښي پنبي رپیدلي My legs were giving way from exhaustion. **2** to sway, oscillate; flap; flutter (of banners) **3** to shudder **4** to soar (of birds)

رپیدنه rapedóna *f.* رپیده rapedə́ *m. plural* **1** trembling, quivering; shivering **2** swaying, oscillating; fluttering (of banners)

رت rat *tautological with used as an intensifier with names of colors* رت تور jet black

رتبوی rutbaví fitting for a rank (of a salary, etc.)

رتبه rutbá *f. Arabic* rank, grade; post; job, position د لوی سفیر په رتبه in the rank of ambassador

رتی ratój *f.* **1** rati (the red seed of Indian licorice, used as a measure of weight) **2** weight in rati equal to eight barley corns **3** *figurative* a drop یوه رتی وینه drop of blood

رتی پتی rəte-póte **1** scattered, thrown about **2** carelessly cut up

رت rəṭ [1] **1.1** obvious, evident رته مبالغه obvious exaggeration **1.2** bold, impertinent (of a person) **1.3** complex, confused **1.4** brusk, rude رته خبره brusk comment, rude word **1.5** ill-bred **1.6** unsuitable رت ویل to speak plainly ډبري رتي مه وایه Don't babble on, it's not fitting. **2.1** completely, quite; very **2.2** evidently

رت rəṭ [2] ☞ رد

رتوالی rəṭjā́ *f.* ☞ رتیا

رتل raṭál *transitive* [*past:* راته يي و] **1** to berate, tell off **2** to censure **3** to drive off, banish **4** to drive (cattle)

رتمت rəṭmə́t ☞ رډبېل رت مت

رتن raṭə́n spotted

رتنه raṭə́na *f.* **1** abuse **2** censure

رتوالی rəṭvā́laj *m.* **1** boldness, impertinence **2** complication, confusion **3** bruskness, rudeness **4** lack of breeding, bad breeding **5** obviety, apparentness

رتول rəṭavə́l *denominative, transitive* [*past:* رت یې کړ] to complicate, confuse

رتونکی raṭúnkaj **1** *present participle of* رتل **2** *m.* **.1** hostile critic; negator; skeptic **2.2** muddle-headed person

رته¹ ráṭa *f.* spot, mark

رته² ráṭa *f. singular of* رت¹

رتېدل rəṭedə́l *denominative, intransitive* [*past:* رت شو] to become complicated, become confused

رجا radzhā *f. Arabic* hope, aspiration

رجال ridzhā́l *m. Arabic masculine plural of* رجل

رجب radzháb *m. Arabic* **1** Rajab (seventh month of the lunar year) **2** *m. proper name* Rajab

رجحان rudzhhā́n *m. Arabic* **1** advantage; superiority; preponderance پر نورو باندي رجحان لرل to surpass others, be higher than others **2** *law* preferential right of acquisition **3** profit, advantage **4** tendency, bent

رجز radzház *m. Arabic* rajaz (a poetic meter used to create a warlike atmosphere)

رجستري radzhistarí رجستري مکتوب radzhistarí registered رجستري مکتوب registered letter رجستري کول to send by registered mail

رجعت radzh'át *m. Arabic* departure, retreat; withdrawal from battle

رجل radzhúl *m.* [*plural:* رجال ridzhā́l] *Arabic* person, man; important personality د دولت رجال state figures; nobility, grandees فکري رجال great minds, great thinkers

رجوع rudzhú' *Arabic* **1** و چا ته رجوع کول to appeal to someone appeal to someone **2** return **3** renunciation (of responsibility, an agreement, etc.)

رجول radzhavə́l *transitive dialect* ☞ رژول

رجولیت radzhulijā́t *m. Arabic* **1** maturity **2** manhood

رجه radzhá *f.* **1** rope, cord **2** drawing **3** custom, tradition, law

رجېدل radzhedə́l *intransitive dialect* ☞ رژېدل

رچ¹ rach *m.* **1** *technology* reed (of a loom) **2** decor; furnishings; goods and chattels **3** *dialect* tool (of production); (machine) lathe

رچ² ruch *m.* wish, desire

رچکی rachə́kaj *m.* skein, hank of yarn

رچڼی racháṇaj *m.* lathe-operator

رچه¹ rúcha *f.* ☞ رچ²

رېچه² richá *f.* ☞ رېچه

رېچن riché-riché ☞ رچي رچي

رځه rə́dza *f.* road

رخ rəts lame, limping

رڅیکبل ratsikkhə́l رڅیکابري [*present:* رڅیکابري ratsekkhə́l *transitive* رڅي یې کېښ :past] *Western* to drag, trail, ford

رح *abbreviation* رحمة الله علیه rahmát ullā́hi alė́jhi *religion* May God's mercy be upon him! May God be merciful to him!

رحلت rahlát *m. Arabic* leaving, departure رحلت کول to depart this world, die

رحم¹ rahm ráhəm *m.* mercy, compassion پر چا رحم کول، په چا رحم کول to pity someone رحم لرل to be merciful په یتیم باندي یې رحم راغئ He pitied the orphan.

رحم² rahím rihm *m. Arabic* uterus, womb

رحمان rahmā́n *Arabic* **1** merciful **2** *m. proper name* Rahman (especially the seventeenth century poet Abdurrahman)

رحمانه rahmā́na *f. proper name* Rahmana

رحماني rahmā́ní divine, heavenly

رحمت rahmát *m. Arabic* **1** mercy, sympathy رحمت کول to pity, have mercy on **2** *proper name* Rahmat

رحمدل rahmdíl **1** sympathetic **2** *m. proper name* Ramdil

رحمن rahmā́n *Arabic* ☞ رحمان

رحمة الله rahmatullā́ *Arabic* **1** ☞ رح **2** *m. proper name* Rahmatulla

رحمېدل rahmedə́l *intransitive* [*past:* و رحمبده] to take pity on, have mercy on

رحیل rahíl *m. Arabic* ☞ رحیل¹

رحیم rahím *Arabic* **1** merciful, kind, gracious (an epithet of God) **2** *m. proper name* Rahim

رحیم الله rahimullā́ *m. Arabic proper name* Rahimulla

رحیمه rahimá *f. Arabic proper name* Rahima

رخ¹ rakh *m.* cutting, slicing

رخ² rukh *m.* face

رخ³ rukh *m. chess* rook

رخ⁴ rukh *m.* ☞ سیمرغ

رخام rukhā́m *m. Arabic* alabaster د رخام ډبره alabaster

رخاوت rakhāvát *m. Arabic* inertia, enfeeblement, apathy

رخپین rakhpín *m.* رخپین rakhpin *m.* soup made with buttermilk

رخت rakht *m.* **1** decor, furnishings **2** fabric, textile, cloth **3** silk cloth **4** *agriculture* plow beam **5** harness

رختباب rakhtbā́b *m.* cotton textiles, cloth

رختخواب rakhtkhā́b *m. dialect* bed-clothing

رخچینه rakhchína *f.* Middle-Eastern style skullcap

رخدار rakhdā́r rifled, threaded (of a gun) توپک rifle

رخسار rukhsā́r *m. poetry* cheek, face

رخصت rukhsát *Arabic* **1** *m.* **.1** parting, leavetaking; له یو بل څخه رخصت to take leave of, bid farewell رخصت غوښتل to ask permission to leave **1.2** authorization to leave **1.3** leave, vacation د ناجوړی special (i.e., extraordinary) leave ضروري رخصت sick leave **2** *predicative* زه نو رخصت یم I shall leave. I am going away.

رخصتول rukhsatavə́l *denominative* [*past:* رخصت یې کړ] **1** to send on leave, authorize to go away **2** to dismiss (upon conclusion of a task, for vacation time); offer leave to **3** to send, dispatch (troops, etc.) **4** to discharge, fire

رخصتي rukhsatí *f.* [*plural:* رخصتي rukhsatə́j *plural:* رخصتي گاني rukhsatigā́ni] **1** completion of a task; departure from work **2** departure, exit **3** leave; school vacation

رخصتېدل rukhsatedə́l *denominative, intransitive* [*past:* رخصت شو] to leave 1 رخصت سم؟ May I go? 2 to take one's leave 3 to be dismissed (upon completion of a task, for school vacation); curtail a task ښوونځی پر درې بجې رخصتېږي School ends at three o'clock.

رخصتېده rukhsatedə́ *m. plural* 1 departure, leaving 2 leavetaking 3 dismissal (on completion of schoolwork, for vacation); curtail class work

رخن rəkhə́n رخندوکی rəkhəndúkaj envious

رخنه rakhná *f.* crack; breach; break

رخه rə́kha *f.* envy; malevolence رخه کول to envy; harbor spite, nourish spite

رخی [1] rəkháj *m. regional* envious person; spiteful critic; rival

رخی [2] rakháj *m.* exit opening (of a reservoir)

رخیل rkhəjə́l *transitive dialect* ☞ خریل

رد [1] rad radd *Arabic* 1 *m.* .1 refusal (of a proposal, of helpful intercession, etc.) 1.2 rejection (of a candidacy) 1.3 repelling (a blow, an attack) 1.4 negation, denial; refusal; objection 1.5 dismissal (from a job, etc.) رد کېدل *compound verb* ☞ رد کول *compound verb* ☞ ردېدل 2.1 refused, turned down (of a job, good offices, etc.) 2.2 rejected (of a candidacy) 2.3 repelled (of a blow, an attack) 2.4 dismissed (from a job, etc.) *idiom* رد خلق rád-i the dregs of society

رد [2] rad *m.* side (direction of movement)

ردالعمل rad-ul-'amál radd-ul'amál *Arabic* ☞ ردعمل

ردخ radóts *m.* left-handed person

ردعمل radi'amál *m.* raddi'amál 1 reaction, reacting 2 ☞ رد [2] 1

ردوید rad-və-bád *m.* abuse, cursing

ردوبدل radubadál *m.* raddubadál *Arabic* 1 confusion 2 quarrel ردوبدل کېدل to be submitted to discussion

ردول radavə́l raddavə́l *denominative, transitive* [*past:* رد یې کړ] 1 to reject (a proposal, good-offices) 2 to reject (a candidacy) 3 to repel (a blow, an attack) 4 to deny; turn down; object 5 to dismiss (from a job)

رده radá *f.* 1 row, line, rank 2 layer, course (in a clay wall) 3 work done by the day 4 *figurative* cause, reason, basis

ردي radí raddí rejected, unfit ردي کاغذ spoilage

ردېدل radedə́l *denominative, intransitive* [*past:* رد شو] 1 to be rejected, be turned down (of a proposition, good-offices, etc.) 2 to be turned down (of a candidacy) 3 to be repelled (an attack, a blow) 4 to deny, turn down

ردیف radíf *m. Arabic* 1 row; category 2 order, sequence په ردیف د اساس in alphabetic order 3 follower 4 *literature* radif (the riming word of a poem) 5 *history* rider mounted behind a horseman

رډ [1] rəḍ 1 protruding (of eyes) 2 cheeky, bold رډ کتل to look cheekily, look boldly 3 stubborn

رډ [2] rəḍ ☞ رت [1]

رډبډ rəḍbə́ḍ 1 directly, straight-off, bluntly رډبډ ویل to speak straightforwardly, talk bluntly 2 obviously, evidently رډبډ پنبمانه to openly sympathize

رډپرډه rəḍpərə́ḍa ☞ رډبډ

رډسترگی rəḍstə́rgaj 1 pop-eyed, goggle-eyed 2 bold-faced

رډول rəḍavə́l *denominative, transitive* [*past:* رډ یې کړ] to protrude, goggle (eyes)

رډی [1] rəḍáj raḍí pop-eyed; goggle-eyed

رډی [2] raḍə́j *f.* oily rag (for cleaning rifles)

رډي [3] rə́ḍi *feminine plural of* رډ [1]

رډېدل rəḍedə́l *denominative, intransitive* [*past:* رډ شو] 1 to be pop-eyed, be goggle-eyed 2 to persist in 3 to be cheeky, be impertinent

رذالت rizālát *m.* رذاله razalá *f. Arabic* baseness, lowness, vileness

رذائل razāíl *m. masculine plural Arabic of* رذیله

رذیل razíl *Arabic* base, vile

رذیلانه razilāná 1 base 2 vicious

رذیله razilá *f. Arabic* [*plural:* رذیلی razilé *Arabic m. plural:* رذائل razāíl] base action, vile deed

ررى rarə́j *f.* flower of the Indian lilac

رز raz *m.* vineyard

رزاق razzák *m. Arabic* 1 *religion* the All-high; God 2 *proper name* Razzaq

رزړ razə́ṛ 1 *m. plural* Razar (tribe) 2 *m.* Razar (tribesman)

رزق rizk *m. Arabic* [*plural:* ارزاق arzák] nourishment, daily bread; food رزق رسول to feed, nourish *idiom* a خپل رزق په لغته وهل to yawn at, wink at something b to miscalculate, make an error in counting c to display carelessness

رزم razm *m.* epic poetry

رزمته razmáta *f.* sustinence

رزمک razmák *m.* Razmak (city, Waziristan)

رزمي razmí 1 *literature* epic 2 warlike

رژند razhə́nd 1 dropping (of leaves) 2 falling (of hair)

رژول razhavə́l *transitive* [*past:* وی یې رژاوه] 1 to drop (foliage) 2 to shed (wool, fur, feathers at molting time), molt 3 to pour, pour out; spill 4 to strew, empty out; spill 5 *technology* to found, cast, mold

رژون razhún *m.* رژونه razhavə́na *f.* 1 fall, autumn 2 molting time 3 pouring out, spilling 4 emptying out, spilling out 5 *technology* casting, moulding, founding

رژېدل razhedə́l *intransitive* [*past:* ورژېده] 1 to drop, fall (of leaves) منی دئ، د ونو پاڼی رژېږي It is autumn, and the leaves are falling from the trees. 2 to fall out (of hair) 3 to molt, shed (of animals, birds) 4 to crumble (of something friable) 5 to fall into ruins (of age), etc. 6 to flow, flow out; spill out 7 to run out, spill; get spilled

رژېدنه razhedə́na *f.* رژېدنه razhedə́ *m. plural* 1 falling (of leaves) د ونو د پاڼو رژېدنه the Fall 2 falling out (hair) 3 molting, shedding (of animals, birds) 4 crumbling (of something friable)

رژيم rezhím *m.* regime, order, structure

رس [1] ras *m.* **1** provisions **2** delivery of provisions to troops **3** arrival

رس [2] ras *m.* hair-dye made from the root of *Amomium anthorhizum*

رسا rasā́ rəsā́ **1.1** attaining something, achieving something **1.2** penetrating, profound (of a mind, thought) **1.3** exact, precise رسا ویشتل کول to shoot accurately **2** *f.* long sabre

رسالت risālát *m. Arabic* prophetic mission

رسالدار risāldā́r *m.* ☞ رساله دار

رساله risālá *f. Arabic* [*plural:* رسالي risālé *Arabic m. plural:* رسائل rasāíl] **1** brochure; booklet; tract **2** cavalry **3** *history* cavalry squadron

رساله دار risāladā́r *m.* commander of a cavalry squadron

رسام rassā́m *m. Arabic* artist, designer

رسامي rassāmí *f.* drawing هغه په رسامي کښي ماهر دئ He has talent for drawing.

رسائل rasāíl *m. Arabic plural* ☞ رساله

رسائي [1] rasāí *f.* ☞ رسېده 5

رست rust rust درست خته clay

رستاق rustā́ḳ *m.* Rustak (city)

رستگاري rastagārí *f.* rescue, deliverance, liberation

رستم rustám *m. proper name* Rustam

رستم خېل rustamkhél **1** *m. plural* Rustamkhejli (tribe) **2** *m.* Rustamkhejl (tribesman)

رستوران restorā́n *m.* restaurant

رسته rastá *f.* **1** line (trade) **2** shop, shift **3** branch

رسخت ruskhát *m.* ☞ رخصت

رسد rasád *m.* **1** portion, share **2** provisions **3** harvest time

رسدرساني rasadrasāní *f.* supplying of provisions

رسليک raslík *m.* receipt, voucher, quittance

رسم [1] rasm *m. Arabic* [*plural:* رسمونه rasmúna *Arabic plural:* رسوم ruśum] **1** custom, tradition رسم کول to observe custom, follow tradition **2** duty; tax گمرکي رسم ورواج customs, formalities, procedures **3** ceremony drawing; portrait تزيني رسمونه pattern, ornamental design رسم ايستل، رسم کښل، رسم کول to draw

رسم [2] rasə́m *colloquial present tense of* رسېدل

رسم [3] rasm *m.* grain cleaned by winnowing

رسماً rásmán *Arabic* officially

رسم الخط rasm-ul-khát *m.* rasm-ul-khátt *Arabic* **1** calligraphy **2** written language **3** spelling, orthography

رسمگر rasmgár *m.* artist

رسماول rasmawə́l *denominative, transitive* [*past:* رسم يي کړ] to draw

رسمي rasmí *Arabic* **1** official په رسمي ډول officially, ceremonially رسمي جريده official gazette, official journal **2** official (of a language) **3** nominal, rated رسمي اجوره official pay rate

رسميت rasmiját *m. Arabic* [*plural:* رسميات rasmiját] officialdom; state of being official په رسميت سره پيژندل to recognize officially د رسمياتو په اساس formally

رسمېدل rasmedə́l *denominative* [*past:* رسم شو] to be drawn

رسوا rusvā́ disgraced رسوا کول to disgrace, shame رسوا کېدل to be disgraced, be shamed

رسوايي rusvāí *f.* shame, disgrace

رسوب rusúb *m. Arabic* **1** precipitation, sediment **2** sedimentation, alluvium

رسوبي rusubí sedimentational, alluvial

رسوخ rusúkh *m. Arabic* **1** stability, firmness, steadfastness **2** *figurative* authority, good reputation خپل رسوخ ساتل to preserve one's reputation

رسول [1] rasúl *m. Arabic* **1** prophet **2** *proper name* Rasul

رسول [2] rasavə́l *transitive* **1** [*past:* وېي رساوه] **1.1** to deliver; transport; purvey; خان رسول to reach **1.2** to bring **1.3** to allow to ripen **1.4** to cause, inflict (e.g., harm, damage) خلل او ويجار رسول to inflict damage صدمه رسول **a** to inflict damage **b** to damage something **1.5** to train (personnel, staff, etc.) **2** *m. plural* **1** delivery; purveyance transport د اوبو رسول water supply **2.2** causing, inflict (e.g., damage, harm) **2.3** training (personnel, etc.) *idiom* په سر رسول to bring to a conclusion په مصرف رسول to use, employ, spend

رسولی rasvalə́j *f.* rasalə́j **1** corn, callus **2** swollen gland **3** tumor; lump

رسوم rusúm *Arabic masculine plural of* رسم

رسومات rusumā́t *masculine secondary plural of* رسوم

رسی [1] rasə́j *f.* **1** rope, cord **2** *figurative* bonds, ties

رسی [2] rasí *present tense of* رسېدل

رسی [3] rasáy *computer science* access

رسيد rasíd *m.* [*plural:* رسيدونه rasidúna *Arabic plural:* رسيدات rasidā́t] **1** receipt; arrival; delivery **2** written receipt (for delivery of sth); quittance رسيد کول to sign for something upon receipt د رسيدونو کتابچه receipt book د رسيداتو کتاب delivery-record book

رسيد raséd *past stem of* رسېدل

رسيدات rasidā́t *Arabic masculine plural of* رسيد

رسيدگي rasidagí *f.* **1** inspection, control **2** *investigation* **3** reconsideration (of a case)

رسېدل rasedə́l *intransitive* [*present:* رسېږي *present:* رسي *past:* ورسېد *past:* ورسېده] **1** to reach; attain; arrive; come to ښار ته رسېدل to get to the city, arrive in town درورسېدم! I'll go to your place! پر چا را to overtake someone **2** to be received (mail, documents, etc.) **3** پر... پوري رسېدل، تر ... پوري رسېدل، و... ته رسېدل to go up to, extend to **4** to reach (of a sound) **5** to be due, be owing to, get (by inheritance) و ده ته د ګټي څلرمه برخه رسېږي A fourth of the profit was due him. **6** to come due, come (time period) د تگ وخت راورسېده The time to depart has come. **7** to understand, grasp, comprehend زه ورسېدم چه ... I understood that ... ته به پخپله ینه You yourself will look into this fully. پري ورسېږي **8** to ripen mature (of fruit, etc.) **9** to rise (of dough) **10** to ripen, become ripe **11** to be trained *idiom* رسېدل خپل مقصد ته رسېدل، په خپل مطلب رسېدل to attain a goal, get what one is after د زره تر مراده رسېدل to get that

which is desired په سر رسېدل to finish, be completed د يو شي په
مصرف رسېدل to be used in the manufacture of something; be used
for something د ځپله لاسه رسېدل to punish oneself

رسېدنه rasedə́na *f.* ☞ رسېده ¹ rasedə́ *m. plural* **1** arrival, coming **2**
arrival (of mail, documents, etc.) **3** extension **4** expiration (of a
term), coming (of) **5** understanding, comprehension, grasp **6**
ripening, maturing (fruits, etc.) **7** condition or state of being
trained

رسېده ² rasedə́ *imperfect plural of* رسېدل

رسېده ³ rasedá *imperfect plural of* رسېدل

رسېده ⁴ rasidá **1** mature, ripe **2** adult, grown-up **3** trained

رسېدگي rasidagí *f.* ☞ رسېدگي

رسي کوډ rasi kóḍ *computer science m.* access code

رسي والا rasəjvālā́ *m.* rope seller

رش ¹ rash *m.* **1** sawdust **2** crumbs **3** dirt **4** pus **5** ☞ گرمکي

رش ² rash *m.* cream

رشاد rashád *m. Arabic* **1** *religion* true faith; the right way **2**
correctness **3** *proper name* Rashad

رشادت rashādát *m. Arabic* courage, bravery رشادت ښودل to display
courage, demonstrate bravery

راشتلی rashtə́laj *m.* ☞

رشتونی rishtúnaj ☞ رښتين

رشته rishtá *f.* **1** thread **2** *biology* filament; feeler, antenna **3** kind
of parasitic worm; suture **4** *figurative* ties, bonds يوه قوي تينگه
رشته strong bonds

رشته داري ¹ rishtadārí *f.* relations, extended family

رشته داری ² rishtadā́raj *m.* relative

رښتيا rishtiā́ *f.* ☞

رښتياني rishtiānáj ☞

رښتين rishtín ☞ رښتين

رښتينجا rishtinjā́ *f.* رښتينوالی rishtinvā́laj *m.* ☞

رښتينه rishtína **1** *feminine* ☞ رښتينه **2** *feminine singular of* رښتين

رشد rushd *m. Arabic* **1** growth رشد کول to grow **2** maturity د هغه
فکري رشد the maturity of his thoughts

رشدي rushdí رشديه rushdijá *Arabic* middle, intermediate رشدي
مکتب middle school

رشقه rishḵá *f.* lucerne (grass)

رشک ¹ rashk *m.* envy د هغه کسانو په طبيعي ژوند مي رشک راغئ، د هغه
کسانو په طبيعي ژوند ماته رشک راغئ I envy the free life of these
people.

رشک ² rəshk *m.* manage; scab

رشکه rishḵá *f.* ☞ رشقه

رش لری rəshlə́raj *m.* bath-house attendant

رشوت rishvát *m. Arabic* bribe رشوت اخيستل، رشوت خورل to take a
bribe رشوت ورکول to give a bribe, bribe

رشوت خور rishvatkhór *m.* رشوتخور bribe-taker, corrupt official

رشوت خوري، رشوتخوري rishvatkhorí *f.* bribery, bribe-taking,
corruption

رشوه rishvá *f. Arabic* ☞ رشوت

رشه ¹ rə́sha *f.* **1** custom, tradition **2** personality, character

رشه ² rə́sha *f.* food, provisions

رشه ³ rə́sha *f.* cream

رشه ⁴ rashá *f.* **1** pile of corn, grain (on the threshing floor) **2**
threshing

رشي ¹ rə́shi *feminine plural of* رشه ¹,²,³

رشي ² rashé *feminine plural of* رشه ⁴

رشيد rashíd *Arabic* **1** manly; valorous, brave **2** *m. proper name*
Rashid

رښ raḵh *m.* juice; extract

رښتنگلوي raḵhtəngalví *f.* رښتنگي riḵhtinagí *f.* correctness, right;
justice

رښتننج raḵhtənə́naj *m.* **1** proof **2** checking, investigation رښتننی
کول a to prove پر رښتننی کول b to check, investigate

رښتنی ¹ riḵhtináj rəḵhtənáj ☞ رښتين

رښتنی ² rəḵhtəní *f.* faith; veracity

رښتون riḵhtún ☞ رښتين

رښتونی riḵhtúnaj **1** sincere, veritable, true زما ټولي خبري رښتوني دي
riḵhtúni I am telling the truth. **2** honest

رښتيا riḵhtjā́ **1** *f.* truth, verity رښتيا ويل to speak the truth چه رښتيا
ووايم … چه ده همدا رښتيا to tell the truth; I have to admit that I …
The way it is is this; Truth to tell رښتيا په indeed, in actuality **2**
really and truly کاشکي رښتيا خوب وای! Oh, if it only were only a
dream! **3** *attributive* رښتيا خبره ده چه the way it is, is this تول رښتيا
رښتيا خبره دا ده Why don't you tell the whole truth? خبره ولي نه کوي؟
truth to tell; the truth is that رښتيا حال ويل to tell it the way it was
رښتيا کېدل to try to justify, come true

رښتياگلوي riḵhtjā́glaví *f.* **1** sincerity **2** dedication

رښتياگو riḵhtjā́gó **1** truth to tell **2** ☞ رښتياگوی

رښتياگوی riḵhtjā́gój veracious

رښتياگو ¹ riḵhtjā́nó ☞ رښتياگو

رښتياني riḵhtjā́náj genuine, sincere يوه رښتياني قصه the genuine truth
هغه رښتياني او ستر ليکوال دئ He is a really great writer.

رښتياوالی riḵhtjāvā́laj *m.* correctness, veracity

رښتيا وينکی riḵhtjā́ vajúnkaj correct, right

رښتين riḵhtín **1** faithful, dedicated; sincere **2** true, right **3** correct,
veritable

رښتينواله riḵhtinvā́la *f.* رښتينتيا riḵhtintjā́ *f.* rightness, trueness;
correctness, veracity

رښتينگلوي riḵhtingalví *f.* ☞ رښتيا گلوي

رښتينه riḵhtína *f.* truth, fidelity, correctness

رښتيني riḵhtináj ☞ رښتين

رښک rəḵhk *m.* mark, line

رښکه rə́ḵhka *f.* **1** ☞ رښک **2** stripe

رښکی rəḵhkáj *f.* **1** stripe **2** tape, ribbon; braid, lace

رښېدل rəḵhedál *intransitive* [*past:* ورښېده] to be frightened (of);
recoil in fear

رصد rasád *m. Arabic astronomy* observation

رصدخانه rasadkhāná *f.* observatory

رضا rizā́ *f.* razā́ *Arabic* **1.1** *f.* wish, desire; will خپله رضا کوئ do as you wish په خپله رضا according to one's own wishes خوښه او رضا سره voluntarily *compound verb* څوک رضا کول convince, persuade someone هغه مي رضا کړي ده I convinced her **1.2** *m. proper name* Riza **2** *predicative* **.1** pleasing, likeable دا داسي کار وکه I don't like this matter. زما رضا ندئ **2.2** satisfied چه دوی له تا رضا وي Behave so that they will be satisfied with you.

رضاکار rizākár *m.* razākár *m.* **1** volunteer **2** amateur (in art); a fancier

رضا کارانه rizākārāná razākārāná **1.1** voluntary **1.2** amateur **2** voluntarily

رضامندي rizāmandí *f.* رضایت rizāját *m. Arabic* satisfaction; gratitude د هغو څخه يي رضامندي وکړه He expressed his gratitude to them.

رضائي rizāí ورور foster, half-brother

رطب ratb rutb *Arabic* **1** green; fresh **2** *m.* **.1** green foliage **2.2** ripe figs

رطل ratl *m. Arabic* ratl (measure of weight)

رطوبت rutubát *m. Arabic* **1** dampness; moisture **2** showers (of rain, snow)

رعایا ru'ājā́ *m. Arabic of* رعیت

رعایت ri'āját *m. Arabic* **1** execution, observance of something د مقرراتو رعایت کول to execute decisions *compound verb* رعایتبدل *compound verb* ☞ رعایت کېدل to be observed **2** respect (for the law)

رعایتول ri'ājatavól *denominative* [*past:* رعایت یي کړ] to execute, observe د غذائي رژیم رعایتول to observe a diet, keep to a diet

رعب ru'b *m. Arabic* رعب داد ra'bdāb *m. regional* **1** horror, fear **2** greatness **3** strength, force

رعد ra'd *m. Arabic* thunder

رعنا ra'nā́ *Arabic* beautiful; nice-looking

رعنا زبا ra'nāzebā́ *f.* yellow dogrose, afghan dogrose, *Rosa Lutea*

رعناگی ra'nāgáj *m.* bluethroat (a kind of bird)

رعیت ra'ját *m. Arabic* [*plural:* رعایا ru'ājā́] **1** subject; nationals; entire population **2** farmer; peasant; non-tenant farmer (in India) **3** *history* the territory of Britain په رعیت ملک کښی in British India; on British territory

رعیتي ra'jatí *f.* nationality, allegiance; citizenship

رغ ¹ ragh clear, evident

رغ ² ragh *m.* punishment, retribution

رغ ³ ragh *m.* ☞ راغه

رغا raghā́ *f.* **1** medical treatment **2** sewing; needle-work, embroidery

رغاو rəghā́v *m.* break or rupture in relations

رغاوه raghāvə́ **1** *imperfect of* رغول **2** *m. plural* ☞ رغاو

رغاونيز rghāvníz splendid, sumptuous (of things)

رغبت raghbát *m. Arabic* desire, aspiration رغبت کول to wish for something; aspire to something

رغتیا raghtjā́ *f.* ☞ روغتیا

رغدی rəghdaj bright guy, smart fellow

رغرند rghərónd **1** rolling **2** *m.* slope, incline

رغرول rghəravól *transitive* [*past:* و یی رغراوه] **1** to open (the eyes) هري خوا ته سترګي رغرول to look all around, look about **2** to turn, move, turn over تېره رغرول to roll along, roll (somewhere else) *idiom* اوبه خوله رغرول to rinse the mouth out

رغړی رغړی سترګي rghəŕj: protruding eyes

رغرېدل rghəredól *intransitive* [*past:* و رغړیده] **1** to open (of eyes); be open **2** to turn over; roll along, roll to another place اوخ په اوخ رغړېدل to toss and turn ☞ رغنتل

رغړېده rghəredó *m. plural* **1** opening (the eyes) **2** turning, moving, turning over

رغنت ¹ rghəkht *imperfect of* رغنتل

رغنت ² rghəkht *m.* **1** rolling, rolling down **2** floundering around

رغنت پته rəghə́kht paṭá *computer science f.* scroll bar

رغنتل rghəkhtól *intransitive* [*present:* رغړي *past:* و رغنت] **1** to roll, roll down **2** to turn, move, turn over; flounder around

رغلی rghəláj *m.* hearth; iron tripod (for a kettle)

رغندی rghə́ndaj *m.* lower end of the gullet

رغو raghó *oblique plural of* راغه

رغوس rghus *m.* black kid (goat)

رغوست rgust *m.* black color, color black

رغول raghavól *denominative, transitive* [*past:* روغ یي کړ] **1** to sew **2** to cure (of), treat (medically); heal **3** to repair, correct, set rights **4** to form, create (new words)

رغون raghún *m.* **1** medical treatment **2** deliverance

رغونه raghavóna *f.* **1** sewing, needle-work **2** curing, treatment, healing **3** healing (of wounds), mending **4** repair, correction **5** formation (of new words)

رغه raghá *f.* ☞ راغه

رغی ¹ rəgáj *m.* ☞ رغونه

رغی ² ragáj **1** shallow (of a vessel) **2** *m.* saucer

رغی ³ rgáj *f.* soot, lamp-black

رغبدل raghedól *denominative, intransitive* [*past:* روغ شو] **1** to be sewn **2** to be given medical treatment, be healed, be cured; make a complete recovery from **3** to mend (of a wound) **4** to be repaired, be fixed **5** to be formed (of a word) **6** to be broken off (e.g., of ties) د خپله څخه نه رغبدل not to break off with kin

رغبدن raghedán *m.* رغبدنه raghedə́na *f.* **1** sewing, needle-work **2** medical treatment, recovery; healing **3** mending (of a wound) **4** repair; correction, setting right **5** a construction **6** breaking off (ties) *idiom* د زخمي زړه رغبدن comfort, consolation

رف raf *m. Arabic* shelf for belongings

رفاقت rafākát *m. Arabic* **1** sympathy, empathy **2** comradeship; friendship رفاقت یی سره وننیت They became friends. **3** journeying together, accompaniment د چا سره رفاقت کول **a** to work together with someone; cooperate with someone **b** to accompany someone

رفاه rifãh *f. Arabic* well-being, prosperity مجلس رفاه *madzhlís-i* The Economic Counsel (in Afghanistan)

رفتار raftãr *m.* **1** treatment, manner (towards) **2** conduct رفتار كول *a* to treat, behave towards د چا سره ښه رفتار كول to treat someone well **b** to conduct oneself, operate, act **3** flow, current (of a stream) **4** *military* march, attack; compassion **5** movement, travel (of a vehicle, etc.) د لارى رفتار تېز نه و The truck proceeded slowly. **6** gait, walk

رفرندم referendúm *m.* referendum

رفريجرتر rifridzheretãr *m.* refridzherátor refrigerator

رفع raf'a *f. Arabic* **1** discontinuance; surmounting, elimination; getting rid of **2** satisfaction, fulfilment (of requirements, needs) رفع كول *compound verb* **a** to discontinue, cease; overcome, eliminate, remove, get rid of **b** to satisfy, fulfill (requirements, needs) د چا اړيكي رفع كول to satisfy someone's needs تنده رفع كول to quench thirst رفع كېدل *compound verb* **a** to be discontinued, cease, end; be eliminated **b** to be satisfied, be fulfilled (needs, requirements)

رفعت rif'at *m. Arabic* **1** high position; high office; dignity **2** promotion, ascent, rise

رفع دفع ráf'a-dafa *f.* **1** regulation, adjustment **2** punishment, reprisal په رفع دفع د روښانيانو During the reprisals against the Roshani

رفعه ráf'a *f.* ☞ رفع

رفقا rufaќã *Arabic masculine plural of* رفيق

رفل rafl *m. regional* rifle

رفو rufú *m. Arabic* darning; mending, repair (minor) of garments رفو كول to darn, mend, effect minor repairs (to clothing)

رفوگر rufugár *m.* tailor who does minor clothing repair

رفيده rafidá *f.* cloth gloves (for extracting bread from the oven)

رفيق rafiќ *m. Arabic [plural:* رفيقان rafikãn *Arabic plural:* رفقا rufaќã] **1** comrade; friend; traveling companion **2** *proper name* Rafik

رفيقه [1] rafiќã *f.* female friend; comrade (used together with the name)

رفيقه [2] rafíќa *oblique of* رفيق

رفيقي rafiќí *f.* ☞ رفاقت

رقابت raќãbát *m. Arabic* **1** competition; rivalry آزاد رقابت free competition **2** contest *idiom* د تسليحاتو رقابت، تسليحاتي رقابت the arms race

رقاص raќќãs *m. Arabic* **1** dancer **2** pendulum (of a clock)

رقبه raќabã *f. Arabic* area, territory; zone د آستريا رقبه territory of Austria د ځنگلونو رقبه wooden area; forested area

رقت riќќãt *m. Arabic* **1** sensitivity **2** sympathy, compassion; commiseration

رقت انگېز riќќatangéz رقت آور riќќatãvár touching, affecting; pathetic

رقص raќs *m. Arabic* dance رقص كول *a* to dance **b** *figurative* to flash (light-rays)

رقص ځاى raќsdzãj *m.* dance floor; area set off for dancing

رقصول raќsavól *transitive [past:* وي رقصاوه] to make dance, dance

رقصي raќsí pertaining to dance, dance-, dancing-

رقعه ruќ'a *f. Arabic* note د مېلمستيا رقعه invitation عذريه رقعه *uzrijá* note of apology

رقم raќám *m. Arabic [plural:* رقمونه raќamúna *Arabic plural:* ارقام arќãm] **1** numeral; sign **2** sum **3** kind, type; aspect څه رقم What kind? د بل رقم of a different kind or sort, every conceivable sort of **4** *history* royal decree

رقه ruќá *f.* ☞ رقعه

رقيب raќíb *Arabic* **1** *m.* rival; contestant, competitor **2.1** rival; competing **2.2** contending

رقيبانه raќibãná **1** rival, competing **2** contending

رقيق raќíќ *Arabic* **1** liquid, diluted **2** rarefied

رقيمه raќimá *f. Arabic* letter, message

رقيه ruќќijá *f. proper name* Rukkiya

رک ruk rǝk clear; open; frank رک سرى direct, straightforward or sincere man

ركاب rikãb *m. Arabic* stirrup, stirrups

ركابى rǝkãbaj *m.* ☞ ركېبي

ركات rǝkãt *m. religion* rakat (the fixed Moslem prayer ritual)

ركاټ rikãṭ *m.* ☞ ريكاړه

ركروغ rǝkrógh ☞ روغجوړ رك روغ

ركشا rikshã *m.* rickshaw

ركشاسايكل rikshãsãjkl *m.* pedicab (rickshaw powered by a bicycle)

ركنه [1] rakkh *m.* ☞ ركنبه rǝkkha *f.* **1** track, trail, trace, sign **2** branch (of the economy) **3** path

ركنبه [2] rikkhã *m.* ☞ ركشا

ركعت rak'át *m. Arabic* ☞ ركات

ركن rukn *m. Arabic [plural:* اركان arќãn] **1** support, pillar, column **2** member (of an organization) **3** organ (of an enterprise, institution)

ركو ruko *f.* ركوع ruku' *f. Arabic religion* genuflexion, deep bow made during namaz (i.e., a Moslem prayer)

ركود ruќud *m. Arabic* **1** depression **2** dead lock (in talks)

ركېب rǝkéb *m.* ☞ ركاب

ركېب تسمه rǝkebtasmá *f.* stirrup strap

ركېبي rǝkebãj *m.* ركېبى rǝkebãj *f.* small dish; saucer

ركيك rakík *Arabic* indecent (words)

رگ rag *m.* **1** vein; artery; blood vessel د رگ كلكېدل *medicine* arteriosclerosis رگ وهل *a* to let blood **b** to vaccinate (smallpox) **c** *euphemism* to take care of "natures needs" محمود ولاكه بيا رگ ووهي Mahmud will not survive. **2** *mining* vein **3** *biology* species **4** *botany* vein, rib (of a leaf) د زړه رگونه *d* heart-strings زړونو رگونه خوځول to move, disturb the heart or the soul (of song, music) رگ پالل to maintain communications with the wife's relatives

رگوړى rigóṛaj *m.* weakling (of a child)

رګه rága *f.* **1** way, road ولي جان رګه پسي رااخيستي وه Vali-jan followed me. **2** track, print (foot) د یو شي رګه اخيستل to track something down

رګی ¹ ragáj *m.* intimacy; relationship رګي چلول, رګي کول to become related to; become close, become intimate with رګ ☞ رګی پالل and رګ پالل

رګي ² ragí **1** injured, hurt لاس مي رګي سوئ دئ I hurt my hand. **2** worn out, tired out (from hard work)

رګی ³ ragə́j *f.* difficult road

رم ram **1** fearful, timorous **2** *m.* **.1** fear, fright **2.2** shying, jumping to one side

رمباره rambā́ṛa *f.* **1** bellow; bleating رمباري وهل to bellow; beat **2** tsound of a siren

رمبکه rambə́ka *f.* shoots, greens غنم لا رمبکي دي The wheat has just sprouted.

رمبکی ¹ rambəkáj *m.* bellowing

رمبکی ² rambəkáj *m.* rural policeman, part-time constable

رمبوسی rambosáj *m.* **1** musk **2** musk-cleer

رمبه rambá *f.* **1** ☞ برمه **2** ☞ رمبی

رمبی rambáj *m.* **1** *agriculture* hoe, chopper رمبی کول, رمبی وهل to weed **2** leather-cutting knife

رمت ramə́ṭ *tautological with* روغ

رمز ramz *m.* Arabic [*plural:* رمزونه ramzúna *Arabic plural:* رموز rumúz *plural:* رموزات rumuzā́t] **1** secret ته چوک په رمز بنه پوهول to initiate someone into a secret **2** hint, allusion **3** stenography **4** riddle

رمزنویسي ramznavisí *f.* **1** stenography **2** cryptography, secret writing

رمضان ramazā́n *m.* Arabic **1** Ramadan (the ninth month of the lunar year; the month of the Fast); **2** *personal name* Ramadan, Ramazan

رمند ramə́nḍ ☞ برمند

رموز rumúz *m.* Arabic plural from رمز

رموزات rumuzā́t *m.* Arabic second plural from رموز

رمول ramavə́l *transitive* [*past:* و یې رماوه] **1** to drive the cattle to pasture **2** to frighten

رمه ramá *f.* flock (of sheep, goats), herd

رمه وال ramavál *m.* **1** cattle breeder **2** wholesale buyer, cattle buyer

رمی ¹ rə́maj *m.* usually plural **1** mucus **2** diarrhea, dysentery

رمی ² ramáj *paired word with* روغ

رمی ³ ramáj *f.* ☞ رمی ¹

رمی تون rəmajtún *m.* hospital

رمیدل ramedə́l *intransitive* [*past:* و رمبده] **1** to go together, go in a herd (to the pasture) **2** to be frightened, be startled (or, for a horse, to shy) **3** to wander; roam

رمیده ramedə́ *m. plural* **1** freight, startling (of a horse) **2** roaming, wandering

رمیز rəmíz *m.* ☞ رمز

رناګي ranāgáj *m.* ☞ رعناګي

رنبی rambáj *m.* ☞ رنبي

رنت rant *m.* رنټ ranṭ *m.* rent, income (from real estate, land, investments, etc.)

رنج randzh *m.* torment, suffering

رنجرومه randzhrúma *f.* ☞ رنجوني

رنجک randzhák *m.* **1** fine powder; priming device, touchhole رنجک الوزول to ignite the priming device; **2** primer, fuse رنجک والوت the rifle misfired

رنجک دان randzhakdā́n *m.* fire pan (the receptacle for the priming of a gun in a flint rifle)

رنجکی randzhakə́j *f.* powder horn (or powder flask)

رنجنونی randzhənúnaj *m.* رنجوني randzhúnaj *m.* mascara box

رنجه rə́ndzha *f.* **1** small stripe (fabric) **2** rag

رنځ randz *m.* **1** sickness, ailment; **2** consumption, tuberculosis; رنځ شوی consumptive, tubercular; **3** distress, offense

رنځره randzṛə́ *plural* tar

رنځړی randzə́ṛaj رنځمن randzmə́n رنځور randzúr **1.1** sick, ill **1.2** distressed, pained رنځوری زره grief, affliction **2** *m.* patient, sick person

رنځورتون randzurtún *m.* clinic

رنځورغاړی randzurghā́ṛaj sickly, unhealthy

رنځورول randzuravə́l *denominative, transitive* ☞ رنځول

رنځوري randzurí *f.* ill-health; sickliness له رنځوری راپاڅیدل to recover, get better

رنځوریدل randzuredə́l *denominative, intransitive* [*past:* رنځور شو] to fall ill (usually with tuberculosis)

رنځول randzavə́l *transitive* [*past:* و یې رنځاوه] **1** to distress, hurt **2** to make ill

رنځیدل randzedə́l *intransitive* [*past:* و رنځېد] **1** to grieve; be offended; be upset **2** to contract tuberculosis

رند rənd rind **1.1** negligent; careless **1.2** depraved **2.1** fast-liver, playboy **2.2** depraved person **2.3** cheat, rogue

رندر rundar *f. dialect* ☞ ورېندار، ورېنداره

رندکه randə́ka *f.* jet, stream (of water)

رنده randá *f.* rəndá plane (carpenter's tool)

رندي rindi *f.* **1** dissolute life; dissipation **2** trickery, swindling

رندي خانه rindikhānā *f.* brothel

رنډ rənḍ **1** *m.* persistency, doggedness رنډ کول a to display persistency b to entreat, prevail upon **2** dogged; insistent

رنډیدل ranḍedə́l *denominative, intransitive* [*past:* رنډ شو] to persist, be dogged

رنګ rang *m.* **1** color, coloring هلک د رنګه ډېر تور و The boy was very dark-skinned. رنګ يې سپین وتنبتید He grew suddenly pale. په رنګ خرابیدل a to fade b رنګ بایلل to fade بدرنګ bloodstained وینو رنګ to turn out to be false (e.g., of reports) رنګ ورکیدل a to fade, lose color b to be missing, disappear **2** paint, dye رنګ ورکول to paint, dye, color **3** ink **4** shoe-polish; wax **5** manner, way, procedure رنگ ده؟ In what way? How? دغه رنگ thus, in this way همداسي رنگه This is the way. Here's the way. **6** kind, type; aspect رنگ په رنگ، رنگ پرنگ، رنگ رنگ of every kind, various, every conceivable, all kinds of بل رنگ پیداکول to accept another method, change, alter; be transformed انقلابي رنگ ورکول to revolutionize **7** *figurative* brilliance; charm, attractiveness *idiom* د چا رنگ الوتل to spread false rumors رنگ اچول to be embarassed; feel shy; be ashamed of someone د چا رنگ بدول to shame someone, disgrace someone رنگ بدبدل، رنگ ژبړبدل to disgrace oneself, cover oneself with shame د چا رنگ ښه کبدل to become well-known, become famous رنگ ورکبدل to disappear, get lost

رنگارنگ rangāráng **1** various, variegated **2** particolored; many colored, motley

رنگارنگي rangārangí *f.* diversity; diversity of colors

رنگ آمېزي rangāmezí *f.* **1** selection of colors; color scheme; coloration; gamut of colors **2** embellishment

رنگ پنگ rangpáng stained (with blood, etc.)

رنگټ rangə́ṭ weeping; sobbing; whimpering رنگټ وهل to weep; sob; whimper

رنگدار rangdā́r ☞ رنگین

رنگرېز rangréz *m.* dyer

رنگرېزي rangrezí dyeing

رنگړۍ rangṛáj rangeṛáj **1** sparse; scattered **2** rare, seldom رنگړۍ وبښته sparse or thin hair **3** loose **4** beaten down (by hail); fallen, beaten down, lodged (of crops) رنگړۍ کول **a** to thin out, weed out (crops) **b** to loosen, hoe **c** to beat down (hail); knock down (crops) رنگړۍ کبدل **a** to be thinned out, weeded out (crops) **b** to be loosened **c** to be knocked down; be lodged (crops) *idiom* رنگړۍ باران freezing rain

رنگژړۍ rangzhã́raj disgraced

رنگمال rangmā́l *m.* house painter, decorator

رنگوټ rangúṭ *m. regional* recruit, rookie

رنگول rangavә́l *denominative, transitive* [*past:* رنگ یې کړ] **1** to color, paint, decorate **2** to clean with shoe-polish, wax

رنگون rangún *m.* Rangoon

رنگه rangá colored; colorful د سینما رنگه فلم color film *idiom* رنگه فلزات non-ferrous metal

رنگه ránga *combining form* colored سور رنگه red

رنگه لیدانی rangálidā́nay *computer science m.* color monitor

رنگی rangáj ¹ ☞ رنگړۍ

رنگي rangí ² *f.* painting, coloring

رنگی rángaj ³ ☞ رنگه

رنگیځ rangidz ¹ ☞ رنگېز

رنگبدل rangedә́l *denominative, intransitive* [*past:* رنگ شو] **1** to be painted, be colored **2** to be cleared with shoe-polish, wax

رنگېز razgíz **1** beautiful; colorful **2** bright

رنگین rangín **1** colored; multi-colored, varicolored **2** colorful, bright **3** dyed, decorated

رنگین چاپگر rangínchápgár *computer science m.* color printer

رنگيني ranginí *f.* colorfulness; brightness; beauty

رڼه rә́na *f.* traingular section of land

رڼ raṇ ¹ *m.* hide, skin, pelt

رڼ ruṇ ² ☞ رون ¹

رڼا raṇā́ ruṇā́ **1** *f.* [*plural:* رڼاوي raṇā́vi *plural:* ruṇā́vi *plural:* رڼاګاني raṇāgā́ni *plural:* ruṇāgā́ni] **.1** light, radiance تته رڼا dim light رڼا ورکول to gleam, radiate **1.2** flash (of a gunshot, etc.) **1.3** illumination طبیعي رڼا کول، طبیعي رڼا natural illumination, natural light برقي رڼا، د بجلی رڼا electric light; electrical illumination رڼا کول *compound verb* to light up, light (electric lightbulb); illuminate رڼا کبدل *compound verb* to brighten; light up په برق وسیله سره رڼا کېږي to illumine with electricity **1.4** brightness **1.5** *figurative* flash, ray, gleam **1.6** *proper name* Runa **2** *attributive regional vice* رڼه¹ **2** *attributive* به رڼا ورځ، د رڼا ورځ bright day د رڼا اچول in broad daylight هغه واقعاتو په رڼا کبنې In the light of these occurrences په واقعاتو باندي رڼا اچول to throw some light on the situation د سترګو رڼا سبزل to weaken or deteriorate the vision

رڼا نوستونکی raṇā́ nustúnkaj illuminating رڼا ګروپ reflector (light house, beacon)

رڼائي raṇā́i *f.* illumination (of a city)

رڼايي سپنسیز مزي raṇājí spaṇsíz mázi *computer science f. plural* fiber optic cable

رڼغوني raṇəghúne *f.* dim, weak light; gleam

رڼکی raṇakáj ¹ *m.* mammiform bone

رڼکی raṇakáj ² *m.* **1** crystal **2** mica

رڼول raṇavә́l *transitive* [*past:* وي یې رڼاوه] **1** to light up; illuminate; illumine **2** to polish; burnish **3** to open wide, open up (the eyes) **4** to ignite, light, see fire to

رڼوني raṇunáj *m.* clear water

رڼوونکی raṇavúnkaj **1** *present participle of* رڼول **2** *m.* polisher

رڼه raṇá ¹ *feminine singular of* رون ¹

رڼه rə́ṇa ² *f.* ☞ ریځه

رڼی raṇaj ¹ *m.* orchid

رڼی raṇé ² *feminine plural of* رون ¹

رڼبدل raṇedә́l *intransitive* [*past:* ورڼبده] **1** to light up; shine **2** to be polished

رو rav ¹ *m.* **1** motion, movement د رو ګودر پیدا کول to find a ford **2** flock of quails **3** way, track, path **4** resolution (of a problem) *idiom* ورینی رو beforehound, in good time د خبري رو بدلول to direct the conversation in another direction

رو ru ² *m.* ☞ روی ¹

رو ro ³ *f.* ☞ روح

رو ro ⁴ *f.* aluminum

رو ro ⁵ *Eastern* ☞ ورو

روا ١ ravā **1** permitted, allowed; acceptable, accepted روا کول to permit, allow روا کېدل to be permitted, be allowed; be accepted روا ګڼل، روا لرل to consider as allowable, deem permissble; regard as acceptable **2** legal, just **3** correct

روا ٢ rvā́ *f.* ☞ ورا

روابط ravābít *Arabic masculine plural of* رابطه

رواج ravā́dzh *Arabic* **1** *m.* **.1** walking, going, circulation **1.2** sale **1.3** custom; tradition رواج لرل **a** to be accepted; be prevalent **b** to be in motion; be popular, move well (of goods) رواج مېندل to be disseminated; take root; penetrate **2** *attributive* **.1** accepted; widespread **2.2** marketable (goods)

رواجول ravā́dzhavál *denominative* [*past:* رواج يې کړ] **1** to put into circulation **2** to sell **3** to introduce a custom, inoculate; disseminate

رواجي ravā́dzhí **1** accepted, generally accepted; widespread **2** popular, marketable (of goods)

رواجېدل ravā́dzhedál *denominative, intransitive* [*past:* رواج شو] **1** to be in circulation; circulate **2** to be saleable **3** to become customary, be inoculated; be widespread, be disseminated

روادار ravādā́r **1** approving; recognizing روادار کېدل to approve, recognize, agree **2** gracious, merciful ☞ پېرزو

رواداري ravādārí *f.* approval; recognition

رواش ravā́sh *m.* edible rhubarb

رواشه ډوډۍ ravā́sha ḍoḍə́j lavash (a square flat loaf resembling Armenian bread)

راولپنډي ravālpinḍí *f.* Rawalpindi

روان ١ ravā́n rəvā́n **1** going; moving; proceeding somewhere **2** flowing; running **3** flowing; connected (of verses) **4** fluent (in language) په پښتو رواني خبري کول to speak Pashto fluently **5** carrying on, conducting (of disputes, conversations, battle) **6** effective (of a law) *idiom* روان کول the current year روان نشته ، سکون everything flows along, everything is changing هر شي زوان دئ

روان ٢ rvān *vice* وران

روانشناسي ravānshināsí *f.* **1** knowledge of the temperament, customs and life of a people **2** psychology

روانګي ravangi *f. regional* **1** movement, progression **2** departure, going away

روانول ravānaval *denominative, transitive* [*past:* روان يې کړ] **1** to set out; move; start up (a car) **2** to take, carry away (with one) زه يې د خانه سره کورته روان کړم He took me to his house. **3** to learn by heart

روانه ravāná **1** going, proceding; bound for روانه کول to direct (to, at); send, despatch; transport; transfer روانه کېدل to get under way; set out; transfer, relocate **2** *f.* passport

رواني ١ ravāní *f.* **.1** smoothness (of verse) **1.2** smooth, fluent reading **2** *attributive* beginning to learn (of a child)

رواني ٢ ravāní *m. plural* ☞ لوهاني

روانېدل ravānedál *denominative, intransitive* [*past:* روان شو] **1** to get under way; move; start up; depart, go away; sail away; leave **2** to

flow, flow through **3** to be about, turn on (of a speech) په خبره ... دي موضوع روانه شوه چه The talk was that ...

روانېده ravānedə́ *m. plural* **1** departure, leaving; sailing; setting out, embarkation **2** flowing through

روايت rivāját *m. Arabic* [*plural:* روايات rivājāt] **1** tradition, legend, narration په روايت سره according to legend **2** tradition

روب ١ rub *m. military* aiguillette, aglet

روب ٢ rob *m.* mouthful, swallow (of water)

روبرو rubarú face to face; opposite facing

روپو rupó *oblique plural of* روپۍ

روپوش runúsh *m.* rupósh coverlet, blanket

روپۍ rupə́j *f.* **1** rupee (monetary unit in India and Pakistan, and also formerly in Afghanistan) **2** money په روپو رانيول to purchase روپۍ باشل **a** to be generous, be munificent **b** to throw money about

روټ roṭ *m.* short bread

روټاک roṭā́k **1** careless; negligent **2** niggardly, stingy

روټاکتوب roṭāktób *m.* روټاکوالی roṭakvā́laj *m.* **1** carelessness; negligence **2** niggardliness, stinginess

روټه róṭa *f.* روټۍ roṭə́j *f.* **1** bread (usually of barely) ډبله روټه loaf of bread **2** food, victuals روټۍ ته کښېناستو *regional* He sat down to dine.

روټۍغپ roṭəjgháp gluttonous

روجايي rudzhāí *f.* sheet

روجه rodzhá *f. dialect* ☞ روژه

روځ rvadz *f. Western* [*plural:* روځي rvádzi] day بله روځ on the following day يوه روځ once, one day يوه روځ yesterday پرون روځ after په لرو روځو sometimes په دې نژدي روځو کي one morning سهار several days روځ په روځ from day to day په لس روځي for ten days روځ **a** لويه روځ دخوا by day يوه روځ تر مينځ in a day, after a day holiday **b** نوي روځ Sunday New year, Nevruz **c** *religion* Judgement Day له بدي روځي unfortunately روځ يې وګرزبده His luck changed. روځ نه درلودل to idle, loaf روځ ګډول to not enjoy life (because of too much emphasis on work)

روځن raudzán *m.* ☞ مکن

روځباره rvadzbā́ra *f.* daily wages

روځ تېری ١ rvadztéraj losing time to no purpose

روځتېري ٢ rvadzterí *f.* loss of time

روځنی rvadzanáj *Western* daily; everyday; diurnal روځني اخبار daily newspaper د کارونو روځني ترتيب، د کارونو روځني پروګرام the order of the day, the schedule for the day روځني ژوند daily life

روځ و شپه rvadz-o-shpá *f.* a day and a night, twenty-four hour period

روح ruh *m. Arabic* [*plural:* روحونه ruhúna *plural:* روحان ruhā́n *Arabic plural:* ارواح arvā́h] **1** spirit عسکري روح warlike, martial spirit د دوستي له روح سره in the spirit of friendship د روح غذا spiritual nourishment د سپين بيري روح والوت the old man took heart; the old man cheered up **2** soul **3** breeze, zephyr

روحاً rúhán *Arabic* spiritually; morally

روحاني ruhaní *Arabic* **1** *m.* [*plural:* روحانيان ruhānijā́n *m. Arabic m. plural:* روحانيون ruhānijún] **.1** clergyman **1.2** *plural* clergy **2** *attributive* .1 spiritual, ideological, high-principled (of a leader) **2.2** intellectual, mental; religious

روحانيت ruhāniját *m. Arabic* **1** spirituality, incorporeality **2** ecclesiastical rank, spiritual office په روحانيت شاملېدل to accept ecclesiastical office **3** the spiritual life **4** sanctity

روح پرور ruhparvár **1** invigorating, bracing روح پرور نسيم breeze, zephyr **2** inspiring, vivifying, encouraging, life-giving

روح پېژندونکى ruh pezhandúnkaj *m.* psychologist

روحنواز ruhnaváz inspiring روحنوازه آهنگ cheerful or inspiring melody

روحي ruhí *Arabic* **1** spiritual, religious, moral **2** mental, psychical روحي حال spiritual condition روحي خپورتيا spiritual, mental, psychic disorder روحي تحليل psychoanalysis

روحيات ruhijā́t *m. Arabic plural* psychology

روحياتي ruhijātí **1** spiritual, intellectual, psychical **2** spiritual, intellectual, psychological

روحيه ruhijá *f. Arabic* spirit, moral, spiritual condition, mood, morale

روخ ¹ rokh *m.* side

روخ ² rokh *Eastern* appropriate, fitting

روخ ³ rukh *m.* opposition روخ کول to show opposition, oppose

روخى rókhaj *m. Western* side (in competition, etc.)

رود ¹ rod rud **1** river; small stream ووړ رود brook **2** *figurative* stream, flow (of tears)

رود ² ravd *imperfect of* رودل

رود ravd *past stem of* رودل

رودبار rodbā́r *m.* **1** flood-plain of a river **2** strait

رودباري rodbārí رودباري مځکه land which is watered by a river, land periodically inundated

رودخانه rodkhāná *f.* channel or bed of a river

روداد rudā́d *m.* ☞ روداد لیکل روی داد to illuminate

رودل ravdál rəvdál *transitive [present:* روي رود یی و *past:* rəví *past:* rod یی و] **1** to suckle (the breast) **2** ☞ ربل

رودنگ rodáng *m. botany* madder, *Rubia tinctorim*

رودنه rəvdə́na *f.* suckling (the breast)

رودونى ravdúnaj *m.* motherless lamb

روده ¹ ravdá *f.* **1** way, road **2** sign; trace, track

روده ² ravdə́ *m. plural* suckling (at the breast)

رودي rodí watered by a river رودي مځکه land watered by a river

رودېشيا rodeshijā́ *f.* Rhodesia

روړه róḍa *f.* large intestine

روړه مست roḍamást *m.* indigent, beggar, one who begs for bread

رودېشيا roḍeshijā́ *f.* ☞ رودېشيا

رور ror *m. dialect* ☞ ورور

رورا rorá *m.* Brother!; Friend!; Buddy!

رورو ¹ ravráv *regional* from time to time; sometimes

رورو ² roró *dialect* gradually, slowly

رورولى rorválaj *m.* rorvālí *f. dialect* ☞ وروروالى

روري roṛi *f. dialect* ☞ روري خوري به کو ، حساب تر ميانځ ورورې *proverb* It pays to be thrifty.

روړى roṛáj *m.* piece of rubble, piece of brick; adobe brick, piece of quarry stone

روز ¹ roz *m.* life, existence د هغه د لاسه زه روز نه لرم He makes life impossible for me.

روز ² rvaz *f. dialect* ☞ روخ

روز roz *combining form* day روزنامه a diary b journal (trade, business)

روزافزون rozafzún getting larger every day, growing

روزانه rozāná **1** *f.* daily pay **2** daily, everyday; commonplace روزانه کار و بار everyday problems; life's vanities **3** *adverb* daily

روزگار rozgā́r *m.* **1** time, epoch, century **2** existence, life **3** occupation; work

روزل rozə́l *transitive [past:* و یې روزه] **1** to educate **2** to develop (the mind, abilities, etc.) **3** to raise (sheep, etc.) **4** to care for (children, the sick); look after (children, a patient) **5** to train, prepare (personnel), nurse, foster

روزمره rozmará **1** daily, everyday; usual, commonplace د ژوند روزمره کارونه life's cares **2** daily, each day, everyday

روزنامچه roznāmchá *f.* **1** diary **2** journal (trade, business)

روزنامه roznāmá *f.* newspaper

روزنامه نگاري roznāmanigārí *f.* journalist (female) په روزنامه نگاري گوتي پوري کول to work as a journalist

روزنتون rozəntún *m.* safeguarding motherhood and babydom

روزنځای rozəndzā́j *m.* rozə́ndzáj *m.* **1** animal farm, livestock farm, nursery **2** fish-pond **3** educational institution

روزنه ¹ rozə́na *f.* **1** education, upbringing **2** development (of an ability, skill, etc.) بدني روزنه physical development; physical exercises ذهني روزنه intellectual development, education **3** raising (sheep, etc.) د پسه روزنه sheep-raising **4** care (of children, patients, etc.); looking after, nursing (children, patients) **5** training (personnel)

روزنه ² rozaná *f.* **1** window, skylight; opening (in a roof) **2** doors (of a car, a cupboard)

روزونکى rozúnkaj **1** *present participle of* روزل **2** *m.* tutor, educator

روزه ¹ rozá *f.* ☞ روژه

روزه ² rozə́ *imperfect of* روزل

روزه ³ rozá *imperfective imperative of* روزل

روزه دار rozadā́r *m.* ☞ روژتي

روزي ¹ rozí *f.* **1** daily bread, subsistence; wages روزي گټل to earn subsistence **2** fate, portion; success

روزي ² rózi *present tense of* روزل

روزي خور rozikhór *m.* **1** animate, living being; man, human being

روزي رسان rozirosán *m.* روزي گر rozigár *m. religion* God

روژتي rozhatáj *m. religion* man who is observing Ramadan

روژه rozhá **1** *f.* **1** fast (among Moslems), Ramadan, abstinence from food روژه نيول، روژي نيول to observe روژه ماتول to break a fast a fast, fast **1.2** Ramadan (the tenth month of the lunar year) **2** *predicative* fasting مونږ روژه وو We fasted.

روژه مات rozhamā́t *m.* روژه ماتی rozhamā́taj *m.* **1** breaking a fast, termination of a fast **2** food which breaks a fast

روږد rugd **1** used to; accustomed to; familiar with, feeling at home with **2** tame, domesticated (animals)

روږد توب rugdtób *m.* روږد تیا rugdtjā́ *f.* روږوالی rugvā́laj *m.* custom; domestication (of an animal)

روږدول rugdavә́l *denominative, transitive* [*past:* روږد یې کړ] **1** to draw into **2** to train, tame (an animal)

روږدی rugdáj ☞ روږد

روږدېدل rugdedә́l *denominative* [*past:* روږد شو] **1** to train oneself, get accustomed to, familiarize oneself with **2** to be trained, be domesticated (of an animal)

روژه rogá́ *f. dialect* ☞ روژه

روبړي بوبړي rógi-bógi chopped up, cut into pieces

روس rus *m.* **1** Russian (person) **2** Russia

رؤسا ruasā́ *Arabic masculine plural of* ریس

وروست rost *Eastern* ☞ وروست

روستاړی rustā́ṛaj *m.* crupper (harness piece in shape of leather loop passing under a horses tail)

روست والی rostvā́laj *m.* ☞ وروست والی

روستول rostavә́l *denominative, transitive* ☞ وروستول

روسته rústa *dialect* ☞ وروسته

روستی rustáj rvustáj rvəstáj *dialect* ☞ وروستی

روستبل rustebál **1** behind, after all **2** *m.* rear, back, hinder part

روستېدل rostedә́l *intransitive* ☞ وروستېدل

روستینی rustináj *dialect* ☞ وروستی

روسي ¹ rusí **1** Russian روسي ژبه the Russian language **2.1** *m.* [*plural:* روسیان rusijā́n] Russian (person) **2.2** *f.* Russian, Russian language

روسی ² rusáj **1** *feminine singular of* روسي ¹ **2** *f.* Russian (female)

روسیه rusijá *m.* Russia شوروي روسیه، سوېت روسیه Soviet Russia سپینه روسیه Belorussia

راویش ravísh *m.* **1** way of acting, conduct **2** way, fashion, mode **3** method, means د علم روش scientific method فلسفي روش philosophic methodology **4** gait **5** step

رووشان ró-shān *dialect vice* وروشان gently, softly

روشان roshán روښان

روشناس rushinā́s **1** *m.* acquaintance **2** well-known

روشنفکر roshanfíkr **1** educated; intellectual **2** *m.* **.1** intellectual [*plural:* روشنفکران roshanfíkrā́n] **2.2** the intelligentsia **2.3** educator

روشني roshaní *f.* light, radiance

روښان roķhán **1.1** luminous, bright, radiant **1.2** educated; intellectual **1.3** brilliant, outstanding (of speech) **1.4** lucid (of the mind) د روښان ذهن خاوند دئ His mind is lucid. روښان کول **2** *m. history* Roshan (nickname of Bayazid Ansari, founder of the Roshani sect)

روښانتیا roķhāntjā́ *f.* ☞ روښاني ²

روښانځون roķhandzún *m.* ☞ روښاني ¹

روښانول roķhānavә́l *denominative, transitive* [*past:* روښان یې کړ] **1** to light, ignite **2** to light up په سره رنا روښانول to illumine **3** to explain, elucidate, clear up; throw light upon (e.g., a question, a problem) **4** to enlighten (the mind)

روښانه roķhā́na **1** enlightened په دې روښانه عصر کښي in our enlightened age **2** *f. proper name* Roshana

روښاني ¹ roķhāní *m.* roķhānáj *history* Roshanite, follower of Roshan (Bayazid Ansari)

روښاني ² roķhāní *f.* clarity; elucidation

روښانېدل roķhānedә́l *denominative, intransitive* [*past:* روښان شو] **1** to light up, catch fire روښان شوي اعلامونه illuminated signs **2** to brighten **3** to be explained, be elucidated, be cleared up; have light thrown on (e.g., a question, problem) **4** to be educated, receive knowledge

روښان roķhán ☞ روښن

روښنای roķhnáí *f.* **1** light, radiance د ستورو روښنايي the radiance of the stars روښنايي اچوونکی دستگاه to illuminate searchlight **2** brilliance, brightness د خپل عقل د روښنايي په وسیله Thanks to his brilliant mind.

روښه roķhá́ *f.* halvah

روښه وال roķhavā́l *m.* seller of halvah or sweets

روضه rauzá *f. Arabic* **1** garden; flowerbed **2** tomb of a saint

روغ rogh **1** healthy, sound, unharmed تل روغ پاتي کېدل to be always healthy, be ever robust د روغ رنځور (ناروغ) خبري سره کول to inquire of one another about the health of relations روغ بدن پاچاهي ده sound mind in a sound body **2** in good order, in good working order, sound **3** healthy, sane

روغبړ roghbáṛ *m.* exchange of greetings د لاسو روغبړ، د لاسونو روغبړ handshake د چا سره روغبړ کول to exchange greetings with someone, greet someone

روغتون roghtún *m.* hospital, clinic; health-care facility

روغتیا roghtjā́ *f.* health عامه روغتیا، د روغتیا ساتنه public health, sanitation د روغتیا د ساتني تشکیلات public health organs د روغتیا وزارت to make a complete recovery, get well ميندل Ministry of Public Health

روغتیاوال roghtjāvā́l *m.* **1** *military* chief of the directorate of military medicine **2** medical inspector

روغجوړ regh-dzhór healthy, fit روغجوړ دي غواړم! I wish you good health! Good health to you!

روغجی róghdzáj *m.* ☞ روغتون

روغ رمټ rogh-raməṭ روغ رمی rogh-rəmáj روغ موټ rogh-moṭ quiet healthy, hale and hearty, fit

روغلیک roghlík *m.* **1** peaceful transaction **2** peace treaty

روغن roghán *m. usually in compounds* **1** lard, fat **2** grease; (polishing) wax; lubricant

روغنداغ، روغن داغ roghandā́gh *m.* saucepan

روغني roghaní 1 greased with a lubricant; waxed, cleaned; cleaned روغني بوټونه cleaned slippers 2 *technology* yielding oil, oleaginous روغني مواد oils

روغنيات roghanijā́t *m. plural* oils, fats

روغ نيتي roghnijatí *f.* amicable relations, benevolent relations

روغوالی roghvā́laj *m.* ☞ روغتيا

روغوبړ roghubár *m.* ☞ روغ وبړ

روغول roghavál *denominative, transitive* [*past:* روغ يې کړ] 1 to pacify, conciliate 2 ☞ رغول

روغوندې róghunde *Eastern* gently

روغه rógha *f.* 1 peace, concord, friendship سره روغه کول to be reconciled with, get along with one another په روغه سره in peace and harmony د چا سره پوره روغه لرل to be in full agreement with someone د چا په بنګابښ روغه کول to be reconciled through someone's mediation 2 state of being easy to get one with 3 health په روغه healthy, sound په روغه ستنبدل to return safe and sound

روغه rógha² *feminine singular of* روغ

روغه غوښتونکی rógha gukhtúnkaj peaceful, peace-loving

روغه کوونکی rógha kavúnkaj *m.* mediator, arbiter

روغبدل roghedál *denominative, intransitive* ☞ رغبدل

روف rauf *Arabic* 1 good, kind 2 *m. proper name* Rauf

روک rok¹ 1 *m.* .1 cash money روک ورکول to pay cash 1.2 he who pays or is paid in cash 2.1 honest, just 2.2 honorable 2.3 pure, unadulterated; genuine

روک ruk² *dialect* ☞ ورک

روړکی rokáj¹ ☞ وروړکی

روگ rog *m.* 1 strap (of a sandal); lace 2 belt; girdle 3 worm-gear, drive-screw (of an oil press)

روگ بوگ rógi-bógi روگي بوگي کول روگ بوگ کول to tear one another's clothing (in the course of a fight); rip the clothing during an attack on a person (of a dog)

روگرداني rugardā́ní *f.* 1 deviation د قانون څخه روگرداني کول to break the law 2 disagreement; opposition

روږه rvə́ga rvúga *f. dialect* ☞ ورږه

رول rol¹ *m.* role مهم رول بازل، مهم رول بازي کول، مهم رول لوبول to play an important role رول ادا کول to execute, play a role

رول rol² *m.* 1 road-roller 2 roll (of a paper etc.) 3 ride (on a horse)

رول rul³ *m.* ruler

روم rəvə́m¹ *first person, present tense singular of* رودل

روم rum² *m. history* 1 Byzantium 2 Turkey د روم بحيره Mediterranean Sea 3 Turkish Seljuk Sultanate

روم rom³ *m.* روما romā́ *f. & m.* Rome

روماتيزم rumā́tízm *m.* rheumatism

رومال rumā́l *m.* 1 towel 2 napkin

رومان román *m.* novel

رومانليکوال románlikvā́l *m.* رومان ليکونکی، رومان ليکوال román likúnkaj *m.* novelist

روماني rumāní¹ 1.1 ☞ رومن 1.2 Romanian 2 *m.* Romanian (person)

روماني romāní romantic, romantical

رومانيا rumānijā́ *f.* رومانيه rumāniá *f.* Romania

رومن román romi' 1 Byzantine 2 overseas, foreign رومي رومن tomatoes 3 Roman, Latin رومن حروف Latin alphabet بانجن

رون run *m.* thigh, femur ☞ ورون

رونتگن rontgán *m.* رونت گن x-ray د رونتگن متخصص roentgenologist

رواندا ruandā́ *f.* Ruanda

رواندی ravəndáj ravandí suffering from diarroea

روند raund *m. regional* 1 beat, regular tour; patrol, patrolling 2 *sports* round 3 turn

رونړ run̓ *regional* ☞ رون¹

رونړه rúna *m. plural regional* ☞ ورونه

رونق ravnák *m. Arabic* 1 brilliance, radiance; beauty 2 prosperity *Eastern* سوداگری ښه رونق لاره Trade has prospered. 3 animation, lively movement په ښار کښي رونق ښکاربده Lively movement was noticed in the city.

رون ruṇ¹ *m.* رونه runá *f.* رڼه raṇá *f. m.* [*plural:* رانه rā́nə *m. plural:* رون ruṇə *f. plural:* روني rúṇi *f. plural:* رڼي raṇe] 1 light, transparent, pure رونه چينه clear spring, pure spring روني سترگي clear eyes 2 bright, brilliant; radiant 3 shining 4 of the first water (diamonds) *idiom* په رون تندي cordially رون گيغ دا يو dawn He has a lucid mind. رون ذهن خاوند

رون rauṇ² *m. regional* 1 cartridge, round رون او بم اورول to subject to gunfire and bombardment 2 ☞ روند

رونا ruṇā́ roṇā́ *f.* ☞ رڼا

رونائي ruṇājí *f.* light; luminescence; brilliance زورور رونائي لرل to emit a strong light, shine (of an electric light bulb)

رونکی ruṇakáj *m.* ☞ رڼکی¹

رونگه rúṇga *f.* temple

رونوالی ruṇvā́laj *m.* ☞ رڼا

رونول ruṇavál *transitive* ☞ رڼول

رونول rauṇavál *denominative, transitive* [*past:* رون يې کړ] to regulate, adjust, put in order

رونه rúṇa *plural Eastern* ☞ ورونه

رونه سترگه rúṇa stárga *f. astronomy* Venus

روني ruṇáj *m.* polishing, buffing

رونبدل ruṇedál *intransitive* ☞ رڼبدل

رونبدل rauṇedál *denominative, intransitive* [*past:* رون شو] to go right, come right, work out well

رؤوس ruús *m. Arabic plural of* رأس

روول rəvavál *transitive* [*past:* و يې رواوه] to suckle, breast feed

رووی rováj¹ *m.* drying room, barn for drying grain

رووی róvaj² *m.* bag, knapsack (for bread)

روه roh *m. history* mountainous part of Afghanistan in Baluchistan

روهلی rohiláj *m.* 1 Afghan 2 mountaineer

روهی roháj rohí 1 mountain, of the mountains 2 *m.* mountaineer

روهبدل rohedál *intransitive* ☞ روهبدل

روهېله rohelá *m. plural* **1** mountaineers, mountain men **2** Afghans

روهيلی rohiláj *m.* ☞ روهلی

روی ¹ ruj *m.* **1** face **2** cause, reason; grounds ددې اطلاع له رويه according to this communication ددې له رويه from this point of view لدې رويه in this respect

روی ² rә́vaj *m.* **1** evil spirit, imp; demon **2** nightmare

روي ³ rәví *present tense of* رودل

روی ⁴ rә́ve *f.* **1** witch **2** bright and sprightly woman

رويبار rujbár *m.* go-between, matchmaker (between prospective marriage partners)

رويباره rujbә́ra *f.* matchmaker (female)

رويباري rujbārí *f.* negotiations of a go-between (for prospective couples); role of a go-between (for a couple)

رويبند rujbánd *m.* face-veil (for a female)

رويت ruját *m. Arabic* **1** seeing with one's own eyes, scrutiny, contemplation; vision **2** reasoning, reflection, understanding

رويجايي rujdzhāí *f.* ☞ روجايي

روبد rved *Western separable part of the verb* اروبدل

رويداد rujdā́d *m.* **1** incident, occurrence سرحدي رويدادونه border incidents **2** record, minutes (of a meeting)

رويدار ¹ rujdā́r **1** respected, esteemed **2** *m.* important person

رويدار ² rujdā́r *m.* ☞ رويداد ²

رويداري rujdārí *f.* **1** respect, esteem; repute; dignity روی داري **2** attention paid to someone **3** flattery, adulation

روبره rәverá *f. dialect* ☞ وربره

رويزه rvezá *f.* maid of honor of the bride (at the wedding)

رويکار rujikā́r **1** working, acting, operating **2** executed, brought about رويکاربدل ☞ روی کار کېدل رويکارول ☞ روی کار کول

رويکارول ¹ rujikāravә́l *denominative, transitive* [*past:* رويکار يې کړ] **1** to act, operate **2** to execute, bring about **3** to carry on (e.g., a controversy)

رويکاربدل ¹ rujikāredә́l *denominative, intransitive* [*past:* رويکار شو] **1** to be in operation **2** to be carried out, come true **3** to be in progress (e.g., a dispute, a controversy)

رويکښ rujkásh *m.* روی کښ rujkáҟh *m.* sheet, cover (for a bed)

رويمال rujmā́l *m. Eastern* kerchief

روين rují̇̄n *m. botany* madder, *Rubia tinctorum*

رويه ¹ ravijá *f. Arabic* **1** mode of action, conduct رويه نيول to conduct oneself, behave, act تاسي کومه رويه نيولي ده؟ How have you decided to act? **2** relationship to someone, something

رويه ² rúja *oblique of* روی ¹

رويهمرفته rujihamraftá in general, in sum ... رويهمرفته ويلای سو چه In general, we can say that ...

روجي rojí *present tense of* رودل

روبدل ruedә́l *intransitive* [*past:* و روبده] to quarrel, start an argument, squabble

رهايش rahāísh *m.* residence په هوټل کښی رهايش لرل to stay in a hotel رهايش، رهائش

رهبر rahbár *m.* **1** guide د چا سره رهبر کېدل to accompany someone **2** leader

رهبري rahbarí *f.* **1** accompaniment **2** leading, leadership د چا رهبري کول **a** to accompany someone, conduct someone **b** to lead someone

رهته ráhta *f.* ráháta *dialect* rest, peace

رهټ rahát́ *m.* ☞ ارهټ

رهدار rahdā́r striped, in stripes (of material)

رهزن rahzán *m.* ☞ راهزن

رهگذر rahguzár *m.* **1** traveler; passerby **2** road, way; course (of a ship, etc.) *idiom* د ... له رهگذره because of, in view of

رهن rahn *m. Arabic* deposit, pledge, mortgage د رهن سند deposit receipt, pawn ticket

رهنما rahnumā́ *m.* ☞ راهنما *and* راهنمای

رهنمائي rahnumāí *f.* ☞ راهنمائي

رهني rahní *Arabic adjective* depository; mortgage رهني بانک mortgage bank

رهوال rahvā́l *m.* trotter (i.e., horse)

رهه rә́ha *f.* aluminum

رهي rahí rә́hí going; setting out رهي کول **a** to set out **b** to dispatch, send رهي کېدل **a** to proceed, start out هغه خپل کورته را رهي دئ He will head for home. **b** to be bound for, move out (to, for)

رهبدا rahedā́ *f.* dispatch, departure; driving off (cattle)

رهيسو rahísu *Western past and present of* رهي کېدل vice رهي سو

رهيسي rahísi *Western past and present of* رهي کېدل vice رهي سي

رهيل ¹ rahél *m.* lectern for the Koran

رهيل ² rәhél *m.* ☞ ربل ¹

رهينه rahijá *f.* object which is pawned or pledged

ری ¹ re *f.* the name of the letter ر

ری ² raj *m.* **1** thought; consideration ری وهل to think, consider ښه ری ووهه Think it over thoroughly **2** price, valuation

ريا ¹ rijā́ *f. Arabic* hypocrisy, pretence د ريا رنگونه په ځان منبل to play the hypocrite, dissemble

ريا ² rajā́ *f.* rәjā bray (of an ass)

رياست rijāsát *m. Arabic* **1** supremacy, leadership, presidency, chairmanship د ... تر رياست لاندي under the leadership of; with (so and so); at the head رياست کول to hold sway; preside; direct **2** presidium **3** (chief) directorate د اردو رياست directorate of military manpower د قبايلو رياست، رياست قبائل Chief Directorate for Tribal Affairs *rijasat-i* chief directorate for tribal affairs د تشريفاتو رياست protocol department **4** rectorship; deanship **5** principality (in India); state (in the U.S.)

رياشه rijā́sha *f. dialect* **1** ☞ رشه ⁴ **2** provisions, victuals

رياض rijā́z *m. Arabic* **1** ☞ روضه **2** Er-Riad, Riad (city) **3** *proper name* Riaz

رياضت rijāzát *m. Arabic* **1** asceticism; abstinence **2** selfless devotion **3** training (physical)

رياضت کښ rijāzatkáҟh *m.* رياضتي rijāzatí *m.* **1** aesthete **2** zealot

رياضي rijāzí *Arabic* mathematical د رياضي تصاعد پر اساس اضافه توب کول to increase in an arithmatical progression علوم رياضي exact sciences

رياضيات rijāzijā́t *m. Arabic plural* mathematics, the mathematical sciences

رياکار rijākā́r *m.* 1 hypocrite; sanctimonious person 2 two-faced, affected

رياکاري rijakārí *f.* hypocrisy, two-facedness; sanctimoniousness

رباکتور reāktór *m.* ریباکتور atomic reactor اتومي ریباکتور

رباکتیف reāktíf 1 *m.* reagent 2 reactive

ريال rijā́l *m.* real (silver Iranian coin worth 1/100 of a gold pehlevi)

ریالیزم reālízm *m.* ☞ ریالیزم

رباليستي realistí realistic

ریالیزم reālízm *m.* realism سوسياليستي ریالیزم socialist realism

رببار rebā́r *m.* rǝjbār رويبار ☞

رببار rebā́ra *f.* rǝjbāra رويباره ☞

رببارى rebā́rí *f.* rǝjbāri رويباري¹ ☞

ربغ rebə́dz *m.* besom, broom

ربغ بوټی rebǝdzbútaj *m.* kochia (used in the manufacture of brooms)

ربغى rebǝ́dzaj *m.* sweeper, janitor

ربل rebdə́l *transitive* ☞ ربل

ربېدون rebdún *m. botany* Tesota undulata (a kind of tree)

ربز rebə́z *m.* ☞ ربغ

ربزوالا rebǝzvālā *m.* broom-seller, broom peddler

ربل rebǝ́l 1 [*past:* وي ربه] to reap, harvest (grain) غنم په لور ربل to harvest wheat with a scythe چه کړي هغه به ربي *proverb* As you sow, so shall you reap 2 *m. plural* harvesting, reaping (of grain)

ربوند rebǝ́nd ☞ ربوند

ربونده rebǝ́nda *f.* ☞ ربونده

ربونکى rebúnkaj *m.* reaper

ریتاړه ritā́ṛa *f.* strip, ribbon ریتاړي ریتاړي کول to tear into strips ریتاړه کېدل to turn to rags, tear (of old, worn-out clothing)

ریچ پڼس richpéx̌ *m.* fine-tooth comb

ریچن richə́n lousy, lice-ridden, full of nits

ریچه richá *f.* 1 nit (louse-egg) 2 small piece, shred ریچې ریچې کول to tear into shreds

ریحان rajhā́n rihā́n *m. Arabic* basil, Ocimum basilicum

ریخ rikh *m.* 1 diarrhea 2 feces, dropping ریخ وهل ☞ ریخل 3 kind of children's game

ریخانګه rikhā́nga *f.* ☞ ریتاړه

رېخت rekht *m.* external appearance, outward look

ریخل rikhə́l *transitive* [*past:* وي ریخل] to excrete liquid excrement; suffer from diarrhea

ریخن rikhə́n suffering from diarrhea

ریخه ríkha *f.* ☞ ربېنه²

ریخى rikháj 1 ☞ ریخن² *m.* diarrhea (of cattle)

ریخى ríkhaj² *m.* sluice gate of a water-storage reservoir (for release of water on to irrigated land)

رېد red کول to germinate; bud; sprout

رېدوان redvā́n *m.* ☞ ربېدون

رېدى redáj *m.* 1 field poppy 2 tulip 3 *proper name* Redaj رېدى ګل Redaj Gul

رېړ reṛ *m.* row, line; file

رېړم reṛə́m *m.* coral

رېړى reṛáj *m.* ram with a star-shaped flash on the forehead

رېز rez¹ *m.* twittering (of birds); warbling (of a nightingale) مرغان رېز کوي The birds are twittering.

رېز riz² *m.* landship د واورو رېز avalanche

رېز rez³ 1 small; petty 2 torn (to pieces) رېز رېز او ټکرټکر کول to tear to bits 3 *combining form* pouring, spilling خون رېز bloody, sanguinary

رېزش rezísh *m.* head-cold

رېزګى rezgə́j *f.* crumb; bit; grain

رېزمرېز rezmaréz رېز و رېز rez-u-réz torn

رېزمه رېز rezmaréz chopped up, crushed رېزمه رېزکول to tear, cut (carelessly) up

رېزه rezá *f.* 1 small piece, crumb رېزه رېزه ground up; chopped up رېزه رېزه کول to grind up; hack, chop; crumble 2 small game

رېزه کوهستان rezá kuhistā́n *m.* Reza-Kuhistan (district, Parvan Province)

رېزه ګیري rezagirí *f.* small-game hunting

رېژون rezhún *m. dialect* ☞ رژون

رېژېدل rezhedə́l *intransitive dialect* ☞ رژبدل

رېګ reg *m.* broom

رېږد regd *m.* shivering; trembling, quivering د بېري رېږد اخیستل to tremble in fear

رېږدان regdā́n *m. Eastern* shivering, trembling

رېږدله regdə́la *f.* earthquake

رېږدند regdǝ́nd shivering, trembling

رېږدول regdavə́l *transitive* [*past:* وي رېږداوه] 1 to shake (from fever) 2 to shiver, tremble, shudder

رېږدلا regdelā́ *f.* shivering; trembling, shuddering په رېږدېدا راوستل to cause to shiver; throw into a state of shivering

رېږدېدل regdedə́l *intransitive* [*past:* ورېږدېده] 1 to shiver, shake لاس رېږدېدل to shike, writhe په تبه کښې رېږدېدل His hands are shaking. یې رېږدي in fever 2 to sway, writhe

رېږدېدا regdedə́ *m. plural* ☞ رېږدېدا

رېږوى régvaj *m.* bleating (of sheep) رېږوى کول to bleat

رېسرچ risárch *m.* scientific research رېسرچ او څېړني کول to carry out scientific research

رېش resh *m.* method of spinning

رېش rish *m. combining form* beard رېشخند mockery; irony سپین ریش white-bearded

رېشخند rishkhánd *m.* ridicule; irony رېشخند وهل a to ridicule someone په چا باندي رېشخند وهل b to speak ironically about someone

رېشخندي rishkhandí *f.* ridicule د چا رېشخندي کول to make a laughing stock of someone; ridicule someone

ريشل reshә́l *transitive* [*past:* وي يې ريشه] تار ريشل to spin to spin yarn *idiom* په سبز کنبي يې لا پوني نه وه ريشلي He only made a beginning.

ريشه ¹ reshá *f. dialect* ☞ رشه ⁴

ريشه ² rishá *f.* cotton; fiber د ريشي ډبره asbestos

ريښتيا rikhtjá *f.* ☞ رښتيا

ريښم rekhә́m *m.* reẖm *plural* silk

ريښمانگی reẖmãngáj *regional* جامي ريښمانگي silken silk dress

ريښمگر reẖәmgór *m. regional* silkworm breeder

ريښمگري reẖәmgarí *f.* sericulture

ريښمين reẖmín silk, silken

ريښه ¹ reẖá *f.* ríẖa 1 root, rootlet د يو شي ريښبني ايستل to eradicate something په يو شي کښي ريښبنه لرل to implant هر ځای ته ريښبني غځول to be rooted in something 2 fibre ريښبني ريښبني کول to tear in shreds 3 basis 4 *grammar* root, stem *idiom* د احمد ريښبنه وخته Ahmed's clan died out. د چا ريښبنه کښل to slay to a man; wipe out the entire clan

ريښه ² rékha *f.* embroidery on the edge of the collar (of a woman's dress)

ريفورم refórm *m.* reform

ريکارد ¹ rikárḍ *m.* ريکارډ rekárḍ *m.* 1 record (gramophone) 2 recording (film, gramophone disk) ريکارډ کول *compound verb* to record (on film, disk) ريکارډ کېدل *compound verb* to be recorded (on film, disk)

ريکارډ ² rikárḍ *m.* rekárḍ record د ... ريکارډ درول to establish a record ريکارډ ماتول to break a record

ريکارډگيري rikarḍgirí *f.* recording (on film, disk)

ريکلام reklám *m.* advertisement

ريکياويک rekijãvík *m.* Rejkavik

ريگ reg *m. plural* 1 gravel 2 sand ريگ روان Regiravan (an isolated terrain feature near Charikar with moving sands)

ريگا rigá *f.* Riga

ريگستان registán *m.* 1 stoney desert 2 Registan (various districts)

ريگماهي regmahí *m.* regmãháj skink (a kind of lizard)

ريگي regí sandy ريگي غونډی dune, barkan, sandy hill

ريل ¹ rel *m.* 1 railroad د ريل تپسن railroad د ريل سرک railroad station, railroad terminal د ريل پټلی railroad line 2 train زره پوش armored-train 3 rail

ريل ² rәjә́l *transitive* [*present:* رائي *past:* وي يې ريل] to bray (of an ass, donkey)

رياليزم rializm *m.* ☞

رياليستي rialistí realistic

ريل گاډی relgáḍaj *m.* railroad train

ريلوني relúnaj *m.* ☞ رودوني

ريم rim *m.* 1 pus 2 sediment; precipitation

ريمان rimán *m.* low quality ruby

ريمن rimón *m.* 1 purulent, suppurating 2 impure

رينده rindá *f.* harness-maker's knife

رينگټ ringԥ́t *m.* ☞ رنگټ

رينگه ¹ rínga *f.* file, column

رينگه ² rínga *f.* 1 sobbing 2 croaking (of frogs) رينگه کول a to sob b to croak (of frogs)

رينه riná *f.* awl

ريني renáj reddish-brown, chestnut (of the coat of cattle)

ريودل revdә́l rijaudә́l *transitive* [*past:* وي يې ريود] to raise, raise up

ريودوژنېرو rio-do-dzhanéró *f.* Rio-de-Janerio (city)

ريوړی revṛáj *f.* kind of candy made of sesame oil and sugar

ريوگراندي rio-gránde *f.* Rio Grande River

ريوون revún *m.* pen used when milking ewes

ريوند revánd sloping, slanting, inclined دا ځای ريوند دئ There is an incline here. ريونده لاره a road with a considerable slope

ريونده revánda 1 *feminine singular of* ريوند 2 *f.* slope, declivity 3 aslant, slantwise

ريوي rijaví *Arabic* pulmonary ريوي التهاب inflamation of the lungs

ريويزيونزم revizionízm *m.* revisionism

رئيس raís *m. Arabic* [*plural:* رئيسان raisán *Arabic plural:* رؤسا ruasá] 1 head, chief رئيس الوزرا chairman of the council of ministers د جمهور رئيس president of the republic د اداري رئيس director of the administrative department 2 mayor (of a city) 3 director 4 rector, dean 5 ruler, prince

رئيسه rajisá 1 *f. Arabic for* رئيسه هئيت *presidium, ruling body* د صدر رئيسه هئيت a chairman of the presidium b chairman of the governing body, head of government 2 princess

رئي ¹ rәjí ☞ رهي

رئی ² rajáj *m.* rhubarb

ړ

ړ rá ṛe 1 the seventeenth letter of the Pashto alphabet 2 the retroflex (cerebral) "ṛ"

ړا rá *f.* the name of the letter ړ

ړانځوه ṛãndzṛó *m.* ṛãnzṛó *m. plural* tar

ړانده ṛãndә́ *m. plural of* ړوند

ړبن rәbә́n *m.* namby-pamby, namby-pamby person

ړپ ṛap *m.* 1 friable, crumbly soil 2 thick layer of dust (on the road) 3 sticky mass; mucilage 4 thick syrup 5 splash (of water) 6 clicking (with the tongue) 7 coagulating blood; blood clot

ړپ ړپ ṛapṛap *m.* splash (of water, etc.)

ړپند ṛapә́nd soft and moist (e.g., of soil)

ړپول ṛapavә́l *transitive* [*past:* وي يې ړپاوه] 1 to disturb, cause ripples (on the surface of water) 2 to paddle (laundry) 3 to click (the tongue)

ړپېدل ṛapedә́l *intransitive* [*past:* وړپېده] 1 to be disturbed, be covered with ripples (of the surface of water), splash 2 to lap (water), splash 3 to swing back and forth, be unsteady (in gait)

ړپېده ṛapedә́ *m. plural* 1 splashing (in water, of water) 2 swaying, rocking unsteadily (gait)

رت [1] ṛat disproportionately large رته ږيره **a** broad and thick beard **b** coward **c** scoundrel

رت [2] ṛat *m.* ☞ رت

رتګيرى ṛatgíraj *m.* رتى ږيرى ṛatajgíraj *m.* **1** bearded man **2** coward **3** scoundrel

رټ ṛaṭ *m.* orange, the color orange

رچ ṛach dangling; trembling; shivering

رچند ṛachə́nd shaky, unstable

رچول ṛachavə́l *transitive* [*past:* و يې رچاوه] **1** to shake, sway **2** to tremble; rock; move unsteadily

رچدل ṛachedə́l *intransitive* [*past:* ورچده] **1** to shiver, shake **2** to dangle; rock, move unsteadily

رخبنى ṛakhbənáj *m.* bed-frame

رزول ṛazavə́l *transitive* [*past:* و يې رزاوه] to treat cattle medically, heal (with the aid of oil, etc.)

رزدل ṛazedə́l *intransitive* [*past:* ورزيد] to be treated medically, be healed (with oil, etc., of cattle)

رزيدنه ṛazedə́na *f.* رزيده ṛazedə́ *m. plural* medical treatment or healing of cattle (using oil, etc.)

رقول ṛaḳavə́l *transitive regional* [*past:* و يې رقاوه] **1** to agitate; mix; stir (paddle) **2** to push, push slightly **3** to trounce, thrash, beat; beat up **4** to agitate with a paddle, churn about (laundry, with a paddle, stick)

رک ṛak ☞ رچ

رکول ṛakavə́l *transitive* ☞ رقول

رکدل ṛakedə́l *intransitive* ☞ رچدل

رمبزيزه ṛambəzíza *f.* ☞ رمبزبره

رومبنى ṛumbanáj ☞ رومبنى

رومبى ṛumbáj ☞ رومبى

رمبزبره ṛumgéga *f. agriculture* cow which has calved for the first time

رنبوسه ṛambósa *f.* thin gruel

رنجه ṛəndzhá *f.* root of a tooth which remains in the socket

رند ṛund ☞ روند

رندتوب ṛandtób *m.* رندتيا ṛandtjá *f.* رندښت ṛandə́kht *m.* ☞ روندتوب

رندکى ṛandəkáj nearly blind

رندو ṛandó oblique *plural of* روند

رندکى ṛandukáj ☞ رندکى

رندول ṛandavə́l *denominative, transitive* [*past:* روند يې کړ] to blind, make blind خپل دښمن يې قصداً روند کړ He blinded his enemy.

رندون ṛandún *m.* blindness

رنده ṛandá *f.* **1** *singular of* روند **2** [*plural:* رندي ṛandé *plural:* رنديانی ṛandijắni] blind woman

رندى ṛandáj *m.* blind man

رنددل ṛandedə́l *denominative, transitive* [*past:* روند شو] **1** to become blind, lose one's sight **2** to be blinded پلار ئي په روپو پسې رندده His father was blind to his hope of receiving money.

رندده ṛandedə́ *m. plural* blinding, dazzling; blindness

رنگ ṛang **1** wrecked, destroyed; spoiled **2** disorded (of affairs) **3** cancelled **4** liquidated, disbanded (of an organization)

رنگ بنگ ṛang-báng **1** intoxicated, made drunk **2** acting, speaking in an extravagant, grandiose manner

رنگتوب ṛangtób *m.* رنگوالى ṛangvắlaj *m.* **1** disintegration, collapse; ruin **2** disorder (in affairs); undermining (society) **3** cancellation **4** liquidation, disbanding (of an organization)

رنگول ṛangavə́l *denominative, transitive* [*past:* رنگ يې کړ] **1** to destroy, turn into ruins **2** to mess up (affairs); undermine (society) **3** to cancel **4** to liquidate, disband (an organization)

رنگه بنگه ṛánga-bánga *feminine singular of* رنگ بنگ

رنگى [1] ṛangáj *m.* weeping, sobbing

رنگى [2] ṛangáj **1** thin **2** rarified, liquid

رنگى [3] ṛangə́j *f.* silk turban, silk kerchief

رنگبدل ṛangedə́l **1** *denominative, intransitive* [*past:* رنگ شو] **1.1** to be destroyed, be ruined **1.2** to have an accident **1.3** to be in disorder (affairs); o be undermined (society) **1.4** to be cancelled **1.5** to be liquidated, disbanded (organization) **2** *m. plural* ☞ رنگبده

رنگبده ṛangedə́ *m. plural* **1** destruction **2** disorder (of affairs); undermining (society) **3** liquidation, disbanding (organization) **4** cancellation **5** collapse, ruin

وراندې ṛvắnde *dialect* ☞ رواندي

روز ṛuz *m.* thin gruel

رمبزبزه ṛumbəzíza *f.* ☞ رمبزبره

رومبنى ṛumbáj رومبنى ṛumbənáj رومبى **1.1** first په رومبي سرکي at first **1.2** former, past; ex- **1.3** ancient; of old **2** earlier, prior; already رومبى هغه ما رومبنى وويل چه ... I already said that ... راغئ He came earlier. He came beforehand. رومبنى څه موده some time ago

رمبزبره ṛumgéga *f.* ☞ رمبزبره

رومبى ṛumbáj ☞ رومبى

روند ṛund **1** *m.* [*plural:* رانده ṛāndə́ *f. singular:* رنده ṛandá *f. plural:* رندي ṛandé] **1.1** blind په يوه سترگه روند و He was blind in one eye. په رندو سترگو حرکت as though blind, blindly په رانده شان to walk gropingly or blindly **1.2** dark **1.3** rude, impolite **2** *m.* blind man روند د خداى نه څه غواړي؟ دوه سترگي! *Western proverb literal* What does the blind man ask of God? Two eyes! *figurative* He/she only dreamed of this. *idiom* رنده چرګه soup

روندتوب ṛundtób *m.* روندتيا ṛundtjá *f.* روندوالى ṛundvắlaj *m.* **1** blindness **2** blinding, dazzling, blindness **3** *figuratives* darkness, rudeness

روندول ṛundavə́l *transitive* ☞ رندول

روندبدل ṛundedə́l *intransitive* ☞ رندبدل

ره ṛə *m. dialect* ☞ زره

رى [1] ṛaj *m.* ram

رى [2] ṛe *f.* the name of the letter ړ

رى [3] ṛəj a cry used in driving cattle

ری ṛaj ṛe *diminutive noun suffix* خسری blade of grass

ڼيمباخه ṛimbákha *f.* old clothes, rags

رينگري ṛingṛáj *m. dialect* sparse growth of trees

رينگی ¹ ṛingáj *m.* tray or tablecloth with refreshments

رينگی ² ṛingáj *m.* ☞ رنگی ¹

رينگي ³ ṛingí *m. plural* household utensils; household goods, chattels

ز

ز zā ze **1** the eighteenth letter of the Pashto alphabet **2** the number 7 in the abjad system

زا ¹ zā *f.* time for giving birth to young (of certain animals), calving time of cattle

زا ² zā *f.* **1** percolation of water **2** moisture, dampness د زا ايستلو سيستم drainage system

زا ³ zā *f.* name of the letterز

زابر zābúr *m.* drainage ditch

زابل zābúl *m.* زابلستان zabulistan *m. history* Zabulistan (name of ancient country in present-day Afghanistan, the native land of the epic hero Rustam) د زابل ولايت Zabul Province

زابه zābə́ *imperfect tense of* زبل

زاج zādzh *m. plural* ☞ زاک

زاخيل zākhél **1** *m. plural* the Zakhejli (tribe) **2** *m.* a Zakhejl tribesman

زاد ¹ zād *m. Arabic* stores, provisions, supplies

زاد ² zād *combining form* -born پري زاد fairy-born, spirit-born

زاده zādá *combining form* becoming, being born شاهزاده crown prince, prince

زار ¹ zār *m.* ☞ څار

زار ² zār *m.* czar

زار ³ zār **1** *m.* complaint **2.1** sad, sorrowful, woeful **2.2** weeping, sobbing; crying out **2.3** poor, unhappy; pitiful, insignificant

زار ⁴ zā́r *combining form* جبه زار swamp

زاربوتی zārbútaj *m. botany* wild rue, *Ruta graveolens*; harmal, *Peganum harmala*

زارخند zārkhánḍ *m.* ☞ زهرخند

زارزار zārzár *m.* **1** cries, groaning **2** sob, sobbing زارزار ژړل **a** to sob, shed tears, wail **b** to bewail د خپلي لور په حال به يې زارزار ژړل She mournfully bewailed the fate of her daughter.

زارزنگی zārzangə́j *f. botany* colocynth, bitter apple, *Citrillus colocynthus*

زارع zāré *m. Arabic* [*plural:* زارعين zāre'ín] agricultural worker, hired hand, field laborer

زارمری zarmə́raj ill-fated, ill-starred

زارول zāravə́l *denominative, transitive* ☞ څارول

زاره zārá *f.* **1** ☞ زهره ¹ **2** liver *idiom* ده زاره به چاودله He became very angry.

زهره ترکی ¹ zāratrákaj **1** dead; croaked **2** ☞ زاره ترکی

زهره ترکي ² zāratrakí *f.* ☞ زاره ترکي

زاره چاودی zārachávdaj sad, sorrowful

زاري ¹ zārí *f.* rārə́j **1** request; entreaty; supplication **2** lamentation, complaint زاري کول **a** to entreat; obtain by begging, get by pleading; beg of, pray, implore **b** to lament, complain of

زاري ² zāré *plural of* زاره

زاريدل zāredə́l ☞ څاريدل *denominative*, intransitive

زارمبوج zāṛəmbúj *m.* زارنبی zaṛúmbaj *m.* odor of burned cloth

زارند zāṛə́nd missing from the herd or flock, stray (of cattle)

زاړه ¹ zāṛə́ **1** *masculine plural of* زوړ زاړه شيان **a** old thing **b** old clothing **2** *oblique singular of* زوړ ¹

زاړه واړه zāṛə́-vāṛə́ *m. plural* both young and old

زاړه والا zāṛəvālā́ *m.* old-clothes merchant

زاړي ¹ zā́ṛaj *m.* **1** corn shoots; crops **2** sucker, adventitious growth

زاړي ² zā́ṛe *f.* cow which has ceased to give milk

زاړه لوغي zaṛəjlvághe *f.* ☞ زره لوغي

زازو zāzú **1** willy-nilly, against one's will **2** without fail, certainly

زازي zāzí *m. plural* ☞ څاځي

زاږه زاړه وایه zāɡ́ə children

زاغ ¹ zāgh *m. plural* **1** alum **2** vitriol

زاغ ² zāgh *m.* crow, raven

زاغاوی zāghāvə́j *f.* cormorant (the bird)

زاغچکه zāghcháka *f.* daw, jackdaw

زاغچه zāghchá *f.* **1** gull **2** daw

زاغزوغ zāghzúgh *m.* gossipmonger

زاغزوغي zāghzughí *f.* gossip, talk زاغزوغي کول to gossip, tittle-tattle

زاگ zāg *m. plural* ☞ زاغ ¹ سپين زاگ alum

زاگی zāɡ́əj *f.* shepherd's cloak

زاله zā́la *f. dialect* ☞ څاله

زام zām *a combination of the preposition* زه *and the verb* وايم *colloquial* I suppose, I say; it should be, probably ته زام نه وي I suppose, I say; it should be, probably تللئ؟ You probably did not go?

زامبيا zāmbijā́ *f.* Zambia

زامن zāmə́n *masculine plural of* زوی ¹

زامه zā́ma *f.* jaw پورتنی زامه upper jaw لوړه زامه lower jaw ننداندنی زامه to speak indistinctly, mumble *idiom* تر زامي لاندي کول jaw زامي to stint, be greedy, be stingy ترله تپرول to get hold of یو شی تر زامي کول

زان zān ☞ څان

زانډوری zānḍóraj *f.* upper jaw

زانغولی zāngholáj *m.* hoe, mattock

زانگ zāng *present stem of* زنگل ¹

زانگنه zāngə́na *f.* rocking, swinging

زانگو zāngó *f.* [*plural:* زانگوواني zāngóvi *plural:* زانگوگاني zāngogā́ni] **1** cradle, swing, rocking chair په زانگو کښيني to swing in a cradle, rock in a cradle, swing or hammock **2** small raft **3** native place, cradle of something

زانگي zā́ngi **1** *present tense of* زنگل ¹ **2** *vice* زنگيري ☞ زنگېدل

391

زانو zānú *m.* knee په زانو وهل to kneel په زانو کښېنستل to get down on the knees, kneel; genuflect

زانه zānə́ *imperfect tense of* زنل

زاني zāní *m. Arabic* adulterer, libertine

زانيه zānijá *f.* adulteress, woman of loose moral character

زاڼه zā́ṇa *f.* female crane (the bird)

زاڼی zā́ṇaj crane (bird)

زاڼیه zā́ṇja *f.* ☞ زاڼه

زاو zāv ☞ ځاو

زاوزات zāvzā́t *m.* زاوزاد zāvzā́d *m.* generation, progeny, clan بشري زاوزات the human race, humanity

زاوزو zāvzú زازو

زاولۀ zāvlə́ 1 lazy 2 *m.* lazy person

زاولنه zāvlə́na *feminine singular of* زاولن

زاوله zā́vla *f.* ☞ ژاوله

زاويه zāvijá *f. Arabic* 1 angle قائمه زاویه right angle حاده زاویه acute angle منفرجه زاویه obtuse angle د انعکاس زاویه angle of reflection د سقوط زاویه angle of incidence 2 slope, declivity

زاویه گر zāvijagár *m.* goniometer

زاه zāh *f.* ☞ زا²

زاهد zāhíd *Arabic* 1 *m.* [*plural:* زاهدان zāhidā́n *plural:* زاهدين zāhidín *Arabic plural:* زهاد zuhhā́d] aesthete, hermit; zealot 2 devout person, pious person

زاهدي zāhidí *f.* aestheticism, the hermit's life

زاه کشي zāhkashí *f. technology* drainage

زايپه zājipá *f.* wife, married woman

زائد zaíd *Arabic* 1 added on, increased 2 extra, superfluous

زائر zāír *m. Arabic* [*plural:* زوار zuvvā́r *plural:* زائرين zāirín] devotee, pilgrim, visitor to a shrine, etc.

زايشگاه zājishgā́h *m.* maternity home, lying-in hospital

زائل zāíl *Arabic* 1 disappearing, vanishing 2 setting (of heavenly bodies) زائل کول *compound verb* ☞ زائلول

زائلول zāilavə́l *denominative, transitive* [*past:* زائل یې کړ] 1 to bring to naught 2 to eliminate, destroy, get rid of 3 to ruin 4 to wear out (clothing)

زائلېدل zāiledə́l ☞ زائل شو *denominative, intransitive* 1 to disappear, vanish 2 to set (of celestial objects) 3 to be removed, be annihilated, be eliminated 4 to perish 5 to be worn out (clothing)

زائنیزم zājanízm *m.* Zionism

زائي zā́ji *m. combining form plural used in names of tribes* احمد زائي the Akhmadzai

زبات zbāt 1.1 proven, established 1.2 firm, stable, protracted 2 *m.* favor, grace, attention

زباتل zbātə́l *transitive* [*past:* وي یې زباته] to do a favor for; show consideration

زباد zbād ☞ زبات

زبادول zbadavə́l *denominative, transitive* ☞ ثابتول

زبادون zbādún *m.* affirmation; confirmation; attestation; proof, evidence

زبادېدل zbādedə́l *denominative, intransitive* ☞ ثابتېدل

زبان zabā́n zubā́n *m.* tongue, language (usually employed as the second element of a compound word) پارسي زبان Farsi-speaking, Farsi-speaker پښتو زبان Pashto-speaking, Pashto-speaker حال پوهول zabān-i to explain by signs or gestures

زبان آور zabānāvár eloquent

زباندان zabāndā́n *m.* language expert; linguist; polyglot

زبانداراز zabāndarā́z rude, cheeky, bold in speech

زبانزد zabānzád on everbody's lips, repeated by all د هر خاص او عام زبان زد و His name is one everyone's lips.

زبانشناسي zabānshināsí *f.* linguistics

زباني zabāní 1 oral 2 orally, in words زباني ویل a to transmit oral instructions b to issue a verbal order

زبده zubdá 1 *f. Arabic* the best, choice part of something 2.1 best, choice 2.2 outstanding

زبر zabár zabór 1 *m.* .1 top 1.2 zabar, fatha (supralinear vowel-marking for the phoneme /a/) 2 upper

زبرجد zabardzhád *m. Arabic* 1 Topaz 2 chrysolite

زبردست zabardást 1.1 potent, strong; powerful 1.2 authoratative 1.3 superlative 1.4 skillful, expert 1.5 venerable 1.6 high (of a mountain range), lofty 1.7 immense (of a crowd) 1.8 remarkable, splendid زبردسته تماشه a splendid spectacle د چا زبردست استقبال کول to arrange a luxurious reception for someone 2 *m.* .1 strong man 2.2 skilled person, expert person 2.3 *proper name* Zabardast

زبردستي zabardastí *f.* 1 potency, strength; might 2 authoritativeness زبردستي کول to oppress 3 superiority 4 skillfulness 5 venerability

زبرگ zbərg 1.1 large, big, great, huge 1.2 grown-up, adult; old 1.3 distinguished 1.4 holy, sacred زبرگه میاشت the month Rajab 2 *m.* forefather, ancestor ☞ بزرگ

زبرگي zbərgí *f.* ☞ بزرگي

زبل zabə́l *transitive* [*past:* وي یې زابه] to strike, befall (of misfortune, etc.)

زبله zábla ☞ ځبله

زبون¹ zəbún *m.* tasting, sampling (e.g., of food) زبون وهل to try, sample, taste

زبون² zabún *Arabic* 1 insignificant; despicable 2 weak, feeble, helpless حال یې زبون شو He has grown weak. 3 unhappy

زبون³ zəbún *m. dialect* ☞ زبان

زبون وهلئ zəbún vahə́laj 1 quiet, taciturn; dumbstruck (by fear) 2 hungry

زبوني zabuní *f.* 1 insignificance, mediocrity 2 weakness, feebleness, helplessness

زبه¹ zba *f. Eastern* 1 nanny goat 2 ☞ وزه

زبه² zə́ba *f. dialect* ☞ ژبه

زبی zəbə́j *f. dialect* ☞ ژبی

زبرگي zbergáj *m.* 1 moan (of a sick man) 2 cry, groaning

زبښ zbeǩ *m.* absorption, soaking up; blotting up

زبښل zbekhál *transitive* [*past:* زبيښنه وي] 1 to suck; suck around (candy); soak up, take up; absorb 2 to swallow 3 to press (to) په to press to one's breast; embrace لاس زبښل خپله غبر کښي to press to one's breast; embrace kiss the hand 4 to knead, mash; press down 5 *figurative* to torment something

زبښند zbekhánd absorbing, taking up, blotting up

زبښنه zbekhána *f.* ☞ زبښ

زبلل zbelál *transitive* ☞ زبښل

زبينگي zbingáj *m.* gore, gusset (in a dress)

زپل zapál *transitive* ☞ زيل

زپلتوب zapáltób *m.* depression, low-spiritedness; exhaustion

زجر zadzhr *m. Arabic* oppression, crushing down, weighing down

زحل zuhál *m. Arabic astronomy* Saturn

زحمت zahmát *m. Arabic* 1 effort, labor ديوکار زحمت پر ځان اخيستل to take upon oneself the effectuation of some matter سختي او زحمتونه په ځان اخيستل to be subjected to privations and dificulties زحمت ايستل، زحمت کبل، زحمت ويستل a to try, strive b to endure difficulties *proverb* بي زحمته راحت نشته، په زحمت پسي راحت دئ Work brings complete satisfaction. There is no happiness without work. 2 worry; constraint, burden

زحمت کښ zahmatkásh ☞ زحمت کښ

زحمت کښي zahamatkashí *f.* 1 industry 2 endurance

زحمت کښ zahmatkáǩh زحمت وبستونکي zahmát vestúnkaj 1.1 industrious 1.2 hardy 2 *m.* worker, laborer

زحمتي zahmatí depressed, grieved

زخت zəkht ☞ زبت 1

زخم zakhm *m.* wound, wounding کاري زخم a mortal wound زخم کول to inflict a wound, wound

زخم zakhm 2 *m.* whirlpool

زخمي zakhmí wounded زخمي کول to wound زخمي کبدل to be wounded

زخمي کبده zakhmikedá *m.* injury, wounding

زخن zəkhán 1 knotty 2 warty

زخه zókha *f.* 1 knot 2 bump; growth 3 wart زخه ختل to appear (of a growth, a wart) 4 *regional* front sight (of a rifle) تر زخه لاندي راوستل to sight, take aim

زخه خبل zakhakhél 1 *m. plural* the Zakhakhejli (a subdivision of the Afridi tribe) 2 *m.* Zakhakhejli (tribesman)

زخرا zakherá *f. colloquial* ☞ ذخيره

زد zad 1 *m.* 1 blow د چاقو زد a knife stroke, stab 2 skirmish, clash 3 effect, influence; consequence زد کول a to strike b to affect, influence, be influential

زد zəd 2 *m.* 1 ford 2 ☞ ضد 3 damage

زدايت zadāját *m.* ☞ زاوزات

زدان zardán *m. plural* ☞ ځدران

زده کړه zdákṛa *f.* ☞

زدوخورد zadukhúrd *m.* skirmish, clash, encounter; battle

زدويل zdojál *transitive* [*past:* زدوو وي] زدوول zdoval *transitive* [*past:* زدويه وي] 1 to grate, grind (e.g., roots) 2 to scrape, clean off

زده zda 1 learned by heart, learned; mastered, grasped زده کول to study; come to know; learn, memorize د چا څخه يو شی زده کول to learn something from someone چا ته يو شی ور زده کول to teach someone something زما بنه حساب زده دئ to learn, master زده کبدل I can read well. ستا اوبازي زده ده؟ Do you know how to swim? پښتو زده ده؟ Do you know Pashto?

زده zadá 2 1 beaten down, beaten up 2 oppressed

زده کرودزي zdakródzáj *m.* school, academy, educational institution

زده کرونکي zdakṛúndkaj *m.* زده کروني zdakṛúnaj *m.* ☞ 1

زده کړه zdákṛa *f.* studies, learning; studying زده کړه کول to study, engage in studies د چا څخه زده کړه کول to learn from someone اقتصادياتو زده کړه کول to study economics

زده کړي zdakṛáj 1 *m.* pupil, student

زده کړئ zda kóṛəj 2 learned; acquired through study

زده کړي zdakṛáj 3 *f.* [*plural:* زده کړياني zdakṛəjáni] pupil, student (female)

زده کړه کونه zdakavóna *f.* ☞

زده کونکي zda kavúnkaj 1 *m.* pupil, student; university student

زده کونکي zda kavúnke 2 *f.* pupil, student (female); university student (female)

زدي zadáj *f.* ☞ سدی

زر zar 1 *m. plural* 1 precious metal; silver; gold سره زر gold سپين زر pure gold نگه زر، کره زر، چاندي زر silver 2 riches, wealth; money

زر zər 2 *m.* [*plural:* زرونه zərúna *plural:* زرگونه zərgúna *plural:* زرها zərhá] *numeral* thousand يو زر (one) thousand دوه زره two thousand پنځه زره five thousand *colloquial* (one) million

زر zər 3 ☞ زر very quickly زر تر زره ژر sooner or later زر وي که وروسته

زراعت zirā'át *m. Arabic* agriculture; agronomy د زراعت فاکولته the agronomy department (of a college) زراعت کول to work in agronomy, be engaged in agriculture

زراعت پيشه zirā'atpeshá working in agriculture, agronomy

زراعتي zirā'atí agricultural; agronomy; agrarian زراعتي آفتونه pests and diseases of crops زراعتي اقتصاد the economics of agriculture زراعتي مملکت an agrarian country زراعتي ماشينونه agricultural machines

زرامی zrāmáj *m.* drop

زرب zrab *m.* 1 hard frost 2 pomp 3 external appearance

زربرخ zarbarákh *m.* 1 talc 2 mica 3 foil

زربيانگ zarbjáng *m.* 1 tanner's scraper 2 scraper, drawknife

زرپ zrap *m.* ☞

زرپښ zarpáǩh *m.* ☞ زرگ

زرپرلی zarperólaj ☞ زرخيد

زرتشت zartúsht *m.* Zarathustra, Zoroaster

زرتشتت zaratushtát *m.* Zoroastrianism

زرغ zərdz 1 brown, dark brown زرغي سترگي brown eyes 2 chestnut

زرنۍ ¹ zə́rdzəj *f. plural* ☞ زرني

زرځى zərdzáj *m.* ☞ زرزى

زرخرید zarkharíd [*past:* زرخریده مـّحکه] acquired (as contrasted to inherited); acquired land (i.e., through purchase)

زرخیز zarkhéz zarkhíz 1 gold-bearing, auriferous 2 rich, lavish 3 fruitful

زردار zardā́r 1 rich 2 *m.* rich man

زردآلو zardālú *m.* [*plural:* زردآلوگان zardālugán *plural:* zardālā́n] apricot, dried apricot

زردشت zardúsht *m.* ☞ زرتشت

زردکه zardə́ka *f.* carrot

زردوم zardúm *m.* powerful poison

زرډانگی zərḍā́ngaj *m.* three kilometers

زرز zərz زرغ *dialect* ☞ زرغ

زرزپو zarzpó *interjection* bang

زرزري ¹ zarzarí 1 *f.* dress with gold embroidery 2.1 golden (hue) 2.2 blond

زرزري ² zərzarí hurried; hastening

زرزى zərzáj *m.* kind of sheep with red ears

زرشاه zarshā́h *m. proper name* Zarshah

زرشوى zarshój *m.* prospector, gold prospector

زرشویي zarshují *f.* gold mining

زرع zár'a *f. Arabic* sowing, crops

زراعتي zar'í ☞ زراعتي

زرغا zarghā́ 1 green 2 fresh, blooming

زرغاله zarghā́la *f.* 1 lying-in or puerperal woman; forty days after childbirth 2 cow who has just calved

زرغون zarghún 1 زرغونه zarghuná *f. m.* [*plural:* زرغونه zarghunə́] *f.* [*plural:* زرغوني zarghuné] .1 green, verdant 1.2 fresh, new, flourishing 2 *m. proper name* Zarghun

زرغونتوب zarghuntób *m.* زرغونتیا zarghuntjā́ *f.* 1 greenery, vegetation 2 prosperity

زرغونمازو zargunmāzú *m.* nutgall, oak gall

زرغون والی zarghunvā́laj *m.* ☞ زرغون توب

زرغونول zarghunavə́l *denominative* [*past:* زرغون يې کړ] 1 to plant with trees and gardens 2 to make fresh, make flowering, make flourishing 3 to aid in growth, facilitate growth 4 to water (as a river) 5 to grow, cultivate 6 to paint, color, dye green 7 to make happy 8 to develop

زرغونه ¹ zarghuná 1 *feminine singular of* زرغون! زرغونه شې May you prosper! 2 *proper name* Zarghuna

زرغونه ² zarghunə́ *masculine plural & oblique singular of* زرغون

زرغونیدل zarghunedə́l *denominative* [*past:* زرغون شو] 1 to germinate 2 to become fresh, become new, become flourishing 3 to grow, germinate 4 to grow prettier, flourish 5 to flourish 6 to develop

زرغونیده zarghunedə́ *m. plural* 1 growth, germination 2 prosperity 3 development

زرغونیز zarghuníz *m.* plant

زرغه zárgha *f.* 1 sluggishness 2 laziness

زرک zərk *m.* red-legged partridge

زرکاڼی zərkā́ṇaj *m.* touchstone

زرکبی zarkabə́j *f.* ferrule of the staff of a banner

زرکوبي zarkobí *f.* gold-beating; engraving on gold

زرکوړى zərkuṛáj *m.* nestling of a red-legged partridge

زرکه zə́rka *f.* 1 red-legged partridge 2 *proper name* Zarka

زرگر zargár zargə́r *m.* goldsmith, jeweller

زرگرایه zərgrā́ja thousandfold

زرگرکاڼی zargarkā́ṇaj *m.* touchstone

زرگري zargarí *f.* goldsmith's trade, goldsmith's work

زرگل zargúl *m. botany* African marigold

زرگنډي zargaṇḍí *f.* silver embroidery

زرگونه zərgúna 1 *plural of* زر ² 2 ☞ زرگرایه

زرگونی zərgúnaj thousandfold

زرل zarə́l zərə́l *transitive* [*past:* زاره يې] to gild, cover with gilt

زرلښته zarlə́khta *f. proper name* Zarlashta

زرلگ zərlə́g *m. botany* club moss, Lycium

زرم zərə́m *ordinal* thousandth

زرمت zurmát *m.* Zurmat (district)

زرمشر zərmáshr zərmə́shər *m.* 1 *history* commander of a thousand men 2 *regional colloquial* colonel

زرنباد zurunbā́d santonic, wormseed root

زرنج zarándzh *m.* Zaranj (city)

زرنځي ¹ zərə́ndzi *f. plural* ☞ زرني

زرند گړی zrangā́ṛaj *m.* ☞ ژړند گړی

زرنده zránda *f. dialect* ☞ ژرنده

زرندۍ zrandə́j *f.* basement

زرنگ ¹ zaráng *m.* maple

زرنگ ² ziráng quick, agile, bright, lively

زرنگار zaringā́r decorated or adorned with gold

زرنگي zirangí *f.* liveliness, agility, efficiency

زرنه ¹ zrə́na *f.* ☞ زرني

زرنه ² zə́rnə *m. plural* ☞ زرنه

زرني zarní zarə́ní *f.* زرني زرنۍ zəranə́j *f.* 1 scrutiny; spying په زرني کتل to scrutinize fixedly 2 espionage زرني کول a to scrutinize; spy upon b to find out about, reconnoiter

زرنیخ zarníkh *m.* arsenic

زرڼه zərṇa *m. plural* tar, pitch

زرڼي ¹ zərṇi *f. plural* sticky and malodorous silt, mud; slime

زرڼي ² zaraṇáj 1 leprous 2 ignorant

زرو ¹ zə́ro oblique *plural of* زر ² په زرو زرو a thousands b by thousands

زرو ² zaró *f. proper name* Zaro

زرو ³ záró oblique *plural of* زر ¹

زروالی zərvā́laj *m.* ☞ ژروالی

زروبول zarabavə́l *transitive* [*past:* زروباوه يې] to gild, cover with gilt

زروبیدل zarobedə́l *denominative; intransitive* [*past:* زروب شو] to be gilded, be covered with gilt

زرویلئ zarojə́-ləj gilded

زره ¹ ziréh *f.* armor plate; shirt of mail, armor

زره ² zə́ra *f.* ☞ زر

زره ³ zə́ra زر تر زره very quickly, without delay

ذره ⁴ zaṛá *f.* ☞

زرها zərhā́ *plural of* زر ² په زرهاو زلمیان thousands of young men زرهاو کتابونه thousands of books

زرهپوښ، زره پوش zirehpókh زرهپیښ zirehpókh **1** armored; dressed in a coat-of-mail, clad in armor زرهپوش موټر armored car **2** *m.* **.1** armored car **2.2** armor-clad warrior

زرهدار، زره دار zirehdā́r armor-clad; armored

زری ¹ zə́raj *m.* ☞ ځُری

زري ² zarí **1** woven of gold threads **2** gold

زری ³ zarə́j *f.* food sufficient for өne night

زری ⁴ zraj wise, intelligent

زریځ zarídz ☞ زرین

زریز ¹ zaríz *m. medicine* croup

زریز ² zəríz **1** *m. history* commander of 1,000 men **2** thousandth لس زریز ten-thousandth

زري زرکه zarí zə́rka *f.* monal (the female Himalayan pheasant)

زرین zarín **1.1** golden د لمر زریني پلوشي the golden rays of the sun **1.2** gilded, gold-colored; blond **1.3** embroidered in gold زرینه خولۍ skullcap embroidered in gold **2** *m. proper name* Zarin

زرامبو zṛāmbó dessicated, dried in the sun, jerked

زرامبوی zṛāmbúj *m.* smell of burned cloth

زرامبو zṛān ☞ زران

زرپ zṛap *m.* narcissus

زرتوب zaṛtób *m.* زرتیا zaṛtjā́ *f.* old age, declining years

زرخن zəṛkhə́n rancid (e.g., of oil)

زرختوب zəṛkhəntób *m.* زرخنوالی zəṛkhənvā́laj *m.* rancidity, rankness

زرخنول zəṛkhənavə́l *denominative, transitive* [*past:* زرخن یې کړ] **1** to cause to be bitter and malodorous **2** to spoil, deteriorate the quality (of food products)

زرخنبدل zəṛkhənedə́l *denominative, intransitive* [*past:* زرخن شو] **1** to become rancid **2** to spoil

زرخوړی zəṛkhúgaj depressed, dispirited

زرښت zaṛə́kht *m.* **1** old age; antiquity **2** aging **3** decrepitude, dilapidation

زرغی ¹ zərghə́j **1** vacillating, indecisive **2** *m.* improvement of appetite (in a patient who is recovering)

زرغی ² zərghə́j *f.* vacillation, indecisiveness

زرکوټی zaṛkúṭaj *m.* rags, worn-out clothing

زرگوټی zəṛgóṭaj *m. diminutive* heart *idiom* زرگوټی دې ورووبست You have frightened him.

زرگوټی ² zəṛgúṭaj *m.* ☞ زروکی

زرگی zəṛgáj *m.* **1** *diminutive* heart زرگی مي وريت شو I was worn out. **2** (Dear) son! (address of a father to a son)

زرن zəṛə́n manly, bold, brave, valiant

زرند zəṛánd زوند zuṛánd ☞

زوږندول zəṛandavə́l *transitive* ☞ زوږندول

زوږندبدل zəṛandedə́l *intransitive* ☞ زوږندبدل

زوږ zṛo *oblique plural of* زره ¹

زوږ zaṛó *oblique plural of* زوږ ¹

زوتیا zaṛvā́laj *m.* ☞ زوتیا

زوه ور zṛəvár زوور ☞

زوورتوب zṛəvartób *m.* زوورتیا zṛəvartjā́ *f.* **1** bravery, valor, manliness, boldness زوورتوب کول to be brave **2** courage

زووږمه zṛogmá *f.* **1** odor of burnt rags **2** scorched rag applied to a wound

زووکی zaṛúkaj *m.* **1** clothing; dress **2** cloth panel (of a banner) **3** *dialect* old rag, tattered cloth

زوول zaṛavə́l *denominative* [*past:* زوو یې کړ] **1** to wear out **2** to age

زووږمه zṛumbáj *f.* زوومبی zṛumba *f.* ☞ زوومبه

زره ¹ zṛə *m.* **1** heart; soul **a** په زره سره with the heart (to feel) **b** attentively د زره کوښښبنونه the sparking, activation, etc., of aspiration د زره له کومي wholly from the heart, from a pure heart, from the depths of the soul; completely sincerely د زره د پاسه چرته without wanting to, unwillingly د زره حال ویل to bare the soul *proverb* زره ځي هلته پښنی هم ځي Wither the heart is attracted, thence the feet will go. *Eastern proverb* د زره و زره ته لارده، زره په زره پوهېږي Heart gives tidings to heart. د مور زره په ځوی او د ځوی زره په دیوال *Eastern saying* The son repays his mother's love with ingratitude. په زره کوږ، په خوله خوږ *saying* Honey on the lips, but ice in the heart. چه په زره یې غم د یار وي، څه به خوب کا؟ *Eastern proverb* If there is longing in the heart for the beloved one, how can one sleep? چه د زره مینه یې نه وي، مین یې مه کړي د ملا په تعویذونو *Eastern proverb* You can't force kindness. **2** bravery, valor, courage gallantry, daring د لوی زره خاوند brave person; daredevil زره کول to display valor, exhibit manliness سل زوونه یوکول to take courage, take heart **3** wish, desire **4** feeling, love زره چه مین شي *proverb* ښایست نه غواړي، خوب چه راشي بالبنت نه غواړي When love comes, indeed beauty will not be necessary, and you will desire sleep, but will not request a pillow. **5** stomach **6** interior part of something, core, center زره اچول **a** to fear, be frightened of, be afraid of; worry, be alarmed **b** to fall into confusion **c** to be melancholy, miss; be dejected زره اخیستل **a** to be discontented, be dissatisfied; be disillusioned **b** to take close to one's heart **c** to get out of the habit of **d** to refuse, not consent to زره مي اور اخلي I am very thirsty. I am tortured by thirst. I suffer from the heat. زره اړېدل to be distressed, be upset د چا زره اوچتول *Eastern* to cheer someone up **a** زره بدېدل to take offense; grow angry **b** to quarrel زره پخېدل to worry about; grieve for; to suffer زره په یو شي پخېدل to sympathize with someone's misfortune or grief زره پرته کول **a** to cease to want cheer, cheer up **b** to make glad, gladden; give great pleasure زره پورته کېدل **a** to be satisfied, be glad, be merry **b** to feel sick, feel nauseous **c** د ... څخه زره پورته کېدل to grow cool to someone or something; cease to love someone or something زړه **a** زړه په زړه پوهېدل to be intitiated into the inner secrets of another **b** to share all one's thoughts په زړه ترل **a** to get accustomed to, become attached to **b** چا زړه تشول to trust someone, rely on someone **a** to get very angry, be beside oneself **b** to speak directly, speak openly, speak without reservations, be frank زړه توربدل **a** to be distressed, be upset; be saddened, be grieved **b** to feel hostility, cease to love کله کله له ځانه مي زړه تور شوئ دئ Sometimes I was opposed myself. زړه مي توري تکي شو څوکار مي پاى ته ورساوه I was completely worn out when I finished work. زړه مي پر توري تکي شو I became very sorry for him. زړه مي پر چا تور دود کېدل to sympathize with someone, feel really sorry for someone زړه تکېدل to vanish (of desire) زړه چاودل **a** to die (of heartbreak) **b** to be disturbed, be distressed زړه چول to labor, toil زړه مه خوړل، زړه مبنل کېدل to be pained, grieve ☞ زړه ښکېدل خوره Don't be upset. زړه خورل کېدل to become ill with tubercolosis زړه خوربدل *khvagedál* to be worn out, be exhausted زړه خوربدل to be satisfied, get pleasure from, experience pleasure; be moved to ستا په خبرو مي زړه خوږ شو It was nice to have talked with you. زړه پر سنک پرخوربدل *khugedál* to feel pity for someone, pity someone خواركي مي زړه خوربري I feel very sorry for that poor devil Sanak. زړه دربول **a** to be afraid, experience fear, fear **b** to display indecisiveness ولاړشه، زړه مه دربوه! Proceed more boldly! زړه ډاډه کېدل to calm دربېدل to quail, blench, hesitate, vacillate د چا زړه لاس ته راوستل I calmed down. زړه مي ډاډه شو attract or incline someone to one's side ☞ زړه رببل د چا زړونه رببل to do something nice for someone; oblige someone; not زړه ساتل disturb someone زړه پر چا سپکول **a** to grow very angry at someone; be beside oneself; vent one's spleen on someone **b** to speak one's mind, openly, without reserve زړه مي پري سپک کړ *Eastern* I told him everything without holding back. زړه په سرول to have one's wishes realized; have a feeling of satisfaction; be satisfied احمد د خپل کتاب په میندلو زړه سوړ کئ Ahmad rejoiced at finding his book. **b** to quench the thirst زړه سړبدل **a** to be quenched (of thirst) **b** to be attained, be realized (of desires) **c** to have a feeling of satisfaction **d** to grow cold, cool to someone or something د کاره to پر چا زړه سول، پر چا زړه سوړ شو This work bores me. مي زړه سوړ شو sympathize, feel sorry for someone زړه مي ورباندي وسو I felt sorry for him (her, them). زړه شکول to grow cool, indifferent to something زړه شین کېدل **a** to be upset, be disturbed **b** to grow cold, cool to something **c** to get exhausted, become worn out زړه **a** زړه بنه کول to worry، د چا زړه کبنل زړه ښنوېدل ☞ ښنکل to rejoice, experience joy **b** to amuse oneself, have fun, have a good time وى و کار ته زړه to enjoy one's thoughts زړه په خبره بنه کول to make up one's mind د څخه زړه صبرول to patiently endure separation from someone زړه غوربول to cheer up د چا زړه غوربول to quail, play the coward, be afraid د چا زړه کبنل to dishearten someone زړه غوربېدل to fear, be afraid of د چا زړه کبنل to frighten, put fear into someone زړه د گوگله کبنل، زړه د گوگله راکبنل

---

a زړه د گوگله درکبنل، زړه د گوگله ورکبنل to frighten or scare someone to death زړه دي د گوگله را ځخه وکبن You scared me to death. **b** to disappoint somebody, captivate somebody محبوبا يي زړه د گوگله to be زړه پر کبنبنستل He was charmed by Mahbuba. کبنلئ دئ zealous, be painstaking; show zeal زړه کورت کورت کېدل to wish very much, wish for or desire something strongly; زړه کېدل to desire زړه مي هم کبري He doesn't want to work. زړه يي کارته نه کبري *saying* I am in a state of indecision. I want to او ساړه مي هم کبري and at the same time don't want to. زړه گرزبدل **a** to reconsider, change one's opinion **b** to convert to another faith زړه گروبدل to fall in love زړه لگبدل، د احمد زړه گرو شوئ دئ Ahmed fell in love. زړه to grow calm; satisfy oneself, become convinced چا زړه لگبدل to lose heart, play the زړه لوبدل، د چا زړه لوبدل to be generous coward زړه ماتول *Eastern* **a** to dissuade from something **b** to discourage ځما زړه يي مات کړ He dissuaded me. زړه ماتبدل، د چا زړه ماتبدل **a** to be dissatisfied **b** not to have the wish or intention, not to wish زړه مربدل، د چا زړه مربدل to feel apathy to something, be indifferent to something; be sated with something په چا زړه منبل کبدل، د چا زړه منبل کبدل to want something very much پوري زړه مبنتل **a** to love someone **b** to believe someone, trust زړه مبندل someone زړه منل to believe, trust, have confidence in زړه په ننوتل to fall in love زړه نبنتل to dare, venture زړه و يو کار ته نيول to compose oneself, cease to worry, come to one's senses زړه ورته پخبدل to decide on something زړه ورل to nourish enmity toward someone چا ته زړه ورکول to encourage someone زړه وبنل to win someone's heart, captivate, charm; attract زړه وبنل **a** to be satisfied with something **b** to tolerate something, endure something زړه ولاربدل to wish, want, have the desire زړه وهل **a** to mistrust someone; have doubts about someone; mistrust someone's word **b** to pall on, bore **c** to evoke revulsion, sicken **d** to despair of په دي *Eastern* to زړه وبستل Don't be distressed about that کبنبي زړه مه وهه frighten, scare زړه يخول to calm down; grow cool toward په چا to زړونه بندي کول to arrange for someone's election زړونه اینبودل captivate, charm زړونه رببل **a** to set the teeth on edge (with something sour, tart) **b** to give pleasure دا نغمه زړونه رببي This melody consoles the soul. زړه ته پربوتل **a** to believe something ځما I don't believe it. I can't believe this. **b** ☞ زړه ته نه پربوځي زړه ته to profoundly lament; feel deeply; be زړه ته غم اچول، لوبدل melancholy, grieve پر زړه زور تبرول to act against one's desires پر **a** زړه مالگي پاشل، پر زړه مالگي تویول، پر زړه مالگي دورول to open or exacerbate (old) wounds of the heart; evoke cruel, unpleasant recollections **b** to console someone hypocritically په زړه اور لگبدل Everything is په زړه مي اور لگبري څه اوبه راکه زړه اور اخیستل ☞ burning inside, give me water. په زړه خورل to collect oneself په زړه to vacillate, doubt; disbelieve someone's words په زړه پوري توربدل کبدل to be nice, be kind, be pleasant ... په زړه يي وخوره چه It came into his head that ... په زړه کبني خیره درلودل to have a suspicion, suspect زړه کبدل، په زړه راکبدل، په زړه درکبدل، په زړه ورکبدل، په زړه suspect گرزبدل، په زړه راگرزبدل، په زړه درگرزبدل، په زړه ورگرزبدل، په زړه لوبدل، په

زړه رالوبېدل، په زړه درلوبېدل، په زړه ورلوبېدل، a to remember, recollect b to guess, estimate په گوتي زړه وهل to exacerbate (old) emotional wounds; evoke painful, unpleasant thoughts and recollections په زړه کښي خوړل کېدل Don't torment my soul. په زړه کښي مي گوتي مه وهه *Western* په زړه کښي زهيرېدل *Eastern* to endure silently; be disturbed at heart but not show it په زړه کښي غل کېدل to play the hypocrite; play up to په زړه کښي لاس گرزېدل to feel uneasiness, worry, be alarmed, be troubled زوی مي نن نه دئ راغلئ، په زړه کښي مي لاس گرزي My son did not arrive today; I am worried. په زړه کښي نقش کول a to imprint on the heart b to remember well, learn by heart دغه زما خبري بايد په زړه کښي نقش کړې! Remember my words well! تر زړه وينې څخېدل to bleed (usually of the heart); be terribly disturbed, grieve د زړه اور سړول a to quench thirst b ☞ زړه په سړول د زړه په زور تلل، زړه اور سړېدل to scarcely move, drag along with difficulty, drag oneself along د زړه ايستل، د زړه څخه ايستل to put out of one's head, forget د زړه زنگ اخيستل، د زړه زنگ ايسته کول، د زړه زنگ لېري کول to calm down, make to forget oneself, ones troubles, etc. چا ته د تر زړه د وينې څخېدل ☞ زړه څخه وينې څخېدل زړه غوته خلاصول، چا ته د زړه تولي غوتي خلاصول to pour one's heart out, open up to someone د زړونو رگونه خوڅول to charm, captivate زړه وينې خورل a to take a lot of trouble for a person; take care of, worry about someone b to grieve د بېلتون له لاسه د زړه وينې خورم The separation tormented me. د زړه کول to do something with love, put one's heart into work, work with enthusiasm د زړه د کومي څخه د زړه لمبه مړه کول، د زړه لمبه وژل to put one's heart into a job, work with spirit, work with enthusiasm د زړه لمبه مړه کېدل ☞ د زړه څخه وتل to be forgotten د زړه په سړول to be quenched (thirst) د زړه نه ولی پرېکېدل to suffer, torment oneself, be distressed د چا زړه دپاره ويل د زړه څخه ايستل، د زړه ايستل *Eastern* ☞ وېستل to comfort someone د زړه غوته هوراېدل to cease to envy someone زړه مي په زړه کښي دئ خبري مي I planned to play a dirty trick on him. زړه يي د وينو مي په اوبه نه سکي I don't trust him. I can't rely on him. ور سره مي زړه دئ His heart bled. He was quite distraught. زړه کښي دئ ؤک شو He likes me. پلار مي په دوه زړه کښي دئ My father vacillates; he doesn't know how to act, what to decide upon. زړه يي خورا نرئ سوي دئ He is quite touchy. He is very sensitive. زړه يي د سړي همسايه شو His heart sank. His heart skipped a beat. زړه يي سپين دئ He's a simple chap. He is a naive soul. د دغه سړي زړه لکه درياب دئ He is a bighearted man. دغه زړه تش پاتي شو He was disillusioned. زما د داسي مجلسو څخه زړه نه راڅي I do not feel at home with people like that. *Eastern* په زړه يي څنگل ولاړ دئ He is cruel. His heart has hardened. زما زړه هم تينگ نشو، په ژرا شوم I couldn't restrain myself, and began to sob. زړه يي نرئ نرئ کېدو، وړي و He was so hungry that he had stomach cramps. د مرغۍ زړه ؤک و Murgi was very much saddened. زړه دئ ټول لره! Don't worry! Be calm!

زړه ² zaṛá 1 *feminine singular of* زوړ ¹ په زړه دوستي old friendship زړه اوسبدل to live in the old way or in the traditional style 2 *f.* old woman

زړه ³ zaṛá *m. Western vocative of* زوړ زړه سړيه! زړه! Hey, old man!

زړه بداوی zṛəbadávaj *m.* dislike, hostility یو تر بل زړه بداوی پیدا کول to dislike one another, feel hostile to one another

زړه بدوالی zṛəbadwálaj *m.* 1 enmity, hostility 2 dissatisfaction

زړه پاڅوونکی zṛə pātsavúnkaj invigorating, enlivening

زړه پوري zṛəpuri 1 pleasing; attractive; nice 2 interesting 3 heartfelt, sincere

زړه ترکی zṛətrákaj ¹ distressing; sad, mournful

زړه ترکي zṛətrakí ² *f.* distress; sadness, melancholy

زړه تورن زړه توری zṛətoráj zṛətorə́n 1 dissatisfied 2 indifferent, apathetic د چا نه زړه تورن کېدل a to be dissatisfied with someone; be offended by someone b to grow cool toward, be indifferent to someone

زړه ټکی zṛətə́kaj *m.* intimate secret; testamentary desire (wish states in a will)

زړه چوونکی zṛə chavavúnkaj heartrending زړه چوونکی آواز heartrending cry

زړه ستړی zṛəkhastá ☞ زړه خسته

زړه خلاصی zṛəkhlásaj glad, jolly, rousing

زړه خوريني zṛəkhvərínaj distressed, saddened

زړه خوږی zṛəkhúgaj ¹ ☞ زړه سواندی ¹

زړه خوږي zṛəkhugí ² *f.* ☞ زړه سواندي ²

زړه ږغی zṛəḍə́ghaj ¹ ☞ زړه تورن

زړه ږغي zṛəḍəghí ² *f.* 1 repulsion 2 indifference, apathy

زړه راښکون zṛərākhkún *m. regional* attractiveness, fascination, charm

زړه راښکوونکی zṛə rākḥúnkaj ☞ زړه وړونکی

زړه راپوونکی zṛə rapavúnkaj disturbing, enrapturing; thrilling

زړه ستړی zṛəstə́raj 1 tired, exhausted 2 sad

زړه سواندی zṛəsvándaj ¹ 1 kind, responsive, sympathetic, compassionate 2 solicitous

زړه سواندي zṛəsvándí ² *f.* 1 goodness, kindness, responsiveness, sympathy, compassion 2 solicitude د چا سره زړه سواندي کول a to have sympathy toward someone, sympathize with someone; feel sorry for someone b to care for, be solicitous of someone

زړه سوروالی zṛəsoṛwálaj *m.* coolness, indifference د چا سره زړه سوړوالی لرل to grow cold toward someone

زړه سوی zṛəsávaj grieved, disturbed; unhappy, suffering

زړه شین zṛəshín زړه شيني zṛəshínaj 1 irate, wrathful 2 sad, mournful; distressed 3 angry, offended ده ده له لاسه زړه شين یم I am angry with him. I am offended by him. د کار څخه زړه شين یم I have lost interest in the work.

زړه غلوونکی zṛə ghulavúnkaj tempting زړه غلوونکی شیونه zṛə ghulavúnki temptation

زړه غوخوونکی zṛə ghutsavúnkaj depressed, sad; gloomy

زړه غوښتی zṛəghúkhtaj 1 attractive, interesting 2 wanted, desirable

زړه کښونکی zṛə kkhúnkaj ☞ زړه وړونکی

زړه لوغی zaṛá lvághe *f.* milch cow with a yearling calf

زړه ماتوالی zṛəmātválaj *m.* **1** exhaustion **2** discontent **3** discontent

زړه ماتوونکی zṛə mātavúnkaj grieving; sad (of thoughts)

زړه مینتی zṛəməkhátaj favorite, beloved

زړه نازړه zṛənāzṛə́ unwillingly, involuntarily, reluctantly

زړه ور zṛəvár **1** courageous, brave, daring, bold; fearless په بی پروائی زړه ور desperately brave زړه ور کېدل to be courageous, be brave, be bold **2** courageously, bravely, boldly **3** *m. proper name* Zravar

زړه ورتوب zṛəvartób *m.* زړه ورتیا zṛəvartjá *f.* valor, courage, boldness, fearlessness; daring په زړه ورتوب courageously, bravely, boldly

زړه وروول zṛəvaravól *denominative, transitive* [*past:* زړه وریې کړ] **1** to act bravely, act boldly, act courageously **2** to cheer up; hearten, put courage into someone

زړه وړونکی zṛəvṛúnkaj زړه وړونی zṛəvṛúnaj **1** pleasing, attractive **2** beautiful, fine, lovely, entrancing, captivating, charming

زړی [1] zə́ṛaj *m.* **1** seed, pit (e.g., watermelon, muskmelon, cantaloupe); stone (of a fruit) **2** kernel, core **3** *technology* core **4** basis, nucleus

زړی [2] zəṛáj *m. medicine* jaundice

زړیدل zaṛedál *denominative, intransitive* [*past:* زوړ شو] **1** to age, grow old **2** to wear out, become decripit **3** to get out of commission, fall into ruins **4** to become obsolete, become outmoded دا فکر زوړ شوئ دئ This idea is already outmoded.

زړیده zaṛedə́ *m. plural* **1** aging **2** wear; decrepitude; deterioration

زړی لوغی zaṛé lávghza *f.* ☞ زړې لوغزه

ززغولي zazghúli *f. singular* cracklings

زړ [2] zig *regional* ☞ زیر

زړگی [1] ziggáj *m.* ☞ زیرگی

زړول [2] zigavál *transitive* ☞ زیرول

زړه [1] zigá *feminine singular of* زړ

زړه [2] zigé *m. plural of* زړ

زړی [1] zgaj *m.* calloused portion of the sole of a camel's foot

زړي zigé *feminine plural of* زړ

زړیدل [2] zigedál *intransitive* ☞ زیریدل

زست zist *m.* ☞ زیست

زشت zisht **1** ugly; vile, unsightly, misshapen **2** bad, foul, evil **3** hareful; despicable

زشکله zə́shkəkla ☞ ځنبكله

زبنا zəkhá *f.* sesame

زبنت [1] zəkht very; exceedingly زبنت ډېر very much زبنت ښه very good زبنت لوی very big, huge زبنت ډېر تاثیر لرل to exercise very strong influence زبنت ډېر فرق لرل to differ strongly

زشت [2] zəkht ☞ زشت

زبنته [1] zə́khta ☞ زبنت اختلافات زبنته زیات دئ The contradictions were very great.

زبنته [2] zə́khta *feminine singular of* زبنت [2]

زبنتیل zəkhtejə́l *intransitive* [*past:* ویې زبنتیه] **1** to shame **2** to embarrass, inhibit **3** to hurt, offend

زبنتیینه zəkhtejə́na *f.* insult; affliction

ځنبكله zákhkála ☞ ځنبكله

زبنا zə́khá *f. regional* ☞ زبنا

زعامت za'āmát *m. Arabic* leadership د چا تر زعامت لاندي، د چا د زعامت لاندي under someone's leadership

زعفران za'afarán *m. Arabic plural* saffron

زعفراني za'afarāní **1** *adjective* saffron **2** yellow, yellow color

زعیم za'ím *m. Arabic* [*plural:* زعیمان za'imán *Arabic plural:* زعما zu'amá] **1** head, leader **2** president, chairman; responsible person

زغ [1] zəgh *m.* ☞ جغ

زغ [2] zəgh *m.* sound of meat sputtering (in a frying pan)

زغاره zghára *m.* millet-flour bread

زغاست zghāst *m.* raid, descent, attack *idiom* په زغاست لاندي کول to outdistance

زغاستل zghāstál *intransitive* ☞ ځغستل

زغاسته zghāstə́ *m. plural* zgästa *f.* ☞ ځغاسته

زغاله zaghālá *f.* lump or piece of dough

زغبندی zəghbandáj *m.* ☞ جغونډی

زغر [1] zighír *m. plural* **1** flax **2** flaxseed د زغرو تبل، د زغرو غوړي flaxseed oil

زغر [2] zghər *m.* ☞ زغره

زغرد zghard **1.1** fast, quick, swift, agile, smart **1.2** gallant; brave, courageous **2.1** quickly, swiftly, soon, smartly **2.2** bravely, courageously په زغرد ویل to speak straight, speak without beating around the bush **3** *m.* **.1** speed; quickness, swiftness **3.2** bravery, courage

زغردتوب zghardtób *m.* زغردتیا zghardtjá *f.* زغردوالی zghardválaj *m.* **1** speed; adroitness, quickness **2** bravery, courage

زغردول zghardavál *denominative* [*past:* زغرد یې کړ] to speed up, hasten

زغرلی zghərə́láj **1.1** *history* dressed in chain mail or armor **1.2** armed, mailed زغرلی موټر armored automotive vehicle **2** *m. history* armored warrior

زغروبی [1] zgəróbaj *m.* troublemaker

زغروبی [2] zgəróbaj *m.* talisman; amulet

زغرووی zghəróvaj *m.* watchman (for a melon field)

زغره zghára *f.* armor, chain mail *idiom* زغره غوټه tight and strongly knotted knot

زغرلی zghərjālaj ☞ زغرلی

زغرد zghaṛd ☞ زغرد

زوغرنڅه zughṛə́ndza *f.* ☞ زوغرنڅه

زغستل zghəstál *intransitive* ☞ ځغستل

زغل zghal *m.* race

زغلا zghalá *f.* raid, descent, attack زغلا کول to effect a raid, attack

زغلول zghə́lavál **1** *transitive* ☞ ځغلول **2** *m. plural* races د اسونو زغلول horse races

زغلی zgalí *present tense of* زغستل

زغلیدل zghaledál *intransitive* [*past:* وزغلیده] to run; rush along, tear along موټر ګړندی زغلیده The automobile speedily rushed along.

زغلیده zghaledə́ *m. plural* run, running زغلیده رازغلیده bustle

زغم zgham *m.* 1 patience ☞ زغم تېرول 2 absorption; blotting up, taking up 3 digestion, assimilation (of food) 4 suppression (of desire); abstinence

زغمل zghaməl *transitive* [*past:* وي يې زغامه] 1 to endure, bear, tolerate; stand خپل قهر زغمل to restrain anger 2 to absorb, take up 3 to digest, assimilate (food) 4 to take (medicine) 5 *physics* to exclude (light)

زغمناک zghamnák endurable

زغمون zghamún *m.* 1 endurance 2 patience زغمون لرل *a* to be hardy *b* to have patience

زغمېدل zghamedál *intransitive* [*past:* وزغمبد] 1 to be borne, be put up with 2 to be absorbed, be taken up, be blotted up 3 to be digested; be assimilated (food)

زغمېده zghamedə́ *m. plural* patience, restraint

زغن zaghán kite (the bird)

زغوپر zghupár *m.* misfortune, disaster زغوپر وهلئ a sufferer, one who has fallen into disaster or distress

ژغورل zghorál *transitive dialect* ☞ ژغورل

زغومی zghúmaj *m.* whirlpool, maelstrom

زغونډی zghunḍáj *m.* ☞ جغونډی

زغه zgḥə *m.* ☞ غز

زفت zift *m.* 1 resin, tar, pitch رومي زفت asphalt 2 gum

زقوم zakúm *m.* zakḳúm *Arabic* 1 upas tree, *Antiaris toxicaria* 2 bitter stuff, poison

زک zək *m.* [*plural:* زکان zəkā́n] inflated skin (used for river crossings)

زکات zakā́t *m. Arabic religion* 1 zakat (tax on property for aiding poor Muslims) 2 purification; purity, righteousness

زکام zukā́m *m. Arabic* head cold; catarrh of the upper respiratory passages

زکاوت zakāvát *m. Arabic* purity

زکات zakā́t *m. Arabic* ☞ زکات

زکريا zakarjā́ *m. proper name* Zakariah

زکندان zəkandán *m.* ☞ ځان کندن

زکوات zakavát *m. Arabic plural of* زکات

زکه zə́ka ☞ ځکه

زکي zakí *Arabic* 1 pure, righteous, pious 2 devout

زگ ¹ zag *m.* ☞ ځگ ¹

زگ ² zig *Eastern* ☞ زېر ²

زگال zəgál *m.* bread (e.g., crumbled up in buttermilk)

زگروا zgarvā́ *f.* ☞ زگبروی

زگ گری zaggə́raj *m.* oil press

زگول zagavál *transitive* [*past:* وي يې زگاوه] to froth

زگېدل zagedál *intransitive* [*past:* وزگېده] to foam, froth

زگرووی zgervā́j *m.* groan, moan, sigh زگبروی کول to groan, moan, sigh

زگېرل zgeṛál *transitive* [*past:* وي يې زگېړه] to baste, tack (sewing technique)

زل ¹ zə́l *m.* 1 time, occasion 2 blow, shock په يو زل *a* at once *b* with one blow ☞ ځل ¹

زل ² zə́l *m.* horse-cloth ☞ ځل ²

زل ³ zal *m.* tempering, annealing

زلال zulā́l *Arabic* clear, pure, translucent زلالي اوبه clear water, spring water

زلاند zə́lā́nd ☞ ځلاند

زلپی zə́lpəj *f.* 1 link for a door chain 2 door chain 3 sword knot

زلخوږتوب zə́lkhuģtób *m.* زلخوږتیا zə́lkhuģtjā́ *f.* زلخوږي zə́lkhuģí intense hunger

زلخوږی zə́lkhúģaj very hungry, hungry as a wolf

زلزلا zalzalá *f. Arabic* earthquake, temblor; oscillation 2 shock

زلنت zaləkht *m.* ☞ ځلنت

زلفه zúlfa *f.* [*plural:* زلفي zúlfi *usually plural plural:* زلفیاني zulfijā́ni] curls, ringlets, locks of hair پریشاني زلفه loose-hanging hair

زلفی zulfə́j *f.* ☞ زلپی

زلکېدل zalkedál *intransitive* [*past:* زلکبدل وزلقبده *past:* وزلکبده] to sparkle, shine

زلل zə́lál *m.* 1 slip, blunder, false step; error 2 short weight 3 harm; damage; loss زلل رسول to inflict harm; cause damage

زلما zalmā́ *f.* youth

زلمکی zalmakáj 1 young 2 growing, sprouting زلمکی کبدل to germinate, sprout

زلموتی zalmótaj *m.* youth, lad, stripling

زلمی ¹ zalmáj 1 *m.* .1 [*plural:* زلمي zalmí *plural:* زلمیان zalmijā́n] youth, lad, young man هغه خو زلمی دئ He is already a grown lad. 1.2 eligible bachelor, young man د واده زلمی eligible bachelor 1.3 *proper name* Zalman 2.1 young, youthful زلمی کول to rejuvenate; make young, make hale and hearty زلمی کبدل to become a youth, grow (of a boy) 2.2 new; fresh 2.3 tender

زلمی ² zalmáj 1 *f.* girl 2 *feminine singular of* زلمی ²

زلمیتوب zalmitób *m.* youth

زلمیکوټ zalmajkóṭ Zalmajkot (settlement near Gerat)

زلند ¹ zə́lə́nd ☞ ځلاند

زلند ² zə́lánd 1.1 imperious, commanding, masterful 1.2 oppressive; cruel, tyrannical 2 *m.* aggressor

زلوبی zalobə́j *f.* ☞ ځلوبی ²

زلوچه zalochá *f.* rug

زلول zalavál *transitive dialect* ☞ ځلول

زلونه zalvaná *f.* ☞ زولانه

زله zilá tired

زلېچه zelechá *f.* rug, rugs used as bedding

زلیخا zulajkhā́ *f.* zulejkhā́ *proper name* Zuleika

زلېدل zaledál *intransitive dialect* ☞ ځلبدل

زلینه zə́lína *f. abusive* trollop, strumpet, streetwalker

زم ¹ zam *m.* wound, injury; hurt

زم ² zəm *Eastern a combination of the pronoun* زه *and the conjunction* هم خو زم وایم I also; and I said so too

زما zmā *pronoun* **1** *oblique of* زه زما څخه near me, from me; زما سره with me **2** *possessive* my زما کور my house زما کتابونه my books *idiom* زما دي وي؟ What's this to do with me? زما يي پري څه! Oh-oh, I swear! زما دي وي که دي پريږدم! Oh, oh, I don't allow you!

زمام zimā́m *m. Arabic* **1** reins of government; power, authority; governing, government **2** reins

زمامدار zimāmdā́r *m.* **1** ruler **2** leader

زمامداري zimāmdārí *f.* **1** government; authority **2** leadership

زمان zamā́n *m. Arabic* **1** ☞ زمانه په زمان او مکان time and place زمان زمان at times, at periods **2** *proper name* Zaman

زمانه zamāná *f.* **1** time, period له پخوا زماني، له پخوا زماني څخه، له خو زمانه from ancient times; from olden days زمانو زمانو راهيسي some time تر ډيرو زمانو پوري a long time, extended time په نن زمانه in our time په يوه زمانه کښي one time; some time په زمانو زمانو دوام کول to last, continue for a long time **2** century, epoch **3** world, creation **4** fortune, fate

زمانه سازي zamānasāzí *f.* time-serving

زماني zamāní **1** temporal **2** chronological **3** *grammar* pertaining to tense or time زماني قيد adverb of time

زمبر zambā́r [1] *m.* harrow

زمبر zambá́r [2] *m.* loud voice زمبر کښل to shout

زمبر zambá́r [3] *m.* thick (dense) woods; thicket, copse

زمبک zumbák *m.* ☞ زنبک

زمبل zambál *transitive* ☞ ځمل

زمبور zambúr *m.* **1** pincers; tongs **2** ☞ زنبور

زمبولی zambólaj *m.* follicle, utricle

زمبه zámbá [1] ☞ زنبه

زمبه zámba [2] *f.* زمبی zambáj *m.* winking

زمبدل zumbedál *intransitive* [*past:* وزمبيده] to shake, oscillate, rock

زمبل zambél *m.* basket په زمبل کښي اينبودل to put into a basket

زمرچی zmarbacháj *m.* **1** tiger cub **2** lion cub

زمرد zamurrúd [1] *m.* emerald

زمرد zamarrúd [2] *m.* icicle

زمرک zmarák *m. proper name* Zmarak

زمرکټی zmarkaṭáj *f. dialect* **1** tigress **2** lioness

زمرلای zəmarlā́j ☞ زمريالی

زمره zumrá *f. Arabic* **1** sort, category په دغه زمره کښي including **2** the masses; crowd

زمری zmaráj [1] *m.* [*plural:* زمري zmarí *plural:* زمريان zmarijā́n] **1** tiger **2** lion **3** ☞ اسد **4** brave man, valiant man **5** *proper name* Zmaran زمري *zmarí* د زمري لکی ته ګوته وروړل the lion's share د زمري برخه **a** to fan dormant sedition **b** to bring unpleasantness on oneself

زمری zmaráj [2] *f.* tigress, lioness

زمريالی zmarjālā́j **1.1** military, warlike, martial **1.2** courageous, brave, valorous **2** *m.* **.1** warrior, soldier, trooper **2.2** a brave, courageous man

زمرين zəmarín *m.* **1** hard freeze, intense cold spell **2** dew **3** Hades, Hell, the Nether Regions

زمزم zamzám *m. Arabic* well in Mecca (near the Kaaba)

زمزموربلی zamzmogólaj weakened by wounds

زمزمه zamzamá *f. Arabic* **1** rumor, talk **2** singing, tune, melody زمزمه کول to sing, break into song

زمکه zmə́ka *f. Eastern* land, earth د زمکي خاوند landowner ☞ ځمکه

زمکي zmə́ke [1] *Eastern plural of* زمکه

زمکی zmakə́j [2] زمکی غوښنه mushroom

زمن zəmán *m.* زمنه zámna *f.* task, obligation

زمند zamánd **1** *m. plural* the Zamandi (tribe) **2** *m.* Zamand (tribesman)

زمنه پوهی zámnapóhaj زمنی zamnáj intelligent; conscientious; comprehending; quick on the uptake

زموخ zmokh zmukh زموخت zmokht zmukht **1** sharp, harsh **2** crude, rough **3** *figurative* severe

زموختیا zmokhtjā́ *f.* زموخوالی zmokhvә́laj *m.* **1** sharpness, harshness **2** rudeness, roughness **3** *figurative* severity

زموږ zmug *pronoun Western* ☞ زمونږ

زمول zmol **1** faded, withered **2** tarnished, dull **3** *medicine* numb, mortifying **4** unhappy **5** helpless, powerless, weak **6** bedridden (of a patient)

زمولتوب zmoltób *m.* زمولتیا zmoltjā́ *f.* زمولوالی zmolvә́laj **1** fading **2** state of being tarnished or dried up **3** *medicine* necrosis **4** powerlessness, weakness

زمولول zmolavál [*past:* زمول يي کړ] **1** to cause to fade **2** to make unhappy **3** to weaken; make powerless, make helpless

زمولی zmólaj **1** powerless, helpless **2** unhappy

زمولېدل zmoledál *denominative, intransitive* [*past:* زمول شو] **1** to fade, wither; wilt **2** to grow dim **3** to weaken, become weak, lose strength

زمونږ zmung zəmung **1** *oblique of* مونږ څخه زمونږ at me, with me, from me **2** *posessive pronoun singular & plural* our

زمونږه zmúnga *pronoun dialect vice* زمونږ

زمی zә́maj [1] *m. dialect* ☞ ژمی

زمی zmә́j [2] *f.* زمی zəmә́j *botany* saltwort, *Salsola*

زمبر zmer *m.* زمبرنه zmerә́na *f.* guard, guarding

زمبری zméraj *m.* custodian

زميندار zamindā́r **1** agricultural زميندار خان landowner **2** *m.* **.1** farm owner; farm landlord **2.2** peasant farmer

زمينداري zamindārí *f.* **1** landed estate; country estate, farm estate **2** *agriculture* زميندارۍ کول to be engaged in farming

زمينداور zamindāvár *m.* Zamindavar (district) ☞ کجکي زمين داور [2]

زميندوز zamindóz *regional* underground زميندوز ګاډي subway

زمينه zaminá *f.* **1** background; basis, foundation د مفاهمۍ زمينه پيدا کول to find a basis for agreement **2** grounds, conditions, circumstances زمينه برابرول، زمينه تيارول، زمينه آماده کول to create conditions, establish grounds **3** field, branch

زميني zaminí land, terrestrial زميني هدف terrestrial object, feature *idiom* توت زميني wild strawberries

زنا zinā́ *m. Arabic* adultery; fornication زنا كول to commit adultery; fornicate

زناديقه zanādiḳá *m.* زناديق zanādíḳ *Arabic plural of* زنديق

زنار zunnár *m. Arabic* 1 زنار zunnár *m. history* coarse belt (which Christian subjects of Muslim governments were obliged to wear) 2 sacred cord (which Brahmins wear across the shoulder)

زنازه zanāzá *f. dialect* ☞ جنازه

زناكار zinākár *m.* adulterer; seducer

زناكاره zinākára *f.* adulteress; seducer

زنانه zanāná 1.1 female, feminine, woman's زنانه كميس woman's dress 1.2 effeminate 2 *f.* .1 women 2.2 women's half of the house; harem 2.3 woman

زنانه خانه zanānakhāná *f.* the women's half of the house; harem

زنبر zambár *m.* ☞ زمبل

زنبق zambáḳ *m.* زنبك zambák *m.* zambə́k *m.* 1 lily 2 iris, yellow flag, blue flag 3 tassel; pompom 4 sharp-pointed beard 5 embroidery, decoration (on a dress)

زنبل zambə́l *transitive* ☞ حُمل

زنبور zambúr *m.* 1 wasp; bee 2 pincers, press, vice 3 ☞ زنبورك

زنبوردار zamburdár *m.* beekeeper, apiarist

زنبورداري zamburdārí *f.* beekeeping

زنبورك zamburák *m. history* small cannon (carried on a camel)

زنبه [1] zambá hirsute (of the body)

زنبه [2] zə́mba *f.* winking زنبل كول to wink

زنبل zambə́l *m.* ☞ كچكول

زنجير zandzhír *m.* ☞ زنجير

زنچخى zənchúkhaj *m.* chin

زنځ zandz *m.* alum

زنځه zə́ndza *f.* centipede

زنځي [1] zə́ndzi *f. plural* slime; mud

زنځى [2] zəndzə́j *f.* feminine adornment in the form of ringlets

زنځي [3] zə́hdzi *plural of* زنځه

زنځير zandzír *m.* chain; manacles, handcuffs

زنځيري [1] zandzirí 1 pertaining to chains or handcuffs *military* زنځيري خپاره an extended line of riflemen at the time of an attack زنځيري خط a type of stenography 2 mad, insane

زنځيري [2] zandzirí *m. literal* with a broken chain; *figurative* insane, crazy

زنخ zanákh *m.* زنخدان zanakhdán *m.* chin

زنخول zankhvál *m. anatomy* diaphragm

زند zand *m.* the Zend (the translation and commentary on several parts of the Avesta in the Pehlevi language)

زندان zindán *m.* prison; dungeon د پوروړو زندان debtor's prison

زنداني zindāní *m.* prisoner, person under arrest; captive زنداني كېدل to be imprisoned, be under arrest

زندرك zandə́rák *m.* lower jaw

زندقه zandaḳá *f. Arabic* 1 *f. religion* fire-worship 2 heresy; atheism, unbelief

زندگاني zindagāní *f.* زندگي zindagí *f.* life, existance

زنده باد zindabā́d Long live … !

زنده جان مال zindadzhā́n living زنده جان cattle

زندى zəndáj *f.* noose, lasso زندى اچول *compound verb* a to hang someone b to suffocate someone, strangle someone

زنديق zindíḳ *m. Arabic* [*plural*: زناديقه zanadiḳá *Arabic plural*: زناديق zanādíḳ] 1 *religion* fire-worshipper 2 heretic, atheist

زندى zəndáj *m.* ☞ زوندى

زنزاوى zanzávaj *m.* 1 drops of water 2 drop

زنزل zanzavə́l *transitive* ☞ خنځول

زنزه zə́hza *f.* ☞ زنزه

زنزي [1] zə́nzi *plural* mud; slime

زنزي [2] zə́nzi *plural of* زنزه

زنزېدل zənzedə́l *intransitive* [*past*: وزنزيده] to flow down; to drip; to flow, leak, pour, stream

زنغلاى zanghə́láj *m.* strip of material sewn to the frayed edge of (Middle-Eastern type bell-bottom) trousers

زنكدن zankadán *m. regional* death throes, state of being on the verge of death

زنگ [1] zang *m.* 1 bell برقي زنگ electric bell 2 chime, small bell زنگ وهل a to ring b to jingle

زنگ [2] zang *m.* rust زنگ كول، زنگ نيول، زنگ وهل to be covered with rust, oxidize زنگ كېدل to rust

زنگ [3] zang *m.* hard frost, extreme cold

زنگانه zangānə́ *oblique of* زنگون

زنگبار zangbár *m.* Zanzibar

زنگ زده zangzadá rusty, rusting, rusted, covered with rust

زنگل [1] zangə́l *transitive* [*present*: زانگي *past*: وزنگېده] to rock, swing, rock to and fro

زنگل [2] zangál *m. dialect* forest, woods د يوه زنگله منظره a forested landscape ☞ خنگل

زنگن zangə́n 1 rusty, rusted, rust-covered 2 dirty, slovenly

زنگنى zanganə́j *f.* gore or gusset reaching to the knees (of trousers)

زنگ نيوونكى zang nivúnkaj rusting, rust-covered

زنگورى zangúraj *m.* bunch of grapes

زنگوگرافي zingogrāfí *f.* typefounding

زنگول zangavə́l *transitive* [*past*: و يي زنگاوه] 1 to rock, rock to and fro 2 to rock (e.g., a cradle); lull by rocking

زنگوله zangulá *f.* zangolá handbell, gong

زنگوله والى zangolavā́laj *m.* curliness, curlyheadedness

زنگولى [1] zangolə́j *f.* melancholy, sadness

زنگولى [2] zangulé zangolé *plural of* زنگوله

زنگون zangún *m.* زنگانه zangānə́ *oblique* [*plural*: زنگونونه zanganúna] knee زنگون كېدل *compound verb* a to get ready to fire; aim b to get to work vigorously; work hard c to let a chance slip by, take a false step, fail, fall behind in work زنگون لگول to kneel زنگون وهل a to bang one's knees, regret, deplore, be distressed b to submit, surrender په زنگانه كښېنول to bring to the knees زنگون پک *obsolete military* From a kneeling زنگون كېږد!

position! (as a command) *idiom* زړه ته زنګنونه ورکول to suffer, be tormented

زنګي [1] zangí *m.* artistic dancer, skillful dancer

زنګي [2] zangí *m.* 1 Black (person) 2 native of Zanzibar

زنګېدل [1] zangedól *intransitive* [*past:* وزنګبده] 1 to rock, sway 2 to be rocked, be lulled (child, cradle)

زنګېدل [2] zangedól *intransitive* [*past:* وزنګبده] to jingle, clank

زنل zanól znól [*past:* وي زانه] 1 *botany* to graft, engraft 2 to push into, shove into 3 to pierce, punch a hole in

زننه zanóna *f.* 1 *f. botany* graft, grafting 2 pushing in, shoving in, insertion 3 piercing, punching (hole in)

زنه [1] zóna *f.* chin له ناکامۍخخه لاس پر زنه کښېنستل to be depressed, fall into a depression, hang the head څوک تر زنه نیول، څوک تر زني نیول to beg, entreat someone

زنه [2] zna *f. botany* saltwort, *Salsola*

زنه [3] zaná *f.* dye (special type used to stain leather after tanning)

زنهار zinhár 1 unconditionally 2 Look out! Watch out! Careful!

زنغوزه zaŋghozá زنغوزی zanghozáj *m.* pine nuts

زنکی [1] zoŋkáj *m. dialect* juvenile ☞ ژنکي [1]

زنکی [2] zaŋǝkáj *f.* caraway

زنی [1] zóŋaj *m.* boy, young lad

زنی [2] zóŋaj *m.* ☞ زونی

زنیه لار zaŋjalár *f.* custom of barring the way of the bridegroom near the bride's village (with a view to obtaining a ransom)

زو [1] zo ☞ زوکول

زو [2] zo *dimunitive* son! د پلانکي زو! Hey, sonny!

زو [3] zu *m.* piece of brick

زو [4] zov *imperfect tense of* زوول [1]

زوا zvā *f.* supplication, fervent entreaty

زواحق zavāhík *m. Arabic plural zoology* reptile

زوار zuvvár *m. Arabic plural of* زائر

زواک zvāk *m. dialect* life ☞ ژواک

زواگر zvāgór *m.* person seeking forgiveness

زوال [1] zavál *m. Arabic* 1 destruction, decline; dying out 2 loss 3 decline or setting of the sun at dusk

زوال [2] zavál *m.* ☞ زول [1]

زوبل zóból *dialect* ☞ ژوبل

زوتول zavtavól *denominative, transitive* ☞ ضبطول

زوج zaudzh *m. Arabic* 1 pair, something occuring in pairs 2 married couple, spouses

زوجي zaudzhí *Arabic* 1 paired, composing a pair 2 marital, pertaining to marriage زوجي تعلقات marital relations

زوجیت zaudzhiját *m. Arabic* marriage, matrimony

زوخلول zukhlavól *transitive* ☞ څكلول

زوخلېدل zukhledól *intransitive* ☞ څكلېدل

زود zud 1 quickly, hurriedly, soon 2 *combining form* زود هضم easily digestible (of food)

زودات zavdát *m.* ☞ زاوزات

زود رنجه zudrándzha hot-tempered, irascible; touchy

زوول [1] zodól *transitive* ☞ زوول [1]

زودهضم zudházm easily digestible (of food)

زودي zudí *f.* speed, celerity, haste

زور [1] zor *m.* 1 strength, force, might په زور by force, forcibly په وچ a strongly زوره a strongly په زوره زوره a strongly, د توري او توپک په زور by force of arms b very loudly زور اخیستل to be forceful زور کول to try, apply force a to try with all one's might b to overcome دوه زوره کول a to try with all one's might b to overcome ناجوړی زور لگول Illness overcame him. زور په وکئ a to employ efforts; use force b to deal with (matters) زور نیول to try و یو کار ته زور to try و یو کار ته زور to strengthen, reinforce something زور وهل to force one's way through, break a way through for one's self 2 help د متو په زور by means of physical force 3 coercion, compulsion; violence پر چا He emphasized that … په دې خبره یې زور واچاوه … to compel someone *idiom*

زور [2] zvar *m.* 1 zabar, fatha (vowel signs) 2 top زور زبر وبستل *Eastern* to look over carefully; inspect from head to toe ☞ زبر

زور [3] zavór *m.* 1 grief, affliction, confusion, upset; concern, worry 2 cares, trouble(s); agitation, anxiety, unrest

زور [4] zur *m.* opening (of a potter's wheel)

زور [5] zur thin sound, delicate sound

زوراستري zorāstrí *f.* Zoroastrianism

زورآور zorāvár 1 strong, powerful; mighty 2 energetic 3 populous (of a city)

زورتوب zurtób *m.* زورتیا zurtjā́ *f.* good sound

زوردار zordár strong, powerful, mighty

زورزیاتی zorzjātáj *m.* oppression, violence

زورطلبه zortalába requiring great strength دپر زورطلبه کارونه کول to be engaged in heavy physical labor

زورق zavráḳ *m. Arabic* 1 boat, launch 2 gondola (of a balloon)

زورقي zavraḳí 1 pertaining to a boat 2 pertaining to a pontoon

زورکی zvarakaj *m.* zvar kaj zvarakaj (vowel sign for the phoneme ه /a/)

زورگیر zorgír 1.1 demanding, insistent 1.2 unyielding, insistant 2 *m.* usurper

زورل zoról *transitive* [*past:* وي یې زوره] 1 to torture, oppress 2 to bore, bother 3 to curse, reprove 4 to compel

زورلی zoróle *f.* cursing, abuse زورلي کول to curse, abuse

زورنه zoróna *f.* 1 oppression; pressure, stress 2 bawling out, telling off; cursing out 3 coercion

زورتوب zurvắlaj *m.* ☞ زورتوب

زورور zoravár zoravár 1 strong, mighty, powerful 2 strong, very great; stormy زورور باد strong wind زورور سېلاو storm-lashed floodwaters 3 prominent, outstanding زورور سندرغاری a prominent singer 4 beautiful, excellent زوروري سندري جوړول to compose beautiful songs 5 strong bright (light)

زورتوب zoravtób *m.* زوروتیا zoravartjā́ *f.* زوروالی zoravarvắlaj strength, power, might

زورول zavravól *transitive* [*past:* وي یې زوراه] 1 to grieve, upset 2 to torture 3 to oppress

زوركی zvarakā́j *m.* ☞ زوره کی

زوري zorī́ *f.* strength, might

زوریدل zavredól *intransitive* [*past:* و زوریده] **1** to grieve for, be disturbed, be grieved **2** to be pain-wracked, suffer

زور¹ zoṛ **1** *f.* زړه zaṛá *m.* [*plural:* زاړه zāṛə́ *f. plural:* زړي zaṛé] **1.1** old, ancient زوړ اثر زوړ بنار old man زوړ ښار old city monument of antiquity **1.2** old, ancient; worn; secondhand, used **2** *m.* old man

زوړ² zvaṛ **1** *m.* slope, declivity, incline, descent **2** *attributive* gently sloping, uneven لوړ زوړ an uneven place ☞ خوړ

زوړ پوړ zoṛ-póṛ old, ancient; worn; used

زوړتوب¹ zoṛtób *m.* **1** old age, declining years **2** antiquity; superannuation

زوړتوب² zvaṛtób *m.* slope, declivity, incline, descent

زوړتیا¹ zoṛtjā́ *f.* ☞ زوړتوب

زوړتیا² zvaṛtjā́ *f.* ☞ زوړتوب

زوړښت zoṛə́ṣht *m.* ☞ زوړتوب¹

زوړکی zoṛə́kaj *m.* ☞ زوړکی

زوړند zvaṛə́nd pendent, hanging سر زوړند head hanging dejectedly

زوړندول zvaṛəndavól *denominative* [*past:* زوړند یې کړ] to hang, suspend

زوړندی zvaṛəndáj *m.* basket containing food products (hung high to protect the contents from mice and cats)

زوړندیدل zvaṛəndedól *denominative* [*past:* زوړند شو] to be hung, hang

زوړوالی¹ zoṛvā́laj *m.* ☞ زوړتوب¹

زوړوالی² zvəṛvā́laj *m.* ☞ زوړتوب²

زوړول zoṛavól *transitive* ☞ زوړل

زوړی¹ zvəṛáj *m.* ☞ زوړ²

زوړی² zavṛáj *m.* load; burden, cargo

زوړیدل zoṛedól *intransitive* ☞ زړیدل

زوز zoz *m.* [*plural:* زوزان zozā́n] *plural botany* camelthorn (the bush)

زوزات zavzā́t *m.* زوزاد zavzā́d *m.* ☞ زاوزات

زوزکودی zozkudáj *m.* temporary (hunter's, trapper's) cabin (constructed of thorn brush)

زوزگوړی zozguṛáj *m.* زوزگوړی zozgvuṛáj *f.* manna (dried, edible exudate) of the camelthorn bush

زوزجانه zozjā́ṇa *f.* clumps of thorn bushes

زوږ¹ zvag *dialect* **1** *m.* **.1** noise; hubbub; din; uproar زوږ کول to make a noise, cause an uproar زوږ مي تر غوږ شو I heard the noise. دا څه شور او زوږ دئ؟ What's that noise? **1.2** anxiety; distress **1.3** hunger; want **2.1** lost **2.2** disordered, deranged

زوږ² zvəg *m.* bitter taste, bile, gall

زوږتلانگه zvagtalā́nga *f. dialect* echo

زوږم zvagə́m *m.* ☞ وږم

زوږناک zvagnā́k noisy

زوږوزوږ zvag-u-zvúg *m.* زوږه زوږه zvága *f. dialect* ☞ زوږ¹

زوږیدل zvagedól *intransitive dialect* [*past:* و زوږیده] to make noise, make a roar (of a crowd)

زوش zoḵh *m.* ☞ جوش

زوښا zoḵhā́ *f.* sweetened syrup (of unabi and other berries); jelly

زوښول zoḵhavól *transitive* ☞ جوشول

زوښه zoḵhá *f.* ☞ زوښنه

زوغرنځه zughṛə́ndza *f.* pistachio (tree, nut) yielding a tannic substance, buzunchu

زوک¹ zuk *m.* **1** labor; effort, striving **2** concern, worry

زوک² zok *m.* hardened earth of a karez or Afghan irrigation well or ditch system

زوکړه zókṛa *f.* **1** birth د زوکړي پر وقت at birthday د زوکړي سالگره birthday **2** *biology* artificial propagation **3** fertilization صناعي زوکړه artificial fertilization (insemination)

زوکړی¹ zókəṛəj born نوی زوکړئ هلک newborn baby boy

زوکړي² zókṛi *plural of* زوکړه

زوکلول zuklavól *transitive* [*past:* و یې زوکلاوه] to torment, torture

زوکلیدل zukledól *intransitive* [*past:* و زوکلیده] to be tormented, be tortured

زوکول zokavól *transitive* [*past:* و یې زوکاوه *past:* زوي یې کړ] **1** to give birth to, bear **2** to give birth to, serve as a reason for

زوکونه zokavə́na *f.* birth

زوکونکي zokavúnke *f.* woman in or approaching childbirth, parturient woman

زوگ¹ zvag *m. Eastern* ☞ زوږ

زوگه¹ zúga *f.* ☞ زوله

زول¹ zavál *m.* yarrow, milfoil

زول² zul *m.* **1** ☞ خول **2** cold; cold winds

زول³ zol *m.* **1** ☞ کولک **2** worry, concern

زولال zulā́l *m.* aggressor; oppressor; user of force

زولاندی zulā́ndaj oppressive, repressive

زولانه zavlā́na *f.* [*plural:* زولني zavlané] handcuffs, manacles, chains *idiom* د اسارت زولني ماتول to throw off the chains of slavery *idiom* د چا استقلال ته زولني اچول a to deprive someone of the possibility of independent action b to deprive someone of independence

زولن zavlə́n purulent, festering زولن کېدل to fester, become purulent

زولنه zavlaná *f. Eastern* ☞ زولانه

زوله¹ zolá *f.* household belongings; furnishings, goods and chattels

زوله² zóla *f.* **1** long bag (for transport of cargo on a camel) **2** old-style silk-lined shirt **3** any very large object

زوله زوله zóla-zóla huge, enormous (of an object) زوله زوله کېدل to be huge, be enormous (of an object)

زولی¹ zoláj *m.* felt bag (for transporting skin bags of oil on camelback)

زولی² zoláj *f.* ☞ خولی

زولي زنبیلي zóli-zanbéli *f. singular* rags, old clothes

زوم¹ zum *m.* **1** son-in-law **2** groom

زوم² zvam **1** scanty, insufficient; small **2** diminished, decreased زوم کول to subtract, diminish زوم کېدل to diminish, decrease, become scanty, run short

زومبا zómbā *f.* Zomba (city)

زومبک zumbǝ́k *m.* ☞ زمبک *astronomy* ستوري the Pleiades

زومبکی zumbǝkáj *m.* 1 small pompom; tassel 2 pendant earring

زومتوب ¹ zumtób *m.* state of being a son-in-law or groom; state of being a newly-married man

زومتوب ² zvamtób *m.* زومتیا zvamtjā́ *f.* insufficiency, want

زوم خیل zumkhél *m. plural* 1 son-in-law's kinfolk or tribe; son-in-law's relations 2 bridegroom's kinfolk or tribe; bridegroom's relations

زومگاری zumgāṛáj *m.* best man (for a groom)

زومگی zumgáj *m. affectionate* son-in-law

زومل zumál *m.* promise

زومنه ¹ zvámna *f.* soup, chowder

زومنه ² zvámna *f.* loss, damage

زوموالی ¹ zumvālaj *m.* ☞ زومتوب ¹

زوموالی ² zvamvālaj *m.* ☞ زومتوب ²

زومول zvamavál *denominative* [*past:* زوم يې کړ] to remove, do away with

زومی ² zumǝ́j *f.* ☞ زمی

زومبدل zvamedǝ́l *denominative* [*past:* زوم شو] to disappear, vanish

زومی کنده zumǝjkánda *f.* meadow, pasture

زون zǝván ☞ زولن

زونبه zúmba *f.* wink, winking; blink, blinking

زوند zvand *m. dialect* ☞ ژوند

زوندون zvandún *m. dialect* ☞ ژوندون

زوندی zvandáj *dialect* ☞ ژوندی

زوندی zunḍáj *m.* 1 pompom, tassel 2 pendant

زونډیگر zunḍigár *m.* زونډیگر zunḍigǝ́r زونډی والا zundiválā́ *m.* braid maker, gold-lace maker

زونگه zúnga *f.* 1 hum, buzz 2 echo, replication (of sound), reverberation, repetition (of sound) چا ته زونگه ورسول to let someone know, inform someone

زونی zúni ☞ ځيني

زونی zúṇaj *m.* seed (e.g., of a melon, watermelon)

زووب zǝbób *m.* 1 percolation, soaking through 2 wetting

زوول ¹ zovǝ́l [*past:* زو يې زووه *and* و يې زووه] to bear, give birth to

زوول ² zovǝ́l *transitive* ☞ ژوول

زوولودژیست zoolodzhíst *m.* zoologist

زوولودژی zoolodzhí *f.* zoology

زوولی zovǝ́laj born

زوونکی zovúnke *f.* parturient woman, woman in childbirth

زوونه zovǝ́na *f.* birth د زوی زوونه the birth of a son

زوه zǝ́va *f.* pus زوی کول to suppurate (a wound)

زوی ¹ zoj zuj *m.* [*plural:* زامن zāmǝ́n] 1 son ديني زوی، نيولئ زوی foster son د زوی بنادي the celebration of the birth of a son زوی mama's boy 2 young (of animals)

زوی ² zǝ́vi *feminine plural of* زوه

زوبرگی zvǝrgáj *m.* ☞ زگبروی

زویک zojék *m.* زویکی zojǝ́kaj *m. diminutive* son, sonny

زوی مړی zojmǝ́raj zújmǝraj *m.* a man whose son has died زوی مړی کول to deprive of a son زوی مړی کېدل to lose a son

زوی نيو zujnív *m. dialect* foster son

زوی والی zojvǝ́laj *m.* زوی ولی zojvalí *f.* sonship

زه ¹ zǝ *first person singular, oblique* 1 I (the subject of the action of intransitive verbs in all tenses and of transitive verbs in the present and future tenses) هم زه namely me, wit me زه ځم I am going. زه کار کوم I am working 2 me (the object of the action of intransitive verbs in ergative constructions) زه يې ووهلم He (they) beat me. They beat me.

زه ² za *dialect* ☞ ځه ²

زهد zuhd *m. Arabic* selfless devotion, asceticism, aloofness زهد کول to be a selfless devotee, be an ascetic; hold oneself aloof from this world

زهر zahr *m.* زهر záhǝr *plural* poison, bane; toxic substance په خوراک to زهر ورکول to poison food, put poison in food کښی زهر اچول poison, envenom څوک په زهرو وژل to poison someone

زهرا zuhrā́ *f. regional* ☞ زهره ²

زهرالود zahrāhlúd poisonous; poisoned

زهرخند zahrkhánd *m.* malevolence, malicious pleasure in the misfortune of others په زهرخند سره gloatingly, with malicious pleasure at another's ill-fortune

زهردار zahrdā́r poisonous; poisoning; poisoned

زهرموره zahrmorā́ زهرمهره zahrmuhrā́ *f.* bezoar

زهرناک zahrnā́k ☞ زهردار

زهروي ¹ zuhraví venereal امراض زهروي venereal disease

زهروي ² zahraví poisonous, toxic

زهره ¹ zahrá *f.* 1 bile 2 gallbladder 3 *figurative* mainlines, bravery, courage, valor *idiom* زهره چودل a to be frightened b to be very disturbed

زهره ² zuhrá *f. astronomy* Venus

زهره ترکی ¹ zahratarákaj grieving څوک زهره ترکي کول to torture someone زهره ترکي کېدل a to be unsuccessful; try in vain b to be strongly disturbed

زهره ترکی ² zahratrakí *f.* 1 death 2 torment, suffering; strong grief

زهري ¹ zahrí ☞ زهردار

زهري ² zuharí *Arabic* venereal

زهریت zahriját *m.* toxicity; poisonousness, noxiousness (of air)

زهریله zahrilá *regional* ☞ زهردار

زه گذاری zehguzāri *f.* laying eggs, depositing of eggs (of insects)

زه گیر zehgír *m.* 1 notching of a bow (for fastening the bowstring) 2 fingerboard (of a stringed musical instrument)

زهوب zǝhób *m.* زهوب zahúb 1 pus 2 mucus, secretion

زهوزاد zǝhozād *m.* ☞ زاوزات

زهول zǝhavál *transitive* [*past:* و يې زهاوه] 1 to exhaust, wear out 2 to use up 3 to remove, eliminate 4 to grieve

زهه zahá 1 worn-out 2 vanished 3 distant

زهېدﻝ zəhedә́l *intransitive* [*past:* و زهېده] **1** to grow thin; become emaciated **2** to become worn out; get tired **3** to vanish **4** to wear oneself out

زهیر zahír **1** gaunt, emaciated **2** weak, powerless; ill; tired **3** saddened, grieved په خورا زهیر وضيعت کېدﻝ in a sorry state of affairs **4** pining for someone

زهیرتوب zahirtób *m.* زهیرتیا zahirtjá *f.* زهیروالی zahirvā́laj *m.* **1** exhaustion, state of being worn out **2** weakness, powerlessness; weariness **3** sadness, longing; grieving د زهیرتوب خبره ده چه sadly, worthy of compassion

زهیروﻝ zahirvә́l *denominative* [*past:* زهیر یې کړ] **1** to exhaust, wear out **2** to make weak, make powerless; drain, deplete **3** to grieve, sadden

زهیرېدﻝ zahiredә́l *denominative, intransitive* **1** to become exhausted **2** to get tired **3** to become sad, become distressed

زې ¹ ze *f.* the name of the letter ز

زی ² zəj *f.* extended family, clan

زی ³ zaj *m.* **1** posterity, descendants **2** *combining form* tribe, tribal subdivision **a** احمدزي akhmadzí Akhmadzai (subdivision of various tribes) **b** akhmadzáj *m.* Akhmadzaj (tribesman)

زې ⁴ ze *combination of the pronoun* زه *and* یې *Eastern* که زې پرېږدم یې if I leave him

زی ⁵ zaj *m.* ☞ ژی ¹

زی ⁶ zəj *f.* ☞ ژی

زیا zjā *f.* **1** memory **2** notification زیا نیوﻝ to inquire about, ask about somebody **3** knowledge, wisdom

زیات zjā́t zijā́t **1** much; highly; more ډېر زیات very much تر هر څه زیات most of all, نور هم زیات still more, all the more زیاته frequently, repeatedly په زیاته all the more since; یو کار پر بل زیات بلل، کومه چاره پر له حده زیات excessively especially په زیاتو to prefer one to another **2.1** many; numerous بله زیاته بلل in many places په زیات مقدار in a large quantity زیات خلق ګڼل many think that ... many suppose that ... **2.2** largest, greatest زیات حد the maximum, limit زیاته توجه کوﻝ to pay more attention to something

زیات توب zjāttób *m.* ☞

زیاتره zjātára great part, majority په مونږ کښې زیاتره کسان many of us; the majority of us زیاتره خلق ور باندي خبر دي The majority of us know this.

زیاتیګر zjātvál *m.* ☞

زیاتوالی zjātvā́laj *m.* **1** increase; rise; growth څلور چنده زیاتوالی four times **2** plurality **3** intensification **4** surplus د دریابو د اوبو زیاتوالی flood, high water **5** addition, increment

زیاتوب zjātób *m.* ☞ د رایو زیاتوالی د معاش زیاتوالی increase in wages په زیاتوب by a majority of votes

زیاتوﻝ zjātavә́l *denominative, transitive* [*past:* زیات یې کړ] **1** to increase; raise **2** to multiply **3** to add, add to something غواړم ... I wish to add that ... **4** to intensify, strengthen **5** to develop زراعت زیاتوﻝ to develop agriculture

زیاتی ¹ zjātáj *m.* **1** increase; raise **2** addition, augmentation **3** violence, force په چا زیاتی کوﻝ to oppress someone *idiom* په خبرو کښې ډېر زیاتی کوﻝ to be too obstinate, be overly stubborn

زیاتي ² zjātí zijātí **1.1** over and above that, besides that, aside from that; moreover بل زیاتی شي ته اړ دی نه زیاتي besides this; moreover نه یم I need nothing more. **1.2** usually, ordinarily **2.1** superfluous زیاتي مواد **a** garbage **b** discharge **2.2** spare, reserve (of things) **3** already

زیاتېدﻝ zjātedә́l *denominative, intransitive* [*past:* زیات شو] **1** to increase; rise **2** to be added to, augment **3** to grow, intensify **4** to exceed, excel

زیاتیګر zjātigár *m.* زیاتوال zhātvál *m.* agressor

زیاد zijā́d *Arabic* ☞ زیات

زیادآب zijādā́b full, flood, having a high water-level

زیادت zijādát *m. Arabic* ☞ زیاتوالی

زیادوﻝ zijādavә́l *transitive* ☞ زیاتوﻝ

زیادېدﻝ zijādedә́l *intransitive* ☞ زیاتېدﻝ

زیار zjār *m.* endeavor, effort; labor په لوی زیار with great effort, with great labor زیار ایستل، زیار کښل to endeavor, strive, labor; make efforts دا کار د یو شي زیار په ځان منﻝ to personally undertake work ډېر زیار غواړي This work requires great diligence.

زیار ایستونکی zjār istúnkaj **1** assiduous; zealous, industrious **2** *m.* worker

زیارت zjārát *m.* zijārát *Arabic* **1** pilgrimage, visit to holy places **2** visit, call زیارت کوﻝ **a** to make a pilgrimage, visit holy places **b** to call on, visit د مور او پلار زیارت کوﻝ to visit relatives **c** espistolary **c** to vouchsafe to read (a letter) **3** ☞ زیارت ګاه *idiom* د زیارت روغ Thursday

زیارتغاخهی zjāratghā́khaj *m.* Ziarat Gakhaj (principal town, Momand Province)

زیارت ګاه zijārātgáh *m.* place of pilgrimage; shrine, holy place

زیارسی zjā́rsaj **1** agile, quick **2** bright

زیار کښونکی zjār kkhúnkaj **1** assiduous, zealous; industrious **2** *m.* a worker

زیار کښي zjārkakhí *f.* زیارنه zjārә́na *f.* endeavor; zeal, fervor, industry

زیاړه zjā́ṛa *f.* abuse زیاړي کوﻝ to swear, curse

زیان zjā́n zijān *m.* **1** damage, loss, harm زیان مېندﻝ to suffer, receive damage or injury; suffer loss **2** loss زیانونه *military* casualties

زیانکار zjānkár **1** harmful, detrimental **2** *m.* pest, vermin

زیان کاري zjānkārí *f.* damage, injury, detriment زیاري کوﻝ to harm

زیانمن zjānmә́n **1** suffering, receiving damage, suffering a loss زیان من کېدﻝ to suffer, receive damage, suffer a loss **2** ruinous

زیانوﻝ zjānavә́l *denominative, transitive* [*past:* زیان یې کړ] **1** to inflict damage **2** to cause an abortion, abort

زیاني zjāní **1** ☞ زیانمن **2** *f.* woman who is having an abortion

زيانېدل zjānedál *denominative, intransitive* [*past:* زيان شو] **1** to suffer, suffer damage, suffer loss **2** to be injured **3** to be aborted (of a fetus)

زيب zeb *m.* **1** adornment, furnishings **2** beauty, elegance

زيبا zebā́ **1** beautiful; well-dressed; elegant **2** *f.* kind of pattern on a skullcap of the Middle-Eastern type

زيباک zebā́k *m.* Zebak (district, Badakshan)

زيب النسا zebunnisā́ *f. Arabic proper name* Zebunnisa

زيبائي zebāī *f.* beauty, elegance; attractiveness

زيبو zebó *f. endearment form from* زيب النسا Zebo

زيتون zajtún *m. Arabic* olive, olive tree د زيتون غوري olive oil

زيتونه zajtúna *f.* ☞ زيتون

زيتونه zajtúna *f. proper name* Zajtuna

زيج zidzh *m. Arabic* astronomical tables; astronomical calendar

زيد zajd *m. Arabic proper name* Zejd *idiom* که زيد وي که عمر وي someone or other, any او که بكر

زير zir *m.* ☞ خير

زبر zer *m.* zir **1** bottom, lower part **2** zer, kasra (vowel sign)

زير zir *m.* zer *music* **1** high tone; high note **2** thin string (giving a high note)

زيراستر zerastár *m.* lining

زيربغلي zerbaghalí *f.* a small drum

زيربنا zerbanā́ *f. philosophy* basis

زيرجامه zerdzhāmá *f.* pants

زيرخانه zerkhāná *f.* **1** cellar, basement. **2** adobe house; dugout

زيرخول zerkhól *m.* primer end of a cartridge case

زيردست zerdást **1.1** dependent (on); subject (to); subordinate; junior (to) **1.2** submissive (to) **2** *m.* **.1** subordinate **2.2** *history* a vassal

زيرزميني zerizaminí **1** underground, subterranean **2** *f.* ☞ زيرخانه

زيرک zirák **1.1** quick on the uptake, clever; inventive, resourceful **1.2** sharp-witted **1.3** efficient, adroit **2** *m.* **.1** *proper name* Zirak **2.2** Zirak (a branch of the Durrani tribes)

زيركي ziraki *f.* **1** cleverness, quick-wittedness; inventiveness, resourcefulness **2** sharp-wittedness **3** efficiency, adroitness

زيرگى zergáj *m.* ☞ زگبروى

زيرل zeral *computer science* compress, to compress

زيرلب zeriláb softly, in a whisper زيرلب ويل to whisper

زيرمه zérma *f.* **1** preparation; stockpiling, reserve د كال زيرمه the reserve for a year **2** supply زيرمه كول a to stockpile, create reserves b to supply **3** concern, care **4** mission, message, commission **5** visit, call

زيرمه تون zermatún *m. military* supply directorate, quartermaster department

زيرمه خور zermakhór *m.* partisan, follower

زيرمه سات zermasā́t *m.* warehouseman

زيرمه وال zermavā́l *m. military* chief of supply

زيرنى zerənáj stagnant, foul (e.g., of water)

زير و بم zir-u-bám *m.* high and low notes, extremes ربابه زير و بم راوستل a to strike chords on the rebab b to disturb, strike a sensitive note د نغمو په زير و بم كښي ځان هېرول to be engrossed in music

زير و زبر zer-u-zabár زير و زبر كول to examine closely

زيره zirá *f.* caraway

زيرى zéraj *m.* **1** (joyous, pleasant) news, tidings پر چا زيرى كول، چا ته زيرى ورول to convey (joyous) tidings to someone; congratulate someone **2** dandelion **3** spiderweb (flying in the air)

زيرى ziré *plural of* زيره

زيرى گمى zerajgáraj *m.* ☞ زيرى وال zerajvál *m.* man bringing good news; harbinger of good tidings

زير zjar **1** yellow; reddish blond زير رنگ pale (of the face) رنگ دي ولي زير دئ؟ What makes you pale? **2** *m.* yolk (of an egg)

زير zeṛ *m. plural* brass

زيرانكه zjaṛānáka *f.* **1** yellow wagtail **2** ☞ زيركه

زيرپوستى zjarpóstaj yellow-skinned

زيربخلى zjaṛzbekhálaj **1** yellow **2** pale, grown pale **3** thin-looking, pinched-looking

زيركه zeṛóka *f.* zéṛka yellow bunting, *Emberiza bruniceps*

زيرگل zjaṛgúl *m.* **1** dandelion **2** *proper name* Zjargul

زيروالى zjaṛvā́laj *m.* **1** sallow complexion **2** paleness

زيرول zjaṛavál *denominative* [*past:* زير يې كړ] **1** to make yellow; color yellow **2** to make pale

زيره zjáṛa *f.* swearing, abuse زيري كول to abuse, swear at

زيره zjáṛa *feminine singular of* زير

زيرى zeṛáj *m.* **1** *medicine* jaundice **2** yolk (of an egg)

زيرى zjaṛój *f.* disgrace زيري كول a to shout, cry out b to defame, revile

زيرى zjaṛáj **1** yellow **2** pale

زيرېدل zjaṛedál *denominative, intransitive* [*past:* زير شو] **1** to yellow; be colored yellow **2** to grow pale **3** to ripen (of grains, etc.)

زيگ zeg *m.* birth

زيگ zig *m.* زيره zigé زيگه zigá *f. m.* [*plural:* زيگه zigá زيگى zigé] **1** hard, firm, stiff **2** crude, rough; unfinished **3** sharp (of a retort) **4** steep, perpendicular; inaccessible **5** direct, frank (of a person) **6** uncomely, ungainly **7** stern, cruel **8** rude (of words)

زيگتوب zigtób *m.* زيگتيا zigtjá *f.* ☞ زيروالى

زيگده پگده zégda-pégda *f.* appearance, beginning, origin

زيگه zégga *f. astronomy* zodiac

زيگى ziggáj *m.* hedgehog

زيگى ziggój *f.* female hedgehog

زيگمه zégma *f.* eyelid

زيگنتون zegəntún *m.* lying-in home

زيگنځى zegəndzáj *m.* birthplace; homeland

زيگنده zégənda **1** *f.* **.1** *figurative* source, spring, wellspring **1.2** fruit, result, outcome زيرنده كول a to give birth to b to form, create (e.g., words) **1.3** *grammar* ☞ مصدر *attributive* زيرنده ځای a low marshy place, water-filled hollow

زبرندی zegəndáj **1** fruitful **2** productive, resulting

زبروالی zigvālaj *m.* **1** firmness, hardness, stiffness **2** rudeness, roughness **3** sharpness **4** directness, frankness

زبرول ¹ zegavól *transitive* [*past:* و يي زبراوه] **1** to give birth to, bear **2** to create

زبرول ² zigavól *denominative, transitive* [*past:* زبر يي کړ] **1** to harden, make stiff **2** to make rude, rough **3** to tighten

زبره ¹ zigá *feminine singular of* زبر ²

زبره ² zigə́ *m. plural of* زبر ²

زبربدل ¹ zegedól *intransitive* [*past:* وزبربد] **1** to be born **2** to appear, arise, begin **3** to flow out, ooze out (of water)

زبربدل ² zigedól *denominative, intransitive* [*past:* زبر شو] **1** to get hard, become firm; grow stiff **2** to grow crude, become rough **3** to be sharp **4** to be direct, frank **5** to be embittered against someone; be in a temper **6** to get down, work; set briskly to work *idiom* د بوډا غوني زبر شو باندي The old man was stupified. زبر شو My hair stood on end.

زبربدلئ zegedóləj **1** having been born (newly-born) نوی زبربدلی کوچنی newborn, infant **2** arising, appearing, beginning

زبربدنه zegedóna *f.* زبربده zegedə́ *m.* **1** birth **2** appearance, rise, beginning, origin

زیست zist *m.* life, existence زیست کول to live, exist

زیست باهمي zist-i-bāhamí *f.* coexistence

زیگ ² zig *Eastern* ☞ زبر

خْیگر zigár *m.* ☞ خْیگر

زیگوالی zigvālaj *Eastern* ☞ زبروالی

زیگول ² zigavól *transitive Eastern* ☞ زبرول

زیگبدل ² zigedól *intransitive Eastern* ☞ زبربدل

زیل ¹ zájl *m.* zájəl kind, sort, type په زیل زیل خواره various dishes څه زیل؟ What kind?

زیل ² zil *m.* zel **1** cord (for tying up a person under arrest) **2** stubbornness, obstinacy

زیل ³ zajl *m.* ☞ زبلی

زیلاند zíländ *m.* نوی زیلاند New Zealand

زیلچه zilchá *f.* small rebab

زبله zelá *f.* **1** tendril (of a plant, runner) **2** branch (of a tribe)

زبلی zelə́j *f.* **1** tendril (of a plant) **2** rootlet **3** *medicine* scrofula

زیم zjam *m.* moisture; dampness زیم کول to grow damp

زیمت توب ziməttób *m.* embarassment, shame

زیمته zimətá being ashamed, ashamed زیمته کول to shame زیمته کېدل to be ashamed

زیمجن zjamdzhón ☞ زیمن

زیمکښ zjamkə́ẖ *m.* drainage canal

زیمناک zjamnā́k moist, damp زیمن کول to moisten

زیمنه zjamóna *f.* moist soil

زیم والی zjamvālaj *m.* moisture; dampness

زین ¹ zin *m.* saddle زین کول، آس زین کول to saddle زین اینېودل to saddle *compound verb* to saddle (a horse)

زین ² zajn *m. Arabic* decoration, furniture, appointments

زینبه zajnába *f. proper name* Zainab

زین پوښ zinpóẖ *m.* **1** cover (for a saddle) **2** saddlecloth; horse-cloth

زینت zinát *m. Arabic* decoration, furniture, appointments

زینتي zinati **1** adorning **2** decorative زینتي بوټي decorative plants

زین ساز zinsā́z *m.* saddler; harness-maker

زینکوگرافي zinkogrāfī *f.* manufacture of moveable type

زینگر zingór *m.* crowd, mass, multitude

زینگی zingáj *m. sports* throw over the thigh (in wrestling)

زینول zinavól *transitive* [*past:* زین يي کړ] to saddle

زینه ziná *f.* **1** stairway; flight of stairs حرکت زینه برقي lift, elevator د بېری زیني ladder کوونکي زینه escalator **2** stage, level

زبور zevár *m.* decoration; valuables, jewels; appointments, furniture زبور تړل to adorn oneself; adorn with jewels

زبوره zevára *f. proper name* Zevara

زی ⁴ زئي ¹ zəjé *combination of the pronouns* زه *and* يي ☞ زی

زئي ² zəjí *f.* clan, family, descent, origin دئ په زئي څوک دئ؟ What is his family origin?

زهیر zəjír ☞ زئیر

زهیرول zəjiravól *transitive* ☞ زئیرول

زهیربدل zəjiredól *intransitive* ☞ زئیربدل

ژ

ژ zhe the nineteenth letter of the Pashto alphabet

ژاپون zhāpón *rare* Japan

ژاخ zhākh *m.* dense forest

ژاخو zhākhú plain, homely, ugly (of a person)

ژاخه zhākhá *f.* thicket of bushes

ژارغالی zhārghálaj *m.* nomads' temporary dwelling place dug into the ground

ژاړ ¹ zhāṛ *m.* ☞ جاړ

ژاړ ² zháṛ *present stem of* ژړل

ژاړندوک zhāṛəndúk *m.* cry-baby (of a person)

ژاړنده zhāṛónda *f.* spring from which water dribbles out

ژاړه ¹ zhā́ṛ *imperfective of* ژړل

ژاړه ² zhā́ṛa *imperfective imperative of* ژړل

ژاله ¹ zhāla *f. Eastern* ☞ جاله

ژاله ² zhālá *f.* hail

ژامبېل zhāmbél *m.* jawbone

ژامه zhā́ma *f. Eastern* jaw کوزه ژامه بره ژامه upper jaw, maxilla د ژامي غاښ lower jaw, mandible ژامي گرېږدي molar دیخني يې دواړه His teeth were chattering from the cold.

ژاندارم zhāndā́rm *m.* gendarme

ژاندارمه zhāndārmá *f.* gendarmerie د حدودو ژاندارمه د border guard ژاندارمي قوماندان chief of the gendarmerie (in a province)

ژانه zhāná *f.* flattery, toadyism, sycophancy ژانه کول، ژاني کول *compound verb* to flatter; fawn (upon)

ژاني zaānáj *m.* **1** flatterer **2** toady, lickspittle, sycophant

ژاولٸن zhāwlə́n **1.1** sticky; sticky; resinous **1.2** irresolute, hesitant, listless, languid, spiritless **2** *m.* nincompoop; irresolute person, milksop

ژاوله zhā́wla *f.* **1** resin; gum **2** cud ژاولي ژوول *compound verb* **a** to chew the cud **b** *figurative* to talk nonsense, foolishness; talk rubbish, talk through one's hat ژاولي مه ژوه! Don't talk nonsense! **3** rosin, colophony

ژباړون zhbāṛún *m.* ژباړونکی zhbāṛúnkaj *m.* translator (from one language into another)

ژباړه zhbā́ṛa *f.* translation (from one language into another); paraphrasing

ژباوٸن zhəbāwún *m.* **1** flatterer, sycophant **2** intriguer, plotter; dodger

ژبپوه zhəbpóh *m.* ژب پوهاند zhəbpohánd *m.* **1** linguist **2** translator (from one language into another)

ژبپوهٸنه zhəbpohə́na *f.* linguistics

ژب پوهنه zhəbpezhandə́na *f.* ☞ ژب پوهنه

ژب پٸژندونکی zhəbpezhandúnkaj *m.* ☞ ژبپوه

ژب دود zhəbdód *m.* grammar

ژب ښوونه zhəbxhodə́na *f.* teaching (one's native) language

ژبغړاند zhəbghəṛánd *m.* ژبغړاندی zhəbghəṛándaj child who is beginning to talk ژبغړاندی کٸدل *compound verb* to begin to talk (of a child) زما زوی اوس ژبغړاندی سوئ دئ My son is already talking.

ژبٸن zhəbə́n promised, given (one's) word

ژبنی zhəbəná́j linguistic

ژبٸور zhəbawár ☞ ژبه ور

ژبونکی zhəbunkaj *m.* **1** gore, gusset (in a dress) **2** collar **3** insert in a bodice embroidered in gold

ژبون وهٸلی zhəbunwahə́laj struck dumb from fear

ژبه zhə́ba *f.* **1** *anatomy* tongue لویه ژبه ، هلکی ژبه ، حلقي ژبه uvula **2** language (as means of intercourse) پښتو ژبه ، د پښتو ژبه the Pashto language انگرٸزي ژبه the English language پردی ژبه ، foreign language خارجي ژبه regional dialect کورنی ژبه national language حکومتي ژبه state language د خبرو اترو ژبه official رسمي ژبه official language دفتري ژبه colloquial language state language ژبه رسمي گرڅول to recognize as the state language د underworld language اودخيلي ژبه native language مورنی ژبه in other words د ژبې پر سر baby's babble ماشوم وړه وړه ژبه flattery په خپله ژبه (to know or learn) by heart د لباس ژبه in (one's) native language ژبه اړول *compound verb* to retract one's word, go back on one's word ژبه بدلول *compound verb* **a** to retract one's word **b** to be insolent **c** to chatter, babble, talk nonsense ژبه ترل *compound verb* to become silent; lapse into silence, stop talking ژبه تلول *compound verb* to chatter, babble, engage in idle talk ژبه چلول *compound verb* to smack (one's) lips ژبه ساتل *compound verb* to talk; babble, to work the tongue ژبه بنورول *compound verb* to be silent, utter not a word ژبه کٸبل *compound verb* to speak; say **a** to dare (to) **b** to bawl, scream, yell, shout, shriek, wail (usually of women) ژبه کول *compound*

verb **a** to be insolent **b** to argue; dispute **c** to promise, give one's word to someone **d** to start talking (of a child) لواړه ژبه کول *compound verb* to speak indistinctly, mumble, mutter هدٷو ژبه یې وچه شوه He was left speechless. ژبه ماتول *compound verb* to break a promise د چا ژبه نيول *compound verb* to silence somebody ژبه ورکول *compound verb* **a** to promise, give a promise **b** to come to an agreement with someone پر ژبه *Eastern* We became silent حُمونږ ژبې واوښتي په پښتو ژبه سره خبري کول *compound verb* to mention انگرٸزي ژبې ته راایستل to translate into English (in) Pashto د یوي to be forgotten خه شی چه زړه یې احساس کوي ، هغه له ژبې څخه لوٸدل He tells everything that he is feeling. **3** pointer (of scales or a balance) ژبي مي وربنستان وکړل *idiom* I am fed up with it, I am sick and tired of it, I have had it upto my ears.

ژبه کی zaəbakə́j *f. anatomy* uvula

ژبه ناست zhə́banāst well-known to everybody, talk of the town, topic of general conversation

ژبه ور zhəbawár **1** eloquent, expressive **2** having a sharp tongue, sharp-tongued **3** using foul language

ژبه ورتیا zhəbawərtjá́ *f.* **1** eloquence **2** impudence, impertinence, insolence, cheek **3** foul language, ribaldry

ژبه ورکی zhəbawə́rkaj ☞ ژبه ور

ژبی zhəbə́j *f.* **1** *anatomy* tongue **2** tongue (of flame) **3** gore, gusset (in a dress) ژبی لوٸدل *idiom* **a** *medicine* croup **b** to lecture someone at length, preach at length

ژبينکی zhbínkaj *m.* gore, gusset (of a dress)

ژدوٸل zhdojə́l *transitive* ☞ ژوول

ژدوٸنه zhdojə́na *f.* cud

ژر zhər quickly; soon ژر تر ژره very soon! ژر راسه! Come here right away! ژرکٸدل *compound verb* to hurry, rush, hasten ژر شه! *compound verb* to (be in a) hurry, make haste Hurry up! ژر شو He hurried.

ژرپژٵر zhərpəzhár quickly; urgently

ژرتیا zhərtjá́ *f.* speed; velocity

ژرگه zhə́rga *f.* ☞ پلوڅه

ژرلٵک zhərlə́k *m. botany* matrimony vine, boxthorn, *Lycium*

ژرندگٵری zhrandagə́raj *m.* miller

ژرنده zhránda *f.* mill (water) بخاري ژرنده steam wind-mill بادي ژرنده (-powered) mill لاسي ژرنده hand mill غنم په ژرنده اوړه کول to grind wheat in a mill د چا په ژرنده اوړه کول *idiom* **a** to grind wheat at somebody's mill **b** *figurative* to get to know someone well; ژرنده کبنبنول *idiom* **a** to make someone a miller **b** *figurative* give a person no rest درد په ژرنده کبنبنولی The pain doesn't give him any respite. پر ژرنده کبنبنستل *idiom* **a** to become a miller **b** *figurative* to fail to find relief. د ژرندي د دوو پلونو تر مينځ *idiom* between a rock and a hard place

ژرنده گری zhrandag ə́raj *m.* miller

ژرندیغاښ zhrandighá́xh *m. anatomy* molar

ژرنگ zhrang *m.* peal, ringing, chime

ژرنگانٵی zhrangānáj *m.* handball, bell, cymbal

ژرنگول zhrangawól *transitive* ☞ شرنگول

ژرنگهار zhrangahár *m.* peal, ringing; chime

ژرنگېدل zhrangedól *intransitive* ☞ شرنگېدل

ژروالى zhərwálaj *m.* speed; velocity

ژره zhóra *f.* ژرې zhərəy 1 thorn, prickle; thorn tree 2 hawthorn

ژر zhaṛ *Western* 1 *m. plural* brass 2.1 yellow ژر پول penny, brassware 2.2 pale د ژرو گلو باغ *idiom* darling, sweetheart ☞ زېر

ژړا zhaṛá *f.* 1 crying, weeping په ژړا خه نه to start to cry په ژړاکېدل It's no use crying over spilt milk. په ژړا کبري، په تشه ژړا خه نه کبري شه *Eastern* He began to cry. له ژړا سره ویل ، په ژړا کښي ویل to speak in a whining voice 2 complaint چاته ژړاکول to complain to someone 3 whining, whimpering 4 lamentation 5 galipot (on a mulberry tree)

ژران zhaṛán 1 whining 2 complaining

ژرانده zhaṛánda Muharram (the first month of the lunar year) د ژراندي ورځي ، ژراندي ورځي the first ten days of Muharram

ژرانک zhaṛānúk *m.* cry-baby

ژرانکه zhaṛánka *f.* ژرانه blue-headed wagtail, *Motacilla flava*

ژربخون zhaṛbakhun yellowish

ژررنگى zhaṛṛángaj yellow

ژرغو zhaṛghú ژرغونکى zhaṛaghúnkay *dialect*, ژرغونى zhaṛaghúnay whining, whiny

ژړل zhaṛól 1 [و یې ژړل ، و یې ژاړي *present:* ژاړي *past:* ژاړه] (without a direct object) to cry, weep نو ولي یې ژړل؟ Why was she crying? په چغو ژړل to howl, roar, bellow 2 (with a direct object) to mourn something خپل قسمت ژاړي He bemoans his fate.

ژرندوک zhaṛəndúk ژرندوکى zhaṛəndúkay 1 whining, whiny 2 *m.* cry-baby

ژرنده zhaṛónda *f.* ☞ ژرانده

ژروالى zhaṛwálaj *m.* yellowness, yellowish-ness

ژروژمه zhaṛuzhamá yellowish

ژړول zhaṛawól *transitive* [*past:* و یې ژراوه] to make cry; bring to tears بېلتون ژړولم ، بېلتانه ژړولم Parting made be sad.

ژړوونکى zhaṛawúnkaj touching, moving, stirring

ژرغونى zhaṛaghúnaj ژره غونه zhaṛagúna ☞ ژره غونى

ژړى zhaṛáj 1 1 yellow; very yellow 2 *medicine* jaundice, icterus

ژرى zhaṛáj 2 *f.* 1 ☞ جرى 2 mirage

ژړېدل zhaṛedól 1 *intransitive* [*past:* وژړېده] to cry, weep

ژړېدل zhaṛedól 2 *denominative, intransitive* [*past:* ژړ سو] 1 to yellow, to become yellow گلان ژړ سول The flowers turned yellow. 2 to turn or become pale هغه تکه ژړه سوه She blanched

ژړېدونکى zhaṛedúnkaj 1 *present participle from* ژړېدل 1 سترگي running eyes, teary eyes

ژړېدونکى zhaṛedúnkaj 2 *present participle from* ژړېدل 2

ژړېده zhaṛedó *m.* 1 weeping, crying 2 mourning, bemoaning

ژژگى zhəzhgáj *m.* hedgehog

ژغ zhəgh *m.* 1 yoke 2 *figurative* yoke (as a symbol of oppression, etc.)

ژغ zhəgh *m.* squeak, creak ژغ او پغ ، ژغ او پغ کول squeak, creak ژغ او پغ کول *compound verb* to squeak, creak

ژغا zhəghá *f.* ☞ ژغهار

ژغنشى zhaghtsój *f.* needle(s) (of a conifer)

ژغورل zhghərál *transitive* ☞ ژغورل

ژغل zhaghál *m.* ☞ بغل

ژغنډ zhghanḍ *m.* notch; cut; indentation ژغنډ ورکول ، ژغنډ جوړول *compound verb* to make a notch, cut, score, serrate

ژغنډکى zhghənḍókaj *m.* 1 cut; notch; groove, slot 2 *military* notch of a rear sight

ژغنډه zhghanḍó *m.* ☞ ژغنډ

ژغورځاى zhghordzáj *m.* ژغورځاى zhghórdzáy *m.* refuge, asylum, sanctuary, shelter

ژغورل zhghorál *transitive* [*past:* و یې ژغوره] 1 to defend, protect, guard خان ژغورل *compound verb* a to defend oneself b to beware of, be careful of; to refrain, abstain from 2 to warn, caution (against)

ژغورنه zhghoróna *f.* defense; guarding, protection د خان ژغورنه self-defense

ژغورى zhghoráj *m.* defender

ژغونډى zhghundáj *m.* 1 ☞ جغوندى 2 *abusive* viper, spiteful person

ژغههار zhəghəhár *m.* squeak, creak ژغهار کول *compound verb* to squeak, creak

ژغهاى zhəgháj *m.* stretcher, litter (made of branches)

ژگه zhga *f. dialect* wife

ژلى zhaláj *f. Western* ☞ بلى

ژمگنى zhəmgənáj winter, winter's, wintry

ژمگورى zhəmgóraj *m.* winter camp; winter dwelling

ژمنه zhámna *f.* promise ژمنه کول *compound verb* to promise

ژمنى zhəmənáj winter, winter's, wintry

ژمى zhómaj *m.* winter په ژمي ، په ژمي کښي in winter تور ژمى *idiom* the first twenty-five days of winter (when there is still little snow) سپین ژمى *idiom* the period from the sixty-sixth through the ninetieth day of winter (when winter has really settled in)

ژن zhən *adjectival suffix* ☞ جن

ژندره zhandərá *f.* 1 lock 2 apparatus for straightening used shell cases

ژندرى zhandráj *f.* wiredrawing bench

ژنرال zhenrál 1 *m.* general 2 general ژنرال قونسل general consul

ژنگ zhang withered

ژنگوره zhəngóra *f.* ☞ ژمگورى

ژنگورى zhangúraj *m.* cluster, bunch (of grapes)

ژنوسید zhenosíd *m.* genocide

ژنیو zhinéw *m.* Geneva

ژنکى zhəṇkáj 1 *m.* youth, lad, adolescent boy, young man

ژنکى zhəṇkáj 2 *f.* teenage girl, adolescent girl, girl

ژنى zhóṇaj 1 *m.* 1 young man, lad, adolescent 2 fiancé

ژنى zhaṇáj 2 *f.* 1 gut, intestine 2 string (made of gut) 3 bow string

ژنيتوب zhaṇitób *m.* adolescence; youth

ژواک zhwāk *m.* life, existence ژواک خوړلی elderly مرګ او ژواک life او ژواک کول *compound verb* to live

ژوبل zhóbəl wounded; injured, hurt; crippled, mutilated, maimed

ژوبلتوب zhobəltób *m.* ژوبل تیا zhobəltyā *f.* wounding many times, covering with wounds; mutilation

ژوبلول zhoblawə́l *denominative, transitive* [*past:* ژوبل یې کړ] **1** to wound, cripple, injure, hurt **2** to harm, injure; inflict damage; سترګي ژوبلوي The sun blinds the eyes.

ژوبلېدل zhobledə́l *denominative, intransitive* [*past:* ژوبل شو] **1** to be wounded; be hurt; be crippled **2** to suffer

ژوبله zhóbla *f.* wound, injury

ژوبلېده zhobledə́ *m. plural* wound(ing); mutilation

ژور zhawór, zhawár, zhəwór **1** deep; ژور کوهی deep well **2** with ruts and grooves, with pits and bumps ژور کول *compound verb* or ژوروبدل *compound verb* or ژور کېدل *compound verb* or ژورول *compound verb* to make deep **3** wise; intelligent **4** deep, serious, solid, substantial; ژور فکر profound idea

ژورتوب zhawərtób *m.* ژورتیا zhawərtyā *f.* **1** depth **2** hollow, depression

ژورغاښی zhawərghā́khaj *m.* depression in the front tooth of a horse (by which its age is judged)

ژورغالی zhawərghā́laj *m.* **1** small pit, little hole **2** *agriculture* hollow, hill, hole

ژورلېگی zhawərlégaj *m.* ژورلېنگی zhawərléngay *m. anatomy* popliteal fossa

ژورمېچ zhawərméch *m. technology* plumb line, plumb bob

ژورنال zhurnā́l *m.* magazine

ژورنالیست zhurnālíst *m.* journalist

ژورنالیستي zhurnālistí **1** journalistic **2** *f.* journalism

ژوروالی zhawərwā́laj *m.* **1** depth **2** depression; pit; hollow, cavity; dent

ژورول zhawərawə́l *denominative, transitive* [*past:* ژور یې کړ] to deepen, make deeper; make a depression

ژوره [1] zhwə́ra **1** *f.* .1 depth **1.2** pit, hole; depression; hollow, cavity; dent **2** *feminine singular of* ژور

ژوره [2] zhawúra *f.* leech ژوره اچول ، ژوره لګول ، ژوره نښلول *compound verb* to apply leeches, put on leeches

ژوري zhawóri *plural of* ژوره [1,2]

ژورېدل zhawəredə́l *denominative, intransitive* [*past:* ژور سو] to go deep into; go deep down; project into

ژورېدنه zhawəredə́na *f.* depression, hollow

ژوژ zhwazh *m.* ☞ ببوژ

ژولیده zholidá **1** tangled, muddled, confused **2** disheveled, tousled, rumpled

ژوند zhwand, zhwənd *m.* **1** life, existence د ژوند جگړه ، د ژوند دپاره the struggle for life ژوندکول ، ژوند لرل *compound verb* to live, exist تر ډېره عمره په یو له بله د دوستی ژوندکول to live amicably یوه ژوله ژوندکول to live a boring life **2** animation, liveliness,

vivacity د ژوند په ښو او بدو شریکه وه She shared with him both joys and sorrows.

ژوندانه zhwandānə́ *oblique singular of* ژوندون

ژوندپوهه zhwandpóha biology

ژوندوبه zhwandobə́ *f. plural folklore* water of life

ژوند و ژواک zhwand-u-zhwā́k *m.* life, existence خوشحال ژوند و ژواک joyful life

ژوندون zhwəndún *m.* life, way of life د ژوندانه میزان standard of living گډ ژوند coexistence د ژوندانه جگړه struggle for existence ژوند کول *compound verb* to live, exist; be found, live, breed (of animals) ژوند تریخول *compound verb* to be the bane of (someone's) existence

ژوندی zhwandáj **1** living, live, alive ژوندی دئ که مړ؟ Is he alive or is he dead? **2** lively, active, mobile; energetic **3** animated, lively (e.g., of correspondence) ژوندی کول *compound verb* **a** to animate, revive, resurrect; revitalize, resuscitate **b** to save, rescue, come to soneone's aid **c** to encourage, reassure, cheer (someone) up ژوندی کېدل *compound verb* **a** to rise again, come to life; be restored to life **b** become animated **c** to be saved, be rescued **4** undercooked (of pulses) ژوندی دي وي افغانستان! Long live Afghanistan! ژواند vanished

ژوندیتوب zhwanditób *m.* vivacity, liveliness; animation

ژوندی کېده zhwandajkedə́ *m. plural* **1** resurrection, reanimation; revival, rebirth **2** saving, rescuing

ژوول zhowə́l **1** *transitive* [*present:* ژویي *past:* و یې ژووه] **.1** to chew; chew well, masticate **1.2** *figurative* to chew over, think over, mull over, reason out **2** *m. plural* **.1** chewing, masticating **2.2** *figurative* thinking, mulling over, reasoning out

ژوه zhə́wa live! long live! stay alive!

ژوی [1] zhə́waj **1** lively, animated **2** *m.* animal; living being, creature

ژوی [2] zhoj *present stem of* ژوول *and* ژویل

ژویل zhojə́l *transitive* ☞ ژوول

ژوین zhuán *m.* ژوئن June

ژویه zhója *imperfective imperative of* ژوول

ژی [1] zhaj *m.* [*plural:* ژي zhi *and* ژیان zhiyán] **1** wineskin **2** bagpipes

ژی [2] zhəj *f.* **1** edge د پاڼ ژی edge of a precipice, verge of disaster **2** side د ماکو ژی side of a boat **3** side of the road, shoulder **4** border, edging, selvage **5** border, edge (of a forest) **6** string **7** bowstring ژی باندي کول to tighten bowstring ژی کوزول to loosen bowstring **8** *math* chord

ژی [3] zhe *f.* the name of the letter ژ

ژیاره zhibā́ra *f.* ☞ ژباره

ژیبه zhéba *f. dialect* ☞ ژبه

ژیړ zhjrr **1** *m. plural* **.1** brass **1.2** bile, gall **2.1** yellow; reddish, red-haired **2.2** pale ژیړ گرځېدل *compound verb* **a** to turn yellow **b** to turn pale ژیړ کول *compound verb* ☞ ژیړول ژیړ کېدل *compound verb* ☞ ژیړېدل

ژړانکه zhjaŕánka *f.* ☞ ژیړانکه

ژيربخ‍ن zhjaṛbəkhə́n yellowish

ژيرنگ zhjaṛráng yellow, yellow-colored ژيره reddish beard

ژيرسري zhjaṛsáre f. yellow-headed wagtail

ژيرگل zhjaṛgul m. ☞ زيرگل

ژيروالی zhjaṛwắlaj m. ycllow(ish)ness

ژيروـل zhtaṛawə́l denominative, transitive [past: ژير يي کر] to make yellow, color yellow

ژيره¹ zhjáṛa 1 f. .1 yellow(ish)ness 1.2 medicine jaundice 2 feminine singular of ژير²

ژيره² zhjáṛa f. 1 shame, disgrace 2 insult 3 mockery پر چا ژيره اړول ، وچا ته ژيره اړول a to shame someone, disgrace someone b to insult someone 4 to mock someone, make fun of someone ژيري کول compound verb a to shame, disgrace, defame b to insult; scold, rail at, heap abuse on c to mock, make fun of

ژيری¹ zhjaṛáj 1 m. medicine jaundice 2.1 yellow ژيری تبه malaria 2.2 pale ژيری ژيری کتل to lick one's lips (watching someone eat)

ژيری² zhjaṛə́j 1 f. ☞ ژرانکه 2 feminine singular of ژيری¹

ژيرېدـل zhjaṛedə́l denominative, intransitive [past: ژير شو] 1 to yellow, become yellow 2 to pale, become pale

ژيرېدنه zhjaṛedə́na f. ژيرېده zhyaṛedə́ m. plural 1 yellowing, turning yellow 2 pallor, paleness

ژيرين zhjaṛín brass

ړ

ړ ge the twentieth letter of the Pashto alphabet; retroflex ر

ړد gd present stem of اينبودل

ړدن gdən m. plural millet د ړدنو ډوډۍ millet bread

ړدون gadún 1 m. plural Gaduni (a tribe) 2 m. a Gadun (member of the Gadun tribe)

ړرينگري gərengə́ri m. plural ☞ ړله گرکی

ړړۍ gaṛə́j f. ☞ ړلۍ

ړبړ gag m. coal dust

ړغ gagh m. Western sound; voice; cry, shout په لوړ ړغ loudly ته بغ کول ، پرچا باندي ړغ کول to call to someone پيره والا راباندي ړغ The sentry called to me. نه چا بغ راته وکړ No one called to me. ور بغ يي کړه! He summoned them to (come to) him بد ړغ وهل idiom a to render poorly (fat, lard) b to worsen the patient's condition

ړغانځه gghándza f. flea

ړغ بندی gəghbandáj m. agriculture yoke pin, plug in the ox-yoke

ړغرـل ggharə́l transitive [past: و يي ړغرل] to listen to someone sympathetically

ړغرول gharawə́l transitive ☞ ژغورل

ړغرۍ¹ gghari f. agreement, consent

ړغری² gghraj m. film on the teeth

ړغگغري gaghgəghə́raj m. ☞ ړله گرکی

ړغبغه gaghgaghá f. handbell; cymbal

ړغگغۍ gaghgəghə́j f. 1 hull on a grain of wheat 2 tamarisk leaf

---

ړغل gghal m. 1 sludge; (ice) 2 gravel

ړغن gaghə́n ړغن کېدل compound verb a to spoil, turn rancid (of oil) b to suffer, get into trouble احمد رغن سو A misfortune befell Ahmed.

ژغورل gghorə́l transitive Western ☞

ړغ و ړوغ gaghugúgh m. noise, shouting, uproar, hubbub

ړغاول gaghawə́l transitive [past: و يي رغاوه] 1 to sing 2 to play (a musical instrument) 3 to compel (someone) to talk, make (someone) be heard 4 to make noise چاته رغول to shout to someone

ړغېدـل gaghedə́l 1 intransitive [past: ورغبده] .1 to sound, resound (of sounds) 1.2 to talk, to speak; converse; express oneself 2 m. plural sound(ing), phonation

ړغېدونکی gaghedúnkaj 1 present participle of رغبدل 2 sound رغبدونکي سينما talking pictures

ړغيز gaghíz 1 vocal (e.g., the vocal chords) 2 clear, ringing توري linguistics vowel

ژغبلوه gghelwá f. pointless argument

ړله گرکی galagárkaj m. soft hail, snow pellets, graupel, tapioca snow

ړلۍ galə́j f. hail

ړمنځ gməndz f. plural رمنځي comb

ړمنځول gməndzawə́l denominative, transitive [past: رمنځ يي کړ] to comb سر رمنځول compound verb to comb one's hair وبنبتان رمنځول to comb the hair

ړمنځېدـل gməndzedə́l denominative, intransitive [past: رمنځ سو] to comb one's hair

ړمنځ gmundz f. ☞ رمنځ

ړمونځول gmundzawə́l transitive ☞ رمنځول

ړمونځی gmundzáj m. technology reed (in a loom)

ړنگ gang m. bell (e.g., door bell, telephone ringer, electric bell), handbell

ړنگوری gəngúraj m. cluster, bunch (of grapes)

ړو go ستا په سر ړو خدای رو! really I swear by your head!

ژواک gwāk m. ☞ ژواک

ړوبړ gwag m. noise, din, racket دا څه ړوبړ دئ؟ What kind of noise is that? ړوبړ بغ racket

ړوغ gugh m. paired word with بغ بغ و ړوغ noise, uproar, hubbub, shouting

ژوند gwand m. ☞

ژوندون gwandún m. ☞

ژوندی gwandáj ☞

ړنگ gung m. echo

ژوی¹ gə́waj ☞

ړوی² gəwáj m. witness

گی¹ gə́j f. ☞

ړی² ge f. name of the letter ړ

ړيرخيړلی girkhṛəjə́laj with shaven beard, clean-shaven

ريره girá f. beard د ريرو خاوندان bearded man ريره اوږدول ، ريره bearded man لويه ريره ساتل to grow a beard پربنبودل to grow a thick and bushy beard ‫ د احمد په ږيره كي اوس ويشتلي پيدا سوي دي‬ Ahmed's beard is touched with gray ‫ږيره خريل‬ *compound verb* **a** to shave (one's) beard **b** *figurative* to disgrace oneself ‫ږيره دي وخريله سه!‬ *idiom abusive* You can go to hell! ‫په ګرده عالم كي مسعودږيره وخريله‬ Masoud made a spectacle of himself in public ‫احمد د ولي ږيره باد كړه‬ Ahmed dishonored Wali ‫ږيره په درواغو سپينول‬ *idiom* **a** to languish in ignorance **b** to be idle, loaf ‫ږيره دي په درواغو سپينه كړي ده‬ You haven't learned anything ‫ږيره كړول ، ږيره ښنورول‬ *compound verb* to beg for something ‫د ږيري څخه اخيستل ، پر بربت اچول‬ to do clumsily ‫ږيره ور سړى‬ a bearded man **2** *m.* ‫ږيره ور‬ giṛawər, giṛawə́r **1** bearded

‫ږيرى‬ [1] giṛáj *m.* elbow; elbow joint

‫ږيرى‬ [2] giṛə́j *f.* thin hull of maize

‫س‬

‫س‬ [1] sin the twenty-first letter of the Pashto alphabet; the numeral 60 in the abjad system

‫س‬ [2] *abbreviation of* ‫سؤال‬

‫سا‬ sā *f.* [*plural:* ‫ساوي‬ sā́wi *and* ‫ساگاني‬ sāgā́ni] **1** breathing, respiration ‫سا اچول‬ take a breath ‫سا اخيستل‬ *compound verb* **a** to breathe **b** to hold one's breath **c** *figurative* to get into trouble, have a misfortune **d** *figurative* to fall into poverty ‫سا يي بنده سوه‬ His breathing stopped. ‫سا ختلئ‬ **a** choking, suffocating **b** at (one's) last breath ‫سا سول، سا ختلئ‬ to be sitting in sadness ‫سوگل‬ *compound verb* to tire, become tired, be short of breath, be out of breath ‫سا كبنل ، لنده سا كبنل‬ *compound verb* to breathe, ‫سا پر لنده اخيستل‬ **a** to breathe intermittantly **b** to be short-winded, be short of breath ‫ژوره سا كبنل‬ to breathe deeply ‫سا لرل‬ *compound verb* to breathe, live ‫سا نيولئ كورته راغئ‬ He came home out of breath. ‫په سا وهل‬ get into the windpipe, to stick in the throat ‫اوبه مي په سا ووهلي، وتوخيدم‬ I choked on the water. ‫په سا كبني مار‬ to be scared to death **2** stench, stink, heavy smell ‫سا تلل، سا ولاړيدل‬ *compound verb* to smell bad, to stink; come from, issue from (of a heavy smell) **3** air ‫د چا سا ايستل، د چا سا كبنل‬ to kill someone ‫ساه‬ ☞

‫س ، ا‬ *abbreviation of* ‫سردار اعلى نشان‬ bearer of the order of "Sardar-I ala"

‫ساوو‬ sāú ☞

‫سابق‬ sābíq *Arabic* **1** former, past ‫سابق سزايافته‬ *regional law* having a previous conviction **2** previous, foregoing

‫سابقاً‬ sābíqán *Arabic* before, formerly, in the past, in former times, in the old days, at one time

‫سابقه‬ sābiqá *f. Arabic* [*m. plural Arabic* ‫سوابق‬] **1** the past **2** precedent **3** length of service, experience, seniority ‫په خدمت كښي‬ ‫اوږده سابقه لرل‬ to have long work experience **4** experience **5** past history, pre-history (of an issue) **6** prefix

‫سابندي‬ [1] sābandí *f.* **1** shortness of breath; labored breathing **2** asthma

‫سابندى‬ [2] sābándaj **1** suffering shortness of breath **2** *m.* asthmatic

‫سابنى‬ sābənáj *m.* ☞ ‫سابه والا‬

‫سابين‬ sābún *m.* ☞ ‫صابون‬

‫سابو‬ sābú *m. Panicum colonum* (a plant used to make mats)

‫سابودانه‬ sābudāná *f. colloquial* ☞ ‫ساگودانه‬

‫سابون‬ sābún *m.* ☞ ‫صابون‬

‫سابه‬ sābə́ *m. plural* vegetables; greens ‫د سبو برابرول‬ stocking up on vegetables ‫د تورو لاندي سابه سابه كبدل‬ to be hacked by sabers

‫سابه خرڅونكى‬ sābə́ khartsawúnkaj *m.* ‫سابه والا‬ *m.* greengrocer, dealer in green vegetables

‫ساپټ‬ sāpə́ṭ quite, totally, completely, entirely ‫ساپټ لبوني‬ out of one's mind

‫ساپي‬ [1] sāpí *m plural* **1** Sapi (a tribe) **2** *m.* Sapi

‫ساپي‬ [2] sāpí *f.* ☞ ‫صافي‬

‫ساپيدل‬ sāpedə́l *intransitive* ☞ ‫صافيدل‬

‫سات‬ [1] sāt *m.* **1** *colloquial* ☞ ‫ساعت‬ **2** ☞ ‫ست‬

‫سات تبري‬ sātterí *f. colloquial* ☞ ‫ساعت تبري‬

‫ساتل‬ sātə́l **1** *transitive* [*past:* ‫وي يي ساته‬] **.1** to defend, protect; guard, watch over ‫ځان ساتل‬ *compound verb* **a** to defend oneself, protect oneself **b** to beware of, guard against ‫د چا څخه ځان ساتل‬ to be careful **1.2** to keep, keep safe, protect ‫خپلي خبري ساتل‬ **a** to keep a secret **b** to speak cautiously **1.3** to keep (e.g., lifestock) **1.4** to keep intact, keep in (good) order **1.5** to nurse, take care of, look after **1.6** to reserve, keep, save up ‫د ځان دپاره ساتل‬ to reserve for oneself **1.7** to bring up, rear, educate ‫خپل زامن ښه ساتي‬ He is doing a good job raising his sons. **1.8** to keep, have (e.g., a cook, a servant) **1.9** to maintain (e.g., communications) **2** *m. plural* ☞ ‫ساتنه‬

‫ساتلوالى‬ sātəlwā́laj *m.* safety, state of good preservation, inviolability; material well-being, material security; protectedness, security

‫ساتندوى‬ sātandúj, sātəndój **1** *m.* **.1** defender; patron, sponsor; guard, keeper, custodian **1.2** *religion* God, Savior **1.3** protector **2** defending, protecting; guarding

‫ساتنگي‬ sātangí *f.* labored breathing

‫ساتنه‬ sātə́na *f.* **1** defense, protection; safeguarding; protecting ‫د ځان‬ ‫د ساتني دپاره جگړه كول‬ to conduct defensive combat **2** maintaining in (good) order (e.g., a road) **3** care, caring for (a sick person, one's clothing, etc.)

‫ساتو‬ sātú *m.* **1** keeper, custodian **2** hospital attendant, orderly

‫ساتول‬ sātúl *m.* large knife (butcher's); cutter, chopper; hatchet

‫ساتونكى‬ sātúnkaj **1** *present participle of* ‫ساتل‬ **2** *m.* ☞ ‫ساتندوى‬ [1]

‫ساتي‬ sā́ti *present tense of* ‫ساتل‬

‫ساتبري‬ sāterí *f. colloquial* ☞ ‫ساعت تبري‬

‫ساتين‬ sāṭín *m. Eastern* satin

‫ساچ‬ sāch *m.* pink starling

‫ساچمه‬ sāchmá *f. usually plural* ‫ساچمي‬ shot (for a shotgun)

‫ساحه‬ sāhát *m.* ☞ ‫ساحه‬

ساحر sāhir *m. Arabic* sorcerer, wizard; magician

ساحرانه sāhirāná enchanted, magic

ساحره sāhirá *f. Arabic* sorceress, witch, magician, enchantress

ساحري sāhirí *f.* witchcraft, sorcery; wizardry, magic

ساحل sāhil, sāhél *m. Arabic* [*plural:* ساحلونه *and Arabic* سواحل] bank, shore; seashore, seacoast

ساحلي sāhilí shore, coastal ساحلي خط shoreline ساحلي اوبه coastal waters

ساحه sāhá *f.* 1 space, area 2 *figurative* arena, field, sphere په عملي ساحه کښې in practice د اقتصاد په ساحه کښې in the field of economics

ساخت sākht¹ *m.* 1 manufacture; production 2 design 3 structure, construction

ساخت sākht² *m.* morocco (leather)

ساختگي sākhtsgí 1 *f.* deception, hypocricy; forgery, falsification ساختگي کول *compound verb* a to deceive, dissemble b to forge, counterfeit, falsify 2 man-made, artificial, simulated; counterfeit, false, falsified

ساختمان sākhtmā́n *m.* 1 design; arrangement, layout 2 structure ساختمان ارتجاعي elasticity جيالوجي ساختمان geological formation 3 construction

ساختماني sākhtmā́ni construction

ساخته sākhtá 1 made, arranged 2 fabricated; contrived; counterfeit, false, forged

ساخته کار sākhtakā́r *m.* counterfeiter, forger, falsifier

ساخته کاري sākhtakārí *f.* forgery, fake, falsification

ساخلو sākhláw *m. history* garrison

ساخولی sākhwúlaj mild, complaisant, obliging

ساخه sākhá *f.* 1 deafening noise 2 calamity, disaster, misfortune 3 *religion* Judgment Day, Doomsday

ساد sād 1.1 honest 1.2 honorable, estimable 1.3 reliable, faithful 2 *m. regional* head of the house شل شپې د ساد ، يو پکښې د غل *proverb Eastern* a thief also has luck (*literally:* twenty nights for the head of the house, one night for a thief)

سادات sādā́t *m. plural Arabic of* سيد

سادگي sādagí *f.* 1 simplicity; unpretentiousness; primitiveness 2 artlessness, credulity, *naïveté* په سادگي کښې out of simple-mindedness سادگي کول *compound verb* to act directly

سادو sādú *m.* 1 swindler, cheat 2 flatterer

ساده sādá 1 simple, uncomplicated; unpretentious, artless; primitive ساده لار simple way په ساده الفاظو in plain words 2 simple-minded, credulous, naïve 3 short-witted, intellectually limited 4 pure, without contaminants 5 beardless, clean-shaven 6 humble, of modest means (of a house, etc.) 7 banal, trite, commonplace, petty, vulgar

ساده sā́da *feminine singular of* ساد

ساده توب sādatób *m.* ☞ سادگي

ساده دل sādadíl simple-minded, credulous; naive

ساده دلي sādadilí *f.* simple-mindedness, credulousness; *naivete*

ساده روی sādarúj beardless, clean-shaven

ساده کار sādakā́r *m.* 1 worker who does simple work 2 apprentice

ساده کاري sādakārí *f.* simple work, work that does not require job skills

ساده گي sādagí *f.* ☞ سادگي

ساده لوح sādalúh simple-minded, artless; credulous; naive

ساده لوحي sādalauhí *f.* simple-mindedness; credulousness; naivete

سادين sādín *f.* 1 plowland, plowed field 2 virgin soil سادين کول *compound verb* to plow (up), till سادين کېدل *compound verb* to be plowed (up), be tilled نه د دين شو او نه د سادين *proverb* neither one thing nor the other

ساډو sāḍú *m.* [*plural:* ساډوان] braggart, boaster

ساډوب sāḍúb upset, annoyed; depressed, despondent ساډوب کېدل *compound verb* to be upset, be annoyed; be depressed

ساډوبي sāḍubí *f.* state of being upset, distress; depression, despondency

ساډه sā́ḍa *f.* ساډه سوډه bragging, boasting ساډه وهل *compound verb* to brag, boast

ساډوی sā́ḍój *f.* lazy and stupid woman

سار sār¹ *m.* good news, glad tidings

سار sār² *m.* ☞ څار

سار sār³ *m.* buzzard (the bird)

سارا sārā́ *f.* 1 steppe; desert 2 rural areas

ساراشین sārāshín *m.* steppe dweller; nomad

ساراگښت sārāgákht *m.* ساراگښت ته تلل *compound verb* to heed nature's call

سارا شین sārājí *m.* ☞ سارایي

ساربان sārbā́n *m.* ☞ ساروان

ساري توب cārtób *m.* سارتیا sārtyā́ *f.* ☞ ساري توب

سارجنټ sārdzhánṭ *m. regional* sergeant

سارق sāríq *m. Arabic* 1 thief 2 plagiarist

سارقه sāriqá *f. Arabic* thief

سارکه sāróka *f.* pink starling (locust-eater)

سارمکۍ sārmǝkǝ́j *f.* سارمه sā́rma *f.* سارمی sārmǝ́y *f.* orach, mountain spinach, *Atriplex hortensis*

سارنده sārindá *f.* سارنگ sāríng *m.* سارنگۍ sāringǝ́y *f.* kind of violin

ساروان sārwā́n *m.* camel driver, cameleer, camel herdsman

ساروج sārúdzh *m.* cement

ساره sārá¹ *oblique of* سور په ساره درې کروه three kurukhs wide (about 10 kilometers)

ساره sārá² *f.* ☞ سارا

ساری sā́ri¹ *m.* ☞ څاري

ساری sārí² *Arabic* communicable, infectious ساري مرضونه communicable diseases ساري شفاخانه، ساري روغتون hospital for infectious diseases

ساری sā́raj³ 1 equal, equivalent 2 *m.* equal, match ساري نه لرل to have no equal داسي سری دئ چه ساري یي نشته He has no equal. دا دوه هلکان ساری دي These two boys are equal. د هغه څخه زما ساری واخله Settle accounts with him for me.

ساري توب sāritób *m.* equality

سار sāṛ dying, being killed (of crops, from frost, drought, etc.)

ساره sāṛə **1** *m. plural* cold (weather), frost نن ساره دي It is cold today. **2** *m. plural and oblique singular of* نن مي ډېر ساره کېږي I feel very cold today. په سوړ تر ساره سيوري لاندي in the cool shade *proverb* ترخه، ساره او تاوده ګالل in a cold place يوه ساره ځای کښي to experience much in life د سترګو ساره *idiom* delight (of my eyes), consolation

ساره تاوده sāṛə-tāwdə́ *m. plural* onion soup

ساړی sāṛə́j *f.* ساري sāṛí sari (Indian women's dress)

ساز saz¹ *m.* **1.1** equipment, gear ساز او وسله accouterments **1.2** harness **1.3** saz (musical instrument) **1.4** music د ساز آله musical instrument ساز وهل، ساز کول *compound verb* to play (a musical instrument) **1.5** lift (construction) **2.1** made, manufactured **2.2** in good repair, unbroken **2.3** well, healthy ساز يم I am healthy. **2.4** proper, fitting; appropriate; suitable; pertinent, apt, to the point دا سازه نده That is not the right way. **2.5** in agreement, in conformity with something **2.6** being in good order; settled, arranged کاري يي ساز نه دئ Things are not going well for him. **2.7** correct, right دا سازه خبره ده That is true. **2.8** business-like, efficient, sensible (of a person)

ساز sāz² making, fabricating something ساعت ساز watchmaker

سازش sāzísh *m.* **1** compact; agreement; deal; compromise سازش کول *compound verb* to come to an agreement; enter into a deal, make a compromise **2** *Eastern* plot, conspiracy

سازش کار sāzishkā́r *m.* conciliator; double-dealer

سازشي sāzishí conciliating; accomodating, easy-going, easy to get along with

سازښت sāzə́kht *m.* harmony, consent, agreement

سازمان sāzmā́n *m.* organization; enterprise, production facility

سازنده sāzandá, sāzindá *m.* **1** musician **2** creator, builder

سازوباز sāzubā́z *m.* furnishings (e.g., of a room), furniture

سازوسامان sāzusāmā́n *m.* furnishings; equipment, outfit, accouterment

سازول sāzawól *denominative, transitive* [*past:* ساز يي کړ] **1** to manufacture, make; build; create; draw up (a plan, a design) **2** to write (a book); compose (a song) **3** to sew **4** to repair, fix; adjust, arrange **5** to prepare, (make) ready سفر ته ځان سازول to prepare for a trip **6** *ironic* to spoil, ruin, wreck; upset, frustrate, foil کار مو خوک سره سازول We frustrated them in this matter ورته ساز کړ to reconcile with someone

سازي sāzí¹ **1** *f.* ☞ سازش **2** *m. regional* musician

سازي sāzí² *f.* manufacturing, production طياره سازي aircraft manufacturing

سازېدل sāzedól *denominative, intransitive* [*past:* ساز شو] **1** to be built; be manufactured, be produced نوي لار سازېږي a new road is being built **2** to be repaired, be mended, be put right **3** to get running smoothly, come right, turn out all right **4** to be written, be in writtenform **5** to prepare for, get ready for (e.g., a trip) **6** to

suit, fit; be just right سره سازېدل *proverb* to be reconciled, reconcile oneself

سازېده sāzedə́ *m. plural* **1** manufacturing; building **2** fixing, adjusting, getting organized

ساطع sāti' *Arabic* sparkling, twinkling, shining

ساطور sātúr *m. Arabic* ☞ ساتول

ساعت sā'át *m. Arabic* **1** hour يو نيم ساعت an hour and a half په شل ساعته کښي in twenty hours **2** clock, watch **3** time لږ ساعت پس after some time ساعت په ساعت from time to time په دي ساعت *instantly* هم په هغه ساعت instantly دپر ساعت just now دا ساعت هم a a long time b hourly; constantly, continuously څه لږ ساعت وروسته after some time دلږ ساعت ګرځېدو نه پس having taken a little walk بيا نه جاروځي تېر to have a good time ساعت تېرول بد ساعت accident ساعت په بهرته *proverb Eastern* You can't turn back the clock.

ساعت تېري sā'atterí *f.* **1** pastime, entertainment ساعت تېري کول to have a good time **2** delight, joy

ساعت جوړوونکی sā'át dzhoṛawúnkaj *m.* ساعت ساز sā'atsā́z *m.* watchmaker

ساعت سازي sā'atsāzí *f.* manufacturing of watches

ساعت والا sā'atwālá *m.* watchmaker, watch vendor

ساعي sā'í **1** assiduous, diligent; careful, thorough, painstaking **2** *m.* adherent, zealot

ساغر sāghár *m.* cup, goblet

ساغري sāghrí *f.m.* **1** croup (of a horse, donkey) **2** shagreen, shagreen leather

ساق sāq *m. Arabic* **1** shin, shank **2** boot top **3** stem, stalk

ساقچه sāqchá *f.* pedicle

ساقط sāqit *Arabic* **1** falling **2** annulled, having lost force, having become invalid له حکمه ساقط ګڼل to consider invalid هغه قرارداد د اعتبار څخه ساقط دئ This agreement is null and void.

ساقطول sāqitawól *denominative, transitive* [*past:* ساقط يي کړ] to annul, declare null and void

ساقطېدل sāqitedól *denominative, intransitive* [*past:* ساقط شو] to be annulled, lose force, become invalid

ساقه sāqá *f. Arabic* stalk; stem

ساقي sāqí *m. Arabic* wine waiter

ساقي نامه sāqināmá *f.* bacchanalian song

ساک sāk¹ *m. singular & plural history* Saki tribe

ساک sāk² *m. plural* ☞ ساگ

ساک پاک sāk pāk very pure ساک پاک وو It was very clear.

ساکت sākít *Arabic* **1** (keeping) silent; taciturn **2** quiet, calm, tranquil

ساکټ sākáṭ *m. electrical engineering* socket, outlet, receptacle

ساکښ sākákh **1** *m.* animal **2** breathing **3** animated

ساکښ والی sākakhwā́laj *m. grammar* quality of being animate

ساکن sākík *Arabic* **1.1** immobile; immovable, motionless **1.2** calm, tranquil; quiet ساکن کېدل *compound verb* to fall silent, settle down, compose oneself **1.3** *physics* static **2** *m.* **.1** resident, dweller, inhabitant **2.2** *linguistics* provided with the diacritical mark sukun

ساکن والی sākinwǻlaj *m.* peace, calm; quiet

ساکی sākáj *m.* start of blooming of the roses

ساگ sāg *m. plural* greens, vegetables

ساگله sāglá *f.* copper boiler, cauldron

ساگڼی sāgṇáj *m.* **1** dish of rice and vegetables, vegetable ragout **2** dish, plate

ساگودانه sāgudāná *f.* sago

ساگېڼی sāgeṇáj *m.* ☞ ساگڼی

سال¹ sāl *m. plural* sand; gravel

سال² sāl *m.* year

سالار sālár *m.* head, leader

سالارزی sālārzí *m. plural* **1** Salarzai (a tribe in Badzhaur) **2** *m.* a Salarzay

سالب sālíb *Arabic* negative

سالخورده sālkhurdá elderly; old, aged يو سالخورده سړی old man

سالدانه sāldāná *f. medicine* leishmaniasis, oriental sore

سالک sālík *Arabic* **1** going **2** *m.* **.1** traveller **2.2** mystic on the path to knowing God

سالگره sālgirá *f.* anniversary, year, date of an event

سالگشت sālgásht *m. agriculture* fallow land

سالم sālím *Arabic* **1.1** healthy, unharmed, safe **1.2** good **1.3** happy, satisfactory; successful **1.4** safe **1.5** correct, right په سالم ډول **2** *proper noun* Salim سالم عقل sound mind

سالم الاعضا sālim-ul-a'zǻ *Arabic* healthy سالم الاعضا اشخاص healthy people

سالمانه sālimāná satisfactory, happy, successful

سالن sālán *m.* ragout

سالندی¹ sālandí *f.* **1** short wind **2** asthma **3** labored breathing (with pneumonia)

سالندی² sālándaj **1.1** suffering from shortness of breath **1.2** being out of breath, puffing and panting **2** *m.* asthmatic

سالنگ¹ sāláng *m.* ☞ سالن

سالنگ² sāláng *m.* Salang (pass) د سالنگ وات the road over the Salang (pass)

سالو sālú *m.* silk kerchief, silk shawl; veil سالو په سر کول to throw a kerchief or veil over one's head

سالواله sāluwǻla *f.* **1** girl in a shawl or veil **2** *folklore* sweetheart, beloved, darling

سالن sālón *m.* salon, room د خوراک سالون dining room د مطالعې reading room سالون، د مشروباتو سالون bar د لوستلو سالون

سالوېدور sālwedór *m.* El Salvador

ساله sālá *used with numerals* څلور ساله four-year يو ساله one-year-old

سالی sāláj *m.* ☞ سالن

سالیانه sālijāná **1** yearly, annual **2** *f.* annual pay, yearly salary

سامان sāmǻn *m.* **1** household things, utensils; property; baggage **2** equipment; gear; materiel د برق سامان electrical equipment جنگي

سامان، د حرب سامان military equipment **3** things, stuff, belongings, goods **4** harness **5** ☞ سامانه

سامانه sāmāná *f.* pomp, splendor, pomposity

سمبال sāmbǻl ☞ سمبال

سمبالول sāmbalawǝl *denominative, transitive* ☞ سمبالول

سامبولی sāmbólaj one not wearing trousers

سامراج sāmrádzh *m. regional* imperialism

سامراجي sāmrādzhí *regional* imperialistic (of policy, etc.)

سامع sāmí' *m. Arabic* **1** listener, auditor **2** *plural* سامعان audience, listeners

سامعه sāmi'á *f. Arabic* hearing, sense of hearing سامعه کول *compound verb* to listen

سامعه نوازي sāmi'anawāzí *f.* to delight someone with gossip ☞ د چا سامعه نوازي کول

ساموا sāmoǻ *f.* Samoa

سامي¹ sāmí *Arabic* **1** Semite **2** Semitic (e.g., language)

سامي² sāmí *Arabic* tall, high, elevate, exalt

سامی³ sāmáj *f. Eastern* the client's side (which is paying taxes to a district chief)

سان¹ sān *m.* ☞ صحن²

سان² sān *m.* **1** parade, inspection (of troops) تر سان تېرول، سان نيول *compound verb* to organize a parade, make an inspection (of troops) سان ورکول *compound verb* **a** to take part in a parade **b** to conduct an inspection (of troops) **2** (numerical) strength (of an army); bringing up to and maintaining strength (of an army)

سان³ sān *m.* whetstone, grindstone, hone

سان پولو sān-páulu *m.* Sao Paulo

سانتو دومينگو sānto-domingó *f.* Santo Domingo

سانتي sāntí *f. abbreviation of* سانتيمېتر

سانتياگو sāntjāgó Santiago

سانتيمېتر sānṭimétr *m.* centimeter

سان هوزې sān-dzhozé *m.* ☞ سان هوزې

سانچه sānchá *f.* **1** mold **2** template, pattern **3** matrix

سانحه sānihá *f. Arabic* [*m. plural* سوانح sawāníh] incident, happening, adventure; event

ساندو sāndú **1** mourning **2** *m.* weeper, mourner

سانده sǻnda *f.* groan(ing), moan, weeping, crying, mourning ساندي ويل *compound verb* to mourn

ساندو sāndú *m.* brother-in-law (husband of wife's sister)

سانده¹ sānḍá *f.* skink (lizard)

سانده² sānḍǝ́ *m.* breeding bull, stud water buffalo

سانده³ sānḍá *f.* female water buffalo in heat

ساندي sānḍí seeking refuge, seeking asylum ساندي کېدل *compound verb* to seek refuge, seek asylum

سانس sāns *m.* sauce, gravy

سن سالوېدور sānsālwedór *m.* San Salvador

سانس سکرېت sānskrít *m.* Sanskrit

سانسور sānsúr *m.* censorship ترسانسور لاندي نيول to institute censorship over something

سان فرانسسكو sān-fránsísko *m.* San Francisco

سانگه sánga *f.* 1 bough, branch 2 off-shoot, branch 3 lance, pike, spear 4 caravan (on horses); party of travelers (mounted)

سانگی sāngə́j *f.* wooden pitchfork

سان مارينو sān-mārinó *f.* San Marino

سان هوان sān-huā́n *m.* San Juan

سان هوزې sān-hozé *m.* San Jose

ساني sāní ¹ *m.* 1 *history* inspector for maintaining army strength (under Ahmed-Shah) 2 ☞ سان ²

ساني sāní ² calico, cotton, (made) of cotton (of fabrics)

سان sāṇ *m.* 1 stallion 2 bull, breeding bull, stud bull

ساو sāw *m. history* tax, duty, assessment

ساون sāwáṇ *m. regional* savan (the fourth month of the Indian calendar: July-August)

ساوو sāwú 1 noble 2 *m.* master, owner

ساووتوب sāwutób *m.* nobility, nobleness

ساويسا sāwisā́ *f.* confidence, assurance, certitude

ساه sā *f.* ☞ سا

ساه پوهنه sāhpohə́na *f.* psychology

ساهر sāhír *Arabic* not sleeping, being awake

ساه كبن sāhkáḵ *m.* ☞ ساكبن

سالنډي sāhlanḍí ¹ *f.* ☞ سالنډي ¹

ساه لنډى sāhlánḍaj ² *m.* ☞ سالنډى ²

ساهو sāhú 1 animated, lively 2 civilized 3 free 4 ardent, fervent, passionate, fiery (of feelings)

ساهوكار sāhukā́r *m. Eastern* usurer, money-lender

ساه ويسا sāhwisā́ *f.* ☞ ساويسا

ساى sāj *m.* hollow, depression, ravine

سايبيريا sājbírjā *f.* Siberia

سايپروس sājprús *m.* Cyprus (the island and the country)

ساير sāír *Arabic* سائر 1 other 2 *m. plural military* privates

سايره sājrá *f.* goldfinch

سازميكي sājzmikí seismic

سايس sāís *m. Arabic* سائس groom, stableman

سايق sāíq *Arabic* سائق 1.1 drive on, urge forward 1.2 leading 1.3 prompting, urging, inducing, impelling 2 *m.* driver, drover

سايكالوجست sājkālodzíst *m.* psychologist

سايكالوجي sājkālodzí *f.* psychology

سايكل sājkál *m.* bicycle سايكل چلول *compound verb* to ride a bicycle

سايكلون sājklón *m.* cyclone

سايگون sājgón *m.* Saigon

سايگي sājagí type of currant (dried in the shade)

سايل sāíl ¹ *m. Arabic* سائل 1 beggar, mendicant, cadger 2 suppliant, supplicant; petitioner

سايل sāíl ² *Arabic* سائل 1 liquid, fluid 2 *m.* [*plural:* سوايل ، سوائل] liquid, fluid

سايله sāilá *f. Arabic* suppliant, supplicant; petitioner

ساينتست sājnṭíst *m.* scientist; naturalist

سائنس sájans *m.* ساينس science; the exact sciences; natural science, natural history د ساينس فاكولته mathematics and physics department د لومړي ساينس elementary knowledge of natural science طبيعي ساينس a physics b natural science, natural history

ساينسپوه sājanspóh *m.* ساينسدان sāyansdā́n *m.* 1 scientist 2 naturalist

ساينسي sājansí scientific; relating to the exact sciences ساينسي مبتكرات scientific problems

سايه sājá *f.* 1 shade, canopy; cover د خپلي سايي څخه بېرېدل to be afraid of one's shadow 2 *figurative* protection, patronage د چا په سايه كښي لوېدل a to be under the protection of someone په سايه كښي لوېدل pampered, be spoiled b to be dependent, not be independent 3 canopy 4 awning 5 gnome

سايه دار sājadā́r shady

سايه وان sājawā́n *m.* 1 canopy 2 awning 3 umbrella, parasol, sunshade

سب sab *m. Arabic* defamation; insult, outrage سب ورکول *compound verb* to defame, shame, dishonor

سبا ssbā́ 1 *m.* .1 tomorrow د سبا ورځ tomorrow په سبا the next day, on the morrow, the next morning 1.2 morning د سبا سترگه the morning star, Venus سباته a the next day b the next morning سبانه بل سبا to stay over-night 2 tomorrow شپه سباکول the day after tomorrow زه سبا سهار ځم I am going tomorrow morning.

سبابه sabbābá *f. Arabic* سبابه گوته index finger

سبات sbāt ¹ *m.* room; veranda

سبات sbāt ² *m.* ☞ اثبات

سباتول sbātawə́l *denominative, transitive* ☞ اثباتول

سبارون sabārúṇ *m.* dawn, daybreak

سباستوپل sebāstópól *m.* Sevastopol

سباگون sabāgún *m.* سباوون sabāwún *m.* dawn, daybreak د سباگون خواته by morning سباگون شفق dawn

سباله sabā́la ☞ سبا ، سباته

سباناری sabānāráj *m.* breakfast سباناری کول to have breakfast

سبايي sabājí 1 *attributive* morning سبايي مال a early morning b early in the morning 2 in the morning

سبب sabáb *m. Arabic* [*plural:* سببونه sababúna *and Arabic* اسباب asbā́b] 1 cause, reason له دي سببه ، له دغه سببه for this reason; اصل سبب څه بل شی و in reality, in fact, there was another reason نوهم دغه سبب دئ چه ... ، په همدغه سبب سره ،هم دا سبب دئ چه for this very reason په دوه سببه for two reasons د روپو د نشتوالي په owing to the lack of money ... له دي سببه چه because... 2 د باد په سبب with the aid of the wind means

سبت sabát *m.* mother-of-pearl

سب تراپيكي sabtrāpikí subtropical سب تراپيكي سيمه the subtropics

سبحان subhā́n *m. Arabic* 1 thank God, God be praised, glory to God 2 *proper noun* Subkhan

سبحان الله subhānalláh *Arabic interjection* oh Lord, oh God

سبحانه subhānahú *Arabic religion* praises to the Most High!

سبد ssbád *m.* **1** basket **2** *technology* cradle, bucket

سبر¹ sábər *m.* **1** cypress د سبر ونه cypress **2** arborvitae

سبر² sábər *m.* ☞ صبر¹

سبره sábra *f.* cypress سمه سبره، دنګه سبره، نبغه سبره a slender and shapely cypress

سبز sabz **1** green; fresh; young **2** swarthy, dark-complexioned

سبزبرګ sabzbárg *m. history* tax on agricultural crops

سبزوار sabzwár, sabzawár *m.* ☞ شين ډند

سبزواری sabzwāráj **1** Sabzawar **2** *m.* native or resident of Sabzawar

سبزه sabzá **1** *f.* **.1** greens, grass **1.2** fluf, fuzz (on the chin of a youth) **2** swarthy, dark-complexioned

سبزه خورک sabzakhurák *m.* skylark

سبزه زار sabzazár *m.* meadow, grass plot, glade, clearing

سبزي sabzí *m. plural* greens, vegetables د سبزیو پټی garden

سبزي کار sabzikár *m.* gardner, vegetable grower

سبزي کاري sabzikārí *f.* **1** vegetable gardening, vegetable growing **2** vegetable garden

سب سټېشن sabsṭéshan *m.* substation

سبق sabáq *m. Arabic* [*plural:* سبقونه sabaqúna *and Arabic* اسباق asbáq] lesson; studies د سبق کوټه class سبق اخیستل *compound verb* to take lessons د معلم څخه سبق اخیستل to study with a teacher د چا سره سبق ضبطول *compound verb* to learn a lesson by heart تا خپل سبق ویل to study with someone و چاته سبق ویل to teach someone په کم جماعت کښي سبق وایه؟ Have you learned the lesson? سبق یادول ، سبق په یادول In what class is he studying? *compound verb* to learn a lesson by heart پر سبق کښېنول to send to school

سبق آموز sabaqāmúz instructive

سبقت sabaqát *m. Arabic* priority د چا علمي سبقت منل to recognize someone's priority in science

سبقي sabaqí **1** relating to lesson **2** *m.* student, pupil زما سره سبقي دئ schoolmate

سبک¹ sabk *m. Arabic* **1** school; trend (e.g., literary school) **2** good style, language

سبک² subúk ☞ سپک¹

سباناری sabanāráj *m.* ☞ سباناری

سبڼه sabóṇa *f.* satisfaction سبڼه کول to be satisfied

سبو sabó *oblique plural of* سابه

سبوس sabús *m. singular & plural* **1** bran **2** rice husks

سبوناکه sabunáka *f.* rice kasha with green vegetables

سبوڼج sabóṇaj *m.* leavened dough

سبیره sabirá *alliterating word with* سکه سکه سبیره ورور می دئ⁵ He is my (own) brother.

سبیل sabíl *m. Arabic* **1** path, road **2** means, way **3** treating, entertaining

سپ sap 2. **1** *interjection* smack **2** finished, completed سپ کول *compound verb* to finish, complete سپ کېدل *compound verb* to be coming to an end, be nearing completion

سپا sapá ☞ صفا

سپاچه sapāchá *f.* **1** awning **2** bench **3** platform, dais **4** low mound of earth along the sides of a peasant house

سپاخه spákha *f.* type of needlework

سپارتاک spārták *m.* almondleaf willow branch, whip, lash

سپارښت spārə́kht *m.* سپارش sipārísh, supārísh *m.* سپارښتنه spārəkhtə́naf **1** order **2** commission, errand, assignment, mission د سپارښت کاغذ letter of recommendation سپارښته پر ځای کول to carry out an assignment **3** application, intercession سپارښتنه کول *compound verb* **a** to recommend someone **b** to intercede for someone

سپارل spārál **1** *transitive* [*past:* و یي سپاره] **.1** to give an assignment, assign a mission to, entrust **1.2** to pay in, deposit (e.g., money in a bank) **1.3** to hand over; transfer, convey **1.4** to bury, inter پر سپارنه **2** *m.* ☞ Farewell! خدای می سپارلی یې! ، په خدای می سپارلی یي

سپارلي¹ spārlí *f.* **1** horseback riding د سپارلي اسباب harness سپارلي کول *compound verb* to go in for horseback riding **2** retinue; cavalcade

سپارلي² spārlaj, spārólaj *past participle of* سپارل

سپارنځی spārə́ndzáj *m.* storehouse, depot, warehouse, place for storage

سپارنه spárna *f.* **1** order **2** commission, errand, assignment **3** handing over; transferring, conveying

سپاره¹ spára *f.* plowshare

سپاره² sipārá *f. religion* each of the thirty chapters of the Koran

سپاره³ spárə́ **1** *m. plural and oblique singular of* سپور سپاره سئ Mount up! (command) **2** *m.* **.1** crew **2.2** passengers

سپاره⁴ spárə́ *imperfective of* سپارل

سپاره⁵ spārá *imperfective imperative of* سپارل

سپاري supārí *m. singular & plural* betel nut

سپاریتیر spāritír *m.* plow beam

سپاس sipás *m. religion* praising, glorifying د چا سپاس ویل to glorify someone

سپاس نامه sipássnámá *f.* letter of thanks; written greeting to someone marking an event or occasion سپاس نامه ویل to read (out) such a written greeting

سپانچه spānchá *f.* ☞ سپارچه

سپاند spānd *alliterating word with* سپک

سپانده spánda *f.* Syrian rue, wild rue

سپانه spāṇə́ *imperative of* سپنل

سپاه sipáh *m. history* army, forces

سپه سالار sipāhsālár *m.* ☞ سپاه سالار

سپاهي spāhí, sipāhí *m.* fighting man, warrior; soldier خاصه سپاهیان *history* Guards هر سپاهي د خپله اسه *Eastern* police د پولیس سپاهي *proverb Eastern* all are dissatisfied with their fate موږ دئ (*literally:* every soldier is tired of his horse)

سپاهي توب spāhitób, sipāhitób *m.* military art, military affairs

سپاهي خانه sipāhikhāná *f. regional* barracks

سپاهي ګري spāhigarí, sipāhigarí *f.* ☞ سپاهي توب

سپاهي ګوتی spāhigláзaj *m.* tin soldier, toy soldier

سپاهي spājí, sipājí *m.* ☞ سپاهي سپايي

سپت sipát *m. colloquial* ☞ صفت

سپتامبر siptámbr *m.* سپتمبر *m.* September

سپوخسه spúkhza *f.* ☞

سپخول spəkhawə́l *transitive* [*past:* وي يې سپخاوه] 1 to untie (e.g., a knot) 2 to rip open, rip up

سپخېدل spəkhedə́l *intransitive* [*past:* وسپخېده] 1 to come untied, come undone (e.g., of a knot) 2 to be ripped up, be ripped open 3 to open (of the eyes of a puppy at birth)

سپر ¹ spár, sipár *m.* 1 shield 2 forecarriage (of an artillery piece)

سپر ² sapár *m.* ☞ سفر

سپرت spirít *m. plural* alcohol د موټر سپرت gasoline

سپرتیا spartjā́ *f.* horseback riding

سپرخول sparkhawə́l *transitive* ☞ سپخول

سپرخی ¹ spərkháj *m.* 1 awl; needle for sewing burlap 2 knitting 3 linchpin

سپرخی ² sparkháj dry, hard, tough

سپرغه spórgha *f.* 1 well (e.g., the shaft of a *kahriz*) 2 pit, hole; foxhole 3 type of pattern 4 small island, islet

سپرغی spərghə́j *f.* spark د اور سپرغی الوزي Sparks are flying off the bonfire.

سپرک sparák *m. botany* larkspur, delphinium, *Delphinium Zalil* (yields a yellow dye)

سپرکښ siparkákh *m.* brave man, courageous soul, brave spirit

سپرلنی ¹ sparlanáj *m.* rider, horseman

سپرلنی ² sparlanáj *Eastern* Spring

سپرلو sparló *f.* سپرلی *f.* riding (horseback); driving د سپرلی ډاگ hippodrome سپرلو وهل ، سپرلو ویستل بایسکل سپرلو bicycle riding *compound verb* to go in for horseback riding په سپرلو تلل to rush along on horseback دی خورا ښه سپرلو وهي He is a very good horseman. د سپرلو الوتکه passenger plane

سپرلی sparláj *m. Eastern* Spring

سپرمغ spərmə́gh *m.* fat (e.g., in soup)

سپرمغی spərmeghə́j *m.* 1 spark 2 ☞ سپرمغ

سپرمینه saparmajná *m. plural regional military* sappers, combat engineers

سپرو sparó *oblique plural of* سپور ¹

سپرول sparawə́l *denominative, transitive* [*past:* سپور یې کړ] 1 to help someone mount a horse; seat someone in a car 2 to wind (on a spool or bobbin) اوبه پر سپرول to let water onto a field, irrigate a field

سپرونه sparawə́na *f.* helping (someone) to mount a horse; seating (someone, in a car, etc.)

سپره ¹ sapára *f.* ☞ صفره ²

سپره ² suprá *f* ☞ سفره

سپره ³ spará *feminine singular of* سپور ¹

سپره ور sparawár broad, wide, broadened, widened

سپریت spirít *m. plural* alcohol, spirits

سپرېدل sparedə́l *denominative, intransitive* [*past:* سپور سو] to seat oneself, get on or into (e.g., on a horse, into a car, etc.); ride (on something)

سپرېدونکی sparedúnkaj 1 *present participle of* سپرېدل 2 *m.* passenger; rider, horseman

سپرېده sparedə́ *m. plural* boarding, putting aboard; riding, driving

سپر spəṛ open, opened out, unfolded

سپړل spəṛə́l *transitive* [*past:* وي يې سپړود] 1 to turn around, swing around 2 to open (the eyes, e.g., of a new-born puppy) 3 to strip, disassemble, dismantle, take to pieces 4 to rip up, rip open 5 *figurative* to elucidate, ascertain عوامل راسپړل to get an understanding of the cause

سپړود spəṛód *present stem of* سپړل

سپړی spaṛə́j *f.* wooden bolt (which fastens the plowshare to the plow beam)

سپږمه spəgmá *f.* nostril

سپږن spəgə́n *Eastern* lousy

سپږه spə́ga *f. Eastern* louse سپږي نه وازده وباسي *proverb* He is awfully stingy.

سپږی spəgə́j *f.* aphid, plant louse

سپښته spə́khta *f.* 1 ankle; pastern 2 *figurative* basis, foundation 3 *figurative* the real but hidden cause سپښته اړول *compound verb* to give away secret, betray a trust

سپغزه spə́ghza *f. anatomy* pubis

سپق sapáq *m.* ☞ څپق

سپک ¹ spək, spuk 1 light, lightweight سپک ټانک light tank سپک ماشینګن light machine gun 2 weak, slight 3 light, easy سپک کار an easy matter 4 insignificant, contemptible, shabby, wretched چاته سپک کتل، چاته په سپک نظر کتل worthless person، سپک سړی چاته په سپکه سترګه کتل to treat someone with disdain, view someone with contempt, hold someone in contempt, despise someone

سپک ² səpák *m.* measure of length equal to the width of four fingers

سپکاوی spəkā́waj *m.* 1 disrespect 2 insult چاته سپکاوی اړول to insult someone, demean or belittle someone 3 meanness 4 insignificance, contemptuousness

سپکتوب spəktób *m.* سپکتیا spəktyā́ *f.* ☞ سپکوالی

سپک سپاند spək-spánd worthless, contemptible

سپکوالی spəkwā́laj *m.* 1 light-weight, flimsy, trivial 2 insignificance, contemptibility 3 humiliation; insult د چا سپکوالی کول to insult; humiliate, belittle

سپکول spəkawə́l *denominative, transitive* [*past:* سپک یې کړ] 1 to facilitate, make easy 2 to insult; humiliate, belittle, demean زه يې He insulted me. ځان سپکول *compound verb* to abase oneself, grovel دوی پنښي سپکي کړي وي *idiom* They were hurrying.

سپکونه spəkawə́na *f.* 1 making lighter, easing, facilitating 2 insult(ing); humiliating, demeaning, belittling

سپکه ¹ spə́ka 1 *feminine singular of* سپک سپکه خبره، سپکه خوله offensive word سپکه خبره کول *compound verb* to insult 2 *f.* 1.

چاته سپک اپول، چاته سپک ، چاته سپک lightness, light weight **2.2** ☞ سپکوالی؛ ويل to insult someone **3** nonsense, rubbish

سپکېدۇل spəkedə́l *denominative, intransitive* [*past:* سپک شو] **1** to become light, lose weight **2** to be insulted, be humiliated **3** to suffer humiliation, be humiliated

سپکېدنه spəkedə́na *f.* **1** reducing (of weight) **2** offense, insult; humiliation

سپگن spəgə́n *Eastern* ☞ سپرن

سپل اغزی spəlaghzáj *m. botony* caltrop, puncturevine, *Tribulus terrestris*

سپلگ spiləg *m.* fat (goat, beef)

سپلگه spə́lga *f.* mica

سپلم spələ́m *m.* **1** ☞ سپيرلم **2** gossip, gossiper, tale-teller

سپلمه spə́lma *f.* turtledove

سپلمی spəlmáj *m.* horse with a star on its forehead

سپلمی spəlmáj *f. botony* calotrope, *Calotropis procera*

سپلنی spələnáj *m. usually plural* سپلني spələní the seeds of the Syrian rue or the wild rue; seeds of the ispand سپلني کول *compound verb* **a** to burn Syrian rue **b** *figurative* to sacrifice ترتادي سپلني سم! I am ready to die for someone ترچاسپلني کبدل to die for you! د سپلني ملخ grasshopper

سپم spam *m.* **1** eye (of a needle) **2** hole (for an earring) دا شی د ستنی تر سپم وزي that's a great rarity

سپما spamá *f.* **1** thrift, economy سپما کول *compound verb* to save, conserve, use sparingly, economize **2** economics

سپمۇک spamúk thrifty, economical

سپمۇل spamawə́l *transitive* [*past:* وي يي سپماوه] **1** to save, conserve, use sparingly, economize **2** to spare something هيڅ ڈول زيار نه to spare no effort د هيڅ ڈول فداکاري څخه ځان نه سپمۇل to make any sacrifice

سپمی spamáj ☞ سپمۇک

سپمېدۇل spamedə́l *intransitive* [*past:* وسپمېده] to be saved, be used sparingly, be kept in reserve

سپنخۇری spənkhə́raj *m.* ☞ اوسپنخۇری

سپندخ spandə́kh *m.* **1** large ball of yarn **2** ball **3** dummy calf, stuffed calf (which is put next to a cow so that she will give more milk)

سپندوخه spəndókha *f.* playing ball سپندوخه کول *compound verb* to play ball

سپنگه spə́nga *f.* ☞ سرمه

سپنگی spəngə́j *f.* ☞ سپوربمی

سپن spəṇ *m.* syllable سپن کول *compound verb* to read syllable by syllable

سپنسی spaṇsáj *m.* **1** yarn (cotton) د سپنسيو شيان cotton fabrics **2** thread سپنسي پر نري ځای شلېږي *proverb* It breaks where it is thin, a chain is only as strong as its weakest link **3** *medicine* dracunculiasis

سپنسين spaṇsín cotton سپنسين ټغر reversible rug

سپنکی spaṇkáj *m.* spark

سپنل spəṇə́l *transitive* [*past:* وي يي سپانه] to take apart carefully, parse, analyze

سپنول spəṇawə́l *transitive* [*past:* وي يي سپناوه] to open (buds)

سپنی spə́ṇaj *m.* ☞ سپونی

سپنېدۇل spəṇedə́l *intransitive* [*past:* وسپنېد] to open, come out (of buds), bloom

سپوتنیک sputník *m.* satellite (e.g., earth satellite)

سپوتک spoṭák سپوتکی spoṭákay سپوتی sapúṭay **1** mean, base, foul, vile **2** shallow, superficial; light-minded, frivolous

سپوخسه spókhdza *f.* سپوخڅه spókhtsa *f.* سپوخزه spókhza *f.* سپوخڅه spókhsa *f. anatomy* pubis

سپور spor **1.1** [*f.* سپره، *m. plural* سپاره، *f. plural* سپري] sitting, riding (on a horse, in a car, etc.) سپور سئ Mount up! (as a command) **1.2** wound; planted, put on **1.3** raised, lifted (of water in a canal or irrigation ditch) **2** *m.* rider, man on horseback سپور نغری tripod, trivet

سپور spor **1** stale, old, not fresh (of bread, food) سپوره ڈوڈی stale bread **2** lenten, without meat or milk, lean **3** coarse, improper, indecent (of a word) سپوري ستغي ويل to say insulting things سپور چلم hookah with hashish

سپور spor *m. biology* spore

سپورټ spoṛṭ *m.* سپورت sport *m.* sport, sports د سپورټ جامي gym clothes سپورت سامان sports equipment سپورت کول *compound verb* to go in for sports د سپورټ ښوونکی trainer

سپورټمین spoṛṭmajan *m.* sports lover; sports fan

سپورټي spoṛṭí sporting, sports, athletic

سپورخور sporkhór living on cold food

سپورخولی sporkhúlaj using foul language

سپورسترگی sporstə́rgaj shameless, insolent, impudent, brazen, unconscionable

سپوروالی sporwálaj *m.* **1** staleness, lack of freshness **2** coarseness, rudeness **3** bad taste, lack of taste, tastelessness

سپورۇل sporawə́l *denominative, transitive* ☞ سپرول

سپورۇل sporawə́l *denominative, transitive* [*past:* سپور يي کۇ] **1** to make stale **2** to make lean

سپوره spóra **1** *feminine singular of* سپور **2.1** stale bread; dry crust **2.2** unpleasant word, offensive word

سپوري spóri **1** *feminine plural of* سپور **2** *f. plural* insulting words, offensive words سپوري کول *compound verb* to insult; give offense, offend

سپورېدۇل sporedə́l *denominative, intransitive* ☞ سپربدل

سپوربدل sporedə́l *denominative, intransitive* [*past:* سپور شو] **1** to go stale, become stale **2** to be lenten, be lacking fat

سپوربمی spogmáj *f.* **1** the moon, moonlight د سپوربمی کال lunar year د سپوربمی تندره artificial earth satellite مصنوعي سپوربمی lunar eclipse ډورلسمي سپوربمی full moon سپوربمی ده The moon is shining. د پنڅلسمي سپوربمی نوی سر وهلئ دئ The moon is full. **2** *proper noun* Spozhmay

سپوخځه spóghza *f.* ☞ سپوخڅه

سپوڼ spuṇ *m.* ☞ سپین

سپوڼی spúṇaj *m. medicine* ringworm

سپاه sipáh *m.* ☞ سپاه

سپهر sipahár *m.* **1** evening **2** *military* third watch

سپهره sipahrá *f.* **1** sky, heavens; celestial sphere **2** *figurative* fate

سپه سالار sipahsālár *m.* **1** commander-in-chief **2** marshal

سپی¹ spaj *m.* [*plural:* سپي spi *and* سپیان spiyán] **1** dog; male dog **2** *abusive* dog, son of a bitch څوک سپی کول to rebuke someone, lecture someone, give somone a good dressing down سپی کېدل *compound verb* **a** to be cowardly, be base **b** to be stingy د سپی تور پوست پر مخ غوړول **a** to be shameless **b** to be scanty, be skimpy *proverb* He is an inveterate swindler. سپی د وزګري په بیع خرڅوي (*literally:* he sells a black dog for the price of a billy-goat) خر سپی *proverb* two shoes make a pair (*literally:* a gray dog is brother to a jackal) د ګیدړ ورور دئ to live سپي تر لکی لاندي عمر تېرول worse than a dog په سپي زوی پلار ښکنځلی دئ *saying* on account of a low, dishonest son the father is called name د اوبو سپی otter

سپی² spəj *f.* female dog, bitch

سپیازول spjázawəl *transitive* [*past:* سپیازه یې کړه] to have a miscarriage, miscarry, give birth prematurely

سپیازه spjáza **1** *f.* female, dam (after a miscarriage) سپیازه کېدل *compound verb* to have a miscarriage, miscarry, give birth prematurely **2.1** unripe, green, immature **2.2** premature, prematurely born (of a baby) **2.3** wild, foolish

سپیاکه spijáka *f.* **1** mung bean bread **2** fork

سپیپڼ spipáṇ *m.* white double-flowering rose

سپیتانه spitána *f.* سپی توب، سپیتوب spitób *m.* meanness, baseness, loutishness; squalor, filth سپیتانه کول to behave badly

سپیته spéta *f.* **1** wedge **2** spoke **3** grain tester, grain-grading balance

سپیتی spitáj *m.* scoundrel, villain, rascal

سپیته spitá never, in no case

سپیځل spedzəl *transitive* ☞ سپیڅل

سپیڅ spets ☞ سپیڅلی

سپیڅل spetsəl *transitive* [*past:* و یې سپیڅه] **1** to clean **2** to whiten, bleach **3** to illuminate, light up

سپیڅلتوب spetsəltób *m.* سپیڅلوالی spetsəltyá *f.* spetsəlwálay *m.* **1** cleanness **2** neatness **3** tidying up, cleaning, putting in order

سپیڅلی spetsəlaj **1** clean سپین سپیڅلی perfectly clean **2** genuine, real **3** uncontaminated, pure سپیڅلی کول *compound verb* to clean (rice); to refine (crude oil, etc.)

سپید sapéd white

سپیدار sapedár, spedár *m.* **1** aspen **2** white poplar

سپیدپوستی sapedpóstaj white-skinned

سپیدچه spedchá, sapedchá *f.* type of wheat

سپیدلتیا spedəltjá *f.* سپیدلنه spedlóna *f.* **1** naivete, artlessness **2** narrow-mindedness

سپیدلی spedəlaj **1** naïve; artless, open-hearted **2** narrowminded, unintelligent, limited

سپیده sapedá *f.* **1** whiting, white pigment **2** ☞ سپیدي²

سپیدي¹ sapedí *f.* whiteness

سپیدي² spedé, sapedé *f. plural* dawn سپیدي لا نه وي چاودلي It is not yet daybreak.

سپیدي چاود spedechāwd *m.* سپیدي چاوده *m. plural* dawn, daybreak

سپرخولی sperkhwúlaj **1** using foul language, swearing, cursing **2** *m.* one who uses bad language, a foul-mouthed man

سپرخی sperkháj *m.* ☞ سپرخی¹

سپرکونډکه sperkunḍáka *f.* سپرکونډه sperkúnḍa *f.* crested lark

سپرکی¹ sperkáj *m.* **1** coward **2** scoundrel, villain, rascal

سپرکی² sperkáj grayish; ash-colored, ashen

سپرکی³ sperkəj *f.* omum plant (a medicinal plant)

سپرگل spergəl *transitive* [*past:* و یې سپرگه] to scold, rail at, abuse verbally

سپرگه spérga *f.* crude word, offensive word

سپرلټ sperláṭ **1** dusty, covered with dust **2** *m.* slacker, idler, loafer, goof-off

سپرلکی sperlakáj *m.* two-year-old colt

سپرلم sperləm *m.* fox, vixen

سپرمخی spermákhaj unfortunate, ill-fated; ominous, ill-omened, ill-boding

سپرمرغی spermərgháj *m.* beads of fat (e.g., in soup)

سپرووني sperawúnaj *m.* meal, flour (for rolling dough)

سپیره سپرۀ sperə́ *singular & plural* [*f.* سپېره, *f. plural* سپیري] **1** light gray بی حاصله او سپیره مځکه bare desert سپیره صحرا infertile land ګهیځ morning twiilight **2** dusty, covered with dust **3** dirty, soiled; turbid; stained, spotted **4** deathly pale, sallow (of the color of a face) **5** unfortunate, unhappy, unlucky, ill-fated, ill-stared, hapless **6** ruined, devastated **7** unfit, useless سپیره ډاګ کول *compound verb* to destroy, smash سپیره کول *compound verb* **a** to make dusty, cover with dust **b** to soil, (make) dirty **c** to break, destroy **d** to rob, clean out, loot (a house); destroy utterly سپیره کېدل *compound verb* **a** to be dusty, be covered in dust **b** to get soiled, get dirty; become turbid **c** to be beaten, be destroyed **d** to be robbed, be utterly destroyed **8** without meat or milk, not rich (of food)

سپیره توب sperətób *m.* **1** gray, the color gray **2** *figurative* death, destruction

سپیره شان sperəshān grayish

سپیره مخ sperəmákh **1** low, base, vile, loathsome **2** *dialect* submissive, obedient; ashamed

سپیره والی sperəwálaj *m.* ☞ سپیره توب

سپیزل spezəl *transitive* ☞ سپیڅل

سپیږمه spegmá *f.* nostril

سپی ستوری spistóraj *m.* tiresome person, annoying person

سپیسته spésta *f.* leavened dough

سپېبنته spékhta *f. anatomy* 1 peritoneum 2 pericardium سپېبنته اورل *compound verb* to give away another's secret, tell every little thing about

سپغول speghól *m. botony* psyllium, plantago, ispaghula, *Plantago ispaghula* (a medicinal plant)

سپیگمه spegmá *f. Eastern* ☞ سپېرمه

سپلنی spelanáj *m. usually plural* سپلني spelaní *Eastern* ☞ سپلنی لوگی کول، سپلنی دودول، :سپلنی to cure with wild rue, to smoke with harmel

سپېمتوب spematób *m.* 1 the period of estrus, the time of heat (in a bitch) 2 estrus, heat (in animals)

سپېمه spemá *f.* bitch in heat

سپېمتوب spematób ☞ سپېمه توب

سپین spin 1.1 white سپین کاغذ a white paper b a blank رنگ یی تک له سپینه سپین white as le سپینه دئ لکه واوره Her face is white as snow. white can be 1.2 gray 1.3 clean, bright ورغ په سپینه in broad daylight 1.4 sincere 1.5 moral, chaste; decent, respectable, honest 1.6 innocent, pure, instained, unsullied 2 *m.* .1 gray hair سپین لګېدل to appear (of gray hair), turn gray 2.2 albumin, protein د سترګو سپین، د هګی سپین egg white the white of the eye 2.3 silver د سپینو باهوگان silver bracelets 2.4 the exposed part of the body (e.g., the face, the hands) 2.5 snow 2.6 *proper noun* Spin

سپین باز spinbáz *m.* light-colored hawk or buzzard

سپین بحر spinbáhr *m.* 1 Mediterranean Sea 2 White Sea

سپین برېښ spinbrékh sparkling whiteness

سپین بولدک spinboldák *m.* Spinboldak (a border post)

سپین پگری spinpagráj *m.* cleric, mullah (in a white turban)

سپین پوستی spinpóstaj with white skin, white-skinned, white (of a person)

سپین توب spintób *m.* سپین تیا *f.* whiteness

سپین خولی spinkhwúlaj beardless

سپین دروبی spindróbaj respected, honorable

سپین رنگی spinrángaj white in color, white

سپین دروبی spindróbaj ☞ سپین دروبی

سپین روس spinrús *m.* Belarus

سپین زر spinzár *m. plural* silver

سپین زرلی spinzarálaj silver-plated

سپین زړه spinzáray سپین زړی 1 open-hearted, candid, sincere 2 trusting, credulous

سپین ږیرتوب spingirtób *m.* 1 old age 2 gray hair (in men)

سپین ږیری spingíraj *m.* [*plural:* سپین ږیریان spingiri *and* سپین ږیری spingiriyắn] 1 an old man سپین ږیری کېدل *compound verb* a to age, grow old b to turn gray, become gray 2 elder, village headman, white beard سپین ږیری کول، سپین ږیری نیول *compound verb* to elect a village headman

سپین سبا spinsabắ سپین سبیل الله spinsəbiləlla، سپین سبا درول، سپین سبا کول *compound verb* to empty a house

سپین سپڅلی spin-spetsálaj clean, neat

سپین سترگي spinstərgí *f.* insolence, impertinence, shamelessness سپین سترگي کول *compound verb* to behave insolently, act provocatively

سپین سترگی spinstórgaj 1 insolent, impertinent, shameless سپین سترگی کېدل *compound verb* to become more and more insolent 2 ungrateful, thankless

سپین سرتوب spinsartób *m.* old age, advanced age (of women)

سپین سری spinsáre 1 old, gray (of a woman) 2 *f.* old woman

سپین شان spinshắn whitish

سپین غر spinghár *m.* Spingar, Safedkokh (mountain range)

سپین کب spinkáb *m.* white fish

سپین کپی spinkápaj 1 white as foam 2 bare (of a desert)

سپین کت spinkát *m.* chalk

سپین ککی spinkakáj absolutely white, totally white

سپین کی spinkáj *m.* سپینکی spinkáy abomasum, true stomack (sausage for broiling)

سپینکی spinkój *f.* سپین کی spinkóy piece of suet

سپینکی spinkój *f.* whiting, white pigment

سپین گل spingul *m. proper noun* Spingul

سپینگه spengá ☞ سپېرمه

سپین گئځ spin gaídz *m.* daybreak; early morning, dawn صبا سپین fully dawned گئځ

سپین لمني spinlaməní *f.* chastity, morals

سپین لمني spinlamóne chaste (of a woman)

سپین لمی spinlómaj *m.* ermine (in winter), stoat (in summer)

سپین مخي spinməkhí *f.* 1 honesty, sincerity 2 innocence

سپین مخی spinmókhaj 1 white-faced 2 honest, sincere 3 innocent

سپین نینولی spinninólaj *m.* 1 rice kasha, rice porridge 2 rice drained in a colander

سپین والی spinwáalaj *m.* whiteness

سپین وړری spinwwrógaj white-maned (of a horse)

سپین وزری spinwazáraj white-roofed

سپین وږی spinwágaj *m. Aristida* (a type of grass)

سپین وشمه spinwáshma whitish

سپینول spinawól *denominative, transitive* [*past:* سپین یی کړ] 1 to whiten, whitewash 2 to tin-plate, tin-coat; nickel-plate 3 to grind, polish, buff 4 to clean; skin (an animal), peel (e.g., an apple); flay, skin, dress 5 to bare (the teeth) 6 to resolve an argument, settlle (a question, an issue) 7 to demonstrate one's correctness 8 to ascertain (the truth)

سپین ولی spinwólaj *m.* white poplar, silver poplar

سپینه spína 1 *feminine singular of* سپین 2 *f.* .1 silver coin هغه ډېري سپیني لري He has a lot of money. 2.2 fat on meat 2.3 eggwhite 2.4 resolution (of a problem, issue); settling (of a matter, a deal) سپینه یی ورسره وکړه They settled this business with him. سپینه خبره، سپینه وینا a clear speech b candid expression سپینه ویل *compound verb* to speak directly, speak straight out; speak the truth

سپینه spína *vocative of* سپین [6]

سپینه خاوره spína kháwra *f.* chalk

سپینه لاره spína lára *m. astronomy* Milky Way

سپیني spíni 1 *feminine plural of* سپین 2 *f. plural* **.1** Achilles tendon سپیني یې وتنبنبیدي His legs refused to heed him. سپیني پریکول *compound verb* to throw someone into confusion, fluster someone; weaken someone, deprive someone of strength سپیني پریکیدل *compound verb* to be scared, have the jitters, be frightened **2.2** the fat on meat

سپیني پایخي spíni pājtsé *f. plural* په سپینو پایخو ورکول to give a girl in marriage without the wedding rites

سپینبدل spinedól *denominative, intransitive* [*past:* سپین شو] **1** to turn white, become white **2** to be whitened **3** to be tin-plated; be nickel-plated **4** to turn gray ږیره می سپینه سوه I have turned gray. **5** to be peeled, be shelled **6** to be resolved (of an argument); be settled (of a question or deal) **7** to justify oneself, be confirmed

سپیو spíjo *oblique plural of* سپی [1]

ست [1] sat *m.* **1** invitation (to a meal) د چایو ست کول to invite someone for a cup of tea; ورته می ست کړئ دئ چه سبا می مهلمه سي (have) invited him for dinner tomorrow. **2** honor

ست [2] sat even, smooth

ستا stā *pronoun* **1** *oblique of* ته [3] ستا سره ستا څخه of you with you **2** *possessive pronoun* your(s)

ستاج stādzh *m.* ☞

ستار [1] sitár *m.* sitar

ستار [2] sattár *m. Arabic* **1** patron **2** *proper noun* Sattar

ستار [3] stār *m.* film star, movie star

ستار [4] sitár *m. Arabic* **1** coverlet; counterpane **2** cover, canopy **3** curtain **4** screen

ستاره [1] sitārá *f.* **1** star ستاره پربوتل *compound verb* to fall (of a star) **2** movie star, film star **3** type of fireworks) **4** fate; lot; (good) luck, good fortune

ستاره [2] stārá *f.* fear of someone ستاره لوبدل، ستاره پر لوبدل *compound verb* to be afraid of someone or something; waver, hesitate, vacilate

ستاره شناس sitārashinás *m.* astronomer

ستاره شناسي sitārashinásí *f.* astronomy

ستاري sitārí *m.* sitar player

ستاره stáṛa *f.* peace; reconciliation

ستاژ stāž *f.* length of service ستاژکول *compound verb* to work on a probationary or trial basis, be in on-the-job training

ستاژیر stāžér *m.* probationary worker, on-the-job trainee

ستاسو، ستاسي stāsu, stāso ستاسي stāsi *Eastern pronoun* **1** *oblique case of* تاسي ;ستاسو څخه ستاسو سره by you with you **2** *possessive pronoun* your(s) ستاسو کلی your village ستاسو په ښار کښي in your city

ستاکهولم stākhólm *m.* Stockholm

ستامبول stāmbúl *m.* Istanbul د ستامبول آبنا the Bosporus

ستان stān -stan (suffix denoting a country or place) افغانستان Afghanistan

ستاندار stānadár *m.* coming from a well-known family (especially clerical)

ستانه stāná 1 *f.* **.1** well-known family (especially clerical) **1.2** threshold (of a door) **2** from a prominent clerical family, honorable

ستانه stānə́ *m. plural of* ستون [2]

ستاوندي stāwə́ndi *f. plural* nonsense, heresy, rubbish

ستایش sitājísh *m.* praise; glorification

ستایل stājól 1 *transitive verb* [*past:* وي ستایه] **.1** to praise, laud; glorify **1.2** to mention, call, name **1.3** to call, name په مشهور نوم to glorify someone خوک په بدی ستایل to defame someone **2** *m. plural* praise دا اقدام ډېر د ستایلو وړ دئ This is a very praiseworthy undertaking.

ستاینه stājə́na *f.* **1** praise, praising د چا ستاینه کول to praise someone **2** song; ballad

ستایوال stājwál *m.* panegyrist, eulogist

ستخ stəkh, stukh ☞ ستغ [2] ستخي خبري کول to say unpleasant things

ستخ stəkh backwards, flat on one's back ستخ پربوت He fell backwards.

ستدیوم stadjúm *m.* stadium

ستر [1] satr *m. Arabic* **1** closing; concealment **2** *military* cover, concealment; covered position ستر او اخفا camouflage **3** *figurative* harem; women's side of the house, female quarters; women ستركول *compound verb* to close, conceal, cover; defend; hold in a harem **4** modesty

ستر [2] star *m. anatomy* temple

ستر [3] stər 1 large; large-scale ستر بندر a major port ستره مانئ a large building ستركیدل *compound verb* to enlarge, extend ستركیدل *compound verb* to be enlarged **2** great ستر لیکونکی a great writer **3** deep (e.g., of a well) **4** important, significant (of a business deal, issue)

ستراتوستات strātostát *m.* stratosphere balloon

ستراتېژیکي strātežíki strategic ستراتېژیکي وسله strategic weapon

سترانتیوم strántijúm *m. plural* strontium راډیواکتیف سترانتیوم radioactive strontium

ستراو satráw *m.* **1** fallen fruit **2** fallen leaves **3** juice (fruit)

سترپوښ satrpóx indulging, pandering

سترپوښي satrpoxí *f.* indulgence, pandering

سترتوب stərtób *m.* سترتیا stərtyá *f.* **1** size, magnitude, extent **2** grandeur, power, might **3** importance, significance (of a deal, of an issue or question)

سترغلی stərghólaj *m.* **1** eye-socket, orbit **2** *Eastern* eyelid

سترکوکو stərkokó *m.* white rose

سترګبېڅن stərgbedzhə́n attractive, nice, sweet

سترگتوري ستورتوري كېدل stərgtóraj starving *compound verb* to be hungry, be starving دى دپر و ډوډى ته ستركتورى سو He was very hungry.

ستركخوېړی [1] stərgkhugí, stərgkhwugí سترگ خوبړی *f. medicine* ophthalmia

ستركخوبړی [2] stərgkhúgaj, stərgkhwúgaj سترگ خوبړی *m.* with big eyes; suffering from ophthalmia

ستركرپ stərgráp *m.* twinkling of an eye, instant

ستركک stərgák سترككي *f. plural Eastern* 1 winking ستركک چاته ستركگونه وهل *compound verb* to wink at someone 2 twinkling, scintillation (e.g., of a star)

ستركلينه stərglína *f.* flirting, exchanging glances

ستركن کوکو stərgən kokó *m.* narcissus

ستركنلی stərganəlaj *m.* ☞ ستركلی

ستركور stərgawə́r ☞ ستركه ور

ستركورتوب stərgawərtób *m.* 1 vision, sight 2 keenness of observation

ستركوبړی stərgwə́g *aj* envious; greedy

ستركه stə́rga *f.* 1 eye د ستركي تور a pupil b the apple of one's eye; light of the eyes (endearing address to a son) د ستركي كاسه eyesocket ملالي ستركي، مراوي ستركي languid eyes د ستركي په ښكار eyes full of tears لندې ستركي as much as the eye can see ستركي په بنو in an instant ستركو په رپ كښ*ي proverb* a burden of your own choice is not felt (*literally:* the eyelids are no burden to the eyes) 2 star; planet, د لمر ستركه star د نور ستركه morning star د سهار ستركه the solar disk د نمر ستركه Eastern the sun has risen 3 زنكانه ستركه *anatomy* knee cap راختلى وه *compound verb* to glance, look ستركه اخيستل *compound verb* to be subjected to the evil eye ستركه، ستركه اوبنتل *compound verb* a to await, wait for b to hope لرل *compound verb* to have one's eye on something, covet ستركه پتول *compound verb* a to close the eyes b to have a little nap, take a nap ستركه مي پته كړي نه ده I didn't sleep a wink c *figurative* to close one's eyes to something, show indulgence towards ستركه پيداكول *compound verb* to acquire an eye for ستركه to regain one's sight, see again ستركه سره خورل Western to hate each other, be unable to stand one another ستركه خوربول *compound verb* Western to sleep a little, take a nap ستركه رپول *compound verb* to wink, blink د چا څخه ستركه سوئل، د چا څخه ستركه سول a to be afraid of someone b to pay attention to someone ستركه كول *compound verb* to be frightened, shy (of an animal) د چا څخه ستركه كول، له چا څخه ستركه كول to be afraid of, be scared of someone ستركه وهل ، ستركي لكيدل *compound verb* ☞ ستركه اچول *compound verb* glance at, give a look at ستركي وچاته اړول a to look, to glance at someone b to wink at someone ستركي الوڅي كول to screw up one's eyes, narrow one's eyes, squint د ستركي اوچتول to grow in someone's eyes; justify someone's trust or confidence وچاته ستركي اوچتبدل to look someone right in the face ستركي وراوبنتل a to catch sight of, notice b to

rely on someone, have confidence in someone ستركي بايلل *compound verb* to go blind, be deprived of sight ستركي وچاته It vexes me to look at him. ستركي برگول، ستركي وچاته برگي نيول *compound verb* to scowl, look at angrily ستركي پتول برندول *compound verb* a to close one's eyes b *figurative* to indulge, fail to pay attention, ignore c *figurative* to play the hypocrite, act against one's conscience d *figurative* to repudiate (e.g., a debt) ستركي پتبدل *compound verb* a to be closed, be shut (of the eyes) b to close one's eyes, die, pass away وچاته ستركي پتبدل Western to be angry at someone ستركي نه پورته كول *compound verb* to be ashamed, be bashful, be shy ستركي ور پورته كول *compound verb* a to itch (of the eyes) b to be ashamed ستركي ورلوبړول ☞ ستركي تخبدل *compound verb* a to blindfold someone b Western *figurative* to cheat, dupe (when selling something) ستركي تورول *compound verb* to apply black makeup to the eyes b *figurative* to deceive someone ستركي توربدل *compound verb* a to work with reluctance b to fear, be afraid c to go dark before one's eyes (when mountain climbing, etc.) ستركي تيتي اچول *compound verb* a to lower the eyes b *figurative* to be ashamed, be abashed, be disconcerted ستركي جكي وچاته نيول to wait, await ستركي مي ورته جكي نيولي وې چه رابه سي I awaited his arrival. ستركي وچاته چپه اوبنتل Western to be angry at someone د چا ستركي څارل ، ستركي الوڅي كول ☞ ستركي چوغي نيول Eastern a to follow someone with your eyes b to work under supervision په كټوكتو زما ستركي خيربدل to be shameless; become insolent ستركي وختلي I waited and waited until I was tired of waiting, and I ruined my eyes. دچا ستركي خرول to disgrace or defame someone ستركي خرول *compound verb* to be blinded ستركي خوربدل *compound verb* to go blind, lose one's sight ستركي خوبربدل *compound verb* a Eastern to take a nap, sleep a little b به . . . باندي ستركي خوبربدل be charmed by someone; fall in love with someone, admire someone c په چا باندي ستركي خوبربدل to recognize someone ستركي لرل a to be seeing, have sight, be able to see b to have a head (i.e., to have brains, to be smart); understand c to hope for, expect ترچاپوري مي پري خوبړي شوې He seemed familiar to me. ستركي درنول to be ashamed of someone ستركي نه لرل *compound verb* a to start something bad b to harbor hostile intentions ستركي دربدل to feel enmity towards someone ستركي دربدل *compound verb* a to roll (of the eyes) b to be near death ستركي دومارل *compound verb* Western to lower the eyes, cast down one's eyes (from shame) ستركي پرچا راكبنل to be angry at someone ستركي ربړي كول a to be amazed, be surprised ستركي ربړي ختل to stare (with bulging eyes) b to be angry, pretend being angry ستركي روښانه كبدل a to become clear (of a view) b to rejoice at seeing someone or something ستركي پرچانه رونبدل a to not see enough of, not get enough of looking at someone b to take a dislike to someone ستركي سپخبدل *compound verb* a to open (of the eyes) b to come into the world, be born چه ستركي مي سپخبدلي I have never seen anything like it in دي، داسي شى مي نه دئ ليدلئ

all my born days. سترګي سپينېدل a to be shameless (of a look, glance) b to be waiting impatiently, be worn out with waiting سترګي سرې to become bloodshot (of the eyes) سترګي سرې سرې ختل a to covet something b to envy someone c to harbor enmity کول to someone d to burn with desire سترګي سري کېدل a to be angry, be irritated b to envy سترګي سول، په ... a to pity, feel sorry for or about someone or something سترګي سوځل، په b to envy someone د زیرک په احمد باندي سترګي سوځي Zirak envies Ahmed, Zirak is envious of Ahmed. c to be afraid of someone سترګي شلېدل compound verb to abandon shame and conscience سترګي شني to forget oneself, overstep the سترګي شني کېدل، په چا باندي limits of decency سترګي کنته اچول، سترګي ځورول compound verb a to lower the eyes, cast down or drop one's eyes b to dread, fear سترګي کنته کول to lower the eyes, cast down or drop one's eyes سترګي کنبل compound verb to be angry, become furious, fly into a rage سترګي د لرګو کلکول compound verb to speak openly کول to abandon or cast off shame; become more and more insolent د چا سره سترګي لګول، د عقل to be perspicacious, be wise سترګي لګېدل، پرچا باندي to look at someone سترګي لګېدل to notice someone, take note of someone د چا سترګي سره لګېدل to be on good terms with, live in harmony; be friends سترګي لورول، د زوی په واده کنبي a to show honor and respect to someone ورلورول ده سترګي رالورلې کړې He did me the honor of coming to my son's wedding. b to come to someone's aid, help سترګي لوبېدل to become sunken (of the eyes, owing to starvation, etc.) سترګي مړي a to سترګي مړېدل ;سترګي کنته اچول ☞ اچول، سترګي مړي مړي اړول satisfy hunger; eat to the point of satiety b not to be greedy or stingy سترګي پرچا لګېدل ☞ و یو شي ته د امید a to set (one's) hopes on something سترګي په چا مبنتل سترګي و ... ته نیول to scrutinize, take a good look at; wait for, expect سترګي و یو شي ته to covet something سترګي و حق ته نیول to show the whites of one's eyes, die, pass away سترګي لاري ته نیول to watch the road, wait for someone, be expecting someone سترګي ورکول، to hang one's head; look down, cast down one's راکول، سترګي درکول eyes سترګي وږي کېدل a to be hungry b to be greedy, be stingy, be grasping سترګي ورتلل to be closed, close (of the eyes); fall asleep سترګي وبنتل drop off to sleep سترګي یي سره ورغلي He fell asleep. Eastern to avert one's eyes سترګي رانه نه ویاسي Eastern He doesn't take his eyes off me. سري سترګي ګرځه Eastern Don't be afraid of anyone. و چا ته د کینې په ستر ګه کتل to treat somebody with hostility چاته په to have no special liking for someone چا ته به بده ستر ګه کتل درنه سترګه کتل to respect somebody, treat someone with respect چاته د احترام په ستر ګه کتل چاته په سپکه ستر ګه کتل to despise someone, not respect someone په ښه ستر ګه کتل to treat well په ستر ګو کنبي دچا اغزي کېدل to undertake something bad in relation to someone په ستر ګه بدلګېدل، دچا په ستر ګه بنه نه لګېدل not to be pleasing to someone په غتو ستر ګه بیدېدل a to be negligent, be remiss b to be happy-go-lucky, be care-free په ستر ګو کنبي جګ درېدل a to recall, recollect, see in one's mind's eye b not to forget, (of a good deed)

ستا نېکي مي په ستر ګو کنبي ولاړه ده I will never forget your kindness. په ستر ګو کنبي ختل a to be shameless, be insolent b to irritate someone; pester someone ورته مي په ستر ګو دوند راغئ He drove me into a rage. په ستر ګوکنبي بنورېدل a to imagine, see in one's mind's eye b to be shifty, be restless (of the eyes); loom دچا په ستر ګو کنبي to look steadily at someone, stare at someone په ستر ګو کت اچول to bewitch, put the evil eye on کول د سره ستر ګو لیدل to see for one's self, see with one's own eyes په ستر ګوکنبي ورنوتل، په ستر ګوکنبي راننوتل a to act insolently b to pay ستر ګوکنبي درنوتل with black ingratitude c to renounce, abandon, decline something په ستر ګو کنبي ☞ تر ستر ګو کېدل، ستر ګو ته درېدل، ستر ګو ته درېدل a to meet (someone's) eye تر ستر ګو ګرزېدل b to become loathsome, as if to see in جک درېدل one's mind's eye له ستر ګو لوېدل a to disgrace oneself, bring shame upon oneself; fall in someone's eyes b to become loathsome, become repulsive بده ستر ګه زه دواړو ته په یوه ستر ګه ګورم the evil eye I treat both the same. یوه ستر ګه به دي ژاړي او بله به دي خاندي one doesn't know whether to laugh or cry یوه ستر ګه څلور کول to be all eyes, be on the alert, be on one's guard, keep one's eyes open ستر ګه په لاري یم tete-a-tete ستر ګي په لاري یم I am waiting impatiently. لار ته مي کتل، دوپ ستر ګي مي څلور سوې wore my eye out waiting. ستر ګي مي درپسي څلور سوې I waited for you impatiently. ستر ګي مي مرغی مرغی شوي I could hardly keep my eyes open. ستر ګي یي کوهو ته پرېوتي دي Eastern His eyes have become sunken. ستر ګي مي ورته تیتي نه دي a I am in no way worse than him. b I am in no way obligated to him. یو و بل ته سري ستر ګي They can't stand each other. و احمد ته مي ستر ګي دي I am waiting for Ahmed. ستر ګي یي وهلئ یم He (they) put the evil eye on me. په ستر ګو! Eastern blind as a bat په ستر ګه Gladly! په ستر ګو! ، په دواړو ستر ګو! ، پر دواړو ستر ګو Western باندي ستر ګو کنبي اخیستل a to suffer from the evil eye b to suffer from people's ill-will ستر ګ Eastern with great difficulty په ستر ګ مبنلو تر ستر ګو ته اوبه ورکول، ستر ګو ته غور I see double. ته مي دوه دوه کېږي ورکول Western a to charm, bewitch (by beauty, etc.) b to admire, feast one's eyes on (e.g., sweetheart, girl friend) ستر ګو نه یې وینی څاښي Eastern His eyes were bloodshot. ستر ګو لیدل نه وکړي before daybreak تر ستر ګو دي وګرزم I am prepared to give my life for you! د ستر ګو to lose all sense of shame and conscience د ستر ګو اوبه وتل څخه خاشه نه اخیستل to become stern, become hard-hearted

ستر ګه وال ستر ګه ور stərgawál ستر ګوار stərgawár 1 seeing, with eyes to see 2 big-eyed 3 observant (e.g., a writer)

ستر ګه ورتوب stərgawartób m. vigilance, keenness of observation

ستر ګی stərgój f. 1 (eye)glasses 2 birth-mark, mole 3 pivot (of a door) 4 disease of the eyes (in horses)

ستر ګه وال stərgíz ☞ ستر ګیز

ستر لنگ starlíng m. ☞ ستر لنگ

ستر مني satrmaní f. reclusion, seclusion

ستر ناب stərnáb m. ruler; historical satrap

ستر تیا stərwálaj m. ☞ ستر والی

ستر ونده satrwánda (woman) living in seclusion, in a harem

سترﻩ ‎1‎ satrá *f. Arabic* **1** curtain **2** shawl, veil **3** shelter, cover د اراضي سترﻩ natural cover سترﻩ کول *compound verb* to hide, cover; conceal

سترﻩ ‎2‎ sutrá clean, neat په سترﻩ کاليو کښې neatly dressed

سترﻩ ‎3‎ stə́ra *feminine singular of* ستر ‎3‎

سترى ‎1‎ satráj *m.* **1** small stack **2** bundle, sheaf of ears [of grain]

سترى ‎2‎ satráj *f.* **1** ☞ سترى **2** scratch, abraison

سترﯦدل stəredə́l *denominative, intransitive* [*past:* ستر شو] **1** to be large **2** to grow, increase **3** to be important, be significant

ستري وتري satrí-watrí سترى وتري پرﯦوتل *compound verb* **a** to fall **b** to be defeated, be smashed ستري وتري کول *compound verb* **a** to bring down, overturn, topple **b** to smash, annihilate

سترول stərawə́l *denominative, transitive* [*past:* ستړی يې کړ] to tire out, exhaust

ستړى stə́ṛaj **1** tired, fatigued, exhausted ستړى ستومانه worn out ستړى کول *compound verb* **a** to tire; wear out, exhaust; (over)strain د دﯦنمن دي چاري ډﯦر ستړی کړم This work has made me very tired. a عسکر ستړي کول to wear down the enemy forces **b** to bother someone, pester someone, torment someone, exasperate someone ﺷﺎن ستړى کول، ﺷﺎن ستومانه کول **a** to get tired; become exhausted **b** to toil by the sweat of one's brow ستړى کﯦدل *compound verb* to ge tired; become exhausted **2** ending, coming to an end ستړى ورځ The day is drawing to a close.

ستړيا stə́ṛjá *f.* fatigue, exhaustion ستړيا اچول *compound verb* to rest يو گړى دلته کښېنه ستړيا واچوه Sit here for an hour or so and rest.

ستړﯦدل stəredə́l *denominative, intransitive* [*past:* ستړى شو] to get tired, become fatigued

ستړى مښې stə́ṛaj-máshe *f.* ستړى مشې stə́ṛay-máshe f. greeting د چا سره ستړى مشې کول to exchange greetings with someone

ستغ ‎1‎ stəgh **1** *m.* **.1** sharp rise, steep slope **1.2** road through a mountain pass **1.3** complication, difficulty د حيات ستغ the burdens of life **2.1** astringent خوله ستغه کول to make one's mouth sore **2.2** unpleasant; harsh په ستغه لهجه in a harsh tone **2.3** miserly, stingy **2.4** low, mean, vile **2.5** steep ستغه لار steep road **2.6** harmful; unfavorable **2.7** hateful, odious

ستغ ‎2‎ stəgh *m.* **1** larva (of the gadfly or warble fly) **2** abcess or boil from the gadfly larva

ستغه stə́gha *f.* **1** rudeness, harsh word **2** unpleasantness **3** tonsil

ستکهوم stakhóm *m.* Stockholm

ستگ stəg *m.* pin

ستل ‎1‎ sátl, sátəl *m.* pail, bucket

ستل ‎2‎ satə́l *transitive* [*past:* و يې ستل] **1** to spread; spread out **2** to (make) even, smooth out, (make) level

ستم ‎1‎ sitám *m.* **1** oppression; tyranny; coercion **2** insult, offense ستم کول *compound verb* **a** to oppress **b** to offend, insult

ستم ‎2‎ stam *m.* **1** quickened breathing **2** muscle spasms, contractions (during childbirth, while defecating) ستم وهل *compound verb* **a** to breath with quickened breath **b** to exert oneself

ستم ‎3‎ stam *m.* eye (of a needle)

ستما stamá́ *f.* quickened breathing; shortness of breath, labored breathing

ستمبر sitámbr *m.* September

ستمن ‎1‎ stamə́n **1** hospitable **2** decent, honest, respectable

ستمن ‎2‎ stamə́n fresh, green

ستمى stamáj *m.* ☞ ستم ‎2‎ کول *compound verb* to breathe with quickened breath

ستمﯦدل stamedə́l *denominative, intransitive* [*past:* ستم شو] to pant, breathe heavily ستړى شوئ ستمﯦږي He is tired and is breathing hard.

ستن ‎1‎ stən *f.* [*plural:* ستني stə́ni] **1** needle ستن ﭘﯧﭘل *compound verb* to thread a needle **2** awl **3** pin **4** syringe ستن لگول، ستن to چا ته ستني وهل *compound verb* to give an injection وهل vaccinate someone (against smallpox) **5** post, pole; column; prop, support د بادوان ستن a wooden pole د لرگي ستن mast **6** hand (of a watch or clock) **7** needle (of a conifer) **8** dragonfly **9** *figurative* basis; support ستن او دسمال betrothal

ستناو stənáw delaying, holding back, slowing

ستناوه ‎1‎ stənáwa *f.* respect, esteem

ستناوه ‎2‎ stənāwə́ *imperfect of* ستنول

ستنبه stənbá *m.* ستن به vaccinating, inoculating

ستنځى stə́ndzaj *m.* **1** prison **2** stand, stop, halt

ستندرد standárd *m.* standard

ستندرديزاسيون standardizāsjón *m.* standardization

ستنک stənák *m.* pin

ستنول stənawə́l *denominative, transitive* [*past:* ستون يې کړ، و يې ستناوه] **1** to return, give back **2** to delay someone or something **3** to direct, turn, fix (one's gaze)

ستنه ‎1‎ staná *f.* return په ستنه تلل to go back په ستنه پوري وتل، په ستنه کﯦدل to step back

ستنه ‎2‎ stə́na *f. dialect* ☞ ستن

ستنه ‎3‎ staná *feminine singular of* ستون ‎2‎

ستني ‎1‎ stə́ni *plural of* ستن

ستني ‎2‎ stané *feminine plural of* ستون ‎2‎

ستنﯦدل stanedə́l *denominative, intransitive* [*past:* ستون شو] **1** to return, go back **2** to be delayed; be kept, linger, stay too long پرون Yesterday I was delayed in the city په ښار کښي د ماما کره ستون شوم at my uncle's. **3** to be directed, be turned, be fixed (of one's gaze)

ستو ‎1‎ staw *m.* **1** door **2** pore **3** chink, crack, slit; (small) hole

ستو ‎2‎ sətú *m.* **1** crumb; insignificant amount, bit **2** crushed mulberry

ستوان satwā́n *m. plural* fried ground seeds (e.g., ground peas, crushed mulberry, nuts) *proverb* هم ستوان خوري، هم ﺑﻨﭙﯧﻠﻲ ﺑﻐﻮي He who chases two hares catches neither.

ستوخ stukh ☞ ستغ ‎1‎ ‎2‎

ستوخى stúkhaj *m.* shortness of breath, labored breathing, panting

ستوديو studijó *f.* studio د راډيو ستوديو radio studio

ستور sutúr *m.* draft animal (e.g., mule, horse)

ستورپوه storpóh *m.* astronomer

ستورپوهي storpohí *f.* astronomy

ستورپژواند storpežǎnd *m.* **1** astronomer **2** astrologer

ستورپژندتیا storpežandtjǎ *f.* **1** astronomy **2** astrology

ستوری stóraj *m.* star; planet د قطب ستورو مواصلات astronautics د تلي ستوری the North Star لکیور ستوری comet د میزان ستوری starfish بحري ستوری Libra (the constellation) ستوری پرپوتل **a** to fall (of stars, meteors) **b** *literal & figurative* to roll **c** to suffer failure; change (of one's fortune) د هغه ستوری لوړ و He had a lucky star.

ستوغ 2 stugh ☞ ستغ1

ستوغه stúgha **1** *f.* ☞ ستغه **2** *feminine singular of* ستوغي خبري ستوغ کول to say unpleasant things ستوغي اورېدل to listen to something unpleasant

ستوف stof *m.* plate, slab

ستوک stok *m.* stock(s), supplies; availability (of goods, etc.)

ستوکل stokál **1** insignificant, worthless **2** ill-disposed, wishing ill, bad (of a person)

ستوګه stóga *f.* ☞ استوګه

ستول satawál *transitive* [*past:* و يې ستاوه] to seat, make or have someone sit down

ستومانتیا stomāntjǎ *f.* fatigue, tiredness, weariness

ستومانول stomānawál *denominative, transitive* [*past:* ستومان يې کړ] to tire (out), exhaust

ستومانه stomā́na **1** tired, tatigued ستړی ستومانه کول worn out *compound verb* to tire (out) ستومانه کېدل *compound verb* to get tired, become fatigued **2** disillusionment, disappointment **3** regretting زه په خپلو کړو ستومانه يم I regret what I did.

ستومانه کوونکی stomā́na kawúnkaj tiring, fatiguing; tedious, tiresome, boring

ستوماني stomā́ní *f.* **1** tiredness, fatigue دماغي ستوماني exhaustion *compound verb* to rest **2** regret, ستوماني اچول، ستوماني ايستل repentance **3** reluctance, unwillingness

ستومانېدل stomānedál *denominative, intransitive* [*past:* ستومانه شو] **1** to get tired, become fatigued **2** to repent, regret, rue

ستومی stúmaj *m.* eye (of a needle)

ستون 1 sutún *m.* **1** pole, post **2** *military* column **3** column (e.g., in a newspaper, magazine) **4** column (of a table), paragraph پنځم ستون fifth column

ستون 2 stun [*f.* ستنه، *m. plural* ستانه، *f. plural* ستنې] **1** returning, going back **2** being delayed, lagging, راستون، درستون، ورستون being late ستون کول ☞ ستنول؛ ستون کېدل ☞ ستنېدل

ستونځه stóndza *f.* ستونزه stúnza *f.* **1** anxiety, uneasiness, worry **2** obstacle; difficulties

ستونول stunawál *denominative, transitive* ☞ ستنول

ستونه stúna *f.* return

ستونی stúnaj *m.* larynx له خپګان نه زما ستونی بند شي I have a lump in my throat. د احمد ستونی ډک ډک کېدئ Ahmed got a lump in his

---

throat. په ستوني کنبي درېدل ، په ستوني کنبي منبتل to stick in the throat. د چا په ستوني کنبي لغته اينبودل، د چا په ستوني کنبي پښه اينبودل **a** to hinder, disturb someone; ruin a deal **b** to get stuck in the throat له ستوني تپرول to swallow, gulp

ستنېدل stunedál *denominative, intransitive* ☞ ستنبدل

ستونېدنه stunedána *f.* return

ستنيز stuníz glottal, pharyngeal

ستوني stunístǎk (flat) on one's back, supine ستوني ستخ ستوني ستاک *compound* ستاک پرپوت He fell flat on his back. ستوني ستاک کېدل *verb* to lie down on one's back ستوني ستاک بیده دئ He sleeps on his back.

ستوه stә́wa *f.* knife, dagger

سته 1 stә *m. plural Western* **1** existence, being **2** property

سته 2 sta *Western* is, are; there is, there are ساعت در ښخه سته؟ Do you have a watch? په کور کښي څوک سته؟ Is anyone there in the house? سته دئ (there) is, there are

ستمن stamә́n wealthy, well off, propertied

ستوالی stawā́laj *m.* existence, being

ستي 1 stí, satí burned ستي کول *compound verb* to burn alive ستي کېدل *compound verb* to be burned alive

ستی 2 satә́j *f.* [*plural:* ستياني] sati (a widow who burns herself together with the body of her husband)

ستی 3 stәj *f. botony* fumatory

ستېتوسکوپ stetoskóp *m.* stethoscope

ستېزه 1 stéza *f.* **1** plateau **2** level place on the slope of a mountain

ستېزه 2 stezá *f.* **1** argument, wrangling, squabbling **2** fighting, struggle; enmity **3** injustice ستېزه کول *compound verb* **a** to argue, wrangle, squabble **b** to fight, struggle; quarrel, have a feud with

ستېشن steshán *m.* ☞ ستېشن

ستیل stil *m.* style

سټ 1 saṭ *m.* **1** wooden base of an anvil **2** anvil **3** stump **4** *regional* log (of wood) **5** log **6** *dialect* sudden attack, surprise attack; سټ ورکول to defeat someone

سټ 2 saṭ *m.* ☞ ښټ

سټ 3 saṭ killed, perished سټ کول *compound verb* **a** to ruin, destroy **b** to bring down, fell, chop (e.g., a tree) سره سټ کول to annihilate each other سټ کېدل *compound verb* ☞ سټېدل

سټ 4 saṭ *m.* boiled mung beans

سټاتیک sṭāṭík static

سټار saṭár *m.* **1** tar **2** ☞ سوهان

سټاف sṭāf *m. regional* **1** staff, headquarters **2** staff, personnel

سټاکهالم sṭākhā́lm *m.* Stockholm

سټاله sәṭā́la *f.* supposition, conjecture, surmise, guess په سټاله اخیستل to suppose, surmise

سټرابري sṭrābarí *f.* strawberries; hautbois strawberries

سټراتسفېر sṭrā́tasfér *m.* stratosphere

سټرلنگ sṭarlíng *m.* **1** sterling **2** pound sterling

سټ سمټ سړی sәṭsamáṭ lazy, idle, loafing سټ سمټ slacker, lazybones, idler, loafer

سټ سودا səṭsudā́ *f.* purchase without weighing

ستک ¹ suṭə́k *m.* **1** hammer; sledge-hammer **2** small hammer, mallet, gavel

ستک ² sṭik *m. regional* riding crop, cane

ستک کاري suṭəkkārí *f.* forging, blacksmithing, shoeing

سټکوری səṭkúraj **1.1** burned, chared (of bread) **1.2** wrinkling, puckering **1.3** frozen, stiff with cold **1.4** withered سټکوری کول *compound verb* **a** to sear, scorch, burn **b** to wrinkle سټکوری کېدل *compound verb* **a** to burn **b** to wrinkle **2** *m.* **.1** burned bread **2.2** half-burned log **2.3** root, basis

سټگی səṭə́gaj *m.* small hammer, mallet

سټل səṭə́l *transitive* ☞ کټل

ستماتونی səṭmātúnaj *m.* ستمتونی *m.* woodcutter

ستوپ sṭop *m.* stove, oven

سټ وټ saṭwáṭ killed, perished, annihilated سټ وټ کول *compound verb* to ruin, destroy, annihilate سټ وټ کېدل *compound verb* to perish, be killed; be annihilated

سټور sṭor *m. regional* storehouse; store جنرال سټور department store

سټول ¹ səṭawə́l *denominative, transitive* [*past:* سټ یې کړ] **1** to ruin, destroy **2** to kill, slaughter, annihilate, exterminate

سټول ² sṭul *m. regional* **1** stool **2** small table

سټه səṭa *f.* **1** root **2** base, basis; foundation **3** support, post **4** *Eastern* log په سټه پوهېدل to investigate thoroughly, get to the essence, get at the root

سټی saṭə́j *f.* back of a blade

سټېدل səṭedə́l *denominative, intransitive* [*past:* سټ شو] **1** to be killed, be annihilated **2** to perish, die **3** to be felled (e.g., of a tree)

سټېده səṭedə́ *m. plural* distruction, annihilation; death

سټډيوم sṭédə́jum *m.* stadium

سټېشن sṭeshán *m.* station د برېښنا سټېشن، برقي سټېشن power-generating plant د راډيو سټېشن radio station

سجاده sadzhādá *f. Arabic* **1** prayer rug **2** temple, chapel

سجاده نشين sadzhādanishín *m.* head imam in a holy place

سجايا sadzhājā́ *m. Arabic plural of* سجيه

سجده sidzhdá *f. Arabic* [*plural:* سجدې *and m. plural* سجود] *religion* bowing to the ground, prostrating سجده کول *compound verb* to bow to the ground, prostrate oneself

سجره sə́dzhra *f.* ☞ سرجه

سجع sadzh' *f. Arabic* rhymed prose, rhyming prose

سجل sidzhíl, sidzhíll *m. Arabic* **1** record, register **2** registration form د احوال سجل، د اهاليو سجل registry of vital statistics (e.g., births, deaths, marriages, divorces) **3** service record

سجود sudzhúd *m. Arabic plural of* سجده

سجيوي sadzhijawí inborn, innate, congenital

سجيه sadzhijá *f. Arabic* [*m. plural* سجايا] inborn characteristic, innate quality, natural character د خپلي سجيي پر اساس by one's innate qualities د ډېري لوري سجيي خاوند و He was a man of high morals.

سوچه such ☞ سچ

سچاپ sacháp *m.* fringe

سوچه suchá ☞ سچه

سخ səts thick, dense

سحار sahā́r *m. Arabic* سحر ¹ sahár *m.* dawn, morning twilight; early morning په لوی سحار at dawn نن سحار this morning وختي سحار early in the morning

سحار ¹ sahár ☞ سحار

سحر ² sihr, sehr *m. Arabic* witchcraft, sorcery, magic سحرکول *compound verb*

سحرآمېزه sihrāméza سحرآمېز sihrāméz bewitching, magic(al), miraculous

سحرخېزه saharkhéza arising early, arising at dawn

سحرگاه sahargā́h *m.* ☞ سحرمال

سحرگر sihrgár *Arabic* **1** *m.* sorcerer, magician, wizard, charmer **2** charming, bewitching (of a look or glance)

سحرمال saharmā́l **1** *m.* dawn, daybreak **2** at sunrise, at dawn

سحري sihrí marvelous, magical, enchanting

سخ ¹ səkh *m.* happiness, luck, good fortune, success سخ دي شه! I wish you good luck!

سخ ² sakh ☞ سبر

سخ ³ sakh *interjection* bravo, wonderful, excellent

سخا ¹ sakhā́ *f. Arabic* generosity, magnanimity, liberality

سخا ² skhā **1** rotten, putrid, foul سخاکول *compound verb* to rot, ferment سخاکېدل *compound verb* to rot, putrify, decompose يوه ها *saying* an only son and he was a ne'er-do-well وه، هغه هم سخا وه (*literally:* just one egg, and it was addled)

سخات ¹ sakhā́t *m.* funeral banquet, funeral repast

سخات ² skhāt *m.* miscarriage, abortion; foetus

سخاتوب skhātób *m.* سخاتيا *f.* putridity, rottenness

سخاته skhā́ṭa *f.* flat nose

سختاړېدل skhāredə́l *intransitive* ☞ سختاړېدل

سخافت sakhāfát *m. Arabic* **1** weakmindedness, imbicility, stupidity, obtuseness **2** unconvincingness, unpersuasiveness

سخالين sakhālín *m.* Sakhalin

سخاوالی skhāwálaj *m.* ☞ سخاتوب

سخاوت sakhāwát *m. Arabic* generosity, magnanimity, liberality سخاوت کول to be generous, be magnanimous

سخاورېوه skhā́wga *f. botony* **1** long cyperus; tormentil **2** sweet flag

سخت sakht **1** hard, strong, firm, rigid, stiff **2** hard, arduous, difficult, heavy **3** strict, stern **4** severe, cold سخت ژمی a severe winter **5** stingy, tight, miserly (of a person) **6** rude, harsh **7** heavy, grave, terrible سخت جرم a serious crime **8** persistent, stubborn, hardened, embittered

سختاړ sakhtā́ṛ *m.* **1** boiled rice porridge **2** thin gruel, pap

سختاړول sakhtāṛawə́l *denominative, transitive* [*past:* سختاړ یې کړ] to boil (until) soft (e.g., porridge, gruel)

سختاړېدل sakhtāṛedə́l *denominative, intransitive* [*past:* سختاړ شو] to be boiled soft (e.g., porridge, gruel)

سخت دل sakhtdíl سخت زړی sakhtzə́ṛay cruel, brutal, hard-hearted, heartless, callous

سخت سر sakhtsár 1 steadfast, stable, firm, unshakable 2 persistent, stubborn, insistent 3 tough, having great endurance, having great staying power

سخت سری ¹ sakhtsarí f. 1 steadfastness, staunchness, firmness 2 persistence, stubbornness, insistence 3 endurance, staying power, fortitude

سخت سری ² sakhtsáraj having a stern temper, a stern disposition

سخت گیره sakhtgíra severe, stern; strict, exacting, demanding

سخت مزاجه sakhtmizā́dzha severe, having stern disposition

سختوالی sakhtwā́laj m. ☞ سختي ¹ د زړه سختي cruelty, brutality, savageness, hard-heartedness.

سختول sakhtawə́l denominative, transitive [past: سخت یې کړ] 1 to make hard, make rigid 2 to make severe, harden, embitter 3 to fasten, secure ډبری سختول compound verb to tighten a nut 4 to make difficult

سخته sákhta 1 f. .1 deprivations, difficulties; indigence, poverty سخته په ځان زغمل to endure deprivations 1.2 unpleasantness 2 very, extremely سخته ښه سړی دئ He is a very good man. 3 feminine singular of سخت سخته روغ rainy day

سختي ¹ sakhtí f. [plural: سختي and سختیگان] 1 hardness; cruelty 2 difficulty; trouble, serious position په سختي سره with difficulty په ډېره سختي with great difficulty 3 misfortune, trouble ډېري سختي پری تېری شوي He experienced many deprivations. 4 sternness, severity 5 stinginess, miserliness 6 shortage, need د اوبو سختي lack of water

سختي ² sakhti feminine plural of سخت

سختیا sakhtjā́ f. ☞ سختي ¹

سختېدل sakhtedə́l denominative, intransitive [past: سخت شو] 1 to get hard, become firm, become rigid, stiff; get strong 2 to become difficult; become stressful (of life) 3 to become hard or severe, grow cruel or violent

سخر ¹ skhə́r m. father-in-law (wife's father)

سخر ² skhar 1 m. [plural: سخر] stone, rock 2 petrified, hardened

سخرگنی skhərganə́j f. خسرگنی wife's relatives, wife's family

سخره ¹ skhára f. stone, rock

سخره ² skhə́ra feminine singular of سخر ²

سخره غوټه skhə́ra ghúṭa f. hangman's knot, noose

سخری skharaj stubborn, steadfast

سخړه ¹ sə́khṛa f. embryo

سخړه ² skhə́ṛa f. 1 artel of (ditch)diggers or excavators or navvies (who dig kahrizes) 2 trace (of a plow)

سخکال sakhkā́l dialect ☞ سړ، سړکال ²

سخکوره sə́khkóra f. double-sided ax

سخکی sə́khkaj m. whine of a bullet

سخن ¹ sukhún, sukhán m. [plural: سخنان] word, speech سخن دان smart, intelligent

سخن ² səkhə́n happy; lucky, fortunate

سخن آرا sukhanārā́ eloquent

سخن آرايي sukhanārājí f. eloquence

سخن آور sukhanāwár 1 eloquent 2 m. poet

سخن چین sukhanchín m. gossip, scandal-monger; tattletale

سخن دان sukhandā́n 1 smart, intelligent (of a person) 2 m. poet; man of letters

سخندرکی ¹ skhundurkáj m. ☞ سخوندرکی

سخن سازه sukhansā́za m. 1 gasbag, windbag 2 deceiver, cheat, swindler, liar

سخن فهمه sukhanfáhma clever, bright, quick

سخوار skhwāṛ with or having a flat nose, with a nose like a duck

سخوتن skhutə́n m. hot ashes

سخوټ skhwə́ṭ m. 1 crooked club or cudgel 2 fat male, stout man

سخوختن skhwukhtə́n m. ☞ سخوتن

سخور sə́khəwār happy; lucky, fortunate

سخوښتی skhwə́khtáj m. 1 shuttle (weaver's) 2 corner (of the mouth)

سخوندر skhwandár m. calf, bull-calf

سخوندرکی ¹ skhwə́ndarkáj m. calf

سخوندرکی ² skhwə́ndarkə́j f. سخوندره skhwandə́ra f. heifer

سخه ¹ sə́kha f. 1 malicious joy; malice, spite سخه پخول compound verb to gloat 2 vindictiveness

سخه ² skha ☞ ښخه

سخهار sə́khahár m. 1 rustle, rustling (of the wind) 2 whine of a bullet

سخي sakhí 1 generous, magnanimous 2 m. proper noun Sakhi

سخی ² skhaj m. calf, bull-calf دریابي سخی seal

سخی ³ skhəj f. heifer

سخي توب sakhitób m. ☞ سخاوت

سخیف sakhíf Arabic 1 unconvincing, weak دغه دلایل سخیف دي Those are unconvincing arguments. 2 empty, frivolous, empty-headed, flighty

سد ¹ səd m. 1 consciousness, sense, feeling پر سد کېدل، په سد کېدل to regain consciousness بې سده کېدل to lose consciousness 2 understanding 3 intellect, reason بې سده سری blockhead, dolt, stupid person سد دي په سر کښې دئ که نه؟ Are you in your right mind?

سد ² sad, sadd m. Arabic 1 wall سد سکندر the Great Wall of China 2 dam, weir, dyke 3 curtain 4 obstacle

سدره sádra f. gifts or tributes to a sayyid

سدری sadrə́j vest

سدس suds m. Arabic one sixth (part) of something

سدکاو sədkā́w m. stomach upset, indigestion; diarrhea

سدني sídni m. Sidney

سدو sadó m. proper noun Sado [diminutive of اسدالله]

سدوبد sədubə́d m. consciousness سدوبد څخه ورکول to beat someone senseless, beat until loss of consciousness

سدوزي sadozí, saduzí **1** *m. plural* **.1** the Sadozi tribe (a branch of the Durani from which were drawn the rulers of Afghanistan in the eighteenth and early nineteenth centuries) **1.2** branch **2** sadozáy, saduzáy *m.* a Sadozai [member of the Sadozi tribe]

سدول sadwál *m.* person of small stature; squab (a short squat person)

سده suddá *f. Arabic* **1** hindrance, obstacle **2** bolt, lock (in a door) **3** *medicine* embolism, thrombosis

سده sudá **1** pure, uncontaminated **2** genuine, real

سدی sədəj, sadə́j *f.* century سدیو کېدل to grow old

سدر suḍár **1** *m.* [*plural:* سدران suḍarānand سدر suḍər] wild boar **2.1** bald; balding **2.2** scabby, mangy

سدول sədúl *m.* **1** old ox **2** sluggish listless person, dawdler; lout, oaf

سر sar *m.* **1** head سپین سر gray head سر ته at the head of the bed **a** په خپل سر by one's head (to swear, etc.) **b** spontaneously, by oneself **c** involuntarily, unwittingly **2** *classifier* head (for counting cattle) شل سره مال twenty head of cattle **3** chief, leader; director **4** front part, forepart of something **5** top, topmost part, apex; summit **6** surface د اوبو په سر on water د مځکي پر سر on the ground **7** upper reaches, headwaters, riverhead; source سر ایستل *compound verb* to originate, have its source (of a river) **8** beginning د میاشتي په سر کښني at the beginning of the month له سر څخه مودي، سر له څخه مودي from the very start لومړي سره څخه beginning (from, with)…, starting (from, with) سر له دي سر له نن ورځي ، سر له نن ورځي starting with this issue شماري څخه from today forward سر تر پایه، سر تر پنبو **a** from head to toe, from foot to head **b** from beginning to end, from start to finish **c** له یو تر بل سره all, entirely, completely; absolutely **9** end; edge پوري from end to end **10** end, tip (e.g., of a finger) **11** *figurative* life سر ورکول، سر بایلل to sacrifice one's life in the name of something له سر او مال تېر prepared to sacrifice life and property; که څما د سر امن وي **a** if they preserve my life **b** if they show mercy to me ژوند ځار شه له سره او سر ځار شه له عزته *saying* life is dearer than money, and honor is dearer than life **12** addition, extra, additional payment دا قلم مي د ذهین د قلم سره الیش کئ، شل افغانی مي سر پر ورکړ I exchanged pens with Zaheen and paid him an extra twenty Afghani **13** goods or commodity equivalent (in bartering) سراخیستل *compound verb* **a** to rise up against, rebel against, come out against someone; be obstinate, fail to obey or submit to, resist ده د بادار څخه سر واخیست He stopped taking orders from his boss. **b** to receive something extra, receive extra payment in money (in an exchange) د چا سر اړول to give someone in marriage; celebrate someone's wedding سر آسمان ته رسېدل **a** to be very tall **b** to become conceited, get a big head سر اودل *compound verb* to braid one's hair سر اینودل، سر اینبودل *compound verb* **a** to go to bed **b** to become thoughtful سر پر زنګانه اینبودل to plan, conceive **c** to subordinate oneself to, submit to **d** to lay down one's life for, sacrifice oneself پر وطن سر اینبودل to give one's life for one's country **e** to begin, undertake د خبري سر اینبودل to start a

conversation (about something); to broach a subject **f** to flow together (of rivers) **g** to live together, cohabit with someone سر سر بندول سر بنندل بایلل، سر بازل *compound verb* **a** to close, stopper, cork **b** to become engaged, become a fiancé سر پتول *compound verb* **a** to be lost in thought **b** to be on the alert, prick up one's ears سر پښني کول **a** to shirk, evade, elude, try get out of doing something **b** to (try to) persuade or induce someone to do something سر په سوري کول د چا to hunker down in a slit trench څخه سر پيچل، د چا څخه سر تاوول to come out against someone; contradict someone; fail to obey someone سر تر آسمانه تبرېدل **a** to get a swelled head over **b** to hold a high position سر تکول *compound verb* to worry, fret, torment oneself; suffer **b** د چا څخه ته سر ... تکول to complain, make complaints against someone سر تیتول **a** to lower one's head, hang one's head **b** to submit, resign oneself, bow to, acquiesce سر تیتبدل *compound verb* **a** to disgrace oneself **b** to humiliate oneself, grovel د چا سر ختل to ruin someone, be the undoing of someone; drive someone to his grave سر غړول *compound verb* **a** to hang one's head **b** to hang one's head, be dejected, be sad, grieve **c** to not agree to سر څنډل *compound verb* to shake one's head "no" سر په خلاصېدل، سر په خبره خلاصبدل *compound verb* **a** to perish, pay with one's life **b** د چا سر ختل د چا سره سر خورل سر خورل سر په رسبدل **a** to be possible, be feasible, be realizable, be practicable دا کار سر سره خوري That is feasible. **b** correspond to, conform to, be in keeping with; سر خوربدل to hurt, ache (of the head) سر درلودل، سر لرل **a** to have a good head, have brains **b** to outweigh, be heavier than (about a pan of a balance) **c** to be larger, be more expensive than something) سر راوړل to distinguish oneself, be notable for; accomplish a great feat سر په رسبدل to understand, comprehend something خپل سر سپینول ؟ سر دي په ورسبدئ Do you understand? to live to have gray hair سر بنندل *compound verb* to give one's life for something سر بنورول to sacrifice everything سر و مال بنندل *compound verb* to nod one's head ده سر را بنورولی دئ چه پښتو در بنیم He agreed to teach me Pashto. سر غړول، سر غړول *compound verb* **a** to rise up, rebel; evince rebelliousness **b** to not agree to سر کښنته اچول، سر کښنته غړول، سر کښنته کول *compound verb* **a** to hang one's head **b** humility, submissiveness **c** سر کول ;سر تيتول ره، در، ور to give consent to a marriage **d** to agree to سر کوزول *compound verb* **a** to start something, set about, proceed to, begin to **b** to break (open) (of a boil or abcess) **c** to miss (the mark), be wide of the mark ما نښان سر کئ I missed the target. **d** to braid the hair, make a braid (after shampooing) په ... سر کبدل **a** to set out for, leave (for), go (to) someplace *Eastern* په غرو سر شه He went to the mountains. **b** to go, walk somewhere په باغ را سر شه *Eastern* He went into the garden. **c** to start, strike up (e.g., a conversation) په خبرو سر شه *Eastern* He struck up a conversation. د چا سر گرزول، د چا سر گرځول to confuse, bewilder someone, take away someone's ability to reason sensibly سر به دي وګرزي He is causing you a lot of trouble. سر په ګرزول to get into an argument;

intervene in a quarrel ته سر مه په ګزوه! Don't pay any attention. په چا سر ګرزول to sympathize with someone; be concerned about someone په چا سر ګرځول دی په کار سر نه ګرزوي He isn't worked up about the cause. سر ګرزېدل compound verb to be giddy, be dizzy سر يې ګير کړه! Eastern سر راباندي ګرځي My head is spinning. Charm him! سر ماتول compound verb a to hurt someone's head badly, break someone's head b to puzzle over something, rack one's brains over something c to thirst for, long for, to seek after something d to give in addition, give an extra سر مخ يې ونغبنتل لار Eastern Unnoticed he disappeared. سر نيول to be performed, be accomplished سر نه نيول a to be impossible, be unrealizable b to not agree to سر په لاس کښي نيول to give or surrender oneself wholly to a cause سر نه سره ورتلل، سر نه سره رسېدل to not turn out well, fail to be a success; be unrealizable د دي کار سر نه سره ورځي This is not working out. سر پر ورکول a to lay down one's life, sacrifice oneself b to exhibit self-sacrifice or dedication c to give something in addition, give a little extra سر وهل compound verb a to behead, cut or chop off someone's head b to look for, search for c to appear, rise (of the moon and sun) سر وهلی بر وهلی) a crazy, insane b upset; confused, perplexed سر په تندي وهل، سر په دوارو سر لاسو وهل to grieve, mourn, be sad, to feel bad, be melancholy پر سر اخيستل Eastern یې راته مه وينځه! Don't stick up for him! take on (oneself), shoulder (responsibility for supporting the family, caring for someone); lay on oneself (the burden of cares) د ملګري غم مي پر سر اخيستئ دئ I undertook to help my friend in his trouble. د چا پر سر لاس تېرول پر سر اوبه تېرول to bathe, take a bath to pity, feel sorry for someone, treat with kindness, to be nice to, take tender care of someone پر سرو سره ختل a to crowd b to jam, cram into په سر اخيستل a to get into one's head b to fill (of the teeth) د چا په سر ختل to abuse someone's kindness; take advantage of someone with a less forceful personality ته لاري لاري، په سر وختي You are abusing my kindness په سر بيول، په سر رسول to carry out responsibilities; serve تر سر تپرول to avoid, evade, shirk کار تر سره رسول، سر نيول to find out, worm a secret out of someone تر سر کېدل، تر کار تر سره کول to finish, bring the matter to an end مطلب سره کېدل to be realized, be consumated, be brought to an end کار تر سره رسول ☞ یې تر سره سو His dream came true. سر ته رسول سر ته رسېدل to end, come to an end, be completed, be consumated د خبري و سر ته ونه رسېدي You didn't understand what the point was. د سره کول to fulfill (one's duty); bring (a matter that has been begun) to an end د سره کېدل to be realized, come true (of a desire) سر و جدل وهل to do one's utmost, try as hard as one can, try with all one's strength سر و کړکی کېدل to be at daggers drawn, be at swords' points, quarrel, feud هغوی سره سر و کړکی دي They are mortal enemies. سر زرو کي یې وکړل، سر سته یې وکړل Eastern They got dressed up. سر مي ورته نغري کړ I've racked my brains over him سر په وښنتو نه درنېږي saying a burden of one's own choice is not felt (literally: one's own hair is not a weight on one's head) سري ورته سر ته یې سودا ختلې ده Eastern He ruined this deal. په خولې کم He

د سر په کاسه کي اوبه سره چنبل to feud, quarrel; harbor rabid hatred د سر دپاسه سر شته I will find justice. د سر سترګي خوړل، د سر کسي خوړل to go blind, lose one's sight د سر سترګي وخوري! I wish you would go blind! سر پر سر one after the other a سر په سر even with, on a level with b tie, draw (to play to a) c even, even-steven, without any extra payment (in an exchange) سر تر سره full, complete سر له سره، سر د سره completely, wholly; absolutely په سر directly, personally; -self احمد په سر سره راغلئ Ahmed appeared in person. په يو سر inedpendently, on one's own, personally د سري پر سر courageous, daring; dare-devil تر سر تېر per person, per head (of payment) اوبه یې سر له راغلي He had to yield. یو سر دوه غوړونه quite alone, very much alone یو سر یم I'm all by myself څوک سر پر خپل سر باندي پرېنبودل to not raise any obstacles to someone; give someone complete freedom یو کار تر سر ستا په سر چه خوشي تپرول to leave a matter as is ... I swear to you that... سل سره هغه مما په سر قسم نه خوري He loves me very much. خيشتول، یو نه خريل saying to scatter one's efforts, start many projects and fail to complete them (literally: to lather up a hundred heads and not shave a one) په سر کښي یې مسواک او په بغل کښي یې زما په سر څه اور بل دئ؟ He is a prig and a hypocrite. خنجر Nothing upsets me. په سر یې د د سر سوري یې نشته He doesn't have a patron. He ستا د سر یې فرياد کړئ He is depressed. اوښ انبار پروت دئ complained about you. د چا سره دي سر دئ؟ Whom do you wish to see?

سر 2 sir, sirr m. Arabic [plural: سرونه sirrúna and Arabic اسرار asrár] secret سر ويل، سر ساتل compound verb to keep a secret فاش کول compound verb to divulge a secret

سر 3 sur m. music note; key

سرا 1 sará f. ☞ سره

سراب saráb m. Arabic figurative mirage

سراج sirádzh m. Arabic lamp

سراج sarrádzh m. harness maker, saddler

سراجي sarrádzhí f. harness-maker's craft, trade of harness-making, saddler's craft, trade of saddle-making, saddlery

سراچه 1 sarachá f. small house, outbuilding

سرارو sarārú m. artery

سراسر 1 sarāsár m. juniper

سراسر 2 sarāsár from start to finish; completely, totally, absolutely

سرسري sarāsarí ☞ سرسري

سراسيمګي sarāsimagí f. 1 confusion, perplexity, embarrassment, disarray 2 haste, hurry

سراسيمه sarāsimá 1 confused, perplexed, being in a state of confusion 2 hurrying; bustling سراسيمه کول compound verb a to throw into confusion b to hurry, make someone hurry سراسيمه کېدل compound verb a to lose one's presence of mind, become flustered, get into a state of confusion b to hurry, make haste, bustle

سراښ srákh greedy, miserly, stingy

سراښتوب sráakhtób m. greediness, miserliness; stinginess, cupidity

سرابند srākhə́nd ☞ سرابس

سرابنول srākhawə́l *denominative, transitive* [*past:* سرابس يي کړ] to make greedy, make stingy

سرابنی srākhí ☞ سرابنتوب

سرابنیدل srākhedə́l *denominative, intransitive* [*past:* سرابس شو] to be greedy, be stingy

سراغ surā́gh *m.* **1** search, investigation; questioning, interrogation **2** track, footprint; sign, mark; token سراغ پیداکول، سراغ ایستل *compound verb* **a** to look for, search for; make inquiries **b** to find tracks; discover, find, detect

سراغي surā́ghí *m.* detective

سرافراز sarāfrā́z ☞ سرلوړی

سرافرازي sarāfrāzí *f.* ☞ سرلوړي

سرافسر sarāfsár *m.* garrison commander, post commander

سرانجام sarāndzhā́m *m.* outcome, end, conclusion (of a business deal, an affair)

سرانجنیر sarindzhinir *m.* chief engineer

سرانداز sarāndā́z *m.* **1** back (of a bed) **2** large carpet on the floor

سرانه sarāná *f.* **1** lintel **2** cross-piece

سراو sarā́w *m.* upper reaches of a river, headwaters of a river

سراوره srā́wra *f.* sweets, candy (sent by the bridegroom to the bride's home on the seventh day of the wedding)

سراوړه srā́wṛa *f.* crowd; gathering (of people)

سراهند srāhə́nd ☞ سرابس

سرای sarā́j, srā́j *m.* **1** caravansary, inn **2** large house, detached house د دنیا سرای transitory world (as opposed to the eternal world of the hereafter)

سرایت sirājā́t *m. Arabic* **1** infection سرایت کول to infect; transmit an infection **2** penetration و يو شي ته سرایت کول to penetrate into something; be passed on to something; spread to something, extend to something

سرای خواجه sarā-ji-khodzhá *m.* Sarai-I-Khodzha (populated place north of Kabul)

سرایدار sarā́jdár *m.* سرای دار **1** owner of a caravanasary, innkeeper **2** palace employee

سراېږد sarégd *m.* ☞ سروېږد

سراینی saríkhaj submissive; subjugated, subdued

سرایوالا sarā́jwālā́ *m.* سرای وان sarāywā́n owner of a caravanasary, innkeeper

سرب srab *m.* [1] **1** remedy (against disease) **2** *medicine* treatment

سرب srab [2] deep-red

سرباختن sarbākhtán ☞ سربازي

سربادی sarbādáj **1** mad, senseless **2** talking nonsense

سرباز sarbā́z **1** bold, courageous, selfless **2** *m.* **.1** bold spirit, daredevil **2.2** patriot د وطن سرباز patriot **2.3** soldier

سربازي sarbāzí *f.* daring, boldness, courage, selflessness سربازي کول to exhibit daring, show selflessness د سربازی میدان field of battle

سربانده sarbā́nda *f.* سربانډی sarbā́nday *m.* **1** strip of land at the head of a field **2** upper sloping masonry course of a duval **3**

agriculture balk (a strip of land left unplowed) **4** bridge entrance, bridge approach, the front part of a bridge

سربانډۍ sarbāndə́j *f.* سربانه sarbā́ṇa *f.* **1** traces (of a plow) **2** rawhide strap

سربدال sarbədál **1** suffering from dizziness, experiencing vertigo **2** confused, muddled سربدال کول *compound verb* to confuse, muddle

سربدالتیا sarbədāltjá *f.* سربدالي sarbədālí *f.* **1** dizziness, vertigo **2** (state of) confusion, perplexity

سربدل sarbədál sacrificed

سربډاګه sarbəḍā́ga **1** carefree, light-hearted **2** wasteful, extravagant سربډاګه سړی spendthrift, squanderer, waster, prodigal

سربر sarbúr, sarbár **1** with trimmed branches سربر کول to trim branches **2** *m.* cutting branches, trimming branches

سربراه sarbarā́h getting ready to travel, preparing for a trip; leaving for somewhere سربراه کول to start, set about doing something

سربسته sarbastá **1.1** closed; sealed; stoppered, corked **1.2** whole, unbroken, untouched **2** *f.* **.1** small turban **2.2** triangular scarf, kerchief

سربفلک sarbafalák high, tall (of a mountain)

سربلند sarbulánd, sarbilánd **1** proud, grand, pomous **2** *m. proper noun* Sarbuland

سربلندي sarbulandí *f.* **1** height, elevation **2** pride, pompousness **3** ☞ سرفرازي

سربمهر Sarbamúhr sealed up; under seal

سربند sarbánd **1** *m.* **.1** headband **1.2** chord (used as the base in weaving nets out of straw) **1.3** main gate of an irrigation ditch **1.4** upper reaches, headwaters (of a river) سرينده بازار **2.1** closed closed market **2.2** not having an outlet to the sea

سربه sarbá [1] thick, greasy

سربه srabá [2] *f.* corpse; carrion سربه کول *compound verb* to kill, slaughter

سربي serbí **1** Serb(ian) **2** *m.* Serb

سربر sarbér ☞ سربره

سربرن sarberə́n *figurative* superficial د بحر په سربرنه هوا کښې د اوبو The air over the seal is very humid. زما داسي سربرنه توبس زیات وي خبره نه ده خوښه I don't care for such light-mindedness.

سربره sarbéra **1** from above, above پر عمارت سربره on the building **2** besides something سربره په دې چه besides that **3.1** upper, top; سربره خونه upper room **3.2** to have come out on top, have gained victory; having been victorious

سربیه sarbája *f.* cost, cost price, prime cost

سرپ srəp, sərp *m.* [1] **1** coniferous tree **2** pine tree

سرپ srəp *m.* [2] *plural metallurgy* lead

سرپ surúp [3] **1** completely, entirely **2** only

سرپاږي sarpā́gi *m. plural* [1] **1** Sarpagi (a tribe) **2** *m.* ☞ سرپاږی

سرپاږی sarpā́gaj *m.* [2] facial edema, puffiness

سرپاغي sarpā́ghi, sarpā́ghaj ☞ سرپاږي

سرپټ sarpə́t *m.* سرپته sarpə́ta *f.* ☞ سرپوته

سرپرازه sarparā́za ☞ سرلوړی سرپرازه اوسئ! I have the honor.

سرپرست Sarparást *m.* **1** patron; trustee, guardian **2** leader, manager

سرپرستي Sarparastí *f.* **1** patronage, protection; trusteeship, guardianship **2** guidance, leadership, management سرپرستي کول *compound verb* to lead, guide; direct

سرپرېکړی sarprekə́ṛaj with head chopped off, beheaded

سرپرکمشر sarpaṛkmə́shər *m. military* master sergeant; sergeant major د سرپرکمشر معاون sergeant first class

سرپښتۍ sarpuḳhtə́j *f.* fillet (from the middle portion of a sheep's carcass)

سرپطنوسي sarpatnusí *f.* napkin for a tray

سرپل saripúl *m.* Saripul د سرپل بازار Saripul market (in Kabul)

سرپناه sarpanáh *m.* shelter; refuge, asylum; haven

سرپناهي sarpanāhí *f.* cover, protection

سرپوته sarpúṭa *f.* girl; unmarried woman

سرپوړی sarpóṛaj ☞ سرلوړی²

سرپوښ sarpóḳh *m.* **1** lid, cover **2** valve (of the heart) **3** *technology* cap, head پر خبره سرپوښ اېښودل to hush something up, cover something up

سرپوښلی sarpoḳhə́laj covered, with a roof, with an awning

سرپول srəpawə́l *transitive* [*past:* وي يې سرپاوه] to flap (wings)

سرپه چېړی sarpəcheṛój **1.1** head over heals **1.2** down, downwards, down hill **2** confused, perplexed; stunned هغه سرپه چپړی ولاړ دئ He is stunned.

سرپی srəpáj *m. onomatopeia* sound of birds' wings during flight

سرپېدل srəpedə́l *intransitive* [*past:* وو سرپېده] to flap (wings)

سرپین sərpín lead (made of, containing, or pertaining to the metal lead)

سرت sərát *m.* body

سرتاسره sartāsára سرتاسر from end to end; from edge to edge د دنيا په سرتاسره کښې in the whole world

سرترپايه sartərpā́ja سرترسره sartərsára all, completely, entirely; from edge to edge

سرترلی sartaṛə́laj **1.1** closed سرترلی ډبلی closed box **1.2** sealed up **2** *m.* nomad

سرتروکی sartaṛúkaj *m.* headband

سرترونی sartaṛúnaj covering the head سرترونی دسمال head scarf

سرتمبه sartambá opposing; being stubborn, stubbornly resisting

سرتمبه کي sartambəkí *f.* سرتمبکي obstinacy, stubbornness; persistence

سرتناو sartanáw *m.* string of snares and nets

سرتور sartór **1** uncovered (of the head) سرتور سر bare-headed, hatless **2** defenseless, unprotected سرتوره مه سي! *saying* Long live your husband! (a woman's wish)

سرتوروالی sartorwálaj *m.* shame

سرتورول sartorawə́l *denominative, transitive* [*past:* سرتور يې کړ] to shame

سرتوره sartóra **1** *feminine singular of* سرتور **2** *f.* widow سرتوره کېدل *compound verb* **a** to bare one's head **b** to lose one's husband, be widowed

سرتوره مه سي! *saying* May you live and have a family (a wish expressed by one woman to another)

سرتوري¹ sartorí *f.* **1** shame **2** widowhood

سرتوري² sartóri *feminine plural of* سرتور

سرتورېدل sartoredə́l *denominative, intransitive* **1** [*past:* سرتور شو] to disgrace oneself **2** [*past:* سرتوره شوه] to be widowed, become a widow

سرتيپ sartip *m. history* general

سرتیر¹ sar-i-tír quickly, fast, on the run, in a rush

سرتېر² sartér **1** courageous, brave **2** devoted; selfless

سرتېره sarterə́ pointed

سرتېزه sartéza سرتېز sartéz **1** pointed **2** hot, fiery; hot-tempered, quick-tempered

سرتيته sarṭíta ashamed سرتيته کول *compound verb* to shame, put to shame

سرتيتی sarṭítaj **1** ☞ سرخوړی² **2** *m.* **.1** pig, hog, swine **1.2** *abusive* pig

سرج sardzh *m.* cheviot

سرجماعه sardzhamā'á *m. obsolete* private first class, lance corporal

سرجمع sardzhám' *f.* sum total

سرجه sə́rdzha *f.* **1** frozen snow crust **2** sledding (over the snow) سرجه جوړول *compound verb* سرجه کېدل *compound verb* to toboggan, slide (down a mountain, over the snow, on a board)

سرجي sardzhí of or pertaining to cheviot

سرچپه sarchapá overturned, upended, tipped over

سرچشمه sarchashmá *f.* ☞ سرچینه

سرچمه sarchumá *f.* سرچومې *usually plural* سرچومې shot (shotgun)

سرچینه sarchiná *f.* **1** upper reaches, headwaters (of a river) سرچینه اخیستل have its start (of a river) **2** spring, source (of water) **3** *figurative* source, origin د تودوالي سرچینه heat source

سرځور sardzwóṛ descending, going down

سرځوړه sardzwáṛa *f.* slope, incline

سرځوړی sardzəwaṛáj ☞ سرځوړ

سرځی sardzáj *m.* front part, fore-part

سرخوړي¹ sartsurí, sartswuṛí *f.* shame; embarrassment

سرخوړی² sartsúṛaj, sartswúṛaj **1** being ashamed, being embarrassed **2** with bowed head **3** ashamed

سرخه sartsá *dialect* cold, cool, chilly; very cold, icy

سرخپره sartseṛá immediately, directly

سرخپري sartseṛí *f.* ☞ سرخوړي¹

سرحد sarhád, sarhádd *m. Arabic* [*plural:* سرحدونه sarhadúna *and Arabic* سرحدات sarhadát, sarhaddát] border, limit, boundary; borderland آزاد سرحد band of Pashtoon independent tribes د سرحد محافظ border guard تر سرحد تېرېدل to cross the border, cross a boundary

سرحددار sarhddár *m.* chief of a frontier post

سرحدي sarhadí, sarhaddí **1** frontier, border سرحدي ټانه frontier post **2** demarcation سرحدي کميسيون demarcation commission

سرخ surkh red

سرخاب surkhā́b *m.* ☞ سرخاو

سرخار sarkhā́r *m.* thorny hedge

سرخانه sarkhāná *f.* household tax

سرخانی sarkhānə́j *f.* camel stall

سرخاو surkhā́w *m.* 1 Surkhab (the name of a number of rivers) 2 red duck

سرخ باد surkhbā́d *m.* *medicine* erysipelas

سرخ پوش surkhpósh *m.* *history* Red Shirt

سرخچه surkhchá *f.* type of apricot

سرخ روی surkhrúj respected, esteemed; famous, glorious

سرخ روئي surkhrují *f.* honor, respect; good fame

سرخرینه sarkhrəjóna *f.* shaving the head (of an infant, as a rirual)

سرخس sarkhás *m.* *Arabic* fern ونی وال سرخس tree fern

سرخط sarkhát, sarkhátt *m.* 1 headline 2 foreword, preface

سرخکه sarkháka *f.* pink starling

سرخ وپارسا surkhupārsā́ *f.* Surkhuparsa

سرخود sarkhúd independent

سرخوړلی sarkhwaṛə́laj (who) perished, (who laid down his life

سرخوړوونکی sarkhugawúnkaj tiring, tedious, tiresome, boring, irksome

سرخوړي sarkhugí *f.* سرخوړیدلم sarkhugedə́lm *plural* 1 headache 2 trouble; unpleasantness ده سرخوړي دا This is simply unpleasant.

سرخوش sarkhúsh 1 merry, jovial, vivacious 2 tipsy, having had a little too much to drink

سرخوشي sarkhushí *f.* 1 cheerful mood 2 intoxication

سرخوڼ sarkhóḷ *m.* سرخوڼه sarkhwā́la *f.* crown of a hat

سرخه surkhá 1 pretty, beautiful 2 light bay, chestnut (of a horse's color)

سرخي surkhí [1] *f.* 1 rust (also on the surface of plants) 2 scrofula 3 beauty; high color, blush, glow 4 crimson 5 red coloring, red paint, red dye 6 red ink 7 *figurative* fame, glory

سرخی surkhā́j [2] *m.* light bay horse, chestnut horse

سرخی surkhə́j [3] *f.* 1 fringe 2 edge, selvage

سرخېل sarkhél *m.* tribal leader, tribal chief, head of a clan

سرد sard cold, very cold, icy; frosty, freezing

سردار sardā́r *m.* 1 leader; head; chief; military leader 2 Sardar (a title of the aristocracy); prince د سردار اعلی ننبان the Order of "Sardar-I ala" د سردار عالي ننبان the Order of "Sardar-l ali" 3 *regional* Indian officer; captain 4 *proper noun* Sardar

سردارو sardārú *m.* mercury

سرداري sardārí *f.* 1 supremacy; leadership, management 2 domination سرداري کول *compound verb* a to dominate b to rule over, have dominion over, have sway over

سرداری sardārə́j *f.* *proper noun* Sardaray

سردانه sardāná *f.* sources (of a river)

سردرختي sardarakhtí *f.* 1 fruit 2 part of the garden with fruit trees

سردرد sardárd *m.* headache

سردردي sardardí *f.* trouble, agitation

سردره sardará *f.* upper part of a valley

سردست sar-i-dást 1 being at hand, being available; on hand 2 current, pressing, urgent

سردسېر sardsér *m.* cold zone, cold lands, cold-climate countries

سردوباره sardubārá anew, again, (all) over again

سرده sardá *f.* cantaloupe, muskmelon

سردي sardí *f.* cold, hard frost

سررشته sarrishtá *f.* 1 measure 2 post, job, position 3 tie, connection, relation; junction, combination 4 end, tip (of a thread, string or rope) 5 row, line 6 arrangement, adjustment, organization سررشته کول، سررشته نیول *compound verb* a to take measures b to arrange, adjust, organize

سررشته دار sarrishtadā́r *m.* district finance manager

سررشته داري sarrishtadārí *f.* 1 district financial management 2 job of district finance manager

سرزګی sarzəgáj *m.* piece of leather (with which a jug is tied up)

سرزمین sarzamín *m.* country; territory

سرزنش sarzanísh *m.* reproach, rebuke; reprimand

سرزوره sarzóra سرزوری sarzóray obstinate, stubborn; persistent; recalcitrant

سرزوري sarzorí *f.* stubbornness; persistence; recalcitrance سرزوري کول *compound verb* to be stubborn

سرزواره sarzwā́ra *f.* ☞ سرڅوره

سرژه səržá سرږه sərgá *f.* female mouflon, mouflon ewe

سرسام sarsā́m *m.* 1 delirium; fever 2 meningitis

سرسایه sarsājá *f.* 1 alms (given to the poor when breaking a fast) 2 shawl, veil (given to a newlywed woman by her father on the last day of the wedding)

سرسابز sarsábz 1 green, turning green, blooming 2 fertile سرسبزه fertile land سرسبز کول، سرسبزه کول rich region سرسبزه علاقه مځکه *compound verb* to make fertile, cause to flower

سرسبزي sarsabzí *f.* 1 flowering 2 planting of greenery, planting of trees and shrubs 3 *figurative* prosperity, flourishing

سرسر sarsár [1] *m.* cold hard wind, high cold wind

سرسر sarsár [2] being on the surface or on top سرسر کول *compound verb* to select, pick out (e.g., the larger grain) سرسر کېدل *compound verb* to be selected, be picked out (e.g., of a larger grain)

سرسرتوره sarsartóra bareheaded, hatless

سرسري sarsarí 1 superficial, casual, slipshod 2 external, outward, outer سرسري مظاهرات outward manifestation 3 easy, not difficult 4 happy-go-lucky, carefree, not serious, frivolous, light-minded

سرسیانده sarsjā́nda ☞ سراسیمه

سرشاخي sarshākhí *f.* tax on small livestock

سرشاره sarshā́ra سرشار sarshā́r 1 overfilled, full to the brim; cramed or stuffed with something 2 *poetic* drunken, intoxicated سرشاره کېدل *compound verb* *poetic* to be drunk, be inebriated

سرشاري sarsharí *f.* **1** abundance, plenty, profusion **2** *poetic* intoxication, inebrriation

سرشانه sarshāná *f.* shoulder strap, shoulder piece; epaulet

سرشاهي sarshāhí *f.* measure of weight equal to 14 grams

سرشت sarísht, sirísht *m.* **1** mixture **2** *figurative* nature **3** *figurative* constitution, structure, physical make-up

سررشته sarishtá *f.* ☞ سرشته

سررشته دار sarishtadár *m.* **1** *Eastern* clerk of court **2** ☞ سررشته دار

سرشماري sarshumārí *f.* سرشمېر sarshmér *m.* census (of the population)

سرشوخ sarshókh jovial, jolly, lively, cheerful; mischievous (of a person)

سرښته sariɬhtá *f. dialect* ☞ سررشته

سرطان saratán *m. Arabic* **1** crayfish, crawfish; crab **2** *medicine* cancer, carcinoma **3** the constellation Cancer (Crab); saratan (the fourth month of the solar year; June-July

سرطبيب sartabíb *m.* head physician

سرعت sur'át *m. Arabic* **1** speed, velocity د حرکت سرعت a speed of motion **b** *military* rate of march **2** tempo, pace, rate

سرغ sargh *m.* saddle

سرغاړی sarghā́ṛaj **1** obstinate, stubborn; recalcitrant, unruly; disobedient, naughty **2** *m.* rebel, insurgent, mutineer, rioter; insurrectionist

سرغټ مشر sarghaṭmóshər *m.* commander-in-chief

سرغاړندج sarghṛā́ndaj ☞ سرغاړی

سرغړونه sargharawóna *f.* **1** stubbornness, obstinacy; disobedience **2** mutiny, riot; uprising

سرغشی sargháshaj *m.* cane; rush, reed

سرغندج sarghandáj *m.* سرغنه sarghaná *m.* head, leader سرغندي کسان leaders, chiefs, heads

سرغوچ sarghwóch *m.* sealing wax

سرغوړ sarghwáṛ *m.* pomade

سرغوند sarghúnd *m. medicine* mumps

سرفراز sarfarā́z ☞ سرلوړی ²

سرفرازي sarfarāzí *f.* distinction; high position, greatness

سرفه sarfá¹ *f. Arabic* profit, gain; advantage, benefit

سرفه surfá² *f.* cough

سرقت sariqát *m. Arabic* **1** theft **2** plagiarism

سرقول sariqól *m.* ☞ سرکول ³

سرقوماندان sarqumāndán *m.* commander-in-chief

سرقوماندانيت sarqumāndāniját *m.* high command

سرقه sarqá *f.* ☞ سرقت

سرک sarák *m.* **1** road **2** street پوخ سرک a roadway, pavement **b** لوی سرک highway کوڅنی سرک path(way), walk(way) سرک نيول *compound verb* to leave, set off, start off, hit the road

سرکاتب sarkātíb *m.* secretary د اوراقو سرکاتب archivist; office manager, manager of office work

سرکار sarkār *m.* **1** government مقامي سرکار *history* local government **2** estate, holding(s) **3** *regional* district made up of several tribes **4** chief, leader

سرکار sarkár **1** *m.* business د مطبوعاتو سره سرکارلري He has business with the press. **2** *law* valid, in force, in effect

سرکاري sarkārí **1.1** state, government(al) سرکاري ملازم government worker, government employee, civil servant **1.2** public (of a building, etc.) **2** *f.* management, superintendence

سرکاڼي sarkāṇí sarkā́ṇay **1** *m.* [*plural:* Sarkani (a tribe)] **2** *m.* a Sarkanai (member of the Sarkani tribe)

سرکتابت sarkitābát *m.* position or job of business manager; position or job of head secretary

سرکټ sarkíṭ *m.* circuit (electrical) لنډ سرکټ short circuit

سرکردگي sarkardagí *f.* supremacy, control, leadership; guidance

سرکرده sarkardá *m.* [*plural:* سرکرده گان sarkardagā́n] **1** leader **2** chief, superior; senior (official, etc.)

سرکرده گي sarkardagí *f.* ☞ سرکرده گي

سرکس sirkás *m.* circus

سرکسازي saraksāzí *f.* road building

سرکش sarkásh ☞ سرکښ

سرکشاده sarkushādá open (of a letter) سرکشاده مکتوب open letter

سرکښ sarkáɬh **1** obstinate, stubborn; recalcitrant, unruly; disobedient **2** *m.* horse blanket

سرکښته sarkɬhóta with head bowed, meek, humble سرکښته ځواب ورکول to reply meekly

سرکښي sarkaɬhí *f.* **1** obstinacy, stubbornness; recalcitrance, unruliness; disobedience **2** riot سرکښي کول *compound verb* **a** to be obstinate **b** to riot د چا د فرمان څخه سرکښي کول to fail to obey someone, not obey someone's order

سرکلی sarkaláj *m. Eastern* first haircut (child's)

سرکنده sarkónda headlong سرکنده تربدل *compound verb* to run headlong, without watching where one is going

سرکنډج sarkunḍáj¹ *m.* lock of a child's (hair, left by a vow or solomn promise)

سرکونډی sarkunḍój² *f.* ☞ سرکنډی

سرکنډج sarkunḍój³ *f.* short-haired girl (whose hair has been cut)

سرکنډج sarkanḍój⁴ *f.* bride (fiancee) whose betrothed dies before the wedding

سرکوب sarkób **1** towering above, dominating (an area, a terrain) **2** *m.* overseer, supervisor

سرکوزج sarkúzaj *m.* **1** swine, hog, wild boar **2** *abusive* swine, scoundrel, villain,

سرکوزي sarkuzí *f.* humiliation, abasement

سرکول sarkwól¹ upside down, head over heels سرکول دربدل *compound verb* to stand on one's head سرکول اوښتل، سرکول کېدل *compound verb* to turn sommersaults

سرکول sarkól² *m.* **1** bowl (of a hookah) **2** bucket, hopper (of a mill)

سر کول ³ sarikól *m.* Sarykul (lake in the Pamir mountains)

سرکونډوی sarkunḍə́j *f.* turning sommersaults سرکونډوی کول، سرکونډوی وهل *compound verb* to turn sommersaults

سرکه sirká *f.* vinegar

سرکی ¹ surkáj *m.* whistling, howling (of the wind)

سرکی ² surkə́j *f.* cherries

سرکی ³ sərkə́j *f.* ladybird beetle, ladybug

سرگذشت sarguzásht *m.* 1 adventure, event, happening 2 narrative, story

سرگردان sargardán 1 upset, sad, downcast, aggrieved, distressed; worried, anxious 2 wandering په یو شي پسي سرگردان seeking something

سرگردانول sargardānawə́l *denominative, transitive [past:* سرگردان یې کړ] to disturb, upset, embarrass; to (cause) distress, aggrieve, upset

سرگرداني sargardāní *f.* 1 grief, sorrow 2 confusion, anxiety, uneasiness; distress

سرگرم sargárm 1 enthusiastic (about something) 2 ardent, fervent 3 energetic

سرگرمي sargarmí *f.* 1 keenness, attraction سرگرمي کول *compound verb* to be keen on something, take great interest in something 2 ardor, ferver 3 enthusiasm

سرگروه sarguróh *m.* leader, guide; ringleader

سرگړی sərgə́ṛaj *m.* 1 cypress grass, *Cyperus* 2 beard grass, *Andropogon* (a cereal)

سرگشتگي sargashtagí *f.* vertigo, dizziness, giddiness

سرگشته sargashtá 1 suffering from dizziness or vertigo 2 psychologically ill 3 upset سرگشته کول *compound verb* to confuse, bewilder (someone)

سرگله sargalá *f.* tax on pasturage (per head of livestock)

سرگنگس sargangás ☞ سرگشته 1

سرلوحه sarlawhá *f.* 1 sign, signboard 2 vignette

سرلوړي ¹ sarlwaṛí *f.* honor respect, fame, glory چا ته سرلوړي ورکول to do someone the honor of, honor someone په چا سرلوړي کول to be proud of someone, take pride in someone

سرلوړی ² sarlwáṛaj worthy of honor and respect, deserving of honor and glory چوک سرلوړی کول to honor someone, do someone the honor of سرلوړی کېدل *compound verb* to be awarded with someithing

سرلویي sarlojí *f.* 1 arrogance, swagger; conceit 2 pride سرلویي کول *compound verb* a to be proud of, take pride in اوس خو مو د دوی په توره خو سرلویي کړو We are proud of their courage b to swagger, boast; get puffed up, get conceited, give oneself airs

سرله سره sarləsára anew, once again, (over) again

سرماتوک sarmātúk 1 pugnacious 2 *m.* pugnacious fellow, pugnacious boy, one who is always spoiling for a fight

سرماتوکه sarmātúka *f.* pugnacious woman, pugnacious girl

سرماتی ¹ sarmátaj 1 ☞ سرماتوک 1 2 with hurt head, with bruised head

سرماتی ² sarmātáj *m.* 1 top masonry course of a wall 2 eaves

سرمال ¹ sarmál *m.* rope for tying on a pack (on a pack animal)

سرمال ² sarmál filled to the brim (of a cup, bowl, etc.)

سرمامور sarmāmúr *m.* chief, senior (officer) د پولیسو سرمامور chief of a police department (in a province)

سرماموریت sarmamuriját *m.* police department (in a province)

سرمایه sarmājá *f. economics* capital اصلي سرمایه fixed capital

سرمایه دار sarmājadár 1 *m.* capitalist 2 wealthy, rich سرمایه داره ژبه rich language

سرمایه داري sarmājadārí 1 *f.* capitalism 2 capitalist(ic)

سرمایي surmājí ☞ سرمه ئي

سرمشق sarmáshq *m.* 1 example, model 2 exercise

سرمنبکی sarmuḵhkə́j *f.* lizard

سرمعلم sarmu'allím *m.* 1 senior teacher 2 senior instructor

سرمغزن sarmaghzə́n 1 garrulous, talkative 2 to go out of one's mind (on account of chattering and noise) سرمغزن کول *compound verb* سرمغزنېدل ☞ سرمغزن کېدل *compound verb*

سرمغزنول sarmaghzənawə́l *denominative, transitive [past:* سرمغزن یې کړ] to drive (someone) crazy (with noise, chattering) په ډېرو نارو دي سرمغزن کړم I was stunned by your scream.

سرمغزنېدل sarmaghzənedə́l *denominative, intransitive [past:* سرمغزن شو] to go out of one's mind, lose one's wits, go crazy (from noise, jabbering, etc.)

سرمقاله sarmaqālá *f.* editorial, lead article

سرمنشي sarmunshí *m. history* chief of the king's personal office

سرمه surmá *f.* antimony, stibium

سرمه یي surmají dark blue

سرنا surná *f.* zourna (type of flute)

سرناچي surnāchí *m.* zourna player

سرنامه sarnāmá *f.* 1 address 2 title page

سرنایي surnājí *m.* ☞ سرناچي

سرنجه srə́ndzha *f.* sediment, lees (when melting butter)

سرنگ ¹ suráng, surə́ng *m.* 1 sap, undermining سرنگ وهل *compound verb* to dig a sap, undermine 2 mine د سیند سرنگ torpedo

سرنگ ² suráng *m.* chestnut

سرنگ اچوونکی suráng achawúnke torpedo boat

سرنگ پراني surangparāní *f.* blasting, blasting operations

سرنگون sarnigún 1 overturned, toppled 2 shot down, brought down (of an aircraft) لاله سرنگون fritillaria (a decorative plant)

سرنگی sarangáj *m.* 1 ☞ سرنگ ¹ 2 corridor, passage(way), entrance (hall)

سرنوشت sarnawísht *m.* lot, fate; destiny, fortune د چا په سرنوشت کښي څه تغییر راوستل to influence one's destiny

سرنی ² saranáj upper, located above, from above, from the top, on the surface of something سرنی برخه the upper part (e.g., of a page)

سرنېزه sarnezá *f.* three-edge bayonet; dagger bayonet

سرنیکه sərniká *m.* great-great-grandfather

سرو ¹ sarw *m. poetic* graceful سرو روان stately as a cypress

سرو ² sró, səró *oblique plural of* سور ⁵

سرواخی sarwákhaj obstinate stubborn, recalcitrant

سرواښ sarwā́kh m. سرواښی sarwā́khay m. tether (e.g., for an ox)

سرواندي sarwā́ndi f. plural ☞ سربانده

سرواني sarwānī m. plural 1 Sarvani (a tribe) 2 m. a Sarvanai (a member of the Sarvani tribe)

سروب srob سروپ srop quite, entirely, totally

سروپا sarupā́ سروپای sarupáy 1 m. robe (of honor) 2 from head to toe

سروتن sarután identical, equal (of calculation) سروتن رسېدل compound verb to share equally (when deviding or partitioning property)

سروتکه sarwátka f. ☞ سکروته

سرود saród m. song; melody

سرودگو sarodgó سرودگوی sarodgóy m. 1 singer 2 musician

سرودگویي sarodguí f. singing

سرودي sarodí m. singer

سرور¹ surúr m. Arabic gladness, joy, mirth

سرور² sarwár m. 1 leader, head 2 proper noun Sarvar

سرورخ sarwárkh m. 1 headwork of a canal 2 place where two rivers join, the confluence of two rivers 3 source 4 figurative beginning, first step

سروره sarwára f. proper noun Sarvara

سروري¹ sarwarí f. 1 leadership 2 power, domination

سروری² sarwráj m. ☞ سرباری load (on an animal)

سروزنه sarwázna f. 1 waistband of trousers 2 fringe (on woman's wide trousers)

سروسامان sarusāmā́n m. property; belongings, things

سروشان sarwshā́n stately as a cypress, graceful

سروغل sroghál transitive [past: وي يې سروغه] to put into a difficult situation; perplex, nonplus

سروشان sarwqāmát سروقد sarwqád ☞

سروکار sarukā́r m. relation, connection له ... سره سروکار نه لرل to not have anything to do with …

سروکال sarukā́l all year, the whole year round

سرولم sulám m. beginning د کار سرولم the beginning of the matter پر سرولم کېدل the beginning of the month د میاشتي سرولم idiom to get terribly angry

سرور sarwór m. sweets, candy (brought to the bride's house from the bridegroom)

سروه sárwa f. cypress

سروې sarwé m. 1 research, study 2 geological prospecting د سروې هیئت prospecting party 3 topographic survey

سروېږد sarwégd m. pillow

سروېس sarwés سرويس sarwís m. 1 servicing, service 2 هوايي د موټر د حمل او نقل سرویس automobile transportation airline 3 colloquial bus 4 sports service

سرویل srojál transitive [past: وي يې سرویه] to kill, swat (fleas, etc.)

سره¹ sə́ra f. manure, dung; fertilizer کیمیائي سري chemical fertilizers زمکي ته سره اچول to fertilize the soil

سره² sra f. 1 corpse; carrion 2 sandy knoll; sand hill, dune

سره³ srə 1 m. plural of سور⁵ سره کول compound verb to make red hot, heat to incandescence, make white hot 2 m. plural gold, gold money

سره⁴ sra 1 feminine singular of سور⁵ 2 f. gold coin, gold piece

سره⁵ sará, sə́rá, sərə́ 1.1 together; with each other, with one another; between ourselves; to each other, to one another دوی سره They came together. ﺨﻪ سره وايي؟ راغلل What are they talking about amongst themselves? خورا سره to each other سره یو بل ته بیا به کله سره ووینو؟ They love each other very much. گران دي When will we see each other again? د زامنو يې سره جگړه وسوه His sons have quarrelled سره يوﺨای کول together compound verb to assemble, unify, concentrate سره يوﺨای کېدل compound verb to be assembled, be unified, be concentrated 1.2 completely, entirely زما کالي ببخي سره تکرتکر دي totally All my clothing was torn to shreds. گرده سره درې سره پرېوتل All three fell down. 2 postposition 1 a with, together (indicates compatibility, in combination with the preposition) د یو شي سره together with د خوراک د شیانو سره together with produce b near, at, by (indicates being near something) د کړکي سره at the window c upon, after (used when denoting an action or event, after which something happens or occurs) د راپرېوتو سره upon arriving when falling 2.2 with, with the aid of something (serves to denote the instrument of an action, in combination with the preposition په (په) یو شي سره with the aid of 2.3 according to something, in accordance with …; (as) per in combination with the word سم and the preposition د سم د بین المللي قانون سره by international law د راپور سره سم according to the report 3 forms compound conjunctions with concessive connotation in combination with the demonstrative pronoun دا، دغه، هغه, the preposition له هغه چه ... the conjunction له دغه چه ... له دي چه despite

سره⁶ sará pure, uncontaminated

سره⁷ sará draft (of an ox, bullock)

سرهار surəhā́r m. sound (of the wind)

سره بانجن srə bāndzán m. plural tomatoes

سره زر srə zár m. plural gold; gold pieces

سره غاړه sra ghā́ṛa f. anatomy pharynx

سره غورﺤکه sra ghurdzáka f. 1 large spark 2 bright flame

سره کېده srə kedə́ m. plural 1 frying, roasting 2 melting, (suet, tallow)

سره مخه sra mókha f. medicine erysipelas

سرهوا sarhawā́ suffering from self-importance, conceited; haughty, arrogant, supercilious سرهوا مه گرزه! nonsense, rubbish سرهوا خبره Don't get a swelled head!

سره ور sərawár Eastern ☞ سرور

سره و زرغونه sra-u-zarghuná f. سره وشنه f. rainbow احمد په سره و زرغونه کېني رغنتی دئ idiom Ahmed is quite beardless.

سره وله sra wə́la f. Dzungar willow

سره ورتوب srəwartób *m.* width, breadth; spaciousness

سري ¹ sirrí *Arabic* secret مكاتب سري secret correspondence

سرى ² sráj, suráj *m.* ☞ سره سرى كېدل¹سورى to betray one another

سرى ³ sə́raj *m.* measles

سرى ⁴ sə́raj *m. botany* tamarisk

سرى ⁵ saráj *f.* 1 land-working partnership, joint working of land by two or more poor peasants 2 team of oxen

سرى ⁶ sərəj *f.* 1 head of a hookah 2 scoop

سرى ⁷ srəj *f.* cherry (fruit and tree)

سرى ⁸ sre 1 *feminine plural of* سور⁵ سري اوبنكي hot tears 2 *f. plural* gold pieces; gold

سرياني surjāní Syrian

سريته surjáta *f.* ☞ سوريته

سريخ srikh *m. botany* Mimosa seris (tree)

سري سمبوري surí-səmburí ☞ سوري سمبوري

سرېښ srikh *m.* 1 glue 2 stickiness

سرېښن srikhə́n سرېښناك, سرېښنند sticky; viscous

سرېښنه sríkhna *f. anatomy* femoral head cavity

سرېښنول srikhawə́l *denominative, transitive* [*past:* سرېښ يې كړ] to glue, paste; stick, paste together

سرېښېدل srikhedə́l *denominative, intransitive* [*past:* سرېښ شو] to stick (to, together), adhere (to), be pasted, be glued; cling to

سري صاف sirisāf *m. Arabic* muslin

سريع sarí' quick, fast, rapid, swift

سريع آتش sari'ātásh rapid-firing

سريع السير sari'-as-sájr *Arabic* high-speed, fast

سريعانه sari'āná fast, rapid; hurried, hasty

سري مي sreməj *f.* lentil

سرېنائيكا sirenāikā *f.* Kirenaika

سرېندوال srindawə́l, sərindawə́l *m.* violinist; fiddler

سرينده srindá, sərindá *f.* 1 violin; fiddle سرينده وهل *compound verb* to play the violin 2 *poetic* lyre

سرينده مار srindamə́r, sərindamə́r *m.* ☞ سرېندوال

سري ورخ sariwárkh, sariwarə́kh *m.* 1 upper reaches, headwaters (of a river) 2 start, beginning (of work, of a business deal)

سري ورې sərewəré obvious, patent, evident

سريه sarjá *f.* rising (of the sun) سريه وهل *compound verb* to rise (of the sun)

سرېني sarə́baní *m. plural* Sarbani (a group of Afghan tirbes) ☞ سره بن

سرپ srap *m.* 1 ☞ سپهار 2 *onomatopoeia* sound of the clash of swords

سرپهار srəpəhár *m.* squelching, sloshing (of mud under-foot) سرپهار لرل *compound verb* to squelch, slosh (through mud)

سرتيا sartjə́ *f.* cold; the cool, coolness

سرك sarák *m.* ☞ سرك د اورګاډی سرک; railroad

سرو ¹ saró *oblique plural of* سرى¹

سرو ² saró *oblique plural of* سور¹

سروباج sarobáj *m.* [*plural:* سروبي sarobí *and* سروبيان sarobiyán] earthenware pitcher

سروبي sarobí *f.* Sarobi (region)

سروتى saṛótaj *m.* man, little man, little fellow

سرول saṛawə́l *denominative, transitive* [*past:* سورۍ يې كړ] 1 to cool (off), chill 2 *figurative* to calm, quiet, soothe 3 to slake lime

سره ¹ saṛá, sə́rá *feminine singular of* سور نن ورځ سره ده It's cool today.

سره ² saṛə 1 free, unoccupied, not busy (from work, etc.) 2 completed, fulfilled, carried out

سره بن saṛabán *m.* Saraban (one of the main tribes of the Afghans)

سره كى saṛəkə́j *f.* top, summit, crown (of a tree, of a mountain)

سره لوه saṛalə́wa *f.* سره لوی *f.* fever and chills; fever سره لوی ده He is feverish.

سرى ¹ saṛáj *m.* [*plural:* سري saṛí *and Western* سريان saṛiyə́n] 1 man, person دري سري راغلل Three people came. څوك سرى كول to make someone a man سرى كېدل *compound verb* to become a man 2 husband; man 3 worker; servant 4 lad, young man 5 people; men پر سري درېدل to support someone

سرى ² saṛé, sə́ṛé *feminine plural of* سور

سرى ³ saṛé *m. Western* old chap, old fellow, friend

سرېتوب saṛitób *m.* 1 manliness د سرېتوب شان befitting a man 2 humaneness, humanity

سرېچن saṛechán chilly, sensitive to cold (of a person)

سرېځى saṛídzaj *in combination with numerals* دوه سرېځى two-place, two-seat

سرى خور saṛikhór 1 greedy, stingy 2 *m.* cannibal

سرېدل saṛedə́l *denominative, intransitive* [*past:* سوړ سو] 1 to become cold, cool (down) 2 to catch cold, come down with a cold 3 to quiet down, calm down, compose oneself جنگ سوړ سو fighting ceased

سرېتوب saṛihúkh *m.* ☞ سرى هوښ

سزا sazā *f.* punishment څوك په سزا ورکول و چاته to punish someone د سزا, د سزا وړ, قابل د سزا punishable سزا رسول to teach someone a lesson

سزاوار sazāwár 1 worthy, deserving of something د يو شي سزاوارکېدل to be worthy, deserve something 2 befitting, proper

سزاول sazāwúl *m.* 1 tax collector 2 *history* estate manager, steward

سزاياب sazājāb *Eastern law* convicted, condemned

سزنى sazə́naj *m.* needles (of conifers)

سزاول sazawál *m.* ☞ سزاول

سژ ¹ səž *m.* سژا *f.* sə́žā ☞ سژهار

سژه səžá *f. Western* ☞ سرژه

سژهار səžahár *m.* whine (of bullets)

سږ ¹ səg *m.* ☞ سژ, سژه هار

سږ ² sag current, this (of the year) سږكال the current year د سږكال حاصلات this year's harvest

سږمه səgmá *f.* nostril a تر دوو سرمو كېدل to overeat, eat too much, eat one's fill b to get angry

سرن ¹ səgə́n pulmonary سرن رگ artery

سرن ² sagə́n سرنی current, this (year); of the current year, of this year سرن کال this year

سرژه səgá *f.* ☞ سره

سرژهار səgəhå̃r *m.* ☞ سژهار

سرژج sə́gaj *m.* lung د سرريو ناروغتياوي pulmonary diseases له هغه سرري زره يې د سرري همسايه شو He tortured me. لاسه مي سرري پاخه سوه *saying* His heart skipped a beat.

سسپار saspå̃r *m.* plowshare

سسپارکودی saspārkodáj *m. Eastern* tool bag, tool kit

سسپاره saspå̃ra *f.* ☞ سسپار

سسپور saspór *m.* hoe, mattock

سست sust, səst 1 weak, feeble 2 slow, sluggish; listless, languid; lazy 3 stretched loosely, slack (of a rope, etc.)

سست انکشاف sustinkishå̃f poorly developed, underdeveloped (of a country)

سست پست sust-pust 1 very weak, quite feeble 2 quite listless

سستم sistém *m.* 1 system 2 network (e.g., telephone)

سستوالی sustwå̃laj *m.* 1 weakness 2 inertia, listlessness; laziness, indolence, sloth

سستول sustawə́l *denominative, transitive [past:* سست یې کړ] 1 to weaken, enfeeble 2 to slacken, loosen (a rope, etc.)

سسته sústa 1 *feminine singular of* سست 2 *f. regional* delaying, procrastination; omission په خوراک کښي هيڅ سستي نه کول to not deny someone food

سستي sustí *f.* 1 impotence, weakness 2 sluggishness; listlessness 3 carelessness, negligence د انضباط سستي relaxation of discipline سستي کول *compound verb* a to show weakness, reveal weakness b to reveal negligence, exhibit negligence

سستيت sustiját *m.* ☞ سستي

سستېدل sustedə́l *denominative, intransitive [past:* سست سو] 1 to become weak 2 to be sluggish, be listless; be lazy, indolent 3 to be slackened, be loosened (of a rope, etc.) 4 to fade (away), die out (of a noise)

سسکوره səskóra *f.* rocky terrain

سسلي sisilí *f.* Sicily

سسول sasawúl *transitive dialect* ☞ خڅول

سسی sə́saj *m. botony* saxaul, *Haloxylon*

سشکله sashkála *f.* always, constantly, continually; every time

سڼبنا səḵå *f.* sizzling, sputtering (the sound of meat, etc., being fried or broiled)

سڼبسوره saḵhsóra *f.* hoe, mattock

سڼبکوره səḵhkóra *f.* ☞ سسکوره

سطح sath *f. Arabic* سطحه sátha *f.* 1 surface سطح مرتفع plateau 2 *figurative* level د بحر د سطحي څخه above sea level د ثقافت سطح to raise the cultural level

سطحي sathí *Arabic* 1 surface, superficial سطحي معلومات superficial knowledge 2 groundless, unfounded

سطر sátr, sátər *m. Arabic* 1 line سطر کښل *compound verb* to draw a line; rule, line off 2 line (of print) 3 row, series

سطرکش satrkásh *m.* ruler, straightedge

سطرنج satrándzh *m.* chess د سطرنج تخته chess-board

سطرنجي satrandzhí *f.* shatrandzhi (a rug fabric)

سطري satrí by the line

سطل sátl, sátəl *m. Arabic* bucket, pail

س،ع *abbreviation of* سردار عالي نښان *history* bearer of the order of "Sardar-i ali"

سعادت sa'ādát *m. Arabic* 1 happiness, bliss; prosperity 2 well-being 3 *proper noun* Saadat

سعد ² sa'ādatmán ☞ سعد ²

سعادت مني sa'ādatmaní *f.* 1 happiness; prosperity; success 2 well-being

سعد ¹ sa'd *Arabic* 1 *m.* 1.1 lucky arrangement of stars, lucky star 1.2 favorable sign 1.3 happiness, prosperity 1.4 *proper noun* Saad 2.1 happy, prosperous 2.2 favorable, satisfactory

سعد ² su'úd *m. Arabic* nut grass, coco grass, *Cyperus rotundus*

سعود sa'úd *m.* ☞ سعد ¹

سعودي sa'udí Saudi سعودي عرب، سعودي عربستان، سعودي عربيه Saudi Arabia

سعی sa'ja *f. Arabic* endeavor, effort سعی کول *compound verb* to try, endeavor, strive for سعی او زياړکول to make efforts

سعيد sa'íd *Arabic* 1 happy, fortunate; favorable ته سعيد نه يې your are unfortunate, you are luckless 2 *m. proper noun* Said

سعير sa'ír *m. Arabic* hell, hades

سعيه sá'ja *f.* ☞ سعی

سعيي cá'ji *plural of* سعيه

سغ səgh *m.* 1 whistle, whine (of a bullet) 2 sound of wings (of birds flying) سغ سغ کول *compound verb* a to whistle, whine (of a bullet) b to make a fluttering sound with the wings

سغا səghå̃ *f.* ☞ سغهار

سغل səghə́l *m. medicine* dyspepsia; indigestion

سغول səghawə́l, sughawə́l *transitive [past:* وو يې سغاوه] 1 to pierce; punch a hole in, puncture 2 to fling, hurl, throw 3 to let fly, shoot (a bullet)

سغهار səghahå̃r *m.* 1 puffing, wheezing, snorting 2 whistle, whine (of a bullet) سغهارلرل *compound verb* to whistle, whine (of a bullet)

سغی sugháj *m.* puffing, wheezing, snorting (through the nose)

سغېدل səghedə́l *intransitive [past:* وسغېده] 1 to be pierced, be punctured 2 to whistle, whine (of a bullet)

سفارت sifārát *m. Arabic* 1 embassy 2 duties of an ambassador

سفارتخانه sifāratkhāná *f.* embassy, embassy building; (ambassador's) residence

سفارش sifārísh *m. [plural:* سفارشونه sifārishúna *and Arabic* سفارشات sifārishå̃t] 1 commission, assignment; instructions 2 order سفارش کول *compound verb* a to give an assignment, instruct, commission **b** to order سفارش وركول *compound verb* to order

سفاك saffák *Arabic* **1** bloodthirsty **2** *m.* bloodsucker, extortionist; villain

سفاكي saffākí *f.* **1** bloodthirstiness **2** incurability (of a disease)

سفر safár *m. Arabic* **1** journey, trip; voyage د سفر شيان، د سفر اسباب baggage سفركول *compound verb* to travel, journey په سفرتلل to set out on a journey سفر پخير! ، سفر په خير Bon voyage! **2** wartime **3** *military* campaign **4** *figurative* the final journey, death له دنيا نه يې سفر وكړ He has left this world.

سفرا sufará *m. plural Arabic of* سفير

سفربر safarbár mobilized سفربركول *compound verb* to mobilize

سفربري safarbarí *f.* mobilization عمومي سفربري general mobilization د يوي برخي سفربري partial mobilization

سفرخرڅ safarkhárts *m.* **1** travel expenses **2** travel allowance, travel pay

سفرمينا safarmijná, saparmijná *m. plural regional* sappers, combat engineers د سفرمينا پلټنه combat engineer battalion

سفرنامه safarnāmá *f.* travel diary

سفره sufrá *f. anatomy* anus

سفري safarí **1.1** travel **1.2** field **2** *f.* **.1** journey, trip **2.2** provisions for the road

سفلي suflí *Arabic* **1** lower سفلي غړي the lower extremities **2** low, base, mean

سفليس siflís, sifilís *m.* syphilis

سفوف safúf, sufúf *m. Arabic medicine* powder (a medicine)

سفيد saféd white

سفيدار safedár *m* **1** white poplar, silver poplar **2** wood of the white or silver poplar

سفيدپوش safedpósh **1** dressed in white **2** *m.* rich man, wealthy person

سفيدكوه safedkóh *m.* Safedkokh (the name of various mountain ranges)

سفيده safedá *f.* **1** poplar **2** white (of an egg), egg white **3** whiting, white pigment

سفير safír *m. Arabic* [*plural:* سفيران *and Arabic* سفرا] ambassador سفير كبير، لوى سفير ambassador

سقاو saqáw *m.* سقا saqá *m.* [*plural:* سقاوان saqāwán] water-carrier د سقاو زوى *history* Bache-Sakao

سقاوه saqāwá *f.* **1** swimming pool, pond **2** cold bath

سقر saqár *m. Arabic* hell, nether world

سقف saqf *m. Arabic* **1** ceiling **2** roof **3** *figurative* vault of heaven, firmament

سقف پوشي saqfposhí *f.* ceiling, overhead, cover

سقلات saqlát *m. Arabic* red fabric; purple

سقوط suqút *m. Arabic* **1** fall, collapse سقوط كول *compound verb* **a** to fall **b** to be knocked down الوتكي ته سقوط وركول to shoot down a plane **2** breakdown, disintegration **3** death, destruction, downfall **4** defeat

سقيم saqím *Arabic* **1** sick, unhealthy **2** incorrect, wrong, false

سك¹ suk *m.* ☞ سوك¹

سك² sik *m.* Sikh

سكاتلېنډ skátlénḍ *m.* Scotland

سكارات sakārát *m. Arabic* agony; faint, fainting سكارات موت sakārát-i ... death throes

سكارلاتين skārlātín *m.* scarlet fever

سكاروى skárwaj *m.* pneumonia; pleurisy

سكاره skārə́ *m. plural* [*singular:* سكور] coal د لرگيو سكاره (hard) coal د تپري سكاره، د ډبري سكاره، د كان سكاره charcoal سپين سكاره white coal

سكاره خرڅوونكى skārə́ khartsawúnkaj *m.* سكاره والا *m.* coal seller, coal vender

سكاسه skása *f.* silhouette

سكال sakál *m.* current year, this year

سكالرشيپ skālarshíp *m.* stipend, scholarship, student grant سكالرشيپ وركول to give out a scholarship

سكالو² skāló *f.* ☞ ښكالوه

سكام¹ skām *m.* post, pole

سكام² skām *abbreviation of* ماسكه ويل I did say; you know, you see ☞ سكه² ⁸

سكاندينويا skāndinawijá *f.* Scandinavia

سكاندينويايي skāndinawijājí Scandinavian

سكان skāṇ **1** dark bay (of a horse's color) **2** dark-complexioned, swarthy **3** sunburned, tanned

سكاڼى skāṇáj *m.* chisel

سكاوټ skāuṭ *m. regional* **1** boy scout **2** scout, reconnoiterer

سكته¹ sə́kāta *f.* **1** patience, endurance **2** satisfaction سكته كول *compound verb* to be sufficient, suffice

سكته² saktá *f. Arabic* **1** interruption, stoppage; hitch, hesitation **2** comma **3** becoming torpid, becoming rigid, becoming numb **4** *medicine* insuline

سكوى¹ skídzaj *m.* ☞ سكوى¹

سكر sukr *m. Arabic* intoxicating drink; wine

سكرتر sekretár *m.* سكرتر *m.* secretary

سكروټه skarwáṭa *f.* **1** red smouldering lump of coal **2** spark د اور كوچنى سكروټي ځني الوځي Sparks fly from the bonfire.

سكړك¹ sukṛə́k *m.* cornbread

سكړك² sukṛúk **1** crippled, maimed **2** *m.* cripple سكړك كول *compound verb* to cripple, maim سكړك كېدل *compound verb* to be crippled, be maimed

سكستل skustál *transitive* [*present:* سكلي *past:* و يې سكست] to shear (wool)

سكسول saksawúl *m. botany* saxaul, *Haloxylon*

سكنت¹ skə́kht *imperfect of* سكنتل

سكنت² skə́kht *m.* cutting out سكنت كول *compound verb* to cut, cut out

سکښتل skə́ķhtəl *transitive* [*present:* سکښي *past:* سکښت وي يي] **1** to cut out (a dress) **2** *figurative* to make plans, make suppositions; estimate

سکښته skə́ķhta *f.* cutting out

سکل [1] skəl *transitive* ☞ څنبل

سکل [2] skul *present stem of* سکستل

سکم [1] skam *m.* sack, bag

سکم [2] skəm *present first person of* سکل

سکنجبين sikandzabín *m.* lemon juice with sugar; syrup of vinegar and honey

سکندر sikandár *m. proper noun* Alexander

سکندن skindán *m.* trial, test, taste, sample

سکنده skindá *f.* **1** healing, healing over; scarring, cicatrization (of a wound) **2** joining of disparate parts

سکنډه skunḍá *f.* nip, pinch, tweak

سکنی sakanáj blood, by blood, own

سکڼ [1] skaṇ *m.* cut, cutting out

سکڼ [2] skaṇ ☞ سکان

سکڼ [3] skaṇ *present stem of* سکنتل

سکڼی skaṇə́j *f.* **1** queen bee's cell (in a beehive) **2** handle (of a dish)

سکو [1] sku *m.* ☞ سکوی [1]

سکو [2] sakú *m.* **1** stone bench **2** platform

سکوت sukút *m. Arabic* silence, quiet

سکور skor *m.* [*usually plural* سکاره skārə́] **1** coal (usually charcoal) **2** charred log, smouldering brand په غم کي سوی سکور د چا د خوشحالی اور سکور کول کېدل to torment oneself, be tormented **a** to spoil someone's mood **b** to poison someone's joy

سکورکانی skorkáṇaj *m.* (hard) coal

سکوست skwəst *m.* shearing (of sheep)

سکوستل skwəstə́l *transitive* ☞ سکستل

سکول [1] skwəl **1** *transitive* ☞ سکستل **2** *m. plural* shearing د پسه سکول sheep shearing د سکولو وخت sheep-shearing season

سکول [2] skawə́l *transitive* ☞ څکول

سکول [3] skwul *m. regional* school

سکول [4] skwəl *present stem of* سکوستل

سکولگر skwəlgár *m.* shearer (of sheep)

سکولل skwalə́l *transitive* [*past:* سکوست وي يي] to shear (sheep)

سکوم skum *m.* ☞ سکم [1]

سکون sukún *m. Arabic* peace and quiet, calm, tranquility سکون او آرام ورڅخه ېبول to deprive someone of peace and quiet

سکونت sukunát *m. Arabic* **1** residence سکونت لرل، سکونت کول *compound verb* to live, dwell, inhabit سکونت کېدل *compound verb* to settle (down), take up residence **2** peace and quiet, calm(ness), tranquility; immobility

سکونداره skunḍára *f.* ☞ سکنده

سکونډل skunḍə́l *transitive* [*past:* سکونډ وي يي] **1** to pinch, nip, tweak **2** to pinch something off, pick something off

سکونډه skúnḍa *f.* nip, pinch, tweak

سکوه skə́wa *f.* fork (for winnowing grain)

سکوی [1] skə́wi *plural of* سکوه

سکوی [2] skoj *m.* **1** seam; stitch **2** embroidery **3** anxiety, uneasiness **4** *figurative* kind, stamp, mold; outward appearance, exterior

سکوی [3] skəwáj *m.* tailor

سکویار skojár *m.* tailor

سکویر skwer *m.* public garden

سکویر skwajr *m. regional* landowner, landed gentleman

سکویل skojə́l *transitive* [*past:* سکویه وي يي] **1** to comb; comb out **2** to shear (sheep) **3** to massage, rub

سکوینه skojə́na *f.* **1** combing, combing out **2** shearing (of sheep) **3** massaging

سکه [1] sikká *f. Arabic* coin سکه منل پخپله سکه هرچا په a to persuade someone **b** to impose one's own opinion on someone

سکه [2] sikh *m.* ☞ سک [2]

سکه [3] siká *f. metallurgy* lead

سکه [4] siká, sikká *f. Arabic* outward appearance (beautiful)

سکه [5] saká blood, by blood, own سکه خور own sister (related by blood) سکه ورور own brother (related by blood)

سکه [6] siká **1.1** respected, honored **1.2** serious **1.3** *dialect* dull, obtuse; slow-witted **2** *m.* slow-witted person, dimwit

سکه [7] cáka *f.* taste (of food)

سکه [8] sə́ka **1** ☞ څکه **2** as if, like ما سکه ويل نن به راشي I thought that he would come today.

سکه [9] skə *dialect imperfect of* سکل

سکه [10] ska *Eastern imperfective imperative of* سکل

سکي [1] ski *m. plural* skis سکي کول، سکي وهل *compound verb* to ski

سکي [2] skaj *m.* ☞ سکوی [1]

سکي [3] sikké *plural of* سکه [1, 4]

سکېچ skech *m.* **1** (rough) sketch, free-hand drawing **2** sketch

سکي کوونکی ski kawúnkaj *m.* skier

سکیم [1] skim *m.* sack, bag

سکیم [2] skim *m.* scheme, plan; project, design

سکیندبه skindabá *m.* ☞ سکینده به

سکینده skindá *f. medicine* splint, cast

سکینده به skindabá *m.* osteopath, bone-setter

سگ [1] sag *m.* dog

سگ [2] sag *dialect* ☞ سپر [2]

سگال sigál *m.* **1** imagination **2** suspicion **3** enmity, hatred **4** speech, word

سگرت sigrát *m. plural* cigarettes

سگرټ sigráṭ *m.* ☞ سگرېټ

سگرټ دانی sigraṭdānī *f.* cigarette case, cigar case

سگرټي sigraṭī́ *m. plural* smoker, cigarette smoker

سگرېټ sigréṭ *m.* cigarettes یوه دانه سگرېټ cigarette

سگرېټ والا sigreṭwālā́ *m.* vendor of cigarettes, cigars

سگک sagák *m.* **1** buckle; hook; fastening **2** mole cricket (insect)

سگل sugúl *f.* [*plural:* سگلي sugúli] winter boots made of rawhide

سگلاوو saglāwú *m.* سگ لاهو *m.* otter

سلگی suglə́j *f.* ☞ سلگی

سگوان sagwắn, saguắn *m.* teak tree

سگه ¹ sagá *f.* ☞ سرژه

سگه ² sə́ga *f.* 1.1 means, capital 1.2 profit 1.3 allotment of land 2 *attributive* acquired; gathered; obtained

سگی sə́gaj *m. Eastern* ☞ سبری

سل ¹ sil, sill *m. Arabic* tuberculosis د سبریو سل pulmonary tuberculosis د هډوکو سل tuberculosis of the bones سل ورولوپري He has the onset of tuberculosis.

سل ² sal *m.* raft, float

سل ³ sə́l 1 *numeral* (one) hundred (100) سل او پنځه one hundred five (105) سل زره 80% one hundred thousand (100,000) سل کاله century 2 *m.* [*plural:* سلگونه sə́lgúna, سوونه sawúna and سلها, سلها sə́lhắ] hundred په سل هاو، په سلگونو by the hundreds; hundreds په سل هاو پښتانه hundreds of Pashtoons سل سره خیشتول یو نه خریل *saying* to lather a hundred heads and shave nary a one په سلو کښې و وبسا وړ نه ښکاري Apparently he doesn't deserve complete trust.

سلا salā́ *f.* advice, counsel; instructions د چا څخه سلا غوښتل to ask advice of someone سلا مشوره کول *compound verb* to consult, confer, take counsel سلا ورکول *compound verb* to give advice نو اوس څه سلا کوي؟ What do you advise now?

سلابر salābúr *m.* interest; profit

سلابلا salābalā́ without rhyme or reason; for no reason at all, without cause سلا بلا کارکول to act without thinking

سلاټه salāṭá *f.* 1 cattail root 2 kind of tomato salad

سلاح silā́h *f. Arabic* [*plural:* اسلحه aslihá] weapons, arms, armament سلاح پریښودل to lay down one's arms

سلاح خانه silāhkhānā́ *f.* arms depot, arsenal

سلاح کوټ silāhkláз *m. obsolete* stacks (rifle) سلاح اجراکول to stack arms

سلارزي salārzí *m. plural* 1 Salarzai (a tribe in Badzhaur) 2 *m.* a Salarzaj

سلاره salārá *f.* سلاری salārə́y *f.* 1 striped silk 2 shawl, veil

سلاسوم salāsúm *m.* سلاسم ☞ سلاسون

سلاسل *m. plural Arabic of* سلسله

سلاسون salāsún lynx

سلاطین salāṭín *m. plural Arabic of* سلطان

سلاگری salāgáraj *m.* advisor, counsellor

سلاله sulālá *f. Arabic* 1 dynasty 2 posterity

سلالی salālə́j *f.* ☞ سلاره

سلام salā́m *m. Arabic* 1 regards, greetings شاهي سلام the ceremony of hearing the national anthem سلام اخیستل *compound verb* ☞ سلام اچول سلام بیاکول *compound verb* a to greet someone; welcome b to salute سلام سپارل، سلام ورباندي ویل to convey greetings سلام کول *compound verb* a to greet, welcome b *Eastern* present arms! سلام بیاکول a to send greetings to reply to a greeting b to submit to, resign oneself to c to convey

سلام مي قبول کئ، سلام مي ومنئ Please accept my greetings سلام مي ومنئ greetings. چاته سلامونه کول to bow down low to someone اول سلام بیا کلام *saying* Without greetings there's no conversation 2 peace, calm 3 *m. proper noun* Salyam

سلامالېک salāmālék *m.* 1 exchange of pleasantries; exchange of greetings 2 nut grass, coco grass, *Cyperus rotundus* سلامالېک سره لرل *idiom* to associate with, to be friends

سلامت salāmát *Arabic* 1 *m.* .1 rest, peace, calm, quiet, tranquility امان او سلامت سره complete tranquility 1.2 health 2 *attributive* .1 safe, sound; healthy سلامت اوسی! Good-bye! (on parting); Bless you! (upon sneezing) 2.2 sufficient, enough 3.1 all right, well, safely 3.2 everything as a whole

سلامتیا salāmatjā́ *f.* calm, quiet, tranquility

سلام علیکم salā́m'aléjkum *Arabic* greetings to you (on meeting and parting); hello ما ورسره سلام علیکم وکړل I greeted him.

سلامي salāmí 1 greetings, regards 2 salute (by guns) سلامي کول *compound verb* to salute 3 review of troops د عسکرو سلامي نیول to inspect the troops

سلاو slāw *m.* Slav

سلاوي slāwí Slavic

سلایي sə́lājí, salájí *f.* سلائي *f.* 1 small stick for applying antimony 2 *history* large needle (with which people pierced the eyes of their enemy) 3 vertical axle of a water-lifting wheel 4 rod, stem, spindle

سلب salb *m. Arabic* 1 taking away, depriving 2 denial, negation له چا څخه راحت او اسودگي سلب سلبول *compound verb* ☞ سلب کول to deprive someone of tranquility, violate someone's peace and quiet سلبېدل *compound verb* ☞ سلب کېدل

سلبول salbawə́l *denominative, transitive* [*past:* سلب یې کړ] to deprive, take away

سلبي salbí *Arabic* 1 negative سلبي قوت lack, shortage, deficiency 2 lazy, inactive

سلبېدل salbedə́l *denominative, intransitive* [*past:* سلب شو] 1 to be deprived of 2 to be lost, be forfeited

سلټ salát *m.* 1 shield 2 trench, entrenchment

سلټه sə́ltá *f.* fortification, breastwork, parapet

سلح siláh *f.* ☞ سلاح

سلحشور silahshór 1 *m.* fighting man, soldier سلحشور نجبا knights 2 martial, warlike, bellicose

سلحشوري silahshorí *f.* bellicosity, warlike character سلحشوري لرل *compound verb* to be warlike, be bellicose

سلخ salkh *m. Arabic* last day of the lunar month

سلدراج sildirádzh *m.* men's long underpants, underwear

سلسل بول silsil-i-bául *m. plural* diabetes

سلسلتاً silsilátán *Arabic* 1 at the command of 2 through channels

سلسله silsilá *f. Arabic* [*plural:* سلسلې silsilé *and m. plural* سلاسل salāsíl] 1 consistency; system په سلسله سره، د سلسلې د مراتب له through channels, through the chain of command سلسله ساتل *compound verb* to observe the order of priority 2 session 3 series **4** chain, row, line **5** duration **6** chain (of mountains), mountain range **7** genealogy, pedigree

سلسیوس selsijús *m.* Celsius د سلسیوس ۱۰۰ درجي 100 degrees Celsius

سلطان sultā́n *m. Arabic [plural:* سلطانان sultānā́n *and Arabic* سلاطین salātī́n] **1** king; sultan **2** *proper noun* Sultan

سلطانه saltā́na *f. proper noun* Sultana

سلطاني sultāní king's, regal, royal; sultan

سلطنت saltanát *m. Arabic* **1** kingdom, realm, sultanate **2** royal authority; sultan's power سلطنت کول *compound verb* to reign, rule

سلطنتي saltanatí ☞ سلطنتي دربار سلطاني royal court

سلطه sultá *f. Arabic* **1** power, authority **2** state, power

سلف salā́f *m. Arabic [plural:* اسلاف aslā́f] **1** predecessor, forerunner, precursor **2** ancestor, forefather

سلفر sulfúr *m. plural* sulfur

سل کلن səlkalā́n سل کلنی səlkalanáy centenary, centenial, centuries-old, secular

سلگ səlág *m.* harvested wheat before threshing

سلگی səlgə́j, sulgə́j *f.* **1** death rattle **2** sobbing نری سلگی loud sobbing سلگی وهل، سلگی کول *compound verb* **a** to wheeze **b** to sob د ورځي وروستی سلگی وي The day is drawing to a close.

سلگېدل səlgedál *intransitive [past:* وسلگېده] to snort

سلم selā́m *m. Arabic trade* fixed-term transaction, business deal for the delivery of goods at a specified date

سلم¹ sələ́m *ordinal* hundredth

سلم² sə́ləm *m.* family, tribe

سلمان salmā́n *m. proper noun* Salman

سلماني salmāní *m.* barber

سلمچي silamchí *m.* ☞ چلمچي

سلمشر səlmə́shr *m.* lieutenant of cossacks, cossack squadron commander

سلمه¹ salmá *f.* surprise, astonishment, amazement سلمه کول *compound verb* to be surprised, be astonished, be amazed

سلمه² sələ́ma *feminine singular of* سلم سالگره centenary

سلندر silíndr *m.* **1** cylinder **2** tank, bottle (e.g., for oxygen)

سلنډه slā́nḍa *f.* infertile woman

سلنگ روز silingróz *m. electronic* socket (on the ceiling)

سلواغه salwāghá *f. [plural:* سلواغي salwāghé] **1** bucket, pail د څا په سلواغه اوبه کښل to draw water from a well with a bucket **2** ☞ دلو، دلوه

سلوتري salotrí *m. Eastern* veterinary, veternarian

سلوک sulúk *m. Arabic* **1** mode, manner **2** treatment of someone, behavior in relation to someone سلوک کول *compound verb* to treat someone

سلوکي sulukí pleasant, well-mannered, urbane, polite, courteous

سلول¹ selúl *m. biology* cell

سلول² sulawə́l *transitive* ☞ سولول

سله¹ sála *f.* **1** brick **2** pig, ingot, billet **3** casting

سله² salá *f. botony* awn, beard, barb, seta

سله³ sə́la ☞ سل³

سله ریژی slaréžaj, səlaréžaj *m.* brick maker

سلی¹ saláj *m.* ring

سلی² sólaj *m. dialect* ☞ څلی

سلی³ salə́j *f.* ramrod, ram; spit

سلی⁴ sələ́j *f.* pile, heap

سلیپر salipár *m.* سلي پر **1** slippers **2** *railroad* cross-tie, bridge tie

سلیت¹ səlít full, filled سلیت کول *compound verb* to fill

سلیت² slet *m.* سلبت *m.* **1** slate (board, for writing on) **2** (roof) slate

سلیخ slikh سلبخ slékh, salékh سلیخت slikht سلبخت salékht **1** *m.* **1.1** glue **1.2** viscosity, stickiness **2** sticking, adhering

سلبخ ناک slekhtnā́k sticky; viscous

سلیز səlíz *ordinal* hundredth

سلیس salís *Arabic* **1** clear, intelligible, easy to understand **2** expressive

سلیخت slikht *m.* سلبینت slekht *m.* ☞ سلیخ

سلیقه saliqá *f. Arabic* **1** taste (sense of the fine and elegant) **2** inclination, disposition; attraction

سلیکه slíka *f.* ☞ څریکه

سلیم salím *Arabic* **1.1** peaceful, peaceable; gentle, meek, humble **1.2** well, unharmed, safe **2** *m. proper noun* Selim

سلیم الطبع salim-ut-táb' peaceful, peaceable; gentle, meek, humble

سلیم العقل salim-ul-'aql *Arabic* of sound mind

سلیمان sulimā́n, sulejmā́n *m. proper noun* Solomon; Suleiman کوه سلیمان ، د سلیمان غر Suleiman range

سلیمان خپل sulejmānkhél **1** *m. plural* Suleimankheili (a tribe) **2** *m.* a Suleimankheil

سلیماني¹ sulimāní, sulimānáj *m. Arabic* **1** *history* Suleimani (nickname of Afghans) **2** hoopoe (bird)

سلیمانی² slemānə́j, sulemānə́j *f.* onyx

سلیولوز seljulóz *m.* cellulose

سم¹ sam **1** straight, direct, even سم سرک straight road سم سیخ perfectly straight **1.2** correct, true, real سم کار true cause زما اټکل سم وخوت My supposition proved to be correct. **1.3** honest, decent سم اخلاق decency, honesty **1.4** concordant with something, consonant with something د ... سره سم according to **1.5** accurate, direct سم لگېده direct hit **2** quite, totally, completely سم very good, best په سم ډول entirely correct سم او غر hill and dale سم لاس *regionalism* right hand

سم² sum *m.* hoof

سم³ sam, samm *m. Arabic* poison, venom, toxin

سم⁴ səm *Western present first person singular of* سول²

سما samā́ *f.* ☞ سموالی

سماترا sumātrā́ *f.* Sumatra

سماسه samāsá *f.* patty, pastry

سماع samā' *f. Arabic* **1** listening, hearing out; attention **2** hearing **3** song

سماعت samā'át *m. Arabic regional* hearing, trying (a case) قابل سماعت under the jurisdiction of سماعت کول *compound verb* to hear a case, try a case

سماعه samā́'a *f.* ☞ سماع

سماعي samā'í traditional

سماغ sumágh سماق *m. Arabic* سماک *m.* 1 *botony* sumac 2 *mineralogy* porphyry

سمالیند somālilénd *m.* Somalia

سماو samáw *m.* 1 justice, equity, fairness 2 correctness, rightness

سماوات səmāwát *m.* سماوار *m.* samovar

سماورچي samāwarchí *m.* سماوروالا *m.* vendor of hot tea; tea-house proprietor

سمباخ summákh *m. anatomy* anus

سمبال sambál 1 *m.* .1 finery, decoration, adornment 1.2 arranging, adjusting, settling 2.1 arranged, adjusted, settled 2.2 being at hand, being within easy reach سمبالي ساتل روپۍ to hoard one's money

سمبالول sambālawál *denominative, transitive [past:* سمبال یې کړ 1 *]* to dress up, beautify, adorn سمبالول خان *compound verb* to get dressed up 2 to arrange, adjust, settle 3 to prepare, make ready

سمبالونه sambālawóna *f. plural* 1 decoration, adornment 2 arranging, adjusting, settling

سمبالي sambālí *f.* putting into good order, regulating د کور سمبالي domestic science, housekeeping

سمبالیدل sambāledál *denominative, intransitive [past:* سمبال شو 1 *]* to get dressed up 2 to be arranged, be adjusted, be settled

سمبټه sambáṭa *f.* rice kasha, rice porridge

سمبوري samburí *paired word with* سوري

سموسه samosá *f.* patty with filling, filled pastry

سمبول símból *m.* symbol

سمبه sumbá *f.* 1 pole, staff (for a flag, banner)

سمت samt *m. Arabic* 1 path, way 2 land, place 3 area, region سمت شمالي *history* Northern District of Kabul Province (formerly) Southern Province سمت مشرقي (formerly) Eastern Province

سمت samát 2 sufficient, enough دا چینه سمتي اوبه لري There is enough water in this spring.

سمتره samtará *f.* ☞ سنتره

سمتورۍ samturáj *m.* saber

سمتي samtí, simtí regional, territorial, district

سمټه samáṭa *f.* large turban

سمځ smats *f.* سمځه smátsa *f. [plural:* سمځي smátsi] 1 cave, cavern د سمځي اوسېدونکی cave-men 2 sap, undermining

سمخ səmákh *paired word with* سور

سمخ سترګی sməkhstórgaj impudent, insolent, shameless; audacious

سمدستي samdastí ☞ سم دلاسه

سم دسموني samdəsamúni *f.* ☞ سمنه

سم دلاسه samdəlā́sa سم دم، سمدم samdám 1.1 now, at once, immediately, instantly سمدم روان سول They set out at once. 1.2

directly 1.3 outright, on the spot 2.1 immediate 2.2 direct, even 2.3 rash, hasty 2.4 current (of expenditures)

سمر samár *m. Arabic* 1 story, narrative 2 morning chat

سمرنا smirnā́ *f.* Smyrna *history* Izmir

سمساره samsārá *f.* monitor (a lizard)

سمست samíst *f.* ☞ سمځ

سمساره samsará *f.* ☞ سمساره

سمسور samsór 1 almost ripe 2 fresh, turned green 3 blooming, flourishing

سمسورتوب samsortób *m.* سمسورتیا samsortyā́ *f.* سمسوروالی samsorwálay *m.* 1 ripeness, maturity 2 freshness 3 flourishing 4 planting of greenery

سمسورول samsorawál *denominative, transitive [past:* سمسور یې کړ 1 *]* to make fresh, force to turn green 2 to plant greenery 3 to make blooming, make flourishing

سمسوري samsorí 1 *f.* ☞ سمسورتوب

سمسوری samsóraj 2 *m.* (one's) equal, match

سمسوربدل samsoredál 1 *denominative, intransitive [past:* سمسور شو *]* to ripen, mature 2 to turn green 3 to bloom, prosper, flourish

سمسوربده samsoredá *m. plural* ☞ سمسورتوب د هیواد سمسوربده prosperity of the country

سمښت samákht 1 *m.* smoothing, leveling; straightening

سمښت smákht 2 *m.* envy; hostility, ill-will

سمع cam', sam'á *f. Arabic* hearing

سمک samák *m. Arabic astronomy* Pisces

سم لاسی samlā́saj immediate, pressing, urgent; near, forthcoming سم لاسي اقدام urgent measures

سم دلاسه samləlā́sa ☞ سم له لاسه

سمن samán 1 *m. plural* 1 jasmine 2 lily of the valley

سمن samán 2 *m. Eastern* summons, subpoena (to court); court summons, subpoena سمن جاري کول *compound verb* to subpoena

سمنبویه samanbúja *f.* darling, sweetheart

سمنټ simánṭ *m. plural* cement

سمنټسازي simanṭsāzí *f.* cement production

سمند samánd 1 (of a horse's color) light bay, dun, cream-colored 2 *m.* light-bay horse

سمندر samandár, samundár 1 *m.* 1 sea; ocean 2 *proper noun* Samandar

سمندر samandár 2 *m.* 1 salamander 2 newt, eft

سمندروز samandróz *m.* silk taffeta

سمندري samandarí سمندرریز samandaríz sea; ocean سمندري خلیج buoy سمندري منار lighthouse, beacon

سمندول samanḍól *m. botony* broomrape, *Orobanche*

سمنگان samangā́n *m.* Samangan, Simingan (the ancient name of Haibak) د سمنگان ولایت *history* Samangan Province

سمنگی samangáj *m.* piece of cloth (on which dough is rolled out)

سمنو samanú *m.* malt

سمنه samána *f.* arranging, adjusting سم له سمني، سم د سمني completely

سمواله samwála f. سموالى، سم والى samwálay m. 1 straightness; evenness; smoothness 2 ☞ سمول 2

سموڅ samúts f. dialect cave, cavern

سمور samúr m. Arabic 1 sable 2 marten

سموزروالا samwazarwālá straight-winged (of insects)

سمول samawól 1 denominative, transitive [past: سم يي کړ] 1.1 to (make) level, (make) smooth, straighten 1.2 to improve someone, reform someone; make (someone) conscious of, bring something home (to someone) 1.3 to put right, settle, arrange (e.g., affairs); put in order 1.4 to adjust, smooth (one's dress) 1.5 to put (someone) on the right path 1.6 to lay, train (a gun, cannon), aim (at) 1.7 to regulate, adjust 2 m. plural 2.1 leveling, smoothing, straightening 2.2 correction (of deficiencies) 2.3 putting right, settling, arranging, putting into order 2.4 laying, training (of artillery pieces), aiming 2.5 regulating, adjusting

سمون samún m. 1 ☞ سمول 2 2 reform 3 system, order 4 accordance, conformity, correspondence د ... سره سمون خوړل to correspond (with), conform (to), be in keeping (with) 5 military quartering, billeting

سمونتون samuntún m. military department of housing allowances

سمون وال samunwā́l m. military chief of the department of housing allowances

سمونه samawóna f. ☞ سمنه

سمه sáma 1 feminine singular of سم 1 1.1 نو straight line سمه کرښه ... سمه more correct will be په سمه ... correct, right سمه او ښه داده چه plain; level place, level terrain 2 f. 2.1 plain, flat place, level terrain سمه او غر hills and dales 2.2 correct, right (of a word) 2.3 Sama (region of the Yousufzai land between the rivers Kabul, Buner and Swat)

سمه تخته sáma-takhtá lying on the back سمه تخته پریوتل compound verb to lie on the back; fall flat on one's back

سمى samój f. technology plumb (line, bob)

سميات sammiját m. Arabic 1 poisoning 2 infectiousness

سمېدل samedól denominative, intransitive [past: سم شو] 1 to be leveled, be smoothed, be straightened 2 to come to an awareness 3 to be put right, be settled, be arranged 4 to be trained, be laid (of an artillery piece), be aimed 5 to be regulated, be adjusted

سمېستر siméstr m. semester

سمينار seminā́r m. seminar

سن san m. Arabic 1 year 2 age په وړو سن کښې in childhood

سنا senā́ f. senate د سنا مجلس senate

سنا sanā́ f. botany senna

سناتوريم sanātorjúm m. sanatorium

سنار sunā́r m. goldsmith, jeweller

سنار sanā́r m. sanar (an ancient coin with a value of 15 puls)

سنارى sunārí gold; gilded

سنارى sanārí red, carmine, red in color

سناريو senārijó f. scenario

سناسى sanāsí m. ☞ سنداسى

سنبال sambāl m. ☞ سمبال

سنبالول sambālawól denominative, transitive [past: سنبال يي کړ] سنبالول خان سنبالول compound verb a to prepare for, get ready for b to outfit oneself, set out on a journey 2 to draw up, form (into ranks) 3 to equip, provide with

سنبل sumbúl m. 1 hyacinth 2 giant fennel 3 citronella (grass), Cymbopogon nardus 4 poetic lock, curl, ringlet; curls

سنبله sumbulá f. Arabic 1 astronomy Virgo (the constellation) 2 sumbula (the sixth month of the solar year; August-September)

سنت sunát, sunnát m. Arabic religion 1 sunna سنت اهل Sunni Moslems 2 circumcision سنت کول compound verb a namaz (one of the daily prayers required by Islamic tradition) b سنتول compound verb 3 [plural: سنن] custom, rule سنت اخيستل compound verb to cut, trim (a moustache, beard) وهل

سنتره santará f. tangerine, mandarin orange

سنترى santrí, santarí m. Eastern colloquial sentry, sentinel

سنتول suntawól, sunntawól denominative, transitive [past: سنت يي کړ] religion to perform the ritual of circumcision, subject someone to circumcision

سنتي sunatí, sunnatí f. religion circumcision

سنت ياګو sant-jā́gó m. Santiago

سنتېدل sunatedól, sunnatedól denominative, intransitive [past: سنت شو] religion to undergo circumcision

سنته santá f. 1 face 2 appearance, exterior د احمد توره سنته ده Ahmed is very swarthy.

سنج sandzh m. 1 weight 2 technology load

سنج sundzh desert, deserted, uninhabited; dismal, doleful سنج کول compound verb to devastate, lay waste (to), ravage سنج کېدل compound verb to be deserted, be uninhabited; (become) empty, become deserted

سنج sóndzh m. parapet (on a flat roof)

سنجاب sandzhā́b m. سنجاپ sanjā́p m. squirrel

سنجاغ sandzhā́gh m. سنجاق sanjā́q m. pin د وېښتانو سنجاغ hair-pin

سنجتوب sundzhtób m. سنج تيا sunjtyā́ f. desertedness, emptiness, uninhabitability

سنجش sandzhísh m. 1 thinking over, deliberating, weighing; assessment, rating 2 measuring, measurement, taking stock of 3 valuation; price

سنجوالى sundzhwā́laj m. ☞ سنجتوب

سنجول sandzhawól transitive [past: و يي سنجاوه] 1 to think over, deliberate, weigh 2 to seek, look for; think of, devise, invent; develop (e.g., a plan) يوه چاره سنجول to look for a way out 3 to assess; estimate, calculate ښه او بد سنجول to distinguish good from bad

سنجه súndzha f. desert

سنجېدل sandzhedól intransitive [past: و سنجېده] 1 to be deliberated, be weighed 2 to be sought after, be devised; be developed (e.g., of a plan) 3 be assessed; be estimated

سنجیده sandzhidá **1** considered, thought through, weighed **2** serious, well-founded, reasonable

سنځل sandzól *transitive* [*past:* و یې سنځاوه] **1** to pour out (water, etc.) **2** to vacate, empty

سنځله sandzóla *f. botany* oleaster, *Elaeagnus*

سند ¹ sanád *m. Arabic* [*plural:* سندونه sanadúna *and Arabic* اسناد asnád] **1** document; patent, license; deed, statement د پور سند bond **2** diploma

سند ² sind *m.* ☞ سیند

سند ³ sind *m.* Sind (region around Kararchi, Pakistan) د سند دریاب the Indus River

سندان sindán *m.* anvil

سندخ sandúkh *m.* ☞ صندوق

سندرچي sandərchí ¹ سندرغاړی sandərghā́ray **1** *m.* .**1** singer **1.2** musician **2** singing

سندرغاړې sandərghā́re **1** *f.* singer **2** singing

سندرگوی sandərgój *m.* singer

سندره sandóra *f.* **1** song **2** poem, verse سندري ویل *compound verb* **a** to sing **b** to compose songs

سندړ sandáṛ *m.* large camel

سندله sandalá *f.* locally manufactured cement (of broken brick, lime and vegetable fibers)

سندلۍ sandalə́j *f.* brazier, hearth; sandali ځان په سندلۍ کښې گرمول to warm oneself by the brazier, warm by the hearth

سندنۍ sindanáj ☞ سیندنی

سندوخ sandúkh *m.* ☞ صندوق

سندور sandúr *m.* cinnabar

سندوی sandój *m.* tulip

سندھ sindh *m.* **1** Sind (region around Kararchi, Pakistan) **2** the Indus River

سندي ¹ sindí **1** Sind **2** *f.* Sindhi (the language)

سندی ² sandáj *m.* tulip

سندیافته sanadjāftá one who has received a degree (of higher education); graduated (from college)

سنډ ¹ sənḍ *m.* ginger

سنډ ² sunḍ *m.* ☞ شونډه

سنډ ³ sunḍ *m. plural* **1** viscose, rayon **2** hemp

سنډا sanḍā́ *m.* water buffalo

سنډاسي sanḍāsí, sanḍā́saj *m.* **1** beggar **2** caste of Indian fakirs

سنډل sanḍál *m.* sandal

سنډۀ ¹ sanḍə́ *m.* ☞ د سنډگانو جنگ وه، د کانړو بوټو پکښي قضا راغله سنډا *saying Eastern* when masters fall out, their men get the clout (*literally:* the water buffalo fought, but the grass and stones suffered)

سنډه ² sánḍa *f.* desert hen, desert chicken

سنسکریت sanskrít *m.* Sanskrit

سنفونیه sinfonjá *f.* symphony

سنک sanák *m. proper noun* Sanak

سنکونا sinkoná *f.* bark of the cinchona tree

سینکیا sinkiá *f.* ☞ سنکیا

سنگ ¹ səng *m.* **1** whimpering (of a child) سنگ او پنگ کول whimpering سنگ سنگ کول to whimper **2** whine (of a bullet)

سنگ ² sang *m.* stone (usually in word compounds) سنگ پارس sáng-i-... philosophers' stone سنگ تهداب sáng-i-... foundation سنگ مرمر sáng-i-... marble سنگ مثانه sáng-i-... *medicine* stones (in the urinary bladder)

سنگا səngā́ *f.* ☞ سنگهار

سنگاپور singāpúr *m.* Singapore

سنگار singā́r *m.* adornment, decoration د سنگار کمره، د سینگار خونه dressing room

سنگاربکس singārbáks *m.* dressing case, toilet case

سنگارول singārawól *denominative, transitive* [*past:* سنگار یې کړ] to decorate, adorn

سنگ اندازي sangandāzí *f.* paving roads with crushed stone or gravel

سنگاون singāwán *m.* boat rudder

سنگ بر sangbúr *m.* سنگ تراش sangtarásh *m.* stonemason, bricklayer; lapidary

سنگ تراشي sangtarāshí *f.* stone cutting د سنگ تراشی صنایع processing stone

سنگ تره sangtará *f.* tangerine, mandarin orange

سنگدان sangdán *m.* stomach (in birds), crop, craw

سنگ دل sangdíl cruel, brutal, pitiless, ruthless, heartless, hard-hearted, callous

سنگ دلي sangdilí cruelty, brutality, ruthlessness, heartlessness, callousness

سنگر sangár *m.* **1** breastworks; rampart; fortification (work) سنگر وهل *compound verb* to build fortifications, erect a rampart **2** rock, cliff دوی د یو سنگر ملگري دي They are brothers-in-arms.

سنگرېزه sangrezá *f.* **1** gravel **2** pebbles

سنگرېزي sangrezí *f.* ☞ سنگربزي

سنگ ریشه sangrishá *f.* alabaster

سنگړه sangóṛa *f.* boulder, large rock

سنگزن sangzán ☞ ځنگزن

سنگسار sangsár *m. history* stoning (a form of capital punishment)

سنگشوی sangshoj *f.* washing of rice سنگشوی کول *compound verb* to wash rice

سنگل sangól *f.* ☞ ځنگل

سنگلاخ sanglā́kh **1.1** stony, rocky **1.2** difficult, hard **2** *m.* rocky terrain

سنگوپ sangúp *m.* (turning) somersaults, somersaulting

سنگوټی sangoṭáj *m.* young hare, leveret

سنگورکه sangoráka *f.* iron net for scalding currents or ابجوشه

سنگوړی sangoṛáj chubby, plump

سنگهار sangahā́r *m.* **1** whimpering **2** whistling (of bullets)

سنگې sangér stony, rocky

سنگین sangín **1** *m. Eastern* bayonet سنگین لگول! Fix bayonet! **2.1** stone; paved **2.2** stony **2.3** serious **2.4** *figurative* heavy

سنگين بار sanginbắr *m. military* supply train, unit transport

سنگين دل sangindíl cruel, ruthless, heartless

سنن sunán *m. Arabic plural of* سنت 3 *and* سنه [2]

سنوات sanawắt *m. Arabic plural of* سنه [1]

سنول snawśl *transitive* [*past:* و يې سناوه] to swing, rock, shake

سنه [1] saná *f. Arabic* [*m. plural* سنوات sanawắt] year د وينې زلميانو غورځنگ په ٢٦ سنه په کندهارکښې پيل سو The Awaken Youth Movement started in the year 26 in Kandahar. شمسي سنه solar year قمري سنه lunar year

سنه [2] sunná *f. Arabic* ☞ سنت

سنه مکي sanamakí *m. plural* Alexandria leaf, Alexandria senna

سني [1] sunní 1 Sunn 2 *m.* Sunni (a member of the Sunni branch of Islam)

سنى [2] snəj *f.* woolen thread, woolen yarn

سنياسي sanjāsí *m.* Hindu ascetic; righteous man

سني توب sunnitób *m.* Sunni, Sunnism

سنېدل snedźl *intransitive* [*past:* و سنېده] to swing, rock, fluctuate

سني گال senegắl *m.* Senegal

سني گلوي sunnigalwí *f.* سني والى *m.* Sunni, Sunnism

سڼ [1] saṇ *m.* 1 jute 2 flax

سڼ [2] səṇ *m.* ginger

سڼي sə́ṇi *f. plural* ☞ خڼي

سؤ [1] su' *Arabic* 1 *m.* evil 2.1 bad; evil 2.2 malicious 2.3 ominous, sinister 3 evil, bad سؤاجراات a abuse, misuse b mismanagement

سو [2] sáwa ☞ سوه [4]

سو [3] su *Western* 1 *present perfective first person plural of* شول [2,3] 2 *past of* شول [2,3]

سو [4] so *pronoun* dialect ☞ څو

سو [5] su *dialect* 1 wounded; hurt, injured, bruised 2 emaciated, skinny

سوا [1] swā *f.* fennel, dill

سوا [2] siwấ *Arabic* without, besides, with the exception of

سوا [3] səwấ *f.* extortion

سوابق sawābiq *m. Arabic plural of* سابقه

سوابى swābój *f.* Swabi

سوات swāt *m.* Swat

سؤاجراات su'idzhrā'ắt *m. Arabic plural* 1 abuse, misuse 2 mismanagement

سواحل sawāhil *m. Arabic plural of* ساحل

سواد sawắd *m. Arabic* 1 copy, duplicate تصديق لرونکى سواد، مصدق سواد certified copy, attested copy 2 list 3 copy (of a document) 4 rough draft, rough copy 5 literacy 6 suburbs

سؤاداره su'idārá *f. Arabic* inability to organize, lack of administrative abilities, mismanagement

سواركار sawārkár *m.* 1 rider, horseman; dzhigit (skilled horseman, trick rider); equestrian 2 jockey

سواره [1] swāre *m. Eastern plural of* سور [2]

سواره [2] suwārá *f.* 1 stem, stalk 2 stuble, stubble field

سواري [1] sawārí mounted; cavalry سواري فرقه cavalry division

سوارې [2] suāré *f.* soiree, evening party

سواست swāst *Western second person plural past of* شول [1,3]

سؤاستعمال su'isti'mál *m. Arabic* incorrect use of something; abuse, misuse of something

سؤال su'ál *colloquial* swắl, suwắl *m. Arabic* [*plural:* سوالونه suwālúna *and Arabic* سؤالات su'ālất] 1 question د سؤال اشاره question mark سؤال او ځواب correspondence; conversation; communication چه سؤال هغسي ځواب *proverb* one ill turn deserves another 2 request سؤال کول *compound verb* a to ask b to beg alms

سوالگر swālgár *m.* beggar; cadger

سؤالي suwālí, suālí 1.1 asking, inquiring 1.2 interrogative, inquiring, questioning 2 *m.* .1 beggar; cadger 2.2 usurer

سوان [1] suwắn light, easy

سوان [2] suwắn *m.* ☞ سوهان

سوانح sawānih *m. Arabic plural of* سانحه

سوهان کار suwānkár *m.* ☞ سوهان کار

سوهان کاري suwānkārí *f.* ☞ سوهان کاري

سوانگ [1] swắng, sawắng *m.* 1 disguise, disguising; pretense 2 imitation سوانگ کول *compound verb* a to disguise oneself; pretend, feign, simulate b to imitate

سوانگ [2] suwắng *m.* malt

سوانگى swắngáj *m.* 1 pretender 2 imitator 3 follower

سواني suwāní 1 *f.* lightening, easing; lightness, ease 2 light, easy, lightened, eased, mitigated

سواى swāj *Western* 1 *potential and conditional forms, past tense of* شول [3] دې انکار نسواى کولای She could not refuse. 2 *sometimes used in place of the present* سي

سوب [1] swab 1 ready, prepared عسکر د دفاع دپاره سوب او حاضر دي the troops are prepared for defense. 2 expecting سوب کښېنستل *compound verb* to be waiting, be in readiness

سوب [2] səwáb *m.* 1 ☞ سبب 2 anxiety, worry, alarm, agitation

سوب [3] suwáb *m.* cure, medical treatment; remedy (for an illness)

سوبارى sobắraj *m.* ☞ څوبارى

سوبت sobát *m.* 1 ☞ صحبت 2 song (with instrumental accompaniment) 3 merriment, merry-making, high spirits سوبت کول *compound verb* to have a good time, enjoy oneself 4 monetary collection (for the benefit of pupils in a madrasa)

سوبمن sobmán winning, conquering, prevailing

سوبه [1] sóba *f.* victory سوبه ورل *compound verb* to win, conquer, be victorious

سوبه [2] subá *f.* 1 well, shaft (of a kahriz) 2 arch, span (of a bridge)

سوبه [3] sóba quiet, calm

سوپ sup *m.* entrance (hall), entryway, vestibule, anteroom

سوپارى supārí *m. plural* betel (nut)

سوپراوکسايد suparoksájd *m. chemistry* peroxide

سوپرسونيک supersoník with supersonic speed, having supersonic speed د سوپرسونيک الوتکه a supersonic aircraft

سوپۍ ¹ supáj *m.* male monkey

سوپۍ ² supə́j *f.* monkey, marmoset

سوت sawt *m.* ☞ ثبت

سوترګي sutragí *f.* cleanness; neatness, tidiness

سوتره sutrá clean, neat, tidy

سوترۍ sutrə́j *f. Eastern* string, twine

سؤتفاهم su'tafāhúm *m. Arabic* misunderstanding د دوی په مینځ کښې مینځ هیڅ سؤتفاهم نسته Between them there is complete agreement.

سوتن sutə́n *m.* tracking dog, bloodhound; police dog, work(ing) dog

سوت ¹ sawút *m.* 1 person who guards shephards' things 2 army cook, camp cook

سوټ ² suṭ *m.* suit د شپې سوټ dress coat

سوټبوټ suṭbúṭ 1.1 sullen, gloomy, morose; sour, dissatisfied 1.2 strongly bound, strongly attached څوک سوټ بوټ ترل to make someone very attached (to oneself) 2 wholesale, indiscriminately

سویزرلېنډ swiṭzarlénḍ *m.* Switzerland

سوټک suṭə́k *m.* ☞ ستک ¹

سوټکه suṭáka *f.* corn-cob

سوټکی suṭəkáj *m.* 1 land mark(er), boundry mark(er); border post, frontier post 2 kind of embroidery

سوټکېس suṭkés *m. regional* trunk, suitcase

سوټمار soṭmā́r peddler; hawker

سوټه ¹ suṭá *f. dialect* bread

سوټه ² súṭa *f.* offspring (of animals)

سوټه ³ soṭá *f.* ☞ سوټکه

سوټه مار soṭamā́r 1 pugnacious 2 *m.* pugnacious fellow, one who likes fighting

سوټی ¹ soṭáj *m.* [*plural:* سوټي soṭí *and* سوټیان soṭiyā́n] 1 staff, crook, stick; club, bludgeon, cudgel 2 *agriculture* flail 3 flint 4 male member, penis

سوټی ² soṭə́j *f.* ☞ سوټی ¹ 4

سوجي sudzhí سوجي اوړه semolina

سوچ ¹ such ☞ سوچه

سوچ ² swich *m.* ☞ سویچ

سوچ ³ such *m.* 1 thought, reflection 2 guess, guessing

سوچه suchá 1.1 pure, uncontaminated 1.2 irreproachable, blameness, unstained 1.3 *dialect* unfortunate; ominous, sinister 2 completely, entirely, quite, totally

سوچه والی suchawā́laj *m.* 1 purity, state or quality of being without contaminants 2 irreproachability, blamelessness

سوچي sóchi *m.* Sochi

سوځ swadz *present stem of* سول ²

سوځلی swadzálaj burned down, burned out

سوځند swadzánd 1 burning, smarting, scorching, parching, broiling 2 disturbing, nerve-racking

سوځول swadzawál *transitive* [*past:* و یې سوځاوه] to burn (down, out), incinerate

سوځونکی swadzúnkaj 1 *present participle of* سول ¹ 2.1 igniting, used for starting fire سوځونکی بم incendiary bomb 2.2 sultry, hot, torrid (of the weather)

سوځونه swadzawána *f.* 1 burn, scald 2 burning (down, out), incinerating

سوځېدل swadzedál *intransitive* [*present:* سوځي *past:* و سوځېده] to burn; burn down, burn out

سوځېدنه swadzedána *f.* 1 fire, conflagration 2 burning; combustion

سوځېدونکی swadzedúnkaj 1 *present participle of* سوځېدل 2 *m.* fuel

سوخت sokht *m.* 1 burning 2 combustion 3 *figurative* bitterness

سوخته sokhtá 1 burned (down, out) 2 burned, scorched 3 exhausted, worn-out د چا ځګر سوخته کول to tire, wear someone out

سوخر sukhár *m.* spite, malice; hostility, ill-will

سوخره súkhra *f.* fillet سوخره غوښه meat fillet

سوخړی پوخړی sukhŕáj-pukhŕáj 1 scalded 2 boiled (until) soft سوخړی پوخړی کېدل *compound verb* a to be scalded b to be boiled (until) soft, be overcooked

سوخل sukhál *transitive* ☞ سیخل

سوخوز sawkhóz *m.* sovkhoz, state farm

سوخول sukhawál *transitive* [*past:* و یې سوخاوه] 1 to injure, wound 2 to break, chop, split, pierce, perforate, puncture 3 to stuff with something, fill with something 4 to blow one's nose

سوخېدل sukhedál *intransitive* [*past:* و سوخېده] 1 to hiss (of a boiler) 2 to be pierced, be punctured 3 ☞ سیخېدل

سود sud *m.* 1 a benefit; gain b profit, income, receipts 2 interest سود اخیستل او سود خورل *compound verb* to collect interest 3 usury سود ورکول to practice usury, engage in usury سودا purchases

سودا ¹ sawdā́ *f. Arabic* [*plural:* سوداګاني sawdāgā́ni *and* سوداوي sawdā́wi] 1 concern, anxiety, nervousness د چاته سودا لوېدل to be concerned about someone, worry about someone; become anxious about someone 2 thought, idea سودا وهل *compound verb* to become thoughtful, be lost in thought, to ponder a سودا وهلی worried, anxious b deep in thought, pondering 3 desire, aspiration د چا سودا ایستل to satisfy someone's desire 4 love; strong passion 5 melancholy 6 bile, strong irritation 7 despondent, low spirits, depression

سودا ² sawdā́ *f.* 1 purchase, purchased goods سودا اخیستل *compound verb* to buy something 2.1 trade, commerce; commercial 2.2 trade, deal, sale and purchase سودا کول *compound verb* a to go shopping b to bargain; trade (in), to engage in commerce

سودا ³ sodā́ *f.* ☞ سوډا

سودات sodā́t virtuous; righteous

سوداګر sawdāgár *m.* [*plural:* سوداګر sawdāgár *and* سوداګران sawdāgarā́n] merchant, tradesman, businessman

سوداګري sawdāgarí *f.* trade, commerce

سودان sudā́n *m.* Sudan

سودایي sawdājí 1 maddened, crazy (from love) 2 obsessed (by an idea) 3 melancholy; sad 4 mistrustful, suspicious

سودايي توب sawdājitób *m.* suspiciousness; mistrustfulness

سودخواره sudkhā́ra *m.* usurer

سودگن sudgə́n quiet, calm

سودگنه sudgə́na *f.* peace, rest; calming, quieting, soothing

سودمن sudmánd advantageous; useful; profitable

سودمندي sudmandí *f.* advantage, gain, benefit; profit; advantageousness, usefulness, profitability

سوده [1] sawadá *f.* 1 basket 2 wicker lid, wicker cover

سوده [2] sudá *f.* 1 obstruction, jam 2 *medicine* volvulus, twisted bowels

سوده [3] sudá 1 (finely) ground, powdered سوده کول *compound verb* to grind, crumble finely, mince سوده کېدل *compound verb* to be fine-ground; be finely crumbled, be minced سوده وريجي boiled rice 2 abraded, worn away (of a horse's hoof)

سوده [4] sóda *f.* comfort, comforting, consolation; consoling; quiet, calm, quieting, calming

سوده [5] sudá ☞ سوچه

سوده [6] sodá *f.* soda, sodium carbonate

سودا sodā́ *f.* 1 soda water 2 soda

سودر soḍə́r 1 *m.* .1 wild boar, wild hog; hog, pig 1.2 *abusive* pig, swine 2.1 lazy 2.2 ill-mannered, unpolished, uncouth 2.3 pigheaded, stuborn, willful

سوډره soḍə́ra 1 *f.* swine 2 *feminine singular of* سوډر [2]

سوډه səwáḍa 1 *paired word with* ساوه 2 intrigues, machinations, crafty designs

سور [1] sor *m. Eastern* ☞ پسور

سور [2] sor *Eastern* ☞ سپور

سور [3] sur, sor *m. plural history* 1 Suri Dynasty 2 Suri tribe

سور [4] sur *m.* sur (a variety of karakul)

سور [5] sur [*f.* سره srá, sərá, *m. plural:* سره srə *f. plural:* سرې sre] 1 red, scarlet سور په وينو stained with blood 2 ruddy (of the face) 3 burning hot, incandescent 4 bay (horse's color) 5 ardent سور سور کول او شین کېدل to fly into a rage کافر infidel *compound verb* a to make red, paint red b to fry, roast, broil c to make red hot, make incandesce d to set on, hound, urge on سور راتلل، *compound verb* ☞ سوربدل [1] 6 sterile (of a ram, a billy-goat) سور کور ورکول to give a complete set of furniture in a dowry سور کور راوړل to bring as a dowry complete furnishings (carpets, etc.)

سوراړ surā́ṛ *m.* hot desert

سوراغزی surāghzáj *m. botany Catha edulis* (kind of shrub)

سوران surā́n *m.* 1 simoom 2 *medicine* bulimia

سوراني surāní wailing, howling; screeming, yelling

سورانا surāṇā́ ☞ سوربوني

سورباتينگړ surbāṭingáṛ *m. singular & plural* tomato(es)

سورباد surbā́d *m.* ☞ جوانان

سوربخن surbakhə́n reddish

سوربڼی surbā́ṇaj red, red-haired

سوربوني surbuṇáj 1 red 2 rosy, ruddy

سورپلی surpálaj *m.* سورپلۍ surpalə́j *f.* 1 nettle 2 *regional* velvet bean, *Mucuna pruriens* 3 ☞ سورمل

سورپوستی surpóstaj red-skinned

سورت [1] surát *m.* ☞ صورت

سورت [2] sort *m.* 1 sort, kind, variety, grade, quality, brand 2 sorting, grading سورت کول *compound verb* to sort, grade

سورت بندي sortbandí *f.* سورت کاري sortkārí *f.* sorting, grading

سورتمان sortmā́n *m.* assortment, variety, range

سرجه surdzhá *f.* ☞ سرجه

سورڅاڅکی surtsā́tskaj *m.* species of snake

سورخچوکی surkhəchúkaj *m.* 1 piece of sirloin 2 ruddy man ځان سورخچوکی کول to wash up properly

سورخکه surkhā́ka *f.* snipe

سورخولی surkhúlaj blood-thirsty

سورخه surkhá *f.* variety of wheat

سورخي [1] surkhí *f.* ☞ سرخي [2]

سورخی [2] surkháj *m.* bay horse

سوردلی surdaláj *m.* windhover, kestrel (a bird)

سورسات sursā́t *m. history* provisions (furnished to troops by the population)

سورسانده sursā́nda *f.* سورساندی sursā́nday *m.* 1 mountain flower 2 heather

سورسترگی surstórgaj irritated, angered; angry; irritable

سورسری sursáraj red, red-haired

سورسورکه sursuráka *f.* 1 fireworks 2 strong wind, hurricane

سورشان surshā́n reddish

سورغاړی surghā́ṛaj with a red border (of a shawl)

سورغوړی surghwáɡaj *m.* amaranth, *Amaranthus polygamus*

سؤ رفتار su'raftā́r *m.* bad conduct, bad behavior د مامور سؤ رفتار abuse of power

سورکنډو surkanḍó *f.* ☞ سورکونډو

سورکوکو surkokó *m.* red rose

سورکونډو surkunḍó *f.* girl who cuts her hair (who is not yet betrothed)

سورکی [1] surkáj 1 *diminutive* red; scarlet 2 reddish-brown, rust (-colored) سورکی مېږی red ant

سورکی [2] surkə́j *f.* cherry (the fruit)

سورگل surgúl *m.* red rose

سورگلی surgúlaj *m.* kind of greenery

سورگولغ sur-gulásh rosy and plump

سورل surál *m.* chestnut horse

سورلاسی surlā́saj *m. law* murderer, killer

سورلان surlā́n *m.* wolfhound

سورلکی surlakə́j *f.* redstart (bird)

سورلمنی surlamə́ne *f.* woman who has died in childbirth

سورلن sorlə́n shady

سورلنډ surlánḍ *m.* 1 jackal 2 Surland (a tribe)

سورلنډی surlanḍáj *m.* jackal

سورلنۍ swarlanáj *m.* **1** rider, horseman; cavalryman **2** horse trainer, horse breaker **3** jockey

سورلي swarlí *f.* **1** ride, riding سورلي کول *compound verb* to go in for horseback riding **2** retinue **3** cavalcade **4** passenger **5** rider

سورليمار swarlimár *m.* horseman, rider

سرمايي surmājí سرمه ئي ☞

سورمخي [1] surməkhí *f.* honor, glory

سورمخى [2] surmókhaj rubicund, ruddy (of the face)

سورمړنی surmaṛánaj *m.* cockroach

سورمل surmól *m.* feather grass, spear grass

سورمېږی surmegáj *m.* red ant

سورن sorón shady

سورنا surnā́ *f.* **1** oboe **2** flute

سورناچي surnāchí *m.* oboist, flutist

سورنجان surindzhā́n *m. botony* **1** meadow saffron, autumn crocus **2** merendera (a medicinal plant)

سورنچی surnicháj *m.* pink worm, pink bollworm

سورنگ suráng *m.* **1** sap, undermining **2** tunnel

سورنا surnā́ *f.* سورنا ☞

سورناچي surnā́chí *m.* سورناچي ☞

سوروالی surwā́laj *m.* **1** redness, the color red **2** daybreak, dawn; glow

سورور sorawár wide, broad په سورور جبهه on a wide front

سوروږی surwágaj *m.* red wheat

سورول [1] surawól *transitive* [*past:* و يې سوراوه] **1** to set on, sic on (a dog, etc.) **2** to infuriate

سورول [2] swarawúl *denominative, transitive Eastern* ☞ سپرول

سوره [1] swarā́ *f. history* daughter or female slave who has been given in exchange for a kidnapped wife or daughter

سوره [2] surá *f.* sura (a chapter of the Quran)

سوره [3] surá *f.* ammoniac plant (medicinal plant)

سوره [4] sorá *f.* ☞ سوری [4]

سوره [5] swará *Eastern feminine singular of* سور [2]

سوری [1] surí *m. plural history* the Suri dynasty (in medieval India)

سوری [2] surí *m.* large sack

سوری [3] suráj **1** *m.* **.1** hole, slit; opening, orifice **1.2** burrow, hole **2** full of holes, holey, worn-out, torn سوری کول *compound verb* **a** to stab, pierce; make holes in; punch a hole in د سوری کولو ماشین perforator **b** to dig through, burrow through سوری کېدل *compound verb* **a** to be pierced; wear through; be worn-out, be torn **b** to be burrowed through سوری پیداکول to (try to) find a way out (of a difficult or embarrassing situation, etc.) په سوری ننوتل *compound verb* to seek refuge

سوری [4] sóraj *m.* ☞ د سوری ځایونه سیوری shady spots سوری کول *compound verb* **a** to shade **b** to darken, obscure, black out په سره سوری کول **a** to be concealed, be hidden in the shadows **b** to seek refuge سوری ته اچول to dry in the shade

سوری [5] suráj *feminine singular of* سوری [2]

سوري [6] soré *f. plural* cries, wails سوري کول *compound verb* to cry, wail, shout, howl

سوریا surijā́ *f.* ☞ سوریه

سوریانگه surjā́nga *f.* oriole

سوریته surjáta *f. history* **1** concubine **2** female slave or captive who has borne the master a child

سوربدل [1] suredól *intransitive* [*past:* و سوربده] **1** to become red, turn red **2** to fry, roast, broil **3** to incandesce **4** to get angry, be angry, fly into a rage **5** to undertake a business with zeal **6** to feel shy, be ashamed

سوربدل [2] swaredól *denominative, intransitive Eastern* ☞ سپربدل

سوری سمبوري surí-samb urí all full of holes, riddled with holes

سوری سوری suráj- suráj full of holes, holey

سوریه surijá *f.* Syria د سوریې عربي جمهوریت the Syrian Arabic Republic, SAR

سور soṛ [*f.* سره saṛá, *m. plural:* ساره sāṛó, *f. plural:* سړې saṛé] **1** cold, cool په ساره موسم کښي at the cold times of the year د ده لاسونه ساره دي He has cold hands. **2** cold, indifferent ساره indifference سوړ مزاج coolness, sluggishness, apathy, phlegm په ساره نظر کتل to be cool, be indifferent سوړ زړه ښکاره کول to view dispassionately, regard with indifference **3** unattractive (of a person) **4** stern, severe, cruel **5** lazy

سوړا soṛā́ *m.* **1** awkward man, clumsy guy **2** lazy person **3** coward

سوړبور soṛ-bóṛ sad, saddened, melancholy

سوړبوی soṛbúj *m.* سوړبویي، سوړبوئي soṛbuyí *f.* stink, stench, foul odor

سوړپور sóṛ-póṛ ☞ څوک سوړپور سوړپور سری سوړنگور unsympathetic سوړپور اوبنتل to kill with one blow سوړپور to fall down in a heap سوړپور ولوبد He fell in a dead faint.

سوړتیا soṛtjā́ *f.* ☞ سوروالی

سوړسک soṛsók *m.* [*plural:* سوړسکان soṛsəkán] corn bread

سوړسمخ soṛ-səmókh ☞ سوړنگور

سوړفکره soṛfíkra phlegmatic

سوړمېرج soṛmeráj cold, indifferent

سوړن suṛón **1** lying, false **2** *m.* liar

سوړنگور soṛ-ngóṛ [*f.* ساره نگړه saṛá-ngaṛá, *m. plural:* ساره نگاره sāṛó-ngāṛó, *f. plural:* سړې نگړي saṛé-ngaṛé] quite cold, cold as ice

سوړوالی soṛwā́laj *m.* **1** cold; coolness د هوا سوړوالی fall in temperature **2** *figurative* coldness, indifference

سوړول soṛawól *denominative, transitive* ☞ سپړول

سوړه [1] súṛa *f.* **1** slit, crack; hole **2** burrow **3** precipice

سوړه [2] súṛa *f.* syphilis

سوړي [1] súṛi *f. plural* lie, falsehood

سوړي [2] súṛi *plural of* سوړه [1,2]

سوړی [3] suṛáj *m.* ☞ سوړه [1] سوړی کول *compound verb* **a** to pierce; make a hole **b** to dig, dig through, burrow through

سوړېدل soṛedól *denominative, intransitive* ☞ سپړېدل

سوړیز sawaṛíz free, unrestricted; idle, vagrant

سوړي سمبوري suṛí-sambuṛí ☞ سوری سمبوري

سوز [1] soz *f.* **1** burning **2** woe, sadness; grief, sorrow; melancholy, anguish په زړه سوز spiritual anguish **3** zeal, ardor, diligence راتلل *compound verb* **a** to be animated, be inspired, be full of enthusiasm **b** to get excited

سوز [2] swaz *present stem of* سول [2]

سوزاک sozắk *m.* gonorrhea

سوزان sozắn **1** burning, scorching **2** sad, melancholy, sorrowful

سوزبر sawzbár *m.* ☞ سبزبرگ

سوزش sozísh *m.* سوزښت sozə́kht *m.* **1** burning; combustion **2** agitation, anxiety, uneasiness; care, concern **3** vexation, annoyance, distress; pain

سوزن sozán *m.* needle; pin

سوزناک soznắk ☞ سوزان

سوزنک sozanák *m.* striker, striker pin; firing pin

سوزني suznáj *sozní f.* **1** tape (with which a baby is bound when being swaddled) **2** shawl

سوزول swazawə́l *transitive* ☞ سوځول

سوزه sawzá, sozá *f.* **1** gore, gusset (in a dress) **2** ax

سوزي [1] sawzí *m. plural* **1** greens, vegetables **2** spinach

سوزی [2] sozáj *m.* basket with a small opening

سوزي [3] sawzé, sozé *plural of* سوزه

سوزیدل swazedə́l *intransitive Eastern* ☞ سوځبدل د چا نه سوزبدل to envy someone, be consumed by envy of someone

سوزبده swazedə́ *m. plural* burning

سورمه sogmá *f.* ☞ سرمه

سوسړ [1] susář *m.* dolphin

سوسړ [2] susář *m.* petty thief, pilferer

سوسکبدل suskedə́l *intransitive [past:* و سوسکبده] to tremble, shiver, shake, quiver

سوسن [1] sosán *m. Arabic [plural:* سوسنان sosanắn] **1** lily **2** iris

سوسن [2] sosán leggy, lanky

سوسني sosaní violet, lilac, dark blue سوسني باتینگن eggplant

سوسی susə́j *f.* **1** susi (a striped fabric of cotton or silk) **2** ☞ سیسی

سوسیالست sosiālíst *m.* socialist

سوسیالستي sosiālistí **1** socialist(ic) **2** socialism

سوسیالیزم sosiālízm *m.* socialism

سوسیولودزیکي sosjolodzhikí sociological

سوسیولوژي sosjoloží *f.* sociology

سوسیولوژیکي sosjoložikí sociological

سوشلست sóshalist ☞ سوسیالستي

سوشیالیزم soshjālízm *m.* ☞ سوسیالیزم

سوښتاج [1] swəkhtáj, sukhtáj *m.* corner of the mouth

سوښتاج [2] swəkhtáj *m. textiles* shuttle

سوءعمل su' amál *m. Arabic* **1** evil deed, heinous crime **2** misdemeanor

سوغ [1] sugh, sogh *m.* **1** snuff سوغ کول *compound verb* to take snuff **2** pinch of snuff

سوغ [2] sugh, sogh *m.* ☞ سغ؛سوغ سوغ shaking

سوغات sawghāt *m.* present, gift سوغات کول *compound verb* وراندي کول to give a gift, offer a present

سوغاتي sawghātí gift, present [attributive]

سوغالی soghắlaj, sughắlaj *m.* rabbit hole, hare's burrow

سوغځی sughdzə́j *f.* ☞ سوزی

سوغل soghə́l *intransitive* ☞ سوغبدل [1]

سوغن sughə́n **1** wheezing, snorting, puffing, breathing hard through the nose **2** *m.* snotty person, snot-nosed person

سوغول [1] sughawə́l *transitive [past:* و یي سوغاوه] **1** to draw something up into the nostrils **2** to sniff **3** to wheeze, snort, breathe hard through the nose **4** to cause to sniff

سوغول [2] sughawə́l *transitive* ☞ سغول

سوغبدل [1] sughedə́l *intransitive [past:* و سوغبده] **1** to wheeze, snort, breathe hard and loudly through the nose **2** to sniff

سوغبدل [2] sughedə́l *intransitive* ☞ سغبدل

سوق sawq *m. Arabic* **1** sending, dispatching; direction **2** moving, transferring, shifting (e.g., troops) **3** conducting, waging (combat); leading (troops) سوق او اداره directing, leading, management (of a military operation) د پلیو سوق او محاربه combat regulations for the infantry سوق کبدل *compound verb* **a** to be sent, be dispatched **b** to be transferred, be shifted (of troops)

سوق الجیش sawq-ul-dzhájsh *m.* strategy

سوق الجیشي sawq-ul-dzhajshí **1** *f.* strategy **2** strategic

سوءقصد su' qásd *m. Arabic* attempt (at, on), encroachment (on, upon) سوءقصد کول *compound verb* to make an attempt (on someone's life), attempt to assassinate someone

سوقیات sawqijā́t *m. plural Arabic* **1** sending, dispatching **2** shifting, moving (e.g., troops)

سوک [1] suk *m. [plural:* سوکونه sukúna *and Western dialect* سوکان sukā́n] **1** fist سوک وهل *compound verb* to knead (dough) سوکونه خورل، په سوک وهل to strike with the fist *compound verb* ورکول سوک کول *compound verb* to be beaten (up) to make a fist **2** punch with the fist **3** stump, stub سوک پر یوه شي ایستل to settle or arrange, matters in a careless or slipshod way

سوک [2] siwák *m.* smouldering brand, firebrand, charred log

سوک [3] swak *m.* cold wind

سوکالی sawkālə́j *f.* calm, quiet, peacefulness, tranquillity

سوکري súkre Sucre

سوکړ sukář *m* man with a thin beard and moustache

سوکړک sukṛák *m.* ☞ سوړسک

سوکړه sukṛá *f.* **1** drought **2** crop failure

سوکلی suklə́j *m.* mollycoddle, milksop

سوکموک sukmúk wrinkled سوک موک کښینستل to sit all huddled up

سوکه [1] swáka *f.* charred log

سوکه [2] sawká **1** *f.* rest, peace **2** quietly, gently, slowly سوکه سوکه on the sly

سوکه [3] súka *f.* ☞ څوکه

سوکي [1] súki سوکي په نوکي کول to oppress someone

سوکی² swakáj *m.* nettle

سوکی³ swókaj *m.* د اور سوکی firebrand, smouldering brand

سوکی⁴ səwakój *f. plural* pimples

سوکي موکي súki-múki سوکي موکي کول *compound verb* to tie someone up and give him a beating

سوگ sog *m.* dew

سوگت sawgát stingy, greedy, grasping

سوگر sogár **1** *m.* .**1** braggart, boaster **1.2** miser, skinflint **2** stingy

سوگل sugól *f.* سوگله sugála *f.* سوگلی¹ suglóy *f.* winter footwear

سوگلی² suglój *f.* سلگی

سوگند sawgánd *m.* oath, vow سوگند خورل *compound verb* to swear to, take an oath سوگند ورکول *compound verb* to cause to take an oath

سول¹ sol *m.* reason, intelligence, mind

سول² swəl **1** *intransitive* [*present:* سوځي *past:* وسو] .**1** to burn **1.2** to catch fire, flare up په خپل سر سول to ignite **1.3** to burn oneself **1.4** *figurative* to wither, perish **1.5** *figurative* to pity, feel sorry for درباندي نه سوځي They do not feel sorry for you. **1.6** *transitive* [*past:* وی سو] **a** to burn (down) **b** to destroy ټول مال یی راخُخه یووړ، و یی سوم They took everything I have. **2** *m. plural* .**1** burning د سولو لرگي fuel, د سولو مواد، د سولو خیزونه firewood; fuel **2.2** tanning, baking in the sun **2.3** fire, conflagration

سول³ swəl *intransitive Western* شول¹

سول⁴ sul *m.* greed, cupidity, stinginess, miserliness

سولاغ sulágh *m.* hole; crack, slit

سولاغه sawlághá *f.* سلواغه

سولاند sulánd سولانده sulánda, سولجن swaljón, سولند swalónd **1** greedy, grasping, stingy **2** lustful, lewd, lascivious

سولنده sulánḍa *f.* hollow, depression

سولو¹ swólo *oblique plural of* سول² 2

سولو² swólu *past tense, first person plural of* سول² 1

سولول sulawól *transitive* [*past:* وی سولاوه] **1** to rub; rub in; spread **2** to erase (with an eraser) **3** to wipe, wear out, abrade **4** to saw **5** to sniff at everything اروا سولول *idiom* **a** to fall upon one's food **b** to be a parasite, be a sponger **c** to be greedy, be grasping, be stingy

سوله¹ sóla, súla *f.* peace د سولي په زمانه کښي in peacetime د سولي سیاست a policy of peace سره سوله کول to be reconciled with غوښتني

سوله² swóla *Western imperfect, feminine singular of* سول³

سوله³ swólə *Western imperfect, masculine singular of* سول³

سوله بوله solá-bolá سلا بلا

سوله خواخوونکی sóla khwáxhawúnkaj سوله دوست soladóst, سوله غوښتونکی sóla ghúxhtúnkay peaceable, peace-loving

سولي¹ sóli *plural of* سولي¹

سولي² sulí سولاند 1

سولي³ sulój *f.* **1** gallows څوک سولی ته خِپول د سولی تخت scaffold **a** په سولی کول to hang someone **2** stake (instrument of execution)

---

to hang from a gallows, string up **b** to impale on a stake **3** pole (acrobat's)

سولی⁴ sulój *f.* سیلی²

سولېدل suledól *intransitive* [*past:* وسولېده] **1** to grind off; be obliterated, be effaced; wear out **2** to go to ruin (of the teeth) **4** to be sawed

سوم¹ swam *m.* **1** eye of a needle **2** opening (of an earring)

سوم² swəm *Western past tense first person of* سول² 1

سوم³ swəm *Western past tense first person of* سول³

سوم⁴ sawóm hundredth دوه سوم two-hundredth دری سوم three-hundredth

سوماترا sumátrā *f.* Sumatra

سومالي لِند somālilénd *m.* سومالي لِند somālilénd *m.* Somalia

سومباټور sumbāṭawór سومبور

سومباټی sumbā́ṭaj *m.* **1** (small) hole **2** سومبی

سومباخه sumbākha *f.* سومبته sumbáṭa *f.* **1** hind part, back **2** seat, posterior, rump

سومبروغی sumbrúghaj *m.* **1** door **2** window **3** hatch

سومبری sumbóraj *m.* **1** small door **2** light opening (in the ceiling), skylight

سومبل sumból *transitive* [*past:* وی سومبه] to stab with a pike

سومبور sumbawór broad in the beam, having a large rump

سومبه sumbá *f.* سونبه

سومبی sumbój *f.* **1** *anatomy* anus **2** croup, crupper, hind quarters

سون swun *m.* **1** burning **2** fire, conflagration **3** fuel د هوانوردی سون aviation fuel

سونار sunár *m.* goldsmith, jeweler

سوناري sunārí red, cinnabar

سونبه sumbá *f.* **1** shaft (of a spear) **2** *technology* punch **3** funnel **4** *military* rammer, bore brush

سونټه sunóṭa *f.* سنټه

سونټی مونټی suntáj-munṭáy armless and legless

سونجه súndzha *f.* desert

سونځ sundz frightful, terrible

سوندخ sundókh *m.* سوندک sundók *m.* صندوق

سوندر¹ swandár *m.* سخوندر

سوندر² sundór *m.* sandarac, gum juniper

سونده súnda *f.* **1** envy **2** suspicion; jealousy سونده کول *compound verb* **a** to envy **b** to suspect; be jealous

سوندړ¹ sunḍ *m. plural regional* **1** kenaf, *Hibiscus cannabinus* **2** flax **3** viscose, rayon

سوندړ² sunḍ *m.* dry ginger

سوندوک sunḍók *m.* شوندوک

سوندوک موندوک sunḍók-munḍók *m.* final days of the month of کب، حوت

سوندړ مونډ sunḍmúnḍ taciturn, uncommunicative

سونده súnḍa *f. dialect* شونده

سونډي sunḍí linen (of fabric)

سونگ swang *m.* burning د سونگ مایع مواد liquid fuel

سونګټ sungә́ṭ **1** wrinkled سونګټ کول *compound verb* to wrinkle, pucker **2** numb with cold سونګټ کېدل *compound verb* **a** to wrinkle, pucker **b** to become numb from the cold

سونګټ sungә́ṭ *m.* weeping, crying

سونګټ sungә́ṭ *m.* kind of flat cake baked on a rock

سونګټ-مونګټ sungә́ṭ- mungә́ṭ ☞ سونګټ

سونګل sungә́l *m.* sobbing

سونګن sungә́n whining

سونګوټ sungúṭ ☞ سونګټ

سونګی sungáj *m.* **1** dwarf, pigmy **2** short and stout person

سونګی songáj, sungáj ☞ بونګی

سونګی sungáj *m.* **1** short-eared ram **2** earthenware dough trough, kneading trough

سونه swә́na *f.* ☞ سون

سونه soná *f.* wild duck, mallard

سونه soná *f.* horse fly

سون suṇ *m. plural* ☞ سونډ

سون suṇ *m.* **1** puffing, wheezing, snorting **2** blowing one's nose **3** pinch of snuff سون کول *compound verb* ☞ سونول و چاته سون نه وهل when one is intimidated by someone

سونګه suṇgá *f.* sobbing

سونول suṇawә́l *transitive* [*past:* و یې سوناوه] **1** to clear one's nose, blow one's nose **2** to sniff (e.g., snuff) **3** to suck in, drink in, absorb **4** to inhale, breathe in

سونهار suṇәhā́r *m.* puffing, wheezing, snorting

سونی suṇí **1** viscose, rayon سونی توکران viscose fabrics, rayons **2** سونډي ☞

سونی suṇә́j *f.* lying سونی ویشتل *compound verb* to throw dust in the eyes

سونېدل suṇedә́l *intransitive* [*past:* و سونېده] **1** to smell (of); reach (of an odor) **2** to be inhaled, be breathed in **3** to be sucked in, be drawn in, soak into, be absorbed

سوو sáwo *oblique plural of* سوه

سوو swu *Western past tense first person plural of* سول

سووان suwā́n ☞ سوان

سووخوز sowkhóz *m.* state-run farm

سوور swor *Eastern* ☞ سپور

سوونکی swúnkaj **1** *present participle of* سول **2** hot سوونکي بخارات hot steam

سوونه sawúna *m. plural of* سل

سووه sowá *f.* ☞ سوا

سوه swa hoof

سوه swә *m. plural* **1** burning **2** incinerating **3** loss of crops (from drought)

سوه sowá *f.* decoration; attire, apparel

سوه sáwa *m. plural short form of* سل دوه سوه two hundred درې سوه three hundred

سوه swa *past tense feminine of* سول

سوه swә *past tense masculine of* سول

سوه sә́wa *f. dialect* female hare, doe hare

سوهاګن sohāgә́n *f.* **1** favorite wife **2** young bride (during the nuptials)

سوهان sohā́n *m.* **1** file سوهان کول *compound verb* to file with a file; scrape **2** rasp **3** grater

سوهان کار sohānkā́r *m.* metal-worker, fitter, mechanic; locksmith

سوهان کاري sohānkārí *f.* metal-working; locksmithing

سوهانګی sohāngáj *m.* small file, file

سوهره suhára *f.* incoherent speech, gibberish, ravings

سوی swaj *m.* **1** burning **2** sizzling سوی کول *compound verb* to burn (intransitive) مخ مي سوی کوي My face is burning. **3** *figurative* ardor, zeal, fervor, diligence **4** *figurative* anxiety, alarm

سوی soj *m.* [*plural:* سویان] hare سوی غلی کول rabbit کورنی سوی to plan something in secret

سوی sә́waj **1** *past participle of* سول **2.1** aggrieved, disappointed **2.2** sad, sorrowful, grievous

سوی sә́waj *Western past participle of* سول

سوی swe *f. plural of* سو

سوی sowé *f. plural of* سوه

سوی swe *Western past tense second person singular and third person feminine plural of* سول

سوپت sowét سوپت sowéṭ **1** *m.* the Soviet Union **2** Soviet د سوپت حکومت the Soviet Government سوپت روس Soviet Russia

سوپتر sweṭár *m.* sweater

سوپزرلند swiṭzarlénd *m.* ☞ سویزرلند

سوپتسم sowetísm *m.* Soviet regime, Soviet power

سوپتي soweṭí Soviet

سویچ swich *m.* [*plural:* سویچونه swichúna *and Western* سویچان swichā́n] *technology* switch سویچ کېنبکنبل، سویچ کول، سویچ وهل *compound verb* to switch on (electric current)

سویچ بورد swichbórḍ *m. technology* switchboard

سویدن swídán *m.* Sweden

سویده sә́weda *in place of* سوی ده

سویدي sә́widi *in place of* سوی دي

سویئ دئ sә́wajdәj *in place of* سوی دئ

سویډن swiḍә́n *m.* سوئډن ☞ سویدن

سویډني swiḍaní, swiḍanáj **1** Swedish **2** *m.* Sweden

سویز suiz *m.* د سویز کانال the Suez Canal

سویزرلند suizarlénḍ *m.* سویس **1** *m.* Switzerland

سویس suis *m.* Switzerland

سویس suis *m.* سویز ☞

سوپشل sweshә́l *transitive* ☞ لوشل

سوغالی sojghā́laj *m.* ☞ سوی غالی

سویکه sojáka *f.* suslik, ground squirrel

سویل suwúl *m.* south

سوپلی suwelә́j *f.* ☞ سهپله

سویه sawijá *f. Arabic* **1** level د سویي اوچتول د ژوندانه raising the standard of living **2** equality

سويه ² sojá *f.* seedlings, shoots, sprouts (up to six weeks)

سويه ³ sója *f.* **1** doe hare **2** *Eastern* hare (in general) کورنی سويه **a** doe rabbit **b** rabbit

سه se *numeral* three

سهار sahár *m.* morning لوی سهار شين سهار end of the night سهار دي په خير!، سهار مو په خير towards morning سهار ته daybreak Good morning!

سهار سترگه sahārstérga *f.* morning star; Lucifer (i.e., Venus)

سهارگاه sahārgáh *m.* سهارمال sahārmál *m.* morning, morning time

سهارنۍ saharanáj morning; سهارنی ورځپاڼه، سهارنی جريده morning newspaper

سهام sihám *m. Arabic plural of* سهم ¹

سهامي sihāmí joint-stock (attributive) سهامي شرکت joint-stock company

سه برگه sebargá *f.* clover, red clover

سه تار setār *m.* setar (a three-stringed musical instrument)

سهروردي suharwardí, suhrawardí *m.* Sukhravardiya (the name of an Islamic sect)

سه شنبه seshambá *f.* Tuesday

سه فصله sefaslá yielding three harvests a year

سهل ¹ sahl *Arabic* easy, not difficult په خوړا ښه سهل دی really easy

سهل ² sahól, sehól **1** *transitive verb* [*past:* و يي ساهه] **1.1** to digest (food) **1.2** to endure, suffer **2** ☞ سهنه

سهل الهضم sahl-ul-házm *Arabic* easily digestible, easily assimilated سهل الهضم غذاگاني digestible, light food

سهل انگاري sahlangārí *f.* **1** light-heartedness, light-mindedness, frivolousness; carelessness **2** oversight, omission **3** relaxation, indulgence هيڅ تغافل او سهل انگاري نه کول to not give an easy time

سهلېدل sahledól *denominative, intransitive* [*past:* سهل شو] to be digested (of food)

سهم ¹ sahm *m. Arabic* [*plural:* اسهام ashám *and* سهام sihám] **1** share, part; participation په ... کښي سهم اخيستل to participate, take part, in **2** share (of stock) بي نامه سهم personal share سهم ordinary share

سهم ² sahm *m. Arabic botany* corymb, cyme

سهم ³ sahm *m.* terror, fear سهم کول *compound verb* to frighten, scare

سهمانه sahmāná *f.* ☞ سامانه

سهمدار sahmdár *m.* سهم لرونکی sahm larúnkay *m.* **1** shareholder, stockholder **2** partner د شرکت سهمدار shareholder of a company

سهم گر sahmgár inspiring fear, terror, frightening

سهمناک sahmnák dreadful, terrible; threatening, formidable

سهنه sahóna *f.* **1** digestion (of food) **2** patience, forbearance, endurance

سهو sahw *m. Arabic* **1** mistake; error; miss **2** clerical error, slip of the pen **3** slip of the tongue; error in counting, miscalculation

سهواً sáhwan *Arabic* by mistake, erroneously

سهولت suhulát *m. Arabic* **1** lightness **2** easing, relief **3** security, provision, support (e.g., of military operations) د حرکت سهولت security of movement (of troops)

سهوه sáhwa *f.* mistake په سهوه by mistake, erroneously سهوه کول *compound verb* to make a mistake, err په سهوه لوبدل to be mistaken بنده سهوه لري to err is human

سهه ¹ sáha *f.* ☞ سا

سهه ² sáha *f.* clothesline

سهه ³ sóha *f.* patience, endurance

سهي sahí ☞ صيح سهي کول *compound verb* **a** to look closely at, observe carefully **b** to notice, to spot, observe, remark

سهبدل sahedól *intransitive* [*past:* و سهبده] to suffer, endure, undergo په هيڅ صورت ممکنه نه وه چه و سهبري He is by no means eager to... بي له تا مي زړه نه سهبري I am miserable without you.

سهيل suhájl *m. Arabic* **1** *astronomy* Canopus (the star) **2** south; south-west سهيل وخوت Autumn has come.

سهېله suhéla *f.* سهېلي ¹ saheli, suhelí *f.* سهېلی suhelój *f.* **1** (female) friend; woman of the same age **2** servant girl, woman servant, maid **3** concubine

سهېلي ² suhelí south, southern

سهيم sahím *m. Arabic* **1** participant په يوه کار کښي ځان سهيم گڼل to consider oneself as participating in a cause **2** ☞ سهمدار

سهيمه sahimá *f. Arabic* share, part سهيمه ورکول to pay a share (e.g., to the family budget)

سئ ¹ sój *Western present tense second person plural of* سول ³

سي ² si *m. plural* **1** bran **2** fly eggs

سي ³ si *Western present tense of* سول ³

سي ⁴ se *Western present tense second person singular of* سول ³

سياه sjā *f.* ☞ سيا

سياځه sjádza *f.* ☞ شاځه

سياح sajjáh *m. Arabic* [*plural:* سياحان sayyāhán *and Arabic* سياحين sayyāhín] **1** traveler; wanderer **2** tourist **3** explorer

سياحت sijāhát *m. Arabic* **1** journey, voyage; trip, excursion **2** going around; detour **3** visit, visiting سياحت کول *compound verb* **a** to travel, take a trip, make an excursion **b** to go around; make a detour **c** to visit

سياحه sajjāha *f.* **1** (female) traveler **2** (female) tourist

سياحي sajjāhí *f.* ☞ سياحت

سيادت sijādát *m. Arabic* **1** supremacy, rule, sway; power, authority **2** sovereignty ملي سيادت sovereignty

سيار sajjár *Arabic* **1** wandering سيار ستوری planet **2** mobile, portable سياره شفاخانه، سيار روغتون field kitchen سياره اشپزخانه field hospital

سياره ¹ sjára *f.* **1** shortness of breath سياره يي ده He is short-winded. **2** asthma

سياره ² sajjārá *Arabic* **1** *feminine singular of* سيار **2** *f.* planet

سياست sijāsát *m. Arabic* **1** politics, policy; political line **2** conduct, behavior (of a person) **3** diplomacy **4** management **5** capital punishment, punishment په چا سياست کول to punish someone

سياست پوه sijāsatpóh *m.* سياستدان siyāsatdán politician, political figure

سياست مدار sijāsatmadár **1** *m.* experienced politician; statesman **2** experienced in political matters

سياست وال sijāsatwál *m.* politician

سياسي sijāsí *Arabic* **1.1** political سياسي اقتصاد political economy **1.2** diplomatic سياسي مناسبات diplomatic relations **2** *m.* [*plural:* سياسيون] siyāsiyún political figure, politician

سياسيات sijāsijāt *m. plural Arabic* **1** policy, politics; political issues **2** political science

سياسيون sijāsijún *m. plural Arabic of* سياسي²

سياق sijáq *m. Arabic* **1** order **2** way, method **3** kind, sort **4** style د عبارت سياق turn of speech **5** siak (a particular method of accounting)

سيال sjāl *m.* **1** man of equal status; man of one's own circle; equal **2** rival, competitor

سيالاني sjālāni *plural of* سياله¹

سيالتوب sjāltób *m.* rivalry, competition

سيالداري sjāldārí *f.* **1** unwillingness to lag behind others **2** exchange of gifts (between the relatives of the bride and grroom on the occasion of the wedding)

سياله¹ sjála *feminine of* سيال

سياله² sjála *f.* **1** respite, breather **2** halt سياله كول *compound verb* **a** to pause, take a breather **b** to make a halt

سياله³ sajjālá *f. Arabic* **1** electric current **2** flow, stream

سيالي sjālí *f.* **1** competition, contest **2** unwillingness or reluctance to lag behind others **3** rivalry, competition د چا سره سيالي كول to vie with someone, compete with someone د چا سره سيالي لرل to be the equal of someone; compete with someone

سيانتست sijāntíst *m.* **1** scientist, scholar **2** naturalist

سيانس sijāns *m.* **1** science **2** the exact sciences

سيانسي sijāncí *scientific* سيانسي پوهان scientists, scholars

سياه sijāh **1** black **2** unhappy, unlucky

سياه بخت sijāhbákht unfortunate, unlucky, unhappy, miserable

سياه پوښ sijāhpóḵ *m. history* kafir-siyaposh

سياه چشم sijāhcháshm *m.* hunting bird of the falcon family

سياه چوب sijāhchób *m. botony* cotoneaster

سياه خاك sijāhkhák *m. agriculture* loose smut (caused by the fungus *Ustilago tritici* and *Ustilago nigra*)

سياه دم sijāhdúm *m.* gray duck

سياه روز sijāhróz, sijāhrúz, سياه روزگار siyāhrozgár unlucky, unfortunate; ill-starred, ill-fated

سياه روزگاري sijāhrozgārí *f.* سياه روزي siyāhrozí misfortune; disastrous situation

سياه كوه sijāhkóh *m.* Siyakhkukh (the name of various mountain ridges)

سياه گرد sijāhgírd *m.* Siagird

سياه گوش sijāhgúsh *m.* karakal د سياه گوش پوست karakal hide

سياه لنگي وهلى، سياه لنگي نيولى sijāhlingí *f.* scurvy سياه لنگي with scurvy

سياهه sjāhá, sijāhá *f.* inventory شيان سياهه كول *compound verb* to register something سياهه كبدل *compound verb* to include something in the inventory

سياهي sijāhí *f.* **1** ink سره سياهي black ink **2** blackness

سجب sjab *m.* roof, shelter; refuge, haven

سيب seb *m.* [*plural:* سيبونه sebúna *and* سيبان sebán] apple

سبباستوپول sebāstópol *m.* Sevastopol

سبب زاده sebzādá *m. colloquial* ☞ صاحبزاده

سيبيريا sajbirjá *f.* Siberia

سيپاره sipārá *f. religion* each of the thirty chapters of the Quran

سيپى¹ sipáj *f.* spoon

سيپى² sepáj *f.* teaspoon

سيپى³ sipáj *f.* mother-of-pearl, nacre

سيپى⁴ sipáj *f.* selvage

سيت¹ sit *m. history* Scythian

سبت² set *m.* **1** set (e.g., of crayons) **2** suite (of furniture) **3** instrument, apparatus د راديو سبت radio receiver **4** set of equipment

سپت¹ siṭ *m.* place, seat

سپت² seṭ *m.* **1** money changer **2** (wholesale) merchant **3** banker

سپت³ seṭ *m.* ☞ سپت¹

سپته seṭh *m.* ☞ سپت²

سيجي sidzhí thorough-bred, pure-blooded

سبځل sedzál *transitive* [*past:* وى يې سبځه] to burn (down, up); to incinerate

سيحون sajhún *m. Arabic history* Sayhun; Syr Darya (river)

سيخ¹ sikh *m.* [*plural:* سيخونه sikhúna *and* سيخان sikhán] **1** ram rod, cleaning rod **2** spit (for roasting) **3** switch, twig سيخ وهل *compound verb* to seek, look for, search for

سيخ² sikh **1.1** upright, erect, standing; protruding, jutting out **1.2** stuffed, well packed, full, filled **2** straight, directly ورته سيخ كبدل to get down to business straightaway

سيخ پا sikhpá سيخپا reared سيخ پا كبدل *compound verb* to rear (of a horse)

سيخچه sikhchá *f.* **1** spit (for roasting) **2** *history* bayonet

سيخدم sikhdúm *m.* pintail duck

سيخك sikhák *m.* hairpin

سيخل sikhál *transitive* [*past:* وى يې سيخه] **1** to pierce; puncture; punch a hole in **2** to stuff; pack (with), fill (with) **3** to stuff into, cram into; shove into, push into

سيخلى sikhálaj **1** pierced, punctured **2** stuffed, crammed full, filled; larded

سيخول sikhawál *denominative, transitive* ☞ سيخل

سيخبدل sikhedál *denominative, intransitive* [*past:* سيخ سو] to be stuffed, be crammed full

سید sajíd *m. Arabic* [*plural:* سیدان sayidán *and Arabic* سادات sādát] **1** sayyid (a descendant of the Prophet Muhammad) **2** *proper noun* Sayyid

سیدال səjdál *m. proper noun* Saidal

سیدو sajdó *f.* Saido (the principal city of Swat)

سیده sidá straight, level سیده کول *compound verb* to (make) even, (make) level, straighten

سیر sajr *m. Arabic* **1** walk, stroll, taking a walk **2** motion, course; process; movement **3** detour د سیر خط route; orbit

سیر ser *m.* lot, fate

سیر ser, sir *m.* ser (a unit of weight equal to four charaks, regional – equal to two English pounds) د کابل سیر a Kabul ser (700 grams)

سیر ser, sir satisfied, sated, full (up)

سیراب seráb irrigated, watered; with abundant water حاصل خیزه او سیرآبه دره a fertile and well-watered valley سیرآب کول *compound verb* to fill with water; saturate, soak

سیرالیون sjéra-león *f.* Sierra Leone

سیرت sirát *m. Arabic* **1** way of life; conduct, behavior **2** biography

سیرځی serdzáj *m.* progressive person, leading worker, advanced worker

سیردریا sirdarjá *f.* Syr Darya (river)

سیرزی serzáj *m.* ☞ سپرځی

سیرلی serláj *m.* child taken away from its mother

سیرلی serláj *f.* ☞ سپری

سیرم serúm *m. plural medicine* serum

سیری seráj *f.* pious foundation, property set aside for religious purposes

سیربدل seredál *denominative, intransitive* [*past:* سیر شو] to eat one's fill, eat to satiety, be full, be sated

سیری seráj *f.* ☞ خپری

سیرځل sezál *transitive Eastern* ☞ سپخل

سیرزني sezní *f.* ☞ سوزني

سیرزی sezí *present tense of* سول

سیره sigá *f.* female mouflon

سیستان sistán *m.* Sistan د سیستان ډنډ، د سیستان جهیل Hamun Lake

سیستم sistém *m.* system استعماري سیستم colonial system

سیستماتیکي sistemātíkí systematic, regular

سیسمولوژي sesmoloží *f.* seismology

سیسه sisá *f metallurgy* lead

سیسی siséj *f.* desert hen, desert partridge

سیشن seshán *m. regional* session; sitting

سیطره sajtará *f. Arabic* supremacy, domination, hegemony

سیغان sajghán *m.* سیغان او کهمرد Saigan and Kamerd district

سیف sajf *m. Arabic* [*plural:* سیوف suyúf] **1** sword; saber **2** *proper noun* Saif

سیف sif *m. trade* sif د سیف پلورنه a sif transaction

سیف sef *m.* **1** safety catch (e.g., on a revolver) **2** safe

سیف الله sajfullá *m. Arabic* Saifulla

سیفو sajfó *m. proper noun hypocoristic form of* سیف

سیفون sifón *m.* siphon

سیک sek *m.* power, might سبک ختلی grown weak

سیکرتر sekrəṭár *m.* secretary

سیکره sajkará *f.* **1** percent(age); interest روپی سیکره اخیستل to lend money at interest **2** coarse fabric (in a piece up to 100 gyaz in length) **3** group; society

سیکل sekál *transitive* [*past:* ویي سیکه] **1** to heat (up), warm (up) **2** to fry, roast, grill **3** to make a poultice

سیکن sekán **1** *m.* revulsion, disgust, aversion, repugnance **2.1** satiated, surfeited, sated له ښه خوراکه هم سړی سیکن شي *proverb Eastern* one can be fed up with good food too **2.2** having an aversion to food **2.3** weak, feeble, infirm

سیکور sekəwár strong, powerful

سیکه siká *f. metallurgy* lead

سیگار sigár *m.* cigar

سیگرټ sigréṭ *m.* ☞ سګرټ

سیل sájl, sájəl *m. Arabic* **1** walk, stroll **2** sight, spectacle, show سیل کول *compound verb* **a** to go for a walk **b** to see, look over, examine, survey; be a spectator د ښار سیل کول to see the sights of a city

سیل sil *m.* seal (the animal)

سیل sel *m.* **1** flock سیل کول *compound verb* to fly in flocks, flock together **2** mud flow, turbulent mountain stream **3** freshet, flood **4** downpour, heavy rainstorm

سیلاب siláb *m.* syllable

سیلاب seláb *m.* ☞ سیل په یو د سیلاب غوندي راتلل to rush, gush سیلاب کښې مخ پورته لامبو وهل to go against the current

سیلابي selābí **1** irrigated by flooding (of the soil) سیلابي زمکه flood plain, bottom land, flood lands **2** *figurative* stormy, rough, tempestuous, impetuous, swift سیلابي حرکت impetuous movement

سیلان silán *m.* **1** Ceylon (Sri Lanka) ☞ سری لانکا **2** granite

سیلاني sajlāní, sajlānáj *m.* **1** spectator, viewer **2** traveler, wanderer **3** *proper noun* Sailani

سیلاني silāní Ceylonese (Sri Lankan)

سیلاو seláw *m.* ☞ سیل 2, 3

سیلاوه selāwá *f.* long knife (weapon)

سیلبین sajlbín *m.* سیل کوونکی sayl kawúnkay *m.* spectator, viewer; visitor (e.g., of an exposition)

سیلگری silagárəjl *m.* ☞ سیله گر

سیلو siló *f.* **1** (grain) elevator **2** bread factory, large commercial bakery (in Kabul) د سیلو ډوډۍ European-type bread

سیلون sejlón, selón *m.* Ceylon (Sri Lanka) ☞ سری لانکا

سیلوه sélwa *f.* ☞ سیله

سیله síla *f.* **1** devotion, adherence **2** support, backing, patronage **3** friendship, friendly feelings; goodwill, kindness سیله کول *compound verb* to regard someone with favor, have kind feelings towards someone; stand up for someone

سیله گر silagár *m.* سیلی **1** adherent, devotee; supporter, advocate **2** patron

سیلی ¹ siláj **1** adherent, devotee; supporter, advocate **2** patron

سیلی ² siláj *f.* **1** whirlwind; sand storm, dust storm **2** snow storm, blizzard

سیلی ³ siláj *f.* slap

سیلی ⁴ siláj *f.* cord, line of goat hair

سپلی ⁵ seláj *f.* rennet, starter for cheese

سیم sim *m.* [*plural:* سیمونه simúna *and Western* سیمان simán] **1** wire, conductor, cable پوښل سوئ سیم، عایق سوئ سیم insulated wire **2** wire اغزن سیم barbed wire اتصالی سیم *electronic* fuse **3** silver

سیما simá *f.* appearance, aspect; face, physiognomy حقیقي څهره او سیما true face

سیماب simáb *m. plural* mercury

سیمابی simābí mercury, mercuric

سیمال simál *m. proper noun* Simal

سیم جوش simdzhósh *m.* welding

سیمدار simdár wire, of wire

سیم دوزی simduzí *f.* gold thread, silver thread, purl (for embroidering)

سیمرغ simúrgh *m.* **1** bearded vulture, lammergeier **2** *folklore* simurg (fabled bird)

سیمسار ¹ simsár *m.* ☞ سمساره

سیمسار ² simsár *m.* tradesman who sells various small items

سیمک ¹ simák *m.* knitting needle; spoke (of a wheel)

سیمک ² simák *m. botony* rush

سیم گل simgíl *m.* plastering, plaster (made out of clay and cattail lint) سیم گل کول *compound verb* to plaster the walls

سیمنت simánt *m. plural,* سیمنت simánt *m. plural* cement

سیمه ¹ síma *f.* **1** territory, region, area توده سیمه hot region, subtropics میانه سیمه region of moderate climate **2** territory of a tribe or family اداري سیمي controlled regions (of tribes) **3** (compass) direction **4** shelter **5** zone

سیمه ² semá *f.* **1** ☞ سپیمه **2** ☞ اسپیمه

سیمه څار simatsár *m. military* garrison, post

سیمه وال simawál *m* countryman

سیمه یز simajíz regional, territorial سیمه یز تړون regional pact

سیمي simí **1** wire, سیمي تار metal string **2** made of wire

سیمیا ¹ simijá *f.* magic

سیمیا ² simijá *f.* سیمیان simiyán *m.* noodles, noodle soup سیما توت kind of mulberry tree

سمینار seminár *m.* seminar

سین ¹ sin *m.* ☞ سیند

سین ² sin *m.* the name of the letter س

سین ³ sen *m.* Seine د سین دریاب the Seine River

سپنتري senṭrí *m. regional* sentry, sentinel

سیند sind *m.* **1** river د کابل سیند Kabul River **2** sea د اوقیانوس سیند ocean تور سیند the Black Sea

سیندلاو sindláu *m.* ☞ سگلاوو

سیندمشر sindmáshər *m.* admiral

سیندنی sindanáj marine, maritime, nautical

سینکیا sinkjá *f.* arsenic sulfide ژړه سینکیا yellow arsenic

سینگار singár *m.* ☞ سنگار

سینگاربکس singārbáks *m.* dressing case

سینگاروالـه singārwála *f.* woman who dresses the bride

سینگارول singārawál *transitive* ☞ سنگارول

سینگال senegál *m.* Senegal

سینگاون singāwón *m.* rudder, helm (of a boat, a ship)

سینگته singóta *f.* black-cropped thrush

سینگری singaráj *m.* powder flask

سینگی singój *f.* small sheat fish

سینما sinimá, sinamá *f.* [*plural:* سینماگانی sinimāgáni *and* سینماوي sinimáwi] cinema, movies رنگداره او مجسمه سینما color stereo films سپاره سینما portable movie projector

سینماوالا sinimāwālá *m.* movie theater manager

سینمایي sinimājí cinematographic سینمایي پرده screen سینمایي نوار movie film

سینوال sinwál marine, living in the sea سینوال آس sea horse سینوال ستوری starfish

سینه siná *f.* **1** chest د سیني پرده *anatomy* diaphragm، د سیني پنجره، سینه پراخول chest, thorax سینی صندوق *compound verb* **a** to straighten one's chest **b** to accomplish a feat ما هغه سیني سره ولگاوه I pressed him to my chest. سینه په سینه **a** hand-to-hand **b** having hugged, embraced each other سینه وهل *compound verb* to beat one's chest, swear سینه یي راته ووهله He promised me to do that. پر سینه توري سانگي پخول to struggle to the death, the triumphful end د دښمن په مقابل کښي یي خپلي سیني سپر کړیدي They boldly advanced against the enemy. **2** bowels of the earth په سره سینه calmly سر You سینه وهم I am trying with all my might. د سیني زور دي ډپر دئ are a real worker. سینه په سینه را منتقل کېدل to be passed on from generation to generation

سینه باز sinabáz *m.* **1** mustle thrush, *Turdus viscuvorus* **2** embroidery with holes

سینه بغل sinabaghál *m.* pneumonia

سینه بند sinabánd *m.* **1** chest strap (of a harness) **2** corset **3** bodice **4** belt **5** brassiere, bra

سینه پهلو sinapahlú *m.* ☞ سینه بغل

سینه داغی sinadághaj sad, downcast, dispondent, distressed

سینه سوز sinasóz سینه سوخته sinasokhtá **1** exhausted, worn-out, extremely tired, fatigued **2** dispondent

سینه کباب sinakabáb being worn out with suffering, exhausted

سینی ¹ siní *f.* tray; dish

سینی ² siné *plural of* سینه

سینگال senegál *m.* Senegal

سبو ¹ sew *m.* moisture, dampness, humidity

سبو ² sew *m.* [*plural:* سبوان sewán] apple

سیوران siwrán *m.* **1** canopy **2** awning

سیورن sjorón **1** shady **2** dried in the shade

سیوری sjóraj, séwraj *m.* shade کښی سیوري په in the shade زما د سر

سیوری dear father (address in letters, *literally:* the canopy is over my head) سيورى لرل compound verb to cast a shadow سيورى كول to be shady, give shade

سيول[1] siwíl regional civil سيول نافرماني history civil disobedience (in India)

سيول[2] seúl m. Seoul

سيهي sihí f. colloquial ☞ سياهي

سييرالبون sijérā-león f. Sierra Leone

ش

ش[1] shin 1 the twenty-second letter of the Pashto alphabet 2 the number 300 in the abjad system

ش[2] abbreviation for شمسي

ش[3] 1 ش abbreviation شجاعت همراه 2 شجاعت مند abbreviation شجاعت همراه

شا[1] shā f. [plural: شاگاني shāgáni plural: شاوي shávi] 1 back زما په شا a behind my back b in my absence د.... شاته behind ... زمونه له شا after ... زمونه تر شا after us, behind us شا ته مو after me, behind me مارش! شا military Fall back! (as a command) د شا لوري باد fair wind, favorable wind 2 shoulder شا په شا shoulder to shoulder 3 wrong side, reverse side 4 rear د.... تر شا in the rear د.... تر شا كښنته a reinforcements b rear elements د شا قوت a reinforcements شا تينگول، شا تينگول ☞ شا اړول a to help somebody, support someone b to come to the rescue, be a reinforcement (e.g., in battle) د چا شا په مڼکه راوستل to throw someone (wrestling), overcome و چا ته شا كول to turn one's back on someone, show someone one's back دښمن ته شا كول to run away, retreat شا ورته اړول، شا گرزول ☞ شا ته اړول a to turn one's back; turn around شا گرز! military About face! (as a command) b figuratives to shirk work, loaf on the job شا لگول a to rest one's back (against) b figurative to find support شا شړل to repulse (e.g., enemy troops) ښوك په شا to withdraw, pull back په شا تلل to clap someone on the back (as a sign of approval) شا تپول to load onto the back په شا لويدل to hand back, lag behind حمله په to repel an attack تر شا كول، تر شا كښدل to disregard someone, scorn someone; not pay attention to something دا غم يي شاته و اچولو Eastern He forgot his grief. چا ته شا وركول to help someone, support someone; protect someone idiom د.... پر شا اوبه تربدل to worry, be disturbed

شا[2] shā m. ☞ شاه

شاب shāb m. edged weapon; dagger, double-edged blade

شاباز[1] shābáz m. شاهباز

شاباز[2] shābáz m. شاباس shābás m. small pigtail (worn on the brow by young women)

شاباشى shābāsáj ☞ شاباشى

شاباش[1] shābásh ☞ شاباشى

شاباشى shābāsháj 1 bravo, excellent 2 m. praise; approval چاته شاباشى وركول to praise someone; voice approval of چاته شاباشى ويل someone

شابوتى shābútaj شابوكى shābúkaj hunchbacked, bent, kyphotic

شابېل shābél m. tip, arrowhead

شاپ[1] shāp m. ☞ شاب

شاپ[2] shāp m. ☞ شاف

شاپ[3] shāp m. 1 shop (of a factory) 2 colloquial shop (retail), store

شاپو shāpó f. hat

شاپور shāpúr m. ☞ شاهپور

شاپيانگه shāpjánga f. withania, Withania coagulans (a plant of the solanaciae family which yields a leaven used as a substitute for rennet in cheese-making)

شاپيتى[1] shapiṭáj m. snail

شاپېتى[2] shāpéṭaj m. 1 load; burden 2 shell; cockleshell

شات shāt m. plural honey د دوى په شاتو bee idiom د شاتو مچمچي كبني زهر وي They are insincere.

شاتر shātír m. 1 groom 2 servant who runs alongside his master's horse

شاتماغه shātəmágha f. coquette, flirt

شاتنى shātaní 1 adjective rear, rear-echelon شاتنى خطوط rear-echelon communications 2 behind, located in the rear 3 remote (of a district)

شاتوت shātút m. ☞ شا هتوت

شاتورى[1] shātóraj saddleless, unsaddled (of a beast of burden, pack animal)

شاتورى[2] shātorəj f. plural calumny; fabrication شاتورى كول to calumniate; fabricate, invent

شاته shā́ta behind, from behind regional له شاته نه from behind, behind

شاتپول shāṭapavə́l m. plural praise, approval

شاتوغوب[1] shāṭughtób m. شاتوغوالى shāṭughválaj m. ☞ شاتوغى

شاتوغى[1] shaṭughí f. kyphosis (state of being hunchbacked)

شاتوغى[2] shaṭúghaj شاتيتى shāṭíṭaj شاتيغى shāṭíghaj hunchbacked, kyphotic

شاتينگه shaṭinga f. crop, craw (of birds)

شاتينگى[1] shaṭíngaj m. 1 protector, patron 2 assistant, helper

شاتينگي[2] shaṭingí f. 1 protection, defense, patronage 2 help, assistance

شاتينگي shaṭingi plural of شاتينگه

شادزه shā́dza f. 1 flagstone 2 stone slab

شاخ shākh m. 1 branch; bough 2 offshoot 3 spur (land) 4 department, section 5 railroad spur line, branch line 6 branch (of some central organization)

شاخسار shākhsár 1 branching 2 m. .1 branches 2.2 thicket; grove

شاخص shākhís m. Arabic 1 landmark; marker 2 criterion, index

شاخك shākhák m. feeler, antenna (in insects)

شاخل shākhál m. plural French lentil

شاخه shākhá f. 1 ☞ شاخ 1, 2 2 electric engineering plug 3 rod, bar

شاخه برى shākhaburí f. pruning (of trees) شاخه برى كول compound verb to prune (trees)

شاخپل shākhél *m.* ☞ شاهخپل

شاخپل shākhél *m.* best man

شاد shād 1 joyful, merry, gay 2 *m. proper name* Shad

شاداب shādā́b 1 watered, well-watered 2 fruitful شاداب دره fruitful valley 3 fresh, green

شادانه shādāná *f.* ☞ شاهدانه

شادباش shādbā́sh *m.* congratulation

شادو shado *f.* [*plural:* شادوگاني shādogā́ni *m. plural:* شادوگان shādogā́n] monkey, ape

شادوله shāḍulá *m.* freak, monster, deformed person

شادي shādí *f.* monkey, ape *idiom* د شادي زخم ترينه جوړ شوی This matter has dragged out too long.

شادي shādí *f.* ☞ ښادي

شادوله shāḍóla *f. abusive* 1 mug, ugly face 2 hobgoblin 3 *Eastern* ☞ شاندوله

شاډيندک shāḍindák *m.* swings

شاذ shāz *Arabic* 1 rare, little used (of a word) 2 unusual, extraordinary (of a man)

شاربل shārbál *transitive* [*past:* و یې شاربه *past:* و یې شاربه] 1 to stir, shake up 2 to churn (butter) 3 to hatch out (chicks) *idiom* اوبه شاربل to grind water in a mortar; be engaged in a senseless task

شاربونکی shārbúnkaj *m.* 1 churning (butter) 2 oil press

شارتي shārtí *f. electrical engineering* short circuit

شارتېدل shārtedál *denominative, intransitive* [*past:* شارتي شو] shārtedál *denominative, intransitive* [*past:* شارت شو] *electrical engineering* to short-circuit

شارژدافېر shārzhedāfér *m. diplomacy* chargé d'affaires

چاارژور chaārzhór *m. military* magazine case

شارک shārk *m.* shark

شارو shāró *f.* ☞ ښارو

شاري گر shārigór *m.* singer

شاړ shāṛ 1 lazy; maladroit; sluggish 2 crude, unkempt 3 stern, severe 4 uncultivated (of land)

شاړتوب shāṛtób *m.* شاړتیا shāṛtjā́ *f.* 1 maladroitness; sluggishness 2 rudeness, unkemptness 3 state of being uncultivated (land)

شاړشپاړ shāṛshpāṛ شاړ 1, 2 *m.* 1 lazybones 2.2 boor

شاړول shāṛavál *denominative* [*past:* شاړ يې کړ] 1 to render barren (of land) 2 to make sluggish

شاړه shāṛa *f.* low railing, wall (around the edge of a flat roof)

شاړه shāṛa *f.* 1 land unfit for cultivation 2 uncultivated land; virgin land شاړي مځکي waste land; virgin land شاړه مځکه ودانول to prepare virgin lands for cultivation شاړه مزروعي کول *compound verb* ☞ شاړول

شاړه shāṛə *imperfect of* شړل

شاړي shāṛi *m. plural* ☞ اشاړي

شاړي shāṛi *f. plural of* شاړه

شاړېدل shāṛedál *denominative, intransitive* [*past:* شاړ شو] 1 to grow neglected; be unfruitful (land) 2 to grow lazy; become sluggish

شاړي واړي shā́ṛi-vā́ṛi lazy; sluggish; slow-moving; malardoit, clumsy

شازه shāza *f.* 1 flagstone 2 stone slab د لحد شازه gravestone

شاستر shāstár *m.* the Shastra (the sacred scriptures of Hinduism)

شاسي shāsí *f.* landing gear

شاطر shātír *m.* 1 ☞ شاتر 2 *proper name* Shatir

شاعر shā'iŕ *m. Arabic* [*plural:* شاعران shā'irān *plural:* شعرا shu'arā] poet

شاعرانه shā'irāná poetic

شاعره sha'irá *f. Arabic* poetess

شاعري shā'irí *f.* poetry; poetic work, composition شاعري کول to write verse

شاغاسي shāghāsí *history* master of ceremonies

شاغاسيخپل shāghāsikhél *m. plural* ☞ شاغاسي خپل

شاغل shāghíl *Arabic* 1 attracting someone's attention; drawing someone into something 2 attentive

شاغوټی shāghuṭój *f.* short-toed lark

شاف شاپ shāf shāp *m. medicine* suppository; cotton-flannel bellyband (used to treat infants for colic)

شافع shāfi' *f. Arabic* defender; protector, patron

شافعي shāfi'í *m. Arabic* 1 Shafi'ite (a follower of the religious school of the Imam Shafi'i) 2 *adjective* Shafi'ite

شافه shāfá *f.* ☞ شاف

شاق shāḳ *Arabic* penal, pertaining to imprisonment at hard labor

شاقاسي shāḳāsí *m.* ☞ شاغاسي

شاقاسيخپل shāḳāsikhél *m. plural history* the Shakasikhejli (a clan of the Barakzai and the Muhamedzai who held the hereditary post of master-of-ceremonies)

شاکاسه shākāsá *f.* large bowl

شاکر shākír *m. Arabic* grateful د هغه شاکر اوسه! Be thankful to him!

شاکروپ shākṛúp ☞ شابوتي

شاکلنگه shākulánga *f.* crane (the bird)

شاکوپی shākúpaj ☞ شابوتي

شاکونډۍ shākunḍój wild pear tree, wild pear

شاگرد shāgírd *m.* 1 pupil, student 2 apprentice, journeyman 3 cadet

شاگرده shagírda *f.* pupil (girl)

شاگردي shāgirdí *f.* period of time spent as a student; apprenticeship شاگردي کول a to study; learn a trade b to work as an apprentice

شاگري shāgarí *f.* د زوم شاگري the glorification of the bridegroom at the wedding

شاگرد shāgíŕd *m. Eastern* ☞ شاگرد

شاگم shāgúm good omen, augury; good sign

شاگوړی shāgúṛaj *m.* part of a camel saddle

شاگۍ shāgój *f.* 1 low mountain 2 mountain foothills 3 foot of a mountain 4 tomb

شاگۍ shāgój *f.* assistance, support د چا شاگۍ کېدل to help someone, support someone

شال shāl *m.* kerchief, shawl کشمیري شال *m.* شال پر سر اچول to cover oneself with a shawl, throw on a shawl

شالباف shālbā́f *m.* shawl weaver

شالشوی shālshój *m.* one who launders shawls

شالکی shālakáj *m.* small shawl, kerchief

شالی shālə́j *f.* شالي shālí *f. plural* rice crop, raw rice, unthreshed rice

شالیزار shālizár *m.* شالی زاره shālə́jzāra *f.* ☞ شولگره

شالیکنه shālikə́na *f.* endorsement سپینه شالیکنه blanket endorsement

شالیکونکی shālikúnkaj *m.* endorser

شامپین shāmpén *m. plural* champagne

شامپیون shāmpijón *m.* champion, victor

شامت shāmát *m. Arabic* 1 failure; unhappiness 2 victim of failure; disheartened person

شامتوره shāmatóra *f.* شامتوله shāmatóla *f.* black starling, common starling

شامته shāmatá *f. Arabic* noise, fuss شامته لرونکي گری alarm clock

شامخه shāmə́kha *f.* lining

شامدام shāmudā́m eternally, always

شامکی shāmakə́j *f.* swan

شامل shāmíl *Arabic* 1.1 participating; composed of په یو کار کي شامل گرزول to involve in some matter 1.2 consisting of; composed of و یو شي ته شامل بلل to reckon among, comprehend 1.3 general, universal, comprehensive 2 *m. [plural:* شاملان shāmilā́n *Arabic plural:* شاملین shāmilín] .1 participant 2.2 *proper name* Shamil

شاملات shāmilā́t *m. Arabic plural* communal pastureland, forests, wastelands

شاملول shāmilavə́l *denominative, transitive [past:* شامل یي کي] 1 to contain, comprise 2 to include ځان شاملول to enroll (in school) 3 to enter (on a list)

شاملبدل shāmiledə́l shāmledə́l *denominative, intransitive [past:* شامل شو] 1 to include (in), be contained (by) 2 to participate in something, be a composite part of something د چا په ډله کي شاملبدل to affiliate with someone 3 to be entered, be registered, enroll somewhere

شاملبدونکی shāmiledúnkaj *m.* participant

شاملبده shāmledə́ *m.* shāmiledə́ *plural* 1 inclusion (in an agenda) 2 participation 3 enrollment 4 entry (e.g., on a list)

شامه ¹ shāmmá *f.* 1 smell (sense) د شامي حس sense of smell 2 scent

شامه ² shāmə́ *m. plural of* شوم ¹

شامتوره shāmatóra *f.* ☞ شامه توره

شامی ¹ shāmí *Arabic* 1 Syrian 2 *m.* Syrian (person)

شامی ² shāmə́j *f.* 1 grave 2 tomb 3 cemetery in the mountains

شامیانه shāmijāná *f.* large marquee, large tent (with flat top)

شان ¹ shān *m.* 1 way, manner; type, kind په هیڅ شان under no circumstances د...په شان differently, otherwise په بل شان، بل شان similar (to), like په څه شان ؟ In what way? How? په دي شان In this way, thus په هر شان سره in any way, by any means هغه شان thus دا شان a such a b thus, therefore په ډېر ښه شان سره a very well, carefully b happily,

successfully او که دغه شان ونشي in the opposite case, otherwise 2 a joyous song

شان ² shā'n *m. [plural:* شئون shu'ún *Arabic plural:* شئونات shu'unā́t] prestige, merit, position شان خرابول to undermine prestige

شان ³ shān *m. combining form* like, similar, -ish (as the the second element of compounds) تورشان blackish

شانان shānā́n *m. proper name* Shanan

شانته shā́nta شانتی shā́nte *dialect* 1 like, similar to, such as یو شانته identical; monotonous تیټ شانته rather low, rather short 2 similar; approximate, like همدغه شانته a just the same b precisely the same یو شانته monotonously خبره اوږده شانته شوه The matter has dragged on a bit.

شانټی shanṭə́j *f.* fascine, faggot; millpond

شاندار shāndár 1 magnificent, festive; grandiloquent شانداره منظره majestic sight, majestic panorama, picture 2 outstanding (of success)

شاندوله shandóla *f.* leapfrog

شاندوی shandə́j *f.* ☞ شانتی

شانس shāns *m.* luck; success, good fortune

شانگوری shāngúraj 1 protuberant 2 ☞ شابوتی

شانگه shā́nga *f.* شانگی shāngə́j *f.* pitchforks (wooden, for winnowing grain)

شان مان shānmā́n disturbed, distressed

شانه ¹ shāná *f.* 1 comb 2 *textiles* reed (of loom)

شانه ² shāná *imperfect of* شنل

شانه وانه shāná-vrāná شانه وانه تلل shāná-vrāná to act as proud as a peacock

شانی ¹ shā́ni ☞ شانته

شانی ² shānáj *m. botany* eelgrass, tape grass, valiseria

شاوخوا shāukhvā́ *f.* 1.1 د شاوخوا neighboring شاوخوا ته کتل to look around 1.2 ambience, environment په دغه شاوخوا کښي in this region 2 د کابل شاوخوا ته in Kabul district د... په شاوخوا کښي a around, about something b about something, in relation to something 3 around, round about 4 *attributive* surrounding شاوخوا کلي neighboring شاوخوا کسان surroundings, milieu neighboring settlements

شاور shāvə́r *m.* shower

شاوری shāvə́raj *m.* ☞ نیزوری

شاول shāvúl *m.* shāvə́l *technology* plumb; plumb bob د اوبو شاول sounding lead

شاولي واولي shā́vli-vā́vli 1.1 careless; unstable 1.2 unwise 1.3 disoriented, surprised 1.4 slovenly 2 *m.* negligent fellow, slob

شاه shāh *m.* 1.1 shah, king; prince 1.2 title of the Sayyids (descendants of Mohammed) 1.3 bridegroom on his wedding day; prince, newlywed 1.4 *proper name* Shakh شاه مردان، شاه میران *proper name* Ali (the brother-in-law of Mohammed) 2 *combining form* شاه ځلمی good lad

شاهانه shāhāná royal ذات شاهانه His Highness, the King دربار شاهانه the Royal Court

شاهباز shāhbáz *m.* [*plural:* شاهبازونه shāhbāzúna] **1** mediator **2** [*plural:* شاهبازان shāhbázắn] **a** large light-colored hawk **b** falcon, raptorial bird

شاهباشی shāhbā́sh ☞ شاه باش 1

شاهباشي shāhbāshí *f.* ☞ شاباشي

شاهببنه shāhbəbắna *f. proper name* Shahbibi

شاهپر shāhpár *m.* flight or primary lift part of a bird's wing

شاهپور shāhpúr *m. proper name* Shakhpur

شاهتره shāhtará *botany* fumitory, fumaria

شاهتوت shāhtút شاه توت [*plural:* شاهتوتان shāhtutắn] black mulberry (tree)

شاهتير shāhtír *m.* [*plural:* شاهتيران shatirắn] *technology* beam, rafter

شاهخبل shāhkhél *m. regional* trashman, sweeper; janitor

شاهد shāhíd *m.* [*plural:* اشهاد ashhád] *Arabic* **1** witness شاهد تپرول to produce a witness په چا شاهد تپربدل to produce a witness against someone **2** [*plural:* شواهد shavāhíd] testimony

شاهدانه shāhdāná *f.* hemp

شاهدخت shāhdúkht ☞ شاهزادگی

شاهدوستي shāhdostí *f.* monarchism

شاهده shāhidá *f. poetry* **1** sweetheart, girlfriend **2** witness (female)

شاهدي sháhidí *f.* testimony, evidence of a witness شاهدي کول شاهدي **a** to bear witness, give a deposition **b** to testify شاهدي وبل، ورکول، د یوشي پوره شاهدي ورکول to fully confirm something

شاهراه shāhrā́h *m.* large wide road, highway

شاهرگ shāhrág *m. anatomy* jugular vein

شاهزادگی shāhzādagə́j *f.* princess; royal princess

شاهزاده shāhzādá *m.* prince; royal prince

شاهزادگی shāhzādə́j *f.* ☞ شاهزادی شاه زادی

شاهزوی shāhzój *m.* ☞ شاهزاده

شاهکار shāhkắr *m.* **1** masterpiece **2** feat, accomplishment

شاهکاري shāhkārí *f.* **1** prowess **2** talent, gifts

شاهگري shāhgarí *f.* ☞ شاگري

شاه گل shāhgúl *m. proper name* Shahgul

شاه مسته shāhmásta sprightly, frisky (of a girl)

شاه مبرمنه shāhmermóna *f.* empress; queen

شاهنامه shāhnāmá *f.* Shakname (a work by Firdousi)

شاهنشاه shāhanshā́h *m.* the Shah-an-Shah, the King of Kings (title of the ruler of Iran)

شاهنشاهي shāhanshāhí **1** *indeclinable* pertaining to the Shah-an-Shah, Royal (used for the former government of Iran) **2** *f.* monarchy, the royal house

شاهي shāhí¹ **1.1** royal شاهي دولت kingdom **1.2** monarchial **2** *m.* bodyguard, royal bodyguard

شاهي shāhí² *f.* **1** realm, reign; autocracy **2** shai (a coin equal to 1/6 kran or 5 puls) **3** shai (a kind of silk cloth) **4** *proper name* Shakhi

شاهي خبل shāhikhél *m. regional* ☞ شاهخبل

شاهين shāhín *m.* **1** red-headed sapsan (raptorial bird); the shahin falcon **2** *proper name* Shahin

شاهي ولات shahivalát یا شاهي ولات! Try with all your strength!

شایان shāján fitting, appropriate دا شایان وي as befits one

شاید shājád probably, possibly, maybe

شائع shājí شايع 'shāí *Arabic* **1** published شايع کول to publish لکه چه شایعه شوبده. as they write to be published **2** ordinary, popular

شائعه shāi'á *f. Arabic* [*plural:* شائعات shāi'át] شایعه shāji'á *f.* rumor, talk

شایع shājiá *f. singular of* شايع²

شائق shāík *Arabic* شايق shājík **1** desirous **2** *m.* [*plural:* شائقين shāikin *plural:* شایقین shājiḳin] **.1** enthusiast (of something) **2.1** client

شائي shājí ☞ شاهي²

شب shab *m.* night, evening

شباب shabáb *m. Arabic* youth

شبابي shabābí youthful; pertaining to youth

شبانه روز shabānarúz *m.* 24-hour period د یوه شبانه روز په موده کښي for 24 hours, in the course of a 24-hour period

شباهت shabāhát *m. Arabic* likeness, similarity د ... سره شباهت لرل to be like, be similar to

شببو shabbú *m. botany* **1** cruciferae (a kind of wild mustard) **2** tuberose, *Polianthes tuberosa*

شببينک shabbinák *m.* nightjar, goatsucker (the bird)

شبتل shabtál *m.* شبتله shabtála *f.* Persian pear

شب چراغ shabchirā́gh *m.* **1** carbuncle **2** firefly, glowworm

شبح shábah *f.* شبح shábh [*plural:* اشباح ashbā́h] شبحه shábha *f.* **1** outline; silhouette; contour **2** deduction

شبخون shabkhún *m.* nocturnal attack

شبخيز shabkhéz *m.* one praying at night

شبر shibár *m.* د شبر کوتل the Shibar Pass

شبرغان shibirghán shibirghan *history* district د شبرغان اعلی حکومت

شبری shabaráj one afflicted with nyctalopia (i.e., night blindness)

شبقدر shabḳadár¹ *m.* Shabkadar (city, near Peshawar)

شب قدر sháb-i-ḳadar² *m.* ☞ شوقدر

شبکوري shabkorí *f. medicine* nyctalopia (i.e., night blindness)

شبکه shabaká *f. Arabic* **1** lattice **2** veil; netting **3** net, network (telephone, road, etc.)

شبکه کاري shabakkārí *f.* woodcarving (action)

شبکیه shabakijá *f. Arabic anatomy* retina

شبگير shabgír ☞ شبخون

شب نشيني shabnishiní evening, evening party د شب نشینی جامې evening clothes; evening dress

شبنم shabnám *m. plural poetry* dew

شبو shabó *f.* **1** ☞ شببو **2** *proper name* Shabbo

شبه shabá¹ *f.* jet; agate (the mineral)

شبه shibh² *m.* shabáh *Arabic* ☞ شباهت

شبه جزيره shibhdzhazirá *f. Arabic* peninsula

شبهه shubhá *f. Arabic* doubt, suspicion

شبهه ناک shubhanák dubious suspicious

شبى shbəj *f.* flat cake

شبين shabín *m.* nighttime شبين سحار سو It became light.

شبيه shabíh *Arabic* similar, analogous; comparable ديو شي سره like something, similar to something شبيه، ويوشي ته شبيه

شپ shap *m.* shelter, roof

شپ shap *tautological with* گپ

شپ shəp *m.* pit, abyss

شپارس shpáṛas *numeral* sixteen

شپارس پولى shpáṛaspuláj *m.* coin worth sixteen pul

شپارسم shpáṛasóm *m. ordinal numeral* sixteenth

شپاله shpālə́ *oblique of* شپول

شپانه shpānə́ *plural of* شپون

شپانه غود shpānəghód *m.* ☞ شپنغود

شپړه shpəṛá *f.* shoemaker's knife

شپړ shpəṛ six-fingered

شپږ shpag shpəg *numeral Western* six دېرش شپږ thirty-six

شپږتر shpagtáṛ *m.* board upon which nard is played

شپږخنډى shpagtsənḍíz شپږ خنډيز shpagtsanḍíz **1.1** hexagonal **1.2** hexahedral **2.1** hexagon **2.2** hexahedral

شپږ ډزى shpagḍázaj six-chambered (weapon)

شپږ کروهي shpagkuruhí *f.* vicinity, surrounding country; suburbs د بنار په شپږ کروهي کښي in the suburbs

شپږ گون shpaggún all six, (a group of) six

شپږم shpagə́m *m. ordinal numeral* sixth

شپږمياشتنى shpagmjāshtanáj semiannual; half-yearly

شپږن shpəgə́n shpugə́n lousy, louse-ridden

شپږه shə́ga *f.* louse

شپږى shpəgə́j *f.* plant louse (on wheat)

شپږيکه shpagjaká *f.* one-sixth part of something

شپشتى shpishtáj *m.* hub (of a wheel)

شپگ shpag *numeral Eastern* ☞ شپږ

شپنغود shpanghód *m. botany* lapwing, pewit, green plover, *Vanellus vanellus*

شپنکى shpankáj *m.* herd boy, shepherd

شپنه shpaná *f.* shepherdess

شپنى shpaní *f.* herding شپني کول to herd, herd sheep

شپنى shpanáj *adjective* **1** night, nocturnal **2** evening

شپنى shpané *plural of* شپنه

شپنيان shpanijā́n *plural of* شپه

شپو shapó *f.* hat

شپوږى shpugə́j *f.* ☞ شپږى

شپول shpol *m.* **1** fence شپول تړل to fence in **2** pen (for sheep) **3** aureole (of the moon)

شپون shpun *m.* [*plural:* شپانه shpānə́] shepherd, herdsman

شپونتوب shpuntób *m.* **1** shepherding **2** cattle raising

شپه shpə *m.* [*plural:* شپنيان shpanijā́n] shepherd خوک شپه کول to recruit someone as a shepherd شپه نيول to hire a shepherd

شپه shpa *f.* night تکه توره شپه It's night. It is as dark as pitch. د شپې all night, the whole night through شپه، درسته شپه، کړى شپه د شپې خ، د شپې کوټه، د شپې او د روځي at night د شپې دوړى night's lodging bedroom د شپې د تېرولو ځای supper شپې a on that same b every night c at night, nightly once at night د شپو نه يوه شپه وه چه toward night ته، شپى لره، شپى له the night password شپه پر سر اخيستل د شپې نوم to not sleep the whole night, be wakeful شپه کول to spend the night *idiom* شپې ته روغ ويل to be unable to analyze something; mix up day and night; call black-white *idiom* د عمر شپې تېرول to manage to survive somehow; scarcely make ends meet *idiom* د عمر شپې شمېرل to live out one's allotted span *idiom* توره شپه کېدل to be high (of prices)

شپه تېرى shpatéraj *m.* overnight guest, guest who will stay the night

شپه روڼى shparúṇaj wakeful, alert

شپه روندى shparundí *f.* nyctalopia, night blindness

شپه و ورځ shpavrádz shpa-u-vrádz day and night, 24-hour period شپه ورځ پر ځان يوه کول to live شپې ورځي تېرول to work both day and night

شپيان shupiján *m.* charge, indictment

شپيتم shpetə́m *m. ordinal* sixtieth

شپيته shpetə́ *numeral* sixty

شپيته shpéta *f.* شپيتى shpetáj *m.* شپيتى shpetə́j *f. technology* wedge

شپيځى shpédzaj *m.* lodging for the night

شپيركى shpperkáj *m.* ☞ شپيلكى

شپيړنه shpeṛə́na sloven, slattern

شپيزر shpezár *m.* the end of the night

شپيشترى shpeshtaráj *m.* **1** ☞ شپيته **2** ☞ شپيشتى

شپيشته shpéshta *f.* **1** lucerne (grass) **2** ☞ شپيته

شپيشتى shpíshti *f.* shpíshti *plural* lucerne (grass) *idiom* د خوک شپيشتو پر بناخ خبرول a to take someone in b to incite one person against another

شپيشتى shpéshtaj *m.* blade (propellor, fan, etc.), cog (of a wheel)

شپيلغى shpelagháj ☞ شبرى

شپيلک shpelák *m.* [*plural:* شپيلکونه shpelakúna *Western plural:* شپيلکان shpelakā́n] **1** whistling, whistle شپيلک کول، شپيلک وهل to whistle **2** a whistle

شپيلکى shpelkáj *m.* whistling, whistle شپيلکى کول a to whistle b to sing (of a thrush)

شپيلل shpelə́l *transitive* [*past:* و يې شپيلل] to whistle

شپيلل shpelə́l *transitive* [*past:* شپيلول و يې شپيله shpelavə́l *transitive past:* و يې شپيلاوه] to gnaw; gnaw around; suck around

شپيلى shpeláj *m.* **1** whistling, whistle **2** whistle, siren (of a factory, train) **3** whistle, hum (of the wind)

شپيلى shpeláj *m.* good-for-nothing, cad

شپيلى shpeláj *f.* **1** reed-pipes; fife; flute شپيلى وهل to play the reed-pipes **2** *anatomy* aural opening د غوږ شپيلى aural opening **3** whistling, whistle **4** whistle, whistle (of a factory, train) **5** barrel (of a rifle) *idiom* د لاس شپيلى bone of the forearm او ستوان نغرل

شپیلی وهل دواره نه کیږي *proverb* You can't eat cornmeal and play the flute too.

شپیلی مار shpeləjmā́r *m.* flautist

شپینی shpenáj night, nocturnal شپینی خبره yesterday's conversation

شت [1] shat *m.* die (in children's games) شت وهل، شت ویشتل to draw lots

شت [2] shət speeding along, rolling along

شتا shatā́ ☞ شتاه

شتاب shitā́b *m.* haste; speed

شتابي shitābí *f.* hastiness, haste په شتابی سره hurriedly, urgently شتابي کول to hurry, hasten

شتاتوب shatātób *m.* ☞ شتائي

شتام shtām *m. regional* blank form with seal شتام کاغذ stamped paper

شتاوالی shatāvā́laj *m.* ☞ شتائي

شتاه shatā́h **1** mendacious **2** evil, perfidious **3** garrulous **4** shameless

شتاهه shattā́ha *f.* شتایه shatājá *f.* **1** prostitute **2** impudent woman

شتائي shatā́ī *f.* **1** evil, wickedness **2** shamelessness **3** peevishness **4** obstinacy

شترک shuturák *m.* bittern (the bird)

شترکه shuturáka *f.* شترکي shuturáki *usually plural* **1** jet of water **2** waterfall, cataract شترکه وهل **a** to squirt; gush **b** to spurt **c** to cascade (of a waterfall)

شترمار shuturmā́r *m.* grass snake

شترمرغ shuturmúrgh *m.* **1** stork **2** vulture, buzzard

شترنگ shtiríng *m.* **1** steering gear, rudder apparatus **2** sluice gate

شتري shuturí **1** light brown, beige **2** *f.* camlet (cloth)

شتمن shtəmán ☞ شته من

شتمني shtəmaní *f.* ☞ شته من

شتو shto *oblique of* شته [1]

شتوالی shtəvā́laj *m.* ☞ شته والی

شتومی shtúmaj *m.* pestle

شته [1] shtə *m. plural* **1** existence, being شته کیدل to exist **2** property جنسي شته material goods, property د شته دفتر inventory books شته کول to create, bring about پر شته یې درلودل He was very rich.

شته [2] shta there is; there are; it is, he is احمد شته؟ Is Ahmed here? شته دئ there is, it/he is په دي کور کښ څوک شته که نه؟ Is anybody home?

شته [3] shatá *f.* dill

شته من shtəmán **1** rich **2** *m.* a wealthy man

شته من توب shtəmantób *m.* wealth

شته من مند shtəmánd ☞ شته من

شته مني shtəmaní *f.* wealth

شته والی shtəvā́laj *m.* existence, being د شته والی جنگ the struggle for existence

شتی [1] shatój *f.* **1** knee **2** point (arrow, lance)

شتی [2] shatój *f.* shtój **1** green mold (on walls, etc.) **2** Chlorella (a seaweed) **3** corncob (without kernels)

شتی [3] shatój *f. from* شتا

شتی [2] shte *dialect* ☞ شته

شتمبی shtemój *f.* stone mortar

شتل shaṭál *m.* ☞ شډل

شتلکي shaṭaláki *f. plural* شتلکي کول to writhe, quiver

شتلوالی shaṭalvā́laj *m.* ☞ شډلتوب

شتوپ shṭop *m.* stove, cooker

شته shaṭá corncob

شتیدل shṭedól *intransitive* [*past:* و شتیده] to writhe, shake

شجاع shudzhā́' *Arabic* **1** brave, valorous, manly **2** *m. proper name* Shuja

شجاعت shudzhā'át *m. Arabic* bravery, valor, manliness شجاعت کول to display valor, demonstrate manliness

شجاعتمن shudzhā'atmán ☞ شجاعتمن سړی brave man, hero

شجاعت مند shudzhā'atmánd title given to a major

شجاعتمندانه shudzha'atmandānā́ ☞ شجاع [1]

شجاعت همراه shudzhā'athamrā́h shudzhā'athanarā́ title for a general

شجره shadzhará *f. Arabic* **1** geneology, family tree **2** list of saints

شجیع shadzhí' *Arabic* ☞ شجاع [1]

شتسړلی shtsəṛóláj *m.* chisel

شحم shahm *m. Arabic* fat, internal fat

شحمي shahmí *Arabic* fat, greasy شحمي مواد fats

شخ shakh **1** firm, hard, rigid **2** tight **3** rooted, frozen in place

شخیدل shakhedəl *compound verb* ☞ شخ کیدل شخ کول *compound verb*

شخر shkhaṛ *m.* large flock of birds

شخره shkhóṛa *f.* **1** dispute; conflict; litigation پدې کښې شخره او بحث نشته This is indisputable. **2** battle; clash **3** band, gang

شخص shakhs *m. Arabic* [*plural:* اشخاص ashkhā́s] person, persona, personality فني اشخاص technical specialists *idiom* لمړی شخص *grammar* first person

شخصاً shákhsán *Arabic* personally دی شخصاً مسئول دئ He will bear personal responsibility.

شخصپرستي shakhsparastí *f.* ☞ شخصیت پرستي

شخصیت shakhsijā́t *m. Arabic* [*plural:* شخصیتونه shakhsijatúna *Arabic plural:* شخصیات shakhsijā́t] personality, person خصوصي شخصیت private person حقوقي شخصیت juridical person د شخصیت او پیژندگلوی سند to be a juridical person شخصیت لرل personal identification document

شخصیت پرستي shakhsijatparastí *f.* cult of personality

شخکی shakhkój *f.* small pimple

شخلی [1] shakhláj *m.* hitching post (for cattle)

شخلی [2] shakhuláj *m.* ☞ شخولی

شخند shakhand *m.* ☞ شخوند [1]

شخنه shakhóṇa *f. anatomy* joint

شخوده shukhudá scratched

شخول [1] shkhval *m.* **1** voice (of a bird) **2** rumble; noise; din **3** rustling (of leaves) **4** gurgling (of a brook)

شخول ² shkhvə́l *m.* discomposure, depression

شخول ³ shakhavə́l *denominative, transitive* [*past:* شخ یې کړ] to stretch, draw tight, draw taut, strain

شخولی shkhvə́laj *m.* 1 quiver 2 knapsack, pouch 3 game bag

شخوند shkhvand *m.* chewing, rumination; cud شخوند کول، شخوند a to chew the cud b to masticate (food) وهل

شخوندوهونکی shkhvand vahúnkaj *adjective* ruminant, cud-chewing شخوندوهونکی حیوانات ruminant animal vahunki

شخبدل shakhedə́l *denominative, intransitive* [*past:* شخ شو] 1 to stretch, draw tight 2 to be frozen in place, be rooted to the spot

شخبده shakhedə́ *m. plural* 1 stretching tight, drawing tight 2 torpor, numbness; inability to move (from fear, surprise, etc.)

شد ¹ shud *m.* possibility شد لري چه … It is possible that …

شد ² shad shadd *Arabic* ☞ شدید

شداوه shadāvá *f.* شلاوه shalāvá *f.* kind of water plant

شدائد shadāíd *m. Arabic plural of* شدیده

شدت shiddát *m. Arabic* 1 strength, intensity, intenseness په شدت سره strongly, energetically شدت کول a to intensify, strenghten b to grow more severe, grow colder ژمی شدت کوي Winter is growing severe. جنگ په شدت سره جاري دئ A bitter battle is going on. 2 violence 3 difficulty

شدرو shadráv *m.* noisy dispute (of women)

شدني shudaní possible; attainable

شدویی shudopə́j *f.* ☞ شین توپکه

شدی shidé *f. plural* ☞ شیدی

شدیاره shudjā́ra *f.* plowed field شدیاره مکه plowed field شدیاره کول to plow land

شدید shadíd *Arabic* 1 strong; large شدید تاوان great losses 2 energetic 3 angry, cruel, ferocious 4 tense شدید مرض serious illness

شدیده shadidá *Arabic* 1 *feminine singular of* شدید 2 *f.* [*plural:* شدیدي shadidé] *m. Arabic* [*plural:* شدائد shadāíd] difficulty, problem

شدل shaḍál 1 *m.* [*plural:* شډل shaḍə́l *plural:* شډلان shaḍalā́n] *literal & figurative* 1.1 barren flower شډل کېدل *compound verb* ☞ 1.2 clumsy person; bumpkin; lazy man, apathetic man 2.1 sluggish; lazy; apathetic; slow-moving 2.2 stout, portly, awkward 2.3 unbleached, coarse (of cloth) 2.4 bad, rough (of a road)

شډلتوب shaḍaltób *m.* شډلوالی shaḍalvā́laj *m.* 1 barrenness 2 uncouthness, crudity 3 sluggishness, slow-movingness 4 awkwardness

شډله shadala 1 *feminine singular of* شډل ² 2 unbleached cloth, coarse cloth

شډلېدل shaḍaledə́l *denominative, intransitive* [*past:* شډل شو] to not bear fruit, be barren; be a barren flower

شذوذ shuzúz *m. Arabic* eccentricity

شر ¹ sharr *m. Arabic* 1 malice; spite 2 misfortune, calamity, disaster, evil شر او شور noise, disorder نه شر شته نه شور Complete silence reigns. 3 harm, damage 4 baseness, meaness

شر ² shur *m.* shər shir 1 splash (of water); the noise of rain 2 rustling, rustle

شراب sharā́b *m. Arabic singular & plural* [*plural:* اشربه ashribá] 1 wine 2 spiritous drinks

شراب خانه sharābkhāná *f.* lowly tavern; beer hall

شراب خور sharābkhór *m.* 1 one who loves to drink to excess 2 drunkard

شراب خوری sharābkhorí *f.* 1 drinking to excess; use of spiritous drink 2 drunkenness

شرابي sharābí 1 *m.* drunkard 2 drunk

شرارات sharārát *m. Arabic* 1 villainy 2 lawlessness 3 baseness, vileness

شرافت sharāfát *m. Arabic* 1 nobility 2 honor, merit, virtue 3 respect, glory; esteem

شرافتمآب sharāfatmā́b *Arabic* venerable one (form of address for an ecclesiastic)

شراکت sharākát *m. Arabic* ☞ شرکت

شراکت نامه sharākathāmá *f.* agreement of fellowship or comradeship, agreement or contract of shareholders

شرانداز sharrāndā́z *m.* troublemaker

شرائط sharāít *m. Arabic plural of* شرط

شرائین sharāíjn *m. Arabic plural of* شریان

شربت sharbát *m. Arabic* syrup; sherbet د انار شربت pomegranate syrup

شربت باب sharbatbā́b *m. plural* beverages, drinks

شربل sharbə́l *transitive* [*present:* شاربي *past:* شربل وبی *past:* شاربه ویی] 1 to chop (meat) finely, mince 2 to hatch (chicks)

شربنه sharbə́na *f.* 1 chopping finely (meat) 2 hatching (chicks)

شربول sharbavə́l *transitive* [*past:* شرباوه ویی او] 1 to chop (meat) finely, mince 2 to rock back and forth, oscillate 3 to turn over, stir up

شرب shrab *m.* ☞ شرپ

شریهار shrapā́ *f.* ☞ شرپا

شرپسند sharpasánd sharrpasánd pernicious, obnoxious شرپسند اشخاص obnoxious people; scoundrels

شرپهار sharapəhār *m.* شرپی shrəpáj *m.* 1 splash (of water) 2 lash (of a whip)

شرت shurút کول to throw things around, strew شرت او شپارس کول to throw things around, strew شپارس کول

شرح sharh *f.* شرحه shárha *f. Arabic* exposition; explanation, elucidation; interpretation; description شرح حال shárh-i biography شرح کول *compound verb* to explain, elucidate; describe

شرشائي sharshāí *f.* sharshai (measure of weight equal to one Indian tola, 24 grains)

شرشر shurshúr *m.* 1 noise (e.g., of the wind) د باد په شرشر کار کول to work out in the wind شرشر باد الوزي The wind whistles. 2 gurgling, babbling (of water)

شرشره sharshará *f.* 1 gurgling, babbling (of water) 2 small waterfall

شرشف sharsháf *m. Arab plural* colza oil

شرشوبنده sharshobónda *f.* scolopendra, centipede

شرط shart *m. Arabic* [*plural:* شرطونه shartúna *Arabic plural:* شرائط sharāít] 1 condition د ترون شرطونه the conditions of the agreement شرائط مخكيني preconditions شرط كول *compound verb* to stipulate; provide for شرط كېدل *compound verb* to be conditioned upon; be stipulated بې له كمه شرطه تسليمول to surrender, capitulate unconditionally ولي شرط دا دئ چه ... however, under the condition that ... په دې شرط چه ... provided that د چا without any conditions of any kind 2 bet د چا نه شرط تړل to bet, lay a wager with someone سره شرط تړل to win a bet with someone شرط پوره كول to fulfill the conditions of a wager 3 sign, token, mark

شرطنامه shartnāmá *f.* condition of an agreement, provision of a treaty; condition

شرطوالا shartvālá *m.* bettor

شرطي shartí 1 conditional 2 *abusive* strumpet, trollop

شرطيه shartijá *f. Arabic* lottery

شرع shár'a *f. Arabic* Shariat (Islamic religious law)

شرعاً shár'án according to the laws of Shariat

شرعه shár'a *f.* ☞ شرع

شرعي shar'í *Arabic indeclinable* 1 pertaining to Shariat; according to the law of Shariat شرعي حكم a legal action instituted thru Shariat شرعي محكمه a trial according to Shariat 2 established, in accordance with Shariat; legal شرعي او قانوني ښځه a legal wife

شرغشی sharghasháj *m.* ☞ شلغشی

شرف sharáf *m. Arabic* 1 nobility 2 honor, merit; respect; esteem د لوړ مقام شرف ځانته حاصلول to live honestly په شرف ژوندون كول to receive a high post, obtain an important appointment دا د شرف او فخر باعث دئ This is an affair of honor. This relates to honor. 3 *proper name* Sharaf

شرفا shurafá *m. Arabic plural of* شريف

شرف الدين sharafuddín *m. Arabic proper name* Sharafuddin

شرفتمند sharafatmánd noble; honorable

شرفتمندانه sharafatmandāná 1 noble; honorable 2 virtuous

شرفياب sharfjáb worthy of honor

شرفيابي sharfjābí *f.* reception, audience د چا ملاقات شرفيابي ته راتلل to be received in or granted an audience with someone

شرق sharḳ *m. Arabic* the East شمالي شرق the northeast نژدې شرق the Near East وسطي شرق the Middle East ليرې شرق the Far East د كابل كېنی شرق east of Kabul

شرقاً shárḳán *Arabic* to the east, eastward, in the east

شرقول shraḳavól *transitive regional* [*past:* و يې شرقاوه] to beat; lash په كرورو شرقول to beat with a lash

شرقهار shraḳahár *m. regional* clang (of metal); tapping

شرقي sharḳí *Arabic* 1 eastern شرقي مطالعات Eastern Studies, Oriental Studies 2 شرقي خوراک، شرقي دودی Eastern cuisine 2 resident of the East

شرک shirk *m. Arabic religion* 1 polytheism; paganism 2 unbelief

شرک shrak *m.* 1 knock, tap 2 lash (of a whip) 3 a quickened pulse

شرک shirák *m.* blanket

شركا shurakā *m. Arabic plural of* شريک

شركت shirkát *m. Arabic* 1 fellowship; shirket (i.e., partnership), society, company تجارتي شركت trading company مختلط شركت silent partnership سهامي شركت، انونيم شركت joint-stock company جهازي شركت shipping company 2 participation په يو كار كېنی شركت a to take part in, participate in something b to share (e.g., someone's feelings) زه ستا په خوښی كېنی شركت كوم I share your joy.

شركتي shirkatí pertaining to a shirkat, of a joint-stock company

شركهار shrakahár *m.* شركی shrakáj *m.* 1 knock, tap, rap 2 lash (of a whip)

شرم shárəm *m.* shárm 1 shame, dishonor, disgrace دا د شرم خبره ده It is a shameful affair.... ډېر شرم دئ چه It is a great shame that ... خورا شرم دئ چه ... It disturbs my conscience. I am راته شرم راځي ashamed. *proverb* شرم مي كوت، بخ مي خوت I was ready to sink into the ground from shame. 2 bashfulness; shyness شرم كول to be ashamed شرم لرل to be ashamed, be shy 3 *Islamic law* fine imposed over and above kun (blood money) for the commission of shameful acts in connection with a murder

شرمبی shrambój *f.* ☞ كونجی

شرمدار sharmdzhón شرمسار sharmdár شرمجن sharmsár 1 bashful; conscientious 2 shy, timid

شرمښ sharmə́ḵ *m.* shərmə́ḵ wolf

شرمنكی sharməḵhkój *f.* [*plural:* شرمښكی sharmə́ḵhkój *plural:* شرمښكياني sharmə́ḵhkəjā́ni] lizard

شرمښه sharmə́ḵha *f.* she-wolf

شرمگير sharmgír ashamed, embarrassed

شرمناک sharmnā́k ☞ شرمجن

شرمندتيا sharmandtjá *f.* شرمندگي sharmandagí *f.* 1 shame, disgrace, dishonor 2 bashfulness; shyness 3 diffidence

شرمنده sharmandá shamed of; modest, diffident, shy شرمنده كول to shame شرمنده كېدل to be ashamed of

شرمښ sharmúḵ *m.* ☞ شرمښ

شرمول sharmavól *transitive* [*past:* و يې شرماوه] 1 to shame 2 to disgrace, dishonor خپل قام او تبر شرمول to disgrace one's family ځان شرمول to disgrace oneself

شرمونكی sharmavúnkaj shameful

شرمېدل sharmedól *intransitive* [*past:* وشرمېده] to be ashamed; be embarrased; be diffident

شرمېده sharmedə́ *m. plural* shame, embarrassment

شرمينگي sharmingí *f.* ☞ شرمندگي

شرنگ shrang *m.* 1 *onomatopoeia* sound made by breaking glass, dishware, etc. شرنگ او شرونگ ringing, chime 2 clatter, clanging (e.g., of swords); saber rattling 3 hubbub (of voices) 4 the recitation of lessons by children, aloud په شرنگ سبق ويل to study a lesson by chanting in unison

شرنگا shrangá *f.* ☞ شرنگهار

شرنگانی shrangānáj *m.* شرنگاوو shrangāvú *m.* rattle

شرنگول shrangevál *transitive* [*past:* وي يې شرنگاوه] 1 to jingle (bangles, bracelets, etc.) 2 to knock, rap, rattle 3 to clang, clash (weapons, etc.)

شرنگهار shrangahár *m.* 1 ringing; chiming 2 rustle 3 rustling

شرنگی shrangáj *m.* ☞ شرنگ¹

شرنگېدل shrangedál *intransitive* [*past:* و شرنگېده] 1 to jingle 2 to rustle 3 to rap, knock

شروپ shrup ☞ شرپ

شرورشور sharrushór *m.* vanity

شروط shurút *m. Arabic plural of* شرط

شروع shuru' *Arabic* 1 *f. Arabic m.* [*plural:* شروعات shuru'át] beginning, initiative د مجلس په شروع کښي at the beginning of the meeting له شروع تر آخره پوري from beginning to end بنه شروع a good beginning په... شروع کول، په... باندي شروع کول، پر... باندي شروع کول to begin something, start something, get going at something شروع ميندل to make a beginning, make a start 2 *predicative* having (just) begun شروع کول *compound verb* to begin شروع کېدل *compound verb* to start ډوډۍ شروع کېږي Supper is commencing.

شروع کېده shuru'kedá *m. plural* beginning, undertaking

شرونگ shrung *tautological with* شرنگ

شرهار shurahár *m.* gurgling, noise of water شرهار وهل a to gurgle b to patter (rain)

شری sharaj¹ *m. medicine* measles شری نيولئ sharí one suffering from measles د چا شری کېدل a to appear (of measle rash) b *figurative* to be characteristic, be inherent, be innate

شری sháre² *f. plural medicine* chicken pox

شريان sharján *m.* shirján *Arabic* [*plural:* شرائين sharajín] *anatomy* artery د شرائينو رگونه pulmonary artery د سږيو شريان pulmonary artery

شرياني sharjāní arterial

شرېدل sharedál *intransitive* ☞ شورېدل

شرير sharír *Arabic* 1.1 spoiled; corrupt 1.2 evil; loathsome يو شرير سړی loathsome man; scoundrel, rascal 2 *m.* [*plural:* اشرار ashrár] 2.1 bandit, robber 2.2 scoundrel, rascal

شريعت shari'át *m. Arabic* ☞ شرع a to decide according to Shariat (i.e., traditional Islamic law); try or judge according to Shariat b to institute an action under Shariat

شريف sharíf *Arabic* 1.1 noble, wellborn 1.2 reknown; famed 1.3 *figurative* high 2 *m.* 2.1 *proper name* Sharif 2.2 [*plural:* اشراف ashráf] Sherif (title of the governor of Mecca and of the descendants of Mohammed)

شريفانه sharifāná 1 noble, wellborn 2 glorious, famous; reknown

شريفه sharifá¹ *f. Arabic proper name* Sharifa

شريفه sharifá² *f.* cornice, ledge

شريک sharík *m. Arabic* 1 [*plural:* شريکان sharikán *Arabic plural:* شرکا shuraká] 1.1 companion, comrade 1.2 shareholder 1.3 participant شريک کېدل شريک کول *compound verb* ☞

شريکېدل 2 common, general د دواړو پوله شريکه وه They had a common boundary. په شريکه *adverb* together

شريکول sharikavál *denominative* [*past:* شريک يې کړ] to make a participant in something, involve in something, attract to something په خبرو کښي ئان شريکول to take part in a conversation

شريکه sharíka 1 *feminine singular of* شريک 2 *f.* friend (female) د حيات شريکه lifelong (female) friend

شريکېدل sharikedál *denominative, intransitive* [*past:* شريک شو] to participate in something; be attracted to something, be involved in something

شارېدل ☞ شړکېدل شاړول شاړ کول ☞ شړ

شړپ shṛap *m.* شړپ و شړوپ shṛap-u-khrúp 1 *m.* splash (of waves, pouring water) 2 rustle, (indistinct) noise 3 *onomatopoeia* Slosh!

شړپول shṛapavál *transitive* [*past:* وي يې شړپاوه] to splash, splash about

شړپهار shṛapahár *m.* شړپی shṛapáj *m.* ☞ شړپ

شړپېدل shṛapedál *denominative, intransitive* [*past:* وشپېد] to splash, splash about

شړت shṛat ☞ شړم

شړتول shṛatavál *denominative* ☞ شړمول

شړتېدل shṛatedál *denominative, intransitive* ☞ شړمېدل

شړته shaṛatá *f.* 1 barley; barleycorn 2 small quantity, few

شړشپه shaṛshapá *f.* 1 abatement (e.g., of a storm) 2 fear 3 misfortune, disaster

شړشړی shaṛshaṛáj *f.* ☞ شورشوری

شړشم shaṛshám *m. plural* cole seed, rapeseed د شړ شمو تېل rapeseed oil په تلي کښي شړشم څوک زرغونولی شي؟ *Eastern saying* It's a senseless undertaking.

شړک shṛak *m. regional* شړک shṛak *m.* 1 lash, lashing 2 crash; knock, rap شړق او شروک knocking, crashing 3 noise, uproar (of the wind) شړق باران thunderstorm, downpour

شړکول shṛakavál *transitive* [*past:* وي يې شړکاوه] 1 to lash (with a whip, etc.) 2 to knock, rap (on the door, etc.)

شړکهار shṛakahár *m.* ☞ شړق

شړکېدل shṛakedál *intransitive* [*past:* و شړکېد] 1 to crack, emit a crash; slam (door) 2 noise, hum (wind)

شړکېده shrakedá *m. plural* 1 crash; slamming (door, etc.) 2 noise, hum (wind)

شړل shaṛál *transitive* [*past:* وي يې شاړه] 1 drive, drive through; drive out 2 to fire (a bullet) 3 to send packing, evict

شړلئ shaṛáláj 1 *past participle of* شړل 2 unfit, superfluous

شړم shṛam 1 poorly attached 2 loose-hanging 3 loose, flabby 4 clumsy; slow-moving; lazy, sluggish

شړمتوب shṛamtób *m.* شړموالی shṛamválaj *m.* 1 looseness, flabbiness 2 clumsiness; tardiness; laziness, sluggishness

شړمول shṛamavál *denominative* [*past:* شړم يې کړ] 1 to attach poorly 2 to cause to become loose or flabby 3 to cause to become clumsy or slow; cause to become lazy or sluggish

شرمېدل shṛamedál *denominative, intransitive* [*past:* شرم شو] **1** to be poorly attached **2** to hang loose **3** to grow loose, become flabby **4** to grow clumsy, become slow moving; be lazy, be sluggish

شرنگ shṛang *m.* شرنگار shṛangār *m. regional* hum, whistling شرنگ او شرونگ hum, whistling

شرنه shaṛóna *f.* driving out

شروالی shaṛválaj *m.* **1** ungainliness, awkwardness **2** infertility, barrenness **3** fallowness (of land)

شروبی shṛóbaj *m.* shaṛóbaj **1** watering can **2** spigot (e.g., of a samovar)

شرپ shṛup *tautological with* شرپ

شروتېدل shaṛotedál *intransitive* [*past:* شروتبد و] to come loose, sink (morally)

شرول shaṛavól *transitive* [*past:* یې شراوه] **1** to boil soft (e.g., meat) **2** to soften

شرول shaṛavól *transitive* [*past:* یې شراوه] **1** splash, splash out; spurt, spray

شروم shṛom *m. plural* remains (in the pan) after cooking meat

شرومبی shṛumbé shṛombé *f. plural* churning

شرون shaṛún *m.* شرنه

شروند shṛund شروند غوړونه shamed

شرونگ shṛung *m. tautological with* شرنگ

شره shára *f.* شاره

شرهته shaṛháta *f.* شرته

شرهول shaṛhavól *transitive* شرول

شرهېدل shaṛhedál *intransitive* شرېدل

شری sháṛaj *m. botany* Eremurus (small family of Asiatic herbs in the family Liliaceae)

شری shaṛəj *f.* **1** wooden blanket, flannel blanket **2** rug, plaid **3** a small shawl

شری shaṛəj *f.* hedge mustard, *Sisymbrium* (a medical plant)

شری shaṛí *present tense of* شرل

شرېدل shaṛedál *intransitive* [*past:* و شرېده] **1** to be boiled soft (of meat) **2** to decompose, break down **3** to fall apart

شرېدل shaṛedál *intransitive* [*past:* و شرېده] to splash, spill

شرېدل shaṛedál *denominative, intransitive* شارېدل

شرېده shaṛedə́ *m. plural* **1** boiling soft (of meat) **2** decomposition, breaking down **3** decay, falling apart, dissolution

شرېده shaṛedə́ *m. plural* splashing, splash, spillage

شرېده shaṛedə́ *m. plural* neglect

شری ور shaṛəjvár wrapped up in a shawl or wool wrap

شست shist *m.* shast gunsight اخیستل شست to take aim

شست shast *m.* **1** ring with a mirror (worn by women on the middle finger) **2** thimble **3** fishspear, harpoon

شستی shastaj *m.* **1** chrysanthemum, *Chrysanthemum indicum*

شش shəsh *m.* pendant (on a necklace)

ششت shasht *m.* thimble

ششتی shashtáj *m.* شستی

ششک shishk *m.* **1** shelf **2** awning; arch

شش کروهي shashkuruhí *f.* شپږ کروهي

ششنا shishnā *f.* neighing (of a horse)

ششنل shishnól *transitive* [*past:* یې ششنل] to neigh (of a horse)

ششنی shishnaj neighing (of a horse) ششنی کول to neigh (of a horse)

ششنېدل shishnedál *intransitive* [*past:* و ششنبد] to neigh (of a horse)

ششنېده shishnedə́ *m. plural* neighing (of a horse)

شش و پنج shash-u-pándzh *m.* vacillation, indecisiveness په دې شش وینځ I vacillated, not able to decide. وینځ کېنبي وم

شطارت shatārát *m. Arabic* quickness, agility, efficiency

شطرنج shatrándzh *m. Arabic* chess د شطرنج تخته chessboard شطرنج کول to play chess

شطرنج باز shatrandzhbā́z *m.* شطرنج کوونکی shatrándzh kavúnkaj *m.* chess player

شطرنجي shatrandzhí *adjective* chess په شطرنجي ترتیب in staggered order, staggered

شعار shi'ár *m. Arabic* slogan, motto

شعاع sho'ā́' *f.* shu'ā *Arabic m. Arabic* [*plural:* اشعه ashi'á] **1** ray **2** flash, radiance

شعاعي sho'ā'í radiating شعاعي مواد **a** radiation, emanation **b** rays

شعائر sha'āir *m. Arabic plural of* شعیره

شعبات sho'bā́t *m. Arabic plural of* شعبه

شعبان sha'bā́n *m. Arabic* Shaban (8th month of the lunar year)

شعبده باز shu'badabā́z *m.* **1** conjurer, juggler **2** cheat, swindler

شعبه sho'bá *f.* shu'bá *Arabic* [*plural:* شعبی sho'bé shu'bé *m. Arabic plural:* شعبات sho'bā́t shu'bā́t] **1** section, department, branch **2** wing, offshoot

شعر she'r *m. Arabic* [*plural:* شعرونه she'rúna *Arabic plural:* اشعار ash'ár] **1** poetry **2** verse شعر ویل، شعر کول to write verses, compose verses

شعر sha'r *m. Arabic* **1** hair **2** capillary

شعریه sha'rijá **1** *adjective* capillary شعریه رګونه capillaries **2** *f.* capillaries

شعف sha'áf *m. Arabic* delight, ecstasy

شعله shu'lá *f. Arabic* شغله

شعور shu'úr *m. Arabic* **1** mind, intellect; consciousness په بشپړ شعور in full consciousness و هغه د شعور خاوند He was an intelligent man. سیاسي شعور **2** political consciousness د feeling اضطراب شعور کول to worry

شعوراً shu'úrán *Arabic* purposely, consciously

شعوري shu'urí *Arabic* conscious; intelligent

شعیره sha'irá *f. Arabic m.* [*plural:* شعائر sha'āir] **1** *religion* ceremony, ritual **2** custom

شغ shəgh *m.* **1** noise made by a flock of birds taking off **2** whistle (e.g., of a bullet)

شغا shəghā́ *f.* شغ

شغاشغ shəghāshógh *m.* noise, din, rumbling; rumble (e.g., of train wheels)

شغال shəghā́l *m.* چغال

شغالي ¹ shəghālí **1** low grade, of inferior quality or kind **2** locally produced; handcrafted

شغالى ² shəghālój *m.* **1** breed of camel **2** rifle (handmade)

شغرب shəghrób *m. colloquial* east له شغربه تر مغربه from east to west

شغرغ shəghrágh *m.* troublemaker

شغف shəghấf *m. Arabic* passionate love

شغل shughl *m. Arabic* matter, affair, occupation, preoccupation; work

شغله shughlá *f.* **1** ray د ابكس شغلي X-rays **2** radiance **3** spark

شغنان shughnãn *m.* Shugnan (province)

شغني shughní **1** Shugnanian **2** *m.* .1 a native of Shugnan 2.2 *f.* Shugnanian, the Shugnanian language

شغول shəghavól *transitive [past:* وي شغاوه] **1** to fling, throw, toss **2** *regional* to launch (e.g., a missile)

شغهار shəghahấr *m.* ☞ شغ

شفا shifã *f. Arabic* healing, cure شفا ميندل to make a complete recovery; get better

شفاخانوي shifākhānaví *adjective* hospital, pertaining to an infirmary

شفاخانه shifākhãná *f.* hospital عسكري شفاخانه hospital, infirmary

شفاخانه يي shifākhānaíj *adjective* hospital-, curative شفاخانه يي ښار health resort (city)

شفاعت shafa'át *m. Arabic* **1** protection; intercession شفاعت كول **a** to take someone's part; intercede **b** to be a mediator

شفاعت گر shafā'atgár *m.* **1** protector; intercessor **2** mediator

شفاف shaffấf *Arabic* **1** transparent, translucent **2** very delicate

شفافيت shaffāfijất *m. Arabic* transparency

شفاهي shifāhí *Arabic* oral; verbal شفاهي ادبيت a popular oral composition *folklore* شفاهي امتحان an oral examination *law* شفاهي دلائل oral testimony of the parties

شفتالو shaftālú *m.* peach (tree)

شفر `shifr *m.* cipher, code

شفري shifrí enciphered, encoded

شفعه shuf'a *f. Arabic law* a prior right to acquire something

شفق shafáḵ *m. Arabic* sunset; evening; dusk

شفقت shafaḵát *m. Arabic* sympathy; mercy, compassion; kindness پر چا شفقت كول to pity someone; sympathize with someone; be kind to someone

شفوي shafaví *Arabic linguistics* labial; bilabial

شفي shafí *m. Arabic* savior, rescuer

شفيره shafirấ *f. Arabic* chrysalis, pupa (e.g., of a butterfly)

شفيع shafí' *m. Arabic* **1** protector **2** intercessor

شفيق shafíḵ *Arabic* **1.1** merciful; sympathetic **1.2** loving; tender **2** *m. proper name* Shafik

شق shiḵ shiḵḵ *m. Arabic [plural:* شقونه shiḵúna *Arabic plural:* شقوق shuḵúḵ] **1** half **2** dilemma **3** branch د مدرسي خارجي شق external (i.e., nonresident) studies د مدرسي داخلي شق boarding school

شقاقل shaḵāḵúl *m. Arabic Polygonatum verticillatum* (whorled variety of polygonum, in the buckwheat family)

شقاوت shaḵāvát *m. Arabic* misfortune, calamity; disaster

شقائق shaḵāíḵ *m. Arabic* anemone

شقي shaḵí *Arabic* **1** unhappy, unfortunate **2** pernicious

شقيقه shaḵiḵá *f. Arabic anatomy* temple

شك ¹ shak *m.* shakk *Arabic [plural:* شكونه shakúna] *Arabic [plural:* شكوك shukúk] doubt; suspicion شك راورل، شك كول to doubt, be doubtful په دي كښي هيڅ شك نشته there is no doubt, doubtless دا د شكه وتلي خبره ده It is indisputable.

شك ² shak on end, sticking up

شكار ¹ shikấr *m.* ☞ ښكار

شكار ² shkãr *m. plural* potassium, potash, alkali

شكارگاه shikārgãh *m.* hunting ground; hunting preserve

شكارل shkāról *transitive [past:* وي شكاره] to instigate, set (someone) on (someone else)

شكاره shkāró *oblique of* شكور ¹

شكاري ¹ shukāri *f. plural* ☞ شوكاري

شكاري ² shikārí **1** *adjective* hunting **2** raptorial (of birds)

شكاكيت shakkākijất *m. Arabic* skepticism

شكال shkãl *m.* ☞ ښكل

شكانه shkānó *masculine plural of* شكون

شكاونه shkã́vna *f.* **1** stealing, robbing; thievery **2** cutting-off, isolating

شكايت shiakājất *m. Arabic [plural:* شكايتونه shikājatúna *Arabic plural:* شكايات shikājất] **1** complaint **2** dissatisfaction شكايت كول **a** to complain, lodge a complaint **b** to express dissatisfaction

شكايتنامه shikājatnamấ *f.* complaint (written)

شكر ¹ shúkr *m.* shúkər *Arabic* **1** thanks; gratitude شكر ايستل، شكر to thank دچا شكر كښل to thank someone شكر په ښای راورل to express thanks **2** satisfaction

شكر ² shakár *m. Arabic* ☞ شكره ¹

شكرانه shukrānấ *f.* contribution (e.g., to a mullah)

شكرپاره shakarpārấ *f.* sweet tree-dried apricot

شكرخند shakarkhánd smiling

شكرخوره shakarkhurấ *f.* **1** hummingbird **2** person with a sweet tooth

شكرستان shakaristấn *m.* **1** sugar plantation **2** sugar mill شكرستان افغاني *shakaristán-i-afghaní* an anthology of Afghan literature compiled by Kazi (Moslem judge) Mir Ahmed Shah

شكرگذار shukrguzãr **1** thankful, grateful **2** satisfied

شكرگذاري shukrguzārí *f.* **1** thankfulness, gratitude **2** satisfaction

شكرگنج ¹ shakarganáj *m.* sugarcane plant

شكرگني ² shakarganí *m. plural* honeycombs

شكرلب shakarláb **1** sweet-mouthed (of a beloved) **2** male with a harelip

شكرنج shakarnáj *m.* sugarcane plant

شكرنى shakarnäj *m.* sugarcane plant

شكره ¹ shakára *f.* shakóra sugar (usually granulated) د شكري فيصدي sugariness

شکره ² shikrá *f.* female of a kind of hawk

شکری ¹ shəkráj *m.* powder flask

شکری ² shkəráj *f.* bast basket, woven reed basket

شکری ³ shikaraj *m.* kind of hawk

شکری والا shakarivālā sugary, yielding sugar (of plants)

شکریه shukrijá *f. Arabic* gratitude د بلنی شکریه کول to thank for an invitation شکریه وراندي کول to render thanks شکریه! Thanks!

شکست shikást *m.* crushing defeat, rout شکست خورل، شکست کول to suffer a crushing defeat

شکست خورده shikastkhurdá defeated utterly, suffering a crushing defeat

شکسته shikastá **1** broken up; broken apart **2** *f.* shikasta (i.e., broken) script (cursive handwriting in which manuscripts and sometimes correspondence are written)

شکسته نفس shikastanafás modest

شکسته نفسي shikastanafasí modesty

شک شک shakshák on end, sticking up

شکل shakl *m. Arabic* [*plural:* شکلونه shaklúna *Arabic plural:* اشکال ashkál] type, form, aspect, appearance د ...، په ...، په شکل په شکل او ژبره کي ... in appearance شکل سره in the form of ... ارول، شکل تبديلول a to chance form, alter appearance b to rework, transform **2** drawing, sketch, image **3** figure, subject

شکلاً sháklán *Arabic* in shape, in appearance, in form

شکلی shakáláj *f.* end of a turban

شکمپاره shkampārá *f. Plantago ispaghula* (a kind of plantain)

شکمن shakmán **1** doubting **2** suspicious, dubious

شکمن والی shakmənválaj *m.* suspicion, doubt, dubiousness

شکن shikán *combining form* breaking, breaking apart, fragmenting طياره شکن antiaircraft

شکنجه shikandzhá *f.* شکنځه shikandzá *f.* **1** instrument of torture (rack, stocks, etc.) **2** *literal & figurative* vice **3** torture, torment شکنجه کول to torture, torment **4** bookbinder's press

شکنه shkaná *f.* kind of thick soup made with onion *idiom* د بل په شکنه غوړونه سول، د بل په شکنه غوړونه سوڅل to meddle in the affairs of another

شکنه shkaṇá *f.* **1** female porcupine **2** barren woman

شکور ¹ shkor *m.* ☞ شکری ²

شکور ² shakúr *Arabic* extremely grateful, thankful

شکور ³ shukúr *Arabic* **1** thanking, giving thanks **2** *m. proper name* Shukur

شکورک shakurák په دي خبره شک ورک نه يم I really don't know this.

شکوری shkoráj *m.* small basket

شکوک shukúk *m. Arabic plural of* شک ¹ د دوی په زړو کښي يو ډول شکوک پيدا شوي دي A suspicion creeped into their hearts.

شکول ¹ shkavál **1** to tear, rend خت يي ورته وشکاوه He tore his shirt. **2** to tear off, tear out **3** to dig up; pull out **4** to irritate, open (a wound) **5** to break off, tear off; rip out **6** to rob, burglarize *idiom* پښه شکول to cease going somewhere

شکول ² shakavál *transitive* [*past:* شک يي کړ] to stand on end

شکونه ¹ shkavána *f.* **1** tear, rending, rent **2** disruption, loss of contact **3** uprooting, pulling out **4** breaking off, tearing off, extraction **5** robbery, burglary

شکونه ² shakavána *f.* standing on end

شکون shkuṇ *m.* shkon [*plural:* شکانه shkāṇə *plural:* شکنیان shkaṇiján] porcupine *proverb* شکون که حلال شي، رنگ يي مردار دئ *literal* Even though a porcupine should be declared fit to eat, it will still look unclean. *figurative* You can't wash a black dog white.

شکوه ¹ shikóh *f.* **1** splendor; magnificence **2** grandeur, majesty

شکوه ² shakvá *f.* shikvá *Arabic* complaint شکوه کول to complain

شکي shakí shakkí suspicious, doubting; mistrustful شکي کېدل to be suspicious; doubt something **2** problematic

شکېدل ¹ shkedál *intransitive* [*past:* و شکېده] **1** to tear, rend; be torn, be rent **2** to be ripped out, be extracted **3** to be torn out **4** to be opened, be irritated (of a wound) **5** to be dug out **6** to be robbed, be burglarized

شکېدل ² shakedál *denominative, intransitive* [*past:* شک شو] to stand, be stood upright د سنک بجل شکه شوبده اوس Now Sanak is lucky.

شکېزه shkéza *f.* supports, poles (tent, marquee)

شکبل shkel *m.* ☞ ښکبل

شکبل ² shkelál *transitive dialect* ☞ شکول

شکبلول shkelavál *denominative, transitive* [*past:* شکبل يي کړ] to hobble

شکبلی shkeláj *m.* whistle

شکبلبدل shkeledál *denominative, intransitive* [*past:* شکبل شو] to be hobbled

شگاره shigāra *f.* **1** pregnant **2** with calf

شگرگنی shagaranáj *m.* **1** honeycombs **2** wasp nest

شگری shigráj *m.* powder flask

شگلن shəglán **1** sandy **2** gravelly; granular

شگلنه shəglána *f.* sandy soil **2** ☞ شگلونی

شگلور shəglór sandy

شگلونی shəglúnaj *m. anatomy* sacrum

شگماهی shəgmāháj *m.* skink (a lizard)

شگموبنی، شگ موبنی shəgmúkhaj *m.* emery paper

شگن shəgán ☞ شگلن

شگوفه shigufá *f.* shugufá flower, blossoming شگوفه کبدل to bloom, blossom out

شگون shagún *m.* shugún omen, augury; token

شگه shə́ga *f.* sand ميده شگه غله sand شگه غته gravel, coarse sand شگه quicksand د شگو ډېری a mica b talc دونکی شگي dunes; sand hillock طلا لرونکی شگي، سره زر لرونکی شگي gold-bearing sand, auriferous sand

شگی ¹ shigáj *f.* sandy soil

شگي ² shə́gi *feminine plural of* شگه

شگيرنی shəgirnáj *m.* ☞ شگرگنی

شگيگل shəgigúl *m.* **1** mica **2** talc

شل ¹ shal *m.* 1 pike, javelin, spear, lance 2 staff (with a sharp metal tip)

شل ² shəl 1 *numeral* twenty 2 *m.* [*plural:* شلگونه shəlgúna *f.* *plural:* شلي shə́li] a score دوه شله dwa shále forty درې شله sixty four hundred په شلگونو روپۍ scores of rupees شل کول *compound verb* a to complete some matter, carry something to a conclusion b to effectuate; execute a seemingly impossible task ، ما شل نه کئ te ham wəláka dəğa kar shəl kəi I didn't do this and you also will deal with it in vain. بې ما دي شل نه کړه Without me you achieved nothing. Without me you couldn't deal with this matter. شل کرته! Willingly! Gladly!

شل ³ shal shall *Arabic* paralyzed په پنبو باندي شل دئ His legs are paralyzed. شل شول paralyzed

شل ⁴ shal *m.* staircase

شل ⁵ shal *m.* ram (delivered to the home of the deceased by his relatives)

شلاټه shalā́ṭá *f.* root of the reed mace

شلاغ shallā́gh *m.* 1 lash, scourge, whip 2 slap, buffet, box on the cheek

شلانډه shlā́nḍa *f.* 1 toad 2 agama (a lizard) 3 round-head (a species of lizard of the Agamadae family)

شلاوند shlā́vóṇḍ *m.* شلاون shlā́vóṇ *m.* collective responsibility; collective guarantee

شل ایکیزه shə́likizá *f.* twenty-iki coin

شلبر shaləbə́r *m.* flimsy cloth, thin cloth

شل پلاری shə́lplā́raj ancestry unknown

شل پولی shə́lpulə́j *f.* twenty-pul coin

شلت shlə́t shalə́t ☞ شډول

شلتالو shaltalú *m.* [*plural:* شلتالان shaltālā́n] peach (tree)

شلتی shalatí *f.* unhusked barley

شلخته shə́lákhta *f.* brazen woman, shameless woman

شلخورکه shalkhoráka *f.* giant lizard

شلخی ¹ shalkháj *m.* sorrel (rumex)

شلخي ² shilakhí *regional* blank (of a cartridge)

شل دانه shə́ldāná *f.* pearl necklace; necklace

شلغت shə́lghát deformed, ugly (of things)

شلغشی shalghā́shaj *m.* wild sugarcane, *Saccharum spontaneum, Saccharum sara*

شلغم shalghám *m.* turnip, rutabaga

شلک ¹ shilák *m.* volley; (gun) salute شلک کول to fire a salute شلک ورکول to fire a volley

شلک ² shə́lák *m.* a score شلکه څلور four hundred

شلکه shaláka *f.* laziness, sluggishness

شلکی shilakí spent, fired شلکي کارتوس spent cartridge

شلگ shalág 1 coarsely woven; flimsy (of cloth) 2 *m.* ☞ شلتی

شلگونه shə́lgúna *plural of* شل ² 2

شلگه shalgá *f.* awn, beard (of wheat)

شلگی ¹ shalgáj *m.* 1 javelin; fish spear 2 metal tip 3 pennant

شلگی ² shalgáj *f.* shelf; niche

شلم ¹ shilám shlám 1 *m.* 1.1 partly-filled grain sack 1.2 poorly-tied bundle 1.3 animal with a pendulous belly 2 ☞ شلم کول شرم شرمبدل ☞ شلم کېدل شرمول ☞

شلم ² shə́ləm *numeral* twentieth

شلمدنه shaləmdána *f. botany* salep (dried and ground tubers of Orchis species, used for food and medicine)

شلمشر shə́lməshr *m.* commander of a detachment or group consisting of twenty men

شلمول shlamavól *denominative* ☞ شرمول

شلمبدل shləmedól *transitive* ☞ شرمبدل

شلنډ shlanḍ 1 fat, stout; burly; plump 2 fatted, well-fed

شلنډتوب shlanḍtób *m.* شلنډوالی shlanḍvā́laj *m.* 1 stoutness; burliness 2 state of nutrition

شلنډول shlanḍavól *denominative, transitive* [*past:* شلنډ يي کړ] 1 to make fat, make stout 2 to fatten up, feed up

شلانډه shlā́nḍa *f.* ☞ شلنډه

شلنډبدل shlanḍedól *denominative, intransitive* [*past:* شلنډ شو] 1 to grow fat, grow stout; get heavy, become plump 2 to be fattened up, be well fed

شلنگ shiling *m.* shilling

شلوار shalvā́r *m.* wide Middle-Eastern-style trousers

شل وشل shalushál *m.* شل و شوت shalushút *m.* 1 cripple 2 paralytic

شلول shlavól *transitive* [*past:* ويي شلاوه] 1 to tear, tear apart; break off د اسارت ځنځيرونه شلول to break the chains of slavery 2 to tear off, detach 3 to break off, break apart سياسي روابط شلول to sever diplomatic relations 4 to stop, cease, curtail 5 to break open, force, smash 6 to crack (with the teeth)

شلوم ¹ shlom *m. plural* ☞ شروم

شلوم ² shlavóm *present tense, first person of* شلول

شلومباون shlombāvóṇ *m.* 1 bag in which kurut is pressed or squeezed into a solid mass

شلومبه shlombá *f.* شلومبې shlombé skim milk; sour milk *saying figurative* تشي شلومبي شاربل to grind water in a mortar *literal* to try to shake up or squeeze out sour milk in the air without a bag *figuratively* to engage in a fruitless occupation

شلومب shlomb *m.* ☞ شلومبه

شلونه shlúna *f.* boil

شله ¹ shəmlá *f.* subcutaneous layer of fat (e.g., in sheep)

شله ² shalláh importunate, persistent

شله ³ shə́la ☞ شلي ¹

شلي ¹ shə́li *Eastern* shə́le *plural of* شل 2 اته شلي روپۍ one hundred and sixty rupees

شلي ² shli *m. plural* 1 grain, cereal 2 grains, cereals

شلیته ¹ shə́líta *f.* 1 large sack (e.g., for transporting straw, cotton) 2 purse, pouch

شلیته ² shalíta *f.* 1 leftovers, leftover food 2 old woolen rag; rags, old cloths 3 strumpet, trollop

شلیدل shledól 1 [*past:* و شلېده] 1 to tear, break 1.2 to come off, get detached 1.3 to be severed, be broken, be disrupted (e.g., of

diplomatic relations) **1.4** to stop, halt **1.5** to be smashed **2** *m.*
plural literal break, breach شلېدو د سياسي روابطو a break in
diplomatic relations

شلېدلئ shledáləj **1** *past participle of* شلېدل **2** torn, rent

شلېده shledə́ *m. plural literal* break, breach, severance, disruption

شلیک shilík *m.* ☞ شلک [1]

شلیکی shlikáj *m.* dried apricots

شلیل shalíl *m.* nectarine

شم [1] sham *m.* ☞ شمع

شم [2] sham sticking up, upright

شم shəm *present tense, first person of* شول [1]

شماتت shamātát *m. Arabic* schadenfreude (pleasure in the
misfortune of an enemy)

شماخه shamákha *f.* weed grass

شمار shmár *m.* shumár **1** quantity; numbers, numerical strength;
number په شمار راتلل ... د to be a
component part of ... يو شمار a certain quantity **2** counting, calculation شمار کول to count,
compute, reckon

شمارل shmārə́l *transitive Eastern* [*past:* ويې شماره] to count,
calculate

شمال [1] shimál *m. Arabic* north شماله څخه تر جنوبه پوري from north
to south د کابل شمال ته to the north of Kabul

شمال [2] shamál *m. Arabic* (north) wind و شمال ته اېنودل to ventilate نري شمال لګېده A slight wind was blowing.

شمالاً جنوباً shimālán-dzhunúbán from north to south

شمال شرق shimál-i-shaṛk *m.* شمال الشرق the northeast

شمال شرقي shimālishaṛkí northeastern

شمال غرب shimál-i-gharb *m.* شمال الغرب the northwest په شمال ... د
غرب northwest of ...

شمال غربي shimalígharbí northwestern

شمالي shimālí northern شمالي شرقي northeastern شمالي غربي
northwestern شمالي آسمان بربنډ the northern lights, the aurora
borealis *sámt-i history* سمت شمالي، شمالي خوا the Northern
District شمالي ولايات the Northern Provinces (of Afghanistan)

شمان shəmán *m.* garbage, trash

شماندروز shamāndróz *m.* silk cloth

شمائل shamāíl *m. Arabic plural* **1** innate qualities; innate
properties **2** talents; merits; virtues

شمځی shamdzáj *f.* ☞ شمزی

شماخه shamákha *f.* ☞ شاخه

شمرتی shmə́rti *m. plural botany* fenugreek

شمزی shamzáj *f.* **1** spine, backbone, spinal cord **2** lower back,
small of the back **3** support

شمس shams *m. Arabic* **1** sun **2** *proper name* Shams

شمسي shamsí solar شمسي نظام the solar year شمسي سنه، شمسي کال
the solar system

شمشاد shamshád *m.* **1** spruce, fir **2** box (tree)

شمشتی shamshatáj *f.* turtle, tortoise

شمشمه shamshamá *f.* **1** splendor, brilliance; pomp **2** honor, esteem

شمشو shamshó *f.* ☞ سیخچه

شمشېر shamshér *m.* sword; sabre, cavalry sword

شمشېرکه shamsheráka *f.* support brace used in fixing the plowshare
to the plow beam

شمشېرگر shamshergə́r *m.* **1** cutler **2** armorer

شمعه shám'a *f.* شمع *Arabic* candle

شمعه دان sham'adán *m.* candlestick, candleholder

شمعه ساز sham'asáz *m.* candle maker

شمعي sham'í *adjective* candle

شمکلی shamkaláj *m.* **1** cloth rag (for cleaning millstones) **2** fringe
(for a rug, turban, etc.)

شمکور shamkór blind; suffering from night blindness

شمکوري shamkorí *f. medicine* nyctalopia, night blindness

شمکی shamakáj *m.* **1** common chicory **2** *regional* dandelion

شملانه shəmə́lắna *f.* carelessness, negligence

شمله shamlá *f.* **1** end of a turban **2** edge, selvage, fringe **3**
adornment, pride

شمله دار shamladár fringed

شمن shamán *m.* **1** idol worshipper **2** idol

شمندروز shamandróz *m.* **1** kind of coarse silk-cloth **2** taffeta **3** ☞
سمبال

شموخه shamúkha *f.* ☞ شاخه

شمول shumúl *m. Arabic* participation په شمول ... د with the
participation of ...

شمولیت shumuliját *m. Arabic* participation د چا سره شمولیت کول to
participate with someone in something

شمه [1] shə́ma *f.* tent (usually of black goats' wool) توره شمه a black
tent (of goats' wool) *idiom* شمه سپینول to undertake the impossible
شمه نه سپینېږي *saying literal* A black tent will never be white.
figurative The leopard cannot change his spots.

شمه [2] shumá *f.* juice (squeezed from fruits)

شمه [3] sháma *f.* ☞ شمع

شمه [4] shammá *f. Arabic* odor, smell

شمي [1] shammí *Arabic* **1** olifactory **2** fragrant, odorous, aromatic

شمي [2] shamí *m. proper name* Shami

شمبر shmer *m. Western* **1** quantity; numerical strength; number د
نفوسو شمبر population strength, numbers طبع شمبر، د چاپ شمبر edition (e.g., of a book) په زیات شمبر a in great quantity b a
great quantity په شمبر راتلل ... د to be counted in ... to be included
in the number ... **2** calculation د شمبر علم arithmetic

شمبرل shmerə́l *transitive* [*past:* ويې شمبره] **1** to count, reckon,
calculate **2** to suppose, consider **3** to enumerate **4** to count up,
list by numbers

شمبرنه shmerə́na *f.* calculation, counting

شمبرونکی ماشین shmerúnkaj calculator, adding machine شمبرونکی

شمیم shamím *Arabic* sweet-smelling, aromatic

شمیست shimíst *m.* chemist

شمیمه shamimá *f. Arabic* perfume, sweet smell, aroma

شناخت shnākht *m.* **1** acquaintance, acquaintanceship شناخت لرل to have an acquaintanceship, be acquainted with **2** understanding, intellectual grasp; knowledge **3** recognition, identification **4** *regional* recognition, perception شناخت کول to recognize, identify **5** ability, skill **6** mastery (in the execution of circle dancing)

شناخته ¹ shnākhta **1.1** acquainted **1.2** known, recognized **2** *m.* [*plural:* شناخته گان shnākhtagán] acquaintance, friend

شناخته ² shnákhta *f.* شناختسه shnákhtsa *f.* tombstone inscription, epitaph

شناز shanāz *m.* shināz **1** inflated hide used to cross rivers **2** wineskin, waterskin

شناس shinās *m. combining form* knowing, acquainted with something مردم شناس Orientalist شرقشناس anthropologist

شناسي shināsí *f. combining form* knowledge, understanding مردم شناسي anthropology شرقشناسي Eastern Studies

شناغله shnāghla *f.* **1** syrup made of the fruit of the pistachio tree, *Pistacia khinjuk, Pistacia kabulica* **2** mixture of ground khinjuk and flour

شنالغه shnálgha *f.* dough which has not risen

شناوی ¹ shnāváj *f.* buttermilk, whey

شناوی ² shnāváj **1** with a touch of gray (in the beard)

شنبه shambá *f.* شنبې shambé *f. Western* **1** Saturday **2** *component of a name of the week* چارشنبه Wednesday

شنتی shanṭáj *f.* stone embankment, quay

شندزکی shəndzakáj *f.* شنڅه shóndza shándza *f.* abscess, boil, furuncle

شنځی shəndzáj *f.* ☞ شمزی

شناخته shnákhta *f.* ☞ شناخته ²

شند shand *m.* a kind of falcon or hawk

شندل ¹ shindál *m. plural* ☞ شیندل ¹

شندل ² shindál *transitive* ☞ شیندل ²

شنده ¹ shánda *f.* **1** agitation, excitement **2** calamity **3** desperate undertaking; senseless affair **4** mockery **5** extravagance

شنده ² shində́ *inperfect tense of* شندل ²

شندی ¹ shandaj *m.* star tulip, *Tulipa stellata*

شندي ² shándi *plural of* شنده ¹

شنډ ¹ shunḍ *m.* ginger

شنډ ² shanḍ shəṇḍ **1** barren, sterile وچه شنده **a** completely barren (of land) **b** dry (of a cow) **2** unproductive, not yielding crops **3** fruitless, without result **4** frustrated, unsuccessful

شنډاک shənḍák *m.* kind of children's game played with pebbles

شونډپاره shunḍpārá ☞

شنډتوب shanḍtób *m.* ☞ شنډوالی

شنډکیز چرگ shunḍkíz-chərg *m.* turkey

شنډوالی shandváḷaj *m.* **1** unfruitfulness; sterility **2** unproductiveness; barrenness **3** washout, fizzle **4** failure

شنډول shanḍavál *denominative, transitive* [*past:* شنډ یې کړ] **1** to render sterile **2** to make unfruitful, make barren **3** to cause to be

a fizzle, cause to be a washout **4** to frustrate (plans); bring to naught (efforts)

شنده shánḍa shóṇḍa *feminine singular of* شنډل ²

شنډی shanḍáj **1** fruit of an Indian lilac, *Melia sempervirens* **2** walnut (in the husk)

شنډیدل shanḍedál *denominative, intransitive* [*past:* شنډ شو] **1** to be barren **2** to be unproductive, be of low-yield **3** to be fruitless, be without result **4** to be disrupted, be thwarted (plans); fail; come to naught (of efforts)

شنقار shunḳār *m.* gerfalcon

شنک shanák *m.* cobbling together, pooling resources (e.g., money, etc.)

شنکاړه shənkāṛa *f.* stony soil, barren soil

شنکی shinkáj *m. proper name* Shinkaj

شنگ ¹ shing *m.* ash tree

شنگ ² shəng *m.* **1** peep; soft sound **2** a tiny object, insignificant object; tiny bit

شنگار shəngār *m.* soft sound

شنگال shangāl *m.* ☞ ښنگل

شنگرف shingárf *m. plural* **1** cinnabar (color) **2** red ink

شنگرک shangrák *m.* kind of plant

شنگری ¹ shingráj *f.* ☞ شینگری

شنگری ² shangráj *f.* form for casting pots

شنگرپ shingiríp *m. plural* ☞ شنگرف

شنگره shəngára *f.* girl who has run off with someone against her parents' will

شنگشویه shangshója *f.* cleaning small stones from rice

شنگل shungúl *m. botany* broomrape, *Orobanche*

شنگن shəngə́ṇ *m.* ☞ شگون

شنگهای shanghāj *m.* Shanghai (city)

شنل shanál shənál *transitive* [*past:* شانه یې وی] **1** to seek, look for **2** to search for **3** to grope, rummage **4** to scrutinize, study **5** to explain, check upon, investigate **6** to dig over, hoe up

شننه shanána *f.* **1** search **2** inquiry; raid **3** examination **4** check; investigation **5** digging over; hoeing up

شنو shno *oblique plural of* شین

شنوا shanavá serving

شنواري ¹ shinvārí *plural* the Shinvari (tribe) **2** shinvāráj *m.* Shinvari (tribesman)

شنوالی shənvāḷáj *f.* olive tree; olive (fruit)

شنول shanavál *transitive* [*past:* شناوه یې وی] to rock, vacillate, shake, shiver, tremble

شنه ¹ shna *masculine plural of* شین **2** *m. plural* green forage, fodder (lucerne grass, clover)

شنه ² shna **1** *feminine singular of* شین **2** *f.* grass; hay

شنه پیروي shnə perávi *m. plural* disease of the eyes

شنه توخله shna ṭukhə́lá *f.* whooping cough

شنه خړه shna khə́ra *f.* time before dawn, first light

شنه زرغونه shna-zarghuná *f.* rainbow

شین زمری shnə zmarí *plural of* شین زمری

شنه غاره shna ghā́ṛa *f.* whooping cough

شنه کوتره shna kavtára *f.* grey dove

شنه کېدۀ shnə kedə́ *m. plural* 1 growth, germination 2 origin

شنه لوخړه shna lukhə́ṛa *f.* thick smoke, blue-grey smoke

شنه هریره shna hariṛá *f. botany* the green mirobolan (fruit), fruit of *Terminalia chebula*

شنی shə́naj *m.* 1 ☞ شینی 1 2 tick (bloodsucking) 3 poultry louse

شنی shné *f. plural* pistachio (fruit)

شنی shné *feminine plural of* شین شنی اوبه کول a to make very liquid, make watery b to cook without seasoning or without adding spices (soup, etc.) شنی اوبه کېدۀ to be very dilute, watery شنی په شنی ورکول to lend money at interest

شنبدل shanedə́l *intransitive* [*past:* وي یی شنبده] 1 to tremble, shudder; shake, swing 2 to quiver; to beat, pulsate

شنبده shənedə́ *m.* shnedə́ *plural* 1 growth; generation 2 origin

شنیع shaní' *Arabic* base, vile, nasty

شنبلی shneláj *m.* 1 meadow, glade 2 verdure

شنیونه shnevúna *f.* شنی ونه pistachio (the tree)

شن shaṇ *m.* neighing (of a horse) شن او شون neighing (of horses) شن او شون اچول to neigh loudly

شن shaṇ 1 frightened 2 having lost consciousness, being unconscious

شنا shəṇā́ *f.* ☞ شنهار

شن shaṇshán *m.* rustle, rustling

شنشنی shəṇshəṇáj *m.* 1 chime 2 trinket

شنشوب shaṇshób *m.* washing of rice شنشوب کول to wash rice شنشوب کېدۀ to be washed (of rice)

شنول shəṇavə́l *transitive* ☞ شنول

شنول shəṇavə́l *transitive* [*past:* وي یی شناوه] to make neigh (a horse)

شنهار shəṇahā́r *m.* 1 rustle; rustling 2 neighing (of a horse) 3 ringing, chime 4 noise, uproar, roar د سیند شنهار the noise of river 5 whistle (of the wind)

شنبدل shəṇedə́l *intransitive* ☞ شیشنبدل

شو shu 1 *past tense of* شول 2 *present and future perfective, first person plural of* شول

شو sho *interjection* sho-sho (cry used to halt a donkey)

شواخون shvākhún *m.* shavākhún 1 suffering, torment, torture

شوار shvār spread out, laid out

شواروز shavāróz *m.* shavārúz ☞ شبانه روز

شوارول shvāravə́l *denominative, transitive* [*past:* شواریي کړ] to spread, spread out

شواربدل shvāredə́l *denominative, intransitive* [*past:* شوار شو] to spread, extend, unfold; be spread out

شوار shvār 1 sluggish; slow-moving 2 disorderly 3 crude, rude

شواره shvā́ṛa *f.* unproductive land

شواړي شواړي shvā́ṛi-shvā́ṛi 1 divided into small pieces or shreds; untwisted, undone 2 sluggish; slow-moving 3 ungainly, awkward

شواړي شواړي کول a to undo, unplait b to become sluggish, become slow-moving شواړي شواړي کېدۀ a to become undone, become unplaited b to be sluggish, be slow-moving

شوال shavā́l *m.* Shaval (the western spurs of the Suleiman Mountains)

شوال shavvā́l *f. Arabic* Shawwal (the 10th month of the lunar year)

شواهد shavāhíd *m. Arabic plural of* شهادات

شوبله shóbla *f.* 1 placed trampled down by hooves or feet (e.g., on a battleground) 2 old riverbed 3 drainage canal 4 moist soil, sandy soil

شوبله shóbla *f.* 1 *zoology* centipede 2 tank

شوبی shobə́j *f.* شببو

شوپ shup *m.* snuffling, slurping (when swallowing liquid food)

شوپه shopā́ *m.* ☞ شوپا

شوپرک shaparák *m.* shavparák bat (the animal)

شوپري shoparí *f.* profession of a chauffeur

شوپړ shopə́ṛ *m.* ☞ شوپه

شوپشو shopəshó 1 dispersed, scattered 2 dissipated, squandered شوپشو کول a to disperse, scatter b to dissipate

شوپه shupá *m.* shopá 1 uncircumcized male 2 *abusive* unbeliever, infidel

شوپشو shopəshó ☞ شوپه شو

شوپیان shupijā́n *m.* loss

شوپیانه shupijā́na *f.* calumny, slander

شوتالو shavtālú *m.* ☞ شفتالو

شوتتی shavtátaj *m.* turtle

شوترکی shutárki *f. plural* ☞ شترکي

شوتل shavtál *m. plural* شوتله shavtála *f.* Persian clover

شوته shavtá *f.* mortar of slaked lime, ash, etc. (for stuccoing bathhouses, sheds)

شوتي shávti *f. plural* joke شوتي کول to joke

شوت shuṭ 1 armless 2 legless 3 lame

شوتکه shuṭáka *f.* ear (of corn)

شوت لاسی shuṭlā́saj armless

شوته shuṭá *f.* unripe melon

شوته shúṭa *feminine singular of* شوت

شوتی shúṭaj *m.* armless

شوخ shokh 1 playful, mischievous شوخ هلک mischievous child 2 bold, cheeky; brazen

شوخ چشم shokhcháshm having lively or crafty eyes

شوخ وشخ shokhushákh immodest; brazen

شوخون shokhún *m.* ☞ شبخون

شوخي shokhí 1 *f.* .1 playfulness, mischievousness په شوخۍ سره ویل to joke, speak in a joking tone 1.2 boldness, cheekiness شوخي کول a to be naughty b to act in a bold or cheeky manner 2.1 lively; joking, playful 2.2 cheeky, bold

شوخین shokhín lively, smart, bright; playful, jolly

شودانه shavdā́na *f. anatomy* fontanelle

شودپۍ shodəpə́j *f.* white wagtail (the bird)

شوده [1] shodә́ *m. plural* shodá *f. Eastern* 1 milk تینگ شوده whole milk **a** تا د شودو مور tea and milk د شودو چای سپور شوده skim milk wet nurse **b** adoptive mother 2 milky sap of a plant, latex

شوده [2] shodá stupid; on the simple side

شودپۍ shodapə́j *f. plural* ☞

شودې shodé *f.* shudé *plural dialect* milk *idiom* د شودو نه یې خولې بوی خي *literal* The milk hasn't been licked off his lips yet. *figurative* He is still a child.

شودیاره shudjā́ra *f.* ☞ شدیاره

شودپۍ shodepə́j *f. plural botany* spurge, *Euphorbia*

شودي خرخونکی shodé khartsavúnkaj *m.* شودي والا shodevālá *m.* milkman, milk merchant, dairyman

شودي وریجې shodé vrídzhe *f. plural Eastern* rice kasha cooked in milk

شودنگ shodә́ng *m.* 1 a fool 2 calumny, slander

شور [1] shor *m.* noise, ruckus, sensation, stir شور کول، شور اچول to raise a ruckus, brawl, row 2 commotion 3 experience, feeling د عشق شور amatory emotions, feelings of love

شور [2] shur *m.* shəvúr 1 splash (e.g., of water being poured) 2 peep; low noise شور کول to cheep complainingly (of hatchlings, etc.)

شورا shurā́ *f. Arabic* [*plural:* شوراوي shurā́vi *plural:* شوراگاني shurā́gāni] council (institution) د شوروي سوسیالستي جماهیرو د اتحاد عالي شورا The Supreme Soviet of the Union of Soviet Socialist Republics اقتصادي او اجتماعي شورا The Economic and Social Council (of the United Nations) د امنیت شورا The Security Council (of the United Nations) د قیمومت شورا The Trusteeship Council د افغانستان شورا The Afghan Parliament شورا جوړول to form a council

شوراوک shorābák *m.* شوراوک shorāvák *m.* Shoravak (district between Kelat and Kandagar)

شوربا shorbā́ *f.* ☞ بنوروا

شورپنیر shorpanír *m.* salted cheese, pickled cheese

شورپوشت shorapúsht peevish; violent, unruly

شورش shorísh *m.* rebellion; mutiny; insurrection شورش کول to rebel; instigate mutiny; rise up (in insurgency)

شورشر shorshár *m.* شورشغب shorshagháb *m.* 1 uproar, row 2 agitation, alarm, disturbance

شورش والا shorishvālá *m.* rebel; mutineer; insurgent

شورق shorә́k *m. anatomy* skin of the tongue

شورکی [1] shurkáj *m.* ☞ شورهار

شورکی [2] shorakə́j *f.* brahmin mynah, black-headed mynah, *Temenuchus pagodarum*

شورماشور shormāshór *m.* noise, turmoil; disturbance د کوڅي شورماشور noise of the street

شورمبی shurumbé *f. plural* ☞ شلومبي

شوروا shorvā́ *f.* ☞ بنوروا

شوروفرغا shor-u-ghavghā́ *f.* شوروفریاد shor-u-farjā́d *m.* ruckus and row شوروغوغا کول to cry out, shout

شورول shoravә́l *transitive* ☞ بنورول

شوروغوغا shor-u-havhā́ *f.* ☞ شوروغوغا

شوروي shuraví *Arabic* 1 Soviet شوروي اتحاد thc Soviet Union شوروي حکومت Soviet Government 2 *m.* 1. the Soviet Union 2 [*plural:* شورویان shuravijā́n] a Soviet citizen

شورویه shuravijá *feminine plural of* شوروي

شورهار shorahā́r *m.* 1 noise, splashing (of poured water)

شورهاها shorhāhā́ *f.* ☞ شورشر

شورا shurā́ *f. Arabic* ☞ شورا

شوربدل shuredә́l *intransitive* [*past:* و شوربدي] to pour out, splash out

شور [1] shur *m.* ☞ شورهار

شور [2] shur ☞ شار

شوراʼي shoṛají *m.* funnel (for pouring liquids from one container to another)

شوپړ shuṛpúṛ very dirty

شوړتک shuṛtә́k fine (of cloth)

شورشوړۍ shuṛshuṛә́j *f.* fireworks

شورکی shuṛkáj *m.* ☞ شورهار

شورگی shorgáj *m.* 1 mortar 2 vessel in which butter is churned

شورمبی shurumbé *f. plural* ☞ شلومبي

شوروۍ shuṛavә́l *transitive* ☞ شپړول [1, 2]

شوره shoṛa *f.* shuṛa 1 strainer 2 stopper made of grass 3 old cloths, rag 4 filaments (on the inflorescence of millet, etc.) 5 a large piece of something

شورهار shuṛhā́r *m.* ☞ شورهار

شوری shúṛi *feminine plural of* شور [2]

شوربدل [1] shuṛedә́l *intransitive* ☞ شپردل [1]

شوربدل [2] shuṛedә́l *intransitive* [*past:* و شوربدي] to splash (of water)

شوغردل shughṛedә́l *intransitive* [*past:* و شوغپده] 1 to roll from side to side; to toss (in sleep) 2 to squeak, squeal

شوغکه shughā́ka *f.* beard (on an ear of cereal grain)

شوغول shughavә́l *denominative* [*past:* شوغ یې کړ] to curve, bend; distort

شوغه [1] shughá *f.* stiff wool; stiff hairs

شوغه [2] shughá *f.* ☞ چوغه

شوغی shugháj *m.* 1 sheep or goat with spots on the ears 2 male with a sparse beard

شوغبدل shughedә́l *denominative, intransitive* [*past:* شوغ شو] to bend, curve; become distorted

شوق shauk *m. Arabic* 1 wish, desire, enthusiasm په شوک څوک a to evoke a desire in someone **b** to egg someone on شوق لرل to wish, have a wish, have a desire د سبق او علم شوق لرل to strive for knowledge 2 diligence, zeal, interest د کار سره شوق او

مینه شوق او ذوق love or enthusiasm for a matter or business enthusiasm شوق كول to display zeal, show interest

شوق انگبز shauḵangéz attractive, alluring حسن شوق انگبز وي Beauty attracts.

شوقدر shauḵadár *m.* Shabkadar (the 27th night of the month of Ramadan)

شوقمن shauḵmǝ́n شوقمند shauḵmánd desirous of; wishing for something د هغه فلم د هواخورۍ ډېر شوقمن دي They love walks. د ليدو ډېر شوقمن وم I wanted very much to see that movie.

شوقي shauḵí شوقين shavḵín 1 wishing for; desirous of something; enthusiastic about something 2 *m.* fan, amateur of something د هغه د فټبال شوقي دئ He is a سينما شوقي نه يم I'm not a movie fan. football fan.

شوك ¹ shuk 1 torn off, stripped 2 broken off, torn up; torn to pieces 3 robbed

شوك ² shok *m. medicine* shock

شوكاره shukắra *f. usually plural* شوكاري shukāri 1 scratching 2 scratch, abrasion شوكاره كول to scratch

شوكاڼی shaukáṇaj *m.* 1 soft stone (from which pottery is made) 2 slate, clayey shale

شوكپشوك shukpǝshúk شوك پوك shukpúk cut out, cut up into pieces

شوكت shavkát *m.* shaukát *Arabic* 1 power, greatness; splendor; brilliance 2 *proper name* Shawkat

شوك شوك shukshúk dilapidated, worn-out

شوكمار shukmắr robber, thief, bandit

شوكپشوك shuk-mashúk ☞ شوك مشوك

شوكور shavkór shaukór ☞ شمكور

شوكورۍ shavkóri *f.* shaukóri ☞ شمكورۍ

شوكول ¹ shukavǝ́l *transitive regional* ☞ شكول

شوكه shúka *f.* robbery; burglary; banditry شوكه كول to rob; engage in thievery

شوكي پوكي shúki-púki *feminine plural of* شوك پوك

شوكبدل shukedǝ́l *intransitive* ☞ شكبدل ¹

شوگه shugá *f.* kind of rice

شوگیر shogír *m.* ☞ شبخون

شوگیره shogíra *f.* شوگیرۍ shogiri *f.* vigilance, vigil, watch

شول shvǝ́l *independent perfective of* كبدل *intransitive* 1 [*present:* لویه غلطي وشوه *past:* وشو] .1 to happen, occur, come about څه در باندي شوي دي؟ What happened to you? ... كله داسي هم وشي چه Sometimes it happens that ... 1.2 to occur (i.e., "fall" of rain) تېركال بارانونه ډېر وشول It rained a lot last year. 1.3 to pass (of time) پنځه كاله وشوه Five years went by. 1.4 to take place, be held مجلس وشو A meeting took place. 1.5 to be effected, be completed كار وشو The business was effected. 1.6 to be born د احمد زوی وشو A son was born to Ahmed. 1.7 to arrive (of news, tidings, etc.) 1.8 to get to, disappear; depart (of a person) زما كتاب څه شو؟ Where has my book disappeared to? احمد څه شو؟ Where did Ahmed depart to? 1.9 to arrive, come (season) پسرلی شو Spring has come 2 *an auxiliary and productive verb*

شي *present:* شو *past:* .1 (expresses the perfective aspect of the verb) كبدل *in compound verbs and verbs with prepositional constructions* رهي سو He set out. زخمي شو He is wounded. په چرت كښي شو He fell to thinking. په ژړا شوه She began to cry. 2.2 (forms the perfective aspect in the passive voice) ختكي وخورپ شو The melon has been eaten up. 2.3 (in potential constructions) to be able زه تلای شم I can go. زه لیكلای شم I can write. و به ختلای شم I will be able to arise. 2.4 *past tense third person masculine plural vice* شوه 1

شول ² shul rude, rough

شول ³ shul *compounding word with* شل ³

شولتكی sholtǝkáj *m.* ☞ شورق

شولخ sholákh *m.* ☞ شورق

شولك sholák *m. anatomy* skin

شولكه sholǝ́ka *f.* leech

شولكی sholǝkáj *m.* short coat for a child; jacket

شولگ sholág *m.* ☞ شولك

شولگره sholgára *f.* rice paddy; field under rice cultivation

شولمپی sholǝmpáj *m.* chaff from rice straw

شولو ¹ shólo *oblique of* شولی ¹

شولو ² shvǝ́lu *first person plural past of* شول ¹

شولو ³ shvǝ́lo *dialect vice* شو ¹

شول وابنه، شولوابنه sholvaḵǝ́ *m. plural* rice straw

شول وشل shol wshǝ́l شولوشل sholushál *m.* ☞ شل وشل

شوله ¹ shola *f.* ☞ شولی ¹

شوله ² shvála *f.* knife for trimming a (horse's) hoof

شوله ³ shvála *f. dialect* ☞ شولی ²

شوله ⁴ sholá *f.* watery rice kasha; thin rice gruel

شوله ⁵ shvǝ́la *feminine of* شول ¹

شوله ⁶ shvǝ́lǝ *plural dialect vice* شول ¹

شوله ⁷ shóla Hey, you.

شوله غم shvǝ́laghám *m.* misfortune, calamity, disaster

شوله یز sholajíz *adjective* pertaining to rice-growing, rice growing

شولی ¹ shóle *f.* shóli *plural* raw rice, unprocessed rice سپیني شولی white rice غتي شولی farinacious rice سری شولی red rice نری شولی translucent rice *idiom* د شولو په نرخ غوښنت خرڅول *literal* to sell millet at the price of rice *figurative* to cheat someone

شولی ² shváli *f. plural* د كولمو شولی gripping (stomach) pains

شولی ³ shvǝ́le *feminine plural of* شول ¹

شولی ⁴ sholǝ́j *f.* lazy woman

شوم ¹ shum hungry شوم پاتي كبدل to grow hungry

شوم ² shum *Arabic* 1 unhappy, ill-fated, ill-starred 2 miserly 3 unlucky ځما نصیب شوم و I had bad luck. 4 serious (of a crisis)

شوم ³ shvǝm *first person singular past of* شول ¹

شوم بخت shumbákht unhappy, ill-fated

شومتیا shumtjắ *f.* 1 hunger 2 miserliness 3 misfortune, ill luck

شومړی shumṛé *f. plural* ☞ شلومبه

474

شوم شغال shum-shaghál *m.* **1** wicked, pernicious, or obnoxious man **2** miserly man, miser

شومل shumə́l *transitive* [*past:* شوم یي شومل] **1** to drink in large gulps; drink at one gulp **2** to quickly gulp down (soup)

شومله shomlá old, decrepit; worn-out

شوملي shomlé *f. plural* buttermilk

شوموالی shumvā́laj *m.* ☞

شومول shumavə́l *transitive* [*past:* و يي شوماوه] to compel to drink at a gulp, force to drink in large swallows

شومه ¹ shúma *f.* part or division of the night لومړی شومه the first half of the night دوهمه شومه the time after midnight *dialect* twilight قلاره شومه ده a quiet night

شومه ² shúma *f.* **1** fodder, feed; food, victuals شومه اچول to feed (livestock) شومه حاصلول to obtain food, get nourishment **2** evening meal, supper **3** funeral meal, refreshments served to mourners په خپل پلار يي ښه شومه وکړه He arranged a nice wake for his father د مخکي شومه کېدل to lie on خاورو شومه کېدل to perish the damp ground

شومه ³ shumá *f.* **1** juice, extract (from fruit) **2** meaning, essence of something

شومه دم shumadám *m.* د شپي شومه دم the dead of night

شومی ¹ shúmaj *m.* **1** swallowing **2** swallow شومی کول ☞ شومل

شومي ² shumí *f.* شوميت shumiját *m.* **1** starvation, undernourishment **2** hunger strike (e.g., in order to force payment of a debt) **3** miserliness, avarice, greed

شونټی shonṭəj *f.* shunṭə́j wooden taper, splint of wood used for a light, kindling wood

شونډ ¹ shunḍ *m. plural* ginger

شونډ ² shunḍ *m.* snout, muzzle

شونډا shunḍá *m.* man with a hare lip

شونډان shunḍā́n *m. plural colloquial form from* شونډه

شونډپاره shunḍpārá having a harelip

شونډک shunḍə́k *m.* [*plural:* شونډکونه shunḍəkúna *plural:* شونډکان shunḍəkān] **1** trunk (of an elephant) **2** proboscis (e.g., of a bee)

شونډکی shunḍəkáj ugly, repulsive (of a person)

شونډکيز چرګ shunḍəkíz chərg *m.* turkey

شونډپاره shunḍú ☞

شونډور shunḍavə́r **1** thick-lipped **2** with wide rims (of pottery)

شونډه shunḍa *f.* [*plural:* شونډي shunḍi *plural:* شونډان shunḍā́n] lip شونډي په غاښ کول *literal* to bite the شونډه چیچل lips to bite the lips *figurative* to be surprised, be astounded د فدا شونډه په شنه کېدو Fida's mustaches are beginning to grow. شونډان خرول to **a** grumble at, feel hurt **b** to plan an evil action شونډان يي وچ شوه **a** He was annoyed and fell silent. **b** He became agitated.

شونډیز shunḍíz *linguistics* labial

شونشون shunshún *m.* whistle, howling (of the wind)

شونکی shúnkaj ☞ شوونکی

shungə́ṇ *m.* ☞ شگون

شونه shvə́na *f.* coming into being; realization

شونی shúnaj ☞ شوونکی

شوو ¹ shov *m.* protection; shelter, refuge شوو ورکول to protect; shelter

شوو ² shvu *first person plural participle* ☞ شول ¹

شوونکی shvúnkaj شووني shvúnaj possible, probable; feasible

شووینیزم shovinízm *m.* chauvinism

شوه ¹ shəvá *f.* Sissoo tree, Shishma tree, *Dalbergia sissoo*

شوه ² shavá ☞ شپوه

شوه ³ shvə *m. plural* **1** past tense of شول ¹ **2** *m. plural* possibility, feasibility

شوه ⁴ shva *f. past of* شول ¹

شوه توب shavatób *m.* **1** lowering, descent; descending **2** slope, declivity

شوی shuj *m.* shoj **1** coarse cotton-cloth **2** ☞ الچه

شوی ² shoj cry used to drive bullocks and cows

شوی ³ shə́vaj *past participle of* شول ¹

شوي ⁴ shə́ve *f.* Nim tree, *Azadirachta indica*

شوي ⁵ shve *f. second person singular and plural of* شول ¹

شوئ ⁶ shvəj *Eastern second person plural, past of* شول ¹

شوی ده shə́veda *vice*

شوي دي ¹ shə́vidi *vice*

شوئ دئ ² shə́vajdəj *vice*

شه ¹ shah *m.* ☞ شاه

شه ² shə *Eastern past tense of* شول ¹

شه ³ sha *imperative of* شول ¹

شها shahā́ *f.* beloved

شهاب shihā́b shahā́b *m. Arabic* [*plural:* شهب shuhúb] **1** falling, star **2** meteor, bolide **3** flame

شهاب الدین shihābuddín *m. Arabic proper name* Shahabuddin

شهادت shahādát *m. Arabic* [*plural:* شهادونه shahādatúna *Arabic plural:* شواهد shavāhíd] **1** testimony, evidence تحریری شهادت written testimony, deposition چشم دید شهادت *regional* eyewitness evidence زباني شهادت *regional* oral testimony, oral evidence شهادت ورکول to testify to something **2** martyrdom (for a belief, idea) په شهادت رسېدل to perish, die (for a belief, an idea)

شهادتنامه shahādatnāmá *f.* certificate; testimonial; diploma

شهامت shahāmát *m. Arabic* **1** valor, bravery, courage **2** nobility; noble qualities

شهباز shahbā́z *m.* fretboard (of a rabab)

شهد shā́had shāhd *m. Arabic plural* honey

شهدا shuhadā́ *m. Arabic plural of* شهید **2**

شهر ¹ shahr *m.* city

شهر ² shuhr *m. Arabic* desperate undertaking

شهر ³ shahr *m.* [*plural:* شهور shuhur] *Arabic* month

شهرالعسل shahr-ul-'ásl *m. Arabic* honeymoon

شهرپناه shahrpanā́h *f.* city walls; city fortifications

شهرت shuhrát *m. Arabic* glory, fame د شهرت تنده the pursuit of glory شهرت گټل، شهرت حاصلول، شهرت پیداکول to become renown,

د زر شهرت گټلو مرض vainglory د خاص شهرت میندل to
acquire fame be outstanding

شهرسازي shahrsāzí *f.* town-planning

شهري shahrí city, municipal

شهریار shahrijār *m.* monarch, emperor, ruler, czar

شهریاري shahrijārí **1** monarchic, imperial شهریاري ذات king **2** *f.*
monarchy; reign, realm

شهزادگۍ shahzādagə́j shahzādgə́j *f.* princess

شهزاده shahzādá *m.* prince

شهسوار shahsavár *m.* dashing rider

شهسواري shahsavārí *f.* horseback riding

شهکار shahkár excellent خوندوره او شهکاره کیسه کول to relate a
fascinating tale

شهلا shahlā́ *Arabic* grey-eyed

شهنائي shahnāíj *f.* flute

شهند shahónd kind of falcon

شهنشاهي shahanshāhí *f.* **1** sovereignty **2** empire

شهو shahó *f.* ☞ شها

شهوت shahvát *m. Arabic* lust, concupiscence, sexual desire

شهوت پرست shahvatparást شهوتي shahvatí concupiscent, lustful

شهود [1] shuhúd *m. Arabic* **1.1** presence **1.2** intuition **2** present,
one present or attending

شهود [2] shuhúd *m. Arabic plural of* شاهد

شهور shuhúr *m. Arabic plural of* شهر [3]

شهی shahə́j *f.* ☞ شها

شهید shahíd *Arabic* **1** killed, slain **2** *m.* [*plural:* شهیدان shahidā́n
Arabic plural: شهدا shuhadā́] **.1** martyr (for a belief, idea) شهید
کول a to kill b to disgrace شهید کېدل a to be killed b to die a
martyr's death **2.2** victim (e.g., of a flood)

شهین shahín *m.* **1** kind of falcon **2** beam (of a scale) **3** camel gun

شهین چي shahinchí *m. history* cannon-founder, cannon-maker

شی [1] shaj *m. Arabic Western* [*plural:* شیان shijā́n shəjā́n *Eastern
plural:* شي shi *plural:* شیونه shijúna *Arabic plural:* اشیا ashjā́] **1**
thing, object د مکتب شیان school equipment دا څه شی دئ؟ What is
that? و هیڅ شي ته نه و ار نه دئ nothing, a trifle هیڅ شی نه دئ shi He
wants for nothing. یو شی کول to unify, unite **2** question, problem,
matter **3** [*plural:* شیان shijā́n shəjā́n *plural:* اشیا ashjā́] goods,
commodities د شیانو تولیدي شیان industrial goods تولیدي شیان
commodity products

شي [2] shi *plural of* شی [1]

شي [3] shi *present tense of* شول [1]

شئ [4] she *second person present of* شول [1]

شئ [5] shəj *imperative plural of* شول [1] تېر شئ! Pass along!

شیاخه shiā́dza *f.* ☞ شاخه

شیاطین shajātín *m. Arabic plural of* شیطان

شیان shijā́n *Western plural of* شی [1]

شیب shajb *m. Arabic* **1** grey hair **2** old age, declining years

شیبه [1] shebará *f. medicine* شبره تبه typhus

شیبه [2] shibára *f.* relief; easiness

شبه shebá *f.* **1** instant, wink, twinkling په یوه شېبه کښې in an
instant; instantaneously, instantly **2** moment; time لږ شېبه وروسته
shortly thereafter شېبه په شېبه from time to time بایسته بنه شېبه
fikr وړئ و .He reflected for quite a long time شېبه نیمه پس
somewhat later د دوهۍ خو شېبې mealtime **3** heavy rain, pouring
rain, a downpour په شېبو وریدل to rain buckets

شیت [1] shit ☞ چیت

شبت shet *m.* ☞ شېډ

شیطان shajtā́n *m.* **1** slanderer **2** debauchee; faker **3** ☞ شیطان

شیطان خوت shajtānkhvə́t *m.* ant lion, doodle bug (larva)

شیت په شیت shitpəshít scattered

شیتړ shitə́r *m.* coarse cloth

شیته خوله shítakhvulá shítakhulá with open mouth

شبتۍ shetə́j *f.* **1** tip (of an arrow) **2** ear of maize

شیته shitá́ *f.* ear of maize (not cleaned)

شیخ shajkh *m.* shekh *Arabic* [*plural:* شیخان shajkā́n *Arabic
plural:* شیوخ shujúk *plural:* مشایخ mashājíkh] **1** elder, venerable
old man, sheik **2** spiritual advisor **3** convert to Islam (in India)

شیشر shikhdáv *m.* شیخدو shekhdáv ☞ شیشر

شیخي shajkhí *f.* boasting, bragging د شیخي په ژبه ویل to boast, brag

شیدا shajdā́ **1** crazy, maddened **2** madly in love شیدا پتنگ *poetry* a
lovelorn butterfly

شبدلوبنی shidlokhaj *m.* milk pitcher, milk container

شیدي shidé *f. plural Western* milk وچي شیدي dried milk شیدي
dried milk شیدی مور wet nurse د شیدو مور rice kasha in milk وریجي
milk, yield milk (cow) شیدي ورکول a to give milk b to breast-
feed, nurse *idiom* شیدي سره ایله کول، شیدي سره پربنبول to love one
another شیدي او غوري کبدل to be very friendly, love one another

شیدیاره shidjā́ra *f.* ☞ شیدیاره

شیدی والا shidevalā́ *m.* milkman, dairyman

شیډ sheḍ *m.* lampshade

شیر [1] sher *m.* **1** tiger **2** lion شیر یا گیدړه کبدل *literal* Be either a
lion or a jackal. *figurative* All or nothing. **2** شیر د خدای The Lion
of the Gods (an epithet of the Prophet Ali) **3** *proper name* Sher
شیر افضل Sher Afzal شیر علي Sher Ali

شیر [2] shir *m.* milk

شیرازه [1] sherāzá *f.* **1** order; state of being put in good order,
correctness **2** knots, cords, ligatures (fastening something) **3**
hemstitch, whipstitch, overstitch **4** stitching (bookbindery) **5**
buttress (on the wall of a fort)

شیرازه [2] shirāza *f.* sherā́za sour milk (used as a cooling drink)

شیرازي shirāzí *f.* happiness, joy

شیراني shirāní *m. plural* the Shirani (tribe) **2** shirānáj *m.*
Shirani (tribesman)

شیربیر sherbabár *m.* lion

شیربیره sherbabára *f.* lioness

شیربچه sherbachá *m.* **1** *history* Cub Scout **2** lion cub

شیربرنج shirbiríndzh *m.* rice kasha with milk

شیرچای shirchā́j *m. singular & plural* tea with milk

شیرچائي shirchāi̯ tea blossoms with milk

شبرخان sherkhán *m.* Sherkhan (city) د شبرخان بندر Sherkhan (a river port, formerly Kizil-kala)

شبرخت sherkhát *m.* ☞ شبرخط

شیرخشت shirkhíst *m.* manna or dried sap from the Cotoneaster (a flowering shrub, *Cotoneaster nummularia*)

شبرخط sherkhát *m.* sherkhat (a kind of game) شبرخط کول to play sherkhat

شیرخور shirkhór شیرخوره shirkhóra 1 being nourished with milk شیرخوار هلک a breast-fed child 2 breast-fed child

شیردان [1] shirdā́n *m.* 1 milk jug 2 abomasum (fourth division of the stomach in ruminant animals, a source of rennet)

شبردان [2] sherdā́n شبردهن sherdahā́n *m.* tap, spigot

شبرشاو shershā́v *m.* jeweler's balance

شیرشیرک shirshirák *m.* pasture, meadow

شبرک [1] sherák *m.* blanket

شیرک [2] shirák *m.* unripe maize-grain

شیرکتی shirkaṭə́j *f.* cow which has given milk for a year

شبرکه sheráka *f.* ☞ بنارو

شبرکی sherəkáj 1.1 brave, valorous 1.2 bragging, boastful 2 *m.* 1 brave man 2.2 braggart, boaster شبرکی کېدل to boast

شیرگرم shirgárm warm

شبرم sherám *m. proper name* Sheram

شیرماهی shirmāháj *m.* small fish

شیرمست shirmást 1 suckling (of a male lamb) 2 *m.* suckling

شیرین shirín ☞ شیرین

شیروار shirvā́r *m.* ☞ پی واز

شیروانی [1] shirvānī́ *f.* 1 kind of dress 2 hipped roof

شیروانی [2] shirvānə́j *f.* 1 roof of brush and earth (hipped) 2 child's cloak

شیروشکر shirushakár *m.* 1 close friendship, intimacy 2 kind of silk cloth

شیره [1] shirá *f.* 1 sweet syrup 2 juice د معدي شیره digestive juice 3 buttermilk to which fresh milk has been added 4 sweet gruel (for newborns)

شیره [2] shirá *m.* 1 child at breast, nursling 2 suckling

شیره دار shiradā́r juicy

شیریخ shirijákh *m.* ice cream

شیرین shirín 1.1 sweet 1.2 pleasant; nice; kind, good شیرین کول *a* to make sweet *b* to make pleasant, render pleasant شیرین کېدل *a* to be made sweet *b* to be made pleasant 2 *m. proper name* Shirin

شیرین بویه shirinbujá *f.* licorice root, licorice plant, licorice

شیرین زبان shirinzabā́n shirinzubā́n 1 eloquent; golden-tongued, sweet-tongued 2 affectionate, caressing

شیرینکه shirinā́ka *f.* pimple

شیرین گفتار shiringuftā́r ☞ شیرین زبان

شیرینه shirína *f. proper name* Shirin

شیریني shirinī́ *f.* 1 candy, sweets, delicacies د شیریني صنایع the candy industry 2 sweetness شیریني ورکول to sweeten, sweeten up; *colloquial* to arrange party on the occasion of a betrothal or engagement 3 nectar 4 tip, gratuity 5 eloquence

شیریني باب shirinibā́b *m. plural* sweets, candies

شیریني پز shirinipā́z *m.* confectioner, candy maker

شیریني فروش shirinifurúsh *m.* confectioner, candy merchant

شپر sheṛ having inflamed eyelids, having inflamed eyes

شپرا sheṛā́ squint-eyed, one-eyed

شپراتوب sheṛatób *m.* squint-eyed condition, strabismus

شیشتاوه shishtāvá *f.* cow or sheep giving little milk

شیشتج shishtáj *m.* spoke (of a wheel)

شیشر shishár *m.* black-billed thrush, *Turdus atrogularis*

شیشک [1] shishák *m.* 1 niche, bay, arch; shelf 2 vault, cupola

شیشک [2] shishák *m.* three-year-old ram

شیشکه [1] shishā́ka *f.* witch; (fairy-tale) hag *idiom* د شیشکو نکلونه fables, fairy tales

شیشکه [2] shíshka *f.* 1 twig, shoot 2 narrow stripe, pattern (e.g., on a rug)

شیشگی shishgáj *m.* hedgehog

شیشن shishə́n 1 suckling, nursing (of a male) lamb 2 *m.* lamb; suckling ram

شیشنی shishnáj *m.* neighing (of a horse)

شیشنبدل shishnedə́l *intransitive* [*past:* و شیشنبده] to neigh (horse)

شیشه shishá *f.* 1 looking glass 2 vial 3 heliograph

شیطان shajtā́n *m. Arabic* [*plural:* شیطانان shajtānā́n *Arabic plural:* شیاطین shajātī́n] 1 evil spirit, Satan, devil, demon 2 wretch; mischievous person شیطان خوت ant lion (larva)

شیطان مآب shajtānmā́b *Arabic* 1 satanic, diabolical, devilish 2 base (of a person)

شیطانه shajtā́na *feminine of* شیطان

شیطاني [1] shajtānī́ *f.* 1 ☞ شیطنت 2 satanic, devilish, diabolical

شیطاني [2] shajtā́ni *f. plural of* شیطان

شیطنت shajtanát *m.* 1 dirty tricks, (diabolical) machinations; mean tricks 2 malice, spite 3 joke, prank له شیطنته ډکي سترگي roguish eyes, crafty eyes

شیعه shi'a 1 *Arabic m.* 1 [*plural:* شیعه گان shi'agā́n *m. Arabic plural:* شیعهگان *Arabic plural:* شیع shijá] Shiite 1.2 sect, party 2 *adjective* Shiite

شیعه توب shi'atób *m.* شیعه والی shi'avā́laj *m.* Shiah (movement in Islam)

شبف shef *m.* 1 supervisor 2 chief

شبفته sheftá madly in love

شیک shik smart, chic شیک لباس ostentatious clothes, rich clothing

شیکاگو shikāgó *f.* Chicago (city)

شبکدار shekdā́r checked, checkered

شیگړه shigə́ra *f.* heavy rain, downpour

شیگر shigár *m.* abductor of a young girl from her parents

شیگړه shigə́ra: شیگړه ښځه ☞ متیزه

شلاوه shelāvá *f.* uniform irrigation of land

شپله [1] shelá *f.* **1** shallow gully, depression; hollow low place ژوره شپله canyon **2** dry riverbed

شپله [2] shelá شپله کول to give a sidelong glance

شپله پینگ shelapíng *m.* man fleeing from something; one shirking work

شپلی sheláj **1** dark green **2** *m.* dark-green cloth

شیمي shimí *f.* chemistry

شیمیست shimíst *m.* chemist

شیمیائي shimjáij chemical

شین shin **1** *f.* شنه shna *m.* [*plural:* شنه shnə *f. plural:* شني shne] **1.** sky blue, blue; green شین باغ ، شنه کول green orchard **a** to grow, sprout (plants) **b** to plant with trees and shrubs **c** to make blue, make green; dye blue or green **d** to get a bruise, get a black and blue mark څوک په وهلو شین کول to beat someone black and blue **a** to grow; germinate شین کېدل ، شنه کېدل **b** to flourish (of plantings) **c** to be dyed blue or green **d** to become blue, become green **e** to turn red (from laughter) **1.2** pure, clear (of the sky) نن اسمان شین دئ Today the sky is clear. Today is a clear day. **1.3** sad, mournful زړه به یې شین وي He is feeling blue. **1.4** grey (of an animal's coat), slate grey شنه کوتره the grey dove **2.1** *m. proper name* Shin **2.2** blueness; blue color; verdure, greenness *idiom* شنه ژړا violent weeping شنه ږیره a beard streaked with grey

شین امي shin-amí completely illiterate

شین پاڼی shinpáņaj *m.* water lily

شین پوش shinpósh *m. regional* member of the Muslim League (Pakistan)

شین تتی shintatáj *m.* turtle, tortoise

شین تړی shintáŗaj *m.* cliff-dwelling nuthatch

شین تاغ shintágh *m.* ☞ شین تاغ

شین توب shintób *m.* ☞ شین والی

شین توپی shintopáj *f.* white wagtail

شین توتي shintotí *m.* **1** green parrot **2** roller (bird), Coraciidae

شین تاغ shinţágh *m.* شین تاغی shinţághaj roller (bird), Coraciidae

شین توپکه shinţopáka *f.* شین توپی shinţopáj *f.* white wagtail

شینجاوی shindzhávaj *m.* fading seedling, dying seedling, sapling

شینجکی shindzhakáj *f. Western* ☞ شنځکی

شین چغزی shinchaghzáj *f.* pistachio

شین چمبي shinchambáj *m.* dyer

شین خوتی shinkhúţaj *m.* ☞ شین تاغ

شین خورکه shinkhvaráka *f.* blue agama (lizard)

شیندل [1] shindál *m. plural* **1** cattle droppings **2** dampness

شیندل [2] shindál *transitive* [*past:* و یې شینده] **1** to scatter, strew **2** to sow **3** to sprinkle, spurt, squirt **4** to spread, scatter about, throw about **5** to radiate (light) **6** to expend something; to squander (money) سترگو ته خاوري شیندل to throw dust in the eyes

شینده [1] shində *imperfect tense of* شیندل [2]

شینده [2] shində *m. plural* **1** sowing, crops **2** sprinkling, spraying **3** spreading, throwing about **4** radiation (of light) **5** expenditure of something; squandering (of money)

شیندی [1] shindáj *m.* family of leguminous plants

شیندي [2] shindí *present tense of* شیندل [2]

شین ډنډ shinḍánḍ *m.* **1** green and overgrown pond **2** green valley **3** Shindand (city, formerly Sabzevar)

شین ډولی shinḍavláj *m.* half-withered crops, wilting crops

شینډی shinḍáj *f.* concern, pains, troubles, endeavors

شین رنگین shinrangín dressed in green clothing

شین زمری shinzmaráj *m.* **1** lion **2** brave man, courageous fellow

شین ږیری shingíraj *m.* man with grey streaks in his beard

شین سترگی shinstárgaj blue-eyed

شین سری [1] shinsáraj *m.* yellow wagtail

شین سری [2] shinsáre شین سری هیلی broad-billed duck

شین سورخی shinsurkháj **1** light grey **2** *m.* horse with light-grey coat

شینشوبی shinshóbaj *m.* sage

شین توتي shintotí *m.* ☞ شین توتي

شین غاړی shinghāŗaj *m.* blue throat (the bird)

شین غټ shinghát *m. plural* unripe melons

شین غته shinghátạ *f.* index finger

شین غزی shinghózaj *m.* great tamarisk

شین غوده shinghóda *f.* lapwing (the bird)

شینکلی shinkəláj *f.* twig, sprig, shoot

شین وړم shinkvuŗám *m.* ☞ شین وند [1]

شین کومکه shinkumáka *f.* شین کومه shinkúma *f.* **1** turtledove **2** slate-blue dove, blue-grey dove

شینکی [1] shinkáj **1** green; blue شینکی اسمان blue sky **2** *m.* **.1** grass **2.2** unripe melon **2.3** clay pot (glazed) **2.3** *proper name* Shinkaj

شینکی [2] shinkáj *f.* **1** *singular of* شینکی [1] **2** *f.* **.1** clay pot (glazed) **2.2** *proper name* Shinki

شنه کبده shin-kedə́ *m. plural* ☞ شنه کبده

شینگټی shingə́ţaj *m.* unripe fruit

شینگری shingráj *f.* **1** portico **2** turret

شینگرو پینگرو shingŗó-pingŗó torpid, slow-moving

شینگړه shingə́ṛa *f.* شینگړی shingŗáj *f.* ☞ مټیزه

شینگل shingúl *m.* شین گل *proper name* Shingul

شین گلی shingúlaj *m. botany* broomrape, *Orobanche*

شینگی shingáj *m.* packhorse

شینلی shinláj *m.* ☞ شنبلی

شین مغزی shinmághzaj *m.* شین منڅی shinmándzaj *m.* melon with green pulp

شینوالی shinválaj *m.* **1** blue color شین والی ، **2** growth, sprouting (of a plant)

شینوبره shinvábra blue, green

شینوبی shinóbaj *m.* buttermilk

شینورگی shinvárgaj **1** grey coated (of an animal) **2** blue

شینولی shinvə́laj *m.* white poplar

شینی ¹ shínaj *m.* **1** *medicine* whitlow, felon, paronychia **2** tick **3** louse (bird louse)

شینی ² shiné *dialect feminine plural of* شین

شینیدل shinedól *intransitive* ☞ (شین کیدل) شین

شیو shíjo *oblique of* شی ¹

شیوعی shuju'í *Arabic* **1** communistic **2** *m.* Communist

شیوعیت shuju'iját *m. Arabic* Communism

شیون sheván *m. poetry* sobbing, weeping, crying

شئون shu'ún *m. Arabic plural* **1** *of* شان ² **2** prerogatives د ملت شئون the rights of nations

شئونات shu'unāt *m. second plural of* شئون

شیوه ¹ shevá *f.* **1** matter, deed **2** habits, manners **3** coquetry, flirting

شیوه ² shevá **1** lowered, let down شیوه کول to lower, let down کیدل a to descend, sink; go down مځکه واربه وار پسې شیوه کیږي The road constantly descended. **b** to arrive somewhere عمق ته a to submerge, sink **b** to become absorbed (e.g., in thought) **2** lower down; downwards

شیوه گر shevagár *m.* **1.1** master craftsman, expert **1.2** artisan **2** *adjective* expert, skillful, masterly

ښ

ښ khin khe the twenty-third letter of the Pashto alphabet

ښاپرک khāpərák *m.* ښاپیرک khaperák *m.* bat

ښاپیری ¹ khāperáj *m.* demon, imp

ښاپیری ² khāpərəj *f.* [*plural:* ښاپیریگاني khápərəjāni *plural:* ښاپیریگانی khāpərəjgāni] **1** fairy د سمندر ښاپیری siren; mermaid **2** *proper name* Shahperi

ښاځه khádza *f.* ☞ شاخه

ښاټ khāts *m.* arrogance, conceit

ښاټیدل khātsedól *intransitive* [*past:* و ښاټید] to put on airs; be haughty

ښاخ khākh *m.* **1** branch, twig; shoot; offshoot **2** branch (of a tribe) **3** tributary, feeder stream (of a river) **4** spur, branch (of a mountain range) **5** branch (of an enterprise) **6** field, sphere (of acitivity) ☞ شاخ

ښاخدار khākhdár ☞ ښاخلن

ښاخک khākhák *m.* ☞ شاخک

ښاخلن khākhlón **1** branch **2** branching

ښاخله khākhlá *f.* **1** twig **2** offshoot

ښاخور khakhvór having thick branches

ښاخه khákha *f.* narrow path

ښاخی khākhój *f.* pitchfork

ښاد khād cheerful, joyful, content ☞ ښاد کول ☞ ښادول ښادیدل خدای دي ښاده کړه! ، ښاده شی که! May God bless you! (good wishes to a woman)

ښادان khādán ☞ ښاد

ښادمن khādmn jolly, joyful, exultant

ښادمنی khādmóni **1** *feminine plural of* ښادمن **2** cheerfulness, joy, exultation

ښادنامه khādnāmá *f.* cheerfulness, gladness, joy

ښادول khādavól *denominative, transitive* [*past:* ښاد یې کړ] to gladden, cheer, divert, amuse

ښادي ¹ khādí **1** *f.* joy, gladness, cheerfulness **2** *f.* carousal, celebration; celebration of a family event (e.g., birth, circumcision, wedding) ښادي کول a to have a good time, be cheerful, exult **b** to play, celebrate a wedding **3** *m. proper name* Shadi

ښادي ² khádi *f. plural of* ښاد

ښادیانه khādjāná *f.* **1** joy, gladness, cheerfulness **2** exultation (on the occasion of a wedding, etc.) **3** epithalamium, wedding song

ښادیدل khādedól *denominative, intransitive* [*past:* ښاد شو] **1** to rejoice, be cheerful, have a good time **2** to exult

ښادیدنه khādedóna *f.* joy; gladness; cheerfulness; exultation; carousal (on occasion of a wedding, etc.)

ښار khār *m.* **1** city تر ښار دباندي a out of town (location) **b** out of town (motion) **2** Shar, Khar (city, the admininstative center of Badjaur)

ښارسازي khārsāzí *f.* town planning

ښارک khārák *m.* ښارگ khārág *m.* **1** wooden plug (e.g., for a mill, oil press) **2** *anatomy* jugular vein **3** artery, important route *idiom* د ژوند مهم ښارک a vitally important question

ښارگوټی khārgótaj *m.* small town

ښارنی khāranáj city ښارني خلق city dwellers, urban population

ښارو khāró *f.* **1** minah (bird) **2** beloved, darling (woman)

ښاروال khārvál *m.* **1** mayor, head of municipality, principal officer of a city **2** city dweller

ښاروالی khārválaj *m.* kharvāli *f.* city administration, municipality د ښاروال kharvāli kharvālój ☞ ښاروال

ښاروکی khārokáj *f.* black-headed mynah bird, brahmin mynah bird

ښارونی ¹ khāronáj *m.* male mynah bird

ښارونی ² khāronáj *f.* khārunój *f.* ☞ ښارو

ښاره khārá *f.* **1** small town, large village **2** ☞ اشاره

ښاری khārí kharáj **1** city, urban, municipal ښاري ژوندون city life, urban ways **2** *m.* city dweller

ښاغپ khāgháp *m.* **1** hungry man **2** greedy man, grasping man

ښاغپه khāghápa *f. from* ښاغپ

ښاغل khāghól *transitive* [*past:* ویې ښاغه] **1** to love **2** to esteem **3** to prefer

ښاغلتوب khāghóltób *m.* ښاغلتیا khaghóltjá *f.* **1** esteem, honor **2** preference

ښاغلی khāghóLaj **1.1** dear **1.2** esteemed, honored ښاغلو! ، ښاغلو Sirs! **1.3** pleasing, nice **2** *m.* sir, Mr. گرانو ښاغلیو! حاضرینو! Honored sirs!

ښالمه khálma *f.* stickiness; viscosity

ښالانگ khāláng **1** bandy-legged **2** occupied with something

ښالیځ khālídz ښالیز khāliz **1** fresh; blooming **2** succulent

ښاليزي ḵhālizí *f.* **1** freshness **2** succulence

ښامار ḵhāmár *m.* **1** dragon **2** monster

ښانده [1] ḵhā́nda *f.* knowledge, familiarty, acquaintanceship

ښانده [2] ḵhāndə́ *imperfect tense of* ښندل

ښانک ḵhānák *m.* **1** large wooden trough, wash trough **2** wooden dish **3** peddler's or marketman's wooden high-sided stand د لرگو ښانک wooden vat

ښانکی ḵhānakáj *m.* **1** small trough, wash trough **2** small booth; hawker's tray

ښانگر ḵhāngər *m.* ښانگړ ḵhāngər *m.* sharp leg pains

ښانگور ḵhāngavə́r **1** long-legged **2** lanky ښانگور مېږی long-legged ant

ښانگه ḵhā́nga *f.* **1** leg from the thigh to the instep; lower or nether extremity **2** spur (of mountains) **3** neck of a skin bag

ښانگه ور ḵhāngavə́r ☞ ښانگور

ښانگۍ ḵhāngə́j *f.* pitchfork

ښاوات ḵhāvā́t *m.* kulba of land (a measure of land equal to 50 to 150 dzheribs) ☞ قلبه

ښاول ḵhāvə́l *m.* ☞ شاول

ښاوندی ḵhāvə́ndaj *m.* ☞ سروخ

ښاهرگ ḵhāhrág *m. anatomy* the jugular vein

ښاهه ḵhāhə́ *imperfect of* ښهل

ښاهي ḵhāhí *f.* **1** shahi, shaj (coin worth 1/20 of a kran)

ښايست ḵhājə́st *m.* **1** beauty; attractiveness; charm **2** elegancy **3** adorment ښايست موندل to be adorned

ښايستو ḵhājəstó *f. proper name* Shaisto, Shaista

ښايستوالی ḵhājəstvā́laj *m.* ☞ ښايست

ښايستوکی ḵhājəstúkaj beautiful; nice; pleasing; nice-looking, charming

ښايستوگۍ ḵhājəstogə́j *f. proper name* ☞ ښايستو

ښايسته ḵhājəstá **1.1** beautiful; attractive; nice-looking, cute ځان ښايسته کول to adorn په يو شي ښايسته کول to adorn oneself, be adorned with something ښايسته کېدل to grow prettier **1.2** large, fairly large **2.1** very; well د وزو ښايسته غټه رمه a fairly large herd of goats ښايسته ښه very good, very well وخت مو ښايسته ډېر تېر شو We had a very good time. **2.2** fairly, reasonably **3** *m. proper name* Shaista

ښايستاتوب ḵhājəstatób *m.* ښايسته والی ḵhājəstavā́laj *m.* ☞ ښايست

ښايستوکۍ ḵhājəstagótaj ☞ ښايستوکی

ښايه ḵhája *Eastern imperative of* ښندل *vice* ښيه [1]

ښايي [1] ḵhā́ji *Eastern present tense of* ښنودل *vice* ښنئ [1]

ښايي [2] ḵhā́ji ښايي ḵhā́i **1** it is necessary, one has to, it should, it is required, it is fitting ... تاسو لره ښايي چه you should, you need to ... تا ته دا ښايي چه Now this is what you have to do ... لکه څرنگه چه ښايي as is fitting ... **2** probably, possibly تاسي به خبر ياست چه ښايي You probably know that ... ښايي چه زمونږ معلم به هم راسي ... It is possible that our teacher will come.

ښاېدل، ښايئدل ḵhāedə́l ḵhājedə́l *intransitive* [*present:* ښائي *present:* ښايېري *past:* وښايېدل] *obsolete* **1** to be required, to befit **2** to be in keeping with, to suit

ښايېدنه ḵhājedə́na *f.* ښايېده ḵhājedə́ *m. plural* obligation

ښپه ḵhpa *f. Eastern* leg ☞ پښه

ښپېته ḵhpéta *f.* ☞ شپېته [1]

ښپېتول ḵhpetavə́l *denominative, transitive* [*past:* ښپېته يې کړ] to torture with a sharpened stake

ښپېمان ḵhpemā́n *dialect* ☞ پنپېمان

ښتره ḵhatrá *f.* wooden snow shovel

ښتري [1] ḵhatrí *m. regional* Hindu merchant, Hindu shopkeeper

ښتري [2] ḵhatré *plural of* ښتره

ښتکری ḵhatkaráj *m.* ښتگری ḵhatgaráj *m.* ankle, anklebone

ښچي ḵhche *vice* چه ښه It is good. راغئ ښچي It is good that he has come.

ښځکی ḵhədzakə́j *f. colloquial* wench

ښځلی ḵhadzaláj sorrel, Rumex

ښځمني ḵhədzmə́ni *f. plural* women, female sex

ښځنوکی ḵhədzanúkaj **1** effeminate **2** effete ښځنوکی کېدل a to be effete b to acquire the characteristics of a woman (of a man)

ښځني ḵhədzənáj **1** effete ښځني ژوندون life in comfort **2** feminine, pertaining to women

ښځوکی ḵhədzúkaj ښځونک ḵhədzunák ☞ ښځوکی

ښځه ḵhə́dza **1.1** woman د ښځو ليسه women's gymnasium (secondary school), women's lycée دښځو خيريه ټولنه Women's Philanthropic Society د ښځي و ځای ته رسېدل to mature (of a girl) **1.2** woman, wife ښځه پرېښودل to reject a wife; divorce a wife ښځه کول to deal with someone's wedding ښځه ځني ولارول to marry, take a wife د چا ښځه کېدل to marry (of a woman) **1.3** female (of animals) **2** *attributive* female, feminine sex *idiom* ښځه کېدل to grow cowardly, experience fear, be frightened

ښځيتوب ḵhədzatób *m.* ☞ ښځيتوب

ښځي [1] ḵhədzí *f.* femininity

ښځي [2] ḵhə́dzi *plural of* ښځه

ښځيتوب ḵhə́dzitob *m.* **1** married state (for a woman) **2** female sex

ښځينه ḵhədziná **1** women's, female (of dancing, etc.); lady's (of a hat, etc.)

ښڅرلی ḵhətsərláj *m.* chisel

ښڅياکه ḵhətsjā́ka *f.* swallow (the bird)

ښخ [1] ḵhakh **1** buried **2** interred, entombed (of the dead)

ښخ [2] ḵhakh stiff, hard, firm

ښخخند ḵhəkhánd *m.* ښخخندی ḵhəkhandáj *m.* swamp, quagmire, bog

ښخوالی ḵhakhvā́laj *m.* burial, interment

ښخول ḵhakhavə́l *denominative, transitive Eastern* [*past:* ښخ يې کړ] **1** to bury, inhume **2** to entomb, inter **3** to thrust into, plunge into, pierce

ښخوونگ ḳhakhaváng *m.* ښخوونه ḳhakhavə́na *dialect* **1** burying, inhumation **2** internment, entombment, sepulture **3** plunging into, thrusting into, piercing

ښخوونکئ ḳhakhavúnkəj **1** *present participle of* ښخول **2** *m.* gravedigger

ښخېدل ḳhakhedə́l *denominative, intransitive* [*past:* ښخ شو] **1** to be buried, be inhumed **2** to be entombed, interred **3** to be pierced; stick into

ښخېدنه ḳhakhedə́na *f.* ښخېده ḳhakhedə́ *m. plural* burial, interment, funeral, graveside rites

ښرا ḳhərā́ *f.* prayer calling down misfortune upon someone ښرا کول to wish someone every kind of disaster, curse

ښرغلی ḳhərghaláj *m.* **1** anthill **2** nest (of insects)

ښرکنی ḳhərkanáj *m. Eastern* site of an ancient settlement, ruins of a city

ښرن ḳhərə́n *m.* saline (of soil) ښرنه مځکه saline soil

ښروه ḳharə́va *f.* yew

ښره ḳhara *f.* **1** barren land **2** saline soil

ښره مغه ḳharamágha *f.* saline soil

ښکار ḳhkār *m.* **1** hunting; catching (mining, fishing, etc.) د زرکو ښکار pearl fishing د کبانو ښکار fishing په مرغلرو ښکار birding ښکار وتل to hunt, go hunting **2** game, catch ښکار کول to bag, catch ښکار کېدل to be bagged, caught **3** victim

ښکارځای ḳhkārdzáj *m.* ☞ ښکارغلی

ښکارزن ḳhkārdzə́n ښکارزن ḳhkārzə́n *m.* hunter

ښکارغلی ḳhkārghaláj ښکارگاه ḳhkārgáh *m.* hunting grounds

ښکارند ḳhkārónd **1** well-known; apparent, obvious **2** noticable, visible **3** introducing someone

ښکارندوی ḳhkārəndój ḳhkārəndúj **1** known; apparent, obvious **2** *m.* **.1** one who expresses something **2.2** *proper name* Khkarandoj

ښکارنده ḳhkārónda ☞ ښکارند

ښکاروز ḳhkārúz *m.* agricultural worker, tiller, peasant

ښکاروزتوب ḳhkāruztób *m.* ښکاروزي ḳhkāruzí *f.* agriculture, tilling the soil ښکاروزتوب کول to engage in agriculture

ښکارول ¹ ḳhkāravól **1** [*past:* ښکاره یې کړ] **.1** to show, present (e.g., documents) **1.2** to disclose, reveal **1.3** to make known, expose **1.4** to explain; elucidate; clear up, elaborate **2** *m. plural* ☞ ښکارونه

ښکارول ² ḳhkāravól *denominative, transitive* [*past:* ښکاره یې کړ] to hunt; catch, bag ماهیان په تور ښکارول to net fish *idiom* د چا زړونه ښکارول to charm, entrance, captivate someone

ښکارونه ḳhkāravóna *f.* **1** presentation, submission (of a document) **2** disclosure, revelation **3** exposure, unmasking; clearing up, elaboration

ښکاره ḳhkārá **1** manifest, evident; clear, obvious ښکاره غلطي an obvious error دا هم ... دلیل خو ښکاره دئ The reason is obvious. ... ښکاره ده چه خبره It is also clear that ... **2.1** manifestly **2.2** clearly; openly ښکاره وایو چه ... We openly declare that ... ښکاره کول **a** to show, reveal, prove oneself **b** to ځان ښکاره کول ¹ښکارول

boast, flaunt ښکاره کېدل ☞ **3** in appearance, outwardly, by appearance

د ځان ښکاره کول ښکاره کول *m. plural* ☞ boasting, conceit

ښکاري ¹ ḳhkārí *m.* **1** hunter (of animals and birds) **2.1** *adjective* hunting ښکاري توپک hunting rifle **2.2** raptorial, of prey ښکاري مرغان raptorial birds, birds of prey **2.3** *adjective military* pursuit, fighter ښکاري الوتکه fighter aircraft, pursuit plane

ښکاري ² ḳhārí *present tense of* ښکارېدل

ښکارېدل ḳhkāredə́l *denominative* [*present:* ښکاري *present:* ښکارېږي *past:* ښکاره شو] **1** to become clear, become evident, become obvious **2** to appear to be, seem داسي ښکارېده چه ... It seemed that ... **3** to manifest itself (of a disease) **4** to be visible, appear

ښکالو ḳhkālóf́ *f.* **1** tread **2** whisper **3** dull noise, obscure noise, sound, rustle

ښکالوه ¹ ḳhkālavá *f.* difficulty, obstacle

ښکالوه ² ḳhkālvá *f.* **1** rumble, uproar (of voices) **2** agreement **3** tread د پښو ښکالوه the tread of feet

ښکانځه ¹ ḳhkā́ndza *f.* ☞ ښکنځا

ښکانځه ² ḳhāndzə́ *imperfect of* ښکنځل

ښکتنی ḳhkatanáj *Eastern* د ودانی ښکتنی طبقه the lower floor of a building

ښکته ² ḳhkáta ḳhkə́ta *Eastern* ☞ کښته

ښکته کېده ḳhkáta kedə́ *m. plural* **1** descent **2** landing; loss of altitude **3** reduction, lowering; fall (prices)

ښکته والی ḳhkatavā́laj *m.* **1** descent **2** low place, depression

ښکر ḳhkər *m.* [*plural:* ښکر ḳhkər *plural:* ښکرونه ḳhkərúna *Western plural:* ښکران khkərā́n] **1** horn (of an animal) په ښکر وهل to butt, lift on the horns په ښکر جنگېدل to come to grips in battle, come to blows **2** *medicine* cupping glass ښکر لگول **a** to be gored, be butted **b** to employ cupping glasses **3** powder flask **4** a part of the housing for a set of millstones *idiom* دا هلک بی سره او بی ښکره دئ This child is without supervision. د دي کار سر او ښکر نه دئ معلوم It is not known how this matter will end. ښکر کول to give oneself airs ښکر وهل to oppose, resist

ښکرور ḳhkəravə́r **1** horned **2** *m. abusive* cattle

ښکری ¹ ḳhkəráj *m.* **1** pod (bean) **2** curl, lock

ښکري ² ḳhkərí *adjective* horn, of horn (articles)

ښکری ³ ḳhkaráj *f.* ☞ شکری ²

ښکل ¹ ḳhkul *m.* ښکل کول *compound verb* to kiss

ښکل ² ḳhkə́l *transitive* [*past:* ویې ښکه] *Eastern* **1** to pull out, draw out; drag, extract; drag out, pull out (e.g., a tooth) را ښکل to pull down **2** to drive out (e.g., from a home) **3** to take off (clothing) **4** to strip off, flay (a hide) **5** to drive out; banish, send away **6** to tear away (from work) **7** to recover a debt **8** to write **9** to mark; draw **10** to express, press out (juice) **11** to present, show (e.g., documents) **12** to acquire the means to live, earn a livelihood **13** to receive (wages) **14** to eliminate; dismiss (from a job) **15** to transport a load, carry cargo **16** to dig, excavate an irigation well **17** to invent **18** to introduce (e.g., as a custom) **19** *with a number of nouns forms stable phraseological compounds or bound forms* زیار ښکل to bend efforts; try ښکل بني to lean on (for support) ☞ کښل [2]

ښکلا ښكلا khkə́lā *f.* **1** beauty په ښکلا beautifully دا منظره هيڅ ښکلا نه لري There is nothing attractive in that sight. **2** decoration

ښكلاپوژندنه khkə́lāpezhandə́na *f.* aesthetics

ښكلاكارى khkə́lākārí *f.* decoration; trim (of a building)

ښكلتوب khkultób *f.* ☞ ښكلا

ښكلتيا khkultjā *m.* ☞ ښكلا

ښكلول khkulavə́l *denominative, transitive* [*past:* ښكل يې كړ] to kiss خپل ماشوم يې ډېر ښكلاوه She smothered her child in kisses.

ښكلى [1] khkúlaj beautiful; attractive ښكلى گلالى نوم a beautiful name ښكلي صنايع khkúli the decorative arts ښكلى كول to decorate; embellish, adorn په يو شي ښكلى كېدل to be decorated with something

ښكلى [2] khkə́laj **1** *past participle of* ښكل **2** *m.* **.1** letter, message **2.2** khkə́li fate, destiny

ښكليتوب khkulitób *m.* **1** beauty; attractiveness **2** decoration

ښكلېدل khkuledə́l *denominative, intransitive* [*past:* ښكل شو] to be smothered in kisses

ښكنځا khkandzā́ *f.* cursing, swearing, verbal abuse ښكنځا كول to curse, swear, abuse verbally

ښكنځل khkandzə́l *transitive* [*past:* وى يې ښكانځه] **1** to swear at, curse, abuse someone verbally **2** *m. plural* ☞ ښكنځا چاته ښكنځل كول to thoroughly curse someone out

ښكنځلي khkandzə́li *f. plural* ☞ ښكنځه khkandzə́na *f.* ☞ ښكنځا

ښكول khkavə́l ḵhkavə́l *transitive* [*past:* وى يې ښكاوه] **1** to roll along, roll up **2** to fling, hurl **3** to loosen (a stake, etc.) **4** to shake (a tree)

ښكل [2] khkul *transitive dialect* ☞ ښكل

ښكولول khkulavúl *transitive dialect* ☞ ښكلول

ښكولى khkúlaj **1** ☞ ښكلى [1] **2** good (of morals) ښكولي! Lovable one! Beloved! (as a form of address)

ښكوم khkum *m.* advice, counsel; wish, desire

ښكومى khkúmaj *m.* well-wisher

ښكوى khkuj *m.* **1** way of writing, spelling; written account **2** letter, message

ښكي khke ☞ كښته [2]

ښكېدل khkedə́l *intransitive* [*past:* وښكېده] **1** to slip, slip off **2** fall

ښكېدنه khkedə́na *f.* **1** slipping **2** falling, fall

ښكېل khkel *m.* **1** hobbles ښكېل كول *compound verb* to hobble ښكېل كېدل *compound verb* to be hobbled **2** fraud, cheating

ښكېلول khkelavə́l *denominative, transitive* [*past:* ښكېل يې كړ] **1** to hobble **2** to cheat, defraud

ښكېلېدل khkeledə́l *intransitive* ☞ شكېلېدل

ښكېنى khkenáj **1** downstream, blowing from the south (of a wind) **2** lower **3** southern ښكېنى سړى a southerner (i.e., Indian, Pakistan)

ښل khal *m.* stairway

ښلونه khlóna *f.* pimple, boil

ښندزه khəndza *f.* furuncle ښنځه ختل to appear, erupt (of a furuncle)

ښندل khandə́l khəndə́l *transitive* [*past:* وى يې ښنانده] **1** to make a present; distribute; present **2** to spend په واده كي يې ډېري روپي ښندلې They spent a lot of money on his wedding. **3** to grant, bestow (e.g., a favor) دى ټولو هيڅ فائده ونه ښندله This didn't do any good. All this was useless. **4** to emit (radiation) **5** to exert (influence); effect (an action)

ښندنه khandə́na *f.* khəndə́na **1** gift, bestowal; reward ښه ښندنه good deed; alms ښه ښندنه كول to do good, create good actions **2** expenditure **3** collective gift (e.g., at a wedding)

ښندونى khəndúnaj **1** giving; distributing; generous **2** spending

ښنده khə́nda *f.* **1** excess **2** disaster; misfortune

ښندى khəndə́j *f.* ☞ شندى

ښنزه khə́nza *f.* ☞ ښنځه

ښنغلى khənghə́láj *m. anatomy* femoral socket

ښنك khanák *m.* ☞ ښنك

ښنكى khanákaj *m.* small wooden basket

ښنگ [1] khəng *m.* ash tree

ښنگ [2] khəng *m.* **1** clot of blood **2** frozen earth

ښنگر khəngár *m.* ☞ ښنانگر

ښنگروښ khangrókh *m.* front fastening of a sandal

ښنگورى khəngə́raj khungə́raj *m.* **1** ☞ ښنونگرى [2] *anatomy* anklebone

ښنگسرى khangsáraj *m.* ښنگبر khangkhár *m.* ☞ ښنگسرى وتل ښنغلى to dislocate the hip

ښنگل khangál *m.* saline soil

ښنگلى [1] khangə́ləj *f.* hard soil, soil impervious to moisture

ښنگلى [2] khangə́ləj ښنگلي مالگه salt extracted from nitrous soil

ښنگورى khangorə́j *f.* ☞ متيزه

ښنگى khangə́j *f.* ring (for fastening sheep)

ښنه khna *f.* **1** leg (from hip to sole) **2** iliac bone *idiom* ښنه ښنه كول to saw into pieces

ښنو [1] khu *m. plural Eastern* punk, tinder, amadou

ښنو [2] kho *m. plural of* ښنه [1] ښنو ته بد ويل to discredit, run down

ښنوالى khəvə́laj *m.* ☞ ښنه والى

ښنوانه khvā́na *f.* ☞ ښنون

ښنوبه khóba *f.* water tap, spigot

ښنوبى khvabáj **1** barehanded **2** unarmed

ښنوخل khutkhə́l *transitive* [*past:* وى يې ښنوخه] to make a hole, make an aperture; make a hole in, pierce, perforate

ښنوڅه khútsa *f.* khótsa **1** *medicine* **.1** nettle-rash **1.2** hole, aperture **2** impatient; irritable

ښنودل khodə́l [*present:* ښنئي *past:* وى يې ښنود] **1.1** indicate, show لار تجربي دا خبره ښنودلي ده چه ... to show the way Experience indicated that ... **1.2** to teach, instruct, explain (a task, a lesson) **1.3** to exhort, give instructions **1.4** to teach a good lesson to someone **1.5** to introduce to, acquaint with someone **1.6** to present, submit (a document, etc.) **1.7** to speak, say **2** *m. plural*

☞ بنودنه *idiom* ځان بنودل a to appear, show up b to give oneself airs, become conceited; brag ځان بل راز بنودل to pretend, mask, disguise oneself

ḳhodə́na بنودنه *f.* 1 indication, demonstration 2 study, training, teaching 3 counsel, instruction; showing 4 submission, presentation (document) 5 theatrical presentation

ḳhodə́ بنوده [1] *imperfect of* بنودل ځان يې دوست بنوده to pretend to be someone else

ḳhodá بنوده [2] *imperfect of* بنودل [1]

ḳhor بنور [1] *m.* worry, anxiety جذبات په بنور راوستل to worry, be anxious ☞ شور [1]

ḳhor بنور [2] *m.* 1 nest (of wasps, etc.) 2 anthill 3 honeycombs, beehives

ḳhur بنور [3] *m.* rake, scraper

ḳhorə́ḳht بنورښت *m.* 1 movement 2 vacillation 3 shaking, vibration (from an explosion)

ḳhorəkáj بنورکی *m.* sorrel, Rumex

ḳhormāḳhór بنورمابنور *m.* 1 noise, uproar 2 stir 3 swarm (insects)

ḳhorəmágha بنورماغه *f.* saline, alkaline soil

ḳhorə́n بنورن saline, alkaline

ḳhorə́nd بنورند بنورنده ḳhorə́nda 1 agitating, exciting 2 fluttering, swinging; swinging back and forth 3 moving 4 active, lively (of a man)

ḳhorə́na بنورنه *f.* saline, alkaline soil

ḳhorvá بنوروا *f.* khorvávi [*plural:* بنورواوي] soup د چرګ بنوروا chicken soup

ḳhoravə́l بنورول *transitive* [*past:* وۍ بنوراوه] 1 to trouble, agitate, sway, cause to shake; rock, rock back and forth; shake (a tree, etc.) 2 to move, put in motion 3 to budge 4 to wave (e.g., the hand) 5 to shake up 6 to shake vigorously ځان بنورول to rouse oneself يو شي ته ځان بنورول to acquire something

ḳhorá بنوره [1] *f.* 1 saline, alkaline soil بنوره زمکه saline, alkaline soil 2 fertilizer 3 *botany* saltwort, Salsola 4 saltpeter قلمي بنوره saltpeter

ḳhóra بنوره [2] *imperfective imperative of* بنوریدل [1]

ḳhoramágha بنوره ماغه *f.* saline, alkaline soil

ḳhoranā́k بنوره ناک بنوره یې ḳhoraí 1 saline, alkaline 2 barren, unfruitful

ḳhóraj بنوری [1] *m.* ☞ بنورکی

ḳhoráj بنوری [2] *m.* eye disease of cattle

ḳhorí بنوری [3] *present tense of* بنوریدل [1]

ḳhoré بنوری [4] *plural of* بنوره [1]

ḳhoredə́l بنوریدل [1] *intransitive* [*present:* بنوري present: بنوربېري] [*past:* وبنوریده] 1 to be agitated, heave; reel, oscillate; swing, swing oneself 2 to shiver سره بنوریدل to quiver, struggle (of a caught fish on a line) 3 to move, put into motion سم د ځایه نه I cannot move from the spot. 4 to make a stir ځایه له نه دا واو I really couldn't stir. و بنوربېدم 5 to fiddle around (with something),

root, rummage around (in something) 6 to not come to pass, not eventuate, not come true (of a dream, hope)

ḳhvaredə́l خپریدل [2] بنوریدل *denominative, intransitive Eastern* ☞ خپریدل

ḳhoredə́na بنوریدنه *f.* 1 agitation, stirring 2 *physics* oscillation 3 rocking motion 4 oscillatory motion

ḳhoredúnkaj بنوریدونکی [1] *present participle of* بنوریدل 2 unsteady, shaky

ḳhoredə́ بنوریده [1] *m. plural* ☞ بنوریدنه

ḳhumák بنومک *m.* Murrain disease of donkeys

ḳhuván بنون *m.* olive, olive tree د بنون تېل olive oil, salad oil بنون ونه olive tree

ḳhovə́ndzaj بنوونځی *m.* ☞

ḳhung بنونګ *m.* 1 corner 2 edge, tip (of an object)

ḳhungə́raj بنونګری *m.* hoof (cloven)

ḳhungər بنونګر *m.* numbness of the legs

ḳhúnga بنونګه *f.* ☞ بنونګ

ḳhungáj بنونګی [1] limping

ḳhúngi بنونګي [2] *plural of* بنونګه

ḳhunaláj بنونلی *m.* olive tree orchard

ḳhóna بنونه *f.* ☞ بنون

ḳhovə́l بنودل *transitive* ☞

ḳhovə́ndzáj بنوونځی ḳhovəndzə́j *m.* بنوون ځای *m.* school لومړنی elementary school لومړنی بنوون ځای منځنی بنوون ځای secondary school ثانوي بنوون ځای مسلکي بنوون ځای trade school; school for craftmen

ḳhovúnkaj بنوونکی [1] *m.* 1 teacher 2 trainer

ḳhovúnke بنوونکي [2] *f.* teacher (female)

ḳhovə́na بنوونه *f.* 1 demonstration; showing, displaying 2 instruction, direction چاته لازمه بنووني ورکول to give someone the necessary instruction 3 teaching, instructing د بنووني کال the academic year

ḳhovúnaj بنووني [1] *m.* ☞ بنوونکی

ḳhovə́ni بنووني [2] *m. plural of* بنوونه

ḳhvahavə́l بنویول khuhavə́l *transitive* ☞ بنویول

ḳhvahavə́na بنوهونه khuhavə́na ☞ بنوی والی

ḳhvahedə́l بنویدل khuhedə́l *intransitive* ☞ بنویدل

ḳhvaj بنوی [1] *m.* wooden spade

ḳhvaj بنوی [2] 1.1 smooth (of paper) 1.2 slippery 1.3 beardless 1.4 counterfeit, fake بنویه روپی counterfeit rupee 1.5 hypocritical 1.6 fraudulent, knavish بنوی سری a hypocrite b swindler, cheat 1.7 *figurative* smooth, facile, fluent (of speech, language) 1.8 polished; finished 2.1 smoothly; lightly بنوی تېرول to skip over, scan lightly 2.2 in a slippery way بنوی ژوندون the good life, a life of ease

ḳhvajḳhā́k بنوی بنهاک khvajḳhā́k بنوی بناک disappearing, vanishing بنوی بناک ورکېدل to disappear, vanish

ḳhvajakáj بنویکی *m.* 1 quick man, agile man, efficient man 2 bright man; sly man, clever man 3 swindler, fraud

ښوينداردار ķhvajə́nd ښوينددار ķhvajəndár *Eastern* slippery khvendár ښويند
ښويند ځای a slippery place

ښوينددوكى ķhvajəndúkaj *m.* skating rink; toboggan slide

ښوينددوی ķhvajəndúj crawling, creeping (of animals)

ښوينددوكى ķhvajandáj *m.* ☞

ښوی والى ķhvajvā́laj *m.* 1 smoothness 2 slipperiness 3 agility, quickness, efficiency 4 brightness, slyness, cleverness 5 trickery, fraud, deceit

ښويول ķhvajavə́l *transitive* [*past:* وى يي ښوياوه] 1 to make to slide 2 to skate, slide ځان پر ښويول to slide, skate along on something 3 to misdirect 4 to defraud; deceive someone 5 to polish

ښوی والى ķhvajavə́na *f.* ☞

ښوی ķhvája *f. singular of* ښوی [2] 1

ښوی نالاكه ķhvája-ķhālā́ka 1 having smooth walls 2 impregnable (of a fortress)

ښويدل ķhvajedə́l *intransitive* [*past:* و ښويده] 1.1 to slide 1.2 to skate, glide 1.3 to crawl, creep د سيني په زور ښويدل to crawl, go on all fours 1.4 to slip پښه يې وښويده He slid. He slipped. 1.5 to collapse, cave in 1.6 to err; be deceived 1.7 to go astray 2 *m. plural* ☞ د غونډی ښويدل collapse, cave-in

ښويدنه ķhvajedə́na *f.* ښويده ķhvajedə́ *m. plural* 1 sliding 2 skating, gliding 3 slip, error, mistake, inaccuracy

ښويدونى ķhvajedúnaj *m.* sleigh, hand sled

ښه [1] ķhə ښه ķha *f. m.* [*plural:* ښه ķhə *f. plural:* ښی ķhe] 1.1 good ښه آس a good horse ښه خلک good people ښه كالى a good dress 1.2 good (in various senses) ښه چاره good work د ښه نيت a goodwill mission 1.3 pleasing ښه غږ a pleasant voice 1.4 suitable, fit, appropriate ښه غوندی not bad, quite good دا كار تا ته This matter is not for you. 1.5 advantageous 1.6 healthy ښه يم I'm healthy. ښه كول a to improve, ameliorate د مامورينو حال ښه كول to improve the situation of employees b to display charity د چا سره ښه كول to get along with someone; treat someone well c to correct, adjust, tune up d to restore to health, make well ښه كېدل a to دغه دوا ما ښه كړم This medicine helped me. to improve b to get better c to recover د هغه صحت ښه كېږي He's improving. His health is getting better. d to change for the better (of a person) 2 *m. plural* good, the good, good deed د بدو سرو ! له بدو غوښتو ښه نبوروا وي Do not expect good deeds from evil people. 3.1 very well, all right ښه ... ډير ښه، ډير ښه دئ، خورا ښه very well ... په ښه شان سره، په ښه ډول Well, OK ښه نو ... It is good that ... سو چه I ښه مي په ياد دئ چه ... You have acted well. تا ښه كړي دئ چه understand well how... 4 very much ډير ښه لا still more, much more 5 long ودربدو We stopped there for a long time. *idiom* ښه ايسېدل to like ښه بلل، ښه ګڼل to prefer, consider as better; consider good په چا باندي ښه لګېدل *Eastern* to like someone (e.g., appearance) ! ښه راغلى!، ښه راغلاست Welcome! You خو ښه تر ښه couldn't wish anything better than this. You couldn't imagine anything better. *proverb* د ښو غوښو ښه نبوروا وي! Good meat makes good soup!

ښه [2] ķha 1 *feminine singular of* ښه هوا [1] ښه good weather 2 *f.* 1 good, the good (both abstract and concrete) سنک زما سره ښه وكړه Sanak was good to me. 2.2 advantage, benefit له ښی ويستل to render useless زه به دي هم ښه به ښه درسم I will prove useful to you. دا ښيز هيخ د ښی نه دئ *Eastern* This is an insignificant thing. 2.3 well-being, prosperity 3 good, well دا ښه ده چه ... a It is well that ... b It would be well if ... ; It would be better if ... ښه مياشت So long! Good-bye! Good ښه دي مله شه!، په مخه دي ښه! ☞ صفر [2] luck! خداى دي ښه درولى! May God give you success! I wish you success! د دوى ښه نه ځني راځي They do not like this.

ښها ķhahā́ *f.* 1 good (abstract) 2 mercy, charity

ښهاک ķhhāk *echoic word with* ښوى

ښهانه ķhahā́na *f.* ښهانه ķhahā́ņa *f.* good (abstract); advantage *idiom* په چا پوري ښهانه پربښنبوول to honor someone; show respect for somebody

ښهباز ķhahbā́z *m.* peacemaker, mediator

ښه ترا ķhətarā́ 1 very best 2 better, best موضوع ښه ترا رنه شوه The situation became clearer. The question became clearer.

ښه ترخه ķhətərķhá ښه تره ښه ترينه ķhətā́ra 1 very best, best of all 2 best way of all, best possible, best of all

ښه والى ķhətób *m.* ☞ ښه توب

ښه چاري ķhəchārúkaj ښه چاروكى khəchā́raj virtuous

ښه ځوان ķhə dzvān *m.* 1 generous man, magnanimous man, hospitable man 2 good young man

ښه ځواني ķhadzvānī́ *f.* 1 generosity, magnanimity 2 spirit, mettle, dash

ښهر ķhā́hr ķhā́hər *m.* city

ښه راغلي ķhərā́ghle *f. & m. plural* encounter, meeting; greeting ښه راغلي ويل، ښه راغلي كول to meet; greet

ښه ورځ ķha rvadz *f.* ☞ ښه ورځ

ښهري ķhahrí ķhahráj ☞ ښناري

ښه زري ķhəzəraj *adjective* good, kind ښه زړى ځوان a good lad

ښه سري والى ķhəsarivā́laj *m.* decency

ښه كېدل ķhəkedə́l *m. plural* 1 improvement 2 refinement, perfecting

ښه ګڼل ķhəgaņə́l *m. plural idiom* ستاسي ښه ګڼل او سلا Your kindly advice.

ښهل ķhahə́l *transitive* [*past:* وى يي ښناهه] 1 to curse زوى د مور او پلار ښنهئ دئ The parents cursed their son. 2 to disown, reject, turn away

ښه مايه ķhamājá thoroughbred, aristocratic

ښه مرغ ķhəmórgh *m.* happiness, good fortune له ښه مرغه happily, luckily

ښه مرغي [1] ķhəmərghí *f.* 1 happiness, good fortune 2 greeting, congratulation, well-wishing ښه مرغي ويل to congratulate

ښه مرغى [2] ķhəmárghaj happy, fortunate

ښهنه ķhəhə́na *f.* cursing, imprecation

ښه والى ķhəvā́laj *m.* 1 improvement 2 well-being 3 good (abstract and concrete) د وطن د ښه والي دپاره for the good of the Motherland

4 advantage, benefit **5** good quality **6** adjustment, regulation, tuning **7** recuperation, recover ناروغه ښه والي ته مخ کوؤلئ The patient is recovering.

ښه ورځ ḳha vradz *f.* **1** well-being, sufficiency د ښې ورغ لپدل to live in plenty, flourish **2** holiday

ښه ونه ḳhavə́na *f.* ☞ ښبون

ښی ¹ ḳhaj *adjective* right ښی لاس right hand **a** right side **b** north مخ ښی the face, right (of cloth) ښی گرځ! *military* Right face! (as a command)

ښی ¹ ḳhi **1** *m. plural of* ښی ¹ **2** *indirect singular m. of* ښی ¹

ښی ³ ḳhe **1** *f. plural of* ښه ² **1** ښی منئ good apples **2** *indirect singular feminine of* ښه ¹

ښی ⁴ ḳhe *contraction of* ښه *and the pronoun* یی

ښی ⁵ ḳhe the name of the Pashto letter ښ

ښی ⁶ ḳhaj *f. plural of* ښی ¹

ښیاست ḳhə́jāst *Western second person, present tense plural of* ښبودل

ښیالمی ḳhjā́lme *f. plural* saliva

ښیخ ḳhidz *m.* tarantula

ښیځه ḳhédza *f. botany* yellow eremurus, *Eremurus aurantiacus*

ښیرا ḳherá́ *f.* ☞ ښیره ¹

ښیراز ḳherā́z **1** fresh; cool **2** happy, prosperous, fortunate **3** merry, gay, joyous

ښیرازتوب ḳherāztób *m.* ښیرازتیا ḳherāztjā́ *f.* ښیرازي ḳherāzí *f.* **1** freshness; coolness **2** happiness, prosperity, well-being **3** merriness, joy

ښیرازیدل ḳherāzedə́l *denominative, intransitive* [*past:* ښیراز شو] **1** to grow cooler **2** to be happy **3** to grow, become merry, rejoice

ښیرون ḳherún *m.* wild olive tree

ښیرونه ḳhervə́na *f.* kind of pistachio bush

ښیروه ḳherə́va *f. botany* Cotoneaster (a kind of flowering bush)

ښیره ¹ ḳherá́ *f.* cursing, curse ښیره کول to curse راته یی ډېری ښېری و کړلې He heaped curses upon me.

ښیره ² ḳhirá́ *f.* ☞ شیره ¹

ښیښینه ḳhiḳhá́ *f.* **1** glass **2** vial, small bottle, flask; glass vessel **3** [*plural:* ښیښینی] ḳhiḳhé] glasses, spectacles ښیښینی پر سترگو اچول to wear glasses

ښیښیني ḳhiḳhai *adjective* glass ښیښینی یي نل glass tube, tubing ښیښیني، ښیښینئ

ښیگړه ḳhegə́ra *f.* **1** adventure, benefit د خپلی ښیگړی دپاره for one's own benefit **2** good (abstract and concrete) د چا ښیگړه غوښتل to wish someone well **3** well-being **4** kindness, goodness; consideration ښیگړه کول to display kindness, show consideration **5** improvement **6** virtue هغه د دې ښیگړو خالي و He was devoid of these virtues. He did not possess these qualities. **7** cooperation, help, assistance

ښیگڼوال ḳhegəṇvál *m.* member of a children's organization (ages 12 to 18)

ښیگړه ḳhegə́ṇa *f.* ☞ ښیگړه

ښیهل ¹ ḳhəjə́l *plural Eastern imperfect of* ښبودل

ښیهل ¹ ḳhajə́l *transitive* ☞ ښیهل ¹

ښیهلی ¹ ḳhelá́j *m.* ferment, leaven

ښیبلئ ² ḳhajə́ləj *past participle of* ښبیل ²

ښیبینه ¹ ḳhína *f.* ḳhéna *Eastern* ☞ خوښبینه

ښیینه ² khajə́na curse, cursing

ښیهنه ³ ḳhəjə́na *f.* instruction, training

ښیيني ḳhíne *f.* ښیيني ḳhinə́j *f.* ☞ خوښبینه

ښیيون ḳhəjún *m.* instruction, direction

ښیوونکی ¹ ḳhəjúnkaj *m.* ☞ ښیوونکی

ښیوه ḳhevá *f.* decoration; dolling up, prettying up

ښیيه ¹ ḳhəja *imperfective imperative of* ښبودل

ښیيه ² ḳhəjə́ *Eastern imperfect tense of* ښبودل

ښیئ ḳhə́ji *present tense of* ښبودل

ښیي ḳhə́je *second person, present tense of* ښبودل

ښیئ ³ ḳhə́jəj *Eastern second person plural, present tense of* ښبودل

ښیهل ¹ ḳhejə́l ☞ ښبیل ¹

ص

ص ¹ sā́d the twenty-fourth letter of the Pashto alphabet (pronounced like س (s) and therefore sometimes replaced by the letter س)

ص ² *abbreviation for* صفحه

ص ³ *official abbreviation* صداقت همراه

ص ⁴ *Arabic abbreviation* صلی الله علیه وسلم sallá lahú alájhi wasallám *religion* Peace and blessings of Allah be upon him! (said after the mention of the name of Prophet Mohammed)

ص ⁵ *abbreviation for* صحیح *accounting* correct, verified

صابر sābír *Arabic* patient, tolerant

صابون sābún *m.* soap د صابون جوړولو صابون وهل to soap, lather فابریکه soap factory

صابون پزي sābunsāzí *f.* صابون سازي soap-making

صاحب sāhíb sāíb *m. Arabic* **1** gentleman; sir, mister عالمان صاحبان scientist colleagues **2** possessor, owner د علم صاحبان scientists, learned men صاحب قلم sāhíb-i man of letters **3** *proper name* Sahib, Saib

صاحب جانه sahibdzhā́na *f. proper name* Saibdzhana

صاحب زاده sahibzādá́ *m.* **1** gentlemen **2** Sahibzada (title for a person of distinguished lineage) **3** descendent of some renowned religious personage

صاحب کار sāhibkā́r *m. history* director of an estate

صاحب مرام sāhibmarā́m *Arabic* purposeful, single-minded

صاحب منصاب sāhibmansā́b *m. Arabic* officer صاحبنصاب،

صاحبه sāhibá́ *f. Arabic* **1** lady, madame **2** owner (female), possessor (female)

صاحبي انگور sāhibí variety of large sweet grape صاحبي

صاخه sākhá́ *f. Arabic* **1** sharp sound **2** unpleasantness **3** *religion* Judgement Day

صاد sā́d *m. Arabic* the name for the letter ص

صادر sādir *Arabic* **1** outstanding, outgoing (of documents) **2** pronounced (of the judgement or sentence of a court) **3** issued, promlgated (of an order, resolution) **4** despatched, sent (letters, documents) **5** exported **6** drawn up (bill of exchange, check) صادربدل ☞ صادر کېدل صادرول ☞ صادر کول

صادرات sādirā́t *m. Arabic plural* **1** export **2** export goods د صادراتو سوداگر exporter

صادراتي sādirātí *f.* exports صادراتي مقدار items of export صادراتي مواد export volume صادراتي مقدار export company شرکت exports, export goods

صادرول sādiravól *denominative, transitive* [*past:* صادر يې کړ] **1** to pronounce (a decision, sentence a court) **2** to issue, promulgate (an order, a resolution, etc.) **3** to dispatch, send (letters, documents) **4** to export **5** to draw up (bill of exchange, check)

صادروونکی sadiravúnkaj *present participle of* صادرول د برات صادروونکی drawer (of a bill)

صادره sādirá́ *f. Arabic* **1** *feminine singular and masculine plural of* صادر **2** *f.* outgoing correspondence د صادرې او واردې کتاب the register of incoming and outgoing papers

صادرېدل sādiredól *denominative, intransitive* [*past:* صادر شو] **1** to be pronounced (of a verdict) **2** to be promulgated (of an order, resolution, etc.) **3** to be despatched, sent (of letters, documents) **4** to be exported **5** to be drawn up (bill of exchange, check) **6** to issue from someone; spring from, result from

صادرېده sādiredó́ *m. plural* **1** issuance (of a verdict) **2** promulgation (of an order, resolution) **3** dispatch (of letters, documents) **4** export **4** to be slackened, let out (rope, etc.) **5** drawing up, executing (of a bill of exchange, a check)

صادق sādíḳ *Arabic* **1** veracious, true **2** faithful, dedicated **3** *religious* epithet of the Imam Jafaf

صادق القول sādiḳ-al-ḳául *Arabic* faithful to one's word; veracious

صادقانه sādiḳáná **1** veracious, sincere, true **2** faithfully, sincerely

صاروخ sārúkh *m. Arabic* missile, rocket

صاروخي sārukhí *adjective* missile, rocket

صاعقه sā'iḳá *f. Arabic* lightning

صاف sāf sāp **1** clean, pure, transparent صافي اوبه clean water, pure water, transparent water صافه هوا **a** pure air **b** clean weather د يكشنبي په ورځ هوا صافه وه Sunday the weather was clear. **2** clear, intelligible **3** frank, clear, unequivocal

صاف باطن sāfbātín pure, innocent, chaste (of a look, a person, etc.)

صاف گو sāfgú *m.* frank person, open person, sincere person

صافو sāfó sāpó *indirect plural of* صافي [1]

صافول sāfavól sāpavól *denominative* [*past:* صاف يې کړ] **1** to purify (of adulterants); strain, filter; make clear, make transparent **2** to settle (an account, etc.) **3** to slacken, let out (e.g., a rope) **4** to clear (the way, the road)

صافي [1] sāfī sāpí **1** *m. plural* the Safi (tribe) **2** sāfáj sāpáj *m.* Safi (tribesman)

صافي [2] safī sāpí *f.* **1** purity, transparency **2** clarity, intelligibility

صافي [3] sāfə́j *f.* sāpə́j strainer; filter; colander

صافي [4] sā́fi *f. plural of* صاف [4]

صافېدل [1] sāfedól sāpedól *denominative, intransitive* [*past:* صاف شو] to become clear (of adulterants); be strained; be filtered; be pure, transparent **2** to be frank, be open **3** to be settled (of accounts, etc.) **4** to be cleared (of a road)

صالح sālíh *Arabic* **1.1** good; virtuous; decent; worthy صالحه اشخاص good, decent people; worthy people **1.2** competent; capable صالح مقام competent authority **1.3** pious **2** *m. proper name* Salih

صالحه sālihá́ *f. Arabic singular and plural of* صالح [1]

صالون sālón *m.* sālún hall لوی صالون large hall; conference room

صامت sāmít *Arabic* **1** deaf **2** silent

صانع sāní *m. Arabic* [*plural:* صانعين sāni'ín] **1** artisan, craftsman **2** creator, originator, producer

صائب sāíb *Arabic* **1** purposeful **2** accurate, sharp-sighted **3** correct, appropriate

صائت sāít *Arabic* **1** ringing **2** resounding

صبا sabā́ *Arabic* **1** *m.* **.1** morning باد صبا bā́d-i morning breeze, zephyr د صبا سترگه the morning star, Venus **1.2** the morrow, tomorrow بل صبا the day after tomorrow لا بل صبا in three days د صبا *adjective* **a** morning **b** tomorrow's ... **2** tomorrow, on the morrow ☞ سبا

صباله sabā́la tomorrow

صباناری sabānāráj *m.* صبانهری sabānaharáj *m. regional* breakfast

صبانی sabānáj *Eastern* **1** tomorrow's ... صبانی ورځ tomorrow; on the morrow **2** morning, morning's

صباوت sabāvát *m. Arabic* childhood, youth, adolescence

صبائي sabā́i *f.* morning hours د صبائي په وخت کښي in the morning په صبائي ورځ early in the morning *Eastern* صبائي وختي in a week

صبح subh *m. Arabic* morning صبح صادق dawn, early in the morning صبح صادق دئ Dawn broke.

صبحدم subhdám *m.* **1** morning, early morning **2** in the morning

صبر [1] sábr *m.* sábər patience, tolerance په خورا صبر او طاقت سره **a** very patiently; with enviable patience **b** with great restraint صبر کول **a** to bear, endure **b** to put up with (grief, sorrow) **c** to await, expect د صبر کاسه يې ډ که شوه The cup of his patience overflowed. د صبر مېوه خوږه ده *proverb* Patience is rewarded.

صبر [2] sabír *m.* sabr *botany* aloe

صبرناک sabrnā́k patient, tolerant اوښ خورا صبرناک حيوان دئ The camel is a very patient animal.

صبرول sabravól *denominative, transitive* [*past:* صبر يې کړ] to compel to endure زړه صبرول to endure, bear

صبرېدل sabredól *denominative, intransitive* [*past:* صبر شو] to be patient, be tolerant زما زړه نه صبرېږي I am impatient. I can't wait. I can't stand it.

صبغه sibghá *f. Arabic* **1** faith, religion **2** *religion* baptism, christening **3** nuance **4** nature, characters

صحابت sahābát *m. Arabic* 1 comradeship, fellowship, companionship 2 escort, accompaniment

صحابه sahābá *m. Arabic plural religion* friends and associates of Mohammed

صحاف sahhāf *m. Arabic* 1 bookbinder 2 bookseller

صحافت sihāfát *m. Arabic* 1 the press 2 bookseller

صحافي sahhāfī¹ *f.* 1 bookbinding (the business, craft)

صحافي sihhāfī² *adjective* publishing, relating to the press, printing صحافي وګړي publishing workers

صحبت suhbát *m. Arabic* 1 conversation, discourse 2 intercourse, relations صحبت کول a to converse, talk b to associate with 3 ambience, milieu, society

صحبتي suhbatí *m. Arabic* interlocutor, collocutor

صحت sihhát *m. Arabic* 1 correctness, rightness, veracity صحت لرل to be correct, be right, correspond to reality 2 well-being; health د تولني د صحت ساتنه sanitation انفرادي صحت ساتنه hygiene له خپل صحت a to justify oneself; be confirmed b to recover ميندل سره علاقه لرل to be concerned about one's health, worry about one's health د چا د صحت پوښتنه کول to inquire about someone's health څما صحت خراب و My health has deteriorated.

صحت بخښونکی sihhát bakhkhúnkaj healthful (of climate)

صحت عامه sihhat-i-'āmá *f.* sanitation; health care

صحت مند sihhatmánd healthy, having good health

صحرا sahrá *f. Arabic* 1 barren plain, steppe, desert صحرای کبیر، د صحرا خدمت saheá-ji the Sahara 2 field لویه صحرا، صحرای عظم *military* field service

صحرارو sahrāráv صحرارو موټر land rover, cross-country vehicle

صحراشین sahrāshín *m.* صحرانشین sahrānishín *m. demotic* steppe-dweller, nomad; desert-dweller

صحرانی sahrānáj wild (of birds, animals)

صحرايي sahrājí صحرائي sahrāí 1.1 *adjective* steppe, desert 1.2 wild (of animals) 1.3 field صحرايي توپخانه field artillery 2 *m.* steppe-dweller, desert-dweller; nomad

صحن sahn¹ *m. Arabic* courtyard, yard; area, level land

صحن sahn² *m. Arabic textiles* calico رنګه صحن percale

صحنه sahná *f.* sahná-ji *Arabic* 1 stage, ring, arena, platform صحنه تمثیل stage, ring, arena له صحنې څخه ایستل a to leave the stage b to finish with something or someone; liquidate something 2 sphere, field, walk of life صحنه پرېښودل *literature* to leave the stage, go away 3 picture, sight, appearance دا ډېره غمجنه صحنه ده This is a very sad sight.

صحه shihhá *f. Arabic* ☞ صحت

صحیح sahí¹ ☞ صحیح

صحی sihhí² *Arabic* sanitary; hygienic, health; medicinal صحی پاله health care صحی تشکیلات medical personnel صحی هیئت health care organizations صحی مامورین medical healthcare workers صحی physicians' care; medical services

صحیح sahí *f.* sahíh *Arabic invariable* صحیحه sahíha *f.* 1 precise, true, correct صحیح ترجمه a correct translation صحیح کول to

صحیح کول correct; make more precise; check, verify; clarify *regional* to pick out, single out, keep an eye on someone 2 healthy, sound *idiom* صحیح حرف *linguistics* consonsonant phoneme صحیحه نتیجه a good result صحیح فکر وهل to think soundly, think soberly

صحیح النسب sahihunnasáb *Arabic* pure-blooded, thoroughbred, aristocratic

صحیه sihhijá *Arabic* 1 *feminine singular & plural of* صحی² 2 *f.* official د صحیی وزارت Ministry of Health د صحیی مدیر representative of the Ministry of Health (in a province)

صدا sadá *f. Arabic* 1 sound 2 voice 3 cry, call, summons

صدادار sadādár 1 noisy, resounding (of waves, etc.) 2 sounding 3 *linguistics* voicing, voiced

صدارت sadārát *m. Arabic* 1 chairmanship, leadership 2 *sadārát-i* job or position of prime minister صدارت عظمی the administrative offices of the prime minister

صداقت sadākát *m. Arabic* 1 faithfulness, veracity, devotion د چا صداقت لرل، د چا صداقت کول to remain faithful, be true to, be devoted to someone د چا خدمت په صداقت کول to serve someone faithfully and truly 2 truth, sincerity صداقت و شجاعت همراه *sadākát-va-shudzhā'athampāh* the official title of a major general

صداقتمآب sadākatmáb *Arabic* عالیقدر صداقتمآب the title of advisor or deputy to a minister, etc.

صداقت همراه sadākathamráh official title for a mudir, khan, and other eminent personages

صدد sadád *m. Arabic* intention, wish; goal

صدر sadr *m. Arabic* 1 breast 2 *regional* center (political) 3 governing body (of a society, etc.) 4 leader, chief د پاکستان صدر the president of Pakistan

صدراعظم sadra'zám *m. Arabic* prime minister

صدرالدین sadruddín *m. proper name* Sadruddin

صدرمقام sadrimaķám *m. Arabic* capital (administrative center)

صدره sadrá *f. Arabic* group of dervishes or pilgrims visiting a shrine

صدری sadrój *f.* ☞ سدری

صدف sadáf sadáp *m. Arabic plural* صدفه sadáfa *f.* 1 mother-of-pearl 2 (pearl) shell د مرغلرو صدف pearl oyster

صدفي sadafí *Arabic adjective* mother-of-pearl

صدق sidk *m. Arabic* 1 truth صدق پیدا کول to try to justify oneself; turn out to be true; be confirmed ویل یې کاملاً صدق کوي His words have been confirmed. 2 veracity, sincerity 3 faithfulness, devotion

صدقه sadķá *f.* sadaķá *Arabic* alms, contribution (for a religious purpose) صدقه کول، صدقه ورکول *compound verb* to contribute (for a religious purpose)

صدمه sadamá *f. Arabic* 1 blow 2 harm; damage ویو شي ته صدمه د چا نوم ته صدمه رسول to inflict damage, do harm to someone رسول to damage someone's reputation, disparage someone's good qualities or authority 3 misfortune

صدور sudúr *m. Arabic* **1** going out, departure **2** pronouncement (of a verdict) **3** promulgation (of an order, a resolution) **4** drawing up (of a bill of exchange) **5** export

صدي sadí *f.* صدى sadój *f.* **1** century, 100-year period **2** hundred (collective numeral)

صديق¹ sadíḳ *m. Arabic* sincere friend, true friend

صديق² saddíḳ *Arabic* **1** true, sincere **2** *m. proper name* Siddik

صراپ sarráp *m.* ☞ صراف

صراحت sarāhát *m. Arabic* **1** clarity, precision **2** precisely formulated condition **3** clear instruction, directive

صراحتاً sarāhátán *Arabic* openly, clearly, precisely, definitely

صراحي surāhí *f.* clay pitcher with a long neck

صراط sirāt *m. Arabic religion* road to paradise, way to heaven

صراف sarráf *m. Arabic* **1** money-changer **2** banker

صرافت sarāfát *m. Arabic* thought; intention, motive

صراف خانه، صرافخانه sarráfkhāná *f.* office for money changing, money-changing bureau

صرافي sarráfí *f.* **1** exchange of money **2** profession of money-changing **3** occupation of banker

صرب sarb *m.* **1** a Serb **2** *history* Serbia

صرع sar' *f. Arabic medicine* epilepsy, falling sickness

صرعي sar'í *adjective* epileptic مريض صرعي an epileptic

صرف¹ sarf *m.* [*plural:* اصراف asráf] **1** expenditure, expenses **2** use صرف چاى sarf-i tea-drinking **3** morphology

صرف² sirf sirp *Arabic* **1** only, just, exclusively زه صرف ستا دليدو دپاره راغلئ يم I have come here only for the purpose of meeting with you. نه صرف ... بلکه *Eastern* not only ..., but also **2** flagrant, bald-faced, outright (i.e., lies)

صرف نظر sárf-i-nazár *m.* disregarding, ignoring تر يوشي صرف نظر کول، ديوشي څخه صرف نظر کول to reject something; ignore, pay no attention to something

صرفول sarfavól sarpavól *denominative, transitive* [*past:* صرف يې کړ] **1** to expend, spend **2** to use **3** to show, display (concern)

صرف ونحو sarfunáhv *m. grammar* morphology and syntax

صرفه sarfá *f. Arabic* **1** advantage, benefit **2** savings, economies په يو شي کښي صرفه کول **a** to observe economies in something **b** to limit oneself in something

صرفه بخښونکی sarfá bakhḳhúnkaj economical

صرفه جو sarfadzhú thrifty, economical, careful (about money)

صرفه جو يي sarfadzhuí *f.* thrift, thriftiness, carefulness in money matters

صرفي sarfí *Arabic* **1** grammatical; morphological صرفي قواعد grammatical rules **2** *m.* author of a grammar

صرفيات sarfiját *m. Arabic plural* expenditures, expenses

صرفېدل sarfedól sarpedól *denominative* [*past:* صرف شو] **1** to be spent, be expended, be disbursed **2** to be used, be employed, be used up

صريح saríh *Arabic* **1** clear, precise **2** decisive, categorical (refusal, etc.) **3** flagrant, bald-faced, outright (i.e., lies)

صريحاً saríhán *Arabic* **1** clearly, precisely **2** decisively, categorically **3** clearly, openly, patently

صرير sarír *m. Arabic* squeak (of a pen, of a door)

صعب sa'b *Arabic combining form* difficult, hard صعب العبور difficult to traverse

صعب العبور sa'b-ul-'ubúr difficult to traverse

صعب العلاج sa'b-ul-'ilādzh *Arabic* difficult to cure, صعب العلاجه ناروغي a disease which is difficult to cure

صعب الورود sa'b-ul-vurúd difficult to access, hard to get to

صعوبت su'ubát *m. Arabic* difficulty, straits

صعود su'úd *m. Arabic* **1** lifting, ascent **2** arising, beginning **3** growth, development صعود کول **a** to arise, ascend **b** to spring up (disagreements, etc.) **c** to develop, grow

صعودي sa'udí *Arabic* **1** arising, ascending, springing up **2** Saudi Arabia

صغار sighār *m. Arabic plural* **1** *from* صغير² **2** children

صغارت saghārát *m. Arabic* childhood

صغر sighár *m. Arabic* **1** smallness, insignificance **2** childhood

صغرا sughrá *Arabic* **1** *feminine singular of* اصغر **2** *f. philosophy* the minor premise of a syllogism

صغير saghír *Arabic* **1.1** little, juvenile **1.2** *law* minor, not of age **2** *m.* [*plural:* صغيران saghirán *Arabic plural:* صغار sighār] child, infant

صف saf saff *m. Arabic* [*plural:* صفونه saffúna *Arabic plural:* صفوف sufúf] **1** row, order; rank; file د صف په شکل in rows, in ranks دوفيله صف column of four يوه فيله صف single file, Indian file صف ترل، د نبي لاس صف *Eastern* right flank د صفونه جوړول to draw up in military order

صفا safá *Arabic* **1** clear, transparent صفا اوبه clear water, transparent water **2** clean, neat, tidy **3** clear, precise صفا ويل to speak clearly صفا پښتو ويل to speak Pashto well **4** evident صفا د تېلو د صفا کولو کارخانه oil refinery صفا کول **a** to clean, purify, refine **b** to clarify, make more precise (question, problem, etc.) صفا کېدل **a** to be clear, be transparent **b** to be cleaned, be purified, be refined **c** to be clean, be neat, be tidy **d** to be made more precise; be explained, be cleared up دا خبره بالکل صفا شوه Everything was explained in full. *idiom* په سوله او صفا کښي ژوند کول to live in peace and harmony لاس په چا صفا کول to get the better of, surpass someone

صفات sifát *m. Arabic plural of* صفت

صفار saffár *m. Arabic* **1** coppersmith **2** *history* Saffar (the founder of the Saffarid Dynasty, Yakub ibn-Lejs)

صفاکاري safākārí *f.* **1** purification, refining **2** explanation, making more precise (question, problem, etc.)

صفاوالى safāválaj *m.* **1** purity, cleanliness **2** purification, cleansing **3** tranquility

صفائي safāí *f.* **1** purity, transparency **2** cleanness, neatness, tidiness **3** clearness, preciseness **4** tranquility, peace د زړه صفائي spiritual peace, spiritual tranquility **5** innocence, lack of culpability صفائي

کول a to clean (a room, etc.) b to prove one's innocence 6 tax on real property 7 *regional law* defense وکیل صفائي د defender, defense lawyer صفائي گواه د defense witness

صف بندي safbandí *f.* saffbandí *regional military* drawing up in ranks صف بندي کول to draw up in military formation

صفت sifát *m. Arabic* [*plural:* صفتونه sifatúna *Arabic plural:* صفات sifãt] 1 quality, virtue; peculiarity; distinctive trait; indication ضميره صفت مومدل د تاجر distinctive, characteristic indications to become a merchant 2 description 3 praise د صفت لایق praiseworthy, worthy of praise د چا صفت کول to praise someone 4 *grammar* adjective

صف ترنه saftaṛóna *f.* safftaṛona ☞ صف بندي

صفتي siffatí 1 صفتي کلمه adjective 2 high-quality (of merchandise)

صفحه safhá *f. Arabic* 1 page 2 step, phase د سپوږمی صفحه a lunar phase

صفحه بندي safhabandí *f. typography* imposition, pagination

صفدر safdár brave, valorous, courageous

صفر [1] sífr *m.* sífar *Arabic* 1 cipher, zero, nought تر صفر لاندي below zero (of temperature) 2 nothing, empty spot, vacant position

صفر [2] safár *m. Arabic* Safar (the second month of the lunar year)

صفرا safrã́ *f. Arabic* bile

صفراوي safrãví 1.1 bilious, containing bile 1.2 choleric, easily aroused to anger 2 *m.* choleric man

صفره safára *f. Arabic* ☞ صفر [2]

صفوت safvát *m.* sufvát *Arabic* 1 best, most select part of something 2 quintessence

صفوف sufúf *m. Arabic plural of* صف

صفوي safaví *m. history* 1 Sefevid (the dynasty) 2 *adjective* Sefevid

صفه suffá *f.* 1 dock 2 platform

صفي safí *Arabic* clean, clear, transparent

صفیه safijá *f. Arabic* 1 *feminine singular of* صفي 2 *f. proper name* Safiya

صقلي گر siķligár *m. regional* gunsmith; armorer ☞ صقلي گر

صكوك sukúk *m. Arabic plural* [*singular:* صك sakk] 1 documents 2 checks

صلا salã́ *f.* 1 entertaining 2 verbal invitation 3 summons; appeal مونږ دا صلا و کړه چه ... We came to this decision ... *idiom*

صلات salã́t *m.* [*plural:* صلوات salavã́t] *Arabic* prayer

صلاح salã́ *f.* salã́h *Arabic* [*plural:* صلاحگاني salagãni salahgãni] 1 counsel, advice صلح مصلحت to give advice د چا سره صلاح ورکول کول to take counsel with someone; seek advice of someone 2 well-being 3 morality; virtue 4 interest د مملکت صلاح the interests of the State

صلاح کار salãhkã́r *m.* advisor, counselor

صلاحیت salāhiját *m. Arabic* 1 competence, jurisdiction, authority د ... صلاحیت لرل to have the right to something د صلاحیت مینده کول to receive the right 2 honesty, decency

صلاحیتدار، صلاحیت دار صلاحیت لرونکی salāhiját larúnkaj salāhijatdã́r competent, plenipotentiary, authoritative صلاحیت دار مخای the competent authority صلاحیت دار مقامات the competent authorities

صلاحیت نامه salāhijatnāmá *f.* warrant, mandate; credentials, authority

صلب sulb *m. Arabic* 1 loins; belly; bosom 2 descendents; clan

صلبي sulbí *adjective* blood, direct, immediate (of a descendent)

صلح súlh *f.* súlha *Arabic* peace صلحي مذاکرات د peaceful negotiations د صلح غوښتلو a separate peace جلا صلح، یوازنی صلح a policy of peace صلح په دنیا کښی peace for the whole world همیشه دي وي د دنیا صلح او روغه! Long live worldwide peace! صلحي طرفداران د supporters of peace صلحي جهاني شورا د the World Peace Council [1] سوله ☞ 2 صلح کول، صلح ترل to conclude peace صلح آمیز sulhāméz peace-loving, peaceful د اتومي انرژی صلح آمیز استفاده peaceful uses of atomic energy

صلح پسند sulhpasánd *m.* 1 pacifist 2 peaceable, peace-loving

صلح پسندي sulhpasandí` *f.* 1 peaceableness 2 pacifism

صلح جو suldzhú striving for peace, peace-loving

صلح جویانه sulhdzhujāná peace-loving صلح جویانه نظریات تعقیبول to display peaceableness, love of peace

صلح خواهانه sulhkhāhāná peace-loving صلح خواهانه سیاست a policy of peace

صلح خواهي sulkhãhi *f.* peaceableness, love of peace

صلح غوښتونکی sulh ghuḳhtúnkaj peace-loving

صلح نامه، صلحنامه sulhnāmá *f.* 1 armistice, truce 2 peace treaty 3 deed, deed of transfer

صلحه súlha *f.* reconciliation, peace صلحه کول to conclude a peace صلح ☞ صلحه سره کول to be reconciled with someone

صلحنامه sulhanāmá *f.* ☞ صلحه نامه

صلعم sal'ám *Arabic abbreviation* صلی الله علیه وسلم sallá lahú alájhi wasallám *religion* Peace and blessings of Allah be upon him! (said after the mention of the name of Prophet Mohammed)

صلوات salavã́t *Arabic masculine plural of* صلات and صلوة [*plural:* صلواتونه salavātúna] blessing, benediction

صلات salã́t *m. Arabic* [*plural:* صلوات salavã́t *plural:* صلوة ونه salatúna] prayer

صله silá *f. Arabic* (familial) connection, nearness

صلیب salíb *m. Arabic* 1 cross سور صلیب salíb-i احمر صلیب Red Cross 2 Crusade اهل صلیب áhl-i Christians د صلیب جنگ *history* the Crusades

صلیبي salibí *Arabic* 1 pertaining to the cross صلیبي جنگونه *history* the Crusades 2 *m.* [*plural:* صلیبیون salibijún] *Arabic history* Crusader

صماخ simãkh *m. Arabic anatomy* auditory canal

صمد samád *Arabic* 1 eternal 2 *m.* .1 master, lord, overlord 2.2 *proper name* Samad

صمصام samsã́m *m. Arabic* 1 sharp saber; sharp sword

صمغ samgh *m. Arabic* gum, resin عربي صمغ Arabic gum

صميم samím *m. Arabic* 1 core, pith, heart; interior part 2 sincere, cordial, heartfelt

صميمانه samimāná 1 sincere, heartfelt روابط صميمانه sincere, cordial relations 2 sincerely, cordially

صميمي samimí sincere, heartfelt

صميميت samimiját *m. Arabic* sincerity, cordiality

صنا saná *f.* Sana (city)

صناعت sanā'át sinā'át *Arabic m.* [*plural:* صنايع sanaji' *plural:* صنائع sanāí] 1 art نفيس صنائع، ظريف صنائع fine arts 2 trade; profession د صنايعو مكتب trade school; industrial school 3 industry

صناعتي sanā'atí industrial

صناعي sina'í *Arabic* 1 artificial, synthetic 2 expertly made 3 industrial

صنايع sanājí *m. plural* صنائع sanāí *m. Arabic* 1 *plural of* صناعت 2 ثقيل صنايع، درانه صنايع، سنگين صنايع heavy industry خفيف صنايع لاسي صنايع، د لاس صنايع، كليولي صنايع، سپك صنايع light industry صنايع cottage industry, handicrafts 3 branches of industry

صندق sundúk̨ *m.* sandúk̨ ☞ صندوق

صندقچي sunduk̨cháj *m.* box, casket, case

صندل sandál *m. singular & plural* sandalwood tree, sandalwood

صندله sandalá *f.* sandala (a mixture of clay, vegetable fiber, and wood ash used for plastering floors)

صندلي sandalí *f.* sandal; mangal (a barzier or a metal pan for holding burning coals under a stool, covered by a blanket)

صندوف sandúf *m.* satin

صندوق sandúk̨ *m.* sundúk̨ *Arabic* [*plural:* صندوقونه sandúk̨una *plural:* صندوقان sanduk̨án] 1 trunk; box; chest صندوق كول *compound verb* to place in a trunk, put in a box صندوق كېدل *compound verb* to be placed in a trunk, be put in a box 2 ballot box 3 till د پس انداز صندوق savings bank د معاونت صندوق benefit fund 4 coffin *idiom* د سيني صندوق *anatomy* thorax

صندوقچه sunduk̨chá *f.* box, casket, case; small box, small chest, small case, trunk

صندوقدار sandukdár *m.* cashier, treasurer, bursar

صنعا san'á *f.* ☞ صنا

صنعت san'át *m.* 1 art عالي صنعت fine arts 2 trade, craft; business 3 industry د صنعت خاوند industrialist *idiom* صنعت عسكري the military art; military profession

صنعتكار san'atkár *m.* صنعتگر، صنعت گر san'atgár craftsman, handcraftsman واړه صنعت كاران small local businessmen or handicrafts workers

صنعتي san'atí 1 industrial صنعتي مملكت industrial nation صنعتي كول to industrialize 2 artistic صنعتي شيان industrial goods; manufactured goods

صنف sinf *m.* sanf *Arabic* [*plural:* صنفونه sinfúna *Arabic plural:* اصناف asnắf *plural:* صنوف sunúf] 1 kind, sort; species, genus; category 2 class (in school) 3 *biology* class د مرغانو صنف class of birds 4 shop, shift; (socioeconomic) class كسبي صنف

(socioeconomic) class 5 armed forces' branch or service د هوا صنف the air force, military aviation

صنفي sinfí 1 pertaining to a shop, shift, or socioeconomic class 2 industrial 3 professional, pertaining to a specific class of craftsman (carpenters, metalworkers, etc.)

صنم sanam *m. Arabic* idol, image, object of worship

صنمه sanáma *f. poetry* beloved (woman)

صنوبر sanavbár sanobár *Arabic* 1 pine tree 2 coniferous tree

صنوف sunúf *m. Arabic plural of* صنف

صواب saváb *m. Arabic* 1 fair, just, equitable, the right way to act 2 rightness, innocence صواب لټول to strive for truth, seek justice

صوابديد savābdíd *m.* 1 approval, sanction 2 advice, wish, desire

صوابی svābój *f.* Swabi (city, Peshawar District)

صوات svát *m.* Svat, Swat (district)

صوب saub *m. Arabic* direction, quarter, side

صوبائي subaí provincial, regional

صوبجات subadzhát *m. Arabic plural of* صوبه

صوبه sobá subá subáh *f. Arabic* [*plural:* صوبي sobé subé *m. Arabic plural:* صوبجات subadzhát] province

صوبه دار subahdár *m.* 1 *history* subadar, governor general 2 *colloquial* lieutenant 3 captain

صوبه سرحد subahisarkhád *m. history* northwest border province

صوبېدار subedár *m. regional* ☞ صوبه دار

صوت saut *m. Arabic* [*plural:* اصوات asvất] sound, noise

صور sur *m. Arabic* trumpet (made of a horn), horn

صورت surát *m. Arabic* 1 form, shape په اجمالي صورت in short, briefly 2 face صورت مي ښكل كړه! Kiss me! 3 body; figure روغ د فعل صورت My whole body hurts. تول صورت مي خوږېږي health 4 صورت *grammar* aspect of a verb 5 list; enumeration; entry; record a صورت حال detailed account; detailed statement b report 6 numerator 7 *astronomy* phase د سپوږمي صورت phase of the moon 8 manner; way, kind په دې صورت سره in this way 9 case; situation, circumstance په دغه صورت كښي، په دې صورت كښي in such a case په هر صورت in any event, in one way or another په هيڅ صورت چه وي be that as it may not under any circumstances د ضرورت په صورت كښي in case of necessity صورت a to change one's clothes b to change appearance صورت بدلول a to come to be, come to pass b to happen, take صورت مېندل، صورت نيول place; eventuate دى شي صورت ځانته نيول to turn into something

صورت پرست surátparást *m.* formalist

صوري surí suraví *Arabic* external; formal; apparent, visible

صوف suf *m. Arabic* camlet; wool

صوفي sufí Sufi; dervish-mystic

صوفيانه sufijāná Sufic صوفيانه ژوند Sufic life; the life of a dervish-mystic

صوفي توب sufitób *m.* 1 Sufism 2 mysticism

صوفيه sófijá *f.* Sofia (city)

صوم ¹ sum *m.* ruble

صوم ² saum *m. Arabic religion* fast

صومع sauma' *f.* صومعه sauma'á *f. Arabic* cell; hermit's dwelling په صومع کښي ژوند کول to live as a hermit or recluse

صهونيت sihuniját *m. Arabic politics* Zionism

صياد sajjád *m. Arabic* **1** hunter (of birds and small game); trapper **2** *poetry* captivator of hearts

صيادي sajjádí *m. Arabic* hunting; hunting or trapping trade صيادي کول to engage professionally in hunting or trapping

صيانت sijanát *m. Arabic* support; protection

صيب sajb *m.* seb *colloquial* ☞ صاحب

صيحه sihá *f. Arabic* shout

صيد sajd *m. Arabic* **1** hunting, trapping **2** game; catch

صيدگاه sajdgáh *m.* hunting ground

صيغه sighá *f. Arabic* **1** formula (e.g., for a divorce) **2** form; shape; type د پور په صيغه in the form of a loan **3** grammatical form of a verb, verb form; conjugational paradigm

صيفيه sajfijá *f. Arabic* **1** holiday or summer house outside the city **2** district where there are summer, holiday, or weekend houses

صيفيه نشين sajfijanishín *m.* visitor or resident of a summer cottage, holiday house, or a district in which these are located

صيقل sajḳál *m. Arabic* **1** polishing; buffing **2** point; sharp point صيقل کول *compound verb* **a** to polish, buff **b** to sharpen, bring to a point صيقل کېدل *compound verb* **a** to be polished, be buffed **b** to be sharpened, be pointed

صيقلگر، صيقل گر sajḳalgár *m.* **1** polisher; burnisher **2** grinder **3** *regional* gunsmith

ض

ض zād **1** the twenty-fifth letter of the Pashto alphabet **2** the number 800 in the abjad system

ضابط zābít *m. Arabic* **1** company-grade officer د ضابط وکيل second lieutenant **2** [*plural:* ضابطان، آمر zābitán] آمران ضابطان، کوچني ضابطان field-grade senior officers خورد ضابطان officers **3** *history* leader, ruler

ضابطه zābitá *f. Arabic* **1** law; legislation; code ضابطه ديوان *regional* Code of Civil Law **2** order, discipline د ضابطي لاندي راوستل to introduce order, set to rights **3** memorization, rote learning په ضابطه کښي راوستل to memorize, learn by heart

ضابطي zābití *f.* officer corps

ضاد zād *m. Arabic* the name of the letter ض

ضامن zāmín *m. Arabic* **1** warrantor, guarantor د هغه ضامن يم I'll vouch for him. په دي باره کښي ضامن يم I certify that ... **2** bail, surety **3** deposit, security; guarantee

ضامنه zāminá *f. used with* ضامن 1

ضامني zāminí *f.* ☞ ضمانت

ضائع zāi *Arabic* **1** perished **2** fallen; lost **3** destroyed ضائع کول **a** to ruin **b** to lose **c** to destroy ضائع کېدل **a** to perish **b** to be lost دپر وخت يي پر ضائع شو He spent a lot of time on this. **c** to be destroyed

ضائعه zāi'á *f. Arabic m.* [*plural:* ضائعات zai'át] losses, loss, damage

ضائفه zāifá *f.* zāipá *Arabic* woman, weak sex

ضبط zabt *m. Arabic* **1** seizure (of territory) **2** confiscation; sequestration, seizure (of prosperity) **3** control; restraint; self-control, self-possession با وجود د ډېر ضبطه notwithstanding his restraint په ځان ضبط کول to be restrained, be collected; keep oneself in hand د ضبط نه ځان ايستل to lose self-possession, lose one's cool, lose control of oneself ضبط احوالات zabt-i counterintelligence **4** list (of words, songs, etc.) ضبط کول ☞ ضبطول

ضبطوالا zabtvālá *regional* disciplined; restrained

ضبطورابط zabturábt *m. Arabic* state of discipline

ضبطوالى zabtválaj *m.* seizure, confiscation

ضبطول zabtavál *denominative, transitive* [*past:* ضبط يي کړ] **1** to seize (territory) **2** to confiscate; to sequestrate; put a lien on (property) **3** to memorize, learn by heart **4** to list (words), record a song **5** to pick up (documents)

ضبطي zabtí **1** confiscated **2** *f.* confiscation; sequestration

ضبطېدل zabtedál [*past:* ضبط شو] **1** to be seized (of territory) **2** to be confiscated, be put under lien (of property) **3** to be memorized **4** to be recorded (words, song) **5** to be picked up (document)

ضخامت zakhāmát *m. Arabic* **1** fatness **2** portliness; plumpness

ضخيم zakhím *Arabic* **1** fat **2** burly, portly, plump

ضد [1] zid zidd *Arabic* **1** opposite, opposing **2** *m.* **.1** opposition د...پر ضد، د...په ضد، د...پر ضد باندي، د... په ضد باندي against ديو شي سره anti-air د هوايي حملو د ضد someone, against something د چا سره ضد نيول to oppose, be opposed to something against someone **2.2** malice, spite د هغه سره ضد کوي He harbored malice toward him.

ضد [2] zíd-i zídd-i *combining form* counter-, anti- ضدتانک antitank

ضداستعمار ziddiisti'már zidiisti'már anti-colonial

ضد امپريالستي ziddiimpirjālistí zidiimpirjālistí anti-imperialist

ضدانساني ziddiinsāní zidiinsāní inhuman, misanthropic

ضدتانک zidd-i-tānk zid-i-tānk antitank

ضدعفوني ziddi'ufuní zidi'ufuní *Arabic* disinfection, disinfecting ضدعفوني کول، اوبه ضدعفوني کول **a** to sterilize (water) **b** to disinfect

ضدفاشيست ziddifāshíst zidifāshíst anti-fascist

ضدفاشيستي ziddifāshistí *f.* zidifāshistí anti-fascism

ضدفضائي ziddifāzjí zidifāzjí ☞ ضدهوايي

ضدفيوډلي ziddifeoḍalí zidifeoḍalí anti-feudal

ضدملاريا ziddimalārijá zidimalārijá antimalaria

ضدهوايي ziddihavāí zidihavāí anti-war; antiaircraft

ضدي ziddí **1** opposite, opposing; contrasting **2** spiteful

ضديت zidiját *m. Arabic* **1** opposition, contrast **2** hostility **3** contradiction; antagonism ضديت کول to contradict

ضدين ziddájn *m. Arabic plural of* ضد [2] two antitheses, antipodes

ضراب zarráb *m. Arabic* stamper (of coins)

ضراب خانه zarrābkhaná *f.* mint

ضرب zarb *Arabic* [*plural:* ضربونه zarbúna *Arabic plural:* ضربات zarbắt] **1** blow **2** beating **3** stamping (of coins) وهل ضرب to stamp (coins) **4** *regional* maiming, injury, mulitation ضرب خفيف minor injury ضرب شديد zarb-i serious injury ضرب رسول a to inflict a blow **b** to inflict an injury **5** *math* multiplication د ضرب جدول the multiplication table **6** *grammar* accent, stress

ضرب المثل zarb-ul-masál *m. Arabic* proverb; saying

ضربان zarabán *m.* zarbán *Arabic* beating (heart), pulsation

ضربت zarbát *m. Arabic* ☞ ضربه

ضربول zarbavál *denominative, transitive* [*past:* ضرب يې کړ] to multiply پنځه په دری کي ضرب کئ multiply 5 x 3

ضربه zarbá *f. Arabic* blow, stroke

ضرر zarár *m. Arabic* [*plural:* ضررونه zararúna *Arabic plural:* اضرار azrār] harm, damage, loss ضرر رسول a to harm, inflict damage, inflict loss **b** to grieve ضرر لېدل a to suffer injury, suffer loss, suffer **b** to be grieved, be injured

ضرر رسوونکي zarár rasavunkaj harmful, injurious ضرر رسوونکي حشرات zarár rasavúnki harmful insect ضرر رسوونکي نباتات zarár rasavúnki weeds

ضررناک zararnắk ضرري zararí **1** harmful **2** damaging

ضرور zarúr *Arabic indeclinable* **1.1** necessary, needful ضرور دئ چه It is necessary to ... ضرور جای dzhāj-i toilet, latrine **1.2** urgent, pressing (a matter) **2** necessarily; without fail; of course

ضرورت zarurát *m. Arabic* **1** necessity, requirement, need و چاو ته to be needful of something ضرورت لرل زه شي ته ضرورت لرل I require tea. **2** coercion

ضرورتاً zarurátán *Arabic* **1** perforce **2** without fail, certainly او لزوماً without fail, absolutely

ضروري zarurí *Arabic* **1** necessary, obligatory, inevitable ضروري دئ It is necessary. دا ضروري شی نه دئ چه، دا ضروري خبره ده چه This is really unnecessary. One can really do without this. **2** important ضروري ضروري extremely important

ضروريات zarurijất *m. Arabic plural* objects of prime necessity د سفر ضروريات travel necessities

ضعف za'f *m.* zu'f *Arabic* weakness, powerlessness د زړه ضعف a drop in cardiac activity, cardiac insufficiency ورباندي ضعف راغئ He experienced weakness. *idiom* اخلاقي او معنوي ضعفونه moral instability ضعف کول to grow weak

ضعيف za'íf *Arabic* **1** weak, powerless, impotent ضعيف کول to weaken ضعيف کېدل to become weak, grow weak **2** *m.* [*plural:* ضعيفان za'ifấn] a weak creature

ضعيف الاراده za'if-ul-irādá *Arabic* weak-willed

ضعف za'ifí ☞ ضعيفي

ضلالت zalālát *m. Arabic* error, blunder, deviation from the truth د ضلالت له پښو لاندي کېدل to fall into error, blunder, deviate from the truth

ضلع zíl'a *f. Arabic* [*plural:* اضلاع azlắ] ضلعه zíl'a *f. regional* **1** side **2** border, verge **3** linear measure ضلع بسواسه 2,209 meters

47,183 meters **4** *regional* ضلع جريب 9,879 meters ضلع بسوه province, district **5** state (administrative-territorial unit)

ضم zam zamm *m.* **1** addition; augmentation; supplement **2** *predicative* additional, augmentational; supplemental ديو شي سره ضم کېدل to be added (to), be supplemental to something

ضماد zimắd *m. Arabic medicine* **1** plaster **2** compress تود ضماد poultice, hot compress

ضمانت zamānát *m. Arabic* **1** bail, guarantee; surety ضمانت کول to guarantee د چا ضمانت کول to go bail for, vouch for someone په ضمانت ازادول to release on bail **2** security په ضمانت as security (for)

ضمانت کوونکی zamānát kavúnkaj *m.* bailsman, guarantor

ضمانت نامه zamānatnāmá *f. law* written surety, guarantee

ضمائر zamāir *m. plural of* ضمير

ضمائم zamāim *m. Arabic plural of* ضميمه

ضمن zimn *m. Arabic* **1** middle, midst **2** content د ... په ضمن کښي among, including په دي ضمن کښي moreover; by the way

ضمناً zímnán *Arabic* moreover, this being so; by the way

ضمني zimní *Arabic* **1** implied; indirect **2** fortuitous; collateral **3** detailed

ضمول zamavál zammavál *denominative, transitive* [*past:* ضم يې کړ] to add, join to, supplement, enclose

ضمه zammá *f. Arabic* zamma, pesh (the supralinear sign which indicates the short vowels "u" or "o")

ضمير zamír *m. Arabic* [*plural:* ضميرونه zamirúna *Arabic plural:* ضمائر zamāír] **1** heart, soul د عقيدي او ضمير په امر according to the dictates of the heart **2** intentions, dreams **3** *grammar pronoun* منغصله ضمائر enclitic (unstressed) pronoun متصل ضمير emphatic personal pronoun **4** conscience **5** *personal name* Zamir

ضميران zamirán *m. Arabic botany* basil, *Ocimum basilicum*

ضميمه zamimá *f. Arabic* [*plural:* ضميمي zamimé *Arabic m. plural:* ضمائم zamāím] **1** guarantee, surety, security **2** *biology* appendage **3** supplement

ضوابط zavābít *m. Arabic plural of* ضابطه

ضيا zijắ *Arabic* **1** *f.* brilliance, radiance; light ضيا الملت والدين *history* title of the Emir Abdurrahman Khan **2** *m. proper name* Zia, Zeeya

ضيا zajắ¹ *f. Arabic* loss; ruin

ضياع zijắ² ☞ ضائع

ضيافت zijāfát *m. Arabic* entertaining, refreshments; feast; banquet

ضيف zajf *m. Arabic* [*plural:* ضيفان zajfān *Arabic plural:* ضيوف zujúf *plural:* اضياف azjắf] **1** guest **2** visitor; client

ضيوف zujúf *m. Arabic plural of* ضيف

ضيق ziķ *m. Arabic* **1** narrowness **2** difficulty; constraint **3** cares, troubles

ط

ط toj tā **1** the twenty-sixth letter of the Pashto alphabet (pronounced ت "t" and so is sometimes replaced by the letter ت) **2** the number 9 in the abjad system

طا tā *f. Arabic* the name of the letter ط

طابوت tābút *m. Arabic* coffin

طاخچه tākhchá *f.* ☞ طاقچه

طاس tās *m.* **1** *geography* basin **2** *botany* corolla

طاسبرگ tāsabárg *m.* petal

طاعت tā'át *m. Arabic* **1** obedience چا طاعت کول د to obey (someone) **2** *religion* pious work, pious action

طاعون tā'ún *m. Arabic* plague, pestilence

طاق ¹ tāķ *m. Arabic* vault, cupola; arch

طاق ² tāķ *Arabic* odd (i.e., not even)

طاقت tāķát *m. Arabic* **1** strength, force, power طاقت بدني physical force, strength تر طاقت زيات، تر طاقت بهر، تر طاقت لوړ beyond one's strength; excessive **2** endurance; patience بي له اوبو څخه طاقت نه I cannot do without water. **3** energy طاقت اټومي atomic energy طاقت شمسي solar energy **4** *politics* power **5** troops, armed forces طاقت دريايي د Navy طاقت هوايي Air Force طاقت ... د They are engaged in wrestling. طاقت نه بيرون ماليات اخلي راوړل to deal with something

طاقت نما tāķatnumā́ *f.* ☞ قوت نما

طاقت فرسا tāķatfarsá exhausting

طاقتور tāķatvár powerful, strong

طاقچه tāķchá *f.* niche, bay; shelf

طاقي tāķí *architecture* vaulted, arched; formed as a niche or bay

طالب talíb **1** *m. Arabic* [*plural:* طالبان tālibā́n *Arabic plural:* طلاب tullāb *plural:* طلبه talabá] student **2** seeker (after something; one striving (for something); one trying to attain, thirsting for, requiring something

طالبان tālibā́n *plural* Taliban, Taleban (religious-political movement and group that ruled Afghanistan from 1996-2001)

طالب العلم tālib-ul-'ílm *m.* **1** student **2** student at a Muslim religious school

طالب العلمه tālib-ul-'ílma *f.* **1** student (female) **2** student (female) at an institute of higher learning

طالع tālé' tāli' *Arabic* **1** *f.* fate, destiny; luck, happiness د ده طالع پته ده His fate is unknown. **2** *astronomy* rising (of celestial bodies)

طالعمن tāle'mán tāli'mán طالعمند tāle'mand tāli'mand lucky

طاوس tāús *m. Arabic* **1** peacock **2** *proper name* Taus که هر څومره طاوس ښايسته دئ خو بيا يې هم پنښې توري دي Proverb literal Beautiful though he may be, yet the peacock's feet are black. *figurative* Every rose has its thorns.

طاون tā́un *m.* ☞ طاعون

طاهر tāhír **1.1** pure; spotless, immaculate **1.2** holy **2** *m. proper name* Tahir

طاير taír طاير tajír *Arabic* **1** flying **2** *m.* [*plural:* طير tajr] bird

طائفه taifá *f.* طاجفى tājifá *f. Arabic* [*plural:* طائفي tāifé] *Arabic m.* [*plural:* طوايف tavājif] **1** tribe **2** *biology* order **3** *obsolete* gang, band

طب tib tibb *Arabic singular & plural* medicine, medical treatment طب يوناني eastern medicine

طبابت tabābát *m. Arabic* medical treatment, medical practice د طبابت کار کول to engage in the practice of medicine

طباخ tabbākh *m. Arabic* cook

طباخت tabbākhát *m. Arabic* طباخي tabbākhí *f.* cookery, the culinary arts

طباشير tabāshír *m. Arabic* **1** bamboo sugar **2** chalk; a stick of chalk

طباع tabbā́' *m. Arabic* printer

طباعت tibā́'at *m. Arabic* printing, typographic work

طباعتي tibā'atí *Arabic* typographic, polygraphic طباعتي غلطي misprint طباعتي متخصص printer (one who prints) کتاب ښه طباعتي ښايست لري The book is typographically well executed.

طباف tabbā́f *m.* ☞ طواف ²

طبائع tabbāí' *m. Arabic plural of* طبيعت

طبرق tubráķ *m.* ☞ توبره

طبع tab' *f.* tab'a *Arabic* **1** printing; publication طبع لمړى first edition طبع کول compound verb to print, publish طبع کېدل compound verb to be published, be printed **2** nature, natural order **3** disposition, character **4** talent, ability, natural gifts

طبعاً tab'án **1** by nature **2** naturally **3** of course

طبع آزمائي tab'āzmāí *f.* checking, trial, test

طبعه táb'a *f.* **1** ☞ طبع **2** mood, disposition نن مي طبعه خته ده I am in a bad mood today. Today I am out of sorts.

طبق ¹ tibķ *m. Arabic* conformity, accordance په طبق ... د in accordance with something

طبق ² tabáķ *m. Arabic* tray

طبق ³ tabáķ *m. veterinary* hoof and mouth disease

طبقات tabaķát *m. Arabic plural of* طبقه

طبقات الارضي tabáķāt-ul-arzí geologic, pertaining to the structure of the earth

طبقاتي tabaķatí **1** *adjective* estate (in the historical sense of "class") طبقاتي اختلافات class society طبقاتي تولنه **2** class contradictions طبقاتي جنگ class struggle طبقاتي بېلوالى class differentiation

طبقه tabaķá *f. Arabic* [*plural:* طبقي tabaķé] *m. Arabic* [*plural:* طبقات tabaķát] **1** section (of the population); group (of people); estate **2** class طبقات اجتماعي متضاد antagonistic classes طبقات دوست amicable classes طبقه حاکمه the ruling class طبقه کېنه زحمت workers **3** society; circles (social) طبقي حاکمي ruling circles **4** category; degree **5** stage **6** stage (of a missile) **7** *geology* stratum, bed (of soil) **8** *biology* class

طبقه بندي tabaķabandí *f.* **1** classification; taxonomy د حيواناتو طبقه بندي classification, animal taxonomy **2** differentiation طبقه بندي کول a to classify, systematize b to differentiate

طبل tabl *m.* drum

طبله tablá *f. Arabic* 1 small tamborine 2 wooden platter or tray for fruit

طبليسي tbilísi *m.* Tbilisi (city)

طبي tibbí *Arabic* 1 medical, medicinal; therapeutic طبي مرسته medical, therapeutic aid طبي فاكولته medical faculty (i.e., department of a university) طبي مكتب medical school طبي مواد medications

طبيب tabíb *m. Arabic* [*plural:* طبيبان tabibán *Arabic plural:* اطبا atibā *plural:* اطبه atibbá] doctor, physician, medical practitioner د اسونو طبيب veterinarian

طبيبه tabíba *feminine of* طبيب

طبيبي tabibí *f.* healing, medical treatment, the practice of medicine

طبيعت tabi'át *m. Arabic* [*plural:* طبيعتونه tabi'atúna *Arabic plural:* طبائع tabāi] 1 nature, disposition, character د فعال طبيعت خاوند دئ He is energetic. 2 essence, natural order د طبيعت قوانين the laws of nature 3 mood, temperament ځما طبيعت ډير خوشحاله شو My mood was excellent. طبيعت يې ځای له رانغى *Eastern* He wasn't calmed down.

طبيعتاً tabi'átán 1 naturally 2 by nature; by one's nature

طبيعي tabi'í *Arabic* 1 natural; normal طبيعي منابع، طبيعي پيداوار natural resources طبيعي علوم natural history طبيعي علم natural science په طبيعي ډول naturally, normally طبيعي ورښبنم natural silk 2 understood ده چه طبيعي understandably; naturally 3 spontaneous طبيعي سير drift

طبيعي والى tabi'iválaj *m.* state of nature, natural state; state of normality, normality

طبيعيون tabi'ijún *m. Arabic plural* naturalist, natural scientist, natural historian

طبيله tabelá *f.* stable

طحال tihál *m. Arabic anatomy* spleen

طراح tarrāh *m. Arabic* 1 draftsman 2 ringleader, organizer 3 instigator

طرار tarrár *Arabic* 1 bright 2 articulate; sharp-tongued

طراز tiráz *m. Arabic* 1 decoration, adornment, finery 2 manner, form; method

طراوت tarāvát *m. Arabic* freshness, succulence (of grass, pasturage)

طرب taráb *m. Arabic* 1 gladness, joy, merriment 2 delight

طرابلس الغرب tarabulus-al-gharb *m.* Tripoli (city); Tripolitania

طرح tárh tárha *f. Arabic* 1 plan, draft, draft-plan 2 blueprint, engineering drawing 3 drawing طرح كول *compound verb* a to work out a plan; to make a draft-plan b to draw, execute a blueprint c to draw, sketch طرح كېدل *compound verb* a to be worked out (plan) b to be traced out, be drafted, be executed (blueprint etc.) c to be drawn, be sketched d to be expounded, be clarified

طرحه tárha *f.* ☞ طرح طرحه په طرحه طرح sundry, different, various

طرد tard *m. Arabic* driving out, chasing away, expulsion

طرز tarz *m. Arabic* fashion, mode, manner د حكومت طرز governmental structure, system of government د توليد طرز method of production طرز عمل *tárz-i* conduct, deportment طرز تفكر *tárz-i* way of thinking; thinking, thought په يوه يا په بل طرز *idiom* in one way or another

طرف taráf *m. Arabic* [*plural:* طرفونه tarafúna *Arabic plural:* اطراف atrāf *plural:* طرفين tarafájn] side, party مقابل طرف a opponent b trade contractor

طرفدار tarafdár 1 *m.* partisan, follower, supporter 2 for (in voting)

طرفداري tarafdārí *f.* 1 adherence; partiality 2 support, sympathy د چا طرفداري كول on someone's side to be someone's supporter, support someone د چا د خپلو نظرياتو طرفداري ته راوړل to succeed in inclining someone to one's favor, win someone over to one's side د يو كار په طرفداري دربدل to speak out for something, support something

طرفداري tarafdāri *feminine plural of* طرفدار

طرفه turfá *f. Arabic* novelty

طرفين tarafájn *masculine dual Arabic of* طرف يو له طرفينو څخه one of the parties

طرق turúk *m. Arabic plural of* طريق

طرم turúm *m.* horn, bugle; trumpet

طرمچي turumchí *m.* bugler, trumpeter

طره turrá *f. Arabic* plume (decoration)

طري tarí *Arabic* 1 fresh, new 2 tender, soft

طريق tarik *m. Arabic* [*plural:* طرق turúk] way, road

طريقت tarikát *m.* ☞ تصوف

طريقه tariká *f. Arabic* path, way, manner, mode د ژوند طريقه way of life توليد طريقه method of production په ډېره ساده او اسانه طريقه very simply په علمي طريقه on a scientific basis په عجيبه طريقه سره in a strange manner, strangely, unusually

طراق طراق tarāk-tarāk *interjection* 1 bang, knock-knock 2 *m.* knock په ور طراق طراق كول to knock طراق طراق كول to knock on the door

طشت tasht *m.* 1 tub, trough; large copper basin; bathtub 2 *geography* basin 3 depression

طعام ta'ám *m. Arabic* food, victuals

طعامبه ta'āmbá *f. colloquial* ☞ طعمه

طعامخانه ta'ámkhāná *f.* dining room, mess hall, refectory

طعام نامه ta'āmnāmá *f.* menu

طعمه tu'má *f. Arabic* food, fodder

طعن ta'n *m. Arabic* reproaches, rebukes

طعن آميز ta'nāméz sarcastic, mocking طعن آميز خبري sarcasm

طعنه ta'ná *f. Arabic* 1 rebuke, blame 2 mockery; irony, sarcasm طعنه وركول، طعني وركول to jeer at, ridicule

طغ tugh *m.* 1 pennant, guidon 2 banner

طغيان tughjān *m. Arabic* 1 overflowing of banks, flooding (of a river); high water 2 *figuratives* rebellion, sedition

طغياني tughjāní 1 f. 1. ☞ طغيان 1.2 figuratives excess 1.3 figuratives disturbance, commotion 2.1 stormy طغياني بهبده turbulent flow (of a river) 2.2 figuratives disturbed طغياني كېدل to be disturbed, get into a commotion

طفل tifl m. Arabic [plural: اطفال atfāl] babe, infant

طفلانه tiflāná infantile, child's, pertaining to a child

طفلك tiflák m. baby, infant, young child

طفلس tiflís m. Tiflis (city) ☞ طبليسي

طفلي tiflí f. ☞ طفوليت

طفوليت tufuliját m. Arabic childhood; infancy د طفوليت ورځي childhood years

طفه tafá f. ☞ طائفه

طفيل tufájl m. Arabic 1 parasite, sponger, freeloader 2 biology parasite

طفيلي tufajlí parasitic په طفيلي ژوند ژوندون كول to lead a parasitic life, freeload

طلا tilā́ f. 1 gold طلا سنگي native ore د زرشویی طلا gold dust شگو طلا placer gold 2 tila (a gold coin); ducat

طلاب tullā́b m. Arabic plural of طالب

طلاباب tilābā́b precious metals

طلادار tilādā́r 1 embroidered in gold; stitched in gold 2 gilded

طلاق talā́k m. Arabic divorce د ښځي طلاق اچول to give a divorce to a wife idiom يو شي ته طلاق وركول to part with something

طلاقنامه، طلاق نامه talāk̲nāmá f. certificate of divorce, decree of divorce

طلاقول talākavə́l denominative, transitive [past: طلاق يې كړ] to give a divorce (to a wife)

طلاكاري tilākārí f. gilding, gilt

طلايه tilājá f. regional forward detachment, advance detachment; advance post

طلائي tilā́í 1 gold, of gold 2 golden (color); light-brown; blond idiom طلائي مرغى a happiness, great success b rich yield (ore)

طلب talā́b m. Arabic [plural: طلبونه talabúna Arabic plural: طلبات talabāt] 1 claim; request د يو شي طلب كول to claim something; to request something 2 debt (owed to someone); monetary request 3 regional wages, pay طلب وركول to pay for work

طلب گار، طلبگار talabgā́r 1 requiring, requesting; seeking; desiring 2 m. .1 plaintiff 2.2 creditor

طلب گاري talabgārí f. marriage brokerage (proposing a man as husband)

طلبنامه talabnāmá f. obsolete requirement, request; call

طلبول talabavə́l denominative, transitive [past: طلب يې كړ] to demand, ask for; call (for)

طلبه talabá m. Arabic plural of طالب

طلبه talbá f. hunting lure, decoy, bait

طلبېدل talabedə́l denominative, intransitive [past: طلب شو] 1 to be needed 2 to be called, be summoned

طلسم tilísm m. tilísəm Arabic talisman, amulet طلسم ماتول to annul the efficiency of a talisman, deprive a talisman of its effective force

طلسم والا tilismvālā́ m. magician, wizard

طلسمي tilismí enchanted, spellbound

طلوع tulú' f. Arabic dawn, sunrise

طماع tammā' Arabic greedy, avid

طماغه tumāghá f. hood for a hawk (in falconry)

طمانچه tumānchá f. revolver

طمانيت tamāniját m. rest, tranquillity

طمطراق tumturā́k m. 1 pomposity, bombast 2 splendor, pomp

طمع tám tám'a f. Arabic طمعه tám'a f. 1 avidity, greed طمع لرل to be avid, be greedy 2 expectation, hope د تانه مي دومره طمع نه وه I don't rely on you. I was not confident of you 3 lust, desire د روپو په طمع in pursuit of money طمع كول to desire strongly, be avid for; strive to get something

طن tan m. ton

طناب tanā́b m. Arabic 1 rope; cord 2 tanap (a measure of square area, having various regional values)

طنابي tanābí adjective rope, cord; of rope, of cord

طناو tanā́v m. 1 ☞ طناب 2 belt drive (e.g., for a spinning wheel)

طنبور tambúr m. Arabic tambur (a stringed, long-necked musical instrument resembling a mandolin)

طنطنه tantaná f. Arabic melody

طنز tanz m. Arabic mockery, irony

طنزاً tánzan Arabic mockingly, in mockery; ironically

طنين tanín m. Arabic 1 resonant sound; rumble, hum 2 buzzing (of insects)

طواف tavā́f m. Arabic religion 1 ritual procession or tour around the Kaaba 2 pilgrimage طواف كول to complete a pilgrimage

طواف tavvā́f m. Arabic fruit peddler, water peddler; peddler; one selling products from a stand or tray at a market

طوامير tavāmír m. Arabic plural of طومار

طوائف tavājif m. plural طوائف tavāíf m. Arabic plural of طائفه

طوبره tobrá f. bag, sack

طوپ top m. ☞ توپ

طوپچي topchí m. ☞ توپچي

طوپ سازي topsāzí f. ☞ توپ سازي

طوپوغرافي topoghrāfí f. topography

طور taur m. Arabic [plural: اطوار atvár] manner, mode, way په غير ارادي طور باندي involuntarily a thus, therefore b exactly so همدې طور سره

طور tur m. طور كوه طور kúh-i ... Mount Sinai د طور جزيره the Sinai Peninsula

طوطا totā́ m. parrot

طوطاخيل totākhél 1 m. plural the Totakhejli (tribe) 2 m. Totakhejl (tribesman)

طوطاگركى totāgarkáj m. Eastern swallow

طوطي tutí *m.* parrot *idiom* طوطي يې گونگ شو He fell silent (awhile).

طوغ tugh *m.* togh 1 pennant, guidon 2 banner

طوفان tufā́n tupā́n *m. Arabic* 1 tempest, typhoon, storm; hurricane د ريگ طوفان sandstorm; simoon طوفان راولړ شو A storm arose. د طوفان اخته کېدل The sea was running high. چپو طوفان راپيدا شول to encounter a storm or hurricane 2 flood 3 deep agitation د هيجاناتو طوفان deep stirring, perturbation of feelings *idiom* طوفان کول to excavate the earth, work zealously

طوفاني tufā́ní 1 stormy; blustery 2 encountering a storm, buffeted by a storm 3 worried, agitated 4 assault طوفاني عساکر assault detachments

طوق tauḳ *m. Arabic* 1 necklace 2 neck-ring (of a bird) 3 *poetry* the bounds, ties of love 4 yoke of slavery

طول ¹ tul *m. Arabic* 1 length د موج طول wavelength 2 *geography* longitute شرقي طول east longitude غربي طول west longitude

طول ² tul *m.* tulle

طول البلد tul-al-balád *m. Arabic* meridian

طول الياف tulaljā́f *Arabic* long staple (cotton)

طولاني tulā́ní protracted, extended, prolonged

طومار tumā́r *m. Arabic* [*plural:* طومارونه tumārúna *Arabic plural:* طوامير tavāmír] 1 roll, scroll; bundle (of paper) 2 book 3 list, register

طوی ¹ toj *m. regional* holiday, merriment; wedding

طوی ² toj *m.* the name of the letter ط

طويل tavíl *Arabic* long, lengthy, protracted

طوبله tavelá *f.* 1 stable 2 cattle pen, sheepfold; stall

طهارت tahārát *m. Arabic* 1 purity, cleanliness 2 holiness

طی taj *m. Arabic* 1 folding, rolling up 2 passing through, proceeding طی کول *compound verb* to pass along (a route) طی کېدل *compound verb* to be traversed (of a route)

طيار tajjā́r *Arabic* flying طيار بم pilotless aircraft (weapon)

طياره tajjārá *f. Arabic* aircraft جنگي طياره combat aircraft د رفاقت طياره escort aircraft د هجوم طياره، د پياده قوا طياري assault aircraft *obsolete* a commander of aviation د طياري قوماندان b aircraft commander

طياره ران tajjārarā́n *m.* pilot, flyer; aviator

طياره سازي tajjārasāzí *f.* aircraft construction, the aircraft industry

طياره شکن tajjārashikán *adjective* antiaircraft طياره شکن توپ antiaircraft gun

طياره وان tajjāravā́n *m.* ☞ طياره ران

طياره وړونکی بېړی، طياره وړونکی کښتی tajjārá brunkaj brunkaj aircraft carrier

طياره ويشتونکی tajjārá vishtúnkaj *adjective* antiaircraft

طيب tajjíb *Arabic* 1.1 good; pleasant 1.2 legal 2 *m. proper name* Tajib

طير tajr *m. Arabic* 1 [*plural:* طيور tujúr] bird 2 *plural of* طائر birds, feathered creatures

طيران tajarā́n *m. Arabic* flight *idiom* د افکارو طيران flight of fantasy, flight of the mind

طيش tajsh *m.* anger, rage, wrath

طيف tajf *m. Arabic* 1 ghost; apparition, spectre 2 *physics* spectrum

طيور tujúr *m. Arabic plural of* طير

ظ

ظ zoj zā 1 the twenty-seventh letter of the Pashto alphabet (pronounced as "z" and so sometimes replaced by the letter ز) 2 the number 900 in the abjad system

ظا zā *f.* the name of the letter ظ

ظالم zālím *Arabic* 1 *m.* tyrant, oppressor; dictator 2 *attributive* 2.1 cruel, wicked; savage, pitiless 2.2 tyrannical, despotic 2.3 unjust ظالم بېلتون *folklore* the name of a wicked character in a tale

ظالمانه zālimāná 1 cruel, tyrannical, despotic ظالمانه ترون an unjust treaty 2 cruelly, despotically

ظالمه zalíma *f.* 1 *used with* ظالم 2 *poetry* beloved (female); tormentress

ظاهر zāhír *Arabic* 1.1 apparent, obvious, patent ظاهره برتري obvious advantage, superiority ظاهره ده چه ....، ظاهره خبره ده چه ... It is apparent that ... It is obvious that ... 1.2 external, surface دا ظاهر لري، خو باطن نه This is superficial. This is shallow. This isn't serious. 2.1 obviously, apparently 2.2 externally 2.3 *proper name* Zahir

ظاهراً zāhírán *Arabic* 1 apparently, obviously 2 openly, up front; frankly 3 externally, on the surface

ظاهربين zāhirbín 1 *m.* superficial person 2 superficial, shallow

ظاهربيني zāhirbiní *f.* superficiality, shallowness

ظاهرداري zāhidārí *f.* ظاهرنمائي zāhirnumāí *f.* sham, pretense

ظاهروالی zāhirvā́laj *m.* 1 clarity, obviousness 2 visibility

ظاهرول zāhiravál *denominative, transitive* [*past:* ظاهر يې کړ] 1 to discover, reveal, manifest 2 to express, state خواهش ظاهرول to express a wish, state a desire

ظاهروونکی zāhiravúnkaj 1 *present participle of* ظاهرول 2 *m.* expressor, one who expresses (thoughts, aspirations, etc.)

ظاهره ¹ zāhira *feminine singular of* ظاهر په ظاهره seemingly خو جوره ده She is seemingly in good health.

ظاهره ² zāhirá *f. Arabic m.* [*plural:* ظواهر zavāhír] manifestation

ظاهري zāhirí 1 *adjective* external, exterior; surface ظاهري بنه external appearance ظاهري عالم the outside world, surroundings 2 appearing, seeming 3 apparent, evident

ظاهربدل zāhiredál *denominative, intransitive* [*past:* ظاهر شو] 1 to be discovered, be revealed, be manifested; turn out to be 2 to be expressed, be stated

ظاهربده zāhiredá *m. plural* discovery, revelation, manifestation

ظرافت zarāfát *m. Arabic* **1** humor; sharp-wittedness **2** elegance; grace **3** breeding, civility, courtesy

ظرف zarf *m. Arabic* [*plural:* ظرفونه zarfúna *Arabic plural:* ظروف zurúf] **1** dish; vessel; container **2** *grammar* adverb **3** interval of time, interval د دوو ساعترو په ظرف کښي in the course of two hours **4** *philosophy* form ظرف او مظروف form and content

ظرفي zarfí *grammar* adverbial

ظرفيت zarfiját *m. Arabic* **1** capacity, volume; displacement, tonnage د تولیداتو ظرفیت rate, scope, volume (of work, etc.) **2** volume of production **3** productivity **4** force, power

ظروف zurúf *m. Arabic plural* **1** *of* ظرف **2** *figurative* conditions, possibilities مناسب ظروف تهیه کول to create the appropriate conditions

ظریف zaríf *Arabic* **1.1** sharp-witted, intelligent **1.2** elegant, fine ظریفه صنایع sanají-ji... fine arts, artistic professions **1.3** elegant, charming; gracious **2** *m. proper name* Zarif

ظریفه zarifá *Arabic* **1** *f.* **.1** refined, intelligent speech; witticism **1.2** *proper name* Zarifa **2** *feminine plural of* ظریف [1]

ظفر zafár *m. Arabic* **1** victory, triumph **2** *proper name* Zafar

ظفرطراز zafartaráz victorious, triumphal

ظل zil *m.* zill *Arabic* [*plural:* اظلال azlál *plural:* ظلال zilál] **1** shade **2** patronage, protection

ظلم zulm *m. Arabic* **1** repression, oppression; violence, force, persecution پر چا ظلمونه کول to repress, oppress someone **2** cruelty **3** injustice

ظلماً zúlmán *Arabic* **1** cruelly; despotically **2** unjustly

ظلمات zulumát *m. Arabic* **1** *plural of* ظلمت **2** northern countries

ظلمت zulmát *m. Arabic* [*plural:* ظلمات zulumát] **1** darkness, gloom **2** chaos

ظلم رسیده zulmrasidá oppressed; repressed, persecuted

ظلوم zalúm *Arabic* cruel, tyrannical, despotic

ظن zan zann *m. Arabic* [*plural:* ظنون zunún] **1** opinion; thought **2** proposal, proposition; suspicion

ظني zanní *Arabic* proposed; suspected

ظنین zanín *Arabic* distrustful; suspicious

ظواهر zavāhír *m. Arabic plural of* ظاهره [2] د طبیعیت ظواهر phenomenon of nature, natural phenomenon

ظوی zoj *m.* the name of the letter ظ

ظهر [1] zuhr *m. Arabic* noon

ظهر [2] zahr *m. Arabic* [*plural:* ظهور zuhúr *plural:* اظهر uzhúr] **1** spine, back **2** reverse side, back (of a check, bill of exchange) **3** rear **4** assistance, help

ظهرنویس zahrnavís *m. economics* endorser; person making an endorsement

ظهرنویسي zahrnavisí *f. economics* endorsement (the endorsement on the back of a check)

ظهري [1] zuhrí *Arabic adjective* midday

ظهري [2] zahrí **1** back **2** spinal **3** reverse **4** rear

ظهور [1] zuhúr *m. Arabic* revelation; manifestation; origin; appearance ظهور کول to be discovered, be revealed; be manifested, arise

ظهور [2] zuhúr *m. Arabic plural of* ظهر [2]

ظهورالدین zuhuruddín *m. proper name* Zuhuruddin

ظهیر zahír *m. Arabic* **1** assistant, helper **2** patron, protector **3** *proper name* Zahir, Zaheer

ظهیرالدین zahiruddín *m. Arabic proper name* Zahiruddin

ظهیره zahirá *f. Arabic* noon

ع

ع [1] 'ajn **1** the twenty-eighth letter of the Pashto alphabet **2** the number 70 in the abjad system

ع [2] **1** *abbreviation* عیسوي Christian (in chronology) ۱۹۳۰ ع 1930 A.D. **2** *abbreviation* علیه الرحمه

ع، ا **1** *abbreviation* عالیجاه اخلاص مند the title of **2** حاکم

عابد 'abíd *m. Arabic* [*plural:* عابدین 'ābidín *plural:* عباد 'ubbád *plural:* عبده 'abadá] devout man, religious man, believer

عابر 'ābír *m. Arabic* [*plural:* عابرین 'ābirín] traveler, wayfarer

عاج 'ādzh *m. Arabic* ivory; elephant's tusk د عاج ساحل the Ivory Coast

عاجز 'ādzhíz *Arabic* **1** weak, pitiful, unhappy **2** incapable (of doing something) دیو شي څخه عاجز کېدل to be unable, not be capable of doing something; not be able to cope or deal with something **3** docile, obedient

عاجزانه 'ādzhizāná pitiable, wretched, miserable, insignificant

عاجز مزاجه 'ādzhíz-mizádzha quiet, tranquil (of a person)

عاجزه 'ādzhíza **1** *feminine singular of* عاجز **2** *f.* [*plural:* عاجزاني 'ādzhizāni] poor fellow, poor devil

عاجزي 'ādzhizí *f.* **1** helplessness **2** humility, meekness; obedience زه په ډېري عاجزي دغومره وایم چه ... I dare to say only that ... **3** *idiom* عاجزي کول to beseech; to entreat

عاجل 'ādzhíl *Arabic* **1** hastening, hurrying **2** urgent, hasty **3** quick acting

عادات 'ādát *m. Arabic plural of* عادت

عادت 'ādát *Arabic* **1** *m.* habit, wont; custom د ډېر عمر عادت old custom, old habit د خپل عادت مناسب، سم by habit, usually پر عادت according to one's wont انسان د عادتو بنده دئ د خپله عادته سره *proverb literal* Man is a slave to habit. *figurative* Habit is second nature. دیو شي سره عادت اخیستل، دیو شي سره عادت مېندل، دیو شي له سره عادت نیول to get used to, grow accustomed to something عادت کول to conceive a liking for wine شراب خوړلو سره عادت نیول تاسي په دي ځان عادت کړئ دئ You accustomed yourself to this. This became a habit with you. **2** *predicative* ☞ عادتي عادت کېدل *compound verb* to conceive a liking for, get used to something, get accustomed to something

عادت لرل to have the habit, custom عادت ماتول to violate the custom

عادتاً 'adátán *Arabic* **1** usually, ordinarily **2** by habit **3** *military* At a walk! (as a cavalry command)

عادتي 'ādatí **1** customary **2** habitual

عادل 'ādíl *Arabic* **1** just **2** *m.* [*plural:* عدول 'udul] a just man

عادلانه 'ādilāná just په عادلانه ډول حل كول to act justly, act according to justice **2** justly

عادي 'ādí *Arabic* **1** usual, ordinary, normal په عادي طور usually, ordinarily **2** simple عادي خلگ simple people **3** accustomed to, used to, grown used to something د... سره عادي كول to accustom to something, involve in something ديو شي سره عادي كېدل to get into the habit of, grow accustomed to something **4** walking (of a pace) عادي قدم مارش! *military* Forward march! (as a command)

عار 'ār *m. Arabic* **1** dishonor, disgrace عار گڼل to consider to be a disgrace; disdain to **2** shame

عارض 'āríz *Arabic* **1.1** appearing, arising **1.2** accidental, fortuitous **2** *m.* [*plural:* عارضان 'ārizā́n *Arabic plural:* عارضين 'arizin] plaintiff, petitioner; applicant

عارضه 'ārizá *f. Arabic* [*plural:* عارضي 'ārizé *Arabic m. plural:* عوارض 'avāríz] **1** illness **2** event, occasion, accident **3** hindrance, obstacle *idiom* د مرض ابتدائي عوارض the first signs or symptoms of an illness

عارضه دار 'ārizadā́r broken (of terrain)

عارضي 'ārizí accidental, fortuitous; attendant (as in "attendant circumstances"); concomitant په عارضي ډول by chance, fortuitously; incidentally

عارضين 'ārizín *m. Arabic plural of* عارض 2

عارف 'āríf *Arabic* **1** expert, learned; wise; knowledgeable **2** *m.* **.1** mystic **2.2** *proper name* Arif

عارفانه 'ārifāná **1** competent **2** pious

عاري 'ārí *Arabic* **1** naked, bare, nude **2** deprived of something, free from something, not containing something

عارياتي 'āriyatí ☞ عاریتي

عاریت 'āriját *m. Arabic* **1** temporary use of a thing, taking a thing for temporary use, for rent or hire يو شي عاریت اخيستل *Arabic* شى په عاریت اخيستل to take a thing for temporary use; for rent عاریت وركول، په عاریت وركول to give something for temporary use, rent it out **2** something taken for temporary use, rented, or hired

عاریتاً 'arijátán *Arabic* for a time, for temporary use, for rent

عاریتي 'ārijatí **1** taken for temporary use, rented عاریتي وركول to issue for temporary use, rent out **2** lying, false, fictious عاریتي وېښتان wig

عازم 'āzím *Arabic* **1** setting out, departing د پېښور عازم شو He left for Peshawar. **2** intending (to do something)

عاشق 'āshíq *Arabic* **1** beloved, loving passionately عاشق كېدل to fall, be in love **2** *m.* **.1** in love **2.2** lover, amateur, admirer

عاشقانه 'āshiqāná **1.1** *adjective* love-, impassioned **1.2** passionately loving, in love **1.3** lyric **2** lovingly, passionately

عاشقه 'āshiqá *f.* beloved

عاشقي 'āshiqí *f.* being in love; love عاشقي كول **a** to fall in love **b** to court, make advances to a girl

عاشورا 'āshurā́ *f.* عاشوره āshurá *f. Arabic* the 10th day of the month of Muharram (the anniversary of the death of the Imam Husein) د عاشوري روځ the 10th day of the month of Muharram

عاصي 'āsí *Arabic* **1.1** disobedient, intractable, rebellious **1.2** sinful, culpable **2** *m.* **.1** disobedient person **2.2** rebel; insurrectionist **2.3** sinner, culprit

عاطف 'atíf *Arabic* **1** favorable, gracious, benevolent, kind **2** propitious

عاطفوي 'ātifaví *Arabic* propitious

عاطفه 'ātifá *f. Arabic* [*plural:* عاطفي 'ātifé *Arabic m. plural:* عواطف 'avātíf] **1** sympathy, favor عاطفه او زره سوی responsiveness **2** good graces, benevolence, kindness

عاطل 'atíl *Arabic* **1** inactive, idle, loafing **2** worthless, useless, vain

عافیت 'āfiját *m. Arabic* health, well-being عافیت باشد! Good health to you!

عاق 'āk 'ákk *Arabic* **1** disobedient, intractable, insubordinate (of children toward parents) **2** accused, damned عاق كول to curse (children); disinherit

عاقبت 'akibát *Arabic* **1** *m.* [*plural:* عاقبتونه 'ákibatúna *m. plural:* عاقبتونه 'ákibatúna *Arabic plural:* عواقب 'avakíb] **.1** consequence **1.2** ending; end, denouement, outcome, result **1.3** fate, lot **2** at last, finally *idiom* عاقبت په خير! I wish you success!

عاقبت اندېش 'ákibatandésh farsighted, foresighted, cautious; circumspect

عاقبت اندېشي 'ákibatandeshí *f.* farsightedness, foresightedness; circumspection

عاقد 'akíd *Arabic* **1.1** negotiating **1.2** capable **2** *m. trade* contractor; person concluding a trade deal

عاقل 'ākíl *Arabic* **1** intelligent, sensible, sagacious, wise **2** *m.* **.1** wise man **2.2** intelligent person **2.3** *proper name* Akil

عاقلانه 'ākilāná **1.1** wise, sensible عاقلانه كار a sensible step, prudent step ديو شي عاقلانه استعمال intelligent use of something په عاقلانه ډول sensibly **1.2** able **2.1** wisely, sensibly **2.2** capably

عالم 'ālám *Arabic* **1** *m.* **.1** world, universe, cosmos **1.2** people څو زره عالم پکښې وو There were several thousand people there. **1.3** incalculable multitude, immeasurable quantity, number **2** *attributive* huge, large هلته ډېر عالم سړي وه There were a great number of people there.

عالم 'ālím *Arabic* **1.1** learned **1.2** expert, well-informed, knowing **2** *m.* [*plural:* عالمان 'ālimā́n *Arabic plural:* علما 'ulemá] **.1** learned man **2.2** theologian **2.3** *proper name* Alim

عالمگیر 'ālamgír **1** world, worldwide عالمگیر جنگ world war **2** conquerer of the world, subjugator of the world

عالمگیریت 'ālamgiriját *m.* world domination

عالم نما 'ālimnumā́ *m.* well-read person (in the sense of one who has a precise but mechanical grasp of a discrete body of literature)

عالمي 'ālamí *Arabic adjective* world, worldwide

عالي 'ālí *Arabic* **1** high, higher عالي تعليمات higher education د شوروي مكتب institution of higher learning, institute **2** supreme سوسيالستي جماهيرو عالي شورا the Supreme Council of the USSR **3** ceremonial (of a meeting)

عاليجاه 'ālidzháh *element of the title of* حاكم *and* اعلى حاكم high-ranking

عاليجناب 'ālidzhanáb *m. Arabic* honorable person, noble person, wellborn person

عاليجنابي 'ālidzhanābí *f.* nobility

عالي رتبه 'ālirutbá highly placed عالي رتبه مامورين high ranks, official personages (other than a minister and his deputy) عالي رتبه منصبداران senior officer complement

عاليشان 'ālishán **1.1** reknowned, well-known **1.2** highly-placed **1.3** excellent **2** *element of the title of generals*: His Excellency

عاليقدر 'āliķádr *official element of the title of premier and of generals*: His High Excellency

عاليه 'ālijá *feminine plural of* عالي

عام 'ām āmm *Arabic* **1.1** usual, ordinary دا خبره دبره عامه ده This is the usual thing. **1.2** simple عام خلك simple folk, the common people **1.3** nationwide, common; general, universal عام بازار the Common Market په عامه دنيا كي in the world, in the whole world عام اعتصاب general strike **1.4** general, in general use, public **2** *m.* simple folk, the common people *idiom* په عام ډول سره in general عام له دي نه چه، عام تر دي چه including, inclusively

عام المنفعه 'ām-ul-manfa'á *Arabic adjective* in general use

عام فهم 'āmfáhm *Arabic* عام فهمه āmfáhma understood, simple in concept, popular

عامل 'āmíl *m. Arabic* **1** [*plural:* عاملان 'āmilán *Arabic plural:* عمال 'ummál] agent, designated representative **2** *Arabic* [*plural:* عوامل 'avāmíl] reason, factor **3** [*plural:* عاملان 'āmilán *Arabic plural:* عمله 'ummál *plural:* عمال 'amalá] worker, executer **4** [*plural:* عاملونه 'āmilúna *Arabic plural:* عوامل 'avāmíl] *grammar* preposition or postposition requiring an inflexion **5** *Arabic* [*plural:* عوامل 'avāmíl] *medicine* pathogenic organism

عاملانه 'āmilāná **1** efficient, businesslike **2** energetic په عاملانه ډول **a** efficiently, in a bussinesslike manner **b** energetically

عام مقبوليت 'āmmaķbuliját *m.* popularity

عاموالى 'āmválaj *m.* عاموالى، عام والى **1** the state of being usual **2** prevalence, diffusion **3** spreading, dissemination, wide introduction

عام وخاص 'āmm-u-kháṣ *m.* aristocracy and the peasantry, high and the low (levels of society)

عامول 'āmavól *denominative, transitive* [*past:* عام يي كړ] to disseminate, introduce

عامه 'āmmá *feminine plural of* عام 1

عامه مصرف 'āmmamaṣráf *adjective* consumer-, having wide consumption, usage

عامي 'āmí āmmí *Arabic* **1** uneducated, ignorant عامي سړى ignoramus **2** *m.* ignoramus

عاميانه 'āmijāná **1** vulgar **2** demotic, colloquial عاميانه ژبه colloquial speech

عامبدل 'āmedól *denominative, intransitive* [*past:* عام شو] to be disseminated, be introduced

عانه 'āná *f. Arabic anatomy* pubis

عائد 'āíd عايد 'ājíd *Arabic* **1** relating to, having a relationship to someone, something **2** receiving, incoming (of income)

عائدات 'āidát *m. plural* عايدات ājidát *m. Arabic singular:* عائده income, receipts, revenue return ملي كالني عائدات annual income د عايداتو ماليه income tax عائدات national income

عائداتي 'āidātí عايداتي 'ājidātí *adjective* income, revenue

عايشه 'ajshá *Arabic proper name* Ajsha

عائق 'āíķ عايق 'ājíķ *Arabic* **1.1** hindering, impending **1.2** *technology* insulating **2** *m.* **.1** hindrance, obstacle **2.2** *technology* insulation, nonconductor د برق عائق nonconductor

عائقه 'āiķá *f.* عايقه ājiķá *f. Arabic* [*plural:* عائقي 'āiķé *m. Arabic plural:* عوائق 'avāíķ] hindrance, obstacle

عائلوي 'āilaví *Arabic adjective* family, familial

عائله 'āilá *f. Arabic* family

عبا 'abá *f. Arabic* aba (a woolen water-repellant cape)

عباد 'ibád[1] *masculine plural of* عبد 2

عباد 'ubbád[2] *m. Arabic plural of* عابد

عبادت 'ibābát *m. Arabic* **1** worship (given to God or a god), cult (of a god) **2** prayer د عبادت سندري ritual hymns, chanting د خداى عبادت كول to worship God, pray

عبادتځاى 'ibādatzáj *m.* عبادتخانه ibādatkhāná *f.* عبادتگاه ibādatgáh *m.* temple, place of worship

عبادتي 'ibādatí pious, religious

عبارت 'ibārát *m. Arabic* **1** meaning عبارت له... څخه consisting of كورنى عبارت له پلار، مور، اولاد او نورو خپلوانو څخه ده ...، including ... The family consists of the father, the mother, the children, and the other relatives. **2** phrase, expression; turn of speech; *grammar* sentence په بل عبارت سره، په بل عبارت in other words, phrased otherwise په لنډ عبارت in short **3** style

عباس 'abbás *m. Arabic proper name* Abbas

عباسي 'abbāsí *history* **1** *adjective* Abbasid **2** *m.* an Abbasid

عبث 'abás *Arabic* **1** vain, useless, idle; empty, worthless عبث ويناوي empty words عبث خبري كول يا كاواكي to talk nonsense او الفاظ عبثيدل2 to no purpose, in vain, uselessly, vainly عبث كېدل عبثول كول عبث تلل to turn out to be in vain, be useless, to no purpose زيار يي عبث ولاړ His efforts turned out to be in vain.

عبثول 'abasavól *denominative, transitive* [*past:* عبث يي كړ] to waste, squander (time, etc.)

عبثېدل 'abasedól *denominative, transitive* [*past:* عبث شو] **1** to be in vain, be useless, to no avail **2** to be lost, spent idly (time, etc.)

عبد 'abd *m. Arabic* **1** [*plural:* عبید 'abíd *plural:* عبدان 'ubdā́n *plural:* 'ibdā́n] slave, thrall **2** [*plural:* عباد 'ibā́d] slave of God, a man **3** *element in person names* عبدالباقي Abdul'baki

عبدالاحد 'abdulahád *m. Arabic proper name* Abdulahad

عبدالباقي 'abdulbā́ķi *m. Arabic proper name* Abdulbaqi

عبدالحق 'abdulhák̇k̇ *m. Arabic* Abdulhaq

عبدالحمید 'abdulhamíd *m. Arabic* Abdul Hamid

عبدالحى 'abdulhájj *m. Arabic* Abdulhaj

عبدالرحمان، عبدالرحمن 'abdurrahmā́n *m. Arabic proper name* Abdurrahman

عبدالرحیم 'abdurrahím *m. Arabic proper name* Abdurrahim

عبدالرحیم زي **1** 'abdurrahimzí *m. plural* the Abdurrahimzai **2** abdurrahimzáj *m.* Abdurrahimzai (tribesman)

عبدالرسول 'abdurrasúl *m. Arabic proper name* Abdurrasul

عبدالرشید 'abdurrashíd *m. Arabic proper name* Abdurrashid

عبدالروف 'abdurraúf *m. Arabic proper name* Abdurrauf

عبدالستار 'abdussattā́r *m. Arabic proper name* Abdusattar

عبدالشكور 'abuushshakúr *m. Arabic proper name* Abdushakur

عبدالطیف 'abdullatíf *m. Arabic proper name* Abdullatif

عبدالظاهر 'abduzzā́hir *Arabic proper name* Abduzzahir

عبدالعزیز 'abdul'azíz *m. Arabic proper name* Abdulaziz

عبدالغفار 'abdulghaffā́r *m. Arabic proper name* Abdulghaffar

عبدالغفور 'abdulghafúr *m. Arabic proper name* Abdulghafur

عبدالغني 'abdulghaní *m. Arabic proper name* Abdulghani

عبدالقادر 'abdulk̇ādír *m. Arabic proper name* Abdulqadir

عبدالله 'abdullá abdulláh *m. Arabic proper name* Abdulla, Abdullah

عبدالمجید 'abdulmadzhíd *m. Arabic proper name* Abdulmajid

عبدالنبي 'abdunnabí *m. Arabic proper name* Abdulnabi

عبدالواحد 'abdulvāhíd *m. Arabic proper name* Abdulwahid

عبدالوهاب 'abdulvahhā́b *m. Arabic proper name* Abdulwahab

عبدل 'abdál *m. proper name* Abdal

عبده [1] 'abdá *f. Arabic* slave, bondswoman

عبده [2] 'abadá *m. Arabic plural of* عابد

عبراني 'ibraní ebraní *Arabic* **1** Jewish **2** *m.* Jew

عبرت 'ibrát *m. Arabic* example, lesson for others, edification د عبرت درس اخیستل، دیو شي ٻخه عبرت اخیستل to draw conclusion for oneself, take good note of عبرت وركول to show an example د چه نورو عبرت سي as an edification for others, in order to serve as an example to others

عبرتناک 'ibratnā́k instructive

عبري 'ibrí ☞ عبراني

عبقریت 'abk̇arijā́t *m. Arabic* genius

عبور 'ubúr *m. Arabic* passage, passing; crossing, ford ناقابل عبور impassable *compound verb* عبور كول to pass through or over, to get across

عبور و مرور 'ubur-u-murúr *m.* movement, traffic, run (of transport)

عبوس 'abús *Arabic* **1** stern; strict **2** morose, gloomy

عبوسي 'abusí *f.* **1** sternness; strictness **2** moroseness, gloominess, dismal look, appearance

عبید [1] 'abíd *m. Arabic plural of* عبد 1

عبید [2] 'ubajd *m. Arabic* **1** slave, bondsman; servant **2** believer

عبیدالله 'ubajdullá 'ubajdulláh *m. Arabic proper name* Ubajdulla

عبیدانه 'abidā́na obediently, docilely; humbly; servilely

عبیر 'abír *m. Arabic* **1** fragrance, ambergris **2** *regional* saffron

عتاب 'itā́b *m.* etā́b *Arabic* reproach; censure عتاب كول to reproach; censure

عتیق 'atík̇ *Arabic* ancient, antique; very old

عتیقه 'atik̇á *f. Arabic* antiquities, productions of ancient times

عتیقه شناس atik̇ashinā́s *m.* **1** archeologist **2** antiquarian

د عتیقه شناسي هیئت atik̇ashinā́sí *f.* archeology archeological expedition

عثمان 'osmā́n *m.* 'usmā́n *Arabic proper name plural* Osman, Usman

عثماني 'osmā́ní *Arabic* **1** *adjective* Osmanli, Ottoman امپراطوري، عثماني دولت *history* the Ottoman Empire **2** *m.* Ottoman, Osmanli Turk

ع، ج *abbreviation* عالیقدر جلالتمآب His Excellency (title of ministers and ambassadors)

عجالت 'edzhālát *m. Arabic* haste

عجالتاً 'edzhālátán *Arabic* **1** urgently, hurriedly **2** immediately, at once

عجان 'edzhā́n *m. Arabic anatomy* perineum

عجائب 'adzhāíb *m. Arabic* **1** *plural of* عجیبه [2] **2** miracles, wonders; extraordinary things عجائب المخلوقات **a** wonders, curiosities **b** surprising creations; monsters

عجائبات 'adzhāibā́t *masculine second plural of* عجائب

عجائب گر 'adzhāibgár *m. regional* museum

عجب 'adzháb *Arabic* **1.1** surprising, amazing, astounding عجبه دا ده چه ...It is surprising that عجب لا دا شى دئ چه It is most astonishing of all that ... **1.2** strange **2** *m.* surprise, astonishment عجب! It is astounding! It is surprising!

عجبه 'adzhába **1** *feminine singular of* عجب **2** *f. proper name* Ajaba

عجز 'adzhz *m. Arabic* **1** obedience, docility; submission **2** weakness, powerlessness, lack of strength خپل عجز منل to recognize one's lack of strength or one's weakness

عجله 'adzhalá *f. Arabic* haste, impetuosity

عجم 'adzhám *m. Arabic singular & plural* non-Arabs; Iranians, Persians; Tajiks

عجمي 'adzhamí *m. Arabic singular & plural* **1.1** non-Arabs; Iranians, Persians; Tajiks **1.2** inexperienced; ill-informed **2** *m. military* recruit, rookie, untrained soldier

عجول 'adzhúl *Arabic* quick, smart, bright

عجولانه 'adzhulā́na quick, speedy

عجیب 'adzhíb *Arabic* surprising, strange, unusual عجیبه دا ده strangely عجیب لا دا ده چه ... ، عجیب لا دا خبره ده چه ... It's even surprising that ...

عجیب الشکل 'adzhibushshákl *Arabic* unusual, of strange appearance

عجیبه¹ 'adzhíba *feminine singular of* عجیب

عجیبه² 'adzhibá *Arabic* 1 *feminine singular of* عجیب 2 *f.* [*plural:* عجائب 'adzhāíb] wonder

عداد 'idád *m. Arabic* 1 counting, calculation 2 category, sort

عدالت 'adālát *m. Arabic* 1 justice 2 equity عدالت چلول to administer justice 3 court, tribunal قومي عدالت tribal court فوځي military tribunal مذهبي عدالت ecclesiastical court د عدالت خرڅ *regional* court costs

عدالت پسند 'adālatpasánd just, equitable

عداوت 'adāvát *m. Arabic* hostility; enmity د چا سره عداوت کول، د چا سره عداوت لرل to be or become hostile to someone

عدد 'adád *m. Arabic* [*plural:* عددونه 'adadúna *Arabic plural:* اعداد a'dád] 1 number, amount, numerical strength 2 item 3 *grammar* number

عددي 'adadí *Arabic* numerical

عدس 'adás *m. Arabic* lentil

عدسي 'adasí 1 *f.* lense, optical glass; objective 2.1 lenticular, lense-like 2.2 biconvex

عدل¹ 'adl *m. Arabic* 1 justice, equity 2 equitableness

عدل² 'idl *m. Arabic* half a load; pile; piece (of goods) د مالوچ عدل a bale of cotton

عدلي 'adlí *Arabic* forensic عدلي طب forensic medicine

عدلیه 'adlijá *f. Arabic* justice, equity عدلیه محکمه court, tribunal د بین المللي عدلیه محکمه International Court عدلیي وزارت Ministry of Justice

عدم 'adám *Arabic* 1 *m.* .1 absence په عدم د ... in the absence of 1.2 nonexistence 2 *combining form* non-, anti- عدم انتظام disorder; indiscipline

عدم اخلاق 'adamakhlā́ḳ *m. Arabic* immorality

عدم اطاعت 'adamitá'at *m. Arabic* insubordination, disobedience

عدم اطمینان 'adamitminán *m. Arabic* uncertainty

عدم اعتبار 'adami'tibár *m. Arabic* distrust

عدم اکتشاف 'adamiktisháf *m. Arabic* lack of development, backwardness

عدم التفات 'adamiltifát *m. Arabic* lack of consideration, disdain

عدم انتظام 'adamintizám *m. Arabic* disorder; indiscipline

عدم اهمیت 'adamahammiját *m. Arabic* disdain, disregard, lack of consideration

عدم بلدیت 'adambaladiját *m. Arabic* unfamiliarity, nonaquaintance

عدم تثبیت 'adamtasbít *m. Arabic* instability

عدم تجربه 'adamtadzhribá *f. Arabic* inexperience

عدم تشدد 'adamtashaddúd *m. Arabic* nonresistance to evil

عدم تناسب 'adamtanāsúb *m. Arabic* disproportion

عدم توازن 'adamtavāzún *m. Arabic* lack of equilibrium; unstable equilibrium

عدم توافق 'adamtavāfúḳ *m. Arabic* disagreement, absence of accord; disharmony, dissent

عدم توجه 'adamtavadzhdzhóh *f. Arabic* lack of consideration, disdain

عدم رضایت 'adamrizāját *m. Arabic* displeasure; discontent; dissatisfaction

عدم شمولیت 'adamshumuliját *m. Arabic* nonparticipation; keeping aloof from something

عدم صلاحیت 'adamsalahiját *m. Arabic* 1 incompetence 2 unskillfulness

عدم فهم 'adamfáhm *m. Arabic* incomprehension

عدم مداخلت 'adammudākhalát *m. Arabic* noninterference په داخلي چارو کښي عدم مداخلت noninterference in internal affairs

عدم مساوات 'adammusāvát *m. Arabic* inequality

عدم مصادقت 'adammusādaḳát *m. Arabic* insincerity

عدم موافقت 'adammuvāfaḳát *m. Arabic* discord, dissent

عدم موجودیت 'adammavdzhudiját *m. Arabic* absence

عدم موفقیت 'adammuvaffaḳiját *m. Arabic* failure, failing, unsuccess

عدن¹ 'adán *m. Arabic* Aden (city)

عدن² 'adn *m. Arabic* Paradise, Eden

عدو 'adúv *m. Arabic* [*plural:* اعدا a'dā́] (mortal) enemy, foe, adversary

عدول¹ 'udúl *m. Arabic* 1 deviation; divergence; moving away (from) عدول کول to deviate; diverge; move away 2 insubordination, disobedience

عدول² 'udúl *m. Arabic plural of* عادل 2

عده 'iddiá *f. Arabic* 1 number 2 multitude

عدیل 'adíl *Arabic* even, equal, the same (as)

عذاب 'azáb *m. Arabic* torment, torture د چا څخه په عذاب کېدل to suffer as a result of someone's action څوک په عذاب کول to torture someone

عذابول 'azābavúl *denominative, transitive* [*past:* عذاب یي کړ] to torture, torment

عذابېدل 'azābedál *denominative, intransitive* [*past:* عذاب شو] to be tormented, be tortured سره عذابېدل to languish

عذر 'úzr úzər *m. Arabic* apology, excuse; occasion, cause, reason (for a refusal, etc.) معقول عذر a valid reason عذر راوړل to introduce arguments, give motives for عذر غوښتل to ask for absolution, ask for forgiveness عذر کول *Eastern* to refuse, decline په عذر ویل د چا عذر قبلول to agree with someone's arguments عذر موزر کول to justify oneself by some means; excuse oneself apologize profusely; bring forth all kinds of excuses or reasons

عذرجن 'uzrdzhán ☞ معذور

عذرخواهي 'uzrkhvāhí *f.* request for forgiveness ډېره عذرخواهي کول to apologize profusely

عذرمن 'uzrmán ☞ معذور

عراب 'aráb *m. Arabic plural of* عرب

عرابه 'arābá *f.* vehicle, bullock cart; *military* gun-carriage, caisson

عرابه کښ 'arābákakh draft (of animals)

عراده 'arādá *f. Arabic* **1** wheel **2** carriage **3** *enumerative classifier used in counting cannons, vehicles, carriages, automobiles, trucks*

عراده کېږ 'arādakáǩh ☞ عرابه کېږ

عراق 'irā́ǩ *m.* Iraq

عراقي 'irāǩí **1** *adjective* Iraqi **2** *m.* Iraqi (person)

عرائض 'araíz *m. Arabic plural of* عريضه

عرب 'aráb *m. Arabic* [*plural:* عراب 'arā́b *Arabic plural:* عربان 'urbā́n] Arab, Arabs عرب لیګ، د عربو سعودي Saudi Arabia د عربو جامعه عرب، اتحاد dzhāmi'á-ji The League of Arab Nations بحیره the Arabian Sea

عربستان 'arabistā́n *m.* Arabia سعودي عربستان Saudi Arabia د عربستان بېدیا the Arabian desert

عربه 'arába *f.* Arab woman عربه ښځه Arab woman

عربي 'arabí *Arabic* **1** *adjective* Arabian; Arab, Arabic د عربي مملکتو اتحادیه، د عربي مملکتو تولنه the Arab League د عربي متحد جمهوریت United Arab Republic, the UAR د شام عربي جمهوریت، د سوریا عربي جمهوریت the Syrian Arab Republic **2** *f.* Arabic, the Arabic language

عربیه 'arabijá **1** *f.* Arabia سعودي عربیه Saudi Arabia **2** *feminine & plural of* عربي

عرش 'arsh *m. Arabic* عرش کرسي arshkursí *f. regional* **1** heavens, empyrean **2** throne; *religion* Divine Throne; throne of God

عرش معلا 'arshimu'allá *f.* عرش معلی heavens, empyrean

عرصه 'arsá *f. Arabic* **1** field, arena **2** field of battle, field of combat

عرض 'arz *m. Arabic* report; petition, request عرض کول to report, say respectfully ... دومره باید عرض وکړم چه I can only say that ... و چا ته عرض کېدل to say respectfully د چا په حضور کي عرض کول be reported to someone ... په عرض زه یو عرض لرم I should say ... رسول to report to someone; respectfully inform

عرض 'arz *m. Arabic* **1** width, breadth **2** *geography* latitude شمالي عرض north latitude جنوبي عرض south latitude

عرض 'aráz *m. Arabic* [*plural:* اعراض 'arā́z] **1** symptom **2** chance **3** external characteristic; phenomena which are external to the substance of a subject

عرضاً 'árzán *Arabic* **1** in breadth, in depth **2** diagonally, in cross section

عرض البلد 'arz-al-balád arz-ul-balád *m. Arabic* latitude

عرض بېگي 'arzbegí *m.* official of the chancellery in charge of receiving complaints (in the Ministry of the Court of Afghanistan)

عرضچي 'archí *m.* عرض دار arzdā́r *m.* عرض والا arzvālā́ *m.* petitioner

عرض والی 'arzvā́laj *m.* width, breadth

عرضه 'arzá *f.* **1** supply (of goods, production) عرضه او تقاضا supply and demand عرضه کول *compound verb* to supply (goods); to market عرضه کېدل *compound verb* **a** to be supplied (goods) **b** to be shown, demonstrated (of goods at an exhibition) **2** submission (of a report)

عرضي 'arzí *f.* petition; letter from an subordinate

عرف 'urf *m. Arabic* **1** common law; civil law; secular law (as contrasted to shariat or religious law) **2** custom, habit, wont محلي او خصوصي عرف او عادات local customs **3** *regional* nickname

عرفان 'irfā́n *m. Arabic* knowledge, education

عرفاني 'irfāní cultural, educational

عرفي 'urfí **1** based on civil law عرفي نکاح نامه contract عرفي قباله official record of a divorce **2** usual, based on custom

عرق 'aráǩ *m. Arabic* **1** sweat **2** arrack, vodka **3** distillation product **4** essence *idiom* د گلاب عرق rose water

عرق 'irǩ *m. Arabic* [*plural:* عروق 'urúǩ] **1** family, clan; descent عرق او نژاد family, clan; descent **2** vessel (blood circulatory); vein, artery

عرق النسا irǩ-un-nisā́ *f. anatomy* sciatic nerve

عروس 'arús *f. Arabic* bride

عروض 'arúz *m. Arabic* prosody (a system of versification), poetry

عروق 'urúǩ *m. Arabic plural of* عرق

عریض 'aríz *Arabic* wide, broad

عریضه 'arizá *f. Arabic* [*plural:* عریضي 'arizé *Arabic m. plural:* عرائض 'arā́iz] request, petition د عرائضو مدیر director of the Department of Petitions (for the prime minister)

عریضه چي 'arizachí *m.* petitioner

عریضي 'arizí *f.* width, breadth

عزب 'azáb *Arabic* celibate, unmarried

عزت izzát *m.* honor, glory د عزت نښان the Badge of Honor د ... نومان honored and esteemed people د آب او عزت خلق self-respect چا عزت ورکول to honor someone چا عزت ساتل to show honor; do honor (to)

عزت الله 'izzatullá *m. Arabic proper name* Izatulla

عزت النفس 'izzat-an-náfs *m.* عزه النفس *Arabic* self-respect; sense of honor

عزتمند 'izzatdā́r ☞ عزت دار

عزتمآب 'izzatmā́b civil servants lower than عالیقدر

عزتمند 'izzatmánd عزت ناک izzatnā́k esteemed, honored

عزت همراه 'izzathamrā́ izzathamrā́h *element of the title of generals*

عزرائیل 'azrāíl *m. Arabic religion* Azrail, Angel of Death

عزل 'azl *m. Arabic* dismissal, removal عزل کول *compound verb* to dismiss, remove

عزلت 'uzlát *m. Arabic* solitude, hermit's life عزلت کول to seek solitude, become a hermit, lead the life of a hermit

عزلتي 'uzlatí *m. & f. Arabic* hermit; recluse; hermitess

عزم 'azm *m. Arabic* **1** decisiveness; stubbornness, persistance په عزم پاخه to work persistently, doggedly بې عزم indecisiveness **2** intent; decision کلک عزم firm decision ټینگ عزم کول to make a firm decision

عزیز 'azíz *Arabic* **1** dear, lovable, desired لرل to love; esteem **2** *m.* [*plural:* اعزا a'izzā́] **.1** close friend **2.2** relative **3** [*plural:* عزیزان 'azizā́n] **a** clansmen, relations, kinsmen **b** Brothers! (form of address) **4** *proper name* Aziz

عزیزتوب 'azíztób *m.* عزیزتیا azíztjā́ *f.* ☞ عزیزوالی

عزیزداري 'azizdarí *f.* relationship through marriage

عزیزګلوي 'azizgalví *f.* عزیزوالی 'azizvắlaj *m.* عزیزي 'azizí *f.* **1** kinship relations between an uncle, nieces, or nephews **2** friendship عزیزګلوي کول to love, esteem

عزیمت 'azimát *m. Arabic* **1** exit, departure د عزیمت په لار along the route عزیمت کول to depart **2** resoluteness, resolution

عساکر 'asākír *m. Arabic plural of* عسکر 2

عسر 'usúr *m.* عسرت usrát *m. Arabic* difficulties; straits مالي عسر financial difficulties

عسکر 'askár *m. Arabic* **1** *singular & plural* troops; army **2** [*plural:* عسکران 'askarān *Arabic plural:* عساکر 'asākír] trooper, warrior, soldier

عسکري 'askarí **1.** د عسکري حکومت حال *martial law adjective* army, troop, military عسکري خدمت military service **1.2** martial (e.g., of a song) **1.3** soldierly **2** *m.* trooper, warrior, soldier

عسکریت 'askariját *m.* military service; military profession

عسل 'asál *m. Arabic plural* honey

ع، ش official *abbreviation* عالیشان و شجاعت همراه the title of a فرقه مشر

عشا 'ashắ *f. Arabic religion* **1** evening meal **2** evening

عشاري 'ashārí *Arabic* decimal, tenfold

عشاریه 'asharijá *f.* decimal fraction نه عشاریه پنځه 5.9

عشر 'ushr *m. Arabic* [*plural:* اعشار 'ushắr] **1** tenth part of something **2** tithe (tax)

عشرات 'asharắt *m. Arabic plural* [*singular:* عشره] tenths

عشرت 'ishrát *m. Arabic* entertainment; feast, banquet; merriment, joy عیش او عشرت کول **a** to enjoy life **b** to feast, banquet

عشق 'ishk *m. Arabic* love عشق کول to love; be in love, fall in love د خپل کار سره عشق لرل to love one's work عشق د زور کار نه دئ Love cannot be compelled.

عشق آباد 'ashḳābắd *m.* Ashkabad (city)

عشقبازي 'ishḳbāzí *f.* amorous intrigue; making advances, flirting عشق بازي کول to make advances

عشق پیچه 'ishḳpechá *f. Eastern botany* ivy

عشقي ishḳí love, amorous عشقي آثار love lyric

عشوه 'ishvá *f. Arabic* coquettishness; playfulness

ع، ص official *abbreviation* of عالیقدر صداقت the title of counsellors, deputy ministers, directors of finance, and chiefs of directorates

عصا 'asắ *f. Arabic* staff; cane; baton

عصاره 'usārá *f. Arabic* juice (squeezed out of fruit, etc.), extract

عصاکش 'asākásh *m.* leader, guide

عصافیر 'asāfír *m. Arabic plural of* عصفور

عصب 'asáb *m. Arabic* [*plural:* اعصاب a'sắb] nerve

عصباني 'asbāní *Arabic* **1** nervous; irritable **2** angry with, enraged at

عصبانیت 'asbānniját *m.* عصباني توب ashbānitób *m. Arabic* **1** nervousness; irritability **2** rage, wrath, ire

عصبي 'asabí *Arabic* **1** nervous عصبیه مرضونه nervous affliction, disease عصبي سیستم the nervous system **2** psychic (of phenomena)

عصبیت 'asabiját *m. Arabic* **1** zeal **2** fanaticism **3** intransigence **4** bias, prejudice

عصر 'asr *m. Arabic* [*plural:* عصرونه 'asrúna *Arabic plural:* اعصار a'sắr *plural:* اعصر a'súr *plural:* عصور 'usúr] **1** century, epoch, era **2** dusk, time just before evening **3** prayer at dusk, vesper prayer

عصرانه 'asrāná *f.* evening reception; evening

عصري 'asrí *Arabic* contemporary, modern عصري هوټل a modern hotel عصري کبدل to modernize عصري کول to be modernized

عصریت 'asriját *m. Arabic* **1** modernity **2** novelty

عصري کبده 'asrikedَ *m. plural* modernization

عصریه 'asrijá *f. Arabic* supper, evening meal وروسته یوه عصریه وخورله شوه Supper took place later.

عصفور 'usfúr *m. Arabic* [*plural:* عصافیر 'asāfír] **1** sparrow **2** small bird

عصمت 'ismát *m. Arabic* **1** chastitiy; purity **2** *proper name* Ismat

عصمت الله 'ismatullá *m. Arabic proper name* Ismatulla

عصور 'usúr *m. Arabic plural of* عصر

عصیان 'isijắn *m. Arabic* rebellion; uprising, mutiny

عصیر 'asír *m. Arabic* digestive juices

عضلات 'azalất azulất *m. Arabic* **1** *plural of* عضله 2 **2** musculature

عضلاتي 'azlātí azulātí muscular; physical عضلاتي قوت physical strength عضلاتي کول physical labor

عضلوي 'azalaví azulaví *Arabic* muscular

عضله 'azalá 'azulá *f. Arabic* [*plural:* عضلي 'azalé *plural:* 'azulé *m.* *Arabic plural plural:* عضلات 'azalất *plural:* 'azulāt] muscle د قوي عضلي لرل to be muscular, be brawny بازو عضله biceps

عضو 'uzv *m. Arabic* [*plural:* اعضا a'zắ] **1** *anatomy* member, organ **2** member (of an organization, society); a participant in something

عضوه 'úzva *f. anatomy* member, organ; extremity

عضوي 'uzví[1] *Arabic* organic عضوي کیمیا organic chemistry عضوي مواد organic substances عضوي وران مواد products of decomposition

عضوي 'úzvi[2] *feminine plural of* عضوه

عضویت 'uzviját *m. Arabic* **1** organism ژوندی عضویت living organism انساني عضویت the human organism **2** membership د اکاډیمی د عضویت کاندبد corresponding-member of the Academy په افتخاري عضویت لرل to be a member (of an organization, society) عضویت منل to elect as an honorary member

عطا 'ata *f. Arabic* grant, gift; donation چا ته کول to bestow on someone

عطاالله 'ataullá 'ataulláh *m. Arabic personal name* Ataulla

عطار 'attắr *m. Arabic* dealer in gums and dyestuffs; seller of perfumes or apothecary goods; trader in small grocery items

عطارد 'utaríd *m. Arabic astronomy* Mercury (the planet)

عطاري 'attārí *f.* trade in perfumes, gums, dyestuffs, apothecary, or small grocery items

عطر 'atr itr *m. Arabic plural* **1** perfumes **2** scent, fragrance په عطرو كول to make oneself or something smell sweet or fragrant

عطرآمېز 'atrāméz aromatic, fragrant عطرآمبز بوي scent, fragrance

عطردان 'atrdán *m.* small box or vial for scents

عطركشي 'atrkashí *f.* perfume production

عطري 'atrí 'itrí *Arabic* aromatic; sweet-smelling

عطريات 'atrijắt 'itrijắt *m. Arabic plural* fragrances, aromatic substances; perfumes

عطسه 'atsá *f. Arabic* sneezing

عطف 'atf *m. Arabic* **1** treatment (paying of attention, giving of consideration, etc.) **2** attachment, liking for someone **3** connection; contiguity; association (with) د عطف حرف *grammar* conjunction عطف كېدل *compound verb* to join, unite **4** leaning (towards), sympathy; compassion (for)

عطفول 'atfavól *denominative, transitive* [*past:* عطف يې كړ] to pay (attention), attract (attention)

عطوفت 'utufát *m. Arabic* leaning, bent, disposition

عطيه 'atijá *f. Arabic* gift د طبيعت عطيه natural gift

عظام ¹ 'uzắm uzzắm *Arabic* most high

عظام ² 'izắm *Arabic plural of* عظيم

عظمت 'azamát *m. Arabic* **1** greatness; excellence **2** honor, glory **3** haughtiness, arrogance

عظمى 'uzmā *f. Arabic of* اعظم **1** صدارت عظمى **a** position of prime minister **b** Chancellery, Office of the Prime Minister

عظيم 'azím *Arabic* [*plural:* عظام 'izắm] **1** .1 great, huge **1.2** important, high **1.3** outstanding, famous (e.g., a poet) **2** *m. proper name* Azim *idiom* عظيم دولتونه Great Powers

عظيم الجثه 'azim-al-dzhussá *Arabic* enormous, gigantic

عظيم تره 'azimtára most high

ع، ع *official abbreviation* عاليجاه عزت همراه district chief

ع، ع، ش *official abbreviation* عاليشان و شجاعت همراه نائب سالار title of general

ع، ع، ص *abbreviation* **1** عاليجاه عزت و صداقت همراه title of the province chief **2** اعلى حاكم title of a general

عفت 'ifát *m. Arabic* modesty, chastity, feminine honor

عفريت 'ifrít *m. Arabic* afreet (a powerful evil spirit or gigantic and monstrous demon in Arabic mythology)

عف عف 'af'af **1** *m.* bark (of a dog) **2** *onomatopoeia* bowwow

عفو 'afv *m.* application; petition; pardon, forgiveness عفو غوښتل to ask forgiveness عفو كول to forgive

عفونت 'ufunát *m.* عفونه ufuná *f. Arabic* **1** decay; decomposition **2** infection; contagion د عفوني پر ضد دواوي antiseptic, disinfectant

عفوني 'ufuní **1** rotten, decayed **2** infectious, contagious

عفوه 'úfva *f.* ☞ عفو

عفيف 'afif *Arabic* modest; chaste; maidenly

عقاب ¹ 'uḳáb *m. Arabic* eagle; plains or steppe eagle

عقاب ² 'iḳáb *m.* punishment, retribution

عقائد 'aḳáid *m. plural* عقايد aḳájid *m. Arabic plural* of عقيده

عقب 'aḳáb *Arabic* **1** *m. Arabic* rear; back part of something **2.1** back, backwards **2.2** behind, from behind

عقب نشيني 'aḳabnishiní *f.* retreat; withdrawal عقب نشيني كول to retreat; withdraw

عقبه 'aḳabá *f. Arabic* [*plural:* عقبي 'aḳabé *m. Arabic plural:* عقبات 'aḳabát] danger, dangerous moment, risk

عقبى ¹ 'uḳbā *f. Arabic* **1** the other world, world beyond the grave **2** result

عقبي ² 'aḳabí *Arabic* **1** *Arabic adjective* rear د عقبي مرستي ټولګی rear detachment, reserve **2** behind, rear, back, hind

عقد ¹ 'aḳd *m. Arabic* [*plural:* عقدونه 'aḳdúna *Arabic plural:* عقود 'uḳúd] **1** conclusion (of a treaty) **2** convocation (of a meeting) **3** contraction (of marriage) **4** agreement; treaty; transaction تجارتي عقد تړل، تجارتي عقدونه، تجارتي عقود trade agreements, trade deals **a** to conclude an agreement عقد كول **b** to contract (a marriage) to agree, conclude an agreement

عقد ² 'iḳd *m. Arabic* **1** collar **2** necklace

عقد كوونكى 'aḳd kavúnkaj *m. trade* contractor

عقده 'uḳdá *f. Arabic* **1** knot, tying a knot **2** *anatomy* ganglion, nerve bundle **3** difficulty; hindrance, obstacle, muddled affair **4** speech defect

عقرب 'aḳráb *m. Arabic* **1** scorpion **2** *astronomy* Scorpio (the constellation) **3** Akrab (the 8th month of the solar year; October-November)

عقربک 'aḳrabák *m.* عقربه aḳrabá *f.* hand (of a clock, etc.), indicator

عقر قرحا 'aḳarḳarhắ *f. Arabic botany* **1** Pyrethrum **2** chamomile

عقل 'áḳl áḳël *m. Arabic* [*plural:* عقلونه 'aḳlúna *Arabic plural:* عقول 'uḳúl] mind, intellect; reason عملي عقل practical intelligence له عقل نه بهر inconceivable, چا ته عقل ښودل to teach sense impossible دا خبره نه راځي کبني به عقل ما حُ *Eastern* This isn't sinking into my head. هغه له عقله پياده دئ He is a real numbskull. عقل يي له سره ښکه ځي He's making a fool of himself.

عقل خوځېدلى 'aḳl khvadzedálaj not (mentally) normal, crazy, mad

عقل فروشي 'aḳlfurushí *f.* conceit

عقل مند aḳlmánd ☞ عاقل

عقلي 'aḳlí *Arabic* **1** intelligent; intellectual **2** positive, based on experience or facts **3** psychic, mental

عقليت 'aḳliját *m.* level of intellectual development

عقليه 'aḳalijá *indeclinable* mental, intellectual عقليه مرضونه psychic or mental illness

عقود 'uḳúd *m. Arabic plural of* عقد ¹

عقيدت 'aḳidát *m. Arabic* ☞ عقيده

عقيدتمند 'aḳidatmánd *m.* partisan, supporter of some particular teaching, doctrine, or theory

عقيده 'aḳidá *f.* [*plural:* عقيدي 'aḳidé *m. Arabic plural:* عقائد 'aḳáid] **1** belief عقيده لرل to believe, suppose پر کسان په دي عقيده Many suppose that ... **2** opinion; conviction په زما in my opinion عقيده نيكارول عقيده کول to express an opinion د عقيدي له مخي کار کول to act out of conviction

عقیده مند 'aķidamánd **1** convinced **2** supposing, considering

عقیده مندي 'aķidamandí *f.* conviction

عقیق 'aķíķ *m. Arabic geology* carnelian, sard

عقیقه 'aķiķá *f. Arabic* tuft, fluff (of hair)

عقیم 'aķím *Arabic* **1** fruitless; barren; childless **2** unavailing, futile په عقیم صورت سره ineffectually, futilely **3** unproductive

عقیمول 'aķimavól *denominative, transitive* [*past:* عقیم یې کړ] to render fruitless, render futile د غلیم حمله عقیمول to break the enemy's attack

عکاس 'akkás *m. Arabic* photograph

عکاسي [1] 'akkāsí *f.* **1** photographing د عکاسی کمره camera هوایي عکاسي aerial photography, photogrammetry **2** photographic

عکاسي [2] 'akāsí *f.* acacia

عکس 'aks *m. Arabic* **1** reflection خپل عکس یې په اوبو کښی ولید He saw his reflection in the water. **2** snapshot, photograph عکس نیول to take a photo, photograph **3** contrast, antithesis, opposition د دوی نظریات مطلقاً یو د بل عکس واقع شوی دي Their viewpoints are diametrically opposed. په عکس د هغو، په in spite of this عکس د دي on the other hand, on the contrary عکس سره، په عکس د هغه سره عکس کول *compound verb* to engrave, stamp, reflect

عکس اخیستونکی 'aks akhistúnkaj *m.* photographer

عکس العمل 'aks-ul-'amál *m. Arabic* **1** reaction, reacting **2** reflexes

عکس برداري 'aksbardārí *f.* photographing, photography

علی الاطلاق 'alā-ul-itlāk *Arabic* in general, overall

علاج 'ilådzh *m. Arabic* **1** cure; remedy, medicine; healing د څان علاج کول to receive treatment, undergo treatment **2** way out, means *compound verb* علاجول وکړم دي علاج به اوس ☞ علاج کول Now I am going to settle accounts with you! نو علاج دا دئ چه Now here's a way out (of a situation).

علاج پذیر 'ilådzhpazír curable

علاج نا پذیر 'iladzhnāpazír **1** incurable **2** *literal* incorrigible

علاجول 'ilådzhavól *denominative, transitive* [*past:* علاج یې کړ] **1** to heal, cure **2** to teach someone a lesson; settle accounts with someone

علاقه 'alāķá ilaķá *f. Arabic* [*plural:* علاقي 'alāķé *plural:* 'ilaķé *m. Arabic plural:* علائق 'alāíķ *plural:* علاقات 'alāķát] **1** state of having an interest in; interest, concern; diposition, arrangement د علاقي خاوند interested party **2** په کومه موضوع کښی د علاقي خاوند relation; connection, interest د چا سره علاقه تشکیلول a to establish a relationship with someone د چا سره علاقه لرل a to maintain a relationship with someone **b** to sympathize with someone ته زما سره ډېره علاقه لري You feel for me deeply. **b** to take an interest in someone د چا سره علاقه قطع کول to break off a relationship with someone **3** district, region, territory

علاقه بند 'alāķabánd *m.* gold-lace maker, braid maker

علاقه دار 'alāķadår **1.1** relating to something **1.2** having an interest in something **2** *m. official* alakadar (local headman or senior local official)

علاقه داري 'alāķadārí *f.* **1** interest (state of having an interest in); concern **2** *official* post of alakadar (local headman or senior local official)

علاقه لرونکی 'alāķá larúnkaj interested (having an interest in) علاقه لرونکي دولتونه alāķá larúnki the interested powers علاقه لرونکي کسان alāķá larúnki the interested parties

علاقه مند 'alāķamánd **1.1** interested (having an interest in) **1.2** relating to something; concerned with something **1.3** interested in, keen on **2** *m.* fan, aficionado

علاقه مندي 'alāķamandí *f.* interest; concern علاقه مندي مېندل to evoke interest د یو شي سره علاقه مندي لرل to be interested in something

علام 'allám *Arabic religion* omniscient (one of the epithets of God)

علامت 'alāmát *m. Arabic* [*plural:* علامتونه 'alāmatúna *Arabic plural:* علامات 'alāmát] ☞ علامه [1]

علامه [1] alāmá *f. Arabic* **1** sign; mark, emblem, token **2** symbol, badge **3** signal, sign ترافیکي علامي road signs

علامه [2] 'allāmá *Arabic* erudite, learned

علاوتاً 'elāvátán 'ilāvátán besides, in addition

علاوه 'elāvá 'ilāvá *Arabic f.* **1** addition, augmentation علاوه کول to add, augment **2** besides, furthermore د علاوه د دېنه Eastern علاوه پر دغه above all علاوه پر دي ټولو besides علاوه تر ...Eastern except, besides دوی نه علاوه except them

علائق 'alāíķ *m. Arabic* **1** plural of علاقه **2** interests **3** concern **4** devotion **5** relations, interrelationships د دوستی علائق friendly relations, amicable relations تینگ ثقافتي علائق close cultural ties

علت 'illát *m. Arabic* [*plural:* علتونه 'illatúna *m. Arabic plural:* علل 'ilál] **1** reason, factor په کوم علت له علتو سره for whatever reason there may be **2** illness; indisposition **3** flaw, defect

علتي 'illatí **1** sick, ill; unhealthy **2** defective, having a deficiency, a defect

علف 'aláf *m. Arabic* **1** grass **2** forage

علفچر 'alafchár *m.* علف چر، **1** tax on pasturage **2** pastureland

علفي 'alafí **1** herbaceous **2** hempen; made of hemp fibers, etc.

علک 'ilk *m. Arabic* mastic (a vegetable resin)

علل ilál *m. Arabic plural of* علت

علم [1] 'alám *m. Arabic* [*plural:* علمونه 'ilmúna *plural:* علوم 'ulúm] knowledge; science علم ادب 'ilm-i... literature (as a study) درسي علمونو اکاډېمي academic disciplines, subjects د علومو Academy of علوم اجتماعي social sciences د علومو پوهنځی faculty of Sciences علم physics and mathematics *idiom* د هیڅ چا علم نه راځي No one even knows about this. د علم پگړی یی و ترله He has completed the Medressese (i.e., Moslem theological school).

علم [2] 'alám *m. Arabic* **1** banner, flag; pennant **2** famous man, oustanding man **3** *proper name* Alim

علما 'ulamá *m. Arabic of* عالم [2]

علم الانسان 'ilm-ul-insān *m. Arabic* anthropology

علم التعلیم 'ilm-ut-ta'lím *m. Arabic* pedagogy, educational science

علم الجرائم 'ilm-ul-dzharāím *m. Arabic* criminology

علم الجنين 'ilm-ul-dzhanín *m. Arabic* embryology

علم الروح 'ilm-ur-rúh *m. Arabic* psychology (science)

علم الطبيعه 'ilm-ut-tabi'já *f. Arabic* 1 natural science 2 physics

علم آوري 'ilmāvarí *f.* familiarization, scrutiny, examination

علم بردار، علمبردار 'alambardár *m.* flag bearer

علم دوست 'ilmdóst *m.* patron of science

علم فروش 'ilmfurúsh *m.* pedant

علم فروشي 'ilmfurushí *f.* pedantry

علم وخبر 'ilmukhabár *m.* 1 declaration (customs) 2 *military* certificate of service

علمي 'ilmí *Arabic* 1 scientific علمي فعاليت scientific activity 2 scholarly, academic علمي درجه academic degree

علميت 'ilmiját *m.* learning, erudition د علميت خُنبتن learned man, erudite person

علناً 'alánán *Arabic* openly, publicly

علني 'alaní 1 evident, obvious; open, public 2 frank

علو 'ulúvv *m. Arabic* 1 height, altitude, eminence 2 grandeur

علوفه 'ulufá *f. Arabic* forage; provisions (military)

علوم 'ulúm *m.* علم *plural of* علم [1]

علوي [1] 'ulví *Arabic* 1 high, superlative 2 heavenly علوي اجسام heavenly bodies 3 beyond the clouds

علوي [2] 'alaví *m. Arabic* 1 descendant of Ali 2 Ali-ite, follower of Ali

علويان 'ulviján *m. Arabic plural* heavenly bodies

علويت 'ulviját *m. Arabic* high position

علي 'alí *Arabic* 1 high, most high 2 *m. proper name* Ali حضرت علي the Imam Ali

علی 'alā *combining form* on, according to, in accordance with (as the initial element of Arabic compounds) علی الخصوص especially, particularly, for the most part

عليا 'uljá *feminine singular of* اعلی

علي آباد 'aliābád *m. Arabic* Aliabad (district, Kabul)

عليا حضرت 'ulijāhazrát *f.* Her Highness (title of a queen)

علا الاطلاق 'alā-ul-itláḳ ☞ علی الاطلاق

علی الانفراد 'alānfirád *Arabic* separately, individually

علی الحساب 'alālhisáb *Arabic* according to the account or the count

علی الخصوص 'alālkhusús *Arabic* especially, in particular, for the most part

علی العجله 'alāl'adzhalá *Arabic* hastily, hurriedly

علی المراتب 'alālmarātíb *Arabic official* according to echelon, by command level, in order of subordination

عليت 'illiját *m. Arabic philosophy* causality د عليت ارتباط causal relation

عليحده 'alahidá 'alaidá *Arabic* 1 separate 2 separately

علي شېر 'alishér *m. proper name* Alisher

عليك 'alájka *Arabic* سلام عليك! Greetings to you!

عليك سليك 'alájk salájk *m. Arabic* greeting يو بل سره عليك سليك کول to exchange greetings عليك سليك مو وکړل We exchanged greetings.

عليكم السلام 'alajkumassalám *Arabic* And greetings to you! I give you greeting! (the response to the greeting سلام عليكم)

عليگر، علي گر 'aligár *m.* 1 Aligar (city, India) 2 Aligar (the Moslem university in the city of Aligar)

عليل 'alíl *Arabic* weak, ill

علي مسجد 'ali-masdzhíd *m.* Ali-Masjd (settlement, Khyber District)

عليه 'alijá *Arabic feminine singular of* علی دولت عليه افغانستان davlát-i-'alijá-ji High Afghan Goverment (the official name of Afghanistan)

عليه 'alájhi 'aléjh *Arabic combining form* 1 on him; over him 2 to him عليه الرحمه *Arabic religion* May the mercy of God be unto him!

عم *Arabic religion abbreviation* عليه السلام! 'alajhassalám May he rest in peace!

عماد 'imád *m. Arabic* support; column

عماد الدين 'imāduddín *m. Arabic proper name* Imaduddin

عمارت 'imārát *m. Arabic* building; structure

عماري 'imārí *f. Arabic* palanquin (on the back of an elephant or camel)

عمال 'ummál *m. Arabic plural of* عامل 1, 3 د عمالو وزارت Ministry of Labor د عمالو حزب the Labor Party (in England)

عمان [1] 'omán *m. Arabic* Oman

عمان 'ammán *m.* Amman

عمد 'amd *m. Arabic* design, intent

عمده 'umdá *Arabic* 1 chief, principal 2 *f.* substance, the main thing

عمده فروشي 'umdafurushí *f.* wholesale sales, wholesale trade

عمر [1] 'umr 'úmər *m. Arabic* [plural: اعمار a'mắr] 1 life, human lifetime عمر دئ، تېرېږي in one's life, in one's lifetime په خپل عمر I wish you a long life! ستا عمر دي ډېر وي! Life, time takes its course! عمر لرل، عمر تېرول to live, pass through life 2 time وروسته ترڅو عمر، څو How long ago this was! خونه ډېر عمر وسو چه ...! په عمر پوخ سړی Some little time passed. 3 age عمر وروسته an elderly man د مراني عمر ته رسېدل to come of age, attain majority (of a youth)

عمر [2] 'umár *m. Arabic proper name* Omar, Umar

عمران 'umrán *m. Arabic* [plural: عمرانات 'umrānất] 1 modern conveniences, services and utilities (of a municipality) 2 well-being

عمرانات 'umrānất *m. Arabic* 1 *plural of* عمران 2 construction

عمراني 'umrāní 1 relating to services and utilities modern conveniences 2 *adjective* construction عمراني کارونه، عمراني چاري، د مملکت عمراني پلان the State Plan for Construction

عمري 'umrí 1.1 eternal, constant 1.2 final; conclusive 1.3 life, for life په عمري بند محکومول to sentence to life, imprisonment 2 for life, forever, always

عمق 'umḳ *m. Arabic* [plural: اعماق a'mắḳ] depth

عمل 'amál *m. Arabic* [plural: عملونه 'amalúna *Arabic plural:* اعمال a'mál] 1 business, work, labor د عمل تقسيم division of labor 2 action; act, deed عمل کول to act; take action تا څما په حکم ولي عمل

وﻧﻪ ﻛﺮ؟ Why didn't you do as I told you? عمل د خپلي لاري مل دئ
proverb A good deed will not be forgotten for a lifetime. **3** *math*
operation څلور اصلي عملونه the four operations of arithmetic **4**
history power **5** practice علم او عمل theoretical knowledge and
practice يو خيال د عمل ميدان ته راوستل to bring some idea into
effectual practice **6** operation, action **7** process د احتراق عمل the
process of combustion **8** *biology* function **9** drug addiction **10**
medicine defecation; cleaning out the bowels *idiom* په عمل کښي
in actuality, indeed *idiom* په عمل (۹)بجو ده at nine o'clock

'amálán *Arabic* practically, indeed; clearly, graphically عملاً

'amalbánd *medicine* suffering from constipation, constipated عملبند

'amaldár *m. obsolete* governor, ruler of a province عمل دار، عملدار

'amaldārí *f.* **1** jurisdiction **2** competence **3** عمل داري، عملداري
sphere of authority

'amalgarí *f.* physical work; manual labor عمل ګري

'amalnāmá *f.* **1** protocol, written record **2** deed of عمل نامه
property, deed of ownership of land

'amalá *f. Arabic plural from* عامل 'āmíl **1** team, crew د بېړۍ عمله
crew of a ship د ټانک عمله crew of a tank اور وژونکي عمله
firefighting crew, firemen **2** workers; workforce; employees;
(service) personnel; table of organization; organizational
infrastructure **3** retainers; servants

'amalí amlí **1.1** practical عملي تحصيل practice عملي کول *a* to عملي
bring into practice, effect, put into practical operation **b** to
perform, execute (e.g., a song) عملي کېدل *a* to be put into practice,
be effected; be put into operation, be performed, be executed (of a
song) په عملي توګه practically, indeed, in reality **1.2** practical;
efficient **2** *m.* **.1** smoker **2.2** drug addict

'amalijāt **1** *plural of* عمليت **2** operation, action, activity عمليات
military operation, action د توپخانو عمليات urgent حربي عمليات
measures **3** operation (surgical) د عملياتو مېز operating table **4**
exercise

'amalijātí operational عملياتي

'amalijāt *m.* عمليه amalijá *f. Arabic* process عمليت

'amalikedá *m. plural* putting into practice or effect, عملي کېده
bringing into operation, execution, performance

'amú *m. Arabic* uncle (father's brother) عمو

'amúd *m. Arabic* **1** vertical or perpendicular line; a عمود
perpendicular **2** pole; column; support

'amúdán *Arabic* vertically; plumb, sheer perpendicularly عموداً

'amudí *Arabic* vertical; sheer, plumb, perpendicular عمودي ليکه
a vertical or perpendicular line; a perpendicular

'amudijāt *m. Arabic* verticality; sheerness, plumbness; عموديت
perpendicularity

'umúm *m. Arabic* entire nation, whole population عموم

'umúmán *Arabic* **1** generally; in general **2** in broad areas, in عموماً
circles, in fields

'umumí *Arabic* **1** general, universal; principal, main, chief عمومي
general meeting عمومي مجلس، عمومي مجمع، عمومي غونډه عمومي

تلګراف main telegraph office عمومي کول to disseminate widely,
introduce **2** social, public; nationwide عمومي باغ public garden
عمومي اسامبله general عمومي الوتکه civil aircraft **3** general
assembly عمومي والی governor-general; viceroy **4** world-;
universal عمومي ادبيات world literature *idiom* په عمومي لحاظ in
general, generally

'umumiját *m.* **1** *plural of* عموميت **2** common phenomena عموميات

'umumiját *m. Arabic* **1** community, communality, عموميت
universality **2** popularity عموميت پيدا to be popular عموميت لرل
to obtain popularity, become popular **3** dissemination,
introduction عموميت ورکول to disseminate widely, introduce,
popularize

'imumikedá *m. plural* wide dissemination, introduction عمومي کېده

'ammá *f. Arabic* aunt (father's sister) عمه

'amík *Arabic* **1** deep, profound **2** deeply into something عميق
کېدل to go deeply into, penetrate deeply into something

'an directly; right up to; exactly عن

'unnáb *m. Arabic plural botany* jujube (tree and fruit) عناب

inād *m. Arabic* obstinacy عناد کول to be obstinate, show عناد
obstinacy عناد لرل to be obstinate

'inādí obstinate عنادي

'anāsír *m. Arabic plural of* عنصر عناصر

'anāsirparastí *f.* bowing to the forces of nature عناصرپرستي

'inán *m. Arabic* **1** uzda, rein **2** reins (of government) عنان

'anāvín *m. Arabic plural of* عنوان عناوين

'ināját *m. Arabic* favor, grace عنايت کول to show grace, عنايت
demonstrate favor

'inajatullá inajatulláh *m. Arabic proper name* Inayatulla عنايت الله

'anáb-us-saláb *m. Arabic* solanum, morel عنب الثلب

'ambár *m. Arabic plural* ambergris عنبر

'ambarbúj fragrant, sweet-smelling, aromatic عنبربوی

'ambarí having the color or scent of ambergris عنبري

'ánchi even ☞ ان 2 عن چه

'índu 'índa *Arabic* at, in the presence of, near, around (as the عند
initial element of Arabic compounds) عندالامکان when possible,
when an opportunity offers itself

'ind-ul-iktizā *Arabic* in case of necessity or need عندالاقتضا

'ind-ul-imkán *Arabic* when possible, when the عندالامکان
opportunity arises

'ind-az-zarurát *Arabic* ☞ عندالزوم عندالضرورت

'ind-ul-luzúm insofar as is possible عندالزوم

'andalíb *m. Arabic* **1** blackbird **2** *poetry* nightingale عندليب

'indí *Arabic* **1** subjective **2** made-up, fabricated, fictitious, عندي
imaginary

'unsúr *m. Arabic* [*plural:* عنصرونه 'unsurúna *Arabic plural:* عنصر
عناصر 'anāsír] **1** element کيماوي عناصر chemical elements د
عناصرو جدول elements table **2** composite part; component element
3 (basic, primal) element څلور عنصره the four elements of nature
(earth, water, fire, air)

عنصري 'unsurí *Arabic* elementary, primary, initial; basic (of a rule)

عنعنات 'an'anất *m. Arabic* plural of عنعنه

عنعنوي 'an'anaví traditional

عنعنويت 'an'anaviját *m. Arabic* traditional character, traditional nature

عنعنه 'an'aná *f. Arabic* tradition په عنعنه سره according to tradition

عنعنپسند 'an'an'apasánd adhering to tradition; conservative

عنف 'unf *m. Arabic* 1 oppression, force, violence 2 cruelty, brutality په کمال عنف او شدت exceedingly cruelly

عنقا 'anḳá *f. mythology* phoenix

عنقاوي 'anḳāví uncommon, rare, marvelous

عنقريب 'anḳaríb *Arabic* soon, shortly thereafter, immediately thereafter

عنکبوت 'ankabút *m. Arabic* spider

عنکبوتي 'ankabutí spider-like, arachnoid عنکبوتي حيوانات

عنوان 'invấn unvấn *m. Arabic* [plural: عنوانونه 'invānúna *Arabic* plural: عناوين 'anāvín] 1 title, heading; name, appellation تر عنوان under the name of د تجارت عنوان trading firm 2 address د لاندي addressed to someone 3 method, way, form په عنوان چا under the guise, pretext of; by way of, means of

عنود 'unúd [1] *m. Arabic* stubbornness; obstinacy

عنود 'anúd [2] *Arabic* stubborn, obstinate

عنودانه 'anudāná 1 stubborn; obstinate 2 stubbornly; obstinately

عنه 'ánha *Arabic* from him

عنيف 'aníf *m. Arabic* despot, oppressor

عنين 'innín *Arabic* 1 weak, powerless 2 impotent

عوا avvấ *f. Arabic astronomy* Boötes (the constellation)

عوارض 'avāríz *m. Arabic* plural 1 *from* عارضه 2 folds (accidents of terrain) طبيعي عوارض، د مخکو عوارض relief (natural features) 3 *used for diverse types of monetary collections*

عواطف 'avātíf *m. Arabic* plural of عاطفه

عواقب 'avāḳíb *m. Arabic* plural of عاقبت

عوام 'avấm *m. Arabic* common people

عوام فريب 'avāmfaríb avāmfaréb *m.* demagogue

عوام فريبي 'avāmfarebí *f.* demagoguery

عوامل 'avấmíl *m. Arabic* plural of عامل 2, 4, 5 د توليد عوامل means of production

عوامي 'avamí demotic, pertaining to the common people

عوائق 'avāíḳ *m. Arabic* plural of عائقه

عود 'aud [1] *m. Arabic* return

عود 'ud [2] *m. Arabic* ud, oud (a kind of stringed musical instrument)

عود 'ud [3] *m. Arabic* 1 *botany* aloe 2 stick, staff, rod

عودت 'audát *m. Arabic* ☞ عود [1]

عورات 'aurất *m. Arabic* sexual organs, private parts

عورته 'avráta *f.* ☞ اورته [1]

عوض 'iváz *m. Arabic* substitution, replacement د دي په عوض، د دي in exchange for, instead of, in place of د چا په عوض in place of someone په عوض ورکول to replace

عوضي 'ivzí 1.1 *f.* substitution, replacement د چا عوضي کول to substitute for or replace someone 1.2 *m. regional* deputy 2.1 mutual, reciprocal 2.2 *regional* substitute

عوعو 'av'áv *m.* ☞ عف عف

عهد 'áhd [1] *m. Arabic* 1 promise, obligation; assurance عهد او قول به عهد او قول کول to oblige, obligate 2 by promises, by pledges عهد کول a to promise, obligate oneself; assure b to conclude a treaty ځانه سره يي عهد وکئ He pledged his word.

عهد 'ahd [2] *m. geology* epoch, period د طبقات الارض دريم عهد tertiary period د اول عهد انسانان primitive, primeval people

عهد شکن 'ahdshikán breaking a promise, obligation, or treaty

عهد شکني 'ahdshikaní *f.* breaking of a promise or obligation, violation of a treaty

عهدنامه 'ahdnāmá *f.* 1 written obligation 2 treaty; convention

عهده 'uhdá *f. Arabic* 1 promise; obligation 2 responsibility 3 post, appointment ديوه کار د عهدي څخه وتل، د يوه کار له عهدي څخه وتل، ديوه کار له عهدي څخه را وتل، د يوه کار د عهدي څخه را وتل، تر to deal with some matter عهدي ننه وتل

عهده دار 'uhdadár *m. regional* 1 official, functionary; staff-official 2 noncommissioned officer

عهده داري 'uhdadārí *f.* government service; office, post عهده داري کول to serve

عيادت 'ijādát *m. Arabic* visitation to a sick person د رنځور عيادت کول to visit a sick person

عيار 'ijấr 'ajấr *m. Arabic* 1 assay (of precious metals) 2 touchstone (of a jeweler) 3 standard, criterion

عياش 'aijấsh *m. Arabic* fast-liver, playboy, sybarite

عياشي 'aijashí *f.* enjoyment of life; sybaritism; amusement

عيال 'ajāl ejāl *m. Arabic* family عيال او اطفال kith and kin

عيالدار 'ajāldár *adjective* family-, having a family

عيالي 'ajālí familial, family

عيان 'ajấn 'ejấn *Arabic* obvious, visible, clear عيان کول to show, display عيان کېدل to appear, make one's appearance

عيب 'ajb *m. Arabic* [plural: عيبونه 'ajbúna *Arabic* plural: عيوب 'ujúb] deficiency, defect, flaw په خپل عيب پوهېدل to recognize one's shortcomings خپل عيب د ولي په مينځ او د بل عيب د کلي په مينځ *proverb literal* One's own flaw is a rivulet, that of another is a whole countryside. *figurative* to see a mote in the eye of another, but not a beam in one's own eye *idiom* د چا عيب بنودل to discredit someone a to blame, impute blame عيب لگول، عيب پوري کول b to censure, judge

عيب پوش 'ajbpóḳh concealing flaws, hiding shortcomings

عيب پوښي 'ajbpoḳhí *f.* concealment of flaws, hiding of shortcomings

عيبي 'ajbdzhón ☞ عييجن

عييجو 'ajbdzhó ajbdzhú 1 discrediting someone; saying spiteful things 2 *m.* slanderer; hostile critic

عيب گوی 'ajbgój *m.* slanderer; hostile critic

عيب گيری 'ajbgirí *f.* captiousness

عيب ناک 'ajbnāk flawed, having a flaw, defective

عيبي 'ajbí 1 flawed, having a flaw, defective 2 trainted, imperfect *idiom* په سترگو عيبي شو He became blind. He was struck blind.

عيد 'id *m. Arabic religion* holiday; celebration عيد مو مبارک! Have a happy holiday! Happy Eid! مو مبارک شه!

عيدگاه 'idgáh *m.* large mosque (where celebrations are conducted); place for festivities

عيدي 'idí *Arabic religion* holiday festivity

عيسايي 'isājí ☞ عيسوي isāí

عيسائيت 'isāiját *m.* ☞ عيسويت

عيسوي 'isaví 1 Christian (of chronology), A.D. د عيسوي حساب ۱۸۷۹ کال و It was 1879 according to the Christian chronology. 2 *m.* Christian

عيسويت 'isaviját *m. Arabic* Christianity, Christian faith

عيسی 'isā *m. proper name* Jesus عيسی مسيح Jesus Christ

عيسی خيل 'isākhél *m. plural* 1 the Isakhakhejli (a branch of the Ahmedzai-Gilzai and other tribes) 2 *m.* Isakhejl (tribesman)

عيش 'ajsh *m. Arabic* enjoyment of life; pleasure عيش عشرت, عيش merriment; the good life, life of merriment, pleasure او عشرت خپل عيش او نوش جاري ساتل to live the good life, live a life of pleasure عيشونه کول to enjoy life; enjoy oneself

عين¹ 'ajn *m. Arabic* the name of the letter ع

عين² 'ajn *m. Arabic [plural:* اعيان a'jắn *Arabic plural:* عيون 'ujún] 1 eye 2 source, wellspring 3 essence, essential substance 4 at the height of په عين جنگ کښي ájn-i at the height of the battle 5 kind (as in "payment in kind") په عين حال کي، په عين زمان کي ájn-i at the same time, simultaneously هغه په ځواني کښي مړ سو He died at the height of his power.

عيناً 'jnán *Arabic* 1 precisely, letter-for-letter 2 exactly

عينک 'ajnák *m. regional* عينکه ajnáka *f. usually plural* عينکي ajnáki glasses, spectacles پر سترگو عينکه ايښودل، پر سترگو عينکي to put on glasses اچول

عيني¹ 'ajní *Arabic* 1 eye-, optic, visual 2 one-and-the-same, identical 3 objective عيني حقيقت *philosophy* objective reality 4 material عيني احتياجات material needs, requirements

عيني² 'ajni 3 عين²☞

عينيات 'ajniját *m. Arabic plural* equipment, material

عينيت 'ajniját *m. Arabic* 1 identity, identicalness, sameness 2.1 objectivity, objectiveness 2.2 objectivism

عيوب 'ujúb *m. Arabic plural of* عيب

عيون 'ujún *m. Arabic plural of* عين²

غ

غ ghajn 1 twenty-ninth letter of the Pashto alphabet 2 number 1000 in the abjad system

غ *official abbreviation* غيرت من title of a captain

غاب ghāb *m.* plate

غاپ ghāp *present stem of* غپل

غاپي ghápi *present tense of* غپل

غاتر ghātə́r *m.* mule

غاتول ghāṭól ghāṭúl *m.* 1 poppy 2 tulip 3 *proper name* Ghatol

غاتوی ghāṭój *m.* ☞ غاتول 1, 2

غار ghār *m. Arabic* 1 cave, grotto 2 burrow; den, lair 3 nest (for wasps) 4 anthill

غارت ghārát *m. Arabic* robbery; destruction, ravage, ruin

غارتگر ghāratgár *m.* marauder; bandit, robber

غارتگري ghāratgarí *f.* marauding; pillage, robbery

غارمه ghārmə́ *m. plural* heat, hot weather, sultriness نن ډېر سخت غارمه دئ Today it is very hot.

غارندونه ghārəndúna *f.* غاروزينه ghārozína *f.* round-head (kind of lizard)

غاري¹ ghārí ghāráj gluttonous, voracious, insatiable

غاري² ghārí *regional* knowledgeable, well-informed; knowing a matter, business well

غاريقون ghāriḳún *m.* pileate (capped) mushroom

غاربوجن ghārbodzhə́n *m.* 1.1 fissure (in the skin); ulcer 1.2 suffering from cracking skin; ulcers (behind the ear, between the fingers) 2 ulcerated, cracked, with sores (of the skin)

غاربوجنېدل ghārbodzhənedə́l *denominative, intransitive [past:* غار بوجن شو] to crack, be covered with cracks or ulcers (of the skin)

غارپټی ghārpəṭój *f.* scarf, muffler

غارکی ghārakój *f.* bandolier, ammunition belt

غارگی ghārgój *f.* necklace

غارو ghārú having a long neck, long-necked

غاره ghā́ra *f.* 1 neck په غاره چا ته تر غاره وتل to embrace someone په غاره کي a to embrace (one another) b not to get along ورلوېدل to fall on the neck of, to go to someone in a time of emotional need, hug د احمد خور د ده په غاره کي ورولوېده او و يې ژړل Ahmed's sister fell upon his neck and burst into tears. 2 throat, gullet; pharynx سره غاره larynx, windpipe وچه غاره esophagus غاړي شني غاره خپه کول to strangle غاره تازه کول to clear one's throat a to cry out at the top of one's lungs b to wheeze; lose one's voice په غاره کي لوېدل to grab someone by the throat; fight with someone 3 collar 4 neck (of a vessel) 5 shore, bank لار د رود په غاره غاره تللي ده The road runs along the shore of the river. پوري 6 this (the near) bank دا پوري غاره the other (the far) bank راپوري غاره 7 go along the side د لاري پر غاره ځئ edge; side (of road, etc.) زينبه پر زوی غاره کول a to sing b to be proud (of) غاره وراچول Zainab is proud of his son. a sing b play په غاره ورواچوه! Play a bit on the reed-pipe! (i.e., on the reed-pipe) لوړه غاره *idiom* هسکه غاره (very) proudly لوړا لوړه غاره په خورا haughtily غاره ايستل a to pay off a debt غاره ادا کول to pay a debt b to be content with something زه په دې کتاب غاره نه باسم، نور راکه! This book does not suffice for me; give me another! غاره چا ته to خپله غاره د چا امر ته اينودل to be subordinate to someone be obedient to someone; obey someone's orders غاره و يو شي ته اينودل to acknowledge something د تسليم غاره يې ايني ده They اينودل surrendered. They submitted. غاري اينودل a to bow the head;

غاړه I راپوري ده submit, be subordinate (to) **b** to sacrifice a life have a cold. I have a cough. خلاصول غاړه **a** to carry out a promise **b** to be freed from an obligation د چا غاړي خلاصول **a** to give someone his due **b** to execute someone's will or testament **c** to pay up someone's debt **d** to tell someone the truth ما خپلي غاړي I told him straight out what I thought. خلاصي کړي، ورته ومي ويل غاړي بندول، غاړه بندول **a** to lie **b** to give false testimony; appropriate another's goods په چا بندول خپلي غاړي to live at the expense of another; exploit someone د يو شي څخه غاړه پيچل to refuse to submit to something; refuse to do something غاړي غرونه ورل to carry away, annihilate all in its path (of a hurricane) د اوبنانو غاړي چا نيولي دي saying to have a cold, have a cough له چا نه غاړه غرول **a** غاړه غرول، غاړي غرول Force breaks the straw. to refuse someone **b** to be stubborn, be obstinate **c** to refuse (to do) something يوه وظيفه پر خپله غاړه اخيستل، يوه عهده پر خپله غاړه to take an obligation upon oneself, be obligated اخيستل دا پور ستا پر د چا پر غاړه اخيستل to place responsibility upon, oblige someone اينودل پر غاړه تلل، پر غاړه ژرل You still owe this debt. غاړه پاته سو to consider (one's) wishes; please **b** to sympathize ور په غاړه کول **a** to force (i.e., one's opinions) upon someone مسئوليت ور په غاړه دئ It is his responsibility. په غاړه کنبي اوبه ښکاره کبدل to be very beautiful د چا د غاړي کول **a** to load someone down, put all the work on someone **b** to give someone responsibility د چا غاړي کبدل to burden someone; be a burden to someone له غاړي اړول to be freed from responsibility

غاړه ږغ **ghāṛagágh** *m.* **1** special melody played on the reed-pipe **2** singing (of people, nightingales)

غاړه غوی *f.* غاړه غجي **ghāṛaghaṭə́j** *f.* غاړه غتی **ghāṛaghədzhí** **ghaṛagharə́j** *f.* embraces غاړه غتی کبدل to embrace غاړه غتی راتلل **a** to embrace (one another) **b** to be combined, be linked شاعري او موسيقي يو تر بله سره غاړه غتی ورغلي دي Music and poetry are closely linked.

غاړه ګری **ghāṛagə́raj** *m.* peasant having a joint property boundry with someone

غاړه وړونکی **ghā́ṛa vṛúnkaj** obedient, pliant

غاړي **ghā́ṛi** *Eastern plural of* غاړه

غاړيت **ghāṛít** *m.* deception, shrewd dealing چاته غاړيت ورکول to deceive, cheat someone

غاړي غاړي **ghā́ṛi-ghā́ṛi 1** brim full, full to the top **2** highwater هلمند بيا په ټپو غاړي غاړي راغئ The Gilmend again reached flood-level. **3** embracing

غاز I **ghāz** *m.* [*plural:* غازونه **ghāzúna** *Arabic plural:* غازات ghāzā́t] gas د غاز ضد anti-gas خفه کوونکی غازونه asphyxiating gases د غازاتو تبادله gas exchange

غاز 2 **ghāz** *m.* *history* copper coin, bronze coin; half pice

غاز 3 **ghāz** *m.* viscosity, elasticity (of dough)

غاز درلودونکی **ghāz darlodúnkaj** containing gas; full of gas

غازسازي **ghāzsāzí** *f.* production of gas

غازه **ghāzá** *f.* **1** rouge **2** high color, flush, blush

غازي 1 **ghāzí** *m.* *Arabic* **1** victor **2** *religion* militant (in spreading the Muslim faith), warrior for the faith, crescentader

غازي **ghāzi** gas, gaseous غازي ماسکه gas mask

غاسُل **ghāsúl** *m.* *Arabic botany* saltwort (*Salsola*, used in place of soap)

غابښ **ghāx̌** *m.* **1** tooth د غابښ خوږ، د غابښ درد د مخي غابښونه incisors د غابښ جوړولو موسسه، د غابښ حکيم، د غابښ ډاکتر toothache dentist د غابښونو جوړولو موسسه dentist's office, office where dentures are fitted and dispensed آلوچي مي غابښ برپنبول **a** to set the teeth on edge غابښ ويربپنباوه My teeth are on edge from cherry plums. **b** to tell someone off غابښونه يي پر ټوتل His teeth were falling out. غابښ چيچل **a** to grate, grind the teeth **b** to be patient ثو روځي غابښ وچيچه، کتاب در پيدا کوم Be patient for a few days; I'll get you a book. **c** to become angry مور و زوی ته غابښ چيچل The mother got angry at her son. **d** to threaten someone د هلک لمړي غابښ زبري The child is cutting his first tooth. غابښونه سپينول **a** to smile; grin **b** to toady غابښ کتل to grate the teeth, gnash the teeth **a** to examine a tooth, examine the teeth **b** to determine age (animal's) by examination of the teeth غابښ کنبل to extract a tooth تر غابښ ويل، تر غابښ لاندي کول to bite غابښ لګول to speak through the teeth چه غابښونه وو، نوچيني نه وي *proverb literal* When there were teeth, there were no peas. *figurative* Wealth came too late. **2** cog, tooth (of a gearwheel) **3** blade *idiom* غابښونه ورايستل to cheat, pull the wool over someone's eyes غابښ تودبدل to assuage hunger غابښ يي هم پري تود نه شه *Eastern* It hardly sufficed for a snack. غابښونه تر له تبربدل to skimp, stint غابښونه تر له تبرول to become stingy, become miserly, become niggardly غابښ تبره کول، **a** to have a grudge against someone **b** to hanker after something ويو شي ته ګوتي په غابښ نيول to be suprised at something; be astounded by something

غابښ برهان **ghāx̌burnān** obvious, clear

غابښ ټومبونی **ghāx̌tuṇbúnaj** *m.* toothpick

غابښ چيچک **ghāx̌chichák** pebbly, with pebbles (of rice, etc.); contaminated with stones

غابښ چيچن **ghāx̌chichə́n 1** angry; wrathful **2** ☞ غابښ چيچک

غابښ چيچنه *f.* غابښ چيچي **ghāx̌chicháj** *m.* **1** to grind the teeth **2** censure غابښ چيچنه ورته وکړه! Tell him off!

غابښ سکوی **ghāx̌skój** *m.* food sticking between the teeth

غابښک **ghāx̌hək** غابښو **ghāx̌hú** toothy

غابښمنونی **ghāx̌mx̌únaj** *m.* toothbrush

غابښ وتلی **ghāx̌vatálaj** having loose teeth, with teeth that are falling out

غابښور **ghāx̌avár ghāx̌húr 1** *m.* **.1** rake غابښ وتلی کول *compound verb* to rake, smooth with a rake په غابښ وتلي باندي ځمکه آواړول to smooth out soil with a rake **1.2** pitchfork **2.1** toothed; toothy; serrated **2.2** big-toothed, having prominent teeth

غابښوره **ghāx̌hvára** *f.* *regional* pitchfork

غابښ وله **ghaх̌vəla** *f.* weeping willow

غابښ ولی **ghaх̌hvə́láj** *f.* root of a tooth

غاښونکی ghāx̌havúnkaj *m. Eastern* toothpick

غاښی [1] ghā́x̌haj *m.* **1** crest (of mountain) **2** mountain pass

غاښی [2] ghāx̌hój *f.* ☞ ښاخی

غاښیز ghāx̌híz *linguistics* dental

غاصب ghāsib *m. Arabic* [*plural:* غاصبین ghāsibín] invader, usurper; aggressor

غاصبانه ghāsibāná aggressive; violent

غافل ghāfíl *Arabic* **1** careless, negligent, remiss; absentminded **2** ignorant, uninformed د دې څخه غافل وم I did not know about that.

غافلول ghāfílavól *denominative, transitive* [*past:* غافل یې کړ] **1** to cause to become careless or negligent **2** to indulge, show indulgence (to)

غافلېدل ghāfíledól *denominative, intransitive* [*past:* غافل شو] **1** to be ignorant, be uninformed **2** to be ignorant (of) **3** to be careless; be negligent; be absentminded

غالب [1] ghālíb *Arabic* **1.1** conquering, overcoming; victorious **1.2** prevailing **1.3** more probable غالب گمان دئ، دا غالبه ده چه ... په in all probability, extremely probable ☞ غالب کېدل **2** *m.* victor غالبېدل

غالب [2] ghālíb *m.* ☞ قالب

غالباً ghālíbán in all probability; extremely probable غالباً دا ده چه ... It is most likely that …

غالبانه ghālibāná victoriously

غالبوزک ghālbuzák *m. botany* marsh mallow

غالبوزه ghālbúza *f.* bumblebee; wasp د شاتو غالبوزه bee, honeybee

غالبوزی ghālbúzaj *m.* kind of herringbone embroidery

غالبول ghālbúl *m.* ☞ غال مغال

غالبېدل ghālíbedól *denominative, intransitive* [*past:* غالب شو] to conquer, surmount; overcome

غال مغال ghālmaghāl *m.* row, disturbance غال مغال کول to create a row, make a din

غالوشه ghālvósha *f.* small milk pail

غالغول ghālghúl ghālvoghúl *m.* ☞ غال مغال

غالی [1] ghālój *f.* carpet د غالیو اوډل to weave a carpet غالیو اوډل carpet weaving

غالی [2] ghālé *f.* **1** cheating (at cards, etc.) غالی کول to cheat (at cards, dice, etc.) **2** deceit

غالی [3] ghālí غالېجن ghāledzhón **1** deceitful **2** knavish, dishonest

غالیچه ghālichá *f.* غالیگی ghālichój *f.* غالی گی ghaləjgój *f.* rug

غالیوالا ghaləjvālá *m.* rug merchant

غامض ghāmíz *Arabic* dark, unclear, incomprehensible, enigmatic

غاندنه ghāndóna *f.* ☞ غندنه

غانده [1] ghāndó unpleasant; repulsive

غانده [2] ghāndó *imperfect of* غندل [2]

غاندو ghāndú **1** cowardly; base **2** crawling on the knees, demeaning oneself

غاو ghāv *m.* **1** disturbance; mutiny; riots غاو کول to be in a disturbed state; rebel, mutiny **2** disturbance, din **3** call for help

غاوچی ghāvchí *m.* **1** gatekeeper **2** porter

غاور [1] ghāvír *Arabic* **1** secret, concealed, interior **2** intimate **3** circumspect

غاور [2] ghāvór ☞ غاوره

غاورسی [1] ghāvrósaj *m.* **1** assistant, helper **2** defender, protector

غاورسي [2] ghāvrasí *f.* **1** help, assistance **2** protection

غاوره ghāvóra proud پر خپل عزت باندې ډېر غاوره دئ، په خپل عزت باندې ډېر غاوره دئ They value their reputations highly.

غاوناک ghāvnák noisy, riotous, turbulent

غاوول ghāvavól *transitive* [*past:* و یې غاواوه] **1** to cause to be riotous, noisy, or turbulent **2** to make to cry out

غاوی ghāvój *m.* plaintiff; person seeking justice

غاوېدل ghāvedól *intransitive* [*past:* وغاوېده] **1** to make a disturbance, raise a din **2** to cry out

غایات ghājāt *m. Arabic plural of* غایه

غائب ghāíb غایب ghājíb *Arabic* **1.1** absent, missing **1.2** hidden, concealed **1.3** vanishing, disappearing **2** *m. grammar* third person

غایبانه ghājibāná **1** correspondence (relating to a friendship) غایبانه پېژند گلوي an epistolary (long-distance friendship) **2** by correspondence

غایبداني ghājibdāní *f.* premonition

غایبگو ghājibgú *m.* prophet; prognosticator

غایبگویي ghājibgují *f.* prophesy; prognostication

غایب والی ghājibválaj *m.* **1** absence **2** disappearance **3** invisibility

غایبېدل ghājibedól *denominative, intransitive* [*past:* غایب شو] to disappear, get lost له سترگو څخه غایبېدل to disappear from view, fade from sight

غایت [1] ghāját *m.* ☞ غایه

غایت [2] ghāját *m.* ☞ غائط

غایت الغایت ghājat-al-ghāját *m. Arabic* most important task, very important goal

غائط ghāít *m. Arabic* feces, defecation, excrement غائط کول to defecate

غایطه ghāitá feces, stools, execrement غایطه مواد

غای لمی ghājlóme *f.* stye (on the eye)

غائله ghāilá *f. Arabic* **1** calamity **2** clash, conflict

غایوي ghājaví **1** final; utmost **2** special-purpose

غایه ghājá *f. Arabic* [*plural:* غایي ghājé *m. Arabic plural:* غایات gājāt] **1** goal, task د دې غایي دپاره with this goal **2** limit, boundary, end

غائي [1] ghāí *Arabic* final, last, ultimate

غایي [2] ghājé *f. plural of* غایه

غبار ghubā́r *m. Arabic* **1** dust; puffs of dust **2** fog; steam

غبارآلوده ghubārāludá غباري ghubārí **1** covered with dust, dusty; dull **2** foggy

غبندی ghbándaj *m. anatomy* gland

غبرگ ghbarg **1** double; twofold, duplex غبرگه شپږی double (weight) plaid **2** pair په غبرگ صورت in pairs, two by two **3** repeated,

غبرگي لوني linguistics reduplication *idiom* غبرگ ترکيب recurring
willingly, with all my heart په غبرگو لپمو both daughters

غبرگ ټک ghbárgṭak *m. computer science* double click

غبرگلون ghbarglún *m.* fold, pleat (in a garment)

غبرگوالی، غبرگ والی ghbargválaj *m.* 1 duplication 2 state of being a pair

غبرگول ghbargavól *denominative, transitive* [*past:* غبرگ يې کړ] 1 to double 2 to pair *idiom* خبره غبرگول، جواب غبرگول a to contradict, object b to repeat; duplicate

غبرگولۍ ghbargoláj *m.* 1 twin 2 [*plural:* غبرگولي ghbargolí] twins جوزا ☞

غبرگون ghbargún *m.* 1 answer; rejoinder 2 folding (of clothing) 3 pleat, fold; layer

غبرگونه ghbargavóna *f.* 1 doubling 2 pairing

غبرگوني ghbargúni *m. plural dialect* ☞ غبر گولۍ 2

غبرگه ghbárga 1 *feminine singular of* غبرگ 2 *f.* 2.1 woman who has borne twins غبرگه لگېدل to bear twins 2.2 narrow gully 2.3 handful په غبرگو وېشل to distribute by handfuls

غبرگېدل ghbargedól *denominative, intransitive* [*past:* غبرگ شو] 1 to be doubled, be folded in two 2 to be formed into two files or columns غبرگ سئ! Form fours! (as a command) 3 to be turned toward us, this way, etc. 4 to return راغبرگ شو He returned. 5 to accompany, travel with

غبرگېدنه ghbargedóna *f.* غبرگېده ghbargedó *m. plural* 1 doubling; folding in two 2 forming up in two columns, ranks, or files 3 turning toward us, this way, etc. 4 return 5 accompaniment, traveling together 6 repetition

غبطه ghibtá *f. Arabic* envy

غبغب ghabgháb *m.* 1 double chin 2 dewlap

غبن ghabn *m. Arabic* deceit, cheating, swindle غبن شروع کول to engage in cheating or swindling

غبي ghabí *Arabic* 1 weak-witted; dull-witted; slow (mentally); dull (of intellect) 2 forgetful, absentminded

غپ ghap *m.* غپا ghapā *f.* bark (of a dog)

غپاندی ghapāndaj ☞ غپند

غپل ghapól *transitive* [*present:* غاپي *past:* وې غپل] to bark (like a dog) *proverb literal* سپي غاپي، کاروان تېرېږي The dog barks when the caravan passes. *figurative* That's a lot of hot air. چه ډېر غاپي، نو چیچل نه کوي *proverb* A barking dog never bites.

غپند ghapónd غپندوکی ghapandúkaj barking, yelping (dog)

غپول ghapavól *transitive* [*past:* وې غپاوه] to tease (a dog)

غپه ghupá *f.* ☞ غوته 2

غپهار ghapəhár *m.* bark (of a dog)

غپېدل ghapedól *intransitive* [*past:* وغپېد past: وغپېده] to begin to bark, yap, or yelp

غپېده ghapedó *m. plural* bark, yapping, yelping

غټ ghaṭ 1.1 big, large په غتو گامو with large strides غتي مڼي big apples 1.2 fat, stout, burly, corpulent 1.3 outstanding,

distinguished (men) 1.4 important, serious غته خبره an important question غته وجه important reason, serious reason 1.5 great (of powers) 1.6 loud (of a voice) په غټ آواز loudly 2 *m.* great man; distinguished person; prominent figure; grandee *idiom* غټ جوار maize غټ مازيگر a toward evening b beginning of evening غټ کتل to stare; look boldy غټ ويل a to speak loudly b to brag, boast

غټ ghuṭ ☞ غوټ غټ پرېکړئ ويل to speak in plain terms

غټ باز ghaṭbā́z [1] *m.* large hawk, chicken hawk

غتباز ghaṭbā́z [2] *m.* boaster, braggart

غتبازي ghaṭbāzí *f.* boasting, bragging غتبازي کول to boast, brag

غټ پټ ghaṭpáṭ 1 very big, huge 2 ☞ غټ [1]

غتتوب ghaṭtób *m.* غټتيا ghaṭtjā́ *f.* 1 size 2 greatness 3 distinction

غټرکی ghaṭərkaj *m.* غتری ghaṭóraj *m.* ball, lump, clod

غټ غټ ghaṭgháṭ loudly غټ غټ ويل a to speak loudly b to boast, brag

غټ مشر ghátməshr ghátməshər *m.* 1 chief, head 2 *military* commander-in-chief

غټ نسی ghaṭnásaj potbellied, big-bellied

غټو ghuṭú [1] *m.* Adam's apple

غټو ghā́ṭo [2] *oblique plural* ☞ غټ [1]

غټواله ghaṭvā́la *f.* غتوالی ghaṭvā́laj *m.* 1 size, dimension 2 thickness 3 fullness, burliness; corpulence 4 greatness

غټوکی ghaṭokáj *affectionate* ☞ غټ [1]

غټول ghaṭavól *transitive* 1 *denominative* [*past:* غټ يې کړ] 1.1 to increase; enlarge 1.2 to thicken 1.3 to cause to become fat, corpulent, or burly 2 [*past:* وي يې غتاوه] 2.1 to present; reward (with) زه پلار په کتاب وغتولم Father presented the book to me. 2.2 to extoll

غټوله ghaṭóla ungainly, clumsily built; disproportionate

غټونه ghaṭavóna *f.* 1 increase; enlargement 2 thickening

غټه ghóṭa *f.* dune, barkan

غټه غرنده ghā́ṭa ghərónda *f.* eyeball

غته کولمه ghā́ṭa kulmá *f.* large intestine

غټی ghaṭáj [1] *m.* lump, ball, clod غتی غتی in clods, in lumps غتی کول to crumple, ball up

غټی ghuṭáj [2] *f.* ☞ غوټی [1] *regional* غتی غتی راتلل، غتی غتی راوتل to ooze (of blood)

غتيالۍ ghuṭjāláj 1 possessing a large craw or crop 2 having a dewlap

غټي دانې ghā́ṭi dāné *f. plural* wasp د غتو دانو د ضد واکسین anti-waspbite vaccine

غټېدل ghaṭedól *denominative, intransitive* [*past:* غټ شو] 1 to be increased; get large 2 to become fat 3 to be fat, be plump, be burly; to be corpulent; grow fat, grow plump

غټېدنه ghaṭedóna *f.* غټېده ghaṭedó *m. plural* 1 growth, increase; augmentation 2 thickening

غجره ghádzhra *f. Melia azadirachta* (kind of tree)

غجري ghadzharí *f.* غجری ghadzharój horsecloth

غجکه ghadzhə́ka f. ghidzhak (a kind of violin)

غجکه والا ghadzhəkavālā́ m. ghidzhak player

غوجل ghudzhə́l f. غوجل

غج [1] ghəch ghach m. 1 anger, spite غج لرل to experience anger 2 vengeance; reprisal غج کښل، غج اخيستل to take vengeance on

غج [2] ghəch imitative word for the cry or chirp of a bird غج کول to cry, chirp (of birds)

غجکه ghicháka ghacháka f. ☞ غجکه

غجول ghachavə́l transitive [past: و يې غجاوه] to squeak, crunch (of shears, etc.)

غچه [1] ghúcha غچي ghúchi dialect 1 particle which modifies or softens the force of an imperative غچه لاړ شه! Go away now! Oh go away! 2 interjection oh, ah

غچي [2] ghəchí f. [plural: غچی ghəchə́j plural: غچياني ghəchijā́ni] plural scissors, shears

غحرکی ghadzə́rkaj m. newborn kid

غحزول ghadzavə́l transitive ☞ غزول

غحزول شوی سيميز جال ghadzawə́lshawəy simajíz dzhā́l m. computer science extended LAN (Local Area Network)

غحزونکي ghadzavúnki m. غحزوني ghadzavúni f. plural ☞ غزونه

غحزېدل ghadzedə́l intransitive ☞ غزېدل

غغ [1] ghəts m. dialect 1 revenge 2 anger, spite 3 obstinacy

غغ [2] ghuts dialect ☞ غوت

غوڅکی ghutskáj m. ☞ غوڅکی

غوڅول ghutsavə́l transitive dialect ☞ غوڅول

غوڅېدل ghutsedə́l intransitive dialect ☞ غوڅېدل

غدار ghaddā́r Arabic 1 treacherous, perfidious, traitorous 2 m. traitor, betrayer

غدد ghudád m. Arabic plural of غده

غدر ghádr ghā́dər m. Arabic 1 treachery, treason, perfidy 2 rebellion, mutiny 3 uprising

غدکه ghadáka f. jacket (of cloth)

غدوی ghadój m. bandit, brigand, highway robber

غده ghuddá f. Arabic [plural: غدي ghuddé m. Arabic plural: غدد ghudád] gland

غدی ghadə́j f. Arabic 1 daylight robbery, banditry, brigandage غدی کول to rob, engage in banditry, engage in brigandage غدی اچول to rob 2 regional raid

غدير ghadír m. Arabic lake

غذا ghizā́ f. Arabic [plural: غذاگاني ghizāgā́ni Arabic plural: اغذيه aghzijá] food, victuals, nutriment مقوي غذا high-calorie diet د عقل او فكر غذا spiritual nourishment غذا تيارول to prepare food idiom

غذائي ghizāí Arabic adjective food-; nourishment- غذائي قيمت nutritiousness غذايه مواد، غذائي مواد food, nourishment, provender غذائي خواهش appetite, desire to eat

غذائيت ghizāiját m. nutritiousness

غر [1] غر ghar m. [plural: غرونه ghrúna plural: غرہ ghrə] 1 mountain سپين غر، پښتانه د غره spinghar, Safedkokh mountain Afghans د غره لمن a foot of a mountain b ميز Muflon (kind of wild sheep) تر غره اړول slope of a mountain د غره په سرختل to cross a mountain to climb a mountain, ascend to the summit of a mountain 2 pile, heap (of stones, grain, etc.) 3 giant, titan (of science, etc.) د علم يو لوی غر a great scientist idiom زه در پسي لکه غر ټينگ ولاړ يم Depend upon me as though upon a stone wall.

غر [2] ghur m. goiter

غر [3] ghər m. 1 noise (of transportation) 2 crash (of a collapsing wall) 3 snarling (of a dog)

غرا [1] gharrā́ Arabic brilliant (of speech, etc.)

غرا [2] gharā́ f. thunder, crash; rumble غرا کول to thunder, crash; hoot, honk

غرابات gharābā́t m. Arabic oddity, eccentricity زيات غرابت لرل to be very odd په دې کښي د تعجب او غرابت ځای نشته There is nothing surprising or odd about this.

غراره gharārá f. 1 bag (for transporting loads on a donkey) 2 rags, tatters

غرامات gharāmā́t m. Arabic plural 1 of غرامت 2 reparations

غرامت gharāmát m. Arabic [plural: غرامات gharāmā́t] 1 monetary fine 2 compensation for damages

غران ghrān m. Western ☞ قران [2]

غرانده ghrā́nda f. flame accompanied by smoke

غرانيت ghrānít m. plural granite

غراوو gharāvú m. 1 childish, infantile babbling 2 windbag

غرائب gharāíb m. Arabic plural غرايب gharājíb m. plural 1 of غريبه [1] 2 wonders, unusual things

غرائز gharāíz m. Arabic plural of غريزه

غرب [1] gharb m. Arabic west غرب او شمال northwest، غرب او جنوب southwest

غرب [2] ghrab m. 1 drumbeat 2 crash (of something falling)

غربا [1] ghurabā́ m. Arabic plural of غريب [2]

غربا [2] ghrabā́ f. ☞ غربهار

غرباً ghárbán Arabic to the west غرباً او شرقاً from west to east

غرباوه ghrabāvə́ imperfect of غربول

غربوری gharburáj m. bulldozer

غربول ghrabavə́l transitive [past: و يې غرباوه] 1 to beat (a drum) 2 to thunder, crash

غربهار ghrabahā́r m. 1 continuous drumbeats 2 rumble (of traffic, etc.)

غربی [1] ghrəbáj m. buckle, clasp (of a strap, etc.)

غربی [2] ghrabáj m. ☞ غربهار

غربی [3] gharbí Arabic 1 western غربي او شمالي northwestern سهيلي، غربي او جنوبي southwestern 2 m. European (person)

غربېدل ghrabedə́l intransitive [past: و غربېده] 1 to clatter, rattle, beat (drum) 2 to rumble, rattle (of traffic, etc.)

غربېر gharbér m. hubbub, din, rumble

غربن gharbín m. carbine

غرپر ghərpər *m.* **1** noise, racket, din; disorder **2** stomach-rumbling

غرپرت ghərpárt *m.* idle talk

غرپش gurpásh *m.* ☞ غرپر

غرتک ghərtə́k غرتن gərtən boastful, bragging

غرته ghárta *f.* back, back part of something

غرتي ghárti *f. plural* غرتي کول to speak nonsense, talk rubbish غرتي مه کوه! Don't talk rubbish!

غرتی ghərṭáj *m.* piece, lump (of sugar, etc.); ball, lump; bundle, ball

غرچی ghərcháj *m.* **1** grating (of teeth) **2** crash (of collapsing timbers, beams) غرچی کول to crack

غرچیدل ghurchedə́l ghrəchedə́l *intransitive* [*past:* غرچیده و] **1** to bellow (of a buffalo); bleat (of a goat) **2** to crack (of collapsing timbers)

غرڅپه ghartsapá *f.* **1** flow from the mountains **2** large wave

غرڅن ghartsə́n mountain; mountainous

غرڅنی ghartsanáj **1** mountain (in names of animals) غرڅنی چرگ monal, Himalayan pheasant **2** *m.* ☞ غرڅه 1

غرڅه ghartsə́ **1** *m.* .**1** wild goat **1.2** savage, uneducated person, crude person **1.3** *proper name* Ghartsa **2** ☞ غرڅنی 1

غرز ghraz *m.* ☞ غرب 2

غورځنگ ghurzáng *m. dialect* ☞ غورځنگ

غرزول ghərzavə́l 1 *transitive* [*past:* و يي غرزاوه] to beat, batter, strike, pound

غورزول ghurzavə́l 2 *transitive* ☞ غورځول

غرزی ghərzáj 1 *m.* **1** snarling (of a dog) **2** crack (of a rifle); boom or roar of cannons

غرزی gharzáj 2 *m.* **1** indigenous mountain man; mountaineer, mountain dweller **2** *proper name* Gharzai

غرزیدل ghrazedə́l 1 *intransitive* [*past:* و غرزید] **1** to be beaten; be worn down **2** to rumble, clatter, roar (of traffic)

غورزیدل ghurzedə́l 2 *intransitive* ☞ غورځیدل

غرزیده ghrazedə́ 1 *m. plural* **1** beating **2** rumbling, rumble (of traffic, etc.)

غورزیده ghurzedə́ 2 *m. plural* ☞ غورځیده

غرړل ghərṛə́l *transitive* [*past:* و يي غرړل] to snarl (of a dog)

غرړی ghərṛáj *m.* snarling (of a dog)

غرس ghars *m. Arabic* **1** planting (of vegetation) **2** seedling غرس کول to plant (vegetation) غرس کيدل to be planted (of vegetation)

غرشین gharshín *m.* **1** *plural* Garshini (tribe) **2** Garshini (tribesman) **3** mountaineer, mountain dweller

غرض gharáz *m. Arabic* [*plural:* غرضونه gharazúna *Arabic plural:* اغراض aghrā́z] **1** goal, intent په غرض with the goal (of) د دي وينا شخصي غرضونه This is what I mean by this. نه ما غرض دا دئ چه personal goals, self-serving goals د هغه په هر سلام کښي سل غرضه پټ دي *literal* In each of his greetings, one hundred goals are hidden. *figurative* He is always thinking of his own personal interests. **2** ulterior motive, secret intention **3** malevolence غرض دا چه، غرض دئ چه in brief, in a word

خودغرض gharazmán ☞ غرضمن، غرض من

غرضي gharazí egotistical, self-serving

غرغچ gharghóch *m.* butting غرغچ کول to butt

غرغر ghurghúr ghərghór *m.* grumbling; muttering غرغر کول to grumble; mutter

غرغرانک ghərghərānák *m.* rattle (toy)

غرغرک ghargharák *m.* pulley, block

غرغر gharghár *m.* **1** suffering **2** need, want, distress په غرغر اخته کېدل **a** to suffer **b** to be in need, distress

غرغره gharghará 1 *f.* **1** pulley, block **2** rinsing, garble (of the mouth) **3** roar, bellow (of a camel) **4** cry, wail غرغره کول **a** to raise something by a block and tackle **b** to rinse, gargle **c** to bellow (of a camel) **d** to cry out, bawl

غرغره gharghará 2 *f.* descent, going down (of the sun) د نمر سترگه غرغره شوه The sun has gone down.

غرغری ghərgharáj *f.* wheeze, wheezing sound

غرغښت ghərghə́kht *m.* **1** game, fun, amusement **2** outdoor party for women with games (in a meadow) **3** *history* Ismail (nickname, the second son of Kais Abdurrashid, the eponymous founder of one of the four tribes of the Afghans)

غرغښتي gharghukhtí 1 *m. plural* Gargushti (name of one of the four principal tribes of the Afghans)

غرغښتی gharghə́khtáj 2 *m.* kind of plum

غرغور gharghúr *m.* **1** noise, din **2** wailing, outcry (from fright)

غرغپچکو gharghechkó *m. botany* cotoneaster

غرفه ghurfá *f. Arabic* **1** pavilion (at an exhibition) **2** booth **3** chamber, hall

غرق gharḳ *Arabic* **1** *m.* immersion (in liquid); sinking, submerging **2** *predicative* .**1** immersed (in liquid); sunken, submerged **2.2** sleeping soundly غرق اوده و He slept soundly. **2.3** fascinated by something, immersed in something په خيالاتو غرق وم I fell to dreaming.

غرقاب gharḳā́b *m.* whirlpool, abyss, maelstrom, chasm

غرقول gharḳavə́l *denominative, transitive* [*past:* غرق يي کړ] **1** to immerse (in liquid); sink, submerge **2** to plunge into deep sleep **3** to destroy

غرقیدل gharḳedə́l *denominative, intransitive* [*past:* غرق شو] **1** to be immersed (in liquid); be sunken, be submerged **2** to fall fast asleep **3** to perish, be lost

غرکنو gharkənú *m.* kind of green vegetable (greens)

غرکی ghərkáj 1 *m.* bellow (of a buffalo)

غرکی ghərkáj 2 *m. Russula foetens* (a kind of mushroom)

غرگی ghargáj *m.* hillock

غرمچ gharmach *m.* spring promenade among the flowers in the meadow ☞ غرغنبت

غرمکی gharmakə́j *f.* time just before noon

غرمنی gharmanáj *adjective* noon-, noonday- غرمنی ډوډی light afternoon snack

غرمه gharmá *f.* noon غرمه تکنه precisely at noon; at the hottest part of the day سره غرمه twelve o'clock, noon د غرمی ووڼی afternoon تر غرمی وروسته snack, lunch at noon, in the second half of the day غرمکۍ gharmakə́j *f.* ☞

غرند ghərə́nd غرنداز ghərəndā́z talking nonsense, engage in idle talk

غرنده [1] ghrā́nda *f.* chin

غرنده [2] ghərə́nda *f.* **1** misfortune, calamity; hopeless situation په احمد دنیا غرنده سوه را باندي Ahmed fell into misfortune. Calamity struck me. **2** thunder *idiom* چوک پر غرنده کول to force, coerce, compel, constrain

غرندی [1] ghrə́ndaj *m.* trachea

غرندي [2] ghərə́ndi *plural of* غرنده [2]

غرنگ ghrang *m.* clang, clatter (resulting from the fall of a metallic object)

غرنی gharanáj mountain, mountainous

غروال gharvál *m.* mountaineer, mountain dweller

غروب ghurúb *m. Arabic* sunset, setting of the sun نمر د غروب په حال The sun approached its setting. د غروب و خوا ته in the west; toward the west کښی و

غرور ghurúr *m. Arabic* pride, arrogance; conceit, haughtiness *idiom* ملي غرور *politics* chauvinism

غروړه ghrúra *f.* غروړی ghrúṛaj *m.* **1** *medicine* swelling (of tonsils) غروړي swollen (tonsils) **2** suppressed anger, rage په زړه کي غروړي لرل to nurture anger in one's heart

غروسم gharusám gharosám *m.* غروسمه gharusáma *f.* mountains and valleys

غرول ghəravál *transitive* [*past:* و يې غراوه] **1.1** to make to roar (an animal) **1.2** to cause a rumble or rumbling; cause banging **1.3** to cause to chatter or talk **2** [*past:* و يې غرول] to roar, bellow; snarl

غرومب ghrumb *m.* ☞

غروی ghrə́vaj *m.* palm (of the hand)

غروبنته gharvékhta *f. botany* rush, *Juncus*

غره [1] ghurrá *Arabic* first day of the lunar month

غره [2] ghurrá *Arabic indeclinable* proud; haughty; arrogant

غره [3] ghə́ra *f.* hinder parts, buttocks

غره [4] grə **1** *oblique singular of* غر [1] **2** *plural of* غر [1]

غرهار ghərəhā́r *m.* **1** rumbling, crashing د توپو غرهار the crashing of weapon-fire **2** hum, roar (of an aircraft) **3** idle talk

غره لرونکی grə larúnkaj mountainous غره لرونکي مکچه mountainous terrain, mountainous landscape

غروال ghrəvál *m.* ☞ غروال

غری [1] ghuráj *m.* **1** goiter **2** person with large goiter

غری [2] ghərəj *f.* rash

غرجاسی gharjāsáj *m. dialect* ☞ غراشه

غرب [1] ghreb *m.* sobbing *idiom* ستوني له غربه ډکبدل to be in despair

غریب [2] gharíb ghəríb *Arabic* **1.1** poor; unhappy, unfortunate, wretched خلق غریب poverty **1.2** strange, unusual; remarkable **2** *m.* [*plural:* غریبان gharibā́n *Arabic plural:* غربا gurabá] **1** poor

man **2.2** poor fellow, poor guy **2.3** alien; foreigner **2.4** *regional* quiet man, mild man

غریبانه gharibāná poor, poverty-stricken غریبانه لوازم impoverished circumstances

غریباني gharibā́ni *f. plural of* غریبه [2]

غریب پروری gharibpālə́na *f.* ☞ غریب پالنه

غریب پرور gharibparvár غریب پروره gharibparvára concerned about the poor

غریب پروری gharibparvarí *f.* concern for the poor

غریب خانه gharibkhāná *m.* my home, the home of your humble servant

غریب کار gharibkā́r *m.* peasant going off to seasonal work and other odd jobs

غریب کاري gharibkārí *f.* day laborer, seasonal and odd-job work (in various types of work which peasants usually do)

غریب گوتی gharibgótaj *m.* poor fellow, poor guy

غریبه [1] gharibá *f. Arabic* [*plural:* غریبي gharibé *plural:* غرائب gharāíb] marvel, rarity

غریبه [2] gharíba **1** *f. singular of* غریب [2] **2** *f. of* غریب [2]

غریبي gharibí *f.* **1** foreign land **2** toil; hired labor غریبي کول to strive, toil څه غریبي کوي؟ What are you doing? What are you busy with? **3** ☞ د خواری او د غریبي **4** غریب کاري poverty, want, need په دپره غریبي کښي ژوند کول to be needy, be impoverished ژوند تېرول to live very poorly; drag out a miserable existence **5** martial song (kind of poetic composition)

غرېچی gharecháj *adjective* **1** mountain **2** *m.* mountaineer, mountain dweller

غرېدل ghəredə́l *intransitive* [*past:* وغرېده *past:* وغرېد] **1** to talk rubbish, talk nonsense **2** to roll, peal (thunder) څومره غرېږي هغومره *proverb* Much noise, little sense. نه ورېږي **3** to bang, crash

غرېده ghəredə́ *m. plural* **1** idle chatter, nonsense, rubbish **2** thunder, rumbling, banging

غریزه gharizá *f. Arabic* [*plural:* غریزي gharizé *m. Arabic plural:* غرائز gharāíz] **1** attraction (to), bent (for) **2** instinct

غریزي [1] gharizí instinctive; natural, innate

غریزي [2] gharizé *plural of* غریزه

غرو [1] ghrev *m.* **1** regret **2** outcry, groaning, weeping ☞ غریب [1]

غربو [2] gharév *m.* roar (e.g., of a tiger, a lion)

غری وري ghə́ri-vári pitted, pocked, pot-holed

غربوژن ghrevzhə́n ☞ غربوناک

غربوناک ghrevnák **1** disturbed, distressed **2** weeping

غر ghər *m.* spitting, expectoration د وینی یو غړ غړ کول to spit blood

غراسپی ghiṛáspaj *m.* platform in a tent or pavilion where dishes and utensils are stored

غراسکی [1] ghṛáskaj *m.* main beam (of a house)

غراسکی [2] ghuṛáskaj *m.* ☞ غراسکی

غراشه ghuṛásha *f.* loop, buttonhole (in clothing)

غراندو ghəṛāndú long-necked

غرانگو gharangú having an unpleasant voice; having a nasty sound, sharp

غرانگور gharāngavə́r ☞ غراندو

غرانگه gharā́nga f. 1 weeping; outcry; groaning 2 noisy uproar 3 roar, bellow (of a camel) غرانگي وهل a to weep; cry out; groan b to create a noisy uproar c to roar, bellow (of a camel)

غرانگه gharā́nga f. long-necked (domestic) animal

غرانگي gharāngí ☞ غراندو 2 غرانگو 1

غرانگۍ gharāngə́j f. long-necked pitcher

غرب ghrab m. pomp, splendor

غارېودجن gharbodzhə́n dialect ☞

غرپ ghrap m. ☞ غورپ

غرپر gharpár m. angry cry

غرپل ghrapə́l transitive ☞ غورپیل

غرپول ghrapavə́l transitive [past: یې غرپول] to gulp down, swallow; drink in gulps اوبه غرپول to drink water in gulps

غرپېدل ghrapedə́l intransitive [past: و غرپېدل] 1 to splash (of water) 2 ☞ غورپېدل

غرت ghrat m. sound emitted in swallowing

غرچ ghrach m. swallowing, gulping down, engulfing, ingesting (food)

غرچول ghrəchavə́l transitive [past: یې غرچاوه] to swallow, gulp down, ingest (food)

غرچول ghrəchavə́l transitive [past: یې غرچاوه] to clatter, clash, rattle (firearms)

غرچی ghrəcháj m. ☞ غرت

غرچېدل ghrəchedə́l intransitive [past: و غرچېد] to be consumed, be ingested (food)

غرخکی ghrətskáj m. peals, claps of thunder

غرخکی ghrətskáj m. 1 splinter, chip 2 mote, speck of dust

غرخکی ghuṛátskaj m. regional cloud

غردی ghardáj braided, plaited

غرز ghraz m. noise of a falling object; crash; rumble

غرزا ghrəzá غرزهار ghrəzahár m. noise made by a falling object

غراسپی ghraspáj m. ☞ غرغر

غرغر gharghár m. ☞ غرغر

غرغره gharghaṛá f. ☞ غرغره

غرک ghrək m. 1 envy 2 spite

غرک gharə́k m. غرکه gharə́ka f. butter churn غرک شربل to churn butter

غرل ghaṛə́l transitive; defective [present: غړي past: غنت] to turn, revolve ☞ غنبتل

غرم ghram m. غرمب ghramb m. ☞ غروم

غرمباری ghrumbāráj noise, din د الوتکي غرمباری the roar (motor noise) of an aircraft

غرمبو ghrambó f. splashing of water غرمبو کول to splash with water

غرمبول ghrambavə́l transitive ☞ غروم بول

غرمبی ghrəmbáj m. rumble, rattle (of gun, cannon fire, etc.); rumbling, roar

غرمبېدل ghrambedə́l intransitive [past: و غرمبېده] 1 to resound; hoot, honk 2 to shout, cry out (in rage)

غرن ghrən ☞ غرند

غرنبېدل ghurumbedə́l intransitive [past: و غرنبېده] to peal, crash (of thunder)

غرنجهار ghrəndzhahár m. snarling, growling (of a dog)

غرند gəṛə́nd 1 fading, withering غرند او مراوي بوټي او ګلونه تازه شوي دي The bushes and flowers which had faded have turned green again 2 dull, sluggish 3 depressed, downcast, dispirited غرند کول a to be conducive to fading b to make sluggish c to hold back, retard idiom غرند تېرول to scorn, despise غرند تېرېدل to make allowance ☞ غرندول

غرندتوب ghəṛəndtób m. غرندتیا ghəṛəndtjā́ f. 1 fading 2 dullness; sluggishness

غرندول ghəṛəndavə́l denominative, transitive [past: غرند یې کړ] 1 to cause fading 2 to cause to be dull or sluggish 3 to retard, hold back

غرنده ghəṛə́ndə 1 revolving 2 shaking; rocking 3 rolling 4 located to the side

غرندی gharandáj m. person with an evil eye

غرندېدل ghəṛəndedə́l denominative, intransitive [past: غرند شو] 1 to fade 2 to be sluggish, be lazy

غرندېده ghəṛəndedə́ m. plural ☞ غرندتوب

غرنگ ghəṛáng m. twisting, rolling (up)

غرنگه ghaṛánga f. ☞ غرانگه

غرنگی ghrangə́j f. dewlap (of a sheep, goat)

غرنه ghəṛə́na f. ☞ غرنگ

غرواندی gharvāndáj m. collar

غروسکه ghrúska f. 1 thick smoke 2 rain cloud

غروشتی ghəṛvashtáj mountain almond, wild almond

غروکی ghaṛúke f. small oil-press

غړول gharavə́l transitive [past: یې غراوه] 1 to roll (the eyes) 2 to open (the eyes) سترگي غړول to open the eyes 3 dialect to roll, slide along 4 to breathe weakly

غروم ghṛum m. غرومب ghṛum m. 1 roar (e.g., of a tiger, lion) غروم وهل to roar 2 rattle, clash, rumble (of firearms) 3 peals (of thunder) 4 splash (of a falling stone in water)

غرومبل ghṛumbə́l transitive [past: یې غرومبل] 1 to eat, chew up food making smacking, munching noises 2 to roar angrily (of a tiger, a lion)

غرومبنه ghṛumbə́na f. roar (of a tiger, lion)

غرومبول ghṛumbavə́l transitive [past: یې غرومباوه] to make roar (a tiger, lion)

غرومبهار ghṛumbəhár m. ☞ غرومب

غرومبی ghṛumbáj m. 1 whirlpool 2 ☞ غرومب

غرومبېدل ghṛumbedə́l intransitive [past: و غرومبېد] 1 to roar (of a tiger, lion) 2 to keep rattling, roaring (etc., of gunfire) 3 to keep pealing (of thunder)

غرومبېدنه ghṛumbedə́na f. غرومبېده ghṛumbedə́ m. plural ☞ غرومب

غړوندی [1] gharandáj *m.* 1 animal collar 2 sukun (name of the supra-linear symbol) ☞ جزم

غړوندی [2] ghŕúndaj *m.* neck (of a bottle)

غړونه gharavóna *f.* 1 opening (the eyes) 2 rolling (the eyes)

غړوونی gharavúnaj *m.* slops

غړی [1] gháṛaj *m.* 1 member (of an organization, society); representative; deputy دايمي غړی، اصلي غړی permanent member, active member (of an academy) ملگری غړی، خبريال غړی corresponding member 2 *anatomy* member, organ 3 extremity 4 calf (of the leg) 5 bread baked in layers (esp. by Ismailities) 6 gap in sowing, gap in plowing *idiom* غړی غړی روغبدل، غړی غړی Are you ته را سره ځي؟ هو، زه غړی غړی پروت يم going with me? Yes, indeed. to rejoice پرېوتل غړی تنبتبدل to be thunderstruck, be rooted to the spot (from fear)

غړی [2] ghaŕój *f.* 1 collar 2 neck (of a pitcher, etc.) 3 neck (of an ostrich, camel, etc.)

غړجاکه gharjáka *f.* ☞ غړنگی

غړيټ ghriṭ *m.* betrayal, deceit; cheating

غړېدل gharedǝl *intransitive* [*past:* و غړېده] 1 to whirl, turn, revolve 2 to move, stir 3 to open up (the eyes) 4 to weaken, grow weak

غړېک ghṛek *m.* 1 loop, buttonhole (on clothing) 2 tab (of sandals) 3 handle (of a scythe)

غړېکور ghṛikavór having a dewlap (of sheep)

غز [1] ghaz *m.* tamarisk tree, *Tamarix indica*

غز [2] ghuz *m.* Western [*plural:* غزان ghuzán *Eastern plural:* غزونه ghuzúna] walnut غز ونه د hazelnut tree

غزا [1] ghazá *f. Arabic religion* ghazawat, holy war, war for the faith

غزا [2] ghǝzá وشوه! غزا It doesn't matter!

غزار ghuzár ☞ غوزار

غزارول ghuzāravól *denominative, transitive* ☞ غوزارول

غزاربدل ghuzāredól *denominative, intransitive* ☞ غوزاربدل

غزال ghizál *m.* 1 young gazelle 2 tender creature, graceful creature

غزکرکی ghuzakarkáj *m. regional* dung beetle

غزل ghazál *m. Arabic literature* ghazal, ode, love poem, lyric poem رباعي، rubai, quatrain ديواني غزل one ghazal of a collection 2 ملي غزل song

غزلچي ghazalchí *m.* غزل خوان ghazalkhán *m.* singer who composes ghazals; singer

غزلسرائي ghazalsarāí *f.* ghazal-singing غزل سرائي ويل a to compose a ghazal b to sing a song

غزلنی ghazlanáj *m.* tamarisk fruit

غزلون ghazlún *m. plural* small tamarisk twigs (used for kindling)

غزله ghazála *f.* ☞ غزل

غزنوي ghaznaví 1 *adjective* Gaznevid (i.e., pertaining to the Gaznevid Dynasty) 2 *m. history* Gaznevids (the Gaznevid Dynasty) محمود غزنوي Mahmoud Gaznevi

غزني ghazní *m.* ghaznáj 1 Gazni (city) 2 Gazni District د غزني ولایت Gazni Province

غزنيچی ghaznicháj *adjective* Gazni غزنيچي پوستين Gazni sheepskin coat

غزول ghazavól *transitive* [*past:* وي يې غزاوه] 1 to lay out, stretch out, lay, put down (a communications line, etc.) 2 to awaken (some feeling, etc.) *idiom* يو کار ته لاس غزول to get down to work

غزونه ghazavóna *f.* غزوني ghazavóne *f.* 1 laying down, stretching (a line of communications, etc.) 2 *Eastern* stretching (upon wakening) 3 غزوني کول awaking (a feeling, etc.) a غزونه کول to stretch (upon waking up) b to awaken (feelings, etc.)

غزی ghóaj *m.* stilt, *Himantopus himantopus* (the bird)

غزېدل ghazedól *intransitive* [*past:* و غزېد] 1 to extend, stretch 2 to stretch out (on the bed)

غزېدنه ghazedóna *f.* lying down, stretching out

غژدي ghizhdí *f.* tent, marquee, pavilion

غژکه ghizháka *f. music* ☞ غجکه

غژغوئی ghazhghvajáj *m.* غژگاو ghazhgáv *m.* yak

غږ ghag *m. Eastern* 1 voice, sound غږ ټيټول to lower the voice 2 cry, shout غږ کول to make noise, shout, raise an alarm غږ نه to not utter a sound or a word په يو چا غږ کول to declare a man to be one's fiancé before witnesses (custom in entering into a marriage without the consent of the family) ☞ بغ

غږپوهاند ghagpohánd *m.* phonetician

غږډاک ghagḍák *m.* voice mail

غږکارټ ghagkāṛt *m. computer science* sound card

غږلويونکی ghaglojavúnkaj 1 intensifying sound 2 *m.* loudspeaker

غږمار ghagmár noisy, loud

غږول ghagavól *transitive* [*past:* وي يې غږاوه] 1 to make to sound, pronounce سندري غږول to ring out, resound د دروازي زنگ غږول to sing 2 to play (an instrument) شپيلی غږول to play the reed-pipe

غږېدا ghagedá *f.* 1 sounding 2 singing 3 play, playing (a musical instrument)

غږېدل ghagedól *intransitive* [*past:* و غږېد] 1 to be heard سرودونه to be heard 2 to speak, converse غږېدي د تليفون په to speak on the telephone 3 to ring out (of bells) ذريعه غږېدل

غږېده ghagedó *m. plural* 1 sounding; phonation, sounds 2 talk, conversation 3 ringing (of a bell)

غږيز ghagiz *adjective* 1 vowel غږيز توري vowels, vowel sounds, phonemes غږيز فونېم vowel phoneme 2 sound غږيزي څپي sound waves

غږيگ ghagig dzhāl *m. computer science* voice network

غس [2] ghus *dialect* ☞ غوټ [1]

غسل ghúsl *m.* ghúsǝl *Arabic* 1 ablution 2 bathing

غسل خانه ghuslkhāná *f.* bathroom

غسول [1] ghasúl *m.* ☞ غاسول

غسول [2] ghusavól *transitive* ☞ غوڅول

غسه [1] ghósa *f.* 1 badger 2 honey bear

غسه [2] ghusá *f.* ☞ غصه

غسه ناک ghusanák ☞ غصه ناک

غشا ghishá *f. Arabic* **1** covering; cover **2** *biology* membrane; membranous tissue

غشائه غوشاند ghushájə *m. plural* ☞ غشائي

غشائي ghishāí *biology* membranous

غشک ghəshk *m.* غشلره ghəshlára *f.* **1** disturbance **2** disorder, alarm

غشو ghəshāv *m.* currycomb (for horses)

غشی ghə́shaj *m.* **1** arrow غشی ويشتل to shoot a bow, shoot an arrow from a bow **2** plow beam **3** needle (of a porcupine) *idiom* پر غشی خورل to encounter a disaster, experience calamity پلار چه مړ شو، غشی مي پر څيگر وخوړ څيگر خوړل to be very distressed When father died all the savor went out of life.

غشت ghə́kht *m.* ☞ غنبتنه¹

غنبتل¹ ghəkhtə́l *transitive* [*present:* غړي *past:* و يې غنبته] **1** to roll, twist **2** to wrap up **3** to wind, revolve **4** to roll, swaddle, plait

غوښتل² ghukhtə́l *transitive* ☞ غوښتل

غنبتلوتوب ghəkhtə́ltób *m.* غنبتلتيا ghəkhtə́ltjá *f.* غنبتلوله ghəkhtə́lvála *f.* غنبتلوالی ghəkhtə́lválaj *m.* **1** strength, power **2** influence **3** nutritiousness (of food)

غنبتلی¹ ghəkhtə́laj **1** strong, powerful, mighty; forceful **2** overpowering; surmounting; overcoming; getting over, overwhelming (i.e., fear, depression) **3** quick, efficient, smart غنبتلی کول a to cause to be strong, cause to be vigorous; strengthen, reinforce b to cause to be quick, cause to be efficient غنبتلی کبدل a to be strong, be vigorous; be strengthened, be augmented b to be quick, be efficient c to master, overcome

غنبتلی² ghəkhtə́laj *past participle of* غنبتل¹

غنبتنه ghəkhtə́na *f.* **1** rolling, turning, twisting **2** wrapping **3** turning, revolving **4** rolling up, swaddling, plaiting د غنبتني تار cord, twine

غوښتنه² ghukhtə́na *f.* ☞ غوښتنه

غنبته¹ ghə́khta *f.* small braids on the brow (of a female)

غنبته² ghə́khtə *imperfect of* غنبتل¹

غنبتی ghə́khtaj **1** strong, vigorous **2** twisted, plaited

غصب ghasb *m. Arabic* **1** seizure, appropriation, usurpation **2** confiscation غصب کول a to seize, appropriate b to confiscate

غصبول ghasbavə́l *denominative, transitive* [*past:* غصب يې کړ] **1** to seize, appropriate, usurp **2** to confiscate

غصه ghussá *f. Arabic* **1** grief, affliction غصه به ورتله He was distressed. He was upset. **2** anger, rage ما غصه اوبسکله *regional* I contained my rage. غصه کبدل *compound verb* a to be upset, be distressed b غصه کبري به نه؟ You'll not be upset? b to fall into a rage, become irate

غصه ناک ghussanák **1** grieved, upset **2** angry, enraged

غضب ghazáb *m. Arabic* rage; irritation په ډېر غضب سره irately, with anger په قهر او غضب کبدل to fall into a rage

غضبناک ghazabnák incensed; angry, irritated

غضروف ghuzrúf *m. Arabic* cartilage, gristle

غضروفي غضروف لرونکی ghuzrúf larúkaj غضروفدار ghuzrúfdấr غضروفي ghuzrufí **1** cartilaginous **2** gristly

غضنفر ghazanfár *m. Arabic* **1** lion **2** *proper name* Ganzanfar

غفار ghaffấr *Arabic* **1** All-Forgiving (epithet of God) **2** *m. proper name* Gafar

غفران ghufrấn *m. Arabic religion* total forgiveness, remission of sins

غفلت ghaflát *m. Arabic* **1** inattention, carelessness, neglect; unconcern; neglectfulness **2** sluggishness, stagnation

غفور ghafúr *Arabic* **1** All-Forgiving (epithet of God) **2** *m. proper name* Ghafur

غک ghək *m.* غکا ghəkấ *f.* bleating (of a goat)

غکل ghakə́l *transitive* [*present:* غاکي *past:* و يې غکل] to bleat (of a goat)

غکول ghəkavə́l *transitive* [*past:* و يې غکاوه] to cause to bleat (of a goat)

غکبدل ghəkedə́l *intransitive* [*past:* وغکبده] to bleat (of a goat)

غکبدنه ghekedə́na *f.* bleating (of a goat)

غگ ghag *m. Eastern* ☞ غږ

غگبدل ghagedə́l *intransitive Eastern* ☞ غږبدل

غل¹ gal *m.* [*plural:* غله ghlə] thief, robber, bandit, marauder ته مي غل کبدل You have robbed me. a to be a thief b to do someone a bad turn ډېر ځله مي تويک غل شو I erred several times. پټ غل بادشاه دئ *proverb* You are only a thief if you get caught. د غله ته د غره کبني ځای نشته *proverb literal* Even in the mountains a thief cannot hide. *figurative* Murder will out.

غل² ghul *m. plural dialect* ☞ غول¹

غل³ ghul *m.* ☞ غلغل

غل⁴ ghil *m. Arabic* **1** envy **2** meanness, baseness

غلا ghlā *f.* [*plural:* غلاوي ghlấvi *plural:* غلاگاني ghlāgā́ni] **1** theft, robbery; banditry, brigandage دا بشپړه غلا ده This is regular robbery. د غلا شيان stolen goods, pilfered goods د غلا عادت kleptomania غلا کول a to commit theft, commit robbery b *compound verb* to rob, steal something غلا کبدل a to occur (of a theft) b *compound verb* to be stolen چه غلا يي وشوه، نو څوکبدار يي وساتلو *proverb Eastern literal* They stationed a guard after the theft. *figurative* to lock the barn door after the horse has been stolen په غلا تلل to be stolen, be swiped په غلا ورل to swipe, pinch **2** something secret, something done in secret په غلاغلا by theft چا په غلا in secret from someone *idiom* ځان د مشکلاتو څخه غلا کول to avoid difficulties, circumvent obstacles

غلات ghallā́t *m. Arabic plural of* غله¹

غلاظت ghilāzát *m. Arabic* **1** dirt **2** thickness, density **3** rudeness, sharpness (of manner, speech)

غلاغوندک ghlāghundák *m.* ☞ غلچک

غلاف ghilā́f *m. Arabic* **1** sheath; case; cover د برچي غلاف bayonet case, bayonet sheath د ماشيندار غلاف machine-gun cover **2** envelope, jacket

غلاگرکی ghlāgarkáj *m. regional* robber, thief

غلام ghulā́m *m. Arabic* [*plural:* غلامان ghulāmā́n *Arabic plural:* غلمان ghilmā́n] 1 slave, serf 2 servant 3 *epistolary* your obedient servant 4 *proper name* Gulam

غلامانه ghulāmāná 1 slave-like غلامانه ذهنیت slave-psychology 2 servile, slavish

غلام بچه ghulāmbachá *m.* page (i.e., kind of servant in former times)

غلامول ghulāmavə́l *denominative, transitive* [*past:* غلام یې کړ] to enslave someone

غلامي ghulāmí *f.* slavery, servile state

غلانځور ghulāndzavə́r غلانځور حیوانات mammals

غلانځه ghulā́ndza *f.* غلانزه ghulā́nza *f.* ☞ غولانځه

غلاوزه¹ ghlā́uza *f.* wasp, bee

غلاوزه² ghlā́vza *f.* cow yielding little milk

غلبله ghalbalá *f.* shouts, outcries; rumpus, uproar وهل to shout, cry out; make a din, create a disturbance, cause an uproar

غلبنگی ghulbangə́j *f.* toilet, latrine

غلبه ghalabá *f. Arabic* victory پر چا غلبه کول to conquer, attain victory over someone; prevail over someone; overcome someone د والی پال په لویه کښې غلبه موندل to win a victory غلبه میندل to gain a victory a volleyball match

غلبیل ghalbél *m.* sieve, strainer; sifter غلبیل پاخي، کوزي ته وايي تا کښني دوه سوړي دي غلبیل پاخي، کوزي ته وايي په تا کښني دوه سوړي دي *proverb Eastern literal* The sieve stands up and speaks to the pitcher: "You have two holes." *figurative* The pot calling the kettle black. غلبیل کول full of holes غلبیل غلبیل to make a hole in, pierce غلبیل کېدل to be full of holes, become full of holes

غلبیلوالا ghalbelvālā́ *m.* seller of sieves and strainers

غلبیلول ghalbelavə́l *denominative, transitive* [*past:* غلبیل یې کړ] 1 to strain 2 to put through a sieve or strainer, use a sifter اوبه غلبیلول to waste one's time on something useless, to pound water in a mortar

غلت ghult *m. regional* deceit, cheating (esp. in gambling)

غلتوب ghaltób *m.* thievery, robbery, brigandage

غلجي ghildzhí 1 *m. plural* Gilzai (group of tribes) 2 ghildzháj *m.* Gilzai (tribesman)

غلچک ghalchák *m.* petty thief

غلچکی ghalchakáj 1 *m.* petty thief 2.1 examining stealthily, scrutinizing furtively 2.2 accomplished by stealth غلچکی نظر اچول to spy upon

غلچه ghalchá *m.* galcha, dweller in the Pair د غلچه ژبي the Pair languages

غلخور ghulkhór *m. regional vulgar* liar

غلزي ghə́lzí *m. plural* غلزیان gə́lzijā́n *m. plural* Gilzai, members of the Gilzai tribe

غلشکه ghləshká *f.* hulled wheat

غلط ghalát *Arabic* 1 *m.* [*plural:* غلطونه ghalatúna *Arabic plural:* اغلاط aghlā́t] error, mistake که می غلط نه کئ If I am not mistaken. 2 *attributive, predicative* erroneous, mistaken, untrue,

faulty, defective غلط توری misprint, typographical error دا غلطه خبره ده to be mistaken This is untrue. This is incorrect. پوهېدل په غلطه لار روانېدل to take the wrong road

غلطفهمي ghalatfamí *f.* 1 error, mistake 2 misunderstanding

غلطوالی ghalatvā́laj *m.* erroneousness, incorrectness

غلطول ghalatavə́l *denominative, transitive* [*past:* غلط یې کړ] 1 to confuse, mix up ډاکټر یې مرض غلط کړئ The doctor made an incorrect diagnosis. دا سړی که می غلط نه کئ د احمد ورور دئ This man, unless I am in error, is Ahmed's brother. لار غلطول to go wrong, stray from the path 2 to deceive, lead into error 3 to distract پام په نورو شیانو غلطول to be distracted

غلطه ghaláta 1 *feminine singular of* غلط 2 *f.* error, mistake په غلطه سره mistakenly

غلطي¹ ghalatí *f.* mistake, error طباعتي غلطي misprint, typographical error فاحشه غلطي a gross error *idiom* را نه غلطي وشوه I made a blunder.

غلطي² ghaláti *feminine plural of* غلط 2

غلطیا ghalatjā́ *f.* mistake

غلطېدل ghalatedə́l *denominative, intransitive* [*past:* غلط شو] 1 to make a mistake; go astray, err 2 to miscount, miscalculate 3 to be confused لار را څخه غلطه شوه I strayed from the path. I fell into error.

غلطېدنه ghalatedə́na *f.* غلطېده ghalatedə́ *m. plural* 1 commission of an error; error 2 miscalculation, miscount 3 illusion (optical, etc.)

غل غدوی ghalghadúj *m.* robber, bandit

غلغني ghalghə́kháj *m.* superfluous tooth

غلغل ghulghúl *m.* غلغله ghulghulá *f.* غل غول ghalghúl *m.* noise, uproar; disturbance غلغل کول to raise a ruckus; instigate a riot

غلگی ghalgáj *m.* petty thief

غلمان ghilmā́n *m. Arabic* 1 *plural of* غلام 2 *religion* youths in paradise

غلمی ghalmáj *m.* cockspur (a plant used for soap), *Echinochloa, Anabasis multiflora*

غلمینه ghalmína *f.* wheaten bread

غلنی¹ ghalanáj 1 shirking work, goldbricking 2 thievish (of an animal)

غلنی² ghalanáj *f.* waterfowl, aquatic bird

غلو¹ ghulúv *m. Arabic* 1 excess, extreme غلو کول to be extreme 2 immoderation

غلو² ghló ghəló *oblique plural of* غل¹

غلو³ ghalló *oblique plural of* غله¹

غلوخه ghlávdza *f.* ghlódza bee

غلولول ghulavə́l *transitive* ☞ غولول

غله¹ ghalá *f.* ghallá *Arabic* [*plural:* غلي ghalé *plural:* ghallé *m. plural:* غله جات ghaladzhā́t *plural:* ghalladzhā́t *Arabic plural:* غلات ghalā́t *plural:* ghallā́t] 1 whole-grain bread, grain 2 food, comestibles

غله² ghla *f.* petty thief

غله ³ ghulá *f.* log, billet

غله ⁴ ghlə *plural of* غل ¹

غله ⁵ ghúla *dialect* pal, buddy (informal form of address)

غله ⁶ ghlə ghla *separable parts of the verbs* راتلل، درتلل and ورتلل *in the past tense*

غله باب ghalabáb ghallabáb whole-grain bread, grain

غله بود ghalabúd ghallabúd fruitful, productive (of land)

غله خرڅونکی ghalá khartsavúnkaj *m.* grain merchant

غله خېز ghalakhéz ghallakhéz ☞ غله بود

غله دان ghaladán *m.* ghalladán millwheel casing

غله شگه ghla shə́ga *f.* quicksand

غله فروش ghalafurush *m.* ghallafurúsh grain merchant

غلی ¹ ghulə́j *f.* whirlpool

غلی ² ghalé ghallé *plural of* غله ¹

غلی ³ ghə́laj 1 quiet, tranquil; taciturn غلی تېرول to avoid, get around something by silence, keep mum about something 2 somber, sad, gloomy 3 withdrawn, not frank 4 acting secretly, acting surreptitiously 5 concealing oneself, hiding oneself ځان ورته غلی کول، غلی کښېنستل to conceal oneself, sit in ambush توپ غلی کول a to calm, soothe, make to be quiet b to suppress شورش غلی کول *military* to mine, set mines کول to put down a rebellion c to drive into a corner (in a dispute) غلی کېدل a to grow calm, be soothed, calm down; fall silent; abate b to be hidden, be concealed, be secreted; sit in ambush c to cease, die down, subside 6 extinct (of a volcano)

غلی ⁴ ghle غلی ghləj *the separable part of the verbs* راتلل، درتلل and ورتلل *in the past tense*

غلیا ghə́ljá *f.* silence

غلیان ¹ ghaliján *m. Arabic* boiling د غلیان حد *physics* boiling point د احساساتو غلیان *idiom* agitation

غلیان ² ghaliján *m.* water pipe, hookah

غلیب ghleb *m.* deceit, betrayal غلیب خورل to be betrayed, be deceived غلیب ورکول to betray, deceive

غلی توب ghə́lajtób *m.* silence

غلیچ ghlech strong, healthy

غلی دان ghaledán *m.* ghalledán 1 moneybox 2 till

غلیدل ghuledə́l *intransitive* [*past:* و غلیده] to be deceived, be betrayed ☞ غولېدل

غلیظ ghalíz *Arabic* thick, dense; thickened, condensed

غلی غچی ghə́le-ghə́che *f. plural* evasion, avoidance

غلی غلی ghə́laj-ghə́laj 1 secretly, surreptitiously 2 hiding oneself

غلی غلیا ghə́leghə́ljá *f.* quiet, silence

غلیلاک ghə́lilák *m.* 1 attack 2 crossing, violation (of a border)

غلیم ghalím *m.* enemy, foe, adversary

غلیمانه ghalimáná inimical, hostile; antagonistic

غلیمتوب ghalimtób *m.* غلیمتیا ghalimtjá *f.* enmity; hostility

غلیمه ghalíma *f. feminine of* غلیم

غلیمي ghalimí *f.* ☞ غلیمتوب

غلیواج ghalivádzh *m.* kite (bird)

غلئ ghalaí *f.* ghallaí *regional economics* rent-in-kind

غم gham *m.* ghamm *Arabic* 1 grief, sadness, melancholy; sorrow; misfortunes د چا په غم کښ yearning for someone, missing somebody زمونږ په هر غم کښ شریک و He always sympathized with us in our misfortune. زړه نه مي غم واچولو *Eastern* I grieved deeply. غم غلطول a to dispel melancholy; forget grief; forget sorrows b to be diverted غم گالل to suffer misfortunes; endure unpleasantness پردی غم د واورو سور دئ، پردی غم نیم اختر دئ *proverb literal* Another's grief is colder than snow. Another's grief is almost a holiday. *figurative* Another's grief does not give one pain. په چا غم، په چا اختر *proverb* Grief to some, joy to others. 2 care; concern د چا یوجهان غمونه a whole lot of cares, a mass of worries غم خورل a to be concerned about someone b to sympathize with someone هیڅ غم مه کوه! غم مه خوره! Don't grieve! Don't be sad! Be in no way sad! Don't get downcast! غم ورسره کول to be concerned about someone, be worried about something 3 *history* tax, duty کوری غم head tax, poll tax سری غم dwelling tax غم ورکول to require duty, exact the payment of tax غم غپیول to pay tax, pay duty *idiom* غم غپیول to solve (e.g., a problem), resolve (e.g., a question)

غماز ghammáz *m. Arabic* informer, snitch; slanderer; gossipmonger

غمازک ghamāzák *m.* float

غماز ¹ ghammāzí *m.* ☞ غماز

غمازي ² ghammāzí *f.* informing, act of informing; slander; gossip, scandal

غماشه ghumásha *f.* mosquito, gnat

غمباده ghambādá *f.* tumor in the abdominal cavity

غمبسه ghumbə́sa *f.* bumblebee

غمبوری ghəmbúraj *m.* heap, pile

غمبه ghumbá *f.* ☞ غومبه

غمجن ghamdzhə́n *f.* sad, grief-stricken, upset; sorrowful د پلار د مرگ څخه غمجن کېدل to be saddened by the death of a father *idiom* غمجنه ورځ a bad day b calamity

غمجنوالی ghamdzhənvā́laj *m.* grief, affliction

غمجنول ghamdzhənavə́l *denominative, transitive* [*past:* غمجن یې کړ] to grieve, sadden, upset

غمجنېدل ghamdzhənedə́l *denominative, intransitive* [*past:* غمجن شو] to be grieved, be upset, be saddened

غمچینه ghamchína *m.* whip

غمزپلئ ghamzapə́ləj غم زېلئ ☞

غمخوار ghamkhuár sympathizing

غمخواري ghamkhuārí *f.* ☞ غمخوري

غمخور ghamkhór concerned, caring, attentive, sympathetic, responsive

غمخورگي ghamkhuragí *f.* غمخوري ghamkhorí *f.* concern, care

غمر ghamár *m.* crybaby

غمزپلئ ghamzapə́ləj saddened, grieved; grief-stricken غم زېلئ ☞

غمزن ghamzhə́n *dialect* ☞ غمجن

غمشریک ghamsharík empathetic, sympathetic, responsive

520

غمشریکي ghamsharikí *f.* 1 condolence; sympathy; consolation د غمشریکي خط a letter of condolence 2 responsiveness

غم غلطي ghamghalatí *f.* entertainment, diversion

غم کش ghamkásh concerned, caring حسن غم کش *folklore* Good Hassan (caring about others)

غمجن ghamgín ☞ غمگین

غمگیني ghamginí *f.* grief

غم لړلئ ghamlaṛóləj ☞ غمجن

غمناک ghamnâk sorrowful, sad غمناکي سترګي sad eyes

غمور ghamavór extremely saddened

غمول ghamavól *transitive* [*past:* و یي غماوه] 1 to grieve; sadden 2 to trouble, worry

غمی ghamáj *m.* 1 precious stone in a signet ring 2 seal 3 *proper name* Ghamai

غمېدل ghamedól *intransitive* [*past:* و غمېده] 1 to be burdened, be hampered 2 to be worried 3 to overeat

غمی والا ghamajvâlâ *m.* ring merchant

غنا ghanấ *f. Arabic* wealth; prosperity; property *idiom* ازادي خپله غنا ګڼل to treasure one's freedom

غناشکي ghənấshki *f. plural* 1 slowly flowing water 2 water percolating through a dam or dike

غنایم ghanāím *m. Arabic plural of* غنیمت

غنائي ghināí 1 lyrical; songful 2 pathetic

غمبۀسه ghimbə́sa *f.* ☞ غمبسه

غنجالی gandzhālój *f.* swing (child's toy)

غنځاښی ghundzāḳháj *m. usually plural* غنځاښي ghundzāḳhí sweet bread cooked in butter

غندل 1 ghandál *m.* 1 stalk, stem (of a plant) 2 cartilage (nasal) 3 *proper name* Ghandal

غندل 2 ghendól [*past:* و یي غانده] *transitive* to defame; denigrate, abuse, censure, criticize, run down

غندلغاړه ghandalghâṛa *f.* long neck (of a person)

غندل غاړی ghandalghāṛáj 1 long-necked (person) 2 *m. dialect* handsome youth; stately youth

غندنه ghəndóna *f.* criticism; censure; reproach

غندو ghandú *Western* raving, rambling

غندوی ghandóvaj *m.* watercress

غندی 1 ghundáj *m.* bag, sack

غوندي 2 ghúndi ☞ غوندي 2

غنډ 1 ghunḍ *m. Eastern* timber, beam

غنډ 2 ghunḍ *m. military* regiment هوايي غنډ to mine, set mines د طیارو غنډ aviation regiment

غوند 3 ghunḍ ☞ غوند

غنډاری ghunḍā́raj *m.* ☞ غونډاري 1

غنډایه 1 ghənḍā́ja *f.* freak, monster

غنډایه 2 ghunḍājə́ *m.* 1 juvenile, lad 2 youth assisting a plowman, plowboy 3 freak, monster

غنډژبی ghunḍzhə́baj babbling, speaking with confused articulation ☞ غونډژبی

غنډوسکی ghunḍə́skaj *m. Eastern* ball

غنډک ghunḍák *m.* tarantula

غنډکی ghunḍakáj *f.* 1 hillock; knoll; mound 2 round object; lump, ball

غنډل ghunḍál *m.* ☞ غنډک

غنډمشر ghunḍmáshr *m.* ghunḍmáshər colonel دوهم غنډمشر lieutenant colonel

غنډمشري ghunḍməshrí *f.* rank of colonel ابتدائي غنډمشري، دوهمه the rank of lieutenant colonel لمړی غنډمشري the rank of colonel

غنډ مند ghunḍ-múnd *dialect* ☞ غوند مند

غنډوسکه ghunḍúska *f.* kind of ballgame

غنډول ghunḍavól *transitive* ☞ غونډول

غنډوی ghunḍə́vaj *m.* ☞ غندوی

غنډه 1 ghanḍá́ *f.* kind of melon

غنډه 2 ghúnḍa *f.* stout woman; heavy woman

غنډه 3 ghunḍá́ *m.* ghunḍagán [*plural:* غنډګان ghunḍagán] *regional* hooligan

غنډی 1 ghunḍój *f.* hill; hillock

غنډی 2 ghunḍáj *m.* ☞ غندک

غنډېدل ghunḍedól *intransitive* ☞ غوندېدل

غنزاښی ghunzā́ḳhaj *m.* ☞ غنځاښی

غنکی ghankáj *m. hunting* decoy (for luring quail)

غنګ ghəng *m.* 1 sound made by a metal object 2 echo

غنګا ghəngā́ *m.* echo

غنګوری ghangúraj *m.* ear lobe

غنګهار ghangəhār *m.* 1 ringing; tapping 2 echo

غنم ghanóm *m. plural* wheat د ژمي غنم winter wheat د پسرلي غنم spring wheat لپوني غنم wild rye غنم ښکاره کول او تور غنم rye اوریشي خرڅول *proverb literal* to display wheat, but sell barley *figurative* to pass off one thing as another

غنم رنګ ghanəmráng غنم رنګی ghanəmrángaj غنم غونی ghanəmghúnaj dark-complexioned, bronzed, suntanned

غنم ګره ghanəmgára *f.* wheat field

غنم والا ghanəmvâlâ seller of wheat, wheat merchant

غنمین ghanəmín wheaten

غنمینه ghanəmína *f.* wheatbread, wheaten bread

غنویري ghanvíri *f. plural* young sprouts, shoots

غنه ghóna *f.* 1 thornbush 2 thorn hedge; living fence 3 sharp thorn

غني 1 ghə́ni *f. plural* 1 *of* غنه 2 clumps of thornbushes

غني 2 ghaní 1 rich, prosporous غني کول to enrich غني کېدل to grow rich, become rich 2 *m.* .1 [*plural:* غنیان ghaníjân *Arabic plural:* اغنیا aghnijā́] rich man 2.2 *proper name* Ghani

غنی 3 ghónaj *m.* spider

غنی 4 ghanój *f.* 1 thornbush hedge 2 coral milky cap (mushroom)

غني ترین ghanitarín very rich, richest

غنیمت ghanimát *m. Arabic* [*plural:* غنیمتونه ghanimatúna *Arabic plural:* غنائم ghanāím] 1 bag (hunting), catch (fishing), trophy 2 propitious, favorable occasion, moment وخت غنیمت ګڼل to take advantage of a favorable occasion **3** good, good deed دا کتاب غنیمت دئ This book is a real find.

غڼاسکي ghuṇā́ski *f. plural* غڼاسکي وهل to trudge, drag, trail

غنه ghə́na *f.* غنې ghə́ne *f.* spider د غڼي تار توره غنه spiderweb *dialect* tarantula

غو ghav *m.* kind of shashlik cooked under hot sand in a sheep's stomach

غوا ghvā *f.* [*plural:* غواوي ghvā́vi *plural:* غواګاني ghvāgā́ni *dialect plural:* غوا ghvā] cow ما کله د چا ملاسته غوا هم نه ده پاڅولې *saying literal* I never roused anyone's resting cow. *figurative* I never injured anybody. I am a completely harmless man. *idiom* غوا یې د غوا شرع جوړول لنګه سوه He lucked out. to inflate some matter

غوابيـږی ghvābízhaj *m.* snail

غوارودوني ghvārodúne *f.* round-head (lizard)

غوارـ ghvāṛ *present stem of* غوښتل

غوارڼه ghvāṛə́na *f.* hope

غوابنکی ghvāx̌káj *m.* eye (of a needle)

غواګۍ ghvāgə́j *f.* small cow, little cow

غوالوشه ghvālvásha *f.* milk pail

غوایان ghvajā́n *m. plural* غوایه ghvājə́ *m. plural* **1** *of* غویی **2** horned cattle

غویی ghvajáj *m. dialect* ☞

غویی ghvají *plural and oblique singular of* غویی

غوایتوب ghvajitób *m.* stupidity غوایی توب کول to act stupidly غوایی توب مه کوه! Don't be stupid!

غوایژبه ghvājizhə́ba *f.* غوایی ژبی ghvājizhə́bə́j *f. botany* oxtongue, *Anchusa officinalis*

غوایی سترګه ghvājistə́rga *f.* oxeye daisy, *Chrysanthemum leucanthemum*

غوایی ښکر ghvājix̌kə́r *m.* orchid, *Epipactis palustris*

غوایی والا ghvājivālā́ *m.* owner of an ox

غوباړی ghobā́ṛaj *m.* gadfly, horsefly

غوبانـه ghobānə́ *plural of* غویون

غوباڼی ghobā́ṇaj *m.* ☞ غویاری

غوبری ghobə́raj *m.* cheek

غوبل ghobál *m.* **1** grinding, crushing (with the assistance of oxen) **2** mill, crush, crowd, mass of people jammed together غویل جوړول **a** to arrange a jam (a crowded affair) **b** to behave brutally **3** hot argument, polemic

غوبلول ghobalavə́l *denominative, transitive* [*past:* غویل یې کړ] **1** to grind up, crush د قلبي په غویو غویلول to grind up by means of oxen-power **2** to break up, wear down

غوبلیدل ghobaledə́l *denominative, intransitive* [*past:* غویل شو] **1** to be ground up, be milled (by oxen-power) **2** to be broken up

غوبنه ghobaná *f.* shepherdess

غوبني ghobaní *f.* herding (cattle)

غوبنی ghobanáj *m.* ☞ غویون

غوبنی ghobané *plural of* غوبنه

غوبون ghobún *m.* غوبه ghobá *m.* غوبـه ghobə́ *m.* [*plural:* غوبانه ghobānə́] herdsman, cowherd; drover

غوپول ghupavə́l *denominative, transitive* to dip, plunge into, sink (into) (water or some other liquid)

غوپه ghupá *f.* ☞ غوته²

غوتی ghutáj *f.* powder-horn, powder flask

غوت¹ ghoṭ ☞ غټ¹

غوټ² ghvuṭ ghvəṭ **1** cut off غوټ نیم که! Cut it in half! غوټه to cut, cleave **2** decisive, categorical, definite; conclusively غوټ ماتول to speak decisively, categorically *idiom* خبره کول to rout, smash

غوټ په غوټ ghvuṭ-pə-ghvuṭ ghvəṭ-pə-ghvə́t decisively, categorically, definitely; conclusively غوټ په غوټ ویل to speak decisively, talk categorically

غوټ کوټ ghvəṭ-kvə́ṭ stout and ruddy; picture of health

غوټن ghuṭə́n **1** knotty, in small knots **2** intricate, involved

غوټندی ghuṭə́ndáj **1** plunging (into water or some other liquid); diving; dipping (in) **2** *m.* submarine

غوټو ghuṭú *m.* throat; gullet

غوټول ghvəṭavə́l *denominative, transitive* [*past:* غوټ یې کړ] to make fat, make stout; feed up, fatten up

غوټه¹ ghúṭa **1** *f.* **.1** knot, small knot (in thread, rope) غوټه اچول to tie a knot غوټه کلکول to tighten a knot **1.2** fastener; button خلاصول **a** to untie (a knot) **b** to undo **c** to sort out (a matter) **d** to execute, carry out (something difficult) غوټه خلاصیدل **a** to be untied (of a knot); come undone **b** to be unfastened; come undone **c** to get sorted out (of a matter, affair) **d** to be executed, be accomplished (of something difficult) غوټه کول **a** to link, tie up **b** to tie to **c** to fasten to غوټه کېدل *compound verb* **a** to be tied, be tied up **b** to be tied to **c** to be fastened (to) **1.3** hump (of a camel) **1.4** cone (pine) **2** *predicative* **.1** linked, tied, fastened **2.2** tied to **2.3** fastened (to) *idiom* د زړه په سر غوټه آرزو secret dream د زړه ټولي غوټي سپړل to open up the heart (to), confide one's inner thoughts (to) **a** to wrinkle the brow **b** to make an unpleasant face تندی غوټه کول

غوټه² ghuṭá *f.* **1** plunging (into water or some other liquid); diving غوټه خوړل to dive; be dipped **2** attack, falling upon غوټه کول **a** to be plunged (into water or other liquid); dive; be dipped **b** to attack, fall upon, throw oneself upon someone **c** *compound verb* to plunge, sink into (some liquid or other) غوټه کېدل *compound verb* **a** to be plunged (into some liquid or other, i.e., water); dive; be dipped **b** to attack; fall upon someone غوټه وهل **a**, ☞ غوټه کول **b**

غوټی¹ ghuṭáj *f.* **1** bud **2** drop (of sweat, etc.) **3** navel **4** *proper name* Ghutai *idiom* د ځوانۍ غوټی یې غوړېږي She is becoming a real beauty.

غوټی² ghuṭə́j *f.* scarf, shawl

غوټیالی¹ ghuṭjālə́j *f.* **1** necklace **2** breed of goat having a dewlap

غوټیالی² ghuṭjālə́j *m.* dewlap

غوث ghaus *m. Arabic* **1** help, assistance **2** patron, protector **3** *proper name* Ghaus

غوجر ghodzhár *m.* saline soil

غوجل ghodzhál *f.* غوجله ghodzhála *f.* ghudzhála *f.* cow barn, cowshed; sheepfold

غوچ¹ ghvəch ghuch *m.* ☞ قوچ

غوچ² ghavzh ghuch deep (of a river, a well, etc.)

غوچالی ghavchálaj *m.* غوچانی ghavchánaj *m.* pit

غوچواله ghavchvála *f.* غوچوالی ghuchválaj *m.* depth د بحر غوچواله the depth of the sea

غوچول ghavchavál *denominative, transitive* [*past:* غوچ یې کړ] to deepen, make deeper

غوچه¹ ghavchá *f. agriculture* brood

غوچه² ghúchi غوچي ghúchi *regional* well, so, well that's it

غوچیدل ghavchedál *denominative, intransitive* [*past:* غوچ شو] to deepen, become deeper

غوزاریدل ghudzāredál *intransitive* ☞ غوځاریدل

غوزاریده ghudzāredə *m. plural* ☞ غوځاریده

غوځی ghudzáj *m.* ☞ غوزی¹

غوځ ghvəts ☞ غوت¹

غوڅاوو ghvətsāvu cutting, sharp

غوڅکی ghutskáj *m.* steer

غوڅول ghvətsavál **1** [*past:* غوڅ یې کړ] *denominative, transitive* **1.1** to cut, cut out, cut off **1.2** to sever, interrupt **1.3** to solve, decide (question, problem) نوم غوڅول to choose a name **2** *m. plural* **2.1** cutting, cutting off; hewing off **2.2** severing, interruption **2.3** blow (of a saber); saber-cut *idiom* توره په اصل غوڅول کوي *proverb literal* A chip off the old block. *figurative* Like father, like son. په خپله توره یې ځان غوڅ کړ *saying* He punished himself.

غوڅه ghvátsa *f.* ☞ غوڅیده

غوڅیدل ghvátsedál *denominative, intransitive* [*past:* غوڅ شو] **1** to be cut, be hewn off **2** to be interrupted **3** to be decided, be solved (of a question, problem)

غوڅیده ghvátsedə *m. plural* **1** cutting off; hewing off **2** interruption **3** solution (of a problem, question)

غوښتل ghukhtál *transitive* ☞ غوښتل

غوډل¹ ghoḍál *m.* tarantula

غوډل² ghoḍál *m.* crops before the ears or fruit ripen

غوډلی ghoḍáláj *m.* **1** ear of reed-mace **2** ear of unripe maize (for boiling)

غور¹ ghaur *m. Arabic* discussion; examination; consideration په... کښي غور کول، په... باندي غور کول، پر... باندي غور کول to discuss, examine; consider غور کیدل to be discussed, be examined **2** investigation

غور² ghor *m. history* Ghur, Ghor (province, northern Afghanistan) د غور ولایت Ghur Province

غور³ ghur *m.* **1** goiter **2** burden هغه د غاړي غور شوئ دئ He became a burden. *idiom* غور کول to be ashamed of something

غور⁴ ghur *m.* **1** thunder **2** roar, bellow (of a camel)

غورات ghurát *m. plural* Ghorat (district)

غوراډاپی ghurāḍāpí *f.* bragging

غورانگه ghuránga flame

غوراوي ghwarāwi *f. plural computer science* options

غوربند ghorbánd *m.* Ghorbend, Ghurbend (river, district)

غوربړ ghurbéṛ *m.* **1** crowd **2** herd, flock

غورپژ ghvərpázh *m.* noise, hubbub

غورچي ghurchí *m.* ☞ غوریالی²

غورڅکه ghurzáka *f.* **1** tongue of flame سره غورڅکه flame **2** spark

غورڅنگ ghurdzáng *m.* **1** leap; jump; dash غورڅنگ کول to leap; jump; make a dash په دښمن غورڅنگونه کول to dash, dart at, throw oneself at the enemy **2** breaker, wave زړه یې په غورڅنگ کنپوتئ، His heart fell. زړه یې په غورڅنگ پربوتئ

غورڅول ghurdzavál *transitive* [*past:* و یي غورڅاوه] **1** to throw, fling, hurl; toss غورڅول ځان سیند ته to throw oneself in the river ځان پر چا غورڅول to throw, hurl oneself at someone **2** to take off, doff (e.g., clothing, hat) **3** to miscarry, abort (of an animal) **4** to defer, put off (e.g., an examination or inspection of something) **5** to evoke (e.g., dissent, discord) **6** to cause to fall into (amazement)

غورڅی¹ ghurdzáj *m.* **1** agitation, worry **2** throw, toss **3** unwinding (e.g., of thread) **4** leaps, jumps (in a dance) **5** flood, freshet

غورڅي² ghurdzí *present tense of* غورڅیدل

غورڅئ³ ghvurdzəj Go get 'em! (cry used in battle or in fun)

غورڅي پرڅي ghurdzé-pərdzé *f. plural* efforts, attempts

غورڅیدل ghurdzedál ghvurdzedál *intransitive* [*past:* وغورڅیده] **1** to spring, leap up, jump, come sailing by تر واله غورڅیدل to spring through a channel (of the aryk, i.e., native Afghan irrigation system) **2** to be thrown, be tossed و بلي خوا ته غورڅیدل to be thrown across **3** to gallop, fly away **4** to fall apart, fall; fall out **5** to pound, beat (of the heart) **6** to be thrown off, be cast away; fall off, drop off غورڅیدل بیرته to set back, recede

غورڅیده ghurdzedə ghvurdzedə *m. plural* **1** springing, leaping up, jumping **2** throwing, tossing; throwing off **3** galloping away, flying away **4** falling **5** beating (the heart)

غوررسي ghaurrasí *f.* inspection, investigation

غورزنگ ghurzáng *m.* **1** ☞ غورڅنگ **2** pressure

غورزول ghurzavúl *transitive* ☞ غورڅول

غورزه ghurzá *m. plural* setting (of the sun)

غورزي پرزي ghurzé-porzé *f. plural* ☞ غورڅي پرڅي

غورزیدل ghurzedál *intransitive regional* ☞ غورڅیدل

غورس ghvərs fat, stout غورس کول to get fat غورس کیدل to become fat, stout

غورسول ghvərsavál *denominative, transitive* [*past:* غورس یې کړ] to thicken, fatten

غورسیدل ghvərsedál *denominative, intransitive* [*past:* غورس شو] to be thickened

غورغوشت ghorghúsht *m.* play, fun, amusement

غورغوښتی ghorghuҳtáj *m.* almond tree

غورغۍ ghurghә́j *f.* ring, hoop

غورلندسه ghvərlandә́sa *f.* large flame

غورله انا ghvərlaaná ghvurlaaná *f.* great-grandmother

غورمچ ghvərmә́ch *m.* gadfly, horsefly

غورمه ghaurmá ghormá *f.* roast meat

غورنۍ ghwaranә́j *f.* *computer science* menu

غورنیکه ghvərnikә́ *m.* great-grandfather

غوره [1] ghorá *f.* unripe fruits (used in seasoning for meat dishes) د غوري اوبه green grapes, unripe grapes انگورو غوره juice of unripe grapes; sour seasoning, acidic seasoning

غوره [2] ghvára 1 choice, excellent 2 selected, chosen 3 approved, accepted 4 preferred 5 serious, important; significant غوره کول a to choose, select b to approve, receive, accept c to prefer d to take on, assume (an appearance, a character) غوره کېدل a to be chosen, be selected b to be approved, be accepted

غوره [3] ghúra *f.* boasting غوري کول to boast د سره غوري to butter one another up, say nice things about one another

غوره [4] ghurá *f.* bellow, roar (of a camel)

غوره پوره ghura-purá *f.* bark (of a dog)

غوره چون ghvarachún selected, elected, chosen

غوره کوونکی ghvára kavúnkaj *m.* elector, voter

غوره گل ghoragә́l *m.* thickly-mixed clay (for plastering roofs)

غوره نیا ghvára nijá *f.* great-grandmother

غوره والی ghvaraválaj *m.* superiority, advantage

غوره هار ghurhár *m.* ☞ غرهار

غوري [1] ghurí *m.* ghoráj *m.* dish (on which food is offered)

غوري [2] ghvarí *m. plural* Ghwari (one of the four main branches of the Afghan tribes or supertribes which include the Momandi, the Khaili, the Chamkani, and the Zerani)

غوري [3] ghorí ghoráj *history* 1 *adjective* Ghorid 2 *m.* Ghorid

غوري [4] ghuré *plural of* غوره

غوري [5] ghvári *feminine plural of* غوره [2]

غوریاجه ghorjādzhá *f.* ☞ غوریژه

غوریالی [1] ghurjāláj goiterous

غوریالی [2] ghvərjaláj *m.* 1 joker; clown 2 windbag

غوریانی ghvarjjānáj *m.* cornflower

غوري خېل ghvarikhél *m. plural* Gwarikhejli ☞ غوري [2]

غورېدل ghuredә́l *intransitive* [*past:* و غورېد] چه 1 to thunder, rumble پر غورېږي، دونه و نه ورېږي *proverb* *literal* Thunder in the sky but no rain. *figurative* A lot of noise, but no action. 2 to talk nonsense

غوریز ghvaríz chosen; elected; selected

غورېژه ghurézha *f.* ☞ غوریژه

غوریه خېل ghvarjakhél *m. plural* ☞ غوري [2]

غوړ ghvaṛ 1.1 *adjective* oily, fatty; tallow د کب غوړ مواد fats غوړ پر غوړو تویېږي fish oil *proverb* Oil flows into oil. 1.2 rich دا غوړ سړی دئ He is a rich man. 1.3 good-looking,

handsome غوړه بنځه a good-looking woman, a beautiful lady 1.4 bright (of a flame) 2 *m.* pomade د سر غوړ pomade *idiom* په غوړو او گرمو خبرو لاس ته راوړل to obtain something through flattery

غوړاسکی ghvaṛáskaj *m. Dodonaea burmanniana* (kind of weed)

غوړاشه ghuṛásha *f.* loop, buttonhole (on clothing) غوړاشه ایستل to sew a buttonhole

غوړانځه ghuṛándza *f.* flame and smoke

غوړانگه ghuṛánga *f.* sunbeam, ray of the sun

غوړاو ghvəṛāvú *m.* toady, lickspittle

غوړاوه ghvəṛāvә́ *imperfect of* غوړول [1]

غوړپ ghuṛáp *m.* ghvṛap *m.* mouthful, drink *idiom* د علم د چینې څخه to be introduced to science يو غوړپ کول څان يو غوړپ کول to get dressed up

غوړ پړ ghvaṛ-páṛ very greasy

غوړپکه ghorpáka *f.* occurence, event

غوړپکۍ ghvaṛpәkә́j *f.* buffet, slap in the face

غوړپول ghvaṛpól ghvaṛpavól ghvaṛpavál}[*past:* غوړپ یې کړ] *denominative, transitive* to swallow; drink in gulps

غوړپېدل ghvaṛpedә́l *denominative, intransitive* [*past:* غوړپ شو] to be swallowed, be gulped down

غوړپیش ghvaṛpísh *m.* rage, anger, ire

غوړپکی ghvaṛpekáj *m.* curly-headed lad

غوړځکه ghuṛdzáka *f.* flame

غوړخولی ghvaṛkhúlaj gluttonous

غوړزاخی ghvaṛzākháj *m.* kind of loaf

غوړزگي ghvaṛzә́gi *f. plural* fat, grease

غوړزنگ ghvaṛzáng *m.* غوړزون ghvaṛzún *m.* thick soup with onion

غوړژبی [1] ghvaṛzhә́baj 1 glib-tongued 2 mellifluous in speech; flattering

غوړژبي [2] ghvaṛzhəbí *f.* sweet speeches; flattery غوړژبي کول to flatter, butter up

غوړسترگی ghvaṛstórgaj having beautiful eyes

غوړسکه ghvә́ṛska *f.* 1 thick smoke; fumes 2 thick growth of bushes, underbrush

غوړشکه ghvṛóshka *f.* 1 excessive quantity; multiplicity غوړشکه in crowds, in groups 2 ☞ غوړسکه

غوړگه [1] ghvórga *f.* 1 reed-rush, *Arundo karka* 2 switch; twig

غوړگه [2] ghuṛgá *f.* shin

غوړگی ghvaṛagáj *m.* disease of plants

غوړلنه ghvaṛlána *f.* fat-rendering boiler; fat-rendering pan or kettle

غوړلستونی ghvaṛlastúṇaj *m.* 1 rich man; propertied man 2 estimable person

غوړلوښی ghvaṛlókhaj *m.* 1 fat-rendering vessel 2 impudent fellow

غوړلی ghvaṛlój *f.* young ear of corn (without kernels)

غوړم ghvṛam *m.* 1 rattle (of firearms) 2 roar (e.g., of a tiger)

غوړه مال ghvaṛamál *m.* ☞ غوړه مال

غوړه مالي ghvaṛamālí *f.* ☞ غوړه مالي

غوړمبه ghuṛambá *f.* large intense flame

غوړمرغه ghvaṛmərghá *f.* kind of evergreen grass

غورمربچه ghvaṛməredzhá *f.* cow calving for the first time

غورمبسن ghvaṛmesón ☞ غورپبجن

غورنجه ghvṛándzha *f.* tongue of flame

غورندزاى ghuṛandzáj *m.* pine tree

غوري مواد ghvaṛaní fats غوروني fatty مواد ghvaṛanáj

غوروكى ghvaṛukə́j *f.* blossom, blossoms (of a tree)

غورول [1] ghvaṛavə́l *transitive* [*past:* وي يې غوراوه] **1** to spread, extend, unfold **2** open, open wide **3** to put, set, place نقب غورول *military* to mine, set mines **4** to be conducive to blossoming, stimulate blossoming

غورول [2] ghvaṛavə́l *denominative, transitive* [*past:* غوری يې کړ] **1** to grease, oil, lubricate; butter **2** to make greasy, soil (something) with grease or oil

غورونه [1] ghvəṛavəna *f.* **1** extending, spreading **2** opening, opening wide **3** putting, setting, placing

غورونه [2] ghvaṛavə́na *f.* **1** greasing, oiling, lubricating; buttering **2** making greasy, soiling (something) with oil or grease

غورونى ghvəṛavónaj *m.* bedding, litter

غوره ghvaṛa *feminine singular of* غور [1]

غوره مال ghvaṛamál **1** *m.* toady, sycophant **2** fawning, bootlicking

غوره مالي ghvaṛamālí *f.* fawning, excessive flattery د پردو غوره مالي fawning over foreign things غوره مالي کول to fawn upon, bootlick; flatter excessively

غوره وونى ghvəṛavúnaj *m.* **1** person unfolding or spreading something **2** bedding, litter

غوري [1] ghvaṛí *m. plural* fuel oil; oil, fats (animal); grease د لم غوري sheep's tail fat د کبانو غوري fish oil ژر غوري fuel د ماهيانو غوري، د نباتي غوري vegetable oils *idiom* حيواني غوري animal fats په چا پوری غوري منبل to flatter excessively

غوري [2] ghvaṛí *feminine plural of* غور

غورياشه ghvaṛjā́sha ghoṛjā́sha **1** ☞ غراشه [2] **2** kind of flower

غوريانځکى ghvaṛjāndzakə́j *f.* iris, flag

غوريانه ghvaṛjā́na *f.* blue iris, blue flag

غورېدزن ghvaṛedzhə́n غورپبجن ghvaṛechə́n غوريځ ghvaṛídz greasy, oily, fatty

غورېڅى ghvaṛetsə́j *f.* curls; kinky hair; ringlets

غوريدل [1] ghvaṛedə́l *intransitive* [*past:* و غوريده و *past:* و غوريده] **1** to be spread out, be extended; be spread, be unfolded **2** to fall prone with hands flailing **3** to open, open wide ده تندی نور هم وغوريد He became all the merrier. **4** to open up (of buds) **5** to rejoice, beam with joy **6** to be dispersed, be scattered (of light, rays)

غوريدل [2] ghvaṛedə́l *denominative, intransitive* [*past:* غوری شو] **1** to be oiled, be lubricated; be buttered **2** to be soiled with grease or oil

غوريدلى ghvaṛedə́ləj *past participle of* غوريدل [1] په غوريدلي تندي، a merry b satisfied, content c merrily d with pleasure غوريدلي تندي سره

غوريدنه [1] ghvaṛedə́na *f.* **1** extending, unfolding **2** opening, opening wide **3** budding, putting out buds **4** dispersion, diffusion, scattering (of light, rays)

غوريدنه [2] ghvaṛedə́na *f.* **1** oiling, lubricating; buttering **2** soiling with something oily or greasy

غوريده [1] ghvaṛedə́ *m. plural* ☞ غوريدنه [1]

غوريده [2] ghvaṛedə́ *m. plural* ☞ غوريدنه [2]

غورېژه ghvaṛezhá *f. botany* Indigofera gerardiana (used as a fertilizer)

غوريكى ghvaṛíkaj *m.* soot-covered kettle, sooty boiler

غوري والا ghvaṛí larúnkaj ☞ غوري لرونکى [2]

غوري مست ghvaṛimást *m.* ghuṛimást *m.* thorny sage (medical plant)

غوري والا ghvaṛivālá **1** *m.* oil merchant (of cooking, oil, etc.) **2** oleaginous, oily غوري والا نبات oil-yielding plant

غوز [1] ghoz *m.* fatty covering or integument of intestines or kidneys; internal fat

غوز [2] ghuz *m.* [*plural:* غوزان ghuzā́n] walnut

غوزار ghuzā́r falling down; knocked off the feet

غوزارول ghuzāravə́l *denominative, transitive* [*past:* غوزار يې کړ] to throw down, knock off the feet; overturn, topple over

غوزاريدل ghuzāredə́l *denominative, intransitive* [*past:* غوزار شو] to fall; be thrown down, be knocked of the feet

غوزاريدنه ghuzāredə́na *f.* غوزاربده ghuzāredə́ *m. plural* falling

غوزاړى ghuzā́ṛaj *m.* ☞ غوزه کړکى

غوزبه ghózba *f.* lance-leaved ash, Fraxinus oxyphylla

غوززى ghuzə́zaj *m.* horsefly larva (under an animal's skin)

غوزه ghozá *f.* **1** cocoon **2** boll (cotton) **3** cone (pine) **4** kind of earring

غوزه کړکى ghuzakə́rkaj *m.* dung beetle

غوزى [1] ghuzáj *m.* **1** load, burden **2** armful **3** ☞ غوززى *idiom* غوزی غوزی تلل to march along proudly

غوزي [2] ghúzi *f. plural* jet of water غوزي وهل to spurt out a jet of water

غوزى [3] ghozáj *m.* **1** embrace **2** struggle, wrestling ☞ غبر

غوژه [1] ghvazhá strong, sturdy

غوژه [2] ghozhá *f.* kind of grass

غوژاى ghuzháj *m.* large water-bag

غوږ ghvag *m.* ear د ماهي غوږ شپيلى *anatomy* the acoustic duct په غوږو درودند He has sharp hearing. غوږونه يي تره دي gills غوږونه He is hard of hearing. غوږ دي دئ؟ Do you hear or not? موږ غوږونه اړولي وه چه کله a to listen to b to await (something) We were awaiting news of your arrival. به دي د راتلو خبر راشي غوږونه يي کاڼه واچول، غوږونه يي پری کاڼه واچول، غوږونه يي پری کاڼه کړل a He pretended that he didn't hear. b He didn't agree. د زره په غوږ اوربدل to listen (to), listen attentively غوږ a to hear something; listen to something زه به يي غوږونه وباسم Listen, look! b to eavesdrop, overhear باسه! a I'll pull his ears. b I'll scold him. د چا خبرو ته غوږ ايښنودل to listen to someone's words; listen to someone غوږ کېږدئ! Listen! د

خپل وجدان غوږ اينودل to listen to the voice of conscience، د خپل وجدان عزت ته غوږ اينودل a to pull someone's ears د غوږ پيچل، غوږ تاوول، غوږ مرورل b to give someone a scolding غوږ څارل to eavesdrop, overhear, listen in غوږ يي هم نه رسېږي He didn't turn a hair. He wasn't scared at all. غوږونه خورل to drone on at someone, bore someone تا له مي غوږونه وخوړل I was droning on at you. حُما غوږونه مي درانه شوه I became deaf. I became hard of hearing. غوږ نيول Eastern a to hear, listen پري غوږ شه I heard him. ونيسه! Listen! b to overhear, eavesdrop c to ask forgiveness د چا پر خبره غوږ نيول to turn one's attention to someone's words, reckon with someone د چا خبره پر غوږ اينول، د چا خبره پر غوږ را اينول، د چا خبره پر غوږ در اينول، د چا خبره پر غوږ ور اينول، د چا خبره پر غوږ وهل to instigate, egg on, put someone up to something په غوږ ورکول to speak so that others hear په غوږ هيڅ نه اروي He won't hear a thing. په غوږ کېدل، په غوږ را کېدل، په غوږ در کېدل، په غوږ ور کېدل، په غوږ لګېدل، په غوږ را لګېدل، په غوږ در لګېدل، په غوږ ور لګېدل to reach (of a sound), be heard په يو غوږ يې Are you listening? proverb په غوږ دي لګي؟ It goes in one ear and out the other. په بل يي وباسي او نباسي د چا خبره په غوږو کنښي نيول، د چا خبره په غوږو کنښي نيول to remember someone's words; obey خبره يي په غوږ وهله He did not sustain the conversation. په غوږ کنښي ورته تيلي ووهه! Convince him! Persuade him! دا خبره يي په غوږ واچوله He paid attention to this circumstance. He heeded this. په غوږو کنښي اينول to put on earrings په غوږو کنښي ګوتي نيول ورکول، لمنتي په غوږو کول to ignore, not to listen to someone, not to pay attention to someone دا زما خبره دي په غوږو کنښي نيولي ده؟ Did you remember what I said? و چا ته په غوږو خبره په غوږو کنښي تينګه ونيسه! Remember this well! د چا په غوږ ورکول، و چا ته په غوږو کنښي ورکول to egg someone on کنښي ويل to have a word in someone's ear; have a private word with someone د غوږه يي نژدي کول Tell him! غوږونه سره to converse in whispers خبره له غوږه ايستل a to pay no attention to someone b to forget something idiom زه يو غوږ شوم I pricked up my ears. غوږ خلاصول to open someone's eyes to something د غوږ په لاربنوونه د هغه غوږونه اوس خلاص شول He has only now comprehended. زما په خبره دي غوږونه خلاص شوه؟ Did you understand what I was talking about? غوږ په غوږ تلل to walk abreast د چا سره غوږ په غوږ تلل to walk in step with someone غوږ يي ګاټه، سري بايلود to not lag (in a race, competition) غوږ کېدل saying He miscalculated. د کنفرانس و نتيجي ته غوږ په هوا و waiting for the results of the conference. غوږ لري او سترګي نه لري He is gullible. غوږونه مي ساره to pass away غوږونه پر ارامه کېدل شول، غوږونه مي په قلار شول I became calm. حُما په غوږ نه لګي I can't believe this. I don't believe my own ears. د بدري په غوږ دا خبري نبي These words were not to Badri's liking. خبره تر غوږه ورتبرول نه لګېدي to bring to (someone's) notice د غوږه مي دا خبره ور تبره کړه I let him know. I brought it to his attention. غوږ ورنيول to teach someone a lesson د چا غوږ ته to Pay no attention to his words. غوږ وريسي مه وره لنده ګوته ورورل، د چا غوږ ته لنده ګوته ورورل to oppress someone,

څان تر دوو غوږو په پورو ډوبول، څان تر دوو غوږونو په پورونو ډوبول torment someone پورونو ډوبول to be up to one's ears in debt

غوږايستنه ghvagistə́na f. eavesdropping

غوږايستونی ghvagistúnaj adjective overhearing

غوږاينونی ghvagiḵúnaj obedient

غوږباسي [1] ghvagbāsí f. eavesdropping

غوږباسی [2] ghvagbā́saj loving to eavesdrop

غوږبوچی ghvagbucháj having clipped ears, having cropped ears

غوږپستکی ghvagpastə́kaj m. earlobe

غوږتاو ghagtā́v m. غوږتاوي ghvagtāví f. reprimand

غوږتومبونی ghvagtumbúnaj m. small stick used for cleaning the ear

غوږڅارنه ghvagtsārə́na f. eavesdropping

غوږخورونی ghvagkhvarúnaj sharp (of a sound)

غوږکاسی ghvagkāsáj m. ☞ غوږتومبونی

غوږکنوونی ghvagkaṇavúnaj deafening

غوږکی [1] ghvagə́kaj m. 1 handle (of a vessel) 2 peg (of a guitar, violin, etc.) idiom د زړه غوږکی auricle

غوږکی [2] ghvagakáj f. whispering back and forth

غوږمبوری ghvagəmbúraj m. mammiform bone

غوږمک ghvagmák m. swelling or tumor in the vicinity of the ear

غوږن ghvagə́n hearing about some secret; informed about something; knowing about something

غوږندرویه ghvagəndrója f. sharp word, sharpness

غوږنیوی ghvagnívaj m. eavesdropping غوږنیوی کول to eavesdrop

غوږو [1] ghvagú ☞ غوږور

غوږو [2] ghvagó oblique plural of غوږ

غوږوالی ghvagvā́laj m. earring

غوږور ghvagvór 1 with big ears, big-eared; lop-eared 2 having ears, eared (of a vessel, jug, pot)

غوږوره ghvagavə́ra f. 1 cap with earflaps 2 nightcap with earlaps

غوږوکی ghvagúkaj m. square corner (of a chador, etc.)

غوږول ghvagavól transitive [past: و يي غوږاوه] 1 to force to listen 2 to inform

غوږی [1] ghvagáj m. 1 handle 2 peg (of a guitar, violin, etc.) 3 corner, angle, corner (e.g., of a chador where it meets the ears) 4 mouthpiece د تېلفون غوږی telephone mouthpiece 5 sluice, floodgate (of an irrigation system) 6 rays of sun coming through a cloud; shaft of light; flash of light 7 small field (at the foot of a mountain)

غوږی [2] ghvagə́j f. whisper

غوږچنه ghvagechə́na f. dimple behind the ear

غوږېدل ghvagedə́l intransitive [past: و غوږېد] 1 to listen; percieve; sense 2 to find out; be informed; find out about

غوږېدنه ghvagedə́na f. 1 aural perception 2 notification

غوږیز ghvagíz 1 having ears, having handles (of a vessel, pot, jug) 2 listening

غوشاک ghushā́k m. plural غوشائي ghushā́j m. plural غوشوي ghoshój m. [plural: غوشایه ghoshā́jə] غوشیاري ghushjā́ri m.

غوشئي *plural* ghoshajáj *m.* [*plural:* غوشيان ghushajā́n] cattle dung

غوشپر ghushér *m.* dung pit

غوښت ¹ ghuḵht *m.* ghvəḵht *m.* desire, wish; request

غوښت ² ghoḵht *m. plural* Italian millet, *Panicum italicum*, millet

غوښت ³ ghuḵht *imperfect of* غوښتل *and Western substitute for* غوښته

غوښتپانه ghuḵhtpā́ṇa *f.* notice (of a meeting, conference)

غوښتل ghuḵhtál ghoḵhtál *transitive* [*present:* غواړي *past:* وي يې غوښت] 1 to solicit, request, desire اجازه غوښتل to request permission لوړ قيمت غوښتل to ask a high price 2 to wish, want زه د دي خبري ښکاره غواړم چه کابل ته ولاړشم I want to go to Kabul. زه کول غواړم، زه غواړم چه دا خبره ښکاره شي، زه غواړم چه دا خبره ښکاره کم I want to explain this. 3 to try to get په ټينگه سره غوښتل to importune, insist 4 to call; invite; summon 5 to send for; order 6 to require, be in need of (something) ډېر خرڅ غوښتل to require large expenditures مريض پاملرنه غواړي The patient is in need of care. دا خبره ډېر غور غواړي The problem requires careful investigation. 7 to ask in marriage

غوښتن ليک ghuḵhtənlík *m.* petition, application

غوښتنه ¹ ghuḵhtə́na *f.* ☞ يوه حقه او د زړه غوښتنه secret dream روا غوښتنه lawful requirement, legal requirement

غوښتونکی ghuḵhtúnkaj 1 *present participle of* غوښتل 2 *m.* partisan, supporter

غوښتونی ghuḵhtúnaj 1.1 wishing; desiring 1.2 requiring 2 *m.* partisan, supporter

غوښته ¹ ghuḵhtə́ *m. plural* 1 request 2 desire 3 demand 4 need 5 invitation; summons 6 subscription, written request; order 7 marriage request

غوښته ² ghuḵhtə́ *imperfect plural of* غوښتل

غوښتئ ghúḵhtəj *past participle of* غوښتل

غوښلن ghvaḵhlə́n غوښن ghvaḵhə́n 1 meaty 2 stout, fat; corpulent, portly

غوښور ghvaḵhavə́r 1 ☞ غوښن 2 muscular

غوښورتوب ghvaḵhavərtób *m.* غوښنورتيا ghvaḵhavərtjā́ *f.* 1 meatiness 2 stoutness; corpulence, portliness

غوښه ghváḵha *f.* 1 *usually plural* غوښي ghvā́ḵhi meat د اس غوښي horsemeat وره *regional* د پسه غوښي camel meat د اوښ غوښي poultry د چرگ غوښي، د چرگي غوښي mutton نری غوښه، *regional* veal د خوسي غوښي، د سخوندر غوښي، د کچه سخي غوښي *regional* beef د کب غوښي، د غوائي غوښي، غته غوښه، fish (the meat of fish) د وزو غوښه raw meat اومه غوښه goat meat وچه غوښه dried meat وريته غوښه *dialect* roast meat غوښه اخيستل a to grow fat, grow stout, grow corpulent b to rejoice تويل غوښه a to grow thin b to emaciate, wear out تو يبدل to get thin 2 muscle *idiom* اول وخوره د ځان غوښي، نو بيا خوره د ښکار غوښي *literal* If you want to eat fish, you must get into the water. *figurative* You can't make an omelet without breaking an egg.

غوښور ghvaḵhavə́r ☞ غوښنور

غوښی ¹ ghoḵháj *m.* ☞ غوړی ¹

غوښي ² ghvā́ḵhi *plural of* غوښه

غوښين ghvaḵhín ☞ غوښن

غوطه ² ghutá *f. Arabic* ☞ غوته

غوغا ghoghā́ *f.* ghaughā́ *f.* 1 noise د موجونو غوغا splash of waves 2 cry غوغا کول a to make a noise b cry out 3 disorders, riots; mutiny غوغا جوړول to create riots; raise a mutiny

غوغو gháughau *m.* barking (dog)

غوگ ghvag *m. Eastern* ☞ غوږ

غوگی ghvagáj *m.* plot of land, small piece of land

غول ¹ ghvul *m.* ghvə́l *plural* stools, feces غول کول to defecate

غول ² ghul *m.* ghol *Arabic* demon, evil spirit; monster

غول ³ ghol *m.* 1 detachment, group; crowd 2 herd, flock په غول a by detachments, in groups; in crowds b in herds, flocks

غول ⁴ ghol *m.* hernia, rupture

غولاﻧﺨﻪ ghulā́ndza *f.* ghvə́lā́ndza *f.* 1 udder 2 kind of edible plant

غولاﻧﺨﻪ ghulā́ndza *f.* غولانﺨﻮر larúnkaj *f.* ghulāndza-və́r لرونکی mammal غولانﺨﻪ لرونکی حيوان

غولبگی ghvə́lbagə́j *f.* latrine

غولبه ghulbá *f.* ploughing, tillage, ploughed land ☞ قلبه

غولخور ghvə́lkhór false, lying, mendacious

غولغوله ghulghulá *f.* noise, uproar; commotion

غولک gholák *m.* moneybox

غولکه gholáka *m.* slingshot, catapult

غولمرگ ghulmárg *m.* 1 pus, matter (within an abscessed boil) 2 core of a boil

غولنج ghulə́ndzh *m.* colic

غولنگ gholáng *m.* gland

غولنه ghulə́na *f.* stye (on the eye)

غولول ¹ ghulavál ghvulavál 1 *transitive* [*past:* وي يې غولوه] 1.1 to deceive, gull, trick ځان غولول to be mistaken, deceive oneself 1.2 to lead astray, deflect from the right path 2 *m. plural* deception نظر غولول an optical illusion

غولونه ghulavə́na *f.* ghvulavə́na deception, trickery, swindling, cheating

غولوونکی ² ghulavúnkaj ghvulavúnkaj 1 *present participle of* غولول deceptive غولونکي کالي اغوستل to disguise oneself

غوله ¹ gholá *f.* 1 log, beam, timber 2 measure (for milk, water)

غوله ² ghvə́la *parenthetic word* غوله دا کار ښه نه دئ! truly, in very truth, too bad

غوله کمانه gholakamā́na *f.* slingshot, catapult; sling

غولی ¹ ghólaj *m.* 1 yard, court د انگړ غولی yard, court 2 floor (of a room) د کوټي غولی floor 3 hold, bottom (of a boat) 4 *biology* natural habitat (area where particular plants or animals are found) *idiom* غولی پر چا تنگول to place someone in a hopeless situation (in a conversation, quarrel, etc.); to pin someone to the wall

غولی ² ghuláj *f.* whirlpool, maelstrom; gulf, abyss

غولی ³ gholáj *f.* 1 assemblage, crowd په غولی غولی in crowds غولی کېدل to divide into groups, group 2 flock (of birds) کول to gather in flocks, flock (of birds) **3** irregular troops, detachments of irregular militia

غولېدل ghuledə́l ghvuledə́l [*past:* و غولېده *and past:* غولېد] *intransitive* **1** to be deceived; err **2** to overlook, make an error in counting

غولېدنه ghuledə́na *f.* ghvuledə́na غولېدنه ghuledə́ غولېد *m. plural* **1** deception **2** miscount

غولي ناسته gholinā́sta *f.* visit by the bridegroom-to-be to the home of the father-in-law after the latter has agreed to the marriage

غوماشه ghumā́sha *f.* ☞ غماشه د غوماشو ونه elm tree

غومبار ghumbā́r *f.* thick smoker

غومباره ghumbārá *f.* **1** ancient cannon **2** large swelling (from a blow, sting of a wasp, etc.)

غومبر ghumbə́r *m.* **1** cooing غومبر کول to coo (of doves) **2** calls, cries (of dancers) *idiom* غومبر وهل to pay court to, make advances to

غومبسکه ghumbə́ska *f.* sally

غومبسه ghumbə́sa *f.* wasp

غومبک ghumbák *m. botany* rush

غومبوری ghumbúraj *m.* cheek غومبوري کول ghumbúri *m.* to be chubby-cheeked, be round-faced

غومبوسکی ghumbúskaj *m.* غومبه ghúmba *f.* fatty tumor; tumor, growth; lump

غومبی ghumbáj *m.* tubby youth, chubby lad [1]

غومبي ghúmbi *m. plural of* غومبه غومبي swollen, inflated [2]

غومی ghúmaj *m.* spurge, euphoria

غومېدل ghumedə́l *intransitive* [*past:* و غومېد] **1** to laugh at, mock **2** to threaten

غوناجی ghonādzhə́j *f.* young cow, heifer

غناږه ghunā́ga *f.* sugared fruit

غونج ghvundzh *m.* **1** bag (for transport of straw) **2** sheaf in the field (of wheat, barley, etc.) [1]

غونج ghvundzh ghvə́ndz **1** wrinkled, wrinkled up **2** shriveled (up) [2]

غونجا ghvə́ndzhā **1** lazy **2** flaccid, inert

غونج مونج ghvundzh-múndzh **1** completely wrinkled (up) **2** shriveled (up)

غونجوالی ghvə́ndzhvā́laj ghvundzhvā́laj *m.* **1** wrinkling; shriveling (up) **2** pressure, contraction (of the heart)

غونجول ghvə́ndzhavə́l *denominative, transitive* [*past:* غونج یې کړ] **1** to wrinkle **2** to form into sheaves

غونجی ghundzhə́j *m.* withering of fruits [1]

غونجی ghundzhə́j *f.* young sheep in heat [2]

غونجېدل ghvə́ndzhedə́l *denominative, intransitive* [*past:* غونج شو] **1** to wrinkle up; shrivel up د مخ پوستکي یې سره غونج شوي The skin on his face was wrinkled up. **2** to be compressed, be gripped (of the heart) **3** to fade, wither

غونچه ghunchá *f.* cluster, bunch

غونځاخای ghundzāk̲h̲áj *m.* **1** flat-cake; small white loaf **2** blade of a handmade cotton gin

غونځرکی ghvə́ndzə́rkaj *m.* newborn goat

غونځول gundzavavə́l *transitive* [*past:* و یې غونځاوه] **1** to turn; turn over **2** to oscillate, vacillate

غونځونه ghundzavóna *f.* **1** turning, rotation, turning over **2** oscillation

غونځه ghvə́ndza *f.* hawthorn (tree)

غونځی ghúndzaj *m.* bag, sack

غونځېدل ghundzedə́l *intransitive* [*past:* و غونځېده] **1** to toss about (in sleep) **2** to wriggle, squirm (of worms) **3** to swarm, team **4** to hide oneself (unnoticed) **5** to steal surreptitiously; toss something somewhere unnoticed

غوند ghúnd ☞ غوندې [2]

غوندرکی ghundə́rkaj غوندری ghundə́raj stunted

غونده ghundá *f.* spun wool

غوندی ghundáj *m.* bag د غوندي ستن ghundí... sacking needle [1]

غوندې ghúnde *Eastern* **1** similar, like **2** like, as د تا تا غوندې like us لکه مونږ غوندې like a stone تیږه غوندې like you تیره غوندې، دا یوه عجیبه احمد غوندې ښکاريده *Eastern* He resembles Ahmed. غوندي خبره ده This is quite a strange story. احمد لږي غوندې وریجي ور کړي Ahmed gave him a little rice. [2]

غوندي ghúnde *Western* ☞ غوندې [3]

غوندي ghúndi *the separable part of the verb* اغوستل *in the present tense* [4]

غونډ ghunḍ ghvunḍ **1.1** round, circular, spherical, globular **1.2** collected, concentrated; gathered **1.3** chunky, stocky (of a person) **2** *m.* **.1** ☞ غنډ [2] **2.2** mountain with gently sloping pinnacle **2.3** *medicine* bubo **3** *predicative* **.1** collected, convoked **3.2** acquired **3.3** accumulated **3.4** gathered into a pile (e.g., grain); gathered, piled up together غونډه دنیا *idiom* غونډه مزکه the whole world

غونډاری ghunḍā́raj **1** *m.* **.1** round lump; ball, sphere; round-shaped object غونډاری کول snowball واورو غونډاری *compound verb* to form into a ball, ball up (clay) **1.2** round stone, spherical stone **1.3** bar, ingot (steel) **1.4** shot, projectile **1.5** ball (of yarn, thread) **1.6** tumor, growth, thickening **1.7** bubble **2.1** round; circular **2.2** spherical, convex

غونډاری ghunḍā́rə́j *f.* small flat-cake, small white loaf

غونډال ghwanḍā́l *m. computer science* system

غونډژبی ghunḍzhə́baj ghunḍzhə́baj ghvə́nḍzhə́baj stammering

غونډسر ghvə́nḍsər *m.* rotting leaf

غونډسری ghvə́nḍsáraj ghunḍsáraj round-headed

غونډسکه ghunḍə́ska *f.* ball

غونډک ghunḍák *m.* ghvunḍák artillery battery [1]

غونډک ghunḍák *m.* ghvunḍák tarantula [2]

غونډکمشر ghunḍakmə́shr ghvunḍakmə́shər *m. military* battery commander

غونډکی ghunḍakə́j *f.* **1** tumor, growth, thickening **2** sally **3** *anatomy* pubis **4** small hill; hillock [1]

غوندکی ² ghvəṇḍakáj *m.* **1** pudgy youth **2** front-sight (of a weapon)

غوندل ghvuṇḍál *m.* tarantula

غندلمشر gunḍməshr gunḍmə́shər *m.* ☞ مشر

غندلمشري ghunḍməshrí *f.* ☞ مشري

غوندمند ghunḍ-múnḍ ghvənḍ-mə́nḍ **1** rather round, rather stout **2** stout and ruddy, rubicund

غوندو ¹ ghonḍó *f.* rather full or chubby girl

غوندو ² ghvə́nḍo *oblique plural of* غوند

غوندو ³ ghvə́nḍo *oblique plural of* غونډه

غوندوری ghunḍúraj *m.* ☞ غونډاری ¹

غوندوسکی ghunḍúskaj **1** sphere, globe; ball-shaped lump or mass **2** ball

غوندول ghunḍavə́l ghvənḍavə́l [*past:* غوند یې کړ] *denominative, transitive* **1.1** to assemble; convoke **1.2** to acquire دنیا غوندول to acquire property **1.3** to amass, accumulate **1.4** to collect into a pile (grain) **1.5** to create (material resources, funds) **1.6** to call (to arms) **1.7** to collect (e.g., proverbs, songs) **1.8** to create (conditions) **2** *m. plural* **.1** assembly, muster; convocation **2.2** acquisition **2.3** collection into a pile (grain) **2.4** creation (of material resources, etc.) **2.5** call (to arms); mobilization (of troops) د لښکرو غوندول mobilization

غونډه ghvə́nḍa ghúnḍa **1** *feminine singular of* غوند **2** *f.* **.1** assembly, conference, meeting; session, congress پټه غونډه closed meeting گډه غونډه joint meeting لویه غونډه general meeting مسلکي غونډه production meeting مکمله غونډه plenary meeting, plenum غونډه کول to meet, have a meeting; conduct a conference meeting; sit in a meeting **2.2** hillock, low hill **2.3** round rock, spherical stone **2.4** round clod (of earth); ball (of dough)

غونډهاری ghunḍháraj *m.* swelling; bubo

غونډه مری ghvə́nḍa maráj *f.* gullet

غنډی ¹ ghunḍáj *m.* ☞ غندک

غونډی ² ghunḍáj *f.* **1** hill, hillock; foothill **2** fat girl *idiom* د خپر پر غونډی کېنبنستل to hold oneself apart, not to participate (in quarrels, etc.)

غونډی ³ ghvənḍáj ghunḍáj **1.1** short, thickset; short of stature, petite **1.2** rather stout, rather full **2** *anatomy m.* head (proximal end) of the femur

غونډېدل ghvənḍedə́l ghunḍedə́l *denominative, intransitive* [*past:* غوند شو] **1** to be assembled; be convoked **2** to be acquired **3** to be accumulated; be deposited **4** to be collected into a pile (grain) **5** to be created (of material resources, etc.)

غونډېده ghvənḍedə́ ghunḍedə́ *m. plural* **1** assembly, convocation **2** acquisition **3** accumulation **4** collection, piling up (e.g., grain) **5** creation (of material resources, etc.)

غونزېدل ghunzedə́l *intransitive* ☞ غونڅېدل

غونه ghuná *f.* **1** color, shade, hue (of skin) **2** appearance, external aspect **3** personality; conduct, comportment

غونی ¹ ghúnaj *f.* ghúni *plural* **1** body hair **2** skin غونی زیږېدل *a* to stand on end (of hair) *b* to shrivel from the cold (of skin) *c* to shiver **3** pore

غونی ² ghuné *plural of* غونه

غونی ³ ghunaj *combining form* likeness, similarity ژړغونی yellowish (i.e., like yellow) بدغونی having a low character, depraved

غونېښای ghunekháj good-natured, genial

غون ghuṇ *m.* nasal sound

غوناسکه ghuṇáska *f.* leaping

غوناسکی ghuṇáskaj *m.* غوناشکی ghuṇáshki *f. plural* **1** last gasp, dying breath **2** gurgling (of water)

غونکی ghuṇkáj *m.* ☞ غونهار

غونه ghuṇá *f.* rumble, drone

غونهار ghuṇəhár *m.* nasal speech

غونی guṇáj nasal

غونېدل ghuṇedə́l *intransitive* [*past:* وغونېد] **1** to nasalize, speak through the nose **2** to speak condescendingly

غونېده ghuṇedə́ *m. plural* nasal speech

غونېژی ghuṇezháj *m.* **1** goldbricking, trying to get out of **2** grumbling

غوډل ghvəḍál *m.* ☞ زمبر ¹

غوړه ghvéra *dialect* ☞ غوره ²

غوړبچنی ghvégnaj *m.* ☞ غوړبچنه

غوړبنکی ghvékhkaj *m.* green shoots, greenery, vegetation

غوی گاډی ghvegáḍaj *m. Eastern* bullock cart

غوجلانه ghvəjlā́na *f.* kind of edible plant

غوی لنگ، غویلنگ ghvajláng **1** groin **2** crupper or harness-strap passed under the tail of the animal (in the case of an ox it serves to anchor the load)

غویمند، غوی مند ghvajmə́nḍ *m.* **1** panic, alarm (among cattle) **2** trampling; stamping **3** tramping out a road in the snow (using oxen) **4** annihilation, destruction, ruin **5** flouting, gross violation غویمند کول *compound verb a* to cause a stampede, create a disturbance (among cattle) *b* to trample, stamp *c* to stamp out a road in the snow (using oxen) *d* to annihilate, destroy, ruin *e* to flout, commit a gross violation غویمند کېدل *compound verb a* to be stampeded, be alarmed *b* to be trampled *c* to be tramped out (of a road in snow, using oxen) *d* to be annihilated, be destroyed, be ruined *e* to be flouted, grossly violated **6** assembly, mob

غویمه ghvəjmá *f.* ghvəjəmá female water-buffalo or cow in heat غویمه کېدل to be in heat (of a female water-buffalo or cow)

غوی ghvajáj *m.* [*plural:* غوایه ghvājí *Eastern plural:* غوایه ghvājə́ *Western plural:* غوایان ghvājə́n] **1** bull د قلبي غوی **2** ox *astronomy* Taurus (the constellation) **3** ☞ ثور *idiom* د غوائي سترگه *a* watch (timepiece) *b* botany marguerite, white oxeye *idiom* د غوائي دباندي غابن کېدل to lose all significance; be a mere cog in the machine اوس نو غویی پوست سوئ دئ، په یوه لکی پاته دئ A little bit still remains to be done. غویی کول *compound verb* to subordinate oneself

غه gha *pronoun obsolete* that (one) ☞ هغه [1]

غیاب ghijáb *m. Arabic* absence د چا په غیاب کښی in someone's absence, in absentia

غیابي ghijābí 1 absent 2 in default (of a trial, sentence, etc.)

غیاث ghijás *m. Arabic* 1 help; deliverance 2 *proper name* Ghias

غیب ghajb *Arabic* 1 *m.* .1 secret 1.2 that which is inner, secret, or concealed 1.3 absence 2 hidden, unseen عالم غیب the unseen world ویل غیب to predict, prophesy

غیبت ghajbát *m. Arabic* 1 scandal, backbiting; abuse 2 censure, condemnation د چا غیبت کول a to backbite; discredit; abuse b to censure 3 absence

غیبگو، غیبگو ghajbgú *m.* prophet, seer, soothsayer

غیبگویی، غیب گویی ghajbgují *f.* prophecy

غیبه ghajbá *f.* cleaned cotton; cotton wool

غیبي ghajbí 1 absent 2 hidden, unseen; secret

غیب ghib *m.* funnel (for pouring liquids) ☞ قیف

غیږه ghédzha *f.* 1 ☞ شلبر 2 onager, wild ass

غیر ghajr *Arabic* 1.1 other, different; another تاسی ته غیر له دی … نور څه ندی پاته شوی چه Nothing else remains for you than to … وغیره، او غیره and so forth, and so on, etc. 1.2 standing outside of something دا د دیموکراسی له روحیی نه غیر دئ This contradicts the spirit of democracy. 1.3 another's 2 *preposition* besides, aside from, without غیر له دی besides, aside from غیر له دی besides that, aside from that غیر د څلورو کسانو څخه with the exception of four men 3 *m.* [*plural:* اغیار aghjár] stranger, alien دوی اغیار دی They are strangers.

غیر ghajr *Arabic prefix* non-, without, sans- غیر آزاد not free, dependent

غیرآباد ghajrābád unpopulated, deserted

غیراختیاري ghajrikhtijārí involuntary, forced په غیراختیاري ډول involuntarily, compulsorily

غیرآزاد ghajrāzád not free, dependent

غیراستعمال ghajristi'mál obsolescent, going out of use

غیراصلي ghajraslí changed حالت غیراصلي *grammar* inflected form (of a word)

غیراطرافي ghajatrāfí extraneous, strange

غیرپښتون ghajrpakhtún *m.* non-Afghan

غیرت ghajrát *m. Arabic* 1 feeling or sense of personal worthiness; self-esteem; pride; self-respect له غیرته from pride, out of self-respect 2 zeal, fervor, heat 3 valor, courage; bravery 4 indignation, anger څما غیرت جوش کښی راغئ I became indignant. I got angry. *Eastern* I became indignant. I got angry. 5 modesty غیرت کول، غیرت لرل a to display self-love, show self-respect b to display zeal, show fervor c to display courage, show valor, demonstrate bravery d to be indignant, be (angrily) disturbed e to be modest

غیرتمن gajratmán 1 having a feeling of personal worth; proud; self-respecting 2 zealous, ardent 3 valorous, courageous; brave 4 indignant, (angrily) disturbed 5 modest

غیرت مند ghajratmánd 1 ☞ غیرتمن 2 title of a captain

غیرتناک ghajratnāk ☞ غیرتمن

غیرتنظیم ghajrtanzím incorrect; irregular

غیرتولیدي ghajrtavlidí nonproductive

غیرتي ghajratí 1.1 noble غیرتي او شجاع سړی a noble and courageous man 1.2 assiduous, zealous, ardent 2 *m.* .1 noble man 2.2 assiduous man; zealous man

غیردجانبدار ghajrdzhānibdár passionless; neutral

غیرجنگي ghajrdzhangí *military* non-combatant

غیرچلن ghajrchalán obsolescent, going out of use

غیرحاضر ghajrhāzír absent; non-appearing (for work, class, etc.)

غیرحاضرول ghajrhāziravál *denominative, transitive* [*past:* غیرحاضر یی کړ] to compel to be truant, commit absenteeism څان غیرحاضرول to be an absentee, not to appear (for work, class, etc.)

غیرحاضري ghajrhāzirí *f.* absence, truancy, non-appearance (at work), absenteeism (from class, etc.) د مکتب څخه غیرحاضري absent from class at school

غیرحاضریدل ghajrhāziredál *denominative, intransitive* [*past:* غیر حاضر شو] to be absent; not appear (for work), be a truant, be absentee (class, etc.), play hooky, cut classes

غیرحربي ghajrharbí non-military, civilian, civil

غیرحق ghajrhák ghajrhákk *Arabic* illegal

غیرحقیقي ghajrhakiķí *Arabic* unreal, cut off from reality; fictitious

غیرحکومتي ghajrhukumatí unofficial

غیردایمي ghajrdājimí inconstant, temporary

غیردیني ghajrdiní *Arabic* society, fashionable

غیرذیروح ghajrzirúh *Arabic grammar* inanimate

غیرراضي ghajrrází unsatisfactory

غیررسمي ghajrrasmí *Arabic* 1 unofficial غیررسمي رپوټونه unofficial communication 2 outside of regular duties

غیرذروي ghajrzaraví non-nuclear

غیرزوجي ghajrzaudzhí extramarital

غیرساکښن ghajrsākákh ☞ غیر ذیروح

غیرشرعي ghajrshar'í *Arabic* 1 illegal 2 illegitimate

غیرشعوري ghajrshu'urí *Arabic* 1 irrational; unreasonable 2 unconscious

غیرصحي ghajrsihhí *Arabic* 1 unhealthy 2 unhygienic

غیرضروري ghajrzarurí unneeded

غیرطبیعي ghajrtabi'í unnatural, abonormal, extraordinary

غیرعادلانه ghajr'ādilāná unjust

غیرعادي ghajr'ādí *Arabic* unusual, uncommon

غیرعضوي ghajr'uzví *Arabic* inorganic

غیرعلاقه ghajr'alāķá *f. regional history* zone or region of independent tribes on the northwest Indian frontier

غیرغږیز ghajrghagíz *linguistics* consonantal (of a phoneme)

غیرفطري gajrfitrí *Arabic* abnormal, unnatural

غيرقابل التحمل ghajrḳābil-at-tahamúl *Arabic* intolerable

غيرقابل مقايسه ghajrḳābilimuḳājisá incomparable, matchless

غيرقانوني ghajrḳānuní unlawful; illegal په غيرقانوني ډول unlawfully; illegally غيرقانوني اعلانول to declare unlawful, declare illegal

غيرقبول ghajrḳabúl ineffective, void

غيرقصدي ghajrḳasdi *Arabic* unintentional, involuntary

غيرلښکري ghajrlaḵhkarí peaceful, civil, non-military

غيرمتجانس ghajrmutadzhānís *Arabic* heterogeneous

غيرمترقب ghajrmutarḳḳáb *Arabic* unforeseen; unexpected; sudden

غيرمترقي ghajrmutaraḳḳí backward, unprogressive

غيرمتزلزلانه ghajrmutazalzalāná steadfast, stable, unshakeable

غيرمتعلق ghajrmuta'allíḳ *Arabic* foreign, alien, not related to a matter

غيرمتناهي ghajrmutanāhí limitless, boundless

غيرمحارب ghajrmuhāríb 1 *military* non-combatant 2 non-warring

غيرمحدود ghajrmahdúd *Arabic* limitless, boundless, infinite

غيرمحدوديت ghajrmahdudiját *m.* limitlessness, boundlessness, infinity

غيرمحرم ghajrmahrám *Arabic* alien, strange

غيرمرئي ghajrmar'í *Arabic* 1 unseen; hidden, secret 2 unknown

غيرمساعد ghajrmusā'íd *Arabic* unsuitable, inappropriate

غيرمستقيم ghajrmustaḳím *Arabic* oblique; roundabout, devious په غيرمستقيم صورت سره indirectly

غيرمسلح ghajrmussalláh *Arabic* unarmed; peaceful

غيرمصدق ghajrmusaddáḳ *Arabic* unverified (of a communication)

غيرمطلق ghajrmutláḳ *Arabic grammar* imperfective

غيرمطلوب ghajrmatlúb *Arabic* unwanted; unneeded

غيرمطمئن gajrmutmaín *Arabic* unquiet, insecure

غيرمعمولي ghajrma'mulí unusual

غيرمعياري ghajrmi'jári *Arabic* non-standard

غيرمعين ghajrmu'ajján *Arabic* indeterminate غيرمعين مقدار an indeterminate quantity

غيرمكفي ghajrmakfí *Arabic* insufficient; unsatisfactory

غيرمكشوف ghajrmakshúf *Arabic* unknown, unresearched, uninvestigated

غيرملك ghajrmúlk *m. regional* foreign country, foreign parts; foreign countries, overseas parts

غيرملكي ghajrmulkí *regional* 1 foreign; alien; outland; newly arrived 2 *m.* foreigner; alien, outlander

غيرممتاز ghajrmumtáz *Arabic* unpriviledged

غيرممكن ghajrmumkín *Arabic* impossible, unrealizable

غيرمنتظر ghajrmuntazír *Arabic* unexpected; sudden په ناڅاپي او غيرمنتظر ډول unexpectedly; suddenly, at once

غيرمنجمد ghajrmundzhamíd *Arabic* non-freezing

غيرمنصفانه ghajrmunsifāná unjust

غيرمنظم ghajrmunazzám *Arabic* 1 irregular غيرمنظم لښکرونه irregular troops 2 partisan غيرمنظم جنگ کول to carry on partisan warfare 3 disorderly, irregular

غيرمنقطع ghajrmunḳatí' *Arabic* uninterrupted; tireless

غيرمنقول ghajrmanḳúl *Arabic* غيرمنقولي ghajrmanḳulí immoveable, real (of property) غيرمنقول مالونه real property

غيرموثر ghajrmuassír *Arabic* 1 ineffective, null, void 2 ineffectual

غيرمولد ghajrmuvallíd *Arabic* not producing; unproductive

غيرمهذب ghajrmuhazzáb *Arabic* uncultivated, uneducated, ignorant

غيرنظامي ghajrnizāmí peaceful, civil, civilian, non-military غيرنظامي اشخاص peaceful population غيرنظامي کول to demilitarize

غيرنورمال ghajrnormál abnormal

غيرواضح ghajrvāzíh *Arabic* unclear, foggy

غيرواقعي ghajrvāḳi'í *Arabic* unreal, nonexistent

غيرودان ghajrvadán unpopulated, deserted

غيره ¹ ghjára *f.* wild ass, onager

غيره ² ghajrá *Arabic* other, and the others, et. al. اوپه غيرو کښي as for the rest, in other respects

غيره ³ ghajrá *f. Arabic singular and plural of* غير

غيريت ghajrijját *m. Arabic* 1 change, alteration; distinction 2 oddity, exceptional thing 3 estrangement; extraneousness غيريت محسوسول to feel oneself alien, alienated 4 envy

غبږ gheg *f. m. Eastern f.* [*plural:* غبږي ghégi *Eastern plural:* ghége] 1 embrace, embraces غبږ په غبږ embracing one another د غبږي روغبږ کول to embrace one another په غبږ کبدل to embrace one another (upon meeting) په غبږ پوښتنه کول، په غبږ ستري to embrace mutually, greet one another په غبږ نيول مشي کول to envelop, enclose 2 *figuratives* bosom, lap; surface 3 armful 4 *sports* wrestling په غبږ ورتلل، غبږي نيول، غبږي ايستل to wrestle *idiom* تر غبږ under the armpit د غبږي طفل nursling, nursing child په غبږ کښي گرځول to carry (a child) in the arms

غبږباز ghegbáz *m. sports* wrestler

غبږبازي ghegbāzí *f. sports* wrestling

غبږباس ghegbás *m.* ☞ غبږباز

غبږباسي ghegbāsí *f.* ☞ غبږبازي

غبږروغ بر ghegoghbár *m.* greeting with an embrace

غبږه ghéga *f. dialect* ☞ غبږ د مور په غبږه کښي ور ولوېده She flung herself into her mother's embraces. د مور په غبږه کښي in the mother's arms

غبښ لاسی gheshlásaj armed

غبښي ghesháj *m. dialect* ☞ غښی

غيظ ghajz *m. Arabic* ire, rage

غبگ gheg *m. Eastern* ☞ غبږ

غيل ¹ ghil *m. Arabic* grove, small wood; forest

غبل ² ghel *m.* 1 fending off, evading (a blow) 2 avoidance, shirking

غبلي ghelé *f. plural* 1 flock (of sheep, goats) 2 Wolves and Sheep (the children's game)

غين ghajn *m. Arabic* the name of the letter غ

غينجه ghíndzha *f.* leaping; leaping up

غيور ghajjúr 1 valorous, courageous 2 zealous, earnest, fervent

ف

ف **fe 1** thirtieth letter of the Pashto alphabet (occurs only in loan words; usually pronounced as "p" or "v" and, for this reason, is often replaced by the letter پ or ٠و) **2** number 80 in the abjad system

ف official *abbreviation* قاضي title of a فضیلت مآب ** f**

فابریکه **fābriká** *f.* [plural: فابریکې **fābriké** *m. Arabic* [plural: فابریکات **fābikắt**] factory د فابریکي خُښتن factory owner د برېښنا electric power station فابریکه

فابریکه یي **fābrikaí** *adjective* factory, plant

فاتح **fātíh** *Arabic* **1** *m. Arabic* **.1** victor; conqueror; patron **1.2** discoverer; author, founder **1.3** *proper name* Fatih **2.1** victorious; conquering **2.2** discovering; founding, beginning

فاتحانه **fātihāná 1** victorious, triumphant **2** victoriously

فاتحه **fātihá** *f. Arabic* **1** beginning; opening, introducing **2** first sura of the Koran فاتحه ویل، فاتحه لوستل، فاتحه کول to read the first sura of the Koran; read the prayer for the departed ☞ پاتا

فاتحه خواني **fātihakhāní** *f.* requiem assembly or service among Moslems during which the first sura of the Koran is read

فاجر **fādzhír** *Arabic* **1** depraved, vicious, debauched, corrupt **2** *m.* libertine, debauchee, adulterer

فاجع **fāzhí'** *Arabic* **1** awful, horrible; tragic **2** ruinous; destructive

فاجعه **fādzhi'á** *f. Arabic* [plural: فاجعي **fādzhi'é** *m. Arabic plural:* فجائع **fadzhāí**] **1** tragedy, drama **2** disaster; catastrophe; misfortune

فاحش **fāhísh** *Arabic* **1** excessive, inordinate, monstrous فاحش تقصیر a grave fault **2** shameless; indecent, indelicate **3** gross, scandalous, patently untrue دا فاحشه غلطي ده It is a gross error. **4** sharp, significant **5** outright, arrant (of a lie)

فاحشه **fāhishá** *Arabic* **1** *feminine singular of* فاحش **2** *f.* prostitute

فاحشه گري **fāhishagarí** *f.* **1** excess, state of being inordinate, monstrousness **2** shamelessness, indecency, obscenity **3** prostitution

فاخته **fākhtá** *f.* turtledove

فاخته رنگي **fākhtarángaj** grey, grey-colored; dove-grey فاخته رنگی کپړه grey cloth

فارس **fārs** *m.* **1** Fars (province, Iran) **2** *obsolete* Persia د فارس خلیج the Persian Gulf

فارسي **fārsí** *f.* **1** Farsi, Farsi language فارسي ژبه the Farsi language د کابل فارسي Farsi-Kabuli, Dari **2** *m.* Persian

فارسي بان **fārsibān pārsibān** فارسي زبان **fārsizabān** فارسي زبانه **fārsizabāna 1** Farsi speaker; one who knows Farsi **2** *m.* Tajik; Khazar; Persian

فارغ **fārígh** *Arabic* **1** finishing something; liberated from something **2** unoccupied, free (from business, a matter) فارغ وخت، فارغ ساعت leisure, leisure time هغه لا فارغ نه دئ که وزگار شي، نو در به شي He is

still busy; once he is free, he will come to you. **3** careless, carefree **4** getting detached from or out of something

فارغ البال **farigh-ul-bál** tranquil; free of care, carefree

فارغ البالي **fārigh-ul-bālí** *f.* **1** quiet, peace, tranquility; carelessness, unconcern **2** comfort

فارغ التحصیل **fārigh-ul-tahsíl** *m. Arabic* graduate; one who has completed a course of study

فارغ التحصیلاني **fārigh-ut-tahsíla** *f. Arabic* [plural: فارغ التحصیله **fārigh-ut-tahsilắna** *m. Arabic plural:* فارغ التحصیلات **fārigh-ut-tahsilất**] graduate (girl, woman)

د فارغ التحصیلي **fārigh-ut-tasilí** *f.* completion of studies د فارغ التحصیلی سند التحصیلی شهادتنامه، د diploma, certificate of completion of studies

فارغول **fārighavól** *denominative, transitive* [past: فارغ یې کړ] to free, liberate from something

فارغېدل **fārighedól** *denominative, intransitive* [past: فارغ شو] to be freed from something *idiom* له طبع زه چایو نه فارغ شوم I drank tea. څخه فارغېدل to appear (publication), be issued, be published

فارق **fāríḳ** *Arabic* distinguishing; distinctive فارق علامات distinguishing marks; distinguishing characteristics; distinctive markings

فارقه **fāriḳá** *f. Arabic* hyphen

فارم [1] **fārm** *m.* land-holding, farm تجربوي فارم experimental farm د مرغانو د روزني فارم، د حیواناتو د روزني فارم stock-farm poultry فارم، د روزني فارم poultry farm تعاوني فارم collective farm, kolkhoz کولکتیف فارم، دولتي فارم state collective farm

فارم [2] **fārm** *m.* application; blank form; registration form

فارماکولوژي **fārmākolozhí** *f.* pharmacology

فارمول **fārmúl** *m.* فارمولا **fārmulá** *f.* formula فارمول الجبري algebraic formula ریاضي فارمول mathematical formula

فارمولیزي **fārmulizé** formulated فارمولیزي کول to formulate

فارمه لین **fārmalín** formalin

فارمېشن **fārméshin** *m. military* formation د فارمبشن پرواز to mine, set mines په فارمېشن in formation

فآرنهایت **fāʾrinhájt** *m.* Fahrenheit thermometer

فاروړ **fắrvaṛ** *history* فاروړ پالیسي active policy of British imperialism for Northwest India

فاروق **fārúḳ** *Arabic* **1** perspicacious, sagacious **2** *m. proper name* Faruq

فاریاب **fārjáb** *m.* Faryab (ancient name for the city of Davlatabad) د فاریاب ولایت Faryab Province

فاسدژن **fāsdzhén** *m. chemistry* phosgene

فاسد **fāsíd** *Arabic* **1** spoiled; bad, nasty فاسدي اوبه polluted water فاسده هوا polluted air **2** vicious, criminal *idiom* فاسد په فاسد سره to fight fire with fire دفع کول

فاسدول **fāsidavól** *denominative, transitive* [past: فاسد یې کړ] to spoil, soil something

532

فاسدېدل fāsidedál *denominative, intransitive* [*past:* فاسد شو] **1** to be spoiled, be soiled فاسده شوي هوا polluted air **2** to be vicious, be criminal

فاسدېدونکی fāsidedúnkaj *present participle of* فاسدېدل پژ فاسدېدونکی perishable (of food products)

فاسفور fāsfór *m. plural* فاسفورس fasfórus *m. plural* phosphorus

فاسق fāsíḳ *Arabic* **1** vicious, depraved, debauched; immoral **2** *m.* debauchee, libertine

فاسل fāsíl *m.* ☞ فوسیل

فاسولیا fāsuljá *f.* green bean, haricot bean, French bean

فاسیل fāsíl *m.* ☞ فوسیل

فاسیلي fāsilí fossilized فاسیلي حیوانات fossilized animals

فاش fāsh *Arabic* evident, open, published; declared, announced فاش کول to make known, declare; publish, publicize

فاشیزم fāshízm *m.* fascism

فاشیست fāshíst *m.* fascist

فاشیستي fāshistí **1** *adjective* fascist **2** *m.* Fascist

فاصل fāsíl *Arabic* **1** dividing, separating, detaching **2** demarcational فاصل حد border فاصل خط line of demarcation

فاصلوي fāsilaví *Arabic* فاصلوي نښه hyphen

فاصله fāsilá *f. Arabic* [*plural:* فاصلي fasilé *m. Arabic plural:* فواصل favásíl] **1** interim, interval, space **2** distance **3** partition **4** break

فاصولیا fāsuljá *f.* green bean, haricot bean, French bean

فاضل fāzíl *Arabic* **1.1** learned, educated فاضله ښڅه an educated woman **1.2** excelling **1.3** luxuriant; excessive; superfluous **1.4** supplemental **2** *m.* **.1** [*plural:* فاضلان fāzilán *Arabic plural:* فضلا fuzalá] learned man, scientist; educated man **2.2** ☞ فاضله 1

فاضله fāzlá *f. Arabic* **1** surplus, excess; remainder **2** spare, superfluous فاضله مواد excretion; excrement

فاطمه fātimá *f. proper name* Fatima

فاعل fā'íl *Arabic* **1** active, doing, making; working **2** *m.* **.1** agent **2.2** operator **2.3** worker **2.4** *grammar* agent, person performing the act

فاعل مختار fa'il-i-mukhtár free in one's actions; acting of one's own will, independent

فاعلي fā'ilí **1** active; operational; effective **2** *grammar* ergative فاعلي جمله ergative construction **a** present participle **b** noun of agent

فاعلیت fā'iliját *m. Arabic* **1** state of action **2** activity; operational state; effectiveness

فاق fáḳ *m. Arabic* crack, cleft; opening, aperture; groove; channel, fluting

فاقد fāḳíd *Arabic* deprived of something; having lost something

فاقه fāḳá *Arabic* **1** *f.* **.1** poverty, destitution; need **1.2** hunger, starvation, fasting فاقه کول to be hungry; fast **2** poor, destitute (of a person)

فاقه کښ fāḳakásh fasting, starving; hungry

فاقه کښي fāḳakashí *f.* **1** hunger, fasting **2** starvation

فاکتور fāktór factor

فاکولته fākultá faculty, university academic department د ادبیاتو فاکولته faculty of literature

فال fāl [1] *m. Arabic* **1** divination, fortunetelling, prophesy, فال نیول، فالونه اچول to tell fortunes, practice sorcery; tell the future **2** omen دا یو بختور فال دئ This is a good omen.

فال fāl [2] *m.* diet; abstinence

فالبین fālbín *m.* fortune-teller, palmist فال بین،

فالبینه fālbína *f.* fortune-teller, palmist (female)

فالبیني fālbiní *f.* fortune-telling, palmistry فالبیني کول to tell fortunes, tell the future

فالپښتنه fālpukhtána *f.* ☞ فال کتنه

فالت fált *m. geology* fold

فالتو fāltú **1** *m.* **.1** stock, store (of some objects or other) **1.2** spare part **1.3** *colloquial* reserve (of a military person) فالتو کول to transfer to reserve **2.1** spare فالتو سامان spare parts **2.2** extra, surplus

فالج fālídzh *Arabic* **1** *m.* paralysis فالج شوی a paralytic; an invalid **2** *predicative* paralyzed فالج کېدل *compound verb* to be paralyzed

فالسه fālsá *f.* Grewia asiatica (tree yielding edible fruit and lumber)

فالکتنه fālkatána *f.* فالګیري fālgirí *f.* sorcery, fortune-telling, telling the future

فالوده fāludá *f.* jam

فالېز fāléz *m.* melon field; kitchen garden ☞ پالېز

فالېزکاري fālezkārí *f.* melon cultivation

فامیل fāmíl *m.* **1** surname, family name د فامیل نوم لرل to bear a surname, have a family name ستاسې د فامیل نوم څه دئ؟ What is your surname? **2** family بشري فامیل human race **3** *biology* family باغلي فامیل legumes *idiom* د فامیل چای black Chinese tea

فامیلپالنه fāmilpālána *f.* concern for the family

فامیله fāmilá *combining form* family, familial څلور فامیله ودانی a four-family house

فامیلي fāmilí *adjective* family, familial فامیلي نوم family فامیلي ژوند family life

فانتزي fāntazí *f.* fantasy

فانوس fānús *m.* **1** lantern, lamp لاتین او فانوس lamp with a candle **2** magic lantern

فانه fāná *f.* **1** wedge **2** bolt, catch, lock, bar

فاني fāní *Arabic* liable to decay, perishable; unstable; ephemeral

فائده fāidá *f. Arabic* [*plural:* فائدې fāidé *m. Arabic plural:* فوائد favāíd] **1** use, advantage په دې کښي هیڅ فائده نشته This is completely useless. نوڅه فائده؟ To what use? To what advantage? و... ته فائده رسول، و... ته فائده را رسول to assist, help **2** profit, gain **a** فائده لرل **a** to be useful **b** to yield, produce profit, gain فائده کول **a** to be useful **b** to have material value **c** to be profitable فائده میندل **a** to derive use, derive advantage **b** to derive profit, derive gain د یو شي څخه فائده اخیستل **a** to get use or profit

533

from something **b** to derive advantage د فائده اخیستلو تنده thirst for profit, greed for gain **3** outcome; result

فائده بخش fāidabákhsh **1** useful, having a use; advantageous **2** beneficial

فائده مند fāidamánd فائده ناک fáidanãk **1** useful; advantageous **2** profitable, income-bearing

فایرپروف fãjrprúf **1** fireproof, fire-resistant **2** secure in terms of fire-resistance

فائز fāíz *Arabic* **1** overcoming something; attaining success **2** fortunate, successful

فائض fāíz *Arabic* **1** abundant, abounding in **2** generous

فائق fāíḳ *Arabic* surmounting, superior; superlative

فائقیت fāiḳiját *m. Arabic* superiority فائقیت لرل، فائقیت کول to have superiority

فاینل fãjnál finál د فاینل لوبه the decisive play

فبروری fabruarí *f.* February

فت fut *m.* ☞ فت [1]

فتاح fattáh *Arabic* **1** *religion* He who opens the door of happiness (epithet of God) **2** *m. proper name* Fattah

فت بال futbál *m.* football, soccer

فتح fath *Arabic f.* [plural: فتحي fáthi *Arabic plural:* فتوح futúh] **1** victory; winning, conquest فتح به زمورږ وي We will conquer. فتح به He attained victory. فتح یې بیا مونده پر هغه تمامه سي Victory will be ours. فتح کول **a** to attain victory **b** to subjugate, conquer جنگ فتح کول to win the war **2** *m. proper name* Fateh

فتحمند fatamánd victorious, conquering

فتحنامه fathnámá *f.* victorious communique, victorious report

فتحه fátha *f.* ☞ فتح 1, 2

فتحه fathá *f. Arabic* fatha, zabar (surpralinear symbol used to indicate the short vowel phoneme /a/)

فتحه مند fathamánd ☞ فتحمند

فتحه مندي fthamandí *f.* triumph, victory

فتحیاب fatahjãb ☞ فتحمند

فتراک fitrãk *m.* saddle straps or cords fixed to a saddle and used to tie game, etc.

فتق fatḳ *m. Arabic* **1** *medicine* hernia **2** rupture, tear, strain

فتق بند fatḳbánd *m.* truss (for one suffering from a hernia)

فتنه fitná *f. Arabic* **1** disturbance; commotion; mutiny, rebellion **2** disaster **3** anxiety; unpleasantness فتنه کول **a** to foment mutiny; rebel **b** to harm **c** to cause anxiety, cause unpleasantness

فتنه انگیز fitnaangéz *m.* troublemaker; disrupter, disturber of the peace; instigator

فتنه انگیزي titnaangezí *f.* ☞ فتنه 1

فتنه جو fitnadzhú **1** engaging in machinations, taking part in intrigue **2** *m.* troublemaker; instigator

فتوا fatvá *f.* فتوالیک fatvālík *m. Arabic* ☞ فتوی

فتوت futtuvát *m. Arabic* magnanimity; generous; nobility

فتوح futúh *m. Arabic plural of* فتح

فتوحات futuhãt *m. second plural of* فتح

فتور futúr *m. Arabic* **1** exhaustion; fatigue; weakness; flaccidity په لبمه فتور راوستل to bring to a state of exhaustion, fatigue; weaken فتور راشي The eyesight is weakening. **2** quarrel; squabble; argument

فتوی fatvá *f. Arabic* fatwa, decree, sentence, judgement (decision reached by a Muslim ecclesiastical official on a legal or religious matter) فتوی ورکول to issue a fatwa

فتیله fatilá` *f. Arabic* wick, fuse

فت fuṭ *m.* foot دوه فته two feet [1]

فت fiṭ *regional* fit, suitable د فوغ د پاره فت نه دئ He is unfit for military service. [2]

فتاپت paṭãpát rumbling, roaring موټر فتاپت روان و The car was roaring along at full speed.

فت بال futḅál *m.* **1** football, soccer **2** football, soccer ball د فتپال لویغاړی football player, soccer player

فت نوټ fuṭnót *m.* note, footnote

فت واري fuṭvārí *f. regional* extent, length in feet

فټومو faṭomú paṭomú *regional* damn you; be thou accursed

فټه fúṭa ☞ فټ [1]

فټه ایز fuṭajíz fiṭajíz ۶۰ فته ایزه پایه pillar 60 feet in height

فجائع fadzhāí *m. Arabic plural of* فجیعه فاجعه and

فجور fudzhúr *m. Arabic* debauchery, dissipation

فجیع fadzhí *Arabic* sad, regrettable; tragic

فجیعه fadzhí'á *f. Arabic* [plural: فجیعي fadzhi'e *m. Arabic plural:* فجائع fadzhai'] **1** horror **2** tragic event; tragedy, calamity; misfortune **3** cruelty

فحاش fahhásh *m. Arabic* foul-mouthed person

فحاشي fahhāshí *f.* **1** swearing, cursing, verbal abuse **2** viciousness, corruption; debauchery, depravity **3** prostitution فحاشي کول **a** to swear, curse **b** to be engaged in corrupt acts **c** to be engaged in prostitution

فحش fuhsh *m. Arabic* swearing, foul language, cursing، فحش ویل په فحش اخته کېدل to swear, use foul language, curse

فحوا falivá *f. Arabic* significance, meaning فحوی

فخر fakhr *m. Arabic* **1** glory, honor **2** object of pride په چا باندي فخر کول to take pride in one's origins د خپل لاس په گټو فخر کول to take pride in the fruits of one's labor فخر مي دئ چه ... *official* I have the honor (to) ... په دپر فخر عرض کول چه ... I have the honor to report ... فخر گڼل to consider it an honor, take pride in

فخري fakhrí *Arabic* honorary, honorable

فدا fidã *Arabic* **1** *f.* (exculpatory, sin) offering فدا کول *compound verb* to offer in sacrifice, sacrifice د آزادۍ فدا شو He died for freedom. **2** *f.* self-sacrifice **3** *f.* ransom (for a prisoner) **4** *m. proper name* Fida

فداکار fidãkãr selflessly dedicated, selfless, wholehearted فداکاره ښنځه faithful wife, dedicated wife هغه فداکار دئ He is wholeheartedly dedicated to the work.

فداکاري fidākārí *f.* selflessness; selfless dedication

فدائي fidāí *m.* فدائي fidājí 1 man giving his life for a sacred matter; patriot; man who is selflessly dedicated to an idea 2 man who is dedicated to someone ستا فدائي يم I am dedicated to you. I love you wholeheartedly.

فدراسیون federāsjón *m.* federation د فت بال فدراسیون football federation, soccer federation

فدرال federál فدرالي federali federal; federative فدرال جمهوريت federative republic

فدویت fidaviját *m. Arabic* ☞ فداکاري

فدیه fidjá *f. Arabic* 1 ransom فدیه ورکول to pay ransom 2 *religion* fulfillment of an obligation, discharging of a debt

فدربشن feḍerashán *m.* federation

فرات furát *m. Arabic* 1 Euphrates د فرات دریاب، د فرات سین the Euphrates River 2 fresh water

فراخ farákh broad, expansive, wide

فراخوالی fərākhválaj *m.* ☞ فراخي

فراخول fərākhavál *denominative* [*past:* فراخ یې کړ] to widen, expand, broaden اتکائي نقطه فراخول to widen the bridgehead

فراخه fərákha *f. singular of* فراخ سینه فراخه broad chest

فراخي fərākí *f.* width

فراخېدل fərākhedál *denominative, intransitive* [*past:* فراخ شو] to be broadened, broaden

فرار firár farár *m. Arabic* flight; escape; desertion فرار کول a to flee; desert b *compound verb of* فرارول

فرارول firāravál *denominative, transitive* [*past:* فرار یې کړ] to drive away, take away, lead away; compel to make an escape; force to flee

فراري firārí *m.* refugee, escapee; deserter فراري غل robber, brigand (fleeing from justice)

فراریت firāriját *m.* desertion

فرارېدل firāredál *denominative, intransitive* [*past:* فرار شو] to flee, desert

فراز ¹ firáz *m.* ascent, rise; takeoff فراز کول to evaporate, vanish (of steam)

فراز ² faráz *m.* 1 ascent, rise, upward movement 2 *combining form* سرفراز proud

فراست firāsát *m.* فراسات farāsát *Arabic* 1 perspicacity; quick-wittedness; quickness on the uptake د فوق العاده فراست خاوند دئ He is very perspicacious. 2 smartness; skill, know-how

فراش farásh *m.* فرّاش farrásh *Arabic* 1 servant whose duties are to spread the carpets or floor coverings 2 servant, guard (for a mosque, temple)

فراش باشي، فراشباشي farāshbāshí farrāshbāshí *m.* 1 principal servant, majordomo 2 *history* chamberlain

فراشخانه farāshkhāná *f.* farrāshkhāná storeroom for carpets and rugs

فراشه farásha *f.* farrāsha maid, housemaid

فراشي farāshí *f.* farrāshí work and job of a chamberlain

فراغ farágh *m. Arabic* 1 idleness, lack of occupation 2 termination, completion of work فراغ کول a to be freed from work b to be finished, be completed 3 ☞ فراغت

فراغت farāghát *m. Arabic* leisure time, free time; rest د فراغت روځ free day, day off موقتي فراغت respite

فراق firāķ *m. Arabic* separation, parting

فراک frák *m.* fərák frock coat, tailcoat, tails

فراکسیون frāksión *m.* fraction

فراموش farāmósh farāmúsh forgotten

فراموش کاري farāmushkārí *f.* forgetfulness; absentmindedness

فرامین farāmín *m. Arabic plural of* فرمان

فرانس frāns *m.* France

فرانسوي frānsaví 1 French فرانسوي ژبه French, French language 2.1 *m.* Frenchman 2.2 *f.* French, French language

فرانسه frāsná *f.* France

فرانسیس frānsís *m.* Frenchman

فرانسیسي frānsisí ☞ فرانسوي

فرانک fránk *m.* franc

فراوان farāván firāván فراوانه farāvána firāvána plentiful, abundant

فراورده farāvardá *f.* food product زراعتي فراورده agricultural production

فراه faráh *m.* farráh Farakh (city) د فراه ولایت Farakh Province *idiom* د فراه کانی grindstone, whetstone

فراهم farāhám 1 gathered, assembled, collected فراهم کول to gather, collect, assemble (e.g., information, data) فراهم کېدل to be gathered, be collected, be assembled (e.g., of information, data) 2 together, at the same time

فرائض farāíz *m. Arabic plural of* فریضه

فرجه furdzhá *f. Arabic* 1 slit; aperture 2 dispute; split

فرح بخش farahbákhsh joyful

فرحت farhát *Arabic* 1 *m.* pleasure; joy; comfort, consolation 2 *f. proper name* Farhat

فرخ farrúkh 1 happy, fortunate (of a man) 2 propitious

فرخنده tarkhundá happy, fortunate, propitious

فرد fard *Arabic* 1 *m.* .1 [*plural:* افراد afrád] man, individual; person, human being, party د حکومت فرد government figure 1.2 [*plural:* افراد afrád] warrior, soldier, enlisted man, private 1.3 [*plural:* فردونه fardúna] list register; roster 1.4 one line (of poetry), verse 1.5 [*plural:* فردونه fardúna] individual 2.1 odd 2.2 only, sole, unique

فردا fardá *poetry* tomorrow

فردوس firdaús *m.* heavenly garden, celestial tabernacles, elysian fields

فردي fardí 1 individual; personal فردي انکشاف the development of personality فردي ګټه personal advantage 2 separate (of a family)

فردیت fardiját *Arabic* 1 uniqueness 2 individuality, individualism

فرزانه farzāná 1 wise; learned 2 intelligent

فرزند farzánd *m. poetry* 1 son 2 child

فرزندي farzandí *f.* position of a son په فرزندي اخيستل، په فرزندي نيول to adopt as a son

فرزين farzín *m. chess* queen

فرس farás *m. Arabic chess* knight

فرسخ farsákh *m.* فرسنگ farsang *m.* farsakh (measure of distance equal to 6.8 km.), league, parasang

فرسوده farsudá **1** worn, effaced **2** out-of-date, outdated (of news, data, information) فرسوده کېدل **a** to wear out, become dilapidated **b** to get old, become outdated, grow stale (of news, data, information)

فرش farsh *Arabic* **1** *m.* **.1** bedding, litter; carpet; rug; floor matting **1.2** spreading, strewing (i.e., of material on the floor) **1.3** floor, flooring **1.4** pavement **2** *predicative* covered, spread

فرشبندي farshbandí *f.* **1** paving, covering, bedding, litter **2** pavement material فرشبندي کول **a** to cover, spread, litter **b** to pave

فرښته firishtá *f.* ☞ فرښته

فرشول farshavál *denominative, transitive* [*past:* فرش يې کړ] **1** to cover, spread over **2** to lay (on top of) **3** to pave **4** to face

فرشېدل farshedál *denominative, intransitive* [*past:* فرش شو] **1** to be covered, be spread over **2** to be laid on, be laid on top of **3** to be paved **4** to be faced (with)

فرښتانه firiḵtāná angelic

فرښته firiḵtá *f.* angel هغه فرښته ده She is an angel.

فرصت fursát *m. Arabic* convenient opportunity; convenient time; propitious moment; propitious circumstances ده دي فرصت مي نه و I did not succeed in doing this. ما ته فرصت نشته I don't have the time. فرصت حاصلول to seize an appropriate moment, find an appropriate opportunity, use the occasion (to) بنه فرصت له لاسه ايستل to miss a propitious opportunity فرصت غنيمت ګڼل to take advantage of the occasion و چا ته فرصت ورکول to give someone the opportunity (to) فرصت ته يې کتل They waited for a propitious opportunity. له فرصت څخه استفاده کول to take advantage of the appropriate moment or occasion

فرض farz *m. Arabic* **1.1** debt, obligation پر ځان فرض بلل، پر ځان هغه کار تر سره کول راباندي فرض ګڼل to consider as one's obligation فرض دئ I am obliged to execute this work. **1.2** obligatory religious injunction فرض ادا کول to carry out (a religious) obligation تا خپل فرض ادا کړه *Eastern* You carried out your obligation. **1.3** assumption, guess فرض کول **a** to suppose, guess **2** فرضول ☞ compound verb فرض وکړه چه ... Suppose that ... **b** *compound verb* ☞ فرضول *predicative* obligatory

فرضاً fárzán *Arabic* **1** supposedly, presumably **2** let us suppose, let us presume

فرضول farzavál *denominative, transitive* [*past:* فرض يې کړ] to suppose, presume داسي فرضوو چه ... we suppose ... we presume that ... دا فرض کړه چه ... Just imagine that ...

فرضي farzí *Arabic* **1** supposed, presumed, imagined, imaginary مځکه يو فرضي محور لري The earth has an imaginary axis. **2**

فرضي nominal, fictive, fictitious فرضي نومونه fictitious names **3** required by religion or morals

فرضيات farziját *m. Arabic plural of* فرضيه

فرضيت farziját *m.* ☞ فرضيه

فرضېدل farzedál *denominative, intransitive* [*past:* فرض شو] to be presupposed; be considered دا فرضېدلی شي چه ... It can be suggested that ...

فرضيه farzijá *f. Arabic* [*plural:* فرضيې farzijé *m. Arabic plural:* فرضيات farziját] **1** hypothesis; assumptions, supposition, presumption; presentation **2** *religion* instruction; command

فرع fár'a *f. Arabic m.* [*plural:* فروع furú] **1** branching; offshoot; branch **2** subsidiary **3** development **4** outcome, conclusion **5** derived from something **6** percentage rates (on capital)

فرعاً fár'án *Arabic* partly

فرعون fir'aún *m. Arabic* **1** pharaoh د فرعون مرغه guinea fowl **2** tyranny

فرعوني fir'auní *f.* فرعونيت fir'auniját *m.* **1** haughtiness **2** tyranny

فرعي far'í *Arabic* **1** derived; subsidiary فرعي کوميته auxiliary committee; subcommittee **2** secondary; minor **3** approach (of a road)

فرغانه fargāná *f.* Fergana (city)

فرفر farfár fərfər **1** quickly, swiftly **2** smoothly, tranquilly

فرفره farfará *f.* fïrfirá **1** top **2** revolving object (i.e., door, bookcase)

فرق farḳ *m. Arabic* difference, disparity, distinction فرق لرل to be distinct from ... فرق نلري indifferently, of no matter يو تر بله فرق لرل، يو تر بله سره فرق لرل to differ; be distinct from one's another; be different from one another فرق کول **a** to differ, be distinct **b** to change, alter

فرقان furḳán *m. Arabic* Koran

فرقوي firḳaví *Arabic adjective* group; sectarian; factional فرقوي جګړي clique-formation; sectarianism; fractionalism فرقوي تعصب squabble; dissention

فرقه firḳá *f. Arabic* **1** group; detachment **2** *religion* sect, persuasion **3** faction **4** *military* division

فرقه بندي firḳabandí *f.* فرقه پرستي firḳaparastí *f.* **1** grouping; clique-formation **2** squabble, dissention

فرقه مشر firḳmáshr *m.* firḳmáshər general اول فرقه مشر lieutenant general د ويم فرقه مشر major general ثاني فرقه مشر

فرلانگ farláng *m. regional* furlong

فرم firm *m.* farm firm

فرم² farm *m.* bench; school bench, desk

فرماليته formālitá *f.* formality

فرمان farmán *m. Arabic* [*plural:* فرمانونه farmānúna *plural:* فرامين farāmín] order; decree; document د چا تر فرمان لاندي being subordinate to someone د چا فرمان وړل to execute someone's orders; be subordinate to someone

فرمان بردار farmānbardár submissive, obedient, being subordinate د چا فرمان بردار کېدل to be subordinate, be submissive to someone

فرمان برداري farmānbardārí *f.* obedience, submission, subordination فرمان برداري کول to be subordinate

فرمان دهي farmāndehhí *f.* command, commanding

فرمان وړونکی farmắn vṛúnkaj obedient, submissive

فرمايش farmājísh *m.* ☞ فرمايښت

فرمايشي farmājishí ordered, reserved

فرمايښت farmājə́kht *m.* order فرمايښت ورکول to issue an order, order

فرمايل farmājə́l *transitive* [*past:* و يې فرمايه] *polite form of* ويل **1** to speak, deign to speak شيخ سعدي فرمائي Saadi writes. **2** to order; ordain **3** to condescend, deign to do something دا اظهاري يي وفرمايه ... They deigned to state ... د کابل و خواته يې حرکت وفرمايه They deigned to leave Kabul.

فرمل firmál *m.* Birmal (district, Pakti Province)

فرملي firmalí **1** Birmalian **2** *m.* citizen of Birmal

فرموده farmudá *f.* **1** command, order **2** instruction له ستاسي سم according to your instructions فرمودي سره **3** command, injunction, behest

فرنجل firindzhál *m.* Firinjal (settlement, Gorbend)

فرنگ faráng *m.* European *idiom* باد فرنگ syphilis

فرنگستان farangistán *m. obsolete* Europe

فرنگي farangí farangáj **1** *m.* **.1** Englishman **1.2** European **2.1** English **2.2** European

فرنگۍ farangə́j **1** *f.* **.1** English woman **1.2** European woman **2** *feminine singular of* فرنگي 2

فرنگيتوب farangitób *m.* European manners; imitation of Europeans

فرني firní *f.* [*plural:* فرني گاني firnigani] rice gruel; kind of blancmange of rice flour

فروري farvarí *f.* February

فروزان furuzán *poetry* radiant, shining

فروش furúsh *m.* farósh sale, selling, sales

فروش کار furushkā́r *m.* merchant, seller

فروع dfurú *m. Arabic plural of* فروع

فروعات furu'ā́t *m.* **1** *second plural of* فروع **2** judicial assembly

فرونزي frúnze *m.* Frunze (city)

فرهاد farhā́d *m. proper name* Farhad

فرهنگ farháng *m.* **1** dictionary; lexicon **2** culture

فرهنگي farhangí **1** cultural فرهنگي همکاري cultural collaboration **2** educational

فرياد farjā́d *m.* **1** groaning, crying out, weeping; shout (for help) فرياد نبلول to cry out, yell په فرياد کېدل to grieve over فرياد کول to cry out, raise a rumpus **2** complaint پر چا باندي فرياد کول، چا ته فرياد کول to complain to someone

فريادرس farjādrás *m.* patron, protector; comforter

فريادي farjādí *m.* **1** complaint فريادي چا ته ورتلل to go to someone with a complaint **2** complaining; alarming

فريب faréb firéb *m.* **1** deceit, betrayal, swindling د سترگو او نظر فريب optical illusion حربي فريبونه military strategem فريب خورل to be deceived په چا فريب کول، په چا فريب ورکول to cheat somebody, swindle someone **2** temptation

فريب آميز farebāméz deceitful; mendacious

فريبکاري farebkārí *f.* deceit, cheating

فريبگر farebgár deceitful, mendacious فريبگر سړی cheat, swindler, con man

فريبي farebí *m.* cheat, swindler, con man

فريتون، فري ټون friṭáun *m.* Freetown (city)

فريد faríd *Arabic* **1** incomparable, matchless, unmatched **2** *m. proper name* Farid

فريشانه fareshā́na ☞ پرېشان

فريضه farizá *f. Arabic* [*plural:* فريضي farizé *m. Arabic plural:* فرائض farāíz] **1** religious obligation (fast, prayer) **2** debt, obligation خپله فريضه بلل to consider as one's obligation

فريفته fareftá poetry **1** deceived **2** in love, lovelorn

فريق faríḳ *m. Arabic* [*plural:* فريقان fariḳā́n *plural:* فريقين faiḳájn] **1** *regional* one engaged in a suit بل فريق the opposing side پر فريق the losing side ور فريق the winning side د مقدمي فريقين the litigants فريق اول faríḳ-i plaintiff, complaint فريق ثاني faríḳ-i defendant, accused **2** section, part of something **3** group, detachment

فرېکوېنسي trekvénsi *f. physics* frequency

فرېم frem *m.* **1** frame (of spectacles, glasses, etc.) **2** mounting, framework, hull

فرېوان frevā́n فرېوانه frevā́ba plentiful, abundant

فزيک fizíks *m.* ☞ فزيک

فزيالوژي fizijālodzhí *f.* ☞ فزيولوژي

فزيالوژيک fizijālodzhík فزيالوجيکي fizijālodzhiki ☞ فزيولوژيک

فزيک fizík *m.* physics ذروي فزيک nuclear physics د فزيک اطاق physics laboratory د فزيک د علم پوهاند physical scientist

فزيکپوه fizikpóh *m.* دان فزيک fizikdan *m.* physicist

فزيکه fiziká *f.* ☞ فزيک

فزيکي fizikí physical; natural فزيکي شکل build, frame فزيکي محيط physical and geographic environment

فزيولوژي fizijolozhí **1** *f.* physiology **2** physiological

فزيولوژيک fizijolozhkík فزيولوژيکي fizijolozhiki physiological

فساد fasád *m. Arabic* [*plural:* فسادونه fasāduna *Arabic plural:* فسادات fasadā́t] **1** disturbance; disorder اخلاقي فساد moral dissolution **2** harm; misfortune; evil لوی فساد پيدا شو Great unpleasantness resulted therefrom. فساد جوړول، فساد کول a to cause disturbances, instigate troubles; sow dissent b to harm, spoil

فسادي fasādí **1.1** causing disorders; sowing dissent **1.2** evil, harmful **1.3** troublesome **2** *m.* [*plural:* فساديان fasādiján] troublemaker; plotter, intriguer

فست کلاس fasṭklā́s *regional* **1** first-class **2** of the first class or rank فست کلاس ټکټ first-class ticket

فسخ faskh *m. Arabic* **1** abolition, annulment د قرارداد فسخ abrogation of a treaty **2** breaking, disruption (of a relationship) فسخ کېدل *compound verb* ☞ فسخول فسخ کول *compound verb* ☞ فسخېدل

فسخول faskhavól *denominative, transitive* [*past:* فسخ يې کړ] **1** to annul; dissolve **2** to disrupt, break off

فسخه fáskha *f.* ☞ فسخ

فسخېدل faskhedól *denominative, intransitive* [*past:* فسخ شو] **1** to be annulled, be dissolved **2** to be broken off (of relationships)

فسق fisk *m. Arabic* **1** dissipation, profligacy; immorality **2** violation of religious law, sinfulness فسق کول **a** to dissipate, engage in depravities **b** to violate religious law, sin

فش fash ☞ فاش

فشار fishár *m.* **1** pressure جوي فشار، هوايي فشار atmospheric pressure فشار خونه airtight, pressurized cabin; pressurized chamber په فشار خون مبتلا شو fishár-i high blood pressure; hypertonia He suffered from hypertonia. **2** oppression, violence, pressure, coercion سياسي فشار political pressure, political coercion په چا فشار راوستل to exert pressure, coercion on someone فشار ورول **3** a multiplicity of matters; affairs د کار فشار a program of work, work committment

فصاحت fasāhát *m. Arabic* eloquence; smoothness of speech, elegance of (written, spoken) style

فصحا fushā *m. Arabic plural of* فصيح

فصل fasl *m. Arabic* [*plural:* فصلونه faslúna *Arabic m. plural:* فصول fusúl] **1** time of the year, season **2** epoch, time, period **3** six months, half a year په فصل **a** according to the times, seasons of the year **b** according to half-yearly periods **4** sowing, crops فصل standing crops پسينه فصل grain shoots ولاړ فصل خپتي فصل late crop سمسور فصل nearly ripe grain رنګي فصل a sparse crop اوري فصل spring مئينه فصل early crop د گڼ فصل abundant crop هغه مځکي دوه فصله شوي دي These lands now yield two crops. **5** chapter, section (of a book) **6** solution (of a problem) **7** act (of a play) فصل کول *compound verb* to solve (a problem) فصل کېدل *compound verb* to be solved (of a problem)

فصلانه faslāná *f. regional* harvest tax

فصلي faslí seasonal

فصول fusúl *m. Arabic plural* **1** *of* فصل **2** four seasons of the year

فصيح fasíh *Arabic* **1** eloquent; flowing, pure, clear (speech) **2** *m.* eloquent man

فصيل fasíl *m. Arabic* parapet; breastworks; trench

فضا fazā *f. Arabic* **1** space; expanse; area **2** air, atmosphere تانده فضا pure air, fresh air د مځکي فضا the terrestrial atmosphere خارجي فضا ته الوتنه space flight, flight into outerspace باندیني فضا، خارجي فضا spaceship **3** atmosphere, ambience د خارجي فضا بېړی سياسي فضا the political atmosphere مساعده فضا favorable circumstances **4** yard, courtyard

فضاپيما fazāpajmā **1** *adjective* space فضاپيما بېړی spaceship **2** *m.* astronaut

فضاحت fazāhát *m. Arabic* shame, dishonor په ډېر فضاحت with great shame, ingloriously

فضانورد fazānavárd *m.* astronaut

فضائل fazāíl *m. Arabic plural of* فضيلت

فضائي fazāí **1** aerial فضائي عکسونه aerial photography فضائي پوسته airmail **2** فضائي وزارت Ministry of Aviation فضائي قوه Air Force فضائي پرواز space flight فضائي بېړی spaceship لوړه فضائي چاودنه space high-altitude explosion

فضل fazl *m. Arabic* **1** superiority, perfection; merit, virtue **2** grace; generosity **3** [*plural:* فضول fuzúl] surplus, profit **4** *proper name* Fazl

فضلا fuzalā *m. Arabic plural of* فاضل **1, 2**

فضلات fazalāt *m. Arabic plural* [*plural:* فضله fazlá] **1** excrement, stools; feces; dung فضلات لیري کول to remove dung **2** products of decomposition **3** *physiology* excretion

فضل فروشي fazlfurushí *f.* conceit

فضله fazlá *f. Arabic m.* [*plural:* فضلات fazalāt] waste products, refuse

فضول [1] fuzúl *m. Arabic* فضل

فضول [2] fuzul *Arabic* **1.1** inappropriate, unnecessary **1.2** superfluous; surplus, inordinate **1.3** obtrusive, interfering in another's business **2** *m.* **.1** importunity **2.2** innappropriateness فضول خرخ سری fuzulkhárts extravagant, wasteful **a** prodigal, a spendthrift

فضولي fuzulí **1** *f.* **.1** inappropriateness; misplaced interference **1.2** superfluity; abundance, extremes **1.3** importunity **1.4** wilfullness **2.1** ☞ فضول [2] **2.2** willfull

فضيحت fazihát *m. Arabic* shame, disgrace, dishonor فضيحت کول to shame, disgrace, dishonor فضيحت کېدل to be shamed, be disgraced, be dishonored

فضيحت آمېز fazihatāméz shameful, disgraceful, dishonorable

فضيلت fazilát *m. Arabic* **1** perfection, superiority فضيلت او کمالات perfections **2** erudition **3** [*plural:* فضائل fazāíl] *Arabic* merit, virtue

فضيلت مآب fazilatmāb *m.* title for a judge, qadi

فطر fitr *m. Arabic* first meal eaten after a fast, breaking of a fast

فطرت fitrát *m. Arabic* **1** nature انساني فطرت human nature **2** property, quality, attribute, character **3** predisposition **4** attraction **5** alms distributed after the breaking of a fast

فطرتاً fitrátán *Arabic* by nature, according to one's own nature

فطرتي fitratí **1** ☞ فطري **2** by nature, according to one's own nature

فطري fitrí *Arabic* **1** natural, innate, inborn **2** normal

فطير fatír *Arabic* unleavened (of dough, bread)

فعال fa'ál *Arabic* active, operative, energetic په یوه چاره کښې فعاله برخه اخیستل، په یوه چاره کښې فعاله برخه لرل to take active part in, actively participate in

فعالانه fa'ālāná efficatious, active, effective

فعاليت fa'āliját *m. Arabic* **1** *military* activity; effective action فعاليت کول to act, show activity مشترکه فعاليت to mine, set mines **2** *economics* operation, transaction **3** work, activity په فعاليت **a** په فعاليت راتلل، په فعاليت شروع کول، کښې اچول to put into operation to go into action, act, operate **b** to engage in battle, do combat

فعل fi'l fe'l *m. Arabic* [*plural:* فعلونه fa'lúna *m. Arabic plural:* افعال af'ál] **1** business, affair, activity, operation deed بد فعل کول to act poorly **2** *grammar* verb; verb form فعل لازمي intransitive verb متعدي فعل transitive verb افعال قياسي regular verb سماعي افعال irregular verbs (verbs of archaic conjugation) معاون افعال auxiliary verbs حال فعل fi'li, fé'l-i present tense

فعلاً fi'lán fé'lán *Arabic* at present, at the present time, now

فعلي fi'lí fe'lí **1** present-day, present **2** *grammar* verbal; verbal-derivative **3** active, operative

فغان fighán *m.* **1** cry, groan **2** *interjection* Alas!

فغفور faghfúr *m. history* **1** title of the bogdokhan (sacred ruler), emperor of imperial China **2** porcelain

فقار fakár *m. Arabic* vertebra

فقاريه fakārijá فقاريه حيوانات vertebral

فقدان fukdán fikdán *m. Arabic* **1** absence (e.g., of experience); lack **2** deprivation, loss

فقر fakr *m. Arabic* **1** poverty, destitution; want فقر کول to be destitute; be in want **2** poverty **3** impoverishment **4** alms فقر غوښتل to request alms

فقرا fukará *m. Arabic plural of* فقير

فقرات fikrát *m.* fikarát *Arabic plural of* فقره

فقرالدم fakr-ad-dám *m.* anemia

فقره fikrá *f. Arabic* [*plural:* فقري fikré *m. Arabic plural:* فقرات fikrát *plural:* fikarát] **1** paragraph, item لويه فقره paragraph **2** *grammar* phrase **3** *saying* **4** vertebra

فقط fakát *Arabic* **1** only, just, uniquely **2** that's all, the end (at the end of a letter, recipe, etc.)

فقه fíkh *m.* fíkha *Arabic* **1** *religion* fiqh, theology, jurisprudence **2** knowledge

فقها fukahá *m. Arabic plural of* فقيه

فقه اللغت fíkh-ul-lughát *m. Arabic* etymology

فقهه fíkha *f.* ☞ فقه

فقيد fakíd *Arabic* **1** deceased, departed; official late, fallen asleep in the Lord (of a monarch) **2** irretrievably expended, lost

فقير fakír *Arabic* **1** *m.* [*plural:* فقيران fakirán *Arabic plural:* فقرا fukará] .**1** pauper, poor man **1.2** faqir, traveling dervish **1.3** *proper name* Faqir **2** poor

فقيره fakíra *f. singular of* فقير

فقيري fakirí *f.* **1** poverty, destitution فقيري کول to be destitute; be poverty-stricken; beg **2** hermit's life, way of life of a dervish

فقيه fakíh *m. Arabic* [*plural:* فقها fukahá] specialist in Muslim law, a specialist in shariat

فكاهت fukāhát *m. Arabic* sharp-wittedness, humor; joke

فكاهي fukāhí *Arabic* humorous; jocular فكاهي جملي jokes; anecdotes په فكاهي ډول in joke

فكر fikr *m.* [*plural:* فكرونه fikrúna *Arabic plural:* افكار afkár] *Arabic* **1** thought; meditation; reflection; thoughtfulness ابتكاري initiative, undertaking د فكر ريم way of thinking په دې فكر يم Here's what I think. په دې ټولو کښي پر تا فکر لازم دئ You need to remember all this. په دې کښي بايد ښه فکر وکړو **a** to think One must think this through well. زما خبري واورئ او فکر ورباندي **b** to worry, be anxious ييخ Listen to me and think about it! وکړئ! **b** to worry, be anxious په يو شي to be prudent وراندي فکر لرل Don't worry! فکر مه کوه ! د فکر to think about, reflect on, think over something کښي فکر وهل He became pensive. فکر يي نه وررسبږي He is unable to grasp this. تال وهي لکه ستا په زه په فکر کښي پرپوتم I was deep in thought. فکر چه راځي، داسي نه ده This is not what you think. This is not what you imagine. فکر زغلول، په... فکر زغلول to think something over په فکر لوبدل **a** think up په خپل فکر کښي سنجول **b** to be pensive arrive at the view at the decision; become pensive **2** opinion زما په in my opinion له مونږ سره دا فکر شته چه ... We propose that فکر ستا دا فکر غلط دئ ... You are not right about this. **3** attention په ځما فکر نه و I did not pay attention. I did not فکر سره attentively notice. دومره دي فکر اوسه چه ... فکر مو اوسه چه to pay attention Just don't forget ... فکر يي بحث ته و He kept up with the dispute. ستاسو به فکر وي چه ... You probably noticed that ... دځان په فکر نه to د چا د فکر سلسله پربکول He has no concern for himself. distract someone زما و يو شعر ته فکر شو I remembered one verse. د اشنا کورنی ته فکر وراچول to think about or remember the family of a friend فکر ته راتلل to come to mind, remember

فکراً fikrán *Arabic* in an intellectual sense

فکرمن fikərmán فکرمند fikərmánd pensive; anxious

فکري fikrí *Arabic* **1** pensive **2** psychological; intellectual, philosophical فکري ارتقا intellectual development **3** ideational فکري جريان ideational flow فکري وحدت like-mindedness **4** pertaining to thought فکري خصوصيت intellect

فوکل fokól *m.* ☞ فوکول

فگار figár ☞ افگار

فلات falát *m. Arabic* plateau

فلاح[1] falláh *m. Arabic* fellah, agricultural field worker, peasant, grain farmer

فلاح[2] falá *f.* faláh *Arabic* **1** happiness **2** prosperity, well-being

فلاحت falāhát *m. Arabic* husbandry, grain farming, agriculture

فلاحتي falāhatí agrarian, agricultural

فلاحي falāhí *f.* ☞ فلاح[2]

فلاخن falākhún *m.* sling (weapon)

فلاسفر filásafar *m. regional* philosopher

فلاسفه falāsifá *m. Arabic plural* ☞ فيلسوف

فلاکت falākát *m. Arabic* poverty, need په فلاکت اخته کېدل to become poor, fall into want

فلاکس fláks *m.* falākás *botany* phlox

فلالجست filāladzhíst *m.* philologist

فلالوجي filālodzhí *f.* philology

فلالوجيک filālodzhík philological

فلالين falālín *m.* ☞

فلان fulán *Arabic pronoun* so-and-so, such-and-such

فلانکی flānkáj falānkáj plānkáj palānkáj *m.* ☞ فلانی

فلانل falāníl *m.* flannel

فلانی flānáj falānáj plānáj palānáj *m.* so-and-so (a man)

فلانین falānín *m.* ☞ فلانل

فلیپاین filipájn *m.* فلیپین filipín *m.* Phillipines, Phillipine Islands

فلتر filtr *m.* filter فلتر کول *compound verb* to filter

فلج faldzh *m. Arabic* **1** paralytic فلج د اطفالو poliomyelitis **2** *economics* depression فلج کول *compound verb* to paralyze

فلز filíz *m.* filízz *Arabic* [*plural:* فلزونه filizzúna *Arabic plural:* فلزات filizzát] metal

فلزجوړوونکی filízdzhoṛavúnkaj filízdzhoṛavúnkaj metallurgical

فلزساز filizsáz filizzsáz *m.* **1** metalworker **2** metallurgist

فلزسازي filizsází filizzsází *f.* metallurgy

فلزکاري filizkārí filizzkārí *f.* metal processing د فلزکاری صنایع the metal-proccssing industry

فلزي filizí filizzí metallic فلزي ذخیري metal ore deposits

فلس fals *m.* fils *Arabic* [*plural:* فلسونه filsúna *Arabic plural:* فلوس fulús] **1** scales (of a fish) **2** fils (small Iraqi coin worth 1/1000 of a dinar)

فلستاپ fulwstáp *m. regional* stop فلستاپ کول *compound verb* to make a stop

فلسطین filastín *m. Arabic* Palestine

فلسفه falsafá *f. Arabic* **1** philosophy **2** theory; theorectical bases, theoretical points of view

فلسفه دان falsafadán *m.* **1** philosopher **2** theorectician

فلسفي falssafí *Arabic* philosophical

فلسفیانه falsafijāná philosophical فلسفیانه خبري philosophizing

فلسي falsí squamous, scaly

فلفل filfíl *m.* pepper (the plant)

فلک falák *m. Arabic* [*plural:* افلاک] **1** sky; celestial sphere **2** *astronomy* orbit **3** fate, destiny

فلکس falakás *m.* phlox

فلک شکاف falakshikáf loud, piercing فلک شکافي ناري heartrending cries

فلکي falakí *Arabic* **1** celestial heavenly **2** astronomical

فلم film *m.* **1** film; movie رنگه فلم غږیدونکي فلم sound film color film د فلم اخیستلو hنري فلم artistic film اخباري فلم documentary film **a** to film a movie فلم اخیستل **b** ستودیو، د فلم ستودیو movie studio *m. plural* filming movies د فلم اخیستلو موظف کس movie cameraman د فلم ښکاره کول to show a film **2** photographic film فوتوگراف فلم photographic film

فلمبرداري filmbardārí *f.* filming, shooting د فلمبرداري دستگاه film camera د فلمبرداري hنرمند cameraman

فلم سازي filmsází *f.* production of films, creation of movies د فلم سازی صنعت the film industry

فلمگیري filmgirí *f.* ☞ فلمبرداري

فلنته filintá *f.* carbine; hunting rifle

فلنین falanín *m.* ☞ فلانل

فلوت flut *m. music* flute

فلور flor[1] *m.* flor (a breed of caracul sheep)

فلور flor[2] *m.* flora

فلوربسنت floresánt fluorescing, shining فلوربسنت برقي څراغونه fluorescent bulb, daylight quality lamp

فلوس fulús *m. Arabic plural of* فلس

فلیته falitá *f.* **1** ribbon **2** wick, fuse

فلیته دار falitadár matchlock (of a rifle)

فلبل fulél *m. plural* scented (hair) oil

فم fam *m. Arabic* **1** mouth, orifice **2** entry or upper aperture of the stomach

فن fan *m.* fann *Arabic* [*plural:* فنونه fannúna *Arabic plural:* فنون funún] **1** branch of science; science **2** technology **3** art لطیفه فنون the fine arts

فنا fana *f. Arabic* **1** destruction; death; mortality **2** nonexistence, disappearance; decomposition, transitoriness, perishability فنا کول to annihilate کېدل فنا to disappear فنا کول کمان **a** to be annihilated; perish **b** to hide, disappear **c** to dissolve څوک د فنا په کوهي کښي وراچول to destroy, lead someone to destruction

فنامنا fenámenā *m. plural* phenomena (of nature, etc.)

فنان fannán *m. Arabic* ☞ فنکار

فناناپذیر fanānāpazír **1** inexhaustible فناناپذیر منابع inexhaustible resources **2** imperishable, non-transitory

فندق fundúk *m.* **1** funduk (variety of small nut tree and its fruit, related to the hazelnut) **2** *endearment* lips of the beloved **3** *botany* bud

فنډ fanḍ *m.* fund, stock

فنر fanár *m.* spring, coil spring

فنروالا fanarvālá *adjective* spring

فنري fanarí *adjective* **1** spring **2** elastic فنري پلاستیک resilient or elastic plastic material

فنکار fannkár *m.* creative worker; artist, one active in art

فنکیانگ finkjáng *m.* Pyongyang (city)

فنلاند finlánd *m.* فنلند finlánd *m.* فنلنډ finlə́nḍ *m.* Finland د فنلاند خلیج the Gulf of Finland

فنلند finlénd *m.* فنلنډ finlénḍ *m.* Finland

فنلنډي finlenḍí **1** Finnish **2** *m.* Finn

فنومفن fnomfén *m.* pnomepén Phnom Penh (city)

فنون funún *m. Arabic plural of* فن

فني fanní *Arabic* **1** *f.* [*plural:* فنیه fannija] **.1** technical فني دستگاه technical equipment فني خلګ، فني کسان، فني وګري specialist, qualified workers, technicians **1.2** artistic فني صنعت art (painting, music, etc.); fine arts **2** *m.* [*plural:* فنیان fanniján] specialist

فنیات fanniját *m. Arabic plural* technology

فواد fuád *m. Arabic* **1** heart **2** *proper name* Fuad

فواره favārá favvárá *f. Arabic* fountain, jet, spout, spring

فواصل favāsíl *m. Arabic plural of* فاصله

فوائد favāíd *m. Arabic plural of* فائده

فوائد عامي favāid-i-'āmá *f.* governmental structure د فوائد عامي وزارت فوائدعامه Ministry of Public Works

فوت faut *m. Arabic* **1** decease, death فوت كول to die, pass away **2** loss بې د وخت له فوته not losing any time

فوتوگراف fotográf *m.* photograph

فوتوگرافي fotográfi *f.* ☞ فوتوگرافي

فوتي fautí dead

فوتېدل fautedól *denominative, intransitive* [*past:* فوت شو] **1** to die, pass away **2** to perish

فوتېده fautedó *m. plural* **1** death **2** destruction, ruin

فوت fut *m.* foot فوته ۱۵۰ 150 feet ☞ فټ [1]

فوټبال futbál *m.* football, soccer فوټبال، فوټ بال

فوټبال كوونكى futbál kavúnkaj *m.* football player, soccer player

فوټ نوټ futnót *m.* footnote, note

فوټو fotó *m. & f.* [*plural:* فوټوگان fotogán *f. plural:* فوټوگاني fotogáni] photograph, photographic print

فوټوگراف fotográf *m.* ☞ فوټوگرافي 1, 2

فوټوگرافي fotográfi *f.* **1.1** photography (the art) د فوټوگرافى اسباب photographic equipment د فوټوگرافى ځاى photographic studio د فوټوگرافى لابراتوار photographic laboratory هوايي فوټوگرافى اخيستل aerial photography **1.2** photograph, photographic print **2** photographic

فوج faudzh *m. Arabic* [*plural:* فوجونه faudzhúna *Arabic plural:* افواج afvádzh] army, troops فوج جوړول to gather troops, assemble troops

فوجدار faudzhdár *m. history* military leader, army commander

فوجكشي faudzhkashí *f.* فوج كښي faudzhkakhí *f.* **1** invasion, armed attack **2** campaign

فوځ faudz *m. regional* army troops دريائي فوځ Navy با قاعده فوځ the Regular Army فوځ ماتول to dismiss the army

فوځداري faudzdārí *adjective regional* criminal فوځداري مقدمه criminal case فوځداري حاكم criminal court فوځداري عدالت criminal court judges

فوځي faudzí *regional* **1.1** army; troop; military فوځي منصبدار officer فوځي عدالت military court, court martial فوځي سلوټ كول to salute **1.2** strategic **2** *m.* soldier, trooper; military man

فور faur *m. Arabic* speed, hurry

فوراً fáurán *Arabic* at once, immediately, quickly, urgently

فورت لامي fort-lāmí *m.* Fort Lamy (city, Africa)

فوركاست forkást *m.* weather forecast

فورم form *m.* **1** uniform (i.e., clothing) **2** school uniform

فورماليته formālité *m.* formality

فورمول formúla *m.* formula

فوري faurí *Arabic* urgent فوري خبر ناڅاپه urgently په فوري صورت 'sudden jump, sudden leap forward

فوريت fauriját *m.* فوري والى fauriválaj *m. Arabic* **1** urgency **2** hurry

فوسفور fosfór *m. plural* phosphorus

فوسفوري fosforí phosphoric فوسفوري مواد phosphorous compounds

فوسيل، فوصل fosíl *m.* fossil

فوضويت favzaviját *m. Arabic* anarchy

فوفنا fufaná annihilated, destroyed, exterminated فوفنا كول to annihilate, destroy, exterminate; perish ☞ پوپينا

فوفولزي fufulzí *m.* pupulzí ☞ پوپلزي

فوق fauk *m. Arabic* **1** top, summit **2** from the top, above, up on top

فوق البشر fauk-al-bashár *m. Arabic* superman

فوق العادگي fauk-ud-'ādagí *f.* **1** extraordinariness; urgent in nature **2** unusualness; outstanding

فوق العاده fauk-ul-'ādá *Arabic* **1** extraordinary, urgent فوق العاده احوال extraordinary circumstances **2** unusual, outstanding **3** prominent فوق العاده اشخاص prominent persons

فوق العادگي fauk-ul-'ādagí *f.* ☞ فوق العاده گي

فوقاني faukāní upper, top فوقاني قسمت upper part, upper half

فوقيت faukiját *m. Arabic* **1** ☞ فائقيت فضائي فوقيت air superiority **2** superiority

فوكول fokól *m.* collar

فولاد folád *m.* fulád *plural* steel د فولادو ويلي كول **a** to smelt steel **b** smelting of steel

فولادسازي folādsāzí *f.* steel production د فولادسازى فابريكه، فولادسازى كارخانه steel-annealing, steel-smelting factory

فولادي folādí *adjective* steel *idiom* فولادي غر نړول to get down to rather hard work فولادي اراده an iron will

فولكلور folklór *m.* **1** folklore **2** ethnography

فولكلوري folklorí **1** folkloric فولكلوري مواد folkloric material **2** ethnographic

فونوگراف fonográf *m.* phonograph

فونټيك fonetík *m.* phonetics

فونټيكي fonetikí phonetic

فونټيك fonetík *m.* ☞ فونټيك

فونټيكي fonetikí ☞ فونټيكي

فونم foném *m. linguistics* phoneme

فهرست fihríst *m.* **1** list, enumeration; index, directory; table of contents **2** notice د مجلس فهرست agenda

فهم fahm *m.* pam *Arabic* **1** understanding, apprehension, intelligence **2** intellect, reason

فهمول famavól *denominative, transitive* [*past:* فهم يې كړ] **1** to explain, elucidate, find out; become acquainted د دى اعلاميى څخه دا From this statement it is evident that ... ۇول فهمول كېږي **2** to understand, imagine, conceive

فهمېدل fahmedól *denominative, intransitive* [*past:* فهم شو] to be explained, be found out; have become acquainted څه ترې فهمېدلى What do you understand by this? شى؟

فهيم fahím *Arabic* **1** knowing; intelligent **2** *m. proper name* Fahim, Faheem

في fe *f.* the name of the letter ف [1]

في fi *Arabic preposition-prefix* **1** in; on **2** at, at the time [2]

فياض fajjáz *Arabic* **1** generous, magnanamous **2** *m. proper name* Fayaz

في الجمله fildzhumlá *Arabic* on the whole, in general

في الحال filhál *Arabic* at once, immediately

في الحاله filhála at the present time

في الحقيقت filhaḳiḳát *Arabic* actually, indeed

في المقابل filmḳābíl *Arabic* on the other hand, on the contrary

فيته fitá *f.* 1 ribbon, tape په فيته كبني ترل to rewind a ribbon or tape 2 *adjective* ribbon, tape *idiom* فيته چنجی tapeworm

فيچر fichár *m.* 1 feature article 2 hit (movie)

فبدراسيون federāsión *m.* federation

فبدرالي federālí federal, federative فبدرالي نظام federation, federal system فبدرالي جمهوريت federal republic

فبدرالي feḍerālí ☞ فبدرالي

فبدربشن feḍeréshan *m.* ☞ فبدراسيون

فير fajr *m.* fire; gunfire فير... په، فير كول د توپ فير artillery fire فير كول to fire at, bombard

فبرنگئه feringána *f. regional* Englishwoman

فبرنگی feringáj *m.* ☞ فرنگی [1]

فيرني firní *f.* ☞ فرني

فيروزي firuzí *f.* victory

فيروژه firozhá *f.* turquoise

فبروكانكريتي ferokānkrití *adjective* ferroconcrete

فيزيولوجي fizijālodzhí *f.* فيزيالوژي fizilālozhí *f.* فيزيولوجي fizijolodzhí *f.* physiology

فيزيونومي fizijonomí *f.* physiognomy

فيس fis *m. m.* 1 fee د داخلبدو فيس entrance fee فيس وركول to pay a fee 2 payment بله فيس او اجوري free

في سبيل الله fisabilullá *Arabic* free, for nothing, without payment

فبشن féshán *m.* féshən mode, fashion د فبشن... fashionable فبشن خاوند dandy, young person given to inordinate display in dress, etc.

فبشني feshəní *m.* 1 dandy; fashion plate 2 fashionable, stylish

فيصد fisád *used to express percentages* ۲۰ فيصده سكاره 20% of the coal

فيصدي fisadí 1 *adjective* percent 2 *f.* percent of an allocation in percentage points د في صدي په حساب in percentages

فيصل fajsál *m. Arabic regional* ☞ فيصله

فيصله fajsalá *f. Arabic* decision, resolution; sentence (of a court) په فيصله سره by decision, according to the decision فيصله كول *compound verb* to decide فيصله كبدل to be decided, be resolved (of a question, problem) فيصله صادرول to impose a sentence (of a court) يوي فيصلي ته رسبدل to come to a decision نو بس په دي فيصله دہ؟ Then it has been decided?

فيصله نامه fajsalanāmá *f.* resolution فيصله نامه صادرول to take, accept a resolution

فيض fajz *m. Arabic* [*plural:* فيوض fujúz] 1 abundance; generosity 2 favor, grace د فيض خاوند gracious 3 well-being; success 4 *proper name* Fayz

فيض آباد fajzābád *m.* Fayzabad (city)

فيضان fajazán *m. Arabic* 1 high water, overflow 2 abundance

فيض رسان fajzrasán 1 generous 2 gracious, virtuous

فيض رساني fajzrasāní *f.* 1 generous 2 grace, virtue

فيل fil *m.* elephant [1]

فيل fil *m.* ☞ فيله [2]

فيل fajl *m.* fejl *regional* failure فيل كول to fail (an examination, etc.) فيل كبدل *compound verb* to be failed, be flunked, flunk (an examination, etc.) په امتحان كښي بد بد فيل كبدل to fail an examination resoundingly, bomb out [3]

فيلپايه filpājá *f.* 1 upright; post 2 column

فيلخانه filkhāná *f.* elephant enclosure

فيلدكورس fildkvárs *m.* فيلدكورس fildkvárs *m.* feldspar

فيلدمارشال fildmārshál *m.* field marshal

فيلسوف fajlasúf *m.* filsúf [*plural:* فيلسوفان fajlasufán *plural:* filsufán *plural:* فلاسفه falāsifá] 1 philosopher; thinker 2 theoretician

فيلگوش filgúsh *m.* 1 water pepper, persicary 2 twigs (pastry)

فيلمرغ filmúrgh *m.* فيل مرغ turkey

فيلمرغه filmúrgha *f.* turkey-hen

فيلوان filván *m.* فيل وان، elephant drover

فيلولوجي filolodzhí *f.* philology

فيله filá *f. obsolete* file, ranks په يوه فيله صف! Form a single file! (as a command) [1]

فيله fíla *f.* cow-elephant [2]

فين fajn fine, of high quality (cloths)

فينانسمان finānsmán *m.* financing

فبنال fenál *m. chemistry* phenol, carbolic acid

فبودال feodál *m.* feudal lord

فبودالزم feodālízm *m.* feudalism

فبودالي feodālí feudal فبودالي اقتصاد feudal economy فبودالي حكمران feudal

فبودال feodál *m.* fjuḍál ☞ فبوډال

فبودالزم feodālízm *m.* fjuḍálízm ☞ فبوډالزم

فبودالي feodālí fjuḍálí ☞ فبوډالي

فيوز fjuz *m.* 1 detonation cap; percussion cap 2 safety fuse, cutout (electrical, etc.) فيوز الوزول to burn out (of a fuse), short-circuit

فيوض fujúz *m. Arabic plural of* فيض

فيوضات fujuzát *m. second plural of* فيض

فيوميگبشن fjumigéshan *m. agriculture* fumigation

ق

ق ḳāf 1 thirty-first letter of the Pashto alphabet (primarily occurs in loanwords, Arabic verb-forms, and Turkish words; pronounced as Arabic ك and may be replaced by the letter or even valorized into "kh" or "gh") 2 number 100 in the abjad system [1]

ق *abbreviation of* قمري [2]

ق *military* 1 *abbreviation* قوا 2 *abbreviation* قوماندان [3]

قاب ḳāb *m.* 1 dish; plate 2 kneading trough 3 case, container

قابض k̬abíz *Arabic* **1.1** grasping, seizing; carrying, receiving **1.2** taking, accepting **1.3** *medicine* tying off, clamping **2.1** recipient; examiner, inspector **2** holder, possessor

قابل k̬abíl *Arabic* **1** worthy, deserving of something قابل د سزا deserving punishment, punishable قابل د شي دیو fit for something **2** *a* قابل د قدر acquiring (e.g., some quality) **3** able; gifted; talented worthy, deserving of respect **b** outstanding, exceptional **c** talented **4** knowledgeable, capable **5** *combining form* قابل رحم k̬ābíl-i worthy of pity, piteous

قابل الزرع k̬abil-az-zár' *Arabic* arable (e.g., land)

قابل برداشت k̬abíl-i-bardāsht *regional* patient

قابل توب k̬ābiltób *m.* ☞ قابلیت

قابل رحم k̬abíl-i-rám worthy of pity, piteous

قابل رشک k̬abíl-i-ríshk enviable

قابل عمل k̬abíl-i-'amál practicable, feasible

قابل قدر k̬abíl-i-k̬ádr worthy; valuable

قابله k̬ābilá *f. Arabic* midwife; obstetric assistant

قابله گي k̬ābilagí *f.* midwifery, obstetrics د قابله گی ښوونځی school of midwifery, obstetrics

قابلیت k̬ābiliját *m. Arabic* **1** ability; fitness حربي قابلیت fitness for military service قابلیت تغیر k̬ābiliját-i *biology* variability **2** natural gifts, endowments; talent **3** qualifications

قابو k̬ābú **1** *m.* **.1** strength; force, might قابو کول *compound verb* to curb, restrain, control *a* په قابو کښې کول، په قابو کبني کول to seize, occupy **b** to seize, grab, take by force **1.2** opportunity, favorable occasion قابو میندل to get the opportunity **2.1** curbing; restraining **2.2** on the qui vive; ready for an attack **3** *adverb* precisely, exactly قابو سهار لس بجي وي It was exactly 10 o'clock in the morning. *idiom* لا دوړی ته می قابو نه کبده خو *Eastern* I didn't want to eat yet.

قاپ k̬āp *m.* vice قاف ²

قاپیه k̬āpijá *f.* ☞ قافیه

قات ¹ k̬āt *m.* layer, stratum; sheet, bed, row قات خورل to form folds قاتول ☞ قات کبدل *compound verb* قات کول *compound verb* ☞ قاتبدل

قات ² k̬āt *m.* ☞ قحطي

قاتر k̬ātár *m.* mule

قاتره k̬ātára *f.* jenny, mule (female)

قات کبدونکی میز k̬āt kedúnkaj قاتگی k̬ātagí folding قات کبدونکی folding table

قاتل k̬atíl *Arabic* **1.1** killing, murdering **1.2** murderous; destructive **2** *m.* murderer

قاتول k̬ātavál *denominative, transitive* [*past:* قات یی کړ] to fold; roll up

قاتي ¹ k̬atí **1** hunger **2** shortage, deficiency ☞ قحطي

قاتي ² k̬atí folded (of a mountain)

قاتبدل k̬ātedál *denominative, intransitive* [*past:* قات شو] **1** to be folded; be rolled up **2** to form folds

قاچاق k̬āchāk̬ *m.* contraband; contraband transport (of goods)

قاچاقي k̬āchāk̬í **1.1** contraband قاچاقي مال contraband goods; contraband **1.2** secret, clandestine **2** *m.* smuggler

قاچغه k̬āchúgha *f.* اشخوري قاچغه table knife

قادر ¹ k̬ādír *Arabic* **1.1** mighty, potent **1.2** powerful په... قادر کول to allow to give the possibility or the opportunity (to) په یو شي باندي قادر کبدل to be in a position to do something **1.3** *religion* almighty **2** *m. proper name* Qadir

قادر ² k̬ādr *m.* cadres (of workers)

قادروي k̬ādraví regular, experienced, skilled, trained

قادری k̬ādaráj **1** shortened, hemmed, cut-off **2** *m.* kadaraj (ample Oriental-style robe, long among the Yusufzai and short among the western Afghans)

قادریه k̬ādirijá *f.* Kadiria (Muslim sect, usually Qadiria, a Sufi order)

قادیانی k̬ādijāní *m. plural* Kadiani (Muslim sect)

قار k̬ār *m.* ☞ قهر

قارجن k̬ārdzhán angry

قارغان kārghán *plural of* قارغه

قارغه k̬ārghá *m.* قارگه k̬ārgá *m.* crow

قارون k̬ārún *m. Arabic* Karun (name of a wealthy man, has become a common name)

قاره k̬ārrá *f. Arabic* continent, continental mass, section of the world; dry-land

قاره ویشتونکی راکت k̬ārrá vishtúnkaj intercontinental missile

قاري k̬āří *m. Arabic* [*plural:* قاریان k̬ariján *Arabic plural:* قرا kurrá] kari (reader of the Koran)

قاري دریاب k̬āří the ocean

قاز k̬āz *m.* gander چینی قاز mountain gander

قازاق k̬āzák̬ *m.* ☞ قزاق

قازاقستان k̬āzākstán *m.* ☞ قزاقستان

قازاقي k̬āzāk̬í **1** *adjective* Kazakh **2** Kazakh, Kazakh language

قازان k̬āzán *m.* Kazan (city)

قازه k̬áza *f.* goose

قاسم k̬āsím *Arabic* **1** dividing; splitting up **2** *m. math* **.1** divisor **2** *proper name* Qasim

قاش k̬āsh *m.* **1** saddlebow **2** trigger (of a revolver)

قاشقار k̬āshk̬ár *m.* Kashgar (city)

قاشقاري k̬āshk̬āří k̬āshk̬āráj Kashgar *adjective* قاشقاري تغر *kashgar* rug (type without pile or nap)

قاش قاش، قاشقاش k̬āshk̬āsh *m.* ☞ خشخاش

قاشغه k̬āshógha *f.* قاشوقه k̬āshúk̬a *f.* knife

قاصد k̬āsíd *m. Arabic* **1** runner; courier; messenger **2** death, hour of death

قاصدي k̬āsidí *m.* dandelion

قاصر k̬āsír *Arabic* **1** having a defect, having a deficiency **2** *m.* deficiency, defect

قاضي k̬āzí *m. Arabic* [*plural:* قاضیان k̬āziján *plural:* قضات k̬uzát] **1** qazi, judge **2** expert

قاضي توب قāzitób judgeship; position of judge د قاضي توب عهده the position of judge

قاطر قātír *m.* ☞ قاتر

قاطري قātirí transported by mule (of a cargo)

قاطع ḳāté *Arabic* 1.1 decisive, firm 1.2 unquestionable, indisputable 1.3 convincing 1.4 sharp, cutting 2 *m.* [*plural:* قطاع ḳuttá'] robber, bandit

قاعدتاً ḳā'idátán as a rule, usually, ordinarily

قاعده ḳā'idá *f. Arabic* [*plural:* قاعدي ḳā'idé *m. Arabic plural:* قواعد ḳavā'íd] 1 rule; order په قاعده brought into a state of order, regulated; tuned, adjusted په قاعده اينبودل to bring to order, regulate; adjust, tune 2 *anatomy* base of the heart 3 *math* base of a cone 4 border

قاغمه ḳāghmá *f.* camel-hair cloth (used for outer clothing)

قاغه [1] ḳágha *f. regional* black crow

قاغه [2] ḳágha *f.* ☞ كاغه

قاغى ḳāghój *f.* ☞ كاغى

قاف [1] ḳāf *m.* name of the letter ق

قاف [2] ḳāf *m.* كوه قاف ḳóh-i Kaf Mountains (legendary, supposedly encircling the entire earth; according to tradition the legendary bird the Sumurg dwells there) *idiom* دا د كوه قاف سورى كول دي This is a Herculean labor.

قافله ḳāfilá *f. Arabic* 1 caravan د قافلي مير caravan leader د بېړيو قافله a caravan of boats 2 troop train 3 string of horses

قافله باشي ḳāfilabāshí *m.* قافله سالار ḳāfilasālár *m.* conductor or chief of a cavaran

قافله والا ḳāfilavālā́ *m.* member of a caravan

قافيه ḳāfijá *f. Arabic* rime

قافيه بندي ḳāfijabandí *f.* riming, versifying

قاق ḳaḳ 1 dry, dried out; faded, stale 2 stiff, hard 3 brittle 4 starchy, starched

قاقا ḳāḳá *f. Arabic* 1 quacking 2 croaking, cawing قاقا كول a to quack b to croak, caw

قاقم ḳāḳúm *m. Arabic* ermine, stoat

قاقمه ḳāḳmá *f.* ☞ قاغمه

قال ḳāl *m. Arabic* 1 talk, chatter 2 word, speech

قالب ḳālíb *m. Arabic* 1 form, model 2 template, mold; last (shoe) 3 body 4 exposition (theme, topic)

قالبي ḳālibí 1 cast, poured in a mold 2 stamped, measured (speech)

قال مقال ḳālmaḳā́l *m. Arabic* din, uproar

قالي درياب ḳālí ocean

قاليچه ḳālichá *f.* rug

قالين ḳālín *m.* carpet د قالين اوډلو صنعت carpet weaving

قالين اودنكى ḳālín udúnkaj *m.* قالين باف ḳālinbā́f *m.* carpet weaver, carpet or rug craftsman

قالين بافي ḳālinbāfí *f.* carpet weaving, rug weaving

قالينه ḳālína *f.* carpet

قام ḳām *m.* ☞ قوم

قام پرست ḳāmparást *f.* ☞ قوم پرست

قام پرستي ḳāmparastí *f.* ☞ قوم پرستي

قام پروري ḳāmparvarí *f.* ☞ قوم پروري

قامت ḳāmát *m. Arabic* stature, height; torso, figure, build

قاموس ḳāmús *m. Arabic* [*plural:* قاموسونه ḳāmusúna *Arabic plural:* قواميس ḳavāmís] 1 dictionary 2 ocean

قامي ḳāmí ☞ قومي

قانال ḳānā́l *m. anatomy* channel; tract هاضمه قانال ḳānāl-i digestive tract

قانع ḳāni' *Arabic* 1.1 content, satisfied قانع كول to satisfy په ... قانع a to be satisfied, be contented with something قانع كبدل b to be convinced 1.2 admitting (something) په زره كښي به په دي خبره قانع شي چه In his heart he admitted that he agreed with this. 2 *proper name* Qani

قانون [1] ḳānún *m. Arabic* [*plural:* قوانين ḳavānín] law; canon, regulation د طبعياتو قوانين laws of nature د قانون فن jurisprudence *idiom* نظامي قانون martial law

قانون [2] ḳānún *m.* ganun (kind of goose)

قانوناً ḳānúnán according to law, legally; lawfully

قانون دان، قانوندان ḳānundā́n *m.* legal specialist, jurist

قانون داني، قانونداني ḳānundā́ní knowledge of the law, jurisprudence

قانون ساز مجلس ḳānunsā́z legislative قانون ساز legislative assembly

قانون شكن ḳānunshikán *m.* lawbreaker

قانون گو ḳānungó *m.* قانون گوى ḳānungój *regional* official of the tax directorate (in a district); finance inspector

قانون نامه ḳānunnāmá *f.* regulations د يونو قانون نامه the UN Charter

قانوني ḳanuní *Arabic* 1 legal, based on law قانوني حكومت the legal government په قانوني شكل legally, according to law قانوني ښځه legal wife قانوني كول to legalize, legitimize قانوني قوه لرل to have legal force 2 legislative قانوني مجلس legislative assembly 3 juridical; based on law قانوني مشاور legal advisor 4 *grammar* regular (of a verb)

قانونيت ḳānuniját *m.* 1 lawfulness; legality 2 conformity with the law

قاهر ḳāhír *Arabic* 1 victorious 2 *m.* victor

قاهره ḳāhirá *f.* Cairo (city)

قاه قاه ḳāhḳáh *m.* loud laugh, guffaw په قاه قاه خندل to laugh loudly, guffaw

قائد ḳāíd *m. Arabic* leader, chief قائد اعظم ḳaid-i Great Leader (title of the founder of Pakistan, Jinna)

قائزه ḳāizá *f.* ☞ قيزه

قايق ḳājíḳ *m.* 1 boat, caïque 2 ship, vessel

قائل ḳāíl *Arabic* 1.1 admitting something; agreeing, being in accord with something; being an adherent of something 1.2 convinced of something قائل كول to قائل كبدل ☞ قائلبدل 2 *m.* adherent; follower

قائلول ḳāilavól *denominative, transitive* [*past:* قائل يي كړ] 1 to convince of something; compel to admit something 2 to compel to recognize, force recognition

قائله ḳāíla 1 ☞ قائل 2 *feminine singular of* قائل

قائلېدٙل **ḳāiledǚl** *denominative, intransitive* [*past:* قائل شو] **1** to be recognized, be admitted **2** to be conscious (of) **3** to agree

قائم **ḳāim** قایم **ḳājím** *Arabic* **1** standing, vertical **2** placed on a firm foundation; established **3** stable; insistent, persistent قائم اوسٙبدٙل to persist, insist **4** *math* right په قايمه زاويه قايمه زاويه right angle occupying a right angle (90 degree) **5** *chess* stalemate

قائم مزاج **ḳāimmizādzh** *Arabic* firm, stable, persistent, insistent

قائم مزاجي **ḳāimmizādzhí** *f.* firmness; persistence, insistence

د چا قائم مقام **ḳaimmaḳắm** *m. Arabic regional* **1** deputy قائم مقام کٙبدٙل to replace someone **2** vicar, substitute; legal successor **3** governor-general; viceroy

د چا قائم مقامي **ḳāimmaḳāmí** *f.* replacing, replacement کول to replace someone

قائمول **ḳāimavǚl** *denominative, transitive* [*past:* قائم يې کٙر] **1** to establish سياسي روابط قائمول to establish diplomatic relations **2** to create, found, establish

قائمېدٙل **ḳāimedǚl** *denominative, intransitive* [*past:* قائم شو] **1** to be established **2** to be created

قب **ḳub** *m. regional* hump, deformity

قب **ḳubb** *m.* **ḳub** *Arabic* ☞ قبه

قبا **ḳabā** *f. Arabic* **1** kaba (wide male garment with long sleeves) **2** drop or waist and seat part of trousers **3** dust jacket (of a book)

قباحت **ḳabāhát** *m. Arabic* **1** outrage; vileness, abomination, meanness, baseness **2** indecency, cynicism **3** fault; blunder

قباله **ḳabālá** *f. Arabic* deed of purchase; contract شرعي قباله deed of purchase in accordance with shariat (i.e., Muslim religious law) د قباله document concerning sale بيع وفا قباله *compound verb* to sell, sell at a reduced price

قبائل **ḳabāíl** *m. Arabic plural of* قبيله

قبائلي **ḳabāilí** tribal قبائلي وېش division into tribes

قبح **ḳabh** *f.* **ḳubh** *Arabic* قبحه **ḳubha** *f.* ☞ قباحت

قبر **ḳábər** *m.* **ḳábr** *Arabic* grave

قبرس **ḳibrús** *m.* **ḳubrús** Cyprus (island, state)

قبرستان **ḳabristán** *m.* cemetery

قبرسي **ḳibrusí** قبرساج **ḳibrusáj** **1** *adjective* Cypriot **2** *m.* Cypriot (person)

قبرس **ḳibrús** *m.* ☞ قبرس

قبرکند **ḳabrkánd** *m.* gravedigger

قبرگاه **ḳabrgáh** *m.* ☞ قبرستان

قبض **ḳabz** *m.* **1** acceptance, receipt, receiving **2** tax; impost **3** receipt for something received قبض ورکول to give a receipt **4** seizure, taking over **5** occupation **6** *medicine* constipation

قبضول **ḳabzavǚl** *denominative, transitive* [*past:* قبض يې کٙر] **1** to accept, receive **2** to grab, seize, take **3** to take over; occupy **4** to constipate, render costive

قبضه **ḳabzá** *f. Arabic* **1** haft, lever; hilt, handle (of a sword) **2** ☞ پر قلا باندي قبضه کول، په قلا باندي قبضه کول to seize a 4,5قبض fortress **3** unoccupied land which has been seized **4** ownership, possession *idiom* زما اوبنکي له قبضي ووتي I could not restrain

my tears. په قبضه راورٙل to obtain, gain, earn (e.g., the means of subsistence) د چا په قبضه رسٙبدٙل to fall into someone's hands

قبضېدٙل **ḳabzedǚl** *denominative, intransitive* [*past:* قبض شو] **1** to be compressed, be contracted, be curtailed **2** to be taken over, be occupied **3** to suffer from constipation *idiom* د چا څخه روح قبضېدٙل to fear, be afraid of someone; tremble before someone

قبل **ḳubúl** *m.* holster

قبل **ḳibál** *m. Arabic* **1** presence; party, side **2** authority, power

قبل **ḳabl** *Arabic* **1** in front of, before, earlier than قبل الميلاد B.C., before our era **2** previous, foregoing, early **3** *m.* front, front part of something

قبل **ḳabál** *m.* ☞ کٙبل له قبله because, for the reason (that)

قبل **ḳabál** *Arabic* surrounded, besieged, invested

قبلاً **ḳáblán** *Arabic* earlier, before; beforehand

د قبل التاريخ دوره **ḳabl-ut-tāríkh** prehistoric the prehistoric epoch

قبل الميلاد **ḳabl-al-milád** *Arabic* B.C., before the modern era د قبل الميلاد پنځمه پېړی the fifth century B.C.

قبلول **ḳablavǚl** *denominative, transitive* [*past:* قبول يې کٙر] **1** to accept, receive دعوت قبلول to receive an invitation په شکريه قبلول to receive something with thanks **2** to receive, meet (guests) **3** to consider, recognize **4** to receive, bear, experience محروميت قبلول to experience deprivations ☞ قبولول

قبله **ḳiblá** *f. Arabic* **1** kibla (the direction in which Muslims turn in praying); direction in which Mecca lies **2** westerly direction, west قبله په سهيل southwest **3** temple **4** object of worship; honored person قبله عالم **ḳiblá-ji** Center of the Universe (imperial title), Your Highness

قبله گاه **ḳiblagáh** *m.* **1** Mecca (city) **2** place of worship **3** well-wisher, patron; father

قبله نما **ḳiblanumá** *f.* compass

قبلي **ḳablí** **1** forehanded **2** former, previous

قبلېدٙل **ḳabledǚl** *denominative, intransitive* [*past:* قبول شو] **1** to be received (e.g., of an invitation) **2** to be considered; be recognized **3** to be received, be met (of a guest) **4** to be endured, be experienced

قبلٙده **ḳabledǚ** *m. plural* **1** receiving (e.g., of an invitation) د يوي غوښتني قبلٙده satisfaction of a request **2** recognition; approval **3** reception, meeting (of a guest) **4** enduring, experiencing

قبلېز **ḳblíz** قبلئز **ḳiblaíz** western قبليزه علاقه the western region

قبور **ḳubúr** *m. Arabic* holster

قبول **ḳabúl** *Arabic* **1** *m.* **.1** receiving, reception **1.2** agreement, approval; recognition د قبول جواب affirmative response, assent قبول ور acceptable, permissible **1.3** reception (of guests) **2** *predicative* permissible, acceptable; approved, recognized دا کار مي نه دئ قبول This is not acceptable to me. I do not agree with this. قبلول قبول کول *compound verb* ☞

قبولدار **ḳahuldár** agreed, agreeing, approving قبولدار کٙبدٙل to agree with, approve

قبولول ḳabulavә́l *denominative, transitive* [*past:* قبول يې کړ] **1** to accept, receive په شراکت قبولول to take into partnership **2** to agree with, approve **3** to endure, suffer, bear **4** *economics* to make an acceptance

قبوله ḳabúla *feminine singular of* قبول

قبولي [1] ḳabulí *f.* **1** *economics* acceptance **2** receiving, receipt (of goods)

قبولي [2] ḳabúli *f. plural of* قبول 2

قبولېدل ḳabuledә́l *denominative, intransitive* [*past:* قبول شو] **1** to be received **2** to be approved

قبه ḳubbá *f.* **1** vault, cupola **2** arch **3** niche **4** alcove

قبی ḳubbáj *regional* hunchbacked, kyphotic, suffering from kyphosis

قبيح ḳabíh *Arabic* base, low, shameful

قبيل ḳabíl *m. Arabic* **1** ☞ قبيله **2** tribe; group, clan

قبيلوي ḳabilaví **1** consanguineous, tribal **2** tribal قبيلوي اختلافات tribal difference

قبيله ḳabilá *f. Arabic* [*plural:* قبيلي ḳabilé *m. Arabic plural:* قبائل kabāíl] **1** tribe جنوبي آزاد قبائل the independent Pushtun tribes د قبائلو the tribes of Southern (present-day Paktia) Province د رياست chief directorate of tribal affairs; department of tribes قبائلو مدير plenipotentiary representative, authorized representative for tribal matters (in a province) د قبائلو علاقه، د قبيلو سيمه، د آزادو د قبيلو سيمه the Independent (Pushtun) Tribal Zone **2** *biology* order **3** clan

قبيله دار ḳabiladár *m.* tribal headman, clan headman

قپان ḳapā́n *m.* commercial scales

قپانچي ḳapānchí *m.* weigher, checker

قت ḳat *m.* ☞ قات [1] قت په قت **a** plicated, folded **b** formed into plaits **c** in layers قت کول *compound verb* ☞ قتول

قتار ḳatār *m. Arabic* ☞ قطار

قتاره ḳatāra *f. usually plural* قتاري ḳatāri nonsense, baloney

قتال [1] ḳitā́l *m. Arabic* **1** skirmish, battle, firefight **2** slaughter, bloody battle

قتال [2] ḳattā́l *m. Arabic* murderer, assassin

قتره ḳatrá *f.* morsel (of meat) ☞ قطره

قتغ ḳatágh *m.* food, dish; meat; any entree (fish, soup, etc.) eaten with bread for relish

قتکاڼی ḳutkā́ṇaj *m.* ☞ قرت کاڼی

قتل ḳátə *m.* ḳát *Arabic* murder, killing, homicide قتل عام ḳátl-i slaughter; butchery قتل عمد ḳátl-i massacre د قتل آواز پري وشه They sentenced him to death. قتلول *compound verb* ☞ قتلېدل *compound verb* ☞

قتلان ḳatlā́n *m. regional* massacre

قتل گاه ḳatlgā́h *m.* **1** field of battle; place of slaying **2** execution place, scaffold

قتلول ḳatlavә́l *denominative, transitive* [*past:* قتل يې کړ] **1** to kill, murder **2** to slay, exterminate

قتلېدل ḳatledә́l *denominative, intransitive* [*past:* قتل شو] **1** to be killed, be murdered **2** to be slain **3** to be exterminated, be destroyed

قتول ḳatavә́l *denominative, transitive* [*past:* قت يې کړ] **1** to put together **2** to beat, thrash, beat up

قته ḳitá *f.* playing card

قتی [1] ḳutáj *m.* ball

قتی [2] ḳutә́j *f.* ☞ قطی

قتی [3] ḳatí ☞ قطعي

قتيل ḳatíl *Arabic* murdered; assassinated

قته گوته ḳáta gúta *f.* middle finger

قجري ḳadzharí *f.* horsecloth, saddlecloth; kind of saddlecloth made of thick felt covering the saddle and the horse's forequarters and hindquarters

قجوره ḳadzhúra *f.* date palm

قجير ḳadzhír *m.* vulture; carrion bird

قچر [1] ḳachár *m.* [*plural:* قچران ḳacharā́n *Eastern plural:* قچر ḳachә́r] **1** mule **2** obstinate person, pigheaded person

قچر [2] ḳachár base (person)

قچروالا ḳacharvālá *m. regional* mule drover

قچره ḳachára *f. regional* jenny, mule (female)

قچري [1] ḳacharí *f. regional* court جنگي قچري military tribunal

قچري [2] ḳachә́re *plural of* قچره

قچه گوته ḳácha gúta *f.* little finger, pinky

قچی ḳicháj *m.* group; small group of people

قچي قچي ḳichí ḳichí in a batches; in groups; in small groups of people

قحبه ḳahbá *f.* prostitute

قحط ḳaht *m.* قحطي ḳahtí *f. Arabic* **1** bad harvest, harvest failure **2** insufficiency, deficiency, shortfall **3** hunger, famine

قد ḳadd *m.* ḳad *Arabic* height; altitude; length په قد ميانه of average height مناسب قد ښکلی او trim figure, well-built figure

قدامت ḳadāmát *m. Arabic* **1** priority **2** preference قدامت ورکول to display preference, prefer **3** old age **4** antiquity

قدامت پسند ḳadāmatpasánd loving olden times; conservative

قدامت پسندي ḳadāmatpasandí love for olden times; conservatism

قدح [1] ḳadáh *m. Arabic* goblet, cup

قدح [2] ḳadh *f. Arabic* **1** reproach; censure **2** slander **3** mockery

قدر ḳádər *m.* ḳádr *Arabic* [*plural:* اقدار aḳdār] **1** quantity; measure, degree; dimension, size لر قدر دونه قدر، دا قدر so much some, some quantity د امکان په قدر to the extent of **2** honor, merit د چا د حقوق قدر او مراعات کول to respect someone's rights **3** to value, worth; meaning, importance د علم قدر the importance of science دا ډېر قدر لري This is very valuable. This has great significance. قدر کول to value, know the price قدر پېژندل compound verb قدر کېدل قدرول compound verb to be valued, be recognized (of merits) د چا ته د قدر په سترگه کتل، چا ته د قدر په درنه سترگه کتل to value (highly), respect someone مونږ د دوی دغه زيارت ته د قدر په سترگو We value their efforts. **4** power, might گورو

قدرافزائي ḳadrafzāí *f.* honoring, respect

قدرت ḳudrát *m. Arabic* 1 force, power, might اقتصادي قدرت economic power د خپل توان او قدرت په نظامي قدرت military might اندازه، د خپل توان او قدرت په اندازه سره to the extent of their powers and resources 2 supremacy, sovereignty د دریابي قدرت the sovereignty of the sea 3 power, authority سياسي قدرت political power مطلق قدرت absolutism 4 د دولت عالي قدرت sovereignty لرل قدرت a to have the power, possess the might b to be able, have it in one's power (to do something) 5 nature, universe 6 *religion* God Almighty, Providence 7 *proper name* Qudrat

قدرتاً ḳudrátán *Arabic* by nature; naturally

قدرتي ḳudratí 1 natural په قدرتي ډول قدرتي مناظر landscapes naturally 2 wild (i.e., growing wild, uncultivated) 3 understood دا قدرتي خبره ده This is understood. 4 *religion* divine 5 unconstrained, relaxed (of a pose)

قدردان ḳadrdā́n *m.* judge, expert زه د دوی د زحمت ډېر قدردان يم I value their efforts very much.

قدرداني ḳadrdāní *f.* 1 proper evaluation; recognition of services د چا قدرداني کتل، د قدرداني په سترګو کتل to value someone 2 په ډېره قدرداني کتل to (highly) value someone or something 2 concern for someone 3 celebration in honor of someone

قدرمن ḳadrmán 1 esteemed; valued; valuable زمونږ دوستي د دوی په نظر قدرمن مېلمانه They value our friendship a lot. 2 dear ډېره قدرمنه ده dear guests وقت په مونږ کښې قدرمن دئ Time is dear to us.

قدرول ḳadravál *denominative, transitive* [*past:* قدر یې کړ] 1 to value, treasure 2 to show respect (e.g., to a guest) 3 to praise

قدرة ḳudrátán *Arabic* ☞ قدرتاً

قدري ḳadrí [1] *Arabic* 1 predestined by fate, fatal 2 *m.* fatalist

قدرې ḳádre [2] 1 some, something or other 2 so, so much as زمور مدعا دومره قدري ده چه ... We only affirm that …

قدس ḳudús ḳuds *m. Arabic* holiness, sanctity د قدس بنار بيت ☞ المقدس

قدسي ḳudsí *Arabic* 1 holy, sacred 2 *m.* saint

قدغن ḳadaghán *m.* prohibition, ban قدغن کول to forbid

قدم ḳadám [1] *m. Arabic* [*plural:* قدمونه ḳadamúna *Arabic plural:* اقدام akḍām] 1 step عادي قدم مارش! normal march step عادي قدم موزون قدم parade step, marching at attention a په قدم by step, at a walk b step by step; gradually قدم اخيستل، قدمونه اخيستل په دري قدمه کښې in three paces قدم اخيستل The moon slowly floated across the sky. قدم اينودل to step د چا سره قدم قدم تلل to keep pace with someone په قدمونو کول to pace off 2 measure (taken), action, step 3 dance step *idiom* يو قدم زمکه clod of earth, bit of earth پراخ قدمونه اخيستل to succeed greatly, overachieve

قدم ḳidám [2] *m. Arabic* 1 seniority (in rank, position) 2 antiquity, old times

قدما ḳudamā́ *m. Arabic plural of* قديم ancient peoples; ancestors

قدمچه ḳadamchá *f.* 1 step 2 pace

قدمځای ḳadamdzā́j *m.* latrine, toilet

قدم دار، قدم والا ḳidamdā́r ḳidamvālā́ *m.* senior (in rank, position)

قدمه ḳadamá [1] *f. Arabic* 1 instance, level 2 step 3 echelon 4 detachment

قدمه ḳadáma [2] *oblique singular and short plural of* قدم [1]

قدنما، قدنمای ḳadnumā́ ḳadnumā́j full length قدنمای عکس full-length قدنمایه هنداره pier glass (mirror) portrait

قدوس ḳuddús *Arabic* 1 *religion* Most Holy (epithet of God) 2 *m. proper name* Quddus

قدوقامت ḳadd-u-ḳāmát *m.* build, figure

قدوم ḳudúm *m. Arabic* arrival, advent

قديفه ḳadifá *f.* sheet worn in a public bath ☞ قطيفه

قديم ḳadím *Arabic* 1 ancient, venerable, old 2 *m.* د .1 antiquity قديمه څخه، له قديمه څخه of old; from ancient times; from a very long time ago 2.2 [*plural:* قدما ḳudamā́] ancestor

قديمي ḳadimí ancient, antique, old په قديمي ډول in the old way

قر ḳur *m.* 1 rumbling, eructation (stomach) 2 quacking, cawing 3 rumble (of horses' hooves, etc.) a قرق کول to rumble, eructate (of the stomach) b to quack, caw c to resound, clatter (of horses' hooves, etc.)

قرا ḳurā́ *m. Arabic plural of* قريه

قرابت ḳarābát *m. Arabic* relationship, kinship; nearness, intimacy د چا سره قرابت لرل a to be close to somebody, intimate with someone b to be related to someone

قرابت دار ḳarābatdā́r *m.* 1 relative 2 person who is close or intimate (to another)

قرابتي ḳarābatí 1 related, intimate, close 2 *m.* ☞ قرابت دار

قرابونه ḳarābuná *f.* ☞ قرابين

قرابه ḳarābá *f.* carboy, large flask; flask

قراح ḳarā́h ḳará *Arabic* pure, unadulterated

قرار ḳarā́r *Arabic* 1 *m.* 1.1 peaceful, tranquil قرار ميندل to calm down, calm oneself down 1.2 constancy, stability; firmness 1.3 decision; resolution; conclusion د محکمې قرار decision of the court 1.4 institution, definition, determination د متاركې شرايط په دغه a قرار نيول ... لاندي قرار سره دي. peace treaty conditions are such as … to calm (oneself) down b to be established, be defined, be determined 1.5 founding, foundation, basis, ground د هغي اطلاع په له قراره د according to this communication د هغي اطلاع له قراره د خپل وس په قرار inasmuch as is known د معلوماتو له قراره معلوماتو، They are helping to the extent that they are able. 2 مرسته کوي *predicative* 1. determined, established 2.1 tranquil, quiet قرار They are قرار ناست دي quietly, tranquilly قرار قرار اوسئ! Quiet! sitting quietly. قراري idiom [1] د دي قرار as indicated below; the following, as follows قراره قراري ☞ له څه قراره؟ What kind? Of what sorts?

قراقرم ḳarāḳorúm *m.* ☞ قره قرم

قرارداد ḳarārdā́d *m.* treaty, agreement; contract قرارداد کول to conclude a treaty قرارداد لغو کول to abrogate a treaty, renounce an agreement

قراردادي کوونکی qarārdā́d kavúnkaj *m.* ☞

قراردادي qarārdādí *m.* contractor; subcontractor; supplier

قرارگاه qarārgā́h *m. & f.* qarārgā́ *m.* [*plural:* قرارگاهونه qarārgāhúna *f. plural:* قرارگاه وي *plural:* قراراوي qarārgā́vi] **1** *military* command headquarters, headquarters, staff headquarters **2** center, focus, focal point

قرارنامه qarārnāmá *f.* written decision, resolution in writing

قراروالی qarārvā́laj *m.* **1** constancy, stability; firmness د پول د نرخ قراروالی stability of the currency exchange rate **2** peace, quiet, tranquillity

قرارول qaṛravә́l *denominative, transitive* [*past:* قرار یی کړ] **1** to calm **2** to establish, define ممنوع قرارول to forbid, interdict **3** to stabilize

قراري ¹ qarārí *f.* **1** peace, calm, tranquility, quiet قراره قراري complete calm, utter quiet, tranquility **2** established; agreed, stipulated

قراري ² qarā́ri *f. plural of* قرار 2

قراریدل qarāredә́l *denominative, intransitive* [*past:* قرار شو] **1** to become calm, become tranquil **2** to be established, be defined **3** to be stabilized

قراقرم qarāќorúm *m.* ☞ قره قرم

قراقلی qarāќulí *m. regional* cap (usually caracul)

قراقوم qarāќúm *m.* Kara-Kum (desert)

قرآن ¹ qurán *m.* qorán *Arabic* (the) Koran د قرآن شریف وظیفه کول to read the Sacred Koran قرآن اخیستل، قرآن خورل to give one's oath on the Koran

قران ² ķirán ќrān *m.* kran (Iranian silver coin equal to one rial)

قران ³ ķirán *m. Arabic* rapprochement; intimacy

قرآن خور qurānkhór having the habit or custom of swearing on the Koran

قرانطین qarāntín *m.* quarantine تر قرانطین لاندي نیول to establish a quarantine

قرآني qurāní relating to the Koran

قراول qarāvúl *m.* **1** guard detachment; patrol **2** aiming قراول کول to aim

قراول خانه qarāvulkhāná *f.* guardroom

قراولي qarāvulí *f.* guard; patrolling قراولي کول to guard; patrol

قرائت ķirā'át *m. Arabic* **1** reading **2** chrestomathy; reader د پښتو قرائت a Pashto chrestomathy (collection of readings) قرائت کول *compound verb* to read, read out قرائت کیدل *compound verb* to be read through, be read out

قرائت خانه ķirā'atkhāná *f.* reading room

قرائن qarāín *m. Arabic* **1** *plural of* قرینه **2** conditions **3** suppositions, assumptions **4** *law* circumstantial evidence **5** signs, tokens, clues **6** context

قرب ķurb *m. Arabic* **1** intimacy, nearness; vicinity **2** kinship, relationship

قربان ķurbā́n *m. Arabic* **1** sacrifice; oblation قربان دي شم I am your obedient servant. I am ready to sacrifice my life for you. تا نه قربان، Eastern I am ready to do everything for you. تر چا قربان درنه

کبدل، له چا څخه قربان کبدل to sacrifice oneself for the sake of someone else **2** *proper name* Qurban

قربانگاه ķurbāngā́h *m.* sacrificial altar; altar

قربانول ķurbānavә́l *denominative, transitive* [*past:* قربان یې کړ] to sacrifice, offer as an oblation خپل ژوند قربانول to sacrifice one's life خپل ژوند به تا نه قربان کړم! Eastern I will give up my life for you!

قرباني ķurbāní **1** *f.* sacrifice د ځان قرباني self-sacrifice **2** sacrificial, doomed to sacrifice قرباني کول *compound verb* ☞ قربانول قرباني کبدل *compound verb* ☞ قربانیدل

قربانیدل ķurbānedә́l *denominative, intransitive* [*past:* قربان شو] to be offered as a sacrifice, become a sacrifice, die as a sacrifice

قربت ķurbát *m. Arabic* **1** nearness, intimacy **2** kinship relationship **3** neighborhood, vicinity

قرپوق ķirpú́ќ kirpuk (breed of caracul sheep)

قرت ¹ ķurút *m. plural* kurut (hard cheese, made into a ball from compressed and dried curds)

قرت ² ķurrát *m. Arabic* joy, gladness

قرت کاڼی ķurutkā́ṇaj *m. usually plural* ķurutkā́ṇni pebble, round, flat stone

قرچه گته ќárcha gúta *f. dialect* ☞ قچه گته

قرحه ķarhá *f. Arabic* wound; sore, ulcer

قرساق ќorsā́ќ *m.* korsak (kind of fox and its pelt)

قرش ķurúsh *m.* kurush (Turkish coin)

قرص ķurs *m. Arabic* **1** circle, circlet; disk **2** ingot, bar **3** flat cake

قرض ķarz *Arabic* **1** *m.* loan; debt; grant; credit قرض حسنه ķarz-i interest-free loan اوږد قرض long-term loan; long-term credit د قرض اخیستل، په قرض اخیستل، قرض کول په بوند، debenture قرض سند bond, debenture قرض کول to take out a loan, borrow; receive a grant; make a loan قرض to loan; issue a grant, offer credit قرض ورکول، په قرض ورکول ورل to take on credit **2** on loan, in the form of a loan

قرضدار ķarzdā́r *m.* debtor, one who owes money قرضدار کبدل to be in debt

قرضه ¹ ķarzá *f. Arabic* ☞ قرض

قرضي ¹ ķarzí *adjective* loan (of money)

قرضي ² ķarzé *plural of* قرضه

قرط ķurt *m. Arabic* mouthful

قرطاس ķirtā́s *m.* **1** paper **2** charter

قرطاسیوي ķirtāsijaví stationery قرطاسیوي مواد stationery, office, writing supplies

قرطاسیه ķirtāsijá *f.* stationery, office supplies

قرطاسیه باب ķirtāsijabā́b *m.* **1** documentation **2** forms, samples of paper **3** ☞ قرطاسیه

قرعه ķur'á *f. Arabic* **1** lot په قرعو خرڅول to cast lots قرعه اچول play the lottery **2** paper ballot; ballot (ball) **3** knucklebone, die

قرعه اندازي ķur'aandāzí *f.* balloting قرعه اندازي کول to vote, cast ballots

قرعه بازي ķur'abāzí *f.* lottery

قرعه کشي ķur'akashí *f.* drawing (lottery)

قرغز ķirghíz *m.* Kirghiz

قرغزستان k̩irghizistā́n *m.* Kirghizistan

قرغزي k̩irghizí 1 *adjective* Kirghiz 2 *f.* Kirghiz, Kirghiz language

قرغه k̩arghá *f.* د قرغي بند Karga Dam and Water Reservoir

قرغز k̩irghíz *m.* ☞ قرغز

قرغزستان k̩irghizistā́n *m.* ☞ قرغزستان

قرغيزي k̩irghizí ☞ قرغزي

قرق k̩urúk̩ 1 *m.* .1 prohibition 1.2 reserve, game reserve 1.3 کول confiscation; seizure (of property); to confiscate; seize property 2 *predicative* .1 reserve, reserved 2.2 *regional* confiscated

قرقره k̩ark̩ará *f.* 1 comb, crest (of a bird) 2 plume (of a headgear, usually of crane's feathers) 3 crane (bird) 4 chrysanthemum (pyrethrum)

قرقره k̩urk̩urá *f.* bee-eater (the bird)

قرقری k̩ark̩arā́j *m.* colic (of a horse)

قرقي k̩urkí *f. regional* confiscation; seizure of property

قرقچن k̩ark̩echán ☞ قرقچن

قرمز k̩irmíz *m.* cochineal (insect from which a red dye is made)

قرمزي k̩irmizí red, crimson

قرمساغ k̩uramā́gh *m.* قرمساق k̩uramā́k̩ *m.* 1 base man, scoundrel 2 pimp 3 cuckold

قرمه k̩urmá *f.* roast meat

قرن k̩arn *m. Arabic* [*plural:* قرنونه k̩arnúna *Arabic plural:* قرون k̩urún] 1 century; epoch; conjunction of planets، قرون وسطی، منځوي قرون k̩urun-i the Middle Ages 2 30th anniversary

قرن k̩arn *m. Arabic* horn (animals)

قرنا k̩arnā́ *f. Arabic music* horn, trumpet

قرنطين k̩arantín *m.* ☞ قرنطين

قرني k̩arní *Arabic adjective* horn, of horn

قرنیکه k̩urnikə́ *m. regional* ☞ غورنیکه

قرنیه k̩arnijá *f. Arabic* cornea, corneal covering of the eye

قروت k̩urút *m. plural* kurut (kind of cheese)

قروغ k̩urúgh *m.* قروق k̩urúk̩ *m.* ☞ قرق

قرون k̩urún *m. Arabic plural* ☞ قرن

قره k̩ará 1 black (*used in geographic names and as an element of compounds* قره باغ Karabag District قره قل caracul) 2 *cards* spades

قرهاری k̩urhā́raj *m.* chirping, chattering (magpies)

قره باغ k̩arabā́gh *m.* Karabag (district north of Kabul, name of a number of other populated places)

قره غول k̩araghúl *m.* guard detachment

قره قرم k̩arak̩orúm *m.* Karakorum (mountain range)

قره قل k̩arak̩úl *m.* caracul (sheep)

قره قلچه k̩arak̩ulchá *f.* caracul ewe

قره قلي k̩arak̩ulí 1 caracul قره قلي پوستکی caracul sheep قره قلي پسه caracul sheepskin 2 *m.* caracul sheep

قره قوم k̩arak̩úm *m.* Kara-Kum Desert

قره کلچه k̩arakulchá *f.* ☞ قره قلچه

قره کلي k̩arakulí ☞ قره قلي

قره وانه k̩aravāná *f.* pot, mess tin; small tank, jerry can

قریب k̩aríb *Arabic* 1 close, near 2 *adverb* close, closely a very close, very closely; close up, right smack up to b factually c almost certainly

قریباً k̩aríbán *Arabic* 1 almost 2 closely, close, close by, alongside; not far from

قریبي k̩aribí *f.* 1 closeness, intimacy 2 relationship, kinship

قریحه k̩arihá *f. Arabic* 1 talent د ادبي قریحه لرل، د لیکلو قریحه لرل to have a mastery of the pen 2 initiative د چا له فکر او قریحي څخه to be created on someone's initiative 3 inventiveness

قریش k̩uráish *m. plural* Kuraishi, Kuraishites (Arabic tribe)

قریم k̩irím *m.* Crimean Peninsula

قرین k̩arín *Arabic* 1.1 united; joined, linked 1.2 near, approximate 2 *m.* .1 fellow traveler, traveling companion 2.2 contemporary 2.3 relative 2.4 brother born at a year's interval

قرینه k̩ariná *f. Arabic* [*plural:* قریني k̩ariné *Arabic plural:* قرائن k̩arāín] 1 context 2 sign; basis; indirect, circumstantial evidence 3 indication له قریني څخه معلومېږي چه ... a from the context it is evident that … b insofar as one can judge

قریه k̩arijá *f. Arabic* [*plural:* قریي k̩arijé *Arabic plural:* قرا k̩urā́] settlement; large village

قریه دار k̩arijadā́r *m.* village headman, elder

قړتي k̩ŕə́te *f. plural regional* balderdash; nonsense, absurdity

قرچ k̩urch *m.* ☞ پهلواړی

قرکچن k̩ark̩echán frozen, freezing, benumbed, stiff with cold; dying of the cold

قرمبزي k̩armbze *f. plural regional* nose drippings, snots

قز k̩azz *m.* k̩az *Arabic* raw silk

قزاخ k̩azā́kh *m.* Kazakh (person)

قزاز k̩azzā́z *m. Arabic* 1 sericulturist, one who raises silkworms 2 silk merchant

قزاق k̩azā́k̩ *m.* 1 cossack 2 Kazak (person)

قزاقستان k̩azak̩stā́n *m.* Kazakstan

قزاقي k̩azā́k̩í 1.1 kazakh 1.2 cossack 2 *f.* Kazak, Kazak language

قزل ایاقي k̩izilajā́k̩í *adjective* kizil-ayak (of a kind of rug)

قزل باش k̩izilbā́sh *m. plural* 1 Kizilbashi (people of Turkish origin) 2 *m.* Kizilbash (person)

قزل قلعه k̩izilkal'á *f.* ☞ شبرخان

قزوین k̩azvín *m.* Kazvin (city, Iran)

قساوت k̩asāvát *m. Arabic* 1 hardness, stiffness 2 severity, cruelty 3 rudeness, sharpness

قسب k̩asáb *m.* 1 red silk 2 small turban 3 ☞ کسب

قسط k̩ist *m. Arabic* [*plural:* قسطونه k̩istúna *Arabic plural:* اقساط ak̩sā́t] payment, fee, installment payment; installment system قسط ترل to establish fees, payment on the installment plan قسطونه ورکول to pay on the installment plan

قسط بندي k̩istbandí *f.* payment on the installment plan

قسطوار k̩istvā́r paid on the installment plan

قسم ¹ ḳism *m.* ḳəsm *Arabic* [*plural:* قسمونه ḳismúna *Arabic plural:* اقسام aḳsám] 1 kind, type; category; order هر قسم of every kind, varied, motley, sundry, variegated له هر قسمه څخه every variety of book هغه قسم of such a kind, such قسم قسم of every type, sundry goods په لاندینی قسم سره in the following manner 2 kind, species, breed د كندهار انگور ډېر قسمونه لري There are many varieties of Kandahar grape. 3 part, portion 4 *military* flight یو قسم a to mine, set mines b little, bit په هیڅ قسم in no instance, not in any manner په یو قسم د قسمو in one way or another لكه څه قسم چه ... It's just as though ...

قسم ² ḳasám *m. Arabic* oath; oath of allegiance عسكري قسم military oath قسم اخيستل، قسم خورل to vow, swear; take an oath of allegiance قسم وركول to take an oath; swear

قسماقسم ḳismāḳism of every kind, type; all possible, varied, variegated

قسمت ḳismát *m. Arabic* 1 part; portion 2 division; partition 3 fate, lot, portion; luck قسمت يې نه و He didn't succeed. He had bad luck.

قسماً ḳismátán *Arabic* partly, partially

قسي ḳasí *Arabic* stiff, hard

قسي القلب ḳasilḳálb *Arabic* cruel, cruelhearted

قسيم ḳasím *m. proper name* Qasim, Qseem

قشر ḳishr *m. Arabic* bark; crust; rind; pelt د مځكي قشر the earth's crust

قشري ḳasharí *Arabic* 1 dermal, cutaneous 2 corky, suberous 3 *literal* surface

قشريه ḳishrijá قشريه حيوانات crustacea

قشط ḳisht *m. dialect* ☞ قسط

قشقاش ḳashḳásh *m. botany* poppy

قشلاق ḳishláḳ *m.* village, settlement; winter quarters

قشله ḳishlá *f.* 1 barracks, casern, military barracks 2 deployment of a military unit

قشله گاه ḳishlagáh *m.* military post (permanent)

قشنگ ḳasháng beautiful

قشون ḳoshún *m.* army, troops

قصاب ḳassáb *m. Arabic* butcher په ډېرو قصابانو غوا مرداره وي *proverb literal* Many butchers, but the cow drops dead (i.e., of natural causes). *figurative* Too many cooks spoil the broth.

قصابه ḳasābá *f. Arabic* head kerchief; kerchief

قصابي ḳassábí *f.* 1 occupation of butcher 2 cooling and processing of carcasses قصابي كول *compound verb* a to cool and process (meat) carcasses b to kill brutally

قصاص ḳisás *m. Arabic* bloody vengeance; retribution قصاص اخيستل to avenge

قصائد ḳasáid *m. Arabic plural* ☞ قصيده

قصب ḳasáb *m. Arabic* delicate linen

قصبات ḳasbát *m. Arabic plural of* قصبه

قصبت الريه ḳasabat-ar-rijá *f. Arabic* windpipe, trachea

قصبت المري ḳasabat-al-marí *Arabic* esophagus, gullet

قصبه ḳasbá *f. Arabic* [*plural:* قصبي kasbé *plural:* قصبات kasbát] small town, settlement

قصد ḳasd *m. Arabic* 1 goal, intention, plan, project په قصد with the goal, with the intention, intentionally قصد كول to intend to, plan to یو كار ته قصد كول to get down to do some matter 2 attempt د انتحار قصد كول to attempt to take one's own life

قصداً ḳásdán *Arabic* intentionally, purposely, with the intention, with the goal, premeditatedly

قصدي ḳasdí 1 intended, planned, premeditated 2 forced, affected قصدي خندا forced or affected laugh

قصر ¹ ḳasr *m. Arabic* palace د دلكشا قصر the royal palace Dilkusha (in Kabul)

قصر ² ḳasr *m. Arabic* 1 insufficiency, limitedness 2 curtailment

قصص ḳisás *m. Arabic plural of* قصه

قصور ḳusúr *m. Arabic* 1 omission, blunder د چا د قصور څخه through somebody's fault د هغه څخه لوی قصور شوئ و He was guilty of a big slip. He made a huge blunder. قصور كول to make a slip, commit a blunder 2 flaw, imperfection

قصه ḳissá *f.* ḳisa *Arabic* [*plural:* قصي ḳisé *Arabic plural:* قصص kisás] 1 tale, anecdote, story بس قصه خلاصه شوه! There's an end to the tale! That's all! 2 event, history ورته دغسي قصه پيښه شوه Such a thing happened to them. 3 matter, affair, business قصه اصله قصه دا ده چه This is the way the matter stood. داسي وه The substance of the matter is this ... قصه دا وشوه چه ... The matter came down to the fact that ... زه له دې قصو نه خلاص وم I was saved from all of this. 4 subject, topic 5 *colloquial* quarrel; argument; altercation

قصه خواني ḳissakhāní *f.* telling of tales د قصه خواني بازار the printers' district in Peshawar where Pashto literature is published

قصيده ḳasidá *f. Arabic* [*plural:* قصيدي ḳasidé *Arabic plural:* قصائد ḳasáíd] 1 ode, kasida (ancient Arabic poem having, as a rule, a rigid tripartite structure); panegyric 2 poem قصيده ويل to compose an ode

قضا ḳazá *Arabic* 1 *f.* 1.1 fate د قضا اراده داسي وشوه It was as fate would have it. خان قضا ته سپارل to depend on fate 1.2 chance په قضا by chance په قضا پوري اړه لرل to depend upon chance 2 *predicative* passed (through) سبق قضا كول to go through a lesson قضا مازديگر in the twilight

قضات ḳuzát *m. Arabic plural of* قاضي

قضاكار ḳazākár accidentally

قضاوت ḳazāvát *m. Arabic* 1 court examination 2 verdict; decision; judgment د قضاوتونه jury د خلقو قضاوت the opinion of the people, the opinion of the peoples' court په مسئله باندي قضاوت كول to adjudicate the problem تاسو پخپله قضاوت وكړئ Judge for yourself. 3 job of a judge, the work of a judge 4 *sports* refereeing, umpiring

قضايا ḳazājá *m. Arabic plural of* قضيه

قضائي ḳazāí 1 judicial; court قضائي قوه judicial power, authority خپلي قضائي وظيفي pure qazāí ekhtiārāt jurisdiction; the right to judge اجرا كول to execute the function of a judge 2 chance; fateful, fate

قضيه ḳazijá f. Arabic [plural: قضي kazijé plural: قضايا ḳazājá] 1 judicial trial, case 2 dispute, litigation 3 quarrel 4 happening, event, incident ناوړه قضيه unpleasantness 5 grammar sentence

قطار ḳatār ḳitār Arabic 1 m. Arabic row, line; file; column د غرونو قطار mountain ridge د موټرو قطار motorized convoy قطار كبدل to be arranged in rows; be drawn up in a line or a column; be stretched out in a line په يو قطار اچول to arrange in rows; draw up in a line or in a column 2 predicative placed in rows; drawn up in a line or in a column; stretched out in a line

قطاربندي ḳatārbandí f. arranging in a row or in a column; stretching out in a line

قطاروزمه ḳtārvazmá f. قطاروزنه ḳatārvazná f. bandolier, ammunition belt

قطاري ḳatārí arranged in rows; drawn up in rank; stretched out in a line قطاري موټر truck train, tractor-trailer train

قطاع ḳuttā' Arabic masculine plural of قاطع

قطب ḳútb ḳútəb ḳutub m. Arabic 1 pole شمالي قطب the North Pole د جنوبي قطب the South Pole د قطب ستوری the Pole Star قطب خوا the Antarctic, Antarctica 2 in the north قطب براعظم axis; shaft 3 electrical engineering pole 4 authority, prominent person; leader idiom نیل قطبونه بیل to be diametrically opposed

قطب پله ḳutbpalá regional to the north

قطب نما ḳutubnumā f. compass

قطبي ḳutbí Arabic polar قطبي دائره the polar regions جنوبي قطبي مناطق the Anarctic, Antarctica شمالي قطبي مناطق the Arctic

قطبين ḳutbájn m. Arabic dual (the) poles, North and South Poles

قطر ḳutr m. Arabic 1 diameter; line of the diameter; diametric line نیمائي قطر radius 2 military caliber 3 math diagonal

قطران ḳatrān m. Arabic tar, pitch

قطره ḳatrá f. Arabic [plural: قطري ḳatré m. Arabic plural: قطرات ḳatarāt] drop د وينو قطره drop of blood قطره قطره drop by drop

قطع ḳat' f. 1 chopping off, severance 2 break; interruption; discontinuance قطع كول compound verb to break; interrupt, discontinue 2 مواصلات قطع to break off relations روابط قطع كول to interrupt communications قطع كبدل compound verb a to be interrupted, be broken off; be discontinued د تگ راتگ لاره قطع شوه The communication was interrupted. b to be covered قطع شوي مسافه the distance covered 3 solution, decision (question, problem) 4 format (of a book, a sheet, a page)

قطعاً ḳát'án Arabic 1 decisively, categorically; conclusively 2 obligatorily قطعاً لازمه گڼل to consider absolutely necessary

قطعه ḳit'a f. Arabic [plural: قطعي ḳit'é] 1 piece; part; fragment 2 m. & f. Arabic [plural: قطعات ḳita'āt] part of the world, continent, mainland 3 m. & f. Arabic [plural: قطعات kita'āt] military subunit, unit قطعه احترام د to mine, set mines 4 literature kita (a short poem of 2, 3, or more stanzas with a special rhyming

scheme) 5 playing card 6 piece, item (classifier used in counting letters, illustrations, photos) قطعي عكسونه 9 ۹ photographs قطعه كول compound verb a to divide into pieces or parts; break up b to interrupt, discontinue

قطعه بازي ḳit'abāzí f. gambling with cards, card-playing

قطعي ḳat'í Arabic decisive, categoric; conclusive قطعي فیصله final decision

قطعیت ḳat'iját m. 1 conclusiveness; outcome قطعیت میندل to be concluded 2 categoricalness, decisiveness

قطغن ḳattaghán m. 1 Kattagan (city) د قطغن ولایت history Kattagan Province 2 ☞ قدغن

قطي ḳutí f. [plural: قطی ḳutə́j Western plural: قطیاني ḳutijā́ni] box د قطی خوراک preserves غوښني په قطی کبني اچول to preserve meat

قطیفه ḳatifá f. Arabic ☞ قدیفه

قفر ḳafr m. Arabic desert

قفس ḳafás m. Arabic cage (for birds, etc.)

قفسه ḳafasá f. Arabic shelves; bookcase

قفقاز ḳafḳā́z ḳavḳā́z m. Caucasus

قفقازي ḳafḳāzí ḳafḳāzáj Caucasian

قفل ḳufl m. Arabic ☞ قلف اچول ته ... و to put the latch on, lock by latching

قق ḳuḳḳúk m. قق ققهار ḳuḳḳukahār m. clatter (of hooves of galloping horses)

ققنس ḳaḳnás m. ققنوس ḳaḳnús m. phoenix (the legendary bird)

قلا ḳalá f. [plural: قلاگاني ḳalāgáni plural: قلاوي ḳalā́vi] 1 castle; kala (local kind of large two- or three-story house surrounded by a high fence) 2 fortress, fort ☞ قلعه

قلاب ḳulā́b m. Arabic hood (for a falcon)

قلابند ḳalābánd surrounded, beseiged قلابند كول to surround, beseige قلابند كبدل to be surrounded, be beseiged

قلابندي ḳalābandí f. seige لاس له قلابندی نیول to raise a seige

قلابه ḳulābá f. Arabic 1 hook 2 fishhook

قلابي ḳulābí 1 hooked, bent into a hook 2 crooked, bent

قلات ḳalā́t m. Kelat (city) د قلات ولایت Kelat Province

قلاچ ḳulách m. span (measure made by the hand with the fingers extended)

قلار ḳalā́r m. قرار

قلارتیا ḳalārtjá f. calm, lull

قلاره قلاري ḳalā́ra ḳalārí f. قلاري ḳalārí f. complete silence, tranquility, peace and quiet

قلاش ḳalā́sh 1.1 clever, shrewd, pushy 1.2 dissolute 1.3 useless 2 m. .1 shrewd person, pushy person, scoundrel 2.2 dissolute person, idler 2.3 good-for-nothing (person) 2.4 debauchee, drunkard

قلائي ḳalā́í m. plural ☞ قلعي

قلب ¹ ḳalb m. Arabic [plural: قلوب ḳulúb] heart

قلب ² ḳalb *Arabic* **1** *m.* **.1** transposition of words, inversion **1.2** transposition of letters, metathesis **1.3** transformation, transmutation **2** counterfeit, false

قلب ³ ḳalb broken (of terrain)

قلباً ḳálbán *Arabic* heartfelt, with all the heart

قلب والی ḳalbválaj *m.* **1** counterfeit **2** falsity

قلبه ḳulbá *f. Arabic* **1** plow د قلبي غوایان harnessed oxen (bulls) **2** team of oxen **3** plowed land قلبه ایستل، قلبه کول *compound verb* to plow, plow up, plow over again *compound verb* to be plowed up, be plowed over again **4** kul'ba (measure of land equal to 50 to 150 jeribs)

قلبه کشي ḳulbakashí *f.* **1** plowed land **2** ceremonial or ritual ploughing on the holiday of Novruz

قلبي ḳalbí *Arabic* **1** hearty, cordial, spiritual قلبي ودا spiritual tranquillity قلبي ودا میندل to calm down, become calm **2** secret, intimate, cherished

قلپ ¹ ḳulp *m.* ☞ قلف خولې ته دي قلپ اچولئ دئ You are always silent.

قلپ ² ḳalp ☞ قلب ²

قلت ḳillát *m. Arabic* insufficiency; shortage

قلزم ḳulzúm *m. Arabic* د قلزم بحیره the Red Sea

قلعچه ḳal'achá *f.* small fortress, fort; stronghold

قلع وقمع ḳal'uḳám' *m. Arabic* **1** defeat, rout قلع وقمع کول *compound verb* **a** to rout, defeat, beat **b** to waste, consume (of a disease, grief)

قلعه ḳal'á *f. Arabic* **1** fortress, stronghold **2** fortress, stronghold د اور قلعه، د اطفائي قلعه fire watchtower **3** *used in geographical names* قلعه مرادبیک Kala-ji-Muradbek (settlement north of Kabul)

قلعه بند ḳal'abánd ☞ قلابند

قلعه بیگي ḳal'abegí *m.* commandant of a fortress, commander of a fort

قلعه نو ḳal'a-ji-náu *m.* Kalajinau (city)

قلعي ḳala'í *m. & f. plural* tin د قلعیو معدن tin miners

قلعي گر ḳala'igár *m.* tinsmith

قلف ḳulf *m. Arabic* [*plural:* قلفونه ḳulfúna *Western plural:* قلفان ḳulfán] lock, bolt, latch قلف کول، قلف اچول، قلف لگول *compound verb* to latch, bolt قلف کېدل *compound verb* to be latched, be bolted قلف را خلاصول، قلف خلاصول to unbolt, unlatch په قلف کښې **a** to put a key in a lock **b** to switch on (current, etc.) ☞ کلي ورکول قفل

قلفک ḳulfák *m.* lock *diminutive of* قلف

قلق ¹ ḳalák *m. Arabic* **1** uneasiness, worry, alarm **2** concern

قلق ² ḳalíḳ *Arabic* **1** worried, troubled **2** concerned

قلل ḳulál *masculine plural of* قله

قلم ḳalám *m. Arabic* [*plural:* قلمونه kalamúna *Western plural:* قلمان ḳalamán *Arabic plural:* قلمات ḳalamát *plural:* اكْلام aḳlám] **1** pen, qalam, reed pen قلم writer په د قلم خاوند خودرنگ قلم fountain pen قلم خورل ...written in such a way ...قلم د to be crossed out, be erased د قلم لاندي راوستل to take notes (e.g., on a lecture) په مجله ما

په پښتو هم قلم I read your article in the newspaper. ستا ادبي قلم ولیده لري He even writes in Pashto. د ده قلم ډېر تېزه دئ He wields a sharp pen. He has an incisive style. قلم وهل to be erased, be crossed out **2** *m. & f. Arabic* [*plural:* اقلام aḳlám] items (e.g., of export) د افغانستان د اخراجاتو یو مهم قلم د قره قلي پوست دئ One of Afghanistan's important export items is caracul wool. **3** *m. & f. Arabic* [*plural:* اقلام aḳlám] item, piece (numerative classifier in counting rugs, carpets, etc.) **4** *m. & f. Arabic* [*plural:* اقلام aḳlám] *botany* graft, cutting **5** cutting tool, point tool, chisel *idiom* یو قلم categorically, decisively قلم مخصوص ḳalám-i the secret unit, the special unit (counterintelligence unit within an organization) پر زړه سر قلم to impress, engrave; memorize قلم کول، د زړه پر سر قلم کول کول *compound verb* to cut off the head قلم کېدل *compound verb* to be cut off (of the head)

قلماغ ḳalmágh *m.* Kalmyk (person)

قلماغي ḳalmághí *adjective* Kalmyk قلماغي ژبه Kalmyk, Kalmyk language

قلم تراش ḳalamtarásh *m.* penknife

قلمداد ḳalamdád *m.* **1** enumeration, list **2** entry (into the composition of a list) قلمداد کول *compound verb* **a** to enumerate **b** to include, enter into (a composition, list)

قلمدان ḳalamdán *m.* pencil box

قلمرو ḳalamráv *m.* **1** empire; power **2** state territory **3** authority **4** sphere, field د علومو په قلمرو کښې in the field of science

قلم فرسائي ḳalafursáí *m.* letter, writing قلم فرسائي کول to write

قلمه ḳalamá *f.* ☞ قلم **4**

قلمي ¹ ḳalamí **1** *adjective* manuscript, handwritten قلمي اثار manuscript materials قلمي کتاب a manuscript **2** pertaining to a writing, writing, literary قلمي طاقت literary talent د مجلي قلمي ملگری magazine worker, journalist د مجلي سره قلمي مرسته کول to work on a journal or a magazine **3** *adjective* graft-, grafted

قلمي ² ḳalamé *plural of* قلمه

قلنج ḳulíndzh *m. Arabic* colic

قلندر ḳalandár *m.* kalandar, wandering dervish; hermit, one withdrawn from the world, aesthete

قلندرانه ḳalandaráná **1** pertain to a dervish **2** pertaining to the hermit's life; withdrawn from the world

قلنگ ḳaláng ḳuláng *m.* **1** duty, tax, impost, revenue قلنگ ورکول to pay a duty or a tax **2** gift, tribute (to a sayyid, lord, etc.) **2** ☞ کلنگ ¹

قلنگي ḳulangí fighting (e.g., fighting cock) ☞ کلنگي

قلوب ḳulúb *Arabic masculine plural of* قلب ¹

قلوي ḳilví *Arabic* alkaline

قلویات ḳilviját *m. Arabic plural* alkali

قله ḳullá *f. Arabic* [*plural:* قلي ḳullé *m. Arabic plural:* قلل ḳulál] summit (of a mountain)

قلي ḳulí *m.* **1** slave **2** porter; stevedore; coolie **3** *proper name* Quli

قلیل ḳalíl *Arabic* few

ق.م *abbreviation* B.C., before this era (in calendar calculations) قبل الميلاد ۴۰۰ 400 B.C. ☞

قمار k̲imār k̲umár *m. Arabic* gambling (dice, cards) قمار کول to gamble د قمار مرتکب کېدل to be a gambler قمار وهل to play cards جگړي قمار a reckless or chancy military move

قمارباز k̲imārbāz *m.* gambler; card-player

قماربازي k̲imārbāzí *f.* gambling (at cards)

قمارخانه k̲imārkhāná *f.* gambling house; gambling den

قماش[1] k̲umásh *m. Arabic* 1 goods 2 cloth, textiles (cotton)

قماش[2] k̲imásh k̲umásh *m. Arabic* 1 manners, foibles 2 conduct, morals

قمچي k̲amchí *f.* قمچينه k̲amchína *f.* whip, quirt, horse whip

قمر k̲amár *m. Arabic* 1 moon 2 [*plural:* اقمار ak̲mấr] *astronomy* satellite (of a planet)

قمري[1] k̲umrí *m. Arabic* turtledove

قمري[2] k̲amarí *Arabic* lunar (of calendrical calculations)

قمع k̲am' *f. Arabic* subordination, subjugation, suppression

قمه k̲amá *f.* dagger

قميص k̲amís *m. Arabic* 1 shirt 2 chemist

قميصگى k̲amisgáj *m.* voluminous shirt, gown

قنات[1] k̲anát *m. Arabic* underground irrigation canal

قنات[2] k̲anát *m.* ☞ قناد

قناد k̲annád *m. Arabic* confectioner, pastry chef

قنادي k̲annādí *f.* 1 pastry baking; candy making 2 pastry shop; sweet shop

قناعت k̲anā'át *m. Arabic* satisfaction; contentment د قناعت وړ ځواب to give a satisfactory answer پر يو شي باندي خپل قناعت ښکاره کول ، په يو شي باندي خپل قناعت ښکاره کول to express satisfaction with something د ... سره قناعت کول a to be satisfied with somebody b په ... کښي قناعت کول to be satisfied with something په دي سره قناعت کېدل to be satisfied (with), be content someone (with) something

قناعت بخش k̲anā'atbákhsh satisfactory (e.g., an answer)

قنال k̲anál *m.* ☞ کانال

قناويز k̲anāvíz *m.* 1 coarse silken fabric 2 *proper name* Kanaviz

قنج k̲undzh *m. regional* shrewdness, deception; hypocrisy

قنجوغه k̲andzhughá *f.* saddlebow straps

قنجي k̲undzhí *f. regional* key ☞ کنجي

قند k̲and *m. Arabic* refined sugar د قندو کارخانه sugar refinery د قند ناروغي *medicine* diabetes میده قند powdered sugar قندو شیره molasses

قنداغ k̲undágh *m.* قنداق k̲undák̲ *m.* 1 butt (of a rifle) 2 carriage, caisson (cannon)

قندوز k̲undúz *m.* Kunduz (city, district) د قندز ولايت Kunduz Province

قندسازي k̲andsāzí *f. adjective* sugar-refining د قندسازي فابريکه sugar refinery

قندهار k̲andhár k̲andahár *m.* Kandahar (city) د قندهار ښار Kandahar (city) د قندهار نائب الحکومه گي ولايت history Kandahar Province

قندهارى k̲andhāráj k̲andahāráj 1 Kandaharian 2 *m.* Kahandarian, resident of Kandahar

قندي k̲andí *adjective* sugar, sugary قندي جغندر sugar beet في صد قندي مواد sugariness

قنديل k̲andíl *m. Arabic* 1 chandelier 2 candelabrum 3 throw, toss (of a fowler's net) قنديل کول to be tossed (of a fowler's net) اخیستل to fall like a stone, attack (as a falcon to its prey) *idiom* بحري قنديل jellyfish, medusa

قو k̲u *m.* swan

قوا k̲uvā *Arabic* 1 *m. plural* [*singular:* قوت k̲uvát *f. singular:* قوه k̲uvá] .1 forces خپل ټول قوا all one's forces 1.2 army, troops محرکه قوا fuel برق قوا electric energy 1.3 هوايي قوا Air Forces 2 *f.* [*plural:* قواوي k̲uvāvi] .1 strength مونږ به خپلي گردي قواوي په We strove with all our strength. د قواو توازن balances of forces 2.2 بري قواوي ground troops بحري قواوي the Navy, the fleet *idiom* د طبيعت قوا the forces of nature

قوات k̲uvất *Arabic masculine plural of* قوت[1]

قواره k̲avārá *f.* 1 figure; build 2 exterior, external appearance

قواعد k̲avā'íd *m. Arabic plural* 1 *of* قاعده 2 order 3 *military* drill instruction قواعد کول to mine, set mines 4 grammar; structure of language

قواعددان k̲avā'iddán disciplined (of troops)

قوال k̲avvál *m. Arabic* itinerant singer; storyteller

قوام[1] k̲ivám *m. Arabic* 1 thickness, density; compactness 2 support, prop 3 existence 4 thickening, condensation 5 syrup

قوام[2] k̲avám *m. Arabic* 1 justice 2 truth, sincerity 3 figure, torso

قوامي k̲ivāmí syrupy, syrup-like

قاموس k̲avāmís *Arabic masculine plural of* قاموس

قوانين k̲avānín 1 *Arabic masculine plural of* قانون 2 law; legislation

قواوي k̲uvāvi *feminine plural of* قوا[2]

قواى جى خمسه k̲uvā-ji-khamsá *f.* five sense organs

قواى جى کار k̲uvā-ji-kár *m.* construction brigade; construction unit

قوت[1] k̲uvát *m. Arabic* [*plural:* قوتونه k̲uvatúna *Arabic plural:* قوات k̲uvất *plural:* قوا k̲uvấ] 1 strength, force د قوت خاوند strong man قوت ميندل to become strong, get strong, grow strong حيواني قوت physical strength, brute force 2 forces عسکري قوت the Armed Forces بحري قوت the Navy پوليسي قوت the police force 3 power, state; (central) authority 4 significance, meaning 5 strength, authority زړه قوت willpower; endurance 6 *math* degree, power *idiom* انساني قوت kinetic energy دا فکر په ټولو خلکو All were convinced that that idea would have کښي قوت لري mastery of everyone. د امراضو د مدافعي قوت *medicine* bodily resistance د اولس ملي قوت، د اولس عالي قوت national sovereignty

قوت[2] k̲ut *m. Arabic* [*plural:* اقوات ak̲vất] food, nourishment, subsistence قوت حاصلول to earn a subsistence wage; live at a subsistence level قوت لا يموت subsistence; minimum level of nourishment necessary for existence

قوت الظهر k̲uvat-az-záhr *m. Arabic* reinforcement, support

قوتناک ḳuvatnák strong, powerful

قوت نما ḳuvatnumá *f. math* exponent

قطي ḳutə́j *f.* ☞ قوتی

قوچ ḳuch *m.* ram (often used of one that is belligerent)

قوچق ḳochák healthy, robust

قوده ḳavadá *f.* **1** tuft of grass, etc., of a size to fit the hand **2** bouquet **3** handful

قورغندل ḳurghandál *m. regional* cactus

قورمه ḳormá ḳavrumá *f.* roasted meat (with spices and fruit)

قوریه ḳavrijá *f.* [*plural:* قوریه ḳavrijé *Western plural:* قوریه گانی ḳavrijagáni] **1** seedling **2** nursery (for plants)

قوس ḳaus *m. Arabic* [*plural:* قوسونه ḳausúna *Arabic plural:* اقواس aḳvás] **1** bow (the weapon) **2** *astronomy* Sagittarius (the constellation) **3** Kaus (the 10th month of the solar year, November/December) **4** *math* arc **5** curve (prices, etc.)

قوس قزح ḳaus-i-ḳázh *m.* rainbow ☞ بوی (بوی تال)²

قوسین ḳausájn *m. Arabic dual* brackets

قوض ḳavz *m.* ☞ قبض

قوضتیا ḳavztjá *f.* قوضیات ḳavziját *m.* ☞ قبض 4

قوضول ḳavzavə́l *transitive* ☞ قبضول

کوغالی ḳughā́laj *m. regional* ☞ کوغالی

قوغوش ḳughúsh *m.* hospital ward

قول¹ ḳaul *m. Arabic* [*plural:* اقوال aḳvā́l] **1** word, utterance د خپل قول سره یو شي کول in confirmation of one's words د تائید دپاره to confess to something **2** promise, word of honor زه قول دئ چه … I give my word that … د چا سره قول کول to give one's promise, give one's word to someone, come to an agreement with someone پر خپل قول دربدل، پر خپل قول ټینگ اوسبدل to keep a promise, keep one's word د چا څخه قول اخیستل to exact a promise, require a word of honor from someone

قول² ḳol ḳul *m.* **1** hand; front extremity (of an animal) **2** handle, hilt

قول³ ḳul *m.* lake

قول اردو ḳol-i-urdú *m. military* corps

قلبه ḳulbá *f.*

قول وقرار ḳaul-u-karā́r *m.* agreement; understanding قول وقرار کول to come to an agreement

قوم ḳaum *m. Arabic* [*plural:* اقوام aḳvā́m] **1** people پښتون قوم the Afghan nation **2** tribe, clan په قوم by clan, by descent رحمن بابا په واده يې په خپل قوم مهمند دئ Rahman Baba is of the Mohand Clan. قوم کښې کړئ دئ He married his fellow tribeswoman. **3** resident (of a village, etc.) **4** group of tribes

قوماندان ḳumāndā́n *m.* **1** commander **2** commanding general د عسکري قواو قوماندان troop commander (of a province) **3** chief **4** commandant

قوماندانی ḳumāndā́ni *f.* **1** command (headquarters) د عسکرو اعلی the High Command **2** Directorate of Police, the Police Directorate د کابل قوماندانی Police Headquarters (in Kabul)

قوماندانیت ḳumāndāniját *m.* command (headquarters) د عسکري فرقې Division Command (headquarters)

قوماند ḳumāndá *f.* **1** command (order) په قوماند at the command, upon command **2** commanding (the act)

قوم پرست ḳaumparást *m.* nationalist

قوم پرستي ḳaumparastí *f.* **1** nationalism **2** nationality

قوم پروري ḳaumparvari *f.* concern for the people, concern for the nation

قوماندان ḳumandā́n *m.* ☞ قوماندان

قومي ḳaumí *Arabic* **1** national, people's, popular قومي خدمت serving the people **2** tribal **3** national قومي ژبه national language **4** ethnic

قومیت ḳaumiját *m. Arabic* **1** nationality **2** citizenship **3** tribal affiliation **4** nationalism

قومیدان ḳumajdā́n *m. military colloquial* lieutenant colonel

قونسرو ḳonsérv *m.* قونسروه ḳonservá *f.* conserves

قونسل ḳonsúl *m.* consul

قونسل خانه ḳonsulkhāná *f.* consulate (the building)

قونسلگري ḳonsulgarí *f.* consulate staff (the representation itself)

قونسلي ḳonsulí consular

قونسول ḳonsúl *m.* consul

قوه ḳuvá *f. Arabic* قوة ḳuvát *m. Arabic* [*plural:* قوي ḳuvé *m. Arabic plural:* قوا ḳuvā́] **1** ☞ قوت د ارادي قوه strength of will, willpower **2** authority اجرائیه قوه executive authority مقننه قوه legislative authority **3** *math* power **4** power (ability) د رانیولو قوه purchasing power

قوي¹ ḳaví *Arabic* **1** strong, powerful, mighty قوي کېدل to gather strength, grow strong **2** robust, vigorous

قوه² ḳuvé *plural of* قوه

قوي البنیه ḳavi-al-binjá *Arabic* strong in body

قهار ḳahhā́r *Arabic* Almighty (epithet of God)

قهر ḳahr *m. Arabic* rage, irritation, wrath په قهر in rage, in irritation په قهر کېدل … to grow angry, become wrathful at someone هغه د قهر څخه سره لمبه شو He fell into a rage. په قهر ویل to speak in anger, talk angrily قهر ورتلل to fall into a rage, get angry

قهرجن ḳahrdzhə́n قهرژن ḳahrzhə́n **1** angry; wrathful; enraged **2** hot-tempered, irascible

قهرمان ḳahramā́n *m.* **1** champion **2** hero

قهرمانه ḳahramā́na *f.* heroine د ډرام قهرمانه the heroine of a play

قهرماني ḳahramā́ni *f.* heroism

قهرمن ḳahrmə́n قهرناک ḳahrnā́k ☞ قهرجن

قهرول ḳahravə́l *transitive* [*past:* و یې قهراوه] to anger, irritate; cause to fall into a rage

قهري ḳahrí *Arabic* inevitable, unavoidable

قهربدل ḳahredə́l *intransitive* [*past:* و قهربده] to be angry with, get enraged, become annoyed, get irritated

قهقرا ḳahḳará *f.* قهقرى *Arabic* regression, decay, decline قهقرا کول to retreat (i.e., in the face of difficulties) مخ په قهقرا نيول to bring or lead into decline, decay

قهقرائي ḳahrḳaráī regressive, leading to regression, decline, decay

قهقره ḳahrḳará *f. Arabic* ☞ قهقرا

قهقهه ḳahḳahá *f. Arabic* 1 loud laugh, guffaw 2 squawk (e.g., of a pelican) قهقهه کول a to laugh loudly, guffaw b to squawk (as a pelican) قهقهه وهل to laugh, laugh uproariously

قهوه ḳahvá *f. Arabic* 1 coffee 2 alcoholic drink

قهوه جوړونکى ماشين ḳahvá dzhoravúnkaj coffee mill, coffee grinder

قهوه خانه ḳahvakhāná *f.* coffeehouse, cafe

قهوه يي ḳahvaí *adjective* coffee (color)

قى ḳaj *m. Arabic* 1 vomit قى وهل *compound verb* قى کول to vomit, throw up قى ورتلل to feel nauseous 2 deposit (carbon, etc. on a candle)

قيادت ḳijādát *m. Arabic* seniority; leadership, management د چا تر قيادت لاندي under someone's leadership or management

قياس ḳijā́s *m. Arabic* 1 comparison, analogy په همدي قياس سره analogously پر... قياس کول to compare, put up against دا خبره له قياسه وتلي ده This is senseless. 2 *philosophy* induction 3 hypothesis

قياسول ḳijāsavól *denominative, transitive* [*past:* قياس يي کړ] to compare, put up against, draw an analogy

قياسي ḳijāsí *Arabic* 1 comparative 2 similiar, analogous

قيافه ḳijāfá *f. Arabic* face; appearance, aspect, look په يوه ډپره پرېشانه قيافه having a very distraught appearance

قيام ḳijā́m *m. Arabic* 1 establishment د سولي او امنيت قيام the establishment of peace and security قيام لرل to be established 2 uprising, rising; speech or verbal presentation against someone or something د چا په مقابل کښي قيام کول to instigate an uprising to speak against someone 3 rising 4 maintainance, support د روغتيا قيام maintenance of (good health)

قيام الدين ḳijāmuddín *m. Arabic proper name* Qiamuddin

قيامت ḳijāmát *m. Arabic* 1 *religion* Resurrection Day; the Last Judgement, Judgement Day 2 calamity; disturbance قيامت جوړول to cause a commotion يو قيامت راوستل to raise a ruckus, cause turmoil هغه کتاب قيامتونه کوي This book excites. 3 surprising matter, astounding affair *idiom* گرمى قيامت را کوز کړئ و It has become hellishly hot. پر چا قيامت جوړول to torture someone

قيامت گلى ḳijāmatgúlaj *m. regional* kind of yellow flower

قيپر ḳipór *m. regional* mud, dirt

قينچي ḳajchí *f.* ☞ قينچي

قيد ḳajd *m. Arabic* [*plural:* قيدونه ḳajdúna *Arabic plural:* قيود ḳujúd] 1 prison detention, imprisonment تنهائي قيد solitary confinement 2 shackles, handcuffs, fetters, chain د غلامى قيود ماتول to break the chains of slavery 3 registration on a list; registration 4 *military* guard platoon 5 *grammar* adverb 6 obligation; provision of a treaty قيدول *compound verb* ☞

قيدخانه ḳajdkhāná *f. Eastern* prison

قيدول ḳajdavól *denominative, transitive* [*past:* قيد يي کړ] 1 to imprison 2 to chain, shackle, handcuff 3 to take prisoner, seize 4 to enter on a list, register 5 to isolate, put in solitary confinement

قيدي ḳajdí 1 *m. Eastern* detainee, prisoner, person under arrest 2 *grammar* adverbial

قيدېدل ḳajdedól *denominative, intransitive* [*past:* قيد شو] 1 to be imprisoned 2 to be chained, be fettered, be handcuffed 3 to be taken prisoner, be seized 4 to be registered; be put on a list 5 to be isolated; be put in solitary confinement

قير ḳir *Arabic* 1 *m.* .1 resin, pitch 1.2 tar 2 *attributive predicative* tarred قير کول a tarred road قير سرک *compound verb* قيرېدل قير کېدل *compound verb* ☞

قيراط ḳirā́t *m. Arabic* carat

قيرپاش ḳirpā́sh *m.* machine for asphalting or tarring a road

قيرول ḳiravól *denominative, transitive* [*past:* قير يي کړ] to tar, asphalt (a road)

قيرېدل ḳiredól *denominative, intransitive* [*past:* قير شو] to be tarred, be asphalted قير شوى لار tarred road, asphalted road

قيزه ḳajzá *f.* bridle, halter

قيسرغر ḳajsarghár *m.* Takht-i-Suleiman (mountain)

قيسي ḳajsí *m. plural* kind of apricot

قيشلاق ḳishlā́ḳ *m.* ☞ قشلاق

قيصر ḳajsár *m.* emperor

قيطان ḳajtán *m.* 1 lace 2 cord

قيطوس ḳitús *m. astronomy* Ceta, the Whale (the constellation)

قيف ḳif *m.* funnel; watering can

قيل وقال ḳil-u-ḳā́l *m.* 1 argument, controversy, scandal 2 gossip

قيم [1] ḳijám *Arabic masculine plural of* قيمت

قيم [2] ḳajím *Arabic* 1.1 straightforward, upright, deserving 1.2 valuable 2 *m.* .1 manager 2.2 guardian 2.3 overseer

قيماغ چاى ḳajmāghchā́j *m.* tea with cream عمومي قيماغ چاى ceremonial serving of tea (one of the wedding rituals)

قيمت ḳimát *Arabic* 1 *m.* [*plural:* قيمتونه ḳimatúna *Arabic plural:* قيم ḳijám] .1 price, cost د بازار قيمت، د مال جاري قيمت the market price د خرڅلاو قيمت the purchase price لومړني قيمت the sales price How د دې شي قيمت څونه دئ؟ ... at the price of ... د... په قيمت سره much does this cost? په گران قيمت، په گران قيمت سره at a high price, expensively په هر قيمت سره چه وي regardless of what it cost قيمت کول *compound verb* to determine the price, evaluate قيمت لوړول lower the price قيمت لوړول to raise, knock up the price 1.2 significance, value 2 *predicative* dear, expensive, valuable غله د عسکر حربيه قيمت شي Bread is growing more expensive. *idiom* قيمت the combat readiness of troops

قيمتدار ḳimatdā́r قيمتناک ḳimatnā́k dear, expensive, valuable قيمتداره کتابونه valuable books

قيمت طلب ḳimattaláb cash-on-delivery, COD

قیمتول ḳimatawә́l *denominative, transitive* [*past:* قیمت یې کړ] to value, evaluate, determine the price

قیمته ḳimáta ☞ قیمت 2

قیمتي ḳimatí 1 dear; valuable 2 *f.* dearness, expensiveness

قیمومت ḳajmumát *m.* قیمومیت ḳajmumiját *m. Arabic* guardianship, wardship تر قیمومت لاندي under wardship

قیمه ḳimá *f.* minced meat, ground meat

قینج ḳindzh *m. regional* coquetry, flirtatiousness

قینچي ḳajnchí *f.* 1 scissors قینچي کول *compound verb* to cut with scissors; clip 2 rafter, truss; beam 3 crossbeam, joist *idiom* قینچي ژبه sharp tongue

قینزه ḳajnzá *f. dialect* ☞ قیزه

قیود ḳujúd *m. Arabic plural* قید

قیودات ḳujudát *m.* 1 *second plural of* قیود 2 limitations, restrictions, reservations

قیوم ḳajúm *Arabic* 1 *religion* Unchanging, Immutable, Eternal (an epithet of God) 2 *m. proper name* Qayum

ک

ک ¹ kāf the thirty-second letter of the Pashto alphabet; often replaces ق q in Arabic and Turkic words; pronounced as "k"; the numeral 20 in the abjad system

ک ² *abbreviation of* کنډک ¹

ک ³ k *poetical word in lieu of* که ²

ک ⁴ ka 1 ☞ کاندي ³ 2 *imperative in lieu of* که ¹

کا ¹ kā 1 ☞ کاندي ³ په عالم ځما خبري خلق کا په نژدي لیري Everywhere people are talking about me. 2 ☞ کاوه ³

کا ² kā *f.* ☞ کاه ¹

کابل kābә́l, kābúl *m.* 1 Kabul د کابل دریاب Kabul River د کابل ښار Kabul City د کابل منځه، د کابل وادي the Kabul Valley 2 Kabul Province د کابل ولایت Kabul Province د کابل والي Governor of Kabul Province

کابلی kābláj, kābәláj 1 *attributive* Kabul 2 *m.* resident of Kabul

کابو ¹ kābú near, close کابوکول *compound verb* to bring closer, bring nearer کابوکېدل *compound verb* to come nearer, approach

کابو ² kābú *m.* ☞ قابو

کابوس kābús *m.* nightmare

کابه kābá *f.* ☞ کعبه

کابین ¹ kābín *m.* 1 bride's provision; dowry 2 bride-money, bride-price

کابین ² kābín *m.* booth

کابینه kābiná *f.* cabinet, government

کاپیتالست kāpiṭālíst *m.* capitalist

کاپیتالستي kāpiṭālistí capitalist, capitalistic کاپیتالستي ممالک capitalist countries

کاپیتالسم kāpiṭālísm *m.* کاپیتالیزم kāpiṭālízm *m.* capitalism ☞ کاپیتالیزم

کاپیتالست kāpiṭālíst *m.* ☞ کاپیتالست

کاپیتالیستي kāpiṭālistí ☞ کاپیتالستي

کاپیتالیزم kāpiṭālízm *m.* ☞ کاپیتالیزم

کاپیتالسم kāpiṭālísm *m.* ☞ کاپیتالیزم

کاپر kāpә́r 1 *m.* infidel, non-believer 2 *abusive* faithless, disloyal; base, foul, mean ☞ کافر هغه کاپر سړی دئ He is a scoundrel.

کاپرچت kāpirchát *m.* 1 long knife, short sword 2 poleax

کاپرخولی kāpәrkhwaláj *f. botany* stinkhorn

کاپرگل kāpәrgúl *m.* sunflower

کاپرېل kāprél *m.* tile, tiling د کاپرېل جوړولو کارخانه tile factory

کاپور kāpúr *m. plural* ☞ کافور

کاپه kāpá *f. colloquial* ☞ قهوه

کاپي kāpí *f.* 1 copy 2 number, copy (of a magazine, book)

کاپیتولاسیون kāpitulāsjón *m.* capitulation

کاپیره kāpiṛá 1.1 fat, stout, obese 1.2 strong, healthy 1.3 mean, base, foul 2 *f.* impudent woman, hussy

کاپیسا kāpisá *f.* 1 د کاپیسا ولایت Kapisa Province 2 Kapisa (the ancient capital of the Kushans)

کاپیکاري kāpikārí *f.* copying

کاپي نویس kāpinawís *m.* copyist; copier

کاپي نویسي kāpinawisí *f.* copying, making a copy د کاپي نویسی کاتب copyist

کاتب kātíb *m. Arabic* 1 clerk, office worker 2 second secretary (of an embassy)

کاتبي kātibí *f.* 1 position or work of a clerk or office worker; clerical work, office work 2 position of second secretary (of an embassy)

کاتره kātrá *f.* 1 large bin (for storing grain), corncrib 2 large container (for storing grapes, etc.)

کاتری kātrәj *f.* small sickle

کاتک kāták *m. regional* katak (the seventh month of the Hindu calendar, October-November)

کاتود kātód *m. physics* cathode

کاتولیک kātolík *m.* (Roman) Catholic

کاتولیکي kātolikí (Roman) Catholic

کاته ¹ kātә́ 1 look, gaze, stare 2 viewing, examining; inspection, examination کاته کول to see د چا سره کاته په غلا غلا کاته spying on someone ☞ کتنه

کاته ² kātә́ *imperfect plural of* کتل ¹

کاته ³ kātá *f.* 1 letter 2 notebook, exercise book 3 directions, instructions

کاتلی kāṭláj *m.* shotgun cartridge

کاتول kāṭawә́l *transitive* ☞ کټول

کاتی ¹ kāṭí *m.* tax collector

کاتی ² kā́ṭaj *m.* 1 saddle tree, wooden base of a saddle 2 convict's shackles 3 almond with a hard shell

کاتیاله kāṭjā́la *f.* large irrigation ditch; canal

کاتیری kāṭerәj *f.* small saucepan (for melting butter)

کاج ¹ kādzh *m.* pine (tree)

کاج ² kādzh *m.* buttonhole

کاجر kādzhór having a leukoma, having a cataract, walleyed

کاچ kāch *m.* tip cat (the game)

کاچغه kāchúgha *f.* ☞ کاچوغه

کاچو kāchú *m.* ☞ چاقو

کاچغه، کاچوغه kāchúgha, kāchógha *f.* spoon

کاڅوړی kātsúraj *m.* plant with edible root

کاڅۍ kātsáj *f.* cup of a sling

کاخت kākht *m.* کاختي kākhtí *f.* ☞ د کاخت کال قحط a year of crop failure لوږه او کاخت famine, starvation

کادر kādr *m.* personnel, cadre

کادری kādráj *m.* 1 stomach, crop, craw (of birds) 2 psalterium, third stomach (part of the stomach of ruminants)

کاذب kāzíb *Arabic* 1 false, lying, untruthful 2 *m.* liar

کاذبي kāzibí false, lying, untruthful

کار [1] kār *m.* 1 affair, business, work, pursuit زه په کار لرم I am very busy. ورسره دي څه کار دئ What is your business with him? په احمد مي کار دئ I have business with Ahmed. د هغه کار جوړ دئ He is prospering. کار تر کاره تېر دئ That business is irremediable. د کار، عضوي کار، جسمي کار work, labor, occupation 2 پکار ☞ په کار physical labor ذهني کار intellectual work د کار استاد foreman, team leader, crew chief د کار آلات means of production د کار څښتن employer د کار قدرت a labor force, labor, manpower, hands b capacity for work, efficiency د کار قرار داد labor agreement د کار ورځ work-day د کار په اندازه work hours, work time وخت د یو شي څخه کار اخیستل to use something, employ something, resort to something اجوره wages د یو شي څخه کار اخیستل کېدل to be used, be employed کار پر مخ بېول، کار پر مخ وهل a to set an affair going, get things going b to get down to work, set to work c to conduct the affair successfully کار پربندودل *compound verb* to quit work, walk off the job; retire کار کول *compound verb* a to work, carry out work ستا پلار څه کار کوي؟ What does your father do? b to work, to act, be in actions, function دستگاه ښه کار کوي The apparatus is working well. c to exert action, exert influence; act دا دارو پرې کار نه کوي This medication is not working for him. d to serve as something, replace something, substitute for something e to earn هغه په ورځ کښې لس افغانی کار کوي He earns ten Afghanis a day. کار کېدل *compound verb* to be conducted, be carried out (of work projects) په ښار کښې ډېر ساختماني کارونه کېږي A large construction project is being carried out in the city. کار ورکول *compound verb* a to be of use, benefit, help دا حیله به کار ورنه کي That ruse won't help. b to work, act, function c to serve as something, replace something, substitute for something پر کار کول to carry out, realize in practice, turn into reality پر کار لوېدل to start working, get to work (on) په کار باندي اچول، په کار اچول to put into action, set into motion په کار راتلل to be needed; be used, be applied په خپل کار دربدل، په کار راوړل to use, apply په کار راوړل، په کار لگول، په کار لگېدل، په کار get (down) to work, get to work, start working تر کار لاندي نیول to process, subject to لوېدل processing کار ته تلل to go to work، د کاره ایستل، د کاره غورځول a to

take out of service (machinery, people) b to remove د کار څخه ځان to shirk work له کاره لوېدل، له کاره وتل to go out of service (of machinery, people) چه نه کار هلته دي څه کار؟ *saying* One shouldn't do more than necessary. په کار کي غوټه اچول *saying* to interfere with, throw a monkey wrench in the works کارونه د خدای دي Everything is in God's hands. د دنیا کارونه دي That's how it is.

کار [2] kār *m.* ☞ قهر

کارآزموده kārāzmudá experienced; skillful; skilled, qualified

کاراکاس kārākás *m.* Caracas

کارآگاه kārāgáh 1 ☞ کارآزموده 2 wise

کارآمد kārāmád necessary, needed, useful; suitable; capable

کارول kārāwó *imperfect of* کارول [3]

کارین پیپر kārənpepár *m.* carbon paper

کارین ډی او کسایډ kārənḍajoksájḍ *m.* carbonic acid, carbon dioxide

کاربوراتور kārburátor *m.* carburetor

کاربورانت kārburánt *m.* fuel mixture

کاربولک kārbolík carbolic, phenolic

کاربون kārbón *m. plural* carbon

کارین پیپر kārbonpepár *m.* ☞

کاربونک اېسد غاز kārboník carbon(ic), carbonaceous carbonic acid gas

کاربین kārabín *m.* carbine

کارپات kārpát *m.* کارپاتیان kārpātiján *m. plural* Carpathian Mountains, Carpathians د کارپات غرونه Carpathians

کارت kārt *m.* 1 card; ticket د بلني کارت invitation card اصول file-card 2 calling card

کارتل kārtél *m. economics* cartel

کارتوس kārtús *m.* cartridge, round تش کارتوس، خالي کارتوس، شلخي blank cartridge

کارتوس دان kārtusdán *m.* bandoleer, cartridge belt

کارتو گراف kārtográf *m.* cartographer

کارتوگرافي kārtográfí *f.* cartography

کارتون kārtón *m.* 1 cardboard, pasteboard 2 file folder, document case

کارته kārtá *f.* quarter (part of a city); district, region

کارټون kārṭún *m.* caricature, cartoon

کارجن kārdzhón angry, infuriated

کارجوړه kārdzhóṛa کارجوړی kārdzhóṛaj efficient, businesslike; industrious

کارروائی kārchalawóna *f.* ☞

کارچوب kārchób *m.* kind of patterned fabric

کارخانه kārkhāná *f.* factory, plant; workshop; factory, mill د ماشین د جهاز سازی کارخانه machine-building plant جوړولو کارخانه shipyard د موټر د ترمیم کارخانه automobile repair shops

کارخانه والا kārkhānawālá plant, mill, factory (worker, hand)

کارد kārd *m.* knife

کاردار kārdár *m.* 1 official; government employee, government worker 2 manager (of an estate, etc.) 3 figure (person active and prominent in his or her field)

کارداري kārdārí *f.* 1 position, post, appointment, job 2 management, direction; business management 3 administration

کاردان kārdán 1 experienced; skillful, skilled, qualified 2 learned, knowledgeable, (well) versed (in), competent

کارداني kārdāní *f.* 1 experience, know-how, skill, knack 2 knowledge, condition of being well-informed, competency

کاردیده kārdidá worldly-wise, experienced, having seen the world

کارد kārḍ *m.* ☞ کارت کارډ داخلي د pass

کارروائي kārrawāí *f.* 1 management, direction; business management 2 actions عسكري كارروائي military actions 3 conduct, behavior 4 action, act, deed 5 work; affair, business

کارزار kārzár *m.* 1 battle, combat 2 campaign

کارساز kārsáz 1 ☞ کاردان 2 *m.* organizer

کارسازي kārsāzí *f.* 1 arrangement, organization, settling 2 skillfulness, expertness 3 (business-like) efficiency 4 intrigue

کارستان kāristán *m.* textile mill, shop

کارسموني kārsamúnaj ☞ کاردان

کارشکن kārshikán *m.* vermin, pest

کارشکني kārshikaní 1 pest, harmful 2 *f.* .1 wrecking 2.2 sabotage

کارښت kārə́kht *m.* 1 plant, mill, shop 2 machine tool 3 press (for grapes)

کارتوس kārtús *m.* ☞ کارتوس

کارتوس دان kārtusdán *m.* ☞ کارتوس دان

کارغان kārghán *m.* plural of کارغه

کارغه kārghə́ *m.* [*plural:* کارغان kārghán] raven; crow سیلاني کارغه rook په کارغانو مېزان نیول to doom the deal to failure in advance

کارغه ټونګه kārghə́-ṭúnga *f.* kind of tulip

کارفرما kārfarmá 1 *m.* .1 employer, proprietor 1.2 *regional* manager 2 in charge, giving orders

کارفهم kārfáhm ☞ کاردان

کارفهمي kārfahmí *f.* ☞ کارداني

کارک kārk *m.* cork, stopper

کارکردګي kārkardagí *f.* development (of deposits); extraction (of mineral resources)

کارکن kārkún 1 *m.* .1 employee, collaborator; worker 1.2 figure (person active and prominent in his or her field) 2 experienced; efficient, business-like, practical

کارکني kārkuní *f.* 1 capacity for work 2 (business-like) efficiency

کارکوټی kārkuṭáj *m.* kind of grass

کارکنډی kārkunḍáj *m.* ☞ کالکنډی

کار کوونکی kār kawúnkaj *m.* 1 laborer 2 worker, employee 3 figure (person active and prominent in his or her field)

کارګاه kārgáh *m. & f.* machine tool, machine د نساجي کارګاه (weaving) loom

کارګذار kārguzár 1 carrying out, executing 2 *m.* executor

کارګر kārgár *m.* laborer; worker, employee لایق کارګر skilled worker

کارګري kārgarí worker's, working, labor

کارګوټی kārgótaj *m.* small piece of business, no big deal; little piece of work

کارګه د زرکي kārgə́ *m.* [*plural:* کارګان kārgán] raven; crow کارګه *saying* a wolf in sheep's clothing (*literally:* a crow in peacock's feathers) ☞ کارغه

کارګه ټکی kārgəṭəkə́j *f. botany* wild mallow

کارنامه kārnāmá *f.* 1 exploit, feat, achievement; deed, act هغه د ډېرو کارنامو ښ‍بنتن دئ He became famous for his great achievements. 2 success, achievement لوري کارنامې کول a to accomplish great deeds b to achieve great success

کاروالا kārwālá *m.* worker; laborer

کاروان kārwán *m.* 1 caravan د کاروان مشر caravan leader, caravan guide د کاروان ښ‍بنتن caravan owner 2 stream, file, row, line تر کاروان مخکېني تلل to surpass, outstrip, leave behind

کاروان بوټی kārwānbúṭaj *m. botany Pteropyrum Aucheri* (kind of shrub)

کاروان سرای kārwānsará̃j *m.* inn, caravansary

کارواني kārwāní 1 caravan 2 *m.* member of a caravan

کارروائي kārwāí *f.* ☞ کارروائي

کاروبار kārubár *m.* affair, business; occupation; affairs, matters, things خلک په خپل کاروبار بوخت وو mundane matters د دنیا کاروبار People were busy with their own affairs. د سفر کاروبار یې سم کئ He got ready for a journey.

کاروباري kārubārí 1 business-like, efficient 2 occupational, professional

کاروکیل kārukíl *m.* plowing, tilling, tillage کاروکیل کول *compound verb* to plow and sow

کارول [1] kārawə́l *denominative, transitive* [*past:* کاري یې کړ] to clean (an irrigation ditch, canal)

کارول [2] kārawə́l *denominative, transitive* [*past:* کاري یې کړ] 1 to earn (money) 2 to use, apply 3 to work out, elaborate

کارول [3] kārawə́l *transitive* ☞ قهرول

کاره [1] kārá *f.* ☞ کاري [1]

کاره [2] kārá *f. botany* paspalums, *Paspalum* (kind of grass)

کاره [3] kārə́ *imperfect of* کول [3]

کاري [1] kārí 1 working, laboring کاري وګړي workers 2 necessary, essential 3 energetic; business-like, efficient 4 effective 5 mortal, fatal کاري زخمي سو a mortal wound He was fatally wounded. کاري لګېدل *compound verb* to wound fatally کاري خورل *compound verb* to receive a mortal blow, be struck down 6 fatal, resigned, inevitable

کاري [2] kārój *f.* tall woven basket (for transporting fruit, etc.)

کاري [3] kārój *f.* gulf; bay

کاریانه kārjā́na *f.* weed growing in wheat

کاریدل [1] kāredə́l *denominative, intransitive* [*past:* کار شو] to be clear, be clean (of an irrigation ditch, canal)

کاریدل [2] kāredə́l *intransitive* ☞ پکاریدل

کاریدل [3] kāredə́l *intransitive* ☞ قهریدل

کاریز kāréz *m.* kahriz, underground irrigation canal

کاریزک kārizák *m. regional* ☞ کاهریزه

کاریزکن kārezkán *m.* laborer who digs kahrizis

کاهریزه ☞ .kārezá *f* کاهریزه

1 کاریزی kārezí irrigated by a kahriz

کاهریزه ☞ .kārizój *f* کاریزی .kārizáj *m* کاریزی 2

کاریژه kārezhá *f.* kind of edible plant

کاریس kārijós *m. medicine* caries

کاریکاتور kārikātúr *m.* caricature

کاریگر kārigár **1** *m.* **.1** [*plural:* کاریگر kārigór and کاریگران kārigarán] laborer; worker د بېړۍ کاریگران crew of a ship کاریگر miner **1.2** *regional* blacksmith, farrier **2** industrious, diligent, hard-working هغه خومره کاریگر سړی دئ He is a very industrious person.

کاریگري kārigarí *f.* **1** activity, activities **2** skill, mastery; skilled work **3** skill, knack, dexterity

کارین kārín *m.* mountainous plot of land temporarily used for crops

کارینده kārindá business-like, industrious

کاړ kāṛ *m.* **1** pebbles **2** rocky terrain د سیند کاړ a rocky river-bed **b** coarse gravel **3** rocky desert, pebbly desert **4** *regional* silver mine

کاړساو kāṛsā́w **1.1** plain, homely and with a poor physique (of a person); ugly **1.2** having an elongated face **1.3** melancholy, doleful, sad, dismal **2** *m.* ugly person, freak

کاړکوت kāṛkút bent, distorted

کاړو ☞ .kāṛú کاړو 1

کاړوکوړ kāṛukúṛ *m.* **1** howls, screams, shouts **2** clanging, clinking, clattering (of dishes)

کاړه kā́ṛa *f.* curdled milk 1

کاړه kā́ṛa *f.* **1** learning a lesson **2** method in which guilt or innocence of one suspected of stealing is determined by immersing his hands in boiling water 2

کاړه kāṛá *f.* dish made of flour, oil and greens 3

کاړی kāṛí beaten up, thrashed 1

کاړی 1 kāṛi *plural of* کاړه 2

کاړی 2 kāṛi *plural of* کاړه 3

کاړی 3 kāṛé *plural of* کاړه 4

کاړی 1 ☞ .kāṛój *f* کاړی 5

کاړین kāṛín rocky (of terrain)

کاړینگ kāṛíng squint-eyed, cross-eyed

کاړي واړي کېدل kāṛi-wā́ṛi weakened, weak, limp, flabby *compound verb* **a** to be very tired خان مي داسي کاړي واړي دئ I am very tired. **b** to be lazy, become lazy

کاز kāz *m.* scissors 1

کاز kāz *m.* **1** den, lair **2** cave, cavern (used as shelter for sheep in winter) 2

قاز ☞ .kāz *m* کاز 3

کاز kāz *m.* wish, desire 4

کازمک kāzmík space, cosmic کازمک ریز cosmic rays

کازمن kāzmón **1** famished, starved **2** desiring, wanting د وږی سپوري ډوډۍ کازمن دئ *proverb* a hungry man is glad for a dry crust

کازموگرافي kāzmogrāfí *f.* cosmography

کازمک ☞ kāzmikí کازمکي

کازی خر kāzikhár *m.* wood louse

کنبل 2 kāg *present stem of* کاګ

کاګبل kāgbál *m.* hyena

کنبل 2 kāgólaj *past participle of* کاګلئ

کوډ 2 kāgó *m. plural and oblique of* کاګه 1

کاګه kāgó *m. plural* anise 2

کنبل 2 kā́ga *imperative, imperfective of* کاګه 3

کړل kāgó *imperfect of* کاګه 4

کړل kāgá *imperative, imperfective of* کاګه 5

کوډ ووډ kāgó-wāgó *m. plural and oblique of* کاګه وا‌ډه

کاګه وېلني kāgó-weláni *m. plural* anise

کاسب kāsíb *m. Arabic* [*plural:* کاسبان kasibán *and Arabic* کسبه kasabá] artisan, handicraftsman; workman

کاسبرگ kāsabárg *m. botany* sepal, calyx lobe

کاست kāst *m.* reduction, reducing, diminishing, decrease; loss(es) 1

کاست kāst *m.* caste د کاست اصول the caste system 2

کاسد kāsíd *Arabic* lacking demand, unmarketable (of goods)

کاسکت kāskét *m.* service cap, cap

کاسني kāsní *m. plural* endive (kind of chicory)

کاسوڼی kāsuṇáj *m.* kind of edible plant

کاسه kāsá *f.* **1** cup, basin, tureen, earthen saucer د بند کاسه containment basin of a dam په یو کاسه سره کېنستل to feast at the same table with someone **2** *botany* calyx **3** shell (of a tortoise) د چا ته د سر په کاسه کي اوبه ورکول *idiom* skull سرکاسه *idiom* to cause great unpleasantness, harass, not give someone peace; annoy someone کاسه پرېنښوول، کاسه پرنسکورول، شنه کاسه *idiom* rainbow په کاسه کي نیمه *compound verb* to hush up, drop, cut off (an affair) خپله کاسه په لغته وهل *idiom* کاسه اینښوول to dupe, deceive someone **a** to overlook, miss, let slip by **b** to show carelessness د هري کاسې مچ *idiom* a person who meddles in everything

کاسه گرب kāsagṛáb *m.* tortoise

کاسي kāsí **1** *m. plural* Kasi (a tribe living in the Kvetta region) **2** *m.* Kasai, Kasi 1

کاسی kāsój *f.* cup of a sling 2

کاسیر kāsír debouched, profligate, dissolute, licentious

کاسیره kāsíra **1** *feminine singular of* کاسیر **2** *f.* **.1** debauchee, lewd woman **2.2** good-for-nothing woman 1

کاسبره kāserá *f. regional* penny, copper coin 2

کاسیري kāsirí *f.* debauchery, dissipation

قاش ☞ .kāsh *m* کاش pommel of a saddle 1

کاشکي ☞ kāsh کاش 2

کاشتکار kāshtkā́r *m.* farmer, grain grower

کاشین ☞ .kāshráj *m* کاشری

کاشغر kāshghár *m* Kashghar

کاشف kāshíf *Arabic* **1.1** discovering, detecting; studying, researching د آواز کاشف sound-detecting **1.2** curious, inquisitive **2** *m.* [*plural:* کاشفان kāshifán *and Arabic* کاشفین kāshifín] investigator, researcher; explorer

كاشكي kā́shke *Western interjection* oh, if only, even if

كاشواز kāshwā́z **1** garrulous, boastful **2** disorderly

كاشوازي kāshwāzí *f.* **1** bragging, boasting **2** disorder

كاشوغه kāshúgha *f.* ☞ كاچوغه

كاشي kāshí *m.* [*plural:* كاشي كاري kāshikārí *f.*] tiles; glazed tile; glazed brick

كاشيگر kāshigár *m.* كاشيگر worker who makes tiles; glazer

كاشي گري kāshigarí *f.* كاشيگري manufacture of tiles, of glazed tile; manufacture of glazed brick

كاشين kāshín *m.* [*plural:* كاشينونه kāshinúna *and* كاشينان kāshinā́n] **1** large earthenware washtub; trough د اورو كاشين kneading trough **2** glazed plates and dishes

كاظم kāzím *m. Arabic proper noun* Kazim

كاغ kāgh *m.* cawing (of a raven, crow)

كاغ kāgh **1** wise; sagacious, perspicacious **2** clever, bright

كاغان kāghā́n *m. plural* Kaghan (region in northwest Pakistan)

كاغتوب kāghtób *m.* **1** wisdom; foresight, prescience **2** cleverness

كاغذ kāgház, kāghǝ́z *m.* [*plural:* كاغذونه kāghazúna *and Arabic* كاغذات kāghazā́t] **1** paper د شتام خالي كاغذ clean sheet of paper ردي كاغذ *regional* پوخ كاغذ stamped paper waste paper **a** سپين كاغذ white paper **b** sheet of white paper **c** blank form, form *Western* پر كاغذه ليكل to write on paper د كاغذ كيسه bag, د كاغذ كخوړه **2** letter; note كاغذ كښل *compound verb* to write a letter **3** paper, document د طلاق كاغذ divorce certificate **4** *plural* كاغذونه *and* كاغذات mail, correspondence; papers

كاغذباد kāghazbā́d *m.* kite

كاغذداني kāghazdāní *f.* basket (for papers), wastepaper basket په كاغذداني كي اچول to throw onto the trash heap

كاغذي kāghazí **1** paper, out of paper كاغذي نوټ banknote **2** thin-skinned, having a thin skin or shell **3** *figurative* fictitious

كاغمه kāghmá *f.* kind of woolen fabric كاغمه تغر reversible rug

كاغ والى kāghwā́laj *m.* ☞ كاغتوب

كاغه kā́gha *f.* crow

كاغى kāghǝ́j *f.* jackdaw

كافر kāfir, kāpír *Arabic* [*plural:* كفار kuffā́r] **1.1** *m.* infidel **1.2** kafir, infidel, unbeliever; native or resident of Nuristan before they converted to Islam **2** *figurative* evil, fierce, cruel كافره ښځه witch

كافرستان kāfiristā́n *m. history* the land of the infidels; Kafiristan (present-day Nuristan)

كافركى kāfirkáj *m.* despicable kafir, contemptible infidel

كافرگل kāfirgúl *m.* sunflower

كافري kāfirí **1** *m. plural* Kafirs (peoples inhabiting Nuristan and Chitral) **2** *f.* Kafir, Kafir language

كافري kāfiráj *m.* ☞ كافر 1

كافور kāfúr *m. plural* camphor

كافوري kāfurí **1** camphor **2** *figurative* white, gray (of hair)

كافه kāfá *f.* كافي kāfí *m. plural* coffee كافه جوړول *compound verb* to make coffee

كافي kāfí *Arabic indeclinable* **1** sufficient, enough **2** sufficiently, enough

كافي kāfé *f.* cafe, coffee-house

كاك kāk *m.* **1** small loaf of sweet bread (which is baked in honor of the birth of a son for distribution to children) **2** *dialect* flat cake (baked on a hot stone)

كاك kāk *m.* cork, stopper

كاكا kākā́ *m.* **1** uncle (father's brother) **2** uncle (addressing an elderly man)

كاكادژي kākādzhí *m. regional* ☞ كاكو

كاكاوو kākāwó *f.* cocoa

كاكړ kākáṛ **1** *m. plural, also* كاكړان kākaṛā́n Kakars (a tribe) **2** *m.* a Kakar (a member of the Kakar tribe)

كاكړستان kākaṛistā́n *m.* region where the Kakars settled

كاكړي kākaṛí *attributive* Kakar كاكړي پسونه the Kakar breed of sheep

كاكښنه kākákha *f.* large net (for carrying straw)

كاكښني kākakhí *f.* carrying of straw in a large net

كاكك kākák *m.* ☞ كاكو

كاككش kākkásh *m.* corkscrew

كاكل kākúl *m.* **1** forelock; lock, curl, ringlet **2** (small) crest (of birds)

كاكنج kākándzh *m, plural* **1** millet **2** green bristle grass; Italian millet, foxtail millet

كاكو kākó *m. diminutive* uncle

كاكوتي kākutí *m. plural botany* ziziphora, *Ziziphora chinopodioides*

كاكوړه kākoṛá *f. botany* colocynth, bitter apple

كاكى kākə́j *f.* aunt (uncle's wife)

كاكى kākə́j *f.* beetle

كاگل kāgíl *m.* plaster for walls (made out of straw and clay) كاگل كول *compound verb* to plaster (walls)

كاگل kāgə́l *transitive Eastern* ☞ كنبل

كاگه kāgǝ́ *Eastern* ☞ كاړه

كاگه kāgǝ́ *m. plural Eastern* ☞ كاړه ويلني

كال kāl *m.* [*plural:* كلونه kalúna *and Eastern* كالونه kālúna] year لا وړم كال the year before last وړم كال last year پروسږ كال د three years ago د next year دا كال this year بل كال لمر كال، د سپوږمى كال lunar year قمري كال leap year كيسي كال fiscal year مالياتي كال solar year شمسي كال the hijra year هجري كال from year to year كال په كال annually هر كال، د كاله per year كال او تلين، واړه كال all year د كال ماشوم a one-year-old baby خوا دي په را كلو كلو له for many years already د كلونو كلونو سودا long-standing concern

كال kāl *m.* thorny fence, barbed fence

كالا kālā́ *m. regional* native (of a native of India)

كالبر kālíbr *m. military* caliber

كالبر kālbár bearing fruit every other year

كالبوت kālbút *m.* body; figure تش كالبوت دربدل *idiom* to be dumbfounded; be bewildered

كالتوس kāltús *m.* ☞ كارتوس

كالِدزh kā́lídzh *m.* college

كالخواه kālkhwāh *m.* كالخوا kālkhwā **1** patron **2** steward, estate manager; manager

كالخواهي kālkhwāhí *f.* ☞ كالخواهي

كالخواى kālkhwā́j plenipotentiary; competent, enjoying full rights

كالخواید kā́lkhwājá *m. dialect* ☞ كالخوا، كالخواه

كالخوائي kālkhwā́ī *f.* **1** power, authority كالخوائي كول *compound verb* to exercise power, exercise authority كالخوائي لرل to possess power, have authority كالخوائي وركول *compound verb* to grant power, give authority; authorize, empower **2** management, superintendence **3** will

كالار kālár *m.* collar

كالك kāló́k *m.* **1** unripe fruit, green fruit **2** boll (of the cotton plant)

كالكچو kālakachó *m. plural Western* guza-paya (dry cotton-plant stems)

كالكندى kālkunḍā́j *m.* **1** dastambul (a small-fruited, sweet-smelling musk-melon) **2** *regional* wild field melon, *Cucumis madraspatanus*

كالكوچ kālkúch كال كوچ **1.1** bend, curve, winding **1.2** turn **1.3** *figurative* ruse, trick, subterfuge, cunning, stratagem كالكوچ خورل *compound verb* **a** to bend, wind **b** to turn **c** *figurative* to use cunning, be crafty; be shifty, dodge **2** *figurative* clever, sly, cunning, crafty

كالكوچكه kālkocháka *f.* كال كوچكه **1** sharp turn **2** loop (made by a wild animal that is being pursued) **3** *figurative* ruse, trick, cunning, resourcefulness **4** *plural* كالكوچكي kālkocháke *Eastern* bends, curves, windings

كالكوچن kālkochón **1.1** sly, clever, adroit, dodgy, resourceful **1.2** twisting, winding **2** *m.* sly one, cunning one, dodger

كالكوچه kālkúcha *f. Eastern* ☞ كالكوچ

كالكوچى kālkúchaj ☞ كالكوچن

كالكندى kālkunḍā́j *m.* ☞ كالكندى

كالكه kāláka *f.* boll (of the cotton plant) د كالكي بوټى cotton plant

كالنى kālanáj yearly, annual

كالنى kālanój **1** *feminine singular of* كالنى **2** *f.* annual, yearbook

كالو kā́lo *oblique plural of* كال

كالو kāló *oblique plural of* كالي

كالورى kālorí *f.* calorie

كالوسر kālusár **1** all year, the entire year, the year round **2** in a year, per year, for a year

كاله kāló *oblique singular of* كور د كاله اسباب household belongings كاله ته home, homeward د كاله باندي outside the house په كاله دننه inside the house

كاله kā́la *short form plural and oblique singular of* كال په لس كاله for ten years د كاله for a year

كاله باغ kālabā́gh *m.* Kalabagh (northwestern Pakistan)

كاله پاڼي kālapā́ṇi *f. plural* **1** name of a forest in the land of the Khattaks **2** area teaming with game

كالاج kāláj *m.* [*plural:* كالي kālí] **1** *usually plural* clothing, dress; underwear د لامبو كالي swimsuit تاوده كالي warm clothing د پروتو كالي bed linen د اينوندلو evening dress د شپي كالي clothes كالي اغوستل *compound verb* to get dressed د كالي المارى wardrobe كالي ايستل *compound verb* to get undressed كالي كول *compound verb* to make a dress كالي جوړول *compound verb* **a** to make a dress **b** to buy a dress **2** *regional* decoration; jewel(ry) **3** *regional* tool, instrument; implement **4** *regional* household utensils, goods and chattels **5** thing د سودا گرى كالي goods له خوشحالي په كالو كي نه ځايبدل *saying* to be beside oneself with joy كالي اخيستل *compound verb* to gather up one's things, pack up one's things, depart, leave, go away

كاليبر kālíbr *m.* ☞ كالبر

كالبدل kāledól *intransitive* ☞ كهالبدل

كاليزه kālíza *f.* anniversary د استقلال د كاليزي تجليل celebration of the anniversary of independence د زبريدني كاليزه birthday

كالي مالي kāli-mālí *m. plural* things, household goods and chattels

كاليمانتان kālimāntā́n *m.* Kalimantan (island)

كاليو kālíjo *oblique plural of* كالي

كام kām *m.* ☞ قوم

كام kām *m.* palate

كام kām *m.* desire, will

كاما kāmā́ *f.* Kama (river)

كامبورى kāmbúraj *m.* **1** stalks of colza (remaining after threshing) **2** chopped corn-stalks

كامبله kāmbelá *f. regional botany Rottlera tinctoria* (a dye plant)

كامپ kāmp *m.* camp عسكري كامپ military camp

كامچه kāmácha *f.* little finger, pinkie

كامچتكا kāmchatkā́ *f.* Kamchatka

كامخور kāmkhór *m.* predatory fish

كامران kāmrā́n **1** fortunate; successful, prosperous **2** *m. proper noun* Kamran

كامراني kāmrāní *f.* good fortune كامراني لرل to succeed, prosper

كامره kāmrá, kāmerá *f.* chamber, cell, room د عكاسي كامره camera

كامل kāmíl *Arabic* **1.1** full, exhaustive, comprehensive; complete كامل باور complete trust **1.2** perfect, superlative **1.3** well-informed, well-versed; learned **2** *proper noun* Kamil

كاملاً kāmílán *Arabic* completely; absolutely, quite; fully; wholly

كاملتوب kāmiltób *m.* كاملوالى kāmilwā́laj *m.* **1** fullness, comprehensiveness; completeness **2** perfection, superiority **3** knowledge

كاملول kāmilawól *denominative, transitive* [*past:* كامل يي كړ] **1** to end, finish, complete **2** to make perfect, perfect, bring to perfection

كامله kāmilá *f. proper noun* Kamila

كامليت kāmiliját *m. Arabic* **1** fullness; completeness **2** integrity, territorial integrity

کامبدل kāmiledә́l *denominative, intransitive* [*past:* کامل شو] **1** to be ended, be finished, be completed **2** to be perfected, achieve perfection

کام ناکام kāmnākám **1** without fail, certainly **2** willy-nilly

کامه [1] kāmá *f.* Kama (region in eastern Afghanistan)

کامه [2] kámmá *f.* comma

کامه وال kāmawál *m.* resident of Kama

کامي [1] kāmí ☞ قومي

کامي [2] kámmé *plural of* کامه[2]

کامیاب kāmjā́b **1** successful, enjoying success; good په کامیاب ډول successfully **2** prospering, successful کامیاب کول *compound verb* ☞ کامیابول; کامیاب کیدل *compound verb* ☞ کامیابیدل

کامیا بانه kāmjābāná **1** ☞ کامیاب **2** successfully, well

کامیابول kāmjābawól *denominative, transitive* [*past:* کامیاب یې کړ] to make successful, make prosperous

کامیابي kāmjābí *f.* [*plural:* کامیابی kāmjābә́j *and* کامیابیګانی kāmjābigā́ni] **1** success; achievement په کامیابی سره successfully کامیابی ګټل، کامیابي لاس ته راوستل to make progress **2** victory

کامیابدل kāmjābedól *denominative, intransitive* [*past:* کامیاب شو] to achieve success, prosper, have success په مقصد کامیابدل to reach a goal, achieve that which was desired چه هر کار ته لاس ورته کړي، پکښي کامیابیږي He is successful in whatever he undertakes.

کامیرون kāmerún *m.* Cameroon

کان [1] kān *m.* **1** mine, shaft, pit د زرو کان gold mine د سربو کان lead mine د کانو وزارت ministry of mining **2** د کانو کارګران miners deposit(s), bed, layer **3** ore **4** *figurative* well, fount

کان [2] kān *m.* rush (a grass-like plant)

کان [3] kān *f.* tumor or swelling on the palate (in horses)

کانادا kānādá́ *f. &m.* ☞ کاناډا

کانادائي kānādāí ☞ کاناډائي

کاناډا kānāḍá́ *f. &m.* Canada

کاناډائي kānāḍāí **1** Canadian **2** *m.* a Canadian

کاناري kānārí د کاناري ټاپوګان the Canary Islands

کانال kānál *m.* canal د سویز کانال the Suez Canal

کان پیژاند kān pezhā́nd *m.* کان پیژندونکی kān pezhandúnkaj *m.* geologist

کانتور kántúr *m.* contour, outline

کانتین kāntín *m.* snack bar

کانتار kāntā́r *m.* toad

کانته [1] kānṭá *f.* broom کانته کول *compound verb* to sweep, sweep up کانته کیدل *compound verb* to be swept, be swept up

کانته [2] kānṭá *f. regional* fork (table)

کانتی kānṭә́j *f.* saddle-tree

کانجر kāndzhár *m.* person suffering from a nervous tic

کانجن kāndzhә́n *m.* wooden axle (of a water-lifting wheel)

کاندکتور kānduktór *m.* conductor, bandmaster

کاندم kándәm *first person of* کول[7] *instead of* کوم[2]

کانده kánda *imperative, imperfective of* کول[7] *instead of* کوه[2] هر څه کاندی هغه کانده! Do what you want!

کاندي [1] kándi *dialect present tense singular and plural of* کول[7] *instead of* کوي[3]

کاندي [2] kándi *dialect instead of* کړی[9] خدای دې کاندي! Please God!

کاندی [3] kāndáj *m.* wooden bin; corncrib

کاندی [4] kāndә́j *f.* spoon

کاندي [5] kánde *present tense second person of* کول[7]

کاندید kāndíd *m.* candidate کاندیدان وړاندي کول *compound verb* to nominate candidates

کاندیدول kāndidawól *denominative, transitive* [*past:* کاندید یې کړ] to nominate as a candidate

کانډال kānḍál *m.* crock

کانډوله kānḍóla *f.* species of plant with edible rhizomes

کانډیاتي kānḍjāti *f. singular & plural* colostrum(s)

کانډیال kānḍjál *m. botany* **1** agriophyllum **2** tumbleweed

کانزینمنټ kānzájnmanṭ *m.* parcel, consignment, lot (of goods)

کانسرت kānsért *m.* concert

کانسرو kānsérw *m.* canned food کانسرو شوي میوي canned fruit

کانسوننټ kánsónenṭ *m.* consonant sound

کانغوزک kānghuzák *m.* dung beetle

کانفرانس kānfirā́ns *m.* **1** conference **2** lecture

کانفلور kānflór *m. plural* potato flour

کانکر kānkә́r *m. singular & plural* ☞ کانکریټ

کانکرت kānkrә́t *m.* long-tailed eagle

کانکریټ kánkríṭ *m. plural* concrete د کانکریټو ګزولو ماشین concrete mixer

کانکریټ ریزي kānkriṭrezí *f.* concreting, laying concrete

کانکریټول kānkriṭawól *denominative, transitive* [*past:* کانکریټ یې کړ] to concrete, lay concrete, cover with concrete

کانکړ kānkә́ṛ faded, withered

کان کنونکی kān kanúnkaj *m.* miner

کانکور kānkúr *m.* competition کانکور اعلانول to announce a competition

کانګر kāngár *m.* gravel (beaten into a compact mass)

کانګرس kángrís *m.* congress د هند ملي کانګرس the Indian National Congress

کانګلومرات kānglomerát *m.* conglomerate

کانګو kāngó *f.* ☞ کونګو[2]

کانګه kánga *f.* [*usually plural* کانګي[1] kángi] **1** *Western* vomiting, retching کانګه کول، کانګه وهل *compound verb* to vomit, throw up کانګه به ورشي He vomited. **2** *Eastern* colic

کانګی kāngә́j *f.* echo کانګی کول *compound verb* to reflect sound کانګی کیدل *compound verb* to echo, repeat, be reflected (of a sound)

کانوانسیون kānwānsjón *m.* convention

کانون [1] kānún *m.* **1** hearth, oven **2** focus, center

کانون [2] kānún *m.* canon (a plucked-string musical instrument)

کانونشن kānwánshán *m.* ☞ کانوانسیون

کانه [1] kāná *f.* misfortune; calamity, disaster; trouble په تا څه کاني سویدي؟ What's happened to you?

کانه ² kắna f. 1 edge, edging, border 2 wing feather, wing quill

کانه ³ kānə́ 1 dull; stupid; ignorant 2 rotten, rotten throughout, rotten to the core

کانه ⁴ kānə́ f. imperfect of کنل

کانه ⁵ kānə́ m. plural digging

کانه ⁶ kắna ☞ کنه ⁵

کانه وانه kắna-wắna f. 1 questions 2 altercation, wrangling, squabbling کانه وانه کول compound verb a to question b to wrangle, squabble; argue, dispute

کاني ¹ kāní mineral; ore, mine کاني شیان mineral resources کاني حفریات exploitation (of ore) کاني حوزه mining region

کاني ² kāní 1 dexterous, deft, adroit; skillful, skilled 2 accurate (of a marksman)

کانۍ ³ kānáj one-eyed, blind in one eye

کانۍ ⁴ kānə́j f. 1 straw; blade of grass; thin reed 2 trifle

کانۍ ⁵ kānə́j f. side whiskers

کانۍ ⁶ kānə́j f. textiles reed (of a loom)

کانۍ ⁷ kānə́j f. file

کانۍ ⁸ kānə́j f. 1 needle case (made from the stem of bird feather) 2 reed, rush

کانې ⁹ kāné or else, or, otherwise

کاني واني kắne-wắne f. plural Eastern argument; quarrel; altercation ☞ کانه وانه

کان ¹ kāṇ m. tree of the oak family

کان ² kāṇ m. ☞ کاوړ

کاناو kāṇā́w m. blacksmith's tool

کانڼن kāṇə́n ☞ کانیز

کانه kắṇa f. cluster of cattail

کانه ² kāṇə́ m. plural and oblique singular of کوڼ ²

کانۍ ¹ kắṇaj m. 1 stone, rock; pebbles د فراه چوني کانۍ limestone د برف کوچ کانۍ whetstone د کانۍ کان quarry کانۍ landslide (in the mountains) په کانۍ جوکه و نه لگېده saying Eastern This didn't have any affect on him; like water off a duck's back; (literally: a leech doesn't stick to a stone) کانۍ ايښوول compound verb history to lay down a stone as a sign of an armistice and peace کانۍ ماتول compound verb history to take up a stone to signify that peace has been broken and military actions are being resumed 2 precious stone 3 weight بنیادي کانۍ a weight د تلي کانۍ corner-stone د کانۍ کرښه a stubborn person د کانۍ زړه an implacable and stern person لکه کانۍ کېدل a to be very stingy b to become hardened, become callous

کانۍ ² kāṇə́j imperative plural of کوڼ ⁷ in place of کوئ

کانیټک kāṇiṭák m. stonemason

کانیڼ kāṇídz, kāṇédz کانیز kāṇíz, kāṇéz 1 stony, rocky کانیڅه زمکه stony soil 2 severe; cruel

کانیکرپ kắṇikṛáp m. 1 boulder 2 craftsman who makes millstones 3 children's game

کانۍ کودي kắṇi-kawdi m. plural furniture, household goods

کاني کورم kāṇikuṛám m. کاني کورم kāṇigurám m. Kaniguram (city in Waziristan) کاني کورم ته لوېدل saying to get lost, vanish into thin air

کاواکي له kāwák 1 shallow, hollow, good-for-nothing, useless کاواکي کول خولې ايستل، کاواکي خبري له خولې ايستل to talk nonsense compound verb to mumble, hem and haw 2 clumsy 3 senseless 4 careless, imprudent

کاوچوک kāuchúk m. plural rubber

کاوچوکي kāuchukí rubber

کاوچه kāwchá f. cot

کاوړ kāwáṛ m. anger, fury

کاوړي kāwaṛí m. angry man

کاوړېدل kāwaṛedál denominative, intransitive [past: کاوړ شو] to become angry, be angry, grow furious

کاوش kāwísh m. 1 digging 2 enmity; quarrel

کاوو kāwú m. ☞ کاهو

کاوه ¹ kāwá f. ☞ قهوه

کاوه ² kāwə́ m. plural making, doing

کاوه ³ kāwə́ imperfect of کول ⁷

کاوئ kāwə́j dialect imperfect of کول ⁷ instead of کاوه ³

کاه ¹ kāh f. 1 itch 2 medicine pruritus کاه کول to itch

کاه ² kāh m. plural straw

کاهبر kāhbár m. sack needle

کاهرزه kāhrezá f. wild safflower

کاهڅنت kāhə́kht m. 1 itch 2 medicine pruritus 3 gnashing one's teeth (from anger) 4 swearing

کاهگل kāhgíl m. ☞ کاه گل ¹

کاهل ¹ kāhíl Arabic 1 lazy, sluggish, languid 2 inert, stagnant بحر الکاهل Pacific Ocean

کاهل ² kāhál intransitive [past: و کاهه] to itch

کاهلي kāhilí f. 1 laziness; sluggishness; languor 2 inertness

کاهن kāhín m. Arabic 1 astrologer 2 soothsayer 3 high priest (the high priest of the ancient Hebrews)

کاهني kāhiní f. 1 astrology 2 soothsaying

کاهو kāhú m. lettuce د کاهو گانو غاب salad bowl

کاهي kāhí m. کاهۍ kāhə́j f. gutter; ditch; ravine

کائنات kā'inā́t Arabic 1 m. plural the cosmos, the universe 2 m. plural nature د کائناتو حاکم انسان دئ Man is the master of nature. 3 m. character; nature ځما په کائنات کښي in one's heart

کائناتي kā'inātí 1 cosmic, space, universe 2 natural

کاینه kājəna f. vengeance, revenge

کايي دریاب kājí deep sea

کب ¹ kab m. 1 [plural: کبونه kabúna and Western کبان kabán] fish واړه کبان small fry 2 astronomy Pisces (the constellation) 3 مقصد کب نيول saying to find a needed thing د کب نيول ;حوت ☞

کب ² kub m. abdominal part of an animal carcass; smoked sturgeon belly

کبا kabā́ f. share of the bride money received by the bride's uncle

کباب kabā́b *m.* kebab, roast تکه کباب skewer kebab داشي کباب roast کبابول compound verb ☞ کباب کول ;کباب کېدل compound verb ☞ کبابېدل

کبابول kabābawə́l *denominative, transitive* [*past:* کباب يې کړ] **1** to roast (meat, wild game); to make shashlik **2** *figurative* to torment, harass

کبابي kabābí *m.* **1** kebab shop **2** one who prepares kebab dishes for customers of a kebab shop

کبابېدل kabābedə́l *denominative, intransitive* [*past:* کباب شو] **1** to be roasted (of meat, wild game) **2** *figurative* to be tormented, be harassed

کباپ kabā́p *m. dialect* ☞ کباب

کباره kabā́ṛa *f. regional* junk, old things د کباري د کان men's old clothes shop

کباړی kabāṛə́j *f.* chapan (men's outerwear in the form of a robe with quilted wadding)

کباله kabālá *f.* ☞ قباله

کبډي kabaḍí *f.* name of a game

کبر [1] kibr, kə́bər *m. Arabic* pride, arrogance, insolence, haughtiness

کبر [2] kabr *m.* ☞ قبر

کبرجن kibrdzhə́n, kəbərdzhə́n proud, arrogant, haughty, presumptuous

کبرداغ kabərdā́gh *m.* roast meat (cured or preserved)

کبرژن kibrzhə́n ☞ کبرجن

کبرغان kabərghā́n *m.* کبرغی kabərghā́j *m.* **1** marmot **2** kind of green vegetable

کبرکنی kabrkánaj *m.* gravedigger

کبره kbára *f.* capers (the shrub)

کبریٰ kubarā *Arabic* **1** *feminine of* کبیر **2** kubrā́ *feminine of* اکبر

کبر kabə́r *m.* tethering post, hitching rail

کبک kabk, kawk *m.* keklik (mountain partridge) کبک زري *kábk-i…, káwk-i…* ular, mountain turkey

کبل [1] kabál *m.* reason, cause د دي له کبله for this reason له همدي کبله وو چه because of this that's why

کبل [2] kabál *m. singular & plural* **1** Bermuda grass, *Cynodon* **2** *regional* bent grass, *Agrostis linearis*

کبل ډکی kabalḍákaj *m. regional* ☞ کبل [2]

کبلزار kabalzā́r *m.* lawn; meadow

کبلول kablawə́l *transitive* ☞ قبلول

کبله [1] kabála *f.* ☞ کبل [2]

کبله [2] kabála *oblique singular of* کبل [1]

کبلی [1] kabláj *m.* **1** fawn of a deer **2** sheepskin coat

کبلی [2] kabláj *m.* curlew; snipe

کبلېدل kabledə́l *intransitive* ☞ قبلېدل

کب نيول kab niwə́l *m. plural* fishing

کبنيوونی kabniwúnaj *m.* fisherman

کب والا kabwālā́ *m.* fishmonger, fish merchant

کبودچه kabudchá *f.* kabudcha (variety of caraculs)

کبوره kabóra *f.* **1** juice; sweet syrup **2** jelly

کبوری [1] kaboṛáj *m.* juice of the sugar cane

کبوری [2] kabúṛaj *m.* muscle

کبول kaból *m.* thank-you gift

کبي [1] kabí *f.* rein; halter; bridle

کبی [2] kubáj humpbacked, hunchbacked

کبی [3] kubə́j *f.* ☞ کوبی [2]

کبیر kabír *Arabic* great, big, large; سفير کبير *safir-i…* ambassador

کبیره [1] kabirá *f.* pattern (for cutting out the uppers of shoes)

کبیره [2] kabirá *f.* grave sin

کبیسه kabisá *f. Arabic* leap year د کبیسې کال leap year

کبین kabín *m.* booth, cab, cabin

کپ [1] kap *m.* shaking, quivering; trembling, shuddering

کپ [2] kap *m.* piece, slice, bit (of food) کپ کول، کپ وهل *compound verb* to bite off کپ نيم ډوډۍ پيدا کول to find subsistence

کپ [3] kap *m.* cuff

کپ [4] kap *m.* cup (as a prize) نقره يي کپ silver cup

کپتان kiptā́n *m.* ☞ کپتان

کاپتاليزم kapitalízm *m.* ☞ کاپتاليزم

کاپتالست kapitalíst *m.* ☞ کاپتالست

کپتالستي kapitalistí ☞ کپتالستي

کاپتالسم kapitalísm *m.* ☞ کاپتالسم

کپتان kiptā́n *m.* **1** captain (of a ship) د بېری کپتان ship's captain **2** aircraft commander

کپر [1] kapə́r *m.* uneven place, rough spot

کپر [2] kupr *m.* کفر

کپر [3] kapár *m.* rope made of the fibers of the date palm

کپرا kapṛā́ *f.* ☞ کپره

کپرک kaparák *m.* **1** thin ice **2** alluvial clay, silt

کپره kaparā́ *f.* کپری kapṛə́j, kaparə́j, kuprə́j *f.* ☞ کوپری [1]

کپریل kupríl *m.* tile, tiling د کپریل جوړولو کارخانه tile د کپریل خڼته tile factory

کپړ [1] kapáṛ *m.* **1** thick rope made from cotton; cable **2** tethering rail, hitching post

کپړ [2] kapáṛ *m.* things, stuff, household goods

کپړ [3] kapáṛ *m.* piece of meat, slice of meat

کپړا kapṛā́ *f. regional* ☞ کپړه

کپړکی kapaṛkáj *m.* small tent

کپړه kapṛá *f. regional* **1** fabric, material **2** clothing پاسنی کپړي outer clothes کپړي وېستل *compound verb* to get undressed, undress کپړي بدلول *compound verb* to change clothes

کپړئي kapṛají ☞ کپړه يي

کپړی [1] kapṛáj *m.* shard, broken dish (used as a drinking bowl for birds, etc.)

کپړی [2] kupṛə́j *f.* small wineskin

کپړی [3] kapaṛə́j *f.* wrestling

کپړئي kapṛají cloth, calico (of a book cover)

کپس kapás *m. colloquial* ☞ قفس

کپسول kapsúl *m. medicine* capsule

کپله kapála *f.* **1** little piece **2** sip کپلي وهل *compound verb* to swallow, gulp; eat; eat with gusto

کپن kapán *m.* ☞ کفن

کپنکښ kapankáḳh *m.* **1** thief who steals shrouds **2** scoundrel

کپنول kapanawál *denominative, transitive* [*past:* کپن یي کړ] to cover with a shroud, put a shroud over

کپڼی kapṇój, kapaṇój *f.* **1** trembling; cramp, convulsion **2** spasm کپڼی اخیستل، کپڼی نیول *compound verb* **a** to be nervous, be agitated **b** to have a strong desire **c** to have hatred for someone; hate somebody

کپه kapá [1] *f.* **1** *medicine* powder کپه کول *compound verb* to lick up powder from the palm of the hand **2** pinch of snuff

کپه kapá [2] *f.* tray (for fruit)

کپه kápa [3] *f.* hunk, chunk, piece

کپه kapá [4] *f.* hut; hovel, shack

کپی kapí [1] *f.* ☞ کبي [2]

کپی kupój [2] *f.* **1** small wineskin **2** powder flask

کپی kapój [3] *f.* shoe; shoes

کپی خولی kapəjkhuláj *m.* (small) cuff

کپیدل kapedól *intransitive* [*past:* و کپید] to shiver, tremble; start, flinch

کپیر kapéṛ *m.* crocodile

کت kat [1] *m.* fold, crease, pleat کت کت، پر کت with folds **2** *predicative* folded ☞ قات [1]

کت kat [2] *m.* **1** pile, heap **2** stock, supply, reserve

کت kat [3] *m.* *plural* catechu (extract used in tanning)

کتاب kitáb *m. Arabic* [*plural:* کتابونه kitābúna *and Arabic* کتب kutúb] book درسي کتاب textbook

کتابات kitābát *m. Arabic* **1** the job of a clerk, position of a secretary په اول کتابت مقررېدل to be appointed secretary **2** business correspondence, clerical work خط او کتابت business correspondence

کتابچه kitābchá *f.* **1** notebook, exercise book **2** booklet, brochure د یادداشت کتابچه notebook; diary

کتابخانه kitābkhāná *f.* **1** library; book depository **2** publishing house **3** book trade

کتاب خرڅونکی kitáb khartsawúnkaj *m.* bookseller

کتابدار kitābdár *m.* librarian

کتابداري kitābdārí *f.* librarianship

کتاب فروش kitābfurúsh *m.* bookseller

کتاب فروشي kitābfurushí *f.* **1** book trade **2** row of book stalls (at a street market)

کتاب ګوټی kitābgóṭaj *m.* booklet, brochure

کتابه kitābá *f. Arabic* inscription; epitaph

کتابي kitābí **1** bookish **2** written **3** well-read, educated

کتار kətār *m.* **1** ☞ قطار؛ د ونو کتار avenue **2** queue, line

کتاره kitārá *f.* **1** parapet **2** pale, fencing, palisade **3** grave marker

کتان katán *m. plural Arabic* **1** linen **2** flax د کتان تار linen fiber

کتاني katāní **1** linen; flaxen کتاني ټکران linen fabrics **2** light brown کتاني

کتای katáj *conditional of* کتل [1]

کتب kutúb *m. plural Arabic of* کتاب

کتب katáb *m. Arabic* **1** frame of a camel saddle **2** bag strap, pouch cord

کتب خانه kutubkhāná *f.* library; book depository

کتبي kitbí *Arabic* **1** written **2** bookish

کتره katrá *f.* small piece, little chunk د غوښو کتره small piece of meat کتره کتره in small pieces ☞ قطره

کتری kutráj [1] *m.* ☞ کوتری

کتری katráj [2] shunning

کترینک katrinák *m.* scamp; loafer, good-for-nothing

کتغ katógh *m.* **1** food; hearty food خوږ کتغ sweet food **2** ragout

کتغلی katghaláj *m.* felt blanket for a bullock

کتغن kattaghán *m.* ☞ قطغن

کتک katók *m.* **1** land that yields a good wheat harvest **2** *regional* katak (the seventh month of the Indian calendar in which maize ripens)

کتکت katkát *m.* cackle, cackling کتکت کول *compound verb* to cackle

کتکتی katkátaj *m. anatomy* manyplies, omasum, third stomach (one of the divisions of the stomach in ruminants)

کتل katól [1] **1** *transitive* [*present:* ګوري *past:* کوت وی یی، in an objectless sentence وی یی کتل *or* وی یی کاته] **1.** to look, watch; perceive, see ترشا کتل to look back at, glance behind مونږ یو تر بله وکاته We exchanged glances. په غتو to view, examine, په ځیر کتل to examine closely د سترګو لاندي کتل to scowl (at) بدید *compound verb* to watch with ill-will **1.2** to examine, view, scan ډاکتر رنځور وکوت The doctor examined the patient. **1.3** to meet, see one another احمد مي وکوت I saw Ahmed. سره کتل to meet, see one another **1.4** to look over, look through; read through کتاب یي وکوت He looked through the book. **1.5** to consider (an issue, a question) **1.6** to study **1.7** to look for هغه څه شي ګوري؟ What is he looking for? **1.8** to wait (for), await, expect وتا ته ګوري They are waiting for you. ستاسي ځواب ته ګورم I am awaiting your answer. **1.9** to pay attention to something; take account of, take something into consideration چا ته یي نه کتل He didn't take account of anyone. **1.10** to observe **2** *m. plural* ☞ کتنه saying to be respectful towards someone کوچنیانو ته په مینه ادب کتل کتل to show love for children

کتل kutól [2] *transitive* ☞ کوتل [4]

کتلاک katlák *m.* catalog

کتلای katəláj *conditional of* کتل [1]

کتلمات katalmát *m.* end of a battle, conclusion of combat

کتلمه katlamá *f.* flaky fried flatbread

کتله kutlá *f. Arabic* mass, masses انساني کتله the common people

کتم katm *m.* کتمان kitmán *m. Arabic* concealing د سر کتم keeping a secret

کتمندو katmandú *m.* Katmandu

کتندځی katóndzáj *m.* out-patient clinic, dispensary

کتنه katə́na *f.* **1** considering, examining **2** inspection, examination (e.g., of a patient) **3** point of view, opinion, view **4** meeting, appointment; interview **5** examining, looking through; reading through **6** examination, consideration (of a question, issue) **7** study **8** waiting, expectation **9** verification, check-up **10** checking up on, monitoring **11** attention و يو شي ته کتنه کول to pay attention to something, turn one's attention to something **12** remark, observation, reproof کتني وړاندي کول to rebuke, to reprove **13** survey, review; و اخبارو ته يوه کتنه press review **14** *medicine* analysis د وينو کتنه blood analysis

کتنه ليدنه katə́na-lidə́na *f.* meeting د نجلۍ کتنه ليدنه becoming acquainted with the future bride کتني ليدني becoming acquainted

کاتو katə́ ¹ *oblique plural of* کاته ¹

کتو katə́ ² *Eastern imperative of* کتل ¹ *instead of* کوت ⁵ ما يو اخبار کتو I was reading the newspaper.

کاتودځی katódzáj *m.* **1** spectacle, show, performance **2** out-patient clinic, dispensary

کتول katawə́l *denominative, transitive* [*past:* کت يي کړ] to fold

کتون katún *m. regional* **1** examination **2** awaiting, expecting **3** inspection

کتوندځی katúndzáj *m.* doctor's consulting room

کتونکی katúnkaj **1** *present participle of* کتل **2** *m.* **.1** reader **2.2** observer, commentator سياسي کتونکی political observer **2.3** inspector, ticket-taker

کتونوال katunwə́l *m.* chief inspector, head of the inspection board

کته káta ¹ *f.* packsaddle

کته katá ² *f. imperfect of* کتل ¹

کته káta ³ *regional* ☞ کبنته

کتي káti ¹ *plural of* کته ¹

کتي katáj ² *Eastern* کتي به شي! Let's see!

کتي katáj ³ *m.* measure for milk

کتۍ kutə́j ⁴ *f.* ☞ قطۍ

کتۍ katé ⁵ *f. plural imperfect of* کتل ¹

کتيبه katibá *f. Arabic* frieze with inscription

کتي پتي kə́ti-pə́ti *f. plural* nonsense, tommyrot کتي پتي ويل *compound verb* to talk nonsense, talk rot, talk through one's hat کتي پتي خبري کول to chatter

کتبدل katedə́l ¹ *denominative, intransitive* [*past:* کت شو] to be folded

کتبدل kətedə́l ² *intransitive* [*past:* و کتبد] to cackle

کتيلعل kutilá'l *m.* ☞ کوتي لال

کټ kaṭ ¹ *m.* cot, bed د کټ خادر sleepwear د کټ جامي bedspread کټ ته ختل to go to bed کټ نيول *compound verb* to take to one's bed, become ill

کټ kaṭ ² *m.* **1** deduction, withholding (from wages) **2** exclusion (from a list) کټ کول *compound verb* **a** to deduct, withhold (from wages) **b** to exclude (from a list) کټ کبدل *compound verb* **a** to be deducted, be withheld (from wages) **b** be excluded (from a list)

کټ kaṭ ³ *m.* black pigment, black dye (made from pomegranate rinds)

کټ kaṭ ⁴ کټ کټل **1** big, large **2** thick; fat **3** strong *idiom* to gaze fixedly at, to stare at ☞ غټ ¹

کټ kaṭ ⁵ کټ وهل *compound verb* to laugh loudly, laugh boisterously

کټا kuṭá *f.* loud laughter, boisterous laughter

کټار kəṭár *m.* kind of needlework

کټار kəṭár ¹ *m.* hopscotch

کټار kəṭár ² stubborn, obstinate

کټاره kəṭārá ¹ *f.* dagger, poniard (with a three-edged blade) په ميني د کټارو ژوبل شو *idiom* He was suffering from love.

کټاره kəṭára ² *f.* cow that will not allow itself to be milked

کټاره kaṭará ³ *f.* ☞ کتاره

کټاربدل kəṭāredə́l *denominative, intransitive* [*past:* کټاره شوه] to be obstinate (of a cow)

کټالۍ kuṭālə́j *f.* smelting crucible, melting pot

کټاو kəṭáw *m.* ☞ کتاب

کټبان kaṭbā́n *m.* craftsman who weaves rope netting for beds

کټبون kaṭbún *m.* vegetable fiber used in bed netting

کټپوری kaṭpóraj *m.* rope by which a bed is held together

کټپوز kaṭpúz *m.* muzzle (e.g., for a dog)

کتر kaṭár *m. plural* Katar (a people living in the vicinity of Attack)

کټرکی kuṭárkaj *m.* foal of an ass

کټکټ kəṭkə́ṭ *m.* کټکی ¹ kəṭkáj loud laughter, boisterous laughter په زوره او کټ کټ خندل to laugh loudly, laugh boisterously کټ کټ خندل to laugh loudly, laugh uproariously

کټکی katkáj ² *m.* کټگی katgáj *m.* **1** stool **2** small bed

کټلاگ kaṭlā́g *m.* catalog

کټماله kaṭmālá *f.* silver necklace, gold necklace

کټمټ kaṭmə́ṭ کټ مټ kəṭmə́ṭ exactly, precisely دا سړی کټمټ ستا ورور غوندي دئ This man closely resembles your brother.

کټمل kaṭmál *m.* bug

کټمبره kaṭméra *f.* jackknife

کټمبری kaṭméraj *m.* baby dove, baby pigeon

کټو kaṭə́w *f.* ☞ کټوی clay cooking pot کټو څو چه پر سر را نه سي، نه تويبري *saying* My cup of patience has overflowed, I am exasperated

کټواز kaṭawā́z *m.* Katawaz (region in southern Afghanistan) د ارگون او کټواز سيمي *history* the Katawaz-Urgun areas

کټوټ kaṭwáṭ ☞ گوډ

کټوټکی kaṭóṭkaj *m.* cradle

کټور kaṭúr *m.* hen-pecked husband

کټوری kaṭóraj, kuṭóraj *m.* [*plural:* کټوري kaṭorí, kuṭorí *and Western* کټوريان kaṭoríán, kuṭorján] **1** bowl, chalice; cup, teacup **2** mug, tankard

کټوار kaṭwár *m.* article of trade corresponding to an order or price list

کټوبنی kaṭókhaj *m.* trivet (for a kettle, pot, cauldron)

کتول ¹ kəṭawə́l *transitive* [*past:* کتاوه وی ی] **1** to send on a trip, send (someone somewhere) **2** to drive (a herd) **3** to frighten, drive away (wasps, etc.)

کتول ² kaṭawúl *denominative, transitive* [*past:* کړ یي کټ] *regional* to cross out کتول نوم *compound verb* to remove from a list

کټوله kaṭolá *f.* bride's palanquin

کټ و مټ kaṭ-u-mə́ṭ ☞ کت مټ

کټوه ¹ kaṭə́wa ☞ کتوی

کټوه ² kaṭwá *f.* projecting tip of a turban

کتوی kaṭwə́j *f.* **1** earthenware pot هرچېري اور بل، **2** pot, saucepan کتوی باندي *saying* everyone has his own concerns (*literally:* everywhere there's a fire burning and on it there's a pot) د شر کتوی ماته شوه *saying* the disturbance came to an end

کتوی خټ kaṭwəjtsə́ṭ *m.* sponger, hanger-on, parasite

کټه ¹ kaṭá *m.* ☞ کته باز

کوټه ² kuṭá *m.* ☞ کوټه ⁴

کټه ³ kaṭá **1** large, big کټه گوته thumb **2** bass string

کټهار kəṭahár *m.* **1** (loud) laughter **2** cry of the partridge

کته باز kaṭá bāz *m.* goshawk

کټپیش kaṭapísh *m.* flick, fillip کټه پیش ورکول to give (someone) a fillip

کته چرگه kúṭa chə́rga *f.* hen that has stopped laying

کاټه گوته káṭa gúta *f.* *Eastern* thumb

کوټه مټه kóṭa mə́ṭa *f.* ☞ کټ مټ

کته مهر kaṭaméhr کټه مېر kaṭamér **1** wicked, malicious, bad, evil **2** cruel, severe, harsh, stern

کته مېری kaṭameráj disobedient, refractory, naughty

کټی ¹ káṭi *m. plural* bean stalks (of mung beans, etc., which go into cattle feed)

کټی ² kaṭáj *m.* **1** buffalo calf, young buffalo **2** baby elephant

کټی ³ kaṭáj *m.* stick used to measure milk

کټی ⁴ kaṭə́j *f.* ☞ کتوی

کټی ⁵ kaṭə́j *feminine of* کټی ¹

کټی ⁶ kúṭe, kə́ṭe shout by which people drive away hens, young donkeys, etc. کټی کول *compound verb* **a** to drive away, shoo (hens, donkey colts, etc.) **b** *figurative* to fire someone, give someone the sack; turn someone out

کتېدل kəṭedə́l *intransitive* [*past:* کتېده و] **1** to set out on a journey, start out on a trip **2** to roam from place to place, lead the life of a nomad **3** to fly away, scatter (of wasps, etc.)

کتېدنه kəṭedə́na *f.* **1** setting out on a trip **2** roaming, leading a nomadic life **3** flying away, scattering (of a swarm of wasps, etc.)

کتېر kəṭér *m.* **1** collective work, help, assistance **2** cartel, peasants' cooperative, workers' cooperative

کتېری kaṭerə́j *f.* small saucepan (for melting butter)

کټیک kaṭík *m.* کټیکی kaṭíkaj *m.* currier, tanner

کتېژل kaṭejə́l *transitive* [*past:* کتېیه وی ی] **1** to shear (e.g., sheep) **2** to cut too short, shear too short **3** to cut branches, prune branches

کثافات kasāfā́t *m. plural Arabic* mud, dirt, sewage

کثافت kasāfát *m. Arabic* **1** density, thickness د نفوسو کثافت، د وگړو population density **2** weight, heaviness, onerousness **3** fullness; portliness

کثرت kasrát *m. Arabic* **1** numerical strength, great number, abundance, plenty د نفوسو کثرت overpopulation **2** majority د ارائؤ کثرت majority of votes **3** frequency, frequent use **4** habit, custom

کثیر kasír *Arabic* **1** many, numerous **2** abundant, plentiful, copious **3** frequent, frequently used

کثیرالانتشار kasir-ul-intishā́r large-circulation کثیرالانتشار ورځپانه a large-circulation newspaper

کثیف kasíf *Arabic* **1** dirty, slovenly; soiled, contaminated **2** *physics* dense

کثیفول kasifawə́l *denominative, transitive* [*past:* کړ یي کثیف] to soil, contaminate

کثیفېدل kasifedə́l *denominative, intransitive* [*past:* شو کثیف] to be soiled, be contaminated هوا کثیفه سوی ده The air is polluted.

کج kadzh crooked, curved, bent

کجاوه ¹ kadzhāwá *f.* bubbles (on the surface of water)

کجاوه ² kadzhāwá *f.* **1** seat (on a camel's back, for a bride) **2** motorcycle sidecar

کجاوی ¹ kadzhāwé *plural of* کجاوه ² 1

کجاوی ² kudzhāwe *f. plural* کجاوی ویل *compound verb* to prate, talk nonsense

کجبېری kadzhbéraj *m.* ripple-seed plantain, *Plantago major*

کجک ¹ kadzhák *m.* **1** curls, ringlets of hair on the forehead **2** cock, cocking piece (of a firearm) **3** iron hook (at the end of a goad) **4** late cucumber **5** part of a water-powered mill

کجک ² kadzhák *m. regionalism* name of a bird

کجکل kadzhkál *m.* epileptic

کجکی ¹ kadzhəkáj *m.* **1** lower jaw, mandible **2** small pond, small spring (by the roadside)

کجکی ² kadzhakáj *m.* Kadzhakai (a region, formerly Zamindawar) د کجکي بند the Kajakai Dam

کجل kadzhál *m. plural* **1** antimony, stibium **2** eye makeup (similar to mascara) **3** soot that is added to antimony

کجلی kadzhalí penciled with antimony, darkened with stibium تور کجلي وېښته eyes made up with stibium سترگي jet-black hair

کجلېچ kadzhléch *m.* کجلبچ turn (in a road); bend, curve

کج موزی kadzhmozé *f. plural* boots with turned-up toecaps

کجوالی kadzhwə́laj *m.* curvature

کجور kadzhúr *m.* kind of maize

کجوره kadzhúra *f.* **1** date د کجوري ونه date palm (the tree) **2** date palm د کجورو ځنگل grove of date palms

کجوکل kadzhukúl کج و کین kadzhukín sinuous, winding, twisting, meandering

کجه kadzhá five-year-old, through the fifth year (of a bull)

کجی ¹ kadzháj **1** bowlegged, bandy-legged **2** *m.* troublemaker, seditionist

کجی ² kadzháj *f.* pin, peg (of a plowshare)

کجیر ¹ kadzhír *m.* black griffon (vulture)

کجیر ² kadzhír *m.* tumor on the neck

کجیر ³ kadzhír beautiful, pretty

کجین kadzhín *m. plural* **1** silk waste **2** heavy thread (for sewing blankets, quilts)

کچ ¹ kuch *m. plural* butter

کچ ² kach *m. regional* **1** measure, size کچ کول *compound verb* ☞ کچول ¹ **2** unit of length equal to 28 inches or 0.71 meters

کچ ³ kach *m.* shortcoming, defect

کچ ⁴ kəch short, undersized, dwarfish, shortish

کچ ⁵ kach *m. regional* glass

کچاړی kachāṛáj *f.* institution, office

کچالو kachālú *m.* [*plural:* کچالوگان kachālugán *and* کچالان kachālán] potatoes

کچتوب kuchəttób *m.* childhood

کچر kachár *m.* [*plural:* کچر kachər] mule

کچروالا kacharwālā *m.* muleteer, muleskinner

کچره ¹ kachára, kachóra *f.* **1** mule **2** *regional* lewd lady, depraved woman د چا کچري تورول *compound verb* to play a dirty trick on someone

کچره ² kachrá mixed, intermixed

کچره ³ kəchrá *f. regional* unripe melon

کچري ¹ kichrí *m. plural* kasha, porridge; ragout with rice and beans

کچری ² kachráj *f.* unripe melon

کچری ³ kachré *f.* copper coin

کچري kachári *m. plural* cry of a partridge; cackling کچري وهل *compound verb* to cackle

کچکاسه kachkāsá *f.* bucket (for pouring syrup when making sugar from cane)

کچ کچ kuch kúch cry by which people call a dog

کچکول kachkól. *m.* cup for collecting hand-outs (among the Dervish)

کچکولک kachkolák *m.* کچکوله kachkóla *f.* shell (e.g., of a pistachio)

کچ گر kachgər *m.* land surveyor

کچل kachál bowlegged

کچماچو kachmāchú *m.* deadly nightshade, *Solanum nigrum*

کچنو kuchnó *oblique plural of* کچنی ²

کچنوتی kuchnótaj *m.* ☞ کچنوتوالی

کچنی ¹ kuchnáj **1** small, little کچنی ضابط non-commissioned officer کچنی اختر the tenth month of the lunar year **2** *m.* child, baby, youngster د کچنیان هلکان ، کچنیان children, youngsters کچنیانو مرگ infant mortality ☞ کچنی

کچنی ² kachanój *f.* **1** prostitute **2** female dancer

کچنیتوب kuchnitób *m.* کچنیواله ، کچنیوالی kuchniwāla kuchniwālaj *f.* childhood

کچوالی kachwālaj *m.* meanness, baseness, vile action

کچوت kachút **1** low, mean, base, vile **2** stingy, miserly, greedy

کچوتوالی kuchutwālaj *m.* **1** childhood **2** small quantity, insignificance, negligibility

کچوتی ¹ kuchótaj, kəchótaj **1** small, little **2** *m.* youngster, lad, (young) boy

کچوتی ² kuchóte **1** *feminine singular of* ¹ کچوتی **2** *f.* girl, young girl

کچول ¹ kachawól *denominative, transitive* [*past:* کچ یې کړ] **1** to try on (e.g., clothes) **2** to measure (area); to carry out a land survey **3** to fix boundaries, establish boundaries

کچول ² kəchól *m.* low and flat dish

کچول ³ kachúl ☞ کچل

کچوله kacholá *f.* **1** nuxvomica, poison nut (yields strychnine) **2** datura, thorn apple

کچ ولوی kuch-u-lój *m.* the old and the young

کچونه kachawóna *f.* **1** trying on (e.g., clothes) **2** measuring (an area); land survey **3** fixing boundaries, establishing boundaries

کچه ¹ kácha *f. Western* size, measure کچه نیول *compound verb* to take (someone's) measurements (e.g., for clothes)

کچه ² kachá **1** unripe, green; raw **2** unprocessed کچه څرمني hides **3** dirt, unpaved (of a road) **4** rammed-earth (of a house) **5** adobe کچه خښته adobe brick **6** undeveloped, backward, stupid; immature **7** inexperienced کچه شا گرد novice **8** ashamed کچه کول *compound verb* to shame, put to shame, make ashamed of کچه کېدل *compound verb* to be ashamed; be confused, be embarrassed په زړه کښې کچه کېدل to be ashamed (of) **9** of low breed, of inferior breed **10** insignificant, negligible **11** timid, shy, bashful

کچه ³ kácha cry used to drive away goats کچه کول *compound verb* to drive away (goats)

کچه ⁴ kácha *f.* ☞ کچه گوته

کچهار kachhár *m. regional* ☞ کچر

کچه گوته kócha gúta, kócha gwóta *f.* little finger, pinkie

کچه لنگ kachaláng *m.* name of a disease

کچی ¹ kuchí *m. plural* butter

کچی ² kucháj *m.* foal of a donkey

کچی ³ kacháj bowlegged

کچی ⁴ kóche ☞ کچه ³

کچيري kachére که چيري if, in the case of something; in the event of something, in the event that

کځر kadzór bald; balding

کځلي kədzáli *m. plural* brushwood, dry branches

کځن kadzán, kadzán *m.* blanket

کځ ¹ kats *m.* **1** bottomland, flood-plain of a river **2** tugai (vegetation-covered bottomland), tugai forest **3** *used in geographical names* کجوري کځ، د کجوري کځ the Kadzhuri Valley

کځ ² kats *m.* **1** fabric from which children's caps a sewn **2** piece of cloth that is sewn to the back of the collar of a woman's dress

کځ ³ kats *m.* ceiling

کځخول katskhwál *m.* bran

کتسخوله katskhwála *f.* 1 cloth cap 2 *regional* cap with earflaps

کتسکی katskáj *m.* foal of a donkey

کتسله katsála *f.* manure pile, dunghill

کتسمتسای katsmətsáj *m.* whisper, whispering کښمښی کول *compound verb* to whisper

کتسوړه katsóṛa *f.* 1 bag, purse د لګښت کښوړه pocket money 2 sack د لامبو کښوړه swim bladder

کتسواک katswák *m.* chicken pox کښوک نیولی sick with chicken pox

کتسی katskáj *f.* ☞ کښ

کحل kohl *m. plural Arabic* antimony, stibium

کخ kəkh naughty, bad (when talking to children)

کخړی kakhaṛáj *m.* name of a star

کخکړی kokhkə́raj *m.* ☞ کبنکړی

کخی kəkháj *m.* 1 helminth, intestinal worm 2 swarm of midges

کدالی kudāláj *f.* hoe کدالی وهل *compound verb* to hoe

کدای kadáj *m.* street clothes; long dressing gown, robe

کدای kadáj *m.* kind of frog

کدخدا kadkhudā́ *m.* village elder, village headman; the head of a family

کدخدایي kadkhudājí *f.* job of village elder

کدر kadár *Arabic* 1 not transparent, opaque, cloudy, turbid 2 *m.* .1 turbidity, cloudiness 2.2 grief, sorrow, woe, sadness

کدو kadú *m.* [*plural:* کدوان kaduán] pumpkin رومي کدو summer squash

کدوچه kaduchá *f.* vegetable marrow, summer squash

کدورت kudurát *m. Arabic* 1 confusion, embarrassment 2 unpleasantness, grief, distress د کدورت باعث کېدل to cause unpleasantness, grief, distress

کدوزری kaduzə́raj *m.* pumpkin seed

کدوسری kadusáraj *m.* blockhead, dolt, dunderhead

کدوکاوش kadukāwísh *m.* meaningless work دونه کدوکاوش او ماغزه خوړل to beat the air

کدوگک kadugák *m. medicine* cupping glass کدوگک نښلول to apply a cupping glass

کدبا kaḍbá *m.* [*plural:* کډبانه kaḍbānə́] کډبنای kaḍbanáj *m.* nomad

کډغالج kaḍghā́laj *m.* کډل kaḍál *f.* کوډل kuḍál کډله kaḍə́la *f.* 1 cabin, shack, hut (made of cane or grass) 2 henhouse (made of cane or grass)

کډن kaḍə́n with the family, family, having a family کډن راغلی دئ He came with his family.

کډو kaḍú *m.* [*plural:* کډوان kaḍuán] 1 pumpkin 2 ☞ کدوگک؛ چا د idiom to drive (someone) out of his mind سر کډو کول، څوک کډو کول کډو کېدل *compound verb* a to go out of one's mind, lose one's wits b to be a fool, be an idiot په کډو کي ډبره اچول idiom to carry on a pointless argument

کډوال kaḍwā́l کډوالا kaḍwālā́ 1.1 family, having a family 1.2 roaming, nomadic 2 *m.* .1 nomad 2.2 family man, man who has a family

کډوبار kaḍubár *m.* loading up belongings (among nomads)

کډوری kaḍúraj *m. medicine* cup

کده kádạ *f.* 1 family (among the nomads) 2 nomad's wife 3 nomad's camp کده کول *compound verb* a to roam, lead a nomadic life b to start a family, get married c to move from place to place, lead a nomadic life, resettle کده لرل a to have a family, move from place to place with the family b to be nomad په کده تلل to be a nomad with a family زه له صواته دلته په کده راغلی یم I moved here from Swat. 4 *regional* furniture; household goods and utensils

کده kaḍá *f.* pit, hole; dimple

کدهل kaḍə́l, kaḍə́l, kaḍə́l *m* 1 pit, hole 2 pit filled with water 3 ground prepared for planting rice

کده والا kaḍawālā́ ☞ کډوال

کدی káḍi *plural of* کده

کدی kaḍáj *m.* 1 hollow space under a weaver's loom (where the weaver puts his feet) 2 pit; ditch

کدی kaḍáj *f.* loom

کذاب kazzā́b *m. Arabic* liar

کذب kazb *m. Arabic* lie, falsehood

کر kar 1 *m.* sowing, planting دکر زمکه beet raising د لبلبوکر arable land کرکول *compound verb* to sow, plant 2 field غنم کر wheat field

کر kər *m.* 1 squeak, crackle, crack 2 *onomatopeia* the sound of cloth being ripped

کر kər *m.* runny bowel movements, liquid feces

کر kar deaf

کر kár *regional adverb-forming suffix* خاصکر especially

کرا karā́ *f.* ☞ کرهار

کرا kirā́ *f.* ☞ کراهه

کراب kurā́b *m.* ☞ تبک

کرات karā́t *m. plural Arabic of* کرت

کراچ krāch *m.* clump or clod of earth

کراچی karāchí *f.* ☞ کراچی

کراچی karāchí *f.* Karachi د کراچی دهانه Karachi Bay

کراچی karāchə́j *f.* کراچی karāchí *f.* 1 two-wheeled cart د کراچی لاسي کراچي wheelbarrow دوه لرګي shafts 2 wheelbarrow

کراچیران karāchirān *m.* کراچي وان karāchiwán *m.* carter, drayman

کرار karā́r ☞ قرار کرار کرار a gradually b slowly, quietly, calmly

کراروالی karārwə́laj *m.* ☞ قرار والی

کراروَل karārawə́l *transitive* ☞ قرارول

کراره karaṛá *f.* comb, currycomb آس کراره کول *compound verb* to clean a horse with a currycomb

کراره karaṛa 1 *feminine singular of* کرار 2 *f.* peace, tranquility په کراره a quietly, calmly b gradually, not all at once په کراره سره

کراري karāṛí *f.* ☞ قراري

کراری karā́ṛi *f. plural of* کرار

کراړ krāṛ *literally & figuratively* hard, strong; rigid

کراړک krāṛák *m.* salted cheese

کراړه krā́ṛa *f.* **1** ayran (a kind of yogurt drink) **2** kurut (dried balls of fermented milk or milk curds) **3** pebble; rocky soil

کراړی karāṛə́j *f.* mushroom

کراز krāz *m.* molting (of birds)

کرازي krā́zi *f. plural* lying words, lies

کراږند krāǵónd with a deteriorated state of health

کراږندتیا krāǵəndtjā́ *f.* کراږ ندوالی krāǵəndwā́laj *m.* **1** tension, tenseness **2** feeling of discontent, feeling of dissatisfaction; state of depression

کراږنده krā́ǵənda dissatisfied

کراسپه krā́spa *f.* means of fastening a pack

کراسته krā́sta *f.* thick felt, felting د کراستي ملا بند کېدل to lose all trust, loss all confidence

کراسته گر krāstagár *m.* fuller who makes thick felt or felting

کراسنویارسک krāsnojársk *m.* Krasnoyarsk

کراغ krāgh with sunken eyes

کراکاش karākásh کراکښ karākáḵh **1** pack (of a horse) **2** *m.* carter, drayman, driver

کراکنده krākánda **1** limp, flabby, weak, infirm, feeble; with undermined health **2** impatient

کرام kirā́m *m. plural Arabic* [*singular* کریم¹] all merciful اولیای کرام the higher clergy who have been posthumously canonized

کرامت karāmát *m. Arabic* **1** miraculous power, miracle **2** generosity, mercy

کرامتي karāmatí marvelous, miraculous, wonder-working

کران کران karán-karán *m. regional* croaking, cawing کران کران کول *compound verb* to croak, caw

کرانه karāná *f.* edge, limit له چا څخه کرانه کېدل to avoid, steer clear of someone

کراڼی karāṇáj *m.* [*usually plural* کراڼی karāṇí] ☞ کرلانبي

کراوُل karāwúl *m.* **1** gunsight; laying, aiming کراول ترل، کراول کول، *compound verb* to aim (at) **2** *military* patrol, guard, security detachment کراول نیول changing of the guards کراول وبستل

کراوی kərāwáj *m.* patron, protector, guardian, trustee

کراهت karāhát *m. Arabic* antipathy, aversion, repugnance; dissatisfaction

کراهه kirāhá *f.* **1** hire, rent, lease په کراهه اخیستل *compound verb* to hire, rent, charter په کراهه ورکول *compound verb* to hire out, lease **2** payment for freight, fee for transportation

کراهه دار kirāhadár *f.* renter, tenant, lease-holder

کراهه کښ kirāhakáḵh ☞ کراکش

کراهه وړونکی kirāhá wṛúnkaj کراهه وړونکي بېړی charter(ed) ship; cargo ship

کراهه kirājá *f.* ☞ کراهه

کرایه کشي kirājakashí *f.* carrier's trade د کرایه کشی کار کول to be a carrier (by trade)

کرایه وړونکی kirājá wṛúnkaj ☞ کراهه وړونکی

کرایی kirājí **2** کراهه rented, hired کرایي *f.* ☞ کرائی

کرباس karbā́s *m.* canvas, linen; hand-made cotton cloth

کربانه karbā́ṇá shining black, gleaming black

کربوړک karbuṛák *m.* ☞ کربوړ ک

کربسکه karbúska *f.* cotton

کربشا karbəshā́ *m.* marmot

کربک karbák *m.* ☞ کربوړ ک

کربلا karbalā́ *f. Arabic* Karbala

کربوړک karboṛák *m.* کربوړی karbóṛaj *m.* agama (lizard)

کربشا karbushā́ *m.* marmot

کربولیک karbolík carbolic, phenolic کربولیک لوگی carbon dioxide

کربون karbón *m.* carbon

کربټ karbéṭ **1** bowlegged **2** *m.* rogue, swindler, cheat

کربزن karbezón snotty

کربزي karbézi *f. plural* snot, mucus

کریبین karíbijin د کربین بحیره Caribbean Sea

کرپ krap *m.* **1** champing, chewing; ruminating **2** crunch, crackle

کرپا krəpā́ *f.* ☞ کرپی

کرپال karpál *m.* talker, chatterbox, windbag, gasbag, babbler

کرپالی karpáŀaj *m.* clay that has dried out and become cracked after a mud-flow

کرپان kirpā́n *m.* dagger

کرپتاوه karpatāwá *f.* well bucket

کرپاړه karpā́ṛa *f.* ☞ کرپالی

کرپله karpála *f.* kind of green vegetable

کرپندوکی krapandúkaj *m.* cartilage, gristle

کرپندی krapandáj **1** *m.* **.1** cartilage, gristle **1.2** crunch, crackle **2** crunchy, crackly کرپندی بسکټ crunchy pastry

کرپول krapawól *transitive* [*past:* و یې کرپاوه] **1** to eat noisily, eat with a crunching sound; champ; to chew, masticate **2** to gnash, one's teeth **3** to gnaw

کرپوله karpulá *f. botany* lemon balm, *Melissa officinalis*

کرپی krápaj *m.* **1** crunch, crackle **2** chewing, champing **3** rustling

کرپېدل krapedól *intransitive* [*past:* و کرپېد، و کرپېده] to crunch, crackle, emit a crunching or crackling sound

کرت karát¹ *m. Arabic* [*f. plural* کرتي karáte *and m. plural Arabic* کرات karā́t] time (referring to each occurrence of a repeating or recurring event) یو کرت once, one time څو کرته several times دری *idiom* شل کرته often کرات مرات کرته، څپر کرته three times، دري کرتي with pleasure, willingly, gladly, readily

کرت kurút² *m. plural* kurut (dried balls of fermented milk or milk curds)

کرتب kartáb *m.* **1** action, act, deed **2** practice; exercise; training **3** ability, skill **4** breaking in (a horse)

کرتوت kartút *m.* **1** action, act, deed **2** affair, business, matter

کرته karáta¹ کرت *plural of* څپر کرته often

کرته kurtá² *f.* کرتي kurtáj *f.* jacket; coat; tunic منصبداري کرته military officer's blouse

کورت kruṭ ☞ کورت

کرج kardzh *m.* hunk, chunk, piece (of a watermelon, etc.)

کچ krach¹ *m.* old and well-trained falcon or hawk

کرچ ² krach *m.* strong hoe, Turkestan hoe

کرچ ³ krəch *m.* ☞ کرپ

کرچل ¹ karchál bowlegged

کرچل ² krachál *transitive* [*past:* کرچول وي یي and کرچول krəchawəl *past:* کرپول ☞ 1 کرپول] 2 to emit a scratching (of scissors, etc.)

کرچونی krachúnaj *m.* cartilage, gristle

کرچه krácha *f.* kind of design in a reversible rug

کرچهار krəchəhár *m.* ☞ کرپ

کرچی ¹ krichí *f. m.* kracháj camomile, Roman camomile

کرچی ² kracháj *m.* ☞ کرچونی

کرځ karádz lazy, listless

کرخ kurúkh *m.* Kurukh (inhabited place near Herat)

کرخت karákht 1 severe; cruel 2 stiff from the cold, frozen

کرخولکه karkhuláka *f.* 1 knot on planed wood 2 stump

کرخی ¹ kərkháj *m. regional* ☞ کرښی

کرخی ² kərkháj *f.* bean plant used in livestock feed

کرد ¹ kord *m.* banked up part of a plot of land

کرد ² kurd *m.* Kurd

کردار kirdár *m.* 1 act, deed, action 2 conduct, behavior, manners 3 good deed 4 dowry

کرداري kirdārí doing a good deed

کردبندي kordbandí *f.* banking up a section of a plot of land

کردستان kurdistán *m.* Kurdistan

کردگار kirdagár *m.* God; The Creator (an epithet of God)

کرده kardá *f.* deed, doing

کردی kurdí 1 Kurdish; کردي ژبه the Kurdish language 2.1 *f.* Kurdish (language) 2.2 *m.* Kurd

کرړان karṛán *m. plural* ☞ کرلاني

کرړه kərṛá *f.* posterity

کرړی ¹ kariṛí, kiraṛí *m. plural* ☞ کرلاني

کرړی ² kirṛáj *m.* cricket

کرړی ³ karṛáj *m.* wheelbarrow

کرږه krə́ga *f.* cry, yell, howl, scream کرږي کول، کرږه وهل *compound verb* to cry out, yell, howl

کرس kras *m. onomatopoeia* the crack of wood being split

کرسپه kraspá *f.* thick wool cord; rope

کرستل kristál *m.* crystal

کرسمس krísmás *m.* Christmas د کرسمس ونه Christmas tree

کرسی ¹ kursí *f. Arabic,* کرسی kursə́j *f.* [*plural:* کرسي kursə́j and کرسي گاني kursə́jgā́ni] 1 chair, stool 2 place, seat د نورو په قطار خپله کرسي اشغالول to take one's place among the others 3 rostrum, platform د خطابي کرسی platform 4 deputy's seat (seat in a legislative body) 5 throne 6 empyrean, the heavens, the firmament

کرسی ² karsáj *m.* medicinal plant used in treating the eyes

کرسی نامه kursinā́ma *f.* 1 family tree, genealogical tree, genealogy 2 seniority

کرشتان krishtán *m.* 1 Muslim who has converted to Christianity 2 Christian

کرشمه karashmá *f.* 1 winking 2 flirting

کرشنیل kurshníl *m.* knitting needle

کرښ krə́kh *m.* 1 footstep, footfall 2 footprint

کرښپل kərəkhpál *m.* 1 footprint 2 *figurative* sign, mark, omen

کرښمه karákhmá *f.* ☞ کرشمه

کرښنده kərkhónda *f.* 1 trace; line 2 dragging of the bride on her cloak by the groom's relatives (a wedding ritual)

کرښندی kərkhəndáj *m.* drawing, diagram; plan, design 2 sketch, illustration, figure

کرښنه ¹ krákhna *f.* 1 decorating, painting 2 embroidering 3 pattern, design

کرښنه ² krákhna *f.* forming a circle around a person sick with typhus

کرښنه ³ karkhóna *f.* site of an ancient city; ruins

کرښندی kərkhundáj *m.* 1 stick for fastening a rope (of a pack) 2 iron ring on a saddle girth or bellyband

کرښه kórkha *f.* 1 line سرحدي کرښه، د ډیورند کرښه the Durand Line state border, frontier 2 کرښه راکښل، کرښه کول to draw a line *idiom* په تندي کښي د خوشحالی کرښي expression of joy on someone's face د کرښو وتی لېوني دئ، د کرښو وتلی لېوني دئ He is quite out of his mind.

کرښي ¹ kórkhi *plural of* کرښي کرښه کرښي ruled, lined کرښي کول *compound verb* to rule, line off

کرښی ² kərkháj *m.* ruler, straight-edge; (drawing, sketching)

کرغ ¹ kurúgh *m.* pasture, meadow

کرغ ² kurúgh *m.* 1 ban, interdiction 2 confiscation 3 enclosure 4 preserve, reservation کرغ کول *compound verb* a to ban, prohibit b to confiscate c to declare to be a preserve d to enclose, fence in

کرغچکه karghəcháka *f.* magpie

کرغر karghár *m.* grief, sorrow; feeling upset

کرغروج karghərúdzh *m.* Adam's apple

کرغره karghára *f.* ☞ کرغ

کرغشی karghóshaj rough, coarse, hard, rigid

کرغکهی karghakháj *m.* 1 place where the jaws join 2 lower jaw, mandible

کرغم karghám *m.* ☞ وودی ¹

کرغوچ karghwóch cut off, chopped off

کرغه ¹ kraghá *f.* dry valley دا مځکه وچه کرغه وه This was barren ground.

کرغه ² karghá *f.* meadow, pasture

کرغر karghér *m.* mud

کرغرن karghərən dirty, soiled, contaminated کرغړني اوبه a stagnant water, standing water b polluted water 2 bad (of the air) 3 *figurative* marred (of a life) 4 *figurative* unpleasant, ugly کرغړن کرغړن نبدل ☞ کرغړن کېدل ;کرغړنول ☞ کول

کرغړن توب karghərəntób *m.* dirt, filth, contamination, pollution

کرغړ نول karghərənawə́l *denominative, transitive* [*past:* کرغړن يې کړ] to soil, make dirty, contaminate

کرغړ نبدل karghərənedə́l *denominative, intransitive* [*past:* کرغړن شو] to be soiled, get dirty, become contaminated

کرغېړه karghéṛa *f.* dirt, filth, mud

کرفس karáfs *m. plural* celery

کرک [1] karák *m.* 1 *Western* common quail 2 yellow-legged buttonquail 3 common snipe

کرک [2] kark *m.* 1 rhinoceros 2 rhinoceros hide, rhinoceros leather

کرک [3] karák *m.* whole wheat

کرک [4] kurk *m.* 1 goat's down, under-fur of a goat's 2 cloth made from goat's down, cashmere

کرک [5] krak *m.* 1 furrow 2 wheel track, rut; wheel width

کرک [6] krak *m.* silt that has dried and cracked

کرکاندۍ kərkáṇḍaj *m.* 1 boulder, rubble 2 crushed stone, ballast (road-bed)

کرکانی karkáṇaj testing, assaying, touchstone

کرک بازي karakbāzí *f.* quail fight

کرکتر karáktar *m.* character, nature

کرکټ krikáṭ *m. sports* cricket

کرکتر karákṭar *m.* ☞ کرکتر

کرکجن krakdzhón 1 breathing hatred, malicious په کرکجن آواز ویل to speak with hatred 2 repugnant, revolting, loathsome

کرکدن karkadán *m.* rhinoceros

کرکر kurkúr *m.* cackle, cackling کرکر کول *compound verb* to cackle

کرکرانی kərkərānáj *m.* rattle (baby's toy)

کرکره karkará *f.* 1 crown کرکره وهل *compound verb* to put on the crown کرکره په سر اینبودل to crown someone king 2 plume, feather (hat decoration) 3 demoiselle crane

کرکري [1] kurkurí pock-marked

کرکرۍ [2] kərkəráj *f.* 1 rattle 2 lure, decoy

کرکړی [3] kərkəráj *m.* 1 water-lifting wheel 2 windlass, winch

کرکمن kurkumán *m.* curcuma, turmeric

کرکن krəkán ☞ کرکجن

کرکند krəkánd 1 nasty, offensive, disgusting, repulsive 2 ugly

کرکند karkánd rolling down the mountain (of a rock, etc.) کرکند کول *compound verb* ☞ کرکندول

کرکندول [1] karkanḍawól *denominative, transitive* [*past:* کر کنډ یې کړ] to roll (a stone, etc.) down the mountain 2 to push away, throw, knock down

کرکانډه karkáṇḍa *f.* 1 boulder 2 stone that is hurled at an enemy (from a fortification or from a height)

کرکندیدل [1] karkanḍedól *denominative, intransitive* [*past:* کر کنډ شو] to roll down a mountain (of a rock, etc.) 2 to fall (down)

کرکن karkáṇ *m.* thicket, underbrush, undergrowth, shrub, brush

کرکڼه karkáṇa *f.* 1 wild jujube (with small fruit) 2 shrub, brush

کر کاوونکی kar kawúnkaj *m.* peasant farmer, tiller of the soil

کرکه krəká *f.* 1 disgust, repugnance; loathing, hatred نژادي کرکه racial hatred سره کرکه کول to harbor disgust for one another, hate one another 2 indignation; discontent, dissatisfaction څخه... د a to feel disdain; feel an aversion; له ... نه کرکه کول hate, loathe هرڅوک له تا نه کرکه کوي Everybody hates you. b to be indignant, express dissatisfaction

کرکه ور krəkawór krəkanā́k کرکه ناک disgusting, repulsive, base, vile

کرکي [1] kurkí made of goat's down, cashmere

کرکی [2] karkáj *m.* ass, donkey

کرکۍ [3] karakój *f.* plowshare

کریکټ kríkéṭ *m. sports* cricket

کر کیمه karkímá *f.* cage (for birds and animals)

کرگر kargár *m.* [*plural:* کرگر kargór] farmer, plowman

کرگرتوب kargərtób *m.* کرگتیا kargərtjá *f.* کر گري kargərí agriculture کرگرتوب کول *compound verb* to engage in agriculture, farm

کرگس kargás *m.* cinereous vulture

کول [1] karál 1 *m.* .1 ice 1.2 cream 2 *predicative* frozen (of water, etc.) کول کېدل *compound verb* to freeze, be frozen, be iced over

کول [2] karál *m.* mortar (for grinding medicines)

کول [3] karól 1 *transitive* [*past:* و یې کاره] to sow, seed; plant, set out; cultivatem چه کړې هغه به رببی، څه چه کړې هغه به رببی *proverb* as you sow, so shall you reap 2 *m. plural* sowing; planting, setting out, transplanting

کرلاني karlā́ni *m. plural* Karlani (the fourth branch of Afghan tribes consisting of the Afridi, Khattak, Utmankheil, Dzadran, Vardak, Orakzai, Mangal, Dzadzi, and others)

کرم [1] karám *m. Arabic* 1 kindness, goodness, mercy, generosity, magnanimity پر چا کرم کول to pity someone, have mercy on someone پر ما کرم وکه! Take pity on me! 2 *proper noun* Karam

کرم [2] karám *m.* cabbage گلدار کرم cauliflower

کروم [3] krom *m. plural* ☞ کروم

کرم [4] kirm *m.* worm

کرماچو karmāchú *m.* nut-gall, oak gall

کرمچ kirmích *m.* canvas, tarp, sailcloth, duck

کرمچي kirmichí canvas, duck

کرمز kirmíz *m.* red or crimson pigment or dye

کرم ساگ karamsā́g *m. regional* ☞ کرم

کرم علي karam'alí *m.* کرمعلي *proper noun* Karam-Ali

کرملین krimlín *m.* the Kremlin

کرمنتوب karməntób *m.* insomnia

کرمنگ kurmáng *m.* common pheasant

کرمنوالی karmənwā́laj *m.* ☞ کرمنتوب

کرموند karmúnḍ fingerless, without fingers

کرمه [1] kərmá *f.* 1 index finger 2 little finger, pinkie

کرمه [2] kuramá *f.* Kuram (a region south of Kabul)

کرن krən thin, emaciated

کرنا karnā́ *f.* karnai (a wind instrument similar to a bugle)

کرنج kərándzh *m.* adze used as a pick

کرنچکی krənchəkáj *m.* hoe, mattock

کرند kuránd *m.* emery

کرندوی [1] krandwáj *m.* colored design along the edge of a sack

کرندوی [2] karandój *m.* farmer, agriculturalist

کرندی krəndáj *m.* hoe with a sharp end (for digging carrots, etc.)

کرنډ krənḍ *m.* dried crust, scab (on a wound) کرنډ کېدل *compound verb* to skin over, dry up, be covered with a crust

کرنډۍ karanḏə́j *f.* **1** small shovel, trowel **2** mason's trowel **3** scoop

کرنک karánk¹ *m.* **1** crown of the head **2** part, parting (of the hair on the head)

کرنک karánk² *f.* کرنکه karánka trachea, windpipe

کرنگ karáng¹ **1** blood-stained, bloody **2** frozen; numb from cold

کرنگ karáng² *m.* sowing, planting

کرنگ kuráng³ brown (of the color of a horse)

کرنگول karangawə́l *denominative, transitive* [*past:* کرنگ یې کړ] **1** to stain with blood **2** to cool, chill, freeze

کرنگه karánga *f.* Adam's apple

کرنگېدل karangedə́l *denominative, intransitive* [*past:* کرنگ شو] **1** to be bloodstained **2** to be covered with ice

کرنه karə́na *f.* ☞ کرهنه

کرنېل karnél *m. colloquial* colonel

کرنۍ karṇə́j *f.* small saucepan (for melting butter, fat)

کرو karú *m. regional* karu (a measure of land area)

کروات kurawā́t *m. plural Arabic* blood corpuscles سره کروات red corpuscles, erythrocytes

کرواره karwā́ṛa *f.* gathering up the kernels of grain (on the threshing floor after threshing) کرواړي کول *compound verb* to gather up grain

کروت kurút¹ *m. plural* ☞ قروت

کروت krawt² *m.* **1** envy **2** spite, malice

کروت غوړي kurutghwaṛí *m. plural* dish prepared from dried curd

کروتی krawtáj envious

کروخکی karótskaj *m.* roots of the barberry (used as a medicine)

کرور krór¹, karór *m.* ten million, one-hundred lak دری کروره thirty million

کرور krur² **1** iron **2** strong, firm, hard

کرورول kruṛawə́l *denominative, transitive* [*past:* کرور یې کړ] to make hard, strengthen

کروړه karoṛá¹ *f.* **1** whip, knout with a long handle په کروړو وهل *compound verb* to whip, lash **2** blow of a whip کروړي خوړل *compound verb* to be subjected to a whipping **3** *figurative* push, motivation, incentive, urging پری کروړه شوه that prompted him (to do something) کروړي وهل *compound verb* **a** to lash, switch **b** *figurative* to urge on, make hurry, to hurry someone

کروړه karwáṛa, karúṛa² *f.* blackberries

کروړېدل kruṛedə́l *denominative, intransitive* [*past:* کرور شو] to become hard, become strong

کروزر kruzár *m. military* cruiser

کروسن krawsə́n کر وسند krawsónd, krosónd easily split, easily broken up, brittle, fragile, inflexible, stiff

کروسه karawsá *f.* ☞ کرفس

کروسېد kruséd *m. history* crusade

کروکور karukór deaf and blind

کروکي krokí *f.* kroki, itinerary map, simple sketch of a locality

کرول karawúl ☞ کرول

کروم krom *m. plural* **1** chromium, chrome **2** chrome leather (a grade of leather)

کرومایټ kromā́jt *m.* کرومیت kromít, kromájt chromium ore, chromites

کرون kron *m.* crown, krona (monetary unit)

د کروندې karwandá, karaundá *f.* **1** cultivated land, arable land ور مځکي agricultural land **2** virgin soil **3** agriculture, working the land, plowing **4** plantation د چایو کرونده tea plantation شنه کرونده *idiom* sky, the heavens, firmament

کرونده گر karwandagár *m.* ☞ کرونکی 2

کرونکی karúnkaj **1** *present participle of* کول³ **2** *m.* farmer, agriculturalist, plowman, tiller of the soil

کروه kurúh *m.* کروه kroh *f.* kuruh (about three kilometers) څلوېښت کروه forty kuruh د یوې کروه په مسافه کي within a kuruh

کروي kurawí¹ *Arabic* **1** spherical کروي شی sphere ځمکه کروي ده The Earth is round. **2** round, rounded, roundish

کروی karwáj² *m.* field guard

کروی kərwáj³ awfully much, horribly much

کروي الشکل kurawi-ush-shákl spherical

کروېږه karwéga empty; stupid

کره kará¹ *f.* spade, shovel

کره kurrá² *f. Arabic* sphere د مځکي کره, مځکنی کره, د دنیا کره the globe نیمه کره hemisphere شمالي کره the northern hemisphere کرهٔ نسیمي *idiom* the atmosphere kurrá-yi... the globe کرهٔ مجسمه

کره kára³ *f.* ☞ کرهنه

کره karrá⁴ *f. Arabic* ☞ کرت

کره kará⁵ **1** pure, uncontaminated کره کول *compound verb* to purify, get rid of foreign matter کره کېدل *compound verb* to be pure, be free of impurities **2** selected, choice, picked **3** frank, sincere **4** correct, true, accurate, exact, reliable, trustworthy

کره kará⁶ *oblique singular of* کور¹ زمور کره to us, to our house, to our place; at our house, at our place

کرهاً kárhán *Arabic* unwillingly; against one's will

کرهار kərahā́r *m.* **1** squeak, creak **2** chirping (of the magpie)

کره پندی krapandáj *m.* ☞ کرپندی

کره توب karatób *m.* **1** purity **2** frankness, sincerity **3** correctness, accuracy, reliability, trustworthiness

کرهډ karháḏ¹ blooming, flowering, turning green

کرهډ kurháḏ² *m. plural* fat hen, lamb's quarters, *Chenopodium album*

کره کتنه karakatə́na *f.* criticism, critical attitude

کرهنه karhə́na *f.* **1** sowing, planting; crops للمي کرهني dry-farming crops آوي کرهني irrigated crops **2** agriculture د کرهني مستقل ریاست the main thrust of agriculture د کرهني لیسه agricultural school د کرهني متخصص agronomist

کرهنی karhəṇáj *m.* ☞ کرگر

کره والا karawālá *m.* navy, ditch-digger, excavator

کره توب کره والي karawālí *f.* ☞

کرهه [1] kráha *f.* aversion, disgust, antipathy, loathing کرهه کول *compound verb* to have an aversion (to), loathe

کراهه [2] kirahá *f.* ☞ کراهه

کرهي kirahí hired

کرهېر karhér *m.* ☞ کار

کره یز kurajíz, kurrajíz global کره یز تغوندی global missile

کری [1] karáj *f. colloquial regional* ☞ کراهه

کری [2] karə́j کری karə́j all, entire, whole کری کال all year کری روغ all day کری شپه all night long کری میاشت the whole month

کری [3] karáj *m. regional* ☞ کوری [2]

کری [4] karə́j *f.* 1 eye, ring, annulet; link (of a chain) 2 muzzle (e.g., a dog) 3 bridle 4 beam, girder; log 5 *biology* joint, segment 6 mountain range

کری [5] karə́j *f.* silt (carried in by a mud flow) that has dried out and cracked

کری [6] kuré get away (the cry people use to chase away a dog) کری شه! Get away!

کریاب karjáb 1 neglected, derelict, unused کریابه میره waste land 2 detained, delayed, stopped 3 needy, indigent, poor 4 having gotten into a difficult situation; helpless 5 not having work, unemployed 6 *regional* listless, slack; negligent

کریابول karjābawə́l *denominative, transitive* [*past:* کړ یې کریاب] 1 to neglect, fail to use 2 to detain, delay, stop; obstruct 3 to make needy 4 to put in a difficult situation 5 to leave without work

کریابي karjābí *f.* 1 neglect, disuse 2 obstruction, obstacle; jam 3 need; poverty 4 helplessness 5 being out of work, the absence of work

کریابدل karjābedə́l *denominative, intransitive* [*past:* شو کریاب] 1 to be neglected, be unused 2 to be detained, be delayed; be held up 3 to be in need; live in poverty; be poor, be indigent 4 to be helpless 5 to not have work, remain without work, to be unemployed

کریات kurijə́t *m. plural Arabic of* کریه [2]

کرېب kreb *m.* stirrup

کرېپ krep *m.* crepe (a fabric)

کرېت [1] krit *m.* کرېټ kreṭ *f.* Crete

کرېت [2] kret *m.* basket, crate (for transporting fruit)

کرېچ krich, kirích *m.* saber

کرېچی krichə́j *m.* gnashing of teeth

کرېغ karídz *m.* farmer

کرېدت kredít *m.* credit د کرېدت په حیث on credit کرېدت پرانستل *compound verb* to open a line of credit کرېدت ورکول *compound verb* to extend credit کرېدت کول *compound verb* to give credit

کرېدتي kredití credit کرېدتي قرارداد agreement on extending credit کرېدتي مرسته کول to give credit

کرېدي kredí *f.* ☞ کرېدت

کرېر karér *m.* crushed stone, gravel, road metal

کرېړه kréṛa, kiriṛá *f.* weeds (gathered from a plowed field)

کرېړی [1] kiriṛáj *m.* Salvadora, *Salvadora persica*

کرېړی [2] kəreṛáj *m.* 1 mole cricket 2 woodcock, *Scolopax rusticola*

کرېړی [3] kreṛáj *m.* heavy molasses, thick syrup (from sugar-cane)

کرېز [1] kurajíz, kurrajíz ☞ کره یز

کرېز [2] kuréz, kuríz *m.* molt, molting, shedding of feathers کرېز کول *compound verb* to molt

کرېټ kreṭ *m. medicine* scab

کرېغه kríga *f.* ☞ کرېږه

کرېستل kristál *m.* crystal

کرېستلي kristalí crystal, crystalline, crystallized

کرېش kuréjsh *m. plural* ☞ قرېش

کرېږه krígha *f.* yell, howl, scream, cry, shout کرېږه کول *compound verb* to yell, howl, scream, cry out, shout

کرېکاښ krekákh, karekákh *m.* ☞ کراکښ

کرېکه kríka *f.* ☞ کرېږه

کرېکی karikə́j *f.* woven bin (for storing grain), crib

کرېله karelá *f.* bitter melonn, *Momordica charantia*

کرېلی kureláj *m.* padded jacket, quilted jacket, sleeveless jacket

کرېلیا karelijá *f.* Karelia

کرېم [1] karím *Arabic* 1.1 generous, magnanimous, gracious, kind; merciful, charitable 1.2 generous, liberal, open-handed 2 *m. proper noun* Karim, Kerim, Kareem

کرېم [2] krem *m. plural* crèam د غابنو کریم tooth-paste

کرېم الطبع karimattáb' noble, fine, generous, magnanimous

کرېملین kremlín *m.* the Kremlin

کرېمن kremə́n damp, humid, moist

کرېمنولوژي kriminolozhí *f.* criminal law

کرېمیا krimijá *f.* Crimea

کرېه [1] karjá *f.* 1 order; instructions 2 stern reprimand کریه کول *compound verb* to give instructions; give a stern reprimand

کرېه [2] kurijá *f. Arabic* [*plural:* کریې kurijé and *m. plural: Arabic* کریات kurijə́t] 1 small ball, globule, spherule, bead 2 *anatomy* blood corpuscle

کرېه [3] karíh 1 repulsive, disgusting, base, vile, loathsome, revolting 2 dirty, slovenly

کرېهه karehá *f.* ☞ کراهه

کړ [1] kaṛ *m.* 1 torture, torment; trouble, fuss 2 in lieu of; shortcoming 3 disease

کړ [2] kəṛ, kuṛ *m.* 1 laughter 2 cracking, crackle, crash, knocking, tapping 3 cackle, cackling 4 babbling (baby's, infant's) 5 sputtering, gurgling

کړ [3] kaṛ *m.* 1 residues of chopped straw, chaff, husks 2 starch

کړ [4] kəṛ *past tense of* کړل

کړا kṛā *f.* tcry of the partridge

کړاپ kaṛáp *m.* old and scraggly ox

کړاپی kṛápaj *m.* short distance

کړاڅی kṛátsaj *m.* boy, lad, adolescent

کړاسکه kṛáska lanky, gangling (of a young man)

کراسو kaṛāsú 1 wrinkled, having got wrinkled کراسو مخ يي دئ His whole face was all wrinkled. 2 reduced to ashes, reduced to dust

کراغ [1] kuṛấgh *m. veterinary medicine* hoof-and-mouth disease

کراغ [2] kṛấgh weak, feeble

کراغ [3] kṛấgh, kuṛấgh *m.* raven

کراغ [4] kṛū́gh *regional* protruding, bulging (of eyes) کراغ کراغ bulging (of eyes)

کراغتيا kṛāghtjấ *f.* ☞ کراغندتوب

کراغند kṛāghə́nd exhausted, worn out, haggard

کراغندتوب kṛāghəndtób *m.* کراغندوالی kṛāghəndwấlaj *m.* weakness, feebleness

کراغندول kṛāghəndawə́l *denominative, transitive* [*past:* کراغند يي کړ] to make weak, make feeble, cause to become weak, cause to become feeble; weaken; exhaust, wear out

کراغندبدل kṛāghəndedə́l *denominative, intransitive* [*past:* کراغندشو] to be weak, be feeble; to grow weak; become exhausted, get worn out

کراک kṛāk *m.* 1 pea; spherule the size of a pea 2 pebble placed in a mortar for grinding spices, etc.

کراو kaṛā́n *m. regional* ☞ کراو

کراند kaṛā́nd 1 bewildered, having lost one's head 2 upset, chagrined, distressed

کرانگی kṛā́ngaj squint-eyed, cross-eyed

کراو [1] kaṛā́w *m.* 1 grief, distress, affliction, unpleasantness چا ته کراو ورپبنول to cause someone grief, cause annoyance, cause unpleasantness 2 torture, torment په کراو اخته کول to torture, torment په يو کراو کښي کبدل، په يو کراو کښي اخته کبدل to worry, torment oneself 3 care, concern, trouble د کور او اولاد کراو concern about the family د کراوه ډک ژوندون a life full of troubles

کراو [2] kṛāw *m.* exercise; training

کراوو kaṛāwú industrious, diligent, assiduous, painstaking

کراوه kaṛāwá *f.* ☞ کناوه

کراوي [1] kaṛāwí ☞ کراوو

کراوي [2] kaṛāwé *plural of* کراوه

کرای kṛāj *conditional and potential of* کړل

کرايي kaṛājí *m.* frying pan

کربو kaṛbú *m.* vicious dog

کربه kaṛə́ba *f.* cornstalk

کربزن kaṛbezə́n ☞ کمبزن

کربزي kaṛbézi *f. plural* snot, mucus ☞ کمبزي

کربیکه kaṛbíka *f.* plow handle

کرپ kṛap *m.* 1 crash, crack (noise); knock, tap (noise) 2 squeak, creak (of boots, shoes); flap, flapping sound (of slippers) کرپ او کروپ a crackle, crackling; tapping (e.g., with a cane) b squeaking, crunching (of boots, shoes)

کرپا kṛapấ *f.* کرپار kṛapấr *m. regional* ☞ کرپهار

کرپر kəṛpə́r *m.* incoherent speech

کرپند kṛapə́nd garrulous and malicious (of a person)

کرپندوکی kṛapandúkaj *m.* 1 cartilage, gristle 2 chatterbox, windbag

کرپنده kṛapə́nda *f.* difficult road, rocky road

کرپوز kaṛpúz *m.* camel's bridle

کرپول kṛapawə́l *transitive* [*past:* و يي کړاوه] 1 ☞ کروپول 2 to gnaw (a bone)

کرپه kṛapá *f.* slippery road, rough road

کرپهار kṛapahár *m.* 1 tramping, stamping (of feet) 2 squeak (of boots, shoes); flapping (of slippers) 3 crackle, crackling; tapping 4 booming sound 5 champing

کرپی [1] kṛapáj *m.* 1 ☞ کرپهار 2 scratching 3 rustling 4 idle talk, jabbering

کرپی [2] kṛapə́j *f.* ☞ کرپنده

کرپبدل kṛapedə́l *intransitive* [*past:* و کرپیده] 1 to crack, make a cracking noise, knock, tap له سړو ښخه يي زامي سره کرپیدي His teeth were chattering from the cold. 2 to squeak, scratch, make squeaking sounds (of a pen, boots, shoes) 3 to flap, flip-flop, make a flapping sound (of slippers) 4 to chatter on, jabber incessantly

کرت [1] kuṛə́t *m.* ☞ کرتهار

کرت [2] kṛət *m.* 1 word; statement کرت کول *compound verb* a to say, speak b to promise 2 sound

کرتکی kaṛtə́ki *f. plural* kind of sandal

کرتن kṛətə́n کرتو kṛətú 1 *m.* windbag, chatterbox 2 garrulous, talkative

کرته kṛəta *f.* empty words, chatter, twaddle کرتي کول *compound verb* to engage in idle talk, prate, chatter, babble

کرتهار kṛətahár *m.* cackle, cackling کرتهار کول *compound verb* to cackle کرتبدل *intransitive* [*past:* و کرتبد] to engage in idle talk, prate, babble

کرتو kṛətú wrinkled; crumpled, rumpled

کرته [1] kṛə́ta *f.* 1 ☞ چتي کرتي کول کرته *compound verb* to talk nonsense 2 wrinkle; fold, crease

کرتي [1] kṛə́ti *plural of* کرته

کرتی [2] kṛə́taj *m.* fold, crease; wrinkle کرتی کول *compound verb* to wrinkle, crumple کرتی کبدل *compound verb* to wrinkle, break into wrinkles, knit one's brow; be crumpled

کرچ [1] kṛəch *m.* ☞ کرسهار

کرچ [2] kṛəch *m.* squeal, screech کرچ کرچ کول *compound verb* to whine, yelp (of a whipped dog); yelp, yap

کرچا kṛachấ *f.* کرچار kṛachár *m.* ☞ کرسهار

کرچول kṛəchawə́l *transitive* [*past:* و يي کرچاوه] 1 to chew 2 to grind the teeth, grit the teeth, gnash the teeth

کرچهار kṛəchahár *m.* ☞ کرسهار

کرچبدل kṛəchedə́l *intransitive* ☞ کرسبدل

کرڅ kṛədz *m.* kiln

کرڅو kaṛtsú *m.* saucepan (for melting butter, etc.)

کرخه kaṛə́kha *f.* uneven land, rough terrain (at the foothills of a mountain, hill)

کردار kiṛdár *m.* ☞ کردار

کرده kaṛdá *f.* action, deed, act

کرړی kiṛṛáj *m.* ☞ کرپری [1]

کرز kṛaz skinny, scraggy, starved (of an animal)

کرس kṛas [1] *m.* ☞ کرسهار او کروس کرسهار **a** crackling, chirping **b** noise, din, racket کرس او کروس کول to beat somebody unmercifully

کرس kṛəs [2] barren (of a steppe)

کرسا kṛasā́ *m. & f.* ☞ کرسهار

کرساو kṛasā́w **1** bearded **2** long-faced, having a long face **3** ugly (of a person)

کرسند kṛasə́nd ☞ کروسن

کرسو kəṛ sú *past tense of* کربدل

کرسول kṛasawə́l *transitive* [*past:* و یې کرساوه] **1** to cause to crack, cause to make a noise **2** to cause crackling, cause a noise **3** to raise a rumpus, cause an uproar **4** to beat, strike

کرسهار kṛasəhár *m.* **1** crackle, crackling; knocking, noise; crackling, chirping سیلی سوه، د ونو څانگي ما تبدلي، کرسهار يې خوت A storm came up, the sound of breaking branches was heard. **2** to grit, grind (the teeth) **3** noise, din hubbub **4** quarrel; arguing, wrangling, altercation کرسهار کول *compound verb* **a** to crackle, crack; knock, make a noise **b** to grit, grind (the teeth) **c** to raise a rumpus, make noise, create a hubbub **d** to quarrel, argue, wrangle

کرسبدل kṛasedə́l *intransitive* [*past:* و کرسبده] **1** to crackle, knock **2** to grit, grind (the teeth) **3** to be raised (of noise, a hubbub, etc.) **4** to quarrel, argue

کرشب kaṛshə́b *m.* ravine, hollow between two hills

کرشوپ kaṛshúp, kaṛshə́p **1** *m.* toothless old man **2** toothless کرشپه خوله hollow mouth

کرشپ توب kaṛshuptób, kaṛshəptób *m.* extreme old age, venerable age

کرشوپی kaṛshúpaj, kaṛshə́paj *m.* ☞ کرشپ

کرشوپ kaṛshúp *m.* ☞ کرشپ

کرشوپ توب kaṛshuptób *m.* ☞ کرشپ توب

کرغ kṛəgh numb, benumbed

کرغبچ karghéch **1** bewildered, perplexed, agitated **2** faded, withered **3** numb, benumbed کرغبچ کبدل *compound verb* **a** to be bewildered, be perplexed **b** to wither, fade **c** to lose feeling, grow numb

کرک kṛək [1] *m.* **1** reed **2** *figurative* puny man, weakling

کرک kṛak [2] *m.* **1** large wicker bin (for storing grain), corn-crib **2** bast fibers

کرک kṛak [3] *interjection* boom, bang

کرکاچ kaṛkách *m.* stubbornness, obstinacy

کرکاچي kaṛkāchí stubborn, obstinate

کرکچو kaṛkicháw *m.* noise, hubbub, racket

کرکر kuṛkúṛ *m.* **1** babble, murmur (of a brook) **2** cackle, کرکر کول *compound verb* **a** to babble, murmur **b** to cackle کرکر وهل

کرکری kəṛkəṛáj [1] *m.* **1** water-lifting wheel **2** pulley block of a ferry

کرکری kuṛkuṛə́j [2] *f.* collared turtle-dove کرکری کوتره، کرکری کونتره collared turtle-dove

کرکوالی kṛukwā́laj *m.* cessation of egg-laying (in hens)

کرکومه kaṛkúma *f.* **1** stone trap, pitfall **2** chicken coop, hen-house; storeroom

کرکه kuṛə́ka, kúṛka *f.* brood hen, sitting hen ☞ کرکه کبدل [1]

کرکه kṛə́ka *f.* ☞ کرکه [2]

کرکی kaṛkáj, kaṛəkáj *m.* reed, cane (used to make pens and hookah pipes) [1]

کرکی kəṛəkə́j *f.* **1** window د جهاز کرکی sky-light, porthole **2** store window, showcase; stand **3** *anatomy* mistral valve [2]

کرکی kaṛakə́j *f.* wide dress with gathers (woman's) [3]

کرکی kəṛəkə́j *f.* hatchet (for chopping brush) [4]

کرکبچ kaṛkéch *m.* **1** altercation, wrangling, squabbling; petty intrigues **2** complication, misunderstanding کرکبچونه لیری کول to eliminate misunderstandings

کرکبچن kaṛkechə́n **1** not in order, unorganized, haphazard **2** spoiled; ruined **3** repulsive, disgusting کرکبچن بوی stench **4** tangled, complex کر کبچنه مسئله intricate question, complex issue **5** tongue-tied, inarticulate کرکبچن کول *compound verb* **a** to cause to be unorganized **b** to spoil, ruin **c** to make repulsive, make disgusting **d** to confuse, complicate کرکبچن کبدل *compound verb* **a** to be in disarray, to be unorganized **b** to spoil, be spoiled, be ruined کار مي گرده خراب او کرکبچن سو My business is totally ruined. **c** to be repulsive, be disgusting **d** to become entangled, become complicated

کرکبچو kəṛkechó **1** *f.* **.1** babbling (of a baby) **1.2** butchering a foreign language **1.3** tongue-tied, inarticulate کرکبچو کرکبچو ویل *compound verb* **a** to babble **b** to butcher a foreign language **c** to be(come) tongue-tied **2** ☞ کرکبچن

کرکبچ والی kaṛkechwā́laj *m.* confusion, complication (e.g., of a question or issue)

کرکبدل kuṛəkedə́l *denominative, intransitive* [*past:* کر که شوه] **1** to hatch (baby chicks) **2** to be a brood hen, be a sitting hen, rear chicks

کرکیمه kaṛkimá *f.* cage (for birds and animals)

کرکین kaṛkín cotton

کرکی ورکی kaṛəkaj-wṛəkaj upset, anxious, worried, troubled

کرل kṛəl *transitive prefective aspect of the verb* کول [7] [*present:* اکري] **1** *independent verb* [*past:* اوکړ] **.1** to accomplish, perform something; execute, carry out (a job) ما کار و کړ I did some work. هغه ښه چه ما کولی Ahmed had a good night's sleep احمد و کړل I did everything I could **1.2** to speak, say کړل چه... Ahmed said... **2** *forming verbs consisting of complex and denominative verbs* کړ ☞ کول [7] [2]

کرلاني kaṛlā́ni *m. plural* ☞ کرلاني

کرلو kṛə́lu *past tense first person plural of* کړل [1]

کرلو kṛə́lo *Eastern past tense of* کړل *in lieu of* کړ [4] [2]

کرله kṛə́la *past tense feminine of* کړل [1]

کرله kṛə́la *Western past tense plural of* کړل [2]

کرلئ kṛə́laj *past participle of* کړل *in lieu of* کړئ

کُرَم ¹ kuṛám *m.* pond; lake

کُرَم ² kaṛə́m, kəṛə́m **1** to cut off, chop off; to cut in two **2** wounded **3** badly beaten **4** disfigured, maimed کُرم کُرم disfigured **5** upset, distressed زړه مي کُرم دئ My heart bleeds. **6** bitten, stung (e.g., by a scorpion)

کُرَم ³ kṛəm *present and past tenses first person of* کول ⁷

کُرَمتوب kaṛamtób *m.* **1** trouble, grief, sorrow, woe **2** bite, sting (of a scorpion, etc.) **3** torment, agony

کُرمچه kaṛmácha *f.* little finger, pinkie

کُرمڅى kəṛamtsáj *m.* strap running across the haunches and under the tail, breeching (part of a harness)

کُرمَم karamə́m grief-stricken; pained, distressed; sad, mournful

کُرمنتوب kaṛamantób *m.* کُرمنوالى kaṛamanwálaj *m.* trouble; shock; grief

کُرمنول kaṛamanawə́l *denominative, transitive* [*past:* کُرمن یې کړ] to upset, distress

کُرمنېدل kaṛamanedə́l *denominative, intransitive* [*past:* کُرمن شو] to become upset, be distressed

کُرموالى kaṛamwálaj *m.* ☞ کُرمتوب

کُرمول kaṛamawə́l *denominative, transitive* [*past:* کُرم یې کړ] **1** to cut off, chop off; cut in two **2** to wound **3** to beat mercilessly **4** to disfigure, maim, mutilate **5** to bite, sting (of scorpions, etc.) **6** to upset, distress **7** to come out against someone; interfere, hinder

کُرمه ¹ káṛma *f.* married woman

کُرمه ² kaṛə́ma *feminine singular of* کُرم ²

کُرميازه kaṛmjáza *f.* saliva, slobber (of an animal)

کُرمېدل kaṛamedə́l *denominative, intransitive* [*past:* کُرم شو] **1** to be cut off, be chopped off; be cut in two **2** to be wounded **3** to be badly beaten **4** to be disfigured, be maimed **5** to be distressed, become upset **6** to be bitten, be stung (as by a scorpion, etc.)

کُرمېزن kaṛmezə́n **1** snotty, slobbery **2** *m.* sniveler; slobberer

کُرمېزي kaṛmézi *m. plural* **1** mucus, snot **2** saliva, slobber

کُرن kṛan *m.* **1** action **2** endeavor, labor **3** practice, exercise **4** conduct, behavior

کُرنج kṛandzh *m.* kuṛə́ndzh **1** sobbing (of a child) **2** yelping, squealing (of a dog) کُرنج کول *compound verb* to whine, whimper

کُرنجا kṛandzhá *f.* کُرنجهار kṛandzhahár, kuṛandzhəhár *m.* **1** squeal, cry **2** yelp, squeal (of a dog)

کُرنچ kṛunch *m.* ☞ کُرنج

کُرنچهار kṛunchahár *m.* ☞ کُرنجا

کُرنچى kṛuncháj *m.* ☞ کُرنج

کُرند ¹ kṛənd energetic, efficient, business-like

کُرند ² kəṛə́nd **1** disarranged, disordered; unorganized **2** unsteady, shaky, unstable **3** lax, loose **4** to be in the scabbard (of a saber, a dagger)

کُرندتوب kəṛəndtób *m.* کُرندوالى kəṛəndwálaj *m.* **1** disorder; lack of coordination, lack of organization **2** unsteadiness, instability **3** slackness, laxity

کُرندول kəṛəndawə́l *denominative, transitive* [*past:* کُرند یې کړ] **1** to put into disorder, disrupt, disorganize **2** to loosen, shake loose, make unstable **3** to slacken, make slack, work loose

کُرنده kaṛindá *f.* mucus (secretion)

کُرندېدل kəṛəndedə́l *denominative, intransitive* [*past:* کُرند شو] **1** to be put into disorder, be disrupted, become disorganized **2** to get loose, be unstable **3** to be slack, work loose **4** to hang in the scabbard (of a saber, dagger)

کُرنگ ¹ kṛəng *m.* stick that is fastened to the neck of livestock to prevent them from running

کُرنگ ² kṛang **1** *m.* knocking, ringing کُرنگ او کُرونگ **a** knocking, clanging, clatter (of dishes) **b** noise, din **2** hard, crackling کُرنگه ژمى hard frost کُرنگه خله the coldest winter period

کُرنگ ³ kṛang *m.* ☞ کُرن

کُرنگ ⁴ kṛing ☞ کُرینگ

کُرنگا kṛangá *f.* ☞ کُرنگهار

کُرنگار kṛangár *m.* echo

کُرنگوالى kṛingwálaj *m.* ☞ کُرینگوالى

کُرنگول ¹ kṛangawə́l *denominative, transitive* [*past:* کُرنگ یې کړ] to ring; make crack, make creak

کُرینگول ² kṛingawə́l *transitive* ☞ کُرنگول

کُرنگه ² kṛánga *feminine singular of* کُرنگ ²

کُرنگهار kṛangahár *m.* knocking; jingling (of bells); clinking, clattering (of dishes)

کُرینگ ¹ kṛingáj ☞ کُرنگ

کُرنگى ² kṛangáj *m.* ☞ کُرنگهار

کُرنگېدل ¹ kṛangedə́l *denominative, intransitive* [*past:* کُرنگ شو] to jingle, clatter; crackle

کُرینگېدل ² kṛingedə́l *intransitive* ☞ کُرنگېدل

کُرنلاره kṛanlára *f.* کُرنلار kṛanlár plan; program

کُرنه kṛə́na *f.* کُرن

کُرو ¹ kṛu *present tense first person plural of* کول

کُرو ² kṛo *Eastern past tense of* کول *in lieu of* کَړ ⁴

کُرو ³ kṛo *oblique of* کُره ¹

کُرو ⁴ kaṛú *m.* soup with buttermilk and butter

کارساو kaṛwás **1** ☞ کُرساو **2** *dialect* ☞ کُرساو

کُروب kṛob *m.* کُروبى kṛóbaj left-over soup

کُروبى ¹ kṛóbaj *m.* کُروب kṛób left-over soup

کُروبى ² kṛobáj *m.* hollow, basin

کُروپ kṛup **1** convex; protruding, jutting out; bulging out **2** crooked, bent, hunched **3** having a dent, dented; having a hollow, having a cavity

کُروپوالى kṛupwálaj **1** کُروپ والى kṛuptjá کُروپ تیا kṛuptób *m.* protuberance **2** hump **3** dent, hollow

کُروپول kṛupawə́l *denominative, transitive* [*past:* کُروپ یې کړ] **1** to make convex; bulge **2** to hunch one's back **3** to make a dent; form a depression سرک کُروپول *compound verb* to grade a road

کروپېدل kr̥upedə́l *denominative, intransitive* [*past:* کروپ شو] **1** to be convex, protrude, bulge **2** to become stooped **3** to have a dent; have a depression

کروس kr̥us *m.* noise of a falling tree

کروستي kr̥ostí *m. plural* roasted grain

کروسند kr̥awsónd ☞ کروسن

کروسی kar̥wasáj *m.* [*plural:* کروسي kar̥wasí *and* کروسیان kar̥wāsijā́n] great-grandson

کروسی kar̥wasə́j *f.* [*plural:* کروسي kar̥wasə́j *and* کرواسیاني kar̥wāsijā́ni] great-granddaughter

کرول kar̥awə́l *transitive* [*past:* کراوه یې و] **1** to roast (on a fire) **2** to warm, heat **3** *figurative* to trouble, worry; torment; annoy خان کرول *compound verb* **a** to warm oneself په اور کښي خان کرول to be warmed, be heated **b** *figurative* to be worried, be tormented

کرولی kar̥awólaj *past participle of* خوان کرول کرولی a strong and handsome lad, a fine fellow

کرومبه kr̥ombá *f.* **1** thin varenets (milk baked in an oven and allowed to ferment) **2** whey **3** swill, thin soup

کرومبی kar̥ombáj *m.* bast basket

کرون kr̥un *m.* ☞ کرن

کرونکی krúnkaj *present participle of* کول *in lieu of* کوونکی

کرونگه kar̥ongá *f.* lean and meatless soup, soup without fat or meat

کرونگه kar̥únga *m.* کرونگی karúngaj *m.* waterfall

کرونگی kar̥úngaj *m.* earthenware pot, bowl

کرونه kar̥awóna *f.* **1** roasting (on a fire) **2** warming, heating **3** *figurative* anxiety

کروه kar̥wá *f.* **1** *history* stuffed ox or buffalo used by warriors in the front as a shield **2** piece, chunk په کروه in pieces

کروهول kr̥ohawə́l *transitive* ☞ گروهول

کروهېدل kr̥ohedə́l *intransitive* ☞ گروهېدل

کرومبزن kar̥wezə́n ☞ کرمبزن

کره kr̥ə *m. plural* **1** deed, act, something accomplished دا د کرو ده خپل کره یې وکره He did what he wanted. چاره نه ده this is impossible کره د خدای دي Everything is in God's hands **2** labor

کره kar̥á *f.* **1** ring, circle **2** bracelet (gold, silver)

کره kr̥a **1** *past tense feminine of* کول **2** *imperative perfective of* کول خدای مه کره! God forbid!

کره kə́ra *f.* ☞ کړی

کرهار kər̥ahár, kur̥ahár *m.* **1** knocking, crack, cracking (noise) **2** noise, din (raised by children) **3** cackle, cackling کرهار کول *compound verb* **a** to make a knocking noise; crackle, creak **b** to make noise (of children) **c** to cackle

کرهاند kər̥ahánd upset, disturbed; confused, perplexed, embarrassed

کروړه krə́wr̥ə *m. plural and feminine singular* **1** form; appearance, look, aspect, shape; facial features **2** outward appearance, looks, exterior کوتره په کره کره ډېره برابره ده He is handsome. کره وره یې ښه ده Kawtara was pretty **3** deed, act, action **4** duty, obligation

کرهای kar̥ahā́j *m.* pot, kettle; shallow iron saucepan

کرهی kur̥há *m.* kurhai (a unit of measure equal to one-fourth of اوړی or oka)

کړی kə́r̥aj *past participle of* کول

کړئ kr̥əj *present tense second person plural of* کول

کړي karí *f.* warmed airan with spices

کړي kri *present tense of* کول

کړی kur̥áj *m.* ☞ کوړی

کړی kr̥aj *Eastern conditional and potential forms of* کول دا کار ده ونشو کړی He couldn't do that.

کړی kar̥áj *f.* **1** loop; ring; ringlet; hoop د ماکو کړی oarlock **2** lasso **3** skein, hank **4** *zoology* segment, joint **5** link (of a chain) **6** stanza د پښو کړی کېدل to hamper, impede, restrict someone د اسارت یې کړی ماتول His hair was curled وپښتان یې کړی کړی شول to break the chains of slavery

کړی kar̥ə́j *f.* beam, girder, joist

کړی kur̥ə́j *f.* ☞ کوړی

کړی kə́r̥e *interjection* shoo, scat (cry used to chase away chickens, etc.) کړی کول *compound verb* to chase out, shoo away

کړی kr̥e *present tense second person of* کول

کړیت kr̥it *m.* ☞ کرت

کړیچی kr̥echə́j *f. dialect* ☞ کړپخی

کړیخ kr̥ets *m.* liver fluke (a parasitic worm)

کړیخن kr̥etsə́n having liver fluke (of livestock and humans)

کړیخی kar̥etsáj *m.* fluke (in sheep)

کړیخی kar̥etsə́j *f.* **1** spoon; ladle **2** saucepan (for melting butter)

کړیدل kar̥edə́l *intransitive* [*past:* و کړیده] **1** to be grilled, be roasted (on a fire) **2** to be warmed, warm oneself لمر ته ښنه و کړیدم I warmed myself in the sun **3** to worry; torment oneself **4** to be burned down, to perish

کړیدل kər̥edə́l *intransitive* [*past:* و کړیده] **1** to cackle **2** to move noisily, to rattle

کړیدن kar̥edə́n *m.* کړیدنه kar̥edə́na *f.* **1** grilling, roasting (on a fire) **2** worry; torture, torment **3** atrophy

کړیدنه kar̥edə́na *f.* **1** grilling, roasting (on a fire) **2** worry; torture, torment **3** atrophy

کړیدنه kar̥edə́na *f.* **1** cackle, cackling **2** rattling

کړیدون kar̥edún *m.* ☞ کړیدن

کړیده kə́r̥eda *perfect of* کول *in lieu of* کړی ده

کړیدئ kə́r̥ajdəj *perfect of* کول *in lieu of* کړی دئ

کړیر kr̥er̥ *m.* pod

کړیزن kr̥ezə́n sick, diseased (of livestock)

کړیس kr̥es *m.* pod

کړیسکی kr̥éskaj *m.* ☞ کړیخ

کریغ krigh emaciated, fatigued, exhausted, grown weak

کریغه kr̥ígha *f.* کریکه kr̥íka *f.* noise; howl, cry

کړینگ kr̥ing **1** curved, bent; sinuous, twisting, winding **2** oblique, slanting **3** humpbacked, hunchbacked **4** disfigured, mutilated, maimed, crippled

کرینگ پرینگ kṛing-pṛing bent, curved; sinuous, twisting, winding

کرینگ والی kṛingwálaj m. 1 curvature 2 obliquity, slope, slant 3 the characteristic of being hunchbacked 4 deformity, abnormality

کرینگول kṛingawól denominative, transitive [past: کرینگ یې کړ] 1 to bend 2 to squint, look asquint 3 to hunch, arch 4 to disfigure, mutilate, maim, cripple

کرینگی kṛingáj ☞ کرینگ

کرینگبدل kṛingedól denominative, intransitive [past: کرینگ شو] 1 to be bent 2 to squint 3 to stoop, become bent (over) 4 to be disfigured, be mutilated, be maimed, be crippled

کړی وړی کاره کړی وړی kóṛe-wóṛe completed almost finished, a done deal

کزلاخ kazlákh m. ☞ جل [3]

کژ kazh [1] m. chin لاس یې په کژ وه idiom he was sitting in deep thought

کژ kazh [2] Western ☞ کوږ [2]

کوژدنه kuzhdóna f. dialect کوژدن

کږ kaǵ m. ☞ کوږ [1]

کږوالی kaǵtjã f. ☞ کوږوالی

کږدلی kaǵdaláj f. spider-web, cobweb

کږدی kigdáj, kǝgdáj f. 1 tent, marquee (made of black goat's or camel's wool) 2 bubble (on water)

کږخانگه kaǵkhánga f. stick, mallet (for playing polo, etc.)

کږکه kaǵóka f. 1 magpie 2 crashing, din, rumbling, roar

کږکی kaǵǝkáj [1] m. process on the shoulder blade of a sheep

کږ کی kaǵǝkáj [2] m. disease of soil or old rice soil

کږل kaǵól transitive [past: و یې کاږه] 1 to fear, be afraid of, consider as portending something ominous 2 to hate 3 to condemn; disparage, discredit; defame, pillory

کږلئ kaǵóləj 1 past participle of کږل 2.1 unpleasant; disagreeable, objectionable 2.2 sinister, ominous, portending evil

کږلبچ kagléch 1 m. .1 curvature 1.2 bend, crook; turn کږلبچ کول compound verb to twist, wind, meander (of a river, a road) کږلبچ ورکول compound verb to turn, make a turn 2 sinuous, twisting, winding کږلبچه لار a winding road

کږلبچی kagléchaj 1 m. .1 turn, bend, curve 1.2 reach, stretch of water 2 having a club hand, club-handed

کږندی kagandáj 1 plagued by illness 2 quarrelsome, peevish, cantankerous, shrewish

کږنه kagóna f. fear, apprehension; fear of that which according to superstition portends evil, misfortune

کږوالی kagwálaj m. curvature; sinuousness, sinuosity

کږوبج kagúbaj ill, sick, physically exhausted

کږول kaǵawól denominative, transitive [past: کوږ یې کړ] 1 to bend; twist 2 to bend, stoop, bow ځان کږول compound verb to stoop, bend (over, forward) 3 to refract (light)

کږوبلنی kagwelónaj m. ☞ کاږه وبلنی

کږه kaǵá [1] f. Kazha (populated place in Nangarhar)

کږه kaǵá [2] 1 feminine singular of کوږ [2] 2 f. in lieu of هغه په لار کږه He is walking along a poor path. کږه روان دئ

کوږوور وړه kaǵá-waǵá 1 feminine singular of کوږوور 2 f. difficulty, impediment

کږبدل kagedól denominative, intransitive [past: کوږ شو] 1 to bend, twist 2 to stoop, bend, bow د چا خوا ته ور کږبدل to bow to someone 3 to look down, drop one's eyes 4 to turn 5 to be refracted (of light) 6 figurative to lose one's way, go astray

کږبده kageḍó m. plural 1 bending, twisting 2 bowing, stooping 3 turning 4 refracting, refraction (of light)

کس kas [1] m. person, personage; man تاسي څو کسه یاست؟ How many of you are there? مونږ دري کسه یو There are three of us. انفرادي کسان escorts, accompanying persons ورسره کسان individuals

کس kas [2] m. ravine; hollow, depression

کسات kasã́t m. vengeance, revenge د چا څخه کسات ایستل، د چا څخه کسات اخیستل to take vengeance on someone

کساد kasã́d m. Arabic, کسادي kasãdí f. depression, stagnation

کسب kasb, kásǝb m. Arabic occupation, trade, craft, business کسبول کول compound verb ☞ ته څه کسب کوی؟ What do you do?

کسبت kisbã́t, kǝsbã́t m. Arabic 1 tool-box, instrument case (e.g., of a surgeon, barber) 2 bag with powder and shot (of hunter)

کسبگر kasbgár m. craftsman

کسبول kasbawól denominative, transitive [past: کسب یې کړ] to gain skills, acquire (work) habits, experience; master something

کسبه kasabá Arabic plural of کاسب

کسبي kasbí m. ☞ کسبگر

کسپین káspiján Caspian د کسپین بحیره Caspian Sea

کسات kasã́t m. 1 ☞ کسات 2 spite, anger, malice 3 ☞ قصد

کستوره kasturá f. oyster

کستیج kastídzh m. cut, slit (in sharovary)

کسر kasr [1] m. Arabic [plural: کسرونه kasrúna, Arabic کسور kusúr and کسرات kusurã́t] 1 mathematics fraction عادي کسر common fraction اعشاري کسر decimal fraction د کسر صورت numerator د کسر مخرج denominator 2 lack, shortage; loss, damage 3 deficit بودجي کسر جبرانول to cover a deficit 4 decrease; loss 5 breaking 6 curtailment, reduction, diminishing کسر کول compound verb to be curtailed, be reduced, be diminished کسر کبدل compound verb to shorten 7 mathematics subtraction

کسر kásǝr [2] m. ☞ مقطع [1]

کسرمن kasrmón damaged, having a defect

کسره kasrá f. Arabic linguistics kasra (name of the diacritical mark, which designates the vowel "i" and sometimes "e")

کسری kasrí Arabic fractional کسری عددونه fractions

کسکر kaskór [1] 1 burned (down), scorched 2 stiff with cold, shriveled (from the cold) 3 destroyed 4 burning (from love) 5 tired out, physically exhausted کسکر کول compound verb ☞ کسکربدل [1]

کسکرول compound verb ☞ کسکر کبدل [1]

کسکر kasckór [2] divided into pieces or parts

کسکر ³ kaskár *m.* unclean paddy that remains in grain

کسکرول ¹ [اکسکر يې کړ :*kaskərawə́l *denominative, transitive* [*past] to burn; scorch **2** to destroy **3** to torment, harass, exhaust physically

کسکرول ² kaskərawə́l *denominative, transitive* [*past:* اکسکر يې کړ] to divide into parts, separate into pieces; crush

کسکرونه ¹ kaskərawə́na *f.* **1** burning, incinerating **2** destruction **3** physical exhaustion

کسکرونه ² kaskərawə́na *f.* division into parts or pieces; crushing

کسکرېدل ¹ kaskəredə́l *denominative, intransitive* [*past:* اکسکر شو] **1** to burn; be burned **2** to become numb, shrivel (from the cold) **3** to be destroyed **4** to burn (from love) **5** to be worn out, be physically exhausted; be tired out

کسکرېدل ² kaskəredə́l *denominative, intransitive* [*past:* اکسکر شو] to be divided or split into parts or pieces; to be crushed or pulverized

کسکرېدنه ¹ kaskəredə́na *f.* ☞ کسکرېده ¹

کسکرېدنه ² kaskəredə́na *f.* ☞ کسکرېده ²

کسکرېده ¹ kaskəredə́ *m. plural* **1** burning **2** becoming numb from the cold, shrink from cold **3** destruction, annihilation **4** burning (from love) **5** fatigue; exhaustion

کسکرېده ² kaskəredə́ *m. plural* dividing into parts, splitting into pieces

کسل ksə́l, kasə́l *transitive dialect* ☞ کتل ¹

کسوت kəswát *m.* ☞ کسبت

کسور ¹ kasúr *m.* vengeance, revenge

کسور ² kusúr *m. plural Arabic of* کسر ¹

کسورات kusurát *m. second plural of* کسر ¹

کسوری kasúraj **1** melancholy; sad, sorrowful **2** feeble; helpless, ineffectual

کسوړه kasóṛa *f.* ☞ کخوړه

کسوف kusúf *m. Arabic* solar eclipse, eclipse of the sun

کسه ¹ kisá *f.* ☞ قصه

کسه ² kisá *dialect imperfective imperative of* کسل

کسی ¹ kəsí, kisí **1** *m. plural of* کسی **2** *dialect present tense of* کسل

کسی ² kə́saj *m.* pupil (of the eye) د سترګو کسی خوړل *idiom* to go blind

کسی ³ kisə́j *f.* riddle, enigma

کسی ⁴ kasə́j *f.* ☞ کږ ¹

کسیا kasjā́ *f.* **1** dust **2** haze; fog **3** speck of dust

کسیره kasirá *f.* small coin, (small) change

کسیز kasíz **1** consisting of a certain number of persons لس کسیز a committee of ten (members) **2** intended for a certain number of persons

کش ¹ kash *m.* **1** pull, traction د هوا په کش pneumatic traction **2** tightening په کش نيول to draw a thread taut **3** drawing (when smoking) کش کېدل کشول *compound verb* ☞ کشول کش *compound verb* ☞ کشېدل **4** difficulty; worry, concern, trouble *idiom* وروی ته ډنه کش ورکول to eat with gusto کش او کړپ noise, racket

کش ² kish *m.* beech marten, stone marten, *Mustela foina*

کش ³ kəsh *intejection* kish, shoo, scat (a cry used to chase chickens away)

کش ⁴ kásh *the second part of word formations* کراکش carter, drayman, driver

کشاد kushā́d capacious, spacious, roomy, wide

کشاف kashshā́f *Arabic* **1** discovering, exploring **2** *m.* **.1** *military* scout, reconnoiterer **2.2** boy scout انجمن کشافان anjumán-i... the Boy Scout Organization in Afghanistan **2.3** discoverer

کشافي kashshāfī́ reconnaissance; prospecting, exploratory

کشال kashā́l **1** long, lengthy, extended (in time) په کشاله لهجه خبری کول to speak in a sing-song voice **2** slow, protracted; prolonged خبری يې څه قدر اوږدي او کشالي دي Their conversation went on for some time.

کشاله kashālá *f.* **1** to take out, pull out, extract; drag کشاله کول *compound verb* to carry, pull, drag **2** drawn-out argument, conflict يوه کشاله هواړول to settle an argument **3** difficulty, complication

کشايش kashājísh *m.* existence

کشب kishā́b *m.* کشپ kasháb *m.* tortoise, turtle

کش پش kəshpə́sh *m.* **1** shivering **2** tread, footsteps (sound)

کشت ¹ kasht *m.* assistant leader (in games)

کشت ² kisht *m. Eastern colloquial* payment; dues ☞ قسط

کشت ³ kisht *m.* **1** square (on a chess board) **2** *chess* check کشت ورکول to announce "check"

کشتری kashtarə́j *f.* woven basket, bast basket

کشت زار kishtzā́r *m.* planted or sown field; sowing, planting

کشتم kashtám *m. regional* customs-house

کشتوری kishtoṛə́j *f.* little ship, small craft; boat

کشته ¹ kishtá *f.* dried apricots

کشته ² kushtá *f.* corrosive sublimate; mercuric chloride

کشته ³ kushtá **1** killed **2** extinguished کشته چونه slaked lime کشته کول *compound verb* to slake (lime)

کشتی ¹ kushtí *f.* wrestling

کشتی ² kishtə́j *f.* [*plural:* کشتی kishtə́j کشتياني kishtijā́ni *and* کشتيګاني kishtijgā́ni] ship; boat بادبانی کشتی sailing vessel بخاري steamship چپه يي کشتی rowboat

کشتي راني kishtirānī́ *f.* navigation

کشتيوان kishtəjwā́n *m.* sailor, seafarer

کشر kəshr, kə́shər, kíshər junior, younger هغه ۸ کاله تر ورور کشره ده She is 8 years younger than her brother. کشران ورونه younger brothers کشران شاګردان pupils of the younger classes

کشران kəshrā́n *m. plural* [*singular* کشر] youth, young people

کشراني kishrānī́ *plural of* کشره ²

کشرتوب kəshərtób *m.* کشرتيا kəshərtjā́ *f.* condition of being younger in age, status of being junior in position

کشرنزی kəshranzí **1** *m. plural* Kishranzi (a tribe) **2** kashranzáy *m.* Kishranzai (a member of the Kishranzi tribe)

کشروالی kəshərwā́laj *m.* ☞ کشرتوب

كشروتی kəshroṭáj **1** younger, junior **2** tiny, wee

كشره kə́shra **1** *feminine singular of* كشر **2** *f.* younger daughter, younger sister

كشرى [1] kəshəráj small; younger كشرى خور younger sister

كشرى [2] kashráj *m.* **1** basket **2** kneading trough, dough trough

كشرى [3] kashṛáj *f.* ☞ كشترى

كشرين kəshrín *rare* youngest, most junior

كرشوپ kashṛúp *m.* ☞ كرشپ

كشش kashísh *m.* **1** traction, pull **2** *physics* attraction, gravitation **3** inclination, tendency

كشف kashf *m. Arabic* **1** discovery, finding, detection **2** understanding, knowledge; research, investigation, study **4** exploration, surveying; reconnaissance, intelligence نژدى كشف reconnaissance كشف كول كشفول *compound verb* ☞ كشف كېدل *compound verb* ☞ كشفېدل;

كشف الحال kashfulh ́al *m. Arabic* finding; search, investigation

كشفول kashfawə́l **1** *denominative, transitive* [*past:* كشف يې كړ] **1.1** to discover, find, detect **1.2** to elucidate, ascertain, establish, determine كشفول د مرض سبب to establish the cause of the illness مونږ دا كشف كړى ده چه ... We have ascertained that... **1.3** to understand, comprehend, come to understand, to learn **1.4** to explore, survey, prospect **1.5** *military* to conduct reconnaissance, reconnoiter **1.6** to explore (a country) **2** *m.* ☞ كشف

كشفيات kashfijá ́t *m. plural* **1** search, investigation; exploration, reconnaissance, intelligence **2** discoveries, research, investigations

كشفياتي kashfijātí exploratory, prospecting كشفياتي څېړني prospecting

كشفېدل kashfedə́l *denominative, intransitive* [*past:* كشف شو] **1** to be discovered, be detected, be found **2** to be elucidated, be established, be determined; recognize, discern **3** to be known **4** to be explored, be surveyed, be reconnoitered **5** to be researched, be studied

كشك [1] kashk *m.* thin gruel; soup

كشك [2] kushk *m.* **1** kiosk; pavilion **2** palace **3** Kushka د كشك دره the Kushk Valley

كشك [3] kashík, kishík *m.* guard, watch, escort, protection كشك كول، كشك گالل *compound verb* to guard, stand guard; watch, keep watch, protect

كشكارل kəshkārə́l *transitive* ☞ شكارل

كشكچي kishikchí *m.* watchman, guard

كشكره kəshkára *f.* magpie

كش كش [1] kəshkə́sh *m.* كشكش the sound of footsteps

كش كش [2] kəshkə́sh *m.* كشكش ☞ كش [3]

كشكل kashkál *m.* common coot, *Fulica atra*

كشكول kashkolə́l كشكول kashkawə́l *transitive* ☞ كشول

كاشكي ká́shki, ká́shke ☞ كاشكي

كشمالو kashmālú *m.* [*plural:* كشمالوگان kashmālugán and كشمالان kashmālán] كشمالى kashmāláj *m.* basil

كشمش kishmísh *m.* kishmish, seedless grape, raisin سپين كشمش sabze (a kind of raisin from the kishmish seedless grape)

كشمشي kishmishí raisin كشمشي انگور the kishmish grape (used in making raisins)

كش مكش kashmakásh كشمكش **1** quarrel; argument **2** battle, fight; skirmish, melee; conflict ديپلوماتيك كش مكش diplomatic battle **3** fight, brawl; fuss **4** difficult; state of being upset; a mental struggle كش مكش I lay down distraught. په كش مكش كښي پريوتم struggle كول *compound verb* **a** to quarrel; argue **b** to fight, struggle; fight, brawl; romp, play (nosily) **c** to create difficulties **d** to be distraught, suffer (in one's heart, mentally, psychologically)

كشمير kashmír *m.* Kashmir

كشميره kashmirá *f.* **1** cloth; woolen fabric **2** suit fabric نخي كشميره cotton cloth پشمي كشميره woolen (cashmere) suiting

كشميري kashmiráj **1** Kashmir **2** *m.* Kashmiri (native or inhabitant of Kashmir)

كشونده kushandá *m.* ☞ كشونده

كشو [1] kashú *m.* pea pods boiled in water

كشو [2] kasháw *m.* mongoose

كشور [1] kishwár *m.* region, territory, land, country

كشور [2] kishór *m.* **1** bandage, dressing **2** *regional* ant-eater **3** *regional* caterpillar

كشوري kishwarí civil, civilian كشوري افراد، كشوري كسان civilians كشوري جنگ civil war

كش وكپ kəshukṛáp *m.* كشوكپ **1** sound of footsteps **2** ☞ كشمكش

كش وگير kashugír *m.* struggle, fight; rivalry

كشول kashawə́l *transitive* [*past:* كش يې كړ] **1** to pull, drag; carry را *compound verb* كشول to bring in, drag in; import يو بل سره كشول to reach out for one another **2** to draw, attract **3** to draw out, stretch **4** to carry someone along by force **5** to be inclined, tend towards something; involve in something, enlist, draw into something **6** to drag something out, hamper the implementation of something

كشونده kushundá *m.* **1** extradition of a murderer and his banishment **2** murderer, killer

كشه [1] kə shá *f.* furrow

كشه [2] kə́sha ☞ كش [3]

كشهار kəshahá́r *m.* rustling; rustle كشهار لرل to make a crackling sounds

كشى [1] kasháj *m.* only son

كشى [2] kəshój *f.* **1** pickax, pick-mattock **2** iron ingot, iron pig

كشى [3] kashój *f.* only daughter

كشي [4] kashé *plural of* كشه [1]

كشي [5] kə́she ☞ كشه [2]

كشيدگي kashidarí *f.* كشيده گي

كشيدل kashedə́l *intransitive* [*past:* كش شو] **1** to be pulled, be dragged, be carried **2** to stretch, be stretched كشيدل سره *compound* *verb* to tighten, shrink, contract **3** to stretch, reach **4** to be delayed, be dragged out (in length), be disrupted (e.g., of a business deal)

کشده گی kashidagí *f.* tension; strained position; strained state (of relations)

کښ ¹ kǝkh *m.* rustling, rustle; sound of light footsteps

کښ ² kakh *m.* **1** pulling, attraction **2** drawing (on a cigarette) **3** sigh **4** mange (in sheep) **5** narrow path

کښ ³ ki, ke ☞ کښي

کښ ⁴ kákh ☞ کش ⁴

کښانده ¹ kǝkhā́nda *f.* track of a smoothing harrow, trace of a toothless drag harrow

کښانده ² kakhā́nda agitated, anxious; upset, alarmed زړه کښانده کول to cause the heart to flutter

کښای ² kkhāj *conditional from* کښت

کښت ¹ kǝkht, kikht *m.* seeding, planting; planted field د کښت آلات farm implements کښت کول to harvest, reap کښت ټولول to sow, plant, drill

کښت ² kakht *m.* ☞ قسط

کښت ³ kukht, kakht *m.* **1** gorge, ravine **2** interval, space, gap **3** slit; orifice, opening, aperture **4** square (on a chess board) **5** *chess* mate

کښتزار kikhtzā́r *m.* ☞ کشت زار

کښتگر kǝkhtgā́r *m.* [*plural:* کښتگر kǝkhtgǝr *and* کښتگران kǝkhtgarā́n] farmer, tiller of the soil, peasant

کښتگري kǝkhtgarí *f.* **1** farming کښتگري کول *compound verb* to engage in farming **2** metayage (a form of share-cropping)

کښتنی kkhatanáj **1** lower **2** cited, or given, below

کښتو ¹ kǝkhtó *oblique plural of* کښت ¹

کښتو ² kkhǝ́to *oblique plural of* کښته ²

کښته ¹ kǝkhtá *f.* seeding, sowing, planting

کښته ² kkhǝ́ta, kkháta **1.1** down(wards); below, underneath, downstairs; from below هغه کښته ولاړ و He was standing below. **1.2** lower کښته کول 30 degrees below zero دېرش درجي تر صفر کښته *compound verb* **a** to lower, let down, bring down **b** to lower, reduce, lessen **c** to land (e.g., an airplane) **d** to unload **e** to disembark, put ashore پر غاړه کښته کول to put ashore **f** to exhaust, expend **g** *figurative* to undermine, tsap (morale) کښته کېدل *compound verb* **a** to be lowered, be let down; sink, come down, descend; lose altitude **b** to come down, diminish, decrease, fall **c** to land, make a landing **d** to unload, be unloaded **e** to disembark, get off, get out of **f** to be exhausted, be used up, run out of **g** *figurative* to fall, deteriorate (morale) کښته لوېدل *compound verb* to fall down, hurtle down; descend کښته پورته کېدل *compound verb* **a** to fluctuate, oscillate, rock, swing **b** to move, to stir (of people) **1.3** further south, south of جلال آباد تر کابل کښته دئ Jalalabad is located south of Kabul. **2** attributive (sometimes inflected) **2.1** lower **2.2** lower (in rank), subordinate **2.3** indicated below **2.4** low; low-lying, lowland کښته دښتونه a low place, a depression **2.5** low, mean, base, vile **2.6** low, quiet (of the voice)

کښته والی kkhatatób *m.* ☞ کښته توب

کښته کېده kkhǝtakedǝ́, kkhatakedǝ́ *m. plural* **1** lowering, letting down, descending **2** lowering, lessening, reducing, falling **3** landing, touching down **4** unloading **5** disembarkation, getting off **6** exhaustion, running low on, using up

کښته گر kkhǝtagár ☞ کښتگر

کښته لوېده kkhǝtalwedǝ́ *m. plural* falling down, tumbling down, hurtling down; descending

کښته والی kkhǝtawā́laj *m.* **1** lowering, hauling down, descent **2** low level د دریاب کښته والی the low level of water in the river **3** baseness, meanness, vileness

کښتي ¹ kkhǝtí *f.* baseness, meanness, vileness ځان کښتي ته ورکول to commit foul deeds

کښتي ² kǝkhtí kakhtíz, kakhtíza. arable, tillable; کښتي مکه worked, cultivated (of soil) کښتي مکي plowed field crops

کښتي ³ kikhtǝ́j *f.* [*plural:* کښتی kikhtǝ́j, کښتي گاني kikhtǝjgā́ni *and* کښتياني kikhtijā́ni] boat; vessel

کښتيوان kikhtǝjwǝ́n *m.* **1** boatman **2** sailor

کښبن kakhíkh *m.* **1** propulsive force, thrust (e.g., of a propeller) **2** attraction, gravitation

کښکر kakhkár کښکرکی kakhkǝ́rkaj completely dry, desiccated

کښکرۍ kakhkǝ́raj **1** *m.* **1.1** bubble (e.g., from soap) **1.2** *plural* seasoning **2** ☞ کښکر

کښکولی kakhkólaj *m.* corn husk, corn shuck

کښکی ¹ kǝkhkáj *m.* rustle

کښکی ² kǝkhkáj *f.* reversible rug; doormat, floor cloth

کښکېلی kakhkedǝ́j *f.* spout

کښل ¹ kkhul *m. Eastern* kiss کښل کول *compound verb* to kiss

کښل ² kkhǝl **1** transitive [*present:* کا ړي *past:* وېي کښېن *and Western* وېي کښئ] **1.1** to pull, drag **1.2** to take out, extract; get **1.3** to tear out, pull out **1.4** to mine, extract (minerals, etc.) **1.5** to draw, get (e.g., water from a well) **1.6** to run, build (an irrigation ditch) **1.7** to extract (a tooth) **1.8** to smoke (e.g., a cigarette) **1.9** to take off (clothes) بوت کښل *compound verb* to take off one's coat کوت کښل *compound verb* to take off one's shoes **1.10** to take out, lead out, drive out **1.11** to exile, expel someone **1.12** to recover (a debt) **1.13** to tear oneself away (from the business at hand) له خپله کاره يي وکښلم He tore me away from business. **1.14** to exert, apply (one's efforts, endeavors, etc.) زيار کښل *compound verb* to try, endeavor **1.15** to sketch, draw, depict **1.16** to write کتاب يي کښلئ دئ He wrote a book. **1.17** to steal کښل کېدل *compound verb passive* **a** to be pulled, be dragged **b** to be taken out, be pulled out, be extracted, be acquired **c** to be torn out, be pulled out **d** to be mined, be extracted (of minerals, etc.) **e** to be drawn, be gotten (e.g., water from a well) **f** to be built (of an irrigation ditch) **g** to

582

be extracted (of a tooth) **h** to be smoked (e.g., of a cigarette) **i** to be taken off, be pulled off (of clothes) **j** to be taken out, be led out, to be driven out **k** to be exiled, expelled **l** to be recovered (of a debit) **m** to be torn away (from the business at hand) **n** to be exerted, be applied (of efforts, endeavors, etc.) **o** to be sketched, be drawn **p** to be written **2** *m. plural* ☞ له يو شي څخه ځان کښنه *idiom* to avoid, shun, eschew something ده کار څخه ځان کښل to shirk work کښل ، له يو کار ځان کښل to make answerable in court يو ځای ته ځان کښل to be moved nearer

کښکلول ☞ *transitive* kķhulawál بنکلول [past: و يې کښلاوه] to kiss

کښلئ¹ kķhóləj *past participle of* کښل²

کښلی² kķhúlaj, kuķhólaj beautiful, pretty, handsome; comely

کښلی³ kķhólaj *m. plural* that which is predestined or fated, destiny, fate

کښهندړی kaķhəndóraj *m.* **1** curved stick for securing a pack **2** beam, bar (for tethering livestock), hitching rail

کښندی¹ kķhəndáj *m.* ice-skating

کښندی² kaķhəndáj *m.* farmer, tiller of the soil

کښنه kķhóna *f.* **1** dragging, trailing (e.g., along the ground) **2** pulling out, dragging out, extracting, getting **3** tearing out, pulling out **4** extraction, mining (of minerals, etc.) **5** drawing (up), getting (e.g., water from a well) **6** running, building (an irrigation ditch) **7** extraction, removal (of a tooth) **8** taking off, pulling off (clothes) **9** recovery (of a debt) **10** sketching, drawing; representation, picture **11** writing

کښول kķhawál, kəķhawál *transitive* [past: و يې کښاوه] **1** to pull, drag noisily **2** to compel to pull, compel to drag **3** to compel to sketch, draw **4** to compel to write

کښوندری kəķhwándraj *m.* ☞ کښندری

کښوندی kaķhwandáj *m.* curved pole in the upper part of a tent

کښا kəķhá *f.* **1** tug, trace (of a plow) **2** ☞ کښندری **3** large net for straw

کښهار kəķhahár *m.* ☞ کشهار

کښئ¹ kóķhəj *past participle of* کښل²

کښی² kķhi کي ki *Western*, کي ke *Eastern*, کښي kķhe *Eastern*, *Western* kshi **1** *postposition*, in, into, to, on (in combination with the preposition په or without it (Eastern dialect), used to denote location within something or motion to the interior of something) په لاره کښي along the road په کوڅه کښي on the street په کور کښي in the house **2** *separable verb prefix* کښېنستل to sit down کښېوتل to get into someplace

کښی³ kaķháj, kəķháj *m.* **1** mirab (the person who manages an irrigation system and the procedure for water usage in Central Asia) **2** watchman who stands guard over the crops **3** peasant who is irrigating his crops

کښی⁴ kķhaj *m.* pen (holder, for writing)

کښی⁵ kóķhaj gelded, castrated

کښبېستل kķheistál, kķheəstál *transitive* ☞ کښبي ايستل

کښبياستنه kķheistóna *f.* ☞ کښبي ايستنه

کښبېباس kķhebās *present stem of* کښبېستل

کښبېباسنه kķhebāsóna *f.* ☞ کښبياسته

کښبېباسونکی kķhebāsúnkaj *present participle of* کښبېستل

کښبېتوب kaķhitób *m.* crop guarding, guarding the planted field(s)

کښبېختل kķhekhatál *intransitive* [present: کښبېخبژي *past:* کښبېخوت] **1** to feel ashamed, be ashamed **2** to press, put pressure on

کښبېختنه kķhekhatóna *f.* **1** constraint, uneasiness, shame **2** pressing, putting pressure on

کښبېده kaķhidá *f.* **1** embroidery **2** decoration کښبېده کول *compound verb* **a** to embroider **b** to decorate **3** pattern, design **4** drawing, illustration

کښبېدهکاري kaķhidakārí *f.* embroidery

کښبېده گر kaķhidagár *m.* artist, painter

کښبېده گره kaķhidagára *f.* **1** embroideress **2** artist

کښبېدیار kaķhidjár *m.* artist, painter

کښبېدی kķhedáj *m.* peacock, peafowl

کښبېرد kķhegd *stem of the present tense, perfective aspect of* اېنودل

کښبېرده kķhégda *imperative, perfective aspect of* اېنودل

کښبېنو kķhékho کښبېنود kķhékhod کښبېنوو kķhékhow *past tense stem of* اېنودل

کښبېنوولئ kķhekhowóləj *past participle of* اېنودل

کښبېکبل kķhekķhál *transitive* [present: کښبېکاږي *past:* کښبي يې کښ] **1** to press, crush, squeeze; press in **2** to give a massage, massage, rub

کښبېکښنه kķhekķhóna *f.* **1** pressing, crushing, squeezing, pressing in **2** massage, massaging, rubbing

کښبېکبنل kķhemandál *transitive* ☞ کښبېکبنل

کښبېناست kķhénāst *Eastern past tense of* کښبېناستل

کښبېناستل kķhenāstál *intransitive Eastern* ☞ کښبېنستل

کښبېناسته kķhenāstó *m. plural* ☞ کښبېناستنه

کښبېناستل kķhenastál *intransitive* [present: کښبېني *past:* کښبېناست *Western* کښبېنوست] **1** to sit down, take a seat; sit **2** to live, dwell, inhabit **3** to make a landing, land له خوبه کښبېنستل to get up out of bed د چا سره کښبېنستل to make friends with somebody پر تخت کښبېنستل to ascend the throne

کښبېناستنه kķhenastóna *f.* **1** sitting, seating **2** living, dwelling **3** landing

کښبېني kķhenanáj ☞ کښبېني

کښبېنوست kķhénust *Western past tense of* کښبېنستل

کښبېنول kķhenawál *transitive* [past: و يې کښبېناوه] **1** to seat **2** to settle (in a new place) **3** to plant (plants) **4** to place, locate, put **5** to set up, assemble (equipment) **6** to put (in, into), install, insert (e.g., window panes, etc.) **7** to set down, land **8** to arrest له خوبه کښبېنول to rouse from sleep

کښبېنونه kķhenawóna *f.* **1** seating, setting (someone down to do something) **2** settling **3** planting (of plants) **4** placing, locating, putting **5** setting up, assembling (equipment) **6** installing, inserting (e.g., dentures, window panes) **7** landing **8** arrest

کنبښني [1] kḳhéní *present tense of* کنبښنستل

کنبښنی [2] kḳhenáj **1** low-land (of people who live in lower places compared to others) **2** blowing from below (of the wind)

کنبښواته kḳhewātә́ *m. plural* **1** getting, reaching, ending up, being (e.g., in(to) a difficult position) **2** getting stuck (e.g., in a net) **3** lowering, reducing, reduction **4** penetrating, penetration

کنبښوت kḳhéwut *past tense of* کنبښوتل *in lieu of* کنبښووت

کنبښوتل kḳhewatә́l *intransitive* [*present:* کنبښوزي *past:* کنبښووت] **1** to get (somewhere), be found, find oneself, come to be په دام کنبښ to get caught in a net د چا په لاس کنبښوتل to fall into someone's hands په مشکلاتو کنبښوتل to get into a difficult position **2** to be lowered, descend, come down **3** to burst into, penetrate

کنبښوتنه kḳhewatә́na *f.* ☞ کنبښواته

کنبښوتئ kḳhewátaj *past participle, short form of* کنبښوتل

کنبښور kḳhewә́r *m.* peasant, farmer

کنبښوز kḳhewuz *present tense stem of* کنبښوتل

کنبښیست kḳhéjost *past tense of* کنبښیستل

کنبښووت kḳhéwot *past tense of* کنبښوتل

کنبښیاسته kḳhejāstә́ *m. plural* **1** insertion; putting in; putting into (operation, service) **2** pulling in, dragging in

کنبښیستل kḳhejәstә́l *transitive* [*present:* کنبښباسي *past:* کنبښي یې یوست] **1** to insert; put in; put into (operation, service), introduce **2** to pull in, drag in **3** to subject to something

کنبښیاستنه kḳhejәstә́na *f.* ☞ کنبښیاسته

قصاب kasā́b *m.* ☞ قصاب

کعبه ka'ába *f.* Kaaba (the sanctuary in Mecca)

کغ kәgh caw, caw (the cry of the crow)

کغا kәgā́ *m.* ☞ کغهار

کغاچ kaghách **1** stubborn, obstinate, recalcitrant **2** triangular **3** ill-fitting (of clothes)

کغاچتوب kaghāchtób *m.* کغاچوالی kaghāchwálaj *m.* ☞ کغاچي

کغاچول kaghāchawә́l *denominative, transitive* [*past:* کغاچ یې کړ] **1** to make stubborn, make obstinate **2** to rebel against someone

کغاچي kaghāchí *f.* stubbornness, obstinacy, recalcitrance

کغار kәghā́r angry

کغالی kughāláj *m.* **1** oven **2** pit, hole

کغر kaghár squinting, squint-eyed, cross-eyed

کغهار kәghkáj *m.* ☞ کغهار

کغن kәgh*ә*́n کغند kәghónd hoarse

کغند [1] kәghónd کغن kәghón hoarse

کغند [2] kәghónd *m.* crane (bird)

کغنده kәghónda *f.* hoarse

کغهار kәghahā́r *m.* croaking

کغیدل kәghedә́l *intransitive* [*past:* و کغیده] **1** to croak **2** to become hoarse, speak in a hoarse voice

کف [1] kaf, kaff *m. Arabic* **1** palm (of the hand) **2** foot د کوټي کف room floor

کف [2] kuf *m.* ☞ چف

کف [3] kuf like, similar (to), resembling

کف [4] kaf *m.* foam, froth

کفار [1] kuffār *m. plural Arabic of* کافر

کفار [2] kifār *Arabic* non-believing, unbelieving (as a noun infidel, atheist)

کفارت kafārát, kaffārát *m. Arabic* کفاره kafārá *f. Arabic religion* expiation of guilt, atonement for sins کفارت ورکول *compound verb* to expiate guilt, atone for sins کفارت کول *compound verb* to repent of one's sins

کفاف kafā́f *m. Arabic* **1** subsistence **2** sufficiency

کفالت kafālát *m. Arabic* deputizing; performance of (one's) duties, substitution, acting for

کفایت kifāját *m. Arabic* **1** sufficiency د ... دپاره کفایت کول to suffice, be sufficient **2** skill; ability, knack

کفتان kiftā́n *m. colloquial* captain پولیسي کفتان *regional* district police chief

کفتر kaftár *m.* ☞ کوتر [1]

کفچه مار kafchamā́r *m.* cobra

کفدار kafdā́r foamy

کفر kufr *m. Arabic,* کفران kufrā́n *m.* **1** unbelief; atheism **2** blasphemy کفر کول *compound verb* to blaspheme **3** *figurative* indecent act دا څه کفر خو نه دئ! It's no sin! **4** *figurative* ingratitude

کافرستان kufristā́n *m.* ☞ کافرستان

کفسجه kafaschá *f.* grille, lattice, bars

کفن kafán *m. Arabic* shroud, winding sheet سور کفن *idiom* to die in battle کفن خیرل *idiom* to escape from the claws of death کفنونه کنبل *idiom* **a** to swindle, to cheat when selling (something) **b** to charge an exorbitant price

کفن دزد kafandúzd *m.* **1** cemetery thief, grave robber **2** fleecer, flayer

کفیل kafíl *m. Arabic* deputy د صدر اعظم کفیل deputy prime minister د مدیر کفیل acting department chief

کک [1] kak *m.* **1** particle, crumb **2** blade of grass

کک [2] kak *m.* sugar-cane molasses

کک [3] kuk *m.* onion

ککر kakә́r *m.* wasps' nest

ککره [1] kakә́ra, kakára *f.* skull

ککره [2] kakára *f.* log thrown across an irrigation ditch; small bridge, footbridge

ککری [1] kukráj, kakráj *m.* puppy

ککری [2] kakarә́j *f.* **1** skull **2** crown (of the head) **3** top, peak, summit (of a mountain) پر ککرئ اور بلیدل *idiom* to be in great grief, experience keenly, mourn تر ککری دود ختل *idiom* to be greatly upset, be mightily discouraged

ککری [3] kukrә́j *feminine of* ککری

ککری [4] kakrә́j *f.* stones (of the urinary bladder)

ککر kakə́ṛ, kakáṛ 1 dirty, soiled, polluted 2 aggravated, weighed down by something; stricken (by grief, etc.) 3 having become passionately fond of, keen on something 4 defiled, profaned, impure, vile ککر سړی sordid person

ککرتوب kakəṛtób *m.* ککروالی kakəṛwálaj *m.* 1 dirt; pollution 2 baseness, meanness, vileness, infamy

ککرول kakəṛawə́l *denominative, transitive* [past: کک یې کر] 1 to soil, make dirty, pollute 2 to aggravate, weigh down with something 3 to defile, profane

ککره kakə́ra 1 *feminine singular of* ککر 2 *f.* prostitute

ککړي kakáṛi [1] *f. plural* ککړي وهل *compound verb* a to cackle (of a hen just before laying) b to call (of a partridge)

ککړي kakə́ṛi, kakáṛi [2] *f. plural of* ککر

ککړی kakúṛj [3] *m.* sweets, confections (prepared on the occasion of the lambing of sheep and goats)

ککړیدل kakəṛedə́l *denominative, intransitive* [past: کک شو] 1 to make oneself dirty, get dirty 2 to be aggravated, be weighed down, burdened by something; be stricken (by grief, etc.) 3 to take to, become keen on 4 to wallow (in impurities) 5 to be defiled, be profaned, be polluted; په بده ورغ ککړیدل *idiom* to fall into poverty

ککښ kakə́x *m.* re-roofing

ککن kakə́n *☞* ککر

ککنکی kakənkáj *m.* kind of plover

ککوبای kəkobáj *m. ☞* گلاب

کاکوره kakóra *f.* colocynth, bitter apple

ککوری kakóṛaj [1] *m.* 1 small loaf of bread 2 flat cake that is baked on hot rocks 3 disk (of the moon, sun) د نمر ککوری the solar disk 4 *music* phonograph record د ککورو باجه phonograph

ککوری kakúṛaj [2] *m.* adolescent boy, teenager, juvenile

ککوی kakúj [1] *m.* hoopoe

ککوی kakə́wáj [2] *m.* lapwing

کاکه káka *f.* corpuscle (blood) د وینو سپیني ککی white blood corpuscles

ککی káki [1] *plural of* ککه

ککی kakáj [2] *m.* baby boy, babe in arms, infant

ککی kəkáj [3] *m.* kind of silk embroidery

ککی kakə́j [4] *f.* baby girl, babe in arms, infant

کگلېچ kagléch *m. Eastern ☞* کربلېچ

کگوالی kagwálaj *m. ☞* کربوالی

کگول kagawúl *transitive Eastern ☞* کربول

کگه‌وگه kagá-wagá *f. Eastern ☞* کربه وړه

کگه‌ول kagawúl *transitive Eastern ☞* کربول

کگی kagé *Eastern* 1 *feminine plural of* کبوړ [2] 2 kind of embroidery

کگېدل kagedə́l *intransitive Eastern ☞* کربېدل

کل kal [1] *m.* cake, oil-seed cake (used as fodder)

کل kal [2] 1 bald; balding 2 mangy, scabby 3 *Eastern* shaven

کل kul, kull *Arabic* 1 all, the whole of 2 general, universal; total 3 *m.* .1 the whole, all, everything 3.2 the collective

قلعه *☞* kalā́ *f.* کلا

قلابند *☞* kalābánd کلابند

کلابندېدل kalābandedə́l *denominative, intransitive* [past: کلا بند شو] to be besieged, be encircled

کلاچه kalāchá *f.* small fortress, stronghold; small village

کلاچي kulāchí *f.* Kulachi city (in the vicinity of Dera Ismail Khan)

قرار *☞* kalár کلار

کلاس klās *m.* 1 class (in school) د اکابرو کلاس courses to eliminate illiteracy 2 class (category, sort) د لومړي کلاس واگون first-class railroad car

کلاسیسیزم klāssisízm *m.* classicism

کلاسیفیکېشن klāsifikéshán *m.* classification کلاسیفیکېشن کول *compound verb* to classify

کلاسیک klāsík classical

کلاسیکي klāsikí 1 classical 2 school, educational (of books, textbooks, manuals) 3 class

کلاغي kalāghí *m.* headband (women's)

کلال kulāl *m.* potter کلال په مات کندول کښني اوبه څکي *proverb* potter drinks water from a cracked pitcher

کلاله kulālá *f.* stigma (of the pistil)

کلالي kulālí [1] *f.* pottery د کلالی څرخ potter's wheel

کلالي kulālé [2] *plural of* کلاله

کلام kalā́m *m. Arabic* 1 word; speech د چا کلام پرېکول to interrupt someone 2 literary work 3 poetic creation 4 *grammar* word group, collocation; phrase د کلام جز part of speech

کلا ماتونکی kalā́ mātawúnkaj siege کلا ماتونکي آلات siege gun

کلام الام kalám-alám نه کلام ویل او نه الام to speak not a word

کلان kalán large; senior

کلانتر kalāntár *m.* foreman; village elder, village headman

کلانکار kalānkắr arrogant, conceited, haughty; putting on airs

کلان کاري kalānkārí arrogance, haughtiness; conceit; putting on airs کلان کاري کول *compound verb* a to put on airs b to swagger

کلاور kalāwúr *m. ☞* کراول

کلاوه kalāwá *f.* skein, hank; ball, clew انجره کلاوه tangled ball زما څخه اوس د کلاوې سر ورک دئ، نه پوهېږم چه څه وکم *idiom* I am in total confusion.

کلاوه‌پېچ kalāwapéch *m.* reel

کلاجي kəlājí کلايي kəlājə́n 1 tin, stanic 2 *m. plural* tin

کلب kulúb, klab *m.* club

کلپ kúlp, kúləp *m. ☞* قفل [1]

کلپ kalp [2] 1 steep, with steep slopes, cliffy, craggy; almost inaccessible, difficult to access 2 broken terrain, rugged country 3 brutal, savage, bitter, violent کلپ جنگ a fierce battle کلپ مردک اورول to subject to intense fire

کلپ kaláp [3] *m.* club

کلپ جوړوونکی kulp dzhoṛawúnkaj locksmith; metal-worker

کلپکی kulpákaj *m.* small lock

کلپول kulpawə́l *denominative, transitive* [past: کلپ یې کر] to lock

کلپي kalpí *f.* duplicity, double-dealing, hypocrisy کلپي کول *compound verb* to engage in double-dealing, be duplicitous

کلپیدل kulpedál *denominative, intransitive* [*past:* کلپ شو] to be locked (up)

کلت kulát, kalút *m.* seeds of horse gram, *Dolichos biflorus*

کلتور kultúr, kaltúr *m.* 1 culture ملي کلتور national culture د کلتور وزیر minister of culture 2 agriculture culture; crop

کلتوري kulturí cultural کلتوري روابط، کلتوري مناسبات cultural ties کلتوري هیئت a delegation of cultural workers

کلجو kaldzháú *m.* naked barley, hulless barley

کلچ klach *m.* bag for carrying soil

کلچر kalchár *m.* culture افغاني کلچر Afghan culture

کلچري kalcharí cultural; cultured

کلچه kulchá *f.* 1 pastry, biscuit; bun 2 bar of soap

کلچه پز kulchapáz *m.* baker

کلچیي kulchají turnip-like کلچیي پیاز onions

کلخوز kolkhóz, kalkhóz *m.* kolkhoz, collective farm

کلخوزي kolkhozí, kalkhozí 1 kolkhoz, collective-farm 2 *m.* kolkhoz worker, collective farmer ښځه کلخوزي female kolkhoz worker

کلداره kaldãra *f.* Indian rupee

کلرک klark *m. regional* clerk, office worker, employee, official, functionary, bureaucrat

کلسیوم kalsijúm *m.* calcium

کلغچکه kalghəcháka *f.* magpie

کلغه kalghá *f.* ☞ کرغه¹

کلاغي kələghãj *m.* ☞ کلاغي

کلف kulf *m.* lock دروازې ته کلف ور اچول to lock the door دروازه کلف ده the door is locked

کلفت¹ kulúft thick, heavy; dense سخت او کلفت گرزول to make thicker, thicken; condense

کلفت² kilíft *m.* Kelif

کلفک kulfák *m.* door bolt

کلک klak 1 hard, rigid, solid, firm; dense 2 strong, durable 3 steadfast, steady, staunch 4 stingy, miserly 5 hard, severe, harsh; coarse, rough; cruel, brutal په وچ کلک زور with brute force 6 strong, fierce, violent کلکه بمباري fierce bombardment, heavy bombing 7 having great endurance (of an animal) 8 firm (of a hope, conviction) موږ کلکه عقیده لرو We are firmly convinced. 9 deep, profound (of feelings, etc.) 10 close (of a connection, tie) د چا سره کلک روابط لرل to have a close connection, maintain close relations with somebody 11 solid, reliable (of scientific work)

کلک پلک klak-plak very firm, very strong, very durable

کلک پوست klakpóst crustacean کلک پوسته حیوانات crustaceans

کلکتوب klaktób *m.* ☞ کلکوالی

کلکته kalktá *f.* Calcutta

کلکتیا klaktjã *f.* ☞ کلکوالی

کلکسیون kaleksjón *m.* collection

کلکل kalkál *m.* کلکل 1 idle or futile argument, wrangling, squabbling 2 noise, din

کلکواگی klakwãgaj hard-mouthed (of a horse)

کلکوالی klakwãlaj *m.* 1 hardness, rigidity, solidity 2 strength, durability 3 steadfastness, steadiness, staunchness 4 stinginess, miserliness 5 severity, harshness 6 intensity, ferocity 7 endurance (of animals) 8 depth (of feelings, etc.)

کلکول klakawál *denominative, transitive* [*past:* کلک یې کړ] 1 to make firm, harden 2 to thicken; condense; ram, tamp, pack 3 to strengthen, consolidate; fasten, secure 4 to lock (a door, etc.) 5 to staunchly defend something راکلکول، درکلکول، ورکلکول 6 *compound verb* to complicate, burden زړه کلکول *idiom* to control oneself, restrain oneself

کلکونه klakawéna *f.* 1 condensation; ramming, tamping 2 strengthening, consolidating, securing 3 locking (a door, etc.) 4 complicating, burdening

کلکه kláka 1 *feminine singular of* کلک 2 *f.* 2.1 hard soil; hard ground 2.2 zeal, exertion; energetic د ... سره په کلکه مجادله کول to conduct a fierce battle

کلکي¹ klakí *f.* ☞ کلکوالی

کلکي² kláki *feminine plural of* کلک

کلکیدل klakedál 1 *denominative, intransitive* [*past:* کلک شو] 1.1 to be firm, be hard; harden, get stronger; thicken, congeal, set 1.2 to condense, be condensed, be rammed, be tamped 1.3 to be strengthened, be consolidated, be fastened, be secured 1.4 to be locked (of a door, etc.) 1.5 to exhibit persistence په دې خبره ولي دومره کلکیږي؟ Why are you so insistent on this? 1.6 to be stingy, be miserly 1.7 to be severe, be stern, be cruel, be brutal 1.8 to be intense, be fierce, be frantic 2 *m. plural* ☞ کلکیدنه

کلکیدنه klakedéna *f.* کلکیده klakedé *m. plural* 1 hardening, solidifying; congealing, setting; condensing 2 strengthening, consolidating; fastening, securing 3 perseverance, persistence 4 stinginess, miserliness 5 cruelty, severity 6 ferocity د رگو کلکیدنه *medicine* hardening of the arteries

کلکین kilkín *m.* ☞ کړکی¹

کلگی kələgáj *m.* 1 crown (of the head); top of a tyubeteika (an embroidered skullcap worn in Central Asia)

کلل kalál *transitive* [*past:* و یې کاله] to measure (distance)

کللتوب kaləltób *m.* measure, measurement (of distance)

کلم kalám *m.* ☞ قلم

کلمات kalimãt *m. plural Arabic of* کلمه²

کلماغ kalmãgh walking gracefully

کلمک kələmák *m.* variety of grape

کلمول kəlamawál *denominative, transitive* [*past:* کلم یې کړ] *agriculture* to vaccinate

کلمه¹ kulmá *f.* gut, intestine ړنده کلمه appendix غټه کلمه large intestine ډکه کلمه mutton sausage

کلمه² kalimá *f. Arabic* [*plural:* کلمي kalimé *and m. plural: Arabic* کلمات kalimãt] 1 word دخیل کلمات borrowed words د کلماتو ترکیب

word-formation وراني كلمي errata **2** speech **3** *religion* symbol of faith, credo كلمه ويل to pronounce the Islamic credo

كلمه وتنه kulmá watə́na *f.* hernia

كلمبدل kəlamedə́l *denominative, intransitive* verb [*past:* كلم شو] *agriculture* to be vaccinated

كلن kalán year پنځه كلن five-year اوه كلن seven-year

كلندج kulándzh *m.* ☞ قلنج

كلنډ kulánḍ *m.* stick (which is fastened to the neck of livestock)

كلنگ [1] kaláng *m.* **1** dowry **2** presents from the bride to the husband's relatives **3** tribute, tax

كلنگ [2] kuláng *m.* [*plural:* كلنگان kulangán] **1** fighting cock **2** crane (bird) **3** hoe, mattock **4** cock, cocking piece (of a firearm)

كلنگر kulangár *m.* Kulangar

كلنگي kulangí **1** fighting كلنگي چرگ fighting cock **2** long-legged (of a person); leggy, lanky **3** *figurative* cocky, pert

كلنه kalə́na *f.* measure, measurement (of distance)

كلنى [1] kalanáj *Eastern* kulanáj **1** yearly, annual كلنى بودجه annual budget پنځه كلن How old is your son? **2** ☞ كلن زوى دي څو كلنى دئ؟ كلن پلان five-year plan

كلنى [2] kələnáj *Eastern* kalanáj **1** existing for so much time **2** since when

كلينيك kliník *m.* ☞ كلينيك

كلينيكي klinikí ☞ كلينيكي

كلو [1] kaló *oblique plural of* كال [1] د كلو څخه وروسته له ډېرو with years كلو after many years

كلو [2] kə́lo *oblique plural of* كلى [1]

كلو [3] kalú *m.* shrike (bird)

كلواخه kalwā́tsa *f.* material compensation for murder

كلوب klúb, kulúb *m.* كلوپ klúp, kulúp club

كلوټ kalóṭ black; swarthy; black-haired

كلوټى kəlóṭaj *m.* small village, hamlet

كلوچ kluch **1** *m.* crusts of bread that remain on the walls of the oven **2** wrinkled

كلوچول kluchawə́l *denominative, transitive* [*past:* كلوچ يې كړ] to wrinkle; rumple, crumple

كلوچى klocháj *m.* distaff, spinning wheel

كلوچبدل kluchedə́l *denominative, intransitive* [*past:* كلوچ شو] to wrinkle, become wrinkled; become rumpled, become crumpled

كلوروفارم klorofā́rm *m.* chloroform

كلورى kalorí *f.* calorie

كلورين klorín *m.* chlorine

كلوشه kalósha *f.* ☞ كلوبنه

كلوښته kloḳtá, klóḳhta, kalóḳhta *f.* **1** tuft (of grass) **2** wisp (of hair, wool) **3** tousled hair **4** tangled wool, snarled wool **5** knout, whip, lash (made of plant fibers)

كلوښتهور kloḳhtawár **1** tousled (of the hair) **2** tangled, snarled (e.g., of wool)

كلوبنه kalā́wḳha *f.* galosh

كيلوگرام kilográm *m.* ☞ كيلوگرام

كلول kulúl, kalól *m. plural* grass pea, *Lathyrus sativus*

كلول kalawə́l *denominative, transitive* [*past:* كل يې كړ] **1** to cause balding, cause to become bald, promote baldness **2** to shave ږيره كلول *compound verb* to shave one's beard

كلوله kululá *f.* something round, object of rounded shape يو معاهده كلوله كول to cancel an agreement, abrogate a treaty

كلومتر kilométr *m.* ☞ كيلومتر

كلونه kalúna *plural of* كال [1]

كلوو kalúw *m.* anise

كله [1] kə́la, kála **1** when? كله راځي When will you come or arrive? كله راسي؟، كله راهيسي؟ Since when? **2** some time, some day; ever; one day; sometimes دا سړى ما كله ليدلئ دئ I once saw this man ... د هغه كله ... since the time that... كله since then د كله راهيسي چه **a** كله نه كله from time to time كله كله often ډېر كله as soon as كله sometime **b** from time to time نور كله (at) another time كله هر Now he sits down - now he stands up. كښېني، كله ولاړېږي always هيڅ كله never **3** really? خو دا دا خبره كله منله؟ Could he really agree to that? هر كله راسي! Welcome! I am glad to see you!

كله [2] kalá head كله پز dealer of boiled sheep's heads and feet

كله پز kalapáz *m.* dealer of roasted feet and heads of animals

كله پنډى kalapəṇḍə́j *f.* mumps

كله غوچك kalaghuchák *m.* kalaguchak (a variety of grape)

كله منار kalaminár *m. history* pyramid of the skulls of enemies killed in battle

كله ناكله kalanā́kala **1** some time, some day **2** from time to time, at times

كله نى [2] kələnáj ☞ كلنى

كله يى kalají *m. plural* tin

كلي [1] kilí *f.* [*plural:* كلى kiləj كلياني kilijā́ni *and* كلي گانى kiligā́ni] د برق د انتقال كلي plug د اتصال كلي electrical switch key

كلي [2] kulí *f.* rinse, rinsing

كلي [3] kullí *Arabic* [*f. plural:* كليه kullijā́] **1** general, common په كلي ډول سره، په كلي طور سره in general اصول general provisions كلي نظريې generalization **2** full, absolute كلي اعتماد full confidence

كلى [4] kə́laj *m.* village د كلي سړى ... *kə́li...* peasant د كلي ښڅه ... *kə́li...* peasant woman د كلي مشر ... *kə́li...* village elder د چا سره كلى كول **a** to live in the same village with someone, be someone's fellow-villager **b** *figurative* to share joys and sorrows with fellow-villagers كلى كور كول to associate with one's neighbors, interact with fellow-villagers

كلى [5] kaláj polled, hornless

كلى [6] kaləj *f.* **1** corn, callus, callosity **2** place that has been rubbed raw; *veterinary medicine* gall

كلى [7] kiləj *plural of* كلي [1]

كلى [8] kaləj *feminine singular of* كلى [2]

كلى [9] kələj *f.* crested lark

کلۍ ¹⁰ kalə́j *f.* **1** slice (e.g., of watermelon) **2** bud **3** chopping of sausage meat

کلۍ ¹¹ kále *interjection* shoo (cry used to shoo birds away form planted fields)

کليات kullijā́t *m. plural Arabic* **1** complete collected works **2** general proposition, general conclusion په کلیاتو کښې on the whole **3** fundamental principles

کليبر kalíbr *m.* gauge; caliber

کلبچ klech strong, tough (of thread); spun, twisted

کلبچول klechawál *denominative, transitive* [*past:* کلبچ یې کړ] to spin, twist (of thread, yarn, etc.)

کلبچېدل klechedə́l *denominative, intransitive* [*past:* کلبچ شو] to be spun, be twisted

کليدان kəlidā́n *m.* bolt, latch (e.g., of a door)

کلېدل kaledə́l *denominative, intransitive* [*past:* کل شو] to become bald, grow bald

کلیز kalíz **1** *m.* notebook-calendar **2** year پنځلس کلیز fifteen-year

کلیسا kalisā́ *f.* Christian temple, church د کلیسا اهل په churchmen کلیسا کښې شاملېدل to become a priest

کلیشه klishá cliché, stereotype

کلیمشر kəlimə́shr *m.* کلي مشر village elder, village headman

کلین kalín *m.* yearly pay (for work), yearly wages

کلینر kilinár *m.* **1** driver's assistant **2** greaser, lubricator

کلینک kilinák *m.* tongs, pincers; handle

کلینیک kliník *m.* clinic

کلینیکي klinikí clinic, clinical

کلیو kə́lijo *oblique plural of* کلی ¹

کلیوال kəliwál ☞ کلیوالی

کلي والا kəliwālá *m.* villager, peasant

کلیواله kəliwála *f.* peasant woman

کلیوالي ¹ kəliwālí *f.* affiliation by birth or residence with the same village; association for the purpose of mutual aid of people born in the same region but who are living elsewhere

کلیوالي ² kəliwā́li *plural of* کلیواله

کلیوالی ³ kəliwā́laj **1** village, rural کلیوالی واحد rural commune **2** *m.* peasant, villager خپل کلیوالی fellow-villager

کلیه kullijá **1** *feminine and plural of* کلی ³ **2** *f.* **.1** general proposition, thesis; axiom **2.2** sum, total

کم ¹ kəm, kum *interrogative-relative pronoun* what, which (of a number of others, of many) کم یو؟ کوم وخت چه Which of them? کوم ¹ ☞ Since when? د کم وخته څخه؟ د کمه وخته څخه؟ when

کم ² kam **1** small, little, insignificant; not many, few هېوادونه few countries په کمه بیه at a low price په کمه درجه راضي to be content with little زه سینما ډېره کمه ګورم I rarely go to the movies. **2** little, few, a little, some, negligible کم نه کم، کم له at least کم نه دئ هغه په هیڅ کم نه دئ less than something دیوشي څخه کم He is in no way inferior to others. کم a little (bit); little by little **3** little, not کم آبه a with little water, b not juicy (of fruit)

کم ³ kamm *Arabic* quantity کم او کیف په لحاظ د in quantity and quality, in terms of quantity and quality

کم ⁴ kəm *present tense first person of* کړل *in lieu of*

کماً kámmán *Arabic* quantitatively, in quantitative terms

کم آبه kamába **1** with little water, shallow **2** not juicy (of fruit)

کم آبي kamābí *f.* **1** shoals; insufficient water **2** lack of juiciness (of fruit)

کماچو kamāchú *m. botany* nightshade

کم ازکم kamazkám minimally, at least

کم استعداد kamisti'dā́d of scant ability, devoid of talent

کم استعمال kamisti'mā́l little-used, rare

کم اصل kamásl of low pedigree, of lowly origin or birth, low-born

کما في سابق kamāfisābíq *Arabic* as formerly, as before, as usual

کمال ¹ kamāl *Arabic* **1** *m.* [*plural:* کمالونه kamālúna *and Arabic* کمالات kamālā́t] **.1** perfection; completeness صاحب کمال *sāhíb-i...* having achieved perfection **1.2** talent **1.3** *proper noun* Kamal **2.1** perfect; full **2.2** highest

کمال ² kamā́l *m.* ☞ کماله

کمال بوتی kamālbúṭaj *m.* ☞ کماله

کمال دار kamāldár ☞ کمال ¹ **2** کمال سې! *saying* I wish you all the best!

کمالزي kamālzí **1** *m. plural* Kamalzi (the tribe) **2** *m.* Kamalzai

کماله kumālá, kamālá *f.* **1** hay plant, *Prangos* (grown for feed) **2** giantfennel, *Ferula Jaeschkeana*

کمالي kamālí excellent, superb; luxurious, posh کمالي سامان luxury items

کمان ¹ kamā́n *m. regional* ☞ کماند

کمان ² kamā́n *m.* **1** bow (weapon) **2** arc; arch; vault, dome

کمانچه kamānchá *f.* **1** kamancha (kind of violin) **2** small bow (for combing cotton) **3** *music* bow

کماند kamā́nd *m.* command د چا تر کماند لاندي under the command of someone د فوځ کمال کول to command an army, be an army commander

کماندر kamā́ndár *m.* کماندر kamā́nḍár *m. regional* commander

کم انکشاف kaminkishā́f little-developed, poorly-developed

کما نکین kamānkákh *m.* bowman, archer

کمان کښې kamānkakhí *f.* shooting with bow and arrow

کمانګر kamāngár *m.* craftsman who makes bows for shooting

کمانه kamāná *f.* winding, bend (of a river)

کمانۍ kamānə́j *f.* spring

کمايي kamā́í *f.* کمائي pay, wages کمايي کول *compound verb* to earn; obtain (the means for existence)

کمباري kumbārí *f.* pottery, potter's workshop or studio

کمبتۍ kambatə́j *f.* thimble for the thumb

کم بخت kambákht unfortunate, unlucky, destitute

کم بختي kambakhtí *f.* misfortune

کمبر ¹ kambár *m. colloquial* ☞ کمر

کمبري ¹ kambarí bitter orange; orange

کمبرۍ ² kambráj *m.* bitter orange, *Citrus aurantium*

کمبرۍ ³ kumbə́raj *m.* ☞ کومبر

کمبرین kámbriján *gelogy* Cambrian

کمبل kambál *f.* کمبله kambála *f.* **1** reversible rug, coarse carpet تر خپله کمبله پينه مه غوّوه، د خپلي سره پنبي غزوه *saying* to cut one's coat according to the cloth **2** cloak **3** woolen blanket; traveling rug د...کمبله ټولول *proverb* **a** to finish, complete something **b** to weaken influence د مريي توب کمبله ټوله شوه The time of slavery is past.

کمبلۍ kambaléj *f.* **1** butterfly **2** small variegated reversible rug

کمبو kambú *m.* netting for straw (made of woolen thread)

کمبوت kambút *m.* ☞ کمبود

کمبوتي kambutí *f.* ☞ کمبود[1]

کمبود kambúd **1** *m.* **.1** shortage, lack, deficiency, deficit د کاغذ د کمبود له امله because of a shortage of paper **1.2** incomplete set **1.3** vacancy **2** insufficient; lacking

کمبودي kambudí *f.* ☞ کمبود[1]

کمبوديا kambodjá *f.* Cambodia ☞ کمپوچيا

کمبه kambá *f.* bin, corn crib; barn, granary

کمبله kambelá *f.* monkey-face tree, *Mallotus phillipinensis*

کمپ kamp *m.* camp

کمپار kampár *m.* potter

کمپالا kampālá *f.* Kampala

کمپاني kampāní *f.* company خارجي کمپاني foreign company

کمپرادور komprādór *m.* comprador, intermediary

کمپرېسور kompresór *m.* compressor

کمپینگ kámpíng *m.* life in tents, camp life

کمپني kampaní *f.* ☞ کمپاني

کمپو kámpú *m.* *regional* camp

کم پیدا kampajdá uncommon, rare

کمپوټ kampóṭ *m.* کمپوټ kampóṭ *m.* **1** stewed fruit, compote **2** canned fruit

کمپوچيا kampuchijá *f.* Kampuchea

کمپوډر kampuḍár *m.* *regional* ☞ کمپوډر

کمپوزیشن kampozíshn *m.* composition

کمپوست kompóst *m.* compost, fertilizer

کمپوونډر kampaunḍár *m.* pharmacist, druggist

کمپوونډري kampaunḍarí *f.* pharmaceutics; the work of a pharmacist

کمپینگ kámpíng *m.* ☞ کمپینگ

کمتر kamtár[1] *f.* *dialect* dove, pigeon

کمتر kamtár[2] **1** little, few **2** smaller, less

کمتره kamtára *f.* *dialect* female pigeon, dove

کمتري kamtarí *f.* a little, a bit; insufficiency, inadequacy

کمتوب kamtób *m.* کمتیا kamtjá *f.* trifle, insignificance

کم جایداد kamdzhājdád land-starved, land-hungry

کم جایدادي kamdzhājdádí *f.* land shortage, land hunger

کم جرأت kamdzhur'át shy, timid, timorous, cowardly

کم جرأتي kamdzhur'atí *f.* timidity, timorousness, cowardliness کم جرأتي له ځانه لري کول to struggle against shyness, overcome shyness

کم جنسه kamdzhínsa of low pedigree; low-grade, low-quality

کمچ kamách *m.* tent pole

کمچتکا kamchatká *f.* Kamchatka

کمچه kamácha *f.* **1** long pole (for tying livestock) **2** stretcher made of poles (for carrying a dead person)

کمچه گوته kamácha gúta *f.* fourth finger, ring finger

کمڅۍ kamtséj *f.* *dialect* plait, tress, braid (woman's)

کم حجمه kamhádzhma compact, of small size

کم حوصلگي kamhawsilagí *f.* flabbiness; apathy; lack of initiative, lack of enterprise

کم حوصله kamhawsilá flabby; apathetic; lacking initiative, lacking the spirit of enterprise

کم خرڅ kamkhárts **1** economical, cheap **2** of modest means کم خرڅ بالانشین cheap but good

کم خرڅي kamkhartsí *f.* **1** cheapness, low prices **2** shortage of means, scantiness of means **3** lack of exactingness, lack of high standards

کم خوبي kamkhobí *f.* insomnia, sleeplessness د کم خوبي ناروغي insomnia

کم خور kamkhór کم خوراک kamkhorák **1** eating little, underfed **2** moderate, restrained in food

کم خوري kamkhorí *f.* **1** malnutrition **2** moderation, restraint in food

کم خون kamkhún anemic

کم خوني kamkhuní *f.* anemia

کم ذات kamzát **1** doing manual labor **2** occupying a low status (in society)

کم ذاتي kamzátí *f.* baseness, meanness, mean act

کمر kamár[1] **1** *m.* precipice, slope; steep cliff, vertical mountainside د کمره په سر ولاړ **a** standing on the edge of a precipice or chasm **b** *figurative* old man **2** waist کمربند belt, sash

کمر kamár[2] skewbald (of the color of horses, etc.)

کمربسته kamarbastá **1** belted, girdled **2** prepared for a journey **3** at (someone's) service, prepared to serve (someone)

کمربند kamarbánd *m.* **1** belt, sash **2** *technology* drive belt

کمرچن kamarchín gathered in at the waist

کمرشکن kamarshikán **1** shattering, crushing **2** ruinous

کمرغالی kamarghálaj *m.* cave, cavern, grotto

کمرکه kamaráka *f.* *regional* cupboard

کمرکیسه kamarkisá *f.* powder pouch (worn at the waist)

کمرگل kamargúl *m.* lichen

کمرنگه kamránga کم رنگ kamráng **1** pale, dim, dull; faded کمرنگه رڼا dim light **2** weak (of tea)

کم روڼ kamrúṇ کم روڼا kamruṇá subdued, pale; dim; weak کم روڼ څراغ dim lamp

کمره kamrá[1] *f.* *regional* room د جهاز کمره cabin, stateroom د خوراک کمره dining room

کمره kamará[2] *f.* camera د عکاسي کمره camera

کمره kamára[3] *f.* capers

کمره kamára[4] *f.* married woman

کمره kamára[5] *feminine singular of* کمر[2]

کمری ¹ kamaráj *m.* rice husks

کمری ² kamráj *m.* (small) scoop

کمزور kamzór weak, feeble, infirm کمزور کېدل *compound verb* ☞ کمزوربدل

کمزورتیا kamzortjá *f.* ☞ کمزوروالی kamzorwǻlaj *m.* ☞ کمزوري ¹

کمزورول kamzorawə́l *denominative, transitive* [*past:* کمزور یې کړ] to weaken د اقتصاد له لحاظه کمزورول to weaken the economy

کمزوري ¹ kamzorí *f.* weakness, debility, infirmity د ځمکي کمزوري fallow land

کمزوری ² kamzóraj ☞ کمزور د مفصلو خبرو څخه ځان کمزوری وینم I am unable to answer the question in detail

کمزوربدل kamzoredə́l *denominative, intransitive* [*past:* کمزور شو] to weaken, grow weak

کمسل kamásl ☞ کم اصل

کمسور kamsór not broad, narrow

کمسومول komsomól *m.* Komsomol (Young Communist League)

کمسومولي komsomolí 1 Komsomol (of or pertaining to the Komsomol) 2 *m.* Komsomolets (a member of the Komsomol)

کمسی kamsə́j *f.* plait, tress, braid (woman's)

کمیشنر kamíshinár *m.* commissar عالي کمشنر، های کمشنر high commissar

کم طاقته kamtāqáta کم سا kam saa kamtāqát weak, infirm, feeble طاقته کېدل *compound verb* a to weaken, grow weak b to surrender, yield

کم عقله kam'áqəla 1 foolish, stupid; unreasonable, unwise; weak-minded, imbecile 2 *m.* fool, foolish person

کم عقلتوب kam'aqltób *m.* کم عقلي kam'aqlí *f.* foolishness, stupidity; imbecility کم عقلي مه کوه! Don't act foolish!

کم غوښی kamghwǻkhaj meager, lean, emaciated, gaunt, wiry, sinewy

کم فرصته kamfursáta busy, having no free time

کم فرصتي kamfursatí *f.* being busy, lack of leisure time

کم فکره kamfíkra not serious, frivolous, ill-considered, not well thought through

کم فکري kamfikrí *f.* lack of seriousness, frivolousness, lack of due consideration, poorly thought through د کم فکری څخه کار اخیستل to show thoughtlessness

کم فهم kamfáhm 1 slow-witted, dull, slow-to-grasp 2 not very conscientious; irresponsible

کم فهمي kamfahmí *f.* 1 slowness, dullness; slow-wittedness 2 irresponsibility

کم قدر kamqádr devoid of value, of little value, not valuable

کم قدري kamqadrí *f.* condition of being of little value

کم قوت kamquwát 1 feeble, weak, infirm; low-powered 2 not productive, not efficient, of low efficiency 3 sterile, infertile

کم قوت والی kamquwatwǻlaj *m.* ☞ کم قوتي

کم قوته kamquwáta ☞ کم قوته

کم قوتي kamquwatí *f.* 1 weakness, infirmity 2 low efficiency 3 sterility, infertility

کم قیمته kamqimáta cheap, inexpensive

کم قیمتي kamqimatí *f.* low prices, cheapness

کمک kumák *m.* 1 help, support; assistance, good offices د چا سره د کمک څخه ځان نه سپمول to render assistance to someone کمک کول to fail to render aid 2 grant, grant-in-aid, allowance

کمکلی kamkəláj کمکوټی kamkóṭaj tiny, wee, diminutive

کمکي ¹ kumakí 1 *m.* assistant 2 auxiliary کمکي فعل *grammar* auxiliary verb

کمکی ² kamkáj 1 small, little کمکی اختر ☞ اختر کمکی هلک youngster, young child 2 *m.* 1 child, baby 2.2 *plural* کمکیان kamkiyán children

کمکیتوب kamkitób *m.* کمکینه kamkína *f.* کمکي والی kamkiwǻlaj m. childhood; nonage

کم گوی kamgúj taciturn, reticent, silent, uncommunicative

کمل kamál *m.* horse cloth, horse blanket

کم له کمه kamləkáma at least, at minimum

کم ما یه kammājá not having sufficient capital, insolvent, bankrupt

کم محنت kammihnát lazy; unconscientiously

کم مهارت kammahārát having poor skills, unskillful, not expert

کمنترن komintérn *m. history* COM intern (Communist International)

کمند kamánd *m.* 1 lariat, rope with a loop, lasso 2 rope ladder 3 hobble

کمندری kaməndráj 1 undersized, shortest, stunted 2 weak, feeble

کم نصیبه kamnasíba unlucky

کم نصیبي kamnasibí bad luck

کم نظره kamnazára having weak eyesight, near-sighted, myopic

کم نوره kamnúra dim, dark سترگي یې کم نوري سوې Everything went dark before his eyes.

کمڼ kamə́ṇ withered, wilted; faded

کمن والی kaməṇwǻlaj *m.* wilting, withering; fading

کمنول kaməṇawə́l *denominative, transitive* [*past:* کمن یې کړ] to promote wilting, contribute to withering

کمنبدل kaməṇedə́l *denominative, intransitive* [*past:* کمن شو] to wither; fade; droop

کمو ¹ kə́mo *oblique plural of* کم ¹

کمو ² kámo *oblique plural of* کم ²

کمواک kamwák کمواکی kamwákaj 1 weak, low-powered 2 not of high quality

کمواکي kamwākí *f.* 1 weakness, low power 2 low quality

کموالی kamwǻlaj *m.* 1 insufficiency; insignificance 2 reducing, lessening

کم وبیش kam-u-bésh more or less

کموده kamóda *f.* [*usually plural* کمودي kamódi] rice kasha with spices

کم وزیات kam-u-ziját more or less

کمول ¹ kumól *m.* stork

کمول ² kamawə́l 1 *denominative, transitive* [*past:* کم یې کړ] .1 to lessen, curtail, reduce 1.2 to lower, reduce (e.g., prices) 1.3 د ....

خُخه کمول to subtract **1.4** to soften, mitigate (e.g., a punishment) **1.5** to diminish, denigrate (someone's dignity, authority, etc.) **2** *m. plural* **.1** lessening, curtailing, reducing **2.2** lowering (e.g., prices) **2.3** د ... خُخه کمول subtraction **2.4** mitigation (e.g., of a punishment); diminishing, denigrating (dignity, authority, etc.)

کموله ¹ kamóla *f.* fine, glassy rice

کموله ² kumóla *feminine of* کمول ¹

کمونست komuníst, kommuníst **1** *m.* communist **2** communist(ic)

کمونستي komuní, kommuní **1** communist(ic) کمونستي جامعه communist society کمونستي ګوند، کمونستي پارتي، کمونستي حزب communist party **2** *m.* communist

کمونسټ komuníṣt, kommuníṣt *m.* ☞ کمونست

کمونیزم komunízm, kommunízm *m.* communism

کمه ¹ kə́ma, kúma *feminine singular of* کم ¹

کمه ² káma **1** *feminine singular of* کم ² په کمه smaller **2** *f.* trifle, insignificance

کم همته kamhimmáta timid, timorous, cowardly

کم همتي kamhimmatí *f.* timidity, timorousness, cowardice

کمي ¹ kamí *f.* **1** reduction, lessening **2** insufficiency, shortage د چاکمي پوره کول to satisfy someone's needs

کمي ² kamí *Arabic* quantitative, numerical کمي تغییرات *philosophy* quantitative change

کمي ³ kamáj *m.* **1** lessening, curtailing, reducing کمی کول *compound verb* to be lessened, be curtailed, be reduced په ... کنبي کمی راتلل، کمی راتلل to be lessened, be curtailed; be insufficient **2** shortage; scarcity د رسن کمی food shortage **3** pinching, infringement, constraint, limitation د خان کمی بلل to consider it a humiliation

کمیابه kamjába rare, seldom encountered

کمیابي kamjābí *f.* rarity

کیمیايي kimjāí ☞ کمیايي

کمیت kamijját *m. Arabic* quantity, number د کمیت تغییر په کیفیت سره transition from quantity to quality

کمیته kamitá *f.* **1** committee **2** commission مداومه کمیته permanent commission د اعتبار نامو کمیته credentials committee

کمیتي ² kamijatí ☞ کمي

کمیته kamiṭá *f.* ☞ کمیته

کمبدان kumedán *m. regional* **1** chief of police **2** *colloquial* major

کمېدل kamedə́l *denominative, intransitive* [*past:* کم شو] **1** to be lessened, be curtailed, be diminished **2** to lose weight **3** to be lowered, be reduced (e.g., of prices) **4** د ... خُخه to be subtracted **5** to be softened, be mitigated (of a punishment); be diminished, be denigrated (of someone's dignity, authority, etc.)

کمېدنه kamedə́na *f.* کمېده kamedə́ *m. plural* **1** lessening, curtailing, reducing شهرت یي مخ په کمبدو دئ His fame is fading. **2** loss of weight **3** fall, reduction (e.g., of prices)

کمېډي komeḍí *f.* کمېډي komeḍí *f.* comedy

کمبرون kamerún *m.* Cameroon

کمیس kamís *m.* [*plural:* کمیسونه kamisúna *and Western* کمیسان kamisán] shirt لاندي کمیس undershirt; slip په کمیسه کنبي نه خایېدل *idiom* to be beside oneself with joy, be overjoyed (*literally:* to not have enough room in one's shirt) کمیسونه زیات خیرل *idiom* to be senior in age (*literally:* to tear up more than shirts) انسان کله په مته کنبي خایېږي او کله په کمیسه کنبي نه خایېږي *proverb* in life anything can happen, there are joys and sorrows

کمیسار komisár *m.* commissar سرحدي کمیسار border commissar

کمیساریت komisārijját *m.* commissariat

کمیسر komisár *m.* ☞ کمیسار

کمیسه کار komisakár *m.* agent, broker د نقلیه کمیسه کار forwarding agent

کمیسیان kəmisján *m. plural* decoration on a dress (made from gold-colored leather)

کمیسیون komisjún *m.* commission

کمیشن kamisshán *m.* **1** trade commission, commission operation **2** *regional* officer rank; the officers

کمیشنر kamishinár *m.* authorized agent; representative د.م.م. کمیشنر representative of the UN (United Nations)

کمیشن کار kamishankár *m.* agent, broker

کمیشن کاري kamishankārí *f.* commission operations د نقلیاتو کمیشن کاري transport and forwarding operations

کمیک komík comical, funny

کمین ¹ kamín ☞ کمینه د عمر او سن کمین younger

کمین ² kamín *m. Arabic* ambush

کمین توګ kamintóg **1** low, mean, base **2** vulgar, coarse

کمینه kaminá **1.1** small, insignificant, unimportant **1.2** humble, meek, submissive, obedient **1.3** *regional* mean, base, low **2** *regional, abusive* scoundrel!, villain!

کمیني kaminí *f.* humility, meekness, submissiveness

کم یو kəm jáw ☞ کم یو راغلئ دئ Someone has arrived.

کمجونسټ kamjuníṣt *m.* ☞ کمونست

کمجونستي kamjunistí ☞ کمونستي

کمجونیزم kamjunízm *m.* ☞ کمونیزم

کن ¹ kán digging, carving کاریز کن worker who is digging irrigation ditches

کن ² kún doing, making کار کن hard-working; worker, collaborator

کنات ¹ kanát *m.* ☞ قنات

کناټور kunāṭawə́r having a broad rump, having a wide posterior, having fat buttocks

کناټی kunāṭj *m.* seat, posterior کناټی خوڅول buttock

کنار kanár *m.* **1** land, place **2** arms, embrace

کناره kanārá, kinārá *f.* land, place د چا څخه کناره نیول خان to avoid گوښه او کناره ژوند کول to live in seclusion کناره نیول to keep aloof

کناره ګیري kanāragirí *f.* voluntarily stepping aside; non-participation

کناړ kunāṛáj *m. dialect* butcher

کناز knāz *m.* prince

کنال ¹ kanál *m.* kanal (a measure of area equal to ¼ jareeb; 1 jareeb = 22 yards)

کنال ² kanā́l *m.* **1** canal **2** *figurative* channel; instance, authority

کناوېز kanāwéz *m.* **1** taffeta (a silk fabric) **2** cotton cloth

کنايت kināját *m. Arabic* کنايه kinājá *f. Arabic* **1** hint; indication **2** allegory; metaphor

کنپل kanpál *m.* first footprint

کنترول kanṭról *m.* **1** monitoring, supervision, checking, inspection, control د کنترول آلي monitoring instruments **2** relating, governing د ترافيک کنترول traffic regulation **3** steering, controlling (an airplane etc.) **4** subordination, compliance; keeping in check, keeping under control د کنترولہ خارجيدل a to get out of control b to get out of compliance ☞ کنترولول ;کنترول کول *compound verb* بيا يې کنترول له واکه ووتئ ;کنترولېدل ☞ *compound verb* کنترول کېدل He lost self-control.

کنترولر kanṭróler *m.* inspector, controller

کنترولېدل ¹ kantrolawə́l *denominative, transitive* [*past:* کنترول يې کړ] **1** to monitor, to supervise, to check, to inspect, to control **2** to regulate **3** to steer, to drive, to control (an aircraft, etc.) **4** to subordinate, to make compliant, to keep in check, to keep under control

کنترولي kantrolí monitoring, checking, inspection, control

کنترولېدل ² kantroledə́l *denominative, intransitive* [*past:* کنترول شو] **1** to be monitored, be checked, be inspected, be controlled **2** to be regulated **3** to be driven, be steered, be controlled (of an aircraft, etc.)

کنترول kanṭról *m.* ☞ کنترول

کنترولول kanṭrolawə́l *transitive* ☞ کنترولول

کنترولېدل kanṭroledə́l *intransitive* ☞ کنترولېدل

کنټکين kanṭkín cotton

کنج ¹ kandzh *m.* **1** coquetry, flirtation **2** clowning, affected airs, grimacing, making faces **3** scorn, disdain کنج کول *compound verb* **a** to flirt, behave coquettishly **b** to clown, grimace, make faces **c** to scorn, disdain

کنج ² kundzh *m.* corner; secluded nook

کنجاره kundzhārá *m.* oil cakes (used as livestock feed)

کنجت kundzhə́t *m. plural* sesame

کنجپوړ kandzhapóṛ *m.* crab

کنجدي kundzhídi *f. plural* sesame

کنجر kandzhór shameless, imprudent, unfit

کنجری kandzhṛáj *f.* shameless woman; strumpet, trollop

کنجغوت kandzhaghwút narrow and dark

کنجک ¹ kandzhák *m.* ☞ کجک ¹

کنجک ² kandzhák *m.* **1** pole with a hook on the end for dragging a roller (during threshing) **2** hook

کنجک ³ kundzhák *m.* ☞ د کنجکو غوړي کنجکه sesame seed oil, tahini

کنجکاوي kundzhkāwí curiosity علمي کنجکاوي inquisitiveness

کنجکه kundzhóka *f.* **1** cowry (a shell used as money) **2** penny, brass farthing د يوې کنجکي زيان insignificant loss

کنجکی kandzhakáj *m.* **1** pin **2** lower jaw, mandible **3** elephant driver's hook, mahout's hook

کنجلک kundzhulák rumpled, crumpled

کنجن ¹ kandzhán crushed, ground, pulverized

کنجن ² kandzhə́n coquettish

کنجواله kandzhwā́la *f.* conceit, complacency, smugness

کنجوړه kandzhoṛá *f.* ☞ کنجاره

کنجوس kandzhús **1.1** stingy, miserly **1.2** mean, base, foul **2** *m.* miser, skinflint

کنجوسي kandzhusí *f.* **1** stinginess, miserliness **2** meanness, baseness, mean act

کنجوغه kandzhughá *f.* strap at the rear saddletree for attaching something

کنجول kandzhawə́l *transitive* [*past:* و يې کنجاوه] **1** to spoil, pamper someone **2** to describe in glowing terms, shower praise on someone (thereby baiting the others) **3** to bid up, drive up the price of something

کنجي ¹ kundzhí *f.* کنجی kundzhə́j *f.* [*plural:* کنجی kundzhə́j *and* کنجياني kundzhijā́ni] *literally & figuratively* key گری له کنجي ورکول to wind a timepiece

کنجی ² kundzhə́j *f.* [*plural:* کنجياني kundzhijā́ni] water pitcher, water jug

کنجبيل kandzhejə́l *transitive* ☞ کنجول

کنځا kandzā́ *f.* curse, oath, swear-word; swearing, abusive language کنځاوي کول، کنځا کول *compound verb* to swear

کنځری kandzəráj *m.* manna (on the cotoneaster) ☞ شيرخشت

کنځړ kandzáṛ *m.* blanket

کنځکی kandzəkáj *m.* main beam of a tent (to which the ribs are attached)

کنځل ¹ kandzə́l **1** *transitive verb* [*past:* و يې کانځه] to scold, rail at, abuse verbally **2** *m. plural* abuse, bad language, swearing کنځل کول *compound verb* to swear, abuse verbally

کنځول ² kandzál *m.* ☞ کنځل

کنځله ¹ kundzə́la *f.* sesame

کنځله ² kandzə́la *f.* [*usually plural* کنځلي kandzə́li] verbal abuse, bad language, swearing کنځلي کول *compound verb* to swear, abuse verbally

کنځول kandzúl *m.* (over)coat, top-coat

کنځه kándza *f.* index finger

کند ¹ kand *m.* **1** ravine; gorge **2** crack **3** pit **4** honeycomb کند جوړول *compound verb* to build a honeycomb

کند ² kənd, kind *m.* **1** rags **2** dress of a fakir or dervish, rags, tatters

کند ³ kund *literally & figuratively* dull

کند ⁴ kand *m.* ☞ قند

کنداغ kandā́gh, kundā́gh *m.* butt, stock (of a firearm)

کندال kandā́l *m.* igniter, primer (of a firearm)

کندانۍ kandānə́j *f.* sugar bowl

کندپوخ kindpókh *m.* ragamuffin, ragged fellow

کندره kándra, kándara *f.* ravine; hollow, depression کندری کودری extremely rugged terrain

کندری [1] kandóraj *m.* crock

کندرج [2] kandráj *m.* plain

کندغالی kandghā́laj *m.* ravine, hollow, gully; precipice

کندکی kandəkáj *m.* yashmak border (embroidered with silk)

کندل [1] kundíl *m. proper noun* Kundil

کندل [2] kandól, kindól *transitive* [*present:* کني *past:* و يې کند] to dig کيندل ☞

کندلوښی kandlóxhaj *m.* sugar bowl

کندو [1] kandú *m.* [*plural:* کندوان kanduā́nand کندوگان kandugā́n] **1** bin, corn-crib (woven and coated with clay) **2** storehouse (for grain)

کندو [2] kandó *oblique plural of* کنده [1] ځان د فنا په کندو اچول to fall, sink into obscurity

کندوری [1] kanduráj *m.* **1** small bin, small corn crib **2** case, box, chest

کندوری [2] kandóraj *m.* crock

کنده [1] kándá *f.* **1** ravine; hollow, depression **2** pit, cavity; precipice, abyss **3** common grave **4** *figurative* precipice, gulf, abyss, chasm د تباهی کندي ته لوېدل the abyss of war د جگړي کنده to perish; slip over a precipice د کندي جام *proverb* the sun

کنده [2] kundá *f.* **1** log **2** butt, stock (of a firearm) **3** plow beam **4** post, column پنبه تر کنده ختل to become engaged to, exchange rings with

کندهار kandhā́r *m.* ☞ قندهار

کندهاري kandhārí **1** *m. plural* Kandhari (a subdivision of the Safi tribe) **2** kandhāráy *m.* a Kandharai

کندی [1] kundí *f.* polishing, glazing (cloth)

کندی [2] kandáj *m.* **1** neighborhood of a village بر کندی the western part of a village کوز کندی the eastern part of a village **2** crock

کندی [3] kundáj *m.* woolen rope, woolen cord

کندی [4] kandé, kándi *plural of* کنده [1]

کندی [5] kandé *plural of* کنده [2]

کندی دار kandidā́r *m.* village elder; foreman

کندی کودری kándi-kudóri *f.* کندی کوندی kándi-kúndi *f. plural* broken land, rough terrain

کندبل kandél *m.* **1** ditch **2** earthenware dish

کند [1] kanḍ *m. plural* **1** gum, resin **2** ☞ قند **3** کندراتي ☞

کند [2] kanḍ *m.* small piece, small chunk (of sugar, etc.) کند کند in pieces

کند [3] kunḍ *m.* widower

کندا kunḍā́, kanḍā́ **1** thick-lipped **2** having a harelip **3** with a broken or broken off horn (of livestock)

کنداتي kanḍā́ti *f. plural* colostrums

کنداس kunḍās, kanḍās **1** toothless **2** *m.* toothless, mumbling old man

کنداستوب kunḍāstób *m.* کنداستیا kanḍāstjā́ *f.* کنداسوالی kunḍāswā́laj *m.* absence of teeth, toothlessness

کندال kanḍā́l *m.* **1** earthenware bowl **2** vat, tub (for dyeing) **3** laundry tub

کنداله kanḍālá *f.* **1** firing chamber (of a flintlock firearm) **2** flowerpot **3** pot (for melting butter)

کنداو [1] kanḍā́w *m.* break, breach; slit

کنداو [2] kanḍā́w **1** defective **2** polled, hornless

کندتون kunḍtún *m.* widowhood

کندر kanḍár, kanḍór *m.* **1** ruins **2** passageway made in a wall by robbers کندر وهل *compound verb* to dig a passageway **3** dwelling place of goblins and ghosts

کندری kanḍóraj *m.* burdock that has gotten stuck in the wool of sheep

کندک [1] kanḍák *m.* **1** battalion د مخابري کندک communications battalion نقلیه کندک transport battalion **2** part of a herd of sheep or goats numbering up to three hundred head **3** part of something

کندک [2] kanḍók *m.* **1** hunk, chunk یو کندک ډوډۍ piece of bread **2** fragment

کندکپر kanḍkapár *dialect* ☞ کندوکپر

کندکمشر kanḍakmóshr *m.* major

کندکي [1] kanḍakí battalion

کندکی [2] kanḍəkáj *m.* hard, frozen piece of something, lump, clod

کندکین kanḍkín cotton

کندلی kanḍaláj *f.* **1** large burdock **2** ☞ کندری

کندو kanḍáw **1** *m.* **.1** (mountain) pass **1.2** excavation, hollow; gap (in a wall) په دېوال کښي کندو کول to make a hole in a wall **1.3** tooth, cog, lug **2** pitted, scratched; pierced

کندواله kanḍwālá *f.* **1** ruins کندواله کول *compound verb* to destroy **2** the site of an ancient town

کندور kanḍúr *f.* fat or grease that is used to soak paper that is to be used instead of glass

کندوری [1] kanḍóri *m. plural* gum, resin

کندوری [2] kanḍúraj *m* distance between the thumb and index finger

کندوسکي kanḍúski *m. plural* ear of maize with husks on

کندو کپر kanḍ-u-kapár **1** scattered, strewn, diffused **2** broken **3** chipped, notched کندو کپر کول *compound verb* **a** to scatter, strew; spread **b** to break, crush **c** to make notches in, chip کندو کپر کېدل *compound verb* **a** to be scattered, be strewn; be spread **b** to be broken **c** to be chipped

کندو کندو kanḍáw-kanḍáw chipped کندو کندو ږمونږ toothless teeth

کندوکی kanḍúkaj *m.* small piece; slice

کندول kanḍól *m.* **1** earthenware bowl, clay mug **2** toothless person **3** *figurative* lunar disk **4** crock د صبر کندول یې ډک شو *proverb* one's patience is exhausted

کندوله kanḍóla *f.* flowerpot

کندولی kanḍoláj *m.* **1** small earthenware scoop **2** small bowl, small handleless drinking cup **3** drinking bowl (for birds) **4** crock

کندووالی kanḍawwā́laj *m.* break, breakthrough, breach

کنډوول kanḍawawǝ́l *denominative, transitive* [*past:* کنډو یې کړ] **1** to chip, make chips, make notches in **2** to break, chop off a little piece of something

کنډوی kanḍówaj *m.* small piece; slice

کنډوبدل kanḍawedǝ́l *denominative, intransitive* [*past:* کنډو شو] **1** to be chipped, chip **2** to be broken, be chopped (off)

کنډه [^1] kanḍa *f.* **1** balance, scale (used by pharmacists, jewelers) **2** balance or scale pan د تجربې په کنډه تلل to verify experimentally

کنډه [^2] kanḍá *f.* source of a river

کنډه [^3] kúnḍa *f.* د کونډې دوه غوایي وه، یو وت نه، بل ننوت نه *saying* there's no way out (*literally*: a widow had two oxen, one wouldn't go out, the other wouldn't come in)

کنډه [^4] kunḍá *f.* hook

کنډه [^5] kǝnḍá *f.* statue, sculpture

کنډی [^1] kanḍój *f. hunting* **1** blind (hiding place for hunters) **2** trap hole

کنډی [^2] kanḍój *f.* ☞ کنی

کنډی [^3] kunḍój *f.* wooden cup, wooden bowl, wooden saucer

کنډیاله kanḍjála *f.* **1** stall, stable (for livestock) **2** ruins

کنډي کپری kanḍé-kapóre *f. plural* **1** uneven, very rugged terrain **2** bumpy road

کنرکی kanórkaj *m.* roast made from dried meat

کنړ kunáṛ *m.* Kunar (river and region) د کنړ دره the Kunar Valley کنړ ولایت Kunar Province

کنړی kunaṛí Kunar کنړی وریجي Kunar rice

کنزاینمنت kanzǝ́nmenṭ *m.* **1** consignment of goods **2** bill of lading

کنزل kanzǝ́l *transitive* ☞ کنځل [^1]

کنزله kunzǝ́la *f.* ☞ کنځله [^1]

کنزه گوته kánza gúta *f.* fourth finger

کنس kans confused, embarrassed, perplexed; stunned, surprised

کنست kǝnóst *m.* digging; excavating

کنستر kunastár *m.* dregs

کنستک kanǝsták *m.* miser, skinflint

کنستل kǝnastǝ́l *transitive* ☞ کیندل

کنسته kunsǝ́ta *f.* ☞ کونسته

کنسرت kansért *m.* concert

کنسروه kanserwá *f.* canned food

کنسکتوب kanǝsktób *m.* کنسکتیا kanǝsktjá *f.* stinginess, miserliness

کنسکی kanǝ́skaj **1** stingy, miserly **2** mean, base, foul

کنسنترات konsentrát *m* concentrate

کنسوی kunsówaj ☞ کون سوی

کنشت kunísht *m.* temple

کنښت kanǝ́kht *m.* ☞ کنست

کنغاره kǝnghā́ra *f.* pelvis

کنغښی kanghǝ́khaj *m.* ☞ کرغښی

کنف [^1] kanáf *m. Arabic* [*plural:* کنفونه kanafúna *and Arabic* اکناف aknáf] **1** land, place; environment, neighborhood **2** edge, border, selvage

کنف [^2] kanáf *m.* kenaf, *Hibiscus cannanbinus*

کنفدراسیون kanfederāsjón *m.* confederation

کنفرانس kanferā́ns *m.* **1** lecture, report کنفرانس ورکول *compound verb* to make a report **2** conference د کنفرانس اطاق conference hall **3** stage performance

کنفکشنری kanfekshanarí *f.* **1** confectioner's shop **2** confectionery

کنکرک kankǝrák frozen

کنکره kunkrá *f. medicine* trachoma

کنکړی kankóraj *m.* crust of bread that has stuck to the wall of an oven

کنکوک kankúk *m.* kite

کنگاش kangā́sh *m. history* tribal council

کنگال [^1] kangāl lone, solitary, single

کنگال [^2] kangā́l *m.* washed (clean) dishware

کنگالول kangālawǝ́l *denominative, transitive* [*past:* کنگال یې کړ] to wash up, rinse (plates and dishes)

کنگالونه kangālawǝ́na *f.* washing, rinsing (of dishes)

کنگالي kangā́li rinsed کنگالي اوبه dishwater

کنگالېدل kangāledǝ́l *denominative, intransitive* [*past:* کنگال شو] to be washed (of dishes)

کنگخړ kangkhǝ́ṛ, kangakhǝ́ṛ *m.* کنگخړه kangakhǝ́ṛa *f.* **1** chips and brushwood **2** wood that has been washed ashore by a river

کنگر kangír *m.* pumice

کنگرخل kangirkhál *m.* leavings, leftovers; remnants of straw

کنگره [^1] kangará *f.* pieces of ice, sludge (on a river)

کنگره [^2] kangrá, kungurá *f.* **1** turret **2** merlon **3** wall with loopholes **4** embrasure, gun port **5** plume (on a helmet) **6** decoration, ornamentation (on a crown) **7** summit (of a mountain) **8** upper part of a wall **9** tooth, cog (of a wheel)

کنگره [^3] kangrá *f.* congress; conference, convention حزبي کنگره party congress

کنگره [^4] kangrá *f.* trachoma

کنگری [^1] kangráj, kungráj *m.* puppy; cub

کنگری [^2] kangrój *f.* **1** built-in cupboard; niche **2** grating at the top of a wall

کنگرزی kangrezáj *m.* **1** echo په غره کښي کنگرزی شو an echo resounded in the mountains **2** ringing in the ears په غوږو کښي می My ears are ringing. کنگرزی شو

کنگړ [^1] kangáṛ *m.* narrow bracelet; bracelet, hoop (among the fakirs, etc.)

کنگړ [^2] kangáṛ *m.* ☞ کنگرخل

کنگړ [^3] kangáṛ *m.* ☞ کنگل

کنگړی kangṛáj *m.* hail

کنگزتون kingztáun *m.* Kingston

کنگس [^1] kangás *m.* narcissus

کنگس [^2] kangás *m.* stumbling کنگس خوړل *compound verb* to stumble

کنگل kangál, kangól **1** *m.* ice کنگل نیول *compound verb* to freeze, become covered in ice **2.1** frozen, stiff from the cold; covered with ice **2** hardened كنگل كول كنگلول; compound verb ☞ كنگل كبدل compound verb ☞ كنگلبدل

كنگۇلزى kangə́lzaj *m.* glacier

كنگلۇنى kanglə́naj *m.* icehouse (cellar)

كنگلول kangalawə́l *denominative, transitive [past:* كنگل يې كړ] **1** to freeze **2** to make hard, solidify

كنگلبدل kangaledə́l *denominative, intransitive [past:* كنگل شو] **1** to become frozen, freeze; become covered with ice; become stiff with cold **2** to harden, become hard

كنگۇڼ kangə́ṇ *m.* ☞ كنگۍ¹

كنگۇ kangú *m.* saffron

كنگوره kangorá *f.* edging, trimming (of a veil, etc.)

كنگوسى kangúsaj *m.* ☞ كنگس

كنگوله kangolá *f.* earthenware dish (for the long-term storage of grapes)

كنگه kə́nga *f.* tombstone

كنگي¹ kángi *m. plural* dung, excrement

كنگۍ² kangə́j *f.* ☞ كنگه

كنگوله kanginá *f.* ☞ كنگوله

كنل kinə́l, kənə́l *transitive* ☞ كيندل

كنوانسيون konwānsijón *m.* convention

كنوباى kənobáj *m.* dregs, leftovers, orts

كنود¹ kənód *imperfect of* كنل

كنود² kənód *m.* digging

كنودل kənodə́l *transitive* ☞ كيندل

كنوخى kənóχhaj *m.* saddle

كنول kanawúl *transitive Eastern* ☞ كيندل

كنونكى kanúnkaj **1** *present participle of* كنل **2** *m.* engraver

كنه¹ kaná, kə́na *f.* tick

كنه² kaná *f.* edge, selvage (of material, a shawl)

كنه³ kúna *f.* bottom د ‏‎پوى كنې لاندي تياره وي *proverb* to be unable to see beyond the end of one's nose (*literally:* at the bottom of a lamp it is dark)

كنه⁴ kúna *f.* ☞ كونه²

كنه⁵ kaná, kanə́ *intensifying particle* ته ځې كنه؟ Well, are you coming or not? وخكه كنه! But I also came to him. زه هم ورغلم كنه Now drink! هو كنه! Yes, indeed! كنه وي in a different way

كنكينا kinakiná *f.* quinine

كنې¹ kiní, kəní *present tense of* كنل

كنې² kəné *present tense second person of* كنل

كنې³ kané كه نه يې differently, in a different way, else, otherwise راځه كنې زه ځم You'd better go or else I'll leave.

كنبرى kanerí *f.* canary

كنيزه kaníza *f.* **1** maidservant, housemaid **2** concubine

كنيسه kanisá *f.* temple

كنيكبر kunikabár *m.* crab

كنين kunáín *m. plural* quinine

كنيه kunijá *f. Arabic* nickname, sobriquet

كڼ kəṇ *m.* snivel, snot

كڼاخه kaṇā́kha *f.* **1** cinereous vulture, black griffon **2** black crow

كڼاوه kaṇāwá *f. [usually plural* كڼاوې kaṇāwé] sandals with wooden soles

كڼتيا kəṇtjā́ *f.* deafness

كڼلغ kəṇlúgh *m. plural* Karluki (a Turkish people)

كڼوټكى kaṇótskaj a bit deaf, a little hard of hearing

كڼول kaṇawə́l *denominative, transitive [past:* كوڼ يې كړ] to deafen; cause to become deaf, make deaf

كڼونه kaṇawə́na *f.* making deaf

كڼه kaṇá, kəṇá **1** *feminine singular of* كوڼ² **2** *f. [plural:* كڼياني kaṇijā́ni] deaf female

كڼوټكى kaṇhóts كڼ هوخ

كڼه ورغه kaṇá, wə́rgha *f.* raven

كڼي¹ kə́ṇi *f. plural* snivel, snot

كڼي² kaṇáj *m.* **1** textiles warp (of fabric) كڼى جار ايستل، كڼى جارول tighten the warp **2** the constellations Ursa Major and Ursa Minor (Big Dipper and Little Dipper)

كڼي³ kaṇáj *m. botany* bindweed

كڼى⁴ kaṇə́j *f.* woodencup

كڼې⁵ kaṇé *feminine plural of* كوڼ²

كڼيا kaṇjā́ innumerable, countless, numberless كڼيا زره thousands

كڼيباف kaṇajbā́f *m.* ☞ كڼيوالا

كڼبدل kaṇedə́l *denominative, intransitive [past:* كوڼ شو] **1** to become deaf, grow deaf **2** to stop (sounding, e.g., of a bell)

كڼيوالا kaṇajwālā́ *m.* weaver of carpets and reversible rugs

كو¹ kaw *m.* hump (of a camel)

كو² ku *present tense perfective aspect first person plural of* كړل, *in lieu of* كړو

كو³ ku *interjection* Would you believe it; How do you like that; Well, I'll be

كواتى kwatə́j *f.* ☞ كواتى

كواټ kwāṭ *m.* three- or four-year-old camel that is being used to carry loads for the first time

كواټگاى kwāṭagáj *m.* three-year-old camel

كواټه kawāṭá talkative, garrulous

كواټۍ kwāṭə́j *f.* hole (for playing ball)

كوارچه kawārchá *f.* wicker basket

كوارسيت kwārsít *m.* كوارسيت kwārsít *m. mineralogy* quartz

كواره kawārá *f.* large and narrow basket for grapes

كواړه kwāṛá *f.* city gates, the gates to the city

كواړى kawáṛaj *m.* pick

كوازه kawāzá *f.* scaffolding

كواغۍ kwāghə́j *f.* ☞ كاغى

كواكب kawākíb *m. plural Arabic of* كوكب

كوال kawál *m.* ☞ كهول

كواللمپور kuā́la lumpúr *m.* Kuala Lumpur

كواله kawālá *f.* ☞ قباله

كوامنتاگ kwāmintā́ng *m.* Kuomintang (Guomindang)

كواندى kawā́ndaj *m.* decorated headband of a camel (bearing the bride on the wedding day)

كوانۍ kwā́ṇəj *f.* name of a children's game

كواى كواى kəwā́j-kəwā́j imitation of the cry of the jackal

كوب kub, kwab 1 *m.* hump 2 humpbacked

كوبا kubā́ *f.* Cuba

كوبالت kobā́lt *m. plural* cobalt

كوباى kobā́j *m.* guinea pig

كوبايي kubāī́ كوبائي 1 Cuban, Cuba's 2 *m.* Cuban, inhabitant or native of Cuba

كوبړ kubə́ṛ withered, faded

كوبلكه kobalā́ka *f.* mushroom

كوبى ¹ kubā́j *m.* cog of a water-lifting wheel

كوبى ² kubā́j *m.* tablecloth with food, refreshments

كوبى ³ kubā́j humped, having a hump (of a bull, camel, etc.)

كوبى ⁴ kobā́j *f.* 1 bladder 2 stomach that is stuffed with pieces of the dried fat of sheep's tails (kept for winter) 3 cupola, dome

كوپ ¹ kop *m.* fast run, running fast كوپ اچول، كوپ كول *compound verb* to run fast, rush

كوپ ² kup 1 humpbacked, bent, stooped كوپ كېدل *compound verb* 2 *m.* hunchback ☞ كوپېدل

كوپا kopā́ *m.* donkey ambler, donkey pacer

كوپال kopā́l *m.* wicker seat

كوپان kopā́n *m.* camel's hump

كوپراتيف koperātíf *m.* cooperative

كوپرېشن koperéshan *m.* organizing in a cooperative

كوپر kopə́ṛ *m.* high hat (worn by Turkmen women)

كوپره kopṛa *f.* coconut; the kernel of the coconut, copra

كوپړى ¹ kopṛə́j *f.* skull

كوپړى ² kupṛə́j *f.* small wineskin

كوپړى ³ kopəṛáj *m.* fossula below the knee

كوپله ¹ koplá *f.* 1 northern skylark 2 *regional* crested lark

كوپله ² kopála *f.* clumsily sewn chokemen; chokemen that fits like a sack

كوپلى koplə́j *f.* saddletree

كوپن هاگن kopenhā́gn *m.* Copenhagen

كوپنى kopaṇə́j *f.* 1 urinary bladder 2 bubble خوله كوپنى كول to draw air into the mouth

كوپول kupawə́l *denominative, transitive* [*past:* كوپ يې كړ] to arch, hunch, make hunched

كوپه ¹ kopá *f.* haircutting كوپه كول *compound verb* to cut (the hair)

كوپه ² kopá *f.* niche in a wall for a lamp

كوپى ¹ kopí *f.* copy

كوپى ² kupáj *m* hunchback

كوپى ³ kopáj *m.* milk pail

كوپى ⁴ kupə́j *f.* powder flask

كوپى ⁵ kupə́j *f.* hunchback

كوپى ⁶ kopə́j *f.* 1 saddle-tree 2 small wineskin used for oil 3 the husk of an acorn

كوپېدل kupedə́l *denominative, intransitive* [*past:* كوپ شو] 1 to stoop; become bent over 2 to bend, curve

كوپېک kopék *m.* kopeck

كوت ¹ kot *m.* sawhorse, stand, rack (for stacking firearms)

كوت ² kwət, kawt 1.1 fold, pleat, crease 1.2 wrinkle 2 *m.* 2.1 pleated 2.2 wrinkled; creased 2.3 taut, braced, drawn in (of the belly, abdomen) كوت كول *compound verb* a to make folds, create pleats b to wrinkle; crease c to tighten, draw in (the belly, abdomen) كوت كېدل *compound verb* a to be pleated b to wrinkle, break into wrinkles c to be taut, be braced, be drawn in (of the belly, abdomen)

كوت ³ kot *m.* long cavity where nomads put their lambs in the winter

كوت ⁴ kawt gouty

كوت ⁵ kot *imperfect of* كتل ¹

كوتار kawtā́r 1 busy, occupied with something 2 enveloped, seized, gripped

كوتان kotā́n *m.* 1 pelican 2 ☞ كوت ³

كوتاه kotā́h short; كوتاه كول *compound verb* to shorten, reduce; curtail, abbreviate كوتاه كېدل *compound verb* to be shortened, be reduced, be curtailed, be abbreviated

كوتاه بين kotāhbín 1 near-sighted, myopic 2 short-sighted, unforeseen, improvident

كوتاه بيني kotāhbiní *f.* 1 myopia 2 improvidence, lack of foresight, short-sightedness

كوتاه فكر kotāhfíkr short-sighted, improvident, superficial, shallow; unreasonable, unwise

كوتاه قد kotāhqád, kotāhqádd short, of short stature, undersized, dwarfish

كوتاهي kotāhí *f.* 1 a trifle, a little bit 2 brevity 3 shortage 4 omission, neglect

كو تحواله دار kothawāladár *m. history* sub-ensign

كوتر ¹ kawtár *m.* pigeon, dove

كوتر ² kutə́r *m.* large muskmelon with ribs

كوترام kotrā́m having accumulated, gathered, having crowded together; driven together كوترام كول *compound verb* to drive together into one place

كوترغاړى kawtarghā́ṛaj *m.* kind of taffeta

كوتركى ¹ kutə́rkaj *m.* trap, snare (for birds, made of goat horn)

كوتركى ² kutrakáj *m.* little puppy

كوترم kotrám ☞ كوترام

كوتره ¹ kawtára *f.* 1 female pigeon, female dove 2 pigeon, dove قاصده كوتره wild pigeon كورنى كوتره domestic pigeon صحرايي كوتره carrier pigeon ملاكي كوتره tumbler-pigeon 3 *proper noun* Kawtara

كوتره ² kotrá 1.1 shredded, cut up, broken 1.2 beaten, thrashed, beaten up كوتره كول *compound verb* a to shred, cut b to thrash, beat up 2 *f.* chopped greens (stems, stalks etc. as fodder)

کوتري ¹ kawtári *plural of* کوتره ¹

کوتری ² kutráj *m.* puppy

کوتری ³ kawatráj *m.* door jamb

کوتړه kutṛá *f.* bosom

کوتغالی kwətghā́laj *m.* place on the slopes of a mountain or hill that is illuminated by the sun, place where the sun is hottest

کوتک ¹ kuták, koták *m.* **1** stick, cudgel, club **2** shepherd's crook; تش کوتک brute force

کوتک ² koták *m.* back of the head, occipital

کوت کوت kwət, kwət **1** pleated **2** wrinkled, creased

کوتل ¹ kotál *m.* steep mountain-pass road موټر د کوتل سرته راوخوت The car climbed to the pass.

کوتل ² kotál *m.* spare horse, reserve horse; a horse that is being led

کوتل ³ kotál crop-eared

کوتل ⁴ kutə́l *transitive* [*past:* و يې کوته] **1** to cut, chop (e.g., meat) **2** to kill, slaughter

کوتلځی kutə́ldzáj *m.* slaughterhouse, abattoir

کوتنه ¹ kutə́na *f.* **1** cutting, chopping (e.g., meat) **2** killing, slaughtering

کوتنه ² kotaná *f.* short trousers (for girls)

کوتڼه kutə́ṇa *f.* female pelican

کوتو kutú *m.* pin-tailed sandgrouse, *Pterocles alchata*

کوتور kwətawár with gathers, gathered; کوتور خت shirt with gathers

کوتول kwətawə́l *denominative, transitive* [*past:* کوت یې کړ] to make pleats, pleat

کوتونی kutúnaj *m.* dressed-out lamb (or ox, sent by the bridegroom to the bride's house for the wedding feast)

کوته اندیش kotahandésh careless, imprudent, incautious; improvident

کوته اندیشي kotahandeshí *f.* carelessness, imprudence; improvidence

کوتی ¹ kútaj, kwútaj *m.* **1** corner, nook **2** dimple (on the cheek or chin) **3** fossula below the knee

کوتی ² kútaj *m.* puppy, puppy dog

کوتی ³ kutə́j *f.* box

کوتی ⁴ kúte cry by which people call a puppy to come

کوتی لال kutilā́l *m.* Daphne, *Daphne oleoides*

کوت ¹ koṭ *m.* small fort

کوت ² koṭ *m.* **1** small village, small settlement **2** *used in place names,* e.g., پښتونکوټ Pushtunkot

کوت ³ koṭ *m.* **1** sawhorse, stand, rack (for stacking firearms) **2** pile, heap **3** supply, reserve د ډوډۍ کوت grain reserves

کوت ⁴ koṭ *m.* **1** overcoat, topcoat لوی کوت overcoat لنډ کوت short coat **2** jacket

کوت ⁵ kwəṭ *m.* cackle, cackling کوټ کوټ کول *compound verb* to cackle

کوت ⁶ kuṭ *m.* alloy of iron, lead, copper, tin, gold, silver, etc.

کوتبند koṭbánd *m* coat hanger کالي پر کوت بند باندي ځورول to hang the clothes on a hanger

کوتخه ¹ kuṭə́kha *f.* **1** fur hat with ear flaps **2** muzzle (e.g., for a dog)

کوتخه ² koṭə́kha *f.* **1** poor little room **2** garden shed

کوترکی kuṭə́rkaj *m.* foal of a donkey

کوترنډ koṭránḍ besieged, dug in a fortress

کوتک kuṭák *m.* ☞ کوتک ²

کوت گارډ koṭgā́rḍ *m. regional* guard room

کوتگی koṭgáj *m.* small fort

کوتل kuṭə́l *transitive* [*past:* و يې کوته] **1** to pound; crush **2** to beat, strike; to beat severely **3** to chop (e.g., meat) **4** to thrash, thresh

کوت مرشل koṭmárshál *m. regional* military court, military tribunal

کوتمشر koṭmə́shər *m.* ☞ کوتوال

کوتنه ¹ koṭána *f.* female pelican

کوتنه ² kuṭə́na *f.* **1** pounding; crushing **2** beating, beating up **3** chopping (e.g., meat) **4** thrashing

کوتنی ¹ kwəṭanə́j *f.* **1** name of a children's game **2** small heap

کوتنی ² koṭanə́j *f.* **1** poor little room, little room, closet **2** small house, hut, peasant's house **3** hunting blind

کوتوال koṭwā́l *m.* chief of police

کوتوالي ¹ koṭwālí **1** *m.* chief of police **2** *f.* police administration

کوت والی ² kwəṭwā́laj *m.* hatching, brooding (of chicks)

کوتور koṭawár large-headed, macro-cephalous

کوتول kwaṭawə́l, koṭawə́l *denominative, transitive* [*past:* کوټه یې کړ] to gather, assemble

کوتونکی ¹ kuṭúnkaj *present participle of* کوتل

کوتونکی ² kwaṭawúnkaj *present participle of* کوتول

کوته ¹ koṭá *f.* **1** room د کتلو کوته، د ملاقات کوته، د ناستي کوته living room د دوډۍ کوته، د دوډۍ خورلو کوته، د طعام کوته dining room د کار کوته، د چاري bedroom د خوب کوته pantry خورلو د شیانو کوته classroom د ښیینو کوته د سبق کوته، د لوستلو کوته study room کوته hothouse د کتابوکوته library (in a house) **2** ward (in a hospital) **3** house with a flat roof **4** cell (of a honeycomb) **5** cabin, stateroom **6** shaft of a (water) well

کوته ² kwáṭa *f.* **1** pile, heap کوټه کول *compound verb* to put into a pile, gather into a heap; pile up, heap up د خوارکي موادو ذخیري کوټه to establish food supplies کوټه کېدل *compound verb* to be put into a pile, put in a heap; be gathered up **2** mass, bulk (of a substance) **3** hillock, hill

کوته ³ kwə́ṭa having stopped laying (of a hen)

کوته ⁴ kuṭə **1** from the breed of mongrels or sheep-dogs (of dogs except for hunting dogs, or hounds) **2** *m.* dog; mongrel, watchdog

کوته ⁵ koṭá **1** false, counterfeit **2** dull, limited; stupid کوټه کول *compound verb* **a** to falsify, counterfeit **b** to make stupid کوټه کېدل *compound verb* **a** to become counterfeit, false بخت یي کوټه شو His luck has betrayed him. **b** to become stupid, foolish **3** not giving milk (of cattle)

کوته ⁶ kuṭá *f.* boulder

کوته ⁷ kuṭá *imperfective imperative of* کوتل

کوته توب koṭatób *m.* **1** fake, forgery, counterfeit **2** dullness, narrow-mindedness; stupidity

کوته غویی koṭá ghwajáj *m* non-working ox

کوتگی ۲ koṭagə́j *f.* ☞ کوتنی کوته نی koṭanə́j *f.* ☞ کوتی ۲

کوته والی koṭawắlaj *m.* ☞ کوته توب

کوتهه koṭhá *f. dialect* ☞ کوته ۱

کوتل kuṭí *present tense of* کوتل

کوتی ۲ kwáṭi *plural of* کوته ۲

کوتی ۳ kwáṭi *feminine plural of* کوته ۳

کوتی ۴ koṭáj *m.* [*plural:* کوتی koṭí *and* کوتیان koṭiǰắn] 1 head (of an animal) 2 *abusive* noggin

کوتی ۵ kúṭaj *m.* little donkey, the foal of a donkey

کوتی ۶ kwaṭáj *m.* wooden bin, crib

کوتی ۷ kwə́ṭaj *m.* corner

کوتی ۸ koṭə́j *f.* 1 palace, villa 2 building د دار الحکومگی کوتی governorship building 3 bank office 4 *history* trading station, trade office and settlement of European merchants 5 goods warehouse

کوتی ۹ kúṭe *f. feminine of* کوتی ۲

کوتی ۱۰ kúṭe cry by which people drive awayl a young donkey کوتی کول *compound verb* to drive a young donkey away

کوتی ۱۱ koṭé *plural of* کوته ۱

کوتیالی kuṭǰālə́j *f.* 1 crucible (of a jeweler, etc.) 2 blast furnace

کوتی تانی koṭəjtāné *f. plural regional* litigiousness, malicious litigation

کوتی والا koṭiwālắ *m.* ☞ کله پز

کوثر ۱ kawsár *m. Arabic* 1 spasm of the masticator muscles 2 gust of cold wind; streams of cold air

کوثر ۲ kawsár *m. Arabic religion* Kawsar (the name of a spring or well in Paradise)

کوجرکی kodzhə́rki *f. plural* vertebrae

کوچ ۱ kuch, kwəch *m. plural Eastern* butter

کوچ ۲ koch, kuch *m.* roaming; migration کوچ کول *compound verb* a to roam; migrate b to set out, start for, set off for c to go away, get out کوچ که Get out! په کوچ بمول to lead away

کوچ ۳ kauch *m.* couch; sofa فنروالا کوچ innerspring sofa

کوچ ۴ kawch empty, hollow

کوچت kuchə́ṭ *m.* small child

کوچت توب kuchəṭtób *m.* کوچت والی kuchəṭwắlaj *m.* childhood

کوچخول kuchkhól *m.* hood, cowl

کوچکارل kuchkārə́l *transitive* [*past:* کوچکاره یی و] to call a dog

کوچ کوچ kuchkúch cry by which people call a dog

کوچ لاغ kuchlắgh *m.* کوچلاغ sheepfold, sheep pen

کوچلانه kuchlắna *f.* skin for keeping butter

کوچلنه kwuchlaná *f.* کوچلنه kuchlaná *f.* butter dish

کوچمال kochmắl, kuchmắl *m.* 1 driver of pack animals 2 guide of a caravan, troop column guide 3 time of moving camp (of nomads)

کوچندی kuchanḍáj *m.* young one, young of

کوچنوتکی kuchnoṭə́kaj tiny, wee

کوچنوتی kuchnóṭaj کوچنی kuchnáj 1.1 little, small, diminutive; insignificant هلک کوچنوتی little boy کوچنی کوته small room

کوچنوتی کول *compound verb* to make small, make insignificant; diminish, lessen سترگي کوچنی غوندي کول to squint چا ته په کوچنوتی نظر کتل to make light of someone's role په کوچنی خبره متاثر کېدل to be upset over trifles 1.2 small, short ... کوچنی کوچنی گامو *kuchní kuchní...* with small steps 2 *m.* baby, small child کوچنیان children د کوچنی څخه تر لویه from the youngest to the oldest, young and old alike

کوچنی واله kuchnitób *m.* ☞ واله

کوچنی ژبیز kuchnəjzhəbíz *linguistics* uvular

کوچنی والی kuchniwắla *f.* کوچنی والی kuchniwắlaj *m.* 1 childhood 2 small size

کوچوان kochwắn *m. regional* coachman, driver; cabman, drayman

کوچوتی kuchúṭaj small, little; tiny, wee

کوچومرغی kuchumurghə́j *f.* yellow wagtail

کوچه ۱ kawchá *f.* cobra

کوچه ۲ kochá, kuchá *m. plural* boiled whole grain (wheat, etc.)

کوچه ۳ kuchá *f.* disease of the donkey

کوچه ۴ kawchá *f.* kind of spoon; ladle

کوچی ۱ kuchí *m. plural* butter د کوچو جوړولو ماشین butter churn

کوچی ۲ kocháj 1.1 nomadic 1.2 migratory (of birds) 2 *m.* nomad

کوچی ۳ kocháj, kucháj *m. anatomy* Achilles' tendon

کوچی ۴ kúchaj *m.* small donkey, young donkey

کوچی ۵ kochə́j *f.* short felt robe

کوچی ۶ kochə́j, kuchə́j *f.* swallow (bird)

کوچیانی kochiǰāní nomadic, nomad's کوچیاني ژوند nomadic lifestyle

کوچیتوب kochitób *m.* roaming, wandering, leading a nomadic life د کوچیتوب ژوند nomadic lifestyle

کوچېدل kochedə́l *intransitive* [*past:* و کوچېده] to roam (like nomads); migrate, move to a different place

کوچینی kuchináj ☞ کوچنی

کوزېدل kudzedə́l *denominative, intransitive dialect* ☞ کوزبدل

کوخ kwats *m.* stack of firewood

کوخر kawtsár, kawtsər *m.* 1 wing 2 (book) cover

کوخره kawtsará *f.* [*usually plural* کوخړی kawtsaré] ☞ کناوه

کوخک kawtsák *m.* ☞ کڅوک

کوخکی kutskáj *m.* young donkey, donkey foal

کوخو kotsáw *m.* sleeveless felt gown

کوخه ۱ kutsá *f.* street; کوچنی کوخه side street

کوخه ۲ kwátsa *f.* 1 garbage dump, trash heap 2 place near a trivet where fuel is piled

کوخه ۳ kwatsá *f.* endeavoring; کوخه کول *compound verb* to try, endeavor

کوخه بندي kutsabandí *f.* barricade

کوخه درب kutsadráb *m.* کوخه ډب kutsaḍáb *m.* کوخه ګرد kutsagárb *m.* tramp, vagrant. vagabond, hobo, homeless person

کوخه ګردي kutsagardí *f.* vagrancy, vagabondage

کوخه ګنبت kutsagắkht *m.* ☞ کوخه درب

کوخه وال kutsawắl *m.* neighbor on the same street

کوتسۍ kawtsə́j *f.* braid, plait, pigtail ده دي کوشۍ اوږدي دي She has long braids سرکوشۍ‌کول *compound verb* to make braids, plait one's hair

کود kud *m.* fertilizer; عضوي کود زراعتي کود organic fertilizer کیمیاوي کود chemical fertilizer

کوداخېل kodākhél *m. plural* the Kodakheil (a branch of the Momands)

کودالۍ kodālə́j *f.* ☞ کدالی

کودتا kudətā́, kudetā́ *f.* revolution, coup d'etat یوه کودتا جوړول to carry out a revolution, stage a coup

کودرکی kawdə́rkaj *m.* کودری kawdə́raj *m.* shard, potsherd, fragment

کودرک kudŕak *m.* muscular stomach of birds, gizzard

کودری kawdə́raj *m.* ☞ کودری

کودک kodák *m.* child, baby

کودکستان kodakistā́n *m.* kindergarten

کودله kodála *f.* ☞ کوډخه

کودن kawdə́n dull, limited; stupid, imbecile

کودن والی kawdənwā́laj *m.* dullness, narrow-mindedness; stupidity; imbecility

کوده kawdá *f.* 1 tuft (of grass); small sheaf (of wheat, etc.) 2 small stack; rick, shock

کوده kodá *f.* loose edge of an irrigation ditch

کودی kawdáj *m.* great-great-grandson

کودی kawdáj *m.* 1 smoked potsherd, fragment 2 earthenware pot څوک په کودي کبنی حلالول *idiom* to kill someone without a knife; destroy, ruin

کودیک kawdík *m.* earthenware pot

کوداخېل koḍākhél *m. plural* ☞ کوداخېل

کوډبېلی koḍbeláj *m.* dormouse (rodent)

کوډخه koḍə́kha *f.* hut, cabin, shack, hovel, shanty

کوډر koḍə́r *m.* curved shovel

کوډغاله kuḍghā́la *f.* کوډغالی kuḍghā́laj *m.* ☞ کوډخه

کوډکه kuḍə́ka *f.* antitank pit

کوډګډ koḍgáḍ charming, possessing charm

کوډګر koḍgár *m.* [*plural:* کوډګر koḍgə́r and کوډګران koḍgarā́n] 1 magician; sorcerer 2 shaman

کوډګره koḍgára *f.* 1 magician; sorceress 2 shaman

کوډل kuḍə́l *f.* ☞ کوډخه

کوډلوبی koḍəlóbaj *m.* conjurer; juggler

کوډله kuḍála *f.* ☞ کوډخه

کوډلۍ kuḍaláj *f.* shanty, hovel, small hut

کوډوۍ koḍwə́j *f.* earthenware bowl, earthenware saucer

کوده kóda *f.* [*usually plural* کوډی kóḍi] charms, witchcraft, sorcery, magic کوډی‌کول *compound verb* to conjure, practice witchcraft

کوډی koḍáj *m.* magician; sorcerer

کوډی kuḍə́j *f.* 1 hut, cabin, shack, hovel, shanty تر مځکي لاندي کوډی dug-out 2 summerhouse, pergola

کوډۍ kawḍə́j *f.* cowry (a shell used as money in India and other countries) د پېغورونو کوډی کېدل *proverb* to become the talk of the town

کوډیکه koḍíka *f.* neck of a wineskin

کور kor *m.* [oblique singular کاله kālə́] 1 house, dwelling په کور، زه پرون کور وم at home I was at home. پر کارونه لرم I have much to do at home. مجبور سوم چه کور پاته سم I had to stay home. کور په کور from house to house کور ته homeward د کاله د کور طبیب family doctor د کور خلګ lodgers د کور سمبالول، د کور سمبالی housekeeping د کارونه domestic affairs د کورونو جوړولو فابریکه group of house-building enterprises کور سره Eastern beside the house کور ډاگ‌کول، کور سپېره‌کول to destroy, ruin کور ډاگ‌کېدل، کور سپېره‌کېدل، کور مسجدکېدل to be destroyed, be ruined; go to pot کور دي ډاگ‌سه! *idiom* May you rot in hell! کور دي ودان‌سه! May your house prosper! کور وهل *compound verb* to rob, plunder اول خپل کور جوړول to look after oneself first 2 square on a chessboard; division (of a table) 3 د مچیو کور honeycomb cell beehive 4 family (especially the female half) د کور سر head of the family د کور خڅنتن a family man (as contrasted to a bachelor) د کاله ټول غړي، د کاله ټول اعضا all family members کور دي خراب شه! *idiom* a Curses on your house! کور کول، د کور کېدل، د کور خاوند کېدل b May you remain wifeless! to get married, start a family 5 country, motherland 6 (social) environment, surroundings; circle سره په کور کبنی between us د ناوي کور in government circles حکومت په کور کبنی 7 dowry utensils and furniture given to the bride as a dowry

کور kwár, kəwár *m. plural* grapes د کورو باغ vineyard کور پاخه سول The grapes have ripened. کوروخانګي پرېکول to prune a vine

کور kur *m.* croaking کور‌کول *compound verb* to croak, make croaking noises

کور kwər *m.* wet soil, swampy, marshy place

کور kor *m.* crab

کور kwar equal, identical, the same as

کور kor blind

کور kor *m.* ☞ کورجای

کورا kurā́ *f.* د کورا رود Kura River Kura River

کوراړی kurā́ṛaj *m.* allotment, plot of land; (garden) bed

کوراړی korā́ṛaj interned; under house arrest

کوراکور korākór from house to house, house by house کوراکور جنګونه civil war

کوربانه korbānə́ *plural of* کوربه

کوربل korbál *m.* کوربله korbála *f.* groans, moans, groaning, moaning; howling; wailing کوربیل‌کول، کوربیل وهل *compound verb* to moan, groan; howl; wail, cry, weep

کوربنه korbaná *f.* housewife

کوربن kawarbə́n *m.* vineyard

کوربه korbá *m.* [*plural:* کوربانه korbānə́] 1 master of the house 2 head of the family, a married man, family man

کوربه توب korbətób *m.* homeownership; having a family

کورپچه kurpachá *f.* small mattress

کورپشا korpəshá homeless

کوربه [1] korpá *f.* aftermath, aftergrowth, aftercrop (a second growth or crop in the same season)

کوربه [2] korpá *f.* haircut; shearing (sheep) کوربه کول *compound verb* to cut (someone's hair); shear (sheep)

کورت kwərót *m. plural* kurut (hard dried balls of fermented milk or milk curds)

کورتک kurták *m.* ☞ اوگره

کورت ماچي kwrət-máchi *f. plural* soup with noodles and kurut

کورتوبه kurətobó *plural f.* kurtobá whey that remains when making kurut (used as a medicine)

کورته kurtá *f.* کورتۍ kurtój 1 jacket 2 dress

کورتي kúrte cry by which people drive sheep to the watering place

کورتین kwrətín made of kurut

کورټ kuráṭ, koráṭ, kwraṭ quite, utterly, perfectly; by no means, not at all

کورجای kordzháj *m.* place in a tent or house where clothing and blankets are stored

کورجی kurdzháj *m.* old hawk

کورچوړ korcháwṛ *m. abusive* scoundrel, villain

کورچوړی korcháwṛaj *m.* ☞ کوړواگی

کورخوری korkhóraj *m.* ☞ کوړواگی

کورخه kwərkhá *f.* 1 okra 2 haricot, kidney bean

کورداري kordārí *f.* connection, relation, contacts, dealings, intercourse د چا سره کور او کورداري کول to maintain good neighborly relations with someone

کوردره kordərá *f.* narrow path across a field

کوردنبله kordumbalá *f.* carbuncle

کورد ډيپلوماتيک kor diplomátík *m. plural* diplomatic corps

کورډيلر kordilér *m.* Cordilleras د کورډيلبر غرونه Cordilleras

کورډيناسيون kordināsjón *m.* coordination

کورډاگی korḍágaj *m.* person without shelter, homeless person

کوړړا korṛá *m.* 1 call of a crane 2 croaking

کوړړیدل kurṛedól *intransitive [past:* و کوړړیده] 1 to make a sound like the call of the crane 2 to croak, make croaking noises

کورزو kurzó *f.* special ax for chopping brushwood

کورزومی korzúmaj *m.* one who lives with his wife's parents

کورس [1] kurs *m.* 1 course; courses يو کلن کورس annual courses 2 course (textbook) لنډ کورس short course

کورس [2] kors coarse (of fabric)

کورس [3] kors *m. regional* dish (food)

کورسپړی korspéṛaj utterly destroyed

کورسیکا korsiká *f.* Corsica د کورسیکا جزیره Corsica Island

کورشگۍ korshagój *f.* closet

کوړکهkaj kurə́khkaj *m.* red mineral paint for dishes

کورغ [1] kwrəgh *m.* sophora (a pernicious weed)

کورغ [2] kwrəgh, kurúgh *m.* ☞ قرق

کورغالی kurghálaj *m.* small plot amidst large fields

کورغول kwrəghawól *denominative, transitive [past:* کورغ یې کړ] to declare to be a reserve, be designated a preserve

کورغی [1] kurgháj *m.* earless ram

کورغی [2] korgháj *m.* allotment of land, plot of land

کورغبدل kwrəghedól *denominative, intransitive [past:* کورغ شو] to be protected (by law), be made a preserve

کورک [1] korák *m.* 1 grain or fruit that has failed to ripen owing to disease 2 small pomegranates

کورک [2] kurk *m.* cloth made from goat's under-fur, cashmere

کورک [3] korák *m.* large bin for storing grain, corncrib

کورکشه kurkəshá *f.* first egg to be laid by a hen

کورکمان kurkamán *m.* کورکمن kurkamán *m.* curcuma, turmeric

کورکوډۍ korkuḍój *f.* hovel, hut, shack

کورکور kurkúr *m.* ☞ کور کور

کورکورانه korkorāná 1 blind 2.1 blindly 2.2 spontaneously

کورکورکه kurkuráka *f.* Chinese turtle-dove, *streptopaelia chinensis*

کورکوري [1] kurkurí pock-marked

کورکوری [2] kurkuráj *m.* powdered brick (used for cleaning metal dishes)

کورکوری [3] kurkuráj *m.* male turtle-dove

کورکوری [4] kurkuráj *f.* pin-tailed sandgrouse, *Pterocles alchata*

کورکوری [5] kurkurój *f.* hard clayey soil that absorbs water poorly

کورکوپی [6] kurkuṛój *f.* bee-eater (bird)

کورکوڼی kurkuṇáj *m.* medicinal plant (used to treat intestinal worms)

کورکی [1] korakáj *m.* 1 small house 2 name of a children's game کور د احمد کور کورکی شو *compound verb* to ruin someone Ahmed's affairs have deteriorated. دا کور هم کورکی لري *saying* This business is not all that simple.

کورکی [2] korákaj *m.* young donkey

کورکی [3] kurkáj *m.* ☞ کورهار

کورکی [4] kurkáj *m.* 1 shallow well 2 shallow shaft of an irrigation ditch in a field

کورکی [5] korəkáj *m. [plural:* کورکي korəkí *and* کورکیان korəkijā́n] round-sheep dung with brushwood (a kind of fuel)

کورکی [6] korakój *f. feminine of* کورکی [2]

کورگډی korgáḍaj *m.* ☞ کوړواگی

کورگوټ korgwóṭ curved; winding, twisting

کورگی korgáj *m.* utensils and furniture (bride's dowry)

کور گیري korgirí good-neighbor relations, neighborly relations

کورل korál *m.* Coral د کورل بحیره the Coral Sea

کورلی kurláj 1 *m.* hare 2 having a short tail, short-tailed

کورم kurám *m.* ☞ کورمه

کورمانه kormāná *f.* housekeeping, domestic science

کورمک kurmák thin, skinny, emaciated

کورمنگ kurmáng *m.* pheasant

کورمه kuramá *f.* Kuram (river, river valley, and region)

کورن korón looking after, or taking care of, one's family

کورنځی korandzə́j *f.* **1** weakness, lethargy **2** ☞ کوربل

کورنده kuránḍa *f.* alfalfa stubble

کورنډۍ kuranḍə́j *f.* bag with agricultural implements

کورنش kurnísh *m.* low bow چا ته کورنش کول to bow low to someone, greet someone with great respect

کورنگی kurəngáj *m.* young donkey

کورنی koranáj **1.1** domestic کورني حيوانات domestic animals کورني سوی rabbit **1.2** internal کورنی اقتصاد housekeeping کورنی بازار internal market **1.3** family کورنی دود او دستور family manners and customs **2** *m.* stay-at-home

کورنی ² koranə́j *f.* **1** family **2** birth, stock; dynasty, house شاهي کورنی king's family, king's lineage د بارکزو کورنی the Barakzai Dynasty انساني کورنی human race, mankind **3** *biology* family **4** group, detachment

کور ¹ koró *oblique plural of* کور

کورواکی korwǎkaj **1** standing at the head of the household, of the family **2** *m.* head of the family

کوروال korwál *m.* ☞ کوربه

کوروالا korwālǎ **1** family, familial **2** *m.* **.1** family man **2.2** family member

کورواله korwǎla *f.* **1** ☞ **2** neighborly relations, good-neighbor relations

کوروالی korwǎlaj *m.* **1** housekeeping **2** responsibilities of the husband in the family, the duties of the father and husband کوروالی کول *compound verb* to keep house; be the head of the family **3** living together, cohabitation

کورودانه korwadǎna *f.* housewife

کورودانی korwadānáj *m.* gratitude کورودانی کول، کورودانی ویل *compound verb* to thank

کور ورانونکی kor wrānawúnkaj **1** ruinous **2** pernicious, fatal; disastrous, destructive

کوروراني ¹ korwrāní *f.* ruin, destruction

کوروراني ² korwrǎnaj *m.* ☞ کورواگی

کوروکورو kurú-kurú cry by which people call a donkey to come

کوروکهول kor-u-kahól, korwəkahól *m.* family

کورولي korwalí *f.* **1** ☞ کوروالی **2** neighborly relations, good-neighbor relations

کوره ¹ kurá *f.* **1** furnace **2** blast-furnace **3** brick kiln **4** fire box (part of a furnace)

کوره ² kawára *f.* *botany* capers

کوره ³ korá **1** destroyed, annihilated **2** crossed off a list کوره کول *compound verb* **a** to destroy, obliterate **b** to cross off, delete from a list

کوره ⁴ kurá, korá **1** unbleached (of fabric) **2** new, not-yet-washed

کورهار kurahǎr *m.* **1** croaking **2** the sound of a hookah

کوری ¹ kurí *f.* **1** heel (footwear) **2** snowshoes

کواری ² kawári *plural of* کوره ²

کوري ³ kwə́ri, kúri, kúre go away کوري کول *compound verb* to drive away (a dog, donkey)

کوری ⁴ kwaráj *m.* barberry stems (used as medicine)

کوری ⁵ kwaráj, koráj *m.* **1** net (of wool or plant fibers, for carrying hay, watermelons, and domestic utensils) **2** braided muzzle (for livestock) کوری اچول *compound verb* **a** to fawn on, curry favor with **b** to expect a present from someone

کوری ⁶ koráj *m.* salt-cellar

کوری ⁷ kawráj *m.* کورۀ kurə́j *f.* **1** large pile of un-thrashed grain **2** hillock, knoll

کوری ⁸ kwaráj *m.* cockleshell

کوری ⁹ kawráj *f.* wooden milk pail

کوریا korejǎ *f.* Korea

کوریځ kurídz *m.* molting (of birds)

کوریر kurír *m.* courier سیاسي کوریر diplomatic courier

کوریز kuríz *m.* ☞ کوریځ

کوری غم korighám *m.* tax levied on each house

کوریل kuríl Kuril; د کوریل جزیری the Kuril Islands

کوریه korejá *f.* ☞ کوریا

کور ¹ kuṛ *m.* **1** leprosy **2** infectious disease, contagious disease

کور ² kwaṛ *m.* shaft of a butter-churn staff or beater

کور ³ kuṛ *m.* **1** gurgle, gurgling (of water) **2** grumbling, rumbling (in the stomach)

کور ⁴ koṛ inclined, tilted کوړول کوړ کور ² *compound verb* ☞ کوړیدل ² *compound verb* ☞

کوراغ koṛǎgh *m.* ☞ تبک

کوړا کوړا koṛǎ-koṛá twisted, twirled (of one's moustache)

کوړت kwṛət *m.* cackle, cackling کوړت کول *compound verb* to cackle

کوړتک kuṛták *m.* thin gruel of flour, butter and sugar

کوړخ kuṛəts *m.* dug out in the steppes (for livestock)

کوړکوړ kuṛkúṛ *m.* gurgle, gurgling (of water)

کوړکوړۍ kuṛkuṛə́j *f.* laughing turtle-dove

کوړکه kwṛəka *f.* hen that has stopped laying

کوړکی ¹ kuṛáj *m.* allotment of land, plot of land

کوړکی ² kuṛáj *m.* ☞ کهار

کوړکی ³ kuṛakáj *f.* [*plural:* کوړکي kuṛakí *and* کوړکی گانی kuṛakəjgǎni] **1** snares (of horn) **2** barrow made of two poles (for moving brushwood)

کوړم kwṛám, kwuṛám **1** standing (of water) کوړمي اوبه stagnant water **2** *m.* pond; deep lake د کوړم کښی کبدل to disappear without a trace, vanish into thin air

کوړمگی kwuṛamgáj *m.* small pound, small lake

کوړمن kwəṛmə́n sick, diseased

کوړمه koṛmá *f.* family; birth, origin, stock

کوړنځ kwṛəndzh *m.* کوړنچ kwṛənch *m.* **1** sob, sobbing (of a baby) **2** yelping, yapping; (of a dog); yelp (of a dog)

کوړنچا kwṛənchǎ *m. & f.* ☞ کوړنچهار

کورنچول kwṛənchawól *denominative, transitive* [*past:* کورنچ یې کړ] to cause to whine, make yelp (of a dog)

کورنچهار kwṛənchahǻr *m.* کورنچی kwṛənchȧj *m.* yelping, yapping (of a dog)

کورنچېدل kwṛənchedól *denominative, intransitive* [*past:* کورنچ شو] to whine, yelp (of a dog)

کورنگ kawṛáng lanky, ungainly, awkward

کورول [1] kuṛawól *transitive* [*past:* وْ یې کوړاوه] to cause gurgling, make gurgle

کورول [2] koṛawól *denominative, transitive* [*past:* کوړ یې کړ] to tilt, incline

کوروی kuṛwȧj *m.* 1 measure of weight for wheat equal to 2.5 lbs 2 basket made of cattail

کوره [1] kwǻra *f.* pile, heap (of un-thrashed grain or vegetables) کوره کول piles, heaps *compound verb* to gather into a pile, heap up; کوره کېدل *compound verb* to be piled up, be heaped up

کوره [2] kawṛá *m.* squabble, trouble-maker

کوره [3] kawṛá *f.* brushwood

کوړه [4] koṛá *f.* hole (for a ball game)

کوروی [1] kuṛȧj *m.* ☞ کوروی

کوروی [2] kawṛȧj *m.* wooden mortar

کوروی [3] koṛȧj sloping, slanting (of a mountain)

کوروی [4] koṛȧj *m.* calf

کوروی [5] koṛȧj 1 *regional* leprous 2 *m.* gangrenous wound; abscess

کوروی [6] koṛȧj *f.* 1 kori (a measure of weight equal to [1/4] اوبی or 7.5 lbs) 2 twenty pieces (when counting logs, pelts, etc.) کوړی کول، کوړی کوړی کول *compound verb* putting twenty pieces together 3 kind of embroidery

کوروی [7] koṛȧj *f.* 1 small stack or pile of wheat sheaves 2 coiled up snake 3 hobble for camel's knees

کوروی [8] kawṛȧj *f.* penny, farthing; dinar

کوروی [9] koṛȧj *feminine singular of* کوروی [5] 1

کوریت kuṛít 1 wrinkled, creased 2 crumpled

کوړېدل [1] kuṛedól *intransitive* [*past:* و کوړېد] to gurgle

کوړېدل [2] koṛedól *denominative, intransitive* [*past:* کوړ شو] to bend over, to stoop

کوروی-کوروی kuṛȧj-kuṛȧj 1 *f.* small stack 2.1 winding, twisting, meandering کوړی کوړی کول *compound verb* a to make winding, make sinuous b to pack or stow with ropes کوړی کوړیکېدل *compound verb* to twist, wind, meander 2.2 wavy (of the hair) 2.3 uneven, rough (of terrain)

کوریکه kuṛíka *f.* brood hen, sitting hen

کورینگ kuṛíng ungainly and stooping

کورینگېدل kuṛingedól *denominative, intransitive* [*past:* کورینگ شو] to stoop

کوز kuz 1.1 lower 1.2 cited below 2 down, downward کوز کتل *compound verb* a to look down b to feel nausea c *figurative* to be ashamed, lower one's eyes

کوزپلی kuzpólaj weak, feeble

کوزده kuzdá *f.* ☞ کوژده

کوزده وال kozdawȧl betrothed, engaged; young man, bridegroom

کوزرگی kuzargój *f.* کوزری kuzaṛój *f.* small earthenware pitcher

کوزغالی kuzghǻlaj *m.* 1 dirty crock 2 feeding rack, water bowl (for dogs, chickens)

کوز گوری [1] kuzgorí *f.* dishonor, shame, disgrace د کوز گوری خبره ده This is a shameful business.

کوز گوری [2] kuzgóraj ashamed

کوزمیک kozmík ☞ کوسمیک کوزمیکه بېړی space ship

کوزنی kuzanȧj 1 lower کوزنی لغمان Lower Laghman Region 2 following (below)

کوزوالی kuzwǻlaj *m.* slope, decline, declivity

کوزوپاس kuz-u-pǻs up(wards) and down(wards)

را کوزول [1] kuzawól *denominative, transitive* [*past:* کوز یې کړ] *compound verb* to lower, to let down سر کوزول *compound verb* to hang one's head, lower one's head 2 to disembark, put ashore, put down, to put off 3 to unload 4 to land (e.g., a plane)

کوزه [1] kuzá *f.* earthenware jug with a long neck کوزه اخیستل *idiom* to become an adult

کوزه [2] kúza *feminine singular of* کوز [1]

کوزه [3] kawzá *f.* ☞ قبضه

کوزي [1] kúzi *f. plural of* کوز [1]

کوزی [2] kuzój *f.* small pitcher

کوزي [3] kuzé *plural of* کوزه [1]

کوزیانه kozjǻna *f.* first acquaintance of the bridegroom with the family of the bride

کوزېدل kuzedól 1 .1 را *denominative, intransitive* [*past:* کوز شو] کوزېدل *compound verb* to be lowered, be let down, descend 1.2 to disembark, be put ashore, be put off (e.g., a train) 1.3 to be unloaded 1.4 to go down to the water (of ducks) 1.5 to land, be landed (i.e., of a plane) 2 *m. plural* ☞ کوزېدنه

کوزېدنه kuzedóna *f.* کوزیده kuzedó *m. plural* 1 descent, lowering 2 landing, putting ashore, disembarking 3 unloading 4 going down to the water (of ducks) 5 landing (e.g., an airplane)

کوژدن kozhdón *m. & f.* کوژده kozhdá *f.* betrothal, engagement کوژدن کول *compound verb* to betroth

کوژک kozhák Kozhak; د کوژک غر the Kozhak (mountain) range

کوژه kozhá *f.* breaking of a fast; failure to observe a fast 2 *m.* breaking a fast; failing to observe a fast

کوږ [1] kog *m.* [*plural:* کاږه kāgǿ *and* کاږیان kāgijǻn] hyena

کوږ [2] kog [*f.* کږه kagá, *m. plural:* کاږه kāgǿ, *f. plural:* کږی kagé] 1 crooked, bent کوږ خط crooked کوږ او کین curve 2 squinting, squint-eyed 3 inclined, tilted 4 bending (over), bent (over, down), bowed (down) 5 bulging کاږه تاویلات *idiom* idle talk کوږ *saying* a sin confessed is half forgiven, a fault مغزی توره نه پربکوي confessed is half redressed احمد و هر چا ته کوږ مغزی واروي Ahmed tries to ingratiate himself with everyone.

کوربل kogbál *m.* hyena

کوربتوب kogtób *m.* کوربتیا kogtjã *f.* ☞ کوربوالی

کوربسترگی kogstárgaj squint-eyed, cross-eyed

کوږل [1] kugól, kwagól *transitive* [*past:* کوږ یې و] to strive, toil; strain oneself

کوږل [2] kogól *transitive* [*past:* کوږ ه یې و] to peel; shell, hull

کوربمغزی kogmághzaj wicked, malicious, vicious

کوربنگوری kogangúraj *m.* snake melon, tarra

کوربوالی kogwãlaj *m.* 1 curvature 2 bend, crook 3 slight cast in the eye, mild strabismus, walleye (divergent strabismus) 4 inclination 5 protuberance, prominence

کوږ وکین kog-u-kín, kogwəkín ☞ کوربوور

کوربول kogawól *transitive* ☞ کربول

کوږوور kog-wóg 1 [*f.* کاربه واربه kagá-wagá *m. plural:* کاربَوور kāgə́-wāgə́ *f. plural:* کربی وربی kagé-wagé] very crooked 2 in all directions, at random پر لاري کوربوور تلل to walk lunging from side to side

کوبره [1] kwagá *f.* effort, diligence, zeal

کوبره [2] kwagá *imperfective imperative of* کوږل [1]

کوبربدل kwagedól *intransitive* ☞ کبربدل

کوس kos *m.* kettledrum; cymbals

کوستاریکا kostārikã *f.* Costa Rica

کوسره kawsará *f.* shoe

کوسری [1] kawsóri *f. plural botany* khinzhak with a thin shell

کوسرِی [2] kawsaré *plural of* کوسره

کوسموس kósmós *m.* space, the cosmos

کوسمیک kosmík space, cosmic

کوسنگ kwusáng *m.* grains of wheat that are left on the threshing floor after threshing (they are picked up by poor people)

کوسه kosá *m.* [*plural:* کوسه گان kosagãn] *folklore* kosa (a man with a thin beard or a beardless man)

کوسی [1] kosáj *m.* [*plural:* کوسیان kosijãn] felt robe; coat made of thick felt; wool chapan (a long-skirted caftan)

کوسی [2] kawasáj *m* great-grandson

کوشالی koshālãj *m.* pelvis

کوشان kushãn ☞ کوششی

کوشان kushãn *m. history* Kushan (dynasty)

کوشانی [2] kushānī 1 Kushan 2 *m.* ☞ کوشان

کوشتوری kushturáj *f.* late(-ripening) small watermelons

کوشش koshísh, kushísh *m.* ☞ کوبنبن

کوششی koshishí diligent, assiduous

کوشبر kawshér *m.* 1 soldering; welding 2 compensation

کوشبرول kawsherawól *denominative, transitive* [*past:* کوشبر یې کړ 1] to solder; weld 2 to sew together; join, splice

کوشبربدل kawsheredól *denominative, intransitive* [*past:* کوشبر شو 1] to be soldered; be welded 2 to be sewn together; be joined, be spliced دوی زړونه سره کوشبر شول *idiom* their hearts flowed together, their hearts beat as one

کوبنار kawkhár *m.* shoemaker who makes soft-soled heelless leather shoes

کوبنان kukhãn ☞ کوششی

کوبنت kwəkht *m.* 1 fold, plait, crease 2 (traveling) rug (used for carrying things) 3 canyon, deep and narrow valley

کوبنبن kokhə́kh *m.* 1 endeavor, effort; diligence, zeal یې فایدی compound verb کوبنبن کول، کوبنبن لرل futile attempts to try, endeavor, to display diligence, zeal 2 striving, aspiration

کوبنکه [1] kawkháka *f. sports* back heel (a move in wrestling)

کوبنکه [2] kawkhóka *f.* peg driven into a wall to which to tie livestock

کوبنل kukhól *transitive* [*past:* کوبنه یې و] to write, inscribe

کوبنلی kukhólaj *dialect* beautiful

کوبنه [1] kãwkha *f.* [*usually plural* کوبنی kãwkhi] women's shoes; soft-soled heelless leather shoes; low shoes, oxfords

کوبنه [2] kawkhá *f.* ☞ کبندری

کوغ [1] kwagh *m.* toad

کوغ [2] kugh 1 stooped, being bent over کوغ کول *compound verb* to bend 2 sunken, collapsed, fallen in کوغی سترگی sunken eyes

کوغاتی koghátaj *m.* کوغالی kughãlaj *m. dialect* 1 small hole, pit 2 depression in porridge into which butter is poured 3 oven, kiln (for firing brick and lime) 4 hovel, hut, shack

کوفت kuft *m.* blow, stroke د زړه کوفت *idiom* despondency, dejection, low spirits, depression

کوفته koftá, kuftá 1.1 chopped (e.g., of meat) 1.2 beaten 2 *f.* small meatballs

کوک [1] kok *m.* cry, howl کوک وهل *compound verb* to yell, howl

کوک [2] kok *m.* coke د کوک سکاره coking coal

کوک [3] kok *m.* 1 winding up (clocks, etc.) 2 tuning (a musical instrument)

کوک [4] kuk *m.* common wild leek, wild onion

کوک [5] kuk earless (of a ram)

کوکا kokã *m.* uncle (address to an older man)

کوکاره kukãra *f.* 1 cry, howl; groaning, moaning; whine, whimpering کوکاري کول، کوکاري وهل *compound verb* a to cry, howl b to whine, whimper (of a dog)

کوکانی kukãnaj *m.* name of a star

کوکائین kokāín *m. plural* cocaine

کوکب kaukáb *m. Arabic* [*plural:* کوکبونه kaukabúna *and Arabic* کواکب kawākíb] star, heavenly body; planet

کوکبی kawkabí space, cosmic; interplanetary کوکبی مواصلات astronautics

کوکچه kokchá *f.* Kokcha

کوکره [1] kukrá *f.* wooden part of a camel saddle

کوکره [2] kukrá *f.* [*usually plural* کوکری kukré] *medicine* trachoma

کوکری kukráj, kukuráj *m.* puppy

کوکړ kukór *m.* 1 long pole with which coals are stirred (in an oven or kiln for firing brick, etc.) 2 kind of pea with small kernels

کوکوړی kukóṛaj *m.* **1** ☞ کوکوړی ¹ **2** large flat cake that is baked on the day a child begins walking unaided (usually the cake is rolled after the child and then distributed to the poor)

کوکړی ² kukṛáj *f.* butterfly

کوکړی ³ kokṛé *f. plural* **1** edge of thick felt **2** wool from which the designs on a mat are made

کوکس koks *m.* coke

کوکسسازي kokssāzí *f.* coking

کوکله koklá shriveled up from the cold

کوکنار koknář *m.* opium poppy (the head)

کوکڼه kukə́ṇa *f.* butterfly; moth

کوکڼی kokaṇə́j *f.* vase (for flowers)

کوکو ¹ kukú, kokó **1** *m.* flower, little flower **2** *children's speech* clean

کوکو ² kukú *m.* cooing (of doves) کوکو وهل *compound verb* to coo

کوکو ³ kawkáw *m.* din and shouting (of children)

کوکوبه kukobá *f.* کوکوبای kokobáj *m.* rose oil

کوکوپیښ kukupə́ḳh *m.* hoopoe

کوکوړی kokóṛaj *m.* ☞ کوکوړی ¹

کوکوشتکه kukushtáka *f.* کوکو کوتره kukúk -awtára *f.* turtle-dove

کوکوگډی kukugeḍə́j *f.* bunch of flowers, bouquet

کوکول kokawə́l *denominative, transitive* [*past:* کوک یې کړ] to wind up (clock, watch, phonograph, etc.)

کوکولالا kokolālá *m.* older brother

کوکومرغه kukú-murghə́ *m.* ☞ کوکوشتکه

کوکومیو kukumjáw *m.* owl

کوکوواوا kukuwāwā́ *f. children's speech* pretty and bright dress

کوکوونه kokowə́na *f.* ☞ کوکی ونه

کوکه ¹ kúka *f.* shout, yell کوکي وهل *compound verb* **a** to shout, howl, yell **b** to glorify, make famous د درخو د ښایست کوکي ولاړي The fame spread of the beauty of Durkho.

کوکه ² koká *f.* **1** kind of beads **2** box, case, crate (for transporting fruit)

کوکي ¹ kúki *f. plural of* کوکه ¹

کوکی ² kukáj *m.* leek

کوکی ³ kokáj *m* boy, little boy

کوکی ⁴ kawəkáj *m.* **1** small iron trowel (for scraping off dough that has stuck to the sides of bowls) **2** ladle, soup ladle

کوکی ⁵ kokáj *f.* **1** little flower **2** pieces of colored mirror (which children play with) **3** my little flower, my dear little one, (address to a child)

کوکی ⁶ kokáj *f.* sorrow, grief, anguish

کوکی ⁷ kokáj *f.* (little) girl, baby

کوکی ⁸ kokáj *f* **1** kiss **2** cheek

کوکی ⁹ kokáj *f.* spider

کوکی ¹⁰ kokáj *f.* butterfly

کوکیالی kokjāláj figured, patterned, parti-colored, variegated (flowery, florid of fabric)

کوکیانه kokjấna *f.* flower garden

کوکیځ kawkídz *m.* bend of a wall

کوکي خېل kukikhéjl **1** *m. plural* the Kukikheili (a subdivision of the Afridi) **2** *m.* Kukikheil

کوکېدل kukedə́l *denominative, intransitive* [*past:* کوک شو] **1** to be tuned (of a musical instrument) **2** to be wound up (of a clock, etc.)

ټولي سترگي د دوی پلو کوکي شوي دي، ټولي سترگي د دوی پلو ته کوکي شوي دي *idiom* all eyes were upon them

کوکی گوته kokój gwóta *f.* index finger, forefinger

کوکی وله kokój wóla *f.* ☞ کوکي ⁵

کوکی ونه kokój wúna *f.* false acacia

کوگ ¹ kog *m. Eastern* ☞ کوږ ¹

کوگ ² kog *Eastern* ☞ کوږ ²

کوگل ¹ kogə́l, kogál *m.* rib cage

کوگل ² kwagə́l *transitive Eastern* ☞ کوږل ¹

کوگی kogə́j *f.* **1** (little) mouth (a baby's) **2** kiss

کوگیر kawgír *m.* ☞ کوکی ³

کول ¹ kol *m.* **1** lake **2** pond **3** ford

کول ² kul *m.* earth that is thrown up when digging a canal

کول ³ kawál *m.* poison

کول ⁴ kol *m.* ☞ کهول

کول ⁵ kul *m.* person of the same age (plural, persons or children of the same age)

کول ⁶ kwəl standing on one's head

کول ⁷ kawə́l *transitive* [*present:* کوي یې کاوه *past imperfective* کاوه یې perfective* کړ یې و] **1** independent verb [*past:* و یې کړ] **1.1** to do, make, carry out, perform, accomplish کار کول *compound verb* to work, toil څه باید وکو؟ What were you doing? What is to be done? **1.2** to conduct, carry out (trade, war, etc.) د چا سره تجارت کول to engage in trade with someone **1.3** to treat, deal with someone د دي سړي سره به څنگه کوو؟ How to treat this person کوه چا چه و به شي په تا *proverb* one good (or ill) turn deserves another **1.4** to take دا هغه قلم دئ چه ما درکاوه او تا نه کاوه This is the pen that I gave you but you didn't want to take it. ښڅه کول *compound verb* to take a wife, get married **1.5** to put on, wear نوی درېشي کوه to wear a new dress today **1.6** to get, obtain; take لرگي له کمه کوي؟ Where did you get the firewood? **1.7** to arrange, conduct (e.g., a meeting) اجلاس کول، جلسه کول *compound verb* to call a meeting; meet **1.8** to be necessary دا کتاب څه کوي؟ What do you need this book for? **1.9** ☞ کول 1.2 **1.10** to force someone to do something دی په هغو باندي محنت مزدوري کوي They worked for him as farmhands. **2** *forming verbs as part of compound and denominative verbs* [*past:* کړ, the verb agrees with the object of the action] جارو کول *compound verb* to conquer استیلا کول *compound verb* to sweep دعوت کول *compound verb* to invite *with the pronouns* را، در، ور *means to give (first, second, or third person). but can stand in free combinations:* راکول to do (something for the first person) درکول to do (something for the second person) ورکول to do (something for the third person) تیلیفون به درکوم I will call you

كول كېدل kul *passive voice* to become, be, grow **3** *m. plural* **.1** deeds, acts, achievements نو اوس څه كول په كار دي؟ What is it that ought to be done now? **3.2** conducting, carrying on (trade, war, etc.) **3.3** treatment of someone **3.4** putting on, wearing **3.5** getting, obtaining **3.6** arranging, conducting (e.g., a meeting) **3.7** utterance, statement ... اوس دا خبره د كولو ده چه it should be mentioned that…, it must be noted that…

كول ^{2} kul *transitive dialect* ☞ ښنكل

كولا ^{1} kolá *f.* Kola د كولا جزیره نما the Kola Peninsula

كولاخ kuláts *m.* ☞ قلاچ

كولاك kulák rich peasant

كولاى ^{7} kawəláj *Western conditional and potential of* كول كه تا كار كولاى if you would work كار كولاى شي he can work

كولبه kulbá *f.* ☞ قلبه

كولپ kúləp *m. dialect* ☞ قفل

كولپک kulpák *m.* bolt (of a door)

كولپكى kulpəkáj *m.* cuff (e.g., on a shirt sleeve)

كولپول kulpawál *denominative, transitive* [*past:* كولپ يې كړ] to bolt, lock (e.g., the door)

كولپي kulpé *f.* kind of needlework

كولپۍ kulpə́j *f.* earthenware kneading trough, dough trough

كولپېدل kulpedál *denominative, intransitive* [*past:* كولپ شو] to be bolted, be locked (e.g., of a door)

كولپېدنه kulpedána *f.* كولپېده kulpedá *m. plural* locking, bolting

كولتور kultúr *m.* ☞ كلتور

كولتوري kulturí ☞ كلتوري

كولخوز kolkhóz *m.* kolkhoz, collective farm

كولخوزچي ^{1} kolkhozchí *m.* kolkhoznik, member of a collective farm, collective farmer

كولخوزچۍ ^{2} kolkhozchə́j *f.* [*plural:* كولخوزچي kolkhozchə́j *and* كولخوزچیاني kolkhozchəjáni] woman member of a collective farm, (woman) collective farmer

كولخوزي kolkhozí kolkhoz, collective farm

كولك ^{1} kolák *m.* **1** opening in the roof for the escape of smoke **2** chimney, smoke stack (factory, etc.)

كولك ^{2} kolák *m.* [*plural:* كولكان koləkán *and* كولكونه koləkúna] orbit, eye socket سترگي يې په كولكو لوېدلي His eyes are sunken.

كولكتيف kollektíf **1** collective **2** *m.* collective

كولومبو kolómbó *f.* Colombo

كولمبیا kolumbijá *f.* Colombia

كولمه ^{1} kolmá *f.* ☞ كورمه

كولمه ^{2} kulmá *f.* ☞ كلمه ^{1}

كولند ^{1} kolánḍ *m.* كولنډى kolanḍáj *m.* ☞ كلند

كولنگ kuláng *m.* pick (ax)

كولو kawálo *Eastern imperfect of* كول ^{7} *in lieu of* كاوه ^{3}

كولول kulawál *transitive* [*past:* و يې كولاوه] **1** to roll, move (by rolling) هندوانه كولول *compound verb* to roll a watermelon **2** to topple, overturn **3** to burn (with acid)

كولولو kululú *m.* **1** larva of the ant lion **2** bogeyman (a fantastic being which people use to frighten children)

كولونته kolontá *f.* cord (of a snare)

كولوني koloní *f.* colony

كوله ^{1} kolá *f.* cartridge case

كوله ^{2} kəwála *f.* spreading stalks of wheat for threshing

كوله ^{3} kulá *f.* howl (of a dog)

كوله ^{4} kawála *imperfect feminine of* كول ^{7}

كوله ^{5} kuwála *f.* earthenware vessel in which dried camel dung is burned

كوله ^{6} kolá *f.* ☞ كولا

كوله بوله kóla-bóla *f.* words of sympathy, compassion

كوله را kolerá *f.* كولرا cholera

كولاى ^{1} kawəláj *Eastern conditional & potential of* كول ^{7} ☞ كولاى

كولى ^{2} koláj *m.* helmet

كولى ^{3} koláj *m* earthenware bin for storing grain

كولى ^{4} kawláj *f.* narrow path along a stony mountainside

كولیار koljár *m.* kachnar, orchid tree, *Bauhinia variegata*

كولېدل kuledál *intransitive* [*past:* و كولېده] **1** to roll, roll over **2** to fall, be overturned **3** to be burned (with acid)

كولېده kuledá́ *m. plural* **1** rolling **2** toppling, overturning **3** burning (with acid)

كوم ^{1} kum, kom *pronoun* **1** what, which (interrogative-relative) كوم كوم؟ Which كتاب را ته راكوئ؟ Which book are you giving me? كوم كوم دي؟ I have many proofs. And what are they exactly? **2** some, some kind of; one, a certain (indefinite) كوم يو some kind of

كوم ^{2} kawám *present tense first person of* كول ^{7}

كوماچ ^{1} kumách *m.* wheat grains of milky-wax ripeness

كوماچ ^{2} kumách *m.* ram's stomach wrapped in cleaned intestines and boiled

كوماچ ^{3} kumách *m.* large piece of unleavened bread

كوماندو komāndó *f. Eastern* diversionary landing team or detachment

كومبار kumbár *m.* potter

كومبائن kombájn *m.* combine

كومبړ kumbáṛ **1** *m.* hole دا بړستن كومبړ كومبړ شوې This blanket is full of holes. **2** holey; full of holes كومبړ كول *compound verb* to make holes in كومبړ كېدل *compound verb* to become holey

كومړى kumṛə́j *f.* bur caught in the wool of a sheep

كومك komák *m.* ☞ كمك

كومك كوونكى komák kawúnkaj auxiliary كومك كوونكې تولگی ... kawúnke… auxiliary detachment

كومكي ^{1} komakí auxiliary كومكي فعل auxiliary verb

كومكى ^{2} kumakáj *f.* turtle-dove

كومن kumán faded, withered; rotten, decayed

كومنتیا kumənṭjá *f.* كومن والى kumənwáلaj *m.* withering; decaying

کومنول kuməṇawə́l *denominative, transitive* [past: کومن یې کړ] to promote withering; rot, cause rotting; let rot

کومنونه kuməṇawə́na *f.* fading; rotting

کومنیدل kuməṇedə́l *denominative, intransitive* [past: کومن شو] to wilt; rot

کومنیدنه kuməṇedə́na *f.* کومنیده kuməṇedə́ *f. plural* withering; rotting

کومول kumól *m.* **1** stork **2** *regional* stilt-walker

کومه kumá¹ *f.* pebbles (the game)

کومه kúma, kóma² *feminine singular of* کوم¹

کومه kawə́ma³ ☞ کوم²

کومه kúma⁴ *f.* کومی kúmaj¹ *m.* **1** oral cavity, mouth cavity **2** central part of something; depth د بحرونو او اوبو په کومه کښې the ocean depths **3** small depression in a hearth (for fuel) د زړه له کومي خخه مبارکي در کوم *saying* I congratulate you wholeheartedly دي کیسې زما د روح کومي ولرزول *kúmi...* This story moved me to the depths of my soul.

کومي kúmi¹ *f. plural of* کوم¹

کومی kumáj² *m.* hump (e.g., of a camel)

کومیته komiṭá *f.* committee

کومیدي komedí **1** *attributive* comic, comedy **2** *f.* comedy

کومیک komík comic, comical کومیک لیکونکی humorist

کومینترن komintérn *m. history* the COM intern, the Communist International intern

کوم یو kum jaw *indefinite pronoun* some, some kind of, a certain

کون kaun *m. Arabic* **1** world, the universe مادي کون the material world دوه کونه *religion* both worlds, this world and the next world **2** being existence

کوناټ kunáṭ *m.* **1** blunt end of an egg **2** bottom (of a jug, pitcher, etc.)

کوناټور kunāṭawə́r **1** having a broad rump, having a wide posterior, having fat buttocks **2** cowardly, faint-hearted

کوناټي kunāṭí¹ buttocks کوناټي هډ *anatomy* sacrum

کوناټی kunāṭáj² *m.* ☞ کناټی

کوناری kunāráj *m.* butcher

کوناس káunā́s *m.* Kaunas

کوناستی kunāstáj¹ *m.* **1** first time a child sits down on his own **2** lifting a patient following an illness

کوناستی kunāstáj² *f.* child's chair

کوناکری konā́kri *m.* Conakry

کونتر kuntár *m.* ☞ کوتر¹

کونتره kauntára *f.* ☞ کوتره¹

کونتی kuntáj *m.* wall washed by a stream

کونتی konṭáj *f.* **1** shepherd's crook **2** cane with a curved knob

کونج kundzh *m.* **1** corner **2** bend, crook د ماغزه کونجونه convolutions of the brain **3** tip, end چاته د سترگو په کونج کتل to look askance at someone

کونجاره kundzhā́ṛá *f.* oil-cakes (used as fodder)

کونجت kundzhə́t *m. plural* ☞ کنجت

کونجری kundzhəráj *m.* stenciling on a wall

کونجر kundzhár *m.* greengrocer

کونجک kundzhák *m.* little corner, nook

کونجکه kundzhə́ka *f.* cockleshell

کونجلغ kundzhələ́gh crumpled; wrinkled

کونجي kundzhí¹ *f.* [*plural:* کونجی kundzhə́j *and* کونجي گاني kundzhigā́ni] key (to a lock)

کونجی kundzháj² bent, stooping; aged

کونجی kundzhə́j³ *f.* stone from which millstones are made

کونجی kundzhə́j⁴ *f.* **1** drinking bowl (for birds in a cage) **2** ladle, dipper

کونځله kundzə́la *f.* sesame

کونځی kauntsə́j *f.* ☞ کوښی

کوندازه kundā́za *f.* cup, handle-less cup

کونداغ kundā́gh *m.* ☞ کنداغ

کندروزی kundrúzaj *m.* **1** red pepper **2** *medicine* bulimia

کوندری kundráj *m.* **1** small pit, hollow, depression **2** board, piece of leather (for rolling out dough) **3** front side of a blanket, right side of a blanket

کوندریزی kundrézaj *m.* intestinal disease of sheep

کوندړی kundúṛaj *m.* small pit, hollow, depression

کوندس kundə́s *m.* clay quarry, clay pit

کونده kundá¹ *f.* ☞ کنده²

کونده kundá² *f.* plow beam

کونده kundá³ *f.* cessation of pain

کوندي kundí¹ *f.* cleaning a gold-trimmed skullcap (by bread, paste, etc.)

کوندی kundáj² *m.* string, cord (for tying up sacks)

کوندی kundáj³ **1** winding, twisting; coiling, wriggling **2** bending down; writhing کوندی کېدل *compound verb* **a** to wind, twist **b** to writhe

کوندی kundáj⁴ *m.* rope of a sling

کوندي kundé⁵ *plural of* کونده¹, ², ³

کونډ kwanḍ¹ *m.* lambing, lambing time for sheep

کونډ kwanḍ, kwunḍ² *m.* widower

کونډ kwanḍ³ *m.* top, summit (of a mountain)

کونډ kwanḍ⁴ *m.* menstruation په کونډ کښې کېدل to menstruate

کونډا kunḍā́ *m.* large earthenware trough

کونډاله kunḍālá *f.* **1** flower vase **2** dish in which hashish is prepared

کونډتوب kwanḍtób *m.* کونډتون kwanḍtún *m.* کونډتیا kwanḍtjā́ *f.* widowhood

کونډغالی kwanḍghā́laj *m.* **1** cabin, hut; tacky little house **2** run-down sheep pen (in the mountains)

کونډکي kunḍə́ki¹ *m. plural* **1** brushwood, wind-fallen twigs and branches **2** short hair

کونډکی kunḍakáj² *f.* widow

کونډلژغ kunḍlazhə́gh *m.* ☞ ژغوندی

کونډلی kunḍaláj *f. botany* variety of acacia with thorns

کوندتوب کوندوالی kwəndwálaj *m.* ☞

کوندوکي kundúki *m. plural* ☞ کوندکي[1]

کوندول kunḍawə́l *transitive* [*past:* و یې کوندواوه] to pound (rice in a mortar)

کوندوه kunḍawa *f.* tablecloth

کونده[1] kwə́nḍa, kúnḍa *f.* widow کونده کېدل *compound verb* to be widowed, become a widow

کونده[2] kúnḍa *f.* 1 fishing rod 2 hook, fish-hook 3 hook; cramp iron, crampon

کونده[3] kunḍá *f.* spring, brook, stream

کوندي[1] kwə́nḍi *plural of* کونده[1]

کوندي[2] kúnḍi *plural of* کونده[2]

کوندی[3] kunḍáj *m.* 1 man who has been unable to take vengeance on his blood enemy 2 weak enemy کوندی کېدل a to be unable to take vengeance on a blood enemy b to be a weak enemy

کوندی[4] kunḍáj 1 hornless (of livestock) 2 cut, shorn, cropped بریت کوندی کول to trim a moustache 3 shortish, undersized

کوندی[5] kunḍə́j *f.* wooden bowl

کوندی[6] kunḍə́j *f.* ☞ کوندلی

کوندی[7] kunḍə́j *feminine singular of* کوندی[4]

کوندي[8] kunḍé *plural of* کونده[3]

کوندېدل kwənḍedə́l, kunḍedə́l *denominative, intransitive* [*past:* کوند شو] to be widowed, become a widow

کونړ kunáṛ *m.* ☞ کنړ

کونړي[1] kunaṛí ☞ کنړي

کونړی[2] kunaṛə́j *f.* earthenware pot for sour milk

کونسترگی kunastə́rgaj *m.* diaper

کونسټ kunsə́ṭ 1 *m.* .1 bread that is baked in hot ashes 1.2 bread that has fallen in the ashes 1.3 tree stump 1.4 tree trunk; base of a tree trunk 2.1 burned, charred 2.2 wrinkled 2.3 grown stiff with cold 2.4 paralyzed

کونسته kunsə́ṭa *f.* foundation کونسته دي وخېژه! *idiom* May you rot in hell!

کونسل[1] konsúl *m.* consul

کونسل[2] káunsil *m.* council

کونسل خانه konsulkhāná *f.* consulate (the premises)

کون سوی kunsə́waj sore seat, sore posterior (when horseback riding)

کونسی kaunsə́j *f.* braid, plait, tress (hair)

کونغو kunghú *m. anatomy* sacrum

کونک kunák *m.* 1 end, the back part of something 2 blunt end of an egg 3 end of an irrigation ditch

کونکشن konakshán *m. electronics* connection کونکشن کول *compound verb electronics* to connect

کونکی[1] konkáj ☞ کمکی[1]

کونکی[2] kawúnkaj *present participle of* کول[7] *in lieu of* کونکی

کونگ kung, kwung *m.* northern eagle owl; large owl

کونگاري کول، کونگاري kungə́ri *f. plural* howling (of a dog) کونگاري وهل *compound verb* to howl

کونگچ kungə́ch *m.* echo

کونگره kongrá *f.* trachoma

کونگری kungráj *m.* puppy, young dog

کونگر kungáṛ *m.* 1 foundation (of a building) 2 custom in the event of repeated deaths of children in a family that an earring is put on the newborn and alms are distributed

کونگو[1] kungú *m.* owl

کونگو[2] kongó *f.* Congo د کونگو رود the Congo River

کونگه kungá restless; worried, anxious, uneasy

کونگی kungáj *m.* owl

کونوېژر konwéjər *m.* conveyor

کونه[1] kawə́na *f.* 1 deeds, achievements 2 conducting, carrying on (trade, war, etc.) 3 treatment of someone 4 putting on, wearing

کونه[2] kwə́na, kúna *f.* 1 anus 2 bottom (of a dish) 3 the lower end (of a cane, walking stick) 4 rear, the rear part of something

کونه سترگی kunastə́rgaj *m.* ☞ کونسترگی

کونه سوی kwənasə́waj *m.* burned food کونه سوی کېدل to be burned (of food)

کونه غری kwənaghə́raj *m.* pelvis

کوني[1] kwə́ni *plural of* کونه[2]

کونی[2] kawunáj, kunáj *m.* lime

کونی[3] kunáj *m.* tick (dog, sheep)

کونی[4] kwə́naj *m.* burned food

کونی[5] konə́j *f. anatomy* auditory canal

کونیخی knítsaj, kunítsaj *m.* ring of cattail (a kind of support)

کونیز kuníz کونیز ټوپک *regional* breech-loading shotgun

کونی کاتر kunikātə́ṛ *m.* کونی کبر kunikabə́r *m.* crab

کونیکشن konekshán *m. electronics* connection, contact

کونین[1] kunájn *m. plural* ☞ کنین

کونین[2] kaunájn *dual Arabic from* کون *religion* two worlds, "this world and the next world"

کون[1] koṇ *m.* large tick (dog, cattle)

کون[2] kuṇ, koṇ [*f.* کنه kaṇá *m. plural:* کانه kāṇə́ *f. plural:* کنی kaṇé] deaf کون یا روند کېدل *idiom* a کون او روند کېدل to pretend to be deaf غوږونه کانه اچول to be deceived b to look through one's fingers (at something), fail to notice (something), ignore (something)

کون توب kuṇtób *m.* کون تیا kuṇtjā́ *f.* deafness

کونکی kuṇkə́j *f.* small window in a wall between two rooms

کون والی kuṇwálaj *m.* deafness

کونول kuṇawə́l *transitive* ☞ کنول

کونی[1] kuṇə́j *f.* 1 earthenware bowl 2 feeding dish (for birds) 3 game of lunki (*literally:* holes) 4 lunka (hole, for the game) 5 knee cap

کونی[2] koṇə́j *f.* dark and windowless room

کونی[3] kauṇə́j *f.* half a nut

کونیدل kuṇedə́l *intransitive* ☞ کنیدل

کونیک kuṇík *m.* bedbug, chinch

کوو [1] kwaw *m.* hump

کوو [2] kawú *present tense first person plural of* کول [7]

کوو [3] kawó *dialect imperfect of* کول [7] *in lieu of* کاوه

کوکی kawúkaj *m.* ladle, soup ladle

کوونکی kawúnkaj *present participle of* کول [7]

کووبدی kuwédaj *m.* shield (of a target)

کوه [1] koh, kuh *m.* mountain د بابا کوه *kóh-i…* the Kohi Baba Range کوه سفید *kóh-i…* the Kohi safed range کوه سلیمان *kóh-i…* the Sulaiman Mountains (Range)

کوه [2] kawá *imperfective imperative of* کول [7]

کوهاټ kohā́ṭ *m.* Kohat

کوه بند kohbánd mountainous کوه بنده علاقه mountainous region

کوه پیمایي kuhpajmāī́ *f.* mountaineering, mountain-climbing

کوهدامن kohdāmán *m.* Kohdaman (region north of Kabul)

کوهړ kuhə́ṛ *m.* whip

کوهسار kohsā́r *m.* ☞ کوهستان [1]

کوهستان kohistā́n, kuhistā́n *m.* **1** mountainous country; uplands; mountainous terrain **2** Kohistan

کوهستاني kohistānáj, kohistā́ni **1.1** mountainous کوهستاني وطن mountainous country **1.2** Kohistani کوهستاني ژبه Kohistani (the language) **2** *m.* one who lives in the mountains, mountain-dweller

کوه طور kohitúr *m.* Mount Sinai

کوه قاف kohiqā́f *m.* ☞ قاف [2]

کوه گردي kohgardí *f.* mountaineering, mountain-climbing

کوه نورد kohnawárd *m.* mountain-climber, mountaineer, Alpinist

کوهي [1] kohí, kuhí **1.1** mountainous افغانستان یو کوهي هیواد دئ Afghanistan is a mountainous country **1.2** wild کوهي ناک wild pear **2** mountainous کوهي شاهین rusty-headed falcon (the central Asian subspecies of peregrine falcon)

کوهی [2] kuṇáj *m. Eastern* [*plural:* کوهي kuhí *and* کوهیان kuhijā́n] **1** well **2** shaft د زني کوهي shaft د کانو کوهي *idiom* a dimple on the chin څوک چه کوهي کیني، کوهي کښني لوېري *saying* He that mischief hatches, mischief catches.

کوئ [1] kawəj *conditional & potential forms of* کول [7] *in lieu of* کولای

کوي [2] kawí, kəwí *present tense of* کول [7]

کوی [3] kə́waj, káwaj *m.* smallpox چا ته د کوی خال وهل، چا ته د کوی خال وهل to inoculate for smallpox

کوی [4] kuwáj, koj *m.* itch کوی کول *compound verb* to itch

کویبیشف kujbishéf *m.* Kuibyshev

کویت kuwájt *m.* Kuwait

کوټه kweṭá *f.* Quetta

کوېدل kəwedə́l *intransitive* [*past:* و کوېده] to cry, call (of an owl)

کوېدن kwedə́n *f. dialect* ☞ کوېدن زه کوېدن می شوې ده I am engaged (to be married)

کوېدی kwedáj *m.* person who delivers the bride to her husband's house in a palanquin

کوېزه kwíza, kwéza *f.* scaffolding

کوېښل [2] kwex̌ə́l *transitive dialect* ☞ کښل

کوني کاتر kojkabár *m.* ☞ کوی کبر

کویل [1] kojə́l *transitive* [*past:* و یې کویه] to comb

کویل [2] kojl *m.* spool, bobbin, reel د سیم کویل spool, bobbin, reel

کوئله [1] kojlá *f. regional* coal

کوېله [2] kuwelá *f.* koil, Indian cuckoo

کوېلی [1] kwélaj *m.* ☞ کوېنی

کوېلی [2] kweláj *m.* ☞ کووکی

کوین kawín *m.* hoe, mattock

کوینه kawína *poetic present tense of* کول [7] *in lieu of* کوي

کوېنی kwénaj, kojínaj *m.* burned food

کوئو پراتور kooperātór *m.* cooperator

کوئو پراتیف kooperātíf *m.* cooperative

کویه kujá *f.* moth

کویی kujáj *m. dialect* well

که [1] ka **1** *imperative of* کړل *in lieu of* کړه [2] **2** *dialect in lieu of* کاندی [1]

که [2] kə *past tense of* کړل *in lieu of* کړ [4]

که [3] ka, kə **1** *conjunction* **.1** or (as interrogative) څي که پاتیږې؟ دلې وې که تللئ وې؟ Were you here or did you leave? نور څه که ووینم او که ونه وینم Will I see something or not? **1.2** or (disjunctive conjunction) په چهارشنبه که په پنجشنبه کښني on Wednesday or Thursday **1.3** if (conditional conjunction) که چیري! که خدای کړل If he will come! که هغه راغئ! If God grants! او که نه وي otherwise که نه وي، که نوي in the event if **1.4** although, though (concessive conjunction) که ته ژاړې که خاندې، It may break you, but you really must do this. که مري که چوي دا به کوي که څه هم... مگر although که څه هم، که هر څو، که هر څه nevertheless... که څه هم مي دا ټکر خوښ نه و، وامي خیست Although I didn't like this cloth, I bought it. **2** *interrogative-relative particle* (English lacks such a particle) زه پر تاسي یو ناز کوم که یې اخلي؟ I want to ask you about something; would you agree? که دي دغه Would you explain this problem to me? مسئله راوبنووله؟ که ډېر که ل whether little or much که نه ☞ کنه [5]

کهار [1] kahā́r *m.* ☞ کوېدی

کهار [2] kahā́r *m.* ☞ کهر

کهاره kahārá *f.* ☞ کواره

کهاړه kahā́ṛa *f.* rope ring (a type of archery target or a support for a dish)

کهال kahā́l **1.1** lazy **1.2** inert, sluggish, passive, listless **2** *m.* **.1** lazy person, idler **2.2** sluggish, passive person

کهالول kahālawə́l *denominative, transitive* [*past:* کهال یې کړ] **1** to make lazy; promote laziness **2** to develop inertia

کهاله [1] kahā́la *feminine singular of* کهال

کهاله [2] kahālə́ *oblique singular of* کهول

کهالي [1] kahā́li *f.* **1** laziness کهالي کول *compound verb* to be lazy, idle one's time away, loaf **2** yawning; stretching کهالي اچول *compound verb* to yawn; stretch oneself

کهالي [2] kahā́li *feminine plural of* کهال

کهالېدٙل kahāledál *denominative, intransitive* [*past:* کهال شو] **1** to be lazy, be idle **2** to be sluggish, be passive, be listless

کهتر kihtár little, small, smaller, lesser

کهتري kihtarí *f.* trifle, insignificance

کهر kahár light chestnut (horse's color)

کهربا kahrubā́ *f.* amber

کهربايي kahrubāī́ amber

کهرکۍ khiṛkə́j *f. regional* window د سترگو په کهر کو ليدل *idiom* to see with one's own eyes

کههٙخت kahə́kht *m.* grief, distress; anxiety, uneasiness

کهکشان kahkashān *m. plural* the Milky Way

کهل والی kahalwā́laj *m.* ☞ کهول والی

کهمرد kahmárd *m.* Kamard

کهٙند kuhánd, kohánd old, ancient, decrepit

کهندل kohandíl *m. proper noun* Kohandil

کهند khand *m.* ☞ قند

کهنگ kuháng, koháng *Western* ☞ کهند

کهنگه kuhánga tall, high کهنگه پېغله plump tall and well-grown girl

کهنه ¹ kohná old, ancient

کهنه ² kahə́na *f.* capacity کهنه لرل to contain, hold, accommodate

که نه ⁵ kəná ☞ کنه

که ني ³ kə-ní که نه وي or else, otherwise ☞ که

کهوټ khoṭ *m. regional* small fortress, fort ☞ کوټ ¹

کهٙول kəhól, kahól *m.* **1** family; birth, origin, stock, generation, lineage زلمی او زینبه سره کهول کړل to marry, get married زلمی او زینبه سره کهول کور سوه Zalmay and Zainab got married. **2** family, origin, lineage (in the names of tribes) جاني کهول the Janikheili

کهول والی kaholwā́laj *m.* کهولي kaholí *f.* family affairs; domestic matters

که ¹ kahá *f.* nausea

که ² kahá *f.* scratching; itch که کول *compound verb* to feel an itch

کهۍ ¹ kaháj *m.* ochre

کهۍ ² kaháj *m.* sedge

کهۍ ³ kaháj *m.* کهۍ kaháj ³ *f.* fascine (bundle of brushwood to protect the channels of rivers and canals from erosion)

کهۍ ⁴ kaháj *m.* ditch

کهۍ ⁵ kaháj thin, emaciated

کهۍ ⁶ kaháj *f.* small ax, little hatchet (for chopping brushwood and shrubs)

کهۍ ⁷ kaháj *f.* **1** mattock, pickax **2** shaft of a millstone

کهېدٙل kahedál *intransitive* [*past:* و کهٙده] **1** to feel nausea, be nauseated **2** to be unsteady, reel, stagger, be unsteady on one's feet **3** to grow weak; pine away

کهېدٙنه kahedə́na *f.* کهٙده kahedó *m. plural* **1** nausea **2** reeling, staggering **3** weakness, weakening

کئ ¹ kəj *present tense second person plural of* کول *in lieu of* کوئ

کي ² ki *present tense of* کول *in lieu of* کوي

کي ³ ki *Western,* ke *Eastern* ☞ کنبي

کی ⁴ kaj *m.* **1** king **2** hero

کې ⁵ ke *present tense second person of* کول *in lieu of* کوې

کې ⁶ ke *contraction of the conjunction* که *and the pronoun* يې کې څوک د رانيولو خواهش لري نو را دي سي If someone wants to buy them, let him present himself کې کتل ... When he glanced (at)...

کې ⁷ ke *Western contraction of the postposition* کي *and the pronoun* ئي دا بکس واخله، په موټر کې کښېږ ده Take this box and put it in the car.

کياژه kajādzá wilted, faded

کيارۍ kjāṛáj *f.* د گلانو کياري (garden) bed ☞ parterre (of a park)

کياٙزه kajā́za *f.* saliva

کياست kijāsát *m. Arabic* perspicacity

کيامت kjāmát *m.* ☞ قيامت

کياني kajāní kingly, regal

کې ايستل keistál *transitive Eastern* ☞ کښېنستل

کې ايسته keistə́ *m. plural Eastern* ☞ کښېنياسته

کېبٙر kebár *m.* iron fork

کېبل kebl *m.* cable زېر زميني کېبل underground cable

کېبل گذاري keblguzārí *f.* laying cable

کيپ kip *m.* ☞ قيف

کېپ تٵون keptā́un *m.* Cape Town

کېپي kajpí *m.* drunkard, reveler

کېټ ket *m.* faith, belief, religion

کېټو kitó *f.* Quito

کېته kéta open کېته خوله open mouth

کېټلۍ keṭláj *f. regional* **1** tea-kettle **2** pan, saucepan

کېج kedzh **1** hard **2** fibrous, stringy (of overripe vegetables) **3** tightly wound, tightly twisted (of rope)

کېجٙلۍ kedzhə́laj **1** stingy, miserly **2** unpleasant (of a person)

کېجٙم kedzhə́m *m.* saddlecloth

کېچ kech *m.* shawl made of cotton material ☞ کبش ²

کېچٙټ kechə́ṭ *dialect* young, under-age

کيچړۍ kichṛáj *m.* dish of rice and beans with dried curd

کيچړي kicháṛi *f. plural* mud, dirt

کيچۍ kicháj small, little

کېټ kets *m.* grave

کېټسکٙنۍ ketskə́naj *m* grave-digger

کېټسٙۍ ketsə́j *f.* ☞ کيسه ¹

کيخه kíkha *f.* mosquito

کيخۍ kíkhaj *m.* worm; intestinal worm; ascarid (e.g., pinworm, roundworm, etc.)

کېدٵی kedā́j *conditional & potential form of* کېدٙل دا هم کېدای سي چه ... it is also possible that... داسي کېدای شي چه ... it can happen that...

کېدٙل kedál *intransitive verb* **1** independent verb [*present:* کېږي *past:* وسو، وشو *imperfect:* کېده]. **1.** to occur, take place, happen دپر ... کله داسي کېږي چه it often happens that... **1.2** to be found, be, bred; sprout په ننگرهار کښي گني کېږي Sugar cane grows in

Nangarhar; بدن په کابل کښي کښي کېږي Millet is grown in Kabul. **1.3** to be conducted (i.e., trade) **1.4** to be carried out, be conducted په هغه علاقه کښي د ساختمان کار کېږي Construction work is being carried out in this region **1.5** to go, to come down (of precipitation) زورور د بارانونه کېږي It is raining hard. **1.6** to total, come to, amount to تکر قيمت پنځه کلداري دئ، چه پنځه ويشت افغاني کېږي The price of the material is five Indian rupees, which amounts to twenty-five Afghani. **1.7** to take place, happen, to occur مگر کېږي چه ځيني وخت … However, it sometimes happens that… **1.8** to be possible, be feasible هر راز چه کېږي by any means **1.9** to be (by kinship) هغه د زرغوني سکه خور کېدله She was Zarghuna's blood sister. **1.10** [*past:* شو،سو] to be born **2.1** *auxiliary and formant verb in compound verbs and in verbs with prepositional phrases* [*present:* کېږي *past:* شو] to become, turn into طبيب کېدل *compound verb* to become a physician ښه کېدل *compound verb* to get well, recover مړ کېدل *compound verb* to die لېونی کېدل *compound verb* to go crazy, go out of one's mind اداره کېدل *compound verb* to manage اصلاح کېدل *compound verb* to improve, get better, reform, mend one's ways په کار کېدل to be used, be applied **2.2** *as an auxiliary verb forms the passive voice of verbs of imperfective aspect* ليدل کېدل to be able to be seen; be observed

کېدلای kedəláj *conditional & potential form of* کېدل *in lieu of* کېدای

کېدنه kedəna *f.* **1** ☞ کېده¹ **2** possibility, feasibility

کېدو¹ kedó *oblique plural of* کېده¹

کېدو² kédu *dialect present tense first person plural of* اينېودل *in lieu of* کېنبېرد دو of

کېدونکی kedúnkaj **1** *present participle of* کېده² ☞ کېدونی

کېدونی kedúnaj possible, feasible ته نه هيڅ کار کېدونی نه دئ You are not fit for anything. مونږ دا کار کېدونی نه گڼو We consider that to be impracticable.

کېده¹ kedə *m. plural* **1** accomplishment, fulfillment, completion **2** growth, growing; cultivation **3** carrying out, executing (e.g., a work project) **4** fall, falling (of precipitation) **5** possibility, feasibility, practicality

کېده² kdeə *imperfect of* کېدل

کېده³ kedá *f. imperfect of* کېدل

کېده⁴ kéda *Eastern imperative perfective aspect of* اينېودل *in lieu of* کېنبېرد ده

کېدئ¹ kédəj *Eastern imperative perfective aspect plural of* اينېودل

کېدی² kédáj *Eastern conditional & potential forms of* کېدل *in lieu of* کېدای of

کېدي³ kedé *imperfect feminine plural of* کېدل

کېډېت kedéṭ *m. regional* cadet (student at a military academy)

کير kir *m.* rice milk porridge

کيرانه kirāṇá *f.* groceries

کيرړی kirṛáj *m.* mole cricket

کيرکها kírkha *f.* ☞ کرکنه

کير کيرک kirkirák *m.* halcyon, kingfisher

کېروزن kerozín *m. plural* kerosene

کېرۍ kerə́j *f.* rim (of a wheel)

کېر keṛ *m.* **1** tamarisk hedge; living green-fence **2** pen, fold, corral (for livestock) **3** sweep of branches **4** wicker curtain that serves simultaneously as a door **5** paling, fencing; palisade

کړ کېچو kiṛkichú *f.* ☞ کېر کيچو

کېړه¹ keṛá *f.* **1** wicker netting of young tamarisk (serves to cover the ceiling) **2** ☞ کېر **3** wicker bin, corn-bin

کېړه² keṛá *f.* iron ring (that fastens plowshares together)

کېړه گی keṛagáj *m.* deep wicker basket

کېړۍ keṛə́j *f.* leather sandals; heel-strap sandals

کېړۍ گری keṛəjgáraj *m.* shoemaker who makes sandals and heel-strap sandals

قيزه kajzá *f.* ☞ قيزه

کيژ kezh *m.* ☞ کيج

کېږ keg *present tense stem of* کېدل

کېږد kegd *Eastern present tense stem perfective aspect of* اينېودل *in lieu of* کېنبېرد

کېږدئ¹ kégdə́j *dialect perfective aspect imperative plural of* اينېودل

کېږدی² kegdə́j *f.* nomads' (black) tent

کېږلی kegə́laj despised; oppressed

کېږه¹ kegá *f.* irrigated land that is ready for plowing کېږه مځکه arable land

کېږه² kéga *imperative imperfective aspect of* کېدل

کېږئ¹ kégəj *present tense second person plural of* کېدل

کېږي² kégi *present tense singular and plural of* کېدل

کېږي³ kége *present tense second person of* کېدل

کيس¹ kajs *m.* Kais (the legendary progenitor of the Afghans)

کېس² kes *m.* honor, glory کېس دي کم شه! *saying* May you live in shame! (a curse)

کېسپين késpijan Caspian کېسپين غدير Caspian Sea

کيسر kajsár *m.* person who frequently shivers and has a fever

کيسه¹ kisá *f* tobacco pouch; bag

کيسه² kisá *f.* ☞ قصه

کيسه³ kesá *f.* small ax, little hatchet (for chopping brush)

کيسه بر kisabúr *m.* pickpocket

کيسه بري kisaburí *f.* petty thievery

کيسه ليکونکی kisá likúnkaj *m.* short-story writer, writer of novellas

کيسي¹ kajsí *m. plural* ☞ قيسي

کيسی² kisə́j *f.* ☞ کيسه¹

کيسی³ kisə́j *f.* **1** riddle, enigma, charade کيسی وراچول to pose a riddle د کيسی ځواب ورکول to solve a riddle **2** story, event داخه کيسی ده؟ What's the matter?

کيسې⁴ kisé *plural of* کيسه¹

کيسې⁵ kisé *plural of* کيسه²

کيسې⁶ kajsé د کيسی غر the Sulaiman Mountains

کيش¹ kish *interjection* kish

کيش² kesh *m.* **1** faith, belief, religion **2** manner, style, characteristic, quality

كِش ³ kesh *m.* **1** cotton blanket; lap robe; shawl **2** old-style colored patterned silk cloth

كِشبافي keshbāfī *f.* making of blankets, shawls or lap rugs د كِشبافي شيان blankets, shawls, etc.

كِشپ kishə́p *m.* tortoise

كِشک kishə́k *m.* **1** sentry **2** protection; guard

كِشكارل kishkārə́l *transitive* ☞ شكارل

كِشكره kishkára *f.* **1** magpie **2** *regional* nutcracker (the bird)

كِشكيش kishkísh *interjection* ksh-ksh

كِشو kisháw *m.* tortoise

كِشينيو kishinéw *m.* Kishinev

كِښ kiḳh, keḳh *imperfect of* كنبل

كنبكل keḳhkə́l *transitive* ☞ كنبل

كنبود kéḳhol *Eastern past tense perfective aspect of* اينبودل *in lieu of* كنبينود

كنبول keḳhwə́l *transitive* ☞ اينبول

كنبى ¹ kiḳhái *m.* **1** intestinal worm, parasitic worm **2** castrated animal

كنبى ² kiḳhə́i *f.* gnat, insect; small worm

كيغاچ kighāch *m.* diagonal plowing, diagonal tilling

كيف ¹ kajf *m. Arabic* **1** intoxication; pleasure, enjoyment, satisfaction د محبت په كيف intoxicated with love **2** quality, characteristic

كيف ² kijéf *m.* Kiev

كيف آور kajfāwár amusing, diverting, affording pleasure

كيفر kajfár *m. Arabic* retribution, punishment

كيفي ¹ kajfī *Arabic philosophy* qualitative له كمي نه كيفي تغييراتو ته the law of the transition from quantity to quality د انتقال قانون

كيفي ² kajfī *Arabic* **1.1** intoxicated, drunk **1.2** intoxicating **2** *m.* drunkard; reveler

كيفي ³ kéfī *f.* café, coffeehouse

كيفيت kajfiját *m. Arabic* **1** the circumstances of the case; position, condition **2** description مفصل كيفيت راكول to describe in detail د لغت معنوي كيفيت the semantics of a word

كيفيتي kajfijatí ☞ كيفي ¹

كيک ¹ kajk *m.* ☞ كيكه

كيک ² kek *m.* plum-cake

كيكاړي kékā́gi *present tense of* كنبكل

كيكر kikár *m.* كيكر kikár *m.* kikar, *Acacia modesta*

كنبل kekkhə́l *transitive Eastern* ☞ كنبل

كيكوړى kikóṛai *m.* flat cake, scone, small loaf of bread

كيكه kájka *f.* flea كيكه په پرتا گه كي لوېدل *idiom* to become agitated, begin to worry

كيگالي kigā́li *m.* Kigali

كيل ¹ kil, kel *m.* **1** furrow **2** rut

كبل kel *m.* tugs of a plow (part of the harness for a plow pulled by an ox or a horse)

كيلک ¹ kilák *m.* ☞ جغ لندى

كيلک ² kelák *m.* **1** hobble **2** braid for attaching the saber grip to the scabbard

كيلو kiló *f.* kilo, kilogram

كيلوات kilowā́t *m.* كيلووات kilowā́t *m.* kilowatt

كيلوگرام kilogrā́m *m.* كيلوگرم kilográm *m.* kilogram

كيلومتر kilométr *m.* kilometer

كيلومتري kilometrí *f.* distance in kilometers په 5 كيلومتري كښي five kilometers

كيلووات kilowā́t *m.* ☞ كيلوات

كيله ¹ kíla, kilá *f.* **1** furrow **2** groove, slot, cut, opening **3** kila (a measure of area, about 40 jareebs) *idiom* ځما جامې كيلې شوي وي My clothes became rumpled.

كيله ² kilá *f.* fortress ☞ قلعه

كيله ³ kelá *f.* banana, banana tree

كيله گى kilagáj *m.* Kilagai (an inhabited place north of Kabul)

كيلي ¹ kilí *f.* key (to a lock) ☞ كلي ¹

كپلى keláj *m.* corn (on the foot), callosity

كيليما نجارو kilimāndzhāró *f.* Kilimanjaro Mountain

كيماوي kimāwí *Arabic* chemical

كيمپ kemp *m.* camp

كيمخ kimúkh *m.* ☞ كيمخت

كيمخت kimúkht, kimə́kht *m.* shagreen leather

كيمخواب kimkhā́b *m.* brocade د كيمخواب جامه brocade dress

كيمره kemrá *f.* camera

كيمنډل kemanḍə́l *transitive Eastern* ☞ كنبل

كيمه kemá *f.* leather bucket which collects the vegetable oil running from the press

كيميا kimijā́ *f.* **1** chemistry عضوي كيميا organic chemistry غير عضوي كيميا inorganic chemistry عمومي كيميا general chemistry زراعتي كيميا agricultural chemistry **2** alchemy

كيميابوتى kimijābútaj *m.* dittany, burning-bush كيميابوتى كېدل *idiom* to become rare; be almost unattainable

كيميا پېژندونكى kimijā́ pezhandúnkaj *m.* chemist

كيمياخانه kimijākhāná *f.* chemical laboratory

كيميادان kimijādā́n *m.* chemist

كيمياگر kimijāgár *m* alchemist

كيمياگري kimijāgarí *f.* alchemy

كيمياوي kimijāwí **1** chemical كيمياوي كارخانه chemical plant كيمياوي تركيبات chemical combine **2** *m.* chemist

كيميائي kimijā́ī كيميوي kimijawí chemical

كين ¹ kin *m.* ☞ كينه ¹

كين ² kin *present tense stem of* كيندل

كښن ³ ken *Eastern present tense stem of* كنبنستل

كنا kenā́ *f.* kanna

كنباستل kenāstə́l *intransitive Eastern* ☞ كنبنستل

كنباستون kenāstún *m. dialect* sitting

كنباسته kenāstə́ *m. plural Eastern* **1** sitting; seating د كنباستو خونه living room, parlor **2** sojourn **3** landing

كناوه kenāwə́ *imperfect of* كنبول

کېنتن kentán *m.* Canton (Guangzhou)

کېنتی kenţáj *m.* toddler, chubby little boy

کنج kindzh *m.* coquetry ☞ کنج

کیند kind [1] *m.* dervish's rags

کینده kind [2] *imperfect of* کيندل

کيندل kindә́l *transitive* [*present:* کيني *past:* و يې کيند] to dig

کیندنه kindóna *f.* digging

کيندی kindáj *m.* mattock, hoe

کيندی kinḍә́j *f.* form; last (of a shoe, boot)

کينشاسا kinshāsā́ *f.* Kinshasa

کينگاري kingā́ri *f. plural* yells, howls

کينگری kingrә́j *f. plural* crushed stone, gravel

کينل kinә́l *transitive* ☞ کيندل

کنپنول kenawúl *transitive Eastern* 1 to seat 2 ☞ کنپنول

کينه kiná [1] *f.* malice, spite; fury, anger; vindictiveness کينه لرل to harbor malice

کينه kína [2] *f.* nit

کينه کينه kinakiná *f.* quinine

کينه گر kinagár کينه ور kinawár vindictive, revengeful, malicious

کيني kiní [1] *present tense of* کيندل

کبني kéni [2] *Eastern present tense of* کبناستل

کينيا kenijā́ *f.* Kenya

کنبډه keneḍá *f. regional* Canada

کنبډي keneḍí *regional* 1 Canadia 2 *m.* a Canadian

کين kiṇ left; کين لور the left side ! کينه خوا گور Dress left, dress (a command) د کين گرځ! To the left, about face! (a command) د کين لاس گند *politics* left, left-wing, leftist کين لاس گند left-wing party, leftist party

کينى لاسی kiḍlā́saj *m.* کينى kiṇáj *m.* left-handed person, left-hander, a lefty, southpaw

کيو kíjew *m.* Kiev

کنبواته kewātә́ *m. plural Eastern* ☞ کنبواته

کيوبا kjubā́ *f.* Cuba

کيوبائي kíubāi 1 Cuban 2 *m.* Cuban, a Cuban

کنبوتل kewatә́l *intransitive Eastern* ☞ کنبوتل

کنبوتنه kewatóna *f.* ☞ کنبوتنه

کيوتو kiotó *f.* Kyoto

کنبيوتی kewátaj *Eastern* ☞ کنبيوتی

کيوټيکس kjuṭíks *m.* nail polish د نو کونو په کيوټيکس سره کول to manicure

کبوغ kewúdz *Eastern present tense stem of* کنبوتل

کيوشو kjushú *m.* Kyushu کيوشو جزيره Kyushu Island

کيها kajhā́ د کيها مړکېدل to die long ago

کيهان kajhā́n *m. poetry* the world, the universe

کيهان نورد kajhānnawárd *m.* astronaut

کيهاني kajhāní world; space, cosmic فضا کيهاني the cosmos د کيهاني فضا تسخير opening up outer space

کوي kəjí [1] *dialect present tense of* کول [7] *in lieu of* کئي

کيى kajáj [2] *m.* reed from which قلم is made

کبنپيستل kejəstól *transitive dialecticism* ☞ کبنپيستل

گ

گ gāf gāp the thirty-third letter of the Pashto alphabet (in Eastern Pashto, the letter and sound are often confused with ږ g; it is also written ګ)

گابون gābón *m.* Gabon

گاتری gātráj *m.* 1 small chopper 2 saw-edged knife

گواتل gātә́l *transitive* ☞ گواتل

گات gāṭ [1] *m.* impost, dues, payment گات اخيستل to collect tax, take in dues

گات gāṭ [2] *m.* ☞ گاته

گات gāṭ [3] *m.* shears, clippers

گات gāṭ [4] *m.* boulder

گاتلی gaṭláj *f. regional* package, bundle

گاته gāṭá [1] *f.* thick mass left after cooking cheese

گاته gāṭá [2] 1 thick, thickening, condensing (of a liquid) گاته کول to thicken, become thick 2 drying up, dessicating گاته کېدل a to become thick b to dry up (of an irrigation well)

گاته gāṭa [3] *f.* 1 manure pile 2 pebble

گاته gāṭa [4] *f.* ☞ گاټي [1]

گاته gāṭә́ [5] *imperfect of* گټل

گاټی gā́ṭaj [1] 1 *m.* eyeball 2 sphere, pebble (for throwing from a catapult or sling) 3 hailstone

گاټي gā́ṭi [2] *f. plural* 1 dry (sheep) dung 2 soiled wool (on a sheep)

گاټی gāṭә́j [3] *f.* 1 pebble placed in the bottom of a water pipe (tobacco pipe) 2 ☞ گاټي [1] 2 3 pebble

گاټی gāṭáj [4] *m.* ḡaṭí *usually plural* kind of game

گاټی gāṭáj *m.* tax collector

گاچ gāch *m.* 1 pen (for sheep) made of thornbush 2 kind of patterned cloth

گازره gādzóra *f.* ☞ گازره

گاخ gāts *m.* Italian millet

گادړ gāḍór ugly, unattractive

گادی gāḍój *f.* anal orifice

گادر gā́ḍər *m.* girder; beam

گاډو gā́ḍo *oblique plural of* گاډی [1]

گاډه gā́ḍa *f. regional* train د ربل برقي گاډه ، د ربلوي برقي گاډه electric train

گاډی gā́ḍaj [1] *Eastern* 1 cart, bullock cart 2 train د اور گاډی د train گرندی railroad station د وري گاډی 3 automobile گاډی تپسن truck گاډی passenger car

گاډی gāḍój *f.* [*plural:* گاډياني gāḍəjā́ni] carriage, cart, wagon د بني carriage, horse-drawn خلور اربه يي گاډی rickshaw ادمانو گاډی conveyance گاډی اخيستل ، گاډی نيول to hire a carter

گاډی بان gaḍəjbā́n *m.* ☞ گاډی والا

گاډۍخانه gāḏəjkhāná *f.* **1** premises or outdoor workshop where carts, wagons, carriages, etc., are made **2** yard, open area where carters or draymen work

گاډۍ والا gāḏəjvālā́ *m.* ۔وان gāḏəjvān *m.* coachman, drayman, carter

گاډۍواني gāḏəjvāní *f.* work of a carter or coachman گاډیواني مي زده ده **a** I work as a carter. **b** I know how to drive a carriage.

گار gār¹ *m.* **1** expenditure **2** loss; damage

گار gā́r² *m.* *suffix used to form the name of an actor or agent* گناه گار sinner توبه گار repentant sinner, penitent

گاراج gārā́dzh *m.* garage

گارد gārd *m.* ۔ گارډ gārḏ *m.* **1** guardhouse, guard-building **2** *regional* guard شاهي گارد Imperial Guard, Royal Guard, Life Guard د احترام گارد honor guard

گارډر gā́rḏər *m.* ۔ گاډر

گارکنۍ garkanə́j *f.* wretched hut, hovel

گارلیک gārlik *m.* draft

گارمن gārmán harmful; noxious گارمن لوگی noxious, poisonous gases

گارنیزون gārnizón *m.* garrison د گارنیزون وظائف garrison service

گاروټی gārotáj *m.* system of irrigation wells (for a vineyard)

گارول gāravə́l *denominative, transitive* [*past:* گار یې کړ] **1** to spend, squander **2** to inflict damage, cause loss

گاره gā́ra¹ *f.* **1** gravel **2** heap of cut sugarcane

گاره gārá² *f.* cave, grotto

گاره gā́ra³ *f.* *feminine of* گار

گاري بگاري gā́ri-bagā́ri cut up into pieces, chopped up گاري بگاري کول to cut up into pieces, chop up

گاریدل gāredə́l *denominative, intransitive* [*past:* گار شو] **1** to be spent, be squandered **2** to be wasted, be lost **3** to turn out to be in vain

گاري واري gā́ri-vā́ri ۔ گاري بگاري

گاړ gāṛ *m.* **1** pebbles **2** place abounding in springs

گاړبوزی gaṛbúzaj *m.* ۔ گاړ گوزی

گاړوتی gaṛvútaj¹ *m.* thread coming out of the center of a ball (of threads)

گاړګوتی gaṛgútaj gaṛgvútaj² **1** *m.* .**1** disheveled hair **1.2** sheep stomach prepared in a special way **2** tangled, entangled گاړگوتی کول to tangle, entangle گاړگوتي کېدل to be tangled, be entangled

گاړ گوتیدل gaṛgutedə́l gaṛgvutedə́l *denominative, intransitive* [*past:* گاړ گوتي شو] **1** to get tangled, become entangled **2** to become tousled, become disarrayed

گاړگوزی gaṛgúzaj *m.* span

گاړه gā́ṛa¹ *f.* dregs (of fermented, boiled, or sour milk, etc.) نه گاړه وخټل، نه غبلي پوول *literal* to not lick the dregs, not pasture the sheep *figurative* to hold oneself aloof, not to interfere

گاړه gāṛá² *f.* corral, fold (for sheep, on the open plains)

گاز gāz *m.* ۔ غاز

گازره gāzə́ra *f.* carrot

گازولین gāzolín *m.* gasoline

غازي gāzí² ۔ غازي

گاش gāsh *m.* ۔ گاړه²

گاښ gāḵh *m.* *dialect* ۔ غابن

گاف gāf gāp *m.* name of the letter گ

گاگره gāgrá *f.* **1** gravel **2** mixture of gravel and mortar

گاگرینه gāgrína *f.* pebbles, shingle

گاگیر gāgír superficial, not serious, frivolous (of a person)

گاگیرتوب gāgirtób *m.* گاگیرتیا gāgirtjā́ *f.* superficiality, lack of seriousness, frivolity

گاگیرول gagiravə́l *denominative, intransitive* [*past:* گاگیر یې کړ] superficial, unserious, frivolous

گاگیریدل gāgiredə́l *denominative, transitive* [*past:* گا گیر شو] to make superficial, make frivolous

گاگېرنه gāgéṛna *f.* guttersnipe, slut, slattern

گاگېړی gāgeṛáj **1** stupid **2** dirty, sloppy, slatternly گاگېړی کېدل **a** to be stupid **b** to be dirty, be sloppy, be slatternly

گالس galís *m.* suspenders

گالل gālə́l *transitive* [*past:* وي یې گاله] **1** to keep, preserve, protect **2** to experience, endure, suffer زحمتونه گالل to experience difficulties غم گالل to suffer grief **3** to suffer (loss, damage)

گاله gālə́¹ *imperfect tense of* گالل

گاله gā́la² *imperfective, imperative of* گالل

گام gām *m.* **1** step, pace شمېرلي گامونه careful steps گام په گام step by step, gradually گام اچول ، گام اخیستل ، گام پوره کول to pace, step, move out **a** چټک گامونه اخیستل to pace quickly **b** to develop rapidly; move forward اساسي گامونه پورته شوي دئ Great successes have been accomplished. گام اېښودل to step in, go in, enter گام کول *compound verb* ۔ په منظوم گامو تلل گامول to walk with measured step, pace off **2** [*plural:* گامونه gāmúna] په گامو کول to pace off gait, step, pace تر یوه لوی خنډ گام اړول to overcome a great obstacle گام تراړول to withdraw from something; reject something, refuse something

گامسکټ gamiskát *m.* گامسکوټ gamiskóṭ *m.* curtain material

گامور gāmavór **1** long-legged; lanky **2** گامور having long strides

گامول gāmavə́l *denominative, transitive* [*past:* گام یې کړ] to measure, measure by paces

گامه gā́ma *f.* *regional* pace (as a unit of measure) دوه گامي زمکه about a meter of land

گامیدل gāmedə́l *denominative, intransitive* [*past:* گام شو] to be measured in paces

گامیدنه gāmedə́na *f.* گامیده gāmedə́ *m. plural* measurement in paces

گامېخه gāmékha *f.* buffalo-cow

گان gān *m. plural suffix used for nouns ending in a vowel* تارو moutain goat تاروگان moutain goats

گانا gānā́¹ *f. regional* song

گانا gā́nā́² *f.* Ghana

گانټو gānṭú *m.* coarse unbleached calico

گانجۍ gāndzhə́j *f. regional* stand, support

گاند gānd نن گاند in our days

گانده gāndá 1 *m. plural* .1 future, futurity 1.2 tomorrow, the morrow 2 future, next; coming

گاندۍ gāndə́j *f.* ☞ گاندۍ 1

گاندوزی gānḍúzaj *m.* ☞ ګربوزی

ګاندوله ganḍolá *f.* squatting ګاندولي وهل to squat

ګاندولی ganḍoláj *m.* man's jacket; high-collared jacket

گانده ¹ ganḍə́ *m. plural* needlework, embroidery

گانده ² gānḍə *imperfect tense of* ګنډل

گانده ³ gánḍa *f.* cord used to hold up wide Oriental-style trousers

گاندۍ ¹ gānḍə́j *f.* 1 pole or shaft used to set a Persian waterwheel in motion and to which bullocks or camels are attached 2 shaft (of an oil press) 3 wagon shaft (to which the horse is harnessed)

گندۍ ² gānḍə́j *f.* beehive

گانزه gánza *f.* third finger, ring finger

گانگر gāngár *m.* ambience, environment; habitat

گانگوړ gāngvóṛ گانگوړ کول gāngvóṛa nasal to compel to speak through the nose گانگوړ ویل to speak through the nose, speak nasally

گانگوړی gāngvóṛaj 1 *m.* stammerer, stutterer 2 stuttering, stammering

گانۍ ¹ gānə́j *f.* 1 collar (for a calf) 2 lime pit, pit, vat (for slaking lime, etc.)

گانی ² gāní *m.* time when the sun has risen a quarter of its apparent diameter above the horizon

گانی ³ gā́ni gā́ne *f. plural Eastern suffix for nouns ending in* ی،و moزوعگاني question, theme غواگاني cows *and* ع،غوا cow موضوع questions, themes

گانل ganə́l *transitive* [*past:* وي ګانه] to dress up someone, adorn someone

گانه ¹ gāṇá *f.* pawn, pledge; mortgage ګانه اینبودل to mortgage (real property) ګانه کول *compound verb* to mortgage (real property) ګانه کیدل *compound verb* to be mortgaged (of property)

گانه ² gāṇá *f.* adornment, decoration *idiom* دعلم په ګانه ښایسته کیدل to attain knowledge, be learned

گانه ³ gaṇə́ *imperfect tense of* ګنل

ګانه اخیستونکی gāṇá akhistúnkaj *m.* ګانه وال ganavā́l *m.* mortgagee (lender of money to a mortgagor, the holder of a mortgage)

ګانه ورکوونکی gāṇá varkavúnkaj *m.* mortgagor (one who has mortgaged a piece of property)

ګانه ييره gāṇajíga *f.* something which has been pledged, pawned, or mortgaged; mortgaged property

گانۍ gāṇə́j *f.* press (for making oil, etc.)

ګانیوال gaṇəjvāl gāṇivāl *m.* 1 oil manufacturer 2 owner of a cane press (for processing sugarcane)

گاو gāv *m. combining form* bullock, bull, ox

گاوچو gāvchú *m.* kind of stretcher with netting

گاوخانه gāvkhāná *f.* cowshed, byre

گاودم gāvdúm tapered at the end, conic (i.e., tapering like a cow's tail)

گاور gāvár *m.* anger, rage, ire

گاوز gāvə́z *m.* deer

گاوزبان gāvzabā́n *m.* ox-tongue, *Anchusa officinalis* (a medicinal plant)

گاوزه gāvə́za *f.* doe

گاوله gắvla *f.* 1 slipper 2 *regional* soft leather shoe (used by nomads)

گاولي گنډونکی gắvli ganḍúnkaj *m.* shoemaker

گاومیخ gāvmékh *m. Western* buffalo

گاومیخه gāvmékha *f. Western* buffalo-cow

گاوند gāvánḍ *m.* 1 neighbor, fellow townsman 2 *regional* neighborhood, vicinity زه ستا د ګاوند ډېر خوشحال یم I am very glad that you are my neighbor.

گاوندتوب gāvənḍtób *m.* neighborhood د دوی په ګاوندیتوب کښې in harmony with the fact that they are neighbors

گاوندۍ gāvənḍáj *m.* 1 neighbor 2 *attributive* neighboring دوه دوستانه او ګاوندي مملکتونه two neighboring and friendly countries

گاوندیتوب gāvənḍitób *m.* ګاوندي ګلوي gāvənḍigalví *f.* neighborliness, neighborhood, vicinity ښه ګاوندیتوب ، ډنه ګاوندیتوب good-neighbor relations په خپل ګاوندیتوب کښې in the neighborhood of

گاون gāvə́n *m.* songs and dancing (as performed by women)

گاوکۍ gāvukə́j *f.* method of plaiting hair and the braids themselves

گاویز gāvéz *m.* large knucklebone (for gambling)

گاه gāh *m.* 1 time ګاه ګاه sometimes, at times, now and then 2 *combining form* place, premises, abode, e.g., قرارګاه staff, headquarters (in earlier borrowed compounds it is regarded as feminine e.g., دستګاه lathe machinist's bench)

گاهر gāhár *m. m.* [*plural:* ګاهرونه gāharúna *f. plural:* ګاهري gāhári] herd of cattle

گاهو gāhú *m.* herdsman, drover

گاهي ¹ gāhí *f.* dccp wound, sore

گاهي ² gắhe once, ever, anytime ګاهي ګاهي sometimes, now and then, occasionally ... ، ګاهي ... now ..., now ..., sometimes ..., sometimes ..., گاهي یې داسي واقعه نه وه لیدلي He never saw anything like it.

گای gāj *m. Western* word of honor, promise پر خپل ګای درېدل to keep one's word, keep one's promise ګای کول to give one's word, give one's promise, promise

گائډ gājḍ *m. regional* guide, conductor

گایل ¹ gājíl gājə́l *regional* wounded ګایل کول to wound گایل کېدل to be wounded

گایل ² gājíl gājə́l *transitive* ☞ ګواتل

گایدل gājedə́l *intransitive* [*past:* وګایید] to speak

گب ¹ gab fat and ruddy, portly, burly

گب ² gəb *m.* bud, fetus, embryo

گبر gabr *m.* Zoroastrian, fire-worshipper

گبره gábra *feminine of* گبر

گبرۍ gabráj *f.* garter (for socks, stockings)

گباړه gabára *f.* large stone, block (capable of being carried)

گبنۍ gabanáj *f.* ☞ گپنی

گبه gába *f.* ☞ گبر

گبین gabín *m. plural regional* ☞ گبینه

گبینخانه gabinkhāná *f.* apiary, bee garden

گبین ژاوله gabinzhávla *f.* wax, beeswax

گبینه gabiná *m. plural* comb-honey; honeycombs دگبینو د مچيو روزنه apiculture, the raising of bees

گبنی gabenáj *m.* beehive, bees' nest; comb with honey

گپ gap *m.* talk, conversation گپ جوړول to carry on conversation گپ لګول to conduct a talk

گپاوو gapāvú garrulous, talkative

گپ شپ gapsháp *m.* conversation, talk دوی په گپ شپ بوخت وو They were talking. گپ شپ لګول to talk, conduct a talk

گپ ¹ gápa *f.* ☞ گپ

گپه ² gapá *f.* 1 cupped hand (as a measure) 2 ball (of clay) 3 chopped reed (the cattail)

گپی ¹ gapí *f.* گپاج gapáj *m.* briddle; rope used instead of reins

گپی ² gapáj *m.* left-handed person, southpaw, lefty

گتکه gatká *f.* slaking or reduction of mercury (by means of lead, tin, and other similar metals)

گتکی gatkáj *m.* ballgame

گتلکه gutlóka *f.* marriagable girl

گتلی gatláj *f.* breed of sheep

گتمه gutmá *f.* 1 ring, signet ring 2 loop 3 clasp, buckle 4 thimble (leather)

گتمۍ gutmáj *f.* ring, signet ring

گته gúta *f.* ☞ گوته

گټ ¹ gaṭ *m.* [*plural:* گټونه gaṭúna *plural:* گټان gaṭán] *Western* 1 cliff; reef; rock reef 2 *dialect* stone څوک په گټو ویستل to stone someone to death 3 dark storm cloud

گټ ² guṭ *m.* ☞ گوټ ¹,²

گټات gaṭát *m.* victory; win

گټره gaṭrá *f.* bundle; bunch, sheaf

گټکه gaṭká *f.* 1 fencing 2 foil, rapier

گټکی ¹ gaṭkáj *m.* 1 low cliff 2 boulder, stone

گټکۍ ² gaṭkáj *f.* crushed stone, ballast

گټل gaṭál *transitive* [*past:* و يي گاته] 1 to earn 2 to acquire, obtain, get خپل استقلال گټل ، آزادي گټل to attain independence; obtain freedom 3 to derive benefit, obtain advantage; gain 4 to derive profit, obtain revenue 5 to win, gain the upper hand بری گټل to gain a victory, carry the day

گټمن gaṭmán ☞ گټور

گټمه gutmá *f.* ☞ گتمه

گټمۍ gutmáj *f.* thimble

گټندوکی gaṭandúkaj ☞ گټندوی

گټندوی سری دئ گټندوی gaṭəndúj 1 earning a lot of money (one who) He earns a lot. 2 *m.* breadwinner

گټنګوی gaṭəngúj *m.* protector, patron; savior, deliverer

گټنه gaṭəna *f.* 1 earning 2 obtaining, attaining, getting 3 deriving benefit, advantage; gaining 4 deriving profit, income, revenue 5 gaining a victory

گټو ¹ gaṭú *first person present tense plural of* گټل

گټو ² gáṭo *oblique plural* گټه ¹,³

گټو ³ gaṭó *oblique plural* گټ ¹

گټو ⁴ guṭó *oblique plural* گټ ²

گټور gaṭavár 1 useful, advantageous گټور نصیحتونه useful advice, counsel 2 profitable, lucrative

گټورول gaṭawárwól *verb* to optimize

گټه ¹ gáṭa *f.* 1 earnings, wages د کور گټه ، د لاهور گټه *proverb* د خپلو متو Wages are good wherever one is in Lahore or at home. گټه پره خوړه او ښه وي *proverb* One's honest earnings are precious. 2 benefit, advantage د فرد گټه ، فردي گټه personal benefit, personal advantage د متقابله گټو په اساس under mutual advantageous conditions 3 profit, income, revenue تر سره گټه تود تاوان ښه دئ *proverb* Better to suffer loss than to have a dishonest profit. حلاله a گټه کول to earn b بی ګاره گټه unearned income گټه legal profit to derive benefit, obtain advantage c to receive profit, get revenue a د یوه شي څخه گټه اخیستل ، د یوه شي څخه گټه وړل to derive benefit, or advantage from something b to derive profit or revenue from something a گټه رسول ، گټه ورکول to yield benefit, yield advantage b to show a profit, show a return 4 good, welfare ، اجتماعي گټه د تولنې په گټه the general welfare عامه گټه for the good of society 5 interest خپله گټه تعقیبول to pursue one's own interests

گټه gaṭá *f. regional* clip of ten cartridges

گټه gáṭa *f.* round stone; round pebble; cobblestone د غره گټه cliff

گټه ګوته gáṭa gúta *f.* middle finger

گټه من gaṭamán ☞ گټور

گټه وته gáṭa váta *f.* 1 earnings, wages احمد د ګټې وټي شو Akhmad has begun to earn wages. 2 benefit, advantage 3 profit, income, revenue

گټی ¹ gaṭáj giṭáj *f.* 1 round pebble, rounded stone 2 stones (in the urinary bladder)

گټی ² giṭáj *m.* anklebone

گټیالی gaṭjālaj ☞ گټندوکی

گټبر gaṭér *m.* winding road through a mountain pass

گټین gaṭín 1 stony, rocky 2 *adjective* stone گټین پل stone bridge

گټینه gaṭína *f.* rocky terrain

گج gadzh *m.* plant with fibrous roots which are used for rope and for medicinal purposes

گجرکی gadzhárkaj *m.* gambling using pebbles for counters or markers

گجری gadzhráj *m.* گجری gadzhráj *f.* sphere or ball of gold or silver (jewelry)

گجوله gadzholá *f.* medicine made of barley for treating ailing camels

گجوي gadzhávi *f. plural* latex, milky juice (from plants)

گجو یينه gadzhojína *f.* bread from barley and wheat

گچ gach[1] *m. plural* lime, gypsum, alabaster; paraffin containing oil which cannot be pressed out پاخه گچ slaked lime

گچ gach[2] *m.* mongrel, hybrid

گچ gach[3] *m.* ☞ گچ[2]

گچ gəch[4] *m.* raw spot on a camel's groin

گچ بتی gachbaṭáj *f.* oven for calcining gypsum or alabaster

گچگر gachgár *m.* specialist in alabaster work

گچل gachál *transitive* [*past:* و يې گاچه] to measure

گچ لرونکی gach larúnkaj lime, gypsum

گچ مالي gachmālí *f.* coating with gypsum, alabaster, etc.

گچوگول gachugól *m.* confused, dismayed, perplexed, or flustered person

گچول gachúl[1] *m.* vagrant

گچول gachavál[2] *denominative, transitive* [*past:* گچ يې کړ] to measure

گچولي gachulí *f.* vagrancy

گچه gácha *f.* scope, measurement, size گچه کول to measure کېدل to be measured

گچي gachí gypsum, lime, alabaster

گځاري gədzāri *m. plural* ☞ گځاري[2]

گځ gəts *Eastern* left گځ لاس left hand د چا گځ لور ته on someone's left *idiom* گځه خوا south

گځی gatsáj *m.* left-hander, southpaw, lefty

گد gd *Eastern present stem of* اينبودل *vice*

گدا gadá *m.* [*plural:* گدايان gadāján] destitute, needy, poverty-stricken

گداگر gadāgár *m.* pauper, beggar

گداگري gadāgarí *f.* pauperism, poverty, beggary گداگري کول to go begging, be destitute

گدام gudám godám *m.* depot, storage depot, dump د اذوقي گدام food-supply storage depot دمهماتو گدام ammunition dump, ammunition depot د غلي گدام grain elevator

گدامخانه gudāmkhāná *f.* warehouse, depot, base

گدامدار gudāmdár *m.* warehouse manager, base manager

گدای gadáj *m.* ☞ گدا

گدايگر gadājgár *m.* pauper, destitute person بوډائي گدايگر destitute or poverty-stricken old man

گدائي gadāí *f.* ☞ گداگري

گدر gudár *m.* 1 ford, river-crossing place په دریاب بې گدره گډېدل *proverb literal* If you don't know where the ford is, don't go into the river. *figurative* Look before you leap. 2 watering hole (for cattle, animals) په گدر پوري وتل to cross a ford 3 place on the shore of a stream where water is obtained 4 dock, landing

گدره gudára *f.* 1 roofing timber 2 joist, beam

گدر gudár *m.* rag

گدری gadráj *f.* گدله gadála *f.* dervish's robe made of scraps of cloth

گدم gudám *m.* cerebral thrombosis, apoplectic stroke

گدور gadór low, worthless, base (of a man)

گده gadá *f.* bunch, bundle; sheaf

گدی gadáj[1] *f.* 1 meeting, conference 2 throne, dais 3 *technology* cushion, bolster 4 collar (for a horse, camel)

گدی gadáj[2] *f. abusive* strumpet, trollop

گډ gəḍ[1] *m. Eastern* 1 ram, sheep 2 wild sheep

گډ gaḍ[2] 1 mixed, intermingled 2 flowing together (e.g., of a stream, river) 3 common, mutual گډه اعلامیه mutual communique سوله غوښتونکی a communal life گډ ژوند، گډ ژوندون b coexistence گډه مرسته peaceful coexistence گډ بازار common market گډ اقدام mutual assistance گډ اقدام common activities, mutual operations په گډه کار کول to work together, mutually, in concert په چا ورگډ together, work in concert associating with, maintaining relations with someone دوی په خپل مینځ سره گډ دئ They are conversing. 4 participating in something, busy with something په کار گډ دئ They are busy with work. 5 different, varied 6 interfering in something 7 breaking out (of an epidemic), flaring up

گډ guḍ[3] ☞ گوډ[2]

گډا gaḍá[1] *f.* dancing, the dance, dance

گډا gəḍá[2] *f.* basin

گډبنه gəḍbaná *f.* shepherdess

گډبه gəḍbá *m.* [*plural:* گډبانه gəḍbānə] *Eastern* shepherd

گډتوب gaḍtób *m.* گډتیا gaḍtjá *f.* ☞ گډوالی

گډر giḍár *m.* ☞ گېډر

گډره giḍára *f.* ☞ گېډره

گډری gaḍáraj *m.* rooster, cock

گډښت gaḍ́kht *m.* ☞ گډوالی

گډکی gaḍkáj *m.* stroller or small wheeled device which a child can use to assist him in walking while holding on

گډل gaḍál *m.* 1 harrowing (of a rice field) 2 kneading, softening (clay) گډل کول a to harrow (a rice field) b to knead, soften (clay)

گډلون gaḍlún *m.* ☞ گډون

گډن gaḍán *Western* lively, energetic

گډندی gaḍandáj *m.* ☞ گډوال

گډو gaḍú *m.* smoke, something to smoke

گډوال gaḍvál *m.* dancer, professional dancer

گډوالی gaḍvālaj *m.* 1 mixing, intermixing 2 flowing together (e.g., of a river, stream) 3 communality, mutuality 4 participation 5 variety

گډوډ gaḍ-vád 1.1 mixed, intermixed; all tangled up, muddled up 1.2 disordered, disturbed, messed up 1.3 confused, unclear 1.4 destroyed; defeated گډوډېدل ☞ گډوډول گډوډ کېدل، گډوډ کول ☞ pell-mell *idiom* زړه یې گډوډ شه His consciousness was clouded. *idiom* گډه وډه ږیره grey beard

گډوډتوب gaḍvaḍtób *m.* ☞ گډوډی[1]

گډوډږیری gaḍvaḍgiráj *m.* man of advanced years whose beard is growing grey

گډوډی ¹ gaḍvaḍvā́laj *m.* ☞ گډوډوالی

گډوډول gaḍvaḍavə́l *denominative, transitive* [*past:* گډوډ يې کړ] **1** to mix, intermix; tangle, muddle **2** to disturb, violate, disrupt **3** to confuse, complicate **4** to destroy, defeat

گډوډی gaḍvaḍáj *m.* gaḍvaḍí *f.* **1** muddle, confusion, mix-up **2** disorder, derangement (of functions, etc.)

گډوډي gaḍvəḍe *f. plural* ☞ گندكي

گډوډېدل gaḍvaḍedə́l *denominative, intransitive* [*past:* گډوډ شو] **1** to be mixed together, be intermixed; be tangled up, be muddled up **2** to be disordered, be violated, be disrupted **3** to be confused, complicated **4** to be destroyed, be defeated

گډوډېده gaḍvaḍedə́ *m. plural* **1** mixing together, intermixture; tangling up, muddling up **2** disorder, violation, disruption **3** confusion, lack of clarity **4** destruction; defeat

گډوری gaḍúraj gaḍóraj *m.* **1** *m. regional* lamb **2** *dialect* ram of the fatty-tailed breed

گډوزی ¹ gaḍózaj *m.* ☞ گاړ گوزی

گډوزی ² gaḍvə́zaj *m.* troublemaker; good-for-nothing

گډوکی ¹ gəḍúkaj *m.* lamb

گډوکی ² gaḍúkaj *m.* ☞ گډوال

گډول ¹ gaḍavə́l *denominative, transitive* [*past:* گډ يې کړ] **1** to mix, intermix **2** to engross, immerse **3** to let down (to the water), launch (a ship) **4** to put into operation, set in motion **5** to take someone at his word *idiom* ځان گډول to participate in something, interfere in something په چا ځان ور گډول **a** to affiliate oneself, join with someone **b** to associate with someone, consort with someone په عسکري خدمت کښي ځان گډول to enter military service

گډول ² gəḍavə́l *transitive* [*past:* و يې گډاوه] to compel to dance

گډول ³ guḍavúl *transitive Eastern* ☞ گوډول

گډوله gaḍolá گډولیزه gaḍolíza **1** *f.* **.1** flour ground from various cereal grains **1.2** medley, jumble **2** *attributive predicative* mixed together

گډون ¹ gaḍún *m.* **1** mixture; blend **2** participation گډون کول ، گډون لرل to participate, take part **3** meeting with someone **4** meeting, conference **5** intercourse, relationship **6** community

گډون ² gaḍún **1** *m. plural* Gadun (a tribe) **2** *m.* Gadun (tribesman) ☞ ردون

گډون کوونکی gaḍún kavúnkaj *m.* participant

گډونکی gaḍúnkaj *m.* ☞ گډوال

گډونوالا gaḍunvālā́ *m.* خپل گډون والا person of one's own circle

گډونه ¹ gaḍavə́na *f.* mixing, intermixing

گډونه ² guḍavə́na *f.* mixing, confusing

گډونی ¹ gaḍúnaj *m.* ☞ گډوال

گډوني ² gaḍúne *f.* ballet dancing

گډوه gaḍvá *f.* copper pitcher (for ablutions, washing)

گډوی gaḍváj *m.* ☞ صراحي

گډه ¹ gə́ḍa *f. Eastern* **1** sheep د گډي غوښه *regional* mutton **2** disparaging old woman, coward

گډه ² gáḍa **1** *feminine singular of* گډ ² **2** *f.* intercourse, relations, links

گډه امي gáḍa amə́j *f.* dance common to men and women

گډه گډوله gáḍa-gaḍolá *f.* disorganization, maladjustment, defects

گډهل gaḍhál *m.* **1** bucket **2** tub **3** ☞ هل

گډه وډه gáḍa-vā́da *feminine singular of* گډوډ

گډه هل gaḍahál *m.* **1** depression, low place **2** land on which rice is grown, rice paddy

گډی ¹ gəḍáj *m.* aggressive ram

گډی ² gaḍáj *m.* **1** feast; party **2** company, society

گډی ³ guḍáj *m.* cripple

گډی ⁴ gaḍáj *m.* person of mixed blood

گډی ⁵ gəḍə́j *feminine of* گډی ¹

گډی ⁶ gaḍə́j *f.* throne

گډی ⁷ guḍə́j *f.* **1** crippled woman **2** doll

گډي ⁸ gə́ḍi *plural of* گډ ¹

گډي ⁹ gáḍi *feminine plural of* گډ ²

گډی چرگ guḍáj chərg *m.* hoopoe

گډېدل ¹ gaḍedə́l *denominative, intransitive* [*past:* گډ شو] **1** to be mixed together, be intermingled **2** to dip into, be absorbed in **3** to be launched (into water, of a boat) **4** to flow into د کنړ رود د کابل په سیند کښي گډېږي The Kunar River flows into the Kabul River. **5** to intersect, join (of a road) **6** to go into action, be put into operation **7** to participate in something, be included in something, be a composite part of something (society, etc.); join in **8** to break out, become widespread (of an epidemic) **9** to get into, trespass (on another's land, of cattle) **10** to get into (e.g., of a predator in relation to a herd) **11** to interfere in something د خلکو په خبرو مه گډېږه Do not interrupt the conversations. **12** to captivate with conversation آوازه گډه He began to talk again. *idiom* دی بیا گډ شو It was rumored. Rumors spread. *idiom* یوې لاري ته ورگډېدل to set out on the road

گډېدل ² gəḍedə́l *intransitive* [*past:* وگډېده] to dance

گډېدل ³ guḍedə́l *intransitive* ☞ گوډېدل

گډېدنه ¹ gaḍedə́na *f.* ☞ گډېده ¹

گډېدنه ² gaḍedə́na *f.* ☞ گډېده ²

گډېدنه ³ guḍedə́na *f.* mixture, mixing

گډېدون gaḍedún *m.* ☞ گډون ¹

گډېدونکی ¹ gaḍedúnkaj *present participle of* گډېدل ¹

گډېدونکی ² gəḍedúnkaj **1** *present participle of* گډېدل ² **2** *m.* dancer

گډېدونکی ³ guḍedúnkaj *present participle of* گډېدل ³

گډېده ¹ gaḍedə́ *m. plural* **1** mixture, mixing, intermixing **2** absorption, plunging into **3** launching (into water, a ship) **4** flowing together, flowing into **5** joining, intersecting (roads) **6** spreading (epidemic) **7** participation **8** going into operation, going into action *idiom* د بازار گډېده a crowd at the market

گډېده ² gəḍedə́ *m. plural* dancing, dances

گډېده ³ guḍedə́ *m. plural* mixing, mixture

گډېر gaḍér *m.* **1** ☞ گډون ¹ **2** bundle (of hay, grass)

گډېره gaḍéra 1 *f. dialect* .1 ☞ گډوله 1.2 ☞ گډون 2 gaḍeró mixed, intermixed گډپره کول to mix, intermix گډپره کېدل to be mixed, intermixed

گډ پکه gaḍéka *f.* 1 crutch 2 brace, support (of an axle, spinning wheel)

گډپله gaḍelá *f.* 2 ☞ گډپره 1 ☞ گډوله 1

گډېلۍ gaḍelə́j *f.* cushion

گډي وډي gáḍi-váḍi *feminine plural of* گډو یو خو گډي وډي مي ولیکلي I wrote down several broken phrases.

گذار guzár *m.* 1 blow, shock, shove 2 leap, bound 3 attack, beating 4 injury 5 crossing, passage; ford گذار کول ☞ گذارول 1 6 once, one day

گذارش guzárísh *m.* [*plural:* گزارشونه guzārishúna *Arabic plural:* گذارشات guzārishā́t] event د دنیا گذارشات world events, events in the world

گذارل guzārə́l *transitive* [*past:* و یې گذاره] 1 to say (a prayer) 2 to effect, carry out, complete

گذارنه guzārə́na *f.* 1 saying, carrying out (of a prayer-ritual) 2 completion, effecting, carrying out to a conclusion

گذارول 1 guzāravúl *denominative, transitive Eastern* [*past:* گذار یې کړ] 1 to hit, strike 2 to throw, toss, pitch 3 to attack, beat, thrash 4 to injure 5 to cross, pass over; ford

گذارول 2 guzāravə́l *transitive dialect* ☞ گذارل

گذاره guzārá *f.* behavior, treatment دخلقو سره دگذاري فن a courtesy دوی د b sociability د چا سره ښه گذاره کول to treat someone well گذاره خو ډېره سخته ده Their life is very hard.

گذاریدل guzāredə́l *denominative, intransitive dialect* [*past:* گذار شو] 1 to be said, be carried out, be effected (a prayer, prayer ritual) 2 to be completed, be accomplished, be effected

گذر guzár *m.* ☞ گدر

گذران guzrā́n *m.* 1 life, existence اجتماعي گذران public life گډ گذران a life in common, life together b coexistence گذران کول to live, exist 2 means or resources for existence

گذشت guzásht *m.* 1 privilege, concession; condescension یو گذشت کول to give a privilege; grant a concession 2 passing, proceeding 3 conduct

گذشته guzashtá 1 past 2 *m.* [*plural:* گذشتگان guzashtagā́n] .1 forefather; forerunner 2.2 the past

گر 1 gər *m. onomatopoeia* 1 the sound of cloth ripping or being torn 2 rumbling (of a carriage, etc.)

گر 2 gar *m.* 1 destitution, calamity 2 suffering

گر 3 gə́r gár *m. suffix used to form a noun of actor* بزگر peasant, farmworker کوډگر sorcerer

گړاتۍ gərātə́j *f.* short felt jacket

گراته grā́ta *f.* dung dried and pressed into round form (used as fuel)

گراج garā́dzh *f.* garage

گراربج grā́rbaj *m.* clavicle

گراف grāf *m.* 1 graph; chart; table; outline plan 2 data

گرافیت grāfít *m.* graphite

گرافیک grāfík *m.* 1 graphic table, graphic display 2 graph

گرافېم grāfém *m. linguistics* grapheme

گرالبه grā́lba *f.* گرالبي gralbi *m. plural* collar, neckband (clothing) *idiom* گرالبه ترل to preserve one's honor

گرام grām *m.* gram

گرامافون grāmāfún *m.* gramafun *m.* gramophone, record player

گرامر grāmár *m.* grammar

گرامرپوه grāmárpóh *m.* گرامر لیکونکی grāmár likúnkaj *m.* grammarian

گرامري grāmarí grammatical د ژبي گرامري تشکیل the grammatical structure of a language

گرامي girāmí 1 dear, valuable 2 esteemed

گران grān 1 dear, valuable, expensive 2 burdensome, heavy, oppressive په ډېره گرانه with great difficulty دا هیڅ گرانه نده This is not at all difficult. 3 favorite, dear گرانه ورورو! Dear brother! Dear friend! ښوک پر ځان گران بلل I love my father. زه پلار په ما گران دئ to hold someone dear 4 esteemed گران گڼل to esteem 5 په قندهار In Kandahar, snow is a rare occurrence. کنبي واوره په گرانه اوري گرانبدل ☞ گران کېدل ، گرانول ☞ گران کول

گرانات grānā́t *m.* garnet (the mineral)

گران بها girānbahā́ grānbahā́ 1 dear, valuable, precious 2 priceless, without price

گرانت grānt *m.* 1 donation, grant د گرانت په توگه in the form of a grant 2 subsidy

گرانتوب grāntób *m.* گرانتیا grāntjā́ *f.* ☞ گرانت

گرانټ grānṭ *m.* ☞ گرانت

گرانتي garāntí *f.* guarantee د گرانتی لاندي with a guarantee

گرانښت grānə́kht *m.* 1 love د مېني گرانښت ، د وطن گرانښت love for the Fatherland 2 dearness, expensiveness 3 difficulty, complication 4 value

گران فروشي girānfurushí *f.* grānfurushí speculation, sale at speculative prices

گران مایه girānmajá grānmajá valuable, dear

گرانوالی grānválaj *m.* ☞ گرانښت

گرانول grānavə́l *denominative, transitive* [*past:* گران یې کړ] 1 to become dear, rise in price 2 to make difficult, hamper, complicate 3 to cause to become nice, attractive, or favored هلک چه په خبرو راشي ورځ په ورځ ځان گرانوي When a child begins to talk he becomes dearer every day.

گرانه grā́na *f.* 1 *singular of* گران 2 *vocative of* زما گرانه! My dear! 3 *f.* difficulty

گراني 1 grāní *f.* 1 dearness, expensiveness 2 obstacle, hindrance, difficulty

گراني 2 grāni *f. plural and oblique singular of* گران نه په ما گراني! No Dear!

گرانیدل grānedə́l *denominative, intransitive* [*past:* گران شو] 1 to become dear, rise in price اوړه ډېر گران شوه Flour has become very expensive. 2 to get more difficult, become complicated, become

618

harder خبره گرانېږي The problem is getting more complex. **3** to catch the fancy of, become attractive to تا راباندي گران شوی You have become dear to me.

گرانېندهٔ grānedә́ *m. plural* ☞ گرانېنت

گراور grāvúr *m.* **1** engraving, print **2** photograph

گراوگوږ gərávgóṛ *m.* stomach rumbling

گراوند grā́und *m. combining form regional* area, plot, site

گرای grāj *m.* time دری گرايه thrice, three times

گربت gurbә́t *m.* eagle

گربته gurbә́ta *f.* female eagle

گربړه garbáṛa *f.* **1** hummocky land **2** clod of soil **3** large rock

گربشوڼ garbashóḷ unevenly, poorly woven cloth

گربل gurbә́l *transitive* ☞ گرمل

گربه gurbá *m.* cat

گربه خورک gurbakhurák *m.* catnip, *Nepeta cataria* (a medicinal plant)

گربت garbéṭ *m.* barley bread

گربينج garbináj *m.* honeycombs

گرت gurә́t *m.* grut **1** space between the thumb and index finger **2** fork (of a tree) *idiom* په گرت ځايول to put someone under pressure

گرج grədzh *m.* grudge, rancor گرج کول to nurse a grudge, harbor a grudge

گرجستان gurdzhistә́n *m.* Georgia

گرجن grədzhә́n rancorous, vindictive

گرچاپېره girchāpéra گرچاپېر girchāpér ☞ گبر چاپېر

گرځ [1] gərdz **1** *short form of the imperfective imperative of* گرځېدل vice ; گرځئ شاگرځ! *military* About face! (as a command) **2** *m.* turn

گرځ [2] gərdz *present stem of* گرځېدل

گرځمان gərdzmā́n گرځن gərdzә́n گرځنده gərdzә́nda گرځند gərdzә́nd **1** rotating **2** wandering, roaming گرځند خرځونکی گرځنده خرځونکی peddler, vendor, itinerant salesman **3** traveling **4** traveling about, journeying گرځمن خلک travelers

گرځندوی gədzəndúj **1** *m.* **.1** traveler **1.2** tourist **2** traveling, strolling

گرځنده تيليفون gardzandá ṭilifū́n گرځنده ټيليفون gardzandá ṭelifū́n *m. computer science* cell phone, mobile phone

گرځندی gərdzəndáj **1** *m.* **.1** wheel **1.2** turn, turning, fork **2** mobile گرځندی سينما portable movie projector

گرځنج gərdzənáj *m.* **1** bend, turn **2** skein (of woolen thread, yarn)

گرځول gərdzavúl *transitive* ☞ گرزول

گرځون gərdzún *m.* vomit; vomiting په ما د گرځون دوره راغله I vomited. I became sick to my stomach.

گرځدل gərdzedә́l *transitive Eastern* ☞ گرزېدل

گرزیده [2] gə́rdzedóna *f.* گرځده gərdzedә́ *m. plural* ☞ گرځبدنه

گرد [1] gard *m.* **1** dust; dust standing in a column in the air د خاورو گرد puffs of dust dusty گرد پاکول **a** د چا د بوتو گرد وهلئ to clean someone's boots **b** to be a bootlicker, toady **2** fog, mist

گرد [2] gərd all, entire گرده دنيا the whole world روخ گرده all day, the whole day, the day long

گرد [3] gərd *Western* round گرد کول گرد to make spherical or round په ميدان کښي خلک سره گرد سوي وه The people crowded into the square.

گرداب girdā́b *m. literal* whirlpool, abyss

گردآړی gərdā́ṛaj *m.* clay or stone sphere (for playing a game in which this sphere is tossed into a hole)

گرداگرد girdāgírd around, from all sides

گردان gardā́n *m.* **1** *grammar* inflection; conjugation; declension **2** learning by heart; repetition (of lessons)

گردانک gardānák *m.* ☞ پلپتن

گردانول gardānavә́l *denominative, transitive* [*past:* گردان یي کړ] **1** *grammar* to inflect; conjugate; decline **2** to commit to memory, learn by heart, repeat (a lesson) *idiom* د ميني درسونه گردانول to experience the pangs and tribulation of love

گرداني gardāní *f.* **1** inflecting; changing termination **2** inflectional

گردانبدل gardānedә́l *denominative, intransitive* [*past:* گردان شو] **1** *grammar* to be inflected; be conjugated; be declined **2** to be learned by heart, be repeated (of a lesson)

گرداو girdā́v *m.* ☞ گرداب

گرداورد girdāvárd around د مځکه پر لمر گرداورد گرځي The earth revolves around the sun.

گرداوی girdā́vaj *m. dialect m.* ☞ گرداب

گردباد girdbā́d *m.* waterspout

گردجن gardzhә́n گردخن gardzón **1** dusty, dust-covered **2** foggy

گردچاپېره girdzhāpéra گردچاپېر girdzhāpér around, about د مځکي نه around the گردچاپېره الوته a flight around the earth دکلي نه گردچاپیره around the village

گردسره gərdsərá fully, entirely, quite

گردش gardísh *m.* گردښ gardíkh *m.* **1** stroll, ramble; trip د مځکي چاپيره گردش کول to make a trip around the world **2** circulation د مالو گردش circulation of goods, turnover د گردش څخه لوبدل to go out of circulation **3** turning, turning point

گردشگاه gardishgā́h *m.* place for strolling, park

گردک [1] gərdák roundish

گردک [2] gurdák *m.* axe

گردکه [1] gərdáka *f.* circle

گردکه [2] gərdáka *f. singular of* گردک [1]

گردکی gərdəkáj roundish

گردله girdalá *f.* snowstorm, blizzard

گردمخی gərdmә́khaj round-faced

گردن gardán *m.* neck

گردنه gardaná *f.* mountain pass

گردني [1] gərdә́ni gərdә́ne *f. plural Eastern* visit by a fiancé to a bride-to-be گردني کول ، گردنو ته تلل to call on the bride-to-be (of a fiancé)

گردني [2] gardaní *f.* horse-collar padding

گردنۍ gardanə́j *f.* **1** bandolier, ammunition belt **2** a slap on the nape (of the neck)

گردو gradú *m.* axe (for cutting bushes, shrubbery)

گردوالی girdválaj *m.* roundness, sphericality, spherical form

گردومه gardumá *f.* habitat, ambiance

گردون gardún *m.* **1** wheel **2** chariot **3** vault of heaven **4** *figurative* fortune, fate

گردوني gərdúni *f. plural* ☞ گردنۍ[1]

گرده[1] gardá *f.* **1** pollen **2** fine hashish

گرده[2] gə́rda *f. singular of* گرد[3]

گرده[3] gə́rda **1** all, whole **2** fully, quite

گرده افشاني gardaafshāní *f.* گرده فشاني gardafshāní *f.* pollination

گرده ورده gə́rda-vórda around, about

گردۍ gərdáj **1.1** round, spheroidal **1.2** rather short and fat **2** *m.* **.1** femoral bone **2.2** fat man

گردیز gardéz *m.* Gardez, Gardiz (city)

گردی شکل gərdajshákl round, circular

گرزول[1] gərravə́l *transitive* ☞ رغمول

گرزول[2] gurravə́l *transitive* [*past:* وي ګرزاوه] **1** to make growl, cause to snarl **2** to cause a crash (noise)

گرړی[1] girráj **1** roundish **2** *m.* rim, felloe (of a wheel)

گرړی[2] gərráj dented, chipped, toothed

گرړی[3] gərráj *f.* **1** wheelbarrow **2** millstone

گرړیدل[1] gərredə́l *intransitive* ☞ رغمیدل

گرړیدل[2] gurredə́l *intransitive* ☞ ګپیدل

گز[1] garz *m.* ☞ گرد گز وهلی covered with dust

گز[2] gurz *m.* guráz *m.* **1** club **2** pod, capsule (of poppy)

گز[3] gə́rz *short imperfective imperative form of* گرزول vice گرڅ

گز gərz *present stem of* گرزیدل

گرزانده gərzā́nda گرزاند gərzā́nd **1** rotating **2** pacing

گرزانده gərzāndá *f.* dry cow, barren sheep

گرزن[1] garzə́n dusty لار گرزنه dusty road

گرزن[2] garzán *m. botany* pistil

گرزند gərzə́nd ☞ گرڅند and گرڅنده

گرزندۍ gərzəndáj *m.* **1** top **2** kind of cradle; carousel **3** turning fork **4** antechamber (for servants) **5** whirlpool, abyss

گرزنی gərzánaj *m.* **1** spindle **2** antechamber, reception area **3** whirlpool, abyss

گرزول gərzavə́l *transitive* [*past:* و یي ګرزاوه] **1** to turn, turn around, twirl **2** to drive around, take around **3** to carry, carry around, convey **4** to lead somebody, take someone **5** to carry (by vehicle), deliver **6** to put in (by digging) an irrigation well, etc. **7** to make something, turn into something; transform **8** to move, put into motion **9** to put into action, put into operation; exploit, execute **10** to alter, rework **11** to turn (e.g., an automobile) **12** to reflect (light, etc.) **13** to beat off, repel (e.g., an attack) **14** to hinder, not allow, prevent د کوچنی د مکتب خڅه گرزول to not send a child to school **15** to avert, stave off یوه بلا گرزول to avert calamity **16** to break, train away from (bad habits, etc.) **17** to

restrain (from some action, etc.) **18** to prevent, cause a rethinking of intended action **19** to disseminate (rumors, talk) **20** to be sick, belch, vomit د چا د خان د انعام وړ گرزول to confer an award **20** *idiom* ښه ور گرزول to return good for good

گرزون gərzún *m.* **1** vomiting, nausea گرزون کول to vomit, be sick to the stomach **2** turning, turning point

گرزیدل gərzedə́l **1** *intransitive* [*present:* گرزي *past:* وگرزیده] **.1** to revolve, turn about, spin **1.2** to whirl سر مي گرزي My head is spinning. **1.3** to be transported, be carried away **1.4** to be carried, be conveyed **1.5** to stroll, saunter; pace; wander **1.6** to take a trip, ride, travel, journey **1.7** to make rounds, go all around ډاکتر په ټولو کوټو کي وگرزیدئ The doctor made the rounds of all the wards. **1.8** to put through, excavate (an irrigation well system, etc.) **1.9** to turn off, turn (to the side) **1.10** to move, go into motion **1.11** to be put into motion, go into action, go into operation; be operated, be executed **1.12** to act, work د برق فابریکه په سکرو گرزي The electric power station works on coal. **1.13** to be changed, be remade **1.14** to be reflected (of light, etc.) **1.15** to be repulsed, be thrown back (attack, etc.) **1.16** to be deducted, be held back **1.17** to be detained **1.18** to hold fast, stand firm (from some action or other) **1.19** to break of, train away from (a bad habit, etc.) **1.20** to envelop, surround (of darkness, night) **1.21** to spread (of talk, rumor) خوله په خوله گرزیدل را گرزیدل to be transmitted from mouth to mouth **1.22** to become ممکن گرزیدل to become possible پیلوټ گرزیدل to become a pilot مجبور گرزیدل to be obliged, be forced, be constrained **1.23** to associate with someone **1.24** to drop in on, visit کله کله خو راگرزه Drop in on us some time. **1.25** to be transformed, be changed, be transmuted بل گرزیدل to be transformed, be changed, be transmuted **1.26** to reject, repudiate (a viewpoint, point of view) **2** *m. plural* ☞ گرزیده[2] *idiom* پرتا و گرزم! Illness upon myself! (said to a sick person) *idiom* یو شي پسي گرزیدل **a** to be occupied with something **b** to attain, strive to get something **c** to strive after something, seek something دا به ستا په خیال کښي نه وي در گرزیدلي چه ... You really did not think of the fact that … ; It didn't enter your head that … پر خان گرزیدل to gain strength, gain courage

گرزیدنه gərzedə́na *f.* ☞ گرزیده[2]

گرزیده[1] gərzedə́ *imperfect tense of* گرزیدل

گرزیده[2] gərzedə́ *m. plural* **1** revolution; rotation; turning **2** delivery **3** supply, delivery **4** stroll, walk **5** trip, journey **6** round, rounds **7** digging, excavation, putting through (of an irrigation well, tunnel, etc.) **8** turning, turning off (to the side or in some direction of a road) **9** movement, travel **10** run, scheduled trip (of a truck, car) **11** going into operation; exploitation, execution **12** action, operation, work **13** change, remaking **14** reflection (light, etc.) **15** deduction, withholding **16** detention **17** spreading (talk, rumor) **18** change, transformation, transmutation **19** refusal, rejection, repudiation (of a viewpoint, point of view) **20** orbit, circuit

گرج garage *m. Eastern* ☞ گرگ [2]

گربل gərgə́l *transitive* [*past:* وي گربه] **1** *Western* to scratch **2** *dialect* to tear, tear to pieces **3** *dialect* to tear off گربل کېدل **a** to be scratched, be abraded گربل شوئ ځای scratch, abrasion **b** *dialect* to be torn, be torn apart **c** *dialect* to be torn off

گربه gə́rɡa *f.* scratch, abrasion

گربی gərɡáj *m.* ☞ گربه

گربېبل gərgejə́l *transitive* ☞ گربل

گرست grast *m.* digging up, digging over

گرستی grəstáj *m.* spade (for digging over, turning over, piling up soil)

گرشک gríshk *m.* giríshk Garish (city)

گرفت giríft *m. regional* **1** taking; seizing **2** grasp **3** *figurative* criticism, critique

گرفتاره giriftā́r giriftā́ra **1** taken, caught, seized; taken prisoner; arrested **2** gripped by emotion, seized by some feeling; undergoing something; experiencing something گرفتار کول ☞ **to fall ill** په مرض گرفتار کېدل ، گرفتارول په مشکلاتو گرفتار کېدل experience difficulties, be in a difficult position

گرفتارول girigtāravə́l *denominative, transitive* [*past:* گرفتاری کړ] **1** to catch, grasp, seize; take prisoner; arrest **2** to grip (of some feeling, emotion)

گرفتاري giriftārí *f.* **1** arrest; seizure **2** state of being occupied **3** care, concern

گرفتارېدل giriftāredə́l *denominative, intransitive* [*past:* گرفتار شو] **1** to be caught, be seized, be taken; be taken prisoner, be arrested **2** to experience something, feel something **3** to be gripped, be seized (by some feeling, emotion)

گرکانده garkā́nḍa *f.* ☞ گرگنده

گرکی garkáj *m.* **1** rattling, clattering (of a carriage) **2** noise of a hand mill **3** sound made by ripping cloth

گرگ [1] gurg *m.* wolf

گرگ [2] garg *m. medicine* mange, scabies گرگ نیول to suffer with mange, itch, or scabies

گرگاډوی gargāḍój *f.* wheelbarrow

گرگوټه gargóṭa *f.* old woman

گرگچوی gargachój *f.* dried length of vine

گرگر gərgər تلل to walk hunched, walk bent over

گرگه [1] girgirá *f.* groats گرگه کول to husk groats

گرگه [2] gurgurá *f.* **1** *botany Reptonia buxifolia* **2** blackthorn

گرگه [3] gargə́ra *f. medicine* whooping cough

گرگه [4] gərgə́ra *f.* hand mill

گرگه [5] girgirá *f.* poorly prepared field

گرگزوړی gargzóṛaj *m.* maize embryo

گرگس [1] gargás *m.* vulture

گرگس [2] gargás *m.* ☞ کوگل [1]

گرگل [1] gargál *m.* itch; mange; scabies گرگل کول **a** to have the itch, have scabies *compound verb* **b** to scratch vigorously (e.g., the skin)

گربل [2] gargə́l *transitive dialect* ☞ گربل

گرگله gargolá *f.* vortex, waterspout

گرگنده gargánḍa *f.* beam, log

گرگڼه gargə́ṇa *f.* liver infested by liver flukes (in cattle)

گرگو gargó *f.* **1** confusion **2** epizootic, murrain, cattle plague (sheep)

گرگوښنه gargókha *f.* badger

گرگه gárga **1** *f.* beam, log **2** *f.* stump **3** *m.* man with a stable or firm character **4** *f. Russula foetens* (a kind of mushroom) **5** *f.* saddletree (frame of saddle)

گرگی [1] gargáj *m.* **1** lazy ox, lazy bullock **2** child's game

گرگي [2] gárgi *Eastern* gárge *f. plural of* گرگه

گرگی [3] gargə́j *f.* stump; block, blockhead

گرگی [4] gərgáj *m.* skeleton

گرلات garlā́t *m.* shard, potsherd

گرلاڅه gərlā́tsa *f.* netting (for holding straw)

گرلنډ gərlanḍ fat, plump, stocky, full-figured

گرم [1] gərúm *m.* ☞ گروم [1]

گرم [2] gərúm *m.* grove of trees

گرم [3] gram **1** guilty, culpable زه گرم نه یم I am not guilty. گرم گڼل to consider guilty, consider culpable, blame, adjudge culpable **2** accused, inculpated **3** experiencing the pangs of conscience

گرم [4] garm **1** warm; hot; sultry گرم اقلیم hot climate گرم هیوادونه hot lands, warm lands **2** warm (of clothing) **3** irascible, passionate, hotheaded گرم بحث heated argument هغه په خبرو گرم راغئ He began to speak animated. He became animated. گرمي گرمي خبري to speak heatedly, talk in a quick-tempered way **4** lively; animated بازار گرم دئ Lively commerce was conducted. گرم مجلس a lively meeting

گرمانه gramāná *f.* fine, punishment

گرمتره garmtára extremely hot, warm; sultry

گرمتیا gramtjā́ *f.* fault, guilt

گرمټ [1] gərmə́ṭ *m.* **1** spear, lance **2** point, spike

گرمټ [2] girmə́ṭ *m.* drill auger (carpenter's tool)

گرمجوشي garmdzushí *f.* heat, warmth; enthusiasm, elan په دا سره گرمجوشي **a** hotly, heatedly **b** decisively; with fervor گرمجوشي کول to greet someone warmly or cordially

گرمسېر garmsér *m.* گرم سپل garmsél *m.* **1** warm countries, subtropics د گرم سپر ممالک subtropics, countries with a subtropical climate د گرم سپر وني subtropical cultures **2** Garmser (district, southwest Afghanistan)

گرماکه garmáka *f.* گرمگي garmáki *usually plural* **1** heat rash **2** acne

گرمل gurmə́l gramə́l *transitive* [*past:* و یي گرمه] **1** to whipstitch; sew with large stitches, baste **2** to gather (sewing), make gathers

گرملی gurmə́laj **1** tacked; basted **2** gathered (sewing)

گرمنه gurmə́na *f.* **1** tacking; basting **2** gathering (sewing)

گرم والی [1] garmavā́laj *m.* heat, hot weather د هوا گرم والی heat, hot weather

621

گرموالی ‎² gramvắlaj *m.* ☞ گرمتیا

گرموز gurmúz **1** unpleasant, sour **2** morose, gloomy

گرموزي gurmuzí *f.* **1** persnicketiness **2** gloominess, moroseness

گرمول ‎¹ gramavál *denominative, transitive* [*past:* گرم یې کړ] to blame, accuse, censure, condemn

گرمول ‎² garmavál *denominative, transitive* [*past:* گرم یې کړ] **1** to warm, heat, heat up ځان په سندلۍکښې گرمول to warm oneself at a sandali **2** to encourage, inspire; fascinate, allure

گرموونکی ‎¹ gramavúnkaj *present participle of* گرمول ‎¹

گرموونکی ‎² garmavúnkaj **1** *present participle of* گرمول ‎² **2** *m.* heating device

گرمه ‎¹ gráma *f.* **1** *singular of* گرم ‎³ **2** *f.* **.1** condemnation, censure **2.2** fault, breach

گرمه ‎² garmá *f.* **1** variety of early melon **2** early vegetables

گرمه ‎³ gármа *f. singular of* گرم ‎⁴

گرمي ‎¹ garmí *f.* **1** heat, warmth; hot weather هوا مخ په گرمی ده The weather is becoming warmer. گرمي مي کېږي I am hot. **2** heat, warmth, zeal **3** fervor **4** height, peak دبحث په گرمی کښې at the very height of the dispute **5** liveliness (e.g., of trade) **6** venereal disease

گرمي ‎² grámi gráme *Eastern feminine plural of* گرم ‎³

گرمي ‎³ gármi *Eastern* gárme *f. plural of* گرم ‎⁴

گرميانه garmijāná *f. medicine* febrifacient

گرمېدل ‎¹ gramedál *denominative, intransitive* [*past:* گرم شو] **1** to be guilty, be culpable **2** to be condemned, be censured

گرمېدل ‎² garmedál *denominative, intransitive* [*past:* گرم شو] **1** to warm, warm up, heat up **2** to be encouraged, be inspired **3** to get excited, become impassioned

گرمېدنه ‎¹ gramedə́na *f.* guilt

گرمېدنه ‎² garmedə́na *f.* **1** heating, heating up, warming **2** inspiration; fascination **3** fervor **4** height, peak (as in the height of his anger)

گرمېده ‎¹ gramedə́ *m. plural* ☞ گرمېدنه ‎¹

گرمېده ‎² gramedə́ *m.* ☞ گرمېدنه ‎²

گرنانۍ gərnāṇój *f.* children's game with potsherds

گرنج grandzh *m.* metallic sound

گرنجانی grandzhānáj *m.* handbell

گرنجول grundzhavól *transitive* [*past:* وى یې گرنجاوه] to wrinkle (the forehead) تندى گرنجول to wrinkle the brow

گرنجهار grandzhahā́r *m.* ringing, chime

گرنجی ‎¹ grandzháj *m.* ringing sound, peal

گرنجی ‎² grundzháj *m.* wrinkle په تندي یې گرنجي دئ *grundzhí* His brow is wrinkled. His brow is furrowed.

گرندوکی garəndúkaj *m.* currycomb

گرندی grəndáj *m.* special knife used in bookbinding work

گرنده garə́ṇḍa *f.* **1** ☞ گرگه ‎² **2** *Carissa carandas, Carissa spinarum* (the bush and its berry)

گرنۍ gərṇój *f.* ☞ گرنانی

گرو giráv *m.* gráv **1** deposit, security د گرو مال pawned property, mortgaged property گرو کول *compound verb* to pledge, pawn, mortgage په گرو اخیستل to take in pawn, assume a mortgage گرو اینیودل mortgaged, pawned **2** *predicative* mortgaged, pawned

گروب ‎² gurúb *m.* ☞ گروپ

گروبی grúbaj *m.* pit

گروپ ‎¹ grup *m.* group; team ساکن گروپ *linguistics* consonant cluster

گروپ ‎² gurúp *m.* electric light bulb, incandescent light bulb د رڼا لوستونکی خلی گروپ reflector of a lighthouse or beacon سمندري گروپ د تباشیري بنیینو گروپ searchlight frosted light bulb گروپ

گروت grot *m.* **1** handshake **2** bundle, fascicle

گروتی groṭáj *m.* unleavened bread

گروړبی gróṛbaj *m.* phlegm

گروزی grúzaj *m.* ☞ گرېوزی

گروس grus *m.* dugout

گرول garavál *transitive* [*past:* وى یې گراوه] **1** to scratch; scratch all over ځان گرول to scratch oneself **2** to engrave; inscribe or make a woodcut گرول کېدل *passive voice* **a** to be scratched; be scratched or abraded all over **b** to be engraved, be inscribed, be cut *idiom* د ورځ کار کوم کړی *idiom* کړی ورځ کار کوم د سر گرولو ته نه یم خلاص ځان گرولو ته نه یم خلاص I work all day long; I do not have a free minute.

گرولبی grólbaj *m.* ☞ گروپبی

گروم ‎¹ grum *m.* **1** grief, sorrow, woe گروم کول to grieve, sorrow, be distraught about زړه یې دگرومه ډک شي Don't grieve! گروم مه کوه! He began to grieve **2** consumption, tuberculosis

گروم ‎² grum *m.* tumor, growth, gall (on a tree)

گروم ‎³ gáravəm *first person present tense of* گرول

گرومجن grumdzhán sad, sorrowful

گرومول grumavál *denominative, transitive* [*past:* گروم یې کړ] to disorder, derange

گرومېدل grumedál *denominative, intransitive* [*past:* گروم شو] to be grieved, be disordered, be deranged

گرومېده grumedə́ *m. plural* grief, pain, distress, disorder, derangement

گرول ‎¹ gravavál *denominative, transitive* [*past:* گرو یې کړ] to pawn, mortgage

گرول ‎² grovál *transitive* ☞ گرول

گروه ‎¹ grávа **1** *f.* clavicle; wishbone (birds) **2** button loop **3** collar, neckband

گروه ‎² guróh *m.* crowd; company

گروه ‎³ groh *m.* creed, denomination

گروهن grohə́n good, kind

گروهنه grohə́na *f.* **1** goodness, kindness **2** ☞ گروهبده

گروهول grohavál *transitive* [*past:* وى یې گروهاوه] **1** to threaten, frighten **2** to win over to one's side

گروهېدل grohedál *intransitive* [*past:* وگروهېده] **1** to be frightened; fear, be scared, be afraid of **2** to be won over to someone's side, join somebody, unite with someone **3** to be attracted (to something); adore, worship **4** to trust someone **5** to honor, esteem, have a reverent attitude toward

گروهېدنه grohedə́na *f.* گروهېده grohedə́ *m. plural* **1** fear, fright, terror **2** enthusiasm; adoration, worship **3** belief, creed **4** honor, esteem; reverence

گروي ¹ grə́ve *f.* ☞ گروه ¹

گروى ² garváj *m.* moan, moaning, groaning

گروي ³ giraví mortgaged, pawned

گروي دار giravidár *m. regional* ☞ گانه وال

گروبدل gravedə́l *denominative, intransitive* [*past:* گرو شو] to be mortgaged, be pawned

گروپدل gərvedə́l *transitive* [*past:* و يې گروپره] to inquire about, query about, ask about

گروپړن gərvegə́n *m.* slitting the pelt of a sheep to remove the hide whole

گروپړنه gərvegə́na *f.* **1** inquiry, query, questioning پوښتنه گروپړنه questioning, investigation by questioning; finding out by detailed cross-examination or questioning **2** examination (of a patient) **3** more precise definition, amplification, complete explanation

گرو پړونکی gərvegúnkaj querying, inquiring, questioning

گرویل grojə́l *transitive* ☞ گرول

گروئنلبند grojnlénd *m.* Greenland

گروېبدل groēdə́l *intransitive* ☞ گروهبدل

گره garə́ *f.* pit in which sugarcane, etc., is buried and stored گره کول *compound verb* to bury (sugar cane, etc.) in a pit

گرهار gərahár *m.* **1** noise of ripping cloth **2** roaring noise of an earthquake

گرهو garhó *f.* insulting words

گړى ¹ gərə́j snaggletoothed (having sharp, uneven teeth)

گرى ² girə́j *f.* peg, pin (of a door)

گرى گرى gərə́j *f.* ☞ گروه ¹

گړي ¹ garí *suffix used to form abstract nouns of the feminine gender* سوداگري trade

گرى ² gáraj *m. suffix used to form nouns of agent* لوگری reaper

گریب grib *m.* hump (of a camel)

گربان grebán *m.* ☞ گرپوان

گرپتی gəreṭə́j *f.* altercation, wrangling, squabble, argument

گرپدر gredar *m. technology* grader

گرپدل gəredə́l *intransitive* [*past:* وگرپده] **1** to itch, scratch oneself **2** to be engraved, be carved, be cut into wood **3** to crumble, fall down (of the ceiling)

گریزي guruzí *f. adjective* contraband د گریزي مال contraband goods گریزي سوداگري contraband trading

گریس gris *m. technology* grease, lubricating grease

گرپگړی gəregə́raj *m.* fine hail, sleet

گرین ¹ grin *m.* breast

گرین ² gərín *m.* twisted thread (of 1-2 strands)

گرینډی grində́j *f.* elongated woven basket for transporting loads on a camel

گرینگپج gringédzh *m.* greengage (a kind of plum)

گرین لپند grinlénd *m.* Greenland

گرین هوس grinháus *m.* greenhouse, cold frame

گرپوان greván *m.* collar, neckband د چا گرپوان ته لاس اچول to grab someone by the collar, take somebody by the scruff of the neck *idiom* په خپل گرپوان کتل **a** to look into one's heart **b** to reflect, think a bit د چا گرپوان را خپرل ، د چا گرپوان در خپرل ، د چا گرپوان ور خپرل to disgrace somebody, defame someone گرپوان څیربدل to disgrace oneself سر يې په گرپوانه کښي ښکته کړئ و He grew sad. He hung his head down. د چا سره لاس او گرپوان کبدل to come to blows, to grapple, quarrel with someone

گرپوه ¹ gréva *f.* ☞ گروه ¹

گرپوه ² grivá *f.* (button) loop (on clothing)

گرپبل gərejə́l *transitive* ☞ گرول

گرپبنه gərejə́na *f.* **1** scratching intensively **2** engraving; wood carving, making of woodcuts

گړ ¹ gar *m.* **1** fortress; stronghold, castle; asylum **2** *used in geographic names* خوشحال گر Khushalgar (city)

گړ ² gəṛ *m.* **1** speech; sound **2** muttering **3** sound(s), phonation گړ او گوړ ، گړپ ☞ گړکول **a** to say, utter **b** to mutter **c** to sound

گړ ³ gaṛ *m.* gold spangles, sequins (ornaments for the hair)

گرا گوړ grā *f.* گرا

گرپچند gráchaj ☞ گرپاچی

گرا گوړ gaṛāgúr *m.* talk; conversation, colloquy گرا گوړ کول to chat; talk, converse

گرپب graḅ *m.* **1** crashing; slamming (of a door, etc.) **2** hubbub, ruckus گرپب او گرپوب ☞ گرپوب **3** dispute **4** wooden mousetrap **5** mouthful, swallow

گرپبا grabā́ *f.* ☞ گرپبهار4

گرپباوو grabāvú ☞ گرپند

گرپبڼ gərḅə́ṛ *m.* **1** chatter; talk, conversation **2** hurly-burly, confusion

گرپب گرپوب grabgrúb *m.* **1** idle talk, chatter **2** slamming (of a door, etc.)

گرپبند grabə́nd garrulous, loquacious, talkative

گرپبنده ¹ grabə́nda *f.* place where boulders are plentiful

گرپبنده ² grabə́nda *f. singular of* گرپند

گرپبنى grabənə́j *f.* rocky terrain

گرپبو grabú **1** talkative **2** mendacious

گرپبوزه gaṛbóza *f.* shivering; shuddering

گرپبوزی gaṛbózaj *m.* span

گرپبول grabavə́l *transitive* [*past:* و يې گرپباوه] **1** to slam (door, etc.) **2** to cause to chatter

گرپبهار grabəhár *m.* **1** idle talk **2** noise, crashing, rattling, rumbling **3** slamming (door, etc.)

گربېدل grabedə́l *intransitive* [*past:* وکړبېده و *past:* وگربده] **1** to talk emptily, talk nonsense **2** to slam (of doors, etc.) **3** to crash; rumble; rattle **4** to be shaky, be tottering, dangle loosely

گربېدلی grabedə́laj talkative, loquacious

گربېدنه grabedə́na *f.* گربده grabedə́ *m. plural* idle talk, chatter

گربزن gaṛbazə́n dirty, unpleasant, slovenly, nasty

گرپر gəṛpə́ṛ *m.* disturbance, agitation

گرچ grəch *m.* **1** noise made in swallowing **2** rattling, crashing, clattering

گرچاوو gəṛchāvú *m.* best man, groom's man (of a groom-to-be, presenting him with bread dough)

گرچند grəchə́nd dangling, swinging; shaking back and forth

گرچول grəchavə́l *transitive* [*past:* ویې گرچاوه] to rumble, rattle something

گرچچه grə́cha *f.* vain quarrel, empty dispute

گرچهار grəchahā́r *m.* گرچی grəchaj *m.* rumbling, rattling

گرچېدل grəchedə́l *intransitive* [*past:* وگرچېده] to thunder, rumble, rattle

گرد¹ gaṛd *m.* dust

گرد² gəṛd round

گردور guṛdaur *m.* races ☞ گرو دور

گردی¹ gaṛdáj *m.* **1** whirl of a spindle **2** short person (male)

گردی² gaṛdáj *m. dialect* bit of thread

گردی³ gəṛdáj *f.* ring

گردی⁴ gəṛdáj *f.* short person (female)

گرز¹ graz *m.* **1** thunder, peal of thunder **2** crunch; crash گرز او گروز crashing, thundering

گرز² garz *m.* ☞ گرد¹

گرزا grazā́ *m. & f.* ☞ گرزهار

گرزگروز grazgrúz *m.* noise, crashing, thundering

گرزول grəzavə́l *transitive* [*past:* ویې گرزاوه] **1** to beat, thrash ډول گرزول to beat a drum **2** to quarrel with somebody, wrangle with someone

گرزهار grazahā́r *m.* گرزی grazáj *m.* **1** slamming (of a door, etc.) **2** noise, hubbub, crashing **3** thunder, peal of thunder

گرگر gaṛgár *m.* roaring (of a camel)

گرگوتی gaṛgutáj *f. dialect* ☞ گاڼگوتی²

گرگوزه gaṛgóza *f.* **1** shaking, chill **2** trembling, quivering گرگوزی راوستل to cause to quiver or tremble

گرگی gəṛgáj *m.* **1** sphericle **2** shaft

گرماچی gəṛmācháj *m.* stand in the form of a ring (for pots and other vessels)

گرماگر gəṛmāgár *m.* noise, ruckus, hubbub

گرمب gramb *m.* گرمبا grambā́ *f.* گرمبهار grambahā́r *m.* گرمبی grambáj *m.* crashing, cracking (of firearms, etc.)

گرنج¹ grəndzh *m.* ringing (of handbell, coins)

گرنج² guṛə́ndzh *m.* **1** loud noise, hubbub **2** whisper, whispering گرنج اچول to whisper

گرنجانی grəndzhānáj *m.* handbell; bell

گرنجاوو grəndzhāvú *m.* rattle

گرنجول grəndzhavə́l *transitive* [*past:* وی گرنجاوه] **1** to clang, beat on iron **2** to knock, make resound

گرنجهار grəndzhahā́r *m.* گرنجی grəndzháj *m.* ringing, pealing گرنجی کتار children's game

گرنجېدل grəndzhedə́l *intransitive* [*past:* وگرنجبده] to ring

گرند gəṛónd **1** glib-tongued دی پر گرند سری دئ He is glib-tongued. **2** smart, bright

گرندوالی gaṛandvā́laj *m.* د تگ گرندوالی quickness, speed, speed of movement

گرنده¹ grandá *f.* disease or ailment of the spleen

گرنده² gəṛónda *f. singular of* گرند

گرندی¹ gaṛandáj grandáj **1** quick, speedy **2** high speed گرندی بېړی high-speed ship گرندی موټر passenger car, passenger vehicle **3** urgent, emergency گرندی اقدامونه grandí gaṛandí emergency measures **4** quick, smart, efficient; lively, agile; energetic **5** skillful, able

گرندی² gaṛəndáj *f.* gecko (lizard)

گرندیتوب gaṛandajtób grandajtób *m.* گرندی والی gaṛandajvā́laj grandajvā́laj *m.* **1** quickness, velocity, speed **2** high velocity **3** smartness, efficiency; liveliness, agility

گرنگ¹ gaṛáng *m.* **1** precipice; abyss **2** sheer cliff **3** crater **4** gulf, abyss په گرنگ کښی غورځول to throw into the abyss, cast into the gulf

گرنگ² grəng *m.* snots

گرنگن grəngə́n گرنگوش grəngósh گرنگوک grəngúk snotty, snot-nosed (of a child)

گرنی gəṛanáj *linguistic* speech, vocal, verbal, oral

گرو¹ guṛó *m. proper name* Guro

گرو² gəṛú *m.* hookah

گرواز gaṛvā́z broad, wide, spacious

گروب¹ grub *tautological with* گروب

گروب² gəṛób boiled soft; watery گروب کول to overcook, make watery گروب کېدل to be overcooked, be watery

گروبر gəṛvəbár *m.* chatter, idle talk; talk, conversation گروبر کول to chat, talk idly; talk, converse

گروبن gəṛobə́n **1** slovenly **2** snot-nosed

گروبول grubavə́l *denominative, transitive* [*past:* گروب یې کړ] to pull down, wreck, mess up, destroy

گروبی¹ guṛobáj *m.* syrup (of sugarcane molasses); sweet syrup; sherbet

گروبی² gróbaj *m.* phlegm

گروبی³ gəṛobáj *m.* **1** water leaking from an irrigation well system **2** stagnant water

گروبېدل grubedə́l *denominative, intransitive* [*past:* گروب شو] to be pulled down, be wrecked, be messed up, be destroyed

گروپر gəṛupə́r *m.* ☞ گرپر

گرودځه gəṛúdza *f.* breast which has gone dry (in a nursing mother)

گروز gruz *tautological with* گرز¹

گراول gəṛavә́l transitive [past: وي يي گراوه] to compel to speak

گروندج garvándzh m. Western 1 stand (for a pot, etc.) 2 platform 3 game

گرونجي garvandzhój f. frame or stand for water jars

گرونگه gaṛungá f. waterfall, cataract

گره guṛá f. 1 cane sugar 2 molasses, treacle

گرهار gəṛəhár m. disconnected speech

گره بره gárabaṛa f. greeting د چا سره گره بره کول to inquire after the health of, greet someone

گره بنده gaṛabánda f. large cave in the mountains

گرهي⁴ gaṛhój f. Eastern ☞ گړی

گړی¹ gaṛáj m. Western hour; time څه گړی وروسته ، څه گړی پس after some time په گړی from hour to hour, with each passing hour

گړی² gaṛáj m. 1 pitcher, jar (for water) 2 jug with hide stretched over it (i.e., a kind of drum) ☞ کوزه¹

گړی³ gaṛój f. 1 hour, about an hour, some time یوه گړی وروسته after some time په هغه گړی at once, immediately 2 [plural: گړی زما گړی ورانه ده garəjgáni] watch د لاس گړی wristwatch My watch stopped running correctly. 3 period of time equal to about 24 minutes

گړی⁴ gaṛój f. small fortress, fort, castle

گړی⁵ gaṛój f. 1 puddle 2 pond 3 place rich in springs 4 bottom of a valley or gully 5 hollow in a rock filled with rainwater

گړی⁶ gárəj m. suffix forming a noun of agent جرنده گړی miller

گړیال gaṛjál m. 1 wall or standing clock with bells or gong 2 gong

گړي بړي gáṛi-báṛi f. plural conversation, talk

گړی جورونکی gaṛáj dzhoṛavúnkaj m. regional watchmaker

گریچ grich m. difficult road

گریده gaṛedá f. ☞ گړبده

گړبدل gəṛedól intransitive [past: و گړبده] 1 to speak; utter; have a talk, conduct a talk په راز مسائلو کښي گړبدل to speak of this and that 2 to narrate, tell a story (of a book) 3 dialect to talk idly, talk nonsense, talk rubbish

گړبده gaṛedó m. plural speech, speeches په گړبده کښي in conversation, during the conversation

گړی ستن gaṛəjstón f. watch hand, clock hand

گړی گر gaṛəjgór m. watchmaker

گړبگینه gəṛegína f. cracklings, burnt scraps of meat

گړبل gəṛajól [past: وي يي گړايه] transitive verb to undermine a wall in order to destroy it

گرینگ gring m. snots

گرینگن gringón snotty گرینگن سری whimperer, milksop

گرینگي¹ grínge f. plural Eastern snots

گرینگی² gringáj m. handbell

گریوال gaṛivál m. گړيوال گړي وال man who buys sour milk in jugs in outlying villages and sells them in the city

گړی والا¹ gaṛəjvālá m. watch seller, clock seller

گړی والا² gaṛəjvālá m. seller of jugs

گز¹ گز شاه د شاه گز the gaz m. gaz, gyaz (measure of length) gáz-i Royal gaz (about 1.066 meters) د جریب گز the land-measurement معمار گز gáz-i gaz (73.8 centimeters) د معمار گز the construction gaz (83.8 cm or 3 feet) مریع گز a square gaz idiom د توپک گز ramrod, cleaning rod

گز² gəz m. rolling

گزار guzár m. blow کول گزار to strike

گزارل guzārә́l transitive ☞ گذارل

گزارول¹ guzāravól denominative, transitive ☞ گذارول

گزارول² guzāravól denominative, transitive ☞ غوزارول

گزاري¹ gazári f. plural 1 siftings (grain), bran 2 ground ears (of grain)

گزاري gazári m. plural chewing tobacco

گزاربدل guzāredól denominative, intransitive ☞ غوزاربدل

په گزانه صورت خرڅول gazāná by the gaz (unit of measurement) to sell by the gaz

گزانه فروشي gazānafurushí f. retail sale of textile materials

گزبره gazbóra f. good-quality coarse silk

گزبوتي gazbúṭi f. plural ceiling covering

گزک¹ gazák 1 m. suppurating, purulent (of a wound because of chill, infection) گزک اخیستل to suppurate, be purulent گزک شوئ پرهار abscess 2.1 suppurating, purulent (of a wound) 2.2 nipped by the frost, frostbitten

گزک² gazák m. 1 snack taken with wine 2 hunting bait (for a trap)

گزک پانه gazakpáṇa f. botany plantain

گزکه gazáka f. trap, snare

گزکي gazáke f. plural Eastern suppuration, purulence (of a wound)

گزلک gazalák m. ricochet, rebound گزلک کول to ricochet, rebound, bounce off

گزمزی guzmúzaj Eastern gloomy

گزموي gazmaví adjective military patrol گزموي عسکر to mine, lay mines

گزمه gazmá f. patrol

گزن guzón m. paralytic گزن وهل to paralyze, strike with paralysis

گزول gazavól denominative, transitive [past: گزي يي کړ] to measure in gaz

گزیاري gazjári m. plural ☞ گزاري²

گزبدل gazedól denominative, intransitive [past: گز شو] to be measured on gaz

گز¹ gag m. regional 1 wasps' nest, beehive 2 honeycombs

گگ gag 1 on in years, elderly; having grey streaks 2 piebald, spotted گگ کبدل a to be on in years, be elderly; grow grey, get grey streaks b to be spotted, be piebald 3 heterogeneous 4 unripe (of fruit) 5 growing around, starting to sprout (with hairs)

گگ³ gəg m. knock, creak, squeak

گگکه gigáka f. magpie

گگکی gagkáj m. ☞ گرهار

گگوبنتي gagvekhtí f. 1 streaks of grey 2 mature, ripe age

گروپنبنتی ² gagvékhtaj having hair with streaks of grey, to be on in years, being elderly

گرهار gəgahár m. knocking, creaking, squeaking

گری جؤهرو گری گری کتل a to regard with embarrassment b to regard with distress or chagrin

گڅ gəs dialect ☞ گس

گستاخ gustákh cheeky, rude; impudent, familiar, insolent

گستاخي gustākhí f. cheekiness, rudeness; impudence, familiarity, insolence گستاخي کول to be cheeky, be rude; be impudent, be overly familiar; act familiarly, behave insolently

گستره gastára f. heifer

گسڼه gusṇá f. ☞ گوسڼه ¹

گسه ¹ gasá f. 1 ricochet, bouncing off, rebounding گسه ورکول to ricochet, rebound 2 blow, shove, push گسه خوړل to stumble against گسه وهل a to start to beat, knock into; strike b to shake; shove, push 3 pole used to stir cane syrup

گسه ² gə́sa dialect feminine singular of گس

گسی gasáj m. ☞ گڅی

گسیا gasjā́ ground, machined, ground off; worn, effaced گسیا کول to grind, machine, grind off; wear down, efface گسیا کېدل to be ground, be machined, be ground off; be worn, be effaced

گسیاوالی gasjāvā́laj m. machining, grinding, grinding off; effacement; wear, wear and tear

گشت gasht m. 1 stroll گشت ته وتل to go for a stroll 2 round; circuit گشت وهل ، گشت کول a to stroll, take a walk b to make a round 3 to make a circuit, turn

گشتي gashtí m. 1 scout, soldier on patrol 2 adventurer

گڨت gəkht m. ☞ گشت

گڨکی gəkhkáj m. ☞ گرهار

گوڼی gúkhaj ☞ گوڼی

گفتار guftár m. speech, conversation, talk گفتار او کردار word and deed

گفتگو guftugú m. guftugó f. گفتگوی guftugúj guftugój m. conversation, talk, discussion گفتگو کول to converse, talk په دي باره کښي ډېر گفتگو شوئ دئ Much has already been said about this.

گگ gag m. wasps' nest

گگر gagár gagór 1 m. .1 blacksmith 1.2 strongman 2.1 brawny, muscular, strong گگر سړی a giant; person in the pink of health 2.2 potbellied 2.3 huge

گگروالی gagərvā́laj m. strength, force

گگروڅه gagrótsa f. dialect ☞ گگروڅه

گگره gagrá گگړی gagrój f. shirt with an opening at the breast

گگروڅه gagródza f. گگروزه gagróza f. shiver, trembling گگروڅو وهل to tremble (from cold, fever) گگروڅو نیول to be seized by shivering, be gripped by trembling

گگړه gagṛá f. 1 crushed stone, ballast 2 decisive man

گگړی gagóṛgi f. plural fried bits of the tail of the fatty-tailed sheep

گگو gəgú m. nightmare

گوگوشتو gugushtú m. & f. ☞ گوگوشتو

گگی gagój f. thick woolen thread

گل ¹ gul m. [plural: گلان gulán plural: گلونه gulúna] 1 flower; rose د گل دنباله peduncle گلونه لگول Eastern to place flowers in a vase په فاطمي پوري گل to be very beautiful گل بي منبلي Fatima is very beautiful. Fatma is a fabulous beauty. گل په خپل بوتي اغزیه نه وي proverb There is no rose without thorns. لگه د انګر بنه بنکاري proverb The rose has its place on the bush. گل ډېر نادر خیز دئ saying This thing is as rare as a fig blossom. 2 used to form flower names گلاب rose 3 medicine cataract 4 deposit formed by combustion, candle snuff گل کول a to flourish, bloom بادام گل کړئ دئ The almond tree has bloomed. گل کېدل compound verb b to extinguish, put out 5 regional Monday 6 pattern 7 reward for good news 8 proper name Gul ستا خبره دې په گل بدله شي saying literal May your speech be flower. figurative I am sorry to interrupt you.

گل ² gal m. 1 large hailstones 2 first snow on the mountain peaks

گل ³ gil m. 1 clay رازي گل clay په غوره گل آوارول to plaster with clay 2 mud, dirt

گل ⁴ gul m. 1 oil cake 2 variety of flour د اورو گل fine-ground flour

گلاب guláb 1 m. plural rose water د گلاب گل kazanlyk rose 2 m. rose

گلابتون gulābatún m. lace, galoon; braid, ribbon

گلاب چشم gulābcháshm m. hawk, raptorial bird of the hawk family

گلابی ¹ gulābáj m. gulābí m. barber, hairdresser

گلابي ² gulābí adjective rose, pink (color) گلابي مخ a rosy little face

گلاپ gulа́p m. 1 ☞ گلاب 2 proper name Gulab

گلارگین glārgín rude, crude; uneven, rough

گلاس gilás m. 1 glass د شرابو گلاس goblet 2 mug (often wooden)

گلاسگو glāsgó f. Glasgow

گلالی ¹ gulāláj 1 pretty, attractive; good-looking, nice; beautiful 2 m. proper name Gulalaj

گلالی ² gulālój f. proper name Gulalaj

گلالیتوب gulālajtób m. attractiveness; quality of being good-looking; beauty

گل انار gulanár 1 pomegranate color, colored like pomegranate 2 m. proper name Gulanar

گل اندام gulandа́m tender

گل اندامه gulandáma f. proper name Gulandama

گلانه gulāná f. reward given to the bearer of good news

گلاڼی gulāṇáj dialect rose, rosy, pink (of color)

گل اوب gulób m. watering down wheat (at threshing time)

گلائي gulāí f. sheaf (of rice)

گلباغ gulbágh m. Gulbagh (suburb, Kabul)

گل ببری gulbabráj m. chadra having a pattern in silk

گلبخور gulbakhór m. catnip, catmint, Nepeta cataria (a medicinal and essential oil-bearing plant) گربه خورک ☞

گل بدن 1 gulbadán ☞ گل اندام 2 *m.* red silk with a narrow white stripe

گلبدین gulbudín *m. proper name* Gulbudin

گل بشره gulbashrá *f. proper name* Gulbashra

گلبرگ gulbárg *m.* petal

گلبوتی gulbútaj *m.* rosebush; rose plant

گل بهار گلبهار gulbahā́r *m.* Gulbahar (settlement, district)

گلپوش gulpósh rosy, iridescent گلپوشي آرزوگاني happy dreams, pleasant dreams

گلپي gulpí *f.* cauliflower

گلتوب gultób *m.* flowering, blooming

گلټ gilə́ṭ *m. plural* ☞ گلپت

گلپتول giləṭavə́l *transitive* ☞ گلپتول

گلپتی giləṭaj *m.* ☞ گلپتی

گلپتپدل giləṭedə́l *intransitive* ☞ گلپتپدل

گلچهره gulchehrá *f.* 1 beauty 2 *proper name* Gulchera

گلچین gulchín 1 *m.* gardener 2 gatherer of flowers

گلدزري guldzarí *f.* target

گلخانه gulkhāná *f.* greenhouse

گلخن gulkhán *m.* hearth; heater (in a bathouse, etc.)

گلخی gulkhə́j *f.* small stove in which children bake carrots

گلخینگی gulkhingáj *m.* sage

گلدار guldā́r 1 varicolored, multicolored, variegated, patterned (cloth) 2 intricately decorated 3 *botany* flowering گلدار نباتات flowering plants گلدار كرم flowering cabbage, cauliflower

گلدان guldā́n *m.* flower bed, flower plot

گلدانی guldānə́j *f.* flowerpot; flower vase

گلدسته guldastá *f.* bouquet

گلدم guldúm *m.* white-cheeked bulbul, *Molpastes leucogenys*

گلدوزي gulduzí *f.* 1 embroidering, embroidery گلدوزي كول to embroider 2 patterned embroidery

گلد gləd shaven-headed, shaven

گلډانگ gulḍā́ng گلډانگ سپی bulldog

گل رخ گلرخ gulrúkh 1 red-cheeked, rosy-cheeked, ruddy 2 *f. proper name* Gulrukh

گل رخسار gulrukhsā́r *m.* ☞ گلرخ 1

گل رنگ گلرنگ gulráng 1 red; rosy, pink په وينو گلرنگ شوئ bloody 2 *m. proper name* Gulrang

گلرو gulrú 1 *poetry* rosy-faced 2 *f. proper name* Gulru

گلرېز gulréz *m.* kind of firework

گلزار gulzár *m.* 1 flower bed 2 flower plot

گل زیری گلزجاړی gulzjā́ṛaj *m.* ☞ گلخړی

گلساز gulsā́z *m.* craftsman making paper flowers

گلستان gulistā́n *m.* 1 rose garden; flower garden 2 Gulistan (name of various settlements, towns, etc.)

گلسرک gulsarák *m.* mountain finch, brambling *Serinus pusillus*

گلیسرین gliserín *m.* glycerine

گل سنگ گلسنگ gulsáng *m.* lichen

گل شاه gulshāh *proper name* Gulshah

گل شكره gulshəkára *f.* ☞ صفر 2

شگي گل گلشگی gulshəgáj *f.* ☞ شگي گل

گلشن gulshán *m.* flower bed

گل عذار gul'izā́r rosy-cheeked

گلف golf *m. sports* golf

گل فام gulfā́m rosy, pink (color)

گل قند gulkánd *m.* 1 rose (flower) jam or preserves 2 lump sugar ground up with rose petals (a medicine)

گلگ gulák *m. proper name* Gulak

گلكار gilkā́r *m.* bricklayer; mason; construction worker

گلكار gulkā́r *m.* craftsman specializing in wall-tracery designs

گلكاري gilkārí *f.* construction trade, masonry

گل كاري gulkārí *f.* wall-traceries

گل كرم gulkarám *m.* flowering cabbage, cauliflower

گل كرنه gulkarə́na *f.* flower growing

گلگشت gulgásht *m.* flower bed, flower plot

گلگل galgál *m.* putty, caulking گلگل وهل to putty, caulk

گل گلاب gulgulā́b gul-i-gulā́b *m.* گل گلاپ gulgulāp *m.* rose سپین گل گلاب white rose

گل گلاچی گل gulgulāchigúl *children's speech* we won, our side won, winners

گلگون gulgún 1 scarlet; pink, rose; ruddy 2 *poetry* rose-like

گلگي giləgáj *m.* calf

گل لښته gullákhta *f. proper name* Gulashta

گل مښخی gulmākhə́j *f.* ☞

گل ماله gilmālá *f.* trowel, smoother گل ماله كول *compound verb* to smooth (e.g., an earthen floor)

گلماهی gulmāháj *m.* trout

گلمكی gulməkə́j *f. proper name* Gulmaki

گلمل gə́lmə́l soiled, dirty

گلملتوب gə́lmə́ltób *m.* dirtying, besmirching

گلملول gə́lmə́lavə́l *denominative transitive* [past: گلمل یې کړ] to soil, dirty, besmirch

گلملپدل gə́lmə́ledə́l *denominative, intransitive* [past: گلمل شو] to be soiled, be dirtied, be besmirched

گل مېخ gulmékh *m.* 1 large-headed nail 2 button 3 bolt

گل مېخی gulmekhə́j *f.* silver decoration in the form of a botton or nailhead (on the sleeves of women's garments)

گل مېر gulmír *m. proper name* Gulmir

گل انار گل نار gulnā́r *m.* ☞

گلنار گلناره gulnā́ra *f. proper name* Gulnar

گل نما gulnumā́ *f.* گل نمائي gulnumāí *f.* kaleidoscope

گلو gilā́v *m. botany Mimosa scandens* (a kind of mimosa)

گلو gulú *m.* 1 throat; gullet 2 neck

گلو gulā́v *m.* pin which secures the axle of a millstone

گلو gul guló *masculine proper name, affectionate from* گل 1 8

گلو gulo *oblique plural of* گل 1

گلو giló *oblique plural of* گل 3

گلو giló *oblique plural of* گله

گلو ⁸ galó *oblique plural of* گله ¹

گلواره galavára *f.* sack for a horse's load, pack

گلوانډ gulvānḍ *m.* cord used to tie the neck of a skin bag of Ajran

گلوبند gulubánd *m.* 1 necktie, cravat 2 necklace

گلوبیول globijúl *m.* corpuscle, blood corpuscle

گلوکوز glukóz *m. plural* glucose

گلول ¹ galavól 1 *transitive* ☞ گال 2 *m. plural* patience له خبره گلولو ووته Patience was exhausted.

گلول ² gulovól *denominative, transitive* [*past:* گل یې کړ] to extinguish (fire, candle, etc.)

گلول ³ gólavól *denominative, transitive* [*past:* گل یې کړ] to plaster with adobe

گلوله باري gululabārí *f.* firing, fire, gunfire

گلونه ¹ gulvóna *f.* ☞ کوکی ونه

گلونه ² gulúna *plural of* گل ¹

گلونه ³ galavóna *f.* patience

گلوه galváh *m.* kind of quail

گلوي galví *f. suffix used to form abstract nouns* ورور گلوي brotherhood, fraternity

گله ¹ gilá *f.* 1 complaint 2 reproach; censure ویل چا ته څه گله ده There is nothing to reproach others for. گله کول a to complain د درده یې گله کوله He complained of the pain. گوښه کول to complain bitterly b to reproach

گله ² galá gallá *f.* 1 flock; herd (of horses, deer); flock (of birds); herd of horses (with mares and one stallion) 2 horse farm

گله ³ gíla cry used to drive calves

گله ⁴ gúla *oblique singular and imperative of* گل ¹

گله ⁵ gulá *f. proper name* Gula

گله آمیز gilaāméz complaining; querulous

گله گرکی galagərkáj *m.* large grainy snowflakes

گله گوسه gilagusá *f.* bitter lamentations, complaints

گله من gilamán complainer گله منه یم له خپله یاره I am complaining about my beloved (a lovey-dovey complaint)

گله وان galaván gallaván *m.* herder, shepherd

گلی ¹ galój *f. Eastern* ☞ ډلی

گلی ² guláj *m.* seizure accompanied by convulsions and loss of consciousness; convulsions (of a mother or child at time of birth); epilepsy

گلی ³ gulí ruddy (of an apple)

گلی ⁴ gilé *plural of* گله ¹

گلی ⁵ gal gallé *plural of* گله ²

گلیا galjá melted, fused

گلبټ gleṭ 1 *m. plural* .1 plating with tin, tinning 1.2 gilt, gilging 2 gilded, plated with gold

گلبټ گر gleṭgór *m.* tin-plater

گلبټول gleṭavól *denominative, transitive* [*past:* گلبټ یې کړ] 1 to tin-plate 2 to gild

گلبټی gileṭáj *m.* kind of rifle

گلبټیدل gleṭedól *denominative, intransitive* [*past:* گلبټ شو] 1 to be tin-plated 2 to be gilded

گلبدل ¹ galedól *intransitive* [*past:* و گلبده] to melt, fuse

گلبدل ² guledól *denominative, intransitive* [*past:* گل شو] to extinguish

گلبري galerí *f.* gallery

گلبگه gólegá *f.* unplowed land

گم gum *usually in compounds* lost, disappeared, vanished

گما gumá́ *f.* wild goat

گمارل gumāról *transitive* [*past:* و یې گماره] 1 to nominate, appoint, designate و کار ته گمارل to assign to work *passive* گمارل کبدل to be assigned 2 to direct (beams, rays etc.) 3 to summon, conscript to something

گمارلئ gumārólaj assigned, nominated, designated (for)

گمارونکی gumārúnkaj 1 *present participle of* گمارل 2 *m.* chief

گمارونی gumārúnaj designating, appointing, nominating

گماشته gumāshtá *m.* agent, authorized representative

گمان gumáń *m.* 1 suspicion, doubt پ چا باندی ستا گمان دئ؟ Whom do you suspect? تر گمان لاندي راتلل to be under suspicion 2 thought, opinion, supposition په دي گمان چه ... suppose that ... غالب گمان دا دئ چه ... One supposes that ... گمان کبږي چه ... In all probability ته دا گمان مه کوه چه ... Don't think that ... a گمان کول to suspect b to suppose, assume پر چا د یو شي گمان کول to presume someone guilty of something

گمبت gumbát *m.* ☞ گنبته

گمبته gumbáta *f.* ☞ گنبته

گمبیا gambijá́ *f.* Gambia

گمراه gumráh 1 strayed from the path; erring گمراه کول to lead from the path; lead astray 2 *m.* heretic

گمراهی gumrāhí *f.* 1 error 2 heresy

گمرک gumrúk *m.* [*plural:* گمرکونه gumrukúna *Arabic plural:* گمرکات gumrukāt́] customshouse د گمرک محصول customs duty د گمرک د محصولو معاف not subject to duty, tariff-free, duty-free د گمرکاتو عمومي مدیریت the Main Customs Administration

گمرک ځای gumrukdzáj *m.* customshouse

گمرک والا gumrukvālá́ *m.* customs official

گمرکي gumrukí 1 *adjective* customs گمرکي محصول customs duty گمرکي دود دستور customs barriers گمرکي بندیزونه customs formalities له گمرکي محصولاتو نه معافي لرل not to be subject to duty; be duty-free پر ... ډپر گمرکي محصول اچول to be subject to high duties پر ... ډپر گمرکي محصول غورځول to be subject to high duties گمرکي رسم او رواج پخایول to go through customs 2 *f.* customs examination

گم گام gumgáḿ on the sly, on the QT, secretly

گمنام gumnáḿ forgotten, unknown

گمنامی gumnāmí *f.* oblivion; the unknown د گمنامی کنده oblivion

گمنځ gumóndz *f.* گمنز gumónz *f. dialect* ☞ ږمنځ

گمه ¹ gamá́ *f.* pit used as a trap

گمه² گُما *gúma f.* secret په گمه کي وهل to do something on the sly, keep secret

گن¹ *gan m.* kite

گن² *gan m.* 1 machine gun 2 sprayer

گن³ *gən m.* bloodsucking tick (in cattle)

گنانگول *gunāngól m.* wild spinach

گناوي *gunā́vi feminine plural of* گناه¹

گناه *gunāh f. & m.* [*plural:* گناوي *gunā́vi f. Eastern m.* گناهونه *gunāhúna*] 1 *religion* sin لویه گناه کبیره گناه *gunāh-i* a capital sin گناه کول to sin 2 guilt, fault; offense; breach (of conduct) دتحریک په دې کښي زمونږ کومه گناه نشته We are not guilty of this. This is not our fault. خپله گناه پر بل اچول to put one's own fault on another; put blame on another

گناهگار گار گناهگار *gunāhgā́r* 1 *m.* sinner 2.1 *regional* guilty ته گناهگاری یې که بیگناه؟ Do you plead guilty or not? 2.2 sinful

گناهگاري گاري *gunāhgārí f.* sin, trespass; transgression

گنائي *ganāí f.* millrace

گنبت *gumbát m.* jump; leap گنبت وهل to jump; leap

گنبته *gumbáta f.* گنبد *gumbád m.* cupola, arch

گن بوت *ganbót m. military* gunboat

گنتي *gintí f. regional* evening roll call گنتي اخیستل to conduct evening roll call

گنته *gaṇtá f. regional* 1 watch, clock 2 hour نیمه گنته half an hour

گنتی *gaṇṭój f. regional* bell

گنج¹ *gandzh m.* 1 treasure 2 treasure-house, treasury 3 bread market 4 alms cup (among dervishes)

گنج² *gundzh m.* angle, corner *idiom* په ټولو گنجه دنیا کښي in the whole world, in all corners of the terrestial sphere

گنج³ *gundzh* ☞ گنجی⁴

گنجان *gundzhā́n* spacious, capacious

گنجایش *gundzhā́jísh m.* 1 capacity, cubic context; tonnage د بازار گنجایش the scope or capacity of the market 2 place, location *idiom* دا دلته گنجایش نه لري This is no place to speak of that. It is inappropriate.

گنجرخی *gandzhárkhaj m.* calibrated rod for measuring the output of water

گنجره *gandzhára f.* titmouse, chickadee

گنجلک *gundzhulák* 1 wrinkled 2 crumpled گنجلک کېدل a to be wrinkled, be puckered b to crumple

گنجول *gundzhavól denominative, transitive* [*past:* گنج یې کړ] 1 to wrinkle, knead 2 to anger 3 to reproach

گندزه *gúndzha f.* ☞ گونځه

گنجی¹ *gandzháj f. zoology* vulture, buzzard

گنجی² *gandzháj* 1 mangy, scabby 2 *m.* corn embryo, grain embryo with sparse kernels

گنجی³ *gandzháj f.* 1 woolen jacket 2 skein, hank (of yarn)

گنجی⁴ *gundzháj* 1 puckered, wrinkled 2 contorted, crumpled

گنجبدل *gundzhedól denominative, intransitive* [*past:* گنج شو] 1 to wrinkle up, crumple 2 to get angry 3 to grow old, get creased, become wrinkled

گنجبفه *gandzhifá f.* 1 pack, deck (of cards) 2 card-playing

گنچه *ganachá f.* thorny sage

گنځپه *gandzópa f.* 1 fox 2 *dialect* dormouse

گنځه *gə́ndza f.* third finger, ring finger

گند¹ *gund* 1 *m.* .1 gang, party 1.2 subdivision, sept (of a tribe) 1.3 grouping 2 equal

گند² *gənd m.* patchwork coat worn by dervishes

گند³ *gind m.* ☞ گیند

گند⁴ *gunde Eastern* ☞ گوندي

گند⁵ *gand m.* brushwood

گنداو *gandā́v m.* 1 stagnant water, foul-smelling water 2 Gandav (name of various settlements and districts)

گندبازي *gundbāzí f.* conflict between or among groups

گندپرستي *gundparastí f.* factionalism

گندپوښ *gəndpókh m.* ragamuffin

گندکي *gandáki f. plural* spoiled raisins, rotten raisins

گنده گي *gandagí f.* ☞ گندگي

گندنا گندنه *gandaná* گندنا *gandaná f.* leek

گندولی *gandolój m.* 1 woman's sleeveless dress 2 short sleeveless coat; sleeveless jacket or blouse

گنده¹ *gundá m.* old man grown wise through living

گنده² *gə́nda f.* patchwork coat, ragged coat worn by dervishes

گنده³ *gínda f.* ☞ گینده

گنده⁴ *gandá* 1 dirty 2 smelly, malodorous 3 rotten 4 base, low

گنده⁵ *gundá* coarse, thick

گنده⁶ *gəndá f.* annual payment to a barber made by an entire village on pre-agreed terms

گندهارا *gandhārá f. history* Gandhara

گنده گي *gandagí f.* 1 dirt 2 stink, stench 3 rottenness, corruption 4 baseness

گندي¹ *gundí f.* clique-formation, cliquishness

گندي² *gundáj m.* partisan of some group or other; adherent, follower

گندي³ *gundí f.* 1 adherency, partisanship, persuasion گندي لرل to have a party; have followers, have adherents 2 rivalry گندي کول to create a party b to compete, vie 3 ☞ سیالي

گندي⁴ *gúndi gúnde* ☞ گوندي²

گندیمار *gundəjmā́r m.* partisan, follower, adherent

گندیماري *gundəjmārí f.* ☞ گندبازي

گند¹ *gaṇḍ m.* 1 edging of a garment 2 clay edging for the rim of a millstone

گند² *gaṇḍ tautological with* لند

گند *gaṇḍ present stem of* گنډل

گنډپور *gaṇḍapúr* 1 *m. plural* the Gandapuri (tribe) 2 *m.* Gandapur (tribesman)

گنډکپ *gaṇḍkáp m. Eastern* pickpocket, cutpurse

گنډل ganḍál *transitive* [*past:* وي گانډه] 1.1 to sew; sew on; mend په خياط کالي گنډل to have a tailor make a dress 1.2 to link; unite; join to; attach to 1.3 to rivet, attract (e.g., the gaze, view) 2 *m. plural* .1 sewing, needlework د گنډلو ماشين sewing machine 2.2 linking; uniting; joining together; attaching to *idiom* خوله گنډل to keep mum, be silent

گنډم ganḍám *first person present tense of* گنډل

گنډنه ganḍána *f.* sewing, needlework

گنډنی ganḍanáj *m.* blouse with gathers

گنډو ganḍú *first person plural present tense of* گنډل

گنډولی ganḍoláj *m.* ☞ گنډونی

گنډون ganḍún *m.* sewing, needlework د گنډون ستن sewing needle

گنډونکی [1] ganḍúnkaj 1 *present participle of* گنډل 2 *m.* tailor

گنډونکې [2] ganḍúnke 1 *f. present participle of* گنډل 2 *f.* dressmaker

گنډونی ganḍúnaj ☞ گنډونکی [1]

گنده gánḍa *f.* 1 upper part of baggy Middle-Eastern trousers through which is passed a cincture or ochkur گنده تړل to tighten the cincture 2 knot (in thread, etc.) کلکي گنډي گنده کول to tie a knot په خپلو گوتو پرانيستل to overcome difficulties (by oneself) 3 node (on a stalk)

گنده تل ganḍatál *m.* asafetida

گنډهبر ganḍhér 1 *m.* .1 bitter taste 1.2 aristolochia, birthwort, *Ristolocia rodaphne* (a poisonous plant); *dialect Rhazia stricta* (a plant used in cheese making as a leaven) 1.3 *plural* poison 2 very bitter

گنډهبري ganḍherí *f.* ☞ گنډهبری [2]

گنډی [1] gunḍáj *m. usually plural* گنډي gunḍí grain ear remaining on the stalk after threshing

گنډی [2] ganḍáj *m.* ☞ گنډولی

گنډی [3] ganḍáj *f.* short jacket of wool or felt

گنډي [4] gunḍí *f.* 1 collar (of clothing) 2 selvage (of material) 3 cord 4 button

گنډي [5] ganḍí *present tense of* گنډل

گنډياره ganḍjā́ra *f.* wild (weedy) rye

گنډيال ganḍjā́l *m.* ☞ مکری [1]

گنډبر ganḍér *m.* poison

گنډبرمری ganḍermaráj *f.* antidote (for poison)

گنډبرن ganḍerán poisonous

گنډبری [1] ganḍeráj *m.* oleander

گنډبری [2] ganḍeráj *f.* cleaned and cut pieces of sugarcane (used for food)

گنر gənár *m.* senile and decrepit ox

گنز gunz *f. dialect* ☞ رمنځ

گنزه gúnza *f. dialect* ☞ گونځه

گنس gans ☞ گنگس [3]

گنستوب ganstób *m.* گنستيا ganstjā́ *f.* گنس والی gansválaj *m.* stunning, deprivation of consciousness

گنسول gansavál *denominative, transitive* [*past:* گنس يې کړ] to stun, deprive of consciousness

گنسونه gansavóna *f.* stunning, deprivation of consciousness

گنسبدل gansedál *denominative, intransitive* [*past:* گنس شو] to be stunned, be deprived of consciousness

گنسبده gansedá *m. plural* loss of consciousness, senselessness

گنکپ gankáp *m.* ☞ گنډ کپ

گنکي ganakí stunned, deprived of consciousness

گنگ [1] gang *m.* invitation to a betrothal

گنگ [2] gəng stunned, deprived of consciousness

گنگ [3] gung mute, dumb گنگ کول to render mute گنگ کېدل to become mute

گنگا gangā́ *f.* the Gang (River) د گنگا درياب ، د گنگا سيند the Gang River

گنگرو gungrú *m.* small bell, handbell; chime

گنگړي gungrí *m. plural* ☞ گنگړی [2]

گنگړ gangár *m.* ☞ گنگر [1]

گنگړه gangará *f.* sufferings, trials, tribulations په گنگړه اخته کېدل to worry about, work beyond one's powers

گنگړی [1] gingráj *m.* chime

گنگړي [2] gungrí *m. plural* boiled grain of pulse, wheat; grain steeped in water

گنگس [1] gangás *m.* narcissus

گنگس [2] gangós *m.* turn, twist; rotation, revolution

گنگس [3] gangś gangós stunned, deprived of consciousness گنگس گنسبدل ☞ گنگس کېدل گنسول ☞ کول

گنگستوب gangstób *m.* گنگستيا gangstjā́ gangəstjā́ *f.* ☞ د گنستوب سر گنگستوب ، dizziness

گنگسول gangsavál *denominative* ☞ گنسول

گنگسبدل gangsedál *denominative, intransitive* ☞ گنسبدل سر يې گنگس شو His head was spinning. He was dizzy.

گنگلو gənglú *m.* turnip

گنگو gangú *m.* saffron

گنگوری gangúraj *m.* bunch of grapes

گنگوړه gangorá *m.* گنگوړ gangor ☞ گانگوړه گانگوړ

گنگ وسنگ gungusúng taciturn, silent

گنگوسه gangosá *f.* sound, utterance

گنگوسی gangusáj *m.* 1 hubbub (of conversation) 2 tread, tramp 3 whisper 4 rustle (of leaves, etc.)

گنگوماښام gangumāk̄ám *m.* twilight, dusk

گنگه بنارو gúnga k̄āró گنگه مينا gúnga majnā́ *f.* waxwing (the bird)

گنگی [1] gangáj *m.* mute, dumb person

گنگي [2] gángí *m. plural* feces, defecation, excrement

گننی ganánaj *m.* nursling lamb (ram)

گنه [1] ganá *f.* knucklebone (for gambling)

گنه [2] ganá *f.* gannā́ ☞ گنی [1]

گنه [3] gunáh *f.* ☞ گناه

گنه [4] guná *f.* sign, token

گنهار gunhár *m.* pot-herb, *Amaranthus paniculatus, Amaranthus polygamus*

گنه درب ganadráb *m.* گنه درو ganadráv *m.* **1** first mowing of lucerne or clover **2** unripe mulberry

گنهگار gunahgár *m.* sinner, culprit

گنهگاروٙل gunahgāravə́l *denominative, transitive* [*past:* گنهگاري يې کړ] to censure, condemn, blame

گنی ¹ ganáj *m.* sugarcane

گنی ² gənaj *m.* **1** beehive **2** wasps' nest

گنی ³ gané *dialect* **1** perhaps **2** like **3** isn't it so

گنی ⁴ ganə́j *f.* suffix for nouns expressing kinship relationships پلار گنی paternal relatives

گنبری ganerə́j *f.* ☞ گنبری ²

گن ¹ gən *m.* snuffling, noisy breathing گن گن nasal

گن ² gaṇ **1** thick, dense گن ځنگل a thick forest گنه ونه a dense tree, tree with a dense crown گن وېښته thick tresses **2** heavy, deep, profound, dense گن سيوری deep shadow **3** shady هغه باغ گن دئ This garden is shady. In this garden is much shade. **4** multitudinous, numerous گن شمېر a great quantity گنه فاميل، a large family گن اکثريت the overwhelming majority گن خلق crowd, mass of people **5** thickly populated, populous گن نفوس dense population **a** گن گن کېدل ② گنېدل ☞ گن کبدل گنوٙل ☞ گن کوٙل to be rendered very thick, be made dense **b** to walk to and fro; move purposelessly **6** dull, cloudly (of the sky) **7** common, frequent (of phenomena)

گنا gəṇá *f.* **1** snuffling, noisy breathing **2** muttering, mumbling

گن بوت gaṇbót *m. military* gunboat

گنتوب gaṇtób *f.* گنتيا gaṇṭjá *f.* ☞ گنوالی

گنرسنی gaṇrásnə́j *f. plural* multimedia

گن کپ gaṇkáp *m.* pickpocket, cutpurse

گنگٙن gəngə́n *m. plural* hubbub, ruckus, noise, uproar

گنوٙل gaṇə́l *transitive* [*past:* و يې گانه] **1** to consider, suppose; regard, estimate حکومت دا گڼل to consider someone ill ښوک مريض گڼل Take ته دا خبره رښتيا وگڼه ... چه The government considers that … my word for it. خان ته ښه گڼل to have a high opinion of oneself نور هم په دې ډول وگڼه and more in this same vein, etc. and so forth *passive* گڼل کبدل to be considered, be regarded سپک گڼل کبدل to be not highly regarded; be held in low esteem; be scorned **2** *Eastern* to count, count up

گننه gaṇə́na *f.* **1** supposition; scrutiny, examination; evaluation **2** *Eastern* counting, counting up

گننی gaṇənáj *m.* ☞ گڼني

گن والی gaṇválaj *m.* **1** frequency **2** thickness, density **3** shadiness **4** multiplicity **5** density of population, populousness

گنوٙل gaṇavə́l *denominative, transitive* [*past:* گڼ يې کړ] **1** to render frequent **2** to thicken, make dense **3** to make shady, shade **4** to make numerous **5** to populate thickly, populate

گنون ganún *m.* **1** enumeration (objects); counting; listing, inventory **2** opinion; supposition, assumption

گنه ¹ ganá *f.* issue (of a magazine, etc.)

گنه ² gána *f. singular of* گن ²

گنه ³ ganá ☞ گڼی ³

گنه ⁴ ganá **1** *imperfective imperative of* گڼل **2** one might say; it can be said

گنهار gəṇahár *m.* nasal voice

گنه بوز gəṇabúz *m.* decisive and bold man

گنه خور gaṇakhvár *m.* rich pastureland

گنه گونه gaṇagúna *f.* **1** crowd; hurly-burly; assemble; age **2** flock (of birds) **3** number, figure

گنی gané **1** *second person present of* گڼل **2** *adverb* really, perhaps (or similar denoting hesitation or doubt) گنی پښتون نه يې؟ Surely you are not a Pashtoon?

گنيال ganjál *m.* digital

گنيال ليديز ټيکلی ganjál lidíz ṭikaláj *m.* DVD (digital video disk)

گنېدل ¹ gəṇedə́l *intransitive* [*past:* وگنېد] **1** to breath heavily and noisily through the nose **2** to speak nasally

گنېدل ² gaṇedə́l *denominative, intransitive* [*past:* گڼ شو] **1** to be plentiful, be profuse, be frequent; grow thickly **2** to be shady **3** to be numerous **4** to be thick, be dense **5** to be thickly populated, be populous

گنېش gaṇésh *m.* weak and sickly man

گنيه ganjá *f.* deposit, pledge, mortgage

گنيه وال ganjavál *m.* mortgage holder; pledgee, pawnee

گو go *Eastern* ☞ درو

گواتٙل gvātə́l *transitive* [*past:* و يې گواته] to wound

گواتنه gvātə́na *f.* wound, wounding

گوا تېمالا gvātemālá *f.* Guatemala (state, city)

گواته guvā́ṭa *f. regional* pile of dried dung cakes, manure

گواتی guvā́ṭaj *m.* owl

گوا چه gvá che so to speak, as if

گوادر gvādár *m.* Gvadar, Gwadar (port, Persian Gulf)

گوار ¹ guvā́r guā́r goā́r *m.* [*plural:* گوارونه guvārúna *plural:* guārúna *plural:* goārúna *Eastern f. plural:* گواری guāre] herd of cattle

گوار ² gavā́r *m. dialect* boor; oaf

گواری ¹ guvārí *m. plural* **1** the Guvari (a people of India) **2** peasant

گواری ² gavārə́j *f.* bag for transporting soil

گواښ gvākh *m.* **1** separation (of quarreling parties); mediation, intervention گواښ کوٙل to separate (in a dispute), pacify someone **2** threat دوی په گواښ پيل وکړ They resorted to threats.

گواښ گرندی ¹ gvākhgrəndáj *m.* ☞ گواښ گری

گواښ گرندي ² gvākhgrandí *f.* intervention, arbitration گواښ گرندي کوٙل to intervene, act as an arbitor, act as a third-party judge

گواښ گری gvākhgə́raj *m.* umpire, arbitor, third-party judge

گواښل gvāḵhəl transitive [past: وي گواښه] 1 to pacify to separate (disputants) 2 to threaten 3 to persuade 4 to prepare or train for something

گواښندوی gvāḵhəndúj m. ☞ گواښ گری

گواښول gvāḵhavəl denominative, transitive [past: گواښ يې کړ] to pacify, appease, separate (disputants)

گواښېدل gvāḵhedəl intransitive [past: و گواښېدل] 1 to threaten 2 Eastern to prepare, get ready for something, decide (to do something) له ډېري مودې نه دي خبري ته گواښېدم چه څه ليکل په کار دئ A long time ago I decided to write something about this problem.

گواکي guāke as though, as if, like

گوال gvāl m. 1 reach, stretch (of a river) 2 bend (of a mountain range) 3 gently sloping drop

گوانچه gavānchá f. kind of harrow used to level off land under cultivation

گوانډ gvānḍ m. suburb

گوانډگري gvānḍgarí f. گوانډگلوي gvānḍgalví f. neighborhood

گوانډي gvánḍe ☞ گواکي 1

گوانډی gvānḍáj dialect 1 m. neighbor 2 neighboring

گواه gavāh m. witness گواه کول compound verb to summon as a witness

گواهي gavāhí f. testimony, witness testimony گواهي ورکول، گواهي اداکول to give evidence

گواهيلنه gavāhilə́na f. giving of evidence, testimony

گواهيلونی gavāhilúnaj m. witness

گواهيورکونه gavāhivarkavə́na f. گواهي لنه ☞

گوبلکه gobaláka f. mushroom, fungus

گوبی gobí 1 f. regional cauliflower بند گوبی head of cabbage

گوبی góbi 2 f. د گوبی بيدیا ، د گوبی صحرا the Gobi Desert

گوبیر gobír ☞ گوپیر

گپ gup 1 m. 1 astronomy Venus 2 bank of clouds

گپ gop 2 m. hump (of a camel, yak)

گپ gup 3 m. gulp, mouthful

گپړی gopṛáj m. leather patch (on a skin bag)

گوپیر gopéṛ 1 elderly 2 m. old man

گوتکی gvətkə́j f. ☞ گوتگی

گوتگوتی gvətgutáj mocked, humiliated گوتگوتی کول to mock, humiliate

گوتگی gvətgə́j f. signet ring, ring

گوتلکه gvətláka f. girl given in marriage in order to stop a blood feud

گوت منډی gvətmanḍé f. 1 pointing a finger 2 censure; reproach; judgment

گوتمو gvətmáv m. گوتمه gvətá f. ☞ گتمه

گوتمی gutmə́j gvutmə́j f. small ring, small signet ring

گوته gúta gvə́ta gvúta f. 1 finger دې کار ته يې گوتي واچول He got down to work. گوته پر اينبودل a to point to, indicate with the finger b to seize for oneself c to point out deficiencies, point the finger at گوته ښندول to fall into the hand of, meet گوته راتلل to point

گوته لگول the finger at Eastern to make a thumbprint (instead of a signature) د چا سره گوتي لگول to fight with someone, scratch somebody up و یو شي ته گوتي ورورول to touch, touch upon لمر په چه د گوتي ځای مومي نو سوک You don't hide the truth. گوته نه پټېږي پکنني ورمندي proverb literal If he finds room for a finger, he puts his whole fist in. figurative Give him an inch and he takes a mile. د یوه لاس گوتي هم فرق لري proverb In a single family, everyone is living a different life 2 gvúta góta Eastern signet ring, ring د گوته په لاس کول to wear a ring سرو زرو گوته gold ring د مير گوته يې He has a prince's ring on his finger. figurative He does nothing. He is laying about. 3 measure (the width of a finger, about one centimeter) idiom ځمونږ تر منځ گوته ده We are not closely related to them. idiom شيطان گوته راکړه Its the devil's own work. idiom بل ته گوته ښنه ځي ، ځان ته نه ځي It is more visible from the side. idiom تياره دومري ډېره ده چه د لاس گوتي نه It is pitch-dark. idiom گوته چيچل to regret, deplore, grieve idiom گوتي تري وباسه Eastern idiom a Leave him in peace. b Don't have anything to do with that matter. idiom په گوته کېدل a to become renown b to become a laughingstock idiom د حيراني پنځه گوتي په خوله ننيستل to be very thirsty Eastern idiom گوته په خوله کښني نيول to be astounded, be surprised, be stunned گوته په غاښ idiom گوته په غاښ کول to be surprised, be astonished د چا نواقصو ته گوته نيول idiom to point out somebody's faults, indicate someone's shortcomings idiom د چا سره گوتي ماتول a to quarrel with someone b to bargain with somebody, trade with someone idiom توره گوته په چا پوري مينبل to blame someone, slander somebody idiom یو گوته رباب وهل to play the rabab a little idiom گوتي په ...وهل، په ...گوتي وهل a to interfere in some matter b to put in order; repair په ځان گوتي وهل پر ځان گوتي وهل to dress up, array oneself (in)

گوتی gvatáj 1 m. measure for powder

گوتی gvə́te 2 f. signet ring, ring

گوته gúti gúte gvə́ti 3 plural of گوته

گوتی gotí 4 Gothic گوتی ډول Gothic style

گوتی gotə́j 5 f. Eastern ☞ گوتی

گوتیک gotík گوتی 4 ☞

گوت guṭ gvəṭ 1 [plural: گوټان guṭān plural: گوټان gvəṭān] 1 angle چوخ نيغ گوټ obtuse angle پلن گوټ right ارت گوټ acute angle گوټ په گوټ کښني کښپښناستل to get oneself into a corner 2 region, district د هېواد په گوټ گوټ کښني in different areas of the country 3 hiding place د یوازي توب په گوټ کښني قرار نيول to find peace in seclusion گوټ ماتول to commit a burglary by breaking in

گوټ guṭ 2 m. 1 mouthful, swallow یو گوټ اوبه a mouthful of water اوبه گوټ گوټ څښکل to drink water in gulps 2 piece (of food) یو گوټ کول to swallow د ... نه یو گوټ to take a swallow

گوټ goṭ 3 m. 1 bobbin; reel 2 chess pawn 3 dolt, blockhead

گوټک guṭák 1 m. corner

گوټک goṭák 2 m. technology pulley, block

گوټکه goṭáka 1 f. ☞ گوټله

گوتکه ² goṭká *f.* savings, economy measures

گوتل guṭál *transitive* [*past:* ويې گوته] 1 to swallow 2 *Eastern* to drink 3 *Eastern* absorb

گوتله goṭlá *f.* skein, hank (of yarn)

گوتلۍ goṭláj *f.* child's pacifier made of cloth (sometimes dipped in a liquid)

گوتناسته gvətnásta *f.* seclusion, the life of a hermit

گوتناستی gvətnástaj *m.* hermit, anchorite

گوتنه guṭána *f.* swallowing

گوتوالی goṭválaj *m.* bluntness, limitedness, scantiness

گوتول ¹ goṭavəl *denominative, transitive* [*past:* گوت يې کړ] to blunt, dull

گوتول ² guṭavəl *denominative, transitive* [*past:* گوت يې کړ] to swallow

گوتی ¹ guṭáj *m.* set square

گوتۍ ² goṭə́j *f.* backgammon board

گوتی ³ góṭaj *m. diminutive suffix* کتاب گوتی little heart زړه گوتی booklet

گوتېدل goṭedəl *denominative, intransitive* [*past:* گوت شو] to become dull, become blunt

گوتیز guṭíz *combining form* angular څلور گوتیز four-cornered, quadrangular

گوتین guṭín gvətín angular

گوجر gudzhár gudzhə́r *m.* 1 shepherd, herder 2 cattleman 3 Gudzhar (nationality) 4 *proper name* Gudzhar

گوجرکی gudzhórkaj *m.* vertebra

گوجره gudzhára *f.* 1 *feminine of* گوجر 2 dairymaid

گوجک godzhák *m.* unleavened bread

گوجی gudzháj *m.* 1 shell; cockleshell 2 snail shell 3 pine cone 4 cataract

گوځن gudzə́n *m.* paralysis گوځن وهلئ paralytic, one suffering from paralysis

گوخی gutsáj *m.* kind of edible mushroom

گوډ godá *m.* ☞ گوډه

گوډاره gudára *f.* clip on the back of the head; a cuff, punch

گوډال godál *m.* trou-de-loup; tank-trap (covered and camouflaged)

گوډام godám *m.* ☞ د اغلاطو گودام گدام piling up of errors

گوډر gudár *m.* ☞ بې گودره په اوبو نه to wade, ford گدر په گودر کېدل گوډر proverb literal If you don't know the ford, do not enter the water. *figurative* If you can't stand the heat, get out of the kitchen.

گوډره gudará *f.* ☞ گدره

گوډر ¹ gudóṛ *m.* 1 small piece, bit گودر گودر in bits, pieces, fragments 2 rag 3 rubbish

گوډر ² gudóṛ *m.* old cow

گوډروالا gudóṛvālá *m.* rag-and-bone man, junkman

گوډره gudáṛa *f.* skinny old woman

گوډړی gudáṛəj *f.* gudə́ṛj patchwork coat of a dervish

گوډه godá *f.* cellar which is not equipped for human habitation

گوډی gudə́j *f.* godə́j doll

گودي پران gudiparán *m.* kite

گوډ ¹ goḍ *m. regional* weeding گوډ کول to weed

گوډ ² guḍ gvəḍ 1.1 lame گوډ کېدل گوډ کړ to grow lame 1.2 injured 2 *m.* cripple, invalid, disabled د جگړې گوډ disabled war veteran

گوډا ² goḍá *m.* 1 doll 2 ☞ گوډی

گوډاگی goḍāgáj *m.* doll, puppet

گوډاگی پالنگر gūḍāgáj pālangár *m. computer science* proxy server

گوډانه goḍána *f.* 1 bosom 2 pocket; pouch, purse هر يو خان ته گوډانه ډکوي *proverb literal* Everyone stuffs his own pockets. *figurative* Everyone takes care of himself. 3 sheet onto which fruit is knocked from the tree 4 storage bag (for belongings)

گوډبانی goḍbāṇáj *m.* porter (carrying a hunter or travelers belongings)

گوډبه goḍbá *m.* special worker who digs irrigation wells and tunnels

گوډتوب gvəḍtób *m.* گوډتیا guḍtjá *f.* 1 lameness 2 state of being disabled

گوډچکی guḍchákaj *m.* گوډکی guḍakáj *m.* small bag, little sack

گوډگر goḍgór *m.* [*plural:* گوډگر goḍgó́r *plural:* گوډگران goḍgəráu] weeder

گوډل guḍál *m.* cattle run, cowpen

گوډوالی gvəḍválaj *m.* ☞ گوډتوب

گوډول guḍavə́l *denominative, transitive* [*past:* گوډ يې کړ] 1 to cripple, wound پنه گوډول to injure the leg 2 to paralyze

گوډه guḍá *f. dialect* knee

گوډی ¹ gúḍaj *m.* 1 leather traveling bag; knapsack 2 neck of a skin water-bag 3 young embryo ear (of corn, maize)

گوډی ² guḍáj *m.* cripple, disabled person

گوډی ³ guḍáj *f.* doll

گوډی ⁴ goḍáj *m.* small scythe, reaping hook (for weeding)

گوډی ⁵ goḍí *m.* worker engaged in weeding

گوډیاری guḍjapārə́j *f.* 1 small water-skin 2 hot-water bottle

گوډېدل guḍedə́l *denominative, intransitive* [*past:* گوډ شو] 1 to be crippled 2 to grow lame

گوډیکه guḍjáka *f.* 1 crutch 2 small doll, dolly 3 leg of a distaff

گذارول ² guzāravə́l *transitive* ☞ گذارول

گدر guzár *m. Eastern* ☞ گدر

گور ¹ gor *m.* grave, tomb د گور په غاړه ولاړېدل to be at the edge of the grave, have one foot in the grave; be at death's door وچي غاري گور ته تلل ، وچي غاري په گور کښې پرپوتل to go to the grave without having enjoyed accumulated wealth

گور ² gur 1 thick; dense, compact په ونو گور وات avenue 2 thick, branchy, spreading, shady 3 abundant (of fruit) 4 foggy; cloudy 5 dark (of a storm cloud) 6 swarming with something, teeming with something گوربدل ¹ گورول ☞ گوربدل ¹ گورکول

گور ³ gur *m.* rumbling at the time of an earthquake; dull noise

گور ⁴ gvar *m.* rival or opponent who is equal in strength

گور ⁵ gor gloomy, somber

گور ⁶ gavár *m.* ☞ گورم ¹

گور gor *present tense of* کتل[1]

گوراځه gorā́dza *f.* rags, tatters

گوراډۍ gurā́ḍə́j *f.* plain girl, plain Jane

گوراگور gorāgór quick, adroit; lively, sharp

گوربت gurbə́t *m.* eagle

گورت[1] górt *m.* web

گورت[2] gvurə́t *m.* ☞ گرت

گورت پاڼه gort pā́ṇa *f.* web page

گورتوب gurtób *m.* ☞ گوروالی

گورتوب gvartób *m.* ☞ گورتیا[2]

گورتیا[1] gurtjā́ *f.* ☞ گوروالی

گورتیا[2] gvartjā́ 1 opposition, counteraction 2 rivalry

گورجه gurdzhá *f.* red plum *idiom* گورجه مخ ruddy face

گورجی gurdzhə́j *f. obsolete* woman's slippers

گورجی سپی gurdzhə́j spaj *m.* setter, pointer (bird dog)

گورستان goristā́n *m.* cemetery; graveyard

گورکښ gorkā́kh *m.* Indian badger

گورکفن gor-kafán *m.* 1 obsequies, funeral service 2 funeral expenses

گورکن gorkán *m.* gravedigger

گورکی[1] gurkáj *m.* ☞ گورهار

گورکي[2] gorkí *m.* د گورکي ښار Gorki (city)

گورگټۍ gorgaṭə́j *f.* badger

گورگوره gvurgúra *f.* 1 ☞ گرګره 2 blackberry bush

گورلځ gurlā́dz سور گورلځ سړی ruddy man

گورم[1] gorə́m *m.* gorám herd of cows or buffalo

گورم[2] górəm *first person singular present tense of* کتل[1]

گورمل gurmə́l *transitive* ☞ گرمل

گورمبدل gurmedə́l *intransitive* [*past:* وګورمبد] 1 to growl, roar; bellow 2 to carry on disagracefully, conduct oneself in an unseemly fashion (at home)

گورنډه gorā́nḍa *f.* 1 hovel, shack 2 old neglected tomb 3 cattle shed

گورنر gavərnár *m.* 1 governor 2 director; member of management د گورنرانو هیات the management (of a company)

گورنر جنرال gavərnár dzhenerā́l *history* governor-general (the viceroy of India)

گوروالی gurvā́laj *m.* 1 thickness; denseness, compactness 2 thickness, branchiness, shadiness 3 abundance, plenteousness 4 fogginess; cloudiness

گوروان gorvā́n *m. Western* shepherd; drover

گوروانکه gorvānā́ka *f.* starling

گوروانه gorvā́na *f.* shepherdess

گورواني gorvā́ni *f.* profession of shepherd, shepherding

گورول[1] guravə́l *denominative, transitive* [*past:* گوری کړ] 1 to make thick, make dense, make compact; thicken 2 to make thick, make branchy, make shady 3 to make abundant, make numerous 4 to make foggy, make cloudy

گورول[2] guravə́l *transitive* [*past:* ویې گوراوه] to reproach, censure

گوره[1] gorā́ *m.* [*plural:* گوره گان goragā́n] *regional* 1 English soldier 2 Englishman

گوره[2] gorá *f.* sawdust, metal filings

گوره[3] góra *imperfective imperative of* کتل[1] گوره چه! Be careful! Look out!

گوره[4] gúra *f. singular of* گور[2]

گوره[5] gorá *f.* gurá gully; rut, groove

گوره[6] gvə́ra *f.* brand, trademark (on goods)

گوره[7] gorá هر گوره in every possible way, very

گورهار gurahár *m.* 1 rumble, rumbling 2 tread, tramp 3 growl, growling 4 reproaches

گوره خر gorakhár *m.* wild ass, onager

گورهنده gorhánda *f.* 1 rough, uneven ground 2 gully, ravine 3 pit 4 ☞ گورنډه

گوره ییز توپک gorajíz گوره ئیز gorajíz *regional* English Martini-Henri rifle

گوری[1] guráj *m.* ☞ گوره[2]

گوری[2] gorí *f.* deceit, fraud, cheating (in gambling) گوری کول to deceive, cheat, defraud (in gambling)

گوری[3] gavrə́j *f.* groats

گوري[4] góri *present tense of* کتل[1]

گوریجن goridzhán cunning; deceptive

گوربدل[1] guredə́l *denominative, intransitive* [*past:* گور شو] 1 to be thick, be dense, be compact; get thick, grow dense 2 to be thick, be branchy, be shady; to grow in great profusion (of vegetation) 3 to be foggy, be cloudy 4 to swarm, teem with something

گوربدل[2] guredə́l *intransitive* [*past:* وگوربد] 1 to behave in a disgraceful manner 2 *Eastern* to grumble, mutter

گوریلا gorilā́ *f.* gorilla

گوریلایي gvarilājí partisan, guerrilla گوریلایي جنگ guerrilla warfare

گوریمار gorimár *m.* confidence man, cheat, deceiver

گوری موری[1] guráj-muráj 1 sudden 2 unexpected گوری موری یې ونیو They seized him without warning.

گوري موري[2] góri-móri precisely, exactly

گوړ[1] guṛ stomach-rumbling (in cattle)

گوړ[2] goṛ *m.* ☞ گوره[6]

گوړ[3] goṛ *m.* weeding of sugarcane

گوړ[4] goṛ *m.* gully

گوړا[1] goṛā́ *m. Melia indica* (a kind of tree)

گوړا[2] goṛá *f.* device for levelling land under cultivation, kind of harrow

گوړابۍ goṛābə́j *f.* 1 small waterfall 2 spray of water 3 children's game

گوړاخر goṛākhár *m.* ☞ گوره خر

گوړاکو guṛākú *m.* 1 wasps' nest 2 high-quality tobacco

گوړباهۍ goṛbāhə́j *m.* maelstrom, gulf, abyss

گوړدانې gvəṛdāné *f. plural* roasted wheat kernels over which black molasses has been poured

گوردم gvərdám *m.* boards, lumber; beam

گوردور goṛdáur *m. regional* races, horse races د گوردور ميدان horse racetrack

گوړکه guṛáka *f.* skein, hank (yarn, thread)

گورماچ guṛmách *m.* ram's stomach cooked together with intestines, head, and feet

گورمار gvərmár *m.* craftsman who makes sugar of sugarcane

گورنج guṛnádzh *m.* maelstrom, gulf, abyss

گوروبی gvəṛobáj *m.* **1** sugarcane molasses syrup **2** stagnant water

گوړه gvə́ṛa *f.* gvúṛa molasses, treacle *idiom* گوړي غوندي کېدل to be friends, love one another د گوړي غوندي لېدل څوک to love someone

گوړی ¹ guṛə́j *f.* sap (of a plant, a tree) د څوز گوړی a dried sappy exudate on the camelthorn bush

گوړی ² guṛə́j *f.* **1** wad (of cotton) **2** skein (of yarn)

گوړی ³ guṛə́j *f.* **1** green shoots of the camelthorn bush (used as cattle feed) **2** roasted maize kernels

گذار guzár *m.* ☞ گذار

گذارول guzāravə́l *transitive* ☞ گذاړول

گذاره guzārá *f.* ☞ گذاره

گذاربدل guzāredə́l *denominative* ☞ گذاربدل

گوزلېکه gozleká *f.* trifle; minute particle

گزموز guzmúz ☞ گرموز

گزموزی guzmúzaj *m.* ☞ گزمزی

گوزن ¹ gavázn *m.* reindeer

گوزن ² guzə́n *m.* گوزن guzə́ṇ *m.* گوزند guzə́nd *m.* paralysis

گوزندو guzaṇdú *m.* wood-boring beetle

گوزوی guzváj *m.* ox used for ploughing, etc., draft animal

گوزه gaváza *f.* fallow deer, doe

گوزی guzə́j *f.* twisted woolen thread

گوسره ¹ gosṛá *f.* ☞ گوسنه ورکول to beat someone, give a clip on the back of the head گوسره وهل to beat with the fist

گوسنه ¹ gosə́na *f.* clip on the back of the head, cuff, punch

گوسنه ² gōsṇa *f.* gvə́sṇa kind of snake

گوسه ¹ gávsa *f.* boulder

گوسه ² gusá *f. tautological with* گله

گوش فيل gosh-i-fíl *m.* twigs, twiglets (pastry)

گوشاک goshák *m.* گوشکه goshāka *f.* گوشکی goshakə́j *f. military* telephone receiver; sound-locator

گوشمالي goshmālí *f.* reprimand, dressing-down

گوشن gushə́n *tautological with* شين

گوشي goshí *f.* capitation tax on cattle گوشي اخيستل to exact a capitation tax on cattle

گوښت guķht *m. religion* instructions of a saint, teaching of an ecclesiastic

گوښته goķhtá *f.* Goshta (town, Momands)

گوښه goķhá **1** *f.* **.1** corner, nook, cozy place **1.2** sector **1.3** ☞ **2.1** cozy, secluded گوښه څای cozy corner **2.2** secluded **2.3** isolated **2.4** rejecting something; standing aside; relinquishing something گوښه يې کړ He took him aside **a** to take

aside. **b** to seclude, isolate **c** to relinquish something گوښه او کناره **b** to be secluded څان گوښه کول **a** to lead a secluded life څان د نورو to reject something; stand aside; relinquish something د اجتماع څخه څان گوښه to maintain a private residence څخه گوښه کول to be unsociable د چا څخه څان گوښه گوښه کول to assiduously avoid someone

گوښه نشين goķhanishín *m.* hermit; anchorite; recluse

گوښه نشيني goķhanishiní *f.* hermit's life; anchoritism

گوښه والی goķhvә́laj *m.* **1** seclusion **2** isolation **3** refusal of something, rejection of something

گوښی گوښی gvúķhaj gúķhaj **1** separate, private; alone separately, particularly هر يو گوښی گوښی each taken separately **2** separately, particularly, specially دا گوښی ګنبېرده Put this aside (in a separate place). گوښی کول to separate, isolate to be separated, be isolated **3** only, just

گوښېدل guķhedə́l *denominative* [*past:* گوښی شو] to be separated, be isolated; be secluded

گوگ gog **1.1** empty, vacant **1.2** hollow **2** *m.* **.1** cavity **2.2** chamber (of the heart)

گوگرد سازی gugirdsāzí *f.* match production د گوگرد سازی فابريکه match factory

گوگړ ¹ gugə́ṛ *m. plural* **1** matches **2** sulfur د گوگړو تېزاب sulfuric acid د گوگړو کان sulfur mine

گوگړ ² gugáṛ decrepit; old; weak

گوگړ ³ gogóṛ *m.* ☞ گوگل

گوړگه goṛgá *f.* cooked, roasted

گوگل ¹ gogál gogə́l *m.* **1** ☞ کوکل **2** hull, fuselage (of an aircraft)

گوگل ² gogíl *m.* gum resin

گوگل ³ gogíl *m. plural* ☞ گوگړ

گوگلای gogláj *m.* [*plural:* گوگلی goglí *plural:* گوگليان goglijә́n] **1** supporting trellis for grapevines, brace **2** stand (for storing bedclothes)

گوگن gogə́n **1** empty, vacant **2** hollow

گوگن والی gogənvә́laj *m.* **1** emptiness, cavity **2** hollow, hollowness

گوگو gugú *m.* ☞ گوگلی

گوگور gogəvúr *m.* kind of mountain flower

گوگوشتکه gugushtə́ka *f.* turtledove

گوگوشتو gugushtú *m. & f.* **1** turtledove **2** gurgling of liquid poured from the neck of a jug

گوگول gogavə́l *denominative, transitive* [*past:* گوگ يې کړ] **1** to make vacant, make hollow, hollow out, gouge out **2** to erode (of river banks)

گوگلی gogáj *m.* ☞ گوگلی

گوگېدل gogedə́l *denominative, intransitive* [*past:* گوگ شو] **1** to be empty, be vacant, be hollow د دي وني څخه گوگ شو A hollow formed in this tree. **2** to be eroded (of a riverbank)

گول ¹ gol *m.* **1** ox standing in the center of the threshing floor (during threshing) **2** dolt, lunkhead

گول ² gol *m. sports* goal

گول ³ gul *m. regional* victim, sacrifice

گول ⁴ gul *m.* ☞ گل ¹

گلمېخ gulmékh *m.* ☞ گل مېخ

گلو ¹ gulú *m.* ☞ گلو ²

گولو ² goló *oblique plural of* گوله

گولو ³ goló *oblique plural of* گولۍ

گولول gulavól *transitive* [*past:* وی یې گولاوه] to upset, stir up trouble; cause disturbance 2 to (unauthorizedly) divulge a secret

گوله golá *f.* 1 piece, bit گوله تېرول ، گوله وهل to swallow, gulp down گولۍ وهل to swallow thirstily, gobble up 2 stirrup strap 3 pill, tablet محمود په یوه گوله ډوډۍ قدرت نه لري Mahmud is unable to earn his livelihood. د احمد a to be very avaricious گوله تر ستوني نه تېرېدل Ahmed is extremely tightfisted. b to stick in the throat

گوله باروت golabārút *m.* ☞ گوله بارود gulabārúd *m. plural regional* 1 munitions 2 ammunition

گوله باري gulabārí *f.* gunfire; bombardment گوله باري کول to fire upon; bombard

گولۍ golój *f.* 1 bullet د توپکو گولۍ bullets د توپ گولۍ shell; shot گولۍ ویشتل to shoot 2 pill, tablet 3 spheroid

گولي پنج gulipándzh *m.* river crab

گولېدل guledól *intransitive* [*past:* وگولېد] 1 to break out, develop (of trouble, dissension) 2 to be divulged (of a secret)

گمان gumán *m.* ☞ گمان

گماڼو gumáňḍ *m.* گماڼو gumáňḍu *m.* mushroom, toadstool

گمبت gumbát *m.* گمبته gumbáta *f.* cupola, arch

گمبزي gumbazí cupola-ed, arched

گومبوري gumburáj *m.* cheek

گمبۍ gumbój *f.* protuberance, bulge; bump, lump

گومل gomál *m.* د گومل دره the Gomal Passage

گومنځ gumóndzh *f. dialect* ☞ ږمونځ

گون ¹ gəván *m.* ☞ ماخی

گون ² gún *suffix forming adjectives with the meaning of "several times as much or as many"* درې گون double; twofold دوه گون triple شل گون 20 apiece

گونټه gonṭá *f.* chess pawn

گونج gundzh ☞ گنجی ⁴

گونجل gundzhól *transitive* [*past:* وی یې گونجه] to wrinkle, crumple

گونجلک gundzhulák ☞ گنجلک

گونجکۍ gundzhəkáj *m.* cupboard (for dishes)

گونجول gundzhavól *denominative, transitive* ☞ گنجول

گونجه gúndzha *f.* crease; pleat

گونجی gundzháj ☞ گنجی ⁴

گونجېدل gundzhedól *denominative* ☞ گنجېدل

گونجي گونجي gúndzhi-gúndzhi wrinkled; crumpled

گونځه gúndza *f.* ☞ گنجه د اوبو په مخ گونځي ripple on the surface of water

گوند gvund *m.* gvənd ☞ گنډ ¹

گند بازي gvəndbāzí *f.* gundbāzí ☞ گنډ بازي

گند پرستي gvəndparastí *f.* ☞ گنډ پرستي

گوندري gundráj *m.* small group

گونده ¹ gavandá *f.* large sack

گونده ² gundá *m.* experienced and strong man, worldly-wise man

گوندي ¹ gundí *f.* gvundí ☞ گنډي ¹

گوندي ² gúnde *Eastern* gúndi maybe, possibly, apparently گوندي تر غرمې پوري راشي خدای Perhaps he will come before noon. گوندي وکي چه maybe, God willing

گوندي ³ gúndaj *m.* large double sack

گندیمار gvəndəjmắr *m.* gundəjmắr ☞ گندیمار

گندیماري gvəndəjmārí gundəjmārí *f.* ☞ گندیماري

گونډه gonḍá *f.* 1 bent knee (of a camel) 2 kneeling گونډه کول a to hobble (a camel) b to clasp the knee گونډي وهل a to kneel b to persist به گونډو کېدل to kneel گونډه ورته وهل to be stubborn, persist, be inflexible

گونز gúnz *f. dialect* ☞ ږمنځ

گونزه gúnza *f.* ☞ گونجه

گونگ gvəng gung ☞ گنگ ²

گونگټ gungóṭ *m.* dung beetle, scarab

گونگرو gungrú *m.* silver handbell

گنگړي gungṛí *m. plural* ☞ گنگړي ²

گونگو gungú *m.* 1 bush having dark-yellow wood 2 saffron 3 wild safflower 4 pale face

گنگوشی gungútsaj *m. dialect* ☞ گنگوشی

گونگوري gungúraj *m.* bunch, cluster (of grapes)

گنگوړه gunguṛá ☞ گانگوړه and گانگور

گونگوړی gungvúṛaj *m.* ☞ وینگالي

گنگوسی gungvusáj *m.* gungosáj ☞ گنگوسی

گونگو ماښام gungú māḵẖám twilight, dusk

گونگه روژه gúnga rozhá گونگه ینگه gungajəngá *f.* complete silence, absolute silence

گونگۍ ¹ gungáj *m.* 1 eagle owl 2 owl *idiom* مگر دوی د گونگي په شان گوړه و خوږه ، خو څوک نه شوه پوه It is like casting pearls before swine.

گونگۍ ² gungáj dumb, mute

گونگۍ ³ gúngaj *m.* bunch (of grapes)

گونه ¹ gúna *f.* 1 color 2 face, complexion 3 kind, type; order

گونه ² gúna gúnaj *suffix* گوني ☞ گون ²

گوني ¹ guné *f.* leather patch on the counter of slipper

گونۍ ² gonój *f.* sack

گونیا gunjấ *f. & m.* triangle (drawing)

گونیه gonjá *f.* ☞ گوني ¹

گوڼ guṇ *m.* weevil

گواټه guvắṭa *f.* ☞ گوهاټه

گوه guh *m.* 1 feces, stool 2 slag

گوهاټه gohāṭá *f.* pile of dried dung cakes

گوهار guhár gohár *f. & m.* گوهاره gohára *f.* herd of cattle

گوهر gohár *m.* 1 precious stone 2 nature, essence 3 flash, gleam (of a saber)

گوی ¹ gəváj *m.* small low mountain pass

گوی ² goj *m.* polo ball

گوی ³ goj *m. plural* dung cake; dried dung

گوی ⁴ goj *m.* **1** ox that works well in harness **2** millwheel lever

گوی ⁵ goj *m.* garrulous person; chatterbox

گویا gujā́ gojā́ **1** as though, like, as it were گویا کېني ، گویا که as though, like, as if چه consequently, therefore, accordingly **2** گویان ☞

گویان gujā́n gojā́n speaking, conversing د خپلې ژبې گویان speaking in the native language

گویانا gviānā́ *f.* Guiana

گویر gojár *m.* gəvír herd of cattle (20-30 head)

گویږ gəvég *m.* questioning

گویږل gvegól *transitive* [*past:* و یې گویبره] to question

گویک govjók *m.* woman's high-heeled slipper

گویول gojavól *denominative, transitive* [*past:* گوی یې کړ] to train an ox to the plow

گویه gója *f.* crumpledness, state of being crumpled

گویې gojé *f.* nonsensical babbling, chattering

گهبراو ghabráv *regional* alarmed هغه گهبراو شه He became alarmed.

گهبراهټ ghabrāháṭ *m. regional* trepidation, worry, alarm گهبراهټ سره ویل to get alarmed, express alarm

گوهر gohár *m.* گوهر ☞

گهړی ghaṛój *f. regional* **1** watch, clock **2** hour

گهړیال ghaṛjā́l *m. regional* د گهړیال مناره گړیال clock tower ☞

گاه گه gáh-gáh گاه گه ☞

گهنټه ghanṭá ghinṭá *f. regional* **1** hour نیمه گهنټه half hour **2** gong, bell گهنټه غږول to ring a bell, strike a gong

گهنټي ghanṭí *f. regional* bell گهنټي غږول to ring, ring a bell

گهنه ghaná *f.* گانه ☞ ¹

گهواره gahvārá *f.* cradle; bassinette

گهور ghur گور ☞ ²

گهیغ gahídz *m.* گهیز gahíz *m.* morning گهیغ زه ورغلم I came to him in the morning.

گی ¹ gəj *f.* cord (for sewing sacks)

گی ² gáj *diminutive suffix forms nouns* زړگی little heart

گیا gijā́ *f.* گیاه ☞

گیان gijā́n *m.* Gian (town, Khost)

گیانا gijānā́ *f.* Guiana

گیا gijā́ *f.* gijā́h *f.* gjjā́h *m.* **1** grass وچه گیاه hay **2** fodder

گیائي gijāí *adjective* vegetable گیائي رنگونه vegetable dyes

گیبای gebáj *m.* baggy Middle-Eastern style trousers with narrow cuffs (for married women)

گیت git **a** to do something unseemly on the quiet; cheat someone **b** to ignore someone's request or order **c** to take off, cop out, run out

گیتار gitár *m.* guitar

گیتارست gitāríst *m.* guitarist

گیتس getís *m.* garters, suspenders

گیټ geṭ *m. regional* gate

گیتکی ¹ giṭkój *f.* گیتی ☞ ¹

گیتکی ² giṭkáj *m. regional* گیتی ☞ ³ 1

گیتی ¹ giṭój *f.* pastern (of a horse)

گیتی ² geṭój *f.* hank, skein (of thread, yarn)

گیتی ³ geṭój *f.* giṭój **1** round flat stone **2** pebble which is placed in a hookah

گیتی ⁴ geṭój *f.* shot, ball (rifle); buckshot گیتی والا توپک getəjvālā́ گیتی والا shotgun

گیچ ¹ gich *m.* [*plural:* گیچان gichán] shards of broken pottery, etc., used in children's games

گیچ ² gich senseless, unconscious, fainting گیچ او منگ senseless, unconscious, fainting

گیچه gichá *f.* گیکه gikhá *f.* **1** garbage, remains of food **2** oil cake, waste products; flax straw, hemp straw

گیدانه gidā́na *f.* گوانچه ☞

گیدړ gidáṛ *m.* gidə́ṛ **1** jackal په زړه کښې یې گیدړ ناست دئ *literal* A jackal sits in his heart. *figurative* He is afraid. He is apprehensive (of exposure, arrest). **2** dog-fox **3** sly fox, shrewdie

گیدرباغ gidaṛbā́gh *m.* solanum, morel

گیدروده gidaṛvadə́ *m.* rain during sunshine

گیداره gidā́ṛa *f.* vixen, she-fox

گیدړی gidaṛój *f.* **1** toadying **2** senseless laughter گیدړی خندل to laugh without reason

گیدی ¹ gidáj *m.* gedáj *regional* donkey

گیدی ² gedí stupid گیدی خر donkey, ass

گیدی ³ gedój *f.* she-ass

گیدبنگ geḍbáng گیدو geḍú **1** potbellied, big-bellied **2** gluttonous, voracious

گیدر giḍár *m.* گیدړ ☞

گیدور geḍavár big-bellied, big with child

گیده géḍa *f.* **1** belly, stomach گیده مړول to eat large quantities په گیده وړی دئ He is fed, clothed, and shod گیده موړ او په تن پټ He is not greedy. گیده مي لاندي ده ، راباندي نه ده hungry. گیده غورزول to abort, miscarry خپله گیده غوړه ساتي He loves to treat himself. He has a sweet tooth. د گیدي مین دئ **a** He is very gluttonous. **b** He loves to eat. په گیده یې رسی تکبړي He ate a lot. **2** interior, center, depth د تیارو د گیدي نه یو څوک راووت Someone came out of the darkness.

گیدور geḍavár گیدور ور ☞

گیدی ¹ geḍáj *m.* **1** armful, bundle (of firewood) **2** sheaf of grass carried on the back *idiom* گیدی کېدل to unite for the attack

گیدی ² geḍój *f.* **1** bouquet **2** bunch (of grass, etc.) **3** small sheaf

گیر ¹ ger **1.1** enclosed with a fence **1.2** surrounded; besieged **1.3** stuck, bogged down گیرول ☞ **2** *m.* catching, capturing; catch *idiom* اوس گیر یې! Now you're caught! Got you!

گیر ² gír *m.* hairpin

گیر ³ gír *combining form* seizing, catching, getting ماهي گیر fisherman, catcher of fish

گرا ¹ gerá quick, smart, efficient

گیرا ² girá 1 f. .1 paper clip; hitch 1.2 small hook 1.3 vice with a screw 2 seizing; catching

گرچاپېر gerchāpér Eastern around له ښهر نه گرچاپېر around the city

گیر گیره girgirá f. ☞ گرگره ¹

گیرنده girandá 1 attractive 2 gripping; fascinating

گیرودار girudár m. struggle د ژوند گیرودار the struggle for existence

گیراول giravól گېراول geravól denominative transitive [past: گیر یې کړ]
1 to seize, grab, catch 2 to confine, imprison (e.g., in a cell, a cage) 3 to surround, beseige 4 to surround with a fence, fence in 5 Eastern to catch هغه باران گېره کړه The rain caught her.

گیره ¹ girá f. sack for transporting loads on a donkey

گیره ² gíra Eastern ☞ ږیره

گېره ³ géra f. singular of گېر ¹

گیری ¹ giráj f. 1 interior envelope of a maize ear 2 hangnail

گیری ² geráj m. rim, felloe (of a wheel)

گیردل giredól geredól denominative, intransitive [past: گیر شو] 1 to fall (into the clutches, net, etc.) 2 to stick, get stuck

گیز gíza suffix used to form adjectives نوت بانک گیز افغاني سل a 100-Afghan banknote

گیگاکه gigáka f. magpie

گېس ges m. 1 gas د گېس رڼا زهریله گېسونه toxic gases گېس لگول to turn on the gas 2 [plural: گېسونه gesúna] gas lamps

گېسو gesú m. curl; braid

گیگابایټ gigābájṭ m. gigabyte

گیگاهارتس gigāhārṭs m. gigahertz

گیگیاني ¹ gigijāṇí m. plural the Gigijani (tribe) 2 gigijāṇáj m. Gigijani (tribesman)

گبل gel rushing along

گیلاس ¹ gilás m. cherry tree

گیلاس ² gilás m. ☞ گلاس

گبلن gelán m. gallon (liquid measure)

گبلول gelavól denominative, transitive [past: گبل یې کړ] to roll (a ball, sphere)

گیله gilá f. complaint

گیله امېز gilaaméz adjective querulous, complaining

گیله گی giləgáj m. ☞ گلگی

گبلدل geledól denominative, transitive [past: گبل شو] to roll along (of a sphere, a ball)

گیلیگی giligáj m. calf

گیم gim m. 1 precipice 2 depression or hollow in a river valley

گبنتری gentráj f. regional roll call

گبنته genṭá f. regional 1 hour 2 watch, clock

گبنته گر genṭagár m. regional clock tower

گبنټی ¹ genṭáj f. skein, hank (yarn, thread)

گبنټی ² genṭáj f. hoe, mattock

گیند gind m. [plural: گیندان gindán] 1 ball 2 math sphere

گینده gínda f. stitching, quilting گینده کول to stitch, quilt

---

گبندی geṇḍáj m. regional 1 rhiniceros 2 history rhinoceros-hide shield

گینگری gingṛáj m. ☞ گنگری ¹

گینی ¹ gináj f. oil press

گبنی ² gené dialect like, resembling

گینی ³ giní f. گینبا ginéjā f. Guinea

گبننی geṇṇaj m. anatomy uterus, womb

گبنه geṇá f. adornment, decoration; appointments; dress, attire د ناوې گبنه ورپوري کول to array the bride, dress the bride

گیوتین gijotín m. guillotine

گیول gəjavól transitive [past: و یې گیاوه] to plait, plait together; braid

گئیغ gaídz 1 m. morning 2 in the morning

گیول gəjajól transitive ☞ گیول

گبیونی gejúnaj m. woolen thread (for tying up bags, etc.)

ل

ل lām 1 the thirty-fourth letter of the Pashto alphabet 2 the number 30 in the abjad system

لا ¹ lā 1.1 still, yet, up to now ته لانه یې تللئ؟ Haven't you left yet? دوې روځي لانه وي تللي چه هغه راغئ It has not been two days yet since he arrived. د مخه تر دې لا even before this 1.2 used with qualitative adjectives to indicate a greater degree of the characteristic denoted, still more, etc. لا لږ لا still less, even less دغه ختکی خوړ دئ او هغه لا خوړ دئ به ښه وي It will be still better. This melon is sweet, but that is still sweeter. 1.3 still more, yet more (in supplement to something) ما به لا یو ښه ویل I had decided to say yet more, but ... او ډېري څوکي یې (د 2 participle even هندوکش) په دوبي لا د واورو څخه ډکي وي Many of its peaks (the Hindu Kush) are snow-covered even in summer.

لا ² lā f. ☞ لای ¹

لا ³ lā a prefix with nouns which have a temporal meaning, and used with the word بل forms adverbs, and adverbial phrases with the general meaning of "after" لا بل گهیغ the day after tomorrow

لا ⁴ lā Arabic negative prefix non-, un-, in- لابیان indescribable, inexpressible

لاابالي lāabālí careless, not careful, not serious, scatterbrained

لااقل lāaḳál Arabic at least, at the very least

لاانتها lāintihā Arabic boundless, endless

لاانتهائیت lāintihāiját m. Arabic boundlessness, endlessness

لابدي lābadí lābudí Arabic obligatory, unavoidable, indispensable دا یو لابدي کار دئ This is unavoidable.

لابراتوار lāborātuár m. laboratory

لابراتواري lāborātuārí adjective laboratory لابراتوري تجربه laboratory experiment

لابیرنت lābirínt m. labyrinth

لابل صبا lābál sabā Eastern لابل گهیغ lābál gahídz the day after tomorrow

لابوري lābóri f. plural extravagant praise, toadying

لابيان lābajắn *Arabic* indescribable, inexpressible

لاپاز lāpáz *m.* La Paz (city)

لاپزن lāpzán *m.* braggart, boaster

لاپسي lāpasé still more اصرار يې لاپسي زيات شو He became all the more insistent.

لاپوک lāpúk boastful په يوه لاپوکه بغ ويل to speak boastfully, boast

لافي lāpi ☞

لاتري lātarí *f.* lottery دلاتري يوه نمره *latráj* a lottery ticket

لاتعد lātu'ádd *Arabic* innumerable, incalculable

لاتويائي lātviānjí ☞

لاتويه lātvijá *f.* ☞

لاته lắta لاته ورمه شپه three nights ago لاته ورمه کال three years ago لاته ورمه ورځ three days ago

لاتين lātín *m.* Latin, the Latin language

لاتيني lātiní *adjective* 1.1 Latin لاتيني امريکا Latin America 2.1 *m.* the Romans 2.2 Latin, the Latin language

لاټ ¹ lāṭ *m.* heap, pile

لاټ ² lāṭ *m.* ☞ لارو

لاټکی lāṭkáj *m.* unripe ear of maize in its covering

لاټو lāṭú *m.* 1 ☞ لاډو ² 2 shrike (the bird)

لاټه lāṭə́ *imperfect of* لټل

لاټپن lāṭén *m.* lantern د خاورينو تېلو لاټپن a kerosene lamp لاټپن او فانوس candle lamp

لاثاني lāsāní *Arabic* matchless, incomparable

لاجبر lādzhbár *m. colloquial* ☞ لاجورد

لاجواب lādzhaváb *Arabic* not finding words for an answer; not having an answer لاجواب سو He did not find words to answer.

لاجورد lādzhvárd *m. plural* lazulite, lapis lazuli د لاجورد معادن deposits of lapis lazuli

لاجوردي lādzhvárdi 1 made of lazulite, of lapis lazuli 2 sky blue; azure

لاژهره lāzháɣra لاچاره lāzhắra ☞ ناچار

لاچاکه lāchắka *f.* breed of dog with sparse fur

لاچي ¹ lāchí *m.* ☞ لاچکه

لاچي ² lāchí *m. botany* cardamon

لاچۍ ³ lāchə́j *f.* ☞ لاچی

لاځواب lādzaváb 1 ☞ لاځواب کول to compel to be silent 2 indisputable, irrefutable

لاخار lātsār 1 helpless 2 incurable

لاخاري lātsā́rí *f.* 1 helplessness 2 incurability

لاحقه lāhiḳá *f. Arabic grammar* 1 suffix 2 ending

لادباد lād-bád *m.* support, stand دومره يې وتکولم چه له لاده باده يې وکېنلم They beat me so badly that I could not stand.

لادو lādú *m.* ☞ لاډو ²

لادنگ lādə́ng *m.* lanky fellow, lanky person

لاډو ¹ lāḍú *m.* broad mountain slope broken by ravines

لاډو ² lāḍú *m.* 1 rind, shell (of an opium poppy capsule) 2 top (the toy) 3 *figurative* blockhead, dolt

لاډونی lāḍúnaj *m.* block, log, blockhead

لاډيز lāḍíz stupid, dull

لار lār *f.* [*plural:* لاري lắri] 1 road, path, way په لار کښي، پر لاري on the road, on the way, en route اسفالت شوي لار asphalt road سمه لار *literal & figurative* straight road لویه لار، لو لار main highway, highway, high road ليري لار long road; circuitous way په ليري لار to take the long way round نژدي لار the shortest route نيمه لار halfway, mid-journey د لاري خرابي the period of bad roads د لاري ملګري traveling companion, fellow traveler خرڅ travel expenses د (له)لاري through, via, by way of د جلال آباد له لاري via Dzhelalabd 2 method; means بله لار داده چه ... another way such as ... د محکمي له لاري by legal means په اصولي لار in legal form 3 trajectory دګولي لار the trajectory of a projectile 4 part (in the hair) د ويښتانو لار part (in the hair) د لار ايستل to make a part (in the hair) a لار پيداکول، د ځان دپاره لار پيدا کول to proceed لار پربکول to find the road, find the way b *figurative* to find a way out لار ترل to cut a road through د يوه تعقيبول to proceed along a certain route a لار غلطول to lose one's way, stray from the path b *figurative* to err, go astray لار ميندل to search out a means لار نيول a to go along the road مونږ همدغه لار ونيوه We went along that exact route. b د چا سره لار نيول to rob c to be on good terms with someone هغه زما سره هيڅ لار نه نيسي چا ته He disagrees with me. a د چا ورخخه ورکه سو He lost his way. He strayed from the path. b He got lost. d to bar someone's way a لار وهل to walk along the road, ride along the road نن مو څلور کروه لار ووهله Today we travelled 4 kuruhs (i.e., about 3 kilometers). b to commit robbery, rob c to bar the way, the road d د چا لار وهل *figurative* to lead astray شيطان يې لار ووهله Satan led him astray په خپله لار تلل a to go on one's way, continue on one's road b to set out for home د لاري سره په لار تپروتل to miss one another, pass without meeting د لاري بنويول to seduce, lead astray, divert from the proper path لار او ليکه را بنودل، لار او ليکه په ښودل، لار او to be led astray چاته په لار ازغي to give instruction, guidance; instruct; ليکه ور ښودل to impede, harm, play a dirty trick on someone ما ټولي لاري چاري ليدلي کتلي I have seen everything. I have experienced it all. لار کتل to await, wait

لاربه lārbá *m.* [*plural:* لاربانه lārbānə́] traveler, wayfarer

لارپنه lārpáṇa *f.* ☞ لارليک

لار پرېکوونکی lār prekavúnkaj high-speed

لارډ lārḍ *m.* Lord دلارډانو مجلس the House of Lords

لارښودنه lārḳhodə́na *f.* ☞ لارښوونه

لار ښوونکی lār ḳhovúnkaj 1 indicating the way 2 *m.* .1 guide; conductor 2.2 mentor; leader; chief

لارښوونه lārḳhovə́na *f.* 1 instruction, precept; leadership 2 commentary (on a law)

لارښوونی lārḳhovúnaj *m.* 1 guide; conductor 2 guidebook

لارغه lárgha 1 *f.* hindrance, impediment 2 ليري لارغه long ago, a long time ago

لارقطار lār-ḳatár *m. military obsolete* column of route

لارلباري lārləbārí *f.* scream, yell

لارليک lārlík *m.* **1** *military* column of route **2** pass; safe-conduct **3** passport

لارنسوماركش lārénsu-mārkish *m.* Lorenço-Marques (city, Mozambique, now called Maputo)

لارموند lārmūnd راوټر rāwṭór *m. computer science* router

لارنيونه lārnivéna *f.* brigandage, robbery

لارنيونكى lār nvinúnkaj *m.* highway robber, brigand

لارو lā́ro *oblique plural of* لار [1]

لارو lāró oblique *plural of* لاري [2]

لاروا lārvā́ *f.* larva (of an insect)

لاروركى lārvrékaj **1** going astray, losing one's way **2** getting lost

لارووني lāravúnaj *m.* ☞ لاروى

لار وهنه lārvahéna *f.* **1** proceeding, going on the road **2** robbery, brigandage

لار وهونكى lār vahúnkaj *m.* لاروهوني lārvahúnaj *m.* **1** traveler, wayfarer **2** robber, brigand

لاروى lāraváj *m.* traveler; passerby

لاره lā́ra [1] *f. Eastern* ☞ goat trail *idiom* د وزي لاره لار چه لاره the wrong way راسته لاره د اوسپني لار railroad د مهربي the correct route بده لاره ښوول wiggle room, room for maneuvering to show someone a bad example لاره كتل to await, wait for someone

لاره lārə́ [2] *imperfect of* لرل

لاره lārá [3] *f.* melody

لاره lārə́ [4] *oblique singular of* لور [1] شان د لاره په crescent-shaped لاربنوونه lārakhovúna *f.* ☞ و چا ته لاره ښوونه کول لاربنوونه to instruct someone; supervise someone

لارى lāráj [1] *m.* ☞ لاروى

لاري lārí [2] *f.* [*plural:* لارى lārój *plural:* لاري گاني lārigāni] truck, lorry

لاري lāri [3] *plural and oblique singular of* لار on the way, en route; on the road

لاري lāre [4] *plural of* لاره [1]

لاريغ lārídz لاريز lāríz striped

لاري لاري lā́ri-lā́ri scattered, strewn; dispersed

لاري والا lārivālā́ *m.* truck driver, lorry driver

لاړ lāṛ [1] *m.* ☞ لړ

لاړ lāṛ [2] *Eastern vice* ولاړ لاړ نه شه He hasn't left. He didn't go.

لاړ lāṛ *present perfective stem and past of* تلل [1]

لاړل lāṛə́l *Eastern vice* ولاړل

لاړلي lāṛə́le *f. past plural of* تلل [1]

لاړن lāṛə́n *Eastern* ☞ لاړو [2]

لاړو lāṛú [2] *m.* ditherer

لاړو lāṛo [3] *Eastern vice* ولاړو

لاړه lāṛə́ *plural Eastern vice* ولاړل

لاړى lā́ṛaj [1] *m.* rafter, beam

لاړي lā́ṛi [2] *f. plural* saliva لاړي يې وچي شوي His mouth has dried up.

لاړى lāṛj [3] *f.* the heel of a plow shaft

لاړي lā́ṛe [4] *f. plural Eastern vice* ولاړي

لاړى lāṛaj [5] *Eastern conditional form of* تلل [1]

لاړجن lāṛedzhén *m.* **1** ☞ لارو [2] **2** *botany* portulaca

لازم lāzím *Arabic* necessary, needful لازم دئ چه it is لازمه ده چه necessary, one must, one should *Arabic* تاسي ته لازمه ده چه ډاكتر ته ولاړسئ You need to go to a doctor. لازم گڼل to consider necessary, think needful

لازماً lāzímán *Arabic* it is obligatory; it is necessary

لازم الاجرا lāzím-ul-idzhrā́ *Arabic* obligatory in execution دابه لازم د الاجرا وي It is necessary to do this without fail.

لازموالى lāzimválaj *m.* necessity, obligation

لازمول lāzimavél *denominative, transitive* [*past:* لازم يې کړ] to compel, oblige; demand something

لازمه lāzíma [1] *f. singular of* لازم

لازمه lāzimá [2] *Arabic* **1.1** *f. singular of* لازم **1.2** *plural* necessary, needed, appropriate (things) **2** *f.* a necessary thing ☞ لوازم

لازمي lāzimí **1** necessary, needed **2** unavoidable **3** *grammar* intransitive (verbs)

لازمبدل lāzimedél *denominative, intransitive* [*past:* لازم شو] to be obligatory, be necessary; be needed; be required

لازوال lāzavál *Arabic* eternal, unfading, non-transient

لاس lās *m.* **1** hand په لاس from hand to hand; hand in hand, alongside کين لاس hand-to-hand combat **2** side لاس پر لاس جنگ on the left side; on the left **3** *figurative* influence, authority د ته هغه ډېر لاس وورلاندي دئ He has great influence. I am in لاس مي و ورلاندي دئ his power. **4** set, suit (of bedclothes, clothing) لس لاسه دريشي ten suits of clothing, ten suits **5** assistance, help, aid لاس اچول **a** پرخه to take, appropriate, take along هغه د بل چا پر مال لاس to get to پرخه لاس اچول He took the property of another. **b** to work on something, get down to something **c** په ځه لاس اچول meddle in something څما په کارو لاس مه اچوه Don't meddle in my affairs. **d** چاته لاس اچول to fight with someone; be free with one's fists **e** ... د to take liberties with someone څخه لاس کارگرانو د کار څخه لاس to cease, throw up (e.g., work) **a** اخيستل The workers stopped work. ما د چلم څخه لاس واخيست I واخيست knocked off smoking a hookah. **b** to renounce something **c** to leave someone in peace زما څخه لاس واخله Leave me in peace. لاس to stretch out the hand, چاته لاس اوږدول **a** لاس اوږدول to help لاس ناولی ايستل **b** خه ته لاس اوږدول to encroach on something *literal figurative* to dirty one's hand لاس پر خوله اينبودل to keep silent د چا لاس را ايله کبدل، د چا لاس در ايله کبدل، د چا لاس ور ايله کبدل **a** to be untied (of the hands); receive freedom **b** to get out of, get rid of something لاس بر کېدل to be able to do something, be in a position to do something په تکت اخيستلو مو لاس برنشو We weren't able to get a ticket. په يوه کار لاس بندول to be engaged in some kind of work په يوه کار لاس بندېدل to be occupied in some sort of work لاس پربولل to lose a brother **a** to wash the hands **b** د لاس پرېکبدل *figurative* to wash the hands of, withdraw from ... خڅه لاس پربولل

something لاس پوري کول، په ... لاس پوري کول to get down to
something (work) دپه مي لاس تنگ دئ I am in great need.
لاس تپرول، په لاس تپرول، توربدل to receive no thanks for a good turn
a to smooth, run the hand over b *figurative* to
indulge someone c to rob د چا پر سر لاس تپرول to caress, pet
someone د چا لاس چلبدل to regret, grieve لاس پر سر تکول to work,
labor لاس خلاصبدل، په چا لاس ځندل to wave the hand, to beckon
کار ته مي لاس خلاصبدل to reconcile a matter with someone's help
لاس نه دربري I can't wait to get to work. I can't bear not to work.
د دغه مال لاس بر کبدل ☞ لاس رسبدل لاس اخيستل ☞ لاس راټولول
لاس اخيستلو لاس نه رسي He is not in a position to buy these goods.
... ته لاس غځول، لاس غځول، و ... ته لاس غځول a *literal* &
figurative to stretch out a hand to someone b to give alms c to
infringe, trespass (on someone's rights, property, etc.) د ... څخه
لاس تر زني کښېناستل، لاس تر زنه د ... څخه لاس اخيستل لاس کښبل
کښبناستل a to be depressed, be sad b to be idle, sit with empty
hands, be unemployed څه ته لاس کول a لاس کول to get down to
doing something b د چا سره توري ته لاس کول to resort to the sword
figurative to help someone دپر لاس کبئ دئ زما سره يي لاس کول
helped me a lot. c to give a hand! لاس کړه! Give me your hand!
لاس پر سر کول، لاس په سر کول، د...څخه لاس په سر کول، د ... څخه لاس
کول a to reject something b to tear away (from work etc.)
لاس پر سر کبدل a to refuse something b to disturb or divert (from a
matter) يو لاس to run aground; get in a pickle لاس په خوله کبدل
کبدل a to lose one's hands b to be united لاس لرل a to participate
in something b to know (how to do) something; look into
something هغه په طب کښي هم ښه لاس درلود He understands
medicine well. c to have authority, have the strength, have the
influence لوی لاس لرل to have great significance, play a large role
لاس لگبدل، په چا سره لاس لگول to fight with someone لاس لگبدل
to be due from someone, be owing from somebody ديو
شي د چا څخه لاس لندول to deprive someone of something, not
authorize somebody to use something لاس مبنل to regret, grieve
a to لاس نيول، to find (a means, method, etc.) لاس موندل
tie the hands, bother, trouble ستا لاس چا نيولئ دئ؟ Who is
troubling you? b د چا څخه پر ... لاس نيول to cover with the hand c
figurative to leave someone in peace! لاس ما نه ونيسه!
Leave me in peace! د چا لاس نيول a to become someone's success
b to be a murid (i.e., a postulant in a dervish order) لاس پر خوله
لاس پر غوږو نيول، لاس پر خوله ايښوول ☞ نيول to close the eyes to
چا ته لاس ورکول a لاس ورکول something; not interfere in any way
to give someone one's hand b د ... سره لاس ورکول to stretch out
the hand (in help etc.) c د ... سره لاس ورکول to unite; join (forces)
د چا سره د دوستي لاس ورکول to stretch out the hand of friendship to
someone, make friends with someone ښه شي ته لاس
لاس را ورته کول to set out to do something, undertake something
په ... لاس ورل، لاس ور ورل، لاس در ورل to touch, concern لاس ورل
لاس پربول ☞ لاس وينځل to obtain something or someone ورل،
لاس تري ووينځه *Eastern* Don't waste your time on him. Don't pay

any attention to him. a لاس وهل، لاس پکنبي وهل to touch b to put
in order په خپل سر باندي لاس وهل to get one's head together, get
one's thinking straight c to interfere, intervene in something په
کورنيو چارو کښبي لاس وهل to intervene in internal affairs d to seize
something; infringe upon something, trespass on something e to
steal لاسونه په ږيره راکښنل a to stroke the beard b *figurative* to
promise لاسونه سره ورکول to exchange handshakes لاس تر لاسه تلل
to walk hand in hand لاس لاس کول to cut, chop into pieces,
dismember لاس پر لاس کبدل to transfer from hand to hand لاس
a to be deprived of one's share b to end up empty- ناولی وتل
handed پر لاس اوبه تپرول، پر لاس اوبه را تپرول، پر لاس اوبه در تپرول، پر
پر لاس اوبه ور تپرول to invite someone; entertain someone as a guest
په لاس کښبي اخيستل، په لاس کښبي to nurse, care for a child لاس لويول
خپله عهده يي په لاس a to take in hand b to begin, commence لاس
په لاس کښبي واخيسته He undertook the fulfillment of his obligation.
راتلل a to fall into the hands; be gotten, be obtained b to arrive (of
information, documents etc.) په لاس خلاصبدل to deal with a matter
with someone's help د چا په لاس کول په لاس خلاصبدل to put on, don (gloves)
د چا تر لاس لاندي لپرل to send with someone (e.g., letters, money)
to be subordinate to someone لاس ته راتلل a to come, arrive
(of news, information, etc.) b to (try to) get لاس ته، لاس ته راورل
a to gather, collect, راوستل to get, receive تر لاسه کول
compile b to seize c to receive (e.g., pay) د بل و لاس ته کتل to
expect help of others د لاسه ايستل، له لاسه ايستل a to lose
something b to stop, quit (e.g., work) د خپله لاسه ببربدل to fear to
make a mess of something (in the heat of the moment) د چا د لاسه
خلاصول to liberate from someone's power or authority, from
someone's influence د خپله لاسه رسبدل to punish oneself د لاسه کول
a to take, seize قلم يي راڅخه د لاسه کئ He took my pen. b to get,
obtain کړه د to succeed; be carried out د لاسه کبدل، د چا د لاسه کبدل
a to disappear, له د لاسه وتل، د لاسه وتل If I am able to. لاسه مي کبري
vanish b to be freed from someone's influence له لاسه ورکول to
lose something; be deprived of something اول لاس in the first
instance, for the first time *idiom* د لاس آله، د چا د لاس آله a tool in
someone's hand, a pawn (or puppet) in someone's hand *idiom* د
لاس گټه revenue for work performed د نبي لاس گنډ the innocent
party خلاص لاس freedom of action که په پور وي که په لاس on
credit or for cash له لاس کښبي مي څه نشته *Eastern* I am penniless. له
دیخ له لاسه، د لاسه on account of, because of, for the reason that
لاسه، دیخ د لاسه because of the cold ستا د لاسه because of you,
because of your fault دوه لاسه دوه پښي *Eastern* a all by oneself b
poor as a church mouse لاس په لستوني دئ، کلی دغه دئ Here is the
village; give me your hand. د چا سره لاس او گربوان کبدل to wrestle,
fight with someone پر لاسو او پښو پربتول، پر لاسو او پښو را پربتول، پر
لاسو او پښو در پربتول، پر لاسو او پښو ور پربتول to beseech on the knees,
ask for forgiveness; implore دا کار د چا د لاسه پوره نه دئ This is too
much for anyone (to do) *proverb* لاس چه مات شي، غاړي ته راشي
When in distress one always thinks of one's friends. لاسونه غورځول
to squander money په پراخ لاس ژوند کول to live in grand style

لاس اړی lāsáṛaj needy, in want

لاس انگی lāsangə́j *f.* throwing a stone from palm to palm (as a kind of game)

لاس باړه lāsbaṛá *f.* payment for work

لاس بری lāsbáraj 1 victorious, conquering 2 *m.* conqueror

لاس پراخی lāsprákhaj generous, having an open nature

لاس پرانیستی lāspranístaj gracious, well-inclined

لاس پړک lāspṛák *m.* hand-clapping, applause

لاسپۀلاس lāspə́lās لاس په لاس lāspə́lās 1 from hand to hand 2 for cash 3 without delay, at once

لاس پلی lāspaláj *m.* trifle (money)

لاس پوری کول lāsporikavə́l *m. plural* beginning, initiation, commencement

لاس پیلی lāspelé *f. plural* mittens, gloves

لاس تړلی lāstaṛə́laj with folded hands *idiom* لاس تړلی دریدل to stand with clasped hands; stand in an obedient attitude

لاس تنگه lāstánga لاس تنگی lāstángaj needy *a* to لاس تنگه کیدل be in need *b* to suffer a loss [1]

لاس تنگی lāstangí *f.* 1 need, want 2 impecuniousness [2]

لاستور lāstavár لاستورگی lāstavə́rgaj having a handle, hilted, hasped

لاستوره lāstavóra *f. dialect* ladle, dipper

لاسته lāstá *f.* direction, side, quarter, region [1]

لاسته lásta *vice* لاس ته *☞* لاس [2]

لاستی lástaj *m.* 1 handle, hasp, hilt د یوم لاستی handle of a spade 2 bouquet د گلو لاستی a bouquet of flowers 3 *electrical engineering* knife switch د سویچ لاستی knife switch

لاستره lāstéra *f.* smoothing, pressing لاس تبره کول to smooth, press, run the hand over

لاستیک lāstík *m.* rubber

لاسخه láskha *f.* ownership, possession

لاس روغبړ lāsroghbáṛ *m.* handshake

لاس سره lāssrə́ *m. plural* 1 use, advantage 2 profit; revenue; receipts 3 payment for work 4 decoration of the hands with henna (prior to a wedding)

لاس کتوی lāskatóvaj لاس کوڅی lāskútsaj لاس کوزی lāskúzaj subordinate, dependent

لاس کونی lāskvunáj *m.* armlet, oversleeve

لاس گته lāsgáṭa *f.* use, advantage

لاس گرزی lāsgərzáj 1 sale by peddling, peddling 2 by peddling

لاس گری lāsgə́raj *m.* assistant, helper

لاس گیر lāsgír *m.* captive

لاس لاندی lāslándaj subject to; dependent, subordinate لاس لاندی خلق subordinates

لاس لاندیوالی lāslāndiváľaj *m.* 1 abasement 2 subjugation

لاس لونی lāslvúnaj *m.* washbasin, washstand, basin (for washing the hands)

لاس لیک lāslík *m.* signature لاس لیک کول *compound verb* ☞ لاس لیک کیدل لاسلیکول *compound verb* to be signed

لاسلیکول lāslikavə́l لاسلیکول *denominative* [past: لیک یې کړ] to sign, affix a signature

لاسلیکیده lāslikedə́ *m. plural* د تړون لاسلیکیده the signing of a treaty

لاس ماغو lāsmāghú *m.* glove, mitten, gauntlet

لاس مبنل lāsmukhə́l *m. plural* condolence, regret; expression of condolence, regret

لاس مندون lāsmaṇḍún *m.* interference

لاس موښی lāsmúkhaj *m.* ☞ لاس وچ

لاس نجت lāsndzhə́t *m.* document

لاس نیولی lās nivə́laj 1 caught 2 with bound hands لاس نیولی راوستل to deliver someone by force

لاس نیونه lāsnivə́na *f.* turning to for advice, help, or cooperation هر چا به تری لاس نیونه کوله Everyone turned to him for advice.

لاس نیوه lāsnivə́ *m. plural* 1 support, help, assistance 2 comfort, consolation

لاس نیوی lāsnívaj *m.* 1 IOU, receipt for debt 2 obedience to someone; motion to something د پیر لاس نیوی کول recognition of a pir (i.e., teacher) by a murid (i.e., dervish-postulant) 3 help, support بی وزلو لاس نیوی assistance to the needy

لاس و پښی lāsupkhé *f. plural* لاس و پښی تکول *a* to worry, be troubled *b* to hurry لاس و پښی غورځول *a* to suffer *b* to suffer from impatience; burn with the desire (to); be impatient (to) لاس و پښی ورکول، *a* to bustle, fuss *b* to be tormented، لاس و پښی سره ورکول *a* to grow weak; grow enervated, lose strength *b* to be tormented لاس وپښی وهل، د یوه کار دپاره لاس وپښی to try, strive د لاس و پښو کار کول to be engaged in physical labor *idiom* لاس و پښی پرته ده She is lying stretched out

لاسوچ lāsvúch *m.* لاس وچونی lāsvuchavənáj *m.* 1 kerchief 2 napkin; towel

لاس ورکړه lāsvárkṛa *f.* 1 handshake 2 an expression of obedience or submission

لاس وزری lāsvzáraj *m.* assistant, helper

لاس ولونی lāsvlúnaj *m.* ☞ لاس لونی

لاسوند lāswánd *m. computer science* document

لاسوندی lāsvandáj *m.* document, receipt [1]

لاسوندی lāsvandáj *m.* لاس وندی lāsvandáj *m.* bead bracelet [2]

لاس وهل lāsvahə́l *m. plural* لاس وهنه lāsvahə́na *f.* 1 interference, meddling 2 trespassing, infringement 3 robbery

لاس وهونکی lās vahúnkaj *m.* thief

لاسه lása *oblique of* لاس

لاسي lāsí 1 *adjective* manual, hand لاسي بم hand grenade لاسي صنایع handbag 2 *adjective* handicraft کڅوړه، لاسي جب handicraft industry 3 counterfeit [1]

لاسي lāsí *computer science* hand-held [2]

لاسي کمپیوټر lāsi kampjūṭə́r *m. computer science* notebook computer

لاس یوی lāsjaváj *m.* 1 unification 2 unity; agreement

لاش lāsh *m.* corpse, dead body

لاشعور lāshu'úr *Arabic* 1 unconscious 2 slow-witted

لاشعري lāshu'urí 1 subconscious 2 unconscious 3 slow-witted

لاشعوريت lāshu'uriját m. Arabic 1 the subconscious, non-realization 2 unconscious 3 slow-wittedness

لاشوړه lāshoṛá f. Cordia dichotoma (a kind of plant)

لاشه lắsha f. ☞ لشكه

لاښ ¹ lāḵ̣ı m. 1 steep precipice; sheer cliff 2 fissure or crevasse in a mountain

لاښ ² lāḵ̣h m. 1 ☞ لاښ 2 garden, orchard, or melon field in which the fruit has been picked

لاښ كول compound verb ☞ لاښ كبدل لانبول compound verb ☞ لانبدل

لانبول lāḵ̣havəl denominative, transitive [past: لاښ يې كؚ] to gather, pick (fruit)

لاښه lāḵ̣hə́ still better, better still

لاښي lắḵ̣hi f. plural fruit which remains unpicked after the harvest

لانبدل lāḵ̣hedə́l denominative, intransitive [past: لاښ شو] to be picked, be gathered (of fruit)

لاعلاج lā'ilā́dzh Arabic incurable

لا علمي lā'ilmí f. regional ignorance

لاغرضه lāgharazá disinterested, unselfish

لاغو lāghú m. skillet for heating butter, cooking oil

لاغورنيكه lāghvurnikə́ m. great-great-grandfather

لافاني lāfāní Arabic imperishable, eternal

لافوک lāfúk m. braggart, boaster; bigmouth

لافه lắfa f. usually plural لافي lắfi bragging, boastfulness لافي وهل to boast, brag

لاقيد lāḵ̣ájd Arabic 1 apathetic, depressed; impassive 2 negligent, careless

لاک lāk m. plural 1 varnish, lacquer 2 sealing wax لاک كول compound verb to be sealed up with sealing wax

لاكن lākín Arabic contrastive conjunction however, but, on the other hand زه ځم لاكن دی نه ځي I am going, but he isn't.

لاكولكره lākúlakáṛa f. ring finger, third finger

لاكي lākí 1 varnished, lacquered 2 the color of sealing wax; dark red

لاگ lāg m. credit transaction; a deal made with a tradesman on credit

لاگوس lắgós m. Lagos

لاگي ¹ lāgí m. dependable contractor, reliable contractor

لاگي ² lāgí f. retail trade

لال lāl 1 m. .1 ruby; Badakhshan garnet پيازي لال amethyst 1.2 a variety of grape 1.3 the color red 1.4 kind of bird 1.5 proper name Lal 2 crimson

لالا lālā́ m. 1 form of address for an older brother 2 form of address used by children to adults 3 form of address to an unknown man

لالا ناوي lālā́ nắve f. form of address for the wife of an older brother

لالاورمه ورځ lắlāvəṛma vradz f. the day before yesterday, day before

لالپوړه lālpuṛá f. Lalpura (town in the country of the Momands)

لالټين lālṭén m. searchlight دستي لالټين flashlight

لالج lālə́dzh m. لالچ lālə́ch m. noise, uproar

لاره lālará regional ☞ راته ¹

لالک lālə́k m. لالكو lāləkó diminutive of لال

لالگی lālgáj m. necklace of very small beads

لالن lālán 1 dear, favorite 2 m. lover, sweetheart

لالو lāló f. dear, darling

لاله ¹ lālá f. 1 tulip 2 poppy

لاله ² lála Eastern ☞ راته ¹

لالهاند lāləhānd لالهانده lāləhānda dismayed; sad, upset, (emotionally) pained

لالهاندول lāləhā́ndavə́l denominative, transitive [past: لالهاند يې كؚ] to sadden, distress, cause pain, pain

لالهاندي lāləhāndí f. sadness, distress, pain

لالهاندبدل lāləhāndedə́l denominative, intransitive [past: لالهاند شو] to be distressed, be saddened, be strongly pained

لاله رخ lālarúkh poetry pink-cheeked

لاله زار lālazár m. tulip bed

لاله سر lālasár m. red-headed pochard (a kind of wild duck)

لاله سری lālasráj m. Falco chicquera (a raptorial bird)

لالی lālā́j 1 dear, beloved; darling 2.1 sweetheart, lover 2.2 pet name for a tiny child 2.3 proper name Lalai

لام ¹ lām m. the name of the letter ل

لام ² lām m. regional 1 march 2 file, rank, row لام ترل to be drawn up in battle order

لاما lāmā́ m. religion Lama

لامب lāmb present stem of لمبل

لامبات lāmbā́t m. 1 refined sugar 2 fruit drop (candy)

لامباتي lāmbātí adjective sugar, sugared

لامبرده lāmburdá above-mentioned, aforesaid

لامبل lāmbə́l transitive ☞ لمبل

لامبنه lāmbə́na f. swimming

لامبو lāmbó f. [plural: لامبووي lāmbóvi] 1 swimming 2 bathing لامبو وهل a to swim b to bathe

لامبوزن lāmbozə́n 1 m. swimmer 2 floating, buoyant

لامبوزنه lāmbozə́na f. swimmer (female)

لامپه lāmpá f. lamp

لامحاله lāmahālá Arabic 1 inevitable, without fail; absolutely, indubitably 2 at least

لامحدود lāmadúd Arabic unlimited, unbounded په لامحدود ډول unboundedly, limitlessly

لامده lāmdə́ masculine plural of لوند

لامذهبي lāmazhabí f. atheism

لامزروع lāmazrú' Arabic uncultivated, untilled مخكي لامزروع uncultivated lands

لامسه lāmsá f. Arabic touch

لامكان lāmakán Arabic 1 without domicile, homeless 2 ubiquitous

لاكلام lāmkalám m. a bit of a word, a little word د چا سره لاكلام كول to have a little word with someone

لامله lāmála for the reason that ..., because ته د څه لامله دا کار کوي؟ Why are you acting so?

لاممکن lāmumkín *Arabic* impossible; nonexistent

لانبو lāmbó *f.* ☞ لامبو

لانبوزن lāmbozə́n *m.* ☞ لامبوزن

لانبوزنه lāmbozə́na *f.* ☞ لامبوزنه

لانجه lāndzhá *f.* 1 care, concern; worry د گمرک لانجي پريکول to undergo the Customs formalities 2 quarrel, friction, disagreement; dissent, discord

لانجه مار lāndzhmár *m.* 1 unpleasant customer 2 peevish person

لاند lā́nde *obsolete* ☞ لاندي²

لاندستون lāndistún *m.* bed; straw mattress, mattress; bedding

لاندنى lāndináj 1 lower 2 following, standing below په لاندني ډول lāndiní a as indicated below b in the following manner

لانده lāndə́ *masculine plural of* لوند

لاندى lā́ndaj¹ *m.* dried meat د لاندي غوښي dried meat, jerky

لاندى lā́ndi lā́nde² *Eastern* 1 down, downward; below 2 *suffix* under له پنبو لاندي *Eastern* underfoot تر ميز لاندي under the table لاندي lower floor د تأثر لاندي under the impression 3.1 په لاندي کرښو کښي the lower floor منزل 3.2 the following in the following lines, verses 3.3 subordinate 3.4 oppressed, degraded هغه سړى خوار دئ او لاندي دئ He is poor and oppressed. خوک لاندي د چا حق لاندي کول to overcome; subordinate; subdue b to seize, conquer, occupy c to cover, flood (with water, etc.) اوبو ډېره to trample or flout someone's rights مځکه لاندي کړه The water flooded a large area. d to shove or place under something e *literal & figurative* to catch up with someone لاندي کېدل a to be subordinate, be subdued b to fall under something; find oneself under something c to sink (into water) تر ... لاندي نيول، تر to overthrow something or someone خه تر تعليم لاندي نيول to teach تبصري لاندي نيول to comment upon شي له لاندي ايستل to pull out, get out, draw out from under something

لاندي باندي lā́ndi-bā́ndi 1.1 up and down 1.2 upwards and downwards 1.3 upside down, topsy-turvy 2 overturned لاندي باندي کول to overturn کاغذونه لاندي باندي کول to turn or leaf through documents چا ته لاندي باندي کتل to look over from head to foot; inspect *idiom* خه خبره سره لاندي باندي شوه A quarrel broke out.

لاندده lāndedə́ *m. plural* wetting; dampening; moistening

لاندستون lāndistún *m.* ☞ لاندي ستون

لاندينى lāndináj lower, bottom مخ lining

لاندو lāndú *m.* instant, moment

لاندپس lāndȩ́s *m.* 1 cassia, *Cassia fistula* 2 melon of elongated shape

لانگه lā́nga *f.* 1 kind of rope netting for a bed 2 rope part of a cot

لانه lā́na *f.* saltwort, *Salsola kali*

لانى lā́ṇaj *m.* 1 لارى¹ 2 jet, spurt, stream

لاوا lāvā́ *f.* lava (volcanic)

لاوارث lāvārís *Arabic legal* escheated (reverted to the state because of lack of heirs, etc.)

لاوالېتا lāvaletā *f.* La-Valletta (city)

لاورمه شپه lāvȩ́rma shpa *f.* the day before yesterday

لاورمه ورځ lāvȩ́rma vradz *f.* three days ago

لاورېز lāvríz *m.* kind of stitching and embroidery

لاوس lāós *m.* Laos ☞ لاهوس

لاونده lāundə́ ☞ لاوند

لاوند lāvə́ṇḍ *m.* لاون lāvúṇ *m.* lāvə́ṇ *m.* 1 thick soup (of buttermilk, flour, and onions) 2 meat relish made of buttermilk

لاوه lāvá *f.* ☞ لاوا

لاهم lāhəm still

لاهو lāhú 1 floating, sailing 2 plunged (into water, etc.) a لاهو کول to launch into water, set afloat (timber, etc.) b to plunge, dip (into water, etc.) c to wash away; erode (soil) a لاهو کېدل to sail; sail forth; set sail b په ماکو لاهو کېدل to be plunged (into water, etc.) c to be eroded, washed away (soil) d to give over (to thought) د فکر په درياب لاهو کول to compel to think things over

لاهوت lāhút *m. Arabic* 1 divinity, divine nature 2 theology, theological science

لاهوتي lāhutí divine *religion* په لاهوتي مقام fallen asleep in the Lord

لاهور lāhór *m.* Lahore

لاهوس lāhós *m.* Laos

لهه lā́ha *f.* ☞ لهه¹

لاهه lāhé² *f.* Gaaga (city)

لاى lāj¹ *m.* tuck, pleat, fold; layer, sheet

لاى lāj² *m.* 1 silt, mud 2 sediment, deposition

لايبېريا lājbirijā *f.* Liberia

لايتجزا lājatadzhazzā́ لايتجزي lājatadzhazzí *Arabic* indivisible; inseparable لايتجزا جز inseparable, integral part

لايتناهي lājatanāhí *Arabic* infinite, endless, boundless د آسمان لايتناهي فضا the fathomless blue of the sky

لا ئحه lāihá *f.* لايحه lajihá *f. Arabic f.* [*plural:* لايحي lāihé *Arabic m. plural:* لوايح lavāíh] plan; draft law; proposed law

لايدرک lājudrák *Arabic* incomparable, inscrutable

لايزار lājzā́r *m.* swamp, bog

لايزال lājazál *Arabic* eternal, immortal

لايسنس lāisáns *m.* license, authorization

لايعني lāj'aní *Arabic* scatterbrained وينا لايعني nonsense, drivel

لايق lājík لائق lāík *Arabic* 1 worthy, deserving of something د انعام لايق to deserve a reward 2 meriting something د نشان سره لايق worthy of a medal 3 befitting, fit هغه د دي کار لايق نه دئ He is not fit (suited) for this work.

لايقوالى lājiķvā́laj *m.* لايقي lāíķí *f.* ☞ لياقت

لايموت lājamút *Arabic* 1 sufficient for nourishment 2 immortal

لاين lājn *m.* ☞ لين

لاينحل lājanhál lājanháll *Arabic* 1 insoluble, unresolved 2 undecomposable; insoluble

لاينفک lājanfák lājanfákk *Arabic* inseperable, unbreakably bound, linked, bonded

لاينقطع lājanḳatí' *Arabic* uninterrupted, continuous; unceasing

لب ¹ lab *m.* [*plural:* لبونه labúna *Western plural:* لبان labā́n] **1** lip; lips; mouth **2** speech **3** shore لب دریا lab-i ... Labi-darya (the name of an embankment in Kabul) *idiom* لبونه پری کول to not regret something د لبه راتلل all leave, exeunt omnes د لبه تلل all enter; enter all

لب ² lubb *m. Arabic* **1** hearth **2** core, pith, heart **3** the heart of the matter **4** the choice or best part of something

لباب lubā́b *m. Arabic* **1** core, pith, heart **2** the choice or best part of something

لباس libā́s *m. Arabic* [*plural:* البسه albisá] **1** clothing ملي لباس national costume په بل لباس changed (clothing) **2** pretense *idiom* د لباس ژبه flattery, adulation

لباسي libāsí **1.1** pretended, false; hypocritical لباسي خلق hypocrites **1.2** disguised, fake **2** *m.* toady, flatterer; liar, hypocrite

لبډر ləbaḍár fat and clumsy, deformed

لبرالسم liberālísm *m.* ☞ لیبرلسم

لبریزه labréza full to the brim لبریزه پیاله a full cup

لبړه lábṛa *f. dialect* worry; complication څه لبړه پیښه شوی ده Some complication developed.

لبغری ləbaghə́raj **1** poor, destitude **2** penniless

لبلبو lablabú *m.* beet د قند لبلبو sugar beet

لبنان lubnā́n *m.* Lebanon

لبناني lubnāni lubnānáj **1** Lebanese **2** *m.* Lebanese (person)

لبنیات labanijā́t *m. Arabic plural* milk products, dairy products د لبنیاتو صنعت the dairy industry د لبنیات فارم dairy farm

لبوزی labúzaj *m.* **1** mountain ledge; peak **2** small mountain with a sharp summit

لبۍ ləbáj *m.* kind of bird trap

لبیک labbájk *Arabic* I obey! At your service!

لپاره ləpā́ra *suffix* ☞ د پاره

لپانډی ləpā́nḍaj *m.* لپانکي ləpā́nkaj *m.* round flat stone (used in games)

لب خټ laptsə́ṭ fruitful (of land); productive

لپړ ¹ lapáṛ *m.* **1** pitch-and-toss (the game) **2** flat pebble used in pitch-and-toss **3** drawing to determine first pitch in the game **4** shivering لپړ وهل to shiver, shake (e.g., from cold)

لپړ ² lapə́ṛ *tautological with* لغ *and* لغړ

لپړک ləpəṛák *m.* ☞ لپړ ¹ **4**

لپړل lapṛál laparə́l *transitive* [*past:* و یې لپړل] to draw lots for first turn at a game

لپړو lapṛú boastful, garrulous

لپړی ¹ lapṛáj *m.* slush; mud, silt

لپړی ² lapṛí **1** *present tense of* لپړل **2** Let's draw lots! (to see who is first to take a turn in a game)

لپکی ¹ lapakáj *m. diminutive of* لپه

لپکی ² lapakə́j *f.* wooden scoop (measure used by a miller)

لپوس lapús impoverished

لپه lápa *f.* **1** handful اوبه په لپه کښي اخیستل to take up water in cupped hands **2** palm, open hand لپه په مخ را تبرول to bring the hand to the face **3** *figurative* small group, bunch, handful

لپۍ ləpáj *m.* pound

لپیت lapit *m.* whey (remaining after the formation of cheese)

لتاړ latā́ṛ **1** subject to, exposed to something; staggered, startled by something په غم لتاړ staggered by grief; sorrowful پر مشکلاتو باندي لتاړ وو They ran into difficulties. **2** destroyed, exterminated **3** spoiled **4** ruined **5** overwhelmed; crushed; trampled **6** sluggish, awkward, clumsy

لتاړول latāṛavál *denominative, transitive* [*past:* لتاړ یې کړ] **1** to subject to something, expose to something; surprise by something, stagger by something په غم لتاړول to cause to fall into grief **2** to destroy, exterminate **3** to spoil د چا ژوند لتاړول to poison someone's life **4** to ruin **5** to crush, trample

لتاړیدل latāṛedál *denominative, intransitive* [*past:* لتاړ شو] **1** to be subjected to something, be exposed to something; be staggered by something, be surprised by something **2** to be destroyed, be exterminated **3** to be spoiled **4** to be ruined **5** to perish, expire لتاړ شه! May the devil take you! Drop dead! **6** to be trampled, be trodden, be crushed

لت پت latpát soiled, besmirched, polluted, splashed لت پت کول **a** to defile **b** to soil, dirty لت پت کیدل **a** to be defiled **b** to be soiled, be dirtied

لتموس litmús *m.* litmus

لتوانیا litvānijā́ *f.* Lithuania

لتوانیائي litvānijā́jí **1** Lithuanian لتوانیائي ژبه the Lithuanian language **2** *m.* Lithuanian (person)

لتویا latvijā́ *f.* Latvia

لتویائي latvijā́jí **1** *adjective* Latvian **2** *m.* Latvian (person)

لته ¹ láta *f.* region, disrict; zone; country

لته ² latá *f.* kicking, a kick لته وهل to kick, strike with the foot لتي تکول to flounder about په لته وهل **a** to thrust back with the foot **b** to reject, spurn something

لته بند latabánd *m.* Lataband (the name of a number of mountain passes and settlements)

لټ ¹ laṭ *m.* **1** axis, axle; axle of a Persian waterwheel **2** fish weir **3** bolt (of a rifle)

لټ ² laṭ **1** lazy; sluggish, apathetic **2** *m.* a lazybones

لټا laṭā́ *f.* searches, investigations

لټاړول laṭāṛavál *transitive* ☞ لتاړول

لټاړیدل laṭāṛedál *intransitive* ☞ لتاړیدل

لټاني laṭā́ni *plural of* لته ⁴

لټ پت ¹ laṭpát ☞ لت پت

لټ پت ² laṭpát لټ پت کول to search out, seek diligently لټ پت کیدل to be sought; conduct diligently (of searches, investigations)

لټپتۍ laṭpaṭáj *f.* kind of dove

لټ پر لټ laṭpərláṭ *Eastern* لټ په لټ laṭpəláṭ from side to side لټ پر
لټ پر لټ اوښتل، لټ پر لټ کېدل to turn from side to side; twist and turn (in
bed); sleep fitfully لټ پر لټ کول a to seek, search for b to keep
turning about

لټاپیر laṭapér *m.* 1 sacks-on-the-mill (children's game) 2 piling up 3
battle, engagement 4 attack پر دښمنانو لټاپیر جوړول to defeat,
exterminate the enemy لټاپیر پر چا جوړول to attack someone

لټتوب laṭṭób *m.* لټتیا laṭṭjá *f.* laziness

لټرى laṭaráj *f.* French bean

لټکه¹ laṭə́ka *f.* ☞ لندۍ³

لټکه² laṭə́ka *f.* blunt saber

لټکه³ laṭká *f.* trigger (of a rifle)

لټل laṭə́l *transitive* [*past:* و يې لاته] 1 to jump, arise 2 to leap up

لټند laṭə́nd 1 ransacking 2 uneasy, suspicious

لټوالى laṭvắlaj *m.* ☞ لټتوب

لټول¹ laṭavə́l [*past:* و يې لتاوه] 1 *transitive* .1 to seek, search for 1.2
to search around; look around; rummage 1.3 to check, investigate
1.4 to trouble, alarm 1.5 to inspect, make an inspection; check
out 2 *m. plural* ☞ لټون

لټول² laṭavə́l *denominative, transitive* [*past:* لټ يې کړ] to render
lazy, render sluggish, render apathetic

لټون laṭún *m.* لټونه laṭavə́na *f.* 1 searches, investigations 2
interrogations لټون کول a to seek and search b to interrogate 3
investigation 4 inspection, inspecting, check

لټونگر laṭūṅgár *m.* لټوونی laṭavúnaj *computer science* browser

لټونکى laṭavúnkaj 1 *present participle of* لټول¹ 2 inquisitive (of
mind)

لټه¹ láṭa *f.* 1 effort, endeavor 2 aspiration, desire 3 searches,
investigations لټه کول to search, investigate

لټه² laṭá *f.* bleached calico

لټه³ laṭá *f.* depression; psychic experience

لټه⁴ láṭa 1 *feminine singular of* لټ² 1 2 *f.* lazy woman

لټاپیر laṭapér *m.* ☞ لټاپیر

لټي láṭi *feminine plural of* لټه¹,⁴

لټیا laṭjá *f.* laziness

لټیدل¹ laṭedə́l *intransitive* [*past:* و لټېده] 1 to stand up, arise 2 to
be scared (e.g., of wasps)

لټیدل² laṭedə́l *denominative, intransitive* [*past:* لټ شو] to grow
lazy, become sunk in sloth

لټیره laṭerə́ 1 idle, loafing لټ او لټېره بنیادم idler, loafer 2 *m.* .1
tramp, hobo 2.2 idler, loafer

لټینگر laṭiṅgə́r *m.* grasshopper

لج ladzh *m.* لجاج ladzhắdzh *m. Arabic* stubbornness, obstinacy د
لج خره کول mulish obstinacy لج کول to be stubborn, be obstinate

لچ ləch *m. medicine* ophthalmia

لچر lachár light-minded, frivolous, scatterbrained

لچرتوب lachartób *m.* لچرتیا lachartjá *f.* light-mindedness, frivolity

لچرکی lachárkaj 1 stubborn, obstinate 2 light-minded, frivolous 3
cheeky, bold

لچري lacharí *f.* 1 stubborness, obstinacy 2 light-mindedness,
frivolity 3 cheek, nerviness 4 angry mood or nature

لچک lachák *m.* black kerchief (the ends of which are used by
women to cover the face)

لچک دار lachakdắr wearing a kerchief (of a woman)

لچن ləchə́n having sore eyes

لځانه lədzána *vice* ☞ ځان له ځانه

لخ ləts 1 naked, nude; bare لخ پیخ، لخ لپړ completely naked 2 open,
uncovered 3 impoverished, ruined 4 *figurative* clear, apparent,
evident

لخساوو lətsāvú discovering, seeking out, ascertaining

لخ پخ ləts-pə́ts ☞ لخ لپړ

لختوب lətstób *m.* لختیا lətstjá *f.* nakedness; nudity, bareness

لخ سر lətssár with bare head, with uncovered head, bareheaded

لخ لپړ ləts-lapə́ṛ لخ لغړ ləts-laghə́r 1 completely naked, stark naked
2 bare naked

لخ والى lətsvắlaj *m.* nakedness, bareness, nudity

لخول lətsavə́l [*past:* لخ يې کړ] *denominative, transitive* 1 to bare,
uncover; strip naked توري يې لخي کړي They bared their swords. 2
to open, open wide 3 *figurative* to clarify, explain 4 to rob

لخه lə́tsa *feminine singular of* لخ 1

لخیدل lətsedə́l *denominative, intransitive* [*past:* لخ شو] 1 to be
denuded, be bared; strip to the skin 2 to be opened, be opened
wide 3 *figurative* to be clarified, be explained 4 to be robbed

لخیدنه lətsedə́na *f.* لخیده lətsedə́ *m. plural* 1 denudation, baring;
stripping bare 2 opening, opening wide 3 explanation,
clarification 4 robbing

لحاظ lihắz *m. Arabic* 1 point of view, viewpoint د لوی والي په لحاظ
in magnitude, in scope 2 attention ډېر لحاظ کول د ... to pay great
attention to someone or something د يوه شي لحاظ نه کول to ignore,
not allow for; pay no attention to something 3 relation په سياسي
لحاظ in a political relation په دي لحاظ in this regard په خصوصي
لحاظ in particular په عمومي لحاظ on the whole a د څه په لحاظ
with the purpose of ... b with a view to ...

لحد láhd *m.* لحد láhəd *m. Arabic* [*plural:* لحدونه lahdúna *Arabic
plural:* لحود luhúd *plural:* الحاد alhắd] 1 grave 2 niche in the
side of a grave into which the body is placed

لحظه lahzá *f. Arabic* 1 glance, look 2 moment, instant

لحن láhn *m.* لحن láhan *m. Arabic* [*plural:* لحنونه lahanúna *Arabic
plural:* الحان alhắn] 1 tone (of speech, utterance); intonation د نياز
لحنونه جگول to move by entreaty, entreat 2 tune; melody, song,
singing

لحود luhúd *masculine plural Arabic of* لحد

لحيم laím *m.* لحيم lahím *m. Arabic technology* soldered joint, soldering

لخت افزار lákhtafzắr *m. computer science* firmware

لخر lakhə́r *m.* half pound

لوخره lukhára f. ☞ لوخړه

لخک ləkhák m. peg, pin (of a door)

لخکي ləkhakí sparse (of plant shoots)

لخلخه lakhlakhá f. aromatic ointment

لوخه lúkha f. ☞ لوخه

لد ¹ ləd m. cattle dung mixed with mud

لد ² lad m. 1 netting (for putting a load on a camel) 2 hem

لدړه ladə́ṛa f. 1 load, pile 2 great quantity, amount

لدغه ləvdágha vice لدغه کبله، لدغه جهته له دغه because, for this reason لدغه قسمه شيان such things

لدي ləvdé vice لدي سببه له دي for this reason, because of this

لډ laḍ m. 1 load 2 net (for transporting hay, straw)

لډامی ləḍámaj m. silk kerchief (used to cover the face of a newborn child)

لدړ ladə́r m. 1 vagrant, tramp 2 lazybones, idler, loafer 3 old clothes 4 carpet dealer

لډو ¹ laḍḍú m. regional kind of candy

لډو ² laḍú m. [plural: لډوان laduán] dung (of donkeys, horses)

لډه láḍa f. bundle of straw or hay

لذا lizá Arabic because, for this reason

لذت lazzát m. Arabic 1 enjoyment, pleasure 2 pleasant taste

لذيذ lazíz Arabic pleasant; tasty, appetizing

لر lar m. 1.1 descent (from a mountain), incline 1.2 failure, defeat 2.1 lower, low-lying, living in the canyon or valley لر پښتون Pushtuns living in India and Pakistan 2.2 conquered, subdued

لربر larbár 1 up and down 2 overturned, upset لربر کول to overturn, upset لربر کېدل a to be overturned, be upset b figurative to be disturbed

لرز larz m. shivering, chill; shudder

لرزان larzán m. shivering, shaking; shuddering (because of something)

لرزی larzáj m. cuffs or sleeve coverings (leather or cloth, used in the haying season)

لرشين larshín m. fecal matter (in an animal's gut)

لرغن largə́n 1 uneasy 2 unable to sleep; suffering from insomnia

لرغون larghún m. 1 olden times; anitiquity 2 formerly, earlier, before

لرغونپېژندنه larghunpezhandə́na f. archaeology

لرغون پېژندونکی larghún pezhandúnkaj m. archaeologist

لرغونتوب larghuntób m. ☞ لرغونوالی

لرغونتون larghuntún m. neologism archaeology

لرغونوالی larghunvãlaj m. 1 antiquity, olden times 2 olden days, the old days

لرغونی larghúnaj 1.1 former, preceding 1.2 pristine, past, very ancient, olden لرغونی پایتخت the ancient capital 2 m. ancestor

لرګبنا largbaná f. of لرګبنه

لرګبه largbá m. [plural: لرګبانه largbānə́] 1 wood-cutter 2 firewood dealer

لرګی ¹ largáj m. 1 staff, cane د لاس لرګی walking stick 2 wood, timber; construction lumber د ودانی لرګی largí construction timber په لرګیو پوښل، په لرګیو باندي پوښل wooden house د لرګیو کور to sheathe with planking د لرګیو جوړولو صنعت the woodworking industry 3 log, billet 4 plural largí firewood

لرګی ² liragáj m. dialect earlobe

لرګي والا largi'khartsavúnkaj m. ☞ لرګي خرخونکی

لرګین largín 1 wooden لرګینه لاره small pier 2 thin, emaciated, boney

لرګي والا largivālá m. dealer in firewood

لرل larə́l transitive [past: ويي لاره، درلود يې] 1 to have, possess, own ورور لري؟ Do you have a brother? ساعت لري؟ Do you have a watch? اغېزه لرل to have influence 2 m. plural .1 owning something 2.2 the presence of something

لرنه larə́na f. 1 ☞ لرل 2 2 property, substance

لرونکی larúnkaj 1 present particle of لرل 2 m. .1 owner, proprietor 2.2 bearer (of a check)

لرونه larúna plural of لور ¹

لرویه lərúja ☞ له رويه

لره ¹ lara imperfective imperative of لرل

لره ² lará Eastern suffix ☞ ته ⁴ چا لره whose, for whom ما لره Mine, to me, to me! ده لره ورکئ! Go to him!

لری ¹ láraj m. defeat

لری ² lə́raj m. anatomy stomach of a ruminant; entrails; paunch (first stomach of a ruminant)

لری ³ líri lə́ri Eastern lə́re 1 far, distant, remote لری خپلوان distant relatives 2 له لري د لري نه far away, afar د لري نه from afar, from far away لري ايستل to withdraw, move away غان لري اچول to send away, remove د چا څخه غان لري to avoid an answer خبره لري ايستل to shun someone ارتياوي لري a to remove, take away لري کول ستوماني لري کول a to satisfy requirements, meet needs کول to rest b to open (e.g., a door) c to take off, remove (e.g., clothing, shoes) d to take away, remove e to deduct, subtract, take away دا شی لري کئ! Take this thing away! زموږ لري کبدل to depart, leave خڅه لري سوي You have left us. لري سه! Go away! Depart! Beat it! سره لري لوبدل They have gone away. لري لوبدل a to end up far away b to depart; separate oneself from لري ليدل to foresee; anticipate, be farsighted

لری ⁴ larí present tense of لرل

لرې ⁵ laré second person present tense of لرل

لرې ⁶ lári f. plural of لر ²

لری ⁷ lə́ri plural of لری ²

لریتوب liritób ləretób m. لري والی lirivālaj lərevālaj m. 1 remoteness, distance; removal 2 distance, space, interval; range, distant place 3 alienation

لری وشتونکی líri vishtúnkaj lə́re vishtúnkaj long-range (of a weapon)

لړ lar m. 1 line, row 2 series د مشکلاتو یو لړ series of difficulties یو لړ مثالونه among other measures taken نورو اقداماتو په لړ کښي to introduce a number of examples راوړل 3 mountain chain, a range لړغون mountain chain 4 lock (of hair) 5 tape, braid, binding لړ کول compound verb a to draw up in a line b to string, thread لړ کېدل compound verb a to be drawn up in line b to be threaded, be strung

لړاک laṛák cheeky, brazen; wild, violent; quarrelsome

لړاوو laṛāvú agressive, bellicose

لړائي laṛāí f. engagement, battle

لړبکه laṛbaká f. 1 shudder, chill; shivering 2 woe; sadness, grief

لړپرلړ laṛ-pər-láṛ in layers, in rows

لړپه laṛə́pa f. 1 property; riches 2 something obtained at no effort; a trove, find

لړز laṛz m. لړزان laṛzán m. ☞ لړېکه 1

لړزنده تبه laṛzánda fever

لړزول laṛzavə́l transitive [past: ويي لړزاوه] 1 to cause shaking, cause shivering; to make tremble 2 to cause vibration 3 to swing, rock 4 figurative to trouble, worry 5 figurative to shake up, shock

لړزوني laṛzúnaj m. ailment of camels characterized by coughing

لړزه laṛzá f. ☞ لړېکه 1

لړزه ترزه laṛzá-taṛzá f. shock; misfortune, disaster

لړزېدل laṛzedə́l intransitive [past: و لړزېدل] 1 to shiver, shake; shudder; quiver 2 to vibrate 3 to swing, rock 4 figurative to be troubled, be worried 5 figurative to be shocked, be shaken up

لړشين laṛshín m. ☞ لرشين

لړل laṛə́l transitive [past: ويي لاړه] 1 to soil, dirty 2 to encrimson (with blood) 3 to besmirch, sully 4 to shake up, stir, agitate, intermix 5 to blend with something 6 to dig, burrow into something 7 to expose to something; stagger (of grief) 8 to torment

لړلئ laṛə́ləj 1 past participle of لړل 2 immoral لړلئ سړی a dirty personage, a good-for-nothing

لړم ¹ laṛám m. [plural: لړمان laṛamán] 1 scorpion 2 ☞ عقرب idiom، ډبري اړوي د لړم خوی لرل to be pernicious, be noxious idiom لړمان غواړي He's asking for trouble.

لړم ² laṛə́m first person present tense of لړل

لړماچ laṛmách m. لړماښ laṛmāx̌ m. ☞ لرمون

لړمانه laṛmānə́ plural oblique singular of لرمون

لړم بالبنت laṛambālə́x̌t m. borer (moth)

لړم بوټی laṛambúṭaj m. Doronicum (a plant which heals scorpion bites)

لړمزی laṛmə́zaj m. to string (pearls)

لړمکه laṛəmáka f. لړمکۍ laṛamkə́j f. medicine nettle rash لړمکه to be covered with nettle-rash, urticaria زلمی و قندهار ته لړمکه کېدل پروت دئ Zalmai is longing to be in Kandahar.

لرمون laṛmún m. oblique singular [plural: لړمانه laṛmānə́ plural: لړمونونه laṛmunúna] 1 bowels, intestines, innards, guts (of an animal) 2 figurative depths idiom خپل لړمون خوړل to be tormented

لړمي ¹ laṛə́mi f. لړمۍ laṛəmə́j f. plural ☞ لړمکه

لړمی ² laṛamə́j f. caterpillar

لړو ¹ laṛú ☞ لړوچتو

لړو ² laṛú first person plural present tense of لړل

لړوبېلر laṛ-və́-belár لړوپټو laṛo-pəṭó messed-up, disordered

لړوچتو laṛó-chaṭó 1 unfit, base (of a person) 2 extravagant

لړوچر laṛochúr m. extravagance

لړوختو ¹ laṛutsatú m. food, food-products

لړوختو laṛutsatú 1.1 greedy, avid 1.2 unfit, base 2 m. good-for-nothing, base fellow

لړومج laṛúmaj strongly desiring, greedy for something

لړه ¹ lára f. 1 enmity; quarrel; flight, row 2 battle, engagement

لړه ² lə́ṛa f. 1 fog, mist لړه ښکته The fog fell. The fog moved in. 2 dusk

لړه ³ lāṛa f. 1 series 2 column; file 3 ridge ☞ لړ

لړه ⁴ laṛá imperfective imperative of لړل

لړه غومی laṛaghúmaj m. robbery; theft لړه غومی کول to rob

لړۍ ¹ laṛə́j f. 1 necklace 2 series; file لړی لړی in rows, one after another 3 sequence

لړي ² lə́ṛi plural of لړه ¹,³

لړي ³ lə́ṛi plural of لړه ²

لړي ⁴ laṛí present of لړل

لړۍ ⁵ laṛə́j f. ☞ چارګل

لړئ ⁶ laṛəj present tense second person plural of لړل

لړيال laṛjál m. computer science index

لړېڅی laṛetsáj m. ladle, dipper

لړېزم laṛezə́m m. dish made of rhubarb and flour

لړېزنګ laṛezáng m. stick used in mixing chewing tobacco

لیزبن lízbón m. لیزبون lízbón m. Lisbon (city)

لزج lazídzh Arabic gluey, tacky, sticky

لزګین lazgín 1 m. Lezgin (nationality) 2 adjective Lezgin, pertaining to the Lezgin people

لزوم luzúm m. Arabic necessity, need, requirement

لزوماً luzúmán Arabic through force of necessity; in event of need

لزومي luzumí 1 necessary, needful, required 2 immutable, unalterable لزومي امر an order which is subject to strict execution

لزوميت luzumiját m. necessity, need, requirement

لژند ləzhə́nd 1 mixed with something 2 soiled; dirtied 3 bloody, bloodstained, encrimsoned (with blood) په وینو لژند لاس a bloody hand لژند کول a to mix something; add something b to bloody, encrimson

لژیون lezhión m. legion

لږ ləg 1.1 small, insignificant; scanty لږي اوبه راوړه bring some water 1.2 not numerous, few لږ ځله rarely, not often 1.3 short, unprotracted لږه مده short period, short term 2.1 little, a little bit; some لږي ورځي پس after a few days, after a few days have passed; recently تر لږه پوري very little لږ تر لږه at least, at the very least; the very least, minimally لږ ځخه a tiny bit, wee bit لږلږ a little bit, a little at a time 2.2 دا ډېر لږ لیدل کېږي This is very rarely observed.

لږ ارتقا ləgirtiḳā́ underdeveloped (of a country)

لږتوب ləgtób m. لږتیا ləgtjā́ f. ☞ د قیمتو لږوالی لږتوب lowering of prices

لږچکي ləgchə́ki لږڅکي ləgtsə́ki 1 a little bit, very little, a slight amount 2 to some degree

لږ خوری ləgkhóraj blind

لږشاني ləgshāni لږغوندي lə́gghundi ☞ لږچکي

لږکوټی ləgkúṭaj very small, insignificant, tiny

لږاکی ləgakə́j f. minority, the lesser part

لږګوټی ləggúṭaj ☞ لږکوټی

لږوالی ləgvā́laj m. 1 deficiency, insufficiency, shortage د اومو موادو لږوالی a shortage of raw materials 2 lowering, lessening 3 trifle, insignificance; scarcity

لږوبه ləgóba f. water shortage

لږو ډېر ləgu-ḍer 1 more or less 2 to a certain degree, to a certain extent

لږول ləgavə́l denominative, transitive [past: لږ يې کړ] 1 to decrease, curtail 2 to subtract, take off 3 to weaken خپل کوښښ لږول to weaken or decrease one's efforts 4 to offer (in trade) at the lowest price

لږون ləgún m. 1 shortage, deficiency 2 decrease, curtailment

لږونه ləgavə́na f. decrease, curtailment, lowering

لږونکی ləgavúnkaj 1 present participle of لږول 2 m. supplier asking the lowest price

لږه شاني ləgashā́ne ☞ لږچکي

لږه کی ləgakə́j f. ☞ لږکی

لږی lə́gáj m. ☞ لږېدنه

لږي lə́gi f. plural of لږ

لږېدل ləgedə́l denominative, intransitive [past: لږ شو] 1 to be decreased, be curtailed 2 to be scarce, grow thin, be infrequent ډزی لږی شوي The shots became more infrequent.

لږېدنه ləgedə́na f. 1 lessening, curtailment, lowering د تولید لږېدنه curtailment of production 2 weakening, slacking; underestimation

لس las numeral 1 ten لس کاله ten years هغه لس لس روپۍ يې ورکړي He gave them ten rupees apiece. 2 m. [plural: لسها lashā́ plural: لسګونه lasgúna] a group of ten objects په لسهاو by tens په دې ورستیو لسګونو کلونو کښ for the past decade 3 consisting of ten

لسان lisā́n m. [plural: لسانونه lisānúna Arabic plural: السنه alsiná] tongue, language

لساني lisā́ni Arabic 1 linguistic, pertaining to language 2 verbal, oral لساني ادبي اثار folklore

لس بېله lasbelá f. Lasbela (district, Beludzhistan)

لس پولی laspulə́j f. ten-pul coin

لست list m. list; register لست ترتیب کول to draw up a list, compile a list

لستوني lastóṇaj m. lastúṇaj Western sleeve لستوني راغنتل a to roll the sleeves up; really get down to work لاس په لستوني lastóṇi to know well enough to shake hands with idiom مار ته په لستوني کښی څای ورکول to harbor a snake in own's bosom

لسته lastá f. 1 quarter, area, country 2 fourth, fourth part of something

لسکی lasakə́j f. cards the ten (of a suite)

لسګون lasgún ☞ لسیز

لسګونه lasgúna m. plural ☞ لس

لسم lasə́m ordinal numeral tenth لسم باب tenth chapter

لسمشر lasmə́shər m. 1 foreman 2 colloquial sergeant

لسي lasí 1 f. group of ten objects 2 ten each, ten apiece لسي خرڅول to sell for ten rupees each

لسي lasí f. 1 skimmed milk 2 strained whey drink used as a cooling drink

لسی lə́sáj m. man, person, personality

لسیز lasíz adjective decimal

لشکرګاه lashkargā́h m. Lashkargah (city)

لشکه lashə́ka f. 1 sting (of a wasp, scorpion, etc.) 2 beard, awn (of grain) 3 splinter, fragment 4 chip

لشکي lashəkí bearded, awned (of plants)

لشکي lə́shki f. ☞ لړکی

لشماتي lashmātí 1 warm (of water) 2 wetted, moistened, lubricated with something

لشه lashá f. ☞ لشکه

لښته lā́khta f. 1 twiglet, withe; brushwood د لنبتو جونګره brushwood cabin (used by fishermen) 2 bar (e.g., of iron)

لښتی lakhtə́j f. earring لنتی په غوږو کول to put on earrings

لښتی lakhtə́j f. dancer (female)

لښتی lakhtáj m. 1 brook, rivulet; small irrigation channel 2 line, mark idiom له سترګو نه یې د اوښکو لښتی روان شو Rivulets of tears flowed from his eyes.

لښتی lakhtáj m. 1 dancer 2 acrobat 3 prestidigitator; juggler

لښتی lā́khti plural of لنبته

لښتیال lā́khtjāl m. computer science table

لښکر lakhkár m. [plural: لښکرونه lakhkarúna Eastern f. plural: لښکري lakhkáre] 1 troops; army منظم لښکر regular army 2 detachment of warriors (of a tribe) پر چا لښکر کول to attack someone; send a detachment to attack someone 3 a flock (of locusts); horde 4 a bank (of clouds) 5 proper name Lashkar

لښکر ځای lakhkardzā́j m. military camp; military post

لښکرکشي lakhkarkashí f. لښکرکښي lakhkarkakhí f. campaign, march لښکر کښی کول to go out on the march

لښکرکوټ lakhkarkóṭ m. لښکرګاه lakhkargā́h m. 1 ☞ لښکرګای 2 Lashkargah (city)

لښکري lakhkáre f. plural Eastern ☞ لښکر

لښکري lakhkarí 1 adjective military, army لښکري خدمت military service, service in the army 2 m. servicemen; trooper, warrior

لښکی lakhkáj m. medicine lancet, scalpel

لښکي lə́khki ☞ لړ ☞ لړخه

لښل lkhəl intransitive [past: ولښه] to wander, lead the nomadic life

لنلول lkhə́laval *transitive* [*past:* لنلاوه و يي] **1** to compel to lead the nomadic life, make to roam **2** to resettle

لبننه lkhə́na *f.* nomad (female)

لبنونى ləkhúnaj *adjective* **1** draft, pack **2** roaming, wandering

لطافت latāfát *m. Arabic* **1** elegance, grace **2** tenderness **3** goodness, kindness; well-wishing **4** wit, wittiness

لطايف latāíf *m. Arabic masculine plural of* لطيفه

لطف lutf *m. Arabic* **1** goodness; kindness; favor لطف وفرمايه **a** be good, be kind **b** Have mercy **2** pleasure, enjoyment د . . . څخه لطف اخيستل to enjoy something

لطفاً lútfan *Arabic* nicely, kindly

لطيف latíf *Arabic* **1.1** pleasant, nice لطيف جنس the feminine sex **1.2** clever, sharp-witted **2** *m. proper name* Latif

لطف اندازي lutfandāzí *f.* attention, care, good behavior

لطيفه latifá *f. Arabic* [*plural:* لطيفي latifé *Arabic m. plural:* لطايف latāíf] joke, witticism; anecdote

لعاب lu'áb *m. Arabic* **1** saliva لعاب ايستل to expectorate **2** mucus **3** enamel

لعابي lu'ābí *adjective* **1** saliva, salival لعابي غده saliva gland **2** mucous **3** enamel

لعل la'l *m.* **1** ruby لعل پيازي amethist د لعل معادن ruby deposits ☞ لال **2** *m. proper name* Lal

لعلج la'láj *m. proper name* Lalaj

لعن la'n *m.* لعنت l'anát *m. Arabic* damnation, perdition پر چا لعن ويل، په چا لعن ويل to curse, damn, condemn someone په دي تا لعن شي! Damn you!

لعنتي la'natí damned

لعين la'ín *Arabic* ☞ لعنتي

لغات lughát *Arabic masculine plural of* لغت

لغاز ləghā́z *m.* mockery

لغازي ləghāzí mocking; derisive

لغت lughát *m. Arabic* [*plural:* لغتونه lughatúna *Arabic plural:* لغات lughā́t] **1** word د لغاتو مجموعه vocabulary **2** speech; expression **3** dictionary **4** glossary

لغت دان lughatdā́n *m.* lexicographer

لغت شناسي lughatshināsí *f.* lexicography

لغته laghā́ta *f.* kicking, rebelling لغتي وهل to kick, rebel په لغته وهل to be ungrateful قبر په لغته وهل idiom to kick to foil death لغته خورل to incur damage or injury

لغړ ləghə́r laghə́r **1** naked; bare لغړ سيم bare wire **2** pure, unadulterated **3** pure, indigent

لغړ اوښ ləgəṛukh *m.* breed of short-wooled camel

لغړتوب ləgəṛtób *m.* لغړتيا ləgəṛtjā́ *f.* nakedness; nudity, bareness

لغړل lghəṛál *transitive* ☞ نغرل

لغړکي ləghə́ṛki *f. plural* sheeps' feet (without meat)

لغړ ندوکى ləghəṛundúkaj rolling; rotating

لغړول ¹ lgəṛavál *transitive verb* [*past:* لغړاوه و يي] **1** to roll; rotate **2** to knead (e.g., dough) **3** to dry out (e.g., felt)

لغړول ² ləghəṛavál *denominative, transitive* [*past:* لغړي يي کړ] **1** to bare, denude, undress **2** to launch into the world

لغړه ləghə́ra *female singular of* لغړ پينتو پښتو pure Pashto

لغړى ¹ ləghə́raj all but naked

لغړي ² ləghə́ri *m. plural* ☞ دلغړو څواونه لغړکي soup made of bones

لغړي ³ ləghə́ṛi *feminine plural of* لغړ idiom لغړي سترگي shameless eyes

لغړيدل ¹ lghəṛedál *intransitive* [*present:* لغړي *past:* ولغړيده] **1** to roll along; rotate **2** to be kneaded (of dough) **3** to be dried out (of felt)

لغړيدل ² laghəṛedál *denominative, intransitive* [*past:* لغړ شو] to uncover oneself, strip oneself; get undressed

لغړيده ¹ lghəṛedə́ *m. plural* **1** rotation **2** kneading (of dough) **3** drying out (e.g., of felt)

لغړيده ² laghəṛedə́ *m. plural* stripping, baring; undressing

لغز laghz *m.* ☞ لغزش

لغزش laghzísh *m.* **1** sliding **2** *figurative* failure

لغزن laghzán *literal & figurative* slippery

لغزيدل laghzedál *intransitive* [*past:* ولغزيده] to slide; slip

لغښت lghə́kht *imperfect of* لغښتل

لغښتل lghə́khtál *intransitive* ☞ لغښيدل ¹

لغکه laghā́ka *f.* variety of unawned barley

لغکي laghə́ki awned, bearded (of cereal grains)

لغم laghm *m.* **1** mine, landmine لغم وروزل to explode a mine **2** mining, undermining, sapping لغم وهل to mine, undermine, sap ☞ نغم

لغمان laghmā́n *m.* Lagman (district) د لغمان ولايت Lagman Province

لغمکه laghəmā́ka *f.* muzzle (calves, kids)

لغو laghv *Arabic* **1** *m.* **.1** abolition, annulment; cancellation لغو لغو او منسوخ کېدل compound verb to abolish, annul, renounce کول (a treaty) compound verb to be abolished, be anulled **1.2** nonsense **2** meaninglessly, uselessly وقت لغو تېرول to lose time for naught

لغورن laghorə́n ləghvəṛə́n **1** dirty, unclean لغورنه هوا polluted air **2** slovenly, sloppy **3** amoral; unscrupulous لغورن سړى an unclean person, dirty personality

لغورنول laghvəṛənavál *denominative, transitive* [*past:* لغورن يي کړ] **1** to dirty, besmirch **2** to make slovenly, sloppy

لغورنيدل laghvəṛənedál *denominative, intransitive* [*past:* لغورن شو] **1** to be dirtied; be spoiled, be besmirched **2** to become sloppy, slovenly

لغونى lghunáj *m.* clay pot

لغوه lághva *f.* ☞ لغو

لغوي lughaví *Arabic* **1** lexical, lexicographic; pertaining to the literal meaning of a word لغوي پانگه vocabulary **2** philological

لغويات laghvijā́t *m. Arabic plural* empty words, nonsense, balderdash

لفاظي laffāzí *f.* garrulousness, gabbiness

لفافه lifāfá *f. Arabic* **1** folder; cover, wrapper **2** envelope, official letter

لفت lift *m.* لفټ lifṭ *m.* **1** lift, elevator د لفت په واسطه ختل to go up in an elevator **2** hoist

لفتنان liftenā́n *m.* لفټننت liftenánt *m. military* lieutenant

لفظ lafz *m. Arabic [plural:* لفظونه lafzúna *Arabic plural:* الفاظ alfā́z] **1** word; expression **2** vocalization of a word **3** form (of a literary work)

لفظي lafzí *Arabic* **1** literal **2** verbal, oral **3** pronounced **4** relating to form (of a literary work) لفظي واحد lexical unit

لقا liḱā́ *f. Arabic* meeting, rendezvous

لقب laḱáb *m. Arabic [plural:* لقبونه laḱabúna *Arabic plural:* القاب alḱā́b] **1** title, rank **2** nickname لقب وركول **a** to give a title; confer a rank **b** to give a nickname چاته د ملګري لقب وركول to call someone a friend

لقمان luḱmā́n *m. proper name* Lokman

لقمه luḱmā *f. Arabic* morsel (of food)

لقه luḱā́ *m.* **1** braggart, boaster **2** bully, brawler, troublemaker **3** good-for-nothing

لک lak *m. [plural:* لکونه lakúna *plural:* لکها lakhā́] lak, 100,000 په لکونو خلق 200,000 دوه لکه hundreds of thousands of people

لک lak **1** established, installed, placed **2** standing upright, upright **3** straight, vertical **4** stiff, unbending

لک ښک laktsák upright, standing upright لک ښک کول غوږونه to move the ears back and forth (of a horse) لک ښک کېدل to prick up (of the ears)

لکړه lakáṛa *f.* **1** cane; staff د جنګك لکړه fishing rod **2** pole (telegraph, etc.) *idiom* د لکړي ځوکه لګېدل **a** to get out of a difficult situation; come out alright; land on one's feet **b** to be able to cope with د لاس لکړه کېدل to become an aid or helper

لکړه lákṛa *f.* roast lung (meat)

لکړی lakaráj thin as a stick, emaciated, puny

لکزمبرگ lukzambúrg *m.* لکسمبرگ luksambúrg *m.* Luxembourg (city)

لک لک laklák *m. Arabic* stork

لکلمی lakaləmáj *m.* لکمونی

لک لبونی laklevanáj agitated, alarmed, scared

لکمونی lakamúnaj *m.* rump (of a bird); sacrum

لکمه ləkā́ma *vice* ☞ له کمه کم

لکنت luknát *m. Arabic* stammering, stuttering د ژبي لکنت لرل to stutter, stammer

لکوبوک lakvəbúk uneven, broken (of terrain)

لکوتی ləkutī́ *Eastern* some, a little, little bit ☞ لرکوتی

لکوری lakóraj *m.* kind of fruit

لکول lakavəl *denominative transitive [past:* لک يې کړ] **1** to install, place, set up (a mast, a tent, etc.) **2** to raise, hoist (a flag) **3** to place vertically, drive into **4** to plant (trees)

لکوموتیف lokomotíf *m.* locomotive

لکه láka ☞ لک

لکه ləka **1** like, similar to, as لکه غر like a mountain, similar to a mountain لکه د نور کله as before, as previously لکه چه ... similar to, as, just like لکه دمخه وویل as was known لکه معلومه چه سوه as was known لکه څنګه چه ... similar to ..., as ... **2** for example, namely **3** such as, as if

لکه lakı *m. Eastern* ☞ لک

لکه laká *f.* spot, stain

لکها lakhā́ *masculine plural of* لک **a** په لکهاو by hundreds of thousands **b** hundreds of thousands

لکه دار lakadár **1** spotted, stained, soiled; spattered **2** spotty, spotted د چا شرافت لکه دار کول spotted fever, typhus لکه داره حما to disgrace, bring shame upon, cover someone with shame

لکی lakə́j *f. [plural:* لکی lakə́j *plural:* لکیانی lakijā́ni] **1** tail لکی بنورول، لکی په لکی single file, Indian file, one after the other وهل **a** to wag the tail (as a dog) **b** *figurative* to toady, fawn; flatter extravagantly **2** tail unit, empennage (aircraft) **3** caudal fin (of a fish)

لکی دار lakəjdár caudate, having a tail

لکي لرونکي laḱedā́ra ☞ لکی داره

لکېدل laḱedə́l *denominative, intransitive [past:* لک شو] **1** to be established, be installed, be set up **2** to place in an erect position, stand vertically **3** to be planted (of a tree)

لکې لرونکې تبه laḱé larúnke spotted, speckled, spotty spotted fever, typhus

لکی وال lakəjvál لکیور lakəjvár caudate, having a tail ستوری comet

لگ lag ☞ لک

لگ ləg *Eastern* ☞ لږ

لگ lag *present stem of* لګېدل

لگاو lagā́v *m.* **1** strong blow, shove, push **2** outlay, expenditure

لگاوو lagāvú **1** extravagant **2** *m.* prodigal, squanderer, spendthrift

لگاوول lagāvavə́l *denominative transitive* to beat up; thrash; hit

لگاوه lagāvə́ *imperfect of* لګول

لگاوېدل lagāvedə́l *denominative, intransitive [past:* لگاو شو] to be beaten up

لگت lagə́t *m.* ☞ لگنت

لگړ lagáḍ *m.* lgaḍ hollow, depression; gully, shallow gully

لگړ lagáṛ *m.* kind of hawk

لگنت lagə́kht *m.* **1** outlay, expenditure, expense انکشافي لگنت capital investment لگنت کارول د چا په لگنت at someone's expense to incur expenses **2** consumption (of fuel, etc.) د لگنت خونه storeroom (for food products)

لگلگ laglág *m.* stork

لگم lagə́m *Eastern first person present tense of* لګېدل

لگن lagán *m.* ☞ لگن کول لگنت کول **a** to spend, expend **b** to consume

لگن lagán *m.* copper basin

لگن سری lagansáraj big-headed, macrocephalous

لگول ¹ lagavә́l *transitive* [*past:* وېي لگوه] 1 to set in motion, put into operation; turn on (e.g., a radio) 2 to utilize, use, employ 3 to consume; expend, spend روپي لگول to spend money 4 to turn on (water) 5 to light (e.g., candle, lamp) اور لگول to ignite 6 to unite; join, connect, fasten to; link يو تر بله سره لگول to join one to another 7 to touch, reach something لاس په دېواله لگول to reach out and touch the wall with the hand 8 to bump into something, hit something 9 to fell (with a bullet, etc.) *idiom* پته لگول to track down, shadow دکان لگول to open a shop دېره لگول to set up or take down a tent or marquee; pitch a camp ډيل لگول to drag out, postpone (the solution to a problem, a meeting, etc.) زور لگول to employ force قلف لگول to lock, bolt گلونه لگول to place flowers (in a vase, etc.) مېز لگول to set the table

لگول ² lәgavә́l *denominative transitive Eastern* ☞ لړول

لگنت lagún *m.* ☞ لگنت

لگوونی lagavúnaj *m.* kindling, splinter, chips

لگه بوگه lagabugá disorderly, incoherent

لگه درگه lága-darә́ga *f.* the trampling of feet

لگي lagí *colloquial present tense of* لگېدل

لگيا lagjā́ 1 busy, occupied with something? ته په څه کار لگيا يې؟ What are you busy doing? په خپل تحصيل لگيا يم I'm studying, I'm doing homework په څه لگيا to assign a task to someone لگيا کول کېدل, څه شي ته لگيا کېدل to be occupied with something, set to work at something, get down to something **a** to د چا سره په خبرو لگيا کېدل talk a lot to someone **b** to carry on a conversation; conduct talks 2 chattering, talking a lot چپ شه! دا څه لگيا يې؟ Be still! What are you going on about? په يوه خبره لگيا يئ He keeps repeating the same thing over and over again.

لگيا توب lagjātób *m.* state of being occupied, busy, state of being loaded with work

لگېدل lagedә́l *intransitive* [*present:* لگېږي ، لگي *past:* ولگېده] 1 to be put in motion; operate (of a car, etc.) 2 to be busy, be occupied with something; get to work on something 3 to be consumed, be spent, be expended روپي ولگېدي The money has been spent. 4 to be utilized, be employed; serve for some purpose 5 to catch fire څراغ ولگېد The lamp په اور باندي لگېدل to start to burn, flare up began to burn. 6 to burn, burn up 7 to touch something; reach out and touch something lightly 8 to brush against something; hit against something 9 to bump into something; jump onto something; stumble on something موټر له دېواله سره ولگېد A car crashed into a cellar restaurant. 10 to stick, adhere to; be joined to; be attached to 11 to grapple, struggle with someone 12 to engage in a battle or skirmish; join battle 13 to be installed (of a pane of glass) 14 to reach, attain something 15 to carry, be heard (of sound) 16 to blow, waft (of wind) باد نه لگېدئ Windless weather remained. 17 to be struck, be hit (of a goal, target) 18 to be struck down (by a bullet, etc.); be wounded په ټوپک ولگېد *Eastern* He was struck down by a bullet. 19 to notice, take note of زمونږ په نظر ولگېد چه ... We noticed that ... 20 to suit,

دواړه سره لگي conform They suit one another. 21 to infringe, trespass on something 22 to act upon or influence something په ما باندي لوږه لگېري I want to eat. 23 to act against someone; harm or injure someone 24 to get down to (work etc.)

لگېده ¹ lagedә́ *m. plural* 1 expenditure, consumption 2 igniting 3 burning up, consuming by fire 4 hitting (of a target), striking down and destroying something د بمانو سم لگېده a direct hit by a bomb 5 use, utilization, employment 6 touching, touching lightly 7 bumping into 8 blowing, wafting (winds) 9 fitness, suitability, appropriateness 10 action or influence upon someone

لگېده ² lagedә́ *imperfect of* لگېدل

لل ¹ lal *m.* force, stength

لل ² lal mute, dumb

لل ³ lә́l *transitive obsolete* [*present:* لي *past:* وېي له] to pronounce, speak سلام لل to greet شاهدي لل، گواهي لل to give evidence, testify

لل گل lalgál struck down, overcome, stunned لل گل کېدل to be struck down, be overcome, be stunned

للل lalә́l *transitive* ☞ لل ³

للمه lálma *f.* dry-farming land, arid-farming land

للمي ¹ lalmí *adjective* pertaining to dry-farming للمي غنم dry-farmed wheat

للمی ² lalmә́j *f.* ☞ للمه

للمي کاري lalmikārí *f.* dry-farming agriculture

للو ¹ laló *f.* cradlesong, lullaby چاته للو ويل، چاته للو کول to lull someone

للو ² lalú shallow, unserious, superficial (of a person)

للوپتو lalopató *f.* 1 flattery, adulation 2 a way of passing time

للو للو lalo-laló *f.* ☞ للو ¹

للون ¹ lalún *m.* weeding, weeding out للون کول to weed, weed out

للون ² lalún *m.* speech; utterance

للونول lalunavә́l *denominative, transitive* [*past:* للون يې کړ] to weed, weed out

للونېدل lalunedә́l *denominative, intransitive* [*past:* للون شو] to be weeded, be weeded out

للی lalә́j *f.* ☞ للو ¹

للېدل laledә́l *intransitive* [*past:* ولليد] 1 to be astounded, be stunned 2 to grow dumb, become dumb

لم ¹ lәm *m.* [*plural:* لمونه lәmúna *plural:* لمان lәmán] 1 fatty tail (of certain breeds of sheep); tail 2 caudal part, termination of something 3 rear, back, hinder part *idiom* په لم خطا ايستل to deceive, hoodwink, lead around by the nose

لم ² lәm *vice* لولم ☞ لوستل

لمار lamář *m.* kerchief (given at a betrothal)

لماری lmářaj *m.* ☞ نماری

لماست lmāsә́t ☞ ملاست

لماستل lmāstә́l *intransitive* ☞ څملاستل

لماستون lmāstún *m.* ☞ لمس

لمانځل lmāndzál transitive [past: لمانځه و یې] 1 to esteem, show honor, show respect 2 to honor, bow to 3 to treat with affection, caress

لمانځنه lmāndzә́na f. honor, esteem په لمانخه with honor; respect د لمانخه ... in honor of someone or something; as a symbol of respect or honor د ... لمانخنه کول to value, esteem

لمانخه ¹ lmā́ndza f. millwheel axle

لمانخه ² lmāndzә́ imperfect of لمانخل

لمانخه lmāndzә́ oblique singular of لمونخ

لمانځي lmāndzí washed, laundered; clean لمانخي کول a to launder, wash b to clean (e.g., clothes) لمانخي کېدل a to be laundered, be washed b to be cleaned (of clothes)

لمانه ² lәmā́na vice ما له مانه ☞

لمباوه lambāvә́ imperfect of لمبول

لمبر lambár m. 1 number د ترتیب لمبر ordinal لمبر کول compound verb to number لمبر کېدل compound verb to be numbered لمبر ورباندي وهل to assign a number اول لمبر لرل to have primary signficance, have primary importance 2 evaluation, grade

لمبر ¹ lumbár m. obsolete 1 foward, front, the front part of something 2 bow, prow (of a ship)

لمبر ² lumbár m. male fox, dog fox

لمبره lumbára f. female fox, vixen

لمبرى ¹ lumbṛáj ☞ لمرى

لمبل lambál transitive [present: لامبي past: لمبل و یې] to bath, wash (oneself)

لمبلدزای lambә́ldzáj m. bath, (enclosed) bathing area

لمبو lambó f. لامبو ☞

لمبور lambúr m. 1 well-shaft of an irrigation system 2 pickaxe (for digging an irrigation shaft, canal)

لمبورچي lamburchí m. kariz (i.e., Afghan irrigation well) digger

لمبول lambavә́l transitive [past: په وینو لمباوه و یې] to bathe, wash لمبول to bathe in blood

لمبه lambá f. 1 flame لمبه کول to fan the flame; kindle a fire په لمبو راتلل to flame up, catch fire; flare, blaze لمبه کېدل to flame 2 summer heat, sultriness هوا سره لمبه وه Sultry weather set in.

لمبی lambáj m. 1 candle 2 lamp

لمبېدل lambedә́l intransitive [past: ولمبېده] 1 to bathe, wash (oneself) په وینو کښي ولمبېدل to be bathed in blood 2 m. plural ☞ لمبېده

لمبېده lambedә́ m. plural bathing, washing د لمبدو وند swimming pool, swimming bath

لم پوست lәmpóst m. skin of the tail

لمتک lәmṭák m. good-for-nothing, cad

لم جندى، لم جوندى lәmdzhunḍáj m. rump; sacrum

لم چر lәmcháṛ having a docked or bobbed tail

لمتسوکى lәmtsukáj m. لم جندى ☞

لمخه lәmtsá f. armful of firewood

لمتساى lamtsáj [plural: لمخي lamtsí plural: لمخیان lamtsiján] felt; large piece of felt

لمحه lamhá f. Arabic blink, moment, instant د لمحي وروستى the last moments, final moments

لمدبل lamdabál m. ☞ لندبل

لمده lamdá 1 Eastern feminine singular of لوند 2 watery elements; sea

لمدبدل lamdedә́l intransitive ☞ لندبدل

لمدبده lamdedә́ m. plural ☞ لندبده

لمدى lәmәdáj m. ☞ لم جندى

لمر lmar m. Western sun نن لمر دئ Today is a sunny day. خه شي لمر ته The sun is baking. زېرى لمر دئ The sun has set. اچول to put in the sun, place in the sun, dry something out in the sun لمر ډرک to set (of the sun) لمر پرپوتل، لمر غوټه کول، لمر لوېدل to rise (of the sun) لمر په دوو ګوتو نه پټېږي وهل، لمر خیره کول proverb You can't shut off the sun with two fingers. لمر زپر شو It has gotten to be past noon. لمر و غر سره تلل to become evening, begin to get dark لمر يوه نېزه کېدل to approach (of the end of the world) تر لمر بنکاره clearly, clearer than clear تر لمر سپینه کول to speak directly, talk without evasion دا کار تر لمر سپین دئ This is clearer than clear. This is as clear as God's daylight. لمره کول a to annihilate, destroy, murder; complete, terminate some matter

لمرپرواته lmarprevātә́ m. plural 1 sunset; setting د لمر پریوتو سره سم at sunset m. the west, western countries 2 m. West د لمر پرېواته ملکونه Western countries

لمر تندره lmartándra f. solar eclipse a to annihilate, destroy, murder b to complete, terminate some matter

لمرتګ lmarṭág m. 1 noon 2 equator

لمرخرک lmartsrә́k m. 1 sunrise 2 dawn 3 ray of the sun

لمرخرکى lmartsә́rkaj 1 sunny (of a side) 2 m. kind of light-colored snake; Emperor Snake

لمرخرک lmartsrík m. لمرخرىکه lmartsríka f. ☞ لمرخرىک

لمرخاته lmarkhātә́ m. plural 1 sunrise 2 د لمرخاته ملکونه Eastern countries m. the East د لمر ختو له خواخه from the east, from an eastern direction

لمر ختیخ lmarkhatídz لمر ختیز lmarkhatíz 1 eastern (of a direction, side) 2 m. East

لمرګلى lmargúlaj m. sunflower

لمر لرونکى lmar larunkaj sunny خای the sunny side

لمر لوېده lmarlvedә́ m. plural ☞ لمرپرېواته

لمر لوېدیز lmarlvedíz 1 western 2 m. West

لمرمخى lmarmә́khaj m. 1 sunflower 2 beautiful

لمرنى lmarә́náj sunny; solar لمرنى کال solar year

لمرى lmaráj dried in the sun

لمريز lmaríz ☞ لمرنى

لمر lamәṛ m. steep precipice; a fissure

لمرزیز lumәṛzíz m. 1.1 first fruit 1.2 firstborn (animals) 2 firstborn

لمرنى lumaṛanáj 1 first, initial لمرنى پلا the first time 2 former 3 first priority (of a task) 4 primary لمرنى زده کړه primary education 5 primitive لمرنى ټولنه primitive society

653

لمړی ¹ lumṛáj **1.1** first په لمړی سر کښني from the beginning, in the beginning د لمري سره ښخه in the first months په لمړيو مياشتو کښني from the very beginning **1.2** primary (school) **2** at first, at the beginning; for the first time **3** *m.* beginning دجگړي د لمړيه څخه from the beginning of the war

لمړی ² lumṛə́j *feminine singular of* لمړی ¹ **1** لمړی خور the third month of the lunar year

لمړی ³ lmaṛə́j *f.* ☞ نمړی ¹

لمس lams *m.* motivation; instigation

لمسنالۍ lamsnā́ləj *f. computer science* touchpad

لمسول lamsavə́l *transitive* [*past:* لمساوه ويې] **1** to motivate; instigate **2** to cause, stimulate

لمسون lamsún *m.* ☞ په لمسون باندي لمس by teaching

لمسوونی lamsavúnaj *m.* instigator

لمسه lamasá *f.* ☞ چا ته لمسه ورکول لمس to incite someone, egg on

لمسی ¹ lmasáj *m.* [*plural:* لمسي lmasi *plural:* لمسيان lmasiján] *Western* grandson

لمسی ² lamsáj *m.* ☞ لمخی

لمسی ³ lmasə́j *f.* [*plural:* لمسی lmasə́j *plural:* لمسياني lmasijáni] *Western* granddaughter

لمسېدل lamsedə́l *intransitive* [*past:* ولمسېد] to be motivated, be incited, be instigated, be egged on

لمسېده lamsedə́ *m. plural* ☞ لمس

لمغړی ¹ lamghaṛə́j *f.* **1** cunning, guile, ruse **2** swindles, intrigues لمغړی کول **a** to use cunning, entrap, cheat **b** to intrigue, engage in intrigues **c** to swagger about

لمغړی ² ləmghəraj **1** shrewd; cunning **2** *m.* **.1** sly, cunning person; dodger **2.2** schemer, cheat **2.3** flatterer

لمغړی ³ ləmghəṛə́j *f.* rump; sacrum

لم غوته ləmghúta with tail tied up (of a military, war, or cavalry horse) لم غوته سپاره cavalry horse, warhorse لم غوته اس mounted warriors, cavalrymen, swordsmen, warriors *idiom* لم غوته ايستل to drive out of the house with disgrace, kick someone out راوستل to show someone in at once پر لم غوته سپرو اوښتل *proverb* He has met his match.

لمکه lumə́ka *f.* snares, traps و چاته لمکه ايښنودل to set a trap for someone

لم گنډی ləmganḍáj *m.* لم گوری ləmgúṛaj *m.* لم گونډی ləmgúnḍaj *m.* **1** rump; sacrum **2** (little) tail

لملېټ lamléṭ *m.* lemonade

لمن lamə́n *f.* [*plural:* لمني lamə́ni] **1** border, hem, skirt (of a dress) **2** base (of a mountain) **3** the lower edge (of a tent, marquee) **4** the limit (of the sky) **5** extent, expanse **6** spread, diffusion, sphere of use *idiom* تشه لمن *figurative* with empty hands, having nothing for one's pains د چا لمن پر سر اړول، د چا لمن پر سر اوښنتل to bring shame upon oneself دسولی خپله لمن پراخول to spread, diffuse تحریک خپله لمن پراخوي to expand the peace movement لمن اچول to خپله لمن to avoid someone لمن غونډول، لمن ټولول to be depressed

خپرول to become widespread (of a custom, etc.) *Western* لو لمن لرل to be generous, be magnanimous اوږده لمن لرل to be disseminated (of the order of the day) د ښه شي لمن لنډېدل to be completed, be ended و چا ته لمن نيول to pursue, go after someone د چا لمن نيول to implore, beseech someone; beg forgiveness of someone د خپلي اختلافاتو اور ته لمن وهل to continue one's speech خبري لمن نيول stir up contradictions تر لمني لاندی کول to protect, take under one's roof

لمنځ ¹ lmandz *m.* bachelor, single man

لمنځ ² lmandz *m.* **1** respect, esteem **2** praise

لمنځل lmandzál *transitive Western* ☞ لمانځل

لمنځنه lmandzə́na *f.* ☞ لمانځنه

لمنځه ¹ lmándza *f.* pine tree

لمنځه ² lmándza *Western short plural of* لمونځ پنځه لمنځه the five namaz (i.e., five Islamic obeisances and prayers)

لمنگی lamangə́j *f.* kind of embroidery stitching لمن گی، لمنگی

لمنه lamə́na *f. dialect* ☞ لمن

لمور ləmavár fat-tailed (of sheep)

لموره lmorá *f.* forage, hay, straw (in wisps)

لمونځ lmundz *m.* [*plural:* لمونځونه lmundzúna *plural:* لمنځونه lməndzúna] *Western* namaz (i.e., prayer) لمونځ کول to perform a namaz, to pray (in the prescribed Islamic way)

لمونځ گذار lmundzguzár *m.* praying, performing a namaz لمونځ گذار،

لمسل lmesə́l *transitive* [*past:* ولمسه ويې] to write, inscribe

لنبره lanbára *f.* bare floor, uncarpeted floor

لمبول lambavə́l *transitive* ☞ لمبه

لمبه lambá *f.* ☞ لمبه

لمبېدل lambedə́l *intransitive* ☞ لمبېدل

لنځي lándzi *f. plural* prayer, supplication

لند lund ☞ لوند

لندبل landabál *m.* **1** freshness **2** humidity, dampness د هوا لندبل the humidity of the air **3** food, dish

لندن landán *m.* ☞ لندن

لندوالی landválaj *m.* liquid; dampness, humidity

لندول landavə́l *denominative transitive* [*past:* لوند يې کړ] to make damp; wet, moisten; dampen

لنده ¹ lindá *f.* ☞ لیندی

لنده ² landá *feminine singular of* لوند لنده مېوه fresh fruits لنده هوا humid air

لیندی ¹ lində́j *f.* ☞ لیندی

لندی ² landáj *m.* main irrigation canal, channel, ditch

لندېدل landedə́l *denominative, intransitive* [*past:* لوند شو] to dampen, wet; moisten; soak

لندېده landedə́ *m. plural* wetting; dampening; soaking

لند land **1** short لنډ پتلون shorts **2** brief, quick په لنډه quickly, soon **3** concise, compressed **4** په لنډه توگه، په لنډه صورت، succinctly په لنډو کالو کښني next, immediate (of time) in the next few years, in a few years خو لنډه دا چه، لنډه يې دا چه in a word, briefly speaking

کان لنډ تنگ کول a to shrink, shrivel b to limit oneself in something

لنډاک lanḍā́k shortsighted, myopic; foolish

لنډاکتوب lanḍāktób *m.* لنډاکي lanḍākí *f.* shortsightedness, myopia; foolishness

لنډبزري lanḍbazə́raj *m.* kind of hawk

لنډپاری lanḍpāraj *m.* inconstant or unreliable friend

لنډتوب lanḍtób *m.* 1 shortness; conciseness 2 closeness, a short distance

لنډغر lanḍaghár *m.* 1 ☞ لنډه هر 2 having a bobbed or cropped tail

لنډفکره lanḍfíkra shortsighted, superficial

لنډکی lanḍakáj *rather short* يو لنډکی مثال به راوړم I will present a small example.

لنډکی lanḍakə́j *f.* shallow irrigation shaft

لنډگنډ lanḍgánḍ 1 hasty, disputed لنډوگنډ نيول to grab (momentarily), snatch 2 short, brief

لنډلار lanḍlār *m. computer science* shortcut

لنډلار غورنی lanḍlār ghwaranə́j *f. computer science* shortcut menu

لنډلار کيلي lanḍlār kilí *f. computer science* shortcut key

لنډ ليدونکی lanḍlidúnkaj myopic, shortsighted

لنډن lanḍán *m.* London (city)

لنډوالی lanḍwáləj *m.* 1 brevity د لنډوالي دپاره for the sake of brevity 2 nearness, shortness of distance

لنډور lanḍavár ☞ لنډاک

لنډوکی lanḍúkaj rather short, bobbed

لنډوگنډ lanḍugánḍ 1 very short, rather short 2 briefly speaking, in a word

لنډول lanḍavə́l *denominative transitive* [*past:* لنډ يي کړ] 1 to shorten, make shorter 2 to curtail, lessen, compress 3 to explain briefly, summarize

لنډون lanḍún *m.* لنډونه lanḍavə́na *f.* 1 shortening 2 curtailment, lessening, compression 3 brief explaination, summary 4 settlement (of some matter)

لنډه lanḍá [1] *f. anatomy* sacroiliac; lumbar part of the spine, small of the back

لنډه lánḍa [2] *feminine singular of* لنډ نو لنډه يي خلاصه کړم briefly speaking *idiom* لنډه منډه کول to display shortsightedness

لنډه کاز lanḍəkā́z *m.* white goose

لنډه هر lanḍahór *m.* 1 vagrant, tramp 2 hooligan, ruffian 3 *abusive* good-for-nothing

لنډی lanḍáj [1] 1.1 short; stumpy 1.2 bobbed; with a cropped tail (of a horse) 1.3 *figurative* brazen (of a person) 2 *m.* .1 short person, shrimp 2.2 *personal name* Landaj

لنډی lanḍə́j [2] 1 *feminine singular of* لنډی 2 *f.* folk melody; a kind of poetry or versification with seven or eight syllables to a line

لنډی lanḍáj [3] *f.* 1 kind of adder 2 *dialect* kind of lizard

لنډی lánḍi [4] *feminine plural of* لنډ

لنډی lanḍé [5] *plural of* لنډه [1]

لنډی lánḍe [6] a combination of the adjective لنډه *and the* preoposition لنډې دا ده يي *in short, speaking briefly*

لنډېدل lanḍedə́l *denominative, intransitive* [*past:* لنډ شو] 1 to shorten; become shorter 2 to become curtailed, lessened, compressed 3 to be expounded in brief 4 to get close *idiom* د هغه لاس لنډ شو They limited his rights.

لنډېده lanḍedə́ *m. plural* 1 shortening روځي په لنډېدو شي The days are growing shorter. 2 curtailment, lessening, compression 3 short exposition, summary 4 growing nearer, approaching

لنډيز lanḍíz lanḍéz *m.* 1 ☞ لنډېده 2 solution (of a problem) 3 summary, short exposition; thesis 4 report 5 list

لنډی سين lanḍáj sin *m.* لنډی سيند lanḍáj sind *m.* Swat (river)

لنډی کوتل lanḍáj koṭál *m.* Landikotal (border point, Pakistan)

لنډی مار lanḍáj mār *m.* kind of adder

لنگ lang [1] lame

لنگ lung [2] *m.* 1 breechclout لنگ وهل wear a breechclout 2 shorts; bathing trunks

لنگتون ləngtún *m.* 1 childbirth, parturition 2 calving (the dropping of young by animals) 3 lying-in-home; obstetrical clinic

لنگته lingáta *f.* backheel (in wrestling) a لنگته اچول، لنگته ايښودل to give someone a backheel trip b to do something bad to someone

لنگر langár *m.* [*plural:* لنگرونه langarúna *f. Eastern plural:* لنگري langáre] 1 anchor لنگر اچول to drop anchor لنگر اخيستل to hoist anchor, haul anchor 2 weight (of a clock) 3 almshouse, refuge, asylum (run by a sheikh, pir) 4 *figurative* slope, declivity

لنگرگاه langargáh *m.* landing, dock (for ships); port; harbor

لنگری langrə́j *f.* 1 kneading trough or vessel 2 deep metal or pottery bowl

لنگس langə́s *m.* narcissus

لنگواله ləngvā́la *f.* ☞ لنگتون 1, 2

لنگوت langót *m.* لنگوته langotá *f.* 1 turban 2 bath towel

لنگور langór *m.* span (space between thumb and forefinger when extended)

لنگول ləngavə́l *denominative, transitive* [*past:* لنگه يي کړه] to impregnate; make pregnant

لنگون ləngún *m.* parturition, children د مبرو لنگون lambing

لنگون خوږ ləngunkhvóg ləngunkhúg spasms, cramps, pangs

لنگه lánga [1] *f.* 1 rope net (for bedsprings) 2 rope (for hauling water out of an irrigation shaft) 3 *figurative* support, aid

لنگه lə́nga [2] *f.* 1 woman in childbirth 2 calving, giving birth to young لنگه غوا a milking cow, cow which has come fresh (giving milk as a result of recent calving)

لنگی lungə́j *f.* ☞ لونگی [1]

لنگېدل ləngedə́l *denominative, intransitive* [*past:* لنگه شوه] 1 to be delivered (of a child); give birth 2 to calve, kitten, drop young (or similar term used to denote the birth of young in specific animals)

لنگېده ləngedə́ *m. plural* childbirth, parturition د لنگبدو درد birth pangs, birth pains, contractions (during childbirth)

لنوکی lənúkaj *m.* pompom (sewed to the bodice of a dress)

لو ¹ lau *m.* lav mowing, reaping, hay-making, harvesting لو او لور reaping لو گډ و to be reaped, be mowed, be harvested The harvest was in progress.

لو ² lav *m.* long tendril of a grapevine

لو ³ lu *m. plural* 1 smoke 2 fumes لوگي کول ☞ لو کول

لو ⁴ lo *f. Western singular of* لوی vice لو خبره لویه bragging فایده a great advantage

لو ⁵ lo *f. no plural* 1 desire 2 appetite

لوا livā *f.* [*plural:* لواوي livāvi] *Arabic military* brigade

لوات lvāt open (e.g., of eyes)

لواتېدل lvātedə́l *denominative, intransitive* [*past:* لوات شو] to open (e.g., of the eyes)

لواحق lavāhíḱ *m. Arabic plural* ☞ لاحقه

لوار luár *m.* Loire (river)

لوار lvāṛ 1 massive, huge لوار اوره coarse-ground flour لوار غنم unground wheat 2 unpolished, uncouth 3 stiff, hard 4 thick, coarse 5 rude, cheeky لوار رغبدل to speak rudely, act cheekily

لوارتوب lvāṛtób *m.* 1 massiveness 2 rudeness, coarseness 3 stiffness, hardness 4 rudeness, cheekiness

لوارگی lvāṛgáj *m.* ☞ لندي کوتل

لوارتوب lvāṛválaj *m.* ☞ لواروالی

لوارول lvāṛavə́l *denominative, transitive* [*past:* لواري کړ] 1 to make massive, make huge 2 to make crude, make coarse 3 to make stiff, make hard 4 to act rudely, act cheekily

لواريدل lvāṛedə́l *denominative, intransitive* [*past:* لوار شو] 1 to be massive, be huge 2 to become rude, become coarse 3 to be stiff, hard, get hard 4 to be rude, be cheeky

لوازم lavāzím *m. Arabic plural* 1 necessary objects 2 *military* supply د لوازمو مدیر chief of supply; quartermaster

لوازمات lavāzimā́t *m. second plural of* لوازم

لوامشر livāmə́shər *m.* livāmə́shr *military* brigadier-general

لواندا luāndā́ Luanda (city)

لوانه lvā́na *f.* shaft of a kariz or irrigation tunnel (the upper part of which is paved with gravel)

لواور lavāvə́r *m.* scythe, sickle ☞ لور ¹

لوایح lavāíh *m. Arabic plural of* لایحه

لوائي lvājí *f.* dawn

لوباتل lobātə́l *transitive* [*past:* و یې لوباته] to compel to take an oath

لوبان lubā́n *m.* incense, frankincense

لوبتک lobaták *m.* variety of wheat

لوبتکه lobatáka *f.* reel

لوبتوکان lóbṭūkā́n *m. computer science* joystick

لوپاجوند lópajwánd *m. computer science* hyperlink

لومتن lómátin *m. computer science* hypertext

لوبت lavbáṭ *m.* ☞ لوپت

لوبدزی lóbdzáj *m.* ☞ د کوچنیانو لوبغی لوبغالی children's playground

لوبغارتوب lobghāṛtób *m.* sport; games

لوبغاری lobghā́ṛaj 1 mischievous, playful (of a child) 2 *m.* .1 mischief-maker, naughty child 2.2 player; sportsman 2.3 artist لوبغاري کوتره a kind of pigeon

لوبغالی lobghā́laj *m.* stadium

لوبگر lobgár *m.* 1 player 2 confidence man, cheat

لوبول lobavə́l *transitive* [*past:* و یې لوباوه] to play ډولکي لوبول to beat the drum رول لوبول to play a role

لوبونه lobavə́na *f.* play

لوبونی lobavúnaj *m.* toy

لوبه lóba *f.* 1 play; fun د لوبو آله card-playing د پاني لوبه toy لوبه ورل، لویي کول to play, have fun لوبه کول to win a game, come out on top in play 2 joke; humorous song 3 fencing 4 sport; games د سپرلی لوبه trick riding (on horseback)

لوبیا ¹ lobjā́ *f.* 1 French beans, haricot-beans 2 beans

لوبیا ² lubijā́ *f.* Libya

لوبدل lobedə́l *intransitive* [*past:* و لوبیده] 1 to be carried away by a game 2 *literal & figurative* to be a toy, serve as a plaything

لوپ lup *m.* trick, ruse لوپ کول to contrive, manage

لوپته lupaṭá *f.* 1 woman's shawl, veil 2 *figurative* cover, covering (snow, etc.)

لوپ-لوپ lúpa-lúpa disheveled (of hair)

لوت lavt flaccid, weak پنبه لوته اینودل a to stumble b to act precipitately

لوتبه lotə́ba *f.* typhus

لوت ¹ luṭ *m.* 1 robbery لوت ورل، لوت اخیستل to rob 2 a raid

لوت ² loṭ *m.* banknote, currency; paper money

لوتباز luṭbāz rapacious, predatory

لوتپاټ luṭpā́ṭ *m.* robbery

لوت پوټ ¹ luṭ-púṭ completely pillaged لوت پوټ کول to plunder, loot لوت پوټ کېدل to be cleaned out by robbery

لوت پوټ ² loṭ-póṭ لوت پوټ کول to stick out, throw out (something)

لوتکه loṭká *f.* a handleless jug

لوتکی ¹ loṭkáj *m.* [*plural:* لوتکي loṭkí *plural:* لوتکیان lotkijā́n] hearth composed either of three stones on which cooking vessels are supported, trivet, or sometimes a small pillar of baked clay, three of which are used to form a tripod for supporting the iron dish on which cakes of Afghan bread are made

لوتکی ² loṭkáj *m.* a kind of pot used on Persian waterwheels

لوت لوت loṭ-lóṭ لوت لوت اونېتل a to sway, rock rhythmically b to be visible, loom

لوتمار luṭmár *m.* 1 robber, marauder 2 ☞ لوته مار

لوتماري luṭmāri *f.* robbery, brigandage

لوتماله luṭmālá *f.* scraper; harrow

لوت میری luṭmíraj *m.* robber chieftan, gang leader

لوتن loṭə́n *m.* kind of dove

لوتنه luṭə́na *f.* ☞ لوتونه

لوتول luṭavə́l *denominative, transitive* [*past:* لوت یې کړ] to rob, pillage; clean someone out by robbery

لوتونه luṭavə́na *f.* robbery, pillage

لوټه ¹ lúṭa *f.* clod, clod of earth *idiom* لوټي لوټي کول *compound verb* to destroy, ravage *idiom* خان په لویه لوټه خېژول to give oneself airs, have a swelled head, think a lot of oneself

لوټه ² loṭá *f.* small jug; small bucket

لوټه مار luṭamár *m. agriculture* mallet, tamper

لوټي luṭí ruined, impoverished

لوټېدل luṭedə́l *denominative, intransitive* [*past:* لوټ شو] to be robbed, be pillaged, be cleaned out by thieves

لوټېری luṭeráj *m.* vagrant; robber

لوجستیک lodzhistík *m.* logistics (as a science)

لوچک luchák 1 shabby, having sparse hair (of a dog) 2 *m.* .1 tramp, vagrant 2.2 landless or homeless peasant; a lonely man 2.3 [*plural:* لوچکان luchakā́n] the poor

لوچه ¹ luchá ☞ لوچک

لوچی luchə́j *f.* twigs (pastry)

لوخ luts ☞ لوخ ښاخونه bare boughs

لوخ پوخ کېدل lutspúts to roll over the ground

لوخ سر lutssár bareheaded, with uncovered head

لوچک lutsák ☞

لوخکه lutsáka *f.* naked child, unclothed doll

لوخکی ¹ lutskáj flattering, smooth-tongued, insincere

لوخکي ² lutsáki *plural of* لوخکه

لوخول ³ lutsavə́l *denominative, transitive* [*past:* لوخ يې کړ] 1 to strip naked, strip bare 2 *agriculture* to strip a vine *idiom* پنبه لوخول to look for work

لوخه lvátsa *f.* entertaining guests arranged in turn

لوخي پوخي lótsi-pótsi *f. plural* 1 wails, supplications 2 throwing, tossing لوخي پوخي کول a to suffer profoundly b to toss about c to writhe in hysteria 3 rolling on the ground (of horses) 4 floundering 5 playing, fun (children)

لوخېدل lutsedə́l *denominative, intransitive* [*past:* لوخ شو] to undress, bare oneself ☞ لخېدل

لوح lauh *m. Arabic* [*plural:* الواح alvā́h] 1 board upon which letters are written 2 board or tablet used by schoolboys to write upon

لوحه lauhá *f. Arabic* 1 ruler, straightedge 2 tablet, chart 3 screen 4 placard, poster هنري لوحه a picture

لوخړول lukhṛavə́l *transitive* ☞

لوخړه lukhára *f.* thick smoke لوخړه جگه شوه Thick smoke was arising. توده لوخړه puffs of smoke and flame

لوخه lúkha 1 bulrush, *Pencillaria spicata* 2 *Juncus effusus* (a kind of soft reed)

لوخی lókhaj *m. Eastern* ☞ لوبنی ¹

لودانه lodā́na lavdā́na *f. Western* gutter, drainpipe

لودره ¹ lovdára *f.* stitch لودره کول to take a stitch

لودره ² lodə́ra *f.* tug (rope or chain trace) of a plow

لودل lodə́l lavi *transitive* [*present:* لوي *past:* و یې لودل] to confirm, testify, give evidence

لودن lodán *m.* side, direction *idiom* لودن ورکول a to get lost, disappear b to go wrong, be deflected from the path, be deflected from the right way

لودنه lodə́na *f.* confirmation; testimony, giving of evidence

لوده lodá *m.* [*plural:* لودگان lodagā́n] dolt, fool, bonehead, boob

لودي ¹ lodí *m. plural* the Lodi (tribe, dynasty) 2 lodáj *m.* Lodi (tribesman)

لودیان ¹ lodjā́n *m. plural* ☞ لودي 1

لودیان ² lodjā́n *m. plural* constellation of two stars appearing in the morning in the southeast

لودین lodín *m. plural* ☞ لودي

لودسپیکر laudspikár *m.* loudspeaker, amplifier

لوده loḍá *m.* ☞ لوده

لور ¹ lor *m.* [*plural:* لورونه lorúna *plural:* لرونه larúna] sickle *idiom* لور په لوټه اچول to be engaged in a purposeless matter *idiom* لور په لوټه تېرول to grind water in a mortar

لور ² lor *m.* side, direction لور په لور on all sides; everywhere د لوره from all sides

لور ³ lur *f.* [*plural:* لوڼي lúṇi *dialect plural:* لوراني lurā́ne *plural:* لورگاني lurgā́ni] daughter دیني لور foster daughter د چا د لور پوښتنه کول to court, ask (someone's daughter) in marriage

لور ⁴ lur *m.* Lur (a people)

لور ⁵ laur *m.* ☞ لورونه

لورستان luristā́n *m.* Luristan

لورغی lorgháj *m.* young ram (lamb) given to a shepherd as a form of payment

لورگ ləvárg *m.* gopher

لورگی lorgáj *m.* reaping knife, chopper

لورم lvarə́m *m.* لورن lvarə́n *m.* [*plural:* لورند lvarə́nd] *botany* madder

لورنه lavrə́na *f.* kindness, goodness, benefaction لورنه غوښتل to ask forgiveness لورنه کول to do a kindness, have pity

لوروځ lo rvadz *f. Western religion* Judgment Day, the End of the World

لورول lavravə́l *transitive* [*past:* و یې لوراوه] 1 to consider worthy, favor someone 2 to do good, show kindness, demonstrate mercy

لوری ¹ lóraj *m.* side, direction له بل لوري lóri from the other side د چا لوری نیول to show support to someone, support someone

لوری ² lúri *imperative of* لور ³

لوربدل lavredə́l *intransitive* 1 to be worthy, deserve, merit 2 و لوربد to grant, allocate someone something (e.g., from one's property) ولوربده

لوربزه lavréza *f.* kind of embroidery stitching

لورین lavrín good; considerate, obliging; kind

لورینه lavrína *f.* 1 goodness; consideration, courtesy 2 recognition of someone's right

لوربیل lavrejə́l *transitive* ☞ لورول

لوړ loṛ 1 stake, picket 2 pestle

لوﺭ lavə́r *m.* 1 cane; walking stick 2 truncheon, baton 3 stake; picket

لوﺭ lvəṛ lvaṛ *literal & figurative* 1 high لوﺭ مقامات higher echelons 2 mountainous, elevated, lofty لوﺭ او ﺧﻮﺭ a uneven, broken (terrain) b mountains and valleys په لوﺭ اوﺧﻮﺭ over mountains and valleys 3 loud (of a voice) په لوﺭ ﺑﺮﻍ ويل to speak loudly 4 above-mentioned, above-cited 5 outstanding (of a feat, etc.) لوﺭي ﻛﺎرﻧﺎﻣﻲ outstanding feats د لوﺭ ﻓﻜﺮ ﺧﺎوﻧﺪ intelligent man, thoughtful man چاته لوﺭ ﻛﺘﻞ to regard someone with condescension

لوﺭاوي lvəṛā́vaj *m.* 1 ascent; movement upward 2 honor, respect

لوﺭﺗﻮب lvəṛtób *m.* لوﺭﺗﺠﺎ lvəṛtjā́ *f.* ☞ لوﺭواﻟﻰ aviation لوﺭﺗﻴﺎ ﻧﻴﻮل to climb, gain altitude

لوﺭﺗﻨﮕﻰ چوﻛﻰ lvəṛtsángaj having supports armchair

لوﺭرﺗﺒﻪ lvəṛrutbá high-ranking

لوﺭﻗﺪ lvəṛḳád strapping, tall

لوﺭﻗﻴﻤﺘﻪ lvəṛḳimáta dear, expensive

لوﺭﻛﻰ [1] lvəṛakáj *m.* fatha, zabar (a supra-linear sign indicating the short a vowel)

لوﺭﻛﻰ [2] loṛəkáj *m.* 1 pipe, tube 2 roller, cylinder 3 roost 4 flick (of the finger on the brow)

لوﺭﻛﻰ [3] lavṛəkaj *m.* truncheon, baton

لوﺭل loṛə́l *transitive* [*past:* وﻱ يﻲ لوﺭل] to vow, take an oath

لوﺭﻣﺎزدﻳﮕﺮ lvəṛmāzdigár *m.* لوﺭﻣﺎزﻳﮕﺮ lvəṛmāzigár *m.* the time just before evening; four o'clock P.M.

لوﺭﻧﻪ loṛə́na *f.* vow, oath

لوﺭﻧﻰ lvəṛanáj upper

لوﺭو loṛú *m.* man given to oaths

لوﺭواﻟﻪ lvəṛvā́la *f.* لوﺭواﻟﻰ lvəṛvā́laj *m.* 1 height, elevation 2 rise, increase (of prices, taxes, etc.) 3 altitude په ۲۰۰۰ ﻣﺘﺮ لوﺭواﻟﻪ ﻛﺒﻨﻲ lvəṛvā́li at an altitude of 2,000 meters 4 development, progress 5 ascent اﻧﺘﻬﺎﺋﻲ لوﺭواﻟﻪ aviation ceiling (a.c.)

لوﺭول [1] lvəṛavə́l *denominative, transitive* [*past:* لوﺭ يﻲ ﻛﺮ] 1 to raise, elevate 2 *figurative* to lift د ﻋﺴﻜﺮو ﻣﻌﻨﻮﻳﺎت لوﺭول to raise the morale of an army 3 to erect, build (e.g., a wall) 4 to develop, promote progress

لوﺭول [2] luṛavə́l *transitive* [*past:* وﻱ يﻲ لوﺭاوه] to peel, strip, flay (e.g., a hide) د ولﻲ پوﺗﻜﻲ لوﺭول to peel the bark from a willow

لوﺭول loṛavə́l *transitive* [*past:* وﻱ يﻲ لوﺭاوه] to make or take an oath

لوﺭه lóṛa *f.* oath, vow لوﺭه ﻛﻮل to take an oath, swear لوﺭه ﺳﺮه اﭼﻮل to exchange vows

لوﺭه lvə́ṛa *f.* lvaṛa 1 altitude, elevation; mountainous terrain; plateau ﻣﺰارﺷﺮﻳﻒ پﺮ لوﺭه دئ Mazari-Sherif is located on the heights. 2 *feminine singular of* لوﺭ [3]

لوﺭه loṛá *f.* gully; temporarily dry gulch

لوﺭه loṛá *f.* Lora (river, Beludzhistan)

لوﺭه ﺩﺯوﺭه lvə́ṛa-dzvára *f.* لوﺭه ژوره lvə́ṛa-zhavára lvə́ṛa-zhavára *f.* 1 ascent and descent 2 broken terrain

لوﺭي [1] lvəṛí *f.* 1 altitude above sea level 2 promotion (e.g., in service) ﺳﺘﺎﺳﻲ لوﺭي ﻏﻮاړم *espistolary* I wish you success.

لوﺭى [2] lóṛaj *m.* ☞ لوﺭﻛﻰ [2]

لوﺭي ﺩﺯوﺭي lvəṛi-dzvári *plural of* لوﺭه ﺧﻮره

لوﺭﻳﺪل [1] lvəṛedə́l 1 [*past:* لوﺭ شو] *denominative, intransitive* 1.1 to arise, elevate oneself 1.2 to receive a promotion 1.3 to rise, be extolled 1.4 to be preferred 1.5 to rise, increase (of price, taxes, etc.) 1.6 to improve (of quality) 1.7 to develop, flourish 2 *m. plural* ☞ لوﺭﻳﺪه [1]

لوﺭﻳﺪل [2] luṛedə́l *intransitive* [*present:* لوﺭي *past:* و لوﺭﻳﺪه] to be flayed off (of hide, etc.); peel off in layers; fall off in layers

لوﺭﻳﺪﻧﻪ lvəṛedə́na *f.* لوﺭﻳﺪه lvəṛedə *m. plural* 1 rise, height 2 raise, promotion (in service, job) 3 extolling 4 preference 5 rise, increase (in prices, taxes, etc.) 6 improvement (in quality) 7 development, flourishing; progress 8 arrival, appearance

لوﺭﻳﺰ lavəṛíẓ *m.* wanderer, vagrant

لوﺭﻳﺰه lavṛíza *f.* kind of sewing or stitching

لوﺭي ژوري lvəṛi-zhavári *plural of* لوﺭه ژوره

لوﺯ lavz *m.* word, promise, agreement لوﺯ ﻛﻮل، لوﺯ را ﻛﻮل، لوﺯ در ﻛﻮل ﺧﭙﻞ لوﺯ ﻣﺎﺗﻮل to give one's word, promise, agree لوﺯ ورﻛﻮل to break one's word, break one's promise, violate one's agreement ☞ ﻟﻔﻆ

لوﺯﻧﺎﻣﻪ lavznāmá *f.* accord, agreement

لوﺯه [1] lavzá *f. Arabic* 1 almond 2 tonsil

لوﺯه [2] lúza *f.* honeybee

لوﺯه [3] lúza *f.* pine sapling

لوﺯي [1] lavzí *Arabic adjective* 1 almond 2 *f.* rhombus

لوﺯي [2] luzáj *m.* wall

لوﺯي lavzé *plural of* لوﺯه [1]

لوﺯي lúzi *plural of* لوﺯه [2, 3]

لوﺯي lvə́zi *separable part of present of* اﻟﻮﺗﻞ

لوژ lozh *m.* loge (in a theater, etc.)

لوﮔﻨﺪه lvagónda *f. medicine* uterine cyst

لوﮔﻪ lvága *f.* hunger; famine د لوﺭي ﻏﺎﺑﻨﻮﻧﻪ ﺗﻮدول to relieve hunger لوﺭه پﺮ دوی ﻏﺎﻟﺒﻪ شوه Hunger overtook them.

لوس los *m.* loess

لوﺳﺎﻛﺎ lusā́kā́ *f.* Lusaka (city)

لوس اﻧﺠﻠﺲ los-ándzhilos *m.* Los Angeles

لوﺳﺖ [1] lvast *m.* lvəst 1 learning; studies 2 reading لوﺳﺖ او ﻟﻴﻚ reading and writing 3 lesson ﺗﺮ لوﺳﺖ the final lesson

لوﺳﺖ [2] lvast lvest *imperfect of* لوﺳﺘﻞ [1]

لوﺳﺖ [3] lost *m.* vomiting, nausea

لوﺳﺖ [4] lust *imperfect of* لوﺳﺘﻞ [2]

لوﺳﺘﺎﻧﯽ lvəstānə́j *f.* female teacher of girls

لوﺳﺘﺨﺎی lvəstdzáj *m.* لوﺳﺘﺨﻰ lvə́stdzáj *m.* 1 classroom; auditorium 2 courses

لوﺳﺘﻞ [1] lvastə́l 1 *transitive* [*present:* لولﻲ *past:* وﻱ يﻲ لوﺳﺖ] 1.1 to read, read through 1.2 to read out (a declaration, etc.) 1.3 to teach چاته درسوﻧﻪ لوﺳﺘﻞ to teach someone, give lessons to

لوستل somebody د منطق درسونه یې طالبانو ته لوستل He taught the students a course in logic. **2** *m. plural* ☞ لوست [1]

لوستل [2] lustə́l *transitive* [*present:* لوني *past:* ویې لوست] **1** to pour, strew, scatter; sprinkle, pour (on) **2** to spray; splash

لوستل [3] lostə́l *transitive* [*past:* ویې لوست] to vomit, throw up

لوستلئ [1] lvastə́ləj *past participle of* لوستل [1]

لوستلئ [2] lustə́ləj *past participle of* لوستل [2]

لوستلئ [3] lostə́ləj *past participle of* لوستل [3]

لوستلي [4] lvastə́li *m. plural* lesson (read through, gone through)

لوستنه lvastə́na *f.* reading; reading through

لوستنه lustə́na *f.* **1** sprinkling; pouring over **2** splashing; sprinkling upon

لوستنه lostə́na *f.* vomiting, nausea

لوستون lvastún *m.* lvustún ☞ لوست [1]

لوستونکی [1] lvastúnkaj **1** *present participle of* لوستل [1] **2** *m.* **.1** reader **2.2** student

لوستونکی [2] lustúnkaj *present participle of* لوستل [2] د لوستونکی ګروپ رڼا beacon; lamp

لوستونکی [3] lostúnkaj *present participle of* لوستل [3]

لوستونی lvastúnaj clear; legible (of handwriting)

لوستون lvastún *m.* sleeve د لوستون خولې cuffs

لوسته [1] lvastə́ *m. plural* ☞ لوستنه [1]

لوسته [2] lustə́ *m. plural* ☞ لوستنه [2]

لوسته [3] lostə́ *m. plural* nausea, vomiting

لوستی [1] lvástaj lvə́staj educated, well-read; literate

لوستئ [2] lvástəj ☞ لوستلئ [1]

لوشکی lushəkáj *m.* rice porridge with warm milk

لوشل lvashə́l lvəshə́l *transitive* [*past:* ویې لوشله] **1** to milk **2** *figurative* to wring out

لوشونکی [1] lvəshúnkaj **1** *present participle of* لوشل **2** *m.* dairyman, milker

لوشونکې [2] lvəshúnke **1** *present participle of* لوشل **2** *f.* milkmaid

لوشي lúshi *f. plural* black mud; slime, ooze

لوبنتل lvə̣khtə́l *intransitive* ☞ لوبېدل [2]

لوبتی [1] loḵtáj *m.* lvaḵhtáj wild almond (the tree or its fruit)

لوبتي [2] loḵhə́ti *f.* لوبنلوني loḵhlúni *f. plural* slops, dirty water (dishwater)

لوبنه lóḵha *f.* **1** custom (moral) nature, character **2** virtue, quality

لوبنی [1] lóḵhaj *m.* **1** dish, dishware; jug, pot چینی لوبنی lóḵhi silicates; porcelain dishware **2** pottery لوبني او لرګی lóḵhi tableware

لوبني [2] lóḵhi *plural of* لوبنه

لوبنینه loḵhína *f.* slops

لوطي lutí *m. Arabic* **1** playboy; dissolute male, debauchee **2** homosexual

لوطیانه lutijāná **1** dissolute, debauched **2** indecent, obscene

لوظ lauz *m.* word (of honor), promise لوظ کول, لوظ را کول, لوظ در کول to give one's word, promise لوظ پوره کول to keep one's word لوظ ورکول not to keep one's word په لوظ ملامت کېدل

لوغ lvagh *m.* yield of milk

لوغرن lughərə́n **1** slightly burnt **2** dirty, soiled; sooty

لوغرول lughṛavə́l *transitive* [*past:* ویې لوغراوه] **1** to roll in the dust **2** to soil, smirch

لوغړېدل lughṛedə́l *intransitive* [*past:* ولوغړېده] **1** to roll in the dust, grovel in the dust **2** to be soiled, be smudged

لوغزه lvághza *f.* cow or goat which is giving milk

لوغسنه lvaghsə́na not permitting itself to be milked (of a cow, goat)

لوغل lvaghə́l *transitive* [*past:* ویې لوغله] to milk ☞ لوشل

لوغول lughavə́l *transitive* [*past:* ویې لوغاوه] **1** to roll (into the earth) **2** to trample

لوغېدل lughedə́l *intransitive* [*past:* ولوغېده] **1** to be rolled (in or into the soil or earth) **2** to be trampled

لوک [1] lok *m.* camel in its fifth year

لوک [2] luk *m.* meteor

لوکات lokā́ṭ *m.* lavkā́ṭ the Japanese medlar (a fruit from a bush of the rose family)

لوکړ lukáṛ *m.* ☞ منډاوو

لوکس luks **1** *m.* **.1** luxury لوکس هوټل first-class hotel **1.2** luxuriance, splendor په ډېر لوکس ژوند luxuriantly, excellently لوکس مالونه luxury articles **2** *attributive* luxuriant, excellent

لوکسمبورګ luksambúrg *m.* Luxembourg (city)

لوکښ lukáḵh *m.* pipe (stove)

لوکوتی lukótaj *Eastern* ☞ لړکوتی

لوکوموتیف lokomotíf *m.* locomotive engine برقي لوکوموتیف electric engine

لوګ log *m. regional* people

لوګ جن lugdzhə́n smoke-filled, smoky, impregnated with smoke

لوګر [1] lavgór *m.* reaper

لوګر [2] logár *m.* Loga (province, river) د لوګر ولایت Logar Province

لوګری lavgóraj *m.* ☞ لوګر [1]

لوګړ logáṛ *m. agriculture* **1** scraper **2** harrow

لوګن lugə́n **1** smoking **2** sooty; smoky

لوګه lóga *f.* desert land unfit for cultivation

لوګی lugáj *m.* **1** smoke لوګی کول **a** to smoke **b** to burn up **c** to smoke, envelop in smoke **2** gas

لوګی تاوان lugí tāvā́n *m. history* household tax

لول lval lvə́l *present stem of* لوستل [1]

لولپاند lulapānd لولپه lulapá *obsolete* **1** burned up, scorched, cremated **2** destroyed **3** burning لولپاند کول **a** to burn down, burn up, scorch **b** to destroy **c** to torture, torment لولپاند کېدل **a** to burn; be scorched, be burned up **b** to be destroyed **c** to be tortured

لولکی [1] lolakáj *m.* round stick

لولکی [2] lolakə́j *f.* **1** butterfly, moth **2** piece of sweet dough formed into a tube then fried in oil and used as a pacifier

لولمن lolamə́n *f.* generosity, good-heartedness

لولنده loləndá skimming along, rolling, swaying, falling

لولو [1] lulú *m.* scarecrow

لولو ² loló *f.* bracelet

لولول lvalavól *transitive* [*past:* وي يې لولاوه] 1.1 to cause to read 1.2 to teach; instruct 2 *m. plural* ☞ لولونه

لولونه lvalavóna *f.* 1 teaching, instruction 2 education

لوله lolá *f.* 1 spool of thread 2 package, bundle 3 tube لوله کول *compound verb* to roll into a tube (e.g., a sheet of paper) 4 *anatomy* tract (e.g., the digestive) لوله کباب kebab made of spiced ground meat patties

لوله کشي lolakashí *f.* pipe-laying

لولۍ lolә́j *f.* prostitute

لولي توب lolәjtób *m.* prostitution

لمبر ¹ lumbáṛ *m.* fox, dog-fox

لمبر ² lumbә́ṛ ☞ لمړی

لومبړه lumbára *f.* she-fox, vixen

لومړنۍ lumṛanáj ☞ لمړنی

لومړی lumṛaj ☞ لمړی

لومړی خبري lumṛáj khabәri *f. plural* preface, foreword

لومشر lomәsh r *m. history* head (of government, etc.)

لومکه lumáka *f.* ☞ لمکه

لومني lomәní *f.* arrogance, conceit

لومه ¹ lúma *f.* ☞ لومی

لومی ¹ lumә́j *f.* net, snare

لومي ² lomé *f.* Lome (city)

لون laun *m. Arabic* [*plural:* لونونه launúna *Arabic plural:* الوان alvә́n] 1 dye; color 2 look; aspect

لوان laván *present stem of* لوستل

لومبر lumbә́ṛ *m.* ☞ لمبر

لومبړه lumbә́ra *f.* ☞ لومبړه

لونته lunṭá bobtailed; cropped

لونتی مونتی lunṭáj-munṭáj tailless and earless

لوند lund *m.* لنده landá *f. m.* [*plural:* لانده lāndә́ *f. plural:* لندي landé] 1 damp, wet, moist لنده هوا damp air 2 juicy (of fruit) 3 fresh (of fruit)

لوندخیشت lund khisht لنده خیشته landá khishtá *f. m.* [*plural:* لانده خیشته lāndә́ khishtә́ *f. plural:* لندي خیشتي landé khishté] soaked through, soaking wet

لوندر lavandә́ṛ good-for-nothing, useless

لندوالی lundvә́laj *m.* ☞ لندوالی

لندول lundavól *denominative, transitive* ☞ لندول

لندیدل lundedól *denominative, transitive* ☞ لندیدل

لوند lavánd 1 *m.* .1 bachelor 1.2 rake, playboy 1.3 outsider, man from the outside (not having the right of access to the woman's side) 2 single, bachelor

لونډتوب laandṭób *m.* bachelor life

لونډتیا lavanḍtjá *f.* 1 immodesty 2 dissipation, debauchery

لونډه lavánḍa *f.* immodest woman

لونګ laváng *m.* cloves (flower, spice)

لونګ بوتی lavangbútaj *m. botany* basil

لونګجن lavangdzhә́n aromatic, sweet-smelling

لونګۍ ¹ lungә́j *f.* 1 longi (a strip of silk or cotton cloth used as a belt), girdle 2 turban 3 veil

لونګی ² lavangә́j *f.* kind of rice

لونګین lavangín *m.* garland of pinks لونګین هار the garland of pinks (i.e., a gift of the bridgeroom to the bride)

لونل lunә́l lavanә́l *transitive* ☞ لوستل ² پسرلي پر مخکه و لونل ګلونه Spring has bedecked the earth with flowers.

لونم lunә́m lavanә́m *first person of* لوستل ²

لونه luná *f.* boil, carbuncle; abscess

لوني ¹ luní lavaní *present of* لوستل ²

لونی ² lúnaj speaking, pronouncing

لونیدل lunedól *intransitive* [*past:* ولونیدل] to be strewn, be spread about, be sprinkled around

لونیک lúnník *m. botany* honesty (garden flower with large purple flowers and transparent capsules)

لونه lúṇa *f. plural regional* لوني lúṇi *f. plural of* لور ³

لوورۍ lovә́raj *m.* 1 the Holy One 2 in whose name one swears

لوول ¹ lovә́l [*past:* و يې لووله] شاهدي لوول to testify, give evidence

لوول ² lavavól *denominative, transitive* [*past:* لو يې کړ] to reap, harvest (grain)

لوولور lav-u-lór *m.* reaping, harvesting (grain); haying-time; harvest work

لوونه lavavóna *f.* reaping the harvest

لووی lóvaj *m.* witness لووی غوښتل to summon a witness

لوه ¹ lә́va *f.* water in swampy soil

لوه ² loh *f.* 1 appetite زما لوه ولاړه شوه I developed an appetite. راولل to evoke or cause an appetite (to arise) 2 raising, nurturing; growing 3 attraction, inclination

لوهار lohә́r *m. Eastern* blacksmith

لوهارخانه lohārkhānā *f.* smithy, forge

لوهاني ¹ lohāní *m. plural* the Lohani (tribe) 2 lohānáj *m.* Lohani, Lohanaj (tribesman)

1 لوهاني lohāní *m. plural* ☞ لوهاني

لوهټ lohә́ṭ *m.* ☞ لوبټ

لوهړه luhә́ra *f.* ☞ لوخړه

لوهن lohә́n causing an appetite (to arise); tasty, appetizing

لوهه lóha *f.* ☞ لوه

لوهیدل lo'edól *denominative, intransitive* ☞ لوبیدل

لوی ¹ lavj *m.* [*plural:* لویان lavijә́n] reaper; hay-gatherer

لوی ² lavә́j *f.* soot

لوی ³ lavә́j *f.* reaper (female)

لوی ⁴ lә́vaj *m.* cutting edge of a saber

لوی ⁵ loj luj 1.1 large, great, huge لوی ډنډ lake 1.2 loud, piercing 1.3 adult, grown لوی سړی grown man 1.4 eminent, great لوی کڼل، لوی بلل to regard as great; extoll 1.5 exalted, venerable 1.6 important, significant لوی شرط an important cicumstance 2.1 adult د لویانو کورسونه courses for adults 2.2 great man 2.3 grandee, exalted personage; rich man 2.4 (tribal) chief, chiefman لوی اختر a Muslim holiday celebrating the Sacrifice of Abraham د

لوی اختر میاشت the twelfth month of the lunar year (in which the Feast of Sacrifice falls) لوی حکومت regional High Court لوی جج province لوی دښمن a sworn enemy لوی رنغ typhoid fever لوی زړه a bravery b endurance, staying power لوی منشي secretary-general په لوی لاس a wittingly b definitely

لوی ⁶ láve f. ovine tuberculosis

لوی ⁷ lavə́j f. payment to a (female) reaper

لوی ⁸ lə́ve f. milk cattle

لویت lojā́t m. primogeniture

لوپت lvet m. monal pheasant, Himalayan pheasant

لویځی lvédzáj m. crash site (of an aircraft)

لوېدل ¹ lvedə́l [past: ولوېده] intransitive 1 to fall; go down 2 to settle (of precipitate, deposit) 3 to flow into (of a river) 4 to set (of celestial bodies) لمر ولوېده The sun set. 5 to be, lie, be disposed 6 to be, turn out to be مفید لوېدل to turn out to be useful د یو کار مانع لوېدل to be an impediment to something 7 to come, arise (of thoughts); appear, arise (of suspicion) 8 to occupy (a job, a post) 9 to be set, be put, be placed (in motion, operation) 10 to be deprived of something 11 to fall down, sink 12 to cost, come to (of goods) ارزانه لوېدل to be cheap 13 to fall, decrease (of a tax) مالیات پرتجارانو لوېږي The merchants are taxed.

لوېدل ² lavedə́l [past: ولو شو] intransitive to be mowed, be reaped, be removed

لوېدلی lvedə́ləj 1 past participle of لوېدل ¹ 2 backward (of countries)

لوېدنه lvedə́na f. ☞ لوېده ¹

لوېده ¹ lvedə́ m. plural 1 falling, going down 2 settling (of precipitation, deposits) 3 flowing into (of a river) 4 setting (of the sun) 5 arising, appearance 6 decline (moral)

لوېده ² lvedə́ imperfect plural of لوېدل ¹

لوېدیځ lvedídz 1 m. the west 2 western لوېدیځه نړی the West, the countries of the West

لوبرند lvegə́nd m. freeloader, parasite, do-nothing

لوبرنده lvegə́nda f. anatomy 1 fontanelle 2 temple

لوبرنه lvegə́na f. sponging, freeloading, parasitism, scrounging

لوبره lvéga imperfective, imperative of لوبدل ¹

لویس los lóis los m. loess د لویس خاوره loess, loessal soil

لوبشت lvesht f. [plural: لوبشتي lveshti] span یوه لوبشت خاوره، یوه a span of land یوشی لوبشت کول compound verb ☞ لوبشت مځکه لوبشتول

لوبشتکی lveshtəkáj m. dwarf, midget, pigmy

لوبشتول lveshtavə́l [past: لوبشت یې کړ] denominative, transitive to measure by or in spans

لوبشتنک lveshtenák m. ☞ لوبشتکی

لوبنت lojə́kht m. 1 growth, development د نباتاتو لوبنت growth of a plant 2 size, magnitude

لوی کالیبر lojkālíbr large caliber

لوبگند lvegə́nd m. ☞ لوبرند

لوبگنده lvegə́nda f. ☞ لوبرنده

لوی لوی lvəjlvə́j bitterly, violently لوی لوی ژړل to weep bitterly, cry violently

لوی ناب، لویناب lojnā́b m. history governor general

لوی نابي lojnābí f. province

لوینه ¹ lojə́na f. 1 maturity, manhood; adulthood 2 magnitude, great size

لوینه ² lvína f. stone trap (for catching birds)

لوی والی lojvā́laj m. ☞ لوینه ¹

لویل ¹ lojavə́l [past: لوی یې کړ] denominative, transitive 1 to increase, enlarge 2 to raise, grow 3 to extoll 4 to intensify (e.g., sound)

لویل ² lvajavə́l transitive [past: وی یې لویاوه] to lower, let down

لویونه lojavə́na f. 1 increase, enlargement 2 raising, nurturing; growing 3 extolling 4 intensification (e.g., noise, sound)

لویه lója feminine singular of لوی ⁵ لویه جرگه the loja jirga لویه ورځ to ☞ لوروځ

لویي lojí f. 1 greatness, grandeur د زړه لویي nobility لویي غوښتل to strive for greatness 2 arrogance, conceit لویي کول to be arrogant, to grow conceited

لویدل lojedə́l [past: لوی شو] denominative, intransitive 1 to increase, grow large 2 to grow 3 to mature, become adult 4 to be nutured; be reared 5 to be extolled 6 to be intensified, intensify (of sound)

لویده lojedə́ m. plural 1 increase 2 growth, development 3 growing up, becoming an adult

له ¹ lə preposition 1 used with or without the suffix or postposition 1a څخه، نه from (to designate the direction from whence something comes or the source or place from whence it comes) له تا،له تا څخه from thee 1b له بامه from the roof له کوره from home of (to designate the person or thing to which something else belongs or to which it relates) له تاسي you have, your's 1c from, for (to indicate the reason or the basis for something) له دي کبله، له دي لامله because of this, for this reason له غمه ژاړم I am weeping from sorrow. 1d on, upon (to indicate physical contact, touching, or contiguity with something, someone) له دېواله ویشتل to strike the wall, hit the wall 2 used to express the comparative and superlative degree له واوري سوړ colder than snow 3 with (used independently or in combination with the postposition, indicates the combination or accompaniment of something, or someone with something, or someone else) له ملگري سره with a friend یو له بله with one another idiom له پاره ددي چه in order that, in order to; because

له ² la postposition vice ته ماله راشه! Come to me! ژمي له for the winter; in winter; toward winter را له to us, to me ښوونځی له in school; to school

لهجوي lahdzhaví linguistics 1 articulatory 2 dialectic لهجوي اتلس dialectic atlas لهجوي خصوصیات dialectic peculiarities

لهجه lahdzhá f. Arabic 1 accent, pronunciation 2 dialect; mode of speech; local speech په ملي لهجه اشعار لیکل to write verses in a popular spirit **3** tone په ډېره خوږه لهجه ویل to speak very affectionately, in an affectionate tone لهجه پسته کول to soften one's tone

لهجوي لهجه ئي lahdzhaí ☞

لهذا lihazá *Arabic* for this reason, as a consequence of this

لهر lahár *m.* **1** impetuosity; rapidity, quickness, liveliness **2** squall; squally wind

له رویه lərúja according to, in accordance with something, in conformity to something

لهړ lahə́ṛ *m. geography* deep and wide basin

لهړی lahaṛáj *m.* **1** beam, girder **2** footbridge; log

له سره ləsára **1** quite, decisively **2** anew, again, from the beginning له سره کول to repeat (said or done again)

له ښکي ləx̌ké ☞ له لاندي

له کمه ləkə́ma where from

له لاندي lə́lā́ndi from below, from under something

لهلپاند lahlapā́nd ☞ لولپه

له لیري lə́líri from after, from far away

له مخه ləmə́kha forward; ahead له مخه شو He went forward.

لهو lahv *m. Arabic* play, fun; entertainment وخت په لهو تېرول to enjoy oneself, have fun

له واره ləvára at once, immediately; suddenly, in a flash

له ورا ləvará له ورایه ləvrā́ja from afar

لهه láha *f.* **1** silt; mud **2** slime

لهه ژن lahazhə́n **1** silty, muddy **2** slimey

له یوه مخه ləjavə́ lába له یوه مخه ləjavə́ mə́kha **1** fully, quite **2** in succession, running

لی ¹ laj *m.* ☞ لای

لي ² li *present tense of* لل ³ دا یې پر فداکاری شاهدي لي This testifies to their selflessness.

لئ ³ ləj *second person present tense plural of* لوستل *vice* لولئ

لیا ljā *dialect* ☞ لا ¹

لیار ljār *f.* لیاره ljā́ra *dialect* ☞ لار د سولي له لیاري کول to resolve something by peaceful means

لیاړي ljā́ṛe *f. plural* ☞ لاړي

لیاشه ljā́sha *f.* ☞ لشکه

لیاقت lijā́ḳát *m. Arabic* **1** qualification; fitness; suitability **2** merit; virtue اخلاقي لیاقت moral qualities **3** ability; talant عادي لیاقت ordinary abilities علمي لیاقت scientific abilities **4** wisdom; intelligence **5** *proper name* Liakat, Liaqat

لیبرالسم liberālísm *m.* liberalism

لیبرالیست liberālíst *m.* liberal

لیبرالیستي liberālistí liberal لیبرالیستي نهضت liberalism; liberal trend, liberal tendency

لیبرویل librvíl *m.* Libreville (city)

لببل lebál *m. regional* label, tag *idiom* پر چا باندي لببل لگول to put a label on someone

لیبوزه lebúza *f.* ledge (of a mountain)

لیبیا libijā́ *f.* Libya

لیپړی ¹ lepṛáj *m.* ☞ لای ²

لیپړی ² lipṛáj exhausted, worn-out

لیپزیگ lajpzíg *m.* Leipzig

لی په لی lajpə́láj confused, perplexed, stunned

لیت ¹ lit **1** smooth, slippery; worn **2** polished, burnished

لیت ² lit *m.* Hymalayan pine, Pinus excelsa

لیتاړه litā́ṛa *f.* rags, old clothes; tatters

لیت پیت ¹ lit-pít completely worn, ground off; absolutely smooth

لیت پیت ² lit-pét bespattered, besmirched

لیتر litr *m.* liter

لیتړی litə́raj scattered, thrown around

لیتواني litvāní لیتوانیائي litvanijā́í **1** Lithuanian لیتواني ژبه the Lithuanian language **2** *m.* Lithuanian (person)

لیتوگرافي litogrāfí *f.* lithography

لیتول litavól *denominative, transitive* [*past:* لیت یې کړ] **1** to rub, grind **2** to rub off; to smooth out; to grind off **3** to polish, burnish

لیتېدل litedə́l *denominative, intransitive* [*past:* لیت شو] **1** to be rubbed, be ground **2** to be rubbed off; be smoothed out; be ground **3** to be burnished, be polished

لټ leṭ *m.* Latvian (person)

لیټاړه liṭā́ra *f.* ☞ لیتاړه

لیټ پرلیټ liṭpərlíṭ **1** turned head over heels **2** disorders, riots

لیټویا leṭvijā́ *f.* ☞ لتویا

لټی ¹ leṭáj *m.* hard clay

لټی ² leṭə́j *f.* thin gruel, porridge

لیچ ¹ lech *m. anatomy* **1** forearm **2** stock (of a rifle)

لیچ ² lich *m. conjunctivitis* لیچ نیولئ one suffering from conjunctivitis

لیچکی lechkáj *m. diminutive of* لیچ ¹

لیچن ¹ lichə́n suffering from conjunctivitis

لیچن ² lajchán *m.* lichen

لیچه lécha *f.* ☞ لیچ ¹ څه شي ته لیچي رغبنتل to prepare for something

لیچی ¹ lecháj *m.* **1** jamb (of a door) **2** *textiles* winding, twisting (wool, cotton)

لیچی ² lechə́j *f.* sheeps' trotters (a food item)

لیڅ lets *f.* لیڅه létsa *f. Western* [*plural:* لیڅي létsi] forearm, ulnar bone *idiom* لیڅي غړول او په کار شروع کول to get to work, get down to work

لیڅی letsə́j ball of yarn

لید ¹ lid *m.* sight په تیاري کښي لید کول to see in the dark

لید ² lid *imperfect* ☞ لیدل

لید ³ líd *m.* کتنه katə́ná *computer science* view

لیدانی lidā́naj مونیتور mūnítọr *m. computer science* monitor

1. لیدل lidə́l **1** *transitive* [*present:* ویني یې و *past:* لید یې و *past:* لیدل وي] to see, notice, discover هغه مي نه دئ لیدلئ I did not see him. **1.2** to see one another, meet together with someone; visit someone **1.3** to experience, endure نقصان لیدل to suffer damage **1.4** to receive (e.g., an award) لیدل کېدل a to be noticed, be observed ډېره لر لیدل

... شوي دي چه a It has rarely been observed that ... b to be seen د غرونه سلسله له ليدل کېږي The range of mountains is seen from afar. c to be recognized ليدل کېدل لازم to be considered or recognized as necessary 2.1 m. plural sight د ليدلو قوت sharpness of vision 2.2 scrutiny, observation 2.3 meeting, rendezvous 2.4 examination, familiarity, acquaintance, visit

ليدل کتل lidə́l-katə́l m. plural ☞ ليدل 2, 3, 4 تر بيا ليدلو کتلو! Until we meet again!

ليدلئ 1 lidə́ləj past participle of ليدل

ليدلي 2 lidə́li m. plural seen, experienced

ليدلي 2 lidə́na f. 1 ☞ ليدل 2 2 ليدنه

ليدني lidə́ni f. plural ordeal, difficulties, adversities; experiences

ليدون lidún m. meeting, talk, conversation

ليدونکى lidúnakaj 1 present participle of ليدل 2 m. viewer

ليده 1 lidə́ m. plural ☞ ليدل ستا د ليدو د پاره راغلئ يم I came to see you.

ليده 2 lidə́ plural imperfect of ليدل

ليده پيده lidə́-pidə́ knowing well; wittingly

ليده ور lidəvár insolent, cheeky

ليدي 1 lidé f. plural imperfect of ليدل

ليدئ 2 lidəj Western ☞ ليده 2

ليډر liḍar m. leader, chief; manager

ليډرشيپ līḍarshíp m. ليډري liḍarí f. management; leadership work

ليډريت liḍərét m. short editorial

لبر ler m. 1 arch-shaped framework, frame (of a lipped roof) 2 gully

لبربنه lerbaná f. used with لبربون

لبربون lerbún m. لبربه lerbə́ m. [plural: لبربانه lerbānə́] shepherd (of a flock of lambs)

لبرگي lergə́j f. lobe (of the ear)

ليرليد lirlíd m. binoculars; spyglass

لير ليدونکى lir lidúnakaj ليرليدى lirlídaj 1 farsighted; keen-sighted سترگي مي ليرليدي نه دي My eyes see poorly. 2 figurative perspicacious

لبرنه lerə́na f. لبرنى lerənə́j f. gutter around a lipped roof (for runoff of rain)

ليرو 1 liró indirect plural of ليره

ليرو 2 líro indirect plural of ليري

لبروغه lervágha f. payment in kind to a shepherd

لبرونى lerúnaj m. suckling (male) lamb without a mother

لبروونى leravunáj m. driftwood (on a riverbank) لبروونى ټولول to gather brushwood (on the bank)

لبره 1 lerá f. ☞ لبر 1

لبره 2 léra f. hollow between two mountains

ليره 3 lírá f. lira, pound, pound sterling

لبري 1 lerí m. plural herd of lambs

ليري 2 líri لري líre 1 ☞ ليري خټه the Far East د ليري څخه from afar, from far away 2 far, far away له څانه ليري اچول to fling away, toss away ليري کول a to remove, dismiss b to strip off (a hide)

ليري کېدل a to withdraw b to disappear ليري لوبدل to end up in a distant place ليدل ليري to foresee

لبرژ 3 lerə́j f. narrow path

ليري توب liritób m. distance; remoteness, farness

ليري ليدونکى líri lirúnkaj ليرليدونکى

ليري والى lirivā́laj m. ☞ ليري توب

لبر ler m. ☞ لر

لبزم lezám embarrassed, confused, ashamed لبزم کول to embarrass لبزم کېدل to be embarrassed

لبزمي lézmi f. plural ☞ لبرمى

لبرد legd m. 1 despatch, sending off 2 migration لبرد کول a to set out on the road b to move, migrate

لبرد راليرد ligdrāligd computer science transmission

لبردل legdə́l intransitive [past: و لبرده past: و لبردل] 1 to set out, pack up and march 2 to resettle, move on 3 to move

لبردول legdavə́l transitive [past: و يي لبرداوه] to dispatch; send out; send 2 to resettle, compel to migrate 3 to move or transport something from one place to another

لبردى legdáj m. pack animal, transport animal

لبردبدل legdedə́l intransitive ☞ لبردل

لبرغندى legghandáj m. senior person in a nomad camp

لبرل legə́l transitive [past: و يي لبره] to send, send out, despatch, send on the way

لبرلڅای legə́l-dźáj m. address, destination

لبرمي 1 léghmi f. plural 1 flattery; toadying 2 begging, entreaty; supplication

لبرمى 2 legmáj m. flatterer; toady

لبرنه legə́na f. dispatching, sending

لبرونکى legúnkaj 1 present participle of لبرل لبرونکى شخص dispatcher 2 m. dispatcher

ليس 1 les m. lajs 1 lace 2 galloon

ليس 2 lejs m. ☞ ليس نايک

ليسانس lisā́ns m. 1 diploma, degree د حقوقو ليسانس law degree 2 license (degree roughly equivalent to master's degree)

ليسانسه lisānsá m. university graduate (holder of a license)

ليست list m. list

ليسک lisák m. kind of Karakul wool

ليس نايک lejsnāík m. regional corporal

ليسه lisá f. lycee; training institute; secondary school عسکري ليسه Officer's Training School

لبشبور leshbór m. torn dress

لبشکه leshə́ka f. dialect ☞ لشکه

لبنن leҳ m. migration, nomadic movement, nomadic camp

لبنبل 1 leҳə́l transitive [past: و يي لبنبنه] 1 to load (cargo, etc.) 2 intransitive [past: ولبنبنه] to migrate

لبنبل 2 leҳə́l transitive [past: و يي لبنبنه] to lick, smack the lips

لبنبنگ leҳháng m. ☞ لبنن

لبنبول leҳhavə́l transitive ☞ لبردول

لېښېدل lekhedə́l *intransitive* ☞ لېږدل

ليطر litr *m.* liter

ليک lik *m.* **1** letter, correspondence ليک لوست reading and writing د ليک ماشين typewriter د ليک مديريت secretariat د ليک مېز desk ليک ليکل to write a letter سره ليک لېږل to correspond with **2** the written language **3** script, type عربي ليک Arabic script **4** *military* column

ليکانی likā́naj *m.* fountain pen; pen

ليک بکس lik bakás *m. computer science* mailbox

ليکبڼه likbáṇa *f.* ليکبڼې likbáṇi *plural computer science* font, fonts

ليک پاڼی likpā́ṇaj *m.* **1** writing paper **2** sheet of paper

ليک دود likdód *m.* rules of writing, orthography

ليک ښود likkhód *m.* **1** teaching to write; the rules of composition **2** clerical work

ليکل likə́l **1** *transitive* [*past:* و يې ليکه *Western past:* و يې ليکل *past:* و يې ليکئ] to write; describe **2** *m. plural* writing, handwriting په ليکلو کښې in writing

ليک مرستونکی lik mrastúnkaj *m.* **1** collaborator **2** coauthor

لېکمن lekmə́n *m.* participant, member, shareholder

لېکن lekín *Arabic contrastive conjunction* but, yet, moreover

ليکنه likə́na *f.* **1** article; written piece, piece of writing **2** letter په ليکنه سره in written form د ليکنو مديريت secretariat, office **3** description **4** inscription

ليکنی likə́naj *m.* ☞ ليکانی

ليک نيوونی lik niwū́naj *computer science* mail recipient

ليکوال likvā́l *m.* writer; author (of an article, a book) د ليکوالانو اتحاديه The Writer's Union

ليکواله likvā́la *f. used with* ليکواله مېرمن ليکوال author (female)

ليکوالي likvālí *f.* **1** work of a writer, literary work د ليکوالی ډګر ته راوتل to embark on a literary profession **2** pertaining to a writer, literary په ادبي او ليکوالي ميدان کښې in the literary profession

ليکونکی likúnkaj **1** *present participle of* ليکل **2** *m.* **.1** writer; author (of an article, a book) **2.2** clerk, scribe; copyist **2.3** office worker

ليکونی likúnaj *m.* clerk, scribe; copyist

ليکه [1] líka *f.* **1** line (of writing, type) **2** line (ruled, printed) سمه ليکه a straight line کږه ليکه a curved line ليکه لار a straight road ماته ليکه a broken line ليکه کښل، ليکه ايستل to draw a line **3** *botany* rib **4** row, rank **5** *military* line; row; clumn ليکه کول **a** to mine, set mines **b** to form in a column ليکه کښل، ليکه کېدل **a** to be drawn up in line **b** to be formed in a column يوه ليکه تلل to march in a column پر اوبو ليکي کښل to be engaged in meaningless work; grind water in a mortar د لېږد ليکه پسي نيول to proceed along the route of migration

ليکه [2] likə́ *m. plural* writing

ليکه [3] likə́ *imperfect of* ليکل

لېکه [4] leká *f.* **1** sharecropping په لېکه اخيستل to rent farmland on a half-and-half basis په لېکه ورکول to lease land to a sharecropper on a half-and-half basis **2** share, portion, part of something

ليکی [1] likáj *m.* book

ليکي [2] líki *f. plural of* ليکه

ليکي لرونکی líki larúnkaj striped, having stripes (e.g., cloth)

ليګ lig *m.* league مسلم ليګ the Muslim League (one of the political parties of Pakistan)

لېګل legə́l *transitive Eastern* ☞ لېږل

ليګه ligá *f.* plot of wasteland

ليګي ligí *m.* member of the Muslim League

ليلا، ليلى [1] lajlā́ *f. Arabic* **1** *proper name* Leila (in particular, the beloved of Madzhnun) **2** dear, beloved

ليلام lilā́m *m.* auction trading; competitive bidding ليلام کېدل *compound verb* ☞ ليلامېدل

ليلامول lilāmavə́l *denominative, transitive* [*past:* ليلام يې کړ] to sell by auction; sell by competitive bidding

ليلام چي lilāmchí *m.* auctioneer

ليلامي lilāmí **1** sold at auction, sold in competitive bidding **2** ready-made (clothing)

ليلامېدل lilāmedə́l *denominative, intransitive* [*past:* ليلام شو] to be sold at auction, be sold by competitive bidding

لېله [1] léla *f.* custom, ways

ليله [2] lajlá *f. Arabic* night

ليلي [1] lajlí *Arabic* **1** nocturnal **2** *proper name* Leili

لی لی [2] laj-laj ugh, nasty, don't put that in your mouth, or similar expression (used to a child to indicate that something will taste unpleasant or be harmful)

ليلېدل liledə́l *intransitive* [*past:* وليلېده] **1** to grow thin, lose weight **2** to wear oneself out, worry oneself sick

ليليه lajlijá *Arabic* **1** nocturnal; evening ليليه ليسه evening school **2** *f.* **.1** dormitory **2.2** boarding school **3** after-work sanatorium

ليم lajm *m.* **1** soldering, brazing **2** coating, plastering (walls) ليم کول *compound verb* **a** to solder, braze **b** to plaster ليم کېدل *compound verb* **a** to be soldered, be brazed **b** to be plastered, be coated, be stuccoed

ليما limā́ *f.* Lima (city)

ليم جوشي lajmdzhushí *f.* welding

لېمڅی lemtsáj *m.* ☞ لمڅي

ليمو [1] limú *m.* lemon د ليمو اوبه lemon juice

لېمو [2] lemó *indirect plural of* لېمه

ليموناد limonā́d *m.* lemonade

ليمويي limuí lemon; lemon-colored

لېمه le-mə́ *m. plural* eyes *idiom* پر غبرګو لېمو به درسم I will call on you with pleasure. په دواړه لېمو کار کول to work, putting one's heart into it

لين lajn *m.* line (e.g., communications) هوائي لين **a** overhead line (e.g., telephone) **b** airline د برق لين electric-pole line د سمندري جهازونه لين shipping line

لېنا lenā́ *f.* Lena (river) د لېنا سيند the Lena River

لينيت liníit *m. plural* lignite د لينيتو سکاره brown coal

لېندزکه lendzə́ka *f. dialect* ☞ نانځکه

ليندکۍ lindakə́j *f.* 1 small arch, bow 2 trigger (of a gun) 3 bow (for a musical instrument) 4 plinth *idiom* ليندکۍ کېدل to bend, wind, turn

لين دوان lajndavā́n *m.* line-layer (telephone, etc.)

لين دواني lajndavā́ni *f.* laying a line (telephone, etc.)

لينده lindá *f.* ليندۍ lində́j *f.* 1 bow (the weapon) 2 trajectory; arc (of a circle) 3 hoop, handle 4 *astronomy* Sagittarius (the constellation) 5 bow (for a musical instrument) 6 bracket 7 cocking-piece د توپک لينده cocking-piece (of a rifle) 8 jet (of water) 9 winding ditch; winding gully 10 *anatomy* ulnar bone *idiom* لينده کېدل to make a bend (of a river)

ليندۍ lində́j² *m.* inflorescence of reed-mace or cattail

لپن دېن lendén *m. regional* exchange, barter

لينډا lenḍā́ لپنډه lenḍə́ bald

لينډۍ lenḍə́j *feminine of* لينډا

لينگاته lingā́ta *f.* لنگټۍ lengṭə́j *f.* ☞ لنگته

لپنگور lengavə́r long-legged

لپنگی lengáj *m.* leg from the thigh to the sole

لپننگراد leningrā́d *m.* Leningrad (city)

لپنني leniní Leninist

لپننيزم leninísm *m.* Leninism

لينوتايپ linotā́jp *m.* linotype

لاين lajn *m. regional* ☞ لين

لېو lev *m.* plastering, coating; stucco لېو کول *compound verb* a ☞ لېو کېدل *b figurative* to be covered (e.g., with clouds) لېوبدل *compound verb* a ☞ b to press oneself to someone, snuggle up

لېوال levā́l 1 thirsting (for a meeting, knowledge, etc.) 2 loving د وطن لېوال a lover of the homeland, a patriot

لېوالتوب levāltób *m.* لېوالتيا levāltjā́ *f.* 1 thirst, strong desire (for a meeting, knowledge, etc.) 2 desire, lust

لېوالول levālavə́l *denominative, transitive* [*past:* لېوال يې کړ] to attract someone; evoke strong desire

لېواليدل levāledə́l *denominative, intransitive* [*past:* لېوال شو] 1 to desire strongly, thirst for 2 to burn with love, lust after

لېوان levā́n *masculine plural of* لېوه¹

لېوبچی levbacháj *m.* wolf cub

لېوتنانت جنرال levténānt dzhanrā́l *m. regional* lieutenant-general

لېور levár *m.* [*plural:* لېورونه levrúna levarúna] brother-in-law (husband's brother)

لېورځوی levərdzój *m.* لېورزوی levərzój *m.* son of a brother-in law (husband's brother), nephew by marriage

لېورزۍ levərzə́j *f.* daughter of a brother-in law (husband's brother), niece by marriage

لېوړۍ levŗə́j kind of halvah made with corn oil

لېوکټی levkaṭáj *m.* wolf cub

لېوپولدوېل leopoldvíl *m.* Leopoldville (city)

لېول ləjavə́l¹ *transitive* [*past:* وې يې لياوه] 1 to train, school, instruct [*past:* وې يې لياوه] 2 to instigate, prompt; influence, egg on to something

لېول lévəl² *m.* level, spirit level

لېول کاري levə́lkārí *f.* levelling, surveying

لېونتوب levantób *m.* madness, insanity د لېونتوب مينه crazy love

لېونتون levantún *m.* psychiatric hospital

لېونسدی levansə́daj unbalanced, abnormal

لېونغړتای levanghŗə́taj talking idly, talking nonsense, talking drivel

لېونغړی levanghə́raj ☞ لېونسدی

لېونه ləjavə́na *f.* training, instruction

لېونی levanáj 1 mad, crazy, insane, lunatic لېونی کول to drive mad لېونی کېدل to go mad 2 *m.* [*plural:* لېوني levaní *plural:* لېونيان levanijā́n] a madman, lunatic

لېوول levavə́l *denominative, transitive* [*past:* لېو يې کړ] to plaster, apply stucco

لېوه levə́ *m.* [*plural:* لېوان levā́n *plural:* لېوگان levagā́n] wolf

لېوه levá² *f.* she-wolf

لېوېدل levedə́l *denominative, intransitive* [*past:* لېو شو] to be plastered, be stuccoed

ليه lijá¹ *f.* tamarisk

ليه lijə́² 1.1 useless, good-for-nothing, worthless ليه کول to render useless, bring to naught ليه کېدل to be useless 1.2 unrestrained 2 just, only

ليه lijáh³ *Arabic* 1 covered; hidden 2 high, noble

لېيل lejə́l *transitive* [*past:* وې يې لېيل] to give evidence, testify

م

م mim¹ 1 the thirty-fifth letter of the Pashto alphabet 2 number 40 in the abjad system

م² *abbreviation of* مسيحي Christian, A.D. ۱۴۱۲م 1412 A.D.

م³ *abbreviation of* ماشيندار

م⁴ mi, me *pronoun* ☞ مي

م⁵ əm, mu *in lieu of* مو³ کورم چيري دئ؟ Where is your house?

م⁶ əm *suffix of ordinal numerals* (after the vowels يم) لسم tenth ۳م فصل third section دوهم، دويم second

م⁷ əm *verbal inflectional ending for first person singular* خم I am going. وايم I am speaking.

م⁸ əm, um *in lieu of* هم²

م⁹ ma, mə *abbreviated form of negation* مه! مکوه! Don't!

ما mā¹ *f.* (bed-)curtains, tent section, shelter half, ground sheet

ما mā² *oblique form of the pronoun* زه 1 me (as the object of the action with transitive verbs in present and future tense forms) راغئ چه ما وويني He came to see me. 2 I, me (used as the subject of the action in an ergative construction) ما کتاب ورکړ I gave him the book. ما وخندل I burst out laughing. 3 me (used with prepositions and postpositions) a ما پسې، په ما پسې on me ما باندي، په ما باندي

after me **b** about me ما پوري Eastern **a** to me **b** above me ما ته،

له ما in me په ما کښي، په ما کي Eastern to me ما له،ما لره ،ما له

ما near me; from me لا څخه، ما نه، له ما نه Eastern for me ما دپاره

under me سره Eastern with me ما لاندي Eastern like me ما غوندي Eastern

مأ **mā** *f. Arabic* water; juice, sap

ما [3] **mā** *in Arabic borrowings* that; that which ما تحت that which is
below or downstairs

مآب **maāb** *m. Arabic* **1** shelter, refuge **2** *in titles* جلالت مآب his
Excellency

ما باندي **mā́ bānde** *Eastern* ☞ ما [2] [3]

مابت **mābát** *m. colloquial* ☞ محبت

مابعد **mābá'd** **1** *m.* continuation **2** after, later (on), then د جنگ ما
بعد زمانه the post-war time or period

مابقي **mābaqí** *f. Arabic* remainder, rest

مابوب **mābúb** *m.* ☞ محبوب

مابوبه **mābubá** *f.* ☞ محبوبه

مابی **mābə́j** *f. proper noun* Mabibi

مابین **mābájn** *m. Arabic* interval, middle, midst د دوو هیوادو په مابین
کښي between two countries د ملت په مابین کښي in the nation په
دي ما بین کښي meanwhile له ما بينه څخه وتل to disappear

مابيني **mābajní** middle, central د ښار په ما بيني برخه کښي in the center
of the city ما بيني امريکا Central America

ما پسي **mā́ pase** ☞ ما

ماپخين **māpk̲h̲ín** *m.* noon; time from two to four p.m. وروسته تر
ماپخين in the afternoon اخير ماپنين towards evening

ماپوري **mā́ pore** *Eastern* ☞ ما [2, 3]

مات **māt** **1** broken ماته ليکه، مات خط ماته چوکۍ broken chair
mathematics broken line **2** split (of firewood) **3** crumbled **4** cut,
sliced (into chunks, shares) **5** cracked **6** killed, slaughtered,
knifed **7** cracked, chapped **8** slaked, quenched (of thirst) **9**
changed (of money) **10** disrupted, wrecked, spoiled, frustrated (of
plans) **11** cancelled, annulled, abrogated, broken (of a contract,
agreement, etc.) **12** disbanded, dissolved (of an organization, etc.)
13 routed beaten, smashed, shattered, defeated **14** destroyed **15**
broken out (of sweat) **16** broken open, forced **17** *physics*
refracted (of light) **18** *figurative* struck, astonished, amazed,
astounded **19** *figurative* weak, helpless زما مات قلم د طبيعت ښکلا
نه شي ترسيمولای My feeble pen is unable to convey the beauty of
nature. **20** dim, pallid (of light) مات گوډ ☞ او گوډ مات دوړ اندي
خه شوی؟ تگ اراده یي ماته وه He had to give up on his intention of going
further. په مات زړه کار کول خه to do something unwillingly
colloquial What's up?

ماتاوی **mātāwə́j** *f.* attic, attic room, garret

ماتحت **mātáht** *Arabic* **1** *m.* **.1** that which is below **1.2** subordinate
ماتحتان subordinates **2.1** being below, being under **2.2** lower;
subordinate (of a military unit, etc.)

ماتحت الشعور **mātaht-al-shu'úr** *Arabic* subconscious, instinctive په
ما تحت الشعور کښي subconsciously, instinctively

ماتحتي **mātahtí** *f.* subordination

ماتریالیزم **māterjālízm** *m. philosophy* materialism

ماتریالیست **māterjālíst** *m. philosophy* materialist

ماتریالیسم **māterjālísm** *m. philosophy* materialism

ماتقدم **mātaqaddám** *Arabic* preceding, previous, former

ماتکبده **mātkedə́** *m. plural* ☞ ماتوالی

مات گوډ **māt-gúḍ** *regional* **1** tumbledown, fallen-to-pieces;
destroyed **2** fallen into decay **3** broken (of language) په ماته گوډه
انگرېزی گپني in broken English

ماتم [1] **mātám** *m. Arabic* mourning ماتم يي و They were in
mourning. د چا په مرگ ماتم کول to mourn (for) someone

ماتم [2] **mátamu** *colloquial contraction of* ماته *and the pronoun* مو
ماتم څه پریښني؟ What have you left (for) me?

ماتمخانه **mātamkhāná** *f.* house of prayer (among the Shiites)

ماتمی **mātə́maj** *m.* compensation, payment, defrayal (of damages)
ماتمی اخیستل to receive compensation

ماتوالی **mātwǎlaj** *m.* **1** breaking **2** defeat **3** fatigue ماتوالی راباندي
راغلی دئ I am feeling worn out. **4** depression, despondency **5**
medicine fracture

ماتوره **māturá** *f.* rocky soil, stony soil

ماتور **mātl** *m.* mason

ماتول **mātawól** *denominative, transitive* [*past:* مات یي کړ] **1** to break
2 to beat **3** to split (firewood) **4** to crumble دوډی ماتول to
crumble bread **5** to cut (into pieces, parts) **6** to crack (open, e.g.,
nuts, almonds) **7** to kill, slaughter, knife, tear to pieces لبوه يو پسه
مات کړ A wolf killed the sheep. **8** to slake, quench (thirst) **9** to
change (money) **10** to disrupt, wreck, spoil, frustrate (e.g., plans)
11 to annul, cancel, abrogate (a contract, etc.) **12** to break (a law,
the silence, etc.) **13** to dissolve, disband (an organization, etc.) **14**
to rout, smash, crush, defeat **15** to destroy طلسم ماتول to nullify
the effect of a charm **16** to break open, force **17** *physics* to
refract (light) مينه ماتول *idiom* to reciprocate

ماتومی **mātúmaj** *m.* commission

ماتونه **mātawóna** *f.* **1** breaking, fracturing; hurting or bruising badly
2 splitting, chopping (of firewood) **3** cutting (into hunks, chunks,
parts) **4** cracking (nuts, almonds) **5** break, split, crack **6** slaking,
quenching (of thirst) **7** changing (money) **8** disruption (e.g., of
plans) **9** abrogation, violation (of a treaty, agreement, etc.) **10**
dissolution, disbandment (of an organization, etc.) **11** crushing,
inflicting defeat **12** abolishment **13** breaking open, forcing **14**
physics refraction (of light)

ماته [1] **mā́ta** **1** *feminine singular of* مات [1] **2** *f.* **.1** ☞ ماتی [1] **2.2** crack,
split

ماته [2] **mā́ta** *f.* prey (i.e., birds of prey) ماته کول to hunt for food (of
birds of prey)

ماته [3] **mā́ta** ☞ ما [2] [3]

ماته خوا **mā́ta khwā** **1** *f.* **.1** smashed-in side (of a vehicle, etc.) **1.2**
smashed or routed flank **1.3** *figurative* grief; grieved, distressed

په ماته خوا کار کول to work without spirit, unwillingly, in a slipshod manner

ماتي [1] mắte *f.* 1 defeat, rout ماتي ورکول *compound verb* to rout, defeat 2 retreat ماتي غوره کول *compound verb* to retreat خوړل، ماتي کول، ماتي ميندل *compound verb* a to suffer a defeat b to retreat 3 lethargy, fatigue 4 anxiety, uneasiness

ماتي [2] mắti *feminine plural of* مات ١ او گوډي trouble, something wrong

ماتېدل mātedə́l *denominative, intransitive* [*past:* مات شو] 1 to be broken, break; be hurt, be bruised badly 2 to crumble, be crumbled 3 to be cut (into pieces, parts) 4 to be quenched (of thirst) 5 to be changed (of money) 6 to be disrupted, be spoiled (of plans) 7 to be abrogated, be broken (of a contract, treaty, agreement, etc.) 8 to be dissolved, be disbanded (of an organization, etc.) 9 to be routed, be smashed, be crushed; suffer defeat 10 to be destroyed 11 *physics* to be refracted (of light) 12 to stick (of a thorn, burr) 13 to go down, shrink (of a swelling) 14 to break (out) (of sweat) په ما يخي خولې راماتي شوې I broke out in a cold sweat.

ماتېدونکی mātedúnkaj 1 *present participle of* ماتېدل 2 fragile, brittle

ماتېده mātedə́ *m. plural* ☞ ماتوالی

ماتبرياليزم māterjālízm *m. philosophy* materialism

ماتبرياليست māterjālíst *m. philosophy* materialist

ماتبرياليستي māterjālistí *f. philosophy* materialistic

ماتس mātús *m.* lump, bump, knob (from a blow); swelling

ماتور mātawə́r with a clean-shaven chin

ماتوره māṭóra *f.* 1 indigestion 2 overeating

ماتوی māṭwə́j *f.* 1 woman's gold ornament worn on both sides of the forehead 2 lock, curl, ringlet

ماتي [1] mā́ṭi *m. plural* whiskers, sidewhiskers

ماتی [2] māṭə́j *f.* large and wide-mouthed jug; earthenware pot

ماثره māsará *f. Arabic* [*plural:* ماثري māsaré *and m. plural: Arabic* مآثر māā́sír] exploit, feat; deed, act

ماجب mādzhíb *m.* ☞ مواجب

ماجت mādzhə́t *m. colloquial* mosque

ماجد mādzhíd *Arabic* famous, noted

ماجر [1] mādzhár *m.* 1 cemetery fence 2 line of demarcation, border, boundary

ماجر [2] mādzhír *m.* ☞ مهاجر

ماجرا mādzharắ *f.* 1 adventure, venture ماجرا غوښتل *compound verb* to engage in adventures 2 incident, happening, occurrence

ماجراجو mādzharādzhú ماجراجوی mādzharādzhúj 1 *m.* .1 adventurist 1.2 adventure seeker 2 adventurist(ic), adventure (movie, etc.)

ماجراجويانه mādzharādzhujāná adventurist(ic), adventuresome

ماجراجويي mādzharādzhúji 1 adventurism 2 love of adventure

ماجرا mādzharắ ماجرا لټوونکی mādzharắ ghukhtúnkaj لټوونکی latawúnkaj 1 adventurist(ic) ماجرا غوښتونکی ماهيت) m. .1 adventurer 2.2 adventure seeker

ماجراغوښتونکی mādzharāghukhtúnkaj 2 adventurism

ماجور جنرال mādzhór dzhinrā́l *m. regional* major general

ماچلوژ māchlə́j *f.* cartridge case

ماچونګن māchungə́n *m.* cricket (insect)

ماچي mắche *m. plural* noodles; vermicelli

ماچين māchín *m.* 1 چين و ماچين Indochina چين و ماچين China and Inochina 2 *obsolete* China

ماچي والا māchewālắ *m.* noodle vendor

ماڅني mắ dzine ماڅخه mắ tskha ☞ ما 2, 3

ماښختن mātskhután *m. dialect* ☞ ماښتن

ماحصل māhasál *m. Arabic* 1 result د تجربو ماحصل the results of the experiments 2 harvest

ماحول māhául *m. Arabic* surroundings, environment بېروني ماحول external environment

ماخذ mākház *m. Arabic* 1 base, basis 2 source (of information, etc.) 3 barrowing

ماخستن mākhustán 1.1 time from eight o'clock in the evening until midnight تېر ماخستن in the evening اول ماخستن the time around eight o'clock in the evening 1.2 namaz (one of the daily prayers required by Islamic tradition, performed before retiring for the night) 2 late in the evening, towards night

مأخوذ mākhúz *Arabic* 1 borrowed or taken from somewhere 2 seized, arrested 3 accused, charged; defendant

ماخوذېدل [1] mākhuzedə́l *denominative, intransitive* [*past:* مأخوذ شو] to be borrowed, be taken from somewhere 2 to be siezed, be arrested 3 to be accused, be charged د عدالت د توهين په جرم ماخوذېدل to be charged with being in contempt of court

ماخي mākhə́j *f.* camel's thorn, *Alhagi camelorum*

ماد mād *colloquial* ☞ مامد ماد علي Mamad Ali

مادتاً māddátán *Arabic* 1 materially; in a material way 2 in essence, essentially

مادګي mādagí *f.* 1 latch 2 *botany* gynoecium

مادل [1] mādíl *m.* ☞ موادل

مادل [2] mādél *m.* model

مادنګی mādangáj lazy; listless

مادون mādún *Arabic* lower, standing below; subordinate, lower, junior (in rank or position)

ماده [1] māddá *f. Arabic* [*plural:* مادي māddé *and m. plural: Arabic* مواد mawádd] 1 material, substance خوږه ماده *botany* nectar 2 *philosophy* matter 3 subject; question 4 article (e.g., of a treaty, contract) 5 material (side of) life 6 pus, matter 7 *physics* mass, body

ماده [2] māddá *f.* female ماده حشره a female insect

مادي [1] māddí *Arabic* 1 material مادي مصارف material expenditures 2 *m.* مادیون māddijún *philosophy* materialist

مادي [2] mādí *history* Median (of or pertaining to the Medes, Media, or the language)

مادیانه mādjắna *f.* mare, young mare, filly

مادیت mādditját *m. Arabic* [plural: مادیات] **1** materiality **2** *philosophy* materialism د تاریخ مادیت historical materialism **3** material side of life

مأذون māzún *Arabic* **1** having received permission; permitted مأذون کېدل to be permitted **2** authorized

مار [1] mār *m.* serpent, snake زنگي مار grass snake د اوبو مار، آبي مار، مار خوړلی د رسي نه ببرېږي rattlesnake, مار خوړلی، مار عینکي د cobra پري نه ببرېږي *proverb* Once bitten, twice shy. مار ته په لستوني کښې *proverb* to cherish a serpent in one's bosom د مار سره څای ورکول غزېدل to vie with a powerful (man)

مار [2] mār *m.* ☞ مهر

مار [3] mắr one who tries something داره مار robber

مارافسون mārafsún *m.* snake charmer

ماراباغ mārbágh *m.* mosquito trap plant

ماربچوری mārbachóraj *m.* ماربچوری mārbachóraj *m.* young snake

مارپیچ mārpéch **1.1** winding; twisted; spiral مارپیچ لار winding road **1.2** spiral په مارپیچ ډول spirally **1.3** sinuous, serpentine **2** *m.* **.1** spiral **2.2** coil (of pipe)

مارپیچه [1] mārpechá *f.* kind of embroidery

مارپیچه [2] mārpéchá *feminine singlular of* مارپیچ

مارتنیک mārtiník *m.* Martinique

مارجری mārdzaráj *f.* **1** bongardia, *Bongardia chrysogonum* (used for snakebite) **2** antidote

مارچ mārch *m.* March

مارچوبه mārchubá *f.* asparagus

مارخور mārkhór *m.* screw-horned goat, markhor

مارخورکه mārkhuráka, mārkhwaráka *f.* short-toed snake-eagle, *Circaetus gallicus*

ماردندن mārdandán *m.* ☞ جمدر [2]

ماردنگی mārdangáj *f.* candlestick دلوگي ماردنگی smoke pot

مارسېل mārsél *m.* مارسېلز mārsélz *m.,* مارسیلیا mārsilijá *f.* Marseilles

مارش [1] mārsh *m.* march; advance, progress; campaign په مارش سره مارش کول *compound verb* to move, shift عادي مارش to march دروبدل on the مارش مارش double قدم مارش! Forward, march! (as a command)

مارش [2] mārsh *m.* march; hymn ملي مارش national anthem

مارشال mārshál, mārishál *m.* marshal

مارشل لا mārshallá *f. regional* martial law

مارغان mārghán *masculine plural of* مارغه

مارغه mārghá *m. Eastern* ☞ مرغه [1]

مارغیت mārghit *m.* deceit, fraud, swindle

مارغیتل mārghitál **1** sly, cunning; knavish **2** *m.* rogue, swindler, cheat; deceiver, imposter

مارفین mārfín *m. plural* morphine

مارک mārk *m.* mark (monetary unit, postage stamp, and trademark)

مارکسیست mārksíst *m.* ☞ مارکسیست

مارکسیستي mārksistí ☞ مارکسیستي

مارکسیزم mārksízm *m.* مارکسیسم mārksísm *m.* Marxism

مارکسیست mārksíst *m.* Marxist

مارکسیستي mārksistí Marxist, Marxian

مارکونډی mārkunḍáj *f.* caltrop, *Tribulus*

مارکه mārká *f.* ☞ مارک

مارکیت mắrkeṭ *m.* market د دنیا مارکیت world market کو بهرنی مارکیت، داخلي مارکیت domestic market common market خارجي مارکیت foreign market

مارکېتنگ mắrketíng *m.* sale, marketing

مارگرڼی mārgírṇe *f. plural* مارگنزری *f. dialect* ☞ مالگینی

مارگیر mārgír *m.* snake catcher

مارل mārᶞl *transitive* ☞ گمارل

مارلی mārᶞlaj *m.* employee, worker; agent

مارمهی mārmāháj *m.* ☞ مارمهي

مارمورا mārmorắ *f.* Marmara د مارمورا بحیره Sea of Marmara

مارمولک mārmulák *m.* gecko (lizard)

مارمهی mārmaháj *m.* **1** eel **2** loach (fish)

مارویات mārupất *m.* lentil

ماره mắra *f.* robbery, pillage, plundering

ماری داری māré-dāṛé *f. plural Eastern* robbery, pillage, plundering ماری داری رااخیستل to engage in robbery

ماړوب māṛób *m.* abundantly irrigated land

ماړوندی māṛwandáj *f.* ☞ مروندی

ماړه māṛᶞ *masculine plural of* موړ [1]

ماړی هاړی mắṛe-hắṛe *interjection* My goodness! Horrors!

مازاد māzắd *m. Arabic* surplus, excess

مازپخین māzpᶍhín *m.* ☞ ماپنین

مازختن māzkhután *m.* ☞ ماسختن

مازدیگر māzdigár **1.1** time after the noon hour, afternoon; time towards evening; evening مازدیگر په همدې ورځ dusk زیری مازدیگر on that very evening د مازدیگر په۴ بجو at four o'clock in the afternoon, at 4 p.m. ورځ مازدیگر شوه It was getting dark. د مازدیگر لوږ مازدیگر و evening reception بلنه It was approaching evening. **1.2** namaz performed after the noon hour **2** afternoon; towards evening; in the evening

مازدیگرنی māzdigaranáj evening مازد یگرنی دعوت evening reception مازد یگرنی گرځېده evening walk

مازغه māzghᶞ *m. plural* ☞ idiom د چا مازغه خوړل ماغزه to bother someone; exhaust someone, exasperate someone مازغه یې رانه وبنکل He wore me out with his questions.

مازو māzú *m.* gallnut, gall

مازوت māzút *m. plural* mazut, black oil, fuel oil

مازې mắze **1** only **2** ☞ محض

مازیگر māzigár ☞ مازدیگر

مازیگرنی māzigaranáj ☞ مازدیگرنی

ماسپخین māspᶍhín *m.* ☞ ماس پنین

ماستاوه māstāwá *f.* soup flavored with sour milk

ماسته māstᶞ *m.* sour milk (milk baked in an oven and allowed to ferment)

ماستر mā́sṭər *m.* **1** mister **2** teacher

ماسخوتن، ماس خوتن mās khután, māskhután *m.* ماس ختن māskhután *m.*

ما سره mā́ sara *Eastern* ☞ ما [2, 3]

ماسکه [1] māsiká *f. Arabic* delaying force, restraining force **2** forces that maintain health **3** cheerfulness, liveliness

ماسکه [2] māská *f.* mask غازي ماسکه gas mask

ماسل māsíl *m.* ☞ محصل

ماسوا māsiwā́ *Arabic* excepting; with the exception of ماسوا ديوه سړي څخه except (for) one person

ماسه māsá *f.* (unit of) weight equal to twenty grains

ماسي [1] māsí *f.* [*plural:* ماسي گاني māsigā́ni] aunt (mother's sister)

ماسۍ [2] māsə́j *f.* leather stockings worn under boots

ماش māsh *m. plural* mung beans گرگره ماش crushed mung beans

ماشأالله māshalláh, māshaallā́h *Arabic interjection* bravo, well done; (may) God keep him

ماشله māshlá, māshalá *f.* ماشوړه māshoṛá *f.* **1** skein, hank (of thread) **2** *figurative* tangle (of contradictions)

ماشوق māshúq ☞ معشوق

ماشوم māshúm **1** *m.* infant; child هغه وخت زه ماشوم وم I was a child then. **2** innocent, inexperienced, unsophisticated

ماشوم توب māshumtób *m.* childhood, childhood years

ماشومه māshúma **1** *feminine singular of* ماشوم **2 2** *f. plural:* ماشوماني māshumā́ni (little) girl

ماشه [1] mā́sha *f.* mosquito

ماشه [2] māshá *f.* ماشۍ māshə́j *f.* trigger ماشه کشول to pull the trigger

ماشۍ mā́shaj *m.* mosquito; midge

ماشين māshín *m.* [*plural:* ماشينونه māshinúna *and Western* ماشينان māshinā́n] **1** machine د گنډلو ماشين sewing machine د ليکلو ماشين typewriter د ماشينونو سپټ collective machinery د ليکنې ماشين, زراعتي ماشينونه، فلاحتي ماشينونه farm machines **2** motor, engine څلور ماشينه الوتکه four-engine aircraft **3** apparatus, instrument د ډوي ماشين (stove) burner

ماشينخانه māshinkhāná *f.* **1** Mashinkhana (a factory in Kabul) **2** plant, enterprise, factory

ماشيندار māshindár *m.* machine gun

ماشينري māshinərí *f.* equipment, machinery

ماشين شاپ māshinshā́p *m.* plant; workshop, shop

ماشينکار māshinkár *m.* ماشين کار **1** mechanic **2** machinist, engineer

ماشينگره mashingára *f.* ماشين گن māshingán *m.* ماشين گڼ māshingáṇ *m.* machine gun

ماشيني māshiní **1** machine, mechanical; mechanized **2** factory, industrial, manufacturing ماشيني توليدات **a** industrial production **b** manufactured goods ماشيني ټوټې factory-made fabric ماشيني کول *compound verb* to mechanize ماشيني کېدل *compound verb* to be mechanized

---

مابنام māk͟hā́m **1** *m.* evening د مابنام په وخت کښي in the evening, at eventide تياره مابنام شو Night fell. **2** in the evening تېر مابنام late in the evening

مابنام ستوری māk͟hāmstóraj *m.* evening star (i.e., Venus)

مابنامي، مابناج māk͟hāmí, māk͟hāmáj **1** *indeclineable* evening مابنامي بلنه evening party مابنامي ستوري evening star (i.e., Venus) **2** *m. zoology* bat

ماضي māzí *Arabic* **1** past, last, bygone **2** *f.* **.1** past ليري ماضي the distant past د ماضي حالات the concerns of bygone days **2.2** *grammar* [*plural:* ماضي گاني māzigā́ni] past tense استمراري ماضي past continuous قريبه ماضي the past perfect بعيده ماضي the present perfect

ماضي پرستي māziparastí *f.* cult of the past, cult of antiquity

ماعدا mā'adā́ *Arabic* besides, except (for)

ماغزه māghzə́ *m. plural* **1** brain د سر ماغزه brain **2** bone marrow **3** seed, kernel, core (of fruit) **4** insides, heart, middle **5** mind, wit, intellect د علي شبر ماغزه سياسي ماغزه لرل to understand politics *idiom* **a** گډوډ وه Alisher's head began to spin. **b** Alisher almost went out of his mind. ☞ د علي ماغزه يې خراب شوي وه *Eastern* He ما غزو کښي يې خلل دئ، په ماغزو کښي يې خلل دئ His brain went dull. هغه ماغزو ته دا خبره نه ورځي *Eastern* He has gone out of his mind. په يو کار ماغزه ايستل، په يو کار ماغزه چپه *Eastern* He cannot comprehend this. کېدل **a** to be overtired from something **b** to exert incredible effort; demonstrate tremendous diligence in something چا ته ماغزه ورچپه و کول to drive to distraction, drive out of one's mind (by noise, arguing, etc.) و احمد ته مي ماغزه وخوټېده I got frightfully mad at Ahmad. ماغزه تکړه ساته! Look sharp!

ماغوت māghút *m. plural* ☞ ماقوت

ما غوندي mā́ ghunde *Eastern* ☞ ما [2] 3

مافوق māfáuq *Arabic* **1** higher, superior (in position, rank, grade) **2** *m.* **.1** chief, senior in point of service **2** *plural* مافوقان māfauqā́n chief, heads, those in authority

مافوق الطبيعي māfauq-at-tabi'í *Arabic* supernatural

مافيها māfíhā́ *f. Arabic* that which is in it; (which is) contained in it دنيا ومافيها the world with all that exists in it

مافي الضمير māfizzamír *m. Arabic* innermost secret; hidden purpose; ulterior motive

ماقبل māqábl *Arabic* **1** past, former, previous, preceding د جنگ ماقبل زمانه pre-war period **2** *m.* past, bygone times

ماقوت māqút *m. plural* kissel; kind of sweet dish made of starch; pudding

ما کره mā kará *Eastern* **1** at my house **2** to my house, to my place ما کره راځه! Come to my house!

ما کي mā́ ke *Eastern* ☞ ما [2] 3

ماکم، ماکمه mākám *m.* mākáma *f. colloquial* ☞ محکم

ماکو [1] mākú *m.* [*plural:* ماکوگان mākugā́n *and* ماکوان mākuān] **1** shuttle (in a loom) **2** boat, canoe

ماکو [2] mākú **1** *m. plural* Maku (a tribe) **2** *m.* Maku

ماکو [3] māú *m.* ☞ مشکی

669

ماکول mākúl *m. Arabic* edibles, food

ماکولات mākulát *m. plural Arabic* food products; victuals, foodstuffs, provisions

ما کی mǻ ke *Eastern* ☞ ما ^{2, 3}

مال ¹ māl *m. Arabic* [plural: مالونه mālúna and Arabic اموال amwál] **1** (personal, movable) property مال او جایداد personal and real property **2** goods د تجارت goods د سواد گری مال تجارتي مالونه consumer goods مال اوبه کول، مال ویلي goods استهلاکي مال to sell goods **3** livestock لس دوولس مالونه ten - twelve head of cattle **4** *figurative* property, capital, fortune **5** wealth مال یوه *saying* to cast property to the wind اگی کول او د دبواله ویشتل

مال ² māl *m.* time ☞ مهال

مال ³ māl tame(ed), domesticated; meek; humble

مال ⁴ mál one who smears, one who spreads; one who fulls (felt) نمدمال felter

مآل ⁵ ma'ál *m. Arabic* **1** sense, meaning, essence دا د ژوندانه مآل گڼل to see in this the meaning of life **2** end, outcome

مالاً ¹ mālán *Arabic* in a material way, in a financial way

مآلاً ² ma'álán *Arabic* consequently, hence; as a result; in the end

مالاخیت mālākhít *m.* malachite

مال التجاره māl-ut-tidzhará *f. Arabic* goods

مالامال mālāmál **1** overfilled, full to the brim مالامال کول *compound verb* to overfill مالامال کېدل *compound verb* to be overfilled, overflow **2** drenched (in blood) **3** abundant, plentiful, copious

ما لاندې mǻ lānde *Eastern* ☞ ما ^{2, 3}

مآل اندېش ma'ālandésh farsighted

مالایه mālājá *f.* ☞ مالایه

مالایی mālājí ☞ ملایي

مالت mālát *m. colloquial* ☞ محله

مالته málta, māltá *f.* Malta

مالته māltá *f.* blood orange, red-pulp Malta orange

مالچر mālchár *m.* مال څر، مالغرمال چر māltsár *m.* pasture

مال حال mālhál *m.* household goods, belongings

مال خانه mālkhāná *f. regional* warehouse

مالیخولیا mālkhuljá *f.* ☞

مال دار māldár **1** well-to-do; wealthy **2** *m.* **.1** breeder, cattle breeder مال دار کوچیان nomad (cattle) breeder **2** rich man

مالداری māldārí *f.* **1** cattle breeding, animal husbandry د مالداری استحصالات، د مالداری محصولات animal husbandry products **2** riches, wealth, solvency

مالزمه mālzimá *f. Arabic* **1** material (e.g., construction materials) **2** articles, accessories, materials (for the office, etc.)

مالستان mālistán *m.* Malistan region

مالش mālísh *m.* مالښ mālíkh *m.* **1** friction **2** rubbing, massage **3** fulling (making felt) مالش کول *compound verb* **a** to rub, massage **b** to full (felt)

مالفروشي mālfurushí *f.* sales, marketing د مالفروشي شعبه sales department, marketing department (in the shirketi)

مالک mālík *m. Arabic* **1** owner, holder, proprietor **2** landowner; landed gentleman لوی مالکان large landowners, owners of large estates د مځکي کوچني مالکان small landowners **3** employer, boss

مالکانه ¹ mālikāná *f.* fee or assessment that is paid to landowners

مالکانه ² mālikāná **1.1** landowner's, landowners' مالکانه حاصلات land rent **1.2** one's own, ownership **2** having property rights

مالکنډی mālkunḍáj *f.* مال کنی، مالکنی mālkuṇáj *f.* caltrop (a weed)

مالک والی mālikwálaj *m.* ownership (property, etc.)

مالکه mālíka *f.* lady; housewife, wife

مالکیت mālikiját *m. Arabic* **1** ownership, possession **2** property شخصي مالکیت personal property خصوصي مالکیت private property دولتي مالکیت government property د مځکي مالکیت landed property

مالگبه mālgbá *m.* [plural: مالگبانه mālgbānə́] salt vendor

مالگذاري mālguzārí *f. regional* **1** land tax, ground rent **2** land that is subject to taxation, taxable land **3** payment of taxes; taxation

مالگروبی mālgrobáj *m.* container in which salt is dissolved (when kneading bread dough)

مالگنتوب mālgəntób *m.* salinity, saltiness

مالگنول mālgənawə́l *denominative, transitive* [past: مالگن يې کړ to salt; pickle; corn

مالگنی mālgənáj *m.* مالگنی malgəṇáj *m.* saltcellar, saltshaker

مالگوبی mālgobáj *m.* salt solution

مالگه málga *f.* **1** salt د ډوډی مالگه table salt غرنی مالگه rock salt مالگه اچول *compound verb* to sprinkle salt, salt **2** *figurative* attractiveness په مالگه سری pleasant and charming person د چا پر زخمو مالگه اچول *idiom* to rub salt on someone's wounds پر زړه مالگه ورتویول *idiom* to cause to be upset, cause pain, cause distress

مالگه والا mālgawālá *m.* salt vendor

مالگین mālgín salt مالگین غدیر salt lake

مالگینتوب mālgintób *m.* **1** saltiness, salinity **2** attractiveness

مالگینول mālginawə́l *transitive* ☞ مالگنول

مالگینی mālginí ☞ مالگین توب

مالگینېدل mālginedə́l *denominative, intransitive* [past: مالگین شو to be salted; be corned

مالگینی mālgíne *f. plural* name of a children's game

مال مواشي mālmawāshí *m. plural* cattle, livestock خپل مال مواشي به يې څرول He was grazing his cattle.

مال والا mālwālá *m.* **1** owner of goods **2** owner, proprietor

مالودج mālúdzh *m. plural* مالوچ mālúch *m. plural dialect* **1** ginned cotton **2** absorbent cotton, cotton batting

مالوچول māluchawál *denominative, transitive* [past: مالوچ يې کړ to gin cotton

مال ورونکی mālwrúnkaj freight, cargo مال ورونکي بېړی freighter

مالوف mālúf *Arabic* **1** customary, usual **2** grown accustomed to, grown used to

مال ومنال māl-u-manál *m.* property, belongings, fortune

مالوي mālawí *m.* Malawi

ماله māلá *f.* **1** putty knife **2** harrow ماله كول *compound verb* **a** to harrow **b** to persecute ماله كېدل *compound verb* **a** to be harrowed **b** to be persecuted **3** weaver's brush

ما لد mā́ la ☞ ما 2, 3

ماله كښ māلakáķh *m. regional* harrier (the bird)

مالي [1] māلí *m.* loader, stevedore, longshoreman; manual laborer, unskilled workman

مالي [2] māí *m. regional* gardener; truck gardener, truck farmer ☞ ماليار

مالي [3] māلí *Arabic* **1** property **2** financial, fiscal; money, monetary مالي كال fiscal year روان مالي كال، جاري مالي كال the current fiscal year

مالي [4] māلí *f.* Mali

مالي [5] māلí *paired word with* كالي

مالي [6] māله *colloquial* time چرگ بانگ مالي with the roosters, at the crack of dawn ☞ مهال

ماليات māلijā́t *m. plural Arabic* taxes; duties, assessments ماليه وركول *compound verb* to pay taxes, pay duties ☞ ماليه

ماليات وركونكى māلijā́t warkawúnkaj *m. m.* taxpayer

مالياتي māلijātí tax; fiscal مالياتي سيستم tax system

ماليار māljā́r *m. regional* gardener; truck gardener, truck farmer

ماليخوليا māلikholijā́ *f.* **1** melancholy; anguish, distress, depression **2** madness, insanity

مالېدل māledál *denominative, intransitive* [*past:* مال شو] to be tame(d), be domesticated; be meek

ماليده māلidá *f.* rich flat cake sprinkled with sugar (for treating guests in connection with reaching an agreement, deal)

مالېزي māلezí *f.* Malaysia د ماليزي اتحاديه Malaysia Union

مالېكول mālekúl *m.* molecule

مالېكولي mālekulí molecular

مالېكيول mālekjúl *m.* ☞ مالېكول

ماليه māلijá *f. Arabic* [*plural:* مالیي māلijé *and m. plural: Arabic* ماليات māلijā́t] **1** tax; duty ماليات مستقيم direct taxes غير مستقيم ماليات indirect taxes پر مدخکو ماليات income tax پر عایداتو ماليات land tax جگېدونكي ماليات progressive tax ماليات اخيستل *compound verb* to levy a tax ماليات ټاكل *compound verb* to institute a tax, set a duty ماليات لگول *compound verb* to impose a tax or duty **2** financial department **3** finances, finance د ماليي وزارت the ministry of finance **4** excise, excise tax, duty

ماليه ده māلijadéh *m.* taxpayer

ماما māmā́ *m.* **1** uncle (mother's brother) **2** old boy, old chap (as a familiar form of address)

ماماجي māmā́dzhí *m. regional,* **1** *hypocoristic diminutive of* ماما uncle **2** uncle (as a familiar form of address to male of one's father's generation)

ماماخېل māmākhél *m. plural* **1** uncle's family **2** Mamakheil (inhabited place near Jelalabad)

ماماغواگى māmāghwāgə́j *f.* **1** wood louse **2** aquatic sow-bug

مامته māmatá *f.* **1** fence around a plowed field **2** fenced-in plowed field

مامد māmád *m. colloquial proper noun* Mamad

مامسى māmasə́j *f.* pear

مامک māmə́k *m.* مامكو māməkó *m. hypocoristic diminutive of* ماما uncle

مامله māmilá *f.* ☞ معامله

مأمن mā'mán *m. Arabic* shelter, refuge, asylum د خپل تسليت مأمن لټول to seek a safe haven

مامنكوټ māmankóṭ *m.* ☞ مأمن

مامور [1] māmúr *Arabic* **1.1** authorized; having received instructions, having received orders **1.2** sent on business, sent on TDY; assigned, appointed مامور كول *compound verb* ☞ مامورول مامورېدل *compound verb* ☞ كېدل **2** *m.* [*plural:* ماموران māmuā́n *and Arabic* مامورين māmurín] **.1** government employee, government worker; official د مامورينو مديريت personnel department **2.2** ministry representative (in a region)

مامور [2] māmúr ☞ معمور

مامورول māmurawə́l *denominative, transitive* [*past:* مامور يې كړ] **1** to authorize; give instructions, give directions **2** to send on a business trip, send on TDY **3** to assign, appoint (to a job) **4** to establish, set up

ماموره māmúra **1** *feminine singular of* مامور māmurá[1] **2** *f. Arabic* woman official; woman manager

ماموريت māmurijā́t *m. Arabic* **1** position, job; service; post مهم ماموريت important post ماموريت نيول to occupy a position, hold a post **2** mission, assignment **3** business trip, TDY **4** appointment (of officials) **5** police directorate

مامورېدل māmuredál *denominative, intransitive* [*past:* مامور شو] **1** to be authorized **2** to be sent on a business trip, go on TDY **3** to be appointed, be named (to a job) **4** to be established, be set up

ماموس māmús thick; viscous

ماموسى māmusə́j *f.* ☞ مامسى

مامول [1] māmúl *Arabic* **1** expect **2** *m.* hope, expectation

مامول [2] māmúl ☞ معمول

مامولک māmulák *m.* male wagtail

مامولکه māmuláka *f.* female wagtail

مأمون māmún *Arabic* **1** ensured; guaranteed **2** safe (of a road, etc.) **3** freed, liberated

ماموند māmúnd **1** *m. plural* Mamunds (a tribe) **2** *m.* Mamund

ماموئي māmují *f.* unpitted dried apricots

مامي [1] māmí *f.* [*plural:* مامى māmə́j *and* ماميگاني māmigā́ni] aunt (uncle's wife)

مامى [2] māmə́j *f. hypocoristic diminutive of* مامي [1] auntie

ماميره māmirá *f.* Wallich's Geranium, *Geranium wallichianum* (medicinal plant)

مانا [1] mānā́ *f.* ☞ معنىٰ

مانا [2] mānā́ resembling; similar

مانجو māndzháw *m.* ☞ ماجر [1]

مانجه [1] māndzhá *f.* military music; bravura music

مانجه [2] māndzhá *f.* kite string

مانجی māndzháj *m.* member of a wedding train (specifically, a participant in the groom's train)

مانچستر mánchəstər *m.* Manchester

مانئپنین māndzpḳhín *m. dialect* ☞ مازپنین

مانځل māndzə́l *transitive* ☞ نمانځل

مانځه māndzə́ *m. oblique of* مونځ

مانځی māndzáj *m.* axle, shaft (of a hand-operated mill)

ماندت māndát *m.* mandate

ماندره mándra *f.* 1 rope, cord (of a tent) 2 runner (of a plant)

ماندگي māndagí *f.* 1 tiredness, fatigue, exhaustion 2 *dialect* indisposition; sickness, ill health

مانده [1] māndə́ *m.* [*plural:* ماندونه māndúna *and* مندونه mandúna] wide ravine

مانده [2] māndá 1 tired, weary; exhaustion مانده کېدل *compound verb* to grow weary, get tired; become exhausted 2 thin, emaciated زه ډېر مانده یم I've gotten very thin. 3 *dialect* sick

ماندېت māndét *m.* ☞ ماندت

ماندینه māndiná *f.* wife ماندینه کول *compound verb* to take to wife, marry

مانده [1] mánḍa *f.* footprint, track

مانده [2] mánḍə́ *imperfect of* منډل [1]

مانړج mānṛáj *m. dialect* ☞ مانی [1]

مانزه mānzə́ *oblique singular of* مونز

مانش mānsh *m.* English Channel بحیرهٔ مانش buhayrá-yi... the English Channel

مانع mā́ni' *Arabic* 1 blocking, preventing, hindering 2 *m.* [*plural:* موانع mawāni'] .1 obstacle مانع کېدونکي نه رفع an unsurmountable obstacle د... مانع گرزېدل، د... مانع لوېدل، د... مانع واقع کېدل to be an obstacle مانع راوستل *compound verb* to create obstacles 2.2 *military* obstacle, barrier, obstruction

مانع سازي mā́ni'sāzí *f. military* construction of obstacles

مانفسټو mānifesṭó *f.* manifesto

مانگو māngó *f.* mango

مانگی māngáj *m.* ☞ مانگی

مانوره mānewrá *f.* 1 *military* maneuvers مانوره کول *compound verb* to conduct maneuvers 2 stratagem, clever trick

مأنوس mānús *Arabic* 1 grown accustomed (to), become familiar (with) د یو شي سره مأنوس کېدل to grow accustomed to something, become familiar with something 2 habitual, usual, customary; ordinary

مأنوسیت mā'nusiját *m. Arabic* habitualness

مانه [1] māná *f.* 1 blame, censure 2 murmur, grumble; complaint مانه کول *compound verb* to grumble, complain

مانه [2] mānə́ *imperfect of* منل

ما نه [3] mā́ na *Eastern in lieu of* له مانه ☞ ما [2]

مانی mānə́j *f.* ☞ مامی

مانیلا mānilá *f.* Manila

مانگج māngáj *m.* 1 boatman 2 sailor

مانو [1] mānú *m.* ☞ مانگی کنیي معلومېري، بنه مانو د طوفان په وخت *saying* It is during a storm that we learn who is a good sailor.

مانو [2] mānú *m.* myrtle

مانوگج mānugáj *m.* sailor; seafarer

مانه mānə́ *f.* ☞ مانه [1]

مانی [1] mānə́j *m.* 1 grief, distress; being upset 2 offense, insult, affront 3 tiff, disagreement مانی کول *compound verb* a to distress, upset b to offend, insult c to provoke a tiff, cause a falling out

مانی [2] mānə́j *f.* [*plural:* مانی mānə́j *and* مانی گانی mānə́jgā́ni] 1 palace; mansion 2 building, structure; multistory house; detached house اسماني مانی skyscraper 3 *figurative* building, structure سپینه مانی *idiom* the White House

مانهجن mānədzhə́n 1 upset, distressed 2 insulted, offended; dissatisfied

مانهجني mānədzhəní *f.* 1 being upset, grief, distress 2 insult, offense, affront

مانهچغ mānechə́gh *m.* swing

مانهگر mānegár 1 ☞ مانی جن 2 touchy, quick to take offense

مأوا mā'wá *f. Arabic* shelter, refuge, asylum

ماورأ māwará *Arabic* 1 on the other side; from behind د اورېخو له ماورأ نه from behind the clouds; behind the clouds 2 located on the other side of something 3 ultra-, super-, trans- ماورأ بنفش ultraviolet

ماورأ لطبیعه māwarā-ut-tabi'á *Arabic* supernatural

ماورأ البحار māwarā-al-bihár *Arabic* overseas

ماورأ الطبیعي māwarā-at-tabi'í supernatural ماورأ الطبیعي قوت supernatural strength

ماورأالنهر māwarānnáhr *m. Arabic history* Mawerannahr (the name of the area between the Amu-Darya and the Syr-Darya rivers during the Middle Ages)

ماورای بحار māwarā-ji-bihár overseas

ماورای بنفش māwarā-ji-banáfsh ultraviolet (of rays)

ماورأ جو māwará-ji-dzháw *m.* ماورأ فضا māwará-ji-fazá *f.* space, cosmos

ماورأ جوي māwará-ji-dzhawí *Arabic* space, cosmic

ماورای حمره māwará-ji-hamrá *Arabic* infrared

ماورای قفقاز māwará-ji-qawqáz *m.* Transcaucasus, Transcaucasia

ماورأ کسپین māwará-ji-kaspiján Transcaspian

ماولولئ māwalwaləy *computer science* readme

ما ولولئ دوتنه mā walwaləy dawtəná *f. computer science* readme file

ماولج māwláj *m.* ماولج māwlə́j *f.* bushing in the upper millstone through which passes the shaft of the nether, or lower, millstone

ماوه māwá *f. dialect* 1 ephedra (a medicinal plant) 2 coil (pipe)

مأوئ [1] mā'wá *f. Arabic* ☞ مأوا

ما وي mā ² we *in lieu of* ماويل I say…

ماه ¹ māh **1** *m.* month; moon له ماه په ماه from month to month **2** *used as the first part of word compounds* ماه پيکر **a** beautiful **b** handsome man, good-looking boy **c** sweetheart, beloved

ماه ² māh *m. regional* magkh (the tenth month of the Indian calendar)

ماهانه māhāná **1** monthly **2** monthly, every month

ماهبيبي māhbibí *f. proper noun* Mahbibi

ماه پيکر māhpajkár **1** beautiful **2** *m.* .1 handsome man, good-looking boy **2.2** beloved, sweetheart

ماه جبين māhdzhabín *poetic* with forehead white as snow

ماهر māhír *Arabic* **1** skillful; able, capable; skilled, trained ماهر کارگر skilled worker **2** *m.* [*plural:* ماهران māhirán *and Arabic* ماهرين māhirín] master of his trade; specialist; expert

ماهرانه māhirāná **1** skillful, masterly; talented, gifted **2** skillfully, masterly; ably, finely

ماهرو māhrú *f. proper noun* Mahru

ماه روی māhrúj moonfaced; handsome

ماه رويه māhrúja **1** *feminine singular of* ماه روی **2** *f.* beautiful woman, good-looking girl, beauty

ماهوار māhawár monthly ماهوار رپوټ وركول to submit a monthly report, present a report for the month

ماهواري māhawārí monthly, by the month, per month

ماهوت māhút *m.* cloth

ماه وش māhwásh *poetic* like the moon, moonlike

ماهی māháj *m.* [*plural:* ماهيان māhí, ماهيان mājān *and* ماهيان mājấn] fish بحري ماهيان ocean fish د خوړو او وبو ماهيان freshwater fish ماهي نيول fishing د ماهيانو روزنه fishing الوتونکي ماهيان flying fish *compound verb* to fish, catch fish د شا غوندي د ماهي protuberant, bulging

ماهي پر māhipár *m.* ماهيپر Mahipar (a waterfall on the Kabul River) د ماهي پر تونل the Mahipar Tunnel

ماهي پشت māhipúsht **1** convex **2** profiled, shaped, graded خيابان ماهي پشت جوړول to grade a road

ماهيت māhiját *m. Arabic* essence, substance, gist, nature; quality, characteristic

ماهي شناس māhishinás *m.* ichthyologist

ماهي شناسي māhishināsí *f.* ichthyology

ماهي غوږ māhighwág *m.* cockleshell, mussel

ماهي گير māhigír, māhajgír *m.* fisherman

ماهيگيري māhigirí *f.* fishing, fishing operation, fishery د ماهيگيري کول، د ماهيگيري کسب کول *compound verb* to be engaged in commercial fishing ماهيگيري بېړۍ fishing boat

ماهيان mājān *m.* **1** *plural of* ماهی **2** kind of women's adornment in the form of gold fish or flowers

ماچي mā́jche *f. plural* ☞ ماچي

مايحتاج mājahtā́dzh *m. Arabic* **1** that which is needed, that which is required **2** necessity

مايع mājí' *Arabic* **1.1** liquid, flowing **1.2** smooth, flowing (of sound) **2** *f. & m.* [*m. plural Arabic* مايعات mājiʿā́t] liquid, fluid خړه مايع cloudy fluid

مايع کريستال خدل mājí' krisṭál khodál *computer science* LCD (Liquid Crystal Display)

مايکروفون mā́jkrofón *m.* microphone

مايل mā́il, mājíl *Arabic* مائل **1** slanting, inclined; sloping په مايل ډول slantingly **2** to be inclined (to) **3** desiring something مايل کېدل *compound verb* **a** to be inclined to (do) something **b** to desire something مريض خوب ته مايل شي The patient is drowsy. *idiom* سروالي ته مايل with a reddish hue

مايلاً mā́ilán *Arabic* مائلاً mājílán aslant, slantingly; obliquely

مايملک mājamlák *m. Arabic* property

ماينه mājná *f.* married woman ماينه کول *compound verb* to give in marriage ماينه کېدل *compound verb* to get married (of a woman)

مايوب mājúb *colloquial* ☞ معيوب

مايوپ mājóp shortsighted, nearsighted, myopic

مايوپ والی mājopwā́laj *m.* shortsightedness, myopia

مايوس mājús *Arabic* desperate, without hope; disillusioned, disappointed مايوس کېدل *compound verb* to despair, lose hope; become disillusioned, become disappointed

مايوسانه mājusāná **1** desperate, hopeless **2** unfavorable (of results)

مايوسي mājusí *f.* مايوسيت mājusiját *m.* **1** despair مايوسي ته لار مه Don't despair! ورکوه! **2** disillusionment, disappointment **3** unfavorableness (of results); inconsolability

مايه ¹ mājɞ́ *m.* long-wooled two-humped camel

مايه ² mājá *f.* **1** rennet; yeast; ferment, liven **2** basis, essence **3** capital; fund ☞ سرمايه **4** nest egg **5** hole (for a game)

مائي māj *m.* May

مباح mubáh *Arabic* **1** *religion* permitted, permissible **2** legitimate, licit; generally accepted

مباحت mubāhát *m. Arabic* **1** permissibility **2** accessibility

مباحث ¹ mubāhís *Arabic* **1** *m.* .1 debater **1.2** opponent, critic **2.1** disputing **2.2** objecting; opposing, critiquing

مباحث ² mabāhís *m. plural Arabic of* مبحث

مباحثه mubāhasá *f. Arabic* **1** debate, discussion; dispute **2** argument مباحثه شروع شوه بحث An argument flared up.

مباحي mubāhí *f.* ☞ مباحت

مبادا mabādā́ God forbid!; lest; what if…

مبادرت mubādarát *m. Arabic* starting, beginning, setting down (to work, to the business at hand) مبادرت کول *compound verb* to start to work, set to work

مبادله mubādalá, mubādilá *f. Arabic* barter; exchange; substitution د an exchange of views د افکارو مبادله barter د جنس په جنس مبادله exchange rate نرخ مبادلي کول *compound verb* to be changed, be exchanged

مبادي mabādí *m. Arabic plural* **1** *of* مبدأ **2** fundamentals, principles, bases; foundations په اعلیٰ مبادیو کښي به یې خبري کولې He spoke of lofty matters.

مبارز mubāríz *m. Arabic* [*plural:* مبارزين mubārizín] brave soldier, valiant warrior; fighter for a cause د آزادی مبارزین، ملي مبارزین fighters for national liberation

مبارزه mubārizá, mubārazá *f. Arabic* **1** fight, struggle سياسي مبارزه political struggle اقتصادي مبارزه economic struggle د ملي خپلواکي طبقاتي مبارزه، د طبقاتو مبارزه ، struggle for national liberation افکارو مبارزه ideological د طبقاتو تر منځ مبارزه class struggle struggle د ژوندون مبارزه کول the struggle for existence *compound verb* to struggle (for), fight (for) د سولي دپاره مبارزه کول to fight for peace **2** single combat **3** campaign انتخاباتي مبارزه (pre)election campaign

مبارک mubārák *Arabic* **1.1** blessed; happy, fortunate زه اختر تاسو ته مبارک شه! *Eastern* مبارک موسه وايم! Happy holiday! نوی کال دي مبارک شه! Congratulations! I wish you happiness! Happy New Year! **1.2** successful دا خو ډېر مبارک کار دئ This is a very good thing. **2** *m.* **.1** respected person **2.2** lucky man

مبارکباد mubārakbād مبارک باد I congratulate you. Congratulations. **2** *m.* ☞ مبارکبادي

مبارکبادي mubārakbādí *f.* مبارکي mubārakí *f.* **1** congratulations د چا ته د... مبارکبادي ورکول، مبارکبادي تلګرام congratulatory telegram، د چا ته د... مبارکبادي وراندي کول، چا ته د... مبارکبادي ویل to convey د مبارکي عرض کول congratulate someone on... congratulations **2** blessing(s)

مبالات mubālát *m. Arabic* attention, concern, care

مبالاتي mubālātí attentive, thoughtful, considerate

مبالغ mabālígh *m. plural Arabic of* مبلغ[1]

مبالغه mubālaghá *f. Arabic* **1** exaggeration مبالغه کول *compound verb* to exaggerate **2** hyperbole

مبالغه آمېز mubālaghaāméz **1** exaggerated; inflated مبالغه آمېزه بيانات exaggeration **2** hyperbolical

مباني mabāní *m. plural Arabic of* مبنا

مباهات mubāhát *m. Arabic* pride, fame په يو شي فخر او مباهات کول to take pride in

مبايعه mubāja'á *f. Arabic* [*m. plural:* مبايعات mubāja'át] purchases, procurement د مبايعاتو رياست the directorate for state purchases

مباينت mubājinát *m. Arabic* discrepancy, disparity, lack of correspondence, divergence; contradiction

مبتدئ mubtadá *f. Arabic* [*plural:* مبتدا ګاني mubtadāgáni *and* مبتداوي mubtadáwi] مبتدا **1** principle; basis; essence **2** *grammar* subject (of a nominal sentence)

مبتدي mubtadí *Arabic* **1.1** initial, elementary **1.2** beginning, beginner **2** *m.* **.1** novice, tyro; pupil **2.2** founder

مبتذل mubtazál *Arabic* **1** banal, trite, stale, hackneyed **2** base, vile

مبتکر mubtakír *Arabic* **1** original **2** *m.* [*plural:* مبتکرين mubtakirín] initiator, innovator, originator, pioneer

مبتلا mubtalá *Arabic* **1.1** plunged into something, gripped by something; possessed by something په غم مبتلا overcome with grief **1.2** gotten into trouble, come to grief **1.3** injured; stricken

(by an illness) **1.4** grieved, saddened, distraught مبتلا کول *compound verb* **a** to plunge into something; seize something **b** to subject to something; plunge into something **c** to strike (of an illness) مبتلا کېدل *compound verb* **a** to be plunged into something **b** to be subject(ed) to something **c** to be stricken (by an illness) **2** *m.* [*plural:* مبتلايان mubtalāján] **.1** patient **2.2** victim

مبحث mabhás *m. Arabic* [*plural:* مباحث mabāhís] **1** part, section, chapter (book) **2** subject, topic; theme **3** problem; subject of an argument or discussion **4** treatise

مبحوث عنه mabhus'ánha *m. Arabic* **1** subject of an argument, point of a discussion **2** subject, topic, line (e.g., of research)

مبدأ mabdá *f. Arabic* [*m. plural: Arabic* مبادي mabādí] **1** starting point; origin **2** principle **3** standard, criterion (e.g., of time)

مبدل mubaddál *Arabic* **1** transformed, changed, reformed **2** altered **3** upset, depressed, despondent

مبذول mabzúl *Arabic* abundant, plentiful

مبذوليت mabzuliját *m. Arabic* abundance, plenty, plentiful ness

مبرا mubarrá *Arabic* **1** saved, spared (from disease, illness, etc.) **2** free of suspicion, above suspicion مبرا کول *compound verb* **a** to save (from illness, etc.) **b** to acquit مبرا کېدل *compound verb* **a** to be saved, be spared (from a disease, illness, etc.) **b** to be acquited

مبرز mabráz *m. Arabic* latrine, lavatory, restroom عمومي مبرز restroom

مبرهن mubarhán *Arabic* shown, demonstrated, proven; elucidated

مبسوط mabsút *Arabic* **1** extended, spread out, stretched out **2** *figurative* extensive, vast, detailed, thorough مبسوطه وينا wordy speech **3** satisfied, contented, cheerful

مبصر[1] mubassír *m. Arabic* [*plural:* مبصرين mubassirín] **1** observer **2** inspector, checker **3** commentator

مبصر[2] mubsír *m. Arabic* **1** expert **2** clairvoyant

مبصر[3] mubassár *Arabic* obvious, visible, noticeable

مبعوث mab'ús *Arabic* **1** sent, dispatched **2** *m.* messenger, envoy مبعوث کېدل *compound verb* to be a messenger (of prophets)

مبغوض mabghúz *Arabic* hateful, repulsive ناخوښ او مبغوض شعور مبغوض پیدا کول to come to hate, conceive a hatred for

مبلغ[1] mablágh *m. Arabic* sum د پادشاهي درخرخ مبلغ *idiom* civil list

مبلغ[2] muballígh *m. Arabic* [*plural:* مبلغين muballighín] **1** preacher مذهبي مبلغ missionary **2** propagandist

مبنا mabná *f. Arabic* مبنئ mabná *f.* basis, foundation

مبني mubní, mabní *Arabic* based on something, grounded in something

مبهم mubhám *Arabic* **1** unclear, indefinite; doubtful **2** innermost, concealed, secret

مبهوت mabhút *Arabic* **1** surprised, astonished, amazed **2** delighted, carried away

مبهوتانه mabhutāná *Arabic* **1** astonished, amazed **2** in amazement

مبهوم mabhúm *Arabic grammar* indefinite (of pronouns) مبهوم ضمير indefinite pronoun

مبيض mubajjíz *m. Arabic* copyist, typist, one who makes fair copies

مبيعه mabi'á *f. Arabic commerce* forward contract, provisional sale

مبين mubín *Arabic* 1 obvious, clear 2 *religion* true

ميکونه mápdzūna *computer science abbreviation of* مهمي پوښتني او ځوابونه FAQs

ميلر maplár *Arabic* scarf, muffler

متابعت mutāba'át *m. Arabic* following (the orders, instruction, etc) of someone; being subordinate, obedience; adherence د چا متابعت کول to follow someone; be subordinate, obey someone د چا متابعت او پيروي کول

متأثر muta'assír *m.* 1 moved by something; under the influence of something; subjected to the influence of something; having sensed something 2 grieved, saddened; upset, distraught متأثر کول *compound verb* ☞ متأثرول a to make an impression on someone b to sadden, cause grief متأثرکېدل ☜ متأثرېدل

متأثرېدل muta'assiredə́l *denominative, intransitive* [*past:* متأثر شو] 1 to be subject to the influence of something; be under the impression of something; sense something 2 to be sad, grieve 3 د ... خه متأثرېدل a to suffer from something b to take offense, take umbrage at someone

متأخر muta'akhkhír *Arabic* 1.1 modern, contemporary متأخر شاعر modern poet 1.2 (the) latest, (the) newest 1.3 lagging (behind) 2 *plural:* متأخرين muta'akhirín contemporaries, people of our time

متأذي muta'azzí *Arabic* 1 grieved, saddened 2 experiencing annoyance, having disappointment

متار matár *m.* [*plural:* متارونه matārúna *and* Western متاران matārā́n] log, billet; tree trunk with branches removed د اتکل متار to judge the amount of something by eye, eye, eyeball وراچول

متاركه mutāraká *f. Arabic* 1 leaving; stopping, ceasing 2 armistice د متاركي قرارداد armistice agreement

متاز mutáz متازه mutáza *colloquial* ☞ محتاج

متازي mutāzí *f. colloquial* need, want

متأسف muta'assíf *Arabic* 1 regretting, feeling sorry; sad متأسف کېدل *compound verb* to regret, be sorry; be sad, be grieved, be distressed زه پر تاسو متأسف يم I feel sorry for you.

متأسفانه muta'assifā́na unfortunately متأسفانه دا ممکنه نه ده Unfortunately, this is not possible.

متاع matá' *f. Arabic* (trade) goods; property; things تجارتي متاع (trade) goods يوه متاع بازار ته ايستل to bring goods to market دا راز متاع نن خريدار نه لري Right now, there's no demand for this product.

متألم muta'allím *Arabic* 1 suffering 2 grieved, distressed, saddened دوى متألمه او غمجن دي They are sad and are grieving.

متالورجي metālurdzhí 1 *f.* metallurgy 2 metallurgical متالورجي صنايع metallurgical products

متالورجيست metālurdzhíst *m.* metallurgist

متالورجيکي metālurdzhíkí metallurgical

متأمل muta'ammíl *Arabic* thoughtful, attentive, careful

متأمن muta'ammín *Arabic* 1 (being) defended; (being) guarded 2 secured, guaranteed

متان ¹ metán *m.* methane

متان ² matán *Arabic* hard, solid, steadfast, firm, unswerving, unbending

متانت matānát *m. Arabic* 1 hardness, solidity, inflexibility; constancy; self-restraint, tenacity, endurance; persistence د متانت self-restraint, tenacity, endurance قوه په متانت سره ويل to underscore, stress, single out 2 stability

متأهل muta'ahhíl *Arabic* married متأهل کسان family people, married folks

متبادل mutabādíl *Arabic* alternating; variable

متباقي mutabāqí *Arabic* remaining, rest of

متباين mutabājín *Arabic* contrasting; differing; different دوى بو له بله سره متباين او جلا دي These are different things.

متبحر mutabahír *Arabic* erudite, knowing the field well متبحر عالم erudite person

متبدل mutabaddíl *Arabic* changeable, unsteady هر شى متبدل وي Everything changes.

متبرک mutabarrák, mutabarrík *Arabic* 1 blessed, holy 2 happy, blissful

متبصر mutabassír *Arabic* 1 perspicacious; farseeing 2 circumspect, discrete; acting with caution, very carefully

متبوع matbú' *Arabic* dominating, commanding; sovereign متبوعه حکومت central government

متبوعیت matbu'iját *m. Arabic* 1 sovereignty 2 dominion, sway, rule, supremacy

متتبع mutatabé' *Arabic* 1.1 researching, investigating 1.2 inquisitive, searching 2 *m.* [*plural:* متتبعين mutatabe'ín] researcher, investigator

متجاور mutadzhāwír *Arabic* neighboring; adjoining, bordering; adjacent, contiguous

متجاوز mutadzhāwíz *Arabic* 1 *m.* aggressor 2.1 violating the borders 2.2 exceeding something; going out of bounds 2.3 aggressive (of a bloc)

متجاوزانه mutadzhāwizāná 1 aggressive متجاوزانه سياست aggressive policy 2 aggressively

متجاوزي mutadzhāwizí aggressive

متجاهل mutadzhāhíl *Arabic* pretending to be a know-nothing, feigning being an ignoramus

متجدد mutadzhaddíd *Arabic* 1 progressive, advanced 2 *m.* advanced worker, leading worker

متحاب mutahā́b, mutahább *Arabic* friendly, amicable متحابه دولتونه، متحابه هيوادونه friendly nations

متحارب mutahāríb *Arabic* warring, belligerent, (being) in state of war متحارب ممالک the warring countries

متحد muttahíd *Arabic* 1.1 combined, united متحد کول *compound verb* to combine, unite سره متحد کېدل *compound verb* to be combined, be united 1.2 unanimous, concordant ! بنه متحد او متفق

اوسئ Live in harmony! **1.3** united, common متحد محاذ a united front **2** *m.* [*plural:* متحدین muttahidín] allies

متحداً muttahídán *Arabic adv.* ūnanimously, by common consent; in accord (with); in harmony

متحدالشکل muttahidushshákl *Arabic* general, common; uniform متحدالشکل به لرل to have a common character

متحدالشکلانه muttahid-ush-shaklāná homogeneous, uniform, identical, same

متحدالمآل muttahid-ul-ma'ál *Arabic* **1** *m.* circular (letter) **2** stereotypic(al) (of a phrase)

متحدالمرکز muttahid-ul-markáz *Arabic* concentric

متحدانه muttahidāná in common, jointly, together متحدانه زیارونه ایستل to make joint efforts; act together

متحده muttahidá *Arabic feminine singular & plural of* متحد متحده ممالک، د امریکا متحده اضلاع the United States of America

متحرک mutaharrík *Arabic* **1** moving, mobile متحرکه جگړه mobile warfare متحرک کېدل *compound verb* to move, shift متحرک کول *compound verb* to move, be moved, shift, be shifted **2** *m.* *linguistics* letter with a diacritical mark (over or under it)

متحرکیت mutaharrikiját *m. Arabic* mobility

متحکم mutahakkím *Arabic* imperious, peremptory, despotic

متحکمانه mutahakkimāná imperious, peremptory په متحکمانه لهجه کېني خبري کول to speak with an imperious tone

متحمل mutahammíl *Arabic* **1** bearing (responsibility); responsible **2** enduring, undergoing or suffering د خرڅو متحمل کېدل، د متصارفو متحمل کېدل to bear the expenses

متحول mutahawwíl *Arabic* **1** transformed, reformed **2** changeable, variable; changing متحول حالت *biology* lability

متحیر mutahajjír *Arabic* amazed, astonished, struck متحیر کېدل *compound verb* to be amazed, be astonished, be struck

متخاصم mutakhāsím hostile, enemy('s); feuding, quarrelling متخاصم طبقات hostile classes

متخاصمانه mutakhāsimāná hostile, enemy('s)

متخالف mutakhālíf **1** different **2** various, diverse **3** opposite, contrary, opposed, countervailing

متخصص mutakhassís *Arabic* **1** *m.* [*plural:* متخصصین mutakhas-sisín] specialist, expert **2** adapted, accommodated; special, specialized

متخصصه mutakhassisá *Arabic* **1** *f.* specialist **2** *feminine singular of* متخصص **2**

متخیل mutakhajíl *Arabic* **1** fantasizing **2** *m.* visionary, dreamer

متداول mutadāwíl *Arabic* frequently used, common, in common use

متدرج mutaddarrídzh *Arabic* gradual

متدرجاً mutaddarrídzhin *Arabic* gradually د سیند هري غاړي ته متدرجاً د ونو بڼونه جګ سوېدي *idiom* Along the banks of the river gardens rose on ledges.

متدین mutadajín *Arabic* religious, pious, devout یو متدین believing

متذبذب mutazabzíb *Arabic* indecisive, uncertain

متذکر mutazakkír *Arabic* **1** remembering, recollecting **2** reminding, resembling, reminiscent of

متر matər *m.* ☞ متره

متر metr *m.* meter یو متر تکر (one) meter of cloth مربع متر square meter, m²

مترادف mutarādíf *Arabic* **1.1** synonymous مترادف لغات synonyms **1.2** following one after the other **1.3** rhythmic **1.4** equal meaning **2** *m.* synonym

مترالیوز mitraljóz *m. Arabic* machine gun

مترانه mitrāná **1** by meters, by the meter **2** *m.* metric area

مترتب mutarattíb *Arabic* **1** brought or put into (good) order; adjusted **2** classified

مترجم mutardzhím *m. Arabic* [*plural:* مترجمان mutardzhimā́n *and Arabic* مترجمین mutardzhimín] translator, interpreter, dragoman

متردد mutaraddíd *Arabic* **1** indecisive, vacillating, having doubts لر متردد شو He began to hesitate. **2** changeable, variable **3** wandering

مترصد mutarassíd *Arabic* **1** observing **2** *m. military* observer, spotter

مترغزي matróghzi *f. plural* cerebral membranes

مترقي mutaraqqí *Arabic* **1** advanced, progressive مترقي قواوي progressive forces **2** successful, prosperous; flourishing مترقي ژوند prosperity, well-being **3** developed (of a country, language, etc.) لر مترقي poorly developed **4** following, next **5** rising (of prices)

مترو metró *f.* metro, subway, undergroud

متروک matrúk *Arabic* **1** abandoned, deserted **2** obsolete, gone out of use

متروکات matrukā́t *m. Arabic plural* inheritance, inherited property

متروکه matruká *f. Arabic* divorced woman, divorcée

متروکه matróka *f.* **1** knout; whip **2** kind of snake د هوا متروکي *idiom* gusts of wind

متروکېدل matrukedə́l *denominative, intransitive* [*past:* متروک شو] **1** to be abandoned, be deserted **2** to become obsolete, go out of use

متره mátra *f.* **1** curdled milk; curds, cottage cheese **2** precipitates, sediment

متره mátra *f.* **1** force, strength **2** feeling, sensation د ځانمني متره egoism د شخصیت متره

متره matrá almost unobtainable متره کول *compound verb* to cause to be almost unobtainable متره کېدل *compound verb* to be rare, be almost unobtainable **2** scanty, poor; insufficient **3** annihilated; exhausted; vanished

متري metrí metric متري سلسله the metric system

متری matráj *m.* small leather bag for koumiss

متریز metríz meter شلمتریز twenty meters long

متریک metrík ☞ متري

متڼ matə́ṛ, mutə́ṛ *m.* blockhead, fool, dunderhead

متزلزل mutazalzíl *Arabic* 1 shaking, trembling متزلزل کېدل *compound verb* to shake, tremble 2 shaken متزلزل ايمان shaken faith

متساوي mutasāwí *Arabic* equal, equaling

متساوي الساقين mutasāwi-as-sāfájn *mathematics* isosceles

متسلسل mutasalsil *Arabic* continuous, uninterrupted (of an action)

متشابه mutashābéh *Arabic* 1 similar, analogous 2 *m.* [*plural:* متشابهات mutashābehā́t] .1 homograph 2.2 homonym

متشبث mutashabbís *Arabic* 1 enterprising و... ته متشبث کول to undertake something 2 *m.* entrepreneur, business owner

متشبک mutashabbík *Arabic* being interlaced, becoming entangled, being closlely interwoven

متشتت mutashattít *Arabic* 1 dispersed, scattered 2 scattered, strewn 3 published in various organs of the press

متشکر mutashakkír *Arabic* grateful, thankful

متشکل mutashakkíl formed, shaped, consisting of متشکله برخه، متشکل جز constituent part

متصادف mutasādáf coinciding, concurring متصادف کېدل *compound verb* to coincide

متصادم mutasādíd conflicting; contradicting, contradictory to something متصادم کېدل *compound verb* to collide, come into collision

متصاعد mutasā'íd *Arabic* 1 *mathematics* cumulative 2 growing, developing 3 rising, ascending

متصدي mutasaddí *Arabic* 1 occupying a leading post or position 2 *m.* .1 entrepreneur 2.2 publisher (of a magazine)

متصرف mutasarráf taken, captured, occupied

متصرفات mutasarrafā́t *m. plural Arabic* 1 seized countries, occupied countries 2 property, holdings, possessions

متصف muttasíf *Arabic* characterizing, being noted for something متصف کول، متصف په *compound verb* to characterize, distinguish متصف کېدل *compound verb* to be characterized by something, be distinguished by something

متصل muttasál *Arabic* adjacent; contiguous; adjoin, bordering on افغانستان په شمال ختيځ کښې په چين پوري متصل دئ In the northeast, Afghanistan borders China. يو په بل پوري متصله سلسله، د واقعاتو يو idiom inseperably connected things, unbroken chain (of events) د ... سره متصل following

متصور mutasawwár *Arabic* 1 imaginary, conceivable; seeming 2 supposed, conjectural; probable, likely; planned, projected متصورکېدل *compound verb* a to conceive, imagine b to suppose; be planned, be designed

متصوف mutasawwíf *Arabic* 1 studying Sufi mysticism 2 *m.* Sufi, mystic

متصوفانه mutasawwifā́ná Sufi; anchoretic متصوفانه ژوند asceticism

متضاد mutazád, mutazádd *Arabic* 1.1 opposite, contrary, opposed; contradicting, contradictory; contrasting متضادي قواوي opposing forces متضاده معنىٰ opposite meaning متضادي راى لرل to be of the

opposite opinion دا د شرف متضاد وي That is incompatible with honor. 1.2 antagonistic 2 *m. linguistics* antonym

متضرر mutazarrír *Arabic* having suffered, having sustained متضرر کېدل *compound verb* to be suffered

متضمن mutazammín *Arabic* 1.1 containing, including 1.2 meaning, signifying 2 *m. law* guarantor

متظاهر mutazāhír *m. Arabic* demonstrator

متعادل muta'ādíl *Arabic* balanced, equal

متعارف muta'āríf *Arabic* 1 familiar, acquainted سره متعارف کول to acquaint someone (with) 2 usual, ordinary, commonplace متعارف حقيقت well-known truth 3 nominal

متعاقب muta'āqíb *Arabic* 1 immediately next; continuous, unbroken 2 consecutive, successive 3 following, (right) after

متعاقباً muta'āqíbán *Arabic* 1 following 2 successively

متعاقد muta'āqíd *Arabic* negotiating, concluding an agreement

متعال muta'ál *Arabic religion* Most High

متعاهد muta'āhíd *Arabic* 1 negotiating an agreement دواړه متعاهدي خواوي the contracting parties 2 *m.* contractor; supplier

متعجب muta'adzhdzhíb *Arabic* being astonished, being amazed متعجب کېدل *compound verb* to be astonished, be amazed ناخاپه متعجب کېدل، ناخاپه ډېر متعجب کېدل to be astonished

متعدد muta'addíd *Arabic* numerous

متعدي muta'addí *Arabic* 1 assaulting, attacking, encroaching, infringing, aggressive 2 *grammar* transitive (of verbs) 3 *medicine* infectious, contagious, communicable متعدي مرضونه contagious

متعذر muta'azzír *Arabic* 1 difficult to show or prove 2 difficult, virtually impossible

متعرض muta'arríz *Arabic* 1.1 attacking, aggressive 1.2 dissenting (from something; disagreeing (with something) 2 *m.* [*plural:* متعرضين muta'arrizín] aggressor

متعرضانه muta'arrizā́ná 1 aggressive 2 aggressively

متعصب muta'assíb *Arabic* 1.1 fanatical, fanatic متعصب سړى fanatic 1.2 stubborn, obstinate 2 *m.* [*plural:* متعصبين muta'assibín] fanatic

متعفن muta'affín 1 rotting, decomposing متعفن کېدل *compound verb* to rot, decompose 2 stinking, fetid

متعلق muta'allíq *Arabic* 1.1 belonging to someone; relating to someone 1.2 connected with something, involving something 2 *m.* .1 relation, regard, respect د نورو اشخاصو په متعلق in relation to other people 2.2 *plural* متعلقان muta'alliqā́n everybody at home, whole family, household

متعلقات muta'alliqā́t *m. Arabic plural* 1 accessories, appurtenances 2 vassal relations

متعلم muta'allím *Arabic* pupil, schoolboy; student

متعلمه muta'allimá *f. Arabic* [*plural:* متعلمات muta'allimā́t] pupil, schoolgirl; (female) student

متعهد muta'ahhíd *Arabic* **1.1** being committed, being obliged متعهد کول *compound verb* to oblige متعهد کېدل *compound verb* to be obliged **1.2** stipulated by contract **2** *m.* contractor; supplier

متعهدله muta'ahhidléh *m. Arabic* contractor

متعين muta'ajjín appointed, designated; determined; established, set

متغير mutaghajjír *Arabic* **1** inconstant, changeable; variable متغير کول *compound verb* to vary متغير کېدل *compound verb* to vary, be varied **2** differing; varying **3** agitated, uneasy **4** irked, irritated, angry

متفاوت mutafāwít *Arabic* **1** differing; different **2** outstanding, being distinguished, being notable (for something) په متفاوته اندازه to differing degrees سره، په متفاوتو درجو سره

متفرج mutafarrídzh *Arabic* **1** *m.* viewer, spectator, onlooker **2** having a good time, enjoying time off from work

متفرد mutafarríd *Arabic* **1.1** single, solitary, individual **1.2** unique, nonpareil; original **2** *m.* eccentric (of a person)

متفرع mutafarré' *Arabic* **1** derivative متفرع کول *compound verb* to derive from somehing متفرع کېدل *compound verb* to be derived from something **2** ramified

متفرق mutafarríq *Arabic* **1** various, different **2** scattered, dispersed, difused **3** separated, separate

متفرقه mutafarriqá *Arabic* **1** *feminine singular & masculine and feminine plural of* متفرق **2.1** various items, diverse articles, all sorts of things **2.2** *f.* various expenditures د متفرقي خرځ various expenditures

متفق muttafíq *Arabic* **1** agreeable (to), unanimous متفق کېدل *compound verb* to come to an agreement ☞ متحد **2** *m.* [*plural:* متفقين muttafiqín] co-participant, collaborator **2** ally

متفقاً muttafíqín *Arabic* in accord, unanimously, by common consent; together, jointly; in concert

متفق الرای muttafíq-ur-ráj *Arabic* unanimous, agreed; solidary الرایی کېدل to be in agreement with somebody

متفق علیه muttafaqalájhi *Arabic* coordinated, agreed-on, not causing disagreement متفق علیه رسم الخط a common orthography

متفقین muttafiqín *m. plural Arabic* **1** *of* متفق **2** *history* countries of the Entente, Entente

متفکر mutafakkír *Arabic* **1** pensive, thoughtful; deep or lost in thought; meditating, pondering; thinking دپر متفکر شو He became thoughtful. **2** *m.* thinker; ideologue

متفکرانه mutafakkirāná **1** pensive, thoughtful **2** pensively, thoughtfully

متفلسف mutafalsíf *Arabic* philosophizing متفلسف نقاد faultfinder

متقابل mutaqābíl *Arabic* **1** opposite, contrary **2** head, contrary, coming from the opposite direction; counter- متقابل یرغل counteroffensive متقابله حمله counterattack د یو شي سره متقابل کېدل to contradict something **3** mutual, joint, reciprocal متقابل احترام mutual respect متقابل ارتباط interconnection متقابله مرسته mutual aid په متقابل ډول mutually متقابل تاثیر، متقابله اغېزه interaction

متقابلاً mutaqābílán *Arabic* mutually, reciprocally متقابلاً گټور mutually beneficial

متقارب mutaqāríb *Arabic* **1.1** coming nearer, getting closer **1.2** near, close متقارب لغات words that are close in meaning **2** *m. poetry* mutakarib (one of the meters in poetry)

متقاعد mutaqā'íd *Arabic* **1** being on pension, in retirement, retired **2** *m.* **.1** veteran **2.2** pensioner, retiree متقاعد کېدل *compound verb* to retire, go on pension

متقدم mutaqaddím *Arabic* **1.1** preceding; former **1.2** old, bygone; ancient **2** *m.* predecessor, forerunner, precursor

متقلب mutaqallíb *Arabic* **1** changeable; inconstant, fickle **2** *m.* cheat, swindler, rogue, rascal خوک متقلب گڼل to consider someone (to be) a cheat

متکامل mutakāmíl *Arabic* **1** improving; evolving **2** perfect, excellent, superlative, first-rate

متکبر mutakabbír *Arabic* haughty, arrogant

متکبرانه mutakabbirāná haughty, arrogantly

متکفل mutakaffíl *Arabic* responsible (having responsibility) for something متکفل گڼل *compound verb* to considered responsible for something

متکلم mutakallím *Arabic* **1** speaking, conversing **2** *m. grammar* first person

متکي muttakí *Arabic* basing, being based on something; relying on something متکي کېدل *compound verb* to be based on something; rely on something

متل matál proverb, adage; saying یو متل تېرول to cite a proverb

متلاش matlásh *m.* cluster of rhubarb

متلاشي mutalāshí *Arabic* going to ruin, falling to ruin; tumbling down

متلون mutalawwín *Arabic* **1** variegated, motley, many-colored **2** unstable, inconstant, changeable; unsteady, shaky

متلي matalí well-known, generally-known; proverbial

متمادي mutamādí *Arabic* long, lengthy, prolonged

متمایز mutamājíz *Arabic* being notable for, outstanding

متمایل mutamāíl *Arabic* متمائل **1** bowing, leaning, bending **2** inclined to something, disposed to something متمایل صفات propensities ... ته متمایل کېدل *compound verb* to be inclined towards something

متمتع mutamatté' *Arabic* enjoying, using, making use of something

متمدن mutamaddín *Arabic* cultivated, cultured, educated, civilized

متمرد mutamarríd *Arabic* **1** resisting, rebellious **2** *m.* [*plural:* متمردین mutamarridín] mutineer, rebel, insurgent

متمرکز mutamarkáz *Arabic* concentrated متمرکز کېدل *compound verb* to be concentrated متمرکز پلان *idiom* unified, general plan

متملق mutamallíq *Arabic* **1** flattering, obsequious **2** *m.* [*plural:* متملقین mutamalliqín] flatterer

متمم mutammím *Arabic* **1** supplementing; completing **2** *m.* **.1** supplement, addition **2.2** epilogue, afterword

متمه mutammimá *Arabic* **1** *f.* supplement, appendix to something **2** *feminine singular of* متمم

متمول mutamawwíl *Arabic* **1** well-to-do, wealthy, prosperous متموله ژبه rich language **2** *m.* [*plural:* متمولين mutamawwilín] rich man

متن [1] matn *m. Arabic* [*plural:* متنونه matnúna *and Arabic* متون matún] **1** text **2** middle, center (of a road, etc.) **3** content, context

متن [2] matn *Arabic* ☞ متين

متنازع mutanāzí' *Arabic* arguing; bringing suit, litigating

متنازع فيه mutanāza'uifíh *Arabic* disputable, debatable, controversial

متنازع فيها mutanāza'uifihá *Arabic feminine singular of* متنازع فيه متنازع فيها فيصله controversial question

متناسب mutanāsíb *Arabic* proportional, commensurate; symmetric(al); proper, suitable د ... سره متناسب commensurate with something اعضا يي متناسب دي He has a fine phisique.

متناسب الاعضا mutanāsibula'zā *Arabic* slender, well built, of fine physique

متناقض mutanāqíz *Arabic* contradictory, conflicting; contradicting, being at variance with

متناوب mutanāwáb *Arabic* **1** alternating په متناوب ډول in turn **2** *mathematics* infinite

متنگ matáng *m.* hoe, mattock

متنوع mutanawwí' *Arabic* heterogeneous, diverse; different

متواتر mutawātír *Arabic* **1** repeated periodically; reiterated, multiple; repeated متواتر انقسام *biology* repeated cell division **2** spread by word of mouth

متوازن mutawāzín *Arabic* **1** balanced, steady, calm **2** even, uniform متوازن پرمختگ even development *a* په متوازن صورت کښي steadily, calmly *b* evenly, uniformly

متوازي mutawāzí *Arabic* **1** parallel **2** parallel, in parallel

متواضع mutawāzí' *Arabic* quiet, mild, submissive; gentle, meek

متوالي mutawālí *Arabic* unbroken, uninterrupted, continuing په متوالي ډول continuously

متوجه mutawadzhíh *Arabic* **1** paying attention; attentive; favorable, disposed **2** turned, directed, aimed **3** relating to something متوجه کول *compound verb* to turn, direct, aim ځان ته متوجه کول to draw attention to oneself متوجه کېدل *compound verb a* to be attentive, pay attention *b* to be turned, be directed, be aimed ضرر به ده ته He will incur damage. متوجه شي مسئوليت ورته متوجه کېږي It is their (his) responsibility.

مبتود metód *m.* ☞ مبتود

متورم mutawarrím *Arabic* distended; swollen, inflated

متوسط mutawassít *Arabic* **1** middle, medium په متوسط ډول on average متوسط تولیدات the average output يو متوسط کور middle-income house متوسطه تجارت مکتب commercial school متوسط طبقه the middle class **2** of average quality يو متوسط هوټل an average hotel

متوسط السير mutawassit-us-sájr *Arabic* medium-range, of medium range متوسط السير راکت a medium-range missile

متوسل mutawassíl *Arabic* resorting to something, turning to something متوسل کېدل *compound verb* to resort to something

متوطن mutawattín having settled, having taken up residence; having been naturalizcd متوطن کول *compound verb* to repatriate

متوقف mutawaqqíf *Arabic* **1** having come to a standstill; stagnant **2** depending, being in dependence متوقف کېدل *compound verb a* to come to a standstill, be delayed in developing, go through stagnation *b* to depend, be in a state of dependence

متولد mutawallíd *Arabic* **1** born, come into being **2** taken place

متولي mutawallí *m. Arabic* **1** guardian of a holy thing **2** executor (of a will)

متون matún *m. Arabic plural* **1** *of* متن [1] **2** monuments of language, literary monuments

مته [1] matә́ *m. singular & plural* wild boar

مته [2] matá *f. commerce* receipt by the merchant of the cost of the goods in parts, payment on the installment plan

متهاجم mutahādzhím *Arabic* assaulting, attacking

متهم [1] muttahám *Arabic* **1.1** accused, indicted د جنایت متهم accused of a crime **1.2** suspected; accused, defendant متهم کول *compound verb* ☞ متهمول **2** *m.* accused

متهم [2] muttahím *Arabic* **1** suspecting **2** *m.* [*plural:* متهمين muttahimín] accuser, prosecutor

متهمول muttahamawә́l *denominative, transitive* [*past:* متهم يي کړ] **1** to accuse, charge, indict **2** to suspect

متهمېدل muttahamedә́l *denominative, intransitive* [*past:* متهم شو] **1** to be accused, be indicted, be charged **2** to be suspected

متهيج mutahajjádzh *Arabic* excited by something په يوه بي اهميته شي متهيج کېدل to get irritated at trifles

متی matáj adroit, agile, sharp, bright, smart

متيازن mәtjāzә́n suffering from incontinence

متيازي mәtjāzi, mutjáe *f. plural Eastern* urine متيازي کول *compound verb* to urinate

متيزځک mәtiztsák *m. medicine* **1** diabetes **2** weakness of the urinary bladder

متيقين mutajaqqín *Arabic* sure, convinced متيقين کېدل *compound verb* to be certain, be convinced; satisfy oneself

متين matín *Arabic* **1** strong; powerful **2** durable; firm, hard متين اساس lasting basis متين عزم firm decision

مټ [1] mәṭ *m.* [*plural: Western* مټان mәṭā́n *and* مټونه mәṭúna] **1** hand; forearm د مټ نه نيول to take by the hand **2** force, power د مټه په زور by physical force **3** *military* flank په وچ مټه په وچ مټه گټل *idiom* to beat the enemy in a fair fight په خپل مټه ځان ساتل *idiom* to suport make a fortune by one's own labor oneself

مټ [2] maṭ, mәṭ *m.* **1** effort په مټ يي کورته ځان ورساوه He made it home with difficulty. په مټ يي نمری له ستوني تېره کړه He choked down a piece. **2** speed, haste مټ کول *compound verb* **a** to make efforts, try, endeavor **b** to hurry, rush

مټ [3] muṭ *m.* [*plural:* مټان muṭắn] **1** fist; hollow of the hand, handful اوس نو متان متان تینگول *idiom* to prepare for something تینگ که چه خو Get ready; we're leaving right away.

مټ [4] maṭ *m.* **1** dust (on the road) **2** silt

مټ [5] maṭ *m.* large earthenware jug

مټ [6] maṭ ☞ کټ مټ

متاک maṭắk *m.* **1** nut with a hard shell **2** short horn (of a gazelle) **3** species of thorny tree

متاکه maṭáka *f.* **1** blister, bump (from an insect bite) **2** swelling, tumor

متاکي [1] məṭắki *f. plural* ☞ گزاري

متایي miṭājí *f.* sweets, candy

مټ ټر məṭṭáṛ *m.* مټ ترونی məṭṭaṛúnaj *f.* **1** bracelet **2** armband

متخ maṭə́kh *m.* grasshopper

متر [1] miṭár, meṭár *m.* **1** meter **2** *technology* counter

متر [2] maṭár, muṭár *m. plural regional* field pea, *Pisum sativum*

متري miṭrí, meṭrí meter, metric

متک [1] maṭák hard, firm, hard-to-crack

متک [2] muṭák *m.* onanism, masturbation متک وهل *compound verb* to masturbate

متکر maṭkár angry, cross

متکور maṭakwə́r **1** having a hard shell **2** *figurative* stingy (of a person) **3** *figurative* shameless, impudent (of eyes) **4** lightly toasted (of unripe heads of wheat, ears of maize) **5** with shedding kernels (of an ear of maize)

متکي [1] maṭakí *f.* wheat with hard kernels, duram wheat

متکی [2] mátkaj *m. diminutive of* متا [2]

متکی [3] məṭkáj *m.* **1** bracelet worn above the elbow **2** armlet on the forearm

متکی [4] maṭkáj *m.* small earthenware jug

متکی [5] muṭkə́j *f.* piece, bit, slice (food)

متن maṭə́n **1** dusty **2** silty

متور məṭór suffering from constipation (of livestock)

متونگه məṭúnga *f.* **1** blister, bump **2** swelling, tumor

مته [1] miṭá *f.* orange

مته [2] mə́ṭa *f.* post; column

مته [3] mə́ṭa خاوره مته potter's clay

مته [4] mə́ṭa *oblique singular of* مته [1]

مته [5] mə́ṭa *f. dialect* **1** hand **2** forearm **3** force د فعالیت متي idiom to begin the business, get started on the business وریوري کول خپلي متي ازمیبل *Eastern* to test one's strength په متي hardly راور سبدم I barely made it.

مته [6] mə́ṭa *f.* dust ☞ مټ [4]

مته [7] mə́ṭa *f.* earthenware pot for froth (in melting butter)

مته [8] maṭá lazy; languid, listless, limp

مته کور maṭakəwúr **1** *m.* roasted ears of unripe wheat, toasted ears of corn مته کورکول *compound verb* to roast ears of unripe wheat, roast ears of corn **2** ☞ متکور

مته والی maṭawắlaj *m.* laziness; languor, intertia, listlessness

متي [1] mə́ṭi *plural and oblique singular of* مته [5]

متي [2] maṭí *f.* laziness; languor, intertia, listlessness

متي [3] muṭí *f.* share of the winnings (in a game)

متي [4] mə́ṭi *plural of* مته [5]

متي [5] mútaj *m.* handle

متي [6] muṭáj *m.* wind

متي [7] maṭə́j *f.* jug in which butter is churned, butter churn

متیایي mitjājí *f.* ☞ متایي

متیخ maṭídz *m.* ☞ متیز

متبر məṭér *m.* assault, sudden attack متبر کول *compound verb* to attack, swoop down on

متیز maṭíz *m.* man who has abducted someone else's wife or daughter

متیزه maṭiza *f.* female who has eloped with her lover متیزه کبدل *compound verb* to elope, run off with her lover

متین maṭín clayey, argillaceous متینه مځکه clay soil متینه خاوره loam

متینگی maṭingáj **1** worthless, good-for-nothing; base, vile **2** *m.* son born out ot wedlock, bastard

مثال misál *m. Arabic* example, model د مثال په ډول for example د خبري د مثاله وایم *compound verb* to cite an example د مثال په توگه ویل say by way of illustration to cite by way of example

مثانه masāná *f. Arabic* urinary bladder د لامبو مثانه swim bladder (in fish)

مثبت musbát **1** proven, established; reliable, trustworthy; confirmed مثبته معلومات reliable information **2** accurate, exact musabbatá... the exact sciences **3** positive, favorable مثبته ځواب a positive reply مثبته رایه ورکول to vote for

مثبتیت musabatiját, musabbatiját *m. Arabic* **1** definitness; state or quality of being established **2** positiveness **3** *philosophy* positivism

مثقال misqál *m. Arabic* misqal (a measure of weight equal to 4.6 grams, or 1/24 of خورد)

مثل [1] misl *m. Arabic* [*plural:* امثال amsál] **1** similarity, likeness په دیو شي په مثل گنل to liken to something **2** د...مثل resembling د مکتوب مثل copy of a letter **3** *regional* folder with files

مثل [2] masál *m. Arabic* [*plural:* امثال amsál] example, model

مثلث musallasás *Arabic* **1** *m.* triangle ډوله مثلث triangular **2** triple

مثلثات musallasát *m. plural Arabic* trigonometry

مثلثي musallasí *Arabic* triangular مثلثي منشور triangular prism

مثمر musmír *Arabic* **1** fruitful, fertile, fruit-producing, fruit-bearing **2** fruitful, successful

مثنوي masnawí *f. Arabic poetry* masnavi (a verse form)

مثنیٰ musanná *Arabic* 1.1 double, doubled 1.2 having two dots (of a letter) 2 *f.* .1 duplicate 2.2 *grammar* dual number

مجادلوي mudzhādalawí related to fighting diseases, medical; therapeutic مجادلوي عملیات therapeutic measures مجادلوي ټیم medical detachment

مجادله mudzhādalá *f. Arabic* [*plural:* مجادلې mudzhādalé *and m. plural: Arabic* مجادلات mudzhādalā́t] 1 argument; quarrel; discord, strife 2 fight, struggle د سره استعمار سره مجادله the struggle against red colonialism د زراعتي آفاتو په ضد مجادله combating agricultural pests مجادله کول *compound verb* a to argue; quarrel b to fight, struggle 3 conflict

مجار madzhā́r *m.* Hungarian, Magyar

مجارستان madzhāristā́n *m.* Hungary

مجارستاني madzhāristā́ní 1 Hungarian, Magyar 2 Hungarian, Magyar

مجاري madzhārí *m. plural Arabic of* مجرا¹

مجاز¹ mudzhā́z *Arabic* 1.1 having the right 1.2 allowed, permitted مجاز کول *compound verb* ☞ مجازول 2 *m.* secondary school graduate, high-school graduate

مجاز² madzhā́z *m. Arabic* metaphor, allegory

مجازات mudzhāzā́t *m. Arabic* punishment

مجازاً madzhā́zán *Arabic figurative* allegorically

مجازاتول mudzhāzātawə́l *denominative, transitive* [*past:* مجازات یې کړ] to punish

مجازاتېدل mudzhāzātedə́l *denominative, intransitive* [*past:* مجازات شو] to be punished

مجازول mudzhāzawə́l *denominative, transitive* [*past:* مجاز یې کړ] 1 to admit (to work, etc.) 2 to permit, authorize

مجازي madzhāzí *Arabic* figurative, allegoric د خبري مجازي معنیٰ figurative meaning of a word

مجال madzhā́l *m. Arabic* 1 possibility; occasion ... ته مجال ورکول to give the possibility بحث ته مجال ورکول to give grounds for an argument 2 force; power; authority 3 courage

مجالس madzhālís *m. plural Arabic of* مجلس

مجامع madzhāmé' *m. plural Arabic of* مجمع

مجاني madzhdzhāní *Arabic* free (of school), tuition-free

مجاور mudzhāwír *Arabic* 1 contiguous; adjacent 2 *m.* .1 mujavir (person who guards a tomb, sepulcher of a holy man and who lives next to it) 2.2 sexton, sacristan

مجاورتوب mudzhāwirtób *m.* responsibilities of a mujavir

مجاهد mudzhāhíd *Arabic* 1 exerting effort, endeavoring 2.1 zealot, adherent; advocate, champion 2.2 fighter for the faith 2.3 fighter; activist د قوم مجاهد national figure

مجاهدات mudzhāhadā́t *m. plural, Arabic of* مجاهده

مجاهدانه mudzhāhidāná fighting; energetic, active

مجاهده mudzhāhadá *f. Arabic* [*plural:* مجاهدي mudzhāhadé *and m. plural: Arabic* مجاهدات mudzhāhadā́t] 1 effort, endeavor; zeal;

diligence, assiduity 2 fighting for the faith 3 struggle (political, etc.) د آزادی مجاهده، د آزادی غوښتلو مجاهده fight for liberation

مجبر mudzhbír *Arabic* 1 compelling, coercing, forcing 2 irresistable; insuperable, insurmountable مجبر احوال، مجبر اسباب، مجبر سبب، مجبر علتونه insurmountable obstacles

مجبور madzhbúr *Arabic* obliged; compelled, forced د چا امر ته مجبور obliged to obey someone مجبور گرزول *compound verb* to oblige; force, compel له مجبوري ورځي تسلیم شول They had to surrender.

مجبوراً madzhbúrán *Arabic* obligatorily, inevitably, against one's will, compulsorily

مجبورتیا madzhburtjā́ *f.* necessity, inevitability; state or condition of being under compulsion

مجبورول madzhburawə́l *denominative, transitive* [*past:* مجبور یې کړ] to coerce, compel, make, force په یو کار مجبور، دي ته مجبور make (someone) do something د زور له لاري څوک مجبورول to force someone

مجبوري madzhburí 1 necessary, essential, inevitable; forced مجبوري ناسته *aviation* emergency landing 2 *f.* necessity, inevitability, state or condition of being under compulsion د مجبوري څخه، د out of necessity خو مجبوري وه ... However, it was necessary to... مجبوري له مخي There was no other way out ...

مجبوریت madzhburiját *m. Arabic* necessity مجبوریت و There was no other way out.

مجبورېدل madzhburedə́l *denominative, intransitive* [*past:* مجبور شو] to be compelled تر شا کېدو ته مجبور شول They were compelled to retreat.

مجتمع mudzhtamí' *Arabic* having gathered, having assembled

مجتهد mudzhthahíd *Arabic* 1 *m. religion* mujtahid, legal scholar (of Islamic law) 2 zealous, fervent

مجد¹ madzhd *m. Arabic* glory, pride قومي او ملي مجد national pride

مجد² mudzhíd, mudzhídd *Arabic* 1 assiduous, diligent 2 importuning for something

مجدد mudzhaddád *Arabic* renewed; new; repeated د ښار مجدد تعمیر restoration of a city

مجدداً mudzhaddádán *Arabic* again, anew, afresh, all over again مجدداً انتخابېدل to be re-elected

مجذوب madzhzúb *Arabic* 1.1 fascinated, enthralled, inspired 1.2 frenzied; overcome with religious zeal; exalted, ecstatic 1.3 mad, crazy; feeble-minded 2 *m.* holy man, saint

مجذور madzhzúr *m. Arabic mathematics* square of a number

مجرا¹ madzhrā́ *f.* [*plural:* مجراگاني madzhrāgā́ni *and m. plural Arabic* مجاري madzhārí] 1 riverbed, channel خپله مجرا بدلول to change course (of a river) 2 tributary 3 canal 4 current 5 water(-supply) pipe, water main 6 line (for electricity)

مجرا² mudzhrā́ *Arabic* brought to fulfillment; fulfilled مجرا لرل to fulfill, bring to fulfillment

مجرایي madzhrā́ji مجرایي سیمه water collection (system) (of a canal)

مجرب mudzharráb *Arabic* well-tried, experienced

مجربت mudzharrabiját *m. Arabic* experience, degree or state of experience, proficiency

مجرد mudzharrád *Arabic* **1** bare, naked **2** pure, unmixed **3** absolute **4** *grammar* momentary aspect (of verbs) **5** abstract په مجرد د رسپدو سره د هغه چه *idiom* as soon as مجرد د رسپدو سره immediately upon arriving

مجرم mudzhrím *Arabic* **1** *m.* [*plural:* مجرمان mudzhrimán *and Arabic* مجرمين mudzhrimín] criminal د جگړي مجرم war criminal **2.1** criminal, felonious **2.2** guilty

مجرمیت mudzhrimiját *m. Arabic* guilt, culpability د مجرمیت شعور feeling of guilt

مجروح madzhrúh *Arabic* wounded, injured

مجره madzhrá *f.* gift, present و... ته مجره کول to give a gift to ...

مجري mudzhrí ¹ *Arabic* **1.1** executive **1.2** implementing, realizing **2** *m.* doer, executor

مجرئ madzhrá ² *f. Arabic* ☞ مجرا ¹

مجزئ mudzhazzá *Arabic* **1** separated, disconnected, dismembered **2** singled out, set apart; separate, detached

مجستریت madzhistrét *m. regional* justice of the peace

مجسم mudzhassám *Arabic* embodied, materialized

مجسمول mudzhassamawól *denominative, transitive* [*past:* مجسم یي کړ] **1** to embody; personify **2** to depict, describe, reflect

مجسمه mudzhassamá *f.* **1** statue; monument **2** embodiment, personification مجسمه تراشل *compound verb* to embody مجسمه کره کرۀ مجسمه *idiom* ☞ kurrá-yi... globe

مجسمه ساز mudzhassamasáz *m.* sculptor

مجسمه سازي mudzhassamasází *f.* sculpture, modeling

مجسمیدل mudzhassamedól *denominative, intransitive* [*past:* مجسم شو] **1** to be embodied, be personified **2** to be depicted, be described, be reflected **3** to come to light, manifest itself, be visible, appear (of difficulties, etc.)

مجک madzhák *m. proper noun* Majak

مجلا mudzhallá ¹ *f. Arabic* مجلئ reference; information; certificate, document

مجلا madzhallá ² *f.* ☞ مجله

مجلات madzhallát *m. plural Arabic of* مجله

مجلد mudzhallád *Arabic* bound (of a book) مجلد کېدل *compound verb* to be bound

مجلس madzhlís *m. Arabic* [*plural:* مجلسونه madzhlisúna *and Arabic* مجالس madzhālís] **1** conference, session, assembly; meeting عمومي مجلس general assembly, general session **2** parliament; mejlis (in Iran, Turkey); chamber, house مجلس مشوره majlís-i... consultative assembly مجلس اعیان majlís-i... senate مجلس وزرأ majlís-i... national council مجلس شورا majlís-i.... council of ministers مجلس لښکري military tribunal **3** company (of guests) مجلس گرم شو The company became animated. **4** circle; society, company سیاسي مجلسونه diplomatic circles **5** party, reception, soiree مجلس کول *compound verb* a to arrange a

conference, hold a meeting **b** to sing مجلس جوړول *compound verb* to arrange a party

مجلسي madzhlisí *m.* **1** musician and singer **2** narrator (of folktales), storyteller

مجلسین madzhlisájn *m. Arabic dual number* both chambers, both houses (senate and council)

مجلل mudzhallál *Arabic* **1** splendid, magnificent, majestic; luxurious مجلله بنگله grand building **2** sweeping, broad (of plans, etc.)

مجلوب madzhlúb *Arabic* **1** attracted (to), drawn (to, into), enlisted (in) **2** imported

مجلون madzhlún *m. colloquial* ☞ مجنون

مجله madzhallá, mudzhallá *f. Arabic* magazine, periodical, journal

مجلئ mudzhallá ¹ *f. Arabic* مجلا ¹ reference; information; certificate, document

مجلي madzhallé ² *plural of* مجله

مجمجه madzhmadzhá in vain, for nothing, to no purpose, uselessly, futilely

مجمر madzhmár *m. Arabic* brazier (for burning rue and incense), censer

مجمع madzhmá' *f. Arabic* [*m. plural:* مجامع madzhāmé'] **1** assembly د مجمع رئیس assembly chair(person) عمومي مجمع general assembly **2** company **3** gathering, crowd, assemblage

مجمع الجزایر madzhma'-ul-dzhazāir *Arabic* archipelago

مجمل mudzhmál *Arabic* **1.1** brief, concise, summary مجملي خبری په مجمل ډول سره to speak briefly, concisely کول briefly **1.2** short **2** *m.* ☞ اجمال

مجملاً mudzhmálán *Arabic* in brief, concisely مجملاً لیکل *compound verb* to summarize, recapitulate (what has already been written)

مجموع madzhmú' *Arabic* **1** gathered, collected, all, whole, entire **2** *f.* total, sum

مجموعاً madzhmú'án *Arabic* cumulatively, as a whole, in all, altogether

مجموعه madzhmu'á *f.* **1** total, sum کلي مجموعه grand total **2** network, system **3** collection, anthology, almanac **4** collective **5** gathering, crowd, assemblage د خلقو مجموعه gathering of people ستورو مجموعه star cluster **6** complex (of enterprises, etc.)

مجموعي madzhmu'í *Arabic* **1** collected; aggregate; general **2** gross **3** final, bottom-line (e.g., balance)

مجمه madzhmá *f.* **1** tray **2** street vendor's tray

مجنون madzhnún *Arabic* **1** crazy, insane **2** *m.* **.1** madman **2.2** *proper noun* Majnun (specifically, the hero of the legend of "Laila and Majnun") د مجنون وله *idiom* ☞ مجنون بېد

مجنون بېد madzhnunbéd *m.* weeping willow

مجنونیت madzhnuniját *m. Arabic* madness, insanity

مجوز mudzhawwáz ¹ *Arabic* **1** permitted, authorized **2** legalized

مجوز mudzhawwíz ² *Arabic* **1** permitting, authorizing **2** *m.* authorization, permission

مجهز mudzhahház *Arabic* **1** outfitted; fully equipped; rigged; supplied **2** armed **3** trained, prepared (of a person); armed with knowledge, educated

مجهزول mudzhahhazawól *denominative, transitive* [*past:* مجهز یې کړ] **1** to equip, outfit **2** to arm ځان مجهزول *compound verb* to arm (oneself)

مجهزیدل mudzhahhazedól *denominative, intransitive* [*past:* مجهز شو] **1** to be equipped, be outfitted **2** to arm (oneself), be armed په توپو مجهزیدل to be armed with cannon

مجهول madzhhúl *Arabic* **1.1** mysterious; unknown **1.2** lazy **1.3** *linguistics* passive (of a sound) مجهوله ضمه او کسره، مجهول واو، مجهوله یا، مجهوله یې the so-called madjhul sounds "o" and "e" **1.4** *grammar* passive مجهوله صیغه the form of the passive voice **2** *m.* **2.1** passive voice **2.2** *mathematics* unknown (quantity)

مجهولات madzhhulát *m. plural Arabic* [*singular:* مجهول] **1** unknown quantities, unknowns **2** vague questions; unsolved problems

مجهولیت madzhhuliját *m. Arabic* uncertainty, obscurity

مجی madzhój *f.* female camel, she-camel

مجید madzhíd *Arabic* **1** glorious, famous, celebrated, renowned **2** *m. proper noun* Majid, Mejid, Majeed

مچ mach, much *m.* [*plural:* مچان machán, muchán] **1** fly; horsefly **2** front sight (of a gun) پر هغه باندي مچ نه پرېږدي چه کښیني *idiom* He protects him in every way possible.

مچ much *m.* bending the legs (when walking) مچ خورل *compound verb* to bend (of the legs, when walking)

مچبنک machbaṇák *m.* ☞ مچ بنک

مچپرانگ machpṛáng *m.* spider

مچچکی machuchkáj *m.* fly larva, maggot (growing in a wound)

مچخ machókh *m.* pedestrian locust

مچخټی machókhti *f. plural* ☞ مچچکی

مچخړي machkhóṛi *m. plural* fly eggs

مچر machár, machór *m.* twig, sprig; shoot, sprout

مچردانۍ machardānój *f. plural* ☞ مچړی

مچرکی machórkaj *m.* twig, sprig

مچرج machrój *f.* مچړی muchaṛój *f.* bed curtain (for protection from mosquitoes), mosquito netting

مچشر machshár *m.* مچشرونی machsharúnaj *m.* **1** fly swatter **2** fly net (on a horse's nose)

مچغنه machghána *f.* ☞ مچلوغزه

مچک machák *m.* [*plural:* مچکان machakán] **1** staff, crook (shepherd's) **2** hook (for bending down tree branches)

مچک machák *m.* larva (fly, etc.), maggot

مچکه macháka *f. children's speech* kiss

مچکی machakí kind of gun

مچگیرک magirák *m.* spider

مچلوغزه machlóghza *f.* sling; slingshot **a** د مچلوغزي ډبری کول to throw far away **b** to be rid of someone

مچمچی machmuchój *f.* ☞ مچی مچ

مچنوغزه machnúghza *f.* ☞ مچلوغزه

مچنگړی machəngáṛaj *m.* shoemaker, boot maker

مچنوالا machənwālá *m.* shoe merchant, seller of footware

مچنه machóṇa *f.* shoe, slipper

مچو machó *f. children's speech* kiss

مچو muchó *oblique plural of* مچی

مچواژی machwázhaj *m.* **1** ☞ مچ شړ **2** insecticide for flies; flypaper; fly agaric

مچوړی machóṛe *f.* stocking

مچوغنه machóghna *f.* مچوقنه machóqna *f.* ☞ مچلوغزه

مچول machawól *denominative, transitive* [*past:* مچ یې کړ] to kiss

مچونه machawóna *m.* kissing

مچوونی machawúṇaj *m.* ☞ مچ شړ

مچه mácha, mócha *f.* kiss د چا څخه مچه اخیستل to kiss someone مچه ورکول *compound verb* to kiss someone مچه راکه! Kiss me! Give me a kiss!

مچه mócha *oblique singular of* مچ

مچي máchi *plural of* مچه

مچی muchój, machój *f.* bee نر مچی د گبینو مچی، د شاتو مچی bee د مچیو روزل، د شاتو مچیو روزل، د مچیو ساتنه beekeeping, apiculture د شاتود مچیو a beehive د مچیو کور، د شاتو مچیو کور swarm کورنی

مچیمار machimár *m. regional* fisherman, angler

مځکنی mdzəkənáj land; ground; earth's, earthly مځکنی قوه ground troops

مځکوال mdzəkwál *m.* farmer, agriculturalist

مځکه mdzóka *f.* **1** earth مځکه د مځکي خاوند بایري virgin land **a** ground water د مځکي لاندي اوبه، د مځکي لاندي اوبه farmer د مځکو حاصلات ground rent **a** harvest, yield **b** soil productivity د نویو مځکو ابادول opening up new lands **2** soil **3** floor د خوني مځکه the floor (of a room) **4** territory مځکه پربکول *compound verb* to take a path, make a way نن مو دري کروه مځکه پر مځکه کړې Today we walked three kurukh (about 11 kilometers). چا مځکه سور تیخی کول to give it hot to someone, to turn up the heat on someone وجاته مځکه گرول to come to someone acknowledging one's fault احمد ته مځکه ځای نه ورکوي Ahmed is not finding his place. **a** مځکه پر چا باندي یوه الغه کول to persuade someone by your arguments **b** to press on, put pressure on someone یو گړی ودرېږه، پر مځکه مځکه دي راباندي یوه الغه کړه Wait a bit; don't rush me so. *idiom* to be ashamed; be nervous, be ready to vanish into the ground from shame **a** په مځکه ننوتل to disappear, vanish into thin air (*literally:* into the ground) **b** to become confused, become nervous په مځکه خولی لگول Get lost! په مځکه ننوزي! *idiom* **a** to be greedy, be grasping, be avaricious **b** to strain every nerve **c** to lament, grieve (over) تر مځکه ایستل to scold someone, really put someone to shame احمد ته یې داسي خبره وکړه چه تر مځکه یې ویوست He spoke to Ahmed such that the latter was ready to disappear into the ground. تر مځکه وتل to be ready to disappear into the ground out of shame د چا امر مخکي ته پرېښودل to fail to take account of someone's will د ده نفوذ پر مخکه لوېږي His influence is waning. و مخکي ته کتل، سترگي مخکي ته نيول to hang one's head; feel ashamed, be flustered; lower one's eyes د مخکي to die, be dying مخکي سر يو کول to run all over looking زني کېدل for something په اورلگيتو پسي مي د مخکي سر يو کئ I was run off my feet looking for matches. د مخکي سر خُني ورکول idiom a to beat someone up احمد يي دونه وواهه چه د مخکي سر يي خُني ورک کئ They beat Ahmed so badly that he felt as if he were going to die. b to knock someone down, run someone off his feet د مخکي سردي You have run me off my feet. د مخکي سر را خُه raخاته ورک کئ ورک دئ idiom a I became exhausted. b I don't know what to begin doing. د مخکي په سر نه پوهېدل idiom a to be struck, lose one's head b to be enfeebled څوک د مخکي سره سمول to beat someone senseless د مخکي پر idiom to die د مخکي په غېږ ورتلل د مخکي په نغم کي اوبه بهول idiom to be an old fox, be a crafty person تر پېنو لاندي مخکه مه گوره، لېري حد ته گوره proverb to be farsighted, learn to look ahead (literally: Don't just look at what's under your feet: look far ahead.) مخکه هغه سوځي چه په مخکي کي proverb Where there's smoke, there's fire. اور پر بل وي سيوری، په اسمان کښي ستوری نه لري saying He has neither a shadow on the ground nor a star in heaven.

مخکه پېژندونکی mdzə́ka pezhandúnkaj m. geologist

مخکه کېندونکی mdzə́ka kendúnkaj excavator ماشين excavator, power shovel

مخه mádza in lieu of مه څه

مترک matsrák m. مترکه mətsə́rka f. 1 gecko 2 small lizard

مڅوڅک mətsotsák m. 1 baby gazelle, young gazelle 2 thing dear to the heart, cherished thing

مڅوڅکی matsótskaj m. name of a medicinal plant

محاذ mahā́z, muhā́z m. Arabic [plural: محاذونه mahāzúna and Arabic محاذات mahāzā́t] front متحد محاذ، متحده محاذ، يو واحد محاذ، مشترک محاذ united front

محاذي muhāzí Arabic 1 opposite 2 parallel

محارب muhāríb Arabic 1.1 military combat; line; drill 1.2 belligerent محارب ممالک belligerents, participants in war 2 m. [plural: محاربين muhāribín] fighting man

محاربات muhārabā́t m. plural Arabic of محاربه

محاربوي muhāribawí Arabic military combat; belligerent قابليت combat efficiency

محاربه muhārabá f. Arabic [plural: محاربي muhārabé and m. plural: Arabic محاربات muhārabā́t] battle, fight, action, combat د مقابل محاربه advanced-guard action پېشدار محاربه meeting engagement محاربه جاري ده A battle is going on. هوايي محاربه air combat

محاسب muhā síb m. Arabic [plural: محاسبان muhāsibā́n and محاسبين muhāsibín] 1 accountant, bookkeeper 2 costing specialist, specialist in cost and price analysis

محاسبوي muhāsabawí 1 bookkeeping, accounting 2 account

محاسبه muhāsabá f. [plural: محاسبي muhāsabé and m. plural Arabic محاسبات muhāsabā́t] 1 accounting 2 accounts فني محاسبه technical assessment 3 calculation 4 calculation, computation; counting, tallying

محاسن mahāsín m. plural Arabic 1 praiseworthy qualities, virtues 2 good deeds

محاصر muhāsír Arabic 1 besieging, blockading 2 m. [plural: محاصرين muhāsirín] one who is besieging

محاصره muhāsará f. Arabic siege, blockade, encirclement اقتصادي محاصره economic blockade محاصره کول compound verb to lay siege to, blockade, surround, encircle محاصره کېدل compound verb to be besieged, be under siege, be blockaded, be under a blockade, be surrounded, be encircled

محاط muhā́t Arabic 1 surrounded, encircled افغانستان په وچه محاط دئ Afghanistan is a land-locked country. 2 girded

محافظ muhā́fíz Arabic 1 guarding, protecting محافظه قطعه guard battalion محافظ کنډک guard 2 m. [plural: محافظان muhāfizā́n and Arabic محافظين muhāfizín] watchman, guard د سرحد محافظ border guard

محافظت muhāfazát, muhāfízát m. محافظه muhāfazá, muhāfizá f. 1 guard; protection محافظت کول compound verb a to guard; protect b to preserve 2 conservatism

محافظه کار muhāfazakā́r 1.1 conservative 1.2 old-fashioned, outmoded 2 m. conservative

محافظه کارانه muhāfazakārāná 1 conservative 2 conservatively

محافظه کاري muhāfazakārí f. conservatism

محافل mahāfíl m. Arabic plural 1 of محفل 2 circles, spheres حاکمه محافل mahāfíl-i... (the) ruling circles ادبي محافل، محافل حاکمه literary circles

محاکات muhākā́t m. Arabic expressiveness, picturesqueness

محاکم mahākím m. plural Arabic of محکمه[1]

محاکمه muhākamá f. Arabic [plural: محاکمي muhākamé and m. plural: Arabic محاکمات muhākamā́t] 1 trial, court examination; court; legal action, lawsuit تر محاکمي لاندي نيول to try, judge 2 decision, decree, verdict, judgement

محال[1] mahā́l, mahā́ll m. plural, Arabic of محل

محال[2] muhā́l Arabic impossible, unlikely داسي ژوندون محال دئ One ought not to live this way. امکانه څخه به هم لېري وي While this is possible, it is difficult to implement.

محالات muhālā́t m. plural Arabic [singular: محال[2]] absurdity, nonsense, rubbish

محاوروي muhāwarawí 1 colloquial, conversational; phraseological 2 idiomatic 3 dialect, dialectal

محاوره muhāwará, muhāwirá f. Arabic [plural: محاوري muhāwaré, muhāwará and m. plural: Arabic محاورات muhāwarā́t, muhāwirā́t] 1 talk; conversaton; oral speech د پښتو ژبي ښه محاوره لري He speaks Pashto well. 2 turn of speech, phrase, locution, expresson; idiom 3 dialect

محاوره يي محاوروي muhāwarají ☞

محب muhíb, muhíbb *Arabic* 1 loving, affectionate 2 *m.* friend

محبت muhabát, muhabbát *m. Arabic* 1 love; attachment, affection محبت كول *compound verb* to feel love (for); feel affection (towards) 2 caress, endearment 3 *proper noun* Muhabbat

محبت آمېز muhabatāméz, muhabbatāméz 1 friendly, amicable 2 caressing, tender, sweet; soft; affectionate, fond

محبوب mahbúb *Arabic* 1 beloved, dear 2 pleasant, nice

محبوبا mahbubā́ *f.* sweetheart, beloved, dear (one)

محبوب القلب mahbub-ul-qulúb *Arabic* 1 beloved by all 2 *m.* everyone's favorite

محبوبه mahbubá *f.* ☞ محبويا

محبوبيت mahbubiját *m. Arabic* 1 pleasantness; attractiveness 2 popularity محبوبيت لرل a to be pleasant, be attractive b to be popular د ټولو خلقو محبوبيت لرل to be everyone's favorite

محبوس mahbús *Arabic* 1.1 arrested, imprisoned 1.2 enclosed (e.g., in parentheses) 2 *m.*[*plural:* محبوسين mahbusín] person under arrest, prisoner, convict

محبوسول mahbusawól *denominative, transitive* [*past:* محبوس يي كړ] 1 to arrest, imprison 2 to enclose (e.g., in parentheses)

محبوسېدل mahbusedól *denominative, intransitive* [*past:* محبوس شو] 1 to be arrested, be imprisoned 2 to be enclosed (e.g., in parentheses)

محتاج muhtā́dzh *Arabic* needy, indigent; poor

محتاجول muhtādzhawól *denominative, transitive* [*past:* محتاج يي كړ] 1 to force, compel 2 to put into difficult material circumstances

محتاط muhtā́t wary, circumspect, cautious, careful له ضرورته زيات محتاط too careful محتاط صورت اختيارول to be wary, be cautious

محتال muhtā́l sly, cunning

محترق muhtaríq burning; combustible, inflammable; explosive

محترم muhtarám *Arabic* 1.1 respected, honorable, venerable 1.2 sacred (of the law) د چا حقوق محترم بلل to respect a person's rights 2 *m.* respected person

محترماً muhtarámán respectfully, with deference

محترمانه muhtaramāná 1 respectful, deferential 2 respectfully, deferentially

محتسب muhtasíb *m. Arabic* 1 one who keeps watch on morals and the observance of customs; guardian of morals 2 market overseer, market supervisor

محتكر muhtakír *m. Arabic* speculator, profiteer

محتمل muhtamíl *Arabic* 1 possible, probable, likely 2 patient, having great endurance 3 mobile; portable

محتوي muhtawí *Arabic* containing

محتويات muhtawiját *m. Arabic* 1 content; contents د سند محتويات the content of the document د كتاب محتويات the content of the book 2 content, degree د آزوتو محتويات the nitrogen content

محجوب mahdzhúb *Arabic* 1 covered (by a veil) 2 solitary, secluded 3 modest; shy, bashful

محجوبيت mahdzhubiját *m. Arabic* 1 reticence 2 seclusion 3 modesty, shyness

محجور mahdzhúr *Arabic* forbidden, prohibited, not permitted

محجوز mahdzhúz *Arabic law* 1 deprived of rights 2 seized, attached, sequestered (of property, etc.)

محجوزيت mahdzhuziját *m. Arabic law* 1 deprivation of rights 2 seizure, attachment, sequestration (of property, etc.)

محدب muhaddáb *Arabic* protruberant, prominent, bulging

محدود mahdúd *Arabic* limited

محدودوالى mahdudwā́laj *m.* ☞ محدوديت

محدودول mahdudawól *denominative, transitive* [*past:* محدود يي كړ] 1 to limit 2 to localize (a war, etc.)

محدوديت mahdudiját *m. Arabic* 1 scantiness (e.g., of resources) 2 limitation, restriction

محدودېدل mahdudedól *denominative, intransitive* [*past:* محدود شو] to be limited

محذور mahzúr *m. Arabic* 1 fear, apprehension 2 obstacle

محراب mihrā́b *m. Arabic* 1 niche in an interior wall of a mosque indicating the direction to Mecca 2 altar; praying

محرر[1] muharrír *m. Arabic* 1 author; writer 2 newspaper worker 3 editor 4 secretary (of an editorial board) 5 one in charge of a department of an editorial board

محرر[2] muharrír *Arabic* written out, written; drawn up په حامل محرر سند document for the bearer

محررات muharrarā́t *m. plural Arabic* papers, documents

محرز muhráz *Arabic* kept, preserved, safeguarded

محرقه muhriqá *f.* typhus ☞ تيفو د محرقي مرض typhus

محرك muharrík *Arabic* 1.1 moving, motive محرك قواوي driving forces 1.2 stimulating, invigorating محرك اقليم healthy climate 2 *m.* 1 [*plural:* محركات muharrikā́t] engine, motor برقي محرك electric motor آلي محرك mechanism; device 2.2 [*plural:* محركات muharrikā́t] stimulus, impulse, motive; incentive 2.3 [*plural:* محركان muharrikā́n *and Arabic* محركين muharrikín] pioneer, leader, initiator; instigator, inciter د جنگ محركين instigator of war, warmonger 2.4 [*plural:* محركان muharrikā́n *and Arabic* محركين muharrikín] activist; advocate, champion, standard-bearer د آزادى محركين champion of freedom

محركه muharriká *f.* motive, inducement, stimulus

محرم[1] mahrám *m. Arabic* 1 close relative or trusted servant who has access to the women's side of the house محرم اقربا close relatives 2 spouse 3 close friend

محرم[2] muharrám *Arabic* 1.1 forbidden 1.2 sacred 2 *m.* muharram (the first month of the lunar year)

محرمات muharramā́t *m. plural Arabic* [*singular:* محرمه[2]] forbidden things, that which is forbidden

محرمانه mahramāná 1 secret 2 secretly, confidentially

محرمه[1] mahráma *feminine to* محرم[1]

محرمه‎ muharráma **1** *feminine singular of* محرم‎ **2** *f.* muharram (the first month of the lunar year)

محرميت‎ mahramiját *m. Arabic* intimacy; faith, trust

محروس‎ mahrús *Arabic* kept, preserved, (safe)guarded

محروقات‎ mahruqā́t *m. plural Arabic* fuel; combustibles محروقاتي منابع‎ mahruqātí fuel منابع محروقاتي‎ fuel resources

محروم‎ mahrúm *Arabic* **1** deprived of something; not having something, not possessing something *a* د یو شي څخه محروم پاته کېدل‎ to be deprived of something *b* not to be awarded something **2** treated unfairly, made destitute; offended; unfortunate **3** forbidden

محرومول‎ mahrumawə́l *denominative, transitive* [*past:* محروم یې کړ‎] to deprive (of something) څوک د ژوندون نه محرومول‎ to deprive someone of life, take away someone's life د بیان د آزادي څخه محرومول‎ *a* to take away freedom of speech *b* to revoke (a mandate, a right) ستر گو څخه محرومول‎ *d* to blind, deprive of sight **2** to treat unfairly, make destitute; offend; make unhappy

محرومي‎ mahrumí *f.* محروميت‎ mahrumiját *m.* **1** deprivation; loss; lack of something **2** destitution; need

محرومېدل‎ mahrumedə́l *denominative, intransitive* [*past:* محروم شو‎] to be deprived of something, forfeit something د حقوقو څخه گردو‎ محرومېدل‎ to be deprived of all rights **2** to be treated unfairly, be made destitute; be unhappy, be unfortunate

محزون‎ mahzún *Arabic* pained, grieved; sad, despondent

محسن‎ muhsín *Arabic* **1** charitable, philanthropic **2** *m.* **.1** benefactor, philanthropist **2.2** *proper noun* Muhsin

محسوب‎ mahsúb *Arabic* reckoned (with), taken into account; (being) taken into consideration

محسوبول‎ mahsubawə́l *denominative, transitive* [*past:* محسوب یې کړ‎] to take into account, consider

محسوبېدل‎ mahsubedə́l *denominative, intransitive* [*past:* محسوب شو‎] to be taken into account; be considered

محسوس‎ mahsús *Arabic* perceptible, tangible, palpable; sensible, felt; apparent, marked, appreciable; ponderable په یوه محسوس ډول‎ markedly محسوس کول‎ محسوسول‎ *compound verb* ☞ محسوسېدل‎ *compound verb* ☞

محسوسات‎ mahsusā́t *m. plural Arabic* [*singular:* محسوس‎] sensations, feelings

محسوسول‎ mahsusawə́l *denominative, transitive* [*past:* محسوس یې کړ‎] to feel, sense

محسوسېدل‎ mahsusedə́l *denominative, intransitive* [*past:* محسوس شو‎] to be felt, be sensed

محشر‎ mahshár *m. Arabic* **1** confusion (of feelings) **2** bustle, turmoil; Babel **3** *religion* place where people will gather on the Day of Judgement

محشور‎ mahshúr *Arabic* **1.1** associating with someone **1.2** *religion* risen, resurrected **2** *m.* [*plural:* محشورین‎ mahshurín] acquaintance, friend

محصل‎ muhassíl *m. Arabic* [*plural:* محصلان‎ muhassilā́n *and Arabic* محصلین‎ muhassilín] **1** conqueror **2** tax collector **3** pupil; student

محصله‎ muhassilá *f. Arabic* [*plural:* محصلات‎ muhassilā́t] pupil, school girl; (female) student, coed

محصور‎ mahsúr *Arabic* **1.1** besieged, blockaded, encircled **1.2** limited, constrained **2** *m.* [*plural:* محصورین‎ mahsurín] one who is beseiged; one who is encircled

محصورول‎ mahsurawə́l *denominative, transitive* [*past:* محصور یې کړ‎] **1** to lay siege (to), blockade, encircle **2** to limit, constrain

محصول‎ mahsúl *m. Arabic* [*plural:* محصولونه‎ mahsulúna *and Arabic* محصولات‎ mahsulā́t] **1** production, product د کار محصول‎ product of labor صنعتي محصولات‎ manufactured goods کالنی محصول‎ annual output **2** harvest, crop, yield ربل شوئ محصول‎ cut crop ولاړ محصول‎ standing crop **3** tax, duty (e.g., postal); payment گمرکي محصول‎ customs **4** excise, excise duty

محصولات‎ mahsulā́t *m. Arabic plural* **1** *of* محصول‎ **2** receipts; tax revenues د دولت محصولات‎ government taxes

محصولدار‎ mahsuldā́r **1** productive **2** wealthy (i.e., of a country)

محض‎ mahz *Arabic* **1.1** pure, uncontaminated **1.2** plain, simple محض سړی‎ یو‎ a simple or ordinary person **1.3** empty, useless (of a dream, etc.) **2** په محض لیدو‎ only scarcely having caught sight of محض په دې چه‎ only because

محضر‎ mahzár *m. Arabic* **1** presence **2** meeting, gathering عمومي محضر‎ لوی محضر،‎ general meeting

محضي‎ mahzí **1** exceptional **2** exceptionally

محظور‎ mahzúr *Arabic* forbidden; illegal

محظوظ‎ mahzúz *Arabic* **1** delighting (in), reveling (in) **2** satisfied (with); glad, joyous یو شي‎ cheerful له مزي څخه محظوظ ژوندانه‎ د‎ څخه محظوظ کېدل‎ *a* to take delight in something *b* to be pleased, be glad

محفظه‎ mahfazá *f. Arabic* **1** box **2** *military* cover (of a mine) **3** *biology* shell, cover, coat, membrane

محفل‎ mahfíl *m. Arabic* [*plural:* محفلونه‎ mahfilúna *and Arabic* محافل‎ mahāfíl] circle, club, group اجتماعي محافل‎ society

محفل بازي‎ mahfilbāzí *f.* clannishness, cliquishness

محفوظ‎ mahfúz *Arabic* **1** kept; guarded, protected **2** remembered; memorable, never-to-be-forgotten **3** preserved **4** safe, protected

محق‎ muhíqq *Arabic* **1** just, fair, right **2** well-grounded, well-founded

محقانه‎ muhiqqāná **1** just, fair **2** justly, fairly

محقر‎ muhaqqár *Arabic* contemptible, despicable محقره کوټه‎ *idiom* hut

محقق‎[1] muhaqqíq *Arabic* **1** investigating, researching محقق مؤرخ‎ *a* keen historian **2** *m.* [*plural:* محققین‎ muhaqqiqín] **.1** investigator, researcher **2.2** thinker

محقق‎[2] muhaqqáq *Arabic* **1** proven, demonstrated, established محققه ده چه‎ ... *a* It has been proven that… It has been shown that… *b* undoubtedly, without doubt محقق کېدل‎ *compound verb* to be proved, be shown, be established محققه شوه چه ... It has been proven that… It has been shown that… 2 true, correct

محققاً muhaqqáqán *Arabic* undoubtedly, without question, for sure, certainly

محک mahák, mahákk *m. Arabic* 1 touchstone 2 standard, criterion; standard of weights and measures

محکم makám, mahkám, muhkám *Arabic* 1 strong, firm, durable 2 locked

محکمول makamawól, mahkamawól 1 *denominative, transitive* [*past:* محکم يي کړ] to strengthen, consolidate, fortify 2 *m. plural* strengthening, consolidating, fortifying

محکمه¹ mahkamá *f. Arabic* [*plural:* محکمې mahkamé *and m. plural: Arabic* محاکم mahākím] 1 court, tribunal خصوصي محکمه tribunal نظامي محکمه military tribunal عالي محکمه Supreme Court بين المللي عالي محکمه International Court ابتدايي محکمه trial court د مرافعي محکمه appellate court 2 *regional* department, institution, agency

محکمه² makáma, mahkáma, muhkáma *feminine singular of* محکم

محکمي¹ mahkamí *f.* strength, durability; degree strengthening, quality of reinforcement

محکمي² makámi, mahkámi, muhkámi *f. plural of* محکم

محکمې³ mahkamé *plural of* محکمه¹

محکمېدل makamedól, mahkamedól *denominative, intransitive* [*past:* محکم شو] to be reinforced, be strengthened

محکوک mahkúk *Arabic* 1 engraved, etched 2 carved, fretted

محکوم mahkúm *Arabic* 1.1 condemned, sentenced 1.2 subjugated; subordinate(d); subject to 1.3 guided, directed; dependent 2 *m.* .1 accused, defendant 2.2 subject, citizen د فنا محکوم *idiom* mortal

محکوم به mahkum-ui-bíh *m. Arabic law* amount paid by the losing party to the plaintiff, damages

محکوم عليه mahkum-ui-aléjh *m. Arabic* 1 one sentenced, condemned one 2 *m.* .1 *law* losing party 2.2 *grammar* subject

محکوم له mahkumlahú *m. law* person who has won his case in court

محکومول mahkumawól *denominative, transitive* [*past:* محکوم يي کړ] 1 to condemn, blame, reproach, censure 2 to sentence, pronounce a sentence 3 to compel, force, coerce

محکوميت mahkumiját *m. Arabic* 1 condemnation; sentence د محکوميت صورت verdict 2 condition of being subject to; dependence د محکوميت ژوندون a dependent life

محکومېدل mahkumedól *denominative, intransitive* [*past:* محکوم شو] 1 to be condemned, be sentenced په دايمي حبس محکوم شو He was sentenced to imprisonment for life. په مرګ محکومېدل to be sentenced to death 2 to be forced, be compelled, be coerced

محل mahál, maháll *m. Arabic* [*plural:* محلونه mahalúna, mahallúna *and Arabic* محال mahál, maháll] 1 place; locality د استوګني محل (place of) residence 2 palace

محلل muhallíl *Arabic* 1 dissolving 2 analyzing 3 aiding digestion

محلم muhallám *Arabic* 1 softened, made soft 2 boiled soft, overcooked

محلمېدل¹ muhallamedól *denominative, intransitive* [*past:* محلم شو] to be softened, be made soft 2 to be boiled soft, be overcooked وضعيت محلم شو *idiom* The situation has become less tense.

محلوج mahlúdzh *m. Arabic* ☞ مالوچ

محلول mahlúl *Arabic* 1 dissolved 2 *m.* solution د دوا محلول mixture

محله mahallá *f. Arabic* [*plural:* محلي mahallé *and m. plural: Arabic* محلات mahallát] quarter, neighborhood, district (of a city)

محلي¹ mahallí *Arabic* local محلي صنايع local industry محلي عمليات ,اقدامات military local operation محلي اخ وډب جاري Local fighting is taking place.

محلي² mahallé *plural of* محله

محليت mahalliját *m. Arabic* 1 disconnectedness, disassociation; isolation, solitariness 2 local significance محليت لرل a to have local significance b to have authority locally

محمد muhammád *Arabic* 1 lauded, extolled; deserving of praise 2 *proper noun* Muhammed, Muhammad

محمدزي muhammadzí 1 *m. plural* Muhammedzai (a tribe living to the north of the Kabul River and also a branch of the Durranis) 2 muhammadzáy *m.* Mukammedzai

محمدي muhammadí *Arabic* 1 Moslem, Mohammedan, Islamic 2 *m.* Moslem, Mohammedan

محمول mahmúl *Arabic* 1 loaded; burdened (as a pack animal) 2 *m. grammar* predicate په مبالغه محموله خبره *idiom* a strong exaggeration

محمولات mahmulát *m. plural Arabic* [*singular:* محموله] freight, cargo

محنت mahnát *m. Arabic* 1 labor 2 effort; diligence محنت کول *compound verb* a to labor, work b to try, endeavor, be diligent, be assiduous

محنتي mihnatí industrious, diligent; assiduous

محو mahw *m. Arabic* anihilation, destruction; demolition محوکول *compound verb* to anihilate; destroy; demolish محوکېدل *compound verb* to be anihilated, be destroyed; be demolished ☞ محوه

محور mihwár *m. Arabic* 1 axis مځکه پر خپل محور څرخېږي The earth rotates about its axis. 2 *technology* shaft 3 *politics* axis

محوري mihwarí 1 participating in the Axis محوري دولتونه the Axis nations 2 *m.* [*plural:* محوريان mihwariján] member of the Axis, participant in the Axis (i.e., Germany, Italy, and Japan during WWII)

محول muhawwál *Arabic* 1 laid, placed; assigned, entrusted 2 handed over, delivered 3 altered, changed 4 carried, moved, shifted

محوله muhawalá *f. Arabic commerce* bill of lading

b محويدل máhwa *f.* ☞ محو محوه کېدل *compound verb* **a** ☞ محو to be shaken محوه شوم This news shook me د دې خبري په تاثر کېني محوه شوم up.

محويت mahwiját *m.* **1** anihilation; death, destruction د محويت کندې to ruin, destroy, anihilate ته اچول **2** strong shock

محير [1] muhajjír *Arabic* **1** astonishing, surprising; wonderful, marvelous **2** struck, stricken محير کېدل *compound verb* to be surprised; be amazed; be astonished

محير [2] muhajjár *Arabic* embarrassed, flustered, confused; shaken

محير العقول muhajjír-ul-uqúl *Arabic* amazing, wonderful, striking, startling محير العقول حوادث wonders محير العقول کوښښونه exceptional efforts

محيط muhít *Arabic* **1** surrounding; encompassing; enveloping بحر محيط báhr-i... ocean **2** *m.* .**1** surroundings, environment طبيعي محيط natural conditions اجتماعي محيط social milieu **2.2** full stretch, full grasp (of the arms), embrace **2.3** wide open space(s), scope د سمندر لوی محيط the wide expanse of the ocean **2.4** circle, circumference د دايري محيط *mathematics* circle, circumference **2.5** society, club, association, circle ستاسي په محيط کېني **a** in your country **b** in your circle (of friends and associates **2.6** *figurative* atmosphere, situation د صميميت په محيط کېني in an atmosphere of sincerity

محيطي muhití **1** surrounding محيطي تودوالی ambient temperature محيطي وضعيت environment, situation, conditions **2** relating to the environment, concerning the surroundings **3** relating to a circle **4** local

محيل muhíl *Arabic* **1** sly, cunning, wily **2** *m.* swindler, cheat

مخ [1] mə́kh *m.* [*plural:* مخونه məkhúna *and* Western مخان məkhā́n] **1** face مخ سور ruddy face مخ په مخ **a** face to face **b** in private, confidentially زر زر His face gives him away. مخ يې شاهدي ورکوي مخ مي لاس او کړو *regional* I washed up quickly. **2** side, edge شمال مخ په پورته، مخ په لوره turned to the north, facing north مخ په لاندي down, downward(s) په مخ *attributive* up, upward(s) advanced, leading پر مخ، په مخ، په مخ کي، تر مخ forward, ahead مخ په وراندي، په وراندي تلل to go forward, advance **3** top, surface د سړک په مخ on the road د مځکي پر مخ on the ground اوبه مخ په بره خيژي The sky is clouded. اريځی د اسمان مخ نيسي The water is rising. **4** *mathematics* bound **5** seat (e.g., of a chair) **6** page **7** face, right side (e.g., of fabric) **8** upper (for shoes) **9** blade (e.g., of a saber, knife) **10** *figurative* honor; fame; reputation; authority; influence دغه ډېر مخ دئ He has great authority. مخ لرل to have, authority, enjoy influence مخ اړول، مخ ور اړول *compound verb* **a** و چا ته مخ اړول to turn towards someone **b** د هيڅ راز زيار څخه مخ نه to renounce something دوی شي نه مخ اړوي They don't stop for any difficulties. **c** د... د پاره و چا ته مخ اړوي to put in a good word for someone **d** to run, save oneself by running مخ اوبنتل، مخ پرته کېدل to become ugly مخ پتول *compound verb* to cover the face, wear a veil مخ تورول to avoid something له يو شي څخه مخ په شا کېدل

compound verb to disgrace, defame, put to shame; slander خپل مخ He disgraced himself. مخ يې تور شو He covered himself يي تور کړ with shame. مخ خر گندول *compound verb* to appear, seem د چا نه مخ زبر راستنول *compound verb* Eastern to turn (around) کېدل to be embarrassed, be flustered, change countenance upon seeing someone مخ سپينول *compound verb* to rehabilitate oneself, prove one's innocence مخ غوړيدل، مخ پرچاغوړيدل ، مخ لگيدل، مخ پرچا لگيدل، د چا مخ کتل to go out of one's mind to satisfy someone's request; accept someone's apology مخ کول *compound verb* **a** to arise, originate مشکلاتو مخ کړئ دئ Difficulties have arisen. **b** to pay attention هغه زما مخ نه کوي He does not listen to me. هيچا مخ نه کوي He is the same with everyone. مخ کېدل *compound verb* ☞ مخامخبدل مخ پر يو کار کېدل to begin, start doing something په دې موسم د غرو واوري مخ پر ويلېدو سي At this time of year the snow in the mountains begins to melt. مخ گرزول *compound verb* **a** to repel, fend off (e.g., an attack, a raid) **b** to renounce something, repudiate something **c** to be over (of an illness, etc.) **d** to turn away; turn; not to pay attention, fail to pay attention احمد ښه دئ، د مخ گرزيدل **a** to live in plenty مخ يي گرزي Ahmed lives well; he is not in need. **b** to lose beauty د... څخه مخ گرزيدل **c** to cool down, grow cold towards someone or something مخ ليدل *compound verb* Eastern to venture to ask د چا مخ ماتول **a** not to مي پري نه ليدو I didn't venture to ask him. accept someone's apology **b** not to honor someone's request **c** to reject someone's mediation د چا وخواته مخ نيول *compound verb* **a** مخ نيول to turn to someone; address someone, appeal to someone **b** د چا مخ نيول to curb, control someone, keep someone in check **c** to cover the face (with a veil) **d** to head for, make one's way (to, towards) د چا سره مخ ورل **a** to be friends with, be on friendly terms with **b** to be attentive to someone, be considerate of someone مخ to urge on, hurry on څوک پر مخ وهل to refuse, deny someone وهل پر مخ ببول *compound verb* to continue, press on, push forward (e.g., an offensive) پر مخ تلل *compound verb* **a** to advance, move forward **b** to develop, progress **c** to be missing, disappear, vanish په بل مخ اړول *compound verb* **a** to turn **b** to dig again, dig anew **a** to have in په مخ کي لرل مخامخول په مخ کول *compound verb* ☞ mind, mean **b** to foresee له مخه کېدل to go forward و مخ ته اينبودل to acquire dishonestly په تور مخ گتل to put in front دپت مخ رقص *idiom* masquerade سپين مخ **a** innocent, not guilty **b** innocence, guiltlessness په سپين مخ راتلل to come with a clear conscience مخ **a** at once, immediately, instantly **b** continuously, uninterruptedly په يو مخ باران اوربده It rained incessantly. مملکت مخ The country is developing. مخ په لاري کول **a** to be on په انکشاف دئ the safe side, be overcautious د چا د مخه کېدل to be under someone's power مخ پر صحرا نيول، مخ پر غرو نيول to go out of one's ستا د لاسه به مخ پر صحرا ونيسم You'll drive me mind, go crazy crazy. ويل ته دي مخ، وهغه ته شا ده *Eastern* You are partial to him. د مخ يې *Eastern* He is utterly powerless. د مخه يې پچه هم نه اوري He is a lucky one. د مخ يي رنا ده تياره ده He is a failure. د مخ پوست

پر مخ نری کېدﻞ to be mild, be gentle, be yielding, be pliant; soften پر مخ کّﻪ، تر شا ګوره، تر شا کتل to be careful, be cautious *saying* Go ahead, but keep your eyes peeled. یوه خبره په هر مخ سره اړول to think something over, راواړول، یو سؤال په هر مخ سره اړول راواړول consider something carefully! مخ پناه کوئ! Beat it!

مخ [2] makh *m. technology* pager

مخابرات mukhābarā́t *masculine plural Arabic of* مخابره

مخابراتي mukhābarātí *Eastern* relating to communications

مخابره mukhābará *f. Arabic* [*plural:* مخابرې mukhābaré *and m. plural: Arabic* مخابرات mukhābarā́t] **1** communication, report, news report **2** communications د مخابرې مرکز communications office مخابره تلگرافي telephone communications تلیفوني مخابره telegraph communications د مخابراتو وزارت the ministry of communications مخابره کول *compound verb* to trasmit, report مخابره کېدﻞ *compound verb* to be transmitted, be reported

مخابره چي mukhābarachí *m.* communications man, signals man, communications worker

مخارج makharídzh *m. Arabic plural* **1** *of* مخرج **2** expenses, expenditures; costs مولد مخرج production costs

مخازن makhazín *m. plural Arabic of* مخزن

مخاصم mukhāsím *m. Arabic* (the) enemy

مخاصمات mukhāsamā́t *m. Arabic plural* **1** *of* مخاصمه **2** hostile actions

مخاصمت mukhāsamát *f. Arabic* [*plural:* مخاصمات mukhāsimā́t مخاصمه mukhāsamá مخاصمي mukhāsamé] enmity, hostility, animosity, antagonism مخاصمات کول *compound verb* to feud with, quarrel

مخاطب [1] mukhātáb *m. Arabic* **1** one who is being addressed, one to whom a speech is addressed څوک مخاطب کول to turn to someone, address someone **2** *grammar* second person **3** *commerce* one who executes a commission, contractor

مخاطب [2] mukhātíb *Arabic* **1** *m.* orator **2** speaking, addressing

مخاطبه mukhātabá *f.* [*plural:* مخاطبي mukhātabé *and m. plural: Arabic* مخاطبات mukhātabā́t] **1** speech **2** conversation **3** exchange of speeches

مخاطره mukhātará, mukhātirá *f. Arabic* risk, hazard, danger

مخاطي mukhātí *Arabic* mucous, mucilaginous, slimy مخاطي پرده mucous membrane

مخالف mukhālíf *Arabic* **1.1** counteracting, opposing, resisting **1.2** opposition مخالف حزب opposition party, opposition **1.3** contradictory **a** to oppose something, act د يوشي څخه مخالف کېدﻞ against something **b** to contradict something د دوی نظریي یو له بلي **a** vote مخالفه رایه They have opposite opinions. سره مخالفي دي against, a nay vote **1.4** opposite, contrary, opposed پر مخالفه خوا on the opposite side د سیند په سمت کښي مخالف حرکت کول to go against the current **2** *m.* [*plural:* مخالفان mukhālifán *and Arabic* مخالفین mukhālifī́n] enemy د خپلي آرزو نه مخالف against my wishes

مخالفت mukhālifát *m. Arabic* **1** opposition, counteraction, resistance **2** insubordination; disobedience **3** opposition **4** objection د چا په مخالفت څه ویل to disagree, contradict someone **5** contrast **6** contradiction مخالفت کول *compound verb* **a** to offer resistance, resist **b** to disagree, contradict **c** to contradict, gainsay

مخالفول mukhālifawə́l *denominative, transitive* [*past:* مخالف یي کﺉ] to turn (someone) against someone څوک څان له مخالفول، څوک څان ته مخالفول to turn (someone) against oneself, antagonize (someone)

مخامخ məkhāmə́kh **1.1** opposite, across from; facing, in front of; face to face مخامخ مو in front of us زما کور ته مخامخ د احمد کور دﺉ Ahmed's house is opposite mine. **1.2** directly, immediately که تل د لمر پرپوتو وخوا ته مخامخ سفر وکړو ... If one goes straight west ... مخامخ پر دښمن باندي حمله کول to attack the enemy head-on **2.1** opposite, contrary مخامخ دیوال the opposite wall **2.2** immediate, direct **2.3** clashing, conflicting with something دوی د خطر سره مخامخ دي Danger threatens them.

مخامختوب məkhāməkhtób *m.* **1** opposition; encounter **2** collision, clash

مخامخول məkhāməkhawə́l *denominative, transitive* [*past:* مخامخ یي کﺉ] **1** to place face to face **2** to set up a confrontation **3** to organize a reception or party **4** to compare (e.g., for purposes of verification) **5** to confront (a fact, etc.)

مخامخي məkhāmə́khí *f.* ☞ مخامختوب

مخامخېدﻞ məkhāməkhedə́l *denominative, intransitive* [*past:* د چا سره مخامخېدﻞ شو] **1** to collide with, clash with **2** to meet to meet with someone, to encounter someone **3** to stand face to face **4** to be confronted **5** to be compared (e.g., for purposes of verification) **6** to encounter (e.g., difficulties); find oneself facing (a fact, etc.) د مقاومت سره مخامخېدﻞ to encounter resistance بېړی د طوفان سره مخامخ شوه The ship was caught in a storm.

مخاوي məkhāwáj **1** respected, esteemed **2** equal, equivalent

مخاویتوب məkhāwajtób *m.* respect, esteem

مخبر mukhbír *m. Arabic* **1** correspondent د باختر د آژانس مخبر Bakhtar news correspondent **2** informant **3** agent **4** informer

مخ پټي [1] məkhputí *f.* wearing the veil, covering the face

مخ پټی [2] məkhpútaj *m.* **1** shawl **2** veil *Eastern* د مخ پټی موسم وه That was at the beginning or at the end of winter.

مخ پټی [3] məkhpútaj *m.* variety of rice

مخپټه məkhpúṭe (one who is) covering or hiding her face under a shawl

مخ پورته məkhpórta up, upwards

مخ په مخ məkhpəmə́kh face to face مخ په مخ کول *compound verb* to bring face to face مخ په مخ کېدﻞ *compound verb* to come face to face

مخ پېتک məkhpeṭák, məkhpeṭə́k *m.* **1** uncovering the face of the bride **2** examination of a newborn

مختار mukhtā́r *Arabic* **1.1** plenipotentiary مختار وزارت diplomatic mission مختار وکیل envoy مختار وزیر person having a full power of attorney **1.2** selected **1.3** independent **2** *proper noun* Muhtar

مختارول mukhtārawə́l *denominative, transitive* [*past:* مختاري يي کﺉ] **1** to authorize, empower **2** to give free rein, give a free hand

مختاري mukhtārí *f.* مختاريت mukhtāriját *m. Arabic* **1** freedom of choice **2** independence, free will

مخترع mukhtarí' *m. Arabic* [*plural:* مخترعين mukhtari'ín] **1** inventor **2** constructor, builder

مختص mukhtás, mukhtáss *Arabic* specific

مختصر mukhtasár *Arabic* **1.1** short, abbreviated; compressed په مختصرو الفاظو کښي briefly **1.2** unimportant, of small import **1.3** small مختصر هسپیتال small hospital **1.4** modest مختصر لوازم modest circumstances **2** *m.* resumé

مختصراً mukhtasárán *Arabic* briefly, in brief, in short

مختگ mǝkhtág *m.* progress, development د صنایعو مختگ the development of industry

مختل mukhtál, mukhtáll *Arabic* **1** disrupted, brought into disorder, violated **2** spoiled, damaged

مختلط mukhtalát *Arabic* **1** mixed, intermixed مختلط کول *compound verb* to mix, intermix مختلط کېدل *compound verb* to be mixed, be intermixed **2** component, compound **3** summary; combined **4** mixed, combined; coalition مختلط شرکت joint stock company

مختلف mukhtalíf *Arabic* various, diverse, different یو د بل څخه مختلف differing

مختلف النوع mukhtalifunnáw' *Arabic* heterogeneous; of diverse sorts; of different makes

مخ تلوني mǝkhtlúnaj going forward, advancing

مختنق mukhtaníq *Arabic* **1** damped down, muffled, deadened **2** smothered, strangled **3** curtailed, limited (of rights) مختنق کول *compound verb* **a** to damp down, muffle **b** to smother, strangle **c** to curtail, limit (rights) مختنق کېدل *compound verb* **a** to be damped down, be muffled **b** to be smothered, be strangled **c** to be curtailed, be limited (of rights)

مختورن ² mǝkhtorǝ́n ☞ مختوری

مخ توري ¹ mǝkhtorí *f.* **1** shame, disgrace **2** guild **3** crime

مختوری ² mǝkhtóraj **1** disgraced **2** ashamed **3** guilty **4** criminal

مخ تولي mǝkhtolí falling down over the face (of a lock or ringlet of hair)

مختوم makhtúm *Arabic* **1** sealed **2** completed, concluded **3** *linguistics* ending in…, which ends in…

مختومېدل makhtumedǝ́l *denominative, intransitive* [*past:* مختوم شو] **1** to be completed, be concluded **2** *linguistics* to end in

مختون makhtún *Arabic religion* subjected to circumcision, circumcised

مخته mǝ́khta **1** forward مخته بیول *compound verb* to lead forward **2** in front of, ahead of

مخ تي mǝ́khte *abbreviation of the words* مخ ته دئ ولاړ یار مخ ته یې محمد Before him stands Yar Muhammed.

مخدر mukhaddír *Arabic* **1** narcotic **2** *m.* narcotic, dope

مخدوم makhdúm *m. Arabic* master, lord, ruler, sovereign

مخرب mukhríb *m. Arabic* **1** *military* destroyer (ship) **2** destroyer, wrecker

مخرج makhrádzh *m. Arabic* مخرجونه makhradzhúna [*plural: and Arabic* مخارج makhārídzh] **1** way out, outcome **2** the organs of speech **3** pronunciation **4** *mathematics* denominator

مخروب makhrúb *Arabic* destroyed, demolished; devestated, wasted مخروبه ځمکه ruined

مخروبه makhrubá *f.* ruins

مخرېوند makhrewánd *m. computer science* forward slash (\)

مخروط makhrút *Arabic* **1.1** turned (on a lathe) **1.2** conical **2** *m.* cone

مخروطي makhrutí *Arabic* **1** conical په مخروطي شکل cone-shaped **2** narrowing at the end, becoming narrower at the end

مخ روني ¹ mǝkhruṇáj *m.* **1** ☞ مخ پټک **2** gift on the occasion of uncovering the face of the bride **3** smoothing over a misunderstanding, settling a misunderstanding

مخ روني ² mǝkhrúṇaj **1** honest, irreproachable **2** intelligent, clever, sensible

مخزن makhzán *m. Arabic* [*plural:* مخزونه makhzanúna *and Arabic* مخازن makhāzín] **1** depository, storehouse **2** arsenal, depot د جبه خاني مخزن ammunition dump **3** treasure-house **4** reservoir (of a lantern) **5** tank **6** (water) reservoir د اوبو مخزن reservoir **7** *anatomy* the pelvis of the kidney

مخ سپيني ¹ mǝkhspináj *m.* innocent appearance; nonparticipation in, being not implicated in مخ سپيني کول to feign disinterest in something

مخ سپيني ² mǝkhspínaj ☞ مخ روني ²

مخسره makhsará *f.* ☞ مسخره

مخ ښکاري mǝkhḳhkārí *f.* **1** uncovering the face of the bride **2** gift to the bride at the time of uncovering her face

مخصوص makhsús *Arabic* **1** special; peculiar (to) **2** special, especial یو کار دڅان دپاره مخصوص کول to specialize in something مخصوص قلم special unit **3** specific (e.g., specific gravity or specific weight)

مخصوصاً makhsúsán *Arabic* **1** especially, inparticular **2** purposely, on purpose, especially

مخصوصيت makhsusiját *m. Arabic* special feature, peculiarity, specificity

مخطط mukhattát *Arabic commerce* cancelled (of a check)

مخفف mukhaffáf *Arabic* **1** lightened, eased **2** abbreviated, curtailed

مخفف نويسي mukhaffafnawisí *f.* cursive (writing)

مخفي makhfí *Arabic* **1** concealed, covert, secret په مخفي راز in secret مخفي کول *compound verb* to conceal, hide **2** illegal

مخفيانه makhfijāná **1** concealed, covert, secret **2** secretly, covertly

مخ کاته mǝkhkātǝ́ *m. plural* ☞ مخ پټک

مخکتنه mǝkhkatǝ́na *f.* attention to someone

مخکښ ¹ mǝkhkáḳh *m.* **1** head, chief, leader **2** herd leader (of goats)

مخکښ ² mǝ́khke ☞ مخکښي

مخ کښنته راکښل ☜ مخکښنته məkhkkhə́ta down, downward مخ کښنته to pull down, haul down

مخکښني mə́khke 1.1 forward 1.2 in front of, before ورته مخکښني in front of him مخکښنی تلل compound verb a to go forward, advance; be on the offensive b to succeed, have success مخکښنی کول compound verb a to move forward, progress b to foster success; develop c to present, submit (e.g., a report) d to mention, remind 1.3 before, earlier مخکښنی له دي نه چه رخصت شو... before parting, before leaving له ټولو څخه مخکښنی first of all یوه ورځ مخکښني د دي نه on the eve of this 1.4 already مخکښني مو وویل... We (have) already said that... 2.1 former, previous 2.2 forthcoming, coming, future مخکښني کال the coming year

مخکښني توب məhketób m. leadership

مخکښني والی məhkewə́laj m. 1 forward movement, movement ahead 2 progress; development

مخکښنی məhkináj ☜ مخکښني

مخکی məhkáj[1] m. even and gentle slope of a hill

مخکي mə́khki, mə́khke[2] ☜ مخکښني

مخکښنی məhkináj 1 front, forward; advanced, progressive مخکښنی ټولگی advanced units 2 progressive, modern 3 former, past 4 preliminary مخکښنی شرط precondition

مخل mukhíl, mukhíll Arabic disrupting something; hindering something; violating something

مخلص mukhlís Arabic 1.1 sincere 1.2 sincerely (in letters) 2 m. [plural: مخلصان mukhlisə́n and Arabic مخلصين mukhlisín]. 1 sincere friend 2.2 proper noun Muhlis

مخلصانه mukhlisāná sincerely, openheartedly

مخلوط makhlút Arabic mixed, intermixed; contaminated مخلوط کول compound verb to mix, intermix مواد alloys مخلوط کول compound verb to be mixed, be intermixed

مخلوع makhlú' overthrown, deposed from the throne

مخلوق makhlúq Arabic 1 created 2 m. [Arabic plural: مخلوقات makhluqə́t and مخلوقونه makhluqúna] creation

مخليد makhlíd m. computer science preview

مخ مخی məhmə́khaj two-faced, hypocritical, characterized by duplicity

مخمس mukhammás Arabic 1.1 fivefold, quintuple, quinary 1.2 mathematics pentagonal 2 m. . 1 muhammas (a stanza of five hemistiches) 2.2 mathematics pentagon منظم مخمس regular, pentagon

مخمصه makhmasá f. Arabic 1 exhaustion, emaciation; dystrophy 2 difficulty

مخمل makhmál m. Arabic velvet

مخملی makhmalí 1 velvet 2 soft, tender, velvety

مخمور makhmúr Arabic 1 drunk, inebriated 2 langorous (of eyes) په وینو مخمور idiom bloodthirsty

مخنی məhnáj ☜ مخکښني

مخنیوی məkhniwáj m. 1 مخ نیوی covering the face مخنیوی کول compound verb to cover the face (of a woman when a man comes into her presence) 2 removal, elimination; prevention; struggle د ناروغیو مخ نیوی disease prevention 3 banning, barring

مخ وچونی məkhwəchúnaj m. towel

مخور məkhawór 1 respected, honored 2 influential, authoritative 3 obliging

مخوري məkhawrí f. 1 respect, esteem 2 influence, authority 3 helpfulness, obligingness

مخوریز məkhawaríz Eastern 1 influential, authoritative, prestigious 2 respected, esteemed

مخوف makhúf Arabic frightful, terrible, sinister

مخوکه makhúka f. Eastern 1 ☜ مښوکه 2 muzzle, snout

مخه mə́kha[1] f. 1 direction ستا مخي ته a in front of you, before you b towards you د چا مخي ته to meet going towards someone د باد مخه گرگېدلي ده The wind has changed direction. 2 way, path 3 basis, foundation, grounds د... له مخي on the basis of something د پلان له مخي according to (the) plan د خپلو تجربو له مخي on the basis of one's experience 4 front part, front of something 5 surface 6 level 7 attention چا ته مخه ورکول give attention to someone مخه و یو شي ته ګرزول to pay attention to something a شي مخه بندول، د یو شي مخه ګرزول، د یو شي مخه نیول to stop, call a halt to, suppress د پیشرفت مخه نیول to call a halt to an offensive b د سیلاب مخه نیول to struggle with something, combat something flood control c to prevent, hinder something d to set out for somewhere, start for somewhere د ښار مخه نیول to set out on the road to the city د ښار وخواته مخه نیول to head out for the city مخه بندبدل compound verb to be stopped, be halted د دیښمن خپله عسکرو مخه بنده شوې ده The enemy's advance was stopped. مخه کول compound verb a Eastern hold one's ground set out for, head for somewhere خپلي دبري ته مخه کول to set out for home b to turn to the side c to use, handle something d to show respect د استقبال دپاره د چا مخي ته راوتل په مخه ورتلل to come across مخي له را تلل، مخي له در تلل، مخي له ور تلل to go to meet someone زه یې مخي له تللئ یم I was on my way to meet him. le مخي to come across له مخي in the afternoon! په مخه موینه! Bon voyage! د ورځي د مخي مخه دي خپله Have it your way. کال ته to deal with something کېدل He has passed his twelfth year. د ژوند و ۱۲ یې مخه سوه د یوشي و مخي ته دربدل not to be afraid of something

مخه mukhá[2] f. ☜ موخه

مخه mə́kha[3] oblique of مخ

مخکخه məkhakhá f. farewell, parting, leave-taking هغه مخه ښي ته مخه ښه کول compound verb to راغلئ و He came to say good-bye. say farewell ورسره مي مخه ښه وکړه I said good-bye to him.

مخي mə́khi[1] oblique of مخ[1]

مخي mukháj, məkháj[2] 1.1 equal, identical, same 1.2 similar, resembling 2 m. . 1 equal 2.2 rival

مخی mukhój 1 *feminine singular of* مخی په ټول کلي کي يې دښايست مخی نه وه In the whole village there was no beauty equal to her. 2 *f.* girl given in marriage to a tribe or family in exchange for a bride taken from them (avoiding payment of bride-price) مخی غوبنتل *compound verb* to seek to marry a girl from a tribe or family in exchange for a bride given to them

مخی توب mukhajtób *m.* 1 equality of position 2 contrasting, comparing 3 competition

مخي ته واته məkhitawátə́ *m. plural* reception, party

مخیل mukhajjál *Arabic* imagined, invented, made up, concocted, fabricated

مخیلات mukhajjalā́t *m. plural Arabic* chimera; fabrication, invention, fantasy, fancy

مخیله¹ mukhajjilá *f. Arabic* imagination, fantasy

مخیله² makhilá *f. Arabic* arrogance, insolence, presumption, haughtiness

مخیم mukhajjám *m. Arabic* camp

مد mad, madd *m. Arabic* 1 *linguistics* madda (the sign of length ~ above the letter alef) 2 length, duration 3 lengthening, drawing out 4 rising tide, incoming tide

مداح maddā́h *m. Arabic* panegyrist, eulogist, extoller

مداخل madākhíl *m. plural Arabic of* مدخل

مداخلت mudākhalát *m.* مداخله mudākhalá *f. Arabic* 1 interference, meddling 2 intervention مداخلت کول *compound verb* a to interfere, meddle b to carry out an intervention 3 relation, connection

مدار¹ madár *m. Arabic* 1 circle; circumference 2 *astronomy* orbit مدارته the Earth's orbit د مځکي مدار د مدار برابرېدل to go into orbit مدار toتوغول to put into orbit 3 *geography* tropic 4 axis 5 starting point, initial position, point of departure 6 basis

مدار² madár *m.* مدارا mudārá *f. and* مدارات mudārā́t *m. Arabic* 1 civility, courtesy, urbanity د چا مدار کول to be civil, be courteous, be well-mannered with someone; show attention to someone 2 patience

مدارج madārídzh *m. plural Arabic of* مدرج

مدارک madārík *m. Arabic plural* 1 *of* مدرک¹ 2 mental capabilities, intellectual faculties, intellect, reason

مداري¹ madārí, mudārí *m.* juggler, conjurer

مداري² madārí orbital مداري الوتنه orbital flight

مدافع mudāfí' *Arabic* defending مدافع وکيل attorney for the defense

مدافعت mudāfa'át *m.* مدافعه mudāfa'á, mudāfi'á *f. Arabic* 1 defense د ... د to د خخه مدافعت کول minister of defense د مدافعي وزير defend to defend oneself 2 *law* the defense د خان خخه مدافعت کول counsel's speech 3 preservation (of plants) د مدافعي قوه، د مدافعي قوت *idiom medicine* resistance (of an organism)

مدافعه وي mudāfa'awí *Arabic* مدافعي mudāfa'í defensive مدافعه وي اتحاد defensive alliance مدافعه وي اقدامات measures to control the diseases and pests of agricultural animals and plants مدافعه وي قوت resistance

مدال medā́l *m.* medal

مدام mudā́m *Arabic* 1 invariable, constant, permanent 2 always, constantly

مدامي mudāmí 1 uninterrupted, constant په مدامي ډول always 2 eternal, perpetual

مداوم mudāwím *Arabic* 1.1 constant, permanent, invariable مداومه کوميته standing committee 1.2 diligent, industrious 2 *m.* [*plural:* مداومان mudāwimā́n *and Arabic* مداومين mudāwimín] student

مداومت mudāwamát *m. Arabic* constancy, unchangeability, invariability, immutability په يو شي مداومت کول to defend something; persist in something

مداومتي mudāwamatí constant, immutable, invariable

مدبر mudabbír *Arabic* 1.1 gifted 1.2 efficient, businesslike 2 *m.* leader, head

مدبرانه mudabbirāná cautious, careful; judicious, wise ښه مدبرانه سياست a wise policy

مدت¹ muddát *m. Arabic* ☞ مده پس له څه مدته after some time

مدت² madát *m. colloquial* ☞ مدد

مدتگار madatgár *m.* ☞ مددگار

مدح madh *m. Arabic* praise; lauding, extolling; panegyric د چا مدح کول to praise, laud, glorify someone

مدح خوان madhkhā́n *m.* panegyrist; praiser, lauder

مدخل madkhál *m. Arabic* [*plural:* مدخلونه madkhalúna *and Arabic* مداخل madākhíl] 1 entry, entrance 2 admission, matriculation (e.g., in a school) 3 participation 4 income, receipts

مدخول madkhúl *m. Arabic* profit, revenue

مدد madád *m. Arabic* 1 aid, assistance, support, help مدد راغوښتل to call for help د چا سره مدد کول to help someone 2 strengthening, reinforcement 3 financial aid, grant, scholarship مدد ورکول *compound verb* a to render aid, give support b to give financial aid, give a scholarship

مدد خرچ madadkhárch *m.* مدد خرچي madadkharchí *f.* grant, allowance

مدد خواه madadkhā́h *m.* one who is calling for help

مددگار madadgár 1 *m.* .1 assistant; accomplice 1.2 ally 1.3 defender, patron 2 assisting, furthering, helping

مددگاري madadgārí *f.* assistance, help, good offices

مدرج madrádzh *m. Arabic* [*plural:* مدارج madārídzh madradzhá] *f. Arabic* degree; stage, level د ترقی لوړ مدارج حاصول to reach a high level of development

مدرس mudarrís *m. Arabic* [*plural:* مدرسان mudarrisā́n *and Arabic* مدرسين mudarrisín] 1 teacher, instructor, lecturer 2 professor

مدرسه madrasá *f. Arabic* 1 school داخلي مدرسه boarding school 2 madrasa, Islamic religious school 3 school, trend, movement (e.g., in art)

مدرسیه madrasijá *Arabic* school مدرسیه ژوند school life

مدرک¹ madrák *m.* [*plural:* مدرکونه madrakúna *and Arabic* مدارک madārík] 1 document that serves as evidence or proof 2 source (e.g., of revenue, income) له دې مدرکه for this line item of income

مدرک² mudrík *Arabic* understanding, comprehending مدرکه قوه intellect

مدرن modérn modern, contemporary; newest, latest

مدعا mudda'á *f. Arabic* **1** claim; demand **2** subject of an argument; a suit, claim **3** assertion, statement خو، ...مدعا دا چه It can be asserted .... چه دا مدعا... **4** purpose, meaning خپله مدعا صفا ښکاره لري؟ What do you have in mind? **5** thought کول to state one's thoughts clearly

مدعا گر mudda'āgár demanding, exacting; insistent, persistent

مدعو mad'úw, mad'úww *m. Arabic* [*plural:* مدعوین mad'uwín, mad'uwwín] invited person, guest

مدعي mudda'í *m. Arabic* **1** plaintiff **2** prosecutor **3** rival **4** claimant **5** advocate, supporter, adherent, follower

مدعیٔ mudda'á *f. Arabic* ☞ مدعا

مدعي العموم mudda'í-al'umúm *m. Arabic* **1** prosecutor general **2** public prosecutor

مدعي العمومیت mudda'í-al-'umumiját *m.* prosecutor's office

مدعیٔ به mudda'ābíh *m. Arabic law* **1** disputed property **2** object of a claim

مدغاسکر madaghāskár *m.* Madagascar

مدغم mudghám *Arabic* **1.1** assimilated مدغم کول *compound verb* to assimilate سره مدغم کېدل to be assimilated **1.2** covert, secret **2** *m.* letter with a tashdid

مدفن madfán *m. Arabic* place of burial; grave; cemetery

مدفوع madfú' *Arabic* **1** discarded, thrown out مدفوعه مواد **a** refuse, waste **b** excrement **2** rejected, turned down, repudiated مدفوعه کول *compound verb* **a** to discard, throw out, throw away **b** to reject, turn down, repudiate

مدفون madfún *Arabic* **1** (of a deceased) buried, interred **2** buried

مدقق mudaqqíq *Arabic* **1** researching, investigating; checking, verifying **2** [*plural:* مدققان mudaqqiqán *and Arabic* مدققین mudaqqiqín] researcher, investigator

مدگاسکر madagāskár *m.* ☞ مدغاسکر

مدلل mudallál *Arabic* **1** proven, supprted by proofs or evidence; well-founded مدلل کول *compound verb* ☞ مدللول **2** meaning, sense, substance, essence

مدللول mudallalawól *denominative, transitive* [*past:* مدلل یې کړ] to confirm; prove; give reasons for

مدني madaní *Arabic* **1** civilized, cultured, refined, educated مدني انسان a person of culture مدني روابط cultural contacts مدني دنیا the civilized world **2** civil مدني قوانین، مدني قانونونه civil legislation مدني حقوق civil rights

مدنیت madaniját *m. Arabic* civilization, culture

مدور mudawwár *Arabic* round; spherical, globe-shaped مدور شکل پیدا کول to grow round

مدون¹ mudawwán *Arabic* gathered together into a collection or divan

مدون² mudawwín *m. Arabic* compiler (of a collection, divan)

مده muddá *m. Arabic* **1** time; term, period of time په دي مده کي meanwhile په دي دومره ډېره مده کي for a short while په لږه مده کي for such a lengthy period of time هغه ډېره مده ژوندی و He lived a long time. **2** length, duration, continuance ☞ موده¹

مده خېل madakhél **1** *m. plural* Madakhels (a tribe) **2** *m.* Madakhel

مدهش mudhísh *Arabic* terrifying, frightful, awful, horrible

مدهوش madhúsh *Arabic* **1** scared, firghtened; bewildered, perplexed مدهوش کېدل *compound verb* to be frightened; be bewildered **2** cold, unfeeling; unconscious **3** intoxicated, drunk

مدیترانه mediterānā *f.* **1** Mediterranean Sea د مدیتراني بحیره Mediterranean Sea **2** coastal area of the Mediterranean Sea

مدید madíd *Arabic* **1** long, protracted, prolonged **2** slow, lingering, long and drawn-out

مدیر mudír *m. Arabic* **1** director, manager, administrator د بانک مدیر bank director د مکتب مدیر principal تدریسي مدیر اجرایي مدیر academic dean د قشلي مدیر garrison commander **2** editor (of a newspaper) **3** ministry representative, authorized agent (in the provinces)

مدیره mudirá *Arabic* **1** managing, directing, running **a** مدیره هیئت directorate; board; (board of) directors, management **b** editors, editorial office, editorial board **2** *f.* (female) director, manager د ښځو د لیسي مدیره principal of a girls' school

مدیري mudirí *f.* management; superintendence

مدیریت mudiriját *m. Arabic* **1** directorate; department عمومي مدیریت directorate د لوازماتو مدیریت office; archive د اوراقو مدیریت quartermaster corps د ماډورینو مدیریت personnel department د تحریراتو مدیریت secretariat **2** the position of director; job of supervising **3** editor (the position or job)

مدینه madiná *f. Arabic* Medina ☞ مدینه مبارکه، مدینه المنوره Medina

مډل miḍl *regional* middle, medium مډل سکول high school

مدیترانه meḍiterānā *f.* ☞ مدیترانه

مذاق mazáq *m. Arabic* **1** taste, sense of taste **2** interest د خپل مذاق مطابق، د خپل مذاق په لحاظ to his taste دا د مذاق خبره ده That's a matter of taste.

مذاکرات muzākarāt *m. Arabic plural* **1** *of* مذاکره **2** talks, negotiations مذاکره کول *compound verb* to conduct negotiations

مذاکره muzākará, muzākirá *f. Arabic* [*plural:* مذاکري muzākaré *and Arabic* مذاکرات muzākarāt] **1** discussion, د تر مذاکرې لاندي نیول to discuss something, talk something over **2** *plural* talks, negotiations مذاکري لاندي نیول

مذاهب mazāhíb *m. plural Arabic of* مذهب

مذکر muzakkár *Arabic grammar* **1** masculine, of masculine gender مذکره کلمه a word of masculine gender **2** *m.* **.1** masculine gender **2.2** [*plural:* مذکرات muzakkarát] noun, word of masculine gender

مذکروالی muzakkarwálaj *m. grammar* masculine gender

مذکور mazkúr *Arabic* **1** above-mentioned, above-named مذکور کول *compound verb* to mention, refer to **2** *m.* **.1** conversation, talk **2.2** communication **2.3** content of a document

مذمت mazammát *m. Arabic* condemnation, blame, reproach; abuse, reviling مذمت کول *compound verb* to condemn, blame, reproach

مذموم mazmúm *Arabic* condemned, blamed, censured, reproached

مذهب mazháb *m. Arabic* [*plural:* مذهبونه mazhabúna *and Arabic* مذاهب mazāhíb] **1** religion, faith, dogma **2** teaching, doctrine **3** school, trend, movement **4** custom **5** mazhab (school of Islamic religious law) حنفي مذهب hanifism مذهب لرل *idiom* to be brave ببرک هيڅ مذهب نه لري *idiom* Babrak is a big coward. د چا مذهب ليدل to test someone's courage مذهب وربښکاره کول to show bravery

مذهبي mazhabí **1** religious, denominational, sectarian; spiritual مذهبي مقتداگان priests **2** *m. regional* Sikh

مر¹ mar *m. Arabic* every fifty articles (in counting), five tens

مر² mur, murr *m.* myrrh

مر³ mr *present stem of* مړل

مراتب marātíb *m.* **1** *plural Arabic of* مرتبه circumstances, details, particulars د تبریک مراتب فرمایل to offer congratulations

مراجع¹ murādzhi' *m. Arabic* [*plural:* مراجعین murādzhi'ín] **1** client; patient; visitor **2** petitioner

مراجع² marādzhí' *m.* **1** *plural Arabic of* مرجع **2** authorities تقنینیه legislative bodies مراجع

مراجعت murādzha'át *m. Arabic* **1** return له يو ځايه مراجعت کول to return from somewhere وکابل ته يې مراجعت وکړ He returned to Kabul. **2** appeal (to), application (to, for) (for a reference, for information) د مراجعت کتاب reference book که و تاريخ ته مراجعت وکړو … If we turn to history …

مراجعه murādzha'á *f. Arabic* ☞ مراجعت

مراجعین murādzhi'ín *m.* **1** *plural Arabic of* مراجع¹ **2** the public, people

مراحل marāhíl *m. plural Arabic of* مرحله

مراحم marāhím *m. plural Arabic of* مرحمت

مراد murád *m. Arabic* **1** desire; goal د زړه تر مراده رسېدل to achieve the realization of one's goal **2** sense, meaning **3** object, article مراد يي دا چه The main point is that… **4** *m. proper noun* Murad

مرادبخته murádbákhta *f. proper noun* Muradbahta

مرادف murādíf *Arabic* **1.1** corresponding (to) **1.2** synonymous مرادف لغات synonyms **2** *m.* synonym

مرادمن مرادمند murādmán murādmánd (having) reached one's goal, (having) realized one's desire

مرادېدل murādedál *denominative, intransitive* [*past:* مراد شو] **1** to have in mind, mean **2** to be realized

مراسلات murāsalāt *m.* **1** *plural Arabic of* مراسله **2** (items of) mail **3** reader (a book for self-education in language and literature)

مراسله murāsalá *f. Arabic* [*plural:* مراسلي murāsalé *and m. plural: Arabic* مراسلات murāsalāt] **1** letter **2** correspondence

مراسم marāsím *m. plural Arabic* **1** ceremonial, ceremony **2** rites, rituals **3** celebration د مراسمو جشن مراسم پر ځای کول to celebrate د مراسمو سالون assembly hall د مراسمو سالون اندازت salute

مراعات murā'át *m. Arabic* **1** attention; care, maintenance **2** respect **3** observance د روغتیا پوره مراعات کول to observe the rules of hygiene د... مراعات کول **a** to give attention **b** to take something into account **c** to respect someone or something **d** to observe (e.g., cleanliness)

مرافعه murāfa'á *f. Arabic* appeal د مرافعي لیکونکی clerk of court د مرافعي محکمه district مرافعي وکیل lawyer, defense attorney د مرافعي قاضي، د مرافعي د محکمي قاضي court, appellate court مرافعه غوښتل appellate court judge *compound verb* to appeal, lodge an appeal, appeal the decision of the court

مرافعه طلب murāfa'ataláb *Arabic* entering an appeal, appealing مرافعه طلب کېدل *compound verb* to appeal, appeal the decision of the court

مرافعه طلبي murāfa'atalabí *f.* lodging an appeal, appealing the decision of the court

مرافقت murāfaqát *m. Arabic* escort, accompaniment

مراقب murāqíb *Arabic* **1.1** observing **1.2** monitoring, checking **2** *m.* [*plural:* مراقبان murāqibān *and Arabic* مراقبین murāqibín] **2.1** observer **2.2** examiner, inspector

مراقبت murāqabát *m. Arabic* **1** verification of performance; observation, supervision; monitoring, inspection د نرخو مراقبت price controls د یوشي مراقبت کول to follow, observe something تر مراقبت لاندي نیول to be under observation, be monitored **2** guardianship **3** observing, keeping; taking something into account **4** contemplation

مراقبه murāqabá *religion* fear of God

مراقید marāqíd *m. plural Arabic of* مرقد

مراکز marākíz *m. plural Arabic of* مرکز

مراکش marākásh *m.* Morocco

مراکشي marākashí **1** Moroccan **2.1** *m.* Moroccan (male) **2.2** *f.* Moroccan (female)

مرام marắm *m. Arabic* goal, task; program, plan د پلان مرام tasks of the plan يو مرام ترسره کول to carry out the plan, realize the program

مرامنامه marāmnāmá *f.* **1** *politics* program; platform **2** charter (of a society)

مرانده mrắnda *f.* **1** thin rope, cord, twine **2** tent rope **3** thread **4** *figurative* heartstrings

مرانگور mrāngór *m.* wood bug (on the mulberry tree)

مراوده murāwalá *f. Arabic* friendly relations; intercourse, contact, communication د چا سره مراوده پیدا کول to establish friendly relations with someone د چا سره مراوده لرل to maintain friendly ties with someone تجارتي او اقتصادي مراودي لرل to maintain economic and commercial ties

مراوه mrāwá *f.* crossbeam of a water-raising wheel to which the trough or race is attached

مراهق murāhíq *m. Arabic* young man, youth, adolescent

مراهقوالی murāhiqwắlaj *m.* youth

مربا murabbắ *f. Arabic* preserves, jam

مربع murabbá' *Arabic* **1.1** square متر مربع square meter, m^2 مربع سطح، مربع مخ a square **1.2** quadrangular **2** *m.* square; quadrangle

مربع شانته murabba'shánta مربع شکله murabba'shákla quadrangular-shaped, square-shaped

مربعي murabba'í square مربعي منشور *mathematics* square prism

مربوط marbút *Arabic* **1** constrained; united; combined; joined, connected **2** په ... پورې relating to something; concerning something مربوط کول papers relating to the case مربوطي پاڼی *compound verb* ☞ مربوطېدل ☞ مربوط کېدل مربوطول **3** proper, appropriate مربوط مقام proper channels, appropriate authorities **4** subordinate, attached

مربوطات marbutát *m. plural Arabic* **1** holdings; areas, regions د ولايت مربوطات هرات the regions of Heart Province **2** sphere of action

مربوطول marbutawól *denominative, transitive* [*past:* مربوط يې کړ **1**] to join, annex; fasten, attach; tie, bind together **2** *military* to attach توپونه په غونډ مربوطول to attach artillery to a regiment **3** *figurative* to relate to something; tie, link with something

مربوطيت marbutiját *m. Arabic* connection, dependence

مربوطېدل marbutedól *denominative, intransitive* [*past:* مربوط شو **1**] to be joined, be annexed; be fastened, be attached; be connected (with), involve **2** *military* to be attached (to) **3** to relate to something, concern, involve something

مربوطين marbutín *m. plural Arabic* relative, relation د مړي مربوطين *law* relatives of the deceased

مربي murabbí *m. Arabic* [*plural:* مربيان murabbiján *and Arabic* مربيون murabbiján] **1** educator, tutor **2** patron, protector, sponsor

مرت mərt *m.* **1** myrtle **2** baby powder

مرتب murátáb, murattáb¹ *Arabic* **1** put in (good) order, put right مرتب ژوند an orderly life په مرتب ډول ساتل to keep in order **2** regular, systematic **3** regulated **4** developed, worked out (e.g., of a plan, program)

مرتب murattíb² *Arabic* **1.1** putting into (good) order; putting right **1.2** developing, working out (e.g., a plan, program) **2** *m.* [*plural:* مرتبان murattibán *and Arabic* مرتبين murattibín] **.1** organizer **2.2** creator, originator

مرتباً murattábán *Arabic* in order, in succession, one after the other; regularly; systematically

مرتبانه martabána *m.* glazed jug

مرتبط murtabít *Arabic* **1** closed, covered مرتبط لوښی covered dish **2** communicating **3** constrained

مرتبول muratabawól, murattabawól *denominative, transitive* [*past:* مرتب يې کړ **1**] to put into (good) order, put right, adjust **2** to regulate **3** to develop, work out (e.g., a program); create, prepare

مرتبه martabá *f. Arabic* [*plural:* مرتبې martabé *and m. plural: Arabic* مراتب marátíb] **1** rank, grade **2** degree **3** dignity, quality,

merit, virtue **4** *mathematics* order of magnitude (of numbers) په مرتبو سره *idiom* much, far, by far

مرتبېدل muratabedól, murattabedól *denominative, intransitive* [*past:* مرتب شو **1**] to be put into (good) order, be put right, be adjusted; be regulated **2** to be developed, be worked out (of a plan or program) **3** to be created, be readied **4** to be achieved, be reached (of a goal) هيڅ نتيجه يي پري مرتبه نه شوه *idiom* This did not yield any results. فايدي ورباندي مرتبېږي This gives certain advantages.

مرتجع murtadzhí' *Arabic* **1** *m.* [*plural:* مرتجعين murtadzhi'ín] reactionary **2** reactionary

مرتد murtád, murtádd *m. Arabic* **1** apostate **2** renegade, traitor, turncoat مرتد کېدل *compound verb* **a** to renounce, abandon (one's) faith **b** to become a renegade, be a traitor

مرتدوالی murtadwálaj *m.* **1** apostasy **2** desertion, treason

مرتضیٰ murtazá *Arabic* The Chosen One (epithet of Ali)

مرتفع murtafí' *Arabic* high, elevated, lofty

مرتقي murtaqí *Arabic* highly developed

مرتکب murtakíb *Arabic* **1** committing a crime **2** sinning

مرتهن murtahín¹ *m. Arabic* **1** mortgagee, pawnee **2** usurer, moneylender

مرتهن murtahán² *m. Arabic* pledge, pawn, pawned object

مرثيه mursijá *f. Arabic* **1** elegy **2** funeral oration **3** mourning

مرجان mardzhán *m.* **1** *plural* coral **2** *proper noun* Mardzhan

مرجانه mardzhána *f. proper noun* Mardzhana

مرجاني mardzhání coral

مرجح muradzhdzhíh¹ *Arabic* **1** preferring **2** *f.* preference

مرجح muradzhdzháh² preferable

مرجحاً muradzhdzhíhán *Arabic* preferably, preferentially

مرجع mardzhá' *f. Arabic* [*plural: m. & f.* مراجع marádzhí'] **1** authority **2** addressee **3** source (of a book, a journal, etc.)

مرجونا mardzhuná *m.* **1** pochard **2** pearl diver, pearl fisher

مرجيون mardzhiwán *m.* **1** diver **2** pearl diver

مرچ mrəch, mərch *m. plural* pepper سره مرچ red pepper تور مرچ black pepper

مرچک mərchák *m.* مرچکی mərchakáj¹ *m.* **1** red pepper د مرچکو seasoned with (lots of) pepper **2** irascible person, hot-tempered person لکه مرچک تک سور شو *idiom* He flared up. He got red as a lobster.

مرچکی mərchakáj¹ *m.* مرچک mərchák **1** red pepper **2** irascible person, hot-tempered person

مرچکی murchəkáj² *m.* oleander

مرچل murchál *m.* [*plural:* مرچلونه murchalúna *and Eastern f. plural:* مرچلي murchále] **1** ☞ سنگر **2** platform for shooting wild waterfowl **3** ditch

مرچه murchá¹ *f.* termite, white ant

مرچه murchá² *f.* rust (on iron)

مرچه murchá³ *f.* ☞ مرچل

مرغ marádz *m.* ☞ مرض

مرڅک mərtsák *m.* small lizard

مرشی martsáj *m.* ☞ مبرشی

مرشي توب martsitób *m.* emnity, hostility, animosity

مرشینگ martsíng *m.* 1 trowel 2 *dialect* pincers, tongs

مرحبا marhabā́ *Arabic* Welcome! زما دي درته مرحبا وي! I welcome you.

مرحله marhalā́ *f.* [*plural:* مرحلي marhalé *and m. plural Arabic* مراحل marāhíl] 1 stage, period; level, degree; phase ابتدايي مرحله initial stage کيفي مرحله qualitative degree پخواني مرحله the stage passed through اخري مرحلي ته رسېدل status quo ننني مرحله to approach the end 2 run; stage; stop a په لمړۍ مرحله کښ at the first stage b in the first leg (e.g, when traveling, between the first two stations or stops) c at the first stop d at once, immediately, right now

مرحمت marhamát *m. Arabic* [*plural:* مراحم marāhím] kindness, mercy پر چا باندي مرحمت کول to show kindness to someone; show mercy to someone

مرحوم marhúm *Arabic* deceased

مرخنی markhaṇáj *f.* jujube, *Ziziphus jujuba*

مرخپری markheṛáj *m.* mushroom

مرد [1] mard *m.* 1 man, male; person 2 brave man, courageous man, brave spirit 3 brave, noble, and decent person, real man يا دست مرد يا پای مرد *saying* … dást-i… pā́y-i… Either fight or run.

مرد [2] mərd *m.* knitted bone

مردار murdā́r 1.1 dead مرداري غوښي carrion 1.2 foul; unclean, dirty مرداري اوبه turbid water a مردار ډند swamp b cesspit, cesspool c *figurative* quagmire 1.3 bad, nasty, unpleasant, vile, mean, base, foul; wretched مردار ژوند a wretched life 2 *m.* مردار سړی scoundrel, villain مرداربدل *compound verb* ☞ carrion, dead flesh, a dead thing مرداري داني *medicine* herpes; shingles احمد تمام عمر په مردارو اوبو کښي ولاړ وي All his life Ahmed has been playing dirty tricks. Ahmed is an inveterate scoundrel.

مردارخواره murdārkhā́ra مردارخوار murdārkhā́r مردارخور murdārkhór 1 feeding on carrion (of animals) 2 *m. figurative* bribe-taker, grafter

مرداردانه murdārdānā́ *f. medicine* herpes; shingles

مردارسنگ murdārsáng *m.* massicot, lead monoxide, litharge, lead oxide

مردارول murdārawə́l *denominative, transitive* [*past:* مردار يې کړ] 1 to dirty, soil 2 to defile, profane *idiom* د نورو سپېن کالي ور مردارول to lay the blame on others

مرداره murdā́ra *f.* carrion; dead body, corpse

مردارهډی murdārhə́ḍaj *m.* donkey, ass, hinny

مرداري murdārí *m.* 1 dirt; nastiness; pollution, corruption 2 abomination, nasty thing, loathsome thing, vileness, meanness مرداري کول *compound verb* to act in a vile manner, behave atrociously, act underhandedly; play a dirty trick on

مرداربدل murdāredə́l *denominative, intransitive* [*past:* مردار شو] 1 to die (of animals) 2 to soil oneself, get dirty 3 to be defiled, be profaned

مردانه mardāná 1.1 courageous, brave 1.2 man's, men's (of clothes) 2 *f.* courage, bravery 3 courageously, bravely, like a man

مردانه ځای mardānadzáj *m. regional* hujra, men's house, house in the village where men gather or where guests stay

مردانگي mardānagí *f.* courage, valor

مردرو mardráw *m.* 1 parapet 2 breastwork

مردک mardə́k, mardák *m.* [*plural:* مردکونه mardəkúna, مردکان mardəkā́n *and* مردک mardák] cartridge; bullet; shell, round په زره high-explosive bomb سوري کوونکي مردک armor-piercing shell د مردک لار *military* trajectory مردک اچول، مردک اورول *compound verb* to fire on, shell

مردکه mardə́ka *f.* 1 ball (for playing lunki) مردکي کول to play lunki 2 fragment, splinter, shard

مردکي [1] mardə́ki *plural of* مردکه

مردکی [2] mardakáj *m.* 1 ☞ مردک 2 ☞ مردکه

مردکۍ [3] mardakə́j *f.* 1 ☞ مردک 2 ☞ مردکه

مردم mardúm *m. plural* people; the world, mankind, humanity

مردم آزار mardumāzár, mardumāzára 1 oppressing, oppressive 2 *m.* oppressor

مردن murdán *m.* death; dying

مردندان mardandā́n *m.* rye grass

مردود mardúd *Arabic* outcast, rejected, repudiated; damned, cursed, accursed

مردوي mardwí *f. biology* seed, sperm

مرده [1] mardá *f.* millstone axle

مرده [2] murdá 1 dead, deceased 2 *m.* [*plural:* مردگان murdagā́n] (dead) body, corpse

مرده رنگ murdaráng deathly pale

مرده سنگ murdasáng *m.* 1 lead oxide 2 white lead (a pigment)

مردي [1] mardí *f.* ☞ مړانه

مردي [2] mardí *f.* ☞ مردوي

مرزا mirzā́ mirza, scribe, clerk; secretary

مرستونه mrastwə́na assistance, cooperation, working together, support

مرستوال mrastwā́l *m.* ☞ مرستيال 1.1, 1.4

مرستون mrastún *m.* 1 shelter, refuge, almshouse, poorhouse 2 ☞ مرستيال 1

مرستونی mrastúnaj 1 helping; supporting, cooperating; auxiliary 2 *m.* assistant مرستونی سیند *idiom* tributary

مرسته mrásta *f.* 1 help, aid, assistance, support, cooperation اقتصادي مرسته economic aid اخلاقي مرسته، معنوي مرسته moral support صحي مرسته medical assistance بېغراضانه مرسته unselfish assistance مادي مرسته material aid د مرستي پیسي mutual assistance گډه مرسته a subsidy, grant-in-aid b donation in the form of money د چا په مرسته a with the help of, with the support of someone, with someone's cooperation b in collaboration with someone چا ته خورا to render someone great assistance يو تر بله سره ډېره مرسته رسول د مرستي لاس ورغزول to help each other to extend the hand of assistance د یو کار دپاره مرسته کول to further something 2 collaboration, cooperation سره مرسته کول a to aid, assist, show support, support, contribute (to) الوتکو د پیاده عسکرو سره مرسته وکړه aircraft acted in coordination with the infantry **b** to collaborate, cooperate د مجلي سره قلمي مرسته کول to collaborate in the magazine **3** textbook, training aid

مرستی mrastáj *m.* **1** person who is rendering assistance; assistant **2** *figurative* favorable factor د ژوند لوی مرستی لمر دئ The sun is the great source of life.

مرستيال mrastjál **1** *m.* **.1** assistant; deputy **1.2** apprentice **1.3** supporter, adherent, advocate **1.4** guardian, protector, patron **1.5** textbook, training aid **2** assisting, working with, contributing to

مرستياله mrastjála *feminine of* مرستيال

مرسل mursál¹ *Arabic* **1** sent, dispatched **2** *m.* messenger, envoy **3** prophet **4** missionary

مرسل mursíl² *Arabic* **1** sending, dispatching مرسله دستگاه radio transmitter مرسل ستیشن sending station **2** *m.* sender

مرسل اليه mursalalájh *m. Arabic* addressee, receiver, recipient

مرسله mursalá¹ *f. Arabic* [*plural:* مرسلي mursalé *and m. plural: Arabic* مرسلات mursalát] **1** message; letters **2** sending, dispatching

مرسله mursilá² *f. Arabic* (radio)transmitter د مرسلي تهسن transmitting radio station

مرسومات marsubát *m. plural Arabic geology* deposits

مرسول marsúl *Arabic* sent, dispatched; addressed

مرسوله marsulá *f. Arabic* item of mail; parcel; package, packet

مرسینگ marsíng *m.* ☞ مرځینگ

مرشد murshíd *m. Arabic* **1** murshid, spiritual tutor, mentor, director of pupils **2** teacher, preceptor

مرصع murassá' *Arabic* sprinkled with precious stones, decorated with jewels تاريخ مرصع tāríkh-i... "Tarikh-i murassa" (the title of a history of the Afghans written by Afzal-Khan Khattak)

مرض maráz *m. Arabic* [*plural:* مرضونه marazúna *and Arabic* امراض amráz] **1** illness, disease ساري مرض infectious disease د مرض تشخيص diagnosis **2** trouble, misfortune **3** ويروسي مرض *figurative* evil, vice

مرضي marzí¹ *Arabic* **1** pleasant; affording satisfaction; satisfying **2** *f.* **.1** satisfaction **2.2** desire, will; wish, inclination د مرضی پرخلاف in spite of (one's) desire ستا مرضي! as you choose, as you please, as you like

مرضي marazí² *Arabic* **1** sick, unhealthy; infirm, sick, feeble; delicate, sickly, morbid **2** pathological; pathogenic

مرطبانه martabán *m.* ☞ مرتبانه

مرطوب martúb *Arabic* **1** damp, wet, moist; moistened **2** blossoming, healthy

مرطوبول martubawól *denominative, transitive* [*past:* مرطوب يې کړ] to dampen, moisten, wet

مرعي mar'í *Arabic* **1** observed, kept, performed **2** common, generally used

مرعي الاجراً mar'ij-ul-idzhrá *Arabic* subject to being carried out, subject to being observed

مرغ mərgh¹ *m.* omen, augury بد مرغ bad omen ښه مرغ، نېک مرغ good omen د ښه مرغه ورځ lucky day د ښه مرغه څخه fortunately له بده مرغه، د بده مرغه unfortunately

مرغ mragh² *m.* **1** large stone being used in weight-lifting exercises; weights, dumbbells **2** fortunetelling with stones مرغ اچول *compound verb* to cast stones (in telling fortunes) مرغ نيول *compound verb* to tell fortunes from stones, read stones

مرغ mrəgh³ *m.* hearth made of clumps of earth (in the shape of a cone)

مرغ murgh⁴ *m.* bird

مرغاب murgháb *m.* Murgab (river)

مرغابی murghābə́j *f.* د مرغابيو ښکار duck hunting

مرغاچکه murghāchə́ka *f.* small pearl

مرغاو murgháw *m.* ☞ مرغاب

مرغباز murghbáz *m.* lover or handler of fighting birds

مرغ پلاو murghpaláw *m.* pilaf with chicken

مرغهتانه marghə́tána *f.* **1** dung beetle **2** dung ball **3** *dialect* eyeball د سترگي مرغتانه eyeball

مرغچچي marghəchíchaj *m.* [*usually plural* مرغچچي marghəchíchi] *botany* Our Lady's Tears, Job's Tears

مرغاچکه marghachə́ka *f.* ☞ مرغه چنه

مرغچي mərghəcháj *m.* necklace of Venetian (artificial) pearls

مرغړی maṛgharáj *m.* **1** gland **2** fatty tumor, lipoma

مرغړین margharín ☞ مرغلين

مرغ زار marghzár *m.* مرغزار meadow

مرغستوری mraghstóraj *m.* Jupiter

مرغسنه marghasə́na *f.* small cloud مرغسنه ده The sky is covered with light clouds.

مرغک mərghák *m.* **1** pin, peg (door, millstone) **2** disease of camels مرغک وتل *compound verb* **a** to come out (of a pin, peg) **b** to suffer a dislocation of the thighbone (of the hip) **c** to become sick (of camels)

مرغلره marghalə́ra *f.* **1** pearl **2** *proper noun* Margarita, Margalira مرغلري پاشل *idiom* to spread pearls of oratory

مرغلين marghalín twisted بنه مرغلين تارونه thread هر چا ته خپل مزی مرغلين دئ *proverb* Everyone thinks his own rope is strong.

مرغمري murghmurí *f.* epizootic disease of hens

مرغمی marghə́maj *m.* ☞ مرغومی

مرغوب marghúb *Arabic* **1** pleasant, attractive, nice **2** of good quality, high-quality

مرغوبيت marghubiját *m.* **1** pleasantness, attractiveness **2** high quality

مرغوتانی marghutáne *f.* anointing of a newborn with dough and oil

مرغوڅی marghútsaj *m.* ☞ مرد که

مرغوړتیا marghuṛtjá *f.* arrogance, haughtiness, loftiness

مرغوړنه marghuṛə́na *f.* مرغوړي marghuṛí *f.* arrogance, haughtiness, loftiness مرغوړي کول to put on airs

مرغوړي marghuṛí¹ *f.* arrogance, haughtiness, loftiness مرغوړي کول *compound verb* to put on airs

مرغوړی ² marghúṛaj *m.* arrogant person, conceited person

مرغوزی marghuzáj *m.* nestling, fledgling

مرغول marghúl, marghól *m.* مرغوله marghulá, margholá *f.* **1** locks, curls, ringlets **2** trill, warble; modulation

مرغومکی marghúmkaj *m.* **1** little billy-goat **2** name of a children's game

مرغومی ¹ marghúmaj *m.* **1** young goat **2** Capricorn (the constellation) د مرغومي مياشت Jadi (the tenth month of the solar year – December-January) **3** name of a children's game

مرغومۍ ² marghúme *f.* little nanny-goat

مرغه ¹ murghэ́, mərghэ́ *m.* [*plural:* مرغان murghán, mərghán] bird (often a bird of prey) د مرغانو خواره کوچنوتی مرغه little bird, birdie bird feed

مرغه ² marghá *f.* **1** Bermuda grass **2** any grass that produces turf or sod

مرغه ³ marghá *f.* مرغه چنه marghachэ́na lawn, grass plot

مرغه کاری marghakārí *f.* **1** laying out or seeding a lawn **2** sodding the ground

مرغي ¹ mərghí *f.* *used as the second element in word compounds* بدمرغي misfortune

مرغی ² mərgháj *m. diminutive* little bird, birdie مسافر د سبل مرغی *idiom* That's a migratory bird—here today, دئ، نن دلې صبا بل ځايي there tomorrow. هيڅ د مرغی لاره پرې نه ښودل not leave the smallest loophole

مرغی ³ mэ́rghaj *used as the second element in word compounds* بدمرغی unfortunate, unhappy

مرغی ⁴ murghэ́j, marghэ́j **1** bird, little bird, birdie بنده کړي مرغی decoy **2** *plural* birds **3** *proper noun* Murgi سترگی مرغی مرغی کښدل *idiom* **a** to stick together (of the eyes when one is drowsy or nodding off) **b** to be dazzled

مرغۍ ⁵ marghé *plural of* مرغه ²,³

مرغی پل murghэjpál *m.* pea vine, *Lotus corniculatus*

مرغېچی murghecháj *m.* boy who chases birds away from a seeded field; crop guard

مرغیخانه murghikhāná *f. regional* poultry yard, fowl run, hen house, chicken coop

مرغېدل mərghedэ́l *intransitive* [*past:* و مرغبده] to have (the) luck, be lucky

مرغی ډوډۍ murghəjḍoḍэ́j *f. botony* wild mallow

مرغېړی margheṛáj *m.* ☞ مرغوی

مرغی کڼی murghəjkaṇáj *m.* broomrape (a weed)

مرغیڼا marghiṇā́ *m.* idler, slacker, loafer, lazybones

مرفق mirfáq, marfáq *m. Arabic* **1** profitable thing; benefit, advantage, gain **2** handy thing, device, contrivance, gadget **3** elbow

مرفقیت mirfaqiját *m.* utility, advantage

مرقد marqád *m. Arabic* [*plural:* مرقدونه marqadúna *and Arabic* مراقد marāqíd] tomb; grave

مرقعه muraqqq'á *f. Arabic* **1** album **2** memorandum book, notebook

مرکانتیلزم merkāntilízm *m.* mercantilism

مرکچی marakāwú *m.* ☞ مرکاوو

مرکب ¹ murakkáb *Arabic* **1.1** mixed, compiled; constituent; consisting of something **1.2** complex, compound مرکبه کلمه *grammar* compound word مرکب فعل *grammar* denominative verb مرکبه جمله، مرکب عبارت *grammar* compound or complex sentence **2** make-up, structure

مرکب ² markáb *m.* **1** riding animal (horse or camel) **2** ship, vessel **3** saddle

مرکبات murakkabā́t *m. Arabic plural* **1** *of* مرکب ¹ **2** 2 *grammar* compound words **3** *chemistry* compounds

مرکبدل murakabedэ́l, murakkabedэ́l *denominative, intransitive* [*past:* مرکب شو] to be formed (of compound words, verbs, etc.)

مرکچی marakchí *m.* **1** representative, delegate **2** Jirga member **3** matchmaker **4** deputy **5** interlocutor

مرکز markáz *m. Arabic* [*plural:* مرکزونه markazúna *and Arabic* مراکز marākíz] center مرکز ثقل *physics figurative* center of gravity د دایرې مرکز *mathematics* center of a circle جنگي مرکزونه military bases د حکومت مرکز the capital (of د کابل په مرکز in Kabul (city) اجتماعي مرکز، دپتولني مرکز village club د ښپني مرکز scientific research center صحي مرکز first-aid station خپل حواس يو مرکز ته راغونډول to collect one's thoughts

مرکزی markazí *Arabic* **1** central مرکزي بانک central bank **2** middle

مرکزیت markaziját *m.* **1** central position **2** centralizaton, concentration **3** centralism

مرکند markánḍ *m. regional* gullet, throat له مرکنده نيول to seize by the throat

مرکنډۍ markanḍэ́j *f.* **1** occipital bone; occiput **2** upper cervical vertabra **3** *dialect* throat

مرکوال marakawāl *m.* **1** member of a delegation or group **2** matchmaker

مرکوز markúz *Arabic* **1** erected, hoisted, established; driven into **2** concentrated

مرکه maraká *f.* **1** delegation; committee, commission **2** conversation; talks, negotiations مرکه لږ ځه اوږده شوه The conversation was a bit drawn out. **3** meeting, conference مطبوعاتي مرکه press conference د چا سره مرکه کول **a** to converse with someone **b** to confer with someone **4** matchmaking مرکه ورکول *compound verb* to send matchmakers **5** soviet, council (an organ of governmental authority) د پښتو مرکه city council د بلديې مرکه *idiom history* Afghan circle, Afghan club (for philology)

مرکه چی marakachí **1** *m.* ☞ مرکچی **2** *m.* interlocutor **3** matchmaker

مرگ marg *m.* death مرگ او ژوند، مرگ اوژواک، تور مرگ life and death مرگ مفاجات sudden مرگ نيولئ dying, moribund مرگ murder death مرگ دي مهلمه شه! Drop dead! په مرگ محکومېدل to be sentenced to death د مرگ په خوب بيدېدل idiom **a** to die, be dying **b** to sleep a deep sleep **c** to exhibit negligence, show carelessness خان مرگ ته ور کول He was incurably ill. وه مله يې ناروغي د مرگ to risk (one's) life مرگ حق دئ، خلاصي تري نشته *Eastern* You can't escape death. د هغه دپاره مرگ لويه ده چه He is not afraid of death. په مرگ يې وئيسي، په تبه به راضي شي *saying* When death threatens you'll be glad for the fever. هلته کار د خره له مرگه ډېر دئ *idiom* There's a lot of work there. د مرگ په بستره on one's deathbed

مرگانه margāná **1** mortal, lethal, deadly **2** mortally مرگانه زخمي کېدل to be mortally wounded

مرگانۍ margānáj, margāní being near death په مرگاني ژول mortally

مرگبار margbā́r مرگ بار threatening with death

مرگټ margā́t *m.* place where Hindus bathe the deceased

مرگ ژواک marg-dzhwā́k *m.* ☞ مرگ ژواک

مرگ‌ری margə́raj *m. dialect* ☞ ملگري 1

مرگ ژواک marg-zhwā́k *m.* مرگ ژواک marg-gwā́k *m. dialect* **1** life and death **2** *figurative* joy and sorrow

مرگ ماهي marg-i-māhí *m. botony* mullein, *Verbascum*

مرگ موش marg-i-músh *m.* arsenic

مرگو margó *f.* **1** loss of cattle (from disease), epizooty **2** epidemic د مرگو دښت Dasht-i Margo (desert, southwestern Afghanistan)

مرگوټی margótaj *m.* ☞ مرگی 1

مرگوڼی marguṇáj *m.* forge

مرگی margí **1** fatal, mortal, deadly

مرگی margáj **2** *m. diminutive of* مرگ د مرگي آواز death cry مرگی راغئ چيغه پر چا کول to threaten someone with death Death came.

مرله marlá *f. regional* marla (a measure of area equal to about 4 square meters)

مرلۍ murláj *f.* reed pipe (snake catcher's)

مرم mrəm *present tense first person of* مړل

مرمت maramā́t, marammát *m. Arabic* **1** repairing, mending **2** curing, treating, (medical) treatment د چا مرمت کول *idiom* to deal with someone

مرمت کاري maramatkārí, marammatkārí *f.* repair, repair work

مرمر marmár *m. singular & plural* marble سنگ مرمر sáng-i... marble د مرمرو تيږي marble slabs

مرمرکاري marmarkārí *f.* marble facing

مرمري marmarí **1** marble, marbly مرمري کاڼی، مرمری ډبره marble

مرمری marmə́raj **2** *m.* maize at the milk-wax stage of ripeness

مرمرين marmarín marble, marbly

مرموز marmúz *Arabic* **1** secret, mysterious مرموز حکايات fairy tales **2** classified secret, secret **3** unrevealed, latent, hidden; not manifest

مرمي marmí *f. Arabic* [*m. plural:* مرميات marmijā́t] shell, projectile

مرند mrand *m.* dam, weir; millpond

مرنده mránda *f.* girl who is not permitted to marry into another clan or family because of enmity مرنده کښېنستل to stay unmarried because of enmity between tribes or families (of a girl)

مرڼی maraṇáj *f.* purslane, portulaca, rose moss

مرو marw *m.* **1** Merv (city) **2** *history* Mary (city)

مروان marwā́n *m. Arabic proper noun* Marvan

مروت muruwwā́t *m. Arabic* **1** generosity, magnanimity **2** valor, courage مروت کول *compound verb* **a** to show magnanimity, demonstrate generosity **b** to display courage, show valor

مروت marwā́t **1** *m. plural* Marvats (the tribe) **2** *m.* Marvat **3** *plural m.* Marvat (the region of the Marvat tribe)

مروت marwā́t *m.* **1** bends, twists, meanders **2** folds, creases **3** screw

مروت marwā́t *m.* rest, peace, calm, quiet

مروج murawwídzh *Arabic* **1** spreading, promoting sales, marketing **2** *m.* patron, sponsor, protector

مروج murawwā́dzh *Arabic* widespread, usual, common مروج پولونه money in circulation مروج نرخ fixed prices

[مروج شو murawwadzhedál *denominative, intransitive* [*past:* to be widespread, be widely accepted; spread widely

مرود murúd *m.* ☞ امروت

مرور murúr *m. Arabic* **1** passing, passage **2** course, duration, exiration (of time, a term, a period) په مرور د دې زماني upon expiration of this time, after this په مرور د زمان in time, in due course; law by prescription **3** affibility, urbanity; attention, consideration

مرور marawə́r, marawúr, marawár offended, treated badly زما نه مرور دئ He bears a grudge against me. مرور کول *compound verb* to offend, treat badly مرور کېدل، خان مرور کول *compound verb* to resent someone

مرورتوب marawartób *m.* مرورتیا marawərtjá *f.* offense, injury, resentment

مروروالی marawərwā́laj *m.* **1** ☞ مرورتیا **2** passion **3** fit of irritation; flash anger, fit of rage

[مرور یې کړ :marəwarawə́l *denominative, transitive* [*past* مرورول to offend someone, hurt someone's feelings, treat someone badly, insult someone

مروري maruri, marorí *f.* مروری maroráj *m.* **1** chamomile, matricaria **2** *regional botany* Helicteres isora

[مرور شو :marawəredál *denominative, intransitive* [*past* مرورېدل **1** to take offense, take umbrage, be hurt, resent **2** to grieve, be sad

مرور maróṛ *m.* **1** bends, twists, meanders **2** cramp, convulsion ورکول *compound verb* **a** to bend **b** to have a cramp, writhe (in pain)

[او یې مروړه :mroṛál *transitive* [*past* مروړل **1** to roll up; crumple; crush **2** to fracture, wrench, sprain (an arm) **3** to torment, harass **4** *figurative* to stifle, suppress (the spirit)

مروره ¹ mroṛá *f.* oil-soaked rag, cleaning patch (for cleaning firearms)

مروړه ² mróṛa *f.* bump, swelling (from an insect bite)

مروړه ³ mroṛə́ *m. plural* **1** rolling up; crumpling, wadding **2** fracturing, spraining (arms) **3** tormenting, harassing **4** stifling, suppressing (of the spirit)

مروړه ⁴ mroṛə́ *imperfect of* مروړل

مروړۍ mroṛáj *m.* colic, shooting pain

مرونډۍ marwanḍə́j *f.* kochia, Vitex negundo (yields a dye)

مروي ¹ marwí *adjective* of Merv, of Mary

مروۍ ² marwə́j *f.* chamomile

مره ¹ mra *imperative, imperfective aspect of* مړل

مره ² mra *used in* دومره، څومره، هغومره

مرهټه marhaṭá *m.* **1** Mahrat **2** state or nation of the Mahrats

مرهم marhám *m. Arabic* **1** plaster; ointment, liniment مرهم پری *Eastern* اينبودل to apply a plaster **2** *figurative* balm, consolation, comfort

مرهوتي marhotí *f.* ☞ مروړه ²

مرهون marhún *Arabic* **1** obliged, obligated, grateful to someone د چا مرهون کېدل to be grateful to someone **2** ...د to be dependent on something **3** pawned مرهون مال pawn مرهون پور a debt that is secured by pledged property خپل ژوند ستا مرهون بولم *idiom* My life belongs to you.

مرهونه marhuná *f. Arabic* pawn, thing pawned

مرئ ¹ mraj *present tense second person plural of* مړل

مري ² marí *f. Arabic* esophagus

مري ³ mri *present tense of* مړل

مرى ⁴ mraj *m.* ☞ مریى

مري ⁵ marə́j *f.* **1** throat د چا مري خپه کول، وچه مري، سره مري larynx د په ننبتي مري ويل to speak in a hoarse voice چا په مري گوتي اينبودل to take someone by the throat، څوک د مري څخه نيول **2** Adam's apple

مرى ⁶ marə́j *f.* **1** small ball **2** bead, beads **3** (glass) beads **4** talisman, charm شونډې يي مري مري کېدلي، خوله يي د ژړا مري مري کېدله *idiom* Her lips were trembling; she was about to burst into tears.

مرې ⁷ mre *present tense second person of* مړل

مريان mrajā́n *plural of* مریى

مريبه mríbə *in lieu of* مري *and* به

مربټی mareṭáj *m.* Mahrat مربټی وهل *idiom* to display bravery

مربجی maredzháj *m.* ☞ مربزی

مريخ marríkh *m. Arabic* Mars (the planet) د مریخ کره the planet Mars

مرید muríd *m. Arabic religion* murid, follower of a Sufi spiritual teacher-master or pir

مريدي muridí *f. religion* muridism مریدي کول *compound verb* to be a murid

مربزی marezáj *m.* مربزی maregáj *m.* entertainment on the occasion of the birth of a son مربزی کول *compound verb* to entertain, arrange an entertainment on the occasion of the birth of a son

مريض maríz *Arabic* **1** *m.* sick person, patient تذکرهٔ مریض tazkirá-yi... certificate of illness; medical certificate of unfitness for work, sick list **2** unhealthy, diseased (organ)

مریضي marizí *f.* illness, sickness, disease د مریضی رقعه declaration of illness (given by an employee) د مریضی سند medical certificate د مریضی په سبب برطرف سوئ excused from work because of illness

مربله mərelá *f.* **1** auspicious occasion, propitious occasion **2** turn

مریم marjám *f. Arabic* ☞ مریمه

مری ² marə́j-marə́j ☞ مری

مریمه marjáma *f. proper noun* Mariam, Maria

مرینډۍ mrinḍə́j *f.* **1** armful (of straw, hay) **2** bunch, small bouquet (of flowers)

مرینوس marinós, merinós *m.* ☞ مېرینوس

مرینه mariṇá *f.* **1** uncut strip (of a field) **2** unplowed field **3** meager crop, crop not yielding a harvest **4** unfinished business, unfinished work **5** confused affair, involved business **6** patch

مریه mrajə́ *m.* مریی mrajáj *m. [plural:* مریان mrajā́n *and* مریونه mrajúna*]* **1** slave **2** man, God's slave

مریي توب mrajitób *m.* slavery

مرېبل mərejə́l *transitive [past:* وي يي مرېبل*]* **1** to rinse **2** to filter, strain

مړ .1 ¹ məṛ *[f.* مړه mṛa *m. plural:* مړه mṛə *f. plural:* مړي mṛe*]* dead, deceased, passed away يا مړ يا مور *saying* It's all or nothing. **1.2** extinguished, gone out **1.3** flabby, limp, listless, feeble **1.4** standing, stagnant (of water) **1.5** sterile, barren, fruitless مړه مځکه mṛa... barren ground مړ کول *compound verb* **a** to kill, do away with **b** to exterminate, destroy **c** to extinguish, put out رونایي ورمره کول to put out the light **d** to exhaust, overwork (someone) له لوبي دي مړ کړ You starved him. **e** to torment, harass, exasperate له دپره غمه دي مړ کړم I miss you terribly. **f** to frighten, scare, frighten (someone) to death **g** to shame, put to shame, make ashamed of ځان مړ اچول مول ☞ مړ کېدل to pretend to be dead, feign death ځان مړ کول to commit suicide **2** *[plural:* مړه mṛə*]* dead person, corpse, the deceased د مړه خبره په مړه پسي ولاړه *saying* Whatever the deceased said it has gone with him. د مړه مال په مړه *saying* The deceased's property follows him. د مړه تر خوله پسي څي لوېدل *idiom* to get cold (of food); get stale مړه شپه *idiom* the night before a holiday

مړام mṛām **1** withered, faded, drooped **2** listless, lazy **3** flowing slowly (of water)

مړامتوب mṛāmtób *m.* مړامتیا mṛāmtjā́ *f.* **1** withering **2** inertia, listlessness **3** laziness

مړامجا mṛāmdzhā́ *m.* **1** listless person, lazy person **2** person who is pretending to be weak and feeble, one feigning weakness and feebleness

مړامول mṛāmawә́l *denominative, transitive* [*past:* مړام يې کړ] **1** to promote fading, contribute to fading **2** to make (someone) an idler, loafer, lazybones

مړامبدل mṛāmedә́l *denominative, intransitive* [*past:* مړام شو] **1** to wither **2** to be listless, be lazy **3** to perish

مړانه maṛā́na *f.* **1** courage, valor, bravery, heroism په مړانه کول *compound verb* to display courage, bravery, valor ده په مړانه ښه نوم گټلى دئ He was renowned for his bravery. **2** maturity, virility هلک مړاني وهلئ، هلک مړاني وهلئ دئ The boy has become a man. **3** generosity, magnanimity

مړاو mṛāw ☞ مړام

مړاوتیا mṛāwtjā́ *f.* ☞

مړاوول mṛāwawә́l *transitive* ☞ مړامول

مړاوی mṛā́waj **1** withered, faded **2** listless; lazy; *passive* مړاوی کول **3** sleepy (of the eyes) ☞ مراوبدل ☞ مراوی کبدل ☞ مراومول **4** dispirited, depressed, despondent, woebegone

مړاوی توب mṛāwajtób *m.* ☞ مړامتوب

مړاوبدل mṛāwedә́l *intransitive* ☞ مړامبدل

مړپوړ mәṛpóṛ [*f.* مړه پړه mṛapṛá, *m. plural:* مړه پړه mṛәpṛó *f. plural:* مړي پړي mṛepṛé] dead, departed, deceased; dead animal

مړت mәṛtә́t listless; lazy; *passive*

مړتوب mәṛtób *m.* ☞ مړتیا¹

مړتون mәṛtún *m.* cemetery, burial ground, graveyard

مړتیا¹ mәṛtjā́ *f.* **1** listlessness; laziness **2** death, dying

مړتیا² maṛtjā́ *f.* satiety, satiation ☞ موړتیا

مړتک mәṛták *m.* basting, tacking; basting thread, tacking thread

مړجوړا maṛdzhuṛā́ mean, vile, lowdown

مړجونی mәṛdzhúnaj **1** faded, drooping, withered **2** near death, dying, on the verge of death

مړځ maṛádz *f.* female quail, quail hen کرکری مړځ yellow-legged buttonquail, *Turnix tanki*

مړڅپن mәṛtsapә́n **1** wilted, withered **2** perished, killed, lost

مړڅپی mәṛtsápaj spiritless, listless; lazy

مړخندی¹ mәṛkhandáj *m.* smile

مړخندی² mәṛkhándaj smiling

مړخوبه mәṛkhóba sleeping like a log, being dead asleep

مړخوږک mәṛkhuẓák tubercular, consumptive

مړخوږی mәṛkhúgaj *m. Western* patient with tuberculosis; consumptive patient

مړخوږي mәṛkhugí *f.* tuberculosis, consupmtion

مړخولی mәṛkhúlaj *m.* indecisive person, ditherer, milksop

مړ maṛ *m.* **1** ☞ مرد¹ **2** saint; spiritual teacher, preceptor

مړدان maṛdā́n *m.* Mardan (city near Peshawar)

مړدک mәṛdák *m.* [*plural:* مړدک mәṛdә́k] bullet; cannonball

مړدکی maṛdakáj *m.* ☞ مړد ک

مړدن muṛdán *m.* ☞ مړدن

مړدې máṛde listen here, friend! مړدې عصمت! Listen here, Ismat!

مرز maṛә́z *m.* common quail

مرزباز maṛәzbā́z *m.* lover of quail fights

مرزگه mṛә́zga **1** scraggy, emaciated, not suitable for slaughter (of sheep, goats, etc.) مرزگي غوښي lean meat **2** *f.* worthless horse, worn-out horse, plug, jade

مرزه maṛә́za *f.* female quail, quail hen ښځه مرزه quail hen

مرژواند mәṛzhwā́nd مرژواندی mәṛzhwā́ndaj **1** half-alive, half-dead; neither alive nor dead مرژواند کول to beat someone to within an inch of his life په ډېرو وهلو یې مرژواند کړئ He was beaten half to death. **2** dying **3** faded, withered, lifeless, limp

مرسترگی mәṛstә́rgaj **1** sly, cunning **2** shameless, brazen, impudent, insolent, impertinent

مرستون mṛastún *m.* **1** cemetery, graveyard; eternal peace **2** tower of death (among the ancient Persians)

مرشومه mәṛshúma *f.* commemorative feast, funeral repast (arranged at the home of the deceased by his relatives and friends during the three days following the death) مرشومه کول *compound verb* to arrange a commemorative feast

مر شوی maṛ shә́waj (who has) died, passed away

مرښت maṛә́kht *m.* **1** saturation; satiety, satiation **2** *figurative* satisfaction

مرغکی mәṛghakә́j *f. botony* rush

مرغنډی mәṛghanḍә́j *f.* discord, dissension

مرغون mәṛghún مرغونجا mәṛghundzhā́, مرغونجی marghundzháj **1** wilted, faded **2** lazy مرغون کبدل *compound verb* **a** to fade, droop, wither **b** to grow lazy, become lazy

مرغونی mәṛaghúne *f. plural* colocynth, bitter apple; wild watermelon

مرغبجن mәṛghedzhә́n مرغبژن mәṛghechә́n مرغبژن mәṛghezhә́n **1** half alive دی مرغبجن غوندي و He was scarcely alive. **2** faded, wilted **3** torpid **4** sad, melancholy (eyes, a look) **5** pale (of the face)

مرغونجی mәṛkandí ☞ مرکندي

مرکونه mәṛkawә́na *f.* murder, assassination

مړل mṛә́l *intransitive* [*present:* مري *past:* مړ شو *and* ومړ] **1** to die, pass away **2** to die out, go out, be extinguished, die down **3** to come to a standstill, end, cease, die, fade away **4** to be emaciated, be physically exhausted, be worn out **5** to worry about, torment oneself, exhaust oneself with له غمه مړ شو He exhausted himself with grief. **6** to frighten, frighten to death **7** to be struck dumb, be speechless, be dumbfounded, be stupified هم در څخه مرم، هم درپسي *saying* When you aren't here I long for you; when you are with me I die from you: can't live with you and can't live without you

مرمزک maṛmәzák *m.* marmazak (a variety of sweet apple)

مرمند mәṛmánd *m.* ☞ مروند

مرنتوب maṛantób *m.* ☞ مړانه

مرنی¹ maṛanáj **1.1** courageous, bold, valorous, brave **1.2** capable (academically) **1.3** skillful, able ☞ ماهر **2** *m.* **.1** hero, brave man, bold spirit, daredevil **2.2** academically gifted person **2.3** expert **2.4** skilled craftsman

مړنۍ ² maṛanə́j *feminine to* مړنی ¹

مړو ¹ maṛó *oblique plural of* مړه

مړو ² mṛo *oblique plural of* مړ

مړو ³ maṛó *oblique plural of* موړ ¹

مړواک məṛwắk *m.* مړواکی məṛwắkaj *m.* executor (of someone's will)

مړوالی ¹ məṛwắlaj **1** death **2** cancellation, state of being cancelled (e.g., of a postage stamp)

مړوالی ² maṛwắlaj *m.* saturation; satiety, satiation

مړوب maṛób **1** watered, given to drink (of animals) **2** watered, irrigated (of fields, etc.)

مړوبول maṛobawə́l *denominative, transitive* [*past:* مړوب يې کړ] **1** to water, give to drink (animals) **2** to water, irrigate (e.g., fields)

مړوبېدل maṛobedə́l *denominative, intransitive* [*past:* مړوب شو] **1** to have something to drink; quench, slake one's thirst **2** to be watered, be irrigated

مړوچ maṛwách powerful, strong

مړوچتوب maṛwachtób *m.* مروچ توب force, strength, power

مړوخوا mṛokhwắ *f.* north

مړخولی məṛkhúlaj **1** taciturn, silent, untalkative **2** shy, bashful

مړوس mṛus *paired word with* بروس

مړوسه máṛosá *f.* stucco decorations, plaster decorations (on doors, walls, and in niches)

مړوښه maṛóẍha *f.* married woman

مړوښي maṛóẍhí *f.* marriage, matrimony, family life

مړوکی mṛókaj *m.* roll of dough that is thrown into the fire in order to safeguard against the evil eye

مړول ¹ maṛawə́l *denominative, transitive* [*past:* موړ يې کړ] to satiete, sate خپل ځان مړول *compound verb* to be full, be sated, eat one's fill حاجتونه مړول *idiom* to satisfy one's needs

مړول ² maṛawə́l *denominative, transitive* [*past:* مړ يې کړ] to extinguish, put out, snuff out

مړولونی məṛwlúnaj (who is) washing the deceased

مړوند maṛwánd *m.* **1** wrist **2** hand هر کار په خپل مړوند سره ته رسول to do everything with one's own hands

مړوندۍ maṛwandə́j *f.* ☞ مروندۍ

مړونه ¹ maṛúna *plural of* مړه

مړونه ² maṛawə́na *f.* saturation, satiety, satiation

مړونی maṛúnaj mortal, deadly, fatal مړونی قبر (the) grave

مړونکی maṛawúnkaj saturating; feeding, giving food to the point of satiety

مړه ¹ maṛá old chap, old fellow, old boy, lad, laddie ☞ مړه

مړه ² móṛa *f.* shawl; lap robe; blanket

مړه ³ mṛə *plural & oblique singular of* مړ

مړه ⁴ mṛa *feminine of* مړ

مړه ⁵ maṛá *feminine of* موړ ¹

مړه پره mṛəpṛá *m.* **1** *plural of* مړ پر مړه پره ² mṛapṛá *feminine singular of* مړ پر

مړه تبه mṛa tə́ba *f.* fever with a not very high temperature, low-grade fever that is extremely exhausting for the patient; subfebrile condition

مړه خوا ¹ maṛakhwắ **1** *f.* satiety, satiation **2** *attributive* **.1** full, sated **2.2** content, satisfied مړه خوا نظر contented look

مړه خوا ² mṛakhwắ unwillingly, reluctantly

مړه خوايي maṛakhwājí *f.* **1** satiety, satiation **2** pleasure, satisfaction

مړه خوږ mṛəkhwə́g *m. plural* **1** tuberculosis, consumption **2** *regional* dropsy

مړه خوګ mṛəkhwə́g *m. regional* dropsy

مړه خوی maṛakhój *m.* rich, high-calorie food

مړهکه məṛháka *f.* wasting fever; consumption

مړهکی məṛhákaj sick with a wasting fever; consumptive

مړه کبده mṛəkedə́ *m. plural* **1** dying **2** extinction; dying away, dying down شمع مړه کبدو ته نژدي ده The candle will soon go out.

مړهکه mṛalúne *f.* مړهی تبه maṛhəjtə́ba *f.* ☞ مړه لونې

مړی ¹ móṛaj **1** murdered, killed, slain; dead **2** *m.* **.1** deceased **2.2** corpse, dead body د مړي جسد corpse

مړی ² maṛáj *m.* thick log of wood beneath a millstone that bears its shaft

مړی ³ muráj *m.* ram, male sheep

مړی ⁴ maṛáj *f.* **1** piece يوه مړی ډوډی piece of bread **2** drink, mouthful, sip, gulp **3** food; bread a سپوره مړی dry bread, stale bread b dry food يوه مړی ډوډی مونږ ته رسبده We earned our daily bread. د چور و چپاو مړی گزبدل to be subjected to plundering

مړې ⁵ mṛe *feminine plural of* مړ

مړې ⁶ maṛé *feminine plural of* موړ ¹

مړې ⁷ móṛe *feminine singular of* مړی ¹ **1**

مړېدل maṛedə́l *denominative, intransitive* [*past:* موړ شو] **1** to become sated, eat one's fill **2** *figurative* to grow cold towards, lose interest in something **3** *figurative* to be satisfied (of requirements, etc.) سترګي می د هغې په لیدو نه or زه یې په لیدو نه مړېږم مړېږي *idiom* I can never see enough of her.

مړېدنه maṛedə́na *f.* **1** satiety, satiation; saturation **2** plenty, abundance

مړېده maṛedə́ *m. plural* **1** saturation **2** *figurative* cooling off towards, losing interest in something

مړېستان məṛestắn *m.* مړېستون məṛestún *m.* cemetery, graveyard

مړېکه maṛéka *f.* ☞ مړهکه

مړینه mṛína *f.* **1** death, demise مرګ او مړینه کول to pass away غوارم او نه بدنامي *saying* Better death than disgrace. **2** mortality, death rate د ورو مړینه infant mortality

مړیي ¹ məṛjají sheep, sheep's, ovine; ram, ram's مړیي غوښه mutton مړیي مستې sour sheep's milk

مړی ² muṛjáj 1 sheep's, ram's 2 *m.* .1 sheepskin 2.2 mutton tallow

مز muz *m.* payment (for grinding flour, etc.)

مزاج mizādzh *m. Arabic* 1 character, temperament; disposition 2 health status دا خبره یې په مزاج بده لګیږي *idiom* He doesn't like that.

مزاج پرسي mizādzhpursí *f. regional* ☞ احوال پرسي

مزاجي mizādzhí 1 *medicine* organic 2 caprice, whim

مزاح muzáh *f. Arabic* 1 joke; prank 2 parody

مزاحم muzāhím *Arabic* 1 blocking, preventing, hindering 2 feeling shy, diffident or nervous, awkward 3 causing anxiety, causing uneasiness

مزاحمت muzāhamát *m. Arabic* [مزاحمونه muzāhamatúna *and* مزاحمات muzāhamāt] constraint, uneasiness, difficulty, embarrassment

مزادګي mazādgáj *m.* two-year-old camel

مزار ¹ mazār *m. Arabic* [*plural:* مزارات mazārāt] tomb, grave, mazar; place of worship, place of pilgrimage

مزار ² mazār *m. abbreviated form of* مزارشریف

مزارستان mazāristān *m.* cemetery

مزارشریف mazār-i-sharíf *m.* Mazar-i-Sharif د مزارشریف نایب الحکومګي *history* Mazar-i-Sharif Province, دمزارشریف ولایت

مزارع ¹ muzāri' *m. Arabic* farmer, agriculturalist, tiller of the soil

مزارع ² mazāri' *m. plural Arabic of* مزرعه

مزاري mazārí *colloquial* Mazar, of or pertaining to Mazar; Mazar-i-Sharif, of or pertaining to Mazar-i-Sharif

مزایا mazājā *m. & f. plural Arabic of* مزیت

مزایده muzājadá *f. Arabic* selling by auction; auction

مزبله mazbalá *f. Arabic* trash heap, garbage pile; dump

مزبور mazbúr *Arabic* aforementioned, aforesaid, above-mentioned

مزج mazdzh *m. Arabic* 1 mixture, blending, merger 2 solution مزج کېدل، یو د بل سره مزج مزجول مزج کول *compound verb* ☞ *compound verb* to mix, blend

مزجول mazdzhawól *denominative, transitive* [*past:* مزج یې کړ] 1 to mix, blend 2 to dissolve

مزخرف muzakhráf, muzkharáf *Arabic* 1 deceptive, false, lying, mendacious 2 absurd, ridiculous, preposterous; senseless, foolish 3 coarse, rough; tawdry (of decoration, ornamentation)

مزخرفات muzakhrafāt *m. plural Arabic* 1 absurdity, nonsense 2 bragging, boasting

مزد muzd mazd *m.* payment for work; wages مزد ډېرول to raise someone's pay تر مزد یې شکرانه ډېره ده، تر مزد یې شکرانه زیاته کړه، تر مزد یې شکرانه ډېره کړه gift given as a token of gratitude (for work done) that is worth more than the earnings

مزدک muzdók *m.* 1 enclosed place 2 mosque

مزدګري mazdgáraj *m.* miller

مزدور mazdúr *m.* 1 hired worker, wage worker; day laborer; unskilled laborer; farm laborer, hired hand 2 loader, carrier, coolie

مزدور ساتل 3 servant *compound verb* to keep a servant 4 worker بې شته مزدوران، د مزدورو ډله، د مزدورانو ډله the proletariat

مزدورکار mazdurkār *m.* 1 worker, working man 2 worker, employee

مزدوره mazdúra *f.* (female) worker

مزدوري mazdurí *f.* 1 work for hire; day work; working as or being a farm laborer 2 hard physical labor, unskilled work مزدوري کول *compound verb* a to work for hire; work as a day laborer; work as a farm hand b to do hard physical labor, do unskilled labor 3 pay for work, wages 4 payment, fee, compensation (e.g., to a doctor) 5 labor, work د مزدوري محصول product of labor

مزده mazdó, muzdó *m. singular & plural* miller, millers

مزرعه mazra'á *f. Arabic* [*plural:* مزرعي mazra'é *and m. plural Arabic* مزارع mazārí'] 1 sowing, sown field 2 farm مزرعه نمونه mazra'á-yi... demonstration farm

مزروع mazrú' *Arabic* مزروعي mazru'í sown, planted مزروع سیمه sown or planted area, area under crops; cultivated area

مزري ¹ mazərí *f.* sandals made from dwarf palm leaves

مزري ² mzaráj *m. Eastern* tiger غټ مزری، شین مزری lion ☞ زمری

مزري ³ mazə́raj *m.* dwarf palm tree

مزري ⁴ mzarə́j *f.* 1 tigress 2 lioness

مزري توب mzaritób *m.* bravery

مزرینه mazrína *f.* article made from the leaves of the dwarf palm مزرینه خولۍ a hat made of dwarf palm leaves

مزغاړي muzghā́rj *m.* 1 small wineskin 2 tobacco pouch 3 small bag (for antimony)

مزغي mazgháj *m. dialect* ☞ مغزی ¹

مزکه mzə́ka *f. dialect* 1 land, ground خرابه مزکه wasteland 2 floor ☞ مځکه

مزګټو mazgaṭə́w *m.* earthenware pot that is set into the ground near a mill and into which tips for the miller's assistant are tossed

مزل mazál *m.* passage, transition; run; stage, distance between stops ښار د پنځو میلو مزل دئ د الوتکو مزل flight distance The city is at a distance of five miles. مزل کول، مزل وهل *compound verb* a to travel b to go, drive, ride; follow ټوله شپه مو مزل وکړ We rode all night. c to flow (of a river) ☞ منزل

مزلځای mazaldzáj *m.* rabat, caravanserai

مزله mazalá *f.* ☞ منزله

مزمار mazmā́r *m.* kind of flute

مزمزه mazmazá *f. Arabic* movement, agitation, oscillation, fluctuation

مزمن muzmín *Arabic* chronic مزمن مرض chronic illness مزمن بحران perpetual crisis

مزور ¹ muzawwár *Arabic* false, spurious, fake, counterfeit, sham

مزور ² muzawwír *m. Arabic* 1 liar 2 falsifier

مزه ¹ mazá *f.* 1 (pleasant) taste په مزه خوړل to eat with satisfaction 2 interest دا ډېره د مزي قصه ده This is an interesting story. مزه خوړل to lose all interest in 3 pleasure مزه اخیستل *compound verb* a to

703

taste, try, partake (of) **b** to obtain pleasure, get satisfaction مزه كول، مزه راكول *compound verb* to be to one's taste; afford pleasure, be pleasant دا به مزي كوي That will be very pleasant. مزه لرل ته ډېره مزه راكوي I like the rural life. **a** to have a pleasant taste **b** to afford pleasure, give satisfaction, be pleasant مونږ په مزه او په خوند وگرځېدو We took a very pleasant walk. په مزه *idiom* lively, animatedly, gaily

مزه ² mə́za *f. computer science* cable

مزه دار mazadā́r مزه ناك mazanā́k **1** tasty; sweet, aromatic **2** pleasant مزه دار مازیگر pleasant evening **3** interesting, attractive

مزى ¹ mə́zaj, múzaj *m.* **1** wire; conductor د تېلفون مزى telephone wire مزى تپرول *compound verb* to lay wire, wire; install wiring د تېلفون مزى وهل، مزى وهل to install a telephone **2** thread **3** lisle thread **4** tent rope **5** bowstring **6** selvage, edge (of fabric) **7** *figurative* bonds, ties (e.g., of friendship) د دوستانه روابطو مزي تينگول to strengthen the bonds of friendship

مزى ² mə́zaj, mázaj **1** firm, stable **2** musclular, stalwart, hefty **3** prompt, quick, expeditious مزى كول *compound verb* **a** to strengthen, reinforce **b** to cause to be prompt, make quick

مزى ³ mazé *plural of* مزه

مزيت mazijā́t *m. Arabic* [*plural:* مزيتونه mazijatúna *and Arabic* مزايا mazājā́] superiority; quality, merit, virtue

مزى تاوونكى mə́zaj tāwawúnkaj *m.* rope-maker

مزید mazíd *Arabic* **1** addition; increase **2.1** additional, supplemental مزید معلومات additional information **2** increased; added, supplemented

مزيدار mazedā́r *dialect* ☞ مزه دار

مزین muzajján *Arabic* decorated, embellished مزین گزول *compound verb* to decorate, embellish, adorn

مژده muzhdá *f.* joyful news, glad tidings

مږ ¹ mag *m.* [*plural:* مږونه mgúna, magúna *and* مږه mgə مږان magā́n] **1** ram, male sheep **2** mouflon; arkhar

مږ ² mug *present stem of* منبل

مږك ¹ mugák, məgák *m.* mouse مږك په غار نسواي ننوتلاى، جارو يې په لكۍ پورې غوټه كئ *saying Western literally* The mouse wouldn't crawl into its hole, and, what's more, it tied a broom to its tail. *figurative* Don't bite off more than you can chew. د دوى په كور كښي *saying* There's nothing in the house. د مږك لكۍ نه سپره كېده (*literally:* In the house a mouse couldn't get his tail dirty.) د مږك غار په نه شايي غوښتل، د مږك غار په نه شاهي غوښتل *saying* to wish the earth would open up and swallow one (out of shame; *literally:* Ready to buy a mouse hole for nine shahi.)

مږك ² mūgák *m. computer science* mouse

مږك باز mugakbā́z *m.* common buzzard (bird)

مږك تڼى mū́gák tə́ṇə́j *f. computer science* mouse button

مږك جړ mugakdzhár *m.* arsenic

مږك خور mugakkhór *m.* ☞ مږك باز

مږك رانه mugakrā́na *f.* mousehole, mouse burrow

مږك كيڼه تڼى mūgák kiṇa tə́ṇə́j *f. computer science* left mouse button

مږكورى mugakúraj, m6gakúraj *m.* baby mouse, young mouse

مږك لنډلار mūgák landlā́r *m. computer science* mouse shortcut

مږك وهونكى məgák wahúnkaj **1** *m.* common kestrel (bird) **2** ☞ موشگيرك

مږل mugə́l *transitive* ☞ منبل

مږم múgəm *first person present of* منبل

مږور mgor *f. dialect* ☞ نږور

مږوى məgwáj *m. dialect* ☞ موږى

مږه ¹ mə́ga *f.* **1** rat; large field mouse **2** calf (of the leg)

مږه ² mgə *plural of* مږ

مږ كورى məgakúraj *m.* ☞ مږه كورى

مږمه məgemá *f.* مږبمه كېدل *compound verb* to be in head (of a ewe)

مس ¹ mis *m. plural* cuprite, red copper ore خړ مس gray copper ore شنه مس cuprite, cuprous oxide سره مس copper glance, chalcocite د مسو كان copper deposits

مس ² miss *f.* miss (title)

مسا masā́ *f.* smile په مسا ويل to say with a smile

مسابقاتي musābiqā́ti competition, competitive مسابقاتي عمليات competitive competition

مسابقه musābiqá *f. Arabic* [*plural:* مسابقې musābiqé *and m. plural: Arabic* مسابقات musābiqā́t] **1** contest, competition د چا د مسابقې جواب ويل to enter a competition with someone **2** rivalry مسابقه كول *compound verb* **a** to conduct a competition **b** to compete (with) شر كتونه يو له بله سره مسابقه كوي The companies are competing with one another. د تسليحاتو مسابقه، تسليحاتي مسابقه *idiom* arms race

مسافر musāpə́r *m.* ☞

مسافر توب musāpərtób *m.* ☞ مسافرت

مساجد musādzhíd *m. plural Arabic of* مسجد

مساح massā́h *m. Arabic* land surveyor

مساحت masāhát *m.* مساحه masāhá *f. Arabic* **1** area; surface; space د مساحه مكتب topographers' school د مساحه مدير chief of the topographic department (in a province) **2** land surveying, setting boundaries مساحه كول *compound verb* to measure (land, area); conduct a (land) survey

مساعد musā'íd *Arabic* favoring, promoting; favorable, suitable مساعده فضا favorable circumstance يو شي ته په مساعد نظر كتل to regard something favorably

مساعدت musā'idát *m. Arabic* مساعدوالى musā'idwā́laj *m.* **1** promoting, furthering, assistance, help, favoring مساعدت كول *compound verb* to promote, further, render assistance, favor **2** favorability (of circumstances) **3** suitability, fitness كه وخت مساعدت وكړي *idiom* If time permits.

مساعدول musā'idawə́l *denominative, transitive* [*past:* مساعد يې كړ] to make favorable, make suitable; assist, render aid; further, promote, favor

مساعدېدۀل musā'idedә́l *denominative, intransitive* [*past:* مساعد شو] to be favorable, be appropriate, be suitable

مساعي masā'í *f. plural Arabic of* مسعي [2] [*m. plural:* مساعیات musā'ijā́t] effort; endeavor تشریک مساعیات joint efforts

مسافت masāfā́t *m. Arabic* ☞ مسافه

مسافر musāfír, musāpir *m. Arabic* [*plural:* مسافران musāfirā́n *and Arabic* مسافرین musāfirín] traveler; wayfarer

مسافرت musāfarā́t *m. Arabic* [*plural:* مسافرتونه musāfaratúna *and Arabic* مسافرات musāfirā́t مسافري musāfirí *f.* journey; voyage د مسافراتو مخصوصه پانه tourist permit

مسافره musāfíra *feminine to* مسافر هغه ښځه بل ښارته مسافره شوه She went to another city.

مسافرېدۀل musāfiredә́l *denominative, intransitive* [*past:* مسافر شو] to set out on a trip, depart

مسافه masāfā́ *f. Arabic* [*plural:* مسافي masāfé *and m. plural: Arabic* مسافات masāfā́t] distance; interval; space, span له مګکي ☞ له مګکي څخه تر ټولو نژدې مسافه apogee څخه تر ټولو ليري مسافه perigee ☞ مسافه اندازه کول to measure (the) distance

مسألت masa'lā́t *m. Arabic* ☞ مسئله

مسالمت musālamā́t *m. Arabic* 1 pacification; calming, quieting 2 peace; reconciliation د چا سره مسالمت کول to be reconciled with someone خبره تر مسالمت په ډول فیصله کول to decide a question by peaceful means

مسالمت آمیزه musālamat-āméza مسالمت آمیز musālamat-améz peaceful; peace-loving مسالمت آمیزه گډ ژوند peaceful coexistence

مسالمت کارانه musālamatkārāná 1 peaceful, peace-loving مسالمت کارانه فیصله the peaceful resolution of an issue 2 peacefully, peaceably

مسالمه musālamá *f. Arabic* ☞ مسالمت

مساله masālā́ *f.* 1 seasoning, relish; spice د طعام مساله spice 2 material(s) د جوړښت دپاره مساله construction materials ☞ مصالح [1]

مسأله mas'ālā́ *f.* ☞ مسئله [2]

مساله باب masālabā́b *m. plural* مساله جات masāladzhā́t *m.* spice(s)

مساله یي masālají marinated, pickled مساله یي کب pickled fish

مسام masā́mm *m. Arabic* [*plural:* مسامونه masāmmúna, *Arabic* مسام masā́m, masā́mm *and* مسامات masāmmā́t] pore, body pores

مسامحه musāmahá *f. Arabic* connivance, winking at; carelessness, negligence, laxity

مسامحه کاري musāmahakārí *f.* don't-care attitude towards one's work, negligence, laxity

مساند masāníd *m. plural Arabic of* مسند [1]

مساوات musāwā́t *m. Arabic* equality مادي مساوات property equality د چا سره د مساوات په اقتصادي مساوات economic equality پنه دریدل to be on an equal footing with someone

مساوي musāwí *Arabic* 1 equal; same; equivalent په صفر مساوي equal to zero په مساوي ډول مساوي حقوق equal rights on equal principles مساوي ارزش لرل to be of equal worth 2 *sports* tie, draw

مساویانه musāwijāná 1 equal, same 2 on equal principles, equally

مساوي والی musāwiwā́laj *m. mathematics* equality, equation

مسائل masā'íl *m.* مسائل *plural Arabic of* مسئله

مس بار misbā́r *m.* 1 copper alloy; tombak (a copper-zinc alloy) 2 borer, drill, auger

مسبب [1] musabbáb *Arabic* conditioned (by), causing something

مسبب [2] musabbíb *Arabic* 1 being conditioned (by), causing something 2 *m.* .1 instigator; perpetrator; inciter, firebrand 2.2 [*plural:* مسببات musabbibā́t] stimulus, motive, inducement

مسبوق masbúq *Arabic* 1 already informed, warned 2 passed, surpassed, overtaken, left behind

مست mast 1.1 drunk, intoxicated 1.2 excited, flushed (with) مست آس fast horse 1.3 rapid, wild (a river, stream) 1.4 lively, quick 1.5 proud 1.6 passionate, ardent; furious, violent, unrestrained 1.7 wild, excited (of an elephant in heat) 2 *m. proper noun* Mast په عشق مست *idiom* besotted with love

مستاجر mustādzhír *m. Arabic* [*plural:* مستاجران mustādzhirā́n *and Arabic* مستاجرین mustādzhirín] renter, leaseholder, tenant, lessee

مستانه mastāná 1.1 drunk, intoxicated 1.2 excited, flushed (with) 1.3 lively, quick 1.4 experiencing rapture, ecstasy 2.1 drunkenly 2.2 excitedly, flushed 2.3 lively, quickly 2.4 rapturously, ecstatically

مستاوه mastāwá *f.* rice soup flavored with sour milk

مستبد mustabā́d, mustabā́dd *Arabic* 1 despotic مستبد حکومت despotism 2 *m.* despot, tyrant

مستیا mәstapā́ *f.* name of a game

مستتر mustatár *Arabic* 1 closed, secret; covered, muffled 2 meant, understood (of a word)

مستثمر mustasmír *m. Arabic* exploiter

مستثنأ mustasnā́ *Arabic* 1.1 excluded مستثنأ گڼل، مستثنأ پیژندل to exclude د عسکري خدمت څخه مستثنأ excused from military service 1.2 exceptional, special 2 *f.* [*m. plural Arabic* مستثنأات mustasnāā́t] exception

مستثناوالی mustanāwā́laj *m.* exclusiveness

مستثنأ mustasnā́ *Arabic* ☞ مستثنأ

مستحب mustaháb, mustahább *Arabic* 1 beloved, favorite, pet, pleasing; approved 2 desirable

مستحصل mustahsál *m. Arabic* product

مستحضر mustahzár *Arabic* informed له یو شي مستحضر کېدل to learn about something

مستحق mustahíq, mustahíqq *Arabic* deserving, worthy; having the right to something; deserved; (as an honorific) honored د استراحت مستحق having the right to rest مستحق گڼل to consider to be deserving مستحق گڼل کېدل to be worthy of something

مستحکم mustahkám *Arabic* secured, strengthened

مستحکمي mustahkamí *f.* 1 securing, strengthening 2 reinforcement

مستحیل mustahíl *Arabic* impossible, improbable

مستخدم mustakhdám *Arabic* **1** *m.* [*plural:* مستخدمین mustakhdamín] employee, office worker حربي مستخدم (military) serviceman **2** being in service

مستدام mustadǻm *Arabic* **1** long, lengthy **2** eternal, perpetual

مستدل mustadál *Arabic* (well-)founded, valid, sound; proven, demonstrated

مستراح mustarǻ, mustarǻh *f. Arabic* restroom, toilet, latrine د تلویث مستراح sanitation, waste water treatment

مسترد mustarád, mustarádd *Arabic* **1** returned, received back **2** recapture (e.g., of an inhabitied place) **3** rejected, turned down, declined مسترد کول مستردول *compound verb* ☞ مسترد کبدل *compound verb* ☞ مستردبدل

مستردول mustaradawól, mustaraddawól *denominative, transitive* [*past:* مسترد یې کړ] **1** to return, give back **2** to recapture, take back, retake (i.e., an inhabited place) **3** to reject, turn down, decline

مستردبدل mustaradedól, mustaraddedól *denominative, intransitive* [*past:* مسترد شو] **1** to be returned, taken back; be returned **2** to be captured, be retaken (e.g., of an inhabited place) **3** to be rejected, be declined

مستري mistrí *m.* **1** master, skilled craftsman **2** artisan, workman

مستریح mustaríh *Arabic* quiet, calm, tranquil

مستري خانه mistrikhāní *f.* shop, workshop

مستزاد mustazǻd *Arabic* **1** increased, augmented **2** *m. literature* mustazad (special verse form in which to each line there is added a short supplementary line having its own rhythmic pattern)

مستشار mustashǻr *m. Arabic* **1** counsellor د سفارت مستشار Counsellor of Embassy **2** consultant

مستشرق mustashríq *m. Arabic* Orientalist, Asianist

مستشعر mustasha'ír *Arabic* comprehending, knowing something و یو کارته مستشعر کبدل to examine, scrutinize, go deeply into a matter په ... مستشعر کول to give to understand something

مستطاب mustatǻb *Arabic* **1** highly honored, greatly revered **2** fine, beautiful, excellent, magnificent

مستطیل mustatíl *Arabic mathematics* **1.1** oblong, elongated **1.2** rectangular **2** *m.* rectangle

مستطیلي شکله mustatilshákla مستطیلي mustatilí rectangular, right-angled

مستظرف mustazríf *Arabic* **1** refined, elegant **2** representational, figurative مستظرفه صنایع مدرسه the fine arts د مستظرفه صنایعو مدرسه school for the arts

مستعار musta'ǻr *Arabic* **1** borrowed مستعار نوم pseudonym **2** used in a figurative way, figuratively

مستعجل musta'dzhíl *Arabic* **1** urgent; pressing, rush **2** speeded up, accelerated

مستعد musta'íd *Arabic* **1** capable, able; talented **2** prepared, trained, ready **3** disposed towards something

مستعفي musta'fí *Arabic* retiring, going into retirement, applying for retirement, sending in one's resignation

مستعمر ¹ musta'mír *m. Arabic* colonizer, colonialist

مستعمر ² musta'már *Arabic* colonized

مستعمرات musta'marǻt *m. plural Arabic of* مستعمره

مستعمراتي musta'marātí **1** colonial مستعمراتي محصولات، مستعمراتي واردات colonial goods **2** *m.* colonist

مستعمره musta'mará *f. Arabic* [*plural:* مستعمري musta'maré *and m. plural: Arabic* مستعمرات musta'marǻt] colony د مستعمرو وزارت history The Colonial Office (in Great Britain) د مستعمراتو وزیر minister of colonial affairs

مستعمره چي musta'marachí *m.* colonizer

مستعمل musta'mál *Arabic* used, applied in general use; having been in use, formerly in use or used; secondhand مستعملي اوبه *idiom* stagnant water

مستعملول musta'malawól *denominative, transitive* [*past:* مستعمل یې کړ] **1** to use, apply, employ **2** to wear (clothes, etc.)

مستعملبدل musta'maledól *denominative, intransitive* [*past:* مستعمل شو] to be used, be applied, be employed

مستغرق mustaghráq *Arabic* **1** sunken, immersed **2** sunk, drowned

مستغني mustaghní *Arabic* **1** not in need of something دا مقاله د اصلاح څخه مستغني نه ده This article still needs to be corrected. **2** rich, well-to-do **3** independent, self-reliant له یو شي څخه مستغني کول to free from something

مستفید mustafíd *Arabic* benefiting from, profiting by, making use of something ☞ د یو شي څخه مستفید کبدل مستفیدبدل

مستفیدبدل mustafidedól *denominative, intransitive* [*past:* مستفید شو] to use, utilize something

مستقبل mustaqbál *Arabic* **1** future مستقبل فعل future tense form of a verb مستقبله زمانه future tense **2** *m. grammar* **1.** future tense **2.2** future, futurity په لنډ مستقبل کښي in the near future

مستقبلتوب mustaqbaltób *m. grammar* future tense

مستقل mustaqíl, mustaqíll *Arabic* **1** independent, self-reliant دا کار تر هغه مستقل دئ This matter does not depend on him. مستقل گرزبدل render independent مستقل مدیر head of department د زراعت مستقل ریاست chief directorate of agriculture **2** detached, non-integrated په مستقل ډول زده کړه special مستقل کنډ ک detached battalion **3** self-education

مستقلاً mustaqíllán *Arabic* independently, on one's own

مستقلانه mustaqilāná, mustaqillāná **1** self-reliant, independent **2** on one's own, independently

مستقل مزاجه mustaqilmizǻdzha, mustaqillmizǻdzha self-reliant, independent (of a person)

مستقیم mustaqím **1** straight مستقیم خط straight line **2** direct, immediate مستقیم انتخابات direct elections **3** staunch, loyal

مستقیماً mustaqímán *Arabic* directly, immediately

مستک masták *m.* **1** rye grass **2** grass pea, *Lathyrus sativus* (causes the disease lathyrism in humans)

مستکی mastakáj *m.* salty kurut (dried balls of fermented milk or milk curds)

مستلزم mustalzím *Arabic* **1** entailing, causing, requiring something **2** cause, factor

مستمري mustamirrí *f. Arabic* **1** retirement benefit, pension مستمري تنخواه، مستمري معاش pension **2** increment, bonus

مستملک mustamlák *Arabic* **1** owned by **2** *m.* [*plural:* مستملکونه mustamlakúna *and Arabic* مستملکات mustamlakát] .**1** dominion, property holding **2.2** colony

مستملکات mustamlakát *m. plural Arabic* **1** ☞ مستملک[1] **2** colonies

مستملکه mustamlaká *f. Arabic* **1** dominion, holding **2** colony

مستند mustanád *Arabic* **1.1** founded, grounded, substantiated **1.2** documented مستند فلم documentary movie **2** *m.* foundation, base

مستوبه mastóba *f.* rice soup laced with yogurt

مستور mastúr[1] *Arabic* **1** closed **2** chaste; modest **3** concealed, secret

مستور mastúr[2] ☞ مسطور

مستورات masturát *f. Arabic plural* **1** *of* مستوره **2** women د مستوراتو شفاخانه women's hospital

مستوره masturá *f. Arabic* [*plural:* مستوري masturé *and f. plural Arabic* مستورات masturát] chaste, modest female

مستوري masturí[1] *f.* chastity; modesty

مستوري masturé[2] *plural of* مستوره

مستوفي mustaufí *m. Arabic* mustoufi, manager of provincial finance

مستوفیت mustaufiját *m. Arabic* managing provincial finance

مستول mastawə́l *denominative, transitive* [*past:* مست یې کړ] **1** to inebriate, intoxicate **2** to excite, arouse **3** to gladden, exhilarate

مستوي mustawí *Arabic* **1** even, smooth (of surface) **2** flat

مستهلک mustahlík[1] *Arabic* **1** consuming **2** *m.* [*plural:* مستهلکین mustahlikín] consumer

مستهلک mustahlák[2] *Arabic* **1** consumed **2** depreciated, settled (of a debt) **3** annihilated, destroyed

مستي mastí[1] *f.* **1** inebriation **2** excitement, arousal **3** exuberance, exhilaration په ډېره مستي خندل to laugh joyfully **4** boisterous, agility, rambunctiousness **5** pride **6** high-spiritedness, ardor **7** frolicking; amusements **8** turbulent flow (of a river), turbulence داوبو مستي freshet

مستي masté[2] *f. plural* boiled fermented milk, yogurt

مستیاره mastjára *f.* wormwood, absinthium, *Artemisia absinthium*

مستبدل mastedə́l *denominative, intransitive* [*past:* مست شو] **1** to drink, booze **2** to get excited, get all worked up **3** to frisk, frolic; make merry

مستر mistár *m.* mister, Mr.

مسجد masdzhíd *m. Arabic* [*plural:* مسجدونه masjidúna *and Arabic* مساجد masájíd] mosque جامع مسجد mosque serving the population of an area

مسجع musadzhdzhá' *Arabic* **1** rhymed مسجع کول *compound verb* to rhyme **2** *f.* rhymed prose

مسح mash *m. Arabic* مسحه *f.* másha **1** stroking, patting **2** touching **3** wiping, rubdown مسح کول *compound verb* **a** to stroke, pat **b** to touch **c** to wipe, rub down سر مسح کول to wipe one's head (during a namaz)

مسخ maskh *m. Arabic* **1** disfiguration, distortion مسخ کول *compound verb* to distort (e.g., fact, reality) **2** metamorphosis, change

مسخر musakhkhár *Arabic* vanquished, brought into submission, conquered

مسخرگي maskharagí *f.* clowning, buffoonery, antics

مسخره maskhará *f. Arabic* ridicule, joke مسخرې وربوري کول to mock دچا د مسخرو شی کېدل to become a laughingstock

مسخره باز maskharabáz *m.* ☞ مسخره چي

مسخره توب maskharatób *m.* ☞ مسخرگي

مسخره چي maskharachí *m.* **1** mocker, joker **2** buffoon

مسخه musakhá ☞ مسیخ

مسدس musaddás *m. Arabic* **1** hexagon **2** stanza consisting of six hemistiches

مسدسي musaddasí *Arabic* hexagonal

مسدود masdúd *Arabic* **1** blocked, obstructed, closed **2** discontinued, suspended مسدود کول *compound verb* **a** to block, obstruct, close **b** to discontinue, suspend مسدود کېدل *compound verb* **a** to be blocked, close **b** to be discontinued, be suspended

مسر məsr *dialect* ☞ مشر

مسرت masarrát *m. Arabic* joy, exuberance

مسرف musríf *Arabic* wasteful

مسري misrí[1] *m. plural* ☞ مصري[1]

مسری misrə́j[2] *f.* folk song verse

مسطح musattáh *Arabic* smooth, even باغ مسطح کول to smooth the soil in the garden

مسطر mistár مسطره mistará *f. Arabic* **1** ruler **2** template (to draw lines with)

مسطور mastúr *Arabic* written

مسطوره masturá *f. Arabic* sample, specimen

مسعود mas'úd *Arabic* **1.1** happy, blessed, fortunate **2** prosperous د چا حالت مسعود کول **a** to make somebody happy **b** to improve a situation **2.1** *m. plural* Masouds (a tribe) **2** *m.* Masoud

مسقط masqát *m. Arabic* **1** impact point **2** birthplace, homeland **3** Maskat

مسک məsk[1] *m.* smile

مسک musk[2] *dialect* smiling

مسکا məská *f. regional* smile

مسکاوو məskāwú مسکاوی məskáway with a ready smile

مسکتوب məsktób *m.* quality of being with a ready smile

مسکتیا məsktjá *f.* kind smile

مسکر muskír *Arabic* inebriating, intoxicating

مسکرات [1] muskirất *m. plural Arabic* [*singular:* مسکر] **1** alcoholic (malty) beverages **2** toast

مسکرات [2] musakkarất *m. plural Arabic* sweets, candies

مسککی məskəkáj *m.* person with a ready smile; vivacious person

مسکن maskán *m. Arabic* **1** residence, abode **2** *trade* domicile

مسکنت maskanát *m. Arabic* poverty, squalor; need

مسکو maskáw *m.* Moscow مسکو اوسېدونکی د Muscovite

مسکوټ miskóṭ *m. regional* officers' mess

مسکوک maskúk *Arabic* hammered, embossed

مسکوکات maskukất *m. plural Arabic* hard cash

مسکول muskawə́l, məskawə́l *denominative, transitive* [*past:* مسکی یې کړ] to make somebody smile

مسکون maskún *Arabic* inhabited, populated مسکون ٻر کزونه inhabited localities

مسکوي maskawí, maskawáj **1** Moscow **2** Muscovite

مسکه [1] mə́ska *f.* woman who had a miscarriage

مسکه [2] maská *f.* butter

مسکی muskáj smiling مسکی کول مسکول *compound verb* ☞ مسکېدل *compound verb* ☞

مسکېدل muskedə́l, məskedə́l *denominative, intransitive* [*past:* مسکی شو] to smile

مسکین miskín *Arabic* **1** *m.* beggar, pauper **2** poor; squalid

مسکینت miskinát *m.* poverty, squalor

مسکینه miskiná *f.* ☞ نسکینه

مسگر misgár *m.* coppersmith

مسگري misgarí *f.* coppersmithing

مسل masə́l [*past:* ده ومسل و یې مسل] to smile He smiled.

مسلح musalláh *Arabic* armed مسلح قوا armed forces مسلح کول *compound verb* to arm مسلح کېدل مسلح کول to get armed *compound verb* to get armed

مسلحانه musallahāná armed مسلحانه اغتشاش *a* mutiny *b* armed rebellion

مسلخ maslákh *m. Arabic* slaughterhouse

مسلسل musalsál *Arabic* **1.1** consistent, systematical **1.2** continuous, having continuity **2** consistently, systematically دا مجله بنه بنه مضامین مسلسل لیکي This magazine regularly publishes interesting articles.

مسلط musallát *Arabic* **1** having gained ownership; dominant; owning **2** dominating مسلط کېدل *compound verb* to dominate, prevail, reign یو مسلط سړی *idiom* a domineering person

مسلک maslák *m. Arabic* **1** occupation, trade, specialty **2** industry **3** *military* branch **4** doctrine, worldview د روښان مسلک worldview, doctrine of Roshan بودايي مسلک Buddhism

مسلکي maslakí *Arabic* **1** professional مسلکي تعلیمات vocational training غیر مسلکي مامورین career officers مسلکي صاحب منصبان civilian employees **2** special مسلکي شعبه special department

مسلم [1] musallám *Arabic* obvious; indubitable; unquestionable دا یو مسلم او منل سوئ حقیقت دئ مسلمه ده چه This is a undoubtedly commonly recognized and indisputable truth.

مسلم [2] muslím, maslím Muslim مسلم لیگ Muslim League

مسلمات musallamất *m. plural Arabic* axioms, indisputable truths

مسلم لیگي maslím-ligí, muslím-ligí **1** belonging to the Muslim League **2** *m.* participant in the Muslim League

مسلمان musalmā́n *m. Arabic* Muslim; Mohammedan

مسلمانه musalmā́na *f.* Muslim woman; Mohammedan woman مسلمانه ښڅه Muslim woman; Mohammedan woman

مسلماني musalmā́ní *f.* Islamism; Mohammedanism

مسلمانېدل musalmānedə́l *denominative, intransitive* [*past:* مسلمان شو] to convert to Islam

مسلمه [1] muslimá *f. Arabic* Muslim woman; Mohammedan woman

مسلمه [2] musalláma *feminine singular of* مسلم [1]

مسلول maslúl *m. Arabic* [*plural* مسلولین maslulín] person sick with tuberculosis

مسله masalá *f.* prayer rug

مسلئ [1] masə́laj *past participle of* مسل

مسلی [2] masaláj *m.* [*plural* مسلیان masaliyä́n] **1** ☞ مصلي [2] regional winnower (worker)

مسلی [3] masalə́j *feminine of* مسلی [1]

مسموم masmúm *masc. Arabic* poisoned مسموم کول *compound verb* ☞ مسموم کېدل مسمومول *compound verb* ☞ مسمومېدل

مسمومول masmumawə́l *denominative, transitive* [*past:* مسموم یې کړ] to poison

مسمومیت masmumiját *m. Arabic* quality of being poisoned

مسمومېدل masmumedə́l *denominative, intransitive* [*past:* مسموم سو] to be poisoned

مسمي [1] masammí *Arabic* porous

مسمی [2] musammấ *Arabic* named, called, nicknamed

مسن musín, musínn *Arabic* old; aged; elderly

مسند [1] masnád *m. Arabic* [*plural* مسندونه masnadúna *and Arabic* مساند masāníd] **1** support **2** throne **3** high position **4** large pillow

مسند [2] musnád *m. Arabic grammar* predicate

مسند علیه musnadaléjh *m. Arabic grammar* subject

مسنون masnún *Arabic* having become customary, having become common practice

مسنه masə́na *f.* smile

مسواک miswák *m. Arabic* **1** toothpick **2** toothbrush پر غاښونو مسواک وهل to brush one's teeth

مسواکي ، مسواکه گوته، مسواکه گته miswáka index finger گوته، مسواکي گته index finger

مسعود masúd ☞ مسعود

مسوده musawwadá, maswadá *f. Arabic* **1** draft, draft note, outline; sketch **1.2** testing, experiment, test, trial د مسودې په ډول as an experiment **1.3** project (i.e., of a law, plan) د قانون مسوده draft law مسوده کول *compound verb* **a** to make a draft, register, draft, sketch **b** to do as an experiment **c** to draw up a plan, formulate a project مسوده کېدل *compound verb* to be done (a draft, project) **2** attempt, experiment **3** draft, bill (e.g., of a law, plan)

مسور [1] maswár *m. botany* safflower, bastard saffron *Carthamus tinctorius*

مسور [2] masúr *m.* variety of lentil

مسول məsawór *transitive* [*past:* و یې مساوه] to make smile, bring forth a smile

مسوه maswá *f.* drained fermented milk

مسویک məsoják *m.* leveret

مسه [1] mása *f.* patting مسه کول *compound verb* to pat ☞ مسحه

مسه [2] mása *contraction of* مه *and* سه

مسهل mushíl *m. Arabic* laxative

مسي [1] misí copper مسي لوښي copper utensils

مسی [2] masáj smiling

مسی [3] masój *feminine singular and plural of* مسی

مسی [4] masój *f.* women's head ornaments

مسیح masíh *m.* مسیحا masihā́ *m. Arabic* Messiah, Christ

مسیحي masihí **1** Christian; of the common era, A.D. (of a calendar) نوی مسیحي کال new year **2** Christian, Christian woman

مسیخ massíkh *Arabic* **1** transformed, transfigured **2** disfigured; distorted

مسېدل masedól, musedól *intransitive* [*past:* و مسېد، و مسېده] to smile

مسېده məsedó *m. plural* smile

مسیر masír *m. Arabic* **1** line, track; route **2** bed, course (of a river) **3** track (of thought)

مسیسیپي misisípi, missisípi *f.* Mississippi د مسیسیپي دریاب Mississippi River

مسئلت mas'alát *m.* مسئله mas'alá *f. Arabic* [*plural:* مسئلي mas'alé *and m. plural: Arabic* مسائل mas'āíl] **1** issue, problem اقتصادي مسائل economic issues **2** task, mission حربي مسئلت combat mission **3** problem **4** *religion* commandment; precepts of a religion

مسئله دان mas'aladā́n *m.* مسئله گو mas'alagú *m.* mentor, adept of religious creed

مسین misín, məsín ☞ مسي

مسینه misiná, məsiná *f.* copper utensils, copperware

مسئول mas'úl **1** responsible د چا په نزد مسئول دئ، چاته مسئول دئ He is accountable to somebody. له یو شي څخه مسئول کېدل to be responsible, be accountable for something; bear responsibility for something **2** *m.* [*plural:* مسئولین mas'ulín] high-ranking official; individual in charge

مسئولیت mas'uliját *m. Arabic* responsibility مسئولیتونه یې ټول په خپله He took full responsibility on himself. له مسئولیت غاړه اختي وو to avoid responsibility و چا ته مسئولیت لرل څخه وتل to be accountable to somebody

مسئولېدل mas'uledól *denominative, intransitive* [*past:* مسئول شو] to bear responsibility; be responsible شخصاً مسئولېدل to be personally responsible

مش məsh *m.* **1** bosom **2** inside pocket

مشابه mushābíh *Arabic* resembling, similar, analogous د دي سره مشابه similar to this

مشابهت mushābahát *m.* مشابهه mushābahá *f. Arabic* resemblance, similarity, analogy دیو شي سره ډیر مشابهت لرل to be very similar to مقایسه او مشابهت .They are very similar یو د بله سره ډیر مشابهت لري کول to compare

مشاته mashātá, mushātá *f.* face; ugly mug, muzzle, snout

مشاجره mushādzhará *f. Arabic* [*plural:* مشاجري mushājaré *and m. plural: Arabic* مشاجرات mushājarā́t] dispute, conflict; feud

مشاد mushā́d, məshā́d **1** ugly, hideous **2** gloomy, bleak

مشاده mushādá *f.* ☞ مشاته

مشار mushā́r *Arabic* indicated, mentioned, said

مشارالیه mushārilájh, mushārunilájh *Arabic* **1** referenced, above-mentioned, said (male) **2** *m.* above-mentioned person, he

مشارالیها mushārilájhā, mushārunilájhā *Arabic* **1** referenced, above-mentioned, said (female) **2** *f.* above-mentioned person, she

مشارالیهم mushārunilájhum *Arabic* **1** referenced, above-mentioned, said **2** *m. plural* above-mentioned persons, they

مشارکت mushārakát *m. Arabic* **1** partnership; company **2** participation په یو کار کېني مشارکت کول to take part in a business

مشاعر mashā'ír *m. plural Arabic of* مشعر

مشاعره mushā'ará *f. Arabic* competition of poets, poetic tournament

مشاغل mashāghíl *m. plural Arabic of* مشغله

مشاق mashshā́q *m. Arabic* **1** instructor **2** coach

مشال mashā́l *m.* **1** torch **2** pine chip **3** torch; leader

مشالداني mashāldāní *f.* **1** torch stand **2** floor lamp

مشاور mushāwír *m. Arabic* **1** counsel, advisor; counselor of embassy **2** consultant فني مشاور science and technology consultant

مشاورت mushāwarát *m. Arabic* ☞ مشاوره

مشاورتي mushāwaratí advisory; consultative

مشاوره mushāwará *f. Arabic* meeting; consultation

مشاوري mushāwirí *f.* position or duties of an advisor

مشاوریت mushāwiriját *m.* consultative office; advisors

مشاهدوي mushāhadawí observed

مشاهده mushāhadá *f. Arabic* **1** examination **2** observation د مشاهدي دقت power of observation مشاهده کول *compound verb* **a** to examine **b** to observe, watch مشاهده کېدل *compound verb* to be observed

مشاهده کوونکی mushāhadá kawúnkaj *m.* **1** observer **2** visitor (e.g., to a museum)

مشاهیر mashāhír *m. plural Arabic of* مشهور famous, renowned, outstanding people; celebrities

مشایخ mashājíkh *m. plural Arabic of* شیخ

مشایعین mushāji'ín *m. plural Arabic* those accompanying a dead body

مشبه mushabbáh *Arabic* being likened; being compared مشبه کول *compound verb* to liken, compare

مشت musht *m.* fist (of a hand) مشت او گریوان کول *idiom* to make variance, mischief between زه ددي احساس سره مشت او گریوان وم I was fighting this feeling.

مشتاق mushtā́q *Arabic* 1.1 craving, yearning something 1.2 loving; in love 1.3 passionate, ardent 2 *proper noun* Mushtak

مشتبه mushtabíh *Arabic* doubtful, ambiguous, unclear, obscure, convoluted

مشترک [1] mushtarík *m. Arabic* [plural: مشترکین mushtarikín] 1 participant 2 subscriber د مجلې مشترک magazine subscriber

a مشترک [2] mushtarák *Arabic* 1 common, joint, shared مشترک لغات synonyms b homonyms مشترک مالکيت joint property 2 mixed

مشترکاً mushtarákán *Arabic* together, jointly

مشتري mushtarí *m. Arabic* 1 client, customer, patron 2 Jupiter (the planet)

مشت زن mushtzán *m.* boxer; fistfighter

مشتعل mushta'íl *Arabic* 1 breaking out, flaming up, flaring 2 *figurative* excited, upset

مشتق mushtáq, mushtáqq *Arabic* derivative

مشتقات mushtaqā́t, mushtaqqā́t *m. plural Arabic* [singular: مشتق] 1 derived words, derivatives 2 *chemistry* derivatives

مشتقول mushtaqawə́l, mushtaqqawə́l *denominative, transitive* [past: مشتق يې کړ] produce, create

مشتقيدل mushtaqedə́l, mushtaqqedə́l *denominative, intransitive* [past: مشتق شو] to be produced, be created

مشتمل mushtamíl *Arabic* containing, comprising; consisting of somebody or something

مشته məshtá, mushtá *f.* beetle (wooden hammer), mallet

مشتبيدل mishtedə́l *denominative, intransitive* ☞ ميشتبيدل

مشخص [1] mushakhkhís *Arabic* 1 distinguishing, recognizing 2 *linguistics* diacritic 3 *medicine* symptomatic

مشخص [2] mushakhkhás *Arabic* 1 definite, isolated, special (of a quality, property) 2 recognized, diagnosed

مشخصات mushakhkhisā́t *m. plural Arabic* [singular: مشخص] 1 indicators 2 distinguishing marks

مشخصول mushakhasawə́l, mushakhkhasawə́l *denominative, transitive* [past: مشخص يې کړ] to isolate, differentiate

مشخصيدل mushakhasedə́l, mushakhkhasedə́l *denominative, intransitive* [past: مشخص شو] to get isolated, be differentiated; diverge, differ

مشدد mushaddád *Arabic* 1 strengthened, reinforced 2 *linguistics* double (of consonants)

مشر mə́shər, məshr 1 senior (in age, position) هيوادپنځه کاله په ذهين باندي مشر دئ Hewad is five years older than Zaheen. د مشر لار د کشر پل دئ *proverb* The path of an older person is a bridge for a younger one. 2 *m.* [plural: مشران məshrā́n, məshərā́n] .1 chief, head, leader د جمهور مشر tribal chief قامي مشر president of republic د کلي مشر village elder جنگي مشر military leader مشر کبدل *compound verb* to appoint head مشر کبدل *compound verb* to become the head; head 2.2 patriarch 2.3 chiefs, leaders,

noblemen; ancestors مشرانو جرگه، د مشرانو جرگه upper chamber of the parliament; council of elders, senate

مشرانه məshrāná *f.* share allotted to the eldest son when something is divided (property, land, etc.)

مشراني məshrāni *feminine plural of* مشر

مشرب mashráb *m. Arabic* disposition, temper

مشرتوب məshərtób *m.* 1 authority, leadership د چا تر مشرتابه لاندي under someone's leadership 2 seniority 3 position of a chairman د دي ټولني په مشرتوب معرفي شو He was nominated to the position of the chairman of this society.

مشرتون məshərtún *m.* authorities, directorate

مشرتيا məshərtjá *f.* ☞ مشرتوب

مشررانزي məshrrānzí 1 *m. plural* Myshranzi (tribes) 2 məshrrānzáy *m.* Myshrranzay

مشرف musharráf *Arabic* 1 dignified; meriting the honor 2 ennobled

مشرفول musharrafawə́l *denominative, transitive* [past: مشرف يې کړ] to dignify; honor ده يوه نشان مشرفول award an order

مشرفبدل musharrafedə́l *denominative, intransitive* [past: مشرف شو] to merit, be honored; have the honor د چا په حضور مشرفبدل be received by somebody

مشرفبده musharrafedə́ *m. plural* bestowing an honor, honoring

مشرق mashríq, mashréq *m. Arabic* 1 east, sunrise 2 East, Orient منځنی مشرق Middle East

مشرقي mashriqí 1 eastern مشرقي افغانستان East Afghanistan مشرقي ولايت، مشرقي خوا Eastern, Jalalabad Province (now Nangarhar Province) 2 *m.* Eastern Province (now Nangarhar)

مشرقي وال mashriqiwā́l *m.* inhabitant of the Eastern Province

مشرک mushrík *m. Arabic religion* infidel; polytheist; idol worshipper; heathen

مشرنزي məshranzí *m. plural* ☞ مشررانزي

مشروالی məshərwā́laj *m.* ☞ مشرتوب

مشروب mashrúb *Arabic* 1.1 given something to drink 1.2 irrigated 2 *m.* [plural: مشروبات mashrubā́t] beverage

مشروپي mashrupáj *m.* striped fabric used to make women's trousers

مشروټي məshroṭáj *m.* 1 precociously mature and smart youth 2 precocious child

مشروط mashrút *Arabic* stipulated, specified په مشروط ډول، په مشروط as agreed مشروط کول *compound verb* to stipulate مشروط صورت کبدل *compound verb* to be stipulated

مشروطه mashrutá *Arabic* 1 *f.* constitution 2 constitutional مشروطه شاهي constitutional monarchy

مشروطيت mashrutiját *m.* 1 constitutional regime, constitutionalism 2 *grammar* conditionality

مشروع mashrú' *Arabic* 1 lawful, legal, permitted مشروع حقوق lawful rights يو حکومت مشروع پيژندل recognized the government *de jure* 2 just مشروع غوښتنه just demand مشروع بلل consider just (e.g., a demand)

مشروعاً mashrú'án *Arabic* lawfully, legally

مشروعیت mashru'iját *m. Arabic* 1 lawfulness, legality 2 justice

مشرولی məshərwalí *f.* ☞ مشرتوب

مشري [1] məshrí *f.* 1 seniority چا ته مشري ورکول elect somebody a leader 2 د مشری حق primogeniture 2 chief position, authority 3 priority د مشری حق لرل have priority

مشری [2] məshráj senior; elder

مشعر mash'ár *m. Arabic* [*plural:* مشاعر mashā'ír] 1 sensation, sense; vision, hearing 2 mind, intelligence مشاعر ذهني mental capacities

مشعشع musha'shí' *Arabic* 1 glittering, resplendent 2 high-flown, grandiloquent

مشعل mash'ál *m. Arabic* ☞ مشال

مشغله mashghalá *f. Arabic* [*plural:* مشغلي mashghalé *and m. plural: Arabic* مشاغل mashāghíl] occupation, business, work د چا په لاس کښې مشغله ورکول to give somebody a job مشاغلو ته to look for a job خان ته مشغله پیدا کول دوام ورکول to go on with the study

مشغول mashghúl *Arabic* engaged, busy (with work, business) مشغول کېدل مشغولول *compound verb* ☞ مشغول کول *compound verb* ☞ د عسکري خدمت مشغولېدل *idiom* subject to military draft

مشغولا mashghulá *f.* مشغولتیا mashghultyá *f.* 1 occupation, business, work, labor د کار او ماغي مشغولا intellectual work مشغولا په وخت کښي زده کړه part-time studies (while keeping a job) 2 entertainment مشغولا کول د مشغولا شیان amusement and games *compound verb* a to be occupied with something b to be entertained, have fun

مشغولول mashghulawəl *denominative, transitive* [*past:* مشغول یي کړ] occupy with something په تاریخ باندي خان مشغولول to be occupied with the study of history ذهنونه مشغولول، د ماغونه مشغولول *idiom* occupy the minds; attract attention

مشغوله mashghulá *f.* مشغولیت mashghuliyát *m. Arabic* ☞ مشغولا

مشغولېدل mashghuledəl *denominative, intransitive* [*past:* مشغول شو] 1 to be occupied, be busy with something د چا په خدمت مشغولېدل serve somebody 2 to be entertained, have fun

مشفق mushfíq *Arabic* 1 kind, kindhearted; gentle 2 *m.* friend

مشق mashq *m. Arabic* 1 exercise, training مشق کول *compound verb* to exercise, train, practice 2 drill ceremony حربي مشق کول undergo drill 3 rigorous drill 4 penmanship, calligraphy sample د لیکلو مشق cursive practice copybooks یوه رقعه پر شاگردانو باندي teach pupils calligraphy مشق کول

مشقاب mashqáb *m.* kneading trough

مشقت mashaqqát *m. Arabic* 1 effort, labor په ډېر زحمت او مشقت with great effort مشقت کول *compound verb* to labor 2 *regional* forced labor; hard labor

مشقي mashqí practice; training

مشک [1] mashk *m.* wineskin

مشک [2] mushk *plural* musk

مشکار məshkár *m.* 1 bird-catcher 2 huntsman; game warden ☞ میرشکار

مشک بد mushkbéd *m.* ☞ مښکوله

مشکک məshkák *m.* 1 small late-ripening and somewhat tart grapes 2 valerian root

مشکل mushkíl *Arabic* 1 difficult 2 *m.* [*plural:* مشکلات mushkilát] difficulty, hardship مالي مشکل financial problems په مشکلات with a great effort په ډېر مشکله with an effort مشکل سره make difficulties مشکلات لیدل، چا ته مشکلات ورپېښول ورته پیدا کول have a hard time doing something پر ټولو مشکلاتو بری میندل overcome all difficulties

مشکلات mushkilát *m. plural Arabic of* مشکل 2

مشکل کشا mushkilkushá resolving difficulties, making things easier

مشکل گذار mushkilguzár rough مشکل گذاره غرنی علاقه a mountain area with limited access

مشکلوالی mushkilwálaj *m.* difficulty; intricacy

مشکلول mushkilawəl *denominative, transitive* [*past:* مشکل یې کړ] to impede, hamper, render difficult

مشکله mushkíla *f.* difficulty, trouble په ډېره مشکله سره with great effort ☞ مشکل

مشکلېدل mushkiledəl *denominative, intransitive* [*past:* مشکل شو] to get difficult, be difficult

مشکنډۍ mushkundə́j, məshkundə́j *f.* musk deer's musk gland

مشکنه məshkə́na *f.* 1 beads (very small) 2 (glass) bead

مشکنیز məshkəníz beaded

مشکور mashkúr *Arabic* 1 laudatory 2 thankful, grateful زه ستا ډېر مشکور یم I am much obliged to you.

مشکوری məshkorə́j *f.* wild weed melon

مشکوک mashkúk *Arabic* suspicious; questionable

مشکوله mashkolá *f.* 1 small wine bag 2 hot water bottle

مشکونډۍ məshkundə́j *f.* ☞ مشکنډۍ

مشکونډي məshkúndi *f. plural* 1 first hair (baby's) 2 curly hair, curls

مشکي [1] mushkí, mushkáj 1 black (of a horse) 2 *m.* .1 black horse 2.2 variable wheatear, *Oenanthe picata*

مشکی [2] mashkáj *m.* water carrier

مشکی [3] mishkáj *m.* hornet without a sting

مشکین mushkín musk مشکین مرک *idiom* a shrew

مشل mashál *m.* ☞ مشال

مشلورگی məshalwárgaj *m.* hair sheep

مشمشه mashmashá *f. medicine* glanders

مشمع mushammá' *f. Arabic* 1 oilcloth 2 linoleum

مشمول mashmúl *m. Arabic* [*plural:* مشمولین mashmulín] attendee (of a meeting, a session)

مشنگ [1] mushúng *m.* مشنگه mushúnga *f.* winter pea

مشنگه [1] mushúnga *f.* مشنگ mushúng winter pea

مشنگه [2] mshə́nga, mashə́nga *f.* 1 small-fruited aromatic melon 2 grass pea, *Lathyrus sativus* 3 ryegrass, *Lolium*

مشنگینه mushəngína *f.* dish made of pea pods

مشو məshú *m.* trousers made of coarse fabric

مشواني [1] məshwāṇí **1** *m. plural* Mishwani (tribe) **2** məshwāṇáy *m.* Mishwanai

مشواڼی [2] məshwāṇə́j *f.* [*plural:* مشواڼي məshwāṇə́y məshwāṇiyā́ni] inkpot

مشورت mashwarát *m. Arabic* ☞ مشوره

مشورتچي mashwaratchí *m.* advisor, consultant

مشورتي mashwaratí advisory, consultative مشورتي رایه لرل participate with a deliberative voice

مشوره mashwará *f. Arabic* council; meeting; consultation د مشوري مشوره چا ته مجلس consultative meeting (in provinces and circuits) کول، مشوره چا ته ور کول to give a consultation; consult somebody; advise somebody

مشوره گر mashwaragár *m.* **1** counselor **2** advisor

مشوره masholóá *f.* reel of thread, skein جړه مشوره، سرگمه مشوره *idiom* tangle جړه مشوره نوره هم جړه کول tangle the issue even more

مشوش mushawásh, mushawwásh *Arabic* **1** disconcerted, upset **2** tangled, intricate مشوش کول مشوش شول *compound verb* ☞ مشوشبدل *compound verb* ☞

مشوشانه mushawashaná, mushawwashaná **1** disconcerted, upset **2** tangled, intricate په مشوشانه ډول **a** excitedly **b** intricately

مشوشول mushawashawə́l, mushawwashawə́l *denominative, transitive* [*past:* مشوش یې کړ] **1** to upset, worry, bother; unnerve **2** to tangle, confuse

مشوشبدل mushawashedə́l, mushawwashedə́l *denominative, intransitive* [*past:* مشوش شو] **1** to be upset; worried; bothered, unnerved **2** to be tangled, confused

مشوق mushawwíq *Arabic* **1.1** stimulating, providing an incentive **1.2** inspiring **2** *m.* **.1** inspirer, mastermind **2.2** [*m. plural Arabic* مشوقات mushawwiqā́t] incentive, motive

مشوکه mashúka *f.* ☞ مښوکه

مشه mashá *f.* ☞ ماشه [2]

مشهد mashhád *m.* Meshhed (Iran)

مشهدي mashhadí, mashhadáj **1** inhabitant of Meshhed **2** *m.* **.1** inhabitant of Meshhed **2.2** one who has been on a pilgrimage to Meshhed

مشهود mashhúd *Arabic* **1** noticed; seen **2** witnessed

مشهور mashhúr *Arabic* known, famous, renowned مشهور ده چه ... It is known that ... مشهور مشهورول *compound verb* to make famous مشهوربدل *compound verb* دوی د خپل حق نه زیات مشهور دي Their fame has been exaggerated. مشهور اغلاط *idiom* gross errors

مشهورول mashhurawə́l *denominative, transitive* [*past:* مشهور یې کړ] **1** to make known, famous **2** to glorify

مشهوريت mashhuriját *m. Arabic* fame; popularity; glory

مشهوربدل mashhuredə́l *denominative, intransitive* [*past:* مشهور شو] **1** to be known, famous **2** to be glorified

مشی məsháj *m. children's speech* **1** thread **2** fish

مشيت mashiját *m. Arabic* **1** wish, aspiration **2** will

مشير mushír *m. Arabic* advisor

مشيمه mashimá *f. Arabic* **1** afterbirth **2** seed lobe

مشين mashín *m. regional* **1** machine, apparatus د بې سیم مشین radio set **2** ship مشین کول *compound verb* to cut (hair), shear with a machine مشین کبدل *compound verb* to get a haircut, have one's hair cut مشین شوی ږیره trimmed beard ☞ ماشین

مشيني mashiní machine, mechanical مشیني طاقت mechanical force

مشئوم mash'ú *masc. Arabic* sinister

مبنا maḳhấ *f.* [*usually plural* مبناوي maḳhā́wi] sheep dung that is stuck to the sheep's coat

مبنتیا mḳhəttjā́ *f.* ☞ مبنتیا

مبنتل mḳhətə́l *transitive* ☞ نبنتل

مبنته mḳhə́ta *f.* ☞ نبنته

مبنتی mḳhətaj **1** adjoining, adjacent; bordering **2** joined to something **3** occupied with something

مبنتیا mḳhətjā́ *f.* **1** contiguity; adjacency **2** being busy, employment

مبنک muḳhk, məḳhk *m. plural* musk ☞ مشک

مبنشکار məḳhkā́r *m.* ☞ میرشکار

مبنکک muḳhkák *m. plural* Indian valerian, *Valeriana wallichiana*

مبنککی məḳhkakə́j *f.* nutgrass, *Cyperus rotundus*

مبنک وږمی muḳhkwágmaj musk

مبنکوله məḳhkwə́la *f.* Egyptian willow, *Salix aegyptiaca*

مبنکی məḳhkáj **1** *m.* **.1** black horse **1.2** variable wheatear, *Oenanthe picata* **1.3** shrew (the animal) **2.1** black; black (of a horse) **2.2** musk

مبنکی muḳhkə́j *f.* aromatic grass

مبنگیرک muḳhgirák *m.* ☞ موشگیرک

مبنل [1] məḳhə́l, muḳhə́l **1** *transitive* [*present:* مړی *past:* و یې مبنه] **1.1** to rub; rub up; rub in **1.2** to wipe dry; wipe clean سترگي مبنل *compound verb* to rub one's eyes **1.3** to wake somebody up **1.4** to plane down **1.5** to full (to increase the weight and bulk of cloth, wool) **1.6** to smear, spread (e.g., butter) په کوچو مبنلی ډوډی bread and butter **2** *m. plural* ☞ لاسونه مبنل مبننه *idiom* to grieve; regret واندارو ته یې زړه مبنل کبري He would like a pomegranate. مبنل *idiom* to search far and wide

مبنل [2] mḳhəl *present verb stem of* مبنتل

مبنلول mḳhəlawə́l *transitive* ☞ نبنلول

مبنلئ [1] muḳhə́laj *past participle of* مبنل

مبنلي [2] mḳhə́li *present tense of* مبنتل

مبننه məḳhə́na, muḳhə́na *f.* **1** rubbing; rubbing in; friction **2** wiping dry **3** wiping clean **4** planing down **5** fulling (increasing the weight and bulk of cloth, wool) **6** smearing, spreading

مبنود məḳhód, muḳhód *m.* **1** ☞ مبننه **2** attempt, effort

مبنوکه maḳhúka *f.* **1** beak **2** spout (of a kettle)

مبنوولی muḳhowə́laj used, used to be

مبنی muḳhí *dialect present tense of* مبنل

مصاب musā́b *Arabic* **1.1** affected (e.g., with a disease) **1.2** stricken by misfortune **2** *m.* [*plural:* مصابين musābín] victim

مصاحب musāhíb *m. Arabic* [*plural:* مصاحبين musāhibín] companion; interlocutor د شاهانه حضور مصاحبين personal advisors of the Afghan king

مصاحبت musāhabát *m.* مصاحبه musāhabá *f. Arabic* 1 conversation; communication د چا سره مصاحبت کول to talk to somebody هغه په صحبت او مصاحبت کښې ښه دئ He is a good conversationalist. 2 interview

مصادر masādír *m. plural Arabic of* مصدر

مصادره musādará *f. Arabic* 1 confiscation 2 fining; fine 3 expropriation مصادره کول *compound verb* a to confiscate b to expropriate مصادره کېدل *compound verb* a to be confiscated, get confiscated b to be expropriated

مصادف musādíf *Arabic* 1 converging دا جشن د تعطيل د ورځې سره مصادف دئ This holiday falls on a day off. 2 meeting with somebody مصادف کېدل a to match, converge b to meet with each other

مصادمه musādamá *f. Arabic* 1 conflict 2 strike, hit 3 collision 4 *military* fight, skirmish

مصارف masāríf *m. plural Arabic of* مصرف

مصارفات masārifất *m. plural of* مصرف expenses, costs فوق العاده مصارفات emergency expenditures

مصافحه musāfahá *f. Arabic* handshake د چا سره مصافحه کول to shake hands with somebody

مصالح masālíh 1 *plural Arabic of* مصلحت 2 materials (construction) د مصالحو د تهيې مديريت construction materials procurement office 3 flavoring, spices 4 plastic

مصالحت musālahát *m.* مصالحه musālahá *f. Arabic* 1 tradeoff, compromise 2 reconciliation; truce, armistice مصالحت کول *compound verb* to accept reconciliation

مصائب masāíb *m. plural Arabic of* مصيبت

مصب masáb, masább *m. Arabic* mouth (of a river)

مصحح ¹ musahhíh *m. Arabic* proofreader

مصحح ² musahháh *Arabic* amended, corrected, proofread

مصحف ¹ masháf *m. Arabic* 1 book, volume 2 compendium, code 3 Koran

مصحف ² musahháf *Arabic* 1 distorted 2 written in error; misspelled

مصداق misdáq *m. Arabic* 1 evidence; testimony د دې شاهد پر مصداق according to this witness 2 clue, piece of evidence 3 meaning مفهوم او مصداق پيدا کول acquire meaning 4 proof of something

مصدر masdár *m. Arabic* [*plural:* مصدرونه masdarúna *and Arabic* مصادر masādír] 1 source, cause; origin 2 *grammar* masdar, verbal noun, indefinite mood, infinitive

مصدق ¹ musaddíq *Arabic* 1 reviewing, confirming, establishing; certifying مصدقه سندونه instruments of ratification 2 *m.* inspector, auditor

مصدق ² musaddáq *Arabic* 1 certified, confirmed; verified 2 *m.* witnessed copy; certified copy

مصدوم masdúm *asc. Arabic* victim

مصر ¹ misr *m. Arabic* Egypt

مصر ² musír, musírr *Arabic* insistent, persistent

مصرا misrất *f. Arabic* ☞ مصرع

مصرانه musiráná, musirrāná 1 persistent; insistent 2 persistently, perseveringly; insistently

مصرح musarráh *Arabic* explained, clarified

مصرحات musarrahất *m. plural Arabic of* مصرح explanations, clarifications

مصرع misra' *f. Arabic* 1 hemistich 2 ☞ لندۍ 2

مصرف masráf *m. Arabic* [*plural:* مصرفونه masrafúna *and Arabic* مصارف masāríf] 1 consumption, utilization په خپل مصرف رسول to use something oneself په مصرف رسېدل to be used, be utilized, be consumed په مصرف خرڅول to use correctly, use for its intended purpose 2 expenditure, cost; expense د شيانو د توليد مصارف production cost د کار مصرف labor consumption تمام شد مصرف cost مصرف کول *compound verb* ☞ مصرفول مصرفېدل *compound verb* ☞

مصرف کوونکی masráf kawúnkaj *m.* consumer

مصرفول masrafawә́l *denominative, transitive* [*past:* مصرف يې کړ] 1 to consume, utilize 2 to expend, spend 3 to spend, invest (e.g., labor)

مصرفي masrafí consumer مصرفي صنايع production of consumer goods

مصرفېدل masrafedә́l *denominative, intransitive* [*past:* مصرف شو] 1 to be consumed, utilized 2 to be spent, expended; be consumed

مصروف masrúf *. Arabic* 1 spent, consumed 2 put to use, utilized 3 occupied په يو کار کښې مصروف کېدل to be occupied with something 4 *grammar* inflection (inflected)

مصروفول masrufawә́l *denominative, transitive* [*past:* مصروف يې کړ] to occupy; involve in a project

مصروفيت masrufiját *m. Arabic* occupation; duty زيات مصروفيت excessive busyness, overload

مصروفېدل masrufedә́l *denominative, intransitive* [*past:* مصروف شو] to be busy doing something زه د يو اخبار په مطالعه کښې مصرف شوم I was busy reading a newspaper.

مصري ¹ misrí *m. plural* سپين مصري a lollipop b refined sugar

مصري ² misrí, misráj 1 Egyptian مصري پونډ Egyptian pound 2 *m.* Egyptian

مصری ³ misrәj *f.* sword made of Egyptian steel مصری توره a sword made of Egyptian steel

مصطفی mustafất 1 chosen 2 *m. religion* 1. Chosen One, Messenger (Muhammed's epithet) 2 *proper noun* Mustafa

مصطکی mastakí *f.* mastic

مصطلح mustalíh *Arabic* 1.1 idiomatic; accepted in the language 1.2 used as a term 2 *m.* [*plural:* مصطلحات mustalihất] 1. idiom 2.2 expression, phrase 2.3 term مخصوص مصطلح special term

مصغر musaghghár *Arabic* **1.1** *grammar* diminutive مصغر اسم diminutive name **1.2** diminished **2** *m.* [*plural:* مصغرات musaghgharát] diminutive name

مصلا musallá *f.* **1** prayer rug **2** suburban square for public prayer

مصلح muslíh aviation **1.1** correcting; reforming **1.2** reconciling; peace-loving, peacefully disposed **1.3** improving **2** *m.* **.1** reformer, transformer **2.2** peacekeeper

مصلحت maslahát *m. Arabic* [*plural:* مصلحتونه maslahatúna *and Arabic* مصالح masālíh] **1** advice; consultation بيا هغه ساعت او هغه يي مصلحت، هغه ساعت، هغه مصلحت When the time comes, we will talk and discuss this. **2** inception د چا په حق کښي بد مصلحت کول to hatch evil plans against somebody **3** usefulness, benefit; interest د وخت مصلحت contemporary challenges اجتماعي مصالح public interest فردي مصالح personal interest مصلحت دا دئ چه It is best to do so. **4** collusion مصلحت کول *compound verb* **a** to confer; consult **b** to negotiate, conspire د مصلحت دپاره دروغ *idiom* a lie to save (someone or something)

مصلحتاً maslahátán *Arabic* deliberately, intentionally; calculatedly; purposely; consciously

مصلحت اندیشانه maslahatandeshāná premeditated, deliberate; intentional

مصلحت اندیشي maslahatandeshí *f.* **1** intentionality **2** intention; design

مصلحتي maslahatí *m.* advisor; confidant

مصلوب maslúb *Arabic* **1** crucified **2** hanged

مصله musallá *f.* مصلی musallá *f.* ☞ مصلا

مصلی[1] musalí *m.* garbage collector; street sweeper, janitor

مصلی[2] musallá *f.* ☞ مصلا

مصنف[1] musanníf *m. Arabic* [*plural:* مصنفان musannifán *and Arabic* مصنفین musannifín] **1** writer; author **2** composer **3** author (e.g., of a design)

مصنف[2] musannáf *Arabic* **1** authored **2** *m.* [*plural:* مصنفونه musannafúna *and Arabic* مصنفات musannafát] composition, work

مصنوع masnú' *Arabic* **1.1** made; processed مصنوع مواد fabricated goods, industrial goods **1.2** artificial, fake, false **1.3** coined, thought up (of a word) مصنوع لغات neologisms **2** *m. & f.* **.1** composition, work **2.2** manufactured item

مصنوعات masnu'át *m. plural Arabic* [*singular:* مصنوع 1] manufactured items, fabricated items, products; industrial goods **2** works, creations

مصنوعه masnu'á *feminine and plural Arabic of* مصنوع

مصنوعي masnu'í **1** artificial مصنوعي ورېنم rayon مصنوعي باران agriculture artificial irrigation مصنوعي ربر synthetic rubber **2** fake, sham, contrived, affected

مصوب mussawáb *Arabic* approved, authorized

مصوبه mussawabá *f. Arabic* decree, resolution, decision مصوبه صادرول to adopt a resolution

مصوت mussawát *Arabic* **1** clear (of a sound) **2** vowel (sound)

مصور[1] mussawír *m. Arabic* painter, artist

مصور[2] maswár *m.* ☞ کاهربزه

مصور[3] mussawár *Arabic* **1** drawn, depicted **2** illustrated

مصوره mussawíra *f.* female painter

مصوري mussawirí *f.* painting (art)

مصیبت musibát *m. Arabic* [*plural:* مصیبتونه musibatúna *and Arabic* مصائب masāyíb] catastrophe, calamity مصیبت کښدل *compound verb* to suffer a catastrophe هر راز مصائب زغمل to tolerate deprivation

مصئون mas'ún *Arabic* **1** protected, guarded, shielded له ... څخه مصئون protected, guarded, shielded **2** possessing immunity, not predisposed (to a disease)

مصئونیت mas'uniját *m. Arabic* **1** integrity, intangibility دیپلوماتیکي مصئونیت diplomatic immunity **2** *medicine* immunity **3** safety

مضار mazár *m. plural Arabic of* مضرت

مضاربت muzārabát *m. Arabic* consignment; selling other people's goods with the profit divided in half between the seller and the owner

مضارع muzārí' *f. Arabic grammar* **1** conditional mood **2** present tense, perfect aspect

مضاعف muzā'áf *Arabic* **1** doubled, double **2** many fold اضعاف مضاعف az'áf-i... hundredfold, many times

مضاف muzáf *Arabic* **1** attached, annexed **2** *m. grammar* dependent member

مضافات muzāfát *m. plural Arabic* [*singular:* مضاف 1] environs, suburbs; adjacent areas

مضاف الیه muzāfalájh *m. Arabic grammar* **1** attribute; apposition **2** object

مضامین mazāmín *m. plural Arabic of* مضمون

مضایقه muzājaqá *f. Arabic* **1** constraint, difficulty **2** straits

مضبوط mazbút *Arabic* **1** solid; robust **2** reinforced **3** absorbed, fixed in memory **4** confiscated

مضبوط طوالی mazbutwálaj *m.* ☞ مضبوطي

مضبوطول mazbutawól *denominative, transitive* [*past:* مضبوط یې کړ] **1** to steady, affix **2** to absorb, fix in memory **3** to confiscate

مضبوطي mazbutí *f.* **1** strength, solidity, robustness **2** state of being reinforced **3** mastering, assimilation **4** confiscate

مضحک muzhík *Arabic* amusing, funny مضحک عبارت بیانول to joke

مضحکه muzhaká *f. Arabic* **1** joke, amusement **2** laughingstock

مضر muzír, muzírr *Arabic* harmful, detrimental مضر مکروبونه harmful germs مضر حشرات insect pests

مضرت mazarrát *m. Arabic* [*plural:* مضار mazár] **1** harm; adverse consequence پر مضارو تمامېدل to harm, inflict damage **2** harmfulness, deleteriousness

مضروب mazrúb *Arabic* **1** *m. mathematics* multiplicand **2** beaten, broken

مضروب فیه mazrubfíh *m. Arabic mathematics* multiplicator

مضطرب muztaríb *Arabic* **1** upset, unnerved, concerned, disturbed **2** facing a predicament

مضمحل muzmahíl, muzmahíll *Arabic* destroyed زړه يې مات او مضمحل شو *idiom* He fell into despondence.

مضمر muzmár *Arabic* concealed, secret, intimate

مضموم mazmúmasc *Arabic linguistics* having the symbol "pesh" or "zamma" (ُ)

مضمون mazmún *m. Arabic* [*plural:* مضمونه mazmunúna *and Arabic* مضامين mazāmín] 1 contents, subject, topic يو مكتوب په دي لاندي مضمون راورسيدئ A letter has arrived whose contents are as follows. 2 article (in a newspaper, etc.); composition اجتماعي مضامين political journalism 3 scholastic subject ديو مضمون درس وركول teach a subject

مضموني mazmuní topical, thematic مضموني حيثيت ساتل keep the plot going

مضيقه maziqá *f. Arabic* predicament; need; straits

مطابع matābí' *m. plural Arabic of* مطبعه

مطابق mutābíq *Arabic* matching, corresponding د ... سره مطابق كېدل according to something or other د خبر په مطابق according to a report د هدايت په مطابق according to the manual

مطابقت mutābaqát *m. Arabic* 1 match, correspondence د ... سره مطابقت لرل to be coordinated with something 2 *grammar* coordination, agreement په جنس مطابقت agreement in gender په عدد مطابقت agreement in number مطابقت لرل to be coordinated

مطابقت نامه mutābaqatnāmá *f.* mandate, instruction (given by voters to their elected representative)

مطاع mutá' *m. Arabic* lord, sovereign

مطالب [1] matālíb *m. plural Arabic of* مطلب

مطالب [2] mutālíb *m. Arabic* creditor, moneylender, loan-holder

مطالبات mutālabāt *m. plural Arabic of* مطالبه

مطالبه mutālabá *f. Arabic* [*plural:* مطالبي mutālabé *and m. plural: Arabic* مطالبات mutālabāt] 1 demand 2 monetary claim; request for payment (of a debt)

مطالبه كوونكى mutālabá kawúnkaj *m.* purchaser, customer

مطالعات mutāli'āt *m. plural Arabic of* مطالعه

مطالعاتي mutāli'ātí research

مطالعه mutāli'á *f. Arabic* [*m. plural:* مطالعات mutāli'āt] 1 reading د مطالعه وسيع مطالعه reading room د مطالعي كوټه، د مطالعي سالون erudition ډيره فراخه مطالعه لري He is an erudite. 2 study, investigation 3 observation 4 review, consideration مطالعه كول *compound verb* a to read b to study, investigate c to review, consider تر مطالعه لاندي نيول to observe, study

مطالعه خانه mutāli'akhāná *f.* reading room, study hall

مطاوع mutāwí' *Arabic* obedient, submissive; subordinate

مطاوعت mutāwa'át *m. Arabic* obedience, submissiveness; subordination د مطاوعت كړى ماتول break the chains of slavery

مطبخ matbákh *m. Arabic* kitchen د مطبخ كوټه kitchen

مطبعه matba'á *f. Arabic* [*plural:* مطبعي matba'é *and m. plural: Arabic* مطابع matābí'] printing house

مطبوع matbú' *Arabic* 1 printed 2 impressed مطبوع كول *compound verb* a to print b to impress

مطبوعات matbu'āt *m. plural Arabic* [*singular* مطبوع] 1 press; printed media 2 printed material (books, newspapers, etc.) د مطبوعاتو مستقل رئيس press department د مطبوعاتو مستقل رياست head of press department

مطبوعاتي matbu'ātí publishing مطبوعاتي ژوند issue date (newspaper, magazine, etc.) د مطبوعاتي ژوندلسم كال 10th year of publication a مطبوعاتي هيئت press representatives, journalists مطبوعاتي خلك delegation of the press مطبوعاتي كنفرانس، مطبوعاتي مركه، مطبوعاتي press conference مطبوعاتي آتشه، مطبوعاتي منشي press conference مصاحبه secretary, press attaché

مطران mitrấn *m.* metropolitan

مطرب mutríb *m. Arabic* 1 musician 2 singer

مطرح matráh *Arabic* 1 *f.* subject of discussion, debate 2 submitted for discussion

مطرد muttaríd *Arabic* 1 subject to a general rule; generally accepted, conventional 2 correct, regular

مطرع matrá' *f. Arabic* suggested topic (of a poetic tournament)

مطروح [1] matrúh *Arabic* compiled; planned

مطروح [2] matrúh *Arabic* [*f. plural:* مطروحه matruhá] 1 excreted, discharged مطروحه مواد discharge 2 released, dropped off

مطرود matrúd *Arabic* exiled, turned away

مطلب matláb *m. Arabic* [*plural:* مطلبونه matlabúna *and Arabic* مطالب matālíb] 1 purpose, intention; wish په خپلو مطالبو رسيدل، مطلب لاس ته راوستل، پر خپلو مطالبو بری ميندل to get one's own way; carry one's point; labor at achieving one's goal 2 demand 3 issue; task اوس په مطلب ورسيدلم And now I come to the substance of the matter. 4 meaning, substance د مطلب خبري important, essential بي مطلبه خبره نه كول to not waste words, talk in earnest 5 topic د مطلب وګای to stray from the point 6 destination مطلب نه ليري لوبدل مطلب يې زه وم to deliver to the destination 7 Matlab ته رسول *idiom* He meant me.

مطلع [1] matlá' *f. Arabic* 1 initial verse, bayt 2 sunrise 3 place of sunrise

مطلع [2] muttali' *Arabic* advised, notified, informed

مطلق mutláq *Arabic* 1 absolute, complete مطلقه آزادي complete freedom په مطلق اكثريت by absolute majority مطلق وكيل empowered; authorized; having a full power of attorney 2 decisive; implacable 3 *grammar* perfect (of aspect) مطلقه ماضي *grammar* past perfect aspect مطلق حال *grammar* present perfect aspect

مطلق العنان mutlaq-ul-'inấn *Arabic* 1.1 free, independent, free in one's actions 1.2 absolute, full 1.3 despotic 2 *m.* philosophy 2.1 autocrat; despot 2.2 the absolute

مطلقاً mutláqán *Arabic* completely, totally; absolutely; at all; in full

مطلقتوب mutlaqtób *m.* مطلقوالي mutlaqwấlay *m. grammar* perfect aspect

مطلقيت mutlaqiját *m.* 1 independence 2 limitlessness 3 fullness of power; absolutism, autocracy 4 abstractness 5 absoluteness

مطلوب matlúb *Arabic* **1** needed, necessary لکه چه مطلوب دي as needed **2** desired مطلوبه نتیجه desired result **3** popular, in demand (of goods) زیاد له مطلوبه اندازي څخه *idiom* matlubá… excessively

مطلوبیت matlubiját *m. Arabic economics* consumer value لرل be needed, required

مطمئن mutmajín *Arabic* quiet; assured مور، مطمئن یوچه … We are sure that…

مطنطن mutantán *Arabic* luxurious, magnificent

مطول mutawwál *Arabic* **1** lingering; plangent **2** extended (of sentence)

مطهر mutahhár *Arabic* **1** pure, purified **2** sacred, holy

مطیع mutí' *Arabic* **1** obedient, docile په مطیع حالت د چا د dutifully امر او فرمان مطیع submissive to somebody **2** subordinate; subject زمور، عزم به مطیع او خم نه شي Our decision مطیع گزیدل submit, obey is steadfast.

مظالم mazālím *m. plural Arabic* [*singular:* مظلمه] **1** oppression **2** insults, injuries, offences

مظاهر¹ muzāhír *Arabic* **1.1** helping, supporting **1.2** showing, demonstrating something **2** *m.* **.1** patron, sponsor **2.2** demonstrator

مظاهر² mazāhír *m. plural Arabic* [*singular:* مظهر¹] phenomena; manifestations; indicators په عملي مظاهرو پیژندل to know people by their deeds

مظاهره muzāhirá, muzāhará *f. Arabic* [*plural:* مظاهري muzāhiré *and m. plural: Arabic* مظاهرات muzāhirát] demonstration مظاهره کول *compound verb* to show, demonstrate د خپل طاقت مظاهره کول to demonstrate one's power

مظاهره چي muzāhirachí *m.* demonstrator

مظاهره کوونکی muzāhirá kawúnkaj *m.* demonstrator

مظروف mazrúf. *Arabic* **1** housed, contained in a vessel **2** *m.* **.1** contents **2.2** *philosophy* content, substance ظرف او مظروف form and substance

مظفر muzaffár *Arabic* **1** victorious, triumphant **2** *m.* **.1** winner, victor, conqueror **2.2** *proper noun* Muzaffar

مظفرانه muzaffarāná **1** victorious, triumphant **2** victoriously, triumphantly

مظفریت muzaffariját *m. Arabic* **1** victory; triumph **2** victoriousness **3** success; successfulness

مظلمه mazlamá *f. Arabic* [*plural:* مظلمي mazlamé *and m. plural Arabic* مظالم mazālím] offence, insult مظلمه یي پر خپله غاره! He has only himself to blame!

مظلوم mazlúm*asc. Arabic* **1** subjugated; oppressed **2** offended; browbeaten; humiliated

مظلومیت mazlumiját *m. Arabic* **1** state of being oppressed **2** state of being cowed, browbeaten; abjection

مظنون maznún *Arabic* **1** suspected, suspect **2** accused

مظنونیت maznuniját *m. Arabic* state of being under suspicion

مظنه mazanná *f. Arabic* **1** thought, opinion **2** assumption, guess; suspicion

مظهر¹ mazhár *m. Arabic* [*plural:* مظاهر² mazāhír] manifestation; embodiment

مظهر² muzhír *Arabic* **1** revealing **2** *m.* mouthpiece, spokesman

معابد ma'ābíd *m. plural Arabic of* معبد

معابر ma'ābír *m. plural Arabic of* معبر

معاد ma'ád *m. Arabic religion* afterworld; paradise

معادل mu'ādíl *Arabic* **1** equal, equivalent; identical; equivalent معادله کلمه equivalent word **2** corresponding to something; comparable to something

معادله mu'ādalá *f. Arabic* **1** equilibrium, balance معادله ساتل maintain equilibrium **2** proportionality, ratio **3** *mathematics* equation

معادن ma'ādín *m. plural Arabic of* معدن

معاذ ma'áz *m. Arabic* shelter

معاذر ma'āzír *m. plural Arabic of* معذرت

معاذیر ma'āzír *m. plural Arabic of* معذار

معارض mu'āríz *m. Arabic* opponent; adversary د فطرت معارض *idiom* unnatural thing

معارضه mu'ārazá *f. Arabic* **1** counteraction, opposition **2** dispute, debate, contestation د ... سره معارضه کول contest something **3** competition

معارف ma'āríf *m. Arabic plural* **1** *of* معرفت **2** enlightenment, education د معارفو وزارت Ministry of Education د معارف مدیر head of the regional education department **3** nobility

معارف خواهي ma'ārifkhāhí *f.* attention to education

معاش ma'ásh *m. Arabic* [*plural:* معاشونه ma'āshúna *and Arabic* معاشات ma'āshát] **1** life, existence **2** means of livelihood, sustenance **3** earnings, wages **4** benefit (for the disabled)

معاش خور ma'āshkhór wage-earner

معاش دهنده ma'āshdihandá *m.* employer

معاشر mu'āshír *Arabic* **1** roommate **2** *m.* [*plural:* معاشران mu'āshirán *and Arabic* معاشرین mu'āshirín] **.1** friend, pal, companion **2.2** cohabitant

معاشرت mu'āsharát *m. Arabic* **1** communication **2** company, society

معاشرتي mu'āsharatí societal, social معاشرتي انقلاب social revolution

معاشقه mu'āshaqá *f. Arabic* **1** (mutual) love **2** love poetry

معاشي ma'āshí *Arabic* **1** worldly; vital **2** *regional* economic

معاصر mu'āsír *Arabic* **1** contemporary, modern معاصر تاریخ modern history **2** *m.* [*plural:* معاصرین mu'āsirín] contemporary

معاف mu'áf *Arabic* **1** exempt (from tax, customs fee, responsibility, etc.) د عسکري خدمت څخه معاف exempt from military duty **2** pardoned; acquitted

معافول mu'āfawál *denominative, transitive* [*past:* معاف یي کړ] **1** to exempt from something **2** to pardon, forgive; acquit

معافي mu'āfí *f.* **1** exemption د معافي روخ day off د معافي امر order of exemption from military duty **2** pardon, forgiveness د معافي

روح *religion* spirit of forgiveness د چا څخه معافي غوښتل ask somebody's forgiveness معافي غواړم، ته مي ونه لیدې I beg your pardon; I did not notice you. معافي زمکه معافي زمکه **a** land given as a gift by the monarch and exempt from taxes **b** land exempt from rent or taxes

معافیات mu'āfijā́t *m. plural Arabic regional* lands exempt from taxes

معافیت mu'āfijā́t *m.* **1** exemption (of customs fee, taxes, etc.) **2** *medicine, biology* immunity معافیت حاصلول acquire immunity **3** pardon

معافېدۀل mu'āfedۀl *denominative, intransitive* [*past:* معاف شو] **1** to be set free, be released **2** to be pardoned, be forgiven

معاقبت mu'āqibā́t *m. Arabic* persecution; punishment

معاکسه mu'ākasá *f. Arabic* counteraction, opposition

معالج mu'ālídzh *Arabic* attendant (of a physician)

معالجوي mu'āladzhawí therapeutic; medicinal طب معالجوي therapeutics; treatment

معالجه mu'āladzhá *f. Arabic* **1** cure; recovery; treatment وریا معالجه free treatment معالجه کول *compound verb* to cure, treat معالجه کېدل *compound verb* to be cured; be treated **2** resolution, consideration, elaboration (of an issue)

مع الواسطه ma'alwāsatá *Arabic* indirectly; not immediately

معاملات mu'āmalā́t *m.* [*plural:* معاملتونه mu'āmalatúna *and Arabic* معاملات mu'āmalā́t معامله mu'āmalá *f. Arabic plural:* معاملي mu'āmalé *and m. plural Arabic* معاملات mu'āmalā́t] **1** deal, transaction (bank, trade) د معاملي خاوند تجارتي معاملت trade deals surety, bondsman **2** trading business معاملت کول *compound verb* to carry out trade operations معاملت کېدل *compound verb* to trade with somebody **3** to be conducted (of trading transactions, trade) **4** dispute, controversy **5** process; action

معامله دار mu'āmaladā́r *m.* contractor, party to a contract د شرکت معامله داران شرکت clients, customers of (a national stockholding company in Afghanistan)

معامله کوونکی mu'āmalá kawúnkaj *m.* ☞ معامله دار

معاند mu'ānid *Arabic* hostile, unfriendly, inimical

معاندانه mu'ānidāná **1** hostile (e.g., of a policy) **2** in a hostile, unfriendly, inimical manner

معاني ma'āní *m. plural Arabic of* معنیٰ

معاودت mu'āwadā́t *m. Arabic* returning to, going back to, coming back to

معاوضه mu'āwazá *f. Arabic* **1** mutual exchange تجارتي معاوضه barter **2** compensation, reimbursement **3** ransom, buyout, payoff, compensation for release of obligation معاوضه کول *compound verb* to compensate

معاون mu'āwín *m. Arabic* [*plural:* معاونان mu'āwinā́n *and Arabic* معاونین mu'āwinín] **1** assistant د جرګي معاون deputy jirga chairman معاون وزارت، د وزارت معاون mu'āwín-i... deputy minister د وزیرانو د شورا لمړی معاون first deputy chairman of the Council of

Ministers **2** deputy district chief **3** tributary (of a river) **4** *grammar* auxiliary verb

معاونت mu'āwanā́t *m. Arabic* support, assistance, help; aid د چا په معاونت سره with artillery د توپخاني په معاونت سره with someone's help طبي معاونت medical assistance support

معاوني mu'āwiní *f.* معاونیت mu'āwiniyā́t *m.* **1** aid **2** position or status of aide

معاهد mu'āhíd *Arabic* negotiating, concluding an agreement

معاهده mu'āhadá *f. Arabic* [*plural:* معاهدي mu'āhadé *and m. plural Arabic* معاهدات mu'āhdā́t] **1** treaty, pact, agreement **2** treatise **3** contract

معائب mu'āíb *m. plural Arabic* deficiencies, defects, flaws معائب ایسته کول to eliminate deficiencies

معاینه mu'ājaná *f. Arabic* **1** examination صحي معاینه، ډاکټري معاینه medical examination د معایني هیئت **a** medical board **b** acceptance team معاینه کول *compound verb* to examine, inspect, see باغ یې معاینه کړ They saw the garden. **2** *geology* prospecting survey

معاینه خانه mu'ājanakhāná *f.* outpatient clinic د حیواني امراضو معاینه خانه veterinary station

معبد ma'bád *m. Arabic* [*plural:* معبدونه ma'badúna *and Arabic* معابد ma'ābíd] **1** temple, place of worship; cathedral **2** sanctuary

معبر¹ ma'bár *m. Arabic* [*plural:* معبرونه ma'barúna *and Arabic* معابر ma'ābír] **1** passage; crossing; move **2** (pontoon) bridge د معابرو مدیریت bridge construction office (in the Ministry of Communal Works)

معبر² mu'abír *Arabic* interpreting, explaining

معبود ma'búd *Arabic* **1** adored, idolized, worshiped **2** *m.* [*plural:* معبودات ma'budā́t] idol

معتاد mu'tā́d *Arabic* habitual, usual معتاد کول to د دیو شي سره accustom, train, inure

معتبر mu'atabár *Arabic* **1.1** respected, trusted; honorable, esteemed معتبر خلق respected people **1.2** influential معتبري ټولني influential circles **1.3** valid (of an agreement, etc.) **2** *m.* [*plural:* معتبرین mu'atabarín] **.1** respected person, solid person **2.2** confidant; proxy **2.3** *proper noun* Muatabar

معتبري mu'tabarí *f.* **1** honor معتبري ګڼل consider an honor, distinction **2** force, validity (e.g., of an agreement)

معتدل mu'atadíl *Arabic* **1** moderate, average **2** proportional, commensurate **3** appropriate, adequate د علومو معتدله درجه adequate scientific training

معتدلانه mu'atadilāná **1** moderate په معتدلانه نظریات moderate views معتدلانه درجه moderately, appropriately **2** moderately, appropriately

معترض mu'taríz *Arabic* **1.1** objecting; opposing **1.2** *grammar* interposing معترضه جمله *grammar* interposing clause **2** *m.* **1.** opponent **2.2** critic

معتزله mu'tazalá *m. plural Arabic religion* Mutazilites (a sect)

معتقد mu'taqíd *Arabic* **1** convinced of something, believing in something ... چه و معتقد دی He was convinced. **2** *m.* [*plural:* معتقدان mu'taqidấn *and Arabic* معتقدین mu'taqidín] believer

معتقدات mu'taqadất *m. plural Arabic* **1** convictions, opinions **2** beliefs

معتکف mu'atakíf *Arabic* pious

معتل mu'tá, mu'tál *Arabic* **1** weak, frail, helpless **2** *grammar* ending in a vowel

معتل الاخر mu'tal-ul-akhír, mu'tall-ul-akhír *Arabic* ☞ معتل

معتمد mu'tamád *Arabic* **1.1** respected, worthy of respect or trust **1.2** veracious, reliable **2** *m.* [*plural:* معتمدین mu'tamadín] **.1** reliable person **2.2** proxy; confidant **2.3** *proper noun* Mutamad

معتنابه mu'tanābíh *Arabic* **1** significant یوه معتنابه اندازه پیسی a significant sum of money **2** serious, important

معجز mu'dzhíz *Arabic* **1** inimitable; miraculous **2** irritating, causing displeasure

معجزه [1] mu'dzhizá *f. Arabic* miracle معجزې ته سترگي نیول hope for a miracle

معجزه [2] mu'dzhiza *feminine singular of* معجز

معجم mu'dzhám *Arabic linguistics* having a diacritic (of a letter)

معجون ma'dzhún *Arabic* **1** mixed, intermingled **2.1** exciting drug mixture (frequently, a narcotic) **2.2** sweets

معدن ma'dán *m. Arabic* [*plural:* معدنونه ma'danúna *and Arabic* معادن ma'ādín] **1** ore علم معدن استخراج ore mining د معادنو ilm-i... mineralogy **2** ore mine; deposit نفتو معادن oil deposit د معادنو وزارت انجنیر mining engineer د معادنو وزارت Ministry of Mining Industry

معدن شناس ma'danshinás *m.* geologist; mineralogist

معدني ma'dani *Arabic* **1** ore **2** mineral معدني شیان، معدني اشیا minerals معدني اوبه mineral water معدني شتمني mineral wealth معدني تیل oil

معدود ma'dúd *Arabic* **1** few in number, scarce **2** *combined with cardinal numerals*

معدودیت ma'dudiját *m. grammar* combination with a numeral or خو

معدوم ma'dúmasc. *Arabic* extinguished; defunct معدوم کېدل *compound verb* to perish; become extinguished

معده mi'dá *f. Arabic* stomach

معذار mi'zấr *m. Arabic* [*plural:* معاذیر ma'āzír معذرت ma'zirát, ma'zarát *m. Arabic plural:* معذرتونه ma'ziratúna *and Arabic* معاذر ma'āzír] pardon, forgiveness; beg pardon له ... څخه معذار غوښتل to ask forgiveness معذار غوښتل

معذور ma'zúr *Arabic* **1** forgiven, pardoned څوک معذور بلل، څوک معذور گڼل forgive, pardon somebody دی معذور وگڼئ! Forgive him! **2** exculpatory **3** upset, distressed **4** helpless, powerless

معذرت ma'zurát *m. Arabic* defect; flaw

معذوریت ma'zuriját *m.* feebleness, helplessness

معراج mi'rấdzh *m. Arabic* **1** ascension **2** highest level, highest stage د کمال معراج ته ترقی a high level of development

د کمال معراج ته رسېدل to bring to perfection رسول achieve perfection

معرض ma'ráz *m. Arabic* exhibition په نمایش معرض for a display

معرفت ma'rifát *m. Arabic* **1** knowledge, study **2** piece of information **3** familiarity, acquaintance **4** mediation, assistance, help ده په معرفت with his assistance

معرفي mu'arrifí *f.* **1** recommendation **2** introduction; acquaintance چاته معرفي کول *compound verb* **a** to recommend, introduce to somebody, acquaint somebody **b** to declare, acknowledge خان معرفي کول to introduce oneself معرفي کېدل *compound verb* **a** to introduce oneself; get acquainted; be introduced to somebody د چا په حضور معرفي کېدل to be introduced to somebody **b** to be known to somebody

معرکه ma'riká *f. Arabic* **1** battlefield, arena **2** battle, fight **3** gathering, assembly **4** meeting; congregation

معروض ma'rúz *Arabic* **1.1** set forth, written down **1.2** reported, submitted **2** *m.* [*plural:* معروضونه ma'ruzúna *and Arabic* معروضات ma'ruzất] report; presentation

معروضات ma'ruzất *m.* **1** *plural Arabic from* معروض 2 **2** address تبریکیه معروضات (written greetings) congratulatory address شکریه معروضات congratulations

معروضي ma'ruzí objective

معروف ma'rúf., mārúf. *Arabic* **1.1** known, renowned; famous **1.2** *grammar* active **2** *m. proper noun* Maruf

معروف خېل mārufkhél **1** *m. plural:* Marufkheils (tribe) **2** *m.* Marufkheil

معزز mu'azzáz *Arabic* honored, worthy, esteemed, respected معزز سړی person held in esteem

معزول ma'zúl *Arabic* **1** removed from office, dismissed, deposed معزول کېدل معزولول *compound verb* ☞ معزول کول *compound verb* ☞ معزولیدل **2** dethroned, overthrown (of a monarchy)

معزولول ma'zulawál **1** *denominative, transitive* [*past:* معزول یې کړ] to remove from office, dismiss, depose; have somebody resign **2** *m. plural* removal from office, disposal, deposition; resignation

معزولېدل ma'zuledál *denominative, intransitive* [*past:* معزول شو] to be removed from office, dismissed from post, be fired, deposed; be forced to resign

معشوق ma'shúq *m. Arabic* beloved, sweetheart, honey

معشوقانه ma'shuqá lovey-dovey, amorous

معشوقه ma'shuqá *f. Arabic* **1** beloved woman, sweetheart, honey **2** mistress

معشوقي ma'shuqí *f.* love; affection

معصوم ma'súmasc. *Arabic* **1.1** innocent معصومه جلکی young girl **1.2** childish **2** *m.* child; innocent baby ☞ ماشوم

معصومه ma'súma **1** *feminine singular of* معصوم 1 **2** *f.* girl **3** *proper noun* Masuma

معصومي [1] ma'sumí *f. Arabic* innocence; sinlessness

معصومي [2] ma'súmi *feminine plural from* معصومه 1

معصومیت ma'sumiját *m.* ☞ معصومي

معصیت ma'siját *m. Arabic* **1** *religion* sin, fault, violation of commandment **2** transgression

معضل mu'zíl *Arabic* difficult, hard, cumbersome; onerous

معضله mu'zilá *f. Arabic* [*m. plural:* معضلات mu'zilất] difficulty, hardship, complication

معطر mu'attár *Arabic* **1** aromatic, sweet-smelling, fragrant **2** perfumed

معطل mu'attál *Arabic* **1** delayed, adjourned, deferred, postponed **2** removed (from office) معطل معطلول *compound verb* ☞ معطل کول *compound verb* ☞ معطلېدل **3** waiting for something **4** idle د فکر معطل پرېښودل not to take the trouble to think, not to think

معطلول mu'attalawәl *denominative, transitive* [*past:* معطل يې کړ] **1** to delay, adjourn, defer, postpone, protract **2** to remove (from office)

معطلي [1] mu'attalí *f.* delay, adjournment, deferment بله معطلي څخه without delay; delay, adjourn, defer, postpone, protract معطلي کول be in no hurry to answer په ځواب کښي معطلي کول get delayed, adjourned معطل پيدا کول deferred, postponed, drag on, drag out, linger

معطلي [2] mu'attáli *feminine plural of* معطل

معطلېدل mu'attaledә́l *denominative, intransitive* [*past:* معطل شو] **1** to get delayed, adjourned, deferred, postponed, drag on, linger **2** to be removed, get removed (from office)

معطلېدۀ mu'attaledә́ *m. plural* **1** delay, adjournment, deferment, procrastination د کنفرانس معطلېدۀ the delay of the conference **2** removal (from office)

معطوف ma'túf. *Arabic* **1** inclined, facing **2** *grammar* connected by a conjunction

معظم [1] mu'zám *Arabic* **1.1** great دول معظم duwál-i... great powers **1.2** important, predominant, significant **1.3** huge, large معظمه قوا major forces **2** *m.* majority, greater part

معظم [2] mu'azzám *Arabic* **1** respected **2** above-mentioned **3** official high (of contracting parties)

معظم له mu'azzamléh *Arabic* ☞ معظم [2]

معقد mu'aqqád *Arabic* difficult, complicated يو معقد حالت quandary

معقم mu'aqqám *Arabic* sterilized; disinfected

معقول ma'qúl *Arabic* **1** rational, prudent, judicious معقول جواب rational answer معقول! This makes sense! **2** acceptable, appropriate, adequate; decent **3** legitimate, valid (of a reason, excuse) **4** convincing معقول دلائل convincing arguments

معقولات ma'qulất *m. plural Arabic* **1** comprehensible, conceivable by the mind **2** rational sciences

معقولیت ma'quliját *m.* **1** intelligence معقولیت لرل to be intelligent **2** civility, politeness, refined manners

معکوس ma'kús *Arabic* **1.1** reflected **1.2** inverted **1.3** *mathematics* inverse, reciprocal **2** *m. mathematics* reciprocal fraction

معکوساً ma'kúsán *Arabic* inversely معکوساً متناسب inversely proportional او همداسي معکوساً and the opposite

معکوسېدل má'kusedә́l *denominative, intransitive* [*past:* معکوس شو] **1** to reflect, be reflected **2** to turn over, be turned over

معلق mu'alláq *Arabic* **1.1** hanging, suspended; dangling معلق پل suspended bridge **1.2** connected to something, related to something په شرط پوري معلق predicated by something **1.3** variable, unspecified **2** *m.* **.1** tumbling **2.2** *aviation* dead loop

معلقه mu'allaqá *f. Arabic* muallaqa (the name of seven famous Arabic pre-Islamic poems)

معلم mu'allím *m. Arabic* [*plural:* معلمان mu'allimán *and Arabic* معلمین mu'allimín] teacher, instructor; mentor سر معلم senior instructor; school principal د معلم روزلو اکاډیمي pedagogical institute

معلمه mu'allimá *f. Arabic* [*plural:* معلمات mu'allimất] female teacher, female instructor; female mentor مشره معلمه female school principal

معلمي mu'allimí *f.* **1** teaching, instruction **2** instructorship

معلول ma'lúl *Arabic* **1.1** sick, unhealthy **1.2** upset; offended **1.3** motivated, justified, stipulated **2** *m.* **.1** invalid, disabled person **2.2** result, consequence

معلولیت ma'luliját *m. Arabic* **1** disease, ill health, state of being unwell **2** state of being justified, stipulated

معلوم ma'lúm, mālúm *Arabic* known, definite زه ماته معلومه ده چه... I am aware that... معلومه How do you know? درته څه معلوم دي؟ It is common knowledge that... ټولوته معلومه ده چه خبره ده چه... Everybody knows that... د معلوم په قرار reportedly کوريي نه I don't know his address. لار درته معلومه ده؟ Do you دئ را معلوم know the way? په معلوم وخت کښي known, certain time

معلومات ma'lumất, mālumất *m. plural Arabic of* معلومه **1** intelligence, information; knowledge د خپلو معلوماتو په اندازه as far په کښي as is known معلومات لاس ته راوړل to get information معلومات ورکول to inform **2** معلومات کول to investigate معلومات اخیستل to inquire about information; reference

معلومات فروشي ma'lumātfurushí *f.* conceit

معلوماتي ma'lumātí **1** informational (of material, etc.) **2** reference

معلومدار ma'lumdár **1** determined, set **2** noticeable **3** well-known معلومداره خبره ده چه... It is known that...

معلوم والی ma'lumwáɫaj **1** fame, renown **2** definitiveness, certainty

معلومول ma'lumawә́l **1** *denominative transitive* [*past:* معلوم يې کړ] **.1** to identify, detect; clarify, find out **1.2** to determine, establish **1.3** to clarify, explain **1.4** to publicize, declare **1.5** to discover, find, detect **2** *m. plural* **.1** identification, detection; clarification **2.2** determination, establishing **2.3** explanation, clarification **2.4** publicizing, declaration **2.5** finding, detection

معلومه ma'lúma **1** *feminine singular of* معلوم **2** ma'lumá *f. plural Arabic of* معلوم

معلومېدل ma'lumedә́l **1** *denominative intransitive* [*past:* معلوم شو] **.1** to turn out, become known معلومه شوه چه... It became known that... څرنګه چه معلومه سوې ده، څرنګه چه معلوم سوی دي... as became known **1.2** to be determined, be established; become definite, become set ... د خبرو يې دا معلومېده چه ... His words suggested that... **1.3** to get explained, become clear **1.4** to be discovered, detected, found د خاوري د تپلو سرچينه معلومه سوېده An oil field has been found. **1.5** to show up, appear څوک را معلوم نشو No one showed up; no one came out to me. **2** *m. plural* ☞ معلومېده

معلومېده mālumedá, ma'lumedá *m. plural* **1** clarification, identification **2** defining, establishing **3** explanation, clarification **4** discovery, detection, finding **5** appearance

معما mu'ammā́ *f. Arabic* [*plural:* معماوي mu'ammāwi *and m. plural: Arabic* معمات mu'ammā́t] **1** riddle; charade **2** *figurative* something enigmatic, inexplicable **3** problem

معماتوب mu'ammātób *m.* mystique; mysteriousness

معماشکل mu'ammāshákl enigmatic

معمار mi'mā́r *m. Arabic* **1** architect **2** builder **3** *figurative* creator

معمارباشي mi'mārbāshí *m.* **1** chief architect **2** site manager

معماري mi'mārí **1** *f.* architecture; art of building د معماري يادگار architectural monument **2** architectural معماري سبک architectural style

معمر mu'ammár *Arabic* elderly, of advanced age معمر کسان elderly people

معمور ma'múr *Arabic* **1** cultivated; tilled **2** prosperous, well furnished **3** abundant (of food for guests)

معموري ma'murí *f.* prosperity, well-being

معمول ma'múl *Arabic* **1.1** usual, customary, common لکه چه معموله ده as is the custom په معمول سره، سم له معمول as is customary ژوند د معمول په شان تېرېده Life went on as usual **1.2** poor, mediocre **1.3** treated; processed; made, manufactured **2** *m.* **.1** common phenomenon **2.2** custom, habit د خپل معمول په مطابق As is one's wont. **2.3** established fee (e.g., to the barber at a wedding)

معمولات ma'mulā́t *m. plural Arabic* manufactured goods; articles **1.3** معمول ☞

معمولاً ma'múlan *Arabic* usually, commonly

معمولي ma'mulí **1** usual, common په معمولي ډول as usual **2** work (of clothes)

معمى mu'ammā́ *f. Arabic* معمٰی ☞ معما مشکله معمٰی daunting task معنا ma'nā́ *f.* معنٰی ☞ معنی

معناً má'nán *Arabic* **1** by implication **2** in reality, actually, in fact **3** morally

معنوي ma'nawí *Arabic* **1** moral, spiritual, mental معنوي کمک moral support معنوي انحطاط moral degradation **2** ideal **3** semantic (of a difference)

معنويات ma'nawijā́t *m. plural Arabic* morale

معنويت ma'nawiját *m. Arabic* [*plural:* معنويات ma'nwijā́t] **1** morale تيت او کنېته معنويت low morale **2** ideality **3** spiritual side

معنی ma'nā́ *f. Arabic* معني ma'ní *f.* [*plural:* معنى وي ma'nā́wi, معنى گاني ma'nāgā́ni *and m. plural: Arabic* معاني ma'ā́ní] **1** sense, essence; meaning معاني علم ílm-i... **a** rhetoric **b** style د دي معنی نو دا ده چه This means that... معنی ورکول *compound verb* to mean, signify; give a دي معنی څه؟ What does this mean?

2 دا لغت په څو معانيو راځي in every sense په ټولو معانيو meaning to په بله معنی in other words idea, thought

1.1 معنادار ma'nādā́r, معنی داره ma'nādā́ra] معنى خيز ma'nākhéz meaningful; significant **1.2** meaning, expressing something **1.3** fraught with meaning **2** pointedly, meaningfully

معول mu'awwíl *Arabic* determined to do something

معهزا ma'ahazā́ *Arabic* at the same time; regardless of; moreover

معهود ma'húd *Arabic* **1** conventional; conditional **2** promised **3** determined, known

معيار mi'jā́r *m. Arabic* **1** measure, benchmark **2** yardstick, criterion **3** standard د سرو زرو معيار gold standard **4** level د ژوند معيار living standard **5** symbol د اصلي کار معيار *idiom* production capacity

معياري mi'jārí **1** standard (of language) **2** standard, accepted, normative معياري اساسونه norms معياري کول *compound verb* to standardize, normalize

معيت ma'iját *m. Arabic* entourage; escort معيت کول *compound verb* to escort

معيشت ma'jshát *m. Arabic* **1** means of subsistence, living **2** life

معين [1] mu'ín *Arabic* **1** *m.* assistant, helper د وزارت معين assistant minister; deputy minister **2** ☞ کمکي 1

معين [2] mu'ajján *Arabic* **1** definite, set **2** designated معين کول *compound verb* **a** to determine, establish **b** to appoint معين کېدل *compound verb* **a** to be determined, set **b** to be designated, get designated **3** to be designed, be intended for somebody

معين توب mu'ajjantób *m.* certainty; state of being preconditioned

معيني mu'ajiní *f.* assistant's or deputy's position

معينيت mu'ajjaniját *m.* **1** certainty; state of being preconditioned **2** *philosophy* determinism

معيوب ma'júb *Arabic* **1.1** ruined, damaged, defective **1.2** crippled, injured, disfigured معيوب سری a disabled person **1.3** unsuccessful, unfortunate **1.4** disgraceful, shameful, ignominious معيوب سلوک unbecoming conduct معيوب کول *compound verb* ☞ معيوب کېدل *compound verb* ☞ معيوبېدل **2** *m.* [*plural:* معيوبين ma'jubín] cripple, disabled person د جنگ معيوب disabled war veteran

معيوب والی ma'jubwā́laj *m.* injury, disfigurement

معيوبول [1] ma'jubawól *denominative, transitive* [*past:* معيوب يې کړ] to ruin, damage **2** to injure, cripple, disfigure **3** to shame, bring disgrace on

معيوبېدل [1] ma'jubedól *denominative, intransitive* [*past:* معيوب شو] to be ruined, be damaged; go bad; be defective **2** to be injured, be crippled, be disfigured **3** to be shamed, bring disgrace on oneself

مغار maghā́r *m. Arabic* مغاره maghārá *f. Arabic* [*plural: f.* مغاري maghāré, *m. plural: Arabic* مغاور maghāwír *and* مغاير maghājír] **1** cave, grotto **2** lair **3** abyss

مغازله mughāzalá *f. Arabic* **1** courtship, flirting **2** writing ghazals, songs (lyrical, love) **3** love poems

مغازه maghāzá *f. Arabic* shop, store د بوټو خرڅولو مغازه ،د بوټو مغازه footwear store مغازه عمومي department store

مغازه دار maghāzadár *m.* مغازه والا maghāzawālá shopkeeper; store owner

مغاک maghāk *m.* **1** pit; depression **2** trench

مغالطه mughālatá *f. Arabic* misunderstanding, mutual miscommunication

مغانه mghāna, məghāna *f.* groin; crotch, perineum

مغاو məghāw *m.* livestock disease

مغاویر maghāwír *m. plural Arabic of* مغاره

مغایر [1] mughājír *Arabic* **1** contradictory; juxtaposed; opposite **2** unacceptable

مغایر [2] maghājír *m. plural Arabic of* مغار

مغایرت mughājarát *m. Arabic* **1** controversy; contradiction **2** discrepancy; difference مغایرت لرل، مغایرت څرگندول *a* to contradict something *b* to diverge, differ

مغتنم mughtanám *Arabic* **1** valuable مغتنم گڼل to place a value on somebody **2** successful, profitable

مغذي mughazzí *Arabic* nutritious; filling مغذي مواد food products

مغرب maghríb, maghréb *m. Arabic* **1** west **2** sundown, sunset **3** west (point of compass) **4** Maghrib

مغربي maghribí *Arabic* **1.1** west, western مغربي ملکونه western countries **1.2** European مغربي لباس خلق European clothing Europeans **1.3** North African **2** *m.* **.1** inhabitant of Maghrib; Moor **2.2** European

مغرض mughríz *Arabic* **1.1** self-serving, opportunistic; greedy **1.2** biased **2** *m.* [*plural:* مغرضین mughrizín] **.1** self-serving person **2.2** biased person

مغرضانه mughrizāná **1** self-serving يو مغرضانه حدس mercenary motive **2** deliberately; in a biased way, in a partisan way

مغرور maghrúr *Arabic* **1** haughty; arrogant; conceited **2** *m.* **.1** braggadocio, braggart **2.2** haughty person

مغرورانه maghrurāná **1** haughty, conceited په مغرورانه ډول ويل to speak arrogantly **2** haughtily, conceitedly

مغروري maghrurí *f.* haughtiness; arrogance; conceit

مغروربدل maghruredál *denominative, intransitive* [*past:* مغرور شو] to be haughty; proud; put on airs

مغز maghz *m.* **1** brain مغز يې بيدار و He was smart. **2** kernel (of a nut, etc.) **3** pulp (of fruit) **4** interior, inside, core د لرگو مغز wood pulp **5** *figurative* contents (e.g., of a book)

مغزن maghzán **1** strong, robust **2** stocky, thickset **3** pithy, meaty (of a book)

مغزی [1] maghzí *f.* مغزی maghzáj *f.* **1** border; edge **2** welting; trim, fringe (of a dress) **3** high soil barrier to contain water in the field

مغزی [2] maghzáj *m.* neck; nape; neck part (of a carcass) لوږه غاړه او *idiom* He walks proudly. په مغزی خبري کول مسک مغزی گرزی maghzí… *a* to be haughty, be conceited *b* to behave tensely; sulk at somebody احمد په مغزی گرزیدل *a* to get upset په مغزی گرزی Ahmed is upset. *b* to sulk, take offence at

مغزی [3] maghzáj *m.* ☞ مغز

مغزی [4] maghzáj *m.* golden trim on shoes

مغشوش maghshúsh *Arabic* **1** mixed; adulterated **2** disturbed, made upset **3** tumultuous (of a people's history); stormy

مغصوب maghsúb *Arabic* occupied, conquered

مغفرت maghfarát *m. Arabic religion* absolution, forgiveness of sins

مغفور maghfúr *Arabic religion* deceased; late

مغل mughál *m.* [*plural:* مغلان mughalán] **1** Mogul د مغلو فوځونه Mogul army **2** ☞ مغول [1]

مغلستان mughalistán *m.* Mongolia

مغلق mughláq *Arabic* **1** unclear, incomprehensible **2** tangled مغلق ځای labyrinth **3** uncertain **4** complicated

مغلواره mughalwāra *f.* مغل والی mughalwālaj *m. historic* tyranny, rule of Moguls

مغلوب maghlúb *Arabic* vanquished, conquered, enslaved; subjugated مغلوب اولسونه enslaved peoples

مغلوبول maghlubawál *denominative, transitive* [*past:* مغلوب يې کړ] **1** to vanquish; subjugate, enslave **2** to overcome مشکلات مغلوبول overcome hardships

مغلوبیت maghlubiját *m. Arabic* **1** state of subjugation **2** defeat **3** depression په مغلوبیت گرفتار کبدل to be depressed

مغلوبیدل maghlubedál *denominative, intransitive* [*past:* مغلوب شو] **1** to suffer a defeat; lose (in sports) **2** to be subjugated, enslaved

مغله mughála *f.* female Mogul

مغلی mughalí ☞ مغولي [2]

مغلیان mughaliján *m. plural history* Moguls

مغلیجا mughulijá *f.* Mongolia د مغلیه د خلکو جمهوریت Mongolian People's Republic

مغموم maghmúm *Arabic* sorrowful; sad ستا په غم مغمومه وه She sympathized with you.

مغمومول maghmumawál *denominative, transitive* [*past:* مغموم یې کړ] to aggrieve, upset, sadden

مغمومبدل maghmumedál *denominative, transitive* [*past:* مغموم شو] to grieve; be sorry, lament

مغني mughanní *m. Arabic* **1** singer **2** musician

مغول maghól *m. singular & plural* **1** mogul **2** ☞ مغل [1]

مغولستان mangholistán *m.* Mongolia

مغوله maghóla *f.* female Mogul

مغولي magholí **1.1** Mongolian مغولي ولسي جمهوریت Mongolian People's Republic **1.2** pertaining to Moguls مغولي کبدل Come over to the Moguls. **2** *f.* Mongolian, Mongolian language

مغیب [1] mughajjáb *Arabic* **1** hidden, invisible **2** *m.* [*plural:* مغیبات mughajjabát] mysterious thing, mystery; secret

مغیب [2] maghíb *m. Arabic* **1** shortage; lack **2** sunset

مغیر [1] mughajír *Arabic* changing

مغیر [2] mughajár *Arabic* that has been changed, changed

مغیلان mughilán *m. Arabic* gum arabic tree

مفاجات mufādzhāt *m. Arabic* **1** surprise attack **2** sudden death

مفاجاتي mufādzhātí 1 sudden, unexpected 2 fatal 3 sudden (death)

مفاخر mafākhír m. plural Arabic glorious deeds; feats

مفاد mufā́d m. Arabic 1 sense, content; meaning 2 interests; benefits مشترک مفاد mutual benefit خپل مفاد ساتل to keep one's interests 3 economics interest

مفاد پرست mufādparást 1 greedy 2 m. greedy person; moneygrubber

مفارقت mufāraqát m. Arabic 1 departure, leave 2 parting, separation

مفاسد mafāsíd m. plural Arabic of مفسده

مفاصل mafāsíl m. plural Arabic of مفصل²

مفاصله mufāsalá f. Arabic 1 break; suspension 2 distance, interval

مفاهمه mufāhamá f. Arabic 1 mutual understanding ښه مفاهمه a good mutual understanding د ښې مفاهمي پر اساس based on mutual understanding 2 agreement; understanding د چا سره مفاهمه کول to reach an understanding with somebody مفاهمي ته رسېدل a to achieve mutual understanding a to come to an agreement, reach an understanding

مفاهيم mafāhím m. plural Arabic of مفهوم

مفت muft 1 free, free of charge 2.1 free په مفته له لاسه ايستل waste for nothing د تعليم مفت انتظام کول ta'alím-i... to organize free schooling مفت شراب قاضي هم خورلي دي proverb Everybody loves things for free. (literally: Even a qazi will drink wine as long as it's free.) 2.2 empty, senseless

مفتاح miftā́h m. Arabic key (to a lock) ☞ کلي 1

مفتح mufattíh Arabic 1 opening, unlocking 2 m. conqueror

مفتخر muftakhír Arabic proud, lofty

مفتخور muftkhór m. freeloader, sponger, parasite

مفت خوري muftkhorí f. sponging, freeloading, parasitism

مفتش mufattísh m. Arabic inspector; auditor; controller د اردو مفتش inspector general of the army

مفتشيت mufattishiját m. Arabic inspection; control د اردو مفتشيت military inspection

مفتوح maftúh Arabic 1 open, opened 2 conquered, subjugated 3 linguistics having above it the fatha vowel point (ﹶ)

مفتون maftún Arabic 1 delighted, enthralled 2 seduced 3 passionately enamored

مفتي¹ muftí m. Arabic mufti (chief judge who rules on controversial issues of Islamic law)

مفتي² múfti feminine plural of مفت 2

مفتي بها muftibahā́ given by mufti (of an explanation)

مفتي گري muftigarí f. position of a mufti

مفرح mufarráh Arabic fresh, refreshing مفرحه هوا fresh air

مفرد mufrád Arabic 1.1 unique; single 1.2 separated, isolated 2 m. grammar singular

مفردات mufradā́t m. plural Arabic [singular: مفرد] 1 articles, sections (e.g., of a report) 2 elements, components, ingredients

مفردوالی mufradwā́laj m. grammar singular, singularity

مفرزه mufrazá f. Arabic detachment, team

مفرط mufrít Arabic excessive, redundant په مفرطه درجه excessively, redundantly

مفرور mafrúr m. Arabic 1 fugitive, criminal 2 deserter

مفروشات mafrushā́t m. plural Arabic [singular: مفروش] furnishings, furniture and carpets

مفروق mafrúq mathematics subtrahend

مفروق منه mafrúq-minhú m. mathematics minuend

مفسد mufsíd Arabic 1 malicious; mean 2 m. .1 rebel; mutineer 2.2 evildoer 2.3 conspirator; inciter

مفسده mafsadá f. Arabic [m. plural: مفاسد mafāsíd] 1 damage; depravity; corruption 2 plots, schemes; machinations 3 outrage 4 mutiny; rebellion اجتماعي مفاسد idiom social evils

مفسدي¹ mufsidí f. 1 rebellion; mutiny مفسدي کول to rebel 2 outrage

مفسدي² mufsidí m. rebel

مفسر mufassír m. Arabic [plural: مفسران mufassirā́n and Arabic مفسرين mufassirín] commentator, reviewer

مفصل¹ mufassál Arabic detailed, close په مفصل ډول in detail, at length مفصل حالات معلومول to question at length

مفصل² mafsíl m. Arabic [plural: مفصلونه mafsilúna and Arabic مفاصل mafāsíl] 1 anatomy joint, articulation د مفاصلو ناروغي rheumatoid arthritis; gout 2 zoology joint, segment

مفصلاً mufassálán Arabic in detail, at length

مفصلي mafsilí Arabic 1 joint مفصلي موارض diseases of the joints 2 zoology articulated, segmented

مفعول maf'úl Arabic 1 made 2 m. grammar object of action; direct object مستقيم مفعول direct object غير مستقيم مفعول، صريح مفعول indirect object مفعول اسم grammar passive participle

مفعولي maf'ulí Arabic مفعولي حالت objective, accusative case

مفغن mufaghghán Arabic afghanized (of borrowed words) مفغن کېدل compound verb to be incorporated into the Afghan language; be afghanized; get assimilated by the Afghans

مفقود mafqúd Arabic missing in action

مفکر mufakkír Arabic 1.1 reflecting; thinking, cogitating 1.2 thoughtful 2 m. [plural: مفکرين mufakkirín] .1 thinker 2.2 intellectual 3 intelligentsia

مفکوره mafkurá f. Arabic [plural: مفکوري mafkuré and m. plural: مفکورات mafkurā́t] idea; thought; concept مفکوره يي واوښته They changed their minds.

مفکوک mafkúk Arabic 1 separated; disconnected 2 untied

مفلس muflís Arabic 1.1 bankrupt; broke 1.2 fallen on hard times, destitute 2.1 bankrupt 2.2 poor person

مفلسي muflisí f. 1 insolvency, bankruptcy 2 poverty, hardship په مفلسي in dire straits

مفهوم mafhúm Arabic 1 understood, comprehended 2 m. [plural: مفاهيم mafāhím, مفهومات mafhumā́t and مفهومونه mafhumúna] .1 sense, content په پراخ مفهوم سره in a broad sense 2.2 concept, idea (e.g., of space and time); comprehension نوي مفهومونه، نوي مفهومات new concepts

مفيد mufíd *Arabic* **1** useful; beneficial **2** meaningful

مفيديت mufidiját *m. Arabic* usefulness; utility; expediency

مقابل muqābíl *Arabic* **1.1** opposite, adverse; subtending (of an angle) مقابل لوری ،مقابل طرف adversary; the opposite side مقابل جانب the other party; party to a contract **1.2** corresponding to something or other **2** *m.* **.1** rival, adversary, enemy **2.2** equivalent, equal amount خپلو خرڅو په مقابل د to cover one's expenditures **2.2** *linguistics* antonym کښني مقابل په ... د **a** compared to somebody or something **b** against; to offset somebody or something **c** instead of something په رايو دبرشو د د بي عدالتۍ په مقابل کښنۍ مبارزه struggle against thirty votes مقابل against injustice په مقابل کښنۍ يي ځواب واوريد ... In response they heard the following ... دې نوي وضعيت په مقابل کښنۍ د status quo پيسو په مقابل کښنۍ for money

مقابلوالی muqābilwālaj *m.* **1** match **2** juxtaposition ...د سره مقابل والی لرل to match something

مقابله¹ muqābalá *f. Arabic* **1** comparison, juxtaposition په يوشي سخته مقابله يي compared to something **2** resistance مقابله کښنۍ They offered strong resistance. د چا سره مقابله وکړه to resist somebody مقابله کول *compound verb* **a** to compare **b** to hold out, endure; cope; master, manage احمد د ټولو سختيو مقابله وکړه Ahmed overcame all hardship. **c** compete (of goods) مقابله کېدل *compound verb* **a** to be compared, be juxtaposed **b** to face, come across something

مقابله² muqābíla **1** *feminine singular of* مقابل **2** *feminine to* مقابل

مقاتله muqātalá *f. Arabic* major battle; combat; fight قتل او مقاتله major battle

مقادير maqādír *m. plural Arabic of* مقدار

مقارن muqārín *Arabic* **1** compared; comparative **2** approximate (of celestial bodies) **3** simultaneous

مقاصد maqāsíd *m. plural of* مقصد

مقاطعه muqāta'á *f. Arabic* **1** break, termination of relations **2** boycott سره مقاطعه کول ...د **a** to break up with somebody, end relations **b** to boycott انتخاباتو سره مقاطعه کول د to boycott elections

مقال maqāl *m. Arabic* speech; remarks

مقاله maqālá *f. Arabic* **1** article **2** speech; remarks; presentation مقاله لوستل *compound verb* to give a presentation

مقام maqām, muqām *m. Arabic* [*plural:* مقامونه maqāmúna *and Arabic* مقامات maqāmāt] **1** place, location مقام کول *compound verb* to settle **2** echelon, agency, authority لوړ مقامات higher authorities د دولتي مقامات ،رسمي مقامات government agencies اداري مقامات governing bodies **3** status, role; position, rank په ... کښنۍ منلئ مقام لرل ځانله to be a recognized authority on something مقام لرل to occupy a special place **4** *music* maqam **5** *music* fret; tune *idiom* implement, realize دپر غوره مقام لرل د عمل په مقام رسول to carry a price; be highly valued (of goods)

مقامي maqāmí, muqāmí topical; local

مقانيزمه meqānizmá *f.* lock (for weapons)

مقاولوي muqāwalawí *Arabic* contractual مقاولوي وجائب contractual obligations

مقاوله muqāwalá *f. Arabic* **1** agreement, contract د بيمي مقاوله agreement, contract of insurance **2** تحريري مقاوله written contract convention **3** transaction

مقاولنامه muqāwalanāmá *f.* agreement, contract د حمل او نقل مقاوله نامه agreement of freight, charter

مقاومت muqāwamát *m. Arabic* resistance سخت مقاومت، کلک مقاومت fierce resistance د بدن مقاومت a body's resistance د چا سره، د يو شي سره مقاومت کول to resist somebody

مقاومه muqāwamá *f.* **1** ☞ مقاومت **2** animosity, hostility

مقايسوي muqājasawí comparative مقايسوي فلالوجي comparative philology, comparative linguistics يوه مقايسوي اشاره کول to make a comparison, compare to something

مقايسه muqājasá *f. Arabic* **1** comparison; juxtaposition د مقايسې درجې degrees of comparison د يو شي سره مقايسه کول to compare, match to something **2** analogy

مقبره maqbará *f. Arabic* mausoleum, burial vault, tomb درنه مقبره sarcophagus

مقبل muqbíl *Arabic* **1** happy **2** *m.* happy person

مقبوض maqbúz *Arabic* gained; occupied (e.g., of a position)

مقبول maqbúl *Arabic* **1** pleasant, attractive **2** acceptable; suitable; fit **3** accepted, customary

مقبوليت maqbuliját *m. Arabic* **1** pleasantness; attractiveness **2** acceptability; suitability **3** marketing (of goods) عمومي مقبوليت ميندل *idiom* to be everyone's favorite, be universally liked

مقتدا muqtadā *m. Arabic* leader مذهبي مقتدا clergyman

مقتدر muqtadír *Arabic* **1.1** strong, mighty مقتدر مملکت a powerful nation **1.2** skillful, able; talented مقتدر ليکوال a talented writer **2** *m.* master, potentate

مقتدي¹ muqtadí *m. Arabic* **1** follower, adept **2** imitator

مقتدی² muqtadā *m. Arabic* مقتدیٰ ☞ مقتدا

مقتصد muqtasíd *Arabic* thrifty, economical

مقتضا muqtazā *f. Arabic* مقتضي¹ muqtazí *f.* necessity, need د حال as necessary په مقتضا سره

مقتضي¹ muqtazí *f.* مقتضا muqtazā necessity, need

مقتضي² muqtazí **1** necessary, needed **2** suitable, fitting

مقتضيات muqtazijāt *m. plural Arabic of* مقتضي¹

مقتول maqtúl *Arabic* killed

مقدار miqdār *m. Arabic* [*plural:* مقدارونه miqdārúna *and Arabic* مقادير maqādí] **1** quantity د پيسي مروجه مقدار، د پيسي جاري مقدار *economics* money supply **2** dose (of a drug) **3** size د اجورې مقدار wage rate **4** measure, unit of measurement **5** amount (of debt etc.)

مقداري miqdārí quantitative

مقدر muqaddár *Arabic* preordained, predetermined هغه چه مقدر و هغه وشول What happened was what was preordained.

مقدرات muqaddarāt *m. plural Arabic* [*singular* مقدر] fates خپل مقدرات د چا سره تړل fate خپل مقدرات د چا سره تړل to tie one's fate with somebody

مقدرت maqdarát *m.* مقدره maqdará *f. Arabic* 1 strength, power 2 potential

مقدس muqaddás *Arabic* sacred مقدسه وظیفه sacred duty مقدس ډوډۍ holy bread مقدس تېل *religion* holy oil

مقدسات muqaddisāt *m. plural Arabic* [*singular:* مقدس] shrines

مقدم muqaddám *Arabic* 1.1 advance; going in front; leading 1.2 former, earlier; previous 1.3 introducing تر کتاب مقدم کول to introduce a book 1.4 preferable مقدم ګڼل to prefer, show preference 2 *m.* head; elder

مقدماً muqaddámán *Arabic* earlier, formerly

مقدمات muqaddamāt *m. plural Arabic* [*singular:* مقدم] 1 preliminary conditions 2 prerequisites; premises 3 beginnings, basics 4 preparation

مقدماتي muqaddamātí 1 preliminary, preparatory د قرار داد مقدماتي صورت draft agreement مقدماتي شرط منل to accept a preliminary condition 2 introductory; introducing مقدماتي خبري introductory word

مقدمه muqaddamá *f.* 1 foreword; introduction; preamble; preface; overture 2 litigation, process, legal action 3 premise 4 confrontation, altercation; مقدمه کول *compound verb* a to litigate b *obsolete* to declare war

مقدمه باز muqaddamabā́z *m. Eastern* litigious person, barrator

مقدمه بازي muqaddamabāzí *f.* barratry, litigiousness; litigation

مقدور maqdúr *Arabic* 1 possible, feasible 2 *m.* .1 possibility, feasibility 2.2 strength, power 2.3 means, money

مقر¹ maqár, maqárr *m. Arabic* location; residence

مقر² muqár *m.* Mokur

مقراض miqrā́z *m. Arabic* scissors

مقرب muqarráb *m. Arabic* near; close, intimate

مقرر muqarrár *Arabic* 1 established, determined 2 appointed مقرر ځای destination 3 intended 4 decided

مقررات muqarrarā́t *m. plural Arabic* [*singular:* مقرر] provisions; decrees, resolutions; rulings

مقرریا muqarartjā́, muqarrartjā́ *f.* 1 establishment, determination 2 appointment

مقررول muqararawə́l, muqarrarawə́l 1 *denominative, transitive* په معلمی مقررول، په معلمی سره [*past:* مقرر یې کړ] .1 to appoint مقررول to appoint an instructor 1.2 to establish, determine 2 *m. plural* .1 appointment 2.2 establishment, determination

مقرري muqararí, muqarrarí *f.* 1 appointment 2 establishment, determination

مقرریدل muqararedə́l, muqarraredə́l *denominative, intransitive* [*past:* مقرر شو] 1 to be appointed, get appointed په یو ماموریت مقرر شو، په [مقرر شو] یو ماموریت سره مقرر شو He got an appointment. 2 to be established, be determined; get established

مقرریده muqararedə́, muqarraredə́ *m. plural* 1 appointment 2 establishment, determination

مقرون maqrún *Arabic* 1 close to something 2 bordering on something

مقسوم maqsúm *m. Arabic mathematics* dividend

مقسوم علیه maqsumaléjh *m. mathematics* divisor

مقصد maqsád *m. Arabic* [*plural:* مقصدونه maqsadúna *and Arabic* مقاصد maqāsíd] 1 goal, intention د سفر په مقصد for the purpose of travel مقصد دي څه to achieve one's goal په خپلو مقاصدو رسېدل ... مقصد می دا دئ چه What do you mean to say? دئ؟ I mean that اصلي مقصد to get what one wants 2 sense د مقصد کب نیول ... sense, essence ... مقصد دا دئ چه The point is that... په دې ټولو the meaning of all this is that 3 خبرو کښي مقصد دا دئ چه destination د مقصد بندر *trade* port of destination

مقصدیت maqsadiját *m.* 1 purposefulness, focus, single-mindedness 2 trend

مقصر muqassír *Arabic* 1 guilty, at fault په مقصر برغ ویل speak guiltily 2 *m.* culprit

مقصود maqsúd *Arabic* 1.1 goal, task 1.2 object 1.3 *proper noun* Maqsud 2 desired, required مقصود ځای ته رسېدل، مقصود محل ته to arrive at one's destination رسېدل د شاه مقصود ډبره *idiom* serpentine (mineral)

مقصوداً maqsúdán *Arabic* definitely; on purpose, deliberately

مقصودي maqsudí desirable, desired مقصودي نتائج desirable results

مقصودېدل maqsudedə́l *denominative, intransitive* [*past:* مقصود شو] to be achieved, be attained; work out, pan out

مقطر muqattár *Arabic* 1 distilled مقطري اوبه distilled water 2 *chemistry* distilled

مقطع¹ maqtá' *f. Arabic* 1 section, profile; size across; cross section د کرې مقطع cross section of a sphere 2 paradigm of a poetic meter; last stanza of a poem

مقطع² muqattá' *Arabic* 1 cut up 2 abridged 3 chanted (of a poem)

مقطوع maqtú' *Arabic* 1 cut off; amputated 2 final; decisive په مقطوع صورت فیصله کول make a final decision

مقعد maq'ád *m. Arabic anatomy* 1 rear, seat 2 anus

مقعر muqa'ár *Arabic* 1 concave 2 sunken 3 bent over

مقفی muqaffā́ *Arabic* مقفیٰ, rhymed

مقل muql *m. Arabic* 1 fruit of dwarf palm 2 *Amyris agallocha* (tree or its resin)

مقلد muqallíd *Arabic* 1 imitating 2 *m.* [*plural:* مقلدین muqallidín] .1 imitator; follower 2.2 actor, comedian

مقلوب maqlúb *Arabic* turned upside down, flipped; overturned; turned inside out

مقناطیس maqnātís *m.* magnet برقي مقناطیس electric magnet

مقناطیسي maqnātisí 1 magnetic مقناطیسي عقرب magnetic needle or arrow 2 magnetic مقناطیسي طریقه hypnotism

مقناطیسیت maqnātisiját *m.* magnetism

مقنع¹ muqní' *Arabic* convincing مقنع دلیل convincing argument

مقنع ² miqná' *f.* مقنعه miqna'á *f. Arabic* veil; bridal veil

مقنن muqannín *Arabic* **1** legislative قوت مقننه legislative power مجلس مقننه legislative assembly **2** *m.* [*plural:* مقننین muqanninín] legislator

مقني muqanní *m. Arabic* **1** sewage remover **2** person who cleans karezes

مقوا muqawwá *f. Arabic* **1** binder **2** cardboard

مقوايي muqawwájí cardboard

مقوله maqulá *f.* [*plural:* مقولې maqulé *and m. plural: Arabic* مقولات maqulát] **1** what was said, utterance **2** saying **3** aphorism, maxim **4** *grammar* category

مقوم muqawwím *m. Arabic* **1** appraiser **2** [*plural:* مقومات muqawwimát] factor; criterion

مقوي ¹ muqawwí *Arabic* **1** reinforcing غذا مقوي nourishing diet **2** restorative, bracing

مقوى ² muqawwá *f. Arabic* مقوٰی ☞ مقوا

مقويت muqawwiját *m.* strengthening (e.g., of health) مقويت وركول *compound verb* to brace, restore

مقهور maqhúr *Arabic* **1** depressed; upset **2** defeated

مقهوريت maqhuriját *m. Arabic* **1** depression, frustration **2** state of being defeated

مقياس miqjás *m. Arabic* [*plural:* مقياسونه miqjāsúna *and Arabic* مقياسات miqjāsát] **1** scale; yardstick; measure د طول مقياسات linear measures د سطحي مقياسات area measures د وزن مقياسات weight measures د اوزانو او مقياسو دفتر Office of Weights and Measures د مقياس تحويلول يو و بل ته measure conversion **2** size

مقياسوي miqjāsawí relative ارزش مقياسوي relative value

مقيد muqajád, muqajjád *Arabic* **1** obliged **2** established, determined **3** tied up, constrained, restrained **4** limited (e.g., of a mind)

مقيدول muqajadawə́l, muqajjadawə́l *denominative, transitive* [*past:* مقيد يې کړ] **1** to obligate ځان مقيدول to pledge, commit oneself **2** to establish, determine **3** to tie up, constrain

مقيدبدل muqajadedə́l, muqajjadedə́l *denominative, intransitive* [*past:* مقيد شو] **1** to pledge, commit oneself **2** to be established, determined **3** to be tied up, constrained

مقيش muqqájsh *m. Arabic* brocade

مقيش دوزي muqqajshduzí *f.* brocade with a pattern

مقيم muqím *Arabic* **1.1** residing; sojourning **1.2** permanent, steady **2** *m.* resident, inhabitant

مكاتب ¹ mukātíb *Arabic* **1** correspondent **2** *m.* correspondent, reporter

مكاتب ² makātíb *m. plural Arabic of* مكتب

مكاتبه mukātabá *f. Arabic* correspondence

مكاتيب makātíb *m. plural Arabic of* مكتوب

مكار makkár **1.1** sly, devious **1.2** lying; hypocritical **2** *m.* cunning person, cheat, fraudster; trickster, swindler

مكاروني makāróni *m. plural* macaroni

مكاره makkára **1** *feminine singular of* مكار **2** *f.* female deceiver, trickster

مكاري ¹ makkārí *f.* cunning, deceit, tricks

مكاري ² makkári *feminine plural of* مكاره

مكاشفه mukāshafá *f. Arabic* **1** discovery, detection **2** exposure **3** inquisitiveness; love of knowledge

مكافات mukāfát *m. Arabic* remuneration, reward; retribution مادي مكافات a valuable reward نقدي مكافات a monetary reward د receive خپلو اعمالو مكافاتو ته رسېدل as a reward مكافات په طور retribution

مكافي mukāfí *Arabic* **1** equal **2** matching, corresponding

مكال makál *m.* jeweler's tools

مكالمه mukālamá *f. Arabic* conversation, interview, talk

مكان makán *m. Arabic* **1** place **2** position, rank **3** lavatory

مكاني makāní local مكاني قيد *linguistics* local dialect

مكبر الصوت mukabbir-us-sáut *m. Arabic* loudspeaker ماشين sound amplifier

مكتب maktáb *m. Arabic* [*plural:* مكتبونه maktabúna *and Arabic* مكاتب makātíb] **1** school, educational institution عالي مكتب institution of higher learning پښتو زبان مكتب a school with instruction in the Pashto language عدديه مكتب college فارسي زبان a school with instruction in the Dari language دري مكتب home school کورنی مكتب elementary school مقدماتي مكتب منځنی مكتب secondary school حربيه مكتب military school **2** mekteb (elementary religious school) **3** school, trend

مكتبي maktabí **1** school مكتبي انډيوال classmate مكتبي زوى a son who is a schoolboy **2** *m.* school student

مكتسب ¹ muktasíb *Arabic* earning; acquiring

مكتسب ² muktasáb *Arabic* **1.1** earned **1.2** acquired, amassed **2** *m.* [*plural:* مكتسبات muktasabát] **.1** earnings **2** acquisition

مكتشف muktashíf *Arabic* **1** inquiring, inquisitive **2** *m.* **.1** inquisitive person **2.2** investigator **2.3** prospector (e.g., of minerals)

مكتوب maktúb *Arabic* **1** written **2** *m.* [*plural:* مكتوبونه maktubúna *and Arabic* مكاتيب makātíb] letter; message

مكتوباً maktúbán *Arabic* in writing

مكتوب نويسي maktubnawisí *f.* correspondence ژوندی مكتوب نويسي lively correspondence

مكث maks *m. Arabic* **1** stay **2** delay, suspension

مكدر ¹ mukaddár *Arabic* **1** polluted, turbid (of water, etc.) **2** gloomy; troubled مكدر کول *compound verb* **a** to pollute, make muddy **b** to disturb, distress

مكدر ² mukaddír *Arabic* **1** muddling (water, etc.) **2** disturbing, distressing

مكر makr *m. Arabic* cunning, ruse; deceit, fraud مكر کول *compound verb* to quibble, cheat; pretend

مكرافون mikrāfón *m.* **1** microphone, mic **2** handset (of a phone)

مكران makrán *m.* Mekran (area in Baluchistan)

مكرجن makrdzhə́n مكار ☞

مكرجنه makrdzhóna ☞ مكاره

مكرر mukarrár *Arabic* repeated, recurring; multiple مكرر توليد recurring performance, repeated performance مكرر يې ويلي دي He repeated himself time and again.

مكرراً mukarrárán *Arabic* repeatedly, on numerous occasions

مكررول mukararawól, mukarrarawól *denominative, transitive [past:* مكرر يي كړ] to repeat

مكرريدل mukararedól, mukarraredól *denominative, intransitive [past:* مكرر شو] to be repeated

مكرژن makrzhón مكار ☞ مكار

مكرم mukrím *Arabic* 1 well-mannered, polite; respectful 2 friendly; hospitable

مكروب mikrób *m.* germ د امراضو مكروبونه pathogenic germs

مكروبي mikrobí microbial مكروبي واكسين vaccine

مكروبيولوژي mikrobiolozhí *f.* microbiology

مكرونه makaroná *f.* macaroni

مكروه makrúh *Arabic* nasty; disgusting; unpleasant; antipathetic مكروه نوم odious name

مكرك makaŕók *m.* 1 lamb collar 2 *technology* collar

مكرن makŕón *m.* sick ram

مكره mákra *instead of* مه كړه چه خدای God forbid... Don't!

مكړي makŕáj *m. botany* Ceratocephalus[1]

مكړي makŕáj *m. [plural:* مكړيان makŕiján *and* مكړي makŕí] 1 tadpole 2 earthworm 3 *dialect* pathogenic element[2]

مكړي makǝŕáj *m.* 1 ☞ مكړک 1 2 pulley, sheave[3]

مكړي makŕáj *m.* handle (e.g., of a bucket)[4]

مكزيک mekzík *m.* Mexico

مكزيكي mekzikí 1 Mexican 2 *m.* Mexican

مكسچر míkschǝr *m.* mixture, potion

مكسور maksúr *Arabic* 1 wrecked; broken 2 *linguistics* the qasra vowel point (ِ)

مكسيكو meksikó *f.* Mexico د مكسيكو ښار, مكسيكو سيټي Mexico City

مكشوف makshúf *Arabic* 1 discovered, detected; explored 2 exposed 3 uncovered, opened, laid bare

مكشوفول makshufawól *denominative, transitive [past:* مكشوف يي كړ] 1 to open, discover; explore 2 to expose, uncover (e.g., shortcomings) 3 to uncover, bare

مكعب muka'áb 1 cubic مكعب متر cubic meter 2 *m. mathematics* cube

مكفن mukaffán *Arabic* shrouded

مكفي makfî *Arabic* adequate, satisfactory

مكلف mukalláf *Arabic* 1 obligated څان مكلف ګرڅول to obligate پري مكلف كول، څان ور باندي مكلف كول to pledge 2 magnificent, gorgeous; luxurious; sophisticated[1]

مكلف mukallíf *Arabic* complicating, hindering, aggravating[2]

مكلفول mukalafawól, mukallafawól *denominative, transitive [past:* مكلف يې كړ] 1 to obligate 2 to appoint; hire (e.g., servant)

مكلفيت mukallafiját *m. Arabic* 1 obligation اخلاقي مكلفيتونه moral duty خپل مكلفيت په څای كول to fulfill one's duty 2 military duty عسكري خدمت مكلفيت compulsory military duty

مكلفيدل mukalafedól, mukallafedól *denominative, intransitive [past:* مكلف شو] 1 to be obliged, be obligated 2 to be appointed; be hired (e.g., servant)

مكمل kukammál *Arabic* 1 perfect, excellent مكمل ترتيبات broad measures 2 completed, finished 3 fulfilled, completed 4 plenary عمومي او مكمل بي وسلي كول a plenary meeting universal disarmament

مكملول mukamalawól, mukammalawól *denominative, transitive [past:* مكمل يې كړ] 1 to complete, finish 2 to fulfill, complete

مكنه makóna مكنه خاوره yellow clay

مكن makán *m.* small window

مكنا makṇá *f.* waterwheel hub

مكنه mǝkṇá *f.* woman's veil

مكي makó *endearing to* 3 مكي

مكوت makúṭ 1 roasted مكوت كول *compound verb* to roast 2 burned

مكوه mákawa *in lieu of* مه كوه

مكه makká *f.* Mecca مكهٔ معظمه Mecca

مكي makkí 1 Meccan 2 *m.* Meccan[1]

مكي makǝj *f.* unleavened flat bread[2]

مكي makkój *f. regional* corn, maize[3]

مكي makój *f. proper noun* Makay[4]

مكياژ makijázh *m.* makeup مكياژ كول *compound verb* to apply makeup مكياژ كېدل *compound verb* to put makeup on oneself مكياژ ليري كول to remove makeup

مكېز makéz *m.* 1 smile 2 coquetry د مكېز كاته coquettish glance مكېز كول *compound verb* to coquet

مكېزګره makezgára *f.* coquette, coquettish woman

مكبره mákega *in lieu of* مه كبره

مكيف mukajíf *Arabic* 1 intoxicating, alcoholic 2 *m. [plural:* مكيفات mukajifất] .1 drug 2.2 alcoholic beverage[1]

مكيف mukajjáf *Arabic* adjusted to something, acclimated to something نوي وطن ته څان مكيف كول to be acclimated[2]

مكين makín *m.* Makin (city, Waziristan)

مګ mǝg *m.* chimney above the hearth[1]

مګ mag *m. Eastern* ☞ مبر[2]

مګازين magāzín *m.* warehouse, storage عمومي مګازين general use storage facility مال مګازين ته سپارل deliver goods to a warehouse

مګر magár *conj.* but, however, only مګر چه ... but ... provided that ..., however, it can happen that... مګر دومره به وي چه ... but it can turn out that... 2 apart, except مګر په لاندي مواردو كنبي except the following cases[1]

مګر magár *m. regional* eighth month of Indian calendar[2]

مګزين magzín *m. regional* warehouse, storage عسكري مګزين military depot.

مګس magás *m.* fly (insect)

مگَک məgák *m. Eastern* ☞ مبرک

مگَنځ magə́ndz *f. dialect* مگنز magə́dz small window ☞ بمونغ

مگَنه magə́na *f.* small window

مگنزیُم magnezijúm *m. plural* magnesia

مگه ¹ mága *f. Eastern* ☞ مبره

مگه ² mə́ga *f. Eastern* ☞ مبره

مغار maghár *m.* ☞ موخی

مگه کوری məgakúraj *m. Eastern* ☞ مبر کوری

مل ¹ mal *m. [plural:* مله mlə *and rear* ملونه malúna] 1 comrade, friend 2 fellow traveler, fellow passenger 3 assistant, helper 4 associate, confederate; accomplice, sidekick, abettor مل کېدل *compound verb* a to be a friend; make friends, become friends b to be a fellow traveler, be a fellow passenger راځه راسره مل شه! Come with me! c to be an assistant d to be associate, be a confederate; be an accomplice, be an abettor 5 supplement, enclosure, appendix د ... په مل as an enclosure خدای دي درسره مل شي! *idiom* May God help you!

مل ² mul *m. plural* wine

ملا ¹ mullá *m. Arabic [plural:* ملايان mullājā́n] 1 mullah 2 scholar, scribe ځان ملا ملا کول *compound verb* to pretend to be a scholar 3 (pagan) priest 4 *plural* ملايان a clergy b scribes; scholars

ملا ² mlā *f. [plural:* ملاوي mlā́wi *and* ملاگاني mlāgā́ni] small of the back; loins د ملا درد spinal column, spine د ملا تیر lumbar pain ملايي خوږیږي He has a backache. ښوک تر ملا نیول to put one's arms around someone's waist ملا سمول stand tall و...ته a د ملا تړل to take up something; get ready for something b to take up arms ملا په چا تړل، د چا ملا تړل to help, assist, provide support to somebody په یو کار پسې ملا تړل to plan, intend; concoct, be up to something د چا ملا ماتول to get ready for a trip د سفر ملا تړل to deliver a crushing blow to somebody رضا یي کړه، ملا یي ماته کړه You can get what you want with kind words. ملايي ماته شوه He exhausted his strength. خپله ملا نه پرانستل endless trouble

ملا ³ malá *f.* friendship

ملازان mullāzā́n *m.* ملابانگ *m.* mullābā́ng azan, call to (morning) prayer ملازان مالی at dawn

ملابست mulābasát *m.* ملابسه mulābasá *f. Arabic [m. plural Arabic* ملابسات mulābasā́t] 1 uncertainty, ambiguity 2 pretense 3 confusion

ملابند mlābánd *m.* ملاپاډه mlāpāḍá *f. and* ملاپټی mlāpaṭə́j *f.* leather belt; sash

ملاتړ mlātáṛ *m.* 1 militiaman; armed guard 2 succor, reinforcement, assistance, support د دوی ملاتړ ته ولاړ دئ He is ready to help them. د یو کار پوره ملاتړ to call for help ملاتړ غوښتل to provide all-out support for something 3 belt کول

ملاتړلی mlātaṛə́laj 1 that has taken up, set about to do something 2 ready, combat-ready 3 ready to help, sympathetic ملاتړلی ورورہ! *idiom* Dear friend!

ملاتړونی mlātaṛúnaj *m.* belt, sash

ملاتري mlātaṛí *f.* support, aid, help ملاتري کول *compound verb* to support, aid, help

ملاتوب mullātób *m.* clergyman's rank; position of a mulla

ملاچرگک mullāchərgák *m.* hoopoe

ملاڅی mlātsə́j *f.* crosspiece (of a spade)

ملاح mallā́h *m. Arabic* 1 boatman 2 sailor

ملاحظات ² mulāhazā́t, mulāhizā́t *m.* 1 *plural Arabic from* ملاحظه considerations; arguments

ملاحظه mulāhazá mulāhizá *f. Arabic [plural:* ملاحظي mulāhazé *and m. plural Arabic* ملاحظات mulāhazā́t] 1 review; examination (e.g., medical) ملاحظات کول *compound verb* a to examine; review b to read 2 respect; politeness

ملاحي mallāhí *f.* 1 navigation, sailing 2 boat transportation 3 marine, maritime, sea

ملاخ malákh *m.* ☞ ملاق

ملاخوږی mlākhwúgaj with lumbar pain

ملاخوږی mlākhwugí *f.* lumbar pain, back pain

ملارگی mlārágaj 1 lazy 2 with lumbar pain

ملاریا malārijā́ *f.* malaria د ملاریا ماشی malaria mosquito, anopheles د ملاریا مریض malaria patient

ملازم mulāzím *m. Arabic* 1 waiting on somebody, serving somebody 2.1 servant 2.2 waiter 2.3 *regional* clerk

ملازمت mulāzamát *m. Arabic* 1 being part of the retinue; waiting (on somebody) 2 services, service, service industry 3 court service 4 عسکري ملازمت military service 5 diligence

ملازمه mulāzimá *Arabic feminine to* ملازم

ملاست mlāst lying

ملاستل mlāstə́l *intransitive* ☞ څملاستل

ملاستنه mlāstə́na *f.* lying

ملاستو mlāstú *m.* sash

ملاسته mlā́sta 1 *feminine singular of* ملاست 2 *f.* lying

ملاشینی mlāshínaj lazy, sluggish

ملاغاښی mlāghā́ḳhaj *m.* vertebra

ملاغه malāghá *f.* ladle

ملاق malā́q *m.* 1 tumbling 2 *aviation* loop ملاق خوړل، ملاق وهل *compound verb* a to tumble b to loop a loop

ملاقات mulāqā́t *m. Arabic* 1 meeting, date د ملاقات کوټه drawing room, living room ملاقات یي ورسره وشو He met (them). 2 conversation, interview د چا سره ملاقات کول a to meet, see somebody b to have a conversation with somebody, to interview somebody 3 visit د ملاقات کارت business card د ملاقات کارډ a business card 2 ملاقاتي mulāqātí 1 visit ملاقاتي کارت، ملاقاتي کارډ a business card 2 visitor د ملاقاتیانو کمره drawing room, reception area

ملاغه mallāqá *f.* ☞ ملاغه

ملاقي mulāqí *Arabic* (something) that one comes across; oncoming د چا سره ملاقي کېدل to come across, to stumble across د فکر او علم He met clever and educated people. خاوندانو سره ملاقي شو

727

ملاک mallāk *m. Arabic* [*plural:* ملاکان mallākān *and Arabic* ملاکین mallākín] landowner, landlord, agrarian لوی ملاک، ستر ملاک a big landlord, a feudal lord

ملاکا malākkā́ *f.* Malay Peninsula

ملاکي mallākí *f.* land ownership

ملاگوري mullāgorí **1** *m. plural* Mullagori (tribe) **2** Mullagorai

ملال malāl *Arabic* **1** *m.* sorrow; grief ورک د دوی د زړه ملال شي! May grief pass them by! خفقان او ملال پیدابول to sadden **2.1** sad; sorrowful; disillusioned; melancholic **2.2** languid ملالي سترگي languid eyes ملال کاته languid look

ملال انگېز malālangéz tiresome; boring; tedious

ملالت malālát *m. Arabic* anguish; blues; dismay

ملاله malā́la **1** *f.* **.1** beauty **1.2** *proper noun* Malala **2** *feminine singular from* ملال

ملالي¹ malā́li *feminine plural from* ملال

ملالي² malā́li *oblique from* ملاله

ملالۍ³ malālā́j beautiful, handsome, pretty

ملا ماتوونکی mlā mātawúnkaj crushing دښمن ته ملا ماتوونکي وهنه ورکول to deliver a crushing blow to the enemy

ملاماتی mlāmā́taj **1** run down, all in, collapsing **2** sluggish, lazy **3** rotten (of a column, etc.)

ملامت malāmát *m. Arabic* **1** reproach, expostulation, rebuke, disapproval, condemnation, denunciation، په لوظ کېنبي ملامت کېږي، په لفظ کېنبي ملامت کېږي He was forced to break his promise. **2** *predicative* at fault; guilty ملامت څوک دئ؟ Who is to blame? هغه دا ده دی یې ملامت وواېه This is not his fault. هغه نه دئ ځان ته یي ملامت He was blaming himself. ملامتول ☞ ملامت کول *compound verb* ملامت گڼل to blame someone

ملامتول malāmatawә́l *transitive* [*past:* ملامت یې کړ] to reproach, censor, reprove, blame, condemn هغه نه ملامتوئ! Don't blame him! خپل ځان ملامتول to blame oneself

ملامته malāmā́ta ملامتي malāmatí *f.* ملامتیا malāmatjā́ *f.* reproach, disapproval, condemnation دوستانو ملامته پر ویله چه ... His friends reproached him for…

ملامتېدل malāmatedә́l *denominative, intransitive* [*past:* ملامت شو] to be condemned, be denounced په دې کار ملامتېږي He is denounced for this.

ملامري mlāmarój *f.* vertebra

ملاني¹ mullānә́j *f.* learned woman

ملانۍ² mlānә́j *f. anatomy* amnion, fetal membrane

ملاو milā́w *regional* converging, matching قدم ملاو کړه! *idiom* March in lockstep!

ملاوستنی mlāwastә́naj *m.* ملاوستی mlāwā́staj *m.* belt, sash

ملاوېدل milāwedә́l *intransitive* [*past:* ملاو شو] *regional* **1** to meet ستا دوست راته ملاو شو Your friend met me. **2** to be granted (time off)

ملاجا malājā́ *f.* Malaya د ملایا شبه جزیره the Malayan Peninsula

ملائک malājík *m. plural Arabic of* ملک⁵

ملایم mulājím ملائم mulāím *Arabic* **1** gentle, tender **2** affectionate **3** moderate, mild (of climate)

ملایمت mulājimát *m. Arabic* **1** gentleness; meekness; tenderness **2** affection **3** moderation, mildness (of climate)

ملایمول mulājimawә́l *transitive* [*past:* ملایم یې کړ] **1** to make gentle, tender **2** to make affectionate **3** to make moderate, mild (of climate)

ملایمي mulājimí *f.* ملایمت ☞

ملایي¹ malājí **1** Malayan **2** *m.* Malayan

ملایي² mullājí *f.* rank of mullah

ملبوس malbús *Arabic* clothed

ملبوسات malbusā́t *m. Arabic plural* clothing, articles of clothing

ملت millát *m. Arabic* [*plural:* ملتونه millatúna *and Arabic* ملل millál *also considered plural*] **1** population of a country; people; nation د متحده ملتو مجلس، د متحده ملتو مؤسسه، د متحده مللو مؤسسه، د ملتونو ټولنه the United Nations د ملگرو ملتو مؤسسه *history* the League of Nations **2** *religion* congregation, flock

ملتان multā́n *m.* Multan (city, Pakistan)

ملتبس multabás *Arabic* **1** mixed, tangled **2** ambiguous

ملت پرستي millatparastí *f.* **1** ☞ ملت دوستي **2** nationalism

ملت دوستي millatdostí *f.* patriotism

ملتفت multafít *Arabic* **1** paying attention to something, noticing something ملتفت کول *compound verb* to draw attention زه دلته تاسي یوي نکتي ته ملتفت کول غواړم I would like to draw your attention to one point. پس له دې ملتفت اوسي In the future, you should pay more attention. ملتفتېدل *compound verb* ☞ ملتفت کېدل **2** attentive

ملتفتېدل multafitedә́l *intransitive* [*past:* ملتفت شو] to pay attention to something, notice something, have a good look at something

ملتقا multaqā́ *f. Arabic* ملتقیٰ **1** juncture, joint **2** confluence (of a river)

ملتوب maltób *m.* ملتیا ☞

ملتوک maltūk *m. computer science* accessory

ملتوي multawí *Arabic* **1** rolled up, coiled, wrapped up **2** twirling, spinning **3** delayed, outstanding (of payment, etc.) ملتوي کول *compound verb* **a** to roll up, coil, wrap up **b** to twirl, spin **c** to delay, be in arrears (of payment, etc.) ملتوي کېدل *compound verb* **a** to get rolled up; get coiled; get wrapped up **b** to spin, revolve, rotate **c** to get delayed, become outstanding (of payment, etc.)

ملتی mәltáj slippery, smooth

ملتیا maltjā́ *f.* **1** escort **2** friendship **3** help

ملت milát *m. regional* minute څو ملته پس، څو ملته باندي a few minutes later

ملجا maldzhā́ *f. Arabic* asylum, shelter

ملح milh *m. Arabic* [*plural:* املاح amlā́h] salt

ملحد mulhíd *m. Arabic* **1** heretic; schismatic; apostate **2** godless person, atheist

ملحدانه mulhidāná heretical; schismatic; apostatic

ملحق mulhaq *Arabic* **1** attached; appended; enclosed **2** adjacent; close, contiguous **3** dependent, depending

ملحقات mulhaqát *m. plural Arabic from* د عمارت او د هغه ملحقه a building and its extensions ملحقات

ملحقول mulhaqawә́l *transitive* [*past:* ملحق يې کړ] to join; attach; append

ملحقېدل mulhaqedә́l *intransitive* [*past:* ملحق شو] **1** to be joined, be annexed, be appended; be enclosed **2** to depend

ملحوظ malhúz *Arabic* **1** likely, possible **2** *m.* [*plural:* ملحوظونه malhuzúna *and Arabic* ملحوظات malhuzất] **.1** likelihood, possibility **2.2** chance; case د هر ملحوظ دپاره چه و for whatever reason, just in case **3** thought, idea

ملحه mílha *f.* ☞ ملح

ملخ malákh, məlákh *m.* [*plural:* ملخان malakhán, məlakhán *and* ملخ malә́kh] locust الوتونکي ملخ migratory locust, Asiatic locust مراکشي ملخ Italian locust, *Calliptamus Italicus* ايتالوي ملخ Moroccan locust

ملخوځي malkhódzi *f. plural* fenugreek seed

ملخوزه malkhóza *f.* fenugreek

ملخوزي malkhózi *f. plural* ☞ ملخوځي

ملخى¹ məlәkháj *m.* locust

ملخى² məlәkháj *m.* **1** hand (of a clock) **2** eleven-cartridge rifle

ملداوي molldāwí **1** Moldavian ملداوي ژبه Moldavian, Moldavian language **2.1** *m.* Moldavian **2.2** *f.* Moldavian, Moldavian language

ملداويا molldāwijá *f.* Moldavia

ملزوم malzúm *Arabic* **1** inseparable; indissoluble, continuous لازم او ملزوم mutually causal; interrelated, interconnected **2** annexed, attached

ملزومات malzumất *m. plural Arabic* **1** necessary things **2** gear

ملزومېدل malzumedә́l *intransitive* [*past:* ملزوم شو] to be inseparable, be inseparably connected

ملطف multíf, mulattíf *Arabic* extenuating, mitigating, mollifying ملطف اثر mollifying effect

ملعون mal'ún *Arabic* damned, cursed

ملغا mulghá *Arabic* annulled, canceled

ملغاسي malghāsí, malghāsáj ملغاشي malghāshí, malghāsháj **1** Malagasy **2** *f.* Malagasy language

ملغلره malghalә́ra *f.* pearl ☞ مرغلره

ملغمه malghamá *f. Arabic* amalgam

ملغود malghód *m.* crook, swindler, flattering deceiver

ملغى **mulghá́** *Arabic* ☞ ملغا

ملفوف malfúf *Arabic* **1.1** wrapped; coiled **1.2** folded; rolled **1.3** related to something **2.1** wrapping **2.2** envelope

ملقب mulaqqáb *Arabic* nicknamed, called

ملک¹ mulk *m. Arabic* **1** state, country **2** region, locality; area

ملک² milk, mulk *m. Arabic* [*plural* ملکونه milkúna *and Arabic* املاک amlất] property; land property; real estate

ملک³ məlә́k *m.* [*plural:* ملکان məlәkán, *dialect second plural:* ملکانان məlәkānán] malik, alderman; clan elder د کلي ملک village elder

ملک⁴ malík *m. Arabic* [*plural:* ملکان malikán *and Arabic* ملوک mulúk] **1** head, leader **2** master, lord **3** tzar, sovereign, king

ملک⁵ malák *m. Arabic* [*plural:* ملائک، ملايک malájak] angel

ملک⁶ malák ☞ ملخ

ملکات malakất *m.* **1** *plural Arabic from* ملکه **2** possessions, domain راسخه ملکات ګڼل consider one's property

ملک الشعراء malik-ul-shu'ará́ *m. Arabic* king of poets (title); poet laureate

ملک الموت malak-ul-máut *m. Arabic* angel of death

ملک پروري mulkparwarí *f. regional* concern about the country, about its prosperity

ملک زاده malikzādá́ *m.* prince

ملک زاده məlәkzādá́ *m.* malik's son

ملک ګير mulkgír aggressive, annexationist

ملکوت malakút *m. Arabic* **1** heavens **2** host of angels

ملکوتي malakutí *Arabic* **1** heavenly **2** wonderful (of a voice, etc.), angelic

ملکه¹ malaká *f. Arabic* [*plural:* ملکي malaké *and m. plural: Arabic* ملکات malakất] **1** mastery, getting the hang of, skill په ... کښې ملکه پیدا کول، په ... کښی ملکه لرل to master something **2** gift, talent

ملکه² maliká *f. Arabic* tsarina, queen

ملکه³ məlә́ka *f.* mistress

ملکه⁴ maláka *f.* angel

ملکي¹ məlәkí *f.* seniority, status of malik or alderman ملکي کول *compound verb* to be a malik, be an elder, be a clan elder

ملکي² malikí *f.* reign ملکي کول *compound verb* to reign

ملکي³ milkí *m. Arabic* landowner

ملکي⁴ mulkí *Arabic* **1** civil, civilian ملکي جرنبل، ملکي برګد، ملکي commander (leader) of tribal militia ملکي لباس فرقه مشر civilian clothes ملکي ماٻورين hospital ملکي شفاخانه civil service ranks ملکي وېش administrative ملکي عسکر militia **2** administrative administrative division

ملکيت milkiját *m. Arabic* **1** ownership د ملکيت حق right of ownership د مځکو ملکيت، د مځکي ملکيت landed property, land ownership a خصوصي ملکيت personal property b private property اجتماعي ملکيت personal property فردي ملکيت; شخصي ملکيت public property, collective property دولتي ملکيت، ولسي ملکيت ، ملي government property **2** dominion, possession ملکيت

ملکيتي milkijatí related to ownership, property

ملګرتوب malgәrtób *m.* ملګرتيا malgәrtjá **1** friendship; companionship **2** escorting **3** support د چا سره ملګرتوب with a to د چاسره ملګرتوب کول، د چا سره ملګرتوب لرل be friends, associate with b to escort somebody c to support somebody **4** agreement, unanimity **5** subscription (to a newspaper, journal, etc.) **6** accompaniment **7** belonging (membership)

ملګري malgərí *f.* ☞ ملګرتوب [^1]

ملګری malgә́raj **1** *m.* **.1** friend, comrade راته گرانه ملګریه! Dear friend! صادق ملګری true friend اداري پوخ ملګری close friend, colleague, coworker **1.2** fellow traveler, fellow passenger **1.3** associate, partner **1.4** ally, adherent ملګري کول *compound verb* **a** د چا سره ملګري کول to send, dispatch with somebody **b** to join, add (e.g., one's voice) د چا ملګری کېدل **a** to get attached to somebody; make friends with somebody **b** to join somebody, unite, connect with somebody **c** to escort somebody د چا ملګری کېدل په یوه نظریه to support somebody's viewpoint; side with somebody **1.5** tributary (of a river) **1.6** attachment **2** *attributive* **.1** escorting, attendant د خپل ملګري هیئت سره with one's entourage دا فکر ده د سره ملګری وي دولت ملګری This thought would not leave him. **2.2** united ملګري ملتونه United Nations هغه د غله ملګري او د کاروان دواړو ملګری دئ *idiom* He talks out of both sides of his mouth. [^2]

ملګرې malgә́re *f.* **1** female friend, female comrade **2** female fellow traveler, female fellow passenger **3** female associate, female partner **4** female ally, female adherent [^3]

ملګریتوب malgəritób *m.* ☞ ملګرتوب

ملل millál *m. plural Arabic of* ملت [^1]

ملل mləl *transitive* [*past:* وېۍ مله] to select a buddy, pair up (in games) [^2]

ملم malám *m.* ☞ مرهم

ملمع mulammá' *Arabic* ☞ ملمه

ململ malmál *m. plural* muslin

ملمه mulammá **1** enameled **2** gilded **3** motley; bright

ملنډه malánḍa *f.* ridicule; mockery په چا ملنډي کول، په چا ملنډو وهل to mock, ridicule somebody په ملنډو ويل to speak mockingly

ملنډي malánḍi *plural of* ملنډه [^1]

ملنډی malanḍáj, malanḍí *m.* **1** jester; clown **2** joker [^2]

ملنډۍ malanḍә́j *feminine to* ملنډی [^1] [^3]

ملنډي وهونکی malánḍi wahúnkaj *m.* tease; mocker

ملسنار milansár *Eastern* outgoing, gregarious

ملنگ maláng *m.* **1** dervish, mendicant fakir **2** ascetic **3** careless person, nonchalant person **4** one in love **5** *proper noun* Malang

ملنگان malangā́n *m.* variety of sedge, *Cyperus elatus*

ملنگتوب malangtób *m.* ملنگي malangí *f.* **1** status of a dervish **2** carelessness; equanimity

ملنگای malangáj *m. proper noun* Malangay [^1]

ملنگۍ malangә́j *f.* large motley-colored watermelon [^2]

ملنگیان malangijā́n *m. botany* Egyptian sage

ملو maláw *m.* bag, sack [^1]

ملو mlo *oblique plural of* مل [^2]

ملو malā́w *m.* ☞ غونج [^3] 1

ملو miláw *regional* ☞ ملاو [^4]

ملواح malwā́, malwā́h *f. Arabic hunting* decoy bird

ملوالی malwā́laj *m.* ☞ ملتیا

ملوب malób *m.* **1** blood and pus **2** sweat

ملوث mulawwás *Arabic* **1** stained, soiled **2** spoiled (e.g., of milk) **3** infected ملوث کول *compound verb* **a** to soil, contaminate **b** to spoil (e.g., milk) **c** to infect ملوث کېدل **a** to get soiled, contaminated **b** to get spoiled (e.g., milk) **c** to get infected

ملودل məlodә́l *transitive* ☞ سپړل

ملودي melodí *f.* melody

ملوک mulúk *m. plural Arabic of* ملک 4 [^1]

ملوک malúk **1** gentle; nice **2** *m.* honey, sweetheart [^2]

ملوک الطوائف muluk-ut-tawāíf *m. plural Arabic* feudals; feudal rulers

ملوک الطوایفي muluk-ut-tawāifí *f.* **1** feudal system, feudalism **2** feudal strife

ملوکانه mulukāná royal ذات ملوکانه king

ملوکه malúka **1** *feminine singular of* ملوک **2** *f.* **.1** beauty **2.2** sweetheart

ملوکیت mulukiját *m.* **1** monarchism, monarchy **2** imperialism **3** empire

ملول malúl *Arabic* dejected, sad

ملونه mlúna *m. plural* ملوني mlúni *m. plural* **1** bridle; reins **2** reins د قواؤ ملونه reins of government; helm of state حکومت ملونه یې په خپل لاس کښې ونیوه He took over control of the armed forces.

ملوېدل milawedә́l *denominative, intransitive* [*past:* ملو شو] to be found

مله mála *f.* steppe plant [^1]

مله mlə *masculine plural of* مل [^2]

مله mla *f.* **1** female friend **2** female fellow traveler, female fellow passenger **3** bridesmaid [^3]

مله malá *f.* ☞ ملواح [^4]

مله mlə *imperfect of* ملل [^5] 2

ملهم malhám *m.* plaster د زړه ملهم، د خوږ ملهم *idiom* comfort; consolation, joy; chicken soup for the soul [^1]

ملهم mulhám *Arabic* inspired [^2]

ملهم mulhím *Arabic* **1** inspiring **2** *m.* inspirer [^3]

ملهمانه mulhimāná **1** inspiring **2** with inspiration, inspiredly

ملي millí *Arabic* **1** national; people's ملي اقتصاد national economy ملي ثروت national wealth ملي مسئله ethnic problem د وینې زلمیانو ملي نهضت *history* The National Movement of Awakened Youth شواری ملي، د ملي خپلواکی مبارزه national liberation struggle ملي شورا shuā-yi... National Council ملي کول *compound verb* to nationalize ملي کېدل *compound verb* to be nationalized, get nationalized د بانک ملي کېدل nationalization of a bank **2** church, faith, denominational [^1]

ملي mli *present tense of* ملېدل [^2]

ملي mli *present tense of* ملودل [^3]

ملي mullә́j *f.* **1** garden radish **2** radish [^4]

ملۍ mle *plural of* مله 3 [^5]

ملیا miljā, maljā encountered; occurring ملیا کول compound verb to bring together, join ملیا کېدل compound verb to occur, be found

ملیار maljár m. regional 1 gardener 2 vegetable grower

ملیارد millijárd m. billion

ملیت millját m. Arabic 1 national sentiment 2 nation; ethnicity د ملیت د غوښتني نهضت national identity ملیت احساس national liberation movement 3 nationality; citizenship نوی ملیت قبلول to change one's citizenship

ملیتاریزم militārízm m. militarism

ملیت پرست millijatparást m. nationalist

ملیت پرستي millijatparastí f. 1 nationalism 2 national sentiment

ملیت خواهي millijatkhāhí f. 1 nationalism 2 national liberation movement

ملیترزم militarízm m. militarism

ملېدل mledál intransitive [present: ملي past: و ملېده] to live, settle, sojourn

ملېریا malerjā f. regional ☞ ملاریا

ملېزي 1 mallezí m. plural Mallezi (tribe) 2 mallezáj m. Mallezai

ملېزیا malezijā f. Malaysia

ملیشي milishí f. ملیشیا milishjā f. regional police (militia)

ملېشیا maleshjā f. ☞ ملېزیا

ملي کول millikawál m. plural ملي کېده millikedá m. plural nationalization

ملي گرام milligrām m. milligram

ملیمتر millimétr m. millimeter

ملین mulajján Arabic mitigated, mollified, softened, soft ملینه ی linguistics diphthong ai

ملیون 1 milljón m. million

ملیون 2 millijún m. plural Arabic nationalists singular ملي 2

ملیونر millijonér m. ملیون والا miljonwālā m. millionaire

ملیوني miljoní, milljoní اته ملیوني ملت eight-million people

م، م abbreviation of ملگري ملتونه

ممات mamāt m. Arabic death د حیات او ممات جگړه دوام لري A life or death struggle is going on.

مماتي mamātí deadly (of struggle)

مماثل mumāsíl Arabic similar, resembling, analogous

ممارست mumārasát m. Arabic experience; practice

مماشات mumāshát m. plural Arabic 1 obsequiousness 2 thoughtful attitude 3 joint merrymaking

مماطله mumātalá f. Arabic 1 delaying (of something that was promised) 2 procrastination, deferral (of payment)

ممالک mamālík m. plural Arabic of مملک

ممانعت mumāna'át m. Arabic 1 obstacle, impediment 2 barrier, obstruction, blockage ممانعت کول a to hinder, impede b to obstruct, block

ممانه mamāṇa f. botany Sageretia brandrethiana (the tree and its fruit)

ممبر mémbár m. regional member (of an organization) ممبر کېدل to be a member of an organization, join an organization

ممبري membarí f. membership

ممتاز mumtáz Arabic 1.1 choice; excellent, superlative, best 1.2 distinctive ممتاز کول compound verb to distinguish, discern په چابک دستی ممتاز کېدل to be distinguished by agility 2 proper noun Mumtaz لوړ او ممتاز هرکلی idiom red-carpet welcome

ممتد mumtád, mumtádd Arabic 1 continuing 2 extended, stretched

ممتنع 1 mumtaní' Arabic refusing, refraining ممتنع رایه ورکول abstain from voting

ممتنع 2 mumtaná' Arabic 1 impossible, unacceptable 2 unavailable, inaccessible, unassailable

ممثل mumassíl Arabic 1.1 reproducing 1.2 expressing, voicing (somebody's feelings, sentiments) 2 m. .1 actor 2.2 mouthpiece (of somebody's feelings, sentiments) 2.3 representative, spokesperson (of a company, etc.)

ممثله mumassíla f. Arabic [plural: ممثلات mumassilát] actress

ممد mumíd, mumídd Arabic 1 promoting, assisting something 2 m. assistant, helper

ممدوح mamdúh Arabic 1 laudable, commendable 2 m. person who is lauded or to whom a laudatory poem is dedicated

ممرېز mamréz m. colloquial spur

ممزوج mamzúdzh Arabic blended, mixed ممزوج او گډ blended, mixed

ممغوړن mámghuṛán dirty

ممکن mumkín Arabic 1 possible تر ممکنه حده پوری as much as possible تر څو چه ممکنه وي possibly ممکنه ده چه insofar as او ورته ممکنه ده چه He can do this. ډېره ممکنه ده quite possible ممکن گرځول to the extent possible تر ممکني اندازې پوری make possible 2 perhaps, maybe ممکن چه هغه بله لار ونیسي He may take another road.

ممکنات mumkinát m. plural Arabic possibilities singular ممکن

ممکنوالی mumkinwālaj m. possibility, feasibility

ممکنول mumkinawál denominative, transitive [past: ممکن یې کړ] to make possible

ممکنېدل mumkinedál denominative, intransitive [past: ممکن شو] to be possible دوی ته به ممکنه شي چه They can do this.

ملایي mumlājí f. مومیائي ☞ مومیایي

مملکت mamlakát m. Arabic [plural: مملکتونه mamlakatúna and Arabic ممالک mamālík] nation, state, country

مملکتداري mamlakatdārí f. statehood

مملکتي mamlakatí state, government مملکتي تشکیلات system of government

مملو mamlú Arabic full, filled

مملوک mamlúk Arabic 1 m. slave 2 being owned by, belonging to

مملوکه mamluká f. Arabic 1 female slave 2 property; belongings

ممنوع mamnú' Arabic prohibited, banned; forbidden ممنوع قرارول compound verb to prohibit, ban دا ممنوع دئ This is prohibited.

ممنوعات mamnu'át m. plural Arabic forbidden, forbidden things [singular ممنوع]

ممنوعي mamnu'í forbidden ممنوعي سمت، ممنوعي سيمه restricted ممنوعي area

ممنون mamnún *Arabic* **1** appreciative, grateful تر ابده به مو خپل ممنون کې We will be grateful to you as long as we live. **2** contented

ممنونيت mamnuniját *m. Arabic* **1** gratitude, appreciation د چا څخه ممنونيت ښکاره کول express gratitude, appreciation to somebody **2** contentment, satisfaction

ممی ¹ məmáj *m.* ladybug

ممی ² mamə́j *f. chilren's speech* sweets, candy, fruit

ممیره mamirá *f.* Buxton's Blue, *Geranium wallichianum*

ممیز ¹ mumajjíz *Arabic* **1.1** differentiating; delimiting **1.2** distinguishing **2** *m.* controller; separating comma (,) in decimal fractions ممیزه اشاره quotation marks د خساري ممیزه *trade* average adjuster

ممیز ² mumajáz *Arabic* differentiated; distinguished

ممیز ³ mamíz *m. plural* sultana raisins سره ممیز red sultana raisins شنه ممیز corinthian raisins, currants ☞ مویز

ممیزه mumajizá *f. Arabic* [*plural:* ممیزي mumajizé *and m. plural: Arabic* ممیزات mumajizát] **1** consciousness **2** distinction, difference, peculiarity **3** advantage

ممیزي ¹ mamízi *f. plural* sultana raisins, raisins

ممیزې ² mumajizé *plural of* ممیزه

من ¹ man *m.* **1** mahn (unit of weight that has different meanings indifferent areas of Afghanistan) د پیښاور من، انګریزي من Peshawar mahn (about 32 kg) د کابل من Kandahar mahn (about 4 kg) تبریزي من Kabul mahn (equals 8 sihrs or 565 kg) **2** area that yields one mahn wheat لس منه مځکه an area that yields ten mahns من په منیا *idiom* **a** to get the knack of; gain experience in something **b** to calm down, relax چه هر قدم به مي کېدۀ من په منیا calm down من من راته ښکاربده، پورته کاوه I had a hard time walking, like I had lead weights on my feet.

من ² mán, mə́n *suffix* ☞ مند

منا maná *f.* **1** hut **2** tower for a watchman who guards a field **3** counter **4** stand, support (for grapevine)

منابع manábi' *Arabic* **1** *masculine and feminine plural of* منبع **2** resources; means تولیدي منابع، تولیداتي منابع resources ثروتي منابع means of production طبیعي منابع natural resources

مناجات munádzhát *m. Arabic* **1** prayer offered while alone, nighttime prayer **2** religious hymn, psalm

مناجاتي munádzhātí *m.* one who prays

منادات munādát *m. Arabic* call, address, proclamation

منادي ¹ munādí *m. Arabic* herald

منادیٰ ² munādā́ *Arabic* **1** proclaimed; declared منادیٰ کول *compound verb* to proclaim, declare **2** *m. grammar* vocative case

منار manár, munár *m.* مناره manārá *f. Arabic* **1** minaret **2** small tower **3** lighthouse

منازعه munāza'á *f. Arabic* [*plural:* منازعي munāza'é *and m. plural: Arabic* منازعات munāza'át] **1** dispute; contentions **2** litigation **3** claim حقوقي منازعات legal disputes; claims د منازعاتو فیصلي رئیس chairman of the board of arbitration (in a province)

منازل manāzíl *m. plural Arabic of* منزل

مناسب munāsíb *Arabic* corresponding; appropriate; suitable; convenient په مناسب، مناسب سره مناسب ځای a suitable place مونږ دا accordingly مناسب ګڼل consider expedient مناسب بلل It is not دا مناسبه نه ده We believed it necessary. چه ویل مناسب seemly. دایي مناسبه و ګڼله چه He found it suitable.

مناسبت munāsabát *m. Arabic* [*plural:* مناسبات munāsabát] **1** connection, relation د جشن په مناسبت in connection with the holiday د چا سره مناسبت لرل have a relationship with somebody **2** match, suitability مناسبت لرل **a** to match, suit **b** to befit, be worthy **3** occasion د یو خاص مناسبت دپاره for a special occasion

مناسک manāsík *m.* **1** *plural Arabic of* منسک ¹ **2** rites of pilgrimage

مناطق manātíq *m. plural Arabic of* منطقه

مناظر manāzír *m. plural Arabic of* منظره

مناظره munāzará *f. Arabic* dispute, disagreement; strife (ideological)

منافات munāfất *m. Arabic* **1** incompatibility; contradiction د... سره منافات لرل to be incompatible **2** discrepancy, difference

منافذ manāfíz *m. plural Arabic of* منفذ

منافرت munāfarát *m. Arabic* disdain; mutual loathing

منافع manāfi' *m. plural Arabic of* منفعت

منافق munāfíq *Arabic* **1** duplicitous **2** *m.* **.1** hypocrite; fake, phony **2.2** enemy **2.3** heretic

منافقانه munāfiqānā́ insincere, duplicitous

منافقي munāfiqí *f.* **1** hypocrisy **2** faithlessness

منافي munāfí *Arabic* contradictory; incompatible د مقصد سره منافي unsuitable language د ادب څخه منافي عبارت incompatible with decency, indecent

مناقشه munāqashá *f. Arabic* **1** argument; quarrel; conflict **2** discussion مناقشه کول *compound verb* **a** to argue, quarrel **b** to conduct a discussion, discuss

مناقصه munāqasá *f. Arabic* tender, competitive bidding

مناقصه کوونکی munāqasá kawúnkaj *m.* bidder

مناقلاتي munāqalātí transportation, engaged in hauling مقامات مناقلاتي transportation organizations

مناقله munāqalá *f. Arabic* [*plural:* مناقلي munāqalé *and m. plural: Arabic* مناقلات munāqalát] **1** communication, transportation, conveyances د مناقلاتو خط a communication line; supply line **2** shipping, hauling, transportation

منال manál *m. Arabic* acquisition

مناني mənānáj tiny, miniscule

مناهي manāhí *m. plural Arabic* مناهیات manāhiját, *singular* منهي prohibitions

منبت munabbát *Arabic* **1** relief; relief decorated **2** *m.* relief

منبت کاري munabbatkārí *f.* relief; relief image

منبر mimbár, minbár *m. Arabic* 1 minbar (pulpit in a mosque) 2 stand; pulpit; podium

منبع manbá', mambá' *f. Arabic* [*plural: m.& f. Arabic* منابع manābí'] source; origin; beginning منبع اخيستل to originate from, flow out (of a river) عايداتي منبع source of revenue, income

منبهات munabbihā́t *m. plural Arabic* analeptics, stimulants

منت minnát *m. Arabic* [*plural:* منتونه minnatúna *and Arabic* منن minán] 1 mercy; favor د اظهار منت په خان منل graciously say; dare say 2 appreciation, gratitude 3 affability; grace 4 request 5 begging, supplication 6 reproach, rebuke په منت لرلي بغ ويل to speak reproachfully زه ستا منت چا ته منت کول a to beg, supplicate پرچا منت کوم I beg you. b to obligate somebody پرچا منت کول، پرچا منت اينږدول a to rebuke, reproach somebody b to demand special gratitude for a favor rendered; believe that somebody owes one a favor زاري او منتونه کول، منت زاري کول to use various entreaties and supplications

منت بار minnatbā́r 1 appreciative, grateful, obliged to somebody د چا منت بار نه دئ He owes no gratitude to anyone. 2 reproached, rebuked

منت باري minnatbārí *f.* appreciation, gratitude د هيچا منت باري نه کول to owe no gratitude to anyone

منتج muntídzh *Arabic* 1 generating, causing 2 finishing, ending in something منتج کېدل a to originate, stem from b to be finished, end in something

منتجه muntidzhá *f. Arabic physics* resultant force

منتخب muntakháb *Arabic* selected, elected منتخب وکيلان elected deputies

منتخبات muntakhabā́t *m. plural Arabic* 1 selected works; readings; anthology 2 excerpts

منت دار minnatdā́r appreciative, thankful; obliged to somebody منت دار زوی your thankful son

منت داري minnatdārí *f.* 1 appreciation, gratitude 2 contentedness

منتر mantár *m.* 1 incantation or prayer purportedly providing protection from snakebites, etc. منتر ويل *compound verb* to conjure, charm, exorcise 2 love potion

منترواال mantarwālā́ *m.* snake charmer

منتشر muntashír *Arabic* 1 diffused, scattered 2 issued, published

منتظر muntazír *Arabic* 1.1 waiting, expecting منتظر اوسېدل، منتظر کېدل to wait, expect زه تاته منتظر وم د I have been waiting for you. چا راتلو منتظر دئ He is expecting somebody. 1.2 duty officer منتظره قطعه duty unit 1.3 hopeful 2 *m.* [*plural:* منتظرين muntazirín] one who waits, welcomes

منتظم muntazím [1] *Arabic* 1 arranging, organizing 2 *m.* 2.1 manager منتظم course manager د کورس منتظم 2.2 custodian د عمارت building custodian 2.3 organizer, sponsor 2.4 administrator

منتظم muntazám [2] *Arabic* 1 orderly, arranged in order; organized 2 regular, systematic 3 symmetrical په منتظم ډول a in an organized manner b regularly, systematically c symmetrically منتظم کول

compound verb to order, organize, systematize b to render symmetrical

منتظماً muntazámán *Arabic* 1 in an organized manner 2 regularly, systematically 3 symmetrically

منتظمه muntazimá *f. Arabic* 1 female manager 2 female head, leader

منتظميت muntazimiját *m.* commandant's office د وزارت منتظميت ministry commandant's office

منتقد muntaqíd *m. Arabic* critic

منتقل muntaqál *Arabic* 1 carried over; hauled 2 transferred, displaced 3 assigned (of rights) منتقل کول *compound verb* ☞ منتقلول منتقلېدل *compound verb* ☞ منتقلېدل

منتقلول muntaqalawál *denominative, transitive* [*past:* منتقل يې کړ] 1 to carry over; haul 2 to transfer; displace 3 to assign (rights)

منتقلېدل muntaqaledál *denominative, intransitive* [*past:* منتقل شو] 1 to be carried over; be hauled 2 to be transferred, be displaced 3 to be assigned (of rights)

منت گذار minnatguzā́r obliging; helpful; accommodating

منت ورونکی minnát wṛúnkaj ☞ منت بار

منتهي muntahí [1] *Arabic* graduating منتهي طالبان graduates

منتهیٰ muntahā́ [2] *f.* منتهیٰ 1 1.1 end, limit, edge 1.2 maximum په لسو ورځو کښې in ten days at most 2.1 finished, completed منتهیٰ کول *compound verb* to finish, complete *compound verb* to get finished, get completed 2.2 maximal 3 extremely, very دا منتهیٰ مهم اکتشاف دئ This is an exceptionally important discovery.

منتي ويدیو montewídeo *m.* Montevideo

منټ mináṭ *m. regional* minute, moment منټ کښې in a minute

منثور mansúr *Arabic* prosaic منثور ادب prose fiction منثور شعر prose poem منثور مضامين prose

منج məndzh, mundzh [1] *m.* 1 rush (fibrous plant) 2 *Saccharum arundinaceum* (plant from which rope is made) 3 Ravenna grass, *Erianthus Ravennae* 4 ☞ مزری [2]

منج mandzh [2] *m.* sleeping accommodations; bed

منج məndzh [3] *paired word to* غونج

منجاري məndzhārā́j *m.* chandler

منجاريتوب mandzhāritób *m.* chandlery

منجاور mundzhāwár *m.* ☞ مجاور

منجر mundzhár, mundzhárr *Arabic* ended, finished, completed منجر کېدل *compound verb* to be ended, finished; reach something; to be over په يو فکر منجر کېدل to arrive at the thought that... دا کار دې ته ... منجر شو چه The bottom line was ...

منجري mandzháre *f.* flower bud, burgeoning bud

منجغی mandzhagháj *m.* منجقی mandzhaqáj *anatomy* vagina

منجل məndzhál 1.1 twisted 1.2 serpentine 2 *m.* 2.1 ☞ منجمله 2.2 barb, tentacle (of a plant)

منجلسي mandzhlisí *m. colloquial* ☞ مجلسي

733

منجله məndzhəlá *f.* **1** support, ring made of grass or wood on which a jug of water is placed **2** pillow placed on the head when carrying loads **3** intertwined wheat stalks

منجمد mundzhamíd *Arabic* **1** frozen; frozen over; iced over شمالي د شمالي برخو منجمد the Arctic Ocean منجمد بحر، شمالي منجمد سمندر نقاط the Arctic **2** congealed; solidified, hardened منجمد کېدل *compound verb* **a** to freeze; ice over **b** to congeal; solidify; harden

منجمله mindzhumlá *Arabic* **1** including; among others **2** as for example **3** on the whole

منجنيق mandzhaníq *m. Arabic* **1** tower **2** ballista; catapult, siege machine; battering ram **3** crane

منجنيقي mandzhaniqí *m.* ballista warrior

منجنيقيت mandzhaniqiját *m. Arabic* ballistics

منجور mandzhawór *m.* ☞ مجاور

منجوړا mandzhuṛá base, mean

منجي ¹ munadzhdzhí *m. Arabic* savior, liberator

منجی ² mundzháj **1** pug-nosed بونجی منجی pug-nosed **2** noseless

منجيت mandzhít *m. botany* madder

منجبدل məndzhedə́l *intransitive* [*past:* ومنجبد، ومنجبده] to fidget

منجبله mandzhilá *f.* ☞ منجله

منځ mandz *m.* **1** middle; middle or inner part of something; medium منځ د لاري a midway, halfway **b** roadway په منځ کښي between, among; in the middle, amongst د منځ چوکۍ the middle chair د ښار د منځ across the town د کال منځ midyear **2** time interval د هغې مودي په منځ کښي during this time in a يوه ورځ تر منځ day د خلورم او پنځم په دي منځ کښي in the meantime; meanwhile تاريخ تر منځ between the fourth and the fifth (date) **3** cavity (of a horn) **4** distance, gap; interval يو شی په منځ کښي پرېکول display a cross section of something په منځ کښي راتلل to wedge in, butt in د ميدان منځ ته راايستل to introduce (e.g., a law) **a** to منځ ته راتلل، منځ ته کېدل، منځ ته drag out into the square **b** to shame داسي پوښتنتي منځ ته راځي to appear, emerge منځ ته را لوېدل Such questions emerge. منځ ته راوړل **a** to deliver, bring in **b** to exhibit, show منځ ته کول **a** to create **b** to receive, obtain; acquire له منځه ايستل، له منځه ورکول، له منځه کښل، له منځه **a** to remove; eliminate له منځه تلل، له منځه وتل، له منځه ورکېدل وړل to disappear, vanish **b** to stay out of something, not interfere into something; avoid something د چا په منځ کښي وېشل to divide between somebody په خپل زمونږ په منځ کښي among us; between us پنه په منځ کښي اېبنوول among one's own, in one's milieu منځ کښي to mediate, act as a go-between

منځالۍ mandzālə́j *f.* middle finger

منځ ته کېده mandztakedə́ *m. plural* emergence, appearance

منځغرى mandzgháraj *m.* gorge, ravine

منځغکي mandzghə́ki *m. plural* kernel, core, nucleus, meat (of a nut, etc.)

منځکنبي mándzkkhi منځ کي، منځ کښي، په منځکنبي between, among; in the middle, amongst پدي منځکنبي meanwhile

منځګرتوب mandzgərtób *m.* ☞ منځګري

منځګري ¹ mandzgərí *f.* منځګر يتوب، منځګري توب mandzgəritób *m.* **1** arbitration; mediation **2** brokerage **3** mediatory role (of money, etc.) **a** منځګري کول to mediate; act as an arbitrator **b** to broker **c** to play a mediatory part (of money etc.)

منځګري ² mandzgə́raj **1** *m.* **.1** arbitrator, mediator **1.2** broker **1.3** means (e.g., of money) **1.4** matchmaker **2** *attributive* منځګري كسان mandzgə́ri… go-betweens

منځګلي mandzgúle *f.* ring finger

منځګوره mandzgorá medium (e.g., of quality)

منځګل mandzg1á1 *m.* ☞ منځګري

منځګوړى mandzgúṛaj middle

منځل مينځل mindzə́l ☞ منخل

منځ لاره mandzlə́ra *f.* منځ لار mandzlấr intersection

منځني mandzənáj **1.1** middle منځني نرخ average price منځني پېړي Middle Ages منځني شرق Middle East منځني اپشيا Central Asia منځني موده time interval منځني جنس neutral gender په منځني اندازه on average **1.2** of average height **1.3** of middling quality **2** fair (grade)

منځوله mandzóla *f.* nest

منځوى mandzwáj منځومي mandzumáj middle منځوى ورور middle brother منځوى خور middle sister منځوى مياشت the month of Zilkada (the eleventh month of the lunar calendar)

منځه ¹ mándza *f.* **1** valley **2** middle side stand of a tent

منځه ² mándza *oblique singular of* منځ

منځه ³ mə́ndza *f.* ☞ لمنځه 1

منځى mandzə́j *f.* **1** easy and smooth slope (at the foothill) **2** center, middle

منځ يالى mandzjāláj middle; average; mean

منځبدل mə́ndzedə́l *intransitive* ☞ منجبدل

منځينه mandziná *f. linguistics* infix

منځيني mandzináj ☞ منځني

منحرف munharíf *Arabic* **1.1** bent; arched; inclined **2** changing; unsteady, impermanent **1.3** unhealthy, weak, sickly **1.4** crooked (of a way) **2** *m.* apostate, defector; deviationist

منحصر munhasír *Arabic* **1** being in the exclusive possession of a single person; monopolistic **2** limited; concerning exclusively a single entity

منحط munhát *Arabic* **1.1** settled; low **1.2** degraded; degenerate **2** *m.* bastard, degenerate

منحل munhál, munháll *Arabic* dissolved, disbanded منحل کېدل *compound verb* to be dissolved, be disbanded

منحني munhaní *Arabic* crooked; curved, bent منحني خط a curved line

منحوت manhút *Arabic* **1** hewn **2** sculptured, chiseled

منحوس manhús *Arabic* ill-fated, unfortunate منحوس تړون notorious treaty د بېکاري منحوسه لمن (heavy) burden of unemployment

منحوسيت manhusiját *m. Arabic* trouble, ill-fate, misfortune

مند ¹ mand *m.* gully, depression

مند ² mənd pug-nosed

مند ³ mánd *suffix* *suffix that forms nouns and adjectives that mean possessing a quality or object* دولتمند rich person; rich *frequently abbreviated to* من

مندانو ¹ mandāṇú *m.* مندارو mandāṛú *m.* 1 flap of a churn 2 cross 3 items connected crosswise

مندانو ² mandāṇú *m.* name of a plant

منداو mandáw *m.* shoulder (of a horse)

مندته mandáta 1 apricot 2 kernel, stone (of an apricot and other fruit)

مندرج mundarídzh, mundarádzh *Arabic* entered; inscribed; included; placed د چک مندرج مبلغ، د چک مندرجه مبلغ the amount written on the check

مندرجه mundaridzhá *f.* *Arabic* [*plural:* مندرجي mundaridzhé *and m. plural: Arabic* مندرجات mundaridzhát] 1 content 2 table of contents

مندرو mandráw *m.* shelf along the wall

مندری ¹ mundráj, məndráj 1.1 scrubby 1.2 short (of height) 1.3 clip-eared 2 *m.* .1 short statured person; shorty, peewee 2.2 dwarf

مندری ² mundráj 1 *f.* .1 petite woman, short woman; shorty 2.2 earring 2.3 pearl 2 *feminine singular of* مندری 1

مندړ ¹ mandə́ṛ *m.* 1 stick to twist the rope to fasten a load 2 pile, log

مندړ ² mandáṛ *m. plural* ☞ مندړ 2

مندسته mandastá *f.* pestle (mortar)

مندکه mandə́ka *f.* 1 pit, kernel 2 nucleus د آتوم مندکه atomic nucleus

مندکی mandə́káj *m.* fallen branches

مندل mundə́l *transitive* ☞ میندل

مندنه mundə́na *f.* ☞ میندنه

مندڼ mandáṇ *m. plural* major section of Yusufzai tribe

مندو ¹ mandáw *m.* Eruca sativa (oleiferous plant)

مندو ² mandáw *m.* ☞ منداو

منده ¹ mində́ 1 *m.* [*plural:* مندیان mindiján] *agriculture* breeder 2 ungelded

منده ² mində́ ☞ مینده 2

مندي mándi *Western plural of* مور 2

مندیا mandjá *m.* threshing (of wheat)

مند ¹ mand *m.* 1 step 2 print (footprint) 3 tree stump 4 snow-crust road; snow road (trail) مند وهل *compound verb* to tramp down a snow road 5 base, support, foundation مند ایستل *compound verb* to undermine, sap 6 source (of evil, etc.) 7 *plural* مندان mandán stubble (of clover, lucerne)

مند ² mund *paired word with* غوند

مند ³ mənd *paired word with* خند

مند ⁴ mənd taciturn, quiet

منداچغ mandāchə́gh *m.* swing (on a shaft)

منداس mandás one-horned

مندانو maṇḍānú *m.* churn

مندڼاوو maṇḍāwú *m.* sled to carry soil مندڼاوو کول *compound verb* to carry on a sled

مندخولی məṇḍkhúlaj, məṇḍkhwúlaj taciturn, speechless

مندر muṇḍár *m.* stump

مندرکی mandə́rkaj *m.* twig

مندکی mandə́kaj *m.* 1 branch stub 2 tree stump; sturdy fellow

مندګک mandəgák *m.* Mandigak (historic place, Kandahar)

مندل ¹ mandə́l *transitive* [*past:* وی مانده] 1 to stick in; jab; thrust in; stuff inside 2 to conceal, hide, hide away 3 to massage, rub in ځان ژوندی په مځکه مندل to bury oneself alive

مندل ² mandál lazy

مندلئ ¹ mandə́laj *past participle of* مندل ¹

مندلی ² mandəláj charred (of a tree)

مندلی ³ mandəláj *m.* shed for sheep that have strayed away from the flock

مندماتی mandmátaj *m.* visit of the bride's house by the groom

مندنه mandə́na *f.* 1 sticking in; jabbing; thrusting in; stuffing inside 2 concealing, hiding, hiding away 3 massaging, rubbing in

مندو mandáw *m.* 1 awning; veranda, terrace, balcony; deck 2 hut 3 gazebo 4 hump (of a camel) 5 ☞ پندغالی ¹

مندوس mandós *m.* 1 ball (of leather or cloth) 2 piece of cloth tied as a hood

مندوسه mandú *f.* large turban

مندوکی məṇḍúkaj *m.* ☞ مندکی

مندولی mandoláj 1 round and small 2 *m.* shorty; tot

منده ¹ munḍə́ *m.* [*plural:* مندان munḍán] 1 branch 2 heel (of a rooster or another bird)

منده ² mə́nḍa *f.* 1 run د مندي لیکه a running strip, a racetrack, a runway په منډه a on the double b willingly په ډېره منډه in a rush منډه وړاندي تلل، په منډه اخیستل *compound verb* to start running مندي کول a to run 2 to run ahead ور منډه کول a to come running ☞ را منډي کول to come running along منډه وهل *compound verb* to run منډي وهل *compound verb* a to stamp one's foot b to run, hustle

منده ³ mə́nḍa ☞ مندل

منده ⁴ mə́nḍa *f. computer science* run

مندهی manḍhə́j *f.* market

مندي ¹ mə́nḍi *plural of* منده ²,³

مندی ² munḍáj *m.* 1 person whose ear has been cut off 2 trimmed tree 3 person without hands or feet, cripple 4 shorty; sturdy fellow 5 ox that is the closest to the center of the threshing ground or the waterwheel (during threshing or raising water)

مندی ³ manḍáj *paired word to* لندی ¹

مندی ⁴ munḍáj *f.* 1 shorty; petite woman, short-statured women 2 woman without hands or feet; cripple

مندی ⁵ manḍáj *f.* ☞ مندهی

مندي تړرې mə́nḍi-tráṛe *f. plural* marches; relocations

مندي رامندي mə́nḍi-rāmə́nḍi *f. plural* running, hustling

منديل manḍíl *m.* (large) turban

منز manz *m. dialect* ☞ منغ

منزايي manzáí *m. plural* منزائي Manzan (branch of the Dzadran tribe)

منزل manzíl *m. Arabic* [*plural:* منزلونه manzilúna *and Arabic* منازل manāzíl] 1 day's march, leg (usually 12 kuruhs کروه or 12,000 camel's steps – 18 km) د منزل وهل *compound verb* a to travel b to go, to ride د سفر منزل قطع کول to travel 2 leg د منزل ضابط *military* staging commandant 3 camp, halting place منزل کول *compound verb* to camp, halt 4 destination منزل مقصود manzíl-i... destination 5 stage, phase 6 residence, facility د منزل تدبير home economics 7 story (building) د دروغو منزل لنډ دئ *idiom* Lies have short legs.

منزلت manzilát *m. Arabic* dignity, rank, status; position قدر او منزلت to be placed high ☞ منزله 1

منزل گاه manzilgáh *m. military* 1 stage point 2 camp site

منزله 1 manzilá *f. Arabic* 1 degree 2 significance د ... په منزله ګڼل to equate with something دا د مهم شي په منزله برېښېږي This seems to be very important.

منزله 2 manzíla *oblique of* منزل

منزله 3 manzilá دري منزله three-storyed

منزلي 1 manzilí residential, domestic

منزلي 2 manzilé *plural of* منزله 1

منزوي munzawí *Arabic* 1 lonely, secluded ګوښه او منزوي ژوند solitary way of life 2 *m.* hermit

منګک mangák *m. regional* 1 mouse 2 rat

منګ کړانه mangakarána *f.* mousehole

منګکه mangáka *f.* mouse (female)

منسک 1 mansák *m. Arabic* rite, ritual, ritualism

منسک 2 minsk *m.* Minsk

منسوب mansúb *Arabic* 1 related, belonging, falling under something 2 *m.* [*plural:* منسوبين mansubín] .1 office worker 1.2 *plural* employees; civilian employees; service staff 3 *plural* relatives, family

منسوبول mansubawól *denominative, transitive* [*past:* منسوب يې کړ] 1 to classify, rank 2 to court; match (somebody in marriage)

منسوبه mansubá *f. regional* bride, betrothed

منسوبېدل mansubedól *denominative, intransitive* [*past:* منسوب شو] 1 to relate, belong 2 to be betrothed

منسوج mansúdzh *Arabic* 1 woven 2 *m.* [*plural:* منسوجات mansudzhát] .1 fabric 2.2 *plural* fabrics, dry goods پشمي منسوجات woolen fabrics کتاني منسوجات cotton fabrics پنبه يي منسوجات linen fabrics

منسوخ mansúkh *Arabic* canceled, annulled قرار داد لغو او منسوخ سوئ دئ The treaty has been annulled.

منسوخول mansukhawól *denominative, transitive* [*past:* منسوخ يې کړ] to cancel, annul

منسوخېدل mansukhedól *denominative, intransitive* [*past:* منسوخ شو] to be canceled, be annulled

منشأ manshá *f. Arabic* 1 source; provenance; origin; starting point له منشأ اخيستل *compound verb* to arise, originate 2 motive دا نه وه چه That's not what I meant.

منشور manshúr *Arabic* 1 promulgated, published 2 *m.* .1 statute; charter د متحده ملتو د مؤسسي منشور، د ملګرو ملتو د مؤسسي منشور United Nations Charter منشور اطلس manshúr-i... Atlantic Charter 2.2 agreement; treaty 2.3 *mathmatics* prism, parallelepiped

منشي munshí *m.* [*plural:* منشيان munshiján] 1 male secretary 2 male office workers 3 male Oriental language instructor (in India – from among the local population) 4 female secretary

منشي خانه munshikhāná *f.* secretariat

منشي ګري munshigarí *f.* 1 duties of a secretary 2 duties of an instructor

منښت manólkht *m.* منښته manólkhta *f.* agreement; acknowledgement منښت کول obedience د مشرانو منښت *compound verb* to acknowledge

منصب mansáb *m. Arabic* position; rank; title

منصبدار mansabdár *m. Arabic* 1 officer 2 official

منصبي mansabí of office (e.g., duties of office); service

منصرف munsaríf *Arabic* 1 impermanent 2 opposing something; avoiding something منصرف کول *compound verb* a to disabuse, dissuade b to distract له ... څخه منصرف کېدل to refuse something 3 *grammar* inflected; conjugated; flexional; inflectional 4 returned

منصف munsíf *Arabic* 1 just منصفه هيئت jury; trial by jury 2 *m.* judge

منصفانه munsifāná 1.1 just; correct; unbiased په منصفانه ډول fairly; justly 1.2 fair (of a price) 2 fairly

منصفي munsifí *f.* trial; court proceedings منصفي کول *compound verb* a to hold a trial; conduct court proceedings b to arbitrate between somebody

منصوب mansúb 1 erected, constructed; mounted 2 appointed, assigned to a position

منصوبيت mansubiját *m. Arabic* 1 structure; setup 2 appointment, assignment to a position

منصور mansúr *Arabic* 1 victorious 2 *m. proper noun* Mansur

منضم munzám *Arabic* joined منضمه انسجه *biology* connective tissue

منطبق muntabíq *Arabic* appropriate; matching; suitable منطبق کېدل *compound verb* to match; suit

منطق mantíq *m. Arabic* 1 logic; logic reasoning 2 talk; conversation

منطقاً mantíqán *adverb* logically, in a reasoned manner

منطق پوه mantiqpóh *m.* specialist in logic; logician

منطقوي mintaqawí *Arabic* regional منطقوي قرار داد regional pact منطقوي اداره regional bureau

منطقه mintaqá, mantaqá *f. Arabic* [*plural:* منطقي mintaqé *and m. plural: Arabic* مناطق manātíq] 1 zone, area ساړه مناطق frigid

زون منطقه توده torrid zone حاره مناطق معتدله زون moderate zone حاره مناطق معتدله منطقه توده tropics 2 band, region

منطقي ١ mantiqí *Arabic* 1 logical, reasoned; consistent نتيجه منطقي … د دي دا ده چه The logical consequence of this is… 2 m. specialist in logic, logician

منطقي ٢ mintaqé *plural of* منطقه

منظر manzár m. *Arabic* 1 looks, appearance 2 sight, spectacle; phenomenon خوندور منظر an agreeable sight 3 landscape; view, scenery

منظره manzará f. *Arabic* [*plural:* منظري manzaré *and m. plural: Arabic* مناظر manāzír] 1 view; landscape; terrain 2 spectacle; scene

منظره دار manzaradár scenic منظره داره دره scenic valley

منظم munazzám *Arabic* 1 regular, systematic په منظمه توگه regularly, systematically منظم اردو regular army اقتصادي منظم اکتشاف planned development of the economy 2 well-managed, organized; orderly 3 neat 4 measured stride

منظماً munazzámán *Arabic* 1 regularly 2 in an organized manner, in an orderly manner, in order 3 neatly 4 in a measured manner

منظور manzúr *Arabic* 1 deemed fit, approved 2 m. .1 goal, task په دغه منظور with this in mind د توليداتو به همدغه منظور to this end دلوپولو په منظور in order to increase production 2.2 sense, meaning … د دي بيان منظور دا دئ The meaning of this declaration is as follows…

منظورول manzurawәl 1 *denominative, transitive* [*past:* منظوري کړ] .1 to authorize, confirm, approve 1.2 to accept (e.g., invitation) 2 *m. plural* approval, confirmation, authorization

منظوري manzurí f. approval, confirmation, authorization د چا په منظوري on somebody's approval د منظوري لوري گرزیدل to be approved, confirmed, authorized

منظوریدل manzuredәl *denominative, intransitive* [*past:* منظور شو] 1 to be approved, confirmed authorized 2 to be accepted (of evidence, deposition, etc.)

منظوم manzúm *Arabic* 1 poetic, written in verses منظوم مضامین poem, poems 2 well-organized; harmonious

منظومه manzumá f. *Arabic* 1 long poem; poem 2 system 3 network (e.g., railroad)

منع mán', mán'a *Arabic* 1 f. ban, prohibition 2 *predicative* banned منع کول *compound verb* a to forbid, institute a ban b to hinder, block c to disallow, prevent له جنگېدو څخه منع کول to prevent a fight d to contain, constrain د دښمن ارخوه را منع کول to pin down enemy flanks د وينې تلل منع کول to stop hemorrhage منع کېدل *compound verb* a to be banned, be forbidden b to encounter an obstacle c to be contained, be constrained, be pinned down د هوا د خرابۍ په اثر منع شوي دي الوتکو عملیات د The weather hinders the aviation activities.

منعقد mun'aqíd *Arabic* 1 convened, gathered 2 concluded (of a treaty, etc.) منعقد کېدل منعقدول *compound verb* ☞ *compound verb* ☞ منعقدیدل

منعقدول ١ [منعقدي کړ mun'aqidawәl *denominative, transitive* [*past:* to convene, gather 2 to conclude (a treaty, etc.)

منعقدیدل ١ [منعقد شو mun'aqidedәl *denominative, intransitive* [*past:* to be convened; get convened 2 to be concluded (of a treaty, etc.)

منعکس mun'akís *Arabic* 1 reflected منعکسه رڼا reflected light 2 overturned 3 inverse; opposite منعکس کول *compound verb* ☞ منعکسیدل منعکس کېدل منعکسول *compound verb* ☞

منعکسول [منعکس یې کړ mun'akisawәl *denominative, transitive* [*past:* 1 to reflect (light, etc.) 2 to overturn 3 to describe (e.g., events)

منعکسیدل [منعکس شو mun'akisedәl *denominative, intransitive* [*past:* 1 to be reflected (of light) 2 to be overturned 3 to find reflection, be described (e.g., of events)

منعه mán'a f. ☞ منع

منفجر munfadzhír *Arabic* 1 exploded 2 explosive، منفجر مواد منفجره مواد explosives

منفذ manfáz m. *Arabic* [*plural:* منافذ manāfíz] 1 orifice 2 pore 3 outlet; manhole 4 vent

منفرد munfaríd *Arabic* 1.1 lonely, solitary; separate منفرد جگړه وال، منفرد جگړه وال نفر a solitary soldier; certain persons منفرد اشخاص individuals 1.2 separate, one-man, individual 1.3 single, bachelor 1.4 special يو منفرد مقام حاصلول to achieve a special status; take a special place 2 m. *politics* independent

منفرداً munfarídán *Arabic* 1 lonesomely, separately 2 separately, individually 3 particularly, specially

منفصل munfasíl *Arabic* 1 separate, divided; not continuous 2 independent (of a person) 3 fired; removed from office, whose resignation has been accepted, who has resigned

منفعت manfa'át m. *Arabic* [*plural:* منفعتونه manfa'atúna *and plural Arabic* منافع manāfí'] 1 use; benefit 2 advantage; profit شخصي منافع personal gain متقابله منافع mutual benefit د چا ته منافع رسول a to benefit somebody b to bring somebody profit 3 interest متضاد منفعتونه opposite interests د متضادو منفعتونو تصادم a clash of opposing interests د چا منافع ساتل to stand up for somebody's interests

منفعت جو manfa'atdzhú 1 mercenary, self-serving 2 m. moneygrubber

منفعت جويي manfa'atdzhují f. 1 speculation 2 profiteering 3 moneygrubbing, avarice

منفعل munfa'íl *Arabic* 1 made, manufactured 2 experiencing, feeling something. 3 upset 4 embarrassed, uncomfortable, shy

منفک munfák, munfákk *Arabic* 1 separate; separated 2 removed, eliminated, displaced, supplanted

منفور manfúr *Arabic* 1 hateful; despicable 2 diagreeable, antipathetic

منفوریت manfuriját m. *Arabic* disgust د چا د منفوریت سبب گرزیدل to disgust

منفي manfí *Arabic* negative منفي ځواب negative answer منفي اغزه a staunch منفي تینگار to affect adversely منفي، منفي اغزه کول resistance b counteraction c refusal د فعل منفي شکل *grammar* negative verb form نه منفي پنځه مساوي څلور Nine minus five equals four.

منقا munaqqá *f. Arabic* ☞ منقیٰ 2

منقاد munqád *Arabic* 1 submissive, obedient یو کار ته منقاد کېدل to submit to something 2 gentle, acquiescent

منقادول munqādawə́l *denominative, transitive [past:* منقادي کړ] to conquer, bring into submission

منقار minqár *m. Arabic* beak

منقبت manqabát *m. Arabic* 1 merit 2 praise, panegyric د چا منقبت ویل to praise, laud somebody

منقبض munqabíz *Arabic* 1 contracted, shrunk 2 constipated

منقبضول munqabizawə́l *denominative, transitive [past:* منقبض يې کړ] 1 to contract, shrink 2 to cause constipation

منقبضېدل munqabizedə́l *denominative, intransitive [past:* منقبض شو] 1 to be contracted, be shrunk 2 to be constipated

منقد munaqqíd *Arabic* 1 *m. [plural:* منقدین munaqqidín] critic 2 criticizing

منقش munaqqásh *Arabic* covered with writing, ornamented

منقطع munqatí' *Arabic* 1 interrupted 2 intersected 3 no longer existing, destroyed; extinct منقطع کول *compound verb* a to interrupt b to intersect c to destroy منقطع کېدل *compound verb* to be interrupted, be suspended a to be cut short, be suppressed c to be destroyed, become extinct

منقل manqál *m. Arabic* brazier, charcoal grill

منقلب¹ munqalíb *Arabic* folded, turned, angled back (e.g., of a tongue); cacuminal

منقلب² munqaláb *m. Arabic* 1 location of a turn 2 outcome, end 3 demise, death

منقله minqalá *f. Arabic* protractor; *technology* declinometer

منقوش manqúsh *Arabic* ornamented with paintings

منقوط manqút *Arabic* designated by a point; provided with a point

منقول manqúl *Arabic* 1 mobile 2 movable (of property) منقول مالونه، منقوله مالونه movable property 3 passed on as tradition 4 told, narrated

منقولات manqulát *m. plural Arabic [singular* منقول] 1 movable property 2 legends; traditions

منقوله manqulá *Arabic feminine and plural of* منقول

منقه munaqá, munaqqá *Arabic* منقیٰ munaqqá 1 pure, purified 2 *f.* red sultanas (variety of large black grapes)

منکر¹ munkír *Arabic* 1 denying, refusing, refuting 2 *m.* person who denies something; adversary; detractor

منکر² munkár *Arabic* 1 denied 2 repudiated; unrecognized 3 chastised, disapproved of; reprehensible

منکرتوب munkirtób *m.* 1 denial; repudiation 2 disapproval, censure

منکرنکیر munkár-nakír *m. Arabic religion* Munkir and Nakir (two angels who, according to Muslim beliefs, interrogate the souls of the dead on their lives and beliefs)

منکرول munkirawə́l *denominative, transitive [past:* منکریې کړ] to make repudiate, force to repudiate something

منکرېدل munkiredə́l *denominative, intransitive [past:* منکر شو] to be denied, be repudiated; deny, renounce, disavow د دې څخه هېڅوک نشي منکرېدلای No one can deny this.

منکسر munkasír *Arabic* 1 fractured; broken 2 saddened, aggrieved منکسر خط polygonal line

منکسر المزاج munkasir-ul-mizádzh *Arabic* sad, sorrowful, melancholic

منکشف munkashíf *Arabic* 1 opened, discovered, revealed دا راز منکشف شو Their secret was out.

منکه¹ manə́ka *conjunction* I swear! (It's true.)

منکه² munaká *f.* ☞ منقه 2

منگ¹ mang *m.* 1 age, years د دېرشو کلویه منگ و He was thirty years old. 2 size, measure, quantity

منگ² mung, mang 1 mute 2 dumbstruck, at a loss for words (from surprise, etc.) منگ تلل، منگ را تلل، منگ در تلل، منگ ور تلل to be dumbstruck, be lost for words, be stunned

منگ³ mang *m.* thick viscous clay, mud

منگچه mangácha *f.* ☞ منگچه

منگار mangár *m.* ☞ منگور 1

منگاره mangára *f.* منگاري mangáre *f. plural* scratch

منگاښه mangáxha *f.* pitchfork for winnowing grain

منگال¹ mangál *m.* large sickle

منگال² mangál *m.* ☞ منقل

منگان mangán *m. plural* manganese

منگتجاره mangtjára *f.* pomegranate (plant)

منگچه mangə́cha *f.* foot, paw (of a predator) منگچي اچول *compound verb* to snatch, grab with the paws, paw

منگر¹ mangár *m. regional* mangar (eighth month of the Hindu calendar)

منگر² mangár ☞ مگر 1

منگرای mangráj *m.* mangrai (small poisonous snake)

منگر mangúr *m.* 1 bedbug 2 tick; mite

منگری mangrə́j *f.* gecko (lizard)

منگریته mangríta *f.* turnip

منگز mangə́z *f. Eastern* ☞ ږمنځ

منگک mangák *m. dialect* mouse

منگل¹ mangál *m.* 1 *proper noun* Mangal 2 *plural* Mangal (tribe)

منگل² mangúl *f. [plural:* منگلي mangúli] ☞ منگول 1

منگل³ mongól *m.* Mongol

منگلوسه manglósa *f.* sedan chair (to carry a bride, etc.)

منگله mangúla *f.* paw, pad, foot (of birds, animals)

منگلی mangulə́j *f.* bead bracelet

منگنی mangənáj 1 autumnal, autumn-like 2 born in the fall (of a litter, offspring)

منگن mungán *m. [plural:* منگني mungə́n *and* منگنان munganán] 1 bedbug 2 tick; mite

منگو mangó stupid; ignorant

منگوتکی mangoṭə́kaj *m.* small jug, small-size pot

منگوتی mangoṭáj *m.* **1** small-size jug, small-size pot **2** waterwheel bucket **3** *figurative* moneybox منگوتی تر چا لاندي کېدل to become rich

منگوچه mangúcha, mangwócha *f.* ☞ منگچه

منگور [1] mangór *m.* adder; blunt-nosed viper

منگور [2] mangúr *m.* blind puppy

منگوروله mangorwóla *f.* asparagus

منگوړ mangwáṛ *f.* ☞ منگړ

منگوړه mangwóṛa *f.* bedbug

منگوړی mangoṛáj *m.* ☞ منگوتی

منگول [1] mangúl *f.* [*plural:* منگولي mangúli] claw; paw منگو لي لګول *compound verb* **a** to take a grip with the claws **b** سره لګول د مرګ to lock horns, get into a fight **c** to claw, scratch د مرګ له منگولو څان *idiom* in the claws of death منگولو ښکار کېدل to get out of the claws of death خلاصول the chains of colonialism; to encroach, infringe on something منگولي نينلول to make an attempt on somebody's life د استعمار منگولي

منگول [2] mongól *m.* Mongol

منگول پاڼی mangulpã́ṇaj *m.* sycamore, *Platanus*

منگوله mangúla *f.* ☞ منگول 1

منگولي [1] mangúli *f. plural* kind of embroidery

منگولي [2] mangúli *plural of* منگول 1

منگولي [3] mongolí **1** Mongolian **2** *m.* Mongol

منگولیا mongolijã́ *f.* Mongolia

منگومی mangomáj *m.* childhood disease characterized by the swelling of gums

منگه múnga *Eastern pronoun* ☞ موږ

منگی mangáj *m.* [*plural:* منگي mangí *and* منگیان mangijã́n] **1** jug د تش منگي آواز ښه خیژي *proverb* An empty barrel rattles the loudest. دا د بل منگي بنوروا ده ... mangí... This is quite another story. This is another kettle of fish. (*literally:* This soup is from a different pot.) **2** jug (musical instrument, i.e., a jug with leather stretched over the top, like a tambourine) **3** clay beehive

منل manэ́l **1** *transitive* [*past:* و یې مانه] **.1** to acknowledge; consent; give consent; approve ده راسره ومنله He agreed with me. هغه زما وینا نه مني زه دا منم د I agree He would not agree with me. ده زما خبره و نه منله to agree with somebody چا خبره منل He did not follow my advice. که تاسي زما منئ و مي منله If you agree with me. بد منل ... چي I acknowledged... I conceded that... *compound verb* to hate; disapprove دا یې بده ومنله He did not like this. ښه منل *compound verb* to approve, find acceptable **1.2** to accept; undertake مصارف یې په ځان ومنل He picked up the tab. یو کار په غاړه منل to undertake something **1.3** to listen to; follow; obey **1.4** to set; establish د چا په سر روپي منل، د چا په سر پیسې منل to put a bounty on somebody's head **1.5** to experience, undergo **1.6** to withstand, support (e.g., a weight, a load) دا پول دېر وزن نه شي منلای This bridge cannot support an excessive load. **1.7** to impose, make acknowledge پر نورو خپله نظریه منل to impose one's opinion

on others منل کېدل *compound verb passive voice* **a** to be acknowledged; be recognized; be approved; get approved **b** to be elected په وکالت منل to be elected a deputy **c** to be accepted, be undertaken **d** to be set, be established **e** to be experienced, be supported, survived **2** *m. plural* ☞ 1-4 مننه دا د منلو خبره ده چي It must be acknowledged. د منلو سر خوڅول to nod one's head in assent

منلتیا manəltjã́ *f.* **1** state of being acknowledged **2** staunchness

منلئ manэ́laj **1** *past participle of* منل منلئ حقیقت a universally acknowledged fact دا منلي خبره ده، دا خو منلي شوي ده It is known that... **2** respected, esteemed ګرما منلي وروره! Esteemed friend! منلي جنابه! Dear sir!

منن minán *m. plural Arabic of* منت

مننه manə́na *f.* **1** acknowledgement, recognition; consent; approval **2** acceptance, undertaking **3** docility, obedience **4** setting, establishing **5** appreciation, gratitude د چا مننه کول to thank somebody

منو manó *m. proper noun* Mano

منوجان manodzhã́n *m. proper noun* Mano-jan

منور munawwár *Arabic* **1.1** lit; illuminated **1.2** enlightened **2** *m.* [*plural:* منورین munawwarín] **.1** member of the intelligentsia **2.2** *proper noun* Munawar **2.3** *plural* intelligentsia, enlightened circles

منوط manút *Arabic* dependent

منونکی manúnkaj **1** *present participle of* منل **2** obedient, docile

منونی manúnaj **1** consenting **2** obedient, docile

منوي manwí *Arabic* assumed; stipulated

منویات manwijã́t *m. plural Arabic* assumptions, intentions

منه [1] mána *short form of* من 2 mnə *oblique singular of* من

منه [2] manáh *m.* ☞ منا

منه [3] miná *f.* dwelling, residence, abode ☞ مېنه

منه [4] maná *imperfective imperative of* منل

منه [5] mána ☞ منع

منهاج minhã́dzh *m. Arabic* **1** high road; wide road **2** *figurative* style; manner

منهدم munhadám *Arabic* destroyed; ruined

منهي manhí *Arabic* forbidden, prohibited (by religion)

منهیات manhijã́t *m. plural Arabic* [*singular:* منهي] prohibitions; forbidden things

مني [1] maní *f.* **1** boast, brag **2** egoism **3** egotism, "me-first" **4** independence

مني [2] maní *f. Arabic* sperm, seed

مني [3] maní *past tense of* منل

منی [4] mə́naj *m.* **1** autumn, fall **2** fall harvest

منی [5] manáj *m.* necklace

منی [6] munáj **1.1** consenting **1.2** obedient, docile **1.3** pious, devout **1.4** temperate, abstemious **2** *m.* **.1** old man, elder **2.2** wise man

منی [7] munэ́j *feminine singular and plural of* منی 1

منياډر maniã́ḍár *m. regional* money order

منېجر manédzhár *m. regional* manager, director (of a factory)

منیر munír *Arabic* illuminating; radiant; luminescent; resplendent

منیز maníz *used as the second part of a word combination that means weighing a certain amount of mans* د غورو لس منیز تیم a ten-man oilcan

منیلا manilá *f.* Manila

مڼه maṇá *f.* **1** apple که شپه تیاره ده، منې په شمار دي *proverb* Even a dark night won't hide a thief. (*literally:* Though the night is dark, the apples have been counted.) **2** hawthorn beads

مڼه غوني maṇaghúnaj *m.* ☞ مرغوني

مو [1] mu *m. plural* congealed soft tallow

مو [2] mu *m.* one hair

مو [3] mu, mo *Western, Eastern* **1** *non-emphatic pronoun form* **1**.1 *used as the object of an action expressed by transitive verbs in the present, past and future tenses* (us) وینې مو؟ Do you see us? سلیم مو بیایي Saleem gives us a ride. **1.2** *used as the subject of an action with transitive verbs in ergative patterns* (we) هیواد مو ولید We saw Hewad. **1.3** *used as possessive pronoun* (our) کتابونه مو Zaheen took our books. **2** تاسي **.1** *used as the object of an action expressed by transitive verbs in the present, past, and future tenses* (you) دوی مو اروي They hear you. **2.2** *used as the subject of an action with transitive verbs in ergative patterns* (you) نه مو دي اروبدلي چي ... Haven't you heard that... **2.3** *used as a possessive pronoun* (your) د ډېري مودي څخه مو مکتوب نه دئ راغلئ There have been no letters from you for a long time.

مواجب mawādzhíb mādzhíb *m. plural and singular Arabic colloquial* **1** stipend, salary **2** *regional* tribal subsidy **3** pension

مواجه muwādzhíh *Arabic* facing somebody or something; standing face to face د سختي او ... د ... سره مواجه کېدل to run into, come across د مشکل سره مواجه کېدل، د مشکلاتو سره مواجه کېدل to run into difficulties

مواجهه muwādzhahá *f. Arabic* **1** face-to-face meeting; confrontation (legal term) **2** presence

مؤاخذه muākhazá *f. Arabic* punishment; prosecution مؤاخذه کول *compound verb* to punish; prosecute

مواد mawád, mawádd *m. plural Arabic of* ماده **1** substances, materials ارزاقیه مواد، خوراکي مواد، خام مواد، اومه مواد raw materials استهلاکي مواد consumer products د خوړلو مواد victuals, foodstuff تعمیراتي مواد manufactured goods; industrial products صناعتي مواد construction materials حربي مواد military gear **2** *law* articles **3** *medicine* pus

موارد mawāríd *m. plural Arabic of* مورد

موازنه muwāzaná *f. Arabic* **1** balancing, maintaining equilibrium, equilibrium خپله موازنه ساتل to maintain balance موازنه د لاسه ایستل، بې موازني کېدل to lose one's balance **2** تجارتي موازنه balance, balance sheet; assets and liabilities statement صحیحه موازنه قائمول trade balance د تجارت موازنه balance, draw up a balance; establish a balance د قواؤ موازنه idiom balance of forces; equilibrium of forces قوتونو موازنه

موازي muwāzí *Arabic* **1.1** parallel **1.2** identical; matching, appropriate په موازي ډول **a** in parallel **b** accordingly, appropriately **2.1** in parallel **2.2** accordingly, appropriately

موازیاً muwāzíján *Arabic* **1** in parallel **2** accordingly, appropriately

موازین mawāzín *m. plural Arabic of* میزان

مواس [1] mawás *m.* **1** gossip, rumormonger; slanderer, libeler **2** telltale; informer, snitch **3** rabble-rouser **4** rebel, mutineer **5** fiend; devil

مواس [2] mawás *m.* **1** protection, guard **2** shelter مواس نیول to hide, find shelter, asylum

مواس [3] mawás *m.* wasp

مواسم mawāsím *m. plural Arabic of* موسم

مواسه [1] məwāsá *f.* fairy tale

مواسه [2] mawása *f.* **1** female gossip **2** female telltale; female informer; female snitch

مواشي mawāshí *m. plural Arabic* livestock

مواصلات muwāsalā́t *m. plural Arabic* communications; supply routes هوائي مواصلات air traffic, airlines

مواصلاتي muwāsalātí **1** communications مواصلاتي لاري communications; supply routes **2** transportation مواصلاتي شرکت transportation company

مواصلت muwāsalát *m.* مواصله muwāsalá *f. Arabic* **1** connection **2** communication, connection **3** date (with one's beloved)

مواضع mawāzí' *m. plural Arabic of* موضع

مواظب muwāzíb *Arabic* **1** caring **2** diligent, assiduous, painstaking **3** taking care of something; looking after something **4** vigilant

مواظبت muwāzabát *m. Arabic* **1** care, concern, custody **2** diligence, assiduousness, studiousness **3** care of something **4** vigilance, alertness

موافق muwāfíq *Arabic* **1.1** appropriate, suitable, favorable; proper **1.2** being in agreement with something موافقه رایه an "aye" vote دغه تصمیمانه په ۶۷ موافقو او ۳ مخالفو رایو تصویب شوه This resolution was adopted with 67 "ayes" against 3 "nays." موافقه رایه ورکول to vote for; vote "aye" موافق کېدل **a** to match, suit **b** to agree with something **1.3** favorable, fair موافق باد fair wind **2** *m.* **.1** match **a** in accordance with the law د قانون په موافق **2.2** supporter

موافقت muwāfaqát *m. Arabic* **1** correspondence د یو شي سره موافقت to correspond to something سره موافقت نه لرل to be a mismatch; disagree **2** arrangement, agreement **3** consent, permit په موافقت کول **a** by agreement with, by permission of موافقت سره to be coordinated, cleared with **b** to agree **4** harmony, consent

موافقت نامه muwāfaqatnāmá *f.* consent (written); agreement

موافقه [1] muwāfaqá *f. Arabic* **1** ☞ موافقت **2** agreement; convention د ماهیگیري موافقت fishing agreement

موافقه [2] muwāfiqa *feminine singular of* موافق

موافقه دوتنه mawāfiqa dawtəná *f. computer science* concordance file

موافقه لیک muwāfaqalík *m.* convention, agreement

مواقع mawāqí' *m. plural Arabic of* موقع

مواقف mawāqíf *m. plural Arabic of* موقف

مواليد mawālíd *m. plural Arabic of* مولود three natural kingdoms (animal kingdom, plant kingdom, mineral kingdom)

موانع mawāní' *m. plural Arabic* [*singular:* مانع] obstacles, difficulties موانع طبيعي natural impediments موانع حل كول to resolve problems موانع ليري كول to remove obstacles

مراعات mawāni'át *second plural of* موانع

مواهب mawāhíb *m. plural Arabic of* موهبه

موبد mobád *m.* Zoroastrian priest

موبل mobl *m.* furniture

موبل سازي moblsāzí *f.* furniture production

د موبيل تېل mobíl lubricating oil

موت maut, mawt *m. Arabic* 1 death; demise 2 destruction

موتور motór *m.* motor, engine د الوتكو موتورونه aircraft engines

موتور لرونكى motór larúnkaj motorized

موتوریزه motorizá 1 motorized 2 *f.* motorized armed forces

موته moth *m. regional* ☞ موت 1

موتيازي mutjáze *f. plural dialect* ☞ متيازي

موټ [1] moṭ *m. plural* mung bean, *Phaseolus aconitifolius*

موټ [2] muṭ *m.* 1 fist 2 hand د موټه له درده څخه شكايت كول، د موټ له درده څخه شكايت كول to complain of pain in one's hand 3 handle, grip 4 handful د دوی د موټه زيار دئ *idiom* This is the fruit of their labors. په موټ او بازو به نه سو ورسره برابر We will not be able to cope with them. ☞ مټ 1, 3

موټ [3] moṭ *paired word to* روغ

موټانه muṭắna *f.* plow handle

موټر moṭár *m.* [*plural:* موټرونه moṭarúna *Western* موټران moṭarắn *and Eastern f. plural:* موټرې moṭáre] 1 automobile, car آتشي موټر fire engine تېزرفتار موټر، خفيف موټر، باري موټر truck باربردار موټر a bus د اوتوبوس موټر، د سرويس موټر، عمومي موټر passenger car زره پوش موټر، زغريالى موټر a dump truck شيانو غورځوونكى موټر an armored car د پوستي موټر a mail truck, a communication truck د موټرو قطار a motorcade; a convoy of trucks د موټر حادثه a car accident تش موټر empty truck موټر چلول موټر ته ختل، په موټر compound verb to drive a car; operate a vehicle د موټر نه كوزېدل، د موټر څخه كېنته كېدل to get into a car كېنې سپرېدل to get out of a car 2 motor; engine د برق موټر electric motor

موټربس moṭarbás *m.* bus

موټرخانه moṭarkhāná *f.* garage

موټردار moṭardár ☞ موتوریزه

موټررو moṭarráw automobile (of a road)

موټرسازي moṭarsāzí *f.* automobile building, automobile industry د موټرسازي فابریكه automobile plant; car factory

موټرسایكل moṭarsájkl *m.* [*plural:* موټرسايكلونه moṭarsājklúna *and Western* موټرسايكلان moṭarsájklắn موټرسايكل moṭarsájkl *m. plural:* موټرسيكلونه moṭarsajklúna *and Western* موټرسيكلان moṭarsajklắn] motorcycle, motorbike

موټركار moṭarkár *m. regional* automobile; motorcar

موټر لرونكى moṭár larúnkaj ☞ موتور لرونكى

موټروان moṭarwắn *m.* driver, chauffeur

موټروان باشي moṭarwānbāshí *m.* garage manager

موټري [1] moṭarí motor موټري ماكو motorboat

موټرې [2] moṭáre *f. Eastern plural of* موټر

موټک muṭák *m.* onanism, masturbation موټک وهل *compound verb* to masturbate

موټگى muṭgáj *m.* small amount; handful

موتور moṭór *m.* ☞ موتور

موتوریزه moṭorizá ☞ موتوریزه

موټه moṭá *f.* 1 tumor 2 gold thread knot

موټى mútaj *m.* 1 fistful; handful يو موټى غنم a handful of wheat 2 palm 3 handle, grip 4 steelyard 5 *history* mutai (unit of length equal to about 10 centimeters) 6 disease affecting pack animals

مؤثر muassír *Arabic* 1.1 efficient; effective 1.2 efficacious, producing an effect 2 *m.* [*plural:* مؤثرات muassirắt] effect, influence, impact

مؤثرانه muassiráná 1 successful, effective 2 successfully, effectively

مؤثروالى muassirwắlaj *m.* مؤثریت muassiriját *m.* successfulness, efficacy; effectiveness

موثق muwassáq *Arabic* credible, veracious; trustworthy د موثقي اطلاع له رویه according to a reliable account

موج maudzh, mawdzh *m. Arabic* [*plural:* موجونه maudzhúna *and Arabic* امواج amwắdzh] wave; billow; choppy sea; ripples; oscillation لنډ موجونه radio waves د بې سيم موجونه short waves موج وهل *compound verb* to roll, billow (e.g., of water surface); oscillate, flutter, wave, undulate; fluctuate

موجب mudzhíb, maudzhíb *m. Arabic* [*plural:* موجبات mudzhibất, maudzhibất *and Arabic* مواجب mawādzhíb] basis, reason, motive په موجب as per, according to; based on something موجب كېدل، د بربادۍ موجب گرځېدل lead to, cause... lead to, cause د راز راز مرضونو موجب گرځېدل to cause various diseases د استثمار موجب گرځېدل to be subject to exploitation موجب د راحت *idiom* convenient, comfortable; accommodating

موجد mudzhíd *Arabic* 1 generating 2 *m.* [*plural:* موجدین mudzhidín] .1 creator, generator; founder 2.2 inventor 2.3 culprit 2.4 factor, motive cause

موجر muadzhdzhár *Arabic* borrowed, loaner, on loan

موجز mudzház *Arabic* 1 abridged; brief موجزه وینا a brief speech 2 *m.* .1 abstract 2.2 summary

موجزه mudzhizá *f.* ☞ معجزه 1

موجود mawdzhúd *Arabic* 1.1 existing, available, at hand 1.2 present, being here 1.3 actual ثابت او واقع او موجود حقيقت irrefutable fact 1.4 current, present موجود كول *compound verb* ☞ .1 2 *m.* موجودېدل moجود كېدل *compound verb* ☞ composition, total number 2.2 availability 2.3 [*plural:* موجودات mujudất, maujudất, mawjudất] creature; organism ژوندي موجودات living beings کوچني موجودات microorganisms, germs مضر موجودات pests 2.4 *proper noun* Maujud

موجودتیا موجودگي maudzhudtjá *f.* mudzhudagí, maudzhudagí, mawdzhudagí *f.* 1 presence 2 availability; available stock (e.g., of merchandise, oil)

موجودوالی maudzhudwắlaj *m.* existence, availability

موجودول maudzhudawə́l *denominative, transitive* [*past:* موجود یې کړ] 1 to set up, create; put together 2 to offer (e.g., a possibility)

موجوده maudzhudá, mawdzhudá *Arabic feminine & plural of* موجود 1 موجوده وخت modern times; modernity

موجودي [1] maudzhudí *f.* 1 ☞ موجودیت 2 *law* bankruptcy estate (in bankruptcy)

موجودي [2] maudzhudi *feminine plural of* موجود 1

موجودیت maudzhudiját *m. Arabic* 1 existence 2 presence; availability 3 available personnel 4 integrity; independence 5 objectivity 6 appearance, establishment; formation of something

موجودیدل maudzhudedə́l *denominative, intransitive* [*past:* موجود شو] 1 to emerge, occur; be established یوه مساعده زمینه موجودیږي A favorable situation is emerging. 2 to be implemented; pan out, work out (of a result)

موجه muwadzhdzháh *Arabic* 1 acceptable 2 respectable موجه اسباب valid reasons, valid excuses 3 plausible (of a pretext)

موجي maudzhí *Arabic* wavy; wave-shaped

موچلی muchlə́j *f.* 1 spent cartridge case 2 earring 3 luring reed (to beckon quails)

موچن گنډونکی mochán gaṇḍúnkaj *m.* cobbler, shoemaker

موچنوالا mochaṇwālā́ *m.* shoe salesman

موچنه mochə́na *f.* 1 shoe زرینه موچنه a gold embroidered shoe 2 shoemaker's wife

موچونوغزه muchunúghza *f.* ☞ مچلوغزه

موچي [1] mochí, muchí *m.* 1 shoemaker; cobbler 2 tanner

موچي [2] mochə́j *f.* shoemaker's wife

موچي گري mochigarí *f.* shoemaking craft

موخی motsə́j *f.* small rock or piece of clay (for a game resembling "heads or tails")

موحد muwahhíd *Arabic* 1 monotheistic 2 *m. religion* monotheist

موخره muakhkhará *f. Arabic* 1 rear part; back 2 afterward; epilogue

موخه mukhá *f.* 1 target; aim 2 goal مشترکه موخه a common goal; a shared goal

موخه دوتنه mūkhá dawtəná *f. computer science* destination file

موخی mukhə́j *f.* two families swapping their girls (in marriage) موخی کول *compound verb* to swap girls between two families (in marriage)

مود mod *m.* fashion نوی مود راایستل to go into fashion مود کېدل be in, be fashionable له موده وتل ، د مود څخه لوېدل be out, go out of fashion د مود سره برابر لباس اغوستل to dress fashionably

مؤدب muaddáb *Arabic* well-mannered; polite دوی مشرته مؤدب وي They treat their elders respectfully.

مودت mawaddát *m. Arabic* friendship

مودرن [1] modérn 1 modern عصري او مودرن سړی دئ a person of modern outlook 2 most recent

مودل modél *m.* model, example

موده [1] mudá, muddá *f.* term; period; time په دې ټوله موده کښي all خه موده پخوا in five years د پنځو کالو په موده کښي this time تر خورا ډېري somewhat earlier په اوږده موده کښي long, a long time د ډېري مودي څخه، له اوږدي مودي راپه for a very long time مودي پوري ډېره موده کېږي چي It's been a long time دې خوا since long ago خه ډېره موده لا نه وه تېره چي ... A short time passed since... د څه مودي څخه، د څو مودي څخه، پس له څه مودي a little later خه موده تېره شوه from a certain moment پس له څه مودي A certain time has elapsed. په ډېره لنډه موده کښي within the shortest time د مودو نه ځما دا خواهش و possible This was my long-cherished dream. د اوږدي مودي پور a long-term loan, credit

موده [2] móda *oblique singular of* مود

مودي [1] muaddí *Arabic* 1 paying, reimbursing 2 *m.* payer

مودي [2] mudé *oblique singular & plural of* موده 1

مودبل modél *m.* ☞ مودول

موډ moḍ *m.* ☞ مود

موډم móḍem *m.* موډم móḍem *computer science* modem

مؤذن muazzín *m. Arabic* muezzin

موذي muzí *Arabic* 1.1 harmful; disagreeable; noxious 1.2 mean 2 *m.* tormentor

مور [1] mor *m.* peacock

مور [2] mor *f.* [*plural: Western* مندي mándi *and Eastern* مېندي ménde] mother خپله مور birth mother, one's own mother او پلار زامن children of the same mother and father, one's own children د شودو مور adoptive mother موري! móri! بي بي! Mother! مور ترمخ رودل from birth د موره زبربدلی *idiom* to be a brave man

مور [3] mur *m.* 1 caterpillar; pest 2 ant

مورا morá *f.* mother, wife of a mullah or a priest

موراک morák *m.* brick layer

مورال morál *m.* morale

موراني morānə́j, murānə́j *f.* rim of a knife's handle

موراوپلار mor-au-plắr *m. plural* parents

موربان morpán *m.* arborvitae

موراوپلار mor-plár *m. plural Eastern* ☞ موراوپلار

مورت murt *m.* myrtle

مورث maurís *Arabic* 1 causing; inflicting 2 *m.* cause

مورچل murchál *m.* ☞ مرچل

مورچنگ morcháng *m.* Jew's harp

مورچه [1] morchá *f.* 1 trench, entrenchment; position د پټو مورچو څخه د ښکاره مورچو څخه اورکول to shoot from covered positions اورکول to shoot from direct positions مورچه نیول to take up position 2 breastwork

مورچه [2] morchá *f.* 1 rust 2 termite

مورچه خور morchakhór 1 corroded with rust, rusted, rusty 2 eaten away by termites

مورچه خورک murchakhurák *m.* wryneck (bird)

مؤرخ [1] muarríkh *m. Arabic* [*plural:* مؤرخان muarrikhā́n *and Arabic* مؤرخین muarrikhín] 1 historian 2 chronicler

مورخ [2] muwarrákh *Arabic* dated, marked with a certain date

مورخانه muarrikhānā́ historical

مورد mauríd *m. Arabic* [*plural:* موارد mawāríd] 1 object, item 2 pretext; basis د استعمال مورد گرزول، د استفادۍ مورد گرزول to use د to be مورد لرل to be used استعمال مورد گرزېدل، د استفادۍ مورد گرزېدل utilized (of an expression, phrase) 3 case, instance په استثنايي موارد کښې in exceptional cases دغه پاس موارد the above-mentioned cases

موررروی morráwaj 1 sucking the mother's breast; nursing (of a baby); suckling (of a baby animal) 2 *m.* .1 suckling 2.2 baby

مورزاده morzādá مورزادی morzádaj congenital; born, inborn هغه مورزاده رند دئ He was born blind.

مورزېږ morzég uterine (of a brother)

مورفولوژي morfolozhí 1 *f.* morphology حيواني مورفولوژي animal morphology نباتي مورفولوژي plant morphology 2 morphological

مورفین morfín *m. plural* morphine

موركه moráka *f.* 1 morkáj, morakáj *f. children's speech* mommy, mom موركي، چای را واچوه! Mommy, pour me some tea!

موركي moráki *Eastern* موركي moráke *oblique singular of* موركه

مورگنی [1] morganáj *m.* relative (maternal)

مورگنۍ [2] morganáj *f.* relatives (maternal)

مورگه morgá *f.* 1 end; edge (e.g., of the sky) 2 ridge, ledge, overhang (of a mountain) 3 hunk (of bread) 4 borer line 5 ledge; lip 6 rim, brim

مورل morál *transitive* [*past:* و یې موره] to force lambs away from ewes; lamb weaning

مورلی murláj *f.* snake catcher's reed

مورم morám *m.* close relative whom one is forbidden to marry ☞ محرم [1]

مورمانسک murmā́nsk *m.* Murmansk

مورمړی mormáṛaj having lost one's mother

مورن morén *m.* moraine

مورنالت mornālát damned

مورنۍ moranáj, moranáj 1 native; maternal مورنۍ ژبه native language, native tongue a مورنۍ هیواد mother country b homeland 2 uterine مورنی ورور uterine brother

موروالی morwā́laj *m.* motherhood

موروپلار mor-u-plā́r *m. plural* parents

موروث maurús *Arabic* موروثي maurusí hereditary; inherited

موروالي morwalí *f.* ☞ موروالی

موره [1] morá *f.* ferment

موره [2] morá *imperfect of* مورل

موري [1] mawrí *m. plural* white wheat

موري [2] móri *Eastern* móre *vocative of* مور [2]

موري [3] morí *present tense of* مورل

موري [4] maurí *m.* leader camel

موري [5] maurí *adjective* Merv, Mary

موري [6] moráj *f.* 1 clay water-pipe 2 flue; chimney 3 oven's ash box, wind box 4 gutter 5 *regional* swear word; curse word, invective

موري [7] mauráj *f.* edge (of a roof); eaves

مورینکه morināka *f.* ☞ مورینه

مورینگه morínga *f.* foster mother

مورینه morína *f.* 1 dam (female) 2 *figurative* basis

مور [1] moṛ [*f.* مړه maṛá, *m. plural:* ماړه mā́ṛә, *f. plural:* مړي maṛé] 1 satiated, full 2 well-off, rich احمد خورا موړ دئ! Ahmed is very rich! 3 satisfied د مړي گېډي شپه او ورغ لیدل *idiom* to be comfortably off, be well provided for

مور [2] moṛ *m.* ☞ موړه 1, 3, 4

موړتیا moṛtjā́ *f.* 1 fullness; satiety 2 wealth, riches 3 satisfaction

موړسترگی moṛstárgaj 1 not greedy 2 pleased, satisfied 3 noble; magnanimous

موړکه [1] móṛka *f.* ☞ موړه

موړول morawál *denominative, transitive* ☞ مړول [1]

موړه [1] moṛá *f.* 1 saddlecloth (under the saddle) 2 packsaddle (of a camel) 3 range (of mountains, waves) 4 edge; lip 5 blockage; long-term constipation 6 stool 7 rampart around a tent 8 kind of embroidery 9 welt from being hit with a twig

موړه [2] muwaṛá, moṛá *f.* tool to clean cotton

موړه والا moṛawālā *m.* saddler who makes packsaddles

موړېدل moṛedál *denominative, intransitive* ☞ مړېدل

موړېده moṛedá *m. plural* ☞ مړېدنت

موز [1] uz *m. dialect* ☞ نمونغ

موز [2] mauz *m. Arabic* banana

موز [3] moz *m.* ispagol, psyllium (medicinal herb)

موزامبیک mozāmbík *m.* Mozambique

موزائیک mozāík *m.* موزائک mosaic

موزع muwazzi' *m. Arabic* salesman, deliverer (of newspapers, magazines, etc.)

موزغاړی muzghā́ṛaj *m.* kohl bag

موزون mauzún, mawzún *Arabic* 1 rhythmic, harmonious 2 well-proportioned; symmetrical 3 suitable, matching, appropriate 4 well-fitting (of clothes) 5 good (of mood) موزون قدم *idiom* cadence, quick time

موزونیت mauzuniját *m. Arabic* 1 rhythmicity; harmoniousness 2 proportionality; symmetry

موزه [1] mozá *f.* 1 high boot 2 feathering (in birds of prey)

موزه [2] muzá, muzé *f.* موزه خانه muzekhānā́ *f.* موزي 1 muzé museum

موزي [1] mozí 1 ☞ موذي 2 *m.* rival (in love)

موزي [2] muzé museum

موزي [3] mozé *plural of* موزه 1

موزیتوب mozitób *m.* lowness, dirty tricks; underhandedness

موزیک muzík *m.* 1 music 2 orchestra موزیک غږول *compound verb* to play music

مؤزیکه muziká *f.* music

موزیگی muzigáj *m.* 1 saboteur 2 rival (in love)

موزیم muzijóm *m.* ☞ موزه

موژ muzh *dialect pronoun* ☞ موږ

موږ [1] mug *Western personal pronoun, first person plural* **1.1** we (as the subject of an action in every tense) موږ ناست یو We are sitting. **1.2** we (as the object of actions with transitive verbs in ergative patterns) موږ یی ولیدو They saw us. **2** *oblique form* **.1** us (as the object of an action expressed by transitive verbs in the present, past, and future tenses and in the imperative mood) سلیم موږ بیایي Saleem gives us a ride. **2.2** we (as the subject of an action with transitive verbs in ergative patterns) موږ کار کاوه We worked. **2.3** us (with prepositions, postpositions, and adverbs) موږ ته to us پر موږ at us له موږ with us, from us **a** په موږ کښ with us, among us **b** within us

موږ [2] mug *present verb stem of* منبل

موربک [1] mugák *m.* ☞ مربک [1, 2]

موربک [2] mugák *m.* muscle; biceps; calf (of a leg)

موربک باز mugakbáz *m.* buzzard (bird)

موربک کوری mugakúraj *m* little mouse

موربل mugә́l *transitive* ☞ منبل

موربي [1] mugí *present tense of* منبل

موربی [2] mogáj, mawgáj *m.* [*plural:* موربي mogí *and* موربیان mogiján, mawgiján] peg; tethering post; lay up

موس [1] mos moss

موس [2] mos موست most thick (of a liquid)

مؤس [1] muassís *m. Arabic* [*plural:* مؤسان muassisán *and Arabic* مؤسسین muassisín] **1** founder; charter member مؤسس اعضا charter members, founders **2** founders ښاغلی پښتون د ویښ زلمیانو مؤسس دئ The founding father of Awaken Youth is Mr. Pashtoon.

مؤسس [2] muassás *Arabic* founded, established

مؤسسه muassasá *f. Arabic* [*plural:* مؤسسي muassasé *and m. plural: Arabic* مؤسسات muassasә́t] **1** enterprise; institution; firm دولتي مؤسسات a state صنعتي مؤسسه an industrial enterprise institution, enterprise **2** organization, facility **3** social institution د مرئیتوب مؤسسه slavery **4** institute (research facility)

مؤسسین muassisín *m. plural Arabic of* مؤسس 1

موسک musk *dialect* smiling موسک کېدل *compound verb* to smile

موسکا muskā́ *f.* smile په موسکا کښ while smiling

موسکوا moskwā́ *f.* Moscow د موسکوا دریاب Moscow River

موسکه múska *feminine singular of* موسک

موسکېدل muskedól *denominative, intransitive* [*past:* موسک شول] *dialect* to smile

موسم mausím, mosә́m, mosím *m. Arabic* [*plural:* موسمونه mausimúna *and* مواسم mawā́sím] season; time of year

موسمي mausimí seasonal موسمي اورښتونه، موسمي بارانونه seasonal موسمي باد monsoon rain

موسوم mausúm *Arabic* called, referred to

موسی [1] musā́ موسیٰ *m. Arabic personal noun* Moses; Musa

موسی [2] mosә́j *f.* ☞ موخی

موسیچه musichá *f.* laughing dove, *Streptopelia senegalensis*

موسی خېل musākhél موسیٰ خېل *m. plural* Musakheils (branch of the Gilzays-Ahmedzays and of the Mangals)

مسېدل musedól *intransitive* ☞ مسېدل

موسیقار musiqā́r *m. music* **1** Pan's flute **2** name of a legendary bird that symbolizes music

موسیٰ قلعه musāqal'á *f.* موسی قلعه Musaqala region

موسیقي musiqí **1** *f.* **.1** music د موسیقي آلات musical instruments د موسیقي دسته orchestra د موسیقي عالي ښوونځی conservatory سنفوني موسیقي symphonic music **1.2** musicality **2.1** musical orchestra **2.2** melodious موسیقي ډله، موسیقي دسته

موسیقي پوه musiqipóh *m.* موسیقي دان musiqidán *m.* **1** musician **2** musicologist

موسیقي والا musiqiwālā́ *m.* musician

موسیو mosjó *m.* monsieur; mister

موسی یي musājí Judaic (of religion)

موش mush *m.* **1** mouse **2** *used as the first part of word combinations* موشگیر **a** kestrel (bird) **b** buzzard

مشغولا mushkhulā́ *f.* ☞

موشخولتیا mushkhultjá *f.* **1** occupation **2** children's games and amusements

موشک mushák *m.* spy, scout

موشکافي mushikāfí *f.* **1** detailed analysis; detailed review **2** perspicacity **3** integrity; scrupulousness **4** censoriousness, cavil, faultfinding

موشکوڼی mushkúṇaj *m.* name of a plant used for brooms

موشکافي mushigāfí *f.* ☞

موشگیر mushgír *m.* موشگیرک mushgirák *m.* **1** kestrel (bird) **2** buzzard (bird)

موشه mushá *f.* black donkey

موبنا muḵhā́ *f.* spreading, applying, smearing, rubbing

موبنانه muḵhāná *f.* airan (drink similar to kefir) goatskin

موبنته moḵhtá *f.* bunch of cut wheat, etc.

موبنتی muḵhә́taj منبتی

موبنکه múḵhka *f.* musk

موبنل muḵhә́l *transitive* ☞ منبل

موبنلي [1] múḵhli *present tense of* منبتل

موبنلی [2] muḵhә́laj *past participle of* موبنل

موبننه muḵhә́na *f.* ☞ مینه

موبنولی muḵhawә́laj *past participle of* موبنل

موبنی múḵhi *present tense of* موبنل

موصوف mausúf *Arabic* **1.1** described **1.2** possessing some quality **1.3** lauded, glorious **1.4** modified **2** *m. grammar* dependent member

موصول mausúl *Arabic* **1** connected, attached **2** relative; relative pronoun

موضع mauzá', mauzé' *f. Arabic* [*m. plural Arabic* مواضع mawāzí'] **1** place, location **2** point د پوپولي موضع یي ونیوله They have taken the Popoli area. **3** *military* position موضع ونیسئ! *idiom* Over the top! (command)

موضوع mawzó', mawzú' **1** *f. and rarely m.* [*plural:* موضوع گاني، موضوعگاني mawzo'gā́ni, *m. plural Arabic* موضوعات mawzu'ā́t and موضوعونه mawzo'úna] **.1** issue; matter د موضوع كيفيت status, situation د ورځي د موضوعاتو په خصوص on a hot topic; on current topics د موضوع پوښتنه كول to find out what's going on, clarify the situation دا موضوع د پروا وړ ده This issue deserves attention. **1.2** topic, plot; content په مختلفو موضوعاتو خبري اتري كول to talk on a variety of topics د مذكراتو موضوع په لاندي قرار ده The agenda is as follows. **1.3** problem; issue د خپلواكي موضوع the issue of independence **1.4** object د بيمي موضوع the object of insurance **1.5** *grammar, philosophy* object; subject **1.6** mission, task; problem تكتيكي موضوع tactical mission **2.1** established موضوعه قوانين established laws **2.2** placed

موضوعه ² mauzu'á *feminine and plural Arabic of* موضو

موظف muwazzáf *Arabic* **1.1** (one) having received an appointment, appointed موظفول ☞ موظف كول officers, officials موظف كسان appointed **1.2** *military* being on active duty **2** *m.* [*plural:* موظفين muwazzafín] clerk, official; manager

موظفول [موظف يي كړ] muwazzafawál *denominative, transitive* [*past:* **1** to appoint, assign to a position **2** to obligate; impose an obligation

موظفيت muwazzafiját *m. Arabic military* active duty

موظفېدل [موظف شو] muwazzafedál *denominative, intransitive* [*past:* **1** to be appointed, get appointed **2** to be obligated, get obligated

موعد maw'íd *m. Arabic* **1** promise **2** prognosis **3** deadline; set time

موعظه mu'azá *f. Arabic* **1** sermon **2** admonition, instruction

موعود maw'úd *Arabic* promised

موفق ¹ muwaffáq *Arabic* **1** successful; lucky; prosperous په ... سره موفق كېدل to achieve success, prosper in something; prove a success **2** favored

موفق ² muwaffíq *Arabic* favoring; assisting, helping

موفقانه muwafaqqāná **1** successful **2** successfully

موفقيت muwaffaqiját *m. Arabic* success, good fortune; achievement ستر موفقيت with great success په ډېر موفقيت a great achievement موفقيت حاصلول، موفقيت مېندل، موفقيت موندل to achieve success; score a success; pull off

موقت muwaqqát *Arabic* temporary په موقت ډول temporarily

موقتاً muwaqqátán *Arabic* temporarily

موقتي muwaqqatí ☞ موقت

موقر muwaqqár *Arabic* **1** respected, esteemed; honorary وقار دروند to carry oneself with dignity **2** serious او موقر ساتل

موقع mauq'á moqá *f. Arabic* [*m. plural:* مواقع mawāqí'] **1** occasion; convenient moment; opportunity په دغسي موقع كښي in such a case د جشن په موقع on the occasion of the holiday د ناكامۍ په موقع in case of failure موقع پر موقع from time to time موقع كتل to look for an opportunity موقع پيدا كول to sneak a chance, get an opportunity و دۍ ته موقع پيدا شوه An opportune occasion arose. دۍ خبري موقع يي برابره كړه چي An opportunity was created for this.

له موقع څخه استفاده كوم I avail myself of the opportunity. **2** circumstances دغه مواقع يي پېژندل They were aware of the circumstances. **3** place موقع نيول to take up space; be situated موقع شناسي پېژندل to observe موقع شناسي mauqashināsí *f.* decorum decorum

موقعه mauqa'á, moq'á *f.* ☞ موقع نو اوس د دې شيانو موقعه نه ده This is no time to deal with these issues. په يوه موقعه in an instant

موقعيت mauqi'ját, mawqi'ját *m. Arabic* **1** situation, position جغرافيائي موقعيت geographic situation **2** timeliness **3** opportune moment; suitable occasion **4** situation

موقف mauqíf, mawqíf *m. Arabic* [*plural:* موقفونه mauqifúna *and Arabic* مواقف mawāqíf] **1** position, point of view خپل موقف يو موقف to elaborate on one's position بيانول، خپل موقف څر گندول to take a certain position په خپل موقف باندي تجديد نظر كول to maintain different بېل بېل موقفونه لرل to review one's position positions **2** circumstances, situation موقف لږ څه اوچت شوئ دئ The situation has somewhat improved. **3** social status اجتماعي موقف installation, setup; unit, piece of equipment **4** parking **5** policy

موقوت mawqút *Arabic* periodic موقوته خپروني mawqu-tá periodicals; periodic publications

موقوف mauqúf, mawqúf *Arabic* **1** forbidden, prohibited **2** terminated, suspended **3** removed (from duties, work) **4** dependent on something; involved with something **5** underpinned, based on something

موقوفول [موقوف يي كړ] mauqufawál *denominative, transitive* [*past:* to forbid, prohibit **2** to terminate, suspend **3** to remove (from duties, work)

موقوفېدل [موقوف شو] mauqufedál *denominative, intransitive* [*past:* to be forbidden, be prohibited **2** to be terminated, suspended **3** to be removed (from duties, work) **4** to depend on something **5** to be underpinned, be based on something

موك mok *m.* bribe; recompense موك اخيستل *compound verb* to take a bribe موك خورل *compound verb* to be on the take موك وركول to give a bribe

موكخور mokkhór *m.* bribe taker

مؤكد ¹ muakkád *Arabic* **1** supported, confirmed **2** emphasized (of a point, a word) مؤكد كول *compound verb* **a** to support, confirm **b** to emphasize (a point, a word) مؤكد كېدل *compound verb* **a** to be supported, be confirmed **b** to be emphasized (of a point, a word)

مؤكد ² muakkíd *Arabic* **1** supporting, confirming **2** emphasizing (of a point, a word)

موكل ¹ muwakkál *Arabic* **1** trusted; authorized; proxy **2** *m.* [*plural:* موكلين muwakkalín] elector; voter

موكل ² muwakkíl *m. Arabic* **1** proxy-giver, grantor **2** client (of a defending attorney)

موكه moká *f.* felt puttees, leggings

موگ mug *dialect pronoun* ☞ مورږ

موگاديشا mogādishā́ *f.* Mogadishu

موگرانده mogrāndá *f.* dormouse; squirrel-tailed dormouse (gnaw)

موگه múga *dialect pronoun* ☞ موږ

موگی ¹ mogáj *m. Eastern* ☞ موږی

مول mol *m.* **1** tip of a turban **2** way of wrapping a turban so it covers one's ears د مول ټوپکی a turban that is wrapped so it covers one's ears

مولا maulā́ *m. Arabic* [*plural:* مولايان maulājā́n] **1** god, lord **2** master

مولانا maulānā́, mawlānā́ *m. Arabic* mawlana; our master (the honorary title of Muslim learned men and theologians)

مولايي mawlāji مذهب مولايي **1.1** master's **1.2** Ishmaelite Ishmaelism **2** *m.* Ishmaelite

مولت molát *m.* ☞ مهلت

مولد ¹ mawlíd *m. Arabic* **1** place of birth **2** birth

مولد ² muwallíd *Arabic* **1.1** producing; generating مولده قواوي power production **1.2** productive **2** *m.* [*plural:* مولدين muwallidín] **.1** producer واره مولدین small producers **2.2** creator د برق مولد *technology* generator

مولد ³ muwallád *Arabic* born, produced

ملدواي moldāwí ☞ ملدوای

ملداویا moldawijā́ *f.* ☞ ملدوایا

مولده muwallidá *f. Arabic and plural of* مولد

مولدیت muwallidiját *m. Arabic* performance; productivity

مؤلف ¹ mu'allíf *m. Arabic* [*plural:* مؤلفین mu'allifín] **1** author, compiler **2** compiler; collector

مؤلف ² mu'alláf *Arabic* **1** composed; put together **2** *m.* [*plural:* مؤلفات mua'llafā́t] composition; work

مولود mawlúd, maulúd *Arabic* **1** born, generated **2** *m.* **.1** birth **2.2** *religion* Prophet Mohammed's birthday **2.3** son **2.4** consequence, result, yield, product منطقي مولود logical consequence **2.5** [*plural:* موالید] mawālíd one of nature's realms

مولودیت mauludiját, mawludiját *m. Arabic* performance; productivity

مولوي mawlawí *m. Arabic religion* mawlawi, learned person

موله molá *f. military* camp; bivouac

مولی ¹ molája *m.* **1** pestle **2** pestle of a hulling machine **3** tree stump

مولی ² mawlā́ *m. Arabic* ☞ مولا

مولی ³ mulája *f.* ☞ ملی

موم ¹ mom, mum *m. plural* wax

موم ² mum *verb stem present of* موندل *and* میندل

مومانه mumāṇá *f.* ☞ ممانه

مومبر mumbár *m. colloquial* ☞ منبر

موم جامه momdzhāmá *f.* **1** oilcloth **2** waxed paper

مومر mumáṛ *m. plural* ☞ مومیایي 1

مؤمن mumín *m. Arabic* [*plural:* مؤمنان muminā́n *and Arabic* مؤمنین muminín] **1** faithful; Muslim **2** *proper noun* Mumin

مومند mománd **1** *m. plural* Momands (a tribe) **2** *m.* Momand

مومو ¹ mómó, múmó *oblique plural of* موم

مومو ² múmu *present tense first person of* موندل *and* میندل

مومي ¹ momí **1** wax **2** waxed

مومي ² múmi *present tense of* میندل

مومي ³ mumí above-mentioned, stated

مومیا momijā́, mumijā́ *f.* **1** mummy **2** ointment

مومی الیهم mumāalejhúm *plural Arabic* above-mentioned (*plural*) مومی الیهم ذوات the above-mentioned persons

مومیایي ¹ momjā́i *f.* مومیائي **1** mineral oil, mineral resin (for the treatment of sprained joints and fractures, etc.) **2** ichthyol **3** embalming

مومیایي ² momjā́i, mumjā́i مومیائي مومیایي جسد embalmed مومیایي mummy *compound verb* to embalm مومیایي کول *compound verb* to be embalmed, get embalmed

مونتاژ montázh *m.* assembly, setup

مؤنث muannás مؤنث *Arabic grammar* **1** feminine gender مؤنثه مؤنث کلمه، مؤنث نوم feminine gender word مؤنث اشخاص females **2** *m.* [*plural:* مؤنثات muannasā́t] feminine gender; feminine gender word

مؤنثتوب muannastób *m.* مؤنث والی muannaswā́laj *m. grammar* feminine gender

مونج ¹ mundzh *m.* ☞ منج

مونځ mundz *m. dialect* ☞ نمونځ

مونځ گوزار mundzguzā́r *m.* (one who is) performing the namaz prayer

موندره mundrá *f.* earring

موندری ¹ mundrā́j **1** of short stature **2** short-eared

موندری ² mundṛə́j *f.* ☞ موندره

موندل mundə́l *transitive Eastern* ☞ میندل

موندنه ² mundə́na *f.* ☞ میندنه

موندنونی mundúnaj accessible, achievable

مونده ² mundə́ *m. plural* ☞ میندنه

موندئ ¹ mundáj *Eastern potential form of the verb form of* موندل *in lieu of* موندای

موندی ² mundáj *m.* [*plural:* موندي mundí *and* موندیان mundijā́n] goat or ram with short ears

موندی ³ mundə́j *f.* she-goat or sheep with short ears

مونډ ¹ munḍ *m.* [*plural:* مونډان munḍā́n] **1** tree stump **2** root **3** source (of evil etc.) **4** foundation, base, basis د لغت اصلي مونډ *idiom* the root of a word

مونډ ² munḍ reticent, quiet

مونډک munḍə́k *m.* **1** small stump (of a tree) **2** branch stub

مونډه ¹ munḍə́ *m.* ☞ منډه

مونډهری munḍhə́raj *m.* compacted area (for games)

مونډهی munḍháj *m.* bull that is closest to the center of the thrashing floor or the waterwheel

مونډی ¹ munḍáj *m.* ☞ منډی

مونډی ² munḍə́j *f.* ☞ منډی

مونډیز munḍíz intricate, complex (of an issue or matter)

مونرویا monrowijā́ *f.* Monrovia

مونز munz *m. dialect* ☞ نمونځ

مونږ mung مونږه múnga *dialect pronoun* ☞ موږ

مونس munís *Arabic* 1 gregarious 2 *m.* intimate friend, close friend

مونسون monsún مون سون *m.* monsoon د مونسون بادونه monsoon winds ☞ موسم

مونش múnish *m.* Munich

مونگ mung *Eastern pronoun* ☞ موږ

مونگ پلی mungpalí *f.* peanuts

مونگه múnga *Eastern pronoun* ☞ موږ

مونوگراف monográf *m.* مونوگرافي monográfí *f.* monograph

موني ¹ munā́j *m.* post on which meat is hung to be air-cured

موني ² múnaj *m.* necklace

موني ³ monā́j *m.* polled goat, hornless goat

موني muṇā́j *m.* plug made of a rag

موهبت mawhibā́t mauhibā́t *m. Arabic* [*plural* موهبتونه mawhibatúna, *Arabic* موهبات mauhibā́t *and* مواهب mawāhíb موهبه mauhibá *f. Arabic plural:* موهبي mauhibé, *m. plural Arabic* موهبات mauhibā́t *and* مواهب mawāhíb] 1 present; gift; offering 2 benefaction, favor 3 gift, talent

موهوم mauhúm *Arabic* 1.1 imaginary, mock, apparent; supposed 1.2 fantastic 2 *m.* [*plural:* موهومات mauhumā́t] 1 fantasy 2.2 superstition; prejudice

موهوم پرست mauhumparā́st superstitious

موهوم پرستي mauhumparastí *f.* superstition; superstitiousness

موی muj *m.* one hair

مؤید ¹ muajjád *Arabic* reinforced; supported

مؤید ² muajjíd *Arabic* 1.1 assisting, helping 1.2 reinforcing 2 *m.* favorable moment

مویز mawíz *m. plural* large black sultanas; raisins سره مویز red sultanas

مواشي maweshí *m. plural* ☞ مواښي

مویښي mawék̈hi *f. plural* 1 tapeworm 2 hemorrhoidal piles

مه ¹ ma, mə *Eastern, Western* 1 *particle* .1 not, don't (negative, prohibitive, emphatic particle; commonly used with verbs of imperfect aspect and conditional or imperative mood; it is sometimes written with the verb) مکوه!، مه کوه! Don't do! 1.2 *postposition* (used for emphasis) ته نن مه ځه! Don't go today! ما مه مي ستړی کوه Don't fatigue me! نه څه پوښتنه کوه مه Don't ask me anything! 2 instead of مه کوه

مه ² ə́ma *suffix feminine of* م ⁷

مهاجر muhādzhír *Arabic* 1 *m.* [*plural:* مهاجرین muhādzhirín] .1 settler, émigré (especially of Muslims who emigrated from India due to the caliphate movement) 1.2 immigrant 2.1 resettling; emigrating, immigrating 2.2 migratory مهاجر مرغان migratory birds

مهاجرت muhādzharā́t *m. Arabic* resettlement; emigration; immigration

مهاجم muhādzhím *Arabic* 1 assaulting, attacking 2 *m.* aggressor

مهار mahā́r, muhā́r *m. Arabic* reins (camel's) مهار کول *compound verb* to bridle (a camel)

مهارپانه mahārpā́ṇa *f. computer science* control panel

مهارت mahārát *m. Arabic* mastery, art; skill, dexterity

مهاراجه mahāradzhá *m.* maharaja

مهارکیلي mahārkilí *f. computer science* control key

مهاري mahārí racing, fast-running (of a camel)

مهال mahā́l *m.* 1 time, season د سهار مهال و چي ذهین راغئ It was morning when Zaheen came. له ده مهاله را و دي خواته since a certain time په راتلونکي مهال کښي in the future, from now on په دي with time په بل مهال recently په تېرېدو د مهال with time وروستي مهال کښي a at this time, now b at دا مهال some time یو ښه مهال other times that time, then همدا مهال دئ چي precisely now, precisely at this time 2 season (of fruit, etc.) د انگورو مهال دوبی دئ Summer is the season for grapes.

مهاڼي mahāṇáj *m.* ferryman; boatman

مهتاب mahtáb *m.* moonlight, moon

مهتابۍ mahtābə́j *f.* kind of fireworks

مهتر mihtár *m.* 1 prince (in particular, the ruler of Chitral) 2 *regional* groom

مهترلام mihtar-lā́m *m.* Mehtarlam

مهتري mihtārí *f.* work of a groom

مهتم muhtammím *Arabic* 1 *m.* .1 observer 1.2 principal; trustee (of a school) 1.3 editor 2 caring

مهجور mahdzhúr *Arabic* 1 abandoned; left 2 forgotten; deserted مهجور حقیقت a forgotten fact; forgotten truth 3 separated له یاره مهجور دئ He is separated from his sweetheart.

مهذب muhazzáb *Arabic* well-bred; well-mannered

مهر ¹ muhr *m.* 1 seal, stamp مهر کول *compound verb* to seal لگول *compound verb* to attach, affix a seal 2 *history* muhr, mogar (gold coin in India) د خاموشی مهر ماتول *idiom* to break silence, violate the silence د خارج مهر یې خرښاوه *idiom* They bragged about their foreign education.

مهر ² mahr *m. Arabic* 1 mahr (bride-price, bride money) 2 mahr (amount of money set aside by the bridegroom for the bride at the marriage ceremony)

مهر ³ mihr *m.* 1 love 2 kindness

مهرباش mihrbā́sh 1 friendly 2 loving

مهربان mihrbā́n, merbā́n, mehrabā́n 1 kind; gracious څنگه مهربان! What attention! هغه مهربان دئ He is kind to me. په ما مهربان دئ your lordship, sir که چیري استاد مهربانه وي ... If the teacher is kind to… 2 gracious

مهرباني ¹ merbāngí, mehrbāngí *f.* ☞ مهرباني ¹ د خدای په مهربانگی سره by the grace of God په مهربانگی سره graciously

مهربانه merbā́na, mehrbā́na 1 *feminine singular of* مهربان ☞ 2

مهرباني ¹ merbāní, mehrbāní *f.* 1 kindness 2 graciousness; mercy مهرباني کول *compound verb* a to be kind b to be gracious مهرباني وکه! Please! Be so kind as to! مهرباني وکئ Thank you!

مهرباني ² mehrbā́ni *oblique of* مهربانه

مهردار muhrdā́r *m.* keeper of the seal

مهردل mihrdíl, mehrdál *m. personal name proper noun* Mihrdil

مهرکن muhrkán *m.* مهرکند muhrkánd *m.* engraver, chiseler

مهرکندي muhrkandí *f.* مهرکني muhrkaní *f.* engraving craft

مهرو mahró *proper noun* Mahro, Mahru

مهره muhrá *f.* 1 shell 2 bead 3 vertebra 4 trowel

مهري muhrí [1] *f.* ☞ موری 2

مهري muhrí [2] sealed

مهلت muhlát *m. Arabic* 1 adjournment, deferment, grace ترسبا پوري مهلت راکړه *compound verb* a to defer, postpone ورکول Postpone this till the morning. b to conclude a truce مهلت غوښتل to ask for deferment 2 respite 3 delay 4 leisure

مهلک muhlík *Arabic* 1 ruinous, deleterious; dangerous; fatal مهلک کار hazardous work مهلک مرض fatal disease 2 crushing, smashing

مهلکه mahlaká *f. Arabic* 1 danger, hazard 2 dangerous place

مهم muhím, muhímm *Arabic* 1.1 important, significant, serious دا کوم شی چي مهم دئ هغه دا دئ چي This is important. دا مهمه خبره ده Here is what's important. تر ټولو نه مهمه دا ده This is what's most important. 1.2 large; major د هوائي قواو مهمه ټولګۍ large aviation units 2 *m.* [*plural:* مهمونه muhimúna *and Arabic* مهمات muhimmát] .1 important matter, enterprise 2.2 campaign, expedition 2.3 danger, hazard; risk

مهمات muhimmát *m.* 1 *plural Arabic of* مهمه 1 2 ammunition, military gear جنګي مهمات munitions 3 needs, requirements

مهمان mihmán *m.* guest

مهمان خانه mihmānkhāná *f. Western* guest room ☞ حجره

مهماندار mihmāndár *m.* 1 mihmandar (government representative who attends to high-ranking foreigners, particularly diplomats, during their stay in the country); master of ceremonies 2 host; one who treats

مهمانداري mihmāndārí *f.* 1 treat; regale; hospitality 2 duties of a mihmandar

مهماندوست mihmāndóst hospitable; generous (of a host)

مهمان نوازي mihmānnawāzí *f.* hospitality

مهمانه mihmána *f.* female guest

مهماني mihmāní *f.* 1 treat; to treat مهماني کول to organize a feast 2 organization of a feast 3 being a guest

مهمترین muhimmtarín most important, largest

مهمل muhmál *Arabic* 1 empty, senseless; absurd مهمل الفاظ meaningless words 2 neglected, ignored مهمل پریښنودل *compound verb* to neglect something; ignore something 3 out of use

مهمند mohmánd 1 *m. plural* Momands (a tribe) بر مهمند mountain Momands کوز مهمند lowland Momands 2 *m.* [*plural:* مهمندان mohmandán, مهمندیان mohmandiyán] Momand

مهمندزی mohmandzí [1] *m. plural* Momanzi (a tribe) 2 *m.* mohmandzáy Momanzai

مهموالی muhimwãlaj, muhimmwãlaj *m.* importance; significance

مهمه muhimmá [1] *f. Arabic* [*plural:* مهمات muhimmát] important, grave matter

مهمه muhímma [2] *feminine singular of* مهم 1

مهمېز mahméz *m.* مهمېزه mahméza *f.* 1 spur 2 goad; pricker

مهندس muhandís *m. Arabic* [*plural:* مهندسان muhandisán *and Arabic* مهندسین muhandisín] 1 engineer سر مهندس chief engineer هوائي مهندس an airplane designer 2 geometrician, specialist in geometry

مهندسي muhandisí *f.* engineering; technology

مهنګا mahangá *regional* dear, valuable

مهنګائي mahangāí *f. regional* value

مهڼ mahə́ṇ *m.* مهڼه mahaṇá *m.* 1 sailor 2 boatman

مهوت maháut *m.* elephant leader

مهی maháj [1] *m.* [*plural:* مهي mahí *and* مهیان mahijã́n] fish

مهی mahə́j, mahí [2] *f.* mung bean

مهی mahé [3] *f. plural* mung beans, *Dolichos pilosus*

مهیا mahjá [1] *f.* flock of sheep

مهیا muhajjá [2] *Arabic* ready-made; manufactured مهیا کول *compound verb* to stock up; produce, prepare

مهیب muhíb *Arabic* frightful; terrible; awesome

مهیج muhajjídzh *Arabic* 1 exciting; stimulating; cheering مهیج بیانات، مهیج اظهارات cheering talk, pep talk 2 *m.* stimulus, incentive

مهیخورک mahikhurák *m.* kingfisher (birds)

مهیرګه mahérga *f.* 1 epilepsy 2 epidemic

مهی ګیر mahajgír, mahigír *m.* fisher

مهی ګیري mahajgirí, mahigirí *f.* fishery

مهین mahín 1 fine; tender 2 smooth; slippery 3 fine, high-quality

مهینه mahiná [1] *f.* monthly salary; monthly pay

مهینه mahiná [2] 1 *f.* early sowing 2.1 early; previous 2.2 ripe, early ripening 2.3 elder; older 3 earlier; previously

می mi, me [1] *Western, Eastern* 1 *non-emphatic indirect form of a pronoun, it cannot start sentence* .1 me (used as the object of an action with transitive verbs in the present and future tenses as well as in the imperative mood) ته می پښتی You are asking me. 1.2 I (as the subject of an action with transitive verbs in an ergative structure) مخکښبي می عرض وکړ چي . . . I have said already that ... 1.3 my (as the possessive pronoun) دا هلک می خوریی دئ This boy is my nephew. اوس می لور چرته ده؟ Where is my daughter now? 1.4 at my place; from me دی می ولاړو اصفهان ته! He left me for Isfahan.

می maj [2] *m. plural* wine سره می red wine

می məj [3] *f. plural* mung bean; kidney beans سري می lentils وېبنتان یې می وریجي شوي وو He became grizzled. His hair became grizzled.

می me, maj [4] *f.* May

می me [5] *Western contraction of the pronouns* می *and* یې نوم می نه یې دئ زده I don't know his name

می me [6] *contraction of the negation* مه *and pronoun* یې می ویبنوه! Don't wake him up!

ميا mjā́, mijā́ *m.* [*plural:* مياگان mjāgā́n, mijāgā́n *and* ميان mjājā́n, mijājā́n] **1** clergyman's title; reverend **2** mister ميا حسين خان Mister Hussein-khan **3** monk

ميا mijā́ *f. dialect* herd (of horses)

ميار mjār *m. dialect* ☞ عيب

ميارن mjārə́n dialect *dialect* ☞ عيب ناک

مياسه mjā́sa *f. dialect* ☞ مياشه

مياشت mjāsht *f.* [*plural:* مياشتي mjā́shti] **1.1** month, د لمر مياشت a month of the solar year قمري مياشت a month of the lunar year مياشتو مياشتو په مياشتو ، په مياشتو for months مياشتي لمرۍ واده د honeymoon نن د مياشت monthly, each month خرومه ده؟ په What date is it today? **1.2** month (*sometimes with* does not decline) په يو څو مياشتي for several months, in a few months مياشت د لمرۍ روڼي ګوره!، مياشت د لمرۍ ورڼي معلومبري *proverb* A month is judged by its first day. (*literally:* A bird is known by its flight.) **2** new moon د سرۍ مياشتي ټولنه the Red Crescent Society

مياشتنۍ mjāshtanáj *m.* monthly

مياشتنۍ mjāshtanə́j *f.* monthly

مياشکوډۍ mjāshkuḍə́j *f.* mosquito net

مياشه mjā́sha *f.* مياشي mjā́shaj *m. Eastern* mosquito د ملېريا مياشه a malarial mosquito; anopheles

مياشي mjā́she *plural of* مياشه

ميان mijā́n *m.* **1** patron (title of saints) **2** descendant of a famous clergyman

ميان mijā́n *m.* **1** small of the back; waist **2** sheath **3** middle هواري مځکي د درياى آمو او هندوکش په ميان کي دي Plains lie between Amu-Darya and Hindukush. د دوى له ميانه فرق نسته *idiom* There is no difference between them. په دا ميان کښې ژمی راغئ، په دې ميان In the meantime, winter has set in. کښې ژمی راغئ

ميانجي ګري mijāndzhí *m.* ميانجي ګراى mijāndzhigáraj

ميانجي ګري mijāndzhigarí *f.* mediation; settling; reconciliation

ميانجي ګراى mijāndzhigáraj *m.* middleman; arbiter

ميانځ mjāndz *m. dialect* ☞ منځ

ميانځنۍ mjāndzinaj ☞ منځنۍ

ميانده mjā́nda *f.* flat rock that pepper, etc., is crushed on

مياندي mjā́nde *dialect feminine plural of* مور

مياني mijāná *f.* ☞ مياني

ميانه mijāná **1** average; moderate سيمه temperate climate area **2** of average height هغه نه دنګ دئ نه مندرى، ميانه دئ He is of average height.

ميانه حال mjānahál ميانه حاله mjānahā́la fairly well-off, neither rich nor poor ميانه حال کسان people who are fairly well-off

ميانه قد mijānaqád ميانه قدى mijānaqá daj of average height

مياني mijāní *f.* Zilqada (the eleventh month of the lunar calendar)

مياني mjānə́j *f. dialect* purse

ميباجد míbājad چي it is necessary; it ought to be

مى پرست majparást *m.* drunkard; fond of drinking

مى پرستي majparastí *f.* drunkenness

ميت majít, majt *m. Arabic* **1** corpse **2** carrion

مېتافيزيک metāfizík *m.* metaphysics

مبتافزيکي metāfizikí metaphysical مبتافزيکي فيلسوف metaphysicist

مېتر metə́r *m.* groom, stableman ☞ مهتر

مېترو metró *f.* subway; metro

ميتل mitál *transitive* [*present:* مېژي ، ميتي *past:* و يى ميتل] urinate

مېتود metód *m.* method علمي مېتود scientific method

مېتوديک metodík **1** methodological **2** methodical

ميته majjíta *f.* ☞ ميت

مېتى metáj *m.* **1** pickaxe **2** stone dresser's hammer

ميتينګ miting *m.* meeting

مېتيؤرولوژي meteorolozhí **1** *f.* meteorology **2** meteorological

مېتيؤرولوژيک meteorolozhík meteorological

مېټ meṭ *m. plural* red ochre

مېټ meṭ *m.* flour bin

ميټا miṭā́ *f.* orange

ميټائي miṭāí *f.* ميټائي sweets; sweet biscuits

ميټر miṭár *m.* **1** meter د بربنا ميټر electric meter د حساب ميټر a cab meter **2** *regional* meter

مېټرک meṭrík *m. regional* enrollment in an institution of higher learning, matriculation د مېټرک امتحان entrance exams

ميثاق misā́q *m. Arabic* [*plural:* مواثيق mawāsíq] **1** agreement; charter **2** promise

ميثاقي misāqí contractual; reached by agreement

مېجر medzhár *m. colloquial* major

مېجر جنرال medzhardzhanrál *m. colloquial* major-general

مېجسترېټ medzhisṭréṭ *m. regional* magistrate

مېچ mech *m.* **1** measure; capacity, size يو مېچ زيات وى somewhat more په يوه مېچ same size, equally tall په هغه مېچ to the same extent تر يوه مېچه پورى to a certain extent **2** measurement, survey په نظر څوک مېچ کول، په نظر څوک مېچول *compound verb* ☞ مېچ کول مېچول to give somebody a dirty look

مېچ mech *m. sports* match; competition د کرکيټ مېچ a cricket tournament د فتبال مېچ a soccer match

مېچ mech *m. computer science* capacity, size

مېچل mechál *transitive dialect* ☞ مېچول

مېچن mechə́n *f.* [*plural:* مېچني mechə́ni] مېچنه mechə́na *f.* hand mill; attrition mill

ميچني michní, michnə́j *f.* Michni (settlement near Khyber)

مېچني mechə́ni *plural of* مېچن *and* مېچنه

مېچنى mechə́naj *m.* turtle

ميچوريني michurewí Michurinite ميچوريني دوکترين Michurin's doctrine

مېچول mechawə́l *denominative, transitive* [*past:* مېچ يى کړ] **1** to measure خونه په قدمونو مېچول to pace the room back and forth **2** to take someone's measurements

مېچونه mechawə́na *f.* **1** measurement **2** taking someone's measurements

مېچه mechá *f.* **1** noodles **2** dodder

مچېدﻞ mechedә́l *denominative, intransitive* [*past:* مېچ شو] to be measured

مېځری medzә́raj *m.* ☞ مبزری

مخ mekh *m.* 1 nail مبخ کوچنی a small nail 2 small peg; peg 3 barb

مبخانه majkhāná *f.* pub, tavern

مبخانیک mekhānī́k *m.* 1 mechanic 2 mechanics 3 railroad engineer

مبخانیکي mekhānikí mechanical مبخانیکي ښوونخی a mechanical-technical school مبخانیکي طلبه students of a mechanical-technical school مبخانیکي انسان a robot مبخانیکي صدمه mechanical damage مبخانیکي کبدﻞ *compound verb* to mechanize مبخانیکي کوﻞ *compound verb* to be mechanized; get mechanized

مبخانیکیت mekhānikiját *m.* 1 mechanism 2 mechanics

مبخچو mekhchú *m.* 1 tree nail; dowel 2 mallet to hammer in a tent's peg 3 hub

مبخزین mekhzín *m. regional* 1 armory 2 storehouse

مبخک mekhák *m.* 1 carnation 2 corn (on one's foot) 3 kind of ornament

می خوار majkhā́r *m.* می خور majkhór *m.* drunkard

می خورگي majkhoragí *f.* drunkenness

مبخوش majkhósh sweet and sour

مبخوﻞ mekhawә́l *denominative, transitive* [*past:* مبخ یې کړ] to nail, fasten with a nail

مبخي مبخي لیک mekhí cuneiform writing

میدان ¹ majdā́n *m. Arabic* [*plural:* میدانونه majdānúna *and Arabic* میادین majādín] 1 public square د بازی میدان recreation ground; sports ground د طیارو میدان، هوائي میدان، د هوابازی میدان an aerodrome, airport 2 field of activity; occupation; arena 3 plain, broad valley (frequently in geographical names) ځاځي میدان Zazi-maydan 4 battlefield 5 staging area میدان خالي کوﻞ، میدان پر ښنوﻞ to give up میدان چغالي کبدﻞ to get rid of one's adversaries میدان ورکوﻞ to gain the upper hand گټﻞ، میدان وړﻞ to give free rein *idiom* a میدان ته راایستﻞ، په میدان راپر بوتﻞ to land to shame, put to shame b میدان ته راغورزوﻞ to expose, unmask (a proposal) د نشر میدان ته راوتﻞ to be printed, be published یو فکر را میدان ته ور داخلبدﻞ to voice an opinion میدان ته کوﻞ to appear in the public arena دی د میدان پهلوان دئ He attracts all the attention.

میدان ² majdā́n Maydan د میدان دره the Maydan Valley

میداني majdāní *f.* square (in a city)

میدوﻞ majdawә́l *denominative, transitive* [*past:* میده یې کړ] 1 to crush, grind; crumble, rub up 2 to grind (grain)

میده majdá 1 *m.* gritty flour; grits 2 finely ground میده اوړه granular flour میده پیسی small change میده حروف small font میده small change میده کبدﻞ میدوﻞ *compound verb* ☞ میده کوﻞ *compound verb* to be reduced to fragments; be ground up

میده بیز majdabíz *m.* small sieve

میده فروش majdafurúsh *m.* chandler

میده گي majdagí *f.* 1 small thing 2 crumbs

میده میده majdá-majdá 1 small 2 crumbled; ground 3 thrashed (of grain) میده میده کوﻞ *compound verb* a to grind, pound; crumble b to thrash (grain) میده اوړه کوﻞ *idiom* to beg, supplicate; talk into; insist

مبدي medí Midian مبدي اقوام Midians

مبدیم mídjum medium (grade)

مبډرډ médṛíḍ *m.* Madrid

مبډﻞ meḍál *m.* medal

مبډیټرانه meḍiṭerāná *f.* Mediterranea د مبډیټرانی بحیره the Mediterranean Sea

میر ¹ mir *m.* 1 mir (a Sayyid title) 2 mir, duke (Uzbek) 3 queen (of bees) 4 senior shepherd

مبر ² mer *m. dialect* Sun

مبر ³ mer *f. dialect* ☞ مور ²

میرا mirā́ *m. proper noun* Mira

میراب mirā́b *m.* mirab (person in charge of water distribution in irrigation)

میرات mirā́t 1 *m.* ☞ میراث 2 *attributive* 2.1 childless 2.2 left without direct heirs 2.3 damned; rotte میرات شه! Be damned!

میراث خوار mirātkhā́r *m.* میراث خور mirātkhór *m.* ☞ میراث خوار

میرات مړی mirātmә́raj 1 abandoned 2 conversational damne مړی تبه! Damned fever!

میراته ¹ mirātá *dialect* ☞ موروث

میراته ² mirāta *feminine singular of* میرات 2.3

میراث mirā́s *m. Arabic* 1 inheritance د میراث حق right of inheritance د میراث محصوﻞ inheritance tax چا ته څخه په میراث اخیستﻞ to receive as inheritance from somebody چا to inherit د یو شي څخه میراث لرﻞ رسبدﻞ to be left as inheritance میراث دي هغه ته پاته سه ، چي هم یې خوری ته میراث ورکوﻞ to bequeath هم پر ژاړی *proverb* Wealth is of no use to a stupid son. 2 heritage روحاني میراث spiritual heritage

میراث خوار mirāskhā́r *m.* میراث خور mirāskhór *m.* 1 heir 2 inheritor; joint heir 3 land tenant with a right to inherit

میراث خوره mirāskhóra *f.* heiress

میراثه mirāsá *f. Arabic* heritage

میراثي mirāsí 1 hereditary; inherited 2 *colloquial* damned خدای دي میراثي که! Damn you! پاتي شي!

میراخور mirākhór *m.* stall master

میران mirā́n *m. proper noun* Miran

میرآو mirā́w *m.* ☞ میراب

میرځری merdzә́raj *m.* میرڅری mirtsә́raj *m.* ☞ مبزری

مبرڅمن mertsmә́n مبرڅن mertsә́n 1.1 hostile 1.2 hateful; mean, vile 1.3 false; mendacious, deceitful 2 *m.* enemy

مبرڅي ¹ mertsí, mirtsí *f.* 1 evil; hostility; spite, rage سره مبرڅي کوﻞ to be feuding 2 *regional* offense, hurt feelings 3 disaster, calamity, grief 4 vexation; chagrin

مبرڅی ² mertsáj *m.* enemy; offender, wrongdoer

مبرڅی ³ mertsә́j *f. from* مبرڅی ²

میرخان mirkhā́n *m. proper noun* Mirkhan

میرخانۍ mirkhānә́j *f.* **1** large turban **2** kind of muslin (for the turban)

میرخېل mirkhéjl *m. plural* Mirkheil (dervish fraternity)

میرزا mirzā́ *m.* [*plural:* میرزایان mirzājā́n] **1** mirza, duke, prince (in combinations, after personal names) **2** mirza, mister (before personal names) **3** scribe, secretary

میرزایي mirzājí **1** prince's; princely **2** *f.* **.1** dukedom **2.2** work or position of a scribe, secretary **3** clothes worn by mirzas

میرسنگ mirsáng *m.* large shell that bath attendants use as a trumpet

میرشکار mirshikā́r *m.* **1** master huntsman, chief hunter **2** chief falconer

میرغاړوه mirghāṛә́wa *f.* name of a plant that bears edible berries

میرغاوډاله mirghāwḍā́la *f.* ☞ ډنډوکی

میر کانتیلیزم merkāntilízm *m.* mercantilism

میرګانی mirgā́naj *m.* marbles (the game or the marbles themselves)

میرګل¹ mirgúl *m. proper noun* Mirgul

مېرگل² mergúl *m.* sunflower

مېرگن¹ mergә́n *m.* epileptic

مېرگن² mergán *m.* **1** Bonelli's Eagle, *Aquila fasciata* **2** skilled huntsman

میرگنج mirgándzh *m.* griffon; vulture

میرگنجی mirgandzháj completely bald; having become bald

مېرگي mergí *f. medicine* epilepsy

مېرگیانی mergjānáj suffering from epilepsy

میرم mirám *m. proper noun* Miram

میرمایي mirmāí *m. proper noun* Mirmayi

میرمجلس mirmadzhlís *m.* toastmaster

میرمجلسي mirmadzhlisí *f.* duties of a toastmaster میرمجلسي کول toastmaster

میرمچی mirmәčáj *f.* queen (of bees)

مېرمن mermә́n *f.* [*plural:* مېرمني mermә́ni] **1** mistress, female owner, lady د مېرمنو ټولنه the lady of the house a د مېرمنو بین المللی نهضت women's association international مېرمن کېدل women's movement to get married, be (become) the mistress **2** madam (form of address) مېرمنو! Dear ladies! دا منطقه د وچ اقلیم مېرمن ده This area enjoys an arid climate.

مېرمنتوب mermәntób *m.* status of a lady, mistress

مېرمنه mermә́na *f.* ☞ مېرمن

مېرنۍ meranә́j *f.* مېرنی مور stepmother

میرو miró *m. proper noun* Miro (term of endearment of میر محمد and other proper nouns start with میر)

میروار mirwā́r *m.* coquetry میروار کول to flirt

مېروزه meróza *f.* name of a plant whose fruit is used to feed silkworms

میروگی mirogáj *m. proper noun diminutive of* میرو

میرویس mir wajs *m. proper noun* Mir Wais (chief of the Ghalzais in the 18th century in Kandahar)

میره¹ mәjrá, majrá *f.* [*plural:* میري majré *and* میري گانی majregā́ne] **1** stepmother میره مور stepmother **2** one of one's father's wives (with regard to the other wife's children)

میره² míra *feminine of* میر

مېره³ majrá, merá *f.* **1** steppe; plain د میوند مېره the Maiwand Plain **2** *regional* nonirrigated land **3** Maira (the area between Attok and Peshawar) **4** grazing land; pasture

میري¹ mirí میري mirә́j *f.* title of a mir; princedom; duties of a tribal chief میري سره ګټل *idiom* to compete تاسي څه میري سره ګټئ؟ What are you fighting about?

میري² majré *plural of* مېره³

میري³ mәjré *plural plural of* میره¹

مېرېزی¹ merezáj, mәjrezáj **1** non-blood related مېرېزی، مېرۍ زی stepbrother **2** *m.* [*plural:* مېرېزي، مېرۍ زي merezí *and* مېرېزیان merezijā́n] non-blood related, stepbrother

مېرېزی² merezáj, mәjrezә́j *f. of* مېرېزی¹ stepsister مېرېزی، مېرۍ زی خور stepsister

مېرېزی meregáj ☞ مېرېزی

مېرینوس merinós *m.* merino sheep

مېرانه meṛā́na *f.* ☞ مېرانه

مېړښتوب meṛokhtób *m.* marriage (with regard to a woman)

مېړنی meṛәnáj ☞ مېړنی

مېړوبنه meṛóәkha *f. dialect* ☞ مېړوبنه پېغله مړوبنه betrothed girl, bride مړوبنه خور married sister

مېړه meṛ **1** *m.* [*plural:* مړونه maṛúna *and* مېړونه meṛúna] **.1** husband, spouse مېړه کول *compound verb* to get married (of a woman) زینبي مېړه وکئ Zaynab got married. مېړه ته ورکول to marry off لور په مېړه کول to marry a daughter off ایا زرغونه مېړه لري؟ Is Zarghuna married? **1.2** brave person, courageous, person; real man مېړونه مړي، نومونه یی پاتېږي *proverb* د توري مېړه a brave man Heroes do not die. **1.3** able and knowledgeable person د قلم مېړه a writer **2** *attributive* brave, courageous, valiant ډېر مېړه سړی دئ He is a very brave person. مېړه مړ که، مړانه یی مه ورکوه *proverb* You may kill a hero, but his fame will live forever.

مېړه توب meṛәtób *m.* **1** ☞ مړانه **2** status, duties of a husband

مېړه مخي meṛәmә́khe man-like (of a woman)

مېز mez *m.* table د دوډۍ مېز dinner table ټوله پر یوه مېز سره راغونډېدو Everyone gathered around the table.

میزان mizā́n *m. Arabic* [*plural:* میزانونه mizānúna *and Arabic* موازین mawāzín] **1** balance, scale **2** equilibrium, balance **3** result د عمومي میزان grand total **4** measure; measurement; amount د صادراتو میزان volume of export **5** Libra (the constellation) **6** mizan (seventh month of a solar year from September 23 - October 22)

میزان الحراره mizān-ul-harārā́ *f. Arabic* thermometer

میزانیه mizānijá *f. Arabic* balance تجارتي میزانیه *economics* trade balance

مېزبان mezbā́n *m.* host (with regard to the guest)

مېزبانۍ mezbāní *f.* hospitality مېزبانۍ کول *compound verb* to offer hospitality, treat

مېزپاسى mezpásay *m. computer science* desktop computer

مېزپوښ mezpókh *m.* tablecloth مېزپوښ غوړول *compound verb* to spread a tablecloth

مېزدار mezdár مېزداره چوکۍ desk (at school)

مېزر [1] majzár *m.* muslin veil

مېزر [2] mezór *m.* barn; granary store

مېزرى mezóraj *m.* dwarf palm

مېزکوټ mezkóṭ *m. regional* officers' mess

مېزګوټى mezgóṭaj *m.* small table

مېزمان mezmān *m.* ☞ مېزبان

مېزمانۍ mezmāní *f.* ☞ مېزبانۍ

مېزوب majzúb crazy, insane

مېژل mezhól *transitive [present:* مېژي *past:* وي مېژل] to urinate

مېږ [1] meg *f. [plural:* مېږي mégi *Eastern* مېږي mége] sheep; ewe د مېږو تربیه sheep rearing پاسنى مېږ a Kabul sheep

مېږ [2] meg *m.* ☞ مېر

مېږتانه megtāná *plural and oblique singular of* مېږتون

مېږره méggra *f.* slightly melted butter

مېږتون megatún *m. [plural:* مېږتانه megtāná] 1 anthill خلک ډېر دي لکه مېږتانه یو پلو بل پلو روان دي People scurry about like so many ants. 2 *Eastern* small house ant 3 *regional* containers that are used to protect food from ants

مېږکمار megakmár *m.* 1 marbled polecat, *Vormela peregusna* 2 mongoose

مېږکۍ megakój *f.* Eurasian wryneck, *Jynx torquilla*

مېږوى megwáj *f. dialect* ☞ موږى

مېږه méga *f.* ☞ مېږ [1]

مېږي [1] mégi *plural Eastern* mége ☞ مېږ [1]

مېږي [2] megí *plural of* مېږى

مېږى [3] megáj *m. [plural:* مېږیان megijān *and* مېږي megí] ant تور مېږى black ant سور مېږى red ant سور مېږى، سورکى مېږى a to have goosebumps; feel creepy b to get rusty (of iron)

مېږى [4] megój مېږى شړى kind of outerwear decorated with embroidery

مېږیانه megjāna *f.* pepper اوږده مېږیانه long pepper

مېږیخور megajkhór *m.* ☞ مېږکى

مېږیمه megemá *f.* مېږیمه

مېس [1] mis *f.* miss (title)

مېس [2] mes *m. regional* ☞ مېزکوټ

مېست mist *dialect* ☞ مېشت [1]

مېسر mujassár *Arabic* 1 accessible دا شیان دوی ته میسر دي These things are available or accessible to them. 2 possible; feasible; practicable

مېسریدل mujasaredól, mujassaredól *denominative, intransitive [past:* میسر شو] 1 to be accessible 2 to be possible; be feasible له هره ځایه چي میسره شي wherever possible 3 to be realized

مېسه majsá *f. passive* standing young crops مېسه غنم sprouting wheat

مېسیون misijón, missijón *m.* mission اقتصادي میسیون economic mission

مېش mesh *f.* ☞ مېږ

مېشت [1] misht, mesht [*f.* مېشته mishtá *m. plural:* مېشته mishtó *f. plural:* مېشتي mishté] living, residing, staying, sojourning; having settled په هوټل کښي چیرته مېشت یې؟ Where do you live? میشت کول He is staying at the hotel. *compound verb* ☞ و مېشتېدل میشت کېدل 1 مېشتول *compound verb* ☞

مېشت [2] misht *m.* technique of kneading dough

مېشتک mishták *m.* مېشتکى mishtakáj *m. dialect* small bag (to deliver grain to the mill)

مېشتول [1] mishtawól *denominative, transitive [past:* مېشته کړل] 1 to house, lodge 2 to transfer to a settled way of life (non-nomadic) 3 to plant (trees)

مېشتول [2] mishtawól *transitive [past:* و یي مېشتول] to knead the dough for a second time; stir

مېشتون mishtún *m.* 1 home, house, lodging 2 settlement

مېشته [1] mishtá 1 *feminine singular of* مېشت [1] 2 *f.* home, residence مېشته کول *compound verb* ☞ مېشتول [1] 1, 2

مېشته [2] mishtó *m. plural of* مېشت [1]

مېشتي mishté *f. plural of* مېشت [1]

مېشتېدل mishtedól *denominative, intransitive [past:* مېشت شو] 1 to live, reside, stay, sojourn; lodge, settle 2 to adopt a settled way of life (non-nomadic)

مېشن mishón, mishán *m.* mission

مېشوانۍ mishwāṇój *f.* ☞ مشوانۍ

مېشه meshá *f.* sheepskin

مېښ mekh *m.* buffalo

مېښبه mekhbá *m.* 1 buffalo herdsman 2 buffalo owner

مېښکار mikhkár *m.* مېښکار

مېښکټى mekhkaṭáj *m.* buffalo calf

مېښ-مېښ mikh-míkh 1 nauseous, nauseated مېښ مېښ کېدل to be nauseous 2 disappointed, saddened

مېښه mékha *f.* buffalo cow

مېعاد mi'ád *m. Arabic* term; deadline

مېکاشیست mikāshíst *m. geology* mica schist

مېکانیزیشن mekānizéshán *m.* mechanization زراعتي مېکانیزیشن agricultural mechanization

مېکانیزم mekānízm *m.* 1 mechanism 2 arrangement, system, organization

مېکانیزه mekānizá mechanized مبکانیزه فارم mechanized farm مبکانیزه قطعات *military* mounted force; vehicle unit

مېکانیکا mekānikā́ *f.* mechanics

مېکده majkadá *f.* ☞ مىخانه مى کده

مېکرافون mikrāfón *m.* ☞ میکروفون

مېکرو mikró *computer science* macro

مېکروب mikrób *m.* microbe, germ

ميكروب شناس mikrobshinás *m.* microbiologist; bacteriologist

ميكروب شناسي mikrobshinaāsí *f.* microbiology; bacteriology

ميكروب وژونكي دوا mikrób wazhúnkaj disinfecting ياشل to disinfect

ميكروسكوپ mikroskóp *m.* microscope

ميكروفون mikrofón, majkrofón *m.* microphone ميكروفون ته دربدل to appear before a microphone

ميگابايت megābǻiṭ *m. computer science* megabyte

ميگاتون megatún *m. Eastern* ☞ ميرتون

ميگزين megzín *m. regional* armory; arms depot

ميگنوليا megnoljā *f.* magnolia

ميگى megáj *m. Eastern* ☞ ميرى

ميل ¹ mil 1 *m.* .1 knitting needle 1.2 barrel, tube (of a gun) 1.3 roasting spit 1.4 stick (for the application of kohl to one's eyebrows, etc.) 1.5 rod 2 rearing (of a horse) ميل كبدل to rear (of a horse)

ميل ² majl *m. Arabic* 1 wish, desire ... ته ميل كول to express a wish آيا ميل لرى چي لږ څه په باغ كښنى قدم ووهو؟ Would you like to have a walk with me in the garden? 2 proclivity, inclination, propensity; sympathy, affection طبيعي ميلونه natural inclinations شرابو ته ميل لرل have a weakness for wine 3 attraction

ميل ³ majl *m.* 1 dirt; mud 2 rust 3 foam; scum

ميل ⁴ mil *m.* mile (1.6 km)

ميل ⁵ mil full, packed ميل كول *compound verb* to fill, pack ميل كبدل *compound verb* to be filled, be packed واله ميل بهبري The freshet began. The snow melt flood began

ميل ⁶ mel *paired word to* تبل مبل يي واچول تبل He poured some oil.

ميلاد milád *m. Arabic* 1 birth 2 *religion* Christmas قبل الميلاد before the common era, before Christ بعد الميلاد common era, after Christ

ميلاد النبي milādannabí *m. religion* Prophet Muhammad's birthday

ميلادي milādí *Arabic* of Christian era, common era, CE (i.e., calendar) ميلادي تاريخ a date according to the Christian calendar

ميلاس melás *m. plural* molasses

ميلان majlán *m. Arabic* 1 inclination, proclivity, sympathy سخت ميلان attraction 2 trend, direction, tendency د ادب نوى ميلان a new trend in literature 3 incline (of terrain) ميلان لرل to flow (of a river)

ميلان لرونكى majlán larúnkaj 1 falling, leaning 2 aspiring to something; intent on something

ميلاو miláw *regional* having occurred, having been found ميلاو كول *compound verb* to search, look for (e.g., a job)

ميلاوبدل milāwedál *denominative, intransitive* [*past:* ميلاو شو] *Eastern* to occur, happen ورته نوكري نه ميلاوبده He could not find a job.

ميلك melák *m.* silk clothing

ميل گاډى melgǻḍaj *m. regional* mail train

ميلمانه melmānə́ *m. plural and oblique singular of* ميلمه

ميليمتر milimétr *m.* millimeter

ملمستځى melmástdzáj *m.* ملمستون melmastún *m.* 1 hotel (state-owned) 2 ☞ مهمانخانه

ملمستيا melmastjā *f.* [*plural:* ملمستياوي melmastjǻwi *and* ملمستياگاني melmastjāgǻni] 1 hospitality په ملمستيا on a visit 2 treat, reception رسمي ملمستيا a party شپي ملمستيا formal reception ملمستياخوړل *compound verb* to help oneself, feast on بيگاته ښُما له پلوه د دوستانو ملمستيا ده In the evening I will be entertaining my friends. د يو شي ملمستيا كول to stand treat, serve something; invite to something نن ما ته هيواد د چايو ملمستيا كړيده Today Hewad invited me to tea. لويه ملمستيا يي وكړه He gave a great feast. ملمستيا وركول *compound verb* to give a party, arrange a banquet د ملمستيا مبلمستيا ئي راكړه He entertained us very well. كالي evening dress

ملمنه melmaná *f.* female guest

ملمه melmá *m.* [*plural:* ملمانه melmānə́] 1 guest څوک ملمه كول to invite somebody over, entertain somebody موږ نن چا ملمانه كړي we are invited نن د چا كره ملمه يم I am visiting somebody today. زه ملمه وم I was on a visit. ملمه كبدل *compound verb* to stay with; be a guest زموږ كور ته ملمه راغلئ He came to visit us. ملمه د كور د خاوند آس دئ، ملمه د كور د كوربه آس دئ *proverb* A guest has to take into consideration his host's actions. د لږ 2 human being, weaker vessel ملمانه سترگه ☞ ملمانه سترگه ساعت ملمه دئ He doesn't have long to live.

ملمه پالنه melmapālə́na *f.* hospitality ملمه پالنه كول *compound verb* to offer hospitality, entertain guests

ملمه پالونكى melmə́ pālúnkaj hospitable د ملمه پالونكى پا يتخت a hospitable capital

ملمه توب melmatób *m.* status of a guest; staying with someone as a guest

ملمه ځى melmádzáj *m.* ملمه ځاى melmádzáj *m.* small hotel

ملمه دوست melmadóst hospitable

ملمه سترگه melmastə́rga *f.* 1 evening star (i.e., Venus) 2 Mercury (the planet)

ملنه melána *f.* she-bear

ملو melú 1 *m.* [*plural:* ملوگان melugān] bear تور مبلو Himalayan bear 2 *f.* [*plural:* مبلوگاني melugāni] she-bear

ملوه melə́wa *f. dialect* grapes

ميله ¹ míla *plural in conjunction with the number of* ميل ⁴ ۵۰ ميل 50 miles

ميله ² milá *f.* 1 rod; post; shaft 2 small stick, block 3 *botany* pistil

ميله ³ melá *f.* 1 folk festival; celebration; picnic د ښځو ميله women's merrymaking 2 fair 3 celebration of an engagement, etc. ورباندي مبلي كول to help oneself to something

ميله ځاى meladzǻj *m.* promenade site, walking area

ميلي ¹ milí *f.* distance in miles په ۱۰۰ ميلى كښني at a distance of 100 miles د ښار په لس ميلى كي ten miles from the city

ميلي ² miláj short-tempered; hot-blooded; temperamental, feisty (of character)

ميلي ³ mile *plural of* ميله 2

مېلي mele⁴ *plural of* مبله

ميليا miljá *regional* 1 collected 2 having occurred

ميليارد miljárd *m.* billion

ميلي گرام miligrám *m.* milligram

ميم mim¹ *m.* name of the letter م

مېم mem² *f.* [*plural:* مېماني memáni] *regional* lady; madam

ميمست majmást *m.* vessel that camel is fed from

ميمنت majmanát *m. Arabic* happiness, well-being, prosperity

ميمنه majmaná¹ *f. Arabic* right flank, right wing (of an army)

ميمنه majmaná² *f.* Maimana د ميمني اعلیٰ حکومت Maimana region

ميمون majmún¹ *m. Arabic* ape, monkey

ميمون majmún² *Arabic* happy

ميموني majmuní monkey's

مېمه méma *f. regional* ☞ مېم

مي مې memé¹ *f. childrens' speech* namaz, prayer

مي مې memé² *f. & m. childrens' speech* 1 breast 2 cry by which the child asks to be breastfed

مي مې memé³ *f. childrens' speech* meh-meh (bleating of sheep and goats) مي مې کول *compound verb* to bleat

مين mаján, majə́n¹ 1.1 enamored; in love مين کول *compound verb* ☞ to make someone fall in love مين کېدل *compound verb* ☞ مينېدل 1.2 liking something; taking an interest in something; fascinated with something 2 *m.* [*plural:* مينان majanán, majə́nán *and* مين majə́n] .1 one in love; lover 2.2 amateur, fan, lover of something هغه د رحمان بابا په ډېوان ډېر مين و He liked poetry by Rahman a lot. د طبيعت مين a nature lover 2.3 *proper noun* Mayan

مين min² *m. military* mine مقناطيسي مين a magnetic mine

مينا miná¹ *f.* 1 enamel; glaze د غاښ مينا tooth enamel 2 blue glass 3 lapis lazuli 4 blue, azure 5 *figurative* blue sky

مينا majná² *m.* 1 myna, *Acridotheres tristis* 2 *poetry* symbol of a beloved girl

ميناتور minātúr *m.* miniature

مين اچوونکی توپ min achawúnkaj *mortar*

مينار minár *m.* ☞ منار

مينارډوله خلی minārḍáula obelisk

مين انداز minandáz 1 mine, mortar 2 *m.* mortar

مينايي minā́í 1 enamel 2 azure; light blue

مينت minát *m.* 1 threat 2 reprimand ☞ منت

مينتابه majantābə́ *Eastern oblique of* مينتوب

مينتوب majə́ntób *m.* crush; fancy; infatuation د مين توب واده کول love marriage په مين توب واده کول marriage for love

مينجر menadzhár *m.* 1 director, manager (of a hotel, etc.) 2 (stage) director 3 leader; chief executive 4 manager, producer

مينجوټ mindzhóṭ *m.* sitting Indian style مينجوټ وهل to sit Indian style

مينجور mindzhawár *m.* ☞ مجاور

مېنچي ménche *f. plural dialect* flat noodles

مينځ mjandz *m.* ☞ منځ

مينځتوب mindztób *m.* status of a female worker, female slave

مينځرکه mindzárka *f.* 1 female slave 2 female worker

منځکبني مينځکبني mjándzke ☞ مينځکبني

مينځگوری mjandzagóṛaj *m.* intermediary; arbiter

منځی مينځگوره mjandzgorá ☞ منځی

کالي مينځل مينځل mindzə́l¹ *transitive* [*past:* و يې مينځه] to wash *compound verb* to wash clothes مخ او لاس مينځل، مخ او لاسونه to خان مينځل، خانونه مينځل to wash one's hands and face wash oneself, bathe 2 *m. plural* bathing, washing د مينځلو washing machine اتوماتيکي دستگاه

منځی مينځني mjandznáj, mjandzanáj مينځوی mjandzwáj, mandzanáj, مينځومان mjandzumā́n, مينځومانه mjandzumā́na middle; average په مينځني کښې middle-class family مينځني کورنی in the meantime

مينځه míndza¹ *f.* [*plural:* مينځي míndzi *and Western* مينځياني mindzijáni] 1 female slave 2 concubine

مينځه míndza² *imperative imperfective form of* مينځل

مينځه mindzə́³ *imperfect of* مينځل

مينځه mjándza⁴ ☞ منځ

مينځه mindzə́⁵ *m. plural* bathing; washing

مينځه گته mjándza gúta *f. Eastern* middle finger

مينځي míndzi¹ *plural of* مينځه

مينځي míndzi² *present tense of* مينځل

مينځياني mindzijā́ni *Western plural of* مينځه 1

ميند mind *imperfect of* ميندل

ميندک mindák *m.* fine opium

ميندکي mindakí *m.* drug addict

ميندل mində́l *transitive* [*present:* مومي *past:* و يې مينده] 1 to find, reveal; discover 2 to obtain; acquire, gain; win 3 to procure, get; attain ميندل کېدل *compound verb passive voice* ☞ مينده² فتح ميندل، ماته to gain a victory; achieve a win شکست ميندل، ماته ميندل to suffer a defeat; fail

ميندنه mindóna *f.* 1 finding, revealing 2 acquisition, gain 3 procuring, getting

مېندو méndo *oblique plural of* مور

مينده mində́¹ *m.* [*plural:* ميندان mindán] *agriculture* breeder; bull; buffalo, goat, ram

مينده mində́² 1 *m. plural* .1 finding, revealing; discovery 1.2 acquisition; gain 1.3 getting, procuring 1.4 achievement 2 found مينده کول *compound verb* a ☞ ميندل b to invent, think of مينده کېدل *compound verb* ☞ ميندېدل a to be found; be detected, be revealed b to be obtained; acquired c to be procured; be obtained d to be invented, thought of

ميندپل mindəpól *m.* 1 ☞ مينده 1 2 *dialect* stud ram

مېندي ménde *plural Eastern of* مور²

مينډ menḍ *m.* camel's straw saddlecloth

مينز mejánz *m. dialect* ☞ منځ

مينوال minawál 1 loyal; devoted 2 merciful; kind

مينوټ minúṭ *m.* 1 outline, draft 2 a copy

مين ويشتونکی توپ min wishtúnkaj top *m.* mortar

مینه ¹ mína *f.* **1** love د هیواد او وطن پاکه او معصومه مینه pure love مینه love for the motherland د ژوند مینه vivacity; love of life مینه سره اخیستل to feel affection for; come to love; fall in love مینه پر خپلو اولادو لرل، مینه to develop a mutual affection د چا مینه نیول to love one's children وخپلو اولادو ته لرل to get to love; fall in love چي د زړه مینه یې نه وي، مینه به یې نه کړي د ملا په تعویذونو *proverb* Love cannot be forced. (*literally:* If there is no love in one's heart, a mullah's incantations cannot make one fall in love.) **2** wish, willingness په ډېره مینه enthusiastically, very willingly وختکي ته مي مینه کېږي like something په یو شي مینه کول I would like some melon. **3** hobby; interest **4** tenderness په چا مینه I زه پري ډېره مینه کوم **a** to love somebody د چا سره مینه کول love him very much. **b** caress مونږ سره یي ډېره مینه وکره He was very gentle to us. **5** empathy; sympathy د ... مینه لرل، د ... سره I لور مي ډېره مینه راسره لرله love **a** مینه لرل My daughter loved me very much. **b** to set store by; hold dear; value **c** to sympathize **d** to be a fan, be interested in هغه د فتبال سره مینه لري He is a football fan. *idiom* **a** to cool down, grow cold د احمد مینه له کاره ماتیدل Ahmed lost interest in work. **b** to be displeased د زړه مینه ماته شوه I am displeased with my son. مي زوی اور سړی to stifle passion (*literally:* pour cold water on the fire of love)

مینه ² majə́na **1** *feminine singular of* مین ¹ **1 2** *f.* **.1** beloved woman **2.2** wife

مېنه ³ ména *f.* **1** motherland, fatherland, homeland **2** area, region, country توده مېنه a hot area **3** lodgings; residence, house, encampment په یو ځای مېنه سازول، مېنه ودانول to build a residence کښېني مېنه نیول to settle, take up residence **4** encampment; camp مېنه بدلول **a** to change residence, move **b** to move one's encampment, move one's camp مېنه کول **a** to build a residence. **b** to halt, set up camp په نوي مېنه اړول **a** to move to a new house **b** to roam to **5** rebate

مېنه دار minadár **1** having been treated kindly **2** appreciative, grateful مېنه دار شوم I am very grateful (to you).

مېنه ناک minanák **1** likeable; nice, sweet (of a person) **2** gentle **3** responsive

مینه وری minawə́raj love; beloved (man); sweetheart

مینیاتور minjātúr *m.* miniature

مینیدل majənedə́l *denominative, intransitive* [*past:* مین شو] to fall in love سره to fall in love with somebody مینیدل to fall in love with each other

میو ¹ májo *oblique plural of* می

میو ² mjaw ☞ میو میو

میور mjawr, majwə́r *m. dialect* peacock, peafowl

میوره mjáwra *f. dialect* peahen

مېوګي ¹ mewgí *f.* money given to relatives for fruit (when getting married)

مېوګی ² mewgáj *m. dialect* leash, tether, halter rope; stake

مېوګی ³ mewagə́j *f.* berry

میومیو کول mjaw-mjáw میومیو *compound verb* **a** to mew **b** to sing (of a quail) **c** *figurative* to suck up to; fawn, grovel

میوند majwánd *m.* Maywand د میوند جنگ the battle of Maywand

مېوه mewá *f.* [*plural* مېوې mewé *and m. plural Arabic* مېوه جات mewadzhā́t] **1** fruit لنده مېوه fresh fruit وچه مېوه dried fruit باغ ډېره مېوه وکړه The orchard gave lots of fruit. مېوه نیول to bear fruit **2** sultana grapes *idiom* د تعلیم مېوي fruit of enlightenment *proverb* د صبر مېوه په مراد پخېږي Everything comes to him who waits.

مېوهار mjawəhár *m.* mewing

مېوه ایز mewaíz *adjective* fruit مېوه ایز شیان fruits and the like

مېوه باب mewabā́b *m.* fruit and berries; fruit

مېوه دار mewadár fruit (of a tree)

مېوه داني mewadāní *f.* fruit bowl

مېوه فروش mewafurúsh *m.* ☞ مېوه والا

مېوه لرونکی mewá larúnkaj *adjective* fruit مېوه لرونکي وني mewá larún-ki… fruit trees

مېوه والا mewawālā́ *m.* fruit merchant

مېوه وېش mewawésh *m.* mutual giving of fruit as gifts (in matchmaking, etc.)

مېوی mewə́j *f.* berry

میه mja *f.* flock of sheep

مئی ¹ maj *m.* May

مئی ² məj *f. plural* mung bean

مئیز ma'íz *m. plural* sultana grapes

مهین majín ☞ مئین

مهینه ¹ majiná *f.* ☞ مئینه

ن

ن ¹ nun **1** the thirty-sixth letter of the Pashto alphabet **2** the number 50 in the abjad system

ن ² na nə *combining form of the negation written with verbs* نکوي، ندئ

ن ³ ən *adjectival suffix* چنجن worm-eaten

نا ¹ nā *negative particle dialect* no نانا! No, no!

نا ² nā *adjective and noun prefix* (indicates the absence of some quality, or indication) un-, in-, non- ناپوره incomplete نا آشنا unknown

نا ³ nā *f. suffix used to form nouns* آبنا strait تنگنا isthmus

نا ⁴ nā *syllable added to the verb in popular poetry* کوینا he does, they do

ناآباد nāābā́d **1** unmastered, not worked ناآباده ملکه virgin land **2** unpopulated, unsettled

ناخبر، ناخبره nāatár ☞ ناتر

ناإجرا nāidzhrā́ *indeclinable* unimplemented, unfulfilled, unexecuted

ناآرامي nāārāmí *f.* **1** alarm, worry قلبي ناآرامي spiritual, mental worry, alarm **2** [*plural:* ناآرامۍ nāārāmə́j] disturbances, disorders

ناأر nāáṛ **1** independent **2** *m.* materially secure man

نازمويلى nāazmujə́laj untested, unproved

نااشتراک nāishtirák *m.* nonparticipation; noninvolvement

ناآشنا nāāshnā نااشنا nāashnā **1** unfamiliar, unknown, strange ناآشنا وطن foreign land ناآشنا لغتونه unfamiliar words **2** strange **3** ignorant about, ignorant of, inexperienced

ناآشنائي nāāshnāí *f.* ناشنايي nāashnāí *f.* ignorance of something; inexperience

ناامني nāamní **1** disturbances, disorders **2** alarming or worrisome situation

ناامېد nāuméd **1** unreliable **2** despairing; discouraged **3** disappointed

ناامېدانه nāumedāná **1** unreliable **2** unreliably

ناامېدي nāumedí *f.* **1** unreliability; despair **2** disappointment

ناانصاف nāinsáf unjust

ناوډلى nāoḍə́laj **1** not in adjustment, not regulated **2** disorderly, untidy

ناوزگار nāuzgár overloaded with work, responsibilities, studies, etc.

نااهل nāáhl ناهله nāáhla **1** ☞ ناآشنا **2** uneasy **3** unworthy, not deserving of something **4** incapable

ناب nāb¹ *m. history vice* لوى ناب ناب نایب governor-general

ناب nāb² *m. Arabic [plural:* انیاب anjáb] molar tooth

ناب nāb³ **1** pure, unadulterated **2** of pure gold

نابابه nābáb نابابه nābába rare, uncommon

نابالغ nābālígh **1** underage, youthful **2** *m.* a minor

ناباوره nābāvára uncertain

نابوبره nābubə́ra ☞ ناخپه

نابرابري nābarābarí *f.* unfitness نابرابري طبیعت د ill-health, indisposition

نابرهو nābarhó ☞ ناخپه

نابړ nābáṛ ☞ ناپړ

نابغه nābighá *m. Arabic [plural:* نوابغ navābigh] genius, man of genius

نابلد nābalád نابلده nābaláda **1.1** unfamiliar with something; inexperienced; ignorant about, ignorant of **1.2** strange, unfamiliar نابلده محیط پر مخ unfamiliar milieu نابلده completely unfamiliar (person) **2** *m.* stranger, foreigner, outlander

نابلدتیا nābaladtjā́ *f.* نابلدي nābaladí *f.* ignorance د نابلدی په وجه یو کار کول to do something out of ignorance

نابوبره nābubə́ra ☞ ناخپه

نابود nābúd **1** bad, unfit, unnecessary; good-for-nothing; useless نابوده زمکه infertile land نابود سړى a good-for-nothing **2** vanished, nonexistent **3** annihilated; ruined; destroyed نابود او محوه کول to annihilate, ruin; destroy

نابودتوب nābudtób *m.* نابودتیا nābudtjā́ *f.* نابودوالى nābudvā́laj *m.* **1** unfitness; worthlessness; uselessness **2** annihilation, ruin; destruction

نابودول nābudavə́l **1.** *denominative, transitive [past:* نابود یې کړ] to spoil, put out of comission **1.2** to annihilate, ruin; destroy **1.3** to remove; eliminate; be saved from something **2** *m. plural* ☞ نابودي

نابودي nābudí *f.* نابودیت nābudiját *m.* **1** annihilation; destruction **2** removal; elimination; deliverance from something

نابودېدل nābudedə́l *denominative, intransitive [past:* نابود شو] to be spoiled; be put out of comission **2** to vanish **3** to be annihilated, be destroyed **4** to be removed, be eliminated

نابوم nābúm ☞ نابلد *and* نابلده

نابیان nābaján inexpressible; unexplainable; inexplicable

ناپ nāp measure, dimensions

ناپاک nāpák **1** unclean, dirty **2** slovenly **3** defiled **4** impious

ناپاکتوب nāpāktób *m.* ناپاکتیا nāpaktjā́ *f.* ناپاکوالى nāpakvā́laj *m.* ☞ ناپاکي¹ **1, 2**

ناپاکول nāpākavə́l *denominative, transitive [past:* ناپاک یې کړ] **1** to soil, dirty **2** to defile

ناپاکي nāpākí¹ *f.* **1** dirt, uncleaness; soiling **2** defilement **3** waste products (e.g., from threshing)

ناپاکي nāpāki² *feminine plural of* ناپاک

ناپاکېدل nāpākedə́l *denominative, intransitive [past:* ناپاک شو] **1** to be soiled, be dirtied **2** to be defiled

ناپام nāpā́m **1** unintelligible, slow-witted **2** inattentive; careless **3** thoughtless; precipitate

ناپامي nāpāmí *f.* **1** unintelligibility, slow-wittedness **2** inattentiveness; carelessness **3** thoughtlessness **4** slip, carelessness, error

ناپایان nāpaján ناپایاو nāpājā́v **1** endless, limitless **2** bottomless, deep

ناپایدار nāpājdā́r **1** unstable, precarious; ephemeral **2** nonpersistent, short-lasting **3** fragile **4** transitory, perishable

ناپایه nāpā́ja ☞ ناپایان

ناپایئ nāpājí *f.* state of being ephemeral, short-lived

ناپروا nāparvā́ careless, feckless

ناپړ nāpáṛ **1** select; excellent **2** important, chief, principal **3** strong; insuperable **4** enormous; voluminous

ناپړانده nāpṛā́nda **1** half-dead, half-alive **2** exhausted, worn-out ناپړانده کېدل to wear oneself out

ناپړیته nāpṛíta *f.* sharp or rude word ناپړیتي ویل، ناپړیتي کول to speak sharply or harshly, be rude

ناپسند nāpasánd **1** unpleasant **2** unacceptable **3** inappropriate, unseemly

ناپکار nāpəkā́r unnecessary, unfit; useless; good-for-nothing

ناپوره nāpurá **1** incomplete **2** unfinished, uncompleted

ناپوه nāpóh **1.1** stupid, unintelligible, slow-witted ناپوه تر دښمنون پوه *proverb* An intelligent enemy is better than a stupid دوست بنه دئ friend. **1.2** unintelligent **1.3** uneducated, ill-informed; ignorant **1.4** irresponsible **2** *m.* **.1** stupid fellow **2.2** ignoramus

ناپوهوالى nāpohvā́laj *m.* ☞ ناپوهي¹

ناپوهه nāpóha *feminine singular of* ناپوه¹

ناپوهي nāpohí *f.* **1** slowness, dullness (of intellect) **2** ignorance, lack of information, benightedness په ناپوهي کول to do something out of ignorance **3** lack of education, illiteracy ناپوهي کول to display ignorance **4** irresponsibility

ناپوهي nāpóhi *feminine plural of* ناپوه

ناپېژندگلوي nāpezhandgalví *f.* ناپېژندگلي nāpezhandgalí *f.* **1** ignorance **2** unfamiliarity

ناپېژندونکی nāpezhandúnkaj unknown; unfamiliar ناپېژندونکی سری stranger, unknown person

ناپېژندوی nāpezhandúj not recognizing

ناپېښه nāpéḳha **1** by chance **2** all at once, suddenly, unexpectedly

ناپېښنه nāpejǿna *f.* disorder, violation of order

ناتاب nātáb weak, powerless, ill

ناتار [1] nātár **1** *m.* **.1** robbery, defeat **2** loss, detriment، ناتار اچول ناتار ناتار جوړول، ناتار کول **a** to rob **b** to inflict damage, harm **1.3** difficulty **1.4** downpour; thunderstorm **2.1** bad, evil, harmful **2.2** unpleasant

ناتار [2] nātár *m.* dish made of sour milk and bread

ناتارگر nātārgár *m.* **1** robber; raider **2** oppressor **3** saboteur, wrecker

ناتجربه nātadzhribá *indeclinable* inexperienced

ناترسه nātársa **1** merciless; hard, severe **2** pitiless

ناتغیر nātaghjír changeless, constant

ناتکمیل nātakmíl ☞ ناتمام

ناتکی [1] nātakáj **1** single, unitary **2** odd (not one of a pair)

ناتکی [2] nātkáj *f.* **1** unitariness **2** quality of being odd

ناتمام nātamám not finished, incomplete, not completed

ناتمامي nātamāmí *f.* incompleteness, unfinished state

ناتوان ناتوانه nātaván nātavǻna weak; debilitated; powerless; without strength ناتوان کېدل to grow weak, weaken

ناتواني nātavāní *f.* weakness, powerlessness, debilitation; lack of strength

ناته nātə́ *imperfect of* نتل

نات [1] nāt *m.* desire; inclination; enthusiasm نات ځني ماتېدل to grow cold, become indifferent to something, cease to be attracted by something

نات [2] nāt *m.* knot (unit of speed)

ناتک nātók *m.* theater, stage

ناتاکلي رسي یاد nātǻkəli rasi jǻd *m. computer science* random access memory (RAM)

ناتکه nātáka agitated, uneasy, alarmed

ناتکی [1] nātəkí *m.* actor

ناتکی [2] nātakí *f.* worry, alarm

ناتکی [3] nātəkáj *f.* pattern, design

ناتکی [4] nātáki *feminine plural of* ناتکه

ناثر nāsír *m. Arabic* prose writer

ناجانه nādzhāṇa ☞ ناکار، ناکاره

ناجائز خرڅونه باید ونکو nādzhǻíz **1** inadmissible; impermissable One must avoid unnecessary expenses. **2** illicit; unlawful

ناجنس nādzhíns **1** alien, foreign, strange **2** not wellborn **3** baseborn

ناجو nādzhú *m.* pine (tree)

ناجوړ خورک ته جوړ، کار ته ناجوړ nādzhór sick, ill, unhealthy, unwell *proverb* He eats like a healthy person, but works like a sick person.

ناجوړتیا nādzhoṛtjǻ *f.* disease, illness

ناجوړه [1] nādzhóṛa ☞ ناجوړي

ناجوړی [1] nādzhóṛaj **1.1** sick, ill, unhealthy ناجوړي خلق sick people, patients ناجوړی کېدل to sicken; fall ill; be indisposed **1.2** weak, sickly **2** *m.* sick person, patient

ناجوړي [2] nādzhoṛí *f.* sickness, disease, illness

ناجه nādzhá *f.* **1** spring, branch **2** edge (e.g., of a boundary strip, irrigation ditch)

ناجی [1] nādzháj *f.* sprig; vine

ناجی [2] nādzhé *plural of* ناجه

ناچ nāch *m.* ☞ نڅا [1]

ناچاپ شوئ nāchāp shǿvəj unpublished, not released from a press ناچاپ شوي آثار shǿvi ... unpublished works

ناچار ناچاره nāchár nāchára **1** compelled ناچار کول to compell ناچار کېدل to be compelled **2** being in a hopeless situation; helpless

ناچاري nāchārí *f.* **1** compulsion **2** hopeless situation; helplessness

ناچ گر nāchgár *m. regional* theater

ناچل ناچله nāchál nāchála **1** going out of circulation (of money) **2** expired

ناچیز ناچیزه nāchíz nāchíza **1** unfit **2** trifling, insignificant زما ناچیزه اثر my modest work

ناځواني nādzvāní *f.* cowardice, faintheartedness ناځواني کول to act the coward, fear, be afraid

ناخ nāts *m.* ☞ نڅا [1]

ناخاپه ناخاپی nātsǻpa nātsǻpe **1** unexpected, sudden ناخاپه پېښنه an unforeseen event, chance occurrence د ناخاپه هجوم په اثر as a result of a sudden attack **2** suddenly, all at once, unexpectedly; unexpected, unaware په ناخاپه دول suddenly, at once, unexpectedly

ناخار ناخاره nātsǻr nātsǻra ☞ ناچار *and* ناچاره

ناخاري nātsārí *f.* ☞ ناچاري

ناخگر nātsgór *m.* dancer; professional dancer

ناخگره nātsgóra *f.* dancer; ballerina

ناخیز ناخیزه nātsíz nātsíza ☞ ناچیز *and* ناچیزه

ناخیزی nātsizí *f.* **1** unfitness **2** triviality, insignificance

ناحق ناحقه nāháḳ nāháḳḳ nāháḳa nāháḳḳa **1.1** unfair, unjust, illicit **1.2** untrue, false, mendacious **1.3** undeserved په ناحق vainly, in vain **2** unjustly, unlawfully

ناحقي nāhaḳi nāhaḳḳí *f.* **1** injustice, unfairness **2** inappropriateness

ناحیه nāhijá *f. Arabic* [*plural:* ناحیي nāhijé *plural:* نواحي navāhí] *Arabic* **1** region; district; province **2** sphere

ناخبر ناخبره nākhabár nākhabára not knowing, uninformed, lacking information

ناختلی nākhatӧlaj not having eventuated; not having results, fruitless

ناخوال nākhvӓl 1 rude; insulting ناخوال سړی boor, ignoramus 2 indecent, inappropriate, unsuitable

ناخوالي nākhvӓli f. plural 1 insult; rudeness ناخوالي کول a to be rude (to) b to harm, hurt; oppress ناخوالي ويل to insult, speak rudely, be rude (to) 2 crime, evil deed

ناخان nākhȧn illiterate; uneducated

ناخانده nākhāndá ناخوانه nākhāna indeclinable not well-read; uneducated ناخوانده خلگ خواننده کول the elimination of illiteracy

ناخواه nākhāh 1 not desiring, unwilling 2 unwillingly, reluctantly, without desire (to)

ناخوښ 1 nākhvȧkh ☞ ناخوبنه

ناخوښتیا 1 nākhvaḳhtjá f. ☞ ناخوښني 1

ناخوښه 2 nākhvȧkha 1 dissatisfied; insulted, offended 2 feminine singular of ناخوښ

ناخوښني 1 nākhvaḳhí f. 1 non-velleity, reluctance ما په ناخوښنی ومنله I reluctantly agreed. 2 dissatisfaction

ناخوښي 2 nākhvȧḳhi feminine plural of ناخوښ

ناخوني nākhuné f. plural 1 vine tendrils 2 kind of eye disorder

نادار nādȧr نادارہ nādȧra poor, lacking possessions نادار سړی poor man, poor peasant

نادارﻱ nādārí f. poverty, need, want

نادان nādȧn 1.1 ignorant, uneducated 1.2 stupid; unintelligent; dull 2 m. ignoramus

نادانﻱ 1 nādāní f. 1 ignorance 2 stupidity, dullness نادانﻱ کول to act unintelligently

نادانﻱ 2 nādāni feminine plural of نادان

نادر nādír Arabic 1 rare, uncommon, extraordinary نادر ښایست rare beauty 2 m. .1 [plural: نوادر navādír] curiosity, marvel 2.2 proper name Nadir

نادرالوجود nādir-al-vudzhúd Arabic rare, unique نادرالوجود فلزات rare metals

نادرست nādurúst incorrect, unseemly, improper

نادره nādirá f. Arabic 1 beauty 2 rare thing, rarity

نادوده nādóda f. نادودي nadodi f. plural ☞ ناخوالی

نادوستانه nādostāná unfriendly; not amicable نادوستانه وضعیت unfriendly relationship; a hostile position

نادیده nādidá 1 invisible 2 unprecedented 3 inexperienced

نار nār m. 1 stalk; trunk 2 sprout, shoot

ناراحت nārāhát disquiet, worried

ناراحتیا nārāhattjá f. disquietude, worry, agitation

ناراست nārȧst 1 crooked, uneven 2 incorrect 3 mendacious, lying 4 wrong 5 dishonest, dishonorable 6 lazy, idle, inactive

ناراستﻱ 1 nārāstí f. 1 unevenness 2 incorrectness 3 untruth, lie, deceit 4 dishonesty, dishonorableness 5 laziness

ناراستﻱ 2 nārȧsti feminine plural of ناراست

ناراض nārȧz discontented, dissatisfied; disagreeing (with)

نارسائﻱ nārasāí f. shortcoming, deficiency; scantness; inadequacy د معلوماتو نارسائﻱ feeblemindedness فکر نارسائﻱ insufficiency of data, of information

ناراض nārizá ☞ ناراض

نارضامندي nārizāmandí f. نارضاوالی nārizāvȧlaj m. dissatisfaction; disagreement د چا نارضامندي راوړل to evoke dissatisfaction د چا نارضامندي سبب گرزیدل to evoke someone's dissatisfaction

نارگل nārgúl 1 m. pomegranate (tree) blossom 2 f. proper name Nargul

نارگیل nārgíl m. ☞ ناریال

نارگیله nārgilá f. water pipe (for smoking tobacco, etc.)

نارنج nārindzh m. plural [plural: نارنجان nārindzhȧn] wild orange, bitter orange نارنج خواره orange

نارنجي nārindzhí indeclinable & adjective orange

نارنهور nārnahúr 1 hungry 2 on an empty stomach

نارو nārú m. 1 parasitic worm, Filaria medinensis 2 filariosis

ناروا nāravȧ 1 not allowed; unsuitable, improper ناروا کارونه that which is forbidden د چا سره ناروا کول to act unjustly to someone; injure someone 2 f. .1 forbidden thing 2.2 improper act

ناروان 1 nāravȧn not flowing, not fluent (speech)

ناروان 2 nārvȧn m. elm tree

ناروغ nārógh 1 ill, unwell 2 m. sick man, patient د ناروغو تذکره a history of illness

ناروغتیا nāroghtjȧ f. 1 illness; indisposition 2 plague, evil, harm; vice د ټولنی ناروغتیاوي societal vices

ناروغوالی nāroghvȧlaj m. discord, dissention (between two people)

ناروغول nāroghavól denominative, transitive [past: ناروغ یې کړ] to cause illness, lead to illness, undermine health

ناروغه nārógha 1.1 indeclinable ill, unhealthy ناروغه کېدل to fall ill, be unhealthy 1.2 feminine singular of ناروغ 1 2 f. sick woman, patient (woman)

ناروغي 1 nāroghí f. [plural: ناروغی nāroghój plural: ناروغي گانﻱ nāroghigȧni] illness داخلي ناروغی internal illnesses عصبي ناروغی neurological illnesses هغه د ناروغی پر بستر پرېووت He took to his bed. He fell ill.

ناروغي 2 nāróghi feminine plural of ناروغه 2

ناروي nārvé f. Norway

ناره nārá f. 1 shout; outcry 2 yell, hollering د اتڼ نارﻱ dance-related singing 3 ethnology announcement, publication (of marriage intentions, etc.) ناره کول a to shout; cry out b to yell, holler c to announce marriage intentions; announce intentions (a woman) without the consent of the father and brother پرچا ناره کول to greet someone with a song a to bawl, yell b ناري کول، ناري وهل to shout, cry out c to sing (of birds) چا ته ناري وهل to call, hail someone

ناری 1 nāráj m. 1 food, meal سبا ناری، د سبا ناری breakfast, lunch ناری کول to breakfast, have lunch 2 غرمي ناری afternoon snack meal sent three days after the wedding by the father to the young newlywed husband

ناري ² nārí *Arabic* **1** fiery **2** explosive **3** hot **4** pertaining to firearms ناریه اسلحه firearm **5** hellish, infernal

ناري ³ nāré *plural of* ناره

ناريالَ nārijál *m.* **1** coco tree, coconut **2** coconut palm

ناري سوري nāré-suré *f. plural* shouts, outcries ناري سوري کول to shout, cry out

نارينتوب nārintób *m.* bravery, valor, courage, manliness نارینتوب کول to display courage, demonstrate bravery; distinguish oneself in battle

نارینه nāriná **1** *indeclinable* **.1** masculine; male **1.2** manly, brave, valorous, courageous **2** *m.* **.1** man د نارینه و دپاره for men, manly **2.2** husband **2.3** brave man, courageous man

نارینه توب nārinatób *m.* ☞ نارینتوب

نارِ nāṛ *m.* stubble field, harvest field

نارام nāṛā́m **1** uncouth **2** disorderly **3** stubborn, intractable

نارامتوب nāṛāmtób *m.* ☞ نارامي ¹

نارامه nāṛā́ma *feminine singular of* نارام

نارامي ¹ nāṛāmí *f.* **1** uncouthness **2** disorderliness **3** stubbornness, intractableness

نارامي ² nāṛāmi *feminine plural of* نارام

نارک nāṛák *m.* **1** ditherer **2** ox not broken to the plow

نارگوره nāṛgóra *f.* ☞ نارِ

نارن nāṛə́n *m.* ditherer

نارنه ¹ nāṛə́na *f.* **1** squawk (of a crane) **2** bray (of an ass)

نارنه ² nāṛə́na *feminine of* نارن

ناره ¹ nāṛa *f.* flower-bearing stem of a plant; stalk, trunk

ناره ² nāṛa *f.* ☞ ناري ¹

ناري ¹ nāṛi saliva ناري پر چا اچول to spit at someone *idiom* د چا ناري ناري یې ومبنتي to flatter someone; toady to someone پر ځان ځخول He was embarrassed and fell silent. He became hesistant and could say no more.

ناري ² nāṛi *plural of* ناره ¹

ناري ³ nāṛə́j *f.* **1** dry stalk **2** stubble

ناري ⁴ nāṛə́j *f.* **1** leather strap (of a plow) **2** leather lace (of a shoe) **3** lasso

ناري ⁵ nāṛə́j *f.* small green valley

ناري ⁶ nāṛi *present tense of* نړل

نارېچن nāṛedzhə́n *m.* ☞ نارن

نارېک nāṛík *m.* ☞ نارک

ناز nāz *m.* **1** splendor **2** airs and graces **3** coquetry, flirtatiousness, affectation **4** whim, desire, wish, request زه پر تاسي یو ناز کوم I have a request for you. د چا ناز اخیستل a to fulfill someone's request ښه دئ، ستا ناز به دي واخلم Good, I will grant your request. **b** to teach someone (a lesson) د چا ناز ورل to please, indulge someone; indulge someone's whims ناز یې پرمځکه نه اچاوه He did not offend them. He granted their wish. **5** comfort; kindness د ناز خندا a flirtatious smile **b** affectionate smile ناز کول a to flirt **b** to behave capriciously **c** to caress **d** to put on airs په ډېر ناز یې وویل He spoke very affectionately. **6** grace; elegance

نازبرداري nāzbardārí *f.* tolerance; indulgence نازبرداري کول to show tolerance; indulge

نازبو nāzbú *m.* botany basil

نازپرور nāzparvár ☞ نازولی nāzdāná نازدانه

نازدکړه nāzdákṛa *f.* lack of training, unpreparedness

نازدکړئ nāzdakə́rəj untrained, unprepared

نازک nāzə́k nāzúk **1.1** slender, fragile **1.2** tender, soft, delicate **1.3** elegant; gracious **1.4** ticklish, delicate; tense وضعیت نازک دئ a tense situation, delicate circumstances په دغسي نازک وخت کښي at such a tense time **2** *m. proper name* Nazuk *idiom* نازک صنف the feminine sex

نازکبدن nāzukbadán **1** shapely, gracious **2** *m.* variety of apple

نازکچه nāzukchá *f.* variety of caracul

نازکوزر nāzukvazár hymenopterous

نازکه nāzə́ka *f.* ☞ نانځکه

نازکي nāzukí *f.* **1** slenderness **2** tenderness, softness, delicacy **3** elegance, beauty, grace

نازل nāzíl *Arabic* **1** tolerance, condescension **2** low (for a price)

نازلت nāzilát *m. Arabic* ☞ نازله

نازلول nāzilavə́l *denominative, transitive* [*past:* نازل یې کړ] **1** to lower **2** *religion* to send down

نازله nāzilá *f. Arabic* ill-luck; disaster, misfortune

نازلېدل nāziledə́l *denominative, intransitive* [*past:* نازل شو] **1** to sink, come down **2** to happen to someone; fall to someone's lot; befall (of ill-luck) دا بلا راباندي نازله شوه! Such a disaster has befallen me! **3** *religion* to be sent down

نازنین nāznín nāzanín **1.1** thin, slender نازنيني شونډي thin lips **1.2** tender, soft, delicate **1.3** elegant, beautiful, gracious **1.4** flirtatious **2** *m.* lover, sweetheart

نازنینه nāznína **1** *feminine singular of* نازنین **2** *f.* **.1** beauty **2.2** sweetheart, lover (woman)

نازور nāzór weak, powerless

نازوکړئ nāzókə̣rəj unborn د نازوکړي قلنگ infant's layette

نازول nāzavə́l *transitive* [*past:* ویي نازاوه] **1** to express endearments **2** to care, care for **3** to spoil, overindulge

نازولی nāzavə́laj **1** delicate, pampered **2** spoiled زوی یې نازولی اموخته کړئ و She has spoiled her son. **3** favorite

نازونخره nāz-u-nakhrá *f.* نازونیاز nāz-u-nijāz *m.* coquetry, flirtatiousness

نازي nāzí *m.* Nazi

نازېدل nāzedə́l *intransitive* [*past:* و نازېده] **1** to flirt, act coquettishly **2** to act capriciously **3** to be carried away by, be delighted with **4** to be proud of په خپل دولت مه نازېږه Don't flaunt your wealth. **5** to give oneself airs

نازېدنه nāzedə́na *f.* نازېده nāzedə́ *m. plural* **1** coquetry, flirtatiousness **2** acting in a capricious manner **3** admiration, delight (in) **4** pride

ناږه nāǵə **1** *m. plural of* نوږ **2** *m. plural* purified oil, refined oil

ناس nās *m. plural* ☞ نسوار

ناساز nāsáz ناسازه nāsáza **1** ill, unwell نه چه ناسازي؟ Are you not ill? **2** unshapely; disordered, maladjusted, out of order

ناسازي nāsāzí *f.* **1** disagreement ناسازي سره بله له یو discord **2** offense, injury

ناسپال nāspál *m.* pomegranate rind

ناست nāst **1** sitting زه ناست یم ته دلته ناست اوسه! Sit here! I sit. I am sitting. **2** inherent, characteristic

ناستهل nāstə́l *separable part of verb* کښېناستل

ناستوگنه nāstógna *f.* ☞ ناسته

ناسته nāsta **1** *f.* **.1** sitting د ناستي ځای seat **1.2** residence, dwelling place; sojourn ناسته لرل to be located, live, sojourn, stay, dwell **1.3** landing (aircraft) د ناستي ځای landing field **1.4** arising from bed ☞ ناسته پاسته **1.5** elimination, defecation ☞ ناسته او ولاړه **2** *f.* *singular of* ناست

ناسته پاسته nāsta-pāsta *f.* ناسته ولاړه nāsta-valára *f.* **1** conduct; habit; disposition **2** social intercourse, relationship د چا سره ناسته پاسته کول to have social intercourse, have dealings or relations with someone

ناستی nāstáj [1] *m.* ☞ ناسته ۱ نه شه و نه رانه ناستی *Eastern* I have not found myself a place. There is no place for me to sit.

ناستي nā́sti [2] *f.* *plural of* ناست

ناسخ nāsíkh *Arabic* rescinding; annulling

ناسره nāsará **1** impure **2** counterfeit, fake

ناسکه nāsaká step-, non-blood ناسکه خور stepsister ناسکه ورونه stepbrothers

ناسم nāsám incorrect, untrue

ناسنت nāsunát **1** unacceptable, improper **2** contrary to religious prescriptions **3** uncircumcised

ناسنجیده nāsandzhidá *indeclinable* **1** not well-considered **2** in an ill-considered manner

ناسوار nāsvár *m. plural* ☞ نسوار

ناسوب nāsváb absent, missing

ناسوت nāsút *m. Arabic* **1** human race, human kind **2** human nature; humaneness, humanness

ناسور nāsúr *m. Arabic* **1** fistula **2** suppurating wound

ناسولټ nāsolə́ṭ ناسونت nāsunát **1** ☞ ناسنت **2** *m.* good-for-nothing

ناسوه nāsavá rude; uncultured, uncouth

ناسي nāsí *f.* ☞ نحس

ناسيونالست nāsionālíst *m.* nationalist

ناشپاتی nāshpātáj *m.* ناشپاتۍ nāshpātə́j *f.* pear

ناشته nāshtá **1** lunch ناشته پر دسترخوان اېنبولده to prepare lunch **2** snack

ناشدني nāshudaní ناشده nāshúda ☞ ناشونکی

ناشر nāshír *Arabic* **1** publishing, releasing for publication **2** *m.* publisher د کتابونو ناشر book publisher

ناشکر nāshúkr ungrateful

ناشکري nāshukrí *f.* ingratitude ناشکري کول to display ingratitude

ناشلېدونکی nāshledúnkaj indissoluble (of links, connections, communications)

ناشناخته nāshinākhtá unfamiliar, unknown ناشناخته لغات unfamiliar words

ناشناس nāshinās unknown, unidentified

ناشولټ nāsholə́ṭ **1.1** deformed, ugly **1.2** absurd, wild ناشولټ کار nonsense *m.* **2.1** boor, uncultivated man **2.2** talker, gossip

ناشولټتوب nāsholaṭtób *m.* **1** deformity; ugliness **2** absurdity, wildness, unrestrainedness (of conduct)

ناشولټه nāsholə́ṭa **1** *f. singular of* ناشولټ **2** *f. usually plural* ناشولټي nāsholáti nonsense ناشولټي کول to talk nonsense, talk rubbish, talk stuff and nonsense

ناشونکی nāshúnkaj impossible, nonexistent, non-feasible

ناشي nāshí [1] *Arabic* proceeding (from), arising (from) له دې ناشي flowing from this, proceeding from this خخه

ناشی nāshaj [2] *m. regional* absorbing, drawing in

نابن nā́kh *m.* fang, canine tooth

نابهاد nākhā́d joyless, despondent

نابهايسته nākhājəstá unattractive

نابهند nākhə́nd نابهنده nakhə́nda unseemly, unwise, incorrect (of conduct)

نابهور nākhór *m.* sal ammoniac

نابهه nā́khə worthless, bad

ناصاف nāsáf dirty, unclean; turbid, murky

ناصافي nāsāfí *f.* mud, dirt, uncleaness د اوبو ناصافی the dirtiness of the water

ناصح nāsíh *m. Arabic* **1** advisor **2** preceptor, mentor **3** close friend, counselor

ناصر nāsír [1] *Arabic* **1** helping, assisting **2** *m.* **.1** assistant **2.2** protector **2.3** *proper name* Nasir

ناصر nāsór [2] **1** *m. plural* Nasir (tribe) **2** *m.* Nasir (tribesman)

ناصري nāsirí *m.* **1** Nasiri (tribesman) **2** ☞ ناصر [2]

ناصواب nāsaváb **1** incorrect, mistaken **2** evil, wicked; sinful

ناطاقت nātākát ناطاقته nātākáta ☞ بي طاقته

ناطق nātíḳ *Arabic* **1** *Arabic* **.1** speaking, having the gift of speech **1.2** *adjective* sound ناطق فلم sound film **2** *m.* [*plural:* ناطقین natiḳin] **.1** orator, public speaker **2.2** announcer

ناطقه nātiḳá *f. Arabic* capacity or ability to speak

ناظر nāzír *Arabic religion* **1** All-Seeing, Seeing (epithet of God) **2** *m.* [*plural:* ناظران nāzirán *Arabic plural:* ناظرین nāzirín] **.1** manager, director د جایداد ناظر estate manager **2.2** observer, viewer **2.3** overseer; supervisor **2.4** *regional* bailiff (officer of a court)

ناظریات nāziriját *m.* administration, board, board of directors

ناظم nāzím *Arabic* **1** regulating; adjusting **2** *m.* **.1** manager; director د کتابخاني ناظم director of a library **2.2** administrator; executive officer **2.3** *history* ruler **2.4** poet; author; writer; compiler **2.5** leader (e.g., of a study group)

ناعاقبت اندیشانه nā'āḳibatandishāná **1** improvident, without foresight; imprudent **2** careless, thoughtless

ناعلاجه nā'ilā́dzha 1.1 forced, compelled 1.2 incurable 2 against the will, willy-nilly

ناعلاجي nā'ilādzhí f. 1 hopelessness (of a situation, resolution of a problem, etc.), unavoidability, inevitability 2 incurability

ناعم nā'ím Arabic soft ناعم حيوانات mollusks; invertebrates

ناغ nāgh m. 1 pride 2 haughtiness, arrogance ناغ کول a to be proud, pride oneself on b to give oneself airs

ناغوختلتوب nāghəkhtáltób m. weakness, powerlessness

ناغوختلی nāghəkhtálaj 1 weak, powerless 2 not tightly twisted (of thread)

ناغبنتلی 2 nāghəkhtaj ☞ ناغبنتی

ناغن nāghə́n f. dialect ☞ نغن

ناغوره nāghvára commonplace, ordinary, usual

ناغه nāghá 1 f. 1.1 fine د چا څخه ناغه اخيستل to impose a fine on someone 1.2 deferment ناغه کول compound verb to defer ناغه کېدل compound verb to be overdue 1.3 failure to appear, absence 1.4 ungerminated seed 1.5 seedling which has not taken root 1.6 bloodshot eyes 2.1 empty, unoccupied 2.2 bloodshot (of the eyes) ناغه وهل to be bloodshot (of the eyes) 2.3 unseemly, improper ناغه کارونه unseemly matters, improper doings

ناغه توب nāghatób m. to impose a fine

ناغه دار nāghadár red from an influx of blood; bloodshot (of the eyes)

ناغېرن nāgherə́n unpleasant ناغېرني پېښي unpleasant events

ناغېري nāgherí f. 1 idleness, loafing 2 gold-bricking, shirking, evasion; ignoring (paying no attention to); complacency ناغېري کول a to loaf, be idle, idle b to shirk, evade something

ناف nāf m. 1 navel, umbilical cord 2 figurative center, focal point

نافذ nāfíz Arabic 1 penetrating, piercing 2 influencing; influential 3 having force; active احکام نافذ کول, قوانين نافذ کول to put into force, into operation

نافذېدل nāfizedə́l denominative, intransitive [past: نافذ شو] to be put into operation

نافرمان nāfarmā́n نافرمانه nāfarmā́na disobedient, intractable

نافرماني 1 nāfarmāni f. disobedience, intractability, insubordination

نافرماني 2 nāfarmā́ni f. plural of نافرمان

نافع nāfí' Arabic useful, beneficial

نافه nāfí f. 1 musk gland of a musk deer 2 stamen

نافهم nāfáhm f. ☞ ناپام

نافهمي nāfahmí f. ☞ ناپامي

نافي nāfí Arabic 1 denying, negating 2 negative

ناقابل nāḳābíl 1 incapable; unfit, unsuitable 2 unworthy

ناقابل الفهم nāḳābilalfáhm Arabic unintelligible, incomprehensible

ناقابل انکار nāḳābíl-i-inkár immutable

ناقابل برداشت nāḳābíl-i-bardásht intolerable

ناقابل بيان nāḳābíl-i-bajān inexpressible, indescribable

ناقابل عبور nāḳābíl-i'-ubúr impassible ناقابل عبور سيند a river without fords

ناقابل فراموش واقعات nāḳābíl-i-farāmúsh unforgettable ناقابل فراموش unforgettable events

ناقابله nāḳabíla f. singular of ناقابل

ناقبول nāḳabúl unacceptable

ناقد nāḳíd Arabic 1 criticizing 2 m. critic

ناقدانه nāḳidāná critical

ناقرار nāḳarār worried, troubled, worrying

ناقص nāḳís Arabic 1 insufficient, incomplete; having a deficiency; defective عقل ناقص stupid, silly, daft; unwise ناقص کول to cause to be deficient, incomplete; make defective ناقص کېدل to be deficient, incomplete; be defective 2 not completed; unsatisfactory ناقص ځواب an unsatisfactory answer

ناقل nāḳíl Arabic 1 transferring, transporting 2 [plural: ناقلان nāḳilā́n Arabic plural: ناقلين nāḳilín] .1 migrant د ناقلينو عمومي مديريت The Resettlement Administration (in the Ministry of Internal Affairs of Afghanistan) 2.2 storyteller 2.3 technology conductor 2.4 medicine carrier idiom تغوندی ناقل missile carrier

ناقرار nāḳalár ☞ ناقرار

ناقله 1 nāḳíla f. singular of ناقل 1

ناقله 2 nāḳilá f. Arabic transport, conveyance

ناقوس nāḳús m. Arabic bell د ناقوس برج bell tower

ناقه nāḳá f. ☞ ناکه

ناک 1 nāk m. plural kind of large pear

ناک 2 nāk adjectival suffix شرمناک shameful خوندناک tasty

ناکاره nākā́ra ناکار nākár 1 bad; unfit ناکار بوټي weeds 2 good-for-nothing; useless 3 unsuccessful, vain 4 lazy 5 worthless 6 ugly, deformed

ناکاره توب nākāratób m. ناکاري nākārí f. 1 unfitness, unserviceability 2 uselessness, valuelessness 3 unsuccessfulness, futility

ناکافي nākāfí insufficient ناکافي غذا insufficient nourishment

ناکام nākā́m 1 .1 unsuccessful; unlucky 1.2 unhappy, unfortunate; hapless 2 m. .1 unfortunate, failure 2.2 need, necessity idiom که گور گران دئ، د مري ناکام دئ figurative Death comes to all men. Death is inevitable.

ناکامتوب nākāmtób m. ☞ ناکامي 1

ناکاموَل nākāmavə́l denominative, transitive [past: ناکام يې کړ] 1 to lead to failure 2 to disrupt (e.g., ideas, thoughts)

ناکامي 1 nākāmí f. [plural: ناکامۍ nākāmə́j plural: ناکامي گاني nākāmigáni] 1 failure; downfall; disruption 2 misfortune, disaster; bitter fate د ناکامي روځي black days

ناکامي 2 nākā́mi f. plural of ناکام

ناکامېدل nākāmedə́l denominative, intransitive [past: ناکام شو] 1 to suffer failure 2 to be frustrated, be unsuccessful

ناکردي nākirdé f. plural 1 malefaction 2 illegal action

ناکس nākás 1 low, base; worthless 2 m. .1 good-for-nothing, cad; worthless man 2.2 coward هر کس او ناکس every Tom, Dick, and Harry

ناکفايتي nākifājatí f. lack of competence (ability to act effectively)

ناكلار nākalā́r ☞ ناقرار

ناكلاري nākalā́ri *f.* worry

ناكلال nākulā́l clumsy, awkward

ناكوړه nākoṛá deformed, ugly

ناكوكه nākóka 1 unhealthy, ill 2 out of tune (of a musical instrument)

ناكه nāká *f.* crocodile

ناگارتوب nāgārtób *m.* ناگارتيا nāgārtjā́ *f.* denial; refusal of something

ناگاره nāgā́ra 1 feigning not to know something, not being informed about something ځان ناگاره اچول to pretend not to know 2 denying, rejecting ناگاره كېدل to deny; reject something

ناگاه nāgā́h ☞ ناڅاپه

ناگاهانه nāgāhāná ناگمان nāgumā́n sudden, unexpected

ناگمانه nāgumā́na 1 suddenly; all of a sudden 2 ☞ ناگاره

ناگوار nāguvā́r 1 unpleasant 2 indigestible

ناگوی nāgój ناگویه nāgója not broken to the plow (of an ox)

ناگه ¹ nāgá *f.* bunch of twisted lucerne grass or straw

ناگه ² nāgáh ☞ ناڅاپه

ناگاهانه nāgahāná ☞ ناگاهانه

نال ¹ nāl *m.* [*plural:* نالونه nālúna *Western plural:* نالان nālā́n] horseshoe نال اچول to lose a (horse) shoe *idiom* پر نال او پر مېخ وهل، پر لم او پر نال وهل to act in concert, act together

نال ² nāl *m.* giant reed, *Arundo donax*

نالائق nālāíḳ unworthy, unsuitable; unfit, worthless يو نالائق هلك a worthless little boy نالائق سړی a good-for-nothing

نالبكی nālbakáj *m.* [*plural:* نالبكي nālbakí *plural:* نالبكيان nālbakijā́n] plate; saucer

نالت nālát *m.* ☞ لعنت

نالتي nālatí *f. colloquial* curse

نالش nālísh *m.* نالښت nāláḳht *m. regional* complaint په چا نالش كول to complain about someone د سر له درد ﺧﺨﻪ به يې نالش كاوه He complained of a headache.

نالگی nālgáj *m.* sapling, seedling; young growing plant

نالوستی nālvástaj 1 illiterate 2 not well-read

نالول nālavə́l *denominative, transitive* [*past:* نال يې كړ] to shoe (a horse)

ناله ¹ nālá *f.* 1 brook; small stream 2 ravine; hollow, depression

ناله ² nālá *f.* moan, cry, wail ناله فرياد moaning, moans and wails

نالی ¹ nālə́j *f.* نالي nālí *f.* [*plural:* نالی گاني nāləjgā́ni] mattress; straw-filled pallet

نالی ² nālé *plural of* ناله ¹,²

نالېدلئ nālidə́ləj 1 invisible 2 unprecedented

نالیكی nālikay *m. computer science* offline

نالينه nālína *f.* slipper with U-shaped metal heel plate

نام nām *m.* 1 name 2 glory; fame; repute *idiom* نام وننگ honor; repute *idiom* د خدای نام! For God's sake! نام خدا! Truly! Really and truly!

ناماتېدونكي nāmātedúnkaj inaccessible, impregnable استحكامونه اوسنگرونه impregnable fortifications

نامانوس nāmānús unusual; uncommon نامانوسه كلمه uncommon word

نامبارك nāmubārák unhappy, unlucky

نام بدي nāmbadí *f.* disgrace, dishonor

نامبرده nāmburdá (above) cited

نامتناسب nāmutanāsíb disproportionate, incongruous

نامتو nāmtú famous, well-known; distinguished

نامتوری nāmtóraj disgraced نامتوری كېدل to disgrace oneself

نامتووالی nāmtuvā́laj *m.* glory دا كتاب د ده د نامتووالي باعث وگرڅېد This book glorified him.

نامحدود nāmahdúd 1 limitless 2 boundless

نامحرم nāmahrám 1 someone else's, another's (from a familiar point of view) 2 foreign, outside 3 not having access to the women's part of the house

نامدار nāmdā́r 1 distinguished, famous, renown 2 well-known

نامداري nāmdā́ri *f.* 1 glory, renown 2 distinction

نامراد nāmurā́d unhappy نامراده كنډه an unhappy widow نامراد زړگی poor soul

نامرادي nāmurā́di *f.* 1 disillusionment 2 state of being inconsolable

نامربوط nāmarbút 1 incoherent; nonsensical 2 alien, having no direct relationship

نامرتب nāmurattáb disorderly, rude

نامرد nāmárd 1 base, low 2 *m.* .1 cad, good-for-nothing 2.2 coward

نامرده nāmárda *feminine of* نامرد

نامردي nāmardí *f.* 1 baseness, lowness 2 cowardice

نامرئي nāmar'í invisible; imperceptible نامرئي اشعه invisible rays

نامرد nāmárd *Eastern* ☞ نامرد

نامړدتیا nāmaṛdtjā́ *f. Eastern* ☞ نامردي

نامزد nāmzád *m.* candidate (i.e., for a degree), aspirant, claimant

نامشروع nāmashrú' illegal, illicit نامشروع ماشومان children born out of wedlock; illegitimate children نامشروعه استفاده misuse of something

نامطبوع nāmatbú' *Arabic* unpleasant; repugnant

نامطلوب nāmatlúb undesirable

نامعقول nāma'ḳúl نامعقوله nāma'ḳúla unfounded, groundless; frivolous; unfounded, baseless

نامعلوم nāma'lúm nāmālúm unknown نامعلوم سړی stranger

نامعين nāmu'aján indefinite, undefined, imprecise

نامكمل nāmukamál ☞ ناقص

ناملائمت nāmulāimát *m.* 1 severity, harshness (of climate, nature) 2 difficulty (of a problem)

ناملموس nāmalmús untouchable ناملموسه طبقه the caste of untouchables

نامكن nāmumkín impossible; improbable دا كار ناممكن دئ This is impossible.

نامكني nāmumkiní *f.* impossibility, impracticability

نامناسب nāmunāsíb **1.1** unseemly; indecent, embarrassing دا نامناسبه خبره ده One should not do this. It isn't nice to do this. **1.2** inappropriate, incongruous **2** *m.* unseemly affair

نامنظور nāmanzúr unacceptable, rejected

نامنکشف nāmunkasháf underdeveloped (of a nation)

نامنویسي nāmnavisí *f.* personnel roster; record په نامنویسی شروع کول to draw up a list of personnel; start a record

ناموافق nāmuvāfíḳ **1** incongruous; incompatible **2** contradictory ناموافق کیدل to contradict something; be unsuitable

ناموافقت nāmuvāfíḳat *m. Arabic* **1** incongruity **2** contradiction

نام ور nāmvár glorious, famous, eminent; renown, distinguished

نام وري nāmvarí *f.* glory, fame; renown

ناموزون nāmauźun **1** discordant, dissonant **2** unseemly

ناموس nāmús *m. Arabic* [*plural:* نوامیس navāmís] **1** honor; good name; reputation, worthiness د لوی ناموس great honor, esteem د خدمت ناموس an affair of honor **2** conscience, conscientiousness **3** law, basic principle د طبیعت نوامیس، طبیعي نوامیس laws of nature **4** purity, chastity **5** female half of a family

ناموس دار nāmusdár **1** honest, decent **2** pure, chaste

ناموسي nāmusí moral ناموسي وظیفه a moral obligation

نامه nāmá *f. regional* **1** name, designation ستا نامه څه ده؟ What is your name? چا نامه سپکول to disgrace someone **2** words **3** letter, epistle **4** message **5** production, book

نامه nāmə́ *oblique indirect singular of* نوم د خدای په نامه in the name of God

نامه nāmə́ *oblique indirect of* نوم لاس په نامه obediently لاس په نامه چا ته دربدل to stand humbly before someone

نامهربان nāmihrbā́n **1** reserved, unfriendly; unkind **2** ungracious, thoughtless toward someone; inhospitable

نامهرباني nāmihrbānī *f.* unkindness, ungraciousness; thoughtlessness to someone

نامه لیکونکی nāmá likúnkaj *m.* نامه نگار nāmanigā́r *m.* correspondent

نامه نگاري nāmanigārī *f.* journalist (female)

نامه وری nāməvə́raj نومری

نامي nāmí **1** by name, called, called by name, designated; having the name of کریم نامی Karim by name **2** renown **3** indicated, rated

نامي nāmé *plural of* نامه

نامبدل nāmedə́l *transitive* نومبدل

نامبر nāmér **1** renowned for her beauty **2** nice, dear

نامبری nāmérāj by name, called, called by name, designated

نامبندگي nāmendagí *f.* despair د نامبندگی توره تیاره complete despair

نامبنده nāménda نامبد

نانا nānā́ *f. children's speech* bit of bread

نانا nānā́ *f. regional* granny

نانا nānā́ *f.* mint

نانائي nānāí *adjective* mint

نان بای nānbā́j *m.* نان وای

نان بائي nānbāí نان وایي

نانپزی nānpazí *f.* bread baking د نان پزی فابریکه bread-baking plant, large-scale bakery

نانځکه nāndzə́ka *f.* **1** toy **2** doll; puppet

ناندری nāndrə́j *f.* **1** argument, quarrel, altercation **2** squabble, fight (among women) **3** ridicule ناندری وهل a to quarrel, have an altercation **b** to squabble (of women) **c** to jeer, ridicule

نانده nāndéh hospitable guests, welcoming guests

نان دهي nāndehí *f.* hospitality

ناندوله nānḍóla *f.* stupid word, nonsense, absurdity ناندولي کول to talk nonsense

نانزکه nānzə́ka *m.* نانځکه

نانغوتان nānghətā́n nanghotā́n disobedient

نانکن nānkín *m.* Nanking (Nanjing)

نانگه nāngə́ *m.* [*plural:* نانگان nāngā́n *plural:* نانگه گان nāngəgā́n] blackberry

نانگه nāngá *f.* honeysuckle

نانوای nānvā́j *m.* نان وایي nānvāí *m. regional* baker

نانوایي nānvāí *f.* **1** bakery **2** bread baking نانوایي کول a to be a baker **b** to work at baking bread

نانای nānáj *children's speech* **1** tiny, weensy **2** teeny-weeny

نانیسا nānisā́ **1** having an aversion to **2** shunning someone **3** cowardly, fainthearted نانیسا کیدل a to have an aversion to **b** to act the coward, be fainthearted

نانیساتوب nānisātób *m.* **1** aversion **2** cowardice, faintheartedness

نانری nāṇə́j *f.* ناری

ناو nāv *m.* hollow, depression; valley

ناواقف nāvāḳíf **1** ill-informed; inexperienced **2** unskillful

ناواقفیت nāvāḳifiját *m.* **1** inexperience **2** lack of skill; state of being poorly informed

ناوتی nāvtáj *f.* chaste woman, woman devoted to her husband

ناوقت nāvákht ناوخت

ناوخته nāvákhta **1** *adjective* late; untimely, not on time ډبر ناوخته very tardily دغه وخت ډبر ناوخته و It was already very late. **2** *adjective* late, untimely ناوخته کول to be late ناوخته کوه مه! Don't be late! ناوخته کیدل ناوختبدل

ناوختبدل nāvakhtedə́l *denominative, intransitive* [*past:* ناوخته شو] to pass (of time)

ناور nāvə́r *m.* [*plural:* ناورونه nāvərúna *Western plural:* ناوران nāvərā́n] **1** water reservoir **2** shallow lake

ناورین nāvrín *m.* **1** mourning **2** grief; misfortune ناورین اچول **3** robbery ناورین جوړول a to cause grief, cause to fall into misfortune **b** to rob

ناوړه nāvə́ṛ **1.1** repulsive; unpleasant ناوړه منظره an unpleasant sight ناوړه رواج a bad habit ناوړه عادت، ناوړه پبښه an unpleasant incident ناوړي خطر a threatening danger **1.2** useless, unfit; unsuitable ناوړه مځکه useless land **1.3** unworthy, improper **1.4** impermissible ناوړه کارونه کول to behave indecently, conduct oneself disgracefully

2 .1 inappropriately **2.2** indecently **2.3** beyond limits, outrageously

ناوړتوب nāvaṛtób *m.* ناوړتيا nāvaṛtjā́ *f.* ☞ ناوړه [1]

ناوړه [1] nāváṛa *f.* **1** unpleasantness **2** indecency; inappropriateness **3** uselessness, unfitness

ناوړه [2] nāváṛa ☞ ناوړ

ناوسه nāvása **1** destitute, having no possessions **2** weak, powerless

ناوسي nāvasí *f.* **1** bankruptcy, insolvency **2** impotence, debility په خپله ناوسي اقرار کول to recognize one's own impotence

ناوقت nāvákt *f.* **1** late; not prompt **2** inappropriate

ناوک nāvák *m.* ناوکی nāvakáj *m.* **1** kind of arrow **2** sting (of a wasp, a bee)

ناوکی nāvakój *f.* [*plural:* ناوکياني nāvakəjáni] **1** daughter-in-law (affectionate) **2** *Western* doll **3** jasmine, *Jasminum revolutum*

ناوگوی nāvagój *f.* ☞ ناوه گی [2]

ناول nāvál nāvál *m.* novella; novel تاريخي ناول historical novel

ناولتوب nāvultób *m.* ناولتيا nāvóltjā *f.* **1** dirt, uncleanness **2** sloppiness, slovenliness

ناولد nāvalád ☞ نابلد، نابلده

ناولست nāvālíst *m.* novelist

ناولی nāvóləj **1** dirty, unclean; unlaved; unlaundered ناولی کوټه a dirty room ناولی کول to soil, besmirch ناولی کېدل to be soiled, be besmirched **2** sloppy, slovenly **3** indecent; inappropriate

ناون nāván nāvón wet, damp, moist

ناونده nāvndó *masculine plural of* نوند

ناوه [1] nāvá *f.* district, province

ناوه [2] nāvá *f.* **1** gutter; drain د بارانه و تنبتهدئ ناوي ته کښېنوست *proverb* Out of the frying pan into the fire. **2** valley **3** avalanche

ناوه گی [1] nāvagój *f.* **1** groove; narrow gutter, channel **2** tubular leaves of several cereal grasses

ناوه گی [2] nāvagój *f.* Navagaj (a part of Badzhura) د ناوه گی خاني the Navagaj Khanship

ناوې [1] nāve *f.* [*plural:* ناوي navi *Western plural:* ناوياني nāvejáni] **1** daughter-in-law **2** young married peasant woman

ناوې [2] nāvé *plural of* ناوه [1,2]

ناوياب nāvijā́t **1 .1** rare, uncommon, choice **1.2** incomparable **2** *m.* rarity, rare thing

ناوېتوب nāvetób *m.* ناوي توب nāvitób *m.* position of daughter-in-law د ناوي تابه مخصوص کالي wedding attire

ناوېده nāvedó *m. plural* married state (of a woman)

ناوېسا nāvisā́ unreliable, not inspiring confidence

ناوي غرک nāvighṛák *m.* keel, breastbone (in a bird)

ناهتخی nāhatsáj sluggish, acting unwillingly

ناهوار nāhavā́r uneven مخ ناهوار uneven surface

ناهوسا nāhosā́ nāhusā́ **1** tired, fatigued **2** uneasy, worried

ناهوسائي nāhosāí *f.* alarmed or uneasy condition

ناهي nāhí *Arabic* forbidding, interdicting

ناهيد nāhíd *m. astronomy* Venus

ناهېرېدونکي کارنامې nāheredúnkaj unforgettable, unfading unfading deeds

ناهيه nāhijá *f. Arabic* [*plural:* ناهيي nāhijé *m. plural:* نواهي nāvāhí] **1** interdiction, ban **2** something forbidden, forbidden thing

ناياب nājā́b rare, hard to find; uncommon

نايابي nājābi *f.* rarity, uncommon thing

نائب nāíb *m.* نايب nājíb *m. Arabic* **1** deputy د رئيس نائب vice-chairman **2** substitute

نائب الحکومگي nāib-ul-hukumagí *f.* **1** governor-generalship; province **2** post of governor-general

نائب الحکومه nāib-ul-hukumá *m. Arabic* [*plural:* نائب الحکومگان nāib-ul-hukumagā́n] **1** governor-general **2** deputy

نائب السلطنت nāib-us-saltanát *m.* نائب السلطنه nāib-us-saltaná *m. Arabic* **1** viceroy **2** regent

نائب سالار nāibsālā́r *m. military* general

نايبگري nājibgarí *f.* نائبي nāibí *f.* نايبي nājibí *f.* **1** post of deputy viceroy or deputy regent د نايبی شورا Regency Council **2** acting tenure of office, deputyship

نايتروجن nājṭrodzhán *m. plural* nitrogen

نايجريا nājdzhirijā́ *f.* Nigeria

نايک nājík *m.* owner, proprietor

نائل nāíl نايل nājíl *Arabic* attaining something په يو شي نائل کېدل to achieve something, attain something

نايينه nājáṇa *f.* wife of a hairdresser, barber

نايونيکوډ nājūnikoḍ *computer science* non-unicode

نائي nāí *m.* [*plural:* نائيان nāíjā́n *Eastern plural:* نا ئيگان nāigā́n] hairdresser, barber

نبات nabāt *m. Arabic* **1** plant; grass د نباتاتو باغ botanical garden **2** herbiculture د نباتاتو تربيه، د نباتاتو روزنه botanist نباتاتو پوهاند sugar, fruit-drop

نبات شناسي nabātshināsí *f.* botanist

نباتي nabātí *Arabic adjective* vegetable نباتي تېل vegetable oil رنگونه vegetable dyes

نبايد nábājad *vice* نه بايد

نبض nabz *m. Arabic* pulse نبض کتل to feel the pulse

نبوت nubuvát *m. Arabic* prophet's role; mission of prophet

نبوغ nubúgh *m. Arabic* genius, talent د نبوغ خاوند a man of genius, genius, distinguished man

نبوي nabaví *Arabic* prophet's; relating to a prophet

نبي nabí *m. Arabic* [*plural:* نبيان nabijā́n *Arabic plural:* انبيا anbijā́] **1** prophet **2** *proper name* Nabi

نبيذ nabíz *m. Arabic* wine

نپتون neptún *m. astronomy* Neptune

نپکه napaká *f.* ☞ نفقه

نپيل napíl *m.* **1** horn of a mountain sheep **2** small clay water-pipe

نتا natā́ *f.* ☞ ندا [2]

نتائج natāídzh *m. Arabic plural of* نتيجه

نتکى natkə́j *f.* nostril pendant (a jeweled decoration like an earring to be worn in a pierced nostril)

نتل natə́l *transitive* [*past:* و یې ناته] **1** to carry off **2** to drive away **3** to abduct **4** to rob; ravage **5** to weaken, undermine forces

نتلى natə́laj **1** *past participle of* نتل **2.1** indifferent, poor (i.e., of health, feelings) **2.2** weak, pitiful **2.3** robbed

ناته náta *f.* **1** nostril pendant **2** large earring **3** wooden plug or pin inserted in nose of camel with cord affixed for leading and controlling the animal

نتيجه natidzhá *f. Arabic* [*plural:* نتيجي natidzhé *m. Arabic plural:* نتائج natáidzh] **1** consequence; result, sum total د دې په نتيجه as a result of this بې نتيجي يې وښندلي This gave good results. **2** outcome, conclusion د دې نتيجه دا نتيجي اخيستل to produce results له دې څخه دا نتيجه The result of this was such that ... وختله چه ... نتيجي ته رسېدل It follows from this that ... لاس ته راحي چه ... to lead to the conclusion **3** *figurative* moral د دې حكايت نتيجه څه ده؟ What is the moral of this story?

نتيجه بخش natidzhabákhsh yielding results, productive, fruitful

نټ naṭ *m.* **1** tightrope walker **2** *regional* acrobat, prestidigitator, juggler **3** confidence man, cheat

نټه¹ naṭá *f.* **1** refusal of something; denial نټه كول to refuse something, deny something ديو كار څخه نټه كول to refuse something, decline something; refute something; deny one's participation in something **2** whim

نټه² naṭa *feminine of* نټ

نثار nisár *m. Arabic* **1** strewing, scattering; showering **2** distribution of money to the population (at holiday time) **3** showering a bride with money or flowers (on the wedding day) نثار كول **a** to scatter, strew; shower **b** to throw money to the population (at holiday time) **c** to sprinkle money or flowers on the bride (on the wedding day) **4** *proper name* Nisar

نثر nasr *m. Arabic* prose

نثرنويس nasrnavís *m.* prose writer

نجابت nadzhābát *m. Arabic* **1** nobility, noble birth **2** decency

نجات nadzhāt *m.* nidzhāt *m. Arabic* saving, rescue, deliverance چا ته د نجات وركول to save, come to the rescue of someone نجات ميندل وركولو دپاره رسېدل to come to the rescue to be saved, be rescued from something

نجاح nadzhā́h *m. & f.* nadzhāh *Arabic* success; good luck

نجار nadzhár *m. Arabic* carpenter; joiner

نجارك nadzhārák *m.* woodpecker

نجاري nadzhārí **1** *f.* carpentry; joinery **2** joiner's; carpenter's

نجاست nadzhāsát *m. Arabic* **1** dirtiness **2** uncleanliness

نجبا nadzhabā́ *m. Arabic plural of* نجيب **2** نجباو اطاق the House of Lords

نجتل ndzhatə́l *transitive* [*present:* نجني *past:* نجت و یې] **1** to set up, pitch (a tent) **2** to hoist (e.g., a flag) **3** to put in, insert

نجتنه nzhatə́na *f.* **1** setting up, pitching (a tent) **2** raising, hoisting (e.g., a flag) **3** inserting, putting in

نجراب nidzhrā́b *m.* Nidzhrab (district)

نجاست nadzhás *m. Arabic* ☞ نجاست

نجف nadzháf *m.* Nedzhef (city)

نجل ndzhə́l *f.* [*plural:* نجلي ndzhə́li] fiancée, bride-to-be; betrothed

نجلتوب ndzhə́ltób *m.* **1** girlhood **2** time after betrothal (before the wedding)

نجلكى ndzhə́lkə́j *f.* [*plural:* نجلكى ndzhə́lkə́j *plural:* نجلكياني ndzhə́lkəjā́ni] little girl, girl, lass

نجلي¹ ndzhə́li *plural of* نجل

نجلى² ndzhə́ləj *f.* [*plural:* نجوني ndzhūni *plural:* نجلياني ndzhə́ləjā́ni] **1** little girl **2** girl, maiden پيغله نجلي spinster

نجلى والا ndzhə́ləjvālā́ *m. plural* relative(s) of the bride-to-be

نجم nadzhm *m. Arabic* [*plural:* نجوم nudzhúm] heavenly body, celestial object; planet

نجم المدارس nadzhm-ul-madā́ris *m.* theological seminary in Khalla (near Jelalabad)

نجن ndzhan *present stem of* نجتل

نجنكى ndzhənakə́j *f. dialect* ☞ نجلكى

نجوړى ndzhoṛáj *m.* scarecrow

نجوم nudzhúm *Arabic* **1** *plural of* نجم **2** *m. plural* astrology; astronomy

نجومي nudzhumí *Arabic* **1** astronomical **2** *m.* astrologer; astronomer

نجونه ndzhúna *dialect* [*plural:* نجوني ndzhúni] *plural of* نجلى²

نجيب nadzhíb *Arabic* **1** wellborn, noble **2** *m.* **.1** [*plural:* نجبا nadzhabā́] nobleman, aristocrat; hereditary gentleman **2** *proper name* Nadzhib (Najib, Najeeb)

نجيب زاده nadzhibzādá *m.* ☞ نجيب **2.1**

نجيبه nadzhibá *Arabic* **1** *feminine singular of* نجيب **1** **2** *f. proper name* Nadzhiba (Najiba)

نچا nachā́ *f.* ☞ نخا¹

نچور nichór *m.* ☞ نخوړ

نچورول nichoravúl *transitive* ☞ نخوړول

نچوړ nichóṛ *m.* ☞ نخوړ

نچوړول nichóṛavə́l *transitive* ☞ نخوړول

نچول nachavə́l *transitive* ☞ نخول

نچه¹ nachá *f.* **1** *textiles* bobbin, spool **2** stem of a water pipe **3** *zoology* new feather (after a bird's molting)

نچه² náchi *vice* نچه ولوبد نه چه I am afraid lest he might fall. اوس راسي Suppose he doesn't come, now.

نچېدل nachedə́l *intransitive* ☞ نخل

نخا¹ natsā́ *f.* dance; (female) dance نخا كول **a** to dance **b** to whirl, twirl **c** to romp په نخا كېدل to begin to dance

نخا² natsā́ *f.* **1** agitation **2** swaying **3** quivering په نخا ګډول **a** to agitate, disturb **b** to rock, sway **c** to quiver (a tree etc.)

نخاوه natsāvə́ *imperfect tense* نخول

نخل natsə́l [*present:* ناخي *past:* نخل و یې] *transitive* to dance *idiom* د چا ډول ته نخل to dance to someone's tune

نخوړ natsóṛ *m. Western* 1 compressing, squeezing 2 wringing, wringing out (e.g., laundry)

نخوړول natsoṛavól *denominative, transitive* [*past:* نخوړ يې کړ] *Western* 1 to compress, press, squeeze 2 to wring, wring out (e.g., laundry)

نخوړېدل natsoṛedál *denominative, intransitive* [*past:* نخوړ شو] 1 to be pressed, be compressed, be squeezed 2 to be wrung, be wrung out (of laundry)

نخول natsavól *transitive* [*past:* و يې نخاوه] to make or cause to dance or whirl about

نخونکی ¹ natsúnkaj *m.* ☞ ناڅګر

نخونکۍ ² natsúnke *f.* ☞ ناڅګره

نخۍ ¹ natsáj *m.* 1 dancer 2 juggler

نخۍ ² natsə́j *f.* ☞ ناڅګره

نخۍ ³ nətsə́j *f.* 1 woolen thread 2 woolen yarn

نخېدل natsedól *intransitive* ☞ نځل

ناخېدونکۍ natsedúnke *f.* ☞ ناڅګره

نحس nahs *Arabic* 1.1 unhappy; unlucky, ill-fated, ill-starred 1.2 ill-omened 2 *m.* unlucky star

نحسي nahsí *Arabic* ☞ نحس 1

نحسيت nahsiját *m. Arabic* ☞ نحوست

نحو nahv *m. Arabic* syntax

نحوست nuhusát *m. Arabic* bad luck, failure; ill luck

نحوي nahví *Arabic* 1 syntactic 2 grammatical

نحيف nahíf *Arabic* thin, emaciated

نخ ¹ nakh *m.* slender vines, branching vines

نخ ² nakh *m.* cotton yarn, cotton thread

نخاس nakhkhás *m. Arabic* 1 profiteer 2 cattle trader 3 *history* slave trader 4 *regional* slave market 5 *figurative* shameful event, disgrace

نخالص nikhālís *regional* pure, unadulterated

نختابي nakhtābí *f.* spinning

نختر nəkhtár *m. Eastern* ☞ ننبتر

نخچه nakhchá *f. figurative* 1 plan; map 2 pattern, tailor's pattern ☞ نقشه

نخره nakhrá *f.* 1 flirtatiousness; coquettish gesture 2 pretense, sham; deceit 3 breach, hole نخره کول a to use cunning, use guile, resort to subterfuges b to make a breach, break through, make a hole *idiom* په نو نخره نه دربدل no ..., not to calm down; to not accept mediation

نخره باز nakhrabáz 1.1 affected; flirtatious 1.2 sham, pretended 2 *m.* sham, pretense

نخره بازه nakhrabáza *f.* flirt (woman)

نخره بازي nakhrabází *f.* 1 affectation; coquettishness 2 hypocrisy, sham

نخړي nə́khṛi *f. plural* flour sprinkled into hot oil

نخس nakhs *m.* نخسان nukhsán *m.* ☞ نقص

نخسی nakhə́saj *m.* spindle rod on which woolen yarn is wound

نخبن nukhákh *m.* hook for taking meat out of a kettle

نخنه nákhkha *f.* 1 sign, mark; label نخبنه کول *compound verb* a to place a mark, sign; label b to designate 2 monument of antiquity دا تاريخي نخنه ده This is an historic monument. 3 target 4 sign, symbol 5 punctuation mark 6 *military* objective, target, aim 7 drawing; chart, plan, schematic (drawing)

نخل nakhl *f. Arabic* date palm

نخلستان nakhlistán *m.* date grove, palm grove

نخوت nakhvát *m. Arabic* 1 hypocrisy, arrogance; conceit 2 splendor, magnificence

نخود nukhúd *m. plural* 1 chickpea 2 nukhud (a measure of weight equivalent to 0.19 grams)

نخودي nukhudí nut-colored, brownish-yellow

نخولېدل nkhuledól *intransitive* [*past:* و نخولېد] 1 to find fault with 2 to be smeared *figurative* to get egg on your face 3 نولېدل

نخي nakhí cotton نخي توتي cotton cloth, cotton textile

ندا ¹ nidā́ *f. Arabic* call; shout; appeal, summons د ندا اشاره exclamation point دا ندا راغله A cry was heard.

ندا ² nadā́ *f. children's speech* 1 candy 2 meal, something to eat

نداپ nadā́p *m.* scutcher of cotton

نداپي nadā́pí *f.* scutching, cleaning of cotton

نداف naddā́f *m. Arabic* ☞ نداپ

ندافي naddā́fí *f.* ☞ نداپي د ندافي فابريکه a cotton-scutching plant

ندامت nadāmát *m. Arabic* repentance ندامت پښېماني کول to repent deeply

ندائي nidājí *grammar* vocative

ندر nə́dar *m.* ☞ نذر

ندرور ndor *f.* [*plural:* ندرندي ndrándi *Eastern plural:* ندرېنده ndrénde *plural:* ندروریاني ndorijā́ne] sister-in-law (husband's sister)

نده náda *vice* نه ده

ندئ ¹ nádəj *vice* نه دئ

ندي ² nádi *vice* نه دي

نديم nadím *m. Arabic* 1 close associate, retainer 2 bosom friend; confidant; close comrade

نذر názr *m.* نذر názar *m. Arabic* نذر *Arabic* 1 present; gift نذر کول ورکول a to present, bestow b to sacrifice, be offered as a sacrifice نذر کېدل *compound verb* to be sacrificed, be offered as a sacrifice 2 vow, promise نذرونه په ځان اينبودل to take a vow, promise

نذرانه nazrāná *f.* 1 gift, gift-offering چا ته نذرانه ورکول to present, make an offering of a gift to someone 2 gifts (exchanged by high-ranking people or princes at a meeting)

نذير nazír *m. Arabic proper name* Nazir

نر nar nər 1 *m.* [*plural:* نر nər *plural:* نران narā́n] 1.1 male (animal) نر بیزو male ape 1.2 man; husband 1.3 stout fellow 2 *attributive* 2.1 masculine, male 2.2 manly, brave نر سړی stout fellow په نره توره ګټل stouthearted woman نره ښځه to take with bravery *Western* پر نر زمري ځل اينبودل to be an inveterate scoundrel

نرتوب nartób *m.* bravery, valor; courage

نرخ narkh *m.* **1** price; official rate, legal price د بازار نرخ market price د نرخ مراقبت the average price متوسط نرخ، منځنی نرخ price نرخ ټاکل to set نرخونه ارزانه کول to lower prices; cheapen نرخونه جگ شوه The prices rose. غنم څه نرخ ورکوي؟ For how much are you selling wheat? **2** *economics* exchange rate رسمي نرخ official rate of exchange د ورځي په نرخ سره the commercial exchange rate بورس نرخ according to the day's rate of exchange نرخ لړبول، نرخ کمول *a* to lower the price *b* economics to lower the exchange rate **3** the norms of Afghan traditional law (adat)

نرخ نامه narkhnāmá *f.* **1** price list, valuation, official price, statuatory price **2** rates (postal, etc.)

نرخی nərkháj *m.* **1** one who establishes a price; valuator **2** one who resolves; arbitrator, umpire, arbiter **3** expert in the norms of Afghan traditional law (adat); judge in Afghan traditional law (adat)

نرد nard *m.* **1** kind of game **2** piece used in this game

نرس nars *regional* **1** *f.* nurse **2** *m.* hospital attendant, orderly نر نرس male nurse, hospital attendant, orderly

نرسری narsarí *f. regional* nursery

نرسنگ nársíng *m. regional* **1** nursing profession **2** care of the sick د نرسري کار کول *a* to work as a nurse *b* to care for the sick

نرسوی nərsəváj *m.* **1** pomegranate rind **2** kind of pomegranate

نرسوئ narsávəj sunburned

نربنځک narkhədzák *m.* نربنځی narkhədzáj *m.* hermaphrodite

نرغوټ narghúṭ *m.* نرغوت narghvə́t *m.* **1** wild cat **2** *botany* kind of eremurus (a small genus of Asiatic herbs of the Liliaceae family)

نرغون narghún *m. dialect* ☞ لرغون

نرغونی narghunáj *dialect* ☞ لرغونی

نرکټا nərkaṭá *m.* large (goat) kid

نر کچور nərkachór *m.* elongated rhizome of the santonic or wormseed root, *Curcuma zeoaria*

نرکاخ nərkákh *m.* **1** arkhar **2** mouflon (wild sheep) **3** goat (flock leader)

نرکی narákaj *m.* mountain pass; col, saddleback

نرکی narakáj *diminutive* thin

نرگاړی nərgā́ṛaj *m. dialect* **1** man **2** husband, spouse

نرگټی nargətáj *m.* ☞ نربنځک

نرگس nargís *m.* nargə́s *m.* narcissus

نرگسی nargəsáj *f.* pomegranate

نرگسی nargəsí colored like a narcissus; like a narcissus *idiom* نرگسی سترگي large eyes (of a beauty)

نرگوس narguvás *m.* small pomegranate

نرگوسه nargúsa *f.* pomegranate tree

نرگوښ nargúkh *m.* **1** fishhook **2** orchardman's hook for harvesting fruit

نرلوخ narlukh *m. plural* cattail head

نرم narm **1** soft, gentle, tender نرم باد، نرم نسیم soft wind, zephyr, نرم تالو breeze په قندهار کي ژمی نرم وي Kandahar has a mild winter. *anatomy* soft palate **2** gentle, mild; softhearted **3** pliant, pliable

نرمچ narmə́ch *m.* gadfly

نرم دل narmdíl نرم زړی narmzə́ṛaj tender, gentle, kind, softhearted; favorable, gracious; indulgent

نرم طبیعته narmtabi'áta نرم گیر narmgír mild-mannered, gentle, meek (of a person)

نرمول narmmavə́l *denominative, transitive* [*past:* نرم يي کړ] **1** to make soft, tender **2** to soften; make softer, mild, compliant سخت زړه نرمول to soften a cruel heart لهجه نرمول to soften the tone

نرمه narmá *f.* soft high-quality silk cloth

نرمي narmí *f.* **1** gentleness, mildness, softness (in address); kindness **2** meekness

نرمي nármi *f. plural of* نرم

نرمې narmé *plural of* نرمه

نرمی narmə́j earlobe

نرمی narmə́j *f. proper name* Narmi

نرمبدل narmedə́l *denominative, intransitive* [*past:* نرم شو] **1** to be soft, be gentle, be tender; become soft **2** to be meek

نرو naró *oblique plural of* نری

نروب naró́b liquid, watery نروب کول to dilute, thin

نروتڅکی narútskaj **1** rather thin **2** somewhat emaciated, drawn

نره nára *f.* nə́ra *singular of* نر 2.2

نری naráj **1** thin, narrow نري سپنسي thin thread نری لار narrow road نری ملا narrow waist **2** emaciated, drawn; gaunt نری سړی a gaunt man **3** watery (of milk, etc.) نری چای watery tea, weak tea **4** light, weak (of wind) نری شمال لگبد A light breeze was blowing. **5** penetrating (of a sound) نری غږ a resounding cry نری ناري وهل to squeal, squeak **6** ticklish (of a problem, question) **7** tender, soft نری زړه يي نری دئ He has a soft heart. **8** delicate نری کول *a* to narrow, taper *b* to emaciate, exhaust *c* to thin, dilute نری کبدل *a* to become narrow, taper *b* to become gaunt *c* to be watery (e.g., of milk) *d* to worry, become worried په دي خبره باندي هغه خبر مو نری غوندي لږ نری شه! Don't worry about this a bit! *idiom* او وربدلئ و We overheard this.

نری naráj *f. singular of* نری وریجي polished rice

نري nári *f. plural of* نر 2.2

نری والی narajtób *m.* ☞ نری توب

نری جوار narí dzhuvár *m. plural* fodder corn

نریځ narídz male, masculine

نری رنځ naráj randz *m.* consumption, tuberculosis

نری زردالو narí zardālú *m. plural* apricots for drying; dried apricots

نرینه nariná ☞ نارینه

نری والی narajvā́laj *m.* **1** fineness **2** narrowing, the narrow part of something

نړ naṛ *m.* one fourth of a dzherib (a measure of land equal to five بسوه bisva)

نړا naṛā́ *f.* cry or roar of an animal

نړیدل ☞ نړانده کېدل نړول ☞ نړانده نړانده naṛā́nda *f.* ruins نړګ naṛg ruined

نړل naṛál *transitive* [*present:* ناړي *past:* و یې نړل] 1 to squawk (of a crane, etc.) 2 to bellow, roar

نړنه naṛə́na *f.* roar, bellow

نړول naṛavál *transitive* [*past:* و یې نړاوه] 1 to destroy; ruin, wreck 2 to topple, overturn

نړونه naṛavə́na *f.* ruin, destruction

نړۍ naṛə́j *f.* 1 world, universe بهرنی نړۍ the extrenal world د نړۍ دوهمه جګړه the Second World War 2 ambiance, environment بشري نړۍ humanity عسکري نړۍ a military environment

نړیچغ naṛechágh *m.* entryway; room; premises

نړیدل naṛedál *intransitive* [*past:* و نړیده] 1 to be destroyed; be ruined 2 to be toppled; be overturned 3 *figurative* to perish; be vanquished

نړیوال naṛəjvál *m. singular & plural* dweller, inhabitant, نړۍ وال dwellers on the world

نړیوال جال naṛəjwál dzhál انترنیټ انترنیت intárniṭ intárnet *m. computer science* internet

نړیوال غځېدلی ګورت naṛaywál ghadzedəlay górt *m. computer science* world wide web (www)

نزاع nizā' *f. Arabic* [*plural:* نزاعګاني nizā'gáni] quarrel, dispute; wrangles د دوی په مینځ کښې نزاع پیدا شوه They were quarreling.

نزاکت nazākát *m.* 1 tenderness; delicacy د نزاکت مراعات delicate treatment, delicate manner 2 elegance 3 ticklishness (of a question, a problem) 4 tension بین المللي نزاکت international tension

نزاله nazālá *f.* ☞ نواله

نزاهت nazāhát *m. Arabic* cleanliness, purity, immaculate state

نزد nazd 1 closely 2 near, close *idiom* د چا په نزد لوی شان او شوکت لرل to stand high in someone's opinion a په نزد د ده according to him b د ده په نزد in his opinion قانون په نزد in relation to the law

نزده nazdá *vice* ☞ نه زده

نزدې nizdé ☞ نژدې

نزدیکي nazdikí *f.* نزدېوالی nizdeválaj *m.* ☞ نژدیکت

نزر nazár *m.* the evil eye نزر کول *compound verb* to put the evil eye on نزر کېدل *compound verb* to have the evil eye put on one ☞ نظر

نزرمات nazarmát *m.* means of putting the evil eye on

نزړه nazṛə́ *m. plural* ☞ ننزړه

نزله nazlá *f. Arabic* cold in the head د نزلي مرض، سرې نزلي head cold د نزلي شکایت *regional* head cold

نزم názəm *m.* pulse نزم کتل to feel the pulse, check the pulse

نزول nuzúl *m. Arabic* 1 descent, lowering, descending 2 falling, recession نزول کول a to descend or lower oneself, come down b to diminish; be diminished 3 settling (of sediment) 4 *economics* discount, discount rate 5 inspiration

نزولي nuzulí *Arabic* 1 descending; coming down 2 degrading; regressing 3 decreasing, falling (e.g., of income, receipts)

نزهت nuzhát *m. Arabic* 1 enjoyment, delight; entertainment; joy, comfort 2 freshness, coolness

نژی nə́zaj núzaj *tautological with* نوی نزی نوی brand new

نژاد nizhád 1 *m.* .1 descent 1.2 breed, race ګډ نژاد crossbreeding 2 *combining form* ترکي نژاد، ترکي نژاده of Turkish descent

نژادي nizhādí 1 relating to descent 2 racial نژادي تبعیض، نژادي توپیر racial discrimination; apartheid

نژتی nzhátaj sticking up; spread wide (fingers)

نژدې nizhdé nəzhdé 1.1 near زموږ کور نژدې دئ Our home is not far away. په دې a near future b *grammar* perfect tense نژدې زمانه په راتلونکي نژدې وخت کښې in recent days; recently نژدو ورځو کښې in the near future دا هلک ډېر را نژدې دئ This boy is my close relative. دا دوه هلکان سره ډېر نژدې like, alike له نژدې څخه from close by 1.2 هغه نژدې و چه ولوېدی، هغه These two boys are very much alike. دي نژدې و چه لوېدلئ وای He very nearly fell. 2.1 about, almost, nearly نژدې ډېرش کاله پخوا It was about ten o'clock. نژدې لس بجي وو about thirty years ago ... نژدې دوې میاشتي کېږي چه It will be و نهارته نژدې almost two months since ... 2.2 near, nearly نژدې کول، سره نژدې کول to bring near; bring together ځان را نژدې کول to approach نژدې کېدل to come near to, draw near, come up to سره نژدې کېدل to come together د کلا په نژدې near the fortress کېدل

نژدیکت nəzhdekát *m.* نژدیکي nəzhdekí *f.* نژدېوالی nəzhdeválaj *m.* 1 nearness (in time and place) 2 approach; convergence

نږدي nágdi *vice* نه ږدي

نږل ngə́l *transitive* [*present:* نږي *past:* و یې نږه و یې نږه *past:* نږل] to sneeze

نږندي ngándi *plural of* نږور

نږور ngor *f.* [*plural:* نږندي ngándi *Eastern plural:* نږېندي ngénde] daughter-in-law

نږول ngavál *transitive* [*past:* وئي نږاوه] to cause to sneeze

نږه nagá *f. singular of* نږور

نږی [1] ngaj *m. Western* sneezing نږی کول to sneeze

نږي [2] ngi *present tense of* نږل

نږې [3] nagé *f. plural of* نږور

نږېندي ngénde *plural of* نږور

نس nas *m.* 1 stomach, belly په نیم نس half-starved د نس شوقي food-lover, glutton, gourmand په ماره نس خوړل to eat one's fill نس خوړل to eat up, devour په تش نس on an empty stomach یو په نس، بل په هوس *proverb literal* One bite in his stomach and he is already dreaming of the next. *figuratively* He is very greedy. He is insatiable. د نسه کبنبنستل to have diarrhea د احمد نس تر خوله Ahmed overate. 2 paunch 3 uterus 4 bed (of a river) 5 وخوت *figurative* depths د مځکي نس، د مځکي دننه نس the depths of the earth 6 lust *idiom* د نس په خوړ تلل to walk with great difficulty

نسا nisá *f. Arabic* [*plural:* نسوان nisván] woman

نساج nassádzh *m. Arabic* cloth

نساجي nassādzhí *f.* weaving; textile production د نساجی صنعت the textile industry د نساجی فابریکه، د نساجی کارخانه textile factory

نسايي nisāí *Arabic* female, women's نسايي مرضونه female diseases, diseases of women

نسب nasáb *m.* 1 descent په نسب او اصل فخر کول to pride oneself on one's descent 2 [*plural:* انساب ansấb] pedigree, genealogy

نسب پېژندونکی nasb pezhandúnkaj *m.* genealogist

نسبت nisbát *m. Arabic* 1 relationship, connection په دې نسبت سره چه ... in view of the fact that ... په هغه نسبت in this connection 2 comparison, likening نسبت و هغه ته، د هغه په نسبت in comparison with him په نسبت سره پخوا ته in comparison with the former د چا ټوکاله پخوا ته in comparison with what was several years ago سره نسبت ورکول to compare with someone 3 proportion, ratio 4 *regional* betrothal

نسبتاً nisbátán *Arabic* relatively; comparatively

نسبتي nisbatí *Arabic* comparative; relative نسبتي اندازه relative dimensions, relative proportions نسبتي نظریه nisbatí the theory of relativity

نسب نامه، نسبنامه nasabnāmá *f.* genealogical tree, genealogical table; genealogy

نسبهی nasbaháj *m.* 1 diarrhea 2 cholera

نسبي [1] nasabí *Arabic* 1 genealogical 2 kindred, related

نسبي [2] nasbí *Arabic* 1 ☞ نسبتي 2 genealogical

نسبیت nasbiját *m. Arabic* relativity د نسبیت نظریه the theory of relativity

نس پرسی naspə́rsaj gluttonous, voracious

نسترن nastarán *m. singular & plural* white dog-rose

نستعلیق nasta'líḳ *m. Arabic* Nastaliq script (Arabic-Persian script developed in the fifteenth century and used mainly for Persian poetical writing)

نستوڼی nastóṇaj *m. Eastern* sleeve لاس په نستوڼي جګړه hand-to-hand combat ☞ لستوڼی

نستوی nastə́vaj *m.* sheet in which bedclothes are wrapped during the day

نسته nə́sta *Western* there isn't, there aren't روپی نسته There isn't any money. احمد دلته نسته Ahmed isn't here.

نسج [1] nadzh *m. Arabic* 1 weaving, cloth making [*plural:* انساج ansấdzh] 2 cloth عصبي نسج neural tissue, nerve tissue

نسج [2] nusúdzh *m. Arabic plural of* نسیج

نسخ naskh *m. Arabic* 1 Neskhi script (regular Arabic cursive script) 2 copying 3 abolition

نس خوړتیا naskhvagtjấ *f.* نس خوړوالی naskhvugvấlaj *m.* diarrhea

نس خوړی [1] naskhugí *f.* abdominal colic

نس خوړی [2] naskhúgaj naskhvúgaj suffering from diarrhea or colic

نسخه nuskhá *f. Arabic* 1 copy, duplicate; copy, specimen; list د دیوان قلمي نسخه، د لاس نسخه the manuscript of a Divan (collection of poetry), a manuscript Divan 2 recipe; prescription

نسر [1] nasr *m. Arabic* vulture

نسر [2] nasə́r *m. plural* chips, brushwood (floating along on floodwater)

نسرین nasrín *m. plural* dog rose

نسغ nasagh *m.* ☞ نسق [2]

نسق nasáḳ *m. Arabic* 1 order, arrangement 2 punishment; capital punishment, execution

نسک nask *m. plural* lentils

نسکار nəskấr *m.* kind of decoration

نسکور naskór nəskór 1 toppled over, overturned 2 brought down, shot down (of an aircraft) 3 disordered, broken down, ruined په ځان نسکور کېدل to become withdrawn, become reserved, become retired into oneself

نسکورول naskoravə́l *denominative* [*past:* نسکور یې کړ] 1 to topple, throw down, overturn 2 to bring down, shoot down الوتکي نسکورول to shoot aircraft down 3 to ruin, wreck 4 to smash, rout (an enemy)

نسکوریدل naskoredə́l *denominative, intransitive* [*past:* نسکور شو] 1 to be toppled over, be overturned 2 to be brought down, be shot down (of an aircraft) 3 to stoop, bend 4 to be disordered, be ruined 5 to be smashed, be routed (an enemy)

نسکیر naskír *m.* 1 close friend 2 relative

نسکیرتوب naskirtób *m.* نسکیرتیا naskirtjấ *f.* نسکیروالی naskirvấlaj *m.* closeness, kinship

نسکیرول naskiravə́l *denominative, transitive* [*past:* نسکیر یې کړ] to bring together, relate, link

نسکیریدل naskiredə́l *denominative, intransitive* [*past:* نسکیر شو] to be brought together, be related, be linked

نسکینه naskína *f.* dish made of lentils نسکینه ټیکله lentil-noodle soup

نسگیر nasgír suffering with diarrhea, suffering with a stomach disorder

نسل nasl *m. Arabic* 1 generation, posterity راتلونکی نسلونه posterity; future generations 2 race; descent دوه رګه نسل mixture, hybrid سوچه نسل a purebred animal 3 clan, tribe 4 issue, increase (of animals) د نسل اخیستلو فارم tribal economy

نسلاً náslán *Arabic* by descent, according to descent

نسل بالنسل nasbinnásl *Arabic* from family to family, from generation to generation

نسلگیري nasligrí *f.* 1 tribal animal husbandry د نسلگیری ریاست the Directorate of Animal Husbandry 2 coupling, mating

نسلي naslí 1 hereditary 2 relating to descent or clan; dynastic 3 tribal, pedigreed, purebred

نسم [1] násəm *Western vice* نه سم

نسم [2] vice نیسم

نسناسته nasnāsta *f.* diarrhea نس ناسته یې ده He has diarrhea.

نسو [1] nasú 1.1 gluttonous 1.2 potbellied *m.* 2.1 gluttony 2.2 paunchy person

نسو [2] násu *Western vice* نه سو

نسو [3] nísu *vice* نيسو

نسوار nasvā́r *m. plural* 1 snuff د نسوارو دبلی snuffbox نسوار کول to take snuff 2 snuff (for sniffing and chewing) نسوار اخيستل to take snuff, dip snuff *idiom* دا خو زما نسوار هم ندئ This is a trifling matter.

نسورداني nasvārdāní *f.* snuffbox

نسوارواله nasārvālā́ *m.* snuff merchant

نسواري nasvāērí 1 dark brown; tobacco-colored 2 *m.* snuff user

نسوان nisvā́n *f. Arabic plural of* نسا

نسواند nasvā́nd greedy, gluttonous

نسوای násvāj *Western vice* نه سوای

نسور nasavə́r ☞ نسو [1]

نسوم násvəm *vice* نه سوم

نسي [1] nási *Western vice* نه سي

نيسي [2] nísi *vice* نيسي

نيسي [3] níse *vice* نيسي

نسي [4] náse *vice* نه سي

نسي [5] nsəj *f.* ☞ نڅي [3]

نسيان nisjā́n *m. Arabic* forgetfulness د نسيان تر پردي لاندي کيدل to forget oneself, be prone to forgetfulness

نسيب nasíb *Arabic* of noble descent, of highborn descent, pedigreed

نسيج nasídzh *m. Arabic* [*plural:* انسجه ansidzhá *plural:* نسج nusúdzh] cloth

نسيم nasím *m. Arabic* 1 light wind, breeze, zephyr; puff, breath (of air) 2 *proper name* Nasim

نسيه nasijá *f. Arabic* credit نسيه اخيستل to buy on credit نسيه خرڅول to sell on credit

نشات nish'át *m. Arabic* ☞ لشه

نشاسته nishaēstá *f.* starch

نشاسته يي nishāstaí starched; starchy, containing starch

نشاط nashā́t *m. Arabic* 1 cheerfulness, joy د ژوند نشاط hearty enjoyment of life, joie de vivre نشاط بندل to inspire joy, gladden 2 courage; liveliness 3 work, activity 4 zeal

نشان nishā́n *m.* ☞ نبنان

نشانچي nishānchí *m.* sniper د نشانچي علامت sniper's badge

نشانزن nishānzán *m.* نشان زن *military* gunner

نشانگاه nishāngáh *m.* gunsight, sight (of a firearm)

نشانه nishāná *f.* 1 sign, token 2 mark 3 badge

نشاني nishāní *f.* 1 sign, token, mark 2 indication 3 code word, code sign, password نشاني کول *compound verb* to initial

نشايسته nishājistá *f.* ☞ نشاسته

نشت nəsht *m.* 1 absence 2 nonexistence ته په نشت حساب وي They haven't taken you into consideration.

نشتر [1] nishtár *m.* scalpel, lancet په نشتر وهل to lance with a scalpel, let blood with a scalpel

نشتر [2] nashtár *m.* ☞ نبنتر

نشتمن nəshtmán destitute, poor

نشتوالی nəshtvā́laj *m.* 1 absence د هغه په نشتوالي nəshtvali in his abscence 2 nonexistence 3 poverty

نشتوکی nəshtukáj stingy, tightfisted

نشتول nəshtavə́l *denominative, transitive* [*past:* نشته يې کړ] to annihilate

نشته nə́shta *Eastern* there isn't, there aren't; (he, she, it, etc.) isn't, aren't يو ساعت مخکبنبي راغلي و اوس نشته He came an hour ago, but he's not here now. روپی نشته There is no money. گوره چه زما کتاب په ميز باندي خو نشته؟ Look and see if my book isn't on the table.

نشتوالی nəshtavā́laj *m.* ☞ نشته والی

نشتيدل nəshtedə́l *denominative, intransitive* [*past:* نشته شو] 1 to be annihilated 2 to disappear, vanish

نشر nashr *Arabic* 1 *m.* .1 publication, issuing 1.2 translation, transmission 2 *predicative* published, printed نشر کول *compound verb* ☞ نشرېدل نشر کيدل نشرول *compound verb* ☞

نشرات nasharā́t *m. Arabic plural of* نشرت

نشراتي nashrātí 1 *adjective* publishing نشراتي موسسه، نشراتي دايره publishing house نشراتي کال year of publication, publication date 2 *adjective* press نشراتي اورگان press organ, organ of the press 3 *adjective* radio-broadcasting نشراتي ستېشن radio station

نشرالصوت nashr-us-sáut *m. Arabic* radio broadcasting

نشرت nashrát *m. Arabic* [*plural:* نشرات nasharā́t] publication د راديو نشرات radio broadcasting, broadcasting

نشرول nashravə́l *denominative, transitive* [*past:* نشر يې کړ] 1 to issue, publish, publicize 2 to transmit; disseminate 3 to emit (rays), radiate

نشره nashrá *f. Arabic religion* public prayer service on the third day after the birth of a child

نشريات nashrijā́t *m. Arabic* 1 *plural of* نشريه 2 radio broadcasting د نشرياتو ستېشن radio station

نشرېدل nashredə́l *denominative, intransitive* [*past:* نشر شو] 1 to be issued, be published 2 to be transmitted, be disseminated 3 to emanate (of rays)

نشريه nashrijá *f. Arabic* [*plural:* نشريات nashrijā́t] publication, issuing of printed matter

نشست nishást *m.* 1 sitting 2 *regional* meeting 3 *regional* landing 4 settling, sedimentation

نشست و برخاست nishást-u-barkhā́st *m.* 1 good conduct; good upbringing; good manners 2 habits

نشم nashm *m.* 1 deceit, trickery, shrewdness نشم کول to trick, cheat 2 *regional* corruptness, debauchery

نشمه nashmá *f.* coquettishness; flirtatiousness

نشمي nashmí shrewd, deceitful, tricky

نشميدل nashmedə́l *intransitive* [*past:* ونشمبده] to flirt

نشنلستيک nashnalistík نشنلستي nashnalistí nationalistic

نشو [1] nushú *m.* nashú *Arabic* 1 growth, development, increase 2 evolution

نشو [2] náshu *vice* نه شو

نشوم náshvəm *vice* نه شوم

نشونما nushú-namā́ *f.* ☞ نشو [1]

نشوو náshvu *vice* نه شوو

نشو ¹ nashv-u-namā́ *f.* ☞ نشوونما

نشه nashvá ¹ *f. Arabic* ☞ نشوه

نه شوه náshva náshvə ² ☞ نشوه

نشوي nashví *Arabic adjective* narcotic نشوي مواد narcotics

نشه nashá *f. Arabic* 1 intoxication په نشه کښي in a drunken state نشه د سره (they) intoxicated نشه وري He was drunk. په نشه کښي وه to sober someone up 2 narcotics, drugs; hashish *idiom* د ورالوزول چا په نشه کښي ورختل to spoil someone's disposition, poison someone's disposition

نشه آور nashaāvár نشه ایز nashaíz 1 intoxicating 2 alcoholic نشه آور مشروبات alcoholic drinks

نشه باز nashabā́z *m.* drug addict

نشه بازي nashabāzí *f.* drug addiction

نشه بندي nashabandí *f. regional* interdiction of narcotics, prohibition of narcotics

نشه خور nashakhór *m.* drug addict

نشه خوري nashakhorí *f.* 1 drug addiction 2 drunkenness

نشئي nashaí 1 drinking هغه نشئي سري دئ He is a drunkard. 2 smoking (narcotic substances) 3 bleary (eyes)

نه شي náshi *vice* ¹ نشي

نه سي náshe *vice* ² نشّي

نشه nashé *plural of* ³ نشّي

نه شئ náshəj *vice* ⁴ نشّئ

نشيب nishéb nashéb 1 *m.* .1 slope, incline 1.2 descent, declivity 1.3 precipice 2 low; gently sloping

نشئت nash'át *m. Arabic* rise, beginning; origin نشئت کول a to arise, spring up; originate b to create

نشي دار nashedā́r *regional* 1 intoxicating, stupefying 2 narcotic

نښان niқħā́n *m.* 1 sign, symbol 2 order, medal نښان ورکول to award a medal د افغانستان ملي نښان the national emblem of Afghanistan 3 target زما ټوپک ښه نښان ولي My rifle fires accurately. 4 arms, symbol, coat of arms د افغانستان رسمي نښان the National Coat of Arms of Afghanistan 5 emblem 6 *regional* flag, banner نښان اوچتول، نښان خپرول ، نښان رپول to raise the flag *idiom* اوس مي غشي په نښان لگېږي! Things are going swimmingly!

نښانچي niқħānchí *m.* marksman; sniper

نښانه niқħā́na *f.* 1 sign, symbol, token 2 target نښانه ويشتل to hit the target

نښاني niқħāní *f.* 1 sign, symbol, emblem نښاني کول a to distinguish b to keep an eye on; note 2 memory, souvenir

نه ښايي naқħāji *vice* نښايي

نښت nқħət *m.* 1 joining, connection 2 contiguity; contact, link 3 relation, relationship, respect نښت لرل a to join, connect b to adjoin, be contiguous to c to have respect to, have a relation to

نښتیا nқħəttjā́ *f.* ☞ نښته

نښتر nəқħtár *m.* [*plural:* نښترونه nəқħtarúna *plural:* نښتران nəқħtarā́n] Himalayan pine, *Pinus excelsa*

نښتره naқħtár *f. proper name* Nashtara

نښتل nқħətál 1 *intransitive* [*present:* نښلي *past:* ونښت] .1 to stick to, stick together; adhere, stick to, place against 1.2 to join, unite; adjoin; border on 1.3 to hit (i.e., a target) مردک په هدف ونښت The bullet hit the target. 1.4 to stick, tie up جاله ونښته The raft got stuck. 1.5 to brush against, touch; bump into پنبه یي له ډبري سره He stumbled on a stone. 1.6 to collide with, meet with, encounter سترگي یي پر هغو ونښتې He noticed them. 1.7 to be commenced, be begun وایي چه نوی پل نښتئ دئ They say that construction on the new bridge has begun. 1.8 to arise, break out; get started جگړه ونښته a The battle was engaged. b War broke out. 1.9 to be busy with, be engaged in something په کار ونښت He was engaged in his work. 1.10 to clash with, quarrel سره نښتل a to wrangle with b to fight c to get tangled up in, get tangled up with ژبه نښتل a to falter (of the tongue) b to stammer 1.11 to fall (into error) پوري نښتل to pester, get on the nerves 2 *m. plural* ☞ نښته

نښتنه nқħətə́na *f.* ☞ نښته

نښتون nқħətún *m.* 1 ☞ نښته 2 being busy, busyness

نښته nқħə́ta *f.* 1 gluing, pasting; adhesion 2 joining, uniting 3 hit, strike 4 sticking, jamming 5 interference 6 collision; skirmish, engagement 7 quarrel, wrangle, dispute

نښتئ nқħə́təj *past participle of* نښتل په دپر نښتئ یم I am very busy. نښتي ژبه ویل to speak stammeringly, stutter

نښتیا nқħətjā́ *f.* ☞ نښته

نښتېڅل nəқħtedzə́l [*past:* و یي نښتبڅه] 1 to squeeze, wring 2 to press, press out 3 to compress; extrude

نښتبڅه nəқħtedzə́ *m. plural* 1 squeezing out 2 pressing out 3 compression; extrusion

نښتبڅل nəқħtezə́l *transitive* ☞ نښتبڅل

نخښه nákħkha *f.* ☞ نخښه

نیښکه nákħka *f. computer science* label

نښل nқħə́l *present stem of verb* نښتل

نښلن nəқħlə́n *m. computer science* attachment

نښلند nəқħlə́nd sticky, adhesive

نښلول nқħə́laval nəқħlaval *transitive* [*past:* و یي نښلاوه] 1 to glue, paste; adhere to; paste under, glue under 2 to tie together, tie to 3 to unite, join to, attach to 4 to undertake, begin; hoist up جنگ نښلول to launch a war 5 to brush against, hook onto 6 to push off, shove off; set on; instigate (e.g., a quarrel, fight) 7 to lure, entice, decoy 8 to invlove, implicate خان نښلول a to implicate in some affair b to set down to serious business

نښلونه nқħə́lavə́na *f.* 1 gluing, pasting 2 tying together 3 joining, uniting 4 *technology* contact

نښلېدل nқħə́ledə́l *intransitive* ☞ نښتل

نښلېدنه nқħə́ledə́na *f.* 1 uniting, unification, joining 2 *technology* contact

نښه nákħa *f.* 1 characteristics, features په نښو یي وپېژاند They recognized him by his features. د ستوریو په نښه لار پیدا کول to find

the road by the stars, get oriented on the way by the stars په نښه
کول to note (a date) **2** trace, remnant د پخواني وخت نښي remnants
of the past **3** target نښه کول *compound verb* **a** to note, make a
note of **b** to aim at نښه کېدل *compound verb* to be noted نښه نیول
to aim, aim at a target نښه می جخته to fire at the target نښه ویشتل
ونه ویشته، را نه خطا شوه I did not hit the target; I missed. **4** model,
pattern **5** emblem **6** sign; signal **7** indication, symptom د ناروغتیا
نښي symptoms of a disease **8** pledge of betrothal (e.g., a kerchief)
9 trademark, model, brand

نښه باز naḳhabåz *m.* sharpshooter

نښه نښانه nåḳha nəḳhåna *f.* feature, characteristic; sign, indication

نښه ویشتونکی nåḳha vishtúnkaj *f.* sharpshooter ښه او پوره ماهر نښه
ویشتونکی expert marksman, sniper

نښبتبځل nəḳhedzəl نښبیزل nəḳhedzəl *transitive* ☞ نښبتبځل

نص nass *m. Arabic* [*plural:* نصوص nusús] **1** manifestation,
evidence **2** exposition; formulation **3** *religion* text (of the Koran)

نصاب nisåb *m. Arabic* **1** beginning, basis; origin **2** merit, virtue **3**
quorum **4** *economics* minimum amount of property subject to
taxation **5** plan, program تعلیمي نصاب plan of study د تعلیم نصاب
training plan

نصارا nasårå *m. Arabic plural of* نصراني **2**

نصایح nasåíh *m. Arabic plural of* نصیحت

نصب nasb *m. Arabic* [*plural:* انصاب ansåb] assembly, installation;
reinforcement; erection, setting up

نصب العین nasb-ul'åjn *m. Arabic* **1** mission, task, goal; installation
صحیح نصب العین the correct installation, correct assembly **2**
purposefulness

نصبول nasbavəl **1** *denominative, transitive* [*past:* نصب يي کړ]. **1.1** to
install, assemble; reinforce; erect, set up **1.2** to dismantle (e.g., a
tent, marquee) **2** *m. plural* installation, assembly; installing;
setting up, erecting

نصبي nasbí *grammar* accusative case نصبي حالت

نصبېدل nasbedəl *denominative, intransitive* [*past:* نصب شو] **1** to be
installed, be assembled; be reinforced, be set up, be erected **2** to
be dismantled (tent, marquee)

نصر nasr *m. Arabic* **1** help, assistance **2** *proper name* Nasr

نصرا nusarå *m. Arabic plural of* نصیر

نصرالدین nasraddín *m. Arabic proper name* Nasruddin ملا نصرالدین
the Mullah Nasruddin

نصرالله nasrullå *m. Arabic proper name* Nasrulla

نصراني nasråní **1** *adjective* Christian **2** *m.* [*plural:* نصرانیان
nasrånjån *Arabic plural:* نصارا nasårå] Christian

نصرانیت nasråniját *m. Arabic* Christianity

نصرت *Arabic* **1** victory, triumph **2** help, assistance

نصرت الله nusratullå *m. Arabic proper name* Nusratulla

نصف nisf *m. Arabic* half

نصف النهار nisf-un-nahår *m. Arabic* **1** meridian **2** noon

نصف قطر nisfḳútr *m. Arabic* radius

نصف کار nisfkår *m. economics* tenant-sharecropper under the half-
and-half system

نصف کاري nisfkårí *f. economics* sharecropping under the half-and-
half system

نصف کره nisf-i-kurrå hemisphere شمالي نصف کره northern
hemisphere جنوبي نصف کره southern hemisphere

نصفین nisfåjn *Arabic dual of* نصف

نصوار nasvår *m. plural* nas, chewing tobacco, nasavar د پزي نصوار
snuff نصوار چنبل ،نصوار کول to chew tobacco *idiom* دا کار زما او
نسوار ☞ ستا نصوار هم نه دئ To us this is a trifling matter.

نصواري nasvårí **1.1** relating to nas (i.e., chewing tobacco) **1.2**
brown; tobacco-colored **2** *m.* nas (i.e., chewing tobacco) user
idiom نصواري سکاره brown coal, lignite

نصوص nusús *m. Arabic plural of* نص

نصیب nasíb *m. Arabic* **1** lot, fate, fortune, destiny د چا په نصیب
کېدل، د چا نصیب کېدل to be someone's destiny, fall to someone's lot
کامیابي زموږ په نصیب شوه We have triumphed. **2** good fortune له
که نصیب می ښه وي If it luckily له ښه نصیبه unluckily بده نصیبه
should be vouchsafed me. If Fate should be kind.

نصیحت nasihát *m. Arabic* [*plural:* نصیحتونه nasihatúna *Arabic
plural:* نصائح nasåíh] advice, counsel و چاته نصیحت کول، و چاته
نصیحت ورکول to advise someone, give counsel to someone

نصیحت گر nasihatgír *m.* advisor, counselor

نصیر nasir *m. Arabic* [*plural:* نصیران nasirån *Arabic plural:* انصار
ansår *plural:* نصار nussår *plural:* نصرا nusarå] **1** helper, assistant
2 accomplice, abettor **3** *proper name* Nasir, Naseer

نضج nazdzh *m. Arabic literal & figurative* maturity, ripeness

نطاق nattåḳ *m. Arabic* **1** orator **2** representative (delivering a
statement) رسمي نطاق official representative **3** announcer د رادیو
نطاق radio announcer

نطفه nuftá *f. Arabic* **1** seed, sperm; embryo په نطفه کښي in
embryo, in the bud **2** posterity **3** *ironic* **3** offspring, progeny, get
(e.g., "the devil's offspring")

نطق nutḳ *m. Arabic* **1** speech, prepared statement د نطق دپاره پر مبز
دربدل to ascend the podium for an address **2** gift of gab

نظار nuzzår *m. Arabic plural of* ناظر هیئت نظارو **a** auditing
commission **b** oversight committee (of a society)

نظارت nazårát *m.* نزارت nizårát *Arabic* **1** observation; surveillance;
supervision تر نظارت لاندي نیول to observe, take under observation
حکومتي نظارت government surveillance **2** monitoring د یوې چاري
نظارت کول to monitor something

نظاره [1] nazårá *f. Arabic* **1** look, glance, regard **2** scene,
appearance, sight, picture

نظاره [2] nizårá *Arabic* نظاره هیئت inspection commission, oversight
commission

نظافت nazafát *m. Arabic* **1** cleanliness, neatness **2** chastity, purity

نظافتي nazåfatí *adjective* sanitary-hygienic, sanitary and hygienic

نظام nizåm *m. Arabic* **1** order; regulations; rules **2** structure;
اقتصادي نظام social structure اجتماعي نظام ,د تولني نظام system

سوسیالیستي نظام capitalism نظام سرمایه داري economical structure socialist strucure **3** *military* formation, forming up تیت نظام forming up for د معایني نظام close order جمع نظام extended order د حرب نظام combat order **4** military service **5** troops; پلی نظام infantry **6** ruler, nizam **7** *proper name* Nizam

نظاماً nizāmán *Arabic military* according to regulations

نظامات nizāmất *m. Arabic* **1** *plural of* نظام **2** statute

نظام حکومت nizām-i-hukumát *m. regional* governmental structure, regime

نظام شمسي nizấm-i-shamsí *m. regional* solar system

نظام عصبي nizām-i-'asbí *m. regional* nervous system

نظام قراول nizāmḳarāvúl *m. military* daily duty-detail, 24-hour duty schedule

نظامنامه nizāmnāmá *f.* **1** *military* regulations **2** standing orders

نظامي nizāmí *Arabic military* نظامي افسران روزونه officers نظامي دربشي military training نظامي عملیات military operations نظامي لوازم arms, armament, weapons نظامي military uniform نظامي مرسته military assistance منصب military rank

نظایر nazāír *m. Arabic* **1** *plural of* نظیر **2** distinguished persons, respected persons

نظر nazár *m. Arabic* **1** look, glance روبنانه نظر clear look, serene look په لمړي نظر کښي at first glance **2** sight تیز نظر keen sight د سترګو نظر یي sharp eyesight نظر کمزوري weak eyesight سترګور نظر His eyesight is good! نظر یي په ځان دئ د تللئ و He went blind. سترګو نظر مي ډېر کم دئ، بي له چشمو هیڅ لیکلئ نه شم *Eastern* My sight is bad; I can't write without glasses. **3** opinion, view, point of view زما په نظر کښي in my view, in my opinion د نظر نقطه point of view دچا په نسبت ښه نظر لرل to have a good opinion of someone **4** relation, comparison نظر و ... ته in relation to …, in comparison with ... د قندهار ښار نظر و کابل ته ډېر کښنته واقع شوئ دئ In comparison with Kabul, the city of Kandahar is situated much lower. **5** observation د متخصصینو تر نظر لاندي under the observation of specialists **6** evil eye, illness caused by the evil eye **7** *proper name* Nazar نظر اچول **a** to look, direct, fasten, throw a glance **b** to direct the attention to, display interest in, be interested in to په اخبار باندي ... ته اجمالي نظر اچول make a survey of ... په اول نظر پېژندل to skim through the newspaper سرسري نظر اچول to recognize at once, recognize at first sight نظر راکښل to attract the glance, attract the attention په ... نظرونه ځغلول to نظر کول **a** to look at, examine, inspect, consider, scrutinize examine, view **b** *compound verb* to give the evil eye نظر کېدل *compound verb* to get the evil eye; suffer from a sickness caused by the evil eye چه نظر نه شي، نظر دي نشي May he (they) not give me the evil eye. I pray they (he) will not give me the evil eye. نظرونه ماتبدل to be released from the evil eye; نظرونه ماتول to be cured of an illness caused by the evil eye زه یي نظر کړم ځکه ناجوړه یم She gave me the evil eye, that's why I'm sick. لیري نظر لرل to have a wide range of interests نظر یي پر احمد ولوېده He glanced at Ahmed. دتوجه نظرونه دځان په لوري اړول to attract attention to oneself

چا ته په درانه نظر کتل، چاته د عزت په نظر کتل، په عزت اوښنه نظر چاته کتل to respect someone, treat someone with respect اکا ته د پلار په نظر to treat an uncle like a father په بد نظر چاته کتل to not be overly fond of someone, not have respect for someone په ښه نظر to look د استفهام په نظر چاته کتل **a** to approve **b** to treat well یو څېز ته د شک په نظر کتل to regard questioningly at someone په نظر لرل، په نظر نیول to have in view, consider, pay attention to په نظر کښي دي چه ... bear in mind that هغه دچا په نظر کښي ورتلل to show oneself, catch someone's eye ... تر نظر لاندي د ټولو تر نظر بد دئ Everyone thinks he is unpleasant. د نظر ته خدعه ورکول to bear in mind, consider, pay attention نیول to create illusions د خلقو د نظر مراعات کول to take people's opinion into consideration *Eastern* له نظره تېرول، د نظر لاندي راوستل to survey, scrutinize, examine له نظره تېرېدل، تر نظر لاندي تېرېدل to be surveyed, be examined, be scrutinized له نظره غورځول to ignore د چا له نظره لوېدل to lose someone's respect, fall in someone's eyes; be deprived of someone's sympathies د خلقو له نظره لوېدلئ دئ People disdained him. People scorned him.

نظر انداز nazarabdáz *m.* circle, sphere

نظر باز nazarbáz **1** *m.* man capable of giving the evil eye **2** flirtatious, throwing playful glances; looking tenderly

نظر بنده nazarbánd نظر بنده nazarbánda **1** interned, detained; arrested نظر بند کېدل to intern, detain; arrest نظر بند کول to be interned, be detained; be arrested **2** charmed, fascinated, captivated

نظر بندي nazarbandí *f.* **1** internment, detention; house arrest **2** charm, fascination; magic, charms

نظر وړونکی nazár vŕúkaj charming, fascinating, entrancing

نظري nazarí *Arabic* **1** theoretical په نظري طرز theoretical **2** optical, visual

نظریه nazaijá *f. Arabic* [*plural:* نظریي nazarijé *m. plural:* نظریات nazarijất] **1** theory اجتماعي نظریات the theory of probability یوه نوي نظریه economic theory, economic studies اقتصادي نظریات وړاندي کول to propose a new theory **2** point of view, opinion, view د چا څخه نظریه غوښتل from this point of view په همدغه نظریه سره to inquire after someone's point of view نظریه ورکول to express one's opinion

نظم nazm *m. Arabic* **1** order; structure; good organization, orderliness **2** poetry; verses, poems دغه نظم او نسق نظم او نسق He wrote this legend in verses. **3** string (of a musical instrument) **4** *proper name* Nazm

نظم و نسق nazm-u-nasák *m.* arrangement; regulation; adjustment; state of adjustment or regulation

نظمي nazmí *Arabic* **1** regulated, in good order **2** poetical

نظمیه nazmijá *f. Arabic obsolete* police د نظمیي نفري *adjective* police

نظیر nazír *Arabic* **1** like, similar **2** *m.* [*plural:* نظایر nazāír] example, model په دنیا کښي نظایر نه لري There is no one like him in the world. دا کتاب نظیر نه لري This book has no equal.

نظیره nazirá *f. Arabic* **1** imitation **2** model, sample

نصیف nazíf *Arabic* neat, clean

نظیفه [1] nazifá *Arabic proper name* Nazifa

نظیفه [2] nazifá *f. singular of* نظیف

نعت na't *m.* [*plural:* نعوت nu'ut] *Arabic* eulogy

نعره na'rá *f. Arabic* 1 shout, cry, scream نعره کول shout, cry out, scream 2 noise ☞ ناره

نعره زن na'razán crying out; screaming

نعش na'sh *m. Arabic* 1 corpse, cadaver 2 stretcher or bier for carrying a corpse

نعل na'l *m. Arabic* 1 horseshoe 2 ferrule of a scabbard ☞ نال [1]

نعلبند na'lbánd *m.* blacksmith, farrier

نعلول na'lavól *denominative, transitive* ☞ نالول

نعمت ni'mát *m. Arabic* 1 charity; donation; good deed په نعمت رسیدل to receive charity نعمت ورکول to show charity, do a great favor 2 good 3 joy, bliss 4 plenty نعمت لرل to live in plenty 5 good food; eats 6 *proper name* Nimat

نعمت الله ni'matullá *m. Arabic proper name* Nimatulla

نعوت nu'út *m. Arabic plural of* نعت

نعیم na'ím *m. Arabic* 1 blissful life 2 *proper name* Naim

نغارچی naghārchí *m.* kettledrummer

نغاره naghārá *f.* 1 kettledrums نغاره ونګول to beat kettledrums (at the gates of a king, emperor, etc., to signal the reception of complaints and requests or petitions) نغاره غږول to beat kettledrums, drum 2 glory

نغارکی nghārakój *f.* old straw mattress

نغارل nghāṛól *transitive* ☞ نغښتل

نغاروني nghāṛúnaj *m.* cloth (in which something is wrapped)

نغاري [1] nghāṛi *present tense of* نغښتل *and* نغارل

نغاری [2] nghāṛój *f.* small straw mattress

نغت nghót *m.* obedience

نغتل nghutól *transitive* ☞

نغته nghóta *f. dialect* ☞ نغوته

نغد naghd ☞ نغده پیسه نقد ready cash

نغده nághda *f.* ready cash

نغدي naghdí ☞ نغدي روپی، نغدي پیسي نقدي ready cash, ready money نغدي پیسي کول to sell for cash

نغر nghar *m.* absorption (of water) نغر کول to absorb (water) نغر کیدل to be absorbed (of water)

نغرتل nghərtól *transitive* ☞ نغرل

نغرښت nghərãkht *m.* swallowing

نغرل nghəról *transitive* [*present:* نغري *past:* و یې نغره] 1 to eat; swallow food 2 to swallow, gulp *idiom* وخوره او ونغره یوه خبره ده Six of one, half a dozen of the other.

نغری ngharáj *m.* 1 hearth, fireplace; heater د پرنګي نغری iron stove برقي نغری electric hot-plate 2 brazier 3 tripod; three-legged pot-stand *idiom* د نغري خاندان a noble and distinguished family (among the Waziri)

نغردل nghərdól *transitive* ☞ نغرل

نغرښت nghəerãkht *m.* ☞ نغښت [1]

نغړندځی nəghṛóndzaj *m.* pine nut

نغز nagghz beautiful

نغښت nghãkht *m.* 1 turning, laying 2 roll, bundle (e.g., of paper)

نغښت nghãkht take whole, all at once, in entirety

نغښتل nghãkhtól *transitive* [*present:* نغاړي *past:* و یې نغښت] 1 to twist, twirl 2 to roll up, wrap; turn, turn off; roll 3 to swaddle, entwine 4 to become enveloped by 5 to coat with, cover 6 to wrap up in ځان په... کښي رانغښنبل to wrap oneself up in ..., get wrapped in ... 7 to dress up in some uniform 8 to avoid, shun, evade

نغلاند naghlãnd nghlãnd 1 hungry 2 insatiable, voracious 3 greedy, grasping; self-interested; rapacious

نغلاند سترګی naghlãndstórgaj greedy, insatiable, grasping

نغلاندی [1] naghlãndaj *m.* 1 glutton 2 greedy and grasping person

نغلاندی [2] naghlãndí *f. plural of* نغلاند

نغلاندی nghalãnde *feminine of* نغلاندی [1]

نغلو naghlú Naghlu (settlement)

نغم [1] naghóm *m.* 1 *military* mine نغم چول to explode a mine 2 undermining نغم کښل to sap, undermine 3 tunnel *idiom* د مخکي په نغم کښني اوبه ببول to be quick on the uptake, be intelligent, be deft

نغم [2] ngham *m.* metal-cutting shapes, snips

نغمه naghmá *f. Arabic* [*plural:* نغمې nagmé *Arabic plural:* نغمات naghmãt] 1 motif, melody; tune; song نغمي ویل to sing, entone a melody 2 *proper name* Naghma

نغمه خوان naghmakhãn *m.* نغمه سرا nagmasará *m.* singer

نغن nghón *f.* naghón [*plural:* نغني nghãni] 1 wheat bread 2 skillet bread

نغند [1] nógənd *m.* 1 loss, damage 2 oppression نغند ور رسول a to inflict damage, cause loss b to oppress

نغند [2] nghand *m.* shortbread

نغی nughánaj 1 labeled, tagged 2 disgraced

نه غواړي nãghvāṛi *vice*

نغوتل nghotól nghutól [*present:* نغوړي *past:* و یې نغوت] 1 to listen to, obey, heed 2 to take advice, be obedient 3 to give directions

نغوته nghóta nghúta *f.* 1 obedience 2 sign, indication 3 advice

نغوره nghóra *f.* boiling, cooking (food)

نغور nghoṛ *m.* fine (monetary)

نغوږ nghog nghugh *present stem of* نغوتل

نغول nghol *m.* 1 drain gutter 2 drainage ditch

نغی [1] núghaj *m.* 1 sign, mark, label, brand 2 mark of shame 3 cutting off, amputation (of an ear, nose, as a form of punishment) نغی اینودل a to single out, mark; label, brand

نغی [2] nugháj ☞ نغی [1]

نفاس nifás *m.* 1 childbirth, parturition 2 postnatal period

نفاست nafasát *m. Arabic* 1 elegance, grace 2 fineness, delicacy په نفاست سره very delicately 3 good quality; high quality, excellent quality 4 luxury

نفاق nifāk *m. Arabic* 1 discord, quarrels, fueds 2 hypocrisy, pretense, sham

نفت naft *m. plural* oil, petroleum د نفتو چيني petroleum deposits, oil-bearing regions د نفتو لوله oil pipeline د نفتو تصفيه petroleum refinement

نفت لرونکی naft larúnkaj نفتي naftí *adjective* oil, petroleum نفتي لرونکي منابع petroleum deposits

نفر nafár *m. Arabic* 1 man, person, human being 2 *numerative classifier used when counting people* لس نفره ten men 3 servant نفر خدمت nafár-i orderly 4 groom, stablehand

نفرت nafrát *m. Arabic* aversion; loathing; indignation نفرت پارول to cause aversion نفرت کول دچا څخه to nurse an aversion toward someone د نفرت په سترګه چا ته کتل to abhor, have an aversion to someone تر مينځ يي نفرت واقع په نفرت ويل to speak with indignation دئ They do not get along.

نفره [1] nafára *used with numerals* پنځه نفره five men; of five men

نفره [2] nafára *short plural of* نفر

نفري nafarí *m. plural* 1 persons, people 2 *military* troops, enlisted personnel د پوليسو نفري police

نفرين nafrín *m. Arabic* 1 curse نفرين کول to curse 2 swearing, abusive language 3 aversion; horror, disgust

نفس [1] nafás *m. Arabic* 1 breathing نفس يي والوت He expired. نفس ختل a to breathe one's last, die b to be at the end of one's strength c to freeze on the spot, die of fright نفس شړل، نفس وهل to breathe heavily, gasp for breath نفس په غاښن نيول to be wracked with pain 2 instant, moment

نفس [2] nafs *m. Arabic* [*plural:* نفسونه nafsúna *Arabic plural:* نفوس nufús] 1 soul, spirit د نفس ګرانښت spiritual purity د نفس پاکوالی egoism پر هر چا خپل نفس ګران وي Charity begins at home. 2 essence, being 3 personality 4 lust, sensual desire نفس وژل to mortify the flesh 5 passion 6 vice 7 hate 8 sperm 9 male sexual organ

نفساني nafsāní *Arabic* 1 sensual, pertaining to the senses 2 mercenary نفساني مقاصد mercenary goals

نفسانيات nafsānaiját *m. Arabic plural* 1 sensitivity; passion 2 lust 3 wrath 4 luxury

نفس کش nafaskásh نفس کښ nafaskákh breathing

نفسي nafsí *Arabic* 1 ☞ نفساني 2 mental, psychological, psychic نفسي کيفيت mental calm, tranquility نفسي خاطر جمعي mental condition نفسي امراض psychic illnesses نفسي علاج psychotherapy 3 egoistic, self-centered

نفسيات nafsiját *m. plural* psychology; state of mind, psyche

نفسياتي nafsijātí mental; psychological

نفسيت nafsiját *m.* subjectivity

نفط naft *m. plural* ☞ نفت

نفطلين naftalín *m. Arabic* naphthalene

نفع náf *f.* náf'a *Arabic* 1 favor; advantage 2 profit خالصه نفع pure profit

نفع دوست naf'dóst *m.* money-grubber

نفع و ضرر naf'-u-zarár *m.* profit and loss

نفعه náf'a *f.* ☞ نفع د يوه کاره څخه نفعه اخيستل to derive profit نفعه لرل a to receive profit b to gain, profit نفعه کول to have an advantage, have a benefit, a gain

نفقه nafaká *f. Arabic* 1 means of subsistence د نفقي وسيلي means of subsistence 2 expenses for food; living expenses د حلال کسب honest wages 3 *law* alimony, maintenance نفقه

نفل nafl *m. Arabic* 1 gift, donation 2 supplementary prayers

نفوذ nufúz *m. Arabic* 1 influence, authority د نفوذ څښتن an influential man د نفوذ لاندي نيول to obtain influence نفوذ پيدا کول to bring under one's influence 2 penetration په يو شي کښي نفوذ کول to penetrate into something

نفوذي nufuzí 1 influential, authoritative 2 passing, allowing to penetrate, allowing to pass (e.g., water)

نفوس nufús *m. Arabic plural* 1 *of* نفس [2] 2 population, inhabitants د نفوسو ډېرښت repopulation د نفوسو اکثريت the growth of population د نفوسو احصائيه census enumeration

نفوس شماري nufusshumārí *f.* census enumeration

نفي [1] nafí *f. Arabic* 1 negation د نفي ادات negative particle په نفي کېني سرخوځول to shake the head in negation 2 refusal 3 banishment; exile نفي کول a to deny b to banish; exile

نفي [2] nafí *Arabic* rejected, turned away

نفير nafír *m. Arabic* copper pipe

نفيس nafís *Arabic* elegant, fine; beautiful; lovely نفيسه صنايع fine arts نفيس معادن precious stones

نفيسي nafisí precious

نفيه nafijá *f. Arabic singular of* نفي [2]

نفئي nafjí *Arabic* negative

نقاب niķáb *m. Arabic* 1 shawl, veil 2 visor

نقاد naķķád *Arabic* 1 *m.* .1 critic 1.2 carping man, captious man 2 critical 2.2 carping, captious

نقادي naķķadí *f.* 1 criticism په شعر او ادب کښي نقادي literary criticism 2 carping attitude, captious attitude

نقارچي naķarchí *m.* ☞ نغارچي

نقاره naķará *f.* naķķará *Arabic* kettledrums

نقاش naķķásh *m. Arabic* 1 painter, artist, sculptor 2 draftsman 3 cartographer

نقاش خانه naķķāshkhāná *f.* art gallery, picture gallery

نقاشي naķķāshí *f.* painting, art دبوالي نقاشي murals, frescoes painting نقاشي کول *compound verb* to be painted; have a picture painted

نقاضت naķāzát *m. Arabic* quarrel; enmity د چا سره نقاضت شروع کول to start a quarrel with someone

نقاط niķát *m. Arabic plural of* نقطه نظامي نقاط military installations

نقاهت naķāhát *m. Arabic* recovery, convalescence

نقائص naķāís *m. Arabic plural* نقايص naķājís *m. plural of* نقيصه

نقائض naķāíz *m. Arabic plural* نقايض naķājíz *masculine plural of* نقيضه

نقب naḳb *m.* *Arabic* **1** *military* mine نقب اچول، نقب غورځول to lay mines, mine **2** sapping; underground trenching

نقب اچوونکی بېړی naḳb achavúnkaj torpedo boat

نقب اخیستونکی بېړی naḳb akhistúnkaj نقب اخیستونکی minesweeper

نقب پاکوونکی بېړی naḳb pākavúnkaj نقب پاکوونکی minesweeper

نقب پران naḳbparán **1** *adjective* explosive; mine **2** sapper's (of troops)

نقب ټوپوونکی naḳb ṭopavúnkaj ☞ نقب اخیستونکی

نقب زن naḳbzán *m.* **1** minelayer, sapper **2** thief operating by tunneling; burglar; thug

نقب زني naḳbzaní *f.* **1** undermining, tunneling; mining **2** theft effected by tunneling; theft by breaking and entering

نقبي naḳbí **1** *adjective military* mine نقبي میدانونه minefields **2** underground, subterranean

نقد naḳd *Arabic* **1** *m.* cash **2** *adjective* cash (of money) په نقد ډول on a cash basis, for cash, on a cash terms

نقداً náḳdán *Arabic* for cash, on a cash account

نقد و جنس naḳd-u-dzhíns *m.* money and goods

نقدي naḳdí *Arabic* **1** *adjective* cash (of money) **2** *f.* cash resources, cash on hand نقدي پلورنه cash sale

نقرائي nuḳrají *adjective* **1** silver **2** white (of an animal's coat)

نقرس niḳrís *m.* *Arabic medicine* arthritis; gout

نقره nuḳrá *f.* *Arabic* **1** silver **2** silver coin; silver money

نقرئي nuḳrají ☞ نقرائي

نقش naḳsh **1** *m.* *Arabic* [*plural:* نقشونه naḳshúna *plural:* نقوش nuḳúsh] .**1** portrayal; drawing **1.2** pattern; illustration د نقش کاغذ wallpaper **1.3** map; terrain map **2** *predicative* drawn; portrayed نقش کول *compound verb* to draw, illustrate *idiom* په زړه کښي نقش کول *compound verb* to learn by heart, memorize, master نقش کېدل *compound verb* to impress itself upon په مغزو کښي نقش کېدل to keep in one's memory

نقش بندي naḳshbandí **1** *f.* pattern **2** *f.* embroidery **3** *f.* decoration **4** *m. religion* Nakshabandi (member of an order of dervishes)

نقش بندیه naḳshbandijá *f.* Nakshabandi (an order of dervishes)

نقش کاري naḳshkārí *f.* embroidery نقش کاري کول to be engaged in embroidery

نقش و نگار naḳsh-u-nigár ☞ نقش

نقشه naḳshá *f.* *Arabic* **1** map په نقشه کښي on a map نقشه کول *compound verb* to plot, draw on a map نقشه کېدل *compound verb* to be plotted on a map **2** drawing, sketch, blueprint د ... نقشه ترل a to draw, conceive, imagine **3** draft plan, schematic drawing **4** plan پنځه کلني نقشه five-year plan نقشه ایستل to draw up a plan نقشې جوړول to construct a plan **5** model

نقشه کښ naḳshakásh *m.* ☞ نقشه کښي

نقشه کشي naḳshakashí *f.* cartography

نقشه کښ naḳshakáḳh *m.* **1** cartographer **2** draftsman

نقشي naḳshí¹ drawn, patterned

نقشي naḳshé² *plural of* نقشه

نقص naḳs *m.* *Arabic* **1** shortcoming, defect, deficiency نقص اصلاح کول to correct defects **2** harm, detriment, loss چا ته نقص رسول to inflict damage on someone نقص کول to suffer loss, bear a loss د فایدې پر ځای نقص اخیستل to suffer a loss instead of making a profit **3** shortage, lack **4** error, mistake

نقصان nuḳsán *m.* *Arabic* **1** ☞ نقص 1, 2 په نقصان خرڅول to sell at a loss نقصان کېدل *compound verb* to be damaged, be spoiled **2** *colloquial* miscarriage, spontaneous abortion

نقصان دار nuḳsāndár نقصان مند nuḳsānmánd **1** harmful, detrimental **2** faulty **3** defective **4** crippled, physically handicapped **5** discredited **6** wasteful, unprofitable

نقصاني nuḳsāní **1** ☞ نقصان دار **2** *colloquial* having had a miscarriage

نقص لرونکی naḳs larúnkaj ☞ نقصان دار 1-4

نقض naḳz *m.* *Arabic* **1** destruction, annihilation; devastation **2** cancellation, liquidation **3** dissolution

نقضول naḳzavól *denominative, transitive* [*past:* نقض یې کړ] **1** to violate قانون نقضول to violate the law, break the law **2** to cancel, liquidate **3** to dissolve

نقط nuḳát *m.* *Arabic plural of* نقطه

نقطه nuḳtá *f.* *Arabic* [*plural:* نقطي nuḳté *Arabic plural:* نقط nuḳát *plural:* نقاط niḳát] **1** point د نبان نقطه point of view د نظر نقطه *military* reference point په نقطه by points, point by point **2** *grammar* period **3** question د ایشېدو نقطه boiling point

نقطهٔ نظر nuḳtá-ji-nazár *f.* point of view د اقتصاد له نقطه نظره from an economic point of view, in an economic sense

نقل naḳl¹ *m.* *Arabic* **1** transfer; move (e.g., of property, equipment) **2** transportation; transporting د مالونو نقل transportation of cargoes **3** conveyance; transference **4** tradition; legend **5** copy **6** copying نقل کول *compound verb* ☞ نقلول a نقل ورکول نقلبدل *compound verb* ☞ to transport (cargo) b to transfer

نقل nuḳl² *m. plural* **1** nukl (sugared fruits); sweets crushed in wine **2** something pleasant, treat

نقلاً náḳlán *Arabic* according to tradition, according to legend

نقل پذیر naḳlpazír *regional* moveable; portable; demountable and transportable

نقلچي naḳlchí *m.* storyteller, folktale narrator

نقل کوونکی naḳl kavúnkaj *m.* ferryman, boatman

نقل گیر naḳlgír *adjective* copy; copying نقل گیر کاغذ copying paper; carbon paper

نقلول naḳlavól *denominative, transitive* [*past:* نقل یې کړ] **1** to transfer; transport (e.g., property) **2** to convey **3** to move مسافر نقلول to carry passengers **4** to resettle **5** to relate, narrate کټ مټ نقلول to transmit exactly **6** to copy

نقلي naḳlí *Arabic* **1** traditional; based on tradition, based on legend **2** copied **3** *adjective* narrative نقلي انشا narration **4** transport, relation to transport **5** fictitious; legendary نقلي قول *grammar* indirect object

نقليات naḳlijā́t *m. Arabic plural* **1** *of* نقليه² **2** transport, transportation, conveyance **3** tradition; legend

نقلياتي naḳlijatí transport, pertaining to transport or conveyance

نقلبدل naḳledә́l *denominative, intransitive* [*past:* نقل شو] **1** to be transported, be conveyed (e.g., of property, equipment) **2** to be transferred, be carried from one place to another **3** to be resettled **4** to be narrated **5** to be copied

نقليه naḳlijá *Arabic* **1** *feminine and plural of* نقلي transport وسيله نقليه transport equipment **2** *f.* [*m. plural:* نقليات naḳlijā́t] **.1** transport د موټرو نقليه automotive transport مصرف نقليي freight **2.2** transport services **2.3** *military* نقليه قطار train; transports خوراكي نقليه food supply train **2.4** payment for shipping, fees for freight

نقوش nuḳúsh *m. Arabic plural of* نقش

نقيب naḳíb *m. Arabic* [*plural:* نقيبان naḳibā́n *Arabic plural:* نقبا nuḳabā́] **1** leader **2** nakib (the chief of a tribe or a community; the chief of the Sayyids, the spiritual head of a guild of craftsmen)

نقيصه naḳisá *f. Arabic* [*plural:* نقيصي naḳisé *Arabic plural:* نقائص naḳāís] deficiency, shortcoming; flaw, blemish, defect نقيصه لیري کول a to eradicate a defect **b** to eliminate a deficiency

نقيض naḳíz *Arabic* **1** contradictory; opposing د یو شي سره نقيض contradicting something **2** *m.* **.1** enemy, foe **2.2** antonym **2.3** opposition, contrast; contradiction

نقيضه naḳizá *f. Arabic* [*plural:* نقيضي naḳizé *Arabic plural:* نقائض naḳāíz] contradiction

نکات nikā́t *m. Arabic plural of* نکته

نکاح nikā́ *f.* nikā́h *Arabic* **1** matrimony, wedlock; marriage, nuptials د نکاح عقد proxy for a father د نکاح پلار the contraction of marriage نکاح کول a to get married, enter wedlock **b** *compound verb* to take as wife په نکاح اخیستل to wed, go through the marriage cermony یوه ښځه یي په نکاح واخیسته He got married. نکاح ترل to give (a daughter) in marriage په نکاح ورکول to go through the wedding ceremony, complete the wedding ceremony **2** betrothal

نکاحانه nikāhāná *f. religion* gratuity given to a mullah for performing the marriage ceremony

نکاحنامه، نکاح نامه nikāhnāmá *f.* marriage contract

نکاحوال nikāhvál *m.* man who is celebrating his wedding

نکاراگوا nikārāguá *f.* Nicaragua

نکاره¹ nakārá ☞ ناکار *and* ناکاره

نکاره² nukā́ra *f.* ☞ نوکاره

نکاري nukā́ri *plural of* نکاره² نکاري کول to scratch

نکان nukā́n *Western plural of* نوک

نکبت nakbát *m. Arabic* ill luck, misfortune; reversal of fortune; failure

نکته nuktá *f. Arabic* [*plural:* نکتي nukté *Arabic plural:* نکات nikā́t] **1** witticism; witty remark نکته ویل to make a witty address هغه پرله پسي نکات وايي He is always witty. **2** circumstances, moment, consideration نازک نکات delicate circumstances

نکته دان nuktadā́n *m.* wit, witty person

نکته سنج huktasándzh **1.1** witty, apt **1.2** penetrating **2** *m.* expert, connoisseur

نکته گیر nuktagír **1** carping, captious **2** *m.* **.1** carping person, pedant **2.2** critic

نکته گیري nuktagirí *f.* **1** faultfinder **2** critic نکته گیري کول a to find fault, carp at **b** to criticize

نکټائي nikṭaí *f.* nekṭā́i necktie

نکرۍ nukrә́dzi *f. plural* ☞

نکریزه nukríza *f.* henna-yielding plant

نکریزي nakrízi *f. plural Eastern* henna د نکریزو شپه the eve of Eid or wedding (when women and children paint their hands with henna) په نکریزو لاسونه سره کول to dye the hands with henna

نه کړ nákәṛ *vice*

نه کړي nákṛi *vice* نه کړي¹

نکړی nákṛaj *Eastern* نکړی شوم I cannot.

نه کړې nákṛe *vice* نه کړې³

نه کړئ nákṛәj *vice* نه کړئ⁴

ناکس nakás ☞ ناکس

نکل nikál *m. plural* nickel

نکل nákә́l *m.* ☞ نقل¹

نکلاوو naklāvú *m.* storyteller, narrator of folktales

نکل کاري nikalkārí *f.* nickel plating نکل کاري کول *compound verb* to nickel-plate

نکلي naklí *m.* ☞ نقلچي

نکول nukúl *m. Arabic* **1** *trade* nonexecution, refusal to execute or pay something **2** protest of a promissary note **3** *law* refusal to give evidence

نه کوي nákavi *vice* نه کوي¹

نه کوې nákave *vice* نه کوې²

نه کوئ nákavәj *vice* نکوئ³

نه که náka *vice* نه که⁴

نکهت nakhát *m. Arabic* fragrance, scent

نکی nakáj *m. anatomy* clitoris¹

نه کي náki *vice* نکي²

نه کې náke *vice* نکې³

نه کئ nákәj *vice* نکئ⁴

نکبده nәkedә́ *m. plural* impracticability د نکبدو چاره an impossible matter

نکیر nakír *Arabic* **1** *m.* negation; rejection **2** negating, rejecting

نگ ang *suffix for abstract verbal nouns* غورځنگ a leap, a jump

نگار nigár **1** *m.* **.1** drawing, illustration, picture, portrait, image د خوني نقش او نگار deocration of a room **1.2** *figurative* idol, heathen image **1.3** beauty **2** *combining form* writing نامه نگار journalist; correspondent

نگاره nigāra *f.* **1** beauty **2** loved one

نگوړ ngāṛ *m. plural of* نگوړ

نگاسه ngā́sa *f.* peep, chirp

نگاشی ngā́shaj *m.* hook, stake, peg on a wall (for tethering cattle)

نگاه nigáh *m.* **1** stare, look, glance **2** observation, surveillance, care نگاه کول to look **b** to observe, survey

نگاهبان nigābā́n *m.* keeper, custodian; guard; protector

نگاهباني nigākbāní *f.* **1** custody, guarding, preserving **2** observation, surveillance, care, concern for someone نگاهباني کول **a** to guard, protect **b** to observe, survey

نگبی ngəbáj *m.* ☞ نگوبی

نگر ngar *m.* row, uproar, hubbub (of birds) نگر کول to raise an uproar, create a hubbub (of birds)

نگران nigarā́n *m.* **1** manager, director (of a school) **2** executive officer فني نگران executive officer for technical matters

نگراني nigarāní *f.* **1** observation, scrutiny, surveillance تر نگراني لاندي **a** under scrutiny, under surveillance **b** under the editorship of **c** under the management of **2** close observation, care, concern

نگړه ngaṛá *f. singular of* نگوړه

نگوړی ngaṛé *f. plural of* نگوړی

نگسی ¹ ngə́saj **1** insignificant; contemptible **2** *m.* laughingstock

نگسی ² ngə́se *f.* **1** laughingstock **2** nonentity, nobody

نگښبی ngəḳháj *m.* small braids on both sides of the brow (of women)

نگل ngə́l *transitive* ☞ نړل

نگلی ngə́laj *m.* ngúlaj *dialect* ☞ نگولی

نگوبی ngubáj *m.* front bow of a saddle

نگور ngor *f. Eastern* ☞ نږور

نگوړ ngoṛ *tautological with* سور نگوړ دغه سور نگوړ پاتي دی This stew is completely cold.

نگوړی ngóṛaj *m.* cucumber

نگوس ngos *m.* **1** cliche **2** photo, snapshot

نگوښ nguḳh *m.* lameness

نگوښبل nguḳhə́l *intransitive* ☞ نگوښبدل

نگوښبول nguḳhavə́l *transitive [past:* و یې نگوښباوه] to make lame

نگوښبدل nguḳhedə́l *intransitive [present:* نگوښبی *past:* ونگوښبد] to limp پنبه یې ژوبله شوې، نگوښبي He has injured his leg and is limping.

نگول ngavúl *transitive dialect* ☞ نړول

نگولی ngólaj ngvə́laj *m.* **1** food, eatables, eats; thick soup; anything that is eaten with bread; meat, fish, milk products, vegetables ډوډی دي له نگولی سره خوړلي ده که سپوره؟ Did you eat only bread or did you have other food? **2** snack

نگونسر nigunsár ☞ سرنگون

نگونی ngúnaj *m.* cupped hand

نگه ¹ nigáh *m.* ☞ نگاه

نگه ² nagá *f. singular of* نوگ

نگهبان nigahbā́n *m.* ☞ نگاهبان

نگهداشت nigahdā́sht *m.* **1** guarding, preservation **2** conservation, saving

نگی ngaj *m.* sneeze, sneezing ☞ نړی ¹

نگېرل ngerə́l *transitive [past:* و یې نگېرل] to think, suppose, imagine

نگین nigín *m.* **1** stone set in a signet ring **2** bezel of the setting (in a signet ring, for the precious stone) **3** ring; signet ring; seal

نگېندي ngénde *Eastern plural of* نگور

نل nal *m. [plural:* نلونه nalúna *plural:* نلان nalā́n] **1** reed; mountain rush, *Arundo donax* د نلو څنگل reed sprouts **2** *technology* tubing نل نبینیبي glass tubing د اوبو نل *technology* water pipe **3** reed pipe نل وهل to play the reed pipes **4** barrel (of a firearm) **5** chimney pipe (of a stove, samovar)

نلام nilā́m *m. regional* ☞ لیلام

نلپېچ nalpéch *m.* stem of a water pipe with its tubing نل پېچ

نلرل nalarə́l *m. plural* absence, lack, want

نل ساز nalsā́z *m.* **1** tinsmith **2** plumber

نلک nilk *m.* plum

نلکه nalká *f.* نلکی nalkə́j *f.* water pipe, water supply pipe

نلگس nalgís *m.* ☞ نرگس

نلگی nalgáj *m.* **1** tubing **2** *anatomy* trachea

نله ¹ nalá *f.* tube, pipe

نله ² nulá nalá *anatomy* ureter

نلی ¹ naláj *m.* **1** femur **2** arm bone; humerus

نلی ² naləj *f.* **1** pipe, tubing **2** stem and tubing of a water pipe (for smoking) **3** empty cartridge **4** bobbin, spool

نلی ³ nalé *plural of* نله ¹,²

نلی ⁴ nalí *plural of* نلی ¹

نم ¹ nam **1** *m.* moisture; liquid **2** wet; moist, damp نم کول to wet, make moist نم کېدل to become moist, become saturated with moisture

نم ² nəm *ordinal numeral* ninth *vice* نهم

نما ¹ namā́ *f. Arabic* growth, growing

نما ² numā́ namā́ **1** *m.* indicator **2** *combining form* indicating something قطب نما compass

نمائڅل nmādzə́l *transitive* ☞ نمانځل

نمائځنه nmādzə́na *f.* ☞ نمانځنه

نماړی nmā́ṛaj *m.* double stitch

نماړستن nmāṛistə́n *f. [plural:* نماړستني nmāṛistə́ni] large needle

نماز namā́z *m.* namaz (worship, prayer, obeisance), Islamic form of prayer

نمازخفتن namāzkhuftán *m. regional* prayer before sleep

نمازل nmāzə́l *transitive* ☞ نمانځل

نمازنه nmāzə́na *f.* ☞ نمانځنه

نمازیگر namāzigár *m. dialect* ☞ مازدیگر

نماسپخین nmāspḳhín *m.* ☞ مازپنین

نماست nmāst *dialect* ☞ ملاست

نماښام nmāḳhā́m *m. Eastern* **1** evening prayer **2** evening په لاره نماښام کېني را باندي نمابنام شو Evening found me on my way.

نمانځي nmāndzguzár ☞ نمائڅي

نمانځل nmāndzə́l *transitive [past:* و یې نمانځه] **1** to raise, nourish, foster, bring up **2** to support, help **3** to praise; extoll; honor **4** to caress

نمانځنه nmāndzə́na f. **1** honor, respect, esteem د چا د نمانځني د پاره in honor of someone **2** nourishing, raising **3** praise دیو کار ډېر نمانځنه کول to praise, lavishly priase something

نمانځوني nmāndzúnaj devout, pious

نمانځه nmāndzə́ indirect singular of نمونځ

نمانځي nmāndzí **1** praying, peforming namaz **2** devout, pious **3** pure, undefiled

نمايان numājā́n **1** evident, apparent **2** obvious, noticeable **3** prominent

نمايش numājísh m. **1** demonstration **2** parade عسكري نمايش military parade **3** presentation; showing, demonstration, making a demonstration, demonstrating د نمايش اطاق exhibition hall **4** showing (a movie) **5** external appearance

نمايشگاه numājishgā́ m. & f. numājishgáh exhibit

نمايشي numājishí **1** adjective spectacle, show **2** ostentatious; revealing **3** demonstration, pertaining to a demonstration

نمائينت numājíќht m. ☞ نمايش

نمايندگي numājandagí f. ☞ نماينده گي

نماينده¹ numājandá m. namājandá **1** representative دائمي نماينده permanent representative د پارلمان نماينده parliamentary representative **2** agent (of a firm)

نماينده² numājandá namājandá representative (female)

نماينده گي numājandagí f. namājandagí f. **1** representation د نماينده گي parliamentarism د چا په نماينده گي حكومت by delagation, in the capacity of someone's representative د چا نماينده گي کول a to represent someone **b** figurative to express, utter something د اضطراب نماينده گي کول to express concern, worry **2** agency; representation; branch (e.g., of a bank)

نيمايه nimājə́ m. ☞

نمبر nambár m. number idiom د اول نمبر ناكامي a big mistake

نمبړى nambəráj m. building up of the soil for melon cultivation

نمبور nambúr m. tunnel or main conduit of a kariz or native Afghan irrigation system

نمبورچي namburchí m. man working in a kariz or native Afghan irrigation system

نمدژن namdzhə́n moist, damp, wet

نمڅى nimtsáj m. ☞ نيمڅى

نمد¹ namád m. felt (strip); felt (piece)

نمد² numd dialect ☞ لوند

نمدار namdā́r ☞ نمدژن

نمدبل namdabál m. ☞ لندبل

نمدساز namadsā́z m. نمد مال namadmā́l m. felt fuller, maker of large felt pieces

نمدوالى numdvā́laj m. dialect ☞ لندوالى

نمر nmar m. Eastern sun د نمر روښنائي sunlight د نمر تېزوالى hot sun د نمر په شان بنكاره The sun was at its zenith. idiom نمر په سر راغلئ و It is as clear as God's day. لمر

نمر پربوآتيز nmarprevātíz western

نمر پربواته nmarprevātə́ m. Eastern **1** singular & plural sunset **2** the West

نمرخاته nmartsrə́k m. نمرخوک nmārkhātə́ m. Eastern **1.1** singular & plural sunrise **1.2** the East **2** from sunrise

نمرختيز nmarkhatíz eastern

نمرگل nmargúl m. sunflower

نمر مخى nmarə́khaj beautiful

نمره numrá f. **1** number **2** degree

نمره زني numrazaní f. numeration, numbering

نمري nmarí m. plural Eastern clothing

نمرېبل nmərehə́l transitive [past: و يې نمرېبل] to wash dishes, rinse dishes

نمر numə́ŗ dialect before, previously; earlier

نمړل nmaŗə́l [past: و يې نمړل] to eat, swallow

نمړى¹ nmaŗə́j f. **1** piece of food; food نمړى كول to eat, swallow **2** piece, slice نمړى كول to cut in bits, cut in little pieces; divide into portions يوه نمړى ډوډۍ وركئ Give him a piece of bread. **3** bread idiom د اور نمړى كېدل to burn up; be a victim of fire يوه غوره They fell heir to a fat sum. نمړى ور برابره شوه

نمړى² numə́ŗaj ☞ نومړى²

نمزدک nmazdə́k m. regional mosque

نمستي namasté f. namaste (Hindu greeting)

نمسى¹ nmasáj m. [plural: نمسي nmasí plural: نمسيان nmasijā́n] Eastern grandson

نمسى² nmasə́j f. [plural: نمسى nmasə́j plural: نمسياني nmasijā́ne] Eastern granddaughter

نمعلوم nam'alúm dialect ☞ نا معلوم

نمك namák m. د هغه دونه نمكونه مو خوړلي دي We have so often enjoyed his hospitality.

نمک حرام namakharā́m **1.1** unfaithful; ungrateful; base **1.2** traitorous, perfidious **2** m. traitor, betrayer

نمک حرامي namakharā́mi f. ، نمكحرامي **1** baseness, lowness; ingratitude **2** betrayal, treason, perfidy نمكحرامي كول a to act basely; repay with ingratitude **b** to betray, commit perfidy

نمک حلال namakhalā́l **1** sincere; devoted; true, faithful **2** decent, honest **3** loyal **4** grateful, thankful

نمک حلالي namakhalālí f. **1** sincerity; devotion; faithfulness **2** decency, honesty **3** loyalty **4** gratitude, thankfulness نمک حلالي كول a to display faithfulness **b** to be thankful, be grateful

نمكسار namaksā́r m. saline soil

نمكين namkín namakín **1** salty **2** witty

نمله namla f. sweat cloth

نمناک namnā́k ☞ نمجن

نمناكي namnākí f. dampness, moisture

نمنځ nmandz m. respect, esteem, deference په ډېر نمنځ ويل to speak very deferentially

نمنځل nmandzə́l transitive ☞ نمانځل

نمنځنه nmandzə́na f. **1** honoring **2** praise, euology; glorification

نمنځونه nmandzúna plural ☞ نمونځ

نمو numúv *m.* namv *Arabic* growth, development د توت وني ډېر ښه نمو پکښني کوي The mulberry tree grows very well there.

نمود namúd *m.* namúd **1** aspect, appearance **2** indicator, indication **3** show, display د ده نمود دپاره **a** for show, ostentatious **b** for the sake of appearances نمود کول to display, demonstrate

نمودار namudár **1.1** apparent, noticeable, obvious **1.2** prominent **2** [*plural:* نموداران namudārán] **.1** model, specimen **2.2** indicator, indication **2.3** symbol

نموداري *f.* namudārí show, display; showing off نموداري کول to stand out (for), make a mark (by)

نمول nmugól *transitive dialect* [*past:* وي نمورده] to comb (the hair)

نمندز nmundz *m.* [*plural:* نمنځونه nmandzúna *plural:* نمونځونه nmundzúna] namaz (Muslim form of prayer), prayer

نمونوي namunaví model, exemplary نمونوي کول to make an example

نمونه¹ namuná *f.* **1** model, example د نموني په ډول in the form of, as a model, as an example د نموني دپاره for example ښوونځی a model school **2** specimen, sample

نمونه² namuná placenta, afterbirth

نمونه³ numúna *plural Western vice* نومونه

نمونیا namuniā́ inflammation of the lungs, pneumonia نمونیا یې شوې ده He contracted pneumonia.

نمه nə́ma *feminine of* نم² نمه میاشت the ninth month

نمي namí *f.* dampness, moisture

نن nən **1** today, now نن شپه tonight نن پرون in our time; lately; these days نن او صبا in recent days نن وي که سبا eigther today or tomorrow **2** *attributive, indeclinable* **.1** as of today, nowadays په نن وخت current affairs د نن ورځي کارونه **2.2** our times نن ورغ at the present time **3** د نن څخه څلور قرنه دمخه four hundred years ago نن سبا کول on that very day تر ننه پوري to drag out, delay, engage in red tape

ننباسي nə́nabāsi *present tense of* ننه ایستل

ننځره nandzṛə́ *m. plural* tar, pitch

نونڅه nunátsa *f.* نونڅه .

ننڅه ننڅه nunətsá-nunətsá to continue to be sick; fail to recover

نداپ nandā́p *m. dialect*

ندارتون nəndārtún *m.* **1** exhibit **2** spectacle, show

ندارچي¹ nəndārchí *m.* **1** spectator, fan **2** [*plural:* ندارچیان nəndārchijā́n] spectators, the audience

ندارچۍ² nəndārchə́j *f.* spectator (female)

ندارځی nəndā́rdzáj *m.* **1** spectacle, show **2** theater

ندارغالی nəndārghā́laj *m.* theater

ندارکړونی nəndārkṛúnaj *m.* ¹

ندارہ nəndārá *f.* **1** spectacle; presentation; show; stage production ندارہ ورکول to give a presentation ندارۍ ښودل to go on stage **2** wedding celebration; merriment **3** survey, view ندارہ کول **a** to admire د سین ندارہ کوي He enjoys the river. **b** to make merry (at a wedding) **c** *compound verb* to look at, watch سپورتي مسابقات ندارہ کول to watch sporting events د فلمو ندارہ کول to attend a film, watch a movie

ندرور nəndrór *f.* ندرور

نندره nandrá *f.* collection of goods (etc., on the part of the relatives on the wedding day as gifts to the groom) نندره ټولول، نندره کول to collect goods نندره ورکول to give money for the wedding (of the family, clan)

ننزړہ nanzṛə́ tar, pitch

ننگور nəngór *f. dialect* نبرور

نن سبا، نن صبا nən-sabā́ nən-sabā́ today and tomorrow; recently

ننکه nanə́ka *f.* pimple, acne

ننکی nənakə́j *f.* **1** pockmark; smallpox **2** pimples, acne

ننگ nang *m.* **1** ننگه¹ خپل ننگ او ناموس گټل to consider as a matter of honor دا د ننگ خبره ده This is a matter of honor. د وطن په ننگ ساتنه ننگ خورل to display valor in defense of the fatherland ننگ ورل to ask for help, seek help from someone **2** modesty **3** shame, disgrace

ننگاڼی nangā́ṇaj *m.* span

ننگاوه nangāvə́ *imperfective of* ننگول

ننگرهار nangrahā́r nəngarhā́r *m.* **1** Nangrahar (province) **2** *history* Nangrahar

ننگرهاری nəngrahārə́j nəngarhārə́j **1** *adjective* Nangrahar, Nangraharian **2** *m.* inhabitant of Nangrahar, Nangraharian (person)

ننگړی nangṛə́j رنگړی

ننگړی شپه nangṛə́j shpa *m.* midnight

ننگبنی nəngakhā́j *m.* dam, weir (of wood, turf)

ننگک nanagák pure, unadulterated

ننگو nangú *m.* ننگانی

ننگوړی nangúṛaj *m.* small-fruited pomegranate

ننگول nangavól *transitive* [*past:* وي ننگاوه] to summon to help, summon to give protection; request patronage

ننگوئ¹ nangavóləj *past participle of* ننگول

نگولی² nangólaj *m. dialect* نگولی

ننگ و ناموس nang-u-nāmús *m.* honor, reputation, good name

ننگه¹ nánga *f.* **1** sense of honor, honor, reputation دی پر ننگه تینگ و He stood up for his honor. **2** protection, support; patronage ننگه ورل to ask protection, ask assistance of someone, seek protection from someone **3** courage, bravery, valor ننگه کول ، خپله ننگه پر ځای کول **a** to defend, give support; offer patronage to **b** to show courage, display valor, demonstrate courage

ننگه² nangá *f.* filtration

ننگیالی nangjālə́j **1.1** honorable, honest **1.2** responsive, keen, sharp, quick **1.3** brave, valorous, courageous **2** *m.* **.1** protector, patron **2.2** hero, brave man, bold person **2.3** *proper name* Nangjalaj

ننگیالی توب nangjālitób *m.* **1** honor **2** valor, courage, bravery

نننی nənanáj today's, current ننني ورځپاڼه today's paper

ننواته¹ nənavātə́ **1** *m. plural* **.1** entry **1.2** entrance **1.3** visit of the fiancé to the bride-to-be before the wedding **2** *past tense plural of* ننوتل

ننواته 2 nənavắta *f.* ننواتي nənavắte *f. plural* ceremonial ritual soliciting forgiveness or assistance ننواته نيول ننواته كول a to conduct the nenavate ritual b to ask forgiveness c to beseech ته زما ننواته ومنه Help me. Do not refuse me help.

ننوب nənób *m.* 1 evaporation 2 percolation; leakage

ننوت nənavót 1 *past tense of* ننوتل 2 *past tense stem of* ننوتل

ننوتل nənavatəl *intransitive* [*present:* ننوزي *past:* ننوت *past:* ننووت] 1 to enter, go in; drop in ننووت را په خونه He entered the room. 2 to ride in, ride into 3 to penetrate 4 to get into منگور په سوري 5 to visit the bride-to-be كنبي ننووت The snake got into a crack. before the wedding (of the fiancé) 6 to seek asylum with someone 7 to interfere ننوتل په خبرو خلگو to break into a stranger's conversation 8 to enter a house; settle in a house as a wife 9 to shrink (of cloth) 10 *computer science* login, to login

ننواتنه 1 nənavatə́na *f.* ☞ ننواته

ننوتوځی nənavatódzáj *m.* entrance (place)

ننوت وزله nanawət wazlá *f. computer science* input device

ننواتون nanawatū́n *m. computer science* log, log on, logging

ننوتونی nənanatúnaj going in, entering (afoot or otherwise)

نن ورځ nənvrádz 1 *f.* this very day 2 today

نن ورځنی nənvradzanáj 1 present, today's, current 2 contemporary

ننول nənavə́l *transitive* [*past:* وي يې ناوه] to strain; purify, filter, distill

ننونی nənavúnaj *m.* 1 sieve; filter 2 strainer 3 colander

ننوت nə́navot *past tense of* ننوتل

ننه ايستل nənavestə́l *transitive Eastern* ☞ ننويستل

ننه 1 nə́na 1 *separable verb prefix expressing movement into something (stressed in the perfective aspect)* ننه ايستل to lodge, accomodate, put into something 2 *may be written in a truncated form* ننوتل to enter, go in

ننه 2 nə́na ☞ نن

ننه 3 nə́na *f.* internal part د مملكت ونني ته in the interior of the country

ننه ايستل nənaistə́l [*present:* ننه يې يوست *past:* ننه يې باسي] 1 to lodge, put into something 2 to introduce 3 to shove into 4 to include 5 to thrust into 6 to thread 7 to insert, fit into

ننه ايستنه nənaistə́na *f.* ننه ايسته nənaistə́ *m. plural* 1 introduction 2 thrusting, shoving into 3 insertion

ننه باسي nənabắsi *present tense of* ننه ايستل

ننه يستل nənajistə́l *transitive* ☞ ننه ايستل

ننی nanə́j *f. children's speech* rice

ننبدل nənedə́l nanedə́l *intransitive* [*past:* ونند] 1 drip 2 trickle, percolate; flow, flow out, flow through 3 to be strained, be purified, be filtered, be distilled

ننبده nənedə́ *m. plural* 1 percolation; flow 2 straining, purifying, filtration, distillation

ننه ايستل nənajistə́l *transitive* ☞ ننه ايستل

ننه ايستنه nənajistə́na *f.* ☞ ننه ايسته

نړول nanavə́l *transitive* ☞ نړول

نړيدل naṇedə́l *intransitive* ☞ نړيدل

نړيده naṇedə́ *m. plural* destruction

نو 1 nu *m.* [*plural:* نوگان nugä́n] umbilicus, navel *idiom* نوي يې ووت He overstrained himself.

نو 2 nav *m.* [*plural:* نوونه navúna] 1 moisture, dampness, wetness 2 pus

نو 3 no so, so that, consequently, then, and for this reason نو چه a in the event that; if b after, as soon as نو ځکه because, for this reason نو دغه دئ چه ... This is why ... اوس به نو ځو Let's go now. ته به نو نه راځي؟ When will you arrive? ته به نو كله راشي؟ What, you aren't coming? نو زه غولبدلئ يم Well, I certainly was fooled. يې د دغه دي وينا ته هيڅ غوږ ونه نيوه Well, they paid no attention to what he said. ښه نو! Okay! Right!

نو 4 no *oblique of* نه 1 *vice* نهو په نو بجو at nine o'clock

نوا navá *f.* 1 voice; noise 2 song, tune; melody; motif 3 means of existence 4 riches, luxury, plenty

نواب navvä́b nuvvä́b *m. Arabic plural of* نائب 1 nabob, rich man 2 *obsolete* governor 3 grandee, prince 4 *proper name* Nawab

نوآباد navābä́d 1 populated; colonized 2 newly constructed 3 newly acquired (of land)

نوآبادي navābādí *f. regional* settlement, colony

نوابغ navābígh *m. Arabic plural of* نابغه

نوابي navābbí *f.* title of a ruler, grandee, or prince

نواحي navāhí *m. Arabic plural of* ناحيه

نواخت navä́kht *m.* tone, phonation نواخت يو رنگه monotony, quality of being a monotone *idiom* دوی په يوه نواخت نه وي They are not alike.

نواخته navākhtá 1 cultivated, fostered; cherished 2 cared for; given affection

نوادر navādír *m. Arabic plural of* نادر 2

نوار navár *m.* nivár 1 tape; ribbon 2 film ثبت شوئ نوار film with sound track 3 beam (of light)

نواره navārá *f. obsolete* dwelling; populated place نواره كول a to populate, settle b to work, cultivate (as land)

نوار nivär *m.* ☞ نوار

نواره 1 navä́ṛa *f. Eastern* virgin soil

نواره 2 nvä́ṛa *f.* sadness, grief, woe

نواړی 1 nvä́ṛaj *m.* double stitch

نواړی 2 navāṛə́j *f.* 1 top of baggy Middle-Eastern style trousers through which a girdle or sash is passed 2 double stitch

نواړي 3 navä́ṛi *Eastern plural of* نواړه 1

نواړي 4 nvä́ṛi *plural of* نواړه 2

نواز navä́z *combining form* caressing (or similar) مهمان نواز hospitable

نوازش navāzísh *m.* caress, endearment, affectionate address نوازش كول to caress نوازش! *regional* Thanks! You are very nice! *idiom* د نوازش فرمان rescript

نوازش نامه navāzishnāmá f. 1 certificate of merit, certificate of good conduct and progress 2 epistolary your kind letter

نوازنده navāzandá m. musician

نوازي navāzí f. 1 fostering, nuturing 2 favor, grace

نواسه navāsá m. grandson

نواقل navāķíl m. Arabic plural of ناقله 2

نواله navālá f. nivālá 1 gift, present 2 good deed 3 portion, part 4 swallow, mouthful 5 food, portion (of food) 6 agriculture concentrate, concentrated fodder

نواله نزاله nəvála-nəzála f. childhood

نوآموز navāmúz m. 1 novice, beginner 2 pupil, student د نوآموزانو for students نوآموز افراد دپاره recruits

نواميس navāmís m. Arabic plural of ناموس

نواهي navāhí m. Arabic plural of ناهيه

نوائب navaíb m. Arabic plural 1 misfortune, disaster 2 accident

نو بالغ naubālígh attaining majority; adult, grown-up, teenager

نوبت nobát m. naubát Arabic 1 turn, in order of turn په نوبت سره، د نوبت په ترتيب in turn, in order of turn هغه خپل نوبت ته منتظر و He waited his turn. نوبت ورته ورسید His turn came. 2 attack, bout (of fever) 3 flourish, march (music usually played at court of high-placed persons) اركسترا د موسیقی نوبت غږوي The band is playing a march. 4 relief, shift; watch 5 figurative death د کښت او کروندي نوبت crop rotation

نوبت چي، نوبتچي novatchí m. novatchí orderly

نوبت خانه novatkhāná f. guardroom

نوبتي nobatí 1.1 usual, routine, regular نوبتي غونډه regular meeting 1.2 alternating 1.3 watch, pertaining to a watch 2 m. member of a watch

نوبر [1] naubár m. early fruits

نوبر [2] naubár m. trail, tasting (of food) نوبر كتل to taste, try something

نوبه nobá f. naubá Arabic ☞ نوبت

نوبهار naubahāŕ m. poetic early spring

نوت not m. music note

نوتریا nutrijá f. nutria

نوټ noţ m. 1 footnote, observation; note, entry 2 note (diplomatic, musical)

نوټ بك noţbúk m. regional notebook

نوټکۍ nuţakə́j f. pattern

نوټول noţavə́l denominative, transitive [past: نوټ يي کړ] 1 to note, make a note in a notebook 2 to note, mark down 3 to make a mark, notch

نوټه noţá f. diplomacy 1 note 2 memorandum

نوټیشن noţéshán m. notation

نوجن navdzhə́n 1 moist, damp 2 purulent

نوجوان naudzhavā́n m. youth, young man

نوچک nauchák navchák 1 m. .1 dew 1.2 youth 2 new, fresh, just appearing

نوچکه naucháka 1 f. girl 2 feminine singular of نوچک 2

نوڅی [2] nútsaj m. Eastern ☞ نوسی

نوحه nauhá f. navhá Arabic crying, sobbing

نوحه خوان nauhakhā́n m. نوحه گر nauhagár 1 m. mourner 2 mourning

نوحه گره nauhagára f. mourner (female)

نوحه گري nauhagarí f. bewailing

نوخول nukhavə́l transitive [past: و يې نوخاوه] to arouse a strong appetite in someone

نوخیدل nukhedə́l intransitive [past: و نوخید] to feel hunger, get very hungry

نور [1] nur m. Arabic [plural: نورونه nurúna Arabic plural: انوار anvā́r] 1 light, radiance; ray (of light) د سترگو نور a Light of my life! Dear! Beloved! b Little son! (as an affectionate form of address) 2 proper name Nur نور محمد Nur Mohammed

نور [2] nvar m. Eastern sun

نور [3] nor 1.1 other, another نور خوک other persons نور كارونه other matters خو نوري ورځي a few days more په نورو الفاظو کښي in other words نور other, varied, various, sundry 1.2 remaining, the rest, what is left پاته نور مبلغ the remaining sum هلته تېره نوره روځ يي He spent what is left of the day there. 1.3 further دغه These talks مذاکري به د تجارتي روابطو د نور پراخوالي دپاره موجب وگرزي served as a means for further broadening of trade relations. 2 m. usually plural another, different, else د نورو چا د خولو څخه out of the mouths of others 3.1 more, still نور هم still more 3.2 in other respects خه نور داسي، خه نور دغسي او داسي نور and so forth, et cetera idiom هر خه هر خه نور شو And so I am leaving. نور نو زه څم Everything has changed. نور پري نه کیږي Eastern One can go further.

نورالدین nuruddín m. Arabic proper name Nuruddin

نورالله nurullá m. Arabic proper name Nurullah

نوراني nurāní Arabic 1 light, clear 2 radiant, luminous; shining, flashing

نوربیا norbjá continuation follows

نمرپربواته nvarpretvātə́ m. plural ☞ نمرپربواته

نورخرکی nvartsrə́kaj m. dialect 1 kind of snake 2 place in the sun, exposed site

نورزائي nurzājí m. plural ☞ نورزي 1

نورزي nurzí 1 m. plural the Nurzai (tribe) 2 nurzáj m. Nurzaj (tribesman)

نورس navrás newly sprouting; young (e.g., of a tree)

نورستان nuristā́n m. Nuristan

نورستاني nuristāní nuristānáj 1 adjective Nuristanian 2 m. Nuristanian (person)

نورسرخي nvarsurkhí f. Eastern sunrise

نورک nurák m. proper name Nurak

نورکله nórkə́la at another time, another time

نورگل nurgúl m. proper name Nurgul

نورلوستونکی nur lustúnkaj shining; gleaming (e.g., of a beacon)

نورمال normā́l normal, ordinary, usual

نورنمائي nurnumā́i *f.* exposition, exposure

نوروز navrúz *m.* **1** day of the spring equinox **2** Navrus (New Year, March 21) د نوروز مبارکي New Year's greetings **3** *proper name* Nawroz

نوروزي[1] navruzí **1** vernal, spring **2** New Year's, relating to Navruz

نوروزی[2] navruzə́j **1** *feminine singular of* نوروزي[1] **2** *f.* weeping willow

نورول noravə́l *denominative, transitive* [*past:* نوريږ کړ] to change, alter

نوره[1] nóra *f. feminine singular of* نور[3]

نوره[2] núra Little Light (an affectionate form of address) ☞ نور[1]

نوري[1] nvarí *m. plural* ☞ نمري

نوري[2] nóri *feminine plural of* نور[3]

نوریدل noredə́l *denominative, intransitive* [*past:* نور شو] to change, alter د تقدیر لیکل نه نوریږي *proverb literal* What is written by fate does not change. *figuratively* What will be, will be.

نوړز nvaṛə́z *m. Eastern* ☞ مړز

نوړزه nvaṛə́za *f. Eastern* ☞ مړزه

نوړول nuṛavə́l nvaravə́l *transitive* ☞ لوړول[2]

نوړی nvaṛə́j *f.* ☞ نمړی[1]

نوړیدل nuṛedə́l nvaṛedə́l *intransitive* ☞ لوړیدل[2]

نوزاد navzā́d **1** newborn **2** *m.* Navzad (district)

نوزی núzaj *m.* grindstone, whetstone, hone

نوږ nog نوږه nagá *f. m.* [*plural:* ناږه nāgə́ *f. plural:* نږي nagé] **1** pure, unadulterated; real, genuine **2** true, sincere **3** pure, clean, decent نوږیدل ☞ نوږ کېدل ☞ نوږول ☞ نوږ کول[2]

نوږل nugə́l *transitive* ☞ نږل

نوږول[1] nugavə́l *transitive* [*past:* وی نوږاوه] to cause to sneeze

نوږول[2] nogavə́l *denominative, transitive* [*past:* نوږ یې کړ] to clean, cleanse

نوږی[1] nugáj *m.* sneeze; sneezing

نوږی[2] núgaj *m.* **1** breed, pedigree **2** property, characteristics

نوږیدل[1] nugedə́l *intransitive* [*past:* ونوږېده] to sneeze

نوږیدل[2] nogedə́l *denominative, intransitive* [*past:* نوږ شو] to be cleaned, be cleansed, be purified

نوس navs *m. colloquial* ☞ نفس[2]

نوستل nvəstə́l *transitive* [*present:* نولي *past:* وی نوست] **1** to pour, strew, sprinkle, scatter **2** to emit (rays)

نوستنه nvəstə́na *f.* sprinkling, strewing

نوسخان nuskhā́n *m.* miscarriage, abortion

نوسخاني nuskhā́ní *f.* woman who has had a miscarriage or abortion

نوسه[1] navsá *f.* moist soil

نوسه[2] nusá key (for a lock)

نوسه[3] nvása *f.* test, trial

نوسی[1] nvasáj *m.* [*plural:* نوسي nvasí *plural:* نوسیان nvasijā́n] *Eastern* grandson

نوسی[2] núsaj *m.* **1** clips (for hair) **2** tongs **3** handle **4** vice

نوسی[3] nvasə́j *f.* [*plural:* نوسي nvasə́j *plural:* نوسیاني nvasəjā́ni] *Eastern* granddaughter

نوسي[4] navsí *colloquial* ☞ نفسي

نوسی[5] nvasí *plural of* نوسی[1]

نوسی[6] núsi *plural of* نوسی[2]

نوسی[7] nvasə́j *plural of* نوسی[3]

نوسه[8] nvási *plural of* نوسه[3]

نوسی[9] navsé *plural of* نوسه[1]

نوسی[10] nusé *plural of* نوسه[2]

نوش nosh *m.* **1** drink, beverage **2** savory food, tasty victuals پر جان نوش-i nósh-i **a** to drink to the health of **b** to taste savory food چا ته نوش ویل to say to someone "Drink, good health!" چا نوش کول to entertain someone (e.g., at tea) **3** enjoyment, delight

نوشادر nushādír *m. plural* ammonium chloride

نوشت navísht *m.* letter نوشت او خوان زده کول to study, learn reading and writing

نوشته navishtá *f.* [*plural:* نوشتجات navishtadzhā́t] **1** something written; letter; document نوشته کول *compound verb* to write په خپل مکتوب کښي یې داسي نوشته کړي دي چه ... In his letter he writes that ... **2** production (written) **3** patterns

نوشل noshə́l *transitive* [*past:* وی نوشل] to drink

نوښنار navḳhā́r *m.* ☞ نو ښنهر

نوښته naviḳhtá *f. Western* ☞ نوشته

نوښخ nuḳhákh *m.* **1** hook **2** fishhook

نوښنهر nauḳhár *m.* Naushera (city, near Peshawar)

نوط not *m.* ☞ نوټ

نوع náv *f.* نووا návā *Arabic m. Arabic* [*plural:* انواع anvá'] **1** species, breed, kind نوع کښني of a different type, various په خپله نوع کښني in one's own way **2** rank, sort **3** *biology* species **4** mode

نوع پالونکی nav'pālúkaj responsive; philanthropic

نوع خواهي nav'khāhí *f.* altruism; humanitarianism

نوع دوستي nav'dostí *f.* humanitarianism

نوعه náv'a *f.* ☞ انساني نوعه نوع mankind

نوعه پرست nav'aparást *m.* altruist

نوعه پرستي nav'aparastí *f.* altruism

نوعیت nav'iját *m. Arabic* **1** attribute, quality **2** particularity, specific character

نوغ nugh *m.* newborn calf

نوغاړی nughā́ṛaj *m.* sprouts of wheat which have become knocked down

نوغتل nughatə́l *transitive* ☞ نغوتل

نوغی[1] núghaj *m.* **1** spot, speck **2** sign, mark; brand, label نوغی اینبودل to mark; brand, place a brand on **3** basis **4** breed, variety **5** kind, type **6** scar, cicatrice, weal *idiom* نوغی لټول to carp نوغی نیول to object

نوغی[2] núghaj *m.* **1** sapling **2** seed **3** progeny; offshoot, scion

نوغي[3] núghi *plural of* نوغي[1,2]

نوغي نوغي núghi-núghi spotty, spotted; having specks, speckled نوغي نوغي کېدل to be spotted, be specked

نوک nuk *m.* [*plural:* نوکان nukā́n *plural:* نکان nukā́n *Eastern plural:* نوکونه nukúna] nail نوکان پرېکول to cut the nails **1** نوک

چه نوک، د نوکانو اخیستل the first cutting of the nails (of a baby) نیول *proverb literal* If he finds a place for his nails he'll put his whole hand in. ﯣای مومي، نو سوک پکښېني ورمندې *figurative* Give him an inch and he'll take a mile. **2** claw, talon **3** insignificant amount, trifle *idiom* نوکان ایستل to try, strive احمد نوکان جنګوي چه جنګ وشي Ahmed is rubbing his fingernails together for others to fight (between themselves). اول نوک ﯣایول، بیا سوک to gradually get one's own, gradually get what one deserves تر نوکانو وينی ﯤﯦدل to feel very unhappy د . . . سره نوک او اوری نوک وهل ﯣ نوک خورل to be indivisible; be one with نوک او اوری کول to make inseparable; indissolubly unite چا نوک د سخره منتل to be successful; have luck, luck out په کار کښبنی نوکان وتل to run up against difficulties in work; be exhausted from work beyond one's strength راﬕه، ولي دي نوک ونيوئ؟ نوک نيول a to stop, get stuck Come, why are you stopping? نوک وهل b to accumulate some money to stumble over چيري يې نوک سور شوئ نه دئ He always had luck. Everything always came out successfully for him. ستا نوک ته هم نه نه سر تر *Eastern* Horror seized him. د نوک قدر نبکي شي کتی *Eastern* He cannot harm you in any way. دي را سره نه ده کړې I have never seen any good from you.

نوکاره nukára *f.* **1** scratching نوکاري کول ، نوکاري لګول to scratch **2** claw, talon

نوکر nokár naukár *m.* **1** servant **2** soldier; trooper **3** vassal

نوکراړی nukráraj *m.* itch, itching of the skin of the arms (from cold) نوکراړی کبدل to scratch oneself

نوکرپیشه naukarpeshá living on service, serving for hire

نوکرﬕي nukrádzi *f. plural dialect* ﯣ نکریزي

نوکرکی nukárkaj tiny, minuscule

نوکروزي nukrúzi *f. plural dialect* ﯣ نکریزي

نوکره nokára naukára *f.* servant, employee (female)

نوکری nukráj [1] *m.* leprosy

نوکری nukáraj [2] tiny, minute, small

نوکری nokarí [3] *f.* **1** service نوکري کول to serve **2** duty د نوکری کتاب duty-roster record-book

نوکری nokári naukári [4] *plural of* نوکره

نوکریوال nokarivál *m.* نوکري والا nokarivālá *m.* person on duty نوکري والا منصبدار duty officer, نوکري وال طبيب physician on duty officer on duty

نوکی núkaj **1** a little, wee bit, some نوکي نوکي اوبه واچوه Pour a little water. **2** a bit نوکي نوکي کول núki-núki to tear, rip to bits پياله ولوېده، نوکي نوکي سوه núki-núki The glass fell and broke into smithereens.

نوک nog *Eastern* ﯣ نوﬔ

نوﬔی nugáj [1] *m. Eastern* ﯣ نوﬔی

نول nul *m.* **1** misfortune, disaster **2** grief, woe, affliction د زړه نول sorrow, grief نول کول to grieve, be upset, grow sad **3** melancholy *idiom* په ﬞپر نول او زول خپله ﬞ‌داره ﬔوله کول to be thwarted; bring to a conclusion with difficulty

نول nol *present stem of* نوستل

نولجن nuldzhán **1** grief-stricken, sorrowful **2** inconsolable

نولجنبدل nuldzhənedál *denominative, intransitive* [*past:* نولجن شو] to grieve, grow sad, get upset

نولژن nulzhán ﯣ نولجن

نولس núlas *numeral Eastern* nineteen

نولسم nulasám *ordinal* nineteenth

نولکی navlakáj **1** cheeky, bold-faced **2** mischievous

نولول nulavál *transitive* [*past:* و يې نولاوه] to upset, grieve; torment

نوله nulá *f.* spout (e.g., of a teapot)

نولی noláj naulág *m.* [1] **1** polecat, ferret, weasel **2** mongoose

نولي nolí [2] *present tense form of* نوستل

نولي nulé [3] *plural of* نوله

نولبدل nuledál *intransitive* [*past:* و نولبد] **1** to pine, grieve, sorrow; be tormented; fall into despair **2** to grow weak, go into a decline

نوم num *m.* [1] [*plural:* نومونه numúna *Eastern plural:* نمونه numúna] **1** name دپلار نوم proper name د شخص خاص نوم **1** name ستا نوم ﯤه شي دئ؟ patronymic ستا نوم ﯤه دئ؟ What is your name? د نامه مبوه from one's own name زما پر نامه in my name په خپل نامه fruit sent to close relatives upon the announcement of a birth and the naming of the newborn د وﬔرو په نامه يوه وينا addressing the population as a whole يو بل ته نوم اخيستل to address one another by first name د نوم پتي to become renowned نوم ايستل، لوی نوم ايستل *Eastern* نوم په امر لیکل to inquire about (a name, address) تپوس کول to issue a document to "bearer" **2** title, designation هندوکش نوم غر the Hindu Kush Mountains تش په نامه a nominal b empty, vacant c نوم اينودل a to نمونه اخیستل to mention, enumerate name b to designate, give a title to نوم حاصلول to receive the name, get the designation د نوم ورکبدل a to be forgotten b to be left without offspring د مشر په نامه یابدل to be designated the senior one **3** name, reputation, renown د لوی نوم خاوند celebrated; celebrity د چا ﯦنه نوم پرېښنودل to leave a good memory (of oneself) د چا نوم سره اینﯚی کبدل to become renowned نوم تلل to be disgraced د چا هميشه نوم يې وﬔاﯤه to become famous نوم ﬔبل، نوم وړل He was forever famous. د نوم دپاره مي نه دئ کړئ I did not do this for glory. **4** *grammar* noun *idiom* په هيﯚ نامه in no way at all د نامه ﬖﯚه لوبدل to be forgotten د چا په نامه کبدل to be asked for in marriage while still a girl

نوم nom *m.* [2] navel, bellybutton *idiom* لاس په نامه in an attitude of obedience

نوم núme ﯣ نومي [3]

نومانده numánda نوماندی numándaj called, named; nicknamed ساون numánda Savun by name نومانده کول to name, call; nickname

نومبر novámbr *m.* November

نومد numd *dialect* ﯣ لوند

نومره numrá *f.* **1** number **2** *military* serial-numbered equipment افرﬕ نومره afrād-i detachment, crew (i.e., gun)

نومﬗ numár ﯣ نومﬗی [2]

نومﬗی numráj ﯣ لمﬗی [1]

نومړی ² numə́raj 1 named; nicknamed 2 mentioned, indicated نومړی کول a to name, designate b to mention, indicate 3 famous, well-known; distinguished

نومل numə́l transitive [past: ونه يي] to designate, name; count, consider

نوملاړی numlā́raj نومور، نوم ور numvár famous, celebrated; distinguished

نوملړ nūmlar m. computer science directory

نوم ورکی numvrə́kaj forgotten

نوم وري numvarí f. celebrity, glory, fame

نوموړی ² numvə́raj نومه ور numavár نومړی ☞ numavə́r

نومې ¹ núme Eastern by name

نومي ² númi present of نومل

نومیالی numjāláj 1 celebrated, popular, famous; well-known, distinguished; renowned 2 m. celebrity, fame

نومبد ¹ numéd imperfect of نومبدل

نومبد ² nauméd ناامبد ☞

نومبدل numedə́l transitive [present: نومبږي past: ونومبده] to be designated, be named, be called خه نومبږي؟ What is your name?

نومبده numedə́ called, named

نومبیل numejə́l transitive [past: نومبیه و يي] to call, name

نون ¹ nun m. the name of the letter ن

نون ² navə́n wet, damp, moist

نونخه nunátsa f. acute phase of a chronic illness

نوند navə́nd nund dialect لوند ☞

نوندوالی nundvā́laj m. لندوالی ☞

نوندول nundavə́l denominative, transitive لندول ☞

نونبدل nunedə́l denominative, intransitive لندبدل ☞

نونس nónas núnas numeral Western nineteen

نونسم nonasə́m nunasə́m ordinal numeral Western nineteenth

نونکی ¹ nunakə́j f. pimples, acne, furuncle

نونکی ² nunakə́j f. cracking of the hoof

نونه núna f. 1 grain; seed 2 foresight (of a rifle)

نونی nunáj m. foresight (of a rifle)

نوو nə́vo oblique plural of نوی ³

نو وارد navvāríd m. newly arrived

نووګری navográj m. kind of bracelet

نوها nauhā́ hungry

نوها توب nauhātób m. hunger

نوی ¹ naváj m. 1 shaft, wheelhorse (in grinding, milling using a horse-drawn device) 2 leader of a herd

نوی ² nuj m. uncle (mother's brother)

نوی ³ nə́vaj návaj 1.1 new; fresh; young نوی خت a new shirt نوی کال new year په نوی مياشت time of the new moon نوی کورونه nə́vi new houses نوی کول a to renew, freshen b to renew, give birth to نوی کبدل a to be renewed, be freshened b to be reestablished, arise 1.2 inexperienced نوی سری a novice 2.1 anew, once again 2.2 recently 3 m. something

new nə́vi زور د نوي په مقابل کښي مغلوب دئ The old gives way to the new.

نوی ⁴ niví nví nəví numeral ninety

نوی ⁵ naváj beginning, inexperienced هغه نوی دئ He is a novice. He is inexperienced.

نوي ⁶ návi vice که نوي نه وي not so, on the contrary

نوي ایستنه návi-istə́ m. plural نوي ایسته nə́ve istə́na f. 1 invention, discovery 2 innovation

نو بالغ nə́vaj-bālígh نوی بالغ ☞

نوی توب nəvaj-tób m. 1 novelty; something new; innovation, new production, invention 2 renewal, restoration 3 revival

نوی چمن nə́vaj-chamán m. New Chaman (city)

نوی ډېلی nə́vaj-ḍeláj m. New Delhi (city)

نوی زبرولئ nə́vaj-zeɣavə́ləj newborn

نوی زبلنډ nə́vaj-zelánḍ m. New Zealand

نویستونی navistúnaj m. 1 inventor 2 innovator

نویسندگي navisandagí f. writing profession; literary activity

نویسنده navisandá 1 knowing how to write خوانده او نویسنده literate m. 2 writer

نه ویشت nəvísht numeral ☞

نه ویشتم nəvishtə́m numeral ☞

نوی کبده nəvajkedə́ m. plural 1 restoration 2 renewal, rehabilitation, revival

نوی ګیني nə́ve giní f. New Guinea

نوبل navél m. 1 earthing up of vines 2 resin from the slashed stem of a vine

نوبلی ¹ navelə́j f. group of relatives of the bride-to-be giving notice of the wedding نوبلی ګرځبدل to go for the purpose of giving notice of a wedding نوبلی لبرل to send relatives to give notice of a wedding

نوبلی ² naveláj m. invitation to a wedding

نویم nvijə́m ordinal nintieth

نوی نزی nə́vaj-nə́zaj brand-new, spanking new

نوی والی nəvajvā́laj m. 1 نوی توب 2 freshness

نویم nəvijə́m numeral نویم ☞

نه ¹ nəh nih numeral nine سل و نه one hundred and nine په نه بجو at nine o'clock نه سوه nine hundred نه زره nine thousand

نه ² na nə negative particle 1 no, not (used in negation, with a negative answer, etc.) تا دغه کتاب لوستلئ دئ؟ نه ، نه مي دئ لوستلئ Did you read this book? No, I didn't read it! نه خیر! No! نه نه! Are you going ته ځی که نه؟ Not under any circumstances! or not? 2 no, not (used as a negation with a predicate verb or verb-predicate, sometimes postpositionally) زه هیڅ وخت نه لرم I have no time at all. دا به کور پاته نه سي She does not stay at home. زه به در I don't know. زه خبر نه یم It will not rain. باران به و نه شي I will not come to you. بیا Eastern They did not go. نه سم I certainly will not remember your name. به د دي نوم به خوله وا نه خلم You have been forgotten. زاري یې قبلبده نه His request went unanswered. **3** neither …, nor … نه ځان ته فايده رسولئ سي او نه بل تر نه He can bring no advantage to himself nor to other people.

نه [3] na *postpostion Eastern* out, out of, from, by, at (used in combination with or without له or د) له ما نه in my possession; from me له هغو نه in their possession; from them له پلار نه in the father's possession; from the father د ښار نه، ښار نه out of the city; from the city د کور نه، کور نه from home; from the house ☞ څخه

نه [4] na un-, non-, in- (or similar negative prefix used with adjectives, participles, and nouns, especially nouns of action) نه هپرېدونکی unforgettable نه پاملرنه، نه توجه inattention

نه [5] na *f. suffix for nouns of action* تېربدنه passing, passage, movement, proceeding

نه [6] na *used in folk poetry to join words ending in a vowel* کوينه he does; they do وايونه we speak ځينه he goes; they go

نه اتیا nəhatjấ *numeral* eighty-nine

نه اتیایم nəhatjájə́m *numeral* eighty-ninth

نهاد nihā́d *m. poetry* nature, substance, essence

نهار [1] nahā́r nihā́r **1.1** hungry; having no breakfast زه نهار وم I have not eaten since morning. **1.2** hungering **1.3** fasting **2** *m.* **.1** starvation **2.2** fast

نهار [2] nahā́r *m.* day

نهار نهور nihā́r-nuhúr on an empty stomach, not having eaten نهور گرځېدل to go hungry, wander hungry

نهاری [1] nahārā́j *m.* naharí *f.* **1** ☞ ناری [1] نهاری کول to breakfast نهاری ورکول to treat to breakfast **2** morning feeding (of cattle)

نهاري [2] nahārí daily نهاري زده کړه the daily occupations, daily duties

نهال nihā́l *m.* niā́l [*plural:* نیالان niālā́n *Western plural:* نهالان nihālā́n *Eastern plural:* نیالونه niālúna *plural:* نهالونه nihālúna] young sapling; seedling, sprout نهال اېښودل to plant a sapling

نهالشاني nihālshāní *f.* planting of saplings, tree planting

نهالول niālavə́l nihālavə́l *denominative, transitive* [*past:* نهال یې کړ] to plant a sapling

نهالي nihālí *f.* niālí [*plural:* نهالی niālə́j *plural:* nihālə́j] mattress, straw pallet

نهام nihā́m **1** hidden, covert; concealed, unseen **2** secret

نهامول nihāmavə́l *denominative, transitive* [*past:* نهام یې کړ] to hide, conceal ځان نهامول to hide oneself, conceal oneself

نهامی [1] nahāmā́j *m.* kind of serious illness of sheep

نهامی [2] nihā́mi *feminine plural of* نهام

نهامبدل nihāmedə́l *denominative, intransitive* [*past:* نهام شو] to be hidden, be concealed د چا له سترگو نهامبدل to be hidden from the eyes, disappear from the field of vision

نهان nihā́n ☞ نهام

نه انکاربدونکی nainkāredúnkaj **1** inalienable (of a right) **2** irrefutable نه انکاربدونکی حقیقت an irrefutable fact

نه اویا nəhavjā́ *numeral* seventy-nine

نه اویایم nəhavjájə́m *numeral* seventy-ninth

نه اهتمام naihtimā́m *m.* inattention, ignoring

نهایت nihājā́t *Arabic* **1** *m.* **.1** limit, extreme degree; end **1.2** goal, limit of desire **2** *attributive* **.1** unusual, remarkable, extraordinary **2.2** high; extreme **3** much; extremely; quite, very نهایت متفکر و He has become very pensive. دپر نهایت unusually much

نه اېل naél wild, untamed

نهائي nihāí نهایي nihājí *Arabic* **1** maximum, final, ultimate; extreme نهائي درجه extreme, highest degree نهائي عقاید extreme views **2** conclusive نهائي پربکړه نه ده شوی This has not yet been conclusively resolved.

نه بدلبدونکی nabadaledúnkaj **1** unalterable; irrevocable (of a process) **2** unshakable, sturdy, firm, inflexible نه بدلبدونکي اراده inflexible will

نه بلوغ nabulúgh *m.* immaturity; state of not having reached legal age

نه بندبدونکی nabandedúnkaj unlimited; inexhaustible طبیعي شته منی nabandedúni … inexhaustible natural resources

نه بېلبدونکی nabeledúnkaj indivisible; indissoluble ارتباط لرل to be indissolubly linked, be bound

نه پنځوس nəhpindzós *numeral* fifty-nine

نه پنځوسم nəphindzosə́m *ordinal numeral* fifty-ninth

نه تبری nata'arúz *m.* ☞ نه تعرض

نه تگ natág *m.* non-arrival; failure to show up

نه توافق natavāfúḱ *m.* divergence, difference, disagreement, dissension; disharmony

نه تیاري natajārí *f.* lack of preparedness, lack of readiness, lack of training

نه تبری nataráj *m.* nonaggression د نه تبري تړون naterí nonaggression pact

نهج nahzh nahádzh *m. Arabic* **1** principle road, superhighway **2** way, mode, method

نه جداکبدونکی nadzhudā́ kedúnjaj inseparable; indissoluble, indivisible

نه چنده nəhchánda ninefold

نه چی nəchi what if …, supposing … ☞ نه [2]

نه ځایبدل nadzājedə́l *m. plural* lack of room, shortage of room

نه څلوېبنت nəhtsalvéḱht *numeral* forty-nine

نه څلوېبنتم nəhtsalvekhtəm *ordinal numeral* forty-ninth

نه څه natsə́ paltry, worthless, trivial *Eastern* ته په نه څه خبره خفه کېږي You are angry over nothing.

نه ختم کبدونکی nakhátm kedúnkaj endless, limitless

نه درجده nadardzhedə́ *m. plural* non-submission, non-insertion, non-inclusion (e.g., of a paragraph in a treaty)

نه دېرش nəhdérsh *numeral* thirty-nine

نه دېرشم nəhdershə́m *ordinal numeral* thirty-ninth

نه ذیروح nazirúh inanimate

نهر [1] nahr náhar *Arabic* [*plural:* نهرونه nahrúna *Arabic plural:* انهار anhā́r] **1** canal **2** river, stream, brook

نهر [2] nahár *regional* ☞ نهار [1]

نه رعایت nari'āját *m.* non-observation (e.g., of a deadline, condition, provision)

نهره nahára *feminine singular of* نهر [2]

نهرى [1] nahráj *m.* ☞ نهاري [1]

نهرى [2] nahrí **1** *adjective* river نهري بېړۍ riverboat **2** irrigated by a canal نهري زمکه *regional* land near a canal; land watered by irrigation system or canal; artificially flooded or irrigated land

نهرين nahrín *m.* **1** Narin (district) **2** nahrájn *Arabic dual of* نهر

نه زړیدونکی nazaṛedúnkaj ageless

نه ستړی کېدونکی nastəṛaj kedúnkaj tireless; unweakened

نشته nə́sta ☞ نسته

نه شپیتم nehshpetə́m *ordinal* sixty-ninth

نه شپیته nəhshpetə́ *numeral* sixty nine

نه شلیدونکی nashledúnkaj unbroken (e.g., ties, communication)

نه ښکاره کول naḳhkārá kavə́l *m. plural* non-presentation (e.g., of a promissory note)

نهضت nahzát *m. Arabic* **1** movement (i.e., social) د آزادي خواهي ملي national liberation movement نهضت، د ملیت غوښتني نهضت **2** development اقتصادي نهضت economic development

نه علاقه na'ilāḳá *f.* indifferent attitude, inattention

نه فناکېدونکی nafaná kedúnkaj unfading; undying; undecaying; deathless

نه قائلیده naḳāíedə́ *m. plural* nonrecognition, non-acknowledgment

نه قبلیده naḳabledə́ *m. plural* refusal (to accept something)

نه قبول naḳabúl *m. economics* refusal to accept a promissory note

نه قبولي naḳabulí *f.* nonacceptance of something; disagreement

نه قناعت naḳana'át dissatisfaction; displeasure

نه کفاف nakafáf *m.* shortage, insufficiency

نه کېدونکی nakedúnkaj impossible, impracticable دا نه کېدونکی کار ښکاري This is impossible.

نه گډون nagaḍún *m.* **1** alienation; unsociability **2** indifference

نه لس nə́hlas *numeral dialect* ☞ نولس

نه لسم nəhlasə́m *numeral dialect* ☞ نولسم

نه لیدونکی nalidúnkaj unseen, unnoticed

نهم nəhə́m *ordinal* ninth

نه مداخلت namudākhalát *m.* noninterference

نه مساعدت namusā'idát *m.* **1** unserviceability **2** unfavorable situation

نه مسئولیت namas'uliját *m.* freedom from responsibility; removal from responsibility

نه مطابقت namutābaḳát *m.* nonconformity (to a pattern, etc.)

نه معلومېدونکی nama'lumedúnkaj **1** imperceptible, unnoticeable **2** invisible (of rays)

نه منل namanə́l *m. plural* disagreement with something; nonacceptance of something

نه موجودگي namaudzhudagí *f.* نه موجودیت namaudzhudiját *m.* absence of something, lack of something

نهماى namanáj *m.* ☞ نهامي [1]

نهنج nahándzh *m.* flower bed

نهنگ naháng *m.* **1** crocodile **2** shark **3** *folklore* whale; leviathan

نه نوی nəhniví *numeral* ninety-nine

نه نویم nəhnivijə́m *ordinal numeral* ninety-ninth

نه وجود navudzhúl *m.* absence, non-presence

نهور nahúr ☞ نهاز [1]

نه ورتگ navartág *m.* non-arrival, failure to show up, nonappearance

نه ورکړه navárkṛa *f.* nonpayment

نهوه nahvá **1** *f.* **.1** fast **1.2** starvation نهوه کول **a** to fast **b** to declare a hunger strike **2.1** fasting **2.2** starving

نهوه توب nahvatób *m.* **1** observance of a fast **2** starvation; starving

نه ویشت nəhvísht *numeral* twenty-nine

نه ویشتم nəhvishtə́m *ordinal numeral* twenty-ninth

نه وېشل کېدونکی naveshə́l kedúnkaj indivisible

نهه [1] nahá *f. dialect* Tuesday

نهه [2] nə́ha nuhə́ *numeral regional* nine

نه هماښتینی nəhamjāshtináj *adjective* nine-month

نهي [1] nahi *f. Arabic* **1** prohibition, interdiction **2** *grammar* prohibitory negative imperative

نهي [2] nahí *f.* nahé *dialect* Tuesday نهي ورځ Tuesday

نهیب nahíb nahéb *m. Arabic* fear, terror, fright

نه یرزن najarzə́n *dialect* unworthy, unfit

نه هېرېدونکی naheredúnkaj unforgettable, not to be forgotten; ineffaceable

نهیل [1] nahél *m.* stuffiness; closeness

نهیل [2] nahíl **1** weak, worn-out **2** disillusioned

نهیلی nahílaj disillusioned

نهیه nahjá *f.* prohibition, interdiction نهیه کول to forbid

نی [1] naj [*plural:* نیان najā́n] **1** reed, rush **2** reed pipe; flute نی وهل **a** to play the reed pipe, play the flute **b** to warble (of a nightingale) *idiom* نی نه ورته وهل to have nothing in common with something

نې [2] ne *particle* ☞ نه [2] د نې پر میدان ناست دئ He insists upon his own. He stands firmly for his own.

نې [3] ne *combination of the negative particle* نه *and the pronoun* یي کتابونه ښه ساتي، نې څيروي یي He treasures the books; don't tear them.

نی [4] náj *m.* nə́j *f. adjectival suffix* پسرلنی vernal, spring

نیا njá *f.* nijā́ [*plural:* نیاگاني njāgā́ni *plural:* نیاوي njā́vi] grandmother دنیا مور great-grandmother دنیا د نیا مور great-great-grandmother

نیابت nijābát *m. Arabic* **1** region governed by a governor-general; position of deputy د سلطنت نیابت regency **2** *administrative* region (in Beludzhistan) ☞ نایب

نیاز njā́z nijáz *m.* **1** entreaty, supplication, request د نیازه ډک الفاظ words full of entreaty **2** vow, promise **3** need, requirement نیاز **4** ☞ ناز **5** *proper name* Niyaz نیاز کول to entreat نیاز ایښودل to dedicate

نيازبين nijāzbín 1 beloved نيازبين زوی beloved son نيازبينه لور beloved daughter 2 pampered, carefully tended نيازبين لويدل to grow up in comfort

نيازبين توب nijāzbintób m. state of being spoiled; delicacy, softness

نيازمن njāzmə́n نيازمند njāzmánd nijāzmánd 1 in want 2 beloved, favorite

نيازمندي nijāzmandí f. 1 need; dependence (material) 2 begging, entreating

نيازه nijāzə́ ¹ plural of نيز ¹

نيازه nijāza ² oblique singular of نياز

نيازه وړی nijāzə́ və́raj 1 borne by the current, carried along by the current 2 m. small pieces of timber, brush, etc., washed to the bank of a stream

نيازي nijāzí ¹ m. friend

نيازي nijāzí ² 1 m. plural the Nijazi (tribe) 2 nijāzáj m. Nijazi (tribesman)

نه ياست nājāst Western vice

نياگانه nijāgāná f. relative of the mother

نياگۍ nijāgə́j f. affectionate 1 granny 2 poverty-stricken old woman

نيال nijāl m. ☞ نهال

نيالگر nijālgə́r m. rice-planting worker

نيالگره njālgə́ra f. nursery; seed plot

نيالگی njālgáj m. 1 seedling, sapling, young tree د نيالگيو اېښنودل a planting of trees نيالگی کښېنول to plant a seedling 2 figurative basis, foundation

نيالي njālí ¹ f. ☞ نهالي

نيالی njāláj ² m. rice seedling

نيالچه nijālichá f. small straw pallet

نيام nijā́m ¹ m. 1 scabbard, sheath توره له نيامه کښل to sheath a sword 2 medicine splint 3 case 4 plow handle

نيام njā́m ² ☞ نهام

نياو njāv ¹ m. regional justice نياو کول to hand down a judgment based on justice نياو موندل to obtain justice

نياو njāv ² m. ☞ نيو ¹

نياواودار njāvādā́r m. regional renter or lessee who is engaged simultaneously in usury

نياوه njā́va ¹ f. compensation نياوه اخيستل to receive compensation نياوه ورکول to compensate

نياوه njāvə́ ² dialect vice نيوه

نياوی njāvə́j just

نياه nijāə́ m. [plural: نيايونه nijājúna نيائي njā́jí m. plural: نيايه گان njājigán] uncle (mother's brother)

نب neb 1 prolonged, extended, continuous په يو نپ continuously 2 sequentially

نبو nibú m. regional lemon

نپال nepāl m. Nepal

نپالي nepālí nepāláj 1 Nepalese 2.1 m. Nepalese (person) 2.2 f. Nepalese (language)

نپتون neptún m. astronomy Neptune

نپون nipón m. Japan

نيت nijāt m. Arabic goal; intention, wish, desire بد نيت evil intention زما نيت دئ چه ښار ته to intend, come to a decision نيت ترل ولاړ سم I have decided to go to the city. نيت کول to intend, plan to, conceive the idea په بد نيت کار کول to intend to, decide to نيت لرل to do something with evil intent

نيټورک کارډ nítwərk kā́rḍ m. computer science network card

نټه neṭa f. date, time, deadline د قوس ۲۰ نټه وه It was the 20th day of the month of Kaus. څه نټه کېږي some time ago نټه حاضر شو Eastern He appeared precisely on the date set. نټه کول compound verb to designate the date, set the deadline نټه ماتول to violate the deadline

نيجر najdzhár m. Niger (river, state)

نيجيريا najdzhirijā́ f. Nigeria

نچ nech ¹ m. 1 stretching oneself نچ ايستل to stretch oneself 2 noose (for birds); trap, snare

نچ njach ² twisted, strong (of thread)

نپچکی nechakáj m. kind of plant

نيچه najchá f. nechá 1 textiles bobbin, spool 2 thin reed 3 tube د تنفس نيچه bronchial tube

نيخۍ nitsə́j f. dialect ☞ انخۍ

نبخڅکی nekhtsəkáj 1 lanky; ungainly (of the figure) 2 m. lanky person

نبخه nékha colloquial abbreviation نه يم خبر I don't know.

نبخۍ nekhə́j f. carpet; rug (of low quality)

نيرنگ najráng m. 1 trick, cunning, guile 2 trick 3 witchcraft, sorcery

نيرنگباز najrangbā́z m. نيرنگ ساز najrangsā́z m. 1 shrewd operator, tricky fellow 2 wizard, sorcerer 3 conjurer, prestidigitator

نيرنگ سازي najrangsāzí f. 1 shrewdness; machinations, intrigues, subterfuges 2 magic, witchcraft, sorcery

نيرو nirú m. & f. plural force, strength, power

نيره nirá f. awl

نيز niz ¹ nez m. flood, inundation; stream, flow نيز ډېر راغئ There was a major flood.

نيز niz ² also, too

نزد nizd ☞ نزد

نزدې nizdé dialect ☞ نزدې

نيزوړي nizavə́ri m. plural ☞ نيازه وړی

نيزه nezá f. 1 pike, spear د ماهي نيزه fish spear, harpoon د نيزو بند a litter made of crossed lances نيزي وهل to beat with spades (in gambling at cards) 2 neza (a measure of length equal to the length of a pike) 3 piece of reed (from which pens are made)

نيزه باز nezabā́z m. participant in the game of nezabaz; horseman زوی يې ښه نيزه باز دئ His son handles the pike well. He is a daring horseman.

نيزه بازي nezabāzí *f.* nezabazi (exercises with the pike or spear as a kind of horsemanship)

نيزه دان nezadắn *m. military* pike holster

نيژدي nizhdé *Western* ☞ نژدي

نيږکى neǵakáj *m.* seed-planting staff

نيږوى neǵváj *m.* first or principal shaft of the native irrigation system

نيس nis *present stem of* نيول

نيست ¹ nest ☞ نښته نست کول to eliminate, destroy, exterminate

نيست ² nist *interjection* grab him; catch him (used when hunting hares)

نيستمن nestmán 1 in want, in need 2 poor peasant

نيستول nestavál *denominative, transitive* [*past:* نيست يې کړ] to eliminate, destroy

نيستي ¹ nestí *f.* nistí 1 need, destitution د نيستي په وخت کښي in case of need هغه په نيستي اخته دئ He is destitute. نيستي په اشخار نه *proverb* Narrow pedantry does not enrich one. 2 annihilation, destruction 3 nonexistence 4 absence of something

نيستى ² nestáj ☞ نښته

نيستيدل nestedál *denominative, intransitive* [*past:* نيست شو] 1 to be annihilated, be destroyed 2 to be absent, not to exist

نيسلم nisálǝm *dialect first person singular imperfect of* نيول 1

نيسه nisá *dialect imperfect of* نيول 1

نيسي ¹ nísi *present of* نيول 1

نيسئ ² nisǝj *imperfective imperative of* نيول 1

نيش nesh *m.* 1 awl نيش جگول to pierce with an awl 2 sharp end, sharp tip 3 thorn, prickle 4 sprout, shoot نيش پياز green onion 5 fang, tusk

نيشتر nishtár *m.* ☞ نشتر ¹

نيشتي níshte *dialect vice* نښته

نيشدار neshdār caustic, biting نيشدار الفاظ caustic remarks په نيشدارو bitingly الفاظو

نيشکر najshakár *m.* sugarcane ☞ گنى ¹

نيشنلزم neshnalízm *m.* 1 nationalism 2 the national liberation movement

نيشنلستي neshnalistí 1 nationalistic 2 *adjective* national-liberation

نيشه neshá 1 *f.* intoxication 2 *predicative* intoxicated نيشه کيدل to get drunk, become intoxicated

نيبن ¹ neḵh *m.* seven-year-old camel

نيبن ² neḵh *m. Western* 1 ☞ نيش 2 prick, stab په نيبن وهل a to prick, stab b to sting c *figurative* to wound, hurt; mock 3 sprout, shoot غنمو نيبن وهلئ a to sprout, send shoots out دئ The wheat has sprouted. b to smoke opium 4 lancet

نيختر niḵhtár *m.* 1 common poplar 2 lancet

نيختوى niḵhtúj *m.* small irrigation system (for a rice field)

نيبنزن neḵhzán 1 stinging 2 pricking

نيبل niḵhál *transitive* [*past:* و يې نيبن] to get stuck in the mud (of a donkey)

نيبنه néḵha *f.* seven-year-old she-camel

نبني ¹ neḵhí *m.* 1 crab 2 crayfish

نبني ² neḵhí 1 sprouting (of an onion) 2 stinging 3 sharp-pointed

نبغ negh 1.1 straight, direct نبغه لار straight road 1.2 erect; vertical a په نبغه directly; vertically b *figurative* immediately, directly د چا سره نبغ ارتباط لرل to be directly connected with someone نبغي خبري کول to speak forthrightly 1.3 steep نبغ غر a steep mountain 2 *m.* piercing (with a pike, bayonet, etc.) نبغ وهل a to stick, jab b to push, shove 3.1 directly نبغ شمال ته ځي They are going directly north. نبغ کتل to look, gaze, stare straight at 3.2 erectly; vertically 3.3 steeply الوتکه نبغه پورته کبري The aircraft proceeds steeply up; it is gaining altitude.

نبغك neghák *m.* shoe nail

نبغكى ¹ neǵakáj *m.* ☞ نبغي

نبغكى ² neghakáj *m.* 1 airs, conceit نبغكى کبدل to put on airs, become conceited 2 ☞ نبغى ¹

نبغ نبغ negh-négh 1.1 directly, straight off 1.2 erectly, upright; vertically 2.1 straight, direct 2.2 standing up, erect *idiom* نبغ نبغ کبدل to put on airs, grow conceited

نبغوالى neghvắlaj *m.* 1 straightness 2 steepness

نبغول neghavál *denominative, transitive* [*past:* نبغ يې کړ] 1 to stand erect; stand straight 2 to stand up straight, straighten up ځان نبغول to straighten oneself up 3 to direct *idiom* ملا نبغول to adjoin

نبغه négha 1 *feminine singular of* نبغ په نبغه straight out, directly 2 *f.* partition

نبغى ¹ negháj *m. anatomy* clitoris

نبغي ² néghi *f. plural of* نبغ ¹

نبغبدل neghedál *denominative, intransitive* [*past:* نبغ شو] 1 to stick up 2 to straighten oneself up, stand up straight

نبك ¹ nek 1.1 kind; good; well پلار يې نبک سړى دئ His father is a kind man. 1.2 good intention نبک نيت په نبکه اراده well-intentioned خپل نبک احساسات يي اظهار کړه He expressed his wishes 1.3 happy, successful 2 *m.* 1 kind man 2.2 pious man 2.3 *proper name* Nek *idiom* د نبکه مرغه happily

نبك ² naják *m.* ☞ نايك

نبكبخت nekakhtár ☞ نبکبخت اختر

نبك انديش nekandésh well-intentioned, well-disposed, benevolent

نبكبخت nekbákht 1.1 happy; lucky, successful 1.2 blessed 2 *m.* 1 old boy (as a familiar form of address) 2.2 lucky man

نبكبختي nekbakhtí *f.* نبک بختيا nekbakhtjắ good luck, success

نبكبين nekbín optimistic پدي موږ په دي کښني نبک بينه يو In this respect we are optimistically inclined.

نبكبيني nekbiní *f.* optimism

نبكپال nekpắl ☞ نبک فال

نبكپر nekpár fast-of-flight; fleet-winged

نبكتائي nektắjí *m.* necktie

نبكچانسه nekchấnsa lucky, successful نبک چانسه پيدا کبدل to be born lucky

نبكخواه nekkhắh *m.* well-wisher

نبک خوی nekkhój نبک خویه nekkhója 1 well-behaved, well-conducted 2 of good character

نبک ذات nekzā́t wellborn

نبک ذاتي nekzātí f. nobility, noble birth

نیکر nikár m. short pants, knickers

نبک عهد nek'ahd 1 conscientious 2 reliable

نبک فال nekfā́l fortunate, happy

نبک کردار nekkirdā́r virtuous

نبک کرداري nekkirdā́rí f. virtue

نیکل nikál m. nilál plural nickel

نبک مرغ nekmárgh نبک مرغه nekmárgha happy; fortunate, successful دا نبک مرغه یم I am happy. I am fortunate. اوبختوره موقع ده This is a lucky occasion.

نبک مرغي [1] nekmərghí f. good fortune, success

نبک مرغي [2] nekmárghi feminine plural of نبک مرغ

نبکنام، نبک نام neknā́m neknā́m famous; esteemed, honored; having a good name, having a good reputation, distinguished

نبکنامي neknāmí f. good name; good repute, good reputation نبکنامي گټل to deserve good repute, deserve a good name

نبک نیت نبک نیتی [1] nekniját neknijátaj 1 loyal 2 benevolent

نبک نیتي [2] neknijatí f. 1 kindness; benevolence 2 goodwill د نبک نیتي په اساس according to goodwill

نبکو nekú ☞ نبک [1]

نبکوټین nikoṭín m. نبکوټین nikoṭín m. plural nicotine

نبکوکار nekukár 1 doing good; benevolent 2 honest (of a person)

نبکوکاري nekukārí f. matter which is meritorious, matter good in itself

نبکویي nekuí f. 1 good, the good 2 beauty, grace

نبکه [1] nikə́ m. [plural: نیکونه nikúna plural: نیکه ګان nikəgán] 1 grandfather 2 head of the clan (among the Waziri and Shivari) 3 forefather د قوم مشر نیکه primogenitor, ancestor ترنیکه forefather, grandfather's grandfather

نبکه [2] néka 1 feminine singular of نبک [1] 2 f. monetary compensation for murder or slander

نبکي [1] nekí f. 1 good, matter of merit نبکي کول to do good, create good را سره یي ډیر نبکي کړیده He has treated me very well. 2 virtue 3 decency 4 reconciliation 5 ☞ نبکه [2] 2

نبکي [2] nekáj m. proper name Nekaj

نیل [1] nil m. plural indigo, blue dye

نیل [2] nil m. Nile (River) د نیل رود Nile River

نیل [3] najl m. ☞ نیبل

نیل [4] nil rearing (of a horse)

نیلاب nilā́b m. 1 Ind (River) 2 Nilab (city on the Ind River)

نیلاتوته nilātutá f. ☞ نیل طوطیا

نیلام nilā́m m. ☞ لیلام

نیلاو nilā́v m. ☞ نیلاب

نیل طوطیا niltutijā́ f. copper sulfate

نیلګاو nilgā́u m. nilgau antelope

نیلم nilā́m m. نیلمني nilmaní m. plural sapphire

نیلو niló f. proper name Nilo

نیلوفر nilufár nilofár 1 m. water lily 2 m. lotus 3 proper name Nilufar

نیلون najlón m. nylon د نیلون جرابي nylon stockings

نیله [1] nilá f. 1 small root, root hairs 2 anatomy capillary

نیله [2] najlá f. cards the nine

نیله [3] nilá 1 blue; dark blue 2 f. root of a plant which yields blue dye

نیله چنار nilá-chinā́r m. white poplar

نیلی niláj 1 m. .1 grey horse 1.2 fast horse 2 grey (of the sky) idiom د خیال نیلی څغلول to be absorbed in daydreams, lost in the clouds

نیلبدل niledál denominative, intransitive [past: نیل شو] to rear (of a horse)

نیم [1] nim 1 adjective half, semi- نیم ساعت half an hour 2 m. half نیم نیم one half each

نیم [2] najə́m a combination of the negative particle نه and the verb copula یم نیم تللئ I was not going. نیم خبر I do not know.

نیم هودی nimaudáj m. ☞ نیم اودی

نیمه nimájə́ m. نیمائي nimaí m. & f. نیمجي nimají m. & f. 1 half; middle, midst د پیړی دوهمه نیمایه the second half of the century د کال په مارچ د میاشتي په اول نیمایه کښی in the first half of the March په سمه نیمایه کښی exactly in the middle 2 attributive half دوي نیمایه برخي two halves نیمایه بیده half asleep نیمایه خلک ولاړل Half of the people have left. په نیمایه کول to divide in halves نیمایه کبدل to be divided in two parts قیمت باندی نیمایه خرڅول to sell at half price

نیمائي دائره nimāí dāirá f. semicircle

نیمائي قطر nimāí ḳutr m. radius

نیمائي کره nimāí kurrá f. hemisphere

نیم بسمل nimbismíl 1 half-slain, half-killed 2 half-dead

نیمبری nimbaráj m. compost pit (in a melon field)

نیم بند nimbánd نیم بندي هګی fried eggs

نیمبولی nimbolé f. نیمبولی nimbolə́j f. plural woman's necklace (made of a gold wire rod strung with glass beads; threaded through the nostril or worn on the neck)

نیمپو nimpú sloping, rickety, ramshackle

نیمتنه nimtaná f. نیمتنی nimtanáj m. 1 sleeveless padded jacket 2 sheepskin vest, sheepskin waistcoat

نیم تود nimtód subtropical

نیمجوش nimdzhósh نیمجوش کول to cook in boiling water, boil or cook in simmering water, simmer, poach

نیمچکی nimchakáj m. wavy pattern (on the edge of a carpet)

نیمچولی nimcholáj m. nomad camp halfway to the next watering site

نیمچه [1] nimchá 1 m. crossbreed, hybrid آس می اصل عربي ندئ نیمچه دئ My horse is not a purebred Arabian, but a mixed breed. 2 m. plural history the Nimcha (Kafiri tribes converted to Islam)

نیمچه [2] nimchá f. short fur jacket

نیم ځانی nimdzā́naj half-alive

نیمتثی nimtsáj *m.* felt, large piece of felt

نیم خام nimkhãm semifinished, partly processed نیم خام شیان semifinished products

نیم خوبي nimkhobí *f.* state of half-sleep د نیم خوبي په حال کښې in a half-sleep state, half asleep

نیم دائره nimdāirá *f.* semicircle

نیم درخت nimdarákht *m.* shrub, bush; group of shrubs, clump of bushes

نیمرڅی nimrátsaj unripe, half-ripe

نیمرسمي nimrasmí semiofficial, quasi-official نیمرسمي آژانس semiofficial agency

نیمرنگ nimráng pale, pale colored

نیم روز nimróz *m.* 1 noon 2 *history* Seistan

نیم روښان nimrokhắn semi-illuminated

نیم رویه nimrujá نیم رویه عکس profile

نیمره nimrá *f.* awning at a gate

نیمزال nimzãl نیمزالی nimzálaj elderly

نیمزالی nimzālə́j *f.* grown daughter

نیمژبي nimzhə́baj stammering

نیمسړی nimsaráj *m.* ☞

نیم سړی nimsaráj *m.* 1 fool, idiot 2 coward

نیم سړی nimseráj *m.* migraine; intense headache

نیم غلامانه nimghulāmãná *adjective* serf, pertaining to serfdom; dependent, subject, vassal

نیم غلامي nimghulāmí *f.* serfdom; vassal

نیم غوړلی nimgharvə́laj half-closed

نیم قطر nimḳútr *m.* radius

نیمکاره nimkára half-and-half نیمکاره زمکه *regional* land rented out on the metayage basis مزکه په نیمکاره ورکول *regional* to rent land on the metayage basis

نیم کره nimkurrá *f.* hemisphere

نیمکښ nimkáẖh نیمکښنه nimkaẖhó نیمکښه nimkáẖha half-open, open slightly ور نیمکښ کول to half open the door, slightly open the door

نیم کله nimkə́lá نیمکله nimkə́lá unfinished, incomplete

نیمکوره nimkorá 1 living in two houses 2 occupied temporarily as a dwelling place (of a house)

نیمکی nimakáj [1] *f.* kind of popular song

نیمکی nimkə́j [2] prattle, babble د ماشوم نیمکی او خوږه ژبه the babble of a child

نیمکی nimakáj [3] *m.* balcony

نیمګانی nimgáṇaj *m.* 1 span 2 kasha made from beans and onions

نیم ګرم nimgárm 1 subtropical نیم ګرمي مُځکي the subtropics 2 warm

نیمګړتوب nimgəṛtób *m.* نیمګړتیا nimgəṛtjã *f.* 1 shortage; need; insufficiency د وګړو نیمګړتیاوي پوره کول to satisfy the needs of the population 2 defect, deficiency, imperfection, flaw 3 shortfall; mediocrity 4 destitution; poverty, want

نیمګړی nimgə́ṛaj 1.1 unfinished, not done کار نیم ګړی پاتي شو The work remained incomplete. نیم ګړی کېدل to remain not fully finished, remain incomplete 1.2 lacking, incomplete 1.3 in the bud, in embryo; unripe, immature 1.4 not of full value, defective; falling short نیم ګړی خبري cripple نیم ګړی سړی nimgə́ṛaj کول to speak indistinctly 1.5 mediocre, second-rate 1.6 halved, partial 1.7 needy, destitute; poor 2.1 not fully, insufficiently 2.2 poorly

نیمګور nimgór نیمګوری nimgóraj *adjective* half په نیمګور قیمت خرڅول to sell at half price

نیمګی nimgáj 1 *adjective* half نیمګی میزان half (quantity) 2 *m.* a half د نونسم قرن په دوهم نیمګی کښې in the second half of the 19th century

نیم مرئی nimmrajáj *m.* peasant, in a state of serfdom and dependence

نیم مرئیتوب nimmrajitób *m.* serfdom; dependence, vassal

نیم مریبه nimmrejá dying in youth

نیم مستقیل nimmustaḳíl semi-independent, semi-dependent

نیمنی nimanáj *m.* vessel (for mixing sour milk with other foods)

نیموالی nimválaj *m.* halving

نیم واول nimvāvál *m.* grammar semivowel phoneme

نیمول nimavə́l *denominative, transitive* [*past:* نیم یې کړ] 1 to divide in half; divide, cut up دا غنم نیم کړه Divide this wheat into halves. 2 to halve

نیمه níma *feminine singular of* نیم [1] 1 نیمه برخه half نیمه ورځ noon شپه نیمه پس after some time پیاله نیمه چای چنبل to have another cup of tea

نیمه nájə́ma *combination of the negative particle* نه *and the verb copula* یمه نیمه خبره I do not know.

نیم هادي nimhādí *m.* physics semiconductor

نیمه بیه nímabája *f.* half price

نیمه جوهر nimadzhauhár semiprecious نیمه جوهر تیږي semiprecious gems

نیمه خوا nimakhvã 1 unfinished, incomplete 2 halved 3 inconstant, unstable 4 not attaining a goal زه هم نیمه خوا وم I also was disappointed نیمه خوا کېدل *compound verb* a to die young b to be unfinished, be incomplete *idiom* نیمه خوا برخه unrealized dreams ستا نیمه خوا پلار your untimely-deceased father

نیمه خوله nimakhvólə́ unclear, indistinct په نیمه خوله ویل to speak indistinctly

نیمه دائره níma dāirá *f.* semicircle

نیمه روځ níma rvadz *f.* noon

نیمه شپه níma shpa 1 *f.* midnight 2 at midnight

نیمه غرمه níma gharmá *f.* time after noon

نیمه غلامي nimá ghulāmí *f.* the system of serfdom; serfdom

نیمه کره níma kurrá *f.* hemisphere

نیمه لار níma lār *f.* halfway point in a journey

نیمه واول nimavāvél *m.* grammar semivowel phoneme

نیم هودی nimhavdáj *m.* set term of use of an irrigation system (communal)

نیمه روځ níma vradz *f.* ☞ نیمه ورځ

نیمی nimáj [1] **1** *m.* half **2** *adjective* half نیمی کول **a** to divide in half **b** to divide up something with someone تر کوره یې لا نیمی لار We were halfway home. نیمی کېدل to divide up, cut into halves

نیمی nimáj [2] *feminine singular of* نیمی [1]

نیمي nimi [3] *feminine plural of* نیم [1] [1]

نیمېدل nimedál *denominative, intransitive* **1** to be divided in halves **2** to be decreased by half

نین najɗn *m.* small piece of meat

نینځکه nindzɗka *f.* ننځکه ninzɗka *f. dialect* ☞ نانځکه

نینک ninák *m.* pupil (of the eye)

نینکه nenɗka *f.* tomtit (the bird)

نینکۍ ninakɗj *f.* small bird of the sparrow family

نینګانی ningɗnaj *m.* span (e.g., of land)

نینګل ningɗl *transitive* [past: و یې نینګه] to crave for, thirst after

نینول ninavɗl *transitive* ☞ ننول

نینونی ninavúnaj *m.* ☞ ننونی

نینوی ninɗvaj *m.* shaft of a plow, handles of a plow

نینه niná *f. usually plural* نیني ورتول، نینه niné parched grain *idiom* نیني کېدل to parch grain نیني نیني کول to be parched (of grains) و یو شي ته نینه نینه کېدل to be burning with desire نینه نینه کېدل to be burning with desire to get something *proverb* دا د اوسپنی نیني چیچل *I* This work is beyond one's strength. د اوسپنی نیني مې وچیچلي I was worn out. I was tired out.

نینېدل ninedál *intransitive* ☞ ننېدل

نینیوالا ninevālá *m.* worker engaged in parching grain

نیو njav [1] *m.* **1** stop, halt **2** pause **3** waiting (for someone)

نیو náju [2] *combination of the negative particle* نه *and the verb copula* یو ... موږ هغه قوم نیو چه We are not such a people as to … We are not such persons as to …

نیو niv [3] *imperfect of* نیول [1]

نیوا nevá *f.* Neva (River) د نیوا سیند the Neva River

نیوای niváj *potential form of the verb* نیول [1]

نیوترون njutrón *m.* neutron

نیورستني njurasteni neurasthenia

نیوز nijóz *m. dialect* flood; inundation; flow (of a river, etc.)

نیوزیلند njuzéland *m.* New Zealand

نیوکه niváka [1] *f.* bride-to-be, fiancée نیوکه ورته کول to marry a girl off to someone

نیوکه niváka [2] *f.* **1** seizure, capture نیوکه کول to seize something, grab something **2** lease, rental

نیول nivɗl **1** *transitive* [present: و یې نیسي past: و یې نیو past: و یې نیوه] **1** to take, seize, grasp له لاسه نیول، تر لاس نیول to take by the hand, grasp by the hand له لمنی نیول to grasp by the hem of a garment د پړي سر نیول to grasp the end of a rope **1.2** to catch, bag (game) مرغی نیول to bag game birds **1.3** to detain غل نیول to detain a thief, arrest a thief **1.4** to hold آس یې ونیسه Hold his horse. **1.5** to occupy, take over هغه ښار عسکرو ونیو، هغه ښار عسکرو

هغه ښار عسکرو ونیو The troops have occupied the city. نیول to occupy a place, settle **1.6** to be backed up, be choked up سیند یخی نیسي The river is choked with ice. **1.7** to give, yield (fruit, etc.) دا ونی ډېره حاصل نیولۍ This tree yielded a lot of fruit. وږي نیول to form ears, form heads (of wheat) **1.8** to put in place, place, locate دا ګړي ډېری اوبه ونیولي This pitcher holds a lot of water. **1.9** to strike, hit, graze (of a bullet) مرمۍ هډوکي نیولئ The bullet grazed a bone. **1.10** to rent, lease **1.11** to hire نوکر نیول to hire a servant پلندۍ نیول to hire a porter **1.12** to strike (of death, illness, etc.) تاسي پرون تبی نیولاست؟ Did you have an attack of the fever this evening? **1.13** to cover, put facing on **1.14** to surround د کابل شاو خوا غرو نیولي ده Kabul is surrounded by mountains. **1.15** to direct, aim توپک مي ورته ونیوه I aimed the rifle at him. **1.16** to make, take (a decision, measures, etc.) **1.17** to set a course (of an airplane, ship) **1.18** to observe (e.g., a fast) **1.19** to gather in, take up نیول کېدل *passive* **a** to be taken, be seized هغه به تر نظارت لاندي ونیوه شي He will be placed under surveillance. **b** to be caught غل ونیول شو The thief was caught **c** to be taken over, be occupied **d** to be placed, be located **e** to be hit (by a bullet) **f** to be rented, be leased **g** to be hired **h** to be covered, be faced **i** to be surrounded **j** to become ill, begin to ache سر مي ونیول شو My head has begun to ache badly. **k** to be directed, be aimed **l** to make, take (a decision, measures) په ښه ډول ترتیبات نیول شوي دي Appropriate measures have been taken. **m** to be observed (of a fast) **n** to be included دغه مسئله د خبرو په اجندہ کښې ونیوله شوه The question was included in the agenda. **o** to be covered (of an opening, hole) **2** *m. plural* **2.1** grabbing, seizing **2.2** catching; arrest **2.3** taking over, occupying **2.4** rental, leasing **2.5** covering, facing **2.6** surrounding **2.7** taking, making (decisions, measures, etc.) **2.8** observation (of a fast) **2.9** gathering in, taking up *idiom* څوک له د پلار ځای نیول to extract an admission from someone take the place of a father ژبه یې ونیوله He bit his tongue. ژبه دي ونیوله شه! He began to stammer. I wish your tongue would be taken out! خبره یې اوږده ونیوله He carried on a long conversation. احمد یې قاتل ونیوه They identified Ahmed as the murderer. ځان عاجز نیول to feign poverty هغه شهرت یې دنیا نیولۍ He was famous the world over. ځان نیولای نشي He cannot restrain himself. لمر تندري ونیو، د ستبشن نیول There was a solar eclipse. رادیو ستبشن نیول to listen to a radio transmission, intercept a radio transmission خوله یې نه نیول کېږي He will not be silent. په خبرو ونیول شو He was drawn into the conversation.

نیولتیا nivɗltjá *f.* seizing, catching, detention; imprisonment; captivity

نیولی njólaj [1] *m.* ☞ نولی [1]

نیولئ nivɗlaj [2] **1** *past participle of* نیول **2.1** sluggish, unenergetic نیولئ a sluggish person **2.2** restrained; muffled نیولئ آواز، نیولئ سری a low voice **2.3** beginning **2.4** narrow, cramped

نیون neón *m.* neon

نیونک nivnák *m.* clips (for holding back hair)

نيونه **nivǿna** *f.* ☞ نيول 2 نيونه كول په باښي to hunt with the aid of a falcon

نيونك **nivúnaj** *m.* ☞ نيوونى

نيوه **nivǿ** [1] *imperfect plural of* نيول 1

نيوه **nivǿ** [2] *m. plural* ☞ نيول 2 نيوه وركول **a** to give way, give in **b** نيوه کېدل to be caught (of a thief)

نيوه **nivá** *f.* handle (of a plow) [3]

نيوئ **nivǿj** [1] *Western imperfect of* نيول 1

نيوي **niví** [2] *vice* نوي [4]

نيويارک **njujǻrk** *m.* New York (city)

نهام **nihǻm** ☞

نهامول **nihaēmavǿl** *denominative, transitive* ☞ نيهامول

نهامېدل **nihāmedǿl** *denominative, intransitive* ☞ نيهامبدل

نئي **nǻje** *combination of the negative particle* نه *and the verb copula* يي

نېبل **najél** *m.* **1** stuffiness, closeness **2** moisture, dampness (of air) **3** wet, raw weather

نېبلجن **najeldzhán** **1** stuffy **2** raw, damp, moist, wet (weather) نيبل جن، نيبلجن

ڼ

ڼ **ṇuṇ** the thirty-seventh letter of the Pashto alphabet (it is not used at the beginning of words, and is pronounced as the retroflex "n")

ڼون **ṇun** the name of the letter ڼ

ڼى **ṇəj** *f. noun suffix* توکڼى spittoon

و

و **vāv** **1** thirty-eighth letter of the Pashto alphabet **2** number 6 in the abjad system

و [2] **vu vo** *verbal copula* **1** *third person singular:* he, it was هغه و? Where was he? **2** *dialect third person plural* دوی ناست و و؟ چيرې They were sitting.

و [3] **va** *Arabic conjunction* and وغيره and so forth, and others

و [4] **və** *preposition* (usually linked with the postposition; in poetry it may be omitted) دا كتاب و احمد ته وركه Give this book to Ahmed.

و [5] **vo** *dialect* ☞ هو [3]

و [6] **ve** *Eastern colloquial vice* وى [6]☞ هغه و ويل He said.

و [7] **vu vo və** *verbal prefix used to form the perfective aspect of simple verbs* **1** *placed immediately before the verb* وتړه! Tie it up! وخوت! وروايه! Speak! He arose! **2** *separated from the verb by several words or particles* و ور و به يي ليږم I will send it to them. به دي نه بخښنم I won't forgive you. **3** *in verbs beginning with* ا *"a" combines with the initial vowel into a single syllable "va"* والوت He flew off. He took off. تو پک دي واخيست؟ هو، وا مي خيست Did you take a rifle? Yes, I took one.

و [8] **u o və** *copulative conjunction, vocalic* (usually in compounds) بندوبست measure (step taken) سره و زرغونه rainbow (or in stabilized compounds) شاوخوا around; environs کاروبار matter, occupation; affairs

و [9] **va wah** *Arabic used in oaths* والله! Oh, Allah!

و [10] **u** *inflectional ending for oblique case of nouns, pronouns, and numerals* سړو ته ووايه Tell the people. په لويو کورونو کښي in big houses د هغو them, their, theirs

و [11] **ó** *m. & f. affectionate diminutive noun suffix* سدو Sado ولو Valo درخو Durkho

و [12] **ú** *augmentative suffix for adjectives* بريتو big-mustachioed خيتو big-bellied

و [13] **u ú** *first person plural verb inflectional ending* کوو We do. ځو We go.

و [14] **o** *dialect third person singular past tense verb inflectional ending in the Khalilo-Momand and several other dialects* وختو (he) ascended, climbed up

وا [1] **vā** *colloquial* **1** *vice* وايي [4] ته به وايي وايه you (singular) speak **2** *almost just as though* واتکه سپينه ده ږيره يي His beard is almost grey.

وا [2] **vā** *hunting* وا کول to train (a hunting bird)

وا [3] **vā** *combination of the verbal prefix* و *and* ا *"a" at the beginning of verbs* والوت He flew away. He took off. وانه خلي I hope he won't take it.

وابستگي **vābastagí** *f.* **1** dependence **2** kinship, relationship

وابسته **vābastá** **1.1** connected with something **1.2** dependent on something or someone **1.3** fastened to someone or something **2** *m.* [*plural:* وابستگان **vābastagán**] **.1** adherent; partisan **2.2** relative

واپس **vāpás** **1.1** last **1.2** returning **2** back واپس رارسېدل to return واپس غوښتل to ask back (a return of something) واپس روانېدل return to one's place home را واپس کېدل، را واپس کېدل، را واپس گرزېدل، را واپس to return, come back په خپلو الفاظو باندي واپس تلل گرزېدل to retract one's words

واپسي **vāpasí** *f.* **1** returning; return **2** *regional military* retreat, withdrawal

واپور **vāpór** *m.* steamboat

وات **vāt** *m.* defect, flaw

واترمارک **vātarmǻrk** *m.* watermark

واته [1] **vātǿ** *m. plural* **1** exit, way out **2** outlet (of a river) **3** departure **4** hatching out (of chicks) **5** swelling, swelling up **6** breaking out (of the bottom of a vessel, dish, etc.) **7** falling out, prolapse **8** dislocation **9** leaving, quitting (a job, etc.); dismissal **10** leaving, dropping out of **11** appearance, publication **12** output (e.g., of production); appearance **13** mining extraction

واته [2] **vātǿ** *imperfect plural of* وتل

وات [1] **vāṭ** *m.* [*plural:* واټونه **vāṭúna** *f. Eastern plural:* واټي **vǻṭe**] **1** road **2** prospect, wide street

واټ [2] **vāṭ** *m. electronics* watt

واتمېچ vāṭméch *m.* واتمېچی vāṭméchaj *m.* range-finder

واتن vāṭə́n *m.* 1 distance, space, interval به مساوي واتن equidistant 2 *math* measurement دري واتنونه the three dimensions (i.e., length, width, height); expanse, area

واتن سنځوونکی vāṭə́n sandzhavúnkaj *m.* واتن ښنودونکی ḵhodúnkaj *m.* sextant

واتی vá̄ṭaj *m.* force, strength, power

واج vādzh *m.* 1 exchange 2 barter goods واج کول to barter, exchange واج ورکول to carry on trade by barter په واج سودا کول barter goods

واجب vādzhíb *Arabic* 1.1 obligatory, compulsory; necessary لوی واجب کول He should be very grateful for this. شکر ورباندي واجب دئ to make obligatory, make compulsory; make necessary 1.2 worthy, fitting 2 *m.* [*plural:* واجبات vādzhibā́t] .1 debt, obligation 2.2 *plural* religious prescription

واجب الرعایه vādzhib-ar-ri'ājá *Arabic* 1 deserving of attention 2 excusable

واجبي vādzhibí *Arabic* obligatory, compulsory; necessary; customary

واخی vá̄tsaj *m.* cheek

واحد vāhíd *Arabic* 1.1 only واحد زوی only son 1.2 single; general; whole واحده قاعده general rule, common rule واحد حکم single general opinion 1.3 definite, determined په یوه واحد وخت کښي in a definite period of time 1.4 separate, individual 2 *m.* .1 unit د monetary unit 2.2 unit (economic, etc.) 2.3 complex, set

واحه vāhá *f. Arabic* oasis سمسوره واحه green oasis

واخ vākh *interjection* alas; oh; ah; eh واخ کول to exclaim, "Oh! Ah!"

واخله vā́khla ☞ واخه 1

واخه 1 vā́kha *colloquial* 1 *perfective imperative of* اخیستل 2 beginning with, counting from ... نه واخه د هندوکش غرونه ټول All of the mountain ranges beginning with Hindu Kush ...

واخه 2 vākhə́ *m. plural Eastern* ☞ وانه

وادار vādā́r compelled وادار کول ☞ وادارول

وادارول vādāravə́l *denominative, transitive* [*past:* وادار یي کړ] to compel, oblige وتلو ته وادارول to force to depart ... په دې وادارول to compel to ...

واده 1 vādə́ *m.* [*plural:* ودونه vadúna] wedding د واده جامي wedding dress د لمري میاشت honeymoon واده کول a *compound verb* ☞ ودول b to get married, celebrate a wedding واده دي کړی دئ؟ Are you married? د خپلي خوښي واده کول to get married, marry for love ودبدل *compound verb* ☞ واده کېدل a forced marriage د ناخوښي واده to marry twice دوه ودونه کول د واده مجلس جوړول to arrange a wedding feast

واده 2 vādá *f. colloquial* ☞ وعده

واده تر vādətár *m.* arranging a wedding, arrangement of a wedding

واده وال vādəvā́l *m.* man celebrating his wedding, man entering into marriage

واده واله vādəvā́la *f.* woman celebrating her wedding, woman entering into marriage

وادي 1 vādí *f.* [*plural:* وادی vādə́j *plural:* وادیگاني vādigā́ni] 1 valley; bed (of a river) 2 oasis

وادي 2 vādé *plural of* واده 2

وار 1 vār *m.* 1 time اول وار the first time; بل وار for the first time دوهم وار another time a second b secondly دوه واره twice; double د دواړو مسلو بحث simultaneously په یو وار سره once more یو وار بیا once more په یوه وار سره کول to discuss two questions at once په وارو وارو frequently, repeatedly; many times, recurrently په وارو زیاتول to increase manyfold وار دواره suddenly, all at once له واره unexpectedly, all of a sudden یو وار at once, abruptly 2 turn یو یو تن په وار وار a gradually b in turn, by turns وار سره، وار په وار in turn, in په خپل وار to go singly in order of turn دننه راتللل order of turn په خپل وار سره in one's own turn وار ایندل a to alternate b to establish a turn یو بل ته یي د خبرو وار نه ورکاوه They interrupted one another. 3 blow د توري وار a sword blow وار کول a to await one's turn b to deal a blow to 4 vengeance, revenge د جنگ په لمري وار کښي to avenge *idiom* وار اخیستل at the beginning of the battle ستا وار کسان people like you وار غوښتل to ask for postponement وار میندل، وار مینده کول to take advantage of the occasion; to find the possibility هیڅ وار مي ندئ خطا I am not at all worried. وار مه خطا کوه Don't worry. وار یي خطا سو He lost his head. دوی وار خطا شو They were embarrassed.

وار 2 vār *m.* laying (of eggs)

وار 3 vár *suffix* used with noun and adjective loanwords denoting possession, endowment with or mastery of a subject or quality امېدوار a hoping, relying on b graduate (holder of the first university degree)

واروپار 1 vārpā́r *m.* ☞ واروپار

وارتل 2 vārətə́l *transitive* ☞ ارتول

وارته vá̄rta thrown

وارث vārís *m. Arabic* [*plural:* وارثان vārisā́n *Arabic plural:* ورثه varasá] heir, successor شرعي وارث legal heir د ورثو په مینځ کښي among the heirs زما وارث خپل زوی دئ My son is my heir.

وارثه vārisá *f. Arabic* heiress

وارخطا vārkhatā́ *predicative* 1 embarrassed; rattled 2 worried 3 stunned, staggered وارخطا کول a to embarrass b to trouble c to stun وارخطا کېدل a to be embarrassed; lose one's self-possession b to be troubled مه وارخطا کېږه! Don't worry! c to be stunned, be staggered

وارخطايي vārkhatājí *f.* 1 embarrassment 2 worry 3 stupefaction

وارد vāríd *Arabic* 1.1 forthcoming; arriving; entering وارد کول ☞ واردبدل ... چه له واردو خبره څخه ښکاره کېږي وارد کېدل From the news that has arrived it is clear that ... 1.2 causal (of damage) 2 *m.* .1 arrival د وارد دمندي لیکه landing strip 2.2 [*plural:* واردین vāridín] importer

واردات vāridā́t *m. Arabic plural* [*singular:* وارده 1] 1 imported goods, imports د واراداتو او صادراتو توازن the external trade balance

2 revenues, receipts 3 *regional* event, incident, happening; occurrence واردات لوی لوی major events *idiom* علمي واردات scientific problems

وارداتي vāridātí import, pertaining to import وارداتي اقلام items of import وارداتي قلمونه items of import

واردکوونکی vāríd kavúnkaj importing

وادوواره vādəvā́ra suddenly, all at once

واردول vāridavə́l *denominative, transitive* [*past:* وارد یې کړ] 1 to import 2 له خارجه واردول، له خارج څخه واردول to import from abroad to note down, enter (e.g., in a journal, on a list) 3 to bring about, cause (e.g., unhappiness, ill luck) 4 to cause, be the reason for 5 to exert (pressure, etc.)

وارده vāridá *f.* 1 *Arabic official* .1 incoming documentation 1.2 incoming mail (from abroad) 2 *feminine & plural of* وارد [1] وارده مکتوبونه incoming correspondence

واردیدل vāridedə́l 1 *denominative, intransitive* [*past:* وارد شو] .1 to be imported 1.2 to be noted down, be entered (e.g., in a journal, on a list) 1.3 to arrive 1.4 to enter, come in 1.5 to arise 2 *m. plural* ☞ واردیده

واردیده vāridedə́ *m. plural* 1 import 2 noting down, entry (e.g., in a journal, on a list) 3 arrival 4 entry, entrance 5 origin

وارد vāṛḍ *m. regional* hospital ward خیراتي وارد hospital charity ward

وارس vārás *m.* inspector

وارسا vārsá *f.* Warsaw

وارسي vārasí *f.* inspection; check; surveillance

واریخت vāríḫt *m.* ☞ اورښت

وارگری vārgə́raj *m.* man who has the right to use something in his turn د ژرندي وارگری څوک دئ؟ Whose turn is it to take his grain to the mill?

وارگه vārgá [1] *f. regional* unseemly affair; inappropriate thing

وارگه vārgə́ [2] *m. plural* ☞ اوربده

وارنټ vāránṭ *m. regional* 1 arrest warrant 2 warrant (e.g., warehouse warrant); customhouse license

واروپار vārvəpā́r [1] *m.* feeling, sensitivity; moral condition

واروپار vārupā́r [2] through, through and through; from both sides

واره vāra [1] *f.* 1 suitable, fitting the occasion واره کول to await the occasion خپلي واري ته گوري He is waiting for an appropriate occasion. واره کول to take advantage of the occasion 2 advantage, profit

واره vāṛə́ [2] *tautological with* خواره

واره vā́ra [3] *oblique singular and short plural of* وار [1]

وارهمن vāramə́n useful, advantageous

واری vā́raj [1] *m.* ☞ وار واری کول a to alternate, take turns b to inflict a blow

واري vārí [2] *m.* sacrifice, victim واري کول *compound verb* to sacrifice

واریانت vārjā́nt vārijā́nt *m.* version

واریز vāríz vāréz periodic, intermittent واریزه تبه intermittent fever

واره vāṛə *m. plural* heel bones

واره vā́ra [2] *pronoun* 1 all, every په وارو پسي after all واره خلگ یي All are saying this. واره همغسي دي They are all that way. 2 as a whole, in their entirety لس واره all ten

واره vāṛə́ [3] *m. plural and indirect singular of* وور [1]

واره خرڅوونکی vāṛə́ khartsa-vúnkaj *m.* retailer

واره زیگه vāṛə́-zigə́ *m. plural* children

واره و زاره vāṛə-və-zāṛə vāṛə́-u-zāṛə́ *m. plural* young and old

واري vā́ri *tautological with* کاري

واز vāz open, wide-open, gaping وازول ☞ واز کول

وازخولی vāzkhvúlaj vāzkhvúlaj 1 wide-open mouth, with open mouth 2 exceedingly surprised, stupefied; stunned وازخولی سری scatterbrained person

وازده vā́zda *f. Eastern* ☞ د نس وازده وازگه internal fat

وازسترگی vāzstə́rgaj 1 with open eyes 2 immodest, shameless

وازکټ vāzkíṭ *m.* ☞ واسکټ vāzkíṭ *m.*

وازگه vā́zga *f.* fat

وازول vāzavə́l *denominative, transitive* [*past:* واز یې کړ] 1 to open, open wide, gape 2 to yawn (mouth, jaws)

وازه vāzə́ *f.* [*plural:* وازي vāzé *plural:* وزي vazé وازونه vāzúna *m.* وزونه vazúna] *m.* 1 measure of length equal to 34 meters (used most frequently in measuring rope) 2 pace (of a horse)

وازه vā́za [2] 1 *feminine singular of* واز 2 *used in geographical names* وازه خوا Vazakhva (place in southern Afghanistan)

وازه خوله vā́za khulá vā́za khvulá stupified, lost one's head وازه خوله کېدل to be stupefied, become disoriented (because of some strong emotion), lose one's head

وازی vāzáj [1] *m.* measurement equal to 28 inches or 71 centimeters

وازي vā́zi [2] *f. plural of* واز

وازېدل vaēzedə́l *denominative, intransitive* [*past:* واز شو] 1 to open wide, gape 2 to yawn 3 to reveal itself, appear, come to light

واژگون vāzhgún overturned, toppled over

واژه vāzhə́ *imperfect of* وژل [1]

واژه vāzhə́ [2] *m. plural* 1 murder, slaying 2 extinguishing, stifling (a fire) 3 suppression (of an emotion, etc.)

واږمه vāgmá *f.* slight breeze; zephyr ☞ وږمه

واست vāst *Western second person plural of the verbal copula* were

واسط vāsít *Arabic* middle, average

واسطه vāsitá *f. Arabic* [*plural:* واسطي vāsité *m. Arabic plural:* وسائط vasāít] 1 mediation د ... په واسطه by means of something واسطه غوښتل to ask for mediation, ask for intercession 2 means 3 reason a په دي واسطه، په دي واسطه سره in this way; thus b for this reason په همدي واسطه therefore 4 patronage, influence

واسع vāsí' *Arabic* expansive, extensive, broad

واسکټ vāskáṭ vā́skíṭ *m.* waistcoat, vest

واسلین vāsilín *m. plural* Vaseline

واسیکه vāsiká urgently, quickly, in an instant

واشنگټن vāshingṭán *m.* Washington

واښ vāx̌ *m.* **1** rope (of wool or hair); lasso **2** *military* sword belt واښ او غاړه کېدل to go to someone with head hanging in guilt or shame of accusation ستا یم واښ، زما یې غاړه! I am at your mercy; اوس مو د کار واښ او غوزی سره وختئ! do with me what you will! واښ او غوزی کېدل *Western* Our deal has fallen through. to be concluded (of work, a matter) اوس مو کار واښ او غوزی شو Well now, we have finished the work.

واښکی ورته vāx̌káj *m.* **1** cord, rope (usually made of wool) غورول *literal* to spread the rope *figuratively* to get ready to take, take up something ته نو واښکی مه ورته غوروه *literal* Do not ready the rope. Don't spread the rope. *figurative* It is not for you to see this thing. یوه ویل *proverb* کور مې تر تا جار! ده واښکی ورته وغوراوه One man said "I sacrifice my house to you!" Another prepared the rope. **2** bunch (of grapes)

واښه vāx̌ə́ *m. plural* grass بې خایه straw سپین واښه hay وچ واښه واښه hay واښه ربېل ، لوی لوی واښه high grass; tall weeds واښه کېدل to mow grass, cut hay په to grow green (of grass) واښه شوي The steepe began to grow green.

واښه والا vāx̌əvālá *m.* merchant or dealer in hay and fodder

واښی váx̌haj *m.* rope, cord

واصف vāsíf *Arabic* **1** describing **2** praising

واصل vāsíl *Arabic* **1** arriving **2** joining واصل کول *transitive* to join واصل کېدل *intransitive* to join

واضح vāzíh *Arabic* evident, obvious; clear, distinct دا یو واضح حقیقت دئ This is the obvious truth. دا بیخي واضحه ده چه ... It is completely clear that ... a په واضح ډول clearly, obviously b distinctly واضح کول to explain, clarify موږ دا واضحه کړه چه ... We explained that ...

واضحاً vāzíhán *Arabic* **1** obviously, evidently **2** clearly, distinctly; precisely

واعظ vā'íz *m. Arabic [plural:* واعظان vā'izā́n *Arabic plural:* واعظین vā'izín] **1** preacher **2** mentor, tutor, instructor

واعظه vaē'izá *feminine of* واعظ

واعظي vaē'izí *f.* preaching, homiletics

واعي vā'í *Arabic* careful, attentive واعي عقل memory; recollection, reminiscence

واغوز vāghóz *m.* Vagoz (settlement)

واف vāf *m.* **1** nightingale **2** *figurative* singer

وافر vāfír *Arabic* **1** abundant, profuse وافر بارانونه abundant rains وافره اوبه period of high water **2** *figurative* extensive, great (of wisdom, etc.)

واق vāk *m.* pochard (species of diving duck)

واقع ¹ vāḳí' *Arabic* **1** located, situated (somewhere) بنگله په یوه غونډۍ واقع ده The summerhouse stands on a hill. **2** happening, occuring هیڅ کار بې a to occur, take place, happen; be واقع کېدل علت او سبب نه واقع کېږي Nothing happens without a reason. b to prove, turn out to be, be found to be موثر واقع کېدل to turn out to be operative, turn out to be effective **3** true دا یو واقع حقیقت دئ This

is a true fact. په واقع کښې بل څه دئ In actuality, this is something else. په خپل ذات او واقع کښې in actuality, in its essence

واقع ² vāḳí' *m. Arabic plural of* واقعه

واقعاً vāḳí'án *Arabic* actually, in actuality, indeed, factually

واقعات vāḳí'ā́t *m. Arabic plural of* واقعه .

واقعات پسندي vāḳí'ātpasandí *f.* **1** realism **2** realistic approach

واقع بیني vāḳí'biní *f.* realism له واقع بیني نه کار اخیستل to approach realistically

واقعه ¹ vāḳí'a *f.* vāḳe'á *Arabic [plural:* واقعي vāḳí'é *m. plural:* واقعات vāḳ'ā́t *plural:* واقع vāḳ'í] occurrence, event, incident, happening, encounter پر هره واقعه for any reason د واقعو لیکونکی chronicler, annalist دغسي واقعات په ژوند کښې ډېر پېښیږي This often happens in life. واقعه یې ورته بیان کړه He told them what the situation was. واقعه او ډکه پېښېدل to befall (of disaster) خو روپی وساته ، یوه واقعه او ډکه به پېښوي سي Save this money for a rainy day.

واقعه ² vāḳí'a *f. singular of* واقع ¹

واقعي vāḳí'í vāḳe'í **1** actual, factual; true; real; concrete, definite په واقعاً ☞ واقعي صورت ، په واقعي صورت سره in reality, actually **2**

واقعیت vāḳí'iját vaḳe'iját *m. Arabic* actuality, reality; concreteness; definiteness دا یو څرګند واقعیت دئ This is the obvious truth. to become actuality, become reality, come to pass میندل

واقف vāḳíf *Arabic* **1** informed; knowing, acquainted هغه مي واقف یم I know him. واقف حال vāḳíf-i experienced واقف کول to acquaint (with), introduce (to) د خطر نه واقف کول to warn of danger واقف کېدل to know, become acquainted **2** *m. regional* acquaintance دوی د هغه زاړه واقفان وو These were his old acquaintances. دا سړی څمونږ واقف و This man was an acquaintance of ours. We knew this man.

واقفیت vāḳifiját *m. Arabic* acquaintance, experience د ... څخه واقفیت لرل to know something; have experience in something

واک vāk **1** *m.* **.1** authority, plenary powers, right مقنینوي واک legislative authority اجرائي واک executive power د واک خاوندان rulers; authorities تر واک لاندي subject (to), dependent (upon) دوی په خپل واک دي They are free to do what they wish. واک ستاسي دئ if it was in my power که زما خپل واک وای our will واک لرل to have a د واکه وتل the authority, have the plenary power, have the right to pass from subordination خوله یې له واکه وتلی ده He said whatever came into his head. He is babbling. b to be beyond the strength (of) **1.2** strength, power واک پر یو شي رسېدل to be in a position to do something a په دې کتاب مي واک نه رسېږي I am not in a position to buy this book. b I am not in a situation to understand this book. د هغې په دې پلنډه مي واک نه رسېږي This burden is too much for me. اوښکي په واک نه وي She could not restrain her tears. She is a crybaby. **1.3** warrant, mandate **2** *combining form with compound adjectives* خپلواک independent, self-sufficient

واکدار vākdár **1** *m.* **.1** leader; ruler د امورو واکدار leaders; rulers; authorities **1.2** boss; manager **1.3** parent, guardian (of a bride, groom) **2.1** sovereign **2.2** competent, enjoying full rights

واکسين vāksín *m.* **1** vaccine **2** shot, inoculation واکسين کول *compound verb* to give a shot واکسين کېدل *compound verb* to get a shot

واکسيناسيون vāksināsjón *m.* واکسينشن vāksineshán *m.* ☞ واکسين 2

واک لرونکی vāk larúkaj 1 *m.* **.1** leader; ruler; representative of the authorities د چارو واک لرونکی vāk larúnki leaders; rulers; authorities **2.1** self-governing **2.2** competent

واکمن vākmə́n *m.* **1** ☞ واکوال 2 **2** king; emperor

واکمني vākmə́ni *f.* ☞ واکوالی

واکوالا vākvālá 1 *m.* **.1** واک والا، واکوالا، واک وال، واکوال leader; ruler; soverign; potentate لوی واکوال *history* an atabeg **1.2** parent, guardian (of a bride, groom) **2.1** independent, self-governing, sovereign **2.2** competent; plenipotentiary; having the right **2.3** leading, governing واکواله جرګه government, leadership, presidium

واکوالی vākválaj *m.* **1** authority, power **2** leadership; administration **3** independence; self-government; sovereignty; state system

واکي vākí *f.* *suffix for derivatives signifying mastery of or endowment with some quality* خپلواکي sovereignty, freedom, independence

واګڼ vāgə́ṇ stunned, stupefied

واګون vāgón *m.* *railroad* **1** car **2** hand trolley, dolly, wagon

واګه vāga *f.* **1** bit; rein; reins **2** rudder; steering wheel **3** *figurative* reins of government د حکومت واګي په خپل لاس کښي نيول، د حکومت واګي په لاس کښي نيول to take the reins of government into one's own hands **4** black woolen sash or belt with tassels

وال vāl *m.* whale

وال vál *m.* *suffix* **1** owner or seller of something بنګړيوال bracelet seller **2** resident of some district بنبروال man from Buna **3** one engaged in some activity ليکوال writer

والا vālá 1 *Arabic* high, most high, great (usually in titles)

والا vāillá 2 *Arabic* **1** *negative conjunction* on the contrary, just the opposite **2** *interjection* truly; really and truly

والا vālá 3 *f.* light taffeta

والا vālá 4 a مجهول (و) والا توري **1** having or possessing something word ending in "o" **2** *m.* owner, proprietor د عقل والا intelligent man ملي جامو والا a man dressed in national costume

والا vālá 5 *m.* *suffix* **1** seller, owner آس والا horse owner ختکی والا melon seller **2** person engaged in some activity نوکري والا duty officer ډوډۍ والا baker

والاحضرت vālā́hazrát *m.* *Arabic* His Highness

والاشان vālā́shā́n *m.* *Arabic* His Excellency

والد vālíd *m.* *Arabic* father, male parent

والده vālidá *f.* *Arabic* mother, female parent

والدين vālidájn *m.* *Arabic plural* parents

والساکټ vālsākíṭ *m.* *electronics* wall socket

والسلام vāssalā́m *Arabic* and that's all

والګا vālgā́ *f.* ☞ ولګا

والګي vālgáj 1 *m.* head cold والګی يې دئ He has a head cold. وهلئ يم I have caught a head cold. vālgí I have a head cold. I have caught a head cold.

والګی vālgə́j 2 *f.* **1** ☞ والی 2 **2** haloxylon root

والله اعلم vāllaha'lamú *Arabic* It is known best to God. God knows best.

واله vālə́ 1 *f.* vālá [*plural:* ولي] irrigation channel تر ولي تېري پوري *literal* to conduct a man through an irrigation tunnel ايستل *figuratively* to wind around one's finger, hoodwink

واله vála 2 *f.* *suffix dialect vice* والی

واله vála 3 *f.* *feminine of* وال

والي vālí 1 *m.* *Arabic* wali, ruler; governor-general (of Kabul Province) عمومي والي governor-general د هندوستان عمومي والي *history* governor-general, viceroy of India

والی vālə́j 2 *f.* earring, earbob د غوږ والی earring, earbob

والی válaj 3 *m.* *suffix for derivative nouns* ښرنګه والی quality سپين والی whiteness معتدل والی moderation

والي بال vālibā́l *m.* vālibā́l volleyball والي بال، واليبال

وام vām 1 *m.* credit; debt; crediting, giving credit to

وام vām 2 *m.* vice بې له بېري او وام وهم without caution, fearlessly

وام vām 3 *colloquial vice* وايم

وان vấn *m.* *suffix* actor, person involved in an action a کښتي وان boatman b sailor موټروان chauffeur, driver

وانا vānā́ *f.* Vana (city, Waziristan)

واند vānd *m.* proposal, intention واند کول to suppose, propose

وانده vấnda *f.* nomad camp; camp وانده کېدل *compound verb* to dispose oneself under the open sky (on the road); be situated under the open sky (on the road)

وانګ vāng *m.* وانګر vāngə́r *m.* pomegranate

وانګي vấngi-vấngi divided into parts; cut up into parts وانګي وانګي کول to divide into parts; cut up into parts وانګي وانګي کېدل to be divided into parts; be cut up into parts

وانمڅه vānmə́tsa *f.* dowry of a bride

وانمود vānamúd *m.* simulation; pretense, hypocrisy

وانو vānó *f.* ☞ وانا

وانه vấṇa 1 *f.* واني usually plural vấṇi tendons (of the foot) واني يې بې وتنبتېدي، واني يي وختي He acted the coward.

وانه vấṇa 2 *f.* pile of ground grain on the threshing floor

وانه vāṇá 3 *f.* ☞ وانا

واو vāv *m.* name of the letter و ؛ مجهول واو the phoneme "o" معروف the phoneme "u" ملين واو the diphthong "au"

واوا vāvā́ 1 *f.* *children's speech* good thing, "num-num"

واوا vā vā́ 2 *interjection* **1** How is this so? Oho! **2** ah ha; bravo; good

واورا vāvrá *m.* vulture, carrion bird

واورجن vāvradzhə́n snowy واورجن پسرلی snowy spring

واوره vávra 1 *f.* **1** snowflake **2** [*plural:* واوري] vávri snow د واوري طوفان snowstorm, blizzard دائمي واوري spring snows د واوري waterfall واوره اوري It is snowing. واورو پېتول to غونډېسکي a lump of snow cover with snow, dust with snow تر واورو لاندي کېدل to be covered with snow *proverb literal* پردى غم له واوري سوړ دئ Another man's grief is colder than snow. *figurative* Another man's grief does not disturb one.

واوره واوره vávra *perfective imperative of* اوربدل [2]

واوره غرى vāvraghəraj *m.* flake (of snow)

واوره نى vāvraṇáj *m.* 1 cellar, icehouse, storehouse for snow (in summer) 2 accumulation of snow in the mountains

واوره والا vāvravālá *m.* seller of snow (in summer)

واوري [1] vávri *plural of* واوره [1]

واوري [2] vávri *present tense of* اوربدل [2]

واورین vāvrín *adjective* snow; snowy واورین غر snowy mountain واورینه هوا snowy weather

واول vāvál *m.* واویل vāvél *m.* vowel خج والا واول stressed vowel

واویلا vāvajlá *f.* واوېلى vāveláj *m. Arabic* groaning, moaning ولي ورپسي دومره واویلا کوي؟ کول Why are you sighing over her? to groan, moan

واه vāh *interjection* bravo; excellent; splendid

واهمه vāhimá *f. Arabic* 1 imagination 2 fear, fright, apprehension, worry د واهمي مرض apprehension واهمي‌دار mistrust, suspicion ما ته دا واهمه راولوېږي چه to frighten, scare واهمه پرېوتل، واهمه لوېدل … I began to fear … I began to become apprehensive lest … دا د دي څخه په واهمه to be afraid, fear, beware of; worry کېني وه چه … She feared that … She was apprehensive lest …

واهه [1] vāhə́ *imperfect of* وهل

واهه [2] vāhə́ *m. plural* ☞ وهنه

وای [1] vāj *interjection* 1 oh (expressing surprise, fright, pain) وای وای وای په تا باندي! Woe betide thee! 2 *m.* وای وای! Oh! Oh! ما له وای وای یي کاوه moaning, groaning He moaned and groaned. وای د دوى پر حال! وکړل I cried out in pain. Woe betide them!

وای [2] vāj *conditional and optative form of the verbal copula* "had," "would be," "would," "should," *etc.* خنګه به ښه وای چه … as وای که ته راغلئ If I had known! که زه خبر وای! would be good که تا ویلي وای if you had said you should come

وای [3] vāj *present stem of* ویل [3]

وایاست vājāst *Western second person plural present of* ویل [3]

وایرنګ vājring *m.* wiring وایرنګ کول to install wiring

وایسرا vājsrá *m. history* viceroy (in India)

وایسراتوب vājsrātób *m.* function or post of viceroy; region ruled by a governor-general

وایم vājəm *first person plural present tense of* ویل [3]

وایه [1] vája *imperative prefective of* ویل [3]

وایه [2] vājá *f.* 1 shame, modesty وایه کول، وایه لرل to be ashamed 2 urgent or necessary thing بې وایي کېدل a to be insolent b to be superfluous

وایه [3] vājə́ *m. plural* 1 utterance 2 reading 3 studies 4 declaration; announcement 5 composition (of verses)

وایه [4] vājə́ *imperfect of* ویل [3]

وایه من vājamə́n ashamed; modest

وائي [1] vājí *f.* 1 sunrise, morning glow 2 sunset, evening glow

وائي [2] vājí pawning (of property)

وايي [3] váje *second person present of* ویل

وائي [4] váji *present tense of* ویل [3]

وایئ [5] vájəj *Eastern second person plural present tense of* ویل [3]

وايي [6] vái *regional* ☞ وای [1]

ویا vabā́ *f. Arabic* 1 cholera ویا ګډه ده، ویا لوېدلي ده Cholera is raging. 2 wholesale deaths, high mortality; epidemic ویا وهلئ a cholera victim

وباسي vúbāsi *Eastern present tense of* ایستل *vice* باسي

ویال vabā́l *m. Arabic* 1 sin; transgression 2 unhealthy climate

وبائي vābāí *adjective* epidemic وبائي امراض epidemic diseases, epidemics

ویره vábra *combining form* -ish, somewhat شین ویره bluish سپین ویره whitish

ویزه vubə́za *f.* moth, clothes moth

ویس vabás That's it. That's all.

وبنکه vubakha *dialect imperative of* بنل

ویلته vəbə́lta ☞ ویله [1]

ویله [1] vabála *Eastern* ☞ بل (یو له بله) *and* ویله باندي one on top of another, in a heap

ویله [2] vabalá *f.* means, way, mode, method

ویله [3] vabalá *f.* dancing

ویننه vabnə́ stubborn, obstinate, pigheaded, bullheaded

وپار vəpár *m.* 1 trade, commerce; trade operations وپار کول to trade, engage in trade 2 commercial credit 3 furniture, decor (of a home)

وپاري vapārí *m.* 1 merchant, trader 2 reliable contractor

ویره vuprá *dialect* ☞ اپره

وت [1] vət vut 1 canyon د خرد کابل وت the Khurdkabul Canyon 2 interval, small increment (distance) 3 tooth, cog 4 crack; cleft

وت [2] vit ☞ ویت

وت [3] vat *dialect imperfect of* وتل *vice*

وتاړه vútāṛə *perfective aspect* تړل

وتاوته vətā́vata *dialect vice* تاته

وتر [1] vatár moist, wet, profusely watered (by rains, etc., of land) وتر کېدل to be moist

وتر [2] vitár 1 *m.* prayer 2 only, unique

وتر [3] vitár *m.* [*plural:* وترونه vitarúna *Arabic plural:* اوتار avtā́r] 1 string; bowstring 2 *math* chord; hypotenuse

وترنري vatərnarí *f.* ☞ ویترنري veterinarí

وتره [1] vátra *f.* 1 moistened land, wet land چه باران وشو، نو زمکه وتره شوه After the rain the soil became moist. 2 *figurative* fertile soil, favorable ground

وتره [2] vatrá *f.* sluice; floodgate

وتري vátəri *f. plural* furnishings (of a house); decor

وتګى vətgáj *m.* vutgáj 1 canyon; hollow 2 flue; smoke conduit

وتل ¹ vatә́l 1 intransitive [present: وزي vúzi past: ووت vúvot past: ووت] often joined with the pronouns را، در، ور. 1.1 to go out, leave, depart له کوټي ووت to leave the room له کوره ووت He left the house. 1.2 to go out hunting به ښکار وتل to go out, leave, depart 1.2 to flow (from, out of), originate (of a river) 1.3 to set out سفر ته وتل to set out on a journey 1.4 to hatch out (of chicks) 1.5 to swell, swell up زما شونډه وتلي ده My lip swelled up. 1.6 to be knocked out, be broken out (of the bottom of a vessel, etc.) 1.7 to tumble out, fall out د هلک غاښ ووت، د هلک غاښ وووت The child's tooth fell out. 1.8 to be dislocated لاس يې له مږونده وتلئ He dislocated his arm. 1.9 to be knocked off, broken off (e.g., of the spout of a teapot) 1.10 to jump off, fall, tumble off 1.11 to break out, come out 1.12 to come off (the rails, etc.); drive off (the road) اورګاډي د اوسپني له لاري وت، اورګاډي د اوسپني له لاري وووت The train went off the tracks. 1.13 to end (in, at), reach (of a road) دا لار چېرته وځي؟ Eastern Where does this road lead? 1.14 to leave, quit (work, service); retire له مأموريت څخه وتل to leave the service, retire 1.15 to pass (of time) د وري مياشت ووته The month of Hamal has passed. 1.16 to drop out of something, leave, depart له يوې ډلې څخه وتل، له يوې ډلي وتل to leave the company, leave the society 1.17 to be excluded from something 1.18 to spring up, begin, arise (of a rumor) دا خبره له کومه ووته؟ Where did this rumor come from? 1.19 to break from, escape from (of words, expressions) خما د خولي نه بې اختياره ووتل. I involuntarily broke out with … 1.20 to turn out, come out to be, prove 1.21 to come out (of printed matter), be published د اصلاح اخبار هره ورځ وزي The newspaper "Islah" comes out daily. کتاب مي سږکال له چاپ نه وتلئ دئ My book was published this year. 1.22 to come out, be released, appear نوي ډول طياري وتلي دي A new type of aircraft appeared. 1.23 to lead to something; flow out of, proceed (from) ددې څخه دا را ووتله چه … This led to the fact that … It came out that … 1.24 mining to extract, mine رنګه فلزات په ډېره اندازه سره وزي Many nonferrous metals are mined. 1.25 to be let by, let slip (e.g., of an opportune moment) 2 m. plural ☞ واته ¹ idiom له لاري وتل to lose the way له کاره وتل to be unfit; become obsolete کار له کاره ووت، کار له کاره وووت The matter is irremediable. 3 computer science to logout

وتلتوب vatәltób m. genius, greatness; outstanding abilities, outstanding talent

وتلئ vatәlәj 1 past participle of وتل 2.1 excellent, of high quality وتلي انگور an excellent grape 2.2 distinguished, exceptional وتلئ ليکوال a distinguished writer سړی وتلئ an exceptional man 3 Eastern conditional and optative form of وتل idiom نه وتلئ او نه نتلئ proverb Neither fish nor flesh. د شک څخه وتلئ undoubted

وتنه vatә́na f. 1 ☞ واته ¹ 2 trust in someone

وتو ¹ vató oblique of واته ¹

وتو ² vató dialect imperfect of وتل vice ووت

وتوځی vatódzaj m. 1 exit (place) 2 outflow (of a lake, pond)

وتول vitavә́l transitive ☞ وېتول

وتون vatún m. ☞ واته ¹

وته ¹ vutá f. 1 street 2 avenue د ونو وتې avenues

وته ² víta f. ☞ وېته

وته ³ vatá f. imperfective of وتل

وته ⁴ vatә́ m. plural dialect ☞ واته ¹

وته ⁵ vә́ta postposition often in poetry ☞ ته ⁴

وتی ¹ vataj m. 1 street 2 opening (of a street)

وتی ² vә́tәj vútәj past participle of وتل vice وتلئ

وتی ³ vataj Eastern conditional optative and potential forms of وتل vice وتلای

وتي ⁴ vaté f. plural imperfect of وتل

وتی ⁵ vuté plural of وته ¹

وتي ⁶ víti f. plural of ووت ²

وتیبدل vitedә́l intransitive ☞ وېتيبدل

وتینبس vútikh obsolete of تنبنتبس

وټ ¹ vaṭ m. ☞ وډ ¹

وټ ² vaṭ m. road

وټ ³ vaṭ m. 1 deficiency; defect 2 objection; protest

وټامن viṭāmín m. regional vitamin

وټانکی vaṭā́nkaj m. agreed upon place of assembly

وټ کټ vaṭkáṭ m. meeting

وټکی vuṭkáj m. flue, smoke conduit

وټندوی vaṭәndój vaṭәndúj economical, thrifty

وټ وټ vaṭvát m. ceaseless weeping, ceaseless tears

وټه ¹ vaṭá f. 1 defect; flaw 2 trade discount, discounted promissory note وټه کول to be discounted

وټه ² vā́ṭa f. 1 economy, thriftiness 2 tautological with ګټه

وټی ¹ vaṭáj m. 1 millrace 2 high part of the channel under which the millrace is installed

وټی ² vaṭáj m. [plural: وټي vəṭi plural: وټیان vəṭijā́n] 1 tassel; pompom 2 silk buttons on a dress (for decoration)

وټي ³ vaṭé plural of وټه ¹

وټي ⁴ vā́ṭi plural of وټه ²

وټی ótaj diminutive suffix کچنوتی small

وثیقه vasiḱé f. Arabic [plural: وثیقي vasiḱé m. Arabic plural: وثایق vasāík] 1 proof, evidence 2 treaty, agreement 3 document, certificate تحریري وثیقه written certification 4 guarantee

و.ج abbreviation ولاشان جلالتمآب (the title of) Governor-General نایب الحکومه His Excellency

ویجاړ vidzhā́ṛ ☞ وجاړ

ویجاړتوب vidzhā́ṛválaj m. ☞ وجاړوالی

ویجاړول vidzhā́ṛavól transitive ☞ وجاړول

ویجاړی vidzhā́ṛaj ☞ وجاړی

ویجاړیدل vidzhā́ṛedól intransitive ☞ وجاړیدل

وجایب vadzhāíb m. Arabic plural of وجیبه

وجد vadzhd m. Arabic 1 delight; rapture په وجد راوستل to bring into rapture 2 ecstasy

وجدان vidzhdān *m. Arabic* conscience خپل وجدان ته خجالت ايستل to feel the pangs of conscience خپل وجدان غولول to strike a bargain with conscience خپل وجدان خرخول to be for sale

وجداناً vidzhdānán *Arabic* morally

وجدان فروشه vidzhānfurúsha base, conscienceless

وجداني vidzhānī moral د چا سره وجداني moral debate وجداني وظيفه moral responsibility وجداني مسئوليت مرسته کول to give someone moral support

وجدانيت vidzhānijāt *m.* conscientiousness; conscience

وجع المفاصل vadzh'aalmafāsíl *m. Arabic* arthritis

وژل vadzhdəl وژل vadshlál *transitive dialect* ☞ وژل

وژله vádzhla *f. dialect* ☞ وژلون

وژنه vadzhóna *f. dialect f.* ☞ وژلون

وجو vadzhó *oblique of* وجه [1]

وجود vudzhúd *Arabic* 1 *m.* .1 existence, being پر وجود راوړل to exist په وجود راتلل، وجود پيدا کول a to show, appear (of looks, etc.) b وجود لرل to come true to exist, be 1.2 being, organism; body ډاکتر زما وجود وکوت The doctor examined me. 1.3 being, individual; person, body 1.4 amount on hand, presence 1.5 male organ 2 *predicative* existing ډېري مختلفي نظري وجودي دي Many different opinions exist. *idiom* يو وجود a unitary whole

وجودي vudzhudí [1] *Arabic* 1 individual, personal 2 essential *idiom* وجودي مذهب، وجودي فلسفه existentialism

وجودي vudzhúdi [2] *f. plural* ☞ وجود [2]

وجوه vudzhúh *m. Arabic plural of* وجه [1]

وجوهات vudzhuhāt *m. second plural of* وجه [1]

وجه vadzhh [1] *f.* vadzhha *Arabic* [plural: وجهي vádzhhi plural: vadzhé plural: وجهي vadzhhé *m. Arabic plural:* وجوه vudzhúh plural: وجوهات vudzhuhāt] 1 reason; cause; basis ددي څه وجه ده؟ What's going on? د دي وجه داده What's the situation? دا څه وجه ده؟ په همدغه وجه دئ چه This is why. له دي وجهي This is the reason. پدي وجه، پدي وجه سره، له دغي وجه نه، له دي This is the reason why. د يخني په وجه for this reason, because of the cold په دپره شنه وجه سره with considerable grounds له دوو وجهو for two reasons په شنه وجه especially 2 side, aspect 3 sum (of money) نقدي وجهي cash, ready cash 4 *grammar* mood 5 external aspect, appearance

وجه vúdzha [2] occiput, nape

وجه vudzhá [3] *f. Western* tendon, sinew

وجهه vádzhha *f.* ☞ وجه [1]

وجهي vadzhhí [1] *grammar* modal وجهي ادوات modal particles

وجهي vádzhhi [2] *f. plural of* وجهه

وجيبه vadzhibá *f. Arabic* [plural: وجيبي vadzhibé *m. Arabic* plural: وجائب vadzhāíb] obligation حقوق او وجائب rights and obligations

وجيزه vadzhizá *f. Arabic* moral (of a tale, etc.)

وچ vəch vuch 1 dry, callous وچه ډوډۍ dry bush a dry bread b bread alone, only bread وچ اودس dry wood وچ لرگي washroom وچ کال dry year, drought year تپ وچ completely dry 2

dry, arid, waterless وچ ډاگ dry plain 3 barren, sterile 4 lean, skinny وچ سړی a lean person, skinny person 5 dried out, faded, wilted وچه غوښه dried fruits وچي مېوي dried vegetables وچ سابه lean meat b dry-cured meat 6 dry, boring, uninteresting 7 unvoiced (of consonants) *idiom* وچ په موچه in vain, to no avail وچ He fears nothing. وچه غوښنه یې ده unpleasant words وچي خبري او لانده سره نغښتل a to lump everything together b to bawl out everyone indiscriminately

وچ ارغوی، وچ اورغوی vuchurghávaj 1 miserly, penurious 2 *m.* miser

وچ په وچه مقابلي ته تيار vuch-pə-vúcha in vain, to no avail شوئ دئ He is resisting in vain.

اوچت vuchát *dialect* ☞ وچت

وچتوب vəchtób *m.* 1 dryness, aridity 2 lack of water, waterlessness 3 sterility, barrenness 4 leanness, skinniness

اوچتول vuchatavál *transitive* ☞ وچتول

وچتوب vəchtjā́ *f.* ☞ وچ تيا، وچتيا

اوچتېدل vuchatedál *intransitive* ☞ وچتېدل

وچر vachár familiar, known

وچ سترگی vəchstárgaj shameless, bold-faced; immodest

وچ غاړی vəchghaṛaj 1 miserly, penurious 2 spoiled (of food because of unclean dishes or pots)

وچکالي vəchkālí *f.* drought سږ وچکالي ده This is a drought year.

وچ کنبی vəchkəkháj *m.* pencil

وچکل vəchkúl *m.* vuchkúl [plural: وچکلان vəchkulān] wether, castrated ram

وچ کلک، وچکلک vəchklák 1 completely dry 2 stiffening with cold 3 thin, gaunt; puny 4 dumbfounded; motionless 5 most pure وچکلک پښتون a pure-blooded Pushtoon 6 stable, inflexible *idiom* a وچکلک درېدل He has completely recovered. هغه وچکلک روغ شو to hesitate in speech b to be rooted to the spot c to be obstinate, insist

وچکل وچکول vəchkúl vuchkúl *m.* وچکولی vəchkúlaj vuchkúlaj ☞ وچکل

وچکی vəchakáj [1] *m.* وچکی vuchakáj *f.* typhus

وچکی vəchakáj [2] *m.* وچکی vuchakáj *f.* 1 peninsula 2 *regional* islet

وچکی vəchakáj [3] thin; gaunt

وچ لبنگی vəchlengáj 1 *m.* thin and tall man 2 lanky, with long and thin legs

وچ موری vəchmóraj 1 *m.* .1 child prematurely weaned 1.2 weanling, young animal that has ceased to suckle 1.3 weakling; runt 2 weaned (of a child, young animal) وچ موری کول to wean (of a child, animal) وچ موری کېدل to be weaned (of a child, animal)

وچ مېږن vəchmegán rather dry

وچن vachán *f.* 1 whitlow, felon, infection of a digit near or under the nail 2 disease of cattle

وچنه vəchána *f.* barren woman

وچوالی vəchvā́laj *m.* ☞ وچتوب، وچ والی

وچوبه vəchóba *f.* **1** waterless valley; unwatered land; dry-farming **2** dry land (as opposed to water) **3** dry spell, drought یوه وچه a severe drought

وچوبی vəchobáj *m.* **1** drought سخت وچوبی severe drought **2** water remaining in a system of irrigation wells and tunnels

وچوړکی vəchóṛkaj thin and weak; puny

وچوکي vəchúki *m.* kindling (chips, etc.); tinder

وچول vəchavəl *denominative, transitive* [*past:* وچ یې کړ] **1** to dry وچول کالي to dry laundry **2** to wipe away (sweat, etc.) **3** to dry-cure, jerk (meat, fish, etc.) **4** to consume, waste

وچ ولخه vəchólskhá vuchvóləkhá **1** *f.* waterless, arid desert **2** astounded, amazed وچ ولخه کېدل to be astounded, be amazed

وچ ولوند vəch-və-lúnd *m.* vuch-u-lúnd [*plural:* وچ ولانده vuch-u-landə́] good and bad, good and ill

وچولی vəchvólaj *m.* vuchvúlaj forehead, brow *idiom* په پراخه وچولی cordially

وچونه vəchavə́na *f.* **1** drying **2** wiping away (sweat, etc.) **3** dry-curing, jerking (meat, fish, etc.)

وچونی vəchunáj¹ *m. medicine* shingles, *Herpes zoaster*

وچوني vuchuní² *m.* lamb up to five moths old, weanling lamb

وچوونی vəchavúnaj *m.* **1** blotting up **2** towel

وچوبلی vəchveláj *m. dialect* forehead, brow

وچه vəcha **1** *f. singular of* وچ **2** *f.* dry land, continent، په وچه کېني د وچي لښکر land and sea سیند او وچه، وچه او لنده on land پر وچه ground troops

وچی باکی vəchibākáj *f.* urge to be sick, feeling of nausea

وچي پوچي vəchi-púchi *f. plural* nonsense, claptrap

وچېدل vəchedə́l *intransitive* [*past:* وچ شو] **1** to get dry, dry out, dry up, become dry (of a river, etc.) رود وچ شو The river dried up. **2** to be dry-cured, be jerked (of meat, fish, etc.) **3** to be paralyzed (of the extremities) لاس یې وچ شو His arm was paralyzed. **4** to be barren قلم یې وچ شو His pen ran dry. خوله دي وچه شه! May you perish! Drop dead!

وچېدنه vəchedə́na *f.* وچېده vəchedə́ *m.* **1** drying; desiccating; drying out, drying up (of a river, etc.) **2** dry-curing, jerking (meat, fish, etc.) **3** paralysis (of the extremities) **4** barrenness, childlessness

وچي کانگي کول vuche-kánge **a** to hiccup **b** to feel an urge to be sick, feel nauseous

وغ vudz *dialect present stem of* وتل

وځوکی vədzúkaj *m.* small burden, bundle

وځي vúdzi *dialect present of* وتل ☞ وزي¹

وټکه vótska vútska *f.* **1** raisin **2** *usually plural* وټکي vótski vútski raisins, sultanas

وټکه vútska² *perfective, imperative* ☞ ټکل

وټکېز vətskéz *m.* وټکېزه vətskéza *f.* frame of a hipped roof

وحداني vahdāní *Arabic religion* one, only, sole; divine

وحدانیت vahdāniját *m. religion* **1** unity **2** monism

وحدت vahdát *m. Arabic* unity وجود وحدت vahdát-i *philosophy* pantheism د فکر وحدت vahdát-i unity of action, collectivism د متضادو وحدت like-mindedness ملي وحدت national unity وحدت *philosophy* unity of opposites

وحش vahsh *Arabic* **1** wild, untamed **2** *m.* wild beast, feral animal د وحشانو باغ zoo, zoological garden

وحشت vahshát *m. Arabic* **1** barbarism; savagery; wildness **2** terror, fear چاته وحشت پیدنبول to frighten someone **3** wasteland, desert **4** solitude, loneliness

وحشتناک vahshatnāk wild, savage; terrifying, horrible, horrifying

وحشه vásha *f. singular of* وحشي

وحشي vahshí **1.1** wild, savage انسان وحشي a savage **1.2** ferocious **2** *m.* **.1** wild beast **2.2** savage **2.3** [*plural:* وحشیان vahshiján] savages, barbarians *f.* **2.4** *f.* [*plural:* وحشیاني vahshiján̄i] wild woman, female savage

وحشیانه vahshijān̄á wild, feral, cruel (of actions, deeds, etc.)

وحشیت vahshiját *m. Arabic* **1** wildness **2** savagery, ferociousness

وحي vahí *f.* revelation, inspiration

وحید vahíd *Arabic* **1** sole; only **2** one **3** *proper name* Wahid, Waheed

وخ vakh *interjection* oh; ah (expressing surprise, fright, pain)

وخامت vakhāmát *m. Arabic* **1** danger **2** difficult situation, threatening situation

وخت vakht *m.* **1** time پر خپل وخت برابر on time, timely; exactly, punctually په یو وخت simultaneously په راتلونکی وخت کېني in time په حاضر وخت کېني at the present time په اوس وخت کېني at present Time passes. .وخت تېرېږي for a long time هغه وخت چه at the time when, when د حرب وخت، د جنگ وخت wartime پر وخت in early times, in the beginning په اول وخت کېني، په لمري وخت کېني timely, opportunely په مناسب وخت کېني in a timely fashion, well in advance په خپل وخت never په هېڅ وخت کي a protracted time, a long time تر زیاته وخته پوري before the war څه وخت؟، کوم وخت؟ چنگ تر وخته پوري at that time کېني کم وخت؟ When? At what time? ځيني وختونه at times, sometimes د وخت د loss of time د وخت زیان for lack of time ترهغه وخته until those times بل وخت ته دي پاته وي Another time! ستاسي پوري to pass وخت تېرول ، وخت اړول I am taking up your time. وخت نیسم وخت را نه نه و I didn't have time. د وخته early, very early (in the morning) سبا د وخته راسه Come tomorrow early in the morning. له ځه وخته په دي خوا some time ago, for some time past تر د هغه وخته څخه چه ... until the time when ... کومه وخته چه ... since the time when ... د وخت بادشاه the then emperor, the emperor at the time هر کار خپل وخت لري .Everything in its time. په دي وختو په دي نژدي وختو کېني recently په هغو اکثره وختونه often There was a time when ... یو وخت و چه in those times ... وختو کېني وخت په وخت، وخت وخت ... from time to time, at times, sometimes ساچان د توتانو پر always, constantly, at any time **2** season هر وخت The starlings fly when the mulberries are ripe. ځو وخته؟ وخت راځي How many times? **3** time (occasion) دوه دري وخته two or three times **4** age, century د ډبري وخت the Iron Age د اوسپنو وخت the Stone Age **5** case, opportunity وخت ته کتل to wait for an appropriate opportunity, bide one's time 6 cattle, food or money sent to the home of a deceased person وخت راورل to send cattle, food or money to the home of a deceased person a few days after the death

وخت نا وخت vakhtnāvákht inopportunely, not on time, tardily; unseasonably

وختي [1] vakhtí early, well in advance; opportunely, very early

وختي [2] vákhti vákhte *Eastern* وختي چه then; at the time when

وختيني vakhtináj 1 former 2 stale (of food)

وخجير vakhdzhír *m.* Vakhdzhir (tributary, Amu-Dara River)

وینکالی vakhkáj *m. regional* ☞ وینکالی

وخم vakhm *m.* fear, terror

وخيم vakhím *Arabic* 1 dangerous; threatening حالات ډېر وخيم شويدي The situation grew menacing. 2 harmful, pernicious 3 unhealthful (of food)

ود vud *m.* vudd *Arabic* وداد vidā́d *m.* friendship; friendliness

ودادي vidādí *Arabic* pedantic; friendly وداديه مناسبات friendly relations

وداع vadā́' *f.* vidā́' leave-taking, farewell د چاسره وداع کول to leave, goodbye, farewell

وداعي vadá'í vidā'í valedictory په وداعي موقع کښي

ودان vadā́n 1 built, equipped 2 well-equipped, improved, comfortable 3 flourishing, thriving, prosperous (of a country, etc.); rich ودان دي وي زموږ وطن! May our Fatherland flourish! 4 inhabited, peopled 5 polished, perfected 6 living somewhere (of a tribe)

ودان ځای vadā́n dzāj *m.* inhabited place; settlement

ودانښت vadānə́kht *m.* structure, building, edifice, construction

ودانول vadānavə́l 1 *denominative, transitive* [*past:* ودان يي کړ]. 1 to construct, build, set up 1.2 to improve 1.3 to facilitate prosperity, facilitate development 1.4 to perfect, polish, improve upon 1.5 to settle, inhabit 2 *m. plural* .1 construction, erection 2.2 improvement 2.3 development 2.4 polishing up 2.5 settling

ودانه vadā́na 1 *feminine singular of* ودان 2 *f.* .1 dwelling; dwelling place 2.2 new construction; new house

ودانی [1] vadāní *f.* ودانۍ vadānə́j *f.* 1 building, edifice, structure د ودانيو صنايع الحاقيه ودانيۍ addition, wing the construction industry 2 construction, building, erection 3 improved construction, amenities 4 prosperity, development 5 improving, polishing up 6 state of being erected 7 abundance, wealth

ودانۍ [2] vadānə́j *m.* ☞ ودانی [1] 6-2

ودانی [3] vadāní *feminine plural of* ودان

ودانېدل vadānedə́l *denominative, intransitive* [*past:* ودان شو] 1 to be built, be erected نوي فابريکي ودانيږي New factories are being built. 2 to be equipped with all services and utilities 3 to flourish, prosper, develop کور دي ودان شه! Thanks! Prosperity to your house! 4 to be improved, be worked over 5 to be settled

ودانېدنه vadānedə́na *f.* ☞ ودانی [1] 6-2

ودرول vədravə́l vudravə́l *transitive dialect* ☞ درول

ودرېدل vədredə́l vudredə́l *intransitive dialect* ☞ درېدل 2

ودرېدونکی vudredúnkaj *dialect* 1 *present participle of* settled (of a tribe)

ودګنۍ vadganə́j marriageable (of a girl)

ودل [1] vudə́l *transitive dialect* ☞ اودل

ودنه vadə́na *f.* growth; growing

ودو vadó *oblique of* واده [1]

ودود vadúd *m. Arabic proper name* Wudud

ودول vadavə́l *denominative, transitive* [*past:* واده يي کړ] 1 to marry, get married لور ودول to give a daughter in marriage زوی ودول to marry off a son 2 to take a wife

ودونه vadúna *plural of* واده [1]

وده [1] váda *f.* 1 growth; growing 2 development جسماني او روحي وده physical and intellectual development جسماني او ذهني وده a to grow; grow up b to grow, develop ته ... وده ورکول a to grow, cultivate b to develop

وده [2] vudá *f.* ☞ هوده

وده [3] vúda *colloquial imperative of* درېدل *vice* ودرېږه halt; stand; wait; stop

ودېدل vadedə́l *denominative, intransitive* [*past:* واده شو] 1 to get married خور ئي په يو غټ سوداګر واده شوې ده Her sister got married to a wealthy businessman. 2 to be given in marriage (of a girl)

ودېده vadedə́ *m. plural* marriage

و دي شي چه vu de shi *chə* possibly, probably, maybe ☞ شول

وديعه vadi'á *f. Arabic* 1 thing put in storage; security, pawning 2 deposit; investment

وډ [1] vaḍ *m.* 1 stubble field, field after the harvest مېږي يي په وډ کښي He let the sheep into the stubble field 2 *agriculture* fallow

وډ [2] vaḍ *tautological with* ګډ

ور [1] var *m.* وره vrə *oblique* [*plural:* ورونه vrúna vrə] د door مېز د ور و ښي خوا ته پروت و The table stood to the right انګړ ور of the door. ور رابېرته کول to open the door ور خلاصول، ور پرانيتل to open the door of the room inwards ور بېرته که! Open the door! ور پوري که! to close the door a bit! ور، ور تړل Close the door! Close the door a little! *idiom* د غره او وره فرق يې وي They have nothing in common. a د لوی ور خاوند hospitable man b sensitive man, responsive man

ور [2] var vər vur 1 *directional pronoun, third person singular & plural* 1.1 a to him; to her; to them b up to him; up to her; up to them c concerning him; concerning her; concerning them d on him; on her; on them 1.2 *functions as a verbally affixed indirect object and precedes the predicate* هلته کور ور جوړ شوئ دئ A house was built for him there. 1.3 to him, to her, to them (with several verbs of motion it indicates the direction of motion) ورسېدل to go into his, her, or their presence; to come into his, her, or their presence پر لسو بجو ښار ته ور ورسېدو We arrived in the city at 10 presence o'clock. ورختل to go up, rise up, ascend ور وخوت He climbed up there. **2** *used as a productive verb prefix* ورکول، ورتلل

ور ³ vár vár *adjectival suffix* زړه ور valorous

ورا ¹ vrā *f.* vurá bridal procession

ورا ² vará *Arabic* **1.1** far, far away له ورا **a** from afar **b** beforehand له ورا ورځ وتاکله شوه The day was set beforehand. د ورا څخه ښکاريدل It is seen from afar. **1.2** beyond, on the other side دې غره نه ورا خوا *Eastern* over on that side of the mountain, beyond the mountain **2** aside from

ورابان vurābā́ṇ *m.* ☞ ورابنی

ورابنی vrābaṇáj *m.* member of a bridal procession

ورابند vrābánd *m.* rope (for pack animal's pack)

وراته vratə́ *m. plural of* وريت ¹

وراثت virāsát *m. Arabic* **1** inheritance, legacy, property received by inheritance **2** heredity

وراثتي virāsatí وراثي virāsí *Arabic* hereditary, inherited

وراځه vrádza *f.* ☞ براځه

واره ¹ vrārə *m.* [*plural:* ورېرونه vrerúna *plural:* وررونه vrarúna] nephew (brother's son)

واره ² vrára *f.* woman who has lost a brother

وراستول varāstavə́l *transitive* ☞ استول

وراسته vrāstə́ *m. plural of* وروست

وراشه vrā́sha *f.* **1** word, words; expression, turn of speech **2** speech, conversation, talk وراشه کول to converse, talk **3** disposition, temper

وراګړی vrāgə́ṛaj *m.* one sworn to or engaged in a blood feud with another family, clan, or tribe

وران vrā́n vərā́n **1** destroyed, defeated, ruined **2** deserted, neglected; uninhabited **3** spoiled, corrupted, put out of commission **4** disordered, wrecked; broken **5** someone or something that has been spoiled, someone or something that has been put out of commission وراني شودي *Eastern* milk which has turned sour **6** sapped (of health) **7** bad, evil وران سړی a bad man, evil man **8** untrue, erroneous ورانه کلمه typographical error **9** one who has had a quarrel or falling out with someone **10** malevolent, ill-disposed

ورانتيا vrāntjā́ *f.* ☞ وران والی

ورانټ varā́nṭ *m. trade* warehouse warrant

ورانښت vrānə́ḳht *m.* ☞ وران والی

ورانکار vrānkár *m.* virānkár **1** destroyer, ravager **2** transgressor, disrupter **3** saboteur, wrecker

ورانکاري vrānkārí *f.* virānkārí **1** destruction; ravaging **2** deterioration **3** sabotage, wrecking

ورانوالی vrānválaj *m.* **1** destruction; massacre; ravaging **2** desolation, neglect **3** deterioration; putting out of commission **4** disorder, disruption (e.g., of equilibrium) **5** disorganization **6** sapping, undermining (of health) **7** quarrel; fight; discord

ورانول vrānavə́l *denominative, transitive* [*past:* وران يې کړ] **1** to destroy, rout; ravage **2** to throw (forcibly), hurl **3** to spoil, put out

of commission **4** to make bad, worsen; complicate **5** to inflict, cause harm, damage **6** to disrupt, ruin; destroy نقشي ورانول to disrupt the plans **7** to disorganize (e.g., work) **8** to undermine (e.g., health) **9** to quarrel *idiom* د چا زړه ورانول to upset someone

ورانه ¹ vrána **1** *feminine singular of* وران **2** *f.* **.1** enmity; hostility **1.2** opposition **1.3** quarrel, dissent

ورانه ² vránə *oblique of* ورون

وراني ¹ vrānáj *m.* **1** harm, damage زيات وراني کول to inflict great harm **2** flaw, defect **3** enmity **4** quarrel; dissent, altercation **5** distrubance **6** destruction; ravaging **7** disorder, upset; disorganization **8** undermining (e.g., of health)

وراني ² vrāní *f.* **1** destruction; ravaging **2** deterioration د هوا وراني bad weather **3** invasion

وراني ³ vrā́ni *f. plural of* وران

ورانېدل vrānedə́l **1** [*past:* وران شو] *denominative, intransitive* **.1** to be destroyed, be crushed, be routed; be ravaged; be disorganized **1.2** to be hurled, be thrown (forcibly) **1.3** to be spoiled, be put out of commission **1.4** to be bad, be worsened, be made more complex **1.5** to be disrupted, be messed up, be disordered **1.6** to be sapped, be undermined (of health) **1.7** to get into a fight په اوبو وراندېدل to quarrel about water **2** *m. plural* ☞ وران والی

ورانېده vrānedə́ *m. plural* ☞ وران والی

ورا ورا vrā- vrā *dialect* straight ahead, opposite

ورايه vrája vərája far, beyond, behind له ورايه from afar نور عمارتونه له ورايه ښکاريدل From afar other buildings were seen.

ورباز vurbā́zə *oblique singular of* ورباز

ورباندي várbāndi ورباندې várbānde *Eastern* **1.1** on him, on her, on it, on them **1.2** for him, for her, for it, for them **1.3** with his help, with her help, with its help; thanks to him, thanks to her, thanks to it, thanks to them شپې او ورځي ورباندي تېروي He lives by means of this. **1.4** concerning him, concerning her, concerning it, concerning them ټول ورباندي ژاړي Everyone mourns him. مونږ علم ورباندي غورکول We know about this. ورباندي لرو to discuss something **1.5** over him, over her, over it, over them هغه لار چه مونږ ورباندي کښته شوو the road over which we came down **2** *postposition* on this, on that

ورباخښل vərbakhḳhə́l *transitive* ☞ بخښل

ورباشه vurbā́sha *f. dialect* grain of barley *idiom* يوه ورباشه a wee bit زه د خپلي خبري نه يوه ورباشه هم اخوا نه اوړم I will not go back on my word for anything.

وربال vurbál *m. dialect* ☞ اوربل ²

وربلی vərbəláj *m.* top flap on Afghan-style pants

وربوز vurbúz *m. Eastern* **1** snout وربوز يي کوډ نيولئ He screwed up his mug. **2** ledge (of a mountain) *idiom* وربوز دي ورک شه! Beat it! Get lost!

وربوزی vərbuzáj *m.* **1** awning of a door **2** hall, entranceway

وربوی vurbój *m.* ☞ ورېوزی ¹

ورپسې várpase **1** after him, after her, after them ورپسې ولاړ سه! Go after him! Go after them! **2** بيا سم ورپسې immediately after him after, afterwards, after this ... وريسي مو ولېدل چه afterwards we saw that ...

ورپورک varporǝk *m.* bolt, bar (of a door)

ورپوري várpori vápore *Eastern* **1** to him, to her, to them **2** after her, after him, after them **3** over him, over her, over them; at ولي دي ورپوري وخندل؟ Why did you laugh at him?

وربه زړه کول var-pǝ-zṛǝkavǝ́l *m. plural* reminder

وربه زړه کېدل var-pǝ-zṛǝkedǝ́l *m. plural* remembrance, recollection

ورت [1] vurt *m.* vǝrt kind of children's game

ورت [2] vurǝ́t *dialect* ☞ وریت [1]

ورتارګه vǝrtárga *f.* ☞ مرداردانه

ورتګ vartág *m.* **1** arrival (at a place distant from the speaker) يي زړه نه غواړي He does not want to go there. **2** visit, call **3** trip **4** *regional* move; nomadic move from one place to another

ورتلل vartlǝ́l [*present:* ورځي *past:* ورغئ] **1** *intransitive imperfect Western* **.1** to go to him, her, or them, set out to him, her, or them, proceed to him, her, or them; thence **1.2** to arrive to him, her, or them, come to him, her, or them; thence *idiom* پر چا ورتلل to attack someone هغه ته د ګډا چل نه ورته He didn't know how to dance. **2** *m. plural* ☞ ورتګ

ورتله vártla *f. imperfect of* ورتلل

ورتول vurǝtavǝ́l *denominative, transitive* [*past:* ورت يې کړ] **1** ☞ **2** to urge on, hurry وریتول

ورته [1] vurtǝ́ *m.* vǝrtǝ́ *plural* wool yarn, spool of wool yarn

ورته [2] várta vǝrta **1** to him, to her, to them; up to him, up to her, up to them ورته راغئ He went up to him. ورته ووايه Tell him. Tell them. **2** near him, near her, near them لوی سپی ورته پروت دئ A large dog is lying near him. **3** in front of him, in front of her, in front of them حاضرين ټول ورته ولاړ شوه The audience stood before him. ورته مخکينی before him, before her, before them

ورته [3] várta resembling, alike, similar سنک محمود ته ورته دئ Sanak resembles Mahmud. يو و بل ته سره ورته دي They are like one another. د ... سره ورته کول to liken

ورته [4] vurtá *f. singular of* ورت

ورته [5] vuráta *tautological with* برته

ورته [6] vartǝ́ *Eastern imperfect of* ورتلل

ورته [7] várta *Western* caught, taken (of fire) اور يې ورته کئ he sets fire to, he ignites (the wood)

ورته [8] várta لاس ورته کول a to stretch out the hand b to set about something جنګ او جدل ته لاس ورته کول to start a quarrel

ورته [9] várta at the door ورته ولاړ دئ He stands at the door.

ورته والی vartaválaj *m.* likeness, similarity د چاسره ورته والی لرل to resemble someone

ورتی [1] vartáj beautiful, good-looking

ورتئ [2] vártǝj *Western imperfect of* ورتلل

ورتبدل vurǝtedǝ́l *denominative, intransitive* [*past:* ورت شو] **1** ☞ **2** *figurative* to be in a hurry, to hurry وریتبدل

ورت [1] vraṭ *m.* flood of tears په ورت ژړل، د ورت ژړل to burst into tears په ورت ژرول to make sob

ورت [2] vǝrṭ *dialect* ☞ رت [1]

ورتر varṭár *m.* bolt, latch

ورتک varṭák *m.* door knocker

ورجو vrídzho *oblique of* ورجي

ورجي vrídzhi *f. plural* rice ☞

ورچاني vurcháne ورچني vúrchǝne *dialect* outside; beyond; out of, from outside of, from out of ورچاني ايستل a to drive out, drive out of; take outside ورچاني راتلل، ورچاني وتل b to carry away with one to go outside, step outside ورچاني ولي نه راځي؟ Why don't you come out? د کړکي څخه ورچاني out, beyond the window (of a railroad car, room, etc.)

ورچنیز vǝrchǝníz external

ورچني vǝrchíne *dialect* ☞ ورچاني

ورځ vradz *f.* [*plural:* ورځي vrádze *plural:* vrádzi] day ورځ بله on the following day ورځ خواره an unpleasant day, bad day, unsuccessful day ورځ ستړي a confusing day, bad day, tiring day ورځ لویه a bright day, clear day b holiday رڼا ورځ، سپينه ورځ Sunday c *religion* Judgment Day, Doomsday ورځ نن today ورځ ډيره by day د ورځي د خوا، په ورځي کښي from day to day هغه ورځي ولاړي The day was very depressing. هغه ورځي ولاړي Those days passed. Those times passed. د ورځي يوه ورځ وه on one fine day ورځ نه يوه ورځ به په خپل مقصد ته ورسپړي One fine day he will attain his goal. د ... ورځ بالا کېدل Day was coming to an end. ورځ بيګاه شوه په اتو ورځو کښي to grow with each passing day (of a child) in a week, in a week's time په پنځلسو ورځو کښي in two weeks ورځ د چا ورځ ګرزېدل to while away the time ورځ ګرزېدل to betray someone; turn away from someone (of happiness, luck) د سنک ورځ ګرزېدلي وه Luck betrayed Sanak. د مبرمنو د نهضت ورځ Women's Day

ورځپاڼه vradzpáṇa *f.* newspaper

ورځپاڼه ليکونکی vradzpáṇa likúnkaj *m.* journalist

ورځچاری vradzchárij *m.* timeserver

ورځلوی vradzlój *m. religion* Judgement Day, Doomsday

ورځيني [1] vradzináj ☞ ورځيني

ورځيني [2] várdzini várdzine ☞ ورڅخه

ورځو [1] vrádzo *oblique of* ورځ

ورځو [2] vrǝ́dzo *oblique plural of* ورځه [1, 2]

ورځو [3] várdzu *first person plural of* ورتلل

ورځه [1] vrǝ́dza *f.* brow ورځه ټولول، ورځي سره کښل to knit the brows, frown د احمد کره ورغلو، ورځي يې وخوړلي We went to Ahmed, but he did not greet us cordially. ورځي يې ورنه شوي He knit his brows. He frowned. په ورځو خبري کول to raise the eyebrows

ورځه [2] vrǝ́dza *f.* tick (of sheep and goats)

ورځه [3] várdza vúrdza vǝrdza *imperfective imperative of* ورتلل

ورځي [1] vrádzi *plural of* ورځ

ورځي [2] vrǝ́dzi *plural of* ورځه [1, 2]

ورځي [3] vǝrdzi várdzi *present tense of* ورتلل

ورځئ [4] várdzǝj *imperfective imperative of* ورتلل

ورځيني vradzináj **1** daily اخبار ورځيني daily newspaper **2** everyday ورځيني چاري everyday affairs **3** day, day's مزل ورځيني a day's drive *idiom* رواج ورځيني شيان existing customs vradziní consumer goods

ورځخه vártsəkha **1** from him, from her, from them; at him, at her, at them; with him, with her, with them; near him, near her, near them كتاب ورځخه واخله Take the book from him. **2** from him, from her, from them (of motion)

ورسک vartsək *m.* ☞ ورثک

ورخېرمه vartsérma adjoining, bordering on, contiguous to, adjacent to, neighboring

ورخ varkh *m.* **1** small stream **2** irrigation channel د پتي ورخ irrigation channels watering a field ورخ پري كول to dig a passage through to an irrigation channel ورخ ترل to close up a passage into an irrigation channel ورخ خلاصول to open up a passage into an irrigation channel **3** sluice gate (of a irrigation channel) **4** dam

ورخاړي vərkháṛaj¹ *m. botany* portulaca

ورخاړي vərkháṛaj² *m.* plague (of sheep and goats), murrain

ورخپوله varkhpúla *f.* method of watering or flooding land

ورختل varkhatə́l *intransitive* [*present:* ورخېژي *past:* وروخوت *past:* وروخاته] **1** to attack **2** ☞ ختل

ورختنی varkhatanáj¹ *m.* predecessor

ورختنی varkhatanáj² *f.* ☞ ورختنی¹

ورخته várkhəta¹ *f.* attack

ورخته varkhatá² in the first place, first of all له ورخته from the very beginning; from the very first

ورخته varkhatá³ *imperfective of* ورختل

ورخړ vərkháṛ *m.* **1** crowd **2** ☞ ورخړه

ورخړله varkhaṛəla *f. dialect* ورخړه varkhóṛa *f.* litter, refuse

ورخیره varkhíra *f.* dirty trick, filthy trick, unpleasantness, mean trick

ورخیزه varkhíza *f.* land watered by an irrigation channel

ورخیمځه varkhímdza *f.* time before noon ☞ غرمكی

ورد vird¹ *m. Arabic* [*plural:* وردونه virdúna *Arabic plural:* اوراد avrád] **1** reading of the Koran in parts **2** daily lesson, daily exercise

ورد vard² *m.* rose, rose tree

ورداشت vardásht *m. trade* obtaining on credit, buying, purchasing د ورداشت كتاب account book

وردغاړي vardəgháṛi charged with, entrusted with (some matter) وردغاړي كارونه اجرا كول to carry out a mission, perform a commission, do an errand

وردك vardák وردگ vardág **1** *m. plural* the Wardagi (tribe) *m.* **2** a Wardag (tribesman) **3** *m. plural* Wardag (a province in the southwest of Kabul) د وردگو ولایت، د وردكو ولایت Wardag Province

وردمخه vardəmə́kha getting down to work on something يو كار ته وردمخه كېدل to get down to work on something

وردي vurdí *f. regional military* uniform

وررسېدل varrasedə́l *m. plural* attaining, attainment (of a goal)

وررسېدلی varrasedə́laj caused زیان ورسېدلی damage inflicted

ورراول vrəravə́l *transitive* [*past:* و يي ورراوه] **1** to tear, tear to pieces **2** to split **3** to tear off

ورراونه vrəravə́na *f.* **1** tearing **2** splitting **3** tearing off

ورربدل vrəredə́l *intransitive* [*past:* وورربده] **1** to tear, get torn to pieces; come unraveled, come apart at the seams; fall apart **2** to split **3** to come unglued

ورربدنه vrəredóna *f.* ورربده vrəredə́ *m.* **1** coming apart at the seams, unraveling (of cloth) **2** splitting **3** getting unglued

ورز vraz *f. dialect* ☞ ورخ

ورزدكول varzdakavə́l *transitive* ☞ زده كول

ورزړ vərzə́ṛ *m. dialect* quail

ورزش varzísh *m.* exercise, physical drill; gymnastics بدني ورزش calisthenics; physical culture بدني ورزش كول to engage in calisthenics

ورزشكار varzishkár *m.* gymnast, athlete شوقي ورزشكار sports fan كسبي ورزشكار professional athlete

ورزشكاره varzishkára *f.* female athlete, woman gymnast

ورزشگاه varzishgáh *m. sports* playing field ورزش گاه، ورزشگاه

ورزشي varzishí *adjective* sport مسابقي ورزشي sports competition

ورزښت varzə́kht *m.* ☞ ورزش

ورزل vrazə́l vərzə́l *transitive* [*present:* ورزني varzóní *past:* و يي ورزه] to crumble; crush; break into pieces; make sausage meat غوښه ورزل to cut up meat ورزلي ور يجي crushed rice, ground rice

ورزنه vrazóna *f.* crumbling, crushing; cutting up in pieces; making sausage meat

ورزو varzó *f.* disgust ورزو كول to have an aversion to

ورزول vrəzavə́l¹ *transitive* ☞ ورزل

ورزول vurzavə́l vərzavə́l² *transitive* [*past:* و يي ورزاوه] to launch (into the air); cause to fly, make to fly; ascend (into the air, e.g., an aircraft)

ورزونه vurzavóna *f.* ascending, ascension (into the air, e.g., an aircraft)

ورزي vráze *plural of* ورز

ورزېدل vrəzedə́l¹ *intransitive* [*past:* وورزېده *past:* وورزبده] to be crumbled, be crushed; crumble; be cut into pieces; be made, be prepared (of sausage meat)

ورزېدل vurzedə́l vərzedə́l² *intransitive* [*past:* وورزبد *past:* وورزېده] **1** to fly, flutter, flit about **2** to rise up, take off (into the air, e.g., an aircraft); fly off

ورزېدنه vrəzedóna¹ *f.* crumbling, crushing; grinding into sausage meat, mincing

ورزېدنه vurzedóna² *f.* flight; takeoff; flitting, fluttering

ورژل vrazhə́l varzhə́l *transitive* ☞ ورزل

ورژنه vrazhóna *f.* varzhóna ☞ ورزنه

ورژون vrazhún *m.* **1** sparseness **2** ejection, throwing, rejection **3** spreading, dispersing *idiom* د گناه ورژون atonement for sin, atonement for guilt

ورژونی vrazhúnaj *m.* kind of kasha, kind of cracked wheat

ورژي vrízhe *f. plural dialect* ☞ وریجي

ورزرگ vrəg *m.* vurəg mane (of a horse)

ورږه ¹ vrə́ga *f.* flea *idiom* دنیا یې لکه وربږي سره وغورځېده His wealth has gone with the wind.

ورږه ² vurgə́ *m.* vargə́ *plural Eastern* beestings, colostrum (the first milk of a cow after calving)

ورساتونی varsātúnaj *m.* doorkeeper, porter

ورسای varsā́j *m.* Versailles د ورسای معاهده Treaty of Versailles

ورستنی vrustənáj ☞ وروستنی ¹

ورسته vrústo vurústo *dialect* ☞ وروسته

ورستوالی vrastvā́laj *m.* rotting; decomposition, decay

ورستول ¹ vrastavə́l *denominative, transitive* [*past:* وروست یې کړ] 1 to rot, decay 2 to wear to rags, bring to a state of being unfit for use (of a currency note)

ورستول ² vərstavə́l *transitive* ☞ استول

ورستون vərstún returning to him (her, them, to that place, or thither)

ورستونول varstunavə́l *transitive* [*past:* ورستون یې کړ] to turn to him (her, them, that place thither, e.g., face, gaze) مخ ورستونول to turn the face to him (her, them, that place thither)

ورسته ¹ vrastá *f. singular of* ورست

ورسته ² vrə́sta ☞ وروسته

ورستی ¹ vrustáj ☞ وروستی

ورستې ² vrasté *f. plural of* وروست ورستې خبري کول to talk nonesense, talk absurdity

ورستبدل vrastedə́l *denominative, intransitive* [*past:* وروست شو] 1 to rot, decompose; decay, go bad 2 to wear out, come to a state of being unfit for use (currency note)

ورسره vársara with him, with her, with them زه ورسره ځم I am going with him (her, them). ورسره with this, along with this, incidentally

ورسک vərsə́k *m.* 1 projection, ledge (of a mountain) 2 turret (of a fortress)

ورسون varsún *m.* advice, counsel

ورسه vársa *imperative perfective of* ورتلل

ورسي ¹ vursí *f.* ☞ ارسي

ورسي ² vársi *Western present perfective of* ورتلل

ورشکست varshikást *m.* failure; bankruptcy

ورشو vərshó *f.* [*plural:* ورشوګاني ورشووي vərshóvi *plural:* vərshogā́ni] 1 pasture 2 common pastureland زمونږ او د هغو ورشو شریکه ده We have pastureland in common with them.

ورشي várshi *present perfective of* ورتلل

ورښ vurə́kh *m.* vrákh wind

ورښتی vrəkhtáj *m.* almond tree

ورښکه vurə́khka *f.* vrə́khka *usually plural* ☞ ورښکي ¹

ورښکي ¹ vurə́khi chill *f.* ورښکي مي کېږي ، ورښکي مي ولاړي شوي I feel shivery. I am getting a fever.

ورښکی ² vrə́khkəj *f.* 1 tape, ribbon, lace 2 cord ☞ ورښکي ¹

ورخودل varkhodə́l *transitive* ☞ بنودل

ورطه vartá *f. Arabic* 1 labyrinth 2 whirlpool, abyss 3 *figurative* difficulties

ورغ vrəgh *m.* 1 conscientiousness 2 feelings, sensitivities ورغ الوتل to lack feelings

ورغاست vərgā́st crushed, ground (of groats)

ورغالی vərghā́laj *m.* 1 ☞ اورغالی 2 heating

ورغانی varghā́ṇaj *m.* 1 flour mixed with oil with which a new mother and infant are anointed 2 act of anointing the mother and child with flour mixed with oil

ورغر varghár *m.* gradient of a stream

ورغړنه vərgharə́na *f.* mud in which livestock (camels, donkeys, etc.) are wallowing

ورغړی vərgharáj *m.* sediment in water; scum

ورغستل vərgastə́l *transitive* [*past:* و یې ورغستل] to hull, crush, grind (groats)

ورغستلي varghəstə́li *m. plural* 1 groats from cracked wheat ورغستلي پخول ، ورغستلي کول to boil cracked wheat groats 2 cracked wheat

ورغلل varaghlə́l vəraghlə́l *past tense of* ورتلل

ورغلئ varaghə́ləj *past participle of* ورتلل

ورغومی vərghúmaj *m.* vurghúmaj ☞ مرغومی ¹

ورغوی vərghə́vaj *m.* vərghávaj 1 palm of the hand د لاس ورغوی palms 2 sole (of the foot) د پښې ورغوی sole of the foot

ورغی ¹ vərghə́j *f.* soot on the ceiling

ورغئ ² varaghəj *past tense of* ورتلل

ورق varák *m. Arabic* [*plural:* اوراق avrā́ḳ] 1 sheet (of paper) [*plural:* ورقونه varaḳúna] 2 document 3 playing card 4 slice

ورقه varaḳá *f. Arabic* 1 letter 2 sheet (of paper) 3 paper, document د راپورت ورقه a written report د هویت ورقه identification card د یادداشت ورقه note, aide-mémoire, memorandum

ورک vrək vurúk *Eastern* 1 lost, strayed 2 lost without a trace 3 forgotten 4 missing, perished 5 stained with sin or vice 6 *figurative* absorbed په فکر ورک indecisive, vacillating

ورک اومتول wūrák ūmtūl *m. computer science* lost data

ورکاندي ² várkāndí *present of* ورکول vice ورکړي

ورکاوه ¹ varkā́və *imperfect of* ورکول

ورکاوی vrəkāváj *m.* 1 loss; waste 2 destruction ورکاوی یې راغئ He is perishing. 3 annihilation

ورکره varkará 1 in his home, in her home; at his home, at her home, at their home 2 to his home, to her home, to their home

ورکړ ¹ várkəṛ *past tense of* ورکول

ورکړ ² varkáṛ *m.* maize chaff, rice chaff

ورکړن varkṛə́n *m.* ورکړنه varkṛə́na *f.* ☞ ورکړه ²

ورکړونی ¹ varkṛúnaj *m.* one who gives something, giver, presenter

ورکړونی ² varkṛúne marriageable daughter ورکړونی خور ورکړونی لور marriageable sister

ورکړه ¹ varkṛə́ *past plural of* ورکول

ورکړه ² varkṛə́ *m. plural* 1 giving, reimbursement; handing (over) 2 granting (e.g., leave) 3 payment, paying, renumeration, pay 4 presentation; donation; gift 5 selling

ورکړه ³ várkṛa *feminine past of* ورکول

ورکړه 4 várkṛa *f.* 1 ☞ ورکړه 2 2 favor, grace 3 giving (of a daughter) in marriage

ورکړه 5 várkṛa *prefective imperative of* ورکول

ورکړه راکړه várkṛa-rákṛa *f.* buying and selling, trade, barter

ورکړئ 1 varkə́rəj *past participle of* ورکول 1

ورکړي 2 várkṛi *present prefective of* ورکول 1

ورکړي 3 várkṛi *f. plural of* ورکړه 4

اورکزي vrəkzí *m. plural* ☞ ورک زي

ورکشاپ varkshā́p *m.* 1 factory د جنګلک ورکشاپ Jangalak Automotive Repair Plant 2 workshop, shop، د ترميماتي ورکشاپ ترميمولو ورکشاپ repair workshop

ورکښي várkẖi *Eastern* várke *dialect* vúrke in him, in her, in them

ورک لاړی vrəklā́ṛaj gone astray, lost the way, off the path

ورکماڼی vrəkmā́naj jolly, gay, merry

ورک مرغه vrəkmərghə́ *m.* phoenix (the legendary bird)

ورک نومی vrəknúmaj unknown, nameless; obscure; forgotten ☞ نوم ورکی

ورکوالی vrəkvā́laj *m.* ☞ ورکېده

ورکوزېده varkuzedə́ *m. plural* descent د کوتل څخه ورکوزېده descent from the pass

ورکول 1 varkavə́l vurkavə́l *transitive* [*past:* ور يې کړ] 1.1 to give, give back or return to him, her, or them; deliver or hand over to him, her, or them و ملګري ته يو کتاب ورکړه Give the comrade the book. نښان ورکول to bestow a medal on 1.2 to grant (e.g., leave) 1.3 to pay, pay for برات ورکول to pay for with a promissary note, pay for with bill of exchange د تار پيسي ورکول to pay by telegram 1.4 to present; bestow 1.5 to sell دا څاتکي په څو ورکوئ؟ How much are you selling these melons for? 1.6 to give (a girl) in marriage 1.7 to relinquish خپل ځای ورکول to give up one's post 1.8 to hit, beat 2 *m. plural* ☞ ورکونه 1

ورکول 2 vrəkavə́l *Eastern* vurukavúl 1 *denominative, transitive* [*past:* هغه کتاب مي ورک کړئ دئ I lost that book. لار ورکول to lose the way 1.2 to eliminate, remove, liquidate نقائص ورکول to eliminate deficiencies 1.3 to destroy, exterminate, annihilate زراعتي آفات ورکول to exterminate agricultural pests ځان په مرګ ورکول to ruin oneself, be one's own undoing 1.4 *colloquial* to take away کتاب ورک کړه! Take the book away! 1.5 to hide, conceal ځان ورکول to hide oneself, conceal oneself 1.6 to drive out, banish someone 2 *m. plural* ☞ ورکونه 1

ورکونه 1 varkavə́na *f.* ☞ ورکړه 1

ورکونه 2 vrəkavə́na *f.* 1 loss, mislaying 2 elimination, endearing; removal; liquidation 3 extermination, annihilation 4 hiding, concealment 5 banishment

ورکه 1 vrə́ka 1 *f. singular of* ورک *f.* 2.1 loss (i.e., of a lost object) 2.2 ☞ ورکونه 2 2.3 destruction

ورکه 2 várka *perfective imperative of* ورکول

ورکي 2 várki ☞ ورکۍ 2

ورکېدل 1 varkedə́l *regional intransitive* [*past:* ورکول شو] 1 to be given, given out 2 to be granted (e.g., leave) 3 to be paid for; be paid out 4 to be bestowed, given as a gift

ورکېدل 2 vrəkedə́l vurukedə́l *denominative Eastern* [*past:* ورک شو] 1.1 to get lost, disappear, go astray چاقو را څخه ورک شوئ دئ My pocketknife has disappeared. 1.2 to perish 1.3 to vanish, disappear 1.4 to be exterminated, be annihilated 1.5 to be eliminated, be removed, be liquidated 1.6 to be taken away, be hidden 1.7 to hide, conceal oneself 1.8 to run away, flee 2 *m. plural* ☞ ورکېده

ورکېده vrəkedə́ *m. plural* 1 loss, disappearance 2 destruction 3 extermination, annihilation 4 elimination, removal, liquidation

ورکئ várkəjí *dialect present of* ورکول

ورگ 1 varg *m.* 1 wool (of a domestic animal) 2 clippings, shearings (from sheep, camels)

ورگ 2 varg *m.* 1 yearling camel يو ورگ yearling camel دوه ورگ two-year-old camel درې ورگ three-year-old camel 2 five-year-old ram

ورگ 3 vrəg *m. Eastern* ☞ ورډ

ورگډ vurgáḍ base, conscienceless ورگډ سړی a base person, a cad; a conscienceless man; a troublemaker

ورگډول vargaḍavə́l *transitive* ☞ گډول 1

ورگډی vargáḍaj *m.* careless man

ورگه 1 várga *feminine of* ورگ 2

ورگه 2 vrə́ga *f.* vurə́ga *Eastern* ☞ ورډه 1

ورگه 3 vurgə́ *m. plural Eastern* colostrum, beestings (first milk after parturition)

ورگی 1 vargáj *m.* small door, small cover, small hatch; window

ورگی 2 várgi *f. plural of* ورگ 2

ورگی 3 vurə́gi vrə́gi *plural of* ورگه 2

ورگينه vargína *f.* braided strap; leather rope

ورل vurál *m.* 1 meditation ورل کول to mediate 2 acceptance of the decision of mediators

ورلاندي várlānde *Eastern* under him, under her, under them

ورلره várlara ☞ ورته 2

ورلښتی vərlaẖtáj *m.* almond tree

ورلگېد vurlagíd *m.* ☞ اورلگیت

ورلول vərlavə́l *transitive* [*past:* ورله يې کړه] to impregnate, fertilize (an animal)

ورله 1 və́rla vúrla 1 foal ورله اسپه a mare in foal 2 pregnant (outside of marriage) ورله کول to impregnate ورله کېدل a to be in foal b to get pregnant, become pregnant (outside of marriage)

ورله 2 várla ☞ ورته 2

ورله انا vərlaānā́ *f.* great-grandmother

ورله توب vərlatób *m.* 1 state of being in foal 2 pregnancy

ورلېدل vərledə́l *denominative, intransitive* [*past:* ورله شوه] 1 to be in foal 2 to get pregnant, become pregnant (outside of marriage)

ورم ¹ varám *m. Arabic* 1.1 swelling, tumor 1.2 abundance 1.3 arrogance, conceit 2 swelled, tumefied, inflated ورم كول to blow out, blow up ورم كيدل to tumefy, blow up, swell up

ورم ² varm *m.* advice, counsel

ورمارګه varmā́rga *f.* varmā́rgə *m. plural* ورمابه varmā́ga *f.* varmāgə́ *m. plural regional* eruption of boils on the face of a child

ورمړ vurmáṛ *m. plural* ☞ اورمړ ²

ورمولی ¹ vurmólaj *m.* diarrhea and vomiting

ورمولی ² varloláj *m.* ferment, leaven (for cheese, farmer's cheese)

ورمېږ vərmég *m.* vurmég *m.* ورمېږه vərméga *f.* vərmég *m. Eastern* back of the head, occiput; nape of the neck ورمېږ كړول to bend down, stoop

ورندارہ varandā́ra *f. dialect* brother's wife ☞ وربنداره *and* ورېنداره

ورنده vurandá *Eastern* rainy

ورنډه vurə́nḍa *f.* attack, raid

ورنس varnís *m.* ورنش varnísh *m. plural* varnish, lacquer

ورنغله varnəghlə́ *vice* ورنه غله ☞ ورتلل

ورنكی vrənkáj *m.* femur, femoral bone

ورنگی vrangáj *m.* light rain, shower

ورنونه vranúna *plural of* ورون

ورنه várna ☞ ورخه *Eastern* ورنه پوښتنه وكړه Ask him.

ورنیكه vərnikə́ *m.* 1 great-grandfather 2 forefather

ورن ¹ vraṇ *m.* coffin

ورن ² vraṇ *m.* channel or bed of a freshet or flood

ورنی vərnáj *m.* diaper, diaper cover

ورو vro 1.1 slowly, quietly, noiselessly ورو ځه Go slowly! Go quietly! 1.2 softly, low ورو خبري كوه! Speak softly! 2.1 slow 2.2 soft, low ورو كول د ورو خبري آواز whisper ورو خبره soft speech a to slow down b to make soft, make low; muffle, make a little more quiet ورو كيدل a to slow down b to be low, be soft; be muffled, be dampened, become a bit quieter

ورودځه vrúdza *f.* brow, forehead

ورود vurúd *m. Arabic* 1 arrival; coming; advent سم د دوی له ورود سره upon their arrival 2 entering; import, importation

ورور ¹ vror *m.* [*plural:* ورونه vrúṇa] 1 brother د تي ورور foster brother سكه ورور one's own brother ديني ورور sworn brother كشر منخوی ورور older brother مشر ورور younger brother middle brother ناسكه ورور stepbrother ورورہ! كه دي ورور دئ Old chap! په مخه دي ګور دئ *proverb literal* Even if he is your brother, the grave lies ahead of you. *figurative* Speak the whole truth. 2 colleague, fellow worker د ورور غوښني خوړل *idiom* to censure

ورور ² varvár *m. dialect* ☞ ولور

ورورکی ¹ vrorkáj *m.* little brother

ورورکی ² vərvərakáj *m.* 1 mirage 2 firefly, glowworm

ورورګلوی vrorgalví *f.* ورورواالی vrorvā́laj *m.* vrorvā́lí *f.* ورورۍ vrorí *f.* 1 brotherhood د ورورګلوی مرسته fraternal assistance 2 relationship, kinship 3 friendship ورورګلوی كول to become friends, live like brothers د ورورۍ حق په ځای كول to extend the hand

of friendship, extend the hand of brotherhood ورورۍ به *proverb* كوو , حساب تر منځه Friendship is one thing, money is another.

ورورل varvṛál *transitive* ☞ وول

وروزه ¹ vrúza *f. dialect* ☞ وروځه

وروزه ² vúrozə *past tense of* روزل

وروزه ³ vúroza *imperative prefective of* روزل

ورور vrug *f.* [*plural:* ورورڍ vrúgi] strip or tape of tanned hide

ویرس vírús *m.* ☞ ویرس

وروست vrost ورسته vrastá *f.* وراسته vrāstə́ vrāstá *m. plural* ورستي vrasté *f. plural* 1 rotten, spoiled; decomposing; bad ووست ختكی rotten melon, spoiled melon ورسته هګی rotten egg 2 worn-out, unserviceable (of a banknote) ورستول ¹ ☞ ووست كول

وروستاری vrustāṛáj *m.* ☞ دمچي

وروستنی ¹ vrustanáj last, latest وروستني خبرونه vrustaní the latest news

وروستني ² vrustaní *m. plural* rear lace of a sandal

وروستو vurústo vrústo *dialect* ☞ ورسته

ورستوالی ¹ vrostvā́laj *m.* rotting; spoiling; decomposition; disintegration

وروستوالی ² vrustavā́laj *m.* ☞ ورسته والی

ورستنۀل vrostanə́l *denominative, transitive* [*past:* ووست یې کۀ] to rot, spoil ☞ ورستول ¹

وروسته vrústa 1.1 after, afterwards, then, thereafter لږ وروسته a little later د اجلاس څخه وروسته یې څه وویل؟ Then what did he say? وروسته د خپلو رایو او نظریاتو تر بنکاره کولو after the meeting له دې وروسته , تر دې after having expressed his opinion and views له دې وروسته وروسته , له دې نه henceforth, after this داسي څخه ونه شي One should not repeat this hereafter. د سفر څخه after the journey 1.2 later وروسته راشه Come a bit later! زه تر تا وروسته راغلم I arrived later than you. a bit later له یوی هفتي په وروسته afterwards وروسته تر هغه in a week, په وروسته كي after a week had passed د دوو میاشتو په finally, at last وروسته two months later, after two months 1.3 from behind, behind وروسته پاته Get up from behind! دی په زده كړه وروسته پاته He fell behind in his studies. 1.4 back دوی په وروسته روان دي They are going back. 2.1 subsequent وروسته زما نه future ... په after 2.2 the following پسي وروسته 2.3 news, latest (of times, discoveries, etc.) په وروسته كلونه كښي in recent years وروسته كول a to be late, be slow, lag b to be وروسته كيدل to delay, postpone postponed c to fall behind 2.4 future د وروسته دپاره for the future

وروسته پاتی vrústapātaj backward (e.g., of a country)

وروسته والی vrustavā́laj *m.* 1 tardiness, delay 2 lag وروسته والی كول to be late, fall behind, lag 3 to fall behind

وروستی vrustáj 1 last, final د دوبي وروستي ورځي the last days of summer وروستی نېټه a later date 2 later 3 *m.* rear, back, back part of something

ووستېدۀل vrostedə́l *denominative, intransitive* [*past:* ووست شو] 1 to rot, go bad 2 to decompose 3 to decay

وروستینبال vrustinbãl *m. dialect* end *idiom* په وروستینبال کي finally, at last

وروغوندې vróghunde very softly

وروک vruk *dialect* ☞ ورک

ورو کوونکی vro kavúnkaj 1 slowing down, retarding *m.* 2 brake

اورول ¹ vuravól *transitive* ☞ ورول

ورول ² varavól *transitive* ☞ ورول

ویرولوژي virolozhí *f.* virology

ورون vrun *m.* [*plural:* ورنونه vranúna] femur; thigh, haunch په ورانه کښي یې ګولی ده A bullet struck his femur.

ګرځنده کمپیوټر وروپاسی wrūnpã́say *m.* لاسي کمپیوټر lãsi kampjūṭǝr gardzandá kampjūṭǝr *computer science* laptop

وروپاسی کمپیوټر wrūnpã́say kampjūṭǝr *m.* laptop computer

وروڼه vrúṇa *plural of* ورور ¹

اورڼی vruṇáj *m.* ☞ اورڼی

ورور vǝrvór *m.* 1 dried meat 2 bride's trousseau

ورورو vrovró slowly, quietly, softly

وروړئ vávrǝj *Western past perfective of* ورول

وره vrǝ *oblique singular of* ور ¹

ورهسته vǝrhista ☞ ورهسته

ورهڼه varhә́na *f.* occupation; trade, craft

ورهول vǝrhavól *transitive* [*past:* یې ورهاوه] 1 to liberate, free, let go 2 to save, rescue, come to the aid of

ورهونه vǝrhavә́na *f.* 1 liberation 2 rescue, deliverance

ورهوونی vǝrhavúnaj 1 liberating, freeing 2 rescuing, saving, coming to the aid of

ورهیدل vǝrhedól *intransitive* [*past:* و ورهیده] 1 to be liberated, be let go 2 to break out, escape (from imprisonment, detention) 3 to be saved from, save oneself

ورهیدنه vǝrhedә́na *f.* 1 liberation 2 flight, escape (from imprisonment, detention) 3 rescue, salvation

ورهیدونی vǝrhedúnaj ورهیدونکی vǝrhedúnkaj 1 liberated, let go 2 rescued, saved

ورهیده vǝrhedә́ *m. plural* ☞ ورهیدنه

ورهیسته vǝ́rhista 1 to him, her, it, them; thence, to that place 2 aside; away, off

وری ¹ varáj *m.* pack; load, cargo د اوښ وری a camel load

وری ² vraj *m.* vuráj [*plural:* وري vri *Western plural:* وریان vrijã́n] 1 young ram, young lamb تندی وری newly-born ram, suckling lamb 2 حمل ² د وري پوستکی lambskin

وری ³ vrǝj *f.* vǝrǝj device for adjusting the bobbin on a distaff or spinning wheel

وری ⁴ vrǝj *f.* young sheep, ewe

وری ⁵ vrǝj *f.* vuráj gum, gums ☞ اوری ⁵

ورې ⁶ vúre cry or call used in herding sheep

وري ⁷ vurí *dialect present tense of* ورېدل ¹

وریا ¹ vǝrjã́ *f.* rain

وریا ² verjã́ *f.* edge, hem

وریت ¹ vrit 1 roasted 2 *figurative* tormented زره یې وریت دئ His heart is tormented.

وریت ² vret obvious, evident, apparent

وریت پیت vrit-pít over-roasted, overcooked, slightly burnt

وریتول vritavól *denominative, transitive* [*past:* وریت یې کړ] 1 to roast, fry 2 *figurative* to torment

وریتونه vritavә́na *f.* 1 frying 2 *figurative* torment, torture

وریته vritá *f.* vuritá 1 *singular of* وریت ¹ 2 roast meat; shashlik د وریته سیخونو وریته shashlik سیخونو کول to prepare a roast; make shashlik

وریتی ¹ vritagǝr *m.* vuritagǝr ☞ وریتی

وریتی ¹ vritáj *m.* shashlik cook and vendor

وریتی ² vrité *f. plural of* وریت ¹

وریتیدل ¹ vritedól *denominative, intransitive* [*past:* وریت شو] 1 to be roasted, be fried, roast, fry 2 *figurative* to suffer; wear someone out د بیلتون په اور کښی وریتیدل to yearn for

وریتیدل ² vretedól *denominative, intransitive* [*past:* وریت شو] to appear, come into sight

وریتیدنه ¹ vritedә́na *f.* 1 roasting, frying 2 *figurative* torment, torture

وریتیدنه ² vretedә́na *f.* appearance, coming into view

وریتیدونی vritedúnaj 1 roasted, fried 2 *figurative* tortured, tormented

وریتیده vritedә́ *m. plural* ☞ وریتیدنه

وریجه vrídzha *f.* grain kernel, grain of rice

وریجی vrídzhi *f. plural* rice غټی وریجي، پنډي وریجي coarse rice, farinaceous rice ایشبدلي وریجي fine polished rice نری وریجي husk rice وریجي کول boiled rice وریجي غوینی pilaf with meat

وریجینه vridzhína *f.* dish made from cooked rice; bread made from rice flour

وریځ vredz *f.* [*plural:* وریځي vrédze] *Eastern* 1 cloud بادونو وریځي above تر وریځو پورته The wind drove away the clouds. سره راوړي the clouds ☞ اوریځ 2 *figurative* darkness; fog د ناپوهی وریځي darkness, ignorance, the power of darkness

وریځه ¹ varjádza *f. dialect* ☞ اریځ

وریځي ¹ vrédze *f. Eastern plural of* وریځ

وریځي ² vrídze *f. plural dialect* ☞ وریجي

ورید varíd *m. Arabic* vein

وریدل ¹ vǝredól varedól 1 *intransitive* ☞ اوریدل 2 *m. plural* fall of precipitation د باران وریدل downpour, rain

وریدل ² varedól *intransitive* ☞ وریدل

وریدي varidí *Arabic* venous (of blood)

ورپرونه vrerúna *m. plural of* وراره

ورپره vrerá *f.* niece (brother's daughter)

ورپرڼ vrerǝ́ṇ *m.* wool spread out for fulling

وریز vǝrjáz *f.* وریزه vréza vréza vuréza *f. dialect* ☞ اوریځ

وریزون vrezhún *m.* small fine things (dropped, strewn about)

وریژي vrízhi *f. plural dialect* ☞ وریجي

وریشل vresól *transitive* ☞ ورېشل

وریشپر vreshpár *m.* harvest

ورېشپر ² vreshpár *m.* uproar, hubbub, din, racket

ورېشل vreshә́l *transitive* [*past:* ورېشه وي] **1** to spin, twist (thread) **2** ورېشل *figurative* to quarrel مه يې راسره ورېشه ☞ Don't quarrel with me!

ورېشونه ¹ vreshә́na *f.* ☞ ورېشون

ورېشون ¹ vreshә́na *m.* spinning, twisting (thread)

ورېشون ² vreshún *m.* **1** inheritance **2** discarded property; something that has gone out of use

وريکهکه vríkha *f.* shoots of wheat

ورېنکی ¹ vrekhkә́j vurekhkә́j *f.* **1** halter (rein attached to a bridle) **2** rear lace of a sandal **3** strip of old cloth

ورېنکی ² vrekhkә́j vurekhkә́j *f.* sprouts, shoots

ورېنم vrekhә́m *m.* silk د ورېنمو چينجی، د ورېنم چينجی silkworm د مصنوعي ورېنم، ساختگي ورېنم، اومه ورېنم raw silk د ورېنمو د چينجيو روزنه viscose سيريکلچر د چينجيو تربيه silk-spinning factory د ورېنمو وېستل د تاولولو فابريکه to be engaged in sericulture

ورېنمين vrekhmín **1** silk ورېنمين تنگی Vreshmin (canyon east of the Kabul Valley over which there is a road to Jelalabad) **2** silky (of hair)

ورېنه vrékha *f.* funeral meal served on the fifth night after a death; alms distributed on the fifth night after a death

ورېغ vregh *m.* dye

وري غوږ vrighvág *m.* *botany* kind of mint, *Phlomis*

ورين vrin open, sincere, frank

ورين تندی vrintandáj **1** cordial, cheerful, affable **2** *m.* cordiality, cheerfulness, affability vrintandí په خوړا ورين تندی د چا سره کتنه کول to accept someone affably, accept someone cordially

ورنداره vrendә́ra ورندار [*plural:* ورنداري vrendә́ri *plural:* ورنداري گاني vrendárigáni] sister-in-law (brother's wife)

ورېنگی vringáj *m.* light rain

وريني vrináj cheerful, glad

وريو vríjo *oblique plural of* ورى ² *oblique plural of* ورى ⁶

ورئيز vurajíz *m.* member of a bridal procession

ورېزه vraéza *f.* vréjza girlfriend of the bride

ور ¹ vaṛ *m.* **1** pockmark **2** scab, crust of a sore **3** infection; cause of an illness ور اخيستل to be infected, catch something

ور ² vaṛ *m. & f.* وړه *f.* **1** proper, appropriate; fit, suitable **2** worthy, deserving of something د اعتبار ور worthy of trust, reliable د افسوس ور worthy of sympathy; deplorable ورللل to consider necessary **a** ور کول to render fit, render suitable **b** to render worthy, render deserving of something **a** ور کېدل to be proper, be appropriate; be suited **b** to be worthy, be deserving of something نو ور ده چه ... for this reason one should له دې جهته دا ور ده چه ... دا ورته ور ده This should be mentioned. دا د يادولو وړه خبره ده they should دا حکايت د اروېدو should You should stay here. دا ور ده چه دلې اوسي هغه د زړه سوي ور دئ It is worth listening to this. One should دا د پېش بيني ور نه و. feel sorry for him. و This could not have been

forseen. **3** well-deserved ور شهرت well-deserved fame, well-deserved reputation

ور ³ vәṛ vuṛ **1** getting the upper hand, conquering, winning ور فريق the winner of the case; the winning party **2** right, guiltless

وور ⁴ vuṛ vәṛ ☞ ور ¹

ور ⁵ vuṛ *m.* use, advantage

ور ⁶ viṛ ☞ ويږ ²

وړاندې vṛánde *Eastern* ☞ وړاندي

وړاندني vṛándәnáj ☞ وړانديني

وړاندون vṛandún *m.* **1** outstripping, passing **2** competition

وړاندي vṛándi *Eastern* vṛánde **1.1** ahead, in front of, before په to move مخ پر وړاندي گام اخيستل forward, ahead پر وړاندي، forward, advance وړاندي ودرېږه Forward! Onward! وړاندي گوره Attention! Dress right! (as a command issued after the order) **a** زموږ عسکر مخ په وړاندي درومي to attack وړاندي درومل، وړاندي تلل Our troops are attacking. **b** to pass, outstrip, go in front **c** to overshoot the mark, over it **d** to be fast (of a timepiece) زما ساعت وړاندي تللئ My watch is fast. وړاندي وروسته little by little, consequently, one by one وړاندي او وروسته راغلو We arrived one after another. **a** وړاندي وروسته کتل to look around **b** to be circumspect, act with caution **a** وړاندي کول to move forward آس Move the چوکی وړاندي که! *chess* to move the knight وړاندي کول chair! **a** پنه وړاندي کول to get down to work **b** to make acquainted, introduce someone **c** to introduce, propose (a resolution, etc.) **d** to bestow, grant اعتمادنامه وړاندي to grant letters of credence استعفا وړاندي کول to send in one's resignation **e** to nominate (as a candidate) **f** to express (viewpoint, opinion) **g** to develop, advance (e.g., a science) **h** to instigate, put up to دا سړی لکه چه چا وړاندي کړئ وي It was as if someone had put him up to it. **i** to create مشکلات وړاندي کول to create difficulties **j** to impel to do something را وړاندي کول to move up to, push up to **a** را وړاندي شه! to go forward, move forward, advance وړاندي کېدل More forward! Go up there! **d** د څخه وړاندي کېدل to outstrip someone **b** to stand in front **c** to precede **d** to come up to, approach **e** to be introduced (a person) **f** to be introduced (into a discussion, etc.), be proposed (a resolution, etc.) **g** to be bestowed, be granted **h** to be developed, move forward (of a science); progress **i** to approach (a question) **j** to arise, be created د هغې ښايست مي سترگو ته وړاندي کېږي I remember her beauty. **1.2** earlier, before مو وويل چه ... وړاندي earlier we said that ... **1.3** then, later هغه وړاندي وويل Then, he said ... **1.4** further, farther, far وړاندي ولاړ It's still two or three miles more. دوه درې ميله وړاندي He went away. **2.1** *attributive* forward, anterior; former ☞ to وړاندي فکر کول **2.2** far وړاندي شرق the Far East *idiom* وړانديني be foresighted, be prudent

وړاندي تگ vṛánditág *m.* **1** movement forward, advance **2** attack **3** outstripping **4** precedence **5** development, progress, success **a** وړاندي تگ کول to move forward, advance **b** to attack **c** to outstrip **d** to precede **e** to develop, make progress, succeed

ورِاندي كوَل vṛā́ndi kavә́l *m. plural* **1** movement forward **2** acquaintance; introduction of someone **3** introduction (to a discussion, etc.); submission, proposal (of a resolution) **4** grant, granting **5** nomination (of a candidacy, etc.) **6** expression (of an opinion, view, etc.) **7** development (science) **8** instigation, putting up to

ورِاندي كېدَل vṛā́ndi kedә́l *m. plural* **1** movement forward **2** precedence **3** approach, drawing near **4** acquaintanceship **5** introduction (to a discussion); proposal (of a resolution, etc.) **6** granting, bestowal **7** development, progress **8** origin, creation

ورِاندينى vṛā́ndiáj **1.1** going forward **1.2** preceding; former; past ورِاندينى كَال last year ورِاندينى ګڼي the preceding issue (of a newspaper, magazine) **1.3** former په ورِاندينى ورځ eve, vigil د ورِاندينى ورځ on the eve of **1.4** *adjective military* forward, advance vṛāndiní ورِاندينى سنګرونه forward positions **2.1** *m.* predecessor **2.2** ancestor

ورِاندي تګ والى vṛāndiválaj *m.* ☞

ورِنګو vṛangó *f. proper name* Vrango

ورِانګه vṛā́nga *f.* **1** ray د لمر ورِانګي راديواكتيف ورِانګي solar rays radioactive rays د روى ورِانګي radiation **2** *figurative* flash, gleam; flashes, gleams

ورِانه vṛā́na *f.* **1** win, winning **2** success **3** rightness

ورِانه پرِانه vṛā́na-pṛā́na *f.* **1** profit and loss **2** winning and losing **3** right and wrong

ورِتوب vaṛtób[1] *m.* ☞ ورِتيا

ورِتوب vaṛtób[2] *m.* ☞ ورِانه

ورِتيا vaṛtjā́ *f.* **1** fitness; suitability, accordance **2** merit, *philosophy* desert **3** high degree of skill (of an athlete, etc.)

ورِجن vaṛdzhә́n infected

ورِغندى vaṛghandáj *m.* ☞ غرِوندى[1]

ورِكوتوب vaṛkutób *m.* ☞ ورِكتوب

ورِكتمن vaṛәktumn *m.* kindergarten

ورِكوتكى vaṛkóṭkaj **1** tiny, minuscule ورِكوتكى هلك child, kid **2** least, slightest ورِكوتكى حركت the slightest movement **3** not great ورِكوتكى غر low mountain, mount ورِكوتكى كلى tiny village, hamlet

ورِكوتوالى vaṛkoṭválaj *m.* childhood په ډېر ورِكوتوالي كښي in early childhood

ورِكوتى vaṛkóṭaj small, little; not great د ورِكوتي قد خاوند دى He is short of stature.

ورِكى vaṛkaj[1] *m.* boy, lad

ورِكى vaṛәkáj[2] ☞ ورِكى[1]

ورِكيتوب vaṛkitób *m.* ☞ ورِكوتوب، ورِكي توب

ورِكينكى vaṛkínkaj ☞ ورِكوتى

ورِكينه vaṛkína *f.* ☞ په ورِكينه واده كول ورِكوتوب to marry when underage

ورِګينا vaṛginá wool rope, hair rope

ورِل vṛәl *transitive* **1** [*present:* ورِي *past:* يو يي وړ] **1.1** to bear, carry, haul, conduct (usually inanimate objects, but also of animate objects if sick or injured) **1.2** to clear away (dishes, etc.) **1.3** to bear or drag away (quarry, game) ليوه پسه يووړئ *Western* The wolf carried away a sheep. **1.4** to carry away (by water) **1.5** *physics* to conduct (heat, electricity) **1.6** to endure (difficulties, etc.) **1.7** to earn, win, receive (award, prize, etc.); get the best of; attain victory دويم لمبر يي يووړئ He got second prize. He got a second place (in exams, etc.). ښه نوم وړل to become famous for, earn a good name ميدان وړل to attain victory, conquer, come out on top ☞ د تيلو ورِنه *and* راوړل *and* درِوړل *and* ورِوړل **2** *m. plural* د برق وړل electric conduction د تودوخي وړلو كښتى oil tanker (ship) وړل heat, thermal conductivity *idiom* زما زيار اوبو يووړئ My efforts turned out to be in vain.

ورِل راوړه vṛә́l-rāṛә́l *m. plural* ☞ وړه راوړه

ورِم vaṛә́m vuṛm previous (of a day, etc.)[1] ورِم كال year before last ورِمه ورځ day before yesterday ورِمه شپه night before last ورِمه مياشت month before last ورِمه مياشت three days ago

ورِم vṛәm *first person present tense of*[2] ورِل

ورِنبى vṛumbáj ☞ ورِنبى

ورِمه vәrma *f.* vúrma *singular of* ورِم[1]

ورِمه ورځنى vәrmavradzináj day before yesterday's, yesterday's ورځني غونډه at yesterday's meeting

ورِن vaṛә́n **1** woolen **2** hairy, hirsute ☞ ورِين

ورِنبى vṛumbáj *Eastern* **1.1** first ورِنبى لس ورځي the first ten days **1.2** former, previous **2** before, formerly; at first

ورِنګ راورِنګ vṛang-rāvṛáng *m.* transport; transporting

ورِنګن vṛangә́n glowing, gleaming, radiant

ورِنګه vṛә́nga *f.* **1** particle **2** dust speck, dust particle

ورِنګى vṛangáj[1] *m.* **1** magnifying glass **2** microscope

ورِنګى vṛangáj[2] ☞ رنګى[2]

ورِنه vṛә́na *f.* conveyance, transport; transportation; transporting

ورِو vaṛó *oblique plural of* وورِ[1]

ورِو vṛo *oblique plural of* ورِه[5]

ورِو vṛu *first person present tense plural of* ورِل

ورِوالى vuṛválaj[1] *m.* ☞ ورِكوتوب

ورِوالى vәṛválaj[2] *m.* **1** ☞ ورِانه **2** advantage

ورِوبى vәṛobáj *m.* mash (for cattle)

ورِوكتوب vaṛuktób *m.* **1** childhood, juvenile years **2** smallness, insignificance

ورِوكتون vaṛuktún *m.* kindergarten

ورِوكوالى vaṛukválaj *m.* ☞ ورِكوتوب

ورِوكى vaṛúkaj[1] **1** small, little; younger ورِوكى هلك boy ورِوكى كول خان ورِوكى to behave like a child **2** not great ورِوكى سيند rivulet ورِوكى غونډى low hillock ورِوكى تيږه pebble **3** not high, low low

ورِوكى vaṛúki[2] *m. plural* **1** bones of the heel **2** tendons of the heel

ورِوكى vaṛúke[3] *f. singular of* ورِوكى[1]

ورِول vaṛavә́l *denominative, transitive* [*past:* ووړ يي كړ] **1** to decrease **2** to break up, reduce in size, grind, crush; chop **3** *figurative* to lower, degrade

ورِومبنى vṛumbanáj first

ورنبی vṛumbáj ورونبی ورومبی vṛumbáj ☞ ورنبی

وړوند vṛund *dialect* ☞ روند

وړونکی vṛúnkaj *present participle of* وړل تیل وړونکي بیړی oil tanker (ship) د تغوندي وړونکي بیړی missile carrier (missile-launch vehicle)

وړونه vaṛavóna *f.* **1** diminution **2** breaking into pieces, making into smaller increments **3** *figurative* abasement

وړونی vṛúnaj ☞ وړونکی

وړه [1] vaṛá *f.* threads attached to the warp from above

وړه [2] vuṛә́ *m. plural dialect* ☞ اوړه [1]

وړه [3] vaṛá *f. singular of* ووړ [1]

وړه [4] vṛә *imperfective plural of* وړل

وړه [5] vṛә *m.* ☞ وړنه plural

وړه [6] vṛa **1** *imperfective singular of* وړل **2** *f. imperfect of* وړل

وړه [7] vṛa *f.* winning

وړه [8] vә́ṛa *f.* fitness, suitability; accordance

وړه [9] váṛa *f. singular of* وړ [2]

وړه [10] vә́ṛa *f. singular of* وړ [3]

وړه پړه vṛapṛá *f.* ☞ وړانه پړانه

وړه راوړه vṛә-rāvṛә́ *m. plural* transport; transporting

وړی [1] vaṛә́j *f. plural singular Eastern* wool د اوښ وړی camel hair د وزو وړی goat hair هراتي وړی Herat wool بادغیسي وړی Badkhyz wool اوبدلي وړی wool cloth د وړیو منځوی وزن shearing اومې وړی raw wool د اودلو فابریکه woolen cloth mill

وړی [2] vúṛaj *m. dialect* ☞ اوړی [1]

وړی [3] vṛi *present tense of* وړل

وړئ [4] vә́ṛəj *past participle of* وړل

وړی [5] vaṛé *f. plural of* ووړ [1]

وړی [6] vṛe *second person present of* وړل

وړئ [7] vṛәj *second person present of plural of* وړل

وړی [8] vṛe *imperfective feminine plural of* وړل

وړی [9] vaṛé *f. plural* ☞ وړه [1]

وړی [10] vaṛáj *m.* pompom, tassle

وړی [11] váṛi *feminine plural of* وړ [2]

وړی [12] vәṛi *feminine plural* **1** *of* وړ [3] **2** ☞ وړه [1] **3** selvage, edge of a rug

وړی [13] úṛaj *m. diminutive suffix* چرگوړی chick; cockerel

وړیا varjá vәṛjá́ **1** gratis, free of charge, free د وړیا په طور gratis, free وړیا اخیستل to take without payment وړیا ورکول to give without receiving payment **2** *regional* cheaply **3** in vain, to no avail وړیا تللل to go for naught

وړیان vaṛján *m.* kind of groats

وړیا والی varjāválaj *m.* **1** absence of payment, quality of being gratis **2** cheapness

وړیدل vaṛedә́l *denominative, intransitive* [*past:* وړ شو] **1** to diminish **2** to be made into smaller increments, be broken up; be broken into pieces **3** to be abased

وړیدنه vaṛedóna *f.* **1** diminution **2** breaking down into smaller increments; breaking up **3** abasement

وړیدونی vaṛedúnaj **1** diminished **2** broken into smaller increments, broken into pieces **3** *figurative* abased

وړین vaṛín **1** woolen وړیني لاس پیلي woolen shirt وړین خت woolen shirt **2** cloth وړین توکر wool-bearing breeds وړین حیوانات روزل to raise wool-bearing stock

وړینه [1] vaṛína *f.* ☞ وړتیا

وړینه [2] vaṛína *f. singular of* وړین

وړیو vaṛájo *oblique plural of* وړی [1]

وز vuz *m.* [*plural:* وزان vuzā́n *plural:* وزونه vzúna] **1** goat **2** wild goat *proverb* چه پلار یې وز نه وي ویشتلي، مور یې غوز نه وي ویشلي If the father does not shoot the goat dead, then the mother cannot divide up the fat.

وزارت vizārát *m.* vazārát *Arabic* [*plural:* وزارتونه vizāratúna *Arabic plural:* وزارات vizārā́t] ministry وزارت خارجه Ministry of Foreign Affairs وزارت داخله Ministry of Internal Affairs د معدنو او صنایعو وزارت Ministry of Mining and Industry د مالئي وزارت، Ministry of Mining and Industry vizārát-i Ministry of Finance وزارت صحیه Ministry of Health وزارت هوایي Ministry of Aviation

وزارت خانه vizāratkhāná *f.* ministry, ministry building

وزارت مختاري vizārát-i-mukhtārí *f.* diplomatic mission

وزبک vuzbák *m.* ☞ ازبک

وزر [1] vazár *m.* [*plural:* وزرونه varzarúna *f. Eastern plural:* وزري vazáre] **1** wing د مچ وزر a fly's wing **b** *figurative* something trivial وزرونه خپرول *figurative* to spread the wings a وزر کول to be winged, be alate (of insects) **b** *figurative* to be conceited, be proud د میږي چه ورکاوی (مرگ) راشي، وزرونه کوي *proverb* Before it dies, the ant acquires wings. پلاني سړی وزرونه کړي دي He has put on such airs. وزر دي وزیږي *literal* May you grow wings! *figuratively* May you grow strong! May you grow powerful! **2** fin **3** hand دواړه وزرونه both hands **4** lifting surface (aircraft) **5** jacket (of a book) **6** support, aid (from relatives); kin بې وزره سړی a helpless man; man who has no support from his relatives دواړه (د) خوک تر وزره یې ختلي He has neither father nor mother. *idiom* د بل په وزر الوتل to take someone under one's wing وزر لاندي نیول *literal* to fly on another's wings *figurative* to avail oneself of another's support; use someone; live on the intellect or work of another

وزر [2] vә́zər *m.* **1** entertainment وزر کول to entertain **2** ☞ فاتحه

وزرا vuzará *m. Arabic plural of* وزیر

وزروالا vazarvālā́ vazarvālá́ winged

وزغان vezghā́n *m.* walnut

وزغی vazghój *f.* boil, furuncle; abscess

وزگار vuzgár vəzgár **1** free, unoccupied (with work); released, fire (from a job); without work, without a job وزگار وخت free time, leisure **2** *biology* nonfunctional

وزگارتوب vuzgārtób *m.* وزگارتیا vuzgārtjá *f.* **1** leisure; idleness; break **2** unemployment کلي وزگارتوب full unemployment جزوي وزگارتوب partial unemployment

وزګارول vəzgāravə́l *denominative, transitive* [*past:* وزګار یې کړ] **1** to release (from work), fire **2** to put out of action, tear away from work **3** to remove له يو کار نه ځان وزګارول **a** to be removed from work **b** to create leisure for oneself د مشکلاتو څخه ځان وزګارول to get out from under difficulties

وزګاري vezgā́rí *f.* idleness; leisure; free time

وزګاريدل vuzgāredə́l *denominative, intransitive* [*past:* وزګار شو] **1** to be released (from work, etc.) دوی نه وزګاريدل They have finished eating. They have eaten. **2** to be idle **3** to be out of the running **4** to find time for something

وزګاريده vuzgāredə́ *m. plural* **1** release (from work) **2** idleness, loafing **3** being out of the running

وزګړی vuzgə́ṛaj *Western* وزګوری vəzgə́ṛaj vuzgúṛaj *m.* kid (goat)

وژل vazə́l *transitive dialect* ☞ وژل

وزله vázla *f.* means, way out بله وزله نشته There is no other way out.

وزم ¹ vazə́m *m.* **1** melody, tune; sound **2** color, complexion (face)

وزم ² vuzə́m *first person present tense of* وتل

وزمه vázma *suffix shade of color* زيړوزمه yellowish

وزمي vazmí melodious

وزن vazn *m. Arabic* [*plural:* وزنونه vaznúna *Arabic plural:* اوزان avzā́n] **1** weight مخصوص وزن specific gravity اتومي وزن ، اتومي وزن atomic weight د وزن پهلوان heavyweight *compound verb literal & figurative* وزن کول to weigh د رانده وزنونه پورته کول to lift weights **2** *poetry* scope

وزنه vazná *f. Arabic* **1** dumbbell; weight **2** ballast

وزنه برداري vaznabardārí *f. sports* weight lifting

وزني vazní *Arabic* **1** heavy **2** weighty, ponderous

وزو ¹ vzo *oblique plural of* وز

وزو ² vúzu *present tense first person plural of* وتل

وزونه vzúna *m. plural of* وز

وزه ¹ vazá *f.* girth; grasp; strap

وزه ² vzá, vuzá *f.* she-goat د انقري وزه angora goat

وزه ³ vúza, və́za *imperative imperfective singular of* وتل

وزه ⁴ váza *f.* ☞ وضع

وزئ ¹ vúzəj *present tense second person plural of* وتل

وزي ² vúzi *present tense first person singular of* وتل

وزي ³ vze *f. plural of* وزه ²

وزۍ ⁴ vúze *present tense second person singular of* وتل

وزيپه ¹ vazipá *f.* alms

وزيپه ² vzipá *f.* thyme

وزير vazír *m. Arabic plural* [وزيران vazirā́n *and Arabic* وزرا vuzarā́] **1** minister; *history* wizier وزير داخله foreign minister وزير خارجه interior minister د حمل او نقل وزير public health minister وزير صحيه transportation minister د مالياتو وزير finance minister د وزير دفاع، defense minister وزير دفاع د وزيرانو هيئت، د وزراؤ هيئت vazír-i... council of ministers, cabinet وزير مختار envoy وزير اعظم vazír-i... prime minister (not in Afghanistan) **2** *chess* queen **3** *proper noun* Wazir

وزيرستان vaziristā́n *m.* Waziristan

وزيره vazíra *f.* **1** female minister **2** minister's wife

وزيره ګوته vazíra gúta *f. regional* ring finger

وزيري ¹ vazirí *m. plural* **1** the Wazirs (a tribe) **2** vazirā́j *m.* a Wazir

وزيري ² vazirí *f.* **1** position (duties) of a minister **2** ministry

وزمه vuzemá *f.* goat in heat وزمه کېدل to be in heat (of a she-goat)

وزيی vuzjáj, vəzjáj goat's وزيی پوتکی a goatskin وزيی غوښه goat meat وزيی شودي goat milk

وژغني vəzghúni *f. plural* goat hair

وژغونيز vəzghuníz made of goat hair

وژل vazhə́l **1** *transitive* [*present:* وژني *past:* وی يې واژه] **1.1** to kill **1.2** to put out; extinguish (fire) **1.3** *figurative* to kill; strangle, suffocate خپل احساسات وژل to suppress one's feelings **2** *m. plural* **1.** killing, murder د چا د وژلو اراده کول to contemplate murder, plan a murder **2.2** putting out, extinguishing (of fire) **2.3** *figurative* suppression, stifling (of feeling etc.)

وژلل vazhlə́l *transitive dialect* ☞ وژل

وژلون vazhlún *m.* وژله vázhla *f. dialect* killing, murder

وژن vazhn *present stem of* وژل

وژنم vázhnəm *present tense first person of* وژل

وژنه vazhə́na *f.* ☞ وژلون

وژني vázhni *present tense of* وژل

وژون vazhún *m.* ☞ وژلون

وژونکی vazhúnkaj **1** *present participle of* وژل **2** deadly, lethal, fatal, deathly وسله وژونکي lethal weapon

وژونکی vazhúnaj ☞ وژونکی ²

وژوه vázhva *f.* gap (between teeth)

وژه ¹ və́zha *f.* occipital depression ☞ وجه ²

وژه ² vúzha *f.* ☞ وژۍ

وژي və́zhi *f. plural* **1** cervical tendons **2** hamstrings

وژۍ ² vuzháj *m.* **1** sinew, string; vein **2** tendon

وږ vag *m.* crown, wreath

وږبی vugbə́j *f.* magpie

وږد vugd *dialect* ☞ اوږد

وږدول vugdavúl *denominative, transitive dialect* ☞ اوږدول

وږدېدل vugdedə́l *denominative, intransitive dialect* ☞ اوږدېدل

وږسترګي ¹ vəgstərgí *f.* greed

وږسترګی ² vəgstə́rgaj greedy, with greedy eyes

وږکی vugkáj *m.* khinjak (a kind of pistachio tree) ☞ خنجک

وږم vágm, vágəm *m.* **1** smell, odor, aroma بې وږمه odorless **2** bad smell, stink وږم لرل to smell (to emanate an odor) **3** evaporation وږم کول to evaporate

وږمک vagmák *m.* slight odor

وږمکی vugmakə́j *f.* moonlight; shining of the moon

وږمول vagmavúl *denominative, transitive* [*past:* وږم يې کړ] to smell زه په باغ ننوتلم، هلته I entered the garden; it was pervaded with fragrance.

وږمه vagmá *f.* **1** fragrance, aroma, pleasant smell ښه وږمه وه **2** slight breeze, zephyr **3** evaporation; vapor

وږمی ¹ vəgmə́j *f.* moonlight; moonbeam

وږمی ² vagmə́j *f.* sense of smell

ورمبدل vagmedәl *intransitive* [*past:* ورمبدل و] to smell, give off a smell (of an odor)

ورده vúga *f. dialect* ☞ هوږه

وږی vágaj [1] *m.* **1** ear of grain ورې کول *compound verb* to come into ear, head up ورې ټولول *compound verb* **a** to collect ears of grain **b** *figurative* to learn from somebody ذهين د هيواد ورې ټولوي Zaheen learns from Hewad. **2** bunch, cluster (of grapes) يو ورې انګور a bunch, cluster of grapes **3** ear of corn, corncob **4** catkin, gosling, pussy (of a willow, etc.) **5** *astronomy* ☞ سنبله

وږی vәgaj [2] **1** hungry; famished; puckish په وږي نس on an empty stomach وږی کېدل *compound verb* to be hungry, be famished; starve برېند له لاري اوري، وږی نه اوري Hunger breaks a stone wall. (*literally:* A naked man turns off the road; a hungry man goes straight ahead.) **2** unsatisfied, unmet (of a need) دوی د روپو او دولت وږي نه دي *idiom* They don't aspire to riches.

وږی vugә́j [3] *f.* iron ring on which is fastened the shaft of a mill wheel or a waterwheel

وږی vugә́j [4] *f.* ☞ اوږی

وږچن vagechә́n *m.* وږي چي vagechí *m.* وږبخاندی vagetsã́ndaj *m.*, وږبخانی vagetsã́naj *m.* man who collects ears of grain (that remain after harvesting)

وږسترګی vә́gajstәrgaj ☞ وږسترګی

وس vas [1] *m.* **1** strength, capability **2** power, will په خپل وس of one's own will, voluntarily; independently زه په خپل وس هلته تلونکی نه يم I shall not go their of my own will. وس چلول *compound verb* to direct, manage زما وس نه چلېږي This is not in my power. د خپله وسه سره سم، سم له خپل وس سره، تر څوچي وس وي، تروسه پوري to the extent of one's power; as much as possible; as much as one can, as best one can له وسه a under the power b subject to تر وس لاندي دا تر وسه تېره خبره ده beyond one's ability دا تر وسه پورته This is beyond my strength. د ده وس نه رسېږي He is incapable. وس کول *compound verb* **a** to try one's best **b** to be able to; be up to; cooperate **c** to pressure, push somebody; persuade پر احمد مي هر څه وس وکئ رانغئ *Western* No matter how hard I tried talking Ahmed into coming, he has not come. **d** *figurative* compete with somebody; match somebody

وس vas [2] *m.* bulimia, abnormal appetite

وس vas [3] *m.* **1** abundance, plenty, profusion **2** population **3** population occupancy

وس vus [4] *dialect* ☞ اوس

وساطت vasātã́t *m. Arabic* **1** mediation **2** intercession د نورو په وساطت سره **a** with mediation by other individuals **b** with intercession by other individuals

ویساه visã́h *f.* ☞ ویساه

وسايط vasā́jit *m.* وسائط *plural Arabic of* واسطه

وسایل vasā́jal *m.* وسائل *plural Arabic of* وسيله

وسپنتوږی vuspәntógaj *m.* file, rasp

وسپنخوړی vuspәnkhә́ṛaj *m.* slag

وسپنه vuspә́na, vuspína, vәspә́na *f. Eastern* iron سپيني وسپنه tin plate

وست vast [1] *m.* **1** benefit **2** small wares; retail trade

وست vust [2] *second part of the verb* راوستل، دروستل *and* هغه یي را نه وست They have not brought him.

وستار vastā́r *m.* commission agent who sells small wares

وستاري vastārí *f.* commission trade in small wares; retail trade

وستری vustráj ☞ د شپې وستري خبرونه وروستی... وستری... latest (evening) news

وستل vastál [1] *m.* square where a village meeting gathers; meeting hall

وستل vustә́l [2] *second part of the verb* راوستل، دروستل *and* وروستل هغه یي را نه وستل They have not brought them.

وستلا vístulã *f.* Vistula

وستون vastún *m.* warehouse

وسته vastá [1] *f.* **1** pond **2** reserve وسته کول to declare a nature reserve وسته ماتول to ignore the prohibition of hunting, poach

وسته vastá [2] *f.* commodity

وسچولا víschulã *f.* ☞ وستولا

وسط vasát *m. Arabic* [*plural:* اوساط awsã́t] **1** middle د جنوری وسط mid-January **2** center

وسطي vastí, vasatí *Arabic* middle; central

وسطا vustã́ *f. Arabic singular & plural of* اوسط وسطی، وسطٰی آسیا āsijã́ji... Middle Asia قرون وسطی ḳurún-i... middle ages

وسع vus' *f. Arabic* **1** capacity, room **2** capability

وسعت vus'át *m. Arabic* **1** widening; propagation **2** growth, development وسعت مېندل to broaden وسعت ورکول *compound verb* **a** to propagate **b** to develop **3** vastness, expanse; spaciousness **4** capacity (e.g., of a market)

وسعت نظري vus'atnazarí *f.* broad view (a person with broad view)

وسعه vás'a *f.* ☞ وسع: په خپله وسعه as best one can

وسکه váska, vúska **1** because; since; for this reason **2** as if, as though

وسکي viskí *f.* whiskey

وسکيزه vaskíza *f.* tent pole

وسلوال vaslavã́l armed وسلوالي قواوي Armed Forces

وسله vaslá *f.* **1** weapons, arms د برید او یرغل وسله داور وسله firearms assault weapons تخریبي وسله destructive ذروي وسلي nuclear arms وسله arms control د وسلو کنترول arms race د وسلو رقابت weapons وسله را اخیستل take up arms, وسله ایښودل to lay down arms, capitulate وسله اغوستل to arm oneself وسله کول to arm بې وسلي وسلي کمول to reduce arms **2** *regional* means وسلي کول to disarm

وسله بند vaslabánd *regional* armed

وسله پال vaslapã́l related to artillery supply and technical logistics

وسله پالي vaslapālí *f.* artillery supply and technical logistics

وسله تون vaslatún *m.* artillery supply and technical logistics directorate

وسله خرڅوونکی vaslá khartsavúnkaj *m.* armorer, arms merchant

وسله دار vasladár armed وسله دار کول compound verb to arm وسله دار کېدل compound verb to get armed

وسله کوټ vaslakóṭ m. pile (for rifles) وسله کوټ کول compound verb to pile arms

وسله لرونکي vaslá larúnkaj armed وسله لرونکي قواوي armed forces

وسله وال vaslaválá 1 ☞ وسله دار 2 m. .1 armorer 2.2 arms seller 3 munitions officer

وسلېدل vasledál intransitive [past: و وسلېده] to break, burst, snap

وسمن vasmán powerful, mighty

وسمه vasmá, vusmá f. 1 botany dyer's woad, Isatis tinctoria 2 indigo (color); henna (black dye) هغه په خپلي ږيري وسمه پوري کوي He dyes his beard black with henna.

وسو vúsu past perfective of سول

وسو vúsu Western 1 past perfective of سول 2 present perfective first person plural of سول

وسواس vasvás m. Arabic 1 doubt, hesitation, uncertainty 2 anxiety, worry وسواس کول compound verb a to hesitate, fluctuate, doubt b to fear, be alarmed, be anxious ته په خپل زړه کښي وسواس مه کوه! Don't worry! 3 temptation, enticement 4 maniac, one possessed

وسواسه vasvāsá f. Arabic 1 enticement, temptation; seduction وسواسه اچول compound verb to tempt, entice 2 hesitation; anxiety, doubt

وسواسي vasvāsí Arabic upset; hesitating; hypochondriac; diffident وسواسي کېدل to be nervous, fidget

وسوسه vasvasá f. obsessive idea

وسه vasá, vassá f. blocks, planks or boughs placed across the main beams of the ceiling

وسه vása f. 1 summer rain 2 monsoon

وسه vása f. dialect ☞ وسع وسه مي نه شي I am not up to it. د هغه دا کار د هر چا د He was unable (to do something). په وسه کښي نه وه وسي نه دئ پوره within one's abilities Not everyone can do this. په خپله وسه abilities

وسي vúsi Western present perfective of سول

وسی vusáj m. dialect ☞ هوسی

وسی vusáj f. dialect ☞ هوسی

وسې vassé f. plural of وسه

وسیع vasí' Arabic vast, spacious, broad وسیع کول compound verb to broaden, expand وسیع کېدل compound verb a increase (of expenses) b to expand

وسیله vasilá f. Arabic [plural وسیلې vasilé and m. plural Arabic وسایل، وسائل vasā'íl] 1 means; way د بانک په وسیله، د بانک په وسیله سره via the bank 2 pretext; reason 3 support, patronage وسیله کول compound verb to help وسیله لرل to enjoy support 4 plural وسائل means (in various meanings) د تولید وسائل means of production د کار وسائل means of subsistence د ژوندانه وسائل instruments of labor د کتلو اوبدلو وسائل conveyances, transportation نقلیه وسائل visual aids

وسیله دار vasiladár m. 1 client 2 ward; protégé

وسیله داري vasiladārí f. dependence

وسیلناک vasilanák 1 enjoying support 2 able to do much

وسیم vasím Arabic beautiful, fine, graceful, dainty

وش vash m. growth, development وش کول compound verb to grow, to develop

وش vəsh m. plural poison ☞ وښ

وشتمار vashtamár m. jester, clown

وشتول vashtavól transitive [past: وو يي وشتاوه] to incite

وشته váshta, vúshta f. joke وشته کول compound verb to joke توقي anecdotes; humor وشتي کول، وشتي وهل compound verb to kid, joke

وشلېگ vahlég m. main prop of a tent

وشم، وشمه vásham، váshma resembling something; like

وشند vahánd m. teenager

وشند vashónd m. young man's daring; young man's prowess, young man's pride

وشنده vashánda f. teenage girl

وشو vúshu dialect vúsho past perfective of شول

وش، وښ vuh vuh interjection oh oh (to express sadness, sorrow, or pain about somebody or something)

وشوله vushvəla ☞ وشوه

وشوه vúhvə past perfective plural of شول

وشوه vúshva past perfective feminine of شول

وشه vúshə Eastern ☞ وشو

وښ vuкh m. plural poison وښ نه پري تلل to fail to affect somebody (of scorpion poison, etc.)

وښته vaкhtá f. 1 variety of large-grain mountain rice 2 women's ornament worn on the chest made of beads or coral

وښتی vaкhtáj m. ☞ 2

وښخور vaкhкhór herbivorous وښخور حیوان herbivorous animals

وښکالی vaкhkǎlaj m. cluster, bunch (of grapes and other fruit)

وښکل vəкhkál, vuкhkál m. dialect ☞ ښکل

وښکه vəкhka f. dialect tear

وښکی vəкhkáj m. 1 corner (of one's mouth) 2 temple

وښکی vaкhkáj m. ☞ وښکالی

وښو vaкhó oblique plural of واښه

وښی vaкháj m. bracelet

وښهیاست vúкhəjāst Western perfective imperative plural of ښنودل

وښجاڼه vaкhjāṇa f. meadow

وښېدل vəкhedál intransitive [past: و وښېبد] to slip out of one's hands (when something is put down)

وښیه vúкhəja perfective imperative singular of ښنودل

وصال visál m. Arabic 1 encounter, meeting; date (with a beloved man or woman) 2 religion demise, death

وصایا vasājá m. plural Arabic of وصیت

وصایت visāját m. Arabic 1 duties of an executor چا ته وصایت ورکول appoint (somebody) an executor 2 guardianship

وصف vasf m. Arabic [plural وصفونه vasfúna and Arabic اوصاف avsáf] 1 quality, property, characteristic امتیازي وصف a distinctive property, feature; difference **2** epithet **3** description, characterization **4** praise; eulogy وصف کول *compound verb* **a** to describe, characterize **b** to praise, eulogize **5** *grammar* adjective

وصفي vasfí *Arabic* **1** descriptive **2** attributive

وصل vasl *m. Arabic* **1** connection وصل کول *compound verb* ☞ to join وصلېدل *compound verb* ☞ وصلول to be connected **2** date, meeting

وصلت vaslát *m. Arabic* juncture, connection, approach وصلت کول *compound verb* to connect, bring together

وصلول vaslavә́l *denominative, transitive* [*past:* وصل یې کړ] to connect, join

وصله vaslá *f. Arabic* **1** patch **2** *grammar* wasla (the name of a diacritic that connects two Arabic words that are pronounced as one) **3** segment; joint

وصلي vaslí *Arabic* connective

وصول vusúl *m. Arabic* **1** arrival; delivery **2** achievement of goal **3** receiving, procurement وصولول *compound verb* ☞ to receive, to obtain وصولېدل *compound verb* ☞ **4** delight

وصولي vusulí *Arabic* obtained, received (of money)

وصولېدل vusuledә́l *denominative, intransitive* [*past:* وصول شو] to be received, be acquired; come in (e.g., of money)

وصي vasí *m. Arabic law* **1** executor **2** trustee, guardian څوک وصي درول، څوک وصي کول **a** to appoint (somebody) executor **b** to appoint (somebody) trustee or guardian

وصیت vasiját *m. Arabic* [*plural* وصیتونه vasijatúna *and Arabic* وصایا vasājá] **1** testament; last will; covenant **2** instruction وصیت کول *compound verb* **a** to bequeath; write a will **b** to give or issue an instructions د چا وصیتونه عملي کول to fulfill somebody's commandments

وصیت نامه vasijatnāmá *f.* will (written) شرعي وصیت نامه legal will, a will according to shariah

وضاحت vazāhát *m. Arabic* clarity, obviousness, distinctness په ډېر وضاحت، په ډېر وضاحت سره very clearly; absolutely obvious; distinctly

وضاعت vazā'át *m. Arabic* humiliation

وضع váz', váz'a *f. Arabic* [*plural* وضعي váz'i *and m. plural: Arabic* اوضاع avzā'] **1** establishing, arranging, placement **2** setting, determination د اجوري وضع setting the amount of salary له مصارفو اقتصادي وضع determination of expenses **3** establishing (e.g., a court of law) وضع کول *compound verb* **a** to establish, arrange, place **b** to set, determine **c** to establish (e.g., a court of law); found **d** to introduce (e.g., a law, a rule) وضع کېدل *compound verb* **a** to be established, be arranged, be placed **b** to be set, be determined **c** to be established (e.g., a court of law); found **d** to be introduced (e.g., a law, a rule) **4** a setup; status, situation اقتصادي وضع economic situation مادي وضع financially, financial situation, materially سیاسي وضع political situation **5** status اجتماعي وضع social status **6** conduct, manner; behavior; treatment د چا پغلي

د چا په نسبت سره وضع غوره کول the girl's taciturnity خاموشه وضع treat somebody coldly **7** position (viewpoint) **8** *grammar* mood د امر وضع indicative mood اخباري وضع imperative mood

وضعه váz'a *f.* ☞ وضع; په موسکی وضعه *regional* with a smile; smiling دا صحیح وضعه ده This is correct. دا طبیعي وضعه ده This is natural.

وضعیت vaz'iját *m. Arabic* **1** circumstances; situation; status; condition اقتصادي وضعیت economic situation حربي وضعیت military situation د حرب وضعیت د کاریگرو وضعیت the status of workers **2** position, attitude **3** *sports, military* posture

وضو vuzú, vazú *m. Arabic* ablutions وضو کول to make ablutions

وضوح vuzúh *m. Arabic* **1** clarity, distinctness **2** clarity, obviousness

وضیع ¹ vazí' *Arabic* **1** base (of feelings) **2** base, mean, villainous

وضیع ² vazí' *f. Arabic* deposit, an amount entrusted to somebody for safekeeping

وطن vatán *m. Arabic* **1** homeland; fatherland, motherland د وطن ساتني دپاره را پر مخ شئ! Forward for the motherland! **2** place of birth, home نا اشنا وطن foreign land د وطن معلومات *regional* studies له وطنه سترګي پناه کول to leave one's native area

وطن پالنه vatanpālә́na *f.* ☞ وطن پرستي

وطن پرست vatanparást **1** patriotic وطن پرست خلګ patriots **2** *m.* patriot

وطن پرستي vatanparastí *f.* patriotism

وطن خواه vatankhāh *m.* patriot

وطن خواهي vatankhāhí *f.* patriotism د وطن خواهي روح patriotic spirit

وطن دار vatandā́r *m.* compatriot; fellow countryman

وطن داري vatandārí *f.* countrymen's association

وطن دوست vatandóst *m.* ☞ وطن پرست

وطن دوستي vatandostí *f.* ☞ وطن پرستي

وطن فروش vatanfurúsh *m.* turncoat; traitor to one's country

وطنوال vatanvāl وطن وال *m. singular & plural* compatriot; countryman; compatriots; countrymen

وطني vataní *Arabic* **1.1** domestic وطني منسوجات domestically produced textile **1.2** political chauvinism لوی وطن وطني تعصب local (of seeds) **1.3** internal وطني خبرونه internal news **1.4** internal communications **2** *m.* **.1** native, indigenous; countryman, compatriot **2.2** native, local, aborigine

وطنیت vataniját *m. Arabic* patriotism د وطنیت روح patriotic spirit

وطواط vatvát *m. Arabic* **1** bat **2** pipsqueak **3** cowardly person, hesitant person

وطواطه vatvā́ta *feminine of* وطواط

وظائف vazā'if *m.* وظائف *plural Arabic of* وظیفه; وظائف الاعضا vazāif-ul-a'zā́ *m. plural* physiology

وظیفتاً vazifátán *Arabic adverb* duty bound; answering the call of duty (service, etc.) هغه خو وظیفتاً مجبور و It was his duty to do this.

وظیفوي vazifaví functional وظیفوي خواص functional characteristics

وظیفه vazifá, vazipá *f. Arabic* [*plural* وظیفي vazifé, vazipé *and m. plural Arabic* وظائف vazāíf] **1** duty, obligation حتمي وظیفه duty,

Pashto-English Dictionary

وظيفه مقدسه fulfillment of one's duty د وظيفي اجراً obligation sacred duty د وظيفي په ډول military duty عسكري وظيفه duty bound (e.g., service duties); under obligation وظيفه كول compound verb to perform one's duty, fulfill one's obligation لرل وظيفه to be responsible وظيفه اشغالول دا زه to take on oneself the obligation خپله وظيفه بولم چي ... I consider it my duty. 2 physiology biology function د اعضاو د وظايفو علم physiology 3 purpose, intent د هنر وظيفه the purpose of art 4 mathematics problem 5 allowance, stipend 6 ration 7 daily prayer 8 daily work

وظيفه دار vazifadár 1 fulfilling one's duty, obligation 2 responsible; authorized(employee)

وظيفه شناس vazifashinás conscientious; (a man) of his word

وظيفه شناسي vazifashināsí f. conscientiousness, awareness

وظيفه لرونكى vazifá larúnkaj 1 present participle of وظيفه لرل 2 officials وظيفه لرونكي كسان، وظيفه لرونكي ماموران obliged

وظيفي vazifí Arabic functional

وعاً vi'á f. Arabic [plural: اوعيه av'ijá] 1 tableware, crockery 2 vessel

وعائي vi'āí Arabic vascular وعائي جريان circulation, blood circulation

وعده va'dá f. Arabic promise د يوي وعده زباني oral promise; word د چا سره وعده كول، د چا as previously promised موږ په خپلو وعدو به وفا وكو We will keep سره وعده ترل our promise. خپله وعده تينگه چا ته عرض كول promise somebody د وعدي خلاف كول، د وعدي بي احترامي كول to break one's پر خپله وعده دربدل، خپله وعده پوره كول to keep one's promise firmly promise هغه به د وعدي پوخ وي He will keep his word. په دري مياشتي وعده idiom for a period of 3 months

وعده خلاف va'dakhlāf, va'dakhilāf breaking one's promise, going back on one's word

وعده خلافي va'dakhalāfí, va'dakhilāfí f. breach of promise

وعده شكن va'dashikán ☞ وعده خلاف

وعده وفا va'davafá true to one's word

وعظ va'z m. Arabic sermon وعظ كول compound verb to preach

وعيد va'íd m. Arabic 1 threat 2 warning

وغه vága f. tapeworm

وغيره vaghajrá Arabic and so on, and so forth, etc.

وفا vafá f. Arabic loyalty, constancy په چا وفا كول to believe somebody وفا يي كول compound verb to keep one's promise راسره وكړه He treated me fairly.

وفات vafát m. Arabic [plural: وفاتونه vafātúna and Arabic وفيات vafajāt] death, demise ده تر وفات وروسته after his death وفاتبدل، وفات كبدل the day of Mohammed's death شريف compound verb to die په څو شپو كښي عبد القادر وفات شو A few days later Abdul-Qader died. مور يي وفات شوه His mother is deceased.

وفادار vafādár devoted; constant

وفادارانه vafādārāná true, devoted; loyal وفادارانه وضعيت a loyal attitude وفادارانه تبريكات idiom sincere congratulations

د وفاداري قسم خورل vafādārí f. fidelity, devotion; loyalty وفاداري كول swear one's loyalty to وفاداري كول compound verb a to be true, be devoted b to behave honestly

وفاق vifáḳ m. Arabic agreement; unanimity

وفاقيت vifāḳiját m. وفاقيه vifāḳijá f. Arabic 1 commonwealth 2 federation, union

وفاوالا vafāvālá ☞ وفادار

وفد vafd m. Arabic 1 delegation, deputation ادبي وفد a writers' delegation 2 the Wafd Party (in Egypt)

وفدي vafdí Arabic 1 Wafdist 2 m. Wafdist

وفرت vafrát m. وفور vufúr m. Arabic 1 plentifulness; abundance د اوبو وفرت abundance of water وفرت كول compound verb a to abound in b to be strong (of a feeling); seize 2 plurality; multitude د تجارت وفرت vigorousness of trade

وفيات vafajāt m. 1 plural Arabic of وفات 2 mortality وفيات لږ دي Mortality is low.

وقار vaḳár, viḳár m. Arabic 1 seriousness, gravitas; presentability ډېر وقار لرل be very serious 2 honor; dignity د چا وقار ته صدمه رسول to offend somebody, humiliate, disparage

وقائع vaḳāi' m. plural Arabic of وقيعه

وقايع نويس vaḳāi'navís m. historiographer, chronicler وقايوي طب viḳājaví preventative preventative maintenance

وقايه viḳājá f. Arabic 1 defense, protection (e.g., of health); prophylaxis 2 prevention 3 safekeeping 4 cover (of a book etc.) وقايه كول compound verb to bind (books)

وقت vaḳt m. Arabic [plural: وقتونه vaḳtúna and Arabic اوقات avḳát] 1 time د هغه وقته څخه since that time په يوه ever کوم وقت 2 a break (in school) تفريحي وقت معين وقت كښي at a certain time تا ته به کوم وقت چا نه وي ويلي چه ... Haven't they ever told you that... ☞ وخت

وقتاً váḳtán Arabic temporarily وقتاً چه when

وقتاً فوقتاً váḳtán-fīvaḳtán Arabic from time to time, at times

وقتي vaḳtí Arabic 1 temporary 2 early ☞ وختي [1]

وقعت vaḳ'át m. Arabic 1 ☞ وقعه 2 significance; importance ويوي خبري ته څه وقعت نه وركول not attach significance to something

وقعه vaḳ'á f. Arabic 1 event; incident; accident 2 struggle; confrontation 3 heat of the battle ☞ واقعه

وقف vaḳf, vaḳúf Arabic 1 m. [plural: وقفونه vaḳfúna, vaḳufúna and Arabic اوقاف avḳáf]. 1 charitable donation (entitling one to the use of proceeds on certain terms) وقف كول compound verb a to bequeath something to charity b to devote to something د يو كار وقف كبدل، ديو كار to devote oneself to a cause دپاره ځان وقف كول compound verb to be devoted to something 1.2 ownership of real estate (without the right of transfer) 1.3 pause, break 2 predicative .1 bequeathed 2.2 devoted

وقف نامه vaḳfnāmá f. charitable donation act; waquf certificate

وقفول vaḳfavál denominative, transitive [past: وقف يي کړ] to bequeath as waquf يو مكتب وقفول to devote, give wakuf to a school دي دپاره د يوه غونډه وقفول to devote one meeting to this

817

وقفه vaķfá *f. Arabic* **1** stop, delay, protraction بېله خُند او وقفې نه without delay, immediately څه قدر وقفه پېښه شوه There was a certain delay. **2** break; pause **3** stagnation, decline اقتصادي وقفه، د اقتصادي فعاليتو وقفه stagnation, decline in the economy; depression **4** breakup, a rupture

وقفي vaķfí *Arabic* waquf

وقفېدل vaķfedә́l *denominative, intransitive [past:* وقف شو*]* **1** to be bequeathed as a waquf **2** to be devoted; get devoted

وقوع vuķú' *m. Arabic [plural:* وقوعات vuķu'át*]* **1** incident; event **2** completion of a transaction **3** onset; emergence **4** *grammar* completion of an action

وقوف vuķúf *m. Arabic* **1** intelligence, mind; wisdom **2** cognition; knowledge علم او وقوف حاصلول *compound verb* to cognize; know

وقوفدار vuķufdár clever; expert, knowledgeable

وقيعه vaķi'á *f. Arabic [plural:* وقيعي vaķi'é *and m. plural Arabic* وقايع، وقائع vaķāí'*]* **1** incident; event **2** fact

وكا vúkā **1** *past tense of* كول⁷ کړل **2** *present perfective of* کړل⁷ كول *in lieu of* وکړي

وكالت vakālát *m. Arabic* **1** authority, powers مخصوص وكالت special rights, special powers په وكالت on somebody's assignment, mandate لرل تام وكالت vakālát-i... to have unlimited authority **2** power of attorney **a** وركول وكالت to give authority; give powers **b** to give power of attorney **3** deputizing **4** deputy's mandate د ملي شورا په وكالت انتخاب شو He was elected a deputy of the National Council. **5** mission, office تجارتي وكالت trade mission; trade agency د ملګرو په وكالت on behalf of (on the instructions of) one's friends زموږ د خوا په وكالت on our behalf وكالت كول *compound verb* to represent somebody, be somebody's authorized representative, agent **6** bar; practice of law

وكالتاً vakālátán *Arabic* **1** on instructions, on assignment; as a representative **2** by a power of attorney

وكالت التجاري vakālat-ut-tudzhārí *f.* trade mission, agency

وكالت نامه vakālatnāmá *f.* **1** power of attorney (document) وكالت نامه ښكاره كول to present a power of attorney **2** authority; power

وكاوه vúkāvә *Eastern past perfective of* کړل⁷ كول *in lieu of* وکړ

وكر vakár *m.* face; image

وكړای vúŗaj *conditional mood, potential form and perfective aspect of* کړل⁷ كول دا يې وكړای شوای چه He succeeded.

وكړو¹ vúkŗu *past perfective first person plural of* کړل⁷ كول

وكړو² vúkŗo *dialect past perfective of* کړل⁷ كول *in lieu of* وكړ

وكړه¹ vúkŗә *past perfective plural of* کړل⁷ كول

وكړه² vúkŗa *past tense feminine of* کړل⁷ كول

وكړه³ vúkŗa *imperative perfective aspect of* کړل⁷ كول

وكړئ vúkŗәj *imperative perfective aspect plural of* کړل⁷ كول

وكړي² vúkŗi *present perfective of* کړل⁷ كول

وكړی³ vúkŗaj *Eastern conditional mood, potential form and perfective aspect of* کړل⁷ كول

وكړې⁴ vúkŗe *past tense f. plural of* کړل⁷ كول

وكښ vúkikh *past perfective of* كښېنل²

وكښنو vúkkho *Eastern past perfective of* كښېنل² *in lieu of* وكينئ

وكلا vukalā́ *m. plural Arabic of* وكيل

وكلی vukléj *f.* wooden mortar

وكم¹ vukә́m *preposition* و *combined with the pronoun* کم خای کم Where to? ته؟

وكم² vúkә́m *present perfective first person of* كول⁷ کړل *in lieu of* وكړم

وكولو vúkavәlo *dialect past perfective of* كول⁷ کړل *in lieu of* وكړ

وكوله vúkavәla *dialect past perfective feminine of* كول⁷ کړل *in lieu of* وكړه

وكوو vúkavu *dialect present perfective first person plural of* كول⁷ کړل *in lieu of* وكړو

وكه¹ váka *f.* craving, appetite

وكه² vúka *imperative mood perfective aspect of* كول⁷ کړل *in lieu of* وكړه³

وكه³ vúkә *dialect past perfective of* كول⁷ کړل *in lieu of* وكړ

وكئ¹ vukáj *Western past perfective of* كول⁷ کړل *in lieu of* وكړئ

وكی² vakáj *m. dialect* ☞ هوكی¹

وكی³ okáj okә́j *diminutive noun suffix* غټوكی a bit older, bit bigger, bit more

وكيښ vúkikh *past perfective of* كښېنل²

وكيل vakíl *m. Arabic [plural:* وكيلان vakilán *and Arabic* وكلا vukalā́*]* **1** proxy holder; representative; authorized agent; agent قانوني وكيل confidant; proxy holder **2** lawyer, defender د دعوا وكيل lawyer مدافع وكيل defender وكيل نيول to hire a lawyer **3** acting (official); deputy د وزارت وكيل deputy minister د باچا وكيل viceroy; in lieu of regent **4** deputy; delegate څوک د يو كار دپاره وكيل كول to authorize somebody; delegate somebody

وكيل التجار vakil-ut-tudzhár *m. Arabic* sales agent, commercial agent

وكيله vakíla *feminine to* وكيل

وكيلي vakilí *f.* ☞ وكالت

وگاټه vúgāṭә *past perfective of* ګټل

وګټه vúgaṭa *imperative mood perfective of* ګټل

وګد vugd *Eastern* ☞ اوږد

وګړی vagә́ŗaj *m.* **1** human being; creature **2** [*usually plural* وګړي vagә́ŗi] people; inhabitants; population افغاني وګړي *vagә́ŗi* Afghan population, the Afghans

وګم vagm *m. Eastern* ☞ وږم

وګمه² vagmá *f. Eastern* ☞ وږمه

وګنه vúgaṇa apparently, probably په مكتوب وګنه دې ته اشاره شوی وه چه ... Apparently, the letter means that...

وګوره vúgora *imperative mood perfective of* كتل **1** look **2** listen up, hey

وګی¹ vágaj *m. Eastern* ☞ وږی¹

وګی² vúgaj, vә́gaj *Eastern* ☞ وږی²

وگیچانی vagajchā́ṇaj *m.* ☞ وربېچن

ول¹ val *m.* **1** coil **2** curl **3** curve, curvature **4** layer, row **5** fold ول كول *compound verb* **a** twist, twine **b** to bend, warp **c** to arrange in rows, arrange in layers, pile up **d** to fold a pleat ول کبدل *compound verb* **a** to be twisted, be twined **b** to be bent, be warped **c** to be arranged in rows, be arranged in layers, be piled up **d** to be folded in a pleat **6** entangling something; freezing (work) ول اچول *compound verb* **a** to make a coil **b** to make a curl **c** *figurative* to throw a monkey wrench into; be uncooperative (at work) **7** price

ول ² vul *m.* mind, intelligence ځان له وله ويستل *idiom Eastern* to act foolishly; be crazy ځان له وله مه باسه ، ځان له وله مه او باسه *idiom* Stop acting foolish!

ول ³ vul *m.* hot wind, sandstorm

ول ⁴ vul *m.* latch (door)

ول ⁵ vul *dialect* **1** cheapness **2** cheap, inexpensive

ول ⁶ vul *paired word to* چل

ول ⁷ vul *colloquial in lieu of* ويل ³ ما ول I thought. تا ول، تا چه ول as if, as though; one could have thought…

ول ⁸ vəl *dialect* **1** past tense third person plural of the copula in lieu of وو or وه **2** the infinitive of the copula "to be"

ول ⁹ vul *present stem of* ويشتل

ولا valá to swear by God ته ولا واخله! ولا اخيستل Swear by God!

ولايت valát *colloquial* ☞ ولايت

ولادت viládát *m. Arabic* **1** birth **2** labor, birth د ولادت پينه delivery, childbirth, parturition

ولادي viládí related to the birth ولادي پينبي labor, delivery

ولادي واستک vládivásták *m.* Vladivostok

ولاړ ¹ valáŗ **1** standing **2** stopped, immobile ولاړ ستوری immobile stars **3** waiting, expecting زه درته ولاړ يم I am waiting for you. **4** standing; still (water) ولاړي اوبه standing water **5** stopped, ceased (of rain, etc.) اوس باران ولاړ دئ The rain has stopped now. **6** based; founded; resting on something **7** *figurative* advocating something, championing something, standing up for something or somebody پوهان پر دي خبره ټينگ ولاړ دي چه ... Scientists advocate the concept of... **8** *in lieu of* ولاړسئ Stand up! (as a command) ولاړ محصول *idiom* standing crops

ولاړ ² vláŗ *Western* **1** *past tense of* تلل ¹ دى مکتب ته ولاړ He went to school. **2** *forms future perfect and imperative perfect from* ولاړ به شي He will go. تلل ¹ سه! Go! Go away!

ولاړتوب valáŗtób *m.* ولاړتيا valáŗtjá *f.* **1** standing **2** stop **3** lull; calm

ولاړ سئ valáŗ səj **1** *imperative perfective plural of* ولاړيدل **2** Stand up! (as a command)

ولاړل vláŗál *Western past tense plural of* تلل ¹

ولاړو ¹ vláŗu *past tense first plural of* تلل ¹

ولاړو ² valáŗo *oblique plural of* ولاړ ¹

ولاړول valáŗavəl *denominative, transitive* [*past:* ولاړ يي کړ] **1** to bring up; make stand, pitch **2** to stop **3** to deliver, bring somebody

ولاړونه valáŗavə́na *f.* ☞ ولاړه ¹ **1**

ولاړه ¹ valáŗa **1** *f.* **1.1** getting up; rise, climb **1.2** standing **1.3** stop, stopping *proverb* د ناستي نه ولاړه، تر ولاړي ښه ده Standing is better than sitting; walking is better than standing. **2** *feminine singular of* ولاړ ¹

ولاړه ² vláŗə́ *Western past tense plural of* تلل ¹

ولاړه ³ vláŗa **1** *Western past perfective feminine of* تلل ¹ **2** *serves to form the future tense and imperative perfect feminine of* تلل ¹ ولاړه راغله You will go. ولاړه به سي Go! سه! *idiom* an opportunity to arrange some matter اوس نو ولاړه راغله نه کېږي The situation is beyond repair.

ولاړه ⁴ vúlāŗə *past tense of* لړل

ولاړي ¹ vláŗəj *Western past tense of* تلل ¹ *in lieu of* ولاړ ²

ولاړي ² valáŗi *f. plural of* ولاړ ¹

ولاړي ³ vláŗe *Western* **1** *past tense second person of* تلل ¹ **2** *past tense plural feminine of* تلل ¹ ښڅي ژر نه ولاړي The women went away after a long while. **3** *serves to form the future perfect and imperative perfect plural feminine of* تلل ولاړي سئ! Go away! ولاړي به سئ You will go away.

ولاړيدل valāŗedál *denominative, intransitive* [*past:* ولاړ شو] **1** to get up, rise تول خلگ ورته ولاړ شول Everyone rose before him. **2** to rise, set out against somebody; rebel و چا ته په جنگ ولاړيدل to wage war on somebody **3** to take up something, set about something; start something **4** to appear, evolve, emerge, develop (of complications, trouble, etc.)

ولاړيدنه valāŗdə́na *f.* ☞ ولاړيده

ولاړيدوني valāŗedúnaj arising, getting up

ولاړيده valāŗedə́ *m. plural* **1** getting up; rising مريض د ولاړيدو شو The sick man began to get up. **2** uprising, rebellion against somebody **3** starting something; setting about something **4** development, appearance, emergence (of complications, trouble, etc.)

ولان vəlán used to something; familiar with something

ولاند vəlánd *m.* person who washes a deceased person

ولانگه vlánga *f.* wooden board (plank) used to wash a deceased person on

ولايت viláját, valáját *m. Arabic* [*plural:* ولايتونه vilájatúna *and Arabic* ولايات viláját] **1** province, region د کابل ولايت Kabul Province شمالي ولايات the northern provinces of Afghanistan **2** state (an administrative territorial unit) **3** position of a governor, regent, governor-general **4** foreign country, abroad, overseas **5** *regional* England ولايت ته روان يم I go to England. **6** holiness

ولايت عهدي vilájat'ahdí *f.* inheriting the throne

ولايتي vilájatí **1** regional, provincial **2** *regional* foreign **3** foreign, European (of goods) ولايتي اوبه *idiom* carbonated water; sparkling water

ولت valt *m.* volt

ولتمتر valtmétr *m.* voltmeter

ولت valkh *m.* ☞ ولت

ولتمبتر valkhméķhr *m.* ☞ ولتمبتر

ولجه vuldzhá, valdzhá *f.* trophy; loot د ولجي مالونه booty ولجه کول *compound verb* captured enemy equipment ولجه کېدل *compound verb* to be captured (as a trophy) ☞ الجه

ولچو válacho *colloquial abbreviation of the phrase* والله خوچه I swear! ولچو قلم را نه کې، نه دي پريږدم I won't let go of you till you give back the pen.

ولچه valachí ولچي valachí, valaché *colloquial abbreviation of the phrase* والله چه I swear! ولچه احمد راغلئ و I swear, Ahmed came.

ولڅه valtsá *f.* taking turns entertaining

ولخه vulkhá *f.* desert

ولد [1] valád *m. Arabic* [*plural:* اولاد avlád] child, kid; son

ولد [2] valád *m.* ☞ بلد

ولدنگ کاري valdingkārí, veldingkārí *f.* welding

ولدوزي valduzí *f.* embroidery in zigzags or curls

ولره vúlara *imperative perfective singular of* لرل

ولړه vúlaṛa *imperative perfective singular of* لرل

ولړه vláṛga *f. dialect* ☞ لوړه

ولس vuləs *m.* **1** people پښتون ولس the Pashtoon people شرقي ولسونه Oriental peoples **2** population; inhabitants د کلي ولس village inhabitants; villagers **3** clan د وردگو ولسونه the clan groups of Wardaks **4** kindred, family

ولس دوست vuləsdóst patriotic

ولسواله vuləsvála *f.* ethnic group, ethnicity

ولسي vuləsí **1** people's ولسي جرگه people's chamber خلک people; people's masses ولسي او عمومي معارف public education **2** national ولسي ژبي national languages ولسي غورځنگ national movement

ولشل vlashəl *transitive* ☞ لوشل

ولشونی vlashúnaj **1** milking **2** *m.* milk bucket

ولکه vúlkha *f.* **1** migration **2** leaving; departure ولنبه کول *compound verb* **a** to move away, migrate away **b** to depart, leave

ولغه valghá *f.* wood pigeon, dove

ولفرام volfrám *m. plural* tungsten

ولکه valká *f.* **1** region; country **2** dominion **3** transfer; handing over to somebody **4** assignment, mission ولکه کول *compound verb* to assign, commission somebody

ولکی vəlkə́j *f.* small root; root (of a plant)

ولگا volgá *f.* Volga

ولگا گراد volgāgrád *m.* Volgograd

ولگرد valgárd *m.* vagrant, tramp

ولگم vúlagəm *present perfective of* لگېدل in lieu of

ولگر valgə́r *m.* **1** appraiser **2** *figurative* firebrand, troublemaker

ولگو valgáw *m.* furnishing (of a house); furniture, utensils

ولگه vláɣga, vúlga *f. Eastern* ☞ لوړه

ولکی [1] vəlgə́j *f.* ☞ ولکی

ولگی [2] vulgé *f. plural* vast deserts

ولل vləl *transitive* [*past:* وويي وله *and* ويي ولل] to wash; wash (clothes), launder

ولم [1] vuləm *present tense first person of* ويشتل

ولم [2] vləm *present tense first person of* ولل

ولم [3] valə́m *the second part of a verb* راوستل *present tense first person*

ولمنه vulmaná *dialect feminine to* لمه [2]

ولموری vulmóraj *m.* diarrhea and vomiting (in a child who had been lying head down)

ولمه [1] valmá *f.* top part of shoes

ولمه [2] vulmə́ *m. dialect* ☞ مبلمه

ولمه [3] vulmá *f. dialect* food

ولنیوس vilnā́ *f.* ☞ ولنیوس

ولنگ [1] valáng *m.* [*plural:* ولنگونه valangúna *and* ولنگان valangán] pomegranate

ولنگ [2] vlang *m.* share, portion

ولنگ [3] vlang *m.* ولنه vlə́na *f.* laundry; washing

ولنیوس vilnjús *m.* Vilnius

ولو [1] való *m.* personal name endearing of ولي [2]

ولو [2] való *oblique plural of* واله

ولو [3] və́lo *oblique plural of* وله [1]

ولو [4] vúlu *present tense first person plural of* ويشتل

ولو [5] vlu *present tense first person plural of* ولل

ولور valvár *m.* [*oblique case* ولوړ valwrə́ *plural:* ولوړونه valwrúna] bride-price, dowry ولور ورکول to pay bride-price

ولوږه vlúga, vlvə́ga *f. dialect* ☞ لوږه ولوږه تپرول to not eat; starve

ولول valvál ول ول **1** folded, pleated **2** curled ولول کوشی curly hair **3** tangled ولول کول *compound verb* **a** to curl **b** to entangle, confuse ولول کېدل *compound verb* **a** to be curled **b** to get entangled, confused

ولوله [1] valvalá *f.* **1** appeal; summons **2** noise; commotion; disarray **3** groan, cry

ولوله [2] vúlvala *imperative perfective of* لوستل [1]

ولونی [1] vlúnaj washing; laundering

ولونی [2] vlúne **1** *feminine of* ولونی [1] **2** *f.* laundrywoman; washerwoman

وله [1] və́la, vúla *f.* willow سره وله Dzungar willow

وله [2] vəlá, vulá, vla *f.* root, small root

وله [3] vlə *m. plural* laundry; washing

وله [4] vulá *f.* truce

وله [5] valá *f.* irrigation ditch ☞ واله

وله [6] vulá *f.* sakman, sakmal (a flock of lambs with ewes)

وله [7] və́la ☞ ورته [2]

وله [8] vúla, və́la *imperative imperfective of* ويشتل

وله [9] və́la, və́lə *colloquial imperative perfective of* لوستل [1]

وله [10] vla *imperative imperfective of* ولل

وله [11] vlə *imperfect plural of* ولل

ولی [1] və́laj *m.* shoulder blade د ولي بار *idiom* burden

ولی [2] valí *m. Arabic* [*plural:* ولیان valijā́n *and Arabic* اولیا aulijā́] **1** respected person; holy man **2** trustee; guardian **3** *proper noun* Wali

ولی [3] valáj, vuláj *m. dialect* kind of tart plum

ولی ⁴ vulə́j *f.* root, small root, small roots

ولی ⁵ vəláj *m.* poplar

ولئ ⁶ vúləj, və́ləj *past participle of* ولل

ولي ⁷ váli *Eastern* vále **1** why, what for, to what end ولي څي Why are you going away? پرون ولي نه وي راغلئ؟ Why didn't you come yesterday? **2** because ولي چه since, because **3** (in response to a question) why not, (with a negative) of course ولي؟ بله برستن سته؟ نسته، هغه ده Is there another blanket? – Of course, here it is.

ولي ⁸ valé *Arabic conjunction* but, however, yet, still ☞ ولېکن

ولي ⁹ valé *f. plural of* واله

ولي ¹⁰ və́li, vúli *plural of* ولی ¹

ولي ¹¹ valí, vulí *plural of* ولی ³

ولي ¹² və́li *plural of* وله ¹

ولي ¹³ vulí, vəlí *present tense of* وېشتل

ولي ¹⁴ vli *present tense of* ولل

ولئ ¹⁵ və́ləj *present tense plural second person of* وېشتل

ولي ¹⁶ valí *suffix of abstract feminine nouns* ورورولي brotherhood

ولي ¹⁷ valí *second part of a verb* راوستل

وليجان vali-dzháṇ *m. proper noun* Wali Jan

ولید vúlid *past perfective of* لیدل

ولېدل vledə́l *intransitive dialect* ☞ لوېدل ¹

ولیدلو ولیده vúlidəlo vúlidə *Eastern past perfective of* لیدل

ولېږي ¹ vlégi *dialect present tense of* ولېدل

ولېږي ² vúlegi *present perfective of* لېږي

ولېشت vlesht *f.* ☞ لوېشت

ولېشتکی vleshtakáj *m.* shorty; Tom Thumb

ولېشه vlésha *f.* battens; boards; thin planks

ولیعهد vali'áhd *m. Arabic* heir to the throne; royal prince

ولېک valék *Arabic*, ولېکن valekín *conjunction* but, however, yet, still

ولېگنده vlégənda *f. Eastern anatomy* temple ولېگندی مي خوږېږي I have a migraine.

ولینعمت valini'mát ولي نعمت *m. Arabic* benefactor

ولیو ¹ və́lijo *oblique plural of* ولی ¹

ولیو ² vulə́jo *oblique plural of* ولی ⁴

ولیو ³ vəlájo *oblique plural of* ولی ⁵

وم ¹ vəm, vum was (first person past of the copula) زه ناست وم I was sitting. تللئ وم I was going away.

وم ² vəm *phonetic variant of the suffix* م خووم which (successive)

ومارگه vumárga *f.* ☞ امارگه

ومان vumắn *m. botany* ephedra

ومانه vúmānə *past tense of* منل

ومړ vúməṛ *dialect past tense of* مړل

ومړی vumṛáj *dialect* ☞ ومبی

ومښت vúməkhət *past tense of* مښنتل

وموند وموندئ vúmund vúmundəj *dialect past perfective of* موندل

ومه ¹ vumə́ *m. plural* ومان

ومه ² vəma she was (first person past of the copula was, feminine)

ومه ³ vəma *feminine of* وم ¹

ونه ¹ vəna *f.* ☞ ونه ¹

ون ² úna *suffix* ☞ ونه ³

ونادیوم vanādijúm *m. plural chemistry* vanadium

ونج ¹ vandzh *m.* exchange, swap, barter

ونج ² vandzh *m.* counter, small table

ونجبده vandzhtjắ *f.* ☞ ونجتیا

ونجړی vandzhə́raj *m.* small counter, small table

ونجول vandzhavə́l *transitive [past:* ونج یې کړ *denominative,* ویې to swap, barter, exchange (something)

ونجبدل vandzhedə́l *intransitive [past:* ونج شو *denominative,* وونجبد] to (mutually) swap, barter, exchange

ونجبده vand *m. plural* swap, barter; exchange

ونخل vənd *transitive* ☞ وینخل

وند ¹ vand *m.* **1** dam, dike; levee **2** moat; trench

وند ² vənd *m.* rags; wipe rags

وند ³ vand *m.* argument; proof, evidence

وند ⁴ vand *imperfect of* وندل

وندر vander, vandə́r *m.* وندرې vandə́re *f. plural Eastern* tether (for sheep, lambs, goats)

وندروند vandrúnd *m.* movement, circulation

وندل vandə́l *transitive [past:* و یې وند] to scold, chide, berate, upbraid, lambaste

وندی ¹ vandanáj *m.* **1** straw twister (a straw rope to tie up sheaves) **2** grass twister **3** tethers; fetters

وندی ² vandáj *m.* string (to tie up a bag, etc.), tie; lace, bead

وندیار vandjắr *f.* ☞ وربنداره, ورېندار

ونډ vanḍ *m.* **1** share of meat, etc., that was bought jointly ونډ کول *compound verb* to separate the carcass into parts, shares **2** assessment, allocation (of tax, fines, etc., per person or per home) **3** land parcel **4** lot, part **5** group of people **6** *military* detachment

ونډوالا vanḍvālắ **1.1** (one) having a share in a joint purchase of meat, etc. **1.2** (one) holding a share, a part, in something **2** *m.* **.1** one who pitches in for a joint purchase of meat, etc. **2.2** (one) holding a share, a part, in something; shareholder, participant

ونډونډ vanḍvánḍ divided into parts ونډوونډ کول *compound verb* **a** to divide into parts, shares **b** to dissect

ونډه ¹ vánḍa *f. Eastern* **1** ☞ ونډ **2** rice crumbs

ونډه ² vanḍá *f.* **1** hay shreds **2** threshed rice

ونډوالا vanḍavālắ *m.* ☞ ونډوالا

ونډی ¹ vanḍáj detailed, do a tour of some type of work (e.g., irrigation, roadwork, because it's one's turn)

ونډی ² vanḍáj *f.* **1** pooling of resources ونډی کول *compound verb* to buy jointly **2** meat, etc., that was purchased jointly د ونډی غوښه meat that was purchased jointly **3** butcher's work, butchering

ونډیمار vanḍəjmár *m.* butcher who chops the meat for participants of a joint purchase scheme

ونډي ونډي vánḍi-vánḍi into pieces, in parts ونډي ونډي کول *compound verb* to divide into parts ونډي ونډي کېدل *compound verb* to be divided into parts

وينځل vinzə́l *transitive dialect* ☞ وينڅل

ونزوېلا venezuə́lā *f.* Venezuela

وينزه vínza *f.* ☞ وينڅه [1]

ونسه vúnisa *imperative perfective of* نيول

ونسي vúnisi *present perfective of* نيول

ونکه [1] vənáka *f.* rhubarb, *Rheum officinale*

ونکه [2] vúnka *colloquial abbreviation of the words* و منه که perhaps, likely

ونکی vənkáj 1 of the same age 2 *m.* peer, mate

ونګره vangrá, vangará *f.* 1 pond 2 pool

ونګه vangá *f.* form, appearance

ونګی vəngə́j *f.* small tree

ونو [1] vúno *oblique plural of* ونه [1]

ونو [2] úno *oblique form suffix* ونه

ونه [1] və́na, vúna *f.* 1 tree; bush اغزنه ونه خوانه ونه thorny bush a young tree وني a fruit tree تر وني لاندي under the tree د مېوو ونه to plant trees کېنبنول 2 stalk (e.g., of wheat) 3 *Western* hindzhak (a kind of pistachio) د وني ژاوله hindzhak oil د وني تبل mastic, a chewing gum made of hindzhak 4 height دنګه ونه tall tree په ونه How tall is he? څومره وي؟

ونه [2] vəná *interjection* egad, oh, oh

ونه [3] úna *plural suffix for masculine nouns that designate inanimate objects and end in a consonant* مېزونه tables ګلونه flowers کورونه houses

ونه ييږ vunajídz ونه ئېز vunaíz tree-like, arborescent

وني [1] və́ni *plural of* ونه [1]

وني [2] vúnaí *m.* wooden framework (on which meat is cured)

ونيسه [1] vúnisa *imperative perfective of* نيول

ونيسه [2] vúnisə *dialect past perfective of* نيول

ونيوال vuniválـ ☞ ونه ييږ

ون vaṇ *m. usually* وڼا vəṇā́ 1 hunting 2 hunting ground

وڼځ vaṇts *m.* assistance in the form of giving a cow, heifer, she-goat, etc. (by the relatives of a young bride in the first years after the marriage)

وڼکه vaṇə́ka *f.* wool edge of felt

وڼی vəṇáj *m.* hunter

وڼيا vaṇjā́ *dialect* ☞ وريا

وڼېوڅي vaṇevútsi running immediately from a kahrez (of water)

وو [1] vo *m. dialect* 1 wind الوزي وو The wind blows. 2 rheumatism

وو [2] vu 1 were (first person plural) موږ هلته وو We were there. دوی چيري وو We were sitting. 2 were (third person plural) شا ګردان ناست وو The students were sitting. 3 *third person singular in lieu of* وه، و که دغه دئ لال Egad, that's Lal.

وو [3] vú, ve *Eastern colloquial in lieu of* يي ويل

وواته vúvātə *past tense plural of* وتل

وواهه vúvāhə *past perfective of* وهل

وواېه [1] vúvāja *imperative perfective of* ويل [1]

وواېه [2] vúvājə *past perfective of* ويل [1]

ووبدل vobdə́l *transitive* وويل vobál *dialect* ☞ اوبدل

ووتو [1] vúvatu *past perfective first person plural of* وتل

ووتو [2] vúvato *Eastern past perfective of* وتل *in lieu of* وت

وود vod *imperfect of* وودل

وودل [1] vodə́l *transitive dialect* ☞ اودل [1]

ووده [1] vudə́ *Eastern* ☞ بيده [1]

ووده [2] vodá *imperfect feminine of* وودل

ووده [3] vodə́ *imperfect plural of* وودل

وودل [2] vodə́l *transitive dialect* ☞ اوډل [1]

ووردِه vurgə́ *m. plural Eastern* ☞ اوربده

وورنی vornáj *m.* diaper

وورول voravúl *transitive Eastern* ☞ اورول [1]

ووره [1] vóra *m.* small cloud ☞ اوره

ووري [1] vorí *present tense of* اوربدل

ووری [2] voráj *m. botany* mustard

ووری [3] vorə́j *f. Eastern* 1 gum 2 (nail) bed ☞ اوری

ووريا vuriā́ *f. Eastern* rain, precipitation

ووربدل voredə́l *intransitive Eastern* ☞ اوربدل [1]

ووربده voredə́na *f.* ☞ اوربده [1]

وورين vorín *linguistics* alveolar (of a sound)

وور [1] voṛ 1 *f.* وره vará *m. plural:* واره vāṛə́ *f. plural:* ووري vaṛé small, little, minor, fine ووِر هلک a boy ووِر کلی a small village A light ووِر ووِر باران دئ He had small eyes. ستړګی يي ووِر ووِر وي rain is falling. ووِر غر small hill 1.2 small, short ووِر عنوان subtitle 1.3 insignificant, minor ووِر کار a trifling matter دی وِرو ووِر خيزونو How attentive he was to such trifling. په ورو ووِر شيانو to deal with trivial matters, to deal with minutiae 1.4 پسي ګرځېدل humble 2 *m.* .1 *[plural:* واره vāṛə́] a baby; toddler; young child 2.2 *plural:* واره vāṛə́ children د ورو پروګرام children's shows schedule *idiom* وره خوله، لوبي خبري He has an insolent tongue.

وور [2] voṛ *imperfect of* وِرل

ووربهيرګر voṛbahírgár *m. computer science* microprocessor

ووڼکی vóṛkaj 1 *m.* baby; toddler; young child 2 small

ووڼګنی voṛganáj *m.* summer harvest

ووڼليد voṛlíd perspicacious; sharp-sighted

ووڼنګوری voṛəngóraj *m. Eastern* summerhouse; summer cottage

ووڼنی voṛənáj *Eastern* summer

ووڼول voṛavúl *denominative, transitive* ☞ وِرول

ووڼه voṛə́ *m. plural dialect* ☞ اوړه [1]

ووڼی vóṛaj *m. Eastern* summer ☞ اوری [1]

ووڼبدل voṛedə́l *denominative, intransitive* ☞ وِربدل

ووزه vúwza *imperative perfective of* وتل

ووګ vog *paired word to* کوډ

ووګد vugd *dialect* ☞ ووړد

ووګده [1] vugdə́ *m. plural of* ووړده

ووګده [2] vugdá *f. singular of* ووړد

ووږه vúga *f. dialect* ☞ هوږه

ووږی vogáj *m. dialect* ☞ هوسی [1]

ووسی [1] vosáj *m. dialect* هوسی

ووسی [2] vosə́j *f. dialect* هوسی

ووښ vukh *m.* back tie of sandals

ووگد vugd *Eastern* ☞ اوږد

ووگی vogáj *m. Eastern* ☞ اوږی [1]

ووله vúvla *imperative perfective of* ويشتل

ووم vum *dialect* ☞ وم

وونډه vúnḍa *f.* herd of camels from a village that are herded by the same shepherd in the steppes or in the mountains; herd of camels

وونه vuná *f.* 1 glitter (of a sword, pearls, etc.) 2 eye disease

وووت və́vot *past perfective of* وتل

وووړی vovə́raj *m.* 1 cobweb in early fall, during Indian summer 2 floating plant seeds 3 *figurative* wanderer, rover

ووها vohā́ *interjection* giddjup

ووهلو vúvahəlo *Eastern past tense of* وهل *in lieu of* وواهه

ووی vúve *colloquial past in lieu of* وويل

ويل vúvajə́l *past perfective of* ويل

ويه vója *f. dialect* egg

ويي vojí *present tense of* وودل

ويست vúvest *past tense of* وېستل

وه [1] və 1 were (third person plural) دوی چيري وه؟ Where were they? دوی ناست وه They were sitting. دوی بنار ته تللي وه They went to town. 2 *Eastern* was (third person singular) ☞ و [2]

وه [2] va was (third person singular, feminine) هغه چيري وه؟ Where was she? هغه کور ته تللي وه She went home. د غرمي يوه بجه به وه It was about one o'clock in the afternoon.

وه [3] va *interjection* 1 hey, look here! وه ورورہ! Hey, buddy! 2 wow (an exclamation of admiration)

وه [4] və *preverb perfective aspect* ☞ و باید وه يي پيژنئ One should know this.

وهاب vahhā́b *m. Arabic* 1 generous giver (God's attribute) 2 *proper noun* Wahhab

وهابي vahhā́bī *Arabic* 1 *m.* [*plural:* وهابيان vahhābiján *and Arabic* وهابيه vahhābijá] Wahhabi, a follower of the Wahhabi sect 2 Wahhabi

وهار vahā́r *m.* seeping water وهار کول *compound verb* to seep (of water)

وهاريدل vahāredə́l *denominative, intransitive* [*past:* وهاري شوی] to seep (of water)

وهب vahb, váhab *m. Arabic* 1 gift 2 forgiveness

وهبي vahbí *Arabic* given as a gift; granted وهبي څيز a present

وهل vahə́l 1 *transitive* [*past:* و يي واهه]. 1. to beat, batter; lash (with a whip) زه يي بې هيڅ ووهلم He gave me a beating for nothing. په سره وهل to give a slap on the back of the head ثت کښي وهل They were fighting 1.2 to fell (trees) 1.3 to chop (wood) 1.4 to stab; cut; kill with a sharp weapon; slash (with a sword, saber) په خنجر وهل to stab with a dagger په توره وهل to slash with a sword 1.5 to

mint (coins) 1.6 to strike, attack, affect (agricultural pests, disease) يخني وهلئ يم I have a cold. 1.7 to smoke چرس وهل to smoke chars (hashish) 1.8 to play (a musical instrument) رباب وهل to play the rabab 1.9 to thrust somewhere 1.10 to touch or coat something (lightly) 1.11 to cover (with a composition) دا مخلوط د دا This composition is applied to various metals 1.12 to travel, overcome, cover (a distance) 1.13 to shoot up (sprouts, etc.) پيازو نبنس وهلئ دئ The onion has sprouted. 1.14 to achieve (e.g., maturity) هلک مراني وهلئ The boy has matured. 1.15 to drive (a horse, a carriage) 1.16 to put on (a turban etc.) پتکی دي ووهه! Put the turban on! 1.17 to cheat, shortchange 1.18 *in combination with nouns, it frequently replaces the verb* کول سپرلی to jump تپوپ وهل to sneeze اتسکی وهل to shout ناری وهل کبدل to ride وهل *passive* a to be beaten, be pummelled b to be felled; get felled (of trees) c to be split (woods) d to be stabbed, be knifed, be slashed e to be minted (of coins) f to be stricken, be attacked, be affected (of agricultural pests, a disease) g to be thrust somewhere h to be coated (with a composition) i to be covered (of a distance) j to be sprouted (of a sprout, etc.) k to be put on (of a turban) l to be cheated, be shortchanged زه په وهنه ☞ خان کښي سره ووهل شوم I was petrified. 2 *m. plural* ☞ وهنه

وهلای vahəlā́j *conditional mood and potential form of* وهل

وهلندای vahlandáj zigzagging; meandering

وهلندی توب vahlandajtób *m.* tortuosity, sinuosity, zigzagging

وهله [1] vahlá *f. Arabic* moment, jiffy په اوله وهله in the first second; at once

وهله [2] vahə́la *f. imperfect of* وهل

وهم vahm *m. Arabic* [*plural:* اوهام awhā́m] 1 apprehension, anxiety, concern; suspicion دوی ډير په وهم کښي وي They are very apprehensive. وهم کول to be concerned, have misgivings د ډار وهم پری غلبه کوي He is scared. 2 imagination وهم لرل a to be apprehensive, be concerned b to imagine 3 misconception 4 whims, quirks

وهمي vahmí *Arabic* 1 imaginary, mock, ostensible; hypothetical په وهمي صورت سره as an وهمي شی falsehood; concoction assumption 2 hypochondriac

وهميدل vahmedə́l *denominative, intransitive* [*past:* وهمي شو] to be apprehensive, be concerned مه وهمبږه! Don't worry!

وهنه vahə́na *f.* 1 beating, battery 2 felling (of trees) 3 chopping (of wood) 4 stabbing, knifing, slashing (with a saber, sword) 5 minting (of coins) 6 being affected by, suffering from (a pest, disease) 7 smoking 8 playing (a musical instrument) 9 thrusting somewhere 10 coating (with a composition) 11 travel, covering (a distance) 12 putting on (of a turban) 13 shortchanging, cheating

وه وه، وهوه وهوا [1] vahvā́ *interjection* hurrah, bravo, atta boy

وهونی جالونه wahūne dzhálūna *m. plural computer science* dial-up networking

وه وه [1] vahváh *interjection* hurrah, bravo, atta boy

وه وه ² va va *folklore* thus it was going (*literally:* was, was)

واویله vahvelá ☞ واویلا

وهیر ¹ vahír *m.* crying, weeping, wailing وهیر کول a to cry, weep b to mourn

وهبر ² vahér ☞ هبر ¹

وهبرغاری vaherghā́raj 1 (one who is) mourning 2 absentminded, forgetful

وی ¹ vә́j *f. Eastern* egg

وی ² vәj *interjection* oh, ah (commonly used by women)

وی ³ vi is, are (third person singular and plural, with the particle به it forms the future tense) حقیقت څنګه چه وي، وي به ن،خو *nevertheless* هر څه چه وي، وي دي in هر توګه چه وي whatever will be, will be any manner

وې ⁴ ve 1 was (second person singular or feminine) 2 were (third person plural: feminine) هغه ښځی چیری وي؟ Where were those women? ښار ته تللي وي They went to town.

وئ ⁵ vә́j *Eastern past tense second person plural copula in lieu of* واست

وې ⁶ ve *colloquial imperfect of* ویل 1 *plural in lieu of* ما وي ته به راشئ I thought you would come. 2 *dialect singular in lieu of* وایه سبق دې وې You were studying.

وئ ⁷ vaj *Eastern conditional mood preferred form in lieu of* وای ²

وې ⁸ ve *contraction of the preverb* و *and pronoun* يې وې ويل He said.

ویار ¹ vjār *m.* 1 envy 2 doubt, mistrust, suspicion 3 in lieu of

ویار ² vjār *m.* ☞ وير

ویاړ vjāṛ *m.* 1 pride له ویاړه دک proudly 2 *regional* conceit; boasting 3 honor د چا په ویاړ in honor of somebody

ویاړجن vjāṛdzhә́n 1 proud 2 bragging; boastful

ویاړل vjāṛә́l *transitive* [*past:* و يې ويارل] 1 to be proud په چا ویارل to be proud of somebody 2 esteem, respect, value په چا باندي ویارل to value freedom 3 to brag آزادی ویارل 4 to be happy, rejoice 5 *dialect* to grin

ویاړن vjāṛә́n ☞ ویاړجن

ویاړنه vjā́ṛna *f.* 1 pride 2 boasting 3 joy, exuberance 4 grin

ویارو ¹ vjāṛú boastful

ویارو ² vjā́ṛu *present tense first person plural of* ویارل

ویاره vjā́ṛa *f.* pride د چا څخه ویاره کول to be proud of somebody

ویاره ² vjā́ṛa *feminine of* مرنده

ویاریځ vjāṛídz honorary

ویال vjāl 1 fresh, young 2 free-and-easy, free

ویالتوب vjāltób *m.* ویالتیا vjāltjá *f.* freshness

ویاله ¹ vjālә́, vjālá *f. Eastern* ☞ واله

ویاله ² vjā́la *feminine singular of* ویال

ویانا vjānā́ *f.* Vienna

ویاند vajā́nd *f.* well-spoken, eloquent

ویبپاڼه webpā́ṇa *f.* گورنځای gorándzāj ګورت ځای górtdzāj *computer science* web page, website

ویب لاګ wiblāg *m. computer science* weblog, blog

ويبه víba *future tense of the copula in laconic sentences in lieu of* وي به 1 will be 2 perhaps, possibly

ويت vit 1 open, gaping 2 insolent, cheeky, shameless

ويت خولی vitkhúlaj, vitkhvúlaj 1 with a gaping mouth 2 yawning 3 open-mouthed (from surprise), stunned 4 curious; inquiring

وټرنری veterinarí 1 *f.* veterinary medicine 2 veterinary

ويت سترګی vitstә́rgaj insolent; shameless, staring

ويت قطاری vitḳatā́raj *m.* ويتکی vitakáj *m. regional* 1 impudent, shameless fellow 2 insolent, bratty (of a child)

ويت سترګی ☞ ويتک viták

ويتنام vitnā́m *m.* Vietnam

وټو vetó *f.* veto د وټو حق the right of veto وټو کول *compound verb* to veto د وټو د حق څخه استفاده کول to use the right of veto

ويتول vitavә́l *denominative, transitive* [*past:* ويت يې کړ] to open, open wide (one's mouth)

ويته víta 1 *feminine singular of* ويت 2 *f.* impudence, insolence, shamelessness

ويتی víte *f. plural regional* incongruity, absurdity

ويتبدل vitedә́l *denominative, intransitive* [*past:* ويت شو] to be opened, be gaping (of a mouth)

وټر veṭár *m. regional* waiter

وټنگ روم véṭingrúm *m. regional* waiting room, lounge

وټو ☞ وټو vetó *f.*

ويجاړ vidzhā́ṛ 1.1 destroyed, obliterated 1.2 uncultivated, unkempt ویجاړه مځکه uncultivated land; wasteland 1.3 upset, disrupted, spoilt, damaged 1.4 ruined (e.g., of health) 1.5 fallen apart, collapsed 2 *m.* harm; damage

ویجاړتوب vidzhāṛtób *m.* ویجاړتیا vidzhāṛtjá *f.*, ویجاړوالی vidzhāṛvā́laj *m.* 1 harm; damage 2 upheaval, disruption 3 deterioration (e.g., of health)

ویجاړول 1. [ویجاړ يې کړ] vidzhāṛavә́l 1 *denominative, transitive* [*past:* to destroy, obliterate 1.2 to neglect, leave untilled 1.3 to upset, disrupt, spoil, damage موازنه ویجاړول to upset the balance مسئله ویجاړول to confuse the issue 1.4 to ruin (e.g., health) 1.5 to break up, facilitate the breakdown or the collapse 2 *m. plural* ☞ ویجاړيده 1

ویجاړه 2.2 ویجاړيده 1. *f.* ☞ ویجاړ vidzhā́ṛa 1 *feminine singular of* 2 *regional* desert; desolate place

ویجاړيدل vidzhāṛedә́l *denominative, intransitive* [*past:* ویجاړ شو] 1 to be destroyed, be obliterated; get destroyed, get obliterated 2 to be uncultivated, be unkempt; uncultivated land; wasteland 3 to be upset, be disrupted, be spoiled; be damaged 4 to be ruined (e.g., of health) 5 to fall apart, collapse

ویجاړيده vidzhāṛedә́ *m. plural* 1 destruction, obliteration 2 lack of cultivation, unkemptness 3 upheaval, disruption 4 ruining (e.g., health) 5 collapse, breakdown; disorganization

ويخ ¹ vikh *dialect* ☞ وينښ

وېخ ² vekh *m. dialect* **1** root **2** foothills (of a mountain) **3** *figurative* basis of something له وېخه وتل ☞ to become uprooted بېخ

وېخته vekhtə́ *m. plural dialect* ☞ وبېنته

ویدول vidavə́l *denominative, transitive [past:* وېده يې کړ*] dialect* **1** to lull; put to sleep **2** to cause numbness (of extremities) **3** *figurative* to make stagnant, make inert

وېده vidá *f. dialect* vidá **1** sleeping وېده کول *compound verb* ☞ وېدېدل *compound verb* ☞ **2** numb, gone to sleep (of extremities) **3** *figurative* stagnant, inert فکر وېده stagnation, inertia **4** *figurative* ignorant

وېده کېده vidəkedə́ *m. plural* putting to sleep, lulling

وېدې vidé *f. plural of* وېده ¹

وېدي vedí Vedic وېدي مدنيت the Vedic civilization ²

وېدېدل videdə́l *denominative, intransitive [past:* وېده شو*] dialect* **1** to sleep, fall asleep **2** to become numb, fall asleep (of extremities) پښه مي کله کله وېدېږي Sometimes my leg goes to sleep. **3** *figurative* to be stagnant, be inert **4** *figurative* to be ignorant, persist in ignorance

ویډیو کارت widjió kā́rṭ *m. computer science* video card

وير vir *m.* **1** mourning, lamenting د چا وير کول to be in mourning for somebody په بدبختي د وير تغرونه ټولول to come out of mourning له وير نه ډک to lament (one's) misfortune **2** grief باندي وير کول sad, mournful **3** complaint, lamentation

وران vajrā́n ☞

ويرانکار virānkā́r *m.* destroyer د موټرو ويرانکار junkyard dealer

ورانول vajrānavə́l *transitive* ☞

ویرانه vajrā́na *feminine singular of* ويران

ویراني vajrāní *f.* ☞ وراني ¹

ویرانېدل vajrānedə́l *intransitive* ☞ ورانېدل

ویرازوی virāwzáj *m.* ☞ ویروسی

ویرجن virdzhə́n **1** mournful, regrettable, sorrowful ويرجنه پېښه an unfortunate incident ويرجنه فکرونه heavy, loss sad thoughts **2** tragic **3** looking sad, grieving

ویردۍ virdə́j *f.* sound of trumpet announcing a halt to movement at night or its resumption early in the morning; ويردۍ وهل to give signals with a trumpet (e.g., of a halt to movement at night)

ویرژړلی virzhaṛə́laj mourning, grieving

ویرژلی virzhə́laj **1** (one who is) in mourning **2** bereaved (of an orphan) **3** sorrowful, sad

ویرګډی virgáḍaj *m.* whiner ويرګډي کېدل *compound verb* to whine, kvetch

ویرګل virgúl *m.* comma

ویرلړلی virlaṛə́laj ☞ ویرژلی

وېرند verə́nd وېرندوکی verəndúkaj *Eastern* **1** cowardly; apprehensive, easily scared **2** *m.* coward ته وبرند يې You are a coward.

ویروس virús وېروس werū́s *m.* **1** *medicine* virus **2** *computer science* virus

ویروسي virusí viral ویروسي مرض a viral disease ¹

ویروسی virosáj *m.* food sent to the relatives of the deceased on the first day after a death ²

وېرول veravə́l *transitive [past:* و يې وبراوه*] Eastern* **1** to scare, intimidate, terrify, appall زه يې ووبرولم They scared me. **2** to scare off

وېرونه veravə́na *f. Eastern* scaring; intimidation; horrification

وېرونکی veravúnkaj **1** *present participle of* وېرول **2.1** dangerous, terrible وېروونکی مرض a dangerous disease **2.2** frightful, scary وېروونکي قصي veravúnki...scary stories وېروونکی ژان a terrifying abyss

وېروه vérva *f.* pear

وېره véra *f. Eastern* **1** fear, fright, apprehension د مرګ وبره ده This may be lethal. وبره کول *compound verb* to threaten وبري تېرول *compound verb* to be afraid, be scared په وبره لوېدل to fear, be scared of, have misgivings about په وبره ويل to speak warily, say cautiously **2** danger, peril; hazard دا وبره پيدا شوه چه ... the danger arose that... وبره دلته ده چه ... the trouble is that ... وبره وبره شته There is a grave danger. ☞ بېره ¹

ویرونکی veranák ☞ ²

وبره وری veravə́ṛaj, veravúṛaj intimidated

ويري vajrí *m.* wild turnip ¹

وبري veré *dialect* there, in that direction ²

وبري vére *plural and oblique singular of* وبره ³

وبرېدل veredə́l *intransitive [past:* و وبرېده*] Eastern* to fear, be scared, be apprehensive هغه له هيچا نه نه وبرېږي He is not afraid of anybody. په زړه کښي وبرېدل to experience misgivings, be worried

وبرېده veredə́ *m. plural Eastern* fright; scare, fear; apprehension

وېر viṛ veṛ *m.* hedge ¹

وېر viṛ **1** open, wide open وبره خوله a gaping mouth **b** *attributive* smiling **2** bewildered, excited **3** laid, spread out وبره اولمه *idiom* fine weather وبره کېدل **a** to clear up (of weather) **b** to arrive (of spring) **c** to calm down ²

وبرخولی viṛkhúlaj ☞ وبت خولی

وورکی vérkaj *m. dialect* ☞

وبرلی veṛláj *f.* halvah

وبرول viṛavə́l *denominative, transitive [past:* وبر يې کړ*]* **1** to open, open up; open wide; lay bare **2** to spread, lay, make (of a bed)

وبره víṛa *feminine singular of* وبر ²

وبریا veṛjā́ *dialect* ☞ وریا

وبرېدل viṛedə́l *denominative, intransitive [past:* وبر شو*]* **1** to be opened, open up; be laid bare **2** to be spread, laid; be made (of a bed); creep (of plants) **3** to spread, propagate

وبرېده viṛedə́ *m. plural* **1** opening up, disclosure **2** spreading

وبز viz *m.* checking of a mat's quality (by dragging it on the ground)

وبزا vizā́ *f.* ☞ وبزه

وبزار vezā́r **1** displeased زه ترې وبزار يم، مخ يې نه وينم I am sick and tired of him. **2** (one who has) cooled down, grown lukewarm to something ☞ بېزار

وبزارول vezāravə́l *denominative, transitive* [*past:* وبزار یې کړ] **1** to pester, nag, make a nuisance of oneself **2** to cause displeasure, disgust

وبزاریدل vezāredə́l *denominative, intransitive* [*past:* وبزار شو] **1** to be displeased; be disgusted **2** to cool down, grow lukewarm to something

ويزه vizá *f.* visa (in a passport) د اقامت ويزه entry visa د خروج ويزه exit visa ويزه کېدل *compound verb* to stamp (a passport) *compound verb* to be stamped (of a passport) ويزه ورکول to grant a visa

وبردن vegdə́n *m.* kind of saddlebag

ويس vajs *m. proper noun* Wais

ويسا vesā́, visā́ *f.* trust ويسا کول پر خپل ځان ويسا self-confidence *compound verb* to trust, put trust in موږ باید پر احمد ويسا وکړو We must trust Ahmed. له تا نه مې ويسا پاڅېده *Eastern* I lost faith in you. پر ځان يې ويسا نه درلوده to trust ويسا لرل He was not sure of himself.

وبساتوب vesātób *m.* reliability

وبسالي vesālí reliable

ويساه visā́h *f.* ☞ ويسا

ويست vist ☞ ويشت ¹

وبست vest ² *past imperfective of* ويستل دوی ترې انتظار وبست چه ... They expected somebody to ...

وبستل vestə́l *transitive Eastern* ☞ ايستل

وبستنه vestə́na *f.* وبسته vestə́ *m. plural* ☞ ايستنه

ويستول vistúl *m.* Vistula (River) د ويستول رود Vistula River

وبسي vési *dialect present perfective of* ورل in lieu of يوسي

ويش vesh *m.* **1** division **2** share of inheritance **3** division (of property, country) **4** wesh (periodical redistribution of land in Afghan tribes) بند وبش bandwesh (allocation of land by the number of male workers) خوله وبش khulawesh (allocation of land by the number of mouths to feed) **5** distribution (of income) وبش کول *compound verb* **a** to conduct division, separation; to divvy up (property) **b** to divide, split (a country) **c** to redistribute land periodically; conduct wesh **d** to distribute (income) **6** border, frontier, limit ګډ وبش shared border ټول کسان بله وبشه *idiom* everybody without distinction

ويش vish *interjection* oh, ouch, oy

ويشت ¹ visht *numeral* twenty (only with digits from 21 to 29) درويشت twenty-three پنځه ويشت twenty five

ويشت ² visht *imperfect of* ويشتل

ويشت ³ visht *m.* target shooting

ويشتل vishtə́l **1** *transitive* [*present:* ولي, *past:* و يې ويشت] **.1** to throw, cast, toss something **1.2** to strike, hit (e.g., with a stone) **1.3** to shoot ځان ويشتل to shoot oneself ټوپک ويشتل shoot with a rifle **1.4** to bring down (with a bullet) **1.5** to hit; bring down **1.6** to drive, urge (a horse) آس ويشتل to race a horse **1.7** to drive (a car etc.) ويشتل کېدل **a** to be thrown, cast **b** to be hit (e.g., with stones) **c** to be brought down, be hit **d** to wound with a shot; put out of action (weapon, etc.) **e** to be driven (of a horse, etc.) **f** to

be driven (of a car, etc.) **2** *m. plural* ☞ ويشتل سپرلی ويشتل *idiom* to go in for riding ځان له مځکي ويشتل ترڅو to beg, beseech چه وويشت نه سې، خبر به نه سې *proverb* One that's been caned is worth two that haven't been.

ويشتلئ vishtə́laj *past participle of* ويشتل زه په زړه ويشتلئ يم I am wounded in the heart.

ويشتونکي vishtúnkaj **1** *present participle of* ويشتل **2** *m.* **.1** shooter **2.2** driver د لاري ويشتونکي a truck driver

ويشته ¹ vishtə́ *m. plural* **1** throwing, casting, tossing **2** striking, beating (stoning) **3** shooting **4** bringing down **5** driving (a car, etc.) نه د تينګي د ويشتو يي، نه د سستي د نيوو، نه د تينګي د ويشتو يي، نه د سستي د نيوو يي *proverb* Neither fish nor flesh.

ويشته ² vishtə́ *imperfect plural of* ويشتل

وبشل veshə́l **1** *transitive verb* [*past:* و يي وبشه] **.1** to divide, distribute په خپل منځ کښي سره وبشل to divide among ourselves (themselves, etc.) ميراث د ورونو په منځ وبشل to divide the inheritance among brothers **1.2** to distribute (e.g., gifts); serve, serve food to guests **1.3** to send out, mail out (invitations) وبشل کېدل *passive voice* **a** to be divided, be distributed **b** to be given out (of gifts) **c** to be sent out, get mailed (of invitations) **2** *m. plural* ☞ وبشل د وبشلو ځانګه division of labor د کارو وبشل allocation department د وبشلو ځای distribution post د اوبو د وبشلو سرحد watershed وبشل کول to be engaged in distribution

وبشله ¹ veshə́la *f.* unleavened flat bread (baked on a frying pan)

وبشله ² veshə́la *imperfect feminine of* وبشل

وبشلئ ¹ veshə́laj *past participle of* وبشل

وبشلي ² veshə́le *f. plural* ☞ وبشله ¹

وبشلي ³ veshə́le **1** *feminine of* وبشلئ **2** *imperfect feminine plural of* وبشل

وبشنه veshə́na *f.* وبشون veshún *m.* **1** division, splitting, distribution **2** giving out, giving away (e.g., of gifts) **3** sending out, mailing (of invitations)

وبشونکي veshúnkaj *present participle of* وبشل د پوستي وبشونکي letter carrier

ويشه ¹ vésha *f.* **1** division وبشه کول *compound verb* to divide, distribute **2** share **3** border

وبشه ² veshá *f. Waziri* beam ☞ بينش

وينږ viḵh **1** alert, awake ترسهاره پوري وينږ وم I was awake till morning. **2** quick-witted; intelligent, bright; clever وينږ هلک a clever and bright young man **3** conscientious, aware وينږ خلک people who are aware وينږ فکر **a** cleverness, brightness **b** consciousness **4** educated **5** active, busy, energetic **6** light (of sleep)

وبنبتان veḵhtā́n *Western plural of* وبنبته مصنوعي وبنبتان wig

وبنبتني veḵhtanáj **1** hair-like, hair-shaped **2** capillary

وبنبتوب viḵhtób *m.* **1** alertness; wakefulness; awakening **2** vigilance **3** cleverness, quick-wittedness **4** conscientiousness د وجدان وبنبتوب *idiom* awakening of consciousness

وېښته veḵhtә́ *m.* [*plural:* وېښتان veḵhtā́n, *Eastern* وېښته veḵhtә́]
hair خورمايي وېښته a hair وېښته هو وېښته hair by hair
brown hair برگ وېښته، گڕ سره وېښته red hair سپين وېښته white hair
وېښته اوتو کول curling iron د وېښتو اوتو کول to curl hair
د وېښتو انتظام، د وېښته اوتو کول to style hair, د a hairdo
وېښتانو ترتيبول a hairstyle يو وېښته ئي لوند نه شو He did not get wet
at all. سر په وېښته نه درنېږي a tiny bit A burden of
one's own choosing does not seem heavy. سر په وېښته نه درنېږي A
head is not burdened with its hair. خولي می وېښتان وکړل I am sick
and tired of repeating. وېښتان می لک لک ودرېدل، وېښتان می جگ
ودرېدل، وېښتان می جگ شول My hair stood on end.

وېښتنيا viḵhtjā́ *f.* ☞ وېښتوب

وېښينول viḵhavә́l 1 *denominative, transitive* [*past:* وېنښ يي کړ]. 1 to
wake up ما سهار وختي وېنښ کئ Wake me up early in the morning.
1.2 *figurative* to awaken وکارته وېنبنول to awaken to activity
قوتونه وېنبنول to awaken the sleeping forces 2 *m. plural* ☞ وېنبنونه

وېنبنونه viḵhavә́na *f.* 1 waking up; reveille 2 awakening

وېنبه vī́ḵha 1 *feminine singular of* وېنښ 2 *f.* reality; the state of being
awake يوه Am I dreaming or is this for real? دا وېنبنه ده که خوب؟
شپه په وېنبنه خوب ويني چه to stay awake all night هغه په وېنبنه خوب ويني چه
… She is daydreaming about …

وېنبنبدل viḵhedә́l *denominative, intransitive* [*past:* وېنښ شو] 1.1 to
wake up زه سهار وختي وېنبنبږم I wake up early in the morning. 1.2
frequently used with the pronoun شو هغه له خوب څخه راوېنبنښ شو He را
woke up. 2 *figurative* to awake

وېنبنبده viḵhedә́ *m. plural* ☞ وېنبنونه

وېنبنبيه vḗḵhəja *contraction imperative perfect from* بنودل *and*
pronoun يي *in lieu of* و يي بنيه

وبگن végán *m. regional* 1 railcar 2 wagon

ويل vajә́l, vajә́l 1 *transitive* [*present:* وايي *past:* و يي وايه *and*
و يي ويل]. 1 to speak, tell, say, talk درته يي څه وويل؟ What did he tell
you? دروغ ويل *compound verb* to tell lies; lie, cheat, چا به څه ويل،
پنتنو ويل، يو له بله سره پنتنو Some said this, others said that. چا به څه
پوچ ويل *compound verb* to twaddle, prattle, to speak Pashto
say empty words څه چه يي ويل هغه يي کول He is as good as his
word. چه ډېر وايي، لږ خبرې proverb If one talks a lot, some of it is
bound to be empty words. 1.2 to read کتاب ويل to read a book
1.3 to teach ما له احمد ځخه سبق وايه to learn سبق ويل I learned
from Ahmed. 1.4 to retell, narrate 1.5 to say, proclaim اطلاع وايي
چه … The message says… 1.6 to inform, name, announce 1.7 to
compose, write (poetry) 1.8 to believe, think ما ويل زه به ولاړ سم I
wondered if perhaps I should go. ويل کېدل *passive voice* a to be
said لکه چه پورته … It is sometimes said that… کله کله ويل کېږي چه
په افغانستان وويل شوه as mentioned above لکه چه پخوا وويل شوه
کښي څو ژبي ويلي کېږي The population of Afghanistan speaks
several languages. b to be read, be read aloud c to be studied, be
researched d to be retold e to be communicated, be named, be
announced رسماً ويل شوي دي چه، رسماً وويل شوه It has been
officially announced that… f to be composed, be written (of

poetry) 2 *m. plural* .1 speech; words; saying; adage د ده په ويلو
according to what he said د ويلو ډپر شيان پيدا شوي دي سره سم
must be said. دا ويل په کار دي چه It should be said. ويل کول to talk
of something 2.2 reading هغه د کتاب ويلو شوق لري He likes to read
books. 2.3 study 2.4 retelling; narration 2.5 message,
announcement *idiom* as if, as though تا به ويل، ته به وا، ته به وايي

ويل [2] vel *m. Western* rudeness, sharp words

ويل [3] vel *m. Western* cheapness; cheapening په ويل کېدنې کېدل a to
become cheaper; go down in value b to sell at a fair price

ويل [4] vel *m.* whale

ويلای vajəlā́j *conditional of* ويل تا به ويلای as if, as though

وبلډېنگ vélḍíng *m* welding برقي وبلډېنگ electric welding

ويلنوس vilnús *m.* Vilnius

وبلنه [1] velә́na *f. dialect* cheapness

وبلنه [2] velә́na *f.* وبلني veláni *m. plural botany* mint خوابره وبلني، کاډه
anise وبلني

ويلوب vilób *m.* lava (volcanic)

ويلول vilavә́l *denominative, transitive* [*past:* ويلي يي کړ] 1 to melt
فلز ويلول to melt metal 2 to melt 3 to dissolve 4 to sell ژړا يي د
فولادو زړه لا ويلاوه *idiom* Her weeping could move to pity even a
heart of stone.

ويلون [1] vajalón *m.* ☞

ويلون [2] vilún *m.* ويلونه vilavә́na *f.* 1 melting, smelting 2 melting
(e.g., of butter) 3 dissolving 4 sales

ويلونکی vilavúnkaj 1 *present participle of* ويلول 2 casting ويلونکی
a foundry کارخانه

وبله [1] velә́, velá *f. dialect* irrigation channel ☞ واله

وبله [2] velá *f.* benefit, advantage

ويلئ [1] vajә́laj *past participle of* ويل [1]

ويلئ [2] vajә́laj *Eastern conditional & potential form of* ويل [1] *in lieu*
of ويلای

ويلی [3] velә́j *m.* osteomyelitis

ويلي [4] vajә́le *contraction of* ويل *and* يي *in lieu of* ويل يي

ويلي [5] vajә́le *dialect imperfect feminine plural in lieu of* ويل [1]

ويلي [6] vī́li 1 molten 2 melted; rendered 3 dissolved 4 melted,
thawed ويلي کول *compound verb* ☞ ويلول ويلي کېدل *compound*
verb ☞ ويلبدل ويلي غوړي سره کېدل *idiom* to become close friends
هيواد او ذهين سره ويلي غوړي دي Hewad and Zaheen are inseparable
friends.

ويلي [7] velé *plural of* وبله [1]

ويلي [8] velé *plural of* وبله [2]

ويلبدل viledә́l *denominative, intransitive* [*past:* ويلي شو] 1 to be
melted 2 to smelt, melt 3 to be dissolved 4 to melt, thaw 5 to
be sold

ويلبدنه viledә́na *f.* ويلبدنه viledә́ *m. plural* 1 melting 2 rendering,
melting (e.g., of butter) 3 dissolving 4 melting د واورو ويلبدنه
thawing 5 sales

وين [1] vin *m.* Vienna

وين [2] vin *present stem of* لیدل

وينا [1] vəjnā́, vajnā́ *f.* [*plural:* ويناگاني vəjnāgā́ni *and* ويناوي vəjnā́vi]
1 speech; words; saying; declaration لوړه وينا a brilliant speech
ترخه وينا bitter words د کتاب مخنی وينا foreword وينا سپکول scolding
وينا کول to give a speech **2** conversation; lecture **3** pronunciation
د وينا اجزا *grammar* part of speech مستقيمه وينا *grammar* direct
speech

وينا [2] vinā́ *f. music* weena هندی وينا Indian weena

وينتيان vjentjā́n *m.* Vientiane

وينځکۍ vindzakə́j *f. diminutive of* وينځه [1]

وينځل vindzə́l *transitive* [*past:* وي يې وينځه] **1** to wash, launder ځان
وينځل *compound verb* to give a bath to; bathe کبدل وينځل *passive
voice* to get washed, get laundered *idiom* د ژوندانه څخه لاسونه وينځل
to despair of life مينځل ☞

وينځلئ vindzə́laj *past participle of* وينځل فضا وينځلي *idiom* fresh air

وينځنه vindzə́na *f.* washing, laundry; bathing

وينځه [1] víndza *f.* female slave د وينځو د خرڅلاو بازار slave market
مينځه ☞ to enslave (of a female), to make a (female) slave نيول وينځه

وينځه [2] víndza *imperative imperfective of* وينځل

وينځه [3] vindzə́ *imperfect of* وينځل

وينځي [1] víndzi *f. plural of* وينځه [1]

وينځي [2] víndzi *present tense of* وينځل

ويند vajə́nd **1** *m.* orator **2** speaker

ويندارہ vindā́ra *f.* اينداره ☞

ويندوکی vajandúkaj garrulous, talkative, loquacious

ويندي vindáj *m.* **1** nosebleed **2** blood disease

ونز veníz *m.* ونس [1] ☞

وينزل vinzə́l *transitive dialect* وينځل ☞

ونزويلا venezuélā́ *f.* Venezuela

ونس [1] venís *m.* Venice

ونس [2] vénus *f.* Venus (the planet)

ونکبنه vinkā́kha *f. medicine* suction cup; cupping glass

وينگ vajáng *m. dialect* **1** words, utterance **2** pronunciation

ونلی venə́laj *m.* وبلني ☞

وينول vinavə́l *denominative, transitive* [*past:* ويني يې کړ] to cause
bleeding

وينه [1] vajnə́, venə́, vujnə́ *m. plural* termite; white ant

وينه [2] vína *f.* [*usually plural* ويني víni, *Eastern* وينه víne] blood
د ويني سپين arterial blood وريدي وينه venous blood شرياني وينه
leukocytes, white blood cells د ويني سره اجزا، د ويني سره اجسام
erythrocytes, red blood cells د وينو د گرزبدني جهاز، د وينو د جريان
blood vessels, blood circulation system د وينو تولبدل، د وينو
hemostasis غونډبده د وينو بانک blood donorship په وينو گډ
congenital; native په وينو رنگ، په وينو لړلئ، سور په وينو، په وينو لړند
red with blood, bloodied هغه د سرې ويني خاوند دئ He is a cold-
blooded person. له غضبه يې وينې په رگو کښې خوټېدي His blood
boiled. په مخ يې د وينو څپي راغلې Blood rushed to his face. د وينو
زما ورسره د ويني شرکت دئ bloodthirsty د وينو تږی bloodshed توبيده
He is my kin. زمور وينه شريکه ده We are blood relatives. د غيرت نه

يي وينه مخ ته راغله *Eastern* His face flushed with shame. وينو ته دي
سترگو يي ويني را اوبنتي تږی ناست دئ He thirsts for your blood.
His eyes became bloodshot. په زره مي ويني اوبنتي My heart is
bleeding. د چاله لاسه ويني *compound verb* to spit blood ويني اچول
احمد وينو اخيستئ دئ one's life is made miserable by somebody اچول
Ahmed is close to death. وينه انجکشن کول to transfuse blood ويني
احمد ته مي ويني وايشبدلي to be angry with somebody و چا ته ايشبدل
I got mad at Ahmed. ويني بهول *compound verb* to shed rivers of
blood د چا وينه تنتبدل to be scared *compound* ويني تويول، ويني رژول
verb to shed blood ډېري ويني توی شوی Much blood was shed. په چا
to energize, encourage يوه نوې او تازه وينه چلول خپلي ويني څکل
grieve د وينو څکو ته دي to suck somebody's blood د نورو ويني څکل
He is your mortal enemy. وينه خوځبدل، ويني بنوئبدل تږی ناست دئ ☞
ويني خورل، ويني اخيستل a to spit blood b to suffer; be tormented
to be cruel د چا ويني سپينبدل to become enraged ويني پر سترگو راتلل
to consider oneself above others د چا ويني سري کبدل ويني سپربدل ☞
and ويني کبل . ويني اچول . ويني وبستل ☞ ويني سپينبدل ويني غورځول
Eastern ويني بنکل *medicine* to bleed (someone) ويني کبپبنستل ☞
وينه يي کبپبني a He has a bleeding. b *figurative* He is ويني اچول
upset. ويني کبدل د چا وينو ته کبپبنستل to wait for somebody's death
to bleed وينه گبپبدل I cut my finger. گوته مي ويني شوه to mix (of
blood); interbreed; crossbreed وينه سره گبپبدل to be
consanguineous; become relatives ويني پر اورغوي نيول to look
death in the eye د چا ويني وچول a to bleed somebody white b to
ruin; to plague somebody ويني وچبدل a to bleed to death b to be
ruined

وينه [3] vajə́na *f.* speech; words

وينه [4] vajná *f.* crystal; glass

ويني [1] víni *Eastern plural of* وينه [2]

ويني [2] víni *present tense of* ليدل

ويني تويول vinitojavə́l *m. plural* bloodshed

وينبدل vinedə́l *denominative, intransitive* [*past:* ويني شو] to bleed; be
cut

ويوړ vújowŗ *dialect past tense of* وړل , *in lieu of* يووړ

ويوړه [1] vújobŗə *dialect past tense plural of* وړل ☞ يووړه

ويوړي vújowŗe *past tense feminine plural of* وړل *in lieu of* يووړي

ويول vajavə́l *causative* [*past:* و يي وياوه] **1** to make speak, talk **2** to
ask questions

ويولون vijolón *m.* violn

ويون vajún *m.* words, utterance; saying

ويونکی vajúnkaj **1** *present participle of* ويل [1] **2.1** reader **2.2** pupil,
student

ويوونه vajavə́na *f.* wish to speak

ويونی vajúnaj (one who is) speaking; a speaker

وبويل vévajəl *contraction of the preverb* و *and the pronoun* يي *and*
verb ويل [1] *in lieu of* و يې ويل

ويه [1] və́ja *f. dialect* egg

ويه [2] vajá *f. linguistics* phoneme

ويي [1] vəjí *dialect present tense of* ويل [1] *in lieu of* وايي

ويی ² vəjáj *m.* **1** word, promise **2** words; utterance **3** saying; byword

ويی بهيرګر vəjáj bahírgár *m. computer science* word processor

ويجدل vajedə́l *intransitive* [*past:* وويده و] **1** to start talking **2** to gab, talk بی ځايه مه ويږده! Stop chattering!

ويجدنه vajedə́na *f.* ويجدو vajedə́ *m. plural* idle talk; blather; chitchat

ويږز vajíz being pronounced

ويل کېدل vejə́l *transitive dialect* ☞ ويل ³ ☞ ويل وييل کېدل ³

ويجنه vejə́na *f.* ويبه vejá *f. dialect* order

وی ئ véje *dialect in lieu of*

ه

ه ¹ hā he hā-ij-havváz **1** the thirty-ninth letter of the Pashto alphabet **2** the number 5 in the abjad system

ه ² abbreviation of هجرت the 1000th year of the hejira (circa 1590)

ه ¹ *Arabic suffix* pronounced as át

ه ² ə́ *m. f.* **1** *adjective and noun ending in the direct form* زړه heart اوږده لرګي long fingers واله irrigation well **2** *adjective and noun ending in the oblique form, and in the masculine singular and the masculine plural direct form* پښتانه of an Afghan, of Afghans

ه ³ a á *f. noun and adjective ending* توره شپه dark night

ه ⁴ á *m. noun ending* همسايه neighbor

ه ⁵ a **1** *ending for oblique case of masculine nouns after* له کوره له out of the house له ښاره out of the city **2** *added to masculine nouns ending in a consonant after numerals* دوه کوره two houses دری کتابه three books

ه ⁶ a á *ending of imperative of verbs* تړه bind, tie وايه speak

ه ⁷ ə *ending of the past perfect and imperfect, the usual ending of the third person singular and plural* (*vice* ل), e.g., تله they went; *in the Western dialect it may also stand after* ل e.g., سوله *vice* سول they became, etc.

ه ⁸ a á *ending of the past tense third person feminine singular* هغه ووته she went out هغه تله they went

ه ⁹ a *optional ending for several verbs (especially in women's speech),* e.g., زه يمه *vice* زه يم

ها ¹ hā *f.* the name of the letter ه های جلي مختفي short "a" or stressed "a" at the end of a word های خفي shwa (zvarakaj) at the end of a word های ساکن the letter ه at the end of a word is used for "a"or "á" های ظاهر ح *colloquial* the letter های حطی، لویه ها *colloquial* the letter ه های هوز، کوچنی ها shwa (zvarakaj)

ها ² hā *f.* egg د ها زير egg yolk د ها سپين egg white ها سپينول to peel an egg, shell an egg ☞ هګی

ها ³ hā ā *demonstrative pronoun colloquial* that; those ها خوا that side, there, on that side ها غاړه that shore, on that shore ها مريض that sick person ... ها نورو ورته وويل چه The others said to him that ... ☞ هغه ¹

ها ⁴ hā *exclamation* **1** yes; good; all right **2** look out; watch yourself ها ګوره چه راتبر نشي Look out! Don't come closer! **3** *interrogative particle* eh, هو

ها ⁵ hā *interjection* ho; oh; well (a cry with which folk songs often begin)

ها ⁶ hā́ *plural suffix for several numerals* په زرهاؤ thousands; by thousands په سل هاؤ hundreds; by hundreds

هاتنه hātə́na *f. Eastern* cow-elephant, she-elephant

هاتي hātí *m. Eastern* elephant *idiom* هغه د هاتي په غوږ اوده نه وه He's not dozing of. He's not day dreaming.

هاجي hādzhí *m.* ☞ حاجي

هادي hādí *m. Arabic* **1** spiritual father, religious mentor **2** *physics* conductor

هار ¹ hār *m.* **1** necklace د مرغلرو هار pearl necklace **2** wreath, garland د ګلو هار wreath, garland

هار ² hār *Arabic* rabid, mad (of a dog)

هار ³ hár *m. suffix used to form onomatopoeic words indicating the repetition or intensification of a sound* شرنګهار resounding, resonance بوږهار honking; hum

هارپ hārp *m.* harp

هارت hrə́t hārə́t ☞ ارت ²

هارتوالی hārtvá̄laj *m.* ☞ ارتوالی hārttjá *f.* هارت والی هارت تيا

هارتول hārtavə́l *transitive* ☞ ارتول ²

هارتېدل hārtedə́l *intransitive* ☞ ارتېدل

هارمونيه hārmonijá *f.* harmonium

هارن hārn *m.* **1** horn, siren (of an automobile) هارن غږول، هارن ورکول to blow the horn, honk, give a signal **2** *music* french horn; bugle

هارود hārúd *m.* Harud (River, western Afghanistan)

هارون hārún *Arabic proper name* Harun, Aaron

هاړ hāṛ *m.* **1** hot season of the year (June and July); Har (the third Hindu month) د هاړ غرمه sultriness, extreme heat **2** haze

هاړه هوړه hā́ṛa-húṛa *f.* **1** hubub, ruckus **2** disorder; hurly-burly, commotion **3** flattery, toadying هاړي هوړي کول to flatter, toady to

هاړي هوړي hā́ṛi-húṛi *interjection* oh, how pleasant

هاسپيټل hāspiṭál *m. regional* hospital

هاسټل hāsṭal *m.* hostel, dormitory

هاسي hā́si hā́se *Eastern* ☞ هسي

هاسي په هاسي hā́se-pə-hā́se *Eastern* in vain, to no avail, for naught

هاشم hāshím *m. Arabic proper name* Hashim

هاضمه hāzimá *f. Arabic* digestion د هاضمي جهاز digestive tract

هاغسي hāghási thus, in this way, therefore

هاغومره hāghómra ☞ هغومره

هاغه há́gha **1** *demonstrative pronoun* that, those له هاغي خوانه from that side, from that direction اوس نو هاغه وخت و چه ... and so the season has come ... **2** *personal pronoun dialect* he ☞ هغه ¹

هاغسي há́ghase ☞ هغسي

هاکي hākí *f.* hockey د هاکي لوبغاړی hockey player د هاکي ټيم hockey team

هاګ hāg *m.* Haaga (city)

هاگۍ hāgə́j *f. singular & plural* ☞ هگۍ هاگی یومخې fried eggs

هال hāl *m.* **1** vestibule; hall; waiting room; foyer **2** *sports* goal post, goal له هال څخه تبرول to kick a goal, score a goal

هالته hā́lta ☞ هلته

هالک hālə́k *m.* ☞ هلک [1]

هالکتوب hāləktób *m.* ☞ هلکتوب

هالکی hāləkáj *m.* ☞ هلکی

هالکینه hālkína *f.* ☞ هلکتوب

هالند hāláni *m.* ☞ هالبند

هالو hāló *interjection* hello

هاله hālá [1] *f. Arabic* lunar halo

هاله hála [2] then, at that time, at that moment چه زه هلته وم نو نو ورور دي هاله راغلی نه و When I was there, your brother did not drop by.

هالي hā́li hā́le *regional* there هالي يې کېږده Put her there. هالي کښېنه Sit there.

هالبند hā́lenḍ *m.* Holland

هالبندي hālenḍí hālenḍáj **1** Dutch هالبندي ژبه hālenḍí the Dutch language **2** *m.* Dutchman, Netherlander

هامون hāmún *m.* plain د هامون دریاچه Lake Hamun

هان hān [1] *particle* **1** ☞ ها [4] په هان خُواب ورکول to answer in an assured manner هان که نه؟ Is it not so? Isn't it true? Yes? **2** *emphatic particle used to strengthen an expression* شکور چیرته دئ Where is Shakur? Wherever is he? هان چیرته دئ؟

هان hān [2] *m.* **1** height (of a man) **2** size, measure

هاند hānd *m.* effort, exertion, zeal; endeavor هاند کول to strain every effort, take great pains په لټون پسې هاند کول to search carefully هاند مې پرې تمام کړ خو نه شو I bent every effort, but nothing came out of it.

هاندوراس hāndurā́s *m.* Honduras

هاندي hāndí diligent, zealous

هانډۍ hānḍə́j *f. regional* cooking pot, stewpan

هانډبوال hānḍewā́l *m.* ☞ انډبوال

هانگري hā́ngri *f.* ☞ هنگري

هانگ کانگ hāngkā́ng *m.* Hong Kong

هانوی hānój *m.* Hanoi

هاڼ hāṇ *m.* similarity, likeness

هاو hāv *interjection* **1** cry used in urging on or stopping a buffalo **2** ah ha; oho

هاوان hāvā́n *m.* **1** howitzer **2** mortar دروند هاوان heavy mortar

هاوانا hāvānā́ *f.* Havana

هاوايي hāvā́i *m.* Hawaii د هاوايي جزيرې the Hawaiian Islands

هاها hāhā́ *f.* **1** shout, uproar, din; turmoil, confusion دا څه ها ها ده؟ What's all this noise? **2** rejoicing **3** loud guffawing ها ها کول، ها ها اچول **a** to make a din, grow noisy; make a ruckus **b** to guffaw

هاها hāhā́ [2] so much for that

هاهو hāhú [1] *m.* ☞ هاها [1]

هاهو hā-hó [2] yes, yes; well yes

هاهولي hāholí *f.* flirting هاهولي کول to flirt

هاهای hāháj *interjection* alas; too bad; a pity

های hāj [1] *f. dialect* ☞ هگی

های hāj [2] *regional* **1** high های تنشن *electrical engineering* high tension **2** supreme, high (e.g., commissar)

های hāj [3] *interjection* alas; ah; woe های زما بدبختي! Ah, how unhappy I am!

های hāj [4] های دئ! There you are! Exactly so!

هايتي hājítí *f.* Haiti

هايدرولوژي hājdrolodzhí *f.* هايدرولوژي hājdrolozhí *f.* hydrology

هايدروژن hajḍrozhín hydrogen

هايدروژني hājḍrozhiní *adjective* hydrogen, pertaining to or affected by hydrogen

هایهای hājháj *interjection* ah; alas; woe های های کول to sigh, exclaim oh or ah های های څه خُومره بد کار وشو! Oh how bad this is! های های که لږ څه مخکښنی راغلئ وای Oh, if you had only come a bit earlier. Why did you not come a little sooner.

هایهوی hājhúj *interjection* **1** ah; alas; woe **2** *m.* noise های هوی کول **a** to regret, deplore; to sigh, say ah or oh **b** to make a fuss **c** to cry "Listen" **d** to shout "Hurrah" (e.g., during an attack)

هايه hājá *demonstrative pronoun dialect* this is it; it's the one

هب hab *m. computer science* hub

هبته habatá **1** useless, futile, vain; good for nothing **2** perished; annihiliated هبته کول **a** to render useless, render futile **b** to spoil, destroy, annihilate هبته کېدل **a** to be useless, be futile; be unsuccessful د دوی ټوله هڅه هبته شوه All of their attempts were unsuccessful. **b** to perish; to be destroyed ☞ ابته

هبته والی habatavā́laj *m.* **1** uselessness, futility; vainness, needlessness **2** nonesense

هبوط hubút *m. Arabic* landing; coming in and landing هبوط کول to land; to come in for a landing

هبه hibá *f. Arabic* gift, bequest هبه کول *compound verb* to grant, bequeath

هبه ډبه hába-ḍába *f.* whooping cough

هبه نامه hibanāmá *f.* settlement, deed

هپ hap swallow, mouthful هپ کول to swallow at once, to gulp down

هپ دپ hapdáp **1.1** quick, agile, adroit, efficient **1.2** hurried **1.3** lost, having lost the way **2.1** unexpectedly **2.2** hurriedly

هپول hapavə́l *denominative, transitive* [*past:* هپ یې کړ] to swallow, swallow down

هپه hapá [1] *f.* help, assistance, support هپه کول to help, support

هپه hapá [2] *f.* **1** striving, aspiration **2** raid, foray هپه کول **a** to strive for, aspire to; be bound for **b** to make a foray **3** detachment (sent to pursue raiders)

هپه hápa [3] *f.* swallow, mouthful

هپه دپه hapá-dapá *f.* effort, endeavor; zeal, diligence هپه دپه کول to strive, bend one's efforts

هپي hapí [1] *f. Western* **1** adder **2** viper, poisonous snake

هپې [2] hapé *plural of* هپه [1, 2]

هپي [3] hápi *plural of* هپه [3]

هتک haták *m. regional* insult د چا هتک کول to insult someone

هتنه hatána *f.* cow elephant, she-elephant

هته hatá *f.* 1 weaver's beam 2 elbow, cubit

هتیات hatját *m.* care, caution, circumspection احتیاط ☞

هتیاتي hatjátí 1 careful, cautious, circumspect 2 *f.* care, caution, circumspection

هتیار hatjár *m.* 1 arms, weapons, armament, equipment 2 apparatus, tool, device هتیار ترل a to prepare for war; arm oneself b to get ready for work

هت [1] haț 1.1 standing; stopping, stock-still 1.2 obstinate 2 *m.* .1 opposition 2.2 disobedience, obstinacy, perversity, stubbornness

هت [2] haț *m.* 1 store, large shop 2 shop

هتال hațál *Eastern* اتال ☞

هتالول hațālavál *transitive* اتالول ☞

هتالېدل hațaledál *intransitive Eastern* اتالېدل ☞

هتکړۍ hațkaṛӘj *f. regional* manacle

هتکل haṭkál *m.* اتکل ☞

هتکلول haṭkalavál *transitive* اتکلول ☞

هتکلېدل haṭkaledál *intransitive* اتکلبدل ☞

هتکي haṭkí *f.* haṭkáj *m.* اتکي [2] ☞

هتکېدل həṭkedál *intransitive* [*past:* وهتکبده] to laugh loudly, guffaw

هتوځی haṭódzáj *m.* هتوزی haṭózáj *m.* اتوځی ☞

هتول [1] haṭavál *denominative, transitive* [*past:* هټ یې کړ *past:* وي یې] 1 to stop, detain 2 to raise, compel, stand or make stand up

هتول [2] haṭavál *denominative, transitive* [*past:* وي یې هتاوه] to cause to guffaw; make laugh

هته haṭa active, energetic هته او سته کول a to make ends meet; do without something for a time b to gamble

هتی haṭӘj *f.* [*plural:* هتی haṭӘj *plural:* هتی گاني haṭəgáni] store, shop

هتېدل [1] haṭedál *denominative, intransitive* 1 to be stopped, be halted, be detained 2 to stand up 3 to arise from bed, wake up 4 to shrink (of cloth)

هتېدل [2] haṭedál *intransitive* [*past:* وهتبد] to guffaw, laugh loudly

هتیوال haṭӘjvál *m.* هتی والا haṭӘjvālá *m.* shopkeeper, merchant

هتیوالي haṭӘjvälí *f.* retail store trade

هجا hidzhā *f. Arabic* 1 syllable 2 painfully slow reading (reading by syllables)

هجائي hidzhāí *Arabic* 1 alphabetic 2 syllabic, consisting of syllables دري هجائي کلمه a three syllable word

هجر hidzhr *m.* هجران hidzhrán *m. Arabic* parting, depature, leaveteaking

هجرت hidzhrát *m. Arabic* 1 resettlement, migration; emigration هجرت کول to resettle, emigrate 2 *history* hejira (the departure of Mohammed from Mecca to Medina; the beginning point for Muslim chronology) 3 *history* resettlement of part of the Afghans from India to Afghanistan in the 1919-1920 period

هجرتي hidzhratí *m.* settler; immigrant

هجرت [1] hidzhrá *f. Arabic* ☞

هجره [2] hudzhrá *f.* ☞

هجري hidzhrí *Arabic* 1 relating to the hegira (i.e., the departure of Mohammed from Mecca to Medina; as the beginning point for Muslim chronology) 2 Muslim chronology هجري سنه a year according to Muslim chronology شمسي هجري کال the solar year of the hegira system قمري هجري کال the lunar system of the "hegira" system

هجرا hidzhrá *m.* هجری hidzhŕáj *m.* 1 eunuch; castrated man 2 pederast

هجگي hidzhgí *f.* reading a syllable one at a time په هجگی ویل to read haltingly, read one syllable at a time

هجو hadzhv *m. Arabic* satire

هجوم hudzhúm *m. Arabic* 1.1 assault; charge, attack د هوايي قوا هجوم attack aviation 1.2 charge 1.3 swarm, plague (of locusts) 2.1 *predicative* abundant; numerous 2.2 swarming, crowding

هجو نویس hadzhvnavís *m.* satirist

هجوه hádzhva *f.* دا شعر یو هجوه ده هجو This poetry is satiric.

هجي hidzhí *f.* painfully slow reading (i.e., one syllable at a time)

هیچ hich هیخ ☞ هچ

هچري hacháre *Eastern* هیچیري ☞ never هجري نه as never before

هخ [1] huts crazy, insane

هخ [2] hits *dialect* هیخ ☞

هتسن hatsӘn هخو hatsú striving, endeavoring, zealous

هخه [1] hátsa *f.* اخه [2] ☞

هخه [2] hátsa *exclamation* get back; stop

هخامنشي hakhāmanshí *history* Achmenid هخامنشي دوره The Achmenid period

هدا hudá *f.* true way, right way; true faith

هداد hudád *m.* هیداد ☞

هدایت hidáját *m. Arabic* instructions, directions, guidance; indication هدایت ورکول to give directions; instruct, teach, guide

هدایت نامه hidájatnāmá *f.* instructions (written), teachings, guidance (written)

هدر hadár *Arabic* 1 *m.* futile, vain loss 2 in vain, fruitlessly, without result

هدف hadáf *m. Arabic* [*plural:* هدفونه hadafúna *Arabic plural:* اهداف ahdáf] 1 target مرمك په هدف ونښت The bullet struck the target. 2 goal, aim, purpose خپل هدف ګرئول to establish one's goal 3 object, mark ځمکنی هدف landmark 4 purposefulness

هدهد hudhúd *m. Arabic* hoopoe

هدیره hadirá haderá *f. Eastern* 1 cemetery, graveyard 2 area, enclosure

هدیه hadijá *f. Arabic* 1 gift, donation, contribution 2 gift to a teacher; teaching fee (to a mullah)

هډ haḍ *m.* 1 bone هډو درد rhematism; rheumatic pain 2 stone (of a fruit) 3 family, clan, descent د هډ دښمني mortal enmity; blood vengeance هډ مي ورسره شریک دئ I am his blood relative. 4

nobility, aristocratic descent هډ ماتول **a** to initiate bloody enmity **b** to display mercy to someone *idiom* پاخه هډ ته رسیدل to attain or reach maturity په هډ می چاره نه لگیږي I am penniless.

هډبند haḍbánd *m.* plaster, label, sticker

هډبندي haḍbandí *f.* هډتر haḍtár *m.* skeleton (of an animal)

هډگود haḍgúḍ *m.* ☞ هډمل

هډماتي [1] haḍmātí *f.* haḍmátaj *m.* **1** enmity **2** *history* compensation for breaking bones

هډماتی [2] haḍmátaj *m.* foe, enemy

هډمل haḍmáḍ *m.* entire skeletal structure; entire body هډمل ماتول to beat up, thrash

هډمرغه haḍmurghə́ *m.* bearded vulture, lammergeier (bird of prey, raptorial bird)

هډو [1] haḍó **1** quite, fully زه یې هډو نه پیژنم I don't know him at all. **2** just, exactly, just now, recently هډو اوس روان وم I just now decided to go. **3** never; not at all; I say (affectionate expression of disbelief, incredulity, etc.)

هډو [2] haḍú esteemed, dear

هډو [3] haḍó *oblique plural of* هډ

هډوال haḍvál *m. dialect* relative

هډواله haḍvála *f.* health (inherited from parents)

هډوالی [1] haḍválaj *m.* **1** boniness **2** strength, force

هډوالی [2] haḍválaj *m.* blood relationship

هډوالي [3] haḍváli *f. plural of* هډواله

هډور haḍavə́r **1** boney **2** thick-set, broad-shouldered **3** strong, robust

هډوکپ haḍukáp *m.* chopper, cleaver; butcher knife

هډوکی haḍúkaj *m.* small bone, bone د هډوکو خوږ rheumatic pain, rheumatism د هډوکو مغز marrow *idiom* د هډوکو امبل یې ورته په غاړه کړ They defamed him.

هډه [1] haḍá *f.* **1** stop; halt; landing, dock د بسونو هډه bus stop **2** base; center; point (e.g., trade) ☞ اوه

هډه [2] haḍḍá *f.* Hadda (settlement near Dzhelalabad)

هډي [1] háḍi *m. plural* **1** tonsils هډي لوېدل throat ailment; angina **2** bone spavin **3** small knot, nodule

هډی [2] haḍáj *m.* metatarsal bone

هډې [3] haḍé *plural of* هډه [1]

هډیره haḍirá *f.* ☞ هدیره

هذا hazá *Arabic demonstrative pronoun* this

هذف hazf *m. Arabic* **1** amputation, severing **2** *linguistics* elision

هذیان hiziján *m. Arabic* **1** delirium **2** ravings

هر [1] har *pronoun* (determinant) each, every, any هر څوک every man, any man هر ځای every place, everywhere, all over, in all places هر کال each year, annually هره میاشت each month, monthly هره ورځ each day, daily هر وار each time هر وخت always, each time, every time; at any time دا جریده په هره دوشنبه نشریږي This newspaper comes out every Monday. په هرو څلورو کالو کښې every four years

هر [2] har *m.* swindler, cheat; traitor

هر [3] hər *m.* bray, hee-haw (of a donkey) هر او پر loud bray (of a donkey)

هر [4] hər **1** *interjection* oh my gosh; well **2** *m.* censure, reproof

هرا horá́ *f.* ☞ هرهار

هرات harát hirát herát *m.* Herat (city) د هرات ولایت Herat Province

هراتی harātáj **1** pertaining to Herat **2** *m.* native or resident of Herat

هراس hirás *m. Arabic* fright, fear, alarm, terror

هراک hrāk *m.* bray, hee-haw (of a donkey)

هراند hərānd **1** fearful; cowardly; shy **2** anxious **3** scared; nervous

هراندوالی hərāndvə́laj *m.* **1** fearfulness; cowardice; shyness **2** anxiousness

هراندول hərāndavə́l *denominative, transitive* [*past:* هراند یې کړ] **1** to scare, frighten **2** to alarm

هراندېدل hərāndedə́l *denominative, intransitive* [*past:* هراند شو] **1** to be cowardly; quail, be frightened; fear **2** to be alarmed, be anxious

هراول harāvúl *m. regional* vanguard

هرتال hartál *m. plural regional* arsenic sulfide, orpiment

هرت harát *m.* ☞ ارهټ

هرتال hartál *m. plural* ☞ هرتال

هرج hardzh *m. Arabic* **1** hindrance, interruption (e.g., at work) **2** disorder, turmoil **3** disturbance, mutiny

هرج و مرج hardzh-u-márdzh *m.* **1** chaos, complete disorder, anarchy **2** confusion, agitation, disturbance

هرچا harchá *oblique of* هرڅوک

هرچرته harchárta هرچیري harchire *Eastern* everywhere, all over, in every place هرچرته چه **a** some time, (or other) **b** all over, wherever, wherever it may be

هرځائي hardzājí *m.* **1** vagrant, idler **2** good-for-nothing, cad

هرځله hardzála **1** each time **2** each and every time, whenever

هرڅنگه hátsənga in every way possible, by any means, by any possible means هرڅه چه وي او هرڅنگه چه وي No matter what happens. In any way that it is possible to do it.

هرڅو hartsó whenever … ; however much …, however … ; be that as it may

هرڅوک hartsók *definite pronoun* each one, anyone, everyone

هرڅومره hartsómra هرڅونه hartsóna in as much as; however much; however هر څومره ژر چه ممکنه ده as quickly as possible; as fast as possible

هرڅه hartsə́ **1** all, everything ما هرڅه چه ویلي دي، رښتیا ده Everything that I said is the truth! هرڅه وشو! That's all! **2** every sort of; no matter how much; all هرڅه چه وي No matter what should happen د هرڅه نه اگاهو، تر هرڅه دمخه all kinds of things, odds and ends هرڅه *regional* first of all, before all else

هررنگه hárranga **1** any, any at all **2** in every way possible, in every shape and form که هررنگه ستړی ستومانه وي No matter how tired he might be.

هرړی [1] hirṛáj *m.* ☞ اړی [1]

هرړی [2] hirṛə́j *f.* ☞ اړی [1]

هرړی 3 hararój *f.* handle (of a plow)

هرزه harzá 1.1 pertaining to litter, trash, etc. هرزه وابنه، هرزه بوټي weeds 1.2 barren, desert, good-for-nothing, worthless 2.1 trifle 2.2 nonsense هرزه ويل to talk rubbish

هرزه برزه harzá-barzá rubbishy, trashy

هرکاره 1 harkārá *m.* 1 courier; messenger; errand boy 2 emissary 3 spy 4 man-of-all work; all-around expert

هرکاره 2 harkārá *m.* 1 iron ladle, iron spoon 2 saucepan with a long handle (used for heating oil)

هرکله harlála harkála 1 always, constantly 2 as soon as; whenever; everytime; when هرکله چه a whenever; every time that ... ; each time that ... هرکله چه راغلي whenever you should come b if, insofar as *idiom* هرکله راشي! Welcome! Always glad to see you!

هرکلاج harkálaj *m.* harkálaj 1 greeting harkóli د هرکلي وینا a welcoming speech پیشنهاد ته هرکلی کول هرکلی کول to meet, greet to welcome a suggestion هرکلی ويل to greet 2 meeting, encounter

هرکی hərkáj *m.* silly laugh, unmotivated laugh

هرگاه hargáh always, constantly

هرگز hargíz *poetic* never

هرگوره hargóra 1 very, extraordinarily, unusually, exceptionally; quite دا به هرگوره د تعجب هرگوره ډېر دئ very much best هغه هرگوره بنه سری دئ It could be quite surprising. He is an exceptionally good man, زه په راتگ هرگوره خوښ شوم I rejoice greatly at his arrival. ماڼی هرگوره بنه ايسي The building is very beautiful. 2 completely, absolutely 3 without fail 4 in any event (with a negation) 5 not at all, in no way; under no circumstances هرگوره مي لاس نه رسېږي I wouldn't involve myself in that for anything.

هرم harám *m. Arabic* [*plural:* اهرام ahrā́m] pyramid

هرمږ hurmə́ṛ *m.* ارمږ

هرمون harmón *m.* hormone

هرنی haraṇój *f.* 1 outburst (e.g., of anger) له ډېره قهره هرنی واخيستلم I was beside myself. I had an outburst of anger. 2 greed

هرومرو harumarú in one way or another; absolutely, unconditionally; without fail تاسي ته دا هرومرو معلومه ده چه ... You must have known that ... You certainly knew that ...

هره 1 hára *f. singular of* هر هره خوا all over, everywhere, in every place

هره 2 hára *oblique of* هر هره چا ته to each one, to every one *oblique of* له هره دولته سره with each government

هرهار hərahā́r *m.* prolonged bray (of a donkey)

هره پلا háraplá each time

هره ورځنی haravradzənáj 1 daily, every day 2 usual, ordinary, workaday

هری 1 hiráj *f.* 1 trick, pretext 2 excuse هری کول a to try to get out of b to excuse oneself

هری 2 həré cry used to drive sheep هری کول to drive sheep

هری 3 huré هوری 1

هری 4 hári *f. plural of* هره

هري 5 hiré *f. plural dialect* ashes, cinders

هریاسه harjása *f.* ground corn (on the threshing floor)

هریان harjā́n *colloquial* حیران

هریان گوټی harjā́n gótaj amazed, startled; stupefied, benumbed; perplexed

هریانی harjāní *f.* 1 amazement, surprise; stupefaction; perplexity 2 state of being oppressed or downtrodden

هربدل həredól *intransitive* [*past:* وهربده] 1 to bray (of a donkey) 2 to bark, yap 3 to speak with irritation

هری رود harirúd *m.* Harirud (River)

هریر hariṛ *m.* kind of blanc-mange (sweet dessert made of a starchy substance and milk)

هریره hariṛá *f.* mirobalan (the dried fruit of *Terminalia chebula*) توره هریره black mirobalan, زیره هریره yellow mirobalan, *Terminalia berica*

هرېړی hareṛój *f.* shaft (of a plow)

هریز huríz *f. dialect* اورېغ

هریو har jav *definite pronoun* each, any, any or either (of two)

هر 1 haṛ *m.* اړوی 1

هړ 2 haṛ *dialect* اړ

هړاند haṛā́nd downcast, sad

هرپی harpój *f.* small box, small case

هریسه harisá 1 boiled soft (of food) هریسه کول to boil soft هریسه کېدل to be boiled soft *f.* 2 harisa (groats with meat)

هزار hazár thousand (mainly used in poetry)

هزارگی hazāragí *adjective* Hazara هزارگي پسونه the Hazara breed of sheep

هزاره hazārá 1 *m.* [*plural:* هزارگان hazāragā́n *plural:* هزاره گان] Hazara 2 *f.* [*plural:* هزاره گاني hazāragā́ni] Hazara woman د هزاره و دره the Hazara Valley 3 *f.* the Hazara (district NW of Pakistan)

هزاره جات hazāradzhā́t *m. plural* Hazarajat

هزاري hazārí *f. history* position of a leader of 1,000 troops

هزل hazl *m. Arabic* joke

هزلي hazlí *Arabic* joking, not serious, comic

هزم hazm *m.* هضم

هزماول hazmavól *transitive* هضمول

هزمېدل hazmedól *intransitive* هضمېدل

هژدات hadzhā́t *m. plural* brass

هسار hisā́r *m.* حصار

هساول hisāravól *transitive* حصارول

هسارېدل hisaredól *intransitive* حصارېدل

هسپانوي hispānaví hispāní 1 Spanish 2.1 *m.* Spaniard 2 *f.* Spanish language

هسپانیه hispānijá *f.* Spain

هسپتال haspitā́l *m.* هسپتال haspitā́l *m. regional* hospital سفري هسپتال a field hospital b mobile dressing station

هسپه haspá *f.* measles *f.* haspá botáj هسپه بوټی plant used to treat measles *f.* اسپه 2

Pashto-English Dictionary

هست **hast 1.1** being, existing **1.2** active; effective **2** *m.* being, existence تر هست یی نښت غوره دئ It would be better if he did not exist (of a wicked person)

هستمند **hastmánd** rich, prosperous; substantial

هستمندي **hastmandí** *f.* wealth; prosperity; riches

هستوگندځۍ **hastogóndzáj** *m.* ☞ استوگنځۍ

هستوگنه **hastógna** *f.* هستوگه **hastóga** *f.* residence, place of residence; dwelling place د هستوگنې ځای **a** dwelling, habitation, residence **b** place of deployment, territoty هستوگنه کول to live, stay, dwell, reside چرته هستوگنه کوي؟ Where do you live?

هستول **hastavól** *transitive* [*past:* و یی هستاوه] **1** to settle, settle down **2** to create, bring into being

هستوي **hastaví** **1** nuclear **2** *figurative* essential

هسته **hastá** [1] *f.* **1** nucleus (e.g., of an atom) **2** *figurative* essence, substance; the main idea or thought, the basic idea or thought **3** central massif (of mountains)

هسته **hísta** [2] ☞ هیسته د دوو هفتو را په هسته هیسته Here it's already been two weeks.

هستیي **hastají** **1** nuclear **2** *figurative* basic, essential

هستي **hastí** [1] *f.* **1** riches; prosperity **2** being, existence هستي لرل to live, exist **3** (living) being

هستي **hasté** [2] *plural of* هسته [1]

هستیا **hastjá** *f.* riches; property د هستیا ژوند the wealthy life, the affluent life

هستېدل **hastedól** *intransitive* [*past:* و هستېد] **1** to live; dwell, reside; be; stay in **2** to come into the world, be born

هستېدونکی **hastedúnkaj** **1** *present participle of* هستېدل *m.* **2** resident, dweller

هسک **hisk** [1] *m.* lot هسک اچول to draw, cast lots

هسک **hask** [2] **1.1** lofty; tall هسک غر high mountain د باغ وني ډېري هسکي دي The trees in the orchard are very high. **1.2** supreme, very high, raised up **1.3** loud; high (in tone, volume) **1.4** proud هسکه غاړه haughtily **1.5** sublime **2** *adverb* **.1** high **2.2** loudly هسک کتل to speak loudly **2.3** proudly هسک رغېدل، هسک ویل to look from high on *m.* **3** sky; height

هسکوالی **haskválaj** *m.* هسکتوب **hasktób** *m.* هسکتیا **hasktjá** *f.* **1** height, altitude **2** lifting, raising; elvation

هسکول **haskavól** *denominative, transitive* [*past:* هسک یی کړ] **1** to lift, raise سر هسکول to lift the head **2** to elevate; make higher **3** to heighten, raise **4** to inflict, deal (a blow) **5** to develop

هسکونه **haskavóna** *f.* lifting, raising; elevation

هسکه **háska** *f.* **1** *singular of* هسک [2] **1 2** height; summit

هسکېدل **haskedól** *denominative, intranstive* **1** to go up, climb هسک شه! Climb up here! Come up here! بیرغ هسک شو The flag was raised. **2** to rise up; become higher **3** to rise up **4** to develop **5** to be carried, be raised (of a saber, etc.)

هسکېدنه **haskedóna** *f.* هسکېده **haskedó** *m. plural* **1** ascent, rising; elevation **2** development

هسکېرلی **haskerólaj** ☞ اسکېرلی

هسي **hási hase** *Eastern* **1.1** thus, in this way هسي نه چه ... What if هسي نه چه ډاروو مرض راشي ... What if the cattle should sicken? **1.2** in vain, fruitlessly, for naught هسي ناست He sits idly. **1.3** for nothing, without payment **2** *demonstrative pronoun* such, such a

هشت و مشت **hasht-u-músht** *m.* **1** gaiety, merriment برائي زمونږ کره Yesterday there was much merriment at our place. خورا هشت و مشت و **2** quarrel, dissention څه هشت و مشت و؟ What was the quarrel about?

هشته **hísta** *dialect* ☞ هسته [2]

هشگونی **hashgúṇaj** angry, severe, stern

هشه **hэsha** a cry to drive donkeys away or driven forth

هنبمه **híkhma** *f.* هاخمه **hákhma** **1** storm cloud; rain cloud هنبمه راپورته شوه A rainstorm broke out. **2** downpour

هونبیار **hukhjár** ☞ هنبیار

هونبیارول **hukhjāravól** *transitive* ☞ هنبیارول

هونبیاري **hukhjārí** *f.* ☞ هنبیاري

هونبیارېدل **hukhjāredól** *intransitive* ☞ هنبیارېدل

هضم **hazm** *m. Arabic* **1** digestion د هضم اعضا the digestive organs **2** absorption, taking in, adoption **3** assimilation (of a people)

هضمول **hamavól** *denominative, transitive* [*past:* هضم یی کړ] **1** to digest (food) **2** to be conducive to digestion **3** to take in; dissolve; to absorb **4** to assimilate (e.g., a people)

هضمي **hazmí** *Arabic* digestive

هضمېدل **hazmedól** *denominative, intransitive* [*past:* هضم شو] **1** to be digested (of food) **2** to be taken in; be dissolved; be absorbed **3** to be assimilated (e.g., of a people)

هغاسي **haghási** **1** thus, in this way څه رنگه چه تاسي گمان کوئ هغسي نه ده The matter is not as you think it is.

هغلته **haghálta** there; thence هغلته چه there, where ... هغلته ولاړو We went (exactly) there.

هغومره **haghúmra** ☞ هغمه

هغو **haghó hughó haghó** *oblique plural of* هغه [1,2] پخوا تر هغو چه ... before ... ; prior to which د هغو بیان ډېر اوږدېږي One needs to discuss this (these things) for a long time.

هغومبره **haghómbra** *dialect* هغومره **haghómra haghúmra** **1** so, such, so much; such a quantity, so much هغومبره سري یی ولي څه کول؟ Why does he need so many people? **2** so, so much څومره چه عمر زیاتېږي The older a man is, the more هغومبره د سري تجربه هم زیاتېږي experienced. Experience comes with age.

هغونبره **haghónbra** *dialect* هغونمره **haghónmra** *dialect* هغونه **haghóna** *dialect* هغوني **haghóni** *dialect* ☞ هغومبره

هغوی **haghój haghúj** *personal pronoun* **1** they **2** them

هغه **hágha** [1] *demonstrative pronoun* (usually not inflected, but sometimes has the oblique *f.* هغي **hэghi**, هغي **haghé** and oblique plural هغو **haghō**) that, those هغه کتاب that book هغه کورونه those houses هغه ښځي those women هغه پلو، هغه خوا that side; there, on that side; to that side هغه ځای there, thence د هغه ځای سري saṛí the dwellers over there هغه څوک چه The one who د هغي ښغلي نوم then, هغه وخت، هغه زمانه کښي په هغه What is that girl's name? څه دئ؟

at that time د هغه وني لاندي *Eastern* under that tree هغه، هغه خبر *thus, in that way هغه دنيا *religion* the other world, the other side

هغه [2] haghá **1** *personal pronoun third person singular and plural m.* **1.1** (*oblique* هغه haghə́, həǵə́) **1.1a** he (as the subject of the action of intransitive verbs in all tenses, and of transitive verbs in present and future) هغه ولاړ he went هغه کار کوي he goes هغه ځي He is working. هغه به يو مکتوب راولېږي He will send us a letter. **1.1b** him (as the object of the action of transitive verbs in the present and future, in rare cases of the past, and also the imperative mode) ته هغه ويني؟ Do you see him! هغه را وبوله! Summon him! هلکانو هغه وواهه The boys beat hum. haghə **1.1c** he, to him (as the subject of the action of transitive verbs in the past tense) هغه يو هغه ووېل He said **1.1d** کتاب واخيست He bought (took) the book. *in combination with prepositions, postpositions, and adverbs* د هغه کتاب his book د هغه دپاره for him **1.2** *f.* (*oblique* هغې haghé) *f.* **1.2a** she (as the subject of the action of intransitive verbs in all tenses and in the present and future of transitive verbs) هغه ولاړه She went away *f.* **1.2b** her (as the object of the action of intransitive verbs in the present and future and sometimes the past tense, and also of the imperative mood) هغه را و بولئ! Summon her! *f.* **1.2c** she (as the subject of the action of transitive verbs in the past tense) هغې کار کاوه She was working, هغې ووېل She said هغې ځواب ورکړ She answered him. **1.2d** for her (in combinations with prepositions, postpositions and adverbs) د هغې دپاره for her د هغې خور her sisters **2** *f. Eastern* that, this د هغه راهيسي haghə since those times سره له هغه چه haghə́ along with that; besides; although, nevertheless پس له هغه haghə́ after this, afterwards, then د هغي په اثر *Eastern* as a result of this, for this reason, because of this د هغي لږدي ورځي کېږي Since then a few days have elapsed. Since those times a few days have elapsed. يو مشکل شته او هغه دا چه ... There is one problem, and that is ... well; it was then, then

هغه دغه haghagaghá *m. plural* one thing and another, all kinds of things, odds and ends هغه دغه کول to give evasive answers; deceive, dupe *idiom* هغه دغه کېدل **a** to spill, scatter **b** disperse

هغه سي hághási *Eastern* hágháse هغسي

هغې [1] haghé **1** *oblique feminine of* هغه [1, 2] ... هغې ووېل چه She said that ... هغې ته ووايه! Tell her! پخواتر هغي before this, up to now **2** *Eastern oblique m. of* هغه [2] عمارت او د هغي ملحقات a building and its extensions تر هغي *Eastern* since

هغې [2] héghi *oblique of* هغه [1]

هفتگي haftagí weekly هفتگي اخبار، هفتگي جريده، هفتگي مجله a weekly, a weekly publication

هفته haftá *f.* week په يوه هفته کښي for a week; in the course of a week د يوې هفتي two times a week په هره هفته کښي دوه ځلي in a week د هفتي ورځ Saturday هره هفته each week

هفته وار haftaíz هفته ايز

هفتگي haftagí هفتگي

هفته واره مجله haftaí weekly هفته ئيز haftaíz هفتئي haftaí هفته وار haftavár a weekly magazine

هک [1] hak surprised, startled, amazed هک تلل to be surprised, be started, be amazed هک حيران dumbfounded

هک [2] hak *m.* wages, payment for work حق

هک پک، هکپک hak-pák **1** startled, amazed in the extreme **2** frightened, dismayed هکپک کول **a** to surprise, startle, amaze **b** to scare هکپک کېدل **a** to be surprised, be startled, be amazed سړی هکپک ور ته پاتي کېږي! This is startling. **b** to be scared

هکتار hiktár *m.* hectare

هکتوليتر hiktolítr *m.* hectoliter

هکتار hikṭár *m.* هکتر

هک پک هک دک، هکدک hak-dák

هکذا hakazá *Arabic* exactly as, just as, in the same way

هکله haklá *f.* په هکله حقله د...concerning ..., about ..., with regard to ... د چا په هکله ليکل to write about someone

هکو پکو hako-pakó worried, anxious

هگ həg *m. Eastern* bear

هگه hə́ga *f. Eastern* she-bear

هگی hagə́j *f. plural* د هگيو چرگي layers, laying hens د هگيو کڅوره ovary پر هگيو هگی اچول to lay eggs د چينجيانو هگی silkworm eggs له هگی راوتل to sit on eggs, hatch out chicks باندي کېنبېنستل to hatch out an egg

هل [1] hə́l *m.* hul **1** shaft (of a plow) **2** plow

هل [2] hal hul hə́l cry of a dervish asking for donations

هلاک halák *Arabic* **1.1** annihilated, destroyed **1.2** killed, slain, perished **2** *m.* **.1** annihilation, destruction **2.2** ruin; death

هلاکت halākát *m. Arabic* death, destruction هلاکت ته رسېدل to perish

هلاکتوب halāktób *m.* هلاکتيا halāktjá *f.* هلاکوالی halakválaj *m.* هلاکت

هلاکول halākavál *denominative, transitive* [*past:* هلاک يي کړ] **1** to annihilate, destroy **2** to kill, slay **3** to distress, kill **4** to weary, exhaust

هلاکوونکی halākavúkaj **2.1** *present participle of* هلاکول **2.1** annihilating, destroying **2.2** fatal **2.3** wearing, exhausting

هلاکي halākí *f.* هلاکت

هلاکيت halākiját *m.* **1** exhaustion **2** tension **3** ruination

هلاکېدل halākedál *denominative, intransitive* [*past:* هلاک شو] **1** to be annihilated, be ruined **2** to perish, die **3** to be distressed, exhaust oneself; kill oneself **4** to be exhausted, be worn out, wear oneself out

هلال [1] hilál *m. Arabic* new moon, time of the new moon

هلال [2] halál حلال

هلالا halālá *f.* commotion, disturbance, noise

هلالي hilālí *Arabic* in the shape of a half moon

هلاهل halāhál *m.* halāhíl *plural* **1** deadly poison **2** deadly, fatal, death-dealing

هلته **hálta 1** there; yonder, thither هلته کښي *Eastern* there هلته کښیبرده Put it over there. **2** then, at that time

هلتي *a combination of the pronoun* يي *and the adverb* هلته وروره Take it over yonder.

هولدر holdár *m.* ☞ هولدر

هلسنكي helsinkí *m. f.* Helsinki

هلک[1] **halə́k 1** *m.* **.1** boy, child هلک كوچني baby, child کوچنیان چه هلک و نه He is still a child! هلک، هلک دئ! children هلک بچه، مور تی نه ورکوي *proverb* If the baby doesn't cry, the mother doesn't give milk. Speak up if you want to be heard د څانه څخه هلک مه جوړوه Don't act like a child. **1.2** lad, youth **2.1** small, slight **2.2** youthful هلک سړی a youth

هلک[2] **halk** *m.* ☞ هلک حلق **a** absence of milk in a diet **b** diet of cold foods without liquids

هلکت **haləkát** *m.* هلكتوب، هلک توب haləktób *m.* هلکوالی haləkvā́laj *m.* childhood, infancy, boyhood د هلكتوب نسبت چاته کول to relate to someone or treat someone as a child, consider someone a child

هلكوټی haləkóṭaj *m.* urchin, ragamuffin

هلکه[1] **halə́ka** *vocative of* هلک[1] 1

هلکه[2] **haləka** *f. singular of* هلک[1] 2

هلکی halkáj *m.* haləkáj **1** boy **2** young lad **3** *regional* dancing boy

هلکینه halkína *f.* ☞ هلكتوب

هل لی **hallə́j** *interjection* aha; oh ho; so that's it

هلم **halə́m** *m.* cress, watercress, *Lepidum sativum*

هلمنت **helmínt** *m.* intestinal worm, parasitic worm, tapeworm

هلمند **hilmánd** *m.* Hilmand د هلمند سیند the Hilmand River

هلواک **halvā́k 1** efficient, quick, smart هلواک كول to hasten هلواک کیدل to hurry, be in a hurry **2** *m.* **.1** haste, hurrying **2.2** greed, avarice

هلواكوالی halvākvā́laj *m.* haste, hurriedness

هلوکان halukā́n *m.* Western plural of هلک[1]

هميالیا himaēlajā́ *f.* همالیه himālajá *f.* Himalayas د همالیا غرونه، همالیي غرونه the Himalayas, the Himalaya Mountains

هلوکان halukā́n *m.* Western plural of هلک[1]

هله[1] **halá** *f.* hallá charge, attack, onset, assault د شپی هله night raid هله كول to attack, assault

هله[2] **halá** hála *f.* **1** urging on **2** *interjection* hurry up there; get a move on هله ژرشه! Go a bit faster there!

هله[3] **hála 1** then, in that case; exactly there, just then; only then مگر دا هله کیږي چه ... هله However, this is only possible when ... هله هله *folklore* at last, finally **2** there

هله گله hálagulá *f.* **1** disturbances, disorders; mutiny **2** هله گله، هله گوله confusion, commotion

هلهله halhalá *f.* **1** rejoicing, exaltation **2** ovation

هله هله **hála-hála** faster; more quickly; get a move on

هلی[1] **halé** ☞ هلته

هلی[2] **halé** hallé *plural of* هله[1]

هلئ[3] **halə́j** hurry up; faster; move a little faster (in addressing many people) هلئ ژغلئ! Run a bit faster!

هلي بلي **háli-báli** *f.* هلي څلي háli-dzáli *f.* **1** uneasiness, worry **2** entreaty **3** effort هلي بلي كول **a** to be uneasy; fret **b** to beseech, entreat **c** to make efforts

هلي دلي hálé-dalé here and there; here there and everywhere

هلي زلي **háli-záli** *f.* ☞ هلي بلي

هلیکوپتر helikoptér *m.* helicopter

هم[1] **ham** *m.* hamm *Arabic* care, trouble, alarm, grief

هم[2] **ham** *Eastern* hum **1** just so, even, likewise, too زه هم ورسره حُم I will also ride with them (him) ته هم هله وې You were also there. **2** namely, precisely, just زه هم ستاسي معلم یم It is I who am your teacher. هم په دغه ټكي at once, right here **3** even, indeed لا اوس هم He even هم په دغه كار كښي تریوه حده كامیاب شوئ هم و and even now attained definite successes in this matter ...هم ...هم... either ... or ... هم یې سكني، هم یې رغوي He himself was a jack of all trades. **4** (with negation) neither ..., nor ...

هم **ham** həm *combining form* co-; mono-; unitary- همكاري cooperation

همای humā́ *m.* ☞ همای

هم اصل **hámasə́l** of the same descent, of one family (of a person)

هماغسي **hamā́ghasi** hamā́ghase *Eastern* **1** *pronoun* very same one, very same ones څه چه وینم هغه هماغسي دئ هم! This is exactly what I see! **2.1** in the very same way, exactly so **2.2** as formerly, as before

هماغلته **hamā́ghalta** in the same place, right there هماغلته اوسه! Stop right there!

هماغومره **hamā́ghomra** insofar as, in the same degree, in the same measure هماغومره لوی و He was just as big.

هماغه **hamā́gha** *demonstrative pronoun* very same one, very same ones هماغه كال in the very same year هماغه لوی غر the highest mountain په هماغه حال كښي in the very same degree په هماغه اندازه in the very same situation, as before *idiom* نو هماغه وجه چه ... for the very reason that ...

همالته **hamā́lta** in the same place, ibidem, ibid

هماهغه **hamahágha** *demonstrative pronoun* same one په هماهغه اندازه in the same measure, in the same degree

هم آهنگ **hamāháng 1** corresponding to, appropriate **2** coordinate with **3** in agreement with; harmonious, in keeping with **4** in sympathy with

هم آهنگي **hamāhangí 1** accordance, correspondence دیو شي سره هم آهنگي لرل to correspond to something **2** coordination (of plans) **3** agreement **4** solidarity

همای **humā́j** *m.* **1** phoenix (it was supposed that a person upon whom its shadow fell would be emperor) د همای سیوری گڼل to consider to be a good omen **2** *folklore* regal bird, bird of paradise **3** vulture, lammergeier (raptorial bird)

همایون **humā́jun 1** august, imperial **2** *m.* *proper name* Humayun

همايوني humājuní august, most high ذات همايوني *official* exalted personage; king; His August Highness

همبره húmbra ☞ هومره

همبهيرگر hambahírgar *m. computer science* coprocessor

همپياله hampjālá *m.* 1 tavern-companion; drinking buddy 2 table-companion

همپيشه hampeshá working in the same profession or trade

همت himmát *m. Arabic* 1 magnanimity, mercy 2 nobility, koral purity; generosity of soul 3 valor, courage, bravery, manliness د همتونه يي کښته شي هغه همت اوچت شه *regional* He grew bolder. Their spirits fell. They became downcast. 4 effort, diligence, fervor; energy 5 firmness, stability همت کول *a* to display magnanimity, display generosity of spirit *b* to show courage *c* to try, strive, to be zealous *d* to display firmness, display stability همت لرل *a* to be magnanimous, be noble *b* to be brave, be manly *c* to be zealous, be forceful *d* to be firm, be stable 6 *proper name* Himmat

همت افزا himmatafzā́ encouraging, inspiring; cheering up

همت افزائي himmatafzājí *f.* encouragement, inspiration; cheering up

همتالوژي hemataēlozhí *f.* hematology

همتناک himmatnā́k 1.1 magnanimous; noble, spiritually generous 1.2 valorous, brave, bold, manly 1.3 fervent, zealous; forceful 1.4 firm, stable 2 *m.* brave man, courageous lad

همتي himmatí [1] ☞ همتناک

همتي himmatí [2] *f.* 1 ☞ همت 2 *combining form a* لورهمتي magnanimity; nobility *b* valor, courage, boldness; manliness

همجنس، هم جنس hamdzhíns *m.* 1 fellow-clansman; relation 2.1 of the same descent; of the same breed 2.2 homogenous; same; of the same kind; of the same quality or value

هم جوار hamdzhavā́r 1 contiguous, neighboring 2 *m.* neighbor

همجوليزتيا hamdzhūlíztjiā́ *f. computer science* justification

همجوليزول hamdzholizwól *computer science* to justify

هم چشم hamcháshm 1 not yielding to someone or something 2 *m.* rival, competitor

هم چشمي hamchasmí *f.* rivalry, competiton هم چشمي کول to rival, compete with

هم‌ځولی hamdzólaj *m.* ☞ همزولی [1]

همخانه hamkhāná 1 living together; living in the same house 2 *m.* neighbor (in an apartment or house)

همخوابه hamkhā́ba *f.* mistress; wife; spouse

هم خيل hamkhél *m.* fellow-tribesman, fellow clansman

همدا hamadā́ *demonstrative pronoun* this very one, these very ones همدا اوس همدا ډول، په همدي شان exactly alike; in the same manner right now همدا نن this very day, precisely today په همدي ځای کښي *a* right there, in that very place *b* at once, right here نو همدا دئ چه ... and this is why ...; for this very reason ... همدا بس دئ چه ... sufficient to say that ... رښتيا همدا ده چه that fact is precisely that ... سبب دئ چه ... همدا Look, the reason is that ...

همدارنگه hamdāranga همداسي hamdā́si همداشان hamdāshā́n 1 homogenous; the same 2 exactly the same, in the self-same manner همداسي نه ده؟ Isn't that the way it is?

همدرد hamdárd *m.* 1 comforter 2 sympathetic, compassionate, empathetic

همدردي hamdardí *f.* sympathy, compassion د چا سره همدردي کول to sympaathize with someone, to express compassion د همدردي په لهجه ويل to speak sympathetically

همدرس hamdárs *m.* schoolmate, classmate; bunkmate, dormitory-mate

همدغسي hamdághasi same, exactly the same, in the same manner کټ مټ همدغسي ده! Exactly so! Just so! Right on!

همدغلته hamdaghálta right here, precisely here

همدغوره hamdaghóra ☞ همدومره

همدغوی hamdaghújj *personal pronoun* they themselves

همدغه hamdaghá *demonstrative pronoun* 1 precisely this, precisely this one, precisely these ones په همدغو ځايو کښي in these exact places 2 this here له همدغه ځايه So that's where it comes from همدغه ډول، همدغه رنگه in the same way, in exactly the same way همدغه کور right now همدغه اوس Look, it's this very house here.

همدغسي hamdághasi hәmdághasi ☞ همدغه سي

همدلته hamdálta right here; in this very place

هم دم، هم‌دم hamdám *m.* sincere friend, true friend

همدومره hamdómra 1 just so much, precisely so much همدومره خبره ده the fact of the matter is ... چه ... همدومره به وايم چه I will say only that ... همدومره بايد پوه شئ Here is what is required that you know. 2 same

همدوی hamdújj *personal pronoun* they themselves; specifically them هغه همدوی دئ چه ... It was they (and no one else).

همدې hamdé *oblique of* همده [1]

همدی hamdáj [1] he (specifically), he himself

همدې hamdé [2] *oblique of* همدا [1]

همډلی hamḍálaj *m.* comrade; chum; schoolmate, classmate

همذات hamzā́t of the same family or clan; identical, one and the same

هم راز hamrā́z *m. poetry* confidant; close friend د چا هم راز، هم راز کېدل to become close friends with someone; to have a close relationship with someone; to be a close or trusted friend

همراه، هم راه hamrā́h *m.* 1 traveling companion, fellow traveler 2 having, possessing, being possessed of (used in titles) ☞ شجاعت همراه

همراهه، هم راهه hamrā́ha *f.* (female) traveling companion, (female) fellow traveler

همرکاب hamrikā́b *m.* traveling companion, fellow traveler

هم رنگ hamráng monochrome, monochromatic

هومره húmra *dialect* ☞ همره

هم ژبه، هم زبانه hamzabā́na ☞ hamzabā́n هم زبانه hamzabā́n

هم زمانه، هم زمان hamzamā́na hamzamā́na 1 synchronic, synchronous, coincident 2 *m.* contemporary

همزولی ¹ hamzólaj *m.* (male) born in the same year as oneself

همزولې ² hamzóle *f.* (female) born in the same year as oneself

همزولی پیغله female-friend (of a female)

همزه ¹ hamzá *m. Arabic* hamza (sign used for the glottal stop)

همزه ² hamzá *m. proper name* Hamza

هم ژبه hamzhóba speaking the same language

همسا hamsā́ *f.* [*plural:* همساګانی hamsāgā́ni *f. plural:* همساوي hamsā́vi] stick; cane; staff

همسایه hamsājá *m.* 1.1 neighbor 1.2 fellow-villager 1.3 tenant, renter (of land) 1.4 vassal tribe, protected client-tribe; protected part of the population among tribes 2 *attributive* neighboring د همسایه و مملکتو سره with neighboring countries

همسایه توب hamsājatób *m.* همسایه ګي hamsājagalví *f.* hamsājagí *f.* 1 neighborhood; good neighborly relations 2 position of a renter of land; position of a client-tribe

همسبق، هم سبق hamsabák̲ *m.* schoolmate, classmate

همسرحد hamsarhád contiguous, bordering

هم سفري hamsafarí traveling companion, fellow traveler

همسنګ hamsáng 1 of the same weight, of the same value 2 *m.* person born in the same year as oneself

هم شکل hamshákl هم شکله hamshákla same, of one form

همشیره hamshirá *f.* nurse

هم صحبت hamsuhbát *m.* 1 interlocutor 2 companion

همصنف hamsínf *m.* schoolmate, classmate

هم عمر ham'úmr *m.* person born in the same year as oneself

همغاړتوب hamghā́r̲tób *m.* agreement; cooperation

همغاړې ¹ hamghā́r̲e *f.* female colleague; female friend

همغاړې ² hamghā́r̲e *m.* colleague; friend

همغسي hamághasi 1 this is the way it is 2 *demonstrative pronoun* it is this one here

همغلته hamaghálta right here

همغمره hamaghúmra *dialect* so much

همغوی hamaghúj they themselves ☞ هغوی

همغه hamágha *demonstrative pronoun* that one there, that very one

هم فکر hamfíkr 1 *m.* person having the same views, like-minded person; partisan, supporter 2 in agreement with the opinions of someone

هم قام hamk̲ā́m *m.* fellow-tribesman, person from the same tribe as one

هم قد hamk̲ad hamk̲ádd of the same height

همقطار hamk̲atā́r *m.* ☞ همكار

هم قوم hamk̲úm *m.* ☞ هم قام

همكار hamkār *m.* fellow-worker, colleague

همكاري hamkārí *f.* 1 cooperation اقتصادي همكاري economic cooperation بين المللي همكاري international cooperation تخنيكي همكاري technical cooperation د چا سره همكاري كول to cooperate with someone 2 *military* joint action by air and by armored forces

هم كام hamk̲ā́m *m.* ☞ هم قام

همكلام، هم كلام hamkalā́m *m.* interlocutor

همكلاج hamkólaj *m.* fellow-villager; person from the same part of the country

همكور hamkór *m.* ☞ همخانه

همكيش hamkísh *m.* co-religionist

همګي hamagí all, everything

هم مذهب hammazháb *m.* co-religionist

هم مركز hammarkáz concentric

هم مسلک hammaslák *m.* colleague, fellow worker هم مسلكان سلاح comrade-in-arms

هم منظم hammunazám symmetrical

هم نام hamnā́m همنامی hamnā́maj 1 bearing the same name 2 *m.* namesake

همنژاد hamnizhā́d having the same descent, having the same origin

هم نشين hamnishín *m.* companion, associate; interlocutor

هم نشيني hamnishiní *f.* society, company

همنوا hamnavā́ 1 in keeping with, in consonance with, harmonious 2 appropriate 3 accompanying

همنوائي hamnavājí *f.* 1 accord, agreement; harmony 2 conformity 3 accompaniment, musical accompaniment 4 (complete) coincidence of points of view

همنوع hamnáu' *m.* 1 fellow clansman, member of the same extended family group 2 member of the same collective as another 3 man, person

همنوعي hamna'ví *f.* commonality د همنوعی احساس a feeling of commonality b humaness, humanity

همنومی hamnúmaj *m.* namesake; one have the same last name

هموار hamvā́r even, smooth ☞ هوار

همواركاري hamvārkārí *f.* levelling, evening out

همواري hamvārí *f.* 1 eveness, smoothness 2 plain

هم وزن hamvázin having the same weight, of equal weight

هم وطن hamvatán *m.* هم وطني hamvataní *m.* fellow-countryman

همه hamá all, every, each

همهغسي hamhághasi 1 *demonstrative pronoun* such a one, such a person or object 2 thus, in such a manner

همهغه، هم هغه hamhághá demonstrative *pronoun* that very one

همه ګير hamagír 1 all-encompassing, taking all in 2 aggressive

همه ګيري hamagirí *f.* width, breadth, wide range

همجاني hamjaní *f.* همياني hamjanój *f. Eastern* purse, pouch

همېش hamésh ☞ همېشه د همېش په شان as if forever

همېشه hameshá 1 always, constantly, eternally د همېشه دپاره eternally, forever; always, constantly د همېشه راسي for a long time, from time immemorial د همېشه نوم ګڼل to immortalize one's name زه همېشه د دي كار مخالف وم I always was against this 2 usual, wonted, eternal

همېشه توب hameshatób *m.* eternity د همېشه توب په ډول forever, for always

همېل hamél *m.* 1 necklace 2 garland د ګلو همېل ورباندي اينبودل to lay a wreath

هومره húmbra ☞ هنبره

هنت hanát *m.* slander, calumny

هنتر hanṭár *m. regional* stallion

هنج həndzh *m. plural* ☞ هنجه

هنجانه hindzhā́ṇa *f.* هنجه hə́ndzha *f.* híndzha *f.* asafoetida bush (a medicinal plant)

هنجی handzháj *m.* short breath هنجی وهل to breath heavily

هند[1] hind *m.* India د هند جمهوريت *history* the Indian Republic د هند اوقيانوس the Indian Ocean

هند[2] hand *m.* measure, size

هنداره hindāra *f.* 1 mirror 2 glass هنداره اينبودل to install glass

هندازيز hindāríz (mirror) smooth

هندچين hindichín *m.* Indochina

هندوستان hindustā́n *m.* ☞ هندوستان

هندسه handisá handasá *f.* 1 geometry تحليلي هندسه analytical geometry ترسيمي هندسه descriptive geometry 2 figure, number, numeral په هندسو in figures, in numbers

هندسي handisí handasí geometric هندسي تصاعد geometric progression هندسي شكلونه a geometric figures b geometric ornament

هندكو hindkó *f.* Hindi, the Hindu language

هندكي hindkí *m. plural* 1 Muslims of Indian descent (living among the Afghans); Indian women hindkáj 2 hindkáj *m.* Muslim of Indian descent

هندو hindú *m.* Hindu هندو د يار د پاره د غوا غوښني خوړلي دي *proverb* The Hindu ate beef for the sake of his friend.

هندواروپائي hinduurupā́i Indo-European (of the language group)

هندوانه hindvāná *f.* hinduvāná melon

هندوانه والا hindvānavālá *m.* hinduvānavālá seller of melons

هندوانۍ hindvāṇáj *f.* həndvāṇáj 1 Hindu woman 2 yellow-headed wagtail, *Motacilla citreola*

هندوبار hindubā́r *m.* place where Hindus congregate or live

هندوچين hinduchín *m.* Indochina

هندوستان hindustā́n *m.* Hindustan

هندوستاني hindustāní hindustānáj 1 Indian 2 *m.* .1 Indian *f.* 2.2 Hindi, the Hindi language

هندوكش hindukúsh *m.* هندوكوه hindukúh *m.* Hindu Kusk د هندوكش غر the Hindu Kush mountain

هندوگرت hindugrát *m.* customs and moral practices of the Indians (Hindus)

هندوه hindáva *f.* həndáva Indian woman

هندويزم hinduízm Hinduism

هنده[1] hínda *f.* mouthful, swallow هنده كول a to swallow, swallow down b to drink in swallows

هنده[2] hánda *f.* ☞ هنده[5]

هندي[1] hindí hindáj 1 Indian هندي كانگرس the Indian National Congress 2 the Hindi language

هندي[2] híndi *plural of* هنده[1]

هندي[3] hádi *plural of* هنده[2]

هندي نژاد hindinzhā́d of Indian descent هندي نژاد خلگ Indian immigrants

هندبال handbā́l *m. sports* handball

هندل handál *m.* crank (for starting a motor) هندل په لاس څرخول، هندل وهل to start the motor of an automobile with a crank

هنډه[1] hinḍə́ *m.* 1 bull, stud bull 2 stallion 3 *agriculture* sire, stud (animal)

هنډه[2] hunḍə́ *m.* wolf

هنډه[3] hə́nḍa *f.* hínḍa 1 opposition; resistance, stubbornness 2 liveliness; forcefulness 3 decisiveness

هنډه[4] hánḍa *f.* 1 member; part of the body 2 part, portion, piece هنډي هنډي كول to tear, tear in pieces *idiom* په كار كښې هنډه هنډه شوم I am very weary of work.

هنډه[5] hánḍa wish, desire; inclination هنډه كول to have a wish, have a desire

هنډى[1] hanḍaj *m.* bail; pack, load

هنډى[2] hunḍə́j *f.* promissary note, bill of exchange

هنډي[3] hə́nḍi hínḍi *plural of* هنډه[3]

هنډي[4] hánḍi *plural of* هنډه[4,5]

هنډيوال handḍajvāl *m.* هنډى وال handḍajvāl ☞ انډيوال

هنر hunár *m.* 1 art 2 expert skill or craftsmanship; talent 3 perfection 4 adroitness; ability, expertise, skill

هنرپيشه hunarpeshá ☞ هنرمن

هنرښودنه hunarḳhodə́na *f.* conceit

هنرمن hunarmán هنرمند hunarmánd 1.1 skilful; inventive 1.2 gifted, talented 1.3 adroit, dexterous 2 *m.* .1 artist; creative worker; (well-known) art personage 2.2 expert 2.3 performing artist

هنرمندي hunarmandí *f.* talents, gifts, artistic gifts

هنرور hunarvár ☞ هنرمن

هنري hunarí relating to art; artistic هنري مكتبونه trends (i.e., of a specific school) of art يو هنري هيئت a delegation of art personages هنري نبوغ، هنري لياقت talent (in art) د ادبي او هنري مجله a literary and art journal هنري نهضت the development of art

هنس hans *m.* 1 goose 2 swan

هنك hanák *m.* mockery

هنكهار hankahár *m.* ☞ هنگهار[1]

هنكى hinkáj *m.* ☞ هنگى

هنگ həng *m.* hing 1 bray (of a donkey) هنگ او ينگ braying of donkey 2 wailing, cring, braying

هنگا həngā́ *f.* ☞ هنگهار[1]

هنگار hangár *m.* hangar

هنگاره həngára *f.* ☞ هنگهار[2]

هنگاري hungārí *f.* ☞ هنگري

هنگاف hangāf́ *m.* cracks in the plastering of a wall

هنگافكاري hangāfkāŕí *f.* patching up or filling up cracks in the plaster of a wall

هنگام hangā́m *m.* time, moment په هنگام كښې in time, in timely fashion نوى هنگام شو the new times (seasons) are approaching

هنگامه hangāmá *f.* **1** crowd, assemblage **2** clamor (e.g., of battle) **3** disorder; chaos, disarray هنگامه سره شوه The disorder was kept within bounds. **4** conflict; struggle

هنگامه خیز ژوند hangāmakhéz troubled, anxious, alarmed هنگامه خیز ژوند a troubled life

هنگامي hangāmí troubled, alarmed, uneasy د هنگامي حالاتونه تېربدل to experience troubled times

هنگر hangár *m.* hangar

هنگري ژبه hungarí hangrí **1** *f.* Hungary **2** Hungarian Hungarian, the Hungarian language

هنگو hangú *m.* Hangu

هنگولا hangolá *f.* **1** howling (of a dog, jackal) **2** wailing, weeping, braying

هنگولل hangolól *transitive* [*past:* و يې هنگولل] **1** to howl (of a wolf, jackal) **2** to weep, wail; bray

هنگهار ¹ hanghár *m.* groaning, moaning (of a patient) هنگهار کول، هنگهار لرل to groan, moan

هنگهار ² hǝngahár *m.* loud cry; bray (of a donkey)

هنگی hingáj *m.* lamentation (of a bride)

هنگېدل hǝngedól *intransitive* [*past:* و هنگېده] **1** to bray (of a donkey) **2** to cry out, wail, howl

هنود hunúd *masculine plural of* هندي ¹

هنوز hanúz yet, hitherto, still

هنه hána *particle* well, yes; yes هنه ، یاد مي شو Yes, yes, I remember him.

هڼ hǝṇ *m.* **1** whinnying, neighing (of a horse) **2** roar, cry, bray (of an ass) **3** loud and unrestrained laughter

هڼهار hǝṇahár *m.* **1** neighing, whinnying (horse) **2** bray, cry (of an ass)

هڼهڼېدل hǝṇhǝṇedól *intransitive* [*past:* وهڼهڼېده] هڼېدل hǝṇdól *past:* [وهڼېده] **1** to neigh, whinny **2** to bray, cry out (of an ass) **3** to laugh loudly or unrestrainedly

هڼېدنه hǝṇedóna *f.* ☞ هڼ

هو ¹ hu *m. Arabic* monster, bogeyman

هو ² hu *abbreviation* هوالله

هو ³ ho **1** *particle* yes خوک پر هو راوستل to persuade, talk into **2** *interjection* **.1** listen; hey هو کول a to affirm, say yes to; assent, acknowledge b to call, cry out to **2.2** hurrah (martial cry during an attack)

هو ⁴ hav cry used to drive a cow

هوا ¹ havā́ *f. Arabic* **1** air; atmosphere د بحر هوا sea air آزاده هوا fresh air مصنوعي هوا conditioned air هوا نوي کول to ventilate (the premises) د زمکي هوا atmosphere, circumterrestrial space رابطه د هوا له لاري ورکړني ایستل aerial communication د کوټي هوا بدلول to air out the room په هوا کول to cause to take off, cause to rise in the air هوا ورکول to cause to evaporate; to volatilize (e.g., benzine) په هوا to ventilate د هوا بدلون، د هوا بدلېده to fly away, rise in the air **2** weather د هوا خرابي a change in the weather د هوا خرابه ده stormy weather

The weather is very bad today. هوا صافه وه The weather has cleared up. **3** [*plural:* havagā́ni] wind د پرهه سخته هوا چلېده A strong wind was blowing. د مازیگر هوا و چلېده Toward evening it became cooler. یخه یخه هوا ولگېده A very cold wind was blowing. هوا او را رسېدلي وه I caught a bad cold. **4** wish, desire د لیدلو هوا کول to want to see هوس a lust, base desire b vainglory ستاسي و مجلس ته مي دپره هوا کېږي I would like very much to sit with you. **5** conceit, arrogance *idiom* د هوا مرغان نالول to be very agile

هوا ² havā́ ☞ های ³ *interjection*

هواباز havābā́z *m.* aviator, flier

هوابازه havābā́za *f.* aviatrix, (female) flier بنځه هوابازه aviatrix, (female) flier

هوابازي havābāzí *f.* **1** aviation تاکتیکي هوابازي tactical aviation د هوابازی شرکت strategic aviation هوابازي ستراتېجیکي airline company د هوابازی میدان airdrome **2** flying business

هواپېژندل havāpezhandól *m.* هواپېژندنه havāpezhandóna *f.* meteorology د هوا پېژندلو ستېشن metrological station

هواپېژندونکی havā́ pezhandúnkaj *m.* meteorologist

هواپیمائي havāpajmaí *f.* aeronautics

هواخواه havākhā́h *m.* **1** adherent, supporter **2** well-wisher

هواخوري havākhurí *f.* walk, constitutional, exercise هواخوري کول to go for a walk, take a constitutional, to exercise

هېواد hivā́d *m.* ☞ هواد

هوادار havādā́r **1.1** spacious **1.2** (well) ventilated; airy هواداره کول to ventilate **2** *m.* **.1** boaster **2.2** one enamored **2.3** adherent, supporter **2.4** well-wisher

هواددوستي hivvādostí *f.* patriotism

هوادنی havādináj ☞ هېوادنی

هوار havā́r **1** even, flat, smooth **2** uniform, alike سا یې هواره ده His breathing is regular. **3** soft, gentle

هوارتوب havārtób *m.* هوارتیا havārtjā́ *f.* **1** evenness, smoothness **2** uniformity

هوارول havāravól *denominative, transitive* [*past:* هواریي کړ] **1** to even out, smoothen; make flat **2** to spread, spread out دسترخوان دلته هوار که Lay the tablecloth here. **3** *figurative* to decide, slove; settle (some matter)

هواره havā́ra **1** *feminine singular of* هوار **2** *f.* plain په هواره کښي The city is located on a plain. بنار پروت دئ

هواربدل havāredól *denominative, intransitive* [*past:* هوار شو] **1** to smooth out, become smooth, even **2** to be made (of a bed)

هواربده havāredó *m. plural* **1** evening out, smoothing out **2** making (beds)

هواشناسي havāshināsí *f.* meteorology

هواگیر havāgír striving, tending upwards; elevated, very high لوی هواگیر کمر a very high cliff *idiom* ځما زره هواگیر شو I took heart.

هوالله huvalláh *Arabic religion* He is Allah, His is God (a formula at the beginning of documents, books, letters)

هوانا havā́na *f.* Havana

هوانگهو huāngho *f.* Huang Ho (Yellow River, China)

هوانما havānumā́ f. weathervane

هوانورد havānavárd m. 1 flyer, aeronaut 2 astronaut

هوانوردي havānavardí f. aviation; aeronautics ملكي هوانوردي civil aviation د هوانوردي ښوونۍ flight school

هوايي [1] havāí Arabic adjective 1 air; aviation هوايي اډه a air base b airdrome; airport هوايي ترافيک، هوايي سرويسونه air traffic, air transportation هوايي عكس airline هوايي خط، هوايي لار، هوايي لين aerial photography هوايي حمله، هوايي يرغل aerial sortie هوايي قوا Air Force; aviation هوايي ملكي رياست Civil Air Fleet Administration 2 adjective flying هوايي پرسونل flight personnel هوايي ښوونۍ flight school 3 free (not captive or domesticated) هوايي کبدل، د سكرو په بخار هوايي مرغان wild birds 4 crazy هوايي کبدل to become crazy 5 futile, vain, useless, senseless, needless هوايي لوله trachea هوايي كيسه swim bladder

هوايي [2] havái ☞ د هوايي جزيرې هاوايي the Hawaiian Islands

هوبره hubará f. kind of crane (the bird)

هوبله hóbla f. means, way; resource بله هويله مي نه درلوده، نو تاسي ته راغلم I had no other resource, and so I came to you.

هو به هو hubahú Arabic precisely, exactly, just as هو به هو دی هم زما د ورور په شان دئ He and my brother are as alike as two drops of water.

هوبي hobí 1 inconstant 2 capricious

هوتک hoták 1 m. proper name Hotak 2 m. plural Hotaki (a Gilzaj tribe) 3 Hotak (tribesman)

هوتكي hotakí m. plural the Hotaki (a Gilzaj tribe) hotakáj m. plural Hotaki tribesman

هوټل hoṭál m. 1 hotel, guesthouse د هوټل خاوند hotel manager; hotel owner 2 restaurant د ووډي هوټل waiter د هوټل خادم dining room

هوټل والا hoṭalvālā́ m. 1 manager or owner of a hotel or guesthouse 2 owner or manager of a restaurant

هوټلي hoṭalí m. 1 waiter 2 hall-porter

هوټي hoṭí m. speedy camel

هود [1] hud m. proper name Hud

هود [2] haud m. ☞ حوض

هودج havdádzh m. howdah, elephant saddle ☞ هوده [2]

هودخيل hudkhél m. ☞ اودخيل

هوده [1] hudá f. 1 charm, incantation, spell هوده كول put a spell on; to drive out spirits د مارانو هوده يې زده ده He knew how to charm a snake. 2 job, post ☞ عهده

هوده [2] havdá f. howdah, elephant saddle

هوده دار hudadā́r m. snake charmer ☞ عهده دار

هوډ hoḍ m. obstinacy هوډ كول a to be obstinate, insist upon; be at variance with b to refuse or reject something هوډ لرل to be obstinate idiom خپل هوډ تر سره كول to get one's own way

هوډسن húḍsan د هوډسن آبناى Hudson's Bay

هوډه hóḍa f. 1 ☞ هوډ 2 firmness, stability په خپله هوډه ولاړ stubborn, obstinate; insisting on one's own way; displaying firmness

هوډى [1] hoḍáj m. 1 stubborn person, mulish man 2 ☞ هوډى [2]

هوډي [2] hoḍí 1 stubborn 2 willful, headstrong; self-willed

هور [1] hor m. dialect ☞ اور

هور [2] hor m. dialect nest

هور [3] hur m. attack, raid, sortie

هور [4] hor m. 1 deer 2 ☞ هوسى [1]

هورا [1] hurā́ far away له هورا from afar, from a distance

هورا [2] hurā́ interjection hurrah

هورتور hortór m. feverish haste د يو كار سره هورتور جوړول to be in an all-fire hurry

هورون hurón m. د هورون غدير Lake Huron

هوره [1] húra f. Houri

هوره [2] hóra f. fallow deer

هوري [1] huré there, thither, over there هوري کښېنه sit down there هوري کښېږده Place (it) over there.

هوري [2] húri hóri way over there هوري کښېنه Sit way over there!

هوري [3] húri plural of هوره [1]

هوري [4] hóri plural of هوره [2]

هوري [5] horáj f. ☞ اورى

هاپه هوړه húṛa f. ☞ هوړه

هوز havváz m. Arabic second group of letters in the abjad system which includes های هوز ز، و، ه the letter هي

هووړه húga f. garlic proverb چه هووړه ونه خوري، د خولې یې بوی نه ځي If you don't eat garlic, you will not smell of garlic.

هوړي [1] hugaj m. kind of wild plant

هوړي [2] húgi plural of هووړه

هوس [1] havás m. Arabic 1 pleasure, amusement 2 desire, wish صرف يو د زړه هوس دئ It is only a whim 3 passion, desire, lust; voluptuousness هوس كول a to have pleasure b to have desire c to lust after هوس پارول arousal of passion

هوس [2] hos Eastern ☞ اوس

هوسا hosā́ husā́ 1.1 calm, peaceful; quiet هوسا ژوند a a quiet life هوسا كول a to calm b to give rest, give peace ځان هوسا كبدل a to calm down b to rest 1.2 comfortable; cosy 2 calmly; quietly هوسا کښېنه Sit quietly.

هوساتوب hosātób m. هوساگلوي hosāgalví f. peace, quiet

هوس انگيز havasangéz alluring, seductive

هوساوالى hosāválaj m. ☞ هوساتوب

هوسايي hosājí f. هوسائي hosājéna f. 1 peace, rest د هوسايني چوكى easy chair د هوسايني ځاى resting place د هوسايي په حال in a tranquil situation 2 well-being, prosperity

هوس پالونكى havás pālúnkaj 1.1 lusting after, passionately desiring 1.2 ambitious 2 m. voluptuary

هوس پرستي havasparastí f. voluptuousness, sensuality, lustfulness

هوسټل hostál m. regional hostel, dormitory

هوسراني havasrāní f. voluptuousness

هوسناك havasnāk ☞ هوس پالونكى

هوسول havasavál [past: وى يې هوساوه] 1 to entice, allure 2 to evoke passion 3 to fill with ambitious thoughts

هوسى [1] hosáj m. kind of gazelle

هوسي ² havasí ☞ هوس پالونکی

هوسی ³ hosə́j *f.* [*plural:* هوسی گانی hosəjgā́ni *plural:* هوسیاني hosəjā́ni] 1 male gazelle 2 antelope

هوسېدل ¹ havasedə́l *intransitive* [*past:* وهوسېده] 1 to wish, desire, want, thirst for ... زړه يې ودي ته هوسېده چه He would like to ... 2 to lust after, strongly desire something 3 to dream about 4 to play with thoughts 5 to enjoy oneself, sport, gambol

هوسېدل ² hosedə́l *intransitive* ☞ اوسېدل

هوسېدنه havasedə́na *f.* هوسېده havadedə́ *m. plural* enjoyment, pleasure

هوسی سترگی hosə́j stə́rgaj gazelle-eyed

هوش hosh *m.* هوښ hukh *m.* هوخ hokh *m. plural* 1 consciousness; feeling 2 reason, mind, intellect, wits د عقل او هوښ خُبنتن in full possession of one's senses پر هوښ کول a to bring back to consciousness b to sober up (*literally and figuratively*) هوښ لرل to be intelligent د هوښنه وتل a to lose consciousness; be deprived of the senses b to lose the mind c to get drunk d to grow proud, grow conceited, grow arrogant 3 attention هوښ کول to be attentive, be careful in one's actions, be circumspect

هوښمن hukhmə́n هوښيار hukhjā́r hokhjā́r 1.1 intelligent; rational, intellectual, wise هوښمن بنده a knowledgeable or learned man; an experienced person 1.2 reasonable, sober, prudent 1.3 knowledgeable 2 *m.* wise man, sage

هوښيارتوب huḵhjartób *m.* هوښيارتيا huḵhjaratā́ *f.* ☞ هوښياري

هوښيارول huhjāravə́l *denominative, transitive* [*past:* هو ښيار يې کړ] 1 to cause to become intelligent or bright 2 to bring back to consciousness

هوښياري hukhjārí *f.* 1 mind, reason, intellect 2 rationality, sobriety; carefulness, circumspection هوښياري کول a to act intelligently, act rationally b to act carefully, act circumspectly

هوښياربدل hukhjāredə́l *denominative, intransitive* [*past:* هوښيار شو] 1 to be intelligent, be rational, be quick-witted 2 to be careful, be circumspect

هوغتله hughálta *dialect* away over there

هوغومره hughúra ☞ هغومره

هوغونه hughóna this much, so much

هوغه hugha hógh *demonstrative pronoun* this away over there, those away over there هوغه څه شي دئ What kind of a thing is this?

هوک huk 1 sunk, submerged, gone down هوک تلل to drown, submerge, go down هوک کول a to drown, scuttle; flood, overflow b to submerge, go down هوک کېدل to drown; be scuttled; be submerged, to go down 2 *figurative* stunned; disordered, upset

هوکايدو hokājdo *f.* د هوکايدو جزيره Hokkaido (Island)

هوکړه hókṛa *f.* 1 agreement; approval, acceptance هوکړه ويل to agree to, approve 2 promise هوکړه کول a to give agreement, consent b to give a promise, promise

هوکلی ¹ hoklə́j *m.* turnip

هوکلی ² hoklə́j *f.* wooden mortar

هوکه ¹ hávka fatigued, tired, exhausted; dead tired (from exhaustion) هوکه کول to exhaust, fatigue هوکه کېدل to grow tired, become fatigued

هوکه ² hoká *f.* ☞ هوکړه

هوکی ¹ hokə́j *m.* 1 agreement, approval د چا په هوکي ... hokí with the consent of someone هوکی اخیستل to get consent هوکی کول to give consent 2 promise 3 betrothal; agreement of the parents to give their daughter in marriage هوکی ورکول to consent to give one's daughter in marriage هوکی وړل to announce a betrothal راوړل to bring the news of the consent of the parents to give their daughter in marriage

هوکې ² hoké *particle & exclamation* yes; of course; all right زه هم پوهېږم Yes, I do know.

هوکی ³ havkáj tired, worn out

هوگه húga *f. Eastern* ☞ هوړه

هول ¹ haul *m. Arabic* horror, fear, terror په هول هول a hurriedly b timorously; cautiously هول کول to be scared, be afraid

هول ² hul *m.* 1 bolt, bar (of a door); catch, latch 2 bolt

هول ³ hul *m.* cry of a dervish asking a donation

هول اخیستونکی haul akhistúnkaj timid

هول اخیستئ haulakhistəj frightened

هولاندي holāndí holāndáj Dutch, Netherlandish

هولدر holdár *m.* 1 socket (lamp) 2 clamp, holder, adapter

هولکی haulakí 1.1 frightened, scared 1.2 alarmed; uneasy هولکي کول a to frighten b to alarm هولکي کېدل a to become frightened, become scared b to become alarmed, be alarmed 2 hurriedly, hastily

هولناک haulnā́k 1 terrible, menacing, dreadful, terrifying, injecting horror هولناک تاریخ a dreadful story, a terrible event 2 frightened, scared, terrified

هولناکي haulnākí *f.* 1 horror, terror 2 timorousness

هومره hómra húmra هومرې hómre so much; so, such, to such a degree

هوموس húmus *m. plural* humus

هومبره hómbra húmbra ☞ هومره

هونگه havánga *f.* mortar (for grinding)

هوڼا hoṇā́ *f.* 1 snare, trap noose (for trapping birds) 2 perch (over a trap or noose for trapping birds)

هووي havvé هووی hovój *interjection* oh, oh, oh; what are you doing

هوهو huhú hohó ☞ های هوی

هوی ¹ huj *m. plural* coal

هوی ² huj *interjection* ouch; ow

هوی ³ hoj *figurative* هوی هوی هوی a traditional cry with which a storyteller punctuates his sung-verse storytelling

هوی ⁴ javə́j *f.* potter's kiln

هویت huviját *m. Arabic* 1 essence, crux 2 identity 3 establishment of identity; identification 4 personality, personal identification د هویت ورقه I.D. papers; personal identification paper, card or document

هویدا huvajdǻ **1** clear, obvious **2** open, apparent **3** proven, indisputable هویدا کول **a** to bring out, make known, elucidate, clear up, explain **b** to prove; make indisputable

هویه ¹ hója *f. dialect* ☞ هګی

هویه ² hója *dialect* ☞ هوغه

هه ha **1** ☞ هوکي ² **2** indeed, really هه دا وڅنه! Come on, drink this up! **3** not on your life; don't even think about it

هی ¹ haj *interjection* too bad; alas هی کول to regret, deplore

هی ² haj **a** هی کول to whip up, drive (a horse) **b** to drive (an automobile) موټر هی که! Step on the gas! Get going!

هی ³ he *f.* [*plural:* هبګاني hegáni] the name of the letter ه

هی ⁴ he *pronoun oblique of* هغه ¹,² د هي خوا from there, from that side or direction

هی ⁵ he *interjection* yes, yes, I hear hear you

هیات hajǻt *m. Arabic* ☞ هیئت

هیبت hajbát *m.* **1** panic, terror, awe هیبت اخیستل، هیبت کول to be frightened چه زه یې ولیدم، نو هیبت واخیست When he saw me, he got scared. **2** sloppy, dirty د مرګ هیبت خورل to be frightened to death هیبت لرل to be afraid, be timorous

هیبتناک hajbatnák terrible, menacing, dreadful, awful

هیپ هی hiphé cry used to drive camels

هیتوبه hajtaubá hajtobá د یو کار څخه هی توبه کول to deny, disclaim; to disavow

هیتي hajití *f.* Haiti

هټ heṭ *m. regional* cap, hat

هټان heṭán *m. plural history* Hittites

هټ پسری heṭpǝsáraj *regional* in a hat, wearing a hat

هیټر hiṭár *m. regional* **1** heating device برقي هیټر electric reflector-heater **2** boiler; kettle (for boiling water)

هیجان hajadzhǻn *m. Arabic* [*plural:* هیجانونه hajadzhānúna *Arabic plural:* هیجانات hajadzhānǻt] **1** disturbance; excitement د هیجاناتو هیجان کول to be greatly distrubed پر هیجان راتلل، په طوفان کښي distrubed پر هیجان راوستل to become distrubed هیجان میندل distrub; to excite **2** wrath, outburst of anger

هیجان راوستونکی hajadzhǻn ravustunkaj disturbing (of a sight)

هیجاني hajadzhāní **1** disturbed; excited **2** disturbing (of an event)

هیجړا hidzṛhǻ *m.* eunuch; castrated male

هیڅ hech *pronoun* ☞ هیڅ

هیڅا hechǻ *oblique of* هیڅوک

هیچری hecháre *obsolete* ☞ هیچري

هچارته hachárta *Eastern* **1** nowhere هغه کتاب مي ډیر ولټاوه مګر هبچرته مي بیا نه موند I looked for the book for a long time, but even so I never found it. **2** nowhere, to nowhere

هیچري hicháre *Eastern* **1** nowhere **2** nowhere, to nowhere **3** never

هیچري héchéri hichiri ☞ هبچرته

هڅګي hedzgí *f.* ☞ هبجګي

هیڅ hita hets *negative pronoun* **1** nothing دی هیڅ نه وایي He doesn't say anything هیڅ نشته There is nothing. هیڅ و نه شو Nothing came of it. It was to no purpose. نور مي هیڅ را نه نیول I didn't buy

anything more. **2** دا په هیڅ شمبرل کبږي This has no value. *attributive* no په هیڅ ډول by no means, in no way هیڅ پروا نشته! It's no misfortune! هیڅ شک نشته چه ... It's beyond doubt that ... له هیڅ خبري څخه هیڅ نه ویرپریم These are trifles. دا هیڅ خبره نه ده I fear nothing. په هیڅ ځای کښني nowhere *idiom* هیڅ وخت never هیڅ په no purpose, for nothing, without any reason

هیڅوک hitstsók *vice*

هیڅ کله hitskála hétskala never زه به هیڅکله دا کار ونه کم I will never do this.

هیڅکي hítske hítske *interjection* kitchy-kitchy-koo (or similar said to make a baby laugh)

هیڅوک hitsók hetsók *negative pronoun oblique* هیچا hichǻ nobody; no one هیڅوک مي و نه لیدل I didn't see anyone. په دي ماڼۍ کښني هیڅوک نه اوسیدل No one lived in this building.

هیڅ یو hits jav *negative pronoun* not a one, no, none

هیداد hidád *m.* **1** penalty; punishment **2** abuse هیداد ورکول **a** to inflict punishment, punish **b** to abuse, curse at someone

هیدروژن hidrozhén *m. singular & plural* ☞ هایدروجن

هیدروژني hidrozhení ☞ هایدروجني

هیدرولوژي hidrolozhí hydrology

هیدرولیک hidravlík hydraulic

هایدروجن hajḍrodzhán *m. singular & plural* hydrogen

هایدروجني hajḍrodzhaní *adjective* hydrogen, hydrogenous

هبډکوارټر heḍkvǻrṭar *m. regional* **1** headquaters **2** board of directors, governing body (of a society)

هبر ¹ her forgotten, forgotten about هبر سبق forgotten lesson نوم یی هبر دئ I forgot his name. هبربدل، هبر کبدل هبرول ☞ را نه هبر دئ

هبر ² hir *m.* kind of stick game

هیرا hirǻ *f. regional* diamond

هبرتوب hertób *m.* هبرتیا hertjǻ *f.* **1** forgetfulness; absentmindedness **2** oblivion

هبرجن herdzhán *m.* forgetful person, absentminded person

هبرړی ¹ hirṛáj *m.* ☞ هبړی

هبرمن hermán *m.* ☞ هبرجن

هیرمند hirmánd *m.* Hilmend (River)

هبرندوکی herandúkaj very forgetful, very absentminded

هبرو heró *m.* [*plural:* هبروګان herogǻn *f. plural:* هبروګاني herogǻni] **1** hero; heroine **2** outstanding person

هبروالی hervǻlaj *m.* **1** forgetfulness; absentmindedness **2** oblivion

هیروشما hiroshimǻ *f.* Hiroshima

هبرول heravál *denominative, transitive* [*past:* هبر یې کړ] **1** to forget دا هبروم چه ... Let's forget about this! راځۍ چه دا هبره کړو! I forgot about ... څه دي هبر کړل؟ What did you forget? **2** to consign to oblivion **3** to not notice; overlook **4** to make forget

هبروونه hevavéna *f.* ☞ هبروالی

هبره ¹ héra *f. singular of* هبر **2.1** oblivion **2.2** forgetfulness; absentmindedness په هبره through forgetfulness, through absentmindedness

هبري ² héri *plural of* هبره ¹

هیري hiré *f. plural dialect* ashes

هېري herí *f.* request for forgiveness هېري کول to request forgiveness

هېري ⁴ hirə́j *m. plural* talk, chatter هېري وهل to talk nonsense, talk rubbish

هېرېدل heredə́l *denominative, intransitive* [*past:* هېر شو] to be forgotten دا خبره مي لا هېره نه شي چه ... How could I have forgotten that ... دا خبري چه هر څه وي خو تېري شوي او هېري شوي All is past and forgotten. نه مي هېرېږي چه ... !زما هېر سوه I forgot! I am not forgetting that ...

هېرېدنه heredə́na *f.* هېرېده heredə́ *m. plural* forgetting

هېر ¹ her *m. no plural form* 1 time 2 one time, once یو هېر once بل هېر a another time b again

هېر ² her *m. plural* floating timber

هېر ³ her *m. dialect* ☞ ایر

هېرمند hiṛmánd *m.* Hilmend (River)

هېړه herá́ *f.* ☞ هېړی ¹

هېړی ¹ heṛáj *m.* long-tailed ram

هېړی ² heṛə́j *f.* long-tailed sheep

هيز hiz *m.* ☞ هجړی

هېزگي hezgí *f.* هجگي کول to read a syllable at a time

هېزم hezám *m.* fuel; firewood

هېزم کش hezamkásh *m.* woodcutter

هیگ hig *m. dialect* bear ☞ یر

هېگه híga *f.* 1 *dialect* she-bear ☞ یره ¹ 2 *medicine* bubo

هیس his *interjection* ☞ هیس هیس

هیسته hísta 1 a bit further; to the side; back; away را هیسته to us, to me; to this side, in our direction; in your direction; in your direction; over here در هیسته to you; in your direction ور هیسته to them, to him, to her; in your direction; this way, over there هیسته کول a to move away b to pull aside, move to one side c د ... څخه to remove from something d to remove, take away, take off e to push, push away, repluse هیسته کېدل a to clear off, go away b to pull away c د ... څخه هیسته کېدل to fire, dismiss d to move off, move away from, withdraw e to push off from, be reflected 2 after د دغه په هیسته باره کور ته هم نه ورتلئ After this he did not go home. 3 forward, ahead

هیسکارل hiskārə́l *transitive* [*past:* و یې هیسکاره] to call (a cow, buffalo)

هیس هیس his-his call to summon a cow or buffalo

هیسي híse hísi ☞ هیسته

هبش ¹ hesh *m.* boiling په هبش راتلل to boil up, begin to boil

هبش ² hesh *m.* Hesh (steppe or dry plain in Badakhshan)

هبشمه heshmá *f. Western* ☞ هبنمه

هبشول heshavə́l *transitive* ☞ ایشول

هی شه hájsha *interjection* alas; too bad

هبشېدل heshedə́l *intransitive* ☞ ایشېدل

هبنب heḵh 1 amazed, surprised, startled, perplexed هبنب کول to amaze, surprise, startle هبنب کېدل to be amazed, be surprised, be startled 2 with steady gaze; with wide-open eyes

هبنب پبنب heḵh-peḵh profoundly surprised, amazed, stupefied هبنب پبنب تلل to be amazed, be stupified

هبنبتوب heḵhtób *m.* هبنبتیا heḵhtjá́ *f.* ☞ هبنبوالی

هبنمه héḵhma *f.* ☞ هبنمه

هبنبوالی heḵhválaj *m.* surprise, amazement, perplexity

هبنبه héḵha *f.* 1 *singular of* هبنب 2 surprise, amazement, perplexity

هیضه hajzá́ *f. Arabic* cholera ویائي هیضه cholera

هبغ hegh hard, tough; strong

هبغ پبغ hegh-pegh very tough, very hard; very strong

هبغ نبغ hegh-negh 1 erect هبغ نبغ کول to be upright, be erect هبغ نبغ کېدل to stick or stand up on end 2 rigidly twisted; motionless

هبغ والی heghválaj *m.* 1 toughness; hardness; strength 2 immobility; state of being in a rigid or twisted position

هیکل hajkál *m. Arabic* ☞ هیکل

هیکارل hajkārə́l *transitive* [*past:* و یې هیکاره] to set on, sic (e.g., a dog)

هیکل hajkál *m.* 1 statue, sculpture 2 flat figurines of people or animals (worn as neck ornaments)

هیکل تراش hajkaltarásh *m.* sculptor, image-maker

هیکل تراشي hajkaltarāshí *f.* sculpture, sculpting

هل hel *m. plural* cardamom

هیلندوکی hiləndúkaj hoping, experiencing hope, trust

هلو heló *interjection* hello

هیله ¹ híla *f.* 1 hope, trust; wish, desire له هیلو ډکي سترگي a look full of hope هیله کول to hope, trust هیله لرل to hope, trust, trust in هیله لرو چه ... We hope that ... هیله ده چه ... There is the hope that ... دوی د کامیابی هیله کوي They hope for success. نور د هیلی مخ It is no use hoping any longer. تور دئ 2 expectation; prospects

هیله ² hilá́ *f.* ☞ حیله ¹

هیله بیله híla-bíla 1 in vain, for naught, to no purpose 2 only just, so much

هیله لرونکی híla larúnkaj nursing a hope or trust (in)

هیلی ¹ hiljə́j *f.* هلهـج heljə́j duck (the bird) پرانگه هیلی pochard توره هیلی narrow-billed teal, white teal

هیلي ² híli *plural of* هیله ¹

هیلي ³ hilé *plural of* هیله ²

هپلیکوپتر helicoptér *m.* helicopter

هپلیوم helijúm *m.* helium

هموگلوبین hemoglobín *m.* hemoglobin

هی ناتار hajnātár *m.* confusion, rumpus هی ناتار جوړ سو a rumpus arose

هینډکی hinḍkáj *m.* ☞ هندکي

هینډه hínḍa *f.* 1 enmity; quarrel, conflict 2 opposition 3 contradiction

هنگ hing *m.* heng 1 groan, sigh 2 bray (of an ass) ☞ هنگ

هنگه hingá́ *f.* ☞ اینگه

هنگهار hengahár *m.* groaning, moans هنگهار کول، هنگهار لرل to moan, groan

هینگی hingáj ☞ هنگی

هین hiṇ *m.* strength, force, power

هینی hiṇáj strong, powerful

هیواد hivắd *m.* هېواد hevắd **1** country, native land په خپل هېواد کښي in one's country, in one's native land مورنی هېواد native country, native land **2** government **3** country, region, clime

هیوادنی hivādináj hevādináj pertaining to the country or the fatherland; native, internal هیوادني خبرونه hivādiní domestic news items; communications about the country

هیوادوال hivādvál *m.* **1** inhabitant of the country **2** fellow-countryman

هیولا hajulā́ *f. Arabic* **1** *philosophy* material, substance **2** monster

هیولائی hajulā́i *Arabic philosophy* material, substantial

هیومس hjúmus *m.* humus

هیون hajún *m.* **1** horse **2** pack-camel **3** freak

هیونه hajúna *feminine of* هیون

هیهات hajhā́t **1** *interjection* alas; woe; too bad **2** mourning for, grieving

هیهی، هی هی hajháj *m.* **1** noisy disorder **2** *interjection* ah; woe; too bad

هیئت haj'át *m.* **1** delegation; commission; organ اجرائي هیئت execeutive organ مختلطه هیئت legislative organ مقننه هیئت combined commission **2** team, crew اطفائیه هیئت firefighting crew **3** apparatus, instrument, system collegium personnel د وزیرانو هیئت ministerial cabinet عسکري عالي هیئت higher military council رئیسه هیئت haj'at-i presidium مدیره هیئت administration, governing body (e.g., of a bank) **4** part; sub-assembly; set د نلو عمومي هیئت a full set of pipes **5** way, manner, form **6** astronomy

هیئت پېژندونکی haj'át pezhandúnkaj *m.* astronomer

ی

ی [1] jā je **1** the fortieth letter of the Pashto alphabet (it is pronounced as the vowel phoneme "y" (in this system "j") before and after other vowels; it also represents the vowel phonemes "i" and "e") ☞ یا [1] **2** the number 10 in the abjad system

ی [2] aj áj *m. noun, adjective and participial suffix* سړی man دوبی summer نری thin نوی new کابلی **a** of Kabul **b** resident of Kabul

ی [3] í *suffix for actor or agent of an action* دوبی laundryman

ی [4] í *f. suffix used for derivative nouns and those denoting professions* دوستي friendship

ی [5] í i *m.* **1** *plural and oblique singular of nouns with the suffix* ی سړی **2** people سړي ویل the man said **2** *nominative plural and feminine and oblique singular of nouns, adjectives, and participles with the suffix* ی [2] *for example:* نوی new (plural adjective); of the new …; concerning the new …, etc.

ی [6] əj *f. noun & adjective suffix* چوکی chair نری thin

ی [7] í *m. suffix for nouns and adjectives formed from the names of countries* چیني Chinese, a Chinese

ی [8] i *Western feminine plural and oblique singular ending for nouns and adjectives in unstressed "a"* سترگي of an eye; eyes

ی [9] é *feminine plural and oblique singular ending for nouns and adjectives in stressed "a"* تختي of a board; boards

ی [10] i í *third person singular and plural personal verb ending in present tense* خي he goes, they go کوي he does, they do

ئ [11] əj aj **1** *second person plural personal verb ending* **1.1** *present and imperative Eastern* تاسي کوئ *Western* تاسي کوی you do, you make **1.2** *present and imperfect Eastern* تاسي تلی *Western* تاسي you were going *Eastern* تاسي وایئ *Western* تاسي وایی you say *Eastern* تلئ **2** *Western personal verb ending, third person singular* زما کتاب چا یووړئ؟ Who took my book?

ی [12] e **1** *personal verb ending, second person singular* ته خي you (singular) go **2** *personal verb ending, third person feminine plural, past tense* دوی چېري وي؟ Where were they (women)?

یا [1] jā *f.* [*plural:* یاگاني jāgā́ni] **1** the name of the letter ی **2** *various forms of the letter* ی *or the various sounds thereof* یای یای مجهول، مجهوله یا the phoneme "e" e.g., تپر past تختی boards یای معروف، معروفه یا the phoneme "i" خي they go; he goes **2.3** تانیثي یای تانیثیه یا the dipthong **2.4** "ه" یای ملین ،ملینه یا the dipthong "aj"

یا [2] jā *disjunctive conjunction* or; either or یا ... یا either … or دا واخله یا هغه واخله Take either this or that.

یا [3] jā *Arabic interjection* hey; ho یا خدایه! Oh, God!

یا [4] jā *dialect* no *vice* یه

یاب jā́b *combining form* receiving, obtaining شرف یاب receiving honors

یابو jābú [*plural:* یابوان jabuā́n *plural:* یابوگان jābugā́n] **1** pony **2** pack horse

یاجوج jādzhúdzh *m. mythology* Gog یاجوج ماجوج Gog and Magog

یاد jād *m.* **1** memory, recollection له خپله یاده ایستل، له خپله یاده وېستل to forget, expunge, put out of memory له یاده وتل to be forgotten دا مو دي په یاد وي We have to remember په یاد راوستل کېدل to remember په یاد ورکول to memorize, learn by heart ور په یاد کېدل، را په یاد کېدل، در په یاد کېدل to recall, recall to mind یاد لرل، په یاد لرل to remember, recollect دا یاد لرل پکار دي چه … One must remember that … په یاد راتلل، له یاده کول to learn by heart **2.1** *predicative* kept in memory **2.2** studied هغه زما خبره دي باید یاده da baid jāda Will you remember what I said to you? وساتل شي چه … One should remember that …

یاد ته نبغ رسی jād tə negh rasáj *computer science* direct memory access

یادداشت jāddā́sht *m.* **1** note, instruction; memo for the record یادداشت کول *compound verb* to note, make a note **2** *diplomacy* note verbale **3** memoir **4** memorandum

یاددهی jāddihí *f.* یادښت jādə́kht *m.* reminder

یادگار jādgár *m.* **1** memorial یادگارونه تاریخي historical memorials **2** memory, recollection **3** souvenir **4** *proper name* Yadgar

یادگیرنه jādgerəna *f.* memory د یاد گیرني ورځ Memorial Day د آزادی د حصول د یاد گیرني ورځ Independence Day

یادلرنه jādlarəna *f.* ☞ یادداشت

یادوبود jādubúd *m.* **1** honoring someone د چا په یادوبود کښي شعر ویل to compose verses in someone's honor **2** (prayer of) remembrance of the dead د چا یادوبود کول to remember someone (in prayer)

یادول jādavəl *denominative, transitive* [*past:* یاد يې کړ] **1.1** to remember, recall زه هغه ملگری یادوم I to recall youth ځلمیتوب یادول have that comrade in mind. دا می صرف د مثال پذول در یاد کړه I suggested this to you only as an example. **1.2** to mention, remind of هغه دا پخوانی پیښني بیا را یادول to recall past events **1.3** to quote کتاب ډېر ځله یادوي He often quotes this book. **1.4** to memorize, learn by heart; master by studying **1.5** to remember in prayer (the dead) **1.6** to name, call په نوم یادول to call by name څوک په بدی سره یادول to curse someone **2** *m. plural* **.1** memoir, recollection **2.2** mention, reminder **2.3** quotation **2.4** memorizing, learning by heart, learning by rote, mastering **2.5** remembering in prayer (the dead)

یادون jādún *m.* ☞ یادول 2

یادونه jādavəna *f.* **1** ☞ یادول 2 **2** note, footnote

یادووني jādavúnaj memorizing; learning by rote

یاده jā́da *oblique singular of* یاد 1

یاده jā́da *f. singular of* یاد 2

یادي jā́di *f. plural of* یاد 2

یادی jādáj *m. obsolete* ☞ یادول 2

یادېدل jādedəl *denominative, intransitive* [*past:* یاد شو] **1** to recall, remember **2** to be remembered; be reminded of **3** to be learned by rote, be learned by heart **4** to be quoted **5** to be named, called په ... سره یادېدل to be named, called **6** to be considered, be counted as, be called **7** to pass for هغه د نېک خوی خاوند یادېده He passes for a man of good character. **8** to be remembered (in prayer ... of the dead)

یادېدنه jādedəna *f.* یادېده jādeda *m.* **1** recollection, memoir **2** mention, reference **3** rote learning, learning by heart **4** quoting **5** remembrance (in prayer, of the dead)

یادېده jādedə́ *imperfect of* یادېدل

یار jār *m.* **1** friend **2** bodyguard (of a prince etc.) **3** assistant, helper **4** lover **5** [*plural:* یاران jārán] **a** friends **b** assistants, helpers **c** bodyguards (of a prince, etc.) څلور یاران *history* first four caliphs (successors of Mohammed) **6** *proper name* Yar *idiom* یار تر کوڅه تبر که، رنگ يي هېر که With heart and eyes cast down.

یارانه jārāna **1** friendly, amicable **2** as a friend, in a friendly manner **3** *f.* **.1** friendship **3.2** love

یاراني jārāní *f.* **1** friendship **2** love یو د بله یاراني شوه They became friends. They grew to love one another.

یارباز jārbáz **1** dissolute **2** *m.* philanderer, lady-killer

یاربازه jārbáza *feminine of* یار باز، ښځه یار بازه **a** flirt **b** dissolute woman

یاربازي jārbāzí *f.* **1** profligacy, dissipation **2** coquettishness, flirtatiousness

یارد jārd *m.* yard (measure of length)

یاردل jārdíl *m. proper name* Yardil

یارډ jārḍ *m.* yard (measure of length)

یارکند jārkánd *m.* Yarkand (river, city)

یارکی jārkáj *m.* little friend, buddy

یارمخچی jārmakhchə́j *f.* short-toed lark

یارو jāró *m. affectionate* 6 یار

یاره jā́ra *f.* **1** woman-friend **2** loved one (a woman) **3** lover (women)

یاره jā́ra *vocative & oblique singular of* یار

یاري jārí *f.* **1** friendship **2** love **3** help, assistance یاري کول **a** to be friend **b** to love **c** to help

یاري jā́ri *plural of* یاره 1

یاری jāráj *m. affectionate* 5 یار

یاري jā́re *m.* old pal (as a familiar form of address)

یاس jās *m. Arabic* **1** despair, sorrow, grief **2** boredom, tedium; **3** sadness

یاس jās *m. plural* lilac

یاست jāst *copula verb, second person plural Western* څوک یاست؟ Who are you?

یاسته jāstə́ *m. plural* **1** drawing out, extraction **2** *imperfect plural of* یستل

یاسته jā́sta *f. dialect* ☞ بیاسته

یاسمن jāsmán *m.* یاسمین jāsmín *m.* یاسمین jāsamín *m. plural* jasmine

یاغي jāghí *m.* rebel, mutineer; insurgent یاغي کول to instigate a rebellion, institute a mutiny د چا نه یاغي کېدل to rise up or rebel against someone

یاغيتوب jāghitób *m.* ☞ یاغي والی، یاغيتوب

یاغیدان jāghedā́n *m.* recurrence of smallpox

یاغیستان jāghistā́n *m. regional* region of independent tribes

یاغیگري jāghigarí *f.* ☞ یاغي والی یاغيگري کول to rebel, start a mutiny

یاغیگر jāghigáṛ *m. regional* **1** ☞ یاغیستان **2** mutineer's country, rebel country

یاغي والی jāghivā́laj *m.* mutiny, rebellion, insurrection, insurgency

یافت jāft *m.* income, cash-flow

یافته jāftá *combining form* receiving, getting تعلیم یافته educated (male)

یاقوت jāḳút *m. Arabic plural* **1** ruby **2** *personal name* Yakut

یاقوتي jāḳutí *adjective* ruby

یال jāl *m.* **1** neck; withers (of a horse) **2** mane

یالتا jāltā́ *f.* Yalta

یالی jāláj *suffix for adjectives formed from nouns* جنگیالی belligerent بریالی victorious

یامه jāmə́ *oblique singular of* یوم

یامېدل jāmedə́l *intransitive dialect* [*past:* و یامېد] to dance

یاندي jā̃ndi *colloquial* ☞ یعني

یانگیکیانگ jāngikjā̃ng *m.* Yangtze (River, China)

یانه jā̃nə́ *plural & oblique singular of* یون

یاور jāvár *m.* 1 assistant 2 *military* adjutant سر یاور aide-de-camp

یاوره¹ jāvára *feminine of* یاور¹

یاوره² jāvára *f.* big-bellied mare

یاوري jāvarí *f.* 1 help, cooperation 2 job or position of an aide-de-camp

یاوندي jāúndé *m.* Yuande

یاوه jāvá 1.1 vain, absurd; futile 1.2 hopeless, good-for-nothing 2 *f.* rubbish

یاوه گوی jāvgój *m.* windbag, idle talker

یاهو¹ jāhú *m. Arabic* 1 *proper name* Jehovah 2 *interjection* oh, God یاهو ویل to call upon God

یاهو² jāhú *m.* kind of owl

یایل jājə́l *transitive dialect* ☞ ویل

یبره jə́bra *adjective* yearling (of a ram)

یبل jábə́l barefooted یبل پښه on the barefoot, on the bare feet

یبله jábla *f. singular of* یبلي

یبلي jabə́li *f. plural of* یبل a bare feet b barefoot

یپلا japlā̃ *colloquial vice* ☞ یو پلا

یتیم jatim *m. Arabic* orphan (fatherless) *idiom* د یتیم د سره نه چیپیري Everyone gives him a hard time.

یتیم توب jatimbób *m.* orphanhood, orphan's lot ستا تر یتیم تابه اوبنکی تویوي One grieves for your orphaned state.

یتیم خانه jatimkhāná *f.* orphanage, institution for orphans

یتیمه jatíma *feminine of* یتیم

یج jadzh rude, cruel, rough

یجه jə́dzha *f. Pinus excelsa* (a kind of pine tree)

یځ ídz یځی ídzaj *suffix* ☞ یز

یخه jatsá *f.* leavings, leftovers

یحیی jahjā̃ *m. Arabic proper name* Yahya

یخ jakh *m. Arabic* 1.1 cold, frost یخ می کېږي I am cold. I am freezing. دا یخ مات شو She has caught cold. وه It has grown a bit warmer. 1.2 ice د یخ جلګه ice field یخ بدونکی ینو ice floe سیندونو یخ ونیو The rivers were covered with ice. The rivers froze over. یخ وېلی کېږي The ice is melting. 2 *attributive* 1. cold, icey, bitter cold یخ یخ بادونه تلل راتلل Cold winds blew all the while. 2.2 cool یخه سیوری cool shade هوا اوس یخه لګېده It became cool. It cooled off. 3 *figurative* calm; satisfied, cool

یخاو jakā́v *m.* cool, coolness په هوا کښې یخاو پیدا شوی وه *Eastern* It has grown cool.

یخبندي jakhbandí *f.* 1 frosts; light frosts 2 freezing of water

یخچال jakhchā́l *m.* د یخچال دوره glacial period

یخچالی jakhchālí 1 glacial 2 *geology* morainal

یخدان¹ jakhdā́n *m.* large trunk bound with iron

یخدان² jakhā́n *m.* یخ زار jakhzā́r *m.* glacier

یخزنی jakhzə́naj 1.1 freezing, stiff with cold; shriveled with cold 1.2 nipped by frost 2 *m.* person afraid of the cold

یخ سوز jakhsóz ☞ یخ زنی

یخمالک jakhmālák *m.* ice-skating

یخني jakhní *f.* 1 cold, frost ورځ په ورځ یخني کېږي With each day it grows colder. یخني مېندل to congeal (of a liquid) پرون ډېره یخني وه Yesterday it was very cold. 2 gravy; sauce (in the form of a liquid condiment for pilaf or stew)

یخوالی jakhvā́laj *m.* د شپو یخوالی cold nocturnal chill

یخول jakhavə́l *denominative, transitive* [*past:* یخ یې کړ] 1 to cool, chill اوبه یخول to chill water 2 to calm, satisfy

یخونه jakhavə́na *f.* cooling

یخه jákha *f. singular of* یخ 2 یخه موچنه golden slippers

یخی¹ jakháj *m.* 1 cold, frost 2 ice دیخي غر jakhí iceberg نیول to be covered with ice, freeze

یخی² jákhi *f. plural of* یخ 2

یخېدل jakhedə́l *denominative, transitive* [*past:* یخ شو] 1 to chill, cool down 2 to freeze, be covered with ice 3 to freeze, be frozen لاس یې یخ سوې دئ His hand froze. His hand was frozen. 4 to be calmed, be satisfied

یخېدنه jakhedə́na *f.* یخېدو jakhedə́ *m. plural* 1 chilling, cooling 2 freezing, covering with ice 3 freezing, frostbite 4 calming, satisfaction

یخی والی jakhajvā́laj *m.* ☞ یخوالی

یدغه jidghá *f.* Idga (a Pamir language)

یدک jadák *m.* spare horse; reserve horse on a lead

یدکبان jadkhbā́n *m.* یدکچي jadakhchí *military* horse-holder (man)

یر jer *m.* ambler (horse)

یربه jarbá *f.* slope, incline, declivity

یرړی jarṛáj *m.* ☞ هېری¹

یرز jarz *m.* 1 worthiness 2 fitness یرز لرل a to be worthy b to be fit

یرزن jarzə́n 1 worthy 2 fit, suitable

یرزه jarzá *f.* price, cost

یرغز jarghúz *m.* jarghā́z ☞ یلغز

یرغکی jarghəkáj *m.* falcon

یرغل jarghál *m.* attack, foray, offensive هوایي یرغل air attack متقابل یرغل counteroffensive, counterattack یرغل کول، مخامخ یرغل to attack, make a foray پر چا یرغل وروړل to attack someone

یرغل jarghál *m.* kavúnkaj 1 conqueror; agressor 2 raider

یرغلگر jarghalgár 1 attacking 2 *m.* ☞ یرغل کوونکی

یرغلگري jarghalgarí *f.* 1 attack, agression 2 foray د یرغلگری یون raid

یرغمال jarghamā́l *m.* یرغمل jarghamál *m.* hostage

یرغه jə́rghá *f.* jurghá 1 to amble په یرغه تلل to go at an amble 2 *m.* ambler (horse)

یرغی¹ jarghə́j *f.* lampblack, soot

یرغی² jarghé *plural of* یرغه

یرق jarák *m.* harness, gear

یرقان jarkā́n *m. Arabic* jaundice

يرمن jirmán يرند jərónd يرندوکی jərəndúkaj **1** cowardly, shy, timid **2** frightened, scared

يرول jiravól *transitive dialect* ☞ وبرول

يره[1] járá *f. dialect* terror, fear

يره[2] jará *interjection* uh-huh; right, indeed

يره[3] jíra *f. dialect* ashes

يره[4] jará *dialect* old pal (as a form of familiar address)

يربدل jiredól *intransitive dialect* ☞ وبربدل

يړ jaṛ *m.* ☞ يرغل

يړی jiṛáj ☞ هپری[1]

يز íz éz *suffix for adjectives & nouns* غوږ ور دوه پتميز big-eared ور recurrent fever واريزه تبه one-anna coin انيز folding door

يزد jazd *m.* يزدان jazdán *m.* God, Lord

يزداني jazdāní divine

يزيد[1] jazíd *m. Arabic* **1** *proper name* Yazid **2.1** wicked, cruel **2.2** damned

يژه jəzhá *f.* root of the pine *Pinus excelsa* (from which pitch is obtained)

يژئ jázhe *f.* wood of the pine *Pinus excelsa*

يږ jəg *m.* bear تور يږ the Himalayan black bear سپين يږ the white bear خو چه يږ مړ نه کړي، پوست يې مه خرڅوه *proverb literal* Don't sell the bear's skin before you kill him. *figurative* Don't count your chickens before they hatch.

يږه[1] jəga *f.* **1** she-bear **2** *medicine* bubo

يږه[2] jagá *f. medicine* cancer

يس jəs ☞ هيس هيس

يستل[1] jastól *f. transitive dialect* ☞ ايستل

يستنه[1] jastóna *f.* ☞ ياسته

يسير jasír *m. Arabic* small, little, easy

يش jəsh *m.* ☞ ايشنا boiling

يشب jasháb *m.* يشم jashm *m. plural* jasper; agate

يشنا jashnā́ *f.* ☞ ايشنا

يشند jashónd boiling; hot يشندي اوبه boiling water

يشول jashavól *transitive dialect* ☞ ايشول

يشبدل jishedól *intransitive dialect* ☞ ايشبدل

يشبدنه jashedóna *f.* ☞ ايشنا

ينبل jəkhól *transitive dialect* يبنوول jəkhodól jəkhovál ☞ ايبنودل

يعسوب ja'súb *m. Arabic* queen bee

يعقوب ja'kúb *m. Arabic proper name* Yakub; Yakob

يعني ja'ní ja'né *Arabic* that is, namely

يغ دغ jaghdágh **1** sticking up **2** rude, crude, hard, harsh

يغمه jaghmá *f.* **1** robbery, pillage **2** spoils, booty

يغنوبي jaghnobí *f.* Yagnobi, the Yagnobi language (a Pamir language)

يقين jaķín *Arabic* **1.1** confidence; conviction کلک يقين firm conviction, unshakeable confidence زه کلک يقين لرم چه ... I am firmly convinced that ... يقين يې راغئ He was convinced He acquired the conviction په چا باندي يقين کول to trust someone د ده

يقين سره ويل کېداى شي چه ... He was convinced that ... يقين وشو One may definitely say that ... زما اوس پوخ يقين راغلئ دئ چه Now I am definitely convinced that ... ده ته دا يقين وشو چه ... He understood that ..., He acquired the convicton that ... **1.2** assurance ستاسي په حضور يقين ورکول to assure someone در کوم چه ... I assure you that ... **2** *predicative* definite, indubitable, indisputable

يقيناً jaķínán *Arabic* definitely, truly, doubtlessly, indisputably

يقين والى jaķinválaj *m.* confidence; conviction

يقيني jaķiní *Arabic* definite, true, precise په يقيني ډول definitely تاريخ يقيني جواب راکوي چه ... History definitely confirms that ...

يک jak *numeral* (usually in compounds) one

يکاولنگ jakāvláng *m.* Yakavlang (district, Daizangi Province)

يکاوه jakāvá *f.* unbroken cloud cover

يک آهنگي jakahangí *f.* unity, cohesion

يکبارگي jakbāragí jakāják يکاجک at once, suddenly; unexpectedly

يکتا jaktā́ *single; one, only

يکتاره jaktārá *f.* a one-stringed musical instrument

يکتائي jaktāí **1** unity **2** singleness

يکتنها jaktanhá alone په يک تنها صورت by oneself

يکجنسي jakdzhinsí *f.* homogeneity

يکجهت jakdzhihát **1** agreed; unanimous **2** *m.* **.1** friend **2** partisan, supporter **3** in accord (with), unanimously

يکجهتي jakdzhihatí *f.* **1** agreement; unanimity **2** friendship

يکدگ jakdág *m.* cottage cheese; cheese

يکدل jakdíl ☞ يک جهت

يکدلي jakdilí *f.* ☞ يک جهتي

يکدم jakdám at once, in the wink of an eye; in a moment

يکرنگي jakrangí *f.* monotony

يکړ jakaṛ **1** solitary, individual **2** only, sole

يکړول jakaṛavól *denominative, transitive* [*past:* يکړ يې کړ] **1** to separate; isolate, seclude **2** to thin out (e.g., plantings)

يکړبدل jakaṛedól *denominative, intransitive* [*past:* يکړ شو] **1** to be thinned out (e.g., of plantings) **2** to be isolated, be secluded

يکسان jaksán **1.1** identically, equally دواړه يکسان پر موږ گران دي Both are equally dear to us. **1.2** also, in the same manner **2** identical, alike

يک ساني jaksāní identity, sameness

يکشنبه، يک شنبه jakshambá *f.* Sunday

يوقلم jakķalám ☞ يک قلم

يکلاجي jaklājí *f.* يکلايي jaklāí *f.* **1** chador, cloak (of a single piece of cloth); mantle **2** overcoat, greatcoat

يکلخت jaklákht يک لخته jaklakhtá **1** at once, immediately; instantly **2** as a whole, fully

يکلنگه jaklingá lever used to draw water from a well کوتل يک لنگه kotál-i-jaklingá Yaklinga (a pass northwest of Kabul)

يکم jakúm *ordinal regional* first

يکنفره jaknafará single-seated يک نفره کټ a single bed

يكنواخت jaknavákht يک نواخته jaknavákhta 1 monotonous 2 homogeneous 3 similar, analogous

يكنواختي jaknavākhtí f. 1 monotony; monotonousness 2 homogeneity 3 similarity, analogy

يکه jaká jakká 1.1 one, only; sole يكه کول to thin out (e.g., plantings) 1.2 one-horse (of a carriage); individual 2 m. .1 only child 2.2 cards ace 2.3 individual soldier, private soldier, trooper 3 element used in place names, e.g., يكه توت Yakkatut

يکه توت jakatút m. jakkatút Yakkatut (suburb, Kabul)

يكهمان ¹ jakahmán lone, lonely (of a person)

يكهمان ² jakhamán similar, alike, analogous

يكي ¹ jakí f. jakə́j 1 history yaki (a small copper coin) 2 farthing, penny ☞ ايكي ¹

يكى ² jakə́j f. velocipede

يكي ³ jakí just, only يكي يواځي پاته يم lonely يكي يواځي I remained all by myself.

يگ jəg m. Eastern ☞ يږ

يگانگي jagānagi f. 1 unity, agreement يگانگي کول to act in concert; to display unity يگانگي لرل to be united 2 singleness; exceptionality idiom دم ديگانگي وهل to promote friendship

يگانه jagāná 1 only يگانه زوی only son 2 rare, exceptional, incomparable, unique 3 agreeable, coordinated, agreed upon, unanimous

يگه ¹ jə́ga f. Eastern ☞ يږه ¹

يگه ² jága f. Eastern disease of horses resulting in hair loss

يگى jagə́j f. kind of children's game

يل jal m. 1 hero 2 champion, upholder

يلاق jalák m. ☞ ايلبند

يلدا jaldá f. longest night of the year

يلدنگ jə́ldáng m. يلدنگ jə́ldáng m. 1 vagrant, tramp 2 poor man, poor peasant

يلغر jalghár m. ☞ يرغل

يلغز jalgház jalghúz bachelor, single; celibate هغه يلغز سړی دئ He is a bachelor.

يلوند jalvánḍ fat and ugly (of a man)

يله ¹ jalá f. swamp, bog

يله ² jalá ☞ ايله

يله دار jaladár m. obsolete scout, reconnaissance man

يله داري jaladārí f. service or job of a scout or reconnaissance man يله داري کول to scout, reconnoiter

يله گرد jalagárd m. [plural: يله گردان jalagərd plural: يله گرد jalagardán] tramp, vagrant

يله گردي jalagardí f. والى ايله jalavālaj m. ☞ يله گردي

يلى jiláj f. dialect ☞ هيلى ¹

يم ¹ jam jamm [plural: يمونه jamuna plural: jammúna plural: يموم jumúm] Arabic ocean, sea

يم ² jəm copula-verb 1 first person singular present tense زه جوړه يم I am well. زه جوړه يم I (f.) am well. 2 I am, I exist

يم ³ jum m. ☞ يوم ¹

يم ⁴ jəm ordinal numeral suffix دويم second اتيايم eighteith

يمال jamál m. avalanche (snow)

يمن ¹ jumn m. Arabic luck, good fortune, prosperity

يمن ² jamán m. Arabic Yemen

يمنول jəmanavə́l denominative, transitive [past: يمن يې کړ] to comfort, calm, console

يمني jamaní jamanáj Arabic 1 Yemeni 2 m. Yemeni (person)

يمنبدل jəmənedə́l denominative, intransitive [past: يمن شو] 1 to be comforted, be consoled 2 to have a good cry

يموم jumúm m. Arabic plural of يم ¹

يمه jə́ma ☞ يم ²

يمه jə́ma f. ☞ يم ⁴

يمين jamín Arabic 1 right (of the side) 2 m. .1 right flank 2.2 right hand 2.3 oath

ين ¹ jen jan m. yen (Japanese monetary unit)

ين ² ájn Arabic suffix for the dual number of nouns, e.g., طرفين the (contracting) parties

ين ³ ín Arabic suffix for the plural number of nouns, e.g., مامورين civil servants

ين ⁴ ín adjective suffix زرين gold, golden ډبرين stone, stoney

ينجه jə́ndzha f. ☞ هنجه

يندره jandrá f. 1 grindstone 2 sharpening wheel

ينده ¹ jínda f. stream, flow

ينده ² jəndə́ m. ☞ اينده ² ينده پسه stud-ram

ينډه jə́nḍa f. 1 stubbornness, obstinacy 2 liveliness, agility

ينسي jenisé f. Yenisei (River)

ينگه ¹ jangá f. 1 polishing tool used by potters for finishing pottery پلکش ☞ 2

ينگه ² jangá tautological with کونگه

ينگي jangí element used in place names, ينگي قلعه Yangi-kala

ينه ¹ jə́na f. dialect ديني چنجى hepatic duct ☞ اينه dialect

ينه ² iná poetry third person present verb ending, ي e.g., ځينه ☞ ځي

ينه ³ iná f. noun & adjective suffix پشمينه cloth; ديرينه old, ancient

ينه ⁴ ína feminine of ين ⁴ زرينه خولۍ the Central Asiatic skull-cap embroidered in gold

يني ¹ jə́ni plural of ينه ¹

يني ² jíni feminine plural of ين ⁴ د لمر زريني وړانگي The golden rays of the sun.

يو ¹ jav jau jo jov oblique يوه juvə́ 1 numeral one يو ځل once, one time يو واري once, one time يو څلور around four, about four يو دوه one or two, a few په يو دم suddenly, at once يو کول a to unite, to join b to nail, sew together (e.g., boards, carpetting) لاس يو کول to be united 2 indefinite pronoun something or other کم someone or other of them کم يو هلک ستا زوی دئ؟ Which of the boys is your son? له يوه ځايه from somewhere or other يو some time, a little while يوه وويل someone said; one of them said 3 m. unit idiom دواړه يو دي both are alike; one and the same, no difference دي يو تول all are identical وي چه يو هر no matter which, any كول ژوند سره يوه په to live separately, live apart

يو ² ju *verb copula* **1** *first person plural present tense* يو جوړ موږ we are well **2** we are, we exist

يو ² jo *indicator of the perfective aspect of the verb* نه مړه گرده يا خو سو، يا پوره بری يو نه سو ورل Either we will all perish, or we will attain victory.

يواتيا javātjā́ *numeral* eighty one

يواتيايم javātjājə́m *ordinal numeral* eighty first

يوازيني javādzinā́j ☞

يوازي javā́dzi *Eastern* javā́dze ☞ يوازي وسيله يواحي The only means.

يواحينتوب javādzintób *m.* ☞ وحدانيت

يواحيني javādzinā́j يوازيني ژوند يواحيني an individual life پښتو "pure Pashto"

يواحيوالى javādzivā́laj *m.* solitude

يواد javā́d *m.* ☞ هيواد

يوار javā́r يو وار وار *vice*

يواريخ javārídz **1** all at once, straight away **2** quite, completely د هغو ليدل يواريخ نا ممکن دئ It is quite impossible to see them.

يوارخيز javарخíz **1** unilateral ډول يوارخيز په unilaterally **2** one sided

يوازي javā́zi javā́ze *Eastern* **1.1** pure, unadulterated; real, genuine يوازي مس pure copper **1.2** alone, solitary زه يوازي پاتي شوم I remained alone كول يوازي a to separate, isolate b to seclude, leave alone كبدل يوازي a to be separated, be isolated b to be secluded, be left alone **1.3** only one, unique يوازي لار the only way يوازي علت the only reason **1.4** individual, personal دغه كسان دي مسئول سره گډه په او يوازي These persons bear personal and collective responsibility. **2** only, solely, just بلكه يوازي نه not only …, but also …

يوازيتوب javāzitób *m.* solitude; seclusion; reclusiveness يوازي توب striving for seclusion, for solitude سلوک توب

يوازيني javāzinā́j **1** personal, individual **2** sole, only **3** pure, unadulterated; real, genuine

يوازيوالى javāzivā́laj *m.* ☞ يوازي توب

يواويا javavijā́ *numeral* seventy-one

يواويايم javajājə́m *ordinal* seventy-first

يوبرابر javbarā́bár **1** same, equal **2.1** identically, equally **2.2** equally, in equal parts

يوبندى javbándaj *m. obsolete* kind of rifle

يوپ jup *m.* diving, sinking كول يوپ to sink, submerge, go under; drown كبدل يوپ to be submerged, be sunk

يوپټه javpaṭā́ single (of a carpet, rug)

يوپلا javplā́ *colloquial* one time, once

يوپينځوس javpindzós *numeral* fifty-one

يوپينځوسم javpindzosə́m *ordinal* fifty-first

يوپدوه javpədvá double, two-fold كول دوه يوپه to double, increase two-fold كبدل دوه يوپه to double, increase two-fold

يوپه يوه javpəjavə́ **1** unexpectedly, suddenly, at once راغئ يو په يو He arrived unexpectedly. **2** one after another

يوپي jupí *f. history* the United Provinces of India

يوتربله javtərbála one after the other, at one another's place; one another

يوجهت javdzhihát agreed, unanimous كبدل يوجهت to agree, come to an agreement

يوجهتي javzhihatí *f.* ☞ يووالى

يوچا javchā́ *oblique of* يوڅوک … دي ويلي چا يو Someone said that …

يوچيري javchíre somewhere

يوځای javdzā́j together د دوی سره يوځای together with them توله يوځای كول to unite, يوځای ووړی خوري They are all eating together. join د چا سره يوځای كبدل a to be united with, join with someone, adjoin someone b to intersect (of routes) c to mate (of animals)

يوځایوالى javdzājvā́laj *m.* **1** unification; joining together د قومونو يوځای والى unification of peoples **2** cohesion, unity **3** combination (of color, sound, etc.)

يوځائي javdzā́i **1** single **2** identical

يوځلي javdzə́li once

يوڅلوېښت javtsalvéќht *numeral* forty-one

يوڅلوېښتم javtsalveќhtə́m *ordinal numeral* forty-first

يوڅو jav tsó *numeral* several, a few پس ورڅي يوڅو after several days يوڅو تنه سړي راغلي دي Several people arrived.

يوڅوک javtsók *indefinite pronoun* someone, somebody, some person

يوڅه javtsə́ *indefinite pronoun* **1** some, some quantity; something, something or other يوڅه مځکه a little piece of land يوڅه يې part of them, some of them يوڅه كول to do something **2** somewhat, to some degree درد يوڅه سپکبري The pain abated somewhat.

يوحزبي javhizbí single (political) party سيستم يوحزبي a single-party system

يوحنا johanā́ *m. Arabic proper name* Joanne

يوخوا بل خوا jokhvā-bə́lkhvā *Eastern* to and from, back and forth, from side to side

يود بل سره javdəbə́lsərā with one another دي نه ساز سره بل يود They do not get along with one another.

يودم javdám **1** immediately, at once **2** immediate

يودوه javdvá *numeral* a few, a couple لرم درسره خبري يودوه I must have a few words with you.

يودوی javdávaj **1** sparse, scattered **2** alone كول يودوی a to scatter, disperse b to seclude كبدل يودوی a to be scattered, be dispersed b to be secluded

يودېرش javdérsh *numeral* thirty-one

يودېرشم javdershə́m *ordinal* thirty-first

يوډزى javḍázaj single-shot (of a rifle)

يو ډل jav ḍal *m.* solid grease, solid fat

يوډول javḍául identical, similar

يور jor *f.* [*plural:* يوني júṇi júṇe] *Eastern* wife of a husband's brother, brother-in-law's wife دا بنځي سره يوني دي These women are married to brothers.

يوراز javráz ☞ يوړول

يورال jurãl Urals د يورال سين the Ural River يورال غرونه the Ural Mountains

يورانيوم jurãnijum *m.* uranium

يورپ juráp *m.* Europe

يورپ پرست jurapparást *m.* partisan of Europe, Westerner

يورپي jurapí يورپيين jurapiján *regional* 1 European 2 *m.* European

يورش jurísh *m.* 1 attack, raid 2 assault

يورشلم jurashalím *m.* Jerusalem

يورنگ javráng يورنگه javránga 1.1 identical, similar, analogous 1.2 monochrome 1.3 sequential 1.4 repetitive 2.1 identically 2.2 uninterruptedly يورنگ سړي راتله People came and went all the time.

يورنگه والى javrangavãlaj *m.* 1 unity, uniformity 2 identity, likeness د عقيدي يورنگه والى unanimity, uniformity of opinion

يوروگواى jurugvãj *m.* Urugvaj (a people)

يورولوژي jurolozhí *f.* urology

يوړه jóvra *f. past tense of* وړل

يوړې jóvre *f. past plural of* وړل

يوز juz *m.* cheetah; hunting leopard

يوزری javazóraj solitary; sole, unique

يوزړه javzṛó unanimous, agreed, in accord يوزړه کېدل to be unanimous, be in agreement

يوزه júza *f.* male cheetah; male hunting leopard

يوژبى javzhóbaj 1 speaking the same language 2 *figurative* true, correct; sincere

يوسپ jusúp *m.* ☞ يوسف

يوسپزي jusupzí *m. plural* ☞ يوسفزي

يوست jost *imperfective past tense of* يستل ډېر زيار يې يوست He tried hard.

يوسترگى javstórgaj one-eyed

يوستوي [1] javəstóve *f.* handful, pinch

يوستوى [2] javastóvaj 1 single; in one layer; unlined 2 *military* single-file په يوستوى قطار! يوستوى ليک single file! Form up in single file! 3 lean, emaciated

يوسف jusúf *m. Arabic proper name* Yusuf, Yosif

يوسفزي jusufzí jusupzí 1 *m. plural* the Yosufzai (a group of tribes) د يوسفزيو علاقه the district of the Yosufzai 2 jusufzáj *m.* jusupzáj Yosufzai (tribesman)

يوسم josóm *first person singular, present tense prefective of* وړل

يوسو jósu *first person plural, present tense prefective of* وړل

يوسه jósa *imperative prefective of* وړل

يوسې [1] jóse *second persson present tense prefective of* وړل خير يوسې! I wish you success! All the best!

يوسي [2] jósi *present tense prefective of* وړل

يوسئ [3] jośój 1 *second person plural, present tense perfective of* وړل 2 *imperative plural perfective of* وړل

يوسيلابي javsilãbi monosyllabic

يوشان javshãn identically يوشان کول to unify, to unite *idiom* په لاس کېني پنځه ګوتي هم يوشان نه دي *literal* Even on one hand all the fingers are different. *figurative* People are all different.

يوشانته javshãnta *indeclinable* identical; similar, like; equal, equivalent د وري په لمري روغ شپه او روغ يوشانته وي On the first day of the month of Hammal the day and night are equal.

يوشان کول javshãnkavól *m. plural* unification, the establishment of uniformity

يوشاني javshãni ☞ يوشانته

يوشپيتم javshpetóm *ordinal numeral* sixty-first

يوشپيته javshpetó *numeral* sixty-one

يوشپيني javspenáj *m.* overnight guest

يوطرفه javtarafá unilateral

يوطرفي javtarafí 1 unilateral (of movement) 2 aside, to the side

يوطور javtóur 1 identical, uniform 2 identically, uniformly

يوقلم 1 in full, conclusively, quite, perpetual (of a prohibition of sth.) 2 categorically 3 at once, straight away

يوقلمه joķlamá *f. military* roll-call د سبا يوقلمه morning roll-call هوايي يوقلمه air-raid alarm

يوکرائن jukrãín *m.* يوکراين jukrãjín *m.* ☞ اوکرائن

يوکسيز javkasíz 1 single-place, for one man, for one person 2 single (of beds, bedrooms) يوکسيز چپرکت single bed

يوکلپتس jukalíptas *m.* eucalyptus

يوکلن javkalán one year, lasting one year يوکلن کورس one year courses

يوکم jav kam *m.* almost, all but يوکم څلوېښت almost forty (39)

يوکى javkój *f.* velocipede

يوگاندا jugãndá *f.* Uganda

يوگوسلاوي jugoslãví Yugoslavian

يوگوسلاويا jugoslãvijá *f.* Yugoslavia

يوگونه javguná somewhat, in some degree, somehow

يولاس javlãs 1 uniting, single, sole 2 homogenous, uniform, identical 3 agreed يولاس کېدل a يولاس او متحد کېدل to be united to be united b to be homogenous, to be identical c to be agreed, to agree d to make friends with

يولاس والى javlãsvãlaj *m.* 1 collaboration, cooperation 2 unity 3 homogeneity 4 agreement, accord, harmony, friendship

يولاف julãf *m.* oats

يولس javólas *dialect* ☞ يوولس

يولسم javólasóm *dialect* ☞ يوولسم

يولورتوب javlortób *m.* support, aid, assistance

يولورى javlóraj *m.* partisan, adherent, supporter

يولوريځ javlorídz يولوريز javloríz unilateral, one-sided

يوله بله javləbála يوله بله سره javləbálasərá one another; to or with one another يوله بله سره پښتو ويل to speak Pashto to one another

يوله بله سره سلام كول to greet one another يوله بله كومك كول to help one another, come to one another's aid

يوليتري javlitrí *adjective* liter نيينه يوليتري one-liter bottle

يوم jum[1] *m.* [*plural:* يومونه jumúna *Western plural:* يومان jumā́n] shovel, spade

يوم jáum[2] *m. Arabic* [*plural:* يومونه jaumúna *Arabic plural:* ايام ajā́m] day

يوم javə́m[3] first (in a count)

يومخ javmə́kh at once, immediately, instantly

يومختوب javməkhtób *m.* يومختيا javməkhtjā́ *f.* sincerity, truth, veracity, frankness, openness, directness

يومخى javmə́khaj sincere, true, veracious, frank, open, direct يومخى سرى a frank, open, truthful or direct man

يومخيز javməkhíz 1 fully, wholly; utterly 2 directly, at once, at one go يومخيز ولاړه All departed.

يومكى jumakáj *m.* shoulder-blade

يومنزله javmanzalá one-story, one storied

يوم والا jumvālā́ *m.* common laborer (esp. one who works with a shovel)

يوموټ javmúṭ 1 required (as of a payment which must be made, or a penalty sum added) 2 at once, immediately, forthwith

يومه javə́ma *f. singular of* يوم[3]

يومي jaumí[1] *Arabic* daily, everyday, commonplace يومي ژوند everyday life يومي امر *military* general order

يومي javə́mi[2] *f. plural of* يوم[3]

يوميه jaumijá *Arabic* 1 *feminine singular of* يومي[1] 2 daily wage, day's pay

يون jun *m.* [*plural:* يانه jānə́] 1 movement, passing, proceding يون كول to move, pass, proceed د سيند يون كول to sail along a river 2 current, flow (of a river) 3 conduct, behavior, manner 4 gait, walk 5 habit; disposition, temper

يوناټاپه javnātsā́pa suddenly, at once, unexpectedly; by chance

يونان junā́n *m.* Greece

يوناني junā́ní junānáj 1.1 Greek, Hellenic يوناني ژبه the Greek language 1.2 pertaining to traditional (Arabic) medicine دى يوناني طب حكيم و He was an experienced "Tabib" (i.e., traditional physician) 2 *m.* .1 Greek, Hellene 2.2 *f.* the Greek language

يونټ juníṭ *m. regional* 1 unit 2 administrative unit د پاكستان غربي يونټ the Western Province of Pakistan 3 *military* small unit (smaller than a regiment)

يونسكو junéskó *f. abbreviation* UNESCO (the United Nations Educational, Scientific and Cultural Organization)

يونفس javnafás in an instant, at once, in one breath

يونل junə́l *intransitive* [*past:* و يونل] 1 to pass, proceed, move 2 to resettle, make a move

يونو junó *f. abbreviation* United Nations

يونس ، يونوس junús *m. Arabic proper name* Yonus; Yona (i.e., Jonah)

يونوي javniví *numeral* ninety-one

يونويم javnivijə́m *ordinal numeral* ninety-first

يونيفورمه يونيفورم juniform *m. regional* يونيفورم junifórm *m.* يونيفورما juniformá *f.* uniform, uniform clothing, tunic د فوځ يونيفارم اغوستل to wear a military uniform

يونيكوډ jūnikoḏ *m. computer science* Unicode

يونيم javním 1 *numeral* one and a half يونيم برابر one and a half times bigger 2 *indefinite pronoun* some, several خلق وائي چه ... Some say that ... 3 sometimes, at times يونيم وخت ځي او راځي From time to time he appears, then he disappears. په يونيم وخت كښې يي شعر وايه Sometimes he wrote verses.

يونيورستي junvársiti *f.* university

يوني júṇi *juṇe Eastern plural of* يور

يوواله javvā́la *f.* يووالى javvā́laj *m.* 1 unity, unification, union 2 harmony, accord, agreement 3 uniqueness, distinction 4 joining together

يوبل javubə́l both that one and the other

يووخت javvákht 1 sometimes, at times 2 sometime, somehow 3 once, one time

يووختي چه javvákhti che 1 when 2 once, one time

يووختيز javvakhtíz 1 extraordinary, unique 2 similar

يوورگ javvárg *m.* yearling camel

يوورگه javvárga *feminine of* يوورگ

يوور jóvur *past tense of* ورل

يوورل jovṛə́l *past plural of* ورل

يووړه jóvṛa[1] *past feminine of* ورل

يووړه jovṛə́[2] ☞ يوور

يووړئ jóvṛəj[1] *Western vice* يوور

يووړې jóvṛe[2] *f. plural of* ورل

يووزري javvazáraj 1 have no relations 2 helpless; alone يووزري سرى a man with no support or help يووزري كېدل to be without assistants, work alone 3 mon-alar; with a single lift surface (e.g., an airplane) يووزري الوتكه monoplane

يوولس javolás *numeral* eleven

يوولسم javolasə́m *ordinal* eleventh

يوورئ jóvəj *past tense Western vice* يوور

يووويشت javvísht *numeral* twenty-one

يووويشتم javvishtə́m *ordinal numeral* twenty-first

يوه jə́va *f.* [*plural:* يوي jə́vi *plural:* يوي jə́ve] *Eastern* plow

يوه javá[2] *f. singular of* يو[1] يوه دوي كول to thin out (plantings) دوى نظريه به سره يوه وي Their viewpoints evidently coincide. *idiom* په يوه او بله كول to dodge, take evasive action, squirm out of *idiom* زما يوه خبره ده My word is firm. *idiom* د چا يوه دوي كېدل to make both ends meet

يوه javə́[3] *oblique singular of* يو[1]

يوه پلا javaplā́ one time, once

يوه خوا javakhvā́ on one side

يوه خوله java khvə́lá in harmony, agreed, unanimous يوه خوله كېدل to agree

852

يوه زرى جُوى javazə́raj sole, only يوه زرى زوى only son

يوه ستوى javastə́vaj 1 alone, solitary 2 sole, only

يوهو johó *interjection* ugh (used to express contempt, revulsion)

يوه ورځې javá vrádze *dialect* once, one time

يوٻ [1] jə́ve *f.* 1 plow 2 plowing يوٻ کول *compound verb* to plow مځکه يوٻ کول *compound verb* a to plow the earth b to engage in plowing يوٻ کېدل *compound verb* to be plowed

يوٻ [2] javé oblique ☞ يوه [2]

يوٻ [3] jə́vi *f.* plural of يوه [1]

يوى [4] joj juj *interjection* oh, ouch (usually used by women) to express surprise, pain, etc.

يوٻ کوونکى jə́ve kavúnkaj *m.* plowman

يو يو jav-jáv 1 alone, by oneself يو يو بيانول to lay out point by point, sequentially دوى يې يو يو ووهل He beat them all up, all by himself. 2 single, unitary

يويه jóvja *f.* ☞ يوه [1]

يه [1] ja *negative particle* no يه ، نه حُم No, I am not going.

يه [2] ja *pronoun Western vice* يې [2]

يه [3] ja *interjection* hey خلقو! يه Hey, you people!

يهود jahúd *m. Arabic plural* 1 Jews 2 Jew

يهودي jahudí 1 Jewish *m.* 2 Jew

يهوديت jahudiját *m.* Judaism, Jewish faith

يې [1] je *f.* the name of the letter ى

يې [2] je ئې e *non-emphatic pronoun, third person singular and plural oblique of* دوى، دا، دى (cannot begin a sentence) 1 he, she, it, they (as the subject of the action of transitive verbs in the ergative construction) خپل کتاب يې واخيست He took his book. She took her book. They took their book. 2 him, her, it, them (as the object of the action of transitive verbs in the present and future tenses) ته يې ويني؟ Do you see him? Do you see her? Do you see

them? 3 his, hers, theirs (as a possessive pronoun) هغه دپر دروغجن سړى دئ حُکه يې زه يوه خبره نه اورم He is a big liar, and therefore I don't believe a word he says. 4a *it may be included in the postposition preceding it* په مکتب کښې يې واچولم کښي He sent me to school. She sent me to school. 4b *it may be included in the form of the verb itself* ويل e.g., وبويل، و يې ويل He said, She said, They said ويلي يې، ويلي He said, She said, They said 5 *it may coalesce with the vowel of the preceding word* ☞ بې and تې and نې

يې [3] je ئې je *verb copula, second person singular present tense* 1 ته لا نه يې تللئ؟ حُوک يې؟ Who are you? Haven't you (he) gone yet? ته لا نه يې تللي؟ Haven't you (she) gone yet? 2 you are, you exist

ئئ [4] joj *verb copula, second person present Eastern* ☞ ياست

ئي [5] ji *verb copula, second person singular & plural present Eastern* ☞ وي [3]

يې [6] je *interjection* hey يې ورورہ! Hey buddy!

يې [7] je (with a protracted or drawn-out pronunciation) yes يې، مکتب ته حُم Ye-e-s, I'm going to school.

يبر jer *m.* caravan

يبروان jereván *m.* Yerevan

ئيړ jiṛ *m.* fleet, flotilla

يبنبل jeḳhə́l *transitive dialect* ☞ اينبودل

ئيلاق jajlắḳ *m.* summer break

ئيم jim *m. dialect* ☞ يوم [1]

يبنه jéna *f.* liver

ئيني [1] jíni *f. plural dialect* blood ☞ وينه [2]

يبني [2] jéni *f. plural of* يبنه

ئيوه jíva *f. dialect* plow حُمکه ئيوه سوه The ground has been plowed.